FINLAND
Helsinki
St. Petersburg
Tallinn
ESTONIA
Nizhniy Novgorod
Volga
URAL MTS.
Riga
LATVIA
Moscow
RUSSIA
LITHUANIA
(RUSSIA)
Vilnius
Minsk
BELARUS
Ural
KAZAKHSTAN
Vistula
Warsaw
Kiev
Kharkov
CARPATHIAN
MTS.
UKRAINE
Dnieper
Budapest
MOLDOVA
Kishinev
Caspian
Sea
ROMANIA
CAUCASUS MTS.
Bucharest
GEORGIA
T'bilisi
Baku
Black Sea
AZERBAIJAN
SERBIA
Danube
ARMENIA
BULGARIA
Yerevan
Sofia
AZERBAIJAN
Skopje
MACEDONIA
Tiranë
Ankara
TURKEY
IRAN
GREECE
Aegean
Sea
Athens
Euphrates
Tigris
SYRIA
Baghdad
CYPRUS
IRAQ
Crete
LEBANON
Beirut
Damascus
Mediterranean
Sea
KUWAIT
Kuwait
Jerusalem
Amman
ISRAEL
JORDAN
Cairo
EGYPT
Nile
SAUDI ARABIA

Western Civilization

The Continuing Experiment

Thomas F. X. Noble
University of Virginia

Barry S. Strauss
Cornell University

Duane J. Osheim
University of Virginia

Kristen B. Neuschel
Duke University

William B. Cohen
Indiana University

David D. Roberts
University of Georgia

HOUGHTON MIFFLIN COMPANY BOSTON TORONTO
Geneva, Illinois Palo Alto Princeton, New Jersey

Sponsoring Editor: Sean W. Wakely
Basic Book Editor: Elizabeth M. Welch
Project Editor: Christina M. Horn
Production/Design Coordinator: Sarah Ambrose
Senior Manufacturing Coordinator: Marie Barnes
Marketing Manager: Rebecca J. Dudley

Chapter opener credits begin on page A-1. Text credits begin on page A-3.

Cover designer: Judy Arisman

Cover image: Bas-relief of Isabella and Ferdinand from Cabildo de la Capilla Real, Granada.

Printed in the U.S.A.

Library of Congress Catalog Card Number: 93-78655

ISBN
Student text: 0-395-55121-8
Examination text: 0-395-69141-9

123456789-VH-97 96 95 94 93

Frontmatter Illustration Credits

p. iv: Claus Hansmann, München; *p. v:* The Art Museum, Princeton University, Museum purchase, Caroline G. Mather Fund; *p. vi:* Alinari/Art Resource, NY; *p. vii:* Archiv für Kunst und Geschichte; *p. viii:* The Board of Trinity College, Dublin; *p. ix:* Altitude, Paris; Musée Archéologique Thomas Dobrée/Giraudon/Art Resource; *p. x:* The John Carter Brown Library at Brown University, Providence; *p. xi:* By kind permission of Marquess of Tavistock and Trustees of Bedford Estate; *p. xii:* Biblioteca Marucelliana, Florence; *p. xiii:* Photographie Bulloz; *p. xiv:* St. Cyril and Methodius National Library, Sofia; *p. xv:* Courtesy of the Trustees of the British Museum; *p. xvi:* Trustees of the Imperial War Museum; *p. xvii:* UPI/Bettmann Newsphotos; *p. xviii:* Patrick Forestier/Sygma.

Brief Contents

Contents

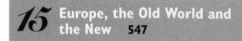

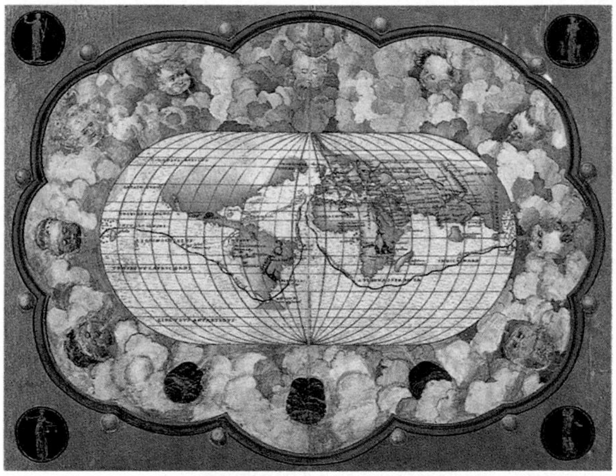

16 The Reformation 581

17 Europe in the Age of Philip II, 1559–1600 619

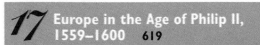

18 Europe in the Age of Louis XIV, ca. 1610–1715 659

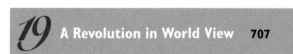

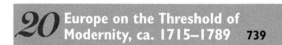

23 The Industrial Transformation of Europe 853

24 New Configurations of Power, 1850–1880 889

25 The Age of Optimism, 1850–1880 921

26 The Coming Conflict, 1880–1914 955

27 War and Revolution, 1914–1919 991

Kaiser u. Volksdank für Heer und Flotte
Frankfurter Weihnachtsgabe 1917
Geldspenden: Theaterplatz 14, Büro 5

Chronologies, Genealogies, and Charts

Documents

Maps

Weighing the Evidence

Preface

The authors of this book are committed teachers who never lost the thrill of being history students. We therefore invite our colleagues on both sides of the desk to see if our experiences with textbooks remind them of their own.

We have taught Western civilization at more than a dozen institutions whose size and mission differ greatly. Like many teachers, we have tried different books, reviewed new or updated books for publishers, examined brochures promising us the book we had always been looking for, and listened to sales representatives explain the strengths of their offerings. We have grown pretty skeptical about claims on behalf of new books. Why, then, have we had the temerity to write one?

Quite simply, we believe that it is possible to do better, for both teachers and students, than has been done before. Miles Davis was once asked what he thought jazz musicians would be playing in ten years, and he said that if he knew that he would already be playing it. We do not claim that we have seen into the future, but we can say with real conviction that we have tried to avoid the mistakes of the past.

The point of a Western civilization textbook is to play a role in a course that will, as a total effort, inform students about the essential developments within a tradition that has powerfully, although not always positively, affected everyone who is alive today. Although each of us finds something to admire in all of the existing books, none of us is fully happy with any of them. We are tired of promises that a given book is "balanced," only to find that it stresses a single kind of history. We regret books that are uneven in their command of recent scholarship. We are impatient with confusing organizational strategies that do not permit adaptation to our syllabuses. We dislike books that are visually unattractive or disconcerting.

After several wide-ranging conversations focusing on what we thought was wrong, we turned, more positively and productively, to a consideration of what we might do to improve the situation. We decided to try very hard to produce a book that is balanced and coherent; that addresses the full range of issues a Western civilization text needs to address; that provides the student reader with interesting, timely material; that is up-to-date in terms of scholarship and approach; and that is handsome to look at—in short, a book that helps the instructor to teach and the student to learn. We kept our common vision fresh through frequent meetings, constant correspondence, critical mutual readings, and expert editorial guidance. Six authors really have come together as one, and because each of us focused on his or her own area of specialization, we believe we have attained a rare blend of competence, confidence, and enthusiasm.

Central Themes

We faced a real challenge in trying to meet the different needs of teachers and students. A case can be made for a "Great Books" approach, but that case fails in the face of the political, legal, institutional, and social heritage of the West. Political history is surely important, but we have all outgrown the old fashioned kings-emperors-popes-generals-diplomats approach of the books that dominated until the 1970s. Social history—from the bottom up—is fascinating, but it often lacks a sense of chronology and of historical change.

Western civilization is a story. We therefore aimed at a strong chronological narrative line. Our experience as teachers tells us that students appreciate this clear but gentle orientation. Our experience tells us, too, that an approach that is more chronological than thematic will leave instructors plenty of room to adapt our narrative to their preferred organization.

For instance, we divide the Roman world in the late second century B.C. and again in the third century A.D. We include a chapter on Late Antiquity that will easily complete a discussion of the ancient world or inaugurate a treatment of the Middle Ages. Chapter 9 treats the Celtic world, Scandinavia, Slavic Europe, Byzantium, and the Islamic world in a way that launches a continuing discussion of these regions both on their own terms and as partners with the European core in the construction of Western civilization. Teachers may, however, elect to omit Chapter 9 without interrupting the basic account of medieval Europe. We give exploration and "discovery" a separate chapter instead of subordinating these issues to Renaissance science or early modern statecraft. We introduce and analyze the industrial transformation in the middle of the nineteenth century, when it was at its highpoint, instead of scattering its account through several chapters. Our twentieth-century chapters reflect the very different understanding that we now have of the historical significance of the world wars, and of the cold war, after the collapse of the Soviet Union. Flexibility and adaptability are evident throughout. Our strategy reflects the best current scholarship, but it also leaves teachers great freedom in deciding where to break for discussions, papers, or examinations.

A chronological narrative that respects the traditional divisions of ancient, medieval, early modern, and modern will inevitably reflect great people and great events. We make no apology for this, and we urge no particular ideology in doing it. Marx was surely right when he said that women and men make history without knowing they are doing so, but it is nonetheless true that Alexander, Charlemagne, Elizabeth I, Napoleon, and Hitler have had a more decisive impact on the development of the West than most ordinary individuals. That is true, but not interesting to teachers or to students until we say why it is true.

This book takes as its point of departure *power* in all its senses: public and private; economic, social, political, and cultural; symbolic and real. We continually ask who had power, and who did not. Through what public and private means was power gained, lost, and exercised in a given time and place? How did people talk about power? What kinds of rituals, ceremonies, or celebrations displayed power? What relationships existed among economic, social, political, and cultural power?

By using power, not old-fashioned high politics, as our organizing principle we believe we have achieved the kind of balance and integration that are frequently promised but seldom attained. We have deliberately avoided putting the occasional paragraph or section on women, children, families, religious minorities, eating habits, or marriage patterns right in the middle of a discussion of something else entirely. We maintain a sustained interest in the history of women, and we discuss such subjects as diet, clothing, or dwellings when Europeans themselves talked about them, or when there were important changes in these areas. Women are not relegated to a separate section in our account of the Middle Ages, for example, but instead are situated in accounts of politics, society, religion, and culture. Nineteenth-century women appear as workers, writers, or political activists and not under a single heading that would deprive them of contextual participation in their own world.

Our focus on power permits a continuous, nuanced treatment of intellectual history. Major thinkers and key intellectual traditions are consistently integrated into the story rather than treated independently as if they were *the* story of Western civilization, or else a sideshow to the main event. Any understanding of Plato and Aristotle, for instance, must begin in the Greek *polis.* Renaissance humanism cannot be understood apart from its late medieval Italian, urban context. We anchor romanticism in its urban, industrial, nationalistic, and politically restless nineteenth-century world, and we treat existentialism as one response to modern war and totalitarianism.

We thought hard about another issue that textbooks usually take for granted: What is the West? This book was conceived and written after 1989, after the end of the cold war and the fall of communist regimes in eastern Europe. Both the West's understanding of itself at any point in time and the historical understanding of the West through succeeding generations have changed in interesting and important ways, never more so than today. Thus, we continually invite our readers to think about the precise object of their study.

Those who reflect on the West at the end of the twentieth century must take account of Islamic minorities in the Slavic Balkans, Turkish workers in Germany, African workers in France, and deeply complicated relations between the northern and southern hemispheres. We look often at the lands that border the historic core of the West, and throughout the text we devote a good deal of attention to relations between the West and the rest of the world.

We ask, finally, that you note the subtitle of the book: "The Continuing Experiment." It was carefully chosen to convey our resolve to avoid a deterministic approach. For students and teachers, an appreciation of continuity and change, of unity and diversity, can foster sympathetic participation in our often bewildering world. We try to give individual actors, moments, and movements the sense of drama, possibility, and contingency that they actually possessed. We, with faultless hindsight, always know how things came out. Contemporaries often hadn't a clue. We respect them. Much of the fascination, and the reward, of studying Western civilization lies precisely in its richness, diversity, changeability, unpredictability.

Distinctive Features

To make this text as accessible as possible to students, we have constantly been aware of its place in a program of teaching. Each chapter begins with a thematic introduction that engages the reader's interest while pointing clearly and in some detail to what will follow. Chronologies help to organize and review major developments. Careful chapter summaries draw together major topics and themes and link the present chapter to the one that follows. To help students strike out on their own to new historical discoveries, we provide for each chapter an annotated reading list of scholarly classics and exciting new works.

In addition to a sound pedagogical framework, and to an engaging full-color design that clarifies and animates the illustrations and text, we have thoroughly integrated all the elements of the book. Our maps, for example, support the text in both traditional and novel ways. Teachers will find "old friends" among them but will make many new acquaintances too. Our diverse array of boxed primary sources—five or six per chapter—are referred to and tightly anchored in the text and support their surrounding discussion. Here again, classic documents are blended with fresh newcomers. Our photographs, many of which have not previously appeared in textbooks, are never merely decorative, and their captions seek to extend the discussions that they complement.

An example may help to illustrate this integration. Chapter 10 recounts the Norman Conquest of England and notes the different views held by the Normans and the Anglo-Saxons of that great event. A picture from the Bayeux Tapestry that shows Harold of Wessex swearing an oath to William of Normandy accompanies the narrative. The caption describes the tapestry and explains the significance of this scene—the Norman view. But the scene also shows William and Harold swearing their oath on relics. One of the boxed documents tells of lords and vassals swearing their oaths on relics, and a passage in the text on the powers of the clergy mentions the clerical control of relics. A particular point is made in several different ways to enhance learning and to promote discussion. Such convergences recur throughout the book.

Another important component of this book is the two-page feature, "Weighing the Evidence," presented at the end of each chapter. These features introduce students to the fascinating variety of sources that historians use and invite them to think critically about the nature of historical information and inquiry. Each opens with a description of the evidence reproduced in the feature—sources ranging from Trojan archaeological artifacts, the Ravenna mosaics, and Renaissance art to eighteenth-century gardens, the layout of the British Museum, and the poetry of World War I—and then discusses how the professional historian examines this evidence to reconstruct the past. When Samuel Butler said that God cannot change history but that historians can and often do, he meant that history itself arises from new or different acts of interpretation. With "Weighing the Evidence," students look over the shoulder of the historian to become active participants in this interpretive process. The sources examined are interesting and instructive in their own right, but the "Weighing the Evidence" features also contribute to the teaching program of the book. As always, they are carefully integrated into the text: there are references to them at appropriate points in the narrative; they themselves contain cross-references where appropriate to other sections or illustrations; and they support on-going discussions.

This book is also flexible in format as well as substantive organization. Because schools use different academic calendars, organize Western civilization courses according to different chronologies, and require or recommend different parts of the course, we issue this book in three formats. There is a one-volume hardcover version containing all thirty-two chapters. There is also a two-volume paperback edition: Volume I contains Chapters 1 to 18 (to 1715), and Volume II contains Chapters 17–32 (from 1560). Finally, there is a three-volume paperback version: Volume A has Chapters 1 to 14 (to 1500), Volume B has Chapters 12–21 (1300–1815), and Volume C has Chapters 21–32 (since 1789).

Volume II opens with a comprehensive introduction that situates the student reader in the late sixteenth century and surveys the course of Western civilization from ancient times to the early centuries of the modern era. This introduction is designed particularly for students who did not take the first semester of the course, or who are new to this book. It should prove beneficial in clarifying terminology and providing points of reference that teachers would like students to know.

At the end of each volume is a fold-out comparative timeline of Western civilization, from prehistory to the present. Bound into the book, this full-color, illustrated timeline is designed to help students review major developments and place them in historical context.

Ancillaries

We have assembled with care an array of text ancillaries to aid students in learning and instructors in teaching. These supplements, including a *Study Guide*, a *Computerized Study Guide, Test Items, Computerized Test Items*, an *Instructor's Resource Manual, Map Transparencies*, a *Videodisc*, and a *Videodisc Guide*, are tied closely to the text and to one another, to provide a tightly integrated program of teaching and learning.

The *Study Guide* and *Test Items* have been written by the same author team—Professors John Moretta and Susan Hult of Houston Community College—to ensure a unified approach to studying and testing. The *Study Guide* contains learning objectives, chapter summaries, multiple-choice questions, key-term identifications, short-answer and essay questions, and map exercises. Correct responses to the questions and answer guidelines for the writing assignments appear at the end of each chapter. The *Study Guide* is published in two volumes, to correspond to Volumes I and II of the text: Volume I contains Chapters 1–18 and Volume II contains Chapters 17–32. The *Study Guide* is also available in a computerized version for use with IBM® PC or compatible computers.* This *Computerized Study Guide* contains text page references for all questions and rejoinders to each multiple-choice question that explain why the student's response is or is not correct.

Each chapter of the *Test Items* offers 40 to 50 multiple-choice questions rated by difficulty and type of skill (factual or conceptual), 20 to 30 key-term identifications, 10 to 15 short-answer and essay questions with answer guidelines, and 1 or 2 map exercises. About one-half of the questions in the *Study Guide* appear in revised form in the *Test Items,* so that teachers may test directly on material studied; these test questions duplicate the substance but never the wording or order of study questions, and they are identified to allow instructors to locate them easily. We also offer a computerized version of the *Test Items,* to enable teachers to alter, replace, or add questions. Each item in the computerized test item file is numbered according to the printed test item file to ease the creation of customized tests. The computerized test item file is available for use with both IBM® PC and compatibles and Macintosh computers.

The *Instructor's Resource Manual,* prepared by Dr. Kevin Kenyon, provides useful teaching strategies and tips for getting the most out of the text. Each chapter contains 5 to 10 teaching objec-

*IBM is the registered trademark of International Business Machines Corporation.

tives based on the learning objectives in the *Study Guide;* a chapter outline; about 5 lecture suggestions; 5 to 8 discussion questions with follow-up inquiries; about 5 collaborative class activities; 10 to 15 writing assignments, including take-home exams, in-class assignments, and term papers; about 10 recommended films and videos, with information about content, length, and distribution; and 5 to 10 suggestions for additional reading, including novels, memoirs, and plays. Many of the exercises and activities draw on or extend the primary sources and Weighing-the-Evidence features located in the text.

In addition, there is a set of 102 full-color *Map Transparencies,* all drawn from the maps in the text, available on adoption.

To add an exciting multimedia component to lectures and learning laboratories, we have created *The History of Western Civilization Videodisc/Videotape/Slide* program. The program allows the instructor to create customized multimedia classroom presentations using this rich collection of visual images. The program is divided into five chronological periods (ancient, medieval, early modern, modern, and Twentieth Century) and contains over 150 still images, 30 animated maps, and motion footage accompanied by period music. A companion *Videodisc/Videotape* instructor's guide provides descriptions, printed bar codes, bar code stickers to create customized lectures, and numeric codes. The program is available at no cost to adopters of the book. Please contact your local Houghton Mifflin representative for more information about this innovative and exciting multimedia program.

Acknowledgments

From the first draft to the last, the authors have benefited from repeated critical readings by many colleagues. We have tried very hard to profit from the vast fund of experience and knowledge that has been placed generously at our disposal. Our thanks to the following instructors:

William S. Arnett
West Virginia University

Jack Balcer
The Ohio State University

Maryann Brink
The College of William and Mary

Steven Fanning
University of Illinois at Chicago

Richard Golden
Clemson University

Johnpeter Grill
Mississippi State University

Gerald E. Kadish
Binghamton University—State University of New York

W. Laird Kleine-Ahlbrandt
Purdue University

Lawrence Langer
University of Connecticut, Storrs

Gregory McMahon
University of New Hampshire

Diane Margolf
University of Charleston

Carol Menning
The University of Toldeo

Terence Murphy
American University

Kathryn Norberg
University of California, Los Angeles

J. Dean O'Donnell
Virginia Polytechnic Institute and State University

William Olejniczak
University of Charleston

Anne T. Quartararo
United States Naval Academy

Roger Ray
The University of Toledo

Kenneth C. Schellhase
Northern Michigan University

Ellen J. Skinner
Pace University

John F. Sweets
University of Kansas

Valerie Warrior
Boston University

Each of us has also benefited from the close readings and valuable criticisms of our co-authors, although we all assume responsibility for our own chapters. Barry Strauss has written Chapters 1–6; Thomas Noble, Chapters 7–11; Duane Osheim, Chapters 12–16; Kristen Neuschel, Chapters 17–21; William Cohen, Chapters 22–26; and David Roberts, Chapters 27–32.

Many colleagues, friends, and family members have helped us develop this work as well. Thomas Noble wishes to thank Linda L. Noble for her patience and kindness over the years devoted to this project. He is also grateful to Elizabeth Meyer, Robert Wilken, and Ian Wood for sharing their knowledge of Late Antiquity and to Wendy Davies for her valuable insights into Celtic history.

Barry Strauss thanks his colleagues at Cornell, who offered advice and encouragement and responded to scholarly questions. In particular, he thanks John Coleman, Judith Ginsburg, Judith Holliday, Peter Kuniholm, Mary Beth Norton, David Owne, Richard Polenberg, Andrew Ramage, Gary Rendsburg, James Weinstein, Jane Whitehead, L. Pearce Williams, and Thomas Vollman. Barry Strauss also thanks his mentor, Donald Kagan, and his family, who offered its support throughout the project. Without the help of Marcia, wife and muse, his chapters would never have seen the light of day.

Duane Osheim wishes to thank his family for accepting the frequent intrusion of this project into the important business of outings, soccer, and holidays. He is also grateful to colleagues at the University of Virginia, whose advice and conversation helped to clarify the many connections between Western civilization and the wider world.

Kristen Neuschel thanks her colleagues at Duke University for sharing their expertise. She is especially grateful to Sy Mauskopf, Bill Reddy, John Richards, Tom Robisheaux, Alex Roland, John J. TePaske, Julius Scott, and Peter Wood. She also thanks her husband and fellow historian, Alan Williams, for his wisdom about Western civilization and his support throughout the project, and her children, Jesse, who began the project, and Rachel, who ended it, for their patience and their joy.

Bill Cohen thanks his wife, Christine Matheu, for her support in this and many other endeavors and his new daughter, Laurel Katherine, whose serene personality allowed him to complete the manuscript. He also extends sincere appreciation to Lance Farrar for his careful reading and thoughtful questions and to George Alter, James Diehl, and David Pace, friends and colleagues in modern European history at Indiana University.

David Roberts wishes to thank Bonnie Cary for her able assistance and J. T. LaSaine, John Morrow, Ronald Rader, William Stueck, and Kirk Willis, colleagues at the University of Georgia, for sharing their expertise in response to questions. He also thanks Beth Roberts for, as always, her support, her interest, and her exceedingly critical eye, and Ellen, Trina, and Anthony, for their college-age perspective and advice.

All the authors wish to thank the thousands of students who helped us to learn and to teach Western civilization. Their questions and concerns have shaped much of this work.

We also wish to acknowledge and thank the editors who did so much to bring this book into being. Elizabeth Welch, our Basic Book Editor, sifted our thoughts, sharpened our focus, and smoothed our prose. Christina Horn, our Project Editor, displayed boundless patience and professionalism as she assembled this book from all its constituent parts. To Jean Woy, Editor-in-Chief for Social Sciences, we are grateful for confidence in this project, and in us. To Sean Wakely, Sponsoring Editor for History, we owe what every passenger owes to the pilot: thanks for a safe trip.

About the Authors

Thomas F. X. Noble

After receiving his Ph.D. from Michigan State University, Thomas Noble has taught at Albion College, Michigan State University, Texas Tech University, and since 1980 at the University of Virginia. He is the author of *The Republic of St. Peter: The Birth of the Papal State, 680–825* and *Religion, Culture and Society in the Early Middle Ages.* Noble's articles and reviews have appeared in the *American Historical Review, Byzantinische Zeitschrift, Catholic Historical Review, Church History, Revue bénédictine, Revue d'histoire ecclésiastique, Speculum,* and *Studi medievali.* He has also contributed chapters to several books and articles to three encyclopedias. Noble has been awarded fellowships by the National Endowment for the Humanities (twice) and by the American Philosophical Society.

Barry S. Strauss

An associate professor of history at Cornell University, Barry S. Strauss holds a Ph.D. from Yale in history. In 1991 he received the Clark Award for excellence in teaching from Cornell. He has been awarded fellowships by the National Endowment for the Humanities, the American School of Classical Studies in Athens, the Killam Foundation of Canada, and Clare Hall, Cambridge. His many publications include *Athens after the Peloponnesian War: Class, Faction and Policy, 403–386 B.C.; Fathers and Sons in Athens; Ideology and Society in the Era of the Peloponnesin War; The Anatomy of Error: Ancient Military Disasters and Their Lessons for Modern Strategists* (with Josiah Ober); and *Hegemonic Rivalry from Thucydides to the Nuclear Age* (co-edited with R. Ned Lebow).

Duane J. Osheim

A Fellow of the American Academy in Rome with a Ph.D. in History from the University of California, Davis, Duane Osheim is a professor of history at the University of Virginia. A specialist in late Medieval and Renaissance social and institutional history, he is author of *A Tuscan Monastery and Its Social World* and *An Italian Lordship: The Bishopric of Lucca in the Late Middle Ages,* as well as numerous studies of religious values and rural life in late Medieval Italy.

Kristen B. Neuschel

Associate professor of history at Duke University, Kristen B. Neuschel received the Ph.D. from Brown University. She is the author of *Word of Honor: Interpreting Noble Culture in Sixteenth-Century France* and articles on French social history and European women's history. In 1988 she received the Alumni Distinguished Undergraduate Teaching Award, which is awarded annually on the basis of student nominations for excellence in teaching at Duke.

William B. Cohen

After receiving his Ph.D. at Stanford University, William Cohen has taught at Northwestern University and Indiana University, where he is now professor of history. Among his many publications are *Rulers of Empire, The French Encounter with Africans, European Empire Building,* and *Robert Delavignette and the French Empire.* His current research focuses on French urbanization.

David D. Roberts

After taking his Ph.D. in modern European history at the University of California, Berkeley, David Roberts taught at the Universities of Virginia and Rochester before becoming professor of history at the University of Georgia in 1988. At Rochester he chaired the Humanities Department of the Eastman School of Music. A recipient of Woodrow Wilson and Rockefeller Foundation fellowships, he is the author of *The Syndicalist Tradition and Italian Fascism* and *Benedetto Croce and the Uses of Historicism,* as well as numerous articles and reviews.

Western Civilization

CHAPTER I

The Ancestors of the West

More than four thousand years ago in Sumer, in what is today Iraq, people had already begun to wonder about the origins of civilization. How did people learn to cultivate "the jewel and ornament of the plain," as a Sumerian poem asks, "the holy furrows . . . [where] grain grows?" How did they learn to live in a "well-supplied" city, "awesome in its appearance," its temples "rich with abundance," its laws "perfected"?[1] Surely, they answered, only the gods could have created civilization.

Today, explanations of the origins of civilization are more diverse and complex. Nevertheless, we can admire people's early investigations of their past, for it is still a difficult subject—and a tantalizing one. There is still much that we do not know, but what we do know is often dramatic and exciting. We know, for instance, that the first modern humans evolved from humanlike ancestors, though scholars debate whether the date was closer to 35,000 or 200,000 years ago. This chapter begins with those first humans and ends with the collapse of the great civilizations of Egypt and western Asia around 1200 B.C. In between came the most momentous inventions in human history: representational art and religion, technological innovation and specialization, settled life and agriculture, and the first villages, from which grew the first cities and kingdoms.

The period studied in this chapter includes both prehistory—that is, time before the invention of writing—and history. Writing appeared last among the complex of characteristics that marks the emergence of civilization: that is, a complex and hierarchical society with formal political and religious institutions, monumental architecture, and significant technological innovation.

Egyptian wall painting depicting Amenhotep III, who holds symbols of pharaonic power.

So characterized, civilization emerged shortly before 3000 B.C. in two great river valleys: the valley of the Nile in Egypt and the valley of the Tigris and Euphrates in what is today Iraq. Two other civilizations emerged before 2000 B.C.*: one in what is today Pakistan and northwest India, the other in northern China. In Europe, the main focus of this book, civilization did not gain a firm foothold until around 2000 B.C., first on the Aegean island of Crete and then on the Greek mainland.

Impressive in their own right, Mesopotamia and Egypt around 3100–1200 B.C. influenced a wide range of early civilizations in the eastern Mediterranean region. Among them are the Hittites and the inhabitants of the Syro-Palestinian city-states, who are studied in this chapter, and the Hebrews and the Greeks, who are studied in Chapter 2.

Origins

The earth is old; modern human beings are young; and civilization is a very recent innovation. In recent years physical anthropologists, archaeologists, geneticists, and biochemists have made great strides in explaining human origins. The subject, nonetheless, is one in which great disagreement still reigns. Each decade seems to bring an exciting new discovery that calls for the reassessment of previous theories.

We can be more certain about the series of processes, beginning around 10,000 B.C., that led to the emergence of civilization by 3000 B.C. Over a period of several thousand years, humans abandoned a mobile existence for a sedentary one. They learned to domesticate animals and cultivate plants. They replaced a hunter-gatherer economy with an agricultural economy. They developed the first towns, from which, over several millennia, slowly emerged complex and centralized social structure.

*We follow the traditional practice in the West of expressing historical dates in relation to the birth of Jesus Christ (actually, to one calculation of his birthdate, because in fact Jesus was not born in 1 A.D.; see page 220). Dates before his birth are labeled B.C. (which stands for *Before Christ*) and dates after his birth are labeled A.D. (*Anno Domini*, Latin for "in the year of the Lord"). A widely used alternate refers to these dates as B.C.E. (Before the common era) and C.E. (Common era).

The First Human Beings

The human family, the hominids, includes not only anatomically modern people but many ancient and extinct species. Some are our evolutionary ancestors; others are branches from a common genealogical tree. Modern human beings—species *Homo sapiens*, subspecies *sapiens* (Latin for "wise, wise human being")—appeared at the earliest about 200,000 years ago and perhaps as recently as 35,000 years ago. There is a range of scholarly opinion about the date, but scholars do agree that humanlike beings are much older.

The earliest ancestors of modern people appeared in the tropics and subtropics of Africa at least 5 million years ago. By about 1.6 million years ago they had evolved into a humanlike creature now known as *Homo erectus* ("upright person"), which migrated out of Africa into Europe and Asia. (Those three continents are sometimes collectively called the "Old World" to distinguish them from the "New World" of the Americas and Australia.) The next important stage in human evolution is the gradual emergence, from separate Homo erectus populations in different places, of various archaic forms of Homo sapiens.

The best known of such archaic people are the Neanderthals. Named for the valley of the Neander River in modern Germany, where their remains were first found in 1856, Neanderthal people lived in Europe and western Asia between about 200,000 and 35,000 years ago. Strong and stocky, with beetle-browed skulls, the Neanderthals were far from being the brutes they are usually imagined. They used stone tools and were among the first people to bury their dead.

Neanderthals, however, were not modern humans. Physically, modern humans have distinctive skulls, with high foreheads and tucked-in faces. Culturally, modern humans would initiate a revolution in hominid behavior that was innovative, inventive, and adventurous. They made the first tools in malleable materials such as bone, antler, and ivory, and not merely in stone; and they produced the first representational art.

These achievements began about 40,000 years ago, the date that some scholars assign, therefore, to the emergence of modern humans. Others, however, separate the biological and cultural changes and have modern people emerging much earlier, about 200,000 years ago.

From the Cave to the Town

The signposts of modern human culture begin to pile up in the late Palaeolithic era (literally, the "Old Stone" age), the period down to about 10,000 B.C., in which stone was the primary medium from which hominids made tools. Art, religion, the desire to control human fertility, technological advance, craft specialization, and warfare all became part of the human scene. Then, after about 10,000 B.C., we see the first evidence that people had learned to domesticate animals and to cultivate plants. They began to live in villages, which soon became walled towns.

Before the emergence of villages, people sometimes built huts, but they frequently lived in caves or rock shelters—hence our notion of the "caveman." Caves offered shelter, could be heated, and made a naturally good vantage point for observing prey. In the late Palaeolithic era, about 30,000 years ago, caves were the site of the earliest representational art. The most spectacular Palaeolithic paintings discovered so far, in 1940, are at Lascaux cave, in southwestern France. European cave paintings of such animals as the bison, horse, reindeer, and woolly mammoth (a huge extinct member of the elephant family with hairy skin and long, upward-curving tusks) attest to early human artistic skill; the presence of abstract shapes attests to an interest in symbols. The cave paintings are perhaps illustrations of myths or attempts to control the environment through magic—that is, to manipulate it supernaturally.

Other early representational art includes skillful engravings on stone of animals, birds, and stylized human females, as well as female figurines carved from ivory or bone. Usually represented with exaggerated breasts or buttocks, the carvings are called Venus figurines, after Venus, the Greco-Roman goddess of love. They might represent an attempt to control fertility through magic.

Venus with a Horn This 18-inch-tall female was carved on a large fallen rock in a rock shelter in France between 22,000 and 30,000 years ago. She holds what may be an incised bison horn. Along with similar figurines, the image may be a symbol of fertility, and represents the skill of late Paleolithic artists. *(Jean Vertut)*

Late Palaeolithic craftsmanship is as impressive as the art. The presence of bone needles and awls (pointed tools for punching holes) implies sewing and therefore clothing. There were stone and bone spear points. So-called spear-throwers (18-inch shafts) allowed a person to throw a spear, hooked onto the end, with great velocity. In Africa, microliths (tiny stone tools) were mounted on handles or shafts to make composite tools.

There is no hard evidence about the way late Palaeolithic society was organized or governed, but organization there was. The existence of late Palaeolithic artists and skilled craftspeople demonstrates specialization of skills and a division of labor. Later myths argue that women were the rulers of prehistoric society; some historians see evidence of matriarchy (literally, "rule by the mother") in the Venus figurines. We do not know what prehistoric families were like—whether nuclear or extended, patriarchal ("ruled by the father"), matriarchal, or egalitarian—but, if we understand the Venus figurines rightly, organizing reproduction, that most basic of family issues, clearly mattered to early people.

Early people were no strangers to warfare. Several hundred thousand years ago, Homo sapiens had learned to make spears and clubs out of wood. Around 10,000 B.C. people developed revolutionary new weapons: the bow and arrows, the sling, the dagger, and the mace (a heavy war club). Spanish cave paintings show that these weapons were used not merely against animals but also against other humans. They also demonstrate the existence of organized troops in columns or lines. One painting shows several followers behind a leader wearing some kind of headdress. A cemetery along the Nile River in the Sudan dating from 12,000 to 4500 B.C. contains numerous human skeletons killed by arrowheads, some with multiple wounds.

Innovations in violence were dwarfed by even greater changes in the economy. About fifteen thousand years ago, humans began to specialize in the plants they collected and the animals they hunted. The logical next step was to learn how to control the environment in order to domesticate plants and animals. People seem to have begun by domesticating dogs, which were useful in hunting. Then they learned to keep sheep, goats, and cattle. Agriculture probably required an even greater imaginative and technological leap. Humans learned first how to grow wheat and barley, then legumes (beans).

Scholars often speak of the domestication of animals and plants as the "Neolithic (literally, "New Stone") Revolution." In truth, the process was evolutionary. It began sometime after 10,000 B.C. in western Asia, in the period of warmer climate following the last Ice Age. By 5000 B.C. agriculturalists and pastoralists were found throughout in the Old World. In Europe, for example, the earliest agricultural settlement, found in Greece, dates to about 6500 B.C. The evidence suggests that domestication was mastered not once but several times, in independent centers throughout the world, from which it spread: a gradual process yet, when we consider that hominids had survived as hunters and gatherers for several million years, a revolution as well.

Perhaps the earliest area of domestication is a zone of land stretching in a crescent shape from what is today southern Jordan in the west around into what is today southern Iran in the east. A region of dependable annual rainfall, scholars call this area the "Fertile Crescent" (Map 1.1). The Neolithic Revolution may have begun after 10,000 B.C. in the hills and valleys in the northern and eastern parts of the crescent (in the Taurus Mountains of Anatolia and the Zagros Mountains of Iran). With domestication came small agricultural settlements, or villages, which were increasingly common after 7000 B.C.

Scholars once thought of Neolithic villages as simple places devoted to subsistence agriculture, with no craft specialization, and as egalitarian societies lacking social hierarchies. In recent years, new evidence and a rethinking of older information have shifted the picture considerably. The Neolithic village site of Çayönü Tepesi in eastern Anatolia, for example, provides evidence of metalworking (of copper) and of specialization of labor (in bead making) from approximately 7000 to 6000 B.C. Other contemporaneous village sites provide evidence of experiments in ironworking and craft specialization in butchering, flintmaking, tanning animal hides, and potterymaking. There was long-distance trade between villages in pottery and in obsidian (a sharp volcanic glass used in tools). Artwork shows men wearing loincloths and headdresses, women wearing pants and halter tops, and both sexes wearing jewelry.

Consider the case of Jericho, in Palestine near the Dead Sea, perhaps the oldest town on earth. A small village around 9000 B.C., by about 7000 Jericho had become a town surrounded by massive walls 10 feet thick and 13 or more feet high. The walls, about 765 yards long, probably enclosed an area of about 10 acres. The most prominent feature of the walls was a great tower 33 feet in diameter and 28 feet high with an interior stairway. Inside the walls was a densely packed population of about 2000 people. Some scholars think Jericho's walls were used for defense; others say their purpose was flood control.

An even larger Neolithic town is Çatal Hüyük in south central Anatolia. Its population

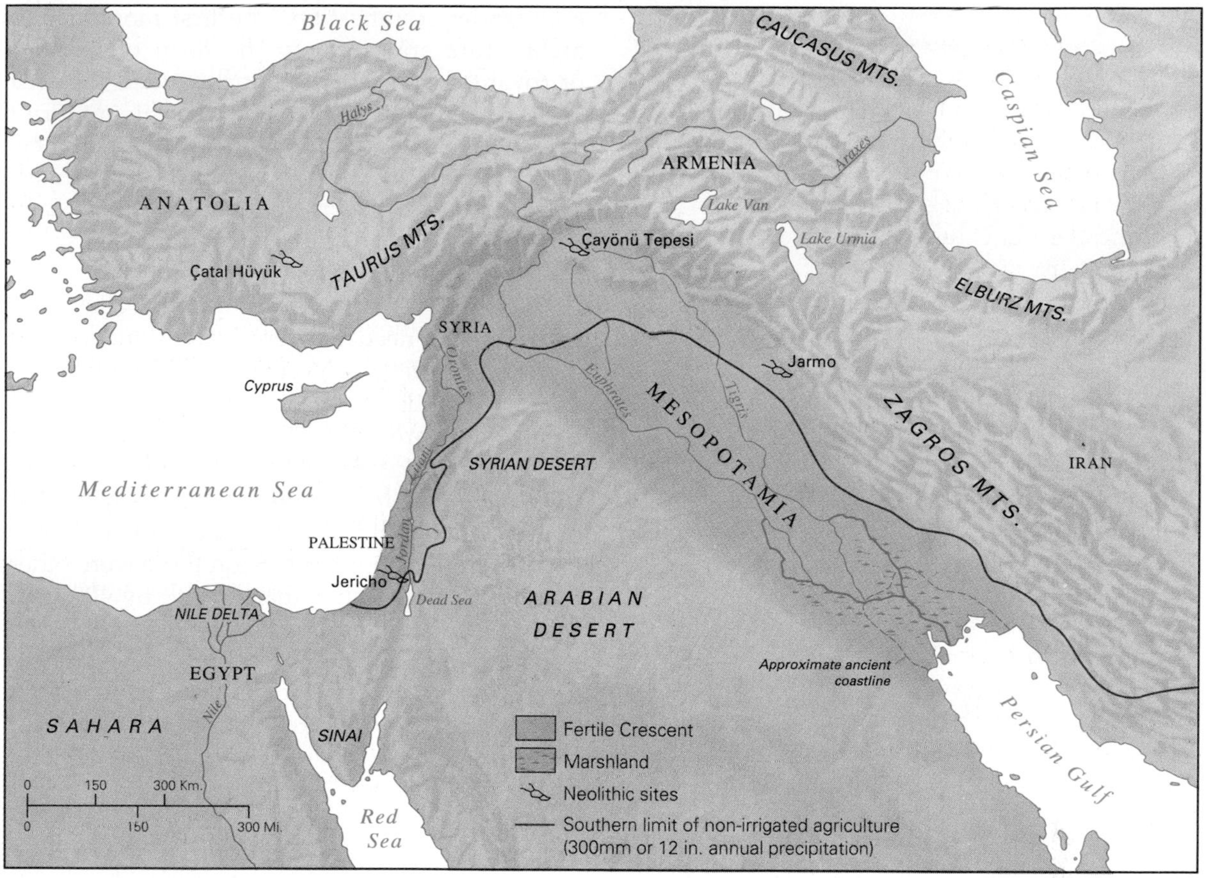

Map 1.1 The Fertile Crescent This map illustrates the geography and annual precipitation of an arc of land in western Asia where the so-called Neolithic Revolution began. Here are found the first known examples of plant and animal domestication and the earliest villages.

of six thousand people in 6000 B.C. made it the largest settlement of the era by far. It was probably a trading center and perhaps a religious shrine. Carbonization from fire has preserved a wealth of artifacts attesting to Çatal Hüyük's sophistication, including fabrics, obsidian mirrors, wooden vessels, and sticks that were used to apply eye makeup.

The Emergence of Civilization

"Civilization" is not easy to define. The Neolithic towns after 7000 B.C. made considerable achievements. A Mesopotamian city-state of around 3000 B.C., however, represents a new phenomenon: a complex society, characterized by considerable social, economic, and class hierarchy. It included formal political and religious institutions. Its monumental architecture created a large, urban space, and technological innovation reshaped its agricultural hinterland. It had developed writing for the purpose of record keeping. There are a number of reasons that the city-states of Mesopotamia are able to be called the first civilization.

Civilization arose in southern Iraq, in the valley between the Tigris and Euphrates rivers, in a region that the Greeks called "Mesopotamia" (literally, "between the rivers"). At around the same time or shortly afterward, civilization also began in the valley of the Nile River in Egypt. Both of these valleys contain alluvial land—that is, a relatively flat tract where fertile soil is deposited by a river.

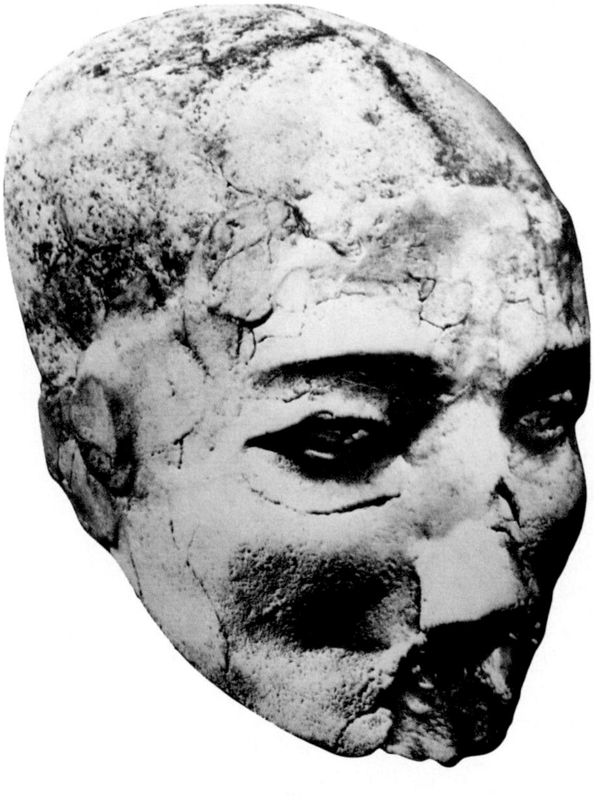

Neolithic Plastered Skull People in western Asia between about 7000 and 6000 B.C. frequently buried bodies beneath the floor of the house, removing the skull. The skulls were exhibited, perhaps to show continuity with ancestors. In this fine, reconstructed example from Jericho, the skull has been filled with clay, its external features molded on with plaster. *(Jericho Excavation Fund, University of London Institute of Archaeology)*

In Mesopotamia, most of the soil was either so dry or so marshy that agriculture would not have been possible without irrigation and flood control—that is, the use of channels, dikes, or dams to control floodwaters and improve the fertility of the land. One Mesopotamian text describes a farmer as "the man of dike, ditch, and plow." Egypt's soil was more fertile, and irrigation, therefore, played a smaller role.

Cities emerged through a slow, incremental process of action and reaction. We do not know the precise order of events, but we do know that agricultural productivity increased greatly, that population grew, that distinct economic classes arose with a high degree of labor specialization and gender stratification. The first monumental architecture appeared, in the form of temples or royal tombs. Government expanded the area of its control. In Egypt one central authority emerged in control of the Nile River Valley. Mesopotamia, in contrast, consisted of numerous city-states—that is, independent units each containing a rural countryside with villages controlled by a capital city.

The growing complexity of river-valley society created a need for cooperation and central direction. Society responded. In Mesopotamia, this response is visible in the ruins of the first temple, built around 5000 B.C. at Eridu, an urban site of about 4 acres. Temple-building demonstrates devotion to a common religious symbol. It is also evidence of the power of central authority to command a labor force. Soon there were other temples at bigger sites than Eridu. By 4000 B.C. temples built on raised platforms had become elaborate, monumental works of architecture—for example, at Uruk (the biblical Erech), which was to be one of the great early Mesopotamian cities. Temple ruins yield up gold, silver, and semiprecious stones.

The fourth millennium B.C. witnessed a series of major technological breakthroughs, including the wheel and the plow. In Mesopotamia, by the period that scholars have named the "Early Dynastic Period" (2800–2350 B.C.), wheeled vehicles were used to transport goods in commerce and to transport warriors to battle. In Egypt, wheeled vehicles were not introduced until around 1650 B.C.

The introduction of the plow made it easier to till the soil and thus to produce food. In the fourth millennium B.C. orchards—of dates, figs, or olives—were also introduced for the first time. Society was growing wealthier and more complex. Pressure grew ever greater on the primitive system of recordkeeping. The result, around 3500 to 3100 B.C., was the invention of writing. Writing was invented for a mixed group of languages, of which the most important was Sumerian. The Sumerians were the first people to leave a written record.

Writing was the child of recordkeeping, so a plausible theory argues. As the complexity of the Mesopotamian economy increased, people needed to take inventories and record transactions. From around 8000 to 3500 B.C. they did so by means of tiny clay or stone tokens that repre-

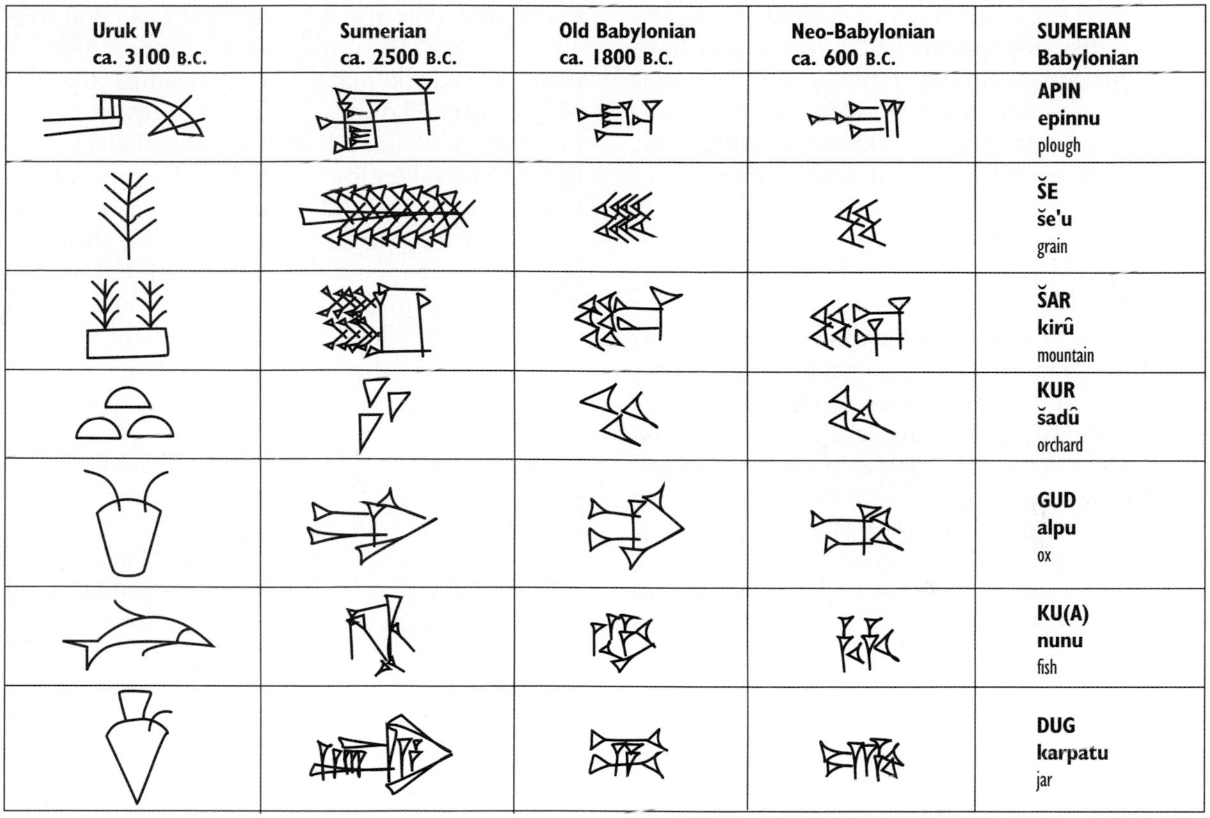
Uruk IV
ca. 3100 B.C.
Sumerian
ca. 2500 B.C.
Old Babylonian
ca. 1800 B.C.
Neo-Babylonian
ca. 600 B.C.
SUMERIAN
Babylonian
APIN
epinnu
plough
ŠE
še'u
grain
ŠAR
kirû
mountain
KUR
šadû
orchard
GUD
alpu
ox
KU(A)
nunu
fish
DUG
karpatu
jar

Figure 1.1 Early Writing The pictographs of early writing evolved into a system of phonetic syllables and abstract symbols. Simplified and standardized, this writing was cuneiform or "wedge-shaped." It was adapted from Sumerian to Babylonian and other languages throughout western Asia. (*Source:* From the Introduction to *Babylon*, by Joan Oates. Copyright © 1979. Used by permission of Thames and Hudson Ltd.)

sented the objects being counted or traded. By 3500 B.C., with 250 different types of tokens, the system had grown unwieldy and people began to use signs to indicate the number of tokens in a given lot. It was a short step to dispensing with the tokens and placing the signs on a clay tablet: the first writing. New words were soon added through pictographs (pictures that stand for particular objects). In time the pictographs evolved into ideograms—that is, abstract symbols that are no longer recognizable as specific objects and thus can be used to denote ideas as well as things.

In the centuries following its introduction, writing became standardized. Sumerian was written on clay tablets with a reed stylus that had a triangular point. Scholars call the signs *cuneiform* from the Latin for "wedge-shaped," a good description of what early writing looks like. In its first centuries, cuneiform was used almost entirely for economic records or commercial transactions; then it was adapted to make brief records of offerings to the gods. By 2350 B.C. cuneiform had evolved into a mixed system of about six hundred signs, most of them phonetic (syllabic), with relatively few ideograms. Writing became flexible enough to record the spoken language. Cuneiform then became an instrument of infinite potential, one that could be used for poetry as easily as for bookkeeping.

An adaptable system, cuneiform became the standard script of various languages of western Asia for several thousand years (Figure 1.1). Compared to a modern alphabet, cuneiform is clumsy, but alphabets were not invented before about 1400 B.C., and they took nearly a thousand years to displace cuneiform. Clumsy it may have been, but cuneiform was writing, and writing is both a catalyst for change and the historian's best friend. Mesopotamia after 3000 B.C. was dynamic, sophisticated, and, best of all, intelligible to us.

Mesopotamia

The people of Mesopotamia after 3000 B.C. flourished and experimented: in government, in cooperation and conflict among different ethnic groups, in law, and in the working out of class and gender relations. Their quest for divine justice laid the foundations on which the Hebrews later built. Their engineering skill, mathematics, and astronomy set ancient science on a grand trajectory. A keen and often bitter awareness of human limitations and vanity, moreover, gives Mesopotamian civilization an appealing, sympathetic quality.

Archaeologists sometimes refer to the third and second millennia in the eastern Mediterranean and western Asia as the "Bronze Age." In this period people mastered the technology of making bronze, an alloy of copper and tin. As a result, bronze frequently replaced stone as a primary material for everyday, practical use. In the first millennium, another new technology was mastered, and iron replaced bronze.

The City-States of Sumer

The Sumerians live. Their independence ended four thousand years ago; their culture and identity were absorbed by foreigners. Yet whenever someone today counts the minutes, whenever a group of people engage in a political debate, whenever someone quotes the law, the Sumerians live, for these are all legacies of that first literate society.

It is ironic that the first cities emerged in southern Mesopotamia, because farming villages came late to this region, about 5300 B.C. The earliest farmers preferred higher elevations, with dependable rainfall, to the hot and dry southern Mesopotamian lowlands. Why they eventually left the highlands for Mesopotamia is unclear. The cause may have been population pressure, competition for good land, or soil exhaustion. Eventually, with the development of a good irrigation system, the immigrants and their descendants turned the marshes and swamps, the dry plains and sand dunes of southern Mesopotamia, into rich farming soil. Nature, nonetheless, was never to be taken for granted in this land of extreme heat, scorching winds, and flash floods. Nor could the people of Mesopotamia afford to ignore the outside world. They depended on foreign trade for minerals and timber while, at the same time, they became uneasily aware that the neighboring peoples of the mountains and deserts welcomed the opportunity to conquer their cities.

The farming settlements of southern Mesopotamia developed into cities. Uruk, the largest, is estimated to have had a population of about ten thousand around 3100 B.C.; by 2700 B.C. that population had grown to about fifty thousand. Present in southern Mesopotamia by 3200 B.C. and perhaps earlier, the Sumerians entered their great age during the Early Dynastic Period (2800–2350 B.C.), when their city-states enjoyed a proud independence. The Sumerians' way of living, their economy, politics, art and architecture, language, thought, and literature—in short, Sumerian culture—dominated southern Mesopotamia for most of the third millennium B.C. Conscious of their unique achievement, they called Mesopotamia simply "the land" (Map 1.2).

It was a land where geography was an obstacle to unification and where the scarcity of fresh water led to quarrels among cities over water rights. Separated from each other by desert and swampland, the twelve Sumerian cities were jealous and particularistic, even though they had much in common: language, literature, arts and sciences, and even religion (no small matter in a society that, as we shall see, was deeply religious). These cities, nonetheless, were rivals—sometimes friendly, often at war—and were always stubbornly independent.

Each city had its own small urbanized area and a larger agricultural hinterland irrigated by canals. Cities traded with each other and with the outside world. They exported grain, dates, and textiles and other worked products in exchange for raw materials, including copper from Oman or Sinai, gold from Armenia or perhaps Nubia (modern Sudan), timber from the mountains east of the Persian Gulf, and carnelian (a reddish mineral used in jewelry) from India. The primary political units of southern Mesopotamia for most of the third millennium B.C., Sumerian city-states were a laboratory of civilization.

How were the Sumerian city-states governed? A Sumerian might respond that they were governed by the gods, for the Sumerians believed that the gods had created everything and owned everything on earth. As historians, we can trace the evolution among the Sumerians of a system in which the temples and the nobility shared power in each city and then a system of monarchy.

In the early Sumerian cities the temple was the focus of loyalty and wielded great economic and political clout. Residents worshiped the city's patron deity at a temple in the center of town. Often the highest building, this temple symbolized the city. Other deities were worshiped in other temples in the city. The temple controlled large landed estates, so the priests, scribes, and other temple officials were a major economic authority. The temple never had a monopoly on power, however, because individual wealthy families formed a separate landed elite.

Ordinary people had a subordinate position. Although usually free, they frequently had to rent land from temple or noble. Some peasants were organized in work bands under foremen. There were also slaves in Sumer, originally captives from the mountains. Slaves formed a small group, much outnumbered by free peasants. Sumerian women worked alongside men in most professions. Priestesses were usually noblewomen from wealthy families.

However influential the temple clergy, individual owners of private property had a considerable amount of political say. What scholars have pieced together from incomplete sources is the existence in each city of a council of elders and an assembly of the people. The council probably was involved in day-to-day governance; the assembly probably was called less frequently. Assemblies appointed and removed kings, approved wars—even over the objection of the council—and served as courts. Membership in the council of elders was probably restricted to the landed elite. The assembly was probably a more open institution. Just how open, we do not know; nor do we know how much freedom of speech existed in the assembly. Thus, it is necessary to be cautious about the claim made by some

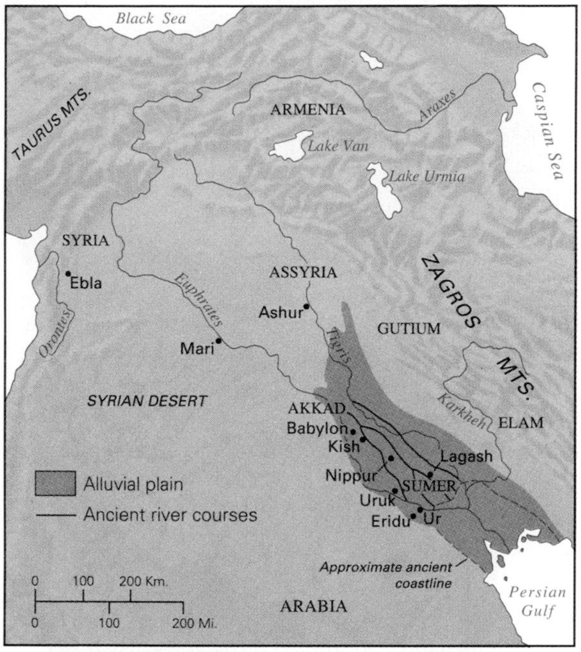

Map 1.2 Mesopotamia In the southern part of the "Land Between the Rivers," as the Greeks called the region between the Tigris and the Euphrates, the world's first urban civilization took root by 3000 B.C.

scholars that the Sumerians enjoyed "primitive democracy." It is nonetheless striking that at the dawn of urban history, city dwellers demanded some say in their government, rather than surrendering all power to priests or king.

By the middle of the third millennium B.C. that freedom had been restricted by the establishment in each city-state of government by a "big man" (*lugal*) or "governor" (*ensi*)—that is, a king or, occasionally, a queen. A military emergency probably led to centralized rule under a monarch. Intercity warfare was chronic, often arising from quarrels over water rights.

The king was first and foremost a warrior. He claimed to be the representative on earth of the gods, a position that gave him general responsibility for his subjects' welfare. Kings accordingly sponsored irrigation works, raised fortification walls, restored temples, and built splendid palaces.

According to a plausible tradition, the earliest Sumerian kings, dating from the period 2700 to 2600 B.C., are Enmebaragesi of the city of Kish, his son and successor Agga, and Gilgamesh of

Akkadian Bronze This stern-faced, life-size cast-bronze head, with its stylized and elaborately ringleted beard and its carefully arranged hair, shows Mesopotamian craftsmanship at its finest. Sometimes said to be Sargon (r. 2371–2316 B.C.) or Naram-sin (r. ca. 2250–2220 B.C.), it was deliberately mutilated in ancient times. *(Claus Hansmann, München)*

Uruk, a hero of epic poetry whom many scholars consider a genuine historical personage. In the cities of Ur and Lagash the king's wife was often a power in her own right. Kish was ruled by Ku-baba (r. ca. 2450 B.C.), the first reigning queen of recorded history.

Sumerian kings also recognized a responsibility for promoting justice. History's earliest known reformer of law and society is Uru-inim-gina, king of Lagash around 2400 B.C. Surviving documents describe Lagash as a society in which wealthy landowners encroached on the temples and oppressed the poor, and royal administrators mistreated ordinary people. The king's aims seem to have been both to correct abuses and to weaken independent sources of power threatening royal authority. Uru-inim-gina attempted to control the bureaucracy, protect the property of humble people, and guard the temples. He also put into effect the first known attempt to control wages and prices. Uru-inim-gina's proclaimed intention was to promote impartial justice, a goal that he expressed in the formula "[the king] will protect the mother that is in distress, the mighty man shall not oppress the naked and the widow." If at the same time he also managed to increase his own power, then so much the better. As it turned out, Lagash was conquered only a few years later. Uru-inim-gina's reforms nonetheless survived as the precedent for a long Mesopotamian tradition of royal lawgiving.

Several warrior-kings attempted to conquer and unite all the Sumerian cities. The most successful was Sargon (r. 2371–2316 B.C.), an unusual figure who rose from obscurity to a high position under the king of Kish before founding his own capital city, Agade. Even more important, Sargon was a native speaker not of Sumerian but of Akkadian.

Conquest and Assimilation

Cities were rarities in the third millennium B.C. Rude and tough, the surrounding peoples of the desert and the mountains coveted Mesopotamia's wealth. Some conquerors came directly from the hinterland to the walls of the city they were attacking, others, like Sargon, rose to power within the context of the warring Sumerian city-states. Both groups were sufficiently impressed by Sumerian culture to adopt a great many Sumerian customs and ideas as their own. The conquering Akkadians, for example, adopted Sumerian religion and wrote Akkadian in cuneiform.

The Akkadians were originally a seminomadic people who lived on the edge of the desert.

Shepherds, they moved their flocks with the seasons. Their language, Akkadian, belongs to the Semitic group of languages, which includes such languages as Arabic and Hebrew. In the fourth millennium B.C. Akkadians had already begun to trickle into the northern Sumerian cities.

The commander of one of history's first professional armies, Sargon conquered all Mesopotamia, and his power extended westward along the Euphrates and eastward into the Iranian Plateau. Recent research suggests that Sargon's armies might have made use of the horse to draw war chariots, thus allowing them to cover much greater distances than earlier forces. Sargon's armies tore down the walls of conquered cities, leaving them defenseless and thereby discouraging rebellion. The old rulers were generally allowed to remain in office because the installation of new men by Sargon might spark local hostility. The Akkadians were satisfied with loose control, as long as they could monopolize trade.

Sargon's dynasty boasted that it reigned over "the peoples of all lands" or "the four quarters of the earth." The Akkadian empire reached its greatest height in the reign of Sargon's grandson, Naram-sin (r. ca. 2250–2220 B.C.), but it did not survive the next reign. Sargon nonetheless proved to be one of western Asia's most influential figures. His ideal of universal empire was one to which future conquerors would lay claim.

Sargon proved adept at using religion to legitimize his rule. A self-made monarch, he was sensitive to the charge of usurpations; indeed, he chose the throne name Sargon (Sharrum-ken in Akkadian) because it means "the king is legitimate." By claiming the status of the gods' representative on earth, Sargon strengthened his authority. He once paraded a defeated enemy in a halter before the temple and priests of Enlil, the chief Sumerian god, confidently proclaiming that Enlil was on his side. Sargon and most of his successors presented themselves as mediators between human beings and the gods, but they usually stopped short of claiming to be gods themselves.

Assimilation was another lasting Akkadian legacy. Although Sargon made Akkadian the official language of administration, he made politic concessions to Sumerian sensibilities. For instance, his daughter Enkheduanna, whom he appointed high priestess at Ur and Uruk, wrote poetry in Sumerian—poetry good enough to be quoted often in later Sumerian texts. She is the first known woman poet. One of Enkheduanna's themes was the union of Sumerians and Akkadians.

MESOPOTAMIA

3500–3100 B.C.	Writing invented
2800–2350 B.C.	Early Dynastic Period
2371–2316 B.C.	Reign of Sargon
2112–2004 B.C.	Third Dynasty of Ur
1900–1600 B.C.	Old Babylonian Period
1792–1750 B.C.	Reign of Hammurabi

(All dates in this chapter are approximate.)

Around 2200 B.C. the Akkadian empire broke up into a series of smaller successor states. The Gutians, raiders from the Zagros Mountains on the eastern border of Mesopotamia, played a major role in ending Akkadian power. Ascendant in eastern Mesopotamia for about a century, the Gutians absorbed Sumerian and Akkadian culture. When Gutian power waned, the Sumerians returned to power under the Third Dynasty of Ur (2112–2004 B.C.). Far from excising all Akkadian influence, the revived Sumerian rulers spoke of themselves as "Kings of Sumer and Akkad." It was a title that would have a long and potent history; for the next fifteen hundred years many of the great kings of western Asia would label themselves, among other things, as "king of Sumer and Akkad." By using this title, the Sumerian kings of Ur showed that they recognized that a composite, common Mesopotamian society was emerging.

This society survived renewed political turmoil around 2000 B.C. Various raiders attacked from the mountains and deserts, and individual cities within Mesopotamia rebelled against Ur. A new kingdom, under the rule of the Amorites, one of the raiding peoples, emerged around 1900 B.C. in southern Mesopotamia. The kingdom of the Amorites, Semitic-speakers, shared Mesopotamian culture and traditions. Babylon, a city in the northern part of southern Mesopotamia, became the Amorite capital. From Babylon, Amorite kings issued cuneiform decrees that, except for being in a Semitic language, might have been drafted by a Sumerian monarch.

The Majesty of the Law

Hammurabi (r. 1792–1750 B.C.) ruled in Babylon about six hundred years after Sargon. Much of his forty-two-year reign was devoted to creating a Mesopotamian empire. A careful administrator who ushered in an era of prosperity and cultural flowering, Hammurabi is most famous for the text known as Hammurabi's Code. Although the work was less a "code" than a collection of verdicts—a kind of treatise on justice glorifying Hammurabi's qualities as a judge—we shall use the familiar name. Hammurabi's Code became both a legal and a literary classic, often copied in later times.

Hammurabi's Code offers a remarkable portrait of Mesopotamian society. The document contains nearly three hundred rulings on topics ranging from family to commercial law, from wage rates to murder. It is a collection of cases rather than of general principles. As such it is very revealing of the pragmatism of Mesopotamian scholarship and science. There was no notion of abstract or universal principles in Mesopotamia; indeed, there was no word for "law."

Hammurabi's Code is often thought of as harsh and early. Harsh it was, but not so early. The earliest known law code was promulgated by King Ur-Nammu of Ur around 2100 B.C., three centuries before Hammurabi, and other codes survive from between Ur-Nammu's and Hammurabi's day. There are many similarities among the codes. As a great reformer, however, Hammurabi prided himself on making changes in the law. In some ways his code was more lenient than earlier documents. For example, family members sold or handed over into servitude because of debt were automatically freed after three years. But Hammurabi's was the first code to include such harsh penalties as bodily mutilation, drowning, and impaling; earlier codes are satisfied with payment in silver as recompense for crime. Hammurabi's Code also introduces the law of retaliation for wounds: "If a man has destroyed the eye of a member of the aristocracy: they shall destroy his eye. If he has broken his limb: they shall break the (same) limb." Children could be punished for the crimes of their fathers. (See the box, "King Hammurabi Dispenses Justice.")

Inscribed in stone and put in a prominent public place, Hammurabi's Code and other Mesopotamian legal texts symbolized the notion that the law belonged to everyone. Although ordinary people could not read, it was possible for them to find a patron who could. Yet Hammurabi's society was anything but egalitarian. There were three classes: slaves, free people who owned land, and *mushkenum* (a subordinate class whose members were legally free but landless and often in a dependent position). Punishments were class-biased: Crimes against a free person received harsher punishment than crimes against a slave or a mushkenum. Debt seems to have been a serious and widespread problem, frequently leading debtors to sell their children, especially their daughters, into slavery. Women could own and inherit property and testify in court. The overall direction of the code, however, is patriarchal: It enshrines the power of the male head of family.

Divine Masters

The Sumerians left their stamp on Mesopotamian religion; the Old Babylonian period (1900–1600 B.C.) was a second era of great religious creativity. Many Sumerian gods arose out of the forces of nature: An, the sky-god; Enki, the earth-god and freshwater-god; Enlil, the air-god; Nanna, the moon-god; and Utu (Semitic, Shamash), the sun-god. Other Sumerian gods embodied human passions or notions about the afterlife: Inanna (Semitic, Ishtar), goddess of love and war; Ereshkigal, goddess of the underworld. The Sumerians were polytheists—that is, they had many gods—and their gods (like the gods of Greece later on) were anthropomorphic, or human in form. Indeed, Sumerian (and Greek) gods were thought to be much like human beings, by turns wise and foolish, except that they were immortal and super-powerful.

We can speak of the Sumerian pantheon—that is, the association of all the Sumerian gods. The Sumerians sometimes envisioned their gods holding an assembly, much like the boisterous

King Hammurabi Dispenses Justice

The Code of Hammurabi, king of Babylon (r. 1792–1750 B.C.), is one of the best-known documents of antiquity. Less a code than a treatise on justice, the text illustrates both the image of himself that the king wished to promote and the class and gender hierarchies of Mesopotamia in the second millennium B.C. The following excerpts are from the preface and body of the text.

[The gods] named me to promote the welfare of the people, me, Hammurabi, the devout, god-fearing prince, to cause justice to prevail in the land, to destroy the wicked and the evil, that the strong might not oppress the weak, to rise like the sun over the black-headed (people), and to light up the land. . . . I established law and justice in the language of the land, thereby promoting the welfare of the people. At that time (I decreed):

128: If a seignior acquired a wife but did not draw up the contracts for her, that woman is no wife.

129: If the wife of a seignior has been caught while lying with another man, they shall bind them and throw them into the water [that is, submit to the water ordeal, with the river as divine judge]. If the husband of the woman wishes to spare his wife, then the king in turn may spare his subject.

170: When a seignior's first wife bore him children and his female slave also bore him children, if the father during this lifetime has ever said "My children!" to the children whom the slave bore him, thus having counted them with the children of his first wife, after the father has gone to (his) fate, the children of the first wife and the children of the slave shall share equally in the goods of the paternal estate, with the first-born, the son of the first wife, receiving a preferential share.

196: If a seignior has destroyed the eye of a member of the aristocracy, they shall destroy his eye.

198: If he has destroyed the eye of a commoner or broken the bone of a commoner, he shall pay one mina of silver.

202: If a seignior has struck the cheek of a seignior who is superior to him, he shall be beaten sixty (times) with an oxtail whip in the assembly.

237: When a seignior hired a boatman and a boat and loaded it with grain, wool, oil, dates, or any kind of freight, if that boatman was so careless that he has sunk the boat and lost what was in it as well, the boatman shall make good the boat which he sank and whatever he lost that was in it.

Source: James B. Pritchard, ed., *Ancient Near Eastern Texts Relating to the Old Testament,* 3d ed., with Supplement (Princeton: Princeton University Press, 1969), pp. 164, 171,173, 175–176.

assemblies of early Sumer. The Sumerians and Akkadians considered Enlil, city-god of Nippur, to be the chief god. The Babylonians replaced him with Marduk, city-god of Babylon.

The keynote of Mesopotamian religion is a certain pessimism about the human condition. It is not surprising that the Mesopotamians, living in a difficult natural environment, regarded the gods with fear and awe. Indeed, they saw their deities as masters or parents who were to be obeyed. Although the gods communicated with humans, their language was mysterious. To understand the divine will, the Mesopotamians engaged in various kinds of divination: the interpretation of dreams, the examination of the entrails of slaughtered animals, the study of the stars (which stimulated great advances in astronomy, as we will see). By building temples,

Ziggurat of Ur Built with a mud-brick core and a baked-brick overlay, ziggurats have not withstood the ravages of time well, but they once dominated the Mesopotamian urban skyline. The ziggurat of King Ur-Nammu of Ur (ca. 2100 B.C.), illustrated here (partially restored), was originally a three-story stepped tower, approached by a triple stair. It is thought there were shrines at the ground level and at the top. *(Robert Harding Picture Library)*

offering prayers and animal sacrifices, and participating in public rituals and processions, Mesopotamians hoped to propitiate their gods.

People expected nothing glorious in the afterlife, merely a shadowy existence. It was thought that with a person's last breath the person's spirit went on a long journey to the Netherworld, a place under the earth. More than one Mesopotamian text describes the Netherworld as the "Land-of-no-return" and "the house wherein the dwellers are bereft of light,/Where dust is their fare and clay their food,/Where they see no light, residing in darkness."[2] The dead resided there permanently, though in some texts their spirits return to earth, often with hostile intent toward the living.

Every Mesopotamian city had its main temple complex, the most striking feature of which was a *ziggurat,* a stepped tower. Constructed originally as simple raised terraces, ziggurats eventually became seven-stage structures. Unlike the pyramids of Egypt, ziggurats were not tombs but "stairways" providing a way for the god to descend from heaven to earth. A typical ziggurat had two temples: a "high temple" at the top, to serve the god in the sky, and a "low temple" for the god to reach the earth. The "low temple" was the chief sanctuary of the city.

Arts and Sciences

From Sumer to Babylon, the people of Mesopotamia were deeply inquisitive. They focused on the beginning and the end of things. "How did the world come into being?" and "What happens to us when we die?" are perhaps the two fundamental questions of their rich literature. The Babylonian creation epic known from its first line as *Enuma Elish* ("When on high") is a poem about the triumph of the gods of order over the forces of chaos. It also commemorates the political ascendancy of Babylon. This poem was recited annually during the New Year's Festival by Babylonian priests. Another important Babylonian literary genre is known as wisdom literature, which responds to life's vicissitudes with pre-

Heroism and Death in Mesopotamia

The **Epic of Gilgamesh** ***sheds light on categories of gender and power in Mesopotamia. Men like King Gilgamesh and his friend Enkidu have heroic adventures and risk death. Women lead quieter lives but are wiser and more realistic, as the following excerpt shows.***

[Beginning lost. Gilgamesh is addressing Siduri, the ale-wife:]

"He who with me underwent all hardships—Enkidu, whom I loved dearly, who with me underwent all hardships—has now gone to the fate of mankind! Day and night I have wept over him. I would not give him up for burial—in case my friend should rise at my plaint—seven days and seven nights, until a worm fell out of his nose. Since his passing I have not found life, I have roamed like a hunter in the midst of the steppe. O ale-wife, now that I have seen thy face, let me not see the death which I ever dread."

The ale-wife said to him, to Gilgamesh: "Gilgamesh, whither rovest thou? The life thou pursuest thou shalt not find. When the gods created mankind, death for mankind they set aside, Life in their own hands retaining. Thou, Gilgamesh, let full be thy belly, make thou merry by day and by night. Of each day make thou a feast of rejoicing, day and night dance thou and play! Let thy garments be sparkling fresh, thy head be washed; bathe thou in water. Pay heed to the little one that holds on to thy hand, let thy spouse delight in thy bosom! For this is the task of mankind!"

Source: James B. Pritchard, ed., *Ancient Near Eastern Texts Relating to the Old Testament,* 3d ed., with Supplement (Princeton, N.J.: Princeton University Press, 1969), pp. 89–90.

cepts that are sometimes simple, sometimes sophisticated. It proved eventually to be a distant influence on the wisdom literature of the Hebrew Bible.

The best-known example of Mesopotamian literature is the *Epic of Gilgamesh.* Frequently translated and adapted by various Mesopotamian and Anatolian peoples, *Gilgamesh* may be a Sumerian work perhaps dating back to about 2500 B.C. An epic poem is the story of heroic deeds, in this case those of Gilgamesh, king of Uruk. Gilgamesh was probably a real historical personage, but the poem primarily concerns his fictionalized personal life, in particular the painful wisdom he gains as he grows from arrogant youth to maturity. The main themes are friendship, loss, and the inevitability of death. Much of the poem discusses Gilgamesh's close relationship with Enkidu, who is first his rival, then his friend, and finally his educator. Enkidu's untimely death makes Gilgamesh aware of his own mortality. Alone, Gilgamesh is incapable of introspection or self-awareness; only through his intense and ultimately tragic friendship with Enkidu does Gilgamesh become aware of himself. The *Epic of Gilgamesh* contains stories that presage the later biblical Eden and Flood narratives; there is little doubt that those narratives found their way from Mesopotamia to the Hebrew Bible. (See the box, "Heroism and Death in Mesopotamia.")

As we have seen in connection with Hammurabi's Code, Mesopotamian thinkers had no concept of abstract or universal principles. They did, however, demonstrate the ability to observe critically, to separate the typical from the particular, and to arrange their thoughts in a logical order. We know, for example, of an Akkadian medical treatise consisting of cases rather than principles, but they are typical rather than particular cases: "a

Relief of King Ur-Nanshe of Lagash This limestone plaque (ca. 2500 B.C.) depicts the king and his children and retinue. The two images of the king show him carrying an earth-filled basket for a building project (upper left) and seated, drinking at a feast, possibly in celebration of the work's completion (lower right). Note the cuneiform inscription and the hole in the center, probably for attaching the plaque to a wall. *(Louvre © Photo R.M.N.)*

man who is feverish and has a burning abdomen" rather than the specific case of so-and-so. Symptoms are arranged according to the part of the body affected, and the ability to observe carefully and to make comparisons and analogies is clear. The description of the course of a particular disease shows a clear awareness of cause and effect. In short, however limited Mesopotamian science seems when judged by later standards, it was a great contribution in its day.

The Mesopotamians made impressive advances in mathematics, astronomy, medicine, and engineering, as well as in divination, which they considered to be every inch a science. The Sumerians had two systems of numeration: a decimal system (powers of ten) for administration and business; a sexagesimal system (powers of sixty) for weights and mathematical or astronomical calculations. Like the Babylonians, we still divide hours by sixty today. Furthermore, our modern system of numerical place-value notation—for example, the difference between 42 and 24—is derived, through Hindu-Arabic intermediaries, from the Babylonian place-value numerical system. The Babylonians were adept at arithmetic and could solve problems for which we would use algebra. A millennium before the Greek mathematician Pythagoras (who claimed to have studied the Mesopotamian tradition) proved the validity of the theorem that bears his name, they were familiar with the proposition that in a right triangle the square of the longest side is equal to the sum of the squares of the two shortest sides. In the first millennium B.C. the Babylonians developed a sophisticated mathematical astronomy (see pages 45–46). As early as the seventeenth century B.C., however, they made systematic, if not always accurate, recordings of the movements of the planet Venus.

In medical matters they demonstrated considerable critical ability, as we have seen. Physicians made advances in the use of plant products for medicines and in very rudimentary surgery. The Babylonians had a simple pregnancy test of moderate accuracy, and they may have been able to perform delivery by cesarean section. They were able to extract an aching tooth. When they became ill, however, most people in Mesopotamia set more store by magic and incantations than by surgery or herbal medicine.

Mesopotamian sculptors, particularly the Sumerians, were adept and sophisticated. They did not produce realistic representations of reality—that was not their purpose. Rather, they aimed at creating symbols of religious piety or political or military power. Sumerian statues tend to be stiff and solemn. The head and face are carved in detail, and the body is neglected and sometimes merely represented by a geometrical form.

The most common type of Mesopotamian sculpture is relief sculpture, in which figures or forms are projected from a flat surface. Steles (upright stone slabs or pillars), plaques, and cylinder seals (small, carved stone or metal cylinders rolled over wet clay to render an impression, often indicating ownership) are all found.

Egypt

From Babylon to the valley of the Nile River, the distance was about 750 miles by way of the caravan routes through Syria and Palestine: close enough to exchange customs, goods, and, if necessary, blows, but far enough for a distinct Egyptian civilization to emerge. As in Sumer, so too in Egypt a great civilization arose in a river valley. Egypt developed writing around 3100 B.C., slightly after Mesopotamia (and possibly under Mesopotamian influence), but was much earlier than Mesopotamia in becoming a unified kingdom under one ruler.

EGYPT

3100 B.C.	Unification of Nile Valley
3100–2695 B.C.	Archaic Period
2695–2160 B.C.	Old Kingdom
2160–1963 B.C.	First Intermediate Period
1963–1786 B.C.	Middle Kingdom
1786–1550 B.C.	Second Intermediate Period; Hyksos
1550–1070 B.C.	New Kingdom

With its unique contributions in religion and politics, and in the arts and sciences, and with its wealth of huge, surviving stone monuments, Egypt has impressed both scholars and lay people as few other ancient civilizations have. In the ancient world, Egyptian culture was distinct but influential, from the spread of such Egyptian notions as a Last Judgment in the afterlife to Egyptian techniques in architecture and sculpture to Christian monasticism, which began in Egypt.

Geography as Destiny

Little did Herodotus, a Greek historian who visited Egypt in the fifth century B.C., know that he was penning one of the great clichés of history when he described Egypt as "the gift of the Nile." Cliché it may be, but Herodotus's statement is hard to surpass for conciseness and accuracy. Ancient Egypt is a product of the unique characteristics of the Nile River (Map 1.3).

Most of Egypt is desert; only about 5 percent is habitable by humans, including a few oases, the Nile Delta, and the Nile Valley itself, which extends about 760 miles from Cairo to Egypt's modern southern border: so-called Upper Egypt, a long and narrow valley nowhere more than about 14 miles wide. North of Cairo, in so-called Lower Egypt, the Nile branches out into the wide, low-lying delta before flowing into the Mediterranean Sea.

The alluvial plain of the Nile was much friendlier to would-be farmers than was the valley of the Tigris and Euphrates. Unlike those

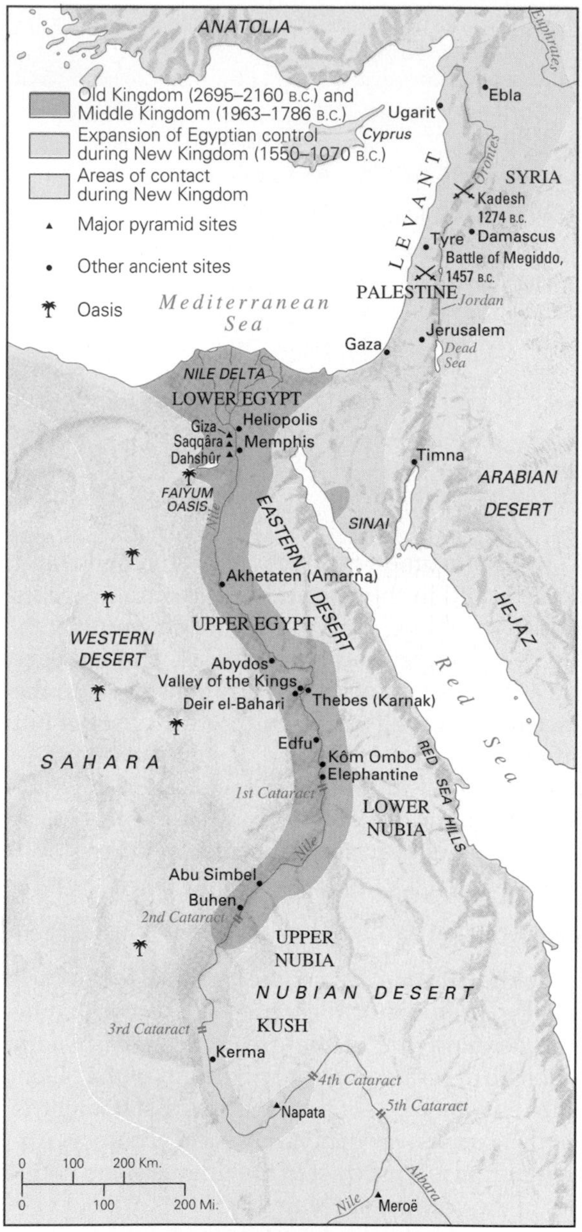

Map 1.3 Ancient Egypt and the Levant The unique geography of the Nile Valley left a stamp on ancient Egypt. Fertile soil made Egypt wealthy, and the surrounding desert led to periods of isolation from nearby African and Asian cultures.

rivers, the Nile was rarely given to damaging floods; its course was remarkably regular and predictable. Its annual floods, which took place between late summer and autumn (in contrast to Mesopotamia's spring floods), were generally benign. As a result, Egyptian agriculture was one of the wealthiest in the ancient world. Bread and beer were the national staples.

Another result of the Nile's fertility was the relative optimism of ancient Egypt's world view. "Hail to Thee, O Nile, that gushest forth from the earth and comest to nourish Egypt!" So proclaims an ancient hymn that indicates the Egyptians' gratitude toward and confidence in the benevolence of the environment. With its plentiful water and fertile land, Egypt did not suffer the chronic warfare that relative scarcity encouraged in Mesopotamia. Nor was Egypt easily reached by invaders. The Nile was cut off by deserts to the east and west, by rapids to the south, and by the Mediterranean to the north.

Egyptian art and literature betray little of the despair over the unpredictability of the universe that developed in the harsher climatic conditions of Mesopotamia. The behavior of the Nile, furthermore, encouraged a static quality in Egyptian ideology. Change seemed virtually impossible. Even death appeared to be a minor event compared with the regularity of the Nile, which may help explain the prominence in Egyptian religion of belief in the afterlife. In addition, the static outlook helped promote the idea of an absolute, all-powerful, and all-providing king—that is, pharaoh.

Storm over Origins

Early Egypt developed a distinctive civilization, with no major invasion for over a thousand years after the beginning of the historical period around 3100 B.C. Just how isolated was early Egypt, however, and just how distinctive was its civilization? A debate has been joined recently about the relationship of Egypt with western Asia, Europe, and the rest of Africa. Before World War II, most Egyptologists tended to see Egypt more as part of the Near East (that is, of the culture of western Asia) than as part of Africa. Many imagined that ancient Egyptians looked much like modern Europeans: as part of "the Great White Race."[3] More recently, with the liberation after World War II of Europe's former African colonies and with the awakening of a growing interest in Africa by African Americans, some people have argued that Egypt was primarily African in character and that the ancient Egyptians were black.

The truth lies in between these two arguments. There was a considerable, perhaps predominant African element in the ancient Egyptian population. But from early times Egypt also had immigrants from western Asia. The result was a mixed population group. Egyptians were generally darker skinned than the ancient peoples of Europe or western Asia but lighter skinned than the peoples of Africa south of the Sahara: they included a considerable variety of skin colors and body types. The farther south in Egypt one went, the more likely one was to see the dark skin and facial features characteristic of black Africans.

Much discussion has focused on the influence of Egypt on ancient Greek civilization, which is usually considered the founding civilization of Europe. Egypt had a limited but significant impact on early Greece, as did the cultures of western Asia. The Greeks borrowed, among other things, Egyptian techniques in architecture and sculpture, Egyptian religious notions, and western Asian artisanship and shipbuilding, poetry and mythology. Much of what the Greeks borrowed, moreover, they transformed into something radically new.

Within Africa itself, Egypt was in continual contact with other regions, particularly the neighboring areas of ancient Libya and Nubia (roughly, the modern Sudan). The people of Nubia, who were black Africans, both borrowed from Egypt and influenced Egypt. Some scholars believe, for example, that the early Egyptian notion of monarchy originated in Nubia. In West Africa certain important institutions—including sacred royalty, the cult of the ram, and belief in the after-life existence of a double of one's physical person—may possibly be of Egyptian origin.

Divine Kingship

Agriculture and settled village life emerged in Egypt around 5000 B.C. By 4000, villages had grown into towns, each controlling a strip of territory. About one thousand years later, around 3100 B.C., the Nile Valley had become one unified kingdom of Egypt. We do not know precisely how this process was carried out. Egyptians writing after 3000 B.C. assumed that the Nile Valley was originally home to two kingdoms roughly corresponding to Upper and Lower Egypt, which, they said, had come into existence by the fourth millennium B.C. Then, around 3100, a certain Menes, king of Upper Egypt, is said to have conquered Lower Egypt and united the two into one combined kingdom controlling the entire Nile Valley.

We do not know how much (if any) of this tradition is true. But it is clear that between about 5000 and 3100 B.C. Egyptian communities up and down the Nile Valley succeeded in clearing local marshes and building local irrigation works, thereby expanding the amount of land under cultivation, which in turn could support a larger population. By 3100 B.C. monumental architecture, writing, and kingship appear, perhaps as indigenous inventions, perhaps borrowed from Mesopotamia and Nubia. For several centuries Egyptians consolidated their institutions. Then, beginning around 2700 B.C., a remarkable and distinctive period of creativity begins, the so-called Third (2695–2600) and Fourth (2600–2500) Dynasties (that is, ruling families) of the Old Kingdom.

The history of third- and second-millennium B.C. Egypt is usually divided into three distinct eras of great prosperity: the Old Kingdom (2695–2160 B.C.), the Middle Kingdom (1963– 1786 B.C.), and the New Kingdom (1550–1070 B.C.). Central authority broke down in the so-called Intermediate Periods between the kingdoms. Broadly speaking, one might characterize the Old Kingdom as a spectacular era of creativity and originality, symbolized by the building of the Great Pyramids; the Middle Kingdom as an era of introspection and literary production; and the New Kingdom as an era in which Egypt's traditional isolation gave way to international diplomacy and expansion.

The early Egyptian government was the first to govern a large territory. Indeed, a chart of Egypt's power structure would be strictly hierarchical, resembling a pyramid, with a broad base of laborers and artisans supporting a commanding elite. The occupant of this high point of power was considered so important that for centuries Egyptians referred to the office rather than to the person, calling it "the Great House": in Egyptian, *per-aa,* or "pharaoh," as the ruler himself (or occasionally herself) was eventually called.

The "Lord of the Two Lands" (Lower and Upper Egypt), to use just one of his several titles, the king in theory owned all the land. In practice

Relief of Sethos I In this delicate work from the limestone temple of Sethos I (r. 1294–1279) at Abydos, the king stretches out his hands toward the god Atum. The king wears the royal headcloth (*nemes*) while the god wears the "Two Mighty Ones," the double crown symbolizing the union of Upper and Lower Egypt. The god holds a scepter, symbol of "welfare," and an *ankh*, symbol of "life." *(Kurt Lange, Oberstdorf)*

Egypt's economy was a mixture of private enterprise and centralized control. The king was thought to watch over Egypt carefully. In the Middle Kingdom, for example, he was represented as a good shepherd, appointed by the sun-god, as one text says, "to keep alive the people and the folk, not sleeping by night as well as by day in seeking out every beneficial act, in looking for possibilities of usefulness." Even sleepless pharaohs needed help, however, and they delegated authority to a large group of officials. Indeed, Old Kingdom Egypt was one of the earliest great bureaucracies. The country was supervised by provincial governors, military commanders, judges, treasurers, engineers, agricultural overseers, scribes, and others. The highest official was the vizier, a sort of prime minister who had more day-to-day power than pharaoh himself.

The essence of good government was what the Egyptians called *ma'at,* whose basic meaning is "order"—in government, society or the universe. *Ma'at* can also mean "truth" or "justice." The god-king embodied what we would call law, but the administration of justice rested mainly on others' shoulders. Egypt had a well-functioning system of judges who heard lawsuits, and it probably also had a detailed law code, although few written laws survive.

Bureaucratic and with claims of absolutism, Egyptian kingship was sacred monarchy. In Mesopotamia, the king claimed to have been appointed by the gods. In Egypt, pharaoh was deemed actually *to be* a god. He was called the "good god" in his lifetime and the "great god" after death. Considered the physical child of the sun-god Re, he was also deemed to be the sky-god Horus, and after dying he became Osiris, god of the underworld. Just as Egyptian myth recounted how the world was created when a god, sitting on a hill, made the waters recede, so pharaoh was thought to make the Nile rise and fall each year. (See the box, "Pharaoh the Divine and Invincible.")

A wall of language and ceremony separated kings from ordinary human beings. Egyptians did not speak "to" the king but rather "in his presence." He was outfitted with a variety of crowns, headdresses, and scepters. Pharaoh's exalted status was apparent on the occasion of a ceremonial "glorious appearance" before his subjects, especially at the Sed festival or jubilee, a celebration of the anniversary of his reign. The most traditional part of the ceremony was the appearance of the king and queen at the palace door on jubilee day wearing special jubilee clothes, but there were other elements of pageantry. The well-documented Sed festivals of Amenhotep III (r. 1390–1352 B.C.), who celebrated three of them, included such grand features as an elaborate procession of boats on the Nile, the assembling of officials and foreign dignitaries standing according to rank, distribution of gifts and a special breakfast (bread, beef, fowl, and beer), and the erection

Pharaoh the Divine and Invincible

Egypt's rulers presented themselves as god-kings. Excerpt (A), a selection from the grave stele of a high official of the Twelfth Dynasty of the Middle Kingdom (ca. 1850 B.C.), states pharaoh's divinity unhesitatingly. Excerpt (B), from an inscription about Amenhotep II (r. 1427–1400 B.C), shows the emphasis that the warrior-pharaohs of the New Kingdom placed on their invincibility in combat—in sport as well as in battle.

(A)

Worship King Nimaatre, living forever, within your bodies and associate with his majesty in your hearts. He is Perception which is in men's hearts, and his eyes search out every body. He is Re, by whose beams one sees, He is one who illumines the Two Lands more than the sun disc.

He is one who makes the land greener than does a high Nile, for he has filled the Two Lands with strength and life. The nostrils are chilled when he inclines toward rage, but when he is merciful, they will breathe the air. He gives food to them who are in his service, and he supplies them who tread his path.

(B)

Strong of arms, one who did not weary when he took the oar, he [Amenhotep II] rowed at the stern of his falcon-boat as the stroke for two hundred men. When there was a pause, after they had attained half an iter's course [about two-thirds of a mile], they were weak, their bodies were limp, they could not draw a breath, while his majesty was (still) strong under his oar of twenty cubits [about 34 feet] in its length. He left off and moored his falcon boat only after he had attained three iters [about four miles] in rowing, without letting down in pulling. Faces were bright at the sight of him, when he did this.

Source: James B. Pritchard, ed., *Ancient Near Eastern Texts Relating to the Old Testament*, 3d ed., with Supplement (Princeton: Princeton University Press), pp. 244, 431.

of festival buildings. (See the feature, "Weighing the Evidence: The Pyramids," on pages 38–39.)

Life and Afterlife

Later peoples, beginning with the Greeks, have assumed that the ordinary Egyptian chafed under royal power. It is true that Egyptians were burdened with a variety of taxes (paid in agricultural produce) and that free people, both men and women, had an obligation of corvée (forced labor) service on public works, from irrigation projects to the pyramids. Sometimes this service caused resentment. We hear of worker discipline maintained by beatings, of fugitives, of the pious hope that there be no corvées in the afterlife, and even, in one unusual case, of a worker's strike.

Most people, nevertheless, probably made their peace with their public burdens. Far from resenting the king's claim to divinity, ordinary people might have been reassured to be ruled by a god. Nor were the pyramid-builders slaves laboring under a tyrant, as Greek writers assumed. In fact, they might have given their labor gladly to raising the man-god's tomb, as an act of faith, just as people centuries later donated time and money to build medieval cathedrals. There were material compensations too: ration supplements for ordinary laborers, steady employment for specialized craftsmen.

Herodotus, that Greek visitor to Egypt, remarked that the Egyptians were the most religious people in the world. Egypt indeed offered a great variety of religious experience, from ritual and festival to ethical teaching to magic. This experience is difficult to summarize, not only because of variations over time and place but because of the tendency of Egyptian religion toward syncretism—that is, to combine mutually opposed beliefs, principles, or practices. For example, Egyptian mythology taught that the sky was a cow or was held up by a god or by a post or was a goddess stretched over the earth. No one was troubled by the inconsistency, as a modern worshiper might be, because it was thought that a fundamental unity underlay the manifold varieties of nature.

In addition to syncretism, Egyptian religion also tended toward henotheism. Monotheism, which is familiar today to Christians, Jews, and Muslims, is the belief in one god and only one god. Henotheists like the ancient Egyptians worship one god without denying the existence of others. For example, the most important Egyptian god was Re, the sun, often called "universal lord." From time to time, Re was syncretized with other gods to create a powerful new god: for example, Re-Atum, a combination of Re and a creator-god; Re-Harakhty, Re-Horus-of-the-Horizon; and Amon-Re, a combination of Re and the invisible, omnipresent Amon. One text even refers to Amon-Re-Atum-Harakhty!

Egypt's polytheistic religion had an abundance of greater and lesser deities, including human, animal, and composite gods. Various animals, from cats and dogs to crocodiles and serpents, were thought to represent the divine. There were innumerable local deities, spirits, and demons as well as gods and goddesses of all Egypt. In addition to Re and his various syncretized forms, important deities included Thoth, the moon-god and god of wisdom; Nut, goddess of the sky; Ptah, who replaced Atum in a separate myth as creator-god; Osiris, who invented agriculture and became lord of the dead; Horus, son of Osiris, a sky-god imagined as a giant falcon; and Isis, wife of Osiris and mother of Horus, a mother-goddess. Temples were numerous and wealthy, though never the central economic institution of the community.

Probably the most striking feature of Egyptian religion was its focus on the afterlife. Unlike the Mesopotamians, the Egyptians believed that death could be an extremely pleasant continuation of life on earth. Hence, they actively sought immortality. The wealthy placed great emphasis on building tombs, decorating them with paintings and inscriptions, and stocking them with cherished possessions for use in the other world. The most cherished possession of all, of course, was the body itself, and the Egyptians provided for its preservation through their mastery of the science of embalming—hence the Egyptian mummies. The Egyptians distinguished between soul and body and believed that part of the soul, the *ka,* was immortal. Unlike later civilizations, however, they were not prepared to jettison the body altogether, believing instead that from time to time the soul desired to return to the body after death. That belief made mummification necessary.

Reserved for the king and his officials in the Old Kingdom, by the Middle Kingdom the afterlife became, as it were, democratized. In the wake of political and social change, Egyptian ideology changed. The Middle Kingdom and the First and Second Intermediate Periods were in many ways an inward-looking and reflective era, one in which materialism was de-emphasized and a sense of common humanity appears. "Even the timid fish shall come to thee," says one text of a First Intermediate Period ruler, "... because thou art the father of the orphan, the husband of the widow, the brother of the divorcee, and the apron of him that is motherless, ... a leader free from covetousness, a great man free from wrongdoing, one who destroys falsehood and brings *ma'at* into being, and who comes at the cry of him who gives voice."[4] (See the box, "Humane Values.")

By the Middle Kingdom, even ordinary Egyptians could live in the afterlife as gods, as long as they could purchase for their graves funerary texts containing the relevant rituals and prayers. The texts emphasize ritual—incantations, magic spells, prayers—as the key to eternal life. Yet from time to time, especially during the Middle Kingdom, there is an impressive insistence on ethical behavior. Created in the likeness of god, men and women must worship the gods and provide for their fellows. A dead person has to appear before the court of a god, usually Osiris, for judgment on his or her life. Before forty-two judges of the underworld, the dead person declares his or her innocence of a variety of sins. The judges then weigh the dead person's heart in the balance against a symbol of *ma'at*, or truth. The sinless are admitted into eternal life in the kingdom of the blessed; the guilty are wiped out.

Egyptian women did not enjoy equal status with men, but they had a considerably greater measure of equality than women in many other ancient societies, particularly in legal matters. A woman could buy or sell, bequeath or inherit, sue or testify in court, all without a male guardian's approval. A married woman retained the status of complete legal independence; she could even own property without her husband's involvement. Outside of the law, women were less free. They sometimes worked outside the home, in agriculture or trade, in the textile and perfume industries, in dining halls, in entertainment, and as priests of various kinds. Women were sometimes managers and sometimes received the same pay as men, but only rarely.

The humane attitudes of the Middle Kingdom were founded on restored order. They were swept away in the period from about 1700 to 1570 B.C., when Semitic-speaking immigrants from Palestine—"Princes of Foreign Uplands," as they were called in Egyptian, or Hyksos, to employ the commonly used Greek term—settled in the delta region and then conquered and ruled much of Egypt. In many ways gentle conquerors, the Hyksos worshiped Egyptian gods, built and restored Egyptian temples, and intermarried with natives. As foreigners, however, the Hyksos were unpopular. Eventually a war launched from Upper Egypt, which had retained a loose independence, drove the Hyksos out.

Ahmose I (r. 1550–1525 B.C.) was the first restored-Egyptian ruler of the New Kingdom. His proved to be a new Egypt indeed. The Hyksos had brought advanced military technology to Egypt, including the horse-drawn war chariot, new kinds of daggers and swords, and the composite bow. Having once tasted foreign occupation, Egypt's new rulers made up their minds to use such weapons in aggressive military campaigns abroad.

Miniature Coffin of Tutankhamon This miniature coffin (8⅞ inches long) is one of four containing the internal organs of the king (r. 1336–1327 B.C.) removed during the embalming process. Made of gold inlaid with colored glass and carnelian, the coffin is typical of the splendor and luxury of the objects discovered in the substantially intact royal tomb. Note the hieroglyphic inscription offering divine protection to the remains. *(Egyptian Museum, Cairo)*

Humane Values

Compilations of wise sayings were popular in Egypt. This text, preserved on a papyrus of around 1450 B.C. and composed at least as early as the Twelfth Dynasty (ca. 1991–1785 B.C.), claims to be the advice of a king of the First Intermediate Period (ca. 2075 B.C.) for his son and successor Merikare. The text reflects the humane and sober values of that era.

Copy thy fathers and thy ancestors. . . . Behold, their words remain in writing. Open, that thou mayest read and copy their wisdom. Thus the skilled man becomes learned. . . .

Mayest thou speak justice in thy own house, that the great ones who are on earth may fear thee. Uprightness of heart is fitting for the lord. It is the forepart of the house [the master's quarters] that inspires respect in the back [the servants' quarters]. . . .

Do not distinguish the son of a man from a poor man, but take to thyself a man because of the work of his hands. Every skilled work should be practised according to the . . . of the lord of a strong arm. Protect thy frontier and build thy fortresses, for troops are of advantage to their lord. . . .

Generation passes generation among men, and the god, who knows men's characters, has hidden himself. But there is none who can withstand the Lord of the Hand: he is the one who attacks what the eyes can see. Revere the god upon his way, made of costly stones and fashioned of metal, like a flood replaced by another flood. . . . Enrich thy house of the West; embellish thy place of the necropolis, as an upright man and as one who executes the justice upon which men's hearts rely. More acceptable is the character of one upright of heart than the ox of the evildoer. Act for the god, that he may act similarly for thee, with oblations which make the offering-table flourish and with a carved inscription—that is what bears witness to thy name. The god is aware of him who acts for him.

Well directed are men, the cattle of the god. He made heaven and earth according to their desire, and he repelled the water-monster. He made the breath of life for the nostrils. They who have issued from his body are his images. He arises in heaven according to their desire. He made for them plants, animals, fowl, and fish to feed them. He slew his enemies and injured even his own children because they thought of making rebellion. He makes the light of day according to their desire, and he sails by in order to see them. . . . For the god knows every name.

Source: James B. Pritchard, ed., *Ancient Near Eastern Texts Relating to the Old Testament,* 3d ed., with Supplement (Princeton: Princeton University Press, 1969), pp. 415–417.

Expansion and Reform

Warlike, expansionist, and marked by a daring attempt at religious reform, the New Kingdom's Eighteenth Dynasty (1540–1293 B.C.) has long held a special fascination for historians. The great warrior-pharaoh Thutmose III (r. 1479–1425 B.C.) symbolizes the dynasty's armed expansion into Nubia and Syria. He fought for twenty years in Syria and Palestine and established Egyptian predominance in the region. Thutmose won his greatest victory during his first campaign, at the battle of Megiddo in 1457 B.C., where Egypt completely defeated the attempt of the Hurrian kingdom of Mitanni to expand southward (see page 29).

Before Thutmose had reached adulthood, his stepmother Queen Hatshepsut served as regent and then assumed the kingship herself (r. 1479–1457 B.C.). Hatshepsut's was the most successful female reign in Egypt until the reign of Cleopatra (r. 51–30 B.C.). Although she led Egyptian armies on campaign to Nubia, Hatshepsut is best known for her less warlike works: at home, public works and temple-rebuilding; abroad, a commercial expedition over the Red Sea to the "Land of Punt" (perhaps modern Somalia, in eastern Africa). As illustrated in words and pictures on the wall of Hatshepsut's splendid, terraced, funerary temple at Deir el-Bahri, the expedition to Punt brought home such exotic objects as incense-bearing trees, ebony, perfume, panther skins, baboons, monkeys, and greyhounds.

As an imperial power, New Kingdom Egypt required an expanded government. There were more officials, more military officers, and more priests than ever before. It was a time of opportunity, of social mobility, and of conflict. Perhaps the most dramatic example of the creativity and quarrels of the era is the so-called Amarna reform, named for a major archaeological site at the modern town of Amarna.

Undertaken by Thutmose III's great-great-grandson pharaoh Amenhotep IV (r. 1352–1336 B.C.), the Amarna reform was a struggle of power and faith. The god Amon-Re had become the chief deity of the New Kingdom. As supporters of the ideology of imperialism, his temple priests were rewarded with land and wealth until their power rivaled pharaoh's own. Amenhotep IV's dramatic response was to forbid the worship of Amon-Re and replace him with the god Aton, the solar disk. Changing his own name to Akhenaton ("pleasing to Aton"), the king ordered the erasure of Amon-Re's name from monuments throughout Egypt. As a further step, Akhenaton created a new capital city in central Egypt at an uninhabited site at the desert's edge: Akhetaton (modern Amarna). The new town had a distinctive culture. Akhenaton's wife, Nefertiti, figures prominently in Amarna art, and she too may have played an important role in the reform.

Sphinx of Hatshepsut Hatshepsut (r. 1479–1457 B.C.) was not the first woman to assume the Egyptian monarchy, but she was the first to have herself represented as a male. In this statue she wears the royal headcloth (*nemes*) and a false beard, and she has the body of a lion. Hatshepsut was also represented as a female, as other artwork attests. *(The Metropolitan Museum of Art, Rogers Fund, 1931 [31.3.166])*

The reform shifted power away from the priests and toward the king, but we need not doubt the reformers' sincerity. Contemporary literature suggests intense religious conviction in Aton as a benevolent god and one who nurtured not only Egypt but all countries. Although the Aton cult focuses on one god, it was not monotheistic but henotheistic. The reformers recognized Re and Akhenaton himself as gods in addition to Aton. Indeed, only Akhenaton and his family were permitted to worship Aton directly; the rest of the Egyptian population was expected to worship the god through pharaoh.

Bold as the reform was, sustaining so dramatic a break with tradition proved impossible. After Akhenaton's death his son-in-law and successor Tutankhaton (r. 1336–1327 B.C.) made a rapprochement with the priests of Amon-Re, which he signaled by changing his name to Tutankhamon. The Amon-Re cult was revived, the Aton cult was abolished, and the city of Akhetaton was abandoned. The priesthood had expanded its power permanently; henceforth, pharaoh's absolutism was not so great as previously.

Arts and Sciences

The Egyptians were superb builders, architects, and engineers. In addition to pyramids and irrigation works, they built numerous other monumental structures: royal tombs, palaces, forts, temples, and obelisks. At their best, Egyptian architects designed buildings in harmony with the unique landscape—one of the reasons for the structures' lasting appeal. Their most original and their most enduring work was done in stone. Stone temples, for example, culminated in the great pillared and monumental structures of the New Kingdom. That period also saw the construction of rock-cut temples, the most famous of which is Ramesses II's (r. 1279–1213 B.C.) project at Abu Simbel: Two chambers were carved out of rock, and in front of the larger chamber were four seated colossi of Ramesses, also carved out of rock. Obelisks were slender, tapering pillars carved of a single piece of stone. Covered with figures and hieroglyphs ("sacred carvings"), and usually erected in pairs in front of a temple, obelisks were meant to glorify the sun.

Throughout history, royal courts have excelled as patrons of the arts; the Egyptian court was one of the first and greatest. Egyptian craftsmen were masters of gold jewelry-work, glassmaking, and woodworking. The major arts are well represented in tombs, which were decorated with rich, multicolored wall paintings, the first narrative painting. There are scenes of the gods, court ceremony, ordinary life, war, and recreation amid the crocodiles and hippotamuses of the Nile Valley. Like so much else in Egypt, painting had a religious purpose. Representations of living people were meant to perpetuate them in the afterlife.

Sculpture was another art form in which Egyptians excelled. Carved in stone, wood, or metal, Egyptian sculpture is a study in contrasts. The body posture is usually rigid and stiff, the musculature only sketchy; the face, in contrast, is often individualistic, the expression full of character and drawn from life. Statues represent kings and queens, gods and goddesses, husbands and wives, adults and children, officials, priests, scribes, animals. Mirroring broader cultural trends, statues of pharaohs undergo a stylistic change from the Old Kingdom, where the royal expression is usually one of majesty and power, to the Middle Kingdom, where the king's face often seems more human and weak. Statues of New Kingdom pharaohs often suggest imperial power, but Amarna sculpture places an unusual emphasis on introspective gazes, and it experiments with the grotesque. Eighteenth Dynasty sculpture often shows a striking interest in feminine beauty and grace.

Ancient Egyptian literature is notable for its variety. Religious subjects, historical and commemorative records, technical treatises in mathematics and medicine, and secular stories survive alongside business contracts and royal proclamations. Egyptian literature is as important for its tools as for its substance. The discovery that the fibers of the papyrus plant could be made into writing material—the word *paper* comes from *papyrus*—would prove to be fundamental for ancient Mediterranean literature. Not only the Egyptians but later the Greeks and Romans and many other ancient peoples wrote on scrolls of papyrus sheets joined together—the precursors of books. Egyptian writing is best known for hieroglyphics, a system of pictures and abstract signs that represent words or ideas. The Egyptians also employed two simplified scripts.

The people who built the pyramids were skilled at arithmetic and geometry. Although not as sophisticated as later mathematicians, Egyptians were able to approximate *pi* (the ratio of the circumference of a circle to its diameter) and to solve equations containing one or two unknowns. Mathematical astronomy never reached the heights in Egypt that it reached in Babylon (see page 45), but the Egyptian calendar was a notable achievement. Based on observation of the star Sirius, the Egyptian calendar, with its 365-day year, approximates the solar calendar. Julius Caesar brought the Egyptian calendar to Rome. Corrected to 365¼ days, it survives to this day (in adjusted form) as the calendar of Europe, the Americas, and much of the rest of the world.

Egyptian medical doctors were admired in antiquity and were in demand abroad. They could set a dislocated shoulder. They had a full battery of splints, disinfectants, sutures, adhesive plasters, elementary disinfectants (from tree leaves), and fatty substances to treat burns. A brilliant treatise, the so-called Edwin Smith Papyrus, demonstrates sophistication and rationalism. Dating from around 1750 B.C., the document claims to be a copy of an original dating from 2700 B.C. (the veracity of that claim is uncertain). In this treatise physicians divide diseases into three categories: treatable, possibly treatable, and untreatable. There are signs of careful observation and tantalizing evidence of postmortem dissection.

Unfortunately, as in Mesopotamia, medical science (at least written medical science) seems to have stagnated after a promising beginning. Although Egyptian doctors distinguished between medicine and magic, they were happy to use magic when all else failed—but usually only then. In a letter of the thirteenth century B.C. to a Hittite king, Ramesses II declines the king's request for an Egyptian physician to treat his sister's infertility. A physician could do nothing, Ramesses explains, because the unfortunate woman was too old to bear children. He goes on to say, however, that an Egyptian magician might be perfect for the job and he has decided to send one.

Widening Horizons: Anatolia and the Levant

The literate river-valley civilizations tend to capture our attention in the third millennium B.C., but we know that city-states were flourishing elsewhere, particularly in the Levant.* Traders that neighbored Egypt, Mesopotamia, and Anatolia, the cities of the Levant were also frequently at the mercy of foreign invasion. The discovery in 1974 of a huge cuneiform archive at Ebla (modern Tell Mardikh) in northern Syria has revolutionized our knowledge of one such city-state in the mid-third millennium B.C. Ugarit (modern Ras Shamra), a cosmopolitan port, flourished in the second millennium B.C.

In the second millennium B.C. the civilized world grew wider and more thoroughly interconnected. New kingdoms appeared, among them the Kassites in Babylonia, the Hittites in Anatolia, and the Hurrians in northern Mesopotamia and Syria. Their expansionist ambitions and those of New Kingdom Egypt made the period from approximately 1500 to 1200 B.C. one of international conflict, both military and diplomatic. It was not only an age of wars and treaties but also one of cultural creativity marked by achievements such as international law, sophisticated historical analysis, and the first alphabet. New kingdoms on the island of Crete (at its height, ca. 1800–1550 B.C.) and on the mainland of Greece (at its height, ca. 1400–1200 B.C.) also became part of the international system (see pages 66 and 67). In the century from about 1250 to about 1150 B.C., however, an unexplained series of economic and demographic disruptions, resulting in invasions and piracy, brought both the international system and its component kingdoms to ruin.

ANATOLIA AND THE LEVANT

2500–2350 B.C.	Cuneiform Texts from Ebla
1650–1450 B.C.	Hittite Old Kingdom
1457	Battle of Megiddo
1450–1380 B.C.	Hittite Middle Kingdom
1380–1180 B.C.	Hittite New Kingdom (Empire)
1400–1200 B.C.	Height of Prosperity at Ugarit
1274	Battle of Kadesh
1250–1150 B.C.	Sea Peoples Invade

The City-States of Syria-Palestine

Most of the documents in Ebla's archive are fragmentary. Nevertheless, the sheer number of them —more than sixteen thousand tablets—has more than doubled the total of known cuneiform documents from the early era of writing (down to ca. 2350 B.C.). Eblaite was a West Semitic language. The work of Eblaite scribes, the texts cover a period of about forty years, probably sometime

*The term *Levant* can be used to refer generally to the territory on the eastern shore of the eastern Mediterranean or, more particularly, to the geographical region known today as Syria and Palestine. In this text, *Levant* is used in the latter sense.

between 2500 and 2350 B.C. Among the writings are the world's earliest known dictionaries.

Ebla was a teeming center of commerce and artisanry. It was a large kingdom, extending over much of Syria, and possibly containing as many as 250,000 people, of whom perhaps 30,000 lived in the city. Successful farmers and sheep- and cattle-herders, Eblaites exported grain and olive oil. Eblaite craftsmen specialized in woolen and linen fabrics and garments and worked-metal objects, including jewelry, daggers, and dishes. Eblaite merchants traded these goods over a wide region from Egypt to Anatolia to western Iran to the lands of the Persian Gulf.

The government fostered trade by negotiating commercial treaties and arranging dynastic marriages. One such treaty between Ebla and Ashur, a city about 435 miles to the east, is the earliest known agreement between two states. When diplomacy failed, Ebla resorted to war, with great success. Ebla's most notable conquest was Mari, a commercial competitor 300 miles downstream on the Euphrates, which tried to block Eblaite trade with Mesopotamia. The defeated Mari was forced to pay tribute and accept an Eblaite governor.

Ebla was ruled by an oligarchy (small elite) headed by fourteen regional governors who were probably also clan elders. The king, a sort of first among equals, was chosen by election rather than inheritance; his power was limited by the oligarchic council. Eblaites seem to have conceived of the state as a large family, the "children of Ebla." The queen and queen mother had significant government authority. The queen had her own properties, administered by officials who answered to her. The queen mother, officially called "the honored mother of the king," had considerable say in the succession.

Attacked by Akkadians around 2300 B.C., Ebla fell to the Amorites around 2000 B.C. It remained a wealthy city, though much diminished in power. Our eyes might now turn to Ugarit, a thriving Mediterranean port of Syria around 1400–1200, as a wealth of documentation indicates. The keynote of Ugarit's history is its cosmopolitanism. As a trading center it linked ships coming from the eastern Mediterranean island of Cyprus or the Anatolian ports with land caravans to Babylonia. Like the later Phoenician cities (see page 46), it was both a middleman and an exporter of its own products such as purple-dyed textiles and metals. The indigenous inhabitants of Ugarit spoke a West Semitic language; their culture and that of large numbers of people in southern Syria and Palestine is called Canaanite (from the Hebrew Bible, which calls Palestine "the land of Canaan"). The merchant community in Ugarit, however, was polyglot, including not only the Canaanite majority but Babylonians, Egyptians, Moabites (a people from the region that is now Jordan), Hittites, and Hurrians, among others.

Canaanite religion in the second millennium B.C. is well attested to in Ugaritic art and texts. Ugarit's gods were anthropomorphic and many in number. The central deities were two divine pairs. One pair (El and Athirat) consists of a king and a queen symbolizing order; the other consists of a storm god and a passionate goddess (Baal and Anat) symbolizing flux and turmoil. El ("god") is a transcendent deity, both the wise creator and the powerful father called "bull." His consort Athirat, called "the progenitress of the gods," is a maternal goddess. In contrast to El, Baal (literally "lord") is present in the natural world. A storm-god, Baal brings rain and fertility but struggles against other forces of nature: Yamm ("the sea"); the desert gods, called the "devourers"; and Mot ("death"), whom not even the gods can conquer. Anat, Baal's sister and perhaps consort, is a violent deity of love and war.

Ugaritic epic and mythic texts contain lessons about the fragility of humans in the divine order. Human prosperity depends on the wisdom and piety of kings and nobles, but they are, alas, imperfect beings. In the *Legend of King Keret,* an epic poem from the fourteenth century B.C., the king fails to fulfill a vow to the goddess Athirat and thus suffers a grave illness that destabilizes his kingdom. The pious are rewarded, and the wicked are punished; but the prayers even of the wicked are heard by El, beneficent ruler of all. Humans suffer in the Ugaritic cosmos, but in the end El hears his children's prayers.

Canaanite religion cast a wide shadow. Baal-worship in the Levant, for example, survived into the first millennium B.C., when it was strong enough to pose a threat to the monotheistic fervor of the Hebrew prophets (see page 52). There is considerable though not unanimously accepted

Relief from Ebla Carved in basalt (a dark volcanic rock) on the side of a sacrificial basin, this sculpture of soldiers and roaring lions comes from the Amorite period (ca. 1800 B.C.). Somewhat coarse in style, it bears witness to the importance of military power in western Asia at the time. *(Aleppo Archaeological Museum. Courtesy, Direction Generales des Antiquités et des Musées)*

evidence that the Greeks absorbed Ugaritic mythology. By far the most influential legacy of Ugaritic culture, however, is the creation of the world's oldest alphabet. Perhaps a wish to set religious documents in writing lay behind the invention of the Ugaritic alphabet; perhaps commercial efficiency was the driving motive. Whatever the cause, Ugaritic scribes in the fourteenth century B.C. invented thirty cuneiform signs as an alphabet to write their Semitic language. It was a true alphabet in that each sign stood for one and only one sound. Later adapted by the Phoenicians and, through them, the Greeks, the Ugaritic alphabet is the source of the English alphabet and most other alphabets in the world today.

The Hittites

How and when the Hittites first came to Anatolia are obscure, but somewhat before 1800 B.C. Hittite personal names appear in contemporary texts. The Hittites spoke an Indo-European language. Nearly half of the world's people today speak an Indo-European language—such as English, French, Italian, German, Greek, Russian, Iranian, and Hindi. Indo-European-speakers probably originated between 4500 and 2500 B.C. in southern Russia, in the region of the Dnieper and Volga rivers. A warlike, mobile, horse-riding people, they emigrated east and west.

The warlike Hittites were masters of the horse. Another source of Hittite power was their control of Anatolia, which they ruled from their city of Hattusas (modern Boghazköy). Rich in minerals and in farmland, Anatolia provided a solid foundation for empire.

Hittite rulers can be securely identified beginning in the seventeenth century B.C. Hittite history is divided into an Old Kingdom (ca. 1650–1450 B.C.) marked by the conquest and consolidation of Anatolia; a Middle Kingdom (ca. 1450–1380 B.C.), a period of retrenchment and loss of territory; a New Kingdom (ca. 1380–1180) characterized by intervention in international politics and then collapse; and finally a Neo-Hittite era (ca. 1180–700) of small successor states. The Hittite empire reached its zenith in the New Kingdom, when it extended into Syria and northern Mesopotamia. It was a time of shifting empires. For instance, after the Old Babylonian (Amorite) dynasty was ended by a Hittite raid, the Kassites, a people from the Zagros mountains of Mesopotamia, took over Babylonia and ruled it for three hundred years (1500–1200 B.C.). The Hurrians carved out the kingdom of Mitanni on the Upper Euphrates around 1500 B.C.

The Old Kingdom Hittite monarch was closer to an Eblaite than to an Egyptian or a Mesopotamian king; he was neither god nor god's representative but rather first among equals. He was supported by an armed, horse-riding nobility who, in return for land, supplied him with troops and mounts. The nobles met in assembly and rendered legal judgments. The power of the nobility spelled trouble for central authority in the sixteenth century B.C., when conspiracy, feud, and assassination came close to destroying the Hittite kingdom. The powerful King Telepinu finally established a secure hereditary succession to the throne around 1500 B.C. In the Hittite New Kingdom the balance of power swung further in favor of the king, who was now addressed as "my Sun" during his lifetime and was deified after death.

Hittite queens and queen mothers had strong and independent positions, as at Ebla. Puduhepa, wife of King Hattusilis III (r. 1278–1250 B.C.), played a memorable role in state affairs. For example, she conducted her own correspondence with the queen of Egypt. Various evidence suggests that Puduhepa was the prime mover in an important religious movement, whereby the Hurrian sun-goddess of Arinna (a shrine near Hattusas) became the chief deity of the Hittite state. The goddess was worshiped as "Queen of the Land of Hatti, Queen of Heaven and Earth, mistress of the kings and queens of the Land of Hatti, directing the government of the King and Queen of Hatti."[5]

Much of Hittite culture is derived from that of the pre-Hittite inhabitants of Anatolia (known as the Hattians) and from the Hurrians, who were in turn influenced by Mesopotamia. Most of the Hittites' gods and mythology were Hattian in origin until the Hittite New Kingdom, when Hurrian influence prevailed. Many scholars have been struck by the Hurrian-derived epic cycle of the god Kumarbi. Kumarbi, father of the gods, seizes power after castrating his father Anu (heaven) and is then replaced by his own son, the weather-god Teshub. A Greek poem of about 700 B.C., Hesiod's *Theogony,* tells almost the same story, down to the details, about the three gods Ouranos (heaven), Kronos (father of the gods), and Zeus (the storm-god). It is likely that the story reached the Greeks by way of Phoenicia, where many Hurrians lived in the later second millennium B.C. Rarely can the historian so clearly trace cross-cultural influence at work.

Although Hittite religion is frequently derivative, the sophistication of Hittite political thought is quite original. Earlier peoples had kept lists and chronicles; Hittite annals are notably livelier, better argued, and more conscious of cause and effect. King Hattusilis I (r. 1650–1620 B.C.), for example, used a historical example to encourage obedience to his decision to disown his rebellious son and choose a new heir. His grandfather had proclaimed an heir, but "his servants and the leading citizens spurned his words and set Papadilmah on the throne." A rhetorical question announces the result: "The houses of the leading citizens, where art thou? Have they not perished?" Nor is Hattusilis unaware of the effect that disowning the disobedient prince will have on the boy's mother:

> Then his mother bellowed like an ox: "They have torn asunder the womb in my living body! They have ruined him, and you will kill him!"[6]

The king explains that he has no intention of mistreating his former heir.

By the reign of Hattusilis III (r. 1278–1250 B.C.), the royal annals are even more sophisticated; they read in parts like a lawsuit, carefully pleading a justification of the king's actions. (See the box, "A Hittite King Analyzes Politics.") Treaties with subordinate states similarly begin with an introduction providing historical background and justifying the relationship sworn to in the body of the text.

The First International System and Its Collapse

The fourteenth and thirteenth centuries B.C. were an era of war and diplomacy among the great powers of western Asia and northeast Africa. Armies and ambassadors routinely traveled across the Syro-Palestinian corridor. For the first time a relatively stable system of competing international powers emerged (Map 1.4). In the Old and Middle Kingdoms, the kings had entrusted the defense of Egypt to border fortifications and a small army. Pharaohs in New Kingdom Egypt, in contrast, pursued a forward defense policy, sending diplomats and, when necessary, large mobile armies into the Levant. Both for Egypt and for other large kingdoms such as that of the Hittites, Syria-Palestine became the battleground for power and influence.

War was one sign of the new international system. War consisted of skirmishes marked by an occasional dramatic battle, such as at Megiddo (1457 B.C.) and Kadesh (1274 B.C.). The latter was a huge battle in northern Syria in which twenty thousand Egyptian troops faced seventeen thousand Hittites. Pharaoh Ramesses II failed to achieve his strategic goal of ending Hittite intervention in Egypt's Syrian sphere of influence. The two powers agreed to share control of Syria-Palestine, as a subsequent treaty attests.

Indeed, treaties are another sign of the international system. Quite a few treaties and letters between monarchs survive in cuneiform archives found at several locations, for example, Amarna. The texts reveal a system of gift-exchange and commerce, alliance and dynastic marriage, subjects and governors, rebels and garrisons. Diplomatic niceties are observed. Kings of other great powers address pharaoh as "brother," while Canaanite princelings call him "my lord and my

A Hittite Warrior This 6½-foot-tall figure was carved on the wall of an entry gate to the city of Hattusas, the Hittite capital, during the New Kingdom period (1380–1180 B.C.). Fierce-looking, vigorous, and outfitted with battle ax, sword, kilt, and possibly mail shirt, he is designed to frighten away both human and supernatural enemies. *(Ankara National Museum)*

A Hittite King Analyzes Politics

King Hattusilis III (r. 1278–1250 B.C.) justifies his rebellion as a provincial governor against King Urhi-Teshub (r. 1285–1278 B.C.), his nephew, and his usurpation of the throne. The text demonstrates the Hittites' mastery of sophisticated political argument.

Thus speaks *Tabarna* [Great King] Hattusilis, the great king, king of Hatti, son of Mursilis, the great king of Hatti, grandson of Supiluliumas, the great king, king of Hatti, descendant of Hattusilis, king of Kussara.

I tell the divine power of Ishtar; let all men hear it, and in the future may the reverence of me, the Sun, of my son, of my son's son, and of my Majesty's seed be given to Ishtar among the gods.

[Hattusilis claims that Urhi-Teshub, jealous of his success, became his enemy.] But out of respect for my brother, I loyally did not act selfishly, and for seven years I complied. But then that man sought to destroy me . . . and he took away from me Hakpissa and Nerikka [territories], and then I complied no more but revolted from him. Yet though I revolted from him, I did not do it sinfully, by rising against him in the chariot or rising against him in the house, but I (openly) declared war on him (saying): "You picked a quarrel with me—you are the Great King, while as for me, of the one fortress you have left me, of just that one fortress am I king. Up now! Let Ishtar of Samuha and the Weather-god of Nerik pass judgment on us." Now whereas I wrote thus to Urhi-Teshub, if someone says: "Why did you previously raise him to the throne, yet now you are writing to him to make war on him?" Yet (I reply) if he had never quarrelled with me, would (the gods) by their verdict have made him lose to me. . . . And because my lady Ishtar had previously promised me the throne, so now she visited my wife in a dream (saying): "I am helping thy husband, and all Hattusas will turn to the side of thy husband." . . . Then I saw great favor from Ishtar. She deserted Urhi-Teshub, and in none other but (her own) city of Samuha she shut him up like a pig in a sty, . . . and all Hattusas returned to me."

Source: O. R. Gurney, *The Hittites*, 3d ed. (Harmondsworth, England: Penguin, 1975), pp. 175–176.

Sun-god" and assure him that they are "thy servant and the dirt on which thou dost tread." Beneath the niceties, there is mundane and regular business: quarrels to be judged, rebellions to be squelched, and even the procurement of "fine concubines" for pharaoh in exchange for Egyptian products and manufactured goods.

As grand as the international system of the late second millennium B.C.was, it did not avoid a crashing end. From Mesopotamia to Greece, from Anatolia to Egypt, one state after another collapsed between about 1250 and 1150 B.C. The resulting period was one of relative poverty and isolation. Surviving evidence is fragmentary, but it suggests that both foreign and domestic problems led to the collapse. Raiders and invaders beset the eastern Mediterranean in this period. Called "Sea Peoples" by the Egyptians, they attacked both on land and at sea. We do not know precisely who they were. There is some evidence of famine and climatic change in some countries, leading to disruption and rebellion. Some states may have overextended themselves in war and thereby bred internal decay. Whatever the cause, one kingdom after another fell in the thirteenth century B.C., from Kassite Babylonia to Hittite Anatolia, from Ugarit to the Egyptian New Kingdom to Mycenaean Greece (see page 67). What followed would prove to be a completely different world.

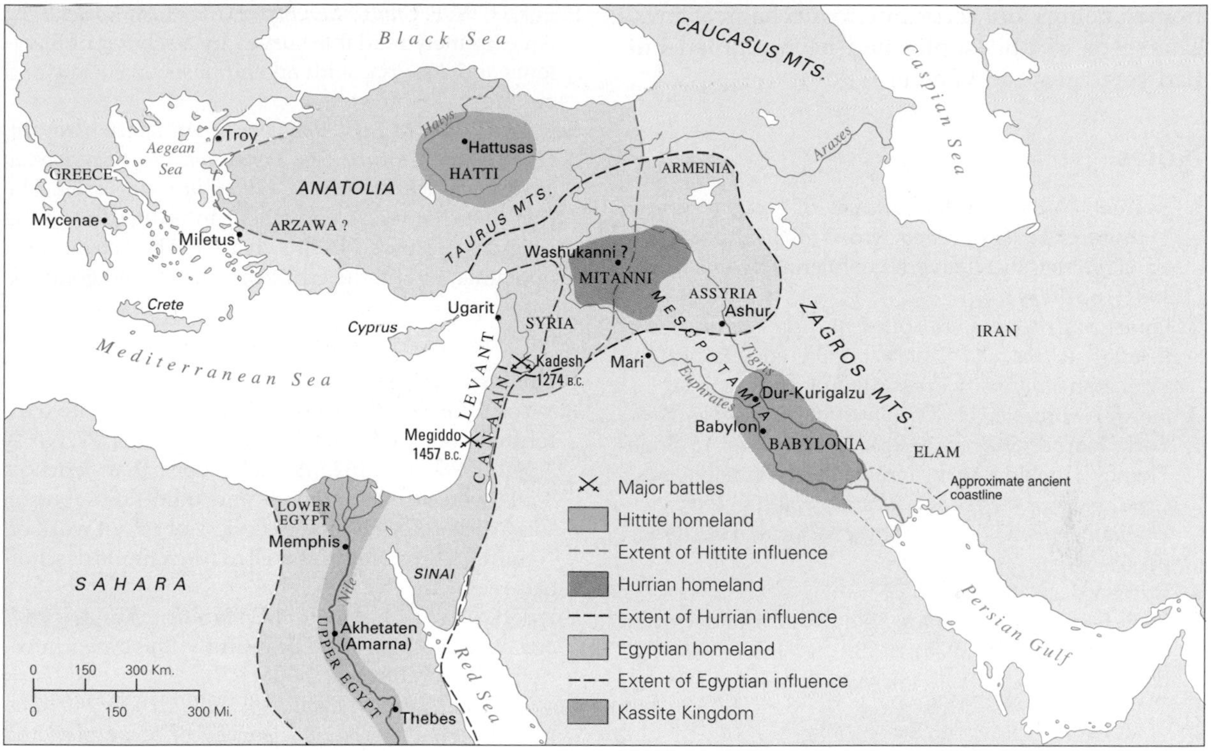

Map 1.4 The International System, ca. 1500–ca. 1200 B.C. In this era of competing kingdoms and city-states, the most dramatic conflict was that between Egypt and the Hittites for control of Syria and Palestine.

Summary

No other period in human history can match the contrasts encountered in this chapter, from the first hominids to the heirs of great kingdoms of Egypt and western Asia after the collapse of the thirteenth century B.C. The legacy of this period, the most creative epoch in human history, almost defies summation. Yet the period was as notable for the questions left unanswered, and the problems left unsolved, as for its achievements. Complex as they were, the various societies of the first two millennia of civilization share a common theme: grandeur of scale. From the vast irrigation works of the Tigris-Euphrates valleys to the grand armies that clashed at Kadesh, from the walls of Uruk to the pyramids, from the towering position of pharaoh to the Akkadian conquest of "the four corners of the earth," from the huge Eblaite archive to the cosmopolitan population of Ugarit, early civilization was a canvas painted with a broad brush.

The relative absence in these civilizations of the notion of the individual and his or her conscience is striking. Gilgamesh, for instance, hero of Mesopotamian epic, is incapable of introspection; his only glimmer of self-understanding comes through comparing himself to his friend Enkidu. Nor did life in Egypt, with its forced labor service and subordination to the state, leave much room for individuality, although the notion of a Last Judgment did at least open a window on individual responsibility. It remained for later ages to redeem the promise of the individual.

It would be the task of later ages too to define the notion of abstract thought. Despite all the scientific achievements of Mesopotamia and Egypt, early thinkers focused on the concrete and specific, without developing the concept of the general principle. To them, nature behaved like human beings, not according to mechanical laws. The seeds of philosophy had been planted but had yet to grow and flower.

Notes

1. Samuel Noah Kramer, *History Begins at Sumer: Thirty-nine Firsts in Man's Recorded History,* 3d rev. ed. (Philadelphia: University of Pennsylvania Press, 1981), pp. 91, 94.
2. James B. Pritchard, ed., *Ancient Near Eastern Texts Relating to the Old Testament,* 3d ed. (Princeton: Princeton University Press, 1969), p. 107.
3. James H. Breasted, *The Conquest of Civilization* (New York: Harper & Bros., 1926), p. 112. Cited in Brian Tierney, Donald Kagan, and L. Pearce Williams, eds., *Great Issues in Western Civilization from Ancient Egypt Through Louis XIV* (New York: McGraw-Hill, 1992), pp. 68–69.
4. Pritchard, p. 408.
5. O. R. Gurney, *The Hittites,* 3d ed. (Harmondsworth, England: Penguin, 1975), p. 139.
6. Ibid., p. 171.

Suggested Reading

General Surveys

Ferrill, Arther. *The Origins of War.* 1985. An excellent introduction to early warfare, though out-of-date on some points.

Frankfort, H., et al. *Before Philosophy: The Intellectual Adventure of Ancient Man. An Essay on Speculative Thought in the Ancient Near East.* 1946. Brilliant essays on the religious and political outlook of people in Mesopotamia and Egypt, contrasting them with the Hebrews and Greeks.

Knapp, A. Bernard. *The History and Culture of Ancient Western Asia and Egypt.* 1988. A clear, concise, and efficient introduction to the basic narrative.

Mallory, John. *In Search of the Indo-Europeans: Language, Archaeology, and Myth.* 1989. A general survey of the current consensus of opinion, arguing that the speakers of the original Indo-European language lived in southern Russia between the Dnieper and Volga rivers around 4500 to 2500 B.C.

Moscati, Sabatino. *The Face of the Ancient Orient: A Panorama of Near Eastern Civilization in Pre-Classical Times.* Trans. from the Italian original. 1962. Although somewhat out-of-date, an unusually lively and ambitious overview from Sumer to ancient Israel, emphasizing the balance of cultural change and continuities.

Neugebauer, Otto. *The Exact Sciences in Antiquity.* 1962. An introduction to ancient astronomy and mathematics.

Saggs, H. W. F. *Civilization Before Greece and Rome.* 1989. An extremely readable survey by a scholar of Babylonia and Assyria, with an emphasis on society and culture.

Seltzer, Robert M., ed. *Religions of Antiquity: Religion, History, and Culture. Selections from The Encyclopedia of Religion, Mircea Eliade, Editor in Chief.* 1989. The first five chapters are excellent introductions to the religions discussed in this chapter. They cover Mesopotamia, Egypt, the Hittites, Canaan, and goddess-worship.

Prehistory

Bar-Yosef, O. "The Walls of Jericho: An Alternative Interpretation." In *Current Anthropology.* Vol. 27, No. 2. April 1986: 157–162. An argument that Jericho's walls were used for flood- and mud-flow–control, this article offers a good overview of recent work on Neolithic chronology, as well as an example of scholarly reassessment.

Gowlett, John A. J. *Ascent to Civilization: The Archaeology of Early Man.* 1984. Beautifully illustrated introduction to prehistory.

Lewin, Roger. *Human Evolution: An Illustrated Introduction.* 2d ed. 1989. A clear survey of a complex and rapidly changing field, with more charts but fewer photographs than the following book.

______. *In the Age of Mankind: A Smithsonian Book of Human Evolution.* 1988. Superb photographs and a readable scholarly text.

Mellaart, James. *The Neolithic of the Near East.* 1975. Though now out-of-date on some points, this remains a good introduction to the subject by the original excavator of Çatal Hüyük. Well-illustrated.

Nissen, Hans J. *The Early History of the Ancient Near East, 9000–2000* B.C. Translated by Elizabeth Lutzeier, with Kenneth Northcott. 1988. A scholarly introduction to the prehistory and the early history of western Asia, with an emphasis on archaeology.

Mesopotamia

Bottéro, Jean. *Mesopotamia: Writing, Reasoning, and the Gods.* Translated by Zainab Bahrani and Marc Van De Mierrop. 1992. A provocative collection of essays arguing that Western civilization began in Mesopotamia; contains a useful glossary.

Jacobsen, Thorkild. *The Treasures of Darkness: A History of Mesopotamian Religion.* 1976. A rich and fundamental introduction.

Kramer, Samuel Noah. *History Begins at Sumer: Thirty-Nine Firsts in Man's Recorded History.* 3d ed. 1981. An engaging tribute to the achievements of early Mesopotamia, though at times perhaps exaggerated.

Lerner, Gerder. *The Creation of Patriarchy.* 1986. A theory of the origins of gender and class hierarchies in

Mesopotamia, with developments in ancient Israel and classical Greece considered as well.

Oates, Joan. *Babylon.* Rev. ed. 1986. A well-illustrated introduction.

Oppenheim, A. L. *Ancient Mesopotamia. Portrait of a Dead Civilization.* Rev. ed. completed by E. Reiner. 1977. A difficult but rewarding introduction to Babylonian and Assyrian cultural history.

Rhee, Song Nai. "Sumerian City-States." In Robert Griffeth and Carol G. Thomas, eds., *The City-State Five Cultures,* 1–30. 1981. A concise introduction, especially good on the economy and environment.

Egypt

Bernal, Martin. *Black Athena: The Afro-Asiatic Roots of Classical Civilization. Vol. 1: The Fabrication of Ancient Greece 1785–1985. Vol. 2: The Archaeological Evidence.* 1987 and 1991. A stimulating and highly controversial argument for the influence of ancient Egypt on ancient Greece. Many scholars agree with the author's arguments on nineteenth-century historians, but few accept his reconstruction of ancient history.

Edwards, I. E. S. *The Pyramids of Egypt.* Rev. ed. 1986. A detailed and well-illustrated introduction, focusing on construction.

James, T. G. H. *Pharaoh's People: Scenes From Life in Imperial Egypt.* 1984. A discussion of Egyptian society in the mid-Eighteenth Dynasty (ca. 1500–1400 B.C.). Subjects include administration, justice, literacy, farming, household architecture, and the domestic economy.

Kemp, Barry J. *Ancient Egypt: Anatomy of a Civilization.* 1991. A sophisticated and up-to-date essay, focusing on archaeology and ideology, best read after a narrative introduction.

Lichtheim, Miriam. *Ancient Egyptian Literature.* 3 vols. 1975–1980. A large selection of translations of Egyptian literary and religious texts.

Metcalf, Peter, and Richard Huntington. *Celebrations of Death: The Anthropology of Mortuary Ritual.* 2d rev. ed. 1991. Includes a fascinating discussion of the pyramids.

Mokhtar, G., ed. *General History of Africa. Vol. 2: Ancient Civilizations of Africa.* Abridged ed., UNESCO General History of Africa. 1990. A good general introduction to the ancient cultures of Egypt, Nubia, Ethiopia, and Libya, among others.

Murnane, William J. *The Penguin Guide to Ancient Egypt.* 1983. Both a travel guide and a sound, basic introduction by a scholar; well illustrated.

Redford, Donald B. *Akhenaten: The Heretic King.* 1984. A highly readable and scholarly account.

Trigger, B. G.; B. J. Kemp; D. O'Conner; and A. B. Lloyd. *Ancient Egypt: A Social History.* 1983. A challenging introduction combining narrative with the analytic approach of the social sciences.

Wilson, John A. *The Burden of Egypt: An Interpretation of Ancient Egyptian Culture.* 1951. Out-of-date on some points, especially on Egypt's earliest history, but still a grand and beautifully written synthesis.

Anatolia and the Levant

Gurney, O. R. *The Hittites.* 3d ed. 1975. A sound introductory survey, with close attention to the sources of evidence.

Macqueen, J. G. *The Hittites and Their Contemporaries in Asia Minor.* 2d rev. ed. 1986. A well-illustrated, thematic discussion.

Pettinato, Giovanni. *Ebla: A New Look at History.* Translated by C. Faith Richardson. 1991. An introduction to the site and its historical significance by the scholar who deciphered Ebla's large royal archive of cuneiform tablets.

Sandars, N. K. *The Sea Peoples: Warriors of the Ancient Mediterranean, 1250–1150 B.C.* 1978. A logical and thorough discussion of the evidence for a complex subject, a case of archaeological detective work; beautifully illustrated.

Weighing the Evidence

THE PYRAMIDS

Many monuments come and go, but not the pyramids of Egypt. The thirty-five major and many smaller pyramids of the pharaonic period were the wonder of the ancient world and are still breathtaking. Best known are the Great Pyramids of Giza—three gigantic, perfectly symmetrical limestone tombs, static and unchanging. Nearly five thousand years since it was built, the pyramid of King Khufu (r. 2589–2566 B.C., better known by his Greek name, Cheops) is still the largest all-stone building in human history.

Built on a base area of 13 acres and rising to a height of 481 feet before its top was damaged, the Great Pyramid of Khufu (rearmost of the three large pyramids in the photo) is magnificent, wondrous, unique: The adjectives pile up. (The central pyramid in the photo is steeper than Khufu's and now taller, but the volume of Khufu's pyramid is greater.) The historian, though, deals not in adjectives but in data. He or she looks at the pyramids and frowns, puzzled. The historian sees the pyramids not as completed monuments but as a monumental problem in construction. How on earth, the historian asks, did the Egyptians build them? Equally important, *why* did they build them?

From the humblest peasant who hauled stone, to the king's son—the individual normally entrusted with the responsibility of managing the site—the pyramid-builders did a heroic job. They had to quarry, drag, and put in place the over 20 million tons of stone contained in the Great Pyramids. Within each pyramid they had to construct a system of tunnels, chambers, vaults, and sliding stone portcullises (grilles) to defend the royal tomb from outsiders. They had to build the complex of tombs, temples, courtyards, statues, pits (containing boats used in the royal funeral), and causeway that stood outside each pyramid. The builders also constructed the nearby Great Sphinx, a human-headed lion carved out of a huge rock outcropping, and perhaps representing Khufu's son king Khepren (r. 2558–2532 B.C.), for whom the second pyramid at Giza was built. The tens of thousands of workers (an educated guess of the number) represented, moreover, a huge challenge in feeding and housing.

The pyramid-builders left almost no written documents about their achievement, but archaeology, fortunately, fills much of the silence. The Great Pyramids stand on a bed of limestone on the west side of the Nile Valley, the very stone used to provide the cores of the buildings, as the still-visible signs of quarrying show. The pyramids were once encased in fine limestone from quarries on the east side of the Nile. Look at the pyramid of Khephren, the central one of the three Great Pyramids illustrated here. Remains of the smooth, limestone outer casing can still be seen near the summit. Stone chippings found seemingly everywhere on the Giza plateau provide a clue about how the individual blocks of a pyramid were put in place. These chippings may have been used to make huge temporary ramps that snaked around and up each pyramid while it was under construction, allowing the builders to haul the blocks into place. When the project was complete, the ramps were torn down.

The workmen's quarters seem at first to have disappeared. On closer inspection, we might locate them under dumps of stone chippings, where remains of one worker's camp were found in the 1970s. Some archaeologists believe that the whole southern edge of the Giza plateau is a vast landfill of ramp and worker-camp debris.

Funerary monuments, the pyramids were to serve as eternal homes for the god-king, who, Egyptians thought, lived on after death. The pyramidal shape beautifully symbolized the king's ascent to heaven on a stairway formed by the rays of the sun. Even so, the vast construction effort would seem to epitomize vanity if its purpose were just to build one man's tomb. We will better understand the pyramids if we see their construction as a way of building a nation.

When the pyramids of Giza were built, the kingdom of Egypt was still young. The power of the king to control the vast area of Lower and Up-

The Great Pyramids of Giza *(Michael Holford)*

per Egypt was still open both to question and to armed revolt. By ordering the construction of an astonishingly large project focused on his person, the king made a statement of his power: an eloquent, simple, and irrefutable statement.

The Great Pyramids symbolized the king's power. Their sheer size demonstrated his ability to organize a vast labor force. Indeed, it has plausibly been suggested that the encampment of workers at Giza represents the largest gathering of human beings to that date. Moreover, the pyramids and the rows of tombs surrounding them reinforced the hierarchical structure of Egyptian society, of which the king was the capstone. Only princes and some officials were given the privilege of erecting a tomb beside the royal pyramids, a privilege that Fourth Dynasty Egyptians viewed as a prerequisite to gaining access to eternal life. The principal royal wives were permitted to be buried in small pyramids of their own, as we see, for example, in the three small pyramids of queens in the foreground of the illustration here.

Did the Great Pyramids succeed in establishing royal authority? The Old Kingdom lasted another three hundred years after the reign of Menkaure (r. 2532–2504), builder of the last of the three Great Pyramids. His successors generally built much smaller pyramids. Some scholars believe they had no choice, because of the crushing costs of construction. In all likelihood, however, pyramid-building stimulated Egypt's economy, fostering prosperity and the spread of craftsmanship. Perhaps Egypt's kings ceased building enormous pyramids because, having made their point, having demonstrated their extraordinary power, it was no longer necessary to do so.

CHAPTER 2

The Book and the Myths: Western Asia and Early Greece

In the sixth century B.C. an obscure prophet—we know him only as "Second Isaiah"—preached a bold message to his compatriots, a conquered people living in exile in Babylon. He told them that Yahweh, their god, was a god of justice and mercy—the one and only true god of the entire world—and that Yahweh had chosen the king of mountainous, backward Persia to conquer western Asia and redeem Yahweh's people. The Babylonians, imperialists who considered their city the center of the universe, might have laughed at the idea that two provincial peoples would divide spiritual and worldly rulership between them. Yet the Persians under Cyrus the Great conquered Babylon in 539 B.C. and a year later proclaimed the freedom of Yahweh's people—the Jews—to return to Palestine and re-establish the Temple to their god in the city of Jerusalem. They did so, and around this time they wrote down their religious and historical traditions in large sections of what would become the Hebrew Bible.

Also in the sixth century B.C., Peisistratus, the ambitious ruler of Athens, a tiny city-state a thousand miles northwest of Babylon, sponsored a literary project to preserve the religious and historical traditions of his people. The literary works whose texts were standardized under his patronage are the *Iliad* and *Odyssey*, the epic poems of Homer, who had composed them more than two centuries before.

Both the Hebrew Bible and the Homeric poems are deeply religious in outlook, but there the similarities end. The Hebrew Bible is monotheistic

Frieze of archers of Darius I (r. 521–486 B.C.) at Susa.

and focuses on the individual's subordination to God. Homer is polytheistic and glorifies the hero, who, though doomed to fail, aspires to godlike achievement. For most scholars the Bible and Homer represent two poles of Western Civilization: the sacred and the worldly, the reverent and the heroic, holy writ and poetic craftsmanship.

The first millennium B.C., therefore, was an era of new and divergent cultural creativity. It was also a period of material innovation. Scholars sometimes call the first millennium the "Iron Age." Thanks to new heating and cooling techniques, metalsmiths produced an alloy of carbon and iron that was harder and more durable than bronze. Iron began to replace bronze in tools and weapons, opening up new technical and military possibilities.

The iron-clad soldiers of Assyria and Persia—to name the most successful examples—established empires that were more systematically organized than were the loose hegemonies of earlier imperialists such as the Akkadians, Hittites, and New Kingdom Egyptians. Guided by Zoroastrianism, a monotheistic and highly ethical religion, the Persian elite ruled a vast, multiethnic empire that stretched from Egypt to modern Pakistan. There was peaceful expansion, too, during the first millennium, through trade and colonization. Great shipbuilders, sailors, and merchants, the Phoenicians traveled as far as Britain and established colonies in the western Mediterranean.

Assyrians, Neo-Babylonians, Phoenicians

Ruthless soldiers, brutal conquerors, and innovative administrators, the Assyrians established an empire in western Asia and Egypt during the eighth and seventh centuries B.C. They were followed in turn by a Neo-Babylonian empire in the seventh and sixth centuries.

Few areas changed hands more often than the hills and coastal plains south of Syria, the area of modern Lebanon, Israel, and Palestine. In the northern part of this region the Phoenicians created a vibrant culture of independent city-states. Neither the Egyptians nor the Hittites ever rebuilt the empires lost to the invasion of the Sea Peoples (1250–1150 B.C.), thereby making it possible for small states to carve out a sphere of independence, as the Phoenicians did. At the height of their prosperity (ca. 1050–750 B.C.) Phoenician merchants and colonizers spread aspects of the advanced civilization of western Asia westward across the Mediterranean.

The Roar of the Lions

The Assyrians, whose homeland was in what is today northern Iraq, spoke a Semitic language. For most of the second millennium B.C. they were a military and mercantile power. They prospered in the metals trade between Mesopotamia and Anatolia, and they were a factor in the balance of power between the Hittites and New Kingdom Egypt. Around 1200 B.C. the Assyrians' state collapsed, but they held on to a small homeland of about 5000 square miles. The toughened survivors emerged with a very aggressive ideology. By expanding in all directions, Assyria ensured security as well as profit.

Assyria's greatest successes came in the eighth and seventh centuries. One by one, states large and small fell—Babylonia, Syria, the kingdom of Israel, Cilicia in southern Anatolia, even Egypt (though Assyrian rule there lasted only a generation). Assyria ruled the two great river valleys of the ancient Near East: the Nile and the Tigris-Euphrates. It was the first state to attain such an achievement. Warrior-kings such as Tiglath-pileser III (r. 744–727 B.C.), Sargon II (r. 721–705), Sennacherib (r. 704–681), and Assurbanipal (r. 668–627) became feared names everywhere.

The Assyrians were warriors. Asshur, their main deity, was a war-god. The key to Assyria's success was its army—from 100,000 to 200,000 men strong—which made an unforgettable impression on observers. The Israelite prophet Isaiah of Jerusalem ("First Isaiah") said of Assyrian soldiers: "[their] arrows are sharpened, and all their bows bent, their horses' hoofs are like flint, their chariot wheels like the whirlwind. Their growling is like that of a lion." (Isaiah 5:28–29). He might have added that Assyrian spearmen, archers, and cavalrymen were equipped with iron weapons and armor. Assyria was the first major state to employ regular cavalry units (rather than charioteers) as the main strike force.

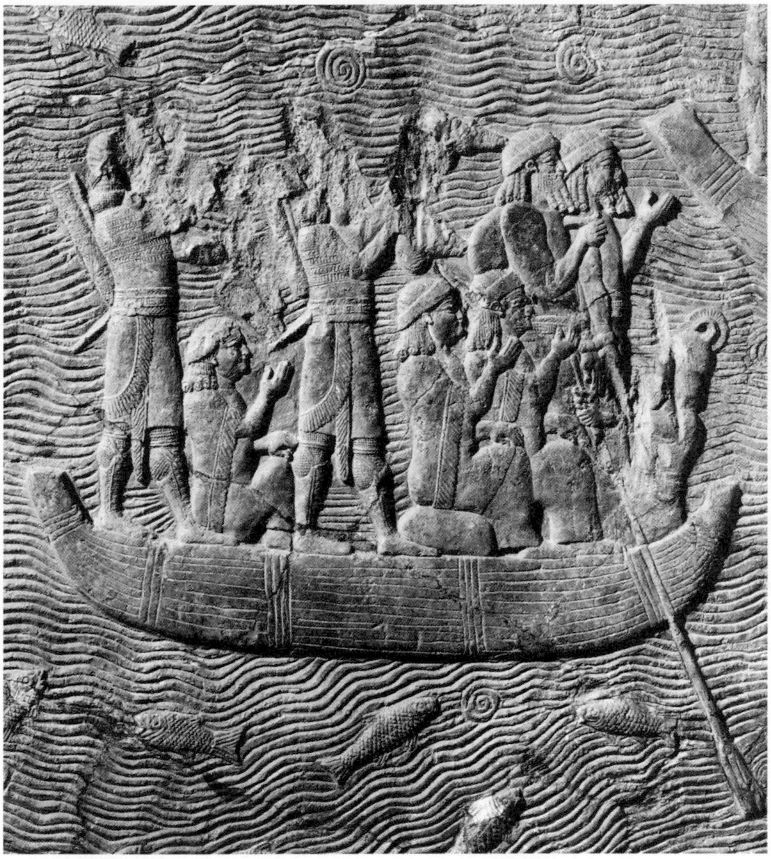

Assyrian Art The sculptured reliefs on the walls of the palace of King Sennacherib (r. 704–681 B.C.) at Nineveh illustrate the relentless expansion of Assyrian military power. This vivid example depicts a royal expedition in the marshes of southern Babylonia. *(Reproduced by Courtesy of the Trustees of the British Museum)*

The Assyrians were excellent engineers, adept at taking walled cities by siege (see the box, "An Assyrian King Attacks Phoenicia and Jerusalem").

The Assyrians displayed superb organizational skills. The central, standing army was supplemented with draftees conscripted from around the empire. Surviving texts document the careful attention that royal agents in the provinces paid to obtaining, maintaining, and distributing horses for the cavalry and chariots. Provinces were kept small to prevent the emergence of separate power bases, and independent-minded nobles were regularly checked by the kings.

The Assyrians were masters at applying a minimum of force with a maximum of brutality. To control the restive subjects of their far-flung empire, the Assyrians met rebellion with ferocious reprisals. Disloyal cities were attacked and, if need be, destroyed. To make sure that everyone understood, the Assyrians set up sculptured reliefs and inscriptions to show, often in gruesome detail, the fate awaiting Assyria's enemies. We see or read of cities burned to the ground; of men flayed alive, even though they had surrendered, and walls covered with their skin; and of piles of human skulls.

The Assyrians engaged in mass deportation. They uprooted the people of a conquered country, resettled them far away—often in Assyria itself—and colonized their land with Assyrian loyalists. Says one royal Assyrian text, in a statement

WESTERN ASIA

ca. 1250–1150 B.C.	Sea Peoples
ca. 1200–1000 B.C.	Israelites settle Palestinian hill country
ca. 1050–750 B.C.	Height of Phoenician city-states
ca. 1020–1004 B.C.	Reign of first Israelite king, Saul
1004–965 B.C.	Reign of David
965–928 B.C.	Reign of Solomon
928–722 B.C.	Divided monarchy (Israel and Judah)
ca. 750–664 B.C.	Height of Assyrian Empire
722 B.C.	Assyrians conquer kingdom of Israel
622 B.C.	Judah accepts "Scroll of the Covenant"
612 B.C.	Conquest of Nineveh
598 B.C.	Neo-Babylonians conquer kingdom of Judah
559–530 B.C.	Reign of Cyrus
550–331 B.C.	Achaemenid Empire
539 B.C.	Cyrus conquers Babylon; permits Jews to return to Palestine
521–486 B.C.	Reign of Darius I
ca. 425 B.C.	Judaean assembly accepts the Torah

echoed by many others, "Bit Amukanni [in Babylonia] I trampled down like a threshing sledge. All of its people and its goods, I took to Assyria." The Assyrians were using mass deportation as early as 1300 B.C., but only under Tiglath-pileser III (r. 744–727 B.C.) did it become a central part of their imperial policy, and it remained so through the reign of Assurbanipal (r. 668–627 B.C.). The so-called Ten Lost Tribes of Israel—the people of the northern Israelite kingdom—were conquered by Assyria in 722 B.C. and transported to Mesopotamia, where they disappear from history.

Assyrian policy was the result of careful calculation. For example, although it is estimated that the Assyrians deported several million people, they deported not whole populations but a carefully chosen cross-section of professions. In that way they ensured themselves a varied subject labor force that included farmers, laborers, and soldiers. They also deported entire families together, to weaken deportees' emotional ties to their former homes. Many deportees were settled in Assyria, where they contributed to the economic and military strength of the empire.

The Assyrian Empire reached its greatest extent with the invasion of Egypt in 667 and 664 B.C., but it had overextended itself (see Map 2.1). Having learned from defeat, Assyria's neighbors had mastered Assyria's military skills. A coalition army of a revived Babylonian kingdom and of Medes (who had formed a powerful state in Iran) conquered Nineveh, the Assyrian capital, in 612 B.C. and defeated the remnants of the Assyrian army in battles in 609 and 605. The Assyrians built a political unit of unprecedented size and efficient administration, but they are primarily remembered for militarism and brutality. Few subjects mourned their passing.

The destruction of Assyria led to a brief political and longer-lived cultural revival for Babylon, whose rulers attempted to revive the glories of Hammurabi's day. For a short period, until the Persian conquest in 539 B.C., the Neo-Babylonian dynasty (founded in 626) and the Medes of Iran were the dominant military forces in western Asia. The Neo-Babylonian dynasty is best known for three things: its prominent place in the Hebrew Bible, the so-called Hanging Gardens of Babylon, and the interest it fostered in astronomy and astrology. As for the Medes, they were an Indo-European-speaking people of western Iran, who rose to power in the mid- to late seventh century B.C. After playing their part in the destruction of the Assyrian Empire, the Medes expanded northward into Armenia and Anatolia. They had already asserted power over the Persians, their Indo-European-speaking neighbors in southwestern Iran (see page 57).

The Neo-Babylonian king Nebuchadrezzar II (Nebuchadnezzar in the Hebrew Bible; r. 605–562 B.C.) conquered the kingdom of Judah (in central Palestine) in 598 and destroyed Jerusalem in 586. He deported many thousands of Judeans to Babylon. Most of the rest of western Asia also fell

An Assyrian King Attacks Phoenicia and Jerusalem

In this inscription the warrior-king Sennacherib describes how he suppressed rebellions in the region of Syria-Palestine in 701 B.C. The king describes Assyrian methods of attacking walled cities and the harsh punishments meted out to the conquered (the Hebrew Bible, in the Second Book of Kings 18:9–19, narrates the rebellion of Hezekiah, king of Judah, from the Israelite point of view).

In my third campaign I marched against Hatti. Luli, king of Sidon, whom the terror-inspiring glamor of my lordship had overwhelmed, fled far overseas and perished. The awe-inspiring splendor of the "Weapon" of Ashur, my lord, overwhelmed his strong cities (such as) Great Sidon, Little Sidon, Bit-Zitti, Zaribtu, Mahalliba, Ushu (i.e., the mainland settlement of Tyre), Akzib (and) Akko, (all) his fortress cities, walled (and well) provided with feed and water for his garrisons, and they bowed in submission to my feet. I installed Ethba'al upon the throne to be their king and imposed upon him tribute (due) to me (as his) overlord (to be paid) annually without interruption. . . .

I assaulted Ekron [a city on Palestine's coastal plain] and killed the officials and patricians who had committed the crime [of rebelling] and hung their bodies on poles surrounding the city. . . .

As to Hezekiah, the Jew, he did not submit to my yoke, I laid siege to 46 of his strong cities, walled forts and to the countless small villages in their vicinity, and conquered (them) by means of well-stamped (earth-) ramps, and battering-rams brought (thus) near (to the walls) (combined with) the attack by foot-soldiers, (using) mines, breeches as well as sapper work. I drove out (of them) 200,150 people, young and old, male and female, horses, mules, donkeys, camels, big and small cattle beyond counting, and considered (them) booty. Himself I made a prisoner in Jerusalem, his royal residence, like a bird in a cage. I surrounded him with earthwork in order to molest those who were leaving his city's gate. His towns which I had plundered, I took away from his country and gave them . . . [to several Philistine kings]. Thus I reduced his country, but I still increased the tribute and the . . . presents (due) to me (as his) overlord which I imposed (later) upon him beyond the former tribute, to be delivered annually.

Source: James B. Pritchard, ed., *Ancient Near Eastern Texts Relating to the Old Testament,* 3d ed., with Supplement (Princeton, N.J.: Princeton University Press, 1969), pp. 287–288.

to Nebuchadrezzar's troops. His most enduring achievement was rebuilding Babylon on a grand scale. In addition to numerous temples, shrines, and altars there was the Hanging Gardens, celebrated by Greek writers. They describe the structure as a large terraced complex that Nebuchadrezzar built for his queen, though it may have been a large plant-covered ziggurat.

Following Mesopotamian tradition, the Neo-Babylonians had a great interest in astronomy, as indeed the Assyrians did as well. The prime motive of Babylonian astronomy was religious—that is, a belief in astrology (the prediction of the future by studying the movement of heavenly bodies). Astrology led to advances in the scientific observation of the heavens. By about 1000 B.C. Assyrians had produced relatively accurate circular diagrams (astrolabes) that showed the positions of the major constellations, stars, and planets over the course of the year. From about

Ishtar Gate, Babylon Under Nebuchadrezzar II (r. 605–562 B.C.) Babylon received a double wall 10 miles long. The massive entryway, a restoration of which is illustrated here, was decorated with glazed, colored bricks showing bulls and dragons. *(Erich Lessing/Art Resource)*

800 B.C. on, Assyrian astronomical observations became particularly careful; by 600 B.C. Assyrian and Neo-Babylonian astronomers could predict solstices, equinoxes, and lunar eclipses.

Astronomy in Mesopotamia reached its heights in the centuries after 500 B.C. The zodiac, a diagram showing the movement of the sun and planets relative to the constellations, was invented in Persian-ruled Babylon in the fourth-century B.C. In the third and second centuries B.C., when Babylonia was under Hellenistic Greek rule, native scientists made great advances in mathematical astronomy, composing tables that could be used to calculate movements of the moon and planets. More sophisticated mathematical astronomy was not produced in the West until the Scientific Revolution of the sixteenth century A.D.

Traders the World Honored

In the Hebrew Bible and in Homer the Phoenicians loom large as merchants and seamen, as "traders the world honored" (Isaiah 23:8). They played a major role in the spread of urbanism and literacy to both shores of the Mediterranean—in Europe and North Africa. Unfortunately, the historical record of the Phoenicians is skimpy, even though they kept records. They wrote on papyrus, which has not survived (papyrus survives only in extremely dry climates such as that of Egypt). Moreover, there has been relatively little archaeological excavation in the area of ancient Phoenicia (Map 2.1). Thus, Phoenician history must be pieced together from scant archaeological remains and from the writings of other ancient peoples.

Phoenician is a Greek term for a people whose civilization was at its height between approximately 1050 and 750 B.C. The word probably refers to the purple dye for which the Phoenicians were well known. Phoenicians were Canaanites, speakers of a Semitic language, and heirs to the civilization that had prospered in Ugarit around 1400 B.C. They refined the alphabet that had appeared in Ugarit by 1300 B.C. (see page 31).

In the mid-second millennium B.C., Canaanites controlled the Levant from Syria to southern Palestine. Beginning around 1200 B.C., however, Sea Peoples, Israelites, and others conquered much of their land. By 1150 B.C. the Canaanites controlled only a narrow strip along the Mediterranean, about 200 miles long and 20 miles wide, in the area of modern Lebanon and northern Israel. They are the people whom historians call "Phoenicians."

Like the Sumerians, the Phoenicians lived in independent and quarrelsome city-states, each consisting of a walled town and a rural territory. The city-states competed over territory and control of commerce. The most important and populous were Aradus, Byblos, Sidon, and Tyre, the greatest of all. Enriched perhaps by refugees from the conquered Canaanite territory, the Phoenician cities began a period of great prosperity around 1150 B.C. Each city was typically governed by a king, who was advised by a council of elders that may have consisted of the leading merchants of the city.

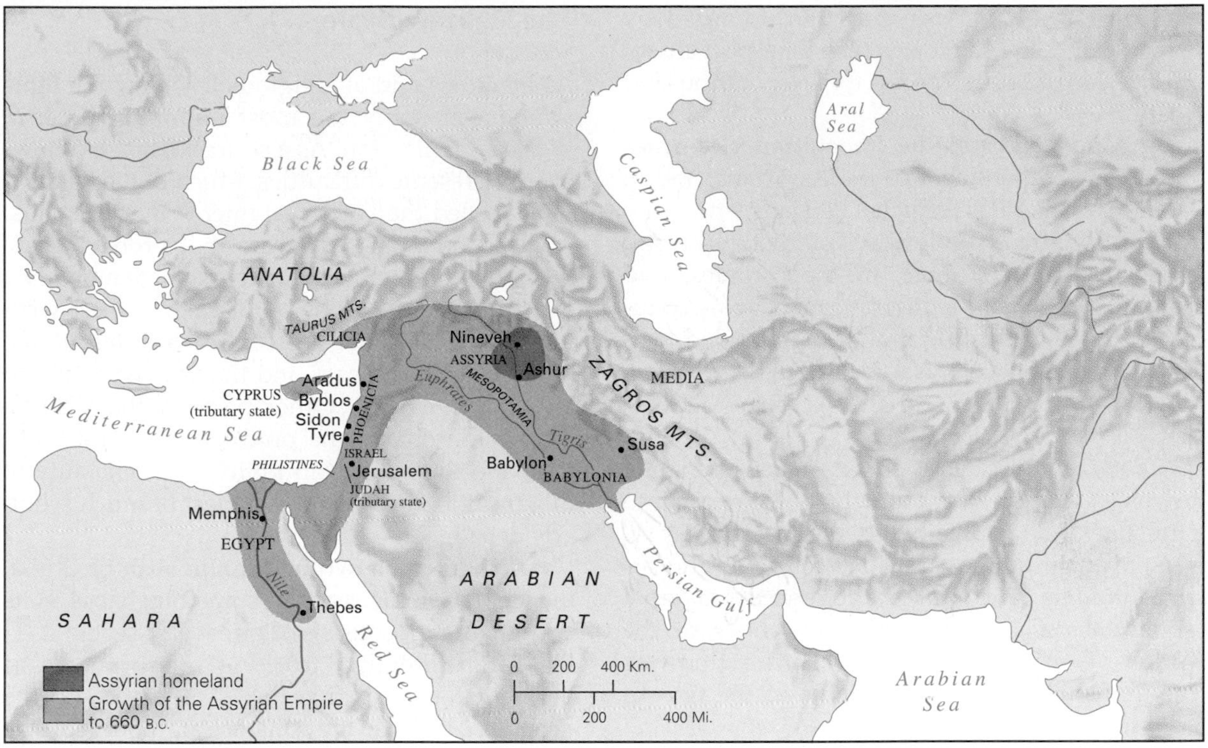

Map 2.1 The Assyrian Empire In their day the Assyrians were the most successful conquerors of the ancient world. In the 660s B.C. their empire extended from the Nile to the Tigris.

Seafarers, merchants, and slave-traders, the Phoenicians served as middlemen between the Mediterranean lands and the caravan routes to Mesopotamia and points east. They were also important craftspeople in their own right. The Phoenicians were known for their use of hardwood and cedar, the latter often made into fine furniture; for purple dye, obtained from local shellfish and used to color textiles; for jewelry and other metalwork; for fine ivories and wooden carvings. They were renowned builders. Important trading partners included Egypt, Cyprus, Greece, Sicily, and Sardinia. King Hiram of Tyre (r. ca. 969–936 B.C.), who provided his city with formidable fortifications, appears in the Hebrew Bible as an ally who provided King Solomon of Israel with wood and workmen for building the Temple in Jerusalem.

Great shipbuilders and sailors, the Phoenicians may have invented the trireme, an oared warship rowed by 170 men on three decks. Around 600 B.C. Phoenician ships accomplished the first known circumnavigation of Africa. Around 450 B.C. they made the first known commercial sailing trip to the British Isles. There are some scholars who think they even reached Brazil. The most lasting Phoenician achievement at sea, however, was the planting of colonies in the Mediterranean, probably beginning in the ninth century B.C.

Phoenicians established colonies for several reasons: to find precious metals, to siphon off excess population, to serve as a refuge. Unlike territory conquered by the Assyrians, Phoenician colonies were settled by people from the home country, who brought their language and customs with them. There were Phoenician colonies in Cyprus, Italy, southern France and Spain, and North Africa, as well as on central and western Mediterranean islands including Malta and the Balearics. Many of the Phoenician colonies eventually became independent states. The greatest

Phoenician colony was Carthage, founded by Tyre around 750 B.C. It was the major port city of the western Mediterranean for over a thousand years.

Around 750 B.C. the Phoenician city-states lost their independence to the Assyrians, and in later years Neo-Babylonians, Persians, and other foreign conquerors followed. But Phoenician culture survived: at home, in the colonies, and among the many Mediterranean peoples influenced by it. The result, though unintended, was that Phoenician colonists exported the civilization of western Asia to the western Mediterranean.

Between 1000 and 800 B.C., when the small towns of Greece were slowly developing into city-states, the sophisticated Phoenicians represented an important outside stimulus. Phoenician traders introduced advanced material goods, slaves, and possibly law codes to the Greeks. Their most significant contribution was the alphabet, which, tradition says, the Greeks adapted from the Phoenicians.

Closer to home, Phoenicians traded with their neighbors to the south, Israel. King Hiram of Tyre (r. 969–936 B.C.), for example, appears in the Hebrew Bible as an ally who provided King Solomon of Israel (r. 965–928 B.C.) with wood and workmen for building the Temple in Jerusalem. Phoenicians and Israelites spoke closely related Semitic languages, but they parted ways on matters of religion, for Israel broke dramatically with Canaanite polytheism.

Israel

In the first millennium B.C. a small, often-conquered people turned imperialism on its head. Human achievement is meaningless, they argued; only the power of divinity matters. There is only one god, they said; all other gods are false. The one true god had revealed himself not to the imperialistic Assyrians but to the less powerful Hebrews—ancient Jews.

The Hebrews, also known as Israelites, had existed as a people since the late second millennium B.C. and perhaps for centuries earlier. Their enduring and influential religion gave rise to Christianity and Islam as well as modern Judaism.

The Hebrew Bible

As literature and as religious teaching, the Bible is unquestionably the most important book in Western civilization. As a source of history, however, it presents difficulties. Much of the Hebrew Bible (called the "Old Testament" by Christians) is based on written sources that probably date back at least as far as the early Israelite monarchy of about 1000 B.C. Some scholars trace these written sources back several centuries earlier, to the religious leader Moses and the laws he is said to have promulgated. Other parts of the Hebrew Bible are probably the product of an oral tradition, and the nature, antiquity, and reliability of that tradition are also the subject of much scholarly debate.

A century or two before the birth of Christ, the Hebrew Bible reached something close to its current form. It consists of three main sections: (1) the Torah (literally "teaching"), also known as the Pentateuch, or five books of Moses; (2) the Prophets, that is, the "historical" books of the early prophets (Joshua, Judges, Kings, and Chronicles) and the books of the later prophets (Isaiah, Jeremiah, Ezekiel, and the twelve "minor prophets"); and (3) the Writings, or Scriptures, various books of poetry, proverbs, and wisdom literature.

The books of the Hebrew (and Christian) Bible are canonical: One by one, each was accepted by established authority as sacred. Two key dates stand out in the canonization of the Hebrew Bible: 622 B.C. and ca. 425 B.C. On the first date, Josiah, king of Judah (see page 52), assembled "the entire population, high and low," to swear to obey "the scroll of the covenant which had been discovered in the house of the Lord" (the scroll probably was Deuteronomy, now the fifth book of the Torah). On the second date, a similar assembly of the people, called by the religious leader Ezra (see page 54), swore to accept the five books of the Torah that had by then been assembled. The introduction of the Torah made its worshipers into what they have been ever since, "a people of the book," as the Muslims would put it many years later. The written tradition and literacy became central to the Hebrews.

The Hebrews are the first people we know of to have a single national history book. That book was written not as secular history but as sacred history. The Hebrew Bible is less the history of Israel than the story of the working out of God's pact, or covenant, with the Hebrews, his chosen people. Its purpose is to inspire faith, righteousness, and national solidarity, not to answer a modern researcher's questions.

Consider the fundamental significance of the covenant. All ancient peoples told stories of their semidivine foundation. Only the Hebrews, however, imagined the nation created by an actual treaty between the people and their god. When the Bible enjoins the Israelites to "love the Lord your God with all your heart and with all your soul" (Deuteronomy 6:5), it is using political language: In the international treaties of the second millennium B.C., *love* was a synonym for "exclusive loyalty."

The central fact of human existence in the Hebrew Bible is God's covenant with the Hebrews. Because of the covenant, history has meaning. History is the story of the success or failure of the Hebrew people in carrying out God's commandments. There is an emphatic focus on the individual: on individual characters taking actions that have moral consequences that unfold over time.

Many of the themes, narrative details, and styles of writing in the Hebrew Bible derive from earlier cultures. The biblical Flood story, for example, seems to be modeled on a similar flood in the *Epic of Gilgamesh.* Biblical poems in praise of God are often similar to Egyptian poems in praise of pagan gods, and biblical wisdom literature often recalls Egyptian or Babylonian parallels. In spite of such borrowings, the Hebrew Bible is dramatically different from its predecessors because it subordinates everything to one central theme: God's plan for humankind and, in particular, for his chosen people—the Hebrews.

The Emergence of Monotheism, ca. 1500–600 B.C.

The earliest nonbiblical evidence of the Hebrews is an inscribed monument of the New Kingdom Egyptian pharaoh Merneptah (r. 1213–1203 B.C.). After a military expedition into Canaan, the pharaoh declared triumphantly that "Israel is laid waste." Scholars disagree about the historicity of the biblical account before this inscription and before archaeological evidence dating from approximately 1200 to 1000—evidence suggesting that Israelite invaders conquered the Canaanite towns of the highlands of Palestine.

Through a combination of the biblical narrative and archaeological evidence, Israelite history after 1200 B.C. is relatively easy to trace. A seminomadic people became settled farmers and shepherds in the hill country of Palestine and then, sometime after 1000 B.C., an urbanized elite slowly began to emerge. Governed at first by tribal leaders, the Hebrews soon adopted a centralized monarchy. Their state was superficially similar to other monarchies of the Levant but developed a unique religious and political ideology.

As for Israelite history before 1200 B.C., archaeology renders the biblical account credible but does not confirm it. If one follows the Bible, Hebrew history began sometime during the period 2000 to 1500 B.C. with the patriarchs, or founding fathers. Abraham, the first patriarch, decided to migrate to Canaan from the city of Harran in northern Mesopotamia. A seminomadic chieftain, Abraham settled on territory north and west of the Dead Sea, where he grazed his herds. His language, Hebrew, was one of the many Semitic tongues spoken between the Mediterranean Sea and the Euphrates River. Seminomadic clans in the region frequently made long migrations in antiquity, so the biblical account of Abraham and his descendants Isaac and Jacob is plausible.

The Bible, however, emphasizes the implausible: Abraham's extraordinary decision to give up Mesopotamian polytheism for belief in one god. This god commanded Abraham to leave Harran; indeed, he made a treaty, or covenant, with Abraham. In return for Abraham's faith, said the god, "As a possession for all time I shall give you and your descendants after you the land in which you are now aliens, the whole of Canaan, and I shall be their God" (Genesis 17:8). Strictly speaking, Abraham was a henotheist rather than monotheist: Although he worshiped only one god, he did not deny the existence of other gods. Nevertheless, he took a giant step on the road to pure monotheism by coming to believe that only one god rules *all* peoples.

The god of Abraham had yet to become the god of all the Hebrews. According to the biblical account, that turning point came about several hundred years later, probably in the reign of pharaoh Ramesses II (r. 1290–1224 B.C.) or

The Sacrifice of Isaac This scene from the mosaic pavement of a synagogue in Palestine (ca. sixth century A.D.) shows the patriarch Abraham, wielding a knife, ready to sacrifice his son. An angel intervened and saved the boy, thus symbolizing the rejection of human sacrifice in the Hebrew Bible. *(Zev Radovan, Jerusalem)*

Merneptah (r. 1224–1214 B.C.). In a time of famine, many of Abraham's descendants had left Palestine for prosperous Egypt. At first they thrived there but eventually were enslaved and forced to build cities in the Nile Delta. Eventually, Moses, a divinely appointed leader, released the Hebrews from bondage in Egypt and led them back toward Canaan and freedom.

The Exodus ("journey out," in Greek), as this movement has been called, is one of the rare examples of a successful ancient slave revolt; it has served as a symbol of liberation ever since. The Exodus is also one of the central events in the history of ancient Israel, because it marked another covenant, this time between the god of Abraham and the entire Israelite people. At Mount Sinai, traditionally located on the rugged Sinai Peninsula between Egypt and Palestine, the Israelites are said to have first accepted as their one god a deity whose name is represented in Hebrew by the letters corresponding to YHWH. YHWH is traditionally rendered in English as "Jehovah," but "Yahweh" is more likely to be accurate. The Israelites accepted Yahweh's laws, summarized by the Ten Commandments. In return for obedience to Yahweh's commandments, they would be God's chosen people, his "special possession; . . . a kingdom of priests, . . . [his] holy nation." The substance of the covenant is unique, but in form and style it bears a certain similarity to the treaties of international diplomacy of the period 1400–1200 B.C. This similarity suggests the genuine antiquity of the biblical tradition (see the box, "The Covenant").

The Ten Commandments are both more general and more personal than the laws of Hammurabi's Code. They are addressed to the individual, whom they commit to a universal standard. They emphasize prohibitions, saying more about what one should *not* do than about what one should do. The first three commandments establish Yahweh as the sole god of Israel, forbid misuse of the divine name, and prohibit any sculpture or image of God. The next two commandments are injunctions to honor one's parents and to observe the seventh day of the week (the Sabbath) as a day free of work. The next two commandments prohibit violent acts

The Covenant

The central event in the history of ancient Israel was the covenant, or treaty, at Sinai between God and his chosen people. In this excerpt from the Book of Deuteronomy, Moses addresses the Israelites just before his death and reminds them of their obligations.

Moses summoned all Israel and said to them: Israel, listen to the statutes and the laws which I proclaim to you this day. Learn them, and be careful to observe them. The Lord our God made a covenant with us at Horeb [Sinai]. . . .

These are the commandments, statutes, and laws which the Lord your God commanded me to teach you to observe in the land to which you are crossing to occupy it, a land flowing with milk and honey, so that you may fear the Lord your God and keep all his statutes and commandments which I am giving to you, both you, your children, and your descendants all your days, that you may enjoy long life. If you listen, Israel, and are careful to observe them, you will prosper and increase greatly as the Lord the God of your forefathers promised you. . . .

What then, Israel, does the Lord your God ask of you? Only this: to fear the Lord your God, to conform to all his ways, to love him, and to serve him with all your heart and soul. This you will do by observing the commandments of the Lord and his statutes which I give you this day for your good. To the Lord your God belong heaven itself, the highest heaven, the earth and everything in it; yet the Lord was attached to your forefathers by his love for them, and he chose their descendants after them. Out of all nations you were his chosen people, as you are this day. So now you must circumcise your hearts and not be stubborn any more, for the Lord your God is God of gods and Lord of lords, the great, mighty, and terrible God. He is no respecter of persons; he is not to be bribed; he secures justice for the fatherless and the widow, and he shows love towards the alien who lives among you, giving him food and clothing. You too must show love towards the alien, for you once lived as aliens in Egypt.

Source: Deuteronomy 5:1–2, 6:1–3, 10:12–19, in *The Oxford Study Bible: Revised English Bible with the Apocrypha* (New York: Oxford University Press, 1992).

against one's neighbors, in particular adultery and killing. The final three commandments regulate community life by prohibiting stealing, testifying falsely, and coveting another man's wife or his goods.

The change in number—from many gods to one god—was perhaps the *least* significant consequence of the monotheism of the Hebrews. Far more important was the new relationship between divinity and humanity. The pagan gods were part of nature, as powerful as the elements but as unpredictable. Israel's god transcended nature. He was the creator and master of nature; he was omnipotent. Whereas the pagan gods were often whimsical or cruel, Yahweh was ethical, just, and merciful. In his supreme and terrible power Israel's god was further removed from human beings than the pagan deities, but in his justice and mercy he was closer: He was both humane and unfathomably suprahuman.

Whether a visionary leader proclaimed monotheism to the Hebrews shortly before 1200 B.C. or whether monotheism emerged centuries later is a matter of scholarly debate. What is undebatable is that ordinary Hebrews had not committed themselves fully to monotheism in 1200 B.C. For centuries afterward, many Israelite worshipers deemed Yahweh their greatest god but not their only god. Unready for the radical innovation that monotheism represented, they carried out the

City of David When David conquered Jerusalem around 1000 B.C. and made it his capital, it was a small, 15-acre town on a steep hill above the valley of Kidron (foreground), outside the walls of today's Old City. His successors expanded the city to include the Temple Mount, once the site of Solomon's Temple, today crowned with the Dome of the Rock, an Islamic mosque. *(Zev Radovan, Jerusalem)*

rituals of various Canaanite deities, whom they worshiped on hilltop altars. Forging a national consensus for monotheism took centuries.

During the twelfth and eleventh centuries B.C., the Hebrews completed the conquest of the Palestinian hill country from the Canaanites. The Hebrews were governed in this period by a series of tribal leaders, or judges, but eventually the military threat posed by the Philistines forced the tribes to accept a centralized monarchy. The Philistines, one of the Sea Peoples, had captured the Palestinian coast in the twelfth and eleventh centuries and posed a serious threat to Israel. The first Israelite king, Saul (r. ca. 1020–1004 B.C.) had some success against them but eventually fell in battle with his son Jonathan. The next king, David (r. 1004–965 B.C.), a former mercenary captain for the Philistines, defeated them decisively.

David was Israel's greatest king. He conquered an empire that extended into modern Jordan, Lebanon, and Syria. David, moreover, conquered the Canaanite city of Jerusalem, which he made into Israel's capital. David's son and successor Solomon (r. 965–928 B.C.) was also a great king, a centralizer who moved from a loose kingship toward a tightly organized monarchy. His most famous act was to build in Jerusalem the Temple whose priesthood and sacrifices became the focus of the national cult of Yahweh. Previously, that focus had been a humble, movable wooden chest known as the Ark of the Covenant.

Solomon represented the high-water mark of the power of the Israelite monarchy. Under his successors the monarchy was split into a large northern kingdom of Israel with a capital at Samaria and a smaller southern kingdom of Judah centered on Jerusalem (Map 2.2). In 722 B.C. the Assyrians conquered the kingdom of Israel. Judah survived, preserving its autonomy first as an Assyrian vassal and then as an independent power.

The religious history of the period of the two kingdoms (928–722 B.C.) and the Judean survivor-state (722–587 B.C.) is marked by an intense drive toward monotheism. The kings of Judah in the seventh century B.C., especially Hezekiah (r. 715–686 B.C.) and Josiah (r. 640–609 B.C.), aggressively attacked the worship of all gods other than Yahweh and all centers of Yahweh-worship other than the Temple in Jerusalem. The kings acted out of conviction and out of the desire to create a sense of community and unity in the face of the threat of outside conquest. They succeeded in making the Temple at Jerusalem the unquestioned religious center of the whole Israelite people, and they began the process of canonizing the Hebrew Bible.

The kings could not have succeeded without the help of the prophets, who were prominent from approximately 900 to 500 B.C. Seers uttering divinely inspired predictions were universal figures in ancient religion. No other culture of antiquity, however, has anything like the Hebrew prophets: charismatic, uncompromising, terrible figures of God's wrath and ultimate forgiveness. The prophets were a reminder of the most radical spiritual teachings of Israel: absolute monotheism, an insistence on righteousness, contempt for materialism and worldly power, love of the powerless. They often supported the kings but did not shrink from confronting authority fearlessly and insisting on uncompromising justice. Among them were Amos, a humble shepherd who preached the superiority of righteousness to ritual; Jeremiah, who prophesied the destruction of Jerusalem as punishment for the people's worship of gods other than Yahweh; and Isaiah, who predicted a new day of universal peace and justice to be inaugurated by a savior.

A characteristic story of the prophets is the confrontation between Elijah, perhaps the most famous prophet of all, and Ahab, king of Israel (r. 871–852 B.C.). Ahab coveted the vineyard of a man named Naboth, but Naboth refused Ahab's offer to buy it. Spurred on by his wife Jezebel, Ahab trumped up charges against Naboth, who was unjustly stoned to death; Ahab then confiscated the vineyard. God sent Elijah to declare to Ahab that, as punishment for committing murder, "dogs will lick [Ahab's] blood" and that of his family (1 Kings 21:19). In a remarkable scene we witness not only Elijah's courage in confronting the king but also the king's abject surrender and repentance before Elijah's spiritual authority. The Western tradition of civil disobedience owes much to the courage of the Hebrew prophets.

Exile and Return

The prophets prepared the people of Judah for survival by correctly predicting ruin and exile and promising that divine providence would guarantee return. The ability of the Judeans to absorb this message was remarkable. Indeed, it needed to be, for between 598 and 582 B.C. the

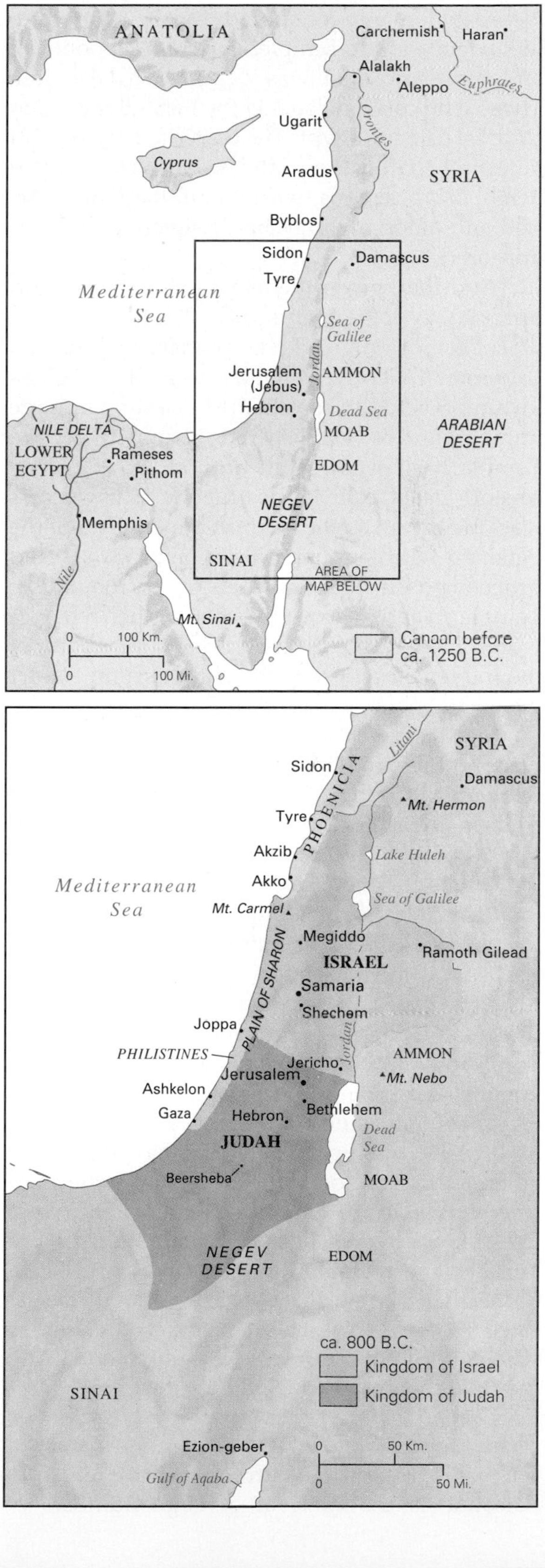

Map 2.2 Ancient Israel The Israelites settled in the Canaanite hill country west of the Jordan River and the Dead Sea after 1200 B.C. (top map). Control of Israelite territory after 928 B.C. was shared between two monarchies (bottom map): the kingdoms of Israel (conquered by Assyrians in 722) and Judah (conquered in 598).

Neo-Babylonians conquered Judah, destroying Jersualem and the Temple. The cultural, political, and economic elite was deported to Babylon. Those who could do so fled the harsh Babylonian colonial rule for Egypt. The dispirited remnant in Palestine shared their land with colonists from neighboring regions, with whom they intermarried and among whom their religion all but disappeared.

And that, given the usual fate of exiled and uprooted peoples in antiquity, should have been that. Yet not only did the remnant of Judah in Babylonian Captivity persevere in its religious loyalty; it actually returned to Palestine in large numbers and re-established its identity there. The Temple itself was rebuilt around 515 B.C., only seventy years after its destruction. This success was due in part to the tolerant imperialism of the Persians, who conquered Babylon in 539 B.C. and proclaimed the freedom of the Jews to rebuild the Temple in Jerusalem. Still, Persian benevolence would have availed little if not for the ability of the Judean elite to keep the faith burning among the exiles.

Statelessness turned many of the exiles inward to their religious traditions, rendering the Babylonian Captivity one of the most creative periods in Jewish history. During the exile the ordinary rituals of Judaism became regularized and widespread: circumcision, keeping the Sabbath, the dietary laws, the annual cycle of festivals. In the absence of king or temple priests, sages and scribes became the leaders of the Jewish community. The exiles, under the impetus of a desire to understand the past, probably put together the Torah in something like its current form. Synagogues ("gatherings" in Greek), modest centers of prayer and study that have been the focus of Jewish worship ever since, may have first emerged in Babylon. At least two important figures kept up the prophetic movement in Babylon: Ezekiel, who preached the restoration of the Temple, and the man known to us only as "Second Isaiah" (Isaiah 40–66). Second Isaiah emphasized the universal aspect of the god of Israel, who could make empires rise and fall and bring the exiles home from far-off Babylon.

Second Isaiah's message is an indication of a second remarkable development in the history of the exiles of Judah. As striking as the return to Palestine is the survival of large numbers of Judeans as an unassimilated people outside of Judah—in other words, as Jews.* For the first time, membership in a community of worship was divorced from residence. Jewish communities flourished in Egypt, Babylonia, and Persia, but the members generally chose not to become Egyptians, Babylonians, or Persians. From the sixth century B.C. on, a majority of Jews lived outside Palestine, and the Jewish Diaspora ("dispersion") became a permanent part of Western history.

Restoring the Jewish community in Judea (the Persian province corresponding to the former kingdom of Judah) did not prove easy. After many difficult years, however, that community was established on a firm and lasting footing under the leadership of two men: the Persian Jewish governor Nehemiah, who arrived in Judea in 445 B.C., and the Babylonian Jew Ezra, who probably arrived a generation later. Nehemiah overcame local and imperial opposition and built a new city wall for Jerusalem, which gave the Jews a secure capital. A priest and scribe, Ezra oversaw the adoption of the Torah by the Judean community (see page 48).

The People of the Covenant

A rough equality, limited government, and the rule of law under God were all fundamental Israelite political notions. According to Israelite belief, humans were made in God's image. Thus, all individuals were equal in a fundamental sense. Whether prince or pauper, all were bound by God's law. A king who disobeyed this law was illegitimate. Indeed, Israel was ambivalent at best about the institution of kingship, which was tolerated as an evil made necessary only by the country's many armed enemies. God's covenant with the Hebrews was a religious contract with political consequences, rendering God the only true king of Israel. Far from being gods themselves or even God's representative, Israel's kings were merely the humble servants.

Israelite egalitarianism was restricted to males. However limited their privileges, women were, nonetheless, accorded considerable honor. Rendered more subordinate than women in other

*Strictly speaking, *Jew* and *Jewish* are anachronistic before the fifth century B.C.

The Mother of Nations

Like the Canaanite epic the Hebrew Bible discusses the importance of reproduction, but it makes the theme both more spiritual and more human. While emphasizing God's plan for humanity, the Bible also offers insight into the human character, and commemorates the role of women as well as men. Consider the case of Abraham and Sarah, ancestors of the Hebrews.

God said to Abraham, . . . "I shall bless [your wife Sarah] and she will be the mother of nations; from her kings of peoples will spring. . . ."

[Three mysterious visitors appear at Abraham's tent.] They asked him where Sarah his wife was, and he replied, "She is in the tent." One of them said, "About this time next year I shall come back to you, and your wife Sarah will have a son." Now Sarah was listening at the opening of the tent close by him. Both Abraham and Sarah were very old, Sarah being well past the age of childbearing. So she laughed to herself and said, "At my time of life I am past bearing children and my husband is old." The Lord said to Abraham, "Why did Sarah laugh and say, 'Can I really bear a child now that I am so old?' Is anything impossible for the Lord? In due season, at this time next year, I shall come back to you, and Sarah will have a son." Because she was frightened, Sarah lied and denied that she had laughed; but he said, "Yes, you did laugh.". . .

The Lord showed favor to Sarah as he had promised, and made good what he had said about her. She conceived and at the time foretold by God she bore a son to Abraham in her old age. The son whom Sarah bore to him Abraham named Isaac. . . . Abraham was a hundred years old when his son Isaac was born. Sarah said, "God has given me reason to laugh, and everyone who hears will laugh with me."

Source: Genesis 17:15–16, 18:9–15, 21:1–6, in *The Oxford Study Bible: Revised English Bible with the Apocrypha* (New York: Oxford University Press, 1992).

ancient societies by law and religious ritual, Israelite women enjoyed a uniquely high status as mothers and partners in running the household.

Israelite women usually could not own or inherit property, as women could in Hammurabi's Babylon; or sue in court, as women could in pharaonic Egypt; or initiate a divorce, as women could in Athens (see page 102). The rise of monotheism meant that the powerful goddesses of other ancient cultures were absent in Israel. Women participated in the rituals of early Israelite religion and the original Temple (ca. 940–587 B.C.) but were segregated in a separate women's courtyard in the rebuilt Temple (ca. 515 B.C.–A.D. 79) and did not take part in temple ritual. Indeed, the perspective of the Hebrew Bible is predominantly male. Consider just two examples. First, of the 1,426 names in the Hebrew Bible, 1,315 are male; only 111 women's names appear, about 9 percent of the total.[1] Second, only males can bear the sign of the Lord's covenant with Israel—that is, circumcision.

Nevertheless, Israelite women enjoyed extraordinary honor as mothers and partners in running the household (see the box, "The Mother of Nations"). The Hebrew Bible states that woman (as exemplified by Eve, the first woman) was created as "a suitable partner" for man (Genesis 2:18, 20). Reproduction and hence motherhood assume great importance in the Hebrew Bible; the Lord enjoins humans to "be fruitful and multiply" (Genesis 1:28). The Bible also commands that children honor both their father and their mother: The two parents are equal in parental authority (Exodus 20:12).

In Israelite society, the primary unit was the rural, peasant household. Because farmers working the rough hill country of Judea and Samaria needed all the help they could get, women and children worked as well as men. Producing many children was an important survival strategy for a small people surrounded by enemies. Israelite women worked in the fields, processed and preserved food, and made clothing. Their role was no less important than that of men, and in one respect it was more important, for women bore and raised children.

The Hebrew Bible sometimes displays sympathy for and insights into the strategies that women used to counter the abuses of male power. In the patriarchal period, for instance, Rebecca thwarts her husband Isaac's plan to give his blessing to their son Esau; she sees that their son Jacob, whom she prefers, obtains her husband's blessing.

Only about a half-dozen women in the Hebrew Bible serve as leaders of Israel, but that is more than in the literature of most other ancient cultures. Deborah (ca. 1125 B.C.), for example, a charismatic Israelite preacher, organizes an army that destroys the forces of a Canaanite commander. Centuries later Esther, a Hebrew woman, becomes the wife of a Persian king whom the Bible calls Ahasuerus, who is probably Xerxes (r. 485–465 B.C.). Esther works ferociously at the Persian court to defeat a conspiracy to wipe out her people, and she saves them. The Book of Ruth (date uncertain) tells the story of a selfless and loyal woman, Ruth, who saves her mother-in-law, Naomi, from ruin and poverty. The Bible celebrates Ruth as Naomi's "devoted daughter-in-law, who has proved better to you [Naomi] than seven sons."

Israelite culture prized women for their cunning, courage, and perseverance—qualities that allowed the people to survive. Military prowess was highly valued in men, but there was appreciation for their inner qualities as well. Schooled in defeat and exile, many Israelites came to the conclusion that "wisdom is better than weapons of war" (Ecclesiastes). Thus, the Hebrew Bible stresses God's primary interest in goodness of soul: "The Lord seeth not as man seeth; for man looketh on the outward appearance, but the Lord looketh on the heart" (1 Samuel 16:7). The god of Israel prizes righteousness above military prowess, sacrifice, or ritual.

One might say that Israelite law reflects a similar tension between power and righteousness. On the one hand, just as Israel's god was omnipotent and jealous, so the law of Israel was meant to be comprehensive and forceful. Capital punishment existed for murder, rape, incorrigible rebelliousness of a son against his parents, adultery by a married woman (both she and her lover were to be executed), a woman's loss of her virginity before marriage, and other offenses. Harsh punishment was mandated for Canaanite towns taken by siege: The entire population was to be killed so as not to corrupt Israel with its religious practices.

On the other hand, by taking intention into account, Israelite law echoes a note already present in Mesopotamia. The so-called Law of the Goring Ox, for instance, allows someone to go unpunished for owning an ox that gores a person to death, unless the owner knew beforehand that the animal was dangerous. If the owner did know, then the owner must be put to death. Israelite law, moreover, demonstrates a belief in the sanctity of human life by prohibiting human sacrifice. An Israelite had to be ready in his or her heart (but *only* in his or her heart) to sacrifice his or her child to Yahweh, as Abraham was willing to sacrifice Isaac when Yahweh so commanded. After ascertaining Abraham's willingness to sacrifice his son, Yahweh freed Isaac from the altar and took a ram as a substitute offering. Western monotheism thus rejected human sacrifice.

Persia

At its height the empire of the Persians stretched from central Asia and northwest India in the east to Macedon and Libya in the west (Map 2.3). Persia's vast empire was loosely governed by a Persian ruling elite and its native helpers. Unlike the iron-fisted Assyrians, the Persians were relatively tolerant and respectful of their subjects' customs. Many of Persia's kings were followers of Zoroastrianism, an ethical religion with monotheistic tendencies. A period of relative peace in most of Persia's domains from the 530s to the 330s B.C. fostered economic prosperity.

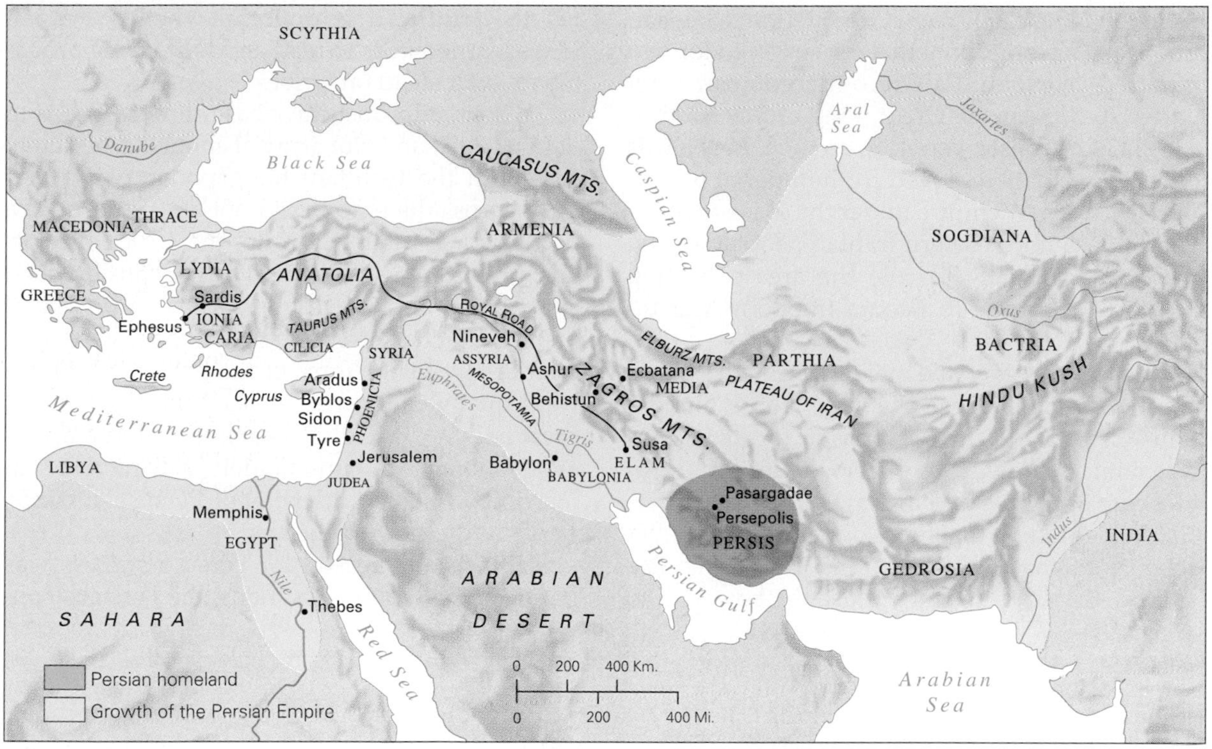

Map 2.3 The Persian Empire Around 500 B.C. the Persian Empire extended from its heartland in southwestern Iran westward to Macedonia and eastward to the northwest region of the Indian subcontinent.

The Persians absorbed much of the culture of the peoples they conquered. Borrowing the administrative methods of the Assyrians and Medes and the long-established officialdom of Babylon, the Persians built a new and durable imperial government. Their official art stressed the unity of the peoples of the empire under Persian leadership. Persian rule represented the greatest success yet in implementing notions of universal kingship dating back to Sargon of Agade (ca. 2350 B.C.). In turn, Persia transmitted the trappings of absolute kingship to later ambitious rulers, from Alexander the Great to the Caesars of Rome and from the Byzantine emperors to the Muslim caliphs.

Building an Empire

Indo-European-speaking peoples, the Medes and the Persians arrived in western Iran around 900 B.C. and perhaps as early as 1500 B.C. The Medes lived in the central Zagros Mountains. The Persians made their homeland farther south in Persis (modern Anshan). Tradition says that Achaemenes established a Persian dynasty, but we do not know if he really existed or when. It is clear that by the late sixth century B.C. the Medes had become the overlords of the Persians. In 550 B.C., however, the Medes were suddenly conquered by the young Persian king Cyrus the Great (r. 559–530 B.C.).

Cyrus the Great built his empire with dramatic speed, conquering most of western and substantial parts of central Asia within twenty years. Within five years of his death in 530 B.C., his son and successor Cambyses (r. 530–525 B.C.) added Egypt and Libya. Cambyses's successor Darius (r. 521–486 B.C.) added northwestern India and Thrace. The frontier regions of the empire, especially Egypt, were often in revolt, and the attempt of Darius and his successor Xerxes (r. 486–465 B.C.) to extend Persian rule to Greece ended in failure (see pages 103–104). The Persian Empire as a whole, nonetheless, survived for two hundred years, until a Greco-Macedonian army under Alexander the Great, king of Macedon (r. 336–323 B.C.), destroyed it. Even then, Persia was only temporarily removed from imperial power. By 246 B.C. a new empire under the dynasty of the Parthians, a northeastern Iranian people, was on the rise, eventually to rule the area extending from Mesopotamia to Bactria (modern Afghanistan).

Let us consider the success of Achaemenid empire, as scholars call the state whose foundations Cyrus laid. The first reason for its success was military prowess. A warrior aristocracy loyal to a core of simple and archaic values ruled Persia. Nobles taught their sons only three things, according to the Greek historian Herodotus (ca. 485–ca. 425 B.C.): "to ride, to use the bow, and to tell the truth." It is doubtful whether Persian kings learned how to read and write; they probably relied instead on scribes.

A solid administrative base allowed Persia to field a huge conscript army of about 300,000 men. Although the resultant hodgepodge of peoples from across the empire did not always fight as a unit, a crack infantry group, the 10,000 Immortals, provided a solid core. The Persians excelled as bowmen and cavalrymen. They made a final break with chariotry and turned the cavalry into the decisive strike force of the battlefield. Persia was equally innovative at sea, building the first great navy. Although Persians served as marines and sometimes as commanders, rowing and seamanship were the domains of Persia's subjects, particularly the Phoenicians.

The second reason for Persia's success was political. Unlike the Assyrians, the Persians con-

Frieze at Persepolis This sculptured relief lines the stairway to the audience hall of King Darius (r. 521–486 B.C.). It depicts Persian nobles, well-groomed and formally dressed, carrying flowers for the New Year's Feast. *(Rony Jaques/Photo Researchers)*

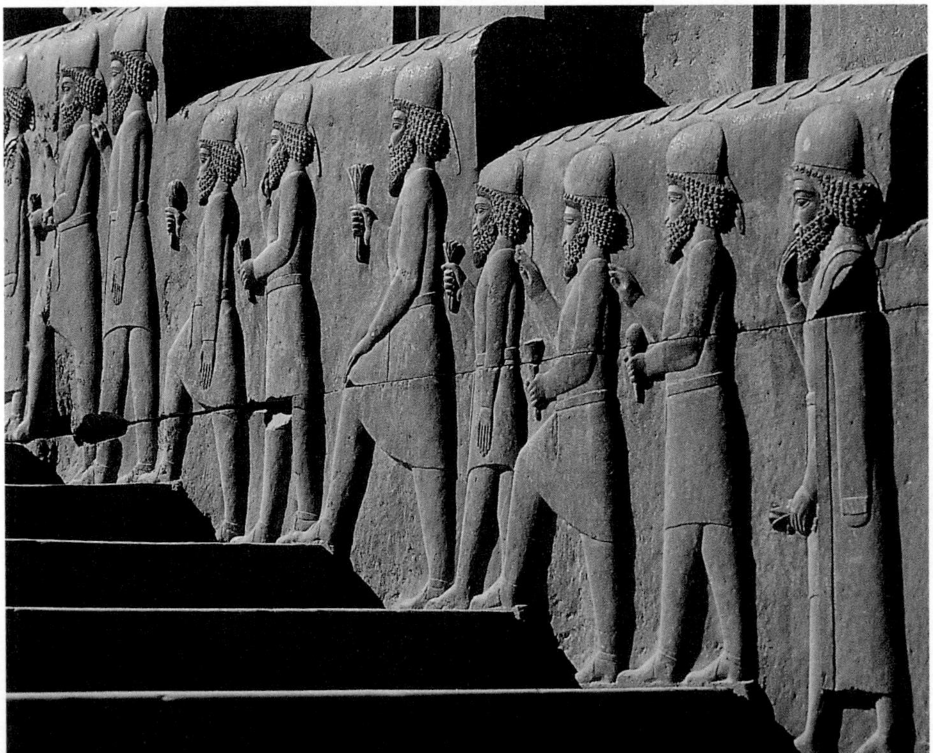

sidered generosity and tolerance to be more effective than terrorism and brutality. As Cyrus prepared to attack Babylon, for example, he portrayed himself as the champion of the traditional Babylonian deity Marduk, the power of whose priesthood had been challenged by the Neo-Babylonian king Nabonidus (r. 556–539 B.C.). As a result, the Babylonians opened the city gates to the Persian army, allowing Cyrus to achieve that greatest measure of military success: victory without a battle. Perhaps the most famous example of Cyrus's departure from Assyrian and Neo-Babylonian imperial policies was his edict of 539 B.C. permitting the Jewish exiles in Babylon to return to Judea. (See the box, "Cyrus and His Subjects' Gods.")

Cyrus's successors sometimes displayed similar diplomatic skill. In the late fifth century B.C., for example, Persia carried out the first explicit balance-of-power policy in Western history. By supporting first one and then another of the Greek city-states in their wars against each other, Persia balanced one enemy against the other and kept them from turning on Persia. This policy protected Persia for the better part of eighty years (413–334 B.C.).

The third reason for Persia's success was its skill at administration and organization. Darius played a crucial role in reorganizing the imperial administration and finances (military-minded Persians sneered at him as a "shopkeeper"). Like the Assyrian Empire, the Persian domain was divided into provinces, which the Persians called *satrapies.* There were twenty satrapies under Darius. Each satrapy was taxed a certain amount in money, horses, and military manpower or ships. Beginning with Darius, the government maintained registries of the sale of slaves, and perhaps of commodities, as a way of collecting taxes. For the first time, taxes could be paid with a stable, official coinage: the gold daric (named after Darius) and the silver shekel. Coins had been invented in the kingdom of Lydia in western Asia Minor in the seventh century B.C. Croesus (r. 560–547 B.C.), Lydia's king, was known for his wealth (hence the expression "rich as Croesus") before Cyrus conquered him in 547 B.C.

The provincial governors, or *satraps,* were powerful, often quasi-independent figures. The empire had many centralizing forces to oppose them, however. Each province had a royal secretary and was visited regularly by traveling inspectors known as "the king's eyes." A network of good roads radiated from the main capital city of Susa and from Persepolis, the capital in Persis proper. The most famous road, the so-called Royal Road, stretched 1600 miles from western Iran to western Anatolia. Covering the whole distance took most travelers three months, but the king's relay messenger corps, for whom a series of staging posts with fresh horse mounts was built along the way, could make the trip in a week.

Another unifying element was prosperity and stability. Darius proclaimed in an inscription that he had fostered the rule of law: "these countries [of the empire] showed respect toward my law; as was said to them by me, thus it was done." Although some scholars suggest that Darius turned the great body of traditional Babylonian case law into a new Persian code for the whole empire, it is clear only that he ordered a codification of Egyptian law. Darius and other Persian kings helped create the conditions for law-abidingness by taking an interest in the economy. Persian roads and a canal connecting the Red Sea and the Nile were open to commercial traffic. The government built irrigation works in Iran and Mesopotamia. It arranged for the transport of fruit trees from region to region, and it may have issued seed grain to estate owners. It ran cottage industries making textiles and rugs, though perhaps only for the royal court.

There was a linguistic aspect as well to centralization. Aramaic, a Semitic language related to Hebrew, was the empire's basic language of commerce and administration. With its alphabetic script, Aramaic facilitated the development of literacy and recordkeeping. Indeed, Aramaic would become the common language of western Asia for over a thousand years, until Arabic replaced it; Jesus Christ was to be its most famous native speaker.

Despite its success, Persia's empire faced several weaknesses. First, Cyrus had bequeathed a legacy as a charismatic war leader. Feeling the need to live up to his example, his successors sometimes undertook overambitious and expensive expeditions that failed, such as wars with the Scythians (a tough nomadic people in Ukraine)

Cyrus and His Subjects' Gods

Although the Persians sometimes used brutal tactics, they preferred to win their subjects' loyalty by gestures of good will, such as winning the favor of the religious leaders. Excerpt (A), a Babylonian inscription, demonstrates the political skill by which Cyrus the Great secured the surrender of Babylon in 539 B.C. without a battle. Excerpt (B), from the Hebrew Bible, records the favor that Cyrus showed to the Jewish exiles in Babylon.

(A)

He [Marduk] scanned and looked (through) all the countries, searching for a righteous ruler willing to lead him (i.e., Marduk) (in the annual procession). (Then) he pronounced the name of Cyrus, king of Anshan, declared him to be(come) the ruler of all the world. . . . And he (Cyrus) did always endeavor to treat according to justice the black-headed whom he (Marduk) has made him conquer. Marduk, the great lord, a protector of his people/worshippers, beheld with pleasure his (i.e., Cyrus's) good deeds and his upright mind (and therefore) ordered him to march against his city Babylon. . . .

I am Cyrus, king of the world, great king, legitimate king, king of Babylon, king of Sumer and Akkad, king of the four rims (of the earth), son of Cambyses. . . .

When I entered Babylon as a friend and (when) I established the seat of the government in the palace of the ruler under jubilation and rejoicing, Marduk, the great lord, [induced] the magnanimous inhabitants of Babylon [to love me], and I was daily endeavoring to worship him. My numerous troops walked around in Babylon in peace, I did not allow anybody to terrorize (any place) of the [country of Sumer] and Akkad. I strove for peace in Babylon and in all his other sacred cities.

(B)

In the first year of King Cyrus of Persia [539 B.C.] the Lord, to fulfill his word spoken through Jeremiah, inspired the king to issue throughout his kingdom the following proclamation, which he also put in writing: The decree of King Cyrus of Persia. The Lord the God of the heavens has given me all the kingdoms of the earth, and he himself has charged me to build him a house at Jerusalem in Judah. Whoever among you belongs to his people, may his God be with him; and let him go up to Jerusalem in Judah, and build the house of the Lord the God of Israel, the God who is in Jerusalem. 1. (to the adherents). Yes, to those (of you) seeking, I shall speak of those things which are to be borne in mind—even by one who already knows—through both praise and worship for the very Wise Master of good thinking and for truth, which things are to be looked upon in joy throughout your days.

Sources: Excerpt (A): James B. Pritchard, ed., *Ancient Near Eastern Texts Relating to the Old Testament*, 3d ed. (Princeton, N.J.: Princeton University Press, 1969), pp. 315–316. Excerpt (B): Ezra 1:1–3, in *The Oxford Study Bible: Revised English Bible with the Apocrypha* (New York: Oxford University Press, 1992).

and the Greeks. Sometimes they insisted on battle when a combination of retreat and diplomacy should have been tried, as when Alexander invaded in 334 B.C. Second, however mild Persian rule, however peaceful and prosperous, it was still rule by foreigners and it still involved taxation. Persian officials, military garrisons, and colonists were found—and were resented—in every corner of the empire. Native resentment, particularly in Egypt, and the independence of certain satraps led to intermittent provincial revolts.

The King of Kings

The exaltation of the Persian king served as a counterweight to rebellious tendencies. The Persian monarch, with his tradition of rough-and-ready soldiery, might seem an unlikely heir of the Mesopotamian divinely appointed king, let alone the divine Egyptian pharaoh. On his tomb, for instance, Darius described himself as "a friend to my friends" as well as a superb horseman, bowman, and hunter. Yet he also declared that he "could do everything," a hint of the grandeur that he injected into court life. From Darius on, the Persian monarch tried to overawe his officials with his despotic splendor.

The "King of Kings," as the Persian monarch called himself, sat on a high, gold and blue throne, dressed in purple, decked out in gold jewelry, wearing unguents and cosmetics, and attended by corps of slaves and eunuchs (castrated men employed in high positions). Although he was not considered a god, he had to be treated worshipfully. Persians spoke of the king's *khvarna,* his "kingly glory," a mysterious aura of power. Anyone who came into the royal presence had to approach him with a bow to the ground, face down. Even when entertaining dinner guests, the king normally ate alone in a separate room, looking at the guests through a curtain. If, after dinner, the king wished to drink with his guests, he would sit on a golden-footed couch while they sat on the floor, and of course he and they would drink wine from separate casks.

Impressive as the court ceremonial was, Persian kings were not absolute monarchs. They were bound by the rule of law and by the considerable power of Persia's proud nobility, on whom they relied to fill the top administrative positions. Competing factions of various viziers, wives, concubines, eunuchs, and sons often brought intrigue and discord to court, especially in the fourth century B.C., a time of frequent rebellion. The kings were nonetheless accustomed to giving commands, and they could act with capriciousness and cruelty when thwarted. Darius I, for example, proudly proclaimed in an inscription that he punished the chief of a rebellion by the Medes with mutilation and impalement and had the other ringleaders flayed. When Darius III (r. 336–330 B.C.) took offense at the remarks of a Greek mercenary adviser, he supposedly seized the man by the belt and handed him over to the royal slaves for execution.

Royal authority was symbolized in the decoration of the great palaces at Susa and Persepolis, a project begun by Darius I and completed by his son and successor Xerxes. The Susa palace, larger of the two, symbolized the universality of the empire by the variety of hands that built it. In an inscription, Darius points out that the cedar for the palace came from Lebanon, brought by Assyrians to Babylon and from there by Carians and Ionians (two peoples native to western Anatolia) to Susa; the gold came from Sardis (western Anatolia) and Bactria; the silver and ebony from Egypt; the ivory from Ethiopia, India, and central Asia. Craftsmen from east and west took part in the construction. The Persepolis palace was smaller but it too displayed the heterogeneity of the empire in its architecture. The palace was placed on a terrace, as in Mesopotamia, but contained columned halls as in Egypt, with Assyrian-style column capitals. Persepolis emphasized the king's vast power by means of a frieze of sculpted relief panels that lined a monumental stairway leading to the palace. The subject is an endless procession of the peoples of the world to do homage to the King of Kings: from the nobility to the Immortals to Median and Persian soldiers to tribute-bearing subjects from the ends of the earth. The overall feeling of the scene is static, as if the Persian Empire would last forever.

Zoroastrianism

One of ancient Persia's most original and important contributions to civilization is religious. From obscure beginnings, Zoroastrianism became the religion of Persia until the Muslim conquest in the seventh century A.D. Although largely extinct in today's Iran, an overwhelmingly Islamic country, Zoroastrianism still survives in small communities, primarily in India. Basic Zoroastrian notions include *dualism* (the notion of a grand conflict between good and evil), *eschatology* (interest in the end of the world), and *soteriology* (belief in a savior). Some scholars argue that these Zoroastrian beliefs influenced similar beliefs in Judaism and Christianity, as well as Roman paganism and Indian Buddhism.

It is easier to describe ancient Zoroastrianism in broad strokes than in detail, partly because the

Relief of Behistun In the mountains of western Iran, high above a main road, an inscription proclaims Darius's legitimacy as Persian king. The sculptured panel pictured here depicts Darius, his weapons-bearers, and conquered rebels, bound at the neck or crushed under his foot, the god Ahura Mazda floating above them. *(Robert Harding Picture Library)*

religion changed radically over the course of its ancient history, partly because relatively little information survives before A.D. 300. This much is clear: The religion was founded by a great reformer and prophet named Zarathustra (Zoroaster in Greek). Zarathustra lived in eastern Iran. His teachings survive in the Gathas ("Songs"), a portion of the Zoroastrian holy book called the Avesta. Some scholars date Zarathustra as late as 550 B.C.; others prefer an earlier date, 750 or even 1000 B.C.

Zarathustra's society was dominated by warriors whose religion consisted of blood cults, violent gods, animal sacrifice, and ecstatic rituals in which hallucinogens were eaten. Zarathustra rejected this religion because it was overly ritualistic and violent. He insisted instead on an inward-looking, intellectual, and extremely ethical religion. He favored ritual ceremonies involving fire, considered a symbol of purity. Like the Jews, Zarathustra was a monotheist, believing in only one god for all people, the supremely good and wise creator of the universe whom he called Ahura Mazda ("Wise Lord"). Unlike the Jews, however, Zarathustra considered the problem of evil to be virtually the central question of religion. If god was one, good, and omnipotent, how could evil exist?

Zarathustra's answer might be called *ethical dualism.* Ahura Mazda had twin children: the Beneficent Spirit and the Hostile Spirit. Each spirit had made a free choice: one for the "truth" and the other for the "lie"—that is, one for good and the other for evil. Every human being faces a similar moral choice between good and evil. "Reflect with a clear mind—man by man for himself—upon the two choices of decision, being aware to declare yourselves to Him before the great retribution," says Zarathustra.[2] Indeed, humanity is caught in a great cosmic struggle in which individuals are free to make a momentous choice. Zarathustra thus endowed humanity with great freedom and dignity. He distinguished between two states of being: the spiritual and the material. The more a person pursued spiritual purity, the greater was the person's ability to choose good rather than evil.

Zarathustra had a linear conception of history. He believed that one day, through an ordeal by fire, Ahura Mazda would judge all the people who had ever lived. Those who had chosen good would be rewarded, and those who had chosen evil would be punished. Then would follow a Last Judgment in which the dead would be transfigured and restored to a glorious bodily existence. There would be, Zarathustra promised, "long destruction for the deceitful but salvation for the truthful." The notion of a savior who would initiate the Last Judgment is an early Zoroastrian belief, if perhaps not a doctrine of Zarathustra himself.

Zarathustra's followers eased his uncompromising rejection of Iranian paganism. Under the leadership of priests, known as *magi* in western Iran, the religion evolved and changed considerably. Lesser deities beneath Ahura Mazda were added to the Zoroastrian pantheon, in part to suit the religion to the needs of the huge, multicultural Persian Empire.

It is tempting to attribute Cyrus's policy of toleration to the ethical teachings of Zarathustra, but it is uncertain whether Cyrus was Zoroastrian. We are on firmer ground with later Persian kings, particularly Darius I, who had an image of himself alongside Ahura Mazda carved on the face of an Iranian cliff. In an accompanying inscription Darius announces: "For this reason Ahura Mazda bore aid, and the other gods who are, because I was not hostile, I was not a Lie-follower, I was not a doer of wrong—neither I nor my family. According to righteousness I conducted myself."[3]

Early Greece to ca. 750 B.C.

When people today think of ancient Greece, they generally think of either the world of the city-states (ca. 700–300 B.C.) or the world portrayed in the *Iliad* and the *Odyssey*, the epic poems of Homer (ca. 800–750 B.C.). Both worlds are products of the first millennium B.C. Civilization, however, flourished in Greece throughout the second millennium B.C., and Homer's works have roots in this earlier era. Most of what we know of this earlier period, called "Aegean Greece" by scholars, is the result of archaeological excavation. In particular, archaeology illustrates the rise and fall of two monument-building, literate civilizations: the Minoan civilization on the island of Crete and the Mycenaean civilization on the Greek mainland (Map 2.4).

GREECE AND THE AEGEAN

2300 B.C.	Greek speakers enter Greek mainland
2000 B.C.	First Minoan palaces on Crete
1800–1550 B.C.	Height of Minoan civilization
1626 B.C.	Eruption of Thera volcano
1550 B.C.	Most Minoan palaces destroyed
1375 B.C.	Palace at Knossos destroyed
1400–1200 B.C.	Height of Mycenaean civilization
1200 B.C.	Mycenaean palaces destroyed
1100–800 B.C.	Greek "Dark Ages"
800–750 B.C.	Homer
700 B.C.	Hesiod

The Minoans

Greece is not an easy land. Mountainous, it contains little cultivable farmland. Although pasture land and forest are more abundant, one-third of the country is entirely unproductive. Most of the farmland, moreover, is to be found in upland plains, which are divided by mountains, making it difficult to concentrate a large labor force to work the land efficiently. There are few rivers. The south enjoys a mild, Mediterranean climate but is quite dry. The north has a Balkan climate of hot summers and cold winters. The indented seacoast provides Greece with many harbors. Greece's geography suggests several recurring features of its history: a contrast between seafarers and mountaineers, a contrast between north

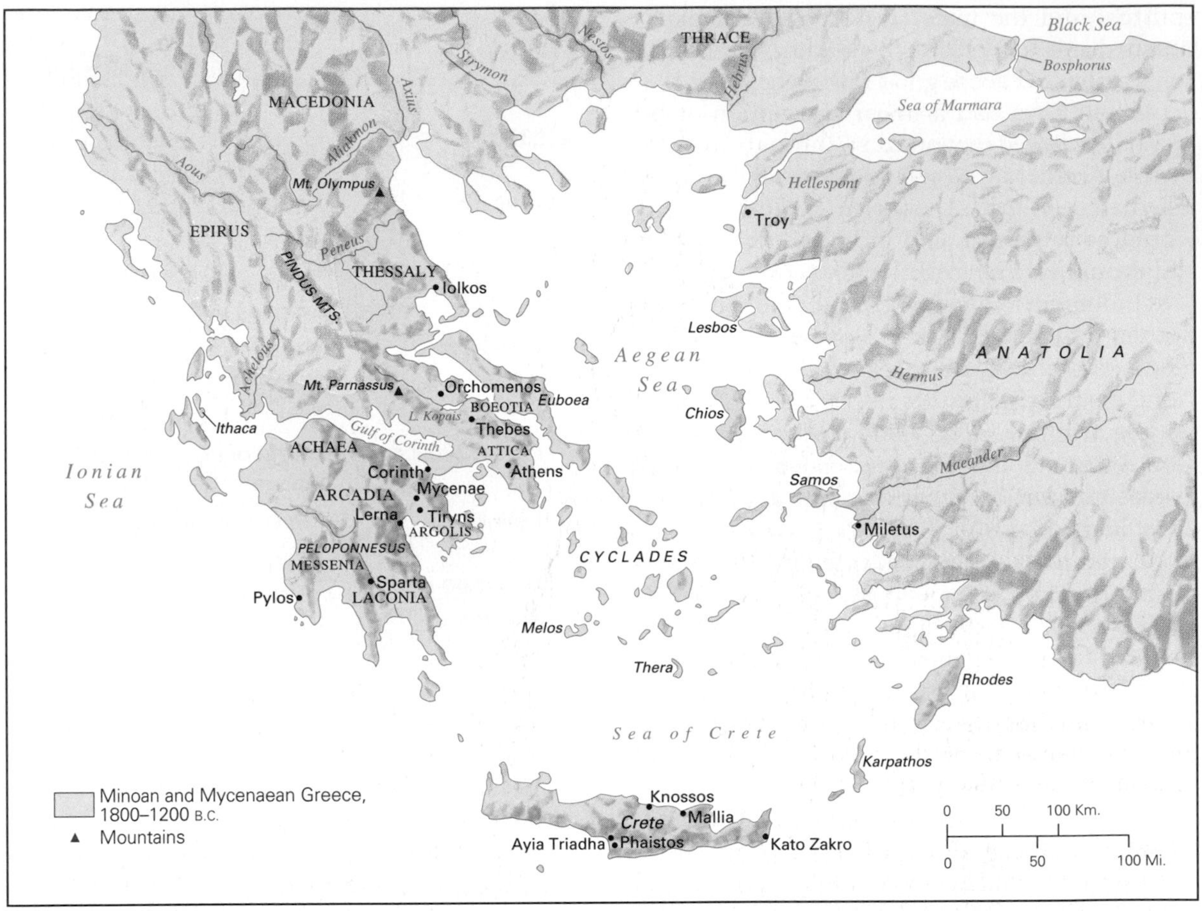

Map 2.4 Aegean Greece The Minoan civilization (height: ca. 1800–1550 B.C.) and the Mycenaean civilization (height: ca. 1400–1200 B.C.) flourished in turn in the second millennium B.C. Aegean region. The center of Minoan civilization was the island of Crete. A mainland people, the Mycenaeans conquered Minoan Crete around 1550 B.C.

and south, and the difficulty of unifying so mountainous a terrain.

Archaeologists have discovered milestones in the emergence of civilization in Greece. The first agricultural villages appeared around 6500 B.C., bronze-making skills after 3000. Between 3000 and 2400 B.C. people living on the Cycladic islands of the Aegean Sea produced exquisitely beautiful marble sculptures and incised terracotta dishes. Both on the islands and the mainland there were small towns, sometimes fortified with stone walls, occasionally containing substantial stone and mud-brick structures.

Just who the early inhabitants of Greece were is a tangled question. Most scholars argue that the inhabitants of Greece before approximately 2300 B.C. did not speak Greek. Around 2300 B.C. there was a large migration into the Greek mainland, perhaps from Anatolia. This migration either destroyed the mainland settlements or occurred in the wake of their destruction. The invaders were the speakers of an Indo-European language that was an early form of Greek. It took them several centuries to establish a high level of material culture on the Greek mainland. In the islands, however, especially on the island of Crete, impressive developments were underway.

Europe's first monumental, literate civilization originated on Crete around 2000 B.C. Its origins are hotly debated. Cretan writing, a syllabary called "Linear A," has survived (we know its language is not Greek, but we do not know what it is). The island of Crete is located on the sea routes between the Greek mainland, Egypt, and Anatolia. The archaeological record contains many signs of trade and cultural contact between Cretans and nearby peoples, from one of whom, perhaps, the Minoans were descended. The evidence is concentrated in Crete's palaces—monumental structures that first appeared at various locations on the island around 2000 B.C. After destruction by earthquake, the palaces were rebuilt on a grand scale, to flourish especially during the period from 1800 to 1550 B.C. Scholars call the palace-builders and their civilization "Minoan," after King Minos of later Greek myth. He was supposed to have ruled a great sea empire from his palace at Knossos.

The Minoan palaces were not merely royal residences but centers of administration, religion, politics, and economics. Minoan palace bureaucrats supervised a large sector of the economy, just as their counterparts did in Ugarit, Egypt, the Hittite kingdom, and other ancient societies. The largest Cretan palace, as well as the first to be excavated, Knossos offers a striking example of Minoan civilization. The main building at Knossos covers three acres, the associated structures an additional two acres. The palace was built around a large central court, 180 feet long by 82 feet wide, that probably was used for public ceremonies. A mazelike structure surrounded the court. The palace had large staterooms, residence quarters, storage rooms, artisans' workshops, and bathrooms, interconnected by corridors, ramps, and stairways. Light wells admitted daylight, and brightly colored frescoes decorated

Palace of Knossos The partially-restored ruins of the main structure at Knossos illustrate the complexity and elaborateness of Minoan architecture. The tapered columns and combination of stone and timber are characteristic features. *(Ekdotike Athenon)*

the walls. Cretan architects were aware of palace architecture elsewhere in the eastern Mediterranean and may have borrowed from it, but precisely who influenced whom remains an open question.

The palaces make clear that the Minoans exploited Crete's considerable natural wealth in agriculture and timber. The stunning artwork, often in precious metal; the sophisticated frescoes; and the vast and elaborate architecture all testify to prosperity. Archaeological and linguistic evidence indicates a widespread Minoan trading network from the Levant to Sicily. A Minoan settlement flourished on the Aegean island of Thera, 70 miles north of Crete. This settlement was destroyed in 1626 (or possibly 1628) B.C. by one of the most violent volcanic eruptions in history. So huge an eruption produced climate changes for several years. The changes are visible in the pattern of tree-rings in ancient wood; that is why scholars can offer so specific a date for Thera's eruption.

From the lack of fortifications around Cretan palaces and the small amount of arms and armor found in burial sites, it appears that the Minoans lived in relative peace. They worshiped a variety of gods and goddesses, often represented in Minoan art, but we do not know their names and functions. Minoan frescoes show that women as well as men played important roles in cult and ritual. The women portrayed by Cretan artists are often beautiful, bejeweled, and elegant; the men, often graceful and athletic. Landscapes and animals are frequently illustrated. In short, Minoan civilization gives an impression of peace, prosperity, and happiness. There is thus a lost-Eden quality about the violent destruction of Minoan civilization. All of the palaces except Knossos

Fresco at Thera This detail of the so-called Fresco of the Ladies shows one of a pair of murals from a shrine. We see a festively costumed woman carrying clothes and ornaments. She is bringing them to a seated woman (not shown), perhaps a goddess. *(The Ancient Art & Architecture Collection)*

were destroyed around 1550 B.C.; Knossos fell around 1375 B.C.

There has been no shortage of theories about the cause of the destruction, but the archaeological evidence strongly supports the notion of an invasion by the Mycenaeans from the Greek mainland. Mycenaean-style artifacts dating from this period have been found in graves on Crete, and thousands of tablets inscribed mostly in an early form of Greek have been discovered in the remains of the final stage of the palace at Knossos. How did the technologically backward Mycenaeans manage to conquer the sophisticated Minoans?

The Mycenaeans

By 1700 B.C. the settlements of the first Greek-speakers on the mainland had begun to grow in size, power, and prosperity. Impressive evidence comes from a series of burial sites in central Greece and the Peloponnesus. The most dramatic are at Mycenae. The royal burials at the site known as Grave Circle B (shafts sunk around 1700 B.C. into the rock of the slope of the citadel hill) contain pottery, weapons, vessels in precious stone, and a death mask made from an alloy of gold and silver. At Grave Circle A (ca. 1700–1600 B.C.) the burials are a treasure house of objects in gold and other precious metals.

How is this dramatic rise in wealth to be explained? Archaeology shows that the Mycenaeans—the term applied to the mainland Greeks of this period—adopted and adapted technology, ideas, and art from their advanced neighbors in Crete, Egypt, Anatolia, and Syria-Palestine. The Mycenaeans traded with these neighbors. They also fought with them, for Mycenaean society was dominated by warrior-kings, raiders who exchanged booty with one another in competitive displays of wealth.

Around 1550 B.C., the mainland warriors achieved their greatest feat: the conquest of Crete. As a result of this conquest, the Mycenaeans adopted a Minoan-style palace economy.

Between about 1400 and 1200 B.C. Mycenaean civilization was at its height. Kings lived in palaces whose storerooms were crammed with treasures. They traveled through their kingdoms on a network of good roads. Mycenaean artists excelled at potterymaking and fresco-painting, metal inlay work and ivory-carving. Mycenaean builders constructed palaces, fortifications, bridges, huge corbelled tombs, and sophisticated drainage works.

Palace officials supervised considerable economic activity, often in minute detail, including agriculture, pasturage, and artisanry. Women and children as well as men were included in the labor force. Our knowledge of the palace economy comes primarily from thousands of clay tablets inscribed by palace scribes around 1200 B.C. They are inscribed in Linear B, mostly an early form of Greek consisting of a combination of syllabary and ideograms.

Abroad, Mycenaean merchants replaced Minoans. They exported wine and scented oils from Sicily to the Levant and brought back metals, ivory, and perhaps slaves. Mycenaean warriors engaged in activities ranging from raids and skirmishes to formal battles.

In the thirteenth century B.C., at the height of Mycenaean power, trouble was brewing for the Mycenaean kings. Palaces at Mycenae and elsewhere were given strong fortification walls. By 1200 B.C., most of the fortified sites had been destroyed. Pylos, which had no walls, was destroyed by fire earlier. Occupation continued on a reduced scale. It appears likely that Mycenaean Greece suffered from a combination of internal weakness and invasion from abroad similar to that of most of the eastern Mediterranean around 1250–1150 B.C., the era of the Sea Peoples (see page 34).

Between Mycenae and the City-States

The term "Greek Dark Ages" has been rendered something of a misnomer as archaeology greatly increases our knowledge of the period from roughly 1100 to 800 B.C. The archaeological evidence suggests a considerable depopulation in Greece from the twelfth through the ninth centuries B.C. It seems that rich and poor alike were worse off than in Mycenaean times.

After the destruction of the palaces around 1200 B.C., Mycenaean culture continued to flicker before finally fading in the early eleventh century. New peoples began to move into central and southern Greece around this time. They probably were the Dorians, speakers of a Greek dialect who came from northern Greece. Their

Lion Gate at Mycenae Carved about 1250 B.C. above the main gate of the citadel's massive walls, the lions—flanking a column, their front paws resting on altars—probably represent royal authority. Inside the walls is Grave Circle B, a royal burial site. *(Dmitrio Harissiadis)*

material culture was rougher and ruder than that of Mycenae's descendants; there is little distinctive about it besides the iron slashing sword and the long bronze fastener. The Dorians usually drove out or enserfed the Mycenaean Greeks, turning much of central and southern Greece into Dorian centers. Among major settlements, only Athens maintained its independence. The city served as an asylum for Mycenaean refugees, many of whom migrated eastward around 1000 B.C. to the Aegean coast of Anatolia, which was destined to become an important center of Greek culture.

Greece from roughly 1100 to 800 B.C. was largely a poor and illiterate society of small towns and low-level agriculture and trade. Nevertheless, it produced notable painted pottery and preserved an oral tradition of poetry handed down from the Mycenaean era. By the end of this period, the Greeks were poised to reach a milestone in narrative artistry in a literary genre: the epic poetry of Homer.

Homer and History

If ancient Greece had had a Bible, the *Iliad* and *Odyssey* of Homer would have been its two Testaments. Only Hesiod, a poet who lived around 700 B.C. and composed two shorter and more didactic poems in the epic tradition (*Theogony* and *Works and Days*), had anything like a comparable influence on later generations. But Greece did not have a Bible. Homer and Hesiod were poets, not priests (as far as we know, the Greek world never had a priestly class comparable to that of Egypt or western Asia). Although their poems inspired, moved, and educated the Greeks—a large part of a Greek boy's education consisted of learning to recite Homer—they were not divine writ.

The Greeks were polytheists, their gods anthropomorphic. The gods of Greece are similar in many ways to the gods of Sumer. They share the foibles and foolishness of humanity but are immortal and far more powerful than humans. The gods figure prominently in early Greek poetry, but they are less powerful than Yahweh, less immediate, and less interested in the inner life of humans. Already, at the beginning of the Greek cultural tradition, there is a tendency toward the belief that "man is the measure of all things," as the thinker Protagoras would say in the fifth century B.C., that became the hallmark of ancient Greece.

The Greek gods of the first millennium B.C. existed in Mycenaean times—offerings to them are recorded on Linear B tablets. Because they were thought to live on Mount Olympus, a 9500-foot-high peak in northern Greece, the Greek gods were called the Olympians. Hesiod's *Theogony* tells the story of the birth of the Olympian gods and their triumph over an older, more primitive generation of deities. The "household" of the Olympians—the early Greek pantheon was conceived of as a noble's household—included Zeus, a sky-god and the "father of gods and men," and his consort Hera; Zeus's brother Poseidon, god of the sea, earthquakes, and horses; Ares, god of war; and Aphrodite, goddess of love. Also in the "household" were Zeus's children: Athena, goddess of wisdom and cunning; Hephaestus, god of craftsmen; Hermes, god of travelers and thieves; Apollo, god of disease and healing; and Artemis, goddess of the hunt, of maidens, and of childbirth. (See the box, "A Greek Goddess Speaks to a Mortal.")

Flawed and sometimes unpredictable, the Greek gods often seem childish, but they are eloquent symbols of the fluctuations of an often hostile natural world. They also embody the values of a warrior society that put a premium on *arete*, or excellence in battle. The heroes in the *Iliad* and the *Odyssey* seek glory through military exploits. They assume that the gods want precisely the same thing and that they will help those mortals whose achievements are most promising. Yet the gods want more. As Homer and Hesiod insist, Zeus, king of the gods, wants justice. Zeus punishes those who do evil—those who, for example, break oaths or give false judgments or violate the laws of hospitality. In the *Iliad*, a Trojan prince named Paris sparks the Trojan War by abducting the beautiful Helen from her husband, the Greek king Menelaus, while he is a guest in Menelaus's household. In return, the Greeks attack Troy. The gods destroy Troy as punishment for Paris's crime. (See the feature "Weighing the Evidence: The Trojan War," on pages 76–77.)

The *Iliad* and the *Odyssey* focus on the Trojan War and its aftermath. The *Iliad* is set in the tenth year of the conflict. The strain of fighting leads to a quarrel between Greek chieftains: Agamemnon, king of Mycenae and the leader of the expedition, and Achilles, the greatest Greek warrior. The most prominent Trojans, King Priam and his eldest son Hector, are less petty but will suffer the greater ruin. The *Odyssey* tells the story of the struggle of the Greek hero Odysseus to return home to Ithaca and to regain his kingship after a twenty-year absence, ten years in the war at Troy and ten years wandering homeward. It also focuses on the loyalty and ingenuity of Odysseus's wife Penelope, who saves the household in her husband's absence, and the maturation of their son Telemachus, who helps his father regain his kingdom.

Homer puts as much emphasis on brains as on brawn; Odysseus, for example, is a man of intelligence and cunning. Homer argues, moreover, that the gods hold human beings to a code of justice, hospitality, and respect for parents. Finally, although the Homeric poems focus on the upper classes—and primarily on the men—the poems have a strain of sympathy for ordinary people and for women. Indeed, they have a general sympathy for failure. Homer's heroes court death and often obtain it. Unlike the psalmist of the Hebrew Bible, a Homeric hero walks alone "through the valley of the shadow of death" (Psalm 23:4); he has no god to redeem him. He knows that the gods ordain human life to be difficult and full of suffering. Human frailty, however, ennobles Homer's heroes.

A Greek Goddess Speaks to a Mortal

The gulf between divine and human is much narrower in the works of Homer than in the Hebrew Bible. In the* Odyssey, *the goddess Athena, disguised as a young shepherd, spars verbally with her favorite mortal, Odysseus, whom she pretends not to know. When she asks his name, Odysseus pretends to be a Cretan trader blown off course. Here, Athena reveals her identity and her admiration for Odysseus's cunning.

At this the grey-eyed goddess/Athena smiled, and gave him a caress,/her looks being changed now, so she seemed a woman,/tall and beautiful and no doubt skilled/at weaving splendid things. She answered briskly:/"Whoever gets around you must be sharp/and guileful as a snake; even a god/might bow to you in ways of dissimulation./You! You chameleon!/ Bottomless bag of tricks! Here in your own country/would you not give your stratagems a rest/or stop spellbinding for an instant?

You play a part as if it were your own tough skin.

No more of this, though. Two of a kind, we are,/contrivers both. Of all men now alive/you are the best in plots and story telling./My own fame is for wisdom among the gods—deceptions, too./Would even you have guessed/that I am Pallas Athena, daughter of Zeus,/I that am always with you in times of trial,/a shield to you in battle . . . ?"

His mind ranging far, Odysseus answered:/ "Can mortal man be sure of you on sight,/even a sage, O mistress of disguises?"

Source: Homer, *The Odyssey,* trans. Robert Fitzgerald (New York: Doubleday, Anchor Books, 1963), pp. 239–240.

Homer's nobles are proud and jealous. In the *Iliad,* for example, when Agamemnon is forced by divine command to return his "prize"—a girl captured in a raid—his honor demands that he take the "prize" of Achilles, his greatest warrior—that is, Achilles' girl. Achilles' response is to sulk in his tent while the Trojans drive his fellow Greeks to near-defeat. In the *Odyssey,* a group of nobles lives off Odysseus's estate in his absence while they wait to see which of them Odysseus's wife (and ostensible widow) might marry. Odysseus's honor demands that he punish them by killing every last one. In both cases, Homer recognizes that the hero goes too far: Achilles' inaction leads to the death of his best friend, and ultimately to his own death; Odysseus's thirst for revenge leads to civil war.

Although Homer was aware of the societal consequences of such actions, he was not a historian. He was a bard, a professional singer of heroic poetry—of songs praising the deeds of the great. Heroic poetry consciously glorifies and magnifies the actions of its subjects. In all likelihood, there is a great deal of tall tale in Homer's stories of Achilles and Odysseus, of Helen and Penelope. We cannot even be sure that these men and women ever really existed.

Indeed, Homer lived neither in the age he sings about nor on the Greek mainland. Homer lived in Ionia (a region of the central western coast of Anatolia), perhaps in the city of Smyrna. Although we do not know just when he lived, it was not until centuries after the Trojan War. One of the more convincing modern theories dates Homer to about 800–750 B.C., a period of increasing change, growth, and ferment in Greece. Some scholars doubt whether there was just *one* Homer and argue that the *Iliad* and *Odyssey* are the works of two different poets. Other scholars deny Homer's existence altogether, arguing that the epics

A Greek Shipwreck This scene, painted on the neck of an Athenian jug in about 725 B.C., may illustrate an incident in the *Odyssey*. The use of abstract, silhouetted figures to tell a story is typical of the Geometric style (900–700 B.C.). *(Staatliche Antikensammlungen u. Glyptothek München)*

are nothing other than the collective product of a long, bardic tradition.

All would agree that the author of the poems worked in a bardic tradition going back to the Mycenaean Age, from which he took stories, details, and language. Most scholars accept the theory that this tradition was oral, not written. Like oral poets elsewhere, Homer and his predecessors composed their poems as they sang them, making use of a stock of stories and formulaic expressions (such as the Greek equivalents of "swift-footed Achilles" and "grey-eyed goddess Athena"). In fact, Homer may have been illiterate.

The oral tradition gave Homer knowledge of a past society that was long gone by his day. Although Homer studs his poems with details of Mycenaean palace life, the ideology of his characters generally reflects the beliefs of his own, post-Mycenaean society.

World of the Heroes

Homer's society resembled a pyramid. At the top was a tiny minority of nobles. Beneath them was the mass of ordinary people, the *demos.* Most people engaged in farming or herding, and for most life was hard.

Homer and Hesiod indicate that the typical Greek community of the eighth century B.C. was ruled by an entrenched, hereditary aristocratic elite group of landowners who proudly called themselves *basileis* (literally "kings"). The basic instruments of government that would exist for centuries in Greece are evident in the *Iliad* and the *Odyssey*: generals, orators, judges, a council, and an assembly. In towns and in the countryside, the basileis dominated the things that mattered to ordinary people: religion, the rendering of justice, and the provision of aid in years of famine. When making decisions about war and peace, a council of elder basileis consulted an assembly of the warriors, that is, the younger basileis. In this arrangement we see a fundamental principle of Greek government: The political community should be composed of the warriors. Because warfare required expensive weapons and leisure time for training, members of the demos were excluded from combat. (See the box, "Homeric Society.")

Members of the demos found it difficult to speak in the assembly. In the *Iliad,* for example, when the Greek army grumbles about King Agamemnon's conduct of the Trojan War, Agamemnon's supporter Odysseus speaks to other nobles gently but strikes members of the demos with his staff, warning them to "sit still and wait for orders from your betters, you who are no warrior and a weakling, counting for nothing in battle or debate."

The main activity of Homer's basileis is warfare. The *Iliad* consists largely of a series of battlefield contests. Homer's heroes are competitive and fearless. The adversaries Hector the Trojan and Achilles the Greek are both willing to die. Hector is the model hero because he fights to defend his parents, wife, and child. Achilles has little interest in family. He prefers death on the battlefield to marriage back home and, by killing Hector, dooms Hector's family. There is a tension in the *Iliad* and the *Odyssey* between the hero as family man and the hero as independent, adventurous, and dangerous youth: between Hector and Achilles, between Odysseus's wanderlust and his need to return home. Indeed, this tension continues as a central theme in ancient Greek culture. In spite of their respect for the power of the father, the Greeks display an ambiguous admiration for youths who assert themselves in the face of patriarchal authority.

Homer does not present women on an equal footing with men but is less misogynistic than the classical culture of the city-states would turn out to be. Homer shows considerable sympathy for women, particularly in the *Odyssey.* Homer's women are weaker than men, but they are neither timid nor helpless. Penelope personifies female resourcefulness: By drawing out interminably her weaving of a shroud for Odysseus's elderly father, she puts the noble suitors off for years. She is as concerned with honor as any Homeric man. By refusing to accept an offer of marriage while Odysseus might still be alive, Penelope does honor to her own good name and to her husband's.

Homeric women play important roles in encouraging men or, in a more complex psychological process, in bolstering a man's courage by playing the foil to his doubts and fears. In the *Iliad,* Hector is emboldened to fight after his wife Andromache begs him not to fight, for her sake and that of their infant son. By taking the burden of hearth and home on herself, Andromache allows Hector to define masculinity as making war. Achilles enjoys a similar relationship with his mother Thetis, as does Odysseus's diffident son Telemachus with Penelope.

Loyalty to the family played an important role in social relations. A person's obligations to kin included the duty to avenge crime or murder. Friendship, cemented by an exchange of gifts, was another important social institution. Even humble peasants prided themselves on hospitality. Nobles cultivated hereditary "guest-friends" in their own and other communities, sometimes building up extensive networks and followings. Unlike the Hebrew Bible, however, Homer does not consider it a virtue to help enemies as well as friends. In Greek morality, enemies were to be treated harshly.

Summary

The first half of the first millennium B.C. was a time of dramatic change. Iron replaced bronze as the primary metal of work and war. New military technology, the frank adoption of brutal and inhumane methods, and improvements in administration led to the creation of the Assyrian Empire, stretching from western Iran to Palestine and briefly even to Egypt. After short-lived hegemonies by Neo-Babylonians and Medes, the Persians established an empire that was larger, better organized, and more tolerant than the empire of the Assyrians. Heirs to Canaanite civilization of the second millennium B.C., the Phoenician city-states expanded across the Mediterranean Sea, less by military conquest than by trade and colonization.

The most important developments of the era, however, were not in commerce, metallurgy, or imperialism but in new conceptions of the nature and meaning of human life. The Persians developed a new religion, Zoroastrianism, that emphasized ethics, the triumph of good over evil, and redemption through a divine savior. The Israelites conquered Palestine and, even after losing it, held on to their identity by means of a tenacious belief in one god. Like Zarathustra, they broke with tradition by insisting that their god

Homeric Society

In the **Iliad**, *the god Hephaestus makes the hero Achilles a shield on which are engraved scenes of contemporary society. This excerpt provides a description of a wedding and a primitive justice system.*

He pictured, then, two cities, noble scenes:/weddings in one, and wedding feasts, and brides/led out through town by torchlight from their chambers/amid chorales, amid the young men turning/round and round in dances: flutes and harps/among them, keeping up a tune, and women/coming outdoors to stare as they went by./A crowd, then, in a market place, and there/two men at odds over satisfaction owed/for a murder done: one claimed that all was paid,/and publicly declared it; his opponent/turned the reparation down, and both/demanded a verdict from an arbiter,/as people clamored in support of each,/and criers restrained the crowd. The town elders/sat in a ring, on chairs of polished stone,/the staves of clarion criers in their hands,/with which they sprang up, each to speak in turn,/and in the middle were two golden measures/to be awarded him whose argument/would be the most straightforward.

Source: Homer, *The Iliad,* trans. Robert Fitzgerald (New York: Doubleday, Anchor Books, 1974), p. 451.

was one, merciful, and just. Omnipotent, God gave history purpose and meaning. The purpose of life, in the Israelite view, was to serve God by acting righteously. The new religion eventually became Judaism. The Jews wrote down their religious and historical traditions in a book that, along with the Christian New Testament, proved to be the most influential single text in the history of the West: the Hebrew Bible.

We know little of the ideologies of the Minoan and Mycenaean civilizations of the second millennium B.C., but their economies and governments seem to be similar to those of the other palace-run states of the eastern Mediterranean. By the first millennium B.C., the Greeks, like the Persians and the Hebrews, had broken with tradition, but with a greater emphasis on the human than on the divine. Homer's epic poems, which had taken shape by the eighth century B.C., focus on the fragile dignity of heroic human actions. Homer idealizes a society of aristocratic warriors seeking honor and glory. Although the Greek gods show favor to heroes, they display no transcendent interest in redeeming human souls. Men and women were doomed to die. Homer's legacy, therefore, was to glorify human heroism while recognizing its fragility. It was a legacy that raised as many questions as answers. In the middle centuries of the first millennium B.C., the Greeks would attempt to provide new solutions to Homer's problems. Their successes and failures still influence the West.

Notes

1. Carol L. Meyers, "Everyday Life: Women in the Period of the Hebrew Bible," in Carol A. Newsom and Sharon H. Ringe, eds., *The Women's Bible Commentary* (1992), p. 245.
2. S. Insler, *The Gāthās of Zarathustra: Acta Iranica,* 8 (Leiden: E. J. Brill, 1975), p. 33.
3. Roland G. Kent, *Old Persian: Grammar, Texts, Lexicon* (New Haven, Conn.: American Oriental Society, 1950), p. 132.

Suggested Reading

General Surveys

Ferrill, Arther. *The Origins of War.* 1985. "Assyria and Persia: The Age of Iron" (65–89) offers a good analytic overview of warfare in the first millennium B.C., before the Greeks.

Knapp, A. Bernard. *The History and Culture of Ancient Western Asia and Egypt.* 1988. Chapters 4 and 5 (135–267) are a clear and concise introduction to the subjects discussed here.

Knox, Bernard. "Myth and Attic Tragedy." In *Word and Action: Essays in the Ancient Theater,* 1–24. 1979. In this stimulating essay, the author discusses the notion of the Jews as a people of the book and the Greeks as a people of myths.

Seltzer, Robert M., ed. *Religions of Antiquity: Religion, History, and Culture. Selections from The Encyclopedia of Religion, Mircea Eliade, Editor in Chief.* 1989. Chapters 6 through 9 are good introductions to Israelite, Iranian, and Aegean religions as well as to Zoroastrianism.

Yadin, Yigael. *The Art of Warfare in Biblical Lands in the Light of Archaeological Study.* 2 vols. 1963. A survey of weapons, armor, fortified sites, strategy, and tactics from the Sumerians on, with an emphasis on Palestine. Superb illustrations.

Assyrians, Neo-Babylonians, and Phoenicians

Bernal, Martin. "First by Land, Then by Sea: Thoughts About the Social Formation of the Mediterranean and Greece." In Eugene D. Genovese and Leonard Hochberg, eds., *Geographic Perspectives in History,* 3–33. 1989. A controversial argument for the political and social originality of Phoenicia's city-states and their influence on early Greece.

Moscati, Sabatino. *The World of the Phoenicians.* Translated by Alastair Hamilton. 1968. A general survey of politics, society, and culture, with more emphasis on the western than on the eastern Mediterranean.

Muhly, James D. "Phoenicia and the Phoenicians." In *Biblical Archaeology Today: Proceedings of the International Congress on Biblical Archaeology. Jerusalem, April 1984,* 177–191. 1985. The author argues that although trade flourished among Greece, Cyprus, and Phoenicia between approximately 1050 and 850 B.C., the Phoenicians did not engage in trade in or colonize the western Mediterranean before 800 B.C. In a scholarly reply (221–223; compare with 226–229), Ora Negbi argues that the Phoenicians were in the western Mediterranean as early as 1100–1000 B.C.

Oates, J. *Babylon.* Rev. ed. 1986. A well-illustrated survey, from the period of Sargon to the Hellenistic Greeks, with a section on Babylon's cultural legacy.

Oded, Bustenay. *Mass Deportations and Deportees in the Neo-Assyrian Empire.* 1979. A detailed study of an appalling practice.

Saggs, H. W. F. *The Might That Was Assyria.* 1984. A readable, introductory history celebrating the Assyrians' achievements.

Israel

Alter, Robert. *The Art of Biblical Narrative.* 1981. By applying the techniques of literary criticism to the Hebrew Bible, the author argues for a much more complex and psychologically subtle world view in that book than is usually thought.

Drane, John. *Introducing the Old Testament.* 1987. An excellent introduction to the archaeology, history, and religion of biblical Israel. Very good illustrations and charts, with a thorough discussion of scholarly controversies.

Johnson, Paul. *A History of the Jews.* 1987. A marvelously readable though at times idealized account by a journalist. The first two chapters treat ancient Judaism.

Meyers, Carol. *Discovering Eve: Ancient Israelite Women in Context.* 1988. A sophisticated analysis combining archaeology, biblical scholarship, feminist theory, and comparative anthropology. The author argues for the existence of a tradition of powerful women in the Hebrew Bible, dating back to the gender equality of early Israelite peasant society.

Negev, Avraham. *The Archaeological Encyclopedia of the Holy Land.* 3d ed. 1990. A valuable and well-illustrated reference book.

de Vaux, Roland. *Ancient Israel.* Vol. 1, *Social Institutions.* Vol. 2, *Religious Institutions.* Translated 1961. A thorough and judicious survey of the literary evidence. Subjects include the family, the state, economics, law, the military, religious sanctions, priests, ritual, and festivals.

Persia

Boardman, John, N. G. L. Hammond, D. M. Lewis and M. Ostwald, eds. *The Cambridge Ancient History.* 2d ed. Vol. 4, *Persia, Greece and The Western Mediterranean, c. 525 to 479 B.C.* 1988. Part 1, "The Persian Empire" (1–286), is an excellent, detailed, scholarly survey of the rise of Achaemenid Persia and the condition of its main provinces.

Cook, J. M. *The Persian Empire.* 1983. A clear and readable introduction, updating Olmstead's book (see below) in the light of recent archaeological discoveries, particularly inscriptions.

Gershevitch, I., ed. *The Cambridge History of Iran.* Vol. 2, *The Median and Achaemenid Periods.* 1985. Contains detailed and scholarly chapters on, among other things, the rise of the Achaemenids, Cyrus, the Medes, sources of evidence, art, architecture, and religion.

Olmstead, A. T. *History of the Persian Empire.* 1948. Out-of-date in some of its findings but still an ambitious narrative history. The prose style is majestic.

Strauss, Barry, and Josiah Ober. *The Anatomy of Error: Ancient Military Disasters and Their Lessons for Modern Strategists.* 1990. An analysis of eight case studies from the ancient world. Several chapters (especially Chapters 1 and 4) discuss Achaemenid Persia.

Greece to 750 B.C.

Barber, R. L. N. *The Cyclades in the Bronze Age.* 1987. A thorough survey of the archaeological evidence.

Beye, C. R. *Ancient Greek Literature and Society.* 2d ed. Chapters 2 and 3 offer a good, brief introduction to Homer.

Chadwick, John. *The Mycenaean World.* 1976. A well-illustrated overview of Greek society around 1400 to 1200 B.C. emphasizing the evidence of Linear B texts. The author was one of the original decipherers of those texts.

Coldstream, N. *Geometric Greece.* 1977. A close examination of the art and archaeology of the period from roughly 900 to 700 B.C.

Desborough, V. *The Greek Dark Ages.* 1972. A thorough and detailed survey of the archaeological evidence for the period between approximately 1125 and 900 B.C.

Finley, M. I. *The World of Odysseus.* Rev. ed. 1978. Essential introductory reading on the historicity, society, and ideology of the Homeric poems.

Graham, J. Walter. *The Palaces of Crete.* Rev. ed. 1986. A detailed analysis of the sites of Minoan Crete, with an emphasis on architecture. Good comparative discussion of Egypt and western Asia. Illustrated.

Griffin, Jasper. *Homer on Life and Death.* 1980. Discusses religion in the epics, with particular attention to Homer's relationship to the literatures of Egypt and western Asia.

Hurwit, J. *Art and Culture of Early Greece, 1100–480 B.C.* 1985. The first two chapters offer a fascinating study of the light that vase-painting and Homeric poetry throw on each other and on early Greek culture.

Starr, Chester. *The Origins of Greek Civilization, 1100–650 B.C.* 1961. Though out-of-date on some points, the book continues to offer a valuable overview, including a provocative discussion of the cultural significance of early Greek vase-painting.

Taylour, Lord William. *The Mycenaeans.* Rev. ed. 1983. A well-illustrated discussion of pottery and chronology, written sources, religion, architecture, art, daily life, war and trade, and the rise and fall of the Mycenaeans.

Vermeule, Emily. *Greece in the Bronze Age.* 1964, new preface 1972. Though written before some important excavations and discoveries of the past thirty years, this is still the best and most thorough overview of Greece from the beginnings to around 1100 B.C.

Weighing the Evidence

THE TROJAN WAR

It is one of the best-known events of antiquity. It is commemorated in works ranging from the *Iliad* and *Odyssey* of Homer to television documentaries. It is recalled in stone, in the ruins of Troy in northwestern Anatolia—one of the most important sites in Mediterranean archaeology. Yet the Trojan War is still mysterious. We are unsure not only when or why it happened but whether it happened at all.

According to Homer, Troy was a prosperous and fortified city ruled by a king, Priam, and engaged in a war against a coalition of warriors from mainland Greece. Ten years of hard fighting ended in the sack and destruction of the city, a scene etched in the Greek imagination. Look at this vase painting, a work from about 490 B.C. by an Athenian artist known today as the Brygos painter. It is a detail of a larger illustration of the sack of Troy. Over a fallen, wounded Trojan man stands a Greek warrior, his sword ready to deliver the death blow. To the Greek's right, a Trojan woman, her hair disheveled, is running away.

The ancients had few doubts about the reality of such scenes or about the actual existence of Troy. Alexander the Great, for instance, in 334 B.C. visited the Greek polis of Troy, which claimed to sit on the site of Priam's city. The Greek scholar Eratosthenes (active 225 B.C.) dated the Trojan War to 1184–1183 B.C. By modern times, however, the city had disappeared, and the Trojan War was considered to be merely the stuff of legend.

Then, in 1829, a 7-year-old German boy received a history book from his father with a picture of Troy in flames. He conceived the lifelong conviction that the Trojan War was a genuine historical fact. Eventually he decided that his mission was to prove it true. By then an adult and a wealthy businessman, he fulfilled his ambition by excavating in Anatolia beginning in 1871. His name was Heinrich Schliemann.

A colorful and stormy man, Schliemann (1822–1890) was to be one of the founders of modern archaeology. Troy, he believed, was located within a large man-made mound about three miles from the Hellespont and about four miles from the Aegean Sea. There, he and several successors excavated. Few scholars doubt that Schliemann discovered Troy. The case of the Trojan War, however, is not so easily settled.

Troy VIIA, House *(Courtesy Archives & Rare Books Department, University of Cincinnati)*

Sack of Troy (detail), Brygos Painter, ca. 490 B.C. *(Erich Lessing/Art Resource, NY)*

For one thing, the excavators discovered nine principal levels of occupation at the site, dating from approximately 3000 B.C. to around A.D. 500. Most archaeologists assign Priam's Troy to the level known as Troy VIIA. This level was destroyed sometime between 1250 and 1225 B.C., which accords with chronological hints in the *Iliad* of a Late Mycenaean context. Also, Troy VIIA was destroyed by fire, which is consistent with a sack by Greek armies. But questions remain: Was the fire caused by war? Did the war last ten years? We have no way of knowing.

Troy VIIA was not the grand city of the *Iliad* but a relatively small and unimpressive place with simple architecture and few signs of luxuries. Look at the photograph of a house in Troy VIIA, one of numerous structures crowded into the space inside the walls. They indicate an impoverished population, perhaps under siege—at least that is what American scholars who excavated at Troy in the 1930s thought. Look at the jars sunk into the floor of the house. The excavators argued that they provided storage for supplies during wartime. Crowded housing and sunken jars are found at other ancient sites, however, and are not proof of war.

Yet few scholars are willing to leave the matter on so uncertain a note. Some historians have pointed out, for example, that Troy VIIA represents a rebuilding of Troy VI after an earthquake and fire. Troy VI seems to have been a large and impressive city. If war destroyed Troy VIIA, perhaps that war began a generation or two earlier, in the heyday of Troy VI—a theory that might explain why Homer describes Troy as being large and splendid. Another theory stems from an archaeological survey in 1992, which found evidence that Troy VIIA was a much bigger city than earlier archaeologists had thought. What they had considered the city wall seems to have enclosed only the acropolis. The outer perimeter of the city was another 1300 feet farther away.

There is much archaeological evidence of Mycenaean Greek trade and settlement in western Anatolia, including Mycenaean pottery at Troy. Perhaps the Greeks did fight a war there, though perhaps the prize was Trojan booty rather than Helen, the kidnapped wife of the Greek king Menelaus. Troy's location might have allowed it to dominate maritime trade. Perhaps the destruction of Troy VIIA was one of countless similar destructions around the eastern Mediterranean in the era of the Sea Peoples (see page 34).

Scholars from other fields are also examining the question. Geologists and hydrologists (students of water and its underground sources) are surveying the Trojan plain to consider the accuracy of Homer's geographic references. Hittite experts point to references in a text from around 1400 B.C. to places called Taruisa and Wilusiya and to a man named Alaksandus—perhaps to be identified as Troy, Ilion (a variant name for Troy), and Alexander (a Trojan prince) and to be taken as suggesting an earlier date for the war.

The facts of the Trojan War are still unverified. We *can* say, though, that as long as Homer's poems survive, the Trojan War will continue to fascinate and intrigue us.

CHAPTER 3

The Age of the Polis: Greece, ca. 750–350 B.C.

Sometime around 550 B.C. the Greek poet Phocylides assessed the relative achievements of his society and its neighbors. Around 1100 B.C. the Mycenaean kingdoms had given way to petty local aristocracies. By Phocylides' day the characteristic political institution of much of Greece was the city-state, or *polis* (plural, *poleis*). A polis was tiny compared to an empire, but Phocylides saw no need for modesty. "A little polis founded on a cliff's edge and governed well," he wrote, "is stronger than senseless Nineveh [the Assyrian capital]."[1] This was no idle boast, for the era of the polis proved to be a defining moment in Western history.

In the mid-first millennium B.C., while the monotheistic religious heritage of the West was first crystallizing in Israel, the philosophical and political heritage of the West was first crystallizing in Greece. Whereas loyalty to God was the central organizing principle of Israel, loyalty to the polis was fundamental to the Greeks. The Greeks saw the polis as an institution in which good people submitted to the rule of good laws. The Phoenicians and other ancient peoples lived in city-states, but it was the Greeks who developed the most radical system of popular government—"power of the people," as they called it, or *demokratia,* from which the word *democracy* comes. Greek writers explored the human soul, but the literary genres in which they excelled—tragedy, comedy, history, and philosophy—never overlooked the centrality of the polis. Not every polis was a democracy, to be sure. Nor did Greek democracy grant equal rights to women, slaves, or immigrants. The same individual freedom that fostered democracy also created factionalism, which expressed itself in frequent wars.

The Charioteer of Delphi, ca. 470 B.C.

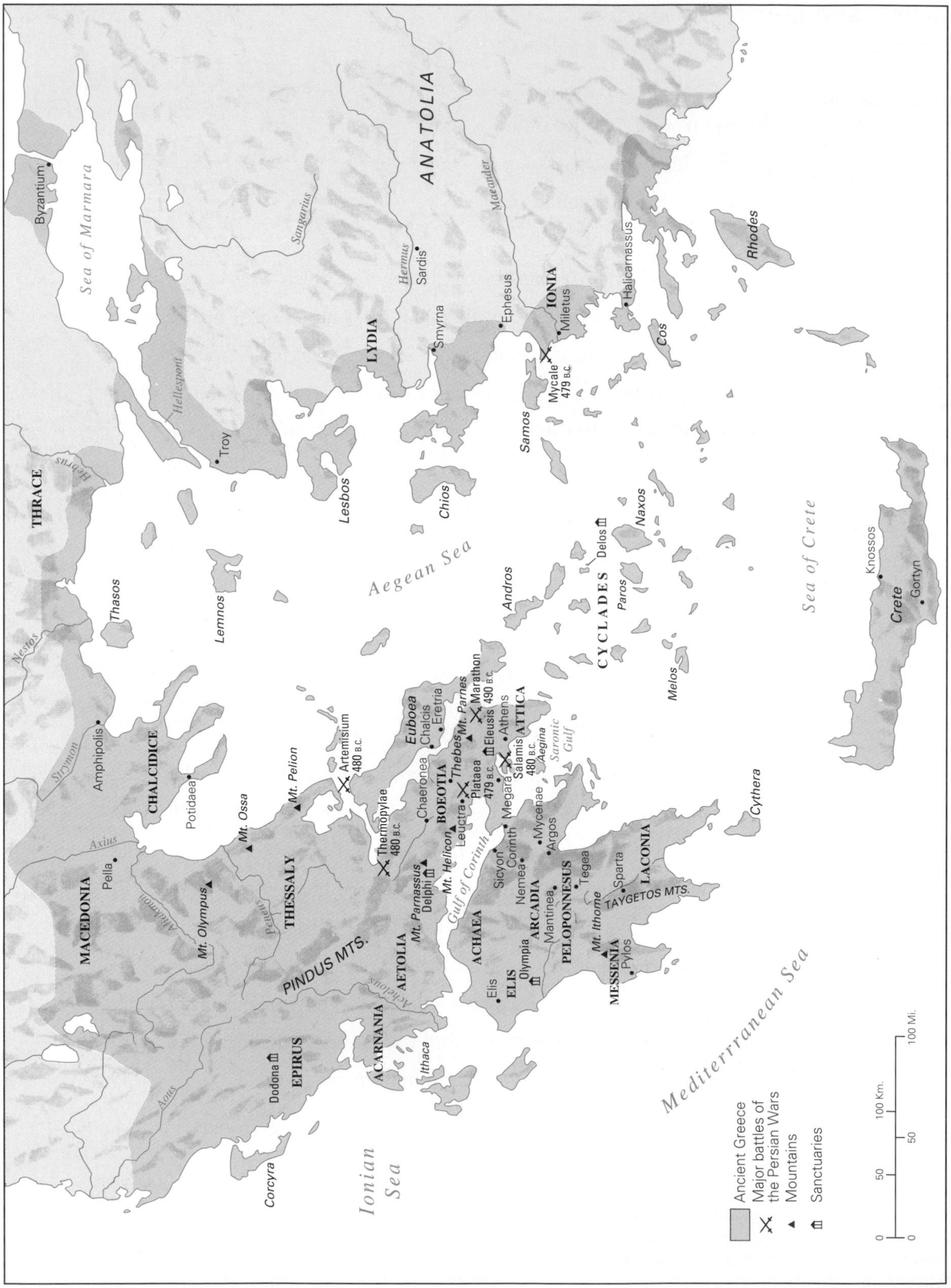
ANATOLIA
Sea of Marmara
Byzantium
Sangarius
Maeander
Hermus
Sardis
Smyrna
Ephesus
IONIA
Miletus
Halicarnassus
Rhodes
Cos
LYDIA
Hellespont
Troy
THRACE
Hebrus
Nestos
Strymon
Thasos
Lemnos
Lesbos
Chios
Samos
Mycale
479 B.C.
Aegean Sea
Andros
CYCLADES
Delos
Naxos
Paros
Melos
Sea of Crete
Knossos
Gortyn
Crete
Cythera
MACEDONIA
Pella
Axius
Haliakmon
Amphipolis
CHALCIDICE
Potidaea
Mt. Olympus
Mt. Ossa
Mt. Pelion
Peneus
THESSALY
PINDUS MTS.
Artemisium
480 B.C.
Thermopylae
480 B.C.
Euboea
Chalcis
Eretria
Marathon
490 B.C.
Mt. Parnes
Thebes
BOEOTIA
Chaeronea
Mt. Helicon
Leuctra
Plataea
479 B.C.
Eleusis
ATTICA
Athens
Salamis
480 B.C.
Aegina
Saronic Gulf
Megara
Mt. Parnassus
Delphi
Gulf of Corinth
Corinth
Sicyon
Nemea
Mycenae
Argos
Tegea
Sparta
LACONIA
TAYGETOS MTS.
Mt. Ithome
MESSENIA
Pylos
PELOPONNESUS
Mantinea
ARCADIA
ACHAEA
Olympia
ELIS
Elis
AETOLIA
Achelous
ACARNANIA
Ithaca
EPIRUS
Dodona
Aous
Corcyra
Ionian Sea
Mediterranean Sea
Ancient Greece
Major battles of the Persian Wars
Mountains
Sanctuaries
0 50 100 Km.
0 50 100 Mi.

Society and Politics in Archaic Greece, ca. 750–500 B.C.

Historians usually call the era in Greek history from roughly 750 to 500 B.C. the "Archaic period." In this context *archaic* refers to the style of sculpture in the two centuries before the "Classical period" (480–323 B.C.). Archaic Greece was a patchwork of hundreds of separate city-states, tribal leagues, and monarchies (Map 3.1). Nevertheless, it displayed a distinctive style and outlook not only in art but also in politics, military arrangements, technology, economics, literature, and religion.

The Archaic period was an era of paradoxes: the simultaneous growth of individualism and a tight community spirit; the emergence of social cohesion despite a continual state of war; the coexistence of deep religious piety and the West's first nontheistic philosophy. The Archaic period was also the point of origin of now-familiar types of government regimes—tyranny, oligarchy, and the first steps toward democracy—and of fundamental notions of citizenship and the rule of law.

Eighth-Century Revival and Expansion

Although on the brink of great achievements, ninth-century Greece was a poor, illiterate society of small towns and low-level trade. Everything began to change in the eighth century. Peace contributed to a sharp population rise, and the economy shifted from herding to farming, a more efficient source of food.

Greek commerce too was expanding. Shortly before 800 B.C., men from the Greek island of Euboea, perhaps following the example of Phoenician merchants and seafarers who had been casual traders in Greece for a century (see page 47), established a trading post in Syria, at Al-Mina on the mouth of the Orontes River (near the modern border between Turkey and Syria). Al-Mina, at the terminus of the chief caravan route from Mesopotamia, was to become the major center of Greek trade with the east for two hundred years. Within a generation, by 775 B.C., Euboeans also established a settlement in the west, on the Bay of Naples in Italy. In both east and west, Greek merchants sought iron and luxury goods; what they offered in return was probably silver (of which ancient Greece had rich deposits) and slaves.

From trading posts, established for commercial purposes, it was but a short step to founding colonies that siphoned off the extra mouths created by population growth. In colonization as in trade the Greeks may have followed the example of the Phoenicians, who had begun establishing colonies probably in the ninth century B.C. Between about 750 and 500 B.C., the Greeks established colonies throughout the Mediterranean and the Black Sea, founding nearly as many cities as already existed in Greece (Map 3.2). Colonization in Italy and Sicily began in earnest around 750 B.C., in the Chalcidice in the northeast Aegean perhaps a generation later, in the Sea of Marmara about 680, in North Africa around 630, and in the Black Sea about 610. In the far west, Massalia (modern Marseilles) was established about 600. Southern Italy and Sicily were especially intense areas of Greek settlement, so much so that the Romans later called the region *Magna Graecia* ("Great Greece"). In the long run, Greek colonization was of great importance for the spread of urban civilization westward, especially into Italy.

Motives for colonization ranged from wanderlust to profit seeking, but the main motive was land hunger. The typical colonist was young; the typical colony was small, consisting of a few hundred settlers. Colonists had to be prepared to fight, for colonies were frequently planted on land belonging to natives. Greek attitudes toward native peoples were complex. Though convinced of their own superiority, the Greeks were happy to trade and intermarry with natives once they had killed or enslaved some and carved out a colony on their land. It is usually assumed that most Greek colonists were male; if so, then the rate of Greek intermarriage with native females must have been high.

Trade and colonization inspired change at home. They made increasing numbers of Greeks

Map 3.1 Archaic and Classical Greece The region of the Aegean Sea was the heartland of Greek civilization around 750–350 B.C. The mountainous terrain, rugged coastline, and large number of islands encouraged political fragmentation.

into seafarers. This was a critical development, for as the historian Thucydides (ca. 455–ca. 399 B.C.) argues, a sea power tends to be more dynamic and innovative than a land power. All trade and conquest redistribute wealth, but seafarers tend to come into contact with new ideas and institutions. In antiquity, ships moved more quickly and cheaply than land transport; thus, seapower tended to accelerate the rate of change.

One important consequence of foreign contact was the introduction to Greece of the alphabet, borrowed from the Phoenicians (who had adapted the Ugaritic alphabet). The first datable examples of the Greek alphabet come from pots from roughly 750 B.C. The alphabet spread rapidly and widely in the next century. No doubt only a small minority mastered writing, but inscribed evidence ranging from misspellings to graffiti to practice exercises shows that a large percentage of the population had a rudimentary knowledge of the alphabet. Some of the most important achievements of Archaic Greece—written poetry, natural philosophy, law codes, and the idea of constitutional and popular government—would have been impossible without the alphabet and the spread of literacy.

Demographic, social, cultural, and economic changes eventually led to political changes. Around 700 B.C. the *basileis,* the elite of landowning, aristocratic families, were still entrenched, as Hesiod shows in his poem *Works and Days.* He calls them "gift-eating basileis," an indication of the bribes they demanded in return for protection or justice. Nor did the *demos* (ordinary people) have any recourse if they were dissatisfied with the basileis, as Hesiod indicates in his fable of

Situation of a Greek Colony Located on a defensible hill overlooking a fertile plain, the Sicilian Greek City of Acragas (Agrigentum) was founded about 580 B.C. Here we see a Doric temple of about 460–440 B.C. and part of the fortification wall that surrounded the city. *(Alon Reininger/Woodfin Camp & Associates)*

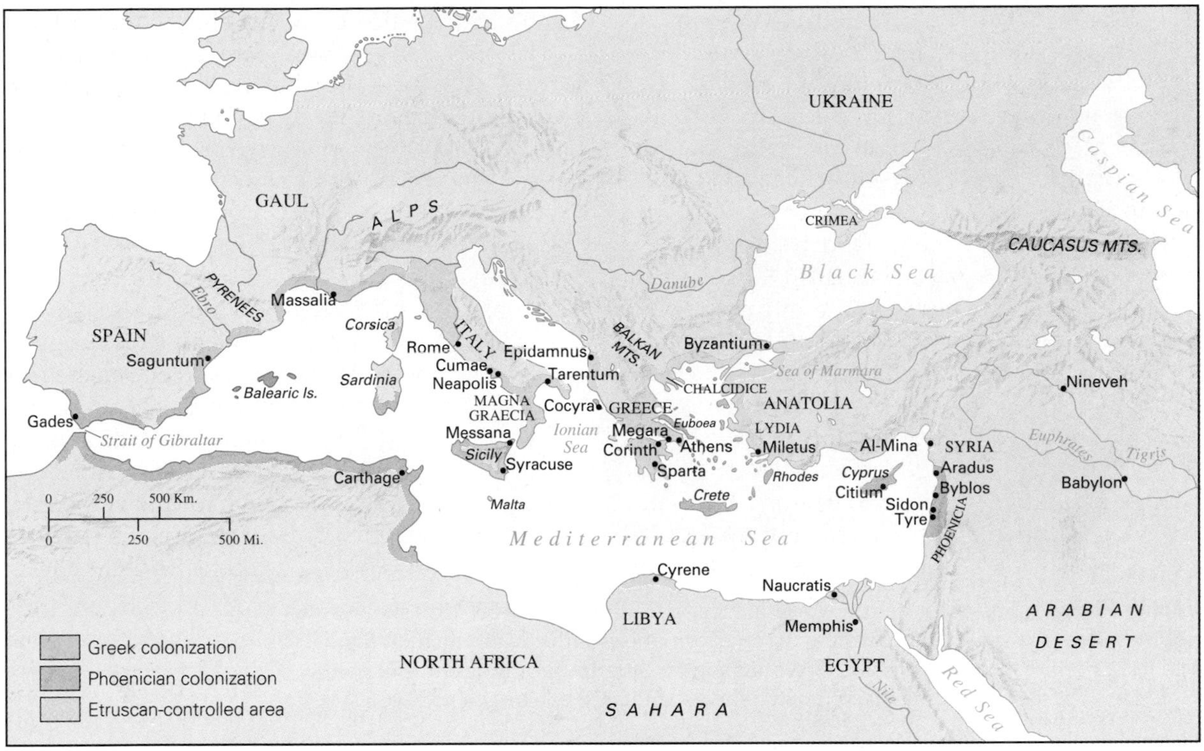

Map 3.2 Phoenician and Greek Colonization Both the Phoenicians (beginning perhaps after 900 B.C.) and the Greeks (beginning around 750 B.C.) established numerous colonies on the coasts of the Mediterranean and Black Seas.

the hawk and the nightingale: "Your master holds you fast,/you'll go where I decide, although you have/A minstrel's lovely voice, and if I choose,/I'll have you for a meal or let you go."[2] Faced with an arrogant aristocrat who demanded a jar of wine or a bushel of wheat in return for a favor, an ordinary person might have felt like a bird in the claws of a hawk. In the changing society of Greece around 700 B.C., however, the power of the basileis was about to give way.

Emergence of the Polis

What made the Greek city-state unique was social cohesion, military technology and formations, and above all, the practice and ideology of citizenship. *Polis* came to denote not just a city but the community as a whole, corresponding roughly to a country or nation. One crude gauge of the centrality of the polis is the words the Greeks derived from it: among them, *polites* (citizen), *politeia* (constitution), *politeô* (to govern), *ta politika* (politics), and *politikos* or *politeuomenos* (politician).

Historians continue to debate the date of the emergence of the polis. In considering this question, one must distinguish between the physical and the ideological community. In physical terms, the polis existed as early as the ninth or even the tenth century B.C. By 800 B.C. walled cities were common in Greece. The intense communal ideology of the polis, however, did not emerge until around 700 B.C.

Most poleis were small, many less than a hundred square miles in size. Athens was one of the largest. Its territory, known as Attica (see Map 3.3), covered a thousand square miles (approximately the size of the state of Rhode Island). It included many villages that had once been autonomous but had come under the authority of the city of Athens, perhaps around 800 B.C. At its

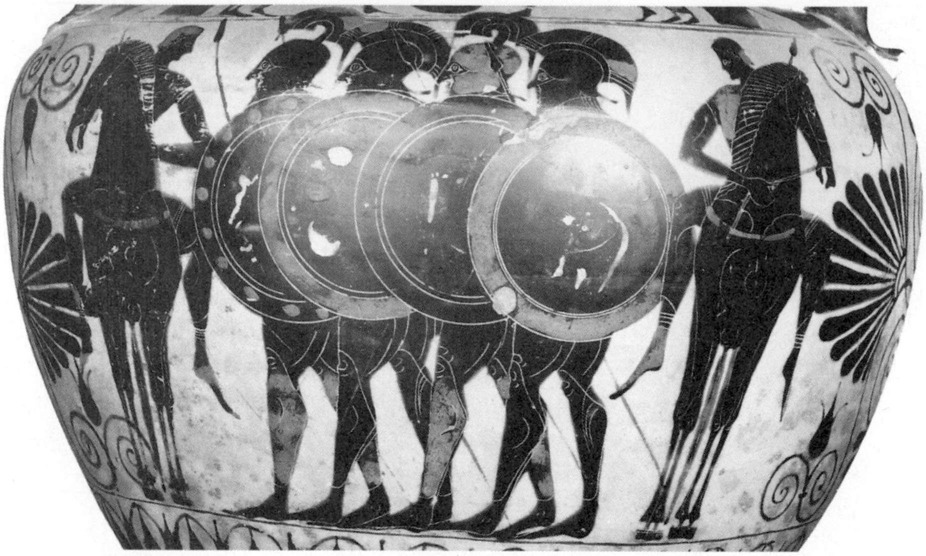

Hoplite Phalanx This black-figure Athenian vase painting (ca. 600–550 B.C.) shows four hoplites (heavily-armed infantrymen) in close formation, with cavalry on their flanks. In real life a hoplite phalanx (formation) would contain hundreds or thousands of men. Note the hoplites' round shields, plumed helmets, and long pikes. *(Louvre © Photo R.M.N.)*

height (ca. 430 B.C.) the population of Athens was about 400,000 (a typical polis contained between 5000 and 10,000 people). The philosopher Aristotle (384–322 B.C.) wrote that an ideal polis should be small enough that the citizens know one another personally.

The polis consisted of two parts: the urban area, which usually was tiny, and the surrounding countryside, where most people lived. From the earliest times, the urban public space included both a defensible hill (preferably with a water supply), called a "high city" (*acropolis*), and a "gathering place" (*agora*) used as a marketplace and for meetings. There was usually at least one temple. After around 500 B.C. stone buildings, including council houses, theaters, covered porticoes, gymnasia, and baths, became increasingly common.

The most remarkable thing about the physical structure of the early Greek polis, however, is just how unremarkable it was. What distinguished the early polis was not its buildings but its ideology. As the poet Alcaeus (born ca. 630 B.C.) puts it, "Not houses finely roofed or the stones of walls well-built, nay nor canals and dockyards, make the polis, but men able to use their opportunity." The cultural and political framework of the polis was in large part the result of a military revolution: the development of the hoplite phalanx.

The Hoplite Phalanx and the Community

The hoplite phalanx was a tightly ordered unit of heavily armed, pike-bearing infantrymen. The phalanx not only became the dominant military force in Archaic Greece, but, with relatively few changes in equipment and tactics, it remained supreme on land in Greece, western Asia, and other Mediterranean regions until its defeat by a Roman legion in 197 B.C. Yet in spite of its importance, the phalanx is an enigma. Questions abound—above all, why men should fight in so uncomfortable and unsophisticated a manner, tightly massed in heavy armor that suited neither Greece's Mediterranean climate nor its mountainous terrain. The key may lie as much in social and cultural history as in military history.

Before the establishment of the phalanx, warfare was dominated by the nobles. Unable to afford equipment, ordinary people did little besides follow the nobles, cheering and throwing stones. Society was changing rapidly, however, and prosperous farmers were no longer content to let nobles monopolize military power. A new, broader-based army emerged, although the poorest men could not afford armor and remained excluded. The heavily armed infantryman (hoplite) of the fighting unit (phalanx) wore bronze armor on his shins and chest and a bronze helmet with only a narrow opening for eyes and mouth. He carried a heavy wooden shield rimmed with bronze, holding it in his left hand. His weapons were a pike—a heavy wooden thrusting-spear with iron tip, at least 9 feet long—and a short, iron stabbing-sword.

An individual hoplite could accomplish little, but when he fought in a phalanx, he was formidable. The men of the phalanx were arranged in close ranks, normally four to eight deep. Soldiers stood together in line, each man's shield overlapping his neighbor's. Hoplite battles were set battles: head-to-head, army against army, all-or-nothing affairs, rather than individual skirmishes or guerrilla raids. Too unwieldy for Greece's mountains, the phalanx fought only in the plains. Battle usually consisted of an initial charge, followed by a grueling contest. The men in the front line pounded the enemy with their pikes while the men in the rear pushed forward. Finally one side would give way. Most of the defeated would escape by running away. A few of their comrades suffered serious wounds; a few died. The winning phalanx would stake its claim to the field by erecting a trophy. By increasing the pool of warriors, the phalanx made warfare more common. For centuries, hoplite battle was virtually an annual occurrence in Greece. War became a way of life.

Aretê, now lamely translated as "excellence" or "virtue," but originally meaning "warrior prowess," was a central concept for the Greeks. In Homer, a warrior fought mainly for personal and familial honor (see page 69). By around 650 B.C. aretê referred also to the community. According to the poet Tyrtaeus (ca. 650 B.C.), the ideal soldier not only fights bravely but "heartens his neighbor by his words." Should he die, his death brings glory not only to his father but also to his city and his countrymen. Although the battlefield remained the favored arena for displays of aretê, the assembly or the council house was increasingly acceptable as an alternative.

Competition characterized both politics and war, and competition, so the Greeks believed, bred aretê. Indeed, Archaic Greece ritualized competition through athletic games that were Pan-Hellenic—that is, all Greece took part. (The word *athletics* comes from the Greek word *athletika,* which means "concerning prizes.") The oldest Pan-Hellenic games were the Olympic games, held once every four years at the shrine of Zeus at Olympia, in the western Peloponnesus. Tradition dates the first Olympics to 776 B.C., but archaeological evidence suggests they began even earlier.

Like most ideals, Tyrtaeus' ideal of military aretê was sometimes honored and sometimes

Practicing for the Games This black-figure amphora (sixth century B.C.), depicts runners and a discus thrower under the supervision of a trainer in the palaestra (training ground). The trainer carries a forked stick, symbol of his office. *(Martin-von-Wagner-Museum at the University of Würzburg)*

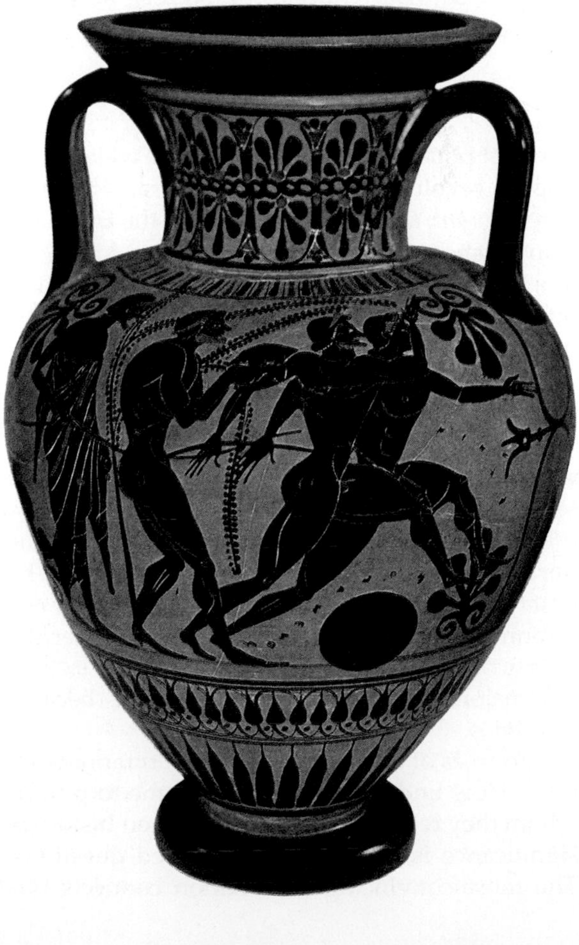

not; it certainly never entirely replaced family loyalty. The phalanx nonetheless fostered the communal spirit of the polis. Hoplite battle was less a matter of individual prowess than of group effort. The polis continued to prize individualism, but not as much as it prized the fulfillment of one's obligations to the community.

As early as about 700 B.C. important public documents were inscribed on stone. Acts of state are attributed not to a personified polis but to the community—for example, not to Thera but to "the Thereans," not to Sybaris but to "the Sybarites." The emphasis is on the plurality. The Greeks came to call the polis a "common thing" (*koinon*). It was a commonwealth. It belonged to its people, not to a few nobles or to a king or a god.

Hoplites were amateur soldiers. Most were full-time farmers outside of the fighting season, which lasted only for the summer months. The notion of the farmer-soldier, important in later political theory, had an immediate, practical effect: Those who fought for society soon demanded a say in governing it.

Tyranny in the Polis

The first political development in the wake of the hoplite revolution was not democracy but tyranny. *Tyrant,* a term borrowed from the East, possibly from Lydia (a wealthy kingdom in Anatolia), originally referred not to an arbitrary and oppressive ruler but rather to a champion of the people. Having overthrown a narrow and entrenched aristocracy, tyrants were at first so popular enough that they did not need bodyguards. *Tyrant* did not become a pejorative word before roughly 550 B.C., when the people soured on the second and third generation of tyrants.

Greek tyranny began in Argos, a polis in the northeastern Peloponnesus, around 675 B.C. The first tyrant was an Argive named Pheidon. By 660 tyranny had spread to nearby Corinth. Over the course of the seventh and sixth centuries B.C., all the major Greek poleis except Sparta became tyrannies.

Sources of evidence for the first tyrannies are poor. How and why the tyrants came to power, whom they represented, and what their historical significance is, are all much-debated questions. The most convincing explanation connects tyranny to the phalanx. At the introduction of the phalanx, most poleis were ruled by the basileis, grown arrogant during their long tenure of power. Hoplites resented their exclusion from office, and once they bore arms, they were in a position to act.

In the seventh century B.C., therefore, men who had been denied political power rose on the shoulders of the hoplites and overthrew a narrow elite. They set up one-man rule, but they did so in the name of a group much broader than the basileis: the prosperous farmers who fought in the phalanx.

Much of what the tyrants did, especially in the first generation, was popular and progressive. They stimulated the economy by founding colonies on trade routes, standardizing weights and measures, and encouraging the immigration of skilled craftsmen from other poleis. Corinth under the tyrant Cypselus (r. ca. 657–625 B.C.), for example, became an exporter of agricultural produce, especially to Magna Graecia, and the wealthiest city in Greece. Tyrants built temples and instituted festivals, provided both jobs and leisure-time activities.

When tyrants passed power on to their sons, however, the second generation tended to rule oppressively. Buoyed by the discontent of the demos, the basileis regrouped and tried to take back power. Thraysbulus of Miletus (ca. 600 B.C.), one second-generation tyrant, advised accordingly: To maintain power, a tyrant should "lop off the tallest ears of grain"—that is, execute or exile aristocrats in order to deny leaders to the opposition. But the tide of discontent was not to be stopped. Few tyrannies lasted beyond the third generation, when they were overthrown and replaced by oligarchy (literally, "rule by the few") or, less often, by democracy (literally, "power of the people"). By 500 B.C. tyranny had disappeared from most of Greece.

Sparta

Located in Laconia, a fertile valley in the south-central Peloponnesus, in the southern part of mainland Greece, Sparta seemed destined by geography for prosperity but not particularly for glory. It was situated not at a crossroads or beside a great harbor but rather by rugged, isolating mountains. Yet Sparta was to be an enormously

An Oracle Establishes Sparta's Government

Tradition says that Lycurgus, founder of the Spartan regime, obtained the blessing of Apollo at Delphi and brought to Sparta a divine pronouncement known as the "Great Rhetra" ("Great Saying"), which underlay the establishment of the Spartan regime. Many historians, however, doubt that Lycurgus ever really existed. And the most that can be said about the Great Rhetra, which is preserved in the writings of Plutarch (ca. A.D. 50–ca. 120), is that it is evidence of what the Spartans believed *about their origins. The tension in the oracle between popular power and central authority is striking.*

Lycurgus . . . brought an oracle . . . from Delphi, which they call a *rhetra.* It goes as follows: "After dedicating a temple to Zeus Skullanius and Athena Skullania, forming *phylai* [tribes] and creating *obai* [districts], and instituting a Council of Elders of thirty including the founder-leaders [kings], then from season to season summon the assembly between Babyka [a bridge] and Knakion [a river] so as to propose and withdraw. But to the people should belong the right to respond as well as power." . . . When the populace was assembled, Lycurgus permitted no one else except the Elders and kings to make a proposal, although the authority to decide upon what the latter put forward did belong to the people. Later, however, when the people distorted proposals and mauled them by their deletions and additions, the kings Polydorus and Theopompus [seventh century B.C.] supplemented the *rhetra* as follows: "If the people should make a crooked choice, the Elders and the founder-leaders are to set it aside"—that is, not to confirm it, but to withdraw it completely and to dismiss the people because they are altering and reformulating the proposal contrary to what was best. Moreover these kings persuaded the city that the god had ordered this supplement.

Source: Plutarch, "Life of Lycurgus," in Richard J. A. Talbert, trans., *Plutarch on Sparta* (Harmondsworth, England: Penguin, 1988), pp. 14–15.

influential model of citizenship and constitutionalism, virtue and communal spirit, austerity and militarism.

The history of Sparta is not easy to write. Sparta was a closed, military society, contemptuous of book-learning, suspicious of foreigners, and secretive toward the outside world. Careful scholarship has dispelled many myths, however. For example, Spartans believed that their unique system had been created at one stroke, by the legendary lawgiver Lycurgus, who is supposed to have lived (according to the most common version) in the eighth century B.C. and whose charter for Sparta was a divine command (see the box, "An Oracle Establishes Sparta's Government"). Nowadays, the scholarly consensus is for gradual innovations in Sparta rather than one, big revolutionary change; for a process beginning around 650 B.C. and continuing for generations. And it is by no means clear that there ever was a Lycurgus. Let us consider the question of origins.

The foundations of Spartan society were laid around 650 B.C., when a three-part class system emerged. Helots, unfree laborers who worked the land and were treated brutally by their superiors, were at the lowest level. *Perioikoi* (roughly, "neighbors"), who were free and locally autonomous but subordinate to the highest class, were above the helots. Spartiates, or Equals, males who monopolized political power and were the only full citizens, were above the perioikoi. We do not know the number of helots, but we do know that they vastly outnumbered the other two classes. When the system began around 650 B.C., there were about nine thousand Equals. Each Equal had the right, after reaching age 30, to attend a legislative and deliberative assembly and to hold public office. Each, moreover, was given a minimum land allotment (wealthy Equals owned additional land), which was worked by helots, thereby freeing the Equal to fight.

Although Sparta seemed like a rigid society by 450 B.C., the idea of sharing power among some nine thousand Equals was quite radical in its day. In contrast to tyranny or to the rule of the basileis, the nine thousand Equals shared a measure of equality in Sparta. What gave them the clout and prestige to do so? Undoubtedly, the Equals were hoplites, the backbone of Sparta's army. In the mid-seventh century B.C., Sparta was even more dependent on its army than was the average polis.

This dependence stemmed from Sparta's treatment of the helots, most of whom were Messenians, the neighboring people to Sparta's west. While other poleis were solving the problems of overpopulation and land shortage by establishing colonies overseas, Sparta's brutal solution was to conquer the fertile territory of Messenia in about 725 B.C. Although the Messenians were Greeks, they were forced to labor for the conquerors. Sparta thus solved its land problem, only to replace it with a security problem. The restive Messenian helots had to be policed, and a dramatic revolt sometime between 675 and 650 B.C. almost succeeded in expelling the Spartans. To keep Messenia, Sparta needed a crack army; to get that, Sparta needed to train, nourish, and glorify its soldiers. The political and economic result was to make all Spartan hoplites into Equals.

In spite of the emphasis on equality, Sparta was no democracy. The ancients classified the Spartan government as "mixed" because it combined elements of monarchy, of popular government, and of rule by an elite few. The assembly of Equals constituted the popular element in the regime, but its powers were limited. Ordinary Equals, for instance, were not encouraged to speak, and voting was conducted by shouting, a far more subjective measure than the show of hands used in the democratic assembly of Athens. Real power was shared among the kings, elders, and ephors (overseers), men generally belonging to a few wealthy families. The two kings (why two is unclear) were less monarchs than commanders of the army and chief priests. A Council of Elders (twenty-eight men plus the kings, for a total of thirty) and a board of five ephors represented the elite few. The council set the assembly's agenda; the ephors had a general supervisory power that permitted them to intervene in all aspects of governance. In reality, therefore, Sparta was an oligarchy.

To maintain control of the Messenian helots, Sparta had to keep up discipline among the Equals. Around 550 B.C. the state established an unusual system of public education for sons of the Equals, the *agoge* ("upbringing"). Its purpose was to ensure discipline, obedience, military preparedness, and total loyalty to the community. The agoge promoted fitness, toughness, and self-discipline.

Austerity was a hallmark of Spartan society after approximately 550 B.C. Spartans' diet was famous for its simplicity. The preferred food was a black broth of pork cooked in its own blood and spiced with salt and vinegar. To discourage consumption, Sparta issued no coins; the official "currency" consisted of heavy and unwieldy iron spits (that is, skewers). Trade with the outside world was avoided because foreign products were believed to be corrupting. Only small numbers of foreigners were admitted to Sparta. Their movements were strictly limited, and they were subject to periodic expulsion.

The life cycle of an Equal boy, as regulated by the agoge, was unique in Greece. At birth, babies were examined by public inspectors. Those who were considered deformed or unfit were "exposed"—that is, abandoned without food or shelter. The victims might die, but they might also be sold into slavery or even secretly adopted. (Other Greeks also practiced exposure of infants but left the matter up to private families.) Surviving children were raised at home up to the age of 7, at which point boys left the family to be boarded with a "herd" of their age mates. Girls did not leave home for barracks. Unlike most Greek girls, they received a public education—limited, however, to physical training, which was thought to strengthen females for childbearing. For the eleven years from age 7 to age 18, a boy went through the rigorous training of the agoge. Boys learned only enough reading and writing for practical ends—for example, for messages to or from military headquarters. On the theory that good soldiers should be strong and silent, Spartans promoted a blunt, concise style of discourse—blunt and pithy, that is, "laconic."

Many boys between the ages of 18 and 20 served in the *krypteia* (secret service), an institution that combined the common Greek practice of initiatory service for young warriors with Sparta's security needs. Boys in the krypteia lived in the hills of Messenia, where they survived by hunting, foraging, and stealing. They spied on the ever-rebellious Messenian helots, whom they could kill with impunity because every year the Spartan state declared war on them. By age 20, all Equals had become hoplites, and they continued to serve in the army until age 60. Supported by helot labor, they devoted full time to fighting and training the next generation.

Men married around age 30, women around 20. Newlyweds were allowed to spend only enough time together to produce offspring. A Spartan male's first loyalty was to his fellow soldiers. Spartan women were relatively more independent than women elsewhere in Greece. Often neglected by their husbands, and having been schooled to assertiveness by youthful physical training outdoors, Spartan women also had the advantage of being able to inherit property, unlike Athenian women.

The aims of the agoge were limited, and it achieved them. Other Greek hoplites were amateurs. Spartan soldiers, in contrast, were effective professionals, dominating land warfare in Greece for several hundred years. Unlike most of the other poleis, Sparta had no walls; the inhabitants claimed that Spartan men were all the defense that was necessary.

Beginning around 550 B.C., Sparta used its military might to build up a network of alliances (dubbed the "Peloponnesian League" by scholars) in the Peloponnesus and central Greece. It may seem paradoxical that a xenophobic society like Sparta became the *hegemon* (literally, "leader") of an extensive alliance system, but in fact Sparta's fear of foreigners may account for its hegemony. The formation of the Peloponnesian League was seen as a preventive strategy to ensure, by intervening in the wider world, that no threat to Sparta would arise on the horizon. Yet Sparta's policy in the league was generally conservative. Major commitments were avoided because of the helot threat in Sparta's rear, because of the danger that austere Spartans might be corrupted by the free-and-easy life abroad, and because of the possibility that a victorious Spartan general might grow too powerful and replace Spartan oligarchy with tyranny.

Spartan Woman This bronze statuette (4¾ inches tall) from Laconia (ca. 530 B.C.) shows a woman running. Unlike other Greek women, elite Spartan women underwent physical education. Although personal freedom was limited in Sparta, women suffered fewer restrictions than their counterparts in democratic Athens did. *(National Archaeological Museum, Athens/TAP Service)*

By around 500 B.C., all of the Peloponnesian poleis except Argos had similar alliances with Sparta, and Thebes came aboard shortly afterward. Allies swore "to follow Sparta wherever it may lead and to have the same friends and enemies." In most cases, the allies either already had oligarchic governments or Sparta made sure that they would. Sparta dominated most allies, but Corinth and Thebes, both military and economic powers in their own right, often engaged in independent policies. Until its breakup in the aftermath of the Peloponnesian War (431–404 B.C.), the Peloponnesian League was the dominant land power in Greece and, after defeating Persia in 480, in the entire eastern Mediterranean.

Sparta exemplified community spirit and respect for law. The people of Sparta, as the historian Herodotus (ca. 485–ca. 425 B.C.) reports a Spartan king as saying, "are free . . . , but not entirely free; for they have a master, and that master is Law, which they fear." Sparta was also an exemplar of equality—limited equality, to be sure, but equality extended to a wider group than ever before in Greece. The notion of the Equals, moreover, contains the germ of the idea of the citizen: a free member of the political community who, unlike a subject, has rights as well as duties. Few other poleis could match the stability and sense of civic duty fostered by Sparta. In the realms of equality and citizenship, however, Sparta was eventually outstripped by Athens. In the realm of liberty, Athens wrote a new chapter in Western history.

Early Athens

Around 650 B.C. Athens's government was in the hands of the basileis of the Attic Plain (Map 3.3), who proudly called themselves the Eupatrids ("well-fathered men"). Nine archons, or magistrates, each chosen for a one-year term, ran the administration, after which they became life members of the Areopagus, a council of elders named for its meeting place on the "hill of Ares." By its prestige, this aristocratic council held the lion's share of power; it was also a homicide court. The demos met in an assembly. Probably from early times on, the assembly had, in theory, supreme lawmaking power, but voting was by shouting, and few people challenged Eupatrid wishes. Athenian society was loosely organized in various groups: "comradeships" (aristocratic clubs), neighborhood associations, burial societies, organizations arranging religious sacrifices,

Banqueting Scene This Corinthian wine-bowl (ca. 600 B.C.) depicts a mythological banquet. The men recline on couches, waited upon by the woman. Banquets and symposia (drinking parties) were among the favorite recreations of Greek aristocrats. *(Louvre © Photo R.M.N.)*

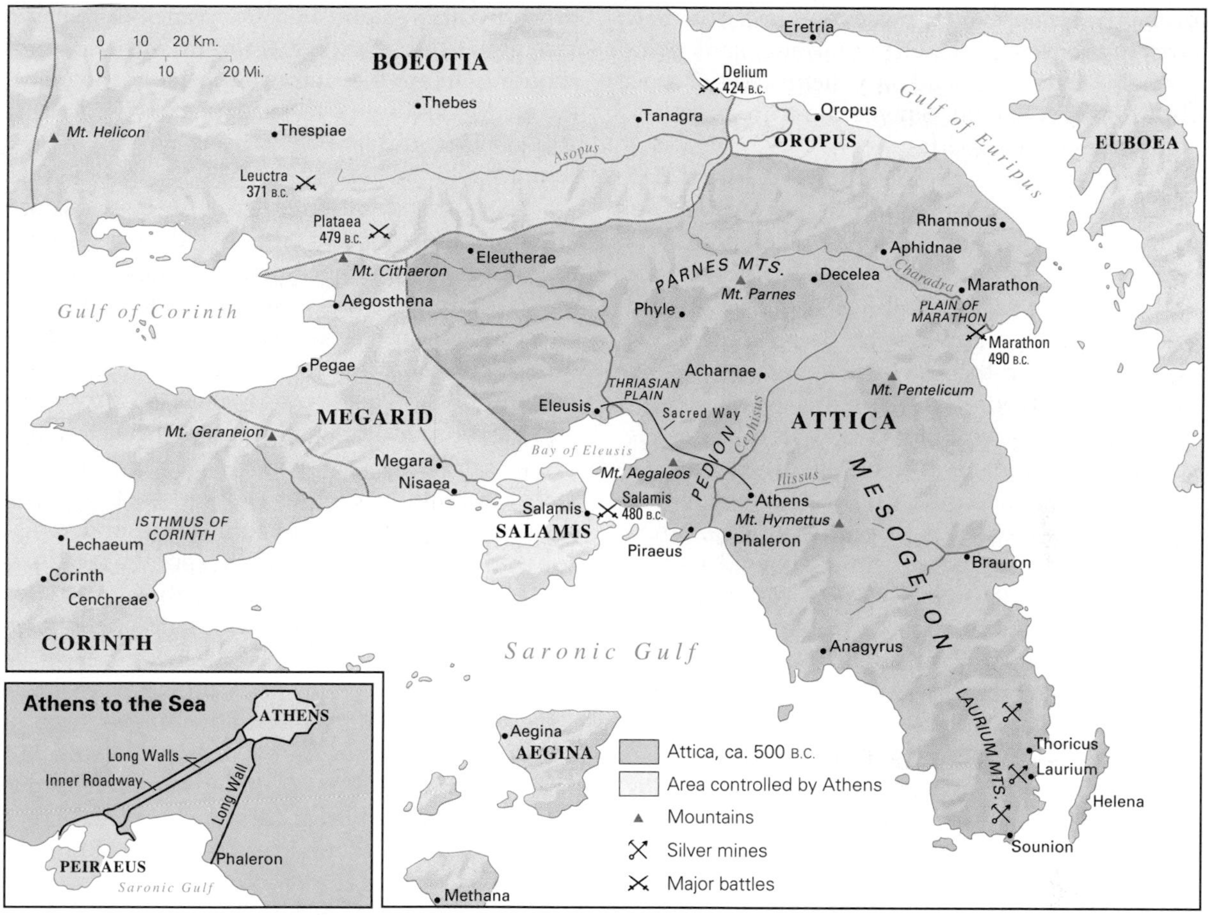

Map 3.3 Attica Mountains and plains alternate in the 1000-square-mile area of ancient Attica. The Long Walls connecting Athens and the port city of Piraeus were built around 450 B.C.

and four so-called tribes based on kinship or residence.

By 632 B.C. aristocratic rule was in trouble at Athens as elsewhere, because of corruption, economic change, and assertive hoplites. In that year one Cylon attempted to establish a tyranny. He failed, but the forces of change kept pressing. In 621 B.C. they forced a codification of the laws, which were then issued in writing. This Code of Draco, named for its main drafter, was famous for its harsh provisions (hence the adjective *draconian*); it was written, as a later commentator observed, "not in ink but blood." Some of its provisions can be reconstructed, but only its homicide law has survived in detail.

The Eupatrids were compelled to publish the laws, which previously, in effect, had been their private possession. Yet Draco's Code seems only to have whetted an appetite for change. The Eupatrids retained a hold on public office, but a wealthy non-Eupatrid elite of hoplites was emerging, grown rich exporting olive oil to Ukraine and shipping grain back to Athens. Some were merchants; most were prosperous farmers. They now wanted political power. As for ordinary Athenians, they typically worked small family farms. Over the years, bad harvests and soil exhaustion had sent many into debt. Those who had pledged their land as collateral became known as *hektemoroi* ("sixth-parters"), probably because they owed one-sixth of their crop to their creditors. Other farmers sank even farther into debt and had only themselves or their children as collateral. Some ended up as slaves, sometimes sold abroad.

Because both rich and poor Athenians had grievances against the Eupatrids, revolution was in the air. Enter Solon (ca. 630–ca. 560 B.C.), who was appointed to the emergency position of sole archon for one year, probably 594 B.C. A Eupatrid who had become a merchant, Solon understood both the old and the new elite, and he was sympathetic too to ordinary Athenians. As his surviving writings show, Solon was a moderate. He could have become tyrant, but he preferred to be a mediator; as such, he said, he "stood with a strong shield before both parties [the common people and the powerful] and allowed neither one to win an unfair victory."[3]

Solon's reforms were comprehensive, spanning both economics and politics. He helped ordinary people by the *seisachtheia*, or "shaking off of burdens," measures that abolished the institution of hektemorage and probably canceled some debts, abolished the practice of making loans on personal surety, and set up a fund to redeem Athenians who had been sold into slavery abroad. Solon disappointed many poor people by refusing to confiscate and redistribute land, but by freeing the hektemoroi, Solon ensured Athens a large class of independent small farmers.

Solon's other economic reforms were aimed at encouraging Athenian trade. To foster production of olive oil, a cash crop, he restricted all other agricultural exports. He changed Athenian weights, measures, and perhaps coins to conform with the most common Greek standard. He also encouraged the immigration of craftsmen to Athens. The result was a trade boom.

Solon made fundamental changes in Athenian government, too. He changed qualifications for office from birth to wealth, a boon to the non-Eupatrid elite. He established four census classes based on agricultural production. Most offices were reserved to men of property, but the poorest class, known as *thetes,* could participate in the assembly and courts. Thanks to Solon, such participation became a more valuable privilege. Solon probably established a Council of 400, which prepared the assembly's agenda. He probably regularized council and assembly meetings, and probably also established the principle that the assembly vote be by the counting of hands, not shouting. In another important change, Solon allowed the assembly to sit as a court to which Athenians could appeal the rulings of magistrates.

Solon's moderation, respect for law, and liberation of the poor and downtrodden are historic milestones. Yet neither Eupatrids nor champions of the poor were satisfied with Solon's middle way. After years of conflict, around 560 B.C. advocates of radical reform finally established a tyranny under Peisistratus (ca. 600–528 B.C.). He and his sons held power for forty of the next fifty years.

Supported by the thetes, the Peisistratids exiled many Eupatrids and confiscated and redistributed their land. Peisistratus kept the façade of Solon's reforms while ensuring that loyal supporters held all key offices. Itinerant judges were appointed to administer justice in the villages of Attica.

A stable regime, the tyranny witnessed prosperity at home and the expansion of Athenian influence abroad. Peisistratus fostered civic consciousness by establishing the Panathenaia, a religious festival held once every four years in honor of Athena, patron goddess of the polis, and by building temples for communal worship on the Acropolis and elsewhere in Athens. When the Persians conquered the Greek cities of western Anatolia in 547 B.C., Peisistratus welcomed migrants, thus bolstering Athenian claims to Hellenic leadership and adding skilled workers to the economy.

Peisistratus's dynasty lasted only two generations. A steadfast opponent of tyrants, Sparta deposed his son Hippias in 510 B.C. Athens's birth and wealth elites were ready to establish an oligarchy, but the way was open for an unexpected development: the emergence of popular government.

The Culture of Archaic Greece

If one trend in Archaic culture was communal solidarity, as reflected in the hoplite phalanx, another was quite opposite: a growing sense of individualism. Increased prosperity and mobility (social, geographical, and political) during the

Archaic period encouraged the breakdown of old ties and left some people with a sense of their uniqueness. An important manifestation of this new consciousness of the self is present in poetry and sculpture.

Archaic religion too underwent superficially opposite trends. While monumental stone temples were being erected and international centers for divination were being built up, Greek thinkers were beginning to move away from divine and toward abstract and mechanistic explanations of the universe.

Revealing the Self: Lyric Poetry and Sculpture

Between approximately 675 and 500 B.C. the dominant Greek literary form was lyric poetry. This form consisted of short poems written in a variety of styles but sharing a willingness to experiment, sometimes by revealing private feelings, sometimes by commenting on contemporary politics (as in the poetry of Tyrtaeus). Epic poetry, by contrast, was longer, grander in theme and tone, and less personal.

Homer never speaks directly about himself, and Hesiod reveals only a few personal details. In contrast, Archilochus of Paros (ca. 700–ca. 650 B.C.), the earliest known of the lyric poets, flaunts the self. Born on the Cycladic island of Paros, Archilochus was the son, perhaps the illegitimate son, of a noble. He was a mercenary soldier (that is, he fought for pay for a foreign country) and a colonist before returning home and dying in a hoplite battle against a neighboring island. The varied subjects of Archilochus's poetry include love, travels, and war. Much of his poetry is satire, sometimes mocking and ironic, sometimes vicious and abusive. He often sets a mood of privacy. Consider, for example, a lonely mercenary described by Archilochus as using his spear to knead bread and to lean on while drinking wine. Archilochus takes an ironic and detached view of hoplite ideals, freely admitting that he once tossed away his shield to escape the battlefield: "And that shield, to hell with it! Tomorrow I'll get me another one no worse."[4]

Sappho of Lesbos (ca. 625 B.C.) is also famous as a private poet, one who composed unmatched descriptions of intimate feelings, among them love for other women. Sappho is one of the few

POLITICS AND SOCIETY IN ARCHAIC GREECE

ca. 750 B.C.	Greek colonization of Magna Graecia begins
ca. 725 B.C.	Sparta conquers Messenia
ca. 675 B.C.	Pheidon becomes tyrant of Argos
594 B.C.	Solon is archon in Athens
ca. 560 B.C.	Peisistratus becomes tyrant of Athens
508 B.C.	Cleisthenes begins reforms in Athens

women poets of antiquity whose work has survived—very little, unfortunately, but enough to show that she was educated, worldly, and versed in politics. Like a modern experimental poet, she uses language self-consciously. Sappho's sensuality comes through in a description of her feelings at seeing a woman whose company she wants, talking with a man: Her heart shakes, her tongue is stuck, her eyes cannot see, her skin is on fire. "I am greener than grass," Sappho writes, "I feel nearly as if I could die."[5]

Sappho discusses female sexuality, a subject that Greek elite culture, dominated by males, tended to ignore. We know little about the sexuality of Greek women or of nonelite males. Among the male elite, romantic love in Archaic and Classical Greece was homosexual love or, to be precise, pederasty ("boy love"). The ideal relationship was supposed to involve a man in his twenties and a boy in his teens. The male elite was, strictly speaking, bisexual. By age 30 a man was expected to marry and raise a family. Perhaps bisexuality prevailed among elite females as well; Sappho, for example, eventually married and had a child.

Another sign of Archaic Greece's interest in the personal is the growing attention paid to the depiction of the human body, both in painting (most of the surviving examples are painted pottery) and in sculpture. Archaic artists displayed increasing skill and sensitivity in depicting the human form. The rich marble deposits in Greek soil gave sculptors promising material; baked clay (terra cotta) and bronze were other common sculptural media.

Early Archaic marble sculpture (seventh century B.C.) was strongly influenced by the way Egyptian sculpture represented the human body. Like Egyptian statuary, early Greek sculpture tended to be formal and frontal. But over the course of the seventh and sixth centuries B.C., Greek sculptors experimented with a greater variety of poses and with increasing realism in showing musculature and motion. This realism, however, was within limits, for the favorite subject of Archaic sculptors was not ordinary people but idealized, beautiful, young people. Typical sculptural forms were the naked young man (*kouros*) and clothed young woman (*kore*), which often served as grave markers or monuments. The goal was to show people not as they were but as they might be.

Religious Faith and Practice

Civilizations came and went in Greece, but the Olympian gods survived, as adapted by successive ages to fit their political and social structures. In the Archaic period, accordingly, the Olympian gods became gods of the polis.

Although the Olympians were worshiped throughout Greece, each polis had its patron deity: Apollo at Corinth, Hera at Argos and Samos, Athena at Athens and Sparta. Each polis had its favorite heroes or demigods: Theseus, the legendary founder of Athens; Heracles (Hercules), a favorite of Dorian cities such as Sparta and Thebes. It was considered important to build a "house"—that is, a temple—for the patron god or at least for his or her statue. The first temples were built of wood; the earliest stone temple, a temple of Apollo at Corinth, was built around 550 B.C.

Temples were rectangular structures with long sides on the north and south, short sides on the east and west, a colonnade around all four sides, and a pitched roof. Temples faced east to catch the sunlight to illuminate the interior, which consisted of two rooms: a small treasury, open to the west, and a larger main chamber, in which a statue of the deity stood. The interior decoration of the temple was simple. Outside, brownish-red roof tiles, painted sculpture above the colonnade and in the pediments (the area between the gables and the front and rear doorways), and terra-cotta roof ornaments created a festive and lively effect. The bare, white ruins seen today are misleading.

The emphasis on exterior rather than interior decoration in a Greek temple reflects the way the building was used. The main ceremony took place outside. A long altar stood in front of the temple and parallel to it. On feast days—and under the tyrants the number of such days was increased greatly, as a sop to the common people—temple priests would sacrifice animals (pigs, goats, lambs, and, on rare occasions, bulls) on the altar. Only the thighs would be burnt for the gods. The rest of the meat would be boiled and distributed to worshipers.

As in other ancient cultures so in Greece divination was an important element of religion. Divination was institutionalized in oracles, places where, it was believed, one could go to consult a god or hero for advice. The deity was thought to speak through the agency of his human servants. Of the various Greek oracles, that of Apollo at Delphi (in central Greece) became the most prestigious and respected. The utterances of Apollo of Delphi were famous among the Greeks for being ambiguous. Different people might interpret them in different ways, and Apollo could always be absolved after the fact if things did not turn out as the listener expected.

The priests of Delphi were regularly consulted by poleis wishing to establish colonies. The priests gave advice about the choice of location and the appropriate patron god or goddess, as well as helping settlers draft new law codes for the colonies. Delphi was also active in the search for new constitutions in the old poleis of Greece. Recall that tradition says that Sparta based its government on a pronouncement of the Delphic oracle (see page 87).

Archaic thinkers pondered the theme of divine justice. In Archaic literature one sees less of the squabblings among the gods than in Homer and more of Zeus's majesty and justice. Although the wicked might seem to prosper, Zeus eventually punishes them or their descendants. "It never escapes him all the way when a man has a sinful spirit; and always, in the end, his judgment is plain," says Solon.[6]

Archaic writers delighted in portraying human emotions, but they had no confidence about the human ability to master emotions. In Archaic literature, people are weak and insignificant; their fortune is uncertain and mutable. The gods are jealous of human success. People who aim too high are guilty of *hybris*—that is, arrogance with overtones of violence and transgression. Hybris brings *nemesis,* "punishment" or "allotment." The safest course is for a person to be pious and humble. (See the box, "The Archaic World View: 'Look to the End'.")

So Archaic religion taught a humbling, even pessimistic, lesson. Yet religious teachings were not always heeded; the pages of Archaic history are full of examples of politicians, generals, athletes, merchants, and artists who aimed high and sought success with seemingly little worry. In Ionia (the territory of the Greek cities along the central western Anatolian coast), one group of Greek thinkers made a radical break with Archaic religion and invented speculative philosophy.

The Origins of Western Philosophy

Abstract, rationalistic, speculative thinking emerged in Greece during the sixth century B.C. The first developments took place in Miletus, an Ionian city. It is often said that the thinkers of Miletus (the Milesians) and their followers in other parts of Ionia invented philosophy, and so they did, but we must be precise about what this means.

The Ionians were not the first to ask questions or tell stories about the nature and origins of the universe; virtually every ancient people did so. Nor did the Ionians invent science. They themselves conducted no experiments. By 600 B.C., moreover, science—including mathematics, astronomy, medicine, and engineering—had been thriving for over two thousand years in Egypt and Mesopotamia, a heritage with which the Ionians were familiar.

The real importance of the Ionians is as transitional figures. Passionately interested in finding order in the universe, they began the movement away from anthropomorphic or divine explanations and toward an abstract and mechanistic explanation of the universe. They themselves did not make a clear distinction between reason and revelation, but they made it possible for later Greek thinkers to do so. Later Greek philosophers were rarely (if ever) atheists, but they took for granted what the Ionians labored to establish: the primacy of human reason.

The Ionians saw themselves as students of nature—*physis* (from which the word *physics* is derived). Although they did not entirely shy away from moral and political questions, it is their interest in natural phenomena that makes the Ionians significant. In their own day, the Ionians were called "wise men" (*sophoi*); to a later generation, they were "lovers of wisdom," *philosophoi* (from which *philosopher* comes).

Thales, the first Milesian thinker, made a name for himself by successfully predicting a solar eclipse in 585 B.C. He is credited with founding Greek geometry and astronomy. Little survives of his writings or those of the other Milesians, but

Athenian Kore This statue of a young woman *(kore)* exemplifies Archaic Greek sculpture's interest in the idealized human form. Note the slight smile, the carefully coiffed hair and the elaborate clothes through which the contours of the female body are visible. The statue would originally have been brightly painted. *(Robert Frerck/Odyssey Productions)*

The Archaic World View: "Look to the End"

Tradition says that Solon visited the court of Croesus (r. ca. 560–547 B.C.), king of Lydia, a wealthy kingdom in western Anatolia. Herodotus contrasts Croesus's power with the modesty of Solon, whom he makes representative of the pessimism and religious faith of Archaic Greece. The gods punish arrogance; today's prince is tomorrow's pauper.

"My lord," replied Solon, "I know God is envious of human prosperity and likes to trouble us; and you question me about the lot of man. Listen then: as the years lengthen out, there is much both to see and to suffer which one would wish otherwise. . . . The total of days for your seventy years is 26,250, and not a single one of them is like the next in what it brings. You can see from that, Croesus, what a chancy thing life is. You are very rich, and you rule a numerous people; but the question you asked me [that is, who is the happiest man Solon knows?] I will not answer, until I know that you have died happily. Great wealth can make a man no happier than moderate means, unless he has the luck to continue in prosperity to the end. Many very rich men have been unfortunate, and many with a modest competence have good luck. . . .

"Now if a man thus favored dies as he has lived, he will be just the one you are looking for: the only sort of person who deserves to be happy. But mark this: until he is dead, keep the word 'happy' in reserve. Till then, he is not happy, but only lucky. . . .

"Look to the end, no matter what it is you are considering. Often enough God gives a man a glimpse of happiness, and then utterly ruins him."

Source: Herodotus, *The Histories,* trans. Aubrey de Sélincourt, rev. A. R. Burn (Harmondsworth, England: Penguin, 1972).

it is clear that he created the first general and systematic theory about the nature of the universe. According to Thales, the primary substance, the element from which all of nature was created, was water. He emphasized the mobility of water and its ability to nourish life.

A reply was not long in coming. Around 550 B.C., Anaximander of Miletus wrote the first known book of prose in Greek, expounding his own philosophy of nature. He attacked Thales for oversimplifying and for failing to do justice to the problem of change. Anaximander accepted Thales' monist assumption—that there was only one primary substance—but he called the substance "the unlimited" or "the undefined" rather than water. According to Anaximander, the universe was in eternal motion, characterized by a conflict of opposites. A third Milesian, Anaximenes, replied that the primary substance might be unlimited but it was not undefined. It was air, whose properties of condensation and rarefaction symbolized the phenomenon of change.

Humble as these theories might seem today, they represent a development of dramatic importance: an open and critical debate among thinkers, each of whom was proposing an abstract and rational model of the universe. Many scholars have speculated about the origins of this development. Why Miletus? Why the sixth century B.C.? There are no sure answers, although certain influences have been suggested. Among them are Miletus' contacts on the trade routes with sophisticated Babylon, the proximity of Ionia to non-Greek peoples and the resulting Milesian appreciation of variety and complexity, and the search for law and order in contemporary Greek political life and its extension to the philosophical plane.

Early Greek philosophy in its second generation moved to other Ionian cities and then migrated westward across the Mediterranean. Heracleitus of Ephesus, who lived around 500 B.C., proposed fire as the primary substance. Although fire was ever changing, it had an underlying coherence. According to Heracleitus, this paradox nicely symbolized the nature of the universe. He summed up the importance of change by the aphorisms "All things flow" and "You cannot step into the same river twice." The universe witnessed a constant struggle of opposites, yet an essential unity and order prevailed. To describe this order, Heracleitus used the term *logos.* This key concept of Greek philosophy is difficult to translate. Among other things, *logos* can mean word, thought, reason, story, or calculation.

Heracleitus' contemporary, Pythagoras of Samos, was both a rationalist and a religious thinker. On the one hand, Pythagoras was a mathematician who discovered the numerical ratios determining the major intervals of the musical scale. It is less certain if, as tradition has it, he discovered the so-called Pythagorean theorem—that in a right triangle the hypotenuse squared is equal to the sum of the squares of the other two sides.

On the other hand, Pythagoras believed that the purity of mathematics would improve the human soul. Just as he had imposed order on the indefinite range of sound between high and low in the musical scale through the use of numbers, so could philosophers understand the entire universe through number and proportion. The resulting knowledge was no mere academic exercise but a way of life. He devoted himself to "observation" or "contemplation"—to *theoria* (from which *theory* comes).

In Croton in Magna Graecia, Pythagoras founded a religious community of men and women. A strict rule of secrecy governed its members. Judging from the little reliable evidence that survives, they abstained from meat and paid much attention to ritual purity. They believed in the kinship of all living things. They also believed in the reincarnation of the human soul, though not necessarily into a human body. According to an anecdote, Pythagoras once stopped a man from beating a dog because he recognized from the barking that the dog was the reincarnation of a friend who had died.

The early Greek philosopher whose work is most fully preserved is Parmenides of Elea in Magna Graecia. Parmenides (b. ca. 515 B.C.) completely distrusted the senses. He believed that reality was a world of pure being: eternal, unchanging, and indivisible, comparable to a sphere. The change that Heracleitus had seen was, to Parmenides, a mere illusion. Parmenides, therefore, is the first Western philosopher to propose a radical difference between the world of the senses and reality. This fundamental strain of Western thought would be taken up by Plato and his followers and then passed to Christianity.

To sum up, in philosophy as in so many other endeavors, the Archaic Greeks were great borrowers and even greater innovators, who left a profound mark on later ages. By the late sixth century B.C., however, Archaic Greece was poised on the brink of revolution that would give birth to the Classical period of Greek civilization.

Classical Athens

The word *democracy* comes from the Greek word *demokratia,* coined in Athens early in the fifth century B.C. *Demokratia* literally means "the power (*kratos*) of the people (*demos*)." A modern democracy is characterized by mass citizenship, elections, and representative government. Athenian demokratia, in contrast, was a direct democracy in which elections were much less important than direct participation; citizenship was narrowly restricted; women were excluded from public life; resident aliens could almost never become citizens; and citizens owned slaves and ruled an empire. Modern democracies tend to emphasize individual rights over responsibility to the community. Athens, in contrast, like any polis, often placed the community first. In spite of the differences, Athenian demokratia established principles that are enshrined in democracy today: freedom, equality, citizenship without property qualifications, most public offices being open to most citizens, and the rule of law.

The Development of Demokratia, 508–321 B.C.

Tyranny often gave way to oligarchy—to government by wealthy men, both Eupatrids and non-Eupatrids. In Athens, however, the Solonian legacy of independent small farmers, the relative weakness of the Eupatrids after Peisistratid rule, and the presence of numerous immigrants created the conditions for revolution. Ironically, a Eupatrid, a member of the Alcmeonid clan by the name of Cleisthenes (d. ca. 500 B.C.), led the revolution.

Cleisthenes' original goal was to take charge of an oligarchy, but the "comradeships," or clubs, that dominated elite politics chose a rival leader instead. At this point, according to Herodotus, Cleisthenes came up with the novel idea of "adding the common people (demos) to his comradeship," although "he had previously ignored them." In other words, Cleisthenes offered political power to the demos. His political rivals responded by calling for Spartan military assistance, but to no avail: Cleisthenes rallied the people to victory. The Athenian triumph proved, in Herodotus' opinion, "that equality is an excellent thing, not in one way only but in many. For while they were under a tyranny, [Athenians] were no better at fighting than any of their neighbors, but once they were rid of tyrants they became by far the best."[7]

Cleisthenes' definition of demos was not all-inclusive. He meant mainly owners of medium-size farms, artisans, and merchants. The poorest Athenians, the thetes, were largely left out. Nevertheless, Cleisthenes laid the foundation for demokratia by establishing the principle that the demos controlled politics. The watchwords of the day were *equality* and *mixing*.

Cleisthenes undermined Eupatrid power once and for all by attacking its local bases of traditional support. By dividing Athenians into ten new tribes (replacing the four traditional tribes), which were further subdivided into 30 regional units (*trittyes*) and about 170 local units (*demes*), Cleisthenes promoted a spirit of equality and of unity. Every Athenian (including immigrants or their descendants, who had been excluded from the old tribes) belonged to a new tribe. Every Athenian hoplite fought with fellow tribesmen in an army now divided into ten tribal units. The tribes also formed the basis of a new Council of 500 to replace Solon's Council of 400. Like the army, the council was divided into ten tribal units, each serving as a kind of executive committee for one of the ten months of the civic year. Each tribe chose its 50 councilmen, who served for annual terms.

The centerpiece of the government was the assembly, some of whose members, emboldened by the new spirit of equality, now spoke up for the first time. The new Council of 500, like the old Council of 400, prepared the assembly's agenda, but assemblymen felt free to amend it. Only the Areopagus council remained a privileged preserve.

The last and most unusual part of the Cleisthenic system was ostracism, a sort of annual *un*popularity contest that received its name from the pieces of broken pottery (*ostraka*) on which the names of victims were inscribed. The "winner" was forced into ten years of exile, although his property would not be confiscated. Ostracism was meant to protect the regime by defusing factionalism and discouraging tyrants; judging by Athens's consequent political stability, it worked.

In 508 B.C. the poorest Athenians had relatively little power in Cleisthenic government. They lacked sufficient financial means to support political activity, sufficient political consciousness, and sufficient self-confidence. These conditions changed by the 450s, rendering Athens a full demokratia. They changed because the oldest principle of Greek politics came to the fore: Whoever fights for the state governs it. To counter the Persian threat against Greece of the 480s (see page 106), Athens built a great navy. Athenian warships were oared ships, triremes, and the core of the rowers consisted of Athenian thetes. Just as hoplites supported new regimes in Greece after 700 B.C., so rowers supported new regimes in Greece after 500.

The Athenian government remained unchanged until 461 B.C. Then setbacks in foreign affairs under conservative leadership gave the leaders of the demos an opening for reform. Ephialtes (d. ca. 460 B.C.) and his young associate Pericles (ca. 495–429 B.C.) turned to the last bulwark of privilege, the Areopagus. They stripped away the council's long-standing supervisory powers over the regime and redistributed those powers to the Council of 500 and the people's court. The decade of the 450s saw another innovation: payment for public service, specifically for jurors, who received a half-drachma (perhaps a half-day's wages) for a day of jury duty. Eventually other public servants also received pay. Conservatives complained bitterly, because they perceived, rightly, that state pay made political activity by poor people possible. State pay was, an Athenian said, "the glue of demokratia."

Demokratia became closely connected with Pericles, who inherited the constituency of Ephialtes after his assassination around 460 B.C. For much of the next thirty years, Pericles dominated Athenian politics. An aristocrat who respected the common people, an excellent orator who benefited from an education in philosophy, incorruptible and a tireless worker, a war leader and a builder in peacetime, Pericles was a political giant. He was frequently elected one of Athens's ten generals: an annual position, one of the few chosen by popular election, and one of the few in which a man might be chosen for more than one or two terms. Under his leadership, demokratia became firmly entrenched as the government and way of life in Athens—so much so that Athenians would shortly speak of demokratia as their "ancestral constitution" and modern scholars would speak of "Periclean democracy."

In truth, demokratia was neither ancestral nor limited to Pericles. Athenian democracy survived, with occasional oligarchic intrusions, for 150 years after Pericles' death. During those years it became more bureaucratic, legalistic, and cautious, but it also became more thoroughly egalitarian.

Bust of Pericles This Roman copy of a fifth-century B.C. original shows Pericles as an ideal leader. His commanding gaze, calm features, and beard suggest maturity and statesmanship. The helmet recalls his military career and also hides his unsightly elongated skull. *(Reproduced by Courtesy of the Trustees of the British Museum)*

How Demokratia Worked

Unlike most modern democracies, Athenian demokratia was direct and participatory. Pericles once claimed that in Athens "people pay attention both to their own household and to politics. Even those occupied with other activities are no less knowledgeable about politics."[8] This is part boast, but only part. Large numbers of ordinary citizens attended the assembly from time to time and held public office or served on the Council of 500 for a year or two. In addition, military service from ages 18 to 59 was universal for men. (See the box, "The Debate on Democracy.")

The instruments of government are easily sketched. The central and commanding institution was the assembly. Open to all male citizens over age 20, assembly meetings were held in the open air, on a hillside seating several thousand on benches. In the fourth century B.C. there was a minimum of forty meetings per year, one about every ten days.

The assembly heard the great debates of the day. It made decisions about war and peace, alliance and friendship; it granted honors and condemnations; it passed decrees relating to current issues and set up commissions to revise fundamental laws. In the assembly great orators such as Pericles and Demosthenes addressed the people, but everyone, however humble, was entitled to speak.

The judicial branch consisted of courts, which, with a few exceptions, were open to all citizens, no matter how poor. Aristotle comments that "when the people have the right to vote in the courts, they control the constitution." Juries were large, commonly consisting of several hundred men chosen by lottery; small juries, it was

The Debate on Democracy

Characters in Greek drama often discuss general principles. In this excerpt from Euripides' tragedy **The Suppliant Women** *(ca. 420 B.C.), Theseus, legendary king of Athens, and a herald from Creon, tyrant of Thebes, debate the merits of democracy.*

Herald
What man is tyrant in this land? To whom/Must I give the word I bring from Creon, ruler/In Cadmus' country [Thebes] . . . ?

Theseus
One moment, stranger./Your start was wrong, seeking a tyrant here./This city is free, and ruled by no one man./The people reign, in annual succession./They do not yield the power to the rich;/The poor man has an equal share in it.

Herald
That one point gives the better of the game/To me. The town I come from is controlled/By one man, not a mob. And there is no one/To puff it up with words, for private gain,/Swaying it this way, that way. . . ./The people is no right judge of arguments./Then how can it give right guidance to a city?/A poor man, working hard, could not attend/To public matters, even if ignorance/Were not his birthright. When a wretch, a nothing,/Obtains respect and power from the people/By talk, his betters sicken at the sight.

Theseus
. . . Nothing/Is worse for a city than a tyrant./In earliest days, before the laws are common,/One man has power and makes the law his own:/Equality is not yet. With written laws,/People of small resources and the rich/Both have the same recourse to justice. Now/A man of means, if badly spoken of,/Will have no better standing than the weak;/And if the little man is right, he wins/Against the great. This is the call of freedom:/"What man has good advice to give the city,/And wishes to make it known?" He who responds/Gains glory; the reluctant hold their peace./For the city, what can be more fair than that?

Source: Adapted from Euripides, *The Suppliant Women,* trans. Frank Jones, in *Euripides IV: The Complete Greek Tragedies,* ed. David Grene and Richmond Lattimore (Chicago: University of Chicago Press, 1958), pp. 73–74.

felt, were easily bribed. After a preliminary hearing, cases were decided in a single day.

The executive consisted of the Council of 500 and some 700 public officials (also, under Athens's empire in the fifth century B.C., several hundred others living abroad). All citizens over age 30 were eligible to serve. Most public officials were chosen by lottery, a system that seemed more democratic than election because rich and poor, talented and untalented, were on an equal footing in a lottery. To guard against incompetents or criminals, Athens made all officials undergo a scrutiny by the council before taking office and an audit after the term. Most magistracies, moreover, were boards, usually of ten men, so even if a bad man managed to pass his scrutiny, he would be counterbalanced by his colleagues. Only generals and treasurers were chosen by election.

Athens had a relatively weak executive. There was no president or prime minister. Its leaders were often generals, but their power rested on their ability to speak persuasively in the assembly. To a striking degree, power was truly in the hands of ordinary Athenians who rowed in the fleet and sat in the assembly and courts. On the local level, every deme had an annually chosen executive and a deme assembly of all citizens.

To a peasant in far-off Marathon (26 miles away), the Athenian assembly might have seemed remote, but his right to speak up in his deme assembly made demokratia real and vivid.

So novel and populist a system of government has not been without critics, either in antiquity or today. Some have charged that the Athenian people were uneducated, emotional, and easily swayed by oratorical tricks. Others say that demokratia degenerated into mob rule after the death of Pericles. Others complain about the lack of a system of public education, which denied many citizens equality of opportunity.

The copybook of Athenian democracy does have some blots in its history, particularly in the heat of wartime. The Peloponnesian War (431–404 B.C.) witnessed several atrocities and judicial murders, among them a massacre on the island of Melos in 416 B.C. After Melos refused to join the Athenian alliance, Athens attacked and conquered the island. All the men were executed, and the women and children were sold as slaves. Yet in its roughly two hundred years of existence, Athenian demokratia was generally stable, law-abiding, and fair-minded.

WAR AND DIPLOMACY IN CLASSICAL GREECE

499 B.C.	Ionians revolt against Persia
490 B.C.	Battle of Marathon
480–479 B.C.	Persian invasion of Greece
477 B.C.	Delian League founded
431–404 B.C.	Peloponnesian War
395–386 B.C.	Corinthian War
371 B.C.	Battle of Leuctra

Metics, Women, Slaves

Another charge against Athenian demokratia is far more serious: that it was democracy for a small elite only. There were never more than approximately 40,000 adult male citizens out of a total population—men, women and children, resident aliens, and slaves—of about 400,000. To become a citizen, at age 18 a boy had to prove that he was the legitimate son of a citizen father and a citizen maternal grandfather. Girls were never officially registered as citizens; although the term "citizen-ess" existed, Athenian citizen women were usually referred to as "city woman." As for resident aliens, whether male or female, they rarely attained citizenship. Athenian ideology emphasized the genetic homogeneity of Athenian citizens; they were, it was claimed, natives from time immemorial, "sprung from the soil itself." In reality, many had ancestors who had immigrated to Athens before 500 B.C., but this fact was glossed over.

In the fifth and fourth centuries B.C. Athens had a large population of foreigners. Some were transient. Others were officially registered resident aliens, or metics. Metics came by the thousands from all over the Greek world and beyond. Some, like Aristotle (a native of a Greek colony in Macedonia), were attracted by Athens's schools of philosophy, but most came because of its unparalleled economic opportunities. Athens's port, Piraeus, was the major commercial center of the eastern Mediterranean (see Map 3.3). Metics could not own land in Athens, and they had to pay extra taxes and serve in the Athenian military. Nevertheless, they prospered in Athenian commerce and crafts.

Athenian women, even those who were citizens, were excluded from politics and played only a humble role in commerce as small retailers. In legal and contractual matters they were almost always required to be represented by a male guardian. They did not have the legal rights of women in Egypt or Mesopotamia or the honor as mothers and household partners of women in Israel. Women generally led restricted lives. Just how restricted, however, is uncertain. We can better answer the question by distinguishing between ideology and practice.

Paradoxically, the more power was distributed among the male citizenry, the more hostile to women's freedom did Athens's citizen ideology become. Greek males believed that the more honor a woman brought the man who won her, the more danger she might bring by tempting outsiders to seduce her. Thus, a prudent man kept his wife secluded. Under a tyranny, it was impossible to guarantee one's wife's safety; in the Greek popular imagination, tyrants liked to show their power by violating their subjects sexually. What made demokratia truly free and egalitarian for males was the ability of every man, even the poorest, to protect his wife. Hence demokratia promulgated an ideology of seclusion for women.

Practice, however, was another matter. As Aristotle asks rhetorically, "how is it possible to prevent the wives of the poor from going out?" Women in poor families could not stay at home because they had to run errands, draw water, and sometimes even help make ends meet. Ordinary houses, moreover, were small and cramped, and in the Mediterranean heat women could not stay inside them all the time. Wealthy women played a large role in Athenian religion, frequently visiting temples and sacred precincts. Women attended public funeral orations in honor of soldiers who had died fighting for Athens. Women probably attended the theater. In short, the seclusion of Athenian women was more ideology than reality. Women were, however, generally excluded from the public space, the center of political, military, and economic power: the assembly, the agora, gymnasia, dockyards, forts, and treasuries.

Yet we occasionally get glimpses, sometimes more, of Athenian women resisting or working behind the scenes to rectify male mistakes. An inheritance case reveals a woman go-between interceding among her quarreling male relations. (See the box, "A Wealthy Woman Gives a Speech.") Greek comedy shows women mocking male pretensions and establishing friendships with each other. A woman who brought a large dowry into a marriage could use it and the threat of divorce to influence her husband (the dowry had to be returned to the woman's father or guardian if there was a divorce). Mothers advised their sons; wives advised their husbands. Despite considerable restrictions, Athenian women were adept at resisting and circumventing male control.

Slavery was widespread in democratic Athens. Some slaves served in agriculture, some labored under miserable conditions in Athenian silver mines, and some were engaged in commerce or the military. Most, however, worked as domestics or in small workshops as, for example, metalworkers or furniture makers. The vast majority of slaves were non-Greek. Most were prisoners of war; some were victims of pirates or debtors from states where, unlike Athens, citizens might still end up in debt-slavery. Thrace (roughly, modern Bulgaria) and Anatolia were the main areas from which slaves came, but some were from North Africa and other Mediterranean regions.

The living conditions of slaves were usually poor and in the silver mines abysmal. Many slaves achieved emancipation, however, and a few rose to positions of wealth and power. A striking and unusual case is that of Pasion (d. 370 B.C.). Originally a slave employee of a banking firm, he bought his freedom and became the wealthiest Athenian banker of his day, as well as an Athenian citizen.

Athenian demokratia lacked many features of modern democracy: a notion of universal human rights, the possibility for immigrants to become citizens, gender equality, the abolition of slavery, and public education. To its small citizen body, however, Athenian demokratia offered extraordinary freedom, equality, and responsibility, and a degree of participation in public life seldom equaled. Demokratia was a model of what democracy could be, but not of whom it could be for.

Struggles for Hegemony

The polis generated community spirit, but that spirit had to compete with a strong and deeply ingrained passion for personal glory and honor. The citizen was often unwilling to make compromises for the public good; the polis recoiled at the thought of sacrificing its honor for the sake of other poleis. The result was a constant struggle in diplomacy and war among city-states, often arranged in leagues under hegemons.

In 500 B.C., Sparta, hegemon of the Peloponnesian League, was the most prominent power of the Greek mainland. Across the Aegean Sea in Anatolia, the Greek city-states had been under Persian rule for two generations, since conquest in the 540s. In 499 B.C., however, events began to unfold that not only would revolutionize that balance of power but would throw the entire eastern Mediterranean into two hundred years of turmoil.

A Wealthy Woman Gives a Speech

Women in classical Athens were supposed to be secluded from men and passive, but they were quite capable of actively intervening in financial and legal affairs. "Against Diogeiton," an oration of about 400 B.C. attributed to the speechwriter Lysias, is a lawsuit between wealthy Athenians over a charge of misconduct as guardian. Diogeiton had married his daughter to his brother Diodotus. When Diodotus died, Diogeiton became guardian to his three young nephews, who were also his grandchildren. Having allegedly embezzled their inheritance, Diogeiton was sued on their behalf by their brother-in-law; but as he explains, first they turned to their mother.

Of the mourning that filled my house at that time it would take long to tell. In the end, their mother implored and entreated me to assemble her father [Diogeiton] and friends together, saying that even though she had not before been accustomed to speak in the presence of men, the severity of their misfortunes would compel her to give us a full account of their hardships. . . . Diogeiton at first refused, but finally he was compelled by his friends. When we held our meeting, the mother asked him what heart he could have, that he thought fit to take such measures with the children, "when you are their father's brother," she said, "and my father, and their uncle and grandfather. Even if you felt no shame before any man, you ought to have feared the gods. For you received from him, when he went on the expedition, five talents [of silver; i.e., a small fortune] in deposit. I offer to swear to the truth of this on the lives of my children, both these and those since born to me, in any place [i.e., temple] that you yourself may name. Yet I am not so abject, or so fond of money, as to take leave of life after perjuring myself on the lives of my children, and to appropriate justly my father's estate." [She goes on to detail Diogeiton's misdeeds, citing specific figures.] Thereupon, gentlemen of the jury, after hearing all the severe things spoken by the mother, the whole company of us there were so affected by this man's conduct and by her statements, . . . that nobody, gentlemen, among us there was able to utter a word: we could only weep as sadly as the sufferers and go our ways in silence.

Source: Lysias, Oration 32: Against Diogeiton, in *Lysias,* trans. W. R. M. Lamb (Cambridge, Mass.: Harvard University Press, 1926), pp. 667–71.

The Persian Wars, 499–479 B.C.

Led by Miletus, the Ionian Greek city-states rose in revolt against Persia in 499 B.C. Athens sent troops to help, but despite initial successes Athens lacked the stomach for a long war and its troops soon departed. The Ionian coalition broke down thereafter, and in 494 B.C. the Persian fleet crushed the Ionian navy. Miletus was besieged and destroyed, but otherwise Persia was relatively lenient in Ionia.

The treatment of Athens, however, was another matter. Imperial powers rarely permit challenges to their authority to go unpunished. In 492 B.C. Darius I sent a large naval expedition to Athens. It was destroyed by a storm, but in 490 he sent a second Persian force of about 25,000 infantrymen and 1200 cavalrymen (with horses) to Marathon, some 26 miles from the city of Athens (see Map 3.3).

The Persians planned to build support in Marathon before marching on to Athens. They were overconfident, however, and let their guard down. Under the general Miltiades (550–489 B.C.), about 9000 Athenians and 1000 allies from the nearby polis of Plataea attacked and won a smashing victory, inflicting 6400 Persian casualties and suffering only 192. (The story, unconfirmed, that a messenger ran 26 miles to the city of Athens with the news, "Rejoice, we conquer!" is the basis for the modern marathon race.) After the battle, Athens experienced a burst of confidence that propelled it to power and glory. If Persia had won, Athens would have acquired neither wealth nor empire, demokratia never would have advanced, and the greatness of the Classical period never would have come about.

Persia sought a rematch. After Darius's death in 486, his son and successor Xerxes decided on a joint land-sea expedition against Athens. He amassed a huge force of several hundred ships and several hundred thousand soldiers and rowers, vastly outnumbering potential Greek opposition. Athens, under the leadership of Themistocles (ca. 525–460 B.C.), prepared by building a fleet of 200 ships. Athens joined Sparta and twenty-nine other Peloponnesian poleis in a Hellenic League of defense, with Sparta in overall command. Most poleis either stayed neutral or, like Thebes and Argos, collaborated with Persia. The Greeks had over 300 ships and about 50,000 infantrymen.

Persia invaded Greece in 480 B.C. and won the opening moves. A small Spartan army under King Leonidas held the narrow pass of Thermopylae in central Greece. With local help, however, the Persians found a way to outflank Leonidas and take both ends of the pass. They crushed the Spartans, who died fighting to the last man (thereby adding to their reputation for courage). After winning a naval victory near Thermopylae, the Persians marched on Athens. Abandoned by its defenders, it was sacked.

The tide then turned. Using the nearby island of Salamis as a base and disinformation as a lure, the Greeks, following Themistocles' strategy, manipulated the Persian fleet into fighting in the narrow straits between Athens and Salamis. The Persians could not use their numerical superiority in this closed space, and the Greeks had the home-base advantage. The result was a smashing Persian defeat under the eyes of Xerxes himself, who watched the battle from a throne on a hillside on shore.

Xerxes and the remainder of the Persian fleet left for home. In retrospect, it was clear that the fleet was vulnerable to Greek attack. Soon it became equally clear how inferior Persia's loosely organized soldiery was to the Greek phalanx. Under Spartan leadership the united Greek army defeated Persian forces on land at Plataea (just north of Attica) in 479 B.C. At about the same time, the Greek fleet defeated a reorganized Persian fleet off the Anatolian coast near Mycale. The victorious Greeks sailed the coast and liberated the Ionians. Not only did Persia fail to conquer the Greek mainland, but it also lost its eastern Aegean empire.

The Rise of the Athenian Empire

Sparta and Athens shared most of the credit for victory: Sparta had made the main contribution on land, Athens at sea. The two powers might have jointly stepped into the vacuum left by Persia's retreat, but Athens had the field to itself. In 477 B.C. Athens became the hegemon of a new security organization, founded on the island of Delos in the Aegean Sea. The dual purpose of the so-called Delian League was to protect Greek lands and to attack and plunder Persian territory. Commander of the league fleet, Athens provided most of the ships and the core of the rowers (the rest were mercenaries). Salaries for the rowers, as well as the cost of building and repairing ships, came from an annual tribute levied on the allies. The number of allies grew from about 150 in 477 B.C. to about 250 in 431 B.C. at the height of the league. Themistocles, the hero of Salamis; Cimon, the son of Miltiades (ca. 507–449 B.C.); and Aristides (ca. 520–ca. 468 B.C.), surnamed "the Just" because of his equitable assessment of the first Delian League tribute, were among the Athenian leaders of the league (Map 3.4).

Fearful as ever of entanglements outside the Peloponnesus, Sparta preferred to leave the Aegean to Athens. Many Spartans nonetheless watched with increasing unease and jealousy as Athenian power boomed.

Athens went from self-confidence and pride to arrogance and overextension. Within a generation, by the 450s, the Delian League was becoming transformed into an Athenian empire. In 454 B.C. the treasury was transferred from Delos to Athens on the excuse that it would be safer there. In the following decades, the allies were com-

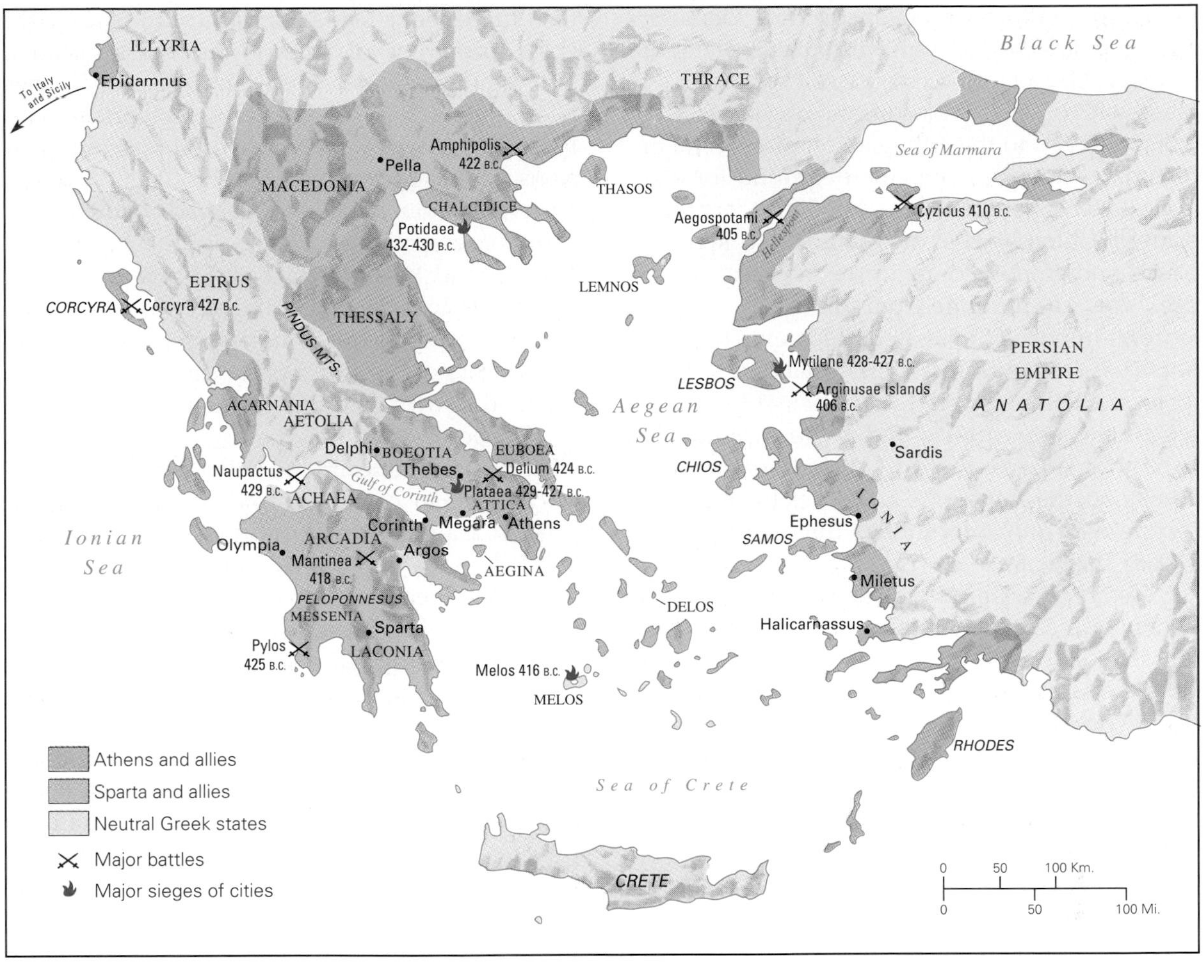

Map 3.4 Greece in the Peloponnesian War During the long and bloody Peloponnesian War (431–404 B.C.), much of the Greek world was divided in two camps: one led by Sparta, the other by Athens.

pelled to send delegations to Athenian festivals, to use Athenian weights, measures, and coinage, and to refer major court cases to Athenian juries.

One by one, beginning with Thasos in 465 B.C., the major allied states rebelled, but Athens crushed each rebellion. Sometimes, after surrender, rebels were executed and their wives and children were sold into slavery. Allied complaints to Sparta stirred fires that were already burning there. A conflict between Greece's greatest land power, Sparta, and Greece's greatest seapower, Athens, began to look all but inevitable.

The Peloponnesian War, 431–404 B.C.

The bloody Peloponnesian War witnessed between 15,000 and 20,000 Athenian battle casualties, not to mention deaths elsewhere or casualties caused by starvation or by a devastating epidemic in the 420s B.C., which killed from one-fourth to one-third of the Athenian population. In addition, this war destroyed the Athenian empire. Finally, the Peloponnesian War demonstrated the Greeks' inability to unite after defeating Persia.

In the Peloponnesian War era, both democratic Athens and oligarchic Sparta sought to promote and enforce their respective ideologies among their allies, though without complete consistency. Democratic Syracuse, for example, was allied with oligarchic Sparta, and oligarchic Mytilene belonged to the Athenian empire. Some unfortunate states became a battleground for ideological debate. In Corcyra (modern Corfu), for example, bloody civil war marked a series of coups and countercoups in the 420s B.C. Athens itself was not immune from dissension and violence. A minority of oligarchs had never been reconciled to demokratia. When Athens began to falter in the Peloponnesian War after 413 B.C., they seized the opportunity and twice installed oligarchy in Athens: first in 411 and again in 404. Each time, the democrats came back to power, the second time only after foreign intervention and a bloody civil war.

Given Spartan supremacy on land and Athenian mastery of the sea, it is not surprising that the Peloponnesian War remained undecided for a decade and a half. The balance of power shifted only after an Athenian blunder. In 415 B.C. Athens adopted the bold plan of attacking Sparta indirectly by a quick raid on Sicily, whose fabled wealth the Athenians hoped to use to reshape the Greek balance of power in Athens's favor. Unfortunately for Athens, Sicily, led by Syracuse, proved to be a formidable foe. The raid became a quagmire and then a disaster, leading to total defeat and thousands of Athenian casualties.

By 412 B.C. most of the Athenian empire was in revolt, and Persia had intervened on Sparta's side—in return for Sparta's restoration of Ionia to Persia, an ironic counterpoint to Sparta's role in driving Persia from Greece in 479. Athens, nevertheless, was sufficiently wealthy and plucky to hold out until 405 B.C., when the Spartans under Lysander (d. 395 B.C.) finally captured almost the entire Athenian fleet in the Hellespont. Athens surrendered the next year.

The Fruitless Wars of the Fourth Century B.C.

Sparta won the Peloponnesian War, but establishing a new Greek order proved beyond its grasp. Trained as soldiers, not as diplomats, never fully reconciled to using seapower, lacking the oratorical skills valued by other Greeks, sure of themselves and contemptuous of others, Spartans made poor leaders. Sparta took over Athens's former naval empire and quickly had a falling-out with its allies. Corinth and Thebes were offended by Spartan heavy-handedness. Persia, meanwhile, faced repeated Spartan invasions of Anatolia to liberate the Greeks, whose surrender Spartans now regretted. United by a common enemy, an alliance of Athens, Corinth, Thebes, and Persia turned on Sparta in 395 B.C. After the indecisive Corinthian War (395–386 B.C.), so named because most of the fighting took place around Corinth, Sparta gave up Anatolia but held its own on the Greek mainland.

Thebes then emerged as Sparta's main rival. Over Spartan opposition, Thebes united the separate city-states of Boeotia under its rule. Brilliant Theban leaders like Epaminondas (d. 362 B.C.) and Pelopidas (403–364 B.C.) inspired victory.

In the meantime, Sparta was suffering from exhaustion and a vast decline in the number of citizens. The original 9000 Equals of the seventh century B.C. were only about 1500 in 371 B.C. The main problem seems to have been greed. Rich Spartans preferred to get even richer by concentrating wealth in fewer hands rather than opening the elite to new blood. The result was military disaster. In 371 B.C. the Boeotian army crushed the Spartans at the battle of Leuctra, killing 1000 men (including 400 Equals) and a Spartan king. In the next few years Boeotia invaded the Peloponnesus, freed the Messenian helots, and restored Messenia to independence, after some 350 years of bondage. It was a fatal blow to Spartan power, but Boeotia too was exhausted and its main leaders were dead. None of the Greek city-states had been able to maintain hegemony.

Nothing better demonstrates the fatal excess of individualism in classical Greece and the absence of cooperative virtues than the wars of the city-states in the fourth century B.C. They did nothing but leave Greece prey to outsiders.

The Public Culture of Classical Greece

Classical Greek culture was public culture, whether in democratic Athens, with its emphasis on public speaking, or in oligarchic Sparta, with its public education. Poets, for example, were not introspective or alienated figures. Rather, to quote the Athenian playwright Aristophanes (ca. 455–ca. 385 B.C.), they were "the teachers of men" who commented on contemporary public debate. Tragedy was performed in a state theater at a state religious festival. All citizens were invited and, in the fourth century B.C., were paid if they attended. Private individuals competed to spend money on productions in order to win public glory. The philosopher Socrates (469–399 B.C.) discussed philosophy in marketplaces and gymnasia. The public, not private individuals, was the major patron of sculpture and architecture.

Public life, accordingly, is the central theme of Classical Greek art and literature. Of tragedy, for example, one might say that regardless of the particular hero or plot, the same character looms in the background: the polis. The Classical historians, Herodotus, Xenophon, and especially Thucydides, have little to say about private life, focusing instead on public affairs. Classical philosophy ranged from biology to metaphysics, but it made politics its central focus.

Religion and Art

A hallmark of Classical culture is the tension between the religious heritage of the Archaic period and the worldly spirit of the Classical period. The Classical period was a time of prosperity, political debate, and military conflict. "Wonders are many on earth, and none more wondrous than man," said the Athenian tragedian Sophocles (ca. 495–406 B.C.). Yet Sophocles was a deeply religious man who also believed that people were doomed to disaster unless they obeyed the laws of the gods. Sophocles mirrored a widespread debate, for he knew his countrymen well. He was

The Parthenon The temple of Athena Parthenos ("the Maiden") on the Athenian Acropolis, the Parthenon was dedicated in 438 B.C. The largest and most complex Doric-style Greek temple, it was built of fine marble. The partially restored ruins symbolize the wealth, power, and greatness of classical Greece. *(William Katz/Photo Researchers)*

not only a popular playwright but a general, state treasurer, priest, and intimate of Pericles.

Classical religion was less sure of itself than its Archaic predecessor. A few people even questioned the very existence of the gods, although most Greeks wanted religion to be adapted to the new age, not discarded altogether. Thus, Athenian religion was tailored to the needs of a democratic and imperial city. In the 440s B.C., under Pericles' leadership, Athens embarked on a vast, ambitious, and expensive temple-building project, using Delian League funds and serving as a large public employment program. Temples were built in and around the city, most notably on the Athenian Acropolis. (See the feature, "Weighing the Evidence: The Parthenon," on pages 118–119.)

Classical sculptors completed the process begun by their Archaic predecessors of mastering the accurate representation of the human body. In anatomical precision, Classical Greek sculpture was the most technically proficient sculpture the world had seen. It was not, however, an attempt to portray humans "warts and all" but rather an idealized portrait of the human form.

To adapt religion to a new age, new cults were introduced. The most popular was the worship of Aesclipius, god of healing. Traditionally a minor figure and considered a son of Apollo, Aesclipius became enormously popular in his own right beginning in the late fifth century B.C. In Athens, worship of Aesclipius was officially inaugurated by the state during the Peloponnesian War. Outside Athens, large shrines to Aesclipius at Epidauros (in the Peloponnesus) and Cos (an island off the Anatolian coast) became pilgrimage centers in the fourth century B.C. for ailing people in search of a cure.

Another religious innovation was the deification of living humans. Greek religion had always recognized heroes as demigods, but nobody had ever seen a hero in the flesh; they had lived, if at all, centuries earlier. At the end of the Peloponnesian War in 404 B.C., however, Sparta's Ionian allies began worshiping the victor Lysander as a god. A decade later, when Athens's power was on the rise again and Sparta's was declining, the same Ionians began worshiping an Athenian admiral instead! Many Greeks were shocked by these cults, deeming it hybris to equate a mortal human with a god.

The Sophists and Socrates

Success in democratic politics required a knowledge of oratory. This demand was met in the late fifth century B.C. by the arrival in Athens of itinerant professional teachers of rhetoric, the art of speaking. They were known as Sophists ("wise men"). Sicilian Greeks invented rhetoric around 465 B.C. by drawing up the rules of argument. For a fee—rarely small and sometimes astronomical—Sophists taught young Athenians the art of speaking. Their curriculum consisted not only of rhetoric but also of the rudiments of linguistics, ethics, psychology, history, and anthropology—in other words, any aspect of "human nature" that might help an aspiring politician. Within a few years most ambitious young Athenians of prosperous families were studying with Sophists.

At their best, Sophists sharpened young minds. Athenian tragedians, historians, and philosophers all benefited from sophistic teaching. Protagoras (b. ca. 485 B.C.), perhaps the best-known Sophist, summed up the spirit of the age in his famous dictum "Man is the measure of all things." This made an appropriate credo for the interest in all things human that is apparent in Classical literature and art. There is, however, a more troubling side to the Sophists. As teachers of rhetoric, they taught respect for success, not for truth. Thus, they acquired a reputation as word-twisters who taught men how to make "the weaker argument defeat the stronger."

Much to the distress of conservatives, Sophists drew a distinction between *nomos,* a word that means "law" or "convention," and *physis,* which means "nature." The distinction had revolutionary potential. In general, Sophists had little respect for the established order. They considered it mere convention. A great man trained by a Sophist might rise above convention and realize the limitless potentialities of his nature: If he overturned democracy to establish a tyranny, so much the worse for democracy. Indeed, the Sophists trained both unscrupulous democratic politicians like the Athenian Alcibiades (ca. 460–404 B.C.) and many of the oligarchs who launched coups d'état against Athenian democracy at the end of the fifth century B.C. As a result, *sophist* became a term of abuse in Athens and remains so to this day.

Classical Greek advances in rhetoric, therefore, were as problematic as they were brilliant. The Sophists had a wide-ranging effect on many different branches of thought. Consider, for example, the work of a great thinker in the Ionian tradition: Democritus (b. ca. 460 B.C.), a native of the northern Greek polis of Abdera but a visitor to Athens. Like many Sophists, Democritus believed that the reality of nature was far more radical than conventional opinion thought. He concluded that all things consisted of tiny, indivisible particles, which could be arranged and rearranged in an infinite variety of configurations. He called these particles *atoma,* "the uncuttable" (from which the word *atom* is derived).

The physicians of the island of Cos are known as Hippocratics, from Hippocrates (b. ca. 460 B.C.), the first great thinker of their school. If they were not directly influenced by the Sophists, they shared many similar habits of thought. Like the Sophists, the Hippocratics were religious skeptics. They considered disease to be strictly a natural phenomenon in which the gods played no part. Hippocratic medicine was noteworthy for its methodology, which emphasized observation and prognosis (the reasoned prediction of future developments). The Hippocratics were the most rigorously naturalistic physicians to date, although their success rate in curing illness was still low.

In the fifth century B.C. not all thinkers welcomed the conclusions of the Sophists. Perhaps their most notable critic, and the greatest of all fifth-century philosophers, was Socrates (469–399 B.C.). Mistakenly considered a Sophist by the public, in 399 Socrates was tried, convicted, and executed by an Athenian court for alleged atheism and "corrupting the young." The Athenian public soon had second thoughts, and the trial of Socrates is usually considered one of history's great miscarriages of justice, as well as one of Athenian democracy's greatest blunders. (See the box, "Socrates' Defense.")

Socrates, in any case, was not a Sophist. He charged no fees, had no formal students, and did not claim to teach any positive body of knowledge. In fact, his basic thesis was negative: the radical ignorance of most people, including himself. His only superiority, he believed, was his awareness of his ignorance. Unlike the Sophists, most of whom were resident aliens, Socrates was an Athenian citizen.

Socrates True to the ironic spirit of Socrates himself, this and similar ancient portrait busts emphasize the philosopher's physical ugliness. His ideas rather than his appearance inspired a large and loyal following. *(Uffizi/Scala/Art Resource)*

Socrates, however, resembled the Sophists in his intense interest in political theory. Like any good Athenian citizen, Socrates served in the military—as a hoplite during the Peloponnesian War. He had his doubts about democracy, which he criticized for inefficiency and for giving an equal voice to the uneducated. He claimed to prefer rule by a wise elite. Nonetheless, Socrates was too loyal an Athenian to advocate revolution. What probably got him into the most trouble was his role as a self-styled "gadfly": Socrates stung the pride of Athens's leaders by demonstrating their ignorance.

Socrates' Defense

In 399 B.C. Socrates was tried on a charge of corrupting the youth of Athens and of believing in deities of his own invention instead of the state gods of Athens. Socrates' defense, as preserved by his pupil Plato, is a stirring description of philosophy as a way of life. His uncompromising stand did not persuade the jury, which voted for his conviction and execution, but his words convey why he was considered an inspiring teacher.

Suppose, then, that you acquit me. . . . Suppose that . . . you said to me, "Socrates, . . . we shall . . . acquit you, but only on one condition, that you give up spending your time on this quest and stop philosophizing. If we catch you going on in the same way, you shall be put to death." . . . I should reply, "Gentlemen, I am your very grateful and devoted servant, but I owe a greater obedience to God than to you; and so long as I draw breath and have my faculties, I shall never stop practising philosophy and exhorting you and elucidating the truth for everyone that I meet. I shall go on saying, in my usual way, 'My very good friend, you are an Athenian and belong to a city which is the greatest and most famous in the world for its wisdom and strength. Are you not ashamed that you give your attention to acquiring as much money as possible, and similarly with reputation and honor, and give no attention or thought to truth and understanding and the perfection of your soul?' And if any of you disputes this and professes to care about these things, I shall not at once let him go or leave him; no, I shall question him and examine him and test him; and if it appears that in spite of his profession he has made no real progress towards goodness, I shall reprove him for neglecting what is of supreme importance, and giving his attention to trivialities. I shall do this to everyone that I meet, young or old, foreigner or fellow-citizen; but especially to you my fellow-citizens, inasmuch as you are closer to me in kinship."

Source: Plato, *The Apology of Socrates,* in Plato, *The Last Days of Socrates,* trans. Hugh Tredennick (Harmondsworth, England: Penguin, 1969), p. 61.

Socrates was trained in the Ionian natural philosophy tradition. He went beyond it, as the Roman thinker Cicero later said, by bringing philosophy "down from the heavens into the streets"; he changed the emphasis from the natural world to human ethics. Like most Greeks, Socrates believed that the purpose of life was the pursuit of aretê. Unlike his contemporaries, however, he did not consider aretê as primarily excellence in battle or in public life but, rather, as excellence in philosophy. One became good by studying the truth, which is part of what Socrates meant by his saying "Virtue (aretê) is knowledge." He also meant that no one who truly understood goodness would ever do evil.

Such an outlook downgrades the importance of willpower or the emotions, but it makes education into the cornerstone of society. Teach people well, according to Socrates, and they will behave morally. Socrates has gone down in history as an inspiring teacher, despite his protestations of not teaching anything. His emphasis was not on research or writing—Socrates refused to write anything down. He believed that truth could be found only in person, not through books; that philosophy requires a verbal give-and-take. His favorite technique was to ask people difficult questions. Pedagogy that relies on questioning is still called the "Socratic method."

Plato and Aristotle

Because Socrates never wrote anything down, we are dependent on others for our knowledge of him. Fortunately, he inspired many students who committed his thoughts to paper. Socrates' most distinguished student, and our most important source for Socrates' thought, was Plato (427–348 B.C.), who in turn was the teacher of Aristotle (384–322 B.C.). Together, these three men laid the foundations of the Western philosophical tradition. They were thinkers for the ages, but each was also a man of his times.

Socrates grew up in confident Periclean days. Plato came of age during the Peloponnesian War, a period culminating in the execution of Socrates. Disgusted, Plato turned his back on public life, although he was an Athenian citizen. Instead of discussing philosophy in public, Plato founded a private school in an Athenian suburb, the Academy. An aristocrat, Plato had a low opinion of democracy, and when he did intervene in politics, it was not in Athens but in far-off Syracuse (in Sicily). Syracuse was governed by a tyranny, and Plato hoped to educate the tyrant's heir in philosophy—a vain hope, as it turned out.

In an attempt to recapture the stimulating give-and-take of a conversation with Socrates, Plato did not write straightforward philosophical treatises but, rather, dialogues or speeches. All of Plato's dialogues have more than one speaker, and in most the main speaker is named "Socrates": sometimes the historical Socrates, sometimes merely a mouthpiece for ideas Plato wished to explore.

A voluminous writer, Plato is not easily summarized. The word that best characterizes his legacy, though, is *idealism,* of which Plato is one of Western philosophy's greatest exponents. Like Parmenides, Plato believed that the senses are misleading. Truth exists but is attained only by training the mind to overcome common-sense evidence. The model for Plato's philosophical method is geometry. Just as geometry deals not with this or that triangle or rectangle but with ideal forms—with a pure triangle, a pure rectangle—so the philosopher could learn to recognize purity. A philosopher would not be misled by, for example, comparing aretê in Athens, Sparta, and Persia; a philosopher would understand the meaning of pure, ideal aretê. No relativist, Plato believed in absolute good and evil.

Philosophy is not for everyone, Plato made clear; only a few people have the requisite intelligence and discipline. In the *Republic,* a dialogue that is perhaps his best-known work, Plato demonstrates the nature of his idealism and its political consequences. He envisioned a society whose elite would study philosophy and attain enlightenment. They would understand the vanity of political ambition, but would nonetheless accept the responsibility of governing the masses. Plato never makes clear precisely why they should accept this responsibility. Perhaps he was enough of a traditionalist, in spite of himself, to consider one's responsibility to one's polis to be obvious. In any case, Plato's ideal state was one where philosophers would rule as kings, benevolently and unselfishly.

Plato explored the details of such a state in the *Republic* and in other dialogues, particularly the *Laws.* It is not clear how wedded he was to individual details; indeed, some of them may have been meant merely to shock or to satirize. An overall picture emerges, however. The ideal state would be like a small polis: self-sufficient, noncommercial, and closed like Sparta, but committed to the pursuit of things intellectual like Athens. Society would be sharply divided into three classes—philosophers, soldiers, and farmers—with admission to each class based on merit rather than heredity. Poetry and drama would be strictly censored. Plato advocated public education and toyed with more radical notions: not only gender equality but the abolition of the family and private property, institutions that he felt led to disunity and dissension.

Plato's ideas have always been controversial but almost never ignored. Even in his own day, most people considered Plato far too radical. The writings of his great student Aristotle were more to contemporary tastes. Originally from Macedonia, Aristotle spent most of his life in Athens, first as a student at the Academy, then as the founder of his own school, the Lyceum. Like Plato, Aristotle wrote dialogues, but none has survived. His main extant works are treatises, largely compilations by students of his lecture notes. One of the most wide ranging of intellectuals, Aristotle had a voracious appetite for knowledge and for writing. His treatises embrace politics, ethics, poetry, botany, physics, metaphysics, astronomy, rhetoric, zoology, logic, and psychology.

Although influenced by Plato's idealism, Aristotle was a far more practical, down-to-earth thinker. His father had been a doctor, which may

"Man Is a Political Animal"

This excerpt from the* Politics *(ca. 325 B.C.) reveals certain basic features of Aristotle's method. An expert logician, Aristotle is a clear and straightforward writer. He is fond of biological analogies, and he believes that each of the parts of nature, like each of the parts of the body, serves a function for the greater whole.

Man is by nature an animal intended to live in a polis [literally, "a political animal"]. . . .

Nature, according to our theory, makes nothing in vain; and a human being alone of the animals is furnished with the faculty of language. The mere making of sounds serves to indicate pleasure and pain, and is thus a faculty that belongs to animals in general. . . . But language serves to declare what is advantageous and what is just and what is unjust. It is the peculiarity of man, in comparison with the rest of the animal world, that he alone possesses a perception of good and evil, of the just and the unjust, and of other similar qualities; it is association in these things which makes a family and a polis.

We may now proceed to add that [though the individual and the family are prior in the order of time] the polis is prior in the order of nature to the family and the individual. The reason for this is that the whole is necessarily prior to the part. If the whole body be destroyed, there will not be a foot or a hand. . . .

We thus see that the polis exists by nature and that it is prior to the individual. Not being self-sufficient when they are isolated, all individuals are so many parts all equally depending on the whole. The human being who is isolated—who is unable to share in the benefits of political association, or has no need to share because he is already self-sufficient—is no part of the polis, and must therefore be either a beast or a god. . . . A human being, when perfected, is the best of animals; but if he be isolated from law and justice he is the worst of all.

Source: Adapted from Ernest Barker, ed. and trans., *The Politics of Aristotle* (London: Oxford University Press, 1946), pp. 5–6.

account for Aristole's interest in applied science and in biology and biological method. Unlike Plato, Aristotle placed great emphasis on observation and fieldwork and on classification and systemization. (See the box, "Man Is a Political Animal.")

Aristotle agreed with Plato about the existence of absolute standards of good and evil, but he emphasized the relevance of such standards to everyday life. Unlike Plato, Aristotle considered the senses important guides; change, he believed, was not an illusion but rather an important phenomenon. Aristotle's view of change was teleological—that is, he emphasized the goal (*telos* in Greek) of change. According to Aristotle, every organism changes and grows toward a particular end and is an integral and harmonious part of a larger whole. The entire cosmos is teleological, and each and every one of its parts has a purpose. Behind the cosmos was a principle that Aristotle called "the unmoved mover," the supreme cause of existence.

Aristotle defined *aretê* as the fulfillment of one's function in the cosmos. The aretê of a horse, for example, was to be strong, fast, and obedient; the aretê of a rose was to look pretty and smell sweet. As for the aretê of a human being, Aristotle agreed with Plato: only the philosopher achieved true aretê. As a pragmatist, however, Aristotle did not imagine philosophers becoming kings. Not that he advocated democracy, which he considered mob rule. Instead, Aristotle advocated a government of wealthy gentlemen who had been trained by philosophers—not the best regime imaginable but, in Aristotle's opinion, the best one possible.

Aristotle may be the single most influential thinker in Western history. His scientific writings were not only the most influential philosophical classic of Greek civilization, and of Roman civilization as well, but remained so during the Middle Ages in the Arabic and Latin worlds. For more than two thousand years there were no serious challenges to Aristotle's intellectual supremacy.

Athenian Drama

Modern comedy and tragedy find distant ancestors in the productions of Athens's theater of Dionysus, named for the god of unrestraint, liberation, and wine. Comedy and tragedy began in religious festivals but quickly became an independent forum for comment on public life.

According to ancient tradition, tragedy was first presented at the Dionysia festival in Athens by one Thespis in the 530s B.C. (hence the word *thespian* for "actor"). The first surviving tragedy dates from the 470s, the first surviving comedy from the 420s. A play in the fifth century B.C. consisted of a chorus and three individual actors who played all the various individual speaking parts. Plays were performed in an open-air theater on the south hillside of the Acropolis. Enormously popular, drama spread all over Greece, and eventually most poleis had a theater.

Classical Athenian tragedy was performed at the annual Dionysia in March. Each playwright would submit a trilogy of plays on a central theme, plus a raucous farce to break the tension

Theater at Delphi Open to the air, an ancient Greek theater contained tiers of stone benches above a circular area where the action took place, behind which backdrops could be erected. The audience often had a view of stirring scenery which, at Delphi, included the temple of Apollo and the valley below. *(Art Resource)*

afterward. Comedies, which were independent plays rather than trilogies, were performed both at the Dionysia and at a separate festival held in winter. Wealthy producers competed to outfit the most lavish and impressive productions. Judges would award prizes for the best plays: a typical reflection of Greek competitiveness.

Tragedy is not easy to define, except generally: a serious play with an unhappy ending. Perhaps a short tag from the playwright Aeschylus can be said to sum up tragedy if anything can: *pathos mathei,* "suffering teaches." The essence of tragedy is what has been called the tragic sense of life: the nobility in the spectacle of a great man or woman failing but learning from failure. In *Oedipus the Tyrant* (ca. 428 B.C.) by Sophocles, for example, the hero kills his father and unknowingly marries his mother. Oedipus cannot escape the consequences of his deeds, but he can react to his fate with dignity and heroism; he can try to understand it. Oedipus loses his power as tyrant and goes into exile, but he retains a degree of honor. It is a moving sight. As Aristotle said, tragedy derives its emotional power from the fear and pity that it evokes and from the purification (*katharsis*) of the senses that it leaves in its aftermath.

The great period of Attic tragedy began and ended in the fifth century B.C. Aeschylus (525–456 B.C.), Sophocles (ca. 495–406 B.C.), and Euripides (ca. 485–406 B.C.) were and are considered the three giant playwrights. Although there were other tragedians, only the works of these three men (or rather a small fraction of their works) have survived. Aeschylus was perhaps the most pious of the three. His plays—notably the trilogy of the *Oresteia* (the *Agamemnon,* the *Libation Bearers,* and the *Eumenides*), the only surviving tragic trilogy, dating from 458 B.C.—take as their central question the justice of Zeus. The subject is the myth of the house of Atreus—in particular, the murder of King Agamemnon by his much-wronged wife Clytemnestra, and her murder in turn by their son Orestes, avenger of his father. Aeschylus casts this primitive saga into an epic of the discovery of justice. Zeus puts an end to revenge killings and institutes the supposed first court of law: the court of the Areopagus in Athens.

Sophocles too was interested in divine justice; he focuses on the relationship between the individual and the community. Heroic individuals have a spark of the divine in them, but by towering over ordinary people, they threaten them. In *Antigone* (ca. 442 B.C.), for example, the heroine refuses to compromise with injustice. Her late brother had committed treason, for which his corpse is denied burial—the standard Greek punishment. Antigone, however, insists on following a higher law, Zeus's law, which demands that all bodies be buried. Turmoil, disorder, and death ensue, but Antigone stays true to principle.

Of the three tragedians, Euripides is the least traditional and the most influenced by the Sophists. His plays reflect the disillusionment of the Peloponnesian War era. Euripides was more impressed by divine power than by divine justice. If the central gods of Aeschylean drama are Zeus the father and Apollo the law-giver, and if Sophocles focuses on semidivine heroes, then Euripides' major deities are Dionysus (also known as Bacchus) and Aphrodite, goddess of erotic passion. In *Medea* (431 B.C.), for example, Euripides dissects the feelings of love, jealousy, and revenge that drive a woman to murder her own children in order to avenge herself on her faithless husband (the children's father). In the *Bacchae* (406 B.C.), an arrogant young king named Pentheus is punished for refusing to recognize the power of Dionysus. When he goes to the hills to spy on drunken women called Bacchae who are worshiping the god, he ends up as their prisoner. Driven to frenzy by Dionysus (Bacchus), the women do not recognize the king; Pentheus' own mother, one of the Bacchae, mistakes him for an animal and kills him.

The changes in tragedy from Aeschylus to Euripides reflect the changes in Athens as first imperial arrogance and then the Peloponnesian War took their moral toll. Aeschylus's confidence in the goodness of the community gives way first to a focus on the individual and then to a fundamental doubt about the possibility of goodness. The civic order, celebrated so confidently at the end of the *Oresteia* (458 B.C.), looks less certain in Sophocles' *Oedipus* (ca. 428 B.C.) and by the time of Euripides' *Bacchae* (406 B.C.) seems terrifyingly weak.

Comedy too was invented in Athens in the Classical period. Like tragedy, comedy offers a moral commentary on contemporary Athenian life. Unlike tragedy, which is usually set in the past and takes its characters from mythology, Athenian comedy (the so-called Old Comedy) is set in the present and pokes fun at politicians and public figures. Whereas tragedy is generally serious and sad, comedy is humorous.

The greatest writer of comedy in the fifth century B.C. was Aristophanes (ca. 455–385 B.C.). His extant plays are lively, ribald, even scatological, and full of allusions to contemporary politics. Aristophanes loved to show the "little guy" getting the better of the powerful and women deflating the pretensions of men. In *Lysistrata* (411 B.C.), his best-known play, he imagines the women of Greece stopping the Peloponnesian War by going on a sex strike, which forces the men to make peace.

Historical Thought and Writing

Herodotus (ca. 485–ca. 425 B.C.) and Thucydides (ca. 455–ca. 399 B.C.) are among the founders of history-writing in the West. This is not to discount the contributions of, for example, the Hittites or Hebrews, or the chronicles, inventories, and genealogies of early Greece. Herodotus and Thucydides, however, are more rationalistic than their predecessors, and their subject matter was war, politics, peoples and customs—what we think of as the stuff of history-writing today. Indeed, the word *history* comes from a word used by Herodotus, *historiai,* meaning "inquiries" or "research."

The works of Herodotus (*The Histories*) and Thucydides (*The Peloponnesian War*) have unifying themes. The theme in Herodotus' *Histories* is the rise and fall of empires. Herodotus sees the Persian Wars as merely one episode in a vast historical drama. Again and again, hardy, disciplined peoples conquered their neighbors, grew wealthy, were corrupted by a life of luxury, and were eventually conquered in turn. Success made people arrogant, driving them to commit injustices, which were eventually punished by Zeus. The breadth of Herodotus' vision is noteworthy. Many Greeks looked down on foreigners, whom they called "barbarians." Herodotus, however, chronicled foreign customs with considerable objectivity. A native of Halicarnassus (a polis on the southwestern coast of Anatolia), Herodotus traveled widely in Anatolia, mainland Greece, Magna Graecia, and Egypt, eventually settling in Athens. He wrote not only about Greeks but also about Persians and Babylonians, Lydians, Libyans, Egyptians, and a host of other peoples in Europe, Asia, and Africa.

Only a child at the time of the Persian Wars, Herodotus gathered information by interviewing older people in various countries as well as by checking what limited written public records existed. Herodotus also wrote about previous centuries, but with uneven accuracy. He could never resist a good story, and alongside solid research are tall tales, unconfirmed accounts, and myths.

Thucydides prided himself on accuracy. He confined himself mainly to writing about an event that he had lived through and participated in: the Peloponnesian War. A failed Athenian general, Thucydides spent most of the Peloponnesian War in exile, carefully observing, taking notes, and writing.

Like Herodotus, Thucydides was influenced by tragedy; he also shows the signs of the sophistic movement, especially in the finely crafted speeches he includes. Thucydides' great theme is the disastrous effect of war on the human soul. He believed that the Peloponnesian War proved that war is a harsh teacher that strips away the veneer of civilization and reveals the savagery of human nature. In Thucydides' opinion, Pericles' Athens had been a high point in the history of civilization. The strain of prolonged war, however, destroyed Athens's moral fiber as well as its empire.

Summary

Western philosophy, science, politics, sculpture, painting, and literary genres such as comedy, tragedy, and history all crystallized in Archaic and Classical Greece. Although the Greeks of this era borrowed much from neighboring cultures, they were remarkably original. The focus of their life was the city-state, or polis. Though small, exclusive, often factionalized, and rarely capable of achieving unity in a large area, the polis may be unparalleled in its ability to foster individual creative genius.

Paradox was the hallmark of the polis, tension a theme in Greek civilization. The Greeks invented democracy while at the same time limiting the freedom of women and immigrants, oppressing slaves, and engaging in imperialism.

While they created magnificent achievements in religious architecture, a portion of their intellectual elite came to the conclusion that the gods were of little importance in explaining the universe. While one leading polis, Sparta, was a paragon of militarism, obedience, and austerity, scorning the life of the mind, another, Athens, prided itself on freedom and cultural attainments.

Athens reached its peak under Pericles, a time of empire, prosperity, and cultural greatness. The three major tragedians were all active, and the sophistic movement was at its most optimistic and progressive. Pericles himself socialized with leading thinkers and sponsored a great building program. Periclean Athens was unique, if not for the sheer concentration of talent, then for the sense that state, cultural elite, and the people were united in a common pursuit. Later times did indeed witness a fall from that state of grace.

Notes

1. Adapted from Richmond Lattimore, trans., *Greek Lyrics,* 2d ed. (Chicago: University of Chicago Press, 1960), p. 23.
2. Hesiod, *Works and Days* in *Hesiod, Theogony, Works and Days: Theognis, Elegies,* trans. Dorothea Wender (Harmondsworth, Eng.: Penguin, 1973), p. 65.
3. Excerpt from a poem by Solon, cited in Aristotle, *Constitution of Athens,* trans. Barry S. Strauss.
4. Charles Rowan Beye, *Ancient Greek Literature and Society,* 2d ed., rev. (Ithaca, N.Y.: Cornell University Press, 1987), p. 78.
5. Ibid., p. 79.
6. Lattimore, p. 19.
7. Herodotus, *The Histories,* trans. Barry S. Strauss.
8. Thucydides, *The Peloponnesian War,* trans. Barry S. Strauss.

Suggested Reading

General Surveys

Beye, C. R. *Ancient Greek Literature and Society.* 2d ed. 1987. A witty and readable analysis from Homer to the Hellenistic era.

Biers, W. *The Archaeology of Ancient Greece: An Introduction,* rev. ed. 1987. A clear presentation of the achievements and variety of archaeological excavation of Greece.

Finley, M. I. *The Ancient Economy.* 1973. A broad and insightful comparison of Greece and Rome and an excellent introduction to the subject.

Forrest, W. G. *The Emergence of Greek Democracy.* 1966. A well-illustrated and vivid introduction to the mainstream interpretation of Greek politics and society from around 800 to 400 B.C.

Green, Peter. *Ancient Greece: An Illustrated History.* 1973. Concise, useful, readable, and beautifully illustrated.

Murray, Oswyn. *Early Greece.* 1980. The best one-volume introduction to the Archaic era, with an emphasis on society and culture.

Pomeroy, S. *Goddesses, Whores, Wives, and Slaves: Women in Classical Antiquity.* 1975. An overview of women in politics and society in Greece, the Hellenistic world, and Rome.

Powell, Anton. *Athens and Sparta Constructing Greek Political and Social History from 478 B.C.* 1988. A lively and scholarly introduction to the social and political history of the two most prominent Greek city-states of the fifth century B.C.

Athens and Sparta

Cartledge, Paul. *Agesilaos and the Crisis of Sparta.* 1987. An introduction to classical Spartan society and politics as well as a specialized study and biography.

Hansen, Mogens Herman. *Athenian Democracy in the Age of Demosthenes.* 1991. A survey that places the political system in its social context.

Humphreys, S. C. *The Family, Women and Death: Comparative Studies.* 1983. Provocative and stimulating essays, influenced by anthropology, on classical Athenian society.

Just, Roger. *Women in Athenian Law and Life.* 1989. A careful examination of the evidence to reconstruct the reality and ideology of women in Athens in the fifth and fourth centuries B.C.

Kagan, Donald. *The Outbreak of the Peloponnesian War.* 1969. The first of a four-volume history of the war, this readable and stimulating book argues, against Thucydides, that the war could have been avoided.

Manville, P. B. *The Origins of Citizenship in Ancient Athens.* 1990. A thoughtful discussion based on comparative anthropology as well as close reading of Greek sources.

Ober, Josiah. *Mass and Elite in Democratic Athens: Rhetoric, Ideology, and the Power of the People.* 1989. A thorough and eloquent argument that Athens was a genuine democracy, in which the people ruled by ensuring that politicians listened to them.

Ste. Croix, G. E. M. *The Origins of the Peloponnesian War.* 1972. A wide-ranging analysis laying blame for the war squarely on Sparta's shoulders.

Strauss, Barry S. *Athens After the Peloponnesian War: Class, Faction, and Policy 403–386 B.C.* 1987. A case study of the interaction of politics and society and of war and peace in classical Athens.

———. *Fathers and Sons in Athens: Ideology and Society in the Era of the Peloponnesian War.* 1993. An examination of the degree to which Athenians imagined the Peloponnesian War as a metaphorical conflict of the generations.

Other City-States and Regions

Legon, Ronald P. *Megara: The Political History of a Greek City-State to 336 B.C.* 1981. An alternative to the usual emphasis on Athens and Sparta, this book examines the fortunes of a small polis astride the land route between Pelopponesus and central Greece.

Salmon, J. B. *Wealthy Corinth.* 1984. An examination of the history of what was perhaps the third most powerful Greek city-state, after Sparta and Athens.

Shipley, Graham. *A History of Samos, 800–188 B.C.* 1987. A political, sociological, and archaeological study of one of the most important of the Greek city-states, an island off the coast of Anatolia.

Society and Culture

Burkert, Walter. *Greek Religion.* 1985. A thorough and logical introduction.

Connor, W. R. *Thucydides.* 1984. A sophisticated and rewarding analysis of an ancient historian using the techniques of literary criticism.

Gould, John. *Herodotus.* 1989. A short and lively essay on the mind of the historian; a fine introduction.

Hanson, Victor Davis. *The Western Way of War: Infantry Battle in Classical Greece.* 1989. This well-written book evokes what fighting in a hoplite phalanx might have felt like.

Hurwit, J. *Art and Culture of Early Greece, 1100–480 B.C.* 1985. A discussion that places art in its societal context.

Irwin, T. *Classical Thought.* 1989. A reliable sketch of the outlines of ancient Greek philosophy.

Lloyd, G. E. R. *Early Greek Science: Thales to Aristotle.* 1971. A thoughtful and readable discussion of science in its social and cultural context.

Morgan, Catherine. *Athletes and Oracles: The Transformation of Olympia and Delphi in the Eighth Century B.C.* 1990. An archaeological and historical study of the role of religious sanctuaries and athletic games in the rise of the Greek polis.

Morris, Ian. *Burial and Ancient Society: The Rise of the Greek City-State.* 1987. A sophisticated analysis of grave sites and what they indicate about the origins of the polis.

Pollitt, J. J. *Art and Experience in Classical Greece.* 1972. An essay on the interrelationship of art, society, and culture in the fifth and fourth centuries B.C.

Wiedemann, Thomas, ed. *Greek and Roman Slavery.* 1981. A collection of translated ancient sources, with commentary.

THE PARTHENON

The Parthenon, completed in 432 B.C., dominates both the skyline of Athens and the historical imagination of the West. The building's fine marble and classical proportions seem to bespeak the free, confident, and united society that one might expect of Periclean Athens, the world's first democracy (see illustration, page 107). A close look, however, suggests a more complex story. The Parthenon's sculpture offers glimpses of the tensions behind the classical façade.

The temple of Athena Parthenos ("the Maiden"), as the Parthenon is formally known, was a public project of Greece's wealthiest city-state, leading naval power, and premier democracy. Athenians spared no expense on its construction. Sculpture included a gold-and-ivory statue of the goddess Athena inside the temple and, on the outside, statuary in each pediment (the triangular space under the eaves) and sculptured reliefs running around the building above the exterior and interior colonnades.

So lavish a program of art demonstrated Athenian wealth but also served an educational purpose: to illustrate basic Athenian values. Because every Athenian male was expected to fight for the city when called on, militant competition is a central theme. Above the exterior colonnade, for example, ninety-two separate panels of relief sculpture depict gods and heroes fighting such foes as giants and centaurs. The sculpture above the interior colonnade is not so easily characterized, however.

The interior sculpture forms a continuous band, or frieze, around the four sides of the building. There are warriors aplenty, primarily cavalrymen but also hoplites and charioteers. See the detail from the west wall. Two riders are illustrated here: one turning and signaling, the other

The Parthenon Frieze, Detail from West Wall *(Courtesy of the Trustees of the British Museum)*

taking control of a rearing horse. Naked youths, they embody the ideal of strong bodies in the service of the polis. The long hair worn by the first rider was popular among the upper classes, a reminder that Athenian cavalrymen were aristocrats.

Not all of the men in the interior frieze are warriors, though, and women too are depicted. See the detail from the east wall. Look at the four women shown here. Like the riders, they are young and in pairs, but there the similarity ends. The women are on foot, clothed, and in solemn procession. The heavy folds of their robes, the hands held at the side, and the expression on the one face that is visible, all suggest calm and decorum.

From both of these pieces we may detect Athenian commonplaces about gender. Young women were expected to be maidenly, reserved, and modest. Their bodies were to be kept private. Young men were expected to be outgoing and assertive. Although men wore clothes in public, they exercised naked in gymnasiums, wrestling-grounds, and stadiums, competing in a healthy activity considered to be good preparation for war.

The historian finds subtler messages in the two scenes. For example, however constrained the role of women, their very presence in the frieze is significant. Women were not permitted to attend the Athenian assembly, but they participated in the rituals and festivals that played so large a role in Athenian public life. Notice, for instance, the two girls shown in the back who carry ritual vessels.

One group of people is notably absent from the frieze: Athenian rowers. The rowers who manned Athens's warships were poor men and the most loyal supporters of democracy. Why are they not depicted on a temple built by vote of Athens's popular assembly, the disbursements for whose construction were inscribed in stone and posted nearby so that any citizen could inspect the way public funds were handled?

The Parthenon Frieze, Detail from East Wall *(The Louvre)*

The answer depends on knowing precisely what the frieze as a whole depicts, but that knowledge—despite the fame of the Parthenon and the relative wealth of documentation from Periclean Athens—is embarrassingly shaky. Most scholars argue that the subject is the Pan-Athenaic procession, held once every four years to honor Athena. The people depicted are said to be the people of Athens—a daring novelty, considering that all previous Greek temple sculpture was restricted to gods, heroes, and mythological figures.

Yet if the scene is the Pan-Athenaic procession, how are we to explain the absence of certain well-known features of that procession—for instance, a large ship model? Some scholars prefer to view the scene as an illustration of a legend from the early history of Athens, a period in which rowers played little role in the Athenian military. Still, there are many nautical motifs in Athenian myth, motifs the Athenians could have chosen to illustrate if they had wished to celebrate the rowers.

Clearly, the Athenians preferred to depict hoplites and horsemen. Some might conclude that Athens was not as democratic as it claimed to be. Another explanation is that Athenian rowers, despite all their political assertiveness, admired the cultural ideal of the hoplite and that conservative traditions died hard even in democratic Athens.

CHAPTER 4

The Hellenistic World

The fourth century B.C. brought the greatest revolution to the Greek world since the rise of the polis four hundred years earlier. Exhausted after a century of warfare, from the 430s to the 330s B.C., the Greek city-states yielded hegemony to Macedon. A northeastern Greek kingdom that had previously been only a fringe power, Macedon rose meteorically under Philip II, until it was the leader of Greece. Although Philip was a brilliant and ambitious general, his son and successor Alexander the Great outstripped him. Alexander led Macedonians and Greeks to control of a region that stretched from Greece and Egypt in the west to Sogdiana (modern Kazakhstan) and what the Greeks called India (today, Pakistan) in the east.

In barely a dozen years Alexander laid the foundations of a new Greek world: the world of the Hellenistic period (323–30 B.C.), distinct in many ways from the preceding Hellenic era (ca. 750–323 B.C.). In Hellenistic times Macedonians and Greeks replaced Persians as the ruling people of Egypt and western Asia. Large numbers of Greek-speaking colonists moved south and east. Governed by Macedonian dynasties, Egypt and the Levant became integral parts of the Greek world and would remain so until the Arab conquest in the seventh century A.D. Greek-speaking kingdoms thrived briefly as far from mainland Greece as modern Afghanistan and Pakistan. At times the new elite was open to natives who learned Greek and adopted Greek ways, but more often the natives were excluded and exploited.

Conquest put huge amounts of wealth into Greek hands. Great new cities were built: Antioch in Syria, Pergamum in Anatolia, Seleucia in Mesopotamia, and, greatest of all, Alexandria in Egypt. Trade increased and

Krater from Derveni, ca. 330. Gilded bronze with silver inlay.

expanded southward and eastward. The scale of political life expanded as well. Federal leagues replaced cities in importance in much of south and central Greece, while monarchies ruled most of the rest of the Greek-speaking world.

Material and political expansion led to unanticipated cultural changes. Hellenistic Greeks were as likely to be subjects of a king or members of a federation as they were to be citizens of an independent city-state. Frequently finding themselves among strange peoples, the Greeks sought comfort in new philosophies, religions, and modes of literary and artistic expression. Science flourished under royal patronage, as did the emerging discipline of literary criticism. The prestige of royal women tended to promote improvements in the overall status of Greek women.

Hellenistic Greeks boasted of having created one world, a common or ecumenical region (from the Greek *oikoumene,* "inhabited [area]"). Yet it was a world reserved on the whole for Greeks; nor was the Greek elite much interested in indigenous culture, with the exception of religion. Greeks adapted and Hellenized a number of Egyptian and Asian deities. The seeds were sown in this era, moreover, for a momentous cross-fertilization between native and Greek religion: Christianity, which emerged from the contacts between Greeks and Jews in Hellenistic times.

Philip of Macedon Found in a Macedonian royal tomb, this miniature ivory head probably portrays King Philip II (r. 359–336 B.C.). Note the rugged features, beard, and war wounds: a scar across the right eyebrow and apparent sightlessness of the right eye. *(Archaeological Museum of Thessaloniki)*

Philip and Alexander

The Hellenistic world was founded by two conquerors: Philip II of Macedon (382–336 B.C.) and his son, Alexander III, known as Alexander the Great (356–323 B.C.). After a century of indecisive warfare among the Greek city-states, Philip conquered them in twenty years; in even less time Alexander conquered Egypt and all of western Asia as far east as modern Pakistan. The legacy of these impressive conquests was a revolution in the history of the Mediterranean.

The Rise of Macedon

Macedon was a border state, long weaker than its more advanced neighbors but capable of learning from them and ultimately of conquering them. Though rich in resources and manpower, Macedon lacked the relatively efficient organization of the polis. Macedon included both tribal groups and cities. Several dialects of Greek were spoken, some unintelligible to southern Greeks, who considered Macedonians barbarians (from the Greek *barbaros,* meaning "a person who does not speak Greek"). Ordinary Macedonians lived rough, sturdy lives. The king and the royal court lived in a sophisticated capital city, Pella, where they sponsored visits by leading Greek artists, writers, and thinkers. Philip confounded Greek stereotypes of Macedonian barbarism by turning out to be a brilliant soldier, statesman, and diplomat—a man of vast ambition, appetite, and energy. A hard drinker, vain, and a man with numerous wives and lovers, he was also an excellent orator and general. Philip's goals were to make himself dominant in Macedon, to make Macedon dominant in Greece, and then, as leader of a combined Greco-Macedonian force, to conquer Persia. He accomplished all but the last.

The instrument of Philip's success was his army, a well-trained, professional, year-round force. Macedon, with its plains and horses, was cavalry country, and Philip made cavalry his main attack weapon. The Macedonian phalanx was meant to hold the enemy phalanx until the cavalry could find a weak spot and attack. Accordingly, Macedonian hoplites carried extra-long pikes to stop the enemy at a distance without engaging him head on. Philip also mastered the technology of siegecraft, raising it to a level unseen since Assyrian days (see page 45).

Philip used his army effectively. After capturing the lucrative gold mine of Mount Pangaeum in Thrace (the region east of Macedon), he turned to the Greek city-states nearby. Olynthus, the most important, fell in 348 B.C. Led by the Athenian Demosthenes (ca. 385–322 B.C.), the main Greek city-states prepared to make a stand. Demosthenes was a superb orator, but his attempts to forge a unified force were too late. By 338 B.C., when an Atheno-Theban army met the Macedonians, Philip had already won over much of the Greek world. His complete military victory at Chaeronea in Boeotia was followed up with a lenient settlement in which all the Greeks except Sparta acknowledged Philip's hegemony. The Greeks would rebel against Macedon more than once, but always in vain, until they fell under the even greater power of Rome. The day was over when the polis could decide the fate of the eastern Mediterranean.

In 336 B.C. Philip was murdered by a disgruntled courtier, and the invasion of the Persian Empire fell to his 20-year-old son Alexander, the new king.

Alexander the Conqueror

Alexander III of Macedon (r. 336–323 B.C.) is as famous in art as in literature, in romance as in history, in Iran or India as in Europe or America. Yet the evidence for the historical Alexander is almost as problematic as that for the historical Socrates or Jesus. After Alexander's untimely death at age 32, contemporaries wrote histories and memoirs, but none has survived. Several good historical accounts, based on earlier texts, are extant, but none was written less than three hundred years after Alexander's day (see the box, "Virtues and Vices of Alexander the Great"). Alexander, moreover, was not only a legend in his own time but a master propagandist. Many of the incidents of his life took place in remote regions or among a few individuals, and they tended to grow with the telling.

Alexander the Great The face of the king (r. 336–323 B.C.) is shown in profile on this coin. Note Alexander's youthful, regular features. He wears a lion's mane on his head and neck, a symbol of Heracles (Hercules), whom the Macedonian royal house claimed as an ancestor. *(Giraudon/Art Resource, NY)*

Still, Alexander's virtues are clear. He was charismatic, handsome, intelligent, and well educated; as a teenager he had Aristotle himself as a private tutor. Alexander was ruthless as well as cultured. He began his reign with a massacre of his male relatives, but he brought a team of Greek scientists along with him on his expedition through the Persian Empire. Although he destroyed peoples and places, Alexander founded twenty cities, one of which, Alexandria in Egypt,

Virtues and Vices of Alexander the Great

Writing in the second century A.D., the historian Arrian composed from earlier accounts what is now the best surviving history of Alexander. A military man himself, Arrian keenly appreciated Alexander's practical skills but was not blind to Alexander's flaws.

Alexander died in the 114th Olympiad, in the archonship of Hegesias at Athens [June 323 B.C.]. . . . He had great personal beauty, invincible power of endurance, and a keen intellect; he was brave and adventurous, strict in the observance of his religious duties, and hungry for fame. Most temperate in the pleasures of the body, his passion was for glory only, and in that he was insatiable. He had an uncanny instinct for the right course in a difficult and complex situation, and was most happy in his deductions from observed facts. In arming and equipping troops and in his military dispositions he was always masterly. Noble indeed was his power of inspiring his men, of filling them with confidence, and, in the moment of danger, of sweeping away their fear by the spectacle of his own fearlessness. When risks had to be taken, he took them with the utmost boldness, and his ability to seize the moment for a swift blow, before the enemy had any suspicion of what was coming, was beyond praise.

Doubtless, in the passion of the moment Alexander sometimes erred; it is true he took some steps towards the pomp and arrogance of the Asiatic kings: but I, at least, cannot feel that such errors were very heinous, if the circumstances are taken fairly into consideration. For, after all, he was young; the chain of his successes was unbroken, and, like all kings, past, present, and to come, he was surrounded by courtiers who spoke to please, regardless of what evil their word might do. On the other hand, I do indeed know that Alexander, of all the monarchs of old, was the only one who had the nobility of heart to be sorry for his mistakes.

Source: Arrian, *The Campaigns of Alexander,* trans. Aubrey de Sélincourt. Rev. J. R. Hamilton. (Harmondsworth, England: Penguin, 1971), pp. 395–396.

later grew into the largest city in the Mediterranean. For all his varied interests, however, Alexander was first and foremost a warrior. Battlefield commander of the Macedonian cavalry at age 18, he devoted most of the rest of his life to warfare.

As a leader of men, Alexander was popular, inspiring, and shared risks with the troops. He knew the value of propaganda, and took pains to depict his expedition to the Greek city-states as a war of revenge for Persia's invasion of Greece in 480 B.C. instead of what it actually was: an act of Macedonian imperialism. He loved the colorful gesture. He began his expedition to conquer Persia in 334 B.C. by sacrificing animals to the gods at Troy, a site evoking Homer's heroes.

On the eve of invasion, Persia vastly outnumbered Macedon on both land and sea. Darius III of Persia was rich, but Alexander's treasury was virtually empty. The Macedonian expeditionary force was short on supplies. The peoples in Persia's multiethnic empire were restive, but so too were Alexander's Greek allies, the mainstay of his fleet. One of Darius's advisers proposed a naval campaign to raise a revolt in Greece and force the Macedonians home. How then did Alexander propose to conquer Persia?

The answer was his faith in the Macedonian army. Although Alexander invaded Anatolia with only about thirty-five thousand men, they were the fastest-marching, most experienced, and most skilled army in the eastern Mediterranean. If Persia would fight the Macedonians in a set battle, Alexander had good reason to be confident of victory—and there was reason to believe that Persia would do just that. Persian elite

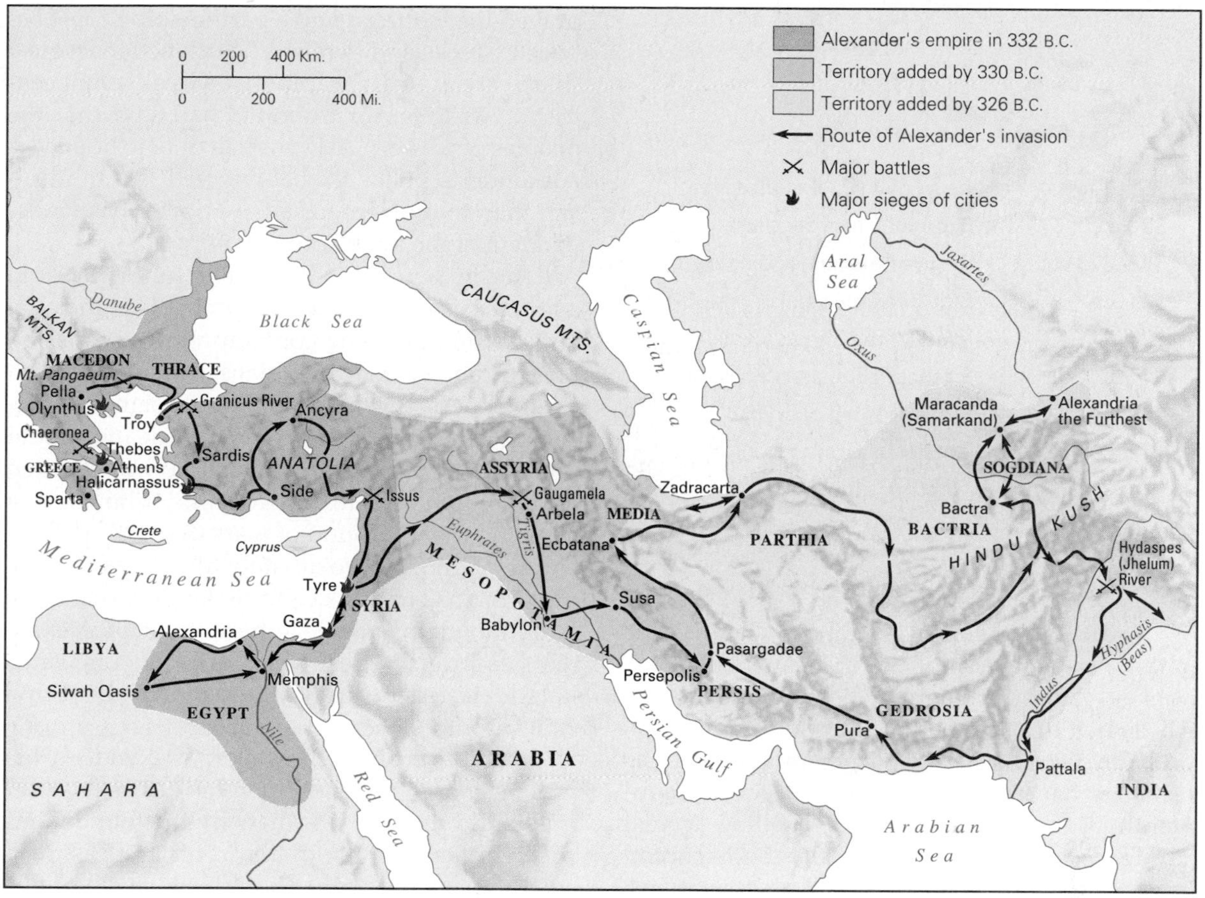

Map 4.1 Conquests of Philip and Alexander Between 359 and 323 B.C., the armies of Macedon conquered first the Greek city-states and then the Persian Empire. Macedonian power extended from Greece and Egypt eastward to modern Pakistan.

ideology impelled the army to face the enemy head-on. Darius, moreover, was a new monarch and a usurper and was under pressure to prove himself in the field. As expected, Macedon crushed the enemy. The war was decided in three great battles: at the Granicus River in Anatolia (334 B.C.), at Issus in Syria (333 B.C.), and at Gaugamela in Mesopotamia (331 B.C.). Darius fled into Iran, was deposed, assassinated, and replaced by a man whom Alexander captured and executed. By 328 Alexander's claim to be king of Persia was sealed with blood and iron.

Having conquered the Persian heartland, Alexander turned eastward (Map 4.1). The last seven years of his career are marked by three themes. First is the continuing and, in Alexander's mind, apparently open-ended military campaign. He pushed his army not only into the eastern parts of the Persian Empire but beyond, into modern Pakistan, which had not been controlled by Persia since the early fifth century B.C. The Macedonians won a major victory there in 326 B.C. near the Hydaspes (modern Jhelum) River over a force employing as many as two hundred elephants. Alexander's infantry suffered considerable casualties before inflicting enough wounds on the elephants to make them uncontrollable. Alexander prepared to continue eastward, perhaps as far as the Bay of Bengal, but his exhausted and homesick men had other plans. They mutinied beside the Hyphasis (modern Beas) River (near the modern Indo-Pakistani border) and forced Alexander finally to turn back. He reached Persia in late 325 B.C.

FOUNDATIONS OF THE HELLENISTIC WORLD

359–336 B.C.	Reign of Philip II of Macedon
338 B.C.	Battle of Chaeronea
336–323 B.C.	Reign of Alexander the Great
331 B.C.	Battle of Gaugamela
322–275 B.C.	Wars of the Successors
312 B.C.	Seleucus I conquers Babylon
304 B.C.	Ptolemy I king of Egypt
276 B.C.	Antigonus Gonatas king of Macedon

The second theme of Alexander's later career is the increasing use of the instruments of despotism. After conquering Persia in 330 B.C., Alexander turned on the Macedonian nobility, probably because he feared potential rivals. His fear may have been well founded, for Macedonian nobles had a tradition of rebelling against strong kings. The years after 330 B.C. are marked by conspiracy trials, purges, and assassinations. The most spectacular took place in 328 in Marakanda (modern Samarkand, located in Uzbekistan) when, after a drunken quarrel, Alexander himself murdered Cleitus, one of his senior commanders.

Another sign of Alexander's growing despotism was his demand for the trappings of Persian kingship. After conquering Persia, for example, he made independent-minded Greeks and Macedonians bow down before him. He demanded that the Greek city-states deify him. "If Alexander wishes to be a god, let him be," was the laconic reply of the Spartans, but Alexander had set a precedent for both Hellenistic monarchs and Roman emperors.

The third theme of Alexander's later career was his novel policy of fusion. After returning from the Indian subcontinent, Alexander began training an army of 30,000 Iranians and dismissed a large number of Macedonian troops. He and his main commanders all married Iranian women. In 324 B.C. Alexander staged a grand banquet in Mesopotomia for 9000, at which he prayed for "concord and a partnership in rule between Greeks and Persians." Such actions were a sharp break with traditional Greek ethnocentrism. Aristotle, for example, had said that the peoples of western Asia were fit only to be slaves. Alexander's policy probably owed less to idealism than to a desire for a new power base independent of the Macedonian nobility.

Alexander died in Babylon in June of 323 B.C., a month before he turned 33, probably of malarial fever, although some contemporaries suspected poison and some historians have suggested drunkenness. Alexander did not designate a successor. His wife, pregnant at his death, would give birth to a son and heir, but he was shunted aside by the Macedonian generals, who began a long and bloody round of wars over the spoils of empire. It took approximately fifty years of fighting, from 322 to 275 B.C., to make clear that three large kingdoms would inherit most of Alexander's empire. The rest was divided among small kingdoms, federal leagues, and independent city-states.

In the long run, however, Alexander's life was far more influential than his death. His conquests did nothing less than lay the foundations of the Hellenistic world. It is ironic to measure in such impersonal terms the achievements of one who, more than most people in history, exemplifies individual success. Whether it was exalting a savior or debunking a hero, much of Hellenistic culture centered on the myth of heroism that Alexander had engendered. Historians who believe the individual is insignificant will rarely have a more challenging counterexample than Alexander.

The Variety of the Hellenistic Kingdoms

Hellenistic political units ranged from multiethnic kingdoms to small, ethnically homogeneous city-states (Map 4.2). The history of the Greek peninsula was marked by a monarchy with republican pretensions and by experiments in federalism and in social revolution. In Asia and Africa, Alexander's successors created a new ruling elite whose upper echelons were reserved for Greeks and Macedonians, whose migration they

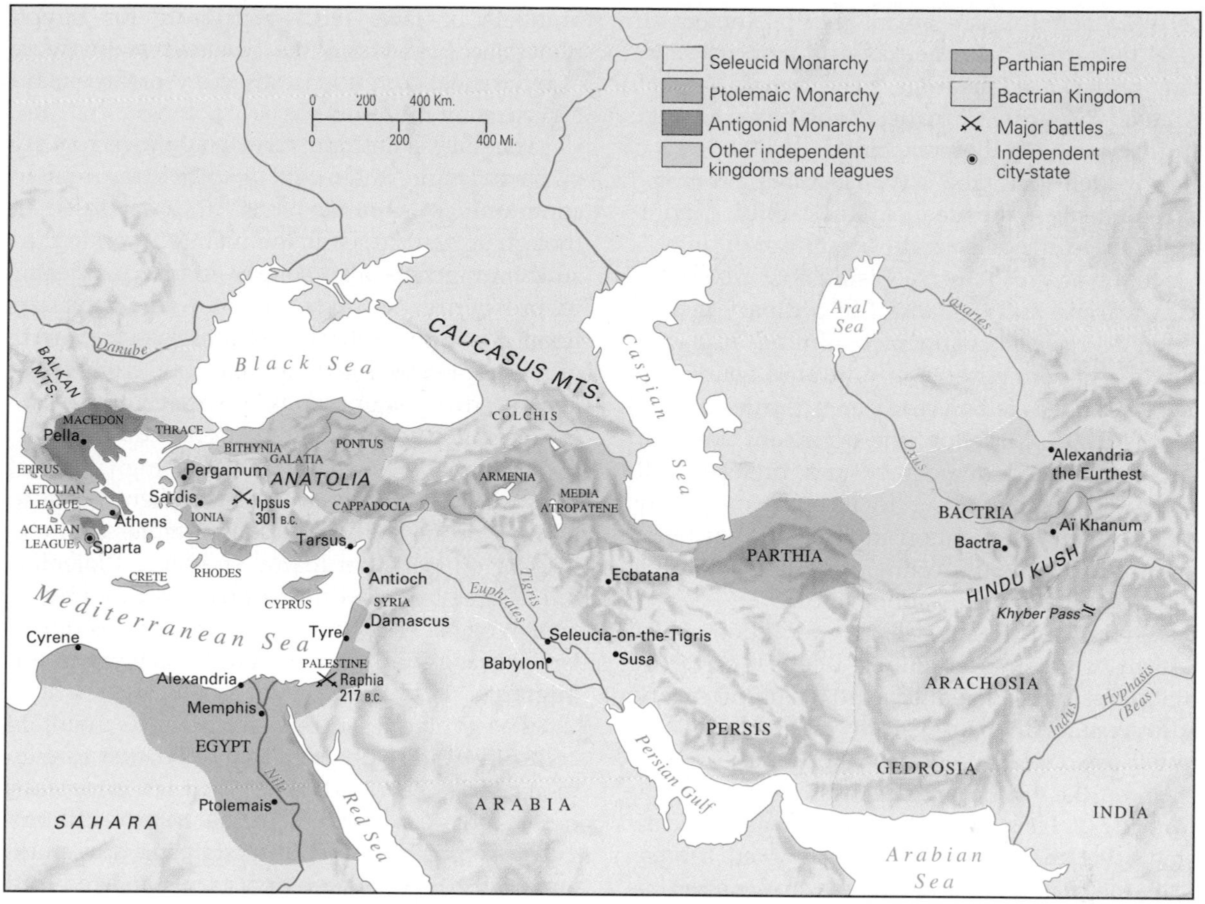

Map 4.2. Hellenistic Kingdoms, Leagues, and City-States, ca. 240 B.C. After Alexander's death, his empire lost its political unity. Great new cities and states arose in the lands he had conquered.

encouraged. There were low- and mid-level administrative positions for native elites, however, particularly if they were willing to learn Greek. The immigrants wanted land, wealth, or adventure. Their paths were eased by a new ideology that identified being Greek less with loyalty to an individual city than with participation in a common Greek civilization.

Although the Hellenistic world became relatively peaceful after 275 B.C., conflict among the kingdoms continued. Generally waged at a low level of intensity, with bribes and diplomacy as weapons, conflict sometimes broke out into major battles. Palestine and the southern Greek mainland and Aegean islands were chronic bones of contention among the large kingdoms. A number of small states emerged in Anatolia, notably Pergamum, whose wealthy rulers were patrons of literature and art, and Galatia, carved out by Celtic invaders from Europe.

Hellenism Redefined

The city-state of the Classical period was particularistic: To be, say, a Theban, one had to be of Theban descent, live in Theban territory, and follow the Theban way of life. Disappointed by the endless wars and fragmentation of the fourth century B.C., Greek intellectuals moved away from particularism. The chief harbinger of things to come was Isocrates (428–338 B.C.), an Athenian teacher of rhetoric. Isocrates redefined the notion of what being Greek meant. He promoted the idea that Greece was not a collection of city-states but, rather, a civilization. "The people we call Greeks," he wrote, "are those who have the same culture as us, not the same blood."[1]

By demoting the city, Isocrates promoted Pan-Hellenism, the ideal of Greek unity. Accordingly, he did not hesitate to support Philip of Macedon against Athens. Disillusioned by incessant warfare and disdainful of ordinary people, Isocrates rejected democracy, aiming instead to create a governing elite of educated gentlemen. Isocrates' ideas fell on ready ears, particularly after his death. Macedon, the dominant power in Greece, disliked democracy and preferred oligarchy, a regime closer to its own monarchy. Macedonian intervention in Greece contributed greatly to a general decline of democracy in the century following Alexander's death.

In the fourth century B.C., redefinition of Hellenism as a common culture made it easier for mainland Greeks to emigrate to far-off places and still consider themselves Greek. Finally, it was now possible for foreigners to become Greek by learning the Greek language and literature. The number of Hellenized foreigners was relatively small, yet their very existence marked a break from the Classical polis, where even a genius like Aristotle could not obtain Athenian citizenship because he was not of Athenian descent.

In the Hellenistic age, Greek eventually replaced Aramaic as the dominant language of the cities and of trade in the eastern Mediterranean. One obtains a sense of the importance of Isocrates' redefinition of Hellenism by considering that one of the most famous Greek-speakers of all antiquity was Paul, the Christian apostle who was born a Jew in Tarsus, a city in southern Anatolia.

Colonialism, Greek Style

Many Greeks and Macedonians emigrated south or east, especially during the third century B.C., but we do not know how many. The few surviving statistics indicate a significant migration but not a mass exodus. By the second century B.C. the colonizing impulse had diminished in Greece and Macedon, but there was a corresponding increase in Jewish emigration. The second century B.C. was a turbulent period in Palestine, and large numbers of Jews left, particularly for Egypt. Ptolemaic Egypt and the Seleucid realm were also the most common destination for Greek and Macedonian migrants.

Whether immigrants to Egypt moved to city or countryside, they tended to live together in communities separate from the natives. Although agriculture was the main economic pursuit, immigrants also sought to realize dreams of prosperity or adventure in trade, industry, finance, administration, or military service. Trade offered opportunities high and low, from shopkeeping (for example, wine merchandise), to skippering a boat that moved grain up the Nile, to investing in such boats. With high interest rates allowed, Egypt was an excellent place to make a profit in moneylending, either on business or on personal loans. The large Ptolemaic bureaucracy offered numerous jobs in administration or tax collection. Because a knowledge of Greek was required, most positions went to immigrants.

The Ptolemies needed soldiers to maintain control of their conquered land. At first foreign mercenaries received generous cash payments; but to create a permanent, hereditary military group living in the countryside, the Ptolemies switched to a policy of land grants and reduced taxes. Farming did not have as high a status in Greek society as soldiering, so, whenever possible, mercenaries hired others to work the land rather than farm it themselves. The middlemen (usually Greeks) often made a handsome profit.

The Seleucids addressed the security and administrative problems of their far-flung realms by establishing over seventy colonies extending to central Asia. Some colonies were civilian, but most were military, composed of retired or reserve soldiers, mostly Greeks or Macedonians. A few were composed of Jews or other non-Greek groups. Colonists received land allotments. Greek-style public buildings were erected, and some cities were laid out according to a rectilinear grid plan reminiscent of the Classical polis. In Greek-speaking colonies, as most of the colonies were, the gymnasium attained a great practical and symbolic importance as both the center of Greek culture and the preparatory school for entry into the elite. The Hellenistic gymnasium offered education in literature, philosophy, and oratory as well as athletics.

Some Seleucid colonies developed into flourishing cities, in which natives as well as colonists were permitted to settle. Native populations were generally added to the Greco-Macedonian core of such cities. Seleucid cities prospered. For example, Greek cities dominated the Syrian coastline and much of Anatolia until the coming of Islam in the seventh century A.D. Greek urbanization should not create the false impression, however, that the Seleucids were motivated by some civilizing mission. They were not. They established colonies to increase their power.

Although Greeks and Macedonians dominated royal bureaucracy and civic government in both the Ptolemic and the Seleucid realms, native elites were not excluded entirely. The Greco-Macedonian conquerors could not have administered the territories they acquired without help from the native people who knew their homelands. The Seleucids did not hesitate to use natives as low- and mid-level administrators: not only as bureaucrats but sometimes even as temple administrators, army officers, and city-governors. In Hellenistic Egypt after about 200 B.C. the number of Greek-speaking Egyptians serving in administration increased, in part because of the drying up of immigration from Greece and Macedon, in part because of the assertiveness of Egyptians in a period of native revolts (see page 132).

An interesting example preserved in papyrus documents is that of an Egyptian named Plenis, who lived in a village in middle Egypt in the late second century B.C. Plenis was a tenant farmer on a royal estate and a priest in a local Egyptian cult. His horizon was not narrow, however; like his father before him, Plenis served as a soldier in the Ptolemaic army. Plenis, moreover, could write Greek as well as Egyptian, and he even used a Greek name: Dionysos, son of Kephalas. The Greek-speaking elite made room for people like Plenis, but the immigrants generally reserved the best positions and privileges for themselves.

Immigration and colonization were not the only sources of new economic opportunities. At the beginning of the Hellenistic era, Alexander turned the huge gold and silver reserves of Persia into coinage and released it onto the market virtually all at once. Although Alexander's action stimulated a rapid inflation lasting about seventy-five years, it also had the positive effect of greatly stimulating commerce. In particular the economy of Hellenistic Egypt became highly monetarized, even on the village level. Barter continued to exist in Egypt, but the widespread presence of money served to stimulate the production and circulation of goods, helping to render Egypt an economic powerhouse. Another stimulus to trade was the creation of large, new Hellenistic cities, especially Alexandria with its great harbors, canals, marketplaces, and infrastructure of banks, inns, courts, and shipbuilding facilities.

During Hellenistic times trade and commerce tended to shift from Greece proper to Anatolia and Egypt. The island of Rhodes, located off the southwest tip of Anatolia, grew into a major trading center, especially for grain. This development was the result of excellent harbors, a location on the merchant routes between Asia, Africa, and southeastern Europe, and a superb fleet. The Rhodian aristocracy grew rich off taxes and

Statuette of an African The tiny bronze (ca. 150–50 B.C.) shows a black youth in the characteristic pose of a Greek philosopher. The fingers of the right hand may have originally held a bookroll. Trade, diplomacy, and war brought black Africans to Hellenistic cities, especially Alexandria. *(Museum of Fine Arts Boston, J. H. and E. A. Payne Fund)*

duties, wisely reinvesting a portion of the profits in naval infrastructure (such as arsenals and dockyards) and in campaigns against pirates. Egypt had many products to trade. Grain was the most important, but textiles, glass, papyrus (from which a kind of paper was produced), and luxury goods were also significant. Egyptian goods were sold throughout the Mediterranean. A network of canals connecting Alexandria to the Nile and the Red Sea beyond also made possible active trading with Sudan, Arabia, and India.

The Seleucid kingdoms controlled rich trade routes to Arabia, India, and central Asia. Commerce was facilitated by good roads, sea travel between the Persian Gulf and India, and a unified royal coinage. The Seleucids traded agricultural goods and manufactured products like textiles, glassware, and metalwork for spices from India and Arabia. In the first century B.C. they even had trade contacts with China, whose silk garments reached the Mediterranean. The kingdom of Pergamum, which stretched inland from Anatolia's northwest coast, exported the agricultural products of the rich hinterland it controlled, as well as the local gray-blue building stone and, as an alternative to Egyptian papyrus, parchment.

Slavery was an important part of the Hellenistic social and economic scene. Although war and piracy were the main sources of enslavement, some people were born into slavery. In Sicily and southern Italy, slaves worked huge plantations, but eastern Mediterranean slaves were commonly found in the household or in administration and in cities rather than in the countryside. Many unfree laborers worked on farms in Egypt and western Asia. Following the pre-Greek traditions of those regions, they were generally tenant farmers tied to kings or potentates rather than outright slaves.

On some plantations, conditions for slaves were bad enough to lead mass uprisings. It was not unusual, however, for domestic or administrative slaves to buy their freedom, sometimes using savings they were allowed to keep, sometimes borrowing money from the master or from friends. Greeks enslaved fellow Greeks, but not without guilty consciences; they often made special efforts to help Greek slaves win their freedom. Even as slaves, therefore, Greeks had special privileges.

Macedon and Greece

Macedon was the last of the three great Hellenistic kingdoms to emerge from civil war after Alexander's death. Not until 276 B.C. was Antigonus Gonatas, grandson of Alexander's general Antigonus the One-Eyed, established firmly on the throne. His Antigonid dynasty lasted about 140 years, until the Roman conquest. Antigonus Gonatas (ca. 320–237 B.C.) devoted himself to internal consolidation and to fighting the attempts of the Ptolemies of Egypt to extend their power to the Greek mainland and in the Aegean; he was successful at both endeavors.

True to the traditions of Macedon, the Antigonids projected an image of simplicity and toughness. Like Philip II and Alexander the Great, Antigonus immersed himself in the culture of the Greek city-states, partly because he admired it, partly because it brought him prestige. As a young man, Antigonus had studied the new school of Stoic philosophy in Athens. As king, he devoted himself to the Stoic dictates of duty, describing his office as "noble servitude" and his diadem as a mere "rag." Antigonus shared the traditional Macedonian ambition to dominate the Greek city-states, but he faced rival powers (see Map 4.2): besides Ptolemaic Egypt, the kingdom of Epirus in northwestern Greece and two new federal leagues in the south, the Aetolians (north of the Corinthian Gulf) and the Achaeans (in the Peloponnesus).

The federal leagues were more tightly organized than Classical Greek military leagues (such as the Peloponnesian League) and larger than the Boeotian League, a fourth-century B.C. federal league, which had covered a relatively small territory. Both permitted some participation by ordinary men but were dominated by the wealthy; they were not democracies. Traditionally mercenaries and pirates, the Aetolians were unrefined but capable of complex political organization. One feature of their league was proportional representation by population in a federal council for constituent cities.

Achaean federalism was the product of a sophisticated urban culture and a more successful political balance between local and federal authorities; accounts of this system would one day influence the founders of the United States.

Achaean citizens enjoyed dual citizenship, local and federal. There was a common federal authority, but constituent cities kept their own constitutions. On the federal level, there were a governing general (both president and commander-in-chief) and ten subordinate magistrates, an executive council, and a general assembly of all citizens over age 30. The assembly met only on extraordinary occasions to discuss war, peace, and treaties. The council was the league's ordinary deliberative body. Assembly meetings alternated from city to city. At these meetings, each city voted as a unit, to prevent the host city from dominating the league numerically.

The most prominent Achaean leader was Aratus of Sicyon (271–213 B.C.), a statesman and general who believed in the rule of law and opposed monarchy, tyranny, and democracy. His ideal was an orderly oligarchy. Under Aratus's leadership the Achaean League became a great anti-Macedonian power, uniting the entire Peloponnesus except Sparta.

Athens, less successful than Sparta in maintaining independence, underwent frequent periods of Macedonian rule. Through a combination of war and diplomacy, however, Athens won periods of freedom from the late fourth to the mid-second century B.C., when all Greece came under Roman rule. Athens remained a vibrant democracy until the late third century B.C., when the oligarchic upper classes finally won the upper hand for good.

Extremes of wealth and poverty, problems of debt, and class conflict challenged Hellenistic Greece. The decline of democracy enabled the wealthy to contribute less to the public good in taxes and to amass private fortunes. The result was sometimes class conflict. Full-scale revolution, however, rarely occurred—in part because the elite sometimes bought off the poor with grain distributions and philanthropy, in part because poor citizens were unwilling to make common cause with slaves, whom they looked down on.

Revolution did briefly show its face in Sparta, thanks to the efforts of two great leaders. After defeat in the fourth century B.C., Sparta became impoverished (see page 106). In the late third century B.C., however, a social revolution was launched from above by Agis and Cleomenes, two Spartan kings working together. Their program included debt relief, a redistribution of land, and a restoration of classical Spartan austerity and equality. Popular in Sparta, the revolution threatened to spread elsewhere. Aratus and the Achaeans went to war to stop it, but a rejuvenated Spartan army won on the battlefield. Desperate, Aratus called in his Macedonian enemies, who crushed Sparta in 222 B.C. and ended the revolution, but Aratus had to agree to give Macedon a toehold in the Peloponnesus. Reformers were active again in Sparta a generation later, but they too were crushed.

Ptolemaic Egypt

The wealthiest, the most sophisticated, and the longest lasting of the Hellenistic kingdoms was Ptolemaic Egypt. One of Alexander's great generals, Ptolemy, son of Lagus (d. 283 B.C.), became governor of Egypt in 323 B.C., and proclaimed himself king in 304. His dynasty lasted until Rome annexed Egypt in 30 B.C., after the suicide of the last of the line, Queen Cleopatra. By contrast, Macedon was absorbed by Rome a century earlier, in 146; Pergamum was annexed in 133; the Seleucid kingdom was annexed in 64. The Ptolemaic kingdom was dominated by a Greco-Macedonian colonial elite that exploited the native inhabitants. The Ptolemies borrowed Egyptian traditions when it suited them, but, except for Cleopatra, they never learned to speak Egyptian.

Unlike the Antigonids, the Ptolemies did not emulate the simple virtues but rather gloried in wealth and grandeur. Ptolemy I showed the way to his successors when he had Alexander's funeral procession hijacked on its way to Macedonia and established a tomb and regular cult in Alexandria—a Greek hero-shrine in the land of the pyramids. Ptolemy I made arrangements to have himself proclaimed "Savior God" after his death; his successors, less reticent, took divine honors while still alive. Another legimitizing tool was the staging of splendid processions in the capital city, Alexandria. Greek states had long sponsored processions, but never on the lavish scale of the Ptolemies (see the box, "An Alexandrian Procession").

The most important Ptolemaic borrowing, however, was the pharaonic tradition of the com-

A Cretan Dream Interpreter in Egypt A painted stele (ca. 200 B.C.) advertises the services of a Greek in Memphis near the temple of Sarapis, a Greco-Egyptian god. The inscription and pediment are Greek, while the pilasters, women, and sacred bull (facing an altar) are Egyptian. *(Egyptian Museum, Cairo)*

mand economy, which the Ptolemies combined with Greek customs of literacy and a monetary economy. The result was a highly complex economy and, for the kings, a highly profitable one. The Ptolemies established a monetary economy with regular coinage and a banking system in place of the previous Egyptian barter system. Putting to use the science of the Museum, the great institute in Alexandria, they sponsored irrigation and land reclamation, the addition of new crops (for example, new varieties of wheat), and the greatly expanded cultivation of old ones (such as grapes for wine). To stimulate trade, they had canals and Alexandria's great harbor built, and they established colonies on the Red Sea.

Their main goal, however, remained exploitation. Most of the people of Egypt made their living in agriculture, either as independent small farmers or as tenants on large estates (some of which were in the royal domain). In either case, the Ptolemies claimed a portion of their produce. Government enriched itself through taxes, rents, demands for compulsory labor, state monopolies (on such diverse items as oils, textiles, and beer), and various internal tolls and customs duties. Up and down the valley and delta of the Nile there were bureaucrats to supervise collection and soldiers in military colonies to enforce their will.

The result was boom times for the elite, under strong kings and queens in the third century B.C. Egypt became the most prosperous part of the Hellenistic world, and Alexandria became the most populous and wealthiest city in the Mediterranean, as well as its literary capital (Map 4.3). In the second century B.C., however, continued economic prosperity was offset by decline among the ruling group. A series of weak kings, the spread of bureaucratic corruption, and the end of Greek immigration created conditions for the reassertion of native Egyptian power.

Native unrest, attested to in the 240s, grew more threatening after the battle of Raphia in 217 B.C., a struggle in Gaza between the Ptolemies and Seleucids for control of Palestine. Raphia was a huge clash of men and elephants—African elephants for the Ptolemies, Indian elephants for the Seleucids. The Ptolemies won, but only because they enrolled thousands of native Egyptians in their army, responding to a shortage of Greek and Macedonian manpower. Emboldened by their new military power, Egyptians engaged in a series of armed revolts that lasted on and off into the 130s.

Papyrus documents describe native resentment of and resistance to Greek hegemony. For instance, a letter writer from the third century B.C. complains of being looked down on as a "barbarian"; he fears "starving to death because I can't speak Greek." Other documents give glimpses of a riot against the Ptolemies in Alexandria late in the third century B.C.; an attempt in 161 B.C. to lynch a worshiper at an Egyptian temple "because," as he wrote afterward, "I am Greek"; the virtual independence of southern Egypt by the early second century B.C.

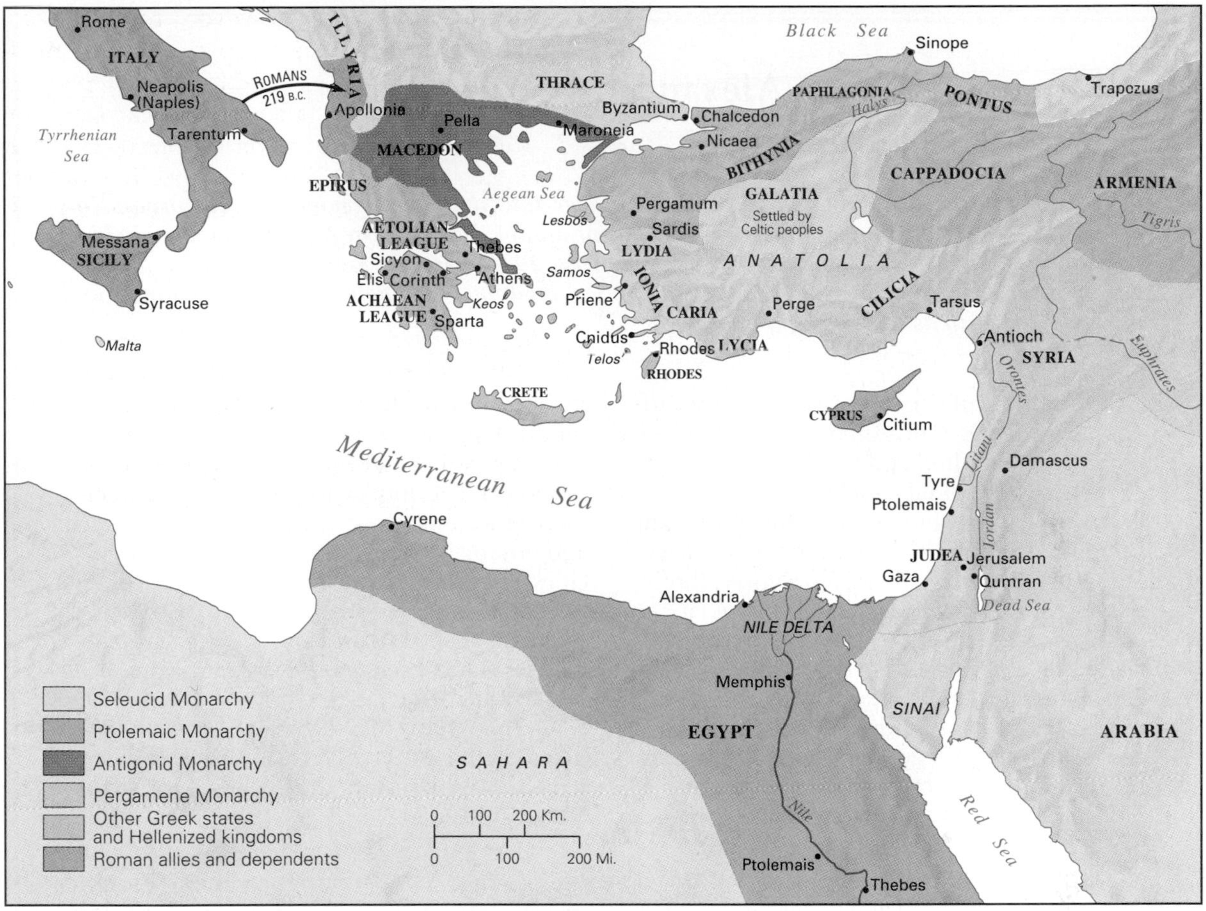

Map 4.3. The Eastern Mediterranean, ca. 200 B.C. The great Hellenistic powers contended for control of this vibrant, turbulent, and prosperous region. Conflict centered on Palestine and the Aegean islands, the rulership of which frequently changed hands.

Wealthy Greeks, sure of their own superiority, displayed only a superficial and limited interest in Egypt. At lower levels of the social scale, however, there is more evidence of native-settler cooperation, especially in the countryside, where intermarriage and bilingualism became common. Many an ordinary Greek became fully assimilated to Egyptian ways. Over the centuries even wealthy, sophisticated, urban Greeks adopted a smattering of Egyptian customs. The Egyptian calendar, Egyptian names, and mummification were all in use. Certain Egyptian literary genres were translated into Greek and became popular: mimes (farces mimicking people and events), folktales, and romances. Around 280 B.C., Manetho, a native Egyptian priest, wrote a guide in Greek to Egyptian history and religion, establishing the standard division of ancient Egypt's dynasties. By 98 B.C. assimilation was evident in the cultural hybrid of a group of 18- and 19-year-old male youths who received traditional Greek military and literary training but prayed to Egypt's crocodile-god.

Seleucids and Attalids

The kingdom founded by Alexander's general Seleucus (ca. 358–281 B.C.) was complex, with shifting borders and inhabitants. The Seleucid kingdom began when Seleucus took Babylon in

An Alexandrian Procession

Processions allowed rulers to advertise their power and to divert the populace. The procession described here by Callixinus of Rhodes, author of a book entitled* On Alexandria, *was held in Alexandria, perhaps in 271 or 270 B.C., as part of the Ptolemaia, an annual international festival sponsored by the Ptolemies. The Ptolemaic kingdom then included Aegean islands and parts of Anatolia as well as Egypt.

After speaking of very many other things and enumerating herds of animals, he [Callixinus] adds: "One hundred and thirty Ethiopian sheep, three hundred Arabian, twenty Euboean; twenty-six Indian oxen, all white, eight Ethiopian, one large white she-bear, fourteen leopards, sixteen panthers, four lynxes, three young panthers, one giraffe, one Ethiopian rhinoceros. Next, on a four-wheeled carriage . . . [various gods]. (Then) statues of Alexander and Ptolemy, wearing ivy-crowns made of gold. [The demi-god] Priapus stood next to them with a golden ivy-crown. [A personification of] the city of Corinth, standing next to Ptolemy, was crowned with a golden diadem. Beside all these were placed a stand for drinking vessels full of golden cups and a golden mixing bowl with a capacity of five measures. This four-wheeled carriage was followed by women wearing expensive clothes and ornaments; they were given the names of cities, some from Ionia [the Aegean coast of Anatolia] and the rest of the Greek cities which were established in Asia and the [Aegean] islands and had been under Persian rule; they all wore golden crowns. . . .

"Though the things that have been mentioned in these processions were many and varied, we have selected only those which contained gold and silver."

Source: M. M. Austin, *The Hellenistic World from Alexander to the Roman Conquest: A Selection of Ancient Sources in Translation* (Cambridge, England: Cambridge University Press, 1981), pp. 361–362.

312 B.C. and ended in 64 B.C. when Syria became a Roman province. There were many, many territorial changes in between. The first three kings ruled a domain stretching from the Aegean to Bactria (modern Afghanistan), but by the early second century B.C. most of the Iranian Plateau and lands eastward had been lost. At its height, in the third century B.C., the Seleucid kingdom had three nerve centers: Ionia (in western Anatolia), with a capital at Sardis; Syria, with a capital at Antioch; and Babylonia, whose capital was Seleucia-on-the-Tigris (near modern Baghdad).

Like Egypt, the Seleucid realms were dominated by a Greek-speaking elite. Unlike the compact Nile Valley with its relatively homogeneous population, the far-flung and multiethnic Seleucid lands presented an enormous administrative challenge. To govern such a conglomerate, the kings took over the Persian system of satraps (provincial governors), taxes, and royal roads and post (see page 59), to which they added an excellent army trained according to Macedonian traditions, a common coinage, and a Hellenistic ruler cult. The Seleucids established Greek and Macedonian colonies across the realm, but they also employed natives as low- and mid-level administrators. Although Greek was the language of the court, Aramaic and Akkadian were frequently used for administration. There even exists an official Seleucid royal seal stamped in cuneiform.

Babylonia, an area of agricultural wealth, cultural sophistication, and strategic significance, was of great importance to the Seleucids. The kings patronized native temples. Archaeological evidence suggests that native Babylonian culture flourished and traditional styles in art and architecture remained strong. The kings encouraged Greek settlement in this important region. In addition to the Greek city of Seleucia-on-the-Tigris, nearby Babylon had a Greek community, complete with gymnasium, agora, and theater, and was probably organized as a polis.

The greatest Seleucid city was Antioch, which became one of the wealthiest and most luxurious of all eastern Mediterranean cities; only Ptolemaic Alexandria outstripped it. The intellectual and artistic capital of Greek Asia in Hellenistic times, however, was not Antioch but Pergamum, in northwestern Anatolia.

The rulers of Pergamum, the Attalid dynasty of kings, carved out a small kingdom that became independent of the Seleucids in 263 B.C. and came into Roman hands in 133 B.C. The Attalids made Pergamum into a showplace of Greek civilization, a would-be second Athens. As in Athens, public building was focused on a steep acropolis. The upper city of Pergamum was laid out on hillside terraces rising to a palace and fortified citadel. One of the terraces housed the famous Pergamum Altar, a huge monument to an Attalid victory over the Celts who first invaded Anatolia in 278 B.C. and whose advance the Attalids checked. They could not, however, stop the Celts from settling in central Anatolia, where they created their kingdom of Galatia.

Pergamum was famous for its sculptors and for a library second only to Alexandria's. Pergamene writers focused on scholarship to the exclusion of poetry, perhaps as a result of the influence of Stoic philosophers, who disapproved of poetry's emotionalism.

Panel from Pergamum Altar This frieze (ca. 180–150 B.C.) decorating the podium of the altar of Zeus illustrates the war of the gods and the giants, imparting a heroic dimension to the battles of the Attalid kings and the Celts. The theme of Greeks and barbarians recalls the sculpture of Athens's Parthenon, suggesting that Pergamum was the successor to Athens as the champion of Greek civilization. *(Art Resource, NY)*

REBELLION AND REFORM	
263 B.C.	Kingdom of Pergamum founded
ca. 246 B.C.	Parthia revolts from Seleucids
ca. 245 B.C.	Bactria gains independence
244–222 B.C.	Reforms of Agis and Cleomenes in Sparta
217 B.C.	Battle of Raphia
167–142 B.C.	Maccabean revolt in Judea

The Greco-Indian Interaction

The Seleucids could not hold on to Alexander's vast eastern domains in the long term. A new Persian dynasty, the Parthians, achieved independence in the mid-third century B.C. and over the next century carved out a huge empire extending westward into Mesopotamia. But to the east, Bactria remained in the hands of the Greeks, though not of the Seleucids. From the mid-third century B.C., an independent Greek Bactria prospered.

Vivid evidence of Greek colonization in Bactria comes from the site of Ai Khanum in northern Afghanistan (its ancient name is unknown). This prosperous and populous city contained many reminders of Greece, among them a gymnasium, theater, and library. A pillar in the gymnasium was inscribed in the mid-third century B.C. with 140 moral maxims from Delphi in Greece, over 3000 miles away.

In the second century B.C., Bactrian kings extended their rule into the Indus River Valley and the Punjab, a region with a modest Greek presence since the fifth century B.C., when the Persians settled Greek mercenaries there. Virtually no literary evidence survives, but monuments and particularly coins demonstrate a certain amount of Greco-Indian cultural interaction. Monuments set up by the great Indian king Asoka (r. ca. 274–232 B.C.) display Greek stone-carving techniques. Some coins from the Greek kingdoms in India during the second century B.C. show bilingual inscriptions in Greek and Indian languages. Their designs include a variety of Indian religious motifs, such as the lotus plant and Lakshmi, goddess of wealth and good fortune.

Asoka tried to convert the Greeks in India to Buddhism and sent Buddhist missionaries as far west as Libya and Greece. The most powerful of the Greek rulers of India, Menander Soter Dikaios, may have converted to Buddhism in the mid-second century B.C. What is certain is Indian admiration for Hellenistic astronomy. One text, for example, says that Greek scientists should be "reverenced like gods."

Bactria was conquered by central Asian nomads in the late second century B.C. The Hellenistic kingdoms of India and Pakistan, however, survived until about the time of Christ, and some Greek communities lasted until the fifth century A.D.

The Alexandrian Moment

In 331 B.C., at the site of a fishing village in the northwestern part of the Nile Delta, Alexander and his advisers marked out the ground plan of a new city. They planned a great eastern Mediterranean trading center to replace Tyre, whose inhabitants had been killed or sold into slavery after the Macedonians took the town by siege in 332 B.C. The new city, called Alexandria, did not disappoint its founders. Grown to a population of a half-million or more by the first century B.C., it was possibly the largest, wealthiest, and most important city in the world. Greeks, Egyptians, and Jews were the largest groups in its cosmopolitan population, but no one would have been surprised to see an Indian or a Celt, an Italian or a Persian.

Under the Ptolemies, Alexandria became one of the great cultural centers of Hellenism. Ptolemaic patronage built and maintained Alexandria's remarkable educational institution, the Museum and Library, which was a flourishing center of literature, literary criticism, and science. Hellenistic culture shone forth in other cities too. Athens remained the capital of Greek philosophy, Pergamum outstripped Alexandria in sculpture and monumental architecture, and Antioch rivaled Pergamum. Alexandria, nonetheless, deserves especially close attention, not least because of the poignance with which Alexandrian literature portrays social change in the elite. Alexandrian writings bespeak both an improvement in the status of women and a disenchantment with traditional notions of the male warrior ideal, as well as an increased interest in emotions and sensitivity.

Other sources round out the picture, attesting to an increase in leisure time, a growth in educational opportunities for both sexes, royal patronage of culture, and the value of even a limited knowledge of Greek literature as the ticket to a job in government service. A schoolbook of the third century B.C., written in Greek on papyrus and found in Egypt, speaks volumes. It includes the Macedonian month-names, numbers up to 25, names of deities and rivers, a verse anthology, and quotations from Homer and Euripides.

The Anti-Epic Temperament

King Ptolemy I in 294 B.C. invited the deposed tyrant of Athens, Demetrius of Phalerum, to found an institution of culture in Alexandria. A writer himself, Ptolemy was no less sincere because the new foundation would bring him prestige and keep his engineers up-to-date on new technology for warfare and agriculture. Demetrius had studied with Aristotle's successor at the Lyceum, Theophrastus (ca. 370–288), a pragmatist interested in compiling and cataloging knowledge.

The new institution was called the Museum (literally, "House of the Muses," the home of the female deities who inspired creativity). The Museum was a residence, study, and lecture hall for scholars, scientists, and poets. One of its key components was the Library, in its day the largest repository of Greek writing in the world. In the third century B.C.—at the height of the Ptolemaic kingdom—the Library contained 700,000 papyrus rolls, the equivalent of roughly 50,000 modern books. Its nearest competitor, at Pergamum, contained less than a third as many rolls.

The Library is one of several indicators of an increase in the size of the Hellenistic reading and writing public. As independence vanished, city-states changed their military training programs for 18- and 19-year-old men into educational programs in literature and philosophy. The names of over a thousand writers of the Hellenistic era survive, and after 300 B.C. anthologies, abridgments, and school texts proliferated.

Although modeled on Athens's Lyceum, the Museum represented a quantum leap from the public culture of the Classical period. The denizens of the Museum were an elite, dependent on royal patronage and self-consciously Greek, as if to set up a barrier against Egyptians. At the Museum, culture was an object of study, not a part of

A Greek-Influenced Indian Statue This figure of a *bodhisattva* ("enlightened one") belongs to the Gandharan school, which was heavily influenced by Hellenistic sculpture. The statue's proportions, facial features and the drapery of its clothing particularly recall Hellenistic motifs, and may be the work of a Greek sculptor. *(Royal Ontario Museum)*

civic life as it had been in Classical Athens. A witticism of Timon, a philosopher from the Peloponnesus who lived in the third century B.C., rings true: "In Egypt, land of diverse tribes, graze many pedants, fatted fowls that quarrel without end in the hen coop of the Muses."

Before we examine Alexandrian literature further, it is worth pointing out how greatly Hellenistic Athenian literature diverged from Classical culture. The greatest Hellenistic Athenian writer, and a figure of international renown, was Menander (ca. 342–292 B.C.). He was the master of a style of comedy called "New Comedy," as distinguished from the "Old Comedy" of Aristophanes that had flourished a century earlier (see page 115). Where Old Comedy was raucous and ribald, New Comedy was restrained; where Old Comedy focused on public matters like war and politics, New Comedy was domestic and private. New Comedy symbolized the turn away from public life in Hellenistic times.

Menander wrote over seventy plays, but only one complete play has survived, *Dyskolos* (*The Grouch*). There are also substantial excerpts from several other plays as well as Roman imitations. The elements of Menander's skill and popularity shine through. Witty and fluent, he preferred stock plots and stock characters: the boastful soldier, the clever slave, the dashing but inept young man, the sweet maiden, and the old miser. Within those limitations, Menander created remarkably realistic and idiosyncratic characters. As a Hellenistic critic asked rhetorically: "O Menander and Life, which of you imitated the other?"

Like Menander, the Alexandrian writers turned from public themes, but in Alexandria the quintessential literary figure was not the playwright but the critic. He was a professional man of letters, as likely to write literary history as poetry. His works tended to be scholarly, even pedantic; they were refined, erudite, subtle—in a word, courtly. Critics prized diversity, novelty, and the exotic over the practical concerns of the city in which they lived. Their work was self-conscious and elitist and often focused on the past. Prime concerns of the critics were establishing a literary canon and standardizing the texts of the canonical authors. Adopted by the Romans, Alexandrian critical standards have influenced the West to this day.

Of the three greatest Alexandrian writers, two—Callimachus (305–240 B.C.) and Apollonius of Rhodes (b. ca. 295 B.C.)—worked at the Library; the third, Theocritus (ca. 300–ca. 260 B.C.), probably lived on a stipend from the Ptolemies. Popular for centuries, Callimachus was probably the most influential, the complete Hellenistic poet. A native of Cyrene who came to Alexandria as a schoolteacher, Callimachus found a position in the Library. There he composed virtually a universal history of all recorded Greek (and much non-Greek) knowledge.

A prolific writer, Callimachus generally preferred short to long poems: "Big book, big evil," he writes. To be sure, Callimachus admired the epic tradition of Homer, but he had revolutionary plans for poetry. Earlier Greek poets were usually austere and public minded; Callimachus preferred the private, the light, and the exotic. "Don't expect from me a big-sounding poem," he writes; "Zeus thunders, not I."[2] Callimachus was expert at the pithy statement in verse, the epigram.

The Causes, Callimachus's masterwork (of which little survives), was at seven thousand lines his one long poem, but it was a collection of brief vignettes rather than a unified narrative. The central theme is the origins of festivals, customs, institutions, and names, many of them obscure. Arcane diction and complex allusions abounded. Only an elite could understand such writing, but Callimachus was an elitist. "I detest all common things," he wrote.

Another major Alexandrian writer was Callimachus's student Apollonius of Rhodes. Tradition says that Apollonius retired to Rhodes after his masterwork, the epic poem *Argonautica* (*Voyage of the Argo*), was poorly received. The subject is the legend of Jason and the heroes who travel on the ship *Argo* to Colchis, at the far end of the Black Sea, in pursuit of the Golden Fleece (the skin of a winged ram). With the help of the Colchian princess Medea, who falls in love with Jason, the heroes succeed and return home safely after numerous adventures.

Apollonius devotes much of the poem to a discussion of the roots of various names, cults, and customs. The main novelty, however, is a fundamental and pervading doubt about the very possibility of heroism. Apollonius's Jason is no Achilles, no Odysseus. Homer describes

Menander A Roman marble relief, based on a Hellenistic original, shows the playwright Menander and three comic masks. The one he holds represents a young man; those on the table are a young woman (left) and old man (right). *(The Art Museum, Princeton University, Museum purchase, Caroline G. Mather Fund)*

Odysseus as "never at a loss"; Apollonius describes Jason as "helpless." Men move the action in the *Iliad* and the *Odyssey*; Jason depends on a woman, Medea, for his success. Indeed, much of the *Argonautica* focuses on Medea and in particular on her love for Jason. With the exception of the works of Sappho, previous Greek poetry generally either ignores female eroticism or presents it in a hostile light. Apollonius's work illustrates both the improved status of women in Hellenistic ideology and the great interest of the age in the inner life of the emotions. All in all the *Argonautica* is less a traditional epic than an anti-epic (see the box, "Jason and Medea").

Like Callimachus, Theocritus, a native of Syracuse, wrote short, polished poetry. He composed thirty-one subtle and refined poems, many highly experimental, conventionally known as idylls. The subjects and styles are eclectic, ranging from minuscule epics to hymns to mimes. The best-known poems, however, focus on country life. They are the first known pastoral poems; indeed, Theocritus probably invented the genre. Theocritus's pastorals explore nature, but always self-consciously, always with the city in mind. His peasants and shepherds are marvelously cultured; they seem more like townspeople on an excursion than like true rustics. Through his Roman admirers, Theocritus's love of nature has exerted a powerful hold on the Western literary imagination.

Outside the Museum, Alexandria had a lively popular culture, much of it Egyptian or influenced by Egyptian models. A glimpse of it is

Jason and Medea

Poet of an age of uncertainty, Apollonius of Rhodes in* Argonautica *challenges traditional notions of heroism and gender. In this scene the hero Jason depends on his lover Medea to capture the Golden Fleece from the monster guarding it. Notice the contrast between the stereotype of woman as spell-caster and the unusual courage and pluck with which the poet endows Medea.

As... [the monster] writhed he saw the maiden take her stand, and heard her in her sweet voice invoking Sleep, the conqueror of the gods, to charm him. She also called on the night-wandering Queen of the world below to countenance her efforts. Jason from behind looked on in terror. But the giant snake, enchanted by her song, was soon relaxing the whole length of his serrated spine and smoothing out his multitudinous undulations.... Medea called to Jason and he snatched the golden fleece from the oak. But she herself stayed where she was, smearing the wild one's head with a magic salve, till Jason urged her to come back to the ship and she left the sombre grove of Ares.

Lord Jason held up the great fleece in his arms. The shimmering wool threw a fiery glow on his fair cheeks and forehead; and he rejoiced in it, glad as a girl who catches on her silken gown the lovely light of the full moon as it climbs the sky and looks into her attic room.

Source: Apollonius of Rhodes, *Voyage of the Argo*, trans. E. V. Rieu. (Harmondsworth, England: Penguin, 1971), pp. 150–151.

afforded in the seven surviving mimes of an obscure writer named Herondas or Herodas. Although written in literary Greek, they discuss commonplace subjects such as shopping for shoes, tourism, lawsuits, and beatings at school, and titillating themes like adultery and prostitution. Lively, bawdy, and funny, filled with the grit of everyday life in the third century B.C., they are a reminder of just how specialized the culture of the Museum was.

Advances in Science and Medicine

The Ptolemies not only reaped practical benefits in military and agricultural technology from their Museum, but became the patrons of a flourishing period in the history of Greek pure scientific inquiry. They also unwittingly promoted a split between philosophy and science that has characterized much of Western culture since. Antigonid patronage of ethical and political philosophy helped keep Athens pre-eminent in those fields. The study of science, in contrast, tended to move to Alexandria. The rulers of Pergamum and, far to the west, Syracuse, a flourishing Hellenistic city in Sicily, were great patrons of science as well. Wealth, improved communications and literacy, continued warfare, and cross-fertilization between Greek and non-Greek traditions, especially Greek and Babylonian astronomy, were all stimuli of Hellenistic science.

Some of the best-known figures of Hellenistic science were mathematicians. In his *Elements*, the Alexandrian Euclid (worked ca. 300 B.C.) produced a systematic exposition of geometry, hugely influential in both Western and Islamic civilizations. Apollonius of Perge in Anatolia (worked ca. 210 B.C.) did brilliant research on conic sections. A Sicilian Greek, Archimedes of Syracuse (287–212 B.C.), did original work on the geometry of spheres and cylinders, calculated the approximate value of pi (the ratio of a circle's circumference to its diameter), and made important discoveries in astronomy, engineering, optics, and other fields. Archimedes was as great an inventor as he was a theoretician. One of the most important of his inventions was the water snail, also known as Archimedes' screw: a screwlike device to raise water for irrigation. Invented by Archimedes during a stay in Egypt, the screw made it possible to irrigate previously barren land, as did the ox-driven water wheel, another Ptolemaic invention.

Advances in mathematics promoted advances in astronomy. Aristarchus of Samos (worked ca. 275 B.C.) is known for his heliocentric hypothesis, which confounded tradition by having the earth revolve around the sun, instead of the sun around the earth. He was right, but Hellenistic astronomy lacked the data to prove his theory, so it was not unreasonable for Hipparchus of Nicaea (worked ca. 135 B.C.) to insist on the centrality of the earth. A great researcher, Hipparchus also discovered the precession of the equinoxes—that is, the slight annual shift in the time of the occurrence of the autumn and spring equinoxes. Eratosthenes of Cyrene (worked ca. 225 B.C.) was saddled with the frustrating nickname of "Beta" (the second letter of the Greek alphabet) because he was considered second best in every branch of study. This "second best" nonetheless calculated through simple geometry an extraordinarily accurate measurement of the earth's circumference.

Hellenistic medicine thrived in Alexandria. Both Greece and Egypt had long-established medical traditions. Greek medicine was more rationalistic, but Egyptian drugs, and possibly Egyptian doctors' knowledge of the eye as well as their emphasis on measuring, helped stimulate Alexandrian medical progress, as no doubt the mere fact of cross-fertilization did. The key to medical advance, however, was the dissection of human cadavers in Alexandria, a first in the history of science. In Greece, as in many ancient societies, religious tradition demanded that dead bodies not be mutilated; but in the frontier atmosphere of early Alexandria, tradition lost much of its force. Although Egyptians did not practice dissection, they did practice embalming, which may have helped Alexandrian Greeks overcome the taboo against cutting open the human body. Ever supportive of research, the Ptolemies provided corpses to Greek scientists for dissection; indeed, they had condemned criminals sent from prison for scientists to dissect alive. The practice, only a temporary one in the early third century B.C., outraged many writers in antiquity, just as today it would be considered an atrocity.

The leading scientific beneficiary was Herophilus of Chalcedon (ca. 320–250 B.C.), a practicing physician in Alexandria. Among his achievements was the recognition (against Aristotle) that the brain is the center of the nervous system, a careful dissection of the eye, the discovery of the ovaries, and the description of the duodenum, which he named (*duodenum* is a Latin translation of a Greek word meaning "twelve fingers," describing the organ's length). In addition, Herophilus developed a detailed theory of the diagnostic value of measuring pulse rates. His contemporary, Erasistratus of Ceos (ca. 330–255), was another brilliant physician who worked either in Alexandria or in Seleucia (the sources are contradictory). His great achievement was a mechanical theory of organic processes such as digestion and of the workings of the vascular system, which he described in impressive detail.

Hellenistic technology has long fascinated and frustrated scholars. The great engineers invented both numerous engines of war and various "wonderworks" to amuse the royal court; among the latter were mechanical puppets and steam-run toys. Given these advances, why did the Greeks achieve neither an industrial transformation, such as was ushered in by the steam engine around A.D. 1800, nor a scientific revolution along the lines of the one begun in the early modern era by such thinkers as Copernicus and Galileo? Historians are not entirely sure but can venture a guess. Greek machine-making technology was not nearly as sophisticated as that of eighteenth-century Europe. The prevalence of slavery in antiquity, moreover, discouraged the invention of labor-saving machines; steam was used only for playthings and gadgets. A related point is the elitist bias of Greek intellectual life. After Archimedes' death, for example, it was claimed that although Archimedes had written copiously on theoretical matters, he never bothered to write about his mechanical inventions because he considered them "ignoble and vulgar."

Perhaps the most important point is the Greek attitude toward nature. Whereas Jews and Christians learned from the Bible that human beings have dominion over nature, thereby making possible the conclusion that it is appropriate to conquer nature, the Greeks thought in far more limited terms. They believed that nature set limits, that a virtuous person tried to follow nature, not conquer it. Thus, Greek engineers were not inclined to make the revolutionary changes that their modern counterparts have promoted.

Aphrodite of Cnidos A 7½-foot-tall marble statue is a Roman copy of an original by Praxiteles (ca. 350–330 B.C.). Perhaps the most famous of Hellenistic female nudes, the statue was housed in a special shrine where it could be viewed in the round to accommodate all the interest it generated. *(Vatican Museums)*

The Individual in Art and Society

Like Hellenistic literature, Hellenistic art attests to changing male attitudes toward women and toward gender issues. The portrait of Jason and Medea in Apollonius's *Argonautica* makes fun of masculine pretensions and celebrates the triumph of female intelligence. It also presents a sympathetic portrait of a woman's romantic desire for a man, as does Theocritus. In the Classical period, depictions of romantic love were generally restricted to male homoeroticism. Accordingly, statues of naked males were common, but women were usually depicted clothed. Hellenistic sculpture, by contrast, affords many erotic examples of the female nude.

There are indications that the Hellenistic Greek male of the elite was much more willing than his Classical predecessor to see lovemaking as a matter of mutuality and respect. Classical vase-painting often depicts heterosexual lovemaking with the mood lusty and explicit. In Hellenistic vase-painting, in contrast, the emphasis is more often on tenderness and domesticity. Hellenistic males often wrote with sensitivity about satisfying a woman's needs and desires. The vogue in Hellenistic art for representations of Hermaphrodite, the mythical creature who was half female and half male, is attributable perhaps not only to the taste for the exotic but also to a notion that the feminine was as important a part of human nature as the masculine.

Many a Hellenistic artist or writer seems to be as interested in emotion as in action and to focus on the inner as much as on the outer life. Callimachus's poem *Hecale,* for instance, ostensibly about the hero Theseus's defeat of the Bull of Marathon (near Athens), actually focuses on Hecale, an old woman who feeds Theseus in her cottage on his way to and from the battle. Hellenistic art often takes women, children, and domestic scenes as its subject, and representations of warriors often focus on their unrestrained emotions rather than on their soldierly self-control.

Hellenistic women enjoyed small improvements in political and legal status and considerable improvements in economic and ideological status. A number of reasons explain these changes. First, Greek women, particularly in the elite, benefited from the spread of monarchy. For one thing, queens and princesses in royal courts had power and prestige that had been denied women in city-states. For another, under monarchy the notion of the independent citizen-warrior was replaced with that of the loyal and prosperous subject. Citizens in the Classical polis had been encouraged to be aggressive and exaggeratedly masculine to the point of misogyny. Subjects in Hellenistic monarchies were meant to cultivate the more passive and reflective virtues of legalism, obedience, and economic enterprise. Because Greek men associated these virtues with women, their respect for female qualities tended to increase. Too, in the new cities, as in many a frontier society, women more often were permitted to inherit and use property than in old Greece.

It was an era of powerful queens: Olympias, Alexander the Great's mother, played kingmaker after her son's death. Arsinoe II Philadelphus was co-ruler of Egypt with her husband (who was also her brother) for five years at the height of Ptolemaic prosperity around 275 B.C. The most famous Hellenistic woman, Cleopatra VII, was queen of Egypt from 51 to 30 B.C. Although she was the lover of two of the most powerful men in the world, the Romans Julius Caesar and Mark Antony, Cleopatra was no exotic plaything. Rather, she was a brilliant and ambitious strategist who nearly succeeded in winning a world empire for her family. (See the feature, "Weighing the Evidence: Images of Cleopatra" on pages 152–153.)

Writers in the new Hellenistic cities often described freedom of movement for women. Theocritus and Herondas, for example, show women going to a temple or a show. Nor did Hellenistic men, even in Athens, obey Pericles' injunction not to speak of good women. In Hellenistic Athens, aristocratic fathers put up a number of ostentatious inscriptions in honor of their daughters who had participated in the cult of Athena. Although women generally continued to need a male guardian to represent them in public, in some situations, at least in Egypt (where the evidence is most plentiful), a woman could represent herself. A woman could petition the government on her own behalf. Widows and mothers of illegitimate children could give their daughters in marriage or apprentice their sons. A few cities granted women citizenship or even permitted them to hold public office. (See the box, "A Seleucid Queen Helps the City of Iasos.")

Some Hellenistic cities admitted women to the gymnasium, previously an exclusively male preserve. Heretofore only Sparta had promoted physical education for women, but by the first century A.D. women were even competing in the great Pan-Hellenic games. Gymnasia were also centers of education in music and reading; one consequence of growing literacy was the re-emergence of women poets and the first appearance of women philosophers in the West. Before dying at age 19, Erinna, who lived on the Aegean island of Telos during the late fourth century B.C., wrote the *Distaff,* a poem in memory of her childhood friend Baucis. This 300-line poem, famous in antiquity, described the shared experiences of girlhood. Hipparchia of Maroneia (b. ca. 350 B.C.), like her husband Crates of Thebes, studied Cynic philosophy. The Cynics, like another philosophical school, the Epicureans, supported a measure of equality between women and men. Hipparchia and Crates led an itinerant life, as popular teachers and the Hellenistic equivalent of counselors or psychologists.

Much of the explanation for the relative freedom of elite women lies in the new economic power of this group. There was probably a connection between one Phile's ability to hold a magistracy in Priene (in Anatolia) in the first century B.C. and her control of the financial resources to build the town a reservoir and an aqueduct. The new cities were generally far less restrictive of women's economic role than classical poleis like Athens had been. In many cities women could sell land, borrow money, and decide whether their husbands could make loans or contracts on the strength of their dowry. Free women could manumit slaves as well.

The role reversals of male and female in Hellenistic art and literature, therefore, are not merely explorations of the unusual. They are important indicators of changing social and cultural trends. Hellenistic women never attained the kind of equality that sometimes exists between men and women today, but they did enjoy genuine though limited improvements in status. Men and women played new roles in a changed,

A Seleucid Queen Helps the City of Iasos

This letter from Queen Laodike III, wife of Antiochus III (r. 223–187 B.C.), was inscribed on a marble stele in Iasos (in southern Anatolia) around 197 B.C. It sheds interesting light on contemporary politics and society.

Queen Laodike to the Council and the people of the Iasians, greeting. Having heard often from my brother [Antiochus, actually her cousin and husband] both what concern he continues to show his friends and allies and how, on regaining your city which had met with unexpected mishaps, he returned freedom to you, and how he introduced laws and other measures to improve your government and bring it to a better condition, I, desiring also to act in conformity with his earnestness and zeal, and for this reason, to institute some benefaction for the poorer citizens but of general utility to the whole people, have written to Strouthion, the administrator, that yearly for ten years he should have brought into the city one thousand measures of wheat and turn them over to (representatives) of the people. You will, therefore, do well by instructing both the treasurers that, on receiving it, they should sell a set amount, and the presidents and whoever else you may designate, that they are to see that the money realized from these (sales) be assigned to dowries for the daughters of the poorer citizens, giving not more than three hundred Antiochene drachmas to each of those to be married; and as for you, should you act toward my brother and our house in general as is proper and be mindful of all our benefactions, I shall gladly endeavor to arrange also other (benefits) which I may think of.

Source: Adapted from Stanley M. Burstein, ed. and trans., *The Hellenistic Age from the Battle of Ipsos to the Death of Kleopatra VII* (Cambridge, England: Cambridge University Press, 1985), pp. 47–48.

complex world. The new Hellenistic philosophies and religions attempted to address that complexity.

The Turn Inward: New Philosophies, New Faiths

The events of the Hellenistic era generated uncertainty: emigration, a trend from independent city-states to monarchies and federal leagues, new extremes of wealth and poverty, and contact with foreign peoples and customs. As literacy expanded, more Greeks than ever before could participate in cultural debate. New philosophies and religions arose to meet new spiritual concerns, generating ideas that would be influential for centuries.

The meeting of Jews and Greeks proved to be just as significant. Challenged by Greek conquest, Greek colonization, and by their own emigration to Greek lands, Jews alternately embraced Hellenism and engaged in resistance, both cultural and armed. In the process, first Judaism and then Hellenism, through the agency of Christianity, were changed forever.

Stoics, Skeptics, Cynics, and Epicureans

Although the polis lost its military and political pre-eminence in the fourth century B.C., philosophy continued to thrive. It was, however, much changed. With the city-state losing significance as a focus of loyalty, and with the Greek-reading public growing in size and geographical extent, Hellenistic philosophy paid less attention than ever before to politics. Moreover, as we have seen, Hellenistic science tended to become a separate discipline from philosophy. What was left as the prime subject of philosophy was ethics, the discovery of the best way to live one's life. The essence of the good life, most philosophers agreed, was finding peace of mind, or freedom from troubles. Hellenistic philosophers won wide followings; indeed, for many people, primarily in the elite, philosophy became a way of life, even a religion.

Several competing philosophical schools emerged. The most popular was Stoicism, with Epicureanism second. Cynicism, never as widespread, was an important precursor of these two doctrines. Skepticism rejected the main philosophies as mere dogmatism and proposed instead a common-sense attitude toward ethics.

The first Cynic was Diogenes of Sinope (ca. 400–ca. 325 B.C.). An exile in Athens, Diogenes developed a philosophy that rejected all conventions. Happiness, he decided, would be found by satisfying one's natural needs with simplicity. Accordingly, Diogenes chose a life of poverty. A beggar in rags, he delighted in shocking conventional morality. Famous for wit and shamelessness, he was nicknamed "Dog" (*kuon*), because the Greeks considered dogs to be shameless animals; his followers were called "Doglike" (*kunikoi,* whence *Cynic*).

Although he founded no school, Diogenes had followers. One of them, Crates of Thebes (ca. 365–285 B.C.), was the teacher of Zeno (335–263 B.C.), who began one of the most important philosophical systems of antiquity: Stoicism. Zeno came to Athens in 313 B.C. from Citium in Cyprus, a multiethnic city; he was possibly of Phoenician origin. Influenced both by Cynicism and by Socratic philosophy, Zeno developed his own doctrines, which he taught in the Stoa Poikile ("Painted Porch," whence the name *Stoic*), a public building.

Like Plato and Aristotle, Zeno sought an absolute standard of good on which to base philosophical decisions. He found it in the divine reason (*logos*), which he considered the organizing principle of the universe and the guide to human behavior. The best life was a life in pursuit of wisdom—that is, a life of philosophy. Only that rare and forbidding figure, the Sage, could truly attain wisdom; ordinary people could merely progress toward it. What was required was study and the attempt to free oneself from all passion.

Stoicism may seem harsh; it is not surprising that *stoical* has come to describe austere indifference to pain. In some ways, however, Stoicism was comforting. First, freedom from passion was meant to bring peace of mind and happiness. Second, unlike Plato, the Stoics were empiricists—that is, they trusted the evidence of the senses. Third, the common share in divine logos entailed a common human brotherhood—led, to be sure, by a Greek-speaking elite. Fourth, the Stoics had a strong practical bent and argued that a good man should play an active role in public life (see the box, "Early Stoic Ethics and Politics").

Like Hellenistic poets or portraitists, the Stoics emphasized the inner life. They believed that intentions matter. This belief was an important Stoic departure from Greek tradition, which tended to emphasize the outcome of an action, whether intended or not. Stoicism also departed from traditional Greek localism, embracing a more cosmopolitan outlook. "This world is a great city, [and] has one constitution and one law," wrote Philo of Alexandria (30 B.C.–A.D. 45), a Stoic and a Jew. Many Stoics believed in a natural law or law of nations—overarching and common principles to govern international relations.

With its emphasis on duty and order, Stoicism became popular with Greek ruling elites, both Macedonian kings and their opponents in city-states and leagues. Stoicism would enjoy even greater success with the Romans, who found its strictures congenial to their own stern morality and who used its concept of a universal state to justify their empire. A great deal of Stoicism was later embraced by the early Christian writers.

Epicurus (341–270 B.C.), an Athenian citizen, founded his philosophical school at around the same time as Zeno founded Stoicism. There were other similarities: Both schools were empiricist and materialist (that is, they tended to trust the evidence of the senses), both sought peace of mind, and both inspired widespread followings. Epicurus, however, taught not in a public place but in a private garden. Whereas the Stoics encouraged political participation, Epicureans

Early Stoic Ethics and Politics

The Roman Marcus Tullius Cicero (100–44 B.C.) studied Greek philosophy in Athens and was influenced by Stoicism, on whose basic ethical and political teachings he sheds light here.

In the case of all the philosophers mentioned, their End of Goods logically follows: with Aristippus [a philosopher from Cyrene, date uncertain], it is simply pleasure; with the Stoics, harmony with nature, which they interpret as meaning virtuous living, i.e., the morally good life, and further explain this as meaning to live with an understanding of the natural course of events, selecting things that are in accordance with nature and rejecting the opposite. . . .

They [the Stoics] hold that the universe is governed by divine will; it is a city or state of which both men and gods are members, and each one of us is a part of this universe; from which it is a natural consequence that we should prefer the common advantage to our own. For just as the laws set the safety of all above the safety of individuals, so a good, wise and law-abiding man, conscious of his duty to the state, studies the advantage of all more than that of himself or of any single individual. The traitor to his country does not deserve greater reprobation than the man who betrays the common advantage or security for the sake of his own advantage or security. This explains why praise is owed to one who dies for the commonwealth, because it becomes us to love our country more than ourselves.

Source: Jason L. Saunders, ed., *Greek and Roman Philosophy After Aristotle* (New York: Free Press, 1966), pp. 113, 125–126.

counseled withdrawal from the rough and tumble of public life. "Calm" and "Live in hiding" are famous Epicurean maxims.

Epicurus' materialism is based on the atomic theory of Democritus (see page 109). Epicurean materialism envisions a thoroughly mechanistic universe. The gods exist but play no active role in events. One need fear neither capricious deities nor an unhappy afterlife, because the soul is merely a combination of atoms that ceases to exist after death. What might be the purpose of life in such an unheroic universe? The answer was the avoidance of pain and pursuit of pleasure. The latter was called "hedonism" (*pleasure* is *hedone* in Greek), but Epicureans meant intellectual pleasure, not the pursuit of food, drink, or sex. Friendship and fraternity were Epicurean ideals—the private analogs, as it were, of Stoic brotherhood.

The Epicureans raised eyebrows and sometimes ire, occasionally coming in for persecution by the state. They were accused of atheism and sensuality. Classical Greek philosophy defined virtue as the highest good. The Epicurean emphasis on pleasure, even spiritual pleasure, seemed perverse to some. Yet Epicureanism was simple, sure of itself, practical, and offered both friendship and a sense of community. It became a popular philosophy, especially among the wealthy.

Skepticism was founded by Pyrrho of Elis (ca. 360–ca. 270 B.C.), a Greek who traveled with Alexander to India. Like Stoics and Epicureans, Skeptics sought peace of mind. They rejected those thinkers' conclusions, however, on the grounds that they were dogmatic—that is, based not on positive proof but merely on opinion (*doxa*). Considering the senses unreliable, Skeptics rejected the common-sense approach of Stoics and Epicureans. In their opinion, one had to suspend judgment on the great philosophical questions. Having done so, a person could accept the customs of the community, avoid politics, and thereby obtain peace of mind. Such a doctrine might appeal to practical people, and, indeed, the main source of Skeptic philosophy is the writing of a Greek physician, Sextus Empiricus (worked ca. A.D. 200).

The Mystery Religions

The traditional Greek religion of the Olympian gods came under attack on every front in the Hellenistic era. First, as the stock of the polis fell, so did that of the Olympians. The Greeks considered specific gods to be embodiments of particular cities. For example, Athena embodied Athens, and Heracles embodied Thebes. After Alexander's conquests, however, the Olympians had to share the spotlight with divinized kings like Alexander himself.

A second attack came from philosophy. Archaic and Classical philosophers had criticized the Olympians as primitive, unsophisticated, and immoral. Hellenistic thinkers stepped up the salvos and reached a wider audience as philosophy became more popular and literacy spread.

A third attack came from science and scholarship. Around 300 B.C., Euhemerus of Messene wrote in his Sacred Scripture that Zeus, Ouranos, and Kronos were not divine beings but merely great kings of the past who were rewarded with divinization, much like a Hellenistic monarch. Debunking the Olympians became a popular literary pastime. For instance, Poseidon was said to be worshiped as the sea-god because he had been the first shipbuilder, and Hades, god of the dead, was said to have invented burial rites.

The Olympians continued to be worshiped at temples, but the rituals seemed ever more hollow and antiquarian. What was to replace them? Of the several new religious movements that marked the age, three stand out: the divinization of kings, the cult of Tyche (Fortune), and the various mystery religions.

Under the Ptolemies and Seleucids, the ruler-worship that Alexander had demanded became standard procedure. Many subjects no doubt considered the divinity of their king or queen merely a patriotic formality; others treated the divinized monarch as something like a patron saint who could intercede for them in heaven. The old Greek city-states, especially the democracies, bristled at ruler-worship. "To transfer to men the honor due to the gods," the Athenian playwright Philippides (active ca. 300 B.C.) wrote, "is to dissolve the democracy."

He might have said much the same about the popular Hellenistic cult of Tyche (Fortune or Luck), often worshiped as a goddess, sometimes as the protective deity of a particular city. The most famous example was the Tyche of Antioch, personified as a statue of a woman wearing the battlements of the city on her head as a kind of crown—a very popular statue, to judge by the many copies found around the Hellenistic world. In the often-confusing expanse of that world, many people felt that only luck could help them.

The third major Hellenistic trend, the mystery religions, addressed spiritual needs similar to those addressed by the philosophical schools: ethical guidance, comfort, release from worries, reassurance about death, and a sense of unity. Unlike philosophies, however, they achieved their goals through the revelation of secret doctrines, or "mysteries," into which worshipers were initiated. Long a feature of Greek religion, mystery cults grew greatly in popularity during Hellenistic times. Consider the cult of Demeter at Eleusis, a town just outside the city of Athens. Demeter was the goddess of fertility. Her daughter Persephone supposedly spent half of the year in the underworld, among the dead, but came back to earth each spring. As told to initiates, the myth symbolized the promise of a blessed afterlife.

Various new mystery religions from outside Greece became even more popular, particularly the Hellenized Egyptian cults of Serapis and of Isis. The Serapis cult was created under Ptolemy I. Serapis was meant to combine Osiris, the Egyptian god of the afterlife, with Pluto, the Greek god of the underworld. Hence, it was an early example of the increasingly common Hellenistic practice of religious syncretism. Despite its roots, Serapis-worship had little appeal to native Egyptians, but the god became popular throughout the Greek world as patron of healing and sailing.

Another traditional Egyptian deity, Osiris's wife Isis, was also turned into a popular Greek and, later, Roman goddess. Called the "Goddess of Ten Thousand Names," Isis was said to symbolize all the female deities of antiquity. Hers was a cult of the afterlife and of the suffering but tender and loving mother; she was particularly popular among women. Thus, under Ptolemaic sponsorship, ancient Egyptian cults were recast and

The Jews Struggle over Hellenism

Greek colonists introduced Hellenic customs to Palestine in the second century B.C. The Jewish response varied greatly, from eager assimilation to violent resistance, as is demonstrated by the following selections from the First Book of Maccabees, written around 100 B.C.

At that time, lawless men arose in Israel and seduced many with their plea, "Come, let us make a covenant with the gentiles around us, because ever since we have kept ourselves separated from them we have suffered many evils." The plea got so favorable a reception that some of the people took it upon themselves to apply to the king, who granted them liberty to follow the practices of the gentiles. Thereupon they built a gymnasium in Jerusalem according to the customs of the gentiles. . . . They joined themselves to the gentiles and became willing slaves to evildoing. . . .

The king [Antiochus IV] wrote to all his kingdom, for all to become one people and for each to abandon his own customs. All the gentiles agreed to the terms of the king's proclamation. Many Israelites, too, accepted his religion and sacrificed to idols and violated the Sabbath. . . .

Many Israelites strongly and steadfastly refused to eat forbidden food. They chose death in order to escape defilement by foods and in order to keep from violating the Holy Covenant, and they were put to death. Indeed, very great wrath had struck Israel. . . .

[An Israelite sacrifices to Zeus.] When [the Jewish priest] Mattathias saw this, he was filled with zeal and trembled with rage and let his anger rise, as was fitting; he ran and slew him upon the altar. At the same time he also killed the king's official in charge of enforcing sacrifices, and he destroyed the altar.

Source: The First Book of Maccabees, in *The Anchor Bible,* vol. 41 (New York: Doubleday, 1976).

spread throughout the Greek-speaking world, circulating such notions as the suffering mother, the Last Judgment, and blessed eternal life after death. Early Christianity was much influenced by such Greco-Egyptian religious notions, but it was more directly the product of debate and ferment within Hellenistic Judaism.

Hellenistic Judaism

Few consequences of Alexander's conquests would have so lasting an impact as the mixing of Greeks and Jews. Before Alexander took Judea from the Persians in 332 B.C., the two peoples had relatively little contact. In the Hellenistic era their fates became intertwined. The Greeks governed Judea and then lost it to a Jewish independence movement; meanwhile millions of Jews settled in Egypt, Syria, Anatolia, and Greece. When the "people of the book" met the people of myth and philosophy, the resulting relationship was one of fascination and hatred, assimilation and violence, conversion and apostasy, Hellenophilia and anti-Semitism. In the end the Romans, successors to the Greeks, destroyed the Jewish state, but the Jewish religion and the Jewish people survived. One might say, moreover, that the Jews forever changed the Greco-Roman soul through Christianity, which had roots in Judaism although it went its own way. Ethical monotheism and a moral code based on intentions and guilt, rather than on actions and shame, triumphed.

Hellenistic Judea was governed first by the Ptolemies until 200 B.C., afterward by the Seleucids, until the establishment of an independent Jewish state in 142 B.C., which came under Roman suzerainty in 63 B.C. The Greeks were not absentee rulers. Rather, they established a large number of Greek colonies in and around Judea, especially under the Seleucids. For many in the Jewish upper classes, the prestige of the dominant culture was irresistible. They abandoned Jewish customs for the Greek gymnasium, theater, and political institutions. With the help of the Seleucid king Antiochus IV Epiphanes (r. 175–163 B.C.), Jewish Hellenizers in 175 B.C. had Jerusalem proclaimed a Greek polis, renamed Antioch, like many a Seleucid city; they even built a gymnasium at the foot of the Temple Mount. In 167 they went further by in effect abolishing Judaism. They outlawed Sabbath observance, prohibited circumcision, and rededicated the Temple to Olympian Zeus.

The traditionalists, however, resisted; aided by the political ineptitude of their opponents, who raised taxes, they rallied the Jewish masses into opposition. Soon a guerrilla revolt began in the countryside, led by the Hasmonean (Maccabee) family of the Maccabees, whose successes are still celebrated by Jews at Hanukkah (see the box, "The Jews Struggle over Hellenism").

The guerrilla movement developed into a disciplined armed uprising, which forced the Seleucids to tolerate an independent state under the Hasmonean dynasty. Religiously conservative at home, the state was expansionist abroad, conquering nearby territories such as the Galilee and forcing their inhabitants to convert to Judaism.

During the struggle over Hellenism, new elements of lasting significance became part of Judaism. First, the Jews developed a literature of spiritual resistance to the foreigner. This literature was apocalyptic—that is, it claimed to reveal dramatic, secret truths. Drawing both on biblical and Mesopotamian traditions, Jewish apocalyptic writing predicted a future cataclysm, when a royal redeemer would evict the foreigner and establish a new kingdom of Israel. The redeemer was often identified with another notion that first became popular in this era: the Messiah (literally, "anointed one"), someone anointed with oil signifying his election as king, a descendant of King David, who would save Israel. Another new aspect of Hellenistic Judaism was martyrdom, the notion of the holy sacrifice of one's life for a religious cause. There was also a growing belief in a final judgment day and resurrection, when God would raise the meritorious dead to live again on earth in their own bodies.

Hellenistic Judaism was far from monolithic. Various sects each proposed its own version of Judaism. Among these sects were the Sadducees ("righteous ones"), a wealthy establishment group for whom the rituals of the Jerusalem Temple were the heart of Judaism. Their opponents, the Pharisees ("those who separated themselves"), insisted on the validity of the oral tradition of interpretation alongside the written law of the Hebrew Bible and the Temple rituals. The Pharisees proposed a kind of democratization of Judaism, emphasizing study and prayer in small groups. A third group was the Essenes, probably to be identified with the Qumran community in the Judean desert (see page 220). As for the Hellenizers, although some were merely place-seekers, others sincerely wished to combine Jewish ethical monotheism with the cosmopolitan spirit of Hellenistic civilization. They wanted, in short, to bring Jewish teachings to non-Jews or Gentiles ("the nations").

Bronze Coin with Menorah This issue of Mattathias Antigone (r. 40–37 B.C.), the last Hasmonean king, is an early example of the use of the seven-branched candelabrum as the symbol of the Jewish people. A similar candelabrum was used in the Temple of Jerusalem. *(Erich Lessing/Art Resource, NY)*

Greek was the common tongue of diaspora Jews, replacing Hebrew and Aramaic. Most Jews of the Hellenistic era lived outside Judea. The diaspora had spread into (among other places) Syria, Anatolia, the Greek mainland, and Egypt, where a strong Jewish presence during the

Persian period grew even greater, particularly in Alexandria. It is estimated that Jews made up 40 percent of the population of Alexandria at the height of Jewish prosperity, in the first century A.D. Tensions simmered between the large Jewish minority and the Greek majority in Alexandria. Greeks found the presence of so considerable a competing community threatening, and they looked down on Jewish dietary laws, circumcision, and other customs. Such attitudes spawned the first anti-Semitic literature as well as sporadic violence that at times broke into riots and persecution.

Summary

Histories of Hellenistic Greece tend to be organized thematically rather than chronologically, a reflection of a period whose individual political actors appear dwarfed by the broad societal trends. The major legacy of the Hellenistic age was its culture. On the elite level, that culture was dominated by Greek-speakers, mostly inhabitants of or immigrants from old Greece and their descendants. The far-sighted Pan-Hellenic ideas of Isocrates smoothed the way for Greeks of different city-states to unite in kingdoms but offered less hope to others. Some natives of the conquered territories were able to learn Greek and join the elite, and some Greeks learned a smattering (occasionally more) of native languages and customs, but the numbers were relatively small. In general, Greeks and Macedonians were the colonial masters; Egyptians, Syrians, Persians, and their neighbors, the conquered peoples.

The most important cultural development of the age was a retreat from a complex of values associated with the citizen-warrior ideal of the Classical city-state. The polis came under the shadow of federal leagues and kingdoms; philosophers questioned the very point of political activity. The hero gave way to the antihero, often a man whose success was dependent on the kindness and love of a woman. The female nude became as important a subject for sculptors as the male nude. Hellenistic women were freer than their predecessors in their movement and their ability to hold property and to have some say in public life.

Stoic philosophers were far more interested in intention than were their Classical predecessors. Yet their interest in the subject pales before that of the Jews, new actors on the Greek stage. Judaism placed an emphasis on the interior dialogue between humans and the divine that was more radical than anything in the Greek tradition. Some Greeks admired Jewish ethics, but few were willing to accept Jewish laws and rituals. Greeks did, however, borrow from other native religions. Hellenistic religion, therefore, was an exception to the general Greek indifference to native culture. The common denominator of the new religious teachings was a close, personal relationship with a savior-god who would guarantee comfort, peace, and eternal life after death.

Ironically, these very doctrines brought their Greek adherents closer to Hellenistic Judaism, which preached righteousness and justice in this life and the hereafter through subordination to the truth of the one and only god. The Jewish doctrine of messianic kingship might even have reminded Greeks of their own ruler cults. Imperceptibly, Hellenic and Hebraic were drawing closer. Under the Roman successor state, Hellenism and Judaism would be combined in a new and powerful form: Christianity.

Notes

1. Isocrates, "Panegyricus," trans. H. I. Marrou, in *A History of Education in Antiquity,* trans. George Lamb (New York: Mentor Books/New American Library, 1956), p. 130.
2. Quoted in Charles Rowan Beye, *Ancient Greek Literature and Society,* 2d ed., rev. (Ithaca, N.Y.: Cornell University Press, 1987), p. 265.

Suggested Reading

General Surveys

Grant, Michael. *From Alexander to Cleopatra: The Hellenistic World.* 1982. A lively and readable introduction, at its best on cultural history.

Green, P. *Alexander to Actium: An Essay in the Historical Evolution of the Hellenistic Age.* 1989. A collection of elegant essays synthesizing scholarship on a wide variety of topics in political, cultural, and social history.

Walbank, F. W. *The Hellenistic World.* 1982. A scholarly introduction by a distinguished historian; particularly good on politics.

Walbank, F. W., et al., eds. *The Cambridge Ancient History,* 2d ed. Vol. VII, Pt. 1, *The Hellenistic World.* 1984. Vol. VIIA, *Plates to Volume VII, Part 1.* New ed. 1984.

An advanced-level survey from Alexander's death in 323 B.C. to the battle of Raphia in 217 B.C.

Philip and Alexander

Badian, E. "Alexander the Great and the Loneliness of Power." In Badian, *Studies in Greek and Roman History,* 192–205. 1964. A brilliant though speculative analysis of the moral costs of Alexander's success.

Cawkwell, G. *Philip of Macedon.* 1978. A short and lively introduction, written in an engaging prose style.

Green, P. *Alexander of Macedon, 356–323 B.C.: A Historical Biography.* 1991. A longer, more detailed study than Hamilton's, written in a polished style.

Hamilton, J. R. *Alexander the Great.* 1973. A reliable and remarkably concise introduction.

Nations and Regions

Bowman, Alan K. *Egypt After the Pharaohs.* 1986. An excellent and highly readable introduction to the social history of the Ptolemaic and later periods.

Ferguson, W. S. *Hellenistic Athens.* 1911. An older book but still a thoughtful, thorough, and delightful narrative account.

Kuhrt, Amelie, and Susan Sherwin-White, eds. *Hellenism in the East: The Interaction of Greek and Non-Greek Civilizations from Syria to Central Asia After Alexander.* 1987. An important collection of essays emphasizing the importance of Mesopotamia to the Seleucid kings and the importance of native elites in Seleucid administration.

Lewis, N. *Greeks in Ptolemaic Egypt.* 1986. An innovative reconstruction of the history of several families, some native and some Greek, across the span of the Ptolemaic period.

Samuel, A. E. *The Shifting Sands of History: Interpretations of Ptolemaic Egypt.* 1989. An extremely useful guide to the variety of modern scholarly appraisals.

Schürer, Emil. *History of the Jewish People in the Age of Jesus Christ (175 B.C.–A.D. 135).* Rev. ed. 3 vols. 1973–1978. A classic and fundamental study, updated by Geza Vermes and Fergus Millar.

Sedlar, Jean W. *India and the Greek World: A Study in the Transmission of Culture.* 1980. A thoughtful and readable study, emphasizing philosophy and religion.

Shimron, Benjamin. *Late Sparta: The Spartan Revolution, 243–146 B.C.* 1972. A detailed, analytical narrative.

Society

Crawford, Dorothy J. *Kerkeosiris: An Egyptian Village in the Ptolemaic Period.* 1971. A fascinating glimpse of local social history.

Grant, Michael. *Cleopatra.* 1972. A very readable biography, well documented and nicely illustrated.

Griffith, G. T. *Mercenaries of the Hellenistic World.* 1935. A lively study of mercenaries as a fighting force and of their background and way of life.

Pomeroy, Sarah B. *Goddesses, Whores, Wives, and Slaves: Women in Classical Antiquity.* 1975. Chapter 7, "Hellenistic Women," is a sound introductory survey of the Hellenistic era.

———. *Women in Hellenistic Egypt from Alexander to Cleopatra.* 1984. A social history that documents women's growing autonomy.

Rostovtzeff, M. I. *Social and Economic History of the Hellenistic World.* 2d ed. 3 vols. 1953. An exhaustive survey by a great and original historian, although many of the conclusions are no longer accepted.

Science, Literature, Religion, and Art

Beye, C. R. *Ancient Greek Literature and Society.* 2d ed. 1987. The last chapter, "The New Athens," is a succinct and lively introduction to the cultural and social trends found in Alexandrian poetry.

Bickerman, Elias J. "The Historical Foundations of Postbiblical Judaism." In Louis Finkelstein, ed., *The Jews: Their History,* 4th ed. 72–118. 1970. A sound, succinct, and stimulating survey of Jewish religion and history from the return from Babylon to the Maccabees.

Ferguson, J. *Callimachus.* 1980. A brief survey of the evidence for Callimachus's works, as well as a discussion of Alexandrian culture and of Callimachus's long-term literary importance.

Hutchinson, G. O. *Hellenistic Poetry.* 1988. A good introduction, with an emphasis on the third century B.C.

Lloyd, G. E. R. *Greek Science After Aristotle.* 1973. An excellent introduction to science and society, with a discussion of philosophy and of scientific culture and institutions as well as of the specific achievements of mathematics and science. Many helpful diagrams.

Long, A. A. *Hellenistic Philosophy: Stoics, Epicureans, Sceptics.* 2d ed. 1986. A concise critical analysis of the main ideas and methods of thought of the major Hellenistic philosophers.

Momigliano, A. D. *Alien Wisdom: The Limits of Hellenization.* 1975. A brilliant, influential, and challenging essay on the interaction of Greeks with other cultures.

Onians, J. *Art and Thought in the Hellenistic Age: The Greek World View, 350–50 B.C.* 1979. An account that emphasizes the reshaping of the classical Greek artistic heritage in a new age.

Von Staden, Heinrich. *Herophilus: The Art of Medicine in Early Alexandria.* 1989. A detailed, scholarly account. The first chapter ("Alexandrian and Egyptian Medicine") is a balanced discussion of the relative importance (or lack thereof) of Egyptian medicine for the early Greek physicians of Alexandria.

Weighing the Evidence

IMAGES OF CLEOPATRA

"Cleopatra's nose: if it had been shorter, the whole face of the earth would have changed," wrote the French philosopher Blaise Pascal (1623–1662). He does Cleopatra an injustice. It was not a pretty face and classical features that enabled her to win the throne of Egypt (r. 51–30 B.C.), to obtain first Julius Caesar and then Mark Antony as ally and lover, and finally to come close to gaining control of the Roman Empire. Intelligence, daring, charm, and extraordinary diplomatic skill account for Cleopatra's success.

Let us consider the queen's manipulation of her public image: no mean task, given the fragility of Ptolemaic power in the first century B.C. Within Egypt, the monarch had to satisfy several different ethnic groups. Most important were the Greeks and Macedonians—who dominated government, the military, and the economy—and the native Egyptian majority. Daughter of Ptolemy XII (r. 80–51 B.C.), Cleopatra was supposed to rule jointly with her brother, but they had a falling-out. She wrested the throne from him and then from another brother and thus had to assert her legitimacy. Also, Ptolemaic Egypt had to project an image of unity to the Romans, who were threatening to annex it as they had the other Hellenistic monarchies.

Bronze Coin of Cleopatra *(Courtesy of the Trustees of the British Museum)*

Cleopatra, like earlier Ptolemaic monarchs, met these challenges by presenting two faces to the world. To the Greeks and Romans she was a Hellenistic monarch; to the Egyptians she was an ancient queen. Look first at the bronze coin of Cleopatra issued at Alexandria probably in the 30s B.C. The queen is shown as a young woman. Her hair, tied in a bun at the nape of her neck, is in the so-called melon style often seen in Hellenistic female portraits. She wears a diadem (royal headband), its ends hanging behind her neck. More commonly worn by Hellenistic kings than by queens, the diadem signifies Cleopatra's claim to authority.

So does the queen's profile. She is portrayed with a prominent chin, a large mouth, and a rugged nose. These features may not be the standard attributes of beauty, but they are precisely the features of coin portraits of Cleopatra's father. By emphasizing Cleopatra's physical similarity to her father, the portrait artist perhaps subtly suggests her right to sit on his throne.

The side of the coin not shown here is far from subtle: Its legend states clearly in Greek, "Queen Cleopatra." The illustration is of an eagle and thunderbolt and a double cornucopia (horn of plenty) entwined with a diadem. The eagle and thunderbolt recall the Greek god Zeus, and the two cornucopias suggest fertility and prosperity. All are recurrent symbols of Ptolemaic royalty. The coin thus portrays Cleopatra as a Greek monarch, the worthy heir of her father. It would have been an effective image in Alexandria, a city dominated by the Greeks and visited by Romans, but not in the countryside, especially south of the Nile Delta, in Upper Egypt, an area that was

Relief of Cleopatra and Caesarion *(Erich Lessing/Art Resource, NY)*

primarily Egyptian. Following dynastic custom, Cleopatra changed her image there.

In Upper Egypt, earlier Ptolemies frequently had been represented in stone in traditional pharaonic style, and they were great restorers of ancient Egyptian temples and builders of new ones. Look at the sculptural relief from the temple of the Egyptian cow-goddess Hathor at Dendera in Upper Egypt. The temple was a monumental structure to whose construction Ptolemy XII had contributed. Cleopatra, his daughter, added an enormous relief on the outside of the rear wall. Carved into the stone are two persons carrying offerings for Egyptian deities. The persons are Cleopatra (left) and her son Ptolemy XV Caesar, who ruled with his mother from 44 to 30 B.C. Alleged to be the illegitimate son of Julius Caesar, Ptolemy XV was commonly known as Caesarion or "little Caesar." At Dendera, however, he and his mother are shown neither as Romans nor as Greeks but as Egyptians.

Look closely at Cleopatra. She wears a long body-hugging robe. On her head is a royal headdress with symbols of the Egyptian gods: the lyre-shaped cow horns and sun-disk of Hathor, the tall plumes of Isis, and the ram's horn of Amon. Caesarion is shown as a pharaoh, wearing the double crown of Upper and Lower Egypt. Mother and son offer incense to the local deities. The small figure between Caesarion and Cleopatra is his *ka,* or soul.

Cleopatra's face is in profile but otherwise has very little in common with her portrait on the Alexandrian coin. Although the features are stylized pharaonic commonplaces, the shape of her head perhaps echoes the elegant and graceful relief portraits of Hatshepsut (r. 1479–1457 B.C.), the most famous female pharaoh before Cleopatra.

Cleopatra commissioned other artworks and monuments in the native style in the Nile Valley. This was the custom of her dynasty, and Cleopatra had absorbed its traditions, but she stands second to none of the Ptolemies in shrewdness and subtlety. She was the only Ptolemaic monarch to learn to speak Egyptian, and she was the only one to come even close to gaining the upper hand over Rome. As the artifacts shown here indicate, she was able to put on an Egyptian face as easily as a Greek one, but she never lost sight of her true interests.

CHAPTER 5

The Rise of the Roman Republic

There are many monuments to the ancient Romans, ranging from amphitheaters and aqueducts to law codes to Spanish, French, and the other languages derived from Latin, the language of the Romans. Practical monuments all, but that is appropriate, for the Romans were a practical people. Virgil (70–19 B.C.), for example, the greatest Roman poet, (see pages 209–210), celebrates not his countrymen's artistry or cultivation but rather their pragmatic accomplishments:

> For other peoples will, I do not doubt,
> still cast their bronze to breathe with softer features,
> or draw out of the marble living lines,
> plead causes better, trace the ways of heaven
> with wands and tell the rising constellations;
> but yours will be the rulership of nations,
> remember, Romans, these will be your arts:
> to teach the ways of peace to those you conquer,
> to spare defeated peoples, tame the proud.[1]

The Romans were innovators in legal science and masters of political mythmaking and propaganda, but they are best known as imperialists. Heirs of Cyrus and Alexander, the Romans turned an Italian city-state into one of the largest empires in history. Rome first conquered Italy and then all the countries of the Mediterranean as well as substantial parts of western Asia and much of Europe. By holding this empire for centuries and by fostering prosperity, Rome planted in what would become Britain, France, Germany, and Spain (among other places), the seeds of the advanced

The Forum,
Rome.

civilizations of the Mediterranean, seeds that would burst into flower centuries later.

Rome is no less important for its influence on the Western civic tradition. Much of the modern vocabulary of politics, from *president* to *inauguration* to *council,* can be traced back to Rome. After an early period of monarchy, Rome was for centuries a Republic (Latin, *res publica,* literally "public thing") before essentially becoming a monarchy again under the Caesars. The Roman Republic was far more hierarchical than Greek democracy. Greek democrats governed themselves; Roman citizens elected their leaders, aristocrats with wide powers of office. To create an effective and stable regime, the elite wisely divided power among separate government bodies, creating a system of checks and balances that tended toward consensus. The elite also manipulated with skill the symbols of authority.

Roman elite politicians sought to control ordinary citizens but in some ways were more flexible than Greek democrats: Unlike Greece, Rome extended its citizenship to a large population, first throughout Italy and then across its entire empire. The modern nation-state with its mass citizenship owes much to Rome. Indeed, although Rome was not democratic, modern democracy—that is, popular government with a large population, whose officials are elected by the people—has roots in the Roman Republic as well as in the Greek city-state.

Fueled by fear, ambition, and greed, Roman expansion generated its own momentum. In tracing it, one shudders at the parallel paths of Roman success and arrogance: at the consolidation of power over huge territories alongside the mounting number of war atrocities, peoples enslaved, and cities destroyed with but little provocation. One also marvels at the irony of the process by which success slowly undermined both the solidarity of Rome's governing elite and the socioeconomic basis of the Roman army. Masters of war and diplomacy, the Romans unknowingly weakened their society with every brick they added to the edifice of empire. One marvels too at the open-mindedness with which the Romans borrowed from other societies, in particular from the Etruscans and Greeks, to whom the Republic owed huge cultural debts. Still more interesting is the shrewdness and generosity with which the Romans shared their citizenship with the elites whom they had conquered, thereby winning their loyalty and strengthening Rome's grip on their territory.

Historians conventionally divide the Republic into three periods: Early (509–287 B.C.), Middle (287–133 B.C.), and Late (133–31 B.C.). This chapter focuses on the rise of the Roman Republic, from the origins of the city of Rome in the early first millennium B.C. to the imperial conquests of the second century B.C. Chapter 6 turns to the collapse of the Republic in the second and first centuries B.C. and the achievements of the Roman Empire in the first three centuries A.D.

The World of Early Italy

Romans in the third century B.C. believed that their city was founded by Romulus, the descendant of immigrants to Italy from far-off Troy. In the first century B.C. a Roman scholar even supplied a precise date for the founding: April 21, 753, by our reckoning.

Although the name "Romulus" supplies a convenient etymology for "Rome," little stock can be placed in the date, the association with Romulus, or the connection to Troy. No history of Rome was written before the late third century B.C., and no history survives before the mid-second century (five and six hundred years after 753 B.C., respectively). In the third century, however, Rome conquered the Greek cities of southern Italy and was captivated by their cultural richness. The Trojan connection was probably invented to give educated Romans a prestigious pedigree that recalled Greek epic but was nonetheless non-Greek.

Archaeology nevertheless provides a kind of confirmation of Roman tradition. Tombs as early as the tenth century B.C. have been found in Rome, but the first evidence of buildings comes from the eighth century B.C. A simple village of farmers and shepherds—a collection of huts—was established then on the Palatine Hill, one of the seven hills of what would be Rome and the place where tradition puts the settlement of 753. Other, similar settlements followed on two or three of Rome's other hills (see inset, Map 5.2).

Archaeological evidence does not mean that we have to accept mythology as history, but it does revive basic questions: What were Rome's origins, and how did Rome grow? The best data are the increasingly detailed archaeological record and elements in ancient historiography that seem to be based on accurate tradition. Many of the details in that historiography are questionable, but the outlines are clear.

Geography and Earliest Cultures of Italy

Italy is a long peninsula, shaped roughly like a boot, extending about 750 miles from the Alps into the Mediterranean (Map 5.1). The Adriatic Sea to the east separates Italy from modern Slovenia and Croatia; to the west, the Tyrhennian Sea faces the large islands of Sardinia and Corsica (and the smaller but iron-rich island of Elba) and the coasts of France and Spain beyond. Across from the "toe" of the Italian boot, and separated from the mainland by a narrow, 3-mile strait of water, is the island of Sicily, large and in antiquity agriculturally rich. Sicily is only 90 miles from North Africa. In short, Italy is centrally located in the Mediterranean and was thus both a tempting target for conquerors and a useful springboard for conquest.

Even within Italy, the prospects for conquest were tempting. The Italian peninsula is divided into a number of distinct geographical regions. In the far north, the high Alps provide a barrier, though not an impenetrable one, to the rest of Europe.

South of the Alps lies some of the ancient Mediterranean's most fertile and metal-rich land. In the north is the rich alluvial plain of the Padus (modern Po) and Adige rivers. Traveling south along the west coast of Italy, one enters in turn the lowland alluvial plains of Etruria (modern Tuscany), Latium (the region of Rome), and Campania (the region of Naples). Each region is fertile, and in antiquity each was a center of agriculture and civilization. Although the Apennine mountains run southward about 800 miles along most of the Italian peninsula (from Genoa through central Italy and then southwest into Bruttium), they are relatively low and contain many passes, facilitating the movement of armies. The upland valleys of the Apennine sustain pasturage and agriculture.

In the middle of the first millennium B.C., Italy was a complex mix of peoples and languages. Etruria belonged to the Etruscans. Campania had been settled mainly by Greek colonists. Latium was home to a number of small Latin-speaking towns, one of them Rome. Of the many other early Italian peoples, two of the most important for Rome would be the Sabines and the Samnites. The Sabines, who alternated among war, cultural interchange, and intermarriage with Rome, lived northeast of Rome in Apennine villages. The Samnites, a better-organized and fiercer military foe, inhabited the southern Apennines. In the fifth century B.C. another important people appeared on the Italian scene: Celts (called Gauls by the Romans), large numbers of whom crossed the Alps and settled in northern Italy after roughly 500 B.C. Most of these various peoples spoke Indo-European languages, of which Latin, the language of the Romans, was one.

Roman House Urns This funerary urn, shaped like an early Roman house, contained the ashes of the dead as well as grave goods. The urn provides evidence of the unsophisticated architecture of Iron Age Rome. *(Werner Forman/Art Resource, NY)*

Rome's location in Latium gave it a central and strategic position in the Italian peninsula. Located 15 miles inland on the Tiber, the largest river on Italy's west coast, Rome was near the sea but far enough away to be safe from sea raiders. The seven hills of the city also offered defensive protection. A midstream island makes Rome the first crossing place upstream from the Tiber's mouth, offering the Romans access north and south.

Latium
0
15 Km.
15 Mi.
Lake Sabatinus
Tiber
Veii
Anio
Tibur
AEQUI
Aro
Gabii
Rome
Praeneste
Tiber
Tusculum
LATINS
HERNICI
Lake Albanus
Anagnia
Ostia
Mt. Albanus
Lake Nemorensis
Trerus
Lavinium
Cora
Ardea
Norba
Tyrrhenian Sea
VOLSCI
Satricum
Privernum
Antium
Roman territory, ca. 500 B.C.
ALPS
VENETI
Adige
Po
Mantua
LIGURES
ETRUSCANS
Spina
Felsina (Bologna)
Ravenna
Faesulae
Arno
Ligurian Sea
Adriatic Sea
ILLYRIA
Volaterrae
Arretium
UMBRI
PICENTES
ETRURIA
Perusia
Populonia
Clusium
Vetulonia
Elba
Volsinii
APENNINES
ETRUSCANS
SABINES
Tiber
Vulci
LIGURES
Alalia
Tarquinii
Veii
Caere
Rome
SAMNITES
Corsica
LATIUM
APULI
LATINS
Capua
CAMPANIA
MESSAPII
Cumae
Neapolis (Naples)
Puteoli
Herculaneum
OSCI
Pithecusae
Pompeii
Tarentum
Bay of Naples
LUCANI
Gulf of Tarentum
Sardinia
Tharros
SARDI
Tyrrhenian Sea
Sybaris
BRUTTII
Carales
Croton
MAGNA GRAECIA
Messana
Panormus
Mediterranean Sea
SICANI
SICULI
Sicily
Acragas (Agrigentum)
Syracuse
Utica
Cape Bon
Hippo Regius
Carthage
NORTH AFRICA
Malta
0
50
100 Km.
0
50
100 Mi.
Etruscans of Etruria
Expansion of Etruscans
Greeks
Carthaginians
OSCI Other peoples

Civilization came later to Italy than to regions farther east. The Neolithic Revolution in Italy is dated to 3500–2500 B.C. (compared to sometime after 10,000 B.C. in western Asia), and the Bronze Age began in Italy about 1800 B.C. (compared to about 3000 B.C. in the east). Separate waves of immigrants brought first Neolithic agriculture and then the Bronze Age to Italy. In the second millennium B.C. most of Italy was settled by the Apenninic people, seminomadic shepherds who drove their flocks up and down the slopes of the mountains with the seasons.

As in Greece and Anatolia, so in Italy the Iron Age began about 1000–800 B.C. The Iron Age brought new peoples to Italy. These newcomers cremated their dead and placed the ashes in urns buried close together in cemeteries, a practice suggesting descent from a similar culture of central Europe, the so-called Urnfield people. From an archaeological perspective, the most interesting Italian Iron Age culture was that of the Villanovans, inhabitants of northern and western Italy and ancestors of the Etruscans. Villanovan graves have yielded elaborate bronze helmets, iron weapons, bone hairpins and combs, and bronze safety pins for fastening clothes.

The Etruscans

The greatest influence on early Rome was that of the Etruscans, the dominant power in Italy between about 650 and 525 B.C. and rulers of Rome itself for about a century. Like the Minoans (see page 63), the Etruscans left a rich artistic legacy that leaves many of the historian's questions unanswered.

The Etruscans first appeared around 800 B.C. Many scholars believe that most Etruscans were Villanovans, with an influential foreign immigrant admixture, probably from Anatolia. Within about two centuries, the Etruscans had organized a loose confederation of twelve city-states centered in Etruria. They grew wealthy from the mining of iron, copper, and silver, from piracy, and from trade. Warlike, Etruscans used navies and heavy-armed Greek-style infantry (the hoplite phalanx) to expand by 600 B.C. into much of central and northern Italy, Corsica, and Elba.

Rome itself fell to the conquerors. Etruscans ruled as Rome's last three kings, traditionally from 616 to 509 B.C. Rome shook off Etruscan rule, but the Etruscan legacy was massive. Even when Rome became a republic around 500 B.C., most symbols of rank, status, and political power were Etruscan in origin. Indeed, virtually all spheres of life in Rome bore signs of Etruscan influence.

Although the Etruscans did not conquer the cultivated Greek cities of southern Italy, they borrowed freely from them. The Etruscans had writing, based on the Greek alphabet, which they shared with the Romans. Etruscan literature included histories and religious treatises, the Romans tell us. None of that literature survives. About ten thousand Etruscan inscriptions have been found, but they are mainly funerary, dedicatory, or religious and contain a limited vocabulary, of which only about half is understood. Apparently Etruscan is neither Indo-European nor Semitic, but its identity is still unknown.

If the Etruscan language were decipherable, it would tell the story of a society of considerable achievements. The Etruscans were excellent engineers, a talent they passed on to the Romans. Etruscans built an extensive network of roads, sewers, bridges, and viaducts (bridgelike structures for carrying roads over valleys) as well as underground tunnels to drain waterlogged ground. They arranged cut stone in well-constructed vaults and arches. The Romans in turn made the arch the hallmark of their engineering and architecture. The Romans also credited the Etruscans with inventing the raised-platform temple and the atrium (central-court) house, both characteristic of Rome.

The considerable effort lavished on grave ritual and on tombs full of rich artifacts indicate that the Etruscans believed in survival after death. The most dramatic ritual was funeral games in honor of the death of the male head of a family. Such games consisted of dancing, horse and chariot racing, boxing, wrestling, and contests between sword-wielding combatants whom the Romans later called gladiators. Fights to the finish,

Map 5.1 Early Italy and Region of City of Rome. Early Italy comprised a variety of terrain and peoples. Rome was located in the central Italian region of Latium. The Alps separate Italy from northern Europe. The Apennine mountain range runs almost the entire length of the Italian peninsula. Much of the rest of Italy is fertile plain.

Etruscan Tomb Painting This wall painting from Tarquinia shows a married aristocratic couple at a banquet. The style of the figures is derived from Greek art, but the depiction of husband and wife dining on the same couch is characteristically Etruscan. *(National Museum, Tarquinia/Scala/Art Resource, NY)*

these contests represented a blood sacrifice to the dead. Today associated with the Roman Empire, these bloody contests were first brought to Rome in the third century B.C.

Etruscan tomb-painters, like many Etruscan artists and artisans, were skilled. The wall frescoes that decorate many tombs frequently display a taste for the styles and mythological motifs of Greek art. Etruscan sculptors, who excelled first in clay and later in bronze, were noted for realism and naturalism, styles that would reappear in Roman sculpture.

As the numerous tombs indicate, the Etruscans were a religious people. The Romans considered them the masters of divination—prediction of the future from the study of animal parts, such as the liver of a sacrificial lamb, or from the study of natural phenomena, such as lightning. Etruscan soothsayers, priests who were highly skilled in divination ("Etruscan science," to the Romans), were often consulted by Rome in times of crisis to supplement the Roman state's own diviners.

Etruscan elite women seem to have enjoyed a higher status than their counterparts in Classical Greece or Rome. Etruscan women kept their own names, and Etruscan children bore the names of both of their parents. In addition, Etruscan elite women were permitted to attend athletic contests in spite of the presence of naked male athletes.

Around 550 B.C. Etruscan land power extended southward to the Bay of Naples, and Etruscan seapower dominated the Adriatic and

Tyrrhenian seas and was poised to expand westward. Although the Etruscans expanded into the Po Valley around 500 B.C., they suffered a decline in power elsewhere from around 525 B.C. on. Rome overthrew the Etruscan kings around 500 B.C. The Greek city of Syracuse, a long-standing rival, crushed the Etruscan fleet in 474 B.C. The Etruscans, moreover, were in the direct path of the Gauls, who attacked Etruria frequently in the fourth century B.C. Finally, the failure of the Etruscan city-states to unite proved fatal against the rising power of Rome. Rome conquered Etruria by 270 B.C. During the following centuries, the Etruscan language and culture slowly disappeared.

Etruscans played a crucial role in urbanizing the city of Rome. Before the Etruscan conquest, Rome was little more than a large village with an agricultural hinterland of about 60 square miles, modest compared to the roughly 1000 square miles of Athens in the Classical period. The earliest Romans mainly pastured sheep, goats, and cattle; some farmed, some fished, and some panned salt at the mouth of the Tiber. By contrast, the Etruscans sponsored building projects—streets, walls, drains, temples, public buildings, a forum (civic center), racetrack—that encouraged the immigration of skilled labor. The Etruscans fostered artisanship and commerce, sponsoring annual trade fairs and providing quarters for foreign merchants.

Having made Rome a true city, the Etruscan kings then turned it into the dominant military power of Latium, the first step on the long road to Roman pre-eminence in Italy and the Mediterranean. By 500 B.C. Roman territory had grown from about 60 to about 500 square miles, about a quarter of the total size of Latium. This size suggests a total population of 30,000 or 40,000, making Rome a fair-size city-state by ancient standards. The backbone of Roman expansion was the Greek-style heavy infantry, about 6000 strong, which the Etruscans introduced.

The Greeks in Southern Italy and Sicily

The Greeks were second only to the Etruscans in their influence on the Romans, and the Etruscans themselves were influenced by Greek civilization. Direct contact with the Greeks brought Rome important elements of its religion, law, and government and strongly influenced both elite culture (from philosophy and poetry to the dining habits of the wealthy) and popular culture (tragedy and comedy).

Roman contact with mainland Greece began in early times and culminated in the Roman conquest of the second century B.C. Before the second century, however, most of Rome's contact with Greeks came from the Greek city-states of southern Italy and Sicily. These cities were prosperous, cultivated, warlike, and—fortunately for the Romans—disunited. Rome conquered them in the third century B.C.

Greeks began to settle Italy as colonists around 775 B.C., drawn first to acquire metals, mainly copper and gold, and later to acquire land on which to settle excess population. Over the next several generations, a string of Greek colonies was planted along the southern Italian coasts and in southern and eastern Sicily (see page 81). Western Sicily was in the hands of Carthage, the great north African trading city and itself a Phoenician colony (see Map 5.1).

Among the most important Greek cities of Italy was Cumae, the one nearest to Rome. Cumae's most famous attraction was the Sibyl, a priestess of the Greek god of prophecy, Apollo. The supposed utterances over the years of various women serving as Sibyl were collected by the Romans around 500 B.C. and kept by priests of the state to be consulted at the command of the senate in times of crisis. Other Greek cities around the Bay of Naples included Puteoli, an important port; Naples itself, a population center and seat of learning; and Pompeii and Herculaneum, much favored later as elite Roman resorts and covered by ash in a volcanic eruption of A.D. 79.

Along the Gulf of Tarentum in the south were such Greek cities as Sybaris, known for its wealthy pleasure-seekers (whence the term *sybarite*); Croton, seat of Pythagoras and the philosophers' community he inspired; and Tarentum itself, a center of artisans and trade. A long-time rivalry between Sybaris and Croton eventually led to Sybaris's destruction without a trace.

Along the east and south coasts of agriculturally rich Sicily, thriving Greek cities included Acragas (Agrigentum), known today for its well-preserved ancient temples; Messana (Messina), a strategic site on the straits facing the mainland;

Female Head from Tarentum This life-sized terra cotta sculpture of the fourth century B.C. demonstrates the wealth and artistry of the cities of Greek Italy and Sicily. The Greeks of the region influenced both Roman and Etruscans. *(Leonard von Matt/Photo Researchers)*

and Syracuse. The greatest city of Sicily and the leading western Greek city, Syracuse won major victories over the Etruscans, Carthaginians, and Athenians before finally losing its independence to Rome in 211 B.C.

Early Rome and the Monarchy

Tradition says that Rome was ruled by seven kings before the foundation of the Republic: three Latins, one Sabine (probably), and three Etruscans. Although the number of kings may be a later invention, there is no doubt about the existence of the monarchy, which leaves its traces in Republican institutions. A form of the Latin word *rex* ("king"), moreover, has been found inscribed on a Roman monument from the early sixth century B.C. The king's power, called *imperium* (from *imperare,* "to command") was very great, embracing religious, military, and judicial affairs.

The king was advised by a council of elders, called the "fathers" (*patres* in Latin) or the "senate" (*senatus,* from *senex,* "old man"). In theory the senate was primarily an advisory body, but in practice it was quite powerful. Senators were often the heads of the most important families in Rome, so the king rejected their advice at his peril. Romans spoke of the senate's *auctoritas,* a quasi-religious prestige resembling the priestly authority held by the Roman father (see page 165). Most senators were patricians, as early Rome's hereditary aristocracy was known. The rest of the people, the bulk of Roman society, were called plebeians. Plebeians were free; most were ordinary people, though some were wealthy. Patricians monopolized the senate and priesthoods, and they did not intermarry with plebeians.

The whole people met in an assembly organized in thirty local units, or *curiae,* hence the name curiate assembly. The assembly's powers were limited. Before becoming law, resolutions of the assembly had to be approved by the patrician senators. When a king died, the senate chose his successor, whom the assembly then acclaimed.

Early Rome was a class-based society, but it was not closed to foreigners. Etruscans, Latins, Sabines, and others came to Rome. Unlike Athenians, who tried to hide the presence of immigrants in their country by a myth of indigenous origins, Romans openly discussed their mixed roots. In early Italy the mix of peoples was too great and the geographical barriers too minor to foster isolated and separate development. Foreigners at first had a subordinate status but gained equality around 550 B.C. Military pressure made it necessary to expand the body of loyal infantrymen, so native Romans decided to incorporate the immigrants into their community—a reform traditionally associated with the Etruscan king Servius Tullius (578–535 B.C.). Servius probably introduced the hoplite phalanx to Rome. Membership in the community, previously based on birth, became determined by residence. Any man with enough property to afford the necessary training and equipment could serve as a hoplite or cavalryman.

In short, like the early Greeks, the Romans moved toward a notion of citizenship based on military service. As in early Greece so in Rome military change bred political upheaval. Within several generations of Servius's reform, Rome went from monarchy to Republic.

Founding the Roman Republic

The traditional date of the overthrow of the Etruscan kings and the establishment of the Republic is 509 B.C. A symbol of revolution in modern times, this event was in fact probably part of a long process rather than a dramatic revolution. The Etruscan monarchy, it seems, suffered a lengthy social, economic, and political decline, hastened by military failure. The institutions of the new Republic were not put in place at once but developed slowly by trial and error. Some scholars reject the date of 509 and put the transition from monarchy to Republic a generation or two later. The traditional story is nonetheless revealing. Let us consider a foundation myth of the Republic and then turn to early Republican society and culture.

A few inscriptions and temple dedications, as well as lists of public officeholders, survive as documents of the Early Republic. For a coherent account, however, it is necessary to turn to the works of Roman historians. Written centuries after the events described, these works embroider the evidence, so we must be cautious.

A Foundation Myth of the Roman Republic

According to the historian Livy (59 B.C.–A.D. 17), the overthrow of the Etruscan monarchy was prompted by the rape of Lucretia, wife of the aristocrat Tarquinius Collatinus, by Sextus, son of the Etruscan king Tarquinius Superbus (r. ca. 534–509 B.C.) (see the box, "The Rape of Lucretia"). Livy embellished the details of the story, which had been preserved for centuries in oral tradition before being written down, yet his version is nonetheless revealing of Roman mores. Livy claims that Sextus was attracted to Lucretia by her modesty: While other wives made merry in their husbands' absence, Lucretia was home spinning wool. Taking advantage of Collatinus's absence, Sextus entered the house as a guest. He then forced himself on Lucretia by threatening to kill her because, he would claim, he had found her in bed with a slave. Ashamed in spite of her innocence, Lucretia incited her husband and his kinsman Lucius Junius Brutus by revealing Sextus's crime and then killing herself with her own dagger. To avenge her, Collatinus and Brutus drove out the kings and established the Republic.

That Rome's mythmakers should found the Republic on the need to avenge a rape may seem strange, but only at first. The main elements of the tale—violence, honor, and family—proved to be of permanent fascination to the Roman elite. Lucretia's honor was literally more important than her life. Centuries later, when Julius Caesar (100–44 B.C.) was asked why he preferred civil war to compromise, he too said that his honor was dearer than his life. The defining feature of Caesar's honor was political prestige, of Lucretia's, chastity, but they shared a devotion to dignity and reputation—fundamental values for both sexes at Rome. The Lucretia story offers other insights into Roman elite mores: the expectation of hospitality among aristocrats, the class bias (adultery by a noble woman was bad enough, but adultery by a noble woman with a slave was unthinkable), and the alleged antithesis between modest Romans and profligate Etruscans.

Lucretia's fate indicates the premium put by Roman nobles on defending family honor and avenging it when necessary. Indeed, family is in many ways the key to Roman society and culture.

The Roman Household

The Latin word *familia* is broader than the English *family*: It connotes slaves, animals, and property, as well as the members of the nuclear family and their ancestors or descendants, and is better translated as "household." The familia was the basic unit of Roman society. A center of both production and consumption, it was also a model of political authority. In theory, though not always in practice, the Roman household was an authoritarian institution governed by a male; thus, the familia is an example of patriarchy.

The legal head of the familia was the *paterfamilias,* the oldest living male—usually the father in a nuclear family, though occasionally the grandfather or, in cases of unusual longevity, the great-grandfather. According to Roman law, the paterfamilias had supreme power within the household. Although he was supposed to call a council of senior male relatives to consult on big decisions, he was not required to follow their advice. He had the right to sell family members into slavery and the rarely used power to kill an errant wife or child. A

The Rape of Lucretia

The historian Livy attributes the founding of the Roman Republic to outrage over the rape of the aristocratic woman Lucretia by Sextus Tarquinius, son of King Tarquinius Superbus. Though of dubious historicity, the story reveals a great deal about Roman attitudes toward gender, honor, and their political implications.

[A guest in Lucretia's house in her husband's absence, Sextus Tarquinius demands that she sleep with him.] But all in vain; not even the fear of death could bend her will. "If death will not move you," Sextus cried, "dishonor shall. I will kiss you first, then cut the throat of a slave and lay his naked body by your side. Will they not believe that you have been caught in adultery with a servant—and paid the price?" Even the most resolute chastity could not have stood against this dreadful threat.

[After being violated by Sextus Tarquinius, Lucretia summons her husband and father.] "In your bed, Collatinus, is the impress of another man. My body only has been violated. My heart is innocent, and death will be my witness. Give me your solemn promise that the adulterer shall be punished—he is Sextus Tarquinius. He it was who last night came as my enemy disguised as my guest, and took his pleasure of me. . . .

"What is due to *him,*" Lucretia said, "is for you to decide. As for me, I am innocent of fault, but I will take my punishment. Never shall Lucretia provide a precedent for unchaste women to escape what they deserve." With these words she drew a knife from under her robe, drove it into her heart, and fell forward, dead.

Her father and husband were overwhelmed with grief. While they stood weeping helplessly, Brutus [aristocrat and family friend] drew the bloody knife from Lucretia's body, and holding it before him cried: "By this girl's blood—none more chaste till a tyrant wronged her—and by the gods, I swear that with sword and fire, and whatever else can lend strength to my arm, I will pursue Lucius Tarquinius Superbus, his wicked wife, and all his children, and never again will I let them or any other man be King in Rome."

Source: Livy, *The Early History of Rome,* trans. Aubrey de Sélincourt (Harmondsworth, England: Penguin, 1971), pp. 98–99.

son, no matter how old, was always legally subject to the authority of a living paterfamilias. Only the paterfamilias, moreover, could own property free and clear. Thus, a 30-year-old man might be under the authority of his paterfamilias and dependent on him for an allowance.

The paterfamilias represented the household to outside authority, both human and divine. He performed regular sacrifices on behalf of the household to its ancestors and gods. A wealthy and aristocratic familia set great store by its ancestors and kin. All patricians and some plebeians belonged to a *gens* (plural, *gentes*), a clanlike kinship group that traced its ancestry back to a purported common ancestor. All Romans had a personal and a family name, and patricians and elite plebeians also had a third name, indicating their gens: for example, Gaius Julius Caesar, whose personal name Gaius was followed by the gens name Julius and the familia name Caesar.

In theory, the paterfamilias was the focus of power in the household, but practice was more complex. The sources are full of indications of fathers' affection, love, and even indulgence for their children. Moreover, Roman women usually married in their late teens and men in their late twenties. Given the low life expectancies, it was common for a man of 25 to have already buried his father. Many, perhaps even most, adult males were independent of a paterfamilias.

Nor was the power of the paterfamilias over his wife or daughter as strict as theory suggests. Unlike men, Roman women never became legally independent, even on the death of a paterfamilias. Instead of receiving a personal name, a daughter was called by the name of her father's gens. For example, Gaius Julius Caesar's daughter was called Julia; if Caesar had had a second daughter, she would have been Julia Secunda ("Julia the Second"). Although fathers were expected to support all male children, they had to support only their first daughter. In other words, they were free to "expose" additional daughters—that is, leave them in the open to die or, as was perhaps more likely, to be adopted or raised as a slave. A father also arranged a daughter's marriage and provided her with a dowry. In theory, again, a most severe relationship, but the evidence suggests considerable father-daughter affection. There are a number of examples of married daughters seeking advice or aid from their fathers.

Most women in early Rome married *cum manu* ("with hand")—that is, they were "handed over" to their husbands, who became their paterfamilias. Even so, Roman wives and mothers had more prestige and freedom than their counterparts in Classical Greece. Legends of early Rome mention some who were peacemakers, negotiators, or (like Lucretia) catalysts of quarrels among men.

The hierarchy of the household was applied to Roman society and politics. Romans conceived of the state as a collection of heads of household, each head competing for honor for his own familia and gens. The imperium (power) of the chief magistrates (a Republican adaptation of the imperium of the king) was analogous to the supreme power of the paterfamilias. An ordinary Roman was expected to obey the magistrates, just as he would obey his paterfamilias.

Shrine of a Wealthy Household This painting from Pompeii shows the spirit of the paterfamilias in a toga, which is wrapped around his head in keeping with Roman procedures of sacrifice. He is flanked by the spirits of departed ancestors. A snake symbolizes fertility. *(Alinari/Art Resource, NY)*

Patrons and Clients

Patron (derived from *pater*) means "defender" or "protector." *Client* means "dependent." Roman society consisted of a pyramidal series of patron-client networks. Most patrons were in turn clients of someone more powerful; only a very few men stood at the top of the pyramid. In the Roman imagination, justice required not equality between patron and client but merely mutual respect. The status of client or patron was hereditary.

Various paths led to the status of client. A peasant in need of help on his farm might ask a wealthy neighbor to become his patron. A manumitted slave became the client of his former owner. A conquered foe often became the client of the victorious general.

Patron and client might help each other in various ways. A patron might provide a client with food or money or land for a dowry. He might settle disputes or provide legal assistance. In return, a client owed his patron respect and service. He escorted his patron in public on important occasions—possession of a large clientele signified prestige and power. If his patron sought political office, the client voted for him. If his patron needed money, the client was obligated to contribute, perhaps to an election campaign or to pay fines or ransoms.

Cloaked in an elaborate language of goodwill, the patron-client relationship was considered to be essentially a matter of *fides* ("good faith" or "trustworthiness"). Romans spoke not of a client submitting to a patron's power but rather of a client "commending himself" to the patron's fides; a patron received his clients into his fides. A patron spoke not of his clients but of his "friends," especially if they were men of standing and substance.

The Romans considered the patron-client relationship to be important and solemn. A patron was supposed to put his clients before kin by marriage; only blood or adoptive relations were to take precedence. The Twelve Tables, a Roman law code of the mid-fifth-century B.C. (see pages 171–172), declares that a patron who defrauds his client is accursed and may be killed with impunity.

Patronage undergirded Roman domestic politics and foreign relations. Although Republican political institutions appeared to work through free elections and popular choice, the obligations of humble clients to wealthy patrons took precedence. If a man's clients grew discontented, another ambitious politician might offer himself as their new patron, and often the result was political change. As for foreign affairs, experience as patrons schooled Roman leaders in treating the peoples they conquered as clients, often as personal clients. Moreover, the Roman state sometimes took foreign countries into its collective fides—much as a patron did a client—thus allowing Rome to extend its influence without the constraints of a formal alliance.

Religion and World View

If we knew nothing about early Roman religion, we could deduce much about it from the familia and patronage. We would expect to find elements of patriarchy and contractualism, and both are indeed present. The task of a Roman priest, whether an official of the state or an individual paterfamilias, was to establish what the Romans called the "peace of the gods." Roman cults aimed at obtaining the gods' agreement to human requests, at "binding" the gods—the Latin term for which is *religio.*

The earliest Roman religion centered on spirits that, the Romans believed, haunted the household and the fields and forests and determined the weather. The Lares, the spirits of departed ancestors, guarded the house, and the Penates watched over the stored grain. The spirit of the hearth was Vesta; of the door, Janus; of the rain and sun, Jupiter (later identified with the Greek sky-god and father-god Zeus); of the crops and vegetation, Mars (later identified with the Greek war-god Ares). The Romans believed that these spirits needed to be appeased—hence the contractual nature of their prayers and offerings. Over the years, as a result of Greek and Etruscan influence, anthropomorphism supplanted Roman animism.

Roman state religion grew out of household religion. Vesta, the hearth-goddess, became goddess of the civic hearth; Janus, the door-god, became god of the city's gates; Jupiter became the general overseer of the gods; and Mars became the god of war. When trade and conquest brought the Romans into contact with foreign religions, the Romans tended to absorb them. The senate screened and sometimes rejected new gods, but by and large Roman polytheism was tolerant.

The Republic sponsored various priestly committees or colleges to secure the peace of the gods. Originally restricted to patricians, the highest priesthoods were opened to plebeians by law in 300 B.C. Although some priesthoods were full-time jobs, most left the officeholder free to pursue a concurrent career as a magistrate or a senator. The two most important priestly colleges were the augurs, who were in charge of divination, and the pontiffs, who exercised a general supervisory function over Rome's numerous rituals, sacrifices, offerings, prayers, temples, and festivals. The chief pontiff, the *pontifex maximus,* was the head of the state clergy. The pontiffs alone controlled the interpretation of the law until the fourth century B.C. The Romans allowed priests to interpret law on the theory that an offense against humans was also an offense against the gods.

There were only two colleges of priestesses: those of Ceres, goddess of fertility and death, and those of the Vestal Virgins. The six Vestals tended the civic hearth and made sure that its fire never went out. They served, as it were, as wives of the whole community, as guardians of the civic household. The Vestals were the only Roman women not under the authority of a paterfamilias. Chosen between the ages of 6 and 10 by the pontifex maximus, they had to remain virgins for thirty years or face death. The Vestals' virtue, like Lucretia's, was considered an index of male honor and so was watched closely.

Although open to outside cultural influences, Romans tended to think of themselves as conservative. Each generation had a vocal and significant old guard that exalted ancestral custom and denounced revolution. Conservatism was fostered by the pride of Rome's noble families, who maintained the memory of their ancestors.

By the Early Republic, class distinctions abounded at Rome. The elite papered over such differences by sponsoring an ideology of simple and austere farmers' virtues—discipline, hard work, frugality, temperance, and the avoidance of public displays of affection even between spouses. Household duties and gender obligations were defined clearly. Women were to be chaste, modest, and practical. Men were to project *gravitas* (weight, seriousness), never lightness or levity. A serious man would display self-control and constancy, the ability to persevere against difficult odds. The masculine ideal was *virtus* (literally "manliness"), which indicated excellence in war and government. The supreme value of the household was *pietas*—devotion and loyalty to the familia, the gods, and the state.

Roman men who attained virtus considered themselves entitled to the reward of *dignitas,* meaning not only public esteem but the tangible possession of a dignified position and official rank—in short, public office. The ultimate test of virtus, however, was war. Let us turn to politics and the military.

Patrician Carrying Two Portrait Busts This first-century A.D. marble statue, a copy of an earlier work, illustrates the upper-class Republican custom of keeping masks of family ancestors. At funerals nobles paraded with the masks and gave speeches praising family traditions. *(Museum of the Palazzo dei Conservatori/Alinari/Art Resource, NY)*

Government and Society in the Early and Middle Republic, ca. 509–133 B.C.

The history of Republican politics is both as simple as the patriarchal framework of the Roman household and as complex as the crosscurrents of affection and manipulation that ran through it. Although Rome had no written constitution, a hierarchical arrangement of public officials and popular assemblies emerged by the third century B.C. Documentation is poor for the earlier period, but later survivals shed some light on earlier practice. Much remains obscure, however, for several reasons. Rome's constitutional forms often mask the realities of elite power and manipulation. Furthermore, perhaps the best source for the mid-Republican constitution, the historian

ROMAN GOVERNMENT AND SOCIETY

753–509 B.C.	Monarchy (traditional dates)
509–287 B.C.	Early Republic
449 B.C.	Law of the Twelve Tables
445 B.C.	Plebeian-patrician intermarriage permitted
367 B.C.	Consulship opened to plebeians
300 B.C.	Highest priesthoods opened to plebeians
287 B.C.	Hortensian Law makes decisions of plebs legally binding
287–133 B.C.	Middle Republic
133–31 B.C.	Late Republic

Polybius (ca. 200–ca. 118 B.C.), a Greek and former hostage who lived in Rome, more or less consciously described the Roman government according to Greek categories, thereby producing considerable distortion.

Political Institutions

Ancient theorists divided Roman political institutions into three branches: executive, legislative, and deliberative. Influenced by the Romans, the American founders adopted a similar division, but with the legislative and deliberative functions combined and a judicial branch added. In Rome, various magistrates of the executive branch administered justice, in addition to their other responsibilities. The Roman senate, which made up the deliberative branch, was far more powerful than the American senate. The Roman legislative branch was made up of several popular assemblies.

The three parts of the Roman constitution, then, were the people, the senate, and the magistrates. Magistrates acted in the name of the "senate and the Roman People"—in Latin, *Senatus Populusque Romanus.* Polybius describes the Middle Republic as a "mixed constitution": the assemblies, a democratic element; the senate, an oligarchic element; and the magistrates, a royal element. Polybius's model of power sharing is elegant but wrong. The institutional structure of the assemblies, the prestige of the senate, the great discretionary power of the magistrates, and, above all, the underlying patronage, conservatism, and class distinctions of Roman society all contributed to the *inequality* of Roman government. Power flowed *away* from the people, at first to the magistrates, who were very strong in the Early Republic, and then to the senate, the dominant power in the government of the Middle Republic.

The magistrates were the executive power. Over the centuries, as Roman government grew larger and more complex, the number of magistrates grew, but certain basic principles remained the same. Magistrates were elected to office by the Roman people; unlike Greek democracy, Rome did not choose its officials by lottery. The magistrates had great power: While in office they could not be prosecuted for their actions. Magistracies were time-consuming jobs but offered no salary, unlike public office in Greek democracy. Election required extensive campaigning, which in turn necessitated many clients. Thus, only a wealthy, elite few could afford to be magistrates. Because the number of magistracies was relatively few, competition for office among the elite was intense. Most magistracies required a minimum age of late thirties or early forties.

Eager for strong, effective magistrates but ever fearful that power might lead to corruption, Rome imposed the principles of collegiality and annuality on its officials. Every magistrate had one or more colleagues, and the tenure of office was only one year. There were thus two consuls, as the chief magistrates were eventually called. Each consul had the power to veto the other's actions, and each held office for only a one-year term. The consuls took over the political and military powers of the king. Each consul had imperium, the power to issue commands and order punishments including execution. But unlike the king, the consuls wielded power temporarily. Reelection was not encouraged and usually could not be sought until ten years had passed after one's first term. An assertive people eventually forced other restrictions on consuls. After 300 B.C., for instance, the consul's power to order executions was limited to military campaigns.

Within the boundary of the city of Rome (a space held sacred), any citizen accused of a capital crime had the right to a trial.

Over the course of the fifth and fourth centuries B.C., other magistracies—praetors, aediles, and quaestors—were developed to assist the consuls. Some praetors served military functions; others were in charge of the administration of justice. Praetors, like consuls, had imperium. Aediles were in charge of policing Rome and supervising marketplaces, commerce, public works, and public games. Quaestors were keepers of the state treasury and quartermasters for the army.

In addition to those annual magistrates were two censors, men who had completed their careers as magistrates and were elected once every four or five years for eighteen-month terms. At first their job was to supervise the census, the military register of citizens that recorded each man's property class. Later the censors began to consider moral as well as financial qualifications and to punish those they considered bad citizens by consigning them to a lower census class. Censors could also expel bad citizens from the senate. The censors became, as it were, supervisors of public morals.

As the Republic's government evolved, adaptability emerged as one of its hallmarks. In times of emergency, for example, the Republic entrusted matters to a single magistrate. The dictator, as he was called, held imperium, and his decisions were beyond appeal; but he held office for only six months. Another sign of flexibility was the practice of promagistracy—that is, of extending a magistrate's imperium past the normal term of office or of temporarily investing a private citizen with imperium. First employed in the fourth century B.C., promagistracy met Rome's needs as a conquering power by greatly expanding the number of men available to serve as commanders or governors away from home.

Like the kings, the consuls were invested with symbols of power. The formal and official public dress of the Roman citizen was the toga, a long, heavy, and expensive garment of fine white wool. It was worn folded on the left shoulder, from which it fell over front and back. The consuls and other higher magistrates wore a toga with a purple hem, the color of royalty. Consuls, praetors, and proconsuls were preceded by attendants carrying the *fasces* (bundles of rods and axes), symbolizing the importance of the chief magistrates and their power to punish and execute. Attendants carried an ivory folding seat, without back or arms, on which magistrates with imperium sat.

The deliberative branch of the Roman constitution consisted of the senate, which guided and advised the magistrates. During most of the Republic the senate consisted of three hundred men. Various methods of choosing senators were employed. In the third century B.C. and later, one became a senator after holding a magistracy. Senators served for life. As former magistrates and as members of a time-honored institution, senators possessed great authority even though, by the Middle Republic, they no longer had the formal power to approve a bill before an assembly could ratify it as law.

Senators made much of their dignified bearing and presence. The sight of a senator in a purple-striped tunic (a symbol of senatorial status), surrounded by clients, must have made quite an impression. Roman authors were fond of the legend of the behavior of some elderly senators who refused to leave Rome when the Gauls captured the city around 390 B.C.—the last time foreigners took Rome for nearly eight hundred years. The senators are supposed to have sat, immobile as statues, rather than show fear.

The senate had the specific powers to receive and send ambassadors and to supervise expenditures. Although the people formally declared war and ratified treaties, the senate was for all practical purposes in charge of foreign policy. The opinion of the senate could be expressed in formal declarations. Meetings were usually held in the senate house in the Forum, the main public square of Rome. Meetings were private, but the doors were kept open.

The legislative branch of the Roman constitution consisted of four popular assemblies. The members of each assembly were Roman men summoned by groups by a presiding magistrate. Reflecting the hierarchical order of Roman society, Roman assemblies were not democratic. In contrast to Greek assemblies, at Rome participants stood rather than sat down and received no salary for attendance. Forced to stand and uncompensated for the time lost from work, the ordinary Roman was unlikely to speak in the assembly, if he participated at all. Discussion was limited, and the patron-client system greatly constrained a client's voting freedom.

Ever conservative, the Romans maintained the curiate assembly, which dated from the period of the monarchy, but consigned it to a largely ceremonial role during the Republic. The centuriate assembly better suited the military oligarchy of the Republic. Based on a military formation (the century was the smallest unit of the Roman army), this assembly offered the façade of popular participation but the reality of control by the wealthy. The centuriate assembly elected consuls and praetors (and, when needed, dictators), voted on laws and treaties, accepted declarations of war and peace, and acted as a court in cases of treason, homicide, and appeals from magistrates' decisions. The assembly, summoned by a trumpet call, met outside the city at dawn on a military parade ground. No discussion was permitted. The assembly was divided according to wealth into census classes of fighting men. The centuries voted in order of wealth. First came the equestrians or cavalrymen, then five classes of infantrymen, and finally the *proletarii* ("breeders"), men too poor to provide their own arms. Because the equestrians and the first class of infantry—the wealthiest men—constituted a majority, in many elections the four remaining classes of infantry and the proletarii did not vote at all.

There were two other assemblies: the council of the plebs and the tribal assembly. The latter became Rome's main legislative body in the third century B.C. To understand its evolution and workings, we turn now to the class conflicts in Rome during the fifth through third centuries B.C.

Conflict of the Orders

Between 494 and 287 B.C., the Early Republic witnessed considerable social and political conflict, usually referred to as a struggle between the patrician and plebeian orders. According to tradition, there were only 136 patrician families in 509 B.C., but they dominated the Early Republic. The plebs, in contrast, were a mass of poor peasants and a small number of wealthy men who were not patricians; there were also plebeian artisans, traders, and shopkeepers, but they were only a tiny part of the population. Wealthy plebeians wanted unrestricted access to high office, from which they had been largely excluded. The mass of plebeians called for relief from debt, for redistribution of land, and for codification and publication of the law. For a century and a half, the two groups of plebeians made common cause, writing an important chapter in the history of political resistance.

This was a crucial era in Republican history. As in Archaic Greece, social conflicts produced political experiment from which relatively stable regimes emerged: oligarchies and democracies in Greece, the Republic in Rome. As Rome reached a domestic political consensus, it presented an ever-stronger military front to its external opponents. By 300 B.C., Rome was ready to grow from being a local power to the dominant state in Italy and then the colossus of the Mediterranean.

Debt loomed large as a problem of Roman society. A form of debt-bondage called *nexum* forced a free man who defaulted on a loan to work off what he owed, often for the rest of his life. Plebeians wanted nexum abolished. Land-hunger was also a widespread problem. The average peasant farm was too small to feed a family, rendering most peasants dependent on public land for farming and grazing. Time and again throughout Republican history, however, public land was occupied by the wealthy, who denied or restricted access to the poor. Their only hope was change.

In the fifth century B.C. the plebs organized themselves as kind of a state within the state, complete with their own assembly (the council of the plebs) and officials (the tribunes of the plebs). The decisions of the council of the plebs, called *plebiscita* (from which *plebiscite* comes), were binding only on the plebs; they did not receive the full force of law for over two hundred years. Plebeian self-confidence and solidarity were nonetheless great. On several occasions during the Early Republic they resorted to secession: the plebs as a whole left the city for the Aventine Hill, where they stayed until their grievances were addressed (see inset, Map 5.2).

There were ten tribunes, elected annually by the plebs. A tribune represented plebeian grievances against the arbitrary power of a magistrate. His house was always open to any plebeian who needed him, and he could not leave the city limits. Inside the city of Rome, a tribune also had the right to veto any act of the magistrates, assembly, or senate that harmed plebeians. In return, the

The Roman Forum Here is a view of the southwestern corner of Rome's central civic space. The remains of temples, arches, and administration buildings are prominent. The rectangular, pitched-roof senate house (upper right) was built in the third century A.D., probably on the site of earlier senate houses. *(Scala/Art Resource, NY)*

plebs swore to treat the tribunes as sacrosanct and to lynch anyone who harmed them.

Around the same time as the creation of the council of the plebs, a tribal assembly also began. As in the council of the plebs, assembly-goers were divided by tribes, but the body represented the people as a whole, including patricians, a powerful force in the assembly thanks to a representation system that heavily favored landowners. The tribal assembly elected lower magistrates and, in the same way as the centuriate assembly, voted on laws and acted as a court of appeals.

Impressive as plebeian activity was, the patricians had formidable resources. Patricians dominated important priesthoods. Thanks to patrician financial aid, patricians' many clients could afford to serve as heavy infantrymen and thereby render support for continued patrician rule. Nevertheless, the plebeians pressed onward, wringing incremental concessions out of the patricians, until finally the patricians decided to neutralize the opposition of the plebeian elite by meeting their main demands. The outcome was a new, combined patrician-plebeian nobility. The patricians had wisely decided to make those compromises to preserve most of their privileges, rather than risk everything on an all-or-nothing exclusionism.

Among the important events in the patrician-plebeian conflict was the publication in 449 B.C. of the law code known as the "Twelve Tables," eventually, if not at first, on twelve bronze tablets in the Forum (see the box, "The Law of the

Twelve Tables"). By modern standards, the code was primitive and illiberal, but its very existence was a plebeian victory. Unfortunately, the modes of legal procedure remained a secret of the pontiffs for another 150 years. The complexity of these procedures ensured that no poor man could go to court without the help of a powerful patron.

Around 445 B.C. the patricians accepted a law that permitted patrician-plebeian intermarriage, a victory for wealthy plebeians. Rather than endure plebeians as consuls, however, patricians suspended the consulship altogether for about eighty years, sharing the consuls' powers among a group of military officers, most of them patricians. In 367 B.C. a compromise was finally reached: A series of laws re-established the consulship and ruled that one consul had to be a plebeian. These laws also provided for short-term relief of debt, a problem worsened by the depradations of the Gauls around 390 B.C. After 367 B.C., additional laws tried to reduce or abolish the rate of interest; nexum was finally abolished in 326 B.C.

After 367 B.C. integration of the patrician and plebeian elites proceeded despite conservative opposition. In 287 B.C. the merging of the orders culminated in a law that made decisions of the council of the plebs as binding as any law. Henceforth there was little distinction between the council of the plebs and the tribal assembly, so the year 287 B.C. has become the conventional starting date of the Middle Republic. Although the patriciate survived and remained prestigious, its importance gradually lessened. The new elite was based on wealth, not heredity. Its members were known as equestrians—men wealthy enough to serve as cavalrymen. The overwhelming majority of Romans remained excluded, as they had been from the patriciate. Equestrians who served in the senate formed the senatorial order, the inner circle of which comprised those who possessed an ancestor who had been consul.

Although ordinary plebeians improved their lot by their exertions, they still faced the twin problems of debt and land-hunger in the Middle Republic. No longer could they depend on wealthy plebeians as champions. Although their problems would come back with a vengeance to haunt the Late Republic, plebeians found temporary relief in the new land that Rome acquired through conquest.

From Italian City-State to World Empire

The Roman elite dealt successfully not only with the domestic challenge from political outsiders, wealthy and poor, but also with foreign challenge. At the beginning of the Republic (ca. 509 B.C.), Roman territory was about 500 square miles, about half of the size of the state of Rhode Island. By 338 B.C. Rome controlled the 2000 square miles of Latium and was moving north into Etruria and south into Samnite country. Three-quarters of a century later, in 265 B.C., Rome controlled all of the Italian peninsula south of an imaginary line from Pisae (modern Pisa) to Ariminium (modern Rimini), an area of about 50,000 square miles (Map 5.2). By 146 B.C., Roman provinces included Sicily, Cisalpine Gaul (northernmost Italy), Sardinia, Corsica, and Spain (divided into two provinces). Once-mighty Carthage was the Roman province of Africa (roughly, modern Tunisia), and once-mighty Macedon was the province of Macedonia, whose governor was also effectively in charge of Greece. The Seleucid kingdom was free but fatally weakened. Rome was the supreme power between Gibraltar and the Levant.

How and why had Rome reached this height from its humble beginnings as a local power in Italy?

Republican Expansion: The Conquest of Italy, ca. 509–265 B.C.

Romans maintained that they conquered an empire without ever once committing an act of aggression. When war was declared, a special college of priests informed the gods that Rome was merely retaliating for foreign injury. The Romans were frequently attacked by others, but Rome often engaged in provocative behavior that left its rivals little choice.

Rome's early conquests reveal many of its lasting motives for expansion. No doubt lust for

Map 5.2 Roman Italy, ca. 265 B.C. Rome controlled a patchwork of conquered territory, colonies, and allied states in Italy, held together by a network of treaties and of roads. The city of Rome (inset) was built on seven hills beside the Tiber River.

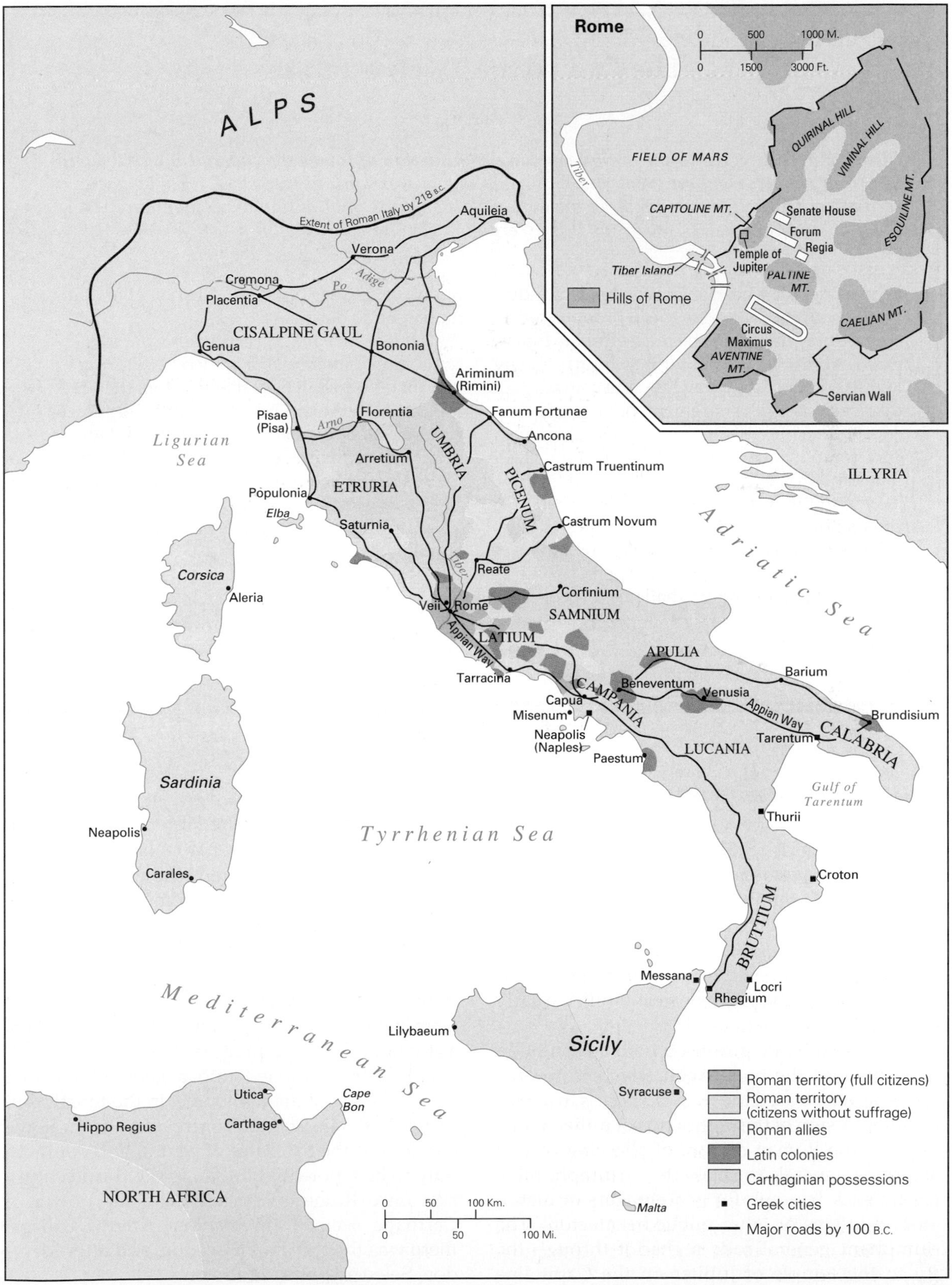
Rome
0 500 1000 M.
0 1500 3000 Ft.
FIELD OF MARS
Tiber
QUIRINAL HILL
VIMINAL HILL
ESQUILINE MT.
CAPITOLINE MT.
Senate House
Forum
Regia
Temple of Jupiter
Tiber Island
PALTINE MT.
Hills of Rome
Circus Maximus
AVENTINE MT.
CAELIAN MT.
Servian Wall
ALPS
Extent of Roman Italy by 218 B.C.
Aquileia
Verona
Adige
Po
Cremona
Placentia
CISALPINE GAUL
Genua
Bononia
Ariminum (Rimini)
Fanum Fortunae
Ancona
Florentia
Pisae (Pisa)
Arno
Ligurian Sea
UMBRIA
Arretium
ETRURIA
PICENUM
Castrum Truentinum
ILLYRIA
Populonia
Elba
Saturnia
Castrum Novum
Adriatic Sea
Tiber
Reate
Corsica
Aleria
Corfinium
Veii
Rome
SAMNIUM
LATIUM
Appian Way
APULIA
Tarracina
Barium
Beneventum
Capua
CAMPANIA
Venusia
Misenum
Appian Way
Brundisium
Neapolis (Naples)
Tarentum
CALABRIA
Paestum
LUCANIA
Sardinia
Gulf of Tarentum
Thurii
Neapolis
Tyrrhenian Sea
Carales
Croton
BRUTTIUM
Messana
Locri
Rhegium
Mediterranean Sea
Lilybaeum
Sicily
Utica
Cape Bon
Syracuse
Hippo Regius
Carthage
NORTH AFRICA
Malta
0 50 100 Km.
0 50 100 Mi.
Roman territory (full citizens)
Roman territory (citizens without suffrage)
Roman allies
Latin colonies
Carthaginian possessions
Greek cities
Major roads by 100 B.C.

The Law of the Twelve Tables

Plebeian agitation led to the formulation and publication of laws by a commission in the mid-fifth century B.C. The first great step in the history of Roman law, the Twelve Tables were inscribed on bronze plaques set up in the Forum. Although its publication was a popular victory, the law was nonetheless severe, as this excerpt on debt shows.

When a debt has been acknowledged, or judgment about the matter has been pronounced in court, thirty days must be the legitimate time of grace. After that, the debtor may be arrested by laying on of hands. Bring him into court. If he does not satisfy the judgment, or no one in court offers himself as surety in his behalf, the creditor may take the defaulter with him. He may bind him either in stocks or in fetters; he may bind him with a weight no more than fifteen pounds, or with less if he shall so desire. The debtor, if he wishes, may live on his own. If he does not live on his own, the person [who shall hold him in bonds] shall give him one pound of grits for each day. He may give him more if he so desires.

Unless they make a settlement, debtors shall be held in bonds for sixty days. During that time they shall be brought before the praetor's court in the meeting place on three successive market days, and the third market day they shall suffer capital punishment or be delivered up for sale abroad, across the Tiber.

On the third market day creditors shall cut pieces [of the debtor's estate or his body]. Should they have cut more or less than their due, it shall be with impunity.

Source: Naphtali Lewis and Meyer Reinhold, eds., *Roman Civilization. Sourcebook I: The Republic,* 3d ed. (New York: Harper & Row, 1990), pp. 109–110; from the Loeb Classical Library.

conquest played a part, as did hatred of outsiders, but self-control and shrewdness were stronger Roman characteristics. Greed, particularly land-hunger, was a perennial theme. Sometimes a domestic political motive was at work, for foreign adventure was a convenient way of deflecting plebeian energies. Perhaps the most significant factors, however, were the personal ambitions of a warrior elite and the prevalence of conflict in early Italy.

Victory in battle promised both a reputation for virtus and the booty with which to reward clients, and it cleared the road to success in a public career. A sign of the high status of military success was the Roman custom of allowing certain victorious generals to celebrate a triumph; there was no such triumph for peacemakers or distinguished judges or other public benefactors. The triumphant general rode a chariot through the city to the temple of Jupiter on the Capitoline Hill. He was accompanied by his troops, by the spoils of victory including famous captives, and by the magistrates and senators (see the box, "A Roman Triumph"). Cheered by the whole state, a general celebrating a triumph might feel that he had indeed outdone his rivals.

The harsh reality of Italian politics also ruled against pacifism. Without the willingness to fight, Rome could neither have won its freedom from the Etruscans nor maintained that freedom. Yet what began as a pragmatic response to present dangers hardened into a habit of meeting even remote threats with force. In the fourth century B.C., having gained control of Latium, Rome considered the Samnites of central and southern Italy to be a potential threat. In the third century B.C., once Rome controlled Italy, the power of Carthage seemed threatening. After Carthage, there was the threat of Macedon, and after Macedon, Seleucid Syria, and so on.

Though flexible and far-reaching, Roman diplomacy sometimes resulted in military engagement. Rome made formal alliances with some states, granting good relations and protection in return for obedience and the supplying of armies or navies when needed by Rome. Short of a formal commitment, however, Rome might accept a state "into its fides"—that is, treat the state as a client. The result was only a moral and not a legal commitment, which sometimes sufficed to frighten any would-be aggressor from Rome's new friend. If not, Rome found itself embroiled in war to prove its trustworthiness as a patron.

Several factors contributed to Rome's extraordinary military success. Roman ideology prized toughness and firmness, the Roman social system instilled obedience, and the competitive ethos raised the stakes for Roman generals. Roman organizational ability and love of order made the Roman military camp a much more regular and systematic place than its Greek counterpart. Beginning in the fourth century B.C., Rome began to reward its soldiers with regular army pay; this and the distribution of conquered land improved morale. Two other points are even more significant: the willingness to adopt foreign military technology and the combination of generosity and firmness with which Rome treated its allies.

The Greek hoplite phalanx came to Rome in the sixth century B.C. At its best on relatively level ground, such as the plain of Latium, the phalanx proved adequate at first. Once the Romans got into mountain fighting, however, as they did in the Apennines against the hill-dwelling Samnites in the mid-fourth century B.C., they found the phalanx wanting. Following a major defeat at the Caudine Forks in 321 B.C., the Romans adopted with great success the Samnites' equipment and tactics.

Unlike the hoplite, the legionary, as the Roman soldier was now called, carried a long, oval body-shield; most legionaries carried a throwing-spear (javelin) instead of a pike, as well as a short sword. Unlike the phalanx, a Roman legion did not fight and maneuver as one thickly massed unit; rather, it contained a loose set of relatively separate and cross-cutting subunits. Legions were drawn up into three lines, organized according to age, experience, and equipment. The tactical unit was the maniple ("handful"), of

Plaque of a Soldier This ivory, one of a pair from Latium dated about 250–200 B.C., provides the best evidence for the dress of a Roman legionary of the Middle Republic. *(Museo de Villa Giula/Art Resource, NY)*

A Roman Triumph

The Roman triumph symbolizes the prestige flowing from military success in Rome; it also demonstrates the senate's attempt to control victorious generals. This description is drawn from the **Epitome** *of Zonaras, a Byzantine historian of the twelfth century* A.D. *Zonaras drew his material on Rome from Plutarch (ca.* A.D. *50–120) and Dio Cassius (second–third century* A.D.*).*

When any great success worthy of a triumph had been gained, the general was immediately saluted as *imperator* by the soldiers, and he would bind sprigs of laurel upon the *fasces* and deliver them to the messengers who announced the victory to the city. On arriving home he would assemble the senate and ask to have the triumph voted him. And if he obtained a vote from the senate and from the people, his title of *imperator* was confirmed. . . .

Arrayed in the triumphal dress and wearing armlets, with a laurel crown upon his head, and holding a branch in his right hand, he called together the people. After praising collectively the troops who had served with him, and some of them individually, he presented them with money and honored them also with decorations. . . . A large part of the spoils also was assigned to the soldiers who had taken part in the campaign. . . .

After these ceremonies the triumphant general would mount his chariot [with his children and relatives]. . . . A public slave . . . rode with the victor in the chariot itself, holding over him the crown of precious stones set in gold, and kept saying to him, "Look behind!" . . . Thus arrayed, they entered the city, having at the head of the procession the spoils and trophies and figures representing the captured forts, cities, mountains, rivers, lakes, and seas—everything, in fact, that they had taken. . . . When these adjuncts had gone on their way, the victorious general arrived at the Roman Forum, and after commanding that some of the captives be led to prison and put to death, he rode up to the Capitol. There he performed certain rites and made offerings and dined in the porticoes up there, after which he departed homewards towards evening, accompanied by flutes and pipes.

Source: From Naphtali Lewis and Meyer Reinhold, eds., *Roman Civilization. Sourcebook I: The Republic,* 3d ed. (New York: Harper & Row, 1990), pp. 230–231; from the Loeb Classical Library.

which there were ten to each line, and thirty to a legion. Each maniple consisted of two centuries (literally "hundreds," although the number of men per century varied), and each century was commanded by a centurion. Legions also contained light-armed troops and cavalry.

A legion marched in a checkerboard pattern, leaving gaps in the lines. In battle each line closed its gaps as it attacked in turn. Unlike hoplites, who engaged the enemy at short range, legionaries first threw their javelins at long range. Then, having broken the enemy's order, they charged and fought with sword and shield. The semi-independence of the maniples, each with its own commander and banner, created a more maneuverable army than that of the phalanx and one better suited for mountain fighting. This advance was no small achievement, for the Greek phalanx had defeated all comers from the fifth century B.C. on. When Rome's legions beat the Macedonian phalanx decisively in 197 B.C., military history entered a new era.

Most major powers in antiquity were bedeviled by rebellions and defections. So were the Romans, but their response was a break with the past. Already the leading power among the Latins under the monarchy, Republican Rome in 494 B.C. formalized its relations with the Latins in an alliance known as the Latin League. Rome was first among equals, but the citizens of even the humblest Latin state had reciprocal rights of intermarriage and commerce with Romans and the right to become a citizen of another state by migrating there. In the fifth century B.C. Rome and its Latin allies fought a long series of wars against rival peoples encroaching on the borders of Latium. Sensing the wisdom of a policy of divide and conquer, the Romans maneuvered their enemies into fighting Rome one by one. The 390s marked two landmarks in this struggle: Rome's capture and destruction of its nearby Etruscan enemy of Veii (396 B.C.) and, only about six years later, a Gallic raiding party's destruction of a Roman army and sack of Rome itself (about 390 B.C.). Rome recovered quickly, but within a generation it had to confront a bitter two-year-long revolt (340–338 B.C.) of the Latins in alliance with the Campanians and various Italian peoples between Latium and Campania.

The year 338 B.C. marked a turning point. Defeated peoples in the ancient world were often executed, deported, or enslaved. Victorious against the Latins, Rome followed a far more generous policy. The Latin League was dissolved. Some of its member states were annexed, and their inhabitants became Roman citizens; others retained independence and alliance with Rome though no longer with one another. The non-Latin allies of the former rebels were also annexed by Rome, but they received the unique halfway status of "citizenship without suffrage." They shared the financial and military burdens of Roman citizenship but also all the rights, except the vote; they also retained the right of local self-government. The settlement of 338 B.C. broke new ground by making it possible for Rome and its former allies and enemies to live together on the basis of relative equality.

The settlement also set a precedent for future Roman expansion. As Rome conquered Italy, a number of privileged central Italian cities (called *municipia*) were given the status of citizenship without suffrage. Others were allowed to retain their independence but were tied to Rome by perpetual alliance. Rome encouraged oligarchy in conquered towns, fostering a community of interests between them and the Roman elite.

If the municipia were the carrots of Roman imperialism, the stick was a network of military roads and colonies crisscrossing Italy, thus allowing Rome to keep an eye on potential rebels. Roman roads allowed the swift movement of troops and linked the growing network of colonies. Colonies were established in strategically vital areas and were peopled mainly with the Roman poor. Together, roads and colonies were a major factor in the consolidation of Roman rule in Italy.

In later years, Italians would complain about treatment by Rome, but compared to the inhabitants of Roman provinces outside Italy, they had a privileged status. Romans too would complain about allied demands for equality, but Rome received from the allies a huge and seemingly inexhaustible pool of military manpower. Manpower was an important factor in Roman victories over the Samnites, Etruscans, and Gauls, all of whom came into the Roman orbit by the early third century B.C. Manpower was decisive in Rome's war (280–276 B.C.) with the Greek general Pyrrhus of Epirus (319–272 B.C.), an adventurer who intervened in southern Italy at the invitation of a Greek city resisting Roman expansion. Although Pyrrhus won battle after battle against the Romans, he was unable to match their willingness to sustain thousands of casualties time and again. Pyrrhus's seeming victories, therefore, turned out to be defeats, which sent him home to Greece disappointed and left us with the expression "Pyrrhic victory."

As for Rome, by 265 B.C. it emerged as the ruler of all of Italy south of the Pisae-Ariminium line. One might say that Rome unified Italy,

ROMAN EXPANSION

494 B.C.	Latin League formed
396 B.C.	Rome destroys Veii
338 B.C.	Latin League dissolved, Roman citizenship extended
312 B.C.	Appian Way constructed
264–146 B.C.	Punic Wars
197 B.C.	Rome defeats Macedonian phalanx
146 B.C.	Rome destroys Carthage and Corinth

The Appian Way Named for the censor Appius Claudius Caecus, who proposed its construction, Rome's first great road was built in 312 B.C., during the Samnite Wars. It originally ran 132 miles from Rome to Capua and was extended an additional 234 miles, probably by 234 B.C., to Brundisium, on Italy's southern Adriatic coast. *(F. H. C. Birch/Sonia Halliday Photographs)*

although Italy was less a unity than a patchwork of Roman territory and colonies and of diverse cities, states, and peoples each allied to Rome by separate treaty.

Rome Versus Carthage: The Punic Wars, 264–146 B.C.

The conquest of Italy made Rome one of two great powers in the central Mediterranean. The other was Carthage. Founded around 750 B.C. by Phoenicians from Tyre, Carthage controlled an empire in North Africa, Sicily, Corsica, Sardinia, Malta, the Balearic Islands, and southern Spain. (The adjective *Phoenician* is *Punicus* in Latin, hence the term *Punic.*) Like Rome, Carthage was run by an oligarchy, but whereas Rome was mainly an agrarian land power, the outlook of the Carthaginian elite was mercantile and naval. Rome had virtually no navy, but Carthage had a great war fleet, a mercantile monopoly of the western Mediterranean, and a major commercial presence in the east.

Carthage was an economic powerhouse. Carthaginian ships traveled to the eastern Mediterranean with minerals from rich mines in Spain, as well as from far-off West Africa and Britain. The Carthaginians were the first Mediterranean people to organize large-scale plantations of slaves for the production of single crops. Even though they zealously wiped out most of Carthaginian elite culture, the Romans did make sure to preserve one Carthaginian classic: a multivolume work on agriculture by Mago. Translated from Punic into Latin by order of the senate, Mago's treatise had enormous impact on Roman landowners, who, with the importation of massive numbers of slaves, adopted the plantation system in Italy (see page 184).

Carthage was a sophisticated and cosmopolitan naval power, boasting generals of extraordinary brilliance, especially in the Barca family, whose most famous member was Hannibal (247–183 B.C.). Carthage might have been a handicapper's favorite at the outbreak of its long wars with Rome in 264 B.C., yet the end result was disaster for Carthage. A combination of Carthaginian weaknesses and Roman strengths accounts for the outcome.

Unlike Rome, Carthage did not have a citizen army. The commanders were Carthaginian, but most of the soldiers were mercenaries and so of questionable loyalty. A second difference in the two states was in the treatment of allies. Rome treated the Italians with considerable respect and tolerance. Carthage showed contempt for its allies, and as a result they had little loyalty toward Carthage and revolted whenever they had the chance. Third, although Carthage's military manpower resources were considerable, they were not so great as Rome's.

At the start of the Punic Wars, Rome had no navy or commanders to match the Barca family but did not suffer from the overconfidence that led Carthage to discount Roman adaptability, tenacity, and ruthlessness. The First Punic War (264–241 B.C.) was fought almost entirely in Sicily. After initial success, Rome realized that it could not win the war without building a fleet. Rome's solution was to capture a Carthaginian warship and use it as a prototype for the Roman navy. Even with a navy, however, the land-loving Romans distrusted the elegant maneuver-and-ram tactics of the sea-going Carthaginians and Greeks. Roman engineers therefore equipped their ships with "ravens," wooden gangplanks with an iron "beak" that penetrated into the enemy's deck. When the Romans engaged the Carthaginian fleet, they threw down the gangplanks, hooked onto enemy ships, and sent Roman soldiers across to fight as if on land.

The long and bloody First Punic War exhausted both sides. In the end Rome won only because the Carthaginian government had had enough. The Carthaginian army in western Sicily under Hannibal's father, Hamilcar Barca (d. 229 B.C.), was still undefeated. At first Rome granted a mild peace treaty, requiring only that Carthage evacuate Sicily and pay an indemnity. Several years later, however, when Carthage was immersed in a mercenaries' revolt, Rome seized Corsica and Sardinia and demanded an additional indemnity.

Forced to give in to these treacherous exactions, Carthage decided to build a new and bigger empire in Spain, beginning in 237 B.C., under Barca family leadership. Spain was inhabited by warlike peoples, but they were no match for Carthage's sophisticated armies. With Spain's rich deposits of silver and copper at its disposal, Carthage was once again a credible threat to Rome. In the mid-220s, an ever-watchful Rome made a treaty with Carthage establishing the Ebro River in northeastern Spain as the boundary of Carthaginian territory. Yet Rome went further, accepting into its friendship the Greek trading

Gold Pendant from Carthage This work from around 500 to 300 B.C. represents the goddess Sekhmet with a lion head, a divine snake, and a solar disk. It was probably used as a protective case for a magic band or amulet. (*Bardo Museum, Tunisia/Martha Cooper/Peter Arnold*)

city of Saguntum, which lay *south* of the Ebro. Though short of a formal alliance, this agreement clearly marked Rome as Saguntum's patron. Emboldened, the Saguntines made themselves a thorn in Carthage's side. In 219 B.C. the new Carthaginian commander, 27-year-old Hannibal Barca, laid siege to Saguntum. With its reputation for trustworthiness at stake, Rome threatened Carthage with war. The enemy was not to be cowed, however. Saguntum fell, and the Second Punic War ensued (218–201 B.C.).

Carthage was willing to risk war because Hannibal had persuaded the home government that he could win a quick, cheap, and easy victory. Because Carthage no longer had a fleet, the Romans felt secure in Italy; Hannibal planned to surprise them by marching overland to Italy, even though the march meant a dangerous passage across the Alps. Hannibal was a tactical genius. He was skilled at ambushes and at the interplay of cavalry and infantry, and he made the enveloping maneuver into a work of art. He reckoned that with his superior generalship he could defeat the Romans in battle and cause them enormous casualties, and he was right. Even without the terrifying weapon of elephants, most of whom died in the harsh climate of the Alps and northern Italy, Hannibal's forces dominated the battlefield. At his victory at Lake Trasimene in Etruria (217 B.C.), Hannibal destroyed a Roman army of 36,000 men; the next year at Cannae in Apulia (southeastern Italy), Carthage gave Rome the bloodiest defeat in its history, killing perhaps 30,000 Romans.

Hannibal incorrectly estimated the result of such victories, however. The Roman elite was both too tenacious and too callous to admit defeat merely because of huge casualties (see the box, "Aftermath of the Battle of Cannae"). The key to Hannibal's strategy, moreover, was to use his victories to destroy the Roman confederacy, but Rome's allies did not revolt as he had expected. There were some significant defections, especially the important Campanian city of Capua; however, most of the allies stood by Rome, both out of loyalty and because of the threat of Roman reprisals. Rome's long-time carrot-and-stick policy in Italy paid off. Roman pragmatism, moreover, showed itself able to deal with crisis. After Cannae, Rome's leadership accepted the policy previously championed in vain by Quintus Fabius Maximus (d. 203 B.C.), who had served as dictator for six months after the defeat at Lake Trasimene. Fabius's was a cautious strategy of harassment, delay, refusal to fight, and attrition. Hannibal was stymied by an enemy who lost battles but refused to surrender.

In the meantime, Rome had bought valuable time to regroup. The fruits of this policy became clear with a series of victories in Spain. The architect of victory was a rising military star, Publius Cornelius Scipio (236–183 B.C.) a Roman who finally understood Hannibal's masterful tactics and succeeded in training his army in them. Invested with extraordinary military powers, Scipio conquered Carthage's Spanish dominions between 210 and 206 B.C. In 204 B.C. he invaded North Africa. Ultimately Hannibal was forced to retreat from Italy and to meet Scipio in battle in 202 B.C. near Zama (in modern Tunisia). It was a hard-fought battle, but the Carthaginians were defeated because of their weakness in cavalry and because of the desertion of their mercenaries. The conqueror of North Africa, Scipio was now surnamed Africanus. As for Hannibal, he played a prominent role in Carthaginian politics for about a decade, until Roman pressure forced him into exile in Syria. In about 183 B.C., after taking part in the Seleucids' unsuccessful war against Rome, he committed suicide rather than face extradition to Rome.

The peace settlement of 201 B.C. stripped Carthage of its empire and reduced it to the status of a local power in Tunisia. Economically, however, Carthage remained enormously prosperous, reviving old fears in Rome of Carthage's political ambitions. In the Third Punic War (149–146 B.C.) Rome mounted a three-year siege under the leadership of Scipio Aemilianus (185–129 B.C.), finally destroying the city of Carthage in 146 B.C. Approximately a century later, Carthage was founded again as a Roman colony and became one of the empire's greatest cities. In the meantime, it was left desolate, its people killed or enslaved.

Rome emerged from the Punic Wars as the greatest power in the Mediterranean. It had acquired new provinces in Sicily, Sardinia, Corsica, Spain, and North Africa (where Carthage's former territory was annexed as the province of Africa). The road to further conquest seemed to lead in all directions.

Aftermath of the Battle of Cannae

Hannibal's victory at Cannae in southern Italy (216 B.C.) was perhaps the greatest defeat ever sustained by Rome. Yet in the end Rome won the war. According to the historian Polybius (ca. 200– ca. 118 B.C.), Roman firmness and resolve in confronting the disaster help explain Rome's general success in war and diplomacy.

After . . . Cannae Hannibal captured the 8,000 Roman soldiers who had been left to guard their camp, . . . he then allowed them to send a deputation to Rome to discuss the matter of their ransom and release. The troops selected ten of their leaders, whom Hannibal sent off, after exacting an oath that they would return to him. One of these men, just as he was going beyond the palisade [wooden wall] of the camp, said that he had forgotten something, and after collecting what he had left behind, once more set out, imagining that since he had returned he had kept his promise and released himself from his oath. On their arrival in Rome, the delegates begged and entreated the Senate not to grudge the prisoners their release, but to allow each to pay three *minae* and return to his people, for Hannibal, they said, had granted this concession. . . . Yet although the Romans had suffered crushing reverses in the war, . . . still, after listening to this plea they neither forgot their dignity under pressure of calamity nor allowed themselves to lose sight of what had to be done. They recognized that Hannibal's object was at once to lay his hands on some money and to sap the fighting spirit of the troops opposed to him by suggesting that even when they were beaten they still had a chance of safety. Therefore the Senate . . . frustrated Hannibal's calculations and all the hopes he had built on these by declining to ransom the prisoners. At the same time they established the rule for their own men that they must either conquer or die on the field. . . . As for the man who had tried to free himself from his pledge by a trick, they put him in chains and sent him back to the enemy. In this way Hannibal experienced less joy from his victory than disappointment, when he saw with amazement the unshaken resolve and the lofty spirit which the Romans showed in their resolutions.

Source: Polybius, *The Rise of the Roman Empire,* trans. Ian Scott-Kilvert (Harmondsworth, England: Penguin, 1979), pp. 351–352.

Victories in the Hellenistic East, ca. 200–133 B.C.

The Second Punic War inflicted a terrible toll on Rome and Italy. Most countries would have savored peace after such an ordeal, but Rome immediately leaped into a long series of wars in Greece and Anatolia. The ostensible origin of the war was the alliance that Philip V of Macedon (r. 221–179 B.C.) had forged with Hannibal after Cannae. In fact, Philip had done little to hurt Rome, nor was he likely to pose a threat in the immediate future. Yet Rome's standing with the Greeks of southern Italy and Sicily might have been diminished by a failure to respond to Philip's provocation. Several smaller Greek states, moreover, had asked Rome to declare war against Macedon in 200 B.C., on the grounds that Macedonian ambitions threatened their security. Such an invitation flattered the Roman elite; in the eyes of many Romans, everything Greek had enormous prestige. Besides, Rome expected a relatively quick and easy victory. It was not disappointed; in 197 B.C. the legions crushed the Macedonian phalanx at Cynoscephalae in central Greece.

This victory was a far cry from the annexation of Macedonian territory. Rome preferred to have

Macedonians and Greeks as clients than to undertake a permanent occupation of their land. In 196 B.C., therefore, a Roman general proclaimed at Corinth that the legions would be withdrawn to Italy and the Greeks henceforth would be free. He meant that they would be "free" within the limits of obedience to Rome. The independent-minded Greeks, however, chafed at Roman domination. They had expected to manipulate the Roman "barbarians" after using them to defeat Macedon.

What followed was a complex interplay. Some Greeks insisted on drawing Rome into their affairs; others feared Rome and sought new allies to balance Roman power. Some Romans resisted the call of Greece; others identified with their Greek friends and began to think in their terms; others were attracted by the prospect of prestige, power, or loot. After several years of intrigue, Rome's Greek opponents managed to provoke an anti-Roman intervention in Greece by the kingdom of the Seleucids. Under Antiochus III (r. 223–187 B.C.) the Seleucids had successfully expanded their power in western Asia and now aimed at European conquests. Antiochus proved no match for Rome, however. Roman forces made short work of the Seleucid enemy, who was driven out of Anatolia as well as Greece. Antiochus agreed to a peace treaty that in effect recognized Roman supremacy in the Mediterranean (188 B.C.).

Rome had hoped to impose a patron-client relationship on Greece and Macedon, thereby avoiding a permanent military presence, but that hope failed. Further political maneuvering in Greece and the ambitions of Philip V's successor as king of Macedon led to another war between Rome and Macedon (171–167 B.C.), settled by a complete Roman victory at Pydna in northern Greece (168 B.C.). Macedon was forced to give up its king and unity and was divided into four separate republics. Two decades later, after additional revolts by Macedonians and Greeks, Rome outlawed even that limited degree of freedom. Macedon became a Roman province in 148 B.C. Greece, not formally a separate province until 27 B.C., was under the thumb of the Roman governor of Macedonia; the leagues uniting separate Greek city-states were abolished. Wherever democracy had survived in Greece, it was replaced with oligarchy. In 146 B.C. Rome destroyed Corinth, one of Greece's wealthiest cities, as a warning against further rebellion. Greece then suffered Roman neglect and taxation for nearly two hundred years.

By annexing Carthage, Macedon, and Greece in the mid-second century B.C., Rome created a dynamic for extending its power around the entire Mediterranean. Before the century was over, southern Gaul was annexed, and Rome had gained a foothold in Asia. The kingdom of Pergamum (northwestern Anatolia) had supported Rome throughout Rome's wars in the east. When Attalus III of Pergamum died without an heir in 133 B.C., he surrendered his kingdom to the Roman people, who made it into the province of Asia. Attalus called his bequest a gift, but in return Rome had to agree not to levy tribute on the Greek cities of the new province. Roman troops, furthermore, were soon dispatched to support the established order against rebellion, an outcome the late king would probably have welcomed.

Two great Hellenistic states remained independent, the Seleucid kingdom and Ptolemaic Egypt. Roman ambassadors and generals frequently interfered in their affairs, however, and no one was surprised when, in the first century B.C., they too were annexed by Rome (Map 5.3).

The Socioeconomic Consequences of Expansion

Expansion led to enormous and unintended changes in Rome's society, economy, and culture. Conquest made wealthy Romans wealthier still, on a scale previously undreamed of. The generals, patrons, diplomats, magistrates, tax collectors, and businessmen who followed Rome's armies made huge profits. By 200 B.C., nonagricultural wealth was a significant feature of the equestrian class. Yet agriculture was more important than ever as a source of elite wealth. In Italy, most profits were in the form of land; in the provinces, not only in land but in slaves, booty, and graft. One of the worst grafters, Gaius Verres,

Map 5.3 Roman Expansion in the Mediterranean, 264–133 B.C. Wars against Carthage and the major Greco-Macedonian powers brought Rome conquests from Spain to North Africa to Anatolia.

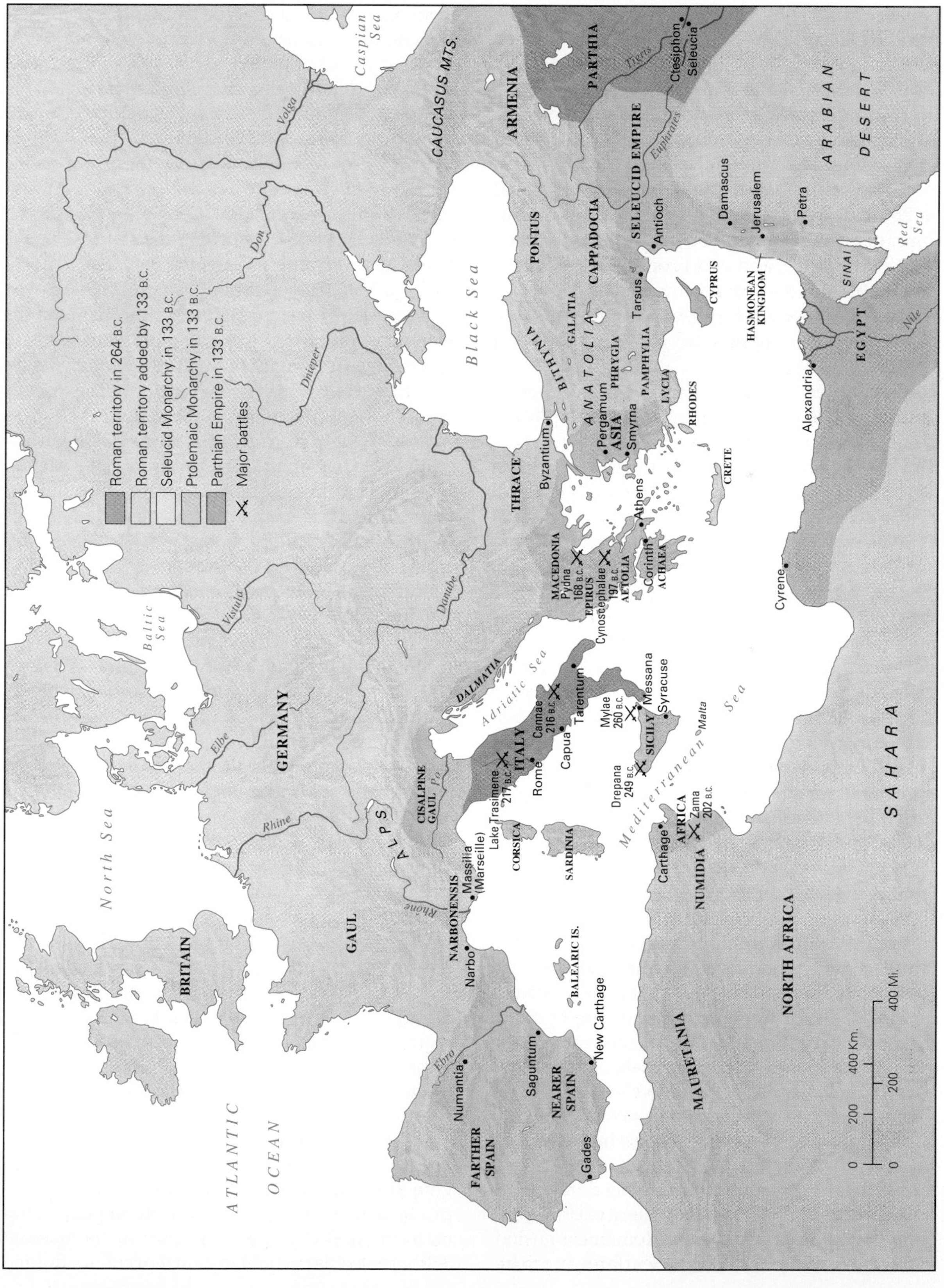

Roman territory in 264 B.C.
Roman territory added by 133 B.C.
Seleucid Monarchy in 133 B.C.
Ptolemaic Monarchy in 133 B.C.
Parthian Empire in 133 B.C.
Major battles
ATLANTIC OCEAN
North Sea
Baltic Sea
Black Sea
Caspian Sea
Adriatic Sea
Mediterranean Sea
Red Sea
BRITAIN
GAUL
GERMANY
NARBONENSIS
CISALPINE GAUL
ALPS
FARTHER SPAIN
NEARER SPAIN
Numantia
Saguntum
New Carthage
Gades
Ebro
Narbo
Massilia (Marseille)
Rhone
Rhine
Elbe
Vistula
Danube
Dnieper
Don
Volga
Po
CORSICA
SARDINIA
BALEARIC IS.
SICILY
ITALY
DALMATIA
Rome
Lake Trasimene 217 B.C.
Capua
Cannae 216 B.C.
Tarentum
Messana
Mylae 260 B.C.
Syracuse
Drepana 249 B.C.
Malta
Carthage
AFRICA
Zama 202 B.C.
NUMIDIA
MAURETANIA
NORTH AFRICA
SAHARA
MACEDONIA
Pydna 168 B.C.
EPIRUS
AETOLIA
Cynoscephalae 197 B.C.
Corinth
ACHAEA
Athens
THRACE
Byzantium
CRETE
RHODES
LYCIA
PAMPHYLIA
PHRYGIA
ASIA
Pergamum
Smyrna
ANATOLIA
BITHYNIA
GALATIA
PONTUS
CAPPADOCIA
Tarsus
CYPRUS
SELEUCID EMPIRE
Antioch
ARMENIA
CAUCASUS MTS.
PARTHIA
Tigris
Euphrates
Ctesiphon
Seleucia
Damascus
Jerusalem
HASMONEAN KINGDOM
Petra
ARABIAN DESERT
SINAI
EGYPT
Nile
Alexandria
Cyrene
0 200 400 Km.
0 200 400 Mi.

governor of Sicily from 73 to 71 B.C., was prosecuted by Cicero (106–43 B.C.), then beginning his oratorical career, for allegedly extorting tens of thousands of pounds of silver from his province. But even Cicero skimmed off several thousand pounds of silver as governor of the province of Cilicia (southern Anatolia) from 51 to 50 B.C.

The first Roman coinage, traditionally dated to 289 B.C., facilitated commercial transactions. Previously, the Romans had made do with barter, uncoined bronze, and cast bronze bars, but now they imitated the workmanship and style of Greek coins. (See the feature, "Weighing the Evidence: Roman Republican Coins," on pages 190–191.)

From their first conquests in Magna Graecia in the third century B.C., Romans began to bring home artists and their works. The trickle of art flowing toward Rome is said to have become a flood when Roman armies entered Greece and Anatolia.

The new wealth and new tastes created a luxury-goods industry in Rome itself, beginning in the third century B.C. Traditionalist opinion was shocked. Not that Rome lacked wealthy households before 300 B.C. Rather, before then Republican ideology had successfully frowned on conspicuous consumption and display. Interest in the arts and letters had been castigated as foreign and corrupting. Although these prohibitions proved impossible to maintain, the elite of the Middle Republic remained champions of conservatism. The most prominent was Marcus Porcius Cato (234–149 B.C.), known as Cato the Censor.

Cato was one of the Republic's "new men." He was the first member of his family to reach the consulship—a rare development, for most consuls of the Middle and Late Republic belonged to families who could boast an earlier consul. Cato championed traditional Roman values of austerity. In 195 B.C., for example, he fought hard, though in vain, to retain a law against the possession of luxuries by women, which had been passed in the crisis of Hannibal's invasion. As censor in 184 B.C., he assessed taxes on luxury goods and slaves at ten times their market value, in order to discourage their use.

Ordinary Romans did not need to be reminded about the virtues of austerity. Unlike the elite, they did not profit from Roman expansion. Indeed, a century of intensive warfare—from the outbreak of the Punic War in 264 B.C. to the destruction of Carthage and Corinth in 146 B.C.—strained the lot of the Roman people to the breaking point. Hannibal's invasion left much of the farmland of southern Italy devastated and Italian manpower considerably reduced. Most people might have rebounded from these problems within a generation or two, if they had not faced other serious troubles.

Conscription had become the norm. The average term of military service between ages 17 and 46 was six years; the maximum term was twenty years. Because experienced legionaries were at a premium, commanders were loath to release them from service. But the longer a man was away in the army, the harder it was for his wife and children to keep the family farm running. With help from a patron, they might be able to make do, though most patrons in fact added to the problem through the introduction to Italy of large-scale agricultural entrepreneurship. Those who sought wealth monopolized Italian farmland, imported huge numbers of slaves, and brought ruin on the free peasantry of Italy.

The last two centuries B.C. witnessed the transformation of Roman rural society from a society of independent farmers to one in which slave labor played a major role. Modern scholars estimate that by the end of the first century B.C. there were 2 or 3 million slaves in Italy, about a third of the peninsula's total population. Prisoners of war and conquered civilians provided a ready supply of slaves. Most worked in agriculture or mining, and their treatment was often abominable; the fewer house slaves were usually better-off.

Wealthy Romans wanted to invest in large landed estates, or *latifundia,* worked by slaves. These estates were either mixed farms (most often devoted to cultivating vines, olives, and grain) or ranches (establishments where animals were raised for meat, milk, and wool). Cato the Censor was a devotee of the latter, arguing that there were only three ways to get rich: "pasturage, pasturage, and pasturage" (see the box, "Cato the Censor on Agriculture"). All a would-be entrepreneur needed was land. Conquests had gained Rome a plenitude of land in Italy. Called public land, it belonged to the Roman people, but an individual was legally entitled to claim about 320 acres as his own. Many entrepreneurs flouted

The Round Temple This elegant, circular, Corinthian-columned structure in the Forum Boarium in Rome, built about 150–100 B.C., is the oldest surviving marble temple in the city. Greek in style, it is an example of Roman borrowing from sophisticated, Hellenistic culture. *(Scala/Art Resource, NY)*

the law, however, and grabbed large chunks of public land for pasturage. They often forced families of absent soldiers off private land, either by foreclosing on debt or by outright violence. Sometimes the families would leave the land for the city, but usually they stayed as tenants.

Before about 170 B.C., poor Romans were sometimes able to find land in colonies. By 170 B.C., however, Rome had established all the colonies in Italy that its security demanded, so that avenue of escape from poverty was closed. A displaced farmer who wanted to compete in the labor market would have found it difficult to underbid cheap slave labor; in any case, Roman ideology frowned on wage labor by citizens. Nor was it practical for a poor farmer to sue a wealthy patron who seized his land, because a plaintiff himself had to bring the accused into court.

The situation of the Italian peasantry was becoming increasingly miserable by the mid-second century B.C. As one modern scholar has put it, "in conquering what they were pleased to call the world the Romans ruined a great part of the Italian people."[2]

The Impact of Greece on Rome and Its Empire

Rome learned much from its new encounter with foreign peoples—and from none more than the Greeks. Wealthy Romans cultivated interests in Greek art, literature, rhetoric, and speculative thought; poor and rich alike enjoyed Greek drama. The simple and frugal elite of traditional Roman ideology began to give way in the third

Cato the Censor on Agriculture

The treatise on agriculture by Cato (234–149 B.C.) is the oldest surviving prose work of Latin literature. In Cato's day, wealthy Romans were buying up or forcing peasants off land all over Italy. These excerpts reveal the elite ideology of gentleman-farming as well as the realities of hard bargaining by landlords and poor living conditions for slaves.

It is true that it would sometimes be better to seek a fortune in trade if it were not so subject to risk, or again, to lend money at interest, if it were an honorable occupation. But our forefathers held this belief and enacted it into law, that while a thief was compelled to repay double, one who loaned at interest had to repay fourfold. From this one may judge how much worse than a common thief they considered the fellow citizen who lent at interest. And when they were trying to praise a good man they called him good farmer and a good tiller of the soil, and the one who received this compliment was considered to have received the highest praise. . . .

When you think of buying a farm, make up your mind not to be eager to buy, and not to spare any exertion on your own part in going to see farms, and not to think it enough to go over them once. The oftener you visit it the more a good farm will please you. . . .

When you come to the farmstead, notice whether there is much equipment for pressing and many storage jars. If there are not, be sure the profit is in proportion. . . . Take care that it is not a farm requiring the least possible equipment and expense. Be sure that a farm is like a man, that however much it brings in, if it pays much out, not a great deal is left. . . .

Clothing for the slaves. A tunic weighing three and one half pounds and a cloak in alternate years. Whenever you give a tunic or cloak to any of them, first get the old one back to make patchwork cloaks of. Good wooden shoes should be given to them every second year.

Source: From Ernest Brehaut, *Cato the Censor on Farming,* in Naphtali Lewis and Meyer Reinhold, eds., *Roman Civilization. Sourcebook I: The Republic,* 3d ed. (New York: Harper & Row, 1990), pp. 474–475, 479.

century B.C. to lovers of the good life. A tension between personal ambition and loyalty to the community had always marked the Republic, and the individualistic spirit of Greek culture did nothing to lessen it.

Before the mid-third century B.C., there was virtually no Roman literature. Writing was generally restricted to commercial and government records and to inscriptions. An oral tradition of songs, ballads, and funeral oratory kept alive the deeds of the famous. In short, the Romans conquered Italy without writing about it.

Contact with the Greek cities brought changes. Large numbers of Roman soldiers in southern Italy and Sicily were introduced to comedy, tragedy, mimes, and sophisticated song lyrics, and many developed a permanent taste for them. It is no accident that the first production of a drama at Rome took place in 240 B.C., the year after the end of the First Punic War. Afterward, the production of such dramas at annual games became standard procedure.

No one could accuse the Romans, however, of rushing headlong into a new age. The authorities continued to have their doubts about theater, which seemed excessively emotional and probably corrupt. They did not allow the building of a permanent theater in Rome until 55 B.C., insisting that the wealthiest city in the Mediterranean make do with makeshift wooden structures. Nor did the Roman elite readily become playwrights or poets. The first gentleman-poet in Rome, Lucilius (180–102 B.C.), did not arrive until the second century B.C., and he was a Latin, not a Roman.

His predecessors, the founders of Latin literature, were all of low social status; little of their work survives. Livius Andronicus (ca. 284–204 B.C.), the first person to translate tragedy and comedy from Greek into Latin, was a Greek freedman (a former slave) from Tarentum. He also translated Homer's *Odyssey* into Latin. His contemporary Gnaeus Naevius (ca. 270–201 B.C.), an Italian from the region of Capua, was a prolific writer whose most important work was an epic account of the First Punic War. This poem, which makes much of the myth tracing Rome's origins to Troy, demonstrates the Roman taste for a sophisticated, Greek-derived foundation myth. Naevius's career also demonstrates the perils of literature, for his lampoon of an aristocratic household is supposed to have earned him prison and then self-exile.

The two great early Latin playwrights are Titus Maccius Plautus (ca. 254–184 B.C.) and Publius Terentius Afer, today known as Terence (ca. 195–159 B.C.). Both of them wrote comedies on the model of the great Greek comic playwright Menander (see page 138). Plautus was an Umbrian and a poor man who learned his Latin at Rome; Terence was a North African slave, educated and freed at Rome. Twenty-one plays by Plautus and six by Terence survive. Plautus's plays are generally earthy and slapstick farces. They are invariably set in Greece, not Rome, in part out of escapism (many were written during the Second Punic War), in part out of the censorial demands of the Roman authorities. They nonetheless reveal much about Roman society. Terence's plays are more subtle than Plautus's, indicating the growing sophistication of Roman theatergoers.

Latin prose developed more slowly than did poetry and drama. The first histories by Romans, composed after the Second Punic War, were written in Greek, for Latin lacked the vocabulary or the audience for history. The works of Quintus Fabius Pictor and Lucius Cincius Alimentus, both Roman senators of the late third century B.C., took the history of Rome down through the Punic Wars. Cato the Censor was the first historian of Rome to write in Latin. His *Origines,* of which little survives, recounted Roman history from the origin of the city to about 150 B.C. The earliest surviving Latin prose work is Cato's *On Agriculture* (see the box on the preceding page).

In the traditional education of a Roman aristocrat, parents and close family friends played the primary role. Although this practice continued, in the second century B.C. wealthy Romans began acquiring Greek slaves to educate their sons in Greek language and literature. Soon Greek freedmen set up schools offering the same subjects; it was not long before similar Latin grammar schools also opened.

One of the forms of Greek literature that appealed most to the practical-minded Romans was rhetoric. Roman orators studied Greek models, and many would say that they eventually outdid the Greeks. Cato was the first Roman to publish his speeches, and he also wrote a book on rhetoric. Both gave impetus to the spread of sophisticated rhetoric in Rome.

Cato's literary output and his knowledge of Greek stand in ironic contrast to his advocacy of simple Roman virtues. Some dismiss him as a hypocrite, but others discern genuine differences between Cato's hesitating admiration for Greek learning and the open enthusiasm with which other members of the elite embraced it. The family of the Scipios, often the butt of Cato's scorn, affords a clear contrast to Cato.

Scipio Aemilianus, conqueror of Carthage in 146 B.C., had a distinguished political and military career. He was also patron of a group of prominent statesmen and soldiers who shared his love of Hellenism. Among the writers whom they supported were the playwright Terence, the poet Lucilius, the historian Polybius, and the Stoic philosopher Panaetius (ca. 185–109 B.C.). The Stoic emphases on duty, wisdom, and world brotherhood appealed both to Rome's traditional ideology and its more recent acquisition of empire.

There was much for Rome to be proud of in Scipio, a man who could effortlessly quote Homer in Greek. There was a disquieting side to him, however. His favorite book was the *Cyropaedia* (*Education of Cyrus*), a philosophical tale by the Athenian Xenophon (428–354 B.C.) about Cyrus, the first great king of Persia. If Rome's leaders were interested in the lives of kings, what did that interest portend for the solidarity of the Roman elite, which had traditionally depended on hostility to monarchy? One might wonder if Rome's devotees of Hellenism had not drunk too deeply at the Greek well of individualism.

Cornelia, Scipio Aemilianus's mother-in-law, did not spend her days at home spinning wool, as Lucretia had done. An educated lover of Hellenism, she wrote letters that existed several hundred years later as examples of elegant Latin prose. Her villa in the resort of Misenum on the Bay of Naples was well known for the distinguished guests whom she received there. When her husband, an outstanding statesman and general, died, Cornelia chose to remain a widow. One of the men who tried to change her mind was no less a figure than the king of Egypt. The widow spent her time managing her own estate and supervising the education of her two sons, the future tribunes Tiberius and Gaius Gracchus (see page 194).

Although Cornelia's privileges were extraordinary, she is nonetheless a reminder of the new possibilities that imperial expansion offered to wealthy Roman women. The conspicuous display of wealth by a wife now might bring status to a husband. Marriage practices changed as well. Because few women were married *cum manu* anymore, that is, handed over to their husbands by their father, a woman's father or nearest male relative, not her husband, was most likely to be her paterfamilias, and a husband's control over his wife's dowry was limited. Furthermore, the farther away the paterfamilias was from her home, the freer the woman might be.

Cornelia is also a reminder of the fundamental conservatism of Roman society. Although we know the years of birth and death of numerous elite Romans of the second century B.C., we do not know Cornelia's. Nor did her literary interests entail any neglect of home and family. Cornelia bore twelve children, though only three of them lived to adulthood (such was the reality of infant mortality even for the wealthiest Romans).

Summary

Republican government, successful imperialism, and the absorption of Greek culture are three outstanding features of the Roman scene in the mid-second century B.C.

In the first centuries of its existence, the Republican oligarchy displayed a remarkable combination of flexibility and stability. It proved able to accommodate not only the competitive instincts of the aristocracy and the newly rich but the land-hunger of the people. The old aristocracy of the patricians opened its ranks to the newly ambitious leaders of the plebeians and also made room in the government for popular representation. The engrained hierarchy of the Roman social and cultural system helped keep politics stable.

The elite channeled popular energies into protecting the young Republic from its numerous enemies in central Italy. Rome consolidated its control of that region by wisely treating its allies with a mixture of firmness and generosity. By extending Roman citizenship, Rome gave them a stake in continued Roman hegemony. Having disposed of its nearest enemies, Rome mounted a quest for absolute security, a quest that led to conquest in Italy and the rest of the Mediterranean. Greed and ambition, as well as fear, were powerful motives of expansion.

The Romans had little native literature of their own, but they knew high culture when they saw it. By the third century B.C. they were well on the way to absorbing and adapting Greek literature and thought. Latin literature began in the second century B.C. Technology and engineering were Roman fortes from early days. Achievements in roadbuilding and shipbuilding were key ingredients of Rome's imperial success.

Having defeated all opponents far and near, Rome seemed to have won absolute security by the mid-second century B.C. Yet its strength was deceptive. Contact with Greek culture liberated the Romans from ruder, peasant ways but also loosened previous restraints. A huge influx of slaves made the acquisition of large estates profitable. The Italian peasantry was already weakened by conscription, and the elite was arrogant from its military success. Thus, it became easy for the strong to confiscate the land of the weak. The result was a growing and dangerous social instability with potential military and political ramifications. At the very moment of triumph, the Republic was in grave danger.

Notes

1. *The Aeneid of Virgil,* trans. Allen Mandelbaum (Berkeley: University of California Press, 1971), pp. 160–161.
2. P. A. Brunt, *Social Conflicts in the Roman Republic* (New York: W.W. Norton, 1971), p. 17.

Suggested Reading

General Surveys

Brunt, P. A. *Social Conflicts in the Roman Republic.* 1971. A fine, non-Marxist overview of the importance of class conflict throughout Republican history.

Cornell, T. J., and J. Matthews. *Atlas of the Roman World.* 1982. A readable introduction to Roman history written by two scholars. The maps and photos are beautiful, among the best available.

Crawford, Michael. *The Roman Republic.* 1982. The best short introduction, sophisticated, lively, and concise.

Heichelheim, F. M., C. A. Yeo, and A. M. Ward. *A History of the Roman People.* 2d ed. 1984. The best introductory textbook, readable and based on up-to-date scholarship.

Kunkel, Wolfgang. *An Introduction to Roman Legal and Constitutional History.* 2d ed. 1973. A survey of the evolution of Roman law in its social and political context from the earliest times to the early Byzantine era.

Early Italy and Early Rome

Bonfante, Larissa, ed. *Etruscan Life and Afterlife: A Handbook of Etruscan Studies.* 1986. A well-illustrated collection of essays on history, economy, art, architecture, coinage, language, daily life, and religion.

Pallottino, M. *The Etruscans.* 1975. An even-handed, well-illustrated introduction.

———. *A History of Earliest Italy.* Translated by Martin Ryle and Kate Soper. 1991. Discusses the current state of the evidence, focusing on 900 to 300 B.C.

Government and Society in the Early and Middle Republic, ca. 509–133 B.C.

Dixon, Suzanne. *The Roman Mother.* 1988. A thoughtful and sophisticated interpretation of the evidence.

Nicolet, C. *The World of the Citizen in Republican Rome.* 1980. An innovative study of civic life focusing on patterns of behavior and structures of thought.

Pomeroy, S. B. *Goddesses, Whores, Wives, and Slaves: Women in Classical Antiquity.* 1976. Chapter VII offers a lively introduction to the women of the Republic.

Saller, Richard P. "Men's Age at Marriage and Its Consequences in the Roman Family." *Classical Philology* 82 (1987): 21–34. A computer-simulated model is used to discuss the impact of the Mediterranean marriage pattern on the Roman family.

Sutherland, C. H. V. *Roman Coins.* 1974. A readable and well-illustrated discussion from the Middle Republic to Late Antiquity.

Watson, A. *Rome of the Twelve Tables.* 1975. An attempt to reconstruct law and society in the Republic of the fifth century B.C.

From Italian City-State to World Empire

Badian, E. *Foreign Clientelae (264–70 B.C.).* 1958. A classic study, vigorously written, of the ways in which the Roman elite transferred its domestic patron-client system to Rome's foreign conquests.

Errington, R. M. *The Dawn of Empire: Rome's Rise to World Power.* 1973. A readable and reliable narrative of Rome's expansion.

Gruen, E. *The Hellenistic World and the Coming of Rome.* 1984. Attuned to the ironies of international affairs, this thoughtful and ground-breaking book argues that the Romans were drawn into domination of the Greek world by the Greeks themselves, not by any grand Roman imperial design.

Keppie, L. *The Making of the Roman Army: From Republic to Empire.* 1984. A sensible and readable reconstruction of the evidence, with particular attention to tactics and organization.

Scullard, H. H. *Roman Politics, 220–150 B.C.* 2d ed. 1973. A good example of the prosopographical approach to Roman politics, a methodology that emphasizes marriage and kinship ties.

Sherwin-White, A. N. *The Roman Citizenship.* 2d ed. 1973. An authoritative work on the varieties of citizenship and their political significance from the earliest times to the Late Empire.

Rome and Its Empire

Brunt, P. A. *Italian Manpower, 225 B.C.–A.D. 14.* 1971. A meticulous and authoritative study of the surviving manpower statistics, most of which are the product of military censuses.

Hopkins, Keith. *Conquerors and Slaves: Sociological Studies in Roman History.* Vol. 1. 1978. A wide-ranging and influential work applying sociological method to history. An excellent study of the impact of empire on the political economy of Italy.

Salmon, E. T. *The Making of Roman Italy.* 1982. A summary of recent research on the peoples of Italy conquered by Rome and of the impact on them of Roman hegemony.

Literature, Religion, Art

Ogilvie, R. M. *Roman Literature and Society.* 1980. A survey of literature in its social context from the Early Republic to the Early Empire. Good bibliographies.

———. *The Romans and Their Gods in the Age of Augustus.* 1970. A good general introduction to Republican religion and its legacy.

Ramage, A., and N. Ramage. *Roman Art: Romulus to Constantine.* 1991. A thorough, readable, and well-illustrated introductory textbook.

Wardman, A. *Rome's Debt to Greece.* 1976. An outline of opinions in Roman literature (from the first century B.C. to the second century A.D.) about Greeks and Greek thought.

Weighing the Evidence

ROMAN REPUBLICAN COINS

Ancient coins are beautiful—beautiful enough to have rooms in museums devoted to them. Once they were practical objects as well. Collectors' items today (and expensive ones), the coins were originally a medium of exchange. That much may be obvious. Less obvious but no less important is the role ancient coins played in public relations. In societies without mass communications, coins were an efficient way for governments to spread a message—especially in cities, the main area of coin circulation. Numismatics (the study of coins) supplements literary evidence, allowing us to reconstruct the past from evidence that people once, literally, held in their hands.

Consider the case of the Roman Republic. A conservative, agrarian state whose elite disdained commerce, the Republic lasted two hundred years without its own coins. Increased wealth, military necessity, and the dictates of prestige finally changed the situation. The Romans began striking coins early in the third century b.c., when military expansion brought Rome into contact with the Greek city-states of southern Italy. Those city-states had been issuing coins for over two hundred years. The Romans, however, made up for lost time in both the quantity and the quality of their issues. Their bronze, silver, and gold coins allowed the Romans not only to buy goods and services in regions of Italy into which they spread their power but also to advertise their new prominence. By issuing coins, the Romans demonstrated as well their ability to master Greek financial, artistic, and communications technologies.

Roman Silver Coin, ca. 269 B.C. *(Courtesy of the Trustees of the British Museum)*

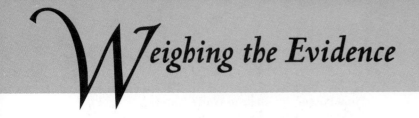

Look first at a silver coin from around 269 B.C., the period when Rome produced its first silver coinage. On the side shown here are a wolf and twin boys. The children are the mythical founders of Rome, the brothers Romulus and Remus, who, according to Roman legend, were abandoned as infants and nursed by a wolf. Notice the word "ROMAN," an abbreviation of *Romanom*, the archaic Latin form of the classical Latin *Romanorum*. This is a coin "of the Romans," in imitation of the inscriptions on southern Italian Greek coins—for example, "of the Neapolitans" on the coins of Naples, a Greek city and Roman ally. The side of this coin not illustrated here shows the head of Hercules as a young man. With his curly hair and diadem, he looks like a Hellenistic athlete; indeed, the style is copied from a coin of Syracuse.

The silver coin, therefore, contains both Greek-derivative and original Roman elements. Why Hercules and the twins and the wolf? Perhaps to announce that, having defeated Pyrrhus and conquered southern Italy, Rome respected Greek traditions but intended to maintain its separate identity—and its power, for Hercules and the wolf were symbols of strength and ferocity.

The silver coin may also have been an advertisement for Quintus Ogulnius, consul in 269 B.C. Twenty-seven years earlier, Quintus and his brother Cnaeus had arranged for statues of Romulus and Remus to be added to the statue of a wolf on the Capitoline Hill in Rome. If the coin commemorates that action, it is an indirect allusion to the glory of the Ogulnius family. Quintus might have preferred to portray himself or another family member on the coin, but tradition limited coin portraiture to gods and heroes. Not until shortly before 100 B.C. would elite Romans illustrate their ancestors on coins—a sign, we may surmise, of a breakdown in group solidarity. But in 269 B.C. that breakdown was more than a century and a half away.

Look now at the gold coin. It was issued sometime between 218 and 216 B.C., early in the Second Punic War, when Hannibal and his army were in Italy, shaking the foundations of the Roman confederacy. We see two soldiers. Each is armed, but their uniforms and features are quite different, suggesting two different nationalities. Both soldiers are touching with their swords a pig held by a young man who is kneeling between them. In a familiar ritual of central Italy, the soldiers are swearing an oath of alliance. According to one ancient interpretation, they are calling on the gods to strike them if they ever violate their oath, just as they struck the pig. On the eve of the battle of Cannae, Rome had every reason to remind its allies of the ties that bound them.

By 216 Hannibal had already inflicted two crushing defeats on Rome's armies in northern Italy. After each battle he ordered the release of captured soldiers from Rome's allies; Roman soldiers remained prisoners. Although Rome's alliance system withstood this attempt to drive a wedge in it, it was prudent of Rome to remind its partners of their obligations.

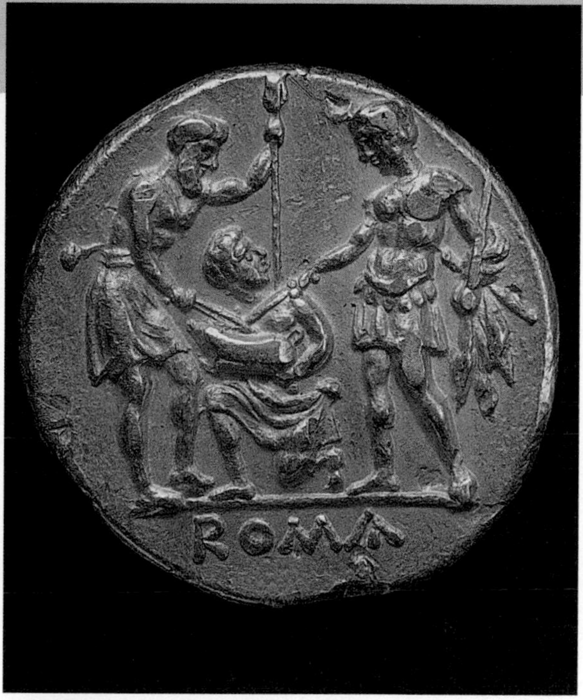

Roman Gold Coin, ca. 218–216 B.C. *(Courtesy of the Trustees of the British Museum)*

Literary evidence suggests that 218 B.C. was the year in which Rome issued its first gold coinage. Even though the coin is gold, Roman finances might have been less then solid. Previously Rome had issued silver coins. The turn to gold might indicate the need to use emergency reserves in the wake of Hannibal's victories.

We may detect in the coin, nonetheless, signs of Roman confidence. The side not illustrated here shows the double-headed god Janus or his son Fontus in what may be a reference to the occasion in 235 B.C. when the doors of the temple of Janus at Rome were closed, as they were only at those few times in Republican history when complete peace reigned. We should also note that the inscription is no longer "ROMAN" but simply "ROMA," not "of the Romans" but "Rome." In a practice beginning around 250 B.C., Roman coins gave up the Greek custom of referring to the people, substituting instead a briefer statement. It was a plain but effective declaration of the power of one city, a power that not even Hannibal's armies could destroy.

CHAPTER 6

Roman Revolution and Imperial Rome, 133 B.C.–A.D. 284

A person born in the Roman Empire in the second half of the first century B.C. would have seen some of the most formidable men and women in human history pass across the scene. Within the space of two generations, Cicero, Julius Caesar, Cleopatra, Augustus, Jesus, and Paul of Tarsus all lived under Roman rule. In the lifetime of our hypothetical Roman, the Roman Republic collapsed in political turmoil and civil war. The lot of the Italian peasantry was miserable, and the provinces were being picked clean by vulturous officials. Yet all began to improve under the rule of Augustus, the first of the Roman emperors.

Augustus took advantage of Rome's war-weariness and of his own superb political instincts to create a new government out of the ruins of the Republic. Like the builders of the Early Republic's constitution, Augustus displayed the Roman genius for compromise. Although he retained the ultimate power, he shared considerable authority with the senate. He made financial sacrifices to feed the urban poor and distribute farms to landless peasants. He ended Rome's seemingly limitless expansion and stabilized the borders of the empire. He began to raise the provinces to a status of equality with Italy. Most important, Augustus initiated an era of peace and prosperity.

The *pax Romana* ("Roman peace"), at its height between A.D. 96 and 180, was an era of enlightened emperors, thriving cities, intellectual vitality, and artistic and architectural achievement in an empire of 50 million or more people. The Roman peace was also an era of considerable spirituality. In the

Pompeii,
Villa of the Mysteries,
ritual scene.

peaceful and diverse empire, ideas traveled from people to people, and the religious beliefs of an obscure sect from western Asia began to spread around the Mediterranean and into northern Europe. The new religion was Christianity.

After 180, Rome slowly passed into a grim period marked in turn by bad emperors, civil war, inflation, plague, invasion, and defeat. After reaching a nadir around 235–253, Rome's fortunes began to improve under a series of reforming emperors. Their works culminated in the reigns of Diocletian (r. 284–305) and Constantine (r. 312–337), who would forge a stronger and vastly different empire (see Chapter 7).

The Revolution from the Gracchi to Caesar, 133–44 B.C.

After 350 years of expansion, a citizen of the Roman Republic in the mid-second century B.C. might have looked forward to a long and happy future for his country, unaware that the Republic was about to begin a century of domestic and foreign unrest that would bring down the whole system. In retrospect, the causes of this revolution are not hard to find. More than a century of intensive warfare—from the outbreak of the First Punic War in 264 B.C. to the destruction of Carthage and Corinth in 146 B.C.—had strained the Roman system to the breaking point. The main sufferers were the ordinary people of Italy—the Roman and allied peasants whose farms were ruined while they were off fighting. The Roman elite was bitterly divided over what to do about the problems of the peasants. One group wanted to redistribute land on behalf of the poor; another group had no sympathy for them. Both groups were willing to exploit the poor for their own ends.

As the population of the city of Rome grew, the provision of a reliable grain supply became a matter requiring government intervention. The factions within the elite, however, were more interested in exploiting the issue for partisan purposes than in finding a solution. Once before, during the struggle between the patrician and plebeian orders in the Early Republic, the elite had been similarly divided and had resolved its differences through compromise (see page 170). The Late Republic, however, was an age of individualism, sophistication, and cynicism; ambitious nobles were no longer willing to subordinate themselves to the community. It was not long before competing armies of land-hungry peasants were marching across Italy.

The Gracchi

Many in the Roman elite were troubled by the military dimension of the agrarian crisis. In modern societies, draftees are often the poorest people. In Rome, military service was a prestigious activity, and putting weapons in the hands of the poor was considered unwise. Thus, a property qualification was imposed on conscripts. As fewer and fewer potential soldiers could afford to own property, however, during the second century it became necessary to reduce the property qualification several times. By 150 B.C. a conscript had to own property worth only 400 denarii—roughly a small house, a garden, and some personal belongings. If the impoverishment of the peasantry continued, Rome would either have to drop the property qualification for the military altogether or stop fielding armies. Clearly, something had to be done.

Into the breach stepped Tiberius Sempronius Gracchus (d. 133 B.C.), one of the ten tribunes for the year 133 B.C. (see the box, "Tiberius Gracchus on Rome's Plight"). The son of Cornelia (see page 188) and a distinguished general and ambassador (whose name Tiberius shared), Tiberius seemed an excellent spokesperson for a group of prominent senators who backed land reform. He proved, however, to be arrogant and overly ambitious. In pursuit of his goals, he deposed one of his fellow tribunes, Octavius, an opponent of reform, and thereby shocked and angered conservatives.

Tiberius's proposed law restored the roughly 320-acre limit to the amount of public land a person could own. A commission would be set up to repossess excess land and redistribute it to the poor, in lots that probably ranged from 9 to 18 acres. These lots were to be inalienable—that is, the wealthy could not buy them back. The former landowners would be reimbursed for improvements they had made, such as buildings or plantings.

Tiberius Gracchus on Rome's Plight

In 133 B.C. Tiberius Gracchus proposed to confiscate from wealthy landowners public land possessed in excess of the legal limit, and to redistribute it to poor Roman citizens. The proposal, and Tiberius's unorthodox methods of getting it passed into law, raised a controversy that led to his murder. Plutarch (ca. A.D. 50–ca. 120) discusses Tiberius's motives and paraphrases one of his speeches.

His brother Gaius recorded in one of his writings that when Tiberius on his way to Numantia [in Spain] passed through Etruria and found the country almost depopulated and its husbandmen and shepherds imported barbarian slaves, he [Tiberius] first conceived the policy which was to be the source of countless ills to himself and to his brother. But it was the people themselves who chiefly excited his zeal and determination with writings on the porticoes, walls, and monuments, calling on him to retrieve the public land for the poor.

. . . Tiberius, fighting for an honorable and just cause with an eloquence that would have dignified even a meaner cause, was formidable and invincible whenever, with the people crowding around . . . , he took his place and spoke in behalf of the poor. "The wild beasts that roam over Italy," he said, "have their dens, each has a place of repose and refuge. But the men who fight and die for Italy enjoy nothing but the air and light; without house or home they wander about with their wives and children. Their commanders lie when they exhort the soldiers in battle to defend sepulchers and shrines from the enemy, for not one of these many Romans has either hereditary altar or ancestral tomb; they fight and die to protect the wealth and luxury of others; they are styled masters of the world, and have not a clod of earth they can call their own."

Source: Plutarch, *Life of Tiberius Gracchus,* in Meyer Reinhold and Naphtali Lewis, eds., *Roman Civilization, Selected Readings,* Vol. 1, *The Republic,* 3d ed. (New York: Columbia University Press, 1990), pp. 251–252.

The proposal was moderate, but wealthy landowners attempted to quash it. Many senators suspected that Tiberius wanted to set himself up as a kind of superpatron, buoyed by peasant supporters. Tiberius's methods disturbed the senate even more than the substance of his proposed law. In addition to deposing Octavius, Tiberius, when the bill became law, intervened in the senate's bailiwicks of foreign affairs and finances by earmarking tax receipts from the new province of Asia to finance land purchases. Finally, Tiberius availed himself of the expedient, of dubious legality, of running for a second consecutive term as tribune. While the tribal assembly prepared to vote on the new tribunes, some senators led a mob to the Forum and had Tiberius and three hundred of his followers clubbed to death.

This shocking event marked the first time in the Republic that a political debate was settled by bloodshed in Rome itself. The ancient sources agree that it was the beginning of a century of revolution. The land commission went ahead with its work, even without Tiberius. His younger brother, Gaius (d. 121 B.C.), was ready to continue Tiberius's work when, in 123 B.C., Gaius became tribune.

Gaius expanded Tiberius's coalition, adding to it supporters from the equestrian order and the urban populace, mainly composed of slaves and freedmen. He gave the plebs cheap grain at subsidized prices. The equestrians were wealthy, landed gentry, similar to senators in most respects except for their failure to have reached the senate; they yearned for political power. A small

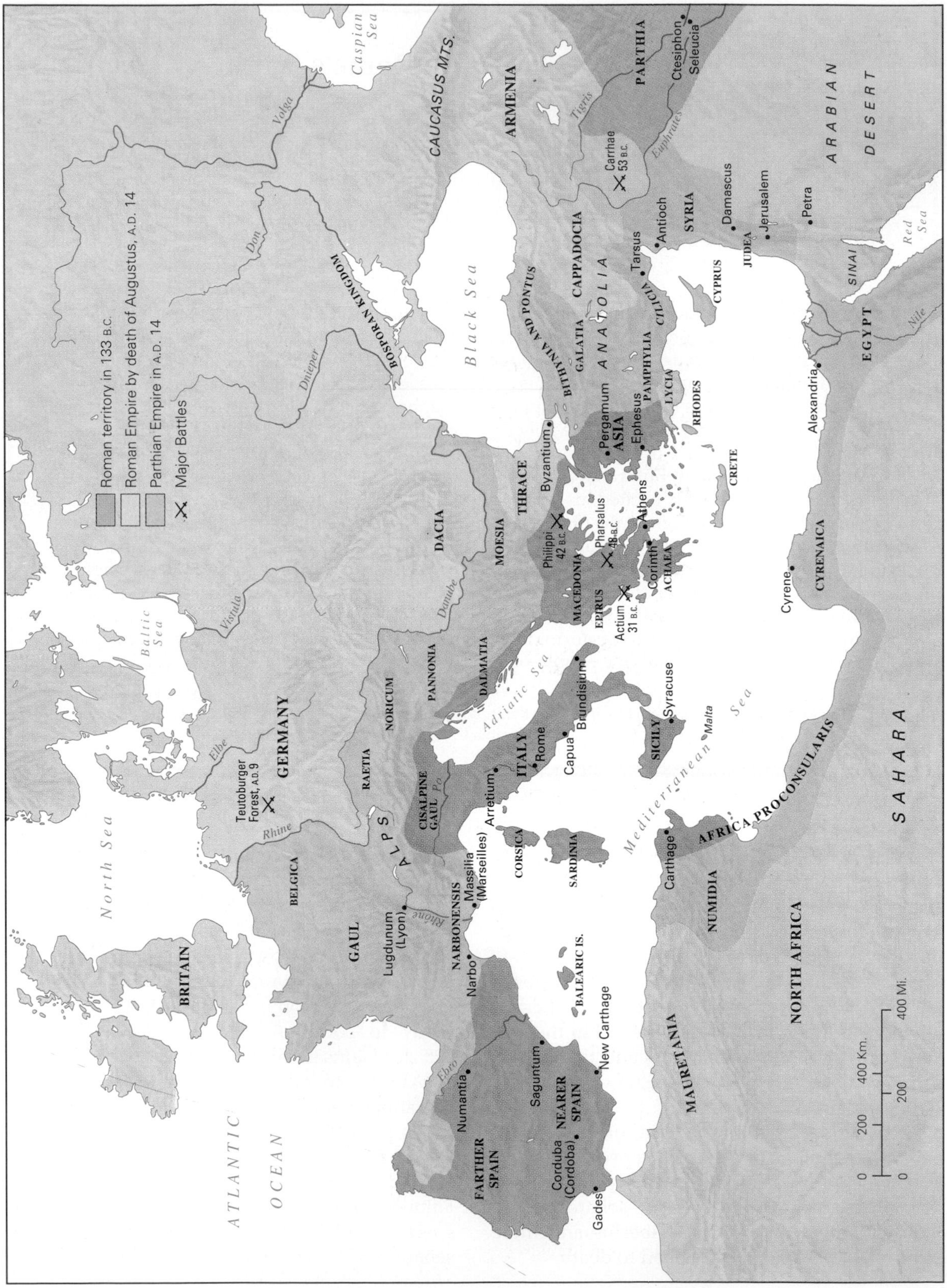
Roman territory in 133 B.C.
Roman Empire by death of Augustus, A.D. 14
Parthian Empire in A.D. 14
Major Battles
North Sea
Baltic Sea
Black Sea
Caspian Sea
Adriatic Sea
Mediterranean Sea
Red Sea
ATLANTIC OCEAN
BRITAIN
GAUL
BELGICA
NARBONENSIS
ALPS
GERMANY
RAETIA
NORICUM
PANNONIA
DALMATIA
DACIA
MOESIA
THRACE
MACEDONIA
EPIRUS
ACHAEA
CISALPINE GAUL
ITALY
CORSICA
SARDINIA
SICILY
BALEARIC IS.
FARTHER SPAIN
NEARER SPAIN
MAURETANIA
NUMIDIA
NORTH AFRICA
AFRICA PROCONSULARIS
CYRENAICA
EGYPT
SINAI
JUDEA
SYRIA
CYPRUS
CRETE
RHODES
ASIA
LYCIA
PAMPHYLIA
CILICIA
ANATOLIA
GALATIA
BITHYNIA AND PONTUS
CAPPADOCIA
ARMENIA
PARTHIA
BOSPORAN KINGDOM
CAUCASUS MTS.
ARABIAN DESERT
SAHARA
Rhine
Elbe
Vistula
Danube
Dnieper
Don
Volga
Tigris
Euphrates
Nile
Rhône
Po
Ebro
Malta
Teutoburger Forest, A.D. 9
Lugdunum (Lyon)
Massilia (Marseilles)
Narbo
Arretium
Rome
Capua
Brundisium
Syracuse
Carthage
New Carthage
Saguntum
Numantia
Corduba (Cordoba)
Gades
Actium 31 B.C.
Corinth
Athens
Pharsalus 48 B.C.
Philippi 42 B.C.
Byzantium
Pergamum
Ephesus
Tarsus
Antioch
Damascus
Jerusalem
Petra
Alexandria
Cyrene
Carrhae 53 B.C.
Ctesiphon
Seleucia
0 200 400 Km.
0 200 400 Mi.

but important group of equestrians was engaged in commerce and tax collection in the provinces. The senate regulated their activities through the so-called extortion courts, which tried corruption cases. Gaius staffed those courts with equestrians. Alluding to the new equestrian power, Gaius remarked, "I have left a sword in the ribs of the senate."

Gaius's ultimate aims are unclear, but the threat Gaius posed to the senate's power is certain. He sponsored an extension of his brother's agrarian law, new colonies, public works, and relief for poor soldiers. Eventually Gaius ran aground on a plan to include the Italian allies as beneficiaries of agrarian reform—a far-sighted notion but one unpopular with the Roman people, who were jealous of their privileges. Denied a third term as tribune in 121 B.C. (he had won a second the previous year), Gaius resorted to force to try to prevent a repeal of his program. The senate responded to his action by passing a declaration of public emergency, empowering the magistrates to use whatever means necessary to protect the state.

With the help of senators, slaves, and mercenaries, one of the consuls had Gaius and 250 of his followers killed. Another 3000 Gracchans were executed soon thereafter. Within a few years, the Gracchan land commission was abolished. It is estimated that approximately 75,000 citizens had been given land. The law, however, was amended to permit the resale of redistributed land, and with the wealthy poised to buy land, the settlers' future was uncertain. The senatorial oligarchy seemed to be back in control.

Appearances, however, proved illusory. Roman politics had become an unstable brew, among whose elements were both the pursuit of personal supremacy and the resort to violence. The crisis of the peasantry continued. In time, it became clear that the Gracchi had divided the political community into two loose groupings. On one side were the *optimates* ("the best people"; singular, *optimas*), conservatives who asserted the rule of the senate against popular tribunes and the maintenance of the estates of the wealthy in spite of agrarian crisis. On the other side were the *populares* ("men of the people"; singular, *popularis*), who challenged the rule of the senate in the name of relief of the poor. The populares were not democrats. Like the optimates they were Roman nobles who believed in hierarchy, but they advocated the redistribution of wealth and power as a way of restoring stability and strengthening the military.

Map 6.1 The Roman Empire in the Late Republic In the years from 133 B.C. to 14 A.D. Rome conquered substantial territories in three continents, adding them to its already large empire.

FALL OF THE ROMAN REPUBLIC

133, 123–122 B.C.	The Gracchi
107 B.C.	Marius abandons property qualification for soldiers
81–79 B.C.	Dictatorship of Sulla
66–62 B.C.	Pompey's conquests in western Asia
60 B.C.	First Triumvirate
44 B.C.	Caesar assassinated
31 B.C.	Octavian defeats Antony at Actium

Marius and Sulla

By 100 B.C. Rome's agrarian crisis had become a full-scale military crisis too (Map 6.1). Roman armies under senatorial commanders fared poorly, first in a war against Numidia (modern Algeria) and then in a series of battles in southern Gaul against Germanic tribes. The situation was saved by an outsider, an equestrian named Gaius Marius (ca. 157–86 B.C.), the first member of his family to be elected consul, for 107 B.C. This "new man" proved to be a great military reformer. Marius streamlined the Roman army: Camp followers were reduced in number, and individual soldiers were made to carry their own equipment. To meet the Germans, who attacked in overwhelming waves, maniples—the tactical subunits of a legion—were reorganized and combined into larger units called cohorts, rendering the army firmer and more cohesive. Most important, Marius abandoned altogether the property qualification for the military. As a result, Roman soldiers were no longer peasants doing part-time military service but rather were landless men making a profession of the military.

Marius was victorious in battle both in North Africa and in Gaul. As a politician, however, he broke with oligarchic solidarity, demanding and receiving six elections to the consulship, unconstitutional though they were. Furthermore, after restoring peace, Marius championed his soldiers by asking in 100 B.C. that land be distributed to them. After violent senatorial opposition, he backed down, but he had rung the death bell for the old, agrarian patron-client system. In early Rome landowners had offered genuine help to their clients among the local peasantry, but no more. Now only military leaders like Marius offered land to the needy. As a result, ordinary Romans, to all of whom the army now lay open, transferred their loyalty from the senate, which the landowners dominated, to their commander.

The Republic was weak, and it became weaker still as a result of two new wars. First, its Italian allies rose against Rome in a bloody and bitter struggle from 91 to 89 B.C. known as the "Social War"—that is, war with the *socii* ("allies"). The allies resented Rome's unwillingness to consult them on major decisions or to share the benefits of empire, even though they provided a large share of Rome's troops. They fought hard, and Rome, in order to prevail, had to concede to them what they had demanded at the outset: full Roman citizenship. The war wrought devastation in the countryside, further destabilizing the Republic.

The other conflict of this period pitted Rome against Mithridates (120–63 B.C.), king of Pontus (northern Anatolia). Mithridates conquered the Roman province of Asia (western Anatolia) and slaughtered the numerous Italian businessmen and tax collectors there. Once again a military man rose to save the day for Rome: Marius's rival and former lieutenant, Lucius Cornelius Sulla Felix (ca. 138–78 B.C.), consul for the year 88 B.C.

The senate assigned Sulla the command against Mithridates, but Marius, elderly but still ambitious, employed a tribune to get a law passed reassigning the command to him. Sulla, supported by his troops, marched on Rome, which he took easily, and annulled Marius's law. The army, not the politicians, held the ultimate authority. Having escaped from Rome, Marius returned in 87 B.C. with his own army, captured the city, and had his opponents killed. He died in 86 B.C., but his allies maintained an anti-Sullan regime in Rome.

Victorious over Mithridates, Sulla returned to Italy in 83 B.C., eager to settle scores. Civil war was followed by proscription—the posting of the names of Sulla's political opponents, as many as 2000 men. Their fate was death, confiscation of their land, and disenfranchisement of their sons. Sulla settled his veterans, about 80,000 men, on land in Italy from which entire communities that had opposed him had been expelled.

Having assumed the long-dormant office of dictatorship—now, unconstitutionally, for life—Sulla attempted to reform the constitution. He aimed to restore the senatorial oligarchy that had ruled before the Gracchi. To this end, he greatly weakened the tribunate by restricting its powers and denying further office to men who served as tribune. He regulated the magistracies to ensure that by the time someone became a military commander or provincial governor, he had been a senator for twenty years and so might display loyalty to the senate. By adding several hundred equestrians, Sulla doubled the size of the senate, from about 300 to about 600 members. The move both defused hostility between senators and equestrians and increased the pool of potential leaders.

The most long-lasting of Sulla's measures was his reform of the courts. He abolished trials before popular assemblies and equestrian-staffed courts. Criminal cases were now heard before one of seven standing courts, whose juries were composed of senators. Although later Roman criminal law evolved considerably, it was founded on Sulla's actions. Generally only wealthy people had access to the standing courts; alleged crimes involving ordinary people were heard before lesser magistrates.

Sulla retired in 79 B.C. and died a year later. His hope of restoring law and order under the senate died with him. He had strengthened the senate, but only at the cost of bloodshed and bitterness. Discontent smoldered among the men whose land he had confiscated. Equally serious, many senators, aspiring to what Sulla had done and not to what he had said, pursued personal power, not the collective interests of the senate.

Pompey and Caesar

New, would-be Mariuses or Sullas now arose. The dominant leader of the seventies and sixties B.C. was Pompey the Great (106–48 B.C.) a brilliant general and a supporter of Sulla. Young Pompey went from command to command: He put down an agrarian rebellion in Italy (78 B.C.) and a rebellion in Spain (77–71 B.C.), cleared the Mediterranean of pirates (67 B.C.), defeated Mithridates again (66 B.C.), and added rich conquests to the empire in Anatolia, Syria, Phoenicia, and Palestine (66–62 B.C.). In the fifties B.C. the tide began turning in favor of Gaius Julius Caesar (100–44 B.C.), another brilliant general and a very clever politician. The son of an obscure patrician family, Caesar had family connections to Marius and his supporters. Caesar's career depended on his brilliant oratory, his boldness, and his sheer talent at war and politics. Caesar conquered Gaul and Britain (58–51 B.C.) and laid the foundations of Roman rule in Egypt (see Map 6.1).

While the elite of the Late Republic struggled to maintain order, ordinary people were struggling for survival itself. Violence had become endemic to rural Italy. It was an era of civil war, in which hostile forces lived on plunder, pilfering crops or animals and emptying storehouses. Many once-prosperous farmers, dispossessed peasants, and runaway slaves alike ended up as brigands or highwaymen. It was also an era of slave revolts, the most serious of which was led by the Thracian Spartacus from 73 to 71 B.C., at a time when Rome also faced major wars in Spain and Anatolia. An able commander, Spartacus beat nine separate Roman armies in two years before finally suffering defeat.

Roman elite women were sometimes pawns, sometimes partners in the political careers of Pompey and Caesar. In 80 B.C., for example, Pompey divorced his first wife to advance his career by marrying Aemilia, Sulla's stepdaughter. Aemilia was not only married at the time but pregnant by her husband. Soon after her divorce and remarriage, she died in childbirth. Caesar took many mistresses, among whom was the queen of Egypt, Cleopatra (69–30 B.C.). Caesar had a penchant for certain Egyptian institutions, such as the Egyptian calendar (see page 200), and he toyed with becoming a monarch himself, an inclination that Cleopatra perhaps encouraged.

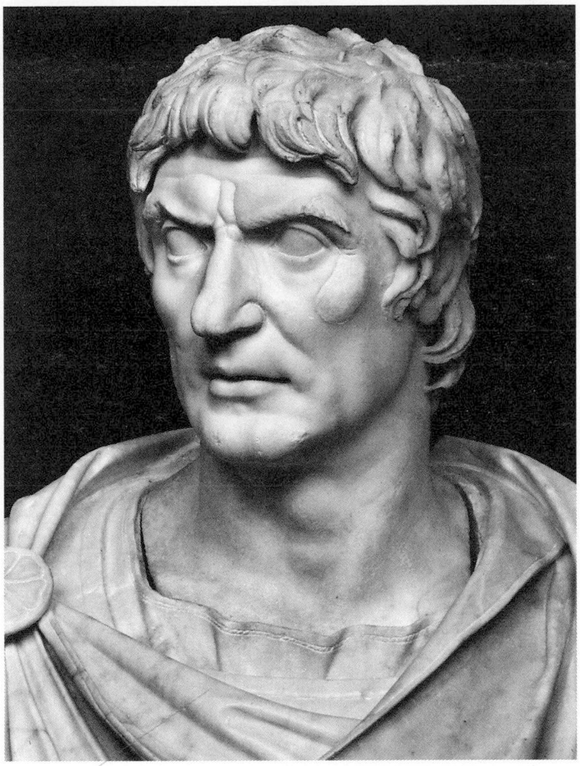

Head of Sulla This grim marble portrait leaves little doubt about the nature of the dictator's power, founded on civil war and mass executions. Note the wrinkles and jowls, characteristic features of the Late Republic's taste for realistic sculpture. *(Staatliche Antikensammlungen u. Glyptothek, München)*

Another of Caesar's mistresses was Servilia, stepsister of Marcus Porcius Cato (Cato the Younger, 95–46 B.C.), great-grandson of the famous censor (see page 184). She was also mother of Brutus, the man who would eventually help murder Caesar.

Pompey was an optimas, Caesar a popularis, but the two of them agreed that they, not the senate or the assemblies, should dominate the Roman state. In 60 B.C. they entered into a pact with a third ambitious noble, Marcus Licinius Crassus (d. 53 B.C.). Known today as the "First Triumvirate," this extraconstitutional coalition was in fact a conspiracy to run the state. Their individual ambitions rebuffed by the senate, each man had an agenda that pooling resources in the triumvirate permitted him to fulfill: for Pompey, ratification of his acts in the East and land for his veterans; for Caesar, who became consul for 59

Coin of Julius Caesar Caesar was the first living Roman to be represented on a coin, a sign both of his power and of the break with tradition that he marked. *(Cabinet des Médailles, Bibliothèque Nationale/Editions Arnaud)*

B.C., a long command with a free hand in Gaul; for Crassus, a rebate for the tax collectors of Roman Asia whom he championed and eventually a command in Syria to make war on Parthia (the revived Persian Empire).

The success of the triumvirate was only temporary. And despite the triumvirate's ultimate failure, its very existence bespeaks the demise of the Republic. Crassus died in an inglorious defeat at Carrhae in Syria in 53 B.C., made symbolically worse by the Parthians' successful capture of Roman legionary standards. Frightened by Caesar's stunning victories in Gaul, Pompey returned to the senatorial fold, now led by Cato the Younger. Cato and his supporters stood for the traditional rule of the senatorial oligarchy. They saw Caesar as a second Marius, a military leader who cared more for his troops and his glory than for the senate. In 49 B.C., ordered by the senate to give up his command in Gaul, Caesar instead marched on Italy with his army. Italy's northern boundary was marked by a tiny stream called Rubicon; when Caesar crossed it, he declared, "The die is cast." Indeed it was, for civil war. Caesar swept to victory against the senate's army, led by Pompey, at Pharsalus in Greece in 48 B.C.; the complete destruction of the senate's forces took until 45 B.C. After Pharsalus, Pompey fled to Egypt, where he found a rude welcome: He was stabbed to death while disembarking.

The years of civil war brought Caesar from Spain to Anatolia. During the fighting he showed the qualities that made him great: speed, adaptability, endurance, and intelligence. He also showed considerable diplomatic skill, offering clemency to any of his enemies who joined him. Caesar was both reflective and literary enough to publish two commentaries on his military campaigns: *On the Gallic War* and *On the Civil War*, the latter appearing after his death. These works sought to glorify Caesar's conquests and justify his decision to wage a bloody civil war.

Back in Rome, Caesar sponsored a vast number of reforms. His political goal was elevating Italians and others at the expense of old Roman families. To achieve it, Caesar conferred Roman citizenship liberally, on all of Cisalpine Gaul (northernmost Italy) as well as on certain provincial towns. He enlarged the senate from 600 to 900, adding his supporters, including some Gauls, to the membership. Caesar's social and economic reforms included reducing debts and founding the first colonies outside Italy, where veterans and poor citizens were settled. He undertook an ambitious public building program in the city of Rome. Caesar's most long-lasting act was to introduce the calendar of 365¼ days, on January 1, 45 B.C. Derived from the calendar of Egypt, it is known as the Julian calendar.

Caesar often flaunted his contempt for republican constitutional formalities. His acceptance of a dictatorship for life offended the old guard, his flirtation with the notion of a monarchy even more so. He took numerous, extraordinary titles and began to institute a religious cult in his own honor. With one eye toward avenging Crassus and another toward equaling the achievements of Alexander the Great, Caesar made preparations for a war against Parthia, but in vain. His ascendancy ended abruptly on March 15, 44 B.C. (the Ides of March by the Roman calendar), when sixty senators stabbed him to death. The assassination took place in the portico attached to the Theater of Pompey, in front of a statue of Pompey himself, where the senate was meeting that day. It had been eighty-nine years since the murder of Tiberius Gracchus.

The assassins called themselves Liberators, believing that they were freeing themselves from tyranny just as the founders of the Republic had done centuries before. Indeed, one of the chief conspirators, Marcus Junius Brutus (ca. 85–42 B.C.), claimed descent from Lucius Junius Brutus, traditional leader of the revolt against the Tarquins that had established the Republic. Like his coconspirator Gaius Longinus Cassius (d. 42 B.C.), Brutus had been a magistrate, military officer, and provincial administrator. Both men thought Caesar's murder was justified by the public interest, but the assassination led only to more years of disorder, renewed civil war, and the threat of tyranny far more severe than Caesar's.

The World of Cicero

Marcus Tullius Cicero (106–43 B.C.) is one of the best-known figures of all antiquity. Like Marius, he was a wealthy equestrian from the central Italian town of Arpinum who, as consul (in 63 B.C.) became a "new man." Cicero was an optimas and defender of the senate, though ready for compromise with the equestrians. He made his name as consul in 63 B.C. by successfully leading the opposition to Lucius Sergius Catilina, a down-and-out patrician who organized a debtors' revolt in Etruria; the army smashed the rebellion.

His intelligence, ambition, literary talents, and study of philosophy and oratory in Greece as a young man enabled Cicero to produce elevated and serious writings. Never as original as Plato or Aristotle, Cicero nonetheless was crucial in making the Latin language a vessel for the heritage of Greek thought. A prolific writer, Cicero produced over a hundred orations, of which about sixty survive; several treatises on oratory; philosophical writings on politics, ethics, epistemology, and theology; poetry (of which little survives); and numerous letters. After his death in 43 B.C. his voluminous correspondence was published with little expurgation. The letters and speeches provide a vivid, detailed, and sometimes damning picture of politics.

Politics in the Late Republic was loud and boisterous. The elite prided itself on free speech and open debate. In the senate, assemblies, and court cases, oratory—sometimes great oratory—was ubiquitous. Few orators in history have matched Cicero's ability to lead and mislead an audience by playing on its feelings. He knew every rhetorical trick and precisely when each was appropriate. His orations are masterpieces of technique, famous for polish, wit, long rolling sentences, and, above all, for emotional power. (See the box, "Cicero Against Catilina.")

Because of increased freedom and greater educational opportunities, during the Late Republic it was possible for elite women as well as men to study oratory. Private tutors were common among the aristocracy, and girls often received lessons alongside their brothers. Girls also sometimes profited from a father's expertise. A particularly dramatic case is that of Hortensia, daughter of Quintus Hortensius Hortalus (114–50 B.C.), a famous orator and rival of Cicero. An excellent speaker herself, Hortensia defied tradition by arguing successfully in the Roman Forum in 42 B.C. against a proposed war tax on wealthy women.

Cicero pilloried one elite woman who enjoyed considerable freedom, Clodia (b. ca. 95 B.C.). Sister of the notorious populist gang-leader Clodius and wife of optimas politician Metellus Celer (d. 59 B.C.), Clodia moved in Rome's highest circles. Cicero accused her of poisoning her husband (the charge was unprovable). She is better remembered from the poems of Catullus (ca. 85–54 B.C.), where she is called Lesbia. In passionate and psychologically complex verse, Catullus describes the ups and downs of their affair, which Clodia eventually ended.

Ordinary people lacked the education or the freedom to express themselves in the manner of a Catullus or Hortensia, but a less civilized means of expression was open to them: the political gang. Brawls and violence between the rival groups of Clodius, a supporter of Caesar, and Milo, a supporter of the senate, became increasingly common in the fifties B.C. As dictator, Caesar abolished the gangs. Meanwhile, among the elite, as Cicero's letters indicate, free speech gave way to gossip, plotting, factionalism, and flattery of Pompey and Caesar. For every man of principle like Cicero, a dozen people were willing to blow with the prevailing winds.

Cicero's works provide evidence of a development in the practice of Roman law. Often unheralded, it was nonetheless of enormous historical importance, for Cicero's contemporaries invented the very notion of the legal expert, a person devoted to explaining and interpreting

Cicero Against Catilina

Of all Cicero's orations, perhaps none is better known than this speech against Catilina, delivered in the Senate in 63 B.C. The consul Cicero argued that Catilina, a senator, was plotting to launch a debtors' revolt.

In the name of heaven, Catilina, how long do you propose to exploit our patience? Do you really suppose that your lunatic activities are going to escape our retaliation forevermore? Are there to be no limits to this audacious, uncontrollable swaggering? Look at the garrison of our Roman nation which guards the Palatine by night, look at the patrols ranging the city, the whole population gripped by terror, the entire body of loyal citizens massing at one single spot! Look at this meeting of our Senate behind strongly fortified defenses, see the expressions on the countenances of every one of these men who are here! Have none of these sights made the smallest impact on your heart? You must be well aware that your plot has been detected. Now that every single person in this place knows all about your conspiracy, you cannot fail to realize it is doomed. Do you suppose there is a single individual here who has not got the very fullest information about what you were doing last night and the night before, where you went, the men you summoned, the plans you concocted?

What a scandalous commentary on our age and its standards! For the Senate knows about all these things. The consul sees them being done. And yet this man still lives. Lives? He walks right into the Senate. He joins in our national debates—watches and notes and marks down with his gaze each one of us he plots to assassinate.

Source: Cicero, *Against Catiline,* in Michael Grant, trans., *Selected Political Speeches of Cicero* (Harmondsworth, England: Penguin, 1977), p. 76.

the law. Complex and intricate, Roman law needed interpretation. Much of it was the work not of legislators but of judges, especially the praetors, who issued annual edicts setting forth how their courts would work. In the Early Republic the pontiffs alone had the right to interpret the law (see page 166), but in the third and second centuries B.C. a group of lay legal interpreters known as jurisconsults emerged. In the first century they became true jurists; their intepretations began to be considered authoritative. Two outstanding jurists of this period were Quintus Mucius Scaevola (d. 82 B.C.), who wrote on the civil law, and Servius Sulpicius Rufus (d. 43 B.C.), an expert on the law of the magistrates. No earlier Mediterranean society had a professional class of legal experts, but no earlier society had faced issues as complex and turbulent. No earlier society had 3 million citizens, as Rome did in the mid-first century B.C. The Western tradition of legal science has its roots in Rome.

Rome's political system, unlike its legal system, did not adapt flexibly to changing circumstances. The disenfranchised of the Late Republic had reasonable goals: land for those who had fought for their country and admission to the senate of a wider group. Yet the old elite resisted both. Cicero's proposed solution was the union of the senatorial and equestrian orders. He also advocated widening the Roman ruling class to include the elite of all Italy. The newly widened ruling class could close ranks and establish *otium cum dignitate,* "peace with respect for rank." Cicero's new order was distinctly hierarchical.

In the turbulent times of the Late Republic, some in the Roman elite turned to Epicureanism. The poet Lucretius (ca. 94–ca. 55 B.C.) describes the Epicurean ideal of withdrawal into the contemplative life in a long didactic epic called *On the Nature of Things*. Most elite Romans, however, including Cicero, preferred the activist philosophy of Stoicism. Cicero put forth a generous view of human brotherhood. He argued that all people share a spark of divinity and are protected by natural law. All therefore have value and importance and should treat others generously. Such ideas would be influential in the new Roman Empire when, under the leadership of Augustus, fair treatment for provincials was a major theme. For Cicero, however, these ideas existed more as theory than as practice.

Cicero did not hide his lack of sympathy for his fellow-citizens who were poor. In one speech he castigated "artisans and shopkeepers and all that kind of scum"; in a letter he complained about "the wretched half-starved populace, which attends mass meetings and sucks the blood of the treasury." Cicero also made his disdain for democracy clear: "The greatest number," he said, "should not have the greatest power."

Elitist as Cicero's views were, he was by no means on the extremist fringe. Cassius, Brutus, and the other Liberators had little interest in even Cicero's limited compromises. Their stubbornness proved to be their downfall, for dispossessed peasants and ambitious equestrians transferred their loyalties to Julius Caesar and, later, to Augustus. One of Caesar's supporters, Sallust (86–ca. 34 B.C.), wrote biting and bitter works of history that indicted the greed and corruption of the optimates, which he blamed for the decline of the Republic. In any case, peace was not restored before the generation of the Liberators was wiped out in renewed civil war and a new generation emerged, weary for peace.

Augustus and the Principate, 27 B.C.–A.D. 68

The assassination of Caesar threw Rome back into turmoil. Civil war followed for the next thirteen years, first between the Liberators and Caesar's partisans and then between the two leading Caesarians. The final struggle pitted Mark Antony (Marcus Antonius, ca. 83–30 B.C.), Caesar's chief lieutenant and successor to the affections of Cleopatra, against Octavian (Gaius Julius Caesar Octavianus, 63 B.C.–A.D. 14), Caesar's grandnephew and adopted son and heir. Although Octavian was younger than Antony, was not a general, and was cursed with poor health, he was a man of unusual cunning and prudence. His forces defeated Antony and Cleopatra at the naval battle of Actium (northwestern Greece) in 31 B.C.; their suicides shortly followed. Octavian spent the next forty-five years healing the wounds of a century of revolution. He did nothing less than lay the foundations of the prosperous two centuries of the Roman peace (Map 6.2).

The Political Settlement

Octavian was both an astute politician and a lucky one. He was lucky in the length and violence of the civil wars. After Actium, most of his enemies were dead, so establishing the one-man rule that he claimed was necessary to restore stability was relatively easy. He was also lucky to live to be nearly 80—he had plenty of time to consolidate his rule. Octavian astutely learned the lesson of Caesar's mistake. He was a cagey man, a careful planner who loved to gamble with dice but never took chances in the game of power. He understood that the Roman elite, however weakened, was still strong enough to oppose a ruler who flaunted monarchial power. To avoid a second Ides of March, therefore, Octavian was infinitely diplomatic, aware that a cooperative senate could aid his rule greatly.

Rather than call himself Dictator, Octavian took the title of *Princeps* ("First Citizen"). From princeps comes *principate,* a term often used to describe the constitutional monarchy of the "Early Empire," the name that historians have given to the period from 27 B.C. to A.D. 192. Four years after Actium, in 27 B.C. the senate granted Octavian the honorific title *augustus,* derived from the verb *augeo,* meaning "to grow." The name suggested prosperity and growth. Another appellation, *imperator* ("commander" and, later, "emperor"), recalled the military might that Augustus (as we shall henceforth call him) could call on if needed.

In 27 B.C. Augustus proclaimed "the transfer of the state to the free disposal of the senate and the people"—that is, the restoration of the Republic. Remembering similar claims by Sulla and Caesar, few Romans were likely to believe this,

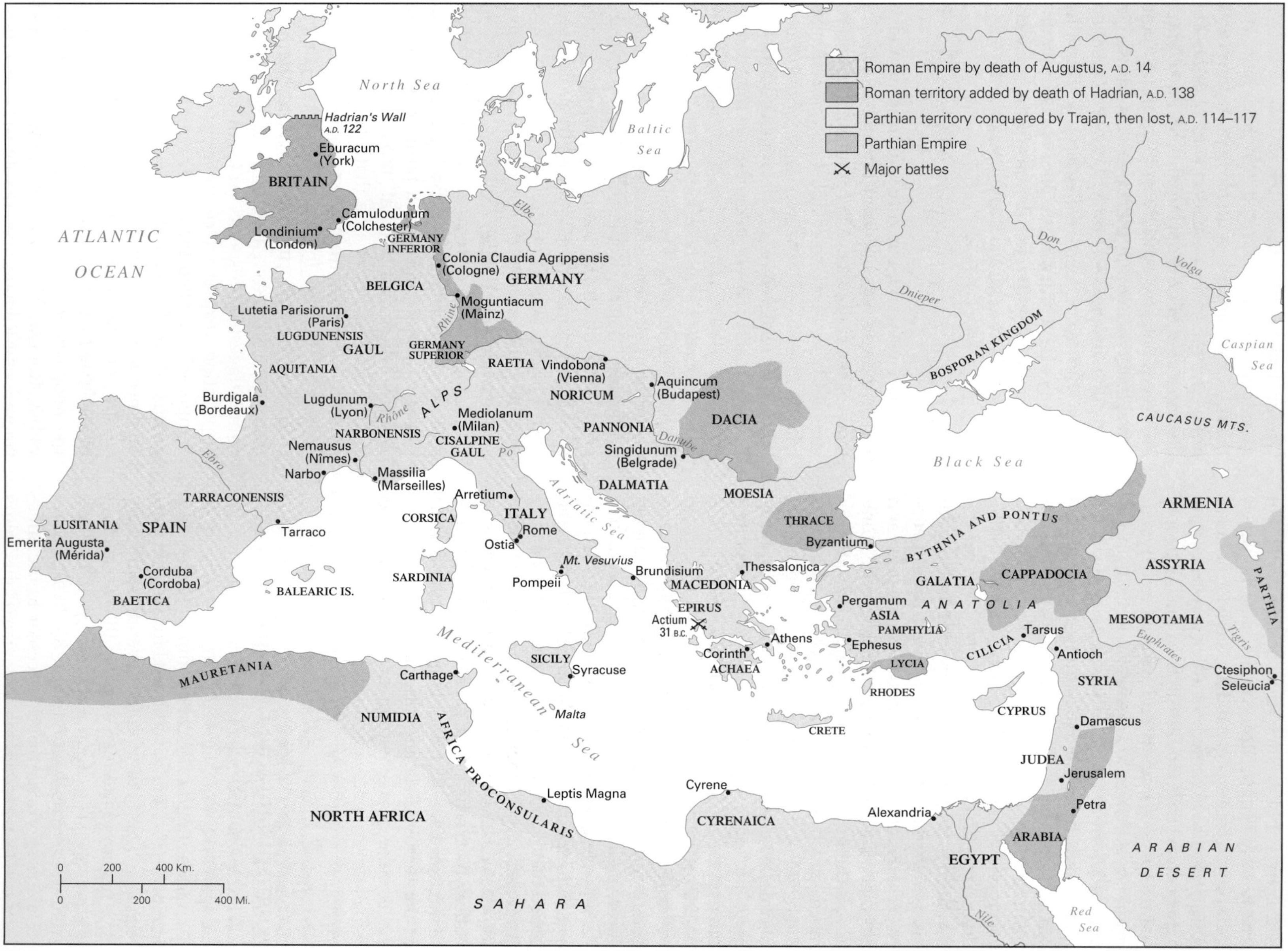
Roman Empire by death of Augustus, A.D. 14
Roman territory added by death of Hadrian, A.D. 138
Parthian territory conquered by Trajan, then lost, A.D. 114–117
Parthian Empire
Major battles
North Sea
Baltic Sea
ATLANTIC OCEAN
Hadrian's Wall A.D. 122
Eburacum (York)
BRITAIN
Camulodunum (Colchester)
Londinium (London)
GERMANY INFERIOR
Colonia Claudia Agrippensis (Cologne)
GERMANY
BELGICA
Moguntiacum (Mainz)
Rhine
Elbe
Lutetia Parisiorum (Paris)
LUGDUNENSIS
GAUL
GERMANY SUPERIOR
AQUITANIA
RAETIA
Vindobona (Vienna)
NORICUM
Aquincum (Budapest)
Burdigala (Bordeaux)
Lugdunum (Lyon)
Rhône
ALPS
Mediolanum (Milan)
NARBONENSIS
CISALPINE GAUL
Po
PANNONIA
DACIA
Danube
Singidunum (Belgrade)
Nemausus (Nîmes)
Narbo
Massilia (Marseilles)
Ebro
TARRACONENSIS
Arretium
DALMATIA
MOESIA
LUSITANIA
SPAIN
Tarraco
CORSICA
ITALY
Adriatic Sea
THRACE
Emerita Augusta (Mérida)
Rome
Ostia
Byzantium
Corduba (Cordoba)
BAETICA
BALEARIC IS.
SARDINIA
Mt. Vesuvius
Pompeii
Brundisium
Thessalonica
MACEDONIA
EPIRUS
Actium 31 B.C.
Athens
Corinth
ACHAEA
Mediterranean Sea
SICILY
Syracuse
Malta
MAURETANIA
Carthage
NUMIDIA
AFRICA PROCONSULARIS
Leptis Magna
Cyrene
CYRENAICA
NORTH AFRICA
SAHARA
Dnieper
Don
Volga
BOSPORAN KINGDOM
Caspian Sea
CAUCASUS MTS.
Black Sea
BYTHNIA AND PONTUS
ARMENIA
GALATIA
CAPPADOCIA
ASSYRIA
PARTHIA
Pergamum
ASIA
ANATOLIA
PAMPHYLIA
Ephesus
LYCIA
RHODES
CILICIA
Tarsus
Antioch
MESOPOTAMIA
Euphrates
Tigris
Ctesiphon
Seleucia
SYRIA
CRETE
CYPRUS
Damascus
JUDEA
Jerusalem
Petra
ARABIA
Alexandria
EGYPT
Nile
Red Sea
ARABIAN DESERT
0 200 400 Km.
0 200 400 Mi.

and few would have wanted the Republic restored in any case; they no doubt appreciated their ruler's tact, however. (See the box, "Augustus: The Official Story.") The new government that emerged, after trial and error, was a partnership between Augustus and the senate—an unequal partnership, in which Augustus held the upper hand, but a partnership nonetheless.

Several things made it work. First, Augustus deftly claimed both consular imperium and tribunician authority without constant election as consul and tribune. He thereby separated his military and civil powers from Republican offices. Second, Augustus dispersed administrative authority to appease various groups and to foster efficient government. An example is his division of the provinces into two categories. To check any new would-be Caesar, he kept for himself the frontier provinces, with the main concentration of armies, as well as grain-rich Egypt. The local commanders were loyal equestrians who owed their success to Augustus. Most of the other provinces continued to be ruled as before by the senate and its promagistrates.

A third and crucial point is that Augustus's senators hardly resembled their predecessors. Unsavory senators enrolled during the civil wars were purged, and the membership of the senate was reduced to about six hundred. The princeps reshaped the Roman ruling class by elevating to the senate large numbers of equestrians, particularly Italians. Where once optimates had monopolized power, now the wealthy classes of Italy eagerly administered the government of the man who had championed their cause.

In order to use the senate as a sounding board, Augustus created a standing committee of magistrates and senators that evolved into an advisory group called the council of the princeps. In ordinary senate meetings, however, the old freedom of speech was gone. What with informers and secret agents, a senator might think twice before speaking.

The popular assemblies fared even worse. To remove all sources of instability, Augustus clamped down on their already limited powers. He made elections a formality by "commending" certain candidates. Over the course of the Principate, the senate gradually assumed the assemblies' legislative function. In other moves against potential instability, Augustus established the city of Rome's first police force and also stationed

Statue of Augustus The emperor Augustus appears here dressed in a toga and holding a scroll, signs of his attention to public affairs. The youthful face and outstretched hand attest to his vigor. (*Louvre © Photo R.M.N.*)

Map 6.2 The Roman World in the Early Empire Many modern cities are built on the site of Roman foundations, evidence of the immense extent of the Roman empire at its height.

Augustus: The Official Story

Not long before his death in A.D. 14, the emperor Augustus arranged for the display in Rome of two bronze tablets containing a record of his achievements. Copies of "the achievements of the Divine Augustus, by which he brought the world under the empire of the Roman people, and of the expenses which he bore for the state and people of Rome" were displayed around the empire. A complete copy survived in the Roman city of Ancyra in Anatolia (modern Ankara, Turkey).

1. At the age of nineteen on my own responsibility and at my own expense I raised an army, with which I successfully championed the liberty of the republic when it was oppressed by the tyranny of a faction. . . .

3. I undertook many civil and foreign wars by land and sea throughout the world, and as victor I spared the lives of all citizens who asked for mercy. 2. [*sic*] When foreign peoples could safely be pardoned I preferred to preserve rather than eliminate them. 3. The Roman citizens who took the soldier's oath of obedience to me numbered about 500,000. I settled rather more than 300,000 of these in colonies or sent them back to their home towns after a period of service; to all these I assigned lands or gave money as rewards for their military service. . . .

20. I restored the Capitol and the theatre of Pompey, both works at great expense without inscribing my name on either. 2. I restored the channels of the aqueducts, which in several places were falling into disrepair through age, and I brought water from a new spring into the aqueduct called Marcia, doubling the supply. . . . 4. In my sixth consulship I restored eighty-two temples of the gods in the city on the authority of the senate, neglecting none that required restoration at the time. . . .

26. I extended the territory of all those provinces of the Roman people on whose borders lay peoples not subject to our government. . . .

27. I added Egypt to the empire of the Roman people. . . .

28. . . . I compelled the Parthians to restore to me the spoils and standards of three Roman armies and to ask as suppliants for the friendship of the Roman people. Those standards I deposited in the innermost shrine of the temple of Mars the Avenger. . . .

35. In my thirteenth consulship the senate, the equestrian order and the whole people of Rome gave me the title of Father of my Country, and resolved that this should be inscribed in the porch of my house and in the Curia Julia and in the Forum Augustum below the chariot which had been set there in my honor by decree of the senate. 2. At the time of writing I am in my seventy-sixth year.

Source: P. A. Brunt and J. M. Moore, eds., *Res Gestae Divi Augusti: The Achievements of the Divine Augustus* (New York: Oxford University Press, 1967), pp. 19–37.

there his own personal guard. Called the praetorians or Praetorian Guard, the name used for a Roman general's bodyguard, the guard would play a role in future imperial politics.

More important for the public good, Augustus established the first civil service for Rome, Italy, and the provinces, embodied in a series of prefectures—or departments—supervising for example, the city watch, the grain supply, the water supply, the building of roads and bridges, tax collection, and the provisioning of the armies. Equestrians were prominent in these prefectures and in the government of the imperial provinces, so they enthusiastically supported the Principate. Freedmen too rose rapidly in what was becoming the imperial bureaucracy.

Augustus: A Skeptical View

Tacitus, a member of the senatorial elite of the Early Empire, looked back to the freedom of the Roman Republic. His* Annals *offer a scathing view of the early emperors, beginning with Augustus, whose reign he discusses briefly.

The violent deaths of Brutus and Cassius left no Republican forces in the field. Defeat came to Sextus Pompeius in Sicily, Lepidus was dropped, Antony killed. So even the Caesarian party had no leader left except the "Caesar" himself, Octavian. He give up the title of Triumvir emphasizing instead his position as consul; and the powers of a tribune, he proclaimed, were good enough for him—powers for the protection of ordinary people.

He seduced the army with bonuses, and his cheap food policy was successful bait for civilians. Indeed, he attracted everybody's goodwill by the enjoyable gift of peace. Then he gradually pushed ahead and absorbed the functions of the senate, the officials, and even the law. Opposition did not exist. War or judicial murder had disposed of all men of spirit. Upper-class survivors found that slavish obedience was the way to succeed, both politically and financially. They had profited from revolution, and so now they liked the security of the existing arrangement better than the dangerous uncertainties of the old regime. Besides, the new order was popular in the provinces. There, government by Senate and People was looked upon skeptically as a matter of sparring dignitaries and extortionate officials. The legal system had provided no remedy against these, since it was wholly incapacitated by violence, favoritism, and—most of all—bribery.

Source: Tacitus, *The Annals of Imperial Rome,* rev. ed., trans. Michael Grant (Harmondsworth, England: Penguin, 1988), p. 32.

The Economic and Social Settlement

The old Roman ruling class made its peace with Augustus, but some never forgave him for ending their ancient privileges. Although Augustus was generally a mild ruler, several of his successors made into the order of the day treason trials, judicial murder, witch-hunts for alleged conspirators, and *damnatio memoriae,* the erasure from the public record of a condemned man's existence. The conservative historian Tacitus (A.D. 55–ca. 117) looked back wistfully to the Late Republic as a golden era of freedom, eloquence, and "the old sound morality." (See the box, "Augustus: A Skeptical View.") Even Tacitus, however, was forced to admit the reality that the Principate was enormously popular with the vast majority of the inhabitants of the Roman world. The reason is simple: Augustus and his successors brought an age of peace and prosperity after a century of disasters under the Late Republic. The sternness of the emperor Tiberius (r. A.D. 14–37), the decadence of Caligula (r. 37–41), and the excesses of Nero (r. 54–68) affected only a tiny minority in the elite; the ordinary person prized the Principate's stability.

The Augustan period was one of affluence, especially in Italy; the other provinces caught up with Italy by the second century A.D. Agriculture flourished with the end of civil war. Italian industries became leaders in exports, among them glass bowls and window panes, iron arms and tools, fancy silver eating utensils and candlesticks, and bronze statues and pots. Italian goods circulated from Britain and Norway to Sudan and eastward to south and central Asia. Augustus stimulated trade by creating the first stable imperial coinage. Brass and copper coins served everyday needs, and there were also gold and silver issues.

The perennial problem of the Late Republic had been land-hunger, which drove peasants into the hands of ambitious generals. Augustus ensured his troops' contentment by compensating 300,000 loyal veterans with land, money, or both, often in new overseas colonies. At first he paid from his own private sources; after A.D. 6 he supported the army from new taxes on the rich. In other words, Augustus made the elite part of a property transfer that they had resisted since the time of the Gracchi. Nevertheless, it should be noted, rural poverty and slavery continued in Italy. In the countryside, only the condition of soldiers and their families was ameliorated, but this improvement was enough to ensure peace.

To end the problem of renegade commanders that had so bedeviled the Late Republic, Augustus reduced the size of the army greatly, gradually cutting the number of legions from over sixty to twenty-eight, around 140,000 men. This reduction freed the Roman economy of a considerable tax burden but left Augustus with only limited opportunity for expanding the empire. In A.D. 9 Rome lost three legions to a native revolt aimed at preventing the consolidation of Roman rule in Germany as far east as the Elbe River. Augustus had to accept the Rhine River as Rome's new German frontier (see Map 6.2).

Imperial defense remained a major issue. The European frontier, with its hostile populations and lack of central authorities to negotiate with, required strong armies. In the more favorable conditions of western Asia and northern Africa, in contrast, Augustus and his immediate successors avoided border conflict by setting up client kingdoms, such as Judea and Armenia, to protect Rome's provinces. With Parthia Augustus negotiated a compromise settlement that failed to expand Roman territory but did achieve the symbolic victory of a return of the legionary standards lost by Crassus at Carrhae in 53 B.C.

The urban poor, many of them freedmen, also benefited under Augustus from a more efficient system of free grain distribution and a large increase in regularly held games and public spectacles—the imperial policy of "bread and circuses" was designed to keep the masses content. Augustus also instituted a vast public works program, which provided jobs for the poor. He prided himself on having found Rome "a city of brick" and having left it "a city of marble."

To promote his ideology of renewal, Augustus sponsored social legislation embodying the old Republican virtues. He passed a series of laws encouraging marriage and childbearing and discouraging promiscuity and adultery. Such legislation was widely disobeyed. In 2 B.C. Augustus felt compelled to make an example of his own daughter, Julia (39 B.C.–A.D. 14), his only child, whose adulteries were the talk of Rome. As punishment she was banished to a barren islet.

Augustus's era marks the beginning of the classical period of Roman jurisprudence, during which the professionalism that had begun to mark Roman law in the Late Republic became a permanent fact. It was probably Augustus who established the practice, followed by later emperors, of granting a few distinguished jurists the exclusive right to issue legal opinions "on behalf of the princeps." He ensured, therefore, that experts guided the administration of justice. The first law school was opened in Rome under Augustus. Roman jurists, many of them provincials, adapted Roman law to the practices of the provinces. Although various provincial legal systems remained in use, the international system of Roman law was also used widely in the provinces.

In religion too Augustus was a legislator and reformer. Many traditional Roman cults had been neglected during the Late Republic. Augustus restored their rituals and priesthoods; he also claimed to have restored all of the eighty-two temples in Rome. In 13 B.C. the senate established the Ara Pacis Augustae (Altar of Augustan Peace), a monument still largely intact. The four sculpted walls of this simple altar depict themes of prosperity, peace, and piety. They show both subjects of Roman myth (for example, Mother Earth, Romulus, and Remus) and Augustus and his family marching to a solemn sacrifice. The altar and the restoration of cults and temples were intended in part to publicize Augustus as Rome's savior.

The Romans deified Augustus after his death, but they would not have tolerated the worship of him as a living divinity. In the provinces, nevertheless, Augustus was so worshiped—both in the East, where the cult of Roma and Augustus grew in popularity, and in the West, where centers of emperor-worship were established at the sites of Lyon and Cologne. Meanwhile, in Italy, associations of freedmen called *augustales* worshiped Augustus's *genius* (spirit), and the civic calendar grew crowded with various festival days celebrating Augustus. The imperial cult of Augustus, an important part of state propaganda until the empire became Christian in the fourth century A.D., was well on its way.

Deification, whether formal or informal, was a heady brew, but Augustus deserved it more than most. He not only had ended the Late Republican era of civil wars but had established the Roman Empire on a completely new footing. Republican institutions had lost their old freedoms, but the emperor and bureaucrats had brought stability. The peace of the Augustan Principate would last, with but few interruptions, for two hundred years. Few people in history have created order so successfully.

The Culture of the Augustan Age

Like *Periclean*, the adjective *Augustan* has come to signify an era of literary and artistic flowering. In both periods there were strong elements of classicism in the arts—that is, an attempt to project canonical, heroic, and idealized values, the values that the self-confident rulers of each epoch wished to promote. Both prose and poetry flourished in Augustus's empire. The emperor and his close adviser Maecenas (d. 8 B.C.) were patrons of a number of important poets, chief among them Virgil (70–19 B.C.) and Horace (65–8 B.C.). The historian Livy (59 B.C.–A.D. 17), who wrote his history of Rome from the founding of the city to 9 B.C. under Augustus, also elicited the princeps's interest in his work. All three men contributed in their writings to the Augustan renewal and rededication of Rome.

In many ways, Virgil speaks for his contemporaries. In the *Eclogues*, poems that, following an Alexandrian model (see page 138), have rustic settings, Virgil describes the miseries of the civil wars and the blessings of peace under Augustus. "A god created this peace for us; for he will always be a god to me," as one character says. In the Fourth Eclogue, Virgil gives vent to messianic sentiments: A child will be born to usher in a restored Golden Age. At the church Council of

Ara Pacis Augustae The Altar of Augustan Peace, contained in a square enclosure about 34 feet by 38 feet and about 23 feet high, and built 13–9 B.C., was reconstructed in the twentieth century. The relief sculpture of the marble walls depicts Augustus's family and mythological symbols of prosperity. (*Art Resource, NY*)

Nicaea in A.D. 325 (see page 238), and later, this poem was given a Christian intepretation. In the *Georgics,* Virgil describes the glories of Italian agriculture, which, thanks to Augustus, could be practiced peacefully again.

Virgil's masterpiece is an epic poem, the *Aeneid,* "the story of Aeneas," the legendary Trojan founder of Rome, or at least of the Latin town from which Rome's founders eventually came. The theme of Rome's founding indirectly celebrates Augustus, often considered Rome's second founder (if Virgil had written an epic directly on Augustus, he would have been constrained in what he could say). The *Aeneid* explores the pain and burden as well as the glory of empire.

If Virgil's work has the grandeur of marble, Horace's poems—*Odes, Epodes, Satires, Epistles,* and *Ars Poetica* (*Art of Poetry*)—are more like finely cut gems. They tend to be polished, highly complex, and less emotional than the *Aeneid.* Like Virgil, Horace explores the themes of war and peace and praises Augustus. "With Caesar [Augustus] holding the lands, I shall fear neither turmoil nor violent death," declares one of the *Odes.* Both Horace and Virgil successfully adapted Greek models and, in the process, created something new. Few writers have had a greater influence on the later Western literary tradition.

Only 35 of the original 142 books of Livy's ambitious history have survived. Livy is both a master storyteller and ironist. His anecdotes of Roman history are remarkably vivid and told in a grand rhetorical style. Like Sallust, he is haunted by the theme of Late Republican decline, but his work is infinitely more hopeful and less bitter than Sallust's. Livy is our major source of evidence for the Roman monarchy and Early Republic. By modern historiographical standards, he is often found wanting. His account of early Rome is long on myth and short on fact. Nevertheless, Livy is not merely an entertaining stylist but a profound thinker on the meaning of history. He embroiders the facts and engages in frank, subjective judgments intended both to inspire patriotism and to inspire reflection on the ironies of history.

Augustus and his entourage were also great patrons of the arts and of architecture, which they considered propaganda tools. They sponsored many major building projects in Rome, from temples to a new Forum of Augustus, the Theater of Marcellus, the Baths of Agrippa, the Pantheon, and the Mausoleum of Augustus. The Augustan era was also a great period of building activity in the provinces, including such monuments as the temple at Nemausus (modern Nîmes) known today as the Maison Carrée, and possibly the Pont du Gard aqueduct, both in southern France.

Augustan sculpture also manifests the themes of peace and plenty. The most common subject is Augustus himself; his statues were ubiquitous throughout the empire. Over the years sculptors experimented with a variety of images, perhaps at Augustus's command. Sometimes he is depicted as an idealized heroic youth, sometimes as a mature soldier in armor, sometimes as a pious Roman priest. Gems, coins, and relief sculpture also celebrated Augustus and his family.

The Julio-Claudians

Augustus had only one child, Julia, from his first marriage, which ended in divorce. In 38 B.C. Augustus took as his second wife Livia (58 B.C.–A.D. 29), who divorced her husband to marry Augustus even though she was pregnant with their second son. She did not bear Augustus children. Seeking a male successor, Augustus used Julia as a pawn in a game of dynastic marriage, divorce, and remarriage, but to no avail. Julia's first two husbands both predeceased her, as did two sons, each of whom Augustus had adopted. In the end, Augustus was forced to choose as successor and as adopted son a man he disliked, Tiberius (42 B.C.–A.D. 37), Livia's elder son.

Livia was among the most powerful women of Roman history. One of Augustus's main advisers, she developed a reputation for intrigue, aimed, so gossip had it, at securing the succession for Tiberius. Livia's enemies accused her of poisoning Julia's husbands and sons, her own grandson Germanicus (a brilliant general whose popularity threatened Tiberius's), and even Augustus himself, who died in bed after a short illness in A.D. 14. Yet when Tiberius finally became emperor, he resented Livia's influence; and when she died, he refused to execute her will or to permit her deification.

From A.D. 14 to 68, Rome was ruled by other emperors from Augustus's family. The dynasty, known as the Julio-Claudians, consisted of Augustus's stepson Tiberius, great-grandson Caligula, grandnephew Claudius, and great-great-grandson Nero. For many elite Romans, this era was one of decadence and scandal and oppression of the old nobility. The main trends of the period were more prosaic. An effective imperial administration grew. Equestrians and freedmen gained an increasing governmental role, while the senate's power declined. Treatment of the provinces improved, and imperial expansion was generally avoided.

The reign of Tiberius (r. 14–37) was marked by intrigue, treason trials, murders, and an increase of the power of the princeps at the expense of the senate. Unpopular with the masses and the elite because he cut back on games and building projects, Tiberius was nevertheless a skilled and prudent administrator. He wisely drew back from war in Germany and Parthia, preferring diplomatic solutions. He reduced taxes and expenditures and promoted honesty among provincial governors.

His successor, his nephew Gaius (r. 37–41), nicknamed Caligula ("Baby Boots"), attempted to elevate himself to the status of a god and to humiliate the senate. He made scandalous behavior into an art form. For example, he appointed his favorite horse not only high priest of a new cult in honor of Caligula the god but also a member of the senate. Caligula raised taxes and trumped up charges of treason in order to confiscate property. He wanted to have his statue erected in the Temple at Jerusalem. He would have had his way, but he was assassinated first, the victim of a high-level Roman conspiracy. After his death the senate debated restoring the Republic, but the imperial family made quite clear the realities of power.

Backed by the Praetorian Guard, Caligula's uncle Claudius forced the senate into naming him princeps. Lame and cursed with a speech impediment, Claudius (r. 41–54) was often the butt of jokes, but beyond that he was a historian, politician, and priest and was fully versed in the cunning ways of his family. An activist emperor, he expanded the imperial bureaucracy with its powerful freedmen; oversaw the construction of an artificial harbor at Rome's silt-clogged port of Ostia; and reconquered Britain, which had fallen out of Roman hands since Julius Caesar's day.

Portrait of Livia This 2½-inch-high onyx cameo of the late first century B.C. is an idealized depiction of Augustus's wife. The braided hair portrays Livia's elegance, while the small mouth and rounded cheeks suggest something of her strength and determination. *(Het Koninklijk Penningkabinet, Rijksmuseum)*

Claudius's death may have been the result of poisoning by his wife and niece Agrippina the Younger (A.D. 15–59); in any case, her son by a previous marriage, Nero, became emperor (r. 54–68). As princeps, Nero's scandalous behavior rivaled Caligula's, and his treason trials outdid Tiberius's. A great fire in 64 destroyed half of Rome. Nero mounted an extravagant rebuilding program afterward, although he was accused of having started the fire so that he could become famous as a builder. Nero found a scapegoat for the fire in the members of a small and relatively new religious sect, the Christians, whom he persecuted.

In contrast to such behavior, Nero provided generally good government for the ordinary people of the empire, and they rewarded him with support. He was unpopular with the senatorial elite, however, and, more serious, he failed to pay all his troops promptly. Confronted with a serious revolt in 68, Nero committed suicide. The next year, 69, witnessed Rome's first civil war in about a century. Three men each claimed the imperial purple after Nero. Finally, a fourth, Vespasian (Titus Flavius Vespasianus, r. 69–79), commander of the army quelling revolt in the province of Judea, was able to make his claim stick. Peace was restored, but not the rule of Augustus's family. Vespasian founded a new dynasty, the Flavians (r. 69–96), which was followed in turn by the Nervo-Trajanic (r. 96–138) and Antonine (r. 138–192) dynasties. The ultimate tribute to Augustus may be that his regime was stable enough to survive the extinction of his family.

The Roman Peace and Its Collapse, A.D. 69–284

Much about Rome in the second century A.D. appears attractive today. Within the multiethnic empire, opportunities for inhabitants to become part of the elite were increasing. The central government was well on its way to granting Roman citizenship to every free person in the empire, a process completed in 212. The emperors emphasized sharing prosperity and spreading it through the provinces. Italy was no longer the tyrant of the Mediterranean, but merely first among equals. This period, the Roman peace, seems particularly golden in contrast with what followed: the disastrous and disordered third century A.D., in which the empire came close to collapse but survived because of a radical and rigid transformation.

The Flavians and the "Good Emperors"

The Flavian dynasty of Vespasian (r. 69–79) and his sons Titus (r. 79–81) and Domitian (r. 81–96) offered good government, and their successors built on their achievements. Unlike the Julio-Claudians, Vespasian hailed not from the old Roman nobility but from an Italian propertied family. A man of rough-and-ready character, when Titus complained that a new latrine tax was beneath the dignity of the Roman government, Vespasian is supposed to have replied, "Son, money has no smell." Unlike his father and brother, Domitian reverted to frequent treason trials and persecution of the aristocracy, which earned him assassination in 96, although the empire as a whole had enjoyed peace and good administration under his reign.

The so-called Five Good Emperors, are Nerva (r. 96–98), Trajan (r. 98–117), Hadrian (r. 117–138), and the first two Antonines, Antoninus Pius (r. 138–161), and Marcus Aurelius (r. 161–180). They are in several ways examples of the principle of merit. Trajan, a Roman citizen born in Spain, was Rome's first emperor from outside Italy. Hadrian and Marcus Aurelius also came from Spain, Antoninus Pius from Gaul. Each of the Five Good Emperors except for Marcus Aurelius adopted the most competent person, rather than the closest blood relative, as his son and successor, thus elevating duty over sentiment. Marcus Aurelius, a deeply committed Stoic, gave full vent to his sense of duty in his *Meditations,* which he wrote in Greek while living in a tent on the Danube frontier, where he fought long and hard against German raids. Antoninus was surnamed "Pius" ("Dutiful") because he was devoted to his country, the gods, and his adoptive father Hadrian.

The Five Good Emperors made humaneness and generosity a theme of their reigns. Trajan, for example, founded a program of financial aid for the poor children of Italy. They also went to great lengths to care for the provinces. Hadrian, a noted lover of Hellenism, lavished attention on Greece, particularly Athens. Both Hadrian and Antoninus Pius contributed generously to buildings in Roman Carthage. These emperors not only commonly received petitions from cities, associations, and individuals in far-off provinces but answered them.

A darker leitmotif in the reign of the second-century emperors was the ever-present problem of border defense. Augustus and the Julio-Claudians had established client kingdoms where possible, to avoid the expense and political dangers of raising armies. Later emperors were inclined to be more aggressive. A new border policy begun under the Flavians was in full operation in the second century A.D.: stationary frontier defense. Expensive fortification systems of walls, watchtowers, and trenches were erected along the perimeter of the empire's border and manned with guards. A prominent example is Hadrian's Wall, which separated Roman Britain from the enemy tribes to the north. Stretching 80 miles, the wall required 15,000 defense troops.

The most ambitious policy was that of Trajan, who crossed the Danube to carve out the new province of Dacia (modern Romania) and who seized on a pretext to invade Parthian Mesopotamia. Although Trajan swept all before him and reached the Persian Gulf, his Parthian campaign was ultimately a disaster. As soon as his army withdrew, Mesopotamia rose in a general revolt, and the Germans followed suit. Trajan's reign marked the empire's greatest geographical extent, but Trajan had overextended Rome's resources. When he died, his successor Hadrian had to abandon Trajan's province of Mesopotamia (see Map 6.2).

Prosperity and Romanization in the Provinces

In general, the Roman peace deepened over the course of the first two centuries A.D. Agriculture, mining, artisanry, and manufacturing continued to prosper, with trade leavening and extending economic expansion. Travel and communications were relatively easy and inexpensive.

The second century A.D., like the Principate generally, was a great age of city life. New cities were founded far from the Mediterranean. Many would be of permanent importance in European history: Cologne (Colonia Claudia Agrippensis), Paris (Lutetia Parisiorum), Lyon (Lugdunum), London (Londinium), Mérida (Emerita Augusta), Vienna (Vindobona), and Budapest (Aquincum). Some of the new cities were veterans' colonies. Some were army camps that grew into towns. Some were market towns that grew by slow accretion.

Whether old or new, cities attracted a large elite population. The Principate was not a domain of country gentlemen, but rather one in which ambitious men wanted to live in great cities, in emulation of the greatest city of the empire: Rome, by Augustus's day a city of perhaps a

Trajan's Arch at Beneventum A marble triumphal arch in southern Italy, this monument (built A.D. 114–117) celebrates both the emperor's military success and his building of a new road. The sculpted relief, one of fourteen decorative panels on the arch, shows Trajan (head missing) distributing food to the children of the poorer citizens of the town. *(Allinari/Art Resource, NY)*

ROMAN PEACE AND THIRD-CENTURY CRISIS

27 B.C.	Augustus establishes principate
ca. A.D. 27–30	Ministry of Jesus
ca A.D. 67	Death of Paul of Tarsus
79	Eruption of Vesuvius
96–180	The "Five Good Emperors"
212	All free provincial inhabitants awarded Roman citizenship
235–283	Period of military anarchy

million people. In cities men competed with each other for positions as magistrates, in imitation of the two consuls, or on the local town council, often called a *curia,* like the senate in Rome; town councillors were called *decurions* and known collectively as the *curial order.* Decurions further competed with each other in lavish expenditures on public buildings in the Roman style, one man endowing a new forum, another a triumphal arch, a third a library, a fourth public baths, and so on. From Ephesus in Anatolia to Colchester in Britain, from Mainz in Germany to Leptis Magna in Libya, a Roman could find familiar government institutions, architecture, and street plans. (See the feature, "Weighing the Evidence: Pompeii,"on pages 228–229.)

The buildings were visible examples of Romanization, although the Romans did not use the term. Roman officials frequently established Roman buildings and monuments or Latin schools for the children of a conquered local elite, but the emperors did not attempt to impose a uniform grid on their subjects. Even if they had aspired to do so, uniformity would have been out of reach, given the size of the empire and the low state of ancient technology. Scholarly estimates of the total population of the empire range between 50 and 100 million people, most of whom lived in the countryside. The small and largely urbanized Roman administration had little direct contact with most people. So, for example, only a minority of the inhabitants of the empire spoke Latin; in the East, Greek was the more common language of administration. Millions of people spoke neither Greek nor Latin. Celtic, German, Punic, Berber, Coptic, Aramaic, and Syriac were other languages commonly spoken in Roman domains. In short, the empire lacked the unity of a modern nation-state.

What then might one mean by Romanization, besides buildings and language? One index has already been suggested: the participation of provincials in the central government, even as emperor. By around A.D. 200, about 15 percent of the known Roman equestrians and senators come from North Africa. By this time, the senate was no longer dominated by Italians but was representative of the empire as a whole.

Participation in government implies another index of Romanization, the extension of Roman citizenship. Pompey and Caesar began the process of enfranchising individuals and communities outside the old borders of Roman Italy. The process continued under the Julio-Claudians and Flavians and flourished under the second-century emperors, who gave magistrates, decurions, or whole cities the privilege of citizenship. Citizens took Roman names reflecting the emperor or promagistrate who had enfranchised them. The provinces were full of Julii, Claudii, and Flavii, among others. They also afford many examples of the juxtaposition of Roman names. The existence of a Roman citizen named Gaius Julius Hannibal, for instance, says something about both the extent and the limits of Romanization.

Finally, in A.D. 212, in a law known as the *Constitutio Antoniana* the emperor Caracalla (r. 211–217) declared all of the free inhabitants of the empire to be Roman citizens. This law was probably less an expression of a yearning for universal brotherhood than of a more prosaic desire to collect increased taxes, for citizens had a heavier tax burden than noncitizens. Nor did universal citizenship mean an end to ingrained Roman social inequality. Rather, privileges previously inherent in citizenship, such as exemption from flogging by officials, now tended to be based on a class distinction, enshrined in private and criminal law: a distinction between *honestiores* (in general, the curial order) and *humiliores* (everyone else). However limited the privileges of citizenship, Caracalla's law was nevertheless a land-

Street Scene, Leptis Magna A wealthy coastal city in what is today Libya, Leptis Magna shows the impact of Romanization in its splendidly preserved architecture. The illustration depicts a paved street, building foundations, and a temple with columns only on the front side, following Roman rather than Greek style. (*Roger Wood*)

mark act. Universal Roman citizenship was a kind of halfway point between ancient empire and modern mass democracy.

Two other institutions were crucial in Romanization: Roman law, with which local elites became familiar, and the Roman army. In antiquity as today, military service had an egalitarian and educational function. A Syrian or Gallic peasant who served in the legions would experience a way of life rooted in central Italy nearly a millennium before. Non-Italians had, and took, the opportunity to rise high in the army or government. This was all to Rome's credit; yet as Italians became a minority in the Roman army, and as ever larger numbers of frontier peoples were recruited, it became conceivable that some day the army might give up its loyalty to Rome.

The Culture of the Roman Peace

In Latin poetry the century or so after the death of Augustus is often referred to as the "Silver Age," a term sometimes applied to prose as well. The implication is that this period was less brilliant than the Augustan era; contemporaries themselves sometimes said as much. It might be fairer to say that the Early Empire never again achieved the self-confidence of the Augustan writers. As the permanence of monarchy and the cycle of good emperors and bad emerged, many in the elite looked back to the Republic with nostalgia and bitterness. Silver Age writing often takes refuge in irony and satire, in epigrammatic pithiness, or in formality or rhetorical flourish. Writing under Trajan, for example, the historian Tacitus pours detailed scorn on the Julio-Claudians and Flavians. Yielding to the inevitable, other Silver Age writers indulged in flattery and obsequiousness toward the emperor.

The Silver Age was an era of interest in antiquities and in compiling handbooks and encyclopedias, an era of self-consciousness and literary criticism. In the first two centuries A.D., Roman writers came from an ever-greater diversity of provinces and backgrounds and wrote for an ever-wider audience, as prosperity and educational opportunities increased. Consider Lucian (ca. A.D. 115–ca. 185), an essayist and satirist. A native of Syria who probably spoke Aramaic before learning Greek, he served as an administrator in Roman Egypt.

Many writers of the era pursued public careers, which offered access to patronage. Tacitus, for instance, rose as high as proconsul of the province of Asia. Prominent literary families emerged, most notably that of Seneca the Elder (ca. 55 B.C.–ca. A.D. 40), a historian and scholar of rhetoric; his son Seneca the Younger; and Seneca the Younger's nephew, the epic poet Lucan (A.D. 39–65).

The family came from Cordoba in Spain; the younger Seneca moved at an early age to Rome, where he became a successful lawyer and wealthy investor. He was well connected enough to be banished in A.D. 41 for alleged adultery with a sister of Caligula. Recalled in 49, he became tutor to the young Nero. When Nero became emperor in 54, Seneca and the commander of the praetorians, Burrus, became his two chief advisers and between the two of them brought good government to the empire. When Burrus died in 62, however, Nero came under the influence of bad advisers, and Seneca was forced into retirement. Three years later Seneca was accused of conspiracy and forced into suicide, as was Lucan.

Seneca the Younger was the major literary figure of his age, a jack-of-all-trades: playwright, essayist, pamphleteer, student of science, and noted Stoic philosopher. Some have criticized his work as lively but insubstantial. Seneca's personal life, in contrast, was made of sterner stuff. He is known for his courageous suicide, in which he opened his veins and bled to death while calmly discussing philosophy (see the box, "Suicide").

A literary career was safer under the Five Good Emperors. Consider Tacitus and his contemporary, the poet Juvenal (ca. A.D. 55–130). Juvenal's *Satires* are bitter and brilliant poems offering social commentary. Juvenal lamented the past, when poverty and war had supposedly kept Romans chaste and virtuous. Amid "the woes of long peace," luxury and foreign ways had corrupted Rome, in his opinion. Critics often blame society's woes on marginal groups. Juvenal, for example, launches harsh attacks on women and foreigners. Tacitus too is sometimes scornful of women. He notes, for example, the charge that Livia had "a woman's lack of self-control."

Tacitus, however, was far from ethnocentric. Few historians have expressed graver doubts about the value of their country's alleged success. For example, Tacitus highlighted the simple virtues of the German tribes, so different from the sophisticated decadence of contemporary Rome. Nostalgia for the Republic pervades his two greatest works, *The Histories,* which covers the civil wars of A.D. 69, and *The Annals* (only parts of which survive), chronicling the emperors from Tiberius through Nero. A masterpiece of irony and pithiness, Tacitus's style makes an unforgettable impression on the reader (see the boxes on pages 207 and 217).

Plutarch (ca. A.D. 50–ca. 120) whose *Parallel Lives of Noble Greeks and Romans* later captured the imagination of Shakespeare, is probably the best-known pagan Greek writer of the first two centuries A.D. Like Livy, Plutarch emphasized the moral and political lessons of history. A careful scholar, Plutarch found his true calling in rhetorical craftsmanship—polished speeches and carefully chosen anecdotes. As in Rome, rhetoric was the basis of much of Greek literary culture in this period.

The Crisis of the Third Century A.D.

The portrait sculpture of the Antonine era (A.D. 138–192) differs significantly from the portrait sculpture of the third century A.D. Antonine sculpture recalls Augustan classicism: busts of the imperial family, for instance, show good-looking, hard-working men and women with regular, often idealized features and thoughtful expressions. In third-century imperial portrait busts, physical features are sharper, chisel-work is coarser, and the uniformities of Greco-Roman classicism give way to diverse local styles. Third-

Suicide

The Romans considered suicide a noble death; members of the elite condemned by the emperor were frequently allowed to take their own life. Anecdotes about famous suicides arose, particularly about women who courageously chose to die with their husbands. This excerpt is set in A.D. 65, when Nero turned on Seneca.

Then Seneca embraced his wife [Pompeia Paulina] and, with a tenderness very different from his philosophical imperturbability, entreated her to moderate and set a term to her grief, and take just consolation in her bereavement, from contemplating his well-spent life. Nevertheless, she insisted on dying with him, and demanded the executioner's stroke. Seneca did not oppose her brave decision. . . . Then, each with one incision of the blade, he and his wife cut their arms. . . .

Nero did not dislike Paulina personally. In order, therefore, to avoid increasing his ill-repute for cruelty, he ordered her suicide to be averted. So, on instructions from the soldiers, slaves and ex-slaves bandaged her arms and stopped the bleeding. She may have been unconscious. But discreditable versions are always popular, and some took a different view—that as long as she feared there was no appeasing Nero, she coveted the distinction of dying with her husband, but when better prospects appeared life's attractions got the better of her. She lived on for a few years, honorably loyal to her husband's memory, with pallid features and limbs which showed how much vital blood she had lost.

Source: Tacitus, *The Annals of Imperial Rome*, rev. ed., trans. Michael Grant (Harmondsworth, England: Penguin, 1988), pp. 376–377.

century emperors are sometimes shown scowling or even looking anxiously into the distance.

The emperors had reason to be anxious. Leaving the relative calm of the second century A.D. behind, the third-century Roman Empire descended into an ever-widening spiral of crisis. Stability first began to slip away during the reign of the last of the Antonines, Marcus Aurelius's birth-son Commodus (r. 180–192), a man with Nero's taste for decadence and penchant for terrorizing the senatorial elite. After assassination and a period of civil war, Septimius Severus, commander of the Danube armies, emerged as the unchallenged emperor (r. 193–211); he founded the Severan dynasty, which survived until 235.

Severan reformers attempted to re-establish the empire on a firmer footing, but they only brought the day of crisis nearer. Septimius and his family illustrate the decentralization of the Roman elite. Descended from Italian immigrants and native Africans, Septimius was born in Roman Libya and spoke Latin with a Punic accent; his wife, Julia Domna, was Syrian. The main theme of his reign was the transfer of power—from the senate to the army and from Italy to the provinces. Those reforms strengthened the empire in an age of increasing border challenges. Septimius's great mistake was indulging in war with Parthia (197–199)—unnecessary war, because the crumbling Parthian kingdom was too weak to threaten Rome. What the war *did* accomplish, however, was to inspire the enemy's rejuvenation under a new dynasty, the Sassanids.

With the assassination of Severus Alexander in 235, the empire began a half-century of one shock after another. The main problem was increased pressure on Rome's frontiers. The Sassanid Persians overran Rome's eastern provinces and captured the emperor Valerian himself in

Head of Trebonianus Gallus This is a detail of a full-length bronze statue that probably depicts Trebonianus Gallus, emperor for only two years (A.D. 251–253) in the troubled third century A.D. The stern gaze and harsh features are often found in the sculpture of the period. (*The Metropolitan Museum of Art [05.30]*)

260. Two Germanic tribes, the Franks and the Goths, hammered the empire from the northwest and northeast.

Ever since the time of Augustus, financial restraint and political prudence had kept Rome's military manpower limited. The result of that limitation, plus fierce resistance by Germans, Britons, and Persians, was little overall expansion of Rome's borders during the Early Empire. The invasions of Roman territory in the third century stretched the system to the breaking point and beyond. To pay for defense, the emperors devalued the currency. The result was massive inflation. As if this were not bad enough, a plague broke out in Egypt in midcentury and raged through the empire for fifteen years, compounding Rome's military manpower problems.

The ability of the empire to rebound from such problems is a tribute to Roman resilience and a sign of the disunity and lack of staying power among the empire's enemies. Recovery began during the reign of Gallienus (r. 253–268), who ended the Frankish threat and nearly polished off the Goths. By 275, the Goths were defeated and the eastern provinces were reconquered. Gallienus excluded senators from high military commands and replaced them with professionals. Moreover, he began a new, more modest policy of border defense. The Romans now conceded much of the frontier to the enemy. They instead used fortified cities near the frontier as bases from which to prevent deeper enemy penetration into Roman territory. They also concentrated mobile armies at strategic points in the rear, moving them where needed.

Gallienus's reforms pointed the way to imperial reorganization, but they were completed by the two great reforming emperors at the end of the third century and the beginning of the fourth: Diocletian (r. 284–305) and Constantine (r. 306–337), subjects of the next chapter. When their work was done, the new Roman Empire of Late Antiquity might have barely been recognizable to a citizen of the Principate.

Early Christianity

Increasing contact between Rome and its western provinces served to plant Roman cities, Roman law, and the Latin language (or its derivatives) in western Europe. As Rome in turn owed much to other Mediterranean peoples, it may be said that the Roman Empire was a vessel that transported ancient Mediterranean civilization to northern and western Europe. No feature of that civilization was to have a greater historical impact than the religion born in Tiberius's reign: Christianity.

Christianity began in the provincial backwater of Palestine among the Jews, whose language, Aramaic, was understood by few in Rome. Christianity immediately spread to speakers of the two main languages of the empire, Greek and Latin, and the new movement addressed the common spiritual needs of the Roman world. By the reign of Diocletian, Christians had grown from the twelve apostles, Jesus's original disciples, to millions, despite government persecution (Map 6.3). In the fourth century A.D., Christianity unexpectedly became the official religion of the entire Roman Empire, replacing paganism—one of the

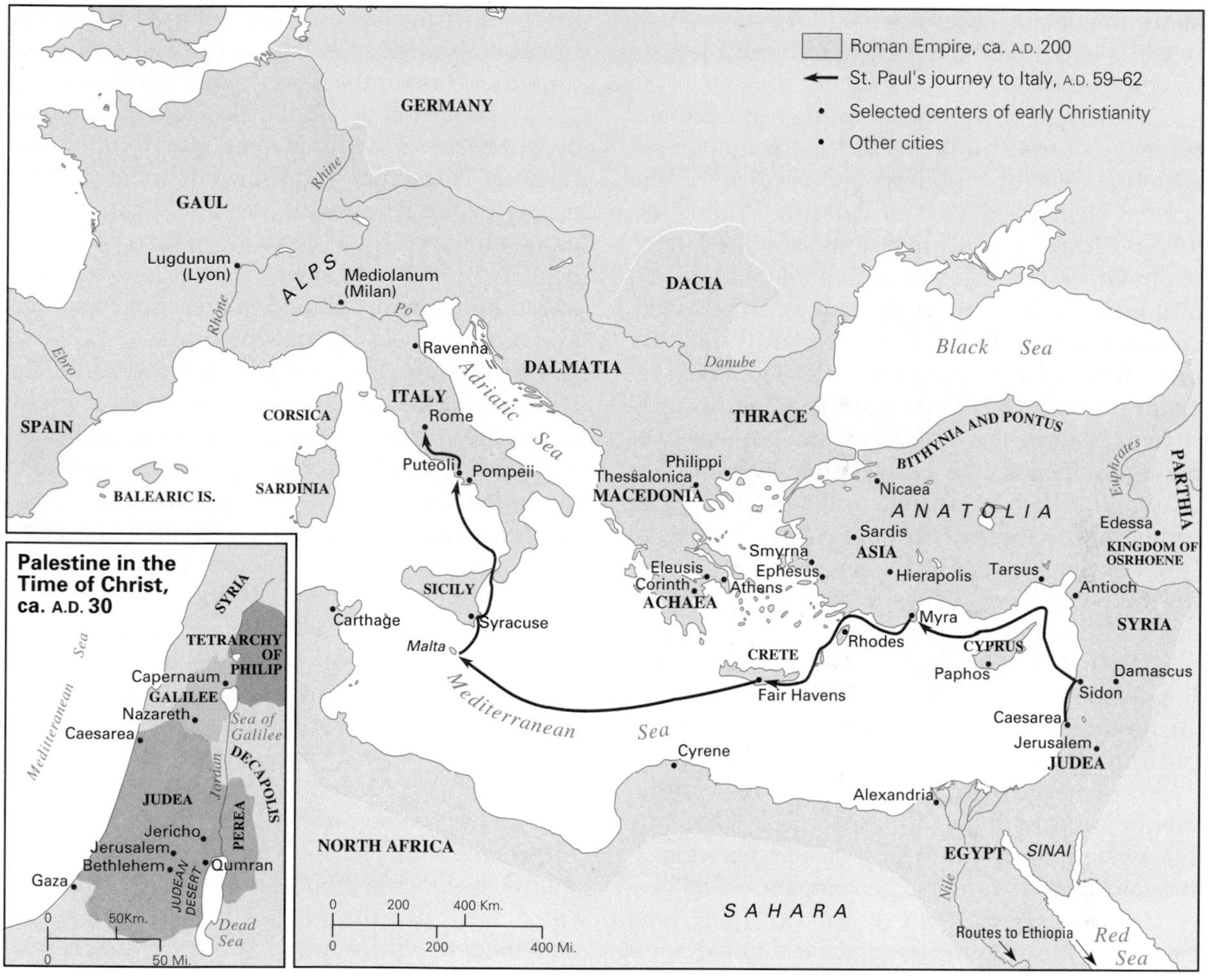

Map 6.3 The Expansion of Christianity to A.D. 200 After its origin in Palestine, early Christianity found its main centers in the Greek-speaking cities of the Roman East. Missionaries like Paul also brought the new faith to the Latin-speaking West, as well as to Ethiopia and Mesopotamia.

most momentous changes in Mediterranean history. We turn to that change in the next chapter; here we consider the career of Jesus and the early spread of the Christian Gospel (literally, "Good Tidings").

Jesus of Nazareth

Christianity begins with Jesus. For all its historical importance, Jesus's life is poorly documented. The main source of information about it is the New Testament books of Matthew, Mark, Luke, and John. Jesus left no writings of his own. Early Christians, however, wrote a great deal. Between the second and fourth centuries A.D. Christians settled on a holy book consisting both of the Hebrew Bible, called the "Old Testament" by Christians, and a collection of writings about Jesus and his followers, called the "New Testament." The account of the Gospel According to Mark, probably the earliest Gospel, was most likely written about forty years after Jesus's crucifixion; several of the letters written by Paul of Tarsus (see page 222) date from the forties A.D.; the earliest pagan sources date from the early second century A.D. and are scanty. Thus, there is much controversy about the details of Jesus's life. But even though much is in dispute, the general import of Jesus's teachings is clear.

Jesus was born a Jew. A speaker of Aramaic, he may have also known at least some Greek, widely spoken by both Jews and non-Jews in the several Hellenized cities of Palestine. To his followers, Jesus was Christ—"the anointed one" (from Greek *Christos*), the man anointed with oil and thus marked out as the king of Israel. They considered him, that is, the Messiah ("anointed one") foretold in the Hebrew Bible who would redeem the children of Israel and initiate the kingdom of heaven. The dynamism and popularity of his teachings led to a clash with Jewish and Roman authorities in Jerusalem, the capital city of Judea, and to the crucifixion. His mission began, however, in a corner of the Jewish world, in the northern region of Galilee, where he lived in the town of Nazareth (see inset, Map 6.3).

Jesus was probably born not long before the death in 4 B.C. of Herod, the Roman-installed client-king of Judea (the date of 1 A.D. for Jesus's birth, a mistaken calculation of Late Antiquity, does not accord with the data of the New Testament). At around age 30 Jesus was baptized by the mysterious preacher John the Baptist; soon afterward Herod Antipas, the Romans' client-king of Galilee, ordered the execution of John. John preached the imminence of God's kingdom, a time of universal perfection, and an end of misery. In preparation, sinful humankind needed to repent. Precisely how much influence John had on Jesus is a matter of debate, as is the question of John's relationship to the religious community of the Essenes. Judaism in the first century A.D. was in a state of creative and turbulent ferment, of which the Essenes are but one example. Indeed, many scholars argue that in this era there was no one normative Judaism, but rather a variety of Judaisms.

The Essenes lived apart from society in pursuit of a new covenant with God. The community at Qumran in the Judean desert, whose history is documented in the Dead Sea Scrolls, ancient texts discovered in 1947, was probably Essene. The tenets of Qumran included frugality, sharing, participating in a sacred communal meal, and avoiding oath-taking. Adherents anticipated the coming of the Messiah and an end of days in which God would punish the wicked. Although Essene doctrine has much in common with early Christianity, early Christians did not withdraw from the world as the Essenes did, but faced it.

There are both similarities and differences between Jesus's teaching and contemporary doctrines of Palestinian Judaism. The most popular group among Palestinian Jews, the Pharisees, focused on the spiritual needs of ordinary folk (see page 149). Pharisees believed that law was central to Judaism but argued that it could be interpreted flexibly, in light of the oral tradition that had grown up alongside the Hebrew Bible. The Pharisees believed in the superiority of spiritual to political matters. They emphasized charity toward the poor. They spoke in parables, vivid allegories that made their teaching accessible.

Jesus argued similarly. Like the Pharisees, moreover, he strongly criticized the pillar of the Jewish establishment, the Sadducees, a small group of priests and wealthy men who saw the Jerusalem Temple and its rites as the heart of Judaism. Like the Pharisees, Jesus rejected the growing movement of the Zealots, advocates of revolt against Roman rule, although there were Zealots among his followers. Yet Jesus was neither a Pharisee nor an Essene. His teaching went further than the Pharisees in rejecting the need to follow the letter of biblical law. Inward purity became the key principle, as reflected in Jesus's statement to his disciples: "Whoever does not accept the kingdom of God like a child will never enter it" (Mark 10:15). Only an adult could become expert in biblical law, but it is probably easier for a child than for an adult to attain spiritual innocence.

Jesus argued that the kingdom of God, which John the Baptist had said was imminent, was actually already beginning to arrive. Jesus, moreover, said that he himself, acting through the direct order of God, could forgive sins. He emphasized the notion of God as a loving and forgiving father. Jesus often spoke in parables and announced himself through miracles, particularly faith healing. He welcomed marginalized groups, such as sinners and tax collectors. As a result, he won a wide following.

Jesus's teaching is typified in the Sermon on the Mount, addressed to his followers in Galilee. He praised the poor and the humble and scorned the pursuit of wealth instead of righteousness. He called for generosity and forgiveness, recall-

Synagogue at Capernaum The reconstructed third-century A.D. synagogue was built over an earlier synagogue, perhaps the one in which Jesus preached and won many followers. A small fishing town on the shore of the sea of Galilee, Capernaum was a center of Jesus's ministry. (*Zev Radovan*)

ing the traditional Jewish Golden Rule—to treat others as one would like to be treated. He said that prayer, fasting, and acts of charity should be conducted in private, not in public, in order to emphasize purity of motive (see the box, "The Sermon on the Mount").

Jesus spoke with conviction and persuasiveness, with "authority," as his followers said. In Galilee they greeted him as king. For some this was a purely spiritual designation; others planned an overthrow of Roman rule, although Jesus rejected that course of action. In any case, his teachings won him hostility from some Pharisees, who considered blasphemous his claim to be able to forgive sins, and from Sadducees stung by his criticisms. Neither group accepted Jesus as the Messiah. By going to Jerusalem, and by timing his visit with the feast of Passover, Jesus ensured the largest possible audience.

Jesus challenged central authority by teaching and healing in the Temple under the eyes of the priests whom he criticized. Nor did Jesus confine his opposition to words: He drove merchants and money-changers away from the Temple precincts by overturning their tables and perhaps even threatening them with a whip. Jesus attracted large crowds of followers, at least some of whom were armed. Sadducee authorities feared trouble, and so did the overlords of Judea, the Romans. The governor, Pilate (Pontius Pilatus), had already endured vehement Jewish objections to the display in Jerusalem of an imperial medallion and of an inscription that seems to have asserted Augustus's divinity. Pilate had no need of further uproar. Temple police and Roman soldiers were called on to arrest Jesus quietly.

Jesus's subsequent trial and execution have always been controversial. The New Testament emphasizes the role of the Jewish leadership and the Jerusalem mob in Jesus's death. Written after the First Jewish Revolt (A.D. 66–77), however, the Gospels may reflect anti-Jewish sentiment in the empire. Crucifixion, the method used to execute Jesus, was a Roman penalty (the traditional Jewish method was stoning) imposed and carried out by Romans. Jesus probably appeared in informal and hurried proceedings before both

The Sermon on the Mount

Preaching and faith healing in Galilee brought Jesus crowds of followers. Matthew presents a speech to the crowds by Jesus, seated on a hillside and surrounded by his disciples. The excerpts include some of Jesus's basic teachings.

"You are light for all the world. A town that stands on a hill cannot be hidden. When a lamp is lit, it is not put under the meal-tub, but on the lampstand, where it gives light to everyone in the house. Like the lamp, you must shed light among your fellows, so that, when they see the good you do, they may praise to your Father in heaven.

"Do not suppose that I have come to abolish the law and the prophets; I did not come to abolish, but to complete. Truly I tell you: so long as heaven and earth endure, not a letter, not a dot, will disappear from the law until all that must happen has happened. . . . I tell you, unless you show yourselves far better than the scribes and Pharisees, you can never enter the kingdom of Heaven.

"You have heard that our forefathers were told, 'Do not commit murder; anyone who commits murder must be brought to justice.' But what I tell you is this: Anyone who nurses anger against his brother must be brought to justice. . . .

"You have heard that they were told, 'Do not commit adultery.' But what I tell you is this: If a man looks at a woman with a lustful eye, he has already committed adultery with her in his heart. . . .

"They were told, 'A man who divorces his wife must give her a certificate of dismissal.' But what I tell you is this: If a man divorces his wife for any cause other than unchastity he involves her in adultery; and whoever marries her commits adultery. . . .

"You have heard that they were told, 'An eye for an eye, a tooth for a tooth.' But what I tell you is this: Do not resist those who wrong you. If anyone slaps you on the right cheek, turn and offer him the other also. If anyone wants to sue you and takes your shirt, let him have your cloak as well. If someone in authority presses you into service for one mile, go with him two. Give to anyone who asks; and do not turn your back on anyone who wants to borrow.

"You have heard that they were told, 'Love your neighbor and hate your enemy.' But what I tell you is this: Love your enemies and pray for your persecutors; only so can you be children of your heavenly Father, who causes the sun to rise on good and bad alike, and sends the rain on the innocent and wicked."

Source: Matthew 5:14–45, in M. Jack Suggs, Katharine Doob Sakenfeld, and James R. Mueller, eds., *The Oxford Study Bible: Revised English Bible with the Apocrypha* (New York: Oxford University Press, 1992), pp. 1271–1272.

the Jewish Council and Pilate. He suffered slow death by crucifixion on Golgotha (Calvary) Hill just outside the city. It was a spring Friday, on the eve of the Passover festival, around A.D. 30.

Paul of Tarsus

According to the Gospel-writers, Jesus died on a Friday and rose from the dead on Sunday, an event commemorated at Easter. He is said to have then spent forty days on earth, cheering his disciples in Galilee and working miracles, before finally ascending to heaven. Heartened, the disciples returned to Jerusalem and spread Jesus's teachings. They preached in synagogues, private households, and even the Temple, and to Greek-speaking as well as Palestinian Jews. Their movement spread in the thirties and forties A.D. throughout Palestine and into Syria. In Jerusalem Christians were known as Nazarenes—that is, followers of Jesus of Nazareth; it was at Antioch that they were first called "men of Christ" (*christianoi*).

It was not clear at first that Christians would form a new religion separate from Judaism. Although Sadducees and Jewish civil officials were hostile, Christians found much support among Pharisees. The Jerusalem church saw itself as the true Israel. Some Christians, however, contemplated a radical break; among them no one was more important than Paul of Tarsus (d. A.D. 67?).

Only Jesus himself played a greater role than Paul in the foundation of Christianity. A remarkable figure, Paul embodied three different and interlocking worlds. Born with the name of Saul, he was a Jew of the Diaspora from the southern Anatolian city of Tarsus. A learned Pharisee, Paul was a native-speaker of Aramaic and knew Hebrew and Greek. His father was one of the few Jews to attain Roman citizenship, a privilege that Paul inherited. Paul's heritage speaks volumes about the variety of the Roman peace, and his religious odyssey speaks volumes more (see Map 6.3).

At first Paul joined in the persecution of the Christians, whom he considered blasphemous. Around A.D. 36, however, he claimed to see a blinding light on the road to Damascus, a vision of Jesus that convinced him to change from persecutor to believer. It was a complete turn-around, a *conversio* ("conversion"), to use the Latin word that would grow so important in years to come. Saul changed his name to Paul and became a Christian.

He also changed what being a Christian meant. The key to Paul's faith was not so much Jesus's life, although that was a model for Christian ethics, as it was Jesus's death and resurrection. Jesus's fate, Paul wrote, offered all humanity the hope of resurrection, redemption, and salvation. Paul retained his belief in Jewish morality and ethics but not in the rules of Jewish law. Following the law, no matter how carefully, would not lead to salvation; only faith in Jesus as Messiah would.

Such doctrines bespoke a break with Judaism, as did Paul's attitudes toward converts. Hellenistic Judaism had long reached out to Gentiles. Some became Jews. Others, scattered throughout the cities of the Roman Empire, were known as "God-fearers"—that is, they accepted the moral teachings of Judaism but refrained from following strict dietary laws and other Jewish rituals. The Jerusalem church baptized converts and considered them Jews, but Paul considered them not Jews but converts in Christ. For Pauline Christians there was no circumcision, no dietary laws, no strict observance of the Sabbath.

From the late forties to the early sixties A.D., Paul tirelessly undertook missionary journeys through the cities of the Roman east and to Rome itself. He aimed to convert Gentiles, and so he did; but many of his followers were Hellenized Jews and "God-fearers."

Paul started Christianity on the road to complete separation from Judaism. Events over the next century widened the division. First, while Pauline churches prospered, departing ever more from Jewish customs, the Jerusalem church was decimated. Jewish authorities persecuted its leaders and, after Rome's suppression of the First Jewish Revolt in A.D. 70, the rank and file of Palestinian Jews rallied to the Pharisees. Second, Jews and Christians competing for converts emphasized their respective differences. Third, although many Jews made their peace with Rome in A.D. 70, enough Jewish-Roman hostility remained to lead to uprisings in the Diaspora in 115 and to the Second Jewish Revolt in 132–135. Both were suppressed by Rome, and Judaism became ever more stigmatized.

Expansion, Divergence, Persecution

Although Jesus's mission was mainly in the countryside, early Christianity quickly became primarily an urban movement. Through missionary activity and word of mouth, the religion slowly spread. It was concentrated in the Greek-speaking East, but by the second century A.D. there were churches in North Africa and Gaul and, beyond Roman boundaries, in Parthian Iraq and in Ethiopia (see Map 6.3).

By around A.D. 200 an orthodox (Greek for "right-thinking") Christianity had emerged. Rooted in Judaism, it was nonetheless a distinct and separate religion finding most of its supporters among Gentiles. A simple "rule of faith," emphasizing belief in one God and the mission of his son Jesus as savior, united Christians from one end of the empire to the other. Christianity attracted both rich and poor, male and female; its primary appeal was to ordinary, moderately prosperous city folk. Believers could take comfort from the prospect of salvation in the next world and in a caring community in the here-and-now. Christians emphasized charity and help for the needy, qualities all too often absent in Greco-Roman society. A Christian writer justly described a pagan's amazed comment on Christian behavior: "Look how they love each other." Most early Christians expected Christ's return to be imminent, upon which he would inaugurate the heavenly kingdom. This belief imparted urgency and excitement to their message.

Early churches were simple and relatively informal congregations that gathered for regular meetings. The liturgy or service consisted of readings from the Scriptures (the Old and New Testaments), teaching, praying, and singing hymns. Baptism was used to initiate converts. The Lord's Supper, a communal meal in memory of Jesus, was a major ritual. The most important parts of the meal were the breaking and distribution of bread at the beginning and the passing of a cup of wine at the end; these recalled the body and blood of Christ. As organizational structures emerged (see page 237), churches in different cities were in frequent contact with each other, discussing common concerns and coordinating doctrine and practice.

As Christianity spread, its troubles with the authorities deepened. For one thing, Christians met in small groups, a kind of assembly that conservative Romans had long suspected as a potential source of sedition. More troubling, however, was Christians' refusal to make sacrifices to the emperor. The Romans expected all subjects to make such sacrifices as a sign of patriotism. The only exception was the Jews, who were permitted to forego the imperial cult because their ancestral religion prohibited them from worshiping idols. The Christians, however, were a new group, and Romans distrusted novelty.

As a result, the emperors considered Christianity at best a nuisance and at worst a threat. Christians were tested from time to time by being asked to sacrifice to the emperor; those who failed to do so might be executed. At times of stress when scapegoats were needed, Christians were sometimes brought to the arena to be fed to the animals. More often, however, Romans tacitly tolerated Christians as long as they kept their religion private. Christians could not proselytize in public places, put up inscriptions or monuments, or build churches. Christianity thus spread under severe restrictions, but spread it did, particularly in the cities of the East. The willingness of martyrs to die for the faith made a strong impression on potential converts. By the late third century there were millions of Christians in the empire, rendering Christianity a minority, but a significant minority.

Mystery Religions

Roman policy toward Christianity by no means reflected an attempt to impose a single, unified religion on the empire. Polytheists, Romans were usually willing to admit new gods to their pantheon, as long as their worshipers took part in the patriotic emperor cult. Roman conservatism, moreover, engendered respect for other peoples' traditional faiths. Although from time to time during Roman history the authorities had tried to expel these faiths from the city of Rome itself, the spread of new religions during the first three centuries A.D. proved irresistible. Besides Christianity and Judaism, the most important were Greek mystery cults, the cults of Isis and Mithras, and Manichaeism. These religions displayed a tendency toward syncretism, often borrowing rites, doctrines, and symbols from one another.

Greek mystery cults included cults of Dionysus, the god of wine, and of Demeter, goddess of grain, who was worshiped at annual ceremonies at Eleusis, a town outside Athens. The "mystery" consisted of secret rites revealed only to initiates. In the case of Demeter, the rites apparently had something to do with the promise of eternal life.

The cult of Isis derived from the ancient Egyptian cult of Isis (see page 147), her brother and husband Osiris, and their son Horus. Its central theme too was eternal life, through the promise of resurrection achieved by moral behavior in this life. Isis, the "Goddess of Ten Thousand Names," was portrayed as a loving mother caring for her son; elements of Isis were later syncretized in the cult of the Virgin Mary. Priests of Isis marched in colorful and at times terrifying parades through the streets of Roman cities, flagellating themselves as a sign of penitence.

Unlike the Isis cult, which appealed particularly to women, the cult of Mithras was in the

Wall Painting of Isis Cult This mural from Herculaneum in Italy shows priests and worshipers participating in a sacrifice to the goddess. Note the sphinxes (background) and ibexes (birds), which call to mind the Egyptian origins of the cult of Isis. *(Museo Nazionale, Naples/Anderson/Art Resource, NY)*

male and especially the military domain. Mithras, a heroic Persian god of light and truth, also promised eternal life. His worshipers believed that Mithras had captured and killed a sacred bull whose blood and body were the source of life. Accordingly, Mithraism focused on bull-sacrifice carried out in a vaulted, cavelike temple called a *Mithraeum.* Initiates were baptized with bull blood and participated in various other rituals, among them a sacramental meal. Their moral code advised a life led in imitation of their hero.

Manichaeism also originated in Persia, but later, in the third century A.D. The founder, the Persian priest Mani, was martyred by conservative religious authorities. His cult recognized not only Jesus but Zoroaster and Buddha as prophets. Manichaeism was characterized by philosophical dualism, which emphasized the universal struggle between good (Light) and evil (Darkness). According to believers, the world had been corrupted by Darkness, but eventually the Light would return. In the meantime, good Manichaeans were to attempt to lead pure lives. Much attention, for instance, was placed on proper diet. Manichaeism was a powerful religious force for two centuries; the great theologian Augustine flirted with it before becoming a Christian.

Summary

Between the second century B.C. and the second century A.D. the Romans changed from a people who had come to destroy into a people who had come to fulfill. At the beginning of this period, the conquered provinces were oppressed by greedy bureaucrats and tax collectors, and Rome's imperial victories nearly ruined the Italian peasantry, who lost their farms while fighting in the Roman army. Members of the Roman elite, rather than displaying that talent for compromise that had made the Republic great, refused to share their wealth with their poor. The poor, however, got their revenge by throwing their support to new patrons, military leaders who raised private armies to win land for their followers and glory for themselves. By the first century B.C. the Republic had collapsed under the weight of political maneuvering, judicial murders, gang warfare, and civil war.

A shrewd and sickly outsider, Octavian, confounded expectations by creating a new empire that would enjoy two centuries of stability; as Augustus, he served as its first emperor. Augustus reconciled the senatorial class by sharing power, but he guaranteed peace by keeping most of the armies in his own hand. He wisely accepted compromise with Parthia and defeat in Germany, reduced military spending, and stabilized the frontiers. He solved the problem of the landless peasantry by raising taxes to provide farms for all veterans. Perhaps most important, he began a new policy toward the provinces, which were slowly raised to equality with Italy. In short, Augustus initiated the prosperous Roman peace, an era lasting until the third century A.D. To survive the crises of that century, it was necessary for Rome to have a bigger army supported by higher taxes collected by a larger bureaucracy, requirements that would shake the social, political, and cultural foundations of the empire, as Chapter 7 discusses.

Literature and the arts flourished alike in the turbulent times of the Late Republic and the peaceful period of the Early Empire. In the provinces, the Roman peace made possible an era of architectural and literary flowering. Rome was a multiethnic empire whose inhabitants increasingly mixed with each other and exchanged ideas. None of these exchanges was more momentous than the emergence of several new religions, one of which would become in Late Antiquity the main religion of the Roman world: Christianity. Without the Roman peace of the Caesars, the Christian Gospel could not have been spread.

Suggested Reading

See also the suggested readings for Chapter 5; several of the works cited there cover the period of Chapter 6 as well.

General Surveys

Beard, Mary, and Michael Crawford. *Rome in the Late Republic.* 1985. An unusual and innovative approach to the subject, emphasizing sociocultural and institutional analysis more than narrative.

Gardner, Jane F. *Women in Roman Law and Society.* 1986. A straightforward survey concentrating on the Late Republic and Early Empire.

Garnsey, Peter, and Richard Saller. *The Roman Empire: Economy, Society, and Culture.* 1987. A thematic rather than chronological introduction by two distinguished social historians.

MacMullen, Ramsay. *Roman Social Relations 50 B.C.–A.D. 284.* 1981. A wide-ranging essay in social history that moves between anecdote and general trend.

Scullard, H. H. *From the Gracchi to Nero.* 5th ed. 1982. A concise and reliable introduction, with an emphasis on political history. Excellent bibliographies.

From the Gracchi to Caesar

Badian, E. *Roman Imperialism in the Late Republic.* 2d ed. 1969. An argument against the economic motivation of Roman imperialism.

Bernstein, Alvin H. *Tiberius Gracchus: Tradition and Apostasy.* 1978. A biography that sees Tiberius as a traditional member of the Roman aristocracy, disaffected by failures in his career prior to 133 B.C. and primarily interested in reform because of Rome's military problems.

Frier, Bruce. *The Rise of the Roman Jurists: Studies in Cicero's pro Caecina.* 1985. A thoughtful analysis of the professionalization of law in the Late Republic and its historical consequences.

Gelzer, M. *Caesar, Politician and Statesman.* 6th ed. Translated by P. Needham. 1968. An incisive, short treatment.

Gruen, Erich S. *The Last Generation of the Roman Republic.* 1974. A detailed analysis of the structure and practices of Roman politics in Cicero's day, arguing against the inevitability of the collapse of the Republic.

Hopkins, Keith. *Death and Renewal: Sociological Studies in Roman History.* Vol. 2. 1983. An argument, against an older view, that the senatorial elite of the Late Republic and Early Empire was surprisingly open to outsiders. Also discusses gladiatorial shows, funerals, mourning, and wills.

Rawson, Elizabeth. *Cicero: A Portrait.* 1975. A sensible, reliable, and readable introduction.

Treggiari, Susan. *Roman Freedmen During the Late Republic.* 1969. An introduction to a fascinating but often overlooked segment of Roman society, including discussions of legal status, careers, political activity, religion, and the family.

Augustus and the Principate

Earl, D. C. *The Age of Augustus.* 1968. A beautifully illustrated introduction to government, society, and religion.

Raaflaub, K., and M. Toher, eds. *Between Republic and Empire: Interpretations of Augustus and His Principate.* 1990. A good selection of the latest scholarly theories and controversies.

Syme, Sir Ronald. *The Roman Revolution.* Rev. ed. 1960. A classic and controversial analysis of Augustus, who, Syme thinks, never seriously shared power with the senate. A work of remarkable literary style.

Wirszubski, C. *Libertas as a Political Idea at Rome During the Late Republic and Early Principate.* 1960. An essay on ideology and practice, with an eye toward the uniqueness of Roman notions of liberty and their difference from modern notions.

The Roman Peace and Its Collapse

Carcopino, J. *Daily Life in Ancient Rome: The People and the City at the Height of the Empire.* 1940. Somewhat out-of-date but a scholarly introduction that is both informative and a pleasure to read.

Luttwak, E. N. *The Grand Strategy of the Roman Empire from the First Century A.D. to the Third.* 1976. A perceptive overview by a nonspecialist of the evolution of strategies of imperial defense from Augustus to the Late Empire.

MacMullen, Ramsay. *Roman Government's Response to Crisis.* 1976. An analytical overview of the third century A.D. with special attention to institutions and society.

Millar, F. G. B. *The Emperor in the Roman World, 31 B.C.–A.D. 337.* 1977. A detailed and informative study of the duties and entourage of the emperor as well as a more general discussion of the Roman imperial government.

Rostovtzeff, Michael I. *Social and Economic History of the Roman Empire.* 2d ed. 1971. A brilliant, ambitious, and original account, although out-of-date and its analysis of the third-century crisis is no longer convincing.

Thompson, Lloyd A. *Romans and Blacks.* 1989. A fascinating study of black Africans and the Roman Empire. Discusses Roman categories of race and ethnicity and contrasts stereotypes and the reality of social relations.

Treggiari, Susan. *Roman Marriage: Iusti Coniuges from the Time of Cicero to the Time of Ulpian.* 1991. An up-to-date and thorough discussion.

Literature, Religion, Art

Chadwick, Henry. *The Early Church.* 1967. An account that covers approximately the same period as Frend's book (see below) but is briefer and more concise and emphasizes theology.

Ferguson, John. *The Religions of the Roman Empire.* 1970. A thorough introductory survey of pagan religions based on both archaeological and literary evidence. Illustrated.

Frend, W. H. C. *The Rise of Christianity.* 1984. A thorough and detailed account from the first century B.C. to the sixth century A.D., emphasizing religion in its social context.

Grant, Michael. *The Jews in the Roman World.* 1973. A good survey of Jews, Romans, and Christians, including a succinct and balanced account of the life and trial of Jesus.

Henig, M., ed. *Handbook of Roman Art.* 1983. A well-illustrated collection of essays by various authors, written for the beginner.

Laistner, M. L. W. *The Greater Roman Historians.* 1963. A good, brief, general survey.

Meeks, Wayne A. *The First Urban Christians: The Social World of the Apostle Paul.* 1983. A social description of early Christianity, very readable and clear.

Russell, Donald. "The Arts of Prose: The Early Empire." In John Boardman, Jasper Griffin, and Oswyn Murray, eds., *The Roman World,* 243–266, 1988. A witty, perceptive, and concise treatment of Greek and Latin prose, excluding history-writing, in the first two centuries A.D.

Shanks, Herschel, ed. *Understanding the Dead Sea Scrolls.* 1992. A very useful collection of introductory essays on a fascinating, much-debated subject.

Weighing the Evidence

POMPEII

We enter their houses uninvited. We retrace their steps as they went about daily chores or stopped to gossip or dodged traffic or worshiped or made love. We even deprive them of the privacy of death. They are the people of Pompeii, famous even two thousand years after they lived—unenviably famous, for they were the victims of a great natural disaster that destroyed nine cities and towns in Roman Campania, of which Pompeii and nearby Herculaneum are the best known. Although most residents escaped, there were deaths, and many tens of thousands of people lost their homes and source of livelihood.

On August 23, A.D. 79, Pompeii and Herculaneum were thriving cities. The next day the volcano of Mount Vesuvius, several miles away, erupted. By August 25 the two towns no longer existed: Pompeii had been buried under more than 17 feet of volcanic ash and pumice stone, Herculaneum under more than 65 feet. Excavations at the two sites, beginning in the 1700s, have unearthed streets and buildings, fine statuary and painting (see pages 192 and 225), fresh-baked loaves of bread in the oven and a dining-room table laden with fish and eggs, and the remains of humans and animals. To many visitors, these sites are a cross between an open-air museum and a graveyard on Halloween. They allow us almost to relive city life in the early years of the Roman Empire, as we may see in two scenes from Pompeii, the more fully excavated of the two cities.

Let us imagine ourselves first near the center of Pompeii, a city spread over 160 acres, surrounded by a wall about 2 miles in circumference. We are at the corner of Stabia and Nola Streets, looking north. A thriving center of cloth manufacture and of trade in wine and olive oil, Pompeii was home to about 10,000 people, with another 20,000 in the surrounding countryside. It is not difficult to see in the mind's eye pedestrians hurrying along the raised, curbed sidewalks visible here. A slave might bring textiles to the cloth-working shop in the house of Vesonius Primus, located up Stabia Street on the west side. A sculptor might bring a bronze family bust to the house of the wealthy banker Lucius Caecilius Iucundus on the east side of the same street.

Corner of Stabia and Nola Streets, Pompeii *(Scala/Art Resource)*

Steps at the corner provided convenient access to vehicles. Pedestrians crossed the street by means of the large steppingstones visible in the foreground, because stepping into the roadway meant risking an encounter with sewage and flowing water. The crossing stones also slowed wheeled vehicles. Without these "speed bumps," they might have moved rapidly along these streets, which, like all of Pompeii's main thoroughfares, were well paved with large stones.

The busy intersection of Stabia and Nola also provides evidence about two other important features of Pompeiian life: water and religion. Numerous public and private wells are found in Pompeii, and an aqueduct brought water to a reservoir inside the walls. Many homes had running water, but the poor depended on the public fountains found at many a corner. Look at the northwest corner of this intersection, where the four stone slabs of such a fountain are visible. Water poured into the basin from the raised stone block in the rear carved with a drunken Silenus, an attendant of the god Dionysus.

Behind the fountain we can see a tall brick tower, one of many neighborhood water towers. The central groove held a pipe bringing water from the reservoir. Smaller pipes carried water to the buildings that stretch northward along Stabia Street. Lining the street are buildings of either brick or rubble masonry, plus a small amount of plaster and wood. Marble was reserved for the wealthy and for public buildings.

Between the fountain and the tower we see a gabled shrine to the gods of the crossroads. Shrines may be found at major corners throughout the city. To Romans, street crossings meant transition. Corners were the home of spirits who, if propitiated, might grant luck and success.

Many Pompeians no doubt prayed to the gods as they ran in flight from the city on August 24, but not all of their prayers were answered. Day turned into night, as the air filled with hot ash and poison gases. Many people died of asphyxiation before they could escape.

Plaster Cast of Skeleton, House of Fabius Rufus, Pompeii *(Alinari/Art Resource)*

Consider our second scene, a room from the house of Marcus Fabius Rufus, located not far from Stabia and Nola Streets. Here excavators found examples of what is a common sight for modern visitors: the outline, in hardened ash, of people who died in flight from Vesuvius's eruption. We see them where they fell. Look at the figure shown here, struggling in vain to get up.

Although the bodies and clothing of the victims eventually decomposed, the moist ash hardened and preserved their shapes, down to the details. By pouring liquid plaster into the cavities where the bodies lay, archaeologists obtained fascinating and grotesque casts. The plaster casts show a virtual cross-section of Pompeii: men and women, young and old, gladiators, slaves, priests, soldiers, rich people (evident from their clothes and jewelry), a beggar holding an alms-sack, merchants, farmers, a goat. There are poignant scenes such as a young couple, a mother and child, and two children holding hands on the road where they lost their way forever. In the atrium of Vesonius Primus's house lies a dog, abandoned by the servants and struggling against its chain. At Herculaneum, skeletons of more than 150 human beings have been found on the beach, waiting, like Vesonius's dog, for help that never came.

CHAPTER 7

The World of Late Antiquity, ca. 300–600

In 1776 a young Englishman, Edward Gibbon, published the first volume of a masterpiece of historical scholarship: *The Decline and Fall of the Roman Empire*. Gibbon claimed that Rome succumbed because of "immoderate greatness" and that the Roman Empire was destroyed by "barbarism and superstition." In the first instance, Gibbon meant that the Roman world suffered from insurmountable internal flaws in its political, institutional, social, and economic life. In the second, Gibbon believed that even as competent rulers sought solutions to Rome's problems, alien peoples (the Germanic barbarians) and alien ideas (especially those associated with Christianity) wrought irreversible transformations in the Roman order. Gibbon's view of Rome's decline and fall long dominated historical thought. Generations of historians shared the idea that the Roman Empire "fell" in the fifth century and with that "fall" the glories of classical civilization gave way to the darkness of the Middle Ages.

Today historians see real achievement in the age where Gibbon saw only decline. How could a world that produced theological writings that would dominate Western thought for fifteen centuries, architectural masterpieces such as the church of Hagia Sophia, or the law books of the emperors Theodosius II and Justinian be seen as moribund? "Late Antiquity," as scholars refer to the period from about 300 to 600, is now seen as an era of political and institutional transformation, of changes in the make-up of the ruling elite, and of the elaboration and dissemination of a Christian culture.

Specifically, this chapter shows how the Roman world responded to the crisis of the third century (see pages 216–218). After the political turmoil of the third century, the fourth and fifth centuries witnessed the emergence of

Baptism of Christ, in circular vault at Baptistery of the Orthodox, Ravenna.

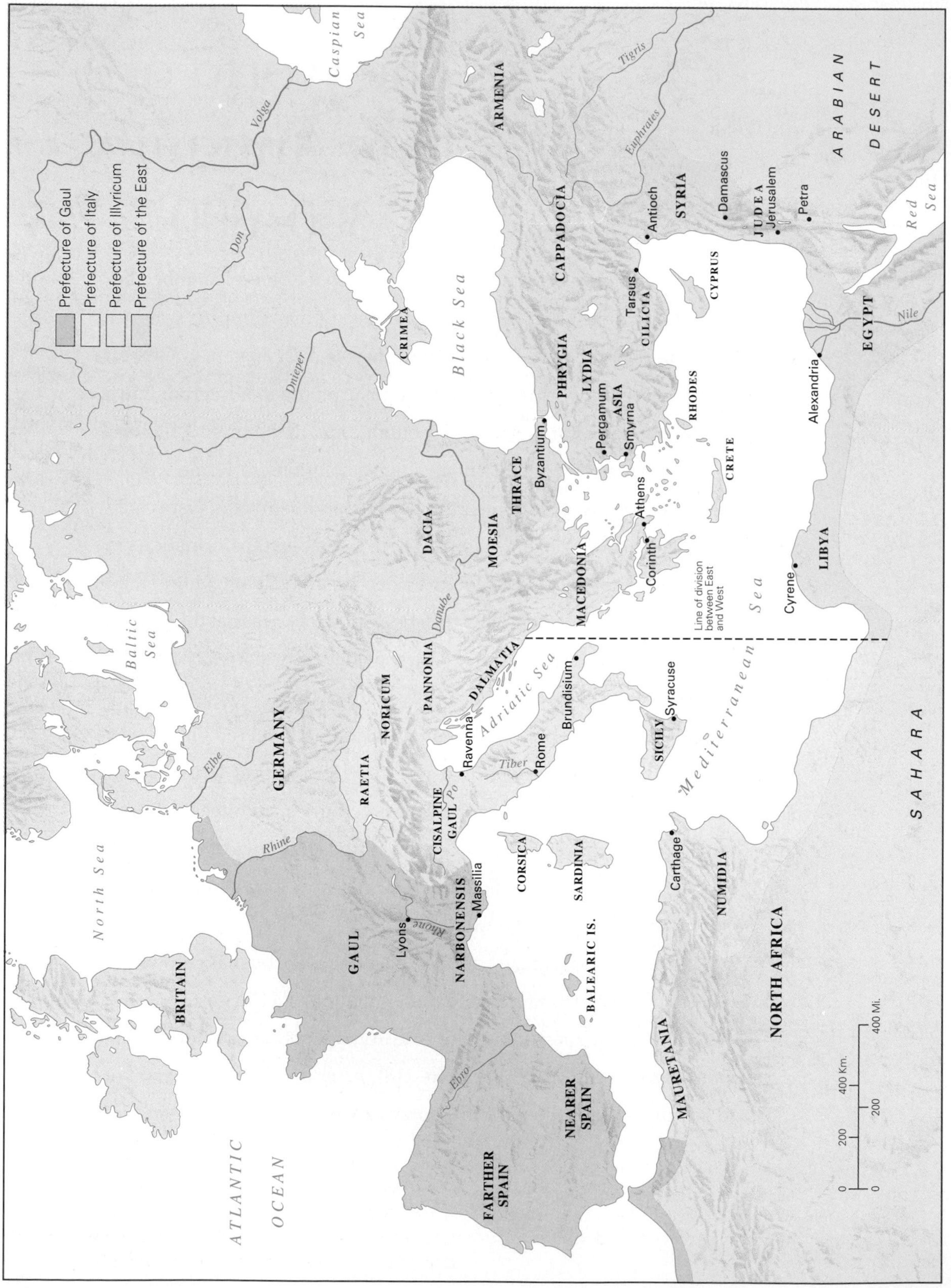
Prefecture of Gaul
Prefecture of Italy
Prefecture of Illyricum
Prefecture of the East
ATLANTIC OCEAN
North Sea
Baltic Sea
Black Sea
Caspian Sea
Adriatic Sea
Mediterranean Sea
Red Sea
BRITAIN
GAUL
GERMANY
RAETIA
NORICUM
PANNONIA
DALMATIA
DACIA
MOESIA
THRACE
MACEDONIA
CRIMEA
ARMENIA
CAPPADOCIA
PHRYGIA
LYDIA
ASIA
CILICIA
RHODES
CRETE
CYPRUS
SYRIA
JUDEA
ARABIAN DESERT
EGYPT
LIBYA
SAHARA
NORTH AFRICA
NUMIDIA
MAURETANIA
FARTHER SPAIN
NEARER SPAIN
NARBONENSIS
CISALPINE GAUL
CORSICA
SARDINIA
BALEARIC IS.
SICILY
Elbe
Rhine
Rhone
Ebro
Po
Tiber
Danube
Dnieper
Don
Volga
Tigris
Euphrates
Nile
Lyons
Massilia
Ravenna
Rome
Brundisium
Syracuse
Carthage
Corinth
Athens
Byzantium
Pergamum
Smyrna
Tarsus
Antioch
Damascus
Jerusalem
Petra
Alexandria
Cyrene
Line of division between East and West
0
200
400 Km.
0
200
400 Mi.

a new style of imperial office and a reformed administration. As Rome responded to threats along its frontiers, Roman society was militarized as never before. The ascendancy of military men, more and more of whom were Germanic, provided a framework for the integration of the Germanic peoples into the administrative structure of the western provinces of the empire. As those forces were transforming the West, the Roman government repeatedly reformed the eastern half of the empire along more traditional lines. Yet everywhere the nature of the elites and the daily lives of most people changed surprisingly little. The paradox of Late Antiquity is that continuity and change worked in tandem.

The triumph of Christianity as an institutional hierarchy, as an increasingly coherent system of thought, and as a set of social principles for organizing human communities is another key achievement of Late Antiquity. The period opens with Christianity suffering its most severe persecution and ends with a dominant faith that was, together with Judaism, the only legally authorized faith in the Roman world.

Responses to the Third-Century Crisis

The third century was an extraordinarily difficult time for the Roman Empire and its rulers. Civil wars and political assassinations were endemic. Peaceful imperial succession was elusive. The frontiers of the empire were always threatened and sometimes breached. The economy was in chaos. As the third century drew to a close, the prospects for the Roman Empire were grim. Nevertheless, the accession of Diocletian in 284 inaugurated more than fifty years of reform that addressed Rome's most serious problems. Those reforms also changed forever the basic nature of the Roman imperial regime. Rome was saved by a Dalmatian peasant's son who rose by talent alone through the ranks of the army to the imperial throne.

The Reforms of Diocletian (r. 284–305)

The Roman Empire was so vast that a single ruler could not deal with its many problems. When Diocletian ascended the throne in 284, the empire had some fifty provinces, which differed greatly in size, population, wealth, strategic importance, and degree of Romanization. The Roman administration traditionally asked for relatively little from its empire, primarily taxes, military recruits, and loyalty. Tax collecting and military recruiting were generally done by local civic authorities with little interference by imperial agents. The imperial administration, made up largely of aristocratic amateurs, numbered only a few hundred men on Diocletian's accession. The Roman Empire was dramatically undergoverned given its size, complexity, and problems.

Diocletian put in place by 293 a regime that historians call the "tetrarchy," or rule by four (Map 7.1). Diocletian first selected an imperial colleague for himself, and then he and his colleague each selected a subordinate official. Diocletian and his colleague were called *augusti,* and the two subordinates were designated *caesares.* The names came from *Caesar,* which was both a family name and a general term for a ruler, and from the special title of *Augustus Caesar.* Diocletian retained the position of senior augustus and concentrated his efforts in the wealthy and populous eastern half of the empire. His aim was to provide colleagues, not equals. The system was meant to provide four men of imperial rank who could lead armies and make decisions in political and administrative matters. Each augustus was to adopt his caesar as his son and heir. In this way, the tetrarchy was intended to provide for orderly succession to the imperial office and to promote experienced, respected men.

Diocletian also addressed himself to an ideological flaw in the Roman imperial system. Ever since the Principate, emperors pretended to be lineal descendants of the Republican magistrates, but their real power was based on the military. Diocletian abandoned the pretense that he was an elected officer of the Roman people. He was addressed as *Dominus,* or "Lord and Master." He

Map 7.1 Diocletian's Division of the Roman Empire Corresponding to the Tetrarchy, the empire was divided into eastern and western halves, and each half was divided into prefectures. Four regions, rulers, and bureaucratic administrations replaced the ineffective rule of one man.

A Contemporary View of Diocletian's Reforms

Historians usually praise Diocletian's reforms, but this passage, from a bitterly hostile Christian writer who hated Diocletian as a persecutor, may actually give the view of the ordinary person.

Diocletian, through both avarice and cowardice, overturned the whole world. For he made three men sharers in his rule; the world was divided into four parts, and armies were multiplied, each of the rulers striving to have a far larger number of soldiers than the emperors had had when the state was ruled by single emperors. The number of those receiving pay from the state was so much larger than the number of those paying taxes that, because of the enormous size of the assessments, the resources of the farmers were exhausted, fields were abandoned, and cultivated areas were transformed into wildernesses. To fill everything with fear, provinces were cut into bits; many governors and more minor offices lay like incubi over each region. Whatever was imposed to maintain the soldiery might have been endured, but Diocletian, with insatiable avarice, would never permit the treasury to be diminished. . . . When he brought about enormously high prices, he attempted to legislate the price of commodities. Thus much blood was spilled, and nothing appeared on the market, and prices soared still higher.

Source: Lactantius, *On the Deaths of the Persecutors,* vii, in *Roman Civilization. Sourcebook II: The Empire,* ed. and trans. Naphtali Lewis and Meyer Reinhold (New York: Harper and Row, 1966), pp. 458–459.

adopted Eastern, especially Persian, habits, such as wearing a jeweled diadem, appearing on an elevated throne, rarely appearing in public and then only amid awe-inspiring ceremony, and requiring those who approached to undergo the ritual humiliation of prostration before him.

Diocletian expanded the imperial administration by doubling the number of provinces and dramatically increasing the number of officials. He added no new territories. Instead, he divided old, large provinces into smaller ones. He then organized groups of provinces into thirteen dioceses and joined the dioceses into four prefectures. To help the augusti and the caesares govern the prefectures, Diocletian equipped each of them with an entourage of military, legal, financial, and secretarial officials headed by a praetorian prefect. By 350 the number of officers from the provincial to the prefectorial level had risen from a few hundred to thirty-five or forty thousand. Diocletian wished to fill the bureaucracy with trained administrators instead of with wealthy senators and equestrians who viewed government service as a means of enriching themselves and enhancing the prestige of their families.

Diocletian's administrative reforms were sensible in principle but costly. By stripping the senatorial order of military and civic responsibilities, they alienated a small but influential group numbering about two thousand. During the Principate, senators had gained enormous wealth, powerful offices, and personal prestige in return for their support of the imperial regime. That wealth, power, and prestige translated into immense private, local influence that endured long after the senators' official power ceased. Around the empire there were also costs. An expansion of the size and duties of the imperial administration necessarily reduced the autonomy of the cities, which for three centuries had been the key components of the imperial system. A day would come when Rome could no longer command the loyalty of the aristocrats or the cities.

Diocletian also attended to Rome's military problems. His major initiative was an attempt to double the size of the army from about 300,000 men, although he was unable to augment it by more than 150,000. The emperor raised conscription levels and began the systematic incorporation of Germans into the army. Military careers had once provided Roman citizenship as well as a secure and decent income. After 212, when citizenship was granted to almost everyone in the empire, the dangers of military life far exceeded the attractions. But noncitizen Germans living along the frontiers were now in the position of noncitizen residents of the empire before 212. The army was attractive to them. Diocletian also built new forts along the frontiers and improved the roads that supplied frontier defenders.

Diocletian's administrative and military reforms were expensive and required a predictable income. Thus, the emperor attempted to regularize the tax system in the empire. A census was held to enumerate the tax-paying public, and the productive value of land was assessed. Each praetorian prefect had to estimate his annual administrative costs; and to raise the necessary funds, he assigned a tax assessment to the men and land in his prefecture. Senators had long been exempt from taxes, and the taxation of business ventures never brought in much revenue. Because more than 80 percent of the population lived outside cities and towns, virtually the whole cost of the Roman system was laid on agriculture, in particular on small farmers. Diocletian's routinization of the tax structure brought in more revenue but also caused hardships. A rising tax burden threatened those who were most vulnerable. With more officials handling vastly greater sums of money, corruption ran rampant. Tax increases and dishonest officials loosened the bonds between subject and emperor. Most people never saw an emperor, but they saw too much of his tax-gouging local minions.

Tax reform was not enough to pay for all of Diocletian's new measures and to address the inflation that had been a critical component of the third-century crisis. In 302, in an attempt to get control of skyrocketing prices, he issued the Edict of Maximum Prices, which froze prices and made many occupations hereditary, largely to keep people from fleeing the countryside. Diocletian wanted a stable economy to finance his reforms, but economic stability was also a desirable precondition to political and social harmony. Unfortunately for Diocletian, prices responded more to economic forces than to imperial commands: They kept on rising. (See the box, "A Contemporary View of Diocletian's Reforms.")

Tetrarchy Ideal and reality are both evident in this sculpture of the tetrarchy. The rulers, depicted equal in size, embrace one another but also bare their weapons—to one another and to the world. *(Scala/Art Resource, NY)*

The Reforms of Constantine (r. 306–337)

Diocletian's careful plans for the imperial succession collapsed almost immediately after his voluntary retirement in 305. When Constantius, Diocletian's western colleague as augustus, died in 306, his troops reverted to the hereditary principle and declared his son Constantine augustus. From 306 to 313 there were often as many as six

THE EVOLUTION OF THE ROMAN EMPIRE

284–337	Reforms of Diocletian and Constantine
313	Edict of Milan grants toleration to Christianity
324–330	Founding of Constantinople
361–363	Pagan reaction of Julian the Apostate
378	Valens defeated by Visigoths at Adrianople
378–395	Reign of Theodosius the Great
408–450	Theodosius II consolidates eastern Roman Empire
410	Visigoths sack Rome
476	Deposition of last Roman emperor in the West
527–565	Reign of Justinian I

men claiming to be augustus somewhere in the empire. From 313 to 324 Constantine shared rule with one man, and from 324 to 337 Constantine ruled alone, with his sons as caesars in various parts of the empire. This compromise between the hereditary and tetrarchal systems persisted for the next two centuries.

For Constantine, consistency with the basic policies of his predecessor was the rule. He had entered the imperial court as a young man in 293, when his father was made augustus, and he later served with his father in Britain and Gaul. He knew the system and maintained the administrative structure that Diocletian introduced. Constantine continued the eastward shift of power begun under the tetrarchy by creating a second imperial capital in the east. He selected an old Greek city, Byzantium, and renamed it after himself, "Constantine's polis" or Constantinople (modern Istanbul). Byzantium's location more than its size, wealth, or fame recommended it. The city commanded the major routes between the eastern and western halves of the empire, overlooked the crucial trade routes to and from the Black Sea region, and was well situated to respond to threats along both the Balkan and the eastern frontiers.

In financial affairs too Constantine's work echoed his predecessor's. He issued a new gold *solidus*, the principal money of account in the Roman world. This coin achieved, and held for nearly a thousand years, monetary stability in the Mediterranean world. A stable currency braked but could not stop the headlong rush of inflation. Constantine did try to acquire new tax revenues by laying a modest levy on senators, who had always been exempt, and on urban shopkeepers and artisans. Both of these taxes were unpopular, and neither brought in much money.

In military affairs, Constantine believed that the long frontiers were too exposed to unpredictable attacks to be held securely, and he expanded the use of mobile field armies. These armies, recruited largely from Germans living along the frontier or even beyond it, were stationed well behind the frontiers so that they could be mobilized and moved quickly. They were given their own command structures, under officers whom the Romans called "Masters of the Soldiers." The praetorian prefects were deprived of their military responsibilities and became exclusively civilian officials. The separation of civilian and military command made sense administratively and politically, because it meant that no individual could combine the command of an army with one of the new and powerful government posts.

Scholars have long debated the strategic and political wisdom of Constantine's arrangements. Moving experienced troops from the frontiers may have invited attacks. Recruiting Germans into the field armies and leaving frontier defenses to German auxiliaries may have created divided loyalties and conflicts of interest. Most Roman provincials had not lived near soldiers. Now the soldiers and the veterans of the field armies became daily companions. One certain result of the reforms of Diocletian and Constantine was the militarization of Roman society, the transformation of the Roman Empire into a vast, armed camp. The financial resources of that empire were now largely devoted to maintaining a military establishment that was expensive, socially diverse, and potentially politically volatile.

Diocletian and Constantine responded with imagination to the political, administrative, military, and economic aspects of the third-century crisis. They also created a new kind of rulership in which a particular style of emperorship was replacing the rule of particular emperors. A monumental statue of Constantine is an indicator of the late antique imperial ideology. Constantine's size serves to emphasize a distance that the viewer cannot articulate but cannot help feeling. It is we who look at him; he does not deign to look at us. The huge statue does not so much depict Constantine as proclaim emperorship. The majesty of Constantine and his long, successful reign stand in stark contrast to the troubles of the third century.

The Legalization of Christianity

Since the first century, Christianity had been making steady progress throughout the Roman world, and by 300 there were Christians in every province. Christianity won converts for many reasons. Basic teachings were important. Another contributor to Christian expansion was a structure that from humble beginnings grew into a vast hierarchical organization. The Roman Empire was rich in varieties of religious experience, but no pagan cult combined compelling teachings with a sophisticated institutional foundation.

The earliest communities of Christians had three kinds of officials whose customary titles in English are *bishop, priest,* and *deacon.* Deacons were clearly subordinate to the other two. Deacons had responsibility for charity and for making arrangements for meetings. Bishops and priests presided at celebrations, preached, and taught. Distinctions between bishops and priests developed over time. Within towns, the eldest priest was gradually accorded precedence and designated "overseer," the literal meaning of *bishop.* As more people converted, as the church acquired property, and as doctrinal quarrels began to cause divisions among the faithful, bishops began to be influential local officials. By the fourth century, even modest towns had bishops. There were more than eighty in Italy alone. By the late fourth century, the bishops in the major cities of the empire were called *metropolitan bishops,* or sometimes *archbishops,* and they had responsibility for territories often called *dioceses.* The Christian church was adapting to its own purposes the administrative geography of the Roman Empire.

Colossal Statue of Constantine This 6-foot-tall head once surmounted a statue more than 30 feet high. Such sculpture displays the distance between the ruler and his subjects. *(Museii Capitolini/Alinari/Art Resource, NY)*

Diocletian will always be remembered for undertaking the last persecution of Christianity, between 303 and 305. We shall never know exactly why he did it. He was a man of conventional piety, and it may be, as even Christian writers later said, that he was truly convinced that the presence of Christians in his army offended his ancestral gods. Diocletian's desire to promote unity may have led him to see the Christians as divisive. Whatever its cause, the persecution was harsh and well planned. Churches were closed, and the Scriptures were collected. Decrees demanded the arrest of the clergy and required citizens to present themselves at a temple for some act of sacrifice. Diocletian's agents had difficulty enforcing his decrees uniformly, and many people had no stomach for an organized reign of terror, so gauging the effect of the persecution is difficult. It certainly did not eradicate Christianity, and it may have drawn favorable attention to the faith by making heroes of its victims, the martyrs whose blood, according to a contemporary, was "the seed of the church."

Constantine was just as interested as Diocletian in promoting the unity of the empire, but he took a different approach. Whereas Diocletian persecuted Christianity, Constantine embraced it. While marching toward Rome to fight for the imperial office to which his father's troops had elected him, Constantine believed that he saw in the sky a cross emblazoned on the sun and accompanied by the words "In this sign you shall conquer." No full explanation has ever been found for the source or depth of Constantine's Christianity or for the actions that he took after seeing this vision. Constantine's mother, Helena, was a Christian. She surely exposed her son to the new faith, but the young Constantine was raised at the court of Diocletian, where he received a traditional pagan upbringing.

Constantine put chi-rho monograms (from the first two letters of *Christos,* "Christ" in Greek) on his soldiers' uniforms and then defeated his rival Maxentius at the Milvian Bridge near Rome in 312. Constantine attributed his victory to the God of the Christians. To show his gratitude, he issued in 313 the Edict of Milan, which made Christianity a legal religion in the empire. In the years ahead, Constantine did more than just treat Christianity as the equal of all other religions. He promoted the Christian church, granting it tax immunities and relieving the clergy of military service. He provided money to replace the books and buildings that had been seized or destroyed in persecutions. He and his mother sponsored vast church-building projects in Rome, Constantinople, and Jerusalem.

Constantine soon discovered that supporting the church could involve considerable risk and distractions. Many quarrels among Christians had gone almost unnoticed when the church and its members could not practice their faith publicly. The Edict of Milan changed all that. Christian heresies almost immediately came to the emperor's attention. *Heresy* comes from a Greek word meaning "to choose." Heretics are persons who choose teachings or practices that persons in positions of authority deem wrong. In Egypt, but eventually in much of the empire, a dispute arose that turned around the central mystery of Christianity itself: the divinity of Jesus Christ. Christian belief held that God exists as three distinct but equal persons: Father, Son, and Holy Spirit.

A priest of Alexandria, Arius (ca. 250–ca. 336), began teaching that Jesus was the "first born of all creation"—that he was conceived by the Holy Spirit, was born of Mary, and was later than the Father in time. Christians had long been stung by the charge that their monotheism was a sham, that they really worshiped three gods. Arianism, as the faith of Arius and his followers is called, sought to preserve monotheism by making Jesus slightly subordinate to the Father. Because Arianism was much easier to understand than Trinitarianism, it won many adherents.

Constantine dealt with religious controversies by summoning theologians to guide him and by assembling church councils to debate issues and promulgate solutions. In 325 at Nicaea (in western Anatolia, just opposite Constantinople) the emperor convened a council of more than three hundred bishops who spoke out against Arius and his teaching. They maintained that Christ was "one in being with the Father," as the words of the Nicene Creed still have it. Arianism did not die at Nicaea, however, and Late Antiquity was never free of doctrinal disputes.

Roman emperors had always been religious officers and had held major priestly offices in the pagan state cults. They were usually deified after death. Constantine, as a Christian, could not claim to be a god, but he did claim to be the specially chosen agent of God. Individual Christians did not object to imperial concern for them because the emperor did not ask to be worshiped. The Christian clergy was happy to have the awesome power of the state brought to bear in favor of the church, as long as the emperor left precise doctrinal formulations to clerics. Constantine's acts were at once radical and traditional.

The Fourth-Century Empire: An Illusory Stability

By 337 stability and good government replaced the turmoil that Diocletian had faced in 284. Reforms had addressed every aspect of the third-century crisis. The key question now was whether the progress achieved by Diocletian and Constantine could be maintained or even advanced. The answer is somewhat surprising. The reforms did not stabilize the empire so much as they provided a stable framework for its gradual transformation.

Imperial Politics: Families and Armies

Constantine had employed a combination of the tetrarchal and dynastic systems. Under him were three caesars, but they were all his sons, and they succeeded him when he died. Constantine's sons had no heirs, and they did not appoint subordinate caesars. When the last of them died in 361, the army turned to Julian (331–363), a nephew of Constantine. Julian was known as a great leader and as a man who looked out for his troops. An attempt was being made to find a legitimate heir to Constantine, not merely a general who would reward the army. Familial and military politics were combining to secure the empire.

Julian ruled for only two years before he was killed fighting in Mesopotamia. He had no heirs and, acting on a long-standing precedent, the army controlled the succession. The choice fell on Valentinian (r. 364–375) and his brother Valens (r. 364–378), who were from the frontier province of Pannonia (roughly, modern Hungary). Valentinian ruled in the west, his brother in the east. Although no one could have predicted it, Valentinian established a dynasty that ruled the Roman world for ninety-one years (364–455).

Events during the years just after the rise of the Pannonians display the stresses in Roman succession. Valentinian assigned his two sons military commands, and their soldiers quickly demanded that they be made augusti alongside their father. The major armies desired to have imperial leaders and patrons of their own. In 378, when Valens was killed in battle, Valentinian's sons sent their brother-in-law Theodosius I (r. 378–395) who had risen through the military ranks in Spain, to the east to maintain order.

Until his own death in 395, Theodosius was the most powerful man in the Roman world, and after his last brother-in-law died in 392, he was Rome's only ruler. He enjoyed the confidence of the people and the army—the former because he was exceptionally competent and honest and the latter because he was an old military man and a superb general. He divided the empire between his two sons without dynastic or military challenge. His branch of the family lived on until the deaths of Theodosius II in the east in 450 and of Valentinian III in the west in 455. Later rulers of the dynasty sometimes ruled alone, sometimes chose colleagues or subordinates. Dynastic and tetrarchal systems were blended effectively. Yet the army's influence was a troubling reminder of the third century.

The army was supposed to protect the empire, not play a role in Roman politics. The military reforms of Diocletian and Constantine were designed to secure effective protection along the frontiers. In the 340s the Romans faced a renewed threat in the east from Persia, where an ambitious shah sought to revive the glories of his ancestors. The Romans did not take this Persian threat lightly, for they knew that in the Persians they faced an old and formidable foe. In the west, Rome faced no single enemy of such proportions, but a lot of relatively minor provocations hastened the army's rise to public prominence.

A serious challenge arose in the Balkans. The Visigoths lived just across the Danube from imperial territory. Since the reign of Constantine they had been "federates" (from *foedus* meaning "treaty") and had been defending a section of the frontier as auxiliary troops. In 376 the Visigoths requested permission to enter the empire, to cross the Danube and settle in the Balkans. They were alarmed about the movement into the Danube basin of the Huns, Asiatic marauders who for some decades had been tormenting the Black Sea region.

Recent years had been difficult for the empire. The Persians had killed Julian in 363, and familial quarrels were disturbing the west. The Romans thus delayed responding to the Visigothic request. Fearful of the Huns, the Visigoths crossed the Danube on their own and then requested permission to settle in the Balkans. Reluctantly, Valens granted permission and said that permanent arrangements would have to be postponed. When the emperor made no progress on settlements, and when local officials began to extort money from the Visigoths, the latter revolted. Valens foolishly marched north to meet them with a small force and was defeated and killed at Adrianople in 378. Theodosius marched east, pacified the situation, and began the process of incorporating the Visigoths into the empire.

Two emperors had been killed in a short time and a third drawn into a frontier dispute. Rulers could not devise a strategy that precluded trouble from Rome's neighbors and enemies. As long as there were military provocations, the role of the army in public life was going to be very great, and military concerns were going to take precedence over civilian ones.

Administrative Successes and Failures

After Constantine there were no massive administrative reforms. The province-diocese-prefecture structure continued to be refined, the number of imperial bureaucrats grew, and the new military organization was maintained. It is among the subtle adjustments to the system that we can see some of the ironies inherent in the process of reform. Two examples are particularly telling.

Valentinian, a soldier raised to the imperial office by the army, wanted to make military careers more attractive and soldiers' lives more comfortable. To achieve his ends, Valentinian proposed to provide soldiers with plots of land and with seed grain. He aimed to supplement soldiers' pay, to tie them more securely to a particular region, and to make them more loyal to him. This creative idea harmonized with earlier military reforms.

Creativity does not assure success, however. Valentinian's program angered the senators, who were still rich and influential. They agitated against the reform because, they said, the emperor was spending too much time worrying about the army, and he was depriving them of lands they desired. The senators also complained that the new program was expensive. They were absolutely right. To pay for land and seed, Valentinian had to raise taxes.

Higher taxes were unpopular all around but especially in the cities, where the burden of collecting them fell on the decurions, the main local officials who composed the town councils. From the time of Valentinian, it becomes possible to trace a steadily declining loyalty to Rome among provincial urban elites. Part of Rome's success under the Principate had been directly tied to the regime's ability to win over local elites all over the empire. Now, a military reform that was perfectly sensible actually provoked suspicion and disloyalty among senators and decurions.

The second example is related to the first. Valentinian's higher taxes created the possibility of greater fraud by officials and greater hardship for ordinary individuals. To protect people against official misconduct, Valentinian introduced officers called "defenders," whose job was to hear appeals against the actions of local officials. Though humane and sensible, this reform angered the decurions, whose decisions were going to be second-guessed by outside agents of the emperor. Not only was their autonomy challenged but their financial security was threatened too. The local curia had to make up any shortfalls in local assessments, and the defenders kept the decurions from squeezing the locals to meet the demands of the treasury or to line their own pockets. Within a generation, this reform was a dead letter. Its failure angered the taxpayers, who had seen in it some protection from the rich and powerful, just as its introduction had disaffected the rich and powerful, who expected the emperor to uphold their interests.

The Futile Quest for Unity

From the time of Augustus, the Roman regime had attempted to promote unity around the cult of the emperor, loyalty to the government, and a common culture. This should not blind us to the fact that the Roman world was huge and diverse. In the time of Constantine, the empire may have numbered some 50 or 60 million inhabitants. Of these, not more than 5 to 10 million lived in towns. Roman government was based on towns. Thus, the actual capacity of the Roman administration to keep track of, to tax, to coerce, and to Romanize the population as a whole was limited.

Even cities, where the Roman presence was greatest, were diverse entities. Their leaders, the wealthy decurions, usually lived in the surrounding countryside and came into town only to conduct personal or official business. Towns were otherwise full of shopkeepers and artisans, teachers and students, locally billeted soldiers, day laborers, domestic servants, entertainers, prostitutes, criminals, and an undifferentiated mass of people who had fled their farms. Some of these people were locals. Others had come from far away. Some people were prosperous. Many lived at the edge of starvation. This complex social mixture made up the late antique Roman Empire.

Unity was hard to achieve even among the elite. For example, the senators, who were increasingly touchy about their loss of power, hated the Pannonian Valentinian and the Spaniard Theodosius. They regarded them as rude, rustic thugs, unworthy of the refined society of Rome. These rulers, for their part, preferred the company of soldiers to that of senators and decurions.

Religious unity could not be achieved either. The Council of Nicaea (325) had tried in vain to eliminate Arianism. Constantine's own son and successor Constantius II (r. 337–361) was an avowed Arian, as was Valens later. For more than forty years, some of Rome's rulers embraced a faith that had been declared heretical. During this time, a Visigothic priest named Ulfilas entered the empire, was converted to Arian Christianity, and returned to spread this faith among his people. When the Visigoths entered the empire in 376, they were considered heretics; but at the time of their conversion, in the 340s, Arianism was the faith of the senior Roman ruler.

Constantine's nephew Julian was called "the Apostate" by his Christian opponents because during his short reign (361–363), he attempted to restore paganism. He forbade Christians to hold most government or military positions or to teach in any school. He did not resort to persecution, however, believing that Christianity could be eradicated by appeals to tradition and by reasoned argument. Obviously, he was wrong and his efforts died with him.

Julian's abortive pagan restoration was echoed a few years later in the affair of the victory altar. Emperor Gratian (r. 375–383), a Christian, removed the altar of victory from the Roman senate. This was a statue of the goddess of victory before which senators usually burned a bit of incense as they passed. Tradition held that this obeisance to victory had for centuries assured the success of Rome's armies. The removal of the altar provoked a cry of anguish from a number of prominent Roman senators, most of whom were still pagan and deeply respectful of Rome's ancient customs. To them, Gratian's act was not so much religious as ideological. He seemed to be turning his back on Roman tradition. Julian's failure, coupled with the senators' inability to get Gratian to change his mind, shows that Christianity in some form was winning over paganism. But in what form? Official policy in this area wavered during the fourth century.

The Development of the Catholic Church

After the Edict of Milan the Catholic church attracted a clear majority of the empire's population (Map 7.2). The Catholic church was Trinitarian in theology, usually aligned with the imperial government, and hierachically organized under the bishops of Rome. The continuing appeal of Christianity's basic doctrines was key in this growth, but so too were imperial patronage and the increasing prominence of the Christian clergy. The rising significance of the clergy, particularly the bishops of Rome, eventually effected

Theodosius Coins, with their wide distribution, were among the most effective means of imperial propaganda. This gold solidus depicts Theodosius I in a typical imperial pose. *(Hirmer Verlag München)*

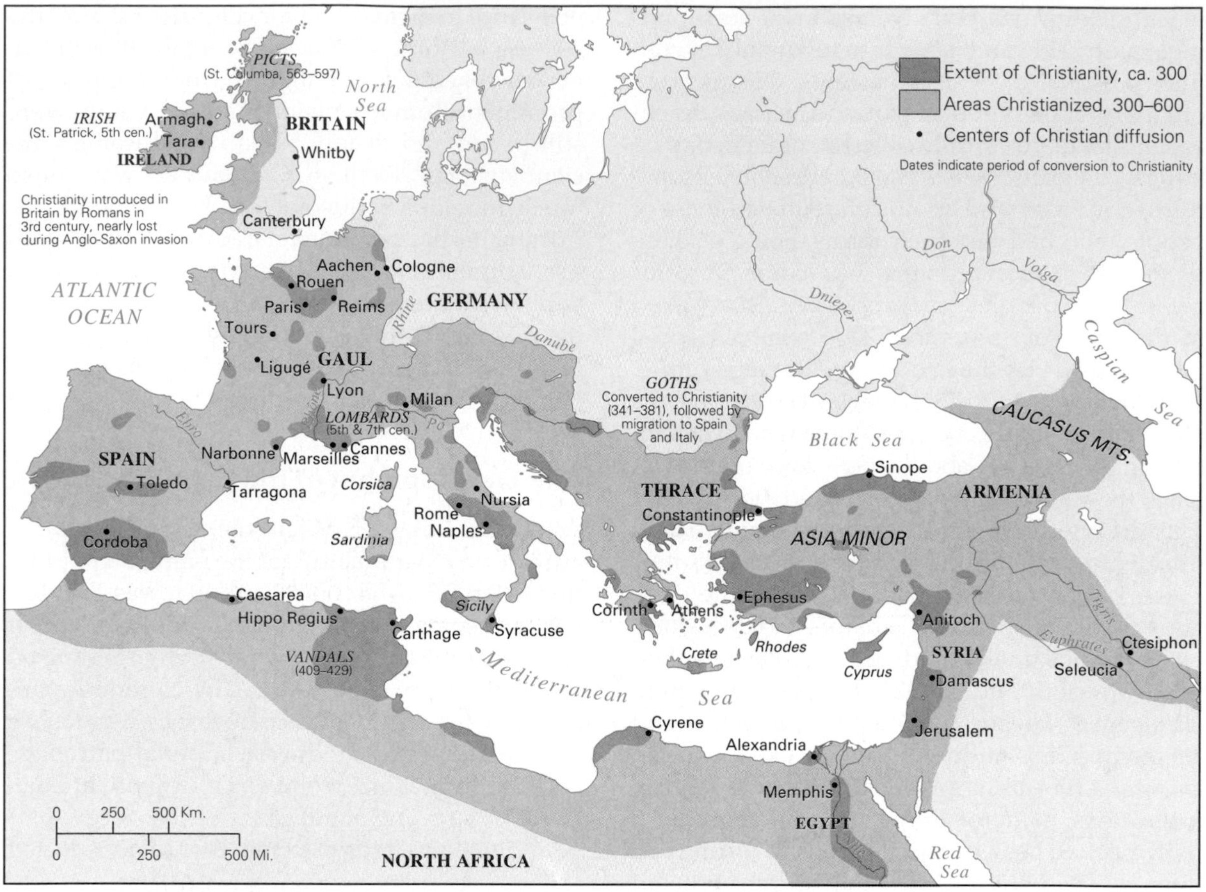

Map 7.2 The Spread of Christianity to A.D. 600 From its beginnings in Palestine (see Map 6.3 on page 219), Christianity, while still illegal, spread mainly in heavily urbanized regions. After Constantine legalized Christianity, the faith spread into every corner of the Roman world.

significant changes in the social and intellectual life, and even in the topography, of late antique towns.

All Christian bishops were understood to be the successors of the apostles. Because Jesus had told the original apostles to "Go forth and teach," it was believed that bishops, as the unique successors to the apostles, continued to possess the teaching authority, the guardianship of doctrine, assigned by Jesus to his original followers. The bishops of Rome coupled this general doctrine of apostolic succession with a particular emphasis on the primacy of Peter (d. A.D. 67?) and created in the fourth and fifth centuries a new, dynamic institution in the Roman world: the papacy.

The New Testament accords a certain respect to Peter among the apostles but provides no clear evidence that he possessed formal leadership. Around the time when the church gained freedom in the Roman world, the bishops of Rome began to advance the idea that Peter had been the official leader of the apostles. Therefore, the bishop who was Peter's successor continued to have leadership of the whole Christian church. By 380 the bishop of Rome, by then regularly addressed as *papa,* or "pope" in English, had become so prominent that Emperor Theodosius required all Christians to believe as the pope did.

Just as a council had been called at Nicaea to address the problem of Arianism, there continued to be church councils. Two principal issues attracted the attention of Christian thinkers and authorities. One of these concerned Trinitarian theology, the branch of theology that tries to explain how God can be triune (three in one). Arianism was the major Trinitarian heresy of antiquity, and the councils of Nicaea and Constantinople (381) pronounced against it. The second struggle concerned Christology, the branch of theology that attempts to understand how Jesus Christ can be both true God and true man. Catholic teaching held that Jesus had two distinct natures. The great Christological heresy of antiquity was monophysitism (literally "one nature-ism"), which maintained that although Jesus appeared as a human, he had only one, divine nature. The Council of Chalcedon (451) condemned monophysitism.

In the later fourth century, and throughout the fifth, popes attempted to impose doctrinal decisions on the councils. Pope Leo I (r. 440–461) was the great theoretician of papal power. His ideas constitute the Petrine theory of papal primacy. According to this doctrine, Peter had not just a moral precedence but a legal primacy among the apostles, and that primacy was explicitly given to him by Jesus. What is more, Leo interpreted apostolic succession as a legal inheritance by the pope of Peter's jurisdictional primacy: As the apostles were teachers, so the pope was the greatest teacher; as the apostles had been the overseers of the early church, so the pope was the overseer of the whole church. Parties already inclined to agree with papal pronouncements were likely to assent to such papal interventions. Opponents not only disagreed with precise papal decisions but also rejected the pope's right to intervene at all.

The rise of the pope in the church as a whole was paralleled by the rise of bishops throughout the empire. By the last years of the fourth century, various ranking members of the social elite were everywhere entering the clergy and rising to its highest offices. This capture of the elite was the final, decisive factor in the triumph of Christianity.

The clergy was an outlet for the talents and ambitions of the elite. For some time, senators had been excluded from military offices and reduced in civilian influence, and decurions were growing dissatisfied with public service. The *episcopal* offices (that is, the office of bishop) was desirable to prominent men for many reasons. It was prestigious. Bishops wore distinctive clothing when officiating, and they were addressed by special titles. These were traditional Roman marks of respect. They had opportunities to control patronage in the way that prominent Romans always had done. They could intervene on behalf of individuals at the imperial court. They came to control vast wealth as the generosity of pious Christians put more resources at their disposal. By the middle of the fifth century, the dominant person in most towns was the bishop, not a civilian official. The bishops, however, were the same persons, from the same families, who had once dominated local society through civic service. In some ways the structure of Roman elite society

Saint Peter This elegant, quasi-imperial bronze statue of Saint Peter enthroned shows how Christians learned to use the techniques of ancient art to broadcast their own message to others. *(Vatican Museums)*

was changing dramatically, but in other ways it was very stable.

One gauge of these changes relates to the topography of late antique towns. The elite had always been responsible for financing most local building projects such as temples, basilicas, forums, and amphitheaters. Such benefactions declined sharply during the third century because of the uncertainty of the times. The fourth century at first saw little building on private initiative, but then came the construction of Christian cathedrals (a bishop's church, from *cathedra,* the chair or seat of the bishop's authority), episcopal residences, baptisteries, and local parish churches. Such buildings as a rule were not placed in the old city centers, which had associations with the pagan past. Instead, they were placed away from town centers and on the edges of populated districts. For the next fifteen hundred years, these Christian centers served as poles around which ancient towns were reconfigured. As the imperial government became less important locally, the existence of an episcopal see (place of a bishop's authority) and building complex usually dictated whether a city survived. The Roman elites built to show pride in their cities and to promote themselves. This did not change in Late Antiquity, but at this time the elites were bishops or rich Christians, and the buildings were cathedrals.

The changed order of things can be readily grasped from an encounter between an emperor and a bishop. Theodosius, in his attempts to discipline the Visigoths after they had defeated and killed Valens, tricked, captured, and killed a few hundred of them. Bishop Ambrose of Milan (339–397), a man of old family, superb education, and wide respect, took it on himself to tell the emperor that he was a member of the church, not its head. Therefore, Ambrose said, because Theodosius had sinned grievously, he had to endure public confession of his guilt and go about in the barren garb of a penitent. This the emperor did. Senators could no longer bend an emperor to their will, but a bishop could.

Santa Maria Maggiore Imagine away the altar canopy and some of the decoration, and this church in Rome is a splendid example of a fifth-century basilica. Note its elegant, harmonious design. Secular buildings of the same time were no longer being built on this scale. *(Alinari/Art Resource, NY)*

Shifting Social Hierarchies

Roman society was hierarchical. From republican times, Rome had been governed by a hereditary class. Although the members of this class affected a style of life that set them apart, they were never a closed caste. First, they did not reproduce themselves very effectively. About two-thirds of the Roman aristocracy was replaced every century—a typical pattern in premodern societies. This meant that there were significant opportunities for social mobility. Second, just as the empire had been born in a social transformation that brought the Italian aristocracy into the Roman governing class, so Late Antiquity was characterized by a social transformation that brought provincial ruling classes and Germans into the framework of power and influence. Social change was always masked as social continuity because when new men reached the top, they tried to embrace the culture and values of those whom they had replaced.

We can characterize the elite by means of three ideals: *otium, amicitia,* and *officium. Otium,* leisure, meant that the only life worth living was one of retreat and composure in which the finer things of life—literature, especially—could be cultivated. *Amicitia,* friendship, implied several things. It could mean the kinds of literary contacts that the thousands of surviving letters from Late Antiquity reveal. Friendship could also mean patronage. The doorstep of every noble household was crowded every morning with a gang of hangers-on who awaited their small offerings and any commands as to how they might do their patron's will. *Officium,* duty, was the sense of civic obligation that the Romans managed to communicate to the provincial upper classes.

Aristocrats governed. They did this in both public and private ways, which are almost impossible to differentiate. Though gradually excluded from key military and administrative posts, nobles did not lose their influence. They used their wealth to win or reward followers, bribe officials, and buy verdicts. Decurions in towns controlled local market privileges, building trades, police forces, fire brigades, and charitable associations. Their public and private means of persuasion and intimidation were immense. In the West, in the growing absence of an imperial administration, Roman public power did not so much "decline and fall" as find itself privatized and localized. Patronage and clientage in Roman society had a benevolent dimension, but they also revealed the raw realities of power.

There was in antiquity an implicit recognition that power was everything and that those who lacked power, whether they lacked money or not, were "poor." On this reckoning, much of the urban population was poor because it lacked access to the official means of coercion and security that the notables enjoyed. Merchants, artisans, teachers, and others were continuously vulnerable because their social, political, or economic position could change drastically at a moment's notice. They lacked the power or connections to protect themselves.

There is no way of estimating the number of the real poor, the destitute, or of describing accurately the conditions in which they lived. It is believed that the actual numbers of urban poor were increasing in Late Antiquity. Poverty and the poor were certainly frequent themes in Christian sermons, and the church described its patrimony as a trust held for the poor. The church provided more frequent, generous, and effective poor relief than ever had been done by ancient institutions. This helps explain a shift in ordinary people's allegiance from magistrates to bishops.

The most numerous citizens of the late antique world can be classed as farmers, but this categorization is not very helpful because it lumps together the greatest landowners and the poorest peasants. Late Antiquity saw a trend in the countryside that continued into the Middle Ages. Freedom and slavery declined simultaneously. Many small, independent farmers, probably people who had long been the clients of local grandees, were actually handing over their possessions—*commending* them is the technical term—and receiving back the use of their former possessions in return for annual rents in money or in kind. They were becoming *coloni,* tenants. Their patrons promised to protect them from lawsuits or from severe economic hardship. More and more, these coloni, formerly clients, were bound to their places of residence and were forced to perform labors or to pay fees that marked their status as less than fully free even though they had not been reduced to slavery. At the same time, many landlords were finding it economically unprofitable to house, feed, care for, and equip slaves. As a result they were manumitting their slaves and elevating them to the status of coloni. Probably there was very little change in the day-to-day lives of the great mass of the rural population, and their position at the bottom of the social hierarchy did not alter.

Christians thought and lived in distinctive new ways. All Christians were sinners, and so all were equal in God's eyes and equally in need of God's grace. Neither birth nor wealth nor status was supposed to matter in this democracy of sin, but Christianity did have hierarchies of its own. The basic offices of the church were hierarchical: popes, patriarchs, archbishops, bishops, priests, deacons. At councils a hierarchy of seniority was observed. In these respects, the structure of the church was very much like that of the secular world.

The church also introduced some novel status distinctions. Holiness, rather than office or achievement, became a badge of honor. Here was a kind of status that could be neither conferred nor withdrawn by anything in this world. And it was not exactly confined to this world. The holy dead were thought to be as present in Christian society as the holy or sinful living. Sanctuaries were dedicated to saints, and people visited the tombs of the saints to pray. Many wanted to be buried near those tombs. Thus, in some ways Christianity produced a society that the ancient world had never known, a society where the living and the dead jockeyed for place in a hierarchy that was at once earthly and celestial.

Inside church buildings another hierarchy could be observed. The front, the apse, was reserved to the clergy. In the nave, the faithful were arrayed in a distinctive ordering. First came the sexually abstinent, then the married, then the penitent. Here was a hierarchy displayed according to sexual practices. In this hierarchy is visible too perhaps the most astonishing achievement, if that is what it was, of the late antique church. It accorded first place to celibate males. In doing so, the church moved women almost outside the social hierarchy. The early church had known deaconesses and possibly priestesses, although the latter disappeared quickly. That the democracy of sin was to be led by celibate males promised future difficulties for women.

From Empire to Kingdoms: The Ascendancy of the Germanic Peoples

The years from the 370s to the 530s were decisive in the history of the Roman Empire in the west. When this period opened, the dynasty of Valentinian was firmly in control. When it closed, the former western provinces of the empire had become a number of Germanic kingdoms, most of which maintained some formal relationship with the eastern Roman Empire. The process that brought the Germanic barbarians into contact with the Romans was an intricate one. Roman policies played as great a role in it as barbarian plans. Many barbarians were peacefully accommodated into the Roman system on essentially Roman terms. The settlement of the Germans illustrates the paradox of continuity and change evident in so many aspects of late antique life.

A Tale of Migrations and Invasions

Few images of the ancient world are more fixed in the popular imagination than the overrunning of the Roman Empire by hordes of savages who ushered in a dark age. For centuries people have spoken of the "barbarian invasions." The Romans inherited the word *barbarian* from the Greeks, who had divided the world between Hellenes, who spoke Greek, and non-Hellenes, who did not speak Greek. Barbarians were literally babblers, foreigners who spoke an unknown language. After the Romans granted citizenship to virtually everyone in the empire in 212, they adopted a Greek-style differentiation between Romans and barbarians. Technically, the latter were just foreigners, but in practice Romans thought barbarians inferior to themselves.

Then there is the idea of invasions. Individual groups of barbarians did invade the empire in various places at different times, but there was never a single, coherent, coordinated barbarian invasion of the Roman world that had well-formulated objectives. The Romans and barbarians did not face one another as declared enemies. Violent confrontations between them occurred, but peaceful encounters were just as common. The Romans had long traded with the Germanic peoples, carried out complicated diplomacy with them, and recruited them into their armies. German veterans were settled in most provinces of the empire, especially in those nearest to the Rhine and Danube frontiers.

The idea of barbarian migrations is sometimes offered as an alternative to invasions. It is equally imprecise. The best source for the early Germans is archaeology. The evidence collected to date makes it clear that the Germans were settled, not migratory, agriculturalists. They lived in villages, farmed the surrounding country, and raised livestock—cattle in particular. If barbarians moved from one place to another, this movement cannot be attributed to migratory habits.

Who were the barbarians? Linguists classify them as belonging to the Germanic branches of the Indo-European family of languages. The Germans can be differentiated from the Celtic and Slavic peoples with whom they shared much of central and eastern Europe, but apart from some minor linguistic variations, it is difficult to distinguish Germans from one another. What are we to make of the profusion of names offered to us by our sources: Franks, Alemans, Saxons, Gepids, Heruls, Vandals, Alans, Visigoths, Ostrogoths, Lombards, Burgundians? These were not discrete ethnic communities. The Romans referred to the German peoples as tribes, but that does not mean that they were descent groups of related people. Every Germanic tribe was a confederation, and these confederations formed, dissolved, and reformed many times. For example, the so-called Visigoths who crossed the Danube in 376 were made up of Visigoths and more than a half-dozen other peoples. The confederations were formed either by powerful leaders who coerced less powerful people to join them or by groups of villages that banded together to protect themselves from aggressive neighbors.

Thinking of the Germanic peoples as polyethnic communities formed in particular political circumstances has two important implications for Romano-barbarian relations. First, it means that we cannot know precisely what form any particular tribe had until it came fully onto the stage of Roman history. In other words, if we do not know what exactly a Burgundian, say, was in 100 B.C., then we cannot say confidently where the Burgundians were. Second, patterns of relations between Germans and Romans went far to determine which Germans would have a knowable history. Some people have a tale that can be told as part of the history of Late Antiquity because Roman writers took account of them, but reconstructing the history of the barbarians before they entered into Roman history is very difficult.

Incorporating the Barbarians

The transformation of the western Roman Empire began as a result of an unexpected set of events involving the Huns, a people from the steppes of central Asia. These nomadic warriors were first mentioned in classical sources in 172, but for the next two centuries they confined themselves to plundering the frontiers of Persia and China. Then, by the middle of the fourth century, they encountered formidable opposition and moved west in search of booty and tribute. In 374 or 375 they fell on the Ostrogoths who lived near the Black Sea. At this juncture the Visigoths requested permission to enter the Balkans. The Huns continued moving west and finally began settling in the Pannonian plain in the 390s.

Until the 420s, the rulers in the East saw the Visigoths as the greater menace; but then the Huns began raiding in the Balkans, preying on trade routes that crossed the region, and demanding tribute from the Eastern emperor. At the same time, a Roman general in Gaul concluded an alliance with the Huns in an attempt to use them as a check on the Burgundians, a federate people who lived in the central Rhineland and were expanding their territories.

In 434 the Huns chose Attila as their king. In return for a huge imperial subsidy, he agreed to cease raiding in the Balkans, and he marched west, having accepted the alliance against the Burgundians. Attila and the Romans together dealt the Burgundians a severe defeat, but Attila saw the weakness of the Roman position and attacked Gaul in 451. The Roman leaders then defeated Attila with a vast network of alliances made up of Romans, Visigoths, Burgundians, and Franks. Attila turned to Italy in 452, even approaching Rome, where Pope Leo I, not the emperor, convinced him to withdraw. Moral preaching and bags of gold from the church's deep coffers were equally persuasive to Attila—

THE BARBARIANS

284–337	Military reforms incorporate more barbarians in army
360s	Appearance of Huns in Black Sea Region
376–378	Visigoths enter Balkans and defeat Valens
410	Visigoths sack Rome
411–418	Settlement of Visigoths in Gaul
430	Vandals seize North Africa
450–550	Angles, Saxons, and Jutes enter Britain
451	Romans, Franks, and Visigoths defeat Huns
486–511	Reign of Clovis: consolidation of Frankish kingdom
507	Franks defeat Visigoths and drive them into Spain
532–534	Justinian's forces defeat Vandals
535–555	Justinian's forces defeat Ostrogoths

plus, although he was a brilliant battlefield commander, he did not have the forces to lay siege to Rome. After returning to Pannonia, Attila died in 454. Before another year was out, the short-lived Hunnic kingdom, largely Attila's personal creation, had vanished. (See the box, "Perception and Prejudice: A Roman on the Huns.")

The history of the Visigoths presents another instructive example of Romano-Germanic relations. They had served as auxiliary troops along the Danube for a long time when they requested permission to cross the frontier in 376. While the central government considered how to deal with them, local authorities sold them food at exorbitant prices and even traded dog meat for Gothic children, who were then enslaved. Barbarians had no monopoly on barbarity. It took until 382 for Theodosius to grant the Visigoths what they had been demanding: land to settle on and a Roman military title—that is, official status—for their king. For decades small bands of Germans had settled inside the Roman frontiers, and barbarians had served loyally in the army. Beginning in the fourth century, most high military officers in the Roman world were barbarians. The only peculiar thing about the Visigoths' situation was that never before had the Romans admitted a whole people, as a people.

For about thirty years the Visigoths struggled to improve the terms of their settlements in the Balkans. Alaric, the Visigothic king after 395, grew tired of unfulfilled promises and of being a pawn in other people's games. He forced matters by attacking Italy.

The Visigothic sack of Rome in 410 was a psychological shock to contemporaries, and it has loomed large for centuries in people's ideas about the "fall" of the Roman Empire. Actually, it was a ploy by Alaric to adjust the terms of his already official status. Alaric died in 410, and his brother took over leadership of the Visigoths. He marched the barbarians north, from Italy into southern Gaul. For good measure, the new Visigothic king captured the western emperor's sister, Galla Placidia, and forcibly married her. However objectionable this act must seem, the Visigoths viewed it as a further demonstration of their loyalty to Rome and their desire to effect a satisfactory new treaty.

In about 418 the Roman government gave in. By the terms of their new treaty, the Visigoths were permitted to settle in southern Gaul, with Toulouse as their base of operations, and were assigned the task of protecting the area from marauding bands of brigands. In return for their service, the Visigoths were given land on which to settle and a portion of Roman tax receipts as pay.

The Visigoths' treaty with Rome made theirs the first Germanic kingdom on Roman soil. From 418 to 451 the Visigoths' king Theodoric I served Rome loyally and earned the respect and admiration of the Gallo-Roman aristocrats among whom he lived. He died fighting against Attila in 451. Between 466 and 484 the Visigothic kingdom in Gaul reached its high point and continued to receive official recognition from Roman rulers. Southern Gaul, one of Rome's oldest and richest provinces, passed from the hands of the Roman bureaucracy and the local nobility into the control of the Visigoths. Nevertheless, from Constantine's first treaty with the Visigoths through the

Perception and Prejudice: A Roman on the Huns

The dread and disgust inspired by the Huns is well captured in this passage. By his comments on the Huns, the Roman historian Ammianus Marcellinus tells us much about his own world.

From the moment of birth they make deep gashes in their children's cheeks, so that when in due course hair appears its growth is checked by the wrinkled scars; as they grow older this gives them the unlovely appearance of beardless eunuchs. They have squat bodies, strong limbs, and thick necks, and are so prodigiously ugly and bent that they might be two-legged animals. Their shape, however disagreeable, is human. They have no use for seasoned food, but live on the roots of wild plants and the half-raw flesh of any animal, which they warm a little by placing it between their thighs and the backs of their horses. They have no buildings to shelter them. They wear garments of linen or of the skins of field-mice stitched together. Once they have put their necks into some dingy shirt they never take it off or change it till it rots and falls to pieces. They have round caps of fur on their heads, and protect their hairy legs with goatskins. They are ill-fitted to fight on foot, and remain glued to their horses, hardy but ugly beasts, on which they sometimes sit like women to perform their everyday business and they even bow forward over their beasts' narrow necks to enjoy a deep and dreamy sleep.

Source: Ammianus Marcellinus, *The Later Roman Empire (A.D. 354–378)*, ed. and trans. Walter Hamilton (Harmondsworth, England: Penguin, 1986), 31.2, pp. 411–412.

continuing recognition by the Romans of Visigothic kings in the fifth and sixth centuries, it was Roman policy more than Visigothic policy that determined the accommodation of this first Germanic kingdom within the framework of the western Roman Empire. At one time or another in the fifth and early sixth centuries, as many as ten different Germanic kingdoms occupied parts of Rome's western provinces. In almost all cases, Roman policies were decisive in the creation of these kingdoms and also in determining which of them survived.

More Kingdoms: The End of Direct Roman Rule in the West

Valentinian III (r. 425–455) was born in 419 and succeeded to the throne as a 6-year-old. Until he came of age, his court was weakened by factional strife, and later his empire, confined to the west, was dominated by military men. On Valentinian's death, the western empire saw a succession of weak nonentities, the last of whom was deposed in 476 by Odoacer, a Germanic general, who simply sent the imperial regalia to Constantinople and declared that the West no longer needed an emperor. This is all that happened in 476, the traditional date for the "fall" of the Roman Empire.

Important events continued to unfold in Gaul. A vast coalition of Romans, Visigoths, Burgundians, and Franks had defeated the Huns. No sooner were the Huns beaten than Roman authorities in the Paris region discovered that the Visigoths were expanding north of the Loire River into central Gaul. To check this advance, the Roman commander in Paris forged an alliance with the Franks. The Franks, long Roman federates, had been expanding their settlements from the mouth of the Rhine southward across

A King and a Bishop: The New Order in Gaul

The power of bishops, the official nature of Frankish rule, and relationships between Clovis and the Gallo-Romans are evident in this letter written to Clovis in 481 by Bishop Remigius of Reims, a Gallo-Roman nobleman.

A strong report has come to us that you have taken over the administration of the Second Belgic Province [the area of Gaul including Paris and the region up to the modern Belgian frontier]. There is nothing new in that you now begin to be what your parents always were. First of all, you should act so that God's judgment may not abandon you. You ought to associate yourself with counselors who are able to do honor to your reputation. You should defer to your bishops and always have recourse to their advice. If you are on good terms with them, your province will be able to stand firm. Encourage your people, relieve the afflicted, protect widows, nourish orphans. May justice proceed from your mouth. Let your tribunal be open to all men. You possess the riches your father left you. Use them to ransom captives and to free them from servitude. Amuse yourself with young men, deliberate with the old. If you wish to reign, show yourself worthy to do so.

Source: J. N. Hillgarth, ed. and trans., *Christianity and Paganism, 350–750: The Conversion of Western Europe* (Philadelphia: University of Pennsylvania Press, 1986), p. 76.

modern Holland and Belgium since the third century. Occasionally the Romans had halted their advance, but usually they had left the Franks alone. They now enlisted the Franks to help stop the Visigoths.

The fortunes of the Frankish kingdom, indeed of all of Gaul, rested with Clovis. He became king of one group of Franks in 481 and spent the years until his death in 511 subjecting all the other bands of Franks to his rule. He gained the allegiance of the Frankish people by leading them to constant military victories that brought territorial gains, plunder, and tribute. The greatest of Clovis's successes came in 507, when he defeated the Visigoths at Vouillé and drove them over the Pyrenees into Spain.

Clovis was popular not only with the Franks but also with the Gallo-Roman population (see the box, "A King and a Bishop"). There were three reasons for his popularity. First, Clovis and the Romans had common enemies: Germanic tribes still living beyond the Rhine and pirates who raided the coast of Gaul. Second, whereas most of the Germanic peoples were Arian Christians, the majority of the Franks passed directly from paganism to Catholicism (see page 259). Thus, Clovis and the Gallo-Romans had a shared faith that permitted Clovis to portray his war against the Visigoths as, at least in part, a crusade against heresy. Third, Clovis eagerly sought from Constantinople official recognition and titles, appeared publicly in the dress of a Roman official, and practiced such imperial rituals as distributing gold coins while riding through crowds of people. The Frankish kingdom under Clovis's family—called "Merovingian" from one of his semilegendary ancestors—became the most successful of all the Germanic realms.

Several little kingdoms emerged in Britain. To meet threats elsewhere, the Romans had begun pulling troops out of Britain in the fourth century and abandoned the island to its own defense in 410. Thereafter, raiding parties from Scotland and Ireland, as well as seaborne attackers, called "Saxons" by contemporaries because some of them came from Saxony in northern Germany, ravaged Britain. Down to the 450s the British continually appealed to the military authorities in Gaul for aid, but to no avail. Then the British tried a desperate gamble. They began to hire bands of Saxons to defend them from their other enemies. By the early years of the sixth century, the hired Saxons had begun to settle down and to form small kingdoms of their own in Britain. Reliable traditions say that England was actually settled by three peoples from northern Germany and southern Denmark: Angles, Saxons, and Jutes. These people, whom we call the Anglo-Saxons (the Jutes left little trace), entered Britain in small groups for a century or more after 450. In the following centuries their tiny kingdoms coalesced into England. Although Britain retained contacts with Gaul, the island had virtually no Roman inheritance.

There were several unsuccessful kingdoms. The Burgundian kingdom that had once prompted the Romans to ally with the Huns was swallowed up by the more powerful Franks in the 530s. The Vandals, who crossed the Rhine in 406 and headed for Spain, went over to North Africa in 429. They were fanatical Arians who persecuted the Catholic population. They refused imperial offers of a treaty on terms like those accepted by other Germanic peoples. And they constantly plundered the islands of the western Mediterranean and the Italian coast, even sacking Rome in 455. The Romans finally exterminated the Vandals in 533.

The Ostrogoths had been living in Pannonia since the 370s, subjects of the Huns for much of that time. They were sent to Italy in 493 by the Romans to remove Odoacer, the man who had deposed the last western emperor in 476. Odoacer had earned the displeasure of the Roman administration by laying hands on the sentimentally significant land of Italy—and by doing so on his own initiative, instead of by Roman directive. The government at Constantinople was familiar with the Ostrogoths' king, Theodoric, because he had been a hostage there for several years. The emperor also wished to remove the Ostrogoths from the Danube basin where they were a potential threat. Sending Theodoric to Italy seemed like a way to solve two problems simultaneously.

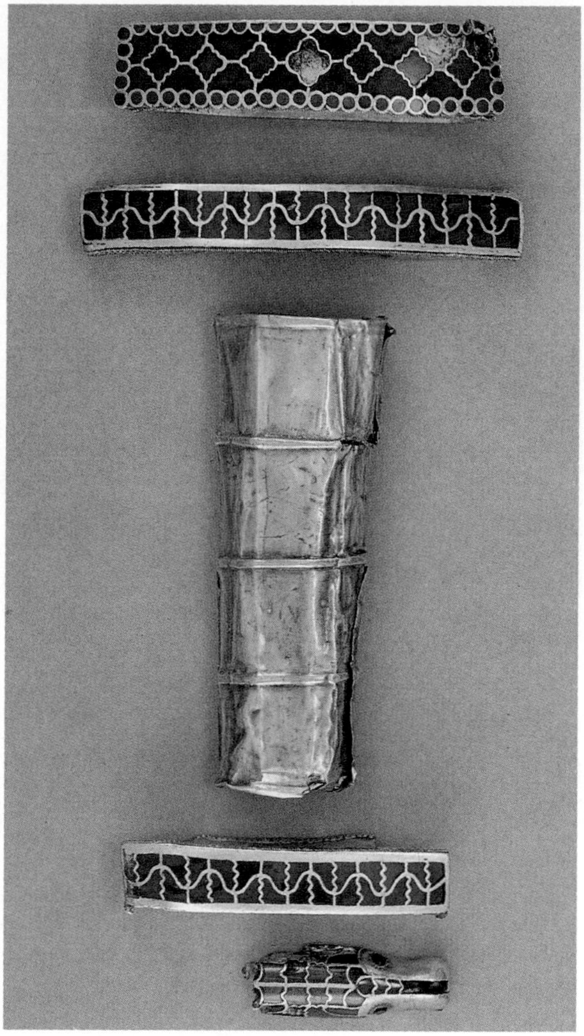

The Sword of King Childeric The tomb of Childeric, father of Clovis, was found in 1639 near Tournai (in modern Belgium). One of its treasures was this sword of exquisite beauty and sophisticated workmanship that shows late antique craftsmanship at its height. *(Bibliothèque Nationale, Cabinet des Médailles)*

Theodoric got rid of Odoacer quickly enough and set up his capital in Ravenna, the swamp-surrounded and virtually impregnable city that had sheltered the imperial administration for much of the fifth century after the Visigothic attack had exposed the weakness of Rome's defenses. Through the force of his personality, and as a result of a series of marriage alliances,

Mausoleum of Theodoric The deeply Romanized Ostrogoth Theodoric designed this classically inspired tomb for himself in Ravenna. The building displays the mixture of the Roman and the Germanic that is prevalent in late Antiquity. *(C. M. Dixon Colour Photo Library)*

Theodoric became the dominant person in western Europe. In Italy he promoted peace, stability, and good government. He won to his service some of the leading men of the time. Still, Theodoric had two strikes against him. One, he and his people were Arians. Two, although the population of Italy was accustomed to having an imperial court dominated by Germans and to having Germanic military men in Gaul as the real powers in the state, they had never been directly ruled by a German, and some of them could not reconcile themselves to Theodoric. Consequently, there were plots between factions in Italy and the imperial court at Constantinople and, by the 420s, Theodoric grew increasingly suspicious and dictatorial. After he died in 526, the government in Constantinople launched an attack on Italy that put an end to the Ostrogothic kingdom but also devastated Italy in twenty years of brutal warfare.

By the 530s the western Roman Empire had disappeared after a process initiated by the entry of the Visigoths into the Balkans in 376. Of all the peoples who had contested for a share of Rome's legacy, only the Franks in Gaul, the Visigoths in Spain, and the Anglo-Saxons in Britain had survived. In some respects the map of the western Roman world was tidier in the middle of the sixth century than it had been at any time since the second (Map 7.3).

Several factors contributed to this outcome. Beginning with Constantine, Rome's best rulers

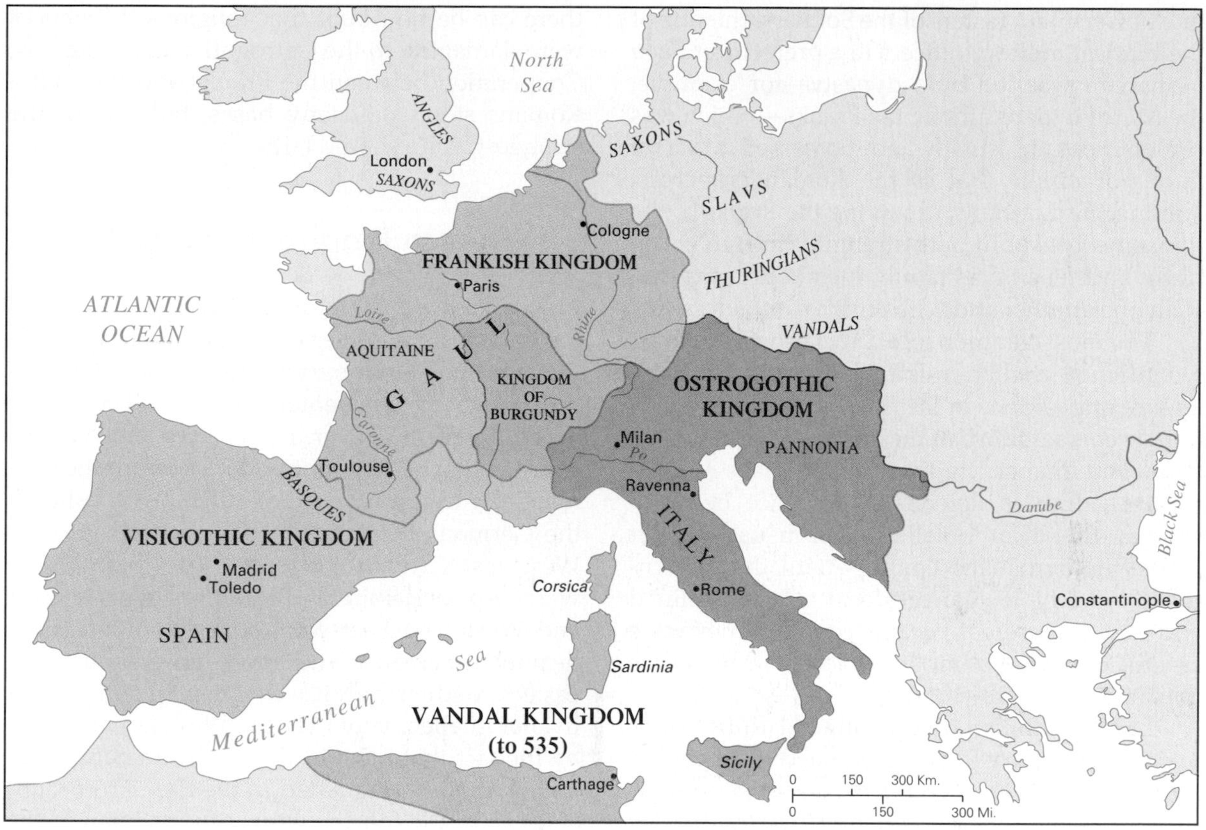

Map 7.3 The Germanic Kingdoms in the Sixth Century By the late sixth century, the western provinces of the Roman Empire (compare Map 6.2 on page 204) had evolved into Germanic kingdoms. Just as provincial boundaries had changed numerous times, the existence and extent of kingdoms were also not permanent.

were resident in and concerned mainly about the East. The Visigoths and other peoples were settled in their own kingdoms on Roman soil, instead of being enrolled in and dispersed among Roman army units. Beginning with Diocletian, the army was increasingly Germanized, and Germanic military men gained high offices in the state. Those leaders often dominated imperial courts and negotiated the series of treaties that submitted former provinces to barbarian peoples. Provincial elites had long been accustomed to having prominent Germans in their midst. The new situation was not unusual to them. Churchmen readily embraced the Catholic Franks and tolerated Arians, such as the Visigoths, who promoted peace and good government without abusing the Catholic population.

The New Old West

The Germanic kingdoms had a great deal in common with one another and were very much like the late Roman Empire, which had been their common tutor. Each realm was led by a king who usually appeared in two distinct guises. To his people, the king was the military leader. The essential bond of unity among each Germanic people was loyalty to the leader, who repaid his followers in booty, tribute, land, judicial protection, and military security. To the Romans, the king appeared as an ally and magistrate. Almost all Germanic kings bore such Roman titles as *consul* or *patrician,* and in these officially conferred titles resided the authority necessary to govern Roman populations. The kings also succeeded to a long line of German Masters of the Soldiers, the title of the highest military officers in a prefecture. Each monarchy was led by a dynasty—for example, the Merovingians among the Franks—which was pre-eminent in wealth and possessed a sacral aura not unlike that of the Roman emperors. Among the Germans, as among the Romans, the dynasties provided both strength through continuity and tension as family members competed with one another and with envious outsiders.

The most common local officials were counts, a combined civilian-military position that made its first appearance in the fifth century. Initially a direct representative of the central government, a count had financial, judicial, and military responsibilities. Just as defenders had once been resented, the local notables, still usually great landowners, disliked counts—until the government's ability to manage local affairs declined and they themselves became counts. Kings were careful to promote important locals to the office of count.

Local administration continued to be based in cities and towns. Taxes continued to be paid to royal governments throughout the sixth century. Provincial populations did not find this policy odd or unjust. Their taxes had always gone primarily to pay for the Roman military establishment, and the monarchies were the heirs of that establishment. Latin continued to be the language of administration. Until the end of Late Antiquity, notaries continued to draw up and to record wills, records of land transactions, and legal documents of all kinds. Major law codes were issued by the Germanic kingdoms, including the Salic Law of the Franks (511), two versions of the Burgundian Code, and several revisions of the Visigoths' laws. These were local adaptations of Roman provincial law. In other words, the legal conditions under which most people lived changed little. It is difficult to find convincing evidence that people's daily lives changed much as a result of the replacement of Roman provinces by Germanic kingdoms.

The Germans generally shared the Christian faith with the provincial populations, but here there were complications. A number of the Germans, chief among them the Vandals, Visigoths, and Ostrogoths, were Arians. Heresy was far from the worst of the Vandals' problems, but there can be no doubt that religious differences were damaging to the Ostrogoths and Visigoths. Cooperation between the Franks and the Gallo-Romans stood on many bases, but one of the strongest was a shared faith.

The Roman Empire in the East

The creation of the tetrarchy separated the eastern and western halves of the Roman Empire administratively. In theory there was only one empire, ruled by one senior augustus. The reality was different, however. The Eastern and Western courts followed different policies toward the Germans, for example. Eastern rulers, who ushered the Germans through the Balkans and into the West, lost virtually no territory to them. There were also fundamental differences between East and West. The East was more populous, more heavily urbanized, and more prosperous. The eastern Mediterranean was Greek in culture and livelier intellectually than the West, as evidenced by the fact that most of the Christian heresies of Late Antiquity originated in the East. From Constantine in the fourth century to Justinian in the sixth, there emerged an eastern Roman Empire that, as the western empire was being parceled out into kingdoms, became the sole heir of the imperial tradition.

Constantinople and Its Rulers

Constantius II (r. 337–361), Constantine's son and successor, began making Constantinople a truly imperial city (Map 7.4). He gave "New Rome" a senate and a set of urban magistrates of its own, placing the city on an equal constitutional footing with old Rome. Constantinople did not have an ancient aristocracy, so Constantius had to create a senatorial order. This he did by promoting prominent and cultivated persons from cities in the eastern half of the empire. Almost immediately rivalries arose between the senates of East and West. From the emperor's point of view, the new situation was satisfactory because there was in Constantinople a harmony of aristocratic and imperial interests.

With the exception of the founder, the ablest members of the dynasty of Valentinian ruled in

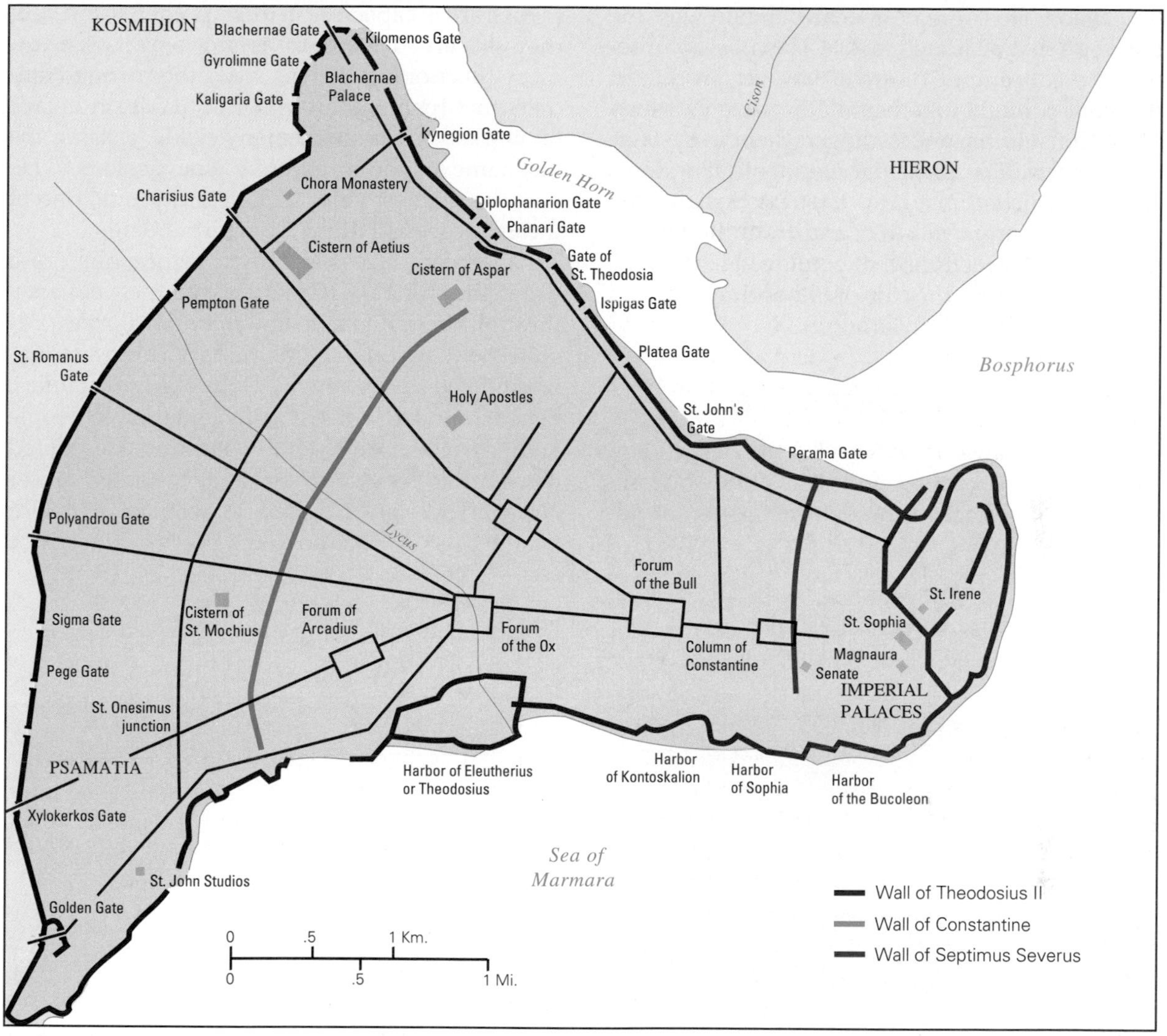

Map 7.4 Constantinople in Late Antiquity Protected by the sea, the Golden Horn, and its massive landward walls, Constantine's new city was an impregnable fortress for a thousand years. Note how the city was equipped with palaces, forums, wide thoroughfares, and other urban amenities. (*Source: The Cambridge Illustrated History of THE MIDDLE AGES*, edited by Robert Fossier, translated by Janet Sondheimer. Copyright © 1989. Used by permission of Cambridge University Press.)

the East. The greatest of these was Theodosius II (r. 408–450), who enjoyed the longest imperial reign in Roman history. Through skillful diplomacy and the occasional application of force, he managed to keep the eastern empire free of serious Germanic incursions and the Persians at bay in Mesopotamia. To protect his capital city, he built on the landward side massive walls whose ruins are impressive even today. He, along with his wife and his sister, promoted learning in the city and both added and beautified important buildings. New Rome did not have the literary and historical associations of old Rome, but it also lacked the pagan connections of the city on the Tiber. Theodosius and his family did much to make the new capital a real intellectual center.

Theodosius' greatest achievement was the law code that he issued in 438. The most comprehensive collection of Roman law yet produced, this code brought together all Roman laws issued since Constantine and arranged them in systematic fashion. The principal Germanic kingdoms were established just after the Theodosian code was issued. From this text, and from the Roman institutional structures that employed it, the Germans were taught the rule of law and regulations for the conduct of daily affairs.

The Reign of Justinian (527–565)

After Theodosius II died in 450, the eastern empire endured seventy-seven years of rule by military men who lacked the culture, vision, or administrative capacity of their predecessors. But they preserved the empire and kept its government functioning. It was from these rough soldiers that Justinian arose. Until his death in 565, he worked tirelessly in many fields, earning the nickname of "the emperor who never sleeps." He was the greatest ruler of Late Antiquity, one of the greatest of all Rome's emperors.

Justinian, like his father before him, rose from the Illyrian (Croatian today) peasantry through the military to the imperial throne. Despite growing up in rural military camps, Justinian showed a wide range of interests and abilities. He surrounded himself with remarkable people and gave them considerable latitude. He flouted convention by marrying a strip-tease dancer named Theodora (d. 548). A woman of intelli-

Theodora This magnificent sixth-century mosaic from Ravenna (it is one of a pair; see page 269) depicts Empress Theodora in all her power and majesty. *(Scala/Art Resource, NY)*

Basic Principles of Roman Law

Roman law is distinguished not only by its particular rules but also by its approach to the subject of law as a whole. These words are from the beginning of Justinian's* Institutes, *his lawbook for students.

Justice is an unswerving and perpetual determination to acknowledge all men's rights. Learning in the law entails knowledge of God and man, and mastery of the difference between justice and injustice. The commandments of the law are these: live honorably; harm nobody; give everyone his due. There are two aspects to the subject: public and private. Public law is concerned with the organization of the Roman state, while private is about the well-being of individuals. [Private law] has three parts, in that it is derived from the law of nature, of all peoples, or of the state. The law of nature is the law instilled by nature in all creatures. The law of all peoples and the law of the state are distinguished as follows. All people with laws and customs apply law which is partly theirs alone and partly shared by all mankind. The law which each people makes for itself is special to its own state. It is called "state law." But the law which natural reason makes for all mankind is applied the same everywhere. It is called the "law of all peoples" because it is common to every nation. The law of the Roman people is also partly its own and partly common to all mankind.

Source: Peter Birks and Grant McLeod, eds. and trans., *Justinian's Institutes,* 1.1–2 (Ithaca, N.Y.: Cornell University Press, 1987), p. 37.

gence, imagination, and great courage, Theodora was one of Justinian's key advisers. Justinian identified and promoted such previously obscure figures as the gifted general Belisarius, the administrative genius John the Cappadocian, and the greatest legal mind of the age, Tribonian. He entrusted two famous mathematicians, Anthemius of Tralles and Isidore of Miletus, with the task of designing the church of Hagia Sophia, which remains his principal monument.

Almost immediately on assuming the throne, Justinian put John the Cappadocian to work reforming an administration that had been little altered in two centuries despite vast changes in the scope of the empire. John worked particularly to secure tighter control of provincial administrators, to ensure a steady flow of tax revenue, and to eliminate official corruption. Tribonian and a commission were assigned the task of producing the first comprehensive review of Roman law since that of Theodosius II in 438. Between 529 and 533 Justinian's code was issued in three parts. The *Code* was a systematically organized collection of all imperial legislation. The *Digest* was a collection of the writings of the classical Roman jurists, the legal philosophers of the Early Empire. The *Institutes* was a textbook for law students (see the box, "Basic Principles of Roman Law"). Justinian's code constitutes the most influential legal collection in human history. It summarized a thousand years of legal work, reigned in the eastern empire for another thousand years, and has affected almost every state and legal system in the modern world.

Not long after undertaking his legal and administrative reforms, Justinian launched an attempt to reconquer the empire's lost western provinces. Belisarius retook Africa from the Vandals and Italy from the Ostrogoths. Justinian also landed an army in Spain to attempt the reconquest of Iberia from the Visigoths. He never had the resources to carry out this task. (See the feature, "Weighing the Evidence: The Ravenna Mosaics," on pages 268–269.)

Although he enjoyed some military successes in the west, Justinian faced constant threats in the Balkans from Bulgars and Slavs and in Mesopotamia from Persians. Costly treaties and humiliating subsidies bought a string of cease-fires but no definitive settlements in these areas. The emperor's campaigns were so expensive that his administrative reforms wound up looking like contrivances to make more money for the emperor to waste. Resentment flared in Constantinople in 532 in violent riots in which mobs coursed through the city demanding the dismissal of John the Cappadocian and other imperial agents. In 542, moreover, the Mediterranean world was visited by plague, one more blow to the empire.

Justinian's religious policy also met with sharp opposition. A genuinely pious man, Justinian legislated frequently on behalf of the church and practiced, along with Theodora, generous charitable benefactions. Still, by both personal conviction and a sense of official duty, Justinian desired religious unity. Although the Council of Chalcedon had condemned monophysitism in 451, Justinian was mildly monophysite, and his wife was enthusiastically so. Justinian tried again and again to find a compromise that would bring all parties together. His church council of 553 assembled amid high hopes but in the end alienated the clergy in Syria, Egypt, and Rome.

Justinian had visions of grandeur, and to give them concrete expression he sought out Anthemius and Isidore. He wished for these great mathematicians to design a church that would be not merely impressive but magnificent. It was to be a representation of the place where heaven and earth touched, the vestibule of heaven. Its symbolic role was to be given regular confirmation by the meeting in this place of the emperor, the patriarch (the archbishop of Constantinople), and the people. There is no evidence that Justinian dictated the form of his church—the church of Hagia Sophia, Holy Wisdom—but the fact that he did not turn to any of the city's regular builders suggests that he was not looking for a traditional basilica.

He got the largest Christian church ever built, but its size is almost the least of its qualities. Hagia Sophia starts from a square just over 100 feet on a side, 70 feet above which are four great arches. Two of the arches are solid and form the nave walls of the church; the other two give way to semi-circular continuations of the nave. Above the main square is a dome that seems to float on a blaze of light. The inside is a riot of color achieved by marble fittings in almost every imaginable hue, by mosaics and frescoes of indescribable beauty, and by the mysterious play of light and shadow. The effect of the whole is disorienting. Space in most basilicas is ordered, controlled, elegant. Space in Hagia Sophia is horizontal and vertical, straight and curved, square and round. The inside is by turns dark and light, purple and green, red and blue. It is indeed as if one has entered a realm that is anchored to this world but that gives access to another one. When Justinian first saw his church in its completed state, he said, "Solomon, I have outdone thee."

It is appropriate that in inspecting his great church Justinian should have looked backward to Solomon, the Hebrew king who built Jerusalem's Temple. In almost all respects Justinian was a traditional, backward-looking ruler. His concern for the administrative minutiae of his empire would have made perfect sense to Diocletian, and his combination of military and diplomatic initiatives would have been understood by Theodosius I, whose namesake, Theodosius II, would have admired Justinian's legal code. In his religious policies, especially in his quest for unity, Justinian drew from a deep well of imperial precedent. Even in his attempt to restore direct rule in Rome's former western provinces, Justinian showed himself a traditionalist.

Christian Culture and Life

A third-century Christian writer asked, "What has Athens to do with Jerusalem?" The culture of Late Antiquity was fashioned as people tried to answer that question. The rise of the Christian intellectual is a key theme in the history of Late Antiquity, as is the nature of the schools, institutions, and communities that fostered cultural changes. Important too is an awareness of the immensity and diversity of a world in which many pagan cultures gave way to many Christian ones.

Hagia Sophia This interior view of Hagia Sophia conveys some sense of the dazzling complexity of this greatest of all late antique buildings. Compare it to Santa Maria Maggiore (p. 244). *(Giraudon/Art Resource, NY)*

Christian culture involved institutions that claimed people's allegiance, communities that nurtured them, ideas that inspired them, and a history that defined them. Christianity grew and spread in the Roman world. It spoke that world's languages, borrowed its philosophical and legal terminology, adapted its administrative structures, reinterpreted its celebrations, and recruited its ablest citizens. The French have a saying: "Plus ça change, plus c'est la même chose"—"The more things change, the more they remain the same." So it was in Late Antiquity, in the realms of government and of religion.

The True Church: Competing Visions

Around 450 a Christian writer said that the Catholic faith was the one believed "everywhere, all the time, by everyone." That is a good, working definition of *Catholicism,* a religious tradition that takes its name from a Greek word meaning "universal." It is no accident that a Catholic church grew up in a Roman world steeped in ideas of universality. The most deeply held tenet of Roman ideology maintained that Rome's mission was to civilize the whole world and bend it to Roman ways.

The Catholic church, in seeking to assume that mission, met opposition on at least two fronts. As a first case, let us look at a quarrel between an emperor and a pope. The popes had been working to gain leadership in the church and to make themselves final arbiters of doctrine. When Emperor Anastasius (r. 491–518) intervened in a quarrel between the Catholics and the monophysites, Pope Gelasius I (r. 492–496) sent a strongly worded letter to Constantinople in which he protested the emperor's intervention. Gelasius told the emperor that the world was governed by the "power" of kings and by the "authority" of priests. Ordinarily, the pope said, the jurisdictions of kings and priests are distinct. If a controversy arises between them, however, then priestly authority must have precedence because priests are concerned with the salvation of immortal souls but kings only rule mortal bodies. Gelasius was telling the emperor to stay out of theology, but he was implying much more. His opposition of the words *power*—meaning mere police power, the application of brute force—and *authority*—legitimacy, superior right—was of great importance. Gelasius was raising the church, with the pope at its head, above the whole secular regime with the emperor at its head.

Gelasius could take this position because he was in Rome where there was no longer an emperor. The pope could also be confident of the unity of the church in the western Mediterranean; in contrast, the East was still riven by controversies. The emperor took sharp exception to Gelasius's arguments, but more pressing business faced him. He could not achieve unity among warring Christian factions, and he had to think about his frontiers more than about the writings of a troublesome priest in old Rome. Christians in the East agreed with Gelasius's views on priestly authority and kingly power only to the extent that they were already opposed to the emperor's theological pronouncements.

This controversy reveals several conflicting visions. Was the church a branch of the state and thus subject to imperial command? The emperor thought so, but the pope denied it. Was the pope the final arbiter of doctrine? Neither the emperor nor the pope's theological opponents were prepared to admit this. Would the pope actually have any real influence in the east? It seemed unlikely. But could the emperor impose his will in matters of religion, in the East or the West, as a practical matter of power or as a theoretical dimension of his office? This seemed unlikely too.

The second case concerns several broad patterns of Christian experience that emerged in Late Antiquity and survive to this day. One of the interesting developments is the emergence of several Christian communities claiming fidelity to a universal—a catholic—tradition. The Latin Christian church in the West was staunchly Nicene and Chalcedonian and took its bearings from Latin church writers. The Orthodox church in the East centered primarily on the emperors and patriarchs, used Greek, and followed Greek Christian writers. The Coptic church in Egypt was monophysite, followed the teachings of the patriarchs of Alexandria, and used the Coptic language. The Jacobite church, a mildly monophysite, Syriac-speaking group, was originally strong in Syria, from where it spread to Mesopotamia and beyond. Each of these churches produced a literature, an art, and a way of life that marked its members as a distinct community. These traditions did not reflect the emergence of something new in Late Antiquity so much as a Christian reinterpretation of very old cultures and ideals.

The Rise of Christian Monasticism

For some people the call of the Gospel was positively revolutionary. They did not wish to work to change this world for the better. They wished to escape this world in order to avoid all that might come between them and the God who was both the source and the goal of human existence. These people were monks who developed a theology and an institution that were among the most creative and long-lived of all the achievements of Late Antiquity. Christian monasticism emerged in Egypt in the last decades of the third century, but the forces that combined to produce monasticism are ancient and universal.

The practice of rigorous self-denial was common to several religious and philosophical sects in antiquity—for example, the Pythagoreans and the Stoics—and was well known among the Jews in the time of Christ, as the Essenes show (see page 220). Widespread opinion held that if one could conquer the desires of the body, one could unite with those beings who were greater and purer than a humanity encumbered by its lusts for food, drink, knowledge, sex, and adventure. Sometimes ascetic practices were adopted by tightly knit groups, sometimes by heroic solitaries.

These traditions met in Egypt in the person of Anthony (d. 356). He was a man who, at about age 20, gave away all his possessions and took up in the Egyptian desert a life of prayer and renunciation. In the desert, Anthony sought to imitate the life of Christ. His spiritual quest became famous, and many disciples flocked to him. Finally, he decided to organize them into a very loose community. Anthony's form of monasticism is called *eremitic,* from the Greek *heremos* for "desert." The name *eremitic,* signifying extreme asceticism and individualism, gives us the word *hermit.*

Pachomius (290–346) created a second form of monastic life. He was a Roman soldier who left the service in 313, was baptized a Christian, and retired to the Egyptian desert, where he studied with a hermit. Eventually Pachomius founded a community of ascetics, and before long his community, and dozens like it, had thousands of members. An anomalous situation had arisen: Literally thousands of people were living alone but together in veritable cities out in the desert. Pachomius wrote the first Rule, or code for daily living, for a monastic community. He organized most aspects of the life of his community by designing a common life based on routines of private prayer, group worship, and work. Pachomius's pattern of monasticism is called *cenobitic,* from the Greek for "common life." The persons living this common life were called *monks,* and the place where they lived this life was called a *monastery.* The head of the community was designated *abbot,* a word meaning "father."

Monasticism spread from Egypt by means of texts such as the *Life of Anthony* (a late antique "best seller") collections of the wise sayings of famous desert abbots, and books written by persons who went to Egypt seeking a more perfect life—among whom were several prominent women, such as Melania (see the box, "Melania the Younger"). The appeal of monasticism grew greater after Christianity gained official status. Those who were attracted to monasticism saw it as a purer form of Christian life, uncorrupted by the wealth, power, and controversy of the hierarchical church. The ascetic life was popular with women for personal reasons and because offices in the church hierarchy were denied to women, whereas positions in monasteries, including that of abbess, provided outlets for female talent.

As monasticism spread from Egypt, it adopted the two basic patterns. To the East, the eremitic pattern was prominent in Palestine and Syria and eventually throughout the Greek-speaking world. Eastern monasticism produced a great legislator in Basil (330–379), who wrote the most influential Rule in the Orthodox church. Generally these monks assembled only for weekly worship and otherwise ate, prayed, and worked alone.

Eremitic monasticism arrived in the West in the person of Martin of Tours (336–397). Like Pachomius, Martin was a pagan Roman soldier who, after his military service ended, embraced both Christianity and asceticism. Even though he was elected bishop of Tours, Martin kept to his rigid life of denial.

An admiring biography kept Martin's memory alive for centuries, but in the West the cenobitic pattern proved more successful than the eremitic. The first great center from which cenobitic monasticism spread was Lérins in the south of Gaul, where a community was founded in 410. The fame of Lérins spread rapidly throughout the western Roman Empire, and men came to it from all over. Lérins attracted many aristocrats, some of whom went on to become bishops and promoters of monasticism.

The most famous monastic founder in the West was Benedict of Nursia (480–545), a middle-class Roman who abandoned legal studies and a potential government career to pursue a life of prayer. Benedict's fame grew so great that he attracted a crowd of followers, and in about 520, at Monte Cassino—80 miles south of Rome, he drew up a Rule. This Rule is marked by shrewd insights into the human personality. It emphasizes the bond of mutual love among the monks and obedience to the abbot. The abbot is assigned

Melania the Younger: The Appeal of Monasticism to Women

The appeal of monasticism was great for men and women, rich and poor, as the career of Melania (383–438) shows. She came from a wealthy Roman family, renounced her possessions, and traveled widely in Italy, North Africa, Egypt, and Palestine, visiting holy men and women. These selected passages from her biography provide glimpses of her life.

Melania was foremost among the Romans of senatorial rank. Wounded by divine love, she had from earliest youth yearned for Christ, and longed for bodily chastity. Her parents, because they were illustrious members of the Roman senate and expected that through her they would have a succession of the family line, forcibly united her in marriage . . . when she was fourteen and her husband, seventeen. [After having two children, Melania persuaded her husband to join her in renouncing the world.] She bridled nature and delivered herself to death daily, demonstrating to everyone that woman is not surpassed by man in anything that pertains to virtue, if her decision is strong. She was by nature a gifted writer and wrote without mistakes in notebooks. She decided for herself how much she should write every day, and how much she should read in the canonical books and in the collections of homilies. Then she would go through the Lives of the fathers as if she were eating dessert. The blessed woman read the Old and New Testaments three or four times a year. The most holy fathers [Egyptian abbots] received her as if she were a man. In truth, she had been detached from the female nature, and had acquired a masculine disposition, or rather, a heavenly one.

Source: Elizabeth A. Clark, ed. and trans., *The Life of Melania the Younger*, cc. 1, 12, 23, 26, 39, *Studies in Women and Religion*, vol. 14 (New York: Edwin Mellen Press, 1984), pp. 27–28, 35, 46, 53–54.

wide powers but is told to exercise them gently. Monks are permitted a reasonable diet and decent, though modest, clothing. Although punishment is provided for, loving correction is preferred. In Late Antiquity the monks of Lérins were the monastic elite of the west, but in later centuries it was Benedict's Rule that dominated monastic life.

Eremitic or cenobitic, East or West, monasticism represented an explicit challenge and a conscious alternative to the civic world of classical antiquity. Monks were assuredly not people who sought to give their lives meaning by service within cities. They went into deserts to serve God and one another. They sought not to acquire but to abandon. Spiritual wisdom counted for more than secular learning, and acknowledgment of their holiness was more important than recognition of their social status.

The Quest for a Catholic Tradition

The Christian clergy attracted not only talented administrators but also gifted intellectuals. As the church became first free and then triumphant, those intellectuals were able to reflect publicly on their faith and its place in the ancient world. The results of their labors produced a coherent tradition that can be called *Catholic.*

Christianity drew much from the pagan and Jewish environments within which it grew, but its fundamental inspiration was the collection of writings called in modern times *The Bible.* In antiquity this material was called *ta hagia biblia* or *sacra biblia,* meaning "the holy books." It was understood to be a collection of sacred writings, and the individual items in that collection had different meanings. From the second century, Christian writers began trying to define a canon, a definitive list of genuine Old and New Testament scriptures. It was widely recognized that until a standard set of Christian sources was defined, there could be no hope of uniformity of Christian belief. This process was not completed until the middle of the fifth century.

While the search was underway for an authoritative list of books, it was also necessary to try to get uniform versions of the books that were being pronounced canonical. The Greek East held to the Greek version of the Old Testament and to the Greek New Testament; but that version was unsuitable in the West, where Latin, not Greek, was the principal tongue. Late in the fourth century, Pope Damasus commissioned Jerome (331–420), a wealthy man who abandoned his luxury for a life of monasticism and scholarship, to prepare a Latin version based on a new translation of the Hebrew Scriptures and Greek New Testament. Jerome's version was called the "Vulgate" because it was the Bible for the "people" (*vulgus*) who knew Latin.

Once a scriptural canon had been identified, there was also a need for a creedal statement that would set down precisely what Christians believed. The councils of Nicaea and Constantinople defined the nature of the Trinity, and Chalcedon formulated the relationship between the human and divine natures of Christ. These central dogmas, or teachings, of the Christian faith were not the only theological issues that arose, however. There were debates about the priesthood, the church, and the problem of human free will. Practical questions came up too. How could Christians fulfill the moral demands of their faith while living in a world whose values were often at odds with church teachings?

Answers to these kinds of questions were provided by a group of Greek and Latin writers who are called the "Church Fathers" and whose era is called "patristic" (from *patres,* the Latin word for *fathers*). In versatility and sheer output they have few rivals at any time. Their intellectual breadth was matched by their elegant style and trenchant reasoning.

THE DEVELOPMENT OF CATHOLIC CHRISTIANITY

ca. 300	Emergence of Christian monasticism
313	The Edict of Milan
325	Council of Nicaea condemns Arian heresy
350–450	Age of the major Church Fathers
380	Theodosius requires Christians to believe as the Pope does
382–392	Jerome prepares Vulgate Bible
451	Council of Chalcedon condemns Monophysite heresy
440–461	Pope Leo I elaborates doctrine of papal primacy
492–496	Pope Gelasius delineates papal and imperial rule

Many Christian writers addressed themselves to the problems of moral living in the world. Ambrose of Milan wrote *On Duties,* a treatise that attempted to Christianize the public ethos that Cicero had spelled out many years before in his book *On Duties.* Cicero talked of citizens' obligations to one another and to the law. He stressed the need for those in places of power and responsibility to be above reproach in the conduct of their personal lives. Ambrose reinterpreted these ideas as duties that Christians owed to one another because of their common worship of God. At about the same time the patriarch of Constantinople John Chrysostom (347–407), one of the most popular and gifted preachers of Late Antiquity (his name means "golden tongued"), bitterly castigated the immorality of the imperial court and aristocracy because by setting a bad example they endangered the souls of their subjects.

No set of thematic categories could be drawn broadly enough to encompass Augustine (354–430). A later Spanish Father, Isidore of Seville, once said that if anyone tells you he has read all of Augustine's books you know he is a

Saint Augustine This depiction of Augustine dictating to a scribe while pupils listen was made in sixth-century Italy. Notice the ecclesiastical garb and tonsures. Note, too, how a Christian scene is placed within a classical architectural frame. *(Staatsbibliothek zu Berlin, Preussischer Kulturbesitz)*

liar. It is difficult to capture the message and the genius of the most influential Christian thinker after Saint Paul. Augustine was born in North Africa to a family of modest means, and he received, at great sacrifice, the best education available. He embarked on a career as a professor of rhetoric. Once he had established himself, he moved on to Rome and then to Milan, which in the fourth century was the unofficial western capital. Augustine fell under the spell of Ambrose and embraced the Christianity that his mother had been urging on him throughout his life. Later Augustine chronicled his quest for truth and spiritual fulfillment in his *Confessions,* a classic of Western literature (see the box, "The Moment of Augustine's Spiritual Awakening"). In 395 Augustine became a bishop and until his death served the North African community at Hippo, and the wider Christian world, with a torrent of writings.

Augustine was not a systematic thinker. He never set out to provide a comprehensive exposition of the whole of Christian doctrine. Augustine tended to respond to problems as they arose. Because he lived in times of constant turmoil, he had opportunities to express himself on a wide array of issues, crucial among which were the relationship between God and humans, the nature of the church, and the overall plan of God's creation.

In the early fifth century some people believed that they could achieve salvation by the unaided operation of their own will. Augustine responded that although God did indeed endow humankind with free will, Adam and Eve had abused their will to rebel against God. Ever since that first act of rebellion there was a taint, called by theologians "original sin," that predisposed humans to continual rebellion, or sin, against God. Only divine grace can overcome sin, and only by calling on God can people receive grace. Here was a decisive break with the classical idea of humanity as good in itself and capable of self-improvement, perhaps even perfection, in this world. According to Augustine, all people were flawed, were sinners, were in need of God's redemption.

Some North African heretics said that sacraments celebrated by unworthy priests were invalid. Augustine believed that the efficacy of the church's sacraments—those ritual celebrations that were considered to be channels for the communication of grace, of God's special aid and comfort to the faithful—did not depend on the personal merit of the minister. A priest or a bishop acted in God's place and through divine grace. Therefore, faith in God was paramount. The church, in this reckoning, was a community of acknowledged sinners that was being led by its clergy in a quest for eternal salvation. Augustine said that God alone was perfect. As in his view of humanity itself, so also in his view of the clergy and of the church, Augustine was emphasizing the almost unbridgeable chasm that separated God from creation. Only God was truly good, and God was a purely spiritual being. Clergy, rulers, churches: These were all human institutions, all more or less good in particular circum-

The Moment of Augustine's Spiritual Awakening

In this passage Augustine relates the moment of his conversion and abandonment of his former life. Notice the role of books and of God in Augustine's memory of the event.

I kept crying "How long shall I go on saying 'tomorrow, tomorrow'? Why not now?" I was asking these questions when all at once I heard the singing of a child repeating the refrain, "Take it and read, take it and read." I stemmed my flood of tears telling myself that this could only be a divine command to open my book of scripture and read the first passage on which my eyes should fall. For I had heard the story of Anthony, and I remembered how he had entered a church while the Gospel was being read and took it as a counsel to himself. In silence I read the first passage on which my eyes fell: *Not in revelling and drunkenness, not in lust and wantonness, not in quarrels and rivalries. Rather arm yourselves with the Lord Jesus Christ; spend no more thought on nature and nature's appetites.* I had no wish or need to read more. It was as if the light of confidence had flooded into my heart and all the darkness of doubt was dispelled.

Source: Augustine, *Confessions*, 8.12, trans. R. S. Pine-Coffin (Harmondsworth, England: Penguin, 1961), pp. 177–178.

stances. But they were not divine any more than God could be found in the idols of the pagan cults.

The sack of Rome by the Visigoths in 410 distressed many people in the Roman world. Some argued that Alaric's seizure of Rome was repayment for Rome's abandonment of its traditional gods. To refute them, Augustine took up his pen to write the most brilliant and difficult of all his works, *The City of God.* This book is a theology of history. It sees time not as cyclical, the traditional classical view, but as linear. There has been a plan in operation, God's plan, since the creation of the world, and that plan will govern all human activity until the end of time. On earth there will always be a struggle between those who call on divine grace, who are redeemed, who are citizens of the City of God, and those who keep to the ways of the world, who persist in sin, who live in the earthly city. One may observe the unfolding of the divine plan by seeing how much of the earthly city has been redeemed at any given time.

Even though the Roman Empire was officially Christian, Augustine refused to identify his City of God with it. Nor would he say that the church and the City of God were identical. What he did say was that the sack of Rome was a great irrelevance because many kingdoms and empires had come and gone and would continue to do so, but only the kingdom of God was eternal and, in the long run, important. To a Roman people whose most cherished belief held that the world would last exactly as long as Rome's dominion, Augustine's dismissal of Rome's destiny sounded the death knell of the classical world view.

Augustine also addressed himself to the problem of education. His was a world where salvation was to be the goal of life, but where people did have to carry on with their ordinary occupations, and where almost the entire educational establishment was pagan in design and content. Education was confined mainly to the elite, who sought schooling partly to orient themselves within their cultural tradition and partly to gain employment, often in the imperial or urban service. This education had three mainstays. Latin or Greek grammar—rarely both—was the first. Augustine, for instance, knew little Greek, and by the sixth century few people in the east knew Latin. The second was rhetoric, once the art of public speaking but now, increasingly, literary criticism. The third was dialectic, or the art of right reasoning. In Late Antiquity public schools were fast disappearing as the need for them slipped away. The imperial service, at least in the west, was all but gone by the sixth century, and the Church Fathers were generally dismissive of the Roman heritage. But the church still needed educated persons, so it provided schools in cathedrals and monasteries.

In a treatise entitled *On Christian Doctrine* Augustine expressed some ideas about education that proved influential for a millennium. He said that everything that one needs to know, not to get or do a job but for salvation, is contained in the Bible. But the Bible, written in learned language, is full of difficult images and allusions. How is an ordinary person to learn what he or she needs to know in order to master this great book? Augustine used the expressive image of "spoiling the Egyptians," borrowed from the account of the Hebrews' Exodus from Egypt, when they took with them whatever they could use. Augustine's attitude to classical learning was that it was useful to the extent that it taught the kinds of things one needed to know in order to read the Bible, to understand it, and to seek salvation. Classical culture had no intrinsic merit. It might give pleasure, but it was equally likely to be a distraction or a temptation to immorality. In education as in all else, Augustine was a realist. He once said, "What we teach is one thing, what we tolerate is another."

Highly influential as well was a treatise *On Divine and Human Readings* by the Italian writer Cassiodorus (ca. 485–580), who had been a loyal servant of Theodoric in Italy. After the fall of the Ostrogothic kingdom, Cassiodorus retired and set up a school of Christian studies. His treatise served as a kind of annotated bibliography of the major writings on school subjects such as grammar, rhetoric, and dialectic, and on biblical commentary.

Cassiodorus agreed with Augustine's idea of "spoiling the Egyptians." He saw that there were no Christian grammars to teach the Latin language, no Christian rhetorical manuals to teach the finer points of writing and speaking, and no Christian dialectics to show how to prove or disprove an argument. These subjects had always formed the core of classical education, and they must still do so in the new Christian world of Late Antiquity. Secular grammars and the like formed Cassiodorus's human readings. These books were preparatory to divine readings, which consisted of the Bible, the commentaries on it, and the writings of the Church Fathers. For centuries schools organized on Augustine's and Cassiodorus's model did an estimable job of preparing the clergy to carry out their functions.

Summary

Late Antiquity, the years from around 300 to around 600, saw the militarization of government. In the west a warrior aristocracy of men whom the Roman world had drawn into service to protect it wound up succeeding the very Romans who had once hired them. Even in the East, the state had to be put on an almost permanent military footing. The content of classical culture was rejected by people who found its myths and immorality repulsive, its philosophy defective, and its ethics imperfect. But the formal aspects of that culture—its languages, its intellectual rigor, its literary devices, its logical subtlety—flourished among Christian writers who appropriated Virgil's beautiful Latin while throwing away his characters and stories. Most people remained farmers and remained poor. Their existence was barely touched by the passing of the classical order. The same kinds of people retained power, wealth, and influence, but now they were more likely to be kings or bishops than prefects or decurions. The paradox of Late Antiquity is the nearly invisible boundary between change and continuity.

What would happen next? In the West, several kingdoms gradually built new structures on their Roman, Germanic, and Christian foundations. In the East, the Roman Empire evolved into the Byzantine. Much that happened in the years between about 600 and 900 was fully rooted in the world of Late Antiquity. Surprising was the emergence of a new people, faith, and society in a previously marginal region, Arabia.

Suggested Reading

General Surveys

Brown, Peter. *The World of Late Antiquity.* 1971. A sprightly and beautifully illustrated interpretation of cultural cross-currents by the most gifted interpreter of Late Antiquity.

Holum, Kenneth G. *Theodosian Empresses: Women and Imperial Dominion in Late Antiquity.* 1982. A fascinating account of the behind-the-scenes roles played by female members of the imperial family in the fifth century.

Jones, A. H. M. *The Decline of the Ancient World.* 1966. This is a chapter-by-chapter abridgment of the author's longer work (see below). The book is not easy going but rewards close study.

———. *The Later Roman Empire, 284–602.* 2 vols. 1964. Despite its age, this massive work remains the best history of the Roman Empire. Its great strength is its detailed treatment of the Roman government.

MacMullen, Ramsay. *Corruption and the Decline of Rome.* 1988. A fascinating assessment of the boundaries between public and private conduct, between legal and illegal behavior.

Matthews, John. *Western Aristocracies and Imperial Court, 364–425.* 1975. A detailed, challenging treatment of the social changes in the western empire in the age of Valentinian and Theodosius.

The Barbarians

Goffart, Walter. *Barbarians and Romans, A.D. 418–584: The Techniques of Accommodation.* 1980. An important, stimulating, and controversial book on how the barbarians were actually integrated into the Roman system on essentially Roman terms.

Heather, Peter. *Goths and Romans, 332–489.* 1991. Less detailed than Wolfram (see below), this book stresses the complexity of Gothic social and political organization in the context of Gothic relations with different Roman authorities.

Musset, Lucien. *The Germanic Invasions: The Making of Europe, A.D. 400–600.* Translated by Edward and Columba James. 1975. Since its first appearance in 1965, this book has become the standard narrative treatment of the movement of the barbarians into the Roman world.

Todd, Malcolm. *The Northern Barbarians, 100 B.C.–A.D. 300.* Rev. ed. 1987. An interesting account of what archaeologists have learned about the barbarians before their entry into the empire. Stresses daily life.

Wolfram, Herwig. *History of the Goths.* Translated by Thomas J. Dunlap. 1988. Not only a history of the Goths, this brilliant book explains current ethnographic thinking about the barbarians.

The Roman Empire in the East

Browning, Robert. *Justinian and Theodora.* Rev. ed. 1987. A readable, reliable, and well-illustrated account of two fascinating people and a remarkable period.

Cameron, Averil. *Procopius.* 1985. The subject of this book was the last great ancient historian. His own tale is interesting, as are his unique perspectives on his world.

Honoré, Tony. *Tribonian.* 1978. This difficult book repays close study by showing how legal thinkers in Justinian's world actually worked. One learns from it a great deal about law in general.

The Development of Christian Culture

Brown, Peter. *Augustine of Hippo: A Biography.* 1969. A penetrating account of the life and world of a man described by the author as possessing "a mind of terrifying acuteness."

———. *The Cult of the Saints: Its Rise and Function in Latin Christianity.* 1981. A lively, imaginative discussion of holy men and women and of their places in this world and the next.

Chitty, Derwas J. *The Desert a City.* 1966. A comprehensive, readable account of monastic origins in Egypt and dissemination to the east.

Cochrane, Charles Norris. *Christianity and Classical Culture.* Rev. ed. 1944. This classic book explains both the borrowings and the oppositions between classical and Christian culture.

Kelly, J. N. D. *Jerome.* 1975. A solid account of the life and work of the Church Father best known for the Vulgate Bible.

Markus, Robert. *The End of Ancient Christianity.* 1990. This stimulating and beautifully written book explores the changing meanings of sacred and secular in the period from 400 to 600.

———. *Saeculum: History and Society in the Theology of St. Augustine.* 1970. A superb account of what Augustine thought about government and society.

O'Donnell, James J. *Cassiodorus.* 1979. A solid treatment of the man whose educational ideas heavily influenced the next several centuries.

Pagels, Elaine. *Adam, Eve, and the Serpent.* 1988. A fascinating but controversial assessment of the evolution of attitudes toward women by the clergy.

Rousseau, Philip. *Pachomius: The Making of a Community in Fourth-Century Egypt.* 1985. A brilliant evocation of the social connections of the early monastic world.

Stancliffe, Claire. *St. Martin and His Hagiographer: History and Miracle in Sulpicius Severus.* 1983. Simultaneously an account of early western eremitic monasticism, and of how we know about it.

Wilken, Robert. *The Christians as the Romans Saw Them.* 1984. This well-written, interesting book gathers the evidence for the pagan reaction to Christianity.

Weighing the Evidence

THE RAVENNA MOSAICS

Propaganda. The word has unsavory connotations. It suggests that someone is trying to convince someone else to do or to believe what is wrong. Actually, the word means only "things to be propagated," a message to be gotten out. The message itself may be good or bad.

When we think of propaganda, we must consider both the message and the medium in which it is conveyed. In antiquity, governments had several means of getting their messages out. Almost all the means were public, visible, striking.

Mosaics are among the most spectacular art forms of Late Antiquity, and in the churches of Ravenna they attained the summit of their propagandistic power. A mosaic is a picture formed by the intricate arrangement of thousands of tiny bits (called *tesserae*) of glass, stone, or metal. An artist created a rough sketch of the intended picture and then laid out the tesserae to conform to the sketch. Next the artist applied wet plaster to a small section of the surface, usually a wall or a floor, that was to receive the picture and then embedded that section's tesserae into the plaster. This process was repeated until the whole mosaic was completed. The result was a durable art form of great beauty and visual interest. In the picture on the opposite page you can see the tesserae and even some of the sparkle produced by the effect of sunlight and candles reflecting off the mosaic.

Mosaics were sometimes placed in private homes by the very wealthy, but more often they were put in conspicuous public places. Churches commonly received them in Late Antiquity. As more of society became Christian, aristocrats in particular were happy to spend lavishly to adorn their places of worship with beautiful decorations. Masses of people saw those decorations, reflected on who had financed them, and pondered the meaning of the image itself.

The greatest patron of all was the emperor. By putting up any work of art, the emperor proclaimed his power and influence. His reach was vast even if he never left Constantinople. Nothing shows this better than the Ravenna mosaics erected by Justinian.

Let us recall the situation. The Arian Ostrogoths had taken over Italy in 493. Ruling from Ravenna, they claimed to be imperial allies and representatives. Down to 535 there were always strains between Ravenna and Constantinople, and in that year Justinian launched the twenty-year-long Gothic War. During and after the war churches were erected as symbols of the imperial restoration.

The mosaic pictured here is located on the left-hand side of the apse, above and behind the altar, in the church of San Vitale in Ravenna. Its central figure is the emperor Justinian. Immediately opposite it is another mosaic (partially reproduced on page 256) focusing on Empress Theodora. San Vitale was a monument to the defeat of the Arian Goths. Any worshiper who raised his or her eyes from the altar saw immediately both Justinian and Theodora. These images made a powerful statement in a city that had been ruled by a Gothic king for thirty-three years. Justinian was leaving no doubt about who was now in charge. Consider too the prominence accorded to Theodora. Justinian really did view her as a partner in his rule.

That the emperor and empress were in charge is indicated in several distinct ways. They are slightly larger and are standing in front of their attendants. They are not quite like the other humans shown in the mosaic. They wear crowns and rich purple—that is to say, imperial—garments. They present gifts: he a gold paten holding the eucharistic bread and she a golden chalice containing the eucharistic wine. Thus the emperor and empress are represented as the donors of the church and as the guarantors of authentic worship.

Justinian tried throughout his reign to promote *homonoia* ("concord"). He tried to reconcile many political and religious factions. Notice the figure to Justinian's left (your right), over whose bald head you can read "MAXIMIANUS." This man

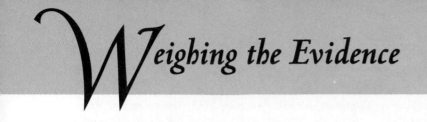

Justinian and His Courtiers, Apse Mosaic, San Vitale, Ravenna *(Scala/Art Resource)*

was the archbishop of Ravenna, a close ally of the emperor and the person responsible both for eradicating Arianism and for reconciling Arians. His prominent position next to the emperor, and the fact that he alone is named, assured everyone of the correct position in religion. And in case anyone needed a further reminder, Maximianus holds in his hand the cross of Christ: There would be no more Arian subordination of the second person of the Trinity to the first.

We may note one more piece of propaganda. Look at the man standing to the left of Justinian and slightly behind him—between Justinian and Maximianus. This is Julianus Argentarius, a wealthy layman who was in all things the emperor's agent in Ravenna. He helped to finance and oversaw the construction of not only San Vitale but also several other churches in Ravenna. His presence signifies homonoia again, this time the traditional concord between the emperor and the elite throughout the empire. Relations between the court and the Italian elite had been very strained under the Ostrogoths. Julianus's presence signaled that all was well once again. Vanity played a role too. Julianus paid for the art, so he had himself included in it.

The church of San Vitale was itself a propaganda statement. Theodoric was buried in a grand octagonal tomb. Justinian's builders chose an octagonal form for San Vitale. This church too is a sepulchre—a shrine for the remains of Saint Vitalis, an early Ravenna Christian who was martyred for the true faith.

In a world without the modern mass media, the media of antiquity served well to broadcast messages to people who understood their real and symbolic language. Recall the images on Hellenistic and Roman coins (pages 152, 190). Look again at the statue of the tetrarchs (page 235), the massive statue of Constantine (page 237), the sculpture of Saint Peter enthroned (page 243). Cassiodorus once said that Rome was "a forest of statues." Every one of them was a propaganda statement.

CHAPTER 8

Early Medieval Civilizations, ca. 600–900

A time-traveler transported back to the Mediterranean world of 600 would almost certainly predict only two heirs to antiquity: the Roman East and the barbarian West. That intrepid wanderer would not be likely to foresee one of the most dynamic developments in the history of Western civilization: the meteoric rise of Islam as a faith and of the Muslims as a people.

In this chapter, three areas and histories, not just two, engage our attention. Remarkable similarities mark the historical development of these three areas. For each, the seventh century was an era of dramatic change, the eighth century an era of reform and consolidation, and the ninth century a time of upheaval. The similarities are not merely chronological. A new imperial tradition developed in each area, a tradition rooted in a particular territory whose people believed themselves to be specially chosen by God and whose rulers defined themselves as God's earthly agents. In all three realms the interaction of local traditions with the Roman past produced new forms of central government that would prove influential for centuries. Commercial ties began to transform the Mediterranean world into a community of peoples who needed to balance mutual interests with bitter rivalries.

After introducing the Muslims, we turn to the reorganized eastern Roman Empire—or Byzantine Empire, as we will call it from now on. Then we discuss the fate of the Germanic kingdoms that were created in Rome's former western provinces and explain why the Frankish kingdom rose to the paramount position in the West.

Jeweled reliquary bust of Charlemagne, ca. 1350. Made to hold fragments of Charlemagne's skull.

The Islamic East

The Arabs, who inhabited much of the area from the Arabian peninsula to the Euphrates River, played a small role in the history of antiquity, and ancient writers took little notice of them. Shortly after 600, a prophet appeared among them preaching a faith old in its basic elements but new in its formulation. Converts to that new faith burst forth with unprecedented spiritual and military fervor, and they conquered territories from Spain to the frontiers of China. Slowly, those lands were gathered into an imperial system with a coherent ideology and government apparatus. Even more slowly, political and cultural elites began forging out of the ethnic, religious, and historical diversity of that vast realm a common culture that was grounded in the teachings of the prophet Muhammad (570–632).

Arabia Before Muhammad

The Arab world in the early seventh century was large and turbulent. The region had long been dominated by the Roman and Persian empires. Arab society itself knew no stable, large-scale political entities. People belonged to close-knit clans, or extended families, that in varying associations formed tribes, the key element in Arab society. In theory, tribes were groups of people tracing descent from a known ancestor. In reality—in this Arabs were like the Germans—tribes were complex associations of relatives, allies, and political or economic clients.

No less complex than its political situation was the region's ethnic and religious composition. The Roman world was overwhelmingly Christian, though there were many kinds of Christians. The Persian realm was officially Zoroastrian, but it had Jewish, Christian, Manichaean, and Buddhist minorities. The Arabs themselves were generally pagans, but Arabia had Jewish and Christian minorities.

The Arab East was also economically intricate and fragile. Bedouins, Arabs who were nomadic pastoralists, provided for their own needs from their herds of sheep and goats, from small-scale trading in towns, and from regular raids on one another and on caravans. There were some farmers, but in most areas soils were too poor and rain too infrequent to support agriculture. Cities supported traders who moved luxury goods, such as spices, incense, and perfumes, from the whole Indian Ocean region and southern Arabia up along caravan routes to the cities of the eastern Mediterranean. These traders formed the economic and political elite of Arabia, and they led the tribes. Mecca, dominated by the powerful tribe of the Quraysh, was the foremost city of Arabia, but competition among cities and tribes was fierce.

A solution to the competition among tribes and towns for control of trade routes was the institution of *harams,* or sanctuaries—places where contending parties could settle disputes peacefully. Usually the founding of a haram was attributed to a holy man whose prestige added to the sanctity of the spot. Mecca was one of the chief harams in Arabia, and its founding was attributed to the Israelite patriarch Abraham and one of his sons, Ishmael. The focus of the sanctuary was the black stone shrine known as the Kaaba. For centuries people from all over Arabia had made pilgrimages to Mecca, to the Kaaba, where a pagan deity was believed to dwell. Muhammad did not appear in a world of calm and stability, and his new religious vision promised even more disruption.

The Prophet and His Faith

Muhammad was born to a respectable but not wealthy or powerful clan of the Quraysh tribe. His father died before he was born, his mother shortly afterward. He was raised by his grandparents and by an uncle. Like many young Meccans he entered the caravan trade. At about age 20, Muhammad had such a reputation for competence and moral uprightness that he became financial adviser to a wealthy Quraysh widow, Khadija (555–619). Although older than Muhammad, she became his wife in 595, and they had a warm and loving marriage until her death.

From his youth Muhammad was a man of spiritual insight. He went into the desert or to caves near Mecca to fast and contemplate. In 610 he received the first of many revelations that commanded him to teach all people a new faith that called for an unquestioned belief in one god, Allah, and an uncompromised commitment to social justice for believers. Muhammad began teaching in Mecca, but he converted few people

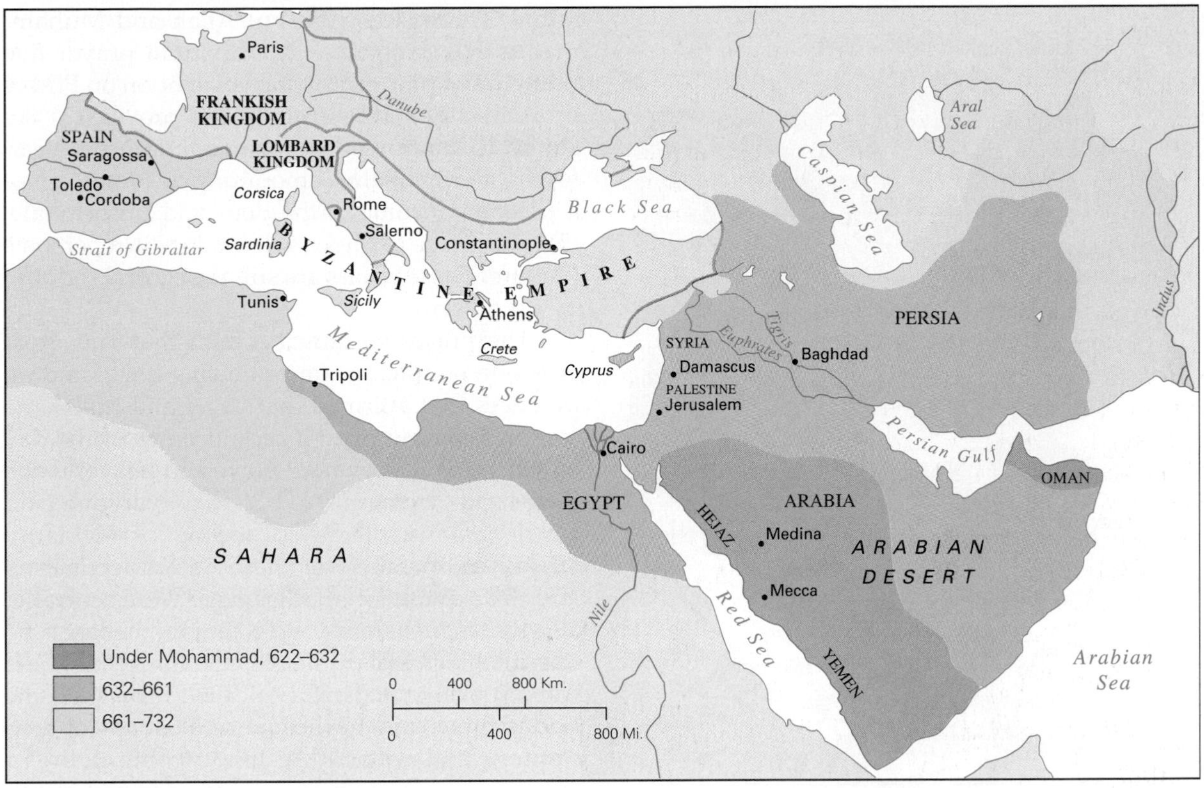

Map 8.1 The Expansion of Islam to 732 This map vividly illustrates the spectacular gains by Islam in the time of Muhammad, under the first caliphs, and under the Ummayyads. Later there were slow, steady gains in Africa, central Asia, and India.

outside his own circle—his wife was his first convert. Some Meccans were envious of Muhammad. Others feared that his new faith and new god might call into question the legitimacy of the shrines in Mecca and jeopardize the traditional pilgrimages to the Kaaba and the trade that accompanied them. By 619 Muhammad's well-connected wife and uncle were dead, and his position was precarious.

At this juncture citizens from Medina, a smaller trading community racked by dissension among pagan Arabs, Jews, and followers of Muhammad, asked Muhammad to establish a haram there. In the summer of 622 small groups of Muhammad's disciples made their way to Medina, and in September Muhammad joined them. His journey from Mecca to Medina, the *hegira,* marks the beginning of a new era, symbolized to this day in the Arab world by a calendar that dates "In the year of the Hegira."

Although Muhammad was fully in control in Medina, Mecca remained the focus of his attention. He had a sentimental attachment to Mecca, but its political and economic importance were critical to his emerging desire to convert all of Arabia. His followers began attacking Meccan caravans and battled with the Meccans several times in the 620s. In 630 Muhammad and many of his followers returned to Mecca in triumph. Muhammad left the Quraysh in control, and he retained the Kaaba as a focus of piety. After making local arrangements, he returned to Medina and set about winning over the Bedouins of the Arabian desert. When Muhammad died in 632, he had converted most of Arabia (Map 8.1).

To what, exactly, had Muhammad and his followers converted? At the most basic level, people were asked to surrender completely to Allah, the one, true God—that is, they were asked to make *al-Islam,* "the surrender." Those who sur-

The Prophet Muhammad This sixteenth-century Persian manuscript portrays Muhammad's night journey to Jerusalem, from where he ascended to heaven. His face is whited-out because Muslims took over the Jewish prohibition against pictorial representation. (*Archiv für kunst und Geschichte, Berlin*)

rendered became *Muslims* and joined the *umma muslima,* a completely new kind of community in which membership depended only on belief in Allah and acceptance of Muhammad as Allah's prophet. All members of the umma were understood to have personal and communal responsibility for all other members. No longer were one's duties confined to a particular clan, tribe, or town. Because of the experience of the hegira, Islam was a religion of exile, of total separation from the ordinary world, and of total dependence on God.

The basic teachings of Islam are traditionally described as "Five Pillars": (1) the profession of faith, "There is no God but Allah and Muhammad is His Prophet"; (2) individual prayer five times daily, plus group prayers at noon on Friday in a *mosque,* a Muslim house of prayer; (3) the sunup to sundown fast for one month per year; (4) the giving of alms amounting to 10 percent of a person's income to the poor and unfortunate; (5) pilgrimage to Mecca at least once in a person's lifetime. These pillars are still the central requirements of Islam.

The pillars sustained a faith that laid great stress on simple, uncompromising belief and on practices that affirmed that belief and built up a sense of community. At certain times of the day all Muslims everywhere bowed in prayer, with their heads facing toward Mecca. Everyone paid alms, creating thereby a feeling of solidarity among all members of the umma. Mecca itself and the experience of pilgrimage were central to all Muslims. There was no elaborate theology, no intricate doctrinal mysteries, and no creed. There was no clergy. Individuals called *imams* led the Friday prayers in the mosque and usually offered sermons that applied Muslim teaching to the issues of the day, but there was no ordained priesthood as in Judaism or Christianity and no hierarchy as in the Christian churches.

Muhammad himself communicated God's teaching to his followers, always insisting that he was transmitting a direct, verbal revelation and not offering his own interpretations. That revelation came in the form of "recitations" that make up the *Qur'an,* the scriptures of Islam. It is not known for certain if there was a definitive collection of "recitations" in Muhammad's lifetime, but not long after his death the Qur'an was put into the form that it has possessed ever since. It is organized into 114 *Suras,* or chapters. The Qur'an contains legal and wisdom literature like the Hebrew Scriptures and moral teaching like the Christian New Testament. (See the box, "The Message of the Qur'an.") The work as a whole, however, develops a unique religious vision.

Initially the Qur'an was interpreted rather freely within the umma, doubtless because there was no clergy to impose a uniform interpretation. After the prophet's death, some people felt the need for an authoritative teaching—as early Christians had felt the need for a canon of Christian scripture and teaching—and their efforts resulted in two important collections. One of these

The Message of the Qur'an

Here are several extracts from the Qur'an. The first is the opening to the text, which one might compare to the Christian Lord's Prayer. The second illustrates the position of Muhammad in the Islamic tradition. The third is a view of the sheer transcendence of Allah.

Sura 1: In the name of Allah, Most Gracious, Most Merciful./Praise be to Allah, the Cherisher and Sustainer of worlds;/ Most Gracious, Most Merciful./ Master of the Day of Judgment./Thee do we worship and thine aid we seek. Show us the straight way, the way of those on whom Thou hast bestowed Thy grace, Thou whose portion is not wrath, and who do not go astray.

Sura 2,136: Say ye: We believe in Allah, and the revelation given to us, and to Abraham, Isma'il, Isaac, Jacob and the tribes, and that given to Moses and to Jesus and that given to all prophets, but we make no difference between one and another of them, and we bow to Allah. *Sura 3,3:* It is He Who sent down to thee [Muhammad] step by step in truth confirming what went before; And he sent down Law and the Gospel before this as a guide to mankind.

Sura 4,171: O People of the Book! Commit no excesses in your religion, nor say of Allah anything but truth. Christ Jesus the son of Mary was an apostle of Allah . . . so believe in Allah and in his apostles. Say not "Trinity" . . . for Allah is one Allah. Glory be to Him for He is exalted above having a son. To him belong all things in the heavens and on earth.

Source: The Holy Qur-an, text, translation, and commentary by Abdullah Yusuf Ali (Lahore, Pakistan: Muhammad Ashrat, 1981), pp. 14–15, 55, 122, 233–234.

was the *sunna,* which means roughly the "good practice"—that is, the customs and habits of Muhammad himself. The second was the *hadith,* the "sayings" of the prophet, presumably the comments he made at different times about how God's revelation was to be understood and applied. The definitive compilations of the sunna and hadith date from the ninth century, and scholars are not sure what portion of them derives authentically from the age of the prophet. Qur'an, sunna, and hadith form the core of a dynamic spiritual message.

Allah's will for Muslims, as revealed in the Qur'an, touches all aspects of life. Lacking elaborate theology and creedal statements, Islam is a religion of practice and allegiance more than of belief. The Qur'an prescribes dietary regulations and personal conduct. Alcohol and gambling are forbidden. Luxury and ostentation are censured. Extreme sexual modesty is enjoined on men and women, and women are expected to remain shut away indoors or to shroud all but their eyes if they appear in public—a custom adopted by the Qur'an from traditional Arab society. The reward for an abstemious life is an eternity of sensual pleasure.

The Expansion of Islam

Muhammad's death brought a crisis. Who or what was to succeed him? In 632 the Meccan elite chose one of their number, Abu Bakr, as *caliph,* or "successor to the prophet." Abu Bakr was elderly, an early convert to Islam, and a former secretary to Muhammad. He and his three successors down to 661 (Umar, Uthman, and Ali) were

THE ISLAMIC WORLD

570–632	The Life of Muhammad
622	The Hegira
632	Election of Abu-Bakr as caliph
632–634	Islamic conquest of Arabia
634	Beginning of Islamic expansion outside Arabia
661	Umayyad Dynasty of Caliphs
750	Abbassid Dynasty of Caliphs

all Meccans, relatives of the prophet by marriage, and early converts. Islamic tradition calls them the "Rightly Guided Caliphs."

Abu Bakr's chief accomplishment was victory in the wars against those, especially Bedouins, who allegedly abandoned Islam. Probably they were only lukewarm Muslims whose commitment did not extend beyond their personal ties to Muhammad. Abu Bakr left his successor Umar a united Arabia (see Map 8.1). Umar began the lightning conquests by the Muslims of much of the Roman and Persian empires. He began the policy of granting choice positions in the expanding caliphate, the Muslim empire, to old converts and of ranking them according to precedence in conversion. As the old elite divided up the new provinces of the caliphate, some of them became *emirs* (governors), and others became lesser administrators. Muslim administrators then collected from all conquered people personal taxes and land taxes. Converts to Islam paid only land taxes. Arab settlers paid no taxes and received salaries from the taxes paid by others. Numerous Arabs profited handsomely from the Muslim conquests.

Umar was murdered by a slave in 644, leaving his successor, Uthman, a huge empire to administer. A great centralizer, Uthman chose emirs, regulated the finances of the provinces, and authorized the preparation of the definitive text of the Qur'an. In attempting to preserve the advantages of the old Meccan elite, Uthman alienated many people, particularly in Egypt, Syria, and Iraq, who had benefited from conquest and who were jealous of their new-found, local wealth and power. Uthman was murdered in 656 and replaced by Ali, whose main goal was to create a truly Islamic government by emphasizing the religious side of the caliph's office as the leader of the umma. Ali was in turn killed by a disillusioned former follower in 661. Years later some Muslims looked back to Ali as the true model for the caliph because he was the prophet's son-in-law, committed to the essential equality of all believers, and stern in his conception of Islam. These Muslims formed the *Shi'a,* the "Party of Ali."

When Ali was killed, the caliphate passed to Mu'awiya, a Meccan whose family had been highly favored since Uthman. He was the governor of Syria and commanded the finest army in the Muslim world. That army assured Mu'awiya's position. From 661 to 750 the Umayyads, as Mu'awiya's family is called, built many of the central institutions that characterized the caliphate until the tenth century.

Greater centralization was instituted. This involved the introduction of a unified coinage, the Arabization of the administration—granting all key positions to Arabs—and taking tight control of provincial governors and taxes. The Umayyads moved the capital of the caliphate to Damascus in their own power base of Syria, more centrally located than the old towns of Mecca and Medina and closer to the militarily active zones in eastern Iran and along the Byzantine frontier in Syria. The Umayyads also presided over the final territorial expansion of the caliphate (see Map 8.1). To the west, North Africa and Spain were taken, and raids were conducted deep into Gaul. In the east, after unsuccessful sieges against Constantinople, the frontier against the Byzantine Empire was moved into the mountains of southern Anatolia and, farther east, campaigns established nominal authority as far as Samarkand and Bukhara (now Kazakhstan, formerly the southern Soviet Union).

It is not easy to account for the astonishingly rapid creation of such a vast empire. Rome's empire expanded for 350 years, but the caliphate reached its zenith in scarcely 100. External factors were important. Byzantium and Persia had financially and militarily weakened themselves in a series of wars that ended just as the caliphate of Umar commenced. Moreover, those two states were exceedingly diverse, and the Muslim armies dismantled them piecemeal. Both old empires, but especially the Byzantine, had deep religious divisions. Coptic Egypt and Jacobite Syria, for example, willingly yielded to the Muslims, who demanded taxes and submission but otherwise left them alone. The Byzantines and Persians tended to depend on static frontier garrisons and large armies that could not be quickly mobilized and moved long distances. The Muslims rarely risked great pitched battles. They preferred a gradually expanding military frontier gained by numerous lightning strikes.

Internal factors were more significant, however. For centuries, raiding and plundering had been a way of life in Arabia, but because Islam forbade Muslims from raiding other Muslims, a new outlet for traditional violence was needed. The prophet himself had believed firmly in the need to expand the faith, and his successors shared that belief. Muslim ideology quickly divided the world into the "House of Islam" and the "House of War." In the House of Islam, the justice of Allah reigned supreme. In the House of War, *jihad,* holy war, was the rule. Christians and Jews, as fellow "Peoples of the Book"—sharers in a scriptural tradition reaching back to Abraham—were spared the choice of conversion or death, but "infidels" were expected to submit and convert. The simple, uncompromising teachings of Islam were attractive, but self-preservation and a desire to join in the material advantages of the new regime were also potent inducements. The Muslim conquests were carefully planned and directed to channel violence out of Arabia, to settle much of western Asia with loyal Muslims, and to permit members of the umma to enjoy vast rewards.

The Abbassid Revolution

The Umayyads were not especially popular, despite their military and administrative successes. Many resented their bureaucratic centralization. Such resentment was acute in areas heavily populated by recent converts who had always disliked the old Arabian elites, and in frontier provinces, where Arab immigrants along with local converts desired autonomy. The secular and opportunistic nature of Umayyad rule also offended pious Muslims. (See the box, "The Failure of the Umayyads.") The opposition came to a head in a series of rebellions that culminated in the naming of a rival caliph, Abu'l Abbas, in 749. In 750 he defeated his Umayyad rival.

The Abbassid period lasted until the thirteenth century. In its earliest phases, especially in the caliphate of Harun al-Raschid (r. 786–809), the Islamic world saw its first golden age. Harun's reign was marked by political stability, economic prosperity, and literary achievements. Abbassid successes are attributable to political acumen and ideological restructuring.

From the frontier, the Abbassids always understood the concerns of the caliphate's provincial populations. Thus, they erected a more international regime. Provincials, especially non-Arabs and recent converts, felt to Islam, to the prophet, and to the prophet's family a loyalty that they could not feel for the old Arabian potentates who had led and initially benefited from the Arab conquests. The Abbassid polity was based on the idea of the fundamental equality of all believers, the common bond of Islam.

Key government posts were given to Iranians and other non-Arabs. Some provincial posts went to members of the Abbassid family, persons who had a certain aura of political and spiritual legitimacy, rather than to Meccan or Syrian aristocrats. Local persons, however, always got some choice positions. The capital of the caliphate was moved to Iraq, but to avoid favoring any existing group or region, the Abbassids built a new city, Baghdad. By addressing regional and ethnic sensitivities in an effective way, they were able to maintain, even extend, the centralized state of the Umayyad period.

The caliphs did not rule the Muslim world by themselves. The daily business of governing was usually in the hands of the *wazir,* who headed the administration, advised the caliph, and often exercised a powerful formative influence on the caliph's children and heirs. The first caliphs chose administrators from loyal Arabs and from experienced Christian subjects. Under the Umayyads the regime was Arabized. Then under Harun al-Raschid the government became international, professional, and hereditary. The chief agency of government was the treasury, which had separate branches dealing with the Muslim alms, with the land and poll taxes paid by subjects, and with the land taxes paid by converts. So sophisticated was this financial machinery that alone among early medieval governments the caliphate could draw up annual budgets. There was also an influential group of palace servants. They did not

The Failure of the Umayyads

This passage from an Arabic chronicle reveals some of the dissatisfaction that the Umayyads aroused.

One day a group of people gathered in the presence of al-Mansur [Abbassid caliph, 754–775], and they spoke of the Umayyad Caliphs, their way of life, their conduct of affairs, and the cause which led to their loss of power. Al-Mansur said, "Abd al-Malik was a tyrant who took no thought for what he did. Sulayman cared only for his belly and his private parts. Umar was a one-eyed man among the blind. The best was Hisham." The Umayyads kept a firm grip on the authority that had been prepared for them, containing it, defending it, and preserving what God had given them, while keeping to the highest and rejecting the lowest of things. This continued until their authority passed to their pampered sons, whose only care was the pursuit of passion and the quest for pleasure in those things which are forbidden by Almighty God. . . . So they discarded the preservation of the Caliphate, made light of Almighty God and the duties of sovereignty, and became too feeble to govern. Then God deprived them of power, covered them with shame, and withdrew His grace from them.

Source: Al-Mas'udi, *Muruj al-Dhahab,* in Bernard Lewis, ed., *Islam from the Prophet Muhammad to the Conquest of Constantinople,* vol. 1 (New York: Harper & Row, 1974), p. 25.

hold important public positions, but their informal influence on the caliph and his family was great. The army was another prominent body within the state.

The central government was linked to the provinces in several ways. In addition to controlling the army and provincial governorships, the caliph employed a network of regular envoys and spies. The court, especially under the Abbassids, drew able young men from all over into the service of the caliph and created hopes among provincial elites that they too might be chosen. In every district and city there were judges, *qadi,* to oversee the application of Islamic law. Qadi were under the authority of the caliph.

The death of Harun in 809 sparked a century of problems. Intense family rivalries touched both the succession to the caliphate and the possession of key provincial positions. The bureaucracy emerged as an influential pressure group, and the palace servants began to foment intrigues. The army became more and more a professional body comprising non-Arabs, especially Turks, hired from the frontiers and beyond because Arabs, enjoying their salaries, declined to serve. The army, the bureaucracy, and the courtiers all had different and conflicting interests and did not hesitate to press their own advantages. Religious divisions persisted, even intensified. Many felt the Abbassids had not gone far enough in erecting a truly Islamic regime. Whole regions took advantage of Abbassid leniency in granting local autonomy and began to fall away. Spain had actually been lost at the time of the Abbassid takeover in 750, when an Umayyad, Abd al-Rahman, erected an independent emirate at Cordoba. North Africa fell away in the mid-ninth century, and by the middle of the tenth century Abbassid power in southern Iraq, Syria, Egypt, and Arabia was negligible. Abbassid caliphs reigned until 1258, but after the early tenth century they had little effective power.

Ironies in the "fall" of the caliphate parallel some of the ironies in the "fall" of Rome. The Arabs spread a culture, a language, and a religion from the Atlantic Ocean to the frontiers of China.

Dome of the Rock This magnificent mosque in Jerusalem (built in 691–692) is the second holiest shrine of Islam—after the ka'aba in Mecca. Muslims believe that Muhammad ascended to heaven from this spot. (*Michael Holford*)

Eventually, however, the Arab regime that accomplished that task became unnecessary to its continuance. In a way, the Arabs were the victims of their own success. They conquered and exploited a world of non-Arabs for the benefit of those who believed in Allah and his prophet, but they gradually converted that world to Islam. As others converted, they could not so easily be exploited or denied opportunities. So the caliphate, like the Roman Empire, gave way to a series of successor states whose parentage is always identifiable.

The Emergence of Islamic Culture

Two currents are apparent in the culture of the Islamic East. One is the religious thought associated with the Qur'an; the other is the assimilation of the Greek heritage. Both were influenced by the eastward spread of Islam that mixed Iranian, Turkish, and even Hindu elements into a culture already rich with Arab, Christian, and Jewish ingredients.

Muslim communities came together for prayer in mosques, the often beautiful buildings usually modeled on the original mosque in Medina. The worshipers arrayed themselves in parallel rows and were led in prayer by an imam. In time the imams started offering interpretations of the Qur'an, and collections of these interpretations began to circulate. Similarly, Muslim judges began to issue opinions on how the Qur'an, sunna, and hadith might be applied to the daily lives of believers. Thus, there grew a body of religious thought.

In 832 an Abbassid caliph endowed the "House of Wisdom," a sort of scholars' academy in Baghdad, and from this point on Muslim scholars had the leisure and wherewithal to begin tackling the corpus of Greek thought, especially the scientific writers. Muslims were proud of their own culture but aware that they had conquered a world with a massive intellectual heritage. The earliest Arab scholars sought mainly to master the learning of the past. They tended to be encyclopedic—that is, to collect and to assimilate huge amounts of information. Works were collected and translated, manuscripts were copied, and libraries were built.

The Byzantine Empire

The century after Justinian's death in 565 was difficult for the eastern Roman Empire. Attacks by Persians, Bulgars, and Muslims, riots and rebellions, and plagues and famines left the empire in a perilous position. In 610 a process of reform and recovery began that had the long-term effect of transforming the eastern Roman regime into one that we call "Byzantine," from Byzantium, the ancient Greek name for the capital city, Constantinople. Before those reforms took hold, however, the eastern Roman state had to fight for its survival.

From the Eastern Roman Empire to the Byzantine Empire

In 610 Heraclius, a gifted, experienced ruler, ascended the throne. He ruled until 641 and set the basic pattern for the rest of the seventh century. That pattern emphasized the eastern, Greek nature of the empire, abandoned military entanglements in the west in favor of security in the east, and initiated institutional reforms designed to take account of new cultural, political, and diplomatic realities.

Heraclius and his successors faced military challenges on two fronts. In the East, Byzantium was the victim of a cruel irony. Between 612 and 619, the Persians conquered Syria, Palestine, Mesopotamia, and Egypt. Heraclius reorganized his military and finances and between 622 and 629 fought a series of campaigns that recovered almost everything. When the unexpected Muslim challenge appeared in 634, Byzantium was exhausted and had no effective response. In the Balkans, the Byzantines enjoyed some successes against Slavs, who had been pushing south for years, and against Avars and Bulgars (peoples related to the Huns), who had settled in the northwestern and northeastern Balkans, respectively. In the West, Spain and North Africa were abandoned to Muslims. In Italy and Sicily, effective imperial authority was minimal, confined to some outposts around Ravenna, Rome, Naples, and Sicily. The west was distant, divided, and distracting. It was clear that the east and the Balkans were critical. The change from the days of Justinian could not be more apparent.

Several cultural indicators point to the emergence of a regime that laid increasing stress on its Greek and Christian roots. For example, the emperors called themselves "Emperor of the Romans," but they did so in Greek. As Justinian had looked to his Latin and Roman roots, so Heraclius and his successors were unashamedly Greek and eastern in their outlook. The emperor saw himself as God's specially chosen and protected agent with full authority over the church and over the religious life of all Christian people. To emphasize the religious foundations of their imperial office, the emperors began putting images of Christ on their coins. In one of his official titles the emperor was "The Thirteenth Apostle." As in the past, the emperors continued trying to solve the age-old Christological and Trinitarian problems.

The emperor's authority and prestige were great within his shrinking empire but negligible in most of Rome's former territories. Heraclius sought religious unity, but his efforts met opposition. For instance, the popes objected to Heraclius's policies, as did most Coptic and Jacobite Christians, who, as noted, offered little resistance to Muslim conquerors who did not interfere with their beliefs. Emperors called church councils that were largely ignored beyond the empire. The differences between Orthodox and other Christians were ever more visible.

The Eighth-Century Recovery

In 717 Leo III became emperor in a moment of acute crisis. Muslim armies had seized most of Anatolia and had laid siege to Constantinople itself. The city would surely have fallen had it not been for the "Greek fire" that made it impossible for the Muslim navy to operate beneath the seaward walls. Leo ruled until 741 and was followed until 775 by his able son, Constantine V. Together they extended the seventh-century focus on the eastern frontiers and on the Greek and Orthodox empire. Although official ideology in the eighth century claimed that the Roman Empire of Augustus was still in existence, under Leo and Constantine a new regime, the Byzantine, was consolidated.

After a century of military reverses, Leo III and Constantine V were often victorious (Map 8.2). They defended Constantinople, recovered Anatolian territory from the Muslims, and checked the advance of the Bulgars. They also completed military reforms that amounted to a major administrative reorganization of the empire. The Romans had always recruited, paid, and equipped soldiers out of tax revenues. In this way Rome procured standing armies along with frontier auxiliaries. Under Leo and Constantine a new system replaced the old order.

Men from frontier regions were recruited and then settled on farms in military districts called *themes.* Each theme, both sea-based naval ones and land-based army ones, stood under a commander who was simultaneously the civil and military chief of his theme. The farmer-soldiers did not pay tax on their lands but discharged their obligations to the state by personal service. Some standing troops were retained, but several thematic armies now constituted the backbone of the Byzantine military.

The system made sense for several reasons. It was less of a drain on the state treasury than the old one. Lower taxes could be levied and a smaller bureaucracy employed to secure revenues. The Byzantine Empire had to defend less territory than Rome had once defended, so armies could be mobilized and deployed locally, rather than moved long distances. The joining of civilian and military rule in a single hierarchy de-

THE BYZANTINE EMPIRE

610–641	Reign of Heraclius
622–629	Successful wars against Persians
634–640	Territorial losses to Muslims
678, 711, 717	Arab sieges of Constantinople
717–741	Reign of Leo III
726–787	Iconoclastic controversy
797–802	Reign of Irene
843	Final restoration of icons

Greek Fire Invented in the seventh century by Callimachus, a Syrian engineer, Greek fire was a mixture formed from petroleum, sulphur, saltpeter, and lime that ignited on contact with water. It was first used to repel the Muslim siege of Constantinople in 678. (*MAS, Barcelona*)

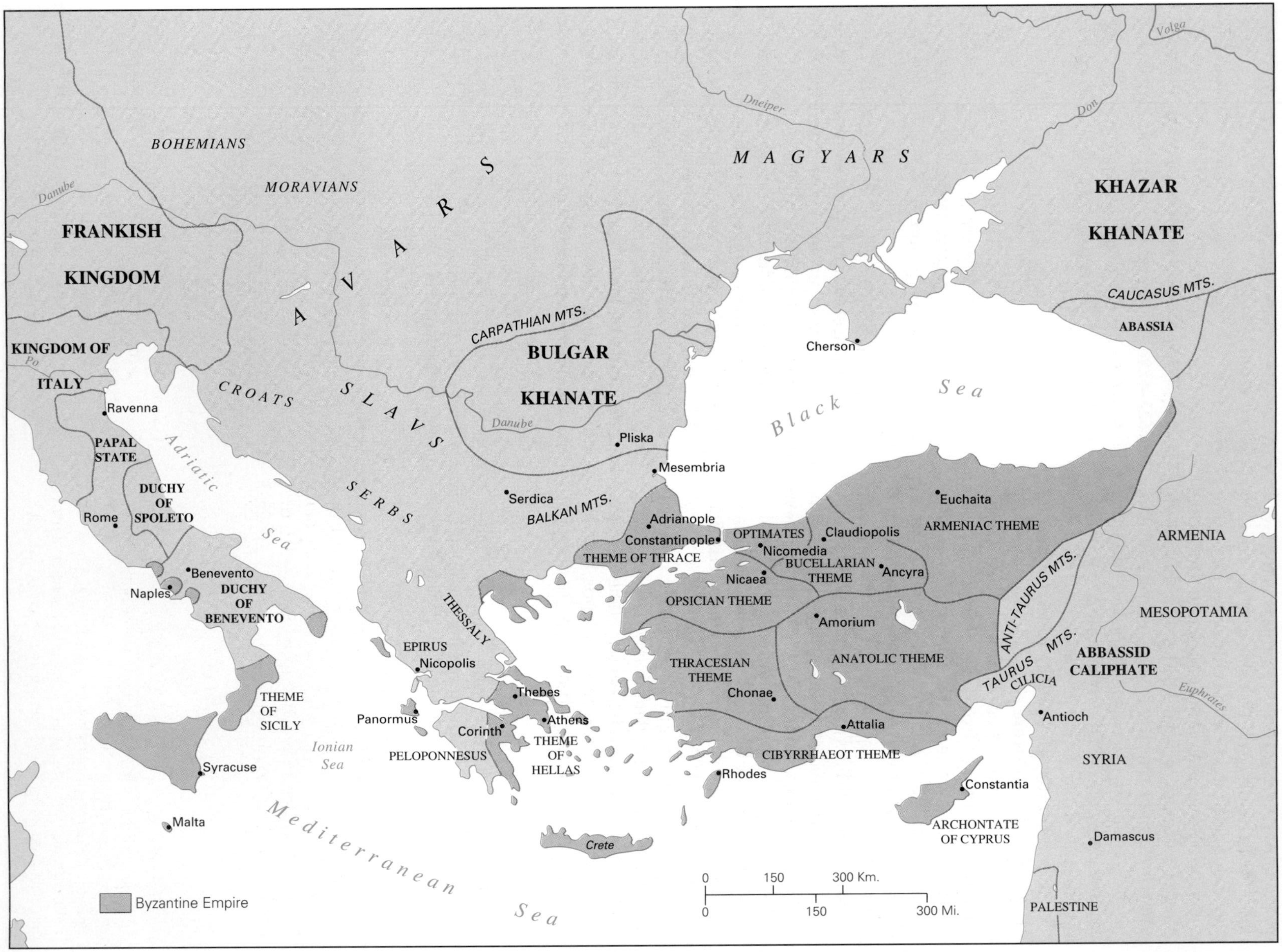
BOHEMIANS
MORAVIANS
A V A R S
M A G Y A R S
KHAZAR KHANATE
FRANKISH KINGDOM
KINGDOM OF ITALY
Po
Danube
Dneiper
Don
Volga
CAUCASUS MTS.
ABASSIA
CARPATHIAN MTS.
BULGAR KHANATE
Danube
Cherson
Black Sea
CROATS
SLAVS
SERBS
Ravenna
PAPAL STATE
DUCHY OF SPOLETO
Rome
Adriatic Sea
Pliska
Mesembria
Serdica
BALKAN MTS.
Euchaita
Adrianople
Constantinople
THEME OF THRACE
OPTIMATES
Claudiopolis
Nicomedia
BUCELLARIAN THEME
Ancyra
ARMENIAC THEME
ARMENIA
Nicaea
OPSICIAN THEME
Amorium
ANTI-TAURUS MTS.
MESOPOTAMIA
Benevento
Naples
DUCHY OF BENEVENTO
THESSALY
EPIRUS
Nicopolis
THRACESIAN THEME
Chonae
ANATOLIC THEME
TAURUS MTS.
CILICIA
ABBASSID CALIPHATE
Euphrates
THEME OF SICILY
Panormus
Thebes
Athens
Corinth
THEME OF HELLAS
PELOPONNESUS
Ionian Sea
Attalia
CIBYRRHAEOT THEME
Antioch
SYRIA
Syracuse
Rhodes
Constantia
ARCHONTATE OF CYPRUS
Malta
Crete
Mediterranean Sea
Damascus
0 150 300 Km.
0 150 300 Mi.
PALESTINE
Byzantine Empire

pendent on the emperor made sense in a state that was continually threatened on all sides.

Leo and Constantine did more than just reform military structures. In 726 Leo issued the *Ecloga,* the first major revision of Roman law since Justinian's. Issuing a law code was a matter of dynastic pride and self-assertion. But where Justinian's *Code* was beyond the capacity of all but the most sophisticated lawyers in Constantinople, the *Ecloga* was "a selection of laws," "an abridgment" whose purpose was to provide a simplified, unified body of law for provincial judges in the Byzantine Empire.

Leo and Constantine initiated far-reaching reforms in an imperial administration little changed since Late Antiquity. Roman administration had consisted of a few very large departments headed by officials who had immense responsibilities and power. The new Byzantine system was characterized by a profusion of departments under officers who had more prestige than actual power and who were more heavily dependent on the emperor. The bureaucracy usually was not a breeding ground for factional squabbles, as in the caliphate. The emperors neutralized the bureaucrats by drawing them by merit from all social classes, paying them well, giving them fancy titles and public recognition, but dividing their responsibilities and curtailing their actual power.

The rulers also promoted religious and cultural unity. The so-called iconoclastic controversy serves as an example of Leo's and Constantine's policies. It was a dispute over icons, paintings of Christ, Mary, and saints. Iconoclasts are those who wish to destroy such images. For a while the emperors themselves were the chief iconoclasts.

Icons began to play a prominent role in Orthodox devotions in the fifth century. Some said that icons served to bring to mind the person depicted and thus helped individuals in their spiritual life. Others felt that icons had theological significance by, for example, affirming the humanity of Christ: If Christ was truly human, then he could be depicted like any other human. By contrast the Jewish and Muslim traditions considered any attempt to depict God as idolatry. Some influential Christian voices also said that any icon was really an idol.

In 726 Leo removed an icon of Christ from the gate of one of the imperial palaces, and for several years he and like-minded clergy agitated against icons. In 731 an imperial decree banned images of Christ or the saints, and thus the iconoclastic controversy arose. Why did an emperor faced with so many threats devote so much energy to this issue?

In the preface to the *Ecloga* Leo portrays himself as an Old Testament king who had a duty to lead his people in the path of righteousness. He seems to have believed quite sincerely that icons were idols and that they provoked God so strongly that God had permitted Byzantium's enemies to prosper. Constantine V, who was much better educated than his father, was opposed to icons for theological reasons. To him, icons laid excessive emphasis on the humanity of Christ—Christological quarrels had not disappeared.

Personal convictions played a role, but public issues were important too. Many famous icons were housed in monasteries. Many monasteries were the object of generous gifts by pious laymen, and many extremely talented people embraced the monastic life rather than serving the state. The emperors had for a long time exercised control over the patriarchs, but they had never really gotten control of the monastic clergy. Attacking icons was in some ways an attempt to make complete the emperor's control of the church.

Iconoclasm had limited success. Many ordinary people cherished icons and ignored imperial policy. The emperors occasionally made an example of prominent iconophiles by exiling or executing them, but most people were left alone. Monks were popular, in some areas as popular as the emperor himself. Attacks on monasteries sometimes backfired. Christians in Egypt or Syria, to the extent they knew about iconoclastic policies, regarded the emperor as a heretic. In Rome, a succession of popes rejected iconoclasm itself and, like their predecessors, wrote to the

Map 8.2 The Byzantine Empire in the Eighth and Ninth Centuries After suffering tremendous territorial losses to barbarians and Muslims, the Byzantine Empire transformed its military, institutional, and cultural structures to create a regime that survived until it was conquered by crusaders in 1204.

Icon of the Virgin Located in a monastery in Sinai, this sixth-century icon was beyond the reach of the iconoclasts. An aloof Mary and Jesus do not meet our gaze. Two soldier saints look right at us and ward us off. Two angels look at the hand of God. *(Reproduced by permission of the Alexandria-Michigan-Princeton Expedition to Mount Sinai)*

emperor to tell him that he had no business interfering in church doctrines. Under papal leadership, Christians in those parts of Italy that still recognized a loose imperial overlordship began to rebel against the emperor's agents. Unity based on religion was an old but elusive ideal for the emperors, as it was for the caliphs.

Ninth-Century Problems

The dynasty of Leo III might have continued indefinitely but for a rapid accumulation of misfortunes in the last decades of the eighth century. Constantine V's promising son Leo IV died suddenly in 780, leaving a 6-year-old son, Constantine VI, and a remarkable widow, Irene (753–803). Shortly after assuming the regency for her son, Irene began planning the restoration of icons. This was a matter of personal conviction with her, but it also owed a lot to an awareness that the controversy over icons had not brought religious or political unity to the empire but had isolated the Byzantine church from all other Christian communities and the Byzantine Empire from all potential allies against Muslims and Bulgars. In 787 Irene convened a church council at Nicaea that pronounced against the iconoclastic decrees.

What Irene could not do was control her frivolous son, who refused to attend to the business of state and trysted with girls who served in his mother's chamber. Exasperated, she blinded him in the very room in which he had been born. Because any physical deformity rendered a person unfit for rule, Irene intended merely to disqualify her son and then to succeed in her own right. Instead, he died from his wounds, and she incurred the name of murderess. From 797 to 802 Irene ruled the empire, but her authority was never really accepted. Many people were horrified at her treatment of her son; others were simply unprepared to accept a woman as ruler. (See the box, "Muslim and Byzantine Insults: A Lack of 'Diplomacy'?") Finally, however, she was the victim of a coup d'état because she could not retain the loyalty of the army or the bureaucracy. The irony in all this is that Irene was able, intelligent, resourceful, and, in truth, the real heir to Leo III.

From the deposition of Irene in 802 until the accession of the brilliant Basil I in 867, the history of the Byzantine Empire is a study in contradictions. There were assassinations and usurpations but also effective rulers. Military successes were recorded but also defeats. The state was always short of cash, and its attempts to raise money angered many people. Religious policy shifted several times too. For example, icons were again outlawed from 815 to 842, with no more effect than in the first period of iconoclasm.

The cultural life of early Byzantium is also riddled with contradictions and ironies. Initially the iconoclastic era was damaging. For obvious reasons, artists could find no patrons, and much of the physical inheritance of the past was destroyed. Architecture fared no better than art. There was too little money or security to finance the building of palaces and churches. The last of

Muslim and Byzantine Insults: A Lack of "Diplomacy"?

This excerpt from an Arabic chronicle reveals something of the attitudes of Muslims and Byzantines toward each other, and of their frontier relations. Notice the mistakes and misunderstandings.

A woman [Irene] came to rule over the Romans because at the time she was the only one of their royal house who remained. She wrote to the Caliphs with respect and deference and showered them with gifts. When her son [Constantine VI] grew up and came to the throne in her place, he brought trouble and disorder and provoked [Harun] al-Raschid. The empress, who knew al-Raschid and feared his power, was afraid lest the kingdom of the Romans pass away and their country be ruined. She therefore overcame her son by cunning and put out his eyes so that the kingdom was taken from him and returned to her. But the people disapproved of this and hated her for it. Therefore Nicephorus [emperor, 802–811] rose against her. . . . He wrote to al-Raschid, "From Nicephorus, the king of Romans, to al-Raschid, the king of Arabs" as follows: "That woman put you in the place of kings and put herself in the place of a commoner. I put you in a different place and am preparing to invade your lands and attack your cities unless you repay me what that woman paid you. Farewell." Al-Raschid replied, "In the name of God, the Merciful the Compassionate, from the servant of God, Harun, Commander of the Faithful, to Nicephorus, dog of the Romans" as follows: "I have understood your letter, and I have your answer. You will see it with your eye, not hear it." Then he sent an army against the land of the Romans.

Source: Abu'l-Faraj al-Isfahani, *Al-Aghani,* in Bernard Lewis, ed., *Islam from the Prophet Muhammad to the Conquest of Constantinople,* vol. 1 (New York: Harper & Row, 1974), pp. 27–28.

the Greek Church Fathers, John of Damascus (ca. 650–ca. 750), ended his career with passionate defenses of icons, but the early iconoclasts produced no distinguished theologians. In the ninth century, the renewal of iconoclasm sharpened the quality of intellectual discussion on both sides of the issue.

When peace and stability prevailed, Byzantine emperors, like Abbassid caliphs, patronized scholars. Byzantine scholars were trying to recapture the same Greek heritage that Muslim scholars were trying to assimilate. Theophilus (r. 829–842) endowed a school in the palace that lasted for centuries as a center of learning. Ironically, its first great teacher was a former patriarch who had been deposed for iconoclasm. The Byzantine church, which had no counterpart in the Muslim world, also promoted learning. The nicknames of some patriarchs—for instance, John the Grammarian and Leo the Mathematician—point to their interests beyond the purely ecclesiastical.

Christian Kingdoms in the West

Several Germanic kingdoms replaced the western provinces of the Roman Empire. Some did not survive the middle of the sixth century, but others, such as the Visigothic, Frankish, and Anglo-Saxon, appeared to have bright prospects. In the West, the seventh century was full of challenges, the eighth century was marked by innovation and accomplishment, and the ninth century was characterized by new challenges and in some areas near collapse. The chronological parallels with the Islamic and Byzantine worlds are striking.

There are other parallels too. The social and political heritages of both the German and the Roman past interacted with Christianity and the Catholic church to produce Christian Europe. Crucial to these developments were the evangelization of the countryside, the spread of an ecclesiastical hierarchy, the shift of papal interests away from the Mediterranean world toward western Europe, and the evolving relationship between royal governments and the Catholic church.

The period between the "fall" of Rome and the appearance of the Carolingian Empire in the late eighth century has been called the "Dark Ages." The term suggests that historians know little about the period or that it was a time of ignorance and superstition. In reality, as much is known about the "Dark Ages" as about the preceding period. The "Dark Ages" was a time of creativity. Regional cultures of real vitality emerged; and the Latin Christian culture on which the intellectual life of Europe was based for centuries took shape.

The Struggles of Christian Spain

After Clovis's victory over the Visigoths in 507, the Visigoths were never able to re-establish dynastic continuity. The result was possibilities for rebellions and usurpations that were more frequent than anywhere else in the West. In addition to internal struggles, Spain faced external threats from the Franks, the Ostrogoths in Italy, and the Byzantines.

The accomplishments of the Visigothic king Leovigild (r. 568–586) seem almost miraculous, given the state of Spain on his accession. He nearly unified the country, and he established a capital (Toledo) and a seat of government—which the Visigoths had been lacking since they lost Toulouse in 507. Leovigild was a good general and a charismatic leader who understood the value of enhancing the royal office. He wore royal vestments, sat on a throne, and issued coins with his own image and name. Leovigild's greatest problem was the Arianism of the Visigothic minority in the midst of the Catholic Hispano-Roman population. An Arian himself, he tried hard to convert Catholics to Arianism but failed. In 589, under King Reccared (r. 586–601), the Visigoths officially embraced Roman Catholicism.

The conversion of the Visigoths permitted close cooperation between the church and the monarchy and placed the human and material resources of the church at the disposal of the crown as it attempted to unite and govern the country. The career of Archbishop Isidore of Seville (560–636) is a prime indicator of those resources. He came from an old Hispano-Roman family, received a fine education, and wrote histories, biblical commentaries, and a learned encyclopedia.

By the mid-seventh century economic prosperity, a high degree of assimilation between Goths and Hispano-Romans, and a brilliant culture marked the high point of Visigothic Spain. The succession problem, however, was never overcome, and a stable central government was beyond reach.

In 710 Muslims from North Africa invaded Spain. Within five years Berbers, native North Africans and recent converts to Islam who were led by Arabs, completed the conquest of much of the Iberian Peninsula, except for the northwest. In 716 the caliph at Damascus introduced an emir who ruled from Cordoba. The emirate of Cordoba struggled to make good its authority over all of Spain but failed to do so. Christians in the rugged mountains of the northwest could not be dislodged, and the Muslims' part of Spain was plagued by the same divisions as the Islamic East: Arab factions against other Arab factions, Arabs against non-Arab Muslims, and Muslims against non-Muslims. The emirate persisted until Ferdinand and Isabella conquered its remnants in the fifteenth century.

Secure in the mountains of northwestern Spain—the region called Asturias (see Map 8.3)—Christian kings built a capital at Oviedo and, in the ninth century, launched attacks against al-Andalus, the Muslim part of Spain. For six hundred years this conflict between Christians and Muslims was the chief dynamic of Spanish history.

Italy and the Papal State

In 600 the Italian political scene was crowded. Several Germanic groups, four Byzantine outposts, and the popes were all contending for power. By the late eighth century, the Franks dominated northern Italy, the popes had created a state in the center, and the Byzantines clung to

Naples and Sicily. That basic pattern then persisted for three hundred years.

After defeating the Ostrogoths, the Romans were in principle masters of Italy, but their attempts to restore order were thwarted by the Lombards, who invaded in 568. These people had long lived in the Pannonian plain, and some of them had served in the Roman armies that defeated the Goths. The Lombard invasion caused the Byzantines to introduce a largely military regime under officers called *exarchs.* Stationed at Ravenna, exarchs appointed civilian and military officers.

The exarchate of Ravenna was weakened by the unwillingness of its population to pay heavy taxes to Constantinople when the receipts were spent in the Balkans and the East instead of against the Lombards. Moreover, Catholic Italy rejected Byzantine Christology and iconoclasm. Gradually the popes organized the defense of central Italy against the Lombards, stood up for the oppressed locals against Byzantine tax collectors, and led the opposition to unpopular theologies. In 751 the Lombard king conquered Ravenna. Muslims conquered Sicily in the ninth century, and Byzantine possessions in Italy were confined to the region around Naples.

Neither numerous nor united, the Lombards were also Arians. The Lombard kings had not systematically organized the conquest of Italy. From their capital at Pavia, the kings dominated the Po Valley, but other Lombards settled elsewhere and created independent duchies in Spoleto and Benevento. Although the Lombard kings converted to Catholicism by 680, formed a strong government, and issued the most sophisticated Germanic law code, they always faced a dilemma. They were weakened because they did not control the people and resources of Spoleto and Benevento. To control those duchies, however, they had to march through either the exarchate or the Roman territory that was increasingly under the authority of the popes.

The strongest Lombard king of the eighth century, Aistulf (r. 749–757), decided to risk the consequences of attacking Ravenna and Rome. He conquered the former but caused the pope to turn to Pepin III, the king of the Franks, for aid and protection. Pepin came to Italy in 755 and 756, defeated Aistulf, and forced him to give to the pope all the lands he had taken from Rome and from Ravenna. A few years later Aistulf's successor reopened hostilities in central Italy. Answering a new papal appeal, in 774 Charlemagne, Pepin's son and successor, defeated the Lombards, deposed their king, and took the Lombard crown for himself.

Crown of King Recceswinth This crown hung over the throne of the Visigothic king Recceswinth (r. 649–672). It symbolized kingship, the power to govern, and marks a stage in the depersonalization of royal rule. (*Museo Archeologico, Madrid*)

The Franks guaranteed to the popes undisputed possession of a substantial territory in central Italy. This first papal state was the culmination of three processes. First, as Roman imperial power declined in Late Antiquity, bishops often became the effective leaders of their towns. This position brought them power and prestige but also burdens. The popes found themselves responsible for Rome's food and water supply, the upkeep of its public buildings, and local charitable services. To pay for these functions, the popes began to organize the efficient bureaucratic administration of the patrimonies, the lands of the Roman church. Long before the 750s, the popes had been the landlords and patrons of many people in Italy, providing essential services formerly handled by the Roman state.

Second, the popes took the lead in protecting many people in central Italy, whether they lived on papal estates or not, from Byzantine taxes and heresy. This effort too forged bonds between the popes and the Italians. Third, eighth-century Rome spawned a justification for papal temporal rule. According to the *Donation of Constantine,* a document written in Rome (probably in the 760s), when Constantine departed Rome for the East, he gave to the pope the authority to rule Rome and the whole West. In reality, no pope ever made such grandiose claims, and no concrete claims were ever based on the *Donation.* But the existence of the document, which was finally exposed as a forgery in the fifteenth century (see page 519), signals a crucial progression from notions of landlordship and protection to direct rule. Thus, while kingdoms and exarchates were collapsing, a papal state was created that survives to this day as Vatican City.

The medieval popes who were simultaneously head of a church and of a state were the heirs of Pope Gregory I (r. 590–604). He came from a senatorial family and held important secular offices before deciding to sell off all his properties and become a monk. His reputation for piety and integrity was so great, however, that the people and clergy of Rome elected him pope. Although Gregory would have preferred a life of monastic retreat, he threw himself into his new responsibilities. He negotiated with emperors and kings, disciplined churches and clerics in the whole West, and began creating and refining the bureaucratic apparatus by means of which popes for centuries would manage their city and patrimonies and later the papal state. Gregory was also a theologian of genius, the last of the Latin Church Fathers. He wrote biblical commentaries, guides for moral living, and a book, *The Pastoral Rule,* which circulated for a thousand years as a guide to how bishops should discharge their duties. Gregory was the founder of the medieval papacy.

The Fate of Far-Off Britain

Britain was less thoroughly Romanized, more quickly abandoned by the Romans, and more deeply influenced by Germanic peoples than any other locality in the west. Around 600 the small Anglo-Saxon kingdoms created in the sixth century took the first steps toward converting to Christianity, transforming Britain into England, and joining England inseparably to the European world (see Map 8.3).

The most successful kingdoms were Wessex, Northumbria, and Mercia. Each had a reasonably large population and territory and opportunities for expansion. Wessex, for example, spread south and west into Devon, Cornwall, and Wales; Northumbria, which began on the North Sea coast, spread west to the Irish Sea and north into lowland Scotland. These kingdoms had ambitious rulers whose wars provided booty, land, and glory for old followers and new recruits.

Foreign connections played a role too. Kent and East Anglia had diplomatic connections with the Franks, and Aethelbert (561–616), the greatest Kentish king, married Bertha, the daughter of a Frankish king. East Anglia's far-flung connections are revealed by a ship burial unearthed near Sutton Hoo in 1939. The ship, either a grave for or a memorial to a king, had been hauled up onto the land, filled with foreign treasures, and buried.

English kings quickly adopted symbolic aspects of rule to legitimize their authority and enhance their prestige. A fine scepter was found at Sutton Hoo, and Northumbrian kings were preceded by banners and a royal standard. Most kings issued coins in their own name. The kings of Northumbria presided in a magnificent wooden hall at Yeavering.

Relations with the church were important also. Two issues proved crucial: the conversion of Britain to Christianity and the development of an ecclesiastical hierarchy. Only a few native Christians survived the invasion of the pagan Anglo-Saxons, and there is no evidence that they ever tried to convert the newcomers. That occurred in two waves, from Rome and from Ireland.

In 597 Pope Gregory I sent a small band of missionaries under a Roman monk named Augustine (d. 604) to King Aethelbert of Kent, whose Christian wife Bertha had prepared the ground for the newcomers. Augustine established his base of operations at Canterbury (literally, "the fortress of the Kent men"). Augustine and his successors had limited success spreading Christianity in southern England, but a new field of influence was opened to them when Ethelberga, Aethelbert's daughter, married King Edwin of Northumbria and took missionaries to her new home. Edwin converted to Christianity, but a pagan reaction followed his death.

In 563 Columba (521–597), a noble Irishman expelled from his country in a political dispute, founded a monastery on Iona, an island off the coast of Scotland. For two generations, monks from Iona spread Christianity in central and lowland Scotland. When later Northumbrian kings turned to Iona for missionaries and bishops, Roman and Celtic Christianity came face to face in Northumbria.

The Christianity brought from Ireland did not differ in fundamental ways from the Roman Christianity imported at Canterbury. Indeed, the Irish were Roman Catholics. But Ireland had been isolated from the intellectual currents of Christianity since Late Antiquity, and its church had developed a number of distinctive local customs. For example, the two traditions used different calendars and thus celebrated Easter on different days. In 664 the Northumbrian king Oswy called a synod at the monastery of Whitby, whose abbess was the former royal princess Hilda (614–680), a champion of Celtic customs (see the box, "Hilda of Whitby," on page 304). At Whitby Roman and Irish representatives debated their positions. Oswy, choosing the universal over the particular, decided for Rome.

In 668 the pope sent to England a new archbishop of Canterbury, Theodore (r. 668–690). He was a Syrian monk who had traveled widely in the East, lived for a time in Rome, gained great experience in church administration, and acquired a reputation for both learning and kindness. He came from Rome but was in many ways an outsider; neither the "Romans" nor the "Irish" in England could easily view him as a partisan. Lacking firm traditions, the church in England was in an administrative shambles. Working tirelessly, Theodore reconciled the conflicting parties, built up a typical Roman ecclesiastical structure, introduced authoritative Roman canon law for the church, and promoted Christian education. Theodore laid the foundations for a unified English church that contributed to the eventual political unification of England.

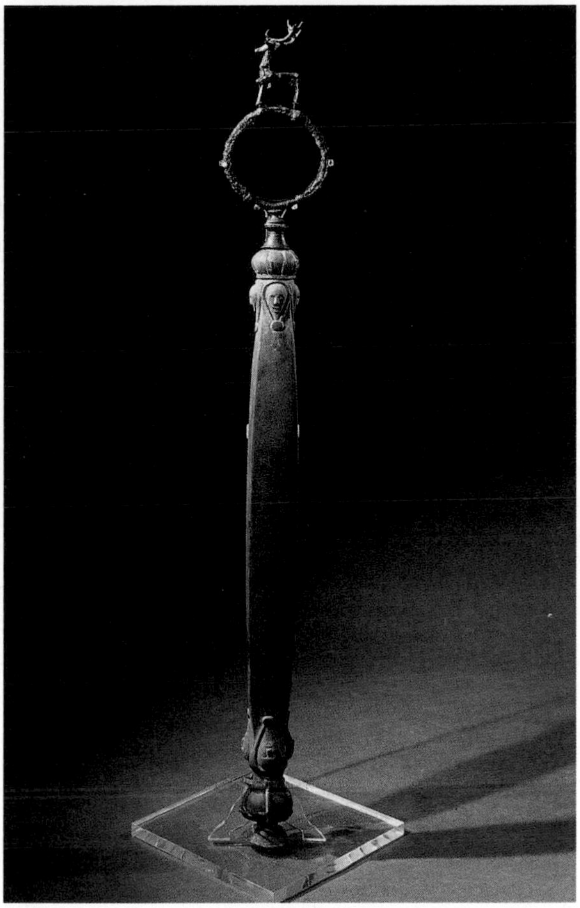

Whetstone from Sutton Hoo This whetstone, the traditional implement for sharpening knives, is surmounted by a stag, a symbol of virility and rulership among northern peoples. It was surely a symbol of the authority of the person commemorated at Sutton Hoo. *(Reproduced by Courtesy of the Trustees of the British Museum)*

Ecclesiastical peace led to the flourishing of monastic life. Monasteries played two important roles in this period. They led the way in bringing Christianity to ordinary people. Despite early gains among kings and nobles, Christianity had barely begun to penetrate the countryside. Monks also maintained international connections, ranging from Ireland to Rome, that attached England to the great intellectual currents of the day and enabled the English to make their own contributions.

After Theodore's school at Canterbury, the most important early center of learning was in Northumbria. There English, Irish, Frankish, and Roman currents flowed together in the monasteries of Lindisfarne, Wearmouth, and Jarrow and in the cathedral school of York. The schools of Canterbury, Lindisfarne, and Jarrow produced some of the most beautiful illuminated manuscripts of the early Middle Ages.

The greatest product of this intellectual tradition was Bede (673–735). When he was 7, his parents performed an act of oblation and gave him to the monastery at Wearmouth. He transferred to neighboring Jarrow and spent the rest of his life there. Bede was a teacher of genius, an erudite scholar, a superb Latin stylist, and a warm human being. His *Ecclesiastical History of the English People,* the most important source for English history from the fifth century to the eighth, did much to identify the Anglo-Saxons as a single English people. His biblical commentaries remained influential all over Europe for centuries. His studies of temporal reckoning popularized the use of A.D. dating, which replaced a bewildering array of local systems.

The career of King Offa of Mercia (r. 757–796) shows the trends in early Britain. His ancestors were pagans, but he was a patron of the church, convener of church councils, and recipient of papal envoys. He dominated all of Britain and was the first to call himself "King of the English." He issued a law code, reformed Mercia's institutions, and signed England's first international trade agreement—with Charlemagne. Unfortunately, after Offa's death, Viking raiders destroyed whatever unity had been achieved.

The World of Charlemagne

The most effective of the early Germanic kingdoms was created by Clovis and the Franks. During the seventh century that kingdom too experienced difficulties but did not disappear. Just as Roman aristocrats had borne the ancient heritage into the Middle Ages, so now a Frankish family, called "Carolingian" from the name of its greatest member, assembled the talent and resources of the Frankish realm in a new way. Charlemagne, the greatest of the Carolingians, reformed his government and church, patronized learning, and resurrected the western empire.

The Rise of the Carolingian Family

The traditional view of the Frankish world sees mostly chaos: When Clovis died in 511, he divided his realm among his sons, and it became clear that several kingdoms would coexist. The Merovingian royal families feuded constantly, sought to expand at one another's expense, and drew their aristocracies into their battles. Trade and intellectual life declined, and the German regions that had been conquered in the sixth century slipped away.

There is another way to view the situation: The *idea* of a single kingdom of the Franks persisted. Kings and aristocrats in the small kingdoms competed for leadership of the realm as a whole. When the king in a region was weak, local nobles struggled to defend the kingdom or to hold it until a minor heir came of age. The flourishing, classicizing culture of late antique Gaul was largely gone, but a creative Christian monastic culture was growing up in all parts of the Frankish kingdom. Monks from the monasteries were accomplishing the difficult task of converting the countryside to Christianity. The seventh century, in other words, was a time when the late antique regime was slowly changing into the medieval regime.

Central to this development was the rise to prominence of the Carolingians. The family appeared in history just after 600 and thereafter monopolized the office of mayor of the palace (sort of a prime minister) to the king in Austrasia (the easternmost kingdom; see Map 8.3). The Carolingians were the noblest and wealthiest family in Austrasia, perhaps in the Frankish world. Within two generations they unified the Frankish realm and increased their own power.

The Carolingians used several methods to accomplish their ends. They formed alliances with powerful noble families in many regions. They waged war against the enemies of the Franks to restore the territorial integrity of the kingdom. Charles Martel (d. 741), Charlemagne's grandfather, led the Frankish forces that put an end to Arab raiding in Gaul, defeating a large force near Poitiers in 732. With booty from their wars, tribute from conquered peoples, spoils taken from recalcitrant opponents, and even lands seized from the church, the Carolingians attracted and rewarded more and more followers until no one, not even the Merovingians, was a match for them. The Carolingians also allied themselves very early with leading churchmen, both episcopal and monastic. They aided missionaries in the work of converting central Germany, thereby expanding Frankish influence in that area.

For more than a hundred years the Carolingians were content with the office of mayor of the palace. Then in 749 Pepin III (son of Charles Martel) decided to send envoys to the pope to ask whether, in the lands of the Franks, it was right that the person who had all the power was not the king. The pope responded that this situation was a contravention of the divine plan. Accordingly, in 751, the last Merovingian king was deposed, and Pepin was elected in his place (r. 751–768). Pepin had prepared his usurpation very carefully with his Frankish supporters, but he appealed to the pope to make it appear that he had become king with divine approval and not by crude usurpation. Hard-pressed by the Lombards in Italy, the pope probably gave Pepin the answer he wanted in order to enlist him as an ally. Three years later the pope visited the Frankish kingdom, crowned and anointed Pepin and his sons (including Charlemagne), forbade the Franks ever to choose a king from family other than the Carolingians, and received a promise of aid in Italy. The Merovingians, after nearly three centuries of rule, had yielded to a new royal dynasty that would last for more than two centuries.

THE GERMANIC WEST

Sixth Century	Franks drive Visigoths into Spain
	Lombards enter Italy
	Franks and then Visigoths convert to Catholicism
	Irish and Roman missionaries initiate conversion of Britain
	Consolidation of Lombard, Visigothic, Frankish kingdoms
	Pontificate of Gregory the Great
Seventh Century	Political struggles in Frankish, Visigothic, and Anglo-Saxon kingdoms
	Lombards fight with popes and Byzantines
	England chooses Roman over Celtic Christianity
Eighth Century	Carolingians become kings in Frankish world
	Emergence of Papal state
	Northumbrian Renaissance
	Offa of Mercia greatest Early Anglo-Saxon ruler (757–796)
	Reign of Charlemagne (768–814)
	Imperial coronation of Charlemagne (800)
	Spain conquered by Muslims
	Lombard kingdom conquered by Charlemagne
Ninth Century	Carolingian Renaissance
	Divisions of the Carolingian empire
	Attacks of Muslims, Magyars, and Vikings

The Empire of Charlemagne

Charlemagne (Carolus Magnus, "Charles the Great," in Latin) was a huge man, and his stature has grown in European history and legend. (See the box, "A Contemporary Portrait of Charlemagne.") Like all great leaders, Charlemagne (r. 768–814) was complex. He spoke and read Frankish, Latin, and some Greek but never learned to write. He promoted Christian morality but perpetrated unspeakable brutalities on his enemies and enjoyed several concubines. Many battles were fought in his name, but he rarely accompanied his armies and fought no campaigns that are remembered for strategic brilliance. Determination and organization were the hallmarks of his long reign, which began in 768.

It took until the mid-780s for Charlemagne to come to grips with his world (Map 8.3). His first major achievement was the articulation of a new

A Contemporary Portrait of Charlemagne

Here is Einhard's description of Charlemagne. Einhard selected suitable passages from **Lives of the Caesars,** *by the first-century Roman historian Suetonius, to build up a picture of Charlemagne that accords well with what is otherwise known about him.*

His body was full and strong, very tall but not more than was fitting, for his height was seven times the length of his feet. His head was round and his eyes, large and piercing. His nose was longer than normal, his hair beautiful, and his expression was happy, even joyful. The power and dignity of his form were very great when he was sitting or standing. His neck was short and thick and his belly stuck out a bit, but the overall fineness of his form veiled these features, indeed his step was firm and all his bearing was manly. His voice was clear but too high for so great a body. His health was good until fevers struck him in the last four years of his life, and at the end he was lame in one foot. . . . He loved foreigners and took great pains in receiving them. He always exerted himself vigorously in riding and hunting. He loved the hot-steam baths at Aachen—they were his reason for his constructing his palace there—and he exercised in the water when he could. No one could beat him in swimming. . . . Sometimes he invited his sons, nobles, and as many as a hundred men into the baths with him. . . . He dressed in the Frankish style. Next to his body he put on a linen shirt and drawers, then hose and a tunic with a silk border. He wore shoes and strips of cloth wound around his legs. In winter he protected his chest and shoulders with a jacket of otter or ermine. He wrapped himself in a blue cloak and wore a sword with hilt and cincture of gold and silver. On festive days or to receive ambassadors, he wore a jewelled sword. The clothes of other peoples, however beautiful, he hated and he only endured to put them on when Pope Hadrian asked him to at Rome.

Source: Einhard, *Vie de Charlemagne,* 4th ed., ed. Louis Halphen (Paris: Société d'Edition 'Les Belles Lettres,' 1967), cc. 21–23, pp. 64–70 (translated and adapted by T. Noble).

ruling ideology in the Latin West. In capitularies—royal executive orders—of 789 Charlemagne required all males to swear an oath of allegiance to him, and compared himself to a biblical king in his responsibility to admonish, to teach, and to set an example for his people. He referred to the people of his realm as a "New Israel," a new chosen people. Interestingly, this chosen people was not exclusively Frankish. No distinctions were to be made among Franks or Bavarians or Saxons. Everyone was to be equal in allegiance to the king and in membership in a sort of Augustinian City of God.

Einhard (ca. 770–840), Charlemagne's friend and biographer, said that Augustine's *City of God* (see page 265) was the king's favorite book. The king understood it to mean that there was a City of God consisting of all right-thinking Christians—the "New Israel"—and a City of Man consisting of pagans, heretics, and infidels. This idea

Map 8.3 The Carolingian World The area over which Charlemagne exerted direct or indirect control was vast. The areas beyond the Rhine and Danube had never been part of the Roman Empire. The Franks made these regions part of European civilization. The Treaty of Verdun (see inset), signed by Charlemagne's grandsons in 843, was the first and most important of several divisions of the Carolingian Empire that resulted in the emergence of France and Germany. The kingdom of Italy and many small territories evolved from the kingdom of Lothair.

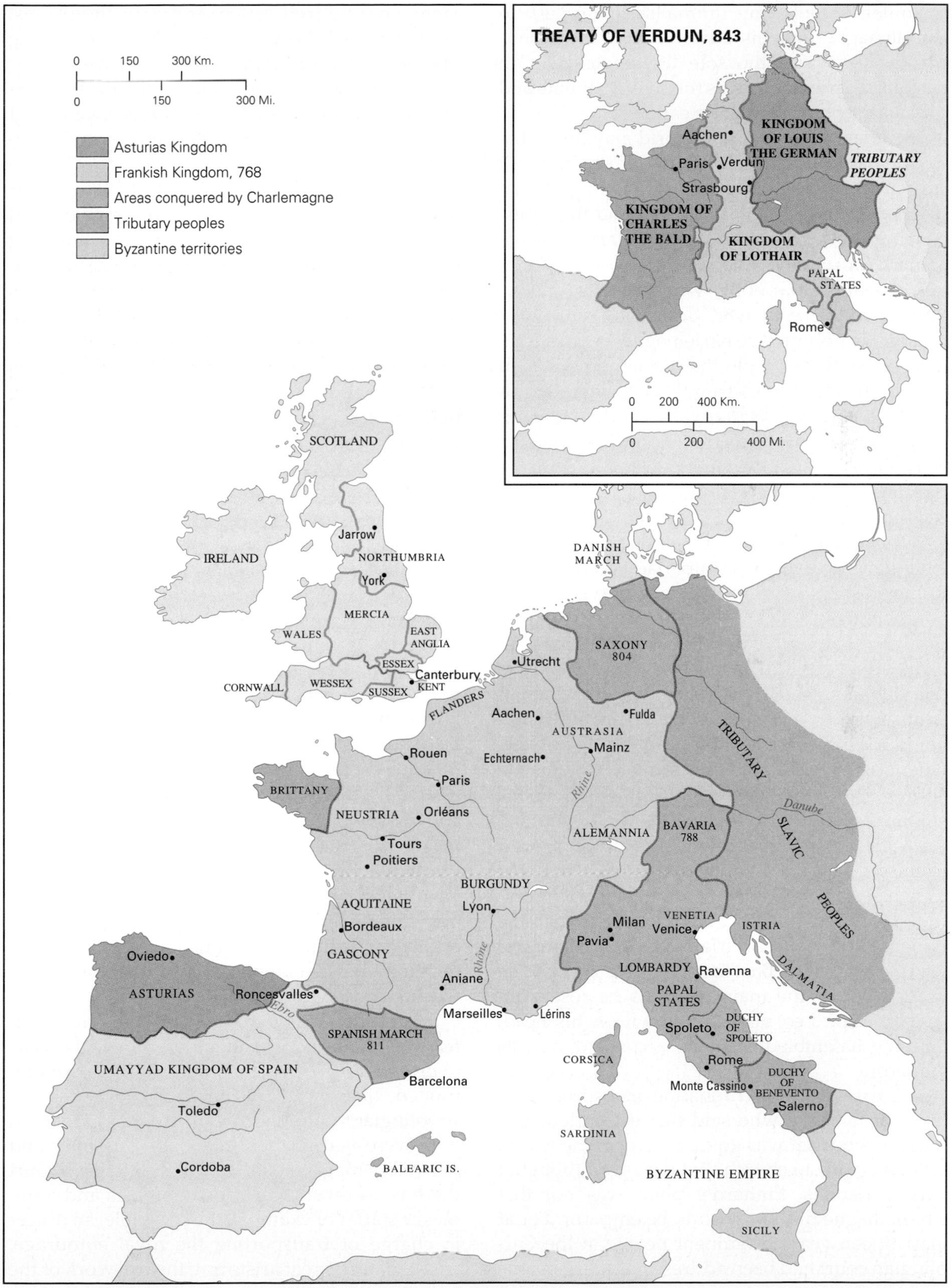
TREATY OF VERDUN, 843
KINGDOM OF LOUIS THE GERMAN
TRIBUTARY PEOPLES
Aachen
Paris
Verdun
Strasbourg
KINGDOM OF CHARLES THE BALD
KINGDOM OF LOTHAIR
PAPAL STATES
Rome
0 200 400 Km.
0 200 400 Mi.
0 150 300 Km.
0 150 300 Mi.
Asturias Kingdom
Frankish Kingdom, 768
Areas conquered by Charlemagne
Tributary peoples
Byzantine territories
SCOTLAND
IRELAND
Jarrow
NORTHUMBRIA
York
MERCIA
WALES
EAST ANGLIA
ESSEX
CORNWALL
WESSEX
SUSSEX
Canterbury
KENT
DANISH MARCH
SAXONY 804
Utrecht
Fulda
FLANDERS
Aachen
AUSTRASIA
Mainz
Rouen
Echternach
Paris
Rhine
BRITTANY
NEUSTRIA
Orléans
TRIBUTARY
SLAVIC
PEOPLES
Danube
ALEMANNIA
BAVARIA 788
Tours
Poitiers
BURGUNDY
AQUITAINE
Lyon
Bordeaux
GASCONY
Rhône
Milan
VENETIA
Venice
ISTRIA
Pavia
LOMBARDY
Ravenna
DALMATIA
Oviedo
ASTURIAS
Roncesvalles
Ebro
Aniane
PAPAL STATES
Marseilles
Lérins
SPANISH MARCH 811
DUCHY OF SPOLETO
Spoleto
CORSICA
Rome
UMAYYAD KINGDOM OF SPAIN
Barcelona
Monte Cassino
DUCHY OF BENEVENTO
Salerno
Toledo
SARDINIA
Cordoba
BALEARIC IS.
BYZANTINE EMPIRE
SICILY

is similar to the Islamic umma (see page 274). To Charlemagne and his advisers, it was obvious that as God was the sole legitimate ruler in heaven, Charlemagne was the sole legitimate and divinely appointed ruler on earth.

Readers in the modern world may think that Charlemagne had crossed a boundary between church and state. It is crucial to understand that to Charlemagne, as to his Muslim and Byzantine contemporaries, no such boundary existed. Church (or religion) and state were complementary attributes of a polity whose end was salvation, not victory in war, domestic security, or personal fulfillment. Charlemagne's ideological legacy was twofold. On the one hand, it created possibilities for bitter struggles later in the Middle Ages between secular rulers and ecclesiastical powers about the leadership of Christian society. On the other hand, it made it hard to define the state and its essential purposes in other than religious terms.

The most disputed event in the reign of Charlemagne was his imperial coronation in Rome on Christmas in 800. It is important to separate how this event happened from what it meant to the participants. In April 799 some disgruntled papal bureaucrats and their supporters attacked Pope Leo III (r. 795–816) in an attempt to depose him. Leo was saved by an ally of Charlemagne and then traveled all the way to Saxony, where the king was with his army. Charlemagne agreed to restore the pope to Rome and, as his ally and protector, to investigate those who had attacked him. No real offenses could be proved against the pope, who appeared publicly in Rome to swear that he had done nothing wrong. Everything was handled to avoid any hint that the pope had been put on trial. When Charlemagne went to St. Peter's Basilica on Christmas Day, he prayed before the main altar. As he rose from prayer, Pope Leo placed a crown on his head, and the assembled Romans acclaimed him as emperor.

Debate over this coronation arises from a remark of Einhard, who said that if Charlemagne had known what was going to happen he would not have gone to church that day, even though it was Christmas. Einhard's point was not that Charlemagne did not wish to be emperor. For at least fifteen years prominent people at the Carolingian court had been addressing Charlemagne in imperial terms in letters, treatises, and poems. What Einhard did mean was that Charlemagne saw himself as a Frankish and Christian emperor. The imperial office dignified his position as leader of the Frankish "Israel." Charlemagne did not wish to be beholden to the pope or to the Romans.

Charlemagne's policies did not change after his coronation. He continued his program of legal and ecclesiastical reform and put the finishing touches on some military and diplomatic campaigns. In 806 he divided his empire among his three legitimate sons; but then two of them died, so in 813 he made Louis his sole heir and successor. Charlemagne outlived most of the friends and companions of his youth and middle age. He outlived four wives and many of his children. Old and alone, ill and lame, he died in early 814.

Carolingian Government

Charlemagne accomplished much through the sheer force of his personality and his boundless energy. But he also reformed and created institutional structures. These helped him to carry out his tasks, guaranteed a measure of permanence to his reforms, and created government patterns that lasted in many parts of Europe until the twelfth century.

The king (or emperor—the offices differed little in practical importance) was the heart of the system. In theory, the king ruled by God's grace and did not have to answer for his conduct to any person. In reality, the king sought consensus through a variety of means. The king controlled vast lands, which gave him great wealth of his own and also the means to reward loyal followers. By controlling appointments to key positions, the king required men to come to him for power, wealth, and prestige.

Carolingian government was amateur but effective. The eastern contemporaries of the Carolingians relied on large numbers of carefully trained, life-long civil servants. In contrast, the Carolingians employed a limited number of men who were tied to them by bonds of family and personal allegiance. At the Carolingian court there were several ceremonial officers and a domestic staff. For example, the constable, an officer in charge of transporting the royal entourage, was usually a great aristocrat; the real work of the office was carried out by others. The treasurer was the keeper of the king's bedchamber, where the royal treasure chest was kept. Several chaplains, whose primary duty was to see to the spiritual needs of the court, kept official records. The queen controlled the domestic staff and the stewards who managed the royal estates.

Local government was mainly entrusted to counts. There were about six hundred counts in the empire and several times that number of minor officials. As in Merovingian times, the counts were at once administrative, judicial, and military officials. Most counts came from prominent families, and the office increased the wealth and importance of its holders. Counts had to promulgate and enforce royal orders and to preside in regular sessions of local courts. Counts got one-third of the fines levied in courts, so the zealous pursuit of justice was in their interest.

The court and the localities were linked in several ways. Under Charlemagne and his successors it became usual for all major officers, whether secular (counts and their subordinates) or ecclesiastical (bishops, abbots), to be *vassals* of the king. In return for their offices and grants of land called *benefices,* vassals solemnly pledged loyalty and service to the king. Vassalage drew on both Roman and Germanic customs. Patron-client ties had always been socially and politically important among the Romans, and the allegiance of warriors to a chief was a key bond among the Germans. But by connecting personal loyalty with public office and material reward, Charlemagne created something essentially new. Only a few thousand men, a tiny fraction of the total population, were vassals at any time. They constituted the political and social elite.

Another connection between the king and his local agents was the assembly that met once or twice a year. At these gatherings, which sometimes had separate secular and ecclesiastical sessions, all free men were to assemble to advise the

Charlemagne's Palace at Aachen In the foreground is the octagonal palace and throne room of Charlemagne's palace at Aachen. It is joined by galleries to the residential quarters in the background. Construction was begun in 788. The models for these buildings were found in Rome and Ravenna. (*Römisch-Germanisches Zentral Museum*)

Charlemagne's Throne, Aachen Palace Chapel Modeled on the biblical description of King Solomon's throne, Charlemagne's throne symbolized the wisdom and justice of the Frankish king who led the new Frankish "Israel." *(Ann Münchow)*

king on matters of great importance, such as war and peace or legal reforms. In practice only the vassals had the means or the interest to ensure their attendance. In these assemblies the capitularies were prepared. Most of the great Carolingian reforms were formulated in these assemblies by cooperation between the king and his most important subjects. The assemblies served to defuse dissension.

The king could also bring his power to bear locally by traveling. The monarchy possessed estates all over the heartlands of the kingdom, and the royal entourage often moved from one place to another. Monasteries and cathedrals had to provide hospitality to the king. As the royal party traveled about the realm, they were able to check on local conditions and to compel local officials to comply with royal wishes.

In 788 Charlemagne began to build a palace at Aachen, and in the last twenty years of his life he was usually in residence there. The later Carolingian rulers all tended to have fixed residences, as did the Byzantines and the Abbassids. In adopting fixed residences and elaborate court rituals, the Carolingians may have been returning to Roman precedents or copying their contemporaries to appear as sophisticated as they. Their actions may also reflect a natural political progression: As a regime incorporates more lands, peoples, and cultural traditions, it tends to become more remote, impersonal, and abstract in the conduct of its business. Elegant courts and intricate rituals enhance the awe felt for a ruler and grant common people symbolic participation in elaborate public acts. It is no coincidence that a key innovation of Charlemagne's reign coincided with his permanent residence in Aachen. In the late 780s he began to send out pairs of roving inspectors, *missi dominici,* envoys of the lord king, to see that royal orders were being observed, that counts were dispensing justice honestly, and that persons of power were not oppressing the powerless.

The Carolingian Renaissance

Charlemagne's reforms culminated in a revival of learning that scholars have named the "Carolingian Renaissance" (*renaissance* is French for "rebirth"). Charlemagne's fundamental ideas are revealed well by the constant use in contemporary sources of words such as *rebirth, renewal, reform,* and *restoration.* Charlemagne, his advisers, and his successors looked back for inspiration to Christian and papal Rome, to Saint Peter and Constantine, and to the Church Fathers. To them, the rebirth of Western society as a "New Israel" was equivalent to the theological rebirth of an individual in baptism. The Carolingians were the driving force behind intellectual growth in their era, and in all areas they subordinated learning to their ideological program.

To accomplish his objectives, Charlemagne required every cathedral and monastery to establish a school. To set up and run those schools he summoned to his court many of the most able and influential intellectual figures of the day: Franks, such as his biographer Einhard; grammar teachers from Italy; Visigoths from the Spanish border, the theologian Theodulf (d. 821) and the monastic reformer Benedict of Aniane (d. 821). His most famous recruit was the Anglo-Saxon Alcuin (735–804), the most learned man of his day and the greatest heir of Bede.

Much of the work of Alcuin and his associates was devoted to the production of textbooks and to the teaching of elementary knowledge. Charlemagne was convinced that people needed to be taught, accurately and intelligibly, the basic truths of Christianity, if he were to accomplish his task of leading them to salvation. A massive effort was undertaken to copy manuscripts of the Bible and of the writings of the Latin Church Fathers. These books, the essential sources for the whole program, needed to be disseminated as widely as possible. The process of copying was facilitated by a new script, Caroline minuscule. (See the feature, "Weighing the Evidence: The Manuscript Book," on pages 306–307.)

It is significant that Charlemagne could attract Alcuin from York, the most renowned school in the West, to head his palace school, just then forming. Charlemagne could place more resources at Alcuin's disposal than anyone else, and he had the will to do so. Alcuin also saw the long-term benefits that would come from his work. No matter how good York was, Alcuin and all his contemporaries must have thrilled at the chance to gather together. Alcuin's pupils spread out in the next generation to create a network of schools that went right on multiplying across the ninth century. That is a powerful legacy. And Alcuin did more than just teach. He wrote learned works and poetry and was for twenty years Charlemagne's most trusted adviser.

With this plan, personnel, and educational network in place, Charlemagne took many concrete steps. He got from Rome a copy of the then-authoritative canon law of the church. In 789, after some years of study by his court scholars, this law was issued for his whole kingdom. In about 786 Charlemagne got from the pope a sacramentary, a service book for worship in cathedral churches, and, again after a period of study, this was imposed throughout the kingdom. Charlemagne sought an authoritative copy of the *Rule of St. Benedict,* and after Benedict of Aniane had studied and commented on it, this Rule was imposed on all monasteries in the kingdom.

Secular reforms mirrored religious ones. Orders were issued regularizing the management of all royal estates. Law codes were updated and made as similar as possible. Not since Rome had governments had either the interest in or the means to promote such centralization. It is striking that in the eighth century the caliphate, the Byzantine Empire, and the Carolingian Empire were engaged in similar centralizing activities.

Versatility was a hallmark of Carolingian learning. There were figures who excelled at history and biography. Biblical studies and theology attracted a lot of attention, and the age produced many poets. One figure who illustrates the best of the age is the Visigoth Theodulf. He came to court in about 785 and served thereafter as a missus, royal adviser, abbot of several monasteries, and bishop of Orléans. He issued important legislation for his diocese. He was the foremost Old Testament scholar of his day and the only one who knew Hebrew. In *The Caroline Books,* he offered the Frankish response to Byzantine iconoclasm. He wrote theological treatises, many letters, and dozens of poems. At Germigny he designed a church that is a masterpiece of early Carolingian architecture.

Carolingian art is a crowning glory of the age. The manuscripts decorated under Charlemagne's patronage and then, for three generations, under the patronage of his descendants and of prominent churchmen show the same combination of elements seen in the career of Theodulf: versatility, respect but not awe for the past, innovation. Several distinct currents produced Carolingian art. Most prominent were the animal and geometric decorative motifs of Irish and Anglo-Saxon art, the elegance, formality, and sense of composition of classical art, basic elements of style from Byzantine painting, actual scenes from papal Rome, and the mysteries of Christian theology. Every element was borrowed, but the finished product was new.

Architecture shows the same trends. Charlemagne's palace complex at Aachen has parallels in imperial Constantinople, papal Rome, and Ostrogothic Ravenna. Workers and building materials were fetched from all over the empire. For basic buildings the Carolingians adapted the basilica. The basilica was fundamentally a horizontal building, but the Carolingians, by altering the western end and façade, added the dimension of verticality. In Romanesque and Gothic architecture this innovation would have a brilliant career (see pages 383 and 420–424).

Charlemagne's legacy was great. Alcuin called him "the Father of Europe." He brought together the lands that would become France, Germany, and northern Italy and endowed them with a common ideology, government, and culture. He provided a model that Europe would look back to for centuries as a kind of golden age. He created a vast, supraregional and supraethnic entity that drew deeply on the universalizing ideals of its Roman, Christian, and Jewish antecedents but that was, nevertheless, original. In one sense the Carolingian Empire represented the final stage in the evolution of the Roman Empire of Late Antiquity, but in another sense the Carolingian Empire was a new kind of regime that pointed to the future.

The Dissolution of the Carolingian Empire

The Carolingian Empire did not outlive the ninth century. Rome's empire lasted much longer, as did Byzantium's and Islam's. All three of these realms were fatally weakened by similar problems, but those problems arose earlier in the Carolingian world than elsewhere. Four issues were critical: geographical and ethnic complexity, the quality and reputation of leadership, political and dynastic strife, and outside attacks.

Size and ethnic complexity contributed to the disintegration of the Carolingian Empire. The empire included many small regions—Saxony, Bavaria, Brittany, and Lombardy, for example—that had their own resident elites, linguistic traditions, and distinctive cultures, which had existed before the Carolingians came on the scene and persist to this day. The Merovingian and Carolingian periods were basically a unifying intrusion into a history characterized by regional diversity. The Carolingians made heroic efforts to build a common culture and to forge bonds of unity. The obstacles were insuperable.

Several of the later Carolingians were rulers of ability. None, however, ruled as long as Charlemagne over so large and diverse a territory. And no other Carolingian evoked such awe in his contemporaries or reverence in posterity.

Another key issue in the breakup of the Carolingian Empire was political and dynastic. The Carolingians regularly tried to create subkingdoms for all their legitimate sons while preserving the imperial title for one of them. This was a creative attempt to concede limited autonomy to particular regions by means of local kingships—for instance in Bavaria, Italy, and Aquitaine—while preserving the "Augustinian" unity of the empire as a whole. Unfortunately, younger sons rarely yielded to their older brothers, and the bonds of loyalty among cousins, nephews, and grandchildren grew slender. Frequent divisions of the empire, or of segments of it, placed local nobilities in the difficult position of changing their allegiance frequently and of jeopardizing their offices and landholdings.

In the Treaty of Verdun in 843 (see the inset of Map 8.3) the three grandsons of Charlemagne—Charles the Bald, Louis the German, and Lothair—divided the empire into three realms: the West Frankish, the East Frankish, and the Middle kingdom. After fierce battles among the brothers, each appointed forty members to a study commission that traversed the whole empire to identify royal properties, fortifications, monasteries, and cathedrals so that an equitable division could be made of these valuable resources. Each brother needed adequate resources to solidify his rule and to attract or hold followers. The lines drawn on the map at Verdun did not give France or Germany its final historical shape. Still, attempts such as that at Verdun to solve political and dynastic crises marked stages in the transformation from a unified Carolingian Empire to smaller successor states.

The final cause of the fragmentation of the empire was a new wave of attacks. In the middle decades of the ninth century, Arabs, Magyars, and Vikings wreaked havoc on the Franks. Based in North Africa and the islands of the western Mediterranean, Arabs attacked Italy and southern France. Magyars, relatives of the Huns and Avars who had preceded them into eastern Europe, were accomplished horsemen whose lightning raids hit Italy, Germany, and even France. Vikings were Scandinavians seeking booty, glory, and political opportunity in Carolingian Europe as institutional consolidation dawned in the northern world. These attacks were unpredictable in time or place and caused local regions to fall back on their own resources rather than look to the central government.

It is no coincidence that the major raids came just as the Carolingians began warring against one another. The forces that were dissolving the Carolingian Empire were intensified by the need to organize defense on a very local level—and by a feeling at the local level that the far-off king and his grand Christian theories of government were of little help in the current crisis.

Carolingian decline should not be exaggerated, however. Amid the tensions among the various Carolingians there always persisted a sense that the empire was a single entity for which all the members of the dynasty bore responsibility. It was in the Carolingian world that the idea of Europe as "Christendom" was born. The idea of a unified Europe is very much alive in the 1990s. On occasion, a Prix de Charlemagne (Charlemagne Prize) is given to a person who has made a great contribution to European unity.

It is also important to realize that the early French and German kingdoms were recognizably Carolingian in their governing structures and ideologies (see Chapter 10). Just as the governing structures of the Roman Empire were inherited by the Germanic kingdoms of the early Middle Ages, so too were key elements of the Carolingian Empire bequeathed to all the regimes that succeeded it. In this respect, the experience of the Carolingian Empire parallels that of the caliphate. There too a huge entity was laid over the top of many older and smaller entities. Each of those regional entities was indelibly marked by Islam, the Arabic language, and the institutions of the caliphs. In the end, the caliphate, like the Carolingian Empire, broke down into smaller units that, although changed in key ways, were true to their own histories. This has been the experience of every multinational empire in the West from Sumer to the Soviet Union.

Charles the Bald From a Bible dedicated to Charles the Bald in about 846, this picture illustrates Carolingian art and ideology. Charles the Bald is depicted with Roman attributes of rule. He is clearly above his clerical advisers. And the hand of God (compare the icon on page 284) points at him. *(Bibliothèque Nationale, Paris)*

Early Medieval Economies and Societies

In economic and social history, the early Middle Ages provides additional evidence of continuity and change. The world remained rural, society was hierarchical, and women were excluded from public power. In rough terms, the Islamic world changed the most, the Byzantine the least, and the West fell somewhere between.

Trade and Commerce

Trade is basically a mechanism to move things from producers to consumers. It may or may not involve market exchanges. The Roman government moved large amounts of goods from the center of the empire to the frontiers to supply their armies. This command process avoided markets but still moved goods from producers to consumers. Roman, Byzantine, and Islamic governments raised taxes in one place, bought goods in another, and then consumed their purchases someplace else without having recourse to markets. Tribute and plunder were also effective exchange mechanisms. The Franks collected tributes in cows from the Saxons. There were diplomatic gifts: A caliph sent Charlemagne an elephant. There was a great deal of exchange with different meanings and values. The commonest exchanges were intensely local.

There were several major trading networks. Mesopotamia was linked by rivers to the Persian Gulf and to both east Africa and south Asia, by land and sea to Byzantium, and by land and rivers to the Black Sea region, Slavic Europe, and the Baltic. Byzantines traded mainly by sea. The whole Mediterranean was open to them, and from the Black Sea they got the products of the Danube basin. The West had many trade routes. The Rhône-Saône river system moved goods, as did the land routes through the Alpine passes. The North and Baltic seas were the hubs of a network that linked the British Isles, the whole of the Frankish north—by means of its rivers—the Rhineland, Slavic Europe, Byzantium, and the Muslim world. The Danube was also a major highway. The major trade networks intersected at many points. Despite religious and ideological differences, Rome's three heirs regularly traded with one another.

Food and other bulk goods never traveled very far because the cost was prohibitive. Most towns were supplied with foodstuffs by their immediate hinterlands, so the goods that moved over long distances were portable and valuable. A caravan of some five hundred camels could move only one-fourth to one-half of the cargo of a normal Byzantine ship. The Muslim world was fundamentally a land empire that had relatively poor roads and primitive wheeled vehicles, so transport considerations were crucial.

Cotton and raw silk were moved to the Mediterranean, where they were made into cloth in, respectively, Egypt and Byzantium. Paper and pottery were moved around the caliphate. Asian spices and perfumes were avidly sought everywhere. The Byzantines traded in silk cloth, fine ivories, delicate products of the gold and silver smiths' art, slaves, and naval stores. Byzantium, with its large fleet, usually controlled the Black and Mediterranean seas but found trade relations difficult to sustain. Reduced in prosperity, the empire could no longer dictate trade terms to subject peoples and competed badly with the Muslims. Trade in the West was partly in high-value luxury goods but mainly in ordinary items such as plain pottery, raw wool, wool cloth, millstones, weapons, and slaves.

Town and Countryside

To think of the ancient world is to think of cities. Thinking of the medieval world brings to mind forests and fields. Actually, from 80 to 90 percent of people in antiquity lived in rural settings, and in the early Middle Ages the percentage was not much higher. What changed was the place occupied by towns in the totality of human life. Fewer government functions were based in towns, cultural life was less bound to the urban environment, and trade in luxuries, which depended on towns, declined.

Towns in the West lost Roman governmental significance but often survived as focal points of royal or, more often, ecclesiastical administration. A cathedral church required a large corps of administrators. Western towns were everywhere attracting *burgs,* new settlements of merchants, just outside their centers. Few western towns were impressive in size or population. Rome may have numbered a million people in the time of Augustus, but it had only about 25,000—one-fortieth of that amount—in 800. Much of the ancient city was unused or given over to gardening. Paris had perhaps 20,000 inhabitants before the Vikings arrived. Even in these reduced circumstances, however, urban building took place. In addition to the large palace complex in Aachen, the Carolingians built smaller palaces in other towns. Several popes were great builders. More than two dozen towns in Carolingian Europe rebuilt their cathedrals. Although society in the West was overwhelmingly rural and agricultural, towns had a role to play in it.

In the Byzantine East, apart from Constantinople, the empire had a more rural aspect after the Muslims took control of the heavily urbanized regions of Syria, Egypt, and parts of Anatolia in the seventh century. The weakening of the caliphate in the second half of the ninth century was a spur to urban growth in the Byzantine Empire. And by the middle of the ninth century, the emperors once again were building palaces and churches in Constantinople. In provincial cities, population growth and urban construction depended heavily on military conditions: Cities threatened by Muslims or Bulgars declined.

The Muslims were great city-builders. Baghdad was created from scratch and was four times larger in area than Constantinople, with a million residents to the latter's 400,000. The most magnificent city in the West was Cordoba, the capital of Muslim Spain. Its population may have reached 400,000, and its great mosque, begun in 785, held 5,500 worshipers, more than any Latin church except St. Peter's. The city had 900 baths, 1,600 mosques (Rome had about 200 churches), 60,000 mansions, and perhaps 100,000 shops. Its libraries held thousands of books when the largest Carolingian book collections numbered a few hundred.

Agriculture nevertheless remained the most important element in the economy and the daily lives of the great majority. Farming primarily meant the production of cereal grains, which provided the breads and porridges that fed most people. Regions tended to specialize in the crops that grew most abundantly in local circumstances and, as noted, there was sufficient exchange to provide for local needs. Animal husbandry was always a major part of the rural regime. English sheep provided wool and meat. In Frankish and Byzantine regions pigs, which were cheap to raise, supplied meat, but for religious reasons—Islam took over the Jewish prohibition against eating pork—pork was almost absent in the Muslim East.

A key development in the West was the appearance of a bipartite estate, sometimes called a "manor." On a bipartite estate, one part of the land was set aside as a reserve (or demesne), and the rest was divided into tenancies. The reserve, consuming from a quarter to half of the total territory of the estate, was exploited directly for the benefit of the landlord. The tenancies were generally worked by the peasants for their own support. The bipartite estate began to appear in the Frankish kingdom around 760. It provided the aristocrats with a livelihood while freeing them for military and government service.

The estates were run in different ways. One landlord might hire day laborers to farm his reserve, paying them with money exacted as fees from his tenants. Another might require the tenants to work a certain number of days per week or weeks per year in his fields. The produce of the estate might be gathered into barns and consumed locally or hauled to local markets. The reserve might be a separate part of the estate, a proportion of common fields, or a percentage of the harvest. The tenants might have individual farms or work in common fields.

Social Patterns

There are certain similarities among the social structures in all three societies. The elites tended to be large landholders, to control dependent populations, and to have access to government offices. There were regional differences too. Scholars had more social rank in Byzantium than they had anywhere else; and churchmen, especially bishops, were powerful in Christian societies but had no counterparts in Muslim ones. Literature, surely reflecting social realities, portrays the cultivated Muslim gentleman in the Abbassid period. This social type, marked by learning, good manners, and a taste for fine things, does not appear in Byzantium or in the West until the twelfth century.

The middling classes show some disparities among the regions. Merchants, for example, often rose through the social ranks to become great aristocrats in Muslim societies. Islamic society often evinced great mobility, because of its restless, expanding nature and because Islamic ideology rejected distinctions in the umma. In Byzantium, traditional Roman prejudices against merchants and moneymaking activities persisted. Thus, there were rich merchants whose wealth gave them private power and influence but who lacked public power and recognition. In the West, merchants were neither numerous nor powerful in the Carolingian period. In some towns, moreover, commerce was in the hands of Jews, always outsiders in a militantly Christian society.

Merchants were not the only people occupying the middle rungs of the social ladder. In all three societies there were central elites and provincial elites. Service at the Carolingian, Byzantine, or Abbassid court counted for more than service in a provincial outpost. It was one thing to be abbot of a great monastery and quite a different thing to preside over a poor, tiny house. The thematic

Labors of the Months From a ninth-century, west-Frankish manuscript, this picture illustrates the labors of the various months of the year. How many of them can you figure out? How do these compare with farm labors where you live? *(Österreichische Nationalbibliothek)*

generals in Byzantium were lofty personages; their subordinates held inferior positions. The vassals of a Carolingian king formed a real aristocracy; their vassals were of decidedly lower rank.

Degrees of freedom and local economic and political conditions shaped the lives of peasants. In all three societies some farmers were personally free and owed no cash or labor services to anyone but the central government. In areas such as Abbassid Iraq, ordinary free farmers led a comfortable life. In the Frankish world, most peasants existed outside the dawning manorial system. They were free, and if they lived in areas of good land and political security, such as the Paris basin, their lives must have been congenial. Byzantine peasants, though free, often lived in areas of military danger, and in some parts of the Balkans they had to eke a living from poor soils. They were highly taxed, and their freedom was small compensation for their economic and personal insecurity. What made all peasants alike was that they were subject to political changes over which they had no control.

At the bottom of the social scale everywhere were slaves. Christianity did not object to slavery itself but forbade the enslavement of Christians. Islam was similar, forbidding Muslims to enslave other Muslims. Slaves therefore tended to be commonest in still-pagan societies—Scandinavia, for example—or in frontier regions where neighboring pagans could be captured and sold. There were more slaves in the Muslim world than in Byzantium, which had, in turn, more than the West.

Women were bound to the same social hierarchies as men. Aristocratic women had opportunities and power that were denied ordinary women. Irene ruled at Byzantium as empress. Frankish and Anglo-Saxon queens were formidable figures in the life of their realms. Carolingian queens managed the landed patrimony of the dynasty, dozens of huge estates with tens of thousands of dependents. The conversion of England to Christianity was fostered by women. Most convents of nuns had aristocratic abbesses who presided over complex enterprises and, often, schools. In the Frankish world aristocratic women secured some learning, and one, Dhuoda, wrote in 841 a manual of advice for her son that conveys biblical and patristic teachings as well as practical wisdom. The Frankish convent at Chelles was a renowned center for the copying of manuscripts. Some Anglo-Saxon nuns owned ships and invested in commercial activities to support their convent. Almost all aspects of the cloth industry were in women's hands. Women had few formal, public roles to play. Their influence, however great, tended to function in the private sphere, rarely revealed to us by sources that stem from the public realm of powerful men.

One example of the problems in the evidence is church roles. Women could not hold priestly office; and although there were deaconesses at Hagia Sophia in the sixth century, they disappeared soon after and had long ago vanished in the West. Religious power could come from office or from personal sanctity. One study of some 2,200 saints from the early Middle Ages finds only about 300 females. It was hard for women to become saints. And if a woman became a saint, her holiness was inevitably described either as "manly"—an extreme ascetic was praised for having the strength and courage of a man—or as beautiful, virginal, and domestic—with female stereotypes. (See the box, "Hilda of Whitby: An English Aristocrat and Abbess.")

The domestic sphere is another difficult realm to enter. The Qur'an permitted a man up to four wives, if he could care for them and would treat then equitably. A Muslim woman, however, was given her dowry outright, and multiple marriages may have meant that relatively more Muslim women could gain a measure of security.

In Byzantium and the West, families rarely arranged marriages for more than one or two daughters. Others remained single or entered convents. The sources hint at female infanticide. Women at all social levels tended to pass from the tutelage of their fathers to that of their husbands. In antiquity a suitor usually paid a fee, a "bride price," to his prospective wife's father and then endowed his wife with "bridewealth," money or possessions of her own. Gradually this practice changed to a system whereby a bride's father paid a dowry to her future husband. Thus, a wife who was cast aside could be left impoverished, for in most places the law did not permit her to inherit land if she had brothers. Females were such valuable property in the marriage market that rape was an offense not against a girl but against her father. A man could divorce, even kill, his wife for adultery, witchcraft, or grave robbing, and then marry again. A woman could usually gain a divorce only for adultery, and she could not remarry. For the vast majority of women daily life was hedged about with legal limitations and personal indignities.

Summary

We have traced three parallel trajectories in the history of the early Middle Ages. A first one is chronological. In the Islamic, Byzantine, and Latin worlds, the seventh century was an age of rapid, dynamic change, the eighth century a time of consolidation and reform, and the ninth century a period of renewed challenges.

A second trajectory is political, religious, and ideological. Three large imperial states were created out of diverse peoples and territories. Each state developed a central government that focused on a powerful leader who was seen as a specially chosen agent of God. Each state erected a system of rule that tied a government capital to its outlying regions. In the Muslim and Byzantine

Hilda of Whitby: An English Aristocrat and Abbess

In the north of England were a few "double monasteries"—communities of both men and women living under an abbess. Hilda was abbess of Whitby, one of the most famous of these. Notice the range of her connections and influence.

She led her life in two equal parts, the first thirty-three years devoted to secular occupations and the second even more nobly devoted to the Lord in monastic life. She was indeed nobly born, the daughter of Hereric, a nephew of King Edwin. . . . When, having abandoned her secular garb, she decided to serve God alone, she went away to the land of the East Angles, whose king was a relative, from where she aimed to travel to Gaul and live as an exile for the Lord's sake where her sister Hereswith, mother of King Aldwith of the East Angles, was already living. But Bishop Aidan called her home and gave her land for a monastery. . . . Later she undertook to found a monastery at Whitby . . . and there she taught righteousness, mercy, purity, and other virtues, but above all peace and charity. . . . So great was her discretion that not only common people but even kings and princes used to come and ask her advice. . . . Those who submitted to her leadership had to study the scriptures . . . and five men from this monastery became bishops.

Source: Venerabilis Baedae, *Historiam Ecclesiasticam Gentis Anglorum,* 4.21, ed. Charles Plummer (Oxford, England: Oxford University Press, 1896), pp. 252–254 (translated and adapted by T. Noble).

worlds, that system was highly bureaucratic; in the Frankish world, the system was more amateur and personal. A religion—Islam, Orthodox Catholicism, or Roman Catholicism—provided the social glue that held each society together and defined the mission of its government. The cultural life of each area was inspired mainly by an attempt to integrate a powerful religious message with older intellectual traditions.

The third trajectory concerns results. In the Islamic and Frankish worlds, large states broke down to leave many smaller heirs. In each instance, changes in the caliber of leadership, unpredictable foreign attacks, and the sheer diversity of the polity pulled the large state apart. The Byzantine Empire, much smaller than the Roman Empire had been, managed to defend its territory. A sense of common and present danger probably helped to preserve the Byzantine state even in the face of severe foreign threats and domestic disputes. Byzantium was not much less complex than the Islamic or Frankish realms, but it was centuries older, and from tradition come strength and confidence.

Traditions, as we have seen, are made up of many components. We have seen too that states may fall but nevertheless leave potent legacies. With these two ideas in mind, we now turn to the lands that lay astride the western European, Byzantine, and Islamic territories. In considering the Celtic, or Scandinavian, or Slavic worlds, we will be asking what contributions they made to Western civilization, how Western civilization influenced them, and, finally, why they did or did not become permanently "Western."

Suggested Reading

General Surveys

Browning, Robert. *The Byzantine Empire.* 1980. Among general histories of Byzantium, this is the most readable and accessible to students.

Collins, Roger. *Early Medieval Europe, 300–1000.* 1991. A balanced and comprehensive narrative stressing political history. Includes a valuable bibliography.

Hodgson, Marshall G. S. *The Venture of Islam: Conscience and History in a World Civilization.* Vol. 1, *The Classical Age of Islam.* 1958. A stimulating, sympathetic interpretation of Islamic origins.

Kennedy, Hugh. *The Prophet and the Age of the Caliphates: The Islamic Near East from the Sixth to the Eleventh Century.* 1986. Detailed but readable, this is the best modern introduction to the emergence and spread of Islam.

Ostrogorsky, George. *History of the Byzantine State.* Rev. ed. Translated by Joan Hussey. 1969. Massive and detailed, this remains the preferred general history.

The Islamic World

Andrae, Tor. *Mohammed: The Man and His Faith.* 1960. First published in 1936, this brief, engaging book remains the best introduction.

Crone, Patricia, and Martin Hinds. *God's Caliph: Religious Authority in the First Centuries of Islam.* 1986. A sensitive discussion of the emergence of the Islamic polity and of the position of the caliphs.

Rahman, Fazlur. *Islam.* 2d ed. 1979. A thoughtful, readable account of the essentials of Islam from Muhammad's time to our own.

The Byzantine Empire

Hussey, J. M. *The Orthodox Church in the Byzantine Empire.* 1986. A standard book by a great authority. Not a thorough survey so much as a series of reflections by the author. Good on the age of iconoclasm.

Kazhdan, A. P., and Giles Constable. *People and Power in Byzantium: An Introduction to Modern Byzantine Studies.* 1982. A series of penetrating essays on politics, ideology, religion, and culture across the whole Byzantine period.

Mango, Cyril. *Byzantium: The Empire of New Rome.* 1980. By a brilliant art historian, this book is especially strong on cultural history.

The Germanic Kingdoms

Campbell, James, ed. *The Anglo-Saxons.* 1982. Brilliant essays and beautiful illustrations.

Collins, Roger. *Early Medieval Spain.* 1983. An intelligent, readable, comprehensive history by a leading authority.

Fell, Christine. *Women in Anglo-Saxon England.* 1984. Interesting and readable, this book concentrates on depictions of women in literature.

Geary, Patrick J. *Before France and Germany: The Creation and Transformation of the Merovingian World.* 1988. A readable narrative, this book makes accessible the best French and German scholarship.

James, Edward. *The Franks.* 1988. By an archaeologist, this wide-ranging study combines the written and material evidence in the best introduction to Merovingian Gaul.

Mayr-Harting, Henry. *The Coming of Christianity to Anglo-Saxon England.* 3d ed. 1991. A fascinating, challenging interpretation of the English and Irish missions and of their impact on English society and culture.

Noble, Thomas F. X. *The Republic of St. Peter: The Birth of the Papal State, 680–825.* 1984. Detailed analysis of the emergence of papal temporal rule, the Franko-papal alliance, and the papal bureaucracy.

Webster, Leslie, and Janet Backhouse, eds. *The Making of England: Anglo-Saxon Art and Culture, A.D. 600–900.* 1991. A breathtaking and magnificently illustrated survey published to accompany a major British Museum exhibition in 1991–1992.

Wickham, Chris. *Early Medieval Italy: Central Power and Local Society, 400–1000.* 1981. A careful reading of the evidence and scholarship as they relate to both public and private power. Difficult but rewarding.

The World of Charlemagne

Ganshof, François Louis. *Frankish Institutions Under Charlemagne.* Translated by Bryce and Mary Lyon. 1970. A technical yet readable account of the Carolingian government and army by the twentieth century's greatest historian of Charlemagne.

Hodges, Richard, and David Whitehouse. *Mohammed, Charlemagne and the Origins of Europe.* 1983. A stimulating reassessment, from archaeological and anthropological perspectives, of many controversial views concerning the end of the ancient world.

McKitterick, Rosamond. *The Frankish Kingdoms Under the Carolingians.* 1983. Dense and difficult but the fullest recent survey of Carolingian history.

Mütherich, Florentine, and Joachim Gaehde. *Carolingian Painting.* 1976. A fine introduction, with beautiful plates, for the student without any substantial art-historical background.

Riché, Pierre. *Daily Life in the World of Charlemagne.* Translated by Jo Ann McNamara. 1978. A highly readable account of how people lived—from what they ate, to their clothing and dwellings, to their customary beliefs and superstitions.

Stafford, Pauline. *Queens, Concubines, and Dowagers: The King's Wife in the Early Middle Ages.* 1983. Entertaining and informative, this book reveals much about the informal channels of power and influence open to women.

Wemple, Suzanne. *Women in Frankish Society: Marriage and the Cloister, 500 to 900.* 1981. A pioneering study, this book is not easy to read but contains much valuable information and interesting interpretations.

Weighing the Evidence

THE MANUSCRIPT BOOK

How long would it take you to copy this whole textbook by hand? We know that it took about a year for two skilled monastic scribes to copy a Bible. Every medieval book was literally a manuscript (from *manuscriptum*, "written by hand"). Manuscripts contain important texts but are also revealing artifacts in their own right.

Codicology and paleography are the sciences of manuscript study. Codicology, the study of books as physical objects, investigates the materials and techniques used to make them. Paleography, the study of handwriting, seeks to read texts and to date and localize surviving books.

Depicted here is a folio (a page) of the Dagulf Psalter, named for the Carolingian scribe who wrote it in 795 on Charlemagne's orders as a gift for Pope Hadrian I (r. 772–795). The rich and powerful often used books as gifts. A psalter is a collection of the 150 biblical Psalms and other canticles—songs or prayers derived from the Bible and used for worship. Can you make out the letters INCIPIUNT CANTICI, at the very top of the page? They mean "Here begin the canticles." The text is the Canticle of Isaiah (Isaiah 12:1–6). Its title is CANTICUM ESAIE PROP ^{h}.

Cathedrals and monasteries usually had *scriptoria*, "writing offices," where scribes and illuminators worked with bookmakers to produce manuscripts. Manuscripts were made from parchment. To make parchment, an animal skin—preferably sheepskin or calfskin—was soaked in a caustic lye solution to remove hair and blemishes, scraped until it was smooth, and then dried on a stretching rack. After drying, the skin was cut to the desired size. The smallest surviving manuscript is 2 inches by 3 inches; the largest is about 36 by 19. The larger the pages, the more costly was the book. One huge Bible produced in Bede's Northumbria required the hides of 500 sheep.

A Quire

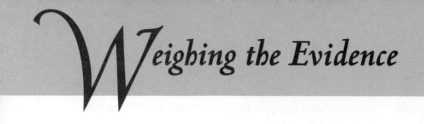

After the parchment was cut and lined—notice how straight and even the lines are on the psalter folio—the bookmaker took four sheets, or folios, of parchment, laid them down together, and folded them, placing the fold at the left, to form a booklet of sixteen pages called a quire—see the drawing. Because the two sides of a piece of parchment differ in color—the "hair side," or outside, is usually darker than the "flesh side," or inside—the quires were arranged so that hair sides faced hair sides and flesh sides faced flesh sides. A manuscript consisted of many quires sewn together.

The first page of the first quire was numbered 1^{r} and 1^{v}, or 1 *recto* and 1 *verso,* meaning 1 "right side" and 1 "turned side." The second sheet was numbered 2^{r} and 2^{v}. Today, book pages are numbered 1, 2, 3, and so on, and books always start with an odd-numbered page on the right side—an inheritance from medieval manuscripts.

Scribes and illuminators received the prepared quires. Scribes wrote text onto the parchment. Illuminators painted beautiful pictures or designs. You have on pages 299, 302, 316, 363, 365, and 404 examples of the magnificent illuminations that were put into medieval books. Most books, however, had no such images at all.

Now you are ready to learn some paleography. We have already deciphered the first two lines of the folio shown here. These lines are written in a "display script." For visual appeal and to facilitate reference, scribes often used different handwritings, colors, or both to highlight first letters, first words, or first lines. Books, like the one you are reading, maintain this tradition. The huge writing—can you make out CONFITE?—marks the beginning of Isaiah's text. It continues,

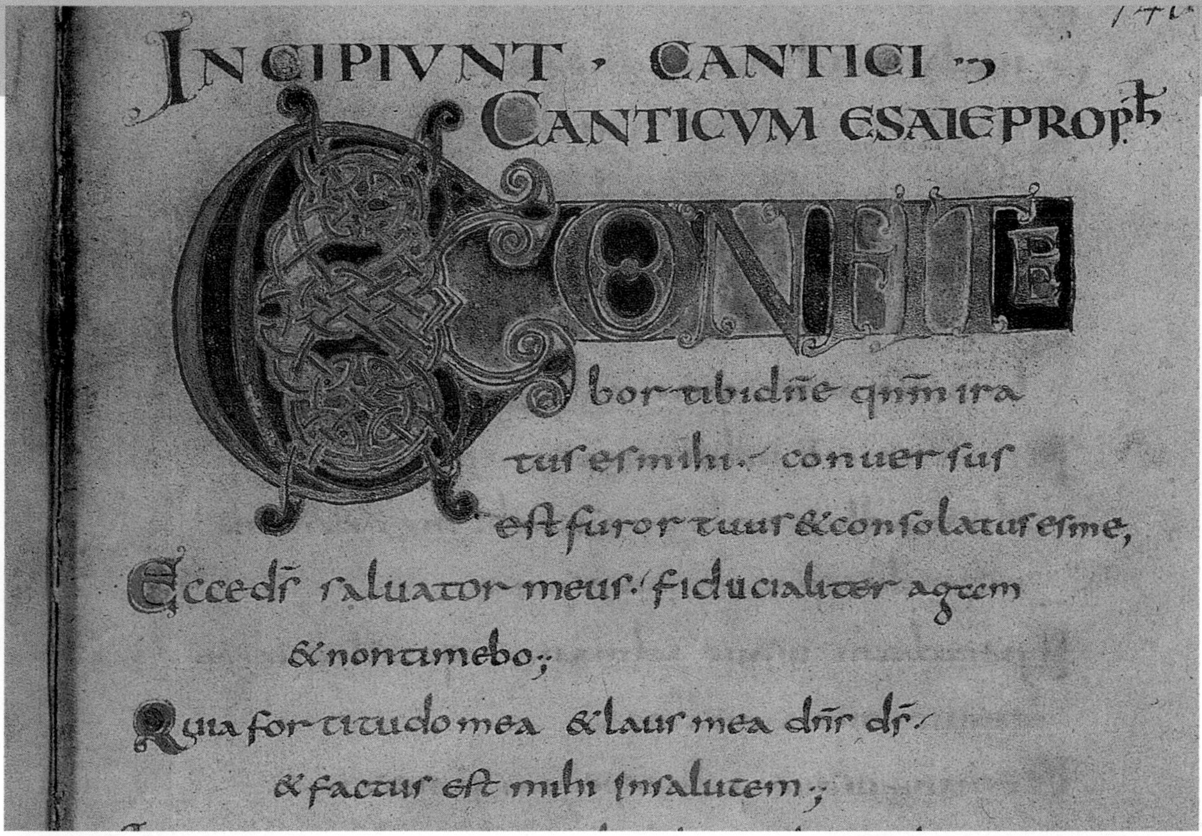

The Dagulf Psalter *(Osterreichische Nationalbibliothek)*

on line four, with *bor tibi dne qum ira*. Line five carries on with *tus es mihi.* *conversus*. Look at line six: *est furor tuus&consolatusesme*. Can you make out the letters yourself?

Several things bear notice here. First, the main script is Caroline minuscule, the new script that accompanied Charlemagne's educational reforms. Because of its clarity, it is the basis for many modern typefaces. Compare the letters in the picture with the ones you are reading.

Second, notice the frequent recourse to abbreviation. Writing was time- and space-consuming, prompting the development of elaborate systems of abbreviation. Can you see, in line four, the letters *dne* with a strike over them, and then the letters *qum*, also with a strike? In this case the words expand to *domine* and *quoniam*. Look at line two, where you see PROP^{h}, shorthand for *Prophetae* ("Prophet"). Also notice the ampersands in lines six, eight, nine, and ten. They stand for *et*, Latin for "and." Note too how the last words in line six run together.

Third, in antiquity, texts had neither breaks between words nor punctuation. As non–Latin-speakers learned to write the language, however, they usually put breaks between the words to facilitate understanding. You can see that most of this text has breaks, except in line six. In lines one, eight, and ten, you can also see a rather curious symbol: ;. It is a full stop, or period.

What else might you learn from a manuscript? Handwriting and systems of abbreviation are distinctive, and specialists use them to date and localize manuscripts. Because parchment was prepared in different ways, some manuscripts can be dated or placed by an analysis of their parchment. Inks differed in chemistry and in appearance and thus help to date and localize books. Styles of illumination and forms of images can also be localized or traced from one scriptorium to another. By knowing when, where, and by whom books were written or illuminated, historians can reconstruct the life and work of intellectual centers that were scattered long ago.

It is estimated that a medieval manuscript without illuminations was worth one year's wages for an ordinary working person. Would you spend a year's wages for a book?

CHAPTER 9

The Frontiers of the Latin West, ca. 600–1300

Twelfth-century French schools advanced the idea of a "Translation of Studies"—their way of saying a development of civilization—from Jerusalem to Athens to Rome to Paris. The persistence of this line of thought has always made it easy to identify Western civilization principally with its core regions: Italy, France, western Germany, and England. These areas were often more populous, more powerful economically and militarily, and more trend-setting culturally than their neighbors. But those neighbors, to whom we now turn, have always been important to the historical experience of the West.

The Celtic lands, Scandinavia, the Slavic countries, Byzantium, and the Islamic world hold a great enveloping mass of peoples who had, and have, complex relations with Europe's core. For example, the Arthurian legends are among the greatest treasures of Western literature. Although they are transmitted mainly in French versions, Arthur was a Celt, and the first people to tell stories about him spoke Welsh and Irish. The military and commercial ventures of the Scandinavian peoples contributed to the gradual movement of the center of Western civilization away from the Mediterranean basin and toward northwestern Europe. There has not been a time from the ninth century to the late twentieth when the Balkans were not a tinderbox threatening the whole West with conflagration. Russia, one of the last of the Slavic realms to emerge, both taught and learned from its Germanic, Byzantine, and Muslim neighbors. From the Middle Ages to the present, Russia has been both a European and an Asian power. As we look at the thirteenth century, we can see that it was Jenghiz Khan much more

Crosier (bishop's staff) from Clonmacnoise, Ireland. Bronze sheet on wood.

than Muhammad who determined that Mesopotamia would finally be more Eastern than Western.

In about 600, the Latin West, Byzantium, and the Islamic lands were about to begin their historic ventures. Each was rooted in the Greco-Roman and Judeo-Christian past. By 1300 the late antique Germanic West had expanded to include Celtic, Scandinavian, and Slavic territories. Dublin, Stockholm, and Prague are Western cities. By 1300 Byzantium had been shattered, first by western Christians, who began as allies and ended as conquerors, and then by Mongols. These successors to the Huns, Avars, and Magyars, called by contemporaries "The Devil's Horsemen," also destroyed the remains of the Abbassid caliphate, left the Islamic world permanently divided, and drew much of the old caliphate away from the Mediterranean and toward Asia.

The Celtic Realms

Jerome (331–420), translator of the Vulgate Bible, once commented on the similarities in the languages spoken in the Rhineland and Anatolia. Those languages were Celtic, and the Celts had been dominant in Europe when the Romans entered the scene in the time of Julius Caesar. The Romans and then the Germans eventually overwhelmed the continental Celts, but Celtic realms in the British Isles survived and exist today. Our focus is on Ireland, Wales, and Scotland, but there were once Celts all over Europe.

Rome held Britain for nearly four centuries but conquered only a portion of south Wales and entertained only diplomatic and commercial relations with Scotland and Ireland. In many respects, the Celtic lands evolved like the Germanic lands on the Continent, although more slowly. Christianity entered the Celtic lands in the fifth century but adopted distinctive local forms in the sixth and seventh centuries. Small, highly personalized political entities grew larger and more territorial. Social hierarchies became more complex and economies diversified, not least because of increasing contacts with the wider European world. Then in the eleventh and twelfth centuries came the watershed event in each Celtic area: the coming of the Normans and the English.

Early Celtic Kingdoms

Each of the Celtic lands is physically distinctive, and geography contributed to their histories in important ways (Map 9.1). Ireland is a small country with a homogeneous population. Relative to its population, Ireland has much fertile land. The climate is mild and damp. Few natural features in Ireland impede the movement of people. From prehistoric times Ireland maintained contacts by sea with Britain and the Continent.

Wales, which has always supported life grudgingly, is a small, rugged land of harsh, unpredictable weather. Ridges of hills running mainly east and west make for limited expanses of good land and difficult communications. Like Ireland, Wales maintained active contacts with all the Celtic realms by sea, in part because the long Welsh frontier with England could be easily crossed only in the extreme north and south. Wales was difficult to unite or to dominate.

Scotland was the least homogeneous of the Celtic lands. Its original Celtic inhabitants were the Picts. The Welsh once occupied portions of the southwest. The Irish conquered the central portions of western Scotland, and the English from Northumbria pushed far up the east coast. Physical diversity rivals human. The highlands are mountainous and inhospitable. Their people have always been fiercely independent. The central zones contain good agricultural land and permit much easier communications. The lowlands have the most fertile land but no protection from the English to the south; for centuries this has been bloody ground.

Three factors influenced the early political history of all the Celtic realms: powerful, ambitious individuals; the church; and the Vikings. The basic unit of power in all Celtic societies was a small territory inhabited and ruled by a single kin group. As in other places from Arabia to France, these groupings consisted of male relatives in a single line of descent, relatives by marriage, unrelated clients, and allies. As many as 150 of these groupings existed in Ireland, each one led by a king. The Scottish *lairds* (lords) and Welsh princes likewise headed families and territories that were small, though larger than the Irish ones.

In the fifth century the O'Neill family from the northwest of Ireland began extending its au-

Map 9.1 The Celtic Lands Rugged terrain, numerous small territories, few cities, easy access to the sea, and powerful English neighbors decisively marked the history of the Celtic peoples.

thority over neighboring regions. In the ninth century men from the southwest rallied much of southern Ireland against the O'Neills and, after a period of near anarchy, Brian Boru (r. 976–1014) became the first ruler to exercise real authority over most of Ireland. Irish tradition regards Brian as the first "national" hero, but he was actually little more than an ambitious, ruthless warrior. For a century after his death his successors, the O'Briens, worked to create a more territorial and less personal kind of kingship.

In Wales, Rhodri the Great (d. 898) and his grandson Howell the Good (d. 950) also moved toward territorial and institutional unity. Howell was the first person to rule most of Wales. He issued coins in his own name and issued a revised code of Welsh law for all under his authority.

Scotland might have been divided between the English and the Irish, but in 685 the Picts defeated the English and removed their effective threat for centuries. From the Irish zone in western Scotland arose Kenneth MacAlpin (r. 843–858), who extended his authority over the Picts as well as over the formerly English lowlands. Kenneth's reign marks the faint beginnings of Scottish unity in fact as well as in legend.

Each of those key figures in Ireland, Wales, and Scotland attracted followers and extended

Howell the Good This picture of Howell, from a manuscript of his laws, depicts him wearing a crown, holding a scepter, and sitting on a tufted throne that looks like a palace. These are key symbols of rule. *(The National Library of Wales)*

his authority by military success. In this they were like the Germanic leaders whom we have already met.

Christianity entered all the Celtic lands in Late Antiquity in circumstances that are shrouded in legend. Each region had famous missionary saints whose lives cannot be told with any confidence. Saint Patrick, who lived in the first half of the fifth century, is the best known. His father was a minor Roman official in the north of Britain, and Patrick spent his adult life as a bishop and missionary in the northern half of Ireland. Probably his see was located at Armagh in Ulster.

The O'Neills, who controlled Armagh, tried hard to get all the Irish to recognize its primacy, seeing this as an effective means of extending their own power. Their plan failed on two counts. First, many of the Irish refused to acknowledge the ecclesiastical authority of Armagh precisely because of its connection to the O'Neills. Second, during the sixth and seventh centuries the tiny political units into which Ireland was divided were often endowed by their leading families with monasteries whose abbots were powerful men who did not seek, or who had been excluded from, secular authority. Ireland had no cities and no regular ecclesiastical hierarchy. Where bishops existed, they often resided in monasteries and were subordinate to abbots. The Irish church was highly decentralized and a bar to national unification, despite the O'Neill efforts.

In Wales several bishoprics eventually arose, but they owed almost nothing to the support of secular political figures. The bishops of St. David's in Dyfed, as the heirs of Wales's semi-legendary patron saint, tried to extend their authority over the whole Welsh church but lacked the power to do so.

In Scotland there were bishoprics in the formerly English south and a primarily monastic organization in the heavily Irish west. In such a diverse land, Scottish kings failed to gain recognition throughout Scotland for a Pictish bishopric at St. Andrews. In the Frankish or Anglo-Saxon kingdoms, the church played a unifying role. In the Celtic lands, in contrast, the churches contributed to disunity.

The Vikings constantly raided both coasts of Scotland and both shores of the Irish Sea from the late eighth century to the early eleventh but produced very different results in the three realms. In Ireland, men from the south made common cause with the Vikings to weaken the O'Neill family. Later, Brian Boru made his reputation as Ireland's liberator from the Vikings. In Wales, as in the Frankish world, constant, local, unpredictable Viking raids contributed to decentralization. In Scotland, powerful men saw the Vikings neither as a means to avoid royal power nor as a justification for uncoordinated local action. Instead, great men rallied around the king in a zealous effort to defend against the outsider. Despite destructive raids, the Vikings contributed to Scottish unity.

England and the Celtic World

In 1066 Duke William of Normandy led a band of adventurers across the English Channel to conquer England, and for two generations after 1066 many more Normans crossed to England. We call these men "Normans" because they descended from Vikings ("Northmen") who in the early tenth century had settled in the West Frankish realm, in the region known afterward as Normandy. Every Celtic realm felt an aftershock of the Norman conquest of England.

Normans began crossing the border into south Wales late in the eleventh century, hoping in that wild country to escape the tight rule of William in England. Some went on their own; others were invited by Welsh magnates who planned to use them as mercenaries against other Welshmen. In this situation, Prince Grufydd ap Cynan turned to Henry I (r. 1100–1135), William's son, and promised allegiance if Henry would recognize his claim to rule all of Wales. Henry agreed, seeing such an alliance as a means of checking the Norman lords who had been entering Wales without getting bogged down in local squabbles. Until 1277 this loose dependence of one great Welsh lord on the king of England persisted.

Finally, urged on by seemingly endless quarrels with the Welsh, Edward I of England (r. 1272–1307) decided to conquer Wales. In 1277 he began a brutal campaign and completed his conquest by erecting and garrisoning castles at strategic positions all over Wales. (See the feature, "Weighing the Evidence: The Medieval Castle," on pages 342 and 343.) He also made his eldest son the Prince of Wales—to this day the official position of the heir to the English throne—and governor of the region. In the fourteenth century English law and institutions were gradually introduced, and the Welsh church was subjected to the authority of Canterbury. Wales was the only one of the Celtic realms to become fully dependent on England.

In Scotland eleventh-century kings seeking to extend their power to the south met Normans coming north. Some of these Normans took service under Scottish kings, but others remained loyal to the family of William. Allegiances became very blurred. Between 1100 and 1260 England and Scotland went to war four times over the question of lordship, but never with decisive results.

Spurred by his successes in Wales and by a sense that he was the rightful overlord of England's neighbors, Edward set out in the 1280s to annex Scotland. In response, Robert Bruce (r. 1306–1328), a dashing knight of Norman extraction, rallied the Scots to his standard. In 1314 he led an army that defeated the much larger force of Edward II (r. 1307–1327) at Bannockburn. In 1328 Robert achieved his life's goal: formal recognition by England, and by rulers all over Europe, of Scotland's independence. The long and bloody wars against the English and Robert's leadership helped to forge a nation out of the disparate and quarrelsome Scots. Of the Celtic realms, only Scotland freed itself from the English.

Ireland falls between the other two. In 1159 King Rory O'Connor turned to Henry II (r. 1135–1189) of England for mercenaries to help

High Cross of Monasterboice The cross of Muiredach, an abbot of Monasterboice in Ireland who died in 922, is a splendid example of a type of monument widespread in the Celtic world. It is covered with excellent sculpture depicting biblical scenes relating to the life of Christ. *(Michael Jenner/Robert Harding Picture Library)*

him consolidate his own position. By 1171 Henry had invaded Ireland because he realized that his hopes of influencing the country through a client ruler were fading as many Norman magnates gained Irish land over whose resources he had no control. Down to the 1250s many "Anglo-Irish," as the settlers from England were called, took over about two-thirds of Ireland. English royal control over them was tenuous at best. An English administration headquartered at Dublin introduced English law and institutions, and the Irish church, though not submitted to Canterbury like Wales's, became episcopal and territorial. Many Irish resisted the Anglo-Irish and in the early 1300s initiated a series of revolts that left England by the end of the fifteenth century in charge of only a small circle of land around Dublin called "The Pale." Ireland "beyond the Pale" was weakened and impoverished irreparably by rebellions against the Anglo-Irish.

Social Distinctions and Economic Expansion

Between 600 and 1300, Celtic societies were hierarchical, and Celtic economies were agricultural. But social structures were not rigid, and the economies were expanding.

Irish and Welsh law codes (comparably early materials do not survive from Scotland) reveal about a dozen gradations of free men. Personal freedom was obviously critical; and, among the free, status differences were very important. Status could be gained or lost easily. The literature of Celtic societies lays great stress on offenses against honor. This emphasis points to a society that was hierarchical and status conscious.

Women in Celtic societies shared status ranks with their menfolk but derived little power or privilege from them. No woman reigned in a Celtic society, and more than once the Scottish nobility changed allegiance rather than face the risk of being ruled by a woman. Saint Brigit (d. 523), Ireland's second patron saint after Patrick, founded Ireland's first and greatest convent of nuns at Kildare. Like the Germanic world, the Celtic realms produced very few female saints. Unlike convents in the Germanic world, Celtic convents were not a usual outlet for the talents and ambitions of aristocratic women. Celtic women were prevented from acting independently at law, and they usually could not inherit land. Irish men frequently had a wife (a woman to produce heirs and cement social relationships), a concubine (a sexual partner who often lived in the man's house for long periods and who might actually monopolize his affections), and a mistress (an occasional and rarely co-resident sexual partner). Men could divorce their wives easily (see the box, "The Furnishings of a Welsh Household"). The church tried hard to sanctify marriage in Celtic societies but had limited success. Celtic literature is full of stories about women of great beauty and cunning but has little to say about women who possessed formal power and influence.

At the other end of the social spectrum were slaves, most often the human booty of warfare. The evidence suggests that slavery was gradually disappearing and serfdom was uncommon in Celtic societies. The number of persons at the bottom of the social ladder, however, seems to have been increasing. In Wales and Ireland the increase owed something to the Norman/English landlords who mercilessly exploited the local peasantry, but it owed more to the absence of primogeniture—the assignment of lands and titles to the first-born son—and the deep-rootedness of partible inheritance among the Celts.

Basically, all legitimate males had a right to an equal share in the family inheritance. This division of property ruined the fortunes of many individuals and whole families. For example, a certain man in Wales succeeded to a sizable estate in the early 1200s, and a century later the estate had been divided among twenty-seven people. In 1286 there were thirteen legitimate claimants to the Scottish throne. Only ecclesiastical establishments, which could inherit but not bequeath because they did not die, stood a good chance of increasing their holdings. Status in Celtic societies was personal and not, in principle, based on wealth. Nevertheless, countless people found themselves so reduced in material resources that they lost both rank and power.

Running counter to the social and legal forces that weakened individuals and groups was a steadily improving economy. From the twelfth century and perhaps earlier, new land was being brought into cultivation. This phenomenon can be observed from Ireland to Byzantium and be-

The Furnishings of a Welsh Household

This passage from the laws of Howell the Good concerns the distribution of household property in case of divorce. The aim was to achieve a nearly even split. Notice the kinds of things a house might hold and who got what.

The husband shall have all the pigs, the wife the sheep. The husband shall have all the horses and mares, the oxen and cows, bullocks and heifers; the wife shall have the goats. . . . All the vessels for milk, except one pail, are the wife's; all the dishes, except one meat dish, are the husband's. One cart and yoke are the wife's. All the jars and drinking vessels are the husband's. Of the bedding, the husband shall have all the bedclothes which are beneath, the wife those which are above. The husband shall have the cauldron, the pillow, the winnowing sheet, the coulter, the wood axe, the gimlet [hole-borer], the fire dog, all the sickles except one, and the gridiron. The wife shall have the pan and the tripod, the broadaxe and the sieve, the ploughshare, the flax and the seed of the flax, and the precious things except gold and silver. If there are any of these (gold or silver) they are to be divided in two equal parts. The products of the loom shall be divided in two equal parts, both linens and woolens. The husband shall have the barn and the grain and whatever is above or in the ground, and the hens and the geese and one cat. The wife shall have the meat that is salted and the cheese that is fresh . . . and the vessel of butter . . . and the ham . . . and as much of the flour as she can carry. Each of them shall have his or her personal clothing, except the cloaks which shall be divided.

Source: Ian F. Fletcher, ed. and trans., *Latin Redaction A of the Law of Hywel* (Aberystwyth, Wales: Center for Advanced Welsh and Celtic Studies, 1986), pp. 58–59.

speaks a rising population and growing prosperity. The majority of Celts engaged in agriculture, particularly the cultivation of cereal grains such as wheat, rye, and oats. Animal husbandry was practiced everywhere too. Irish literature and law are positively full of cows. Personal status, legal fines, boasts, and insults were reckoned in cattle. Sheep were raised everywhere, mainly for wool.

At first the Celtic realms were almost without cities and merchants. The Celts did not inherit Roman cities and for a long time did not need them for government, religious, or commercial reasons. The earliest cities in Ireland were Scandinavian foundations: Dublin, Limerick, Waterford, Wexford. The Vikings, and then the Normans, gave a great impetus to urban growth in Wales. Quite often towns grew up around monasteries or castles introduced by the Normans. Each establishment provided a good-sized, fixed population that could be served by a community of merchants. Moreover, the Vikings and the Normans had far-flung commercial ties that helped to integrate the Celtic realms into a wider zone of economic connections ranging from Scandinavia to the cities of the Continent. The Celts had always exported wool and cloth, slaves, and fish. Imports included luxury goods such as wines and silks. English and Scandinavian intrusions in the Celtic areas, though damaging politically, were commercially beneficial.

Forms of Celtic Culture

Christianity brought with it to the Celtic lands the Latin culture of the Mediterranean world. To promote the understanding of biblical and patristic texts, schools concentrated on grammar. Irish schools, in particular, were renowned for their learning and linguistic competence. Irish scholars were admired for their learning and their com-

The Book of Kells This famous manuscript may have been made at Iona in about 810 but resided for centuries at the monastery of Kells. Depicted here is a "Chi-Rho" page (the first two letters in Christ's name in Greek). The sheer exuberance of the decoration is indescribable. *(The Board of Trinity College, Dublin)*

plex Latin style. Many young Englishmen went to Ireland to study, and several Carolingian schools had Irish masters. After playing an important role in early medieval Europe, Celtic scholarship declined amid waves of Viking, Norman, and English invasions.

In the seventh century Welsh and Irish writers began to compose native stories in their own languages. They produced abundant poetry of a very high order and also histories, saints' lives, and laws. This material represents the earliest, and one of the largest, bodies of vernacular literature from medieval Europe. Few people today study the Celtic languages, but many know of Arthur and his knights and of the star-crossed lovers Tristan and Iseult. Christianity and classical culture influenced every European people, and the Celts added their own ideas to the mix.

Gerald of Wales, a twelfth-century monk and man of letters, said, after he had seen the Book of Kells, that he was sure it was "the work of angels." The book is a Latin Bible decorated in ways never dreamed of in the Mediterranean homeland of both Latin and the Bible. Irish art, best known from paintings in beautiful manuscripts, is intricate, delicate, and moving. Its standard was superb when it burst on the scene in the seventh century, and that high standard was maintained until invasions made life too insecure in Irish religious houses. For centuries thereafter, Irish decorative techniques continued to influence European painters.

The Lands of Scandinavia

Scandinavia, a word that first appeared in Roman writings in the first century, refers to the northernmost Germanic lands that became Denmark, Norway, and Sweden (Map 9.2). Three broad themes mark the historical development of these lands. The first is the paramount role of external relations, whether military, political, or commercial. The second is the slow emergence of centralized states. The third is a rich Old Norse literature, which kept Latin culture in a secondary position.

A consideration of Scandinavia must take geography into account. The sea, not the land, is the great fact. Norway has more than a thousand miles of coastline, and no point in Denmark is more than thirty-five miles from the sea. The Baltic and North seas and the Atlantic Ocean, as well as the numerous islands lying in those bodies of water, are all central to the history of Scandinavia. The sea was a source of food and an avenue for trade, conquest, and adventure.

Denmark is the smallest of the Scandinavian lands but in the Middle Ages was the most powerful. Denmark had plenty of good land, a better climate than Norway and Sweden, and both population and resources exceeding those of its Scandinavian neighbors. Southern and central Norway had mountains in the east and reasonable amounts of arable land in the west but not enough land to support a large population. Northern Norway and northern Sweden were extremely harsh. Sweden was peculiar in two respects. First, much of its best land was often un-

Map 9.2 Scandinavia Poor land and the omnipresent sea invited Scandinavians to adventures abroad and retarded political development at home.

der Danish control, so central Sweden developed instead of the potentially richer south. Second, Sweden faces, and throughout much of its history has looked, to the east. So when Danish and Norwegian Vikings were raiding France and England, the Swedes turned to the Baltic and sailed down Russia's rivers.

Conquest and Commerce Overseas

For about three centuries, beginning in the late eighth century, Scandinavians put their mark all over the map. Raids in England and in the Frankish world played a role in breaking down the power of central governments. By the middle of the ninth century, however, raiding began to give way to permanent settlement. Norwegians established a base at Dublin in 839, and three Viking bands began the systematic conquest of northeastern England in 865. In 862 a Swedish force founded a settlement at Kiev from which the Russian state eventually developed. Between 870 and 930 many Norwegians and some Danes moved to Iceland, creating settlements that continue to this day. In 911 a Norwegian band seized the region of Normandy in western France. In the middle of the tenth century, the emperor at Byzantium had an elite troop of mercenaries, the Varangian Guard, who were Vikings.

Raids and settlement are only one part of this overseas story. Another part concerns politics, diplomacy, and empire building. There were fierce rivalries between the Norwegian settlers in Ireland and the Danish newcomers to England. North German princes wove an intricate web of alliances in Scandinavia to secure commercial advantages in the Baltic. The Swedes once allied with the Poles in an attempt to thwart Danish designs on their land. In the eleventh century the Danish king Cnut made himself king of Norway and of England too (see page 371). He followed his father, who had invaded England in 1013, tempted to do so by the weakness of the reigning king and the successes of Viking raiders since the late 970s. Cnut, who reigned in England from 1016 to 1035, was no barbarian. He was literate and visited the German and papal courts.

Scandinavians also made their presence felt in commerce. Scandinavian merchants were great facilitators of long-distance commercial transactions. Northern traders exchanged furs, timber, amber, and slaves for gold coins and precious objects (jewels, fine metalwork, porcelains) from the Muslim world. From western Europe Scandinavians received coarse pottery, millstones, and weapons (especially Frankish swords) in exchange for the products of their eastern connections. As Europe became increasingly Christian, and as church reform movements imposed dietary restrictions on Catholics, the Scandinavian fishing industry prospered as it prepared and shipped the dried and salted fish that Catholics everywhere ate on a hundred or so meatless days each year.

Political Struggles at Home

Each Scandinavian region entered the historical period with a highly fragmented power structure. Political participation was widely shared within very small areas among free men who assembled regularly in meetings called *Things* to debate issues that were important to the community. None of these little areas imagined itself to have any connection with other areas. There was no conception of a state.

The beginnings of state building in Scandinavia are not easy to describe because of a lack of contemporary evidence. Three forces were certainly critical. One was internal. Within particular areas some men, or some families, came to have greater wealth and power than others. Chieftains arose by attaching men to themselves as a result of successful military activity. This

Oseberg Ship Discovered in 1880, the Oseberg ship was buried in Norway in (probably) the tenth century. The ship belonged to a rich and powerful person, perhaps to a king. It is 21.6 meters long and 5 meters wide. Its crew would have been thirty to forty men. *(University Museum of National Antiquities, Oslo)*

body of retainers, the *hird,* is like the small group of associates around other Germanic rulers. Other men, perhaps not powerful or renowned enough to join the hird, attached themselves as ordinary soldiers to great chieftains. Initially this activity was local, but gradually its scope began to extend to wider areas in Scandinavia and then to the outside world, where we know it as Viking activity. By the late eighth century personal charisma, military prowess and success, and wealth gained from booty and tribute enhanced the position of some chieftains to a position comparable to that of the Germanic leaders living along the borders of the Roman Empire in the fourth and fifth centuries.

The other two forces critical to state building were both external and are almost certainly interrelated. All of Scandinavia was beyond the borders of the Roman Empire and, as far as is known, beyond the reach of Christianity before the eighth century. Rome and the Catholic church both communicated to medieval Europe ideas about central government, public institutions, law, and the ordered routines of complex societies. Scandinavians acquired all these ideas secondhand as they watched the Frankish and Anglo-Saxon states develop nearby and as they became familiar with Christianity.

Christian merchants who settled around northern trading emporia, as well as missionaries sent north by Anglo-Saxons, Franks, and Germans, brought the Catholic faith to these northern lands. By the ninth century Scandinavia began to come to terms with political ideas concerning hierarchies of officialdom, territorial instead of personal rule, court ceremonial, and official documents. Only in the ninth century did a few figures try to turn petty local kingships into powerful and widely respected offices.

In all Scandinavian kingdoms the growth of royal power was impeded by great men who viewed themselves as the equals of the kings who wished to dominate them and by meddling by other Scandinavian rulers. Cnut's successors, for example, lost their control of England and Norway and thereafter could not control the powerful Danish chieftains. By the twelfth and thirteenth centuries, Denmark was regularly at the mercy of the German monarchy and nobility. Norway's monarchy also emerged in the ninth century; but, from about 950 to the end of Cnut's

The Jelling Stone King Harald Bluetooth of Denmark (d. ca. 984) erected this stone with its runic inscription as a memorial to his parents. It reads, "King Harald had this monument made for his father Gorm and his mother Thyri: This was the Harald who won for himself all Denmark and Norway, and made the Danes Christian." *(National Museum, Copenhagen)*

reign in 1035, Norway was under Danish control. After the Norwegian kings had shed the Danish yoke, they patiently and skillfully wore down noble opposition. Their basic technique was to force nobles to join the royal hird, changing them from independent magnates to subservient courtiers. This same tendency could be observed in almost all the monarchies of twelfth- and thirteenth-century Europe.

The scales were definitely tipping to the Crown when in 1319 the reigning king of Norway died without male heirs and the Norwegian throne passed through his daughter to the royal house of Sweden. This third great Scandinavian realm was the last to emerge and the least stable. Denmark's long control of the south was damaging to the Swedish crown as was the relative openness of the eastern Baltic and Russian frontier. As states in western Europe stabilized in the eleventh and twelfth centuries, they put an end to Viking opportunities, but the lands and waters east of Sweden remained uncontrolled for centuries. Swedish nobles could strike out for wealth and adventure and build impressive followings, and there was little the Crown could do to stop this destabilizing behavior.

Where possible, the Scandinavian kings promoted the growth of the Catholic church to enhance their own power. Kings saw bishops as educated, talented allies in the business of building central governments. Norwegian kings were especially successful in incorporating bishops into their hird, where they were able to counter the secular nobility. By 1060 there were eight bishops in Denmark, and in 1103–1104 the city of Lund, in the southern part of Sweden controlled by Denmark, was elevated to an archbishopric, freeing the Danish church from its dependence on German ecclesiastical control. King Olaf of Norway (r. 1016–1028), affectionately remembered by Norwegians as "Saint Olaf," was the first Norwegian king actively to promote the Christianization of his country. Only in 1152 was the seaport of Trondheim made an archbishopric for Norway, independent of Lund and Danish influence.

Life and Literature

Literature written in dialects of Old Norse, the language carried from Norway to Iceland, reveals much of what can be said about Scandinavian society between 600 and 1300. Scandinavia's geography and economy did not initially provide for extremes of wealth and rank. Although nobles did emerge during the Viking period and some slaves could always be found in Scandinavia, most people were farmers and fishermen of modest means who cherished their personal freedom. Free status was almost the only requirement for political participation. The consolidation of states, however, produced a more hierarchical society. By the twelfth century, landed aristocracies existed in all Scandinavian realms as a relatively small number of men came by purchase, coercion, or royal grant into possession of large amounts of land. These landed magnates were the chief obstacles to the growth of royal power.

The coming of Christianity and the consolidation of states did not improve and may even have diminished the roles of women. For example, women had priestly roles in the religion of pagan Scandinavia but not under Christianity. Convents of nuns were centers of cultural life in Frankish and Anglo-Saxon Europe, but female monasticism came late and lightly to Scandinavia. In the traditional northern family, the woman's role was to communicate the family history, as well as medical knowledge and magic. The church, however, frowned on women in teaching roles, so the spread of Christianity may have undermined one of women's key traditional functions in Scandinavian society.

Women had almost no political rights in Scandinavia. They could not speak in meetings of the Thing. At law women could give testimony but not act in their own right. Daughters were under the guardianship of their male relatives, and husbands were responsible for their wives. A daughter could not inherit land if she had brothers; among women, only widows had any real property rights. As states became stronger, and as aristocracies became entrenched, women everywhere in Europe lost the kinds of power and influence that they had possessed when society was local, egalitarian, and fluid.

Scandinavia had writing before it had either literature—Latin or Norse—or Christianity. Museums today are full of stones, sometimes impressively big ones, with strange carvings, or runes, on them. The runic script was used only for inscriptions—for example, for funerary memorials—not for literature. In the twelfth and thirteenth centuries, the introduction of Christianity, contact with Europe, the emergence of more settled politics, and a longing for the old days of free men and great adventures combined to call forth a vast and impressive literature. The two most significant bodies of material are law codes and sagas. The Norse word *saga* means "things said" or "things told" and reveals that the stories began as oral traditions.

Most of the surviving sagas were either written or copied in Iceland. There are two kinds of sagas: historical ones and family chronicles. Historical sagas recount, in a mix of fact and fiction, the great deeds and heroes of the Viking age, as well as the settlement of Greenland and Iceland. Family chronicles relate in both truth and fable histories of great families that were proud of their freedom and independence (see the box, "Gudrun's Dreams, Complex Lives"). The composers of the sagas were wonderful storytellers. In the sagas there is an elegiac tone, a sense of regret at the passing of personal freedom and the old heroic ways.

Having mentioned the presence of this Norse literature, we must note the absence of Latin literature. Christianity came late to Scandinavia, and

Gudrun's Dreams, Complex Lives

The theme of Gudrun's ill-fated love matches is one of the powerful stories in **Laxdaela Saga** *(ca. 1250). In this excerpt, Gudrun asks Gest, a friend of her father, to interpret her dreams. The interpretations give a feel for this saga, for storytelling, and for some big issues in Scandinavia.*

Gudrun was the loveliest woman in Iceland at that time, and also the most intelligent. . . . Gest told her "I can see clearly what your dreams signify. . . . You will have four husbands, and I suspect that when you marry the first one it will not be a love match for you. . . . You will leave him. In your second dream you had a silver ring on your hand; this means you will be married to a second husband, an excellent man whom you will love dearly but only for a short time. I wouldn't be surprised if you were to lose him by drowning. In your third dream you had a gold ring on your hand; this means you will have a third husband, but he will not excel your second to the degree that you think this metal rarer and more precious than silver. I have the feeling that there will have been a change of faith by then, and that this husband will have embraced that new faith [Christianity]. . . . You dreamed that you saw this ring broken in two, and that you saw blood coming from the two pieces. This means that your husband will be slain. . . . In your fourth dream you were wearing a helmet of gold set with precious stones; this means you will have a fourth husband. He will be the greatest chieftain of them all, and he will dominate you completely."

Source: Slightly adapted from *Laxdaela Saga,* translated with an introduction by Magnus Magnusson and Hermann Pálsson (Harmondsworth, England: Penguin, 1969), pp. 118, 121–122.

monasticism, which did so much to foster Latin Christian culture elsewhere, was not a meaningful presence in Scandinavia before the middle of the twelfth century, when royal patronage and an emerging ecclesiastical hierarchy created favorable conditions.

The World of the Slavs

Together with the Celts and Germans, a dozen or so Slavic groups make up the historical peoples of Europe. Rome neither conquered Slavic territory nor enlisted Slavs as federates. In Late Antiquity most Slavs lived above the Carpathian Mountains in what is now Poland. The Slavs, who were settled farmers and not nomads, slowly expanded in the early Middle Ages and colonized large parts of central, eastern, and southern Europe. *Slavs* may serve modern readers as a convenient designation for a number of distinct peoples, but those peoples had no sense of themselves as a single people, and their movements were not coordinated. For discussion it is useful to divide the Slavs into three major groups according to where they settled: western, southern, and eastern Slavs (Map 9.3).

Several features are common to the history of all the Slavic peoples and regions. The key one is a complex pattern of relations with surrounding peoples, whether Germans, Byzantines, Muslims, or Mongols. Another is regional and ethnic diversity. One more is the absence almost everywhere of stable, large-scale political entities.

The Western Slavs

As Slavic tribes moved westward toward the Elbe River in the eighth and ninth centuries, they began to encounter the Franks, who were moving east and asserting their power in Germany. The Franks had no desire to extend their territorial

Map 9.3 The World of the Slavs Slavic states emerged in three clusters called for convenience, and because of linguistic differences, "western," "southern," and "eastern." The Slavs were surrounded by powerful, intrusive neighbors.

control much beyond the Elbe and contented themselves with creating a military frontier from the Baltic to the Danube. In the middle of the ninth century, several Slavic states began to emerge to the east of that frontier.

Moravia, a small land in the valley of the Morava River, rallied around a native duke in the 850s. For a half-century Moravian leaders skillfully avoided conquest by the Germans but finally succumbed in 906 to the Magyars. To the north of Moravia lies Bohemia, which emerged as a coherent political entity in the late ninth century when a local duke forged an alliance between the Czech peoples of Bohemia proper and the Slovaks to the east. (See the box, "Good Saint Wenceslas.") The fragile union of Czechs and Slovaks survived many vicissitudes until its dissolution in 1992. Early in the tenth century an ambitious Polish duke laid the foundations for the kingdom of Poland. It attained cohesion and would have been the most powerful of the west Slavic states if a twelfth-century king had not foolishly divided the kingdom equally among his four sons, weakening it when a number of its neighbors were growing stronger.

The foundations of the Hungarian kingdom were laid when the Magyars were finally defeated by the Germans in 955 and were forced to

Good Saint Wenceslas

Wenceslas of Bohemia (r. 907–929), intended for a monastic career, became leader of his people but was murdered by his brother Boleslav, probably because he (Wenceslas) favored close ties with Germany. He became the patron saint of Czechoslovakia and is remembered in a well-known Christmas carol.

There was a prince among the Czechs by the name of Vratislav, his wife was called Drahomira. And they had a son, their firstborn, whom they baptized and gave the name Wenceslas. Now when he reached the age of tonsuring [about 7], his father, Vratislav, summoned a bishop by the name of Notar, along with his clerics for the tonsuring. . . . Then when his father died, the Czechs appointed Wenceslas, his son, as prince. And Boleslav grew up under him. However, both were young. Thus their mother, Drahomira, fortified the land and ruled the people until Wenceslas came of age. . . . With the grace of God, Wenceslas not only mastered letters but he was perfected in faith. According to the words of the Gospel, he rendered good unto all the poor, clothed the naked, fed the hungry, and received wayfarers. He defended widows, had mercy on the people—the wanting and the wealthy—served those who worked for God, and adorned many churches with gold. For he loved God with all his heart and did, as much as he could, all manner of good things in his life. . . . However, Czech men waxed proud and rose up against their lord Wenceslas . . . and they provoked Boleslav, saying: "Your brother Wenceslas wishes to murder you" . . . and the devil sewed malice in Boleslav's heart to murder him.

Source: Slightly adapted from *The First Church Slavonic Life of Saint Wenceslas,* in Marvin Kantor, ed., *The Origins of Christianity in Bohemia: Sources and Commentary* (Evanston, Ill.: Northwestern University Press, 1990), pp. 61–62.

retreat permanently to their Pannonian bases. In 995 their ruler converted to Catholicism and received a royal crown from the pope. Hungary, with its Magyar leadership and large number of German and Slavic settlers, was—and is—one of the most ethnically diverse states in Europe. During the eleventh century, while neighboring German kings and Byzantine emperors were distracted, a series of able Hungarian kings built an effective state. By the end of the twelfth century, however, excessive generosity to the church and to the nobility severely weakened the monarchy. In 1241 a devastating invasion by the Mongols, fierce Asiatic horsemen who wreaked havoc from Mesopotamia to Germany, disrupted Hungary's political evolution. The ruling dynasty continued until 1301 but much earlier had lost effective power.

Neighbors were a constant preoccupation for the early west Slavic realms. Not one of these states could expand without encountering a more powerful neighbor (see Map 9.3). The Slavic states employed several means to improve their precarious positions. Moravia sought to avoid German domination by turning to Byzantium for Orthodox missionaries. By becoming protégés of the emperor, Moravian rulers hoped to gain an advocate against the German king and to escape the influence of the nearby Bavarian church. Bohemia attempted to play Poland off against Germany and, where Germany itself was concerned, Saxons off against Bavarians. The Poles rejected Orthodox overtures, but—like the Danes and Norwegians—turned directly to Rome for their own archbishopric rather than submitting to German bishops.

The most lasting consequence of this political maneuvering was the mission of the monks Cyril (826–869) and Methodius (805–884), whom the Byzantine emperor sent to Moravia in 863. Merchants, missionaries, and mercenaries had casually introduced Christianity to Slavic lands. Cyril and Methodius set out to convert the western Slavs. They were hindered by all the competing interests in the Slavic lands but still planted a firm base for a distinctive kind of Christianity.

Cyril, a formidable linguist, as a youth had learned something about the Slavic languages in the Balkans. While on his journey to Moravia, he created a script, Glagolitic, to permit the writing down of Slavonic. He also translated portions of the Bible and other Christian works. Later, other Christian texts were translated into Slavonic and thus was born Slavonic literature. Cyril and Methodius agreed with the pope that they would abandon Orthodox Christian practices in return for papal permission to use Slavonic instead of Latin. Church Slavonic, as their literary creation is called, spread widely in the western Slavic lands. However, the fundamental cultural substratum was Latin and Christian, and the dominant cultural influence was German. Eventually even the Glagolitic script disappeared; today, Polish and Czech are written in Latin characters. When monasticism finally penetrated the west Slavic lands, it came from France, Germany, and Italy, not from Byzantium.

The Southern Slavs

When the Magyars settled in the central Danube basin, they carved a divide between the western and southern Slavs. Instead of a great band of Slavic states running from the Baltic to the Balkans, there arose two clusters of Slavs lying to the north and south of Hungary.

The Bulgars, a Turkic people from central Asia, formed the most important of the southern Slavic states and, with Russia, one of the two most important of all the early Slavic states. In the 630s the Bulgars began pushing the Avars from the Danube delta region; then, in the 670s, they in turn faced pressure from the Khazars, another Turkic people who dominated the area from the Caspian Sea to southern Russia. The Bulgars crossed the Danube into Byzantine territory and for most of the eighth century posed a severe threat to the empire. For centuries the Bulgars dominated the northern Balkans and, after their conversion, spread Orthodox Christianity and Byzantine culture.

Their rulers were called *khagans,* and it was Khagan Krum (r. 803–814) who established a hereditary monarchy, negotiated a peace treaty with Byzantium, and took advantage of the Frankish defeat of the Avars to expand his holdings to the west. Krum may be regarded as the founder of the Bulgarian state.

Later Bulgarian rulers made important contributions too. Khagan Boris (r. 852–889) converted to Christianity and, after long flirtations with Rome and Constantinople, decided for the Orthodox faith, but in the Slavonic form introduced by Cyril and Methodius. Boris's conversion may have had genuine spiritual foundations, but it also served as a major step in assimilating the Turkic Bulgar elite with the overwhelmingly Slavic population of Bulgaria.

The greatest Bulgar khagan was Symeon (r. 893–927). He made war on the Byzantines several times to force them to honor, even improve, commercial treaties. The Bulgars sat astride valuable trans-Balkan trade routes and had long dominated the passage of goods along them. Because they needed the vast market of Constantinople, they frequently negotiated the terms of trade with the Byzantines. The more powerful of the two states at any given time usually tipped the balance in its own favor. At one point Symeon dreamed of making himself emperor, and he adopted some elements of Byzantine imperial ceremonial, such as the use of crown, throne, and elaborate titles.

Symeon was a patron of monasticism and learning. Monks had achieved the high point of their influence in the Orthodox world as a result of their leadership against the iconoclasts (see page 283). This triumphant monasticism entered Bulgaria when the khagans decided for Orthodoxy over Roman Catholicism. In Bulgaria, however, the fame of the mission of Cyril and Methodius among the western Slavs, coupled with Symeon's patronage and commitment to Orthodoxy, produced a distinctive tradition. Monasteries translated many works of Christian scholarship into Slavonic and developed a new script, Cyrillic, named for Cyril. Even though its basis was Greek and Orthodox, this Slavonic culture took firm root and was transmitted to other peoples, including the Russians. Cyrillic writing persists to this day in Bulgaria, Serbia, and Russia. Byzantium never exerted the total cultural dominance over Bulgaria that Germany did over the western Slavs.

Unfortunately for the Bulgarians, the Byzantines refused to reconcile themselves to so powerful a neighbor. From 967 to 1018 the Byzantines waged a relentless war against the Bulgars, which resulted in the destruction of the independent Bulgar state. In 1186, after Byzantine power in the Balkans had failed almost completely, a new Bulgarian state emerged, but it was only a shadow of its predecessor.

The western Balkans saw the emergence of several Slavic states. The most important were formed at one time or another by the Slovenes, Croats, and Serbs. Their history almost totally depended on the strength of their neighbors Byzantium, Bulgaria, Hungary. By the middle of the twelfth century, the regions of Croatia and Slovenia had fallen under Hungarian dominance, while Serbia passed under Byzantine control. Through long efforts by the popes, the Venetians, and the Hungarians, the Croatians and Slovenes wound up Roman Catholic, although their books and worship were in Slavonic. The Serbs became Orthodox and Slavonic, with Bulgaria as their dominant influence.

None of these Slavic states in the Balkans expanded very far to the south into Greece. These lands, which had received Slavic settlers in the sixth and seventh centuries, were extensively re-Hellenized by the Byzantines in later centuries. Since the tenth century the Balkan peninsula has had a south that is fundamentally Greek in language and culture and Orthodox in religion and a north that is Orthodox in religion but Slavic in language and culture. Fierce antipathies have always agitated the whole region.

The Eastern Slavs

Troublesome neighbors and the introduction of Christianity were just as important in Russia as in the other Slavic realms. But in Russia these factors worked differently. Russia developed relations of various kinds with powerful neighboring states such as Byzantium, Bulgaria, and Poland. But it was not these organized states but nomads from the steppes—the Mongols—who decisively influenced Russian history.

Vikings, not Slavs, actually founded the earliest Russian state. In the early Middle Ages two trade routes crossed the lands that became Rus-

Twelfth-Century Polish Castle This reconstruction of a castle shows it to have been a combination of earthworks and wooden stockades. Such castles, common in western Europe in the tenth and eleventh centuries, afforded protection to people from a wide area, and permanent dwellings to a few. *(CAF Warsaw/Sovfoto)*

sia. One ran between the Baltic and the Caspian seas by way of the Volga River. The other connected the Baltic and Constantinople by way of the Neva River, Lake Ladoga, the Dnieper River, and the Black Sea. As Slavic farmers were moving slowly eastward into these river basins, they met Scandinavians, mainly Swedes, plying their riverine trade. The Swedes had established several trading stations, notably at Novgorod and Kiev. The Slavic farmers and Scandinavian warrior-merchants had common foes in the steppe peoples—Khazars, Pechenegs, and others—who preyed on them both. In these conditions the Vikings seized control of the Slavs living around their trading stations, fought off the steppe peoples, and laid the foundations for several small states. The Viking leaders were a military elite ruling over a vastly more numerous Slavic population. Much like the Magyars in Hungary or the Bulgars in Bulgaria, the Vikings owed much of their power to effective military leadership in the face of common enemies.

Byzantine and other sources refer to these Viking leaders as "Varangar" or as "Rus," but the name "Russian" became most common. In 882, Oleg, a Viking ruler from Novgorod, extended his authority all the way to Kiev and became the first grand prince of Russia. Ruling from Kiev, the Russian grand princes did not call themselves kings and adopted the title "Tsar," the Russian form of "Caesar," centuries later.

During the tenth century, Russian princes devoted most of their energy to fighting the peoples of the steppes. After notable victories, Vladimir (r. 978–1015) became grand prince and turned Russia into a major state. He made a valuable commercial treaty with Constantinople and also converted to Orthodox Christianity. He received Russia's first bishop from the emperor, seeing as so many others had done that an effective ecclesiastical hierarchy could be a major support to his own rule. To avoid suffocating Byzantine control, however, the emerging Russian church adopted the Cyrillic script and Slavonic writings. Vladimir patronized monasticism and learning and built a huge church in Kiev, which had more than four hundred churches by the end of the eleventh century.

Vladimir attempted to promote peace and security in Russia by sending some of his most unruly nobles to Constantinople as members of the Varangian Guard, while settling others on estates around Kiev to protect it from attack. He also erected a string of fortifications near Kiev. To consolidate his power more widely in Russia, he assigned key posts to eight of his sons rather than to potentially uncontrollable nobles.

Despite Vladimir's efforts, rivalries among powerful nobles, envy of the position of Kiev by other towns, and renewed attacks by the steppe peoples led to a slow decline in Kiev's position and a corresponding rise in the fortunes of Novgorod and Vladimir-Suzdal. These towns also profited from trans-Russian trade and were situated deep enough in the Russian forests to enjoy relative security from steppe peoples.

When the Mongols burst on the scene, they changed Russia as no one had ever done before. The conquering Mongols were a union of pastoral nomads from Mongolia (lands east of the Caspian Sea and north of China) and Turkic soldiers forged by the Mongol Jenghiz Khan (1154–1227). Under his inspired leadership, the Mongols rapidly created an empire that reached from China to the frontiers of Germany. The Mongols first attacked Russia in 1221. In 1237 they took Vladimir-Suzdal, and in 1240 they sacked Kiev. After the death of Jenghiz Khan the Mongol empire split up into several independent khanates. The khanate of the Golden Horde—so named from the golden tent in which the khan presided—dominated Russia until the fifteenth century.

The Mongols granted the Russians considerable local autonomy, but they demanded heavy taxes and—just to remind the Russians who was in control—occasionally carried out bloody raids. The brunt of the taxes fell on Russian peasants, who were thereby impoverished at a time when the living conditions of their western European counterparts were generally improving. Moreover, because the Mongols dominated the trade routes, urban life and the commercial classes declined dramatically.

A lasting consequence of the Mongol attack was the definitive shift of Russia's political center of gravity from Kiev to the north and east. When the Mongols sacked Kiev, Germans and Swedes attacked Novgorod, Russia's remaining trading center. Prince Alexander Nevsky (1220–1263), whose father had been prince of Novgorod, boldly rallied the Russians, defeated both the

Germans and the Swedes, and made a treaty with the Mongols that preserved Russia from dismemberment. Many years later Alexander's successors liberated Russia from the Mongols and created a new Russian state based on the grand duchy of Moscow (see page 498).

Social Realities and the Failure of Central Authority

The Slavic states did not develop effective central governments. One of the key reasons for this failure was that all the Slavic states were at one time or another dominated, sometimes devastated, by powerful neighbors. Two other forces were critical as well. Slavic societies were all diverse ethnically, and neither loyalty to reigning dynasties nor conversion to Christianity created bonds that were strong enough to overcome long-standing tensions. Moreover, ruling dynasties, even strong ones, could not overcome independent aristocratic power and the autonomy of towns.

Writing in the sixth century, the Byzantine historian Procopius spoke of Slavic "democracy." In all likelihood, he was referring to the tribal councils to which all Slavic rulers had to defer. Every Slavic society had a noble class whose powers and status became more well defined as time went along. Nobles were usually great landholders descended from the original settlers or from the conquerors of a particular region. In Russia there were also men of power who made their wealth in trade. In some areas, such as Bulgaria and Russia, there were mixed nobilities, Bulgar and Slav in the first case, Scandinavian and Slav in the second. Regardless of origin, these people had powers that were independent of their rulers, and they guarded those powers jealously.

Every Slavic state was ruled by a dynastic family. Nobilities played varying roles in choosing the particular members of the ruling dynasty who assumed power at any given time. The prince (or duke, or khagan, or king) usually had a body of advisers whose advice he had to follow and from whom he had to select his local officials. Under a powerful ruler, these noble advisers, serving as local officials, were forces for unity; but at the first sign of weakness, they either usurped power or switched their loyalty to the brother, son, or nephew of the ruler. Slavic state forms were primitive in comparison with those of western Europe. With no heritage of Roman or ecclesiastical rule on which to draw, government long remained more personal than territorial, more familial than bureaucratic.

The vast majority of Slavs were farmers, and in early times many Slavic societies had some version of the *zadruga,* the great family. This was a number of people, not necessarily related, who had common responsibility for an agricultural community. The zadruga tended at the local level to moderate social distinctions based on wealth or function and to facilitate ethnic assimilation. As nobilities arose among the Slavs, however, and as rulers became less able to control them, individual farmers declined in both status and relative economic position. By the twelfth and thirteenth centuries many farmers whose ancestors had been free had fallen into personal servitude to members of the nobility, who were able to use their evolving local power to thwart attempts by the central government to control them.

Trade was important in the Slavic world. Cracow in Poland and Prague in Bohemia learned to manage the trade that since antiquity had passed between the Baltic and the Mediterranean. They also facilitated exchange between eastern and western Europe. Russia owes its very birth to the commercial situation of Kiev on the Dnieper River. The Bulgars fought the Byzantines several times to get or to improve commercial relations. The Slavic world was a crucial link in a vast commercial chain that connected Scandinavia, western Europe, central Europe, the Mediterranean, and the Islamic world. Furs, wax, honey, flax, hemp, burlap, hops, tallow, hides, and slaves were exchanged for gold and silver, luxury goods, books, liturgical objects (after the introduction of Christianity), and exotic foods.

Trade concentrated wealth and power in towns. But central governments neither caused nor profited much from urban development. In fact, towns were a centrifugal force in Slavic states. In some areas, such as deeply Romanized Croatia, towns preceded the coming of the Slavs; in other areas the Slavs were responsible for urban development. Almost everywhere, however, towns had councils that represented the community to the ruler and thwarted attempts by rulers to impose their will.

The Byzantine Empire

The history of the Byzantine Empire between the ninth and the thirteenth centuries presents two remarkably different paths of development (see Map 9.4). In politics, war, and diplomacy the period from the accession of Basil I in 867 to the death of Basil II in 1025 marked the Byzantine high point. Then from 1025 until 1204, when Constantinople was captured by an army of western Crusaders, Byzantium experienced a long, steady decline. In the economic and cultural realms, the basic pattern is just the opposite. Although the ninth and tenth centuries show evidence of advance, it was during the eleventh and twelfth centuries that the Byzantine economy reached the summit of its prosperity and the cultural vitality of the empire attained unprecedented levels.

The Macedonian Dynasty

In 867 Basil I usurped the Byzantine throne, laying the foundation for two centuries of rule by an effective, talented dynasty. Basil I (r. 867–886) was a rude Macedonian soldier—loutish, unlettered, and hostile to clerics and bureaucrats. Among his successors, however, there were men who preached sermons, wrote learned books, and reformed laws and institutions. For nearly two centuries, the Macedonian dynasty pursued certain basic policies.

In war and diplomacy, Byzantium had three great areas of concern: the long frontier with the Islamic world; the northern frontier in the Danubian and Black Sea regions, where Bulgars, Russians, and nomadic peoples were threats; and Italy, where commercial relations with Venice, religious ties to Rome, and political control of the south and of Sicily formed the key issues.

Muslim forces had long raided Byzantine Anatolia to capture booty, terrorize the local population, and remind the emperor of his vulnerability. It was Byzantium's good fortune that when the Abbassid caliphate began to weaken in the late ninth century, vigorous leaders took advantage of the situation. In the early tenth century Muslim raids were stopped; then, for the first time since the seventh century, the Byzantines recovered territory in northern Syria, in eastern Anatolia, and in Armenia and Georgia (lying then as now between the Black and Caspian seas). As the tenth century wore on, the Byzantines refurbished their fleet, recovered Crete and Cyprus, and achieved domination in the eastern Mediterranean. By the time of Basil II (r. 976–1025), they ruled more territory in the east than they had ruled since the 620s.

Along the northern frontier, Byzantium faced a series of interrelated problems. Basically, the imperial goal was to keep the incipient Russian state at bay, to control the marauding of nomadic peoples such as the Magyars and Pechenegs, and, above all, to check the Bulgarians. The Byzantines hired Magyars and Russians to attack the Bulgars, manipulated Balkan trade to the great disadvantage of the Bulgars, and forced the Bulgars to receive Christianity from Constantinople, not from Rome. Chafing under this unfair treatment, the Bulgars rebelled often, carrying destructive raids far into the empire. Basil II—"the Bulgar Slayer"—waged year after year of war with the Bulgars and virtually annihilated their ancient kingdom. The Balkans were finally made secure, and the spread of Orthodox Christianity in both the Bulgar lands and Russia considerably extended the cultural reach of Byzantium.

Byzantine dealings with the West were complex, for they touched on three different areas with distinct problems. Relations with Venice, for example, rested on several foundations. From the early ninth century, Venice was the most advanced Christian commercial power in the western Mediterranean. Byzantium regarded Venice as a dependent state and attempted to use it as a conduit for trade with western Europe. In return, Venice received valuable commercial privileges throughout the empire. Byzantium also hoped to use Venice's fleet against the pirates who since ancient times had preyed on Adriatic shipping. Finally, the imperial government hoped to use Venice to influence the Slavic peoples who lived to the west of the Bulgars. In every area, Venice pursued its own interests, rather than behaving like a pawn of Byzantium.

Rome posed an on-again, off-again problem for Byzantium. Although the eastern and western churches were clearly drifting apart, there had been no formal act of separation. The emperors bitterly resented the attempt by the papacy to convert the Bulgars to Roman Christianity, but on other occasions they submitted ecclesiastical issues to the pope for resolution. After 843, iconoclasm was no longer a divisive issue.

For Byzantium, the most important realm in the West was southern Italy, where local magnates persistently encroached on the area of Naples while Muslims from North Africa threatened Sicily (Map 9.4). The Byzantines derived little more than prestige from holding southern Italy and Sicily, but prestige was precious coin in the Byzantine realm. It enhanced the status of the empire among its neighbors and the status of the emperor in his own state.

In imperial politics two issues may be singled out. First, the Macedonian rulers resolved to turn the church into a department of state. Their predecessors had tried to check the independence of the church but had come to ruin because of their iconoclasm. The Macedonians attempted no theological innovations and maintained close cooperation with the patriarchate and the most important bishoprics. Monasteries were placed more firmly under episcopal control, and cenobitic (communal) forms of monasticism were promoted over eremitic (highly individual) ones, again to ensure greater control. To prevent the church from accumulating wealth, strict measures were passed limiting people's ability to donate or bequeath land to the church, and church properties were made liable for many taxes.

The second political issue concerns repeated attempts to break the power of Anatolian aristocratic families. Under the theme system, Byzantium had settled farmer-soldiers on modest plots of land with little or no tax liability (see page 281). Peasants were settled in communal villages that had a single, often high, tax assessment. Over time, because of natural disasters (earthquakes, plagues, famines, locusts), Muslim raids, and outright intimidation, local military officers managed to acquire vast landholdings from peasants who could not meet their tax obligations or from farmer-soldiers who could not afford the costs of service. In some areas these large-scale landowners built up huge military followings of their own. The Byzantine army threatened to become a series of private armies loosely tied to the state. Macedonian legislation created more and smaller themes to limit the power of officers, protected the economic position of small farmers, and brought foreign mercenaries into the military system.

The Dissipation of the Macedonian State

Within a half-century of the death of Basil II in 1025 the Byzantine Empire suffered at Manzikert the most psychologically devastating defeat in its history. That defeat led to a century of decline and to the fall of Constantinople in 1204 to an army of western Crusaders.

Between 1025 and 1071 the empire had no fewer than ten rulers. In almost all aspects of life, individualism drew people's interests and loyalties away from the state. Aristocratic factions sought their own advantage more than that of the empire as a whole. The Macedonian period was prosperous, but wealth tended to accumulate in private hands. Because rich aristocrats paid almost no taxes, the state was unable to profit much from rising prosperity and saw its best efforts to control the aristocracy compromised too. To win over powerful families, honors and offices were multiplied and thus cheapened.

Imperial relations with the Orthodox patriarchate deteriorated during the episcopacy of the willful Michael Cerularius (r. 1043–1058), who sought to break out of the Macedonian mold of pliable churchmen. Cerularius not only made trouble at home but worsened the always tense relations between the imperial court and the papacy. He was determined to impose his will in ecclesiastical matters, even in southern Italy. For decades the use of Latin and Roman Catholic forms of worship had been gaining ground in the region of Naples. Cerularius and the papacy quarreled over jurisdiction in Italy, and when Pope Leo IX (r. 1049–1054) sent a representative to Constantinople in 1054, he and Cerularius excommunicated one another in a fit of rage. These actions inaugurated the schism between the Roman and Orthodox churches that still exists.

In these circumstances two new military threats took on ominous proportions. In southern Italy, meddlesome local notables were eclipsed by a powerful people from western France, the Normans. From their secure bases in southern Italy, the Normans threatened the Byzantines by attacking Sicily and the Balkans. In Anatolia, the Turks emerged as a new threat. In the early eleventh century, large Turkish bands began moving westward from central Asia. Some of these seminomadic warriors entered the service of the caliph, but others independently raided

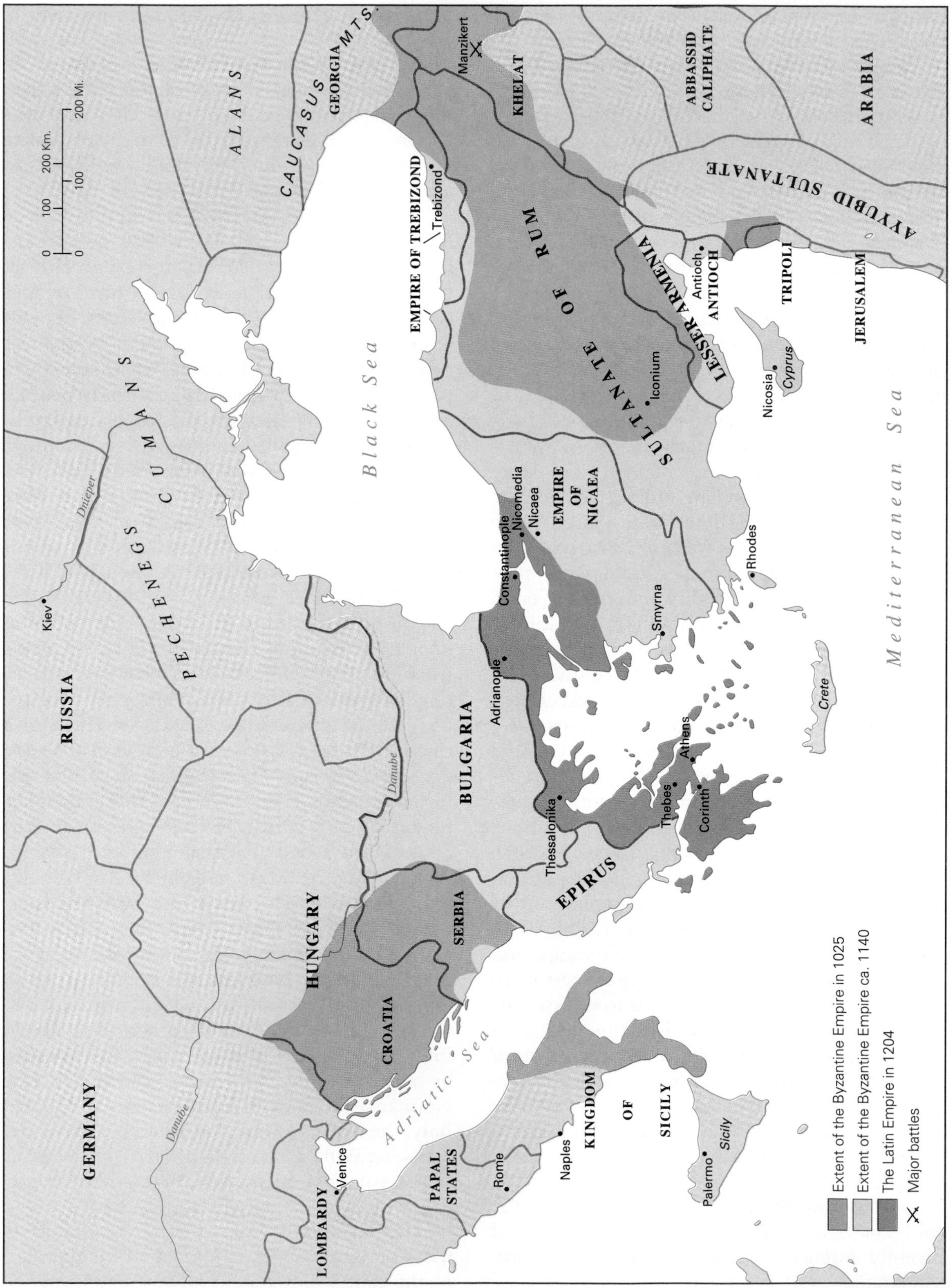
0 100 200 Km.
0 100 200 Mi.
ALANS
CAUCASUS MTS.
GEORGIA
Manzikert
KHELAT
ABBASSID CALIPHATE
ARABIA
AYYUBID SULTANATE
EMPIRE OF TREBIZOND
Trebizond
SULTANATE OF RUM
LESSER ARMENIA
Antioch
ANTIOCH
TRIPOLI
JERUSALEM
Iconium
Nicosia
Cyprus
Mediterranean Sea
Black Sea
CUMANS
PECHENEGS
Dnieper
Kiev
RUSSIA
EMPIRE OF NICAEA
Constantinople
Nicomedia
Nicaea
Smyrna
Rhodes
Crete
Adrianople
BULGARIA
Danube
Athens
Thebes
Corinth
Thessalonika
EPIRUS
HUNGARY
SERBIA
CROATIA
GERMANY
Danube
Adriatic Sea
KINGDOM OF SICILY
Naples
Sicily
Palermo
PAPAL STATES
Rome
Venice
LOMBARDY
Extent of the Byzantine Empire in 1025
Extent of the Byzantine Empire ca. 1140
The Latin Empire in 1204
Major battles

Armenia and Anatolia. Eventually the Byzantine emperor, Romanus IV (r. 1068–1071), felt he had to respond to the humiliation caused by these Turkish incursions. He sent an ill-equipped, untrained army of questionable loyalty to meet the Turkish force. A skirmish near Manzikert (in Anatolia) in 1071 turned into a rout, and Romanus was captured. It seemed that all the achievements of the Macedonian dynasty had been lost.

A decade of confusion followed Manzikert. Then Alexius Comnenus, the head of an important family that led a large aristocratic coalition, was chosen emperor, Alexius I (r. 1081–1118). For more than a century this family ruled the empire and tried to provide effective leadership. Nevertheless, the twelfth century was a time of steady political and military decline.

The Comneni rulers tried to put an end to factional strife and to secure an effective military force. Aristocrats were increasingly assigned grants that made them lords of extensive holdings with dependent peasantries. The holders of these grants had to pay taxes but were allowed to collect substantial revenues from their holdings. The state was thus able to tap rural prosperity without denying aristocrats opportunities to fill their pockets. Usually the holders of grants had to perform military service, but a new army was raised mainly with tax revenues: The emperors hired mercenaries. The government was trying to counter the privatized and localized armies of the eleventh century.

Alexius I was the first Byzantine to seek troops in Latin Europe. Believing that the Turks were vulnerable in Anatolia, he appealed through the pope, Urban II (r. 1088–1099), for mercenaries. He dangled before the pope the hope of a reunion of the eastern and western churches. Alexius, like his twelfth-century successors, did not understand the social and spiritual forces then animating life in western Europe. Only when he got armies of Christian Crusaders bent on liberating the Holy Land from the "infidel" did he discover that he had blundered (see page 384). The Crusaders, for their part, did not understand Alexius and his needs and thought the Byzantines treacherous and dishonest.

Map 9.4 The Byzantine Empire in the High Middle Ages Although powerful and aggressive under the Macedonian dynasty, Byzantium could not, under the Comneni, successfully meet all of the threats it faced.

Problems accumulated in the twelfth century. The grant system actually made the nobles more powerful and less loyal because it confirmed their control of the peasantry at a time when the government was too weak to prevent either abuse of the farmers or tax-dodging. Relations with the West turned increasingly sour because of the first two Crusades (1095, 1144), constant Norman meddling in the Balkans, and vain attempts to reunite the churches. The preferential treatment long accorded Venetian merchants also aroused jealousy in Constantinople and various Italian cities. Emperor Manuel I (r. 1143–1180) erred in his response to these issues. For example, he expelled the Venetians from Constantinople in 1171, thus turning an old, albeit difficult, ally into an implacable foe. To show that he was not militarily impotent, he attacked the Turks in 1176 but was decisively defeated.

After Manuel's death the empire suffered through more than twenty years of civil strife. Contenders for the throne turned to the pope, to the Venetians, to the Germans, and to a crusading army for help in securing the emperorship. The bizarre result of all this importuning was that the Venetians diverted the Fourth Crusade to Constantinople, ostensibly to assist an imperial claimant who would, once recognized as emperor, restore the Venetian position in the capital. Venice could not resist exacting revenge, and some Crusaders decided that Byzantium was a more attractive prize than the Holy Land. In 1204 Constantinople fell not to its historic enemies in the East but to its erstwhile friends in the West.

Various Latin barons, after slaking their thirst for booty, carved the Balkans up into a number of petty principalities and recognized one of their number as a Roman emperor of sorts. This "Latin" empire of Constantinople lasted until 1261, when Byzantines from Anatolia took advantage of Latin disunity to restore Greek rule. The restored Byzantine Empire lasted until Constantinople fell definitively to the Turks in 1453, but it was never again more than a minor player in its own region.

The fall of Byzantium cannot be attributed to Crusaders or to Turks. It was the rulers after Basil II who squandered the Macedonian heritage.

Social and Cultural Progress

Twelfth-century Byzantium witnessed widespread economic advance, in most cases traceable to the eleventh century. Population and agricultural production were growing steadily. Trade was increasing, with more money in circulation. Urban life was recovering. The prosperity was inequitably distributed, however, and it fostered an individualism that worked against the best interests of the state.

All evidence points to dramatic gains in the rural sector of the economy. As nobles acquired larger and larger estates, they had the power and the resources both to command the necessary labor and to bring more land under cultivation. The position of peasants was anomalous. They were more prosperous than ever before but found themselves more legally dependent on their landlords. The prosperity of both nobles and peasants was fueled by population growth and urbanization. In the Balkans, Thessalonika remained important, second only to Constantinople, but Athens, Thebes, and Corinth, unimportant since antiquity, emerged as manufacturing centers for glass, ceramics, and silk.

Empress Zoë The Empress Zoë, shown here with Christ in a mosaic in Hagia Sophia, was for a generation in the eleventh century the dominant figure in Constantinople. She is presenting Christ with a gift for Hagia Sophia. *(Giamberto Vanni/Art Resource)*

Prosperity manifested itself in other ways too. The diet was wider and more sophisticated. Spices and fruits from the Arab world graced Byzantine tables, and foreigners remarked on the amount of meat that Byzantines consumed. Clothing became more elegant for both men and women. New hairstyles—curls on the forehead and waist-length hair for men—marked the wealth and extravagance of the age.

All this prosperity sparked an individualism that ran powerfully against the dominant ideology of the state. The Byzantine world had always maintained the ideal of one ruler, one faith, and one people. Now people were more likely to attach their loyalty to their own town or region, to the nobleman who held the grant for the land they lived on, to the aristocrat who was their cultural patron. People admired hermits, individualistic holy men, rather than cenobites, those who subordinated their will to the abbot and community. Fashion became more individualistic, marked by such curiosities as men going beardless and wearing trousers instead of caftans.

The eleventh and twelfth centuries witnessed the aristocratization of society and the emergence of a corresponding ethos. Traditionally, Byzantine families were nuclear, and the holding of office, whether civil or military, determined social position. Now greater stress was laid on lineage, on birth. Personal, not public, qualities distinguished the aristocrat from other people. At just the time when the government was trying to limit the nobility's actual role in military affairs, the noble ideal was militarized, the pseudowarfare of the tournament was introduced, and quasi-martial pursuits such as polo and the hunt grew in popularity.

The aristocratization of life provided noblewomen with greater scope for activity than ever before. In the patriarchal, nuclear family women were sheltered and protected. The noble families of the eleventh and twelfth centuries, however, provide abundant evidence of powerful, resourceful women. In the 1040s Zoë (980–1050), wife and mother to emperors and a great favorite of the population of Constantinople, was really in charge of the government. Alexius Comnenus attained the throne through the efforts of his mother and then was bedeviled by rumors alleg-

The Character of Alexius Comnenus

Anna Comnena, a keen observer of her turbulent times, created pen-portraits of unusual clarity and interest, such as this one of her father Alexius I.

Alexius was not a very tall man, but broad shouldered and yet well proportioned. When standing he did not seem particularly striking to onlookers, but when one saw the grim flash of his eyes as he sat on the imperial throne, he reminded one of a fiery whirlwind, so overwhelming was the radiance that emanated from his countenance and his whole presence. His eyebrows were curved, and beneath them the gaze of his eyes was both terrible and kind. A quick glance, the brightness of his face, the noble cheeks suffused with red combined to inspire both dread and confidence. His broad shoulders, mighty arms and deep chest, all on a heroic scale, invariably commanded the wonder and delight of the people. The man's person indeed radiated beauty and grace and dignity and an unapproachable majesty.

Source: The Alexiad of Anna Comnena, trans. E. R. A. Sewter (Harmondsworth, England: Penguin, 1969), pp. 109–110.

ing that he listened too much to the advice of women at his court. One of those women was his daughter Anna Comnena (1083–1148), who nearly fomented a civil war in her attempts to secure the imperial succession for her husband. Anna wrote a memoir of her times that is elegant in style and shrewd in insight (see the box, "The Character of Alexius Comnenus"). Other aristocratic women became famous as patrons of artists and writers.

The wealth and individualism that characterized the Byzantine economy and society was also evident in cultural life. Byzantine culture was by definition Greek, but only about one-third of the empire's population spoke Greek as a first language. Thus, it is difficult to generalize about Byzantine culture, although it is safe to say that there were forces for both unity and disunity.

The imperial army, for example, pressed people into a single cultural mold. The Orthodox church was also a powerful force for unity and cohesion. Schools, which existed mainly in Constantinople and the larger towns before the urban resurgence of the eleventh and twelfth centuries, taught only in Greek and offered a curriculum that had changed little since Late Antiquity.

Schools and traditions of learning provide an excellent example of the complexity of the Byzantine situation. Not many people went to school. Women, peasants, and urban laborers—three huge components of the total population—almost never went to school, and very few merchants or aristocrats went on to any form of higher education. Books, hand copied by professional scribes, were costly. A New Testament was worth two months' wages for a working man, and a manuscript of Plato cost two years' wages. Schools and learning were potential unifiers but often served to divide people.

Tenth- and eleventh-century scholars tended to be antiquarians who consciously looked back to the classical past. Some writers resurrected the long-forgotten classical Greek of antiquity. Most people did not have the learning or the leisure to mimic them.

The eleventh and twelfth centuries saw many more writers, accomplished in a variety of genres—biography, history, theology, poetry, romance. The writers of this rich and interesting literature came from various social classes, used everything from classical Greek to "street" Greek, and tended deliberately to avoid the kinds of literary conventions that foster unity among people.

Two figures exemplify the changes that were taking place. Michael Psellus (1018–1096), a high government official, tutor to young emperors, and correspondent with many powerful people, rose by talent and connections at a time when the nobility was trying to limit opportunities for mobility. His vast learning, obtained outside the church, shows what Byzantine schools were capable of. He wrote a historical work dedicated to the idea that history is driven by the character and actions of individuals rather than by divine plans or state destinies. He was interested in science and hoped to promote a rational understanding of the universe, though he was by no means irreligious. Michael encouraged philosophical studies and did much to heighten interest in Plato. Contemporary concerns fascinated him, but so did the ancient heritage.

Opposed to Psellus's worldly views were those of mystics such as Symeon (949–1022), called "the New Theologian." Symeon was abbot of a monastery in Constantinople but suffered exile because of opposition to his religious views. He is called "the New Theologian" to differentiate him from the Greek Church Fathers whose writings had defined eastern Orthodoxy. Symeon initiated the Hesychast movement (the word means "quiet" or "stillness"), which was important in Orthodoxy for centuries. A mystical movement, it stressed the sanctification of the individual rather than the community and intensely private relationships with God instead of the public, liturgical worship that had always been central at Byzantium. In his way, Symeon was just as individualistic as Psellus. He had little place in his scheme for the community. Perhaps it is not surprising that an empire that had lost its sense of community lost its very existence in 1204.

The Islamic World

Between the tenth and the thirteenth centuries, the Abbassid caliphate broke down into distinct regional entities. Religious divisions that contributed to the political disruption of the age appeared, and their effects are still with us. Political and religious changes brought about social, economic, and cultural changes. To put all this a little differently, we can say that unity within diversity is a good characterization of this period. The Islamic faith, the Arabic language, an intellectual tradition rooted in Islamic teachings, and a continuing belief in common membership in the umma (see page 274) persisted in spite of permanent divisions in the political geography of the Islamic world.

The Decentralization of the Islamic State

After 900 the caliphate broke down into three major areas, and each of these in turn split into smaller entities. The old central lands of Iraq and Iran plus their surrounding territories were one area (Map 9.5). Egypt, which often controlled Syria and Palestine, was another. The third area was North Africa and al-Andalus (the Muslim portion of Spain). The two main catalysts for political change were present in all three: military problems and religious strife.

Military problems were both internal and external. Internal problems arose primarily as a result of efforts by rulers to develop effective and loyal fighting forces. Frontier peoples increasingly supplied both troops and leaders. Around 900 the Buyids, a family of mercenary leaders from Iran, entered the service of the caliphs and brought along mercenary troops who were mainly Turkish. In 1045 a caliph who had grown restive under Buyid ascendancy called in the Seljuk Turks, who soon supplanted the Buyids as military leaders. The leaders of the Buyids and the Seljuks assumed the position of sultan, military, and administrative leader of the caliphate. The sultans were respectful of the office of the caliph, but they possessed real power.

In 868 the caliph sent Ahmad ibn-Tulun (r. 868–905), a Turkish servant, to Egypt as its governor. Given the weakness of the caliphs, ibn-Tulun soon made himself independent by building up a mercenary army of his own. Although Tulunid Egypt was peaceful and prosperous, its alien military leaders could not rally sufficient local support to repel an attack by aggressive North African raiders, the Fatimids. In 969 the Fatimids conquered Egypt. By controlling Egypt as well as Palestine and Syria, the Fatimids made themselves completely independent of the caliphate in Baghdad. In the middle of the twelfth century, however, the Fatimids fell from power after a revolt by their largely Kurdish mercenaries, whose greatest leader was Saladin (1138–1193), the man who reconquered Jerusalem from the crusaders

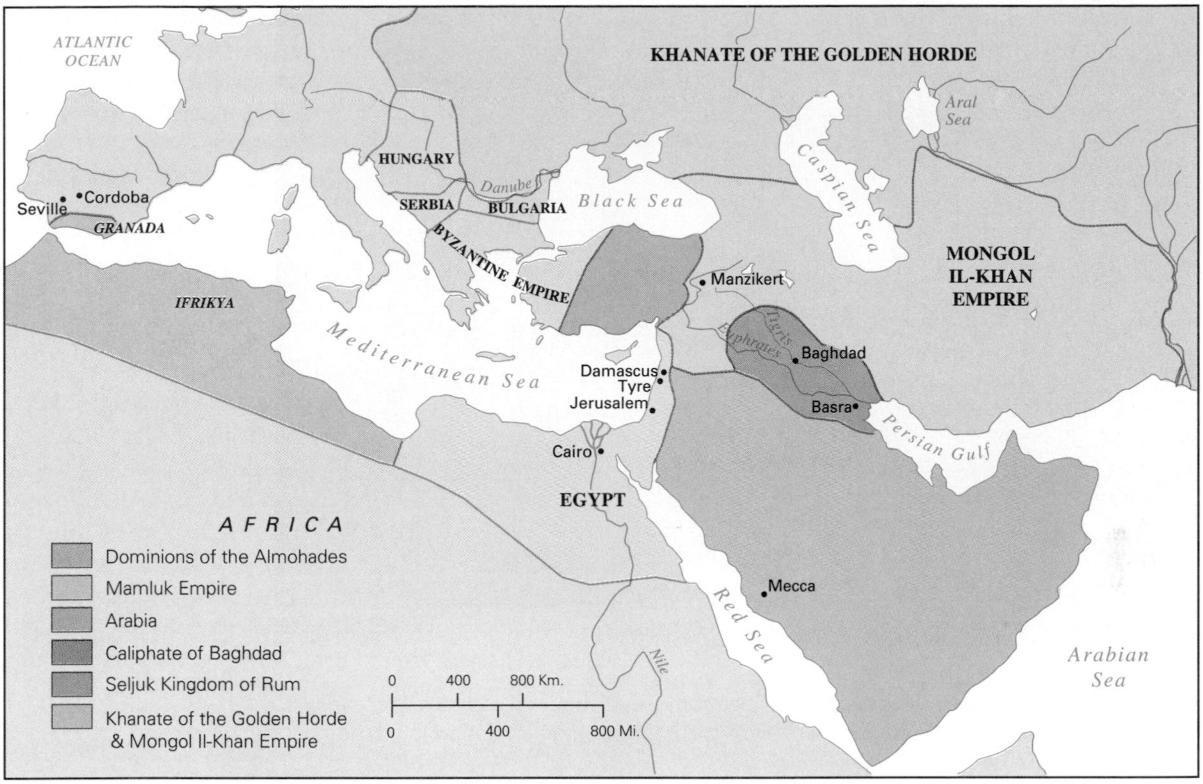

Map 9.5 The Islamic World at the End of the Abbassid Caliphate, 1258 In 1258 the Mongols deposed the last of the Abbassid caliphs. The Mongols could not re-create the vast, Mediterranean-centered empire of Umayyad and Abbassid times. Instead, as they looked deep into Asia, the old caliphate disintegrated.

in 1187. Saladin's successors, in turn, lost power to their mercenaries, Turks called Mamluks, who ruled a more or less independent Egypt until 1517. After the decline of the Fatimids, North Africa experienced generations of local strife fomented by local dynasties and abetted by Muslim rulers in Spain.

External military threats were of several different kinds. In Spain, the Christians launched in the ninth century a war of reconquest that proceeded in on-again, off-again fashion for centuries. Italian cities began sweeping Muslims out of their island naval bases in the Mediterranean. The Byzantines won victories on land and sea until the disaster at Manzikert. In 1095 and 1144 armies of western Crusaders seized lands in Syria and Palestine.

These military defeats were distractions. The invasion of the Mongols was a catastrophe. The armies of Jenghiz Khan wreaked as much devastation on the Islamic world as on Russia. After Jenghiz's death, one horde of Mongols settled down to dominate Russia, but another, based in Iran, tyrannized the caliphate. Mongols deposed the last Abbassid caliph in 1258. The vast Islamic state created within a century of Muhammad's death was gone forever, although Islam continued to win converts. After rejecting Buddhism and Christianity, the Mongols became Muslims.

Religious strife arose during the period of Buyid domination in Baghdad in the early tenth century. Primarily it consisted of bitter enmity between Sunni and Shi'ite Muslims, which spread throughout the Islamic world.

The Shi'ites arose as follows. Some Muslims always believed that the caliphs should be chosen according to strict standards of religious and personal worthiness. Rigorists believed that the only

Ibn-Tulun Mosque, Cairo This beautiful, elegant mosque suggests something of the wealth and power of the Tulunid rulers of Egypt, beginning with Ahmad ibn-Tulun, who was sent to Egypt in 868. *(Carolyn Brown/Photo Researchers, Inc.)*

way to ensure worthiness was to limit the caliphate to the family of Muhammad and, more specifically, to the line of Ali, the husband of Muhammad's daughter Fatima. Adherents of this sect are called the Shi'a, the party of Ali.

Opposed to the Shi'ites were the majority of Muslims, who were henceforth called "Sunni" to emphasize their self-proclaimed adherence to the authentic sunna, the teachings and practice of Muhammad himself. Sunni Muslims accepted the whole line of Umayyad and Abbassid caliphs. Although there were subtle differences among various sunni schools of thought, these differences were in fact narrower than those that had divided Christian sects in Late Antiquity or Roman and Orthodox Christians.

The unbridgeable chasm in the Islamic world was between Shi'ites and Sunnis. Sometimes this religious split had serious political consequences. The regime of the Buyids was fatally weakened by its Shi'ite leanings. The Fatimids in Egypt were militant Shi'ites who, despite brilliant artistic and intellectual achievements, never won widespread loyalty from the Sunni masses.

Unity Within Diversity

Although the caliphate disappeared, there always remained a sense that all Muslims constituted the umma, the community of all believers. Through early Abbassid times there was basically one government and one set of institutions for the umma. In the later Abbassid period, a new ruling ideology was necessary.

In the eleventh century Muslim political thinkers identified three essential components of the caliphal office: legitimate succession to the prophet, direction of the worldly affairs of the believers, and custody of the faith. In the past the caliph could do all these things himself, but now it was argued that he might delegate others to execute these tasks in his name. This theory reflected the irony that the caliphs were becoming increasingly powerless as those who acted in the name of the caliph were most insistent about the caliph's legitimacy.

Caliphs were supposed to be military and government leaders, but in the Islamic world secular affairs were not easily separated from religious ones. Thus, an aura of religious authority always surrounded the caliph. That religious aura led to the bitter fights between Sunnis and Shi'ites about just who was most suited to be caliph, but it also kept emirs and sultans from aspiring to the caliphal office.

Among those who shared the authority of the caliphs we have noted already the sultans, whether Buyid or Seljuk. Such leaders emerged because the caliphs turned to foreign, usually Turkish, mercenaries for their soldiers. These soldiers, who were sometimes slaves, served under leaders to whom they were intensely loyal. They were settled on the land in return for military service, a practice also used by western European and Byzantine governments. Despite political and economic changes, the caliphs were able almost to the end to come up with ways to raise fighting forces. This capability reflects the ingenuity and adaptability of Islamic institutions.

Custody of the faith was increasingly shared by the caliph and the *ulema.* The ulema were elite men in the cities—teachers in schools, preachers of the Friday sermons in the mosques, Islamic lawyers, intellectuals, and the most cultured merchants. The ulema took great pride in their own cities and also in their common Islamic faith and Arabic culture. They formed an international elite that served as a powerful bond of unity.

Like Catholicism and Orthodoxy, Islam produced mystics. These men, called Sufis, wished to approach Allah not so much by study and knowledge as by contemplation and meditation. Sufis were stirred by the same spiritual forces that produced Christian monasticism.

Every town had a qadi, a judge who was trained in law schools whose program of study was almost identical everywhere. These men interpreted the *shari'a,* the Islamic law derived from the Qur'an and the hadith. A common legal culture, which demanded a common standard of public behavior, was achieved in a vast world that included people of numerous ethnic, cultural, and linguistic backgrounds.

The spread of the Arabic language greatly facilitated intellectual exchange in the Islamic world. People spoke everything from Berber dialects in North Africa to Turkish ones in central Asia, but all learned at least some Arabic in order to understand the Qur'an. Because Muslims believed that Allah had communicated directly with Muhammad in Arabic, there was never any question of translating Allah's own words into another language—there was no Islamic Jerome or Cyril. In the Umayyad and Abbassid periods Arabic was the language of administration. All of the great law schools, the institutions that interpreted the shari'a, taught in Arabic. Poetry, history, and other texts, not just religious writings, tended to be in Arabic.

Throughout the Islamic world well-attended elementary schools taught Arabic grammar, and one important category of early Arabic writings was schoolbooks. (One might compare these textbooks to the Latin grammars of early medieval Europe.) The primary responsibility of the teacher was to instruct boys in the Qur'an, hadith, and shari'a. After a pupil had completed a program of study, he received an diploma that spelled out, sometimes in minute detail, who had taught him as well as who, going back generations, had taught his teachers. In formal schooling, the communication of tradition was prized, not innovation or local customs.

Urban Life and Culture

The society and culture of the Islamic world were intimately tied to cities. The largest cities of the Western world were in Muslim lands. Cairo, for example, numbered a million inhabitants in 1300, and Baghdad at its height was nearly as large. No city in Christian Europe had a quarter of that number, with the exception of Constantinople.

The caliphate linked together the two greatest trading basins in the world, the Mediterranean and the Indian Ocean, and provided unprecedented opportunities for mercantile activity. The huge cities of the Muslim world were centers of trade. New products—rice, sugar cane, cotton, watermelons, citrus fruits—passed across long spaces. Because foodstuffs were too bulky and expensive to transport long distances, the commercially driven urbanization of the Islamic world helped to promote agriculture in the immediate environs of great cities. Merchants were thus free to concentrate on spices, porcelains, furs, and other luxury goods. Gold from east Africa flowed into the caliphate, was coined into money, and helped to spur commercial activity. Opportunities for wealth were enhanced, diets became more interesting, and the items of daily life became more diverse.

Most cities were divided into centers and residential quarters. Two building complexes dominated the centers. One was formed by the central mosque and its schools. The other was formed by the great market area. Government cities such as Cordoba, Cairo, and Baghdad also had a major palace complex. Residential quarters surrounded the public areas. Some of the wealthy might live near the market, but small shopkeepers, artisans, and laborers tended to live and work some distance from the center. Domestic architecture in the Islamic world was inward oriented. Façades on the street were plain and unimpressive. Doorways opened on to elaborate entry halls that served both to impress guests and to keep them from seeing into the interior of the house. Privacy was valued highly in family life, perhaps because the dictates of the shari'a made so many other features of life intensely public.

Everything—from business concerns, to religious affiliations, to artistic patronage—tended to be a family affair. Because many families had both urban and rural branches, the city and its hinterland were tied together. In the purely domestic realm women might exercise considerable influence. But Muslim society and culture were male dominated both by shari'a and by long regional tradition. A thirteenth-century jurist, for example, said, "A woman should leave her house on three occasions only: when she is conducted to the house of her bridegroom, on the deaths of her parents, and when she goes to her own grave." When a woman did leave her house, she was veiled and accompanied. The Qur'an proclaimed the essential equality of men and women. Reality, however, was different.

The urban environment, through its schools, mosques, and qadis, gave birth to a rich religious

Islamic Scholars in a Garden From a thirteenth-century Iraqi manuscript, this picture shows literary men in a garden. Beasts are driving a water wheel to refresh them, and a lute player accompanies their poetry with music. *(Bibliothèque Nationale)*

The Autobiography of Avicenna

Avicenna's father was a minor official who tried to provide an education for his son. The family's experiences are revealing of many currents in the Islamic world.

My father was one of those who responded to the propaganda for the Egyptians [the Fatimids] and was counted among the Isma'ilis [a radical religious sect]. He had accepted their teachings on the soul and mind, as had my brother. They often discussed it with one another . . . and they tried to win me over to this doctrine. Sometimes they also used to discuss philosophy, geometry, and Indian arithmetic [that is, arithmetic with the zero] and my father sent me to a certain grocer who knew Indian arithmetic so I could learn it from him. . . . Then al-Natali, who claimed to be a philosopher, was lodged in my father's house in the hopes that I might learn something from him. Before he came I was studying jurisprudence. Under al-Natali . . . I learned the broad principles of logic, but he knew nothing of the subtleties. Then I began to read books and study commentaries on my own until I mastered logic. I also read the geometry of Euclid. . . . Eventually, . . . I busied myself with commentaries on physics and metaphysics, and the doors of knowledge opened before me. Then I took up medicine and began to read the books on this subject. Medicine is not one of the difficult sciences, and in a very short time I excelled in it, so that physicians of merit studied under me.

Source: Bernard Lewis, ed. and trans., *Islam from the Prophet Muhammad to the Capture of Constantinople,* vol. 2, *Religion and Society* (New York: Harper and Row, 1974), pp. 177–179.

culture. But that was not the only intellectual life that emerged in cities. The internationalization of Islamic culture enlivened the rich poetic tradition of the Arabs. The Qur'an was Islam's and Arabic's first prose work, but from the ninth century history and genealogy flourished. The period from the eighth to the tenth century saw the translation of many classical Greek writings into Arabic. The literary works of Greece were almost without influence, but Greek works in philosophy, natural science, and medicine were very influential. Where the Muslim and Latin worlds touched—in Sicily and Spain, for example—Muslims communicated Greek letters to Christians.

Greek learning posed a challenge for Arab thinkers, as it later did for Christians. If truth depended on Allah, and if Allah had revealed all that people needed to know, what was one to make of the abundant knowledge of the Greeks? The first thinker to address himself to this problem systematically was ibn-Sina (980–1037), known to the West as Avicenna. Avicenna believed that basic truths in medicine and other fields could be articulated in terms drawn from Aristotelian philosophy without contradicting divine revelations. (See the box, "The Autobiography of Avicenna.") His position was like Augustine's earlier attitude toward pagan learning: One could take what one needed from it. Some important Arab thinkers disagreed: works of worldly, not to mention non-Arab, thinkers could never be made compatible with Islamic truth.

In the twelfth century ibn-Rushd (1126–1198), a Spanish Arab known in the West as Averroës, defended the way of the Greek philosophers. He said that nothing in the worldly philosophy of Aristotle contradicted the essential truths of Islam and that only a few people were capable of understanding philosophy correctly. Thus, for ordinary people, Averroës maintained, the literal meaning of the Qur'an and the standard interpretations provided in mosques and schools were adequate, but for others, philosophy marked out a path to higher understanding.

Although acceptance or denunciation of Greek philosophy engaged the energies of many thinkers, most people were uninterested in the esoteric disputes of the learned. Practical disciplines such as medicine, astronomy, and language engaged the interest of the cultured urban citizens who were the poets, storytellers, historians, and patrons of artists. Thus, Islamic cultural achievements were both bold and imaginative as well as traditional and conservative.

Summary

Moving from Dublin to Baghdad, we saw not only a great deal of variety but impressive similarities. Between 600 and 1300 governments in the frontiers of the Latin West were becoming more bureaucratic and more impersonal, but everywhere there were tensions between central authority and local interests. Populations were rising and—except in Russia and parts of the Islamic world, where government policies were damaging—prosperity was growing. Social differentiation was becoming sharper. Except in Byzantium and the Islamic world, large-scale kin groupings were giving way to nuclear families as the basic building blocks of societies. Religion continued to play a critical role in forging bonds of unity and in propping up secular institutions. In the Slavic and Islamic lands, however, religion could also be divisive. Official, learned languages did not inhibit the development of vernacular cultures. Indeed, the richest of the vernacular cultures emerged outside the frontiers of the old Roman world. The peoples who lived around the core area of western Europe all had long, complex relations with the region. They contributed money and goods for trade, men for armies, motifs for art, and characters for literature.

Between 600 and 1300 the region now known as "the West" took shape. The Celtic, Scandinavian, and Slavic lands were folded into the West between about 900 and 1300. Byzantium left a huge legacy even though its empire was shattered. Russia was not destroyed by the Mongols, was not converted to Islam, and was not turned outward to Asia.

The profoundest impact in this period was felt by the Muslim world, dominated by waves of Turkish and then Mongolian rulers from the tenth century. Islam grew up in the old Roman world, and for centuries the caliphate hugged the Mediterranean. Before the coming of the Mongols, the deepest roots of Islamic culture tapped into Judaism, Christianity, and Hellenism, but after the thirteenth century Indian and Chinese contributions grew in importance. So it is that much about western Asia now seems familiar to Westerners but much seems foreign and remote. It was, then, in the period between the seventh and the thirteenth centuries that "the West" became both more than and less than the Roman Empire and the Hellenistic world.

The lands that were added—the Celtic realms, Scandinavia, and the Slavic world—remain a permanent part of the story of Western civilization. Later chapters in this book routinely incorporate their histories. Byzantium disappeared, but its cultural legacy in Slavic Europe is immense, and Orthodox Christianity holds the allegiance of millions of people today. The Islamic world split from the West in two senses. First, the Mongols wrenched the center of gravity toward the east. Second, a look at a map of the non-oil-producing regions of western Asia and North Africa today reveals that they are among the poorest areas in the world. Yet in antiquity and in the early Islamic period, those same lands were among the richest and most productive on earth. The rulers of the fragmenting Islamic world of the twelfth and thirteenth centuries destroyed both the wealth and the productive capacities of their lands. It is a bitter irony that when the Muslims defeated the Crusaders and saw Byzantium shrink into insignificance, they lost economic initiative to Europe.

Suggested Reading

The Celtic Realms

Barrow, G. W. S. *Kingship and Unity: Scotland, 1000–1306.* 1981. A solid though unexciting account of a period of decisive change in Scottish history; emphasizes politics.

Byrne, Francis John. *Irish Kings and High Kings.* 1973. A challenging account of early Irish political development.

Chadwick, Nora. *The Celts.* 1970. The best introduction to early Celtic history, society, religion, and culture.

Davies, R. R. *The Age of Conquest.* 1987. A fine, comprehensive history of Wales after the Norman conquest.

Davies, Wendy. *Wales in the Early Middle Ages.* 1982. A complex but stimulating social and economic account.

Henderson, George. *From Durrow to Kells: The Insular Gospel Books, 650–800.* 1987. A valuable introduction to Christian Celtic art, concentrating on manuscripts.

McNeill, John T. *The Celtic Churches.* 1974. The best introduction to the history of Christianity in Celtic lands.

Powell, T. G. E. *The Celts.* 1983. Readable and beautifully illustrated, an especially strong introduction to Celtic culture.

Richter, Michael. *Medieval Ireland: The Enduring Tradition.* 1988. A superb introduction to the controversial history of medieval Ireland.

Smyth, Alfred P. *Warlords and Holy Men: Scotland, A.D. 80–1000.* 1984. A reliable and readable account of the most difficult, because least documented, of all periods in Scottish history.

Scandinavia

Byock, Jesse L. *Medieval Iceland.* 1988. An excellent introduction to Scandinavian society and institutions because so many surviving Scandinavian sources derive from Iceland.

Graham-Campbell, James. *The Viking World.* 1980. A lavishly illustrated introduction to the culture of early Scandinavia.

Jones, Gwyn. *A History of the Vikings.* 2d ed. 1984. The most detailed history of the Vikings in English and the best general introduction to Scandinavian history.

Loyn, H. R. *The Vikings in Britain.* 1977. An interesting account of one of the lands most affected by the Vikings.

Roesdahl, Else. *The Vikings.* 1991. A fascinating book by a distinguished Danish archaeologist, the best introduction to both the Vikings and Scandinavia.

The Slavic World

Auty, Robert, and Dimitri Obolensky. *An Introduction to Russian History.* 1976. Somewhat technical and demanding; the early chapters provide orientation to Russian history and to scholarship on Russia.

Barraclough, Geoffrey, ed. *Eastern and Western Europe in the Middle Ages.* 1970. An interesting, wide-ranging, nontechnical collection of essays by experts on many aspects of east European history and culture.

Dvornik, Francis. *Byzantine Missions Among the Slavs.* 1970. A thorough account, the best introduction to the religious history of the Slavs.

Fine, John V. A. *The Early Medieval Balkans: A Critical Survey from the Sixth to the Late Twelfth Century.* 1983. A solid, current, understandable treatment of a complex subject written by an authority.

Gimbutas, Marija. *The Slavs.* 1971. A readable introduction to Slavic history that provides a valuable introduction to the prehistoric period; heavily archaeological.

Morgan, David. *The Mongols.* 1986. A lively account of the long, complex history of the Mongols and of their impact on their times.

Riasanovsky, Nicholas V. *A History of Russia.* 4th ed. 1984. A standard work whose opening chapters provide a good introduction to medieval Russia.

Vlasto, A. P. *The Entry of the Slavs into Christendom.* 1970. Lengthy and detailed, the best introduction to medieval Slavic history.

Byzantium

Angold, Michael. *The Byzantine Empire, 1025–1204: A Political History.* 1984. Dense, detailed, and uncompromising, a work that will reward the serious and careful reader.

Harvey, Alan. *Economic Expansion in the Byzantine Empire, 900–1200.* 1989. A fascinating and thought-provoking account of Byzantine economic development.

Kazhdan, A. P., and Ann Wharton Epstein. *Change in Byzantine Culture in the Eleventh and Twelfth Centuries.* 1985. A brilliant, entertaining reconstruction of almost all aspects of Byzantine life.

The Islamic World

Abu-Lughod, Janet. *Before European Hegemony: The World System, A.D. 1250–1350.* 1989. An interpretation of the rise and fall of Muslim economic dominance between the Mediterranean and the South China Sea in what is certain to become an influential and controversial book.

Grunebaum, Gustav von. *Medieval Islam: A Study in Cultural Orientation.* 2d ed. 1953. Readable and informative, still the best introduction to Islamic culture.

Hindley, Geoffrey. *Saladin.* 1976. A popular biography of a major and interesting figure.

Hourani, Albert. *A History of the Arab Peoples.* 1991. A readable work by an Arab who tries to interpret the East to the West; the author treats only the Arabs, not all Muslims.

Humphreys, R. Stephen. *From Saladin to the Mongols: The Ayyubids of Damascus, 1193–1260.* 1977. An accessible account of one people and of a period marked by Crusaders, famous heroes, and decisive political changes.

Lewis, Bernard. *The Muslim Discovery of Europe.* 1982. A readable and interesting account of the interactions between Muslims and Europeans.

Weighing the Evidence

THE MEDIEVAL CASTLE

Storybook castles—think of Camelot—figure prominently in almost everyone's idea of the Middle Ages, but the reality was different. Medieval castles were generally small, homely, stark, and uncomfortable. Though not beautiful and romantic, castles were still important.

Castles represent a stage in the history of fortifications. Castles proper were private, residential, and military. A consideration of these three elements will place the castle in historical context and illustrate what historians learn from the impressive ruins that dot the landscape of Europe and the crusader states.

The medieval castle, at its rise in the tenth century, was a private creation. Powerful aristocrats erected castles as their principal dwellings and as a means to secure and extend their political influence. From his castle a lord could dominate a region. The castle also sheltered the lord's immediate dependents temporarily in the event of an attack, and his military retainers more or less permanently.

By the late twelfth and early thirteenth centuries, states, beginning with the French and English monarchies, began to monopolize the possession of castles. Cerreg Cennen, below, was built by a Welsh prince, Lord Rhys (d. 1197), and then seized from his descendants by Edward I of England. Château d'Angers, opposite, was erected by the counts of Anjou but became a garrison of the French monarchy in the thirteenth century. The French word *château* (from the Latin *castellum*) means "great house," signifying the castle's residential purpose. In later centuries, the castle (as château) retained its private and residential nature but lost its military character.

Castles of the tenth, eleventh, and twelfth centuries symbolize well the extreme localization and privatization of power then characterizing Europe. Not surprisingly, as European governments grew stronger in the twelfth century, they suppressed private castles as military entities. Thereafter, as in Roman times, fortresses served essentially public and military purposes. They had resident garrisons, but their purpose was not to be the private residence of a landed lord.

Castles could take many forms. From 900 to 1200 the "Motte and Bailey" form was the most

Cerreg Cennen Castle, Wales *(Michael Holford)*

common. A lord commanded his dependents to dig a circular ditch and to heap the dirt into a mound (the motte). Atop the mound he placed a wooden tower (the bailey). Sometimes there was an elaborate series of mounds, ditches, and wooden walls—look at the picture of the Polish Motte and Bailey castle on page 325—but usually these structures were quite simple.

As siege techniques improved (catapults could hurl projectiles weighing 600 pounds) the wooden building(s) of the bailey began to be replaced by stone. By 1150 or 1200 stone towers (*donjons*, from the Latin *dominium* for "lordship") began to form only the inside portion—the "keep"—of a more complicated structure consisting of walls, towers, and gates. It was not unusual for walls to be 75 or 100 feet high. Because of the growing power of bombarding engines, castle walls had to be thickened often. Towers built at 40- or 50-foot intervals projected beyond the walls so that defenders armed with bows and arrows could fire at attackers along the length of a castle wall. Look at the spacing of the towers in the castles pictured here. Initially towers were square or rectangular, but defenders discovered that round towers—compare those of Cerreg Cennen and Angers—were preferable because projectiles were likely to glance off them.

People needed to enter and leave castles for both hostile and peaceful purposes. Thus castles had gate towers, usually with two gates, one on the outside and one on the inside. Intricate systems of winches, cranks, and counterweights regulated the raising and lowering of the gates. Speedy operation was essential. Some castles had small "sally-ports" from which soldiers could make a rapid dash to attack a besieging enemy.

When possible, lords sited their castles on cliffs, because fewer sides could be attacked and a garrison of modest size could defend the remaining walls. Cerreg Cennen stands 300 feet above a gorge, as you can see from the left side of the picture. The bases of walls or towers were sometimes strengthened by embankments that sloped gently outward. Embankments made the castle walls hard to climb. You can see the embankments at Angers clearly in the photo.

Château d'Angers, France *(Michael Holford)*

Many things can be learned from the castle: the presence of numerous small castles across the countryside—remains of several hundred have been found in France alone—would reveal an extreme decentralization of power in a given place and time. The existence of a few large, strategically sited castles would point to greater central control. Careful mapping of the known locations of castles can tell historians a great deal about the structure of social and political relationships. Castles both contributed and responded to developments in military technology such as more powerful catapults. Stone castles proliferated as Europe grew wealthier and as quarrying technology improved. Castles grew larger as monarchies rather than private individuals built them. Like cathedrals, large, state-funded castles tended to be built by professionals rather than by local laborers. In Chapter 11 you will encounter other examples of the increased professionalization of life in twelfth- and thirteenth-century Europe.

Both fortifications and magnificent dwellings have existed in Western civilization for millennia. The castle, however, met the needs of a politically dominant warrior aristocracy for a private residence with military significance.

SIC RE
SIDET: HAROLD
REX: AN
GLORVM:
STIGANT
ARCHI
EPS

CHAPTER 10

The Expansion of Europe, ca. 900–1150

Spurred by biblical prophecies, hopes and fears gathered expectantly around the turn of the millennium. Shortly after the year 1000 passed without apocalyptic incident, Ralph Glaber, a Burgundian chronicler, wrote these words: "When the third year after the millennium had dawned, churches were to be seen being rebuilt all over the earth, but especially in Italy and Gaul; although most churches were very well constructed and had no need of rebuilding, each Christian community was driven by a true rivalry to have a finer church than that of its neighbors. It looked as though the very world was shaking itself to take off its old age and to reclothe itself all over in a white cloak of churches."[1] Glaber's words signal hope, optimism, progress, achievement. They seem remarkable when we remember that in the late ninth century western Europe was suffering from Magyar, Muslim, and Viking attacks and from political dislocation.

Nevertheless, between about 900 and 1150 Europe's population began one of its longest periods of sustained growth. People brought more land under cultivation, introduced new crops, and made agriculture more efficient. Cities grew in number and size. The tenth century saw the emergence of myriad local communities that were stable and creative. The twelfth century witnessed the re-emergence of centralizing monarchies in England, France, Germany, and Spain.

The church experienced several waves of reform activity. Monastic reformers attempted to improve the education, morals, and spiritual life of religious communities. But the reformers also caused a political and ideological crisis when they challenged the right of rulers to interfere in eccle-

Bayeux Tapestry: Anglo-Saxon nobles and Archbishop Stigand crown Harold of Wessex as king of England.

siastical affairs. A superb vernacular literature began to appear all over Europe, not to challenge but to complement the Latin letters of the schools.

Europeans spread aggressively in every direction. Normans conquered both England and southern Italy. Germans marched east into Slavic Europe. Spanish Christians pushed back the Muslims in the Iberian Peninsula. Armies of adventurers headed east in those remarkable expeditions, the Crusades.

Glaber's words evoke much of this: the energy, rivalry, religious zeal, economic growth, swelling population. *Expansion,* in both the literal and the figurative sense, captures the spirit of the West in the tenth, eleventh, and early twelfth centuries.

Signs of Expansion

Evidence for the economic expansion of Europe abounds but is usually more qualitative than quantitative. No medieval kingdom in the period 900–1150 attempted a complete census (though England came close). Births, baptisms, marriages, and deaths were not systematically recorded. Detailed returns were not kept of the productivity of urban craftsmen or rural farmers. The absence of these records means that we must often draw inferences from a disparate body of evidence.

The Growing Population

The population of Europe began rising slowly in the Carolingian period and may have doubled between 1000 and 1200. From scattered bits of evidence it is possible to suggest that the total population of western Europe was around 30 million in 1000 and from 55 to 60 million in 1200.

In a few regions where family size can be estimated, fertile marriages were producing on the average 3.5 children in the tenth century and from 6 to 7 in the twelfth. All families continued to experience the loss of children. Three queens—those of William the Conqueror, John of England, and Louis VIII of France—lost, respectively 4 of 10, 6 of 14, and 7 of 12 children. The key change is that more babies were being born. People were also living longer than their forebears. Studies of aristocrats, high clergy, and soldiers show that a surprising 40 percent of them were over 40 years old. Male life expectancy was surely longer than female because of the dangers of childbirth, always the great killer of women in the premodern world. The general trend is clear: more babies being born, more infants living into adulthood, more adults living longer.

Other indicators agree. There was no significant plague in Europe between 780 and 1345. On the whole the period was without catastrophic incidents of lack and hunger. Crime was comparatively insignificant as a check on the population and, despite fanciful literary accounts of dozens of men being killed by a single swing of a sword, war carried off few combatants. There is no evidence that sickness was more or less significant than before.

Everywhere in Europe, new land was brought into cultivation (see the box, "The Expansion of Cultivated Land"). More than half of the French documents relating to land in the twelfth century mention *assarting,* the bringing of new land under the plow. Literary texts often tell about knights wandering in a dense forest and then finding a clearing or meadow. Those meadows did not get there by accident. Thousands of acres of forest were felled. Marshes were reclaimed from the sea. Some 380,000 acres were drained along the western coast of France and probably twice that amount of land was drained in both Flanders and England. This activity is inexplicable without assuming a growing number of mouths to feed.

In addition, agriculture was favored by a generally warmer and drier climate through the whole of our period. Not a single vegetable blight was recorded. There was more and also better food. Animals were increasingly reared for their meat. Higher meat consumption meant more proteins in the diet. Beans and other legumes, also high in protein, were more widely cultivated. White grains, especially fine kinds of wheat, replaced poorer cereals in many areas. People of every class and region were almost certainly eating better and living longer and healthier lives.

Technological Gains

The eleventh century was a decisive period in the dissemination of new technologies in Europe. Novelties occurred in agriculture, transporta-

The Expansion of Cultivated Land

These extracts from three German charters show that new land was being brought into cultivation along Europe's frontiers and that people were leaving some areas to seek better opportunities elsewhere.

Frederic, by the grace of God bishop of the church at Hamburg, to all faithful men in Christ, present and future, perpetual blessings. We desire that the contract which the men from beyond the Rhine, called Hollanders, have made with us shall be known to all. Now these men come to find our majesty, requesting the grant of land in our bishopric, until now uncultivated and marshy and useless to the inhabitants of the country, to put it under cultivation. On the advice of our congregation, judging that the thing will be of use to us and our successors, we have given our consent.

Gerungus, by the grace of God bishop of the church at Niessen, to all those present and future. We desire that it shall be known by our congregation now and in the future how I have brought together and established in an uncultivated and almost uninhabited place energetic men coming from the province of Flanders, and how I have given stable, eternal and hereditary possession to them and all their descendants.

Let it be known by the whole congregation, present and future, that I, Wichmann, by the grace of God archbishop of the holy church of Magdeburg, have given to Heribert a village called Pechau, with all its dependencies in field, meadow, woodland and pond for cultivation and to make fruitful, according to the agreement concluded between him and me.

Source: Georges Duby, *Rural Economy and Country Life in the Medieval West,* trans. Cynthia Postan (London: Arnold, 1968), pp. 392, 395–396.

tion, mining, and manufacturing. Technological changes also show us a medieval economy and society that were increasingly interdependent. Agricultural changes came first as a rising population created an increased demand for food that could be met only by new practices. Improvements in agriculture, coupled with others in transport, freed large numbers of persons not engaged in agriculture—urban dwellers, mainly—for other pursuits.

In the Carolingian period, the return on seed—the amount of seed realized for each seed sewn—is estimated at about 3 or 4 to 1. By the late twelfth century this ratio had risen in many areas to 8 or 10 to 1. Given that more land was under cultivation, the overall gains in the food supply were enormous.

The increases can be accounted for in several ways. Horses were more frequently used as draft animals. They were more expensive to acquire than oxen but no more expensive to feed, and they did, in a day, a third or half again as much work. For much less "fuel," horses could haul loads farther and faster than oxen or mules. Thus, fewer men could, with horses, cultivate more land than their predecessors managed with oxen. In addition, they could cultivate the land more frequently and increase yields because more seed would fall on more finely plowed soil. The more widespread use of horses was made possible by the dissemination of the horse collar—older forms of harness suitable for the low-slung, broad-shouldered ox would have choked a horse.

Plows also improved. The light wooden scratch plow used by the Romans was satisfactory for the thin soils of the Mediterranean region but barely disturbed the heavy soils of northern Europe. The invention of a heavy wheeled plow with an iron coulter and a moldboard was a real breakthrough. This plow seems to have been introduced into Carolingian Europe from the Slavic lands, but it was not widely adopted before the eleventh century, perhaps because the expense of its acquisition was not compensated by a growing market for the crops that it could help to produce. The growing availability of iron may have been a factor too. The iron plowshare cut deeply into the soil, and then the moldboard turned and aerated the soil. This heavy plow made it possible for farmers to exploit good soils more fully without exhausting the ground too rapidly.

Soil exhaustion was a constant concern. Spreading manure was the only means of restoring essential nutrients, such as nitrogen. Wider adoption of nitrogen-fixing crops, such as peas and some kinds of beans, retarded soil exhaustion—and also put more protein in the diet. Leaving land fallow was another means of avoiding soil exhaustion. In the early Middle Ages this meant setting aside about half of the arable land every year (the two-field system) or working the land intensively for a few years and then moving on. By the twelfth century three-field schemes of crop rotation were common.

Heavy Wheeled Plow This picture reveals the form of the plow, the horse-collar, and the cooperative labors of many peasants in preparing the fields. (*Bibliothèque Nationale*)

Mill Gears Here we see "undershot" mill wheels (the flowing water passes under them) and also the gears that translate vertical into horizontal motion to turn the grinding stones. (*Bibliothèque Nationale*)

Under the three-field system—another innovation, it seems, of the Slavic world—two-thirds of the arable land saw nearly constant use. The amount of an estate under cultivation rose from 50 to 67 percent. Crop rotation brought other benefits as well. Horses ate oats, but (except in a few places like Scotland) medieval people generally did not. If farmers wished to use horses, they had to dedicate some of their land to growing oats. A three-field rotation allowed some flexibility. Cereal grains were always the staple crop, but as dietary needs and tastes changed, the three-field system permitted much greater variety. Finally, the alternation of winter crops (wheat and rye), spring crops (oats, barley, and legumes), and fallow ensured against a single season of unusually harsh weather.

Surplus produce was intended mainly for the growing towns. To supply that market, improvements in transportation were necessary. Kings often passed laws to secure the safety of highways, and popes three times (in 1097, 1132, and 1179) threatened highwaymen with excommunication. Landlords required their dependents to maintain roads and bridges. Many stone bridges were constructed in France between 1130 to 1170 because wooden bridges were so vulnerable to fire. Indeed, the bridge at Angers (in western France) was destroyed by fire five times between 1032 and 1167.

Keeping the roads safe and passable was one thing. Another was improving the vehicles that traveled on them. Documents and works of art agree that the old two-wheeled cart, drawn by oxen or mules, was giving way to the sturdy four-wheeled, horse-drawn wagon. As the horse collar aided agriculture, so too new systems of tandem harnessing aided transport. The fact that larger quantities of foodstuffs could be moved farther and faster meant that urban communities could be supplied from larger areas. This was a crucial factor in enabling cities to grow and in providing urban residents with a predictable and diverse range of foods.

Transport also moved grain to mills. People in some areas of the Roman world had used water wheels and windmills to grind grain. By the mid-twelfth century no sizable village anywhere would have been without a mill. The construction of elaborate schemes of gearing and of water courses to shoot water over or under a mill grew more sophisticated all over Europe. Producing and transporting increasing amounts of grain would have been pointless without some way to process it.

Evidence from various parts of Europe points to the years after 925 as the beginning of real growth in the mining industry. Notable improvements occurred in both the quarrying of stone and the extraction of metals. Mines were not deep because people lacked the means to keep the shafts and galleries free of water. Still, the exploitation of surface and near-surface veins of ore—principally iron but also tin and silver—intensified, to supply the plowshares, tools, weapons, construction fittings, and coins that were in increasing demand. Stone-quarrying, the commonest form of mining in the Middle Ages, benefited directly from more efficient stone saws and indirectly from improvements in transport. Better techniques in stone-cutting and construction help to explain, for example, the increase in England's stone religious buildings from 60 to nearly 500 in the century after 1050.

Forms of Enterprise

Agricultural specialization became common. Instead of relying on estates or regions to provide for all of their needs, people began to cultivate intensively those crops that were best suited to local conditions. The area around Toulouse, for example, concentrated on herbs from which blue and yellow dyes were made. The central regions of France focused on cereal grains, while the Bordeaux and Burgundy regions turned to viticulture (cultivation of grapevines). Northern Germany specialized in cattle-raising; northern England favored sheep.

Agricultural specialization helps to explain the growth in trade that is discernible everywhere (Map 10.1). Local trade continued to flourish. Italian wines and olive oil, for example, were not produced for far-off markets; they tended to move from countryside to town within a region. The same was true of French or English grains. French wines were much prized, however, especially in England; and certain products, such as English wool and Flemish cloth, were carried far and wide. Salt fish from the Baltic found its way all over Europe. Lumber was routinely traded across the Mediterranean to the wood-poor Muslim world. Spain was a source of warhorses. Southern Europe supplied the northern demand for spices, oranges, raisins, figs, almonds, and other exotic foodstuffs. Caen in Normandy shipped stone, whose color and texture were admired, to England for the construction of churches and monasteries. Rising population, higher productivity, and greater prosperity added up to a larger volume of goods moving farther and more frequently.

The construction and lumbering industries illustrate the expansion and the growing interdependence of economic activities. Both increased employment and income in the predominantly agricultural medieval world. In societies where farming dominates, the labor force may be idle except during planting and harvesting. Stone masons or master builders were highly skilled, but construction provides employment to large numbers of occasional laborers and, through the wages paid to workmen, helps to circulate money through society. Medieval churches, for example, acquired monies from alms and from their lands. Instead of hoarding this money, churches elected to spend it on buildings and thus stimulated much economic activity.

The lumbering industry reveals other facets of medieval economic activity. Before the twelfth century, wood was the main building material, and even after that time it yielded to stone mainly for the church and aristocracy. But wood could be used for things other than buildings—for example, ships. The Venetian shipyards needed about twenty oaks, twenty good-size pines, and fifty or so beeches to make a ship. In the early twelfth century the Venetians were making about ten vessels a year, probably twice the number they had been building two centuries earlier. Whether for shipping or for housing, there was a steadily

Map 10.1 European Resources and Trade Routes, ca. 1100 In an age of expansion, some products were consumed locally but many products moved along increasingly intricate commercial networks.

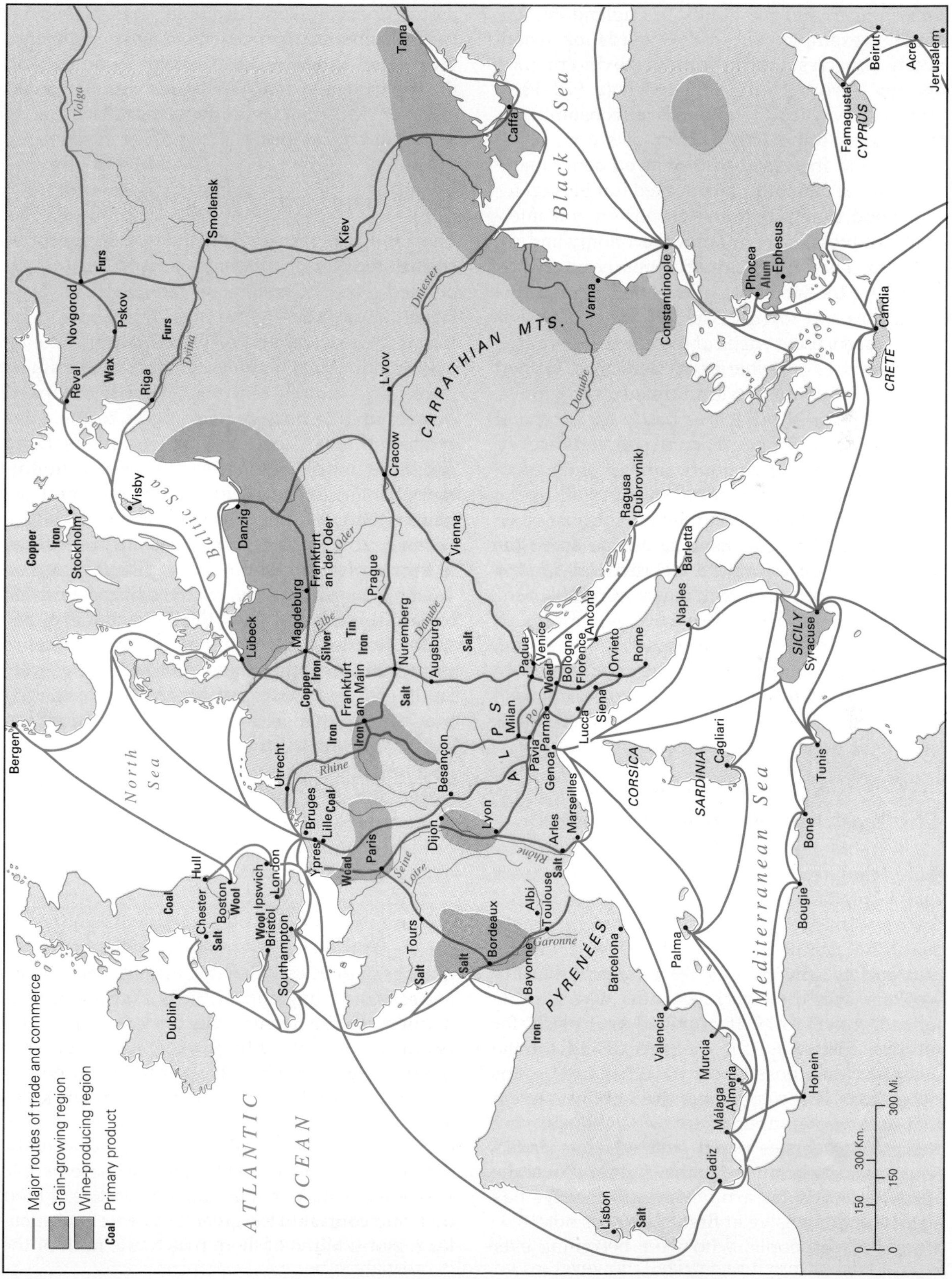

Major routes of trade and commerce
Grain-growing region
Wine-producing region
Coal Primary product
ATLANTIC
OCEAN
North Sea
Baltic Sea
Black Sea
Mediterranean Sea
ALPS
PYRENEES
CARPATHIAN MTS.
CORSICA
SARDINIA
SICILY
CRETE
CYPRUS
Volga
Dvina
Dniester
Danube
Oder
Elbe
Rhine
Po
Seine
Loire
Rhone
Garonne
Bergen
Stockholm
Copper
Iron
Visby
Reval
Riga
Novgorod
Pskov
Wax
Furs
Smolensk
Kiev
Tana
Caffa
L'vov
Cracow
Danzig
Lübeck
Magdeburg
Frankfurt an der Oder
Prague
Vienna
Nuremberg
Augsburg
Salt
Silver
Tin
Frankfurt am Main
Utrecht
Bruges
Coal
Lille
Ypres
Woad
Paris
Dijon
Besançon
Lyon
Arles
Marseilles
Genoa
Pavia
Milan
Parma
Padua
Venice
Bologna
Florence
Lucca
Siena
Orvieto
Ancona
Rome
Naples
Barletta
Ragusa (Dubrovnik)
Varna
Constantinople
Phocea
Alum
Ephesus
Candia
Famagusta
Beirut
Acre
Jerusalem
Syracuse
Tunis
Bone
Bougie
Honein
Cagliari
Palma
Valencia
Murcia
Almeria
Málaga
Cadiz
Lisbon
Barcelona
Bayonne
Bordeaux
Toulouse
Albi
Tours
Dublin
Chester
Hull
Boston
Wool
Ipswich
London
Bristol
Southampton
0 150 300 Km.
0 150 300 Mi.

growing demand for wood. In England, to take another example, about 500 cords of wood, nearly ten acres' worth, were needed to prepare one ton of silver. King Ethelred II (r. 978–1016) alone coined thirty tons of silver, consuming in the process some 15,000 cords of wood. Better mining and increased trade played complimentary roles in demanding increased lumbering.

Wood exemplifies the expansion and interconnectedness of the medieval economy and society. Forests were an important part of daily life, providing the wood for houses, fences, and fuel in villages and towns. Animals, especially pigs, were grazed at the edges of the forest to permit as much land as possible to be dedicated to food crops. Wild animals were hunted in the forest. For aristocrats hunting was partly for sport and partly for food. For poorer rural people, however, wild meat made up a significant part of the regular diet. The forest was also a plentiful source of fruits, nuts, and honey. If the peasants in a given place decided to cut some timber to smelt the king's silver, or to build a wooden wall around their village, or to dispatch masts to Venice or the Baltic, they had some critical choices to make. After the trees were gone, where would they hunt, or graze their animals, or gather their berries? In the very early Middle Ages such choices imposed themselves with little urgency. In Ralph Glaber's world, the urgency was increasingly felt.

The Traditional Order of Society

Alfred the Great (r. 871–899) of England once said that a kingdom needed "men of prayer, men of war, and men of work." By the early eleventh century, it had become almost a cliché in Europe that society consisted of fighters, prayers, and workers. This division reveals the way the elite looked at the world. It provided neat places for warrior aristocrats, for the clergy, and for the peasantry on whose labors the other two groups depended. The clergy and the nobility agreed that they were superior to the "workers," but fierce controversies raged over whether leadership in society belonged to the "fighters" or to the "prayers." The tripartite view of society may seem comprehensive at first, but it was not. It excluded townspeople, who were becoming ever more important. Town residents worked for a living, of course, but only farmers were considered "workers." Where, we may ask, did women fit in the tripartite division? What place was allowed to Jews or Muslims, who in some places were significant minorities?

Those Who Fight: The Nobility

The nobility of the eleventh and twelfth centuries constituted an increasingly closed and well-defined class. Carolingian families had been large, amorphous groupings of people who traced their descent on both the male and the female sides. Such families tended to dominate public and church offices, to hold vast landed possessions, to have regular access to the royal court, and to be fairly open to newcomers. From about the middle of the eleventh century, important changes appeared in the structure and behavior of noble families as political and social life became more local in scope after the breakdown of the Carolingian Empire.

Loose groupings of relatives began to think of themselves as lineages, the descendants of one male ancestor. Such families began to practice primogeniture—the transmittal of all family lands, offices, and titles to the eldest male heir. By purchase, exchange, theft, and intimidation, lineages consolidated their landholdings into compact lordships. At the center of these lands was a castle, and from that castle the family took its name. The sudden emergence in the eleventh century of abundant genealogical writings shows that noble families had a keen sense of their own identity.

The nobility was not yet closed or homogeneous. Fortunes and titles could be acquired quickly in politically volatile areas such as Spain and Norman England or Sicily and along Germany's eastern frontier. In central France and Germany, however, things were more stable, and three levels of nobility can often be discerned.

In the first level were the truly great: kings and other members of royal families, dukes, counts, and frontier lords. In the second were the direct vassals of the great. Many of these people were castellans, persons who built castles of their own and contested the great for power in particular regions. Some of them rose to the rank of the great; others were reduced in power and made dependent on their stronger neighbors. In the third level was a vast and growing class of ordinary knights. These were either the sons of the other two classes or else ordinary free men who owed no service or payments to anyone and were faring badly in the power contests of the age. The consolidation of lineages and of territorial lordships was producing large numbers of men who had noble blood and upbringings, lofty ambitions, but limited prospects. These men, called in contemporary sources "the young," followed adventurers to every corner of the medieval world in search of glory and a livelihood. Some of them joined the retinue of a more powerful man, received cash support and sometimes a fief, and awaited a chance to find an heiress, through whose inheritance a new lineage might be established. These "young" men were often over 40.

Mentioning lords, vassals, and fiefs brings up the subject of feudalism. Charlemagne (see page 291), as one feature of his governing system, had connected personal loyalty (vassalage) with public office and material reward (the benefice or fief). In the tenth and eleventh centuries, versions of this system had spread all over Europe and to almost all levels of society. The result is sometimes called the "feudal system." Many varieties of feudalism existed in Europe from the tenth century to the fifteenth.

Feudalism may be defined as a social and political system wherein public responsibilities and powers that had fallen into the hands of private individuals were fulfilled by men who had sworn personal fidelity to one another. By solemn acts of homage and fealty, a vassal pledged never to do anything that would damage his lord or his lord's interests and also undertook to perform certain services—usually military service and appearance at the lord's court, where important judicial cases would be decided and political decisions made. In return, the lord provided protection—physical, legal, or political—and gave the vassal something of value. From the tenth century, the lord's gift was usually a landed estate, called by modern scholars a *fief* and by medieval texts a *feudum* (whence *feudalism*). (See the box, "Feudal Bonds and Obligations.")

The nobility shows vertical bonds in its hierarchy of vassalic ties and in its command of the peasant population. The nobility also joined in horizontal associations. The retinues of noblemen were a kind of substitute kinship, especially for the "young," who had been cut loose from family ties. Noble groupings often joined in supporting a local monastery, in promoting the cult of a local patron saint, or in enjoying the prayers of its monks. Noblemen frequently fought together and thought of themselves as comrades in arms. Their training in the use of arms and the riding of horses, their clothing, diet, and dwellings—all were similar enough to give them a sense of group solidarity.

A specific ethos, chivalry, belonged to the nobility. Chivalry was a code of conduct for a warrior-aristocracy. Its very name derives from *cheval,* French for *horse,* the classic conveyance of a knight. Today, chivalry is often thought of as either a code of conduct regulating relations between the sexes or the value system behind the romantic image of dashing knights in shining armor saving damsels in distress from fire-breathing dragons. Actually, it prized most highly certain male and militant qualities. Military prowess was the most highly esteemed of chivalric virtues. A knight who was not a great warrior was useless. Literature of the time is full of accounts of battles with immense beasts or of hand-to-hand combat between a single hero and impossible numbers of the enemy.

Open-handed generosity was another key virtue. The truly noble person engaged in sumptuous display to make his power manifest, to show how much he cared for his dependents, and to attract even more followers. Medieval literature is full of rich banquets and stunning presents. In Anglo-Saxon England the king was called "the giver of rings." Knights were deeply concerned about their honor, their reputation. They sought glory, the better to win a lord or a bride. Finally, there was loyalty, the glue that held feudal society together.

But what are we to make of statements such as the following one by William of Malmesbury? William, a twelfth-century English historian, wrote: "They (knights) are faithful to their lords, but swift to break faith. A breath of ill fortune and they are plotting treachery, a bag of money and their mind is changed." Knights, especially the "young," were loyal to their lords when they

Feudal Bonds and Obligations

Duke William of Aquitaine in 1020 asked Bishop Fulbert of Chartres to explain the nature of fealty. The first document is the bishop's idealized view of the mutual obligations of lords and vassals. The second text is a depiction from 1127 of the actual public ceremonies surrounding the feudal bond.

He who swears fealty to his lord ought always to have these six things in mind: what is harmless, safe, honorable, useful, easy, practicable. *Harmless,* that is to say, that he should not injure his lord in his body; *safe,* that he should not injure him by betraying his secrets or the defenses on which he relies for his safety; *honorable,* that he should not injure him in his justice or in other matters that pertain to his honor; *useful,* that he should not injure him in his possessions; *easy,* that he should not make difficult that which his lord can do easily; and *practicable,* that he should not make impossible for the lord that which is possible.

That the faithful vassal should avoid these injuries is proper, it is not for this alone that he deserves his holding; for it is not enough to abstain from evil, unless what is good is done also. He should faithfully aid and counsel his lord, if he wishes to be looked on as worthy of his benefice and to be safe concerning the fealty he has sworn.

The lord ought also to act toward his faithful vassal reciprocally in all these things for if he does not do these things he shall rightly be considered guilty of bad faith.

Through the whole remaining part of the day those who had been previously enfeoffed by the most pious Count Charles did homage to the new count, taking up now again their fiefs and offices and whatever they had before rightfully obtained.

First, they did their homage thus. The count asked the vassal if he were willing to become completely his man, and the other replied "I am willing"; and with hands clasped, placed between the hands of the count, they were bound together by a kiss. Secondly, he who had done homage gave his fealty to a representative of the count in these words: "I promise on my faith that I will be faithful to Count William, and will observe my homage to him completely against all persons, in good faith and without deceit." He took his oath on the relics of the saints.

Source: James Harvey Robinson, *Readings in European History,* vol. 1 (Boston: Ginn, 1904), pp. 184–185, 179–180 (slightly adapted).

could be, but fundamentally they were loyal to themselves.

The nobility governed medieval society. Some held public offices delegated to them by emperors or kings. Virtually all governed also in private capacities, ruling as direct lords over their landed patrimonies and over the people who lived on their lands. Their retinues served as guarantees of their power on the local scene, enabled them to extend their authority at the expense of their neighbors, and protected their lands from attack. The nobility, leaders and followers alike, were supported by the exertions of a vast number of dependents. These people paid rents and fees in both cash and kind and also performed labor services. Their labor freed the nobility for its military, government, and social diversions.

What role was left to noble women in a world of chivalry and feudalism? Convents of aristocratic nuns remained places where women could be highly educated and almost entirely in control of their own affairs. Matilda, daughter of the German empress Adelaide, was abbess of Quedlinburg, mistress of vast estates in northern Germany, and a dominant figure in German politics. Less predictably, Gaita, wife of a Norman prince in Italy, fought in helmet and armor alongside her husband, as did Duchess Agnes of Burgundy. All over France, in the fluid political climate of the tenth and eleventh centuries, women were mistresses of castles and real powers in local politics. By the late eleventh century, however, three developments adversely affected the position of aristocratic women. First, the elaboration of the chivalric ethos defined most key social and political roles as "manly" and thereby excluded women from them. By the middle of the twelfth century it was rare for a woman to hold a castle and unheard-of for one to ride to arms. Second, the consolidation of lineages by aristocratic families occurred simultaneously with a moral campaign by the church to promote monogamous, unbreakable marriage. This situation subordinated women's freedom in the marriage market to the dynastic and patrimonial needs of great families. Third, the spread of feudalism, with its intricate network of personal and proprietary relationships based on military service, tended to deprive women of independent rights over land.

Those Who Pray: The Clergy

Members of the clergy were overwhelmingly noble, but they may be differentiated from lay nobles by virtue of their priestly or monastic offices. As the church promoted its own vision of the tripartite ordering of society, it assigned primacy to the "prayers," to its own leaders. Within the clergy, however, sharp disagreements arose over whether the leading "prayers" were the monks in their monasteries or the bishops who conducted the public business of the church. Ignored in these disagreements between the monastic and secular clergy were the parish priests, drawn often from the lower ranks of society, ill educated, and without a voice in affairs. Whereas in the Carolingian world, the clergy was occasionally an avenue of upward social mobility for talented outsiders, the later consolidation of families began to confine church offices to the younger sons of the nobility. The church, always hierarchical, became in feudal society even more aristocratic in membership and outlook.

In the aftermath of the Carolingian collapse, a great spiritual reform swept Europe. It began in 909 when Duke William of Aquitaine founded the monastery of Cluny in Burgundy on lands that he freely donated. At a time when almost all monasteries were under the domination of powerful local families, Cluny was a rarity because it was freed of all lay and episcopal control and placed under the direct authority of the pope. Cluny's abbots were among the greatest European statesmen of their day and became influential advisers to popes, French kings, German emperors, and aristocratic families.

In the tradition of Benedict of Aniane, Cluny placed great emphasis on liturgical prayer. The monks spent long hours in solemn devotions and did little manual work. Because Cluniac prayer was thought to be especially efficacious, noblemen all over Europe donated land to Cluny and placed local monasteries under Cluniac control. Many independent monasteries also appealed to Cluny for spiritual reform. Sometimes they sent monks to Cluny to observe, and sometimes monks from Cluny visited houses that desired to be reformed. By the twelfth century, hundreds of monasteries were joined in a Cluniac order. Individual houses were under the authority of the abbot of Cluny, and their priors had to attend an annual assembly.

Cluny promoted two powerful ideas. One was that the role of the church was to pray for the world, not to be implicated deeply in it. The other was that freedom from lay control was important if churches were not to be diverted from their spiritual tasks.

In 993 Bishop Adalbero of Metz assisted in the restoration of Benedictine usages in the dilapidated Lorraine monastery of Gorze. Customs at Gorze resembled those at Cluny, and they spread widely in Lorraine, Germany, and England. The Gorze reform was well received by kings and nobles; its aim was not so much to withdraw from the world as to improve it. Monks from the Gorze and Cluniac traditions bitterly criticized clerical immorality and inappropriate lay interference in the church. They preached against clerical marriage and simony, the buying and selling of church offices.

Some people felt that the reforms did not go far enough. They criticized the monastery at Cluny, saying that it had become too opulent and successful, and the monastery at Gorze because it seemed too immersed in worldly affairs. A few were driven by a desire to recapture what they believed to be the way of life of the original apostolic community—a life of poverty, renunciation, and seclusion. Thus, the eleventh and early twelfth centuries saw a proliferation of eremitic experiments in monasticism, especially in Italy, where zealous reformers came into contact with Byzantine ascetics. Other Europeans believed that the apostolic life demanded not only an active life of Christian ministry but also an austere regime of personal renunciation. Cathedral clergy, called canons, in particular, adapted an old rule by Saint Augustine so that they could live an austere communal life and carry out their priestly duties.

The greatest critics of the Cluniac tradition, and the real monastic elite of the early twelfth century, were the Cistercians. In 1098 Abbot Robert left his Burgundian monastery of Molesme because he believed it had abandoned the strict teachings of Saint Benedict. He founded a new monastery at Cîteaux in Burgundy. This house was to follow the Benedictine Rule literally and to refuse all secular entanglements: lands, rents, and servile dependents. So rigorous and poor was the community that it struggled until a young Burgundian nobleman named Bernard (1090–1153) joined in 1112. Three years later Bernard left to found a daughter house at Clairvaux, of which he remained abbot for the rest of his life. Through his writing, preaching, and personal example Bernard dominated the religious life of Europe in the first half of the twelfth century. By the end of the twelfth century there were about 500 Cistercian (from the Latin for *Cîteaux*) monasteries in Europe, and Bernard's own Clairvaux had 700 monks.

With the monastic clergy gaining so much in prestige and visibility, the episcopal clergy countered with its own view of society. Surely, the bishops agreed, spiritual, moral, and intellectual improvement were desirable. Likewise, it was time to end the grossest examples of lay interference in the church. But precisely because so many bishops came from great families and were so well connected, they were less inclined to be rigid about the line of demarcation between lay and clerical responsibilities. In Germany, for example, the king's chapel recruited young noblemen to train them as clerics and to inculcate in them the policies and ethos of the court. Many of these chaplains were appointed to bishoprics and then advanced the king's interests in their new areas of authority. But they were often men of spiritual depth, and they resented what they regarded as monastic carping about their worldliness. By the middle of the twelfth century, bishops, and finally popes too, had imposed on the church a view that monks belonged in their monasteries and that bishops should lead society. After the death of Bernard, monasticism never again enjoyed the prestige or actual power that it had once held.

It was always the special responsibility of the clergy to look after the moral order of the society. In the violent and turbulent world of gentlemen warriors, the church had its own ideas about what a perfect knight should do. The English bishop and scholar John of Salisbury (d. 1180), reflecting on knighthood in the twelfth century, said that it existed "To protect the church, to attack infidelity, to reverence the priesthood, to protect the poor, to keep the peace, to shed one's blood and, if necessary, to lay down one's life for one's brethren."

Turning large numbers of violent young men into servants of the church was a tall order for the clergy, and they had only limited success. One example of the church's success is the military orders. The Knights of St. John, or Hospitallers, and the Knights of the Temple, or Templars, are the major examples, but others existed in Spain and Germany. The Hospitallers started near Jerusalem as a foundation under Benedictine auspices founded by merchants of Amalfi and dedicated to charitable works and care of the sick. Eventually the Hospitallers evolved into a monastic order using a version of the Rule of Saint Benedict and devoted to the defense of pilgrims to the Holy Land. The Templars were men living under religious rule and dedicated to protecting the small states created by the crusaders (see page 385). The military orders measured up

The Knight at Prayer This stained glass window from Chartres depicts the church's idealized conception of one of God's warriors: His sword and pious disposition combat the enemies of religion. (*Sonia Halliday Photographs*)

very well to the clergy's idea of what a perfect knight should be.

The clergy could also regulate disputes in society. For example, when a community was divided by a difficult conflict that demanded resolution, it might turn to the ordeal—a judicial procedure that sought divine judgment by subjecting the accused to a physically painful or dangerous test. An accused person might walk a certain distance carrying hot iron or plunge a hand into a boiling cauldron to pluck out a pebble. The resulting wounds would be bandaged for a set time and then examined. If they were healing, the person was considered innocent; if festering, guilty. The clergy officiated at ordeals before their participation was forbidden by the papacy in 1215.

Clergymen were also the conservators of the relics and shrines where people gained special access to the holiness of the saints. The clergy wrote and preached about the miracles of the saints. Stories told about relics kept in certain places brought people as pilgrims to often far-off shrines to seek healing from illness, injury, or misfortune. The clergy played unique roles in forming and nurturing communities in the world and in interceding for this world with God in the next.

Those Who Work: The Peasants

The peasants, an extremely diverse segment of society, were the "workers" in the tripartite scheme. "Peasants" ranged from slaves to free persons of some substance. Except in frontier zones, where victims were available and religious scruples diminished, slaves were declining dramatically in numbers (as illustrated by the shifts in meaning of the classical Latin *servus* from "slave" to "serf" and of *sclavus*, from "Slav" to "slave"). Serfs, persons bound to the soil, everywhere constituted the majority of the peasants, although their legal and social status differed considerably from place to place. Serfdom was a mixture of economic, juridical, and personal statuses. The serf could be flogged in public, could be set upon by dogs, was excluded from many judicial proceedings, required approval to contract a marriage, and was denied the right to bear arms. Free small farmers, allodists, suffered none of these indignities but rarely lived differently from their less fortunate contemporaries.

The tenth and eleventh centuries were a decisive period in the reshaping of rural society. As lordships of all kinds and sizes formed in the countryside, communities of people were gathered in those lordships. Castles were critical. Powerful men generally sited their castles in close proximity to wood, water, and iron. Sometimes a monastery, rural church, or graveyard also attracted a castle or else grew up near one and helped to anchor a site. The castles were usually earthen mounds surmounted by a wooden dwelling and surrounded by a wooden wall. Only in the twelfth century in northern Europe did stone construction become common.

People from a fairly wide area settled in the vicinity of the castle. Many, originally free, commended themselves to the local lord by handing over their properties and receiving them back in return for rents or personal services. Other people fell into dependent status through military or economic misfortune. What eventually emerged was the manor, an institution wherein a powerful lord controlled the lives of an often large number of dependents. He required payments and services from them and regulated their ordinary disputes. His control was simultaneously public and private.

A minor castellan might control only a small manor and would probably be the vassal of a great lord. A powerful landed lord would generally control many manors and would often give some of them to retainers as fiefs. In other words, the reorganization of the countryside affected the nobility and the peasantry and created parallel sets of vertical bonds of association: Feudal lords and vassals entered into political bonds; lords and peasants entered into economic bonds.

The structure of individual manors, and the dues owed by peasants, varied tremendously across Europe. Certain trends were fairly consistent, however. As the economy expanded, as trade brought more and different products into Europe, and as a more consciously aristocratic lifestyle spread, the nobility began to want disposable cash. Thus, in many places corvées (labor services) were being commuted into cash payments. Peasants were required to pay rent from their own holdings instead of working on the lord's lands. But lords still needed provisions, so they sometimes split peasant payments into cash and kind. Old forms of service could be wholly retained, involving many days per year of work on the lord's demesne, the portion of the manor set aside for the sole benefit of the lord. In such cases, the lord could still extract money from his peasants by requiring them to use his mill and oven and charing them fees.

The trend everywhere was for labor services to diminish. In one region in northern France, twelfth-century peasants owed only three corvées of two days' each for harvesting and haymaking. Elsewhere, peasants might still be required to haul crops to market or to keep roads, bridges, and buildings in repair. On many estates where the menfolk had been largely freed from corvées, the women might still have to work in the lord's house doing laundry, sewing, plucking chickens and geese, cooking, minding dogs, and tending to other household chores.

In the expanding economy of the eleventh and twelfth centuries, the peasants were growing more prosperous, and their lords were constantly seeking new ways to extract the fruits of that prosperity. Peasants thus began to band together to demand that "customs" be observed. These customs were more-or-less formal agreements spelling out the terms under which work and fees would be arranged. In general, life was improving for the peasants in both legal status and living conditions. As early as the twelfth century, France and England saw a movement away from the most onerous forms of serfdom that had existed since Late Antiquity.

The European village was a key product of the tenth and eleventh centuries. People who originally gathered together around a castle began to form a durable human community with many ties. They may have struggled together to forge the customs of the community. Their church and graveyard helped to form a community by tying together the living and the dead and by giving the community a sense of memory and continuity. Peasants generally worked only 250 to 270 days per year, so they had a good deal of time for festivals and celebrations. Births, baptisms, betrothals, and deaths provided opportunities for the community to come together and affirm its mutual ties. Market days and sessions of the lord's court also assembled the village. Villagers needed to cooperate in many of the operations of daily life. They shared tools, plow teams, and wagons. They performed their corvées together. There was much less social differentiation among the peasants than among the nobility, and so less tension.

The status of women in peasant society tended to be, in legal theory and in daily reality, the same as that of men at a time when the status of aristocratic women was declining. Marriage contracts from northern Italy show that brides often entered marriages with a complement of valuable tools. This suggests that peasant women retained some control over their own personal property and also reminds us that the huge gains in rural productivity are almost certainly attributable in part to the work and ingenuity of women. This period was on the whole a good one for the "workers."

Those Left Out: Townspeople and Non-Christians

The tripartite model excluded two important groups of people. In the first group were the increasingly numerous citizens of Europe's growing towns. Obviously people in towns worked; but the prejudices of the aristocracy were rural, so the "workers" deemed necessary to the smooth functioning of the social order were farmers. In the second group were the religious minorities. Muslims were a relatively tiny portion of the population except in Spain and southern Italy, but Jews could be found almost everywhere. Militant Christianity, unleashed by the zeal of religious reformers and evidenced in the military orders and the crusades, made daily life increasingly difficult for non-Christians in Europe.

The central factor in the growth of towns was the rise in the productivity and profitability of medieval agriculture. For the first time there was a regular and substantial surplus that could support an urban population that did not produce its own food. Increased local exchange, coupled with the relentless growth of a money economy, meant there were fortunes to be made and cash to be spent. Some of that cash was spent on luxury and exotic products that increasingly became the objects of far-flung commercial networks. A good part of the cash was spent by rural nobles, who earned it from rents, booty, and the profits of the private exercise of public power. When those nobles moved into towns, they created opportunities for merchants, craftsmen, day laborers, domestic servants, and professional people such as notaries and lawyers. This was particularly true in Europe's most heavily urbanized regions: Flanders, southern France, and northern Italy. The key point is that the growth of the medieval city and of its human community began in the medieval countryside.

Town society was hierarchical, but its structures were new, ill defined, and flexible. Rich people built up gangs of followers who supported them in urban politics, protected their neighborhoods, and occasionally raided the houses of their enemies in the next neighborhood. Relatives, friends, neighbors, persons from a common rural district, or people engaged in similar trades tended to worship together in particular churches, observe certain festivals, and look after one another's families. Tradesmen and craftsmen formed guilds, which started out as dining and burial societies and later became powerful economic forces regulating prices and production standards (see page 408).

In the rapidly changing world of the tenth and eleventh centuries, towns provided numerous opportunities for women. In urban industries such as cloth-making, tanning, laundering, and brewing there is evidence of women managing and even owning enterprises. Apart, perhaps, from finance and the law, distinctions between male and female roles were not so sharp in towns as in rural areas. At least this was true until the later twelfth century, when guilds began to dominate exchange and production and at the same time to limit women's participation.

Sometimes towns owed special allegiance to a bishop, a count, a king, or even the emperor. Frequently that allegiance had its origins in a special grant of freedom purchased by representatives of the town from some higher authority. Rooted in medieval rural society, towns were something new and distinctive.

If urban men and all women stood in an ambiguous relationship to the ideals of the male, rural, aristocratic elite, we can hardly imagine what it must have been like for Jews. Because the Byzantine and Islamic worlds vacillated between persecution and toleration, many Jews migrated to western Europe. Some laymen and many members of the clergy were bitterly hostile to the Jews, but from the time of Gregory I the papacy urged peaceful coexistence and prayers for Jewish conversion. The Carolingians protected the Jews, as did kings in succeeding centuries. Although some Jews in Italy, Spain, and Germany owned farms and vineyards, most Jews settled in cities, where they could live and worship in community with their coreligionists. There was also strength in numbers for people who could at any moment fall victim to persecution.

Jews frequently served as royal advisers in Spain and were often entrusted with sensitive diplomatic missions elsewhere. This service earned them the envy of some Christians, as did their prominence in banking and moneylending. During the tenth century numerous Italian Jews crossed the Alps and settled in Cologne, Mainz, Speyer, Worms, and other growing towns of the German Rhineland. Attacks on Jews increased in the eleventh century, and laws were passed in Spain (1053) and Germany (1084) taking them under royal protection. The religious frenzy unleashed by the First Crusade brought savage attacks on the Jewish communities of Germany and induced many Jews to move to northern France and England. The bishop of Cologne bravely protected the Jews of his city, but sometimes whole communities were wiped out. Twelfth-century Europe was an increasingly difficult place for outsiders.

Germany and the Empire

In the middle of the tenth century Germany was the most powerful state in western Europe (Map 10.2). Two hundred years later Germany was on the brink of collapse. That radical transformation is the most significant political fact in European history in the period 900–1150.

In the face of Viking and Magyar attacks, a series of resolute Saxon dukes built a kingdom, allied with the church, and revived the imperial title. German dynasties proved disastrously short-lived, however, and the monarchy's alliance with the church helped to precipitate the investiture controversy, a crisis in church-state relations. Promising beginnings for the German kingdom yielded meager results.

Unifying the Realm: The Saxon and Salian Rulers

When the Treaty of Verdun assigned the East Frankish Kingdom to Louis the German in 843, it created a new political entity. In the second half of the ninth century, Louis the German and his successors managed to preserve the East Frankish Kingdom and created the possibility of an independent German kingdom. However, just what lands that kingdom would possess was not clear. The Rhine has sometimes been Germany's river, sometimes its western boundary. Germany has no natural frontiers to the east, and incipient Slavic states were jealous of any German advances into their territories.

Germany consisted of several large duchies. Saxony, Franconia, Lorraine, Swabia, and Bavaria—the most important—had a dual historical origin. They were formed of people with distinctive ethnic identities, although their leaders, or dukes, were usually Frankish aristocrats appointed by the Carolingians. As the monarchy weakened amid Carolingian political struggles

Map 10.2 Germany and Its Duchies Throughout the Middle Ages, the chief dynamic in German history was a contest for power between the kings and the dukes.

and foreign invasions, the dukes became the bearers of the German political destiny. In 911 the last legitimate Carolingian of the East Frankish line died, and in 919 the dukes elected Duke Henry of Saxony as his successor.

Henry was the most powerful and the richest of the German dukes. He was chosen precisely because he offered the greatest hope of dealing decisively with the Viking threats in the north and the Magyar attacks in the east and south. Henry I ruled for nearly two decades and was then succeeded by his son, grandson, and great-grandson, all named Otto. These Saxon rulers created a solid German kingdom by consistently

THE SAXON, SALIAN, AND HOHENSTAUFEN RULERS OF GERMANY

SAXONS

HENRY I (r. 919–936)

OTTO I (r. 936–973)

OTTO II (r. 973–983)

OTTO III (r. 983–1002)

HENRY II (r. 1002–1024)

SALIANS

CONRAD II (r. 1024–1039)

HENRY III (r. 1039–1056)

HENRY IV (r. 1056–1106)

HENRY V (r. 1106–1125)

HOHENSTAUFEN

CONRAD III (r. 1138–1152)

FREDERICK I (r. 1152–1190)

HENRY VI (r. 1190–1197)

FREDERICK II (r. 1212–1250)

pursuing a few basic policies: warfare, control of Saxony and of the other duchies, domination of the church, and the acquisition of prestige.

The Saxon dukes had vassals of their own in Saxony, men to whom they had given lands in return for military or administrative service. Their following was augmented by cash payments made possible by ducal control of the silver mines in the Hartz Mountains of Saxony. Henry I (r. 919–936) fought victoriously against the Vikings who were raiding northern Germany, and he initiated Saxony's eastern push into the Slavic lands along the Baltic coast. Otto I (r. 936–973) continued Henry's policies but also raised a pan-German army to meet the Magyar threat. At Lechfeld, near Augsburg, Otto won a decisive victory over the Magyars in 955. At once this battle removed a serious threat to Germany and vastly enhanced Otto's prestige. Otto II (r. 973–983) and Otto III (r. 983–1002) continued the Germany drive to the east into Slavic lands. The Ottonians' successful campaigns attracted more and more followers, who shared in the booty and received land. No one else in Germany could compete with the duke of Saxony as a military leader and as a winner of followers.

In addition to building up a secure power base in Saxony, the Saxon dukes always tried to control one or more of the other German duchies. The German duchies had emerged together out of the late Carolingian world, and the Saxon dukes had not appointed and could not remove any of the other dukes. Sometimes, the Saxons managed to get one or more dukes to swear homage to them as kings of Germany, but this oath was largely symbolic because the other dukes did not owe any specific services to the king. On other occasions, Saxon kings used force to remove another duke and then introduce a member of their own family in place of the duke who had been deposed. There was feudalism in Germany in the sense that all the dukes had vassals, but Germany was not a feudal monarchy because the dukes did not hold their duchies as fiefs granted by the king. The king's inability to control on a permanent basis any region but his own was a continuing weakness in Germany.

Control of the church partly compensated for the absence of central institutions or a hierarchy of vassalic bonds. Bishops and abbots remembered the Carolingian past when crown and church had worked harmoniously for the reform of the kingdom. They willingly supported the king and provided him with able, educated advisers. Many of them, in good Carolingian fashion, saw the king as God's specially chosen agent and believed that it was their responsibility to aid him in the task of governing. The royal chapel, basically the office where documents were prepared and spiritual services were provided for the court, recruited able, ambitious men from all over Germany, trained them, and then sent them back out as bishops or abbots. If the king could not appoint officials in Bavaria, for example, he

Otto III These beautiful examples of early Romanesque painting (see page 383) show Otto III enthroned with crown, scepter, and orb. He is receiving the homage of the four parts of his empire: Slavinia, Germania, Gallia, and Roma. (*Bayerische Staatsbibliotek, München*)

could nevertheless name Bavaria's four bishops. No duke could do this.

Finally, the Saxon rulers were keenly aware of the value of prestige. Symbolic power was only a partial substitute for the lack of central institutions, capitularies, taxes, and other aspects of Carolingian rule, but the Saxons used it for all it was worth. The monarchy was itinerant; it moved about the country. One reason for this mobility was to consume on the spot the resources of various royal estates; another was to make a grand display of the king and his entourage, which sometimes numbered from three to four hundred people. One German nobleman, on his deathbed, warned his son that the quickest way to impoverish himself was to host the king. A royal account says that the court daily consumed 100 pigs and sheep, 100 bushels of corn, 8 oxen, 10 barrels of wine, and 10 barrels of beer. Otto I enjoyed great banquets where he mixed freely and drank liberally with his guests. Otto III preferred to dine alone at an elevated table, in the imperial style. Otto I secured a real prize when he won the hand of a Byzantine princess for his son Otto II. The Saxon rulers attracted learned men to their court, such as the mathematician Gerbert (see page 378), and trumpeted their close association with the abbots of Cluny. Cultural monuments, ranging from beautiful manuscripts to the dawning Romanesque architecture (see page 383), were all patronized by the Saxons. The greatest enhancement of the prestige of the Saxon monarchy, however, came with the restoration of the imperial title by Otto I in 962.

From the middle of the ninth century, Carolingian aristocrats occasionally made themselves kings of Italy, but no one was able to protect or to rule Rome. When Muslims began attacking the city in 844, the popes themselves had to defend the city. In the tenth century the papacy fell into its darkest period. The papacy became the prize in the game of local Roman politics. Things got so bad that one remarkable woman, Marozia (d. ca. 945), was at different times, mother, wife, and mistress of various popes. During these difficult circumstances, Otto

I went to Italy, in 952. He made himself king of Italy and protector of the papacy. He prevailed on the pope to crown him emperor in 962. Few concrete rights came to Otto as a result of his coronation. He got to name some counts and bishops in Italy, to raise some taxes, and to keep south German nobles from meddling in Italy themselves. Mainly, Otto gained immensely in prestige, throughout Germany and the rest of Europe.

What the Saxons could not do was produce a long-lived dynasty. Otto III died without an heir. In 1002 and 1024, distant relatives of the Saxons were elected kings, and the Salian dynasty came to the throne. Based in Bavaria, the Salians often exercised some control of Swabia, but they rarely had any real power in the north, just as the Saxons had usually lacked power in the south. Henry III (r. 1039–1056) was a ruler of real ability and of deep religious piety. Viking and Magyar threats were long past, and the consolidation of the Slavic kingdoms had put a temporary end to Germany's eastward expansion. Lacking military opportunities, and having no more control over the German duchies than his predecessors had won, Henry focused even more than they on control of the church.

Henry saw himself as the church's protector. He also felt that, as God's anointed ruler, he had a duty to control, even to purify, the church. That duty extended all the way to Rome, to which the emperors had paid little attention in recent years. In 1046 Henry was confronted with the scandal of three men claiming to be the legitimate pope. Deeply offended, he removed them all and replaced them with the first of several ardent German reformers. Henry's reign marked the high point of the so-called German imperial church.

The Investiture Controversy

When Henry died in 1056, his son, Henry IV, was a child; and until he came of age in 1066, Germany was anarchic. Moreover, at Rome the reformers introduced by Henry III called for an end to lay investiture (the appointment of church officers by laymen) and to outside interference in the election of popes. These enactments challenged the basis of the German imperial church and attacked a major source of Saxon-Salian prestige. They also signaled that Rome was now taking the lead in church reform. The Salian regime was on the verge of collapse.

When Henry IV came of age, he controlled no duchies, faced a Saxony in open revolt, confronted several bishops who had made themselves independent of royal power, and had little idea of how the papacy would react to him. Henry had a high sense of his royal dignity and a burning desire to restore royal authority. He put down the revolt in Saxony, outmaneuvered most of the aristocrats who opposed him, and restored a good measure of control over the German church.

In 1072 the reformers in Rome elected as pope Cardinal Hildebrand, one of the reformers prominent since the 1050s. He took the name Gregory VII to cover himself with the mantle of spiritual authority possessed by Gregory the Great. Gregory (r. 1072–1085) was a proud, brilliant, inflexible, self-righteous man who thought he understood perfectly well what was wrong with society in his day: Laymen were wrongly in control of too many church offices, and rulers paid too little attention to the pope. Gregory and Henry IV fell into the life-and-death struggle that is usually called the "investiture controversy." The struggle was about the legitimacy of royal and papal rule and the nature of German political and constitutional life.

By 1075 Henry decided to make a show of his restored power by intervening in the selection of a bishop at Milan. His decision came even though the papal court for some two decades had openly opposed such lay interference and Gregory VII had made a series of strong claims about papal rights and powers. Gregory believed that laymen ought to defer to spiritual leaders. Gregory's view was that God had assigned leadership of the whole Christian world to the pope, who was the earthly vicar of Christ, and that kings, emperors, and ordinary officials existed only to do the bidding of the church, led by the pope.

During more than a century of strife among aristocratic factions, the territorial power of the popes had been shattered. But the popes in the eleventh and twelfth centuries, unlike their eighth-century predecessors, did not concentrate on territorial rule. Instead, they turned to tightening as never before the control exercised by the

Henry IV, Duchess Matilda of Tuscany, and Abbot Hugh of Cluny The embattled Henry IV here implores Matilda, a tremendously wealthy landowner and ally of Pope Gregory VII, to intercede with the pope. The powerful abbot of Cluny looks over the scene protectively. Written documents do not portray women's power as vividly as this image does. (*Vatican Library, Rome*)

pope within the church. They used the weapon of excommunication (excluding a person from the sacraments and thus effectively expelling him or her from the church) to coerce persons whom they believed to have violated canon law. They used papal legates, official envoys, to tie the pope to the Western church. The college of cardinals was slowly evolving into a kind of senate for the church. The power of the papacy was expanding as never before.

Henry's view was that he was king by descent from his ancestors and by the election of God and thus had a perfect right—indeed, a profound duty—to supervise the church. But more than principle was at stake for Henry. The German kings had always ruled with the support and cooperation of the church. To ensure that support and cooperation, they had always played a key role in selecting bishops, and they had usually required those bishops to be their vassals. Given Henry's perilous position down to 1075, he simply could not allow the church to slip from his control. (See the box, "The Issues in the Investiture Controversy.")

The Issues in the Investiture Controversy

These two documents illustrate the range of issues involved in the conflict between Pope Gregory VII and Henry IV. The first excerpt is from a long letter written by Henry in 1076. The second is a decree issued by Gregory in 1078.

Henry, king not by usurpation but by the holy ordination of God, to Hildebrand, not now pope but false monk:

Such greeting as this you have merited through your disturbances, for there is no rank in the church on which you have brought, not honor but disgrace, not blessing but curse. To mention only a few notable cases, you have dared to assail the holy rulers of the church, archbishops, bishops, and priests, and you have trodden them underfoot like slaves ignorant of what their master is doing; . . . you have regarded them as knowing nothing, yourself as knowing all things. . . .

We have endured all this in our anxiety to save the honor of the apostolic see, but you have mistaken our humility for fear and have ventured to attack the royal power conferred on us by God, and threatened to divest us of it. As if we had received our kingdom from you! As if the kingdom and empire were in your hands, not God's! For our Lord Jesus Christ did call us to the kingdom. . . . You have assailed me who, though unworthy of anointing, have nevertheless been anointed to the kingdom and who, according to the traditions of the holy fathers, are subject to the judgment of God alone. . . . The true pope Peter exclaims "Fear God, honor the king." But you, who do not fear God, dishonor me, His appointed one. . . .

You, therefore, damned by this curse and by the judgment of all our bishops and ourselves, come down and relinquish the apostolic chair which you have usurped. I, Henry, king by the grace of God, together with all our bishops, say to you: "Come down, come down, to be damned throughout all eternity."

Inasmuch as we have learned that, contrary to the ordinances of the holy fathers, the investiture of churches is, in many places, performed by lay persons, and that from this cause many disturbances arise in the church by which the Christian religion is degraded, we decree that no one of the clergy shall receive the investiture of a bishopric, abbey, or church from the hand of an emperor, or king, or of any layperson, male or female. If anyone shall presume to do so, let him know that such investiture is void by apostolic authority, and that he himself shall lie under excommunication until fitting satisfaction shall have been made.

Source: James Harvey Robinson, *Readings in European History,* vol. 1 (Boston: Ginn, 1904), pp. 279–281, 275 (slightly adapted).

Gregory's response to Henry's action in Milan was to excommunicate him in 1076 and to release his subjects from their oaths of allegiance. Many churchmen and aristocrats abandoned Henry, not so much because they agreed with Pope Gregory but because they relished the opportunity to weaken the king. A meeting of German nobles and papal representatives was arranged to investigate Henry's fitness for the royal office. To forestall the meeting, Henry departed from Germany and met Gregory at Canossa in Tuscany in January 1077. The king stood in the snow before the pope's castle and begged forgiveness from the pope. As a priest, Gregory could not refuse to forgive Henry, and that forgiveness restored the king to the church's good graces and restored his subjects' duty of allegiance.

In Germany, the nobles felt betrayed by Gregory and proceeded to elect a new king. This action enraged Henry, whose ire increased when Gregory said that he would in due course decide between the claims of Henry and his rival. In addition, in 1078 Gregory issued a definitive (earlier pronouncements possessed moral, not legal, force) decree against lay investiture. In response, Henry's propagandists unleashed a torrent of bitterly antipapal writing, the first such campaign in European history, to discredit Gregory. In 1080 the pope excommunicated the king once again, and Henry responded by marching to Rome, chasing Gregory out of the city, and installing a pope of his own who promptly crowned him emperor (which Gregory had refused to do). Gregory, uncompromising to the end, died in exile.

Henry never recovered his position in Germany. Both the material and the moral bases of the German crown were destroyed. What is more, Henry's own sons continually betrayed him. In 1106, Henry V actually deposed his pitiable father, who died within a few months. The reign of Henry V (r. 1106–1125) exposed the flaws in the German system. If the king tightly controlled one or more duchies and the church, and if there was a credible foreign threat, the king could be very powerful indeed. But if one or more of these props were kicked out from under the king, the monarchy threatened to fall. It was unfortunate for Henry IV that, at a particularly difficult moment in German politics, militant churchmen decided to contest royal power and influence in ecclesiastical affairs.

Henry V struggled on for a generation trying to bring the investiture controversy to an end. In 1122 the Concordat of Worms between Henry V and Pope Calixtus II (r. 1119–1124) settled the matter. According to the concordat, Henry agreed that episcopal elections would be free and canonical (carried out according to canon law), and he surrendered investiture with ring and staff, the symbols of the bishop's religious office. Elections were to take place in the royal presence, however, and after the election the king could invest the new bishop with purely secular offices. The concordat was a compromise; but, insofar as it spelled the end of the German imperial church system, it was a victory for the papacy.

KINGS AND WARRIORS

955	Battle of Lechfeld
962	Imperial coronation of Otto I
987	Accession of Hugh Capet in France
1016	Conquest of England by Cnut
1059	Papal-Norman alliance in Italy
1066	Conquest of England by William of Normandy
1072–1085	Pontificate of Gregory VII
1077	Emperor Henry IV at Canossa
1078	Papal Decree against lay investiture
1085	Spanish reconquest of Toledo
1086	Domesday Book
1095	First Crusade
1122	Concordat of Worms

Henry V died without heirs in 1125 and was followed by the dukes of Saxony and of Swabia in succession. The nobles elected these men precisely because they were not powerful. In the early tenth century, the nobles had affirmed the royal principle by electing the most powerful of the dukes as kings. For nearly two centuries, when there were legitimate heirs of suitable age, the nobles had assented to their succession. Now, after three-quarters of a century of turmoil, the nobles elected weak men as kings. Those kings had slender material resources, limited control of the church, and jealous nobles on every side. By the middle of the twelfth century, Germany was weak and disunited.

Shaping the Kingdom

Before about 1050, the majority of Europe's population was ruled, or misruled, by dukes and counts, by bishops and abbots, or by various petty magnates. After the middle of the eleventh century, kingdoms began to have a measurable effect on the lives of most people. In the kingdoms that emerged after the breakup of the Carolingian Empire—France, England, Spain, and Italy—a variety of institutional systems emerged. Amid great local variety, one trend was constant: Personal bonds rather than bureaucratic administrations or abstract notions of allegiance to a state held the kingdoms together. Initially, those institutions were unimpressive, but by the middle of the twelfth century the units of rule were larger, and central governments were more important. In the period 900–1150, both the variety of Europe's government patterns and the size of the individual governments expanded.

The Rise of Capetian France

The Treaty of Verdun (843) created the West Frankish Kingdom, which would evolve into France. In 843, however, it cannot have been clear to anyone what that future France might be like. The twentieth-century French leader Charles de Gaulle is said to have quipped, "It is impossible to govern a country with 325 kinds of cheese." He was referring to France's tremendous diversity.

During the late ninth century and much of the tenth, however, the area suffered cruelly from constant waves of Viking attacks and from repeated failures of the Carolingian family to produce adult heirs to the throne. Chroniclers often quoted the lament of King Solomon: "Woe to thee, O land, whose king is a child."

Royal authority declined sharply because of the weakness of the later Carolingians, but what really damaged the royal office was the emergence of territorial principalities. Whereas Germany produced five major duchies, France saw the appearance of more than a dozen principalities. Some of them had existed before the Carolingians came on the scene: Celtic Brittany in the west, Basque Gascony in the southwest, and Burgundy (formerly a kingdom) in the east. They reemerged, not unlike the German duchies, as districts with some sense of ethnic cohesion and of historical tradition. Normandy, Anjou, Blois, Champagne, and others were products of the years from 850 to 950. Confined largely to the Paris region, the king himself was a territorial prince.

Territorial princes built up their power by taking the traditional "bannal" (from the "ban," the king's right to command) rights of the king into their own hands: the rights to raise armies, hold courts, collect taxes, mint coins, and protect churches. The most successful of these territorial princes then reduced their less powerful neighbors to dependent status by making them swear homage and fealty and perform various services. Many formerly free men sought security in the entourage of powerful neighbors by handing over their possessions and then receiving them back in return for homage and service.

All over the country, territorial princes created vassals who in turn created vassals of their own. These magnates gained manorial rights over the peasantry. Two sets of statistics provide a glimpse into the world of post-Carolingian French politics: (1) In the early tenth century, about 80 percent of all lands donated to churches were allods, lands owned outright, with no obligations attached to them. By the middle of the twelfth century, the number of allods in grants had dropped to 8 percent. (2) In the ninth century, about 10 percent of peasants stood in some form of servile dependency. By 1150, around 90 percent were burdened in some way. Clearly, both land and people had fallen into a widespread network of dependencies. France had become feudal (Map 10.3).

The territorial princes ruled with little reference to the king, and the king had little power over them, but France was not anarchical. Feudalism was a creative response to, more than a cause of, the political disorder of the late Carolingian world. Feudal principalities, when they worked well, as in Normandy and Anjou, could be models of effective local government.

Where did this leave the French crown? The Merovingian and Carolingian tradition was so strong that it never occurred to the French nobles to dispense with the monarchy. In 987, the nobles again ignored the only legitimate Carolingian and turned to a family from Paris that had three times provided kings since 888. The man chosen was Hugh Capet (r. 987–996). No one could have known it at the time, but the Capetian family would rule France in the direct line until the fourteenth century.

The kings had a few real advantages. They possessed a landed patrimony—a demesne—that was minute if compared to the once-vast Carolingian demesne but about equal to the personal

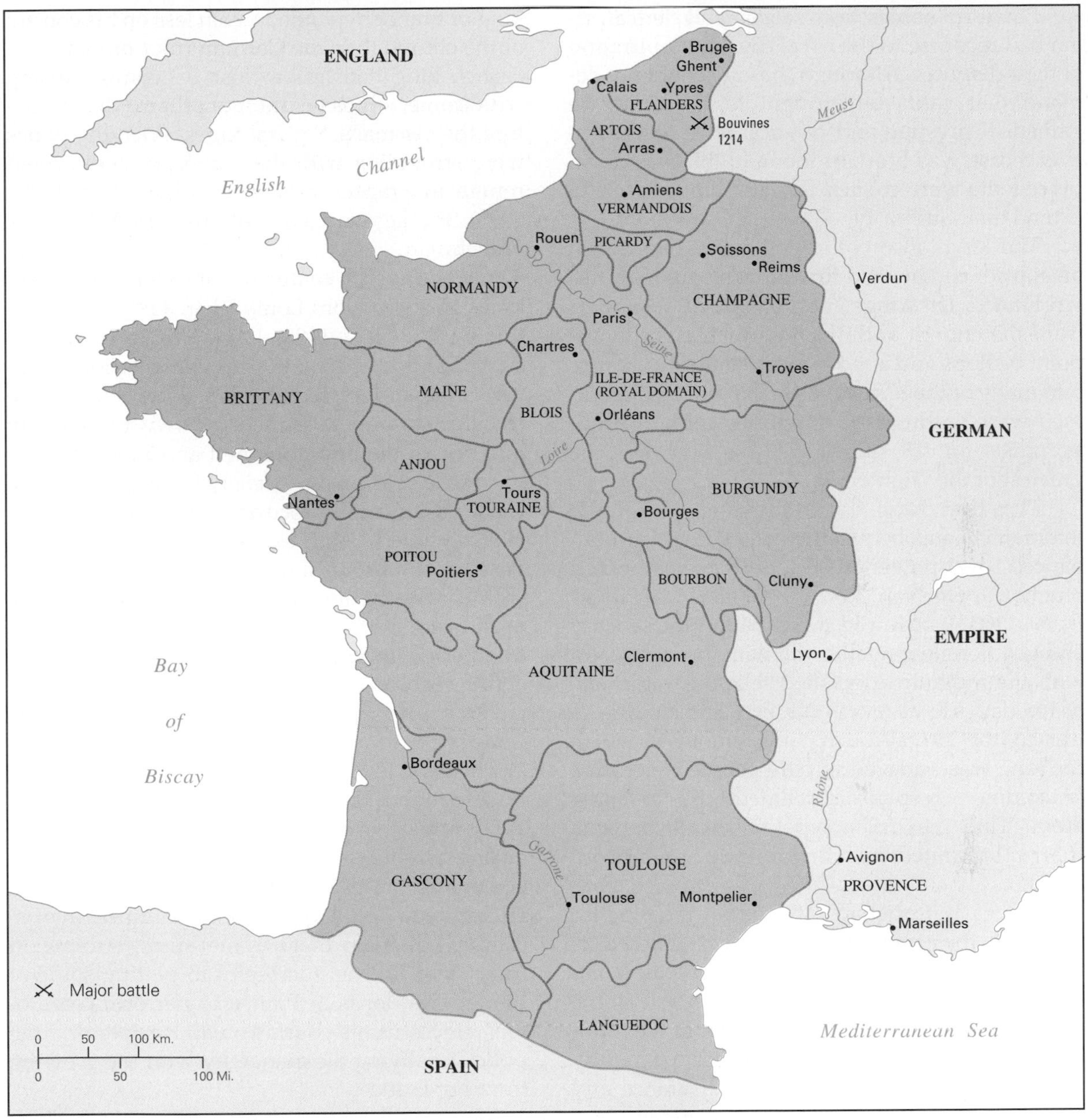

Map 10.3 French Territorial Principalities As the Carolingian West Frankish Kingdom (see Map 8.3, Inset) broke down, and as feudal bonds proliferated, many territories arose under counts and dukes whose struggles to fight off royal control animated French history.

demesne of any of the other great nobles. The Capetian demesne, moreover, was situated strategically in the centrally located Paris basin. In theory all the territorial princes were the king's vassals, and the king received oaths of fidelity from most important noblemen. The early Capetians usually could not force their nominal vassals to perform specific services for them, but no other nobleman could take up the oaths of his peers.

Powerful nobles, both secular and clerical, often had recourse to the royal court for arbitration of their disputes. Although the king could not demand that cases be brought to his court, he gained in prestige and political leverage whenever a case was brought there. In this way, legal precedents were created for later kings to use to extend their authority.

The kings also controlled about two dozen bishoprics and around fifty monasteries in northern France. The kings got great material support from the church and, through their right to appoint bishops and abbots, inserted their influence into many of the territorial principalities. Churchmen were enthusiastic supporters of and propagandists for the monarchy. The king was the greatest of the "fighters."

The first four Capetian kings (987–1108) maintained and bequeathed the throne and enhanced royal power, even if only in small ways. Hugh Capet's son Robert, called "the Pious" (r. 996–1030), acquired a reputation for sanctity and got along especially well with the clergy and with the most distinguished religious reformers of his day. He also was the first French king to display the "royal touch," a ceremony in which the king was believed to cure people of scrofula (a common respiratory ailment) by touching them. This particular type of royal charisma sharply separated the king from any ordinary nobleman.

The early Capetians also began the practice of having their sons crowned and anointed during their own lifetime. When one king died, another one was ready to take over. The role of the nobility in electing kings, very great in the ninth and tenth centuries, had almost disappeared by the twelfth century. In this regard, France and Germany were quite different. In Germany, dynastic failure and papal excommunications afforded the nobility repeated opportunities to engage in kingmaking.

Another early Capetian strength lay in the skillful deployment of alliances and counter-alliances among the territorial princes. The king regularly allied with the dukes of Normandy, for example, because he and they had common rivals in Anjou and Blois.

Finally, the tragedy of the German investiture controversy was not visited on France. The king of France depended much less on his control of the church than the German ruler did, and the French king had less to lose by compromising with Rome, which he did more than a decade before the Germans. Several times when the popes were struggling with the emperors, they found refuge in France, and Pope Urban II (r. 1088–1099), the key successor of Gregory VII, was a Frenchman.

In the twelfth century, France had two gifted kings in succession: Louis VI (r. 1108–1137) and Louis VII (r. 1137–1180). Louis VI was unimpressive as an individual, but his contributions were great. He suppressed the minor nobility in the royal demesne and turned his own principality into one of the best governed and most efficient in France. He made extensive use of the royal touch as a means of focusing loyalty on the king. He promoted Saint Denis (the first bishop of Paris) as a patron saint for France, as well as his shrine in Paris (the Capetian capital), as a way of promoting unity throughout the kingdom. The number of important men who appeared in his court grew steadily, and his coins had a wider circulation than those of any king since the ninth century.

Louis VII began making ceremonial visitations around the kingdom, drawing attention away from the king's lack of real power by focusing attention on the monarchy's grandeur. Capetians and Saxons were alike in this regard. He began to hold larger and more impressive assemblies than any that had met since Carolingian times, and he was successful in getting some of the greatest lords of France to perform ceremonial offices in his court. Louis also initiated the policy of allying the monarchy with the growing towns of France.

Despite their achievements, these two kings ruled a France that was fragile in the extreme. The great nobles were still very powerful. They were royal vassals, but the king had few means at his disposal to coerce them. The constantly shifting network of alliances and counter-alliances had worked well enough for more than a century, but it was no solid basis for effective national government.

Aristocratic, dynastic societies occasionally produce shocking transformations in the political landscape. Louis VII, for example, married the heiress of Aquitaine and at one blow multiplied by several times the amount of land under his direct control. But his new bride, Eleanor of Aquitaine, disliked her pious, abstemious husband almost as much as he disliked her strong, independent temperament. They divorced, and Louis lost all the lands he had gained. Things did not rest there, however. Eleanor quickly married Henry of Anjou, who was about to inherit Anjou, Maine, and Touraine from his father (and who in two years would be crowned King Henry II of England). From his mother Henry would inherit Normandy. Through Eleanor, Henry got Poitou and Aquitaine. Thus, Louis VII was faced with a vassal who controlled about three-fifths of France. What was going to happen to all the patient work of the Capetian kings of France? No one could well have predicted in 1154.

Anglo-Saxon England and the Norman Conquest

At the very time when continental kingdoms were collapsing in the late ninth century, England was unified and put on the offensive by Alfred the Great. In the tenth century Alfred's successors Edward the Elder (r. 899–924), Athelstan (r. 924–939), and Edgar (r. 957–975) constructed a peaceful, well-governed kingdom. All men in the land owed allegiance to the king, and the king could summon all free men to the *fyrd,* the militia. The great men of the realm routinely attended meetings of the *witan,* the royal council that was partly a court of law and partly a political body that resolved disputes among the mighty. The king could issue writs, which were executive orders rather like the Carolingian capitularies. Only the king could issue coins.

All of England was divided into administrative districts called *shires,* and each shire had a royally appointed representative, the shire-reeve, or sheriff. A tax, the Danegeld, first levied on the whole kingdom in times of Viking danger, was beginning to be a routine source of royal income. Alfred's burghs, originally defensive positions in the struggle against the Vikings, were being turned by deliberate royal policy into towns with markets and merchants.

Edward and Athelstan commanded at times the allegiance of various Welsh princes and of the kings in Scotland. Their international position can be seen in their marriages into French princely houses and even into the German imperial family. These kings corresponded with popes, promoted learning, and shared in the spiritual reforms that were sweeping Europe. England's future could not have looked brighter.

In 978 Ethelred II, a boy of about 10, rose to the throne. He has become known as "Ethelred the Unready" (more accurately, Ethelred "of no counsel"), but this label is unfair. Shortly after his accession, England was drawn into the world of northern politics.

King Harald Bluetooth of Denmark was seeking to unify his country and to impose Christianity on the Danes. His methods were brutal, and after 980 gangs of Danish malcontents began raiding the English coast. In 988 Harald's son Swein, a leader of the raiders, deposed his father and took over the kingdom. But he kept on raiding England and joined forces in 991 with Olaf Tryggvason, a mighty warrior. A couple of years later, Olaf went over to the English side, enraging Swein and his followers.

Many people in northern and eastern England, the Danelaw, were of Scandinavian extraction. Their loyalty to Ethelred may have been no stronger than their potential loyalty to Swein, who was no mere Viking adventurer but a crowned king. Ethelred was not much of a soldier at a time when military gifts were needed, and his heavy Danegelds were unpopular. The threat he faced was so great that he fled to Normandy in 1013.

England fell to Swein in 1014 but his sudden death left the consolidation of the conquest to his son Cnut. Cnut ruled England from 1016 to 1035, and his sons after him ruled to 1042. No Viking savage, Cnut was king of Denmark and England and briefly of Norway too. He married Emma, Ethelred's widow, and his own daughter was married to the German emperor. He was a Christian and had visited the pope in Rome. Cnut was one of the most powerful and capable men of his age. In England his rule was purely traditional. England had long enjoyed good government, and he had no reason to change things. He added a few Scandinavian earls, high-ranking aristocrats owing allegiance to the king, but did not purge the Anglo-Saxon aristocracy. Far from being disruptive, the first "Norman Conquest" actually benefited England.

Cnut's sons having died without heirs, the Anglo-Saxons invited the son of Ethelred and Emma, Edward, known as "the Confessor," to become their king. Edward was pious and well intentioned, but he had taken a vow of chastity and would have no heir. The jostling for position among the Anglo-Saxon nobles began almost immediately and was intensified by Edward's penchant for promoting Normans to high position in England (he had spent most of his life in Normandy). What particularly angered some prominent Anglo-Saxons was Edward's promise of his throne to Duke William of Normandy.

When Edward died in 1066, the witan met and elected Harold of Wessex, the most powerful of the Anglo-Saxon nobles, as their king. Norman writers regarded this action as especially vicious because, in their telling, Harold had some years before promised to support William's claim. William began to make preparations to fight for the English inheritance. Harold, meanwhile, had another challenger in the king of Norway and Denmark, Harald Hardrada, who, as king of Denmark, claimed England in succession to Cnut. Harold of Wessex marched north to defeat Harald Hardrada, only to learn that William had landed in the south. Foolishly, he rushed south with a weary army and met William at Hastings. After one day's fighting, England was conquered for the second time in fifty years. The second Norman Conquest left a deep mark on the country.

William "the Conqueror" ruled from 1066 to 1087. Although his power was based on conquest and on a brutal pacification campaign carried out between 1066 and 1071, William always claimed to be the legitimate heir of Edward. His wife was even a distant descendant of Alfred the Great. Conquest gave William an opportunity to do almost anything he could get away with, but English and Norman government provided plenty of precedents for effective rule.

William kept the general allegiance owed by free men to the king. Likewise, he maintained the obligation to serve in the fyrd and to pay Danegeld. He issued writs and jealously guarded his right to a monopoly on minting coins. William got along well with the church. He brought to England as archbishop of Canterbury Lanfranc, an Italian who had been an abbot in Normandy. Lanfranc, an ardent reformer, instituted changes designed to bring the church in England up to contemporary standards in administration and canon law. William controlled his church with an iron hand, but his relations with Pope Gregory VII were generally cordial. Gregory probably did not wish to pick any more fights, and William was a great supporter of Lanfranc's reforms. In many ways, William's takeover, like Cnut's, was purely traditional.

In one critical area, William innovated. He turned most of the estates in England into fiefs and distributed them among the 180 or so greatest of his followers. Each of these vassals held his fief in return for a fixed quota of knights for the royal army. To raise the five thousand total knights required by William, his own vassals had to create vassals of their own. The technical name for this process of vassals creating vassals to help them to perform their service is *subinfeudation*. To make sure that England did not suffer from the kinds of conflicting allegiances that plagued France, William exacted in 1087 the Salisbury Oath. This oath established the principle of liege homage, according to which the king was final lord of all vassals.

William did not give his vassals compact blocks of land. He obviously wished to avoid territorial principalities on the French model. By scattering his vassals' holdings around the kingdom, he kept the vassals from becoming too powerful in any one place, and he more or less forced them to think about national rather than local interests.

William's keen sense of administrative order, along with his desire to know the value of his realm as a whole and the value of the individual segments of it that he had assigned to his vassals, led to the Domesday survey of 1086. Inspectors were sent throughout the country to take the sworn testimony of people everywhere. William sought an enumeration of people, buildings, animals, mills, and anything else of major value. No comparable undertaking was attempted again until the American census of 1790. The surviving records in the *Domesday Book* (named later by critics of the monarchy for the Day of Judgment

BI HAROLD:SACRAMENTVM:FECIT:
VVILLELMO DVCI:
HIC HAROL

The Bayeux Tapestry Probably made at Canterbury to tell the tale of the Norman Conquest from the Norman point of view, this beautiful and huge tapestry (more than 200 feet long) is a monument to the artist's abilities. Depicted here is Harold of Wessex swearing on relics an oath to uphold William's claim to the throne of England. For another view of the tapestry, see page 344. *(Musée de Bayeux/Michael Holford)*

against which there was no appeal) are a precious source of historical information. (See the feature, "Weighing the Evidence: Domesday Book," on pages 388–389.)

William was succeeded by two of his sons, William II (r. 1087–1100), and Henry I (r. 1100–1135), who kept most of their father's system intact while adding some features. Henry carried out major reforms in the financial offices of the monarchy, the Exchequer (so named from the checkerboard table on which accounts were reckoned). He introduced itinerant justices who wandered about the kingdom on regular tours of judicial business. These justices in eyre (a judicial circuit) made it hard for feudal lords to take royal justice into their own hands as their counterparts in France often did. Henry deftly appointed new men as sheriffs and judges. He did not root out the feudal nobility established by his father but instead worked around it.

England, like France, was spared a crisis in relations between monarchy and church. In Lanfranc's successor Anselm, Henry I faced a determined reformer who refused to tolerate lay investiture. Down to 1107, Anselm spent a good deal of time in exile, but in that year he and Henry effected a compromise that anticipated the provisions of the Concordat of Worms.

Henry's only legitimate heir drowned in the English Channel; so when the king died, the barons elected Stephen of Blois (r. 1135–1154), a grandson of William the Conqueror. Henry had tried in vain to get the barons to accept his daughter Matilda as queen. Some barons simply refused to be ruled by a woman, but many feared Matilda's husband, the formidable Count

Geoffrey of Anjou. Most English baronial families still had holdings in Normandy, and the Angevins were old enemies of the Normans. Stephen thus came to the throne in inauspicious circumstances. His reign was marked by factional strife and by constant plotting by Matilda and her supporters.

In 1153 Matilda's son Henry of Anjou prevailed on Stephen to recognize him as his heir. What would this turn of events mean for England? Would Angevin and Norman factions carry on their squabbling? Could anyone undo the damage of Stephen's reign? Would King Henry II be drawn by his vast French holdings to ignore England? It is striking how the decade of the 1150s emerged as a turning point not only for France and Germany but also for England.

The Progress of the Reconquista in Spain

Historians have identified two driving forces in the rich and colorful history of medieval Spain. One is the constant interplay within the Iberian Peninsula of three rich cultures: Christian, Jewish, and Muslim. The other is the bloody experience of several centuries of war along an expanding frontier.

The breakup of the caliphate of Cordoba after 1002 and the emergence of the tiny Muslim kingdoms called *taifas* afforded an unprecedented opportunity to the Christians living in the north of the peninsula. King Sancho I (r. 1000–1035) of Navarre launched an offensive against the Muslims. This war, carried on intermittently until the fifteenth century, came to be called the *Reconquista,* the Reconquest.

The Fortress of Murviedo This magnificent ruin conveys a sense of the fierceness of the frontier war that raged for centuries in Spain. The castle was taken by El Cid in an important battle. *(MAS, Barcelona)*

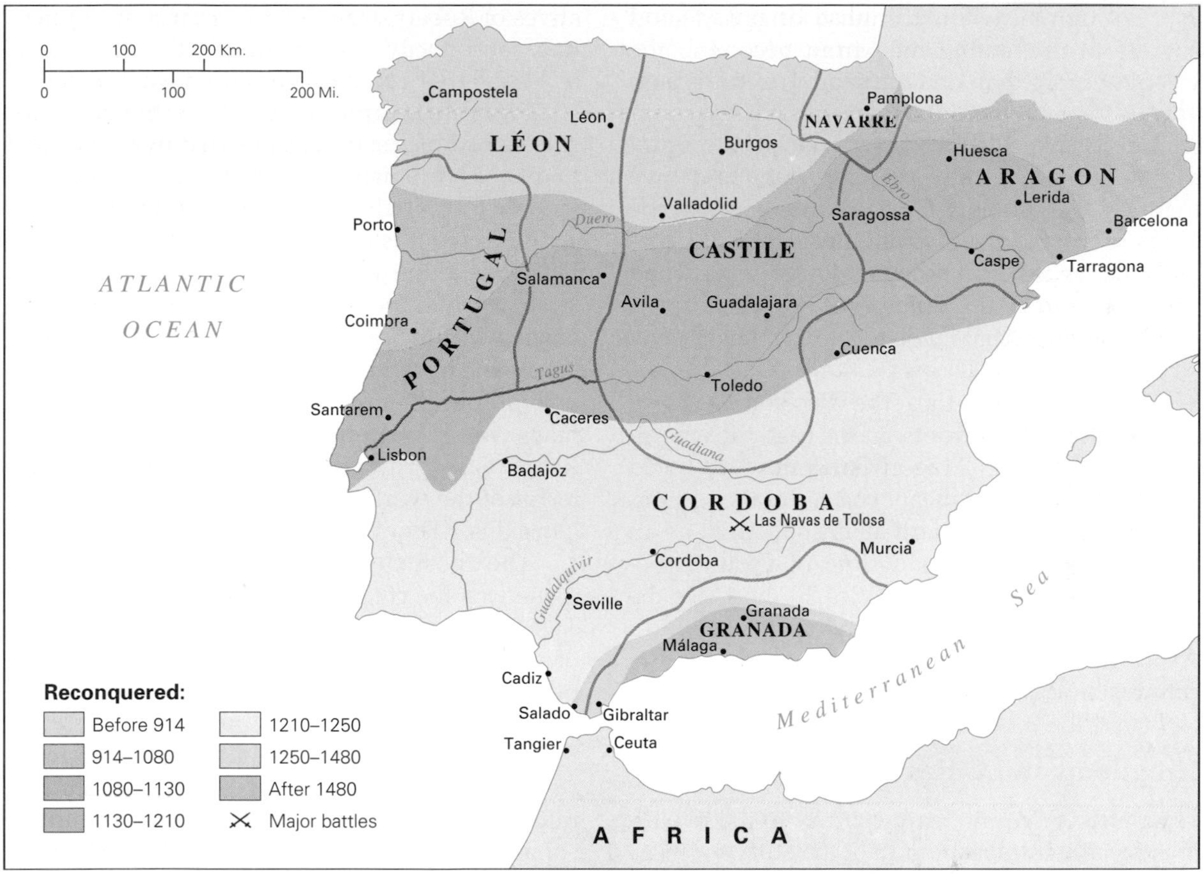

Map 10.4 The Christian Reconquista of Muslim Spain From slow beginnings in the ninth century to the epochal battle of Las Navas de Tolosa (1212), the Christians in Spain pushed back the Muslim frontier and built durable states behind it. *(Source:* David Nicholas, *The Evolution of the Medieval World*. Copyright © 1992. Used by permission of Longman Group UK.)

Before he died, Sancho divided his realm among his sons; thus, the kingdoms of Aragon and Castile arose alongside Navarre. It was Alfonso I (r. 1065–1109) of Castile who really advanced the Reconquista. In 1085 his forces captured the Muslim stronghold and old Visigothic capital of Toledo, an important moral and strategic victory. Alfonso's military successes owed much to the dashing warrior Rodrigo Díaz de Vivar, known as "El Cid" ("the Lord" from the Arabic *sayyid*). Rodrigo was a gifted but slightly unprincipled mercenary who at times fought for the Muslims against the Christians. His career shows just how turbulent Spain then was. Rodrigo's successes, and the reconquest of Toledo, led the retreating Muslims to summon from North Africa militant Muslims who temporarily halted the Christian advance.

Throughout the twelfth century, the Christian states of Spain pressed slowly but relentlessly forward (Map 10.4). The kings, especially the kings of Castile, managed to impose hereditary rule and to exact oaths of allegiance from all their free subjects. As the kingdoms grew and consolidated, the kings tried to make powerful nobles become their vassals. They were more successful on the expanding frontier with Muslim Spain than at home. On the frontier, warriors could be given newly conquered fiefs in return for future military service. At home, in the old kingdoms, the local notables viewed their lands and rights as being independent of royal control.

Through the twelfth century, kings had good success in preventing men from becoming the vassal of more than one lord and in getting their vassals to perform military service. A royal council and judicial institutions also helped to unify the kingdom. To rally the Christians and give them a sense of belonging to a single country, the kings promoted the cult of Saint James of Compostella, Jesus's apostle who allegedly preached Christianty in Spain. In the end, however, it was the Reconquista that made the Spanish monarchy strong.

Down to the 1150s the Reconquista proceeded along three fronts. In the east, the emerging kingdom of Aragon-Catalonia advanced along the Mediterranean coast. In the center, León-Castile pressed hard against al-Andalus. In the west, the nascent kingdom of Portugal became a factor in Iberian politics. In the 1150s the Muslims of Spain once again turned to North Africa for assistance. Help arrived, and the Reconquista was halted again.

Kingdoms and Cities in Italy

The period from the tenth century to the twelfth is especially important in Italian history for three reasons. First, the Germans involved themselves in the affairs of Italy, Rome, and the papacy (see pages 363–367). Second, even before the Norman conquests of England, bands of Norman adventurers began a conquest of southern Italy and Sicily that would result in one of the most dynamic states of medieval Europe. Third, in northern and central Italy in the eleventh century a distinctive type of urban institution began to appear: the commune.

Since the ninth century, the whole region south of Rome had been contested among the Byzantines, the Muslims of North Africa, and local potentates. In 1026 Norman pilgrims bound for the Holy Land landed in southern Italy, where local people invited them to enlist in the fight against the Muslims. By the 1040s the original Normans had been joined by many more who were seeking land and adventure. In 1053 Pope Leo IX (r. 1049–1054) tried but failed to expel the Normans from Italy, and in 1059 Pope Nicholas II (r. 1059–1061) allied with the Norman leader Robert Guiscard (d. 1085). For a half-century, relatives of Robert struggled for control of southern Italy and Sicily; under Roger II "the Great" (r. 1130–1154) a Norman kingdom was created.

From their capital at Palermo, the Normans ruled a complex state that blended Byzantine and Lombard administrative structures with Norman feudalism. In Italy, as in England, the Normans showed a genius for adaptation. Perched advantageously at the juncture of the Latin, Greek, and Arab worlds, the Norman court was more advanced in finance and bureaucratic administration than any of its European contemporaries. No one forgot for a moment, however, that the Normans were first and foremost great warriors. Robert Guiscard's epitaph pronounced him "The terror of the world," and a chronicler said of the Normans, "They delight in arms and horses."

The most dynamic element on the Italian scene was the communal movement (Map 10.5). Two pieces of information help to explain the rise of communes. The first relates to economic expansion. In 1015 Pisa and Genoa undertook a joint attack on Muslim pirates operating from Sardinia. Beginning in the 1060s, the Normans cleared the central Mediterranean of Muslim pirates. When the Seljuk Turks broke Byzantine commercial privileges in the eastern Mediterranean, Venice was quick to take over former Byzantine commerce. By 1100 the Mediterranean was a Latin lake, and Italian merchants were the primary beneficiaries.

The second piece of background relates to political developments in Italian towns. Carolingian towns had been governed by resident counts, and the Germans tried to a degree to maintain this system. The powers of the counts tended to be weak, however, so the Germans relied more on bishops, who were, in Italy as in Germany, key props to the system of imperial rule. But bishops and counts were not alone in holding urban power. Since the late tenth century both bishops and counts had been granting fiefs to local men in order to strengthen their own authority and to procure defense for the town. Gradually these men, whose lands made them wealthy in the expanding economy, moved into the towns and, in turn, enfeoffed other men in the countryside. These lesser vassals were also growing in wealth and moving into towns, where they joined their lords in volatile political factions.

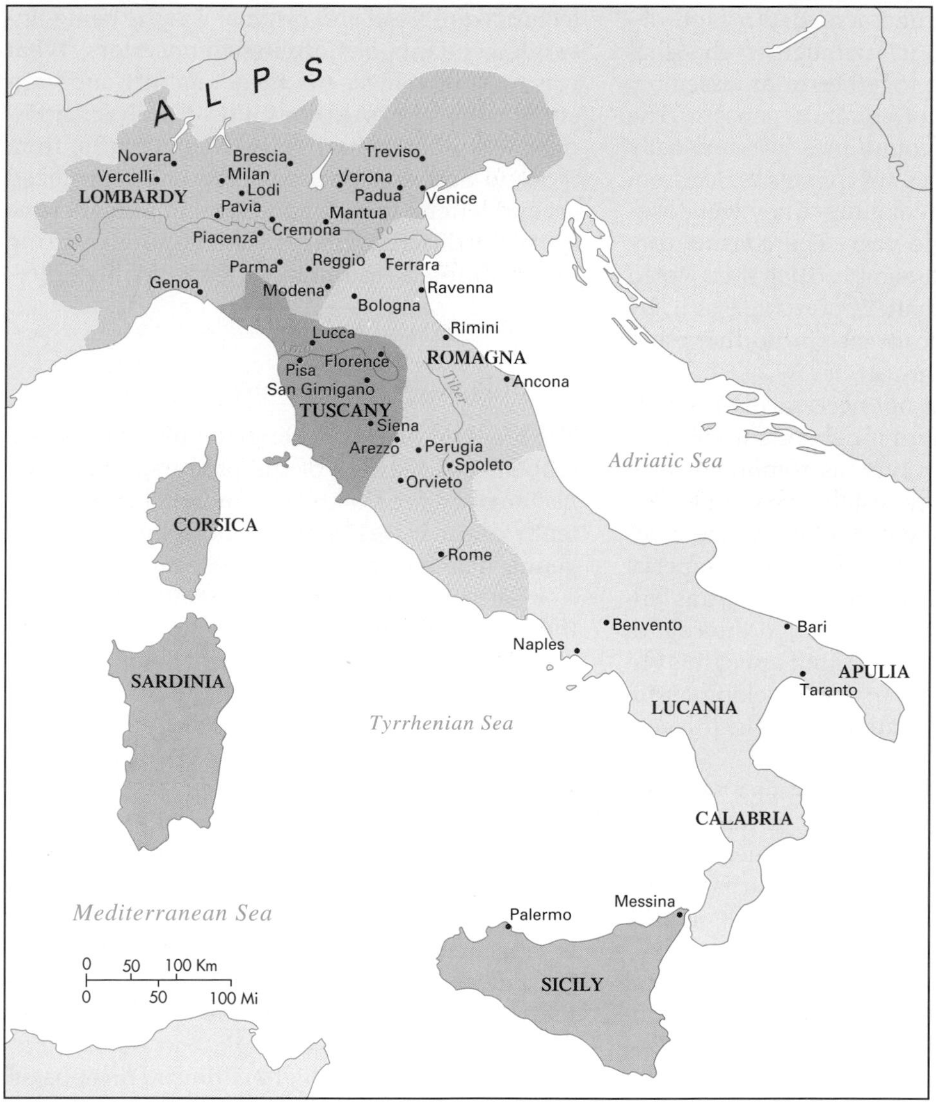

Map 10.5 The Communal Movement in Italy Beginning in the last decades of the eleventh century, towns all over northern and central Italy instituted communal forms of government. In northern Europe, comparable movements existed only in Flanders and parts of northern France.

The death of the German emperor Henry III in 1056 opened twenty years when Italian towns were nearly free of imperial coercion. When his successor Henry IV finally turned his attention to Italy, he tried to govern there by means of bishops. The popes, however, denied him this option, and the rising communal movement compromised other alternatives.

Communes were sworn associations of the local nobility—the vassals of the bishops and counts—and their vassals. A key factor in the rise of communes was reconciliation among violent and competing noble factions. Although commune members swore to uphold one another's rights and called themselves the *popolo,* the people as a whole had nothing to do with the early communes. The commune accorded a high degree of participation to its members in choosing leaders and in coming together in an assembly that voted on matters of common concern. The leaders of the early communes were usually called *consuls*. The number of consuls varied from four to twenty in different cities. They were usually elected for a single year. The consuls proposed matters to an assembly that then voted "yes" or "no" on the matters presented to it. By the 1140s every significant city in northern and central Italy had a commune.

The communes did not necessarily originate as attempts to make cities independent and sovereign. Frequently, however, as communal governments became more established and confident, that is what they did. One by one cities either refused to recognize papal or imperial overlordship or else renegotiated the terms under which they would acknowledge the rule of their historic masters. The working out of this ongoing relationship was a major development in the history of the Italian cities in the twelfth century.

Another important development was the growth of the popolo. Gradually, it came to include more petty rural nobles, some merchants, a few industrialists, and some wealthy artisans and professional men. As a result, political volatility in the cities of Italy remained high.

The Italian commune was a radical political experiment. Everywhere else in medieval Europe, power was thought to radiate downward—from God, the clergy, the emperor, the king. In a commune, power radiated upward from the popolo to its leaders. For several centuries, the Italian city was arguably the most creative institution in the Western world.

Cultural Life in an Age of Expansion

Both tradition and innovation were evident in the cultural life of Europe between 900 and 1150. Church schools remained dominant, but logic replaced grammar at the heart of the curriculum. Cathedral schools began eclipsing monastic ones. Latin letters remained ascendant, but literature in many vernacular languages began to appear in quantity and quality. Romanesque art and architecture were fresh and original despite being lineal descendants of Carolingian ancestors. What was most novel was the sheer quantity and variety of cultural expressions. Post-Carolingian Europe was politically diverse. Many courts, from Sicily to Scandinavia, promoted and patronized art and letters. French and German Romanesque spoke in different voices. The culture of rising towns differed from that of the feudal countryside.

Schools and Latin Letters

The breakup of the Carolingian Empire deprived schools and masters of the patronage that they had enjoyed for a century or more. Therefore, the tenth century was marked more by individual genius than by a program of learning.

Gerbert of Aurillac (940–1003) was perhaps the most distinguished intellect of his age. He left his home in Aquitaine to study in Spain and Italy before settling in Reims, where he was a teacher and then briefly bishop. He attracted the attention of the emperor Otto III and spent some time at the German court, earning appointments as abbot of Bobbio, bishop of Ravenna, and, finally, pope. Gerbert followed Carolingian tradition in being a collector of manuscripts and critic of texts, but he departed from older traditions in his interest in mathematics and in his study of logic.

Fulbert of Chartres (960–1028), Gerbert's finest pupil, elevated the cathedral school of Chartres to the paramount place in Europe. Fulbert wrote letters in elegant Latin and fine poems. He carried on his master's literary interests more than his scientific ones, and well into the twelfth century Chartres remained a major center of literary studies.

Another figure of interest is the aristocratic German nun Roswitha of Gandersheim (d. 970). She wrote poems on saints and martyrs, as well as a story about a priest who sold his soul to the devil. In her mature years, Roswitha wrote Latin plays in rhymed verse based on the Roman writer Terence. In these plays she took tales from Roman and biblical history and used them to convey moral truths.

The eleventh century, more settled and prosperous than the tenth, was more diverse culturally, though it is still hard to detect any coherent program such as the one that characterized the Carolingian Renaissance (see page 296). Law was one field where important initiatives were taken. The increasing sophistication of urban life demanded a better understanding of law. The growing responsibilities of the church called for orderly rules, and the church's frequent quarrels with secular rulers demanded careful delineations of rights and responsibilities. Early in the century Burchard, bishop of Würzburg, produced a *Decretum,* a collection of canon law that was novel for being arranged systematically by topics rather than chronologically. This book was influential for more than a century and heightened reformers' awareness of the law of the church.

By midcentury several major scholars were studying canon law in Italy and France, and they helped to promote the papal view of reform. In Bologna, Irnerius (d. ca. 1130), a transplanted German and protégé of Emperor Henry V, began teaching Roman law from the law code of Justinian (see page 257). This legal work culminated in the publication in 1140 of the *Decretum* of the Bolognese monk Gratian. The most comprehensive and systematic book of canon law ever written, Gratian's work remained authoritative for centuries.

One of the chief accomplishments of the age came about almost by accident. Berengar of Tours (ca. 1000–ca. 1088) wrote a treatise that denied Christ's presence in the Eucharist. This position was heretical. Ordinarily, churchmen would simply have quoted to Berengar various passages from the Scriptures or from the writings of the Church Fathers along with conciliar pronouncements. The evidence, however, was ambiguous. Berengar was finally refuted, at least to the satisfaction of his opponents, by Lanfranc, archbishop of Canterbury during the reign of William the Conqueror. Lanfranc used precise logical argumentation to dispose of Berengar's heretical arguments.

Carolingian schools had focused on grammar, on the basic foundations of language. Now that logic had come to the aid of the faith in one critical case, people were encouraged to apply it all over. Anselm, Lanfranc's successor as archbishop of Canterbury, developed an ingenious proof for the existence of God (see the box, "Saint Anselm on the Existence of God"). The French thinker Peter Abelard (1079–1142) used logic to reconcile apparent contradictions in the Scriptures and in the writings of the Church Fathers. A logical cast of mind is also clearly apparent behind the legal work of Gratian and behind the tightly organized biblical commentaries of the age.

We must not suppose that Anselm and Abelard were skeptics. Anselm's motto was "Faith seeking understanding." Logic was for him the handmaiden of divine truth. He would have agreed completely with Abelard, who said that "Faith has no merit with God when it is not the testimony of divine truth that leads us to it, but the evidence of human reason." Conservatives like Bernard of Clairvaux disagreed. He believed in the absolute primacy of faith and in immediate divine inspiration. To him, logical approaches to divine truth were the height of arrogance. His views were shared in some ways by Hildegard of Bingen (1098–1179), who was well educated, gifted musically, knowledgeable in medical matters, and perhaps the most profound psychological thinker of her age. More than anyone before her, Hildegard opened up for dis-

MONKS AND WRITERS

ca. 900	*Beowulf*
910	Foundation of Cluny
940–1003	Gerbert of Aurillac
962–1028	Fulbert of Chartres
d. 970	Roswitha of Gandersheim
1000–1088	Berengar of Tours
ca. 1033–1109	Anselm of Canterbury
ca. 1050–1150	Emergence of the Romanesque
1079–1142	Peter Abelard
1090–1153	Bernard of Clairvaux
ca. 1095	*The Song of Roland*
1098	Foundation of Cîteaux
1098–1179	Hildegard of Bingen
1140	Gratian's *Decretum*

Saint Anselm on the Existence of God

In his* Proslogion, *a work on logic, Anselm attempted to prove the existence of God. He was contemplating the fool in Psalm 14 who said, "There is no God," and he wondered if it were possible for something to exist in the mind and not also in reality. The fool must have had the idea of God in mind in order to deny God's existence. And if God existed in the mind of even this fool, must not God exist in reality too?

Lord, . . . give me to understand, as far as you can explain, that you exist as we believe, and that you are what we believe. And indeed we believe that you are the greatest thing imaginable. Or is there some other nature? For the fool has said in his heart: "There is no God." But surely that very same fool, hearing what I say: "the greatest thing imaginable," understands what he hears, and what he understands is in his mind, even if he does not understand that it exists. For the existence of the thing in the mind, and understanding that the thing exists, are two different concepts. For when an artist plans what he is going to do, he has it in his mind, but he does not yet understand what he has not yet consummated. But when he has finished the painting, he has it in his mind and also understands that what he has done exists. Therefore, even the fool is convinced that there is something in the mind, than which nothing greater is imaginable, because he understands this, when he hears it, and whatever is understood is in the mind. And surely the greatest thing imaginable cannot be in the mind only, or that very thing, than which a greater cannot be conceived, is a thing than which a greater can be conceived. But that is impossible. There exists therefore, without question, something than which a greater is inconceivable, both in the mind and in reality.

Source: Putnam's Dark and Middle Ages Reader, ed. Harry E. Wedeck (New York: Capricorn, 1965), p. 220.

cussion the theology of the feminine, and the feminine aspect of divinity. She, like Bernard, believed that God was to be found deep within the human spirit, not in books full of learned wrangling.

The future lay with Anselm and Abelard. Anselm was the most gifted Christian thinker since Augustine. He wrote distinguished works on logic, and his theological treatise *Why God Became Man* served for three hundred years as a philosophical and theological explanation of the incarnation of Christ, the central mystery of the Christian faith.

Peter Abelard was a more colorful figure. He argued rudely and violently with all his teachers, though in the end he was probably more intelligent than any of them. He rose to a keener understanding of Aristotle than anyone in centuries, and he developed a sharper sense of both the power and the limitations of language than anyone since the Greeks. He concerned himself with ethics too and was one of the first writers to consider intention to be more important than simple action.

Abelard seduced and then married Heloise, one of his pupils, and he got sufficiently carried away in some of his philosophical speculations that church councils condemned him. He popularized the schools of Paris, however, and attracted to them promising scholars from all over Europe. Once patronage alone had promoted learning, but now equally important was the sheer excitement of the expanding intellectual horizon.

The Death of a Hero

***Beowulf* has been killed by a gruesome dragon after his faithful men proved faithless and abandoned him. Only Beowulf's kinsman Wiglaf stayed by his side. This passage explores the idealism and harsh realities of aristocratic society.**

It was soon after this/That the battle-shirkers came out of the wood,/Ten men together, cowards and vow-breakers/Who had shrunk from throwing a spear in fight/At the hour of their liege lord's heavy need;/But they came in shame carrying their shields,/Their armor of battle where the old man was lying;/Their eyes were on Wiglaf. . . .

Wiglaf spoke, Weohstan's son,/"Many for the sake of one must often/Suffer affliction as we face now./How could we influence our beloved prince,/The keeper of the kingdom, by any advice,/Against his attacking the gold's guardian [i.e. the dragon] . . . /He followed high fate; the hoard is flung open,/Gained at hard cost; overharsh was the destiny/That drove the great king forward to that place . . ." /With ten days' work they had raised the memorial/Of the war-renowned man . . ./Then famous riders rode around the mound,/A dozen all told, of the children of men,/To give voice to their pain, to lament their king,/To utter their elegy, to tell the man's history;/They lauded his bravery, and they praised him chivalrously/For audacious deeds, as should always be—/Man's words should honor his lord and friend,/When his days of living are led to their end./They said he had proved of all kings of the world/The kindest of men and the most humane,/Most gentle to his folk and the most vigilant of fame.

Source: Beowulf, trans. Edwin Morgan (Berkeley: University of California Press, 1967), lines 2845–52, 3076–86, 3159–60, 3169–78, 3180–82.

The Rise of Vernacular Culture

"Clericus, id est litteratus" ("A cleric, that is a literate person"), ran a medieval motto. To know French or to write English did not give one "letters," did not make one a member of the community of scholars. Yet in the period 900–1150 many writers, most of them unknown to us by name, began to write in their native tongues. Their achievement is one of the most important legacies of the age.

The epic poem *Beowulf* is the first true classic of English literature. We do not know who wrote it or when it was written. For a long time scholars confidently assigned it to the eighth century, but now most scholars place it later, in the ninth or possibly in the tenth century. The story focuses on three great battles fought by the hero Beowulf. The first two are against the monster Grendel and Grendel's mother, who have been harrying the kingdom of an old ally of Beowulf's family. The third is against a dragon. *Beowulf* is a poem of adventure and of heroism, of loyalty and of treachery. It treats lordship, friendship, and kinship. Themes of good and evil are sounded throughout. The poem is barely Christian but nevertheless deeply moral. It speaks, in a mature, vigorous, and moving language, to and for the heart of a warrior society. (See the box, "The Death of a Hero.")

Beowulf is the best-known heroic Anglo-Saxon work but by no means the only one. One of the Viking attacks that led to the undoing of Ethelred II was commemorated in *The Battle*

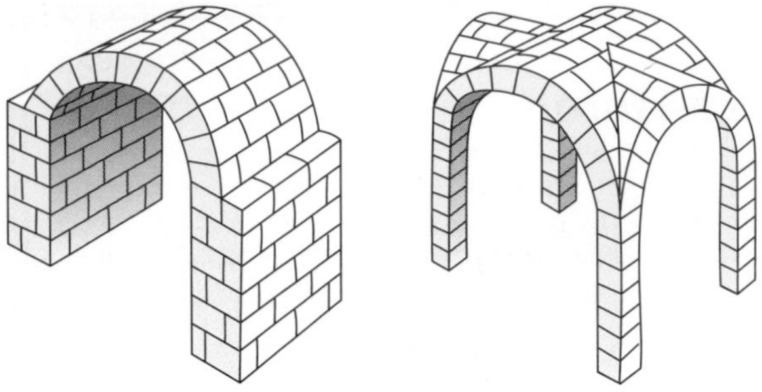

Figure 10.1. The Structure of Romanesque Architecture The basic structural element of Romanesque architecture was the barrel vault, which, when two were joined at right angles, formed a groin vault. These vaults produced great height and strength but gave buildings a massive, fortress-like appearance. (*Source*: Anne Shaver-Crandell, *The Middle Ages* [Cambridge, England: Cambridge University Press, 1982], p. 4. Used by permission.)

of Maldon. There also survive several volumes of elegiac and lyric poetry, mostly on religious themes. Much of this work has great technical merit, and some of it is deeply moving. Also written in Anglo-Saxon were chronicles, legal materials and charters and at least one large collection of homilies. These texts are eloquent testimony to the literary attainments of the "illiterate."

France produced a number of *chansons de gestes*, "songs of deeds," or celebrations of the great. The best is the *Song of Roland*, written around 1100. In 778 Charlemagne's baggage train was raided, and Roland, a count, was killed by some Basques as the Frankish army was returning from a campaign in Spain. By 1100 this obscure event, long kept alive in oral traditions, had been transformed into a heroic struggle between Charlemagne and his retinue and an army of countless thousands of "paynim," who are crude caricatures of Muslims.

Exterior of St. Sernin, Toulouse This fortress-like church (ca. 1080–1120) was paid for by the offerings of pilgrims on their way to shrines in Spain. Its massive walls and numerous colonnades are typical of Romanesque architecture. The form of the building suggests the cross of Christ. (*Jean Dieuzaid, Toulouse*)

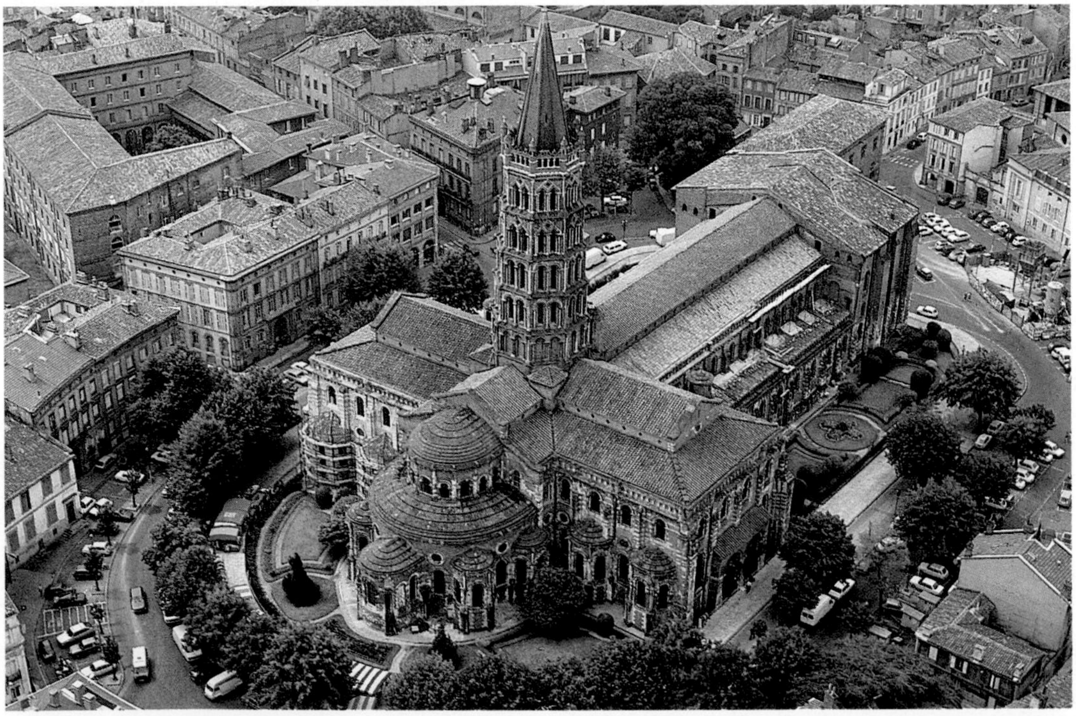

Like *Beowulf, Roland* is a story about loyalty and treachery, about bravery in the face of insuperable odds, about the kindness and generosity of leaders. They take us into a man's chivalric world. Females are all but absent. The two works do not show us personal hopes, fears, or motivations. Everything that we think should be private is made public. What pours forth is the communal ethos and the dominant values of the elite, male social group.

The Romanesque Achievement

Romanesque, "in the Roman style," is a term coined in the nineteenth century to characterize the architecture and, to a lesser extent, the painting of the period from the end of Carolingian art to the full emergence of Gothic art in the late twelfth century. Today scholars define the Romanesque period as extending from roughly 1050 to 1150 and view the Romanesque style as transitional between Carolingian and Gothic.

At several places in Ottonian Germany a return of political stability led to the foundation and reconstruction of churches. Ducal dynasties and women of the imperial family were among the most generous patrons. Pride in their Carolingian inheritance and their new imperial dignity led the Germans to a distinctive architectural style marked by very thick walls, alternating piers and columns in the nave, and galleries. As this architectural style spread all over Europe in the eleventh century, it produced true Romanesque, a style that differed from Roman and Carolingian styles mainly in the greater internal height and space made possible by vaulting (Figure 10.1). To the rectangular elegance of the classical basilica and the height of the Carolingian westworks (see page 297), Romanesque builders added a refined verticality.

Among the distinctive features of Romanesque churches were their wall paintings and frescoes, their sculpture, reliquaries, pulpits, and baptisteries—in short, their exuberant decoration and ornament. Europe's growing wealth and sophistication, and the self-conscious feelings of the church's aristocratic patrons, are very much in evidence. Especially in the south of France, the façades of Romanesque churches provided space for sculpture. The tympanum above doors, a space seen by all who entered, was a favored location. Large-scale sculpture had made a comeback after its almost total absence in the early Middle Ages.

The finest paintings were still in books, in gorgeous illuminated manuscripts, but the court art of Otto III marks a real departure in European painting. (See the paintings on page 363.) The modeling of figures, the overall sense of composition and balance, and the use of space were new. Christian subjects continued to predominate, but the look and feel of imperial German art began to move away from Carolingian traditions.

Interior of St. Sernin, Toulouse The interior space of St. Sernin is high and well ordered, but its typical Romanesque effect—from the barrel vaulting—is that of a tunnel. Massive piers support the gallery level and the roof vaulting above. (*Jean Dieuzaid, Toulouse*)

The First Crusade

In 1096 an army of Christian knights who called themselves pilgrims left Europe to liberate the Holy Land from the infidel. This was the first of many Crusades, so called because the warriors were *crucesignati*, "signed by the cross."

In the early tenth century Europe was still reeling from a ceaseless round of attacks and from the near collapse of its central governing structures. By the late eleventh century, Europe would be an impregnable fortress that had marshaled its resources for an attack on the world around it. What the First Crusade shows us is a Europe of enormous energy, potential, and complexity.

The Background

The background to the First Crusade lies both in the Muslim and Byzantine East and in the Latin West. Three interested parties were involved: the Byzantines, the popes, and the warriors of Europe.

Ever since the emergence of the Turkish threat in the early eleventh century, the Byzantines had been seeking mercenary help. The imperial defeat at Manzikert (see page 329) made their search more urgent and led to appeals to the West. Some troops were rounded up but not enough, so in 1095 Emperor Alexius Comnenus (r. 1081–1118) sent envoys to ask Pope Urban II to lend his support to an appeal for mercenary help against the Turks. To most westerners the Turkish threat to Byzantium was a matter of little consequence. What counted was Turkish depredations along the pilgrim routes to Jerusalem. The popes saw in the plight of the Byzantines and of western pilgrims some opportunities to manifest their leadership of the church. The Orthodox and Roman churches had split in 1054, and the popes very much desired to heal this rift. The popes placed a high value on aiding the Byzantines.

The crusade was perfectly consonant with the ethos of the knights of western Europe. Knights were born and trained to fight. The vernacular literature of the age glorified war and warriors. But churchmen had for some years been advancing an ideal of Christian knighthood that stressed fighting God's enemies and aiding God's people. In the late tenth century there arose, first in France and then in many other places, peace movements called the "Peace of God" or the "Truce of God." These movements sought to prevent war in certain seasons, such as around Christmas and Easter, and on certain days of the week, chiefly Sundays. Peace movements also attempted to outlaw fighting near churches, protect noncombatants, and ameliorate the treatment of enemies and captives. Together the movements constituted a powerful inducement for knights to fight non-Christians outside Europe.

As we noted earlier, the simultaneous rise in population and consolidation of family lineages was producing, especially in France, large numbers of restless, landless "young." These young knights viewed the crusade as an opportunity to do what they did best: fight. In addition to adventure, the crusade provided an opportunity for military glory that might procure advancement back home or a chance to acquire lands and titles far from Europe's highly competitive aristocratic milieu.

The "Pilgrimage" to Jerusalem

Pope Urban II received Alexius's envoys in 1095 and then left Italy for France. He was actually a fugitive because Henry IV controlled Rome. In November at Clermont Urban delivered a moving speech to a vast Christian assembly. He ignored the eastern emperor's appeal for aid and instead promised salvation to soldiers who would enlist in a great struggle to free the Holy Land. The crowd acclaimed his words with a shout of "Deus le vult" ("God wills it").

By 1096 four large armies, which eventually swelled to perhaps 100,000 men—mostly French knights with a smattering of troops from other parts of Europe—assembled under the leadership of the pope's legate. The forces were to rendezvous at Constantinople, where they seem to have expected a cordial imperial welcome and all necessary assistance. Alexius, however, took a rather different view. A rag-tag band of ordinary people preceding the Crusaders had torn through the Balkans like a plague of locusts. Then, the crusading armies themselves sorely taxed the imperial authorities who had to secure their passage from the frontier of Hungary to the gates of Constantinople. Finally, Alexius wanted mercenaries to fight Turks in Anatolia, not armed pilgrims intent on liberating Palestine.

After receiving nominal promises of loyalty and the return or donation of any lands captured, Alexius moved the Crusaders into Anatolia. Almost immediately the Latin army defeated a Turkish force at Dorylaeum, thus earning a valuable, though short-lived, reputation for invincibility. The troops then entered Syria and laid siege to Antioch, which did not fall until 1098. At this point, rivalries among the Crusaders came into the open. One force went to the frontier of Armenia and carved out a principality. One of the ubiquitous Normans kept Antioch for himself. The main army pressed on to Jerusalem and, after a short but fierce siege, conquered it in July 1099. A contemporary soldier described the scene:

> Our men rushed around the whole city, seizing gold and silver, horses and mules, houses full of all sorts of goods, and they all came rejoicing and weeping from excess of gladness to worship at the Sepulchre of our Saviour Jesus, and there they acknowledged themselves his serfs. Next morning they went cautiously up on the Temple roof and attacked the Saracens, both men and women, cutting off their heads with drawn swords.[2]

Godfrey of Bouillon, leader of the troops that had "liberated" Jerusalem, was named "Advocate of the Holy Sepulcher" and became ruler of the Christians in the East. He lived only a short time, however, and was replaced by his brother Baldwin as king of Jerusalem in 1100. The tiny "crusader states" created in the East were reinforced by soldiers and settlers in 1100 and 1101.

Judged on its own terms, the First Crusade was a success. The Holy Land was retaken from the infidel, and the pilgrim routes were passable once more. Entirely uncertain, however, were the prospects of the crusader states, the future course of western relations with Byzantium, and the reaction of the Islamic world once it recovered from its initial shock.

Summary

In 900 the survival of Europe's political, social, and intellectual order was in question. By 1150 Europe was prosperous, confident, and expansive.

Population rose steadily after the ninth century. People everywhere brought new land into cultivation, adopted better agricultural techniques, and improved transportation. Agricultural gains promoted urban growth as some people were freed from farming to undertake commercial and artisanal pursuits. Never before had Europe's economy improved so rapidly.

European society assumed between 900 and 1150 many of the distinctive features that it would bear until the modern period. A landed aristocracy competed with lesser nobles and with urban potentates for power and rank. In a militantly Christian society the clergy had great power and prestige, but it had to struggle continually with envious nobilities and governments in order to maintain its privileged status. Peasants were gaining ground economically and legally, but their position was always precarious.

Governments were growing in power, scope, and sophistication. Kings drew on both the Carolingian past and the innovative spirit of the present to create centralized institutions that were once again effective. There were striking similarities among all the various states of post-Carolingian Europe.

Cultural horizons were expanding too. There were more and better schools than at any time since the Carolingian Renaissance. The curriculum moved beyond an elementary focus on grammar. Vernacular languages were taking their place alongside Latin as sophisticated tools for the expression of complex stories and ideas. Romanesque art represented richness, growth, and novelty.

But everything was fragile. No one in 1150 could have predicted whether the European economy would go on expanding. Cities and their residents might well have taken the lead in social and political life away from kings and landed nobles. Latin letters might have yielded their place to French or English. The death of Saint Bernard in 1153 might have signaled the end of traditional monasticism or an opening for new forms of religious expression. Political crises in England, France, Germany, Sicily, and Spain in the 1150s might have brought a return of political fragmentation, or they might have strengthened the centralizing tendencies in evidence since about 1000. The years after 1150 were creative, but in ways quite different from those between 900 and 1150.

Notes

1. Rodulfus Glaber, *Historiarum Libri Quinque,* 3.4.13, ed. and trans. John France (Oxford, England: Oxford University Press, 1989), pp. 114–116 (slightly adapted).
2. From the Gesta Francorum, trans. August C. Krey, in *The First Crusade* (Princeton, N.J.: Princeton University Press, 1921), p. 257 (slightly adapted).

Suggested Reading

General Surveys

Barraclough, Geoffrey. *The Crucible of Europe: The Ninth and Tenth Centuries in European History.* 1976. Ranging from England to Italy, the author assesses the collapse of the Carolingian order and the beginnings of its replacement by individual states. He takes a more negative view of developments than the one adopted in this text.

Brooke, Christopher. *Europe in the Central Middle Ages.* 1975. This somewhat dated book remains the best introduction in English to a period that has been heavily studied by European scholars.

Le Goff, Jacques. *Medieval Civilization.* Translated by Julia Barrow. 1988. Le Goff, one of France's leading and most original medievalists, offers a comprehensive look at medieval civilization in all its aspects. Fascinating and challenging.

Southern, Richard W. *The Making of the Middle Ages.* 1967. Since its appearance in 1953 this elegant, brilliant, stimulating book has become a classic. It evokes the mentality, society, and politics of Europe from the tenth century to the twelfth.

Feudal Society

Bloch, Marc. *Feudal Society.* Translated by L. A. Manyon. 2 vols. 1964. This is the best-known book by one of this century's greatest historians. Bloch seeks to explain the total history of the post-Carolingian world in terms of the ideals and practices associated with feudalism.

Ganshof, François-Louis. *Feudalism.* 2d ed. Translated by Philip Grierson. 1964. For almost fifty years Ganshof's clear, concise, readable book has been the standard introduction to the essential personal and proprietary aspects of the feudal bond.

Poly, Jean-Pierre, and Eric Bournazel. *The Feudal Transformation, 900–1200.* Translated by Caroline Higgett. 1991. This extraordinarily important book presents a synthesis of all the best French thinking in the past generation or two on social and institutional development, mainly in France.

Reynolds, Susan. *Kingdoms and Communities in Western Europe, 900–1300.* 1984. After exploring the kinds of legal notions that guided community building, this lively book turns to actual communities, ranging from the parish to the kingdom.

National and Regional Histories

Chibnall, Marjorie. *Anglo-Norman England, 1066–1166.* 1986. Focusing on government, institutions, and society, this book is a remarkably effective introduction to a tumultuous century of English history.

Douglas, David C. *William the Conqueror.* 1967. Long, detailed, and challenging, Douglas's book remains the standard against which all biographies of William will be judged.

Duby, Georges. *Medieval France.* 1991. The author of this original and entertaining book is France's leading medievalist. This book is an especially good introduction to his many distinctive ideas about the shaping of French society in the eleventh and twelfth centuries.

Dunbabin, Jean. *France in the Making, 843–1180.* 1985. Readable and interesting, this book describes the making of France's territorial principalities and then shows how a centralized kingdom slowly superseded them.

Fletcher, Richard. *The Quest for El Cid.* 1990. As entertaining and engaging as a detective novel, Fletcher's book seeks both to recapture the historical Cid and to explain literary and historical accounts about him.

Fuhrmann, Horst. *Germany in the High Middle Ages, c. 1050–1200.* Translated by Timothy Reuter. 1986. Beautifully written and translated, this book presents the thought of Germany's leading medievalist.

Gerber, Jane S. *The Jews of Spain: A History of the Sephardic Experience.* 1992. Interesting, lively, and comprehensive—though stronger on cultural than on political developments—this book presents an important history that is too often lost in accounts of Christian and Muslim Spain.

Hyde, J. K. *Society and Politics in Medieval Italy: The Evolution of the Civil Life, 1000–1350.* 1973. More difficult than Waley (see below), this book is a sophisticated introduction to the social complexity and institutional creativity of Italian towns.

Matthew, Donald. *The Norman Kingdom of Sicily.* 1992. This interesting book treats the fascinating personalities and remarkable historical circumstances that made Norman south Italy so distinctive.

Reilly, Bernard. *The Contest of Christian and Muslim Spain, 1031–1157.* 1991. Thorough yet readable and interesting, this book tells how the Reconquista was launched and with what consequences.

Reuter, Timothy. *Germany in the Early Middle Ages, 800–1056.* 1991. This welcome, albeit dense, book covers comprehensively a period never before well treated in English.

Stafford, Pauline. *Unification and Conquest: A Political and Social History of England in the Tenth and Eleventh Centuries.* 1989. The subtitle of this book accurately describes its scope and contents. It is interesting and well written.

Waley, Daniel. *The Italian City-Republics.* 3d ed. 1988. This balanced, nicely written, readily understood book continues to be the best introduction to the incredibly complicated world of Italian urban politics.

Religion and the Church

Blumenthal, Uta-Renate. *The Investiture Controversy: Church and Monarchy from the Ninth to the Twelfth Century.* 1988. Brief, readable, and remarkably comprehensive, this book is the best introduction in any language to the great upheaval.

Lawrence, C. H. *Medieval Monasticism: Forms of Religious Life in Western Europe in the Middle Ages.* 2d ed. 1989. The chapters in this comprehensive, readable book treating Cluny, eleventh-century monastic innovations, and the Cistercians are relevant to this chapter.

Leyser, Henrietta. *Hermits and the New Monasticism: A Study of Religious Communities in Western Europe, 1000–1150.* 1984. Brief, lively, and informative, this book explains the sources and history of the many religious movements that spread throughout Europe, emphasizing the eremitic ideal.

Newman, Barbara. *Sister of Wisdom: St. Hildegard's Theology of the Feminine.* 1987. Interesting and readable, this path-breaking study not only introduces Hildegard but also opens up wholly new ways of thinking about twelfth-century spiritual culture.

Southerm, Richard W. *Saint Anselm: A Portrait in a Landscape.* 1990. The distillation of a life's work by a master historian, this wonderful book introduces not only Anselm but also the intellectual and spiritual life of his world.

Society and Economy

Duby, Georges. *The Early Growth of the European Economy: Warriors and Peasants from the Seventh to the Twelfth Century.* Translated by Howard B. Clarke. 1974. Especially strong on the workings of rural society, this is another introduction to medieval economic history and to the thought of an important, original historian.

Fossier, Robert. *Peasant Life in the Medieval West.* Translated by Juliet Vale. 1988. This is the best introduction to "those who work." Although emphasizing France, the book contributes usefully to an understanding of wider European phenomena.

Herlihy, David. *Medieval Households.* 1985. Stretching from Late Antiquity to the fifteenth century, this engaging book by a master historian treats almost every aspect of the family in its social, domestic, and economic settings.

———. *Opera Muliebria: Women and Work in Medieval Europe.* 1990. This brief and nontechnical book covers most of Europe in the thousand years after about 500. It is full of interesting and sometimes surprising information.

Lopez, Robert S. *The Commercial Revolution of the Middle Ages, 950–1350.* 1971. Lopez's sprightly account of the economic expansion and creativity of this period remains unsurpassed.

Art and Architecture

Demus, Otto. *Romanesque Wall Painting.* 1970. Although the commentary in this book is a little challenging, the pictures are numerous and superb.

Kubach, Hans Erich. *Romanesque Architecture.* 1988. This is a standard introduction to a vast subject by an acknowledged authority. Comprehensive and accessible to nonspecialists.

Zarnecki, George. *Romanesque Art.* 1971. This well-illustrated book avoids jargon and introduces the reader to the rich, complex world of the Romanesque.

Weighing the Evidence

DOMESDAY BOOK

A wit once said, "There are lies, damned lies, and statistics." For all the centuries that precede the preparation of *Domesday Book*, there survives almost no evidence that permits the medieval historian to test that maxim. Even to begin a statistical analysis, one needs data that are abundant, contemporaneous, and commensurable. One needs more than a few isolated cases. The cases cannot be far separated in time, and the types of data must be relatively consistent. Evidence from the earlier Middle Ages rarely meets more than one of those criteria.

Domesday Book, pictured here, and its companion volume, the *Lesser Domesday Book*, contain nearly eighteen hundred pages of detailed information about England in 1086–1087. The books resulted from orders of William "the Conqueror." Here is how the *Anglo-Saxon Chronicle* describes the scene:

> He sent his men all over England into every shire to ascertain how many hundreds of "hides" [units of account] of land there were in each shire, and how much land and livestock the king himself owned in the country, and what annual dues were lawfully his from each shire. He also had it recorded how much land his archbishops had, and his diocesan bishops, and his abbots and his earls and . . . what each landholder in England had in land or livestock, and how much money they were worth. So thoroughly did he have the inquiry carried out that there was not a single hide of land . . . not one ox, nor one cow, nor one pig which escaped notice in his survey. And all the surveys were brought to him.[1]

From other sources we learn that William divided all of England into seven (or possibly nine) circuits that were visited by panels of three or four lay and ecclesiastical notables. The panelists carried with them the surviving records of the Anglo-Saxon kings in order to confirm all revenues owed to the Crown. In addition, all landowners were required to appear before the panels to state their holdings and their value. After the material had been collected and recorded in rough draft, district by district throughout each circuit, all the data were recopied, probably at the royal court, into the surviving books. The material is organized systematically, beginning with towns (though London, the largest, is omitted—it may have been the subject of its own, no-longer-extant, survey) and proceeding to landowners' estates arranged according to size (the king's always come first). Every estate is then described in minute detail.

Historians derive two kinds of information from *Domesday Book*. The first pertains to William and his administration. William came to England in 1066 and found it a prosperous and well-governed country, but he knew little about it. His battles to secure England and to hold his continental possessions were costly. Moreover, as William parceled out England in fiefs to his greatest followers, and as they in turn created fiefs for their own retainers, it was imperative to learn the value of those fiefs. William needed to know what resources were at his disposal.

We may assume from William's claims to all the revenues once paid to the Anglo-Saxon kings that he regarded himself as the legitimate successor to Edward "the Confessor." The use made by William's investigators of Anglo-Saxon royal records is a tribute to the government machinery built up by Alfred "the Great" and his successors. The confirmation of one set of written records by the preparation of another set shows us the growing sophistication of government and the emergence of what historian Michael Clanchy calls the transformation "from memory to written record"—the shift from an overwhelmingly oral to an increasingly written culture.

The survey that resulted in *Domesday Book* helps us to situate William's administration in a longer history. The Romans, the Byzantines, and the Arabs had carried out massive land and re-

1. *The Anglo-Saxon Chronicle*, trans. G. N. Garmonsway (1953; reprint, London: Dent, 1984), p. 216.

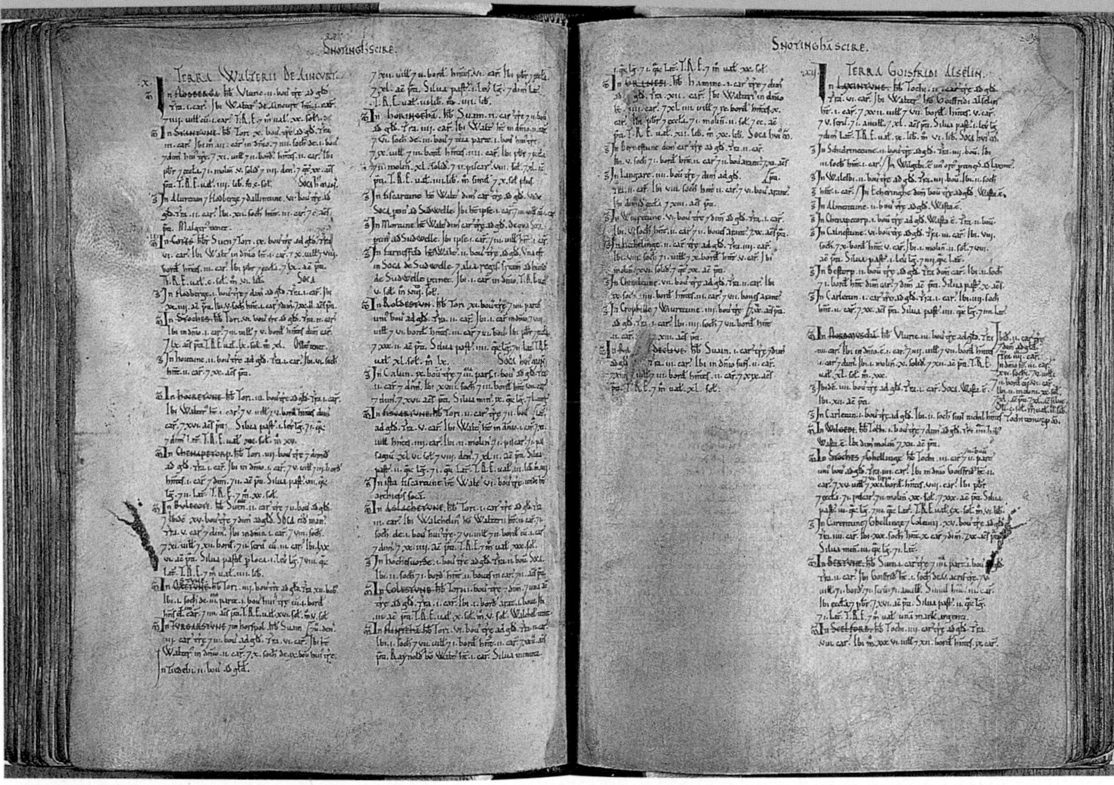

Domesday Book *(Public Record Office, London)*

source surveys, but no European government had undertaken such a venture. In the Carolingian world, the monarchy and some great ecclesiastical establishments undertook surveys of their own holdings, but these were vastly smaller than the kingdom of England. So although we find precedents for William's actions, it is the scale and ambition of his work that remain impressive.

Second, *Domesday* provides historians with a wealth of detail about England. Not everyone was counted, but we can estimate England's population (about 1.5 million) more accurately than we can the population anywhere else in medieval Europe. Social hierarchies are revealed: free people of widely varying status, dependent or servile people, slaves. We also learn the sizes of agricultural holdings, the kinds of crops grown in various parts of England, the types of animals raised, the prevalence of particular animals in one region or another. Likewise, we find rents and manorial dues of all kinds, the cash value of crops and livestock, the value of farms and buildings. These details show us the workings of the English economy. The power and wealth of the church and of the greatest secular magnates are also revealed in detail.

Like the Egyptian pyramids or the Athenian Parthenon, the sheer, tangible existence of *Domesday Book* makes us reflect on the people who produced it. But the data of *Domesday* have provided food for thought since the Anglo-Saxon chronicler first wrote about it. Today those data are regularly entered into computers and analyzed in complex, electronic ways to reveal population distributions and densities, ratios of males and females in the population, and populations relative to particular agricultural regimes, to mention only a few examples. Scholars have also been able to compare the information in *Domesday Book* with similar kinds of information in the very fragmentary land records of Anglo-Saxon England. Such comparisons show continuities and changes in patterns of land-holding and in the sizes of communities, and occasionally reveal the identities of local proprietors over long periods of time. As a result, we know eleventh-century England better than we know any earlier society.

CHAPTER 11

Medieval Civilization at Its Height, ca. 1150–1300

In the mid-thirteenth century, the distinguished canon lawyer Hostiensis calculated that the priestly dignity is exactly 7,644½ times greater than the royal dignity. How Hostiensis arrived at such an astonishing conclusion sheds light on important features of European life in a time of tension and creativity.

Hostiensis was quoting the ancient philosopher-scientist Ptolemy, who claimed that the sun was 7,644½ times brighter than the moon. This allusion points to an interest in science and in scientific texts that had not been conspicuous for a long time. In the period from roughly 1150 to 1300, interest in science was on the increase, and there was a new eagerness to debate the relative values of divine revelation and human reason, of standard authorities and new discoveries.

What has this to do with the sun and the moon? Hostiensis was attempting to lend exactitude to a statement made by Pope Innocent III, who had said that the imperial dignity was to the papal dignity as the moon is to the sun: It is derivative. The problems central to the investiture controversy had not disappeared. Rulers and churchmen across Europe had not yet found a workable basis for their mutual relations. Innocent's metaphors apart, however, the debates began to turn on extremely technical matters of law and jurisdiction, and it was lawyers more than theologians who provided the ammunition for all combatants.

Hostiensis's reckonings, finally, suggest a quest for precision. If *expansion* is a word that captures the spirit of the age between about 900 and 1150, then *precision* is a word that is well suited to the next century and a half.

Chartres Cathedral, south nave aisle. The Creation of Adam.

Ecclesiastical and secular institutions were refined as never before. Legal systems grew more complex. New academic institutions, universities, regularized and professionalized intellectual life. The early twelfth century's interest in logic grew into a rigorous and formal style of reasoning, Scholasticism. Theologians, inspired by Aristotle, defined religious concepts and practices in terms drawn from antique and Arab science—Hostiensis was not alone in this. The Gothic architecture of the age is at base a series of geometric meditations.

Chapter 10 concluded in about 1150 with a series of options. Would there be continuity or change? Would the crises of midcentury be overcome? The answer, as often, is that the forces of both continuity and change were at work.

Germany in 1152 and England in 1154 got new rulers who were ambitious and determined to restore centralized rule. In later generations both countries experienced political success and failure, but England headed in the direction of the nation-state while Germany collapsed. France, meanwhile, charted a steady course of growing royal power.

There are other examples of change in the mid-eleventh century. Bernard and Abelard died. Bernard was the uncrowned king of his age, but monks lost the kind of influence that they had enjoyed for centuries, and mystics yielded to the rationalizing Scholastics. As monks declined in influence, new forms of ascetic life with lay, even female, participation arose to replace them.

Abelard died a condemned, broken man—Bernard had played a role in bringing him down—but his Parisian schools and his dialectical methods won the future, the former as the nascent University of Paris and the latter as the basis for Scholasticism. In 1155 the bishop of Paris laid the foundation for the cathedral of Notre-Dame, perhaps the finest and surely the most famous of all Gothic churches. Within a generation, no one built in Romanesque style.

Latin continued to be the language of government and the church, but from every country in Europe in the second half of the twelfth century a flood of vernacular literature issued forth. The economic trends apparent before 1150 persisted, but now virtually all innovation was in the urban sphere.

The Empire and the Papacy

The century between 1152, when Frederick I ascended the German throne, and 1250, when Frederick II died, was decisive for both Germany and the papacy. Under its new Hohenstaufen dynasty, Germany at first recovered from its early-twelfth-century malaise and then collapsed as its rulers became more interested in Italy than in Germany itself. The papacy battled the German kings, whom they sometimes crowned as emperors, on a wide range of issues and had the satisfaction of seeing an excommunicated Frederick II die without heirs. Meanwhile, unprecedented legal and institutional growth led to the elaboration of the papal monarchy.

Revival of the Empire

After years of near anarchy, many parties in Germany desired a return to stability. In an act of genuine statesmanship, Conrad III in 1152 designated as his successor the powerful Duke Frederick of Swabia instead of his own young son. The dukes concurred. Frederick I (r. 1152–1190), known as Barbarossa ("red-bearded"), achieved a remarkable restoration of the fortunes of the German and imperial crowns. Frederick—strong, athletic, handsome, chivalrous, and intelligent—was the grandest ruler of his generation.

Frederick had some advantages right from the start. He controlled extensive territories in Swabia and, through his wife, in Burgundy (Map 11.1). He was related to the family that controlled Bavaria and Saxony. The German bishops had begun to regret the liberation they had achieved at Worms in 1122, because ducal domination more than compensated for freedom from royal interference. Frederick usually had the support of the most important members of the clergy.

Inside Germany, Frederick pursued one basic policy. He supported the dukes in their attempts to achieve peace and control in their own domains, as long as they agreed to swear homage and fealty to him. Frederick attempted to create a network of vassalic bonds throughout Germany. Vassalic bonds were no substitute for solid institutional control, but they were a start. The best evidence for this is that in 1180 Frederick was able to crush Duke Henry "the Lion" of Saxony,

Frederick Barbarossa This image, perhaps a decent likeness, depicts Frederick as a crusader—note the cross. The orb surmounted with a cross symbolizes the divine and worldly bases of his rule. *(Vatican Library, Rome)*

his most formidable opponent in Germany. Henry had failed to answer a royal summons to serve in the army, and Frederick summoned him to court to answer for this failure to live up to the most basic of a vassal's duties. A century earlier, when Henry IV had tried to establish his authority on firm foundations, shifting coalitions of dukes, bishops, peasants, townsmen, and popes opposed him. This time, such parties either stood aside or actively supported Frederick.

Frederick did have problems in Germany. He made little headway in getting control of his vassals' vassals. There was no Salisbury Oath in Germany. When Frederick brought down a rebellious subject, such as Henry the Lion, he could not claim that subject's fiefs for himself, as was standard practice in France and England. He had to grant those fiefs to others as the price of their support. Having been elected himself, Frederick had only partial success in getting the German nobles to concede early recognition to his son as his successor. Dynastic and electoral principles were still in open competition.

It was in Italy that Frederick's regime nearly came to ruin. After three years spent gaining control of Germany, Frederick went to Italy in 1155 to help the pope crush a communal movement in Rome. The pope was unwilling to tolerate this direct, local challenge to his authority but lacked the power to stop it. As a reward for his trouble, the pope crowned Frederick emperor. Then in 1158 Frederick summoned representatives of the major northern and central Italian cities. He demanded full recognition of his regalian, or ruler's, rights. Even a partial listing of these rights shows the marked difference between the powers of a feudal king and of an emperor. Regalian rights included, in theory, military service; control of roads, ports and waterways, tolls, minting, fines, vacant fiefs, and confiscated properties; appointment of magistrates; construction of palaces; and control of mines, fisheries, and saltworks. Frederick's plans included an extension to Germany of this type of imperial control.

The Italians had no desire to be dominated anew by their northern neighbors, and the popes feared Frederick's growing power in Italy. For nearly twenty years Frederick and the papacy carried on a running battle. More serious for Frederick was the formation in 1167 of the Lombard League, an association of Italian towns under Milan's leadership that opposed the emperor at every turn. In 1176 Frederick led an army to Italy to discipline the Lombard League, but he suffered a devastating defeat at Legnano. In 1183 the Peace of Constance finally resolved the most serious outstanding issues. Frederick and the papacy were reconciled when the emperor gave up his support for an antipope—a pope elected and acknowledged by Frederick and his supporters—and renounced direct control of Rome. The Lombard towns acknowledged a vague imperial suzerainty and paid some fees in recognition but were left largely independent in the conduct of their own affairs.

Despite his troubles in Italy, Frederick was a ruler of real stature. In German legend he is believed to be sleeping under a mountain, to

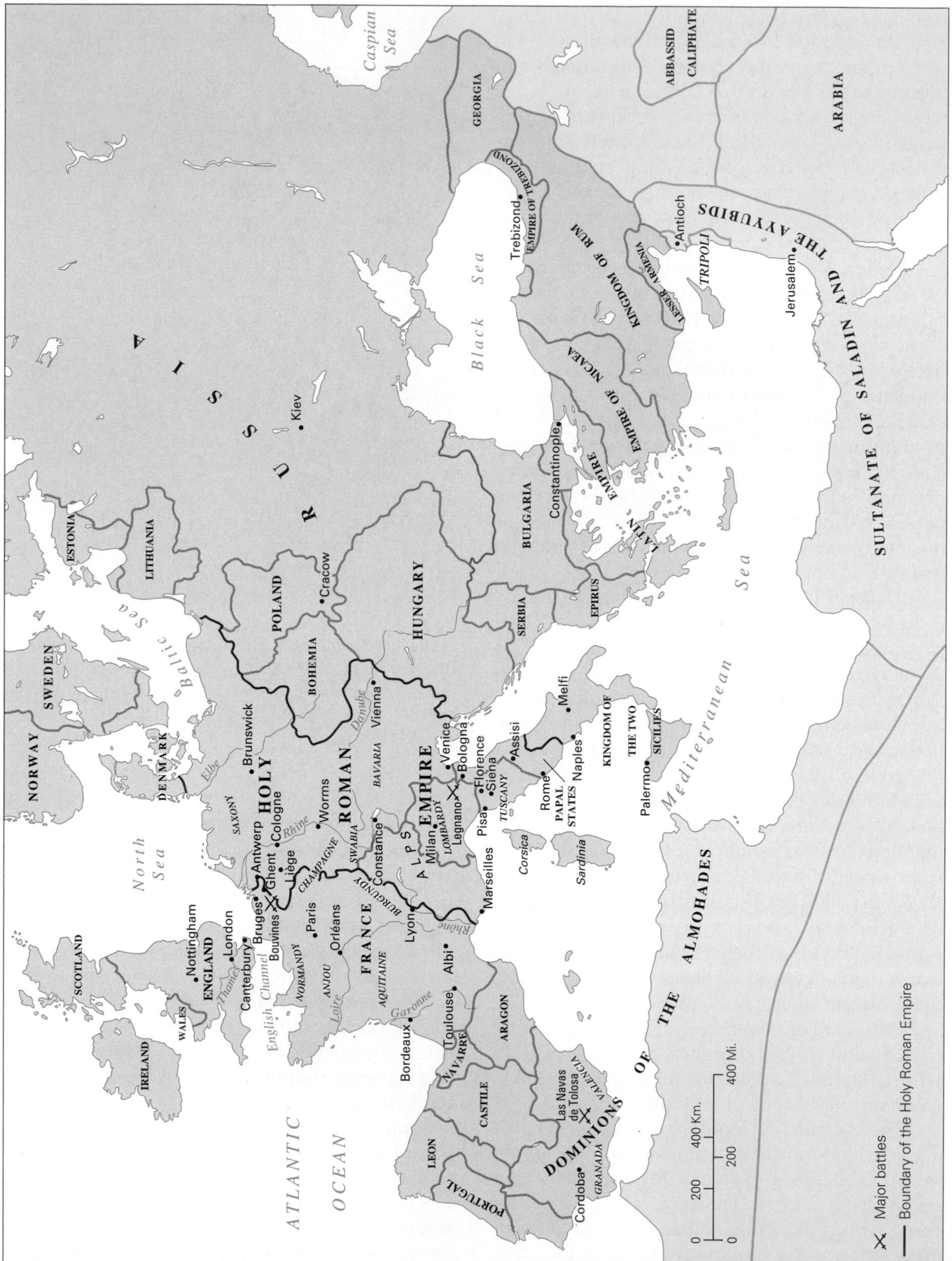

ATLANTIC OCEAN
North Sea
Baltic Sea
Black Sea
Caspian Sea
Mediterranean Sea
English Channel
IRELAND
WALES
SCOTLAND
ENGLAND
Nottingham
London
Canterbury
Thames
NORWAY
SWEDEN
DENMARK
ESTONIA
LITHUANIA
RUSSIA
Kiev
POLAND
Cracow
BOHEMIA
HUNGARY
Vienna
Danube
HOLY ROMAN EMPIRE
SAXONY
Brunswick
Elbe
Antwerp
Cologne
Ghent
Liège
Bruges
Bouvines
Rhine
Worms
SWABIA
BAVARIA
Constance
ALPS
Milan
LOMBARDY
Legnano
Venice
Bologna
Florence
Siena
Pisa
TUSCANY
Assisi
Rome
PAPAL STATES
Naples
Melfi
KINGDOM OF THE TWO SICILIES
Palermo
Corsica
Sardinia
FRANCE
NORMANDY
Paris
Orléans
CHAMPAGNE
BURGUNDY
ANJOU
Loire
AQUITAINE
Lyon
Rhône
Marseilles
Albi
Toulouse
Garonne
Bordeaux
NAVARRE
ARAGON
CASTILE
LEON
PORTUGAL
Las Navas de Tolosa
VALENCIA
GRANADA
Cordoba
DOMINIONS OF THE ALMOHADES
SERBIA
BULGARIA
EPIRUS
Constantinople
LATIN EMPIRE
EMPIRE OF NICAEA
KINGDOM OF RUM
Trebizond
EMPIRE OF TREBIZOND
GEORGIA
LESSER ARMENIA
Antioch
TRIPOLI
Jerusalem
THE AYYUBIDS
SULTANATE OF SALADIN AND
ABBASSID CALIPHATE
ARABIA
0 200 400 Km.
0 200 400 Mi.
Major battles
Boundary of the Holy Roman Empire

Innocent III In this wall painting, the pope wears a tiara, the triple crown that symbolizes his universal episcopate, supremacy of jurisdiction, and temporal rule. Though the greatest of popes, Innocent was also a friend of monks. This painting comes from the Holy Cave at Subiaco near Rome where Benedict began his monastic life. *(Scala/Art Resource, NY)*

awaken when Germany needs him. Frederick's accidental drowning in Turkey on the way to the Third Crusade was a blow to Germany.

Imperial Authority and the Papal Challenge

Henry VI (r. 1190–1197), Frederick's son, was promptly accepted as king in Germany, so he headed straight to Sicily, whose Norman heiress Constance he had married some years before. This trip was a subtle adjustment of traditional policy. Since the tenth century, German rulers had sought in Italy both prestige and resources to apply north of the Alps. But because the Peace of Constance had made Lombardy and Rome difficult to dominate, it made sense for Henry VI to attempt to make Sicily a base for his Italian policy.

It took Henry several years to gain recognition of his authority in Sicily. Then, before the pope would crown him emperor, he had to give assurances that he would not try to control both northern and southern Italy. To buy time for his schemes in Italy, Henry gave the German princes virtual free rein. Suddenly, in 1197, Henry died without having consolidated imperial rule in Italy or royal rule in Germany.

The legitimate heir, another Frederick, was a 3-year-old whose mother, Constance of Sicily, had no standing in Germany and considerable opposition in Sicily from those who thought that she had sold out to the Germans. She made her son the ward of Pope Innocent III (r. 1198–1216). In Germany, counsels were divided. One party favored Hohenstaufen claims and wished to avoid anarchy. Another party preferred ducal rights and an end to Hohenstaufen power.

Once again dynastic instability threatened Germany, affording Innocent an unprecedented

Map 11.1 Europe, ca. 1220 By the early thirteenth century the European states that would exist into modern times were clearly visible, although each would continue to undergo changes. To gain a sense of the evolution of Europe, compare this map with Maps 6.2, 7.3, and 8.3.

opportunity to intervene. Recent popes had occasionally received vassals' oaths from kings of Norway, Poland, Bohemia, Bulgaria, England, parts of Spain, Sicily, and Jerusalem. Papal writings frequently used two metaphors to describe the relationship between secular and ecclesiastical powers. According to one, pope and emperor were like sun and moon—that is, the emperor derived his legitimacy from the pope. According to the other, based on Christ's words, there were "two swords," or two kinds of rule. Both swords, papal supporters believed, were in the hands of the pope. He delegated the secular sword to earthly rulers to protect and advance the church, but secular government had no inherent legitimacy.

The claims of the lawyer-popes (see page 398) to preside over Europe were not meekly accepted by all. In 1157 a papal representative had infuriated Frederick Barbarossa by telling him that the empire was a benefice held of the pope. Frederick Barbarossa had rejected the idea that his imperial dignity came from Rome. He believed that his imperial authority came directly from God and that his actual office was an inheritance from the ancient Romans and from Charlemagne.

The situation after 1197 gave the initiative to Innocent. The pope wished not only to make himself the arbiter of the imperial office but also to keep German power in Italy limited. In return for papal recognition and imperial coronation, Otto of Brunswick (son of Henry the Lion) was prepared to confine himself to Germany. Accordingly, in 1209 Otto was crowned emperor in Rome, but he immediately invaded Sicily, hoping to secure its riches for himself. Innocent responded to this betrayal by excommunicating Otto in 1211 and by crowning his ward Frederick as emperor in 1212. (See the box, "Innocent III on His Rights and Powers.")

Innocent got Frederick II (r. 1212–1250) to swear that he would not attempt to unite Italy and Germany. In 1220 Frederick issued the Statute in Favor of the Princes, which almost totally abandoned regalian rights north of the Alps and left the German princes to themselves. Born in Sicily, Frederick loved the warm climate and cosmopolitan society of the south. He thought Germany cold and dark and Germans dull. All he wanted from the north was a vague recognition of his legitimacy. Frederick's actions stood the old Italian policy of the German rulers since the tenth century on its head. Now an essentially Italian ruler had a German policy.

Frederick cut Germany adrift and then came to ruin in Italy. Almost from the moment of his imperial coronation Frederick was estranged from the papacy. He had promised to go on crusade but constantly refused to depart. That was a serious problem, but the real cause for papal hostility was Frederick's determined effort to unite almost all of Italy.

Frederick's Constitutions of Melfi, based on Norman precedents and issued for Sicily and southern Italy in 1231, shows what he aimed to do everywhere. Frederick planned to institute imperial vicars in all major regions. These were skillful salaried officials appointed and removed at the emperor's will. Under them were to be staffs of experienced officers. Wandering inspectors would supervise the whole system. Unity and uniformity were Frederick's goals. Until his death in 1250 Frederick was constantly hounded by opposition from popes and urban Italians who resented his challenges to their local autonomy.

Frederick has sometimes been seen as a very modern man: secular, rational, calculating. This view is anachronistic. He was a man of his time. He was passionately devoted to both astrology and the cult of saints. He wondered about the immortality of the soul but was no more skeptical than others. His bureaucratic reforms were based on Norman, papal, and Byzantine precedents. Jews, Arabs, and a troupe of dancing girls could be found at his court, for he lived in the most culturally diverse place in Europe, but he remained conventionally Christian.

Frederick's death created different problems in Italy and in Germany. His direct line in Italy had died out by 1268. None of his successors reunited his holdings in Italy or was crowned emperor. In Germany the period from 1250 to 1272 is called the Great Interregnum. The princes could not agree on the promotion of one of their own number, never thought of turning to the Italian heirs of Frederick II, and even invited in outsiders as kings. No German ruler was crowned emperor. Finally, in 1273, Rudolf of Habsburg was elected king of Germany. He failed initially to establish a dynasty, although his family would be prominent in European politics until 1918. The

Innocent III on His Rights and Powers

In this authoritative papal pronouncement from 1202, Innocent explains why he believes the pope has a right and duty to decide who is fit to be emperor.

Among other things certain princes urge this objection particularly, that our venerable brother the bishop of Palestrina, legate of the apostolic see, acted as either an elector [of the emperor] or as a judge of the election. If as an elector, he put his sickle in a stranger's harvest and, by intervening in the election, he seems to have proceeded incorrectly. . . . We indeed by virtue of our office of apostolic service owe justice to each man and, just as we do not want our justice to be usurped by others, so too we do not want to claim for ourselves the rights of princes. We do indeed acknowledge, as we should, that the princes have by ancient custom the right and power to elect a king who is afterwards to be promoted emperor; and especially so since the right and power came to them from the apostolic see which transferred the Roman empire from the Greeks to the Germans in the person of the great Charles. But the princes should acknowledge that the right and authority to examine the person elected as king, who is to be promoted to the imperial dignity, belong to us who anoint, consecrate and crown him; for it is regularly and generally observed that the examination of a person belongs to the one to whom the laying-on of hands belongs. If the princes elected as king a sacrilegious man or an excommunicate, a tyrant, a fool or a heretic, and that not just by divided vote but unanimously, ought we to anoint, consecrate and crown such a man? Of course not. Therefore, . . . we maintain that our legate the bishop of Palestrina . . . did not act as either an elector . . . or as a judge. . . . Rather he exercised the office of one who declared that the king was personally worthy . . . not considering so much the zeal of the electors as the merits of those elected.

Source: Brian Tierney, *The Crisis of Church and State, 1050–1300* (Englewood Cliffs, N.J.: Prentice-Hall, 1964), pp. 133–134.

powerful German state of the Saxons, and the revived state of the Hohenstaufen, had vanished.

Medieval Germany's failure is in some ways more apparent than real. Even today, German-speakers and German lands are scattered all over the map of central Europe. It has never been easy to say just where or what Germany is. Through most of its history, Germany has been both an idea and a confederation of peoples and lands. Germany's medieval failure was really a failure of monarchy. Frederick Barbarossa built up his monarchy in ways very similar to those being used in France and England. What weakened and finally destroyed the medieval German monarchy were the Italian and papal entanglements and the inability of the German royal dynasties to produce heirs.

The Papal Monarchy

The papal power that permitted Innocent III to arbitrate the imperial succession and allowed his successors to break the Hohenstaufen rested on two foundations: ideology and institutions. We can summarize the ideological foundation, discussed here and in preceding chapters, in this way: Clerical and governmental elites elaborated a tripartite theory of social organization that assigned everyone a role in the construction of a Christian commonwealth. All legitimate power and authority in that society came from God. Battles raged over whether kings and emperors (on the one hand) or the priestly hierarchy with the pope at its head (on the other hand) stood nearer to God in a great chain of power. The legacy of the investiture controversy, of the Crusades, and of generations of spiritual reform had given the lead to the priestly power.

The second foundation was institutional. The twelfth-century popes turned resolutely to the refinement of their central government, which grew as never before. The ability of the Roman church to coerce secular rulers and to control local churches reached a high point. The canon law of the church surpassed all other contemporary legal systems in sophistication.

The papacy was an elective monarchy, but electoral procedures rather than dynastic considerations were a persistent problem. In 1059 an election decree had attempted to confine electoral participation to the cardinals but had not specified how many votes were necessary for election: a plurality, a majority, unanimity? The twelfth and thirteenth centuries were filled with contested elections. In 1179 a council decreed that a two-thirds majority was required for election. One problem was solved, but another arose.

Between 1241 and 1305, the papacy was vacant for almost ten years altogether, and once there was no pope for nearly three years. Competing groups of cardinals simply refused to show up for elections, or they left Rome if things were proceeding in a direction they disliked. In 1274 a conclave was used for the first time: Once the cardinals had assembled, they were sequestered until they elected someone. Even so, the system was still abused.

Who were the popes? What were they like? Most of them had been cardinals and had long experience in the government of the church. A very high percentage of the twelfth- and thirteenth-century popes were lawyers, which may explain, in part, their dedication to institutional and legal reforms. Not a single pope from this period has been canonized as a saint. One Englishman was elected; the rest were Roman, Italian, or French. Most were noblemen.

In Rome, the pope presided over the *curia*, as the papal court was called. By the late twelfth century, the fifty-three cardinals, who were increasingly drawn from all over Europe, were the key officers in that court. They sat with the pope in consistory, a small quasi-legislative meeting, and, again with the concurrence of the pope, issued decretals, binding decrees. The cardinals headed the major branches of the papal administration and served as papal legates. In the thirteenth century these princes of the church began to wear their distinctive red hats.

The curia presided over both financial and judicial institutions. Revenues came from the papal lands in Italy, from diverse fees from all over Europe, and from the pious offerings of pilgrims. The judicial institutions administered the rulings of the papal government, heard appeals for dispensations from the ordinary operations of canon law (such as requests for permission to marry from two persons who were closely related), and heard appeals against decisions made by local ecclesiastical courts.

The hearing of appeals from lower courts points to another growing area of activity by the papal government: control of the church throughout Europe. The pope and cardinals had numerous means to work their will. Beginning in 1123, and then again in 1179, 1215, 1245, and 1274, major church councils were called, the largest since the ecumenical councils of Late Antiquity. Until the twelfth century, the popes had called relatively small local councils, but now the great prelates of Europe met on a regular basis. More and more, cardinals, who could be sent out as legates, were regarded as plenipotentiaries—that is they could act as if they were the pope himself. A system of papal provisions enabled the pope to appoint bishops, and sometimes abbots and cathedral canons, all over Europe. In the past, such officers had been elected locally and merely confirmed by Rome. Rome demanded more fees, partly for economic reasons and partly as symbols of central papal authority. Popes promoted the continuous revision and updating of the canon law of the church and shaped that law to emphasize papal prerogatives.

The Roman church also sharpened the tools that it used to make its will felt. Since the early days of Christianity, churchmen had been able to excommunicate a member of the faithful for some grievous offense. Separation from the sacraments of the church had always been a serious punishment. In the Christian Middle Ages, the severity of it increased because the excommunicated person was forbidden *all* social intercourse. Excommunication thus could be politically, socially, and economically disastrous. Another tool was the interdict—a decree that might be directed at a person but more often fell on a region. The interdict brought to a halt the celebration of most sacraments. Its aim was to generate a popular outcry for a particular outcome or remedy.

In the time of Pope Gregory IX (r. 1227–1241) the inquisition was employed for the first time. The increasing incidence of heresy had often resulted in mob atrocities against those suspected of religious deviation. Gregory IX sought to bring a measure of order and legality to the process of identifying and punishing heretics. Just as governments of all kinds had begun to employ wandering inquisitors to learn all sorts of things, he began sending out teams of carefully trained inquisitors to take testimony according to precisely defined rules.

In medieval society a person's religious faith was not a private matter of conscience but a public affair. The aim of the inquisition was to reconcile the wayward, not to punish or execute them. The church could not administer corporal punishment or shed blood, so anyone found guilty by a court of inquisition was handed over to a secular court. Executions for heresy were comparatively rare. Of 945 cases heard in the south of France in 1246, not one resulted in a death penalty; ten years later about 21 of 306 accused heretics were executed.

This ever more bureaucratic and intrusive church related to the laity—to its subjects—in a variety of ways. The line between the clergy and the laity was drawn more sharply than ever before. Many professions—the notariate, law (secular, of course), medicine—were forbidden to the clergy. Lay people were denied any right to preach, to expound on the Scriptures, or to stand in judgment of any offense that a cleric might commit. In the writings of thirteenth-century ecclesiastics, the word *church* usually referred to the institutional entity, to the clergy, and not to the body of all believers. Believers were expected to submit to the clergy in all respects, and effective institutions enforced their submission.

Ideology and institutions were important, but personalities mattered too. Innocent III (r. 1198–1216), for example, was the most powerful man ever to hold the papal office. He came from a minor Italian noble family, received early training in theology and law, and entered the papal administration while in his twenties. His entire life was dedicated to promoting the legal prerogatives of the papacy and the moral improvement of Christian society.

Innocent's struggles with Frederick II, paralleled by conflicts with England (see page 404), are the secular counterparts of the Fourth Lateran Council of 1215. This was the largest, most active council since Late Antiquity. Its numerous rulings on church government made Innocent truly appear as the monarchial head of a church that was itself the key institution in Western society. The council also regulated many aspects of the moral and spiritual lives of ordinary believers and sought to curb heretical movements (see the box on page 413). As a young man Innocent wrote a book, *On the Contempt of the World,* in which he expressed his hope for a life of peace and private contemplation. As an older man he hurled legal thunderbolts at the greatest public figures of the day.

The Evolution of Central Governments

For both France and England the accession of Henry of Anjou in 1154 begged a long list of questions. The second half of the twelfth century saw a reopening of the Reconquista, which signaled dramatic growth in the scope of Spanish royal power. The Italian communal movement experienced important changes, partly from its own dynamics and partly in response to the Hohenstaufen.

Five issues guided most government activity, although their importance differed according to time and place. (1) Frontier problems: In no part of Europe was the exact geographical shape of the eventual state evident. (2) The expanding role of central governments: One constant of the age was a growth in the size, sophistication, and effectiveness of institutions. (3) Relations between rulers and their people: Growing government power often meant that traditional nobilities lost power while obscure men rose to prominence in the service of kings. New representative institutions gave power and voice either to people previously without them or to the formerly powerful in new ways. (4) Relations with the church: This was an old medieval problem, but the growing competence of governments posed old problems in ways that were more practical than theoretical.

(5) Economic issues: Governments found themselves needing more resources at a time when the great expansion of the eleventh and twelfth centuries began to slow.

France

France in 1154 had a king, Louis VII (r. 1137–1180), who had built on the solid work of his predecessors but faced a single vassal, Henry II of England, who controlled more of France than he did. A contemporary writer summed things up:

> The emperor of Byzantium and the king of Sicily may boast about their gold and silken cloth, but they have no men who can do more than talk, men incapable of war. The Roman emperor or, as they say, the emperor of the Germans, has men apt in arms and warlike horses, but no gold, silk or any other wealth. . . . the king of England lacks nothing and possesses everything, men, horses, gold, silk, jewels, fruits and wild beasts. And we in France have nothing except bread, wine and joy.[1]

This passage reveals much about twelfth-century life but somewhat underestimates the resources of the French.

Some of the "joy" that French people felt was attributable to their increasing domination of European culture. The First Crusade was widely seen as a French enterprise. The greatest twelfth-century monastic order, the Cistercian, was French. The aristocracy of England spoke French. There were French quarters in almost all large towns outside France. French was the premier literary language after Latin, and French manners, style, and elegance were admired and emulated everywhere. The architecture that we know as Gothic was then called "the French style."

Although these resources were real, they were also evanescent. Louis VII and his son and successor Philip II (r. 1189–1223)—usually called Philip Augustus—had sturdier bases on which to build, however. They carried on the traditional Capetian policy of controlling the centrally located royal demesne. They continued to associate their sons in their reigns in order to train the heir for rule and stifle any electoral pretensions among the nobility. The "Most Christian Kings of France," as their titles designated them, supported the church and were supported by it in turn. Louis VII began the policy of granting both tangible and moral support to the emerging towns of France.

Louis and Philip even managed to turn the Angevin colossus to their own advantage. For many years, the French king's relations with the great nobles of France had been based less on vassalic bonds than on shifting alliances. While maintaining alliances and extending vassalic ties whenever possible, Louis and Philip became masters at fomenting trouble in Henry's vast continental holdings, usually by setting the Angevin sons against their father and against one another. Philip, in particular, expanded the Capetian demesne. His greatest gains came at the expense of King John of England.

John (r. 1199–1216), son and successor to Henry II, was a vassal of the king of France for all of his father's vast continental holdings. He imprudently ran off with the fiancée of a minor French nobleman, who sued him in the court of Philip Augustus, feudal lord to them both. Philip summoned John to answer for his conduct. When John refused to answer the summons, Philip declared him "contumacious" and his fiefs "escheat" (meaning that the fiefs were to revert to their lord). War was used to settle the matter, and Philip won a resounding victory in 1204.

A decade later Philip confirmed his paramount position by defeating at Bouvines a joint attack on his kingdom by John and Otto IV of Germany, who were both trying to revive their sagging fortunes. One could say that the almost fastidious application of feudal laws had brought the king of France to an unmatched position in his own realm. One could also say that more than two centuries of patient, largely nonfeudal, Capetian policy had permitted the defeat of John of England and the seizure of a large piece of France.

French royal revenues at least doubled between 1180 and 1220. In this, France and Germany differed greatly. The French kings developed substantial revenues internally. When Philip seized the Angevin lands, he did not give them to anyone as fiefs. To govern his new possessions, Philip extended, with some modifications, the old institutions of the royal demesne. Estates on the demesne had been governed by minor noblemen called *provosts,* but after 1204 *bailiffs* were the overseers of the vastly expanded demesne. Bailiffs were non-noble officers, often trained in law, appointed for fixed terms. They had no property or family connections in the territories where they served, and at the end of their term they had to give an account of their work.

Philip was succeeded briefly by his son Louis VIII and then for more than four decades by Louis IX, known as "Saint Louis." Right away it is worth remarking that the prestige of the Capetian dynasty was enough to produce a saint. But if the Capetians had one eye on heaven, they had the other one firmly fixed on France.

Louis VIII (r. 1223–1226) hit on a means of simultaneously governing the old Angevin lands and providing for junior members of the royal family. He divided up some of the former Angevin lands into *appanages* and assigned them to junior members of the royal family. In this way he kept land out of the hands of the nobility and provided resources and responsibility to persons who might otherwise have spent their time plotting against the king.

Louis IX (r. 1226–1270) revived the Carolingian practice of sending wandering officials around the kingdom to check on the work of the bailiffs. He also issued *ordonnances,* the first systematic royal edicts of general application since the Carolingian capitularies. Louis IX abolished serfdom and suppressed private warfare on royal lands. Saint Louis believed that the king's highest duty was the promotion of peace and justice. His reforms made people all over France look to the king rather than to local notables. (See the box, "A Contemporary View of Saint Louis.")

Before the reign of Louis VIII the French monarchy confined its activities to the regions north of the Loire River. Around the year 1200 the Albigensian heresy was discovered in the south of France (see page 412). Religious orders rushed south to meet the threat, French noblemen went adventuring, and the pope preached a crusade. But the Crown refused to be distracted until it had defeated John and digested the Angevin lands that had been swallowed in one gulp. Louis VIII and Louis IX, however, sensing political opportunities and religious duties, finally entered the fray. By the 1250s the Albigensians were beaten. More important, the region of Aquitaine was taken over by the Crown and submitted to royal administration. The Albigensian wars also served the kings of France as a kind of safety valve by draining off some of the land-lust and violence of the nobility.

THE DEVELOPMENT OF STATES, 1150–1300

1154–1189	Reign of Henry II of England
1155	Imperial Coronation of Frederick Barbarossa
1167	Formation of the Lombard League
1170	Murder of Thomas Becket
1176	Battle of Legnano
1183	Peace of Constance
1198–1216	Pontificate of Innocent III
1204	Fourth Crusade
1208	Albigensian Crusade
1212	Imperial Coronation of Frederick II
1212	Battle of Las Navas de Tolosa
1214	Battle of Bouvines
1215	Magna Carta
1215	Fourth Lateran Council
1226–1270	Reign of Saint Louis (Louis IX)
1272–1307	Reign of Edward I of England
1285–1315	Reign of Philip IV (the Fair)
1294–1303	Pontificate of Boniface VIII
1295	First meeting of Parliament

Saint Louis was succeeded by his son Philip III (r. 1270–1285) and then by his famous and important grandson Philip IV (r. 1285–1314), "the Fair." Philip IV began a series of dangerous military and diplomatic gambles to extend his power into Flanders and Gascony.

Flanders was rich and had always been under the authority of the German Empire, which was by now in a shambles. It looked ripe for plucking. Gascony was a major wine-producing region and the last significant part of France not under royal control; treaties had left it under English authority. Philip's quarrels with England's Edward I (r. 1272–1307) were costly to both kings and secured a permanent advantage for neither.

A Contemporary View of Saint Louis

Jean, Sire de Joinville (ca. 1224–1319), accompanied Louis IX on crusade, served as a royal official, and gave evidence in the case for Louis's canonization. In 1309, at the request of Joan of Navarre, wife of Philip IV, he wrote the late king's Life, *from which this excerpt is taken.*

God, in whom he put his trust, preserved him ever from his infancy to the very last. As for his soul, God preserved it through the pious instructions of his mother [Blanche of Castile], who taught him to believe in God and to love Him, and place about him none but ministers of religion. And she made him, while he was yet a child, attend to all his prayers and listen to all the sermons on saints' days. He remembered that his mother used sometimes to tell him that she would rather he were dead than that he should commit a deadly sin.

Sore need of God's help had he in his youth, for his mother, who came of Spain, had neither friends nor relatives in all the realm of France. Because the barons of France saw that the king was an infant, and the queen, his mother, a foreigner, they made the count of Boulogne, the king's uncle, their chief lord, and they looked up to him. After the king was crowned, some of the barons asked the queen to bestow upon them large domains and because she would not the barons assembled at Corbie [north of Paris]. Neither the king nor his mother dared to return to Paris until the citizens of Paris came, with arms in their hands, to escort them. The road was filled with people, some with arms some not, and all cried to our Lord to give him a long and happy life, and to defend him from his enemies. . . .

Many a time it happened that in the summer he would go and sit down in the wood at Vincennes [outside Paris] with his back to an oak, and make us take seats around him. And all who had complaints to make came to him without hindrance. Then he asked them himself: "Is there anyone here who has a cause?" Those who had a cause stood up, and he would say: "Silence all, and you shall be dispatched one after another."

Source: Frederic Austin Ogg, *A Source Book of Medieval History* (New York: American Book Co., 1908), pp. 313–314, 323 (slightly adapted).

They disrupted cross-Channel trade, however, and the Flemish depended on that trade for English wool to supply their cloth industry. Thus, the Flemish rose against Philip in 1302 and humiliated him by defeating the army he sent against them.

Philip's constant need for money to pay for his wars led him to attempt schemes that stirred resentment among various groups in France. He even resorted to seizing the property of the Jews of France and to repudiating his debts to Italian bankers. He died broke in 1314, but there was no reason to think that the impressive gains won by three centuries of Capetian policy would be lost. The kings of France were powerful and respected figures. France itself was paramount in Europe. Paris was evolving into a real capital with commercial interests, government offices, the royal court, and a university (see page 418). The nobility was rich and powerful but also under royal control. The royal family was the most united in Europe. Despite the Crown's debt, prospects certainly looked brighter in 1314 than they had seemed in 1154.

England

Henry II (r. 1154–1189) promptly made it clear that he meant to rule England and also to retain control of his vast continental inheritances. Henry also introduced English rule in Ireland and re-established at least a measure of English authority over Wales and Scotland. Within England, Henry made major changes in the scope and administration of English law.

The Continent proved to be a constant irritant for Henry. In anticipation of the later Capetian appanage system, Henry sought to provide from the Angevin lands individual holdings for his four sons. The boys, however, abetted by their mother Eleanor and by Louis VII and Philip II of France, plotted against their father and against one another. Henry never was able to unify law, institutions, economic practices, or culture in his far-flung "Angevin Empire." Although he was first a French prince, and although he spent more time in France than in England, his greatest contributions were in his island kingdom.

By returning to the practices of the Norman kings and by innovating, Henry fashioned the institutions that turned England into the best-governed kingdom in Europe. His work was like that of his contemporaries. He used men of low or modest means but of great intelligence and careful training to staff government offices. He supported, and usually was supported by, towns and the church in an effort to circumvent the nobility and to expand centers of royal influence. He also kept a sharp eye out for possible sources of revenue.

Henry expanded both the size and the competence of the English government. In the tradition of the Domesday investigators, he carried out two great inquests, one of knight's service and one of sheriffs. The former resulted in a detailed listing of the fiefs of England and of what was owed to the king by them. The latter resulted in the replacement of many of England's sheriffs, the key royal officers in the shires, with men who were more effective and loyal to the king. It was from about this time that the Robin Hood stories arose, with their evocation of the evil, heartless sheriff of Nottingham. In fact, the sheriffs were neither more nor less evil than other men. They were just increasingly effective in doing the king's business.

Henry used judicial institutions to expand royal power and the central government. His objectives were to bring as much judicial activity as possible into royal courts and to diminish the role of the nobles. Through a series of enactments, Henry made it possible for almost anyone to secure a writ that would move a complaint or case into a royal court. Henry also developed a set of rules for handling disputes over the possession of land, one of the commonest areas of legal activity. To handle this business, Henry expanded the system of royal courts. The court of king's bench, for "great men and great causes," and the court of common pleas, for ordinary people and routine offenses, began to sit permanently at Westminster, just outside London and the usual site of the royal court. Since not everyone could go to Westminster, Henry expanded the use of justices in eyre, who went four times a year through every shire to hear cases.

The justice dispensed in Henry's courts was swift and fair, and his courts were popular. Those who felt abused by powerful noble neighbors discovered that by having recourse to royal courts they could get real justice. With royal courts consistently applying a single law in all their sittings, a common law began to grow up throughout the country. No other realm in Europe advanced so far so early on the road to legal unification.

Henry II, ever tidy of mind, desired to bring "criminous clerks"—that is, members of the clergy who had committed crimes—into the royal courts. This policy provoked a howl of protest from Thomas Becket, the archbishop of Canterbury. Thomas held to the traditional church teaching that only members of the clergy could judge other clerics. He said that hauling churchmen into royal courts would expose them to double jeopardy. Becket fled to France for a time. When he finally returned to England, he was murdered before the altar of his cathedral by a group of knights who thought they were doing the bidding of their king. Becket was soon canonized, and Henry had to back down on criminous clerks. The church was still powerful enough to defeat any attempt to diminish its prerogatives.

In 1189 Henry's charismatic, crusading son Richard "the Lionheart" became king and proved in an ironic way the strength of the foundations that the old king had laid. Richard (r. 1189–1199) resided less than ten months in England during his ten-year reign. Mainly, he spent his time harassing Philip II in France and going on the Third Crusade. Back in England the men and institutions put into place by Henry II functioned well in Richard's absence.

When John (r. 1199–1216) succeeded his brother Richard, he inherited some problems and

The Murder of Thomas Becket This is just one of many graphic depictions of the death of Archbishop Thomas before the altar of his cathedral church. *(The British Library)*

quickly created many of his own. Many English noblemen were angry at having been so effectively circumvented by Henry II. The royal treasury was empty. A king's ransom, literally, had been raised to redeem Richard, who had been kidnapped on his way home from the Third Crusade.

John might have stabilized his position, but his loss of Normandy in 1204 was a financial and moral disaster. Still, English institutions were flexible enough that John went right back to work raising money and managed to forge an alliance with Otto IV of Germany. The two rulers planned to attack and divide France. At Bouvines in 1214 Philip Augustus defeated his enemies, and John was humiliated yet again.

Like his father before him, John had severe run-ins with the church. To the intense displeasure of the clergy, John routinely abused episcopal vacancies. When a bishop died, John often withheld permission to proceed to an election and kept the income of the diocese. What really got him in trouble, though, was his refusal to accept Pope Innocent's candidate for the archbishopric of Canterbury. The pope placed England under interdict and excommunicated John. Despite widespread anger and embarrassment, John might have let this quarrel go on indefinitely, but he decided to capitulate in order to win support for the ultimately unsuccessful Bouvines campaign.

In June 1215 some English barons, supported by townspeople and members of the clergy, forced John to affix his name to Magna Carta, the "Great Charter" (the "great" referring to its large size). Its sixty-three clauses spelled out in rather traditional ways the royal prerogatives vis-à-vis vassals, towns, the church, and courts of law. The barons were trying to get the king to acknowledge that he had to obey certain rules, not to destroy the monarchy. Magna Carta's central premise was that everyone, even the king, was under the law; then, in certain perceived areas of ambiguity, it spelled out the law (see the box, "Selections from Magna Carta").

The barons objected to John's abuse of his feudal prerogatives. For instance, as lord, John had rights of wardship. When a vassal died leaving only a minor as an heir, the lord had a right to receive the profits of the fief until the heir came of age and could do homage for it. John regularly prolonged wardships indefinitely to increase his own income.

Another abuse concerned *scutage* (literally, "shield money"). Already in the twelfth century, kings had discovered that their vassals were continually hedging their military service with restrictions. To raise a decent army that would serve for an extended time, the kings began to commute military service into cash payments, scutages, and to hire mercenaries with the cash. Tradition had it that the feudal host—or its money, as it were—could be summoned only in time of emergency. John declared emergencies with alarming frequency and pocketed the money or else squandered it on military disasters in France.

Selections from Magna Carta

These extracts show the practical, political nature of Magna Carta, a document that did not express abstract theories of government, but dealt with concrete, immediate issues.

1. Know that we in the first place have granted to God and by this our present charter have confirmed, for us and for our heirs in perpetuity, that the English church shall be free, and shall have its rights undiminished and its liberties unimpaired.

2. If any of our earls or barons, or others holding of us in chief by knight service shall die, and at his death his heir be of full age and owe relief [a payment for an heir to succeed to a fief], he shall have his inheritance on payment of the ancient relief. . . .

4. The guardian of the land of such an heir who is under age shall not take from the land more than the reasonable revenues, customary dues and services, and that without destruction or waste of men or goods.

7. After her husband's death, a widow shall have her marriage portion and her inheritance at once and without any hindrance; nor shall she pay anything for her dower, her marriage portion, or her inheritance which she and her husband held on the day of her husband's death; and she may stay in her husband's house forty days after his death, within which period her dower shall be assigned to her.

8. No widow shall be compelled to marry so long as she wishes to live without a husband, provided that she gives security that she will not marry without our consent if she holds of us, or without the consent of the lord of whom she holds, if she holds of another.

12. No scutage or aid is to be levied in our realm except by the common counsel of our realm, unless it is for the ransom of our person, the knighting of our eldest son, or the first marriage of our eldest daughter.

16. No man shall be compelled to perform more service for a knight's fee or any other free tenement than is due from it.

38. Henceforth no bailiff shall put anyone on trial by his own unsupported allegation, without bringing credible witnesses to the charge.

39. No free man shall be taken or imprisoned or disseised [dispossessed] or outlawed or exiled or in any way ruined, nor will we go or send against him, except by the lawful judgment of his peers or by the law of the land.

Source: J. C. Holt, *Magna Carta* (Cambridge, England: Cambridge University Press, 1969), pp. 317, 319, 321, 323, 327.

Under John's son, Henry III (r. 1216–1272), and grandson, Edward I (r. 1272–1307), certain problems recurred in England. The king wished to choose his own advisers, but the barons insisted on having some influence in the choices. The king demanded a wide array of taxes and revenues, but barons and townspeople withheld monies except on their explicit approval. The king sought money for an aggressive foreign policy, but people were reluctant to pay. It was clear to everyone that continuous rebellion served the long-term interests of no party. However, until 1295 there was no mechanism for the arbitration of disputes.

As early as 1236 a meeting of the royal council was called a *Parliament,* from a French word that means "talking together." Down to 1295, when the first Parliament in the modern sense met, many different kinds of meetings bore this name. By 1295, Edward I needed money for his wars with Philip IV and with the Welsh and Scots. He also needed a secure means of gaining assent to his statutes, enactments that bear comparison with the ordonnances of Louis IX. The king therefore summoned the barons, bishops and abbots, the knights of the shires, and the burgesses (leading citizens of the towns) to a meeting.

As yet this Parliament had no defined role, no procedures, no fixed membership, and no set times for meetings. Moreover, it was viewed differently by its various attendees. The king saw it as something of a rubber stamp. The barons viewed it as a means of controlling royal excess. The knights and townsmen thought they had gained a means of making permanent the loose alliance that they had enjoyed with the Crown since the twelfth century. Even though no one realized it at the time, the political quarrels of the thirteenth century had resulted in the creation of an institution that would eventually become dominant in the governance of England.

Like Philip IV, Edward I died nearly penniless in 1307. But his family was securely in power, and his country was effectively governed. In Parliament the English had created a potentially national institution. The common law too was a bond that Englishmen shared. Although the aristocracy still spoke French, virtually everyone in the country could speak English. Edward's England had lost many of Henry's overseas holdings but was in decent shape at home.

Spain

By around 1150 the Reconquista in Spain had been halted, not to resume until the early thirteenth century, when Pope Innocent III stirred up crusading zeal. The pope lent encouragement to clerics and nobles in Spain who wished to reopen hostilities against the Muslims. In 1212 a combined Castilian-Aragonese army won a decisive victory at Las Navas de Tolosa, south of Toledo (see Map 10.4). Still more territory was recaptured from the Muslims in the thirteenth century, including the old Islamic capital of Cordoba. The victory of Las Navas de Tolosa was a great turning point in Spanish history. The outcome of the Reconquista was never again in doubt.

In the thirteenth century Spain produced kings of genius, especially James I of Aragon (r. 1213–1276) and Ferdinand III (r. 1217–1252) and Alfonso X (r. 1252–1284) of Castile. These rulers were pious men, genuinely inspired by the ideal of the Crusades, zealous in the promotion of the church. They were also hard-headed rulers. James turned Aragon-Catalonia into the greatest naval power of the western Mediterranean and a formidable economic power too. Ferdinand and Alfonso derived great prestige from their successful wars. Those wars also provided a flow of booty and a supply of lands to reward the Castilian nobles who spent their energy on the frontier, rather than using it to attack the king. Strong central institutions were created. Increasingly professional officers were employed in key government posts, and wandering officials were sent out from the court to inspect the work of local officials. Alfonso issued a major law book, the *Siete Partidas,* for the whole of Castile. These laws were based on Roman law and emphasized royal power. Many aristocrats opposed them vigorously. A representative assembly, the *Cortes,* began to meet on a regular basis. Like the English Parliament, it began as little more than an extension of the royal council, but its role would grow.

Spain was not united in the thirteenth century, but it had evolved into four coherent blocks: a small and impotent Muslim region in Valencia and Granada and three vibrant kingdoms centered on Portugal, Castile, and Aragon. Spain's rulers were effective, and its institutions were evolving like those elsewhere. In the centuries after 711 Spain had looked inward or perhaps out to the Muslim world, but from the thirteenth century Spain was ready and able to play an integral role in European history.

Italy

When Frederick Barbarossa crossed the Alps in 1155, the future of northern and central Italy hung in the balance. If his attempt to introduce tight control had succeeded, the subsequent development of the Italian communes might have been very different. But Frederick's defeat at Legnano in 1176 and the Peace of Constance in 1183 left the Italian cities free to continue their distinctive political evolution.

Although each Italian commune was an entity unto itself, a fairly coherent evolution is evident. By the later years of the twelfth century, the consular communes were still governed by oligarchies of men whose wealth and power came from land, trade, and industry. Merchant interests, however, were growing in prominence at the expense of the landed groups among whom the communal movement had arisen, and ordinary workers were beginning to clamor for participation. The communes were becoming increasingly volatile and violent.

One solution to this crisis was the creation of the *podestà* as a purely local official. In the past, officials bearing this title had sometimes been imperial representatives in towns where imperial power was effective. Now the local oligarchy chose a podestà to serve as a sort of city manager. The podestà often came from the outside, served for a set period (usually six months or a year), and underwent a careful scrutiny at the conclusion of his term. He was expected to be competent not only at ordinary administration but also at military leadership, so that he could police the city as well as defend it. He brought with him a group of seasoned officials as subordinates. Normally, he could not be a property owner in the town, marry into local society, or dine privately with any citizen. By the middle of the thirteenth century, some podestas were becoming virtual professionals. One man, for example, was elected sixteen times in nine cities over a period of thirty-four years, four times in Bologna alone.

The office of podestà did not really solve the crisis of political participation. As early as 1198 in Milan, laborers and workers in the organized trades began to choose so-called captains of the people to watch out for the interests of the less powerful and wealthy citizenry. These officers were originally much like the tribunes of Republican Rome and may have been inspired by them. Like podestas, some captains were local men, and some were outsiders. Their very existence, and their origins outside the local elite, signal the volatility of the urban scene. It is ironic that the Italian cities that had been feudal or episcopal principalities before the rise of the communes passed through a republican phase of wider and wider political participation, only to wind up under strongmen again. Still, republican—that is, participatory—ideology triumphed in the end.

The Podestà in Action The judicial role of the podestà was no less important than his police and military ones. Here, a podestà collects fines from lawbreakers. (*Vatican Library, Rome*)

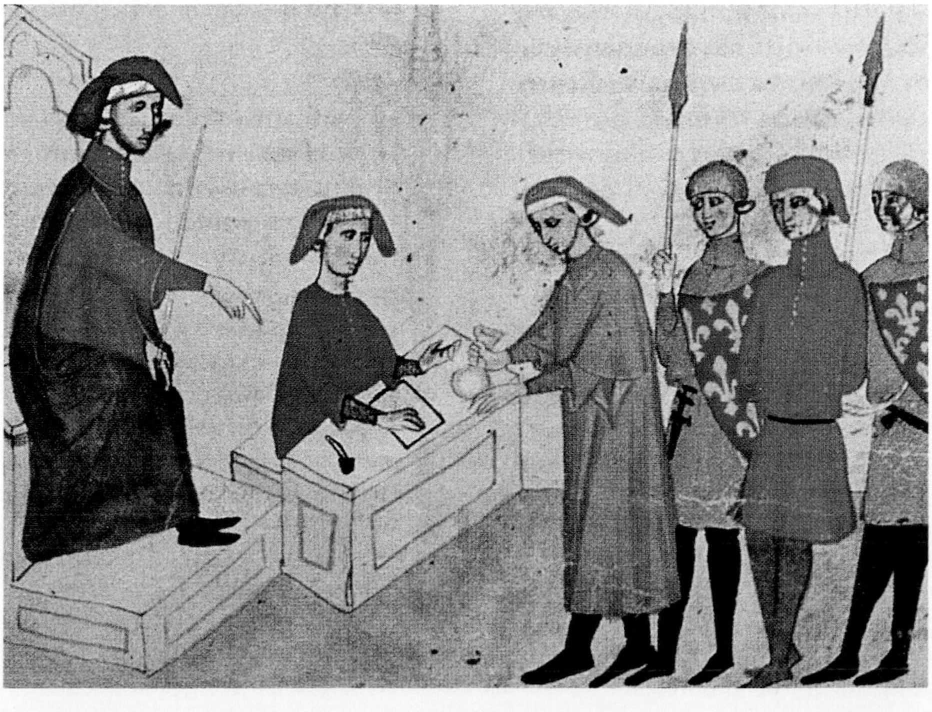

Table 11.1 Population Increases in Italian Cities, 1200–1300

City	1200	1300	Percentage of Increase
Florence	15,000	96,000	+640%
Siena	19,000	52,000	+274%
Pisa	20,000	38,000	+190%

Source: Adapted from Malcolm Barber, *The Two Cities: Medieval Europe, 1050–1320* (London: Routledge, 1992), p. 270.

We have already discussed the changing fortunes of the papal states in central Italy, but a few developments in the south are worthy of note. Once the popes had defeated Frederick II, they decided to look for more pliant allies in the south. In 1266 the papacy called in Charles of Anjou (r. 1226–1285) as king of Sicily and Naples. Charles, a brother of Saint Louis, had received a Capetian appanage in France but longed for greater adventures. He had gone on crusade and had also helped the papacy in its wars against the Hohenstaufen. Charles enjoyed the confidence of the popes, but as an outsider he had little support among any of the diverse ethnic groups of his kingdom. When he moved the capital from Palermo to Naples, he provoked a rebellion in Sicily in 1282, and by 1284 he had to flee. To prevent Charles from regaining his power, some Sicilians turned to the increasingly powerful Aragonese for assistance. For a long time southern Italy was contested between French and Spanish interests, successors to earlier combatants: Byzantines, Muslims, Normans, and Germans.

Economic Life

In the middle of the twelfth century the European economy was in full expansion. By the end of the thirteenth century, that expansion had begun to moderate and, in some areas, to reverse. Decline, however, is not the central theme of economic life. It is more accurate to speak of innovation and adaptation. Urban dynamism supplanted rural creativity. Economic institutions in Europe grew more complex, interdependent, and sophisticated. People began to think in new ways about economic behavior.

The Roles of Cities and Towns

The key population trend was not overall growth but reorganization. Cities were growing as never before. Table 11.1 shows the growth of three Italian cities. Such growth also occurred in cities in Flanders, such as Bruges and Ghent, and in Paris, London, and other cities that were evolving into national capitals. Ghent expanded its city walls five times between 1160 and 1300, a sure sign of growth even in the absence of population figures. Similar forces were operating in the countryside too. In 1100 there about 11 fortified villages outside Florence, but by 1200 there were 205.

Cities were becoming centers for many activities. Governments, which required larger and larger staffs of trained personnel, settled in towns, even when kings continued to ride about the countryside or go off on crusade. The towns of Italy and Flanders, though not national capitals, ruled over extensive hinterlands. Schools and eventually universities (see pages 418–419) were urban institutions. Mercantile, industrial, and legal organizations were based in towns. Ecclesiastical organization was always urban based. Towns began to compete with royal and aristocratic courts as literary centers, and cathedrals, the great buildings of the age, were exclusively urban.

Towns tended to regroup the population, but the people who lived in towns also tended to regroup themselves. For instance, in 1200 Paris had a guild of merchants and four or five craft or trade associations. By 1270 the city had 101 trade and craft guilds, and by 1292 the number had risen to 130.

The guilds had many functions. As towns grew larger and more impersonal, these associations of people engaged in similar occupations fostered a sense of belonging, a feeling of community. Members usually lived in the same areas and worshiped together in a parish church. Growing wealth in general, coupled with fierce pride, produced building competitions whose results are still visible in the often grandiose neighborhood churches that survive in most European towns. The guilds often indulged in elaborate festivals and celebrations, which sometimes turned into drunken debauches that may not have been pleasing to the saints in whose honor they were held. The guilds were also mutual assurance societies. They saw to the funeral expenses of members and provided for widows or orphans.

Mainly guilds were meant to regulate standards of production, to fix prices, and to control membership in their respective trades. A master typically had several apprentices under his guidance as well as one or two journeymen. The apprentices, often teenagers, worked long hours at low pay. Only a few of them advanced to the level of the journeymen, who earned more and who had some hope of becoming masters.

The guilds played important roles in the political life of the towns. The older merchant guilds counted in their membership the urban elite. The newer craft guilds incorporated the workers in the industries that were growing up in cities. The former group had erected the first communes and reserved communal magistracies and council spots for itself. From the late twelfth century, masters in the craft guilds, or their elected representatives, began to demand positions on the city councils. Guilds contributed simultaneously to stability and tension in cities. They controlled ever more tightly the economic, social, and political life of their members. That was stabilizing. But the old merchant elites shared power grudgingly with even the most prominent of the workers. That made for trouble.

The guilds also produced some unintended and negative results. They had a damaging impact on women. As more economic activity came under the umbrella of the guild structures, women were more systematically excluded from guild membership. Usually women could become guild members only as wives or widows. They could not open economic enterprises of their own, although they were workers in many trades. In a growing, diversifying economy, women were denied opportunities by increasingly rigid, professionalized structures.

"City air makes you free" was an old medieval saying. It meant that a person who went to a city would not be under the obligations of manorial society. For the landed aristocrats who went into towns, for members of the clergy or of

The Medieval Guilds In this fanciful English painting, a regal figure benignly watches over a stone mason, who is carving a capital, and a carpenter, who is drilling with an augur. Royal governments often supported prominent townspeople. *(The British Library)*

guilds, towns were indeed places of freedom and opportunity in good times and of relative security in bad times. But as guilds tightened their grip on the urban economy, ordinary people had a hard time finding steady work except in menial positions. Day laborers and domestics were always in demand but were vulnerable to instant dismissal, low wages, and cruel treatment. Some women turned to prostitution, an old profession for which there was growing demand in cities where brides were expected to be virgins and men—required to wait into their late twenties or early thirties to enter a guild and take up a stable position—were relatively old at first marriage. Crime and poverty were byproducts of the growing significance of guilds in cities. The guilds also reinforced professionalism and hierarchy: two phenomena evident in other aspects of twelfth-

and thirteenth-century life. City air did not make people equally free.

Commercial Growth and Innovation

Towns were focal points in commercial networks. Italian and southern French towns gathered the products of the Mediterranean world and moved them north, either up the Rhône Valley and on into northern France or over the central and eastern Alpine passes into Germany. North German, Flemish, and English traders assembled the goods of northern lands and moved them eastward toward central Europe, south down the Rhine, or into the Paris basin. These trade patterns had existed since Carolingian times. New in the mid-twelfth century was the emergence of the Champagne fairs as a meeting point for the commerce of north and south.

Since the early Middle Ages there had been permanent fairs in a few locations and occasional fairs in many places. By the middle of the twelfth century, however, the spices and dyes of the Mediterranean, the wool of England, the furs and linens of Germany, and the leather products of Spain began to be sold in a series of six fairs in the Champagne region of France that lasted seven weeks each. In the first week of each fair the merchandise was put on display; in the last, accounts were settled. The fairs were quiet in November and December because of travel difficulties.

At any time of year, travel was difficult and costly. Few dared to venture across the Alps in the winter, and the northern seas, especially the passage around Denmark, were treacherous in cold weather. Even in the relatively calm Mediterranean, the Venetians refused to send out their trading fleet between November and March. Overland trade was impeded by snow, rain, mud, and highwaymen. Governments tried to restrain robbers, but no one could change the weather. After the road between Pisa and Florence was paved in 1286, it was passable most of the time, but there were not many like it. Because overland trade was so expensive, often multiplying the cost of goods tenfold, transport by water was preferred wherever possible. The freezing of many rivers in the winter, however, brought the movement of people and products to a standstill.

Seaborne trade expanded. The stern rudder, better sails, the compass (in use by 1180), and better navigational charts facilitated sea travel, as did the growing use of larger ships. An Italian fleet sailed to Flanders in 1277, and within a few years the old overland trade routes, and with them the Champagne fairs, began a decline that was not reversed until the invention of the railroad in the nineteenth century.

Changing Economic Attitudes

As medieval society generated more wealth and populations concentrated in cities, people who were relatively well-off became more conscious of those who were less fortunate. Moralists began to argue that the poor were a special gift of God to the rich, who could redeem their own souls by generous charitable benefactions. Most towns established schemes of poor relief. But the numbers of poor people grew so rapidly, particularly in large towns, that they could not be dealt with. Some hospitals, for example, began refusing to take foundlings for fear that they would be deluged with them.

Efforts to alleviate the actual condition of the poor constituted one ethical concern of medieval thinkers, but two issues attracted even more attention. First, theologians and lawyers alike discussed the "just price," the price at which goods should be bought and sold. Christian teaching had long held that it was immoral to hoard food during a famine or knowingly to sell a damaged item. But what was the correct price in ordinary circumstances? A theological view, often dismissed as unrealistic, held that items could be sold for only the cost of the materials in them and the labor absolutely necessary to produce them. A commercial view, often dismissed as immoral, insisted that a fair price was whatever the market would bear, regardless of consequences. A working consensus held that a just price was one arrived at by bargaining between free and knowledgeable parties.

The other ethical issue concerned usury, the lending of money at interest. Christian writers were always hostile to commercial enterprise, and they had plenty of scriptural warrant for their view. Psalm 15 warned that no one can be blameless "who lends his money at usury." The Gospel According to Luke said to "give without expecting to be repaid in full." Luke actually forbade the profit without which most commercial enterprises are impossible. In the twelfth century, churchmen began to be much more assiduous in their condemnations of usury, a practice that had been winked at for centuries.

Prohibitions against usury in a society in full economic expansion produced some remarkably inventive ways to get around the prohibitions. One person might agree to sell another person an item at a certain price and then buy it back on a fixed date at a higher price. Exchange rates between currencies could be manipulated to mask usurious transactions. While some were actually practicing usury, others were trying to find ways to justify it. The commonest defense was that a person who lent money incurred a risk and deserved to be compensated for that risk.

Investment demands credit, and credit requires some recompense for the lender. One way or another, and in the face of deep hostility, credit mechanisms spread in thirteenth-century Europe. They were held up to minute scrutiny by theologians and popular preachers and were found to be evidence of man's sinfulness, acquisitiveness, greed. But all these practices persisted, fueled the continuing expansion of the European economy, and began putting individual profit alongside community interest at the heart of economic thought.

Social and Religious Movements

Twelfth- and thirteenth-century Europe witnessed several social movements unlike anything that had gone before. They involved large numbers of people (both men and women), cut across lines of wealth, status, and occupation, and appeared in many places. Most of these movements had cohesive beliefs, even ideologies, and well-determined goals. They are the first large-scale social movements in European history before the truly mass movements of modern times. They were spurred by the growing intrusions of government and the church, by the unequal distribution of economic growth, and by urbanization.

Heretics and Dissidents

The canon lawyer Gratian (see page 379) defined heresy as a situation where "each man chooses for himself the teaching he believes to be the better one"; that is, he ignores official doctrines. For Gratian and his like-minded contemporaries, faith was not an individual matter. The officers of the church were to decide what everyone else should believe. Unity of belief was crucial in a Catholic ("universal") Christian Europe. In the twelfth century, the church reacted ever more strictly to challenges to its teachings or to its exclusive right to teach.

Heretics did not see themselves as secessionists from the true church. They saw themselves as its only representatives. There was always a degree of popular skepticism. Not everyone believed, for example, that Jesus was born of a virgin, that he was true God and true man, or that God was triune (Father, Son, and Holy Spirit). But such doubts had not previously led to mass defections. Now several factors combined to lead many to reject the teachings and the authority of the church. The quest for the apostolic life—a life of preaching and poverty—attracted perfectly orthodox monks and hermits as well as irreconcilable critics of the wealth, pretension, and power of the clergy. The effort by the church to define its law, theology, and bureaucratic procedures with greater precision drew lines more sharply than ever before between what was, and what was not, acceptable.

Before the middle of the twelfth century, challenges to the church came from men—as far as we can tell the ringleaders were all men—who saw themselves as inspired reformers. Tanchelm of Antwerp, for instance, preached between 1110 and 1115 in the Netherlands. He called churches brothels and clerics whores. He rejected the sacraments and the payment of tithes. Though intemperate, these views represented a fairly coherent program of criticism. But Tanchelm and his band of followers went further. The heretic distributed his hair and nail clippings to his followers as relics of a sort, and in a bizarre public display he married a statue of the Virgin Mary. He seems also to have encouraged his followers to imitate his own sexual license. An obscure priest killed him in 1115. It is not clear that Tanchelm influenced anyone outside his own circle, but right across the twelfth century there were comparable individuals.

Coherent movements of much larger proportions emerged later in the century. In 1173 Peter Valdès, a rich merchant of Lyon, decided to sell all his property, give the proceeds to the poor, and embrace a life of poverty and preaching. Valdès was motivated by the same quest for the apostolic life that had animated the eremitical movement of the eleventh century. But there was a difference: Valdès was a layman. Valdès attracted many followers (known as Waldensians), and in 1179 Pope Alexander III (r. 1159–1181) scrutinized him closely, found his beliefs to be essentially correct, and approved his vow of poverty. But the pope commanded Valdès to preach only when invited to do so by bishops. The bishops, jealous about their own power, extended no such invitations.

Valdès and his "Poor Men of Lyon" went right on preaching and in 1184 were formally declared heretics. Until this point it was not their ideas so much as their appropriation of a clerical office, preaching, that had gotten them into trouble. From this time on, however, the Waldensians became more radical in their attacks on the church. In about 1204 one group of Waldensians was reconciled to the Catholic church; but the majority, which had spread all over southern France and Italy, into Germany, and as far away as Poland, was not reconciled. Waldensian communities exist to this day.

The most serious of the popular heretical movements was that of the Albigensians, as the Cathars of southern France were called. Catharism (from the Greek *katharos,* meaning "pure") refers to the religious descendants of Mani (see page 225) a third-century Persian who taught an extreme dualism that featured polarities in almost all things: good-evil, love-hate, flesh-spirit. Extreme Cathars abstained from flesh in all ways: They were vegetarians and renounced sexual intercourse so as not to produce offspring—that is, more flesh. Cathar ideas had reached the West, probably from Bulgaria, by 1022, when a group of Cathars was burned at the stake in Orléans. By 1144 there were numerous Cathars near Albi, whence the name "Albigensian." After a visit in 1167 by the Cathar bishop of Constantinople, people of every station in the south of France became members of the new church, which, in its own view, was the only true church.

The Catholic church sent isolated preachers against the Albigensians, but with little success. In 1198 and 1203 Pope Innocent III organized systematic preaching tours in southern France, but these too lacked solid results, and in 1208 the pope's legate was murdered by a supporter of the powerful count of Toulouse, who was a Cathar. The killing led to the launching of the Albigensian Crusade, a loosely structured movement that lasted into the 1260s. Its high points were a massacre of the Albigensians in 1244 and inquisitorial campaigns in 1246 and again in 1256–1257. Isolated resisters struggled on into the fourteenth century.

The Albigensians attracted members of the nobility of southern France, perhaps because they feared the increasing domination of Paris and the northern French. Albigensians were staunchly opposed to the clergy of their day, seeing them as rich and corrupt. These teachings helped to draw to the Albigensian cause urban dwellers who resented the wealth and pretensions of the clergy—the same people who followed Peter Valdès.

The Albigensians, like a number of other heretical sects, attracted many women. Unlike the Catholic church, which denied clerical, preaching, and teaching offices to women, the heretical sects tended to be more egalitarian. But the Albigensians, like the Waldensians, were also driven by the same spiritual zeal and desire for ecclesiastical reform that moved many of their contemporaries. They differed from other would-be reformers in that they did not seek to reform the Catholic church from within but departed from it or insisted that they alone represented it. These heretical movements marked the first serious challenge to the ideology of a uniformly Catholic Christendom wherein a person's adherence to the church mattered more than one's ethnicity, class, or occupation. (See the box, "Pronouncements of the Fourth Lateran Council on Heresy.")

Reform from Within: The Mendicant Orders

Traditional monastic orders continued to win adherents, but their interpretation of the apostolic life meant ascetic withdrawal from the world, not pastoral work and preaching. Laymen who wished both to embrace poverty and to preach fell under the suspicion of the ecclesiastical authorities. Early in the thirteenth century a new movement arose, the mendicants (literally beggars). Mendicants were men who aimed to

Pronouncements of the Fourth Lateran Council on Heresy

By 1215 the papacy had become alarmed at the number and strength of the heretical movements in Europe, and it began to take strong measures to counter the dissidents.

3. Convicted heretics shall be handed over for due punishment to their secular superiors, or the latter's agents. If they are clerks [members of the clergy], they shall first be degraded [lose their clerical rank]. The goods of the layman thus convicted shall be confiscated; those of the clergy shall be applied to the churches from which they drew their stipends. . . . If a temporal lord neglects to fulfil the demand of the church that he purge his land of the contamination of heresy, he shall be excommunicated by the metropolitan and other bishops of the province. If he fails to make amends within a year, it shall be reported to the Supreme Pontiff, who shall pronounce his vassals absolved from fealty to him and offer his land to Catholics. . . . Catholics who assume the cross and devote themselves to the extermination of heretics shall enjoy the same indulgence and privilege as those who go to the Holy Land. . . .

7. Further we add that every archbishop and bishop, in person or by his archdeacon or other suitable and trustworthy persons, shall visit each of his parishes, in which there are said to be heretics, at least once a year. And he shall compel three or more men of good reputation, or even, if need be, the whole neighborhood, to swear that, if any of them knows of any heretics or of any who frequent secret conventicles or who practise manners and customs different from those common amongst Christians, he will report them to the bishop; and, unless they clear themselves of the accusation, or if they relapse into their former mischief, they shall receive the canonical punishment.

Source: Henry Bettenson, *Documents of the Christian Church,* 2d ed. (London: Oxford University Press, 1963), p. 133.

preach, to be poor, and to create formal but non-cloistered religious orders. Though similar to the heretics in many ways, they submitted willingly to ecclesiastical authority.

The mendicant phenomenon began when Francis of Assisi (1181–1226), the son of a rich Italian merchant, decided to renounce the wealth and status that were his birthright. He carried out his renunciation in a most public display before the bishop of Assisi in 1206. He stripped himself naked so as to return to his father and to the world all that he had ever received, "that naked he might follow the naked Christ." Francis had gradually grown tired of a life of ease and luxury, but he also experienced a blinding moment of spiritual insight when, by chance, his eyes fell on the passage in the Scriptures where Christ said, "Go, sell all you have, and follow me."

For a few years Francis wandered about begging for his meager sustenance, repairing churches, caring for the sick, and preaching repentance to all who would listen. By 1210 he had attracted many followers, and together they set out to see Innocent III to win approval. After considering the matter for a while, Innocent decided to approve the new order of friars (that is "brothers," from the Latin *fratres*) as long as they would accept monastic tonsure—a sign of submission—profess obedience to the pope, and swear obedience to Francis. The pope was genuinely won over by Francis himself, but he also sensed that by permitting the formation of the Franciscan order he could create a legitimate and controllable repository for the explosive spiritual forces of the age.

Francis prepared a simple rule based on his understanding of the scriptural ideals of poverty, preaching, and service. Alarmed by the vagueness of the first rule and by the extraordinary influx of new members, the papal curia in 1223 prevailed on Francis to write a new rule that stressed order, a hierarchy of officials, and a novitiate—a regularized period of training for new members. Before his death, Francis withdrew more and more from the world, going out into the hills where he celebrated the beauty of nature and his oneness with all creation.

After the death of Francis, his order (usually called "Franciscan," though it is technically the "Friars Minor") split over the issues of property, power, education, and ordination. The movement had begun among laymen, but over time Franciscans were ordained in increasing numbers. Franciscans established schools in most great cities, and by the middle of the thirteenth century some of Europe's greatest intellects were Franciscans. This prominence, like the sacramental power of ordination, was a kind of wealth that Francis had wished to avoid. The real issue of wealth, however, turned on the possession of property. Francis had aimed for both personal and corporate poverty. In the 1230s papal legislation had alleviated strict poverty by permitting the order to acquire houses and property to support its work. Nevertheless, the issue of property continued to spark controversy among the Franciscans.

The other major mendicant order, the Dominican, was the product of very different experiences. Its founder, Dominic de Guzman (1170–1221), was the son of a Spanish nobleman. He became a priest and later a cathedral canon. While traveling, he saw firsthand the Albigensian heresy in southern France, and in 1206 he went to Rome to seek permission to preach against the heretics. The Albigensian Crusade began in 1208, but Dominic's methods were those of persuasion, not coercion.

Albigensian criticisms of the ignorance, indifference, and personal failings of the clergy could never be applied to Dominic and his fellow preachers. Dominic and his followers were supported enthusiastically by the bishop of Toulouse, who saw how useful these zealous preachers of unblemished life could be. In 1215 Dominic, with his bishop's assistance, attempted to form a new order, but by that time Rome had forbidden the creation of new orders for fear of heresy or uncontrollable diversity. Thus, Dominic's "Order of Preachers" (the proper name for the Dominicans) adopted the Rule of Saint Augustine, which many communities of cathedral canons had been using since the eleventh century.

In 1217 Dominic presided at the first general meeting of the order. The Dominicans decided to disperse, some going to Paris, some (including Dominic) to Rome, some to other cities in Europe. Henceforth, the order saw its mission as serving the whole church. Dominican schools were set up everywhere, and the order acquired a reputation for learning and scholarship. The Inquisition was largely assigned to Dominicans. The Dominicans were voluntarily poor, but the order was never rent by a controversy over property as the Franciscans were. Dominic's was a vision of personal, not corporate, poverty. Likewise, as a preaching order, the Dominicans had to be learned and ordained. Franciscan misgivings on these issues did not touch them.

The Franciscan and Dominican orders were both alike and different. Each reflected a widespread desire to emulate the apostolic life of the early church by poverty and preaching. Both were submissive to legitimate authority. Francis's religious vision was the product of a heartfelt need for repentance and renewal. Dominic set out to save the church from its enemies. Francis preached denial, charity, and service. Dominic desired preachers who were sufficiently learned that they could combat the errors of heretics. Both men saw the need for exemplary lives. Francis provided concrete examples for laymen; Dominic wished to avoid the reproaches of the Albigensians, who had adopted lives of simplicity and renunciation. Francis was a more charismatic figure than Dominic, and his apostolate to the urban poor was more compelling. By 1300 Franciscan houses outnumbered Dominican by 3 to 1. Franciscan or Dominican, the mendicants were the greatest spiritual force in high medieval Europe.

Communities of Women

The religious forces that attracted men drew women as well. Traditional orders tended to be hostile to women, however. There was only one Cluniac house for women, and the Cistercians struggled to keep women out of their ranks. The wandering preachers of the twelfth century, without exception, acquired women as followers, but the almost inevitable results were either segregation of the women in cloisters or condemnation of the whole movement.

In 1212 Francis attracted the 17-year-old aristocrat Clare of Assisi (1194–1253), who was fleeing from an arranged marriage. She wanted to live the full life of poverty and preaching that the friars had adopted, and Francis wanted to assist her. Aware that the sight of women begging or preaching would be shocking, in 1214 he gave her and his other female followers a rule of their own. Clare became abbess of the first community of the "Poor Clares." Although cloistered and forbidden to preach, the Clares lived lives of exemplary austerity and poverty and attracted many adherents.

Beguines were communities of women who lived together, devoted themselves to charitable works, but did not take vows as nuns. The Beguine movement arose with the Belgian Mary of Oignies (ca. 1177–1213), who was irresistibly drawn to the ideals of voluntary poverty and service to others. So strong was the pull that she renounced her marriage, gave away all her goods, and went to work in a leper colony. She earned a meager living by spinning.

Groups of Beguines appeared all over the Low Countries, western Germany, and northern France. This was the first exclusively women's movement in the history of Christianity. Beguines sometimes vowed poverty and sometimes did not. They sometimes cloistered themselves into communities and sometimes taught and served the poor and outcast. They neither challenged the officials and teachings of the church nor demanded a right to preach. As laywomen, they did not give rise to scandal as noncloistered nuns would have. They were content to have power over their own lives and communities but not over the wider world around them.

Thirteenth-century Europe knew more female than male mystics, and female mysticism tended to focus on Jesus, especially on His presence in the Eucharist. This is the first religious devotion that can be shown to have been more common to women than to men. Most of the mystics were either nuns or Beguines. As the clergy was defining its own prerogatives more tightly, and excluding women more completely from the exercise of formal public power, female communities provided a different locus for women's activity.

Women who spent their lives in community with other women betray, in their writings and in writings about them, none of the sense of moral and intellectual inferiority that was routinely attributed to women by men and often by women themselves. Women who were in direct spiritual communion with God acquired, as teachers, mediators, and counselors in their communities, power that they simply could not have had outside those settings. These women acquired authority from divine selection, not from office. God alone decided to whom He would reveal Himself in mystical visions.

Beguines and female mystics did nothing to challenge the power or teachings of the church. By granting approbation to these women, the church again appropriated to its own use a potential challenge, just as it did in approving but then cloistering the Clares.

Francis and Clare of Assisi This beautiful, moving Gothic painting by Giotto (late thirteenth century) depicts Francis's funeral cortege passing by Clare's church of San Damiano. Compare this Italian Gothic façade with the French ones on pages 422 and 431. (*Scala/Art Resource, NY*)

The Later Crusades

The factors that produced the First Crusade—papal leadership, a more militant Christianity, religious zeal, surplus soldiers, a spirit of adventure—persisted right through the thirteenth century. Crusading continued to be a popular social movement. People from all over Europe and every social class participated in the Crusades. By 1300, however, the energies long channeled into crusading were being diverted elsewhere, though there was still talk of crusading in Europe after 1500 (Map 11.2).

Crusading was intended to protect the Holy Land and keep open the pilgrim routes to Jerusalem. The creation of the small crusader states in the hostile environment of Syria and Palestine had made continued crusading almost inevitable. In 1138 the tiny crusader state at Edessa on the Armenian frontier fell to a Muslim army, and a shock went through Europe. The pope and Bernard of Clairvaux preached another crusade and persuaded Conrad III of Germany and Louis VII of France to lead it. Unfortunately Conrad and Louis were jealous of one another, and the Second Crusade accomplished little. Its one achievement was an accident. In 1139 an army of English, French, and Flemish soldiers who were proceeding to the Holy Land by sea put in on the Iberian coast and captured Lisbon. This opened a new front in the Reconquista and laid the foundations for the later kingdom of Portugal.

The papacy called for the Third Crusade when Saladin (see page 334) captured Jerusalem in 1187. It is a measure of the force of the crusading ideal that the greatest crowned heads of the day—Frederick Barbarossa, Philip II, and Richard the Lionhearted—answered the call. It must be said, however, that all did so reluctantly, for they had more pressing concerns at home. By 1190 Frederick was dead, and Philip and Richard had returned home to carry on their struggles against one another. Because neither Richard nor Philip would stay in the East to fight Saladin, this crusade merely won access to Jerusalem for pilgrims.

Innocent III was disappointed with the results of the Third Crusade and began calling for another crusade almost immediately on his election in 1198. Popular preachers summoned a mighty host, and the pope and the Fourth Crusade's military leaders engaged the Venetians to construct a fleet of war and transport ships. In less than eighteen months they produced fifty galleys and 450 transports, a tribute to the awesome capabilities of the Venetian shipyards.

Ships, however, were expensive, and the Venetians drove hard bargains. When too few Crusaders and too little money appeared, the Venetians suggested that the Crusaders could discharge some of their debt by attacking a pirate base at Zara on the Dalmatian coast. This idea outraged the pope, but he could do little about it. Then into the camp of the Crusaders came a pretender to the Byzantine throne, who promised that if the Crusaders would help him to claim his patrimony, he would contribute to the cost of the crusade. The Venetians urged the Crusaders to accept this offer, and, to the horror of Innocent III, the Fourth Crusade turned to Constantinople.

Once in Constantinople, the Crusaders learned that their new ally had few friends in the Byzantine capital. The Venetians saw an opportunity to expand business opportunities in the East, and the soldiers welcomed a chance to plunder the Mediterranean's greatest city and to avenge what they regarded as a century of Byzantine perfidy. Thus, the Fourth Crusade captured not Jerusalem but Constantinople. Until 1261, the eastern and western churches were reunited under papal leadership, and substantial tracts of the Balkans fell to western knights under a "Latin Emperor" of Constantinople.

In later decades, popes began to take a more active role in planning Crusades, right down to setting objectives. No pope wanted to lose control of a crusade as Innocent had done, and all popes saw that the liberation of Jerusalem required a solid base of operations in the eastern Mediterranean. Egypt was the objective of the Fifth Crusade (1218–1221) and the Sixth Crusade (1248–1250). Despite a few victories, the Crusaders could not win a secure base. No further crusades to the East were organized in the thirteenth century. In 1291 Acre, the last crusader stronghold, fell and the original crusading era ended.

During the crusading period, the Holy Land was by no means the sole object of Crusaders' attentions. In about 1140 the pope preached a crusade against the Normans in southern Italy, and

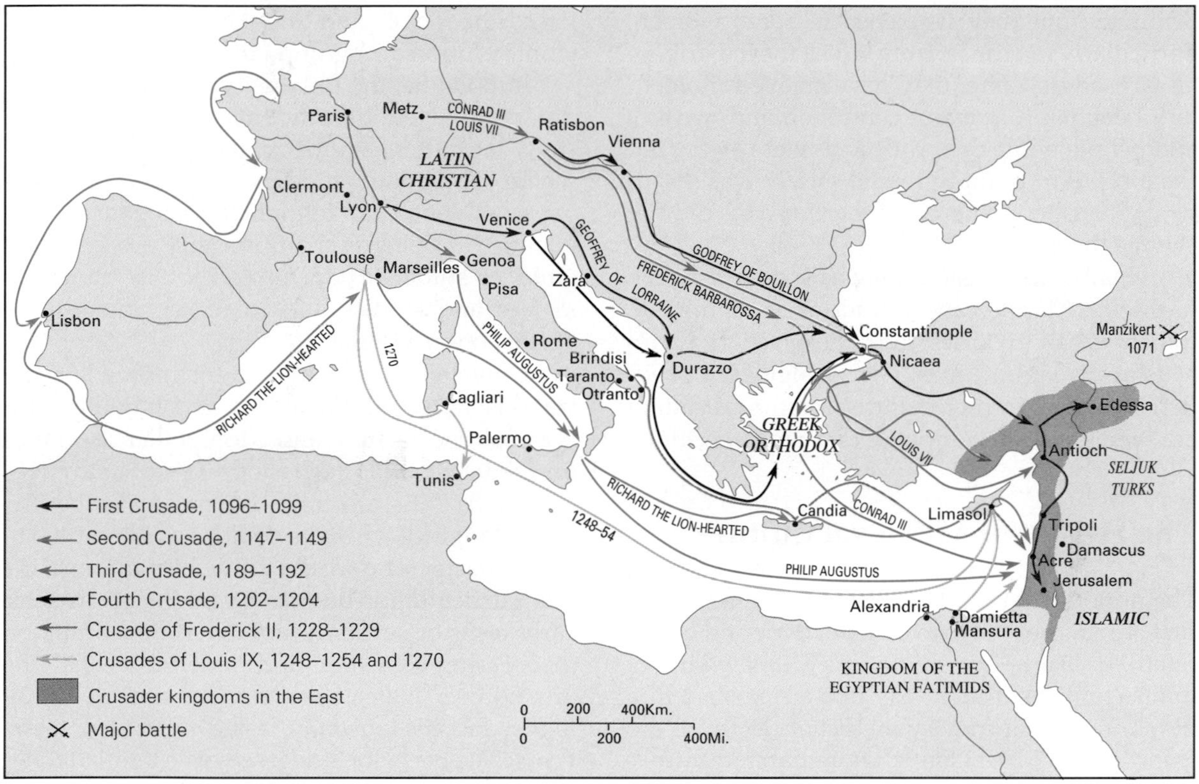

Map 11.2 The Crusades, 1095–1270 The long Western European interest in securing the Holy Land is illustrated by the repeated crusades. Note the numerous routes taken, lands traversed, destinations attained, and points of cultural encounter.

several popes in the thirteenth century, fearful of imperial encroachment, preached crusades against the Hohenstaufen in Italy. In 1147 the papacy authorized a crusade in the Baltic that drove nearly four centuries of German expansion into the pagan Slavic lands to the east of Saxony. And 1208 saw Innocent III's proclamation of a crusade against the Albigensians.

Why did the Crusades end? There are several reasons. By the late thirteenth century, more violence was being directed inward against heretics and political foes of the papacy than outward against the alleged enemies of Christendom itself. Too, as governments became more sophisticated and controlled more of their territories, they began to gain, at the papacy's expense, a near monopoly on the use of violence and greater financial resources. The commercial cities of Italy now needed not so much to open up the Muslim East as to secure comparative advantage over one another. The Christian ideals of poverty, charity, and service, as embodied in the mendicants, were incompatible with warfare. Literary images provide another insight into the decline of the Crusades. After 1300, we are less likely to read about a Christian knight fighting honorably for God and king than about a gentleman of manners seeking the favor of a fair lady.

A balance sheet for the crusading movement as a whole reveals more losses than gains. The Crusades exported many violent men from Europe, but it is not clear that Europe became a less violent place. As a result of the Crusades, relations between Christian Europe and the Muslim world were embittered. The Fourth Crusade mortally wounded Byzantium and worsened the already tense relations between the Catholic and Orthodox churches. Crusading zeal was directed deliberately against heretics and accidentally against Jews. The Crusades did not create anti-

Semitism, but they worsened it. Some women, particularly in France, from which the majority of all Crusaders came, may have enjoyed momentary benefits in terms of control of land, wealth, and people while their husbands were away. But the long-term trend in feudal society was disadvantageous to women, and the Crusades did not change that.

Finally, the crusades may have done as much to disrupt Mediterranean trade as to promote it. Italian urban rivalries took the place of Latin-Muslim-Byzantine ones. That a single new product, the apricot, entered Europe in the crusading era seems small recompense for such huge effort.

The Height of Medieval Culture

The period from 1150 to 1300 is bracketed by the first stirrings of the University of Paris and by the poetry of Dante. Paris points us to a new kind of intellectual institution, the university, and to a new intellectual movement, Scholasticism. Also from France came Gothic art and architecture—elegant, spiritually moving, and logical, just like Dante's works. But Dante, who could write refined Latin, penned his best works in Italian. Italian, French, and German—not Latin—were the languages of the street, though not of the courtroom or lecture hall. Cultural horizons were expanding.

The University

In the early decades of the twelfth century, students gathered wherever there were famous teachers. Gradually, such teachers—figures like Peter Abelard—clustered in a few centers, and the students congregated there as well. The last decades of the twelfth century saw a swarm of masters and students in Paris. Like members of secular guilds, the masters organized. The University of Paris was the result of their efforts.

Several forces drove masters to organize. They wanted to secure their own interests against the bishop's chancellor, the traditional head of all schools in an episcopal city. They wanted to regulate the curriculum that students followed and to prescribe the requirements for entry into their own ranks. Finally, they desired to set the fees to be charged for instruction. By 1209 the bishop of Paris, the pope, and the king of France had granted formal recognition to the university.

In Bologna, the university developed a little differently. Here the students came primarily to study law, after acquiring a basic education elsewhere. These law students were usually older, more affluent, and foreign to Bologna. Consequently, in Bologna the university arose from a guild of students who united to set standards in fees and studies and to protect themselves against unscrupulous masters.

Universities were known for certain specializations: Paris for arts and theology; Bologna for law; Salerno in Italy and Montpellier in France for medicine. Still, the basic course of study was similar. At Paris, a young scholar came to the city, found lodgings where he could, and attempted to find a master who would guide him through the arts curriculum. These boys might be in their early teens or several years older, depending on their earlier education and material means. The arts course, which was the prerequisite to all higher faculties, usually lasted from four to six years. The bachelor's degree was essentially a license to teach, but a bachelor who wished to teach in a university needed to go on for a master's degree. The master's degree required at least eight years of study (including the baccalaureate years), which was completed by a public, oral examination. Some masters went on to become doctors in theology, law, or medicine. A doctorate required ten to fifteen years of study. Medieval academicians were immensely learned.

Student life was difficult. In many ways, students were always foreigners. Although their presence in a town enhanced its prestige, townspeople exploited them by charging exorbitant prices for food and rent. Students' own behavior was not always above reproach. There was surely some truth in the frequently lodged charge that students were noisy, quarrelsome, given to drinking, and excessively fond of prostitutes. Oxford and Cambridge were unique in having residential colleges for students from the very beginning; Paris got one later. Typically, students were on their own.

Students had to work very hard. The arts curriculum demanded a thorough acquaintance with all the famous texts of grammar, logic, and rhetoric. Higher studies added more of Aristotle, particularly his philosophical writings. In theol-

The Law School of Bologna Shown here is the tomb of Cino da Pistoia (1272–1337), a great lawyer and teacher of law in Bologna. The lively sculptures show Cino (above) surrounded by his pupils—note their relative sizes—and Cino's classroom (below). (*Alinari/Mansell*)

ogy, the students had to master the Scriptures, the principal biblical commentaries from patristic times to the present, and the *Book of Sentences*, a theology textbook (ca. 1160) by the Italian Peter Lombard. In medicine, the ancient writings of Galen and Hippocrates were supplemented by Arab texts as well as by observation and experimentation.

The basic method of teaching consisted of the recitation by the teacher of a short piece of a set text, followed by the presentation and discussion of many authoritative commentaries on that text, and concluded by the interpretations and explanations of the teacher himself. Then another passage of the set text was presented and the whole process repeated. This education focused on standard books and received opinions and required students to master large amounts of material. The curriculum nevertheless produced thinkers of prodigious originality.

In principle, universities were open to all males, but in practice they were restricted to those who had the means to attend them. Curiously, mendicant friars became major figures on the university scene. They founded houses of study—residence and dining halls—near every major university. Women were not accepted at universities, either as students or as teachers. It was generally thought, by men, that learning made women insubordinate. Lacking the required formal education, women were furthermore denied entry into the learned professions of theology, law, and medicine, despite the fact that many rural and some urban medical practitioners were women—it was common for women to possess and transmit massive knowledge of folk remedies. The rise of universities is yet another example of how routinization and professionalization cut off opportunities for many people.

Scholasticism

Scholasticism was the intellectual outlook of the medieval schools. That outlook was the product of several related forces. Most important was the Christian tradition. Other forces were the quickening pace of intellectual life occasioned by Latin Europe's encounter with the worlds of Arab and Jewish learning in the era of the Crusades; the need to reconcile natural philosophy, or the claims of reason, with revealed religion, or the realm of faith; and the style of intellectual life that resulted from the twelfth-century fascination with logic.

By the middle of the twelfth century, the Christian tradition had a well-defined set of basic sources—the Scriptures and the authoritative commentators—and two different approaches to the sources. One approach was to rely on divine inspiration, on mystical illumination. This approach to the biblical text was often learned but tended toward the allegorical. The other approach was more concrete and rationalistic and got a potent impetus from the development of logical studies in the twelfth century. The old intellectual struggle within Christian circles between faith and reason was made more acute by the dawning awareness of just how much the ancient Greeks had actually written and by the simultaneous discovery that Arab and Jewish scholars were also struggling to come to grips with that intellectual heritage.

Among many possible problems, we will mention two. First, Aristotle had taught that the universe was eternal and mechanistic. In his scheme of things there was no room for creation or for a benevolent deity who intervened to alter the course of events. Greek science, so obviously right about many things, seemed in this area to contradict fundamental Christian teachings. Second, as Arab and Jewish thinkers looked at natural philosophy and at their own religious traditions, some of them (see the discussion of Averroës on page 339) suggested that the Qur'an or the Hebrew Scriptures contained approximations to truth that were suitable only for persons of limited intellectual ability. Once again, the question was posed: Were the Scriptures true?

The answer of Thomas Aquinas (1225–1274) seemed most effectively to respond to the question. Thomas was the son of an Italian nobleman and a distant relative of Frederick II. A Dominican friar, he was educated at Naples, Cologne, and Paris. In 1252 he began lecturing at Paris and, apart from a few years' service at the papal court, he spent the rest of his life teaching and writing in Paris. A prolific author, his two most famous works are the *Summa Contra Gentiles* and the *Summa Theologiae.* A *summa* was an encyclopedic compendium of carefully arrayed knowledge on a particular subject. Thomas's first summa was addressed to pagan learning, or natural truth—that is, to the kinds of things that any person could know through the operation of reason. His second summa was a summation of the revealed truths of the Christian faith.

Thomas's works are distinctive for two reasons. First, no one before Thomas had so rigorously followed the dialectical method of reasoning through the whole of a field of knowledge, not just a particular problem. For thousands of pages, Thomas poses a question, suggests answers, confronts the answers with objections, refutes the objections, and then draws a conclusion. Then he repeats the process. Second, Thomas carefully distinguished between two kinds of truths. On the one hand were *natural truths,* truths (even theological ones) that anyone can know (or so Thomas thought)—for example, that God exists. On the other hand were *revealed truths,* truths that can be known only through faith in God's revelation—for example, the Trinity or the incarnation of Christ. Thomas maintained that natural and revealed truths simply could not contradict one another because God was ultimately the source of both. If natural truth—for example, Aristotle's contention that the world was eternal—appeared to contradict a revealed truth, then Aristotle was wrong. Thomas was accused by some contemporaries of applying reason too widely, but he actually steered a middle path between intellectual extremes. (See the box, "Thomas Aquinas's Proof for the Existence of God.")

The Gothic Image

One of the most familiar images of the Middle Ages is the inspiring beauty of the Gothic cathedral. It is thus ironic that the word *Gothic* first

Thomas Aquinas's Proof for the Existence of God

This abbreviated account of Thomas's proofs for God's existence illustrates both the working methods of Scholasticism and the character of the* Summa Theologiae. *Aristotelian logic, formal reasoning through syllogisms, is the framework behind the whole system of scholasticism.

[Thomas responds to Anselm.]

Perhaps not everyone who hears this name *God* understands it to signify something than which nothing greater can be thought, seeing that some have believed God to be a body. Yet, granted that everyone understands that by this name *God* is signified something than which nothing greater can be thought, nevertheless, it does not therefore follow that he understands that what the name signifies exists actually, but only that it exists mentally. Nor can it be argued that it actually exists, unless it be admitted that there actually exists something than which nothing greater can be thought; and this precisely is not admitted by those who hold that God does not exist.

[Then Thomas takes another approach.]

It seems that the existence of God cannot be demonstrated. For it is an article of faith that God exists. But what is of faith cannot be demonstrated, because a demonstration produces scientific knowledge, whereas faith is of the unseen. Therefore it cannot be demonstrated that God exists.

[To this, Thomas poses several objections.]

If the existence of God were demonstrated, this could only be from His effects. But His effects are not proportioned to him, since He is infinite and His effects are finite, and between the infinite and the finite there is no proportion. Therefore, since a cause cannot be demonstrated by an effect not proportioned to it, it seems that the existence of God cannot be demonstrated.

[Through abstruse logical reasoning, Thomas refutes this objection, thus proving that God does exist, and then he turns to another argument.]

It seems that God does not exist; because if one of two contraries be infinite, the other would be altogether destroyed. But the name of *God* means that He is infinite goodness. If, therefore, God existed, there would be no evil discoverable; but there is evil in the world. Therefore God does not exist.

I answer that the existence of God can be proved in five ways. The first and more manifest way is the argument from motion. It is certain, and evident to our senses, that in the world some things are in motion. Now whatever is moved is moved by another. . . . Therefore it is necessary to arrive at a prime mover, moved by no other. The second way is from the nature of efficient cause. There is no case known in which a thing is found to be the efficient cause of itself; for so it would be prior to itself which is impossible. Therefore it is necessary to admit a first efficient cause, to which everyone gives the name of God. The third way is from possibility and necessity. If at one time there was nothing in existence, it would have been impossible for anything to have begun to exist; and thus even now nothing would be in existence—which is absurd. Therefore, not all beings are merely possible, but there must exist something the existence of which is necessary. This all men speak of as God. [He continues with ways four and five, and then turns to detailed explanations of all five.]

Source: Anton C. Pegis, *An Introduction to St. Thomas Aquinas* (New York: Random House, Modern Library, 1945), pp. 22–27.

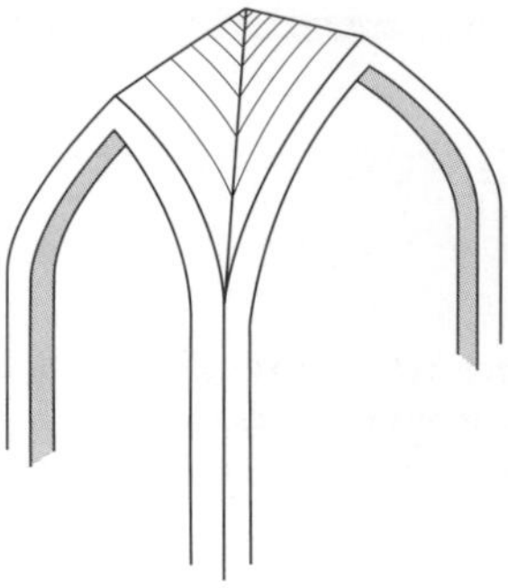

Figure 11.1 The Structure of Gothic Architecture The adaption of pointed arches, an import from the Islamic world, let Gothic builders join structures of differing heights and widths (something that barrel and groin vaulting could not do; see Figure 10.1 on page 382). The resulting structures were high, light, airy, and visually interesting. (*Source:* Anne Shaver-Crandell, *The Middle Ages* [Cambridge, England: Cambridge University Press, 1982], p. 34. Used by permission.)

appeared in the sixteenth century as a term of derision for what was then regarded as an outmoded style so ugly that only the horrible conquerors of Rome, the Goths, could have been responsible for it. The name stuck, but today it simply identifies a period in European architecture, sculpture, and painting that began around the middle of the twelfth century.

Gothic is a French invention. It was Abbot Suger (1085–1151) of St. Denis, a monastery just outside Paris, who, in rebuilding his basilica beginning 1135, consciously sought a new style. He desired to achieve effects of lightness, almost weightlessness, in the stonework of his church and to admit large amounts of light to create a dazzling and mysterious aura on the inside. The Bible often uses images of light to refer to God, and Suger wished to give expression to those images in the house of God for which he was responsible. (See the feature, "Weighing the Evi-

Exterior of Notre-Dame, Paris This most famous of cathedrals (1163–1220) shows all the classic elements of the Gothic style: highly decorated western end, cross shape formed by the nave and transept, flying buttresses to support the walls and roof, side walls that seem like curtains of glass. *(Altitude, Paris)*

dence: The Arts of Chartres Cathedral," on pages 430–431.)

Suger combined a number of elements that had long existed and produced something original. A *pointed arch* is more elegant than a round one; and it permits the joining of two arches of identical height but different widths, which, in turn, permits complex shapes and sizes. The *ribbed vault* is lighter and more elegant than the groin vaults characteristic of Romanesque architecture; it also exerts less stress and facilitates experimentation with shapes (Figure 11.1). Finally, *point support*—basically, the support of structural elements at only certain points—permitted the replacement of heavy, stress-bearing walls with curtains of stained glass. The points of support might be massive internal piers or intricate skeletal frameworks, called *buttresses,* on the outside of the church.

These three elements—pointed arch, ribbed vault, point support—produce a building that is characterized by verticality and translucency. Everything seems to spring upward, and stone surfaces appear so frequently punctured by light as almost to disappear altogether. The desired, and achieved, affect is one of harmony, order, and mathematical precision. It is surely no coincidence that Gothic emerged just as the West was absorbing the recovery of Euclid's mathematical writings and applying the intensely ordered logic of Aristotle to everything from legal problems to theological mysteries.

The Gothic style soon spread in central and northern France. The cathedral of Notre-Dame of Paris was built beginning in the 1150s, and the royal portal at Chartres Cathedral was reconstructed after 1145. Gothic churches could be huge. The interior of Notre-Dame, for example, is 493 feet long and 107 feet high. To avoid a sense of sheer mass, Gothic builders used triple or quadruple elevations inside the buildings and took advantage of point support to pierce the walls at frequent intervals with stained-glass windows. Exterior surfaces were broken up with windows, sculptures, colonnades, and towers. No opportunity was missed to create visual interest and complexity.

The thirteenth century was the most mature period for French Gothic architecture and also the time when Gothic spread most widely throughout Europe. This spread of Gothic may be attributed to the superiority of French masons and stonecutters and also to the tremendous prestige of French culture. By the second half of the thirteenth century there were distinctive Gothic traditions in almost all parts of Europe from Iceland to Poland.

Much Gothic painting, like painting in earlier centuries, was put in books. During the thirteenth century, however, three crucial trends emerged. First, more and more books were made by laymen laboring in workshops as professional bookmakers. Second, rising literacy and invigorated lay piety combined to put many books into the hands of laymen: illustrated Bibles, Psalters

Interior of Notre-Dame, Paris The pointed vaults of the nave produce a verticality that is different in "feel" from the Romanesque (compare page 383). Note the triple elevation, the pointed arches, the ribbed vaulting, the ubiquitous glass that admitted streams of multicolored light. The building can hold 10,000 people. *(Scala/Art Resource, NY)*

(prayer books based on the Psalms from the Bible), Books of Hours (prayer and devotional books for each day), and saints' lives. Book art, in other words, was no longer the preserve of the clergy. Third, a new kind of public painting triumphed.

Stained glass was "painting" only in an indirect sense. Although used in Romanesque churches, stained glass became ubiquitous in Gothic churches. Inspired by sculpture, craftsmen fitted together bits of tinted glass with lead strips in an attempt to create approximations of exterior statuary. Biblical scenes provided the principal stock of motifs. What is particularly impressive is the sheer size of some of the windows that were created. Only Chartres retains much of its original glass. Visitors to Europe today are usually looking at nineteenth-century attempts at restoration.

The builders of the age, like the bookmakers and many sculptors and painters, were professionals who worked to high standards after long periods of training. In this realm of culture, we can see the same tendency to specialization and standardization that we have detected in so many other aspects of life. Important too is the fact that many of these artists became well known and wealthy. In the twelfth century, the workers who remodeled a French cathedral inscribed on their work the words "Not for us, Lord, not for us, but unto Thy name be glory given." A century later, artists usually signed their work.

Latin and Vernacular Culture

Many writers continued to use Latin. University scholars, for example, composed their learned treatises in the ancient tongue, but often in a style that was less rhetorically ornate than that of the classics. Most law books and public documents were still written in Latin, but in a vulgar Latin that was reasonably close to the vernacular in areas where Romance languages (derived from Latin) were spoken. Technical manuals, on farming and animal husbandry, on warfare and armaments, or on law and government—further evidence for the specialization and professionalization of the age—were prepared in Latin too, but in a style that was far more accessible than that of their ancient models. What is most striking, however, is that Latin was rarely used, after about 1200, as the language for serious, original literary compositions.

Here the change from the twelfth century could not be more drastic. Then, theology and poetry, history and biography, and romance and adventure had been written in Latin. Some of this material was serious, but some breathed a light and carefree spirit. Peter Abelard plumbed the depths of his own soul in his *History of My Misfortunes.* His younger contemporary, the Archpoet (d. 1165), wrote poems about drinking and womanizing. These lines are typical of his work:

In the public house to die
    Is my resolution;
Let wine to my lips be nigh
    At life's dissolution:
That will make the angels cry,
    With glad elocution
"Grant this toper, God on high,
    Grace and Absolution!"[2]

No less insouciant were the authors of biting satires such as *The Gospel According to the Silver Marks,* which excoriated the wealth and greed of the papal curia. But this fresh spirit was now largely confined to writings in the vernacular.

The heroic, epic tradition that *Beowulf* and the *Song of Roland* represent did not disappear, but literary energies were applied in new directions. Southern France, in the middle and last decades of the twelfth century, added something new to Western literature: the love lyrics of the troubadours. This poetry, composed by both men and women, profoundly influenced an age and created the literary movement that has long been called "courtly love." Chivalry was initially a code for men interacting with other men. In the world of courtly love, chivalry became an elaborate set of rules governing relations between men and women.

Courtly love had several sources. The classical poet Ovid (43 B.C.–?17 A.D.) who wrote *The Art of Love,* a manual of seduction, was one. Another was the lyrical poetry of Muslim Spain. Ironically, the social world of feudal values such as loyalty and service played a critical role as men became, in effect, love vassals. There was some contribution too from Platonic ideas, particularly the notion that any love in this world could be only a pale imitation of real love. The courtly poets sung of *fin'amours,* a pure love in contrast to the mere lust of the masses. A lover cherished an unattainable lady. He would do anything for the merest display of pleasure or gratitude on her part, as we see in these lines from Bernart de Ventadorn, court poet of the counts of Toulouse in the late twelfth century:

In vain at Ventadorn full many a friend
 Will seek me, for my lady doth refuse me,
And thither shall my wish my way to wend,
 If ever thus despitefully she use me.
On me she frowningly her brow doth bend,
For why? My love to her hath ne'er an end.
 But of no other crime can she accuse me.[3]

Male troubadours placed women on pedestals and worshiped them from afar. Women troubadours took a different line. Women's poems are more realistic, more human, more emotionally satisfying. Castellozza (b. ca. 1200), the southern French wife of a Crusader, idealized not at all when she wrote these lines:

Friend, if you had shown consideration,
meekness, candor and humanity,
I'd have loved you without hesitation,
but you were mean and sly and villainous.

And she did not assign the active role exclusively to the man:

Handsome friend, as a lover true
I loved you, for you pleased me,
But now I see I was a fool,
for I've barely seen you since.[4]

Count William IX of Poitou (1071–1127) was among the first of the troubadours, and his daughter, Eleanor of Aquitaine, brought the conventions of this poetry and point of view to the French and Angevin courts. She and her daughters were the greatest literary patrons of the late twelfth century. The wives of kings and nobles who were frequently away from home maintained stunning courts and cultivated vernacular literature.

The courtly literature of northern France owed much to the troubadour tradition of the south but broke new ground in both forms and content. The romance and the lay were the chief new forms. Both drew on classical literature, the heroic Germanic past, and the Arthurian legends of the Celtic world to create stories of love and adventure. The romance usually develops a complex narrative involving several major characters over a long time. The lay is brief and focuses on a single incident. The most famous twelfth-century writer of romance was Chrétien de Troyes (1135–1183), the court writer of Marie of Champagne, a daughter of Eleanor of Aquitaine. The greatest writer of lays was Marie de France, who wrote at the Angevin court in the 1170s.

The romances and lays explore the contradictions and tensions in a variety of human relationships. Loyalty and honor make frequent appearances. Lancelot, a paragon of knightly virtue, loves desperately his lord Arthur's wife Guinivere. What is he to do? How can he be loyal to his lord, to his love, and to himself? What will he do when a single course of action brings both honor and dishonor? In the epics, speeches are made to swords, to horses, or sometimes to no one in particular; the points being made are universalized. In the romances, real, credible human beings struggle against powerful and conflicting emotional and moral ties. It can be said that never before in medieval literature was there so interesting a depiction of individuals trying at once to do what was expected of them and to do what they wanted.

Although the romances and lays were by no means the preserve of the elite, very little is known about popular literature. One possible exception is the mystery play, which made its first appearance in the eleventh century. The liturgy of the church, which formally re-enacted the life of Christ, was confined to the clergy. But this limitation did not prevent troupes of actors from

SPIRITUAL AND INTELLECTUAL LEADERS OF HIGH MEDIEVAL EUROPE

1135–1183	Chrétien de Troyes
1170–1221	Dominic
1177–1213	Mary of Oignies
1181–1226	Francis of Assisi
1194–1253	Clare of Assisi
1225–1274	Thomas Aquinas
1265–1321	Dante Alighieri

staging, on church porches or village greens, scenes from the life of Christ in simple, direct language. By the twelfth and thirteenth centuries, guilds in many towns sponsored the production of plays commemorating the Christian mysteries. Such plays became a form of popular entertainment as well as an interesting device for teaching elementary Christian ideas.

France led the way in the production of vernacular literature, but by the early thirteenth century centers of romantic poetry were flourishing in Germany and Italy. That French models did not inspire slavish imitation is proved by the master of all vernacular writers, Dante Alighieri (1265–1321).

Dante began as a poet in *la dolce stil nuova,* "the sweet new style" that came from France and captivated Italians. But he moved beyond it in many ways. Dante was a man of extraordinarily wide learning and reading. He served Florence in public capacities and became an exile amid political strife. He wrote a long treatise in defense of the empire—or, really, against the secular rule of the church. But he is best known for one of the masterpieces of world literature, the *Divine Comedy.*

The secret of the *Comedy*'s success is not easy to grasp. It is a long and difficult poem. But it is also humorous, instructive, and moving. In an exquisitely beautiful Italian, Dante took the most advanced theology and philosophy of his time, the richest poetic traditions, a huge hoard of stories, many contemporary events, and a lot of common sense and wove them into an allegorical presentation of the journey of the whole human race and of all people in their own lives.

Accompanied by the Roman poet Virgil, Dante travels through Hell and Purgatory, commenting along the way on the condition of the people he meets. Then, because Virgil is a pagan and only Dante's true love can accompany Dante into paradise, Beatrice, the love of Dante's youth, joins him for a visit to Heaven. The poet's central metaphor is love; the love he feels for Beatrice stands metaphorically for the love God feels for the world. Dante canvasses humanity from the pits of hell, which he reserved for deceivers, to the summit of paradise, where a man inspired by pure love might, despite his sinfulness, dare to look into the face of God.

Boniface VIII and Philip IV: Crisis of Church and State

The years at the turn of the fourteenth century were distinguished by a bitter and protracted controversy between the king of France and the pope. This dispute encapsulates the major themes and particular issues that are discussed in this chapter.

The Issues

In 1294 Philip IV of France and Edward I of England both attempted to collect taxes from the clergy of their respective countries. They were at war in both Flanders and Gascony, their treasuries empty, and their nobilities hostile. In 1296 Pope Boniface VIII (r. 1294–1303) issued the bull (letter) *Clericis laicos* forbidding the taxation of the clergy without explicit papal permission, thereby repeating a decree of the Fourth Lateran Council of 1215. Edward I complied, but Philip responded with a propaganda campaign against the pope in France that was designed to rally popular support for the monarchy. He also issued an edict that forbade the export to Rome of bullion, coin, and valuables from France, an act meant to pressure Boniface by depriving him of vast ecclesiastical revenues.

The king felt he could not permit any power outside France, certainly not one as politically changeable as the papacy, to dictate when he could go to war by denying him valuable sources of income. In 1297 Boniface backed down. In the bull *Etsi de statu* he said that in a dire emergency "the conscience of the king" could decide whether or not to tax the clergy without papal permission.

Philip's edict had affected Rome immediately because the greatest share of papal revenues came from France. Its impact was made all the greater by the precariousness of Boniface's position. An able, intelligent, experienced man, as pope he carried out many important reforms. But the circumstances surrounding Boniface's election were questionable, because his predecessor Celestine V (r. 1294) had resigned to return to a monastery. No other pope had ever resigned (and none has since), and it was not clear whether doing so was strictly legal. Moreover, although Boniface came from an old, rich, powerful family, he was the mortal enemy of several equally well-placed families. Roman factions saw in the dispute with France a fine opportunity to attack the pope.

In 1297 Boniface canonized as a saint Philip's grandfather, Louis IX, implying a reconciliation between Paris and Rome. In 1300 Boniface declared a jubilee year, and Rome was filled with pilgrims, many of them French, and with joyous celebrations. The pope was working hard all the while to heal the rift between France and England so that the resources and energies of Europe could once again be directed against the Muslims. Boniface still envisioned a militant and unified Christian Europe, with him at its leadership, going forth against the enemies of the faith.

In these circumstances, in 1301, Philip IV hauled a minor French bishop before the royal court on charges of heresy, blasphemy, and treason. Perhaps naively, he asked Boniface to concur. Instead, the pope sent the bull *Ausculta, fili carissime* to France. Its language was conciliatory but its message firm: No layman, not even the king of France, should dare to sit in judgment of a prelate of the church. Boniface also summoned the bishops of France to a council to investigate the whole matter. Boniface's actions challenged Philip's authority in two ways. They implied that a power outside France could judge the actions of the French king and limit what he could do inside France. Philip's actions threatened the plenitude of papal power in the church and in Western society.

Philip mounted another propaganda campaign. One of his publicists wrote, "You, noble king, by inheritance above all other princes defender of the faith and destroyer of heretics, can, ought, and are obliged to require and so arrange that the said Boniface be held and judged as an heretic."[5] The spread of lay literacy gave more people access to, and an understanding of, the issues involved in this controversy. Philip called a council of his own to decide if the pope was a heretic. Meanwhile, the pope's enemies in Rome, and also some clergy, were accusing the pope of heresy and questioning the legitimacy of his election.

Pope Boniface VIII This contemporary statue of Boniface by the sculptor and architect Arnolfo di Cambio (d. ca. 1302), who did the original design for Florence's cathedral, depicts this most troubled of popes in majesty. Boniface had enemies, but admirers, too. (*Alinari/Mansell*)

The Outcome

Boniface pressed ahead and held his council in 1302. Few French bishops, and none from the north of France, attended. The council issued the bull *Unam sanctam.* Though fully rooted in the statements of popes going back to Gregory VII, *Unam sanctam* is the most blatant manifesto of papal triumphalism ever issued. Its argument was quite simple. Church and society are one, and the pope is the sole head. Philip responded by sending royal officials to Rome. They joined forces with Boniface's Roman foes and a gang of thugs and then seized and beat the pope at Anagni, his summer residence. Boniface died three weeks later.

A comparison is instructive. Think of Henry IV, shivering in the snow beneath the walls of Canossa castle, begging forgiveness from Gregory VII. Then think of a Roman mob and of the minions of the king of France physically abusing an 80-year-old pope. All of our sources for the events of 1077 are in Latin and were written by clerics. Many sources for the events of 1302 are in French and Italian and were written by laymen. Henry IV was advised by German nobles and members of his family. Philip IV was counseled by lawyers, trained to think of the grandeur of royal power.

Summary

Comparisons between the Europe of 1150 and that of 1300 are instructive both as reminders of what had happened and as suggestions of what was to come. In 1150 Germany was promising, but troubled. It reaped only the trouble. England and France showed great promise too, and they realized much of it. England developed a strong monarchy, a superb legal system, and a significant new institution, parliament. France produced a strong government, a royal saint, and European cultural leadership. But England and France were bitter rivals and had risked financial ruin to pursue their struggle. Foreign conflicts and the quest for funds threatened the position of the monarchy in each country.

The papacy entered the thirteenth century with the powerful Innocent III and departed with the humiliated Boniface VIII. Surely popes would no longer dictate to secular rulers as they had once done. But the church was still a formidable institution, and the pope was its head. Representative institutions seemed to be the order of the day, though as yet few people participated in them and their social and constitutional roles remained to be defined.

For centuries the countryside had driven economic change, but momentum had shifted to cities. Cathedral and monastic schools would never overtake universities, but universities had not spread much beyond England, France, and Italy. Gothic barely existed in 1150, and by 1300 it was about to develop a series of national forms. Scholasticism was just visible in the work of Anselm and Abelard but ascendant in Thomas Aquinas. As the fourteenth century dawned, people all over Europe had reasons to be both hopeful and anxious. They were, in fact, at the start of one of the most turbulent and creative periods in Western history.

Notes

1. Walter Map, *De Nugis Curialium,* 5.5, in John H. Mundy, *Europe in the High Middle Ages* (London: Longman, 1973), p. 387.
2. John Addington Symonds, *Wine, Women and Song: Medieval Latin Students' Songs* (reprint, New York: Cooper Square, 1966), p. 69.
3. James Bruce Ross and Mary Martin McLaughlin, *The Portable Medieval Reader* (New York: Viking, 1949), p. 505.
4. Meg Bogin, *The Women Troubadours* (New York: Norton, 1976), p. 69.
5. Mundy, *Europe in the High Middle Ages,* p. 585.

Suggested Reading

General Surveys

Barber, Malcolm. *The Two Cities: Medieval Europe, 1050–1320.* 1992. Readable, comprehensive, and reliable, this book is an excellent starting point for further explorations.

Mundy, John H. *Europe in the High Middle Ages, 1150–1309.* 1973. A detailed and comprehensive introduction that is readable, witty, and sophisticated.

National Histories

Abulafia, David. *Frederick II: A Medieval Emperor.* 1988. The author's intention is to replace the mythical Frederick with a credible, medieval character.

Arnold, Benjamin. *Count and Bishop in Medieval Germany.* 1991. An exceptionally readable book that gets right to the heart of German local politics and of why it was so hard for kings to build up centralized rule.

Baldwin, John W. *The Government of Philip Augustus: Foundations of French Royal Power in the Middle Ages.* 1986. Massive and detailed yet readable and interesting, this book lays bare how the Capetian system really worked.

Brentano, Robert. *Rome Before Avignon: A Social History of Thirteenth-Century Rome.* 1974. Beautifully written, this book makes the reader feel as if he or she were walking the streets of Rome.

Haverkamp, Alfred. *Medieval Germany, 1056–1273.* 2d ed. 1992. Covering every aspect of German life, this book is the best introduction available in English to the complex history of Germany.

Holt, J. C. *Magna Carta.* 2d ed. 1992. Since its appearance, this has been the standard introduction to the charter and all its problems.

Munz, Peter. *Frederick Barbarossa: A Study in Medieval Politics.* 1969. An entertaining book that is sensitive more to political realities than to abstract theoretical problems.

Nicholas, David. *Medieval Flanders.* 1992. Detailed and comprehensive, this authoritative book introduces a region often mentioned but usually not studied in detail. Offers striking contrasts with Italian developments.

Richard, Jean. *Saint Louis: Crusader King of France.* 1992. The fruit of a lifetime's work by a leading French medievalist, this book is both a detailed account of Louis's life and a compelling introduction to his age.

Strayer, Joseph R. *The Reign of Philip the Fair.* 1980. A half-century in the making, this book is part biography and part analytical history of an age.

Turner, Ralph V. *Men Raised from the Dust: Administrative Service and Upward Mobility in Angevin England.* 1988. A set of six biographies of royal officials, this book provides an interesting explanation of who made the English government work.

VanCaenegem, R. C. *The Birth of the English Common Law.* 2d ed. 1989. Written by a legal historian with a gift for clarity of presentation, this book provides immediate access to perhaps England's greatest legacy to the West.

Warren, W. L. *Henry II.* 1973. The standard biography of the great Angevin, this book is comprehensive, detailed, readable, and entertaining.

Society and Economy

Baker, Derek, ed. *Medieval Women.* 1978. A superb collection of individual essays, some biographical, some analytical, covering the whole medieval period. Unusually coherent and interesting for a collection.

Boswell, John. *Christianity, Social Tolerance, and Homosexuality: Gay People in Western Europe from the Beginning of the Christian Era to the Fourteenth Century.* 1980. Valuable and readable for its own story, this book also shows the consequences for one group of the church's growing awareness of and opposition to differentness.

Keen, Maurice. *Chivalry.* 1984. Among many, many books on this subject, Keen's can be recommended for its balance, readability, and reliability.

Mollat, Michel. *The Poor in the Middle Ages: An Essay in Social History.* 1986. A nice mix of social analysis and theoretical observation, Mollat's book is engaging and instructive.

Shahar, Shulamith. *Childhood in the Middle Ages.* 1990. As in her book on women (see next entry), the author concentrates on the high and late middle Ages in this interesting, readable, memorable book.

———. *The Fourth Estate: A History of Women in the Middle Ages.* 1983. Comprehensive and detailed but less interesting than its subject would suggest, this book slights the early Middle Ages but is solid on the high and late periods.

Religion and the Church

Bynum, Caroline Walker. *Jesus as Mother: Studies in the Spirituality of the High Middle Ages.* 1982. A collection of sparkling essays by a major historian that makes the feminine in religious thought accessible, even central, to any discussion of medieval religion.

Lambert, Malcolm. *Medieval Heresy: Popular Movements from the Gregorian Reform to the Reformation.* 2d ed. 1992. Brilliant and readable, this book is the best history of medieval heresy ever written and one of the best books on medieval religion generally.

Little, Lester K. *Religious Poverty and the Profit Economy in Medieval Europe.* 1978. Readable and entertaining, this book seeks to connect religious, social, and economic ideas ranging from poverty to usury to anti-Semitism.

Moore, R. I. *The Origins of European Dissent.* 1985. A stimulating and sympathetic account of the origins and nature of heretical movements.

Morris, Colin. *The Papal Monarchy; The Western Church from 1050 to 1250.* 1989. Very thorough and detailed, this up-to-date history by a mature scholar is a good starting point for almost any inquiry into ecclesiastical history. Useful bibliography.

Riley-Smith, Jonathan. *The Crusades: A Short History.* 1987. The Crusades have spawned a massive literature. This is by far the best introduction, and its useful bibliography points to the detailed works.

Weighing the Evidence

THE ARTS OF CHARTRES CATHEDRAL

"Images exist so that the unlettered may read in pictures what the lettered read in books." These words of Pope Gregory I provided for a thousand years one justification for Christian representational art. Remember that the Hebrews, and the Arabs after them, forbade such representations. And the Byzantine world suffered through a tumultuous quarrel over sacred art. Nevertheless, Christian art was one of the crowning achievements of the Middle Ages.

Medieval artists attempted to portray biblical stories and theological ideas in paintings, glass, and stone. Before the thirteenth century, paintings were usually confined to books and were seen by very few people. Glass existed in early medieval and Romanesque churches but came into its own in Gothic churches. Sculpture began to appear on the façades of Romanesque churches but achieved unprecedented harmony and beauty on Gothic cathedrals. Unlike manuscript paintings, cathedral arts were public and visible to everyone. They were indeed "Bibles for the poor," as many have called them from the Middle Ages to the present.

But, despite Gregory's assurances, can we actually believe that ordinary, uneducated people—or even professional people who lacked theological training—"read" the statues on the front of a building like Chartres cathedral, whose western portals are shown here? Probably not. In fact, art historians believe that the arts of a cathedral functioned as just one part of a cycle of local teaching, preaching, and celebrating that, taken as a whole, communicated fundamental Christian truths to people and then reaffirmed those truths every time the artistic representations were viewed. Thus the modern historian who wishes to understand the arts of a medieval building must research what was known and taught in a given place at a given time. Some themes are consistent from one place or time to another, but often we find significant differences.

The west front of the cathedral of Notre-Dame ("Our Lady") of Chartres, called the "Royal Portal" because Christ in majesty appears over the central door and because Chartres had associations with the kings of France, tells the story of Christ and his redemption of humanity. The story must be read as a whole and then in detail—right, left, and center.

Notice the twenty-four column-like figures adjoining the three doors. Representations of kings and prophets of the Old Testament, they symbolize the human and spiritual ancestors of Christ. Over the heads of these figures you can see a continuous frieze that tells the Gospel story of the life of Christ.

Now look at the tympanum (large panel) over the door on the right. It shows Mary giving birth, Mary presenting Jesus in the temple, and Mary sitting on a throne with the baby Jesus on her lap. The archivolts—the rows of sculpture surrounding the tympanum—portray figures representing the seven liberal arts. Thus the incarnation of Christ is depicted and interpreted as something that not even all the wisdom of the world is able to grasp.

Turn now to the left door, where Christ is shown ascending to heaven. Beneath him, angels bring promise of a final judgment to the apostles waiting below. The archivolts around Christ contain signs of the zodiac and the labors of the months (turn for comparison to the manuscript painting of the labors of the months on page 302). The scene on the left door teaches that Christ left behind the world of human activity and even the fixed universe created by God, his father. The promise of salvation is offered to humans because Christ suffered and died to redeem them.

Now look at the central door. Here you see Christ in majesty—a representation that art historians call a "Maiestas." The apostles, who teach about Christ, are below him, and figures from the Book of Revelation surround him. This scene provides a glimpse of heaven while reminding people of the judgment they will face.

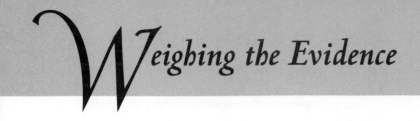

Chartres Cathedral, Western Façade *(Sonia Halliday)*

Historians can connect cathedrals to major cultural trends. For example, written sources tell us that a dramatic upswing in popular devotion to Mary occurred in the twelfth and thirteenth centuries. Artwork devoted to Mary confirms this. These Marian devotions probably reflect women's increasing participation in the spiritual life of the High Middle Ages. By holding up to women the image of pure, maternal, submissive Mary, the church may have been trying to control the excesses of female piety.

Historians also learn about social and economic realities from a study of cathedrals and their arts. The years after about 1140 saw tremendous competition among towns to build larger, finer, more elaborately decorated churches. Chartres sat in the middle of France's greatest grain-growing region, and the rising town had important textile, weapons, and harness manufacturers. It could well afford to rebuild and redecorate the west front in the 1140s and 1150s, and then rebuild the rest of the church after a fire destroyed it in 1194.

The sculpted stone of Chartres can even reveal its secrets to chemists. Specialists can test the stone of Chartres to see where it was quarried. This leads to research into stone-quarrying techniques and research into the methods and finances of transport.

The arts of Chartres also show the interconnectedness of medieval culture. At least three sculptors worked on the western front. One of them also worked at St.-Denis in Paris and another at Étampes in Normandy. The artistic models for Chartres are to be sought in Provence, Burgundy, and Paris.

Look at other examples of medieval art in this book, and see what you can make of them. Do you know enough of biblical history and Christian theology to "read" these images? Can you think of connections between Chartres and medieval France beyond those cited here?

Art and Ideas

Bony, Jean. *French Gothic Architecture of the Twelfth and Thirteenth Centuries.* 1983. Huge, clearly presented, and magnificently illustrated, this is a browser's book as well as a sustained essay by a master of his subject.

Haren, Michael. *The Western Intellectual Tradition from Antiquity to the Thirteenth Century.* 1985. Comprehensive yet brief, readable, and nontechnical, this book is an excellent introduction to Christian philosophy and theology that acknowledges and explains Jewish and Arab contributions.

Jantzen, Hans. *High Gothic: The Classic Cathedrals of Chartres, Reims and Amiens.* 1984. In the voluminous and technically daunting literature on Gothic, this little book can be recommended for clarity, readability, and reliability.

Le Goff, Jacques. *The Medieval Imagination.* 1985. Challenging but rewarding, these essays by a leading historian try to evoke the mental world of a wide array of medieval people.

Mâle, Emile. *The Gothic Image: Religious Art in the France of the Thirteenth Century.* 1958. Since its publication in 1913, this book has attracted admirers and critics. No one doubts its brilliance, readability, or enduring value.

Morris, Colin. *The Discovery of the Individual, 1050–1200.* 1972. Brief and readable, Morris's book has set off much controversy about the definition of individualism and the time of its first appearance in Europe.

Shaver-Crandell, Anne. *Cambridge Introduction to the History of Art: The Middle Ages.* 1982. Brief, carefully illustrated, and clearly written for the nonspecialist, this is an excellent starting point for the student of medieval art and architecture.

CHAPTER 12

The Late Medieval Crisis in Government and Society

In the fourteenth century Europeans sang an old Franciscan hymn, "Day of Wrath, Day of Burning," which described the fear and disorder that would accompany the end of the world and God's judgment of the saved and the damned. The flood, fire, war, and pestilence popularly thought to accompany the final days were certainly prevalent at that time. The end of the Middle Ages (ca. 1300–1500) is often described as a period of continued crisis and decline that brought to an end the growth and expansion of the previous three centuries. In truth, however, the period witnessed both dislocation and growth. In this chapter we discuss the roots of the crisis in the fourteenth century. The economic, social, and political recovery in the fifteenth century is the subject of Chapter 13. The cultural and intellectual changes that accompanied the crisis and recovery are the focus of Chapter 14.

The crises that burdened Europeans were military, political, religious, economic, and social. Between 1337 and 1453, France and England fought what was in effect a world war. The "Hundred Years' War" was primarily fought over English claims to traditionally French lands. At times, however, the German emperor and the kings of Aragon and Castile were drawn into the conflict. Social and political disruptions and the economic burdens of the war allowed the nobles of England and France to limit royal power and made local administration more difficult.

Problems were not simply military or confined to England and France. By 1300 the monarchies, the city-states of Italy, and the papacy had the legal systems, tax structures, and traditions of representation that were to be the

Plunder of the house of a wealthy Paris merchant. From an early-fourteenth-century manuscript.

foundations of modern European government and representative institutions. Here too problems arose that called into question ideas of strong central control. Aristocrats in many parts of Europe challenged the hereditary rights of their rulers. In the towns of Germany and Italy, the patrician classes moved to reduce the influence of artisans and laborers in government, instituting oligarchies or even aristocratic dictatorships in place of more democratic governments.

Questions of power and representation also affected the Christian church as ecclesiastical claims to authority came under attack. Secular governments challenged church jurisdictions. Disputed papal elections led to schism, a split between rival centers of control in Rome and Avignon (a city in what is now the south of France). In dealing with the schism and with more general problems of moral reform, the church hierarchy was challenged by those who argued that authority resided in the whole church and not just with its head, the pope. In the aftermath of the crisis, the church was forced to redefine its place in both the religious and political life of Europe.

A series of economic and demographic shocks worsened political and religious problems. In many respects the fourteenth and early fifteenth centuries marked a pause between the growth and expansion of the high Middle Ages and the growth that was to mark the sixteenth century. Part of the problem was structural: The population of Europe was too great to be supported by the resources available. But the economic decline caused by overpopulation could not be ended because of outbreaks of bubonic plague, which began in 1348. In almost every aspect of political, religious, and social life, the fourteenth and early fifteenth centuries marked a pause in the developments that had characterized the previous century and a half.

England, France, and the Hundred Years' War

A lawyer of King Philip IV of France (r. 1285–1314) observed that "everything within the limits of his kingdom belongs to the lord king, especially protection, high justice and dominion."[1] The political climate of the late twelfth and thirteenth centuries clearly favored the lawyer's claim. Royal officials in England and France generally believed that "liberties"—that is, individual rights to local jurisdictions—originated with the king. But much of the aristocracy in England and France held a contrary view, which limited the king's prerogatives.

When the English king Edward I (r. 1272–1307) instituted his *Quo warranto* proceedings investigating quite literally "by what warrant," or title, individuals claimed jurisdiction in various parts of the realm, he demanded that nobles produce a written charter by which a king had authorized their power. When the earl of Warenne was interviewed, he brandished an old, rusty long-sword and responded to royal officials, "Here, my lords, is my warrant. My ancestors came with William the Bastard [that is, with William the Conqueror in 1066] and conquered their lands with the sword, and by the sword I will defend them against anyone who tries to usurp them."[2] The old earl clearly believed that the rights and traditions of the aristocracy limited even royal attempts to centralize authority.

In the fourteenth and early fifteenth centuries, the old earl's sword rather than the lawyer's brief set the tone of politics in England and France. In that period two English kings would be deposed and murdered, and countless individuals would lose their lives in the series of conflicts now known as the "Hundred Years' War." Internal developments in England and France and the stages of the war itself demonstrate the practical limits of medieval government.

Government in England and France in the Fourteenth Century

Thirteenth-century England appeared to be the very model of a late medieval monarchy. Since the reign of Henry II (r. 1154–1189), English kings had claimed the right to collect subsidies or taxes to administer civil and criminal law in all parts of the monarchy. In France royal rights to taxes and rights of jurisdictions were less well established, but there too, since the reign of Philip II Augustus (r. 1180–1223), royal power had grown steadily. In the fourteenth century matters changed. Philip VI of France died without heirs, and his successor soon faced a long war that brought into question the king's control of most of France. And in England after the death of Edward I in 1307, monarchs found their power limited by forces beyond their control. Fears arising from the growing power of the Crown and the weakness of the king himself brought issues to a head during the reign of Edward II (r. 1307–1327).

In the fourteenth century, the English kings increasingly found themselves unable to control the financial and judicial machinery of their government. By the time of Edward II's accession in 1307, resident justices of the peace were replacing the expensive and inefficient eyre system of traveling justices (see page 403). In theory, they were royal officials doing the king's bidding. In reality, these unpaid local officials were modestly well-to-do gentry who were often clients of local magnates. Justices were known to use their office to carry out local vendettas and feuds and to protect the interests of the wealthy and powerful of their districts. Corrupt judges and sheriffs were a commonplace in popular literature and all too real in the counties of England.

The barons, however, were interested in controlling more than just local justices. Their concerns lay with the Crown as well. Fearing that Edward II would continue many of the centralizing policies of his father, the barons forced the king to accept the Ordinances of 1311, which required a greatly expanded role for Parliament, and especially for the baronage sitting in Parliament. According to the ordinances, the king could no longer wage war, leave the realm, grant lands or castles, or appoint chief justices and chancellors without the approval of the barons in Parliament. The ordinances also required the king to "live from his own patrimony"—that is, from the properties and rights belonging directly to the king. All special taxes or subsidies were to be paid to the public Exchequer rather than into the king's private household treasury. The ordinances stipulated that complaints of abuses by royal officials should be heard by a commission in Parliament. Finally, the ordinances required several of Edward's favorites to be banished from court.

Some of the ordinances were later voided, but the basic principle of parliamentary consent remained central to English constitutional history. In spite of Parliament's power to limit royal acts, kings used Parliament because it had the power to vote new taxes and generally did so when funds were necessary for the defense of the realm—a common occurrence during these centuries. Thus, Parliament grew in power because it usually did what the monarchy asked.

King as Judge People of the Middle Ages believed that jurisdiction and defense of the realm were the highest functions of a king. Philip the Fair called his barons to the court as witnesses to his trial of Robert of Artois. *(Bibliothèque Nationale)*

The barons succeeded in imposing the Ordinances of 1311 because Edward II was a weak and politically naive king. He was easily dominated by a number of adventurers who were widely believed to be the king's lovers. They quickly gained titles and influence through royal favor. The most infamous was Piers Gaveston, a knight from the French province of Gascony, to whom Edward granted the earldom of Cornwall. Jealous barons were able to force Gaveston into exile for a short time, but he soon returned and maintained the king's favor until his trial and execution in 1312. The death of Gaveston solved little. Edward quickly fell under the sway of Hugh Despenser, a knight whose father had been a trusted courtier of Edward I.

FRENCH AND ENGLISH SUCCESSION IN THE FOURTEENTH CENTURY

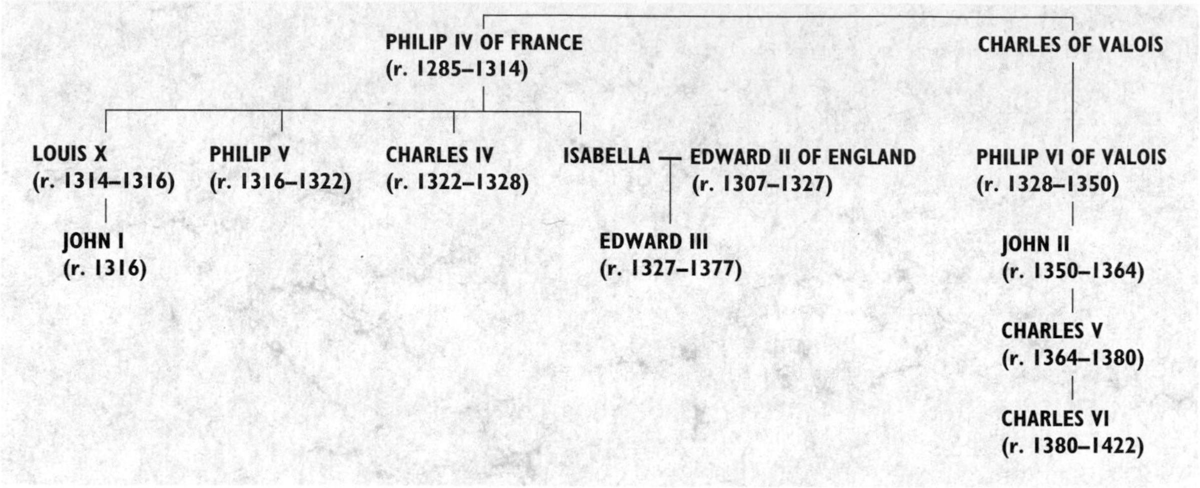

Despenser used his influence to marry the heiress to the duchy of Gloucester and begin the process of creating a personal empire in the south of Wales and of gaining wealth and power in other parts of the realm. While under Despenser's influence, Edward gradually sent most of Despenser's opponents into exile. Queen Isabella and the crown prince went to France, to the court of her brother King Charles IV, in order to negotiate a marriage and to get away from Edward's court. Edward's position steadily deteriorated until he was defeated and captured by a baronial army organized by the queen. After a short regency, his son Edward III (r. 1327–1377) assumed the throne. He was a cautious king, ever aware of the volatility of the baronage.

Observing the civil strife and open rebellion against the king that characterized England in the early fourteenth century, French thinkers prided themselves on the stability of the French monarchy. "The government of the earth," the royal lawyer Jean of Jandun proclaimed, "belongs rightly to the august and sovereign House of France." Nonetheless, the French monarchy in the early fourteenth century also found its prerogatives limited. As in England, there were institutional limits to the power of the kings; and again, as in England, these limits were compounded by events that were to lead to virtual civil war within the kingdom.

The limits of royal power in France were evident in the last years of the reign of Philip IV (d. 1314). Philip's problems will be clear if we compare the *Quo warranto* hearings of Edward I with the situation of Philip IV. Edward initiated the hearings to determine by what right English nobles could claim to hold jurisdictions and titles, implying that all rights ultimately derived from the king himself.

In France, even Philip IV thought of the kingdom of France in a significantly different way. When Philip inquired about his rights in particular areas, he was usually interested in specific economic and judicial claims. No French king could realistically make the English claim that all rights had originated in the person of the king. Although France in the early fourteenth century was the largest kingdom in Christendom, with a population of about 16 million, the king could claim direct jurisdiction over only a small portion of the total. In the villages and castles of the region of Rouergue, for example, the king held jurisdiction over 6090 households, and nobles in the area had rights over 20,412. The county of Flanders and the duchies of Brittany and Aquitaine were virtually autonomous. And the regions of Burgundy, Bourbon, Artois, and Evreux had been granted to the younger sons of the kings as appanages and were virtually autonomous. In all of these areas, justice, taxation, and the army remained in the hands of the local lords.

The French kings, unlike the English kings, did not have the right to collect taxes from all the inhabitants of the realm. To collect money, they had to negotiate individually with each town and each region. The whole process was clumsy and inefficient. And if a threat evaporated before the money was collected, the king could do little to force payment. In 1302, Philip IV called the first meeting of a representative assembly, the Estates General, to explain why he needed taxes for "the defense of the realm." Unfortunately for Philip, the Estates General could listen, but representatives had no authority to grant the taxes. Philip IV and later French kings had to negotiate.

Kings tended to concentrate their demands on the most vulnerable groups. Jews and Italian businessmen could be periodically banished from the kingdom and their assets seized. The king also preyed on relatively powerless or unpopular persons or even on churchmen who could be accused of treason or heresy—crimes whose punishment included the forfeiture of property. Also, kings in the fourteenth century used their right to mint coins to manipulate money to their own advantage. Throughout the fourteenth century, French kings resorted to debasement of currency as a way to solve some of their financial problems. To take one example, between 1295 and 1306 the silver content of French coinage declined by about two-thirds. Needless to say the devaluation of coinage and the expulsion of Italian and Jewish merchants had a profound effect on the French economy.

A series of relatively weak kings during the fourteenth century compounded the structural weaknesses of the French monarchy. Philip IV was succeeded by his three sons, each of whom died without a legitimate male heir. In 1328 the direct Capetian line, which had provided the kings of France since the election of Hugh Capet in 987, finally died out. The last Capetians did produce daughters, but since the fourteenth century it had been accepted that the French crown should pass through the male line only. Thus, the French nobility selected as king Philip of Valois, a cousin of the last king through the male line. He was chosen in preference to the daughters of the last kings and, more significantly, in preference to King Edward III of England, whose mother was the daughter of the late king Philip IV. Philip of Valois was Philip VI (r. 1328–1350).

The Origins of the Hundred Years' War

In 1340 Edward III of England formally claimed the title "king of France." As a grandson of Philip IV, he claimed he was the rightful heir of the last Capetian king. Although Edward's claim to the French throne was certainly part of the reason for the Hundred Years' War, the issue of the crown merely worsened diplomatic and political tensions between the two monarchies. The source of the problems was the long-standing claims of the English kings to territories in France, the fragmented nature of the French monarchy itself, and the volatile nature of international politics.

There were constant tensions in the border lands between Scotland and England (see page 313). When the English intervened in Scotland, as they did disastrously in 1314 and more successfully in the 1330s, the Scots appealed for French aid. Throughout the the late Middle Ages and in the sixteenth and seventeenth centuries, French kings were able to use the Scots' anti-English feeling to their own advantage. Matters in Flanders were more complex. The weaving trades in the large industrial cities of Flanders consumed large quantities of high-quality English wool. But Flemish towns could feed themselves only by importing foodstuffs from France. Both England and France tried to use struggles between the counts of Flanders and their subjects as a wedge against the other. Both Scottish and Flemish affairs fueled the mutual suspicions of the French and the English.

Henry III of England and Louis IX of France had hoped to lay aside the economic and territorial tensions between the two governments by the Treaty of Paris in 1259. In exchange for Henry's rights to traditional Angevin lands (Normandy, Anjou, Maine, Touraine, and Poitou), Saint Louis granted Henry rights to the duchy of Aquitaine, which Henry would hold as a vassal of the French king. Although the treaty had been designed to settle differences between the two monarchies, it created two insoluble problems. First, the French kings claimed that as dukes of Aquitaine, the English kings owed *liege homage*—that is, while kneeling before the French king, they had to swear to provide military aid when-

ENGLAND, FRANCE, AND THE HUNDRED YEARS' WAR

1259	Treaty of Paris grants Aquitaine to Henry III of England as a French fief
1311	English barons force Edward II to accept the Ordinances of 1311
1327	Parliament deposes Edward II
1328	The last Capetian king dies; French nobles elect Philip of Valois king of France (Philip VI)
1340	Edward III of England formally claims the French crown
1346	Battle of Crécy
1356	Battle of Poitiers
1399	Parliament deposes Richard II
1415	Battle of Agincourt
1420	Treaty of Troyes
1422	Charles VI of France and Henry V of England die
1431	Joan of Arc is tried and executed
1453	French armies capture Castillon-sur-Dordogne in the last battle of the Hundred Years' War

ever the French king asked for it. The French king could use liege homage to humiliate the English king and to limit English diplomatic relations with other kingdoms. Second, the treaty implied French sovereignty over Aquitaine, an area in which the French previously had enjoyed little influence. The king of England acknowledged that his duchy was part of France and accepted grudgingly the French claim that Henry's continental subjects had the right to appeal for justice to the French crown.

Relations between the French and the English monarchs finally broke down over the claims of the French monarchs to jurisdiction in Aquitaine and the south of France. In 1324 Charles IV built the fortified town of Saint-Sardos in a disputed border area considered by the English to be a part of their lands. The English destroyed the town's walls, prompting Charles to claim that the duchy of Aquitaine was forfeited to the French crown. The issue was settled in 1327, but suspicions about the ultimate interests of the two monarchs remained. The final straw was the French claim to hear legal appeals of decisions given in Aquitanian courts. To the French kings, these appeals were a normal part of the process of judicial centralization. To the English kings, they were an unacceptable attempt by the French kings to subvert the English monarch's exercise of his own legal jurisdiction and a sign that acknowledging French claims in Aquitaine had been a mistake. In frustration, Edward finally made his fateful claim to the French throne.

Conduct of the War

The Hundred Years' War was a series of short raids and expeditions punctuated by a few major battles and marked off by truces or ineffective treaties. The relative strengths of the two kingdoms dictated the sporadic nature of the struggle. France was far richer than England and had probably three times the population. On at least one occasion the French managed to field an army of over 50,000; at most the English mustered only 32,000. In almost every engagement the English were outnumbered. The most successful English strategy was to avoid pitched battles and engage in a series of quick raids during which they stole what they could, destroyed what they could not steal, and captured enemy knights to hold for ransom.

The war can be divided into four stages (Map 12.1). The first stage, from 1337 to 1360, was characterized by English raids led by the crown prince Edward, later called "the Black Prince" because of the black armor he once wore. The French army rarely prevented English incursions. The few pitched battles were resounding victories for the English, who took advantage of a chivalric ethos according to which, in the words of one French knight, "Who does the most is worth the most." French knights, because of their eagerness to prove their individual merit, were difficult to direct and control. The problem was clear in 1346, when King Philip managed to corner the English army at Crécy. Philip's mounted knights and his hired Genoese crossbowmen were no match for the carefully placed English longbowmen and dismounted knights. A crossbow is a slow but effective weapon when used

Ransoming Captives One English strategy during the first stages of the Hundred Years' War was seizing and ransoming French knights such as Charles of Blois, whose capture is illustrated here. *(Bibliothèque Nationale)*

from a protected position. Caught between rapidly firing English longbowmen and charging French knights who disrupted their position, the French crossbowmen could do little to protect the main part of their army. Driven from the field, the French could not prevent the English reoccupation of the port of Calais, which the English would continue to control until the sixteenth century. The battle of Crécy made the reputation of the crown prince Edward. He defeated and put to flight the cream of French chivalry. (See the box, "The Battle of Crécy.")

The French reformed and rebuilt their army but still were unable to defeat the English. King John of France (r. 1350–1364) intercepted the Black Prince at Poitiers in 1356. Again, a smaller English army in an excellent defensive position was able to use longbowmen to their best advantage. French knights, in their haste to catch up finally with the English army, again charged into a situation that did not favor mounted soldiers. By the end of the battle King John and many of France's most distinguished knights were captives. After long and tortuous negotiations, the French were forced to agree to the Treaty of Brétigny (1360), by which the English gained a ransom of 3 million crowns of gold (equal to the annual revenues of the king in a normal year) for the king and a formal recognition of English rights to Normandy, Maine, and Anjou as well as to the duchy of Aquitaine.

The treaty brought no peace. In the second stage of the war, from 1360 to 1396, the French managed to regain control of much of the land they had lost. The war spilled over into Spain and became truly international. The French allied themselves with Henry of Trastamara, half brother of King Peter "the Cruel" of Castile (r. 1350–1369), in an effort to open a second front against the English. The English, for their part, supported Peter. By the 1380s the war had turned decisively against the English. Edward III and his

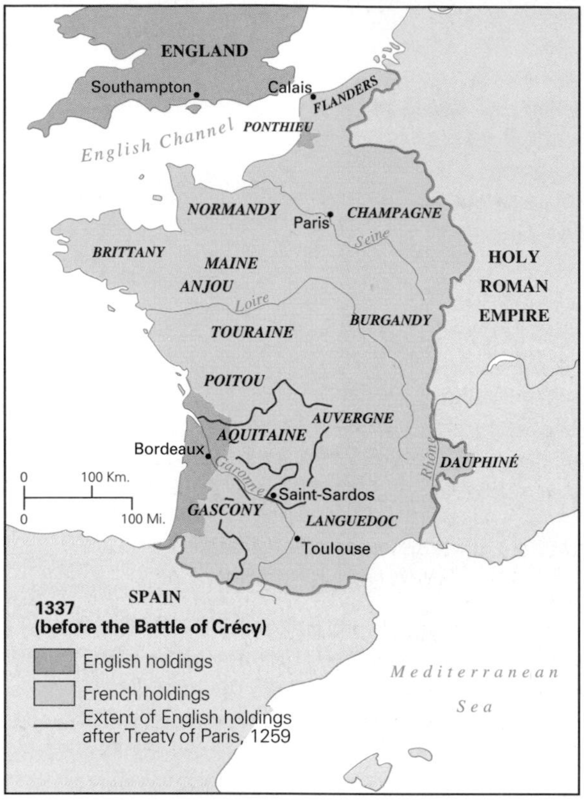
ENGLAND
Southampton
Calais
FLANDERS
PONTHIEU
English Channel
NORMANDY
Paris
CHAMPAGNE
Seine
BRITTANY
MAINE
ANJOU
Loire
HOLY ROMAN EMPIRE
TOURAINE
BURGANDY
POITOU
AUVERGNE
AQUITAINE
Bordeaux
Garonne
Rhône
DAUPHINÉ
0 100 Km.
0 100 Mi.
Saint-Sardos
GASCONY
LANGUEDOC
Toulouse
SPAIN
1337 (before the Battle of Crécy)
English holdings
French holdings
Extent of English holdings after Treaty of Paris, 1259
Mediterranean Sea

ENGLAND
Calais
FLANDERS
Crécy 1346
English Channel
Rouen
NORMANDY
Paris
CHAMPAGNE
Seine
BRITTANY
MAINE
ANJOU
Loire
HOLY ROMAN EMPIRE
BURGANDY
TOURAINE
Poitiers 1356
POITOU
AUVERGNE
AQUITAINE
Bordeaux
Garonne
Rhône
DAUPHINÉ
0 100 Km.
0 100 Mi.
GASCONY
LANGUEDOC
Toulouse
SPAIN
1360 (after the Battle of Poitiers)
English holdings
French holdings
Major battles
Mediterranean Sea

ENGLAND
Calais
FLANDERS
Agincourt 1415
HOLY ROMAN EMPIRE
English Channel
Rouen
Reims
NORMANDY
Paris
CHAMPAGNE
Seine
Domrémy
BRITTANY
MAINE
ANJOU
Orléans
Loire
Bourges
TOURAINE
DUCHY OF BURGUNDY
COUNTY OF BURGUNDY
POITOU
AUVERGNE
AQUITAINE
Bordeaux
Garonne
Rhône
DAUPHINÉ
0 100 Km.
0 100 Mi.
GASCONY
LANGUEDOC
Toulouse
SPAIN
ca. 1429 (after the siege of Orléans)
English holdings
French holdings
Burgundian lands allied with England to 1435
Major battle
Mediterranean Sea

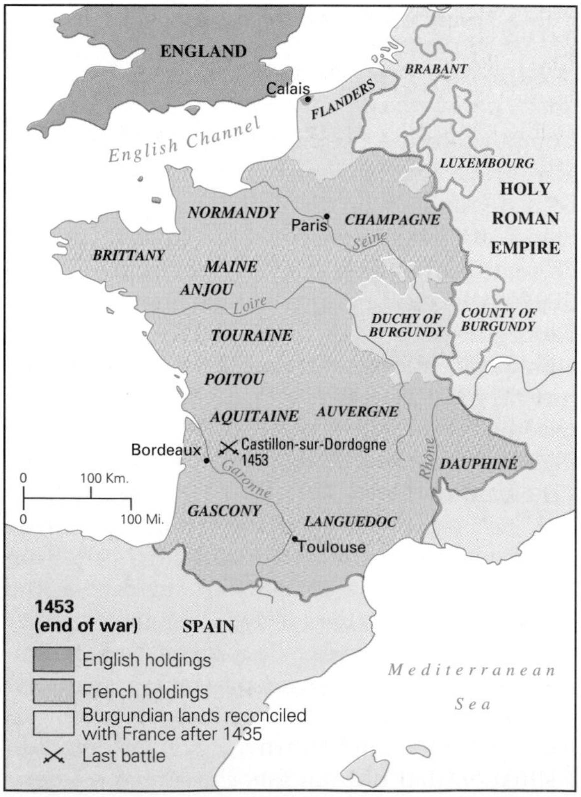
ENGLAND
BRABANT
Calais
FLANDERS
English Channel
LUXEMBOURG
HOLY ROMAN EMPIRE
NORMANDY
Paris
CHAMPAGNE
Seine
BRITTANY
MAINE
ANJOU
Loire
DUCHY OF BURGUNDY
COUNTY OF BURGUNDY
TOURAINE
POITOU
AQUITAINE
AUVERGNE
Bordeaux
Castillon-sur-Dordogne 1453
Garonne
Rhône
DAUPHINÉ
0 100 Km.
0 100 Mi.
GASCONY
LANGUEDOC
Toulouse
1453 (end of war)
SPAIN
English holdings
French holdings
Burgundian lands reconciled with France after 1435
Last battle
Mediterranean Sea

The Battle of Crécy

Jean Froissart (1337–1400) was born into a mercantile family in the county of Hainault, which is now part of France. He became a courtier famed for his verse and eventually for this chronicle, which embodied the highest ideals of late medieval chivalry.

[In pursuit of the English, the king of France finally caught up with them at Crécy.] The king commanded a halt. . . . At this command the leaders halted, but those behind continued to advance saying that they would not stop until they had caught up with the front ranks. . . . Each wanted to outshine his companions, with the disastrous consequences of which you shall shortly hear. . . .

The English, who were drawn up in their three divisions and sitting quietly on the ground, got up with perfect discipline when they saw the French approaching and formed their ranks, with the archers in harrow-formation [concentrated like the spikes on a harrow or rake with the setting sun at their backs] and the men-at-arms behind. . . . [King] Philip came near the place where the English were and saw them, his blood boiled, for he hated them. Nothing now could stop him from giving battle. . . . The Genoese [crossbowmen in the French army] having been marshalled into proper order and made to advance, began to utter loud whoops to frighten the English. The English waited in silence and did not stir. The Genoese hulloa'ed a second time and advanced a bit further, but the English still made no move. Then they raised a third shout, very loud and clear, levelled their crossbows and began to shoot. At this the English archers took one pace forward and poured out their arrows on the Genoese so thickly and evenly that they fell like snow. When they felt those arrows piercing their arms, their heads, their faces, the Genoese, who had never met such archers before, were thrown into confusion.

Source: Jean Froissart, *Chronicles*, trans. and ed. Geoffrey Brereton (New York: Penguin, 1968), pp. 85–95.

son the Black Prince were both dead; the French had taken back much of the land the English had conquered; and the daring English raids no longer produced quick and easy profits. Edward III's grandson Richard II (r. 1377–1399) could not afford the expensive French war and in 1396 signed an unpopular truce. Three years later he was deposed; he died, probably murdered, a year later.

The most fateful shift occurred in the third stage, from 1396 to 1422. Effective French resistance to the English was almost impossible. King Charles VI (r. 1380–1422) of France suffered bouts of insanity throughout his long reign. When he was incapacitated, government practically halted, and political power fell into the hands of dukes of Burgundy and of Orléans, whose political maneuvering led to civil war in France. In 1407, Duke John "the Fearless" of Burgundy assassinated Duke Louis of Orléans, the leader of an anti-Burgundian faction. In response, the Armagnacs, members of the Orléanist faction, began what would be almost thirty years of civil war, during which the French kings remained hostages to one or another faction.

With the aid of the Burgundian factions, the English king Henry V (r. 1413–1422) renewed his family's claim to the French throne. At Agincourt

Map 12.1 England and France in the Hundred Years' War The succession of maps depict both why hit-and-run tactics worked for the English early in the war and why the English were ultimately unable to defeat the French and take control of all of France.

in 1415, the English (led this time by Henry) again enticed a larger French army into attacking a fortified English position, and again a hail of arrows from English longbows shattered the advance. After this brilliant victory, Henry largely abandoned hit-and-run tactics and tried to hold and govern large sections of France. With Burgundian aid, he gained control over Normandy, Paris, and much of northern France. By the terms of the Treaty of Troyes (1420), Henry was to marry Catherine, the daughter of Charles VI, and become the heir to the French throne. A final English victory seemed assured, but both Charles VI and Henry V died in 1422, leaving the infant Henry VI (r. 1422–1461) as heir.

The kings' deaths ushered in the final stage of the war, the French reconquest, from 1422 to 1453. Because the English now claimed to rule France, they could no longer use a strategy of quick raids and profitable ransoming of prisoners. They had to hold the land, and this they could not do.

In 1428, military and political power seemed firmly in the hands of the English and the great aristocrats. Charles VI's successor, the dauphin (or crown prince) Charles, was derisively called "the king of Bourges," after the town south of the Loire where he remained under the protection and virtual control of the Armagnacs. Yet in a stunning series of events, the French were able to reverse the situation. After 1429, they defeated the English, won over the French nobility, and took firm charge of public life in the kingdom. Although part of the transformation resulted from innovations in government, the primary change was the result of a fortunate turn of events.

In 1429, the king with the aid of the mysterious Joan of Arc (d. 1431) was able to raise the English siege of Orléans and begin the reconquest of the north of France. Joan was the daughter of prosperous peasants. Like other late medieval mystics she reported regular visions of divine revelation. Her "voices" told her to go to the king and aid him in driving out the English. For a few months Joan of Arc was the most influential personality at the court of the dauphin Charles. Dressed as a man, she was Charles's most charismatic and feared military leader. She pushed the English and Burgundian forces back toward Paris. With Joan's aid the king was crowned in the cathedral at Reims, the traditional site of French coronations. She was captured during an audacious attack on Paris itself. Charles, however, refused to ransom "the Maid," as she was known, and eventually she fell into English hands. Because of her "unnatural dress" and her claim to divine illumination, she was condemned and burned as a heretic in 1431. A heretic only to the English and their supporters, Joan almost instantly became a symbol of French resistance. Pope Calixtus III reversed the condemnation in 1456; and in 1920 she was canonized: The heretic became Saint Joan, patron of France.

Over the next six years Charles moved against English and Burgundian strongholds. He reorganized his army. At the heart of his forces were paid companies recruited and controlled by his own officers rather than organized by mercenary captains. In the face of growing royal strength, the Burgundians ended hostilities by signing the Treaty of Arras in 1435. The English rejected similar terms; but without allies, they were unable to mount a credible threat to Charles. By 1450 the English had lost all their major centers except Calais. In 1453, the French armies captured the fortress of Castillon-sur-Dordogne in what was to be the last battle of the war. There was no treaty, only a cessation of hostilities.

Impact of the War

The war touched almost every aspect of life in late medieval Europe. It ranged beyond the borders of France as at various times Scotland, Castile, Aragon, and German principalities were drawn into the struggle. French and English support for rival popes prevented early settlement of the Great Schism in the papacy (see page 454). The war and the financial strain of recruiting and paying for armies disrupted the Flemish woolen industry and drained many parts of Europe of capital needed for business investment. The war brought in its wake a rising sense of national feeling in both England and France. It broke the traditional connection between the English and French titled nobilities. In 1300 a large number of the English barons were French in language and origin. By the fifteenth century that was no longer the case. What Edward had begun as a war to retain rights to his family's traditional lands had ended as a foreign war.

By 1400, Anglo-French had ceased to be the language of the English court. Alongside chivalric romances, which owed a great deal to French models, writers in English produced works that had strong social and ethical messages and were firmly anchored in English life. These authors wrote for the literate inhabitants of English towns as well as for the courtiers who surrounded the king and the barons. The greatest of these authors was Geoffrey Chaucer (1340?–1400), the son of a London burgher, who served as a diplomat, courtier, and member of Parliament. Chaucer's *Canterbury Tales* recount the stories told by pilgrims on their way to the shrine of Saint Thomas Becket at Canterbury. The pilgrims and the stories they tell are witty and realistic comments on English society in the late Middle Ages. Typical is the Wife of Bath: "She was a worthy woman all her life, husbands at the churchdoor she had five." After describing her own five marriages, she makes the point that marriage is a proper way to achieve moral perfection, but it can be so only if the woman is master.

War changed the way Frenchmen understood royal rights. A key to French military successes had been the creation of a paid professional army, which replaced the feudal host and mercenary companies of the fourteenth century. The French had come to accept the necessity of regular taxation to raise and maintain a large military force. In the wake of the devastation brought by the English to various parts of France, Frenchmen appealed to royal judicial officials in settling conflicting claims for damages. France was now much more unified than it had been in the opening decades of the fourteenth century.

A final result of the war was a general rise in the level of violence in society. As Henry V casually observed, "War without fire is as bland as sausages without mustard."[3] And because of the highly profitable quick raids, English soldiers ate well. Villages in some parts of France had been sacked and burned every five years. English kings had raised armies by granting pardons to convicted felons who would agree to serve in the king's army. Many who accepted the pardon returned to their native villages looking for revenge against those who had convicted them. And soldiers who did serve often found themselves unpaid during periods of truce. At those times they went in search of work as mercenaries in other parts of Europe. The English mercenary Sir John Hawkwood (d. 1394), finished his life as "ser Giovanni Acuto," a heralded military captain for the Italian city of Florence. Other mercenary captains pillaged freely across Europe. One, a defrocked French priest, specialized in kidnapping municipal officials or even laying siege to entire towns in order to extort money. Truces did not necessarily mean peace in fourteenth-century Europe.

Political Instability in Other States

Political stability, as the Hundred Years' War demonstrated, was not simply an issue of strong versus weak rulers. Several issues slowed the growth of centralized governments and heightened political instability throughout Europe.

Joan of Arc There are no surviving contemporary pictures of Joan, but this sixteenth-century manuscript illumination of Joan as a leader, dressed in armor, shows her as the patriotic symbol of French independence she had become. *(Musée Archéologique Thomas Dobrée/Giraudon/Art Resource)*

Limits on Political Power

No monarch could claim to hold absolute authority. Whether because of financial constraints, legal theory that stated that issues must be approved by those they involve, or a thesis that kings had natural advisers, every king found his powers limited in critical ways by the political community. In the early fourteenth century, military operations depended on money, not on unpaid traditional or feudal voluntary hosts. Across Europe military expenses were devastating. Ten years of war between England and France (1293–1303) cost each side about £1.4 to 1.7 million, at a time when annual income from the king's patrimony in England was normally about £30,000. No king was able to raise the special taxes necessary to pay these expenses, even for defense, without the approval of those who would be expected to pay. English monarchs were able to raise funds through a system of lay subsidies by which all inhabitants of England could be expected to give payments in lieu of actual service. But they had to call a Parliament to do so, and Parliament often demanded concessions before it would grant new taxes. In most other parts of Europe, the right to extraordinary taxes was an issue of debate at the national or provincial level. Times of fiscal or military crisis thus offered the opportunity to wring significant concessions out of a monarch.

It was generally accepted that whoever was affected by a government had the right to approve that government's acts. In Scandinavia and Germany, for example, members of the nobility or even provincial assemblies had the right to acclaim or even elect kings. Part of the English political crisis of the 1320s centered on the complaints of the barons that they, the king's natural advisers, had been frozen out of Edward II's court. Swedish kings in the fourteenth century often heard similar complaints. In the second half of the fourteenth century, representative institutions like the English Parliament, the French Estates General, and the various cortes of the Iberian Peninsula were increasingly called into session. In many countries the nobility, townsmen, and even the peasantry could and did claim the right to sit in these assemblies. Monarchs valued representative institutions as vehicles for the approval of special taxes and as a focus for propaganda. Representatives sitting in these bodies valued the institutions as a locus for airing the grievances of the community.

Royal lawgivers often found themselves restricted in two ways: Certain provinces or territories claimed immunities from interference by a central government; and, because of the expense involved or for political reasons, monarchs often found themselves dependent on unpaid local or regional magnates—the very people the central government needed to control. The issues were raised in most parts of Europe. In Germany many local courts followed their own legal traditions and were immune from imperial oversight. One of the most important acts by a new emperor was the acknowledging of the varieties of immunities and rights that belonged to towns and members of the nobility. In England, arguably the most centralized of the medieval kingdoms, unpaid provincial justices of the peace were usually local gentry as strongly tied to the local nobility as to the king. And to most people the right to judge also implied the right to tax—and the cost of the one often outweighed the benefits of the other.

Joan of Arc's early visions may have urged her to "go to France," yet national feeling or nationalism is a slippery concept that developed very slowly. Rather than speaking of "England," for example, in the late thirteenth and fourteenth centuries it is more proper to speak of a "Plantagenet Empire" that included England, Wales, Ireland, and Aquitaine in southern France. In Germany various institutions could call themselves "of the German Nation," yet people described themselves as speaking Austrian or Bavarian and not German. People in southern France did not consider themselves part of a French monarchy, and their language was not commonly understood in Paris. The same points can generally be made for the rest of Christian Europe. Nationalism and national feeling may be a result of the unrest of the fourteenth century, but they were hardly evident at the beginning of the period.

Spain

The Reconquista conducted by the Christian kingdoms of Portugal, Castile, and Aragon left virtually the whole Iberian Peninsula in Christian hands by the middle of the thirteenth century (see Map 10.4, page 375). Only the tiny kingdom

Baptism of the Moors Although Spain was a land with three religions, the Christian rulers of the peninsula believed that conversion of Muslims and Jews would eventually make the country a Christian society. Increasingly in the Late Middle Ages, baptisms were coerced. *(Jean Dieuzaid, Toulouse)*

of Granada remained a Muslim stronghold. The expansion of Castile in the south cut off the Aragonese from contact with the Moorish frontier and from the possibilities of further expansion and brought the Christian governments into an uneasy confrontation. Cooperation among the Christian kings was possible only when faced by a direct threat of Muslim invasion.

Castile was by far the largest and most powerful of the kingdoms. Under Alfonso XI (r. 1312–1350) and Peter I (r. 1350–1369), Castilians solidified their position as the dominant power on the peninsula. Aided by the French and the papacy, Castilian forces successfully laid siege to the Granadan border fortress of Algeciras between 1342 and 1344. Although the victory did not result in a vast territorial conquest, it did isolate Granada and secure Gibraltar and the south of Spain from the threat of new invasions from North Africa. Without the profits from conquests of new lands, however, Alfonso and Peter found it necessary to raise taxes to pay for their adventures. They were notably more successful with the Castilian Cortes than the French ever were with their provincial assemblies. In 1342 Alfonso XI was granted the *alcabalas,* a 5 percent sales tax that the monarchs continued to collect for much of the fourteenth century. But Alfonso and Peter did face opposition from *hermandades,* or rebellious brotherhoods, made up of townsmen and lower nobles who objected to the king's taxation.

The situation was much different in the kingdoms ruled by the house of Aragon—an empire that at various times included Valencia, Catalonia, Aragon, and the island of Majorca as well as Sicily and parts of what is now southern France. This empire was united only in the person of the king. Each region had its own legal and political system. Thus, in order to collect taxes, the king had to negotiate separately in each region. Additionally, Aragonese claims brought the king into conflict with the French, the papacy, and several of the Italian states. Aragon was a volatile but very powerful Mediterranean empire.

Italy

The Italian peninsula, in comparison to Iberia, seemed a power vacuum for much of the fourteenth century. Northern and central provinces belonged to the kingdom of Italy and thus were part of the Holy Roman Empire (the name that by the fourteenth century was given to the medieval empire whose origin reached back to Charlemagne). Since the death of Frederick II in 1252, however, the empire had largely ceased to exist in Italy. The rest of the northern half of the peninsula was part of the Papal States. One of the shocks of the late Middle Ages, however, was the removal of the papal see from Rome to Avignon in what is now southern France (see page 452). After the departure of popes, papal administrators had only an indirect influence in northern and central Italy. The cities of central and northern Italy were free to create an urban-based political and cultural life remarkably different from that in much of the rest of Europe. As in the twelfth century, what little unity the cities and towns of northern Italy knew was based on a common fear of renewed papal or imperial interference.

The unique situation in Italy is clear from one of the most remarkable political tracts of the fourteenth century, *Defender of the Peace* by Marsiglio of Padua (c. 1275–1342). Marsiglio was a member of a Paduan mercantile family and a Franciscan who had been educated at the University of Paris. In his tract he argued that the popular sovereignty typical of the Italian city-republics was the ideal form for free peoples: "Only the whole body of citizens, or the weightier part thereof, is the human legislator."[4] Citizens, in other words, have the right to make their own laws and see to the maintenance of peace and order in their community. Marsiglio specifically rejected the idea that authority was derived from either pope or emperor. Rectors, mayors, even kings and emperors were, in Marsiglio's view, elected by and responsible to the people: "An elective rule . . . needs no other confirmation or approval." The church, he believed, should be simple and poor like Christ. He condemned the papacy as a usurper of political power. Church properties and jurisdictions, he maintained, should be administered by secular governments, as they usually were in Italian towns. In the early fourteenth century, popular sovereignty was an ideal shared by the townsmen of northern and central Italy.

Marsiglio believed that popular rule brought peace and concord. Unfortunately, in many Italian towns and villages the price of liberty was military and political discord. Through most of the fourteenth century, the towns of central and northern Italy competed uneasily with one another as they attempted to control their own hinterlands and to avoid falling victim to the ambitions of their neighbors. Even at its most peaceful, life in towns was punctuated by cattle raids, attacks on border fortresses, and reprisals aimed at foreign merchants. Wars, the alternative to raids and reprisals, could bankrupt even the strongest town. Milan and Florence were the most dynamic of these towns. Milan sought to control most of the Po Valley, and Florence dominated Tuscany.

The growth and virtual independence of these Italian cities created a volatile political situation that was reflected in a long debate over "peace" or "liberty." The issue of peace was largely a question of internal compromise. The rapidly growing cities housed a broad spectrum of people: feudal aristocrats with values like those of their north European peers; urban patricians whose fortunes depended on urban and rural rents and investments in international trade and banking; artisans and small merchants, many of whom were rapidly enriching themselves; and large numbers of highly mobile, unskilled laborers who moved around in search of employment. Townsmen gathered themselves together in factions based on wealth, family, profession, neighborhood, and even systems of clientage that reached back into the villages from which many of the townsmen had come. In times of unrest, urban nobles who held fortresses and even whole districts in the countryside often called on their peasants to form a band that might rival the town's own militia. Riven with factions, townsmen would often turn control of their governments over to "lords," or "tyrants," sometimes a local noble with a private army. Pinamonte Bonacolsi of Mantua (d. 1293) was typical of many: "He usurped the lordship of his city and expelled his fellow-citizens and occupied their property," according to a chronicler. "And he was feared like the devil."[5] Once firmly in power, tyrants often allowed the town's government to continue to function as it had, only requiring that

Patron Saints Throughout Europe towns as well as countries had patron saints who protected them. As this illustration indicates, the welfare of the town was literally in the saint's hands. *(Scala/Art Resource, NY)*

they should control all major political appointments.

Contrary to the hopes of Marsiglio of Padua, by the early fourteenth century, tyrants were dominating most towns in northern and central Italy. Even in Florence and Venice, the two major exceptions, public life was disrupted by large numbers of new citizens—immigrants drawn by the relatively greater economic opportunities in the towns and recently enriched merchants and speculators who demanded a political voice in government. In 1297, reacting to the presence of so many new citizens, the Venetian government enacted the so-called Closing of the Grand Council. The act guaranteed the political rights of the patriciate, the families who had held office during the late thirteenth century. Although the act initially enlarged the number of families eligible for public office, its ultimate effect was to freeze out recent arrivals. The Venetian patriciate became a closed urban nobility. Political tensions were hidden beneath a veneer of serenity as Venetians developed a myth of public-spirited patricians who governed in the interests of all the peoples, leaving others free to enrich themselves in trade and manufacture.

In Florence, by contrast, political life was convulsed by the issue of new citizens. Violent noble families, immigrants, and artisans of modest backgrounds were cut off from civic participation by the passage of the Ordinances of Justice, which restricted political participation to members in good standing of certain merchant and artisan guilds. Each person elected to office had to pass an informal scrutiny by the Guelf party, an association of old wealthy Florentine families, which saw itself as the protector of the city's political traditions. This traditional practice gave the conservative leaders of the Guelf party a powerful veto over nominations to public offices. The Florentine system guaranteed that real political power remained concentrated in the hands of the great families, whose wealth was based primarily on banking and mercantile investments.

The Holy Roman Empire

The kingdom of Germany and Holy Roman Empire of the late Middle Ages was dramatically different from the empire of the early thirteenth century. After the death of Emperor Frederick II and the extinction of the Hohenstaufen line with the deaths of his sons and grandson, there was a twenty-two-year interregnum (1250–1272) in Germany. Imperial power had rested on lands and castles in southwestern Germany. This stronghold melted away during and after the interregnum as emperors willingly pawned and sold the traditional crown lands in order to build up the holdings of their own families, usually farther to the east. The house of Luxemburg is the most successful example of territorial princes. Emperor Henry VII (r. 1308–1313) and his grandson

Charles IV (r. 1347–1378) pawned and sold lands west of the Rhine in order to secure dynastic claims to the crown of Bohemia and other lands in the east. Two other major dynasties, the Habsburgs in Austria and the Wittelsbachs in Bavaria, and a host of smaller families staked out claims to power and influence in separate parts of the empire. As a result, Germany was becoming a loose collection of territories.

The power of regional authorities in the empire was further cemented by the so-called Golden Bull of 1356. In what is the most important constitutional document of late medieval German history, Emperor Charles IV declared that henceforth the archbishops of Cologne, Mainz, and Trier plus the secular rulers of the Rhenish Palatinate, Saxony, Brandenburg, and Bohemia were the electors responsible for the choice of a new king. The proclamation recognized the major political powers and defined a procedure for election but made it difficult for a family to establish a hereditary right to the crown. After Rudolph of Habsburg's election in 1273 there were fourteen emperors from six different dynasties, and only once, in 1378, did a son follow his father. The contrast between Germany and the monarchies of Iberia, France, and England is striking. In 1350 Germany had no hereditary monarchy, no common legal system, no common coinage, and no representative assembly. Political power was in the hands of the territorial princes.

Scandinavia and Eastern Europe

As in the rest of Europe, in Scandinavia the power of the kings depended to a large extent on their relations to their nobilities and their neighbors. In Denmark, rulers sought accommodations with the nobles and powerful cities of northern Germany. In Sweden and Norway, the situation was complicated by the fact that there was no nobility in the feudal sense of a class of vassals bound to a lord by an oath of homage. Aristocrats were merely leading landowners. Both they and the peasantry were traditionally represented in the Riksdag in Sweden and the Storting in Norway, popular assemblies that had the right to elect kings, authorize taxes, and make laws. King Magnus Eriksson (r. 1319–1365) of Sweden tried to increase royal power by creating a new nobility more closely tied to the Crown and by expanding Swedish influence in what is now Finland and western Russia. Yet because of the cost of his military adventures and his consequent need for revenue, his power remained circumscribed by the interests of the major landholders.

The aristocracies of Scandinavia spoke similar Germanic languages and had close social and economic ties with each other. Thus, it is not surprising that the crowns of the three kingdoms were joined during short periods of crisis. In 1397, the dowager Queen Margaret of Denmark was able to unite the Scandinavian crowns by the Union of Kalmar, which would nominally endure until 1523.

The political fluidity of Scandinavia was also typical of the Slavic East. By the middle of the fourteenth century, however, the duchy of Moscow had emerged as the leading Russian government, unifying neighboring territories in opposition to the Mongols. Farther to the west, the Polish and Lithuanian kingdoms joined their crowns to fend off pressures from the Swedes and the German Teutonic knights in Prussia.

To the south, there was a series of wars that were hardly noticed outside the region but that would have profound consequences in the fifteenth century. The Slavic kingdoms of Bulgaria and Serbia were victims in the struggles of the declining Byzantine Empire and the newly powerful Ottoman Turks. These Turks took their name from Osman, a military leader of the early fourteenth century. Though Muslim, they initially had been invited into the Balkans as allies of the Byzantines. At first the Turks benefited from the factional distrust among the Slavic kingdoms. They quickly adapted the military tactics of their neighbors and came to dominate the Balkans. In 1389 a Turkish army defeated a coalition of Serbs, Bulgars, Bosnians, and Albanians. Later, a league of Hungarian, French, German, and English forces attempted to stem the Turkish advance with the Crusade of Nicopolis in 1396. When Christian knights incautiously charged Turkish positions, they were soundly defeated. The defeat left the Turks poised to take control of the Balkans in the next century.

The Crisis of the Western Church

Early in the fourteenth century the Christian church endured a series of shocks that began a debate about the nature of church government and the role of the church in society. First, the popes moved from their traditional see in central Italy to Avignon. Later, in the wake of a disputed election, there were two and then three claimants to the papal throne. At the same time, the church hierarchy faced challenges from radical reformers who wished to transform the hierarchy of the church. Like the Hundred Years' War, the crisis in papal government involved all the European powers.

Boniface VIII and the Problems of Church Government

In the bull *Unam sanctam* (1302) Boniface VIII declared that there could be no salvation outside the Roman Catholic church and that all political as well ecclesiastical power was derived from the pope. Dissenters, however, had a variety of grievances against the papacy and the church hierarchy. Dante complained in the *Divine Comedy* that Boniface VIII was destroying the church through his avarice. Dante's complaint was shared by all classes. Almost every ecclesiastical controversy or claim to ecclesiastical office seemed to end in court and could ultimately arrive at the papal court, if the litigants could afford expensive appeals. Suppliants needed lawyers, bought innumerable documents, and hired process servers. Many shared Dante's complaint that the papal court was "the place where Christ is daily bought and sold."

Other Italians besides Dante complained early in the fourteenth century that the popes used the diplomatic and military power of the papacy to advance the personal and political goals of their own families rather than to protect the church. Boniface VIII, for example, came from the Gaetani, a middling noble family in central Italy. He viewed his election as an opportunity to secure the fortunes of his relatives, and he quickly transformed his family into one of the most powerful clans in central Italy. A great deal of the hatred directed toward Boniface was based simply on fear of his grasping and violent relatives. Dante, Marsiglio of Padua, and others also criticized the pope as a political leader who used power and influence to prevent unity and peace among the towns and cities of Italy. Dante in a tract called *On Government* and Marsiglio of Padua in *Defender of the Peace* argued that the papacy had no legitimate right to military or political power.

Critics across Europe complained of many of the same problems. They rejected papal claims to be the source of all authority. "Every Lord," said the late-thirteenth-century French lawyer Philippe Beaumanoir, "is sovereign in his own lordship." Papal claims to ultimate jurisdiction and papal defense of clerical immunities were understood by governments as interference in internal affairs. It was controversy over the status of the church that led Boniface to make his extreme claim to political authority in *Unam sanctam*. The response of Philip IV was to send to Rome royal officials who in 1303 teamed with Boniface's Italian enemies in an attack on Boniface in the Roman countryside at Anagni. The French king's objective was to bring Boniface back to France to stand trial for heresy—charges against the pontiff ran from denial of eternal life to sodomy. Philip's agents were unable to hold Boniface and had to retreat to France. The damage had been done, however, for Boniface died a few weeks later.

Although the king's agents were excommunicated for their deeds, Boniface's successors, many of whom were from French-speaking lands, tried to reach an accommodation with Philip. It was, in fact, largely because of Philip that the French archbishop of Bordeaux was elected Pope Clement V (r. 1305–1314). He chose to remain north of the Alps in order to seek an end to warfare between France and England and to protect, to the extent possible, the wealthy religious order of the Templars, which Philip was in the process of suppressing (see page 356). And finally he hoped to prevent the king from carrying through his threatened posthumous heresy trial of Boniface. After the death of Boniface, it was clear that the governments of Europe had no intention of recognizing papal authority as absolute.

The Babylonian Captivity, 1309–1377

Clement's pontificate marked the beginning of a period during which the pope was almost continuously in what is now the south of France. Clement eventually chose to live in Avignon, on the Rhône River in a region that was technically part of the Holy Roman Empire. It was the Italian poet and philosopher Francesco Petrarch (d. 1374) who first referred to a "Babylonian Captivity of the papacy." Recalling the exile of the Israelites and the image of Babylon as a center of sin and immorality, he complained of "this the modern Babylon, heated, raging, obscene, terrible." To Petrarch and to others, the exile of the papacy from its traditional see in Rome stood as an example of all that was wrong with the church.

Although the popes quickly settled at Avignon, it was not immediately clear that the move was to be a long-term change. Only in the 1330s, during the pontificate of Benedict XII (r. 1334–1342), was a new papal palace built and the papal archive moved from central Italy. Over the next two decades the popes created one of the most vigorous and elaborate courts in Europe. It is indicative of the transformation that although the thirteenth-century papal administration required only two hundred or so officials, the bureaucracy grew to about six hundred in Avignon. It was not just the pope's immediate circle that expanded the population of Avignon. Artists, writers, lawyers, and merchants from across Europe were drawn to the new center of administration and patronage. Kings, princes, towns, and ecclesiastical institutions needed to have representatives at the papal court. Papal administrators continued to intervene actively in local ecclesiastical affairs, and revenues that the popes claimed in the form of *annates* (a portion of the first year's revenues from a benefice granted by papal letter), court fees, and provisioning fees continued to grow.

Papal Avignon During the pontificate of Benedict XII the papal palace was begun in Avignon. It became the center of the most brilliant and politically important court in fourteenth-century Europe. *(Altitude, Paris)*

Saint Catherine of Siena Criticizes the Popes in Avignon

Like most of her female contemporaries, Catherine Benincasa (1347–1380) was given no formal education. Nonetheless, because of her piety and spirituality, she was named a "Doctor of the Church"—a title granted only to the most important and influential theologians. She was actively involved in urging the popes to return to Rome and to reform the church. This letter to Pope Gregory XI was probably dictated (Catherine was illiterate) in 1376. It was instrumental in his decision to return to Rome.

My soul longs with inestimable love that God in His infinite mercy will take from you each passion and all tepidity of heart and will reform you into another man by rekindling in you an ardent and burning desire, for in no other way can you fulfill the will of God and the desires of all His servants. Alas, my sweetest Babbo [literally "Daddy"], pardon my presumption in what I have said and am saying—the sweet and primal Truth forces me. This is His will, Father; He demands this of you. He demands that you require justice in the multitude of iniquities committed by those nourished and sheltered in the garden of the Holy Church; he declares that beasts should not receive men's food. Because He has given you authority and because you have accepted it, you ought to use your virtue and power. If you do not wish to use it, it might be better for you to resign what you have accepted; it would give more honor to God and health to your soul.

Source: Robert Coogan, *Babylon on the Rhone: A Translation of Letters by Dante, Petrarch, and Catherine of Siena on the Avignon Papacy* (Potomac, Md., Studia Humanitatis, 1983), p. 115.

Not everyone, however, was comfortable with the situation. During the Hundred Years' War many considered the pope a captive of the French king, and moral complaints were serious. Papal Avignon was the most elegant court in fourteenth-century Europe. Pope John XXII (r. 1316–1334) set the tone for the court. To celebrate the marriage of his grandniece in 1324, he ordered a wedding feast during which uncounted guests consumed 4012 loaves of bread, 8¾ oxen, 55¼ sheep, 8 pigs, 4 boars, and vast quantities of fish, capons, chickens, partridges, rabbits, ducks, and chickens. This repast was topped off with 300 pounds of cheese, 3000 eggs, and assorted fruits and washed down with about 450 liters of wine. Petrarch called Avignon

> [an] unholy Babylon, Hell on Earth, a sink of iniquity, the cess-pool of the world. There is neither faith, nor charity, nor religion, nor fear of God, nor shame, nor truth, nor holiness, albeit the residence . . . of the supreme pontiff should have made it a shrine and the very stronghold of religion.[6]

Many people renowned for their piety, like Saint Catherine of Siena (see the box, "Saint Catherine of Siena Criticizes the Popes in Avignon") and Saint Bridget of Sweden, appealed to the pope to return to simpler ways and to Rome, his episcopal city (see page 485).

Late in 1377, Gregory XI (r. 1370–1378) did return to Rome. He found churches and palaces in ruin and the city violent and dangerous. He would have retreated to Avignon if he had not died a few months later. In a tumultuous election during which the Roman populace threatened to break into the conclave, the cardinals finally elected a compromise candidate who they thought would be acceptable both to the French cardinals and to the Roman mob. Urban VI (r. 1378–1389) was an Italian cleric from a French-controlled part of Italy. He was also violent and intemperate. Many cardinals soon feared for their own safety. Some immediately questioned the legitimacy of the election, which they believed had been conducted under duress. Within months

Map 12.2 Europe and the Great Schism The diplomatic and religious debates over authority in the church came to reflect the geopolitical interests of the governments of Europe. This interrelationship was nowhere more true than in England and France.

they deposed Urban and elected in his place a French cardinal who took the name Clement VII (r. 1378–1394). Urban responded by denouncing the cardinals and continuing to rule in Rome. There were two popes.

The Great Schism, 1378–1417

After some hesitation, western Christians divided into two camps, initiating the Great Schism, a period of almost forty years during which no one knew for sure who was the true pope (Map 12.2). Each side found ready supporters among the states of Europe. During the Hundred Years' War neither the English nor the French could afford to allow the other to dominate the church. The French supported Clement, who eventually resettled in Avignon. The English together with the Italians and most of the German Empire supported Urban, the pope in Rome. Scotland, a mortal enemy of the English, and Castile sided with the French.

The effects of the schism were devastating. Clement inherited the court bureaucracy in Avignon, but only a few areas, notably France, still made all of the customary payments on which that court depended. Urban, the Roman pope, found it necessary to create a court complete with a bureaucracy and a new college of cardinals. Most governments found themselves in a strong position in their negotiations with either of the rivals over ecclesiastical appointments and church taxes. Both papal courts spent what revenues they could generate trying to defeat each other. Moralists and some politicians held out the unrealistic hope that one or the other or both claimants might resign and there could be a new election. But by the 1390s, it was clear that the claimants could not settle the issue themselves.

The crisis gave impetus to new discussions about church government. Debates within the church followed lines of thought already expressed in the towns and kingdoms of Europe. Representative bodies—the English Parliament, the French Estates General, the Swedish Riksdag—already claimed the right to act for the realm, and in the city-states of Italy ultimate authority was thought to reside in the body of citizens. Canon lawyers and theologians similarly argued that authority resided in the whole church, which had the right and duty to come together in council to correct and reform the church hierarchy. The most conservative of the conciliarists said merely that although the pope normally ruled the church on earth, the "Universal Church" had the right to respond in periods of heresy or schism. More radical conciliarists argued that the pope as bishop of Rome was merely the first among equals in the church hierarchy and he, like any other bishop, could be corrected by a gathering of his peers—that is, by a general council of the church.

As more and more churchmen assumed one or another of the conciliarist positions, the rival popes found themselves under increased pressure to end the schism. The issue seemed well on its way to resolution when the two parties agreed to meet in northern Italy in 1408. The meeting, however, never took place, and in retrospect many doubted whether either party had been negotiating in good faith. In exasperation the cardinals, the main ecclesiastical supporters of the rival popes, agreed to call a general council of the church. Meeting in Pisa in 1409, the council deposed both popes and elected a new pope. The council, however, lacked the power to force the rivals to accept deposition, so the only result was that three men were claiming to be the rightful successor of Saint Peter and Vicar of Christ. The outcome of the Council of Pisa demonstrated that the conciliarists, by themselves, would be unable to heal the split in the church. A workable solution would come only when secular rulers were willing to enforce it.

Reunion, Heresy, and Reform

Resolution of the schism was among the items on the agenda of the churchmen attending the council that met in the imperial city of Constance (1414–1417) under the auspices of the Holy Roman emperor.

In 1413 the Holy Roman emperor, Sigismund (r. 1411–1437), faced a religious civil war in Bohemia, the most important part of his family's traditional lands. Bohemia and its capital Prague were Czech-speaking. But Prague was also the seat of the Luxemburg dynasty of German emperors and the site of the first university in the German world. The issue centered on the preaching of John Hus (ca. 1370–1415). As preacher in the Bethlehem Chapel in Prague and theologian at the university, John Hus was the natural spokesman for the non-German townsmen in Prague and the Czech minority at the university. His criticisms of the church hierarchy, which in Prague was primarily German, fanned the flames of Czech national feeling. It was Sigismund's hope that a council might heal the rift within the church of Bohemia. Working energetically, Sigismund managed to get the support of the major European governments and even maneuvered the third papal claimant, John XXIII (r. 1410–1415), into calling a general council of the church specifically charged to deal with reunion, heresy, and reform.

The council's response to the issue of heresy was based on experience with heresy over the previous forty years. In the 1370s John Wyclif (1329–1384), an Oxford theologian and parish priest, began to criticize in increasingly vitriolic terms the state of the clergy and the depredations of the church hierarchy. By 1387 Wyclif's ideas had been declared heretical and his followers were coming under ecclesiastical persecution. Wyclif's criticisms had been especially dangerous because he denied the position of the priest as an intermediary between God and believers. Wycliff believed that the church could be at once a divine institution and an earthly gathering of individuals. Thus, in his opinion, the pronouncements of the church hierarchy had no magisterial status. Wyclif gave that special status to the Scriptures, to the Bible. Wyclif once claimed that he had a number of "poor priests" spreading his doctrines in the countryside. He did gather about himself followers called "Lollards"—or "mumblers," from a Dutch word for Beguines (see page 415). The English clergy were scandalized because the Lollards, who emphasized Bible-reading and popular preaching, allowed women to preach publicly. According to one, "every true man and woman being in charity is a priest."[7]

THE CRISIS OF THE WESTERN CHURCH

1302	Boniface VIII issues *Unam sanctam*
1303	Boniface VIII is attacked at Anagni and dies
1305	Election of Clement V
1309	Clement V moves the papal court to Avignon; beginning of the Babylonian Captivity
1377	End of the Babylonian Captivity
1378	Death of Gregory XI in Rome
1378	Elections of rival popes: Urban VI and Clement VII; start of the Great Schism
1409	Council of Pisa elects a third pope
1414–1417	Council of Constance deposes all three papal claimants
1415	Council of Constance condemns and executes John Hus
1417	Election of Martin V by the Council of Constance; end of the Great Schism

Because of their attacks on the ecclesiastical hierarchy, Lollards were popular among the nobility of England, and especially at the court of Richard II during the 1390s. In the first two decades of the fifteenth century the influence of the Lollards waned, however, and although they continued to exist, they had no great significance.

Wyclif's most lasting impact was probably his influence on John Hus and the Husite movement that he inspired. Following the teachings of Wyclif, Hus attacked clerical power and privileges. By 1403 the German majority in the university had condemned Hus's teaching as Wyclifite, thus initiating almost a decade of struggle between Czechs and Germans, Husites and Catholics. In an effort to break the impasse, Sigismund offered Hus a safe-conduct pass to attend the Council of Constance. The emperor fully expected some sort of reconciliation that would absolve Hus and thus reduce the possibility of civil war in Bohemia. As matters progressed, however, it became clear that the councilors and Hus himself were in no mood to compromise. The council revoked the pledge of safe conduct and ordered Hus to recant his beliefs. He refused. In the end he was condemned as a manifest heretic and burned at the stake on July 6, 1415.

Far from ending Sigismund's problems with the Bohemians, the actions of the council provided the Czechs with a martyr and hero. The Husite movement continued to gather strength. Radical Husites argued that the true church was the community of spiritual men and women. They had no use for ecclesiastical hierarchy of any kind. The German emperors were unable to defeat a united Husite movement. So from 1430 to 1433 the emperor and moderate Husites negotiated an agreement that allowed the Husites to continue some of their practices while returning to the church.The Husite war engulfed all of Bohemia and dragged on until 1436. Bohemia remained a center of religious dissent, and memory of the execution of Hus at a church council would have a chilling effect on discussions of church reform during the Reformation in the sixteenth century.

The council was more successful in dealing with the schism, which to most Europeans was the most pressing issue before it. Gregory XII, the Roman pope, soon realized that he had lost all his support. Although Pope John had convened the council, Gregory was allowed to issue a new call for the council (as a rightful pope should do). His call was immediately followed by his letter of resignation. John still hoped to survive as the one legitimately elected pope, but the council deposed him on May 29, 1415. The council deposed Benedict III (r. 1394–1417), the pope in Avignon, in 1417. The council justified its actions in what was perhaps its most important decree, *Haec sancta synodus* (This sacred synod):

> This sacred synod of Constance . . . declares . . . that it has its power immediately from Christ, and that all men, of every rank and position, including even the pope himself are bound to obey it in those matters that pertain to the faith.[8]

In the minds of the delegates, there was no question where true authority in the church resided: in the whole church.

In the final sessions of the Council of Constance, Odo of Colonna, member of an old Roman noble family, was elected pope of the newly reunified church. Taking the name of Martin V (r. 1417–1431), he presided over an institution that was dramatically different from the church of Boniface VIII.

The issue of reform had a less clear-cut remedy. Critics agreed that the pope no longer behaved like the "Servant of the Servants of Christ" but instead acted like the "Lord of Lords." Cardinals claimed to represent the church at large as counterweights to papal abuse, but as the nobility of the church they and other members of the hierarchy needed multiple benefices to maintain their presence at the papal court. Moreover, both the cardinals and the popes viewed any reforms to the present system as potential threats to their ability to function. The council recognized the need for further reforms. In the decree *Frequens* (Frequently), the council mandated that reform councils had to be called regularly. We are not going to follow this history in detail, but we should note that a council met at Basel from 1431 to 1449 and that many Christians continued to believe that church councils were the best vehicle for reform within the Christian church.

The aftermath of the Great Schism was a general climate of reform and renewal that ecclesiastical leaders had to take into account at all times. No pope could expect to be unchallenged if he made claims of absolute dominion similar to those made by Boniface in *Unam sanctam.* National religious concerns and ongoing interest in conciliar theory remained important aspects of religious life throughout the fifteenth century.

Economy and Society

After nearly three centuries of dramatic growth, European society in 1300 was overpopulated and threatened by drastic economic and social problems. Estimates of Europe's population in 1300 have ranged from about 80 million to as high as 100 million. Levels would not again be this high for over two hundred years. Opportunities dwindled because of overpopulation, war, and epidemics. These shocks brought changes in trade and commerce. Lowered population, deflation, and transformed patterns of consumption also altered the nature of agriculture, which was still the foundation of the European economy. In some parts of Europe the factors responsible for this economic and demographic depression were built into the structure of society itself. At other times or in other places the changes were unforeseeable.

The Subsistence Crisis

People in many parts of Europe were living on the edge of disaster in 1300. Given the low level of agricultural technology and the limited resources available, it was increasingly difficult for the towns and countryside to feed and support the growing population. The nature of the problem varied from place to place. There is evidence of a crisis of both births and deaths. In the towns and villages of Italy there seems to have been a lowered birthrate because of tougher economic times for farmers and laborers. In northern Europe a number of famines dramatically raised mortality rates.

Evidence is clearest in central Italy, but there are indications that throughout Europe the numbers of poor were increasing in the early fourteenth century. Growing numbers of people competed for land to farm and for jobs. Farm size declined as parents divided their land among their children. Rents for farmland increased as landlords found they could play one land-hungry farmer off against another. In many parts of Italy rents and other expenses claimed to one-half or more of the total expected crop. Small farmers living on the margin moved from place to place in search of land to support their families. Many were forced to work as day laborers to make ends meet. But competition for jobs kept wages low; and when taxes were added to high rents and low wages, many peasants and artisans found it difficult to marry and raise families. Thus, because of reduced opportunities brought on by overpopulation, poor townsmen and peasants tended to marry late and have small families.

More dramatic than this crisis of births were the famines that occurred in years of bad harvests. The great famine of 1315–1322 marks a turning point in the economic history of Europe. Wet and cold weather ruined crops in much of northern Europe. Food stocks were quickly exhausted, and mass starvation followed. People died so quickly, English chroniclers reported, that no one could keep up with the burials. At Ypres, in Flanders, 2800 people (about 10 percent of the population) died in just six months. And shortages continued. Seven other severe famines were reported in the south of France during the fourteenth century.

The Black Death

If Europe's problem had merely been one of famine brought on by overpopulation, recovery should have been possible after the population declines brought about by the great famine of 1315–1322. But, because of the arrival of a deadly new pestilence, the economy did not recover. In 1348 bubonic plague returned to western Europe for the first time in almost a millennium. Chroniclers seem clear on the origins of the plague. Genoese traders contracted the plague in Caffa on the Black Sea coast. Infected sailors carried the disease south into Egypt and west to Sicily and then on to Genoa. From there it followed established trade routes first into central Italy and later to the south of France, the Low Countries, England, and finally through the North and Baltic seas into Germany and the Slavic lands to the east (Map 12.3).

The bacillus that caused "the great Mortality," as contemporaries called it, was *Yersinia pestis,* which is still found in certain rodent populations in central Asia, central Africa, and parts of

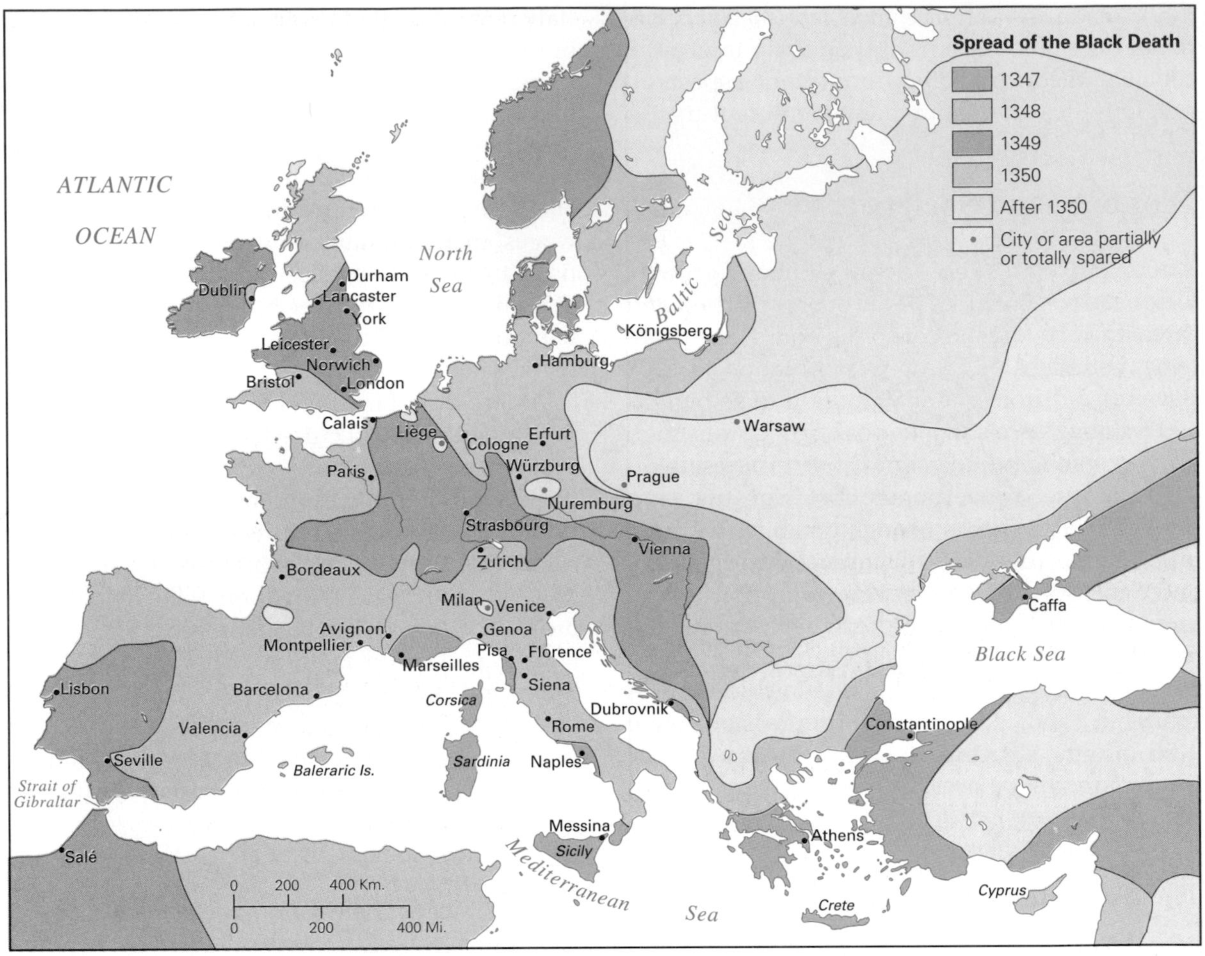

Map 12.3 The Progress of the Black Death The Black Death did not advance evenly across Europe; rather, as is clear from the dates at which it struck various regions, it followed the main lines of trade and communication.

the American southwest. It can pass into human populations when fleas move from a dead rodent host to a human being. In its bubonic form, plague attacks the lymphatic system, bringing painful, discolored swelling under the armpits and in the groin or lower abdomen. If a patient could survive the first days of high fever and internal hemorrhaging caused by the swellings, recovery was possible. No one, however, survived the rarer pneumonic or septicemic forms of plague, which attacked the lungs and circulatory system.

Mortality rates varied, but generally 60 percent or more of those infected died. In the initial infestation of 1348–1351, from 25 to 35 percent of Europe's population may have died. In some of Europe's larger cities the figures may have risen to as high as 60 percent. In Florence, the population probably declined from about 90,000 to 50,000 or even less (see the box, "The Black Death"). And the nearby town of Siena likely fared even worse, with a total mortality of 55 percent in the town and its suburbs.

After the initial outbreak, plague returned again in 1363, and then for three centuries thereafter almost no generation would avoid an outbreak of the plague. Less is known about plague in Muslim lands and in the eastern Mediterranean, but the situation seems to be similar to the European experience. Because plague tended to carry off the young, the almost generational return of plague accounts for the depressed popu-

The Black Death

The plague of 1348 in Florence dominates the popular tales that form the bulk of the **Decameron.** *Giovanni Boccaccio (1313–1375) probably described the plague to emphasize how unusual and irresponsible his protagonists—young men and women who fled Florence, abandoning family and friends—really were. If so, Boccaccio failed miserably. Readers celebrate the fresh and lively irony of the tales. Moreover, Boccaccio's description fits with everything scholars have since discovered about the first infestation of the plague in Italy.*

This pestilence was so powerful that it was transmitted to the healthy by contact with the sick, the way a fire close to dry or oily things will set them aflame. And the evil of the plague went even further: not only did talking to or being around the sick bring infection and a common death, but also touching the clothes of the sick or anything touched or used by them seemed to communicate this very disease to the person involved. . . .

There were some people who thought that living moderately and avoiding any excess might help a great deal in resisting this disease, so they gathered in small groups and lived entirely apart from everyone else. . . . Others thought the opposite: they believed that drinking excessively, enjoying life, going about singing and celebrating, and satisfying in every way the appetites as best one could, laughing, and making light of everything that happened was the best medicine for such a disease. . . . And in this great affliction and misery of our city the revered authority of the laws, both divine and human, had fallen and almost completely disappeared, for like other men, the ministers and executors of the laws were either dead or sick or so short of help that it was impossible for them to fulfill their duties. . . .

Others were of a crueler opinion (though it was, perhaps, a safer one): they maintained that there was no better medicine against the plague than to flee from it. . . . This disaster had struck such fear into the hearts of men and women that brother abandoned brother, uncle abandoned nephew, sister left brother, and very often wife abandoned husband and—even worse, almost unbelievable—fathers and mothers neglected to tend and care for their children as if they were not their own.

Source: Giovanni Boccaccio, *The Decameron,* trans. Mark Musa and Peter Bondanella (New York: New American Library, 1982), pp. 6–10.

lation levels found in many parts of Europe and western Asia until the late seventeenth or eighteenth century.

Lacking an understanding of either contagion or infection, fourteenth-century doctors depended on traditional theories inherited from the Greeks, especially the work of Galen. In Galenic medicine good health was a condition that depended on the proper balance of hot and cold, moist and dry. It was believed that this balance could be upset by corrupt air, the movements of planets, and even violent shifts in emotions. Little could be done about the stars, but many governments responded as did the Italian town of Pistoia, which banned activities, such as the tanning of leather, that produced noxious fumes. And "so that the sounds of bells might not depress the infirm," the town council further limited public mourning of the dead. Without a clear understanding of the biological nature of the disease and lacking modern antibiotics, Europeans were unable to treat plague effectively. Yet in the fifteenth and sixteenth centuries, as the rhythms of the plague infestations became clearer, towns,

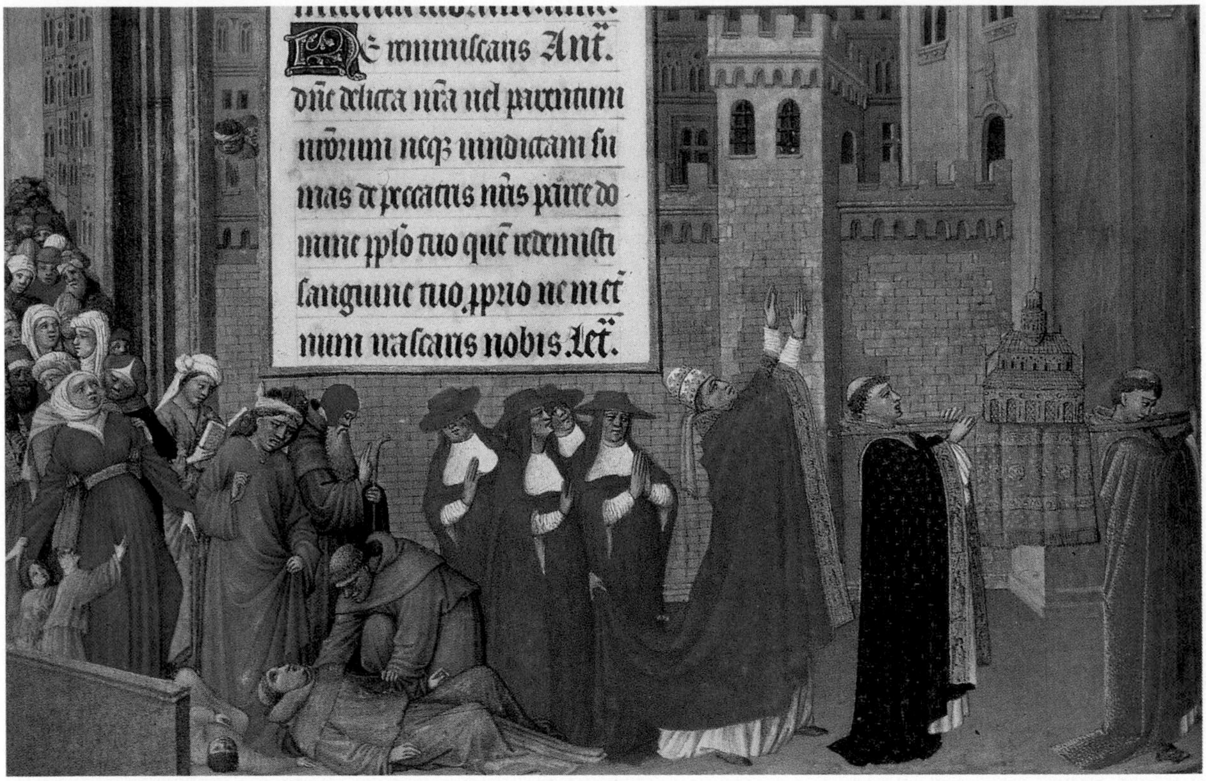

The Black Death This fifteenth-century miniature depicts the procession ordered by Pope Gregory the Great in 590 to end the great plague then ravaging Rome. This was the inspiration for the countless processions during the plague years of the fourteenth through the seventeenth centuries. *(The Bridgeman Art Library, London)*

and later territorial governments, perceived the contagious nature of the disease. The result was attempts at simple quarantines and embargoes to restrict the movement of goods and people from areas where plague was raging.

Alongside medical theory, however, another class of explanations developed. Chroniclers in France, Germany, and Italy reported that many people gave up all hope, eating and drinking without regard to consequences. To others the magnitude of the mortality was such that it seemed to signal the end of the world or at least to be a sign of the severe judgment of God on a sinful world. A traditional religious response was to urge various moral reforms or penitential acts—charitable gifts, special prayers, processions. (See the feature, "Weighing the Evidence: A Painting of the Plague," on pages 470–471.) Women were often thought to be a source of moral pollution and hence one of the causes of God's wrath. In Muslim Egypt women were ordered off the streets; in Christian Europe prostitutes were driven out of towns.

A movement of penitents called "flagellants" arose in Hungary and spread quickly into Germany and across France and the Low Countries. These men and women moved from town to town urging repentance and social and political reconciliation. In an imitation of Christ's life and sufferings, they ritually beat ("flagellated") themselves between the shoulders with metal-tipped whips. (See the box, "Christians, Flagellants, and Jews"). The flagellants, in their quest for a purer, truly Christian society, brought suspicion on all those who were not Christian or were otherwise suspect.

In the wake of the flagellants there were murderous attacks on outsiders, especially lepers and

Christians, Flagellants, and Jews

Froissart's description of the plague provides a striking picture of the religious mentality of late medieval Europe. Here Froissart describes two phenomena that were part of the response to plague in parts of France, Germany, and central Europe: religious processions featuring ritual beating, or flagellation, and massive pogroms against Jewish communities.

In the Year of Grace 1349, the penitents went about, coming first out of Germany. There were men who did public penance and scourged themselves with whips of hard knotted leather with little iron spikes. Some made themselves bleed very badly between the shoulders and some foolish women had cloths ready to catch the blood and smear it on their eyes, saying that it was miraculous blood. . . .

The object of this penance was to entreat God to put a stop to the mortality, for in that time of death there was an epidemic of plague. . . . The penitents of whom I am speaking went in companies from town to town and from city to city and wore long felt hoods on their heads, each company with its own colour. . . .

As soon as the penitents appeared and the news of them spread round, the sect of the Jews contemplated and feared their own destruction, for they had a prophecy made over two hundred years earlier which said in cryptic language: "Knights will come bearing links of iron who will be very cruel, but they will have no leaders and their power and works will not extend beyond the Empire of Germany. But when they come, we shall all be destroyed." Their prophecy came true, for in those days all the Jews were indeed destroyed, though more in one country than in another. The Pope, and the Kings of Castile, Aragon, and Navarre, accepted great numbers of them and laid them under tribute beneath them.

Source: Jean Froissart, *Chronicles,* trans. and ed. Geoffrey Brereton (New York: Penguin, 1968), pp. 111–112.

Jews, who were suspected of spreading the contagion in an attempt to bring down Latin Christian civilization. Like many of the anti-Semitic myths, the stories of Jewish poisoners seemed to arise in the south of France and spread in their most virulent forms to German towns along the Rhine. In many Rhineland towns, the entire Jewish population was put to the sword. In Strasbourg, attacks on Jews even preceded the arrival of plague. Except in a few districts, officials opposed attacks on Jews, lepers, and heretics. After a few months of violence, the flagellants and the leaders of the religious riots were driven from towns.

It was a commonplace among contemporary chroniclers that "so many did die that everyone thought it was the end of the world." Yet even in towns like Florence, where mortality rates were so high, recovery was rapid. Government offices were closed at most for only a few weeks; markets reopened as soon as the death rate began to decline. And within two years tax receipts were back at pre-plague levels. Recovery was quick because the very young and very old were the first to die. Young adults—workers and potential parents—were most likely to survive. European population quickly made good the losses during the first onslaught of plague, but the arrival of the "second pestilence" in 1363 and the nearly generational recurrence of plague in the remainder of the fourteenth and fifteenth centuries (continually carrying off many of the children) guaranteed that general European population levels would stagnate, if not decline.

Patterns of Economic Change

The path taken by the plague approximated the direction of international trade across Europe. The disease moved out of the Black Sea basin toward Alexandria in Egypt and then to Italy—along the routes that brought raw cotton, silk, and spices from East to West. The route of the plague—from Italy through France to England and the Low Countries and only later to Germany and the East—mirrors the fact that in the thirteenth and early fourteenth centuries economic connections between Italy and Germany were less significant than those between England, the Low Countries, and Germany.

The fulcrum of the European economy in 1300 was Italy. Italian merchants sold woolens produced in Flanders and Italy to Arab traders in North Africa, who sold them along the African coast and as far south as the Niger Delta. The Italians used the gold that they collected in payment to buy spices and raw materials in the East, which they resold at the regional fairs of northern Europe.

Because of their expertise in moving bullion and goods and their ready sources of capital, Italian merchants like the Ricciardis of Lucca were ideal bankers and financial advisers to the papacy and European kings, who often needed immediate sources of capital. In the late thirteenth century, members of the Ricciardi family lent vast amounts of money to King Edward I of England to finance his wars. In return they received the rights to collect indirect duties at English ports. Merchants from Cremona, Genoa, Florence, and Siena made similar agreements with the kings of France, Aragon, and Castile and with the papacy. The great merchant-banking houses had agents in most of the cities of Europe. In the course of their operations they developed a network of couriers to move business mail as well as bookkeeping procedures and techniques for the quick transfer of funds over long distances. By the fourteenth century, Italians regularly wrote bills of exchange that businessmen could buy in one part of Europe and redeem in another place and in a different currency.

During the fourteenth century and especially after the coming of plague, a number of these great banking houses fell into bankruptcy. The houses had become weak because they were unlimited partnerships in which the assets of all partners could be seized to cover debts run up by any partner. Many banking houses were also victims of close connections with royal houses. Capital and reserves of the Ricciardis, for example, were seized by Edward I in 1297, precipitating the fall of what was at the time one of Europe's largest businesses. Merchants in France and Castile rightfully feared similar attacks. Their very size was a weakness. It was difficult, if not impossible, for the partners in one concern to keep track of operations stretching from England to the eastern Mediterranean. Also, Italians faced increased competition from local merchants and never managed to penetrate beyond the Rhine in Germany.

In most parts of Europe, prosperity was still tied to agriculture and the production of food grains. In northern and western Europe, foodstuffs were produced on the manorial estates of great churchmen and nobles. These estates were worked by a combination of serfs who owed a variety of labor services and day laborers who were hired during planting and harvesting. So long as population grew, there was a continued demand for produce and a ready supply of relatively inexpensive laborers. But because of wars, famines, and finally plague, those circumstances did not hold in most countries from roughly 1350 to 1480.

Employers found themselves competing for the reduced number of laborers who had survived the plague. In 1351 the English crown issued the Statute of Laborers, which pegged wages and the prices of commodities at preplague levels. According to the statute, regulation was necessary because laborers "withdrew themselves from serving great men and others unless they have living [in food] and wages double or treble of what they were [before the plague]."[9] Even after government attempts to stabilize prices and control wages, most manorial lords still had to pay high wages in order to find laborers. As a result, many large landowners gave up direct farming of their estates and instead leased out lands to independent peasant farmers, who, for the most part, worked their lands with family labor. In southwest Germany some landowners reforested their lands, hoping to take advantage of rising prices for timber and charcoal. In both cases, landlords were reducing their dependence on laborers.

Women at Work Although guild records tended to ignore the contributions of women, many women worked in their husbands' shops. In this miniature, a woman is selling jewelry. Widows often managed the shops they inherited. *(Bibliothèque Nationale)*

Population changes and new markets also had a profound effect on the economies and social relations in European towns. Full participation in the urban economy was normally restricted to those who were "admitted to the freedom of the city"—that is, to citizens. In most towns one could acquire citizenship through inheritance from a citizen father, through the purchase of freedom, or by completing an apprenticeship in one of the town's guilds. Citizenship was essential for participation in public life. But by the late fourteenth century, promotion to master's status and full citizenship in the community were no longer assured. In the aftermath of plague and at a time of lowered population, opportunities for promotion dwindled. For many journeymen in the fourteenth century, there was little chance of promotion to full membership in the guild.

The Popular Revolts

Economic changes and recurring religious and political disruptions unleashed across Europe a wave of violence that was radically different from the violence of previous centuries. Private wars, vendettas, and popular outbursts had broken out in other times, but the violence, drama, and impact of the risings of the fourteenth century remain unique. Some of the revolts seemed directed at the remnants of the old feudal and manorial elites. In that respect they were, as some historians have maintained, merely "a high point in the struggle between landlords and tenants that had been going on at a local and uncoordinated level for at least two hundred years."[10] Urban revolts, however, often seemed to be popular revolutions against exploitation by the patricians and guild masters who dominated local politics and controlled the local economy. In nearly all cases, the popular risings against authorities seem to have been unleashed by the breakdown of the traditional bonds that had been holding society together.

Most Europeans in the fourteenth century were peasants living on isolated farmsteads or in tiny villages of no more than a handful of families. Although farmers could be free or unfree, the distinction was less and less important in the late Middle Ages. In Norway even the lowliest tenants had never been bondsmen. In Italy and Flanders, peasants once had been servile, but by the fourteenth century most were legally free of services and dues owed to a manorial lord. Lords in many parts of England and France retained the rights to labor services at various times of the year as well as the right to payments of death dues and marriage fees. But in areas where population was declining—because of emigration to towns, lower birthrates, or the impact of plague—landlords often found it impossible to enforce these various rights and dues. Desperate for tenants, landlords often allowed farmers to ignore some of the labor or financial services in order to keep them on the land. In areas where the peasantry was legally free, landlords often found it necessary to forgive portions of rents or even to lend money to their tenants in times of need. Landlords also loaned money to tenants to buy seed or draft animals or even to pay the cost of marriages or village celebrations. Thus, when there was a relative shortage of laborers in the countryside, peasants were less easily controlled and exploited than they had been in the past.

Population decline also had serious consequences in the towns of Europe. Because of lower birthrates and higher death rates, late medieval towns needed a constant influx of immigrants in order to expand or even to maintain their population. In York, for example, only one-seventh of those granted citizenship were natives; the others were immigrants. In most parts of Europe the new immigrants came from the surrounding region, but occasionally the new arrivals came from great distances.

Advantages of citizenship were political and economic. Citizenship was restricted to masters in the most important guilds, and it was they who controlled government. In many towns, citizens constructed a system of taxation that worked to their own economic advantage. In Italy this meant a fiscal system of land taxes paid by peasants and indirect taxes that fell heavily on urban workers. In Venice only citizens and patricians were allowed to participate in the lucrative trade with Venice's vast overseas possessions. It was the masters of the most important guilds who were able to define working conditions in the industrialized trades, fields like metal and cloth production. Unskilled laborers and members of craft guilds depended for their economic well-being on personal relationships with powerful citizens who controlled the government and the markets. Peace and order in towns and in the countryside depended on a delicate balance of the interests of the well-to-do and the more humble—a balance easily destroyed by war, plague, and economic depression.

The fragile balance in Flanders broke during the 1330s. Its industrial towns were among the richest in Europe. Although they were under the jurisdiction of the count of Flanders, a French vassal, they were in practical terms independent. They were closely tied to France for the grain and produce necessary to feed their urban population and to England for raw materials for industry. Flemish wealth was based on the manufacture of woolen cloth, which was dominated by the towns of Ghent, Bruges, and Ypres. The members of the weavers' guild were the wealthiest and most powerful single group in Ghent. Opponents of the weavers included conservative patricians living off rents as well as the members of a number of craft guilds.

In 1338, just as the first battles of the Hundred Years' War were being waged, James van Artevelde was elected "captain" of Ghent. Like the tyrants who dominated many Italian towns, he used the office to maintain almost uninterrupted domination of the traditional town council. Although van Artevelde was more a political opportunist than a revolutionary, his popularity rested on the anxiety felt by laborers and artisans. He did require that all guilds should be represented in town government. In this way he earned the enmity of the weavers, who had dominated the city. In addition to war, Ghent and the rest of Flanders also faced a period of depression in the cloth industry. Van Artevelde responded to the crisis by attempting to force the other towns of Flanders into a league dominated by

Peasant Revolts The ruling elites were terrified by the popular revolts of townsmen desiring political participation and peasants wanting an end to various servile dues. These uprisings seemed to challenge the "correct" ordering of social groups. Rulers responded savagely, as in this miniature showing the slaughter of the French peasants, or *jacques*, after their unsuccessful revolt during the Hundred Years' War. *(Bibliothèque Nationale)*

Ghent. Faced with the opposition of the count, hostility from the other towns, and rising discontent in Ghent itself, van Artevelde found himself increasingly isolated. He was assassinated in July 1345, in an act that was as much a personal vendetta as a political statement. Politics in Ghent quickly reverted to its traditional pattern: the well-to-do were again in control.

In the aftermath of war and plague, urban and rural risings broke out in France. Following the French disaster at Poitiers in 1356, Étienne Marcel, provost of the merchants of Paris, mobilized a protest movement. The ordinances that he advocated resembled a French Magna Carta, providing that royal officials should be subject to the Estates General and that the Estates should control taxation. Marcel's power was based on his supervision of Parisian markets and his ability to rally the Parisian masses. Yet his revolution seemed too radical to conservative townsmen in the provinces. His only allies were bands of rebellious countrymen roaming the region around Paris. The rural movement, or *jacquerie* (the name comes from the *jacque*, or jacket, typically worn by the peasants), began in response to long-standing economic and political grievances in the countryside that had been worsened by warfare. The rebels and eventually Marcel himself were isolated and then defeated by aristocratic armies.

Two decades after the defeat of the French rebels, Europe again experienced insurrections. But the risings of the 1370s and 1380s were different from the previous revolts in several significant ways. Political unrest now was much more broadly based than it had been at the start of previous movements. There were political revolutions in many German towns as members of lowly artisan guilds claimed the right to sit alongside patricians in urban governments.

In 1378 a dramatic revolt occurred in central Italy. The city of Florence had grown dramatically in the late thirteenth and early fourteenth centuries. Yet control of the government and the economy remained in the hands of a narrow guild oligarchy. In reaction to a costly war with the papacy, the Ciompi, unskilled workers in the woolen industry, led a popular revolution. The reformers desired to expand participation in government and limit the authority of the guild masters over semiskilled artisans and day laborers. Their demands were conservative enough. They wanted equal access to full memberships in guilds and a more equitable tax system. One of the rebels said they merely wanted to be wealthy like the patricians. To the patricians, however, their demands were unacceptable. Barely six weeks after the Ciompi risings, wealthy conservatives quashed the new guilds and exiled or executed the leaders of the movement, leaving political and economic power even more firmly in the hands of the patricians.

Not long after the destruction of the Ciompi, England was rocked by the Rising of 1381 (often called the Peasants' Revolt despite the fact that townsmen as well as peasants participated). England was seething with unrest by 1380. To continue the war against France, Edward III in 1377 had instituted a poll tax that placed a heavy burden on the common people of England. When he died a short time later, he was succeeded by his grandson, the 10-year-old Richard II (r. 1377–1399), whose government was in the hands of his uncles. To most, it seemed that the fiscal and political problems of England were the responsibility of the king's evil advisers.

In addition to those immediate causes of the uprising, a series of political and economic shocks in the second half of the fourteenth century had called into question old social and economic relationships in England. Because of the failure of the Statute of Laborers of 1351, landlords tried to recoup losses brought on by low rents and low commodity prices by reimposing dues and fines that previously had gone uncollected. In towns, mayors and aldermen who controlled town governments placed economic and political restrictions on newcomers who threatened to swamp the older established families.

The heart of the uprising was a revolt by rural peasants and artisans in the southeast, primarily Kent and Essex. Popular armies led by Wat Tyler (d. 1381), who may have had some military experience, converged on London in June 1381. Sympathetic townsmen let them enter the city, where they executed two of the young king's closest advisers. They demanded legal and economic freedom for the peasantry, suppression of all controls on wages and labor, and confiscation of church properties. In other English towns rebels demanded political participation and economic reforms. Their successes were short-lived. Wat Tyler was murdered during a dramatic meeting with Richard II outside London, and a reaction against the rebels quickly ensued. (See the box, "The Rising of 1381.")

Most of the revolts had few lasting consequences. A series of revolts in Spain, however, had long-lasting and unfortunate effects on Iberian society. In 1391 an attack on the Jews of Seville led to murders, forced conversions, and suppression of synagogues. Violence spread across Castile to Valencia, Aragon, and Catalonia. In the aftermath large portions of the urban Jewish population either converted or moved into villages away from the large commercial cities. The Jewish population in Castile may have declined by a fourth. The Jews who remained in the large cities tended to be moneychangers involved in royal finance. Although the anti-Jewish feelings were expressed in religious terms, the underlying cause was anger over the economic prominence of some Jewish or *converso* (recently converted Jewish-Christians) families. After 1391, anti-Jewish feeling increasingly became racial. As one rebel said, "The *converso* remained a Jew and therefore should be barred from public office."[11] Antagonism against Jews and conversos continued to build until the expulsion of the Jews from Spain in 1492.

Summary

Following several centuries of economic growth and government expansion, the late Middle Ages seems in many ways a century of limits or even of retreat. The costs of government and the com-

The Rising of 1381

The author of this chronicle—probably the most complete account of the English revolt of 1381—seems to have been an eyewitness to the dramatic events in London. Like most literate writers, the chronicler seems more at home with the attitudes and opinions of civil officials and landlords than with the concerns of the "rabble."

Wherefore the commons rose against [the royal] commissioner sent to investigate [rebellious acts in the region] and came before him to tell him that he was a traitor to the king and the kingdom and was maliciously proposing to undo them by the use of false inquests taken before him. Accordingly they made him swear on the Bible that never again would he hold such sessions nor act as a justice in such inquests. . . . They proposed to kill all the lawyers, jurors and royal servants they could find. . . .

[The rebels came to London, where they executed several royal servants. They, and possibly their leader Wat Tyler, forced the king to agree to allow them to deal "with all the traitors against him."] And they required that henceforth no man should be a serf nor make homage or any type of service to any lord, but should give four pence for an acre of land. They asked also that no one should serve any man except at his own will and by means of a regular covenant. . . .

[In a confused melee during meeting with King Richard, Tyler was stabbed.] Wat spurred his horse, crying to the commons to avenge him, and the horse carried him some four score paces and then he fell to the ground half dead. And when the commons saw him fall, and did not know for certain how it happened, they began to bend their bows and to shoot. Therefore the king himself spurred his horse, and rode out to them, commanding them that they should all come before him at the field of St. John of Clerkenwell [a few hundred yards from where Tyler was wounded]. . . .

Afterwards, when the king had reached the open fields, he made the commons array themselves on the west side. . . . [The mayor of London had Wat Tyler] carried out to the middle of Smithfield [a market area on the edge of town] . . . and had him beheaded. . . . And so ended his wretched life. But the mayor had his head set on a pole and carried before him to the king, who still remained on the field. . . . And when the commons saw that their chieftain, Wat Tyler, was dead in such a manner, they fell to the ground there among the corn, like beaten men, imploring the king for mercy for their misdeeds. And the king benevolently granted them mercy.

Source: The Anonimalle Chronicle, in R. B. Dobson, *The Peasant's Revolt of 1381* (New York: St. Martin's Press, 1970), pp. 123, 125, 128, 161, 166–167.

plexity of judicial and military institutions were such that governments had really taken on more than they could manage. The system could work only if kings were strong and charismatic and wars were short and successful. Neither was the case in this period. Weak kings, disputed successions, and unending war made good government difficult if not impossible.

This was as true in church government as in the secular states. The transfer of the papacy to Avignon and the Great Schism raised questions about the nature of ecclesiastical authority. The large number of Christians who supported the Council of Constance demonstrated to all the limits to papal claims to supremacy. They made clear that the papacy needed to refashion its administration, its finances, and its explanation of the pope's role in the church.

Economic and social life in the fourteenth century was disrupted in important ways. Bubonic plague ended widespread population growth. The great mortality and accompanying social disruption intensified the feelings of distrust that many European Christians felt toward outsiders, especially Muslims and Jews. They also added to the strains that many Europeans were already feeling because of war and high taxation. The violent political and social movements that swept Europe, especially after 1350, made clear that many of the old political, social, and economic relationships no longer fit. The crises that began in the first decades of the fourteenth century were largely resolved by the late medieval innovations of the fifteenth century.

Notes

1. Quoted in Charles T. Wood, *Joan of Arc and Richard III* (New York: Oxford University Press, 1988), pp. 56–57.
2. Quoted in Michael T. Clanchy, "Law, Government, and Society in Medieval England," *History* 59 (1974): 75.
3. J. A. Buchon, *Choix des Chroniques* (Paris, 1875), p. 565, as quoted in John Gillingham and J. C. Holt, eds., *War and Government in the Middle Ages* (Totowa, N.J.: Barnes & Noble, 1984), p. 85.
4. Alan Gewirth, trans., *Marsilgius of Padua, Defender of the Peace* (New York: Harper & Row, 1967), p. 45.
5. Salimbene de Adam, quoted in John Larner, *Italy in the Age of Dante and Petrarch, 1215–1380* (New York: Longman, 1980), p. 141.
6. Quoted in Guillaume Mollat, *The Popes at Avignon, 1305–1378* (London: Thomas Nelson, 1963), p. 112.
7. Quoted in Mary Aston, *Lollards and Reformers: Images and Literacy in Late Medieval Religion* (Ronceverte, W.V.: 1984), p. 60.
8. Quoted in Francis Oakley, *The Western Church in the Later Middle Ages* (Ithaca, N.Y.: Cornell University Press, 1979), pp. 65–66.
9. Quoted in Maurice H. Keen, *English Society in the Later Middle Ages, 1348–1500* (London: Penguin, 1990), p. 39.
10. Rodney Hilton in *The English Rising of 1381,* ed. R. H. Hilton and T. H. Aston (Cambridge, England: Cambridge University Press, 1984), p. 3.
11. Quoted in Angus Mackay, "Popular Movements and Pogroms in Fifteenth-Century Spain," *Past & Present* 55 (1972): 52.

Suggested Reading

War and Government

Allmand, Christopher. *The Hundred Years' War: England and France at War, 1300–1450.* 1988. A single-volume summary of the war and its impact on late medieval politics, government, military institutions, literature, and nationalism.

Arnold, Benjamin. *Princes and Territories in Medieval Germany.* 1991. A challenging discussion of German politics and society emphasizing the role of the princes and territorial governments.

Dvornik, Francis. *The Slavs in European History and Civilization.* 1962. A thorough political narrative of the various regions of Slavic Europe.

Guenée, Bernard. *States and Rulers in Later Medieval Europe.* 1985. An introduction to recent research on the general character of government in the Late Middle Ages.

Hay, Denys. *Europe in the Fourteenth and Fifteenth Centuries.* 1966. A well-written introductory survey of politics and society in Europe between 1300 and 1500; coverage of Scandinavia and the Slavic lands as well as the central areas of northwestern Europe.

Henneman, John B. *Royal Taxation in Fourteenth Century France: The Development of War Financing, 1322–1356.* 1971. A challenging discussion of French politics and the development of financial institutions.

Hillgarth, Jocelyn N. *The Spanish Kingdoms, 1250–1516.* 2 vols. 1971. An encyclopedic treatment of the Spanish-speaking kingdoms of Iberia; contains especially good treatments of the position of Muslim and Jewish minorities.

Kaeuper, Richard W. *Justice and Public Order: England and France in the Later Middle Ages.* 1988. A thorough and sophisticated comparison of French and English government that is especially attentive to the social context of government ideals and the limits on the claims of central authorities.

Keen, Maurice H. *English Society in the Later Middle Ages, 1348–1500.* 1990. This recent general introduction to late medieval England covers culture and religion as well as politics.

Larner, John. *Italy in the Age of Dante and Petrarch, 1215–1380.* 1980. Short introduction to the general developments in fourteenth-century Italy, treating but not concentrating on Florence and Venice.

MacKay, A. *Spain in the Middle Ages: From Frontier to Empire, 1000–1500.* 1977. This excellent short introduction to Spain concentrates on the transformation of Spain in the thirteenth century as the Christian kingdoms consolidated their control.

Sumption, Jonathon. *The Hundred Years' War.* 1990. A projected multivolume history of the war. Volume 1,

Trial by Battle, is an excellent narrative of the background diplomacy and the first decades of the war.

Vale, Malcolm G. A. *The Angevin Legacy and the Hundred Years' War, 1250–1340.* 1990. A discussion of the political and diplomatic problems the English kings faced as they tried to integrate Gascony into their realm; covers the many cultural and linguistic ties between the ruling classes of England and France.

Warner, Marina. *Joan of Arc: The Image of Female Heroism.* 1981. An excellent and quite readable book emphasizing the conflicting religious and political opinions about "the Maid."

Religious Schism and Spiritual Life

Banker, James. *Death in the Community: Memorialization and Confraternities in an Italian Commune in the Late Middle Ages.* 1988. An excellent introduction to the functioning of lay brotherhoods in the late Middle Ages.

Bynum, Caroline W. *Holy Feast and Holy Fast: The Religious Significance of Food to Medieval Women.* 1987. A challenging but rewarding book on the unique aspects of fourteenth-century spirituality, it explains why it was most typically found among women.

Crowder, C. M. D. *Unity, Heresy, and Reform, 1378–1460: The Conciliar Response to the Great Schism.* 1977. An anthology containing translations of the major treatises that argued for the authority of the whole church over the pope; includes valuable introductions to the texts that can serve as an excellent narrative of the events of the schism and conciliar movement.

Kieckhefer, Richard. *Unquiet Souls: Fourteenth-Century Saints and Their Religious Milieu.* 1984. A study of the lives of fourteenth-century saints, providing an introduction into the main currents in fourteenth-century spirituality.

Oakley, Francis. *The Western Church in Later Middle Ages.* 1979. The best general history of the church in the late Middle Ages. Oakley gives superior treatments of the Great Schism and conciliarism.

Pantin, William A. *The English Church in the Fourteenth Century.* 1955. The best discussion in English of the Christian church in a national setting, these well-written and accessible essays describe a local church that remained vibrant in spite of plague and religious schism.

Partner, Peter. *The Lands of St. Peter.* 1972. A thorough account of the political and diplomatic initiatives in the Papal States—the area that was the key to the practical power of the papacy.

Southern, Richard W. *Western Society and the Church in the Middle Ages.* 1970. A general introduction to the place of the church in social life in the Middle Ages. There are exemplary discussions of the female religious movements, especially the Beguines.

Tierney, Brian. *Foundations of the Conciliar Theory: The Contribution of the Medieval Canonists from Gratian to the Great Schism.* 1955. The legal and theological issues raised by the schism are discussed in this classic study of the authority of the pope and councils in the structure of the church. A difficult but rewarding book.

Plague and Society

Campbell, B. M. S., ed. *Before the Black Death: Studies in the "Crisis" of the Early Fourteenth Century.* 1991. Debate by a number of historians about the nature and extent of the economic problems of the fourteenth century, including discussion of agriculture and manufacture in the decades before the plague.

Carmichael, Ann G. *Plague and the Poor in Renaissance Florence.* 1985. A work directed at scholars that investigates plague in a specific town, emphasizing the way in which social and economic conditions that preceded the plague conditioned responses to the epidemic.

Geremek, Bronislaw. *The Margins of Society in Late Medieval Paris.* 1987. Description by a noted Polish historian of life in the largest city north of the Alps, including the impact of the deteriorating economic conditions of Parisians.

Hatcher, J. *Plague, Population, and the English Economy, 1348–1530.* 1977. A clear discussion of the effect of declining population on the economy of England.

Miskimin, Harry A. *The Economy of Early Renaissance Europe, 1300–1460.* 1975. Excellent, readable survey of how the economies of various parts of Europe responded to economic decline and plague.

Mollat, Michel, and Philippe Wolff. *The Popular Revolutions of the Late Middle Ages.* 1973. The best survey of the major revolutions of the fourteenth century, emphasizing the local political conditions that brought on the revolutions.

Ziegler, Philip. *The Black Death.* 1971. Although superseded on many specific points, this remains the best single volume on plague in the fourteenth century.

Weighing the Evidence

A PAINTING OF THE PLAGUE

Writers who survived the coming of bubonic plague in 1348 described a world of terror in which things seemed changed forever. Look at this painting, *St. Sebastian Interceding for the Plague-Stricken,* created by the Flemish artist Josse Lieferinxe between 1497 and 1499. One dying man seems to be falling terrified to the ground while a woman bystander in the background screams in alarm. Images of Christ, Saint Sebastian (pierced by arrows), a devil, and a priest seem to indicate that something terrifying and undreamed-of is happening. But what exactly was the terror and what had changed?

The art of the later Middle Ages is an extremely valuable source for understanding social and religious values. As you look at *St. Sebastian Interceding for the Plague-Stricken,* the first step is to understand what men and women in the fourteenth and fifteenth centuries thought about death. After 1400, European Christians often depicted the universality of death in paintings showing the Dance of Death. The motif varies, but typically Death grasps the hands of men and women, rich and poor, noble and peasant, and leads them away. Deathbed scenes were another popular motif. In the late Middle Ages most people believed that at death the good and evil acts committed by an individual were tallied in the Book of Life and the person was granted either eternal life in Purgatory and then Paradise or consigned to eternal suffering in Hell. Judgment scenes often depict the Virgin Mary or another saint pleading before God or contending with the devil or demons over the souls of the dying.

It was essential for people to prepare for a good death. Individuals studied the *artes moriendi,* the arts of dying. A lingering, painful illness was often interpreted as an opportunity for penitential suffering that would be good for the soul. At the point of death, the dying person could confess and receive both absolution for sins and the last sacraments of the church. From that moment on, he or she needed to maintain a calm faith, free from fear. Salvation and eternal life depended on avoiding further sin, especially the questioning of God's forgiveness and mercy. Death was a public event. Clergy, family, religious societies, even neighbors helped the dying person to keep hope. The person might pray, "Virgin Mary, Mother of God, I have placed my hope in you. Free my soul from care, and from Hell, and bitter death."[1]

The concept of a good death is critical to understanding the European response to bubonic plague. To be sure, individuals rarely look forward to death, now or in the Middle Ages. Boccaccio and numerous chroniclers remarked on the suddenness of death and on the lack of priests to hear confession (see the box, "The Black Death" on page 459). Individuals who were healthy in the morning might be dead by nightfall. The suddenness, the lack of preparation for a good death, heightened the dread that accompanied the onset of illness and death.

Medieval Christians turned to patron saints who could represent them before God at the point of death and to stop the onslaught of plague. Three patron saints were especially popular. The Virgin Mary was often shown using her cloak to shelter towns and individuals from arrows carrying pestilence. Saint Roch, himself a victim of plague, was thought to intercede and protect those who prayed in his name. And Saint Sebastian, an early Christian martyr shot with arrows (later understood as symbols of death by plague) was thought to be an especially effective patron during epidemics. In times of plague, people went on pilgrimages to local shrines dedicated to these or local saints, carried images of the saints in processions, and built churches and chapels dedicated to the saints in thanks for deliverance from plague.

With these issues in mind, what do we see in Lieferinxe's painting? The painting portrays an outbreak of plague. We note first the body of the dead person, carefully shrouded. Ideally the

1. Quoted in Philippe Ariès, *The Hour of Our Death* (New York: Knopf, 1981), p. 108.

Lieferinxe: St. Sebastian Interceding for the Plague-Stricken *(Walters Art Gallery, Baltimore)*

dead, like the body in the foreground, were taken to a church and then given a Christian burial. But chroniclers often remarked that so many died, and died so quickly, that no one could be found to bury them properly. In many towns the dead were gathered on carts and hauled to large common graves outside the town. We can see one such cart leaving the castle in the background. In a series of images, then, Lieferinxe shows what mattered most to people. In the foreground is the shrouded body attended by a priest and by other clerics bearing a cross. This person experienced a good death. In contrast, the man who has fallen behind the body is suffering a bad death, one that caught him unawares. He is the object of the concern and grief of those near him. In the sky just above the castle walls, a white-robed angel and a horned, ax-wielding demon contend over the souls of the dead and dying. At the top of the painting, Christ listens to the prayers of Saint Sebastian. The painting thus portrays the impact and horror of plague and also shows the way in which the epidemic might be ended.

Returning to our original question, we find that the terror of epidemic plague was not entirely like a modern panic. Medieval people understood the horror and panic as well as the solutions to the epidemic in terms of traditional religious values: The terror was to be caught unawares.

CHAPTER 13

The Late Medieval Recovery

The shock of plague, war, and economic dislocation subsided in the fifteenth century. Lower rents for farmlands, as well as higher wages brought on by a shortage of workers, changed agricultural production and levels of consumption. Trade and other commercial activity in Northern Europe and the Mediterranean expanded. The virtual monopolies enjoyed by Flemish manufacturers and Italian merchants broke down as new participants appeared. The role played by the Spanish, English, and Germans in commerce grew. Economic life became more complex as the movement of commercial traffic through central Europe increased.

The Christian church responded to the problems of schism, heresy, and reform in important and creative ways. Religious brotherhoods became local forums for spiritual growth and political association. Individual men and women involved themselves in activities that they associated with a Christ-like life. The papacy made changes to its administrative structure and embarked on a cultural and ideological program designed to make Rome once again the center of Christendom. In the wake of schism and conciliar challenges to papal authority, popes created new explanations for their religious authority.

The political institutions of the Continent changed in response to challenges posed by war and unrest. The power of governments grew in the late Middle Ages, as local, regional, and national governments adopted traditional means of control to strengthen military and administrative institutions. In England and France monarchial authority grew as the Crown used the institutions of court and the relationships of clientage to dominate local powers. In other parts of Europe, regional states, such as the duchies of

Members of the court of the duke of Burgundy. From a fifteenth-century miniature.

Burgundy, the dukes of Milan, or the individual territorial governments of the Holy Roman Empire, took control of administration. And by the end of the fifteenth century there were two new powers, the united kingdoms of Spain and the Ottoman Turks, which seemed more dynamic than the older monarchies of England and France.

At the end of the fifteenth century, Europe was a dynamic place.

The Pattern of Economic Recovery

Economic revival in the fifteenth century was the result of several transformations in trade and manufacturing. The European economy no longer moved along an axis between Italy and Flanders. Italian banking techniques spread beyond the Mediterranean, and new networks of trade and finance developed, especially in central Europe. Economic and demographic depression had had a profound effect on agriculture, and a shortage of farmers and laborers left workers in a position to drive hard bargains with landlords. New networks for trade, increased competition, and shifts in demand brought important changes to the cloth industry, the most profitable industry in late medieval Europe.

The Expansion of Commerce

The commercial houses of the fifteenth century tended to be more tightly controlled than earlier business partnerships. The most powerful bank in fifteenth-century Europe was the Medici bank of Florence. Founded in 1397 by Giovanni de' Medici (1360–1429), the bank grew quickly because of its role as papal banker. Medici agents transferred papal revenues from all parts of Europe to Rome and managed papal alum mines, which provided an essential mineral to the growing cloth industry. They took advantage of information gathered from partners throughout Europe to buy and sell silk, woolens, foodstuffs, and even art. Cosimo de' Medici (1389–1464), son and successor of Giovanni, solved the problem of unlimited liability, which had ruined earlier commercial partnerships (see page 462), in a way that allowed for centralized control. Rather than a single partnership, the Medici bank was a series of bilateral partnerships between Cosimo in Florence and easily controlled junior partners in other parts of Europe. Thus, assets in London, for example, could not be seized by creditors to satisfy debts in Barcelona or Bruges.

By the 1430s, the Medicis were easily the wealthiest family in Florence. Always mindful of communal sensibilities, Cosimo de' Medici used his commercial wealth to build a network of friends and neighbors who could be trusted to do his bidding in the volatile world of Italian urban politics. By the middle of the fifteenth century, Cosimo's loans were a wedge in negotiating a settlement of the long-standing rivalry between Florence and Milan. Critics complained that, because of Cosimo's wealth and influence, political decisions in Florence were made in the Medici Palace and not in city hall.

The organizational changes that the Medicis instituted did not eliminate businessmen's dependence on networks of relatives, representatives, and friends. Bankers of the late fourteenth and fifteenth centuries were prolific letter writers. Jacques Coeur (1395?–1456) of France maintained close contact with merchants in Montpellier, Barcelona, the eastern Mediterranean, Bruges, and Paris. After making a fortune trading in southern France, he managed the French royal mint and became the financial adviser of King Charles VII (r. 1422–1461). He put the French monarchy back on a solid financial footing after the Hundred Years' War, becoming in the process the wealthiest individual in France. His wealth and influence earned him jealous enemies. He was accused of murdering the king's mistress, trading with Muslims, and stealing royal funds. His property was confiscated, and he was banished to an island in the Mediterranean, where he died. In his dramatic career, Jacques Coeur demonstrated that Italian merchants were not the only ones who understood international trade.

To manage complex and far-flung enterprises, merchants refined recordkeeping methods. By the mid-fifteenth century, merchants had developed techniques of cost accounting that allowed them to estimate probable returns from a variety of potential investments. Double-entry bookkeeping was popularized in Luca Pacioli's *Summa of Arithmetic Techniques* (1494), the basic text on commercial arithmetic. In addition, merchants wrote handbooks explaining the basics of

Italian Finance The town of Siena in Italy commissioned painted covers for its treasury's account books. This scene illustrates townsmen paying their taxes at the treasurer's bench. The English *bank* comes from the Italian *banco*, or the "bench" on which the merchants transacted their business. *(Scala/Art Resource, NY)*

economics and trade (see the box, "The Efficient Merchant").

Sophisticated accounting methods and handbooks of commerce were essential. Trade occurred in three interrelated areas: Muslim lands and the Mediterranean, central Europe, and northwestern Europe (Map 13.1). Although European traders continued to travel to Damascus, Syria, and to other eastern ports to trade for spices carried from Asia, they were less and less interested in locally produced commodities such as papyrus and silk. By the fifteenth century a number of Italian and French cities had taken up the highly profitable silk trade. The trade in papyrus ended because Europeans acquired the technology necessary to manufacture high-quality rag paper.

Italian expertise was *least* influential in those regions of Europe touching the North and Baltic seas, areas most noted for fishing (a critical source of protein for much of Europe), salt, grain, and furs. The Hanseatic League, an association of over a hundred trading cities centered on the German city of Lübeck, dominated northern commerce. By 1358 it was referred to as a "League of German Cities," and individual merchants could participate only if they were citizens of one of the member towns. League influence reached from London in the west to Novgorod in Russia in the east. Unlike the Mediterranean commercial and banking networks, Hanseatic commerce was quite simple. Merchants depended for their economic influence on the political and military power of the member towns. They created a commercial monopoly over the grain and fur trade in Russia, Poland, and Scandinavia. Norwegians, for example, were forced to concede monopoly control over the export of fish in order to gain the right to buy grain in league-controlled markets.

Hanseatic power depended on a concentration of economic activity in a few easily controlled centers. The league's domination waned in the second half of the fifteenth century as trade diversified. Dutch, English, and even south German merchants took shares of the wool, grain, and fur trade. In the second half of the fifteenth century, towns in the eastern Baltic found that

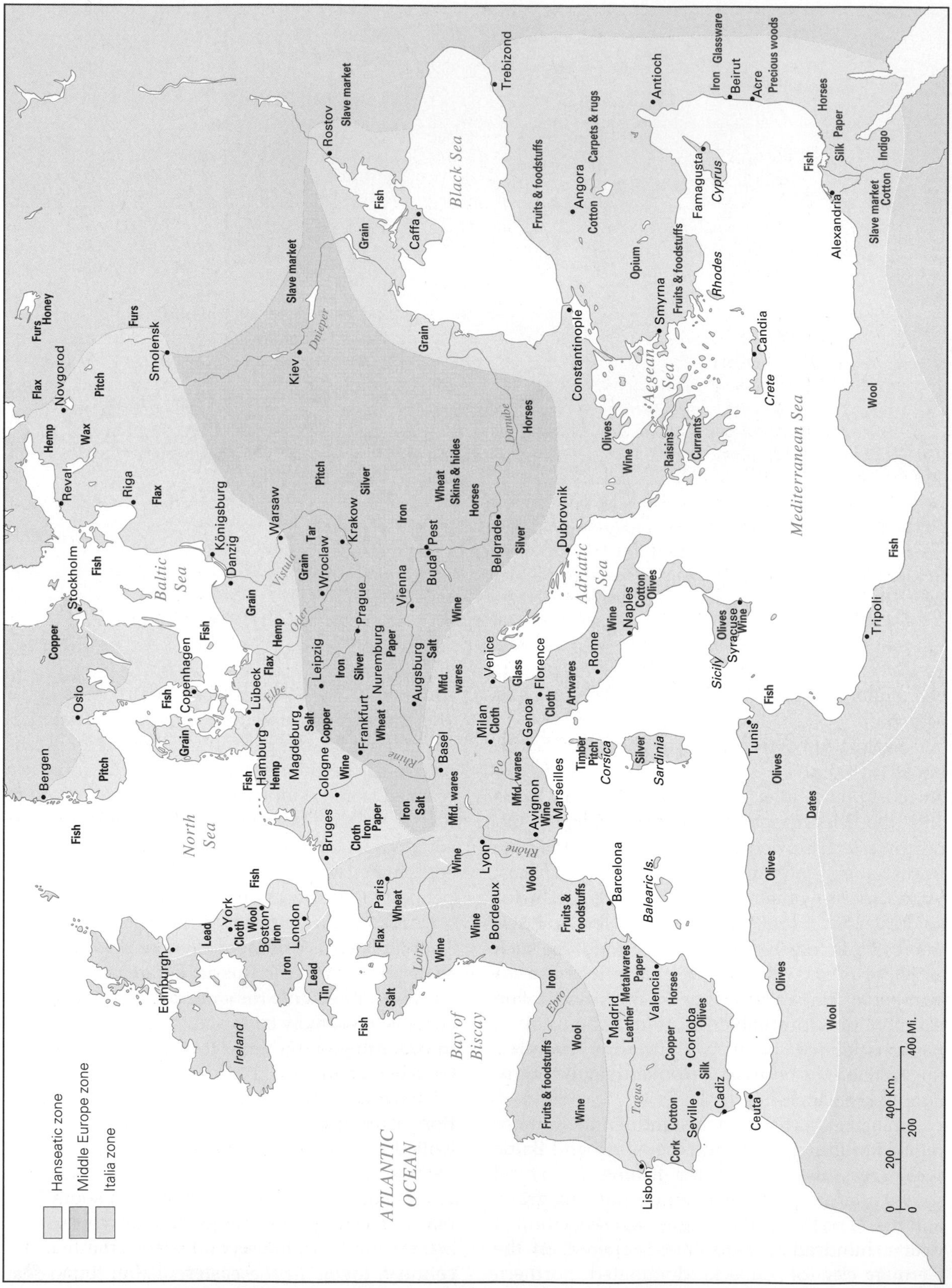

Hanseatic zone
Middle Europe zone
Italia zone
ATLANTIC OCEAN
North Sea
Baltic Sea
Black Sea
Mediterranean Sea
Adriatic Sea
Aegean Sea
Bay of Biscay
Ireland
Corsica
Sardinia
Sicily
Crete
Cyprus
Rhodes
Balearic Is.
Loire
Rhône
Rhine
Elbe
Oder
Vistula
Dnieper
Danube
Po
Ebro
Tagus
Edinburgh
York
Boston
London
Bergen
Oslo
Copenhagen
Stockholm
Reval
Riga
Novgorod
Smolensk
Königsburg
Danzig
Lübeck
Hamburg
Bruges
Cologne
Magdeburg
Frankfurt
Leipzig
Nuremburg
Prague
Wroclaw
Warsaw
Krakow
Kiev
Rostov
Caffa
Paris
Lyon
Bordeaux
Avignon
Marseilles
Basel
Augsburg
Milan
Genoa
Venice
Florence
Rome
Naples
Syracuse
Vienna
Buda
Pest
Belgrade
Dubrovnik
Constantinople
Smyrna
Angora
Trebizond
Antioch
Famagusta
Beirut
Acre
Alexandria
Candia
Tunis
Tripoli
Ceuta
Lisbon
Seville
Cadiz
Cordoba
Madrid
Valencia
Barcelona
Fish
Lead
Cloth
Wool
Iron
Tin
Salt
Flax
Wheat
Wine
Copper
Pitch
Grain
Hemp
Furs
Honey
Wax
Tar
Silver
Paper
Mfd. wares
Glass
Artwares
Timber
Olives
Cotton
Skins & hides
Horses
Slave market
Fruits & foodstuffs
Carpets & rugs
Opium
Raisins
Currants
Glassware
Precious woods
Silk
Indigo
Dates
Metalwares
Leather
Cork
0 200 400 Km.
0 200 400 Mi.

The Efficient Merchant

During the fifteenth century, Italian merchants wrote handbooks discussing the nature of their business and the best ways to protect business. While living in Naples, Benedetto Cotrugli of Ragusa (modern Dubrovnik, Croatia) described the ideal businessman. In addition to praising the dignity of the profession, he discussed the varied nature of business ventures, which he divided into great, modest, and small enterprises.

A great merchant, then, must . . . not keep all money together, but he should distribute it in various solid businesses. . . . That is to say, [suppose] that I am a great and rich merchant in Florence. I acquire an interest in the Altoviti [partnership], whose management is in Venice. . . . And I enter into a partnership in Rome, and . . . into another in Avignon. . . . And according to my lot and substance I keep within my own management 6,000 ducats with which I do business in my own name. . . . And since I have a finger in many places, in solid and planned [investments], I cannot but make out well, for the one makes up for the other. . . .

Those who have a medium amount of money . . . must manage in another way. That is, they must not divide that capital of their own, but keep it solidly tied in one body, except that they may sometimes—yet seldom—make commenda [partnership] contracts of 400 to 500 ducats . . . so that your money may often come back into your hands. . . . [This happens] both because they employ wares which are quickly [disposed of], such as silver, gold, lead, copper, wax, crimson, leather, and the like, and because of the dexterity of mind which they have. . . .

We shall now speak of those who have little money, up to some 500 ducats. They must get personally busy with said money, and . . . [they must] not spread it over several businesses. And they must help the money with personal effort, for if you wish to stand still with so little money you will consume it.

Source: Benedetto Cotrugli, *Della Mercatura et del Mercante Perfetto* (Venice, 1573), 25^{v}–29^{r}, as quoted in Robert S. Lopez and Irving Raymond, eds., *Medieval Trade in the Mediterranean World* (New York: Columbia University Press, 1955), pp. 413–415.

their interests no longer coincided with those of the Rhineland towns that made up the Hanseatic League. Wroclaw (in modern Poland) signaled the nature of the change when it resigned from the league in 1474 to expand trade connections with the south German towns.

Unlike Hanseatic merchants, who depended on political and military power, the south Germans adopted Italian techniques of trade and finance to expand their influence throughout central Europe. Their favored trade routes ran through Nuremberg and farther east to Wroclaw and into Lithuania and were as important as the northern routes controlled by the Hanseatic League. German merchants regularly bought spices in the markets of Venice and distributed them in central and eastern Europe. By the fifteenth century, the townsmen of south Germany also produced linen and cotton cloth, which found ready markets in central and eastern Europe.

The prosperity of Nuremberg, like that of many of its neighbors, rested first on a local marketing network and later on expansion into international trade. The Fuggers of Augsburg, the

Map 13.1 Trade Zones in Europe and the Mediterranean In the fifteenth century, the economic power of the towns of southern Germany, Bohemia, and Poland challenged the Italian-dominated Mediterranean trade and the North Sea trade of the Hanseatic League.

Medieval Bruges The town of Bruges in Belgium was a major trade and financial center during the fifteenth century. English, Italian, and Hanseatic merchants regularly came to the town. Bulk goods such as wool, grain, and fish were loaded and unloaded using cranes like the one in the background. *(Bayerische Staatsbibliothek München)*

most prosperous of the German commercial families, were indicative of the process. Hans Fugger (1348–1409) moved to Augsburg from a nearby village in the 1360s and quickly established himself as a weaver and wool merchant. By the 1470s Jacob Fugger (1459–1525) was a dominant figure in the spice trade and also participated in a number of unusually large loans to a succession of German princes. Loans to the nobility were a wedge allowing the Fuggers to take control of some important copper and silver mines. They became leaders in the Tyrolean silver-mining industry, which expanded dramatically in the late fifteenth century. And in the early sixteenth century they handled all transfers of money from Germany to the papacy. Jacob Fugger's wealth increased fourfold between 1470 and 1500. The Fuggers were indispensable allies of the German emperors. Jacob himself ensured the election of Charles V as Holy Roman emperor in 1519, making a series of loans that allowed Charles to buy the influence that he needed to win election.

Agricultural Change

Merchants in south Germany were in many ways the key new players in European economic life, but innovation and local specialization were also occurring in many other parts of Europe.

Lowered rents and increased wages meant a higher standard of living for small farmers and laborers. Before 1348, when grain prices were high and wages relatively low, most poor Europeans had subsisted on bread or grain-based gruel, having meat, fish, and cheese only a few times a week. A well-off peasant in England had lived on about two pounds of bread and a cup or two of oatmeal pottage washed down with three or four pints of ale; poorer peasants generally drank water except on very special occasions. Lower food prices enabled Europeans to eat more meat and drink more wine, beer, and ale. In the late fourteenth century, adults in parts of Germany may have consumed nearly a liter of wine and a third of a pound of meat along with a pound or more of bread each day. Elsewhere people could substitute an equivalent portion of beer, ale, or cider for the wine. In the late fourteenth century, the consumption of large amounts of meat and fish was common throughout Europe, and harvest laborers were likely to receive about a pound of meat for every two pounds of bread. Hard times for landlords were good times for peasants and day laborers.

To avoid the increased labor costs, many landlords gave up direct farming. Some converted their operations from grain production to raising sheep. Others converted their lands to produce more commercial products: grapes for wine in the regions near Paris, flax for linen in southwest Germany and northern Italy, and trees for lumber in western Germany. The landscape of northern Italy was transformed as town governments and landlords invested heavily in canal projects that created irrigated meadows and pastures and even laid the groundwork for the introduction of rice culture in the sixteenth century. The dukes of Milan introduced commercial forestry and mulberry trees (whose leaves were necessary to feed silkworms) in territories where the land was not really arable.

In eastern Europe, there was increased emphasis on commercial grain farming. In the wake of lowered population in the early fifteenth century, Polish peasants in the duchy of Wroclaw temporarily enjoyed lowered rents and liberation from some dues. In the second half of the fifteenth century, however, landlords were able to take advantage of political and social unrest to force tenants into semifree servile status. In areas where a lord controlled all or nearly all of the available land, peasants had no choice but to accept tenancy on the landlord's terms. This so-called second serfdom created an impoverished work force whose primary economic activity was in the lord's fields. Increasingly in the second half of the century grains raised in Poland and Prussia found their way to markets in England and the Low Countries. Europe east of the Elbe River became a major producer of grain, but at a heavy social cost.

The Transformation of Crafts and Industry

Cloth manufacture, not agriculture, was the part of the European economy that changed most dramatically. First in Flanders, then later in Italy, England, and the rest of Europe, production was moving out of urban workshops and into the countryside. The guilds easily controlled urban workshops and sales in urban cloth markets. In Florence and many other Italian cities masters of the wool guild controlled workers, salaries, and techniques, ensuring that quality, prices, and profit margins remained high. Industries in rural areas tended to be free of controls on quality or techniques. As a result, the production of light, cheap woolens, for which there was a significant demand, moved out of the cities and into the countryside. Rural production, whether in Flanders, Lombardy, or England, became the most dynamic part of the industry.

Rural cloth production, especially in southwest Germany and parts of England, was organized through the putting-out system. Merchants who owned the raw wool contracted with various artisans in the city, suburbs, or countryside—wherever the work could be done most cheaply—to process the wool into cloth. Rural manufacture was least expensive because it could be done as occasional or part-time labor by farmers, their wives, or children during slack times of the day or season. Because production was likely to be finished in the countryside (beyond guild supervision), the merchant was free to move the cloth to wherever it could most easily and profitably be sold; guild masters had no control over price or quality.

Two other developments also changed the woolen trade of the fifteenth century: the rise of Spain as an exporter of unprocessed wool and the emergence of England, long recognized as a source of prime wool, as a significant producer of finished cloth. Spain was an ideal region for the pasturing of livestock. Flocks of sheep regularly moved from mountainous summer pastures onto the plain in the late fall and winter. By the fifteenth century highly prized Spanish wool from Merino sheep was regularly exported to Italy, Flanders, and England. By 1500 there were over 3 million sheep in Castile alone, and revenues from duties on wool formed the backbone of royal finance.

In England, in contrast, an economic transformation was tied to cloth production. Over the course of the late fourteenth and fifteenth centuries, wool exports declined as cloth exports rose. In 1350 the English exported just over 5000 bolts of cloth. By the 1470s exports had risen to 63,000 bolts, and they doubled again by the 1520s. A key to the growth of the English cloth industry was the availability of waterpower, which allowed manufacturers to take advantage of new mechanical fulling mills. A water-driven mill mechanically pounded a mixture of earth, alum, and even urine into the cloth to soften it and increase its weight. Using the mechanical mill allowed a single artisan to full much more cloth than the older methods of working by hand.

The growth of cloth exports furthered the expansion of London. Located on the Thames River and easily reached by sea, the city was ideally placed to serve as a political and economic capital. During the fourteenth and fifteenth centuries, English commerce was increasingly concentrated in the hands of the London merchant-adventurers. Although manufacturing continued to thrive in rural areas, soon after 1500 over 80 percent of the cloth for export was in the hands of the Londoners. This development, coupled with the growth of London as a center of administration and consumption, laid the foundation for the economic and demographic growth that would make London the largest and most prosperous city in western Europe by the eighteenth century.

Industrial changes in the fifteenth century challenged customs and institutions by allowing new entrepreneurs into the marketplace. Patricians in many European towns, however, acted to dampen competition and preserve traditional values. Great banking families like the Medicis of Florence tended to avoid competition and concentrations of capital, because the leaders of rival banks were political and social peers. Not even the Medicis used political influence to create advantages for their own businesses. In northern Europe, governments in towns like Leiden restricted the concentration of resources in the hands of the town's leading cloth merchants. Their aim was to ensure full employment for the town's laborers, political power for the guild masters, and social stability in the town.

Restricting competition to ensure stability within towns reduced the mobility of the laborers. Beginning around 1450, journeymen were less likely to complete the transition from apprentice to master and shopowner. After a number of unsuccessful strikes, journeymen were forced to concede control of the crafts and the terms of labor to the masters. They identified with the associations of journeymen that were springing up to protect the interests of those who now expected to labor all their lives without ever owning their own shops.

Not only journeymen found their economic status challenged. Opportunities for women were significantly reduced. In England, for example, brewing ale had been a highly profitable occasional labor that women combined with the running of a household. Ale soured quickly, so it could not be made in large batches and stored for long periods of time. The introduction of beer, which was easier than ale to store and transport, reduced the demand for ale and provided work for men as beer-makers. At the same time the rights of women to work in urban crafts and industries were reduced. Wealthy fathers were less inclined to allow wives and daughters to work outside the home. Guilds banned the use of female laborers in many trades and severely limited the right of a widow to supervise her spouse's shop. For reasons that are not entirely clear, journeymen objected to working alongside women—perhaps because they now saw their status as employees as permanent instead of temporary. By the early sixteenth century journeymen in Germany considered it "dishonorable" for a woman to work in a shop, even the daughter or wife of the master.

Christianity and the Renaissance Papacy

With the end of the great schism in 1417, the Christian church began a process of individual and institutional reform. More and more people, eager to return religious institutions to their previous levels of discipline, participated actively in religious life. Clergy and laity on the local level desired to change personal behavior as well as the rules governing church institutions. Part of the vigor in Christianity resulted from its ability to express popular ideas of community for a region and even for a nation. But the most profound change may have been the administrative and ideological reconstruction of the Renaissance papacy.

The Contours of Late Medieval Christianity

Despite schism, clerical extravagance, and rising national feeling, the influence of Christianity was not in decline. By the late fourteenth century, Christianity permeated almost every aspect of European life. It provided a definition of belonging and an ideology for public life.

A citizen was first of all a "good [orthodox] Christian," certainly not a heretic, a Jew, or a Muslim. In Spain and France Jews and Muslims needed a special license from the Crown to settle, and they lived under royal protection. Church authorities traditionally had demanded tolerance of Jews, as they did at the Council of Bourges: "The Church protects the Jews, since, it is written, she desires not the death of a sinner." Yet the laity often equated Jews with heretics, and if they were heretics, they need not be tolerated. Franciscans and Dominicans, for all their other virtues, seem to have been leading opponents of toleration. The popular Italian preacher Giordano da Rivalto (1260–1311) assured his Florentine listeners that Jews

> are evil at heart and . . . they would, were they able, crucify [Christ] anew every day and even thus they could not satiate themselves. . . . And behold [it is] God who takes revenge on them in this world, who has brought them into the hatred of all peoples![1]

Giordano did not necessarily incite riots against Jews, but he offered a clear justification for them.

Questions of an individual's salvation and personal relationship to God and to the Christian community remained at the heart of religious practice and theological speculation. Nominalist theologians, the leading thinkers of the late Middle Ages, rejected the key assumption of Scholasticism—that there were universal ideas and generally applicable rules of order for moral life (see page 420). In the words of William of Ockham (ca. 1285–1347), "No universal really exists outside the mind." Truth was to be found in daily experience or in revealed scripture, not in complex logical systems. At the heart is Ockham's method—known as Ockham's razor—that what can be explained with only a few logical speculations "is vainly explained by assuming more."

Nominalist theologians rejected vast logical systems but remained concerned about the role of the individual Christian in securing salvation. They argued that an individual's acts played a crucial role. They believed in a holy covenant in which God would save those Christians who, by means of the church's sacraments and through penitential acts, were partners in their own salvation. Foremost among the pentitential acts was the feeding of "Christ's Poor," especially on important feast days. The pious constructed and supported hospices for travelers and hospitals for the sick. Christians went on pilgrimages to shrines like the tomb of St. Thomas Becket in Canterbury or the church of St. James of Compostela in Spain. They also built small chapels, called chantries, for the sake of their own souls. To moralists, work itself was in some sense a penitential and ennobling act.

Shrines were sites of the miraculous cures and transformations sought by Christians of all social and economic levels. As a young German reported to his relatives early in the sixteenth century, "I vowed to make a pilgrimage to a place one calls Sancta Maria de Loreto [in Italy]. . . . With all my heart I believe it was first God and, after [my vow], this very Sancta Maria de Loreto who protected me from the evil and illness of the plague."[2]

The most common religious practice was participation in religious brotherhoods. Members vowed to attend monthly meetings, to participate in processions on feast days, and to maintain peaceful and charitable relations with fellow members. Religious brotherhoods often played a political role as well. In the south of France, for example, city governments often met in the chapels of the Brotherhoods of the Holy Spirit.

The most typical religious feast of the late Middle Ages was that of Corpus Christi (the "Body of Christ"). The feast celebrated and venerated the sacrament of the mass and the ritual by which the bread offered to the laity became the actual body of Christ. Corpus Christi was popular with the church hierarchy because it emphasized the role of the priest in the central ritual of Christianity. The laity, however, equated Corpus Christi with the body of citizens who made up the civic community.

Kingdoms, provinces, and towns all had patron saints who, believers thought, offered protection from natural as well as political disasters. There were royal saints like Edward of England, Louis of France, and Olaf of Norway, and there were little-known and primarily local saints like Frediano of Lucca in Italy and Eléar in France. Festivals in honor of the saints were a major event in the town or kingdom (see the box, "A Religious Holiday in Florence"). The most revered saint in the late Middle Ages was the Virgin Mary, the mother of Jesus. The most popular new pilgrimage shrines in the north of Europe were dedicated to the Virgin. It was she, the Sienese maintained, who protected them from their Florentine rivals. As the veneration of the Virgin Mary shows, in the late Middle Ages it was not possible to distinguish between religion and society, church and state.

What Christians then did observe was the prominent role that women played in religious life. Holy women who claimed any sort of moral standing often did so because of visions or prophetic gifts such as knowledge of future

A Religious Holiday in Florence

This excerpt from the writings of fifteenth-century historian Goro Dati recounts activities during the Feast of Saint John the Baptist, the patron saint of Florence. The mix of civic and religious interests it describes were typical of Christian life in the towns of Europe.

When springtime comes and the whole world rejoices, every Florentine begins to think about organizing a magnificent celebration on the feast day of St. John the Baptist [June 24].... There are preparations for the horseraces, the costumes of the retinues, the flags and the trumpets; there are pennants and the wax candles and other things which the subject territories offer to the Commune....

At the third hour, there is a solemn procession of clerics, priests, monks, and friars ... and so many relics of saints, that the procession seems endless.... There are many confraternities of men who assemble at the place where their meetings are held, dressed as angels, and with musical instruments of every kind and marvelous singing. They leave from S. Maria del Fiore [the cathedral] and march through the city and then return.

Whoever goes to the Piazza della Signoria on the morning of St. John's Day witnesses a magnificent, marvelous, and triumphant sight, which the mind can scarcely grasp. Around the great piazza are a hundred towers which appear to be made of gold ... [but are actually] wax candles, which have the appearance of golden towers, [they] are the tribute of the regions which in most ancient times were subject to the Florentines.... The lord priors and their colleges [the chief governmental officials] come to make their offerings, accompanied by their rectors, that is, the podestà, the captain [of the people], and the executor.... Then there are offerings by twelve prisoners who, as an act of mercy, have been released from prison ... in honor of St John.

Source: Gene Brucker, *The Society of Renaissance Florence* (New York: Harper & Row, 1971), pp. 75–78.

events or of the status of souls in Purgatory. Reputations for sanctity provided a profound moral authority. The Italian Blessed Angela of Foligno (ca. 1248–1309) had several visions and became the object of a large circle of devoted followers. She was typical of a number of late-medieval female religious figures who on the death of a spouse turned to religion. Like Angela, these women tended to gather "families" around them, people whom they described as their spiritual "fathers" or "children." They offered moral counsel and warned businessmen and politicians of the dangers of lying and sharp dealings. "Oh my sons, fathers, and brothers," counseled Angela, "see that you love one another amongst yourselves ... [and] likewise unto all people."[3]

In the late Middle Ages religious houses for women probably outnumbered those for men. For unmarried or unmarriageable (because of disabilities) daughters, convents were an economical, safe, and controlled environment. Moralists denounced the dumping of women in convents: "They give [unmarriageable daughters] to a convent, as if they were the scum and vomit of the world," was the conclusion of San Bernardino of Siena (1380–1444). The general public, however, believed that well-run communities of women promoted the spiritual and physical health of the community. In a society in which women were not allowed to control their own property and in which women other than queens lacked a role in political and intellectual life, a religious vocation may have appealed to women because it allowed them to define their own religious and social relationships. A religious vocation offered other advantages too. Well-to-do or aristocratic parents appreciated the fact that the traditional gift that accompanied a daughter entering a religious house was much smaller than a dowry.

Some women declined to join convents, which required vows of chastity and obedience to a rule and close male supervision. Margery Kempe (ca. 1373–1439) of Lynn, England, traveled throughout Christendom on a variety of pilgrimages. She left her husband and family, dressed in white (symbolic of virginity), and joined with other pilgrims on trips to Spain, Italy, and Jerusalem. Many other women chose to live as anchoresses, or recluses, in closed cells beside churches and hospitals or in rooms in private houses. Men and women traveled from all parts of England seeking the counsel of the Blessed Julian of Norwich (d. after 1413), who lived in a tiny cell built into the wall of a parish church.

The most controversial group of religious women were the Beguines, who lived in communities without taking formal vows and often with minimal connections to the local church hierarchy (see page 415). In fourteenth-century Cologne, a city of about 50,000, there were over 1200 Beguines working at different crafts. By the early fifteenth century, Beguines were suspect because clerics believed that these independent women rejected traditional religious cloistering and the moral leadership of male clergy and were particularly susceptible to heresy. Critics maintained that unsupervised Beguines held to what was called the "Heresy of the Free Spirit," a belief that one who had achieved spiritual perfection was no longer capable of sin. Rumors of sexual orgies, spread by clerical critics, quickly brought suspect women before local inquisitors. Although some Beguines may have held such a belief in spiritual perfection, the majority certainly did not. But they were feared by an ecclesiastical hierarchy that distrusted independence. (See the box, "The Inquisition of Joan of Arc.")

A more conservative movement for renewal in the church was the Brothers and Sisters of the Common Life founded by the Dutchman Geert Groote (1340–1384). A popular preacher and reformer, Groote gathered male and female followers into quasi-monastic communities at Deventer in the Low Countries. Eventually a community of Augustinian canons was added at Windesheim. Brothers and Sisters of the Common Life supported themselves as book-copyists and teachers in small religious schools in the Low Countries. Members of these communities followed a strict, conservative spirituality that has come to be known as the *devotio moderna,* or "modern devotion." Although they called themselves "modern," their piety was traditional. Their ideas are encapsulated in *The Imitation of Christ,* a popular work advocating a traditional sort of monastic spirituality written by Thomas à Kempis (ca. 1380–1471), a canon of Windesheim. They advocated the contrary ideals of fourteenth-century religious life: broader participation by the laity and strict control by clerical authorities.

The Beguines Like many other lay women of the late Middle Ages, the Beguines were suspected of heresy by the church hierarchy. This miniature depicts Beguines in religious dress and accepting guidance from the abbot of Tournai, the traditionalists' hopeful vision of how things ought to be. *(Bibliothèque royale Albert Ier, Brussels)*

The Rise of National Churches

To reduce the influence of conciliarists, the papacy had been forced to accept compromises on the issues of reform, ecclesiastical jurisdictions

The Inquisition of Joan of Arc

Between January and May 1431 Joan of Arc was investigated by an inquisitorial commission. The minutes of the trial were later translated into Latin and copies were retained by the king of England and the Dominican inquisitor, among others. An important question was whether Joan's acts had any authoritative value: Were her voices from God or the devil? The judges wanted to demonstrate to their own satisfaction that Joan was one of "the sowers of deceitful inventions" of which the Gospels warned. They fully expected that external signs could indicate internal dispositions. She was found guilty and burned alive as a heretic.

The following memorandum is a summation of the commission's case against the maid.

You said that you wore and still wear man's dress at God's command and to His good pleasure, for you had instruction from God to wear this dress, and so you put on a short tunic, jerkin, and hose with many points. You even wear your hair cut above the ears, without keeping about you anything to denote your sex, save what nature has given you. . . . The clergy declare that you blaspheme against God, despising Him and His sacraments, that you transgress divine law, Holy Scripture and the canons of the Church, that you think evil and err from the faith, that you are full of vain boasting, that you are given to idolatry and worship of yourself and your clothes, according to the customs of the heathen.

You have declared that you know well that God loves certain living persons better than you, and that you learned this by revelation from St. Catherine and St. Margaret; also that those saints speak French, not English, as they are not on the side of the English. And since you knew that your voices were for your king, you began to dislike the Burgundians.

Such matters the clergy pronounce to be a rash and presumptuous assertion, a superstitious divination, a blasphemy uttered against St. Catherine and St. Margaret, and a transgression of the commandment to love our neighbors.

And you have said . . . that you know that all the deeds of which you have been accused in your trial were wrought according to the command of God and that it was impossible for you to do otherwise. . . . Wherefore the clergy declare you to be schismatic, an unbeliever in the unity and authority of the Church, apostate and obstinately erring from the faith. . . . [The Inquisitor admonished her,] "You have believed in apparitions lightly, instead of turning to God in devout prayer to grant you certainty; and you have not consulted prelates or learned ecclesiastics to enlighten yourself: although, considering your condition and the simplicity of your knowledge, you ought to have done so."

Source: The Trial of Jeanne d'Arc, trans. W. P. Barrett (New York: Gotham House, 1932), pp. 331–338.

and immunities, and rights to papal revenues. It continued to claim highest jurisdiction, but lay rulers viewed their own religious role as something special. In a parody of a well-known legal maxim that "The king is emperor in his own lands," one theorist claimed, "The duke of Cleves is pope in his own lands."

Lay rulers focused on several issues. They wanted church officials in their territories to be from local families. They wanted ecclesiastical institutions to be subject to local laws and administration. And by the 1470s, it was clear that they wanted to have local prelates named as cardinal-protectors, churchmen who could serve as mediators between local government and the papacy. The most famous of these new political cardinals is Cardinal Thomas Wolsey of England (ca. 1470–1530), an important supporter of King Henry VII and chancellor of England under Henry VIII. Wolsey spent his entire career in royal service.

One of the most important compromises between the papacy and the monarchs was the Pragmatic Sanction of Bourges of 1438, by which the French crown established a claim to a church largely independent of papal influence. The agreement abolished papal rights to annates, limited appeals to the papal court, and reduced papal rights to appoint clergy within France without the approval of the local clergy or the Crown. The Pragmatic Sanction was the first of a number of claims for a unique "Gallican church," a national church free from outside interference. There were similar treaties throughout Europe. Perhaps the most momentous was a bull issued in 1478 by Pope Sixtus IV (r. 1471–1484). It allowed Ferdinand and Isabella of Aragon and Castile to institute the Spanish Inquisition under their own authority (see page 504).

The papal concessions signaled a changed relationship between the papacy and the governments of Europe. With reduced revenues from jurisdictions, annates, and appointments, the papacy of the fifteenth century was forced to derive more and more of its revenue and its influence from its traditional Papal States in central Italy. By the late 1420s, the Papal States produced about half of the annual income of the papacy. In many respects, the fifteenth-century papacy seemed like an Italian lordship rather than the ultimate source of spiritual authority in Christendom.

The Renaissance Papacy

The papacy needed to create a political and ideological counterweight to the centrifugal forces of conciliarism, reform, and local feeling. The political and ideological focus of the revived papacy was Rome and the Papal States. When Martin V (r. 1417–1431) assumed the papal throne, he initially resided in Florence and other parts of Italy, because Romans were still hostile to the return of papal government. By 1450, however, the popes had secured the right to appoint city officials, and they dominated urban policy. They succeeded in pacifying Rome to the extent that they could safely reside almost continuously in the Vatican Palace beside St. Peter's basilica. Once the city was secure, popes rebuilt and reorganized the church and city. Rome became a veritable statement of papal political and religious thought.

The first step in the creation of a new Rome was taken by Pope Nicholas V (r. 1446–1455), a cleric who had spent many years in the cultural environment of Renaissance Florence (see page 522). Hoping to restore Rome and its church to their former glory, Nicholas and his successors patronized the arts, established a lively court culture, and sponsored numerous building projects. Nicholas was an avid collector of ancient manuscripts that seemed to demonstrate the intellectual and religious primacy of Rome. He invited numerous artists and intellectuals to the papal court. He brought the Florentine architect and writer Leon Battista Alberti (1404–1472) to Rome. On the basis of his researches in topography and reading done in Rome, Alberti wrote his treatise *On Architecture* (1452), the most important work on architecture produced during the Renaissance. It was probably under Alberti's influence that Nicholas embarked on a series of ambitious urban renewal projects in Rome, which included the construction of bridges, rebuilding of roads, and even plans for the rebuilding of St. Peter's basilica.

The transformation of Rome had an ideological purpose. As one orator proclaimed, "Illuminated by the light of faith and Christian truth, [Rome] is destined to be the firmament of religion . . . , the secure haven for Christians."[4] Thus, the papal response to critics was to note that Rome and its government were central to all political and religious life. By reviving the style and organization of classical antiquity, the church sought to link papal Rome to an imperial tradition reaching back to Augustus and even to Alexander the Great. Papal restorers rebuilt the earliest Christian churches of the city, emphasizing the literal continuity of imperial authority and apostolic tradition. To papal supporters, there could be only one authority in the church. Early tradition and the continuity of the city itself, they assumed, demonstrated papal primacy.

One particular monument in Rome captures especially vividly the cultural, religious, and ideological program of the papacy: the Sistine Chapel in the Vatican Palace. The chapel is best known for the decoration of the ceiling by the Florentine artist Michelangelo Buonarroti (1475–1564) and for his images of the Last Judgment. The chapel, however, was begun by Pope Sixtus IV in 1475. It was an audience chamber in which

The Sistine Chapel The paintings on the walls and ceiling of the Sistine Chapel in the Vatican tell the Christian story of divine history from creation to the Last Judgment. The sidewalls show the parallels between the life of Moses and the life of Christ. *(Scala/Art Resource, NY)*

an enthroned pope could meet the representatives of other states. In addition it was thought that the college of cardinals would gather in the chapel for the election of new popes.

The decorations done before Michelangelo painted the ceiling reflect the intellectual and ideological values that Sixtus hoped to transmit to the churches and governments of Christendom. Along the lower sidewalls of the chapel are portraits of earlier popes, a feature typical of early churches. More significant are two cycles of paintings of the lives of Moses and Christ, drawing parallels between them. To execute the scenes, Sixtus called to Rome some of the greatest artists of the late fifteenth century: Sandro Botticelli, Domenico Ghirlandaio, Luca Signorelli, and Pietro Perugino. The works illustrate the continuity of the Old Testament and New Testament and emphasize the importance of obedience to the authority of God. The meaning is most obvious in Perugino's painting of Saint Peter receiving the keys to the Kingdom of Heaven from Christ. The allusion is to Matthew 16:18, "Thou art Peter and upon this rock I shall build my church." The keys are the symbol of the claim of the pope, as successor of Saint Peter, to have the power to bind and loose sinners and their punishments.

Directly across from Perugino's painting is Botticelli's *The Judgment of Corah,* which portrays the story of Corah, who challenged the leadership of Moses and Aaron while the Israelites wandered in the wilderness. Corah and his supporters, according to Numbers 19:33, were carried live into Hell. Various popes had cited the implications of the judgment of Corah. Eugenius IV (r. 1431–1437) recalled the fate of Corah when he refused to acknowledge the power of the councils. The pope was bound to oppose the council, he argued, "to save the people entrusted to his care, lest together with those who hold the power of the council above that of the papacy they suffer a punishment even more dire than that which befell Corah."[5]

The popes were not the only people building in Rome. In the late fifteenth century, cardinals of the church and great secular families also patronized architects, builders, and painters, who celebrated the wealth, power, and status of their patrons. The Sienese banker Agostino Chigi (1465–1520) was typical. Although from a modest, non-noble background, Chigi became one of the most influential men in Rome because of his patronage of the arts. He was responsible for the construction and decoration of what is now known as the Villa Farnesina. Popes regularly visited the villa and eagerly attended the lavish banquets for which Chigi was famous. Toward the end of his life he was ennobled by adoption into the family of Pope Julius II (r. 1503–1513).

The effects of papal and private building on the city were profound. Rome grew from a modest population of about 17,000 in 1400 to 35,000 in 1450. By 1517 the city had a population of over 85,000, five times its population at the end of the Great Schism. The papal program was a success. Rome was transformed from a provincial town to a major European capital, perhaps the most im-

Giving of the Keys to Saint Peter Pietro Perugino's painting of Saint Peter's receiving from Christ the keys to "bind and loose" on earth and in heaven illustrates the basis of papal claims to authority within the Christian church. This is the central message of the decorative plan of the Sistine Chapel. *(Scala/Art Resource, NY)*

portant artistic and cultural center of the sixteenth century. Visitors to the Sistine Chapel, like visitors to the papal city itself, were expected to leave with a more profound sense of the antiquity of the papal office and of the continuity of papal exercise of religious authority. Because the building and decorating were being completed as the Protestant Reformation was beginning in Germany, some historians have criticized the expense of the political and cultural program undertaken by the Renaissance popes. But to contemporaries on the scene the work was a logical and necessary attempt to strengthen the church's standing in Christendom.

Reconstruction of the French and English Monarchies

Discussions of governments in fifteenth-century Europe traditionally center on the monarchies of England and France in the period after the Hundred Years' War. Historians frequently use the political experience of those two monarchies as examples of the growth of "New Monarchies"—that is, governments that, because of military exhaustion and the general desire for peace and order, were able to centralize control and create the beginnings of bureaucratic absolute states based on rational calculation. In this approach, the new strength of the French and English monarchies is said to be the result of a new alliance between the middle class and the Crown designed to reduce the strength of the nobility. In truth, politics was not transformed in this period. Although the power of the central government did grow at the end of the fifteenth century, this growth was not based on fundamental changes in the nature of government and law. Continuity with the problems and practices of the past was strong. The key issue was how to control the ambitions and pretensions of the nobility.

The Court of Burgundy

There is no better example of the problems facing government than the experience of the duchy of Burgundy. Although the dukes were French nobles, they maintained an independent foreign policy and were creating a sort of Burgundian state independent of French control. The hostility between England and France during the Hundred Years' War gave rise to the Burgundian dynasty. After gaining control of Burgundy in 1363, Charles of Valois acquired the county of Flanders. He later gained the imperial county of Burgundy and numerous other territories on the border of France and the Holy Roman Empire.

The disparate lands of the Burgundians were united by little more than the power of the Valois family and the prestige of their court. Their subjects spoke French, German, and Flemish. Some were technically part of the kingdom of France; others were subjects of the Holy Roman Empire. The success of the Burgundians depended on the status and influence they gained through their manipulation of the individuals drawn to their circle. They negotiated treaties and marriage contracts with the Germans, the English, and various Italian states, securing a place among the European powers.

The high point of their influence was the court of Philip "the Good" (r. 1419–1467), widely held to be the most brilliant in Europe and a model for the later French, English, Italian, and German courts. Courtiers from Portugal, Italy, and England as well as from France and Germany regularly attended. In 1430, Philip formed the Order of the Golden Fleece, one of a number of aristocratic orders of knights founded in the fourteenth and fifteenth centuries. He took the myths of King Arthur and his knights as his model. Philip wished to imbue his followers with a sense of loyalty and discipline. Knights of the Golden Fleece were not to depart from battle once an engagement was begun, and they were required to go on a pilgrimage if they incurred any form of dishonor. As one bedazzled Englishman said of the Burgundians, "I never heard of anything like it, except King Arthur's court!"[6]

It was Burgundian art and culture that so impressed the Englishman. The cathedral chapter (the association of cathedral clergy) of Cambrai was a virtual conservatory for musicians attached to the court. The Burgundians attracted to Cambrai singers and instrumentalists from France, the Low Countries, England, and Germany. The most famous resident was Guillaume Dufay (1400–1474), a singer and composer who popularized polyphony (music with two or more parts sung or played independently rather than in unison) as well as the use of melodic popular songs in sacred compositions. Dufay traveled in Italy, introducing northern musical tastes to Italian courts.

The Burgundian dukes also drew artists and sculptors to their court. They commissioned a sculptural program by the Dutchman Claus Sluter (1350–1406) at the convent of Champmol, near Dijon, the traditional burial site of the ducal family. Although most of the convent was destroyed in the eighteenth century, Sluter's emotional, free-standing statues of penitents and his baptismal font survive. Weavers of Tournai created decorated tapestries for which the court became famous. Their ornate creations celebrated the Burgundians, their chivalric tournaments, and their hunts.

The most famous artist of the Burgundian court was the Flemish painter and courtier Jan van Eyck (c. 1390–1441), best known for his portraits of courtiers. He painted the Burgundian chancellor with the skyline of Utrecht in the background, and his portrait *Giovanni Arnolfini and His Bride* (1434) combines realistic details of domestic life with symbols of purity and faithfulness. His portraits and sacred paintings were known and appreciated by Italian painters of the Renaissance.

The dukes believed that fine art and lavish ceremony would enhance the figure of the ruling duke himself. The so-called Banquet of the Oath of the Pheasant in 1454 is a famous example of the mingling of art and propaganda. After the fall of Constantinople to the Turks (see page 498), Philip the Good held the banquet to mark his decision to send Crusaders to liberate the city. Recalling the tales of Lancelot and other heroes of medieval literature, the feast celebrated the prominence of the duke of Burgundy in the Christian world. Artists, musicians, and poets took part. Artists constructed and decorated for the duke's banquet a model church large enough to house an organ and musicians. Between courses of the meal, musicians performed popular and sacred songs. The meal and entertainment culminated in a procession in which a female figure (played by a court poet) signifying the mother church pleaded for champions who would free her from the Turks. Then a live pheasant was carried into the hall, and Philip, his sons, and a host of Burgundian nobles vowed on the pheasant to go on a crusade—hence the name for the feast. In spite of the brilliance of the feast and European enthusi-

The Court of Burgundy The court of Burgundy was famous for the tapestries produced for it by Flemish weavers. This scene depicting life at the court probably shows Philip of Habsburg, who inherited the Burgundian lands through his mother. He is surrounded by his courtiers and his wife, Joanna of Spain. *(Rijksmuseum-Stichting, Amsterdam)*

asm for the undertaking, regional and international political problems prevented Philip from ever leading an army to the East.

The feast, the planning for the crusade, and the brilliant court culture were essential to the union of the Burgundian territories. But the duchy was unified only in the person of the duke, and the unexpected defeat and death of Duke Charles the Bold (r. 1467–1477) at the hands of Swiss infantry near Nancy in 1477 ended the Valois Burgundian state. King Louis XI of France moved quickly to take possession of Charles's French lands. Flanders and other Burgundian territories passed to Charles's daughter Mary, the wife of Maximilian of Habsburg. In the sixteenth century, these old Burgundian lands would be the keys to the Habsburg Empire, the greatest power in Europe.

The Recovery of France

The brilliance and independence of the court of Burgundy highlight the troubles of the French monarchy. Royal control still was strongest in the regions closest to Paris. Townsmen saw their responsibilities to the king as significantly limited. They warned him that "you owe [the people of Paris] protection and defense, and they owe you honor and obedience, and what they lack in one relieves them of the obligation of the other."[7] The nobility was similarly suspicious of royal power. During Charles VI's bouts of insanity, the dukes of Burgundy, Berry, and Orléans fought to control the king's person and his government. The aristocratic factions saw their own position as being essential to the stability of the kingdom.

Ducal power was based in the territories that the dukes controlled. As was true of the Valois of Burgundy, many dukes had received these territories as appanages, property or jurisdiction that a king could settle on a younger son in lieu of other claims to royal office. The land usually reverted to the Crown if there was no legitimate male heir, but during most of the fifteenth century territories like Burgundy and Brittany remained outside of royal control.

A key to the ending of the war with the English and the revival of royal power was the changed behavior of King Charles VII (r. 1422–1461). By the late 1430s he had discovered how to handle the political factions in the French court. Through careful appointments and judicious offers of annuities and honors, Charles drew his nobility to the royal court and made the nobles dependent on it. "The court," complained a frustrated noble, "is an assembly of people who, under the pretense of acting for the good of all, come together to diddle each other; for there's scarcely anyone who isn't engaged in buying and selling and exchanging . . . and sometimes for their money we sell them our . . . humanity."[8]

Taking advantage of his prestige and a widespread desire for peace, Charles solidified his power. In 1445, in exchange for a promise that tax rates would remain low, the Estates General offered Charles a perpetual grant of the right to collect direct taxes. With an assured source of income, Charles was able to create Europe's first standing army, which consisted of about 8000 nobles under the direct control of royal commanders. Charles also expanded his judicial claims.

In an effort to end the long-standing feuds and vendettas that marked the preceding century, Charles had ordered in 1429 that heirs should be allowed to inherit as if their families had not been displaced by the English. Yet legal battles over property continued into the 1460s. In part to meet the needs of countless litigants, Charles and his son Louis XI (r. 1461–1483) created new provincial *parlements,* or law courts, at Toulouse, Grenoble, Bordeaux, and Dijon. They also required that local laws and customs be registered and approved by these local parlements.

Royal power continued to grow in the last decades of the fifteenth century. One of Louis XI's advisers noted that Charles VII never had revenues greater than 18,000 francs in a single year but Louis collected 4.7 million. Louis used these vastly increased revenues to intensify pressure on the dukes of Burgundy. (See the box, "Louis XI and the Art of Government.") In 1477, when Charles the Bold was killed, Louis quickly seized the duchy of Burgundy, ridding himself of the greatest independent power in the kingdom. A short time later Louis also defeated the leader of the Armagnac faction. The process of consolidation was completed in 1491 when Charles VIII (r. 1483–1498), Louis's son, married Anne of Brittany, the heiress of the last independent duke of Brittany.

In some ways, the consolidation of the French crown's authority was the result of institutional innovation and reform: the institution of regular taxation, the creation of an army, and the extension of the parlementary system. Yet in many respects the old system had not changed. The appanage system, for example, was not abolished until the 1560s. And the nobles continued to look for opportunities to increase their influence at the expense of the king. During times of crisis or of weak kings, royal power could evaporate rapidly.

England and the Wars of the Roses

Throughout the fifteenth century, threats to order in England stemmed from fears of royal power. The English believed that government should be modest, allowing the king very little room to maneuver. In describing the ideal society in the fifteenth century, one later chronicler wrote that if government was good, "then the noble men shall triumph, the rich men shall live without fear, [and] the poor and needy persons shall not be oppressed or confounded." This meant that any attempt to reduce the role of the nobility as the king's "traditional advisers" or to raise new forms of revenue could easily bring cries of tyranny or abuse of power. Although the English generally agreed that the king could institute new taxes to pay for foreign wars, theorists and parliamentary leaders alike held that the king should live off the income of his traditional rights and properties.

Louis XI and the Art of Government

Philippe de Commines (1447–1511) was a courtier who began his career at the court of the dukes of Burgundy. He astutely recognized the shift of power in favor of the French kings and quickly abandoned the dukes for the royal court, from which he hoped to reap great benefits. In his memoirs, he described life at court. His portrait of Louis XI remains one of the most famous of a fifteenth-century ruler.

Of all the princes I ever knew, the wisest and most dexterous to extricate himself out of any danger or difficulty in time of adversity was my master, Louis XI. He was very humble in his conversation and habit, and the most careful and indefatigable to win over any man to his side that he thought capable of doing him either mischief or service.... He was naturally kind and indulgent to persons of mean estate, and hostile to all great men who had no need of him. No prince was more easy to converse with, or more inquisitive, than he, for his desire was to know everybody he could.... But above all, his great bounty and liberality did him the utmost service; and yet, as he behaved with much wisdom in times of distress, so when he thought himself a little out of danger ... he would disoblige the servants and officers of his court by mean and petty ways, which were little to his advantage; and as for peace, he could hardly endure the thought of it.

Source: The Memoirs of Philippe de Commines, trans. A. R. Scoble (London, 1885), excerpted in Hutton Webster, ed., *Readings in Early European History* (Boston: Heath, 1926), p. 407.

So strong was the antipathy to increased taxation that English kings could not afford a paid bureaucracy, a standing army, or a system of fortresses. To create a bureaucracy or to reward military or political allies, the kings were obliged to offer official positions—positions to which many in the nobility felt entitled by tradition. A successful and charismatic king could hold dissatisfaction in check; but in times of crisis, anger and distrust directed toward the Crown could lead to civil war.

King Richard II (r. 1377–1399) ascended the throne as a child at the death of his grandfather Edward III. Richard recognized the costs of the Hundred Years' War with France and the dangers of noble influence and tried to insulate himself from the peers of the realm by choosing advisers from the lesser nobility and the middle classes as well as from the peerage. But in 1398 he seized the hereditary lands of Henry Bolingbroke, duke of Lancaster and probably the greatest of the magnate leaders. Simmering unrest overflowed. Bolingbroke captured and deposed Richard. Parliament later elected Henry king, Henry IV (r. 1399–1413), the first of the Lancastrian line.

At first the Lancastrians were quite successful. Henry IV avoided war taxes and was careful not to alienate the magnates. Henry V (r. 1413–1422), perhaps the most charismatic of the late medieval English kings, gave the Lancastrians their greatest moments: the victory at Agincourt in 1415 and the Treaty of Troyes in 1420, designed to unify the French and English crowns. Within a decade, however, the French were beginning to force the English out of France, and Henry VI (r. 1422–1461) turned out to be weak-willed, immature, and prone to bouts of insanity.

The infirmity of Henry VI and the loss of virtually all French territories in 1453 led to factional battles called the Wars of the Roses because the red rose was the symbol of the Lancastrian dynasty and the white rose signified the Yorkist opposition. The early skirmishes were a series of feuds and vendettas involving small groups of

ENGLISH AND FRENCH POLITICS IN THE FIFTEENTH CENTURY

1399	Abdication of Richard II; accession of Henry IV
1420	Treaty of Troyes
1422	Deaths of Charles VI of France and Henry V of England
1453	The last battle of the Hundred Years' War
1477	Defeat and death of Charles the Bold at Nancy
1483	Death of Edward IV; death of Edward V and his brother in the Tower of London
1485	Death of Richard III at the battle of Bosworth Fields
1491	Charles VIII reclaims French control of Brittany by marrying Anne of Brittany
1494	Charles VIII invades Italy

nobles in various parts of England as local authority broke down. The source of tension was access to the king's patronage. In an attempt to take control of the situation, Henry VI confronted his rivals. Royal forces initially prevailed against the duke of York, but eventually the duke's son Edward defeated and captured Henry in 1461. Edward of York deposed Henry and claimed the Crown for himself as Edward IV (r. 1461–1483). He faced little opposition because there seemed to be few alternatives.

Like Henry IV almost a century earlier, Edward worked hard to placate the nobility and to stabilize the royal administration. He was obstructed, however, by the actions of his in-laws, the Wydevilles (also called the Woodvilles), an aristocratic family that hoped to enrich itself by seizing all the advantages available to royal relatives. The Wydevilles gained control of many aristocratic fortunes by marrying aristocratic orphans who were under the king's guardianship, thus alienating other families that might have provided spouses for the heirs and heiresses.

At the death of Edward IV, English public life was again thrown into confusion. Edward's sons were still minors, and his widow and her family (the Wydevilles) were widely distrusted. The late king's brother, Richard, duke of Gloucester, led the opposition to the queen. Richard claimed the protectorship over the 13-year-old king, Edward V (r. April–June 1483), and his brother. He seized the boys. They were placed in the Tower of London and were never seen again. An Italian diplomat reported what little was known:

> All the attendants who waited upon the king were debarred access to him. He and his brother were withdrawn into the inner apartments of the Tower proper, and day by day began to be seen more rarely behind the bars and windows till at length they ceased to appear altogether. . . . Whether, however, [the king] has been done away with, and by what manner of death, so far I have not at all discovered.[9]

One of Richard's courtiers later confessed to killing the boys and burying them beneath a staircase, where in 1674 two small skeletons were found.

Richard proclaimed himself king and was crowned Richard III (r. 1483–1485). The new king attempted to consolidate his control at the local level. He withstood early challenges to his authority but in 1485 was killed in the battle of Bosworth Fields, near Coventry, by Henry Tudor, a leader of the Lancastrian faction. Henry married Elizabeth, the surviving child of the late Edward IV. Symbolically at least, the struggle between the rival claimants to the Crown appeared over.

Like Edward IV, Henry VII (r. 1485–1509) recognized the importance of avoiding war and taxation. He also wanted to regain control of the network of patronage by which local officials were appointed and to secure allies for his dynasty. So great was his success that at the time of his death the English monarchy was more powerful than it had been at any time in the previous century. That strength, however, was not based on a transformation of the institutions of government. Like Edward IV, Henry VII controlled local affairs through the traditional system of royal patronage. He also imitated Edward in emphasizing the dignity of the royal office, in imitation of the highly formal court culture of the dukes of Burgundy. Though careful with his funds, he was willing to buy jewels and clothing if they added to the brilliance of his court. As one courtier summed up his reign, "His hospitality was splendidly generous. . . . He knew well how to maintain his majesty and all which pertains to kingship."

Henry's skill in marriage politics gave England ties with Scotland and Spain. He arranged the marriage of his daughter Margaret Tudor to James IV of Scotland and the marriage of his sons Arthur and (after Arthur's death) Henry to Catherine of Aragon, daughter of the Spanish rulers Ferdinand and Isabella.

The English monarchy of the late fifteenth century was not a new departure. The success of Henry VII was based on several factors: the absence of powerful opponents; lowered taxation, the result of twenty-five years of peace under Henry VII; and the desire, shared by ruler and ruled alike, for an orderly realm built on the assured succession of a single dynasty.

The Territorial States

It was not just the power of the great monarchies that grew in the late Middle Ages. In many parts of Europe, provincial governments restored order and stability through the creation of military, administrative, and courtly institutions. From Italy through central and eastern Europe and into Scandinavia, social and political integration was the order of the day. Across Europe, tiny city-states and rural lordships were consolidated into larger and more stable provincial or territorial states.

Transformation of the Italian City-States

By medieval standards, fourteenth- and fifteenth-century Italy was a land of cities. In northern Europe a town of over 20,000 or 30,000 people was unusual. The 100,000 or more people who lived in London or Paris in the fourteenth century made these capitals unlike any other cities north of the Alps. Yet at one time or another in the late Middle Ages, Milan, Venice, Florence, and Naples all had populations nearing or exceeding 100,000, and countless other Italian towns were boasting populations of over 20,000. As a result of the decline of papal and imperial power after 1300, these towns formed numerous small city-republics and petty tyrannies. In the fifteenth century, however, Italy was transformed into a country of territorial powers centered on Milan, Venice, Florence, Rome, and Naples. From the late fourteenth century, these five powers moved to secure neighboring territories and stabilize control over most of the peninsula.

Control of the traditional Papal States was the key to papal independence. Papal administrators worked to regain jurisdiction over towns and regions that had become autonomous and allies of other regional powers. A key element of papal strategy was nepotism, the appointment of relatives to high ecclesiastical and administrative offices. In some ways nepotism was defensible. Popes did need loyal allies to oversee portions of the vast papal bureaucracy and control papal territories in central Italy. But often nepotism went too far. The most infamous excesses were those of Pope Alexander VI (r. 1492–1503), whom contemporaries accused of buying the papal election, poisoning enemies, and exiling opponents he could not kill. Although formally celibate, Alexander freely acknowledged his natural children. He made a series of important dynastic marriages for his daughter, Lucrezia Borgia (1480–1519), and helped his son, Cesare (1475–1507), in an attempt to carve out a state in central Italy. Cesare might have succeeded in creating a new state if he had not been ill at the time of Alexander's sudden death and thus unable to influence the choice of a new pope.

In many respects, the popes were merely following the lead of other major Italian powers. By the early fourteenth century the aristocratic Visconti family had taken control of Milan and secured the title of duke. In the late fourteenth and fifteenth centuries the Viscontis and later their Sforza successors made marriage alliances with the French crown and created a splendid court culture in Milan similar to that of the Burgundians. In a series of wars between the 1370s and 1450s, the dukes of Milan expanded their political control throughout most of Lombardy, Liguria, and, temporarily, Tuscany—the environs of Florence itself. It seemed to many that the Milanese were poised to unify all Italy under their control.

Republican Florence and Venice followed similar policies in dealing with warfare and competition with other states. Although Florentines maintained that they were protecting Florentine and Tuscan "liberty" against the Milanese invaders, their interests went beyond simple defense. Like the Venetians, they wanted to control local and regional trade and to ensure that they were able to claim the locally produced agricultural goods necessary to feed Florence's population. In both Venice and Florence, political leaders paid a great deal of attention to securing the support of the general population. (See the feature, "Weighing the Evidence: A Prospective View of Venice," on pages 508–509.) After a political and diplomatic crisis in 1434 brought on by war and high taxes, virtual control of Florentine politics fell into the hands of Cosimo de' Medici, the wealthiest banker in the city. From 1434 to 1494 Cosimo, his grandson Lorenzo, and Lorenzo's son dominated the government in Florence. Always careful to appease Florentine republican traditions, Medici control was virtually as complete as that of the Viscontis and Sforzas in Milan.

Relations among Milan, Venice, Florence, Rome, and Naples were stabilized by the Peace of Lodi and the creation of the Italian League in 1454. In response to endemic warfare in Italy and the looming threat of the Ottoman Turks in the eastern Mediterranean (see page 498), the five powers agreed to the creation of spheres of influence that would prevent any one of them from expanding at the expense of the others. Despite several short wars, the league managed to avoid large-scale territorial changes from 1454 until 1494. Venice, Milan, and Florence were free to integrate much of northern and central Italy into what would become the Venetian republic and the duchies of Lombardy and Tuscany.

The consolidation of the five powers at the expense of the smaller city-republics was possible because small governments had difficulty paying the costs of defense. Since early in the fourteenth century, forces recruited and led by mercenary captains had dominated the armies of the Italian city-states. To the cost of paying mercenaries was added, in the fifteenth century, the cost of building fortifications capable of withstanding bombardment with cannon. Instead of high thin walls, the new bastions had low, sharply inclined walls with carefully crafted gun platforms designed to catch attackers in a withering cross-fire. Military expenses virtually bankrupted many towns, and anger over taxation to pay for military adventures brought down governments.

The public debt of Florence rose from a half-million florins in 1345 to 3 million florins in 1395, largely because of the expenses of mercenaries and fortifications. Forty years later, war and taxation led to the rise of Cosimo de' Medici as the de facto ruler of Florence. When modern fortifications of Lucca were finally completed in the early seventeenth century, construction had been underway for over a half-century and in excess of 900,000 florins had been spent. In that period, a

The Bastions of Lucca The walls of Lucca show the complex geometrical design that the widespread use of cannons made necessary. Walls were designed to force attackers into zones that could be defended by more than one set of defenders. Such walls, often reinforced by earthworks, were expensive and took decades to complete. *(Biblioteca Statale di Lucca)*

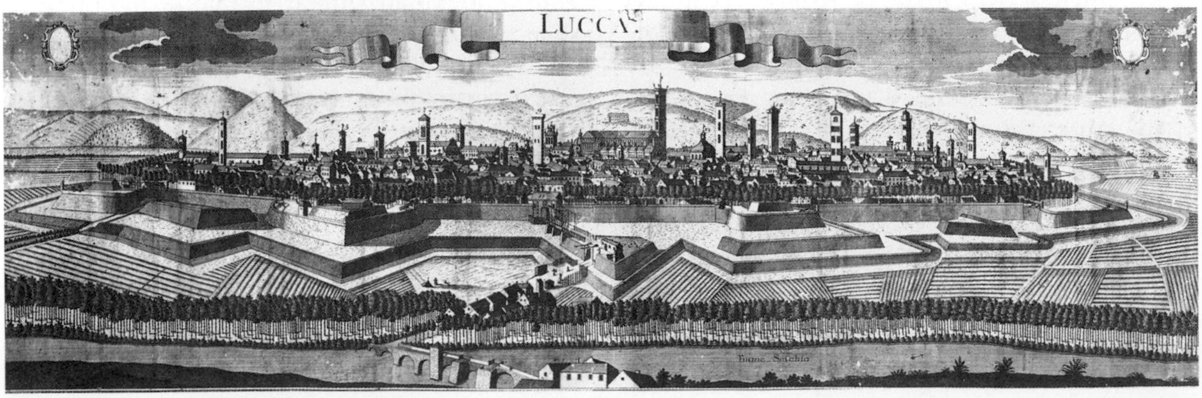

skilled artisan or shopkeeper perhaps earned between 125 and 150 florins a year. Only the very wealthiest city governments could afford to update their fortifications.

The limits of even the territorial states of Italy became clear when King Charles VIII of France invaded Italy in 1494. French kings had hereditary claims to the duchy of Milan and to the kingdom of Naples, but an invitation from Ludovico Sforza of Milan finally enticed Charles to claim Naples. Ludovico hoped that the French would remove from Naples the Aragonese who were opposing his claim to rule Milan. French armies marched across Italy, quickly occupying both Milan and Naples and in the process bringing down the Medici government of Florence. Far from making good on French claims, however, Charles's invasion merely initiated a series of wars that eventually involved the Spanish kings and Holy Roman emperors. The Habsburg-Valois Wars, as they are called, continued for over a half-century, ending with the Treaty of Cateau-Cambrésis in 1559, which left the Spanish kings in control of Milan, Naples, Sardinia, and Sicily (Map 13.2).

The French invasion devastated Italy. Unrest brought on by the invasion allowed Pope Alexander VI to attempt to create a state for his son Cesare in central Italy. In Florence, the war first destroyed the old republic and brought in a new republican constitution. Anti-Medici republicans realized that their previous government had been a sham controlled by the Medicis and their party. Reformers were initially led by the popular Dominican preacher Girolamo Savonarola (1452–1498). In the constitutional debates after 1494, Savonarola argued that true republican reform required a thoroughgoing religious reform of society. Gangs of youth flocked to his cause, attacking prostitutes and homosexuals. Many of his followers held "bonfires of vanities," burning wigs, silks, and other luxuries. As the war continued, and as Florence found itself isolated from its traditional papal and Venetian allies, popular feeling turned against the friar. In 1498, when his followers had lost influence in the government, Savonarola was arrested, tortured, and executed.

The Florentine government that followed attempted to reform administration, build fortresses, and raise a militia, but was unable to save itself from papal and imperial opposition. In 1512 the Medicis returned under papal and imperial protection. First treated as the leading citizens of Florence and as the emperor's allies in central Italy, later the Medicis were named dukes and then grand dukes of Tuscany. The grand duchy of Tuscany remained an independent, integrated, and well-governed state until the French Revolution of 1789. Venice managed to maintain its republican form of government and its territorial state in the sixteenth century; but, like the dukes of Tuscany, the governors of Venice were no longer able to act independently of the larger European powers. Both Naples and Milan were directly ruled by the Spanish kings. Thus, the political integration of the fifteenth century and the impact of the Habsburg-Valois Wars destroyed the tiny city-republics and left the remaining territorial states in a position where they could no longer act independently of foreign powers.

The Triumph of German Provincial Governments

Developments in Germany in the fifteenth century were in many ways similar to those in Italy. As in Italy, political life revolved around towns and regional states rather than around the policies of a monarch. Legal, administrative, and even military initiatives in Germany were not taken by the Holy Roman emperor. There was no single strong imperial dynasty. Relatively weak emperors were chosen alternately from the Luxemburg, Habsburg, or Palatinate dynasties.

There were several reasons for this. Because the emperor's power depended on the power of his family, rulers often pawned imperial rights to castles, market dues, road tolls, and mines in order to invest in properties and rights that belonged directly to their dynasty. Luxemburg and Habsburg emperors gave up traditional imperial rights in southwestern and central Germany in order to gain family lands in the east, in Bohemia and Austria. As a result, imperial claims in most parts of Germany were quite modest. Only with the accession of Frederick III (r. 1440–1493) and the extinction of the Luxemburg family did the Habsburg dynasty begin its domination of the imperial office, which would last until the age of Napoleon. Until 1495 there was no imperial law, and even after 1495 the imperial court in the eyes of most Germans was little more than a court of

Map 13.2 Europe in the Habsburg-Valois Wars Control of northern Italy was essential for both the Habsburgs and the Valois. Italy provided the bridge connecting the Habsburg family's Spanish lands to its German holdings.

appeals. Until the 1490s there was no well-defined imperial diet, or representative assembly, and most imperial attempts to limit feuds and private wars were unsuccessful. In the fifteenth century the Holy Roman Empire was, in effect, a defensive union. The emperor had little direct control over political life in the territories of the empire.

Political and bureaucratic growth tended to occur in the territorial principalities. Laws, taxes, and representative institutions all functioned at the provincial level. As in Italy, the territorial powers took control of many smaller jurisdictions. Because of declining rents and revenues, many imperial knights found it difficult to maintain independent jurisdictions. By 1500, many had been integrated into territorial states. Towns in southwestern Germany faced similar fates. German towns had tried to imitate the Italian city-states by taking control of their surrounding countryside, but only wealthy commercial centers, such as Nuremberg and Augsburg, were strong enough to avoid domination by territorial princes. In many parts of Germany, towns and imperial knights formed leagues to oppose the increased power of the territorial princes, but to little avail. By the 1490s, power within Germany was clearly in the hands of the territorial princes, and within the empire rights and authority were divided between the Habsburg emperor and the territorial princes.

Territorial princes were least effective in what is now Switzerland, where a league of towns, provincial knights, and peasant villages did successfully resist territorial integration. They formed a territorial state of their own. The Swiss Confederation began modestly enough in 1291 as a voluntary association to promote regional peace. Its influence grew significantly when the city-republics of Bern and Zurich joined.

In 1386 forces of the confederation defeated and killed Duke Leopold of Austria, who had claimed jurisdiction over the area governed by the confederation. By the second decade of the fifteenth century, the confederation had conquered most of the traditionally Habsburg lands in the Swiss areas. By the 1470s the Swiss had invented the myth of William Tell, the fearless woodsman who refused to bow his head to a Habsburg official, as a justification for their independent and anti-aristocratic traditions. Their expansion culminated with the battle of Nancy in Loraine in 1477, when the Swiss infantry defeated a Burgundian army and killed Charles the Bold. From then on, the Swiss maintained their independence, and "Turning Swiss" became a battle cry for German towns and individuals who hoped to slow territorial integration.

Aristocrats and Territorial Consolidation in Northern and Eastern Europe

In the fifteenth century, the Scandinavian kingdoms of Denmark, Sweden, and Norway—like the Swiss Confederation—were open to economic and political influences from Germany. Hanseatic merchants traded throughout the area, and German nobles sought to influence political life in the kingdoms. The Scandinavian nobility, however, especially in Denmark, was wary of German interests. Scandinavian nobles tended to intermarry and arrange themselves against the Germans.

The crowns of Denmark, Sweden, and Norway had been united by the Union of Kalmar in 1397, but in the fifteenth century the monarchy was unable to maintain control of the various parts of the kingdom. Monarchs faced opposition by estates composed of nobles and free peasants. Royal power devolved into the hands of political factions composed of provincial nobles and, in Sweden, urban merchants. By 1500, there was little sentiment for a united crown in Norway or Sweden, and in 1523 the Swedes formally rejected union with Denmark.

To the east of Scandinavia, diplomatic and military issues centered on relations between German and Slavic governments. German Teutonic knights controlled Prussia and, under the pretext of converting their pagan neighbors to Christianity, sought to expand eastward against the kingdom of Poland and the Lithuanian state. The conversion of the Lithuanian rulers to Christianity slowed and finally halted the German advance to the east. More serious for the knights was their defeat in 1410 at Tannenberg Forest in Prussia by a Polish-Lithuanian army led by Prince Vytautus (r. 1392–1439) of Lithuania. The reign of Prince Vytautus represented the high point of Lithuanian dominion. He ruled much of modern Poland and western Russia as well as modern Lithuania.

During the fifteenth century Lithuania faced a formidable new opponent, the grand duchy of Moscow. Since the Mongol invasions in the thirteenth century, various Russian towns and principalities had been part of a Mongolian sphere of influence. With the waning of Mongol control, however, the Muscovites annexed other Russian territories. By 1478, Ivan III (r. 1462–1505), called "the Great," had taken control of the famed trading center of Novgorod. Two years later he was powerful enough to renounce Mongol overlordship and refuse further payments of tribute. After marriage to a Byzantine princess, Ivan began to call himself "Tsar" (Russian for "Caesar"), implying that in the wake of the Muslim conquest of Constantinople, Moscow had become the new Rome.

The stability resulting from the rise of Moscow enabled itinerant Russian warriors called *boyars* to transform themselves into landed aristocrats. The boyars came to play a dominant political, institutional, and legal role in provincial society through their control of provincial assemblies, or *dumas.* They used their political power to dominate the countryside and force formerly free peasants into a harsh serfdom from which the Russian peasantry would not emerge until the nineteenth century. It is too early to speak of a Russian national state, yet by 1500 the seeds of Russian dominion were clearly sown.

From Italy through central Europe and into Scandinavia late medieval monarchies were hard-pressed to dominate political life. Yet as the development of the Grand Duchy of Tuscany, the independent feeling of the Swiss states, the rise of Muscovy, and the free peasantry of Scandinavia demonstrate, political order and stability may characterize territorial states as well as centralized monarchies.

Formation of the Ottoman and Spanish Empires

Both in Iberia and in the eastern Mediterranean, political integration in the fifteenth century was brought about by political changes undreamed of a century earlier. The rise of the Ottoman Empire and the unification of Spain created the two powers around which politics and diplomacy would revolve in sixteenth-century Europe.

The Ottoman Turks

In 1453, the Muslim Ottoman Turks breached the walls of Constantinople, killed Emperor Constantine XI (r. 1448–1453), and destroyed the last vestiges of the Byzantine Empire and the Roman imperial tradition that reached back to the emperor Augustus. The sack of Constantinople sent shock waves through Christian Europe and brought forth calls for new crusades to liberate the East from the evils of Islam. It also stirred anti-Christian feelings among the Turks. The leader of the Turkish army, Sultan Mehmed II the Conqueror (r. 1451–1481), was acclaimed the greatest of all *ghazi*—that is, a crusading warrior who was, according to a Turkish poet, "the instrument of Allah, a servant of God, who purifies the earth from the filth of polytheism [i.e., the Christian Trinity]." The rise of the Ottoman Turks led to a profound clash between Christian and Muslim civilizations.

The Turkish threat in the fifteenth century was only one, and perhaps not even the greatest, of the Balkan issues that concerned Christian Europe (Map 13.3). As the power of the Turks advanced, it became clear that a variety of other factors were at play. In 1402 an Ottoman army was defeated by Tamerlane (1336?–1405), the great Mongol Khan whose conquests stretched from Anatolia to China. It took the Ottoman Turks nearly a generation to recover from this defeat. Even as the Turks expanded their area of influence in the Balkans, Christian rulers in Albania, Serbia, Transylvania, and Wallachia saw Turks as only one of the powers they had to fear. Hungarians, Venetians, and Germans also threatened the independence of local rulers. In the 1420s, for example, as the Turks and the Hungarians fought for control of Serbia, the Serbian king moved easily from alliance with one to alliance with the other. By changing religion, rulers often retained their political and economic influence. The Christian aristocracy of late-fifteenth-century Bosnia, for example, was welcomed into Islam and instantly created a cohesive elite fighting force for the Turks. Conversely, as Turkish power in Albania grew, one noble, George Castriota (d. 1467), known by his Turkish name Skanderbeg, recon-

Map 13.3 Turkey and Eastern Europe With the conquest of Constantinople, Syria, and Palestine, the Ottoman Turks controlled the eastern Mediterranean and dominated Europe below the Danube River. The Holy Roman emperors, rulers of Italy, and kings of Spain had to be concerned about potential invasions by land or by sea.

verted to Christianity and became a leading figure in the resistance to the Turks. Only after his death were the Turks able to fully integrate Albania into their empire.

Throughout the fifteenth century there were largely unsuccessful attempts by the papacy and other Christian powers to promote a crusade against the Turks. Neither the Banquet of the Oath of the Pheasant nor the Peace of Lodi and the Italian League of 1454 created a common front against the Muslims. The Italian maritime cities of Genoa and Venice, for example, had trading privileges in Constantinople and Black Sea ports. Neither would actively support a crusade if it adversely affected their trading interests. Similarly, the kings of Germany, Poland, and Hungary tempered their crusading zeal with realistic assessments of how war would affect regional interests. Finally, western aid for eastern Christians was complicated by almost a half-millennium of disagreement between the eastern and western churches over theological issues. The Byzantine emperor John Paleologus (r. 1425–1448) had journeyed to the West in the 1430s in an effort to reunite the two Christian traditions. But the reunion proclaimed at Florence in 1439 was virtually a capitulation by the emperor, because John accepted western views of papal supremacy and the western reading of the Nicaean Creed. The reunion was rejected by most eastern Christians, many of whom preferred living under the Turks to western theological domination.

OTTOMAN TURKS AND THE WEST

1402	Defeat of the Turks by Tamerlane
1439	Reunion of eastern and western churches in preparation for a crusade
1444	Defeat of a Latin crusading army at Varna
1453	Turkish conquest of Constantinople
1454	Formation of the Italian League; swearing of the Oath of the Pheasant in preparation for a crusade to liberate Constantinople
1481	Flight of Ottoman prince Jem to Rhodes

After the defeat of a Latin crusading army at Varna on the Black Sea coast in 1444, the fate of Constantinople was virtually sealed. It was only a matter of time until the Turks took the city. When Mehmed II finally turned his attention to Constantinople, the siege of the city took only fifty-three days. Turkish artillery breached the walls before a Venetian navy or a Hungarian army could come to the city's defense.

After the fall of Constantinople, the Turks worked to consolidate their new conquests. Anatolia was the heart of the Ottoman Empire. Through alliance and conquest, Ottoman domination extended through Syria and Palestine and by 1517 to Egypt. Even the Muslim powers of North Africa were nominally under Turkish control. To the west and north of Constantinople, the Turks dominated Croatia, Bosnia, Dalmatia, Albania, eastern Hungary, Moldavia, Bulgaria, and Greece. Turkish strength was based on a number of factors. The first was the loyalty and efficiency of the sultan's crack troops, the Janissaries. These troops were young boys forcibly taken from the subject Christian populations, trained in Turkish language and customs, and converted to Islam. Although they functioned as special protectors of the Christian community from which they were drawn, they were separated from it by their new faith. Because the Turkish population viewed them as outsiders, they were particularly loyal to the sultan.

The situation of the Janissaries underlines a secondary explanation for Ottoman strength: the unusually tolerant attitudes of Mehmed. Mehmed saw himself not only as the greatest of the ghazi but also as emperor, heir to Byzantine and ancient imperial traditions. Immediately after the conquest of Constantinople, he repopulated the city with Greeks, Armenians, Jews, and Muslims. Religious groups lived in separate districts centered on a church or synagogue, but each religious community retained the right to select its own leaders. Mehmed transferred the capital of the Turkish state to Constantinople. And by building mosques, hospitals, hostels, and bridges, he breathed new life into the city, which he referred to as Istanbul—that is, "the city." In the fifty years following the conquest, the population of the city grew an extraordinary 500 percent, from about 40,000 to over 200,000, making it the largest city in Europe. (See the box, "A European View of the Ottoman Empire.")

At a time when Christian Europe seemed less and less willing to deal with non-Christian minorities, the Ottoman Empire was truly exceptional. Islamic law was tolerant of Christians and Jews as long as they paid a special poll tax and accepted some Turkish supervision. Christian and Jewish leaders supervised the internal affairs of their respective communities. Muslims and non-Muslims belonged to the same trade associations and traveled throughout the empire. Mehmed quickly made trade agreements with the Italian powers in an attempt to consolidate his power. And in Serbia, Bulgaria, Macedonia, and Albania he left in place previous social and political institutions, requiring only loyalty to his new empire.

Mehmed had to tread carefully because the Turks had a number of powerful enemies. The problems that the Ottoman Empire faced were most clear during the reign of Mehmed's son Bayazid (r. 1481–1512). Following Turkish tradition, Mehmed had not chosen a successor but let his sons fight for control. Normally, the successful claimant achieved the throne by doing away with his closest relatives. Bayazid's brother Jem, however, fled into the protective custody of the Knights Hospitallers, a Christian crusading order that controlled the island of Rhodes near the Turkish coast. Jem would live the rest of his life in Christian captivity. In times of crisis, kings and popes would threaten to foment rebellion in Ottoman lands by releasing him. Bayazid also had to worry about the Mamluk Turks, who controlled Egypt and Syria, and the new Safavid dynasty in Persia. Although both were Muslim, they were willing to join with various Christian states to reduce power of the Ottomans. Only in the second decade of the sixteenth century, after Bayazid's son Selim (r. 1512–1520) had defeated the Persians and the Mamluks, were the Ottomans finally safe from attack from the east or south.

The Siege of Constantinople The siege of Constantinople by the Turks required the attackers to isolate the city both by sea and by land. This miniature from the fifteenth century shows the Turkish camps, as well as the movements of Turkish boats, completing the isolation of the city. *(Bibliothèque Nationale)*

The Union of Crowns in Spain

While expanding across the Mediterranean, the Turks came in contact with the other new state of the fifteenth century, the newly unified kingdom of Spain. In 1469 Ferdinand, heir to the kingdom of Aragon and Catalonia, married Isabella, daughter of the king of Castile. Five years later Isabella became queen of Castile, and in 1479 Ferdinand took control of the kingdom of Aragon. This union of crowns would lead to the creation of a united Spain.

The permanence of the union was surprising because the two kingdoms were so different. Castile was much the larger and more populous state. It had taken the lead in the fight to reconquer Iberia and end Muslim rule. As a result, economic power within Castile was divided among those groups most responsible for the Reconquista: military orders and nobles. The military orders of Calatrava, Santiago, and Alcantara were militias formed by men who had taken a religious vow similar to the vow taken by a monk, except that they vowed to fight against the enemies of Christianity. In the course of the Reconquista the military orders assumed control of vast districts. Lay nobles who aided in the Reconquista also held large tracts of land and were very proud of their independence.

Castile's power stemmed from its agrarian wealth. During the Reconquista, Castilians took control of large regions and turned them into ranges for grazing Merino sheep, producers of the prized Merino wool exported to the woolen markets of Flanders and to Italy. To maximize the profits from wool production, the kings authorized the creation of the Mesta, a brotherhood of sheep producers. The pastoral economy grew to the point that by the early sixteenth century there were nearly 3.5 million sheep in Castile. So great were the profits accruing to the Crown from the exporting of wool that all other aspects of the economy were sacrificed to the needs of the Mesta.

Economic power in Castile lay with the nobility, but political power rested with the monarch. Because the nobility was largely exempt from taxation, nobles ignored the cortes, the popular assembly, which could do little more than approve royal demands. The towns of Castile were important only as fortresses and staging points for militias rather than as centers of trade and

A European View of the Ottoman Empire

In the late fifteenth century, Italian governments began to send permanent ambassadors to foreign courts. They were the first governments to do so. Venetian ambassadors quickly earned an international reputation as careful observers of the countries to which they had been assigned. The following evaluation of the Ottoman Empire was written in 1585 by the Venetian ambassador, Gianfrancesco Morosini. It is a combination of shrewd observation and chauvinistic dismissal of a different civilization.

[The Turks] were organized as military squadrons or commando units until 1300 A.D., when one of their number, named Ottoman, a man of low birth, began to build a reputation as a strong and spirited leader. Shrewd and clever, he took advantage of rivalries among his people, attracted many of them to him, and led them in war and conquest, making himself master of various towns and provinces of both the Turks and their neighbors. . . .

They succeed to the throne without any kind of ceremony of election or coronation. But in fact, whichever of the sons can first enter the royal compound in Constantinople is called the sultan and is obeyed by the people and by the army. Since he has control of his father's treasure he can easily gain the favor of the janissaries and with their help the rest of the army and the civilians. . . .

The security of the empire depends more than anything else on the large numbers of land and sea forces which the Turks keep continually under arms. These are what make them feared throughout the world. The sultan always has about 280,000 well-paid men in his service. . . . These include roughly 16,000 janissaries who form the Grand Signor's advanced guard. . . .

The whole empire is inhabited by three groups of people: Turks, Moors [non-Turkish Muslims], and Christians. In Asia and Africa the Moors are more numerous than the Turks, while in Europe the largest number are Christians, almost all of whom practice the Greek rite. There are also many Jews since that is really their homeland, even though they live in it like strangers rather than natives.

Source: J. C. Davis, *Pursuit of Power: Venetian Ambassadors' Reports on Spain, Turkey, and France in the Age of Philip II, 1560–1600* (New York: Harper & Row, 1970), pp. 126, 127, 129, 134–135.

commerce. No force was capable of opposing the will of the monarch. As John II of Castile (r. 1406–1454) explained,

> All my vassals, subjects, and people, whatever their estate, . . . are, according to all divine, human, . . . and even natural law, compelled and bound . . . to my word and deed. . . . The king holds this position not from men but from God, whose place he holds in temporal matters.[10]

The kingdom of Aragon was dramatically different. Although it did manage to take Valencia from its Muslim rulers, Aragon remained smaller and less powerful than Castile. After the conquest of Valencia, Aragon was less involved in the Reconquista. The center of the kingdom was Barcelona, an important trading center in the Mediterranean. In the fourteenth and fifteenth centuries the kings of Aragon concentrated their efforts on expanding their influence in the Mediterranean, south of France and Italy. By the middle of the fifteenth century the Aragonese empire included the kingdom of Naples, Sicily, the Balearic Islands, and Sardinia.

The power of the Aragonese king, in sharp contrast to the Castilian monarchy, was limited because the crown was not unified. The ruler was king in Aragon and Navarre but was count in

Catalonia. Aragon, Catalonia, and Valencia each maintained its own cortes. In each area the traditional nobility and the towns had a great deal more influence than they had in Castile. The power of the estates is clear in the coronation oath taken by the Aragonese nobility: "We who are as good as you and together are more powerful than you, make you our king and lord, provided that you observe our laws and liberties, and if not, not."[11] The distinction with Castile could not be stronger.

The union of the crowns of Aragon and Castile did little to unify the two monarchies. By 1474 Castile and Aragon already had a long history of warfare and mutual distrust. Nobles fought over disputed boundaries, and Castilian nobles felt exploited by Aragonese merchants. Trade duties and internal boundaries continued to separate the two. The two realms even lacked a treaty to allow for the extradition of criminals from one kingdom to the other. Castilians never accepted Ferdinand as more than their queen's consort. After the death of Isabella in 1504, he ruled in Castile only as regent for his infant grandson, Charles I (r. 1516–1556). "Spain" would not emerge in an institutional sense until the late sixteenth century.

Nonetheless, the reign of Isabella and Ferdinand marked a profound change in politics and society in the Iberian kingdoms. The monarchs visited all parts of their realm, reorganized municipal governments, took control of the powerful military orders, strengthened the power of royal law courts, and extended the international influence of the monarchies. Many of their actions were designed to advance the interests of Aragon in the Mediterranean. Ferdinand and Isabella married their daughter Joanna to Philip of Habsburg in 1496 to draw the Holy Roman Empire into the Italian wars brought on by the French invasion. The marriage of their daughter Catherine of Aragon to Prince Arthur of England in 1501 was designed to obtain yet another ally against the French. Those two marriages would have momentous consequences for European history in the sixteenth century.

The reign of Ferdinand and Isabella is especially memorable because of the events of 1492. In January of that year, a crusading army conquered Granada, the last Muslim stronghold in Iberia. In March, Ferdinand and Isabella ordered the Jews of Castile and Aragon to convert or leave the kingdom within four months. In April, Isabella issued her commission authorizing Christopher Columbus "to discover and acquire islands and mainland in the Ocean Sea" (see page 558).

THE UNION OF CROWNS IN SPAIN

1469	Ferdinand of Aragon marries Isabella of Castile
1474	Isabella becomes queen of Castile
1478	Spanish Inquisition is established
1479	Ferdinand becomes king of Aragon
1492	Conquest of Granada; Columbus's first voyage; expulsion of Jews from Spain
1496	Joanna of Castile marries Philip of Habsburg
1501	Catherine of Aragon marries Arthur Tudor of England
1504	Expulsion of Muslims from Spain; death of Isabella; Ferdinand rules Castile as regent for his grandson, Charles I

The conquest of Granada and the expulsion of the Jews represented a radical shift in the Spanish mentality. Until the beginning of the fifteenth century, Spain maintained a level of religious tolerance unusual in Christendom. In the fourteenth century, perhaps 2 percent of the population of Iberia was Jewish, and the Muslim population may have been as high as 50 percent. The various groups were inextricably mixed. The statutes of the Jewish community in Barcelona were in Catalan rather than Hebrew. Conversos, Jewish converts to Christianity, and maranos, Muslim converts, mixed continuously with Christians and with members of their former religions. It was difficult at times to know which religion an individual actually practiced. One surprised northern visitor to Spain remarked that one noble's circle was filled with "Christians, Moors and Jews and he lets them live in peace in their faith."

This tolerant mingling of Christians, Muslims, and Jews was under attack by 1400, however. Complaints came from a variety of sources. Many of the most important financiers and courtiers were Jews or conversos, which in-

The Expulsion of the Jews

Many of the expulsion records explain that the tragedy was "on account of our sins" and to call Jews back to faithfulness. The following anonymous chronicle includes a narrative of the passage of Jews out of Spain and into other lands in the Mediterranean.

And in the year 5252 (1492) the Lord visited the remnant of his people a second time, and exiled them in the days of King Ferdinand. . . . The number of the exiled was not counted, but, after many inquiries, I found that the most generally accepted estimate is 50,000 families. . . . They had houses, fields, vineyards, and cattle, and most of them were artisans. . . . [The] time had become short, and they had to hasten their exodus from Spain. They sold their houses, their landed estates, and their cattle for very small prices, to save themselves. The king did not allow them to carry silver and gold out of this country, so that they were compelled to exchange their silver and gold for merchandise of cloths and skins and other things. . . . Many ships with Jews, especially from Sicily, went to the city of Naples on the coast. The king of this country [King Ferrante II] was friendly to the Jews, received them all, and was merciful towards them, and he helped them with money. The Jews that were at Naples supplied them with food as much as they could, and sent around to the other parts of Italy to collect money to sustain them. . . .

Part of the exiled Spaniards went over sea to Turkey. Some of them were thrown into the sea and drowned, but those who arrived there the king of Turkey received kindly as they were artisans. He lent them money to settle many of them on an island, gave them fields and estates.

A few of the exiles were dispersed in the countries of Italy, in the city of Ferrara, in the counties of Romagna, le Marche, and Patrimonium, and in Rome.

Source: D. Raphael, ed., *The Expulsion 1492 Chronicles* (North Hollywood, Calif.: Carmi House, 1992), pp. 129, 130, 131.

creased tensions among the communities. The most conservative Christians desired a community free of non-Christian influences. All three religious communities thought that there should be distinct dress and behavior among the groups. Christians seemed concerned that many of the conversos were likely to reconvert to Judaism, and the fear of reconversion, or "judaizing," led many to advocate the institution of the Spanish Inquisition.

Inquisitions were well known in many parts of Europe, but the Spanish Inquisition was unique because in 1478 Pope Sixtus IV placed the grand inquisitor under the direct control of the monarchs. Like most Christian rulers, Ferdinand and Isabella believed that uniform Christian orthodoxy was the only firm basis for a strong kingdom. Inquisitors attacked those aspects of converso tradition that seemed to make the conversos less than fully Christian. They were concerned that many conversos and maranos had converted falsely and were continuing to follow Jewish or Muslim ritual. The "New Christians" tended to live near their Muslim or Jewish relatives, eat the foods enjoyed in their former communities, and observe holy days, such as Yom Kippur, the Jewish day of atonement. Over four thousand converso families fled from Andalusia in southern Spain in the wake of the arrival of an inquisitor in 1490.

Because its administration, finances, and appointments were in Spanish hands, the Spanish Inquisition quickly became an important instrument for the expansion of state power. Many in-

The Expulsion of the Jews When the Jews were expelled from the Spanish kingdoms they were able to take little or nothing with them. Many trudged overland to Portugal before finding transportation to North Africa, the Netherlands, Italy, or the Turkish Empire. *(The British Library)*

quisitors used their offices to attack wealthy or politically important converso families both to drive them from public life and to fill the royal treasury, which was where the estates of those judged guilty wound up. "This inquisition is as much to take the conversos' estates as to exalt the faith," was the despairing conclusion of one conversa woman.[12]

Ferdinand and Isabella seem to have concluded that the only way to protect the "New Christians" was to order all Jews who would not convert to leave the kingdom within four months. The order was signed on March 31, 1492, and published in late April after an unsuccessful attempt by converso and Jewish leaders to persuade the monarchs not to implement it.

Many Jews could not dispose of their possessions in the four months allowed and so chose to convert and remain. But it is estimated that about ten thousand Jews left Aragon and that even more left Castile. Many moved to Portugal and then to North Africa. Some went east to Constantinople or north to the Low Countries (see the box, "The Expulsion of the Jews"). In 1504, the expulsion order was extended to include all Muslims.

The economic and social costs of the expulsion were profound. Not every Muslim or Jew was wealthy and cultured, but the exiles did include many doctors, bankers, and merchants. Spanish culture, which had been open to influences from Muslim and Jewish sources, was less so in later centuries. After the expulsion, there was a chasm of distrust between the "Old Christians" and the "New." As early as the first decades of the fifteenth century, some religious orders had refused to accept "New Christians." They required that their members demonstrate *limpieza de sangre,* a purity of blood. By 1500 the same tests of blood purity were extended to a majority of religious and public offices. Thus, by the end of the fifteenth century, the Iberian kingdoms had created more powerful, unified governments, but at a terrible cost to the only area in Christendom that had ever practiced religious tolerance.

Summary

Europe at the end of the fifteenth century was profoundly different from Europe in the middle of the fourteenth century. The complexity of the economy had increased as new patterns of trade and new manufacturing techniques spread throughout Europe. The cloth industry in southern Germany gave rise to new merchant-bankers in towns like Augsburg and Nuremberg. Governments grew stronger as kings, princes, and town patricians used traditional ideas of courtliness and patronage to extend their control.

The strength of government reflected the strength of the person at the center. Military advances, such as new types of artillery and more disciplined armies, in the fifteenth century gave advantages to larger governments; but the experiences of the Italian and German states as well as the duchy of Burgundy demonstrated that regional powers, under certain circumstances, could remain virtually independent of royal control.

In the aftermath of schism and conciliar reform, the church also was transformed in the fifteenth century. The popes who returned to central Italy in the fifteenth century were, like the dukes of Burgundy, adept at using art and literature to explain and magnify their court and their place in Christian society. Art and literature played an important role in the reform and explanation of public life. It is to the role of culture that we now turn.

Notes

1. Quoted in Jeremy Cohen, *The Friars and the Jews: The Evolution of Medieval Anti-Judaism* (Ithaca, N.Y.: Cornell University Press, 1982), p. 239.
2. Quoted in Steven E. Ozment, ed., *Three Behaim Boys: Growing Up in Early Modern Germany: A Chronicle of Their Lives* (New Haven: Yale University Press, 1990).
3. Angela of Foligno, *The Book of Divine Consolation of the Blessed Angela of Foligno,* trans. Mary G. Steegmann (New York: Cooper Square Publishers, 1966), p. 260.
4. Raffaele Brandolini, as quoted in Charles L. Stinger, *The Renaissance in Rome* (Bloomington: Indiana University Press, 1985), p. 156.
5. Quoted in Leopold D. Ettlinger, *The Sistine Chapel Before Michelangelo* (Oxford: Oxford University Press, 1965), p. 105.
6. Quoted in Arthur G. Dickens, *The Courts of Europe* (New York: Crown Publishers, 1977), p. 60 (spelling modernized).
7. Quoted in Bernard Guenée, *Between Church and State: The Lives of Four French Prelates in the Late Middle Ages* (Chicago: University of Chicago Press, 1991), p. 24.
8. Quoted in Peter Shervey Lewis, *Later Medieval France: The Polity* (New York: Macmillan, 1968), p. 15.
9. Quoted in Jeffrey Richards, "The Riddle of Richard III," *History Today* 33 (August 1983): 20.
10. Quoted in Angus MacKay, *Spain in the Middle Ages: From Frontier to Empire, 1000–1500* (London: Macmillan, 1977), p. 137.
11. Ibid., p. 105.
12. Haim Beinart, ed., *Records of the Trials of the Spanish Inquisition in Ciudad Real,* vol. 1 (Jerusalem: The Israel Academy of Sciences and Humanities, 1974), p. 391. Translation by Duane Osheim.

Suggested Reading

Economic Recovery

Abulafia, D. "Asia, Africa and the Trade of Medieval Europe." In *Cambridge Economic History,* 402–473. 1987. A thorough introductory discussion of international trade in the late Middle Ages.

Bridbury, A. R. *Economic Growth: England in Later Middle Ages.* 1975. An account that includes a very accessible discussion of the factors for economic growth in the late Middle Ages.

De Roover, R. A. *The Rise and Decline of the Medici Bank, 1397–1494.* 1966. Based largely on the family's business correspondence, this is the clearest discussion of the business practices of any fifteenth-century bank.

Dyer, C. *Standards of Living in the Later Middle Ages: Social Change in England, c. 1200–1500.* 1989. An account that includes a sophisticated discussion of dietary changes in the wake of population decline and changed commodity prices in the fifteenth century.

Hanawalt, Barbara, ed. *Women and Work in Pre-Industrial Europe.* 1986. Sophisticated case studies of the changing status of women's work in the late Middle Ages in England, France, and Germany.

Hatcher, John. *Plague, Population and Economic Decline.* 1977. An explanation of the complex relationship between plague, population growth, and economic change. This short introduction is designed for students.

Howell, M. C. *Women, Production and Patriarchy in Late Medieval Cities.* 1986. After thoroughly reconstructing guild life in the Low Countries, the author argues that women were frozen out of the cloth industry. A difficult but important work.

Christianity and the Papacy

Cohen, J. *The Friars and the Jews: The Evolution of Medieval Anti-Judaism.* 1982. In a complex, closely argued study, Cohen describes the changed attitudes toward Jews in the thirteenth and fourteenth centuries.

Crowder, C. M. D. *Unity, Heresy, and Reform, 1378–1460: The Conciliar Response to the Great Schism.* 1977. Translations of major political and theological tracts, with clear introductions to the political and intellectual background of the debate. The entire volume is an excellent introduction to the schism.

Ettlinger, L. D. *The Sistine Chapel Before Michelangelo.* 1965. Ettlinger discusses in depth the construction of the chapel, the symbols contained in the scenes, and the religious sources of the symbols. The book includes detailed photographs of the complete Moses and Christ cycles.

Oakley, F. *The Western Church in the Later Middle Ages.* 1979. An excellent introductory survey that discusses the various religious, intellectual, and spiritual currents that colored religious life in the period.

Thomson, J. A. F. *Popes and Princes, 1417–1517.* 1980. This general narrative of the political role of the papacy in the century after the end of the Great Schism is the clearest discussion of papal interests presently available.

French and English Monarchy

Duby, G. *France in the Middle Ages, 987–1460.* Translated by Juliet Vale. 1991. In this general survey, France's most distinguished medievalist concentrates on social and cultural life. Includes excellent pictures, maps, and diagrams.

Goodman, A. *The New Monarchy: England, 1471–1534.* 1988. This is a short introduction to the discussions of the changed nature of monarchy after the Wars of the Roses.

Guenée, B. *States and Rulers in Later Medieval Europe.* Translated by Juliet Vale. 1985. This is the best general introduction to the nature of government in the late Middle Ages. It introduces recent trends in historical research.

Lewis, P. S., ed. *The Recovery of France in the Fifteenth Century.* 1971. The essays in this volume are scholarly case studies discussing the growth in state power in the decade after the Hundred Years' War. Several are difficult but rewarding.

Thomson, J. A. F. *The Transformation of Medieval England.* 1983. This is a general survey of the social, economic, and political development of England in the late Middle Ages.

The Other States of Europe

Christiansen, E. *The Northern Crusades: The Baltic and the Catholic Frontier, 1100–1525.* 1980. This sophisticated but clear history of the expansion of Christian forces into the Baltic includes a discussion of the towns and governments of the fourteenth and fifteenth centuries.

Du Boulay, F. R. H. *Germany in the Later Middle Ages.* 1983. This survey of German history designed for students emphasizes the growth of territorial governments at the expense of the central authorities.

Hay, D., and J. Law. *Italy in the Age of the Renaissance, 1380–1530.* 1989. This accessible general survey of Italian social, political, and cultural life emphasizes the diversity of the states of fifteenth-century Italy.

Moberg, V. *A History of the Swedish People.* Translated by Paul Britten Austin. 1989. This fascinating narrative of Swedish life in the Middle Ages by one of the country's greatest novelists and popular historians is an excellent introduction for the general reader.

The Ottoman and Spanish Empires

Hillgarth, J. N. *The Spanish Kingdoms, 1250–1516.* 1976. This general history by the leading North American historian of Iberia includes sophisticated discussions of the rising distrust of non-Christian groups and the eventual expulsion of Jews and Muslims.

Holt, P. M., Ann Katharine Swynford Lambton, and Bernard Lewis, eds. *The Cambridge History of Islam.* 1970. The essays in this volume provide a general introduction for nonspecialists.

Housley, N. *The Later Crusades: From Lyons to Alcazar, 1274–1580.* 1992. This comprehensive account of crusading history includes an especially good consideration of Christian and Muslim relations in Iberia and the Balkans.

Inalcik, H. *The Ottoman Empire: The Classical Age, 1300–1600.* 1973. A general discussion of the growth of the Ottoman state by Turkey's best medieval historian.

Kamen, H. A. F. *The Spanish Inquisition.* 1966. This passionate introduction to Spain's most controversial institution demonstrates the truth of Lord Acton's observation that "Absolute power corrupts absolutely." Kamen gives an especially clear discussion of court procedures.

MacKay, A. *Spain in the Middle Ages: From Frontier to Empire, 1000–1500.* 1977. This short general introduction to Spain emphasizes the institutional changes that occurred in the late fourteenth and fifteenth centuries.

Weighing the Evidence

A PROSPECTIVE VIEW OF VENICE

Jacopo de'Barbari is said to have made this sketch of Venice in 1500. His rendering is typical of a number of works that show the structure of Italian towns. The artist seems to be sketching from a prospect high above the city; hence, the engraving is called "A Prospective View." If we look carefully at the picture, we can locate virtually every canal, street, and piazza in the city. The detail in the work gives some idea of why fifteenth-century visitors viewed Venice as a terrestrial paradise. Visitors today have the same sensations of delight as they move along the canals or walk the narrow streets and bridges that connect the small piazzas (public squares) and modest parish churches of the city's various districts. The canals mark off what remain of the original islands on which the city was founded in the early Middle Ages. Benefiting from its position as a conduit of trade between central Europe and the Mediterranean, the city grew to a population of over 100,000 people by the fourteenth century, creating the tightly packed neighborhoods revealed in de'Barbari's woodcut. This unique setting has moved countless historians and social commentators to consider how an urban landscape might affect the political and social experiences of its inhabitants.

Many commentators first of all have credited the structure of the city with helping to create Venice's reputation for civic peace. In Florence, mobs could quickly and easily move from neighborhoods to the center of town. In late medieval Venice, any mob intent on violence had to negotiate a number of narrow bridges on its way to the city center, and the authorities could easily defend any one of the bridges. Thus, an obvious effect of Venice's landscape on Venetians was the muffling of dissent. Yet the impact of urban form on the life of citizens was in reality much more complex.

Like most cities of any time, Venice was not a single community but a network of networks. The scene explains the phrase. Notice, for example, the numerous piazzas that were the centers of the nearly sixty parishes into which the city was divided. In the thirteenth and most of the fourteenth centuries, these parishes functioned as small communities, each with a parish church, a public area, local shops, and elected representatives. Parishes often had their own patron saints and public festivals. Most neighborhoods included a complex mix of nobles, merchants, artisans, and the poor, often living on different floors of the same building. These neighborhoods were the fundamental units of the city.

As we study de'Barbari's work, however, our attention returns to what is obviously the focal point of the picture: the area of the Church of San Marco, which was the religious center of the community, the palace of the doge, who was the titular ruler of the city, and the Grand Canal. The image graphically makes the point that local networks built on neighborhood relationships had to compete with the political and ritual connections that tied individuals to the center of the city. The great festivals of the city like the doge's symbolic marriage to the sea, celebrating the city's maritime traditions, and processions in honor of the Virgin Mary (one of the city's patron saints), even the route followed by condemned prisoners, moved from the area of San Marco along the Grand Canal.

As the picture shows, Venice was a great center of commercial activity. Countless ships were anchored just off Piazza San Marco in front of the doge's palace. Cargoes were unloaded and hauled by barge to the warehouses of merchants from Germany as well as from Venice and throughout Italy. Visitors, merchants, and Venetian politicians mingled in the heart of the city.

But the picture hides one social reality of Venice. The network of networks that formed the city was not simply a hierarchy focused on the government. Personal relationships in a local parish were significantly different from those at

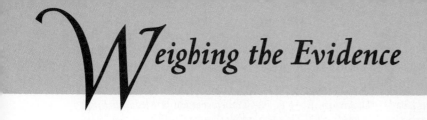

De'Barbari: A Prospective View of Venice (detail) *(Art Resource)*

the city's center. The males of the patrician elite who dominated government used their influence to build up citywide networks of friendship and influence by helping other patricians, middle-class government workers, and even artisans obtain "graces" or favors from the government—lucrative government jobs, the voiding of fines, or help with appeals over taxes.

By the fifteenth century the most important social and political relationships of influential males were rooted in the center of town, in Piazza San Marco. Patrician women, however, created extensive networks of friendship and influence firmly centered on the parishes in which the families lived. Most patricians wanted their wives to remain in the parish, a safe area where they were unlikely to run the risk of public insult or dishonor. Wives were responsible for keeping track of the slaves, servants, and relatives who lived in a great patrician's household. They dealt with local merchants and chatted with other women of all classes on a daily basis when they attended mass at the parish church. It is clear from surviving documents that these patrician women were highly influential in their neighborhoods. In many cases they might be chosen as legal guardians for the children of artisan women they had befriended.

Prospectival views of cities were very popular in the late fifteenth and sixteen centuries, perhaps because townsmen were increasingly aware of the complexity of the urban landscape in which they lived. Like de'Barbari, other artists tried to portray accurately the spaces that made up their towns and the activities that occurred there. In the case of Venice, we see that the shape of the city, its streets and its canals, made it possible for Venetians to move easily from neighborhoods to the city center. Through the work of artists like de'Barbari we recognize something of the complex relationships that were at the heart of life in late medieval cities.

CHAPTER 14

The Renaissance

Between 1300 and 1600, first Italians and later many other Europeans became involved in a series of movements designed to remake radically the culture of Christian Europe. Ignoring many of the positive accomplishments of the previous thousand years, they viewed the recent past as a tragedy from which Europe had to be rescued. To writers interested in literature and moral philosophy the classical world seemed far superior to the world of Scholasticism. In the words of Leonardo Bruni, an influential fifteenth-century writer, "As the city of Rome had perished at the hands of perverse and tyrannical Emperors, so did Latin studies and literature undergo similar ruin and diminution. . . . And Italy was invaded by Goths and Lombards, barbarous, uncouth peoples, who practically extinguished all knowledge of literature."[1] Bruni's feelings were common among artists and writers. They wrote of themselves and their contemporaries as having "revived" arts, "rescued" painting, and "rediscovered" classical authors. They even coined the phrases "Dark Ages" and "Middle Ages" to describe the period that separated classical antiquity from the culture of their own times. In the sixteenth century the painter and art historian Giorgio Vasari described the revival as a *rinascità,* an Italian word meaning "rebirth." And to this day we use the French translation of that word, *renaissance,* to describe the period between 1300 and 1600.

We also use *renaissance* to describe any time of intense creativity and change that differs dramatically from what has gone before. This definition of the word comes to us primarily from the work of the Swiss historian Jacob Burckhardt. In *The Civilization of the Renaissance in Italy* (1860), Burckhardt argued that the creativity and cultural brilliance of the period resulted when Italians suddenly found themselves freed from the medieval

The Duomo (cathedral of Santa Maria del Fiore), Florence. Dome by Felippo Brunelleschi.

restraints of religion, guild, community, and family. Renaissance Italians, he believed, were the first individuals to recognize the state as an autonomous moral structure free from the strictures of religious or philosophical traditions. During the Renaissance, an individual's success or failure in all matters depended on personal qualities of creative brilliance rather than on status in a family, religion, or guild. What Burckhardt thought he saw in Renaissance Italy were the first signs of the romantic individualism and the nationalism that characterized his own society.

Many critics of Burckhardt accept his definition of the Renaissance as a period of brilliance but then argue that, except perhaps in painting and architecture, the culture of Renaissance Europe was in no way superior to the religious, philosophical, and literary culture that preceded or followed it. These critics are in large measure correct. Although the culture of Renaissance Europe was in many ways new and innovative, it had close ties to the ideas of the high Middle Ages and to traditional Christian values.

We cannot answer aesthetic questions of whether Renaissance architecture, literature, and philosophy were actually superior to the culture out of which they grew. We can, however, describe the Renaissance in Europe as an important cultural movement that aimed to reform and renew by making art, education, religion, and political life congruent with their conception of classical and early Christian counterparts. Renaissance men and women misunderstood important aspects of classical culture; nevertheless, their attempts at reform had a profound effect on the development of European culture.

Humanism and Culture in Italy

Logic and scholastic philosophy dominated university education in northern Europe but had less influence in Italy, where education focused on the practical issues of town life rather than on theological speculation. Educated Italians of the fourteenth and fifteenth centuries were interested in the *studia humanitatis,* or humanism. By *humanism,* Italians meant rhetoric and literature—the arts of persuasion—not an ideological or moral program based on religious assumptions about human nature. Poetry, history, letter writing, and oratory based on forms and aesthetic values consciously borrowed from ancient Greece and Rome were at the center of intellectual life.

Humanistic thought in the Renaissance was very much a product of the urban milieu of fourteenth- and fifteenth-century Italy. Italians turned to models from classical antiquity in an attempt to deal with current issues of cultural, political, and educational reform. The humanistic movement began as a belief in the superiority of the literature and history of the past. As humanists discovered more about ancient culture, they were able to understand more clearly the historical context in which Roman writers and thinkers lived. And by the early sixteenth century, their debates on learning, civic duty, and the classical legacy had led them to a new vision of the past and a new appreciation of the nature of politics.

The Emergence of Humanism

Humanism initially held greater appeal in Italy than elsewhere in Europe because culture in central and northern Italy was significantly more secular and more urban than the culture of much of the rest of Europe. Members of the clergy were not likely to dominate government and education in Italy. Quite the reverse: Boards dominated by laymen had built and were administering the great urban churches of Italy. Religious hospitals and charities were often reorganized and centralized under government control. In 1300, four cities in Italy had populations of about 100,000 (Milan, Venice, Florence, and Naples), and many others had populations of 40,000 or more. By contrast, London, which may have had a population of 100,000, was the only city in England with more than 40,000 inhabitants. Even the powerful Italian aristocracy tended to live at least part of the year in towns and conform to urban social and legal practices.

Differences between Italy and northern Europe are apparent in the structure of local education. In northern Europe, education was organized by the church to provide clergy for local churches. In the towns of Italy, education was much more likely to be supervised by town governments to provide training in accounting, arithmetic, and the composition of business letters. In Italy it was common for town governments to hire lay grammar masters to teach in free public schools. They competed with numerous private masters and individual tutors who were prepared to teach all subjects. Giovanni Villani described Florence in 1338 as a city of about 100,000 people in which perhaps as many as 10,000 young boys completed elementary education and 1000 continued their studies to prepare for careers in commerce. Compared to education in the towns of northern Europe, education in Villani's Florence seems broad based and practical and may have been typical of education in the commercial towns of central and northern Italy.

Italian towns were also the focus of theorizing about towns as moral, religious, and political communities. Writers wanted to define the nature of the commune—the town government. Moralists often used "the common good" and "the good of the commune" as synonyms. By 1300, it was common for towns to celebrate the feast day of their patron saint as a major political as well as religious festival. And town governments often supervised the construction and expansion of cathedrals, churches, and hospitals as a sign of their wealth and prestige. Literature of the early fourteenth century tended to emphasize the culture of towns. Dante's *Divine Comedy* is filled with realistic descriptions of his fellow townsmen. Italian historians chose to write the histories of their hometowns. Most, like Giovanni Villani of Florence, were convinced that their towns could rival ancient Rome. The majority of educated Italians in the early fourteenth century, however, were not captivated by thoughts of ancient Rome. Theirs was a practical world in which most intellectuals were men trained in notarial arts—the everyday skills of oratory, letter writing, and the recording of legal documents.

The first Italians who looked back consciously to the literary and historical examples of ancient Rome were a group of northern Italian lawyers and notaries who imitated Roman authors in their poetry and history. Albertino Mussato of Padua (1262–1329) was at the center of the movement of townsmen who adopted classical styles in their poetry and histories. Albertino used his play *Ecerinis* (1315) to tell of the fall of Can Grande della Scala, the tyrannical ruler of Verona (d. 1329) and to warn his neighbors of the dangers of tyranny. He celebrated the independent city-states and urged a renewal of republican values in the cities of the Po Valley. "The rule of justice lasts forever," Albertino concluded, "Virtue soars to heavenly joys."[2] From its earliest, the classical revival in Italy was tied to issues of moral and political reform.

Dante Although banished from Florence, shortly after his death Dante became a symbol of Florentine culture. His portrait was often painted by the town's artists. Boccaccio and other leading humanists wrote biographies of the great poet proclaiming that with his example he had shown how to renew Italian culture. *(Art Resource, NY)*

Petrarch and Early Humanism

Francesco Petrarch (1304–1374), the son of an exiled Florentine notary living at the papal court in Avignon, popularized the idea of mixing classical moral and literary ideas with the concerns of the fourteenth century. His father sent him to study law at the University of Bologna, but Petrarch had little interest in the law. After his father's death he quickly abandoned law for literature. Repelled by the urban violence and wars he had experienced, Petrarch was highly critical of his contemporaries: "I never liked this age," he once confessed. He criticized "the Babylonian Captivity," as he named it, of the papacy in Avignon; he supported an attempt to resurrect a republican government in Rome; and he believed that imitation of the actions, values, and culture of the ancient Romans was the only way to reform his world.

Petrarch believed that an age of darkness—he coined the expression "Dark Ages"—separated the Roman world from his own time and that the separation could be overcome only through a study and reconstruction of classical values: "Once the darkness has been broken, our descendants will perhaps be able to return to the pure, pristine radiance."[3] A brilliant poet and linguist and a tireless self-promoter, he lived his entire life as an example of the way in which classical values could serve as a vehicle for reform. Petrarch's program, and in many respects the entire Renaissance, involved first of all a reconstruction of classical culture, then a careful study and imitation of the classical heritage, and finally a series of moral and cultural changes that went beyond the mere copying of ancient values and styles.

Petrarch labored throughout his life to reconstruct the history and literature of Rome. He learned to read and write classical Latin. While still in his twenties, he discovered fragments of Livy's *Roman History*, an important source for the history of Republican Rome. He annotated and reorganized the fragments in an attempt to reconstruct the form Livy himself had intended. His work on Livy was merely the first step. In the 1330s he discovered a number of classical works, including orations by Cicero, the great philosopher, statesman, and opponent of Julius Caesar. In 1345 he found the collection of letters that Cicero, while in exile, had written to his friend Atticus. These letters, filled with gossip, questions about politics in Rome, and complaints about his forced withdrawal from public life, created the portrait of an individual who was much more complex than the austere philosopher of medieval legend.

Petrarch was and remained a committed Christian. He recognized the tension between the Christian present and pagan antiquity. "My wishes fluctuate and my desires conflict, and in their struggle they tear me apart," he said.[4] Yet he prized the beauty and moral value of ancient learning. He wrote *The Lives of Illustrious Men*, biographies of men from antiquity whose lives he thought were worthy of emulation. He composed an epic Latin poem, *Africa*, about the Roman patrician Scipio Africanus. To spread humanistic values, he issued collections of his letters, written in classically inspired Latin, and his Italian poems. He believed that study and memorization of the writings of classical authors could lead to the internalization of the ideas and values expressed in those works, just as a honey bee drinks nectar to create honey. He argued that the ancient moral philosophers were superior to the Scholastic philosophers, whose work ended with the determination of truth, or correct responses. "The true moral philosophers and useful teachers of the virtues," he concluded, "are those whose first and last intention is to make hearer and reader good, those who do not merely teach what virtue and vice are but sow into our hearts love of the best . . . and hatred of the worst."[5] (See the box, "Petrarch Responds to His Critics.")

Humanistic Studies

Petrarch's program was the inspiration for a broad-based transformation of Italian intellectual life that affected discussions of politics, education, literature, and philosophy. Wherever he traveled in Italy, numerous young scholars flocked to him. His style of historical and literary investigation of the past became the basis for a new appreciation of the present.

Petrarch's program of humanistic studies became especially popular with the wealthy oligarchy that dominated political life in Florence. The Florentine chancellor Coluccio Salutati (1331–1406) and a generation of young intellectuals who formed his circle evolved an ideology of civic humanism. Civic humanists wrote letters, orations, and histories praising their city's classical virtues and history. In the process they gave a practical and public meaning to the Petrarchan program. Civic humanists argued, like Cicero himself, that there was a moral and ethical value intrinsic to public life. In a letter to a friend, Coluccio Salutati wrote that public life is "something holy and holier than idleness in [religious] solitude." To another he added that "The active life you flee is

Petrarch Responds to His Critics

Many traditional philosophers and theologians criticized humanists as "pagans" because of their lack of interest in discovering logical and theological truths and their love of non-Christian writers. In this excerpt from "On My Own Ignorance and That of Many Others," a letter written to defend humanistic studies, Petrarch discusses Cicero and explains the value of his work to Christians.

[Cicero] points out the miraculously coherent structure and disposition of the body, sense and limbs, and finally reason and sedulous activity. . . . And all this he does merely to lead us to this conclusion: whatever we behold with our eyes or perceive with our intellect is made by God for the well-being of man and governed by divine providence and counsel. . . . [In response to his critics who argued for the superiority of philosophy he adds] I have read all of Aristotle's moral books. . . . Sometimes I have become more learned through them when I went home, but not better, not so good as I ought to be. . . . However, what is the use of knowing what virtue is if it is not loved when known? What is the use of knowing sin if it is not abhorred when it is known? However, everyone who has become thoroughly familiar with our Latin authors knows that they stamp and drive deep into the heart the sharpest and most ardent stings of speech by which . . . those who stick to the ground [are] lifted up to the highest thoughts and to honest desire. . . .

Cicero, read with a pious and modest attitude, . . . was profitable to everybody, so far as eloquence is concerned, to many others as regards living. . . . If to admire Cicero means to be a Ciceronian, I am a Ciceronian. I admire him so much that I wonder at people who do not admire him. . . . However, when we come to think or speak of religion, that is, of supreme truth and true happiness, and of eternal salvation, then I am certainly not a Ciceronian, or a Platonist, but a Christian, I even feel sure that Cicero himself would have been a Christian if he had been able to see Christ and to comprehend His doctrine.

Source: Petrarch, "On His Own Ignorance and That of Many Others," in *The Renaissance Philosophy of Man,* ed. Ernst Cassirer, Paul Oskar Kristeller, and John H. Randall (Chicago: University of Chicago Press, 1948), pp. 86, 103, 104, 114, 115.

to be followed both as an exercise in virtue and because of the necessity of brotherly love."[6]

More than Petrarch himself, civic humanists viewed their task as the creation of men of virtue who could take the lead in government and protect their fellow citizens from lawlessness and tyranny. In the early years of the fifteenth century civic humanists praised Florence for remaining a republic of free citizens rather than falling under the control of a lord, like the people of Milan, which was dominated by the Viscontis. In his *Panegyric on the City of Florence* (ca. 1400), Leonardo Bruni (ca. 1370–1444) recalled the history of the Roman Republic and suggested that Florence could recreate the virtues of the Roman state. To civic humanists, the study of Rome and its virtues was the key to the continued prosperity of Florence and similar Italian republics.

One of Petrarch's most enthusiastic followers was Guarino of Verona (1374–1460), who became the leading advocate of educational reform in Renaissance Italy. After spending five years in Constantinople learning Greek and collecting classical manuscripts, he became the most successful teacher and translator of Greek literature in Italy. There had been previously a widespread interest in Greek literature—Petrarch owned a copy of the *Iliad,* though he never managed to learn to read it—and Greek studies had been advanced by Manuel Chrysoloras (1350–1415), who, after his arrival from Constantinople in 1397, taught Greek for three years in Florence. Guarino built on this interest.

Guarino emphasized careful study of grammar and memorization of large bodies of classical history and poetry. He coached students to write orations in the style of Cicero. Guarino believed that through a profound understanding of Greek and Latin literature and a careful imitation of the style of the great authors, a person could come to exhibit the moral and ethical values for which Cicero, Seneca, and Plutarch were justly famous. Although it is unclear that Guarino's style of education delivered the moral training he advocated, it did provide a thorough education in literature and oratory. In an age that admired the ability to speak and write persuasively, the new style of humanistic education pioneered by Guarino spread quickly throughout Europe. The elegy spoken at Guarino's funeral sums up Italian views of humanistic education as well as the contribution of Guarino himself: "No one was considered noble, as leading a blameless life, unless he had followed Guarino's courses."

Guarino's authority spread quickly. One of his early students, Vittorino da Feltre (1378–1446), was appointed tutor to the Gonzaga dukes of Mantua. Like Guarino, he emphasized close literary study and careful imitation of classical authors. But the school he founded, the Villa Giocosa, was innovative because he advocated games and exercises as well as formal study. In addition, Vittorino required that bright young boys from poor families be included among the seventy students normally resident in his school. Vittorino was so renowned that noblemen from across Italy sent their sons to be educated at the Villa Giocosa.

Humanistic education had its limits, however. Leonardo Bruni of Florence once composed a curriculum for a young woman to follow. He urged her to learn literature and moral philosophy as well as to read religious writers. But, he suggested, there was no reason to study rhetoric: "For why should the subtleties of . . . rhetorical conundrums consume the powers of a woman, who never sees the forum? . . . The contests of the forum, like those of warfare and battle, are the sphere of men."[7] To what extent did women participate in the cultural and artistic movements of the fourteenth and fifteenth centuries? Was the position of a woman better than it had been previously? The current of misogyny, the assumption that women were intellectually and morally weaker than men, continued during the Renaissance, but it was not unopposed.

During the fifteenth century, numerous women learned to read and write in Latin as well as in vernacular languages. The plight of two of them indicates some of the limits of humanist thought. Christine de Pizan (1369–1430) was the daughter of an Italian physician at the court of Charles V of France. Her father and later her husband had encouraged her to learn languages and to write. When the deaths of both of these men left her with little money and responsibility for her children, she turned to writing. From 1389 until her death, she lived and wrote at the French court. She composed a short life of Joan of Arc and an instructional book for the education of the crown prince, but she is perhaps best known for *The Book of the City of the Ladies* (1405). In it she added her own voice to what is known as the *querelle des femmes,* the "argument over women." Christine wrote to counter the many writings that characterized women as inferior to men and incapable of moral judgments. She argued that the problem was education: "If it were customary to send daughters to school like sons, and if they were then taught the natural sciences, they would learn as thoroughly and understand the subtleties of all the arts and sciences as well as sons."[8] Christine described in her book an ideal city of ladies in which prudence, justice, and reason would protect women from ignorant male critics.

The limits of Christine's city are evident in the career of Isotta Nogarola (b. 1418) of Verona, one of a number of fifteenth- and sixteenth-century Italian women whose literary abilities were equal to those of male humanists. Isotta quickly became known as a gifted writer, but men's response to her work was mixed. One anonymous critic suggested that it was unnatural for a woman to have such scholarly interests and accused her of equally unnatural sexual interests. Guarino of Verona himself wrote to her saying that if she was truly to be educated she must put off female sensibilities and find "a man within the woman."

Women and Culture Christine de Pizan objected to male denigration of the moral and cultural value of women. This illumination from her *City of the Ladies* shows her ideal society, a place where women, like men, are allowed to study and create. *(Bibliothèque Nationale)*

The problem for humanistically educated women was that there was no acceptable role for them. A noblewoman like Isabella de' Este, wife of the duke of Mantua, might gather humanists and painters around her at court, but it was not generally believed that women could create literary or artistic works of true merit. When women tried, they were usually rebuffed and urged to reject the values of civic humanism and to hold instead to traditional Christian virtues of rejection of the world. Isotta was given this advice when she informed a male humanist friend that she was contemplating marriage. It was wrong, he said, "that a virgin should consider marriage, or even think about that liberty of lascivious morals."[9] Throughout the fifteenth and early sixteenth centuries some women in Italy and the rest of Europe learned classical languages and philosophy, but they became rarer as time passed. The virtues of humanism were public virtues, and Europeans of the Renaissance remained uncomfortable with the idea that women might act directly and publicly. (See the box, "Cassandra Fedele Defends Liberal Arts for Women.")

The Transformation of Humanism

The fascination with education based on ancient authorities was heightened by the discovery in 1416 in the Monastery of Saint Gall in Switzerland of a complete manuscript of Quintilian's *Institutes of Oratory*, a first-century treatise on the proper education for a young Roman patrician. It was found by Poggio Bracciolini (1380–1459), who had been part of Coluccio Salutati's circle in Florence. The discovery was hardly accidental. Like Petrarch himself, the humanists of the fifteenth century scoured Europe looking for ancient texts to read and study. In searching out the knowledge of the past, these fifteenth-century humanists made a series of discoveries that changed their understanding of language, philosophy, and religion. Their desire to imitate led to a profound transformation of knowledge.

A Florentine antiquary, Niccolò Niccoli, coordinated and paid for much of the search for new manuscripts. A wealthy bachelor, Niccolò (1364–1437) spent the fortune he had inherited from his father by collecting ancient statuary,

Cassandra Fedele Defends Liberal Arts for Women

Cassandra Fedele (1465–1558) by the age of 12 had learned Latin and later learned Greek, rhetoric, and history. The Venetian senate praised her as an ornament of learning in the city, but there was no place for an educated woman. She eventually married a provincial physician and was unable to maintain her early prominence, although she occasionally wrote letters and orations. In this oration, which is in the form of a typical defense of liberal studies, she adds her own plea for education for women.

Aware of the weakness of my sex and the paucity of my talent, blushing, I decided to honor and obey [those who have urged me to consider how women could profit from assiduous study] . . . in order that the common crowd may be ashamed of itself and stop being offensive to me, devoted as I am to the liberal arts. . . .

Even an ignorant man—not only a philosopher—sees and admits that man is rightly distinguished from a beast above all by [the capacity of] reason. For what else so greatly delights, enriches and honors both of them than the teaching and understanding of letters and the liberal arts? . . . States and princes, moreover, who favor and cultivate these studies, become much more humane, pleasing, and noble, and purely [through liberal studies] win for themselves a sweet reputation for humanity. . . . For this reason the ancients rightfully judged all leaders deficient in letters, however skillful in military affairs, to be crude and ignorant. As for the utility of letters, enough said. . . . Of these fruits I myself have tasted a little and [have esteemed myself in that enterprise] more than abject and hopeless; and armed with distaff and needle—woman's weapons—I march forth [to defend] the belief that even though the study of letters promises and offers no reward for women and no dignity, every woman ought to seek and embrace these studies for that pleasure and delight alone that [comes] from them.

Source: M. L. King, and A. Rabil, *Her Immaculate Hand: Selected Works By and About the Women Humanists of Quattrocento Italy* (Binghamton, N.Y.: Center for Medieval and Early Renaissance Studies, State University of New York, 1983), pp. 74–77.

reliefs, and, most of all, books. When he died, his collection of more than eight hundred volumes of Latin and Greek texts was taken over by Cosimo de' Medici. It became the foundation of the humanist library housed in the Monastery of San Marco in Florence. Niccolò specified that all his books "should be accessible to everyone," and humanists from across Italy and the rest of Europe came to Florence to study his collection. It would be difficult to overemphasize the importance of the ancient texts collected and copied in Florence. Niccolò's library prompted Pope Nicholas V (r. 1447–1455) to begin the collection that is now the Apostolic Library of the Vatican in Rome. The Vatican library became a lending library, serving the humanist community in Rome. Similar collections were made in Venice, Milan, and Urbino. The Greek and Latin sources collected in these libraries allowed humanists to study classical languages in a way not possible before.

The career of Lorenzo Valla (1407–1457) illustrates the transformation that took place in the fifteenth century. Valla was born near Rome and received a traditional humanistic education in Greek and Latin studies. He spent the rest of his life at universities and courts lecturing on philosophy and literature. Valla was convinced that the key to philosophical and legal problems lay in historical-textual research. Valla's studies had led him to understand that language changes—that it too has a life and a history. In 1440 he published a work called *On the Donation of Constantine.* The *Donation of Constantine* purported to record the gift by the emperor Constantine (r. 311–337) of jurisdiction over Rome to the pope when the capital of the empire was moved to Constantinople (see page 288). The papacy had used the document to defend its right to political dominion in central Italy. The donation had long been criticized by legal theorists, who argued that Constantine had no right to make it. Valla attacked the legitimacy of the document itself. Because of its language and form, he argued, it could not have been written at the time of Constantine:

> Through his [the writer's] babbling, he reveals his most impudent forgery himself. . . . Where he deals with the gifts he says "a diadem . . . made of pure gold and precious jewels." The ignoramus did not know that the diadem was made of cloth, probably silk. . . . He thinks it had to be made of gold, since nowadays kings usually wear a circle of gold set with jewels.[10]

Valla was correct. The *Donation* was a forgery written in the eighth century.

Valla later turned his attention to the New Testament. Jerome (331–420) had put together the Vulgate edition of the Bible in an attempt to create a single accepted Latin version of the the Old and New Testaments. In 1444 Valla published his *Annotations on the New Testament.* In this work he used his training in classical languages to correct the standard Latin text and to show numerous examples of mistranslations by Jerome and his contemporaries. Valla believed that true understanding of Christian theology depended on clear knowledge of the past. His annotations on the New Testament were of critical importance to humanists outside Italy and were highly influential during the Protestant Reformation.

The transformation of humanism exemplified by Valla was fully expected by some Florentines. They expected literary studies to lead eventually to philosophy. In 1456, a young Florentine began studying Greek with just such a change in mind. Supported by the Medici rulers of Florence, Marsilio Ficino (1433–1499) began a project to translate the works of Plato into Latin and to interpret Plato in the light of Christian tradition. Between 1463 and 1469 he translated all of the Platonic dialogues. He was at the center of a circle of humanists who were interested in Platonism and its role in art and society. In 1469 he published the first versions of his *Platonic Theology.*

Ficino believed that Platonism, like Christianity, demonstrated the dignity of humanity. He wrote that everything was connected along a hierarchy ranging from lowliest matter to the person of God. The human soul was located at the midpoint of this hierarchy and was a bridge between matter and God. True wisdom, and especially experience of the divine, could be gained only through contemplation and love. According to Ficino, logic and scientific observation did not lead to true understanding, for humans know logically only that which they can define in human language; they can, however, love things, like God, that they cannot fully comprehend.

Ficino's belief in the dignity of man was shared by Giovanni Pico della Mirandola (1463–1494), who proposed to debate with other philosophers nine hundred theses dealing with the nature of man, the origins of knowledge, and the uses of philosophy. Pico extended Ficino's idea of the hierarchy of being, arguing that humans surpassed even the angels in dignity. Angels held a fixed position in the hierarchy, just below God. In contrast, humans could either move up or move down in the hierarchy, depending on the extent to which they embraced spiritual or worldly interests. Pico further believed that he had proved that there was truth in all philosophies. He was one of the first humanists to learn Hebrew and to argue that divine wisdom was to be found in Jewish mystical literature. Along with others, he studied the Jewish Cabala, a collection of mystical and occult writings that humanists believed dated from the time of Moses.

Pico's ideas were shared by other humanists, who argued that there was an original divine illumination—a "Pristine Theology," they called it—that preceded both Christ and Plato. These humanists found theological truth in what they believed was ancient Egyptian, Greek, and Jewish magic. Ficino himself popularized the *Corpus Hermeticum* (the Hermetic collection), an amalgam of magical texts of the first century A.D. that was mistakenly assumed to date from the age of Moses and Pythagoras. Like the writings of Plato and his followers, Hermetic texts explained how the mind could influence and be influenced by the material and celestial worlds.

THE RENAISSANCE: CULTURE IN ITALY

ca. 1304	Giotto paints the Arena Chapel in Padua
1315	Albertino Mussato presents his play *Ecerinis*
1345	Petrarch discovers Cicero's letters to Atticus
1397	Manuel Chrysoloras arrives in Florence from Constantinople
ca. 1400	Leonardo Bruni writes his *Panegyric on the City of Florence*
1401	Lorenzo Ghiberti receives the commission for the doors of the Baptistery in Florence
1416	Poggio Bracciolini discovers Quintilian's *Institutes of Oratory*
1419	Filippo Brunelleschi's Foundling Hospital in Florence is completed
1427	Masaccio completes his painting of the Trinity in Santa Maria Novella in Florence
1440	Lorenzo Valla publishes his "On the Donation of Constantine"
1444	Lorenzo Valla writes his *Annotations on the New Testament*
1469	Marsilio Ficino publishes his *Platonic Theology*
1474	Andrea Mantegna paints the Camera degli Sposi in Mantua
1478	Botticelli's *Springtime*
1501	Michelangelo's *David*
1508	Michelangelo begins work on the Sistine Chapel ceiling
1513	Niccolò Machiavelli writes *The Prince*
1528	Baldassare Castiglione publishes *The Book of the Courtier*

Along with Hermetic magic many humanists of the fifteenth and sixteenth centuries investigated astrology and alchemy. Hermetic magic, astrology, and alchemy posit the existence of a direct, reciprocal connection between the cosmos and the natural world. In the late medieval and Renaissance world, alchemical and astrological theories seemed reasonable. By the late fifteenth century many humanists assumed that personality as well as the ability to respond to certain crises was profoundly affected by the stars. It was not by accident that for a century or more after 1500 astrologers were official or unofficial members of most European courts. Belief in astrology was not universal, however. Some humanists, like Pico, opposed it because it seemed to deny that humans had free will.

Interest in alchemy was equally widespread though more controversial. Alchemists believed that everything was made of a primary material and that it was possible to transmute one substance into another. The most popular version, and the most open to hucksters and frauds, was the belief that base metals could be turned into gold. The hopes of most alchemists, however, were more profound. They were convinced that they could unlock the explanation of the properties of the whole cosmos. On a personal and religious level as well as on a material level, adepts hoped to take the impure and make it pure. The interest in understanding and manipulating nature that was at the heart of Hermetic magic, astrology, and alchemy was an important stimulus to scientific investigations and, ultimately, to the rise of modern scientific thought.

Political Thought and Machiavelli

The humanists' plan to rediscover classical sources fit well with their political interests. "One can say," observed Leonardo Bruni, "that letters and the study of the Latin language went hand in hand with the condition of the Roman republic." Petrarch and the civic humanists believed that rulers, whether in a republic or a principality, should exhibit all the classical and Christian virtues of faith, hope, love, prudence, temperance, fortitude, and justice. Those qualities were the key to good government and good law. A virtuous ruler would be loved and obeyed. Those virtues were also the key to the preservation of government. The civic humanists viewed governments and laws as essentially unchanging and static. They believed that when change did occur, it most likely happened by chance—that is because of fortune (the Roman goddess Fortuna).

Humanists believed that the only protection against chance was true virtue, for the virtuous would never be dominated by fortune. Thus, beginning with Petrarch, humanists advised rulers to love their subjects, to be magnanimous with their possessions, and to maintain the rule of law. Humanistic tracts of the fourteenth and fifteenth centuries were full of classical and Christian examples of virtuous actions by moral rulers.

The French invasions of Italy in 1494 and the warfare that followed called into question many of the humanists' assumptions about the lessons and virtues of classical civilization. Francesco Guicciardini (1483–1540), a Florentine patrician who had served in papal armies, suggested that history held no clear lessons. Unless the causes of two different events were identical down to the smallest detail, he said, the results could be radically different. An even more thorough critique was offered by Guicciardini's friend and fellow Florentine, Niccolò Machiavelli (1469–1527). After a humanistic education and service from 1494 to 1512 in the anti-Medicean republican government of Florence, Machiavelli developed in a series of writings what he believed was a new science of politics. He wrote *Discourses* on Livy, a treatise on military organization, a history of Florence, and even a Renaissance play (*The Mandrake Root*). He is best remembered, however, for *The Prince* (1513), a small tract numbering less than a hundred pages.

Machiavelli felt that his contemporaries paid too little heed to the lessons to be learned from history. Thus, in his discourses on Livy he comments on Roman government, the role of religion, and the nature of political virtue, emphasizing the sophisticated Roman analysis of political and military situations. A shortcoming more serious than ignorance of history, Machiavelli believed, was his contemporaries' ignorance of the true motivations for people's actions. His play *The Mandrake Root* is a comedy about the ruses used to seduce a young woman. In truth, however, none of the characters is fooled. All of them, from the young woman being seduced to her husband, realize what is happening but use the seduction to their own advantage. In the play Machiavelli implicitly challenges the humanistic assumption that educated individuals will naturally choose virtue over vice. He explicitly criticizes these same assumptions in *The Prince.* He rejects the humanistic belief that human nature is essentially good and that individuals, given an opportunity, will naturally be helpful and honorable. Machiavelli holds to the contrary view, that individuals are much more likely to respond to fear and that power rather than the arts of rhetoric make for good government.

Machiavelli's use of the Italian word *virtù* led him to be vilified as amoral. Machiavelli deliberately chose a word that meant both "manliness" or "ability" and "virtue as a moral quality." Earlier humanists had restricted *virtù* to the second meaning, using the word to refer to virtues like prudence, magnanimity, and love. Machiavelli tried to show that in some situations these "virtues" could have violent, even evil, consequences. If, for example, a prince was so magnanimous in giving away his wealth that he was

Machiavelli In this portrait Machiavelli is dressed as a government official. He wrote to a friend during his exile that each night when he returned from the fields he dressed again in his curial robes and pondered the behavior of governments and princes. *(Scala/Art Resource, NY)*

forced to raise taxes, his subjects might come to hate him. Conversely, a prince who, through cruelty to the enemies of his state, brought peace and stability to his subjects might be obeyed and perhaps even loved by them. A virtuous ruler must be mindful of the goals to be achieved.

Machiavelli expected his readers to be aware of the ambiguous nature of virtue—whether understood as ability or as moral behavior. "One will discover," he concludes, "that something which appears to be a virtue, if pursued, will end in his destruction; while some other thing which seems to be a vice, if pursued, will result in his safety and his well-being."[11]

Like Guicciardini, Machiavelli rejected earlier humanistic assumptions that one needed merely to imitate the great leaders of the past. Governing is a process that requires different skills at different times, he warned: "The man who adapts his course of action to the nature of the times will succeed and, likewise, the man who sets his course of action out of tune with the times will come to grief."[12] The abilities that allow a prince to gain power may not be the abilities that will allow him to maintain it.

With the writings of Machiavelli, humanistic ideas of intellectual, moral, and political reform had matured. Petrarch and the early humanists believed fully in the powers of classical wisdom to transform society. Machiavelli and his contemporaries admitted the importance of classical wisdom but also recognized the ambiguity of any application of classical learning to contemporary life.

The Arts in Italy

Townsmen and artists in Renaissance Italy shared the humanists' perception of the importance of classical antiquity. Filippo Villani (d. 1405), a wealthy Florentine from an important business family, wrote that artists had recently "reawakened a lifeless and almost extinct art." In the middle of the fifteenth century the sculptor Lorenzo Ghiberti concluded that with the rise of Christianity "not only statues and paintings [were destroyed], but the books and commentaries and handbooks and rules on which men relied for their training." Italian writers and painters themselves recognized that the literary recovery of past practices was essential. The Renaissance of the arts can be divided into three periods. In the early Renaissance artists first imitated nature. In the middle period artists rediscovered classical ideas of proportion. In the High Renaissance artists, according to Giorgio Vasari (1511–1574), were "superior to nature but also to the artists of the ancient world" (see the box, "Giorgio Vasari on the History of Art").

The Artistic Renaissance

The first stirrings of the new styles can be found in the late thirteenth century. The greatest innovator was Giotto di Bondone of Florence (d. 1337). Although Giotto had a modest background, his fellow citizens, popes, and patrons throughout Italy quickly recognized his skill. He traveled as far south as Rome and as far north as Padua painting churches and chapels. According to later artists and commentators, Giotto broke with the prevailing stiff, highly symbolic style and introduced lifelike portrayals of living persons. He produced paintings of dramatic situations, showing events located in a specific time and place. The frescoes of the Arena Chapel in Padua (1304–1314) recount episodes in the life of Christ. In a series of scenes leading from Christ's birth to crucifixion, Giotto situates his actors in towns and countryside in what appears to be actual space. More significantly, Giotto manages to capture the drama of key events, like Judas's kiss of betrayal in the Garden of Gethsemane. Even Michelangelo, the master of the High Renaissance, studied Giotto's painting. Giotto was in such demand throughout Italy that his native Florence gave him a public appointment so that he would be required by law to remain in the city.

Early in the fifteenth century, Florentine artists devised new ways to represent nature that surpassed even the innovations of Giotto. The revolutionary nature of these artistic developments is evident from the careers of Lorenzo Ghiberti (1378–1455), Filippo Brunelleschi (1377–1446), and Masaccio (born Tomasso di ser Giovanni di Mone, 1401–c. 1428). Their sculpture, architecture, and painting began an ongoing series of experiments with the representation of space through linear perspective. Perspective is a system for representing three-dimensional objects on a two-dimensional plane. It is based on two

Giotto's Naturalism Later painters praised the naturalistic emotion of Giotto's painting. In this detail from the Arena Chapel, Giotto portrays the kiss of Judas, one of the most dramatic moments in Christian history. *(Scala/Art Resource, NY)*

observations: (1) As parallel lines recede into the distance, they seem to converge; and (2) there is a geometrical relationship that regulates the relative size of objects at various distances from the viewer. Painters of the Renaissance literally found themselves looking at their world from a new perspective.

In 1401 Ghiberti won a commission to design door panels for the baptistery of San Giovanni in Florence. He was to spend the rest of his life working on two sets of bronze doors. The reliefs he created told the stories of the New Testament (the north doors) and the Old Testament (the east doors). In the commissions for the Old Testament scenes, Ghiberti used the new techniques of linear perspective to create a sense of space into which he placed his classically inspired figures. His work made him instantly famous throughout Italy. Later in the sixteenth century Michelangelo remarked that the east doors were worthy to be the "Doors of Paradise," and so they have since been known.

In the competition for the baptistery commission, Ghiberti had beaten the young Filippo Brunelleschi, who, as a result, gave up sculpture for architecture and later left Florence to study in Rome. While in Rome he is said to have visited and measured surviving examples of classical architecture—the artistic equivalent of humanistic literary research. When he returned to Florence, he had a firm sense of the nature of Roman architecture and how its forms could be adapted for

The Doors of Paradise Ghiberti worked on panels for the baptistery from 1403 to 1453. In his representations of scenes from the Old Testament he combined a love of ancient statuary with the new Florentine interest in linear perspective. *(Alinari/Art Resource, NY)*

Florentine life. According to Giorgio Vasari, he was capable of "visualizing Rome as it was before the fall." Brunelleschi's debt to Rome is evident in his masterpiece, Florence's foundling hospital. Built as a combination of hemispheres and cubes and resembling a Greek stoa or an arcaded Roman basilica, the long low structure is an example of how profoundly different Renaissance architecture was from the towering Gothic of the Middle Ages.

In the first decade of the fifteenth century, many commentators believed that painting would never be as innovative as either sculpture or architecture. They knew of no classical models that had survived for imitation. Yet the possibilities in painting became apparent in 1427 with the unveiling of Masaccio's *Trinity* in the Florentine church of Santa Maria Novella. Masaccio built on experiments in linear perspective to create a painting in which a flat wall seems to become a recessed chapel. The space created is filled with the images of Christ crucified, the Father, and the Holy Spirit.

In the middle years of the fifteenth century, artists came to terms with the innovations of the earlier period. In the second half of the fifteenth century, however, artists like the Florentine Sandro Botticelli (1445–1510) added a profound understanding of classical symbolism to the technical interests of Masaccio and Brunelleschi. Botticelli's famous *Birth of Venus* and *Springtime* (1478), both painted for Medici houses, are filled with Neo-Platonic symbolism concerning truth, beauty, and the virtues of humanity. (See the feature, "Weighing the Evidence: The Art of Renaissance Florence," on pages 542–543.)

The high point in the development of Renaissance art was at the beginning of the sixteenth century in the work of several artists throughout Italy. Artists in Venice learned perspective from the Florentines and added their own tradition of subtle coloring in oils. Raphael Sanzio (1483–1520), who arrived in Rome from his native Urbino in 1508, demonstrated that artistic brilliance was not simply a Florentine monopoly. His decorations of the Vatican palaces in Rome included his *School of Athens,* a painting that literally shows the debt of the Renaissance to past learning by portraying the great philosophers of the past as well as contemporary artists. It is in effect the synthesis of the classical learning and artistic innovation for which the Renaissance is famous.

The work of two Florentines, Leonardo da Vinci (1452–1519) and Michelangelo Buonarroti (1475–1564), best exemplifies the sophisticated heights that art achieved early in the sixteenth century. Leonardo, the bastard son of a notary, was raised in a village outside of Florence. Cut off from the humanistic milieu of the city, he desired above all else to prove that his artistry was the equal of the formal learning of his social superiors. In his notebooks he confessed, "I am fully conscious that, not being a literary man, certain presumptuous persons will think they may reasonably blame me, alleging that I am not a man of letters."[13] But he defended his lack of classical education by arguing that all the best writing, like the best painting and invention, is based on the close observation of nature. Close observation

Giorgio Vasari on the History of Art

Giorgio Vasari was a well-known artist and architect at the court of Cosimo de' Medici. Vasari's history of the eminent artists of his day,* The Lives of the Artists *(1550) was an instant success. Vasari saw his volume as telling of arts that were spiritual and religious.

Design is the foundation of both [sculpture and painting], or rather the animating principle of all creative process; and surely design existed in absolute perfection before the Creation when Almighty God . . . directed his creative intellect further, to the clear air and the solid earth. . . . The origin of the arts we are discussing was nature itself. I am sure that although the arts continued to be practiced until the death of the last of the twelve Caesars, their earlier perfection and excellence were not sustained. . . . What inflicted incomparably greater damage and loss to the arts . . . was the fervent enthusiasm of the new Christian religion, . . . not out of hatred for the arts but in order to humiliate and overthrow the pagan gods. Nevertheless, their tremendous zeal was responsible for inflicting severe damage on the practice of the arts, which then fell into total confusion.

[After recounting the destruction of buildings and books of instruction during the wars brought on by the rise of various German tribes, he finds a new beginning in the thirteenth century. . . . He then explains why he considers this story essential.]

Seeing the history of [painting, sculpture, and architecture], artists can also realize the nature of the arts we have been discussing: these, like the other arts and like human beings themselves, are born, grow up, become old, and die. And they will be able to understand more readily the process by which art has been reborn and reached perfection in our times. And if . . . it ever happens at any time that the arts once again fall into the same disastrous decline, then I hope that this work of mine, such as it is, . . . may keep the arts alive.

Source: Giorgio Vasari, *The Lives of the Artists*, vol. 1, trans. George Bull (London: Penguin, 1965), pp. 25, 30, 32, 36–37, 45, 46–47.

and scientific analysis made Leonardo's work uniquely creative in all these fields. Leonardo is famous for his plans for bridges, airships, submarines, and fortresses. There seemed to be no branch of learning in which he was not interested. In painting he developed chiaroscuro, a technique for showing aerial perspective. He painted horizons as shaded zones rather than as sharp lines. "I know," he said, "that the greater or less quantity of air that lies between the eye and the object makes the outlines of that object more or less distinct."[14] It was his analytical observation that made Leonardo so influential on his contemporaries.

Michelangelo, however, was widely hailed as the capstone of Renaissance art. In the words of a contemporary, "He alone has triumphed over ancient artists, modern artists and over Nature itself." In his career we can follow the rise of Renaissance artists from the ranks of mere craftsmen to honored creators, courtiers who were the equals of the humanists. We can also discern the synthesis of the artistic and intellectual transformations of the Renaissance with a profound religious sensitivity.

The importance of Michelangelo's contribution is obvious in two of his most important works: the statue *David* in Florence and his commissions in the Sistine Chapel of the Vatican in Rome. From his youth Michelangelo had studied and imitated antique sculpture, to the point that some of his creations were thought by many actually to be antique. He used his understanding of classical art in *David* (1501). Artists and citizens of

Florence alike hailed the mammoth statue as a masterpiece. Citizens recalled David's defeat of the giant Goliath, saving Israel from almost certain conquest by the Philistines. David became a symbol of the youthful Florentine republic struggling to maintain its freedom against great odds. The statue was moved to a place of honor before the Palazzo Vecchio, Florence's city hall, signifying, as Giorgio Vasari noted, that "just as David had protected his people and governed them justly, so whoever ruled Florence should vigorously defend the city and govern it with justice."[15]

Masaccio's Trinity Masaccio's painting of the Trinity in Santa Maria Novella used the techniques of perspective to create out of a solid wall a space into which he was able to fit representations of the three persons of the Trinity and the patrons of the chapel itself. *(Scala/Art Resource, NY)*

Michelangelo was a committed republican and Florentine, but he spent much of his life working in Rome on a series of papal commissions. In 1508 he was called to Rome to work on the ceiling of the Sistine Chapel. His ceiling frescoes complemented the Moses and Christ cycles along the side walls with scenes from the Creation to Noah and the Flood. In the late 1530s he completed the Christian history begun by Sixtus IV with his painting *The Last Judgment.* In that painting the techniques of perspective and the conscious recognition of debts to classical culture recede into the background as the artist surrounds Christ in judgment with saints and sinners, including in the hollow, empty skin of Saint Bartholomew a psychological self-portrait of an artist increasingly concerned with his own spiritual shortcomings.

Michelangelo's self-portrait reminds us that the intellectual content of the artist's work is one of its most enduring traits. He was a Platonist who believed that the form and beauty of a statue were contained in the stone itself. The artist's job was to peal away excess material and reveal the beauty within. As he noted in one of his poems, it was a process like that of religious salvation:

Just as by carving . . . we set
Into hard mountain rock
A living figure
Which grows most where the stone is most removed;
In like manner, some good works . . .
Are concealed by the excess of my very flesh.[16]

Art and Patronage

The religious passion of Michelangelo's poetry indicates one of the reasons that art was so popular in Renaissance Italy. Art, like poetry, provided a symbolic language through which Italians could reason about the most important issues of their communities. Italians willingly spent vast sums on art because of its ability to communicate social, political, and spiritual values.

Italy in the fourteenth and fifteenth centuries was unusually wealthy relative to the towns and principalities of northern Europe. Despite the population decline caused by plague and the accompanying economic dislocations, per person wealth in Italy remained quite high. Because of

Linear Perspective In this study for a nativity scene, Leonardo da Vinci shows how linear perspective helped the artist compose a work. All lines converge to a single vanishing point. They help the painter create a sense of depth and a spatial relationship among the objects in a picture. *(Alinari/Art Resource, NY)*

banking, international trade, and even service as mercenaries, Italians, and particularly Florentines, had money to spend on arts and luxuries. Thus, the Italians of the Renaissance, whether as public or private patrons, could afford to use consumption of art as a form of competition for social and political status. Increasingly in the fourteenth and fifteenth centuries there was a market for luxuries, including art, and there were numerous shops in which artists could be trained.

Artists in the modern world are accustomed to standing outside society as critics of commonly held ideas. In the late Middle Ages and Renaissance, artists were not alienated critics. In 1300 most art was religious in subject and was created to be displayed in public. Throughout Europe art fulfilled a devotional function. Painted crucifixes, altar paintings, and banners were often endowed as devotional or penitential objects. The Arena Chapel in Padua with its frescoes by Giotto was built and endowed by a merchant anxious to pay for some of his sins.

In the late Middle Ages and Renaissance numerous paintings and statues throughout Italy (and much of the rest of Europe) were revered for their miraculous powers. During plague, drought, and times of war, people had recourse to the sacred power of the saints represented in these works of art. The construction of the great churches of the period was often a community project that lasted for decades, even centuries. These gigantic structures were mixtures of piety, civic pride, and religious patronage. The city council of Siena voted to virtually rebuild its Gothic cathedral of St. Mary, saying that the blessed Virgin "was, is and will be in the future the head of this city" and through veneration of her "Siena may be protected from harm." Thus, it is clear that although the subject of art was primarily religious, the message was bound up in the civic values and ideas of the fourteenth and fifteenth centuries.

The first burst of artistic creativity in the fourteenth century was paid for by public institutions. Communal governments built city halls to house government and to promote civic pride. These buildings contained the jail, the mint, law courts, assembly rooms, and even living quarters for administrators. Towns also reorganized streets, public squares, and the myriad hospitals and lodgings for travelers that dotted the city. In most towns there was a remarkable emphasis on the beauty of the work. Civic officials often named special commissions to consult with a

Lorenzetti: Good Government of Siena Lorenzetti's representation of a community at peace is an accurate representation of Siena itself. Well-dressed youths, busy shops, and peasants were typical sights. Located in the city hall of Siena, the painting reminded the town leaders of the importance of their actions. *(Scala/Art Resource, NY)*

variety of artists and architects before approving building projects. Governments, with an eye to the appearance of public areas, legislated the width of streets, height limits, and even the style of façades on houses.

The cycle *Good Government of Siena* illustrates how Italians used art to communicate political ideas. Painted in the first half of the fourteenth century by Ambrogio Lorenzetti (ca. 1300–1348), *Good Government* combined allegorical representations of Wisdom and the cardinal virtues on one wall with realistic street scenes of a well-ordered Siena on an adjacent wall. Across from the scenes of good government are its opposite, graphic representations of murder, rape, and general injustice and disorder. In this work the government sent a clear political message in a realistic painting that reminded viewers of specific events, times, places, and people. The popular preacher San Bernardino of Siena (1380–1444) made clear the message of Lorenzetti's painting: "To see Peace depicted is a delight and so it is a shame to see War painted on the other wall." And Bernardino's sermon reminded listeners of the conclusions they should draw: "Oh my brothers and fathers, love and embrace each other . . . give your aid to this toil which I have undertaken so gladly, to bring about love and peace among you."[17]

In Florence public art was often organized and paid for by various guild organizations. Guild membership was a prerequisite for citizenship, so guildsmen set the tone in politics as well as in the commercial life of the city. Most major guilds commissioned sculpture for the Chapel of Or San Michele, a famous shrine in the grain market (its painting of the Virgin was popularly thought to have wonder-working powers) and seat of the Guelf party, the city's most powerful political organization. Guilds took responsibility for the building and maintenance of other structures in the city as well. The guild of the cloth merchants paid for the frescoes in the baptistery of St. John the Baptist (the city's patron saint) and commissioned the bronze doors by Lorenzo Ghiberti. The guild of the silk merchants oversaw the selection of Filippo Brunelleschi to design the foundling hospital. Guildsmen took pride in the creation of a beautiful environment, but as the cloth makers made clear in their decision to supervise the baptistery: The work reflected not only on the city and its patron saint but also on the power and influence of the guild itself.

The princes who ruled outside the republics of Italy often had similarly precise messages that they wished to communicate. Renaissance popes embarked on a quite specific ideological program in the late fifteenth century to assert their role as both spiritual leaders of Christendom and temporal lords of a central Italian state. Rulers like the Este dukes of Ferrara and the Sforza dukes of Milan constructed castles within their cities or hunting lodges and villas in the countryside and decorated them with pictures of the hunt or knights in combat, scenes that emphasized their noble virtues and their natural right to rule.

By the mid-fifteenth century, patrons of art works in Florence and most other regions of Italy were more and more likely to be wealthy individuals. Republics, where all families were in principle equal, initially displayed a great suspicion of elaborate city palaces and rural villas. By the middle of the fifteenth century, however, such reserve was found in none but the most conservative republics, like Venice or Lucca. The Florentine merchant Giovanni Ruccelai (1403–1481) stated most clearly his reasons for commissioning art: These "things have given and give me the greatest satisfaction and pleasure because in part they serve the honor of God as well as the honor of the city and the commemoration of myself." Giovanni was responsible for redesigning the façade of his family's palace, constructing across from the palace a loggia, or covered porch, for his relatives to use, and even hiring Leon Battista Alberti to redesign the façade of the great Dominican church of Santa Maria Novella, as Giovanni not so modestly proclaimed on the façade itself.

Florentines and later wealthy families in most other Italian towns built similar palaces. Most also acquired and beautified rural villas to which they could retreat during the heat of the summer. Palaces, gardens, and villas became the settings in which the wealthy could entertain their peers, receive clients, and debate the political issues of the day. The public rooms of these palaces were decorated with portraits, gem collections, books, ceramics, and statuary. Many villas and palaces included private chapels. In the Medici palace in Florence, for example, the chapel is the setting for a painting of the Magi (the three Wise Men who came to worship the infant Jesus) in which the artist, Benozzo Gozzoli (1420–1498), used faces of members of the Medici family for the portraits of the Wise Men and their entourage. The Magi, known to be wise and virtuous rulers, were an apt symbol for the family that had come to dominate the city.

The Spread of the Renaissance

Although the Renaissance began in Italy, by 1500 it was a European-wide phenomenon. Even in the Slavic East, beyond the borders of the old Roman Empire, in Prague and Wroclaw one could find a renewed interest in classical ideas about art and literature. As ideas about the past and its relevance to contemporary life spread, the message was transformed in several important ways. Outside of Italy, Rome and its history did not play the dominant role they played in Italy. Humanists were interested more in religious than in political reform, and they responded to a number of important local interests. Yet the Renaissance idea of renewal based on a deep understanding and imitation of the past remained at the center of the movement. The key to the spread of humanistic culture, however, was the rise of printing, which allowed for the distribution of texts that previously had been available only in Italy.

The Impact of Printing

In the fifteenth century the desire to have and to read complete texts of classical works was widespread, but the number of copies was severely limited by the time and expense of hand-copying, collating, and checking manuscripts. Poggio Bracciolini's letters are punctuated with remarks about the time and expense of reproducing the various classical manuscripts he had discovered. One copy he had commissioned was so inaccurate and illegible as to be nearly unusable. Traveling to repositories and libraries was often easier than creating a personal library. It was rarely possible for someone who read a manuscript once to keep a complete copy to compare with other works.

The invention of printing with movable lead type changed things dramatically. Although block printing had long been known in China and was a popular way to produce playing cards and small woodcuts in Europe, only with the creation of movable type in the 1450s did printing become a practical way to produce books. Johann

Map 14.1 The Spread of Printing Printing technology moved rapidly along major trade routes to the most populous and prosperous areas of Europe. The technology was rapidly adopted in highly literate centers such as the Low Countries, the Rhine Valley, and northern Italy.

Gutenberg (d. 1468) in the German city of Mainz produced between 180 and 200 copies of the so-called Gutenberg Bible in 1452–1453. It was followed shortly by editions of the Psalms. German printers spread their techniques rapidly. As early as 1460, there were printing presses in Rome and Venice, and by 1470 the technique had spread to the Low Countries, France, and England. It has been estimated that by 1500 there were a thousand presses in 265 towns (Map 14.1). The output of the early presses in the first century of their existence was extremely varied. Gutenberg's first mass printing, for example, was of a thousand copies of a letter of indulgence, a remission of penance, for participation in a crusade. Early printers also produced highly popular and profitable small devotional books, abridged collections of saints' lives, and other popular literature, as well as the complete editions of classical authors and their humanistic and theological texts.

There has been a long and complex debate over the impact of printing, but there is general agreement on a number of points. An unexpected aspect of print culture was the rise of the printshop as a center of culture and communication. The printers Aldus Manutius (1450–1515) in Venice and Johannes Froben (d. 1527) in Basel were humanists. Both invited humanists to work in their shops as they edited their texts and corrected the proofs before printing. Printshops became a natural gathering place for clerics and laymen. Thus, they were natural sources of humanist ideas and later, in the sixteenth century, of Protestant religious programs. Printing allowed for the creation of agreed-upon standard editions of works in law, theology, philosophy, and science. Scholars in various parts of the world could feel fairly confident that they and their colleagues were analyzing identical texts. Similarly, producing accurate medical and herbal diagrams, maps, and even reproductions of art and architecture was easier. Multiple copies of texts also made possible the study of rare and esoteric literary, philosophical, and scientific texts in all parts of the world. It became possible to study standard editions of important texts like the Bible thoroughly and systematically.

Humanism Outside Italy

As the influence of the humanist movement extended beyond Italy, the interests of the humanists changed. Although there was a strong religious strain in Italian humanism, public life was at the center of Italian programs of education and reform. Outside Italy, however, moral and religious reform were at the heart of the movement. Northern humanists wanted to reform and renew Christian life. In the aftermath of the Great Schism, Christians continued to desire reform within the church. Critics complained that the clergy was wealthy and ignorant and that the laity was uneducated and superstitious. Northern humanists were involved in the building of educational institutions, in the search for and publication of texts by Church Fathers, and in the writing of local customs and history. In the work of the two best-known humanists, Thomas More and Desiderius Erasmus, there is a sharp critique of contemporary behavior and, in the case of Erasmus, a call to a new sense of piety.

The intellectual environment of the northern Europe into which humanism spread had changed significantly since the thirteenth century. The universities of Paris and Oxford retained the status they had acquired earlier but found themselves competing with a host of new foundations. Most of these universities aspired, as the charter of Heidelburg (1386) noted, "to imitate Paris in all things." Like Paris, almost all had theological faculties dominated by scholastically trained theologians. Nevertheless, the new foundations often had chairs of rhetoric, or "eloquence," which left considerable scope for those who advocated humanistic learning. These new universities, from Bratislava in Slovokia (1465) to Uppsala in Sweden (1477), also reflected the increased national feeling in various regions of Europe. The earliest university in German-speaking lands, the Charles University in Prague (1348), was founded at the request of Emperor Charles IV of Luxemburg, whose court was in Prague. Vienna (1365), Aix (1409), Louvain (1425), and numerous other universities owed their foundation to the pride and ambition of local rulers.

Humanists on faculties of law in French universities practiced the historical study of jurisprudence. Like Lorenzo Valla, they believed that historical and linguistic studies were the best way to learn the law. Italian-trained lawyers introduced what came to be called the "Gallican style" of jurisprudence. Because legal ideas, like language, changed over time, they argued that Roman law had to be studied as a historically created system and not as an abstract and unchanging structure. Humanists like Guillaume Budé (1468–1540) moved from the study of law to considerations of Roman coinage, religion, and economic life in order to better understand the formation of Roman law. The desire to understand the law led other humanist-legists to add the study society in ancient Gaul to their work on Rome and then the law of other societies as well.

Although certain attitudes and values were generally found among humanists everywhere, reform programs had to fit a local context. Roman culture and history held less fascination for the citizens of the Iberian Peninsula, France, Germany, and England than it did for the townsmen of Italy. Humanists outside Italy extended their interests beyond Rome to pre-Roman influences. In Germany, the Roman historian Tacitus's comparison of the noble Germans with decadent Roman patricians gave German humanists an indigenous model of reform. French humanists, deceived by forged texts that purported to indicate Trojan rather than Roman origins for French culture, argued for France's cultural autonomy. Spanish humanists concentrated their interests on Seneca, Lucian, and Quintilian, Roman authors born in Iberia.

The dependence on a pure Latin was also less pronounced outside Italy. Most Italian humanists in the fifteenth century wrote their serious works in Latin. In Spain and France, in contrast, there was a strong tradition of translating the classics into the vernacular.

The new universities often became centers of linguistic studies. Humanistic interest in language inspired the foundation of "trilingual" colleges in Spain, France, and the Low Countries to foster serious study of Hebrew, Greek, and Latin. Like Italian humanists, other humanists believed that knowledge of languages would allow students to understand more clearly the truths of Christianity. Typical of this movement was the archbishop of Toledo, Francisco Jiménez de Cisneros (1436–1517), who founded the University of Alcalá in 1508 with chairs of Latin, Greek, and Hebrew. He began the publication of a vast new edition of the Bible, called the "Polyglot Bible" (1522) because it had parallel columns in Latin, Greek, and, where appropriate, Hebrew. Unlike Valla, Jiménez did not intend to challenge the Vulgate. Rather, he expected to clear up any confusion about the meaning of the Vulgate. The university and the Bible were part of an effort to complete the conversion of Muslims and Jews and reform religious practices among the old Christians.

To the northern humanists, the discovery and publication of early Christian authors seemed critical to any reform within the church. Jacques Lefèvre d'Étaples (1455–1529) of France was one of the most famous of these humanistic editors of early Christian texts. He initially gained fame for his textual work on Aristotle. But after 1500 he concentrated on the edition of texts by the early Church Fathers. The true spirit of Christianity, he believed, would be most clear in the works and lives of those who lived closest to the age of the apostles. Christian humanists inspired by Lefèvre were key players in the later Reformation movements in France. Lefèvre's faith in the value of classical languages was shared by John Colet (1467–1519) of England, founder of St. Paul's School in London. He instituted a thorough program of teaching Latin and Greek aimed at creating scholars who would have access to the earliest Christian writings.

Tensions between the humanists and the advocates of Scholastic methods broke out over the cultural and linguistic studies that were at the heart of the humanist program. Humanists like Pico della Mirandola believed that there were universal moral and spiritual truths in other philosophies and religions. Following Pico's lead, Johannes Reuchlin (1455–1522) of Württemberg embarked on a study of the Cabala, a collection of Jewish mystical writings. Johannes Pfefferkorn, a Dominican priest and recent convert from Judaism, attacked Reuchlin's use of Jewish traditions in the study of Christian theology. Sides were quickly drawn. The theological faculties of the German universities generally supported the Dominican. The humanists supported Reuchlin. In his own defense Reuchlin issued *The Letters of Illustrious Men,* a volume of letters that he had received in support of his position. This work gave rise to one of the great satires of the Renaissance, *The Letters of Obscure Men* (1516), written by anonymous authors and purporting to be letters from various narrow-minded Scholastics in defense of the Dominican. Although the debate was over the validity of Hebraic studies for Christian theology and not over humanistic ideas of reform or wisdom, it indicates the tension and divisions between the humanists and much of the Scholastic community. The early controversies of the Protestant Reformation were initially misunderstood by many as a continuation of the conflicts between humanists and Scholastic theologians over the uses of Hebrew learning.

Thomas More and Desiderius Erasmus

The careers of two humanists exemplified both the strength and the limits of the humanistic movement outside Italy: Sir Thomas More (1478–1535) of London and Desiderius Erasmus (1466–1536) of Rotterdam. After becoming close friends during one of Erasmus's visits to England, the two developed their careers along very different paths. More had been educated at St. Anthony's school in London and became a

Thomas More's Critique of Contemporary Government

The first book of More's* Utopia *records a meeting between an Englishman, Morus, and a mysterious traveler named Hythloday (literally, "a nonsense-peddler"). In their discussions Hythloday presents a powerful critique of contemporary European politics and the problems that a humanist might have at the courts of the powerful.

"Imagine, if you will, that I am at the court of the king of France. Suppose I were sitting in his royal council, meeting in secret session, with the king himself presiding, and all the cleverest counsellors were hard at work devising a set of crafty machinations by which the king might keep hold of Milan, recover Naples, . . . and subdue all Italy. . . . One man urges him to make an alliance with the Venetians for just as long as the king finds it convenient. . . . Another suggests soothing the Emperor's wounded pride with a lavish and agreeable lotion of gold. . . .

"Now at this point, suppose I were to get up again and declare that all these counsels are both dishonorable and ruinous to the king? Suppose I said his honor and safety alike rest on the people's resources, rather than on his own? Suppose I said that men choose a king for their own sake, not for his, so that by his efforts and troubles, they may live in comfort and safety? . . . [After a discussion of a virtuous king he concludes] Such a king will be both a terror to evil-doers and beloved by the good.—Summing up the whole thing, don't you suppose if I set ideas like these before men strongly inclined to the contrary they would turn deaf ears to me?"

[Morus tried to counter Hythloday's points by saying,] "This academic philosophy is quite agreeable in the private conversation of close friends, but in the councils of kings, where grave matters are being authoritatively decided, there is no place for it."

"That is just what I was saying," Raphael [Hythloday] replied. "There is no place for philosophy in the councils of kings."

Source: Sir Thomas More, *Utopia*, ed. and trans. Robert M. Adams, Norton Critical Edition (New York: Norton, 1975), pp. 23–28.

lawyer. A friend of John Colet, he translated Lucian and wrote a humanistic history of Richard III while pursuing his public career. He is most famous for his work *Utopia* (1516), the description of an ideal society located on the island of Utopia (literally "nowhere") in the newly explored oceans. This powerful and contradictory work is written in two books. Book I is a debate over the moral value of public service between Morus, a well-intentioned but practical politician, and Hythloday, a widely traveled idealist. Morus tries to make the bureaucrat's argument about working for change from within the system. Hythloday rejects the argument out of hand. (See the box, "Thomas More's Critique of Contemporary Government.") Thomas More himself seems to have been unsure at that time about the virtues of public service. He was of two minds, and the debate between Morus and Hythloday reflects his indecision. As part of his critique of justice and politics in Europe, Hythloday describes in Book II the commonwealth of Utopia, in which there is no private property but strict equality of possessions, and, as a result, harmony, tolerance, and little or no violence.

Since the publication of *Utopia,* debates have raged about whether More, or we, could ever really hope to live in such a society. Some scholars have questioned how seriously More took this work—he seems to have written the initial sections merely to amuse friends. Yet whatever More's intentions, *Utopia*'s society of equality,

THE RENAISSANCE: CULTURE OUTSIDE ITALY

1405	Christine de Pizan publishes *The Book of the City of Ladies*
1434	Jan van Eyck paints the Arnolfini wedding
ca. 1452	Johann Gutenberg publishes his Bible
1494	Albrecht Dürer leaves on the first of two trips to Italy
1511	Desiderius Erasmus writes *Praise of Folly*
1516	Thomas More writes *Utopia*
1522	Francisco Jiménez de Cisneros's "Polyglot Bible" is completed

cooperation, and tolerance continues to inspire social commentators.

Ironically, More himself, like his creation Morus, soon found himself trying to work for justice within precisely the sort of autocratic court that Hythloday criticized. Not long after the completion of *Utopia,* More entered the service of King Henry VIII, eventually serving as chancellor of England. As a staunch Catholic and royal official, More never acted on utopian principles of peace and toleration. He was, in fact, responsible for persecution of English Protestants in the years before Henry VIII's break with Rome. More's opposition to Henry's break with the papacy and divorce and his refusal to acknowledge Henry as the head of the English church led him to resign his offices. He was eventually imprisoned and executed. More's writing was a stinging critique of political values. He implied that society could be reformed, yet in the period after 1521, his humanism and the ideas of *Utopia* had no influence on his own public life.

Unlike More, who was drawn to the power of king and pope, Erasmus always avoided working for authorities. Often called the "Prince of Humanists," he was easily the best-known humanist of the early sixteenth century. He was born the illegitimate son of a priest in the Low Countries. Forced by relatives into a monastery, he disliked the conservative piety and authoritarian discipline of traditional monastic life. Once allowed out of the monastery to serve as an episcopal secretary, he never returned. He lived and taught in France, England, Italy, and Switzerland. Of all the humanists it was Erasmus who most benefited from the printing revolution. The printer Aldus Manutius invited him to live and work in Venice, and he spent the last productive years of his life at Johannes Froben's press in Basel. He left the city only when Protestant reformers took control of the city government.

Over a long career Erasmus brought out repeated editions of works designed to educate Christians. His *Adiges,* first published in 1500, was a collection of proverbs from Greek and Roman sources. The work was immensely popular, and Erasmus repeatedly brought out expanded editions. He tried to present Greek and Roman wisdom that would illuminate everyday problems. The *Colloquies* was a collection of popular stories, designed as primers for students, that taught moral lessons even as they served as examples of good language. His ironic *Praise of Folly* (1511) was dedicated to Thomas More. An oration by Folly and praising folly, it was satire of a type unknown since antiquity. Folly's catalog of vices includes everyone from the ignorant to the scholar. But more seriously, Erasmus believed, as Saint Paul had said, that Christians must be "fools for Christ." In effect, human existence is folly. Erasmus's Folly first made an observation that Shakespeare would refine and make famous: "Now the whole life of mortal men, what is it but a sort of play in which . . . [each person] plays his own part until the director gives him his cue to leave the stage."[18]

Erasmus's greatest contributions to European intellectual life were his edition of and commentaries on the New Testament. After finding and publishing Lorenzo Valla's *Annotations on the New Testament* (1505), Erasmus embarked on creating a critical edition of the Greek text and a Latin translation independent of the fourth-century Latin Vulgate of Jerome. Like Valla, and unlike Jiménez, Erasmus corrected parts of the Vulgate. He rejected the authority of tradition, saying, "The sin of corruption is greater, and the need for careful revision by scholars is greater also, where the source of corruption was ignorance."[19] What was revolutionary in his edition was his commentary, which emphasized the literal and historical recounting of human experiences. This edition was the basis of later vernacular translations of the Bible during the Reformation.

Underlying Erasmus's scholarly output was what he called his "Philosophy of Christ." Erasmus was convinced that the true essence of Christianity was to be found in the life and actions of Christ. Reasonable, self-reliant, truly Christian people did not need superstitious rituals or magic. In his *Colloquies* he gives the example of a terrified priest who during a shipwreck promised everything to the Virgin Mary in order to be saved from drowning. But, Erasmus observed, it would have been more practical to start swimming!

Erasmus believed that classical and Christian wisdom could wipe away violence, superstition, and ignorance. Unlike More, Erasmus never abandoned the humanistic program. Yet his philosophy of Christ, based on faith in the goodness and educability of the individual, was swamped in the 1520s and 1530s by the sectarian claims of both Protestants and Catholics. Although Erasmus's New Testament was influential in the Reformation, his calls for reforms based on tolerance and reason were not.

Renaissance Art in the North

In the early fifteenth century, while Brunelleschi and Masaccio were revolutionizing the ways in which Italian artists viewed their world, artists north of the Alps, especially in Flanders, were making striking advances in the way they painted and sculpted. Artistic innovation in the North began with changes tied closely to the world of northern courts; only later did artists take up the styles of the Italian Renaissance. Northerners took Italian Renaissance art and fit it to a new environment.

Northern art of the late fourteenth and fifteenth centuries changed in two significant ways. In sculpture, the long, austere, unbroken vertical lines typical of Gothic sculpture gave way to a much more complex and emotional sculpture. In painting, Flemish artists moved from ornate, vividly colored paintings to experiments with ways to create a sense of depth. Artists were striving to paint and sculpt works that more faithfully represented reality. The sculptures of Claus Sluter (1350–1406), created for a family chapel of the Burgundian dukes at Champmol, held a lifelike drama unlike the previous Gothic sculpture. Court painters like Jan van Eyck (c. 1390–1441) in miniatures, portraits, and altar paintings also moved away from a highly formalized style to a careful representation of specific places. In Van Eyck's portrait of the Italian banker and courtier Giovanni Arnolfini and his bride, the image of the painter is reflected in a small mirror behind the couple, and above the mirror is written, "Jan van Eyck was here, 1434." Where Italians of the early fifteenth century tried to recreate space through linear perspective, the Flemish used aerial perspective, softening colors and tones in order to create the illusion of depth.

The influence of Renaissance styles in the north of Europe dates from the reign of the French king Francis I (r. 1515–1547), when Italian artists in significant numbers traveled north. Francis invited Italian artists to his court—most notably Leonardo da Vinci, who spent the last years of his life in France. The most influential of the Italian-style creations in France was doubtless Francis's château Fontainebleau, whose decorations contained mythologies, histories, and allegories of the kind found in the Italian courts. Throughout the sixteenth century, Italianate buildings and paintings sprang up throughout Europe.

Perhaps the most famous artist who traveled to Italy, learned Italian techniques, and then transformed them to fit the environment of northern Europe was Albrecht Dürer of Nuremberg (1471–1528). Son of a well-known goldsmith, Dürer became a painter and traveled first through France and Flanders learning the techniques popular in northern Europe. Then in 1494 he left Nuremberg on the first of two trips to Italy, during which he sketched Italian landscapes and studied the work of Italian artists, especially in Venice. What he learned in Italy, combined with the friendship of some of Germany's leading humanists, formed the basis of Dürer's works, which combined northern humanistic interests with the Italian techniques of composition and linear perspective. Dürer worked in charcoal, watercolors, and paints, but his influence was most widely spread through the numerous woodcuts that he produced on classical and contemporary themes. His woodcut *Whore of Babylon*, prepared in the context of the debate over the reform of the church, is based on sketches of Venetian prostitutes completed during his first visit to Italy.

Numerous other artists and engravers traveled south to see the great works of Italian artists. The engravings they produced and distributed back home made the innovations of the Italians available to those who were unable to travel to the south. In fact, some now lost or destroyed creations are known only through the engravings produced by northern artists eager to learn about Italian techniques.

Portrait of a Black Man Albrect Dürer sketched this portrait in the early sixteenth century, most likely in a commercial center such as Venice or Nuremberg. By that time it was common to show one of the Three Wise Men as black, but such depictions, unlike Dürer's drawing here, were rarely based on portrait studies. *(Graphische Sammlung, Albertina)*

The Renaissance and Court Society

The educational programs of the humanists and innovations in the arts between 1300 and 1550 provided an opportunity for rulers to use culture to define and celebrate their power. Art, literature, and politics merged in the brilliant life of the Renaissance Italian courts. To fully understand the Renaissance and its importance in the history of Europe, we need to examine the uses of culture by governments, specifically investigating the transformation of European ideas about service at court during the fourteenth and fifteenth centuries. We will take as a model the politics and cultural life at one noble court: the court of the Gonzaga family of Mantua.We will also discuss the development of the idea of the Renaissance gentleman and courtier made famous by Baldassare Castiglione, who was reared at the Gonzaga court.

The Elaboration of the Court

The courts of northern Italy interested themselves in the cultural and artistic innovations of the Renaissance artists and humanists inspired by classical civilization, and they closely imitated many of the values and new styles that were developing in the courts of northern Europe, such as the court of Burgundy (see page 488). Throughout Europe, attendance at court became increasingly important to members of the nobility as a source of revenue and influence. Kings and the great territorial lords were equally interested in drawing people to their courts as a way to influence and control the noble and the powerful.

Rulers in most parts of Europe instituted monarchial orders of knighthood to reward allies and followers. The most famous in the English-speaking world was the Order of the Garter, founded in 1349 by King Edward III. The orders were but one of the innovations in the organization of the court during the fourteenth and fifteenth centuries. The numbers of cooks, servants, huntsmen, musicians, and artists employed at court jumped dramatically in the late Middle Ages. In this the papal court itself was a model for the rest of Europe. The popes at Avignon in the fourteenth century already had a household of more than three hundred persons. If one included all the bureaucrats, merchants, local officials, and visitors who continually swarmed around the elaborate papal court, the number was even larger.

Courts were becoming theaters built around a series of widely understood signs and images that the ruler could manipulate. Culture was meant to reflect the image of the ruler. On important political or personal occasions, rulers organized jousts or tournaments around themes drawn from mythology. The dukes of Milan indicated the relative status of courtiers by inviting them to participate in particular hunts or jousts. They similarly organized their courtiers during feasts or elaborate entries into the towns and cities of their realms.

The court was the source of a number of highly remunerative offices. If granting a particular favor was not in the power of a prince, he was expected to send a recommendation on behalf of the suppliant to the person who could grant it. Rulers rarely refused requests outright. To do so would have reduced the image of their power. Italian courts of the Renaissance, for example, devised secret codes that allowed those who received letters from court to know when the ruler was serious and when the recipient could safely disregard an otherwise enthusiastic letter of recommendation.

The late fourteenth and fifteenth centuries were periods of growth in the political and bureaucratic power of European rulers. The increasingly elaborate and sumptuous courts were one of the tools that rulers used to create a unified culture and ideology. At the court of the Gonzagas in Mantua, one of the most widely known of the fifteenth-century courts, the manipulation of Renaissance culture for political purposes was most complete.

The Court of Mantua

An ambassador of the marquis of Mantua once reported that "though he be a small marchese, yet he is a man of quality." The diplomat meant that the Gonzagas were not particularly rich or powerful but they had created around themselves a widely admired court and style of life. Aristocratic values, humanism, and art all played a part in the creation of the Gonzaga reputation.

The city of Mantua, with perhaps 25,000 inhabitants in 1500, was small in comparison with Milan or Venice—the two cities with which it was most commonly allied. Located in a rich farming region along the Po River, Mantua did not have a large merchant or manufacturing class. Most Mantuans were involved in agriculture and regional trade in foodstuffs. The town had been a typical medieval Italian city-state until its government was overthrown by the noble Bonacolsi family in the thirteenth century. Members of the family took control of most of the important communal offices, and friends of the Bonacolsis filled the representative assemblies. The Bonacolsis, in turn, were ousted from the city in 1328 by their erstwhile comrades, the Gonzagas, who ruled the city until 1627.

The Gonzagas faced a problem typical of many of the families who took control of towns in northern Italy. The state they were creating was relatively small, their right to rule was not very widely recognized, and their control over the area was weak. The first step for the Gonzagas was the creation of fortresses and fortified towns that could withstand foreign enemies. The second step was to gain recognition of their right to rule. They had, after all, taken power in a palace revolution. In 1329 they were named imperial vicars, or representatives in the region. Later, in 1432, they bought the title "Marquis" from Emperor Sigismund for the relatively low price of £12,000.

Merely buying the title, however, did little to improve the status of the family. The family's reputation was enhanced by Gianfrancesco (d. 1444) and Lodovico (d. 1478), who brought the Renaissance and the new court style to Mantua. Located in a strategic area between the Milanese and Venetian states, the Gonzagas maintained themselves through astute diplomatic connections with other Italian and European courts and through service as well-paid mercenaries in the Italian wars of the fifteenth and sixteenth centuries. Lodovico served the Venetians, the Milanese, the Florentines, and even the far-off Neapolitans. With considerable understatement Lodovico concluded, "We have worn armor for a long time."

The creation of a brilliant court was an essential part of the Gonzaga program. Early in the Renaissance the Gonzagas involved themselves in the cultural movement of humanism. It was under the tutelage of the Gonzagas that Vittorino da Feltre created his educational experiment in Villa Giocosa, which drew noble pupils from throughout Italy. It would be hard to overestimate the value for the Gonzagas of a school that attracted sons of the dukes of Urbino, Ferrara, and Milan and numerous lesser nobles. The family also called numerous artists to Mantua. Lodovico invited Antonio Pisano, called Pisanello (ca. 1415–ca. 1456), probably the most famous court artist of the fifteenth century. Pisanello created a series of frescoes on Arthurian themes for the Gonzaga palace. In these frescoes Lodovico is portrayed as a hero of King Arthur's roundtable.

Although the Gonzagas never lost interest in the chivalric values of Arthurian romances, they are much better known for their patronage of art with classical themes. Leon Battista Alberti redesigned the façade of the church of Sant'Andrea for the Gonzagas in the form of a Roman triumphal arch. The church, which long had been associated with the family, became a monument to the Gonzaga court just as the Arch of Constantine celebrated imperial power. In the 1460s Lodovico invited Andrea Mantegna (1441–1506) to his court. Trained in Padua and Venice, Mantegna was at that time the leading painter in northern Italy. His masterwork is the Camera degli Sposi (literally, the "room of the spouses"), completed in 1474. It features family portraits of Ludovico Gonzaga and his family framed in imitation of Roman imperial portrait medallions. One scene shows Lodovico welcoming his son, a newly appointed cardinal, back from Rome—proof to all of the new status of the Gonzagas.

The arrival of Isabella d'Este (1494–1539) at court as the wife of Franceso Gonzaga marked the high point of the Renaissance in Mantua. Isabella had been classically educated at Ferrara by the son of Guarino of Verona. She maintained an interest in art, architecture, and music. As a patron of the arts, she knew what she wanted. In one commission she specified the themes and the balance of the work and told the artist to "add nothing." Isabella was also an accomplished musician, playing a variety of string and keyboard instruments. She and others of the Gonzaga family recruited musicians from Flanders as well as Italians to their court. By the end of the sixteenth century, Mantua was the most important musical center of Europe. It was there that Claudio Monteverdi (1567–1643) wrote works that established the genre of opera.

In the fourteenth century Petrarch had complained that however enjoyable feasting in Mantua might be, the place was dusty, plagued by mosquitoes, and overrun with frogs. By the end of the fifteenth century, the Gonzagas had secured for themselves a prominent place on the Italian, and even the European, stage.

Castiglione and the European Gentleman

Renaissance ideas did not just spread in intellectual circles. They also were part of the transformation of the medieval knight into the early modern "gentleman." In 1528, Baldassare Castiglione (1478–1529) published *The Book of the Courtier*, a work in which he distilled what he had learned in his years at the various courts of Italy. Castiglione was born in Mantua, distantly related to the ruling Gonzaga family. He grew up at court and was sent to the Sforza court in Milan to finish his education. He returned home in 1499 to begin a career that would include service in Mantua, Urbino, and Rome. During his career Castiglione met the greatest lights of the Renaissance. While he was in Rome, he became friends with Michelangelo and Raphael as well as with numerous humanistic writers. He died in Spain while on a mission for Pope Clement VII. When informed of his death, the emperor Charles V remarked, "One of the greatest knights in the world has died!" In his life and in his book Castiglione summed up the great changes that had transformed the nature of late medieval chivalry.

The Book of the Courtier reports a fictional series of discussions at the court of Urbino held over the course of four nights in March 1507. Among the participants are the duchess of Urbino, Elizabeth Gonzaga; her lady-in-waiting; and a group of humanists, men of action, and courtiers. In four evenings, members of the circle try to describe the perfect gentleman of court. In the process they debate the nature of nobility, humor, women, and love.

The topics were not randomly chosen. Castiglione explained that he wished "to describe the form of courtiership most appropriate for a gentleman living at the courts of princes." Castiglione's popularity was based on his deliberate

The Gonzaga Dukes of Mantua Ambassadors from throughout Italy wrote to their masters of the brilliance of Mantegna's family portrait of the Gonzagas of Mantua. Mantegna's decoration of the Gonzagas' palace and castle were an ideal form of propaganda for a prince. *(Scala/Art Resource, NY)*

joining of humanistic ideas and traditional chivalric values. Although his topic was the court with all its trappings, Castiglione tells his readers that his models for the discussion are Greek and Latin dialogues, especially those of Cicero and Plato. He was a Platonist. He believed that there was an inborn quality of "grace" that all truly noble gentlemen had. It had to be brought out, however, just as Michelangelo freed his figures from stone. Castiglione held that all moral and courtly virtues existed in tension with their opposites: "no magnanimity without pusillanimity." With numerous examples of good and bad in the world, wisdom could be revealed only through careful imitation, for like the classical authors favored by humanists, Castiglione advises that "He who lacks wisdom and knowledge will have nothing to say or do."[20]

But what Castiglione's readers recalled most clearly was his advice about behavior. Francesco Guicciardini of Florence once remarked that "When I was young, I used to scoff at knowing how to play, dance, and sing, and other such frivolities. . . . I have nevertheless seen from experience that these ornaments and accomplishments lend dignity and reputation even to men of good rank."[21] Guicciardini's comment underlines the value that readers found in Castiglione's work. Grace may be inbred, but it needed to be brought to the attention of those who controlled the court. Courtiers should first of all study the military arts. They had to fight, but only in situations where their prowess would be noticed. Castiglione adds practical advice about how to dress, talk, and participate in music and dancing: Never leap about wildly when dancing as peasants might, but dance only with an air of dignity and decorum. Castiglione further urges the courtier to be careful in dress: The French are "overdressed"; the Italians too quickly adopt the most recent and colorful styles. Reflecting political as well as social realities, Castiglione advises black

Giovanni della Casa on the Perfect Gentleman

Giovanni della Casa (1503–1556), bishop of Benevento and papal bureaucrat, wrote a book about how to get on at court.* Il Galateo (Sir Galahad), *was a practical book of manners, concluding that the courtier should adopt not the most virtuous customs but the customs typical of the court.

You must understand it behooves you to frame and order your manners and doings . . . to please those with whom you live. . . . For you must not only refrain from such things as being foul, filthy, loathsome, and nasty, but we must not so much as name them. . . . It is an ill-favoured fashion that some men use, openly to thrust their hands in what part of their body they like.

Likewise, I like it ill to see a gentleman settle himself to do the needs of nature in the presence of men, and after he had done to truss himself again before them. Neither would I have him (if I may give him counsel), when he comes from such an occupation, so much as wash his hands in the sight of honest company, for that the cause of his washing puts them in mind of some filthy matter that has been done apart. . . .

Besides, let not a man sit so that he turn his tail to him that sits next to him, nor lie tottering with one leg so high above the other that a man may see all bare that his clothes would cover. For such parts be never [dis]played but amongst those to whom a man need use no reverence. It is very true that if a gentleman should use such fashions before his servants, or in the presence of some friend of meaner condition than himself, it would betoken no pride, but a love and familiarity. . . .

We say that those be good manners and fashions which bring a delight or at least offend not their senses, their minds and conceits with whom we live. . . . It is not enough for a man to do things that be good, but he must also have a care he does them with a good grace. And good grace is nothing else but such a manner of light (as I may call it) as shines in the aptness of things. . . . Without which even proportion and measure, even that which is good is not fair.

Source: James Bruce Ross and Mary Martin McLaughlin, eds. *The Portable Renaissance Reader* (New York: Viking, 1953), pp. 340–347, from the 1576 translation by Robert Peterson.

or dark colors, which "reflect the sobriety of the Spaniards, since external appearances often bear witness to what is within."

The courtier always must be at pains "to earn that universal regard which everyone covets." Too much imitation and obvious study, however, lead to affectation. Castiglione counseled courtiers to carry themselves with a certain diffidence or unstudied naturalness (*sprezzatura*) covering their artifice. If courtiers are successful, they will exhibit "that graceful and nonchalant spontaneity (as it is often called) . . . so that those who are watching them imagine that they couldn't and wouldn't even know how to make a mistake." Thus, Castiglione's courtier walked a fine line between clearly imitated and apparently natural grace.

Castiglione's book was an immediate success and widely followed even by those who claimed to have rejected it. By 1561 it was widely available in Spanish, French, and English translations. The reasons are not difficult to find. It was critical for the courtier "to win for himself the mind and favour of the prince." And even those who disliked music, dancing, and light conversation learned Castiglione's arts "to open the way to the favour of princes." Many of the court arts that Castiglione preached had been traditional for centuries. Yet Castiglione's humanistic explanations and emphasis on form, control, and fashion had never seemed so essential as they did to the cultured gentlemen of the courts of Renaissance and early modern Europe. (See the box, "Giovanni della Casa on the Perfect Gentleman.")

Summary

Neither the world of Petrarch nor the world of courts described by Castiglione brought, as Jacob Burckhardt believed, the beginning of modern individualism and creative innovation radically different from the medieval past. Between 1300 and 1600, however, Europe experienced profound cultural innovation in literature, political and social thought, and art.

The impulse for change arose from the belief, shared by thinkers from Petrarch to Machiavelli, that there was a great deal to be learned from study of the Roman past. This was the impulse for humanistic innovations in language, history, and politics. Even revolutionary thinkers like Lorenzo Valla and Niccolò Machiavelli began with the study of classical literature and history. The same transformation is evident among the artists. Early in the fifteenth century, Florentines who experimented with perspective were intent on recovering lost Roman knowledge, and Michelangelo was praised not only for mastering but for going beyond Roman norms.

Issues of reform and renewal were less tied to public life in the monarchies of northern Europe. Moral and spiritual issues were more important. Yet the same movement from imitation to transformation is evident. Erasmus and Dürer assimilated the best of the new art and culture from Italy, but in the *Praise of Folly* and in Dürer's woodcuts the use of past ideas and models was neither simple nor direct.

Innovation depended on the study of the past. As humanists came to know more fully the art and history of Greece and Rome, they recognized the extent to which classical culture represented only one source of legal, historical, or moral understanding. Europeans' recognition of other, often competing, traditions would be tested in the sixteenth century, when they came face to face with a previously unknown world. It is to the geographical discoveries and European expansion that we now turn.

Notes

1. Quoted in Federico Chabod, *Machiavelli and the Renaissance* (New York: Harper & Row, 1958), p. 153.
2. Albertino Mussato, *The Ecerinis,* trans. Joseph R. Berrigan. As quoted in Berrigan, "A Tale of Two Cities: Verona and Padua in the Late Middle Ages," in *Art and Politics in Late Medieval and Renaissance Italy, 1250–1500,* ed. Charles M. Rosenberg (Notre Dame, Ind.: University of Notre Dame Press, 1990), p. 77.
3. Quoted in J. B. Trapp, ed., *Background to the English Renaissance* (London: Gray-Mills Publishing, 1974), p. 11.
4. Quoted in N. Mann, *Petrarch* (Oxford: Oxford University Press), p. 67.
5. Petrarch, "On His Own Ignorance and That of Many Others," in *The Renaissance Philosophy of Man,* ed. Ernst Cassirer, Paul Oskar Kristeller, and John H. Randall (Chicago: University of Chicago Press, 1948), p. 105.
6. Quoted in Benjamin G. Kohl and Ronald G. Witt, *The Earthly Republic* (Philadelphia: University of Pennsylvania Press, 1978), p. 11.
7. Quoted in M. L. King, *Women of the Renaissance* (Chicago: University of Chicago Press, 1991), p. 194.
8. Quoted ibid., p. 222.
9. Quoted ibid., p. 198.
10. K. R. Bartlett, *The Civilization of the Italian Renaissance* (Lexington, Mass.: Heath, 1992), p. 314.
11. Quoted in *The Portable Machiavelli,* ed. and trans. Peter Bondanella and Mark Musa (New York: Penguin Books, 1979), p. 128.
12. Quoted ibid., p. 160.
13. Quoted in *The Notebooks of Leonardo da Vinci,* ed. J. P. Richter, vol. 1 (New York: Dover, 1883 and 1970), p. 14.
14. Quoted ibid., p. 129.
15. Giorgio Vasari, *The Lives of the Artists,* trans. George Bull (Baltimore: Penguin, 1965), p. 338.
16. Julia Bondanella and Mark Musa, eds., *The Italian Renaissance Reader* (New York: Meridian Books, 1987), p. 377.
17. I. Origo, *The Merchant of Prato: Francesco di Marco Datini, 1335–1410* (New York: Knopf, 1957), pp. 155–156.
18. Quoted in A. Rabil, Jr., *Renaissance Humanism: Foundations, Forms, and Legacy,* vol. 2 (Philadelphia: University of Pennsylvania Press, 1988), p. 236.
19. Quoted ibid., p. 229.
20. Quotes of Castiglione are from Baldassare Castiglione, *The Book of the Courtier,* trans. George Bull (Baltimore: Penguin Books, 1967).

Weighing the Evidence

THE ART OF RENAISSANCE FLORENCE

In 1478 or shortly thereafter a member of the Medici family probably commissioned Sandro Botticelli to create the painting *Primavera* (*Spring*). Since its completion, critics have been fascinated by its composition and lyrical qualities. Notice the figures who make up the picture. At the center is Venus, goddess of love. The group to Venus's left tells the classical myth of the return of spring. Zephyrus, the west wind, who brings the fertility and growth of springtime, pursues Chloris, a goddess of fertility. Flowers flow from Chloris's mouth as Zephyrus changes her into Flora, the flower-covered goddess of spring, who stands to her right. These figures are balanced by the group to Venus's right—the three Graces, who are dancing beside the figure of Mercury, the messenger and in this context the god of May. We can easily agree with the critics and connoisseurs who praise the grace and enchantment of Botticelli's mysterious wood filled with dark trees loaded with oranges and his meadow covered with flowers. The work demonstrates Botticelli's great artistic skill and the sophisticated knowledge of classical mythology current in Florence in the last quarter of the fifteenth century. But, you might ask, how much more can it tell us about the culture of Renaissance Florence?

Historians and art historians have struggled to find the best way to use art as a tool in historical studies. In the late nineteenth and early twentieth centuries, art connoisseurs carefully studied brush strokes and coloring so that they could understand and immediately recognize the techniques of the great masters. Modern historians, however, usually approach a work of art in other ways. We can ask "What did the artist mean to paint?" Or we can ask "How does Botticelli's *Primavera* compare to other great works of art, such as Pablo Picasso's *Guernica?*" (see page 1091). But the most fruitful inquiry is "What might Botticelli's contemporaries have noticed in the work?"

To consider what that last question implies, it becomes important to know the social and artistic conventions that might illuminate the meanings in the work, where the work was intended to be displayed, and, finally, how the work comments on the social and cultural interests of the people whom the artist expected to view it. You probably recall that we dealt with some of these issues in Chapter 13 when we discussed the artistic program of the Sistine Chapel. Now let us turn to Botticelli's *Primavera*.

Contemporaries valued Botticelli's brush stroke—that is, his artistic touch. But, surprisingly, they valued just as highly the materials in which he worked. One of the few contracts we have for a work by Botticelli notes carefully the cost and quantities of gold foil and aquamarine blue paint (an expensive and precious color). From this we can see that Botticelli's contemporaries were very aware of color. As Leon Battista Alberti observed critically of fifteenth-century Italians, most people associate gold leaf and deep blue colors with sumptuousness and majesty. Florentines were also very aware of the writings of contemporary humanists—and especially of the humanist belief that classical and Christian wisdom were basically one. Imbuing classical images with contemporary meanings did not seem odd to them. Botticelli's great popularity in Florence actually rested in part on his sophisticated use of classically inspired figures to comment on contemporary issues.

Primavera was meant to decorate the palace of a relative of Lorenzo de' Medici. It was probably designed to be seen by Lorenzo "the Magnificent" himself, who not only held a position of political and economic importance in the city but was a gifted poet and leader of a *brigata*, or company of poets and humanists. The brigata, in fact, was the primary audience for Botticelli's work. Lorenzo and the poets of his circle were actively combining what they believed was the best of

Botticelli: Primavera *(Art Resource)*

their Tuscan culture with the classical philosophy and literature revived by the humanists. Lorenzo once wore on his armor the motto *Le Tems revient*, which loosely translated means "The ages shall be renewed." As we have seen, this renewal was an idea popular among the artists and humanists of Renaissance Italy. In *Primavera* Botticelli uses a number of symbols meant to remind viewers of Lorenzo de' Medici and his cultural interests. Look at the oranges in the trees, for example. They resemble the three balls on the Medici crest. The coming of spring in the person of Flora is precisely the sort of image with which Lorenzo wanted to be associated.

But what of the three Graces? How do they fit into a picture meant to celebrate the merging of old and new in Medicean Florence? For Lorenzo's contemporaries, they may have been the best possible image of the marriage of classical and Tuscan traditions. Lorenzo and his friends knew of the Graces and their association with spring from a variety of classical sources. These particular Graces, however, are Tuscan. The cut of their gowns and their dance would have been recognizable to Lorenzo's friends as typically Florentine. Lorenzo himself had earlier composed a dance, "A Simple Dance Called Venus," which could easily be the dance that they are doing. Next to them stands Venus, the goddess of love. But here she represents spring, flowering (Flora is, after all, the root of the name Florence), and renewal. Her arm is raised in a gesture of invitation. She is inviting us, or, more accurately, the Florentines of Lorenzo's time, to join in a dance of celebration and renewal.

What do we finally see in Botticelli's *Primavera*? It is not simply an imitation of either a classical text or any known classical figure. It seems instead that Botticelli created a sort of visual poem that incorporated numerous themes of classical learning and cultural renewal that were, by the late 1460s and 1470s, widely associated with Lorenzo de' Medici, the cultural and political master of Florentine life. The historian finds in the art of the Renaissance works of great beauty that convey through their materials, composition, and symbols a sense of the values and ideas that animated politics and culture.

21. Quoted in R. W. Hanning and D. Rosand, eds., *Castiglione: The Ideal and the Real in Renaissance Culture* (New Haven, Conn.: Yale University Press, 1983), p. 17.

Suggested Reading

General Surveys

Brown, Alison. *The Renaissance.* 1988. An excellent short introduction to Renaissance art and culture designed for those with little or no background in the field.

Burckhardt, Jacob. *The Civilization of the Renaissance in Italy.* 1860. A classic of nineteenth-century literature as well as the first discussion of the modernity and creativity of the period.

Kelly, Joan. *Women, History & Theory.* 1984. Includes Kelly's famous "Did Women Have a Renaissance?" as well as an essay on the *querelle des femmes.*

King, M. L. *Women of the Renaissance.* 1991. A survey of the social, economic, and cultural experience of women during the Renaissance.

Rabil, Albert, Jr. *Renaissance Humanism: Foundations, Forms and Legacy.* 3 vols. 1988. An excellent and quite accessible introduction to Renaissance humanism.

Particular Studies

Baron, H. *The Crisis of the Early Italian Renaissance.* 1966. The classic discussion of the rise of civic humanism in Florence. Its narrative of the connections between diplomacy and intellectual life is especially clear.

Kohn, Benjamin, and Ronald Witt, eds. *The Earthly Republic.* 1978. An important anthology of writings by fourteenth- and fifteenth-century civic humanists. The general introduction is an especially clear discussion of the rise of civic humanism.

Mann, N. *Petrarch.* 1984. An excellent introduction to Petrarch's life and thought, designed for readers with little prior experience with Renaissance thought.

Skinner, Q. *The Foundations of Modern Political Thought.* Vol. 1. *The Renaissance.* 1978. A survey of political thought that attempts to place thinkers in their social and political context.

Woodward, W. H., ed. *Vittorino da Feltre and Other Humanist Educators: Essays and Versions. An Introduction to the History of Classical Education.* 1897. A volume of essays and documents that are excellent introductions to the Renaissance educational program.

Art and Society in Renaissance Italy

Baxendall, Michael. *Painting and Experience in Fifteenth Century Italy.* 1972. A volume that helps the reader see the art of the Renaissance as it would have been seen in the period.

Hartt, F. *History of Italian Renaissance Art: Painting, Sculpture, Architecture.* 1987. A comprehensive and lavishly illustrated survey of Renaissance art that is sensitive to the social and political milieu in which artists worked.

Letts, R. M. *The Renaissance.* 1992. An excellent introductory essay on the art of Renaissance Italy. Especially good on the innovations of the early fifteenth century.

Panofsky, E. *Renaissance and Renascences in Western Art.* 1969. A difficult but important essay on the concept of Renaissance and on the nature of the differences between the Renaissance and previous periods of creative innovation.

Humanism and Culture Outside Italy

Eisenstein, E. L. *The Printing Press as an Agent of Change: Communications and Cultural Transformations in Early Modern Europe.* 1979. Discussion of the ways in which print culture changed social and intellectual life, rather than the technology of print itself.

Goodman, A., and A. Mackay, eds. *The Impact of Humanism.* 1990. A volume of basic surveys of the arrival of Italian humanistic ideas in the various lands of Europe.

Marius, R. *Thomas More: A Biography.* 1984. A beautifully written biography that questions More's humanistic interests and looks particularly at More's divided feelings about religion and the state.

Murray, Linda. *The Late Renaissance and Mannerism.* 1967. Introductory survey that traces Renaissance themes as they move out of Italy, especially through France, Germany, and Flanders.

Panofsky, E. *Albrecht Dürer.* 1948. The best study of the life and work of Germany's greatest Renaissance artist.

Courts and Castiglione

Dickens, A. G., ed. *The Courts of Europe.* 1977. A well-illustrated collection of essays for the general reader on courts from the Middle Ages to the eighteenth century.

Elias, N. *The Civilizing Process.* 1978. A classic discussion of the transformation of manners and behavior at the courts of Renaissance Europe. Contains difficult analysis but lively descriptions.

Keen, Maurice. *Chivalry.* 1984. A well-written survey of chivalry that includes discussion on the transformation of chivalry at the end of the middle Ages.

Woods-Marsden, J. *The Gonzaga of Mantua and Pisanello's Arthurian Frescoes.* 1988. A broad and well-illustrated discussion of how the artistic interests of the Gonzagas served their social and political needs.

veyotlipan.

CHAPTER 15

Europe, the Old World and the New

In the last decade of the fifteenth century, Portugal and Spain began a series of voyages that eventually carried Europeans to most parts of the world, unifying the already-known "Old World" continents of Asia, Africa, and Europe with a "New World": the Americas and the islands of the Pacific. The story of the first navigators, their technological advances, and the colonies they established may seem straightforward, but students interested in the discoveries and expansion that occurred during the late fifteenth and sixteenth centuries have viewed events in vastly different ways. Accounts of the meeting of the Old World and the New, perhaps more than any other episode of Western history, have been shaded by the perspectives of the writer and the reader. Those who wanted to focus on the transfer of European religion and culture to new lands have viewed Christopher Columbus and the other early explorers as important symbols of the creation of a New World with new values. Those who sought the origins of modern scientific rationalism have believed that Columbus's voyage across the Atlantic Ocean proves that he was a "Renaissance man" who saw through the myths and superstitions of the Middle Ages. However, the descendants of the native peoples who greeted the newly arriving Europeans—the Amerindians, Aborigines, Maori, and Polynesians who lived in North and South America, Australia, New Zealand, and the islands of the Pacific—remind us that the outsiders brought slavery, modern warfare, and epidemic diseases that virtually destroyed indigenous cultures.

Spain commissioned Columbus to sail west because the Portuguese already controlled eastern routes to Asia around the African coast and because certain technical innovations made long open-sea voyages possible.

Cortés and his army, which includes Amerindian allies, are greeted by local leaders during his march to Tenochtitlán.

Thus, as those who celebrate Columbus's achievements have said, the story includes national competition, the development of navigational techniques, and strategic choices. Another aspect of the story, however, is the political, cultural, and military clash that took place in the Atlantic, Caribbean, and Central and South America. The Europeans overthrew the great empires of the Aztecs and Incas, but the transfer of European culture was never so complete as the Europeans thought or expected. The language and customs of the conquered peoples, blanketed by European language and law, survived, though the lands colonized by the Europeans would never again be as they had been before their encounter with the Old World.

The European Background

Over the course of the late Middle Ages Europeans developed the desire and the ability to reach distant lands in Africa and Asia. Three critical factors for the exploratory voyages of the fifteenth and early sixteenth centuries were technology, curiosity and interest, and geographical knowledge. A series of technical innovations made sailing far out into the ocean less risky and more predictable than it had been. The writings of classical geographers, myths and popular tales, and merchants' accounts of their travels fueled popular interest in the East and made ocean routes to the East seem safe and reasonable alternatives to overland travel.

Navigational Innovations

The invention of several navigational aids in the fourteenth and fifteenth centuries made sailing in open waters easier and more predictable. Especially important was the fly compass, consisting of a magnetic needle attached to a paper disk (or "fly") marked off in degrees. The simple compass had been invented in China and was known in Europe by the late twelfth century, but it did not mark off degrees and so was only a rudimentary aid to navigation. By 1500, astrolabes and other devices enabling sailors to use the position of the sun and stars to assist in navigation were also available. An astrolabe allowed sailors to measure the altitude of the Pole Star in the sky and thereby calculate the latitude, or distance from the equator, at which their ship was sailing. Still, until the general adoption of charts marked with degrees of latitude, most navigators relied on the compass, experience, and instinct.

The typical Mediterranean ship of the late Middle Ages was a galley powered by a combination of sails and oars; such a vessel was able to travel quickly and easily along the coast. Because of limited space and the need for a large crew of rowers, galleys were not ideal for long-distance travel. Throughout the Mediterranean, shipbuilders experimented with new designs, and during the fifteenth century the Portuguese and Spanish perfected the caravel. Large square sails efficiently caught the wind and propelled the caravel forward, and smaller triangular sails (lateens) allowed the caravel ship to sail into a headwind. The caravel was larger and needed a smaller crew than the galley, and was more maneuverable than ships with only square sails.

By the 1490s the Portuguese and Spanish had developed the ships and techniques that would make long open-sea voyages possible. What remained was for Europeans, especially Portuguese and Spanish, to conclude that such voyages were both possible and profitable.

Lands Beyond Christendom

The Greeks and Romans had had contacts with the civilizations of Asia and Africa, and in the Middle Ages interest in the lands beyond Christendom had never been lost. In the thirteenth and fourteenth centuries, European economic and cultural contacts with these lands greatly increased. The rising volume of trade between Europe and North Africa brought with it information about the wealthy African kingdoms of the Niger Delta. The Mongols in the thirteenth century opened trade routes to European merchants and missionaries, allowing them to travel eastward along roads formerly closed to them by hostile Muslim governments.

Trade in the Mediterranean also kept Muslims and Christians and Europeans and North Africans in close contact. Europeans sold textiles to Arab traders who carried them across the Sahara to Timbuktu, where they were sold for gold bullion from the ancient African kingdoms of Ghana and Mali located just above the Niger

River. European chroniclers recorded the pilgrimage to Mecca of Mansa Musa, the fabulously wealthy fourteenth-century emperor of Mali. Italian merchants tried unsuccessfully to trade directly with the African kingdoms, but Muslim merchants prevented any permanent contact.

Europeans enjoyed more successful trade connections farther east. The discovery in London of a brass shard inscribed with a Japanese character attests to the breadth of connections in the early fourteenth century. After the rise of the Mongols, Italian merchants regularly traveled east through Constantinople and on to India and China. By the fourteenth century, they knew how long travel to China might take and the probable expenses along the way.

European intellectuals also maintained an interest in the lands beyond Christendom. They had read the late classical and early medieval authors who described Africa, the Indies, and China. The greatest of the classical geographers, Ptolemy of Alexandria, who lived in the second century A.D., was known only indirectly until the early fifteenth century, but medieval thinkers read avidly and speculated endlessly about the information contained in the works of authors from Late Antiquity, such as Martianus Capella, who lived in the fifth century A.D. Martianus preserved fantastic myths and tales along with geographical observations that he had gathered from the writings of Ptolemy and others. He reported, for example, that there were snakes in Calabria that sucked milk from cows and men who became wolves—the earliest mention of werewolves. Martianus assumed that a person who traveled to the south and east of Europe was more and more likely to find wonders. Moreover, it seemed to early geographers that the heat at the equator must be so intense that it would be impossible for life to exist there. By the twelfth century, fictitious reports circulated widely in the West of a wealthy Christian country in the East or possibly in Africa—the fictitious kingdom of Prester John. In the fifteenth century, European Christians looked to Prester John and eventually to the Christians of Ethiopia for aid against the Muslims.

Tales of geographical marvels are epitomized by the *Travels of Sir John Mandeville,* a book probably written in France but purporting to be the observations of a knight from St. Albans just north of London. Mandeville says that he left England in 1322 or 1323 and traveled to Constantinople, Jerusalem, Egypt, India, China, Persia, and Turkey. In the first half of the book he describes what seems to be a typical pilgrimage to the Holy Land. As the author continues eastward, however, the narrative shifts dramatically. Sir John describes the islands of wonders, inhabited by dog-headed men, one-eyed giants, headless men, hermaphrodites. He not only describes his discovery of the lost tribes of Israel but records the location of Paradise. The mixture of fact and fantasy in the *Travels* represents the general level of medieval knowledge of geography. Mandeville reports that the world could be, in fact has been, circumnavigated. He adds that the lands south of the equator, the Antipodes, are habitable.

Mandeville's travels and similar fantastic tales kept alive geographical speculation. They also raised expectations in travelers who actually did venture to the East. Thirteenth-century visitors to central Asia carefully asked their Mongol hosts about the exact locations of these wonders. Columbus, in his dispatches, included reports he had received of an island of Amazons in the Caribbean, and he believed that he had found the rivers flowing from Paradise along the coast of Venezuela.

More reliable information became available in the thirteenth century largely because of the arrival of the Mongols. Jenghiz Khan and his descendants created an empire that reached from eastern Hungary to China (see page 326). This *pax Mongolica,* or area of Mongol-enforced peace, was a region tolerant of racial and cultural differences. The pagan Mongols initially offered Europeans natural allies against the Muslim states as well as a natural target for conversion. In the 1240s and 1250s a series of papal representatives traveled to the Mongol capital at Karakorum near Lake Baikal in Siberia. The letters of papal ambassadors who worked extensively to gain converts and allies for a crusade against the Turks were widely read and greatly increased accurate knowledge about Asia. Other missionaries and diplomats journeyed to the Mongol court and some continued farther east to India and China. By the early fourteenth century, the church had established a bishop in Beijing.

Italian merchants followed closely on the heels of the churchmen and diplomats. The pax

The World Beyond Christendom Medieval Christians believed that wondrous peoples lived beyond the borders of Christendom. Images of headless or one-legged men were usually included in travel accounts. This picture from Marco Polo's *Travels* shows what many Europeans expected to find when they traveled. *(Bibliothèque Nationale)*

Mongolica offered the chance to trade directly in Asia and the adventure of visiting lands known only from travel literature. In 1262 Niccolò and Maffeo Polo left on their first trip to China. On a later journey the two Venetians took Niccolò's son, Marco (1255–1324), who remained in China for sixteen or seventeen years. Marco dictated an account of his travels to a Pisan as they both sat as prisoners of war in a Genoese jail in 1298. The book was widely known. Columbus himself owned and extensively annotated a copy of Marco Polo's *Travels.*

In his account Marco claims that he was an influential official in China; and he may, in fact, be the "Po-Lo" mentioned in Chinese sources as a low-level imperial bureaucrat of Kublai Khan. Marco describes the long, difficult trip to China, his equally arduous return, and the cities and industries he found. He was most impressed by the trade of Ch'nan (modern Hangzhou on the central coast of China)—one hundred times greater, he thought, than the trade of Alexandria in Egypt, a renowned port on the Mediterranean. Marco also visited modern Sri Lanka, Java, and Sumatra. His tales mix a merchant's observations of ports, markets, and trade with myths and marvels—tales of dog-headed men and the kingdom of Prester John.

By 1300 there seems to have been a modest community of Italians in China. By the late thirteenth and fourteenth centuries, Italian traders were traveling directly to the East in search of Asian silks, spices, pearls, and ivory. They and other European merchants could consult the *Handbook for Merchants* (1340) by the Florentine Francesco Pegalotti, which described the best roads, likely stopping points, and the appropriate freight animals for a trip to the East (see the box, "Pegalotti on Travel to the East"). These merchants found that they had cheap access to spices, silks, and even porcelains, which they shipped back to the West. Fragmentary reports of Europeans in the Spice Islands (also known as the Moluccas), Japan, and India indicate that many

Pegalotti on Travel to the East

In his **Handbook for Merchants** *Francesco Pegalotti describes travel to Asia and the commercial customs of the area, demonstrating how usual such travel had become by the 1340s, when his work was published.*

First [of all] it is advisable for him to let his beard grow long and not shave. And at Tana (on the Black Sea coast) he should furnish himself with guide-interpreters, and he should not try to save by hiring a poor one instead of a good one. . . . And besides interpreters he ought to take along at least two good manservants who know the cumanic [Mongol] tongue well. And if the merchant wishes to take along from Tana any woman with him, he may do so—and if he does not wish to take one, there is no obligation; yet if he takes one, he will be regarded as a man of higher condition. . . . And [for the stretch] from Tana to Astrakhan he ought to furnish himself with food for twenty-five days—that is with flour and salt and fish, for you find meat in sufficiency in every locality along the road. . . . The road leading from Tana to Cathay is quite safe both by day and by night, according to what the merchants report who have used it. . . .

Anyone wishing to leave from Genoa or from Venice in order to travel to the said places and journey to Cathay would do well to carry linen . . . without investing in any other merchandise, unless he has a few bales of the very finest linens. . . .

All silver which the merchants carry with them when going to Cathay, the lord of Cathay causes to be withdrawn and placed in his treasury; and to the merchants who bring it he gives paper money, that is, yellow paper stamped with the seal of the said lord, that money being called *balisci.* And with the said money you may and can purchase silk and any other merchandise or foods you may wish to buy.

Source: R. S. Lopez and I. Raymond, eds., *Medieval Trade in the Mediterranean World* (New York: Columbia University Press, 1955), pp. 356, 357, 358.

Europeans in addition to merchants traveled simply for the adventure of visiting new lands.

The Revolution in Geography

The situation changed significantly over the course of the fourteenth century. With the conversion of the Mongols to Islam, the breakdown of Mongol unity, and the subsequent rise of the Ottoman Turks in the fourteenth century, the highly integrated and unusually open trade broke down. The caravan routes across southern Russia, Persia, and Afghanistan were closed to Europeans. Western merchants were once again dependent on Muslim middlemen.

The reports of travelers, however, continued to circulate long after the closing of the trade routes. This new information was avidly followed by Western geographers anxious to assimilate it. Marco Polo's *Travels* and the classical geographical theories of Ptolemy contributed to a veritable revolution in geography in the decades before the Portuguese and Spanish voyages.

In 1375 Abraham Cresques, a Jewish mathematician from the Mediterranean island of Majorca, produced what has come to be known as the *Catalan World Atlas.* He combined the traditional medieval *mappamundi* (or world map) with a Mediterranean portolan. The *mappamundi* attempted to show both spatial and theological relationships. It often followed the O-T form—that is, a circle divided into three parts (⦽) representing Europe, Africa, and Asia, the lands of the descendants of Noah. Jerusalem—the symbolic center of the Christian religion—is always at the center of the map. The portolan, in contrast, was entirely practical. From the late thirteenth century mariners had been developing atlases that included sailing instructions and accurate portrayals of ports, islands, and shallows along with general compass readings. The *Catalan World Atlas* largely holds to the portolan tradition but has more accurate representations of the lands surrounding the Mediterranean.

In the fifteenth century, following Ptolemy's suggestions, mapmakers began to divide their maps into squares marking lines of longitude and latitude. This format made it possible to accurately show the contours of various lands and the relationship of one land mass to another. Numerous maps of the world were produced in this period. The culmination of this cartography was a globe constructed for the city of Nuremberg in 1492, the very year Columbus set sail. From these increasingly accurate maps, it has become possible to document the first exploration of the Azores, the Cape Verde Islands, and the western coast of Africa.

The Florentine mathematician Paolo Toscanelli, in a letter of 1474 to the king of Portugal, included a map demonstrating, he believed, the short distance to be covered if one were to sail straight west first to Japan and then on to China. Not surprisingly, Columbus, after his voyages, observed that maps had been of no use to him. True enough. But without the accumulation of knowledge by travelers and the mingling of that knowledge with classical ideas about geography, it is doubtful whether Columbus or the Portuguese Vasco da Gama would have undertaken the voyages that so dramatically changed the relations between Europe and the rest of the world.

Portuguese Voyages of Discovery

Portugal, a tiny country on the edge of Europe, for a short time led the European expansion. Portugal's experience gives a good indication of the options open to the Europeans as they extended their influence into new areas. Portuguese sailors were the first Europeans to perfect the complex

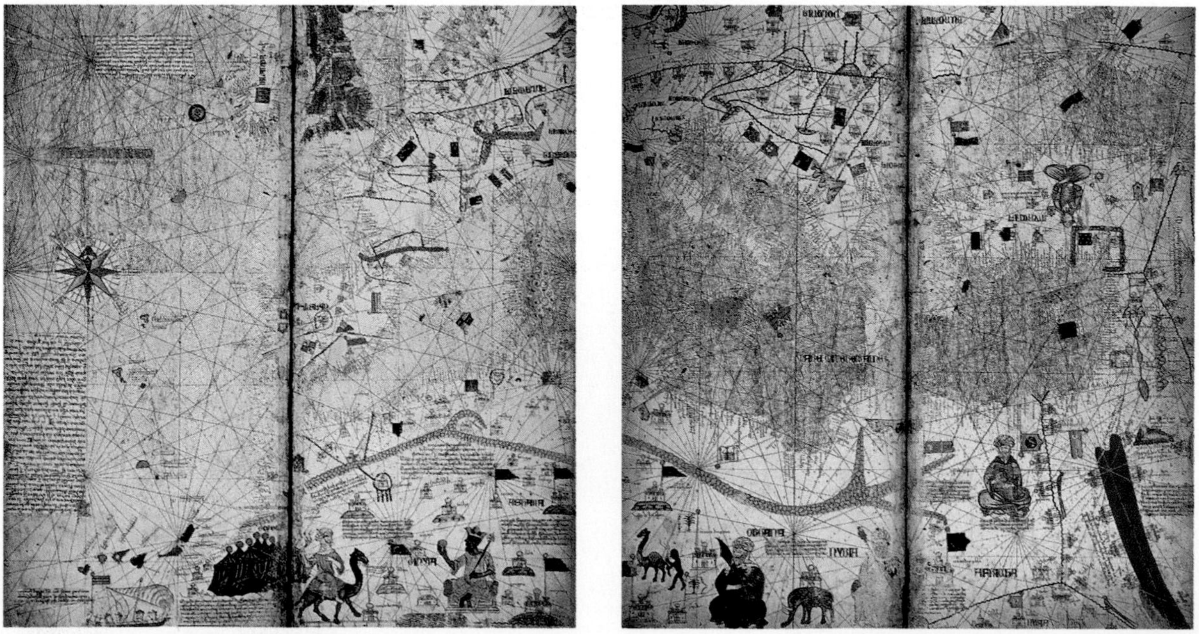

The Catalan Atlas Composed by the Jewish physician Abraham Cresques, this map combined information from classical geographers with navigational information typically found in Mediterranean charts or portolans. Like travelers' tales, the map is not very accurate in depicting the lands east of the Mediterranean. *(Bibliothèque Nationale)*

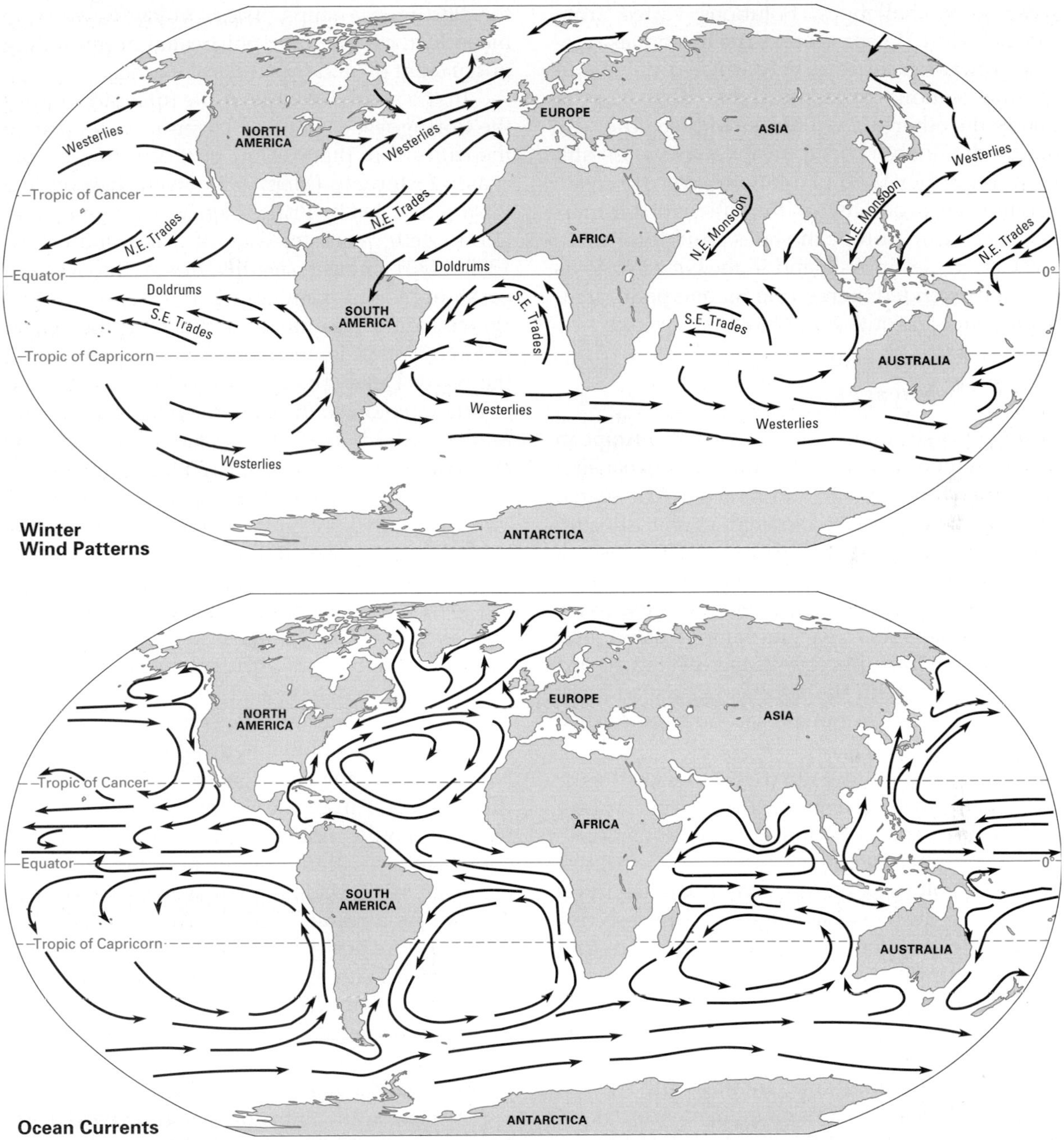

Map 15.1 Winds and Currents Winds and ocean currents move in giant clockwise and counterclockwise circles that limit the directions in which ships can sail efficiently. It was impossible, for example, for the explorers to sail directly south along the entire western coast of Africa.

techniques of using the winds and currents of the south Atlantic, especially along the western coast of Africa (Map 15.1). As they moved down the African coast and later as they tried to compete commercially in Asia, they found that they could not automatically transfer European economic and commercial traditions into new environments. In each new location, the Portuguese faced new challenges. Solutions varied from place to place. In some areas the Portuguese created a network of relatively isolated naval and trading stations to control the movement of goods. In other areas they attempted to create large, dominant Portuguese colonies. In still other areas they used plantation slavery to create commercial products for the international market. The other European states would use these same strategies in Asia and in the New World as they too extended their economic and political interests beyond continental Europe.

The Early Voyages

Portugal, like other late medieval European states, hoped that exploration and expansion would lead to "gold and Christians." The search for Christians was accelerated in the fifteenth century by the growing power of the Ottoman Turks. After the conquest of Constantinople in 1453, Turkish expansion into Syria and Palestine, and Turkish raids reaching into Austria and northeastern Italy, Europeans increasingly hoped for an alliance with the mythical Christian kingdoms of the East to open a second front against the advancing Turks.

For the Portuguese themselves, facing the Atlantic and insulated from the direct Turkish threat, the promise of gold was no doubt more alluring than the search for Christians. The nearest source of gold was well known to late medieval Christians: the African kingdoms of the Niger Delta. The problem for European traders and their governments was that commercial contacts with this wealthy region remained controlled by the Muslim Berber merchants of North Africa. The Portuguese and Spanish hoped to break the monopoly by taking control of the North African coast or by means of a flanking movement along the western coast of Africa.

Actual exploration of the Atlantic had begun long before Europeans recognized the extent of the Turkish threat. By 1350 the Madeiras and the Canaries, groups of islands off the western coast of Africa, regularly were included on European maps. By about 1365 Portuguese, Spanish, and probably French sailors were visiting the Canary Islands. By 1400 the Azores, one-third of the way across the Atlantic, were known and from early in the fifteenth century were regular ports of call for Portuguese ships. These voyages were no mean feat, calling for sophisticated ocean sailing out of sight of land for weeks at a time.

In the second decade of the fifteenth century the Portuguese expansion began in earnest with the capture of the Muslim port of Ceuta on the coast of Morocco (Map 15.2). From then on, the Portuguese, led by Prince Henry "the Navigator" (1394–1460), younger son of King John I (r. 1385–1433), moved steadily down the western coast of Africa. Contemporaries reported that Prince Henry was intent on reaching the "River of Gold"—that is, the Gold Coast of Africa and the Niger Delta. To accomplish this, he directed efforts to colonize the Canaries, the Azores, and Madeira, the largest of the Madeira Islands. He also sponsored a series of expeditions down the African coast, reaching Senegal and the Cape Verde Islands by 1444. The Portuguese quickly established trading stations in the region and soon were exporting gold and slaves to Lisbon.

Prince Henry is often credited with creating a virtual school of seamanship in his court at Sagres on the coast of Portugal, but his efforts at colonization may have had more importance for Portuguese expansion. The islands off the coast of Africa were uninhabited, except for the Canaries, which the Portuguese tried unsuccessfully to wrest from the Spanish. Thus, the Portuguese could not merely establish trading communities within a larger population, for on the Azores and Madeira there was no native population. As a result, by the early 1440s the Portuguese were bringing sheep, seed, and peasants to the hitherto uninhabited Azores and Madeiras, and the Crown was forced to grant extensive lordships to nobles to encourage emigration to the Azores. The islanders survived largely by exporting sheep and grain to Iberia.

A significant transformation occurred on Madeira in the 1440s, when the Portuguese introduced sugar cane to the island. Within a decade sugar was dominating the island's economy. By 1452, there was a water mill for processing the cane, and in the 1470s sugar revenues from

Map 15.2 World Exploration The voyages of Columbus, da Gama, and Magellan charted the major sea lanes that became essential for communication, trade, and warfare for the next three hundred years.

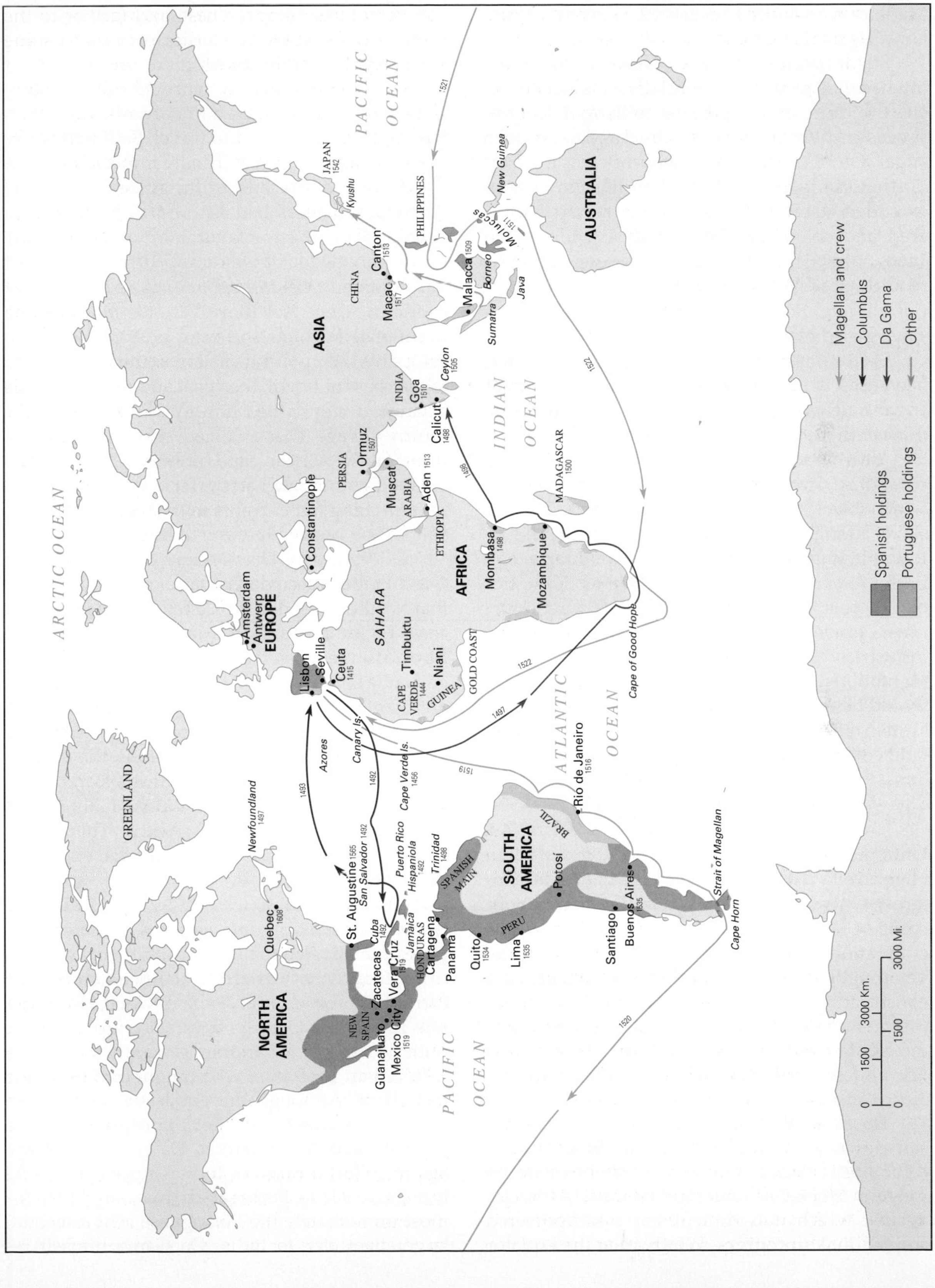
ARCTIC OCEAN
PACIFIC OCEAN
ATLANTIC OCEAN
INDIAN OCEAN
PACIFIC OCEAN
GREENLAND
Newfoundland 1497
NORTH AMERICA
Quebec 1608
St. Augustine 1565
San Salvador 1492
NEW SPAIN
Guanajuato
Mexico City 1519
Zacatecas
Vera Cruz 1519
Cuba 1492
Jamaica
HONDURAS
Hispaniola 1492
Puerto Rico
Trinidad 1498
Cartagena
Panama
SPANISH MAIN
SOUTH AMERICA
Quito 1534
PERU
Lima 1535
Potosí
BRAZIL
Rio de Janeiro 1516
Santiago
Buenos Aires 1535
Strait of Magellan
Cape Horn
Azores
Canary Is.
Cape Verde Is. 1456
1493
1492
1519
1520
1497
1522
1498
1511
1521
1522
EUROPE
Amsterdam
Antwerp
Lisbon
Seville
Ceuta 1415
SAHARA
Timbuktu
Niani
CAPE VERDE 1444
GUINEA
GOLD COAST
AFRICA
ETHIOPIA
Mombasa 1498
Mozambique
MADAGASCAR 1500
Cape of Good Hope
Constantinople
ARABIA
Muscat
Aden 1513
PERSIA
Ormuz 1507
INDIA
Goa 1510
Calicut 1498
Ceylon 1505
ASIA
CHINA
Macao 1517
Canton 1513
JAPAN 1542
Kyushu
PHILIPPINES
Malacca 1509
Sumatra
Borneo
Java
Moluccas
New Guinea
AUSTRALIA
Magellan and crew
Columbus
Da Gama
Other
Spanish holdings
Portuguese holdings
0 1500 3000 Km.
0 1500 3000 Mi.

Madeira constituted nearly 2 percent of the Crown's total income.

Sugar production was capital- and labor-intensive. A great many workers were needed to cut the cane, and expensive mills and lengthy processing were needed to extract and to produce sugar. On Madeira most of the work was done by Portuguese peasants. But when the Portuguese extended sugar cultivation to the newly discovered and colonized Cape Verde Islands in the 1460s, they found that Portuguese peasants would not work voluntarily in the sultry equatorial climate. Soon the Portuguese introduced a slave-based plantation system to produce sugar.

Slaves imported from the Black Sea areas had been used in agriculture since the introduction of sugar cultivation into the Mediterranean in the thirteenth century. The Portuguese themselves had been trading in slaves along the western coast of Africa since the late 1440s—the date from which black slaves appear in Lisbon. African slaves along with slaves from the East could be found in Italy and throughout the Mediterranean in the fifteenth century, most often as domestics or laborers in small enterprises. Since Roman times, however, there had been no slave-based industries on the scale of the Portuguese sugar plantations. Sugar production in the New World would be modeled on the slave-based plantation system perfected by the Portuguese in their island colonies in the Atlantic.

The Search for a Sea Route to Asia

Until the middle of the fifteenth century the Niger Delta remained the focus of Portuguese interest. Only after securing control of the western coast of Africa through the extension of sugar cultivation to Madeira and the Cape Verdes, developing the gold and slave trade in Senegal, and constructing a fortress to control the Volta River (in the modern Ivory Coast) and secure access to most gold-producing areas of West Africa did the Portuguese look seriously at sailing around Africa and discovering a sea route to Asia.

The fifteenth-century sailors who first tried to sail down the coast of Africa faced enormous difficulties. Water and wind currents tend to move in clockwise and counterclockwise circles against which it is difficult for a sail-powered ship to make progress. Winds near the equator generally blow from the east, and farther to the north and south the westerlies prevail. In some zones and at certain times there are pockets of stillness with few breezes to propel ships. A navigator had to find winds and currents moving in the direction he wished to travel. Sailing directly to and from a port was virtually impossible.

By the second half of the fifteenth century, Portuguese sailors had learned to tack along a course, searching for favorable winds and currents. Knowledge of winds and currents allowed Bartholomeu Dias in 1487 to explore the coast of southern Africa (see Map 15.2). He followed the traditional Portuguese routes past modern Angola, at which point he sailed southwest, nearly to the coast of Brazil, then east and north until his exhausted crew asked him to turn back. On the return voyage Dias realized that his ship had rounded the African cape soon named the "Cape of Good Hope." He had perfected the techniques for searching out currents in the Southern Hemisphere and opened the way to India.

A decade after Dias's return from the Cape of Good Hope, Vasco da Gama set sail on a voyage that would take him to Calicut on the western coast of India. Using the information gathered from countless navigators and travelers, Vasco da Gama set sail in 1497 with four square-rigged, armed caravels and over 170 men. He had been provided with maps and reports that indicated what he might expect to find along the eastern coast of Africa. He also carried textiles and metal utensils, merchandise of the type usually traded along the western coast of Africa. This was a trade mission and not really a voyage exploring the unknown.

Da Gama's route was nearly identical to the traditional sailing route favored in later centuries. He traveled to the west and then south until he found the westerlies, the headwinds that carried him beyond the Cape of Good Hope and into the Indian Ocean. He traveled up the coast until he reached Molindi in Mozambique, where he hired an Arab pilot who taught him the route to Calicut. Although the goods the Portuguese traders presented were not appropriate for the sophisticated Asian market, Da Gama did manage to collect a cargo of Indian spices, which he brought back to Portugal, arriving in 1499. Almost immediately the Portuguese sent a second, larger fleet east to India. Da Gama himself returned to India in 1502. From 1500 until the Portuguese lost their last colony in the 1960s, Portugal remained a presence in the Indian Ocean.

The Portuguese in Asia

Trade in the Indian Ocean was nominally controlled by Arabs, but in fact a mixture of ethnic and religious groups—including Muslims, Hindus, Jains, and Nestorian Christians—participated in the movement of cottons, silks, and spices throughout the region. The mixture of trade reflected the political situation. Vasco da Gama's arrival coincided with the rise of the Moguls, Muslim descendants of Jenghiz Khan. By 1530, they had gained control of most of northern India. During the sixteenth century, Mogul influence increased in the south. Throughout the sixteenth century the Moguls remained tolerant of the religious, cultural, and economic diversity found in India. Neither Muslim nor Hindu powers initially recognized the threat the Portuguese represented.

The Portuguese probably encountered some hostility, but there is no reason to believe that they could not have joined this complex mixture of traders. Local rulers collected taxes and ensured political control but otherwise left the various ethnic and religious communities to manage their own trade and manufacture. The problem for the Portuguese was that the products they brought from Europe had little value in sophisticated, highly developed Asian markets. In response to this difficult situation, they created a "Trading-Post Empire," an empire based on control of trade rather than on colonization.

Portugal's commercial empire in the East was based not on colonies and plantations but on fortified, strategically placed naval bases. As early as Vasco da Gama's second expedition in 1502, Portuguese bombarded Calicut and defeated an Arab fleet off the coast of India. This encounter set the stage for Portugal's most important strategist of empire, Alfonso d'Albuquerque (1453–1515), governor-general of Portuguese colonies in India. He convinced the monarchy that the key to dominance in the region was the creation of fortified naval bases designed to permit the Portuguese to dominate the Bay of Bengal and thereby control access to the spices in the Spice Islands. (See the box, "Albuquerque Defends the Portuguese Empire.") By 1510 Albuquerque had captured Goa (on the Indian coast south of Bombay) and Hormuz (controlling access to the Persian Gulf). Later he conquered the sultanate of Malacca on the Malay Peninsula, winning control of the straits that run from the Bay of Bengal to the Spice Islands. By 1600, the Portuguese had created a network of naval bases that reached from Mozambique and Mombasa on the eastern coast of Africa to Goa on the western coast of India and to the island of Macao off the southeastern coast of China (see Map 15.2).

The Portuguese established a royal trading firm, the Casa da India, to control the trade in cinnamon, ginger, cloves, mace, and a variety of peppers. Although their control was far from total, the Portuguese did become significant exporters of spices to Europe. More significant was the creation of the Portuguese Estado da India, or India office, to control Portuguese naval forces, administer ports, and regulate maritime trade. Under the Portuguese system all merchants were expected to acquire export licenses and to ship products through Portuguese ports.

Both the casa and the estado depended for their influence on naval power. Although the Portuguese navy was too small to enforce a complete blockade of clandestine trade, the Portuguese did manage to change the patterns of commerce in the area. Many Asians found it convenient to pay for export licenses and to trade through Portuguese ports. They even found it convenient to ship in European-style vessels and to use Portuguese as the language of commerce.

Spanish Voyages of Discovery

As early as 1479 the Spanish kingdoms had agreed to leave the exploration and colonization of the African coast to the Portuguese. The Castilians concentrated their efforts on what came to be called the "Enterprise of the Indies." The story of the initial stages of this enterprise has led to contradictory conclusions. Many historians have characterized the voyages of Columbus as radical breaks from the medieval past, although they were very much in the tradition of earlier European interest in travel to Asia.

The sailing and exploration necessary to carry out the "Enterprise of the Indies" produced

Albuquerque Defends the Portuguese Empire

In this letter of 1512 to the king of Portugal, Albuquerque, the governor-general of Portugal's colonies in India, informs the king of conditions in the East, explains his strategy, and defends himself against his critics.

You must reduce the power of [the Muslim] rulers, take their coastal territories from them and build good fortresses in their principal places. Otherwise you will not be able to set India on the right path and you will always have to have a large body of troops there to keep it pacified. Any alliance which you may agree with one or other Indian king or lord must be secured, Sire, because otherwise you may be certain that, the moment your back is turned, they will at once become your enemies.

What I am describing has now become quite usual among them. In India there is not the same punctiliousness as in Portugal about keeping truth, friendship and trust, for nobody here has any of these qualities. Therefore, Sire, put your faith in good fortresses and order them to be built; gain control over India in time and do not place any confidence in the friendship of the kings and lords of this region because you did not arrive here with a just cause to gain domination of their trade with blandishments and peace treaties. Do not let anybody in Portugal make you think that this is a very hard thing to achieve and that, once achieved, it will place you under great obligation. I tell you this, Sire, because I am still in India and I would like people to sell their property and take part in this enterprise that is so much to your advantage, so great, so lucrative and so valuable.

Source: T. F. Earle and J. Villiers, eds., *Albuquerque: Caesar of the East* (Warminster, England: Aris and Phillips, 1990), p. 109.

critical information about winds and currents around the world and facilitated later voyages. They also established the basic approaches that the Spanish would follow in their exploration, conquest and colonization of the lands to which they came.

The Role of Columbus

The story of the enterprise begins with Christopher Columbus (1451–1506), a brilliant seaman, courtier, and self-promoter who has become a symbol of European expansion. During the nineteenth century, patriots of the newly created United States of America celebrated Columbus as proof that the discovery and development of North America was not dependent on the British. By the early twentieth century Italian immigrants to North America regarded him as a symbol of Italy's important role in the history of the Americas. And finally, modern historians have celebrated Columbus as one of the great men of the Renaissance who managed to break with medieval myth and superstition. The voyages of Columbus, they have argued, shattered the isolation and parochial vision of the Europeans.

Columbus, however, was not a "Renaissance man" of vision, the harbinger of a new, more rational world. And he certainly was not a bold pioneer who fearlessly did what no others could conceive of doing.

Columbus was born into a modest family in Genoa and spent his early years in travel and in the service of the Castilian and Portuguese crowns. He apparently first put his plans to sail west to Asia before King John II (r. 1481–1495) of Portugal. Only after Portuguese rejection did he approach the Spanish monarchs, Ferdinand and Isabella. His vision seems to have been thoroughly traditional and medieval. Studying information in *Imago Mundi (Image of the World)* (1410), by the French philosopher Pierre d'Ailly (1350–1420), he convinced himself that the distance between the coast of Europe and Asia was much less than it actually is. Pierre d'Ailly had estimated that water covered only about one quarter of the globe. This estimate put the east coast of Asia within easy reach of the western edge of Europe. "This sea is navigable in a few days if the wind is favorable," was d'Ailly's conclusion.

D'Ailly's theories seemed to be confirmed by the work of the Florentine mathematician Paolo Toscanelli (see page 552). Columbus seems to have known of Toscanelli's calculations and even revised them downward. From his own reading of an apocryphal book of the Bible (Esdras 6:42) that reported that only one-seventh of the world was covered with water, Columbus concluded that the distance from the west coast of Europe to the east coast of Asia was about 5000 miles instead of the actual 12,000. Columbus's reading of traditional sources put Japan in the approximate location of the Virgin Islands (it is not surprising that Columbus remained convinced that the Bahamas were islands just off the coast of Asia).

Like Marco Polo before him, Columbus expected to find the marvels reported in the classical sources. In his own journals he recorded reports of islands where women avoided domestic responsibilities and instead hunted with bow and arrow. And he interpreted what he was told in the context of his assumptions. When Amerindians told him of Cuba, he concluded that it "must be Japan according to the indications that these people give of its size and wealth."[1] And on the basis of first-century descriptions, he assured Spanish authorities that King Solomon's mines were only a short distance west of his newly discovered islands. In addition to finding the gold of Solomon, Columbus also expected that by sailing west he could fulfill a series of medieval prophecies that would lead to the conversion of the whole world to Christianity. This conversion, he believed, would shortly precede the second coming of Christ. In Columbus's own view, then, his voyages were epochal not because they were ushering in a newer, more empirical world but because they signaled the completion of the long history of the creation and redemption.

Columbus's enthusiasm for the venture was only partially shared by Ferdinand and Isabella.

OVERSEAS EXPLORATION AND CONQUEST

ca. 1350	The Madeira and the Canary islands are charted
ca. 1400	The Azores are charted
1444	Cape Verde Islands are discovered by Prince Henry the Navigator
1487	Dias is the first European to sail around the Cape of Good Hope
1492	Columbus sails from Spain and discovers the New World
1494	Treaty of Tordesillas
1497	Da Gama sails around the Cape of Good Hope and arrives in India
1501	Vespucci sails along the coast of Brazil and concludes that Columbus had discovered a new continent
1507	Waldseemüller issues the first map showing "America"
1510	Portuguese capture Goa
1513	Balboa crosses the Isthmus of Panama and is the first European to see the Pacific Ocean
1519–22	Magellan's expedition sails around the world from east to west
1519–23	Cortés lands in Mexico, conquers the Aztecs, and destroys Tenochtitlán
1533	Pizarro conquers Cuzco, the Incas' capital
1542	Charles V issues the New Laws
1545	The Spanish discover the silver mines at Potosí

Vasco da Gama was well supplied with large ships and a crew of over 170 men, but Columbus sailed with three small ships and a crew of 90. Da Gama carried extra supplies and materials for trade and letters for the rulers he knew he would meet. Columbus had nothing similar. His commission did authorize him as "Admiral of Spain" to take possession of all he should find, but royal expectations do not seem to have been great.

Christopher Columbus Describes His Discoveries

Columbus's hopes for wealth and titles for himself depended on getting and maintaining the goodwill of Ferdinand and Isabella. After all of his voyages he emphasized his accomplishments and their potential to enrich the Spanish monarchs. Columbus wrote this letter toward the conclusion of the first voyage, which he believed might secure his rights to lordship over all the new territories he found. He was at pains to make clear that what he had found was what one would expect to find on the edge of Asia. In that respect this document deserves to be compared to the later observations of Friar Bernardino de Sahagún on page 574.

In conclusion, to speak only of what has been accomplished on this voyage, which was so hasty, their highnesses can see that I give them as much gold as they may need, if their highnesses will render me very slight assistance; moreover, spice and cotton, as much as their highnesses shall command; and mastic [yellow resin necessary for various adhesives], as much as they shall order to be shipped and which, up to now, has been found only in Greece, in the island of Chios, and the Seignory [of Venice] sells it for what it pleases; and also wood, as much as they shall order to be shipped, and slaves, as many as they shall order to be shipped and who will be from the idolaters. And I believe that I have found rhubarb and cinnamon [both were considered essential for medicine], and I shall find a thousand other things of value, which people I have left here will have discovered, for I have not delayed at any point . . . and in truth I shall have done more, if the ships had served me as reason demanded.

Source: C. Columbus, A. Bernáldez, et al., eds., *The Voyages of Christopher Columbus,* part 1 (London: Argonaut Press, 1930), p. 16.

After a stop in the Canary Islands, the small fleet sailed west. Columbus assumed that he would find the islands of Japan after sailing about 3000 miles. On October 12, about ten days later than he had calculated, he reached landfall on what he believed were small islands in the Japanese chain. He had actually landed in the Bahamas (see Map 15.2). Because Columbus announced to the world he had arrived in the Indies, the indigenous populations have since been called "Indians" and the islands are called the "West Indies."

Columbus established his base of operations on the island of Hispaniola. From one of his ships, which had run aground, he salvaged materials to construct a fortress. He continued his search for Japan, spices, and gold, which he was certain were nearby. By early 1493, he had accumulated a small quantity of gold, some spices, and islanders that he resolved to take back to Spain as proof of his accomplishment. Leaving thirty-nine sailors at his fortress to maintain his claim to these lands, he returned to Spain. (See the box, "Christopher Columbus Describes His Discoveries.")

Columbus returned to the New World three more times—in 1493, 1498, and 1502—exploring extensively in the Bahamas and along the coast of Panama and Venezuela, 800 miles to the south and east of Hispaniola. The enthusiasm his discoveries raised was evident on his second voyage. He oversaw a fleet of seventeen ships with 1500 sailors, churchmen, and adventurers. And Columbus's initial rewards were great. He was granted a hereditary title, a governorship of the new lands, and one-tenth of all the wealth he had discovered.

Columbus reported to the Spanish monarchs that the "Indians" on the islands were friendly and open to the new arrivals. He described simple, naked people, eager, he believed, to learn of Christianity and European ways. The Taínos, or Arawaks, whom he had misidentified, did live simple, uncomplicated lives. The islands easily produced sweet potatoes, maize, beans, and squash, which along with fish provided an abundant diet. Initially these peoples shared their food and knowledge with the newcomers, who they seem to have thought were sky-visitors.

The Spanish, for their part, praised this smiling and happy people. Columbus himself observed that

> they are very gentle and do not know what evil is; nor do they kill others, nor steal; and they are without weapons. . . . They say very quickly any prayer that we tell them to say, and they make the sign of the cross, †. So your Highnesses ought to resolve to make them Christians.[2]

The Spanish attitude changed quickly. The settlers Columbus left at his fortress set an unfortunate example. They seized foodstocks, kidnapped women, and embarked on a frenzied search for gold. Those who did not kill one another were killed by the Taínos.

During succeeding voyages, Columbus struggled to make his discoveries the financial windfall he had promised the monarchs. He was unable to administer this vast new land. He quickly lost control of the colonists and was forced to allow the vicious exploitation of the island population He and other Spanish settlers claimed larger and larger portions of the land and required the Indians to work it. Islands that easily supported a population of perhaps a million natives could not support those indigenous peoples and the Spanish newcomers and still provide exports to Spain. Scholars have estimated that the native population of the islands may have fallen to little more than 30,000 by 1520. By the middle of the sixteenth century, the native population had virtually disappeared.

Columbus remained convinced that he would find vast fortunes just over the horizon. But he found neither the great quantities of gold he promised nor a sea passage to Asia. Even in the face of mounting evidence to the contrary, Columbus maintained that Asia must be just beyond the lands he was exploring. With the islands in revolt and his explorations seemingly going nowhere, the Spanish monarchs stripped Columbus of his titles and commands. At one point he was returned to Spain in chains. After his final trip he still maintained that he had finally found either the Ganges River of India or one of the rivers that flow out of the earthly paradise. Although Columbus died in 1506, rich and honored for his discoveries, he never gained all the power and wealth he had expected. He remained frustrated and embittered by the Crown's refusal to support one more voyage during which he expected to find the mainland of Asia.

Images of the New World This woodcut of Columbus's landing in the New World accompanied an early printed report of his discoveries. Europeans were especially taken by reports of nakedness and cannibalism because both were signs of a lack of law and civilization. *(The John Carter Brown Library at Brown University, Providence)*

In 1501, after sailing along the coast of Brazil, the Florentine geographer Amerigo Vespucci

(1451–1512) drew the obvious conclusion from the information collected by Columbus's explorations. He argued that Columbus had discovered a new continent unknown to the classical world. These claims were accepted by the German mapmaker Martin Waldseemüller, who in 1507 honored Amerigo's claim by publishing the first map showing "America."

Columbus's Successors

Columbus's discoveries set off a debate over which nations had the right to be involved in trade and exploration. Portuguese claims were based on a papal bull of 1481, issued by Pope Sixtus IV (r. 1471–1484), that granted Portugal rights to discoveries south of the Canaries and west of Africa. After Columbus's return, the Spaniards lobbied one of Sixtus's successors, Alexander VI (r. 1492–1503), whose family, the Borgias, was from the kingdom of Aragon. In a series of bulls, Pope Alexander allowed the Spanish to claim all lands lying 400 miles or more west of the Azores. Finally, in the Treaty of Tordesillas (1494), Spain and Portugal agreed that the line of demarcation between their two areas should be drawn 1480 miles west of the Azores, giving the Portuguese rights to Brazil.

Adventurers and explorers worried little about the legality of exploration. Even as Columbus lay dying in 1506, others, some without royal permission, sailed up and down the eastern coasts of North and South America. Amerigo Vespucci traveled on Spanish vessels as far as Argentina while Spanish explorers sailed among the islands of the Caribbean and along the coast of the Yucatán Peninsula. Vasco Nuñez de Balboa crossed the Isthmus of Panama in 1513 and found the Pacific Ocean where the natives living in the region said it would be.

The most important of the explorations that Columbus inspired was the voyage undertaken by Ferdinand Magellan in 1519 (see Map 15.2). Although his motives are unclear, Magellan (1480?–1521) may have planned to complete Columbus's dream of sailing to the Indies. By the 1510s mariners and others understood that the Americas were a new and hitherto unknown land, but they did not know what lay beyond them or what the distance was from the Americas to the Spice Islands of Asia. After sailing along the well-known coastal regions of South America, Magellan continued south, charting currents and looking for a passage into the Pacific. Early in 1520 he made the passage through the dangerous straits (now the Strait of Magellan) separating Tierra del Fuego from the mainland. The turbulent waters of the straits marked the boundary of the Atlantic and the Pacific oceans. Once into the Pacific, Magellan sailed north and west to escape the cold and to find winds and currents that would allow him to continue to Asia. It took almost four months to travel from the straits to the Philippines. During that time, a crew member reported, "We ate biscuit, which was no longer biscuit, but powder of biscuit swarming with worms, for they had eaten the good."[3] The crew suffered greatly from scurvy and a shortage of water and at times had to eat the rats aboard ship to survive. Nevertheless, Magellan managed to reach the Philippines by March 1521. A month later, he was killed by natives.

Spanish survivors in two remaining ships continued west, reaching the Moluccas, where they traded merchandise that they had carried along for a small cargo of cloves. The Portuguese captured one of the ships as it tried to return to the Americas. The other proceeded on through the Indian Ocean, avoiding Portuguese patrols. It continued around Africa and back to Spain, landing with a crew of 15 at Cádiz in September 1522 after a voyage of three years and the loss of four ships and 245 men. No cargo of spices could have been worth the sacrifices. But the significance of the voyage was not the spices but the route established from South America to the Spice Islands. Further, Magellan completed and confirmed the knowledge of wind and ocean currents that European sailors had been accumulating. One of his sailors wrote of him: "More accurately than any man in the world did he understand sea charts and navigation."[4] The way was open for the vast movement of Europeans and European culture into all parts of the world.

Spanish penetration of the New World was different from the Portuguese experience in Asia. The Spaniards established no complex network of trade and commerce, and no strong states opposed their interests. A "Trading-Post Empire" could not have worked in the New World. To succeed, the Spaniards needed to colonize and reorganize the lands they had discovered.

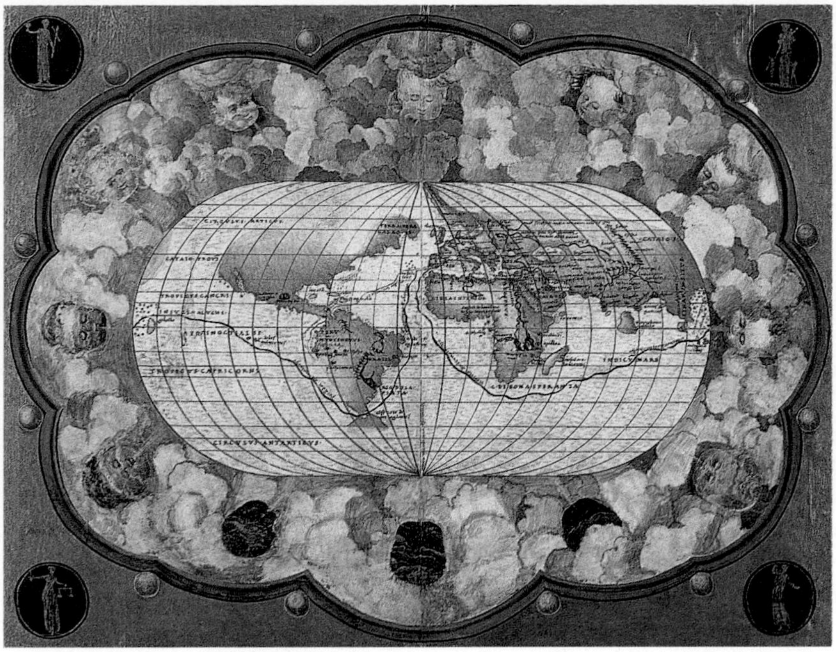

Representations of the World Geographers repeatedly published maps of the world based on the knowledge they had at a given time. Although this map of 1543–1545 accurately depicts the coastlines of Africa and eastern South America, the west coast of the Americas was largely unknown. *(The John Carter Brown Library at Brown University, Providence)*

Spain's Colonial Empire

Between 1492 and 1600, almost 200,000 Spaniards emigrated to the New World. New Spain, as they called these newly claimed lands, was neither the old society transported across the ocean or Amerindian society with a thin patina of Spanish and European culture. To understand the history of New Spain, we will discuss the two major civilizations the Spaniards overthrew, the conquests themselves, and the institutions the Spaniards created in the wake of conquest. We will also discuss the attempts by many of the Spanish to secure fair treatment of the indigenous peoples who had been made part of the Spanish Empire.

The Americas Before the European Invasion

The Spaniards and later their European peers entered a world vastly different from their own. It was a world formed by two momentous events. The first was the creation of the continents of North and South America. North and South America, along with Africa and the Eurasian land mass, were once part of a single super-continent. The breakup of this super-continent left the Americas, Africa, and Eurasia free to evolve in dramatically different ways. From one continent to another, the differences in plants and animals were so dramatic that one eighteenth-century naturalist confessed, "I was seized with terror at the thought of ranging to many new and unknown parts of natural history."[5] The continental breakup occurred millions of years ago, long before the appearance of human beings and many other forms of mammalian life.

The second momentous event was the temporary rejoining of the Americas to the Eurasian land mass by land and ice bridges that allowed Asians to cross over the Bering Strait to the Americas in the period between 30,000 and 10,000 B.C. Their arrival and its timing were momentous for two reasons. These hunter-gatherers seem to have played a significant role in the extinction of several large mammals—mastodons, mammoths, giant buffalo, and even early camels and horses. No easily domesticable large animals remained on the continent. These peoples also arrived in the Americas long before the beginnings of the Neolithic agricultural revolution, which involved the domestication of numerous plants and animals. The agricultural revolution in the Americas occurred around 3000 B.C., perhaps six thousand years after similar developments in the Old World (see page 6). The peoples of the Americas created complex societies, but those societies lacked large domesticated meat or pack animals (the llama was the largest), iron and other hard metals, and the wheel.

By the time of Columbus's arrival, relatively populous societies were living throughout North and South America. Population estimates for the two continents range from 30 million to 100 million—the lower figure is probably more correct. There were complex mound-builder societies in eastern North America and along the Mississippi River and pueblo societies in the deserts of the American southwest, but the greatest centers of Amerindian civilization were in central and coastal Mexico and in the mountains of Peru.

In the late fifteenth century the two most powerful centers were the empires of the Aztecs and the Incas. When the collection of tribes now known as the "Aztec" (or Mexican) peoples appeared in central Mexico in the early fourteenth century, they found a flourishing civilization centered on the cities and towns dotting the Valley of Mexico. Through conquest, the Aztecs united the many Nahuatl-speaking groups living in the valley into a confederation centered on the Aztec capital of Tenochtitlán, a city of perhaps 200,000 people built on an island in Lake Texcoco (Map 15.3). In early-sixteenth-century Europe, only London, Constantinople, and Naples would have been as large as the Aztec capital. The Spanish conqueror Hernán Cortés (see page 566) described Aztec cities "that seemed like an enchanted vision" and that literally rose out of the water of Lake Texcoco. Only Venice could have equaled the sight. The whole valley supported an unusually high population of about a million, fed by farmers who raised a wide variety of crops on farms carefully formed beside canals and in the

Tenochtitlán The Aztec capital was built on an island. Its central temples and markets were connected to the rest of the city and the suburbs on the lake shore by numerous canals. The city and its surrounding market gardens seemed to the Spanish to be floating on water. *(The Newberry Library, Chicago)*

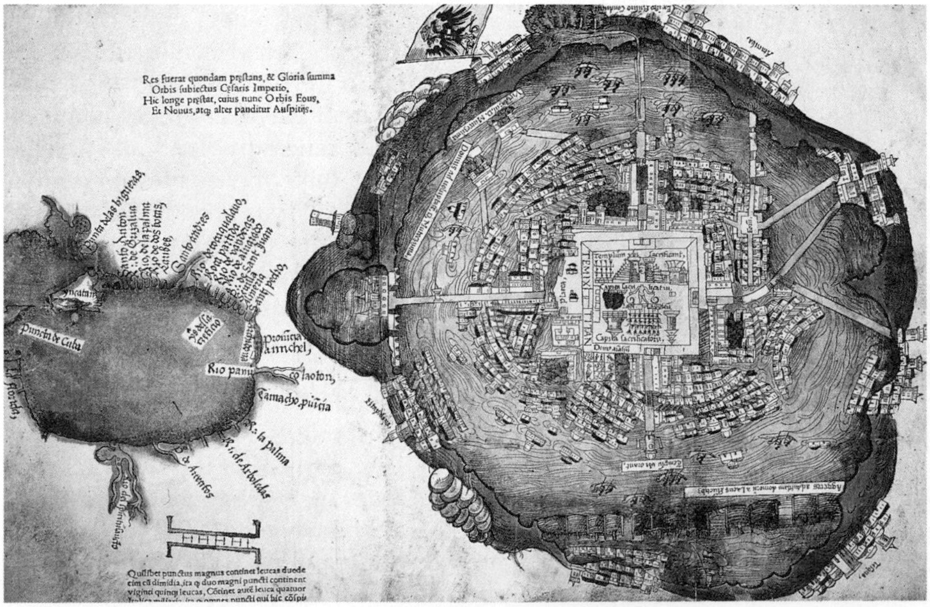

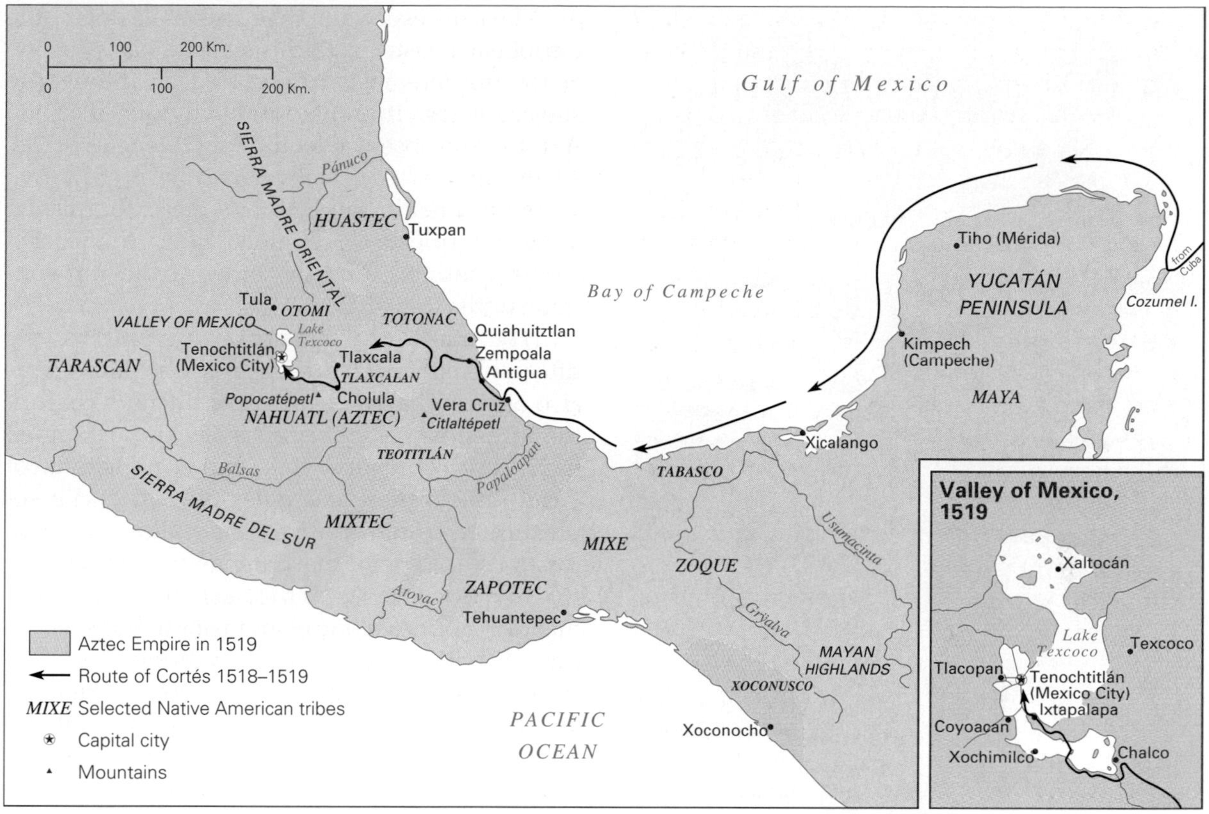

Map 15.3 Mexico and Central America The Valley of Mexico was a populous region of scattered towns, most of which were part of the Aztec Empire. As Cortés marched inland from Vera Cruz toward the valley, he passed through lands that had been in an almost constant state of war with the Aztecs.

marshes on the edge of Lake Texcoco. Using canals along the edge of the lake and other canals in Tenochtitlán itself, merchants easily moved food, textiles, gold and silver ornaments, jewels, and ceremonial feathered capes into the city markets. Spaniards later estimated that 50,000 or more people shopped in the city on market days.

Religion was integral to the Aztecs' understanding of their empire. According to traditions, the first Aztecs who arrived on the island where they would found their capital saw an eagle sitting on a cactus with a serpent in its beak. The eagle symbolized the Aztec war-god Huitzilopochtli; the serpent symbolized Quetzalcoatl, the main god of the peoples already settled in the area. "O Mexicans, it shall be here," said the eagle, foretelling the foundation of the city and the eventual domination of the entire valley by the Aztecs. The Aztecs further believed that the world was finite and that they lived in the last of five empires. It was only continued human sacrifice to Huitzilopochtli that allowed the world to continue. The Aztecs believed that the hearts of sacrificial victims were necessary to sustain their god, to ensure that the sun would rise again each morning. Thus, the Aztecs believed that their continued sacrifice to their god was essential for the continuation of life.

Tenochtitlán was the center of an imperial culture based on tribute. (See the feature, "Weighing the Evidence: A Drawing of Tenochtitlán," on pages 578–579.) Towns and villages under Aztec control paid tribute in food and precious metals. To emphasize that Aztec power and dominance were complete, the Aztecs not only collected vast quantities of maize, beans, squash,

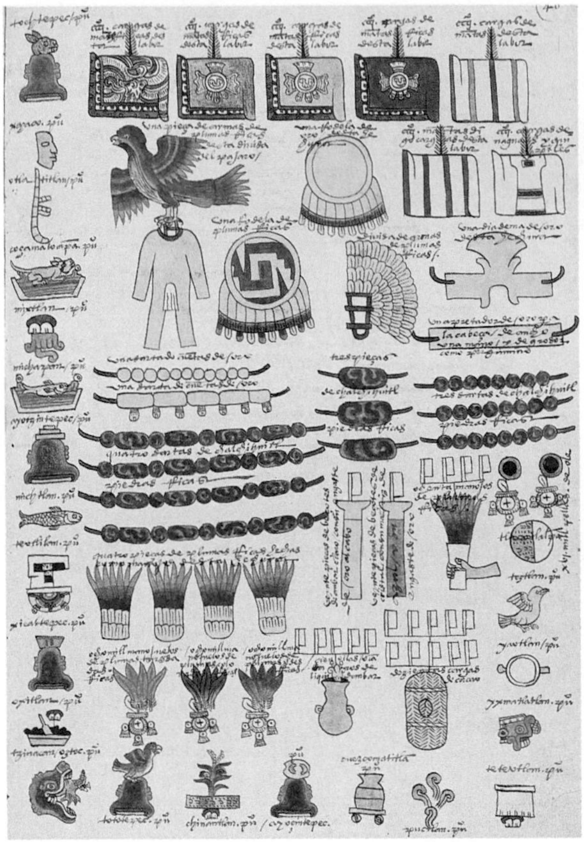

Aztec Culture This is a leaf from the Codex Mendoza, a book detailing the tribute Moctezuma collected annually from subject tribes. In order to understand the codex, Spaniards added the Spanish language equivalent to each pictograph. *(Bodleian Library, Oxford, Ms. Arch. Seld.A.1. fol. 46r.)*

and textiles but demanded tribute in everything down to centipedes and snakes. The most chilling tribute, however, was in humans for sacrifice. When there were no longer wars of expansion to provide prisoners, the Aztecs and their neighbors fought "flower wars"—highly ritualized battles to provide prisoners to be sacrificed. Five thousand victims were sacrificed at the coronation of Moctezuma II (r. 1502–1520) in 1502. Even more, reportedly twenty thousand, were sacrificed at the dedication of the great temple of Huitzilopochtli in Tenochtitlán.

Aztec society was a warrior society that maintained a perpetual state of war with the peoples beyond the mountains that ringed the Valley of Mexico—especially the people along the Caribbean coast. Given this state of war, plus the heavy burdens in tribute placed on the nearby subject cities, it is no small wonder that the Aztecs were obsessed by the contingencies of life. At the end of each calendar cycle of fifty-two years, all fires in the empire were extinguished until fire-priests ascertained that the world would continue. And the Aztec world did continue until August 1523.

The other great Amerindian empire of the fifteenth century, the empire of the Incas, was also of recent origin. During the fifteenth century the Incas formed efficient armies and expanded their control beyond the central highlands of Peru. Fifteen thousand miles of road and a sophisticated administrative system allowed the Incas to create a state that extended from Ecuador to Chile (Map 15.4). As they expanded, they demanded political control and tribute but seem to have been tolerant of local traditions and language. The Incas perfected systems of irrigation and bridge-building initiated by earlier inhabitants of the region. The empire, centered on the city of Cuzco high in the mountains of Peru, was able to sustain a population that may have reached 10 million by the end of the fifteenth century.

Human sacrifice, though not unknown to the Incas, was not an essential part of their religious life. Their state was unsettled, however, by increasingly harsh tax exactions. Under the Inca system, the title *Paca Inca,* or "Great Inca," was inherited by the eldest son of the ruler's principal wife. The ruler's wealth, however, was retained by the rest of his family, who maintained the court as if the ruler still lived. Thus, each new ruler needed money to finance the creation of an entirely new court, and taxes were not only high but continuously increasing.

Both great Amerindian empires, despite their brilliance, rested on uneasy conquests. Subject groups would be willing allies for any invader.

The Spanish Conquests

Hernán Cortés (1485–1546) was ambitious to make something of himself in the New World. Of a poor but aristocratic background from the Extremadura region of southwest Spain, he had gone to the West Indies in 1504 to seek his fortune in the service of the governor of Cuba. The governor gave him a commission to lead an expeditionary force to investigate reports of a wealthy and prosperous Indian civilization. From the very beginning, Spanish authorities seem to have distrusted his aims. He was forced to depart hastily from Cuba to evade formal notification that the governor of Cuba had revoked his commission because of insubordination.

Cortés landed in Mexico at the site of the city he would name Vera Cruz ("True Cross") early in 1519 with a tiny command of 500 men, 16 horses, 11 ships, and some artillery. Aided by a devastating outbreak of smallpox and Amerindian peoples happy to overthrow Aztec control, Cortés and his troops managed to destroy the network of city-states dominated by the Aztecs of Tenochtitlán in two years and lay claim to the Valley of Mexico for the king of Spain. The manner in which Cortés explained and justified his mission can serve as a model against which to measure the adventures of other sixteenth-century Europeans in the Americas.

Cortés, like Machiavelli, believed in the power of truly able leaders (men of *virtú*) to overcome chance through bold acts. Even so, an attempt to capture a city of 200,000 with an army of 500 seems more foolhardy than bold. Cortés seems to have attempted it simply because he found himself with very little choice. With his commission revoked by the governor of Cuba, Cortés arrived on the mainland as a rebel against both the governor of Cuba and the king of Spain. Much of what he did and said concerning the great Aztec empire was an attempt to justify his initial act of insubordination and win back royal support. Cortés burned his ships so that his troops were forced to go with him. Then he founded the city of Vera Cruz, whose town government, which was his own creation, offered him a new commission to proceed inland to Tenochtitlán. He had the good fortune to find Doña Marina, a Mexican woman who was his interpreter and mistress. He also quickly found allies among native groups that for their own reasons wished to see the Aztec Empire destroyed. The allied forces moved toward Tenochtitlán.

The meeting of Aztecs and Spaniards demonstrated the breadth of the chasm separating the Old World and the New as well as the difficulty the one had in understanding the other. At first

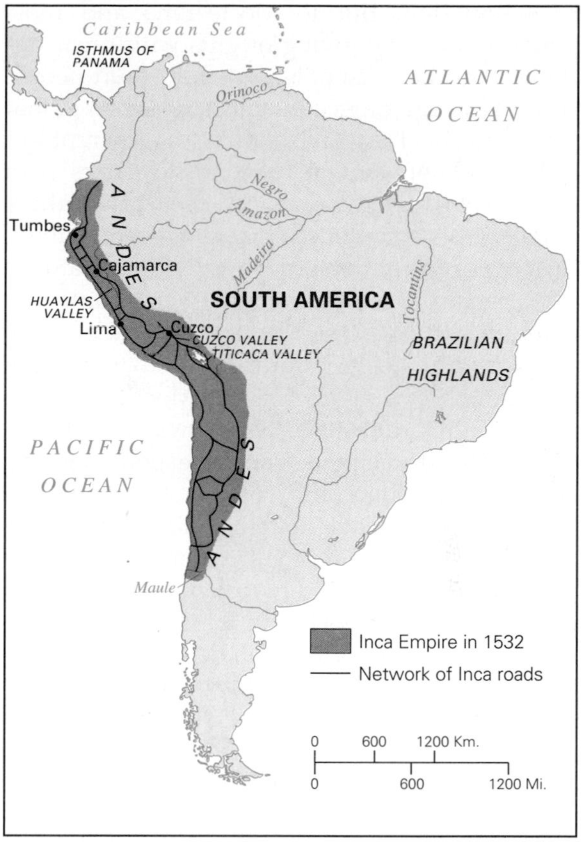

Map 15.4 Peru and Central America The Inca Empire was accessible to the Spaniards only by sea. Spanish exploration and domination brought the destruction of Inca mountain citadels and the transfer of administrative power to the new Spanish city of Lima on the coast.

Moctezuma was unconcerned about the coming of the Spaniards. Later he seems to have attempted to buy them off. And finally he and his successors fought desperately to drive them out of Tenochtitlán. The Aztecs' indecision was caused in large part by the fact that in neither words nor gestures did the two groups speak the same language. Hearing that the Spaniards were marching toward Tenochtitlán, Moctezuma sent ambassadors bearing gold, silver, and other costly gifts, which they presented in a most humble fashion to the Spaniards. To a modern ear the gifts sound like (and have often been interpreted to be) desperate attempts to buy off the invaders. To Cortés, or any European or even Asian resident of the Old World, such gifts were a sign of submission. But to Moctezuma and most Amerindians, the giving of gifts with great humility by otherwise powerful and proud people could be a sign of wealth and status. Seen in that light, Moctezuma's lavish gifts and apparent humility probably demonstrated to the Aztecs' own satisfaction the superiority of their civilization, and Cortés's acceptance of the gifts seemed to indicate his recognition of his own inferior status.

Spaniards later claimed that Moctezuma was confounded by the sudden appearance of these peoples from the East. Cortés reported to the king of Spain that when he first met Moctezuma, the Aztec leader said: "We have always held that those who descended from [the god Quetzalcoatl] would come and conquer this land and take us as his vassals." Later Spaniards explained that the Aztecs believed that Quetzalcoatl, the serpent-god symbolically conquered by Huitzilopochtli, had traveled to the East, promising one day to return and reclaim his lands, thus ending Aztec rule. The Spaniards believed that Moctezuma had been so ambivalent toward them because of his faith in that myth.

There seems to be, however, little truth in either of those stories. Cortés was simply attempting to justify his conquest. There is no surviving pre-conquest source for Moctezuma's supposed confession, and the myth of the return of Quetzalcoatl was first recorded in Spanish and not Indian sources long after the conquest. In truth, neither Cortés nor historians can satisfactorily explain in Western terms Moctezuma's initial response to the Spaniards. Cortés took the Aztec leader captive and began what would be a two-year battle to take control of the city and its empire. Although weakened by the arrival of virulent Old World diseases, the Aztecs continued to fight even as more and more of the subject peoples joined the Spanish forces. The Spaniards cut off food and water to the capital, but still the Aztecs fought.

Different understandings of the rules of war, different traditions of diplomacy, and different cultures prevented the Aztecs and Cortés from reaching any understanding. The peoples of the Valley of Mexico tried to take captives to be sacrificed in temples. The Spaniards, to Aztec eyes, killed indiscriminately and needlessly on the battlefield. Cortés later complained of the Aztecs' refusal to negotiate: "We showed them more signs of peace than have ever been shown to a vanquished people." Thus, to end a war that neither side could resolve in any other way, in 1523 Cortés and his allies completely destroyed Tenochtitlán.

Cortés's insubordination was a model for other adventurers. His own lieutenants later rebelled against his control and attempted to create their own governments as they searched for riches and Eldorado, a mythical city of gold. Later adventurers marched throughout the North American southwest and Central and South America following rumors of hidden riches. Using private armies and torturing native peoples, veterans of Cortés's army and newly arrived speculators hoped to find wealth that would allow them to live like nobles on their return to Spain. Like Cortés, they claimed that they were acting for the monarchy and for Christianity, but in fact they expected that success would justify their most vicious acts.

Francisco Pizarro (1470–1541) was the most successful of the private adventurers. Poor, illegitimate at birth, he arrived in the Americas ambitious for riches and power. After serving in Balboa's army, participating in several slaving expeditions, and helping to found Panama City, Pizarro was prosperous but still not wealthy. Rumors of Inca wealth filtered through to Central America. Pizarro held a small land grant in Panama and was looking for ways to increase his wealth. He and a partner resolved in 1530 to lead an expedition down the west coast of South America in search of the Inca capital. Benefiting from disorganization caused by a smallpox epidemic and ensuing civil war, Pizarro was able to find local allies. Like Cortés, he used numerous Indian allies in his most important battles. Aided by Amerindians eager to throw off Inca domination, he captured and executed the Paca Inca and conquered the capital of Cuzco by 1533. He later built a new capital on the coast at Lima from where he worked to extend his control over all of the old Inca Empire. Pizarro and his Spanish partners seized vast amounts of gold and silver from the Incas. The Spanish eventually discovered silver mines at Potosí, which would be a critical source of revenue for the Spanish monarchy. Resistance to Spanish rule continued into the 1570s, when the last of the independent Inca strongholds was finally destroyed.

Colonial Organization

The Spanish crown needed to create a colonial government that could control the actions of the numerous adventurers and create an orderly economy. Although the Spaniards proclaimed that they would "give to those strange lands the form of our own [land]," the resulting political and economic organization of the new Spanish possessions was a curious mixture of the Old World and the New.

The head of the administration was the monarchy. As early as the reigns of Ferdinand and Isabella, Spanish monarchs had tried to curb the excesses of the explorers and conquerors who traveled in their name. Isabella initially opposed the enslavement of Amerindians and any slave trade in the new lands. Further, they promoted a broad-based debate about the rights of Amerindians and the nature of religious conversion. Royal influence, however, was limited by the sheer distance between the court and the new provinces. It could easily take two years for a royal response to a question to arrive at its destination. Things moved so slowly that as one viceroy ruefully noted, "If death came from Madrid, we should all live to a very old age." Given the difficulties of communication, the powers of local administrators had to be very broad.

By 1535 Spanish colonial administration was firmly established in the form it would retain for the next two hundred years. The king created a Council of the Indies located at court, eventually in Madrid, which saw to all legal and administrative issues pertaining to the new possessions. The new territories themselves were eventually divided into the viceroyalty of Mexico (primarily Central America and part of Venezuela) and the viceroyalty of Peru. Local and regional administrative offices down to municipalities were modeled on the institutions developed in Spain during the Reconquista. Through regional judicial and advisory offices called *audiencias,* viceroys controlled civil and military affairs in their provinces. The government of towns, as in sixteenth-century Spain, was dominated by royally appointed mayors, called *corregidores.*

In Spain, Castilian conquerors completely dominated newly won lands, but in New Spain, royal administrators created Indian municipalities, or districts, in which Spaniards had no formal right to live or work. Government in these municipalities remained largely in the hands of pre-conquest native elites. Throughout the sixteenth century, official documents in these communities continued to be written in Nahuatl. As long as taxes or tribute was paid and missionaries were allowed to circulate, the Spanish government tolerated considerable autonomy in the Indian municipalities.

The problem that most plagued the government was the conquerors' desire for laborers to work on the lands and in the mines that they had seized. From Columbus's first visit, the Spanish adopted a system of forced labor developed in Spain. A colonist called an *encomendero* was offered a grant, or *encomienda,* of a certain number of people or tribes who were required to work under his direction. In theory, the encomendero was to be a protector of the conquered peoples, someone who would Christianize and civilize them. In theory, Indians who voluntarily agreed to listen to missionaries or to convert to Christianity could not be put under the control of an encomendero. If they refused, however, the Spaniards believed they had the right of conquest (see the box, "The Spanish Right of Conquest"). In fact, the conquerors assumed that they were entitled to encomiendas. Cortés himself claimed 115,000 people in Mexico, and Pizarro claimed 20,000 in Peru. In many areas encomenderos simply collected the traditional payments that the pre-conquest elites had claimed. In cases where the subject peoples were forced into mining districts, however, the conditions were brutal.

The pressures exerted by the encomenderos were worsened by the precipitous fall in the indigenous population. On the islands of Hispaniola and Cuba, population decline was primarily due to extreme Spanish demands. Elsewhere, Old World diseases such as smallpox and measles swept through populations with no previous exposure to them. In central Mexico, where we know most about population movements, the pre-conquest population was at least 10 or 12 million and may have been twice that. By the mid-sixteenth century, the native population may have fallen to just over 6 million, and it probably declined to less than 1 million early in the seventeenth century before beginning to grow again.

A large population was essential to the Spanish and the Portuguese when they introduced the

The Spanish Right of Conquest

The Spaniards justified their conquests by arguing that they conquered and enslaved only those people who were unwilling to admit Christian missionaries and therefore were rejecting divine law. Spanish lawyers developed a document that warned natives that a rejection of missionaries would result in conquest. The document, reprinted below, had to be read to people and rejected by them before any conquest would be legal. There is no evidence that it was ever translated into an Amerindian language.

Of all these nations [of the world] God our Lord gave charge to one man called St. Peter, that he should be Lord and Superior of all the men in the world. . . . One of these Pontiffs, who succeeded that St. Peter as Lord of the world . . . made donations of these isles and the *Tierra-firme* [the continent] to the aforesaid King and Queen and to their successors. . . . So their Highnesses are kings and lords of these islands and the land of Tierra-firme by virtue of this donation: and some islands, and indeed almost all those to whom this had been notified, have received and served their Highnesses, and lords and kings. . . . And also they received and obeyed the priests whom their Highnesses sent to preach to them and to teach them our Holy Faith; . . . and you too are held and obliged to do the same. . . . If you do so, you will do well, . . . and we in their name will receive you in all love and charity and shall leave you, your wives, and your children, and your lands, free without servitude, . . . and they shall not compel you to turn Christians. . . . But if you do not do this, and maliciously make delay in it, I certify to you that . . . we shall take you and your wives and your children, and shall make slaves of them, and as such shall sell and dispose of them as their Highnesses may command; and we shall take away your goods.

Source: A. Helps and M. Oppenheim, eds., *The Spanish Conquest in America and Its Relation to the History of Slavery and to the Government of Colonies*, vol. 1 (London: John Lane, 1900–1904), pp. 264, 265, 266.

Old World plantation system to the New World. The Caribbean islands and Brazil were ideal for the production of sugar—a commercial crop in great demand throughout Europe. At first, plantations and mines were worked by Amerindians, but when their numbers declined, the Spanish and Portuguese imported large numbers of slaves from Africa.

Africans had participated in the initial stages of the conquest. Some had lived in Spain and become Christian; indeed, Amerindians termed them "black whitemen." Most Africans, however, were enslaved laborers. African slaves were in Cuba by 1518; they labored in the mines of Honduras by the 1540s. After the 1560s the Portuguese were importing large numbers of African slaves into Brazil to work on the sugar plantations. It has been estimated that 62,500 slaves were imported into Spanish America and 50,000 into Brazil during the sixteenth century. By 1810, when the movement to abolish the slave trade began to grow, almost 10 million Africans had been involuntarily transported to the New World.

The conquerors had hoped to find vast quantities of wealth that they could take back to the Old World. In the viceroyalty of Mexico the search for Eldorado remained unsuccessful. The discovery in 1545 of the silver mines at Potosí in Peru, however, fulfilled the Spaniards' wildest dreams. Between 1550 and 1650 the Spanish probably sent back to Spain 181 tons of gold and 16,000 tons of silver, one-fifth of which was paid directly into the royal treasury. The coordination of the annual treasure fleet from the New World was a major task. Silver and gold from Peru first was shipped up the west coast of Bolivia to

Panama, where it was carried overland to the shores of the Caribbean. There it was again loaded on ships that were expected to rendezvous with the treasure ships from Mexico at Havana before the entire fleet sailed to Spain. The tonnage of precious metals seemed so great to the French scholar Jean Bodin (see page 612) that he held this infusion of wealth responsible for the great inflation that was disrupting the European economy in the late sixteenth century. Bodin overestimated the European-wide impact of the precious metals, but they did represent one quarter of the income of King Philip II of Spain in the 1560s and made him the richest monarch in Europe.

The Debate over Indian Rights

To most conquerors the opportunities for wealth and power need little justification, but the more thoughtful among the Spaniards were uneasy. "Tell me," demanded Friar Antonio Montesinos in 1511, "by what right or justice do you hold these Indians in such cruel and horrible slavery? By what right do you wage such detestable wars on these people who lived idly and peacefully in their own lands?"[6]

Initially the conquerors claimed the right to wage a just war of conquest if Amerindians refused to allow missionaries to live and work among them. Then the conquerors claimed that the native peoples had lost their right to self-rule. From reports of human sacrifice and cannibalism written by Columbus and other early explorers, Europeans concluded that the inhabitants of the New World rejected basic natural laws. To the Europeans, cannibals were less than human and unworthy of even the most basic human rights of property or independent self-government. Juan Ginés de Sepulveda, chaplain of Holy Roman Emperor Charles V, argued in 1544 that the idolatry and cannibalism of the Indians made them, in Aristotle's terms, natural slaves—"barbarous and inhuman peoples abhorring all civil life, customs and virtue" was how he put it. People lacking "civil life" and "virtue" clearly could not be allowed self-government. Other writers commented that nakedness and cannibalism were both signs of the lack of "civility" among the Amerindians. Sepulveda implied that Indians were merely "humanlike," not necessarily human.

Franciscan and Dominican missionaries were especially vocal opponents of views like Sepulveda's. To the mendicants, the Indians initially seemed innocent and ideal subjects for conversion to the simple piety of Christ and his first apostles. In their eyes, Indians were like children who could be converted and led by example and, where necessary, by stern discipline. These mendicants saw themselves as advocates for Indians; they desired to protect the natives from the depredations of the Spanish conquerors and the corruptions of European civilization. The most eloquent defender of Indian rights was Bartolomé de las Casas (1474–1566), a former encomendero who became a Franciscan missionary. Las Casas passionately condemned the violence and brutality of the Spanish conquests. As part of a famous debate with Sepulveda, Las Casas rejected the "humanlike" argument. "All races of

New World Treasure Gold from the New World enriched the church as well as individuals and the monarchy. It was used to create these reliefs for the altar of the Cathedral of Seville. Since Columbus's first voyage, Spaniards had offered gifts of thanksgiving upon their return from the Americas. *(Oronoz, Madrid)*

the world are men," he declared. All are evolving along a historical continuum. It was wrong, he added, to dismiss any culture or society as outside of natural law. Like all other peoples, Indians had reason. That being the case, even the most brutal could be civilized and Christianized. There was, in the view of Las Casas, no argument for natural slavery.

Charles V (who was king of Spain as well as Holy Roman emperor) accepted Las Casas's criticisms of the colonial administration. In 1542 he issued "New Laws" aimed at ending the virtual independence of the most adventurous of the encomenderos. He further abolished Indian slavery and greatly restricted the transfer of encomiendas. At first the European conquerors in Mexico and Peru rejected royal attempts to restrict their rights in the new world, but from the 1540s Indians were protected from the most extreme exploitation.

We should have no illusion, however, that these measures reflected some acceptance of cultural pluralism. The very mendicants who protected Indians assumed that Westernization and Christianization would quickly follow. And in some cases when it did not, as during revolts in the 1560s, the mendicants themselves reacted with a puzzled sense of anger, frustration, and betrayal.

The Columbian Exchange

The conquerors, adventurers, and traders who followed in the wake of Christopher Columbus and Vasco da Gama profoundly altered the Old World and the New. Before 1492 there had been a system of world trade, but now, as the Spanish proclaimed, Europe and especially Spain were at the center of economic and political life. As the Spanish and other Europeans moved throughout the world, they carried with them religions, ideas, diseases, people, plants, and animals—forever uniting the Old World and the New. This amalgamation of culture is known as the "Columbian Exchange."

Crusade for Justice The criticisms of Bartolemé de Las Casas were published widely and accompanied by woodcuts like this one showing the cruelty of the conquerors toward the Amerindians. In response to Las Casas, Charles V passed laws protecting the rights of the indigenous peoples. *(The John Carter Brown Library at Brown University, Providence)*

Disease

Columbus and those who followed him brought not only people to the New World but also numerous Old World diseases. "Virgin-soil" epidemics—that is, previously unknown diseases—are invariably fierce. Although the New World may have passed syphilis to Spain, from which it quickly spread throughout Europe, diseases transferred from the Old World to the New were much more virulent than syphilis. Smallpox spread from Cuba to Mexico as early as 1519. It was soon followed by diphtheria, measles, trachoma, whooping cough, chickenpox, bubonic plague, malaria, typhoid fever, cholera, yellow fever, scarlet fever, amoebic dysentery, influenza, and some varieties of tuberculosis. Disease was the silent ally of the conquerors. During critical points in the conquest of Tenochtitlán, smallpox was raging in the Aztec population. The disease later moved along traditional trade networks. An epidemic shortly before Pizarro's expedition to Peru carried off the Paca Inca and may have contributed to the unrest and civil war that worked to the advantage of the invaders.

Lacking sources, historians cannot trace accurately the movement of epidemic disease or its effect on the New World populations, yet many archaeologists and historians remain convinced that Old World diseases ravaged and disrupted Amerindian populations in eastern North America long before the arrival of European immigrants. In most of the New World 90 percent or more of the native population was destroyed by wave after wave of previously unknown diseases. Explorers and colonists did not so much enter an empty land as an "emptied" one.

It was at least partially because of disease that both the Spanish and the Portuguese needed to import large numbers of African slaves to work their plantations and mines. With the settlement of southeastern North America, plantation agriculture was extended to include the production of tobacco and later cotton. As a result of the needs of plantation economies and the labor shortage caused by disease, African slaves were brought in large numbers. In the Caribbean and along the coasts of Central and South America the Africans created an African-Caribbean or African-American culture that amalgamated African, European, and American civilizations.

Old World in the New This painting of "traditional" Amerindian culture shows animals brought by the Spaniards to the New World. The lives of the Amerindians were changed forever by the introduction of horses, sheep, chickens, and cows, as well as apples, peaches, wheat, and oats. *(From Martínez Compañon,* Trujillo del Peru, *vol. II, plate 77. Courtesy, Harvard College Library)*

Plants and Animals

It became increasingly clear to the Spaniards that the New World had been completely isolated from the Old World (see the box, "The New World and the Old"). The impact of Old World peoples on native populations was immediately evident to all. But scholars have recently argued that the importation of plants and animals had an even more profound effect than the arrival of Europeans. The changes that began in 1492 created "Neo-Europes" in what are now Canada, the United States, Mexico, Argentina, Australia, and

The New World and the Old

In an effort to understand the New World, Friar Bernardino de Sahagún (1499?–1590) interviewed Mexicans about life in Mexico before the arrival of the Spanish. The resulting volume, called the* Florentine Codex *because it now reposes in Florence, is a valuable source on life and religion in Mexico before the arrival of the Spanish. In this excerpt from the* Codex, *the friar reflects on the relation of this world and the European world he had known.

It occurred to me to write here that in the diversity of foods there are scarcely any which resemble ours. It seems that this people had never been discovered until these times, because, of the foods which we enjoy and are enjoying in the regions whence we came, we find none here. We do not even find here the domesticated animals which those of us who came from Spain and all Europe use, from which it appears that [the people] did not come from those regions. Nor had men from those regions come to discover this land, for if they had come from there, they would have come to make them known in other times; from them we would find wheat, barley, or rye, or chicken from there, or horses, or bulls, or donkeys, or sheep, or goats, or other domesticated animals which we utilize, whence it appears that only in these times have these lands been discovered and not before. . . . As to the preaching of the Gospel in these regions, there has been much doubt as to whether or not it has been preached before now. . . . Two trusted religious assured me that in Oaxaca, which is distant sixty leagues to the east of this city, they have some very ancient paintings, painted on deerskin, which . . . seems to me to allude to Our Lady [the Virgin Mary] and her two sisters and to our crucified Redeemer, which they must have derived from ancient sermons.

Source: B. de Sahagún, *General History of the Things of New Spain: Florentine Codex,* part 1, ed. and trans. Arthur J. O. Anderson and Charles E. Dibble (Santa Fe, N.M.: School of American Research, 1950), pp. 96–97.

New Zealand. The flora and fauna of the Old World, accustomed to a relatively harsh, competitive environment, found ideal conditions in the new lands. Like the rabbits carried to the Canary Islands and to Australia, plants and animals alike multiplied.

The most important meat and dairy animals in the New World—cattle, sheep, goats, and pigs—are imports from the Old World. Sailors initially brought pigs or goats aboard ship because they were easily transportable sources of protein. When let loose on the Caribbean islands, they quickly took over. Cattle brought to the New World reproduced just as quickly. In 1587 100 cattle were left untended at Santa Fé de Paraná in Brazil, and twenty years later there were 100,000 in the same region. The spread of horses through what is now Mexico, Brazil, Argentina, the United States, and Canada was equally dramatic. To the list of domesticated animals can be added donkeys, dogs, cats, and chickens. The changes these animals brought was profound. Cattle, pigs, and chickens quickly became staples of the New World diet. Horses enabled Amerindians and Europeans to travel across and settle on the vast plains of both North and South America.

The flora of the New World was equally changed. Even contemporaries noted how Old World plants flourished in the New. Because Old World plants came from a more hostile, more competitive environment, they were able to drive out their New World competitors. By 1555, European clover was widely distributed in Mexico—Aztecs called it "Castilian grass." Other Old World grasses, as well as weeds like dandelion, quickly followed. Domesticated plants like apples, peaches, and artichokes spread rapidly and naturally in the new environment. Early in the twentieth century it was estimated that only one quarter of the grasses found on the broad prairies of the Argentine pampas were native before the arrival of Columbus. Studies of plant life in California, Australia, and New Zealand offer much the same results. The Old World also provided new and widely grown small grains like oats, barley, and wheat.

The new plants and new animals, as well as the social and political changes initiated by the Europeans, pulled the Old World and the New more closely together.

Culture

One reason for the accommodation between the Old World and the New was that the Europeans and Amerindians tended to interpret conquest and cultural transformation in the same way. The peoples living in the Valley of Mexico believed that their conquest was fated by the gods and would bring in new gods. The Spaniards' beliefs were strikingly similar, based on the revelation of divine will and the omnipotence of the Christian God. Cortés, in whitewashing former Aztec temples and converting native priests into white-clad Christian priests, was in a way fulfilling the Aztecs' expectations about their conqueror.

Acculturation was also facilitated by the Spanish tendency to place churches and shrines at the sites of former Aztec temples. The shrine of the Virgin of Guadalupe (north of modern Mexico City) was located on the site of the temple of the goddess Tonantzin—an Aztec fertility-goddess of childbirth and midwives. After numerous healings were reported at the shrine, the Indians quickly began to refer to the Virgin as a goddess. Early missionaries reported that Indians quickly took to Christianity, although investigations later in the sixteenth century raised questions about the depth of their belief. Nonetheless, Christianity quickly became the dominant religion of the peoples of the New World.

The colonists tended to view their domination of the New World as a divine vindication of their own culture and civilization. During the sixteenth century, they set about remaking the world they had found. In the century after the conquest of Mexico, Spaniards founded 190 new cities in the Americas. Lima, Bogotá, and many others were proudly modeled on and compared

Images of the New World Artists and writers quickly incorporated images and ideas about the New World in their work. Albrecht Dürer copied a Portuguese sketch in this illustration included in a traditional European book of illustrations. *(Bayerische Staatsbibliothek, München)*

to the cities of Spain. In 1573 King Philip II (r. 1556–1598) established ordinances requiring all new cities to be based on a uniform grid with a main plaza, market, and religious center. The new cities became hubs of social and political life in the colonies. In these cities, religious orders founded colleges for basic education much like the universities they had organized in the Old World. And by midcentury, the Crown had authorized the foundation of universities in Mexico City and Lima modeled after the great Spanish university of Salamanca. Colonists attempted to recreate in all essentials the society of Spain.

The experience of the Spanish and the Portuguese in the sixteenth century seemed confirmed by the later experiences of the French and English in the seventeenth century. In seventeenth-century New England, the English Puritan John Winthrop concluded, "For the natives, they are nearly all dead of smallpox, so as the Lord hath cleared our title to what we possess."[7] A seventeenth-century French observer came to a similar conclusion: "Touching these savages, there is a thing that I cannot omit to remark to you, it is that it appears visibly that God wishes that they yield their place to new peoples." Political philosophers believed that if there was no evidence that a land was being cultivated by the indigenous people, the rights to that land passed to those who would use and improve it. Thus, colonists believed that they had divine and legal sanction to take and to remake these new lands in a European image.

Summary

Modern historians considering decolonization, economic revolutions in many parts of Asia, and multiculturalism have been changing their ways of thinking about European expansion in the fifteenth century. The achievements of the Spaniards and Portuguese emerged from medieval culture. The expansion of Europe was not the movement of highly developed commercial economies into underdeveloped areas. In Asia, the Portuguese and later the Dutch and English were a military presence long before they were an economic one. In the New World, even as the Spanish conquered people and changed their language, government, and religion, many aspects of Amerindian culture survived in the local Indian municipalities.

The economic, political, and cultural changes brought about by the conquest created a hybrid culture. It is impossible to say whether the economic and technical benefits of the amalgamation of the Old World and the New outweigh the costs. But even those who celebrate the transformation of the New World would probably agree with the conclusions of a native American in the Pacific Northwest: "I am not sorry the missionaries came. But I wish they had known how to let their news change people's lives from the inside, without imposing their culture over our ways."[8] Tolerance, however, was not yet a hallmark of Western societies. Europeans were incapable of allowing others to change "from the inside." The inability to understand and tolerate others was to be a key to the strife created by the other great event of the sixteenth century, the movement to reform church and society.

Notes

1. Quoted in William D. Phillips, Jr., and Carla Rahn Phillips, *The Worlds of Christopher Columbus* (Cambridge, England: Cambridge University Press, 1992), p. 163.
2. Quoted ibid., p. 166.
3. Quoted in J. H. Parry, ed., *The European Reconnaissance: Selected Documents* (New York: Harper & Row, 1968), p. 242.
4. Quoted in Alfred W. Crosby, *Ecological Imperialism: The Biological Expansion of Europe, 900–1900* (Cambridge, England: Cambridge University Press, 1986), p. 125.
5. Quoted ibid., p. 11.
6. Quoted in Mark A. Burkholder, and Lyman L. Johnson, *Colonial Latin America* (Oxford: Oxford University Press, 1990), p. 29.
7. Quoted in Crosby, p. 208.
8. Quoted in Maria Parker Pascua, "Ozette: A Makah Village in 1491," *National Geographic*, October 1991, p. 53.

Suggested Reading

General Works

Crosby, Alfred W. *The Columbian Voyages, the Columbian Exchange, and Their Historians.* 1988. A short pamphlet about historical writing on Columbus and the expansion of Europeans; an excellent place for a beginning student to start.

Curtin, P. *The Tropical Atlantic in the Age of the Slave Trade.* 1991. An introductory pamphlet that is an excellent first work for students interested in the history of slavery and the movement of peoples from Africa to the New World.

Levenson, J. A., ed. *Circa 1492: Art in the Age of Exploration.* 1991. A museum catalog showing art from Asia, Africa, America, and Europe at the time of Columbus includes essays on politics and culture aimed at a general audience.

McNeill, William H. *The Age of Gunpowder Empires, 1450–1800.* 1989. A pamphlet that introduces students to the study of colonial expansion.

Parry, J. H. *The Age of Reconnaissance.* 1981. A classic introductory survey of Portuguese, Spanish, English, and French exploration and conquest to the end of the seventeenth century.

Scammell, Geoffrey. *The First Imperial Age: European Overseas Expansion, 1400–1715.* 1989. As the title implies, this is an introductory survey of European colonial interests through the seventeenth century. The author puts the Spanish and Portuguese explorations in the context of later French and English experiences.

The European Background

Campbell, Mary B. *The Witness and the Other World: Exotic European Travel Writing, 400–1600.* 1988. A literary study of the narratives written by or about travelers, emphasizing especially the interest Columbus had in the reports of previous travelers.

Fernandez-Armesto, Felipe. *Before Columbus: Exploration and Colonization from the Mediterranean to the Atlantic, 1229–1492.* 1987. A well-written and accessible political and institutional narrative, especially valuable on the early Portuguese voyages.

Phillips, J. R. S. *The Medieval Expansion of Europe.* 1988. The best survey of European interest in and knowledge of the world beyond Christendom; especially good on European travelers to the East in the thirteenth century.

Exploration and Empire

Boxer, C. R. *The Portuguese Seaborne Empire, 1415–1825.* 1977. Classic political and institutional narrative of the Portuguese empire; detailed but accessible even to those with little background.

Burkholder, Mark A., and Lyman L. Johnson. *Colonial Latin America.* 1990. A thorough introduction to the conquest and colonization of Central and South America by the Spanish and Portuguese.

Clendinnen, Inga. *Aztecs: An Interpretation.* 1991. A dramatic, beautifully written essay on the Aztecs that shows how daily life, religion, and imperialism were linked.

Elliott, John H. *The Old World and the New, 1492–1650.* 1970. Besides supplying the title for this chapter, these essays are excellent considerations of the reciprocal relations between the colonies and the kingdoms of Spain.

———. *Spain and Its World, 1500–1700: Selected Essays.* 1989. Essays by the greatest living historian of Spain and the New World. The essay on the mental world of Cortés is especially important.

Fuentes, Carlos. *The Buried Mirror: Reflections on Spain and the New World.* 1992. An essay with numerous illustrations, many in color, on the melding of the cultures of Spain and the New World, by one of Mexico's greatest writers. The author's reflections on the merging of Christianity and indigenous religions are particularly valuable.

Hale, John R. *Renaissance Exploration.* 1968. A broad-based introductory survey that emphasizes the technological and geographical innovations that were part of the early voyages.

Moseley, M. E. *The Incas and Their Ancestors: The Archaeology of Peru.* 1992. This general introduction to the Incas includes excellent maps and illustrations.

Phillips, W. D., Jr., and C. R. Phillips. *The Worlds of Christopher Columbus.* 1992. Though written for a popular audience, this is an excellent survey of Columbus and his voyages and an up-to-date summary of recent work on Columbus, maritime technology, and Spanish colonial interests.

Cultural Exchange

Crosby, A. W. *Ecological Imperialism: The Biological Expansion of Europe, 900–1900.* 1986. Discussion of how migrating peoples carried with them plants, animals, and diseases; has an excellent collection of maps and illustrations.

Hanke, L. *Aristotle and the American Indians: A Study in Race Prejudice in the Modern World.* 1959. The most general of Hanke's books about race and prejudice in the Old and New World. Hanke states clearly the philosophical basis of debates over equality from classical Greece to the nineteenth century.

Pagden, Anthony. *The Fall of Natural Man: The American Indian and the Origin of Comparative Ethnology.* 1982. A brilliant, difficult, and rewarding book on the debate over Indians' rights in the sixteenth century.

Smithsonian Institutions. *Seeds of Change.* 1991. This museum catalog has excellent illustrations and introductory essays on the transfer of diseases and plants between the Old World and the New. There is an especially good chapter on religion in the period before the arrival of the Spaniards.

Weighing the Evidence

A DRAWING OF TENOCHTITLÁN

We often say that "history is written by winners," and winners rarely consider the experiences of conquered peoples. To conscientious historians this remains a major problem in the study of the past. What can we know of the Aztecs in the centuries before the Spanish conquest, for example? Cortés and his men painted over temple walls, dressed native priests in white, and began transforming Mexican religion into Christianity. In the process, they burned all the books of the Aztecs, which they associated with idolatry. Tax records, genealogies, and histories were lost along with books of divinations and other religious texts.

The more thoughtful among the Spanish quickly realized that lacking information about the Aztecs and their culture, they could neither rule nor Christianize the Mexicans. To remedy the situation, numerous individuals began collecting information in a manner that many later historians have compared, perhaps overenthusiastically, to modern cultural anthropology. They published their findings in works like the Codex Mendoza, depicted here. Much of what we know about Aztec culture comes from this and similar Spanish-Mexican efforts to preserve knowledge of preconquest life. We can better understand this illustration of the foundation of Tenochtitlán and the problems of collecting information if we consider the composition of the Codex Mendoza itself.

In 1541 Viceroy Antonio Mendoza ordered the compilation of a book about the history, government, and daily life of the Aztecs. Intended for King Charles of Spain as a report on the new lands, the book contains about seventy-one pages of pictures, each accompanied by a page of Spanish text. Mendoza had an Aztec artist paint a collection of traditional historical, religious, and administrative images, re-creating information contained in codices destroyed during the conquest. The meanings of these images were then debated by a group of Nahuatl-speaking Indian dignitaries, who would eventually agree on a narrative that was then translated into Spanish by a scribe. The difficulties of the project are clear from the remark of a frustrated scribe commenting on the hurried and incomplete nature of the last pages of the work: "It was the fault of the Indians, who were slow in coming to agreement."[1]

The scribe's difficulties were the result of the complexity of the written Nahuatl language, which predominated in central Mexico. It combined images that could stand for particular things (pictographs), for particular ideas (ideographs), or for specific sounds. In this respect it was similar to the languages of ancient Mesopotamia (see page 9). Nahuatl symbols rarely created a complete sentence. Rather, they were reminders of histories, tales, and poems familiar to the reader. The image in the lower left represents the city of Colhuacán. We see that the taller figure in a feathered shirt is an Aztec warrior dominating a second warrior. Above the two we see a falling and burning temple, the symbol for conquest. Beside the temple is the symbol for the name Colhuacán. This combination was to prompt the reader to recall or recount to others the story of the Aztec conquest of an important city. It was meant to show the early dominance of the Aztecs.

Such images from the sixteenth century served as a history lesson and a Spanish-Nahuatl dictionary for the Spanish conquerors of central Mexico. If you look carefully, you will see that the Nahuatl figures are clearly identified in Spanish. The central image, for example, is Tenochtitlán itself. The image on the lower right is identified in Spanish as *Colhuacán pueblo*, or "the city of Colhuacán."

Because the codex was a collection of common symbols, it was open to interpretation in different ways by different readers: This fluidity was both its strength and its weakness. We know

1. Quoted in Patricia Rieff Anawalt and Frances F. Berdan, "The Codex Mendoza," *Scientific American* 266 (June 1992): 71.

Codex Mendoza: The Founding of Tenochtitlán *(From* Codex Mendoza, *Ms Arch. Seld.*A.1.*fol. 2r. The Bodleian Library, Oxford)*

from other oral cultures that stories are not usually memorized tales but rather are performances tuned to the interests and prejudices of the audience—in this case the Spanish conquerors. The fluidity of the story is probably what caused disagreement among the Nahuatl-speaking interpreters, especially in sections on culture and daily life.

With this in mind we can return to the image of the foundation of Tenochtitlán. In the center is the glyph or symbol of the city itself. The first settlers on the island in the lake believed that they would found a city in the place where they saw an eagle sitting on a cactus. The border surrounding the images is made up of symbols for each of the fifty-one years in the reign of Tenoch, the first Aztec king. Notice too the division of the city into four parts and symbols for each district. In the quarter on the right we see a skull rack, a grisly reminder that the remains of those sacrificed at the main temples were brought back to the neighborhood of those who had supplied the captive for sacrifice. Skulls like the one in the illustration were posted as proof of local pride and status within the larger community.

The codex shows us how the Spanish came to understand the language and culture of the Aztecs. It also marks the fortunate transformation of violent conquerors into administrators who wanted to understand and even identify with the place they had come to dominate. Like other postconquest attempts to rediscover the nature of Aztec society, the Codex Mendoza suffers from the fact that it was composed almost two decades after the conquest. Yet without it and other early attempts to understand the Mexicans, our knowledge of the Aztecs would be dramatically poorer.

CHAPTER 16

The Reformation

During the sixteenth century, Europe was convulsed by an ever-widening controversy over the nature of Christianity, the relationship between the individual and God, and the role of government in society. The struggle began as an apparently minor theological controversy in Germany—a "quarrel between monks," as the papacy saw it. Debates about salvation quickly widened into arguments about the sacraments—that is, the means by which individuals receive God's grace. By the middle of the century, disagreements had expanded to the point that it was clear that the Christian religion and politics were changed forever. As the controversy continued, the issues spread from questions of theology to those of ecclesiastical and political organization. In the heat of this religious crisis the modern Christian churches, both Protestant and Catholic, were formed.

The Roman Catholic, Lutheran, Calvinist, and Anglican churches all came into being in the sixteenth century. But to speak of "Lutheran" or "Roman Catholic" during the first decades of the Reformation is to ignore the fluidity of the situation in which Europeans found themselves. At first, no one foresaw that the result of the controversies would be separate churches. The reformers of the first half of the sixteenth century shared many characteristics. Almost all emphasized the Bible as the unique source of religious authority and rejected the medieval church's complex view of salvation. Initially, they all rejected any claim of special status or authority for the priesthood.

The medieval church was a political as well as a religious power. Because all of western Europe was considered part of Christendom, all individuals and states were affected by papal rights to appoint bishops and to judge and excommunicate individuals. Further, debates over religion and

The congregation during the sermon. Detail from the altarpiece of a church in Wittenberg, by Lucas Cranach the Elder.

the power and authority of the church did not occur in a political vacuum. Supporters of the church, like Emperor Charles V (r. 1519–1556), gladly would have used force to suppress the new theology, but events conspired to make that unrealistic. In Germany, the emperor faced hostile towns and princes as well as French and Turkish military threats—all of which made action against religious dissidents impossible. In England and Scandinavia, in contrast, monarchs viewed the church as an illegitimate political power and a threat to strong royal governmeı t, and reformers soon found themselves with royal patrons. Elsewhere, especially in eastern Europe, there was no strong central government to enforce religious unity, and a variety of Christian traditions coexisted.

By the second half of the sixteenth century it was clear that there would never again be a single Christian church in western Europe. Political and religious powers concentrated their energies on a process of theological definition and institutionalization that historians call the "Second Reformation," or "Confessionalization." With the changes of the late sixteenth century it becomes appropriate to speak of Roman Catholic, Anglican, and Lutheran as clearly defined confessions, or systems of religious beliefs and practices.

In Protestant and Catholic churches the changes in religion brought about an increased sense of the importance of moral control exercised by religious authorities. Far from freeing the individual, the Christian churches of the late sixteenth century all emphasized correct doctrine and orderliness in personal behavior. The early Protestants may have rejected a sacramental system that they thought oppressed the individual, but the institutions that replaced the old church developed their own traditions of control.

The Reformation Movements

In 1517 a little-known professor of theology at the University of Wittenberg in Saxony began a protest against practices in the late medieval church. Martin Luther had no carefully worked-out idea about the nature of the church and salvation, but his theology struck a responsive cord with many of his contemporaries. Although the various protests resulted in the creation of separate and well-defined religious traditions, the differences among the reformers were not initially as clear as they became in the second half of the sixteenth century. Thus, it is appropriate to speak of "reformation movements" because all the reformers, even the most radical, shared with Luther a sense that the essential sacramental and priestly powers claimed by the medieval church were illegitimate.

Most of the reformers had been influenced by the cultural and literary interests of the humanists. Many had received a humanistic education with its emphasis on literary studies and the study of Latin, Greek, and Hebrew. Although most eventually rejected the general humanistic assumption of the dignity and essential goodness of individuals, they did share with the humanists a faith in linguistic studies of Christian traditions, especially of the Bible. The biblical commentaries and editions of Lorenzo Valla and Desiderius Erasmus (see pages 519 and 534) were the bases for Luther's eventual translation of the New and Old Testaments.

"Protestant" is the label we now use to describe the churches that arose in opposition to the medieval Christian church. It is important to understand, however, that the word *protestant* was originally a political term used to describe German princes who opposed imperial attempts to end a truce between supporters and opponents of the religious reformers in the 1530s. Only later was *Protestant* applied to the resulting churches. The reformers tended to think of themselves as "evangelical reformed Christians." They were *evangelical* in the sense that they believed that authority derived from the Word of God, the Bible. They were *reformed Christian* because their aim was merely to restore Christianity to the form they believed it exhibited in the first centuries of its existence. The process by which the reform movement came to see itself as separate from what we now know as the "Roman Catholic church" began with Martin Luther.

Martin Luther and the New Theology

Martin Luther (1483–1546) seemed to burst onto the scene in 1517, when he objected to the way in which papal indulgences—that is, the remission of penalties owed for sins—were being bought and sold in the bishopric of Brandenburg.

Luther's father, a miner from the small town of Mansfeld, had hoped that his son would take a degree in law and become a wealthy and prestigious lawyer. Martin Luther instead chose to enter a monastery and eventually become a priest.

Throughout his life, Martin Luther seems to have been troubled by a sense of his own sinfulness and unworthiness. According to late medieval theology, the life of a Christian was a continuing cycle of sin, confession, contrition, and penance, and the only way to achieve salvation was to have confessed all one's sins and at least begun a cycle of penance at the time of one's death. Christians lived in fear of dying suddenly without having any chance to confess. The purchase of indulgences, membership in penitential brotherhoods, ritualized charity, and veneration of popular saints were seen as ways to acquire merit and salvation in the eyes of God.

Luther came to believe that the church's requirement that believers achieve salvation by means of confession, contrition, and penance made too great a demand on the faithful. Instead, Luther said, citing the New Testament, salvation (or justification) was God's gift to the faithful. Luther's belief is known as "justification by faith." Confession, contrition, and acts of charity were important products of God's love, but in Luther's opinion, they were not necessary for salvation. Late in his life, Luther explained how he came by these ideas:

> Though I lived as a monk without reproach, I felt that I was a sinner before God with an extremely disturbed conscience. I could not believe that he was placated by my [acts of penance]. I did not love, yes, I hated the righteous God who punishes sinners. . . . At last, by the mercy of God, . . .I gave context to the words, namely, "In it the righteousness of God is revealed, as it is written, 'He who through faith is righteous shall live.'" There I began to understand that . . . the righteous lives by a gift of God, namely by faith. . . . Here I felt that I was altogether born again and had entered paradise itself through open gates.[1]

Although Luther recalled a sudden, dramatic revelation, it now seems clear that his insight developed slowly over the course of his academic career and during his defense of his teachings. Nonetheless, his recollection conveys a sense of the novelty of his theology and the reasons why his attack on the late medieval church proved to be so much more devastating than the complaints of earlier critics.

Martin Luther Although Luther rejected the mediation of saints in religious life, Protestant portrayals idealized Luther, in the same way saints were depicted, in order to emphasize his divine inspiration. *(Woodcut by Daniel Hopfer, 1523)*

Other critics complained of impious priests, an unresponsive bureaucracy, and a church too much involved in matters of government, but the theology that Luther developed struck at the very structure of the church itself. Luther separated justification from acts of sanctification—from the good works or charity expected of all Christians. In Luther's theology the acts of piety so typical of the medieval church were quite unnecessary for salvation, because Christ's sacrifice had brought justification once and for all. Justification came entirely from God and was independent of human acts. Luther argued that the Christian was at the same time sinner and saved, so the penitential cycle and careful preparation for a "good death" were, in his opinion, unnecessary.

Luther also attacked the place of the priesthood in the sacramental life of the church. The church taught that, through the actions of ordained priests, Christ was really present in the bread and wine of the sacrament of Holy Communion. Luther agreed that the sacrament transformed the bread and wine into the body and blood of Christ, but he denied that priests had a role in the transformation. Priests distributed only the bread to the laity, reserving the consecrated wine for themselves—further emphasizing their own special status. Priests, in Luther's view, were not mediators between God and individual Christians. John Wyclif and John Hus (see page 455) had argued against the spiritual authority of unworthy priests. Luther, however, directly challenged the role of the clergy and the institutional church in the attainment of salvation.

In the years before 1517, Luther's views on salvation and his reservations about the traditional ways of teaching theology attracted little interest outside his own university. Matters were very different, however, when he challenged the sale of indulgences. The papacy frequently authorized the sale of indulgences to pay various expenses. Unscrupulous salesmen often left the impression that purchase of an indulgence freed a soul from purgatory. After getting no response to his initial complaints, Luther made public his "Ninety-five Theses." Luther probably posted these theses on indulgences on the door of the Wittenberg Castle church, the usual way to announce topics for theological discussion about the interpretation of the Scriptures and the nature of penance. Luther's text created a firestorm when it was quickly translated and printed throughout German-speaking lands. Luther's complaints about the sale of indulgences encapsulated German feelings about unworthy priests and economic abuses by the clergy. Luther was acclaimed as the spokesman of the German people.

In a debate with a papal representative in Leipzig in 1519, Luther was forced to admit that in some of his positions he agreed with the Czech heretic John Hus. In the Leipzig debate and in the following year Luther responded to his critics and tried to explain more fully the nature of the changes he advocated. Three tracts were especially important. In *Address to the Christian Nobility of the German Nation,* Luther urged the princes to reject papal claims of temporal and spiritual authority (see the box, "Martin Luther's Address to the Christian Nobility of the German Nation"). In *On the Babylonian Captivity of the Church,* he argued for the principle of *sola scriptura*—that is, authority in the church had to be based on teachings found in the Bible. In *On Christian Freedom,* he explained clearly his understanding of salvation: "A Christian has all he needs in faith and needs no works to justify him." Luther was speaking of spiritual freedom from unnecessary ritual, not social or political freedom. This distinction would later be crucial to Luther's opposition to political and economic protests by peasants and artisans.

In 1520, Pope Leo X (r. 1513–1521) condemned Luther's teachings and gave him sixty days to recant. In 1521, Emperor Charles V called an imperial diet, or parliament, at Worms to deal with the religious crisis. Charles demanded that Luther submit to papal authority. Luther, however, explained that religious decisions must be based on personal experience and conscience:

> Unless I am convicted by the testimony of Scripture or by clear reason, for I do not trust either in the Pope or in councils alone, since it is well known that they have often erred and contradicted themselves, . . . I cannot and will not retract anything, for it is neither safe nor right to go against conscience. I cannot do otherwise, here I stand, may God help me. Amen.[2]

The emperor and his allies, however, were firmly in the papal camp. The excommunicated Luther was placed under an imperial ban—that is, declared an outlaw. As Luther left the Diet of Worms, friendly princes took him to Wartburg Castle in Saxony, where they could protect him. During a year of isolation at Wartburg, Luther used Erasmus's edition of the Greek New Testament as the basis of a translation into German of the New Testament, a work that was an influential literary as well as religious work.

The Reformation of the Communities

Luther challenged the authority of the clerical hierarchy and called on lay people to take responsibility for their own salvation. His ideas spread rapidly in the towns and countryside of Germany because he and his followers took advantage of the new technology of printing. (See the feature, "Weighing the Evidence: A Reformation Woodcut," on pages 614–615.) Perhaps 300,000 copies

Martin Luther's Address to the Christian Nobility of the German Nation

Luther wrote this tract to the rulers of Germany to explain the nature of his conflict with the church over ecclesiastical authority. In this excerpt, he makes clear his disagreements with the system of clerical status and immunities that had grown throughout the Middle Ages.

The Romanists have, with great adroitness, drawn three walls around themselves, with which they have hereto protected themselves, so that no one could reform them whereby all Christendom has fallen terribly.

First, if pressed by the temporal power, they have affirmed and maintained that the temporal power has no jurisdiction over them, but on the contrary, that the spiritual power is above the temporal.

Secondly, if it were proposed to admonish them with the Scriptures, they objected that no one may interpret the Scriptures but the Pope.

Thirdly, if they are threatened with a council, they pretend that no one may call a council but the Pope. . . .

Let us, the first place, attack the first wall.

It has been devised that the Pope, bishops, priests, and monks are called the spiritual estate; princes, lords, craftsmen, and peasants are the temporal estate. This is an artful lie and hypocritical device, . . . all Christians are truly of the spiritual estate. . . . As for the unction [anointing with sacred oil] by a pope or a bishop, tonsure [the shaving of the head that marked a cleric], ordination, consecration, and clothes differing from those of a layman—all this may make a hypocrite or an anointed puppet, but never a Christian or a spiritual man. . . . Therefore a priest is nothing, should be nothing, in Christendom but a functionary; as long as he holds his office, he has precedence of others; if he is deprived of it he is a peasant or a citizen like the rest. . . .

The second wall is even more tottering and weak: that they alone pretend to be considered masters of the Scriptures. . . . If our article of faith is right, . . . we are all priests, as I have said, and have all one faith, one Gospel, one Sacrament; how then shall we not have the power of discerning and judging what is right or wrong in matters of faith? . . .

The third wall falls of itself, as soon as the first two have fallen; for if the Pope acts contrary to the Scriptures, we are bound to stand by the Scriptures and to punish and constrain him, according to Christ's commandment.

Source: Beresford James Kidd, ed., *Documents Illustrative of the Continental Reformation* (Oxford, England: Clarendon Press, 1967), pp. 63–65.

of his early tracts were published in the early years of the protest. Luther's claim that the Scriptures must be the basis of all life and his appeal to the judgment of the laity seem to have struck a responsive cord in towns and villages, where councils of local people were accustomed to making decisions based on ideas of the common good. It is also true that townsmen and villagers saw religious and civic life as being inextricably interconnected. For them, there was no such thing as a religiously neutral act.

The impact of Luther's ideas was quickly evident. If the active intercession of the clergy was not necessary for the salvation of individuals, then, according to Luther's followers, there was no reason for the clergy to remain unmarried and celibate, and there was no reason for men or women to cloister themselves in monasteries or convents. Also, maintained Luther's partisans, there was no need to restrict the laity's participation in the sacrament of the Eucharist. Thus, the priest must distribute wine to the laity along with

THE REFORMATION AND COUNTER-REFORMATION

1513–17	Fifth Lateran Council meets to consider reform of the Catholic church
1517	Luther makes public his "Ninety-five Theses"
1518	Zwingli is appointed people's priest of Zurich
1520	Pope Leo X condemns Luther's teachings
1521	Luther appears at the Diet of Worms
1524–25	Peasant revolts in Germany
1527	Imperial troops sack Rome
1530	Melanchthon composes the Augsburg Confession summarizing Lutheran belief
1534	Calvin flees from Paris; Loyola founds the Society of Jesus
1535	The Anabaptist community of Münster is destroyed
1536	Calvin arrives in Geneva and publishes the first edition of *Institutes of the Christian Religion*
1543–63	Council of Trent meets to reform the Catholic church
1555	Emperor Charles V accepts the Peace of Augsburg
1572	Saint Bartholomew's Day Massacre in France
1598	Henry IV of France issues the Edict of Nantes

the bread. With the spread of Luther's ideas came the end of a very visual part of the clerical monopoly. Because Luther's followers believed that penitential acts were not prerequisites for salvation, they tended to set aside the veneration of saints and not to make pilgrimages to the shrines and holy places all over Europe.

Many historians have referred to the spread of these reform ideas as "the Reformation of the Common Man." In Strasbourg, Nuremberg, Zurich, and other towns, ideas about the primacy of the Bible and attacks on clerical privilege were spread by "people's priests," preachers hired by the town government to see to preaching and the care of souls in the community. Many of the most famous reformers initially gained a following through preaching. The message then seems to have spread especially quickly among artisan and mercantile groups, which put pressure on town governments to press for reform. Agitation was often riotous. One resident of Augsburg exposed himself during a church service to protest what he believed was an evil and idolatrous service.

To quell disturbances and to arrive at a consensus within the community, cautious town councils often set up debates between reformers and church representatives. Because the church hierarchy rarely approved of such debates, traditional views were often poorly represented, giving a great advantage to the reformers. The two sides argued over the authority of the church hierarchy, the nature of salvation, and whether papal authority and the seven sacraments could be demonstrated in the Bible. At the conclusion of such a debate, many town governments ordered that preaching and practice in the town should be according to the "Word of God"—a code for reformed practice. In reformed towns, the city council became a council of elders for the church. Thus, civil government came to play an important role in the local organization of the church.

The case of Zurich is instructive. In 1518 the people's priest of Zurich was Huldrych Zwingli (1484–1531), son of a rural official from a nearby village. After a university education, he became a typical late medieval country priest, right down to his numerous mistresses. Yet after experiences as a military chaplain and an acquaintance with the humanist writings of Erasmus, Zwingli began to preach strongly biblical sermons. In 1522 he defended a group of laymen who broke a required Lenten fast to show their disapproval of what they saw as useless ritual. Later in the same year he requested episcopal permission to marry. Early in 1523, he led a group of reformers in a public debate over the nature of the church. The city council declared in favor of the reformers, and Zurich became, in effect, a Protestant city.

Unlike Luther, Zwingli believed that reform should be a communal movement—that town

Map 16.1 Reform in Germany The pattern of religious reform in Germany was complex. Although some territorial princes, such as the dukes of Bavaria, rejected the reform, most free towns, particularly those in the southwest, adopted it.

governments should take the lead in bringing reform to the community. In the years following 1523, the reformers restructured church services, abolishing Mass; they also removed religious images from churches and suppressed monastic institutions. Zwingli further disagreed with Luther about the nature of the sacrament of Holy Communion. Whereas Luther, like Catholic theologians, accepted that Christ was truly present in the bread and wine, Zwingli argued that Christ's presence was merely spiritual. This disagreement created within the movement for reform a division that made a common response to papal or imperial pressure difficult (Map 16.1).

The reform message spread from towns into the countryside, but often with effects that the reformers did not expect or desire. Luther thought his message was an abstract and theological one. Many peasants and modest artisans, however, believed Luther's message of biblical freedom carried material as well as theological meaning.

In many parts of Germany villagers and peasants found themselves under increasing pressure from landlords and territorial princes.

Peasant Freedom The German peasants believed Luther's call for individual freedom of conscience included economic and political freedom. Their revolt of 1525 struck terror in the hearts of German rulers. As this woodcut indicates, the peasant army was lightly armed. Many carried only tools, pitchforks, flails, and scythes. *(Title page of an anonymous pamphlet from the Peasants' War, 1525)*

Taking advantage of changed economic and political conditions, these lords were intent on regaining claims to ancient manorial rights, on suppressing peasant claims to use common lands, and on imposing new taxes and tithes. Like townsmen, peasants saw religious and material life as closely connected. They argued that new tithes and taxes were not just against tradition but violated the Word of God. Using Luther's argument that authority should be based in the Scriptures, peasants from the district of Zurich, for example, petitioned the town council in 1523–1524, claiming that they should not be required to pay tithes on their produce because there was no biblical justification for doing so. Townsmen rejected the peasants' demand, noting that the Bible did not forbid such payments and saying that the peasants should make them out of love.

Demands that landlords and magistrates give up human ordinances and follow "Godly Law" soon turned to violence. Peasants, miners, and villagers in 1524 and 1525 participated in a series of uprisings that began on the borderlands between Switzerland and Germany and spread throughout southwest Germany, upper Austria, and even into northern Italy. Bands of peasants and villagers, perhaps a total of 300,000 in the empire, revolted against their seigneurial lords or even their territorial overlords.

Luther initially counseled landlords and princes to redress the just grievances. As reports of riots and increased violence continued to reach Wittenberg, however, Luther condemned the rebels as "mad dogs" and urged that they be destroyed. Territorial princes and large cities quickly raised armies to meet the threat. The peasants were defeated and destroyed in a series of battles in April 1525. It seems likely that, in response to these rebellions, lords lived in fear of another revolt and were careful not to overburden their tenants. But when it became clear that the reformers were unwilling to follow the implications of their own theology, villagers and peasants lost interest in the progress of the reform. As a townsman of Zurich commented, "Many came to a great hatred of the preachers, where before they would have bitten off their feet for the Gospel."[3]

John Calvin and the Reformed Tradition

The revolts of 1524 and 1525 demonstrated the mixture of messages traveling under the rubric "true, or biblical religion." In the 1530s, the theological arguments of the reformers began to take on a greater clarity, mostly because of the Franco-Swiss reformer John Calvin (1509–1564). Calvin had a humanistic education in Paris and became a lawyer before coming under the influence of reform-minded thinkers in France. In 1534 he fled from Paris as royal pressures against reformers increased. He arrived in Geneva in 1536, where he would remain, except for a short exile, until the end of his life.

Because of the central location of Geneva and the power of Calvin's theology, Geneva quickly replaced Wittenberg as the source of Protestant thought and became a haven for many of Europe's religious refugees. Calvin's ideas about salvation and the godly community rapidly spread to France, the Low Countries, Scotland, and England. Until the end of his life, Calvin was a magnet drawing people interested in reform.

The heart of Calvin's appeal lay in his formal theological writings. In 1536 he published the first of many editions of *Institutes of the Christian Religion,* which was to become the summa of reform theology. In it Calvin laid out a doctrine of the absolute power of God and the complete depravity and powerlessness of humanity.

Calvin believed in predestination, that "the word of God takes root and grows only in those whom the Lord, by his eternal election, has predestined to be his children." Like Luther, Calvin viewed salvation as a mysterious gift of God. Calvin believed that from the beginning of time God had elected those to be saved and those to be damned and that human actions play no part in the divine plan. The elect—that is, the people to whom God graciously grants salvation—freely do good works in response to "God's benevolence." Further, Calvin suggested, the elect would benefit from "signs of divine benevolence," an idea that would have a profound impact on the Calvinist understanding of the relationship of wealth to spiritual life. Calvin believed that good works and a well-ordered society were the result of God's grace. By the seventeenth century, Calvinists widely believed that the elect had a duty to work in the secular world and that wealth accumulated in business was a sign of God's favor. It was an idea nicely adapted to the increasingly wealthy world of early modern Europe.

That connection between salvation and material life, however, lay in the future. The aspect of election that most interested Calvin was the creation of a truly Christian community by the elect. To accomplish this, Calvinists purged their churches of any manifestation of "superstition." Like Zwingli they rejected the idea that Christ was really present in the sacrament of Holy Communion. They rejected the role of saints. They removed from their churches and destroyed paintings and statuary that they believed were indications of idolatry. Public officials were to be "vicars of God." They had the power to lead and correct both the faithful and the unregenerate sinners who lived in Christian communities. In his years in Geneva Calvin tried to create a "Christian Commonwealth," but Geneva was far from a theocracy. Calvin's initial attempts to create a Christian community by requiring public confession and allowing church leaders to discipline sinners were rejected by Geneva's city council, which exiled Calvin in 1538.

On his return in 1541 he sought to institute church reforms modeled on those he had observed in the Protestant city of Strasbourg. Calvin's reformed church hierarchy was made up of four offices: preachers, doctors, deacons, and elders. Preachers and doctors saw to the care and education of the faithful. Deacons, as in the early church, were charged with attending to the material needs of the congregation. The elders became the consistory, a moral and religious court with the power of excommunication. The elders—the true leaders of the Genevan church—were selected from the patriciate that dominated the civil government of the city. Thus, it makes as

John Calvin This image of Calvin in his study is similar to countless pictures of Saint Jerome and Erasmus at work and reminds viewers of Calvin's humanistic education and the role of Christian and classical learning in his theology. *(Lauros/Giraudon/Art Resource, NY)*

much sense to speak of a church governed by the town as a town dominated by the church. The elders actively intervened in education, charity, and attempts to regulate prostitution.

Calvinist churchmen reacted promptly and harshly to events that seemed to threaten either church or state. The most famous event was the capture, trial, and execution of Michael Servetus (1511–1553), a Spanish physician and radical theologian who rejected generally accepted doctrines like the Trinity and specifically criticized many of Calvin's teachings in the *Institutes.* After corresponding with Servetus for a time, Calvin remarked that if Servetus were in Geneva, "I would not suffer him to get out alive." After living in various parts of Europe, Servetus eventually did anonymously come to Geneva. He was recognized and arrested. Calvin was as good as his word. After a public debate and trial, Servetus was burned at the stake for blaspheming the Trinity and the Christian religion.

The Radical Reform of the Anabaptists

Michael Servetus was but one of a number of extremists who claimed to be carrying out the full reform implied in the teachings of Luther, Zwingli, and Calvin. Called "Anabaptists" (or "rebaptizers" because of their rejection of infant baptism), or simply "radicals," they tended to take biblical commands more literally than the mainline reformers. They rejected infant baptism as unbiblical, and they refused to take civil oaths or hold public office, for to do so would be to compromise with unreformed civil society.

The earliest of the radicals allied themselves with the rebels of 1525. Thomas Müntzer (1490–1525) was an influential preacher who believed in divine revelation through visions and dreams. His own visions told him that the poor were the true elect and that the end of the world was at hand. An active participant in the revolts of 1525, Müntzer called on the elect to drive out the ungodly. After the defeat of the rebels, he was captured and executed by the German princes.

Other radicals, such as the revolutionaries who took control of the north German city of Münster, rejected infant baptism, adopted polygamy, and proclaimed a new "Kingdom of Righteousness." The reformers of Münster instituted the new kingdom in the city by rebaptizing those who joined their cause and driving out those who opposed them. They abolished private property rights in Münster and instituted new laws concerning morality and behavior. Leadership in the city eventually passed to a tailor, Jan of Leiden (d. 1535), who proclaimed himself the new messiah and lord of the world. The Anabaptists were opposed by the prince-bishop of Münster, the political and religious lord of the city. After a sixteen-month siege, the bishop and his allies recaptured the city from the Anabaptists in 1535. Besieging forces massacred men, women, and children. Jan of Leiden was captured and executed by mutilation with red-hot tongs.

With the destruction of the Münster revolutionaries in 1535, the Anabaptist movement turned inward. Under leaders like Menno Simons (1495–1561), who founded the Mennonites, and Jakob Hutter (d. 1536), who founded the Moravian Societies, the radicals rejected the violent establishment of truly holy cities. To varying degrees they also rejected connections with civil society, military service, even civil courts. They did, however, believe that their own communities were communities of the elect. They tended to close themselves off from outsiders and enforce a strict discipline over their members. The elders of these communities were empowered to excommunicate or "shun" those who violated the community's precepts. Anabaptist communities have proved unusually durable. Moravian and Mennonite communities continue to exist in western Europe, North America, and even in parts of what used to be the Soviet Union.

Like Luther, all of the early reformers appealed to the authority of the Bible in their attacks on church tradition. Yet in the villages and towns of Germany and Switzerland, many radicals were prepared to move far beyond the positions Luther had advocated. When they did so, Luther found himself in the odd position of appealing to the very imperial authorities whose inaction had allowed his own protest to survive.

The Empire of Charles V

Luther believed that secular authorities should be benevolently neutral in religious matters. In his eyes, the success of the early Reformation was simply God's will:

THE HABSBURG SUCCESSION, 1493–1556

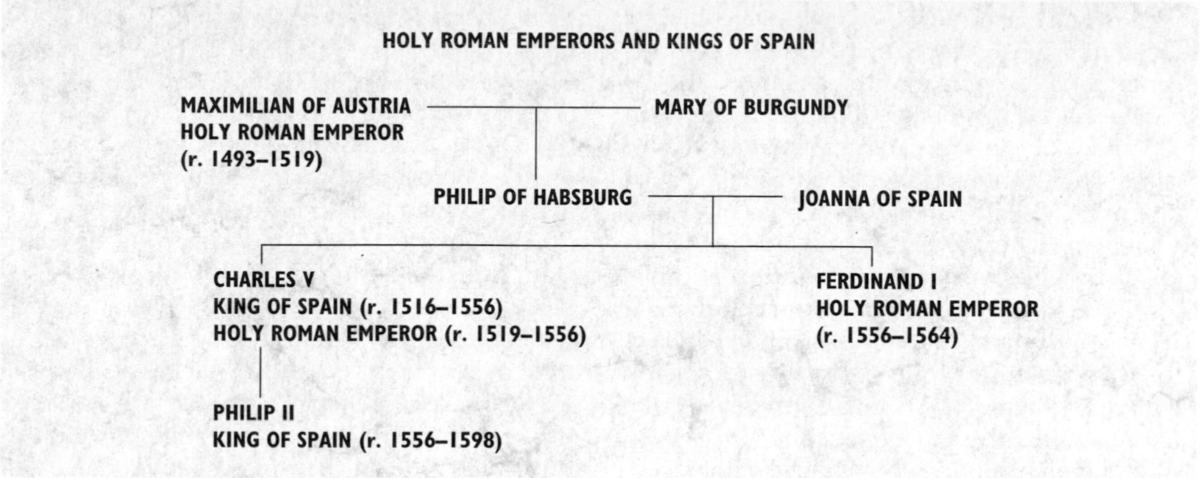

> I simply taught, preached and wrote God's Word; otherwise I did nothing. And while I slept or drank Wittenberg beer with my friends . . . , the Word so greatly weakened the Papacy that no prince or emperor ever inflicted such losses on it. I did nothing; the Word did everything.[4]

As great as the word of God was, Luther must have known that even as he drank his beer, the Holy Roman emperor could have crushed the reform movement if he had chosen to enforce imperial decrees. But attempts to resolve religious conflict became entangled with attempts to hold together the family lands of the Habsburg emperor and political rivalries among the various German princes. The eventual religious settlement required a constitutional compromise that preserved the virtual autonomy of great princes of Germany. The political realities of Europe in the sixteenth century were that political leaders were afraid of the emperor even when he tried to preserve the essential unity of the Christian church.

Imperial Challenges

Emperor Charles V (r. 1519–1556) was the beneficiary of a series of marriages that, in the words of his courtiers, seemed to re-create the empire of Charlemagne. From his father, Philip of Habsburg, he inherited claims to Austria, the imperial crown, and Burgundian lands that included the Low Countries and the Free County of Burgundy. Through his mother Joanna, the daughter of Ferdinand and Isabella of Spain, Charles became heir to the kingdoms of Castile, Aragon, Sicily, Naples, and Spanish America. During the Italian wars of the early sixteenth century, Charles's holdings in Italy expanded to include the duchy of Milan and most of the rest of Lombardy. By 1506 he was duke of Burgundy; in 1516 he became king of Aragon and Castile; and in 1519 he was elected Holy Roman emperor. Every government in Europe had to deal with one part or another of Charles's empire. His chancellor enthused, "[God] has set you on the way towards a world monarchy, towards the gathering of all Christendom under a single shepherd."

Charles seems to have sincerely desired such a world monarchy, but in none of the areas under his control was his authority unchallenged. In Castile, for example, grandees, townsmen, and peasants felt they had grounds for complaint. They objected that taxes were too heavy and that Charles disregarded the Cortes and his natural advisers, the old nobility. But most of all they complained that too many of his officials were foreigners whom he had brought with him from his home in Flanders. Protests festered in the towns and villages of Castile and finally broke out into a revolt called the Comunero (townsmen's or citizens') movement. Between 1517 and 1522, just the time when religious reform was making dramatic advances in Germany, many of the most important towns of Spain were in open rebellion against the Crown. Charles's forces eventually took control of the situation, and by 1522 he had crushed the Comuneros. Between 1522 and 1530, he was careful to spend much of his time in his Spanish kingdoms.

Charles's claims in Italy, as well as his claims to lands in the Pyrenees and the duchy of Burgundy, brought him into direct conflict with the Valois kings of France. Again in the critical 1520s, the Habsburgs and the Valois fought a series of wars. Charles dramatically defeated the French at Pavia in northern Italy in 1525, sacked and occupied Rome in 1527, and became the virtual arbitrator of Italian politics. In the course of the struggle, the Catholic Francis I of France, whose title was "the Most Christian king," found it to his advantage to ally himself with Charles's most serious opponents, the Protestants and the Turks. Francis demonstrated the truth of Machiavelli's dictum that private virtues often play a small role in political and diplomatic life. The Habsburg-Valois Wars dragged on until, in exhaustion, the French king Henry II (r. 1547–1559) and the Spanish king Philip II (r. 1556–1598) signed the Treaty of Cateau-Cambrésis in 1559.

Charles was not the only ruler to claim the title "emperor" and a succession reaching back to the Roman Empire. After the conquest of Constantinople in 1453, the sultan of the Ottoman Turks began to refer to himself as "the Emperor." After consolidating control of Constantinople and the Balkans, Turkish armies under the command of Emperor Suleiman (r. 1520–1566), known as "the Magnificent," resumed their expansion to the north and west. After capturing Belgrade, Turkish forces soundly defeated a Hungarian army at the battle of Mohács in 1526. Charles appealed for unity within Christendom against the threat. Even Martin Luther agreed that Christians should unite during invasion.

The Capture of Belgrade During the sixteenth century Ottoman Turks dominated the Balkans militarily and were a significant force in European diplomacy. They were masters of coordinated attacks combining artillery and infantry. *(Österreichische Nationalbibliothek)*

Suleiman's army besieged Vienna in 1529 before being forced to retreat. Turks also created a navy in the Mediterranean and, with French encouragement, began a series of raids along the coasts of Italy and Spain. The Turkish fleet remained a threat throughout the sixteenth century. The reign of Suleiman in many respects marked the permanent entry of Turkey into the European military and diplomatic system. Turkish pressure was yet another reason why Charles was unable to deal with German Protestants in a direct and uncompromising way.

German Politics

The course of the religious reform was continuously influenced by the political configuration of Germany. In 1500, Germany was much less centralized than France or England. Since 1495, seven electoral princes (three archbishops and four lay princes) and a larger circle of imperial princes claimed the right to representation in the imperial council, and nearly three hundred other towns or principalities claimed various exemptions from imperial control. The emperor's claims in most areas amounted to the right to collect modest taxes on households and individuals, a court of high justice, and the right to proclaim imperial truces. Yet the empire lacked a unified legal system, and the emperor himself had only one vote on the imperial council. In many respects political centralization and innovation were characteristics of individual territories, not of the empire as a whole. The power of the emperor depended on his relations with the towns and princes of Germany.

In the first years after Luther issued his "Ninety-five Theses," he was defended by the elector Frederick of Saxony, who held a key vote in Charles's quest for election as Holy Roman emperor. As long as Frederick protected Luther, imperial officials had to proceed against him with caution. When Luther was outlawed by the imperial Diet of Worms in 1521, Frederick and many other princes and towns refused to enforce the edict against him and his followers unless their own grievances with the emperor and their complaints about the church were taken up at the same time. In 1522 and 1526 the emperor again tried to enforce the ban, but imperial officials were bluntly informed that the towns were unable to conform. At the Diet of Speyer in 1526, delegates passed a resolution empowering princes and towns to settle religious matters in their territories as they saw fit. In effect, this resolution legitimated the reform in territories where authorities chose to follow the new teachings and presaged the eventual shape of the final religious settlement in Germany.

German princes took advantage of the emperor's relative powerlessness and made choices reflecting a complex of religious, political, and diplomatic issues. Electoral Saxony and ducal Saxony, the two parts of the province of Saxony, split over the issue of reform. Electoral Saxony, Luther's homeland, was Lutheran. Ducal Saxony was strongly Catholic. Especially in the autonomous towns, many decisions about religion were often made with an eye on the choices made by neighbors and competitors.

Some rulers made decisions that were even more consciously cynical. The Grand Master of the religious order of the Teutonic Knights, Albrecht von Hohenzollern (1490–1568), who controlled the duchy of Prussia, renounced his monastic vows. Then, at the urging of Luther and other reformers, he secularized the order's estates (that is, he transferred them from church to private ownership), which then became East Prussia, hereditary lands of the Hohenzollern family. In other territories, rulers managed to claim the properties of suppressed religious orders. Even when, as in the case of Count Philip of Hesse (1504–1567), much of the revenue from secularization was used to create hospitals and an organized system of charity, the reforming prince was still enriched.

Some rulers found their personal reservations about Luther reinforced by their fears of popular unrest. Luther's call for decisions based on personal conscience seemed to the dukes of Bavaria, for example, to be a call for attacks on princely authority and even anarchy. In the confused and fluid situation of the 1520s and 1530s, imperial interests were never the primary issue.

The Religious Settlement

With the fading of the Turkish threat on Vienna in 1529, Charles renewed his pressure on the German principalities at a meeting of the imperial diet at Augsburg in 1530. It was for this diet that

The Augsburg Confession In this woodcut of the Augsburg Confession being read to Charles V, the artist has included in the background text and images of the Lutheran teachings on the sacraments and the nature of salvation. In contrast are the images on the left of a papal ceremony and court hierarchy in which, the artist implies, Christ is not present. *(Kunstsammlung Veste Coburg)*

Philip Melanchthon (1497–1560), Luther's closest adviser, prepared the Augsburg Confession, which would become the basic statement of the Lutheran faith. Melanchthon hoped that the document would form the basis of compromise with Catholic powers, but the possibility was rejected out of hand by the imperial party. Charles aimed to affirm his strength in Germany by forcing the princes to end the reform movement and enforce the papal and imperial bans on Luther's teachings.

The Protestant princes responded by forming the League of Schmalkalden. At first, the founders of the league claimed that they were interested in protecting reformed preaching, but the league quickly developed as a center of opposition to imperial influence in general. Eventually Charles and a group of allied princes managed to defeat the league at the battle of Mühlberg in 1547. The emperor was unable to continue pressure on the Protestants, however, because he had depended on the support of some Protestant princes in his battles with the league. As a result, even after military defeat the Protestant princes were able to maintain religious autonomy. In the Religious Peace of Augsburg of 1555 the emperor formally acknowledged the principle that sovereign princes could choose the religion to be practiced in their territories, *cuius regio, eius religio* ("whose territory, his religion"). There were limits, however, for leaders could only remain under papal authority or adopt the Augsburg Confession outlined by Melanchthon (see the box, "The Peace of Augsburg"). Reformed churches associated with Zwingli or Calvin were not legally recognized (Map 16.2).

The Peace of Augsburg

By 1555 it was clear that neither the Protestant princes nor the emperor could defeat the other. In the Peace of Augsburg, the emperor and princes created an agreement designed to end the struggle. It carefully defines the rights and privileges of the rulers but leaves out all the reformers who were not in complete agreement with the Lutherans.

In order to bring peace in the holy Empire of the Germanic Nation between the Roman Imperial Majesty and the Electors, Princes, and Estates: let neither his Imperial Majesty nor the Electors, Princes, etc., do any violence or harm to any estate of the Empire on account of the Augsburg Confession [the declaration of faith of 1530], but let them enjoy their religious belief, liturgy, ceremonies, as well as their estates and other rights and privileges in peace; and complete religious peace shall be obtained only by Christian means of amity, or under threat of punishment of the imperial ban.

Likewise the Estates [governments] espousing the Augsburg Confession shall let all the Estates and Princes who cling to the old religion live in absolute peace and in the enjoyment of all their estates, rights and privileges.

However, all such as do not belong to the two above-named religions shall not be included in the present peace but be totally excluded from it.

Where an archbishop, bishop, or prelate or any other priest of our old religion shall abandon the same, his archbishopric, bishopric, prelacy, and other benefices, together with all their income and revenues which he has so far possessed, shall be abandoned by him without any further objection or delay.

No Estate [government] shall try to persuade the subjects of other Estates to abandon their religion nor protect them against their own magistrates.

In case our subjects, whether belonging to the old religion or to the Augsburg Confession, shall intend leaving their homes, with their wives and children, in order to settle in another place, they shall neither be hindered.

Source: Beresford James Kidd, ed., *Documents Illustrative of the Continental Reformation* (Oxford, England: Clarendon Press, 1967), pp. 363–364.

Shortly after the settlement, Charles abdicated his Spanish and imperial titles. Exhausted by years of political and religious struggle, he ceded the imperial crown to his brother Ferdinand (r. 1556–1564). His possessions in the Low Countries, Spain, Italy, and the New World he ceded to his son Philip II (r. 1527–1598). Charles had believed his courtiers who compared his empire to that of the ancient Romans. He had believed that his duty as emperor was to unite Christendom under one law and one church. But in no part of his empire did he ever command the authority that would have allowed him to unite his lands politically, let alone to re-establish religious unity. In 1558 he died in a monastery in Spain where he retired shortly after his abdication.

The English Reformation

England was closely tied to Germany. Since the twelfth century, large numbers of German merchants lived and traded in England, and there was a major English community in Cologne. Anglo-German connections were especially significant during the Reformation. Reformers from Wittenberg and other Protestant towns had contact with English merchants from London who traded and traveled on the continent. William

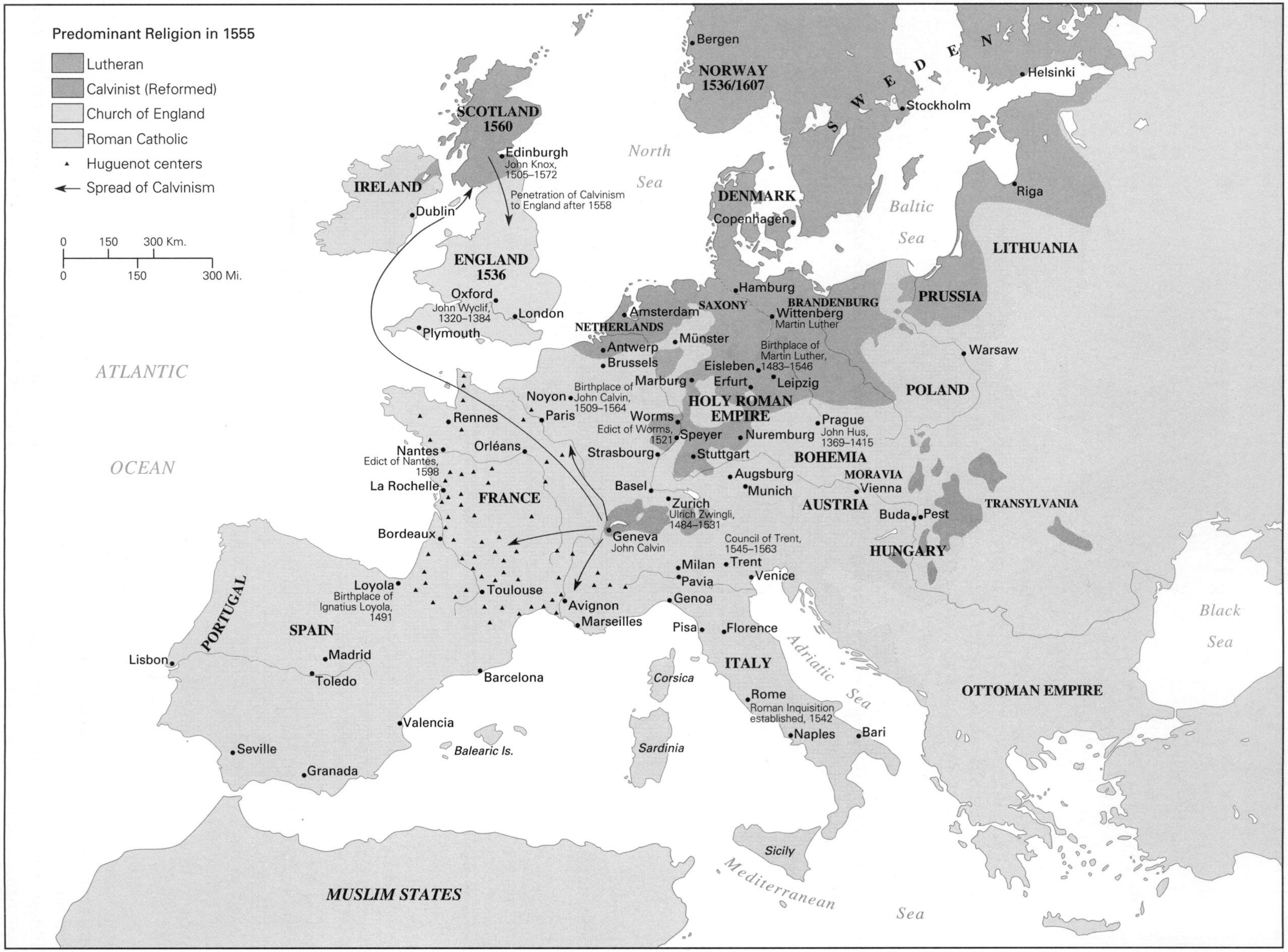
Predominant Religion in 1555
Lutheran
Calvinist (Reformed)
Church of England
Roman Catholic
Huguenot centers
Spread of Calvinism
0 150 300 Km.
0 150 300 Mi.
SCOTLAND 1560
Edinburgh
John Knox, 1505–1572
Penetration of Calvinism to England after 1558
IRELAND
Dublin
ENGLAND 1536
Oxford
John Wyclif, 1320–1384
London
Plymouth
ATLANTIC
OCEAN
North Sea
Bergen
NORWAY 1536/1607
SWEDEN
Stockholm
Helsinki
DENMARK
Copenhagen
Baltic Sea
Riga
LITHUANIA
PRUSSIA
Hamburg
SAXONY
BRANDENBURG
Wittenberg
Martin Luther
Amsterdam
NETHERLANDS
Münster
Antwerp
Brussels
Birthplace of Martin Luther, 1483–1546
Eisleben
Erfurt
Leipzig
Warsaw
POLAND
Marburg
Birthplace of John Calvin, 1509–1564
Noyon
Paris
HOLY ROMAN EMPIRE
Worms
Edict of Worms, 1521
Speyer
Nuremburg
Prague
John Hus, 1369–1415
Rennes
Orléans
Nantes
Edict of Nantes, 1598
La Rochelle
FRANCE
Strasbourg
Stuttgart
BOHEMIA
MORAVIA
Vienna
Augsburg
Munich
Basel
Zurich
Ulrich Zwingli, 1484–1531
AUSTRIA
Buda
Pest
TRANSYLVANIA
HUNGARY
Geneva
John Calvin
Council of Trent, 1545–1563
Trent
Milan
Pavia
Venice
Bordeaux
Loyola
Birthplace of Ignatius Loyola, 1491
Toulouse
Avignon
Marseilles
Genoa
PORTUGAL
SPAIN
Lisbon
Madrid
Toledo
Barcelona
Pisa
Florence
Adriatic Sea
ITALY
Corsica
Rome
Roman Inquisition established, 1542
Naples
Bari
Black Sea
OTTOMAN EMPIRE
Valencia
Balearic Is.
Sardinia
Seville
Granada
Sicily
Mediterranean Sea
MUSLIM STATES

Tyndale (ca. 1494–1536) served as a bridge between the Continent and England. He had a humanistic education in classical languages and began working on a translation of the Bible in the 1520s. Forced to flee London by the church hierarchy, he visited Luther in Wittenberg before settling in Antwerp, where he completed his translation of the New Testament. By 1526, copies of his translation and his religious tracts flooded into England. By the 1520s, Lutheran influence was noticeable in London and Cambridge. To some extent the ground may have been prepared for the reformers by the few surviving Lollards, the followers of Wyclif, who had argued for church reform in the late fourteenth and fifteenth centuries. Lollards, who tended to be literate, were an ideal market for Tyndale's English Bible and his numerous tracts.

As in Germany, institutional change in the church followed from both secular issues and reform ideas. In England, an initially hostile monarch began to tolerate reform ideas when he perceived the papacy as an unbiblical, tyrannical force blocking essential state policy.

Henry VIII Portraits of the king show a handsome man who understood very well the wealth, power, dignity, and majesty that was part of his royal office. *(Lent by Warwick Castle)*

Henry VIII and the Monarchial Reformation

Henry VIII (r. 1509–1547) began his reign as a popular and powerful king. Handsome, athletic, and artistic, he seemed to be the ideal ruler. Henry took an interest in theology and humanistic culture. At first, he was quite hostile to Luther's reform ideas and wrote *Defense of the Seven Sacraments,* which earned him the title "Defender of the Faith" from a grateful Pope Leo X. Throughout his life Henry remained suspicious of many Protestant ideas, but he led the initial phase of the break between the English church and the papacy because of his political problems with the highly orthodox Holy Roman emperor Charles V. The first phase of the English Reformation was thus a monarchial reformation.

Henry VII had initiated closer relations with Spain when he married his eldest son Arthur, prince of Wales, to Ferdinand of Aragon's daughter Catherine. After Arthur's death the future Henry VIII was married to Catherine in 1509. Henry VIII later tried to further the Anglo-imperial alliance when he arranged a treaty by which the emperor Charles V, who was Catherine of Aragon's nephew, agreed to marry Henry's daughter Mary Tudor. But by the late 1520s the Anglo-imperial alliance was broken when Charles, responding to Spanish pressures, renounced the proposed marriage and instead married a Portuguese princess.

Map 16.2 Protestants and Catholics in 1555 Christendom in Western Europe was divided into three major groups. Lutheran influence was largely confined to parts of Germany and Scandinavia, while Calvinist influence spread from Switzerland into Scotland, the Low Countries, and parts of France. Most of the West, however, remained within the Roman Church.

Henry's relations with Charles were further weakened by the king's determination to divorce Catherine of Aragon. Recalling the unrest of the Wars of the Roses, Henry believed that he needed a son to ensure that the Tudors could maintain control of the English crown. By 1527 Henry and Catherine had a daughter Mary but no living sons. Henry became convinced that he remained without a male heir because, by biblical standards, he had committed incest by marrying his brother's widow. As Leviticus 20:21 says, "If a man takes his brother's wife, it is impurity;... they shall remain childless." Henry desired an annulment. Unfortunately for him, Leo X's successor Pope Clement VII (r. 1523–1534) was a virtual prisoner of imperial troops who had recently sacked Rome and taken control of most of Italy. As long as Charles supported Catherine of Aragon and his forces occupied Rome, there would be no possibility of a papally sanctioned annulment of the marriage.

The king's advisers quickly divided into two camps. Sir Thomas More, the royal chancellor and a staunch Catholic, urged the king to continue his policy of negotiation with the papacy and his efforts to destroy the growing Protestant party. Until his resignation in 1532, More led royal authorities in a vigorous campaign against the dissemination of the newly translated Tyndale Bible and against the spread of Protestant ideas. More was opposed and eventually ousted by a radical party of Protestants led by Thomas Cranmer (1489–1556) and Thomas Cromwell (1485?–1540), who saw in the king's desire for a divorce an effective wedge to pry Henry out of the papal camp. Cromwell, who eventually replaced More as chancellor, advised the king that the marriage problem could be solved by the English clergy without papal interference.

Between 1532 and 1535 Henry and Parliament took a number of steps that effectively left the king in control of the English church. Early in 1533 Cranmer was named archbishop of Canterbury. Later in the year Parliament ruled that appeals of cases concerning wills, marriages, and ecclesiastical grants had to be heard in England. In May an English court annulled the king's marriage to Catherine. Four months later, Henry's new queen, Anne Boleyn, gave birth to a daughter, Elizabeth.

Even before Cromwell became chancellor, Henry had attacked absentee clergy, restricted church courts, and prohibited the payment of certain papal taxes. After the split began, the king began to secularize church properties. Parliamentary action culminated in the passage of the Act of Supremacy in 1534, which declared the king to be "the Protector and only Supreme Head of the Church and the Clergy of England" (see the box, "The Act of Supremacy"). Henry meant to enforce his control by requiring a public oath supporting the act. Sir Thomas More refused to take the oath and was arrested, tried, and executed for treason. In some respects, Parliament had acted as an instrument of reform, much like the town councils of the German and Swiss towns that moderated debates over the reform of the church. In England, however, Parliament and perhaps a majority of the laity perceived this monarchial reformation primarily as a political issue.

Cromwell and Cranmer had hoped to use the "King's Great Matter" as a way to begin a Lutheran-style reform of the church. But, though separated from the papal party, Henry remained suspicious of religious changes. Although he continued to object to the parts of the older tradition that he called "idolatry and other evil and naughty ceremonies," he rejected the Protestant understanding of justification and what anti-Protestant critics called "bibliolatry." He complained of radicals who "do wrest and interpret and so untruly allege [novel understandings of Scripture] to subvert and overturn as well the sacraments of Holy Church as the power and authority of princes and magistrates." Between 1534 and Henry's death in 1547, neither the Protestant nor the Catholic party was able to gain the upper hand at court or in the English church. Substantive changes in the English church would be made by Henry's children.

Reform and Counter-Reform Under Edward and Mary

Prince Edward, Henry's only surviving son in 1547, was born to Henry's third wife, Jane Seymour. He was only 10 years old at his father's death. By chance, Edward Seymour, who was Prince Edward's uncle, and the Protestant faction

The Act of Supremacy

As befits a document dealing with the "King's Great Matter," the Act of Supremacy is entirely practical. It makes an interesting comparison with Luther's discussion of clerical authority in his "Address to the Christian Nobility" (see the box on page 585). The Act of Supremacy is the constitutional basis for the subsequent development of the Church of England.

Albeit the King's Majesty justly and rightfully is and oweth [is held] to be the supreme head of the Church of England, and so is recognized by the clergy of their realm in their Convocations; yet nevertheless for corroboration and confirmation thereof, . . . and to repress and extirp all errors, heresies, and other enormities and abuses heretofore used in the same, Be it enacted . . . that the King our sovereign lord, his heirs, and successors kings of this realm, shall be taken, accepted, and reputed to be the only supreme head in earth of the Church of England called the Anglican Church, and shall have and enjoy annexed and united to the imperial crown of this realm as well the title and style thereof as all honours, dignities, pre-eminences, jurisdictions, privileges, authorities, immunities, profits, and commodities, to the said dignity of the supreme head of the same Church. . . . And that our sovereign lord, his heirs, and successors kings of this realm, shall have full power and authority from time to time to visit, repress, redress, reform, order, correct, restrain, and amend all such errors, heresies, abuses, offenses, contempts, and enormities, whatsoever they be, which by any manner, spiritual authority, or jurisdiction ought or may lawfully be reformed . . . most to the pleasure of Almighty God, the increase of virtue in Christ's religion, and for the conservancy of the peace, unity, and tranquillity of this realm.

Source: C. H. Williams, ed., *English Historical Documents, 1485–1558* (New York: Oxford University Press, 1967), pp. 745–746.

were in favor at the time of Henry's death. Seymour was named duke of Somerset and Lord Protector of the young king Edward VI (r. 1547–1553). Under Somerset, the Protestants were able to make significant changes in religious life in England. The Protestant party quickly changed the nature of the Eucharist, allowing the laity to take both bread and wine in the Protestant manner. The process of confiscating properties belonging to chapels and shrines was completed under Edward. In an act of great symbolic meaning, priests were legally allowed to marry; many had already done so. Finally, Archbishop Cranmer introduced the first edition of the English Book of Common Prayer in 1549. The book updated some late medieval English prayers and combined them with liturgical and theological ideas taken from Luther, Zwingli, and Calvin. In its beautifully expressive English, it provided the laity with a primer on how to combine English religious traditions with reform theology. Later, continental Protestants were named to teach theology at Oxford and Cambridge. If Edward had not died of tuberculosis in 1553, England's reform would have looked very much like the changes that occurred in Switzerland and southern Germany.

Protestant reformers attempted to prevent Mary Tudor (r. 1553–1558), Henry's Catholic daughter, from claiming the throne, but Mary and the Catholic party quickly moved into control of the court and the church. Mary immediately declared previous reform decrees to be void. Cardinal Reginald Pole (1500–1558), who

THE ENGLISH REFORM

1509	Accession of Henry VIII
1532	Thomas More, a Catholic, resigns as chancellor of England
1533	Thomas Cranmer, a Protestant, is named archbishop of Canterbury
1534	Parliament passes the Act of Supremacy
1547	Death of Henry VIII; accession of Edward VI and strengthening of Protestant influence
1549	Publication of the Book of Common Prayer
1553	Death of Edward VI; accession of Mary and return of English church to papal authority
1558	Death of Mary; accession of Elizabeth
1559	Parliament passes Acts of Supremacy and Uniformity

had advocated reform within the Catholic church, became the center of the Catholic restoration party in Mary's England. Pole rooted out Protestants within the church. More than eight hundred gentlemen, clerics, and students fled England for the Protestant parts of the Continent. Three hundred mostly humble artisans and laborers were tried and executed by church courts, earning the queen her nickname "Bloody Mary."

The policies of the queen brought about an abrupt return of the English church to papal authority. Most of the English quickly and easily returned to traditional religious practices. Statues were removed from hiding and restored to places of honor in churches and chapels. Although there is no conclusive evidence, the queen's initial successes may indicate that the Reformation was not broadly supported by the people. In fact, the restoration of Catholicism by Mary might have worked if the queen had not died after little more than six years on the throne. At her death there was still no clear indication of what the final settlement of the reform would be in England.

The Elizabethan Settlement

Queen Elizabeth (r. 1558–1603), daughter of Anne Boleyn, succeeded to the throne at the death of her half-sister. The reign of Elizabeth was one of the most enigmatic and successful of English history. She managed to gain control of the various political and religious factions in the country and play off a variety of international powers against each other. She seems to have understood well the necessity of striking a balance between opposing forces.

Her first great problem was a religious settlement. Early in her reign she twice left church services at the elevation of the bread by the priest. Since in Catholic thought it was the action of the priest that made Christ present in the bread, she was indicating symbolically her opposition to a purely Catholic understanding of the sacraments. In the next few years she continued to work for the restoration of many features of her father's and her half-brother's reforms. In 1559 the new Act of Supremacy and an Act of Uniformity reinstituted royal control of the English church and re-established uniform liturgical and doctrinal standards. The Book of Common Prayer composed by Cranmer was brought back, and final changes were made in the liturgy of the church.

Protestants had hoped for a complete victory, but the "Elizabethan Settlement" was considerably less than that. Although figures are lacking, it is likely that a large portion of the English population did not support a return to Henry's and Edward's reforms. After making clear her significant differences with Rome, Elizabeth confounded her most fervent Protestant supporters by offering a number of concessions to Anglo-Catholics. She herself remained celibate, and she ordered the Anglican clergy to do the same—although there was little she could do to prevent clerical marriage. More important, she and her closest advisers allowed a great variety of customs and practices favored by Anglo-Catholics. These matters, the queen's supporters argued, were not essential to salvation, and thus individuals could be allowed to choose. Many of the prayers in the Book of Common Prayer, for example, seemed "papist" to the most radical Protestants. Similarly, many of the traditional clerical vestments and altar cloths remained unchanged.

Elizabeth probably knew that the Protestants had no alternative to supporting her and thus felt free to win back the support of the Anglo-Catholics.

In fact, from the 1570s Elizabeth seems to have been especially concerned to regain control of insubordinate clerics. In these years the main outlines of her religious settlement became clear. She created a reformed liturgy that seemed acceptable to both Protestants and Catholics. At the same time she retained the parish and diocesan structure of the medieval church. She seems to have been most careful to restrict theological debate to the universities.

Toward the end of Elizabeth's reign, Richard Hooker (1554–1600) published his *Laws of Ecclesiastical Polity,* which provides an excellent description of the Anglican (English) church born of the Elizabethan Settlement. England, Hooker maintains, has its own way of handling religious affairs. Theologically it represents a middle way between the traditions cultivated by the Roman church and the more radically biblical religion favored by the Lutherans of Germany and the Calvinists of Switzerland. The Church of England moderated Luther's and Calvin's absolute reliance on Scriptures with history and tradition. In areas where tradition was strong, processions and other pre-Reformation traditions continued to animate village life. In other areas, more austere reformed practices were likely to predominate.

The development of the Anglican church during the reign of Elizabeth was an important part of the political and constitutional changes that were occurring in England during the sixteenth century. One result of Henry VIII's need for a divorce was the increased prestige of the English Parliament as the source of all legal authority within the realm. Only laws created by Parliament were licit. In effect, Parliament, king, and Anglican church had no earthly overlord. The disruptions of the reform period have also been credited with redistributing power at court. The Tudor kings were clearly the center of patronage, power, and influence within the realm. Henry and Elizabeth were especially adept at manipulating parties by granting privileges and titles. Henry and his children seem to have presided over a sizable expansion of the royal bureaucracy. Thus, the restructuring of the Anglican church, with the sovereign exercising religious authority and the archbishop of Canterbury as a royal official, paralleled the expansion of royal power throughout the realm.

Reform in Other States

In England and in the empire of Charles V the success of the new religious ideas depended greatly on the political situation. It would be naive to conclude, as Luther claimed, that "the Word did everything." Yet this complex religious reform movement cannot be reduced to the politics of kings and princes. The issues will be clearer if we survey politics and reform in the rest of Europe, noting whether and to what extent the new ideas took root.

France

Luther's work, and later the ideas of the urban reformers of southwestern Germany and Switzerland, passed quickly and easily into France. Geneva is in a French-speaking area close to the French border. It, like Strasbourg, was easy for French Protestants to reach. Perhaps because of France's proximity to the Calvinists in French-speaking Switzerland or because of the clarity and power of Calvin's *Institutes,* French Protestants were tied more closely to the Calvinists of Geneva than to the Lutherans of Germany.

It is difficult, however, to know how many French Christians were Protestants. At the height of the Reformation's popularity, Protestants probably represented no more than 10 percent of the total population of France. It has been estimated that there were about 2100 Protestant congregations in the 1560s—in a country that had perhaps 32,000 traditional parish congregations. Protestants seem to have been a diverse mix that included two of the three most important noble families at court: the Bourbon and the Montmorency families. Clerics interested in moral reform and artisans who worked at new trades, like the printing industry, also made up a significant portion of the converts. As a group Protestants tended to be of higher-than-average literacy even if they were not necessarily among the most prestigious lords in French society. The Protestant

The Conversion of Jeanne d'Albret

Jeanne d'Albret was the niece of King Francis I and mother of Henry of Navarre, the future Henry IV. In this letter she explains the pressures to remain Catholic and why she chose to become Protestant. After her conversion, her court became a center of the Protestant movement in the south of France.

I am writing to tell you that up to now I have followed in the footsteps of the deceased Queen, my most honored mother . . . in the matter of hesitation between the two religions. . . . [She was] warned by her late brother the King, Francis I, . . . not to get new doctrines in her head so that from then on she confined herself to amusing stories. . . . Besides, I well remember how long ago, the late King [of Navarre], my most honored father . . . surprised the said queen when she was praying in her rooms with the [Protestant] ministers Roussel and Farel, and how with great annoyance he slapped her right cheek and forbade her sharply to meddle in matters of doctrine. He shook a stick at me which cost me many bitter tears and has kept me fearful and compliant until after they had both died. Now that I am freed by the death of my said father two months ago . . . a reform seems so right and so necessary that, for my part, I consider that it would be disloyalty and cowardice to God, to my conscience and to my people to remain any longer in a state of suspense and indecision. . . .

Source: Nancy L. Roelker, trans., *Queen of Navarre: Jeanne d'Albret, 1528–1572* (Cambridge, Mass.: Harvard University Press, 1968), p. 127 (slightly adapted).

population was spread throughout the country. Protestants were well represented in towns; they were probably a numerical majority in the southern and western towns of La Rochelle, Montpellier, and Nîmes. Paris was the one part of the realm in which they had little influence, and their absence in the capital may have been their undoing.

The conservative theologians of the Sorbonne in Paris were some of Luther's earliest opponents. They complained that many masters at the University of Paris were "Lutheran." As early as 1523 Parisian authorities seized and burned books said to be by Luther. But as in Germany, there was no clear understanding of who or what a Lutheran was. The Sorbonne theologians were suspicious of a number of "pre-reformers," including Jacques Lefèvre d'Étaples (1450–1537), who late in life had come to an understanding of justification quite like Luther's. Others were clerics who were intent on religious reform within the traditional structures. Unlike Luther and the Huguenots, these pre-reformers did not challenge the priests' relationship to the sacraments. They were interested in the piety and behavior of churchmen. They never challenged the role of the clergy in salvation. The king's own sister, Margaret of Angoulême (1492–1549), gathered a group of religious persons at her court, even including several reformers (see the box, "The Conversion of Jeanne d'Albret"). But Margaret herself urged that theology be left to scholars; she believed that the laity should stick to simple pieties. Like Margaret, most French Christians had no clear sense that Protestant teachings required a complete break with medieval Christian traditions.

Like previous French kings, Francis I (r. 1515–1547) hoped to extend royal jurisdictions in France and make France an international power. Engaged in the seemingly intractable wars with the Habsburgs, Francis generally ignored religious questions. In 1525, he was taken captive in the wake of a military disaster at Pavia in Lombardy. He was held prisoner for nearly a year, during which time conservatives at the Sorbonne and in Paris moved actively against suspected Protestants. Francis was not initially opposed to what seemed to be moral reform within the church. His own view was that the king's duty was to preserve order and prevent scandal, and at first carrying out that duty meant protecting reformers whom the conservative militants persecuted. The king feared disorder more than he feared religious reform.

On October 18, 1534, however, Francis's attitude changed when he and all Paris awoke to find the city covered with anti-Catholic placards containing, in the words of the writers, "true articles on the horrible, great and insufferable abuses of the Papal Mass." The response of the Parisians was immediate and hostile. They attacked foreigners, especially those who by dress or speech seemed "Lutheran"—that is, German or Flemish. Several months later Francis himself led a religious procession through Paris in honor of the Blessed Sacrament. The "Affair of the Placards" changed Francis's ideas about the sources of disorder. Opposition to traditional religious practices became more difficult and more dangerous. John Calvin himself was forced to leave Paris and eventually France because he feared persecution. Between 1534 and 1560, some ten thousand Protestants fled France, many joining Calvin in Geneva.

Francis I died in 1547, and for the next forty years France suffered from almost unstoppable political and religious turmoil. Francis's son and grandsons proved incapable of controlling the nobles at court. Henry II (r. 1547–1559) was weak willed and easily led by a variety of courtiers. After his accidental death in the celebrations marking the signing of the Treaty of Cateau-Cambrésis, he was succeeded by his three young sons. The sons were thoroughly controlled by their Florentine mother, Catherine de' Medici (1519–1589), who was widely disliked as an outsider and a bourgeois besides. She tried to control the situation by playing one court faction off against another. Thus, she occasionally sought support from the Protestant as well as the Catholic faction.

One faction coalesced around the Guise family from Lorraine in the east of France. The duke of Guise and his brother, the cardinal of Lorraine, quickly became the leaders of a conservative Catholic faction with strong ties to the anti-Protestant leaders of Paris and to the king of Spain. They were opposed by members of the Montmorency and Bourbon families, who had strong connections in the south of France. The Guises were probably the strongest; the Bourbons had the firmest claim to the French crown. Matters took a deadly turn when the duke of Guise loosed a party of soldiers on twelve hundred Huguenot worshipers at Vassy in the early 1560s, killing several dozen. In revenge, Protestants led by the Bourbon Prince Condé assassinated the duke of Guise in 1562. The wave of violence continued into 1563.

This was the first in a series of wars lasting to 1598, usually called the "French Wars of Religion." Some of the violence, to be sure, had a religious origin. Protestants regularly interrupted services and destroyed images that they disdained as idolatrous. Yet it might be more appropriate to see the wars as an extended vendetta between two noble factions—the Guises and the Bourbons—both of whom hoped to defend and even expand their influence at court and in the society at large.

Early in the 1570s the Huguenots seemed to be gaining the upper hand. In a desperate attempt to prevent them from gaining even more influence at court, Catherine de' Medici and Catholic extremists arranged in August 1572 the assassination of Admiral Gaspard de Coligny, the leading Huguenot noble, who was quite influential with the king, Charles IX (r. 1560–1574). On Saint Bartholomew's Day, extremists rushed into a feast celebrating the marriage of the Bourbon Henry of Navarre to the king's sister, massacring most of the Protestant guests. Henry, a cousin and possible heir of the childless king, escaped death by quickly abjuring the Protestant faith and fleeing to the south; he renounced his conversion as soon as he was safely out of Paris. In all, three thousand Protestants were probably killed in Paris and probably ten thousand in all of France.

The Saint Bartholomew's Day Massacre marked a dramatic shift in the fortunes of French

Saint Bartholomew's Day Massacre The murder of Coligny on Saint Bartholomew's Day set off a wave of attacks against Protestants throughout France. The attacks made clear the chasm separating the two groups and the impossibility of a complete Protestant triumph in France. *(Musée Cantonal des Beaux-Arts, Lausanne)*

Protestantism. The Huguenots fought to avenge their martyrs and to protect the territories they still held, but their confidence vanished. Catholics took heart that their country seemed to be cleansed of sacrilege. According to popular Catholic traditions, a miraculous cross in Troyes once again healed the ill, and a hawthorn bush at the Cemetery of the Holy Innocents in Paris was said to have burst into bloom on the day of the massacre.

In political terms the result of the massacre was considerably less than it first seemed. By the late 1570s it was clear to all that Henry III (r. 1574–1589) would have no children and that the Protestant Prince Henry of Navarre was the legitimate heir. When the king was assassinated in 1589, Henry of Navarre was the one remaining viable political leader, and he took the throne. In 1593, to end the civil war, Henry—now Henry IV (r. 1589–1610)—reconverted to Catholicism and began the process of healing the years of war and disorder. In 1598 he issued the Edict of Nantes (named for the city where it was made public), which proclaimed Catholicism to be the religion of the realm, prohibited Protestantism within Paris, but allowed the practice of the reformed religion in certain cities and localities of the kingdom. The Edict of Nantes brought to France religious peace that lasted for nearly a century. In the long run, France was neither converted by Protestants nor cleansed of them. By the close of the sixteenth century many of the French generally agreed with the *politiques,* thinkers who held that religious discord must not be allowed to destroy the fabric of government and society.

Eastern Europe

In some respects, a political vacuum in eastern Europe allowed for the expansion of Protestantism. The church hierarchy was not in a position to enforce orthodoxy. Some rulers were indifferent to religious debates, as were the Muslim Ottoman Turks, who controlled much of eastern Hungary and what is now Romania. Other rulers offered toleration because they could ill afford to alienate any portion of their subject populations.

Protestant ideas initially passed through the German communities of Poland and the trading towns along the Baltic coast. But in the 1540s Calvinist ideas spread quickly among the Polish nobles, especially those at the royal court. Given the power and influence of some of the noble families, Catholics were unable to suppress the various secret Calvinist congregations. During the first half of the sixteenth century, Protestantism was so well established in Poland that it could not be rooted out. Throughout the sixteenth century, Protestantism remained one of the rallying points for those opposed to the expansion of royal power.

The situation was much the same in Hungary and Romania. Among German colonists, Magyars, and ethnic Romanians there were numerous individuals who were interested first in Luther's message and later in Calvinist revisions of the reformed theology. Because no one could hope to enforce uniformity, some cities adopted a moderate Lutheran theology, and others followed a Calvinist confession. By the 1560s the Estates (representative assemblies) of Transylvania had decreed that both religions were to be tolerated. Further, when various radical groups migrated from the west in search of toleration, they too were able to create their own communities in Slavic and Magyar areas.

The Reformation was to have virtually no influence farther to the east, in Russia. The Orthodox church in Russia was much more firmly under monarchial control than was the church in the West. The Russian church followed the traditions of the Greek church, and Western arguments over justification made little sense in Orthodox churches. Given the historic suspicion of the Orthodox for Rome, the Russians were more tolerant of contacts with the Protestants of northern Europe. But there would be no theological innovation or reform in Russia.

Scandinavia

All of Scandinavia became Lutheran. Initial influences drifted north from Germany, carried by Hanseatic merchants and students who had studied at the universities of northern Germany. Yet the reform in Sweden and Denmark even more than in England was a monarchial reformation. In both Scandinavian kingdoms the kings began with an attack on the temporal rights and properties of the church. Changes in liturgy and practice came later as reformers gained the protection of the kings.

Since 1397 in theory all Scandinavia had been united in the Union of Kalmar (see page 450). But early in the sixteenth century the last pretenses of unity were shattered. Christian I of Denmark (r. 1513–1523) invaded Sweden and captured Stockholm, the capital. So great was his brutality that within a few years Gustav Vasa, a leading noble, was able to secure the loyalty of most of the Swedes and in 1523 was elected king of Sweden. Gustav's motto was "All power is of God." Like Henry VIII of England, Gustav (r. 1523–1560) moved carefully in an attempt to retain the loyalty of as many groups as possible. Although he never formally adopted a national confession of faith, the church and Swedish state gradually took on a more Lutheran character. In an effort to secure royal finances, the Riksdag, or parliament, passed the Västerås Ordinances, which secularized ecclesiastical lands and authorized the preaching of the "Pure Word of God." Olaus Petri (1493–1552), Sweden's principal reform preacher, was installed by royal order in the cathedral of Stockholm.

In Denmark the reformers also moved cautiously. Frederick I (r. 1523–1533) and his son Christian III (r. 1534–1559) continued the policy of secularization and control that Christian I had initiated. Danish kings seemed interested in reform as a diplomatic means of attack on the Roman church. It seems that in Denmark the old religion simply suffered from a sort of royal indifference. The kings tended to support reformers as a way to attack the political power of the bishops. The Danes finally accepted the Augsburg Confession, which was becoming the most widely accepted explanation of Lutheran belief, in 1538. The transformation of practice proceeded slowly over the next decades.

In marginal parts of Scandinavia—Finland, Iceland, and Norway—the reform was introduced as a matter of royal policy. Initially there were only a few local reformers to introduce the new theology and practice. In many regions resistance to the monarchial reformation continued for several generations. One valley hidden in the mountains of western Norway continued to follow the old religion for three centuries after its contacts with Rome had been severed.

The Second Reformation, ca. 1545–1600

In the first half of the sixteenth century, the term *Lutheran* applied to anyone who was anticlerical. As Francesco Guicciardini (1483–1540), a papal governor in central Italy, remarked:

> I know of no one who loathes the ambition, the avarice, and the sensuality of the clergy more than I. . . . In spite of all this, the positions I have held under several popes have forced me, for my own good, to further their interests. Were it not for that, I should have loved Martin Luther as much as myself—not so that I might be free of the laws based on Christian religion as it is generally interpreted and understood; but to see this bunch of rascals get their just deserts, that is, to be without vices or without authority.[5]

Guicciardini's remarks catch both the frustration many Christians felt with the traditional church and also the very real confusion over just what it was that Luther had said. In parts of Germany by the late 1520s and across Europe by the 1550s political and religious leaders attempted to make clearer to the peoples of Europe just what *Lutheran, Calvinist,* and *Catholic* had come to mean. Historians term the process of defining and explaining what each group believed, or confessed, the "Second Reformation," or "Confessionalization."

A series of profound changes began in the sixteenth century but continued into the seventeenth century. People began to sort out what it meant to belong to one church instead of to another. Central governments enforced religious uniformity as a way of enhancing the power of the state. In all parts of Europe, religious behavior was altered. Both Protestants and Catholics became more concerned with the personal rather than the communal aspects of Christianity. Many thoughtful people found it impossible to distinguish among the various claims for religious authority. It was easiest to give the power to define religious practice to the government. After the sixteenth century, the nature of Christianity and its place in public life, whether in Protestant or in Catholic countries, was profoundly different from what it had been in the Middle Ages.

Catholic Reform

Historians commonly speak of both a movement for traditional reform and renewal within the Catholic church and a "Counter-Reformation," which was a direct response to and rejection of the theological positions championed by the Protestants. It is certainly true that one can categorize certain acts as clearly challenging the Protestants and other acts as less clearly related to the challenge of reform, but to do so is to miss the point that the energetic actions of the Roman church during the sixteenth century both affirmed traditional teachings and created new institutions better fitted to the early modern world.

The idea of purer, earlier church practices to which the "modern" church should return had been a commonplace for centuries. The great ecumenical Council of Constance early in the fifteenth century had called for "reform in head and members" (see page 456). In 1512, five years before Luther made his public protests, Pope Julius II (r. 1503–1513) convened another ecumenical council, the Fifth Lateran Council (1513–1517), which was expected to look into the problems of nonresident clergy, multiple benefices, and a host of other issues. This tradition of moral reform was especially strong in Spain, Portugal, and Italy, lands where political rulers were either indifferent or opposed to Protestant reforms.

The desire for reform along traditional lines was deeply felt within the church. In the wake of the sack of Rome by imperial troops in 1527, one

Roman cardinal, Bishop Gian Matteo Giberti of Verona (1495–1543), returned to his diocese and began a thoroughgoing reform. He conducted visitations of the churches and other religious institutions in Verona, preached tirelessly, worked hard to raise the educational level of his clergy, and required that priests live within their parishes. Giberti believed that traditional reform and renewal could counter the malaise he perceived. Other reforming bishops could be found throughout Europe.

New religious foundations sprang up to renew the church. The Spanish mystic Teresa of Avila (1515–1582) reflected the thinking of many when she complained, "No wonder the Church is as it is, when the religious live as they do." Members of the new orders set out to change the church through example. The Florentine Filippo Neri (1515–1595) founded the Oratorian order, so named because of the monks' habit of leading the laity in prayer services. Filippo was joined in his work by Giovanni Palestrina (c. 1525–1594), who composed music for the modest but moving prayer gatherings in Rome. Palestrina's music combined medieval plainchants with newer styles of polyphony—creating complex harmonies without obscuring the words and meaning of the text. The popularity of the Oratorians and their services can be measured in part by the fact that oratories, small chapels modeled on those favored by Filippo, remain to this day important centers of the musical life in the city of Rome.

The Catholic reform of the sixteenth century, however, was better known for its mystical theology than for its music. In Italy, France, but especially in Spain, there was a profusion of reformers who chose to reform the church through austere prayer and contemplation. Teresa of Avila, who belonged to a wealthy converso family in Avila, led a movement to reform the lax practices within the religious houses of Spain. Famed for her rigorous religious life, her trances, and her raptures, Teresa animated a movement to reform the order of Carmelite nuns in Spain. Because of her writings about her mystical experiences she was named a "Doctor of the Church," a title reserved for the greatest of the church's theologians.

The most important of the new religious orders was the Society of Jesus, or Jesuits, founded in 1534 by Ignatius Loyola (1491–1556). A conservative Spanish nobleman, Loyola was wounded and nearly killed in battle. During a long and painful rehabilitation, he continuously read accounts of lives of the saints. After recovering, he went on a pilgrimage and experienced a profound conversion.

A Counter-Reformation Saint Saint Teresa of Avila came from a conversa family. She believed that renewal within the Christian church would come through mysticism, prayer, and a return to traditional religious practices. She founded a reformed Carmelite order of nuns to further religious renewal in Spain. *(MAS, Barcelona)*

Loyola initially meant to organize a missionary order directed at the Muslims. The structure of his order reflected his military experience. It had a well-defined chain of command leading to the general of the order and then to the pope. To educate and discipline the members, Loyola composed *Spiritual Exercises,* emphasizing the importance of obedience (see the box, "Ignatius Loyola's Spiritual Exercises"). He prohibited Jesuits from holding any ecclesiastical office that might compromise their autonomy. After papal approval of the order in 1540, the Jesuits' activities were directed primarily to education in Catholic areas and reconversion of Protestants.

Ignatius Loyola's Spiritual Exercises

Loyola intended the spiritual exercises to be a tool for meditation and prayer by which members of the Society of Jesus would grow in faith, understanding, and obedience. Loyola sets out a series of meditations that are to continue over the course of a month, culminating in a series of conclusions about the relations of individual Jesuits to the Catholic church.

The following rules are to be observed in order that we might hold the opinions we should hold in the Church militant.

We should put away completely our own opinion and keep our minds ready and eager to give our entire obedience to our holy Mother the hierarchical Church, Christ our Lord's undoubted spouse.

We should speak with approval of confession to a priest, of the reception of Holy Communion once a year, still more once a month, most of all once a week, the requisite conditions being duly fulfilled.

We should speak with approval of religious orders, and the states of virginity and celibacy, not rating matrimony as high as any of these.

We should approve of relics of the saints, showing reverence for them and praying to the saints themselves.

We should approve of the laws of fasting and abstinence in Lent . . . as well as mortifications both interior and exterior.

We should praise church decoration and architecture, as well as statues, which we should venerate in view of what they portray.

Finally all the Church's commandments should be spoken of favorably, our minds always being eager to find arguments in her defense, never in criticism.

We should be inclined to approve and speak well of the regulations and instructions as well as the personal conduct of our superiors. It may well be that these are not or have not been always praiseworthy; but to criticize them, whether in public utterances or in dealings with ordinary people, is likely to give rise to complaint and scandal rather than to do good. . . .

To arrive at complete certainty, this is the attitude of mind we should maintain: I will believe that the white object I see is black if that should be the decision of the hierarchical Church, for I believe that between Christ our Lord the Bridegroom and His Bride the Church, there is one and the same Spirit, ruling and guiding us for our soul's good.

Source: David Englander, Diana Norman, Rosemary O'Day, and W. R. Owens, eds. *Culture and Belief in Europe, 1450–1600: An Anthology of Sources* (Oxford, England: Basil Blackwell in association with the Open University, 1990), pp. 241–242.

Throughout Europe, Jesuits were famed for their work as educators of the laity and as spiritual advisers to the political leaders of Catholic Europe. In the late sixteenth and early seventeenth centuries they were responsible for a number of famous conversions, including that of Christina (1626–1689), the Lutheran queen of Sweden who abdicated her throne in 1654 and spent the rest of her life in Rome. Jesuits were especially successful in bringing many parts of the Holy Roman Empire back into communion with the papacy. They have rightly been called the vanguard of the Counter-Reformation.

During the first half of the sixteenth century, Catholics joined Protestants in calls for an ecumenical council that all believed would solve the problems dogging the Christian church. But in the unsettled political and diplomatic atmos-

The Council of Trent Delegates from throughout Christendom met in the Cathedral of Santa Maria Maggiore in Trent to deliberate on a response to the Protestants. So many were present that the nave of the church had to be reconstructed in the form of an amphitheater. *(British Museum/The Fotomas Index)*

phere that lasted into the 1540s, it was impossible to find any agreement about where or when a universal council should meet. Finally, in 1545, at a time when the hostilities between the Valois and Habsburgs had cooled, Pope Paul III (r. 1534–1549) was able to open an ecumenical council in the city of Trent, a German imperial city located on the Italian side of the Alps.

It is difficult to overemphasize the importance of the Council of Trent. Reformers within the Catholic church hoped that it would be possible to create a broadly based reform party within the church and that the council would define theological positions acceptable to the Protestants, making reunion possible. Unfortunately for the reformers, conservatives quickly took over the Italian-controlled council.

The Council of Trent sat in three sessions between 1545 and 1563. The initial sessions were clearly meant to mark the boundaries between Protestant heresy and the orthodox positions of the Catholic church. In response to the Protestant emphasis on Scriptures, the council said that the Church always recognized the validity of traditional customs and understandings. Delegates rejected the humanists' work on the text of the Bible, declaring that the Latin Vulgate edition compiled by Jerome was the authorized text. In response to the widely held Protestant belief that salvation came through faith alone, the council declared that good works were not merely the outcome of faith but were prerequisites to salvation. The council rejected Protestant positions on the sacraments, the giving of wine to the laity during Holy Communion, the marriage of clergy, and the granting of indulgences.

Protestant critics often list these positions and conclude that the work of the council was merely negative. To do so, however, is to ignore the many ways in which the decrees of the council were an essential part of the creation of the Roman Catholic church that would function for the next four centuries. The delegates at Trent generally felt that the real cause of the Protestant movement was the lack of leadership and supervision within the church. Many of the acts of the council dealt with that issue. First, the council affirmed Apostolic Succession—the idea that the authority of a bishop is transmitted through a succession of bishops, ultimately leading back through the popes to Saint Peter. Thus, the council underlined the ultimate authority of the pope in administrative as well as theological matters. The council ordered that local bishops should reside in their dioceses, that they should establish seminaries to see to the education of parish clergy, and that, through regular visitation and supervision, they should make certain that the laity participated in the sacramental life of the church. At the final sessions of the council the nature of the Roman Catholic church was summed up in the Creed of Pius IV, which like the Lutheran Augsburg Confession summarized the basic position of the church.

Confessionalization

The labors of the Jesuits and the deliberations of the Council of Trent at midcentury made clear that reconciliation between the Protestant reformers and the Catholic church was not possible. Signs of the recognition of the permanence of the separation were the flight of several important Protestant religious leaders from Italy in the late 1540s and the wholesale migration of Protestant communities from Modena, Lucca, and other Italian towns to Switzerland. These actions signify the beginnings of the theological, political, and social separation of "Protestant" and "Catholic" in European society.

The theological separation was marked in a number of visual and symbolic ways. Churches in which both bread and wine were distributed to the laity during the sacrament of Holy Communion passed from Catholic to Protestant. Churches in which the altar was moved forward to face the congregation but the statuary was retained were likely to be Lutheran. Churches in which statues were destroyed and all other forms of art were removed were likely to be Calvinist. Even matters like singing differentiated the churches. There was in the Lutheran tradition an increased emphasis on congregational singing and on the use of music within the worship service. Countless pastors in the sixteenth and seventeenth centuries followed Luther in composing hymns and even theoretical tracts on music. This tradition would reach its zenith in the church music of Johann Sebastian Bach (1685–1750).

Although Catholics, especially in Italy, did not ignore church music, it was really architecture that distinguished Catholic churches from Protestant churches in the late sixteenth and seventeenth centuries. In Rome, the great religious orders built new churches in the Baroque style. Baroque artists and architects absorbed all the classical lessons of the Renaissance and then went beyond them, sometimes deliberately violating them. Baroque art celebrates the supernatural, the ways in which God is not bound by the laws of nature. Where Renaissance art was meant to depict nature, Baroque paintings and sculpture seemed to defy gravity. The work celebrated the supernatural power and splendor of the papacy. This drama and power are clear in the construction of the Jesuit Church of the Jesù in Rome and especially in Gianlorenzo Bernini's (1598–1680) throne of Saint Peter made for the church of St. Peter in the Vatican. The construction of Baroque churches, first in Spain and Italy but especially in the Catholic parts of Germany, created yet another boundary between an austere Protestantism and a visual and mystical Catholicism.

All of the confessions in the late sixteenth century emphasized education, right doctrine, and social control. In Catholic areas there was renewed concern with private confession by the laity to ensure a proper understanding of doctrine. During this period Charles Borromeo, archbishop of Milan (1538–1584), introduced the private confessional box, which isolated priest and penitent from the prying ears of the community. As early as the 1520s some Lutheran princes had begun visitations to ensure that the laity understood basic doctrine. In Protestant countries pastors used catechisms, handbooks containing instruction for the laity. The first and most famous was by Luther himself. Luther's *Small Catechism* includes the Lord's Prayer, Ten Commandments, and Apostles' Creed along with simple, clear explanations of what they mean. More than Catholic rulers, Protestant rulers used church courts to enforce discipline within the community.

By the seventeenth century, churchmen, like state officials, were intent on enforcing what they understood to be true Christianity. Yet this true religion was much less a public and communal religion than medieval Catholicism had been. Medieval Christians had worried greatly about public sins that complicated life in a community. In the age of confessionalization, theologians—both Protestant and Catholic—worried about the moral status and interior life of individuals. Sexual sins and gluttony now seemed more dangerous than economic sins like avarice or usury.

In all parts of Europe officials of the church were preoccupied with the control and supervision of the laity. Semireligious popular celebrations such as May Day, harvest feasts, and the Feast of Fools had their origins in popular myths and practices that preceded Christianity. Churchmen criticized these celebrations because they seemed to encourage superstition and because they mocked the social and political order with, for example, parodies of fat or ignorant clergy and foolish magistrates.

Religious authorities also were concerned by what seemed to be out-of-control mysticism and dangerous religious practices, especially among women. The impact of the Reformation on the status of women has often been debated. The Protestant position is that the Reformation freed women from the cloistered control of traditional convents. Critics of the Reformation counter that a convent was one of very few organizations that a woman could administer and direct. Women who took religious vows, Catholics point out, could engage in intellectual and religious pursuits similar to those enjoyed by men. The Protestants' destruction of religious houses for women destroyed one of the few alternatives that women had to life in an authoritarian, patriarchal society.

Art and Reform This painting of the intercession of the Virgin Mary in favor of Naples is a typical piece of Counter-Reformation art. It celebrates the power of patron saints and suggests, in the prostrated figures of Luther and Calvin, the powerlessness of Protestantism. *(Alinari/Art Resource, NY)*

In fact, in the late sixteenth and early seventeenth centuries, both Protestant and Catholic authorities viewed with suspicion any signs of religious independence by women. In the first years of the Reformation, some women did leave convents, eager to participate in the reform of the church. Early in the 1520s some women wrote tracts concerning the morality of the clergy. Lutheran and Calvinist theologians, however, argued that a woman's religious vocation should be in the Christian care and education of her family. Religious women in Catholic convents were required to subordinate their mysticism to the guidance they received from male spiritual advisers. Calvinist theologians were similarly suspicious of the theological and spiritual insights of

Protestant women. For the laity in general and for women in particular, confessionalization brought increased control by authorities.

The Authority of the State

One result of the Reformation was the strengthening of state control over religious life. Most magistrates would probably have agreed with the king of Sweden, Gustav Vasa: "These old bishops almost always did great harm to the princes and lords of the kingdom through their disobedient and rebellious actions, parties and companies." Confessionalization certainly allowed magistrates to increase their control over religious institutions.

One reason why the laity allowed monarchs to make extreme claims of sovereignty was simply that after decades of war and unrest, most people were willing to defer on religious questions in order to preserve society from further civil war. One of the theorists of state power was the Frenchman Jean Bodin (1530–1596), who in *Six Books of the Republic* (1576) argued that virtue was to be found in the preservation of peace and justice by a strong, absolute sovereign. *Politiques,* as those who held views like Bodin's were known in France, argued that the nobility was using religion as an excuse to attack the monarchy. Religious doctrine, they concluded, should not be a vehicle for the destruction of government. To the politiques, Henry IV's decision to reconvert to Catholicism to heal the divisions within the state was a just decision.

Many of the politiques put the state first simply because they no longer believed that it was possible to rationally determine the truth in religious matters. Drawing on a philosophical tradition reaching back to the Hellenistic period, these skeptics, both Protestant and Catholic, attacked their opponents by demonstrating that their beliefs were based on experience rather than on reason. "No reason can be established without another reason," the French essayist Michel de Montaigne (1533–1592) concluded; otherwise "there we go retreating back to infinity." Montaigne did not stop there. If we cannot know anything with certainty, he said, it would be folly to make war against or to execute our religious enemies. Tolerance and conformity to public standards seemed the best policy.

Jean Bodin went even further. In *The Dialogue of the Seven Sages,* which he composed in the 1580s, Bodin tells of a meeting in which a Lutheran, a Catholic, a Muslim, a Jew, and a skeptical philosopher debate the nature of religion. The Catholic tends to ignore issues, and the Lutheran makes absolute statements. The Jew and the skeptic seem to have the best of the argument. Whatever Bodin's own views, his dialogue made clear that he like Montaigne was unwilling to believe that people can know absolutely the truth of any religious system. Politiques in most parts of Europe thought that religious truth was a precarious foundation for the fundamental power of the state.

Summary

Throughout the sixteenth century, Europe experienced a number of profound shocks. The medieval assumption that there was a unified Christendom in the West was shattered. The Protestant challenge did not simply attack the institutional structure or the moral lapses as previous heretical movements had done. The early reformers rejected the very nature of the medieval church. Peasants and artisans argued that Luther's message of Christian freedom liberated them from both economic and spiritual oppression.

Monarchies and republics throughout Europe came to view religious institutions and religious choices as matters of state. When faced by theological challenges and cries for moral reform, governments reacted in ways that offered religious change and bolstered the claims of secular government. In England and Sweden, calls for reform resulted in the secularization of church property, which put vast new sources of wealth in the hands of the kings. In the towns of Germany and Switzerland, governments redoubled their efforts to regulate religion and moral life. Thus, both Reformation and Counter-Reformation brought about a significant strengthening of government power.

Ironically, the reforms that Luther and other Protestants advocated on the basis of clear, incontrovertible religious truths eventually led to the suspicion that no truths could be known with certainty. Religious strife led some to conclude that in matters of religion toleration was the only appropriate option. Others concluded that if the truth could not be known, the state must be allowed to make the big decisions. And the states of the seventeenth century were quite willing to do so.

Notes

1. Martin Luther, *Works,* vol. 34 (Philadelphia: Fortress Press, 1955; St. Louis: Concordia Publishing House, 1986), pp. 336–337.
2. Quoted in Steven Ozment, *The Age of Reform, 1250–1550* (New Haven: Yale University Press, 1980), p. 245.
3. Quoted in Robert W. Scribner, *The German Reformation* (London: Macmillan, 1986), p. 32.
4. Quoted in Euan Cameron, *The European Reformation* (Oxford, England: Clarendon Press, 1991), pp. 106–107.
5. Francesco Guicciardini, *Maxims and Reflections (Ricordi),* trans. Mario Domandi (Philadelphia: University of Pennsylvania Press, 1965), p. 48.

Suggested Reading

General Surveys

Bossy, John. *Christianity in the West, 1400–1700.* 1985. A subtle, important essay arguing that the Reformation ended communal Christianity and created in its place a more personal religion emphasizing individual self-control.

Cameron, Euan. *The European Reformation.* 1991. The best recent history of the Reformation, emphasizing the common principles of the major reformers.

Chatellier, Louis. *The Europe of the Devout: The Catholic Reformation and the Formation of a New Society.* 1989. An important study of the reconstruction of Catholic Christianity in the late sixteenth century.

Chaunu, Pierre, ed. *The Reformation.* 1989. A colorfully illustrated general history of the Reformation containing essays on the major events.

Davidson, Nicholas S. *The Counter Reformation.* 1987. A short introduction emphasizing how the accomplishments of the Council of Trent laid the basis for a Catholic revival.

Dickens, Arthur G. and John Tonkin. *The Reformation in Historical Thought.* 1985. A comprehensive survey of debates over the meanings of the Reformation, beginning with the earliest historians and continuing into the twentieth century.

Eisenstein, Elizabeth. *The Printing Revolution in Early Modern Europe.* 1983. A general study of the printing revolution that includes a chapter on the importance of printing in the spread of reform.

Englander, Diana, Diana Norman, Rosemary O'Day, and W. R. Owens, eds. *Culture and Belief in Europe, 1450–1600: An Anthology of Sources.* 1990. A collection of documents illustrating religious and social values and giving an excellent overview of popular reform.

O'Connell, Marvin R. *The Counter Reformation, 1559–1610.* 1974. A very good general introduction to the theology and politics of reform in Catholic Europe.

Ozment, Steven. *The Age of Reform, 1250–1550.* 1980. A clear, well-written introduction to late medieval and Reformation religious ideas, emphasizing the ways in which reformers transformed medieval theological debates.

Schilling, Heinz, ed. *Religion, Political Culture, and the Emergence of Early Modern Society.* 1992. A demanding collection of essays on the organization and regulation of Protestant churches in Germany and the Netherlands, making clear the way in which the new churches disciplined their members.

The Reformers

Bainton, Roland H. *Here I Stand: A Life of Martin Luther.* 1978. First published in 1950 but still an excellent introduction to the life of the reformer.

Bouwsma, William. *John Calvin: A Sixteenth-Century Portrait.* 1987. An important but demanding book on Calvin, emphasizing his debt to the humanist movements of the fifteenth and sixteenth centuries.

Cargill Thompson, William D. J. *The Political Thought of Martin Luther.* 1986. A comprehensive analysis of the political implications of Luther's theological writings.

Dillenberger, John, ed. *Martin Luther: Selections from His Writings.* 1961. An excellent collection of writings that allows readers to follow the evolution of Luther's thought.

McGrath, Alister E. *A Life of John Calvin: A Study in the Shaping of Western Culture.* 1990. An excellent biography emphasizing the definitive role of Calvin's religious thought.

Oberman, Heiko, A. *Luther: Man Between God and the Devil.* 1989. A brilliant, beautifully written essay connecting Luther to prevailing late medieval ideas about sin, death, and the devil.

Potter, George R. and Mark Greengrass, eds. *John Calvin.* 1983. Selections from Calvin's most important works, along with short introductions.

Reformation in Particular Lands

Brady, Thomas A. *Turning Swiss: Cities and Empire, 1450–1550.* 1985. A masterful history of the political and ideological concerns of the townsmen of southwestern Germany.

Weighing the Evidence

A REFORMATION WOODCUT

Erhard Schön's 1533 woodcut "There Is No Greater Treasure Here on Earth Than an Obedient Wife Who Desires Honor" and other broadsheets like it informed and amused Europeans of all walks of life in the late fifteenth and sixteenth centuries. Schön's image of a henpecked husband and his wife followed by others would have been instantly recognizable to most people. The texts along the bottom made clear the message implied in the woodcut itself. But how may we, centuries later, "read" this message? How does the modern historian analyze Schön's broadsheet to investigate popular ideas about social roles, religion, and politics? What do it and similar broadsheets tell us about popular responses to the social and religious tumults of the sixteenth century?

Look at the simple and clear lines of the woodcut. They give a clue about the popularity of broadsheets. They were cheap and easy to produce and were printed on inexpensive paper. Artists would sketch an image that an artisan would later carve onto a block. A printer could produce a thousand or more copies from a single block. Even famous artists like Albrecht Dürer (see page 535) sold highly profitable prints on religious, political, and cultural themes.

Almost anyone could afford broadsheets. Laborers and modest merchants decorated their houses with pictures on popular themes. In the middle of the fifteenth century, before the Reformation, most images were of saints. It was widely believed, for example, that anyone who looked at an image of Saint Christopher would not die on that day.

During the political and religious unrest of the sixteenth century, artists increasingly produced images that referred to the debates over religion. Schön himself made his living in Nuremberg producing and selling woodcuts. He and other artists in the city were closely tuned to the attitudes of the local population. One popular image was entitled "The Roman Clergy's Procession into Hell."

Schön's image reproduced here reflected a worry shared by both Protestants and Catholics: the rebellious nature of women. Evidence suggests that women in the late fifteenth and sixteenth centuries may have been marrying at a later age and thus were likely to be more independent-minded than their younger sisters. The ranks of single women were swollen by widows and by former nuns who had left convents and liberated themselves from male supervision. Thus, it was not difficult for men in the sixteenth century to spot women who seemed unnecessarily independent of male control.

Let us turn again to the woodcut, to see what worried villagers and townsmen and how Schön visualized their fears. Notice the henpecked husband. He is harnessed to a cart carrying laundry. Both the harness and the laundry were popular images associated with women's duties. During popular festivals, German villagers often harnessed unmarried women to a plow to signify that they were shirking their duty by not marrying and raising children. Doing the laundry was popularly thought to be the first duty that a powerful wife would force on her weak-kneed husband. Countless other images show women, whip in hand, supervising foolish husbands as they pound diapers with a laundry flail. "Woe is me," says the poor man, all this because "I took a wife." As if the message were not clear enough, look at what the woman carries in her left hand: his purse, his sword, and his pants (the question "Who wears the pants in the family?" was as familiar then as now). But the woman responds that he is in this position not because of marriage but because he has been carousing: "If you will not work to support me, then you must wash, spin, and draw the cart."[1]

1. Keith Moxey, *Peasants, Warriors and Wives: Popular Imagery in the Reformation* (Chicago: University of Chicago Press, 1989), pp. 108–109; includes a translation of portions of the texts in the broadsheet.

Schön: There Is No Greater Treasure Here on Earth Than an Obedient Wife Who Desires Honor *(Gotha, Schlossmuseum)*

The figures following the cart are commenting on the situation. The young journeyman is asking the young maiden at his side, "What do you say about this?" She responds, "I have no desire for such power." The woman dressed as a fool counsels the young man never to marry and thus to avoid anxiety and suffering. But an old man, identified as "the wise man," closes the procession and ends the debate over marriage. "Do not listen to this foolish woman," he counsels. "God determines how your life together will be, so stay with her in love and suffering and always be patient."

If we think about this woodcut's images and texts, we can understand the contrary hopes and fears in sixteenth-century Germany. Like the young woman, the Christian wife was expected to avoid claiming power either inside or outside the home. Martin Luther concluded that "the husband is the head of the wife even as Christ is head of the Church. . . . Therefore as the Church is subject to Christ, so let wives be subject to their husbands in everything."[2] Authority was to be in the hands of husbands and fathers. But if the good wife was required to avoid power, the good husband was also expected to follow Luther's precepts for the Christian family. As the wise old man observes, the husband must be a loving and forgiving master.

Schön's woodcut and others similar to it should remind you of the "Quarrel over Women" discussed in Chapter 14 (see page 516). The words of the wise man and the young maid bring to mind Christine de Pizan's *City of the Ladies* when they urge love and understanding, but their hopefulness is undercut by the power and immediacy of the image. As the broadsheet makes clear, suspicion of women characterized even the most simple literature of Reformation Europe.

2. Ibid, p. 122.

Collinson, Patrick. *The Birthpangs of Protestant England: Religious and Cultural Change in the Sixteenth and Seventeenth Centuries.* 1988. A series of lectures describing the process by which the Protestant religion was established in England.

Dickens, Arthur G. *The English Reformation.* 1964. A classic, clear discussion of English religion, emphasizing the popular enthusiasm for reform, which Dickens believes is connected to the earlier Lollard movements.

Fenlon, Dermot. *Heresy and Obedience in Tridentine Italy: Cardinal Pole and the Counter Reformation.* 1972. A complex book that argues that there was a strong interest in church reform in papal circles until the middle of the sixteenth century.

Greengrass, Mark. *The French Reformation.* 1987. A short pamphlet to introduce students to the political and religious development of the reformation in France.

Haigh, Christopher, ed. *The English Reformation Revised.* 1987. A collection of essays criticizing Dickens's thesis on the popular basis of reform in England; the introduction is especially useful for following what is still an important debate over reform.

Hsia, R. Po-Chia, ed. *German People and the Reformation.* 1988. A collection of essays that introduce and comment on the various currents of research on the German Reformation.

Moeller, Bernt. *Imperial Cities and the Reformation.* 1972. Three classic essays on why townsmen so enthusiastically responded to the reform message.

Monter, E. William. *Calvin's Geneva.* 1967. A fascinating introduction to life in Geneva during the Reformation, emphasizing that the city was not a theocracy controlled by Calvin.

Moxey, Keith. *Peasants, Warriors, and Wives: Popular Imagery in the Reformation.* 1989. A study of social and religious ideas spread throughout Germany by means of woodcuts; it contains numerous illustrations.

Roper, Lyndal. *The Holy Household: Women and Morals in Reformation Augsburg.* 1990. A study of domestic values in a Protestant city, demonstrating the ways in which reform ideas limited women's religious role to instruction within the family.

Scarisbrick, J. J. *The Reformation and the English People.* 1984. An excellent, clearly written survey of religious practice in England, emphasizing the vitality and popularity of the church on the eve of the Reformation.

Scribner, Robert W. *For the Sake of Simple Folk: Popular Propaganda for the German Reformation.* 1981. A study, illustrated with contemporary woodcuts, that shows how reformers used the new technology of printing to spread popular ideas about reform.

———. *The German Reformation.* 1986. A short introduction for students to the reform in Germany; it has excellent summaries of social and political issues in Germany.

Europe in the Age of Philip II, 1559–1600

An old man sits at his desk. At age 71, he is very old by the standards of the day. He wears spectacles as he pores over the reports and letters that require his attention. (He carries this work with him wherever he travels in his kingdom but is careful not to read in public—lest the sight of a king wearing glasses diminish his majesty in his subjects' eyes.) Near him is a litter on which he can be carried to an adjoining church, where he hears Mass every day without fail. He is so crippled by gout that he cannot walk there himself. He also suffers from recurrent bouts of the malarial fever endemic in Mediterranean Europe. He is Philip II (r. 1556–1598), king of Spain; it is 1598, the last year of his reign.

To contemporary observers, no political fact of the late sixteenth century was more obvious than the ascendancy of Spain. Philip ruled Portugal and much of Italy, the principalities comprising modern Belgium and the Netherlands, and the vast territories claimed by Spain in the New World. Treasure fleets bearing gold and silver from the New World began to arrive regularly during Philip's reign, funding ambitious policies envied and feared by other monarchs.

Philip's position among monarchs was exceptional because Spain was now part of an international trading economy unlike any that had existed in Europe before. The impact of the Spanish Empire and the treasure that poured into Spain was felt throughout Europe, however, and other states profited from both. Moreover, Philip's European territories were typical of others in the political, social, and religious circumstances that prevailed in them. Explosive combinations of religious dissent and political disaffection existed in Philip's principalities in the Netherlands, but similar conflicts

Philip II and his fourth wife in effigy, on top of his tomb in El Escorial.

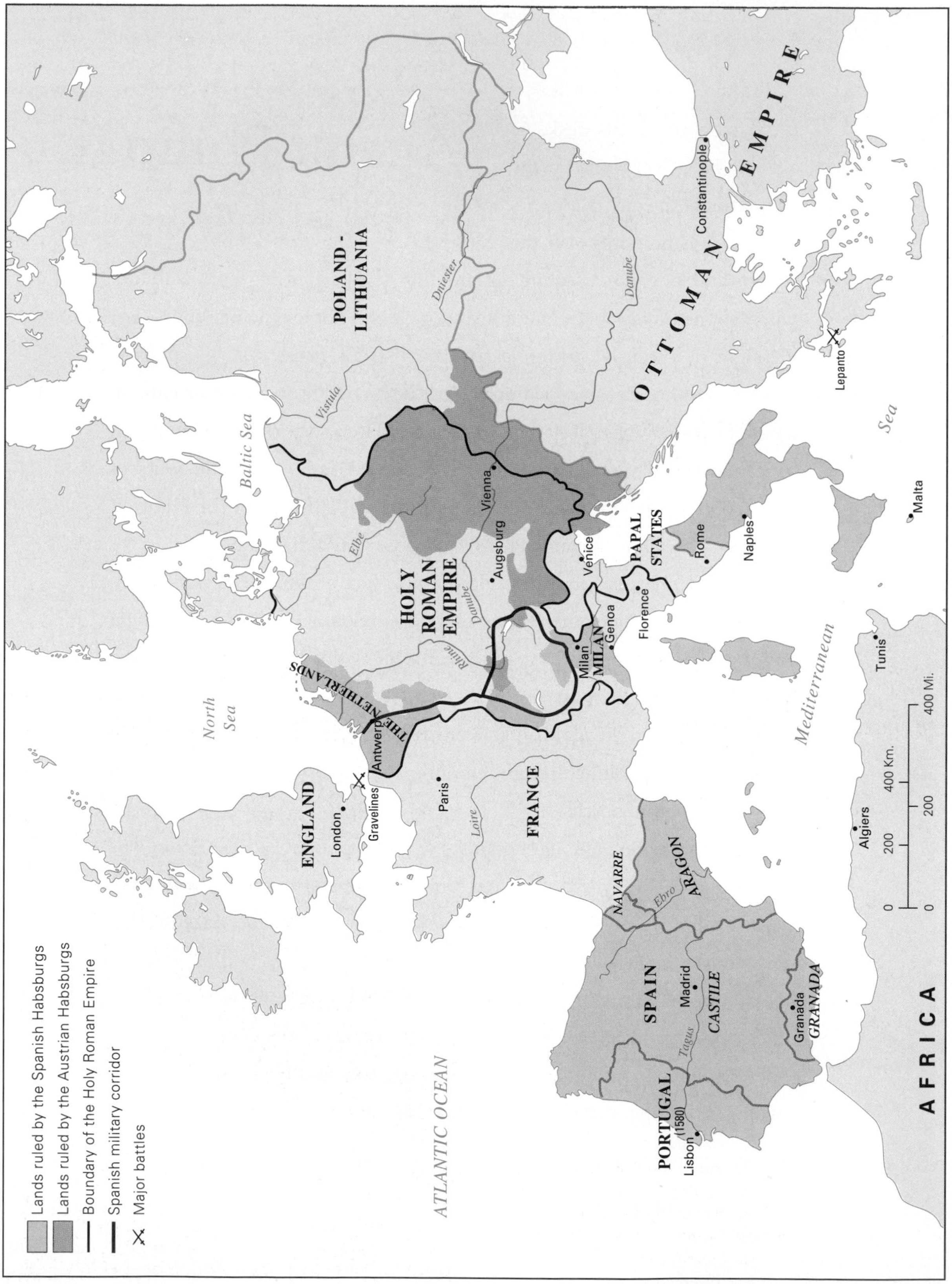
Lands ruled by the Spanish Habsburgs
Lands ruled by the Austrian Habsburgs
Boundary of the Holy Roman Empire
Spanish military corridor
Major battles
ATLANTIC OCEAN
North Sea
Baltic Sea
Mediterranean Sea
ENGLAND
London
Gravelines
Antwerp
THE NETHERLANDS
Paris
Loire
FRANCE
Rhine
HOLY ROMAN EMPIRE
Danube
Elbe
Vistula
Augsburg
Vienna
POLAND - LITHUANIA
Dniester
Danube
OTTOMAN EMPIRE
Constantinople
Lepanto
Venice
Milan
MILAN
Genoa
Florence
PAPAL STATES
Rome
Naples
Malta
Tunis
Algiers
NAVARRE
Ebro
ARAGON
SPAIN
Madrid
CASTILE
Tagus
Granada
GRANADA
PORTUGAL (1580)
Lisbon
AFRICA
0 200 400 Km.
0 200 400 Mi.

were brewing in France, England, and the Holy Roman Empire. Contributing to possibilities for violence was the fact that, throughout Europe, the warrior aristocracy continued to conceive of itself much as its medieval forebears had—as legitimately independent political actors with the right to make war in their own interests. Tensions everywhere were also worsened by economic stress—by rising prices and unemployment—as the century wore on. Like the illnesses that plagued him, Philip's dilemmas as a ruler were commonplace in his day.

A period of tension, even extraordinary violence, in political and social life, the later sixteenth century was distinguished by great creativity in some areas of cultural and intellectual life. Expressed, for example, in the plays of Shakespeare, these works both mirrored and reflected on the tensions of the day, and helped to analyze Europeans' circumstances with a new degree of sophistication.

Imperial Spain and the Revolt of the Netherlands

Philip's father, the Holy Roman emperor Charles V (known as Charles I in Spain), had broken up his cumbersome inheritance before his death. To his son Philip in 1555 and 1556 went Spain, the Low Countries (the Netherlands), the duchy of Milan, the kingdom of Naples, and the conquered lands in the Americas (Map 17.1). Unlike his father, Philip was truly a Spaniard, raised, educated, and given much experience in governing Spain before assuming the throne.

Under Philip's conscientious leadership the Spanish monarchy was able to hold on to most of its wealthy and far-flung possessions despite revolts from within and attacks from without. Yet the revolt in the Netherlands that began early in his reign clearly showed the limits to dynastic rule in such diverse territories. Political power was still highly decentralized, and Philip, like other rulers, could rule effectively only with the cooperation of local elites. Clumsy efforts to adjust this distribution of power in his favor caused Philip to push his wealthiest subjects, in the Netherlands, into revolt.

The Netherlands' conflict illustrated the conditions of political life in this era: towns, provinces, and nobility trying to safeguard medieval liberties against efforts at greater centralization by a ruler, with the added—and very grave—complication of religious division. The revolt also demonstrated the material limits of royal power, for, even with the American riches pouring in, Philip could at times barely afford to keep armies in the field. Extraordinary but also

Map 17.1 The Spanish Habsburgs and Europe Philip II's control of territories in northern Italy permitted the overland access of Spanish troops to the Netherlands and heightened the Spanish threat to France. Lands bordering the western Mediterranean made the sea a natural sphere of Spanish influence as well.

Philip II in 1583 Dressed in the austere black he customarily wore, Philip holds a rosary and wears the Order of the Golden Fleece, an order of knighthood, around his neck. At age 56 Philip has already outlived four wives and most of his children. *(Museo del Prado, Madrid)*

typical, Spain is a revealing window into this period.

Spain at Midcentury

Philip's powers in each of his Spanish kingdoms were circumscribed by the traditional privileges of towns, nobility, and clergy. In Aragon, for example, he could raise revenues only by appealing to local assemblies, the Cortes, which represented nobility and towns. The king did not even have the right to send troops into the region. In Castile, the arid kingdom in the center of the Iberian Peninsula, the king was able to levy taxes with greater ease but only because of concessions that allowed nobles undisputed authority over their peasants. The rural economy of Castile was stunted by this dual oppression by landholders and royal tax collectors. Yet the Spanish Empire became more and more "Castilian" as the reign progressed, with royal advisers and councilors increasingly drawn only from the Castilian elite.

Many of Philip's interests outside of Spain still centered on the Mediterranean, despite the new overseas empire. There were communication and trade of many centuries' standing between Spain and the kingdom of Naples, and there were newer ties with the duchy of Milan and the city-state of Genoa, whose bankers were financiers to the Spanish monarchy. Charles V had tried to secure the western Mediterranean against the Turks at sea and against their client states along the African coast, and Philip was also preoccupied with the Turkish threat.

In the minds of Philip and his advisers, the Turks represented a potential internal threat as well. Philip inaugurated a new wave of persecution of his Muslim subjects, eventually provoking a major rebellion in Granada between 1568 and 1571. The rebels received some help from Muslims in North Africa and were promised aid by the Turkish sultan. After this revolt was crushed, the Muslim inhabitants from Granada were forcibly exiled farther north in Spain.

The City of Antwerp Antwerp was the point of sale for Portuguese spices brought from around Africa, the selling and transshipping center for Baltic goods, including timber, fur, and grain, and the source for manufactured goods such as cloth. *(Musées royaux des Beaux-Arts de Belgique)*

The years of the greatest Turkish threat in the Mediterranean coincided with the beginning of revolt in the wealthy and populous Netherlands. The real jewel among Philip's possessions, the Netherlands had been centers of trade and manufacture since the High Middle Ages (ca. 1100–1300). In at least two of the seventeen provinces, Flanders and Holland, the urban population was approaching an astounding 50 percent of inhabitants. The port of Antwerp in Brabant had become the leading trading center of all of Europe since 1500. The Spanish Empire in America caused dramatic growth in the trading system and thus forged tight economic links between the Netherlands and Spain. To supply its new colonies, Spain demanded increased supplies of timber for ships and grain from Baltic countries and manufactured goods such as cloth from the Netherlands.

The political and economic importance of the Netherlands brought strategic involvement in its wake. Both in northern Italy and along the Netherlands' border, Spain and France had been at war until 1559. England's long competition with France and its important economic ties in the Netherlands led England and Spain to maintain friendly relations until late in the century. Philip's marriage to Mary Tudor, the Catholic queen of England (r. 1553–1558), had been a logical step in that relationship, though the opportunity to return England to Catholicism was an added inducement to maintaining close ties. Even with the accession of the Protestant queen Elizabeth (r. 1558–1603), Spanish-English relations remained cordial until later in Philip's reign, when Spanish-supported Catholic plots against Elizabeth and tighter Spanish control of the Netherlands made Elizabeth begin to fear the power of Spain more than that of France. In 1588, Philip attempted to invade England; afterward, however, he returned to hostilities against France.

Spanish Rule and the First Revolt of the Netherlands

Philip ruled in the Netherlands because through his father he had inherited separate rule of each of the seventeen provinces (Map 17.2). Generally, the States (representative assemblies) of these provinces had agreed to recognize an administrative authority established in Brussels, in the duchy of Brabant. This government included a council of state headed by a representative of the ruler (usually a member of the ruler's family) and councils to administer finances and justice.

Map 17.2 The Netherlands, 1559–1609 The seventeen provinces of the Netherlands were strikingly diverse politically, economically, and culturally. Like his father, Philip was, technically, the ruler of each province separately: he was count of Flanders, duke of Brabant, and so forth.

These provincial States claimed the crucial power to control taxation. They sent delegates to a States-General that met periodically to agree to taxation and other initiatives, but its delegates generally referred back to their provincial States before agreeing to anything. A sort of federal state had thus been devised, but it had many diverse power centers and linguistic variety, including dialects of French, German, and Dutch.

Tension soon arose over Spain's continual demands for money to fight Habsburg enemies.

REVOLT OF THE NETHERLANDS

1559	Peace of Cateau-Cambresis
1561	Philip II attempts to place fourteen new bishoprics in the Netherlands
1564	Netherland city councils and nobility ignore Philip's law against heresy
1566	Calvinist "iconoclastic fury" begins
1567	Duke of Alba arrives in the Netherlands; Margaret of Parma resigns her duties as governor-general
1572	"Second Revolt" of the Netherlands, led by William of Orange, begins
1573	Alba is relieved of his command
1576	Sack of Antwerp
	Pacification of Ghent
1579	Union of Utrecht
1584	Death of William of Orange
1609	Truce is declared between Spain and the Netherlands

In the 1560s, bad harvests and a disruption of the Baltic grain trade owing to wars among the Baltic states brought unemployment and higher prices, which made it difficult to sustain the burden of taxes. Though the 1559 Peace of Cateau-Cambrésis, ending years of fighting with the French on the Netherlands' borders and in Italy, seemed at first a fragile one, the Netherlands nevertheless insisted on the removal of Spanish troops left to guard their frontiers.

They were concerned about money but also about being tightly ruled from afar. Philip II never returned to the Low Countries after 1559. To assist the governor-general, who was his half-sister Margaret of Parma, he left in place a restricted group of ministers and secretaries who were either Spanish themselves or closely tied to the Spanish court. These arrangements were an affront to the local nobles, who had fought for Philip and his father in the wars before 1559 and were accustomed to positions of influence in the council of state. To the nobles' political grievances and wounded honor were added the concerns of townspeople as Philip's religious policy changed from that of his father. For the first time, the hunt for heretics began to be directed at Calvinists from modest and well-to-do families, not just at lower-class dissenters who were usually radical Anabaptists. Punishment began to include not only execution of the individual but also confiscation of family property.

Political and religious tensions rose simultaneously with Philip's attempt in 1561 to add fourteen new bishoprics to the four that had traditionally existed in the provinces. Local nobles opposed the plan because it was decreed with little prior consultation and also because they feared that their own family members, who customarily dominated the church hierarchy, would be passed over for political reasons. Wealthy townspeople, whether Calvinist or not, were also concerned. The new bishoprics represented a concentration of governing power outside of their hands. Moreover, officials in each new bishopric were to act as inquisitors, but the stability of urban economies depended on relative restraint in the prosecution of heresy. In addition, the power of urban elites and nobles alike would be diminished in the provincial States by the addition of new clergy who also had the right to representation there.

The opposition forced Philip to water down his plan for new bishoprics, but tensions continued to rise. Philip would not relax the overall policy of persecution of heretics, despite demonstrations and riots on the occasions of executions for heresy and successful attempts by townspeople to break arrested suspects out of jail. By 1564–1565, municipal councils in the major cities simply stopped enforcing the law against heresy, and leading nobles stopped enforcing it on their estates. In view of their success in the matter of the bishoprics, city elites and nobles were convinced that they could make Philip change this increasingly unworkable policy also.

In the end, events overtook the strained relationship between Philip and his subjects in the Netherlands. What had begun as essentially political dissent, though partly in response to religious problems, turned into a crisis of authority as the religious problem became more acute and caused massive political problems. Encouraged by greater tolerance, Protestants began to hold open-air meetings in large cities throughout the Netherlands in the spring of 1566. The meetings

Elite Fears of Popular Religious Unrest in the Netherlands

In 1566, Calvinists in the Netherlands, urged to action by their preachers, plundered Catholic churches and defied local authorities by holding large public worship services. In document (A), a government agent in a small city reports on the iconoclasm he has witnessed. In document (B), a member of Margaret's government writing to a friend in Spain describes his fears about the effects of the Calvinists' activities.

(A)

The audacity of the Calvinist preachers in this area has grown so great that in their sermons they admonish the people that it is not enough to remove all idolatry from their hearts; they must also remove it from their sight. Little by little, it seems, they are trying to impress upon their hearers the need to pillage the churches and abolish all images.

(B)

The town of Ypres, among others, is in turmoil on account of the daring of the populace inside and outside who go to the open-air services in the thousands, armed and defended as if they were going off to perform some great exploit of war. It is to be feared that the first blow will fall on the monasteries and clergy and that the fire, once lit, will spread, and that, since trade is beginning to cease on account of these troubles, several working folk—constrained by hunger—will join in, waiting for the opportunity to acquire a share of the property of the rich.

Source: Geoffrey Parker, *The Dutch Revolt* (London: Penguin, 1985), pp. 75–76.

grew and became more frequent as many ordinary townspeople now embraced Protestantism for the first time; thousands of people gathered, often arming themselves for their own protection.

During the summer, an "iconoclastic fury" began. Ordinary citizens, sometimes violently but often deliberately and soberly, denuded Catholic churches of the relics and statues deemed idolatrous by Calvinist doctrine. Reflecting the economic strain of these years, food riots also occurred. The two were very different (the participants in food riots carefully targeted grain merchants), but, combined, they raised fears of general unrest in the minds of both the Spaniards and local elites. (See the box, "Elite Fears of Popular Unrest in the Netherlands.") In early 1567, Calvinists seized two towns in the southern Netherlands by force of arms, hoping to start a revolt that would secure freedom of worship. A number of nobles, for their own religious and political reasons, attempted to support a widespread revolt by also taking up arms. Within a few months, Margaret quelled the uprisings with the aid of city governments and loyal nobles, now alarmed for their own power and property. By that time, however, a decision had been made far away in Spain to send in a large force under a Spanish commander—the duke of Alba—and he was already on his way.

But Spanish efforts to control the Netherlands from afar were not to succeed. The duke of Alba arrived in the Netherlands in August 1567 with ten thousand Spanish troops and with not only Philip's agenda but an agenda of his own: Out of favor at court, he wanted a spectacular victory to bolster his standing there. Alba acted like a conqueror rather than as a peacemaker in the Netherlands. He billeted troops in peaceful cities such as Brussels; he set up new courts to try rebels; he arrested thousands of people and executed about a thousand, including townspeople and prominent nobles, Protestants as well as "rebel" Catholics. Finally, Alba began forcibly to collect an unpopular tax that the States-General balked at granting—though they had agreed to other taxes to help pay Alba's costs. In short, Alba repeated every mistake of Spanish policy that had triggered rebellion in the first place. He enforced religious uniformity, which the majority of Catholic population by now may have welcomed, but his highhandedness alienated his potential political allies—the loyal nobility and urban elites.

Margaret of Parma resigned her duties in disgust and left the Netherlands. Protestants from rebellious towns escaped into exile and were joined by nobles who had been declared treasonous for minor lapses of loyalty. The most important of these was William of Nassau, prince of Orange (1533–1584), whose lands outside of the Netherlands, in France and the empire, were out of reach of the Spanish and could fund continued warfare. Thus, a significant community with military capability began to grow in exile. The combined religious and political problems would have been difficult to solve in any case, but Alba's policies created more rebellion than they quashed.

Spanish Reconquest and Dutch Resistance, 1567–1588

In 1572, ships of exiled Calvinist privateers captured about fifty towns in the northern provinces and were welcomed by impoverished and unemployed inhabitants eager to strike a blow at expensive Spanish rule. Shortly thereafter, noble armies led by William of Orange invaded the south. Alba's forces successfully dislodged most of the invaders, partially because assistance from France did not arrive for them. But once again, Alba's brutality worsened the conflict. After his troops were allowed to sack three towns that had surrendered to him—in one instance, murdering all the inhabitants—further surrenders ceased.

From this point on, patterns of conflict that were to characterize the Netherlands for the remainder of the century were in place. The northern provinces, with their remaining outposts, became the center of resistance to Alba and, increasingly, Calvinist strongholds. The Spanish concentrated their efforts in the wealthier southern provinces, which were the center of religious and political resistance up to that point and more vulnerable to French interference.

The success of Spanish efforts depended on the uncertain flow of money from Spain. The war in the Netherlands represents many of the contemporary factors at play—aristocratic privilege, dynastic right, regionalism, and religion. But it also was a stage for the destructive and costly technology of warfare in this period. The bastion, a new kind of defensive fortification that permitted a wide view of the surrounding countryside, had been invented, and now the only way to capture a town or an important castle was to besiege it and starve the defenders out. Where bastions had been incorporated into fortresses, military campaigns consisted of grueling sieges, skirmishes in the surrounding area for control of villages and the supplies they could provide, and occasional pitched battles between besiegers and forces attempting to break the siege. This kind of warfare was extremely expensive because vast numbers of men were required for an effective besieging force, on the one hand, and for garrisoning all the fortresses that controlled farmlands and defended major towns, on the other. It was a stupefying task simply to feed all of these troops, much less to clothe, house, and equip them all. Given the technology of the day, providing bread alone for a force of 30,000 men required a 250-wagon train (plus all the required draft animals) hauling flour, wood for fuel, and bricks to build temporary ovens.

Such success as the Spanish had in the Netherlands owed in large part to innovations in supplying their forces. For example, they devised a system of supply depots where provisions were gathered in advance of the arrival of troops marching north to the Netherlands from the Spanish-held territories in Italy. This "Spanish Road," as it came to be called, enabled the Spanish to send more seasoned troops from other territories north to face the grim conditions of warfare in the Netherlands (see Map 17.1). Yet even under the best circumstances, the army put a great strain on the countryside. There were virtually no separate camps or barracks, so civilians

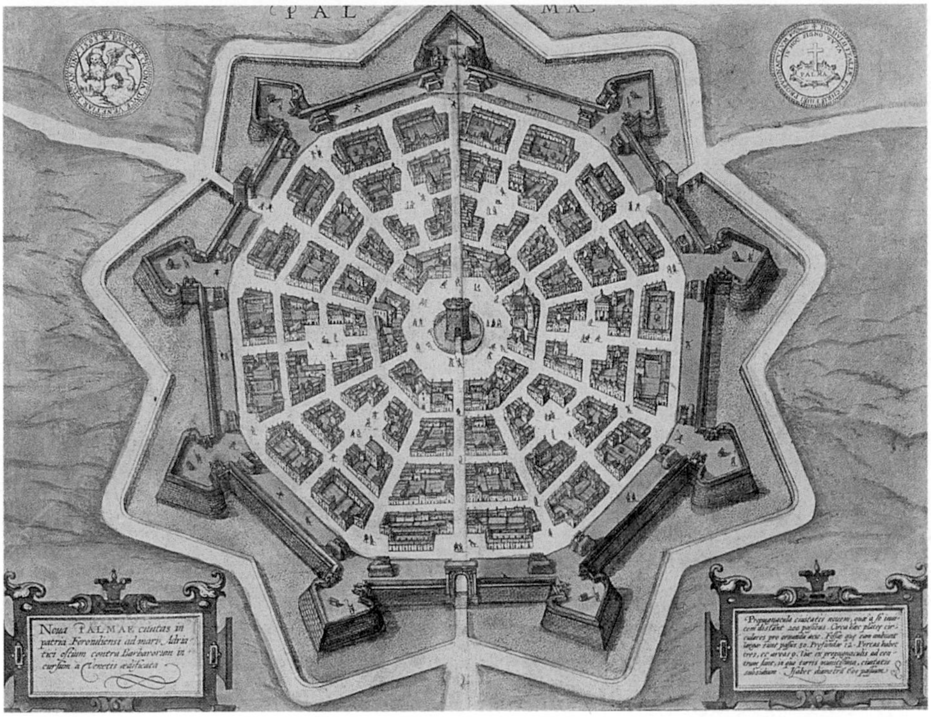

The Bastion Seen here in an example from an Italian fortress, the bastion was the triangular projection from the fortress wall. It enabled defenders to fire on the flanks of besieging forces; lower than medieval fortress walls and reinforced with earth, walls built in this manner were also less vulnerable to artillery blasts. *(Universitäts und Stadtbibliothek Cologne)*

were forced to accept the billeting of troops in their homes. It was impossible to control troops at all times or to prevent the countryside from being plundered.

When, despite American treasure and heavy taxes, Spanish resources faltered and the army of Flanders went unpaid, troops deserted, mutinied, or simply pillaged. From 1572 until 1578, Philip's government was desperately short of funds. Some of his troops in the Netherlands were not paid for more than three years. Several serious mutinies during these years disrupted campaigns against the rebels and also resulted in the loss of political ground in the southern provinces, which were becoming reconciled to Spanish rule. Some of the mutinies were well-disciplined affairs ended by negotiation, but others were riots by an army out of control. The worst occurred in November 1576, when Spanish troops pillaged the hitherto loyal city of Antwerp and massacred about eight thousand inhabitants—remembered in the Netherlands as the "Spanish fury."

Eventually, a large shipment from the Americas renewed Philip's ability to get credit in Europe, but not before the southern provinces had begun to take matters into their own hands. They raised money for citizen armies to protect themselves against the Spanish, and, meeting with unusual resolution in the States-General, they negotiated with the rebel provinces led by William of Orange in the north and concluded the Pacification of Ghent at the end of 1576. It was a treaty agreeing to nonbelligerence on religious grounds and cooperation to drive the Spanish troops out. United by this treaty, the provinces solemnly withdrew allegiance from Philip's representative and invited an Austrian Habsburg prince to be their governor-general.

These fragile beginnings of a self-governing United Netherlands did not last, in part because by 1578 increased shipments of American treasure permitted renewed Spanish belligerence. Also, Philip's new commander, Margaret's son Alexander, duke of Parma, was skilled as both a negotiator and a soldier. As important, tensions within and among the provinces reminiscent of the early years of rebellion began once again to erupt. Calvinist artisans seized control of several cities in Flanders and Brabant, frightening city elites on political and religious grounds simultaneously. Parma took advantage of their fears to woo the Catholic elites of the southern provinces back into obedience to Spain, in return for promises to respect their provincial liberties—and to safeguard their property from troops.

The northern provinces responded in January 1579 with a defensive alliance, the Union of Utrecht. Indeed, Parma might have succeeded in reconquering the northern provinces but for two obstacles. One was the geographical barrier of four rivers that bisect the provinces and impede military maneuvers. The other was the diversion of Spanish resources and attention elsewhere—to attacks on England in 1588 and on France after 1589.

The extent of Parma's military successes later came to define the permanent boundaries of two separate nations, but this was not yet clear. Fighting continued through the 1590s, culminating in 1609 in a truce that still did not recognize the United Provinces—the seven northern provinces—as an independent entity, though in fact they were.

It was a fragile state, an accident of warfare, at first. After the death of William of Orange in 1584, the States General of these seven provinces asked Elizabeth of England for "some lord of quality to become leader and director" of their movement, reflecting the importance of William's leadership of armed resistance to Spain.[1] The commander of the troops that Elizabeth sent to aid the rebels, the earl of Leicester, served ineptly for two years. But there were signs of the strength of the nation to come, in which commercial power would rival aristocratic control. Much of the economic activity of Antwerp had shifted to Amsterdam in the province of Holland because of fighting in the south and a naval blockade of Antwerp by rebel ships. Philip's policies had created a new enemy nation and had enriched it at his expense.

Philip II and the Limits of Power

Relations with Spain's former ally England soured as Elizabeth began aiding the Dutch rebellions and tolerating the use of English ports by the rebels raiding the Netherlands coast. There had also been English attacks on Spanish treasure fleets. For its part, Spain directly supported Catholic resistance to Elizabeth, including a series of plots to replace Elizabeth on the throne with Mary, Queen of Scots. Increased Spanish success in the Netherlands, raids by the Spanish and English on each other's shipping, and Elizabeth's execution of Mary in 1587 prompted Philip to order an invasion of England. A fleet (*armada*) of Spanish warships sailed in 1588.

The Spanish Armada was to clear the English Channel of the enemy in order to permit an invading force—troops under Parma in the Netherlands—to cross the Channel on barges. The plan called for an astounding logistical effort that combined carrying both troops and provisions for an invasion (Parma's troops were only to be a portion of the total) aboard ships primarily designed for naval combat. In the end, it became a dramatic example of the limits of what Philip could achieve with his great ambitions and resources. The English, fighting in their own waters, in ships designed for those conditions, were able to outmaneuver and outgun the Spanish. They attacked and dispersed the Armada off the coast of the southern Netherlands on August 8. Many ships were sunk, and many more sank in bad weather as the Spanish rounded the British Isles and sailed south along the west coast of Ireland (see the box, "The Fate of the Spanish Armada"). Only half of Philip's great fleet made it home. The Spanish Armada utterly failed in its objective.

When Philip died in 1598, he was old and ill, a man for whom daily life had become a painful burden. His Armada had been crushed; he had never succeeded in his aims in the Netherlands. Yet had Philip been so disposed, he could have congratulated himself on many accomplishments of his reign. The Turkish threat to Spain in the western Mediterranean had receded. The Spanish had allied temporarily with the papacy and with Venice—both were concerned with Turkish advances in the Mediterranean—and their com-

The Fate of the Spanish Armada

Even before the fighting began, the ordinary seamen and soldiers aboard the ships in the Spanish fleet suffered from inadequate food and appalling living conditions. After the Spanish defeat, the conditions of the exhausted survivors worsened as they sailed for home. In this document, a Spanish officer, Francisco de Cuellar, describes what happened when his ship, like many others, foundered in stormy seas off the Irish coast. Cuellar eluded capture by English troops in Ireland and eventually reached Antwerp.

The cables could not hold nor the sails serve us, and we were driven ashore with all three ships upon a beach. . . . Within the space of an hour all three ships were broken in pieces, so that there did not escape three hundred men, and more than one thousand were drowned. . . . [The beach] was full of enemies who went about jumping and dancing with delight at our misfortunes; and when any one of our people set foot on the shore, two hundred savages and other enemies fell upon him and stripped him of what he had on until he was left in his naked skin. . . .

[I was thrown up on the beach] . . . and a gentleman came up to me, a very nice fellow, quite naked, and he was so dazed that he could not speak, not even to tell me who he was. . . . I was wet through to the skin, dying of pain and hunger, when there came up two people—one of them armed. . . . Without speaking a word they cut a quantity of rushes and grass, covered us well, and then betook themselves . . . to plunder . . . money chests and whatever they might find, together with more than two thousand [Irish] savages and Englishmen from garrisons nearby.

Source: Colin Martin and Geoffrey Parker, *The Spanish Armada* (New York: Norton, 1988), pp. 239–241.

bined navies had inflicted a massive defeat on the Turkish navy at Lepanto, off the coast of Greece, on October 7, 1571. The spectacular battle had included both sophisticated naval maneuvering and grisly hand-to-hand fighting. The Turks remained a power in the eastern Mediterranean, but their ability to threaten Spain and Spanish possessions in Italy was ended.

Philip could have been particularly proud of some of the results of his policies within Spain. He established a close relationship with his Castilian subjects by establishing his permanent capital (Madrid) and his principal residence, the Escorial, there. The Castilian Cortes had little authority to control taxation, but it was an effective forum for the airing of grievances and thus for the association of nobles and urban elites with the monarchy. Moreover, near the end of his reign, Philip had made inroads into the independence of the kingdom of Aragon.

Aragon presented Philip with twin problems: regional independence and still-feudal noble pretensions. The former meant that local representative assemblies and administrators were accustomed to functioning without much interference. The latter fanned regionalism generally and created unrest among common people subject to the economic and political whims of this ruling class. Noble feuds and peasant rebellions had combined to create virtual anarchy in some areas by the 1580s; moreover, the kingdom became a haven for fugitives from royal justice elsewhere. In 1591 Philip sent in veteran troops from the Netherlands campaigns to establish firmer royal control.

Philip was successful in quashing Aragonese independence because he used adequate force but tempered it afterward with constitutional changes that were cleverly moderate. For example, he did not abolish a powerful executive council of the local Cortes but simply limited its access to tax monies. Finally, he cemented the peace with his Aragonese subjects by doing what he had never done in the Netherlands conflict. He appeared there in person, in the words of a contemporary, "like a rainbow at the end of a storm."[2]

Philip also invaded and successfully annexed Portugal in 1580, thus completing the unification of the Iberian Peninsula. The annexation was assured by armed force but had been preceded by careful negotiation to guarantee that Philip's claim to the throne—through his mother—would find some support within the country. This was old-fashioned dynastic politics at its best. Philip recognized existing Portuguese institutions; Portugal was to be part of the Crown, but its regional identity—like that of Aragon—would remain largely intact. The new resources that Portugal provided—particularly Atlantic seaports—enabled a new rush of imperial ventures; Portugal assisted Spain in naval competition with England and in launching the Armada.

The failures of Philip's policies against England are perhaps the best known to English-speaking people of all of his policies as king. English-speaking historians have often portrayed Philip as a fanatic; but in Spain he is known as Philip "the Prudent," and this title is closer to the truth. Conscientious and diligent to a fault, Philip insisted on reviewing virtually everything himself. His intransigence over religion made the Netherlands' crisis impossible to resolve, but his handling of Aragon suggests that he learned from his mistakes in the Netherlands that flexibility could also be strength. It might be useful to think of Philip dying not a failure but an exhausted success.

Conflict and Continuity in Other States, ca. 1550–1600

While Philip tried to impose his will on the Netherlands, he kept a sharp eye on similar conflicts in France and tried to influence the outcome there in favor of Catholicism and Spanish interests. France was torn apart by civil war from 1562 until 1598, the year Philip died. As in the Netherlands, the conflicts in France had religious and political origins and international implications, and political and religious questions became entangled in ways that made the conflicts almost impossible to resolve.

England experienced no civil wars during this period, but religious dissent challenged the stability of the monarchy. Most peaceful were states in the Holy Roman Empire, where religious diversity on a state-by-state basis had been accepted following the wars between Protestant and Catholic powers in the first half of the century. However, the conflicts of faiths and of political forces had not been definitively solved. Dynastic states in central and eastern Europe—the territories of the Austrian Habsburgs and the kingdom of Poland-Lithuania—remained markedly diverse, both linguistically and religiously, as well as politically decentralized. New challenges would come from resurgent Catholicism, from ambitious rulers eager to mimic Philip II's successes, and from subjects resisting their rulers' dynastic ambitions.

The French Religious Wars

The king of France, Henry II (r. 1547–1559), had concluded the Peace of Cateau-Cambrésis with Philip II in 1559; both monarchs were bankrupt, and Henry was anxious to turn his attention to suppressing heresy. Henry's death in July 1559 from wounds suffered at a tournament held to celebrate the new treaty was a political disaster. Great noble families vied for influence over his 15-year-old son, Francis II (r. 1559–1560). Two brothers of the house of Guise were related to the young king by marriage and succeeded in dominating him. But the Guises faced continual challenges from members of the Bourbon family, who claimed the right to influence the king because they were princes of royal blood and stood next in line to the throne after Henry II's sons. This kind of rivalry made court politics extremely volatile.

The queen mother, the late king's wife Catherine de' Medici (1519–1589), worked carefully and intelligently to balance the nobles' interests, and she sought compromise for the sake of her son's authority. She gained greater authority when, in late 1560, the sickly Francis died and was succeeded by his brother, Charles IX—a 10-year-old for whom Catherine was officially the

THE FRENCH SUCCESSION, 1515–1715

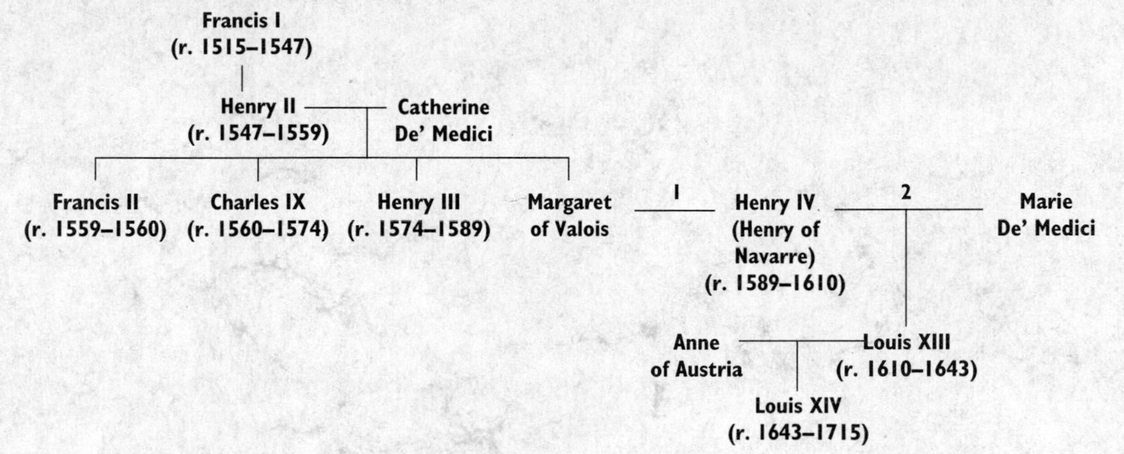

regent. But keeping the conflicts among the great courtiers from boiling over into civil war proved impossible.

One reason for this difficulty was the nature of the conflict among the nobles. In France, as elsewhere, it invariably had a violent component. Noble men went about armed and accompanied by armed entourages even at court. Although they relied on patronage and army commands from the Crown, the Crown depended on their services. Provincial landholdings afforded enough resources to support private warfare, and the nobles assumed a right to wage it.

Another reason for the outbreak of civil war was religious tension throughout France. Public preaching by, and secret meetings of, Protestants (known as "Huguenots" in France) were causing unrest in towns. At court, members of the Bourbon family and other leading nobles had converted to Protestantism and worshiped openly in their rooms in the palace. Catherine decided that the only practical course was at least provisional religious toleration, so she issued a limited edict of toleration in the name of the king in January 1562.

The edict, however, led only to further unrest. Ignoring its restrictions, Protestants armed themselves, exchanged insults and blows with town guards as they traveled to worship, and desecrated Catholic churches. Townspeople of both faiths insulted and attacked one another at worship sites and religious festivals. In March 1562, at Vassy, the duke of Guise's men killed a few dozen Protestants gathered in worship near one of the duke's estates. This incident touched off general fighting because it brought together the military power of the nobility with the broader problem of religious division. Ordinary people fought where they lived, alone or under noble leadership, or joined the main Catholic and Huguenot armies.

The killings at Vassy began the first of six distinct civil wars (though the periods of "peace" between them were troubled also). In some ways, the initial conflict was decisive. The Protestant army lost the principal pitched battle of the war, near Dreux, west of Paris, in December. This defeat ultimately checked the growth of the Protestant movement. It reduced the appeal of the movement to nobles, and the limited rights granted to Protestants in the Crown's peace edict made it difficult for Protestant townspeople to worship, particularly in areas where they were not a majority. But if the Protestants were not powerful enough to win, neither could the Crown decisively beat them.

The turning point most obvious to contemporaries came a decade later. The Protestant

Massacre of Vassy, 1562 This contemporary engraving helped perpetuate the cycle of religious violence by depicting the duke of Guise (B) leading his men in coldly butchering Protestant worshipers. In fact, the Protestants were killed by gunfire after they had pelted Guise's men with rocks when the men tried to disperse the worshipers. Note that Guise's men also rip the poor box (I) off the wall of the church. *(Stadtmuseum Hofgeismar, Department "History of the Huguenots and Waldenses")*

party was still well represented at court by the Bourbon princes and by the very able and influential Gaspard de Coligny, related to the Bourbons by marriage. Coligny pressed for a war against Spain in aid of Protestant rebels in the Netherlands. Alarmed, Charles IX (r. 1560–1574) and his mother authorized royal guards to murder Coligny and other Protestant leaders on August 24, 1572—Saint Bartholomew's Day, according to the Catholic calendar—when all were gathered in Paris to celebrate the royal marriage of the king's cousin, the Bourbon Henry of Navarre, to the king's sister. Coligny's murder touched off a massacre of Protestants throughout Paris and, once news from Paris had spread, throughout the kingdom. Perhaps three thousand people died in Paris and ten thousand in the rest of France.

The Saint Bartholomew's Day Massacre revealed the degree to which religious differences had strained the fabric of community life. Neighbor had murdered neighbor; bodies of the dead, including Coligny's, had been torn apart, mutilated. Gathered in the south of France, the remaining Huguenot forces vowed "never [to] trust those who have so often and so treacherously broken faith and the public peace."[3] Many Catholics also renounced reconciliation. When further war produced the inevitable truces and limited toleration, some noblemen formed a Catholic league to fight in place of the vacillating monarchy.

Another impetus to the breakdown of royal authority by the 1580s was the fact that Henry III (r. 1574–1589), another king of limited abilities who succeeded his brother Charles, was middle-aged and without children. The heir to the throne was the Protestant prince Henry of Navarre, and the assumption of the throne by a Protestant was unimaginable to the zealous Catholic faction at court and to thousands of ordinary Catholics besides. By the end of Henry III's reign, the king had almost no royal authority left to wield. He was forced to cooperate with first one of the warring parties and then with another. In December 1588, he resorted to murdering two members of the Guise family who led the ultra-Catholic faction, and, in turn, he was murdered by a priest in early 1589.

Henry of Navarre, now nominally Henry IV (r. 1589–1610), had to fight for his throne. Facing him were Catholic armies subsidized by the king of Spain, an extremist Catholic city government in Paris, a kingdom of subjects who were tired of war but mainly Catholic, and only meager support from Protestants abroad. Given these obstacles, he was able to force acceptance of his rule only after agreeing to return to Catholicism himself.

After his conversion in 1593, the wars continued for a time, but, after thirty years of civil war, many of his subjects realized that only rallying to the monarchy could save France from chaos. Extreme Catholic nobility and townspeople fought among themselves over the direction to take. The nobility favored acceptance of Henry IV and imposed its will on the citizens of Paris and other cities. Henry succeeded, in part, because of his personal abilities. He was politically astute and a talented general; he was esteemed by warrior society because he was brave, gregarious, and charming.

The civil wars were a crisis for the kingdom of France because of religiously based challenges to royal authority. They also demonstrated the power of the warrior nobility to disrupt the state. Having a strong and able monarch such as Henry IV was part of the solution. By the time Henry IV succeeded in imposing peace within France, nobles were increasingly disposed, for both psychological and practical reasons, to cooperate with him—service to a successful king could be a source of glory. The civil war period thus proved to be an important phase in the continual accommodation of the nobility to the power of the state.

This was by no means the last chapter in the story. Nobles continued to stage full-scale rebellions until the middle of the next century. Neither was the religious problem wholly solved. In April 1598, Henry granted toleration for the Huguenot minority in a royal edict proclaimed in the city of Nantes (see the box, "Henry IV's Proclamation of Religious Peace and Royal Authority.")

The Edict of Nantes was mostly a repetition of provisions from the most generous edicts that had ended the various civil wars. Nobles were allowed to practice the Protestant faith on their estates. Protestant townspeople could worship in at least one town in each administrative district and in other towns where Protestantism had been established during the wars. Protestants were guaranteed access to schools, hospitals, royal appointments, and separate judicial institutions to ensure fair treatment. They were also guaranteed rights of self-defense—specifically, the right to garrisons in about fifty towns.

The problem was that the Edict of Nantes, like any royal edict, could be revoked by the king at any time. Moreover, the provision allowing Protestants to keep garrisoned towns reflected the fact that living peacefully with religious diversity was not yet thought to be possible.

England: Precarious Stability

In Elizabeth I (r. 1558–1603), England—in stark contrast to France—possessed an able and long-lived ruler. Elizabeth was well educated in the humanistic tradition and was already an astute politician at the age of 25, when she acceded to the throne. Religious, political, and constitutional disputes existed in England as elsewhere, but they would not provoke violence on anything like the continental scale during her reign.

Elizabeth came to the throne at the death of her half-sister, Mary Tudor, wife of Philip II. The kingdom had weathered first the short reign of Edward VI (r. 1547–1553) and the establishment of Protestantism and then the short reign of Mary (r. 1553–1558) and the re-establishment of Catholicism. Elizabeth thus faced the urgent

Henry IV's Proclamation of Religious Peace and Royal Authority

In January 1599, Henry IV of France delivered to the Parlement of Paris, the supreme law court responsible for registering royal edicts, the speech from which this excerpt is taken. The Parlement exercised judicial review of royal edicts and was resisting the king's efforts to impose the Edict of Nantes on the war-weary nation.

What I have to say to you is that I want you to verify the Edict which I have granted to those of the [Protestant] Religion. I have done it to bring about peace. I have made it abroad; I want it at home. You should obey me even if there were no other consideration but my station and the obligation of subjects, but you, of my Parlement, have a special obligation. I restored their houses to some, who had been exiled, their faith to others, who had lost it. If obedience was due my predecessors it is still due more to me, as I have re-established the state, God having chosen me to come into this heritage. . . . I know the road of sedition which led [to] the assassination of the late king. I'll take care that it doesn't happen again. I will root out all factions, discipline all seditious teaching. . . .

Those of you who don't want the Edict to pass want war. . . . You are ungrateful to cause me this worry. . . . I am king now, I speak as king and I will be obeyed. Indeed justice is my right hand, but if gangrene sets in it, the left will have to cut it off.

Source: Nancy Lyman Roelker, trans. and ed., *The Paris of Henry of Navarre: Selections from the Memoires-Journaux of Pierre de l'Estoile* (Cambridge, Mass.: Harvard University Press, 1958), pp. 295–296.

problem of reaching a policy of consensus in religious matters—a consensus that could embrace the two extremes of Catholic-like doctrine and practice, which had prevailed under her father, Henry VIII, and Calvinist-inspired Protestantism, which had developed under Edward. True Catholicism was out of the question. The Roman church had never recognized Henry VIII's self-made divorce and thus regarded Elizabeth as a bastard with no right to the throne.

Most important to Elizabeth was a new Act of Supremacy (1559), which would restore the monarch as head of the Church of England. Decisions about doctrine were of less interest to her personally and also were less subject to her control. Elizabeth and most of her ministers were willing to accept some room for maneuver between liturgical practice and personal belief for the sake of defeating the common enemy, Roman Catholicism. For example, a new prayer book, the Book of Common Prayer, incorporated, side by side, elements of both traditional and radical interpretations of communion.

Doctrinal compromise has often been attributed to the forward-looking vision of Elizabeth, but we can be more certain that Elizabeth's contribution to the religious settlement was her firm handling of Catholic-inspired resistance, particularly to the Act of Supremacy. She simply arrested bishops and lords whose votes would have blocked its passage by Parliament.

Over the course of her reign, Elizabeth intervened in a number of foreign conflicts in order to support the Protestant cause, which was central to her own survival. But only slowly did the benefits of Elizabeth's settlements of religious matters reach down to the common people of England. The quality of parish clergy improved, and remnants of Catholic practice were replaced with a common liturgy. By the end of Elizabeth's reign, the Church of England truly existed in more than simply an administrative sense.

Elizabeth I: The Armada Portrait Both serene and resolute, Elizabeth is flanked by "before" and "after" glimpses of the Spanish fleet; her hand rests on the globe in a gesture of dominion that also memorializes the circumnavigation of the globe by her famous captain, Sir Francis Drake, some years before. *(By kind permission of Marquess of Tavistock and Trustees of Bedford Estate)*

The problem of religious dissent, however, was not definitively solved. Catholicism continued to be practiced. Loyal nobility and gentry in the north of England practiced it with discretion. But priests returning from exile beginning in the 1570s, most newly imbued with Counter-Reformation proselytizing zeal, practiced it more visibly. In the last twenty years of Elizabeth's reign, approximately 180 Catholics were executed for treason; two-thirds of them were priests (by 1585, being a priest in itself was a crime).

In the long run, the greater threat to the English crown came from growing tensions with the most radical Protestants in the realm—known (by their enemies initially) as Puritans. Puritanism was a broad movement for reform of church practice along familiar Protestant lines: emphasis on Bible reading, preaching and private scrutiny of conscience and a de-emphasis on institutional ritual and clerical authority. Most Puritans accepted Elizabeth's religious compromise but grew increasingly alienated by her insistence on clerical authority. A significant Presbyterian underground that wished to dismantle the clerical hierarchy of the Church of England began to form in response to the inflexibility of Elizabeth and her leading clerics. Church officials actively persecuted these radical Puritans late in the reign.

Elizabeth's reign saw the beginnings of English expansion overseas. Great interest in overseas possessions and construction of a navy to protect them, however, were in the future; Elizabeth, like all her forebears, felt her interests tightly linked to affairs on the European continent. Her prime interest was in safeguarding the independence of the Netherlands. Philip II's policy in the Netherlands increasingly began to alarm her, especially in view of the weakness of France. She began to send small sums of money to the rebels and allowed their ships access to southern English ports, from which they could raid Spanish-held towns on the Netherlands coast. In 1585, in the wake of the duke of Parma's successes, she committed troops to help the rebels.

Her decision represented a reaction not only to the threat of a single continental power—Spain—dominating in the Netherlands but also to the threat of Catholicism. Spain seemed to have the upper hand in the Netherlands and had threatened her interests—even her throne—in other ways. From 1579 to 1583, the Spanish had assisted the Irish in fighting English domination and were involved in several plots to replace Elizabeth with her Catholic cousin Mary, Queen of Scots. These threats occurred at the height of the return of Catholic exiles to England.

Eventually, in 1588, the English faced the Spanish Armada and the threat of invasion that it brought. The defeat of the Armada was by no means certain to the English. They did not know, for example, how poorly prepared Parma actually was to effect the Channel crossing. Thus, in the wake of victory, a mythology quickly began to build that portrayed Spain as an aggressive Goliath confronting the tiny David of England. But England, in reality, was not the innocent would-be prey; rather, the defeat of the Armada represented one phase of an extended conflict between two kingdoms. Nevertheless, the victory over the Spanish fleet was quite rightly celebrated, for it ended any Catholic threat to Elizabeth's rule.

The success against the Armada has tended to overshadow other aims and outcomes of Elizabeth's foreign policy. In the case of Ireland, England was Goliath to Ireland's David. Since the eleventh century, an Anglo-Irish state dominated by great princely families had been loosely supervised from England, but most of Ireland remained under the control of Gaelic chieftains. Then just as Charles V and Philip II attempted to tighten their governing mechanisms in the Netherlands, so in England did Henry VIII's minister Thomas Cromwell streamline control of outlying areas such as Wales and Anglo-Ireland. Cromwell proposed that the whole of Ireland be brought under English control partly by the established mechanism of feudal ties: The Irish chieftains were to do homage as vassals to the king of England. The great Anglo-Irish families, as powerful as medieval barons, were also to relinquish some of their power to new governing machinery. Under Elizabeth, this legalistic approach gave way to virtual conquest.

Elizabeth's governor Sir Henry Sidney, appointed in 1565, inaugurated a policy whereby Gaelic lords, by means of various technicalities, could be entirely dispossessed of their land. Any Englishman capable of raising a private force could help enforce these dispossessions and settle his conquered lands as he saw fit. This policy provoked stiff Irish resistance, which was viewed as rebellion and provided the excuse for further military action, more confiscations of land, and more new English settlers. Eventually, the Irish, with Spanish assistance, mounted a major rebellion, consciously Catholic and aimed against the "heretic" queen. The rebellion gave the English an excuse for brutal suppression and massive tranfers of land to English control. The political domination of the Irish was complete with the defeat, in 1601, of the very able Gaelic chieftain, Hugh O'Neill, lord of Tyrone, who controlled most of the northern quarter of the island. Although the English were unable to impose their Protestantism on the conquered Irish, to Elizabeth and her English subjects the conquests in Ireland seemed as successful as the victory over the Spanish Armada.

The English enjoyed remarkable peace at home during Elizabeth's reign. However, her reign ended on a note of strain. The foreign involvements, particularly in Ireland, had been very expensive. Taxation granted by Parliament more than doubled during the reign, and local taxes further burdened the people. Price inflation caused by government spending, social problems caused by returned, unemployed soldiers, and other war-related problems heightened popular resentment against taxation.

Financial crisis in England, as elsewhere, automatically brought political strain because the monarchy's usual way to reward loyalty and service by the elite—granting privileges, pensions, and patronage—was hard to continue in the absence of adequate revenues. Elizabeth was extremely adept at balancing the interests and ambitions of her courtiers, and she was renowned for her stinginess, but she could not defy their expectations as a group and still be able to govern. One of her favorite devices was to grant monopolies—the exclusive right to make or trade certain products—which pacified some of her elite subjects while sparking jealousy in others and increasing the prices of products bought by ordinary people. Despite her achievements, therefore, Elizabeth passed two potential problems on to her successors: unresolved religious tension and short-term and structural financial problems.

The Holy Roman Empire: Peace Through Diversity

Through most of the second half of the sixteenth century, the Holy Roman Empire enjoyed an uneasy peace. The Peace of Augsburg (1555) permitted rulers of the various states to impose either Lutheranism or Catholicism in their lands and, for a time, proved to be a workable enough solution to the problem of religious division. Complicating matters, however, was the rise of Calvinism, for which no provision had been necessary in 1555. A number of rulers adopted this newest religion, but the impact of their choices was felt more directly outside the empire than within it. For the most part, there was not a second wave of reforming zeal among the population, and Calvinist rulers chose to support French Huguenots and the Dutch rebels but not to disturb the peace within the empire.

The Habsburgs ruled over a diverse group of territories. Most were within the boundaries of the empire, but many were not German (Map 17.3). Though largely contiguous, the territories comprised independent duchies and kingdoms, each with its own institutional structure. Habsburg lands included speakers of Italian, German, and Czech, as well as other languages. The non-German lands of Bohemia and Hungary had been distinct kingdoms since the High Middle Ages. Most of Hungary was now under Ottoman domination, but Bohemia, with its rich capital Prague, was a wealthy center of population and culture in central Europe.

Unlike the Netherlands, these linguistically and culturally diverse lands were still governed by highly decentralized institutions. Moreover, the Habsburgs made no attempt to impose religious uniformity in this period. In that respect, the Habsburg rulers differed from virtually all of their contemporaries. Ferdinand I (r. 1556–1564), who took over the German Habsburg lands at his brother Charles's abdication in 1556, was firmly Catholic but tolerant of diverse reform efforts within the church, including clerical marriage and allowing the laity to receive both wine and bread at communion. His son Maximilian II (r. 1564–1576) granted limited rights of worship to Protestant subjects within his lands and kept his distance from policies pursued by Catholic rulers elsewhere—most notably, those of his cousin Philip II in the Netherlands. During Maximilian's reign, partly because of his positive leadership and partly because of a lack of persecution, a variety of faiths flourished side by side in Habsburg lands. In this tolerant atmosphere, education, printing, and humanistic intellectual life flourished.

But, given the course of events elsewhere in Europe, this late Renaissance was unlikely to last. The balance began to shift under Maximilian's son, Rudolf II (r. 1576–1612). Rudolf shared the religious style of his father and grandfather. He was an energetic patron of the arts, and sponsored the work of scientists. Yet he was virtually a recluse at his court, pursuing an eccentric intellectual life, and he did not attend carefully to the routine problems of governing.

In any case, the religious balance began to shift on its own in the second half of the century in the wake of the appearance of resurgent Catholicism. Members of the Jesuit order began to appear in Habsburg lands in the reign of Maximilian. Tough-minded and well trained, they established schools and became confessors and preachers to the upper classes. Self-confident Catholicism emerged as one form of cultural identity among the German-speaking ruling classes and thus as a religious impetus to further political consolidation of all Habsburg territories. Ferdinand II (r. 1619–1637) was raised in the atmosphere of reformed Catholicism. He was committed both to tighter rule and to uniformity in matters of religion. Like the English under Elizabeth, Habsburg subjects had enjoyed a period of relative peace in political and religious matters. Now, as in England, the stage was set for conflict of both kinds.

Map 17.3 Territories of the Austrian Habsburgs In addition to the lands constituting modern Austria, Austrian Habsburg lands comprised the Tyrol (modern west Austria and northeast Italy), Carniola (modern Slovenia), part of Croatia, Bohemia (the core of the modern Czech Republic and southern Poland), and Hungary. Most of Hungary had been in Ottoman hands since the Battle of Mohács in 1527.

Stability and Dynamism in Eastern Europe and Central Eurasia

Two states on the eastern frontiers of Europe were crucial players in European affairs in the second half of the sixteenth century: the Ottoman Empire and Russia. Both had interests in Europe as well as to the east, on their Asian frontiers. In the first half of the century, the empire of the Ottoman Turks had reached the practical limits of its expansion with the conquests of Suleiman (r. 1520–1566), known as "the Magnificent." Sporadic fighting between the Ottomans and the Habsburgs along the Hungarian frontier continued in the second half of the century, but the Ottomans' involvement was limited by their rivalry with the Safavid state in Persia. The Ottomans succeeded in extending their territory eastward into modern Iraq, Azerbaijan, and Georgia at Safavid expense.

Despite the Ottomans' many commitments and a succession of weak rulers, their presence in southeastern Europe remained secure, in part because they respected the cultural and religious diversity of their Christian subjects. The Ottomans actually strengthened the Orthodox church, because it was the rival of the Catholic Church, the religion of their Habsburg political rivals. They tolerated Protestants and Jews. Aristocratic and regional independence were factors too: Christian princes, particularly in the Hungarian borderlands, found distant Turkish overlords preferable to closer Habsburg ones. The naval battle of Lepanto (1571) was a setback for the Ottomans. However, control of the western Mediterranean, which this battle decided, was more vital to the Spanish than to the Turks, who quickly rebuilt their navy and re-established supremacy in the eastern Mediterranean.

Although Ottoman power was a constant presence in Europe, the newly proclaimed empire in Russia was the more dynamic state in the second half of the sixteenth century. Ivan IV (r. 1533–1584) was proclaimed "Tsar [Russian for "Caesar"] of All the Russias" in 1547. This act was the culmination of the accumulation of land and authority by the princes of Moscow through the late Middle Ages, when Moscow had vied for pre-eminence with other Russian principalities after the decline of the Kievan state. Ivan IV's grandfather, Ivan III (r. 1462–1505), the first to use the title "tsar," had absorbed neighboring Russian principalities and had ended Moscow's subservience to Mongol overlords.

Ivan IV was the first actually to be crowned tsar and routinely to use the title. His use of the title aptly reflected his imperial intentions, as he continued Moscow's westward push into lands once part of the Kievan state and eastward against the Mongol states of central Asia. Like the Ottomans in the same period, he was more successful against eastern than against western opponents. Two of the three Mongol states to the east and south fell, and the Russians pushed eastward over the Ural Mountains to Siberia for the first time.

Ivan IV as Christian Hero The Russian victory over the Mongol ruler of Kazan in 1552 is memorialized in this picture of Ivan IV trampling Khan Yediger Makhmet, in which the tsar resembles Saint Michael killing a dragon. Ivan did not kill the Khan, and in fact spent much of the battle praying; this image celebrates the conquest as a victory for Christianity. *(From* Kazansky letopisets, *Polnoye Sobraniye Russkikh Letopisey, XIX)*

Competition for control of the regions west and southwest of Moscow was intense, for these regions—modern Beloruss (White Russia) and Ukraine—were controlled by Poland-Lithuania, a dual kingdom at the height of its power (Map 17.4). The duchy of Lithuania had conquered White Russia and Ukraine in the early fourteenth century. A marriage in 1386 had brought it under a joint ruler with Poland, which was now the se-

Map 17.4 Two Empires in Eastern Europe, ca. 1600 Poland-Lithuania dominated the Baltic coastline and its productive hinterland in the sixteenth century, but it would face increasing challenges for control of its eastern territories by the expanding Russian state.

Ivan "the Terrible" Ivan became mentally unstable later in his reign. To his efforts at centralizing governing authority he added extreme despotism. Here, he is depicted as a bloodthirsty tyrant, holding aloft the severed head of one subject, and leading others to their executions. *(New York Public Library, Slavonic Division)*

nior partner in the relationship. Like the union of Castile and Aragon, the union of Poland and Lithuania was initially only dynastic, but, reminiscent of Philip II's efforts at greater unity in Spain, the two states were given a single set of political institutions in the Treaty of Lublin (1569). In other respects, Poland-Lithuania resembled the neighboring Habsburg lands of the era. It was a multiethnic state, particularly in Lithuania, where Russian-speakers predominated. Poland was Catholic but had a large minority of Protestants and Jews. Owing to ties with Poland, Lithuanians themselves were mostly Catholic, but Russian-speakers were Orthodox.

Poland-Lithuania was fortunate in a series of able rulers in the fifteenth and sixteenth centuries and in its size and resources. These resources—including the Vistula and Niemen rivers and the ports of Gdansk and Riga on the Baltic coast—explain much of its attraction for the Russian rulers to the east. These rivers and ports were conduits for the growing trade with the rest of Europe; tolls assessed on the passage of timber, fur, and grain were an important source of income.

But the dual Polish kingdom also had weaknesses. It faced competition for control of the Baltic coastline. Most important, it was an extremely decentralized state subject to strong centrifugal forces, including the ethnic and religious loyalties of its Russian-speaking subjects but also the accustomed independence of its Polish subjects. The king had little control over the nobility; in return for support for his policies, he was forced to grant concessions that weakened urban freedoms and bound peasants to the nobles' estates. The sudden death in 1572 of the very able—

but childless—king Sigismund II (r. 1548–1572) only enhanced the nobles' power. Sigismund's successors would be elected, would have no voice in the succession, and would be closely supervised by noble councilors.

In the empire of Russia, in contrast, Ivan IV was an autocrat. Part of his authority stemmed from his own personality. His willingness to use ruthless methods—including the torture and murder of thousands of subjects—to enforce his will earned for him the name "the Terrible." The practice of gathering tribute for Mongol overlords had put many resources in the hands of Muscovite princes. Ivan IV was able to bypass noble participation and intensify the centralization of government by creating ranks of officials loyal only to him.

A period of disputed succession known as the "Time of Troubles" followed Ivan's death in 1584, but the foundations of the large and cohesive state that he had laid survived this period—and would be ready to challenge Poland again when a strong Russian dynasty re-emerged in the next century.

Society and the State

Like warfare and religious strife, economic change disrupted the lives of communities and individuals. The sixteenth century saw profound economic transformation that, by the end of the century, altered power relations in cities, in the countryside, and in the relationship of both to central governments.

The most obvious economic change was a steady rise in prices, which resulted in the concentration of wealth in fewer hands. Economic change by itself, however, did not spawn all of the social and political change in the era. States made war for religious and dynastic reasons more than for calculated economic advantage. Nevertheless, together, the movements of the economy and the policies of governments created notable shifts in centers of wealth and power.

There was also a marked shift in control of religious practices. Ordinary people were crucial actors in both Protestant and Catholic movements, but established churches increasingly reflected the religious needs of elites—and the elites' desire for authority as well.

Economic Transformation and the New Elites

Sixteenth-century observers attributed rising prices to the inflationary effects of the influx of precious metals from Spanish territories in the New World. Historians now believe that there were specifically European causes for this "price revolution." Steady population growth caused a relative shortage of goods, particularly food, and the result was a rise in prices. Both the amount and the effect of price changes were highly localized, depending on factors such as the structure of local economies and the success of harvests. Between 1550 and 1600 the price of grain may have risen between 50 and 100 percent, and sometimes more, in cities throughout Europe—including eastern Europe, the breadbasket for growing urban areas to the west. Where we have data about wages, we can estimate that wages lost between one-tenth and one-fourth of their value by the end of the century. The political and religious struggles of the era thus took place against a background of increasing want, and economic distress was often expressed in both political and religious terms.

These economic changes affected the other end of the social scale as well. As we have seen, monarchs were making new accommodations with the hereditary aristocracy—with the Crown usually emerging stronger, if only through concessions to aristocrats' economic interests. Underlying this new symbiosis of monarchy and elites were the effects of economic changes that would eventually blur lines between old and new elites and simplify power relationships within the state. Conditions in the countryside, where there were fewer resources to feed more mouths, were growing less favorable. But at the same time more capital was available to wealthy urban or landholding families to invest in the countryside—by buying land outright on which to live like gentry or by making loans to desperate peasants. This capital came from profits from expanded production and trade and was also an effect of the scarcity of land as population and prices rose. Enterprising landholders raised ground rents wherever they could, or they converted land to the production of wool, grain, and other cash crops destined for distant markets.

As a result, a stratum of wealthy, educated, and socially ambitious "new gentry," as these families were called in England, was growing and solidifying. Many of the men of these families were royal officeholders, and they held on to their offices, confident of their wealth and the leisure it made possible. They were increasingly secure in new forms of royal recognition of their status. Where the practice existed, many bought titles outright or were granted nobility as a perquisite of their offices. They often loaned money to royal governments. The monumental expense of wars made becoming a lender to government, as well as to individuals, an attractive way to live off one's capital. The Crown could not do without the new gentry as creditors and as administrators.

No one would have confused these elites with warrior-aristocrats from old families, but the social distinctions between them are less important (to us) than what they had in common—legal privilege, the security of landownership, a cooperative relationship with the monarchy. Indeed, monarchs deliberately favored these up-and-coming gentry as counterweights to independent aristocrats.

City governments also changed character as wealth accumulated in the hands of formerly commercial families. By the end of the century, traditional guild control of government had been subverted in many places. Town councils became dominated by successive generations of privileged families, now more likely to live from landed than from commercial wealth. Towns became more closely tied to royal interests by means of the mutual interests of Crown and town elites. The long medieval tradition of towns serving as independent corporate bodies had come to an end.

Economic Change and the Common People

The growth of markets around Europe and in Spanish possessions overseas had a profound effect on those who had been typical urban producers in western Europe in the Middle Ages. Production of cloth on a large scale for export, for example, now required large amounts of capital—much more than a typical guild craftsman could amass. In many regions, guild members lost political power in towns as the relative importance of their limited scale of production declined, and the guild structure itself began to break down. The decline in market size for traditional artisans meant that fewer and fewer apprentices and journeymen could expect to become master artisans. The masters began to treat apprentices virtually as wage laborers, at times letting them go when enough work was not to be had. The household mode of production in which apprentices and journeymen had worked and lived side by side with the master's family also began to break down, with profound economic, social, and political consequences.

Effects on women workers were particularly dramatic. One of the first reflections of the dire circumstances faced by artisans was an attempt to mitigate competition at the expense of their own mothers, sisters, daughters, and sons. In many cities, widows were forbidden to continue practicing their husbands' trades, though they headed from 10 to 15 percent of households in many trades. Even midwives had to defend their practices, even though as part of housewifery women were expected to know about herbal remedies and practical medicine (see the box, "A Woman Defends Her Right to Practice Healing").

Women had traditionally learned and practiced many trades but rarely followed the formal progress from apprenticeship to master status. A woman usually combined work of this kind with household production, with selling her products and those of her husband, and with bearing and nursing children. Thus, women tended not to be formally involved in or represented by guild structures. Yet they had rarely been formally excluded. Now, in the sixteenth century, such exclusions began regularly to appear in guild statutes. In addition, town governments tried to restrict women's participation in work such as selling in markets, which they had long dominated. Women of this stratum of society thus began to have difficulty supporting themselves if single or widowed and supporting their children. In the changing position of such women, we can see the distress of the entire stratum of society that they represent.

The number and wealth of artisan households were dwindling. Men who in the past could have been apprentices now worked as wage laborers in craft trades wherever they could

A Woman Defends Her Right to Practice Healing

In this document, Katharine Carberiner testifies to the city council of Munich that she does not deliberately compete with male doctors but has skills that might lead other women to choose her rather than male medical practitioners.

I use my feminine skills, given by the grace of God, only when someone entreats me earnestly, and never advertise myself, but only when someone has been left for lost. . . . I do whatever I can possibly do . . . using only simple and allowable means that should not be forbidden or proscribed in the least. Not one person who has come under my care has a complaint or grievance against me. If the doctors, apothecaries or barber-surgeons have claimed this, it is solely out of spite.

At all times, as is natural, women have more trust in other women to discover their secrets, problems and illnesses, than they have in men—but perhaps this jealousy came from that. Undoubtedly as well, husbands who love and cherish their wives will seek any help and assistance they can, even that from women, if the wives have been given up (by the doctors) or otherwise come into great danger.

Because I know that I can help in my own small way, I will do all I can, even, as according to the Gospel, we should help pull an ox out of a well it has fallen into on Sunday.

Source: Merry Wiesner, "Women's Defense of Their Public Role," in Mary Beth Rose, ed., *Women in the Middle Ages and the Renaissance* (Syracuse: Syracuse University Press, 1986), p. 9.

get such work. Many women worked in cloth production, for spinning was a life skill that women learned as a matter of course. Cloth production was increasingly controlled by new investor-producers with large amounts of capital and access to distant markets. These entrepreneurs bought up large amounts of wool and hired it out to be cleaned, spun into thread, and woven into cloth. At every stage, dozens of people were hired as wage laborers in workshops or as pieceworkers in their homes. Thousands of women supported themselves and their children or added to the wages of their laboring husbands in this way. The returns, however, were often meager. Said one woman in Frankfort, "What little I make at spinning will not provide enough even for my bread."[4]

Wealth in the countryside was also becoming more stratified, and the rural economy was changing. In western Europe, the most dramatic impact came from investment in land by the wealthy elite. Countless peasants lost their lands to these "rentiers," who lent them money and reclaimed the land when the money was not repaid. Other peasants were unable to rent land as rents rose, or they were unable to make an adequate living because of the higher cost of land. To survive, some sought work as day laborers on the land of rich landlords or more prosperous farmers. But with the demise of so many opportunities for farming, there was not enough work. Many found their way to cities, where they swelled the ranks of poor. Others, like some of their urban counterparts, coped by becoming part of the newly expanding network of cloth production. They worked as spinners and weavers, sometimes combining this work with a little subsistence farming. However, one bad harvest might send them out on the roads for begging or odd-jobbing; many did not long survive such a life.

In eastern Europe, peasants faced other dilemmas, for their lands had a different relationship to the wider European economy. The more densely urbanized West, whose wealth controlled the patterns of trade, sought bulk goods, particularly grain, from eastern Germany, Poland, and Lithuania. Thus, there was an economic incentive for landowners in eastern Europe to bind peasants to the land just as the desire of their rulers for greater cooperation had granted the landlords more power. Serfdom was now spreading in eastern Europe when precisely the opposite conditions prevailed in the West.

Rebels, Reformers, and Soldiers

The common people of Europe did not submit passively either to economic difficulties or to the religious and political crises of their day. In addition to coping with economic distress in routine ways, both townspeople and countrypeople participated in riots and rebellions to protest their circumstances, particularly when political, religious, and economic tensions reinforced each other. The devastation of civil war in France, for example, was the backdrop to a number of peasant rebellions and urban uprisings.

Former soldiers, prosperous farmers, or even landlords whose economic fortunes were tied to peasant profits might lead rural revolts. If they succeeded, it was in relieving a local problem, such as a local tax burden. Urban protests could begin spontaneously when new grievances worsened existing problems. In a town in central France in 1594, for example, the execution for thievery of a servant whose master was believed to be a thief became the occasion for a demonstration to protest the privilege of the well-to-do. In Naples, in 1585, food riots were provoked not simply by a shortage of grain but by a government decision to raise the price of bread during the shortage. The property of the privileged was sometimes seized, and city leaders were sometimes killed, but these protests generated no lasting political changes and were usually brutally suppressed.

Ordinary people participated in the religious movements of the era. The townspeople of France and the Netherlands played a significant role in the establishment and defense of their "reformed" as well as Catholic religions. Whether Catholic or Protestant, common people took the initiative in attacking members of the other faith to rid their communities of them. At the community level, heretics were considered to be spiritual pollution that might provoke God's wrath or, at least, entice God's flock to stray from the correct path. Thus, ordinary citizens believed that they had to eliminate heretics if the state failed to do so. Both elites and common people were responsible for the hideous violence that sometimes occurred in the name of religion.

Common people drawn from both countryside and towns made up the bulk of all armies. Although nobles remained military leaders, armies consisted mostly of infantry and not of mounted knights. It was ordinary people who defended the walls of towns, dug siege works, and manned artillery batteries. Women were part of armies too. Much of the day-to-day work of finding and preparing food, locating firewood, cleaning guns, and endlessly repairing inadequate clothing was handled individually by women looking after their husbands and lovers among the troops.

Ordinary people fought from conviction and the need for self-defense. Such was the case of Protestants in France who fled their homes in fear and joined the Huguenot armies to defend themselves and their faith. Many other men joined the armies and navies of their rulers because the military seemed a reasonable way of life, given their options. Landless farm hands, day laborers, and out-of-work artisans found the prospect of employment in the army attractive enough to outweigh the dangers of military life. Even if the choice to join up represented merely an escape from destitution, it nevertheless was a choice, as was the decision to remain.

Desertion was common, even among those who believed they were fighting for a cause. Nothing more than the rumor that a soldier's home village was threatened might prompt a man to abandon his post. Battle-hardened troops, such as the Spaniards sent to the Netherlands, could threaten their commanders not only with desertion but with mutiny. A mutiny of Spanish troops in 1574 was a well-organized affair, somewhat like a strike. Whole units of the army mutinied together and found ways to defend themselves while they negotiated with the Spanish command.

Occasionally, mutinies were brutally suppressed; more often, they were successful. Troops received some of their back wages—though often at the price of future mutinies, for rulers lacked resources adequate to sustain their warmaking and money paid out for one need meant not enough for other present and future needs. Most important, desertions and mutinies proved to be crucial in the outcome of wars. Armies could be paralyzed by them after a string of victories that, for the soldiers, had meant many months of hard campaigning. Just when Spain, for example, had seemed most successful, its strategy in the Netherlands ground to a halt.

Religious Institutions and Religious Life

Although ordinary people were crucial to the spread of the reform movements and the resurgence of Catholicism, established churches removed authority from common people wherever religious conflict had already been decided. In Lutheran states in Germany, for example, pastors, backed by a hierarchy of church superintendents and regional church councils, became the instruments of social discipline in local communities, displacing local morals courts that had represented the village communities themselves. Reformed Catholicism also placed ordinary worshipers in a more distanced relationship to authority. By the end of the century, priests were generally far better educated than they had been but were out of touch with traditional religious practices and, in many cases, were alien to the villagers themselves. Whereas in the past a village priest was likely to be a local boy who was educated elsewhere and returned to his home village, now local priests tended to be strangers concerned about orthodoxy, superstition, and "correct" belief, which were not the primary concerns of most villagers.

From this perspective, we can emphasize not the differences among the various competing faiths but rather what they shared. Common to all major faiths of the second half of the sixteenth century was an increasing emphasis on internalized, private piety. Rituals such as communion were still very important, but they were beginning to change character in the wake of a new emphasis by all church hierarchies on internal emotional and spiritual life.

The Council of Trent (1545–1563) had reinforced traditional Catholic belief in the efficacy of the sacraments such as baptism and the Eucharist. But in the decades after Trent, clerics began to insist on a conformity of worship practices. Prayer to local saints was discouraged to emphasize the more distant God and Christ. In an interesting parallel with Calvinist emphases, portrayals of Christ in Catholic art, theological writing, and sermons began to emphasize not the suffering human Christ typical in late medieval art but a stern and remote Christ sitting in judgment. In both Catholic and Protestant practice, correct forms of prayer such as the Lord's Prayer and recitation of the Rosary were stressed.

The emphasis of much of this worship was intended not to celebrate or buttress a sense of Christian community but rather to accomplish a solitary exercise of personal faith. This is an example of cultural change spurred by increasing literacy. Distrust of folk tradition, concern with the proper "text" of prayer, and attention to interior self-reflection are all hallmarks of changes in sensibility brought about by the development of a close relationship with book learning. These changes reflected more the needs and aspirations of the educated upper classes than the needs of ordinary people.

Another example of a shift in religious experience lay in changes in the Catholic notion of penance. The very definition of penance began to change from making restitution for sins (changing one's actions) to feeling genuinely sorry for them. The focus, in other words, shifted from one's relationship to others to one's relationship to oneself. The effect of this shift was to break down community control of religion and leave individuals isolated and more subject to control by church hierarchies.

Further changes in religious practice in both Catholic and Protestant societies concerned attitudes toward charity and treatment of the poor. The medieval notion of charity tied it to everyday life: Charity was spontaneous caring for the family or neighbor. In Catholic doctrine, the exchange was spiritual as well as material. Charity was considered one of the many random ways by

Food and Clothing Distributed by Government Officials Wealthy citizens' wills began to reflect the new definition of charity: Bequests to institutions increased and personal donations to the poor dwindled. *(The British Library)*

which an individual could merit grace and move toward eternal life. Such ideas were anathema to Protestant doctrine, but, interestingly, official Catholic practice concerning charity began to change early in the sixteenth century before the pressure of Protestantism. Official Protestant attitudes toward charity, when they later came into being, closely resembled Catholic ones.

In the second half of the century, public almshouses and poorhouses to distribute food or to care for orphans or the destitute sprang up in towns throughout Catholic and Protestant Europe. In certain ways, these institutions reflected an optimistic vision of an ideal Christian community attentive to material want. But by the end of the century, the distribution of food was accompanied by attempts to distinguish "deserving" from "undeserving" poor, by an insistence that the poor be forced to work to receive their ration of food, and even by an effort to compel the poor to live in almshouses and poorhouses.

From viewing the poor as a fact of life and as an occasional lesson in humility, European elites were beginning to view them collectively as a social (not merely an economic) problem and individual poor people as problems too—in need of collective control and institutional discipline. The establishment of centralized poor relief thus reflected a vision of Christian community in which appearances of the holy were less random and the relationship between religious belief and community order, at least for elites, was increasingly direct.

Society and Culture

Both imaginative literature and speculative writing, such as political theory, bear the stamp of their times. In the second half of the sixteenth century, political speculation often concerned questions of the legitimacy of rulers and of the relationship of political power to divine authority—urgent problems in an age when religious division threatened the very foundations of political order. The form as well as the content of thought reflected its context. Authors and rulers alike often relied on still-prevalent oral modes of communication. Indeed, some of the greatest literature of the period, and some of the most effective political statements, were presented as drama and not conveyed in print. Nevertheless, literacy continued to spread, and striking innovations in literature were due to the increasing opportunities for knowledge and reflection that increasing literacy made possible.

Literacy and Literature

Traditional oral culture changed slowly under the impact of the spread of printing, education, and literacy. (See the feature, "Weighing the Evidence: Signatures," on pages 656–657.) Works of literature from the second half of the sixteenth century incorporate material from traditional folktales, consciously reflecting the coexistence of oral and literature culture. In *Don Quixote,* by Miguel de Cervantes of Spain (1547–1616), the title character and his companion, Sancho Panza, have a long discussion about the subject. The squire Panza speaks in the style that was customary in oral culture—a rather roundabout and repetitive style, by our standards, that enabled the speaker and listener to remember what was said. Cervantes is not necessarily poking fun at this style, for Panza is the sensible character who tries to keep his master, the knight Don Quixote, from acting on his dreams and fantasies. Much of the richness of *Don Quixote* comes from the interweaving of prose styles and topical concerns from throughout Cervantes' culture—from the oral world of peasants to the refined world of court life. The detachment that enabled Cervantes to accomplish this rich portrayal came about from highly developed literacy and the awareness of language that literacy made possible.

The spread of education and literacy in the late sixteenth century had a dramatic impact on attitudes toward literature and on literature itself. The value of education—particularly of the continuing humanist recovery of ancient wisdom—was reflected in much literature of the period. Writers found in humanist education a vision of what it meant to be cultivated and disciplined men of the world. The prolific French humanist François Rabelais (1494?–1553) used this vision to make fun of the irrationalities of medieval Scholastic education and the so-called contemplative yet thoroughly dissolute life of so many clerics. The vision also provided the beginnings of a new self-image for members of the warrior class. As the French religious wars dragged on, some unusually well-educated noblemen wrote works reflecting their propensity to use examples from antiquity to judge and make sense of their own troubled times.

Certain elite women who were able to secure such an education were moved to reflect on their own situation in society. The French poet Louise Labé (1526–1566), writing in 1555, described the benefits of education for women but exaggerated its availability:

> Since the time has come . . . when the severe laws of men no longer prevent women from applying themselves to the sciences and other disciplines, it seems to me that those of us who can should use this long-craved freedom to study and let men see how greatly they wronged us when depriving us of its honor and advantages. . . . Apart from the good name our sex will acquire thereby, we shall have caused men to devote more time and effort in the public good to virtuous studies.[5]

It is customary to regard the French author Michel de Montaigne (1533–1592) as the epitome of the reflective and—most important—*self*-reflective gentleman. Montaigne had trained for the law and became a judge in the Parlement of Bordeaux; he resigned from the court in 1570, however, and retired to his small château, where he wrote his *Essais* (from which we derive the word *essays*), a collection of short reflections that were revolutionary in both content and form.

Montaigne's reflections ranged from the destructiveness of the French wars to the consequences of European exploration of the New World. Toward all of these events and circumstances, Montaigne was able to achieve an analytic detachment remarkable for his day. For example, he noted an irony in Europeans labeling New World peoples "savage," given Europeans' seemingly endless and wanton violence against those "savages" and against each other (see the box, "Montaigne Discusses Barbarity in the New World and the Old"). Who are the real savages, he asked? He deflated pretensions to superiority in his own class of Frenchmen by noting "however high the chair, one is still sitting on one's own behind."

This was Montaigne's greatest achievement—the deep exploration of his own private moral and intellectual life, detached from any vocation or social role (though not detached, of course, from the leisure that his status made possible). The very form of his musings also broke with tradition. He invented writing in the form of a sketch, a "try" (the literal meaning of *essai*), which enabled him to combine self-reflection with formal analysis.

Michel de Montaigne Born into a modest landholding family, Montaigne's abandonment of a prestigious and lucrative career in the provincial Parlement astonished friends and family members. He is pictured here in a seventeenth-century edition of his work. *(Jean-Loup Charmet)*

Historians look for connections between what a writer, artist, or thinker was able to do and the culture within which he or she lived. To appreciate what Montaigne achieved, we should view him in the context of the spread of printing and literacy. We can conjecture that Montaigne had—in addition to his own energy and effort and the resources of leisure— a virtually unparalleled opportunity to reflect on the world through reading the wide variety of printed texts available to him. For the first time, it was possible for the leisured lay reader to juxtapose different events, values, and cultures. Montaigne's writings thus reflect a distancing from his own society and tolerance of others.

His essays also reveal a distancing from himself, and this distancing is also the product of literacy—not simply of the ability to read and write but of the ability to put literacy to use so that one might enjoy long periods of solitude and reflection in the company of other solitary voices contained in books. Montaigne's works mark the beginning of what we know as the "invention" of private life, in which an individual is known more by internal character and personality traits than by social role and past behavior.

Of course, literature was bound up with its contemporary world in other ways as well. Dramatists, poets, and prose writers generally ask profound and in some ways timeless questions about the meaning of human experience; however, the kinds of questions thought important change as society changes. The works of the great English poet and playwright William Shakespeare (1564–1616) still are compelling to us because of the profundity of the questions he asked about love, honor, and political legitimacy, but he asked these questions in terms appropriate to his own day. One of his favorite themes—evident in *Hamlet* and *Macbeth*—is the legitimacy of rulers. He was at his most skilled, perhaps, when exploring the contradictions in values between the growing commercial world he saw around

Montaigne Discusses Barbarity in the New World and the Old

In one of his most famous essays, Michel de Montaigne ironically compares the customs of Native Americans, about whom he has heard, with the customs of his own society.

They have their wars with [other] nations, to which they go quite naked, with no other arms than bows or wooden spears. . . . It is astonishing that firmness they show in their combats, which never end but in slaughter and bloodshed; for, as to routs and terror, they know nothing of either.

Each man brings back as his trophy the head of the enemy he has killed. . . . After they have treated their prisoners well for a long time with all the hospitality they can think of . . . they kill him with their swords. This done, they roast him and eat him in common and send some pieces to their absent friends.

I am not sorry that we notice the barbarous horror of such acts, but am heartily sorry that . . . we should be so blind to our own. I think there is more barbarity . . . in tearing by tortures and the rack a body still full of feeling, in roasting a man bit by bit, having him bitten and mangled by dogs (as we have not only read but seen within fresh memory . . . among neighbors and fellow citizens, and what is worse, on the pretext of piety and religion).

Three of these men (were brought to France) . . . and [someone] wanted to know what they had found most amazing. . . . They said that in the first place they thought it very strange that so many grown men, bearded, strong and armed who were around the king . . . should submit to obey a child. . . . Second (they have a way in their language of speaking of men as halves of one another), they had noticed that there were among us men full and gorged with all sorts of good things, and that their other halves were beggars at their doors, emaciated with hunger and poverty; and they thought it strange that these needy halves could endure such injustice.

Source: Donald M. Frame, trans., *The Complete Essays of Montaigne* (Stanford, Calif.: Stanford University Press, 1948), pp. 153, 155–159.

him and the older, seemingly more stable world of feudal society. Subtle political commentary distinguishes Shakespeare's later plays, written near and shortly after the death of Queen Elizabeth, when political and economic problems were becoming increasingly visible. Shakespeare explored not only the duties of rulers but also the rights of their subjects. In *Coriolanus,* he portrays commoners as poor but as neither ignorant nor wretched; they are in fact fully rational and capable of analyzing their situation—perhaps more capable, Shakespeare hints, than their ruler is. The play is set in ancient Rome, but the social and political tensions it depicts clearly referred to the Elizabethan present.

Shakespeare, Cervantes, and other writers of their day were also representatives of what were coming to be self-consciously distinct national literatures. The spread of humanism added a historical dimension to their awareness of their own languages and to their subject matter: their own society and its past. This kind of self-consciousness is evident in Shakespeare's play *Richard II.* The playwright depicts the kingdom of England, which King Richard is destroying, in terms that reflect the Elizabethan sense of England as a separate and self-contained nation:

This royal throne of kings, this scept'red isle,
This earth of majesty, this seat of Mars,
This other Eden, demi-paradise,

This fortress built by Nature for herself
Against infection and the hand of war,
This happy breed of men, this little world,
This precious stone set in the silver sea,
Which serves it in the office of a wall
Or as a moat defensive to a house
Against the envy of less happier lands,
This blessed plot, this earth, this realm, this England . . .
(*Richard II*, act 2, sc. 1, lines 40–50)

Sovereignty in Image and Word

Drama was the most important art form in the second half of the sixteenth century. Whether produced formally on a stage or in some less structured setting, drama was a favored method of communication because people responded to and made extensive use of oral communication. Dramatic gesture and storytelling to get a message across were commonplace. They underlay the reliance on processions to accomplish the ritual and religious goals of the community.

What we might call "street drama" was an ordinary occurrence: When great nobles entered major towns, a solemn yet ostentatious formal "entry" was often staged. The noble man or woman would ride into the town through its

The Entry of Henry IV into Paris after the Religious Wars The king is depicted here as the magnanimous victor and the residents of the city as both submissive and grateful. This painting memorializes a military triumph in a way that makes the royal victory seem both desirable and inevitable. *(Louvre © R.M.N.)*

main gate, usually beneath a canopy made of luxurious cloth. The event might include staged tableaux in the town's streets, with townspeople costumed and playing various roles in brief symbolic dramas such as David and Goliath, and it might end in an elaborate banquet. A remnant of these proceedings survives today in the ceremony by which distinguished visitors are given "the keys to the city," which, in the sixteenth century, really were useful.

Royalty made deliberate and careful use of dramatic ceremony. Royal entries into towns took on an added weight, as did royal funerals and other occasions. These dramas reinforced political and constitutional assumptions in the minds of witnesses and participants. Thus, over time, we can see changes in the representations of royal power. In France, for example, the ritual entry of the king into Paris had stressed the participation of elites such as the leading guilds, judges, and administrators and had symbolized their active part in governing the city and the kingdom. But in the last half of the sixteenth century, the procession began to glorify the king alone.

In fact, although we can detect only subtle shifts in the exercise of royal power from the beginning to the end of the sixteenth century, we can notice a distinct change in how royal power was represented in drama and painting and, above all, in how political theorists talked about it. The very fact that rulers experimented self-consciously with self-representation suggests that issues pertaining to the nature and extent of royal power were profoundly important and far from settled.

Queen Elizabeth paid a great deal of attention to the image of herself that she fashioned in words and authorized to be fashioned in painting. She had the particular burden of assuming the throne in a period of great instability. Determined not to share her power with a husband, Elizabeth styled herself variously as mother to her people and as a warrior-queen (drawing on ancient myths of Amazon women). She made artful use of the image of her virginity to buttress each of these images—as the wholly devoted, self-sacrificing mother (which, of course, had religious tradition behind it) or as an androgynous ruler, woman but doing the bodily work of man. (See the box, "Elizabeth I Addresses Her Troops.")

More formal speculation about constitutional matters also resulted from the tumult of the sixteenth century. The crisis in the Netherlands ended in the acceptance of Spanish dynastic rule in the southern provinces and the beginnings of an experiment with loosely organized republican rule in the northern provinces. In France, the conflict over royal authority, which was part of the civil wars, took place within a well-established institutional and constitutional tradition and thus provoked a good deal of speculation and commentary. In political theory, then, it is in France where we see innovation in the second half of the sixteenth century.

In French political theory, there is a tension between a medieval understanding of the nature of royal power and a newer view that gave more scope to royal authority. Although there was no actual document, political thinkers commonly referred to France's "ancient constitution." By this term they meant the customary relationship between royal power, which was in principle without limits, and the other bodies within the realm *with* which the crown governed: the aristocracy, the trained judges and bureaucrats, the privileged corporate bodies within towns. In theory, royal authority—particularly in matters of justice, from which all legislative and judicial power springs—was absolute. In reality, it was the "ancient" and customary practice of the collective exercise of sovereignty that weighed most heavily on thinkers before the sixteenth century.

The civil wars in France provided the impetus for energetic reconsideration of the principles and theories underlying royal government. The resulting theories either challenged royal power from a new theoretical position or buttressed royal authority from a new theoretical base. The Huguenot party, not surprisingly, advanced an elaborate argument for the limitation of royal power, particularly after the Saint Bartholomew's Day Massacre. The best-known Huguenot tract (probably authored by the well-educated nobleman Philippe Duplessis-Mornay), *Defense of Liberty Against Tyrants* (1579), advanced the notion of a contract between the king and the people. Under the terms of this contract, obedience to the king was conditional, dependent on his acting for the common good—above all, maintaining and protecting God's true church.

Elizabeth I Addresses Her Troops

The day after English ships dispersed the Spanish Armada, Elizabeth addressed a contingent of her troops. She used the opportunity to fashion an image of herself as a warrior above all but also as the beloved familiar of her people, unafraid of potential plots against her.

My loving people, we have been persuaded by some that are careful of our safety, to take heed how we commit ourselves to armed multitudes, for fear of treachery. But I assure you, I do not desire to live to distrust my faithful and loving people. Let tyrants fear. I have always so behaved myself that, under God, I have placed my chiefest strength in the loyal hearts and good will of my subjects; and therefore I am come amongst you, as you see, at this time, not for my reaction or disport, but being resolved, in the midst and heat of the battle, to live or die amongst you all, to lay down for my God, and for my kingdom, and for my people, my honor and my blood, even in the dust. I know I have the body of a weak and feeble woman, but I have the heart and the stomach of a king, and of a king of England too, and think foul scorn that Parma or Spain, or any prince of Europe should dare to invade the borders of my realm; to which, rather than any dishonor shall grow by me, I myself will take up arms, I myself will be your general, judge, and rewarder of every one of your virtues in the field.

Source: J. E. Neale, *Queen Elizabeth I* (New York: Anchor, 1957), pp. 308–309.

Alternative theories enhancing royal authority were offered, principally in support of the Catholic position though also simply to buttress the beleaguered monarchy itself. The most famous of these appeared in *The Six Books of the Republic* (1576), by the legal scholar Jean Bodin (1530–1596). Bodin was a Catholic but offered a fundamentally secular perspective on the purposes and source of power within a state. His special contribution was a vision of a truly sovereign monarch. Bodin offered theoretical understanding that is essential to states today and is the ground on which people can claim rights and protection from the state—namely, that there is a final sovereign authority. For Bodin, that authority was the king. He recognized that in practice there were limitations—that the king's judgment and discretion would be guided by elites such as judges. However, it was the theoretical grounding for royal authority that interested Bodin.

There is no question that the Huguenot party and Bodin set forth partisan positions in the context of the French civil wars. The importance of both bodies of theory goes beyond their relevance to France, however. Both were important because they were ways of envisioning an open-ended relationship between the ruler and the governed, rather than the government of traditional limits of the medieval period. Contract theory would prove particularly important elsewhere in decades to come as the ruled (usually elites) sought to challenge and limit the power of monarchs. But Bodin's theory of sovereignty was also important to this endeavor in the long run, because it visualized a unitary source of authority, which not the monarch but the people could later claim.

Summary

The extent of Philip II's power and resources were not typical of other monarchs of the day, but the problems of governance that he faced were very typical indeed. As events in the Netherlands, France, and Spain itself demonstrate, political life was both rooted in dynastic power and marked by newly couched challenges to authority. In the Netherlands and elsewhere, religious divisions caused political instability and localized violence as well as outright civil war and revolt against sovereign authority. Many of the problems that plagued Philip II would continue to face rulers around Europe as the next century began. Some would attempt to follow his unswerving opposition to religious dissent—with mixed results.

These rulers would also continue the consolidation of territorial states, which had proceeded in the sixteenth century despite—and at times because of—profound political divisions. The importance of this development was reflected in political theory. But religious and political tumult were to continue against the background of an increasingly complex economy and an increasingly stratified society.

Notes

1. Quoted in Richard Bonney, *The European Dynastic States, 1494–1660* (Oxford, England: Oxford University Press, 1991), p. 161.
2. Quoted in A. W. Lovett, *Early Hapsburg Spain, 1517–1598* (Oxford, England: Oxford University Press, 1986), p. 212.
3. Quoted in R. J. Knecht, *The French Wars of Religion, 1559–1598* (London: Longman, 1989), p. 109.
4. Quoted in Merry E. Wiesner, "Spinning Out Capital: Women's Work in the Early Modern Economy," in Renate Bridenthal et al., *Becoming Visible: Women in European History,* 2d ed. (Boston: Houghton Mifflin, 1987), p. 235.
5. Quoted in Ann Rosalind Jones, "City Women and Their Audiences: Louise Labé and Veronica Franco," in Margaret W. Ferguson, et al., *Rewriting the Renaissance: The Discourses of Sexual Difference in Early Modern Europe* (Chicago: University of Chicago Press, 1986), p. 307.

Suggested Reading

General Surveys

Bonney, Richard. *The European Dynastic States, 1494–1660.* 1991. A recent, rich survey of the period. Good on eastern as well as western Europe but written from an English point of view; thus, it does not consider England as part of Europe.

Elliott, J. H. *Europe Divided, 1559–1598.* 1968. An older but still reliable and readable survey by a leading scholar of Spanish history.

Spain and the Dutch

Elliott, J. H. *Imperial Spain, 1469–1716.* 1963. An older but excellent survey.

Hale, J. R. *War and Society in Renaissance Europe.* 1985. An analysis of war as a function of government and as a part of social, economic, and intellectual life through the sixteenth century.

Lynch, John. *Spain, 1516–1598: From Nation-State to World Empire.* 1991. Another excellent survey.

Parker, Geoffrey. *The Army of Flanders and the Spanish Road.* 1972. A detailed study of Spanish innovations in supplying its armies during the Netherlands' revolt.

———. *The Dutch Revolt.* 2d ed. 1985. The best survey of the revolt available in English.

———. *The Military Revolution.* 1988. A general evaluation of the impact of changes in military technology on land and water from the sixteenth through the eighteenth centuries, by one of the leading historians in the field.

Wedgewood, C. V. *William the Silent.* 1968. A sympathetic biography of the aristocratic leader of the Dutch revolt, which portrays him as a man ahead of his time in his acceptance of religious diversity. Useful for capturing the flavor of the period, though not for its interpretation.

The History of Other States

Mattingly, Garrett. *The Armada.* 1959. A well-crafted and gripping narrative of the sailing of the Armada and all the interrelated events in France, the Netherlands, England, and Spain, told from a decidedly English perspective.

Roelker, Nancy L. *Queen of Navarre: Jeanne d'Albret.* 1968. A scholarly but lively biography of the mother of Henry IV, useful for following events in the religious wars and understanding the rise of Protestantism and the politics at court.

Salmon, J. H. M. *Society in Crisis: France in the Sixteenth Century.* 1975. A dense general treatment of developments in France.

Smith, A. G. R. *The Emergence of a Nation-State: The Commonwealth of England, 1529–1660.* 1984. A good place to start through the immense bibliography on the Elizabethan period.

Sutherland, N. M. *The Huguenot Struggle for Recognition.* 1980. A study of the religious wars, the peace edicts, and their aftermath from the perspective of the Huguenot party.

For central and eastern Europe, see the works by Davies, Evans, and Riasanovsky cited in Chapter 18.

Society, Economy, and Religion

Bossy, John. *Christianity in the West.* 1985. An interpretation of the Reformation period that sees continuities across all faiths.

Braudel, Fernand. *The Perspective of the World.* Vol. 3, *Civilization and Capitalism, 15th to 18th Century.* Translated by S. Reynolds. 1984. A particularly useful volume by this celebrated author of economic history concerning overall patterns in the European and international economies.

Delumeau, Jean. *Catholicism Between Luther and Voltaire: A New View of the Counter-Reformation.* 1977. A new study of the Counter-Reformation that examines popular religious practices as well as official church reactions to Protestantism.

Gutman, Myron P. *Toward the Modern Economy.* 1988. An account of the development of cloth production and the decline of guild manufacture through the early modern period.

Huppert, George. *After the Black Death: A Social History of Early Modern Europe.* 1986. A survey of developments in social and economic history throughout Europe from the fifteenth through the seventeenth centuries. A brief but very usable bibliography will guide further reading.

Wiesner, Merry E. *Working Women in Renaissance Germany.* 1986. An analysis of the role of women in the early modern economy and the conditions of their working lives. Though based on research on Germany, this is the best general treatment of women's work to date.

Literacy, Literature, and Political Theory

Church, William F. *Constitutional Thought in Sixteenth-Century France.* 1969. A survey of sixteenth-century political theory in France.

Eagleton, Terry. *William Shakespeare.* 1986. A brief and highly readable interpretation of Shakespeare that emphasizes the tensions in the plays caused by language and by ideas from the new world of bourgeois, commercial life.

Giesey, Ralph E. *The Royal Funeral Ceremony in Renaissance France.* 1960. One of the earliest studies of royal ceremony in the period.

Greenblatt, Stephen. *Renaissance Self-Fashioning.* 1979. An interpretation of sixteenth-century literature and culture that emphasizes the "invention" of interior self-reflection and self-awareness.

Houston, R. A. *Literacy in Early Modern Europe.* 1988. A general introduction, incorporating the latest scholarship, to the issues of the spread of education and the impact of literacy in Europe.

Kamen, Henry. *The Rise of Toleration.* 1967. This older and rather optimistic study chronicles the slow emergence of secularism and toleration during and after the Reformation.

Kelley, Donald R. *The Beginnings of Ideology: Consciousness and Society in the French Reformation.* 1981. A study of political thought, including but not limited to formal theory, as inspired by the experience of the wars of religion.

Ong, Walter J. *Orality and Literacy: The Technologizing of the Word.* 1982. A synthesis of recent scholarship that concentrates on the psychological and cultural impact of literacy.

Patterson, Annabel. *Shakespeare and the Popular Voice.* 1989. An interpretation of Shakespeare's work that emphasizes his connection to the complex political and social milieu of his day.

Regosin, J. *The Matter of My Book: Montaigne's "Essais" as the Book of the Self.* 1977. One of the leading scholarly treatments of Montaigne's work.

Weighing the Evidence

Signatures

Right now you are staring at words printed on the page of a book. We are so dependent on written communication that we cannot imagine functioning without these symbols. The often-heard warning "Don't believe everything you read" reflects our habit of trusting written information. But what might it be like if words were only fleeting events—spoken and heard in moments of personal interaction—and not things, objects gazed at in silence, easily saved and retrieved?

Let us consider what evidence we have about the spread of literacy in the sixteenth century. Historians have gained a rough idea about what portion of the population was literate in the sixteenth century by counting the signatures on representative samples of legal documents such as wills and marriage contracts. The ability to sign one's name is a fairly reliable indication of literacy in the sixteenth century because then, unlike today, writing was taught in schools only *after* reading was already mastered. For this reason, however, the *lack* of a signature may mask considerable reading ability, for no special significance was attached to learning to write one's name. Sixteenth-century documents are filled with signatures like those reproduced here: the scissors, for a tailor; the arrow, for a fletcher (arrow-maker). Both of the men who made these marks may well have been able to read.

Where documentation is dense, such as in towns, and where the evidence of signatures has been collected, we have profiles of the literacy rates of selected communities. Literacy rates varied widely according to the location of a particular community (remote ones had fewer literate inhabitants) and its economy (certain trades favored literacy; poverty generally worked against it). Overall, men were more literate than women, and western and northern Europeans were more literate than southern and eastern Europeans. In prosperous regions of western Europe, where literacy rates were highest, there was nearly 100 percent literacy, as one might predict, among bureaucrats, officials, and well-to-do townsmen. Among artisans, the rate neared 50 percent. Among peasants, it could be 10 percent or lower.

If we suppose these figures to be accurate, what can we conclude about the impact of literacy on people's lives? Our own reliance on literacy once led us to assume that people in the past would naturally use these skills if they knew how and that literate knowledge—gleaned from books—would quickly replace folk traditions and knowledge communicated orally. But the "signatures" of the tailor, the fletcher, and thousands of others imply that many Europeans lived with partial literacy. And we now realize that the spread of literacy only slowly changed Europeans' reliance on oral communication. Reading and writing supplemented but initially did not replace traditional ways of learning and communicating.

Aristocrats, for example, usually learned to read and write and occasionally were highly educated. But they learned their most valued skills, such as estate management and military expertise, from their older peers, rather as artisan children learned their skills through apprenticeship. Nobles kept copious written records about their landed property but often relied on memory instead of documents to settle disputes. At all levels of society, most reading was done in a group. It was integrated into the common entertainment of storytelling, illustrated in the drawing reproduced here. An evening's storytelling in a household or tavern might include reading aloud but was not fundamentally changed by the inclusion of reading.

Signatures from English Court Depositions *(David Cressy,* Literacy and the Social Order *[Cambridge, England: Cambridge University Press, 1980], p. 60.)*

Tailor **Fletcher**

Joseph Anton Koch: Shepherds Around the Fire *(Staatliche Kunstsammlungen Dresden/Kupferstich-Kabinett)*

There is evidence that people who could read still trusted written material less than, or at least no more than, spoken information. A literate peasant would consult a farmer's almanac, but more for entertainment than for information. His firsthand knowledge of the local climate, crops, and animal husbandry seemed more reliable to him—and was likely to be more reliable—than any text that a distant publisher might provide. Nobles frequently wrote brief letters to each other in which they said little other than "Please trust X, the bearer of this letter." The real message was imparted orally. It was face-to-face communication, built on a personal relationship, that was trusted.

Some of the most dramatic evidence of the persistence of oral culture is in the use of language that is preserved in informal documents such as long letters or the relatively rare memoir. Most people still relied on the repetitive phrasing that is common when language is wholly oral. Thus, even when they wrote words down, they were "thinking" without literacy.

Although we have learned that evidence of literacy does not mean that sixteenth-century people relied on reading and writing the way we do, we are just beginning to understand what their limited reliance on it really meant for their lives and their society. Access to literacy and the use of documents were tools of power and control. Our tailor might be at a disadvantage in a transaction if he could not read the document he signed. However, unlike us, he did not have to rely on documents to establish his identity. And with virtually none of his past recorded in writing, he and other sixteenth-century men and women were free in ways that we are not.

Consider also the tenacity of oral communication. Let us set aside our assumption that written information is superior and try to imagine how powerful oral communication can be. Look carefully at the evidence supplied in the drawing of shepherds gathered around a fire. It dates from the late eighteenth century, when literacy was increasingly widespread and when the persistent oral culture of lower-class people was beginning to be derided in the way that illiteracy is derided today. The cultural gap between literate and illiterate is reflected here in the somewhat derisive representations of the subjects: They are made to seem uncouth. Yet still captured is something of the power of speech and of hearing. Words are events here, and speaker and listeners are active in their parts. The speaker gestures while his companions lean forward attentively to hear and perhaps to argue with him.

In an oral culture, information always is accompanied by sensory input: the sights, smells, and sounds of the person conveying it. And you always know your source. Is it any wonder that common people resisted the "authority" of book learning?

CHAPTER 18

Europe in the Age of Louis XIV, ca. 1610–1715

Toward the end of his reign, the subjects of Louis XIV of France began to grumble that he had lived too long. In fact, he outlived his own son and grandson and was followed on the throne by a great-grandson when he died in 1715. In his own time, Louis was a symbol for the success of royal power in surmounting the challenges of warrior-nobles, in suppressing religious dissent, in tapping the wealth of the nation's population, and in waging war. A period of cultural brilliance early in his reign and the spectacle of an elaborate court life crowned his achievements. At the end of his reign, however, France was struggling under economic distress brought on by the many wars fought for his glory. But, although Louis outlived his welcome, he was then, and is for us now, a symbol of the age that ended with his death.

A few years earlier, in 1701, a man more notorious than famous had died; he too may be considered a symbol of the seventeenth century. The English pirate Captain William Kidd, was executed by British authorities as part of their effort to suppress piracy. His death symbolizes the end of the dynamic phase of European overseas expansion that began with the successes of the Portuguese and the Spanish in the fifteenth and sixteenth centuries. The efforts of private individuals such as William Kidd were integral to Europeans' dominance of trade and establishment of lucrative colonies around the world. The execution of Kidd signaled an effort by European nations to tighten their control of their colonial and trading empires.

The lives of the king and the pirate epitomize two significant developments in European society in the seventeenth century: the increasing consolidation of the nation-state and the growth of overseas trade. Many of

Hall of Mirrors,
Versailles.

the struggles within the consolidating European states, however, traced their origin to the religious and political turmoil of the sixteenth century.

War and Politics

The seventeenth century began with a war in which virtually all the states of Europe participated. In the "Thirty Years' War" (1618–1648), as it is now called, we can see the continuation of conflicts from the sixteenth century—religious tensions, regionalism versus centralizing forces, dynastic and strategic rivalries such as that between the French and Spanish rulers. The war was particularly destructive because of the size of the armies, the burden they imposed on civilian populations, and the degree to which army commanders were out of the control of the states for which they fought. Most of the fighting occurred within the borders of the Holy Roman Empire. Some areas of the empire suffered catastrophic losses in population and productive capacity. As a result of the war, the empire was eclipsed as a political unit by the regional powers within it.

The Thirty Years' War, 1618–1648

The Holy Roman Empire was comparatively peaceful after the Peace of Augsburg halted religious and political wars in 1555. By the early seventeenth century, however, fresh causes of instability brought about renewed fighting. Especially destabilizing was the drive by the Habsburgs—successive emperors and the territorial princes—to reverse the successes of Protestantism both in their own lands and in the empire at large and to consolidate their rule in their diverse personal territories. Politics and religion continued to be thoroughly intermingled.

Both political and religious problems surfaced early in the century. In one incident, in 1606, the aggressively Catholic prince of Bavaria seized an imperial free city in north central Germany, in the wake of religious in-fighting there—a city theoretically subject to no one but the emperor himself. Tensions between Catholic and Protestant states (and among Protestants, for Calvinists and Lutherans were not necessarily allies) were further heightened by a succession crisis. The childless emperor Rudolf II (r. 1576–1612) was aging, and factions of the Habsburg family were seeking allies among the German states to promote their various candidates for the imperial crown.

In 1618 a revolt against Habsburg rule in the kingdom of Bohemia touched off widespread warfare. Bohemia (the core of the modern Czech Republic) was populous and prosperous and had a large Protestant population. Rudolf II had used Prague, its bustling capital, as an imperial capital. Although Catholicism was reclaiming lost ground, Protestants had been confirmed in their rights to worship in the early seventeenth century—significantly, both by Rudolf and by his younger brother Matthias, who hoped to succeed Rudolf as king of Bohemia and as Holy Roman emperor. The crown of Bohemia was bestowed by election, so rival claimants to this wealthy throne needed the acquiescence of the ruling elites, both Protestant and Catholic, of the kingdom.

When Matthias became king of Bohemia and Holy Roman emperor (r. 1612–1619), he reneged on his promise to the Protestants. The Habsburg succession to the Bohemian throne seemed secure, and concessions to Protestant elites seemed less necessary. As in the Netherlands, there was in Bohemia a delicate balance between the regional integrity and Bohemia's expectation of sharing its ruler with other regions. As Philip II had done, Matthias appointed a council of regents that enforced unpopular policies, particularly with regard to religion. The right to build new Protestant churches was denied. Bohemian crown lands were given to the Catholic church.

On May 23, 1618, delegates to a Protestant assembly that had unsuccessfully petitioned Matthias to end these policies marched to the palace in Prague where the hated royal officials met. After a confrontation over their demands, the delegates "tried" the officials on the spot for treason and, literally, threw them out the window of the palace. The incident became known as the "Defenestration of Prague" (the French word for window is *fenêtre*). (The officials' lives were saved only because they fell into a pile of manure.) The rebels proceeded to set up their own government.

The new Bohemian government deposed Matthias's successor as king, his Catholic cousin Ferdinand, and elected a new king in 1619. Ferdinand, however, ruled as Holy Roman emperor (1619–1637). The direct challenge to Habsburg control in Bohemia had implications for the empire as a whole because the new king of Bohemia was a Protestant, Frederick, elector of the Palatinate. Frederick was a Calvinist prince. His territories in west central Germany (called the Lower Palatinate and the Upper Palatinate) carried with them the right to be one of the seven electors who chose the emperor.

Encouraged by events in Bohemia, Protestant subjects in other Habsburg lands asked for guarantees of freedom of worship like those enjoyed by Protestants in Bohemia. This new Protestant success seemed to threaten the religious balance of power in the empire. Other princes saw their chance. Rival claimants to Habsburg rule in Hungary took up arms. The Protestant king of Denmark, Christian IV (r. 1588–1648), who was also duke of Holstein in northern Germany, sought to take advantage of the situation and conquer more German territory.

Foreign powers were also interested in these events. England practiced a pro-Protestant foreign policy, and the English king, James I, was Frederick's father-in-law. Spain's supply routes north from Italy to the Netherlands passed next to Frederick's lands in western Germany, and Spanish interests in the Netherlands were always sensitive to events in the Holy Roman Empire. France's first interest was pursuing its rivalry with Spain; thus, France kept its eye on the border principalities that were strategically important to Spain. In addition, it was in France's interest, much to the disgust of a devout Catholic faction at the French court, to keep Protestant as well as Catholic rulers in the empire strong enough to thwart Austrian Habsburg ambitions.

The revolt in Bohemia thus triggered a widespread war because it challenged Habsburg control in a direct and undeniable fashion and because other Protestant and Catholic princes alike felt their interests to be involved. From the outset, the war was a conflict over the Habsburgs' power in their own lands and about the balance of power in the empire and in Europe (Map 18.1).

By the fall of 1620 a Catholic army was closing in on Bohemia; the army was supported by the duke of Bavaria, who had been offered the Palatinate as a victory prize. On November 8, on a hillside west of Prague, the Catholic force faced a Bohemian army that had not garnered much concrete aid from Protestant allies. The resulting battle of White Mountain was a complete Catholic victory.

THE THIRTY YEARS' WAR, 1618–1648

1618	Bohemian revolt against Hapsburg rule
	Defenestration of Prague
1619	Ferdinand II is elected Holy Roman emperor
	Frederick, Elector Palatine, is elected king of Bohemia
1620	Catholic victory at Battle of White Mountain
1621	Truce between Spain and the Netherlands expires; war between Spain and the Netherlands begins
1626	Imperial forces defeat armies of Christian IV of Denmark
1629	Peace of Lübeck
1631	Swedes under Gustav Adolf defeat imperial forces at Breitenfeld
	Catholic forces sack Magdeburg
1632	Death of Gustav Adolf
1635	Peace of Prague
1643	French defeat Spanish in the Netherlands
1648	Peace of Westphalia

Fighting then became more widespread. The truce between Spain and the Netherlands, established in 1609 (see page 628), expired in 1621, and the nearby Lower Palatinate, now in Catholic hands, offered a staging point for Spanish forces. At this point the Protestant king of Denmark decided to seize more territory, both to give himself greater control over profitable Baltic ports and to defend himself against any Catholic attempt to seize northern German territory. Christian received little help from Protestant allies, however; the Dutch were busy with Spain, and the English were still wary of continental entanglements. The Protestant Swedish were uninterested in furthering Danish ambitions in the Baltic and so provided no aid at all.

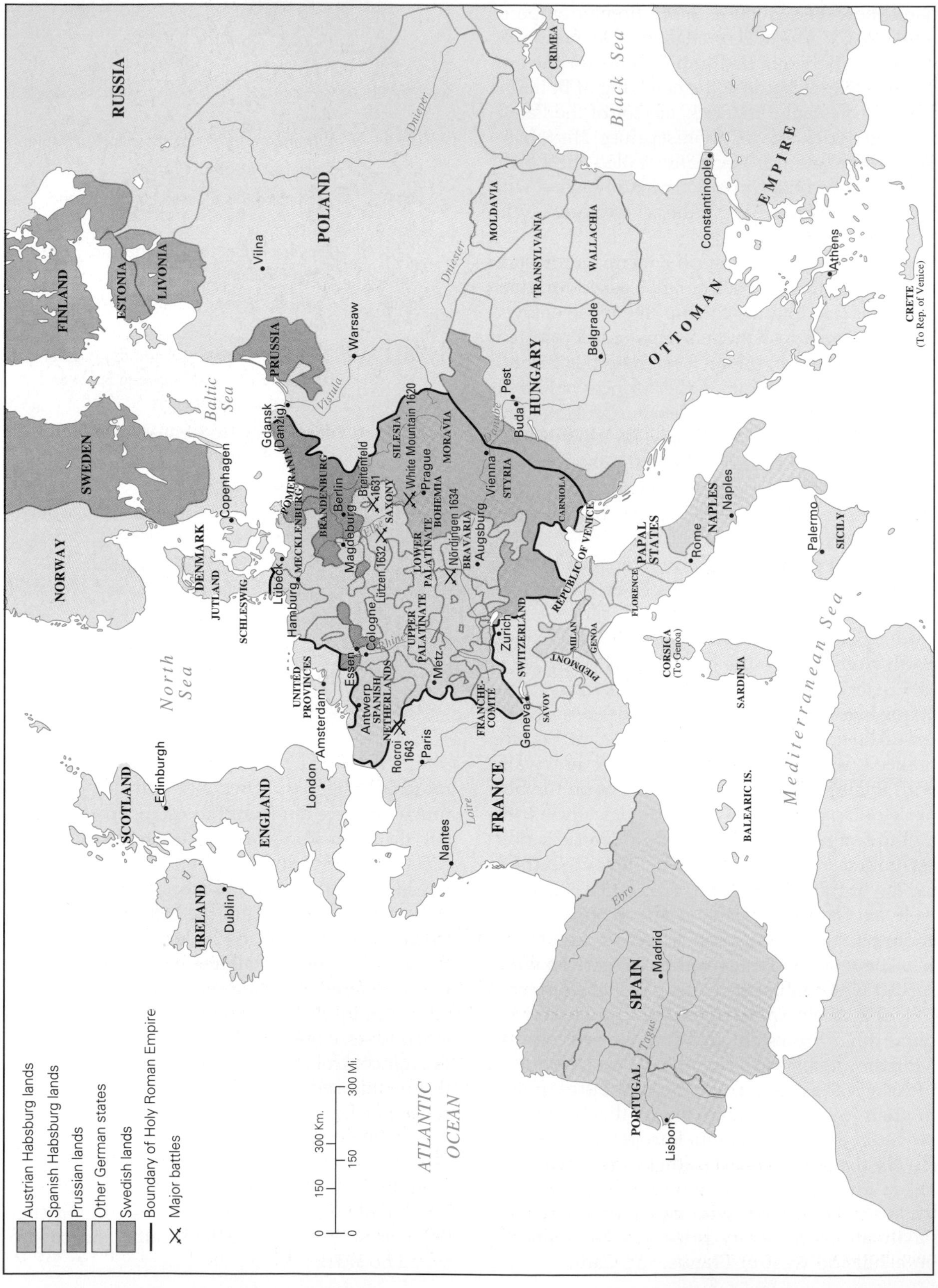
Austrian Habsburg lands
Spanish Habsburg lands
Prussian lands
Other German states
Swedish lands
Boundary of Holy Roman Empire
Major battles
0 150 300 Km.
0 150 300 Mi.
ATLANTIC OCEAN
North Sea
Baltic Sea
Black Sea
Mediterranean Sea
RUSSIA
FINLAND
ESTONIA
LIVONIA
SWEDEN
NORWAY
DENMARK
JUTLAND
SCHLESWIG
POLAND
PRUSSIA
SCOTLAND
ENGLAND
IRELAND
FRANCE
SPAIN
PORTUGAL
UNITED PROVINCES
SPANISH NETHERLANDS
POMERANIA
MECKLENBURG
BRANDENBURG
SAXONY
SILESIA
BOHEMIA
MORAVIA
LOWER PALATINATE
UPPER PALATINATE
BAVARIA
STYRIA
CARNIOLA
FRANCHE-COMTÉ
SWITZERLAND
SAVOY
PIEDMONT
MILAN
GENOA
REPUBLIC OF VENICE
FLORENCE
PAPAL STATES
NAPLES
SICILY
SARDINIA
CORSICA (To Genoa)
BALEARIC IS.
HUNGARY
TRANSYLVANIA
MOLDAVIA
WALLACHIA
CRIMEA
OTTOMAN EMPIRE
CRETE (To Rep. of Venice)
Edinburgh
Dublin
London
Amsterdam
Antwerp
Rocroi 1643
Paris
Nantes
Essen
Cologne
Metz
Hamburg
Lübeck
Copenhagen
Gdansk (Danzig)
Warsaw
Vilna
Berlin
Magdeburg
Breitenfeld 1631
Lützen 1632
White Mountain 1620
Prague
Nördlingen 1634
Augsburg
Vienna
Zurich
Geneva
Buda
Pest
Belgrade
Constantinople
Athens
Rome
Naples
Palermo
Madrid
Lisbon
Dnieper
Dniester
Vistula
Elbe
Rhine
Danube
Loire
Ebro
Tagus

The confusing blend of politics and religion that motivated the Protestant rulers was also evident on the Catholic side. Imperial forces defeated Christian's armies in 1626. Alarmed at the possibility of greater imperial control in northern Germany, Catholic princes led by the duke of Bavaria arranged a truce that led to the Peace of Lübeck in 1629—and to Denmark's withdrawal from the fighting on relatively generous terms.

Christian's rival, Gustav Adolf, king of Sweden (r. 1611–1632), immediately assumed the role of Protestant champion. Gustav, a brilliant and innovative military leader, hoped to gain territory along the Baltic seacoast, but personal aggrandizement also was one of his goals. His campaigns were capped by a victory over an imperial army at Breitenfeld in Saxony in 1631. The tide turned in the favor of imperial forces, however, after Gustav Adolf was killed at the battle of Lützen in late 1632. A decisive imperial victory over a combined Swedish and German Protestant army, at Nördlingen in 1634, led to a general peace treaty favorable to the Catholics: the Peace of Prague (1635).

Large-scale fighting ceased for a time, but the peace was fragile for two reasons. First, the destructive effects of war could not be remedied as easily as treaty provisions could be implemented. Second, France's interest in imperial affairs now intensified.

Where fighting had been concentrated, such as in parts of Saxony, the war caused enormous devastation. In the regions most affected, between a third and half of the inhabitants of rural villages and major towns may have disappeared. Many starved, were caught in the fighting, or were killed by marauding soldiers. The most notorious atrocity occurred in the aftermath of the siege of Magdeburg in 1631. After the city surrendered to besieging Catholic forces, long-deprived soldiers ate and drank themselves into a frenzy, raped and killed indiscriminately, and set fires that totally destroyed the town (killing some of their own ranks in the process). Some victims of war migrated to other regions in search of peaceful conditions and work. Some joined the armies in order to survive. Others formed their own armed bands to fight off the soldiers or to steal back enough goods to live on.

The Horror of War The suffering of civilians at the hands of soldiers is recorded in this contemporary illustration of a firebrand who extorted money and provisions by threatening people's homes with arson. *(From Leonhard Fronsperger,* Von Kayserlichen Kriegsrechten . . . *, vol. 3, fo. LXVIII. Courtesy Harvard College Library)*

Compounding these effects of war were the actions of armies hired by enterprising mercenary generals for whom loyalty to the princes who paid them took a back seat to personal advancement. They contracted to provide, supply, and lead troops and thus were more willing than the princes would have been to allow troops to live "economically" on plunder. All states and commanders strained to pay and supply their troops, but mercenary armies—and their generals—were especially difficult to control.

In any case, the Peace of Prague brought only a temporary peace because French involvement increased. France tried to seize imperial territory along its own eastern border and generously subsidized continued fighting within the empire by

Map 18.1 Europe in the Thirty Years' War The Thirty Years' War was fought largely within the borders of the Holy Roman Empire. It was the result of conflicts within the empire as well as the meddling of neighbors for their own strategic advantage.

channeling monies to Protestant mercenaries there. Fighting dragged on. The Swedes re-entered the war, hoping to obtain territory on the northern coast. In the south, rivals to the Habsburgs in Hungary tried to seize territory. By the end of the war, order had disintegrated so completely in the wake of the marauding armies that both staunchly Catholic rulers and firmly Protestant ones made alliances with religious enemies to safeguard their states. In popular printed literature and court drama alike, the seeming irrationality of the war was condemned.

A comprehensive peace treaty was finally possible after France withdrew its sponsorship of continued fighting. There were domestic reasons for France's withdrawal. Louis XIII (r. 1610–1643) had died, leaving a minor child to rule and to face the burden of war debt. France wanted only a workable balance of power in the empire; more important to France was the continued rivalry with the Spanish Habsburgs for control of territory along France's eastern and northern borders and in Italy. A defeat by France in the Spanish Netherlands in 1643 had convinced Spain to concentrate on that rivalry, and fighting between them continued until 1659.

A series of treaties known as the Peace of Westphalia (1648) ended fighting in the empire. The treaties recognized Calvinism as a tolerated religion within the empire. The requirement that all subjects must follow their rulers' faith was retained, but some leeway was allowed for those who now found themselves under new rulers. The property of those who decided to move elsewhere for religious reasons was protected. In its recognition of religious plurality, the Peace of Westphalia effectively put an end to religious war in the empire. The rights of states, however, were still enforced over the desires of individuals.

In political matters, the treaties reflected some of the recent successes of the Swedish by granting them Baltic coast territory. France gained the important towns of Metz, Toul, and Verdun on its eastern border. Most of the important Catholic and Protestant rulers, such as the dukes of Bavaria and Saxony, extended their territories at the expense of smaller principalities and cities. The son of Frederick—the king of Bohemia—was given the smaller of the two Palatine territories that his father had held. The Upper Palatinate—as well as the right to be a new elector of the emperor—was given to the powerful duke of Bavaria.

Some of the most important political outcomes of the war were not explicitly mentioned in the Peace of Westphalia. No one needed to have them spelled out. One outcome was that the states within the empire would henceforth be virtually autonomous. From this point forward, each major state of the empire would conduct its own foreign policy; the Holy Roman Empire was no longer a meaningful political entity. Another outcome was that the Habsburgs, though weakened as emperors, were strengthened as rulers of their own hereditary lands on the eastern fringes of the empire. They moved their capital from Prague to Vienna, and the government of Habsburg lands gained in importance as administration of the empire waned.

The Military Revolution Continued

Developments in warfare in the seventeenth century were part of the long transition from reliance on brute force to reliance on firepower—that is, from charges of men (often mounted) using swords, knives, and lances to firearms, including artillery and handheld weapons. The seventeenth century saw a further step in the application of firepower to warfare: the use of volley fire, the arrangement of foot soldiers in parallel lines so that one man could fire while another reloaded. Gustav Adolf's victories in the Thirty Years' War and his reputation as a general came from his refinements of volley fire. Gustav amassed large numbers of troops, increased the rate of fire so that a virtually continuous barrage was maintained, and used maneuverable field artillery to protect the massed troops from cavalry charges. Following Gustav Adolf's lead, armies of all the major states adopted these tactics.

These new offensive tactics changed the character of armies and the demands on governments to provide for them. A higher proportion of soldiers became gunners, and their effectiveness lay in how well they operated as a unit. Armies began to train seriously off the field of battle: Drill and discipline were vital to success. The numbers of men on the battlefield increased somewhat, but the total numbers of men in arms supported by the state at any time increased dramatically once the organization to support them was in place. Late in the century, France kept about 400,000 men in arms when at war (which was most of the time).

Despite the new offensive tactics, defensive tactics—such as holding fortresses—often won the day, and pitched battles, such as at Nördlingen in 1634, still tended to be part of sieges. Thus, military strategists took a fresh look at the expensive tactic of besieging fortresses and holding surrounding territory. A general and military engineer designed new fortresses that functioned both as a supply depot and as an impregnable fortification and were to be built at specified distances along France's eastern border.

The new technology, formations, and tactics did not necessarily produce victories more readily than before. Most wars were still won by destroying enemy resources and by wearing down enemy forces. States that tended to matters off the battlefield—especially to recruitment and supply—were most likely to be successful. Louis XIV's victories in the second half of the century are partly traceable to his regime's attention to such matters. From the events of the Thirty Years' War Louis and other rulers learned the importance of supplying, training, and controlling their armies. Whatever the expense, no ruler would again be dependent on great mercenary generals.

State Building and Revolution in the West

The Thirty Years' War brought financial strain and domestic policy conflicts to all participants. Questions about regional autonomy, about the power of elites to contest royal control, and about religion persisted in all the major states of western Europe. Rulers' efforts to raise revenue to carry out aggressive foreign policy sparked protests by common people, who paid most of the taxes, and conflict with elites, who wanted to share in the governing process. In England, the upshot of these conflicts was civil war and the temporary abolition of the monarchy. Common to France, England, the Netherlands, and Spain was a struggle over the nature and limits of central authority.

The Resurgence of France, 1610–1661

Henry IV (r. 1589–1610) successfully brought the French religious wars to a conclusion and extended formal toleration to the Huguenot minority in 1598 with the Edict of Nantes. During his reign, France recovered from long years of civil war. Population and productivity began to grow; the Crown encouraged internal improvements to facilitate commerce. Henry's chief minister, Maximilien de Béthune, duke of Sully (1560–1641), undertook major financial reforms. He succeeded in creating a budget surplus and amassing armaments in anticipation of the Crown's future needs.

Despite these successes, Henry's regime was stable only in comparison with the preceding years of civil war. The power of the great nobility had not been definitively broken. Several leading nobles plotted with foreign powers, including Spain, trying to influence French policy and gain materially themselves. Moreover, the king had agreed to a provision, known as the *paulette* (named for the functionary who first administered it), that allowed royal officeholders not merely to own their offices but also to bequeath those offices to their heirs in return for the payment of an annual fee. Thus, a position in the royal bureaucracy became property like the landed property of the traditional nobility. Guaranteeing the privileged position of royal bureaucrats—particularly the royal judges of the Parlement of Paris, who had recently agreed to the Edict of Nantes only under duress—helped cement their loyalty at a critical time. However, that privileged position made royal officeholders as immune as the warrior-nobility from royal control.

A fanatical Catholic assassinated Henry IV in 1610, leaving his son, Louis XIII (r. 1610–1643), only 9 years old, to face these challenges as well as a return of religious conflict. The problems were worsened by the ineptitude of the regent, Louis's mother, Marie de' Medici (1573–1642). Inexperienced and unskilled politically, she aroused suspicions and stirred up factional strife at court by favoring a staunchly Catholic, pro-Habsburg foreign policy.

In 1621, the king faced a major rebellion by his Huguenot subjects in southwestern France. The Edict of Nantes had granted the Protestant minority significant military power in the form of royally funded garrisons in over fifty towns. But the garrisons for self-defense as well as the right to worship had been granted only in a royal edict, issued (and revocable) at the pleasure of the king. Hearing rumors that the government was going to move against their garrisons, the Protestants felt threatened. Louis himself helped provoke the Huguenot uprising by reimposing Catholicism in a border region near Spain in the Pyrenees, where his ancestors themselves had established Protestantism. He had recently married the daughter of Philip III, king of Spain (known to us, oddly, as Anne of Austria).

The Crown managed the war very badly until 1624, when an ambitious and talented cleric, Armand Jean du Plessis (1585–1642), Cardinal Richelieu, began to exert great influence in the king's circle. In 1628 the king's troops captured La Rochelle, a Huguenot fortress town on the western coast of France. In 1629 the Huguenots accepted the Peace of Alais, which Richelieu had crafted. The treaty was a political triumph for the Crown because it continued the policy of religious toleration but rescinded the Protestants' military and political privileges. It deprived French Protestants of both the means and the motive for further rebellion.

Cardinal Richelieu was perhaps the most talented of all the great ministers who dominated royal governments in the seventeenth century. He intelligently used force or was lenient as necessary to accomplish his goals. *(Chantilly, Musée Condé/Laurie Platt Winfrey, Inc.)*

Cardinal Richelieu was a great executive who knew how to direct his own and others' efforts to maximum effect. He earned the loyalty of the king by conscientiously keeping him informed and carefully managing his sensitive, changeable temperament. There was much opposition to Cardinal Richelieu's policies, but whatever stability Louis's regime achieved was the cardinal's doing.

By 1630 Richelieu ended the challenge of the pro-Catholic party. He persuaded Louis to exile Marie de' Medici, his mother, from court. He also arrested the leaders of this "devout" faction and executed one of them. He could then support German states against the Habsburgs in the Thirty Years' War and, after 1635, intervene directly on behalf of German allies and France's territorial interests against Spain.

Holding sway over the king and achieving control of royal policy proved to be easier than eliminating traditional aristocratic resistance to royal authority, however. There were a number of noble revolts in the 1630s. Several rebel nobles, including France's most talented commanders, were even willing to fight with Spain in order to improve their own bargaining position with the French crown. Richelieu negotiated with some of them and retaliated brutally against others. He took the bold step of executing three nobles for treason—including one from the prominent Montmorency family whose battle wounds were patched up so that he might be executed as an example. Richelieu also used innovative political tools. To undercut noble influence in the provinces, in 1632 he created the office of *intendant.* Intendants were provincial officials who had wide powers for defense and administration.

Rebellions against taxation throughout the kingdom also challenged the control of the Crown and its provincial officials. The burden of taxation on ordinary people increased as the French war effort picked up in the 1630s. Widespread revolts in 1636–1637 and 1639–1640 forced the diversion of royal troops from the wars against Spain. Compounding the misery of crushing taxation was the devastation of war itself along the northern and eastern borders of the kingdom, where much of the fighting against Spain took place.

Richelieu worked zealously and effectively to strengthen the monarchy. But when he and Louis XIII died within five months of each other in 1642–1643, the kingdom again faced unrest as the Crown again passed into the hands of a child, the 5-year-old Louis XIV (r. 1643–1715), and a regent, Anne of Austria (1601–1666). Adept management by Anne for her son and by Anne's chief minister and personal friend Cardinal Jules Mazarin (1602–1666) kept monarchial power intact in the face of three challengers: the Parlement of Paris, the nobility, and the people.

From 1648 to 1652, the regency faced serious revolts. They were led, at first, by the judges of the Parlement of Paris and were the first evidence of dangers to the monarchy stemming from the greater independence royal officers had gained. The Parlementaires objected to loans that the monarchy demanded in exchange for the renewal of the paulette—loans needed to cover rising war costs. They also objected to the creation of the intendants, which undercut the authority of existing provincial bureaucrats. The source of their leverage over the monarchy was their traditional right to register laws and edicts, which amounted to a right of judicial review. Now, the Parlement attempted to extend this power by debating and criticizing government policies.

After a three-month siege of Paris by royal armies in early 1649, the Parlement backed down after winning the guarantee of the paulette without the need for further renewals. The popular unrest that had accompanied the revolt was partially responsible for ending it. Citizens of Paris had barricaded city streets against royal troops. Political pamphlets critical of Mazarin and calling for popular demonstrations at particular times and places were published. The distant memory of the popular government that had seized control of Paris late in the religious wars frightened the Parlementaires into once again becoming pillars of royal authority.

Certain great nobles had supported the Parlementaires and the popular agitation in Paris, and now they and others proceeded to revolt on their own. Access to royal patronage was always hotly contested, and never more so than when an unpopular minister, such as Richelieu or Mazarin, was in control of its distribution. For the next three years, Mazarin and Anne of Austria faced armed revolts throughout the kingdom, led by the greatest princes, coinciding with and supporting continuing popular revolts. For a time, Mazarin was driven into exile. He slowly regained control over the government by using armed force, by winning the loyalty of individual princes through concessions, and through the ineptitude of the rebels themselves.

These challenges to royal power were afterward called the "Fronde"—the name of a children's game of the time—partly to try to diminish their seriousness. They did not succeed because there was no alternative to strong royal power in France. Great nobles were jealous of one another's authority as well as the Crown's and had brought France close to chaos. The Parlement of Paris was a law court, not a representative assembly. Its legitimacy derived from its role as upholder of royal law, and only with great care could it challenge the king on the pretext of upholding royal tradition in his name. Popular rebellions had no national institutional focus, and nervous elites were more likely to quash them than to support them. A strong-willed and able ruler could at least temporarily eclipse challenges to royal power. This is what happened when Louis XIV took over the reins of government at Mazarin's death in 1661.

Crown and Parliament in England

In 1603, Queen Elizabeth died and James VI of Scotland acceded to the English throne as James I (r. 1603–1625) with remarkably little fuss. The son of Mary, Queen of Scots, James had been raised by the Protestant nobility of Scotland who had opposed Mary's rule.

The principal problem facing the English monarchy was financial. There were considerable debts left from the Irish conflicts and wars with Spain. Court life became more elaborate and an increasing drain. Though very intelligent, James lacked administrative ability and a sense of diligence. His own leanings toward extravagance were partly to blame for his financial problems, but so were pressures for patronage from elites. To raise revenue without Parliament's consent the Crown relied on sources of revenue that it had enjoyed since medieval times: customs duties granted to the monarch for life, wardship (the right to manage and liberally borrow from the estates of minor nobles), and the sale of monopolies, whereby a merchant paid the Crown for the right to be sole agent for a particular kind of goods. To these, James added other expedients such as the sale of crown lands and of noble titles, even as he extended traditional means—such as increasing the number of monopolies sold.

These financial measures caused tension among merchants because they interfered with trade and increased the prices of goods, and they created resentments among courtiers competing for monopolies and other perks. Resentments among the nobility were sharpened—and criticism of the court generally was heightened—by James's favoritism of certain courtiers and their families. The chief beneficiary of patronage and the most influential adviser to the king was George Villiers (1592–1628), duke of Buckingham—a powerful but corrupt and inadequate first minister.

James tried to keep the peace with Spain, ending in 1604 the war begun during Elizabeth's reign. But public opinion was suspicious of any policy that seemed to favor Spain. When James's daughter and her husband Frederick, the elector of the Palatinate, were chased out of their new kingdom of Bohemia in 1620, James was forced into a more aggressively pro-Protestant foreign policy. When he finally summoned Parliament for funds, Parliament used the occasion to protest court corruption and the king's financial expedients. Significantly, Parliament did not try to assert its authority against the king in dramatic ways. Rather than legislate changes in the king's finances, the members simply impeached and removed from office two royal ministers. Thus, although political tensions had mounted in James's reign, they were kept within bounds.

Under James's son Charles I (r. 1625–1649), tensions between Crown and Parliament rose. One reason was the growing financial strain of foreign policy as well as the policies themselves. Retaining the unpopular duke of Buckingham as chief courtier and adviser, Charles declared war on Spain and pursued an indecisive but costly foreign policy in France in support of the Huguenot rebels. Many wealthy merchants opposed this aggressive foreign policy, which disrupted trading relationships. Meanwhile, the Crown's reliance on unpopular financial expedients continued and reached a new level of coercion. In 1627, Charles imprisoned certain gentry who refused to lend money to the government.

Problems also swirled around Charles's religious policies. Charles was personally inclined toward "high church" practices: an emphasis on ceremony and sacrament in Anglicanism reminiscent of Catholic ritual. He also was a believer in Arminianism, a school of thought that justified the emphasis on ritual by denying the Calvinist precept of predestination. These emphases highlighted the authority of clerics and the importance of hierarchy and obedience instead of lay control over religion. Charles was intent on fashioning an official religion that would better reflect and justify his claims to power.

William Laud (1573–1645), the most influential religious leader in Charles's reign, was an Arminian. Archbishop of Canterbury from 1633 and thus leader of the Church of England, Laud tried to impose ritual changes in worship, spread Arminian ideas, and censor opposing views. His actions threatened to undermine the religious peace that had allowed "high church" Anglicans as well as fiercely Calvinist Puritans to remain within the Church of England since Elizabeth's reign. Laud also challenged the redistribution of church property, which had occurred in the Reformation of the sixteenth century, and thereby alienated the gentry on economic as well as religious grounds.

Charles's style of rule worsened religious, political, and economic tensions. Like Laud, his chief prelate, he was highhanded and impervious to public opinion. His court was ruled by formal protocol, and access to the king himself was highly restricted—a serious problem in an age when personal access to the monarch was the guarantee of political power. Cold and intensely private, Charles was not a man to build confidence or smooth over political tensions with charm or dexterous political maneuvering.

Struggle over issues of revenue and religion dominated debate in the Parliament of 1628–

1629, which Charles had called to get funds for his foreign policy. In 1628 the members of Parliament presented the king with a document called the "Petition of Right," which protested his financial policies as well as arbitrary imprisonment. Though essentially conservative because it called for a return to previously accustomed governing practices, the Petition of Right nevertheless reflected Parliament's growing determination to check arbitrary royal actions. Charles dissolved the Parliament in March 1629, having decided that the money he might extract from Parliament was not worth the effort.

For eleven years, Charles ruled without Parliament. When he was forced to call Parliament again, in 1640, not only were royal finances in desperate straits but political tension had risen markedly. In the intervening eleven years, Archbishop Laud's religious policies had raised concern and opposition among a wide spectrum of elites as well as among ordinary citizens of London, where his clerical influence was greatest. Moreover, Charles had pressed collection of revenues far beyond traditional bounds. In 1634, for example, he revived annual collection of "ship money"—a medieval tax levied on coastal districts to help support the navy during war. England, however, was not at war, and the tax was levied not only on seaports but on inland areas too. Resistance to the collection of various customs duties, taxes, fees, and fines grew. Refusal to pay became increasingly common in elite circles.

Also important were the immediate circumstances surrounding the summoning of Parliament. Charles needed money to combat a rebellion by his Scottish subjects. Like the Habsburg rulers in Bohemia, Charles tried to rule in Scotland through a small council of men who did not represent the local elite. He also unwisely and unsuccessfully sought to force the Scots, most of whom practiced Calvinist-inspired Presbyterianism, to adopt Anglican liturgy and ritual. In 1639 Charles started a war against them but, lacking men and money, was forced to agree to a peace treaty. Intent on renewing the war, he was forced to summon Parliament to obtain funds.

Politically weakened by military failure, Charles faced Parliament in 1640 and bungled his opportunity to obtain funds and to re-establish a workable relationship with Parliament. This Parliament, now known as the "Short Parliament," met in the spring of 1640. Charles dissolved it after just three weeks, when members questioned the war with the Scots and other royal policies. More politically risky even than dissolving the Parliament—an accepted right of the monarch—was the lack of respect Charles had shown the members—a number of them were harassed or arrested. Mistrust and suspicion fomented by the eleven years in which Charles had ruled without Parliament thus increased.

Another humiliating and decisive defeat at the hands of the Scots later in 1640 made summoning another Parliament imperative. This Parliament is known as the "Long Parliament" because it sat from 1640 to 1660. Charles was forced to agree not to dissolve or adjourn Parliament without the members' own consent and to summon Parliament at least every three years. Parliament abolished many of his unorthodox and traditional sources of revenue and impeached and removed from office his leading ministers, including Archbishop Laud. One royal commander, Thomas Wentworth, earl of Strafford, was executed without trial.

The execution of Strafford shocked many aristocrats in the House of Lords as well as moderate members of the House of Commons. Meanwhile, Parliament, which was controlled by Puritans with various shades of belief, was debating the perennially thorny religious question. A bare majority favored abolition of Anglican bishops and other changes unacceptable to the king. Working people in London, kept apprised of the issues by the regular publication of parliamentary debates, demonstrated in support of that majority. Moderate members of Parliament, in contrast, favored checking the king's power but not upsetting the Elizabethan religious compromise. An event that unified public and Parliamentary opinion at a crucial time—a revolt against English rule in Ireland in October 1641—temporarily eclipsed these divisions.

The fear inspired by this largely Catholic uprising made the broad consensus of anti-Catholicism the temporary driving force in politics. It was widely rumored that Charles would use Irish soldiers against his English subjects. Parliament demanded control of the army to put down the rebellion, and in November the Puritans introduced a document known as the "Grand Remonstrance," an appeal to the people and a long catalog of parliamentary grievances against the king. By a narrow margin it was passed and then published, further setting public opinion in London against Charles. The king's remaining support in Parliament eroded in January 1642, when he attempted to arrest five leading members of Commons on charges of treason. The five escaped, but the attempt set the stage for wider violence. The king withdrew from London, unsure he could defend himself there, and began to raise an army. In mid-1642 the kingdom was at the brink of civil war between royalist "Cavaliers" and parliamentary "Roundheads."

Civil War and Revolution in England, 1642–1660

Fighting broke out in the late summer of 1642. The Long Parliament initiated new taxes to pay for the parliamentary armies. It also restructured the Church of England, eliminating the bishops and calling a national assembly to work out a new religious settlement. Parliament continued to represent a broad coalition of critics and opponents of the monarchy, ranging from aristocrats concerned primarily with the abuses of royal prerogative to radical Puritans eager for thorough religious reform and determined to defeat the king. No one class as a whole favored king or Parliament. As the war continued, divisions within Parliament and among its supporters became increasingly visible.

At first the tide of war favored the royalists. So in the summer of 1643, Parliament sought help from the Scots. In exchange for military aid from the Scots, Parliament agreed that Presbyterianism, the Scottish brand of Calvinism, would become the religion of England.

Meanwhile, Oliver Cromwell (1599–1658), a Puritan member of the Long Parliament and a cavalry officer, realized that the parliamentary forces needed a strong cavalry in order to defeat the king's forces. The eleven-hundred-man cavalry trained by Cromwell and known as the "Ironsides" helped parliamentary and Scottish infantry defeat the king's troops at Marston Moor in July 1644. The victory made Cromwell famous.

In the fall, in Parliament, Cromwell criticized the conduct of the war by the commander-in-chief of parliamentary forces. As a result, sitting members of Parliament were barred from commanding troops (and upper-class control of the army was reduced), and a "New Model Army," rigorously trained like Cromwell's Ironsides, was created.

The New Model Army won a convincing victory over royal forces at Naseby in 1645. In the spring of 1646, Charles surrendered to a Scottish army in the north. In January 1647, Parliament paid the Scots for their services in the war and took the king into custody. In the negotiations that followed, Charles tried to play his opponents off against each other, and, as he hoped, divisions among them widened.

A majority of Parliament wanted peace with the king in return for acceptance of the new church structure and parliamentary control of standing militias for a specified period.

They had begun to fear the more radical groups, particularly those in the army and in London who had supported them up until this point. Most members of Parliament were Presbyterians, Puritans who favored a strongly unified and controlled state church along Calvinist lines. Worship would be purged of "popish" practices, but power would not be shared. These men were increasingly alarmed by the rise of sectarian differences and the actual religious freedom that many ordinary people were claiming for themselves. With the weakening of royal authority and the disruption of civil war, censorship was relaxed and public preaching by ordinary women and men who felt a religious inspiration was becoming commonplace.

More ominous, from the elite perspective, was the presence of organized groups with their own power bases that wanted both religious and political change. Most officers of the New Model Army were Independents, Puritans who favored a decentralized church, a degree of religious toleration, and a wider sharing of political power among men of property, not just among the very wealthy gentry. In London, a well-organized artisans' movement known as the Levelers favored universal manhood suffrage, reform of law, and better access to education in addition to decentralized churches (see the box, "The Levelers Advocate Change").

In May 1647 Parliament voted to disband the New Model Army without paying most

Popular Preaching in England Many women took advantage of the collapse of royal authority to preach in public—a radical activity for women at the time. This print satirizes the Quakers, a religious movement that attracted many women. *(Mary Evans Picture Library)*

of the soldiers' back wages and to offer terms to the king. The army, supported by the Levelers in London, kidnapped the king and in August occupied Westminster, Parliament's meeting place. In November Charles escaped from his captors and tried to raise a new army among his erstwhile enemies, the Scots, who were also alarmed by the growing radicalism in England.

War began again in the north early in 1648 but ended in August with a victory by Cromwell and the New Model Army over the royalist Scots at Preston, in northwestern England. This time, army leaders left nothing to chance. When Parliament, still dominated by Presbyterians, once again voted to negotiate with the king, Cromwell and the army prevented members who favored Presbyterianism or the king from attending sessions. The remaining "Rump" Parliament voted to try the king, and Charles I was executed for "treason, tyranny and bloodshed" against his people on January 30, 1649.

A Commonwealth—a republic—was declared. Executive power resided in a council of state. Legislative power resided in a one-chamber Parliament, the Rump Parliament (the House of Lords was abolished). Declaring a republic proved far easier than running one, however. The execution of the king shocked most English and Scots people. The legitimacy of the Commonwealth government would always be in question, and the tasks of making and implementing policy were made difficult by the narrow political base on which the government rested. Excluded were the majority of the reformist gentry; they had been purged from Parliament. Also excluded were the Levelers and other populist groups. When Leveler leaders published tracts critical of the new government, they were arrested, and new censorship began to be imposed thereafter.

Above all, the government was vulnerable to the power of the army, which had created it. In 1649 and 1650, Cromwell led expeditions to Ireland and Scotland to put down resistance to the new English government. In Ireland, Cromwell's forces acted with great ruthlessness, and English control was advanced by the further dispossession of Irish landholders. Meanwhile, Parliament, unable to agree on systematic reforms, dallied

The Levelers Advocate Change

The Levelers published petitions and proposals for constitutional, economic, and legal reform. Some were addressed to Parliament; others were manifestoes of a more general nature. Excerpt (A), from 1647, reveals some of the social and economic reforms that the Levelers believed should accompany democratic political reforms. Notice the religious inspiration for some of their points. Document (B), from 1649, describes the government envisioned by the Levelers after the execution of the king.

(A)

The oppressive monopoly of merchant-adventurers, and others, do still remain to the great abridgment of the liberties of the people . . . and to the great discouragement and disadvantage of all sorts of tradesmen, sea-faring men and hindrance of shipping and navigation. Also the old tedious . . . way of deciding controversies, or suits in law, is continued to this day, to the extreme vexation and utter undoing of multitudes of families. . . . Likewise, that old but most unequal punishment of malefactors is still continued whereby . . . corporall pains [are] as much inflicted for small as for great offenses, and that most unjustly upon the testimony of one witness, contrary both to the law of God and common equity. . . . Also tithes . . . are still continued, though there be no ground for [it] in Gospel.

(B)

We the free people of England . . . are agreed as followeth, that the supreme authority of England . . . shall be and reside henceforward in a representative of the people consisting of four hundred persons, but no more; in the choice of whom (according to natural right) all men of the age of one and twenty years and upwards (not being servants or receiving alms, or having served the late king . . .) shall have their voices.

Source: Howard Shaw, *The Levellers* (New York: Harper and Row, 1968), pp. 112, 116.

over the one reform that radical elements in the army insisted on: new, more broadly based elections for Parliament. Fresh from his victories in the north, Cromwell led his armies to London and dissolved Parliament in the spring of 1652.

In 1653, some army officers drew up the "Instrument of Government," England's first and only written constitution. It provided for an executive, the Lord Protector; a governing council to assist the Lord Protector; and a Parliament to be based on somewhat wider male suffrage. Cromwell was the natural choice for Lord Protector, and whatever success the government of the Protectorate had was largely due to him.

Unlike many, Cromwell was not averse to compromise. Although he had used the army against Parliament in 1648, he had worked hard to reconcile the Rump Parliament and the army before marching on London in 1652. He believed in a state church, but one that allowed for control, including choice of minister, by local congregations. He believed in toleration for other Protestant sects, as well as for Catholics and Jews, as long as no one disturbed the peace. He was more tolerant of Quakers than most of his peers. Many disillusioned Levelers had joined this religious movement, which claimed fifty thousand adherents a few years after its founding in the early 1650s. The Quakers espoused complete religious autonomy. A congregation worshiped in silence until an "inner light" induced any man or woman present to speak. Quakers were radicals in other ways: They refused all oaths or service to the state, and they refused to acknowledge social rank.

As Lord Protector, Cromwell oversaw impressive reforms in law that testify to his belief in the limits of governing authority. For example, contrary to the practice of his day, he opposed capital punishment for petty crimes. The government of the Protectorate, however, accomplished little because Parliament remained internally divided and opposed to Cromwell's initiatives. Cromwell was challenged by radical republicans in Parliament who thought the Protectorate represented a step backward, away from republican government. In the population at large, there were still royalist sympathizers, and a royalist uprising in 1655 forced the temporary division of England into military districts administered by generals.

In the end, the Protectorate could not survive the strains over policy and the challenges to its legitimacy. In September 1658, Cromwell died of a sudden illness, and the Protectorate did not long survive him. In February 1660, all the surviving members of the Long Parliament rejoined the Rump. The Parliament summarily dissolved itself and called for new elections. The newly elected Parliament recalled Charles II from exile and restored the monarchy. The chaos and radicalism of the late civil war and "Interregnum"—the period between reigns, as the years from 1649 to 1660 came to be called—now spawned a conservative reaction.

Oliver Cromwell Cromwell had seen his family's income decline under the weight of Charles I's exactions. Elected to Parliament in 1628 and again in 1640, he also brought a long-standing religious zeal to his public life. His opposition to the "tyranny and usurpation" of the Anglican church hierarchy first prompted him to criticize royal government. *(In the collection of the Duke of Buccleuch and Queensberry KT)*

The Restored Monarchy and Parliament in England, 1660–1689

Charles II (r. 1660–1685), son of Charles I, returned from exile abroad to claim his throne at the age of 30. He had learned from his years of uncertain exile and from the fate of his father. He did not seek retribution but rather offered a general pardon to all but a few rebels (mostly those who had signed his father's death warrant), and he suggested to Parliament a relatively tolerant religious settlement that would include Anglicans as well as Presbyterians. He was far more politically adept than his father and far more willing to compromise.

That the re-established royal government was not more tolerant than it turned out to be was not Charles's doing but Parliament's. During the 1660s, the "Cavalier" Parliament, named for royalists in the civil war, passed harsh laws aimed at religious dissenters. Anglican orthodoxy was reimposed, including the re-establishment of bishops and the Anglican Book of Common Prayer. All officeholders and clergy were required to swear oaths of obedience to the king and to the established church. As a result, hundreds of them were forced out of office. Holding nonconformist religious services became illegal, and Parliament passed a "five-mile" act to prevent dissenting ministers from traveling near their former congregations. Property laws were strengthened and the criminal codes made more severe.

The king's behavior began to mimic prerevolutionary royalist positions. Charles II began to flirt with Catholicism, and his brother and heir, James, openly converted. Charles promulgated a declaration of tolerance that would have included Catholics as well as nonconformist Protestants, but Parliament would not accept it. When Parliament moved to exclude James from the succession, Charles dissolved it. A subsequent Parliament, cowed by fears of a new civil war, backed down. By the end of his reign, Charles was financially independent of Parliament thanks to increased revenue from overseas trade and to secret subsidies from France, his recent ally against Dutch trading rivals (see page 683).

Underneath this seeming return to prerevolutionary conditions were conditions that reflected the legacy of the revolution that had cost Charles I his head. First, despite the harsh laws, to silence all dissent was not possible. After two decades of religious pluralism and broadly based political activity it was impossible to reimpose conformity; there were well-established communities of various sects and a self-confidence that bred vigorous resistance. Also, anti-Catholic feeling still united all Protestants. In 1678, Charles's secret treaties with the French became known, and rumors of a Catholic plot to murder Charles and reimpose Catholicism became widespread. No evidence of any plot was ever unearthed, though thirty-five people were executed for alleged participation. Parliament focused its attention on anti-Catholicism, passing an act barring all but Anglicans from Parliament itself.

The clearest reflection of the regime's revolutionary background was the power of Parliament. It was able to assert its policies against the desires of the king. Nevertheless, financial independence and firm political tactics enabled Charles to retain a great deal of power. If he had been followed by an able successor, Parliament might have lost a good measure of its confidence and independence. But his brother James's reign and its aftermath further enhanced the power of Parliament.

When James II (r. 1685–1689) succeeded Charles, Parliament's royalist loyalties were at first evident. James was granted customs duties for life and was also given funds to suppress a rebellion by one of Charles's illegitimate sons. Although James never tried to impose Catholicism on England, he did try to achieve toleration for Catholics by decree in two declarations of indulgence in 1687 and 1688. His efforts were undermined by his heavy-handed tactics. When several leading Anglican bishops refused to read the declarations from their pulpits, he had them imprisoned and tried for seditious libel. The jury, however, acquitted them.

James also failed because of the coincidence of other events. In 1685, at the outset of James's reign, Louis XIV in France revoked the Edict of Nantes, which had guaranteed the religious rights of French Protestants since 1598. The possibility that subjects and monarchs in France and, by extension, elsewhere could be of different faiths seemed increasingly unlikely. Popular fears of James's Catholicism were thus heightened early in his reign, and his later declarations of tolerance, though benefiting Protestant dissenters, were viewed with suspicion. In 1688, not only were the Anglican bishops acquitted but the king's second wife, who was Catholic, gave birth to a son. The birth raised the specter of a Catholic succession. In June 1688, to put pressure on James, leading members of Parliament invited William of Orange, husband of James's Protestant daughter Mary, to come to England. William mounted an invasion that became a rout when James refused to defend his throne. James simply abandoned England and went to France. William called Parliament, which declared James to have abdicated and offered the throne to him and to Mary. James eventually invaded Ireland in 1690 with French support but was defeated by William at the battle of Boyne that year.

The substitution of William (r. 1689–1702) and Mary (r. 1689–1694) for James, known as the "Glorious Revolution," was engineered by Parliament and confirmed its power. Parliament presented the new sovereigns with a "Declaration of Rights" upon their accession and, later that year, with a "Bill of Rights" that defended freedom of speech, called for frequent Parliaments, and required subsequent monarchs to be Protestant. The effectiveness of these documents was reinforced by Parliament's power of the purse.

William had wanted the throne of England not for its own sake but to ensure England's support in the Netherlands' ongoing wars with France. Parliament's role in the political process was ensured by William's interests in funding his ambitious military efforts.

The issues that had faced the English since the reign of James I were common to all European states: religious division and elite power, fiscal strains and resistance to taxation. Yet events in England had so far set it apart from the experience of other states in that the incremental assumption of authority by a well-established institution, Parliament, made challenge of the monarchy more legitimate and more effective. Political participation also developed in England more than in other states. In the long run, the strength of Parliament would make easier the task of permanently broadening participation in government.

The Netherlands and Spain

The United Provinces of the Netherlands comprised the seven northern provinces of the Low Countries, which had successfully revolted against Spanish rule in the sixteenth century. From one perspective, the Netherlands, as the provinces are usually called, seems to be at the extreme of decentralization among the European states, since the individual provinces retained much autonomy in theory. In fact, the government of the Netherlands was dominated by informal mechanisms that empowered either the leading merchant families of the city of Amsterdam or their rivals, various members of the noble house of Orange, to determine a collective foreign policy.

In the first half of the seventeenth century, Amsterdam dominated government because of its economic power and political significance. Since the beginning of the Netherlands' revolt against Spain in the 1560s, Amsterdam (in the province of Holland) had become a center of international trade and banking to rival and then surpass Antwerp. A closed circle of wealthy merchant families known as "Regents" dominated politics in Amsterdam and, by means of Holland's representatives to the States General, in the Netherlands as a whole. The chief of the Amsterdam delegation to the States General acted as a sort of head minister and set up and filled the administrative posts that constituted most of the government of the Netherlands. Thus, the government resembled the closed world of privileged officeholders that dominated governments elsewhere. Its unending interest was in conducting a foreign policy that could protect the commercial empire of which Amsterdam was the heart.

The only competition in the running of affairs came from the house of Orange, aristocratic leaders of the revolt against Spain. They exercised what control they had by means of the office of *Stadholder*—a kind of military governorship—to which they were elected in individual provinces. Like the delegates from Amsterdam, members of the house of Orange had private wealth with which to support their political power. Their principal interest was the traditional dynastic one of self-promotion. Therein lay a portion of their influence, for they continued to lead the defense of the Netherlands against Spanish attempts at reconquest—attempts that ended only in 1648 with the Peace of Westphalia. Their power also came from the fact that they represented the only possible counterweight within the Netherlands to the dominance of Amsterdam merchant interests. Small towns dependent on land-based trade or rural areas dominated by farmers and gentry often looked to the Stadholders of the Orange family to defend their interests.

By the last quarter of the seventeenth century, the Regents of Amsterdam had lost control of policy to William of Nassau, who was prince of Orange. The Regents were vulnerable for two reasons. First, they no longer represented the merchant elite of the city because Regent families had been slowly withdrawing from trade to invest in political offices and in financial transactions. Second, they were vulnerable because in 1672 a war had begun with both France and England, two powers that had recently been friendly to the Dutch. England, however, was no longer a dependent trading partner but a rival for overseas commerce, and France was a rival for trade and territory. In these circumstances, the military leadership of the prince of Orange was valued so highly that William of Orange (who assumed the English throne with his wife Mary Stuart in 1689) became an influential presence in Netherlands politics.

The Netherlands was controlled by a privileged few for most of the seventeenth century and was virtually a monarchy led from abroad by the end of the century. Nevertheless, the Netherlands appeared to contemporaries to be an astonishing exception to the normal structures of poli-

Rembrandt: The Syndics of the Cloth Drapers' Guild (1662) In this painting, the last group portrait of his career, Rembrandt depicts the guild members with artful, stylized simplicity. It was Rembrandt's genius also to be able to convey a sense of personality and drama in such commissioned portraits. *(Rijksmuseum-Stichting, Amsterdam)*

tics. In France and other places in Europe, political life was dominated by a court where aristocrats and ministers mingled and conspired and an elaborate ritual of honor and deference glorified the king. The princes of Orange surrounded themselves with splendid trappings, but their court was not the center of political life in the Netherlands. The portraits of the Dutch painter Rembrandt van Rijn (1606–1667) portray the austerity of the merchant oligarchs; theirs was a novel kind of power that could be symbolized without ostentatious display.

The Dutch state seemed all the more distinct and impressive when compared to its former ruler, Spain, which had steadily lost ground since the beginning of the century. Imports of silver declined as the American mines were exhausted and the natives forced to work in them were decimated by European diseases and brutal treatment. Spain's economic health was further threatened by the very success of its colonies: Local industries in the Americas began to produce goods formerly obtained from Spain. The increasing presence of English, French, and Dutch shipping in the Americas provided colonists with rival sources for the goods they needed. Often, these competitors could offer their goods more cheaply than Spaniards could, for Spanish productivity was low and prices were high because of the inflationary effects of the influx of precious metals over the years.

Strategic elements of the Spanish Empire in Europe also broke down. Spanish control of much of the territory between Italy and the Netherlands was challenged by France during the Thirty Years' War. Other Spanish territories, increasingly squeezed for troops and revenue to defend Spanish possessions, revolted. The uprisings reflected economic distress as well as unresolved issues of regional autonomy, primarily in Catalonia and Portugal. The government of Spain was Castilian, and Castile bore the brunt of the financial support of the state. The chief minister to Philip IV (r. 1621–1665), Gaspar de Guzmán, Count Olivares (1587–1645), was an energetic Castilian aristocrat determined to distribute the burdens—and privileges—of government more equitably among the various regions of Spain. His policies provoked rebellions in Catalonia and Portugal. As a result of those uprisings, Olivares resigned in disgrace in 1643.

In Catalonia, the revolt began as a popular uprising against the billeting of troops. It became part of the ongoing war with France when Catalan leaders invited French troops south to defend them and solemnly transferred their loyalty to Louis XIII in the hope that he would respect their autonomy. Spain resumed control only in 1652, after years of military struggle and promises to respect Catalan liberties.

In Portugal, which Spain had annexed in 1580, a war of independence began in 1640, also with a popular revolt. The Spanish government tried to restore order with troops under the command of a leading Portuguese prince—John, duke of Braganza. The duke, however, was the nearest living relative to the last king of Portugal, and he seized this opportunity to claim the crown of Portugal for himself and lead a fight for independence. Although the war dragged on until 1668, the Portuguese under John IV (r. 1640–1656) succeeded in winning independence from Spain.

In the second half of the century, the decline of Spain was vividly symbolized in the person of the monarch himself. Charles II (r. 1665–1700) was physically and mentally feeble, perhaps as a result of all the marriages between close relations among the ruling houses of Europe. Though twice married, he had no heirs; only his cousins in other ruling families of Europe could succeed him. In the last years of the century, the rulers of France, Austria, and England waited for Charles to die and then fought a war over who would be his successor.

The France of Louis XIV, 1661–1715

Louis XIV (r. 1643–1715) was called *le Dieudonné,* "the gift of God," when he was born in 1638, twenty years after his parents' marriage. He began his active reign at a propitious moment. The Peace of the Pyrenees in 1659 had ended the wars with Spain in France's favor and had been capped by Louis's marriage to the Spanish princess, Maria Theresa. More important, he was much better suited to be king than had been his father. He was physically attractive and extremely vigorous; he had been carefully and lovingly coached in his duties by Mazarin and his mother, Queen Anne, rather than neglected as his father had been. Louis XIV would be a diligent king. He put in hours a day at a desk while sustaining the ceremonial life of the court with its elaborate hunts, balls, and other public events.

Louis was determined to end the challenge to royal control reflected in the Fronde, which he had experienced as a personal threat: His mother and mentor had been vilified, and he himself had been shunted about to avoid rebel forces. The government he fashioned was a new combination of traditional patronage relationships and bureaucratic efficiency. He kept the restless aristocracy busy with constant, initially successful, warfare. His emphasis on traditional problems of royal control and military glory led him to successes that other rulers envied and emulated, and the French court became a model of culture and refinement. But Louis also faced the perennial problems of popular revolt and state debt, and he wasted opportunities in the expanding world of international trade.

The Theory and Practice of Absolutism

In the first ten years of his active reign, Louis achieved a degree of control over the mechanisms of government unparalleled in the history of monarchy in France or anywhere else in Europe. He did not invent any new bureaucratic devices but rather used existing ranks of officials in new ways that increased government efficiency and the centralization of control. He radically reduced the number of men in his High Council—the advisory body closest to the king—to include only three or four great ministers of state affairs. This intimate group, with Louis's active participation, handled all policy making. The ministers of state, war, and finance were chosen exclusively from men of modest backgrounds whose training and experience fitted them for such positions. Jean-Baptiste Colbert (1619–1683), perhaps the greatest of them, served as minister of finance and of most domestic policy from 1665 until his death; he was from a merchant family and had served for years under Mazarin.

Several dozen other officials, picked from the ranks of up-and-coming lawyers and administrators, drew up laws and regulations and passed them to the intendants for execution at the provincial level. These officials at the center were often sent to the provinces as short-term intendants on special supervisory missions. This system bypassed many entrenched provincial officials, particularly many responsible for tax collecting, an activity conducive to corruption. The money saved by the more efficient collection of taxes enabled the government to streamline the bureaucracy: Dozens of the offices created to bring cash to the Crown were bought back by the Crown from their owners.

The system still relied on the bonds of patronage and personal service. Officials rose through the ranks by means of service to the great, and family connection and personal loyalty still were essential. Of the seventeen different men who were part of Louis XIV's High Council during his reign, five were members of the Colbert family, for example. In the provinces, important local families vied for minor posts, which at least provided prestige and some income.

At the center, a great deal was achieved in the early years of Louis' regime. Colbert actively encouraged France's economic development. He reduced internal tolls and customs barriers, relics of medieval decentralization. He encouraged industry with state subsidies and protective tariffs. He set up state-sponsored trading companies—the two most important being the East India Company and the West India Company, established in 1664.

Mercantilism, the philosophy behind Colbert's efforts, stressed self-sufficiency in manufactured goods, tight control of trade to foster the domestic economy, and the absolute value of bullion. Capital for development—bullion—was presumed to be limited in quantity. Protectionist policies were believed necessary to guarantee a favorable balance of payments.

This static model of national wealth did not wholly fit the facts of growing international trade in the seventeenth century. Nevertheless, mercantilist philosophy was helpful to France. France became self-sufficient in the all-important production of woolen cloth, and French industry expanded notably in other sectors. Colbert's greatest success was the deliberate expansion of the navy and merchant marine. By 1677 the size of the navy had increased almost six times, to 144 ships. By the end of Louis XIV's reign, the French navy was virtually the equal of the English navy.

A general determination to manage national resources distinguished Louis's regime. Colbert and the other ministers developed the kind of planned government policy making that we now take for granted. Partly by means of their itinerant supervisory officials, they tried to formulate and execute policy based on carefully collected information. How many men of military age were available? How abundant was the harvest? Answers to such questions enabled not only the formulation of sound economic policy but the deliberate management of production and services to achieve certain goals, such as the recruitment and supply of the king's vast armies.

Louis tried to bring the religious life of the realm more fully under royal control by claiming for himself some of the church revenues and powers of appointment in France that still remained to the pope. Partly to bolster his position vis-à-vis the pope, he also began to attack the Huguenot community in France. He offered financial inducements for conversions to Catholicism, then quartered troops in Huguenots' households to force them to convert. In 1685, he declared that there was no longer any Protestant community, and he officially revoked the Edict of Nantes. A hundred thousand Protestant subjects who refused even nominal conversion to Catholicism chose to emigrate.

Despite the achievement of unprecedented centralized control, Louis's regime is poorly described by the term *absolutism,* which historians often apply to it. By modern standards, the power of the Crown was still greatly limited. Neither Louis nor his chief apologists claimed that he was all-powerful, in the sense of being above the law. Louis's foremost apologist, Bishop Jacques Bossuet (1627–1704), asserted that although the king was guided only by fear of God and his own reason in his application and interpretation of law, he was obligated to act within the law. The "divine right" of kingship, effectively claimed by Louis, did not mean unlimited power to rule; rather it meant that hereditary monarchy was the divinely ordained form of government, best suited to human needs.

Absolutism meant not iron-fisted control of the realm but rather the successful focusing of energy and loyalties on the Crown. Louis's own claim to power rested on hereditary privilege, and he safeguarded the hereditary privilege of others. The claim of absolutism worked because the government functioned well in the opening decades of Louis's reign and because his role as the focal point of power and loyalty was both logical, after the preceding years of unrest, and skillfully exploited. Much of the glue holding together the absolutist state lay in informal mechanisms such as patronage and court life, as well as in the traditional hunt for military glory—all of which Louis amply supplied.

Louis XIV Louis, "the gift of God," sponsored artwork at Versailles that not only celebrated royal power but also managed to suggest his own extraordinary qualification for the job of absolute monarch. Louis always believed that his own glory and the interests of the state coincided. *(Michael Holford)*

The King and His Courtiers

An observer comparing the way prominent noble families in the mid-sixteenth and mid-seventeenth centuries lived would have noticed striking differences. The nobility changed in outlook and behavior. By the second half of the seventeenth century, most sovereigns or territorial princes had the power to crush revolts, and the heirs of the feudal nobility had to accommodate themselves to the increased power of the Crown. The nobility relinquished its former independence but retained economic and social supremacy and, as a consequence, considerable political clout. Nobles also developed new ways to safeguard their privilege by means of cultural distinctions. This process was particularly dramatic in France as a strong Crown won out over an independent and powerful nobility.

As literacy became more widespread, and the power of educated bureaucrats of humble origin became more obvious, more and more noblemen from the traditional aristocracy began to use reading and writing as a means to think critically about their behavior and to reimagine themselves as gentlemen rather than primarily as warriors. A sign of Louis's success in taming the aristocracy was the brilliant court life that his regime sustained. Stripped of independent political life, aristocrats lived at court whenever they could, often at great personal expense. There they could participate in the endless jostling for patronage and prestige—for commands in the royal army and for offices and honorific positions at court. Both women and men struggled to secure royal favor for themselves, their relations, and their clients (see the box, "Politics and Ritual at the Court of Louis XIV"). In this environment, new codes of behavior could ensure their political and social distinctiveness. Elaborate rules of courtesy and etiquette regulated court life. Instead of safeguarding one's status with a code of honor backed up by force of arms, the seventeenth-century courtier relied on elegant ceremonial, precise etiquette, and clever conversation. (See the feature, "Weighing the Evidence: Table Manners," on pages 702–703.)

Louis XIV's court is usually associated with the palace he built at Versailles, southwest of Paris. Some of the greatest talent of the day worked on the design and construction of Versailles from 1670 through the 1680s. It became a masterpiece of luxurious but restrained classical styling. The palace gardens, laid out by André Lenôtre (1613–1700), conspicuously celebrated balance and proportion. Colbert channeled pa-

Politics and Ritual at the Court of Louis XIV

This document is from the memoirs of Louis de Rouvroy, duke of Saint-Simon (1675–1755), a favored courtier but one critical of Louis's power over the nobility. Notice his descriptions of court ceremony focusing on the most private moments of the king—an example of Louis's deliberate and exaggerated use of tradition, in this case of personal familiarity among warriors.

The frequent fetes, the . . . promenades at Versailles, the journeys, were means on which the king seized in order to distinguish or mortify courtiers, and thus render them more assiduous in pleasing him. He felt that of real favors he had not enough to bestow. . . . He therefore unceasingly invented all sorts of ideal ones, little preferences and petty distinctions, which answered his purpose as well.

He was exceedingly jealous of the attention paid him. . . . He looked to the right and to the left, not only upon rising but upon going to bed, at his meals, in passing through his apartments, or his gardens of Versailles . . . ; not one escaped him, not even those who hoped to remain unnoticed. He marked well all absences from court. . . .

At eight o'clock [every morning] the chief valet . . . woke the king. At the quarter [hour] the grand chamberlain was called, and those who had what was called the *grandes entrées.* The chamberlain or chief gentleman drew back the [bed] curtains and presented holy water from the vase. . . . The same officer gave [the king] his dressing gown; immediately after, other privileged courtiers entered, and then everybody, in time to find the king putting on his shoes and stockings. . . . Every other day we saw him shave himself; . . . he often spoke of [hunting] and sometimes said a word to somebody.

Source: Bayle St. John, trans., *The Memoirs of the Duke of Saint-Simon on the Reign of Louis XIV and the Regency,* 8th ed. London: George Allen, 1913); cited in Merry Wiesner et al., eds., *Discovering the Western Past,* vol. 2 (Boston: Houghton Mifflin, 1989), pp. 13–14.

tronage to sculptors and painters for work destined for Versailles as well as for other projects. The great range of subject matter in French painting of this period attests to Colbert's success in marshaling talent.

Before Louis's court settled in at Versailles, it traveled among the king's several châteaux in the countryside and in and around Paris, and in that period French court life was at its most creative and productive. Those early years of Louis XIV's personal reign were also the heyday of French drama. The comedian Jean-Baptiste Poquelin, known as Molière (1622–1673), impressed the young Louis with his productions in the late 1650s and was rewarded with the use of a theater in the main royal palace in Paris. Like Shakespeare earlier in the century, Molière explored the social and political tensions of his day. He satirized the pretensions of the aristocracy, the social climbing of the bourgeoisie, the self-righteous piety of clerics. Some of his plays were banned from performance, but most were not only tolerated but were extremely popular with the elite audiences they mocked—their popularity is testimony to the confidence of Louis's regime in its early days.

Also popular at court were the tragedies of Jean Racine (1639–1699), who was for French theater what Shakespeare was to the English: the master of the poetic use of language. His plays, which treated familiar classical stories, focused on the emotional and psychological life of the characters and tended to stress the limits that fate places even on royal persons. The pessimism in

Louis at Versailles Louis XIV (center, on horseback) is pictured among a throng of courtiers at a grotto in the gardens of Versailles. The symbol of the sun appeared throughout the palace; the image of Louis as the "Sun King" further enhanced his authority. *(Château de Versailles/Art Resource)*

Racine foreshadowed the less successful second half of Louis's reign.

Louis XIV and a Half-Century of War

Wars initiated by Louis XIV dominated the attention of most European states in the second half of the seventeenth century. Louis's wars sprang from traditional causes: the importance of the glory and dynastic aggrandizement of the king and the preoccupation of the aristocracy with military life. But if his wars were spurred by familiar concerns about territorial and economic advantage, there was also a new emphasis on state planning and on the management of war itself. Moreover, a sense of a larger national interest behind the economic and polticial motivations for war was dawning.

Louis's first war reflected the continuing French preoccupation with Spain. The goal was territory along France's eastern border to add to the land recently gained by the Peace of Westphalia (1648) and the Peace of the Pyrenees (1659). Louis invoked rather dubious dynastic claims to demand, from Spain, lands in the Spanish Netherlands and the large independent county on France's eastern border called the Franche-Comté (Map 18.2).

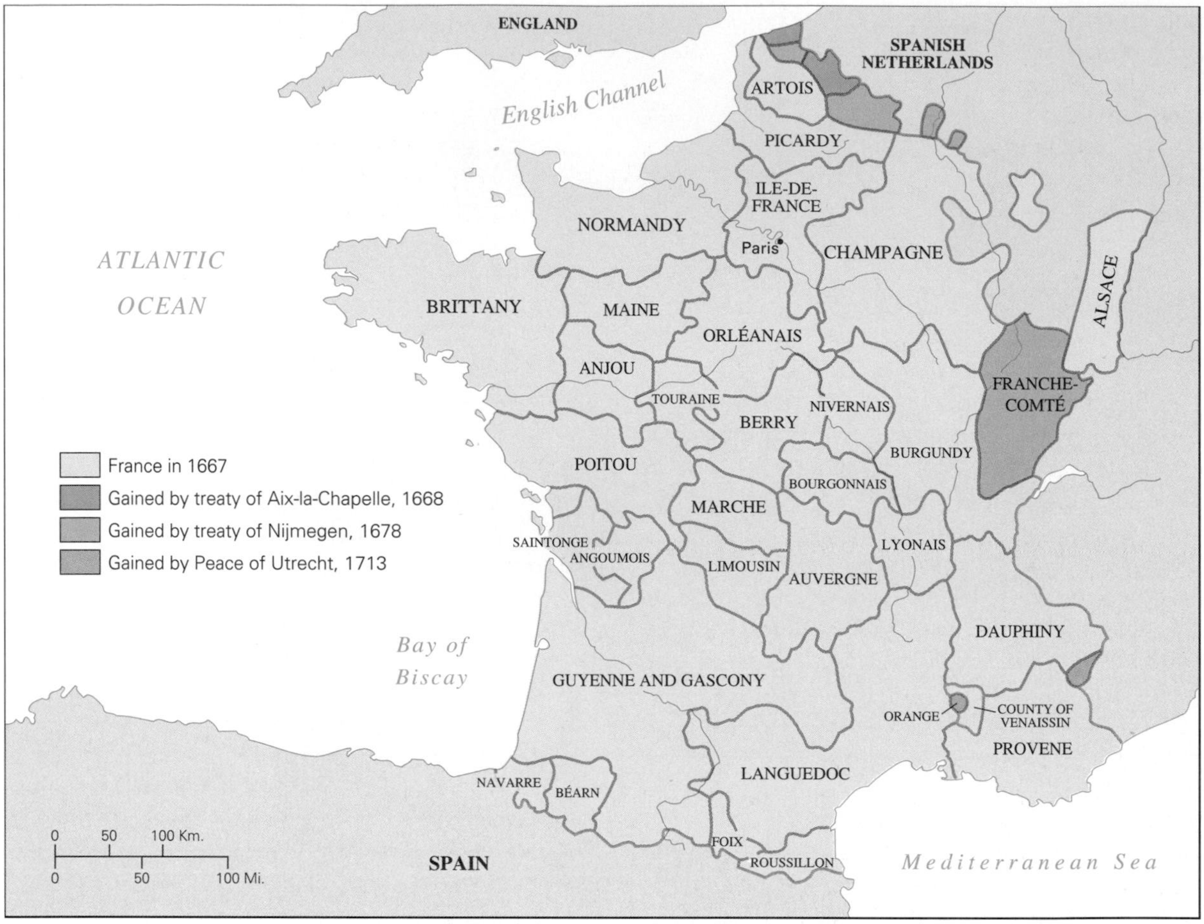

Map 18.2 Territorial Gains of Louis XIV, 1667–1715 Louis's wars, though enormously expensive for France, produced only modest gains of territory along France's eastern and northern frontiers.

War began in 1667. French troops first seized a wedge of territory in the Spanish Netherlands without difficulty and then, in early 1668, occupied the Franche-Comté. The treaty of Aix-la-Chapelle ended the conflict in May 1668. The French retained only some towns in the Spanish Netherlands. Louis had already begun to negotiate with the Austrian Habsburgs over the eventual division of Spanish Habsburg lands, for it seemed likely that the Spanish king, Charles II (r. 1665–1700), would die without heirs. So, for the moment, Louis was content to return the Franche-Comté, confident that he would get it back, and much more, in the future.

Louis's focus then shifted from Spain to a new enemy: the Dutch. The Dutch had been allied with France since the beginning of their existence as provinces in rebellion against Spain in the sixteenth century. The French now turned against the Dutch for reasons that reflect the growth of the international trading economy—specifically the Dutch dominance of seaborne trade. The French at first tried to lessen the Dutch advantage in trade with tariff barriers against Dutch goods. But, after the easy victories of 1667–1668, Louis's generals urged action against the vulnerable Dutch lands. "It is impossible that his Majesty should tolerate any longer the insolence and arrogance of that nation," added the pragmatic Colbert in 1670.[1]

The Dutch War began in 1672, with Louis personally leading one of the largest armies ever fielded in Europe—perhaps 120,000 men. At the same time, the Dutch were challenged at sea by England. The English had fought the Dutch over these same issues, such as trade, in the 1650s; now Louis secretly sent the English king Charles II a pension to ensure his alliance with the French.

At first, the French were spectacularly successful against the tiny Dutch army. Louis, however, presumptuously overrode a plan to move decisively on Amsterdam so that he could preside at the solemn reinstatement of Catholic worship in one of the Dutch provincial cathedrals. The Dutch opened dikes and flooded the countryside to protect their capital, and what had begun as a French rout became a stalemate. Moreover, the Dutch were beating combined English and French forces at sea and were gathering allies who felt threatened by Louis's aggression. The French soon found themselves facing German and Austrian forces along their frontier, and, by 1674, the English had joined the alliance against France as well.

Thanks to well-managed forces and great generalship, the French managed to hold their own against the alliance. The Peace of Nijmegen in 1678 gave the illusion of a French victory. Not only had the French met the challenge of an alliance against them, but the Spanish ceded them further border areas in the Spanish Netherlands as well as control of the Franche-Comté.

Ensconced at Versailles since 1682, Louis seemed to be at the height of his powers. Yet the Dutch War and its aftermath had in fact cost him as much as he gained. Meeting the alliance against him had meant fielding ever-increasing numbers of men—more than 200,000 in arms at one time. Internal reforms in government and finance ended under the pressure of paying for war, and old financial expedients of borrowing money and selling privileges were revived. Other government obligations, such as encouraging overseas trade, were neglected. Colbert's death in 1683 dramatically symbolized the end of an era of innovation in the French regime.

Revocation of the Edict of Nantes in 1685 had won tepid praise from Catholics but angry condemnation from Protestant rulers. Particularly, it worried the English, who since the accession of James II, were a Protestant people with a Catholic king. Louis's unforgiving Dutch opponent, William of Orange, king of England from 1689 to 1702, renewed former alliances against him. The war now known as the "Nine Years' War," or "King William's War," was touched off late in 1688 by French aggression. Louis's troops invaded Germany to claim an inheritance there. In his ongoing dispute with the pope, Louis seized the papal territory of Avignon in southern France. Boldest of all, he helped the exiled James II of England to attempt an invasion to reclaim his throne.

A widespread war had begun, and all the major powers—Spain, the Netherlands, England, Austria, the major German states—were ranged against France. The French also carried the fighting abroad by seizing English territory in Canada. The invasion by James II was decisively stopped, but otherwise the Nine Years' War resembled the later phases of the Dutch War: costly but with indecisive fighting on most fronts.

As in the Dutch War, Louis failed to achieve his initial objectives, but this time there was no illusion of victory. The price of peace was spelled out in the Treaty of Ryswick (1697). Louis had to give up most of the territories in Germany, in the Spanish Netherlands, and in northern Spain that he managed to occupy by war's end. Avignon went back to the pope, and Louis gave up his contentious claim to papal revenues. The terrible burden of taxes to pay for the wars combined with crop failures in 1693 and 1694 caused widespread starvation in the countryside. French courtiers began to criticize Louis openly.

The final major war of Louis's reign, now called the "War of Spanish Succession," broke out in 1702. In some ways it was a straightforward dynastic war in which France and its perennial Habsburg opponent had an equal interest. Both Louis and Holy Roman Emperor Leopold I (r. 1657–1705) hoped to claim for their heirs the throne of Spain, left open at the death in 1700 of the Spanish king Charles II. A will of Charles II gave the throne to Louis's grandson Philip of Anjou, who quickly proceeded to enter Spain and claim his new kingdom. War was made inevitable when Louis renounced one of the conditions of Charles's will by insisting that Philip's accession to the throne of Spain did not mean that he had abandoned his rights to the throne of France. This declaration was an act of sheer belligerence, for Philip was only third in line for the French throne. The Dutch and the English responded to the prospect of a Frenchman on the throne of Spain and the consequent disruption of the balance of power in Europe by joining the emperor in a formal Great Alliance in 1701. The Dutch and English also wanted to defend their colonial interests—the French had already begun to profit from new trading opportunities with the Spanish colonies.

Again the French fought a major war on several fronts at once—including at sea, where they generally lost out to the English navy. Again the people of France felt the cost in crushing taxes worsened by harvest failures. Major revolts inside France forced Louis to divert troops from the war. For a time it seemed that the French would be soundly defeated, but they were saved by the superior organization of their forces and by dynastic accident: The Austrian claimant to the Spanish throne suddenly was poised to inherit rule of Austria and the empire as well, owing to the untimely death of some of his relatives. The English, who were more afraid of a revival of unified Habsburg control of Spain, its colonies, and Austria than of French domination of Spain, began peace negotiations with France.

The Peace of Utrecht in 1713 resolved long-standing political conflicts and helped to set the agenda of European politics for the eighteenth century. Philip of Anjou became Philip V of Spain, but on the condition that the Spanish and French crowns would never be worn by the same monarch. To maintain the balance of power against French interests, the Spanish Netherlands and Spanish territories in Italy were ceded to Austria, which for many decades would be France's major continental rival. The Peace of Utrecht also marked the beginnings of England's dominance of overseas trade and colonization. The French gave to England lands in Canada and the Caribbean and renounced any privileged relationship with Spanish colonies. England was allowed to control the highly profitable slave trade with Spanish colonies.

For France, the costs of Louis XIV's wars was great. Louis added small amounts of territory along France's eastern border (see Map 18.2), and a Bourbon ruled in Spain. But the army and navy swallowed up capital for investment and trade, and strategic opportunities overseas were lost, never to be regained. Louis's government had been innovative in its early years but remained constrained by traditional ways of imagining the interest of the state.

New Powers in Central and Eastern Europe

By the end of the seventeenth century, three states were dominating central and eastern Europe: Austria, Brandenburg-Prussia, and Russia (Map 18.3). After the Thirty Years' War, the Habsburgs' power as emperors waned, and their interest in the coherence of their own territories, which centered on Austria, grew. Brandenburg-Prussia, in northeastern Germany, grew to a position of power rivaling that of the Habsburg state. The rulers of Brandenburg-Prussia had gained lands in the Peace of Westphalia, and astute management had transformed their relatively small and scattered holdings into one of the most powerful states in Europe. Russia's new stature in eastern Europe resulted in part from the weakness of its greatest rival, Poland, and the determination of one leader, Peter the Great, to assume a major role in European affairs. Austria, Brandenburg-Prussia, and Russia would dominate central and eastern Europe until the twentieth century.

The Consolidation of Austria

The Thirty Years' War weakened the Habsburgs as emperors but strengthened them in their own lands. The main Habsburg lands in 1648 were a collection of principalities comprising modern Austria, the kingdom of Hungary (largely in Turkish hands), and the kingdom of Bohemia. According to the Peace of Utrecht (1713), the Spanish Netherlands would also be ceded to Austria and renamed the "Austrian Netherlands." Although language and ethnic differences ruled against an absolutist state along French lines, Leopold I (r. 1657–1705) instituted political and institutional changes that enabled the Habsburg state to be one of the most powerful states in Europe through the eighteenth century.

Much of the coherence that already existed in Leopold's lands had been achieved by his predecessors in the wake of the Thirty Years' War. The lands of rebels in Bohemia had been confiscated

Map 18.3 New Powers in Central and Eastern Europe The balance of power in central and eastern Europe shifted with the consolidation of Austria, the rise of Brandenburg-Prussia, and the strengthening of Russia at the expense of Poland.

and redistributed among loyal—mostly Austrian—families. In return for political and military support for the emperor, these families were given the right to exploit their newly acquired land and the peasants who worked it. Consequently, landlords provided grain and timber for the export market and grain and other foodstuffs for the Austrian armies, and elite families provided the army with officers. This political-economic arrangement provoked numerous, serious peasant revolts, but the peasants were not able to force changes in a system that suited both the elites and the central authority.

Although Leopold had lost much influence within the empire itself, an imperial government made up of various councils, a war ministry, financial officials, and the like still functioned in his capital, Vienna. Leopold worked to extricate the government of his own lands from the apparatus of imperial institutions, which were staffed largely by Germans more loyal to imperial than to Habsburg interests. In addition, Leopold used the Catholic church as an institutional and ideological support for the Habsburg state.

Leopold's personal preoccupation was zealous Catholicism and its re-establishment throughout his territories. Acceptance of Catholicism was made the litmus test of loyalty to the Habsburg regime, and Protestantism vanished among elites. Leopold encouraged the work of Jesuit teachers and members of other Catholic orders. These men and women helped staff his government and administered religious life down to the most local levels. A resurgence of Catholicism, centered on the rather emotional worship of the Virgin Mary, marked these decades. It testifies to the religious workers' success and to the oppressed peasants' need for consolation.

Leopold's most dramatic success, as a Habsburg and as a religious leader, was his reconquest of the kingdom of Hungary from the Turks. Since the early sixteenth century, the Habsburgs had controlled only a narrow strip of the kingdom. Partly because of a temporary lull in other European fighting, Leopold received help from several other states in a Holy League against the Turks and was able to reconquer the kingdom in 1687.

Leopold gave land in the reclaimed kingdom to Austrian officers who he believed were loyal to him. The traditions of Hungarian separatism, however, were strong; and the local nobility, particularly great magnates who for decades had defended the Habsburgs against further Turkish encroachment, retained its independence. The peasantry, as elsewhere, suffered a decline in status as a result of the crown's efforts to ensure the loyalty of elites. In the long run, Hungarian independence weakened the Habsburg state, but in the short run Leopold's victory over the Turks and the recovery of Hungary itself were momentous events. Leopold was able to turn his attention to the vexing problem of the Spanish succession as his reign ended in 1705.

The Rise of Brandenburg-Prussia

Three German states, in addition to Austria, gained territory and stature after the Thirty Years' War: Bavaria, Saxony, and Brandenburg-Prussia. By the end of the seventeenth century, the strongest was Brandenburg-Prussia, a conglomeration of small territories held, by dynastic accident, by the Hohenzollern family. The two principal territories were electoral Brandenburg, in northeastern Germany, with its capital Berlin, and the duchy of Prussia, a fief of the Polish crown along the Baltic coast east of Poland proper. In addition there was a handful of small principalities near the Netherlands. The manipulation of resources and power that enabled these unpromising lands to become a powerful state was primarily the work of Frederick William, known as "the Great Elector" (r. 1640–1688).

Frederick William used the occasion of a war to effect a permanent change in the structure of government. He took advantage of a war between Poland and its rivals, Sweden and Russia, to win independence for the duchy of Prussia from Polish overlordship. When his involvement in the war ended in 1657, he kept intact the general war commissariat, a combined civilian and military body that had efficiently directed the war effort; he thus bypassed traditional councils and representative bodies. He also used the standing army to force the payment of high taxes. Most significantly, he established a positive relationship with the *Junkers*, hereditary landholders, which assured him both revenue and loyalty. He agreed to allow the Junkers virtually total control of their own lands in return for their agreement to support his government—in short, to surrender their accustomed political independence.

Peasants and townspeople were taxed, but nobles were not. The freedom to control their estates led many nobles to invest in profitable agriculture for the export market. The peasants were serfs who received no benefits from the increased productivity of the land. Frederick William further enhanced his state's power by sponsoring state industries. They did not have to fear competition from urban producers because the towns had been frozen out of the political process and saddled with heavy taxes. Although an oppressive place for many Germans, Brandenburg-Prussia attracted many skilled refugees, such as Huguenot artisans fleeing Louis XIV.

Bavaria and Saxony, in contrast to Brandenburg-Prussia, had vibrant towns, largely free peasantries, and weaker aristocracies but were less powerful in international affairs. Power on the European stage depended on military force. Such power, whether in a large state like France or in a small one like Brandenburg-Prussia, usually came at the expense of the state's inhabitants.

Competition Around the Baltic: The Demise of Poland

The Baltic coast was the site for immensely profitable trade between eastern and western Europe and with the western European colonies. This trading system had profound social and political consequences for the states bordering the Baltic in the seventeenth century.

First, it was one spur to war: Sweden and Denmark fought over control of the body of water connecting the Baltic and North seas. Sweden, Poland, and, later, Russia fought for control of the eastern Baltic coastline. Throughout the seventeenth century Poland and Russia fought over grain and timber-producing lands comprising modern Beloruss, parts of modern Russia, and Ukraine.

Second, profits from the production of grain for export in such volume reinforced the power of large landholders, particularly within Poland, where most of the grain was produced. Under the relentless imposition of serfdom, the status of peasants declined, but the economic and political independence of Polish landlords grew. With their enhanced power came increasing independence from the monarchy and disastrous consequences for the Polish state.

When the seventeenth century began, the huge Polish kingdom was in a pre-eminent position. Polish kings had recently seized Livonia (modern Latvia), defended it successfully against Russian attack, and incorporated it into the Polish state, which already included the duchy of Lithuania (modern Lithuania, Beloruss, and Ukraine). Profits from grain fueled a vibrant economy. Gdansk was a booming port city, and industry grew in other major cities such as Warsaw and Cracow.

Internal strains as well as external challenges began to mount, however. The spread of the Counter-Reformation, encouraged by the Crown, as in Austria, created tensions with both Protestant and Orthodox subjects in the diverse kingdom. In Ukraine, communities of Cossacks, nomadic farmer-warriors, grew as Polish and Lithuanian peasants fled harsh conditions to join them. The Cossacks had long been tolerated because they were a military buffer against the Ottoman Turks to the south, but now Polish landlords wanted to reincorporate the Cossacks into the profitable political-economic system that they controlled. Meanwhile, the Crown was involved in several wars. From 1609 to 1612, Polish armies tried but failed to impose a Polish king on the Russians during a dispute over the succession. While aiding Austria in the Thirty Years' War against the Turks, their common enemy, the Poles lost Livonia and other bits of northern territory to the aggressive Gustav Adolf of Sweden.

The Polish crown could not reach consensus with the independent Polish nobility to mount effective counterattacks. Nobles were less interested in further conquests of Baltic territory or in strikes against the Turks than in political and economic links with the West. Beginning in 1648, the Polish crown faced revolt and invasion that it could not counter. In 1651 in a massive rebellion, the Cossacks, with the Crimean Tatars and their Ottoman overlords as allies, defeated Polish armies and established an independent state. In 1654 the Cossacks transferred their allegiance to Moscow and became part of a Russian invasion of Poland that, by the next year, had engulfed much of the eastern half of the kingdom. At the same time, the Swedes, with the assistance of Polish aristocrats acting like independent warlords, seized northern parts of the kingdom.

Polish forces managed to fight back and recover much territory—most important, the western half of Ukraine. But the invasions and subsequent fighting were disastrous. As in the Thirty Years' War, opposing armies devastated the countryside more readily than they destroyed each other. The population of Poland may have declined by as much as 40 percent. Urban economies and cities themselves were in ruins. Poland was a shadow of its former self.

The Catholic identity of the Polish heartland had been a rallying point for resistance to the Protestant Swedes and the Orthodox Russians, but the religious tolerance that had distinguished the Polish kingdom and had been mandated in its constitution was thereafter abandoned. In addition, much of its recovery of territory was only nominal. In parts of Lithuania inhabited by Russian-speaking peoples, the Russian presence during the wars had achieved local transfers of power from Lithuanian to Russian landlords now loyal to Moscow and eager for the rewards of the tsar's service. The elective crown passed in 1674 to a brilliant military commander, Jan Sobieski (r. 1674–1696), known as "Vanquisher of the Turks" for his victories undertaken in a crusading spirit against the Ottomans. Given Poland's internal weakness, however, Sobieski's victories in the long run helped the Austrian and Russian rivals of the Turks more than they helped the Poles. His successor, Augustus II of Saxony (r. 1697–1704, 1709–1733), dragged Poland back into war from which Russia would emerge the obvious winner in the power struggle in eastern Europe.

Russia Under Peter the Great

Shifting the balance of power in eastern Europe and the Baltic in Russia's favor was also the work of Tsar Peter I, "the Great" (r. 1682–1725). Peter accomplished this by military successes against his enemies and by forcibly reorienting Russian government and society toward involvement with the rest of Europe.

Peter was almost literally larger than life. Nearly 7 feet tall, he towered over most of his contemporaries and had physical and mental energy to match his size. He was determined to learn, from the ground up, about the world and about being an effective ruler. He set himself to learning trades—carpentry, dentistry—and he studied soldiering by rising in the ranks of the military like any common soldier. He traveled abroad—incognito when doing so suited his purposes—to learn as much as he could about other states' economies and government. He wanted the revenue, manufacturing output, technology and trade, and, above all, up-to-date army and navy that other rulers enjoyed. In short, Peter sought for Russia a more evolved state system because of the strength it would give him.

Peter initiated a bold and even brutal series of changes in Russian society upon his accession to power. Peasants already were bearing the brunt of taxation, but their tax burden worsened when they were assessed arbitrarily by head and not by output of the land. Even beggars and vagabonds were supposed to pay taxes. Peter's changes also included what amounted to an enforced cultural revolution (see the box, "Peter the Great Changes Russia"). Peter noticed that European monarchs coexisted with a privileged but educated aristocracy and that a brilliant court life symbolized and reinforced the rulers' authority. So he set out to refashion Russian society. He provoked a direct confrontation with Russia's traditional aristocracy over everything from education to matters of dress. He elevated numerous new families to the ranks of gentry and created an official ranking system for the nobility.

Peter's effort to reorient his nation culturally and politically toward Europe was most apparent in the construction of the city of St. Petersburg on the Gulf of Finland, which provided access to the Baltic Sea. In stark contrast to Moscow, dominated by the medieval fortress of the Kremlin and churches in the traditional Russian style, St. Petersburg was a modern European city with wide avenues and palaces designed for a sophisticated court life.

But although Peter was highly intelligent, practical, and determined to create a more productive and better governed society, he was also cruel, ruthless, and authoritarian. The building of St. Petersburg cost staggering sums in money and in workers' lives. Peter's entire reform system was carried out autocratically; resistance was brutally suppressed. Victims of Peter's oppression included his son Alexis, who died after tor-

Peter the Great Changes Russia

Peter the Great's reforms included not only monumental building and a new relationship with elites but also practical changes in education, technology, and administration. Writing about a hundred years after the end of Peter's reign, the Russian historian Mikhail Pogodin (1800–1875) reflected on all the changes Peter had introduced, perhaps exaggerating only the respect Peter earned in foreign eyes in his lifetime.

Yes, Peter the Great did much for Russia.... One keeps adding and one cannot reach the sum. We cannot open our eyes, cannot make a move, cannot turn in any direction without encountering him everywhere, at home, in the streets, in church, in school, in court, in the regiment....

We wake up. What day is it today?... Peter ordered us to count the years from the birth of Christ; Peter ordered us to count the months from January.

It is time to dress—our clothing is made according to the fashion established by Peter the First, our uniform according to his model. The cloth is woven in a factory which he created....

Newspapers are brought in—Peter the Great introduced them.

You must buy different things—they all, from the silk neckerchief to the sole of your shoe, will remind you of Peter.... Some were ordered by him... or improved by him, carried on his ships, into his harbors, on his canals, on his roads.

Let us go to the university—the first secular school was founded by Peter the Great.

You decide to travel abroad—following [his] example; you will be received well—Peter the Great placed Russia among the European states and began to instill respect for her; and so on and so on.

Source: Nicholas V. Riasanovsky, *A History of Russia,* 2d ed. (London: Oxford University Press, 1969), pp. 266–267.

ture while awaiting execution for questioning his father's policies.

The plotting around Alexis was one of several rebellions within the elite that Peter faced. After an earlier rebellion of elite military regiments, which had attempted to depose him in favor of his half-sister, Peter ordered the execution of over a thousand men and the public display of their bodies to inspire submission in others. Peter also faced populist rebellions against the exactions and the cultural changes of his regime. The most serious, in 1707, was a revolt of Cossacks of the Don region against the regime's tightened controls.

The primary reason for the high cost of Peter's government to the Russian people was not the tsar's determination to increase his internal power but rather his ambition for territorial gain. His army and navy were probably his greatest achievement. Working side by side with workers and technicians, many of whom he had recruited while abroad, Peter created the Russian navy from scratch. At first, ships were built in the south to contest Turkish control of the Black Sea; later, in the Baltic. Peter also modernized the Russian army by employing tactics, training, and discipline he had observed in the West. By 1709, Russia was able to manufacture most of the up-to-date firearms its army needed.

Russia was at war virtually throughout Peter's reign. Initially with some success, he struck at the Ottomans and their client state in the Crimea. Later phases of these conflicts brought reverses. Peter, however, was spectacularly successful against his northern competitor, Sweden, for control of the weakened Polish state and the Baltic Sea. The conflicts between Sweden and Russia, "the Great Northern War," raged from 1700 to 1709 and, in a less intense phase, lasted until 1721. By the Treaty of Nystadt in 1721,

Peter the Great This portrait by a Dutch artist shows Peter in military dress according to European fashions of the day. *(Rijksmuseum-Stichting, Amsterdam)*

Russia gained the territory in the Gulf of Finland near St. Petersburg that it now has, plus the territories of Livonia (modern Latvia) and Estonia. These acquisitions gave Russia a secure window on the Baltic and, in combination with its gains of Lithuanian territory earlier in the century, made Russia the pre-eminent Baltic power at Sweden's and Poland's expense.

The Rise of Overseas Trade

The first large-scale ventures overseas were undertaken by the Portuguese and the Spanish in the fifteenth and sixteenth centuries. By the beginning of the seventeenth century, competition from the Dutch, French, and English was disrupting the Spanish and Portuguese trading empires.

During the seventeenth century, European trade and colonization expanded and changed dramatically. The Dutch not only became masters of the spice trade but led the expansion of that trade to include many other commodities. In the Americas, a new trading system linking Europe, Africa, and the New World came into being with the expansion of sugar and tobacco production. French and English colonists began settling in North America in increasing numbers. By the end

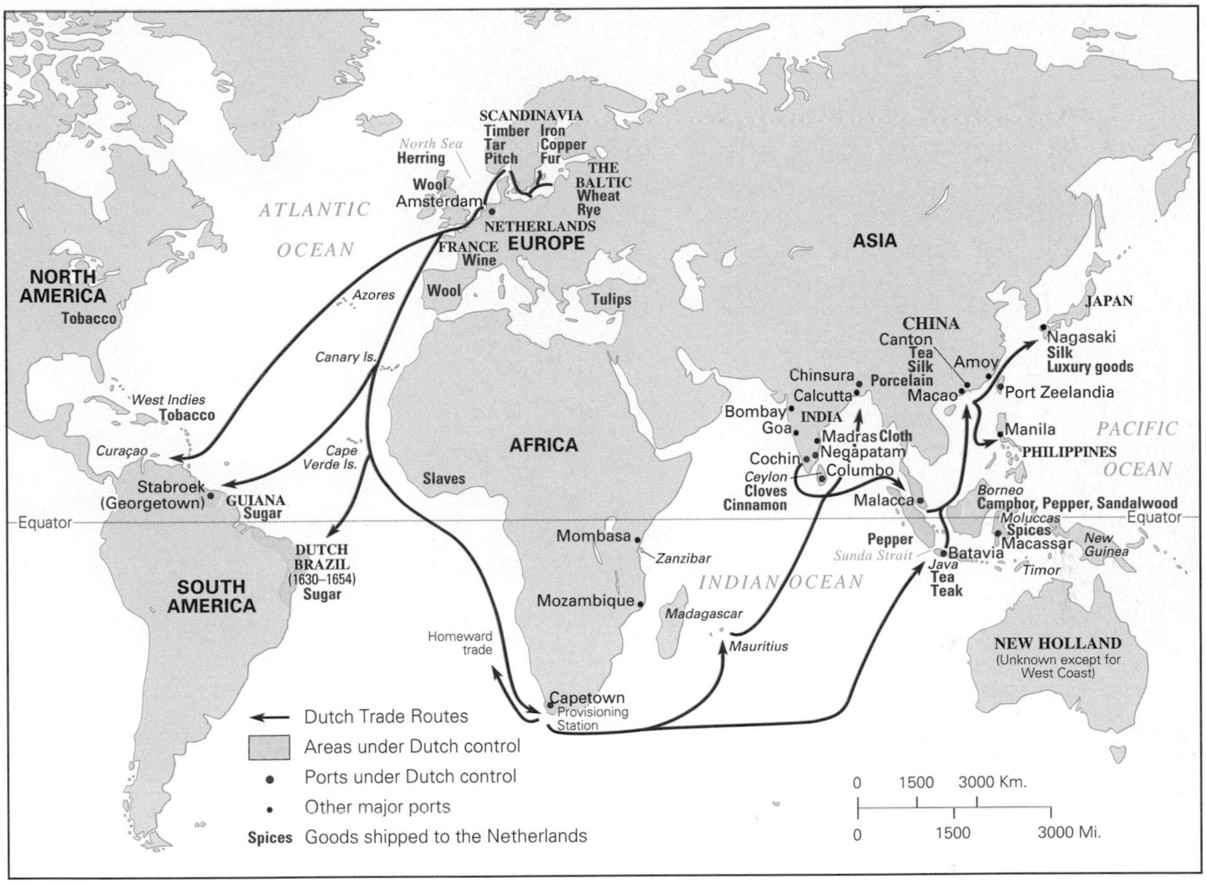

Map 18.4 Dutch Commerce in the Seventeenth Century The Dutch supplanted Portuguese control of trade with Asia as well as dominated seaborne trade within Europe.

of the century, trading and colonial outposts around the world figured regularly as bargaining chips in disagreements between European states.

The Triumph of the Dutch

At the end of the sixteenth century, the Dutch and the English began venturing down the western coast of Africa, around the Cape of Good Hope, and into the Indian Ocean. They were hoping to make incursions into the Portuguese-controlled spice trade with areas of India, Ceylon, and the East Indies. Spain had annexed Portugal in 1580 but the drain on Spain's resources from its wars with the Dutch and French prevented Spain from adequately defending its enlarged trading empire in Asia. The Dutch and, to a lesser degree, the English rapidly supplanted Portuguese control of this lucrative trade (Map 18.4).

The Dutch were particularly well placed to be successful competitors in overseas trade. They already dominated seaborne trade within Europe—including the most important long-distance trade, which linked Spain and Portugal, with their wine and salt, as well as spices, hides, and gold from abroad, with the Baltic seacoast, where these products were sold for grain and timber produced in Germany, Poland-Lithuania, and Scandinavia. The geographic position of the Dutch and the fact that they consumed more Baltic grain than any other area—because of their densely urbanized economy—help to explain Dutch dominance of this trade. In addition, the Dutch improved the design of their merchant

The Dutch Overseas The Dutch East India Company funded trade on such a scale that by 1650 four times as many Dutch ships sailed to the east as Portuguese ships had done during the entire sixteenth century. Depicted here are the headquarters of the company in Bengal, India, in about 1665. *(Rijksmuseum-Stichting, Amsterdam)*

ships to enhance their profits. By 1600 they were building the *fluitschip* (flyship)—a vessel that had a long flat hull and simple rigging and was made from cheap materials—to transport cargo economically.

The Dutch were successful in Asia because of institutional as well as technical innovations. In 1602, the Dutch East India Company was formed. The company combined the government management of trade, typical of the period, with both public and private investment. In the past, groups of investors had funded single voyages or small numbers of ships on a one-time basis. The formation of the Dutch East India Company created a permanent pool of capital to sustain trade. After 1612, investments in the company were negotiable as stock. The enlarged pool of capital meant the risks and delays of longer voyages could be spread among larger numbers of investors. In addition, more money was available for warehouses, docks, and ships. The English East India Company, founded in 1607, also supported trade, but more modestly. It had one-tenth the capital of the Dutch company and did not use the same system of permanent capital held as stock by investors until 1657.

A dramatic expansion of trade with Asia resulted from the Dutch innovations, so that by 1650 the European market for spices was glutted, and traders' profits had begun to fall. To control the supply of spices, the Dutch seized some of the areas where they were produced. Control of supply helped prop up prices, but these gains were somewhat offset by greater military and administrative costs.

The Dutch and English both responded to the oversupply of spices by diversifying their trade. The proportion of spices in cargoes from the East fell from about 70 percent at midcentury to just over 20 percent by the century's end. New consumer goods such as tea, coffee, silks, and cotton fabrics took their place. The demand of ordinary people for inexpensive yet serviceable Indian cottons grew steadily. Eventually, the Dutch and the English diversified their trade in Asia even more by entering the local carrying trade among Asian states. Doing so enabled them to make profits without purchasing goods, and it slowed the drain of hard currency from Europe—currency in increasingly short supply as silver mines in the New World were worked out.

Atlantic Colonies and Trade

In theory, the Spanish colonial empire was a closed trading system controlled by the mother country; in fact, it was vulnerable to incursion by other European states. Spain could not supply colonists' needs at prices low enough to ward off competition from renegade English, Dutch, and French traders. Spanish treasure fleets themselves were an attraction. Competitors all tried to seize treasure ships, and in 1628 a Dutch captain seized the entire fleet. But by then the Spanish economic system and the goals of Spain's competitors had begun to shift.

The limits of an economy based on the extraction of wealth rather than on the production of wealth became clear with the declining output of the silver mines during the 1620s. In response, the Spanish and their Dutch, French, and English competitors expanded the production of cash crops—sugar and tobacco. The European demand for sugar and tobacco, both addictive substances, grew steadily in the seventeenth century, and the demand for spices leveled off.

The plantation system—the use of forced labor to work large tracts of land—had been carried across the Atlantic by the Spanish and Portuguese. The French, English, and Dutch followed their lead and established sugar plantations on the Caribbean islands they held. Sugar production in the New World grew from about 20,000 tons in 1600 to 200,000 tons by about 1770.

While the Dutch were exploiting Portuguese weakness in the eastern spice trade, they were also seizing sugar regions in Brazil and replacing the Portuguese in slaving ports in Africa. Although the Portuguese were able to retake some of their Brazilian territory, the Dutch monopolized the carrying trade, and they became the official supplier of slaves to Spanish plantations in the New World and the chief supplier to most other regions. The Dutch were able to make handsome profits until the end of the seventeenth century, when they were supplanted by the British. A conservative estimate is that approximately 1,350,000 Africans were forcibly transported as slave labor to the New World during the seventeenth century, between a quarter and a third of a million people to work the plantations of each colonial power.

Colonization in North America

From the early sixteenth century, French, Dutch, English, and Portuguese seamen had fished and traded off Newfoundland. By 1630, small French and Scots settlements in Acadia (near modern Nova Scotia) and on the St. Lawrence River and English settlements in Newfoundland were established to systematically exploit the resources of the north Atlantic coasts: timber, fish, and fur. Aware of the great Spanish territorial advantage in the New World, and hoping for treasures such as the Spanish had found, the English, French, and Dutch were ambitious to explore and settle North America (see Map 18.5).

In England, population growth and consequent unemployment, as well as religious discontent, created a large pool of potential colonists. The first of the English settlements to endure in what was to become the United States was established at Jamestown, named for James I, in Virginia in 1607. "Virginia," named for Elizabeth I, the "virgin" queen, was an extremely vague designation for the Atlantic coast of North America and its hinterland.

The Crown encouraged colonization, but a private company similar to the companies that financed long-distance trade was established actually to organize the enterprise. The directors of the Virginia Company were London businessmen. Investors and would-be colonists purchased shares. Shareholders among the colonists could participate in a colonial assembly, though the governor appointed by the company was the final authority.

The colonists arrived in Virginia with ambitious and optimistic instructions. They were to

The Disappointments of the Virginia Colony

In this letter sent to the Virginia Company in 1608, Captain John Smith (1580–1631) explains somewhat angrily that the colony cannot produce the profits that the investors were hoping for. He notes the folly of carrying boats west over the fall line of the Virginia rivers—where, it had been assumed, they might sight the Pacific Ocean as the Spaniards had done in Panama. He reports no sign of the colony of Sir Walter Raleigh, which vanished after settlement in North Carolina in 1587. He also notes the difficulties of extracting wealth and the difficulties of mere survival.

I have received your letter, wherein you write that . . . we feed you but with ifs and ands and hopes, and some few proofs . . . and that we must expressly follow your instructions sent by Captain Newport [the commander of the supply ship], the charge of whose voyage . . . we cannot defray.

For the quartered boat to be borne by the soldiers over the falls, Newport had 120 of the best men. . . . If he had burned her to ashes, one might have carried her in a bag, but as she is, five hundred cannot, to a navigable place above the falls. And for him, at that time to find in the South Sea a mine of gold, or any of them sent by Sir Walter Raleigh, at our consultation I told them was as likely as the rest. . . . In their absence I followed the new begun works of pitch and tar, glass, [potash, and lumber], whereof some small quantities we have sent you. But if you rightly consider, what an infinite toil it is in Russia and [Sweden], where the woods are proper for naught else [and where] there be the help of both man and beast . . . yet thousands of those poor people can scarce get necessaries to live. . . .

From your ship we had not provision in victuals worth twenty pound, and we are more than two hundred to live upon this. . . . Though there be fish in the sea, fowls in the air, and beasts in the woods . . . they are so wild and we so weak and ignorant, we cannot much trouble them.

Source: Philip L. Barbour, ed., *The Complete Works of Captain John Smith (1580–1631),* vol. 2 (Chapel Hill: University of North Carolina Press, 1986), pp. 187–189.

open mines, establish profitable cultivation, and search for sea routes to Asia. The colonists struggled at first merely to survive (see the box, "The Disappointments of the Virginia Colony"). The indigenous peoples in Virginia, unlike those in Spanish-held territory, were not organized in urbanized, rigidly hierarchical societies that, after conquest, could provide the invaders with a labor force. Indeed, the native Americans in this region were quickly wiped out by European diseases. The introduction of tobacco as a cash crop a few years later saved the colonists economically—though the Virginia Company had already gone bankrupt and the Crown had assumed control of the colony. With the cultivation of tobacco, the Virginia colony, like the Caribbean islands, became dependent on forced, eventually slave, labor.

Among the Virginia colonists were impoverished men and women who came as servants indentured to those who had paid their passage. Colonies established to the north—in what was called "New England"—also drew people from the margins of society: Early settlers there were religious dissidents. The first to arrive were the Pilgrims, who arrived at "New Plymouth" (modern Massachusetts) in 1620. They were a community of religious separatists who had originally emigrated to the Netherlands from England for freedom of conscience.

Following the Pilgrims came Puritans escaping escalating persecution under Charles I. The first, in 1629, settled under the auspices of another royally chartered company, the Massachusetts Bay Company. Among their number were many prosperous Puritan merchants and landholders. Independence from investors in London allowed them an unprecedented degree of self-government once the Massachusetts Bay colony was established.

To England, the colonies in North America were disappointments because they generated much less wealth than expected. Shipping timber back to Europe proved too expensive, though New England timber did supply some of the Caribbean colonists' needs. The fur trade became less lucrative as English settlement pushed westward the native Americans who did most of the trapping and as French trappers to the north encroached on the trade. Certain colonists profited enormously from the tobacco economy, but the mother country did so only moderately because the demand in Europe for tobacco never grew as quickly as the demand for sugar.

The colonies' greatest strength, from the English viewpoint, was that the settlements continued to attract people. By 1640, Massachusetts had some 14,000 European inhabitants. Through most of the next century, the growth of colonial populations in North America would result in an English advantage over the French in control of territory. In the long run, however, the size of the colonial communities, their degree of routine political independence from the mother country, and their loose economic ties to England led them to seek independence.

The French began their settlement of North America at the same time as the English, in the same push to compensate for their mutual weakness vis-à-vis the Spanish (Map 18.5). The French efforts, however, had very different results, owing partly to the sites of their settlements but mostly to the relationship between the mother country and the colonies. The French hold on territory was always tenuous because of the scant number of colonists from France. There seems to have been less economic impetus for colonization from France than from England. And, after the French Crown took over the colonies, there was no religious impetus, for only Catholics were allowed to settle in New France. Moreover, control by the Crown forced a traditional hierarchical political organization on the French colonies. There was a royal governor, and large tracts of land were set aside for privileged investors. There was little in North America to tempt people of modest means who were seeking a better life.

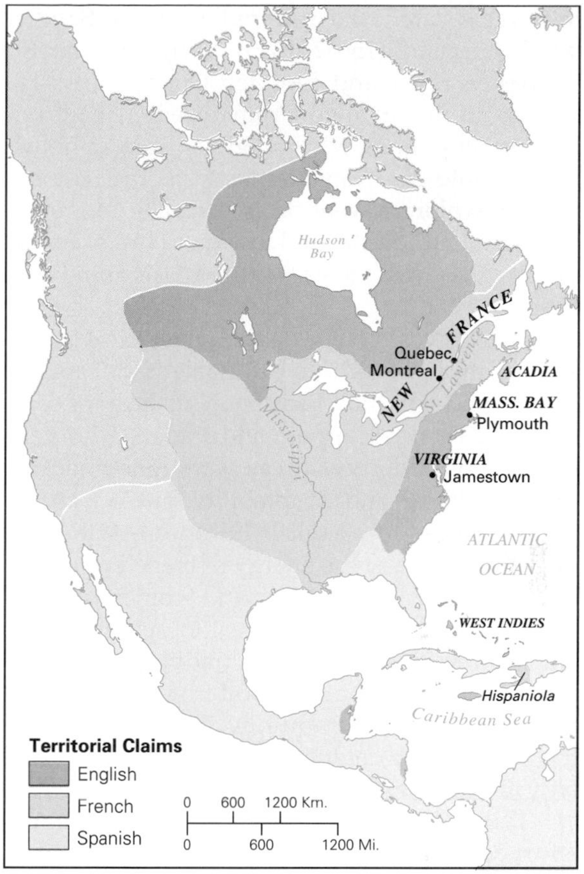

Map 18.5 British and French in North America, ca. 1700 By 1700 a veritable ring of French-claimed territory encircled the coastal colonies of England. English-claimed areas, however, were more densely settled and more economically viable.

The first successful French colony was established in Acadia in 1605. This settlement was an exception among the French efforts because it was founded by Huguenots, not by Catholics. A few years later, the intrepid explorer Samuel de Champlain (1567?–1635) navigated the St. Lawrence River and founded Quebec City. He convinced the royal government, emerging from its preoccupations with religious wars at home, to promote the development of the colony. French explorers went on to establish Montreal, farther inland on the St. Lawrence (1642), and to explore the Great Lakes and the Mississippi River basin.

Such investment as the French crown was able to attract went into profitable trade, mainly in furs, and not into the difficult business of colonization. French trappers and traders who ventured into wilderness areas were renowned for their hardiness and adaptability, but it was not their business to establish European-style communities. Much of the energy of French colonization was expended by men and women of religious orders bringing their zeal to new frontiers. Quebec remained more of a trading station, dependent on shipments of food from France, than a growing urban community. By the middle of the seventeenth century, all of New France had only about 3,000 European inhabitants.

The seeming weakness of the French colonial effort was not much noticed at the time. The French and English competed intensely over fishing in the Atlantic. French and English trappers and traders competed with each other, and there were outright battles between English and French settlements. But for both England and France the major profits and strategic interests in the New World lay elsewhere.

The Dutch experience in North America reveals the degree to which North America was of secondary importance to the plantation profits farther south. In 1624 the Dutch founded a trading center, New Amsterdam, at the site of modern New York City. In 1674 they relinquished it to the English in return for recognition of the Dutch claims to sugar-producing Guiana (modern Suriname) in South America.

The Beginning of the End of Traditional Society

Within Europe, the economic impact of overseas trade was profound. Merchants and investors in a few of Europe's largest cities reaped great profits. The economy became more productive and flexible. Social stratification increased. The growth of the state redirected and centralized economic life, but at a cost to common people. Many people on the margins of economic life were innovative in their efforts to survive but they were increasingly vulnerable to economic forces and state power.

Economic Growth, Social Stratification, and Social Protest

The expansion of overseas trade in the sixteenth and seventeenth centuries had obvious effects in western Europe. Mediterranean trading centers such as Venice and Genoa, once the heart of European trade, did not share in the profits generated by goods now being shipped to and from the New World. Atlantic ports such as Seville—through which most Spanish commerce with the New World flowed—and, above all, Amsterdam, began to flourish.

The population of Amsterdam increased from about 30,000 to 200,000 in the course of the seventeenth century. The great volume of trade centered in Amsterdam made it the ideal place to get credit for business transactions. The Bank of Amsterdam, founded in 1609, became the depository for the bullion that flowed in with trade. Investors deposited funds there. The bank established currency-exchange rates and issued paper money and instruments of credit to facilitate commerce.

All capital cities, not just seaports, grew substantially in the seventeenth century. Increasing numbers of government functionaries, courtiers and their hangers-on, and people involved in trade lived and worked in capital cities. These cities also grew indirectly from the demand such people generated. Courtiers and wealthy merchants demanded services and products, ranging from fashionable clothing to exotic foodstuffs.

In the burgeoning capital cities, medieval forms of city life were eroded and cast aside. Cities were no longer self-enclosed societies dominated by local elites; they were centers of national government and culture. For the first time, cities employed vast numbers of country people. Perhaps as much as one-fifth of the population of England passed through London at one time or another, creating the mobile, volatile community so active in the English civil war and its aftermath. Patterns of consumption in cities reflected the economic gulfs between residents. Most people could not afford to buy imported pepper or sugar. Even in vibrant Amsterdam, poverty was increasing.

Poverty increased in cities because they attracted people fleeing from rural unemployment. Growing central governments increased their tax burdens. Urban demand for grain often caused severe shortages in rural areas. Many rural people, caught in a cycle of debt, abandoned farming and made their way to cities.

Thousands of rural people, particularly those close to thriving urban centers, supplemented their farm income by means of the putting-out system. An entrepreneur loaned, or "put out," raw materials to rural workers, who processed them at home and returned a finished product to the entrepreneur. For example, the rural workers might receive wool to be spun and woven into cloth. The entrepreneur would pay the workers by the piece and then sell the finished product.

In the long run, the putting-out system left workers open to economic vulnerability of a new—more modern—sort. A local harvest failure might not endanger them, but a foreign war or disaster at sea that affected the market for their product might. Moreover, many people could not make ends meet either by farming or from the putting-out system. A young man might find few opportunities for farmwork and no local demand for manufacturing labor.

Peasant rebellions occurred throughout the century as a result of depressed economic conditions and heavy taxation. Some of the revolts were extremely localized and involved limited direct action—seizing the tax collector's grain or stopping the movement of grain to the great cities. Other, more widespread revolts, affected whole provinces and various classes of people and prompted authorities to dispatch armed forces. Participants in a revolt in the French province of Normandy in 1639 included common rural folk, townspeople, and even some local nobles, all of whom were bending under the weight of tax increases to pay for France's involvement in the Thirty Years' War.

An interesting feature of the revolt in Normandy and of many other outbreaks is the inkling they give of the participants' political consciousness. Rebels in Normandy used printing presses to create and circulate "orders" from a mythical leader known as Jean Va-nu-pieds (John Barefoot). The mythical Jean issued orders in the name of the king to rise up against rapacious officials. The use of such a device indicates the rebels' concern about the political legitimacy of their actions. The rebels attacked the abuses of the system, rather than the system itself.

In England during the civil war and Interregnum, religious radicals, driven by their religious convictions, offered new visions of how to organize society. The Levelers advocated broad-based political participation and decentralized, community-run churches. More radical groups expressed different views. For example, the "Diggers" took over areas of uncultivated land and set up model egalitarian communities.

What all of these protesters and actions reveal is that the states of Europe were not reflecting the will or needs of the common people.

The Example of Captain Kidd

In the seventeenth century, increasing numbers of men came to the Caribbean islands, usually to escape the life of a sailor, a settler, or an indentured servant in the New World. Some of them became pirates and used the islands as bases from which to launch raids. Spanish, French, and English ships were all targets, and so were wealthy Spanish colonies.

From the earliest days of exploration, European rulers had given privateers letters of marque, commissions that authorized them to commit acts of war against specific targets—such as Spanish treasure fleets. The Crown took little risk and was spared the cost of arming the ships but usually shared in the profits of plunder. Outright piracy was illegal, but privateering with royal authorization was an acceptable occupation. In practice, the difference between piracy and privateering was small.

The dependence of European merchants, colonists, and governments on overseas trade—not merely on booty—resulted in increasing regulation of privateering and decreasing toleration of piracy by the end of the seventeenth century. As governments' and traders' desire for secure trade began to outweigh their desire for the irregular profits of privateering and piracy, the increasing numbers of pirates with bases in the Caribbean seemed particularly threatening.

The career of the Englishman William Kidd (1645?–1701) illustrates the fate of many pirates and privateers in the second half of the century. When William of Orange assumed the English throne in 1689 and brought England into the Dutch wars against the French, Kidd was recruited as a privateer against the French. He gained enough in booty to retire comfortably in New York in 1691, where he married a local woman of some means. By 1695, however, he was back at sea. He went to England to acquire a commission as a privateer. Although by that time acquiring such a commission was becoming increasingly difficult, Kidd finally gained a letter of marque, after cultivating his contacts at the English court. He was commissioned to hunt down pirates.

Within a few years, Kidd himself was branded a pirate. To survive the long voyage in search of his prey, his ship had to make use of ports of call frequented by buccaneers. Most of the members of his crew were used to the dangers and rewards of the buccaneering life. The crew urged Kidd to seize vessels to which his commission did not entitle him. Kidd raided trading vessels traveling west from English outposts in India. When he returned to port ready to divide his spoils with his sponsors, he found that the English government had decided to make an example of him. The state had drawn a firm line where only a blurred one had previously existed, and was prepared to act forcefully. He was branded a pirate, tried with great fanfare, and hanged at dockside in London on May 23, 1701. Over the next forty years, the concerted action of colonial merchants and governments steadily brought piracy under control, particularly in Atlantic waters.

The Hunt for Witches

In early modern Europe there was a dramatic increase in the persecution of women and men for alleged witchcraft. Approximately 100,000 people were tried and about 60,000 executed. Most of the trials and deaths occurred between 1560 and 1660.

The surge in witch-hunting was closely linked to the aftermath of the Reformation. Certain kinds of witchcraft had long existed in Europe. So-called black magic of various kinds—one peasant casting a spell on another peasant's cow—was common in the Middle Ages. What began to make black magic seem menacing to magistrates, judges, and other authorities was theories linking black magic to devil-worship. Catholic leaders and legal scholars first began to advance such theories in the fifteenth century. By the seventeenth century, both Catholic and Protestant elites viewed a witch not only as someone who might cast harmful spells but also as a heretic. Persecution for witchcraft rose dramatically only after the initial phases of the Reformation were over, and it reflects a continuation of reforming zeal, directed at the traditional forms of folk religion and magic.

So far as we can tell, no proof that an accused person ever attended a devil-worshiping "black" Sabbath was ever produced in any witch trial. Nevertheless, authorities were certain that devil-worship was occurring, so convinced were they that Satan was in their midst and that the folk ways of common people were somehow threatening them.

Contemporary legal procedures allowed the use of torture to extract confessions. Torture or the threat of torture led most of those accused of witchcraft to "confess." Probably willing to say what they thought their captors wanted to hear, many named accomplices or others who were also "witches." In this way, a single initial accusation could lead to dozens of prosecutions. In areas where procedures for appealing convictions and sentences were fragile or nonexistent, prosecutions were pursued with zeal. Prosecutions were widespread, for example, in the small principalities and imperial cities of the Holy Roman Empire, which were virtually independent of all higher authority (see the box, "A Confessed 'Witch' Denies His Confession").

Prosecutions also numbered in the thousands in Switzerland, Poland, France, and Scotland. The majority—perhaps 80 percent—of those convicted and executed in all areas of Europe were women. Lacking legal, social, and political resources, women may have been more likely than men to use black magic for self-protec-

Execution of "Witches" Witchcraft persecution was closely related to other trends of the era: economic insecurity, social and political stratification, and religious fervor. How these conditions resulted in the persecution of women, who constituted 80 percent of the Europeans executed for witchcraft, is also an important part of the story.
(Germanisches Nationalmuseum Nuremberg)

tion or advancement and hence were accused more often than men by their neighbors. Community fear and guilt may account for the fact that many of the accused women were poor. The marked increase in poverty during the late sixteenth and early seventeenth centuries made poor women particularly vulnerable to accusations of witchcraft. It was easier to find such a person menacing—and to accuse her of something—than it would be to feel guilty because of her evident need. The modern stereotype that depicts the witch as an ugly old crone dates from this period.

Christian dogma and classically inspired humanistic writing portrayed women as morally weaker than men and thus as more susceptible to the devil's enticements. Devil-worship was described in sexual terms, and the prosecution of witches had a voyeuristic, sexual dimension. The bodies of accused witches were searched for the "devil's mark"—a blemish thought to be the imprint of the devil. Both Protestantism and Catholicism taught that sexual lust was evil. One theory is that women accused of being witches were victims of the guilt that elite men suffered because of the latter's own sexual longings, which they believed were sinful and might be evidence of damnation. Thus, these men sought to lay blame elsewhere.

The witch-hunts virtually ended by the end of the seventeenth century, as the intellectual fashions changed from religious to scientific thought. Reflecting religious fear and guilt and class divisions, the witch-hunts are central to an understanding of European life in this period. They are both the last chapter in the history of the Reformation and a first chapter in the history of the modern state.

A Confessed "Witch" Denies His Confession

In 1628 Johannes Junius, mayor of the west German town of Bamberg, was tried for witchcraft. The case was unusual because the defendant was a man and a prominent citizen. This document is part of a letter that Junius wrote to his daughter and managed to have smuggled out of prison.

. . . dearly beloved daughter Veronica . . . Innocent have I come into prison, innocent have I been tortured, innocent I must die. For whoever comes into the witch prison must become a witch or be tortured until he invents something out of his head. . . . I will tell you how it has gone with me. [When questioned without torture], I said, "I am no witch, I have a pure conscience in the matter, . . . I'll bear whatever I must."

And then came—God in his highest heaven have mercy—the executioner, and put the thumb-screws on me. . . . Therafter, they first stripped me, bound my hands behind me, and drew me up in the torture [of the strappado]. Then I thought heaven and earth were at an end; eight times did they draw me up and let me fall again, so that I suffered terribly. . . . When at last the executioner [said]: "Sir, I beg you, for God's sake confess something, whether it be true or not . . . for you cannot endure the torture you will be put to; and, even if you bear it all, yet you will not escape . . . but one torture will follow another until you say you are a witch."

And so I begged to be given one day for thought and a priest . . . and at last there came to me [an] idea. I would think of something and say it. It were surely better that I just say it with mouth and words and confess it afterwards to the priest and let those answer for it who compel me to do it. . . . And so I made my confession, as follows; but it was all a lie. . . .

Dear child, keep this letter secret, else I shall be tortured most piteously. . . . Good night, for your father . . . will never see you more.

Source: Alan C. Kors and Edward Peters, *Witchcraft in Europe, 1100–1700: A Documentary History* (Philadelphia: University of Pennsylvania Press, 1972), pp. 253–259.

Summary

The beginning of the seventeenth century was marked by religious turmoil and by social and political upheaval. By the end of the century, the former had faded as a source of collective anxiety, and the latter was largely resolved. Nascent political configurations in the Low Countries, in the empire, and on the frontiers of eastern Europe had evolved into new centers of power—the Netherlands, Brandenburg-Prussia, and the newly powerful Russia of Peter the Great. Most European states had moved from internal division—with independent provinces and aristocrats going their own way—to relative stability. This internal stability was both cause and consequence of rulers' desire to make war on an ever-larger scale. At the beginning of the century, overseas trade and colonization had been the near monopoly of Spain and Portugal; at the century's end, the English, French, and Dutch controlled much of the trade with Asia and were reaping many profits in the Americas.

Beneath these developments lay subtle but significant economic, social, and cultural shifts. One effect of the increased wealth generated by overseas trade and the increased power of governments to tax their subjects was a widening of the gulf between poor and rich. New styles of behavior and patterns of consumption highlighted differences between social classes. Long-term effects of overseas voyages on European attitudes, as well as fundamental change in viewing the world culminating in the development of modern science would have revolutionary effects on Europeans and their cultures. We will now consider the seventeenth century in this, even more startling, light.

Note

1. Quoted in D. H. Pennington, *Europe in the Seventeenth Century,* 2d ed. (London: Longman, 1989), p. 508.

Suggested Reading

General Surveys

Howard, Michael. *War in European History.* 1976. A general study of warfare emphasizing the relationship between war making and state development.

Parker, Geoffrey. *The Military Revolution.* 1988; and Black, Jeremy. *A Military Revolution?* 1991. Two works that disagree about the nature and extent of the changes in military practices and their significance for military, political, and social history. Black tries to refute claims for a dramatic military "revolution."

Pennington, D. H. *Europe in the Seventeenth Century.* 2d ed. 1989; and Bonney, Richard. *The European Dynastic States, 1494–1660.* 1991. Two general histories covering various portions of the century.

The Thirty Years' War and Its Aftermath

Evans, R. J. W. *The Making of the Hapsburg Monarchy.* 1979. A thorough survey of the rise of the Austrian Habsburg state from the breakup of Charles V's empire; emphasizing the importance of the ideology and institutions of Catholicism in shaping the identity and guaranteeing the coherence of the Habsburg state.

Parker, Geoffrey. *The Thirty Years' War.* 2d ed. 1987. A readable general history by one of the best-known military historians.

Vierhaus, Rudolf. *Germany in the Age of Absolutism.* 1988. A concise survey of the development of German states from the end of the Thirty Years' War through the eighteenth century.

England

Aylmer, G. E. *Rebellion or Revolution? England from Civil War to Restoration.* 1987. A useful work that summarizes the important studies on each facet of the revolution; has an extensive bibliography.

Hill, Christopher. *A Century of Revolution, 1603–1714.* Rev. ed. 1980; and *The World Turned Upside Down.* 1972. The first work is a general history; the second, an exploration of Levelers, Diggers, and other groups of lower-class participants in the English revolution.

Stone, Lawrence. *The Causes of the English Revolution, 1529–1642.* 1972. A brief and clear introduction.

France

Beik, William. *Absolutism and Society in Seventeenth-Century France.* 1984. A case study focusing on a province in southern France but nevertheless an important interpretation of the nature and functioning of the absolutist state; has an extensive bibliography.

Briggs, Robin. *Early Modern France, 1560–1715.* 1977. A solid but dense survey.

Goubert, Pierre. *Louis XIV and Twenty Million Frenchmen.* 1970; and *The French Peasantry in the Seventeenth Century.* 1986. Two works that consider political and social history from a broad analytical framework that includes long-term economic, demographic, and cultural data.

Parker, David. *The Making of French Absolutism.* 1983. A good narrative treatment of the period from the late sixteenth century through the establishment of Louis XIV's regime.

Wedgewood, C. V. *Richelieu and the French Monarchy.* 1962. A brief and readable introduction to Richelieu's achievements.

Eastern Europe

Davies, Norman. *God's Playground.* 2 vols. 1982. A densely written survey of Polish history, including political, economic, social, and religious perspectives.

Kliuchevsky, Vasili. *Peter the Great.* Translated by L. Archibald. 1958. A classic work by one of Russia's great historians of the early twentieth century.

Riasanovsky, Nicolas V. *A History of Russia.* 2d ed. 1969. A reliable and readable survey of Russian history from medieval times; has an extensive bibliography of major works available in English.

Early Modern Economy and Society

Bercé, Yves-Marie. *Revolt and Revolution in Early Modern Europe.* Translated by Joseph Bergin. 1987; and *History of Peasant Revolts.* Translated by A. Whitmore. 1990. The first work is a general, comparative survey of revolts and revolutionary movements of all sorts across Europe between 1500 and 1800; the second is a more intensive study of French peasant movements.

Weighing the Evidence

TABLE MANNERS

If you were to sit down in a fancy restaurant, order a juicy steak, and then eat it with your bare hands, other diners would undoubtedly stare and think what bad manners you have. It has not always been the case that table manners meant very much—were able to signal social status, for example. It was not always the case that table manners existed at all in the sense that we know them. How did they evolve? How did they come to have the importance that they do? And why should historians pay any attention to them?

Imagine that you have been invited to dinner at a noble estate in the year 1500. As you sit down, you notice that there are no knives, forks, and spoons at your place at the table, and no napkins either. A servant (a young girl from a neighboring village) sets a roast of meat in front of you and your fellow diners. The lords and ladies on either side of you hack off pieces of meat with the knives that they always carry with them, and then they eat the meat with their fingers. Hunks of bread on the table in front of them catch the dripping juices.

One hundred fifty years later, in 1650, dinner is a much more "civilized" meal. Notice the well-to-do women dining in this engraving by the French artist Abraham Bosse (1602–1676). The table setting, with tablecloths, napkins, plates, and silverware, is recognizable to us. The lady at the extreme right holds up her fork and napkin in a somewhat forced and obvious gesture. These diners have the utensils that we take for granted, but the artist does not take them for granted: They are intended to be noticed by Bosse's elite audience.

In the seventeenth century, aristocrats and gentry signaled their political and social privilege with behavior that distinguished them from the lower classes in ways their more powerful ancestors had felt no need for. Historians have called this the invention of civility. As we have seen, proper courtesy to one's superiors at court was considered essential. It marked the fact that rituals of honor and deference were increasingly taking the place of armed conflict as the routine behavior of the upper classes. Also essential, however, were certain standards of physical privacy and delicacy. Something as seemingly trivial as the use of a fork became charged with symbolic significance. As the actual power of the aristocrats was circumscribed by the state, they found new expressions of status. Since the sixteenth century, new kinds of manners had been touted in handbooks, reflecting changes that already had occurred at Italian courts. During the seventeenth century, these practices became more widespread and opened up a gulf of behavior between upper and lower classes.

Some of the new behaviors concerned bodily privacy and discretion. A nobleman now used a handkerchief instead of his fingers or coat sleeve, and he did not urinate in public. The new "rules" about eating are particularly interesting. Why did eating with a fork seem refined and desirable to aristocrats trying to buttress their own self-image? As any 3-year-old knows, eating with a fork is remarkably inefficient.

Using a fork kept you at a distance—literal and symbolic—from the animal you were eating. Napkins wiped away all trace of bloody juices from your lips. Interestingly, as diners began to use eating utensils, other arrangements about meals changed in parallel ways. Sideboards had been in use for a long time, but pieces of meat were now discreetly carved on the sideboard and presented to diners in individual portions. The carcass was brought to the sideboard cut into roasts instead of unmistakably whole, and it was often decorated—as it is today—to further disguise it.

The new aristocrat was increasingly separated from the world of brute physical force, both in daily life and on the battlefield. In warfare, brute force was no longer adequate. Training,

Table Manners of the Upper Class in the Seventeenth Century *(Courtesy of the Trustees of the British Museum)*

discipline, and tactical knowledge were more important and heightened the importance of rank, which separated officers from the vast numbers of common soldiers (see page 664). Aristocrats now lived in a privileged world where violence was no longer a fact of life. Their new behavior codes signaled their new invulnerability to others. Above all, they worked to transform a loss—of the independence that had gone hand in hand with a more violent life—into a gain: a privileged immunity to violence.

Specific manners became important, then, because they were symbols of power. The symbolic distance between the powerful and the humble was reinforced by other changes in habits and behavior. A sixteenth-century warrior customarily traveled on horseback and often went from place to place within a city on foot, attended by his retinue. A seventeenth-century aristocrat was more likely to travel in a horsedrawn carriage. The presence of special commodities from abroad—such as sugar—in the seventeenth century created further possibilities for signaling status.

It is interesting to note that other personal habits still diverged dramatically from what we would consider acceptable today. Notice the large, stately bed in the same room as the dining table in Bosse's engraving. Interior space was still undifferentiated by our standards, and it was common for eating, talking, sleeping, and estate management all to go on in a single room. The grand bed is in the picture because, like the fork, it is a mark of status. Like virtually everything else, what is "proper" varies with historical circumstance.

Boxer, C. R. *The Dutch Seaborne Empire.* 1965. The standard work detailing the development of the Dutch empire.

Blum, Jerome. *Lord and Peasant in Russia.* 1961. A work that highlights the extension of serfdom in Russia fostered by Peter the Great and other tsars.

Curtin, Philip D. *The Rise and Fall of the Plantation Complex.* 1990. A good starting place for understanding the reasons behind and the significance of Europeans' establishment of plantation agriculture in the New World.

De Vries, Jan. *The Economy of Europe in an Age of Crisis, 1600–1750.* 1976. The single most important work on the development of the European economy in this period, integrating developments within and around Europe with the growth of overseas empires.

Goody, J., Joan Thirsk, and E. P. Thompson, eds. *Family and Inheritance: Rural Society in Western Europe, 1200–1800.* 1976. Essays that constitute a wide-ranging introduction to issues of village and family life throughout the premodern era.

Levack, Brian P. *The Witch-Hunt in Early Modern Europe.* 1987; and Klaits, Joseph. *Servants of Satan.* 1985. Two surveys of witch-hunting in the sixteenth and seventeenth centuries. Levack synthesizes the work of various historians with particular care; Klaits's work is more interpretive.

Parry, J. H. *The Establishment of European Hegemony, 1415–1715.* 1961. A brief introduction to the motives, means, and results of European expansion through the seventeenth century; somewhat dated in its overemphasis on the English in North America but nevertheless a useful overview.

Ritchie, Robert C. *Captain Kidd and the War Against the Pirates.* 1986. A recent work on the communities of castoffs and adventurers that grew up in the Caribbean during European expansion and their place in the Atlantic economic and political worlds.

Sabean, David Warren. *Power in the Blood.* 1984. An innovative series of essays about life in German villages from the sixteenth through the eighteenth centuries; raises questions about the increasing efforts of the state to control village life and the resistance mounted by villagers to these efforts.

Thomas, Keith. *Religion and the Decline of Magic.* 1971. A classic work that traces the changing nature of religious life and the disappearance of magical explanations for things.

Wolf, Eric R. *Europe and the People Without History.* 1982. A survey of European contact with and conquest of peoples after 1400; includes extensive treatments of non-European societies and detailed explanation of the economic and political interests of the Europeans.

CHAPTER 19

A Revolution in World View

As famous as the confrontation between the religious rebel Martin Luther and Holy Roman Emperor Charles V at Worms in 1521 is the confrontation between the astronomer Galileo and the judges of the papal inquisition that ended on June 22, 1633. On that day, Galileo knelt before the seven cardinals who represented the inquisition to renounce his errors and to receive his punishment. His "errors" included publishing scientific propositions that disagreed with views accepted by the church—particularly the view that the earth is stationary and does not spin on its axis and orbit the sun. As Galileo left the cardinals' presence, he is supposed to have muttered, "Eppur si muove" ("But it *does* move").

This seems a wonderful moment of historical drama, but we should be suspicious of it because it oversimplifies historical circumstances. The changes that we know as "the Reformation" and "the Scientific Revolution" were far broader and more complex than the actions of a few individuals whose deeds now seem heroic and larger than life. Galileo, in fact, never made the defiant statement he is credited with.

Moreover, just as we cannot simply credit "heroes" with causing a revolution in scientific understanding, we cannot treat their new scientific views simply as truth finally overcoming ignorance and error. The history of scientific thought is not merely a history of discovery about the world but also a history of explanations of the world. From its beginnings the Scientific Revolution was a broad cultural movement. Copernicus, Galileo, and others contributed important new data to the pool of knowledge, but

Gold-plated globe, made in 1586, and said to have been used by Johannes Kepler.

their even more important collective contribution was a fundamentally new view of the universe and of the place of the earth and human beings in it.

By the end of the seventeenth century, a vision of an infinite but orderly cosmos appealing to human reason had largely replaced the medieval vision of a closed universe centered on earth and suffused with Christian purpose. Religion became an increasingly subordinate ally of science as confidence in an open-ended, experimental approach to knowledge came to be as strongly held as religious conviction. It is because of this larger shift in world view, not because of particular scientific discoveries, that the seventeenth century may be labeled the era of the scientific *revolution.*

The Revolution in Astronomy

Because the Scientific Revolution was a revolution within science itself as well as a revolution in intellectual life more generally, we must seek its causes within the history of science as well as in the broader historical context. Many of the causes are familiar. They include the intellectual achievements of the Renaissance, the challenges that were posed by the discovery of the New World, the expansion of trade and production, the spread of literacy and access to books, and the increasing power of princes and monarchs.

The scientific origins of the seventeenth-century revolution in thought lie, for the most part, in developments in astronomy. Various advances in astronomy spurred dramatic intellectual transformation because of astronomy's role in the explanations of the world and human life that had been devised by ancient and medieval scientists and philosophers. By the early part of the seventeenth century, fundamental astronomical tenets were successfully challenged. The consequence was the undermining of both the material explanation of the world (physics) and the philosophical explanation of the world (metaphysics) that had been standing for centuries.

The Inherited World View and the Sixteenth-Century Context

Ancient and medieval astronomy accepted the perspective on the universe that unaided human senses support—namely, that earth is at the center of the universe and the celestial bodies rotate around the earth. The intellectual and psychological journey from the notion of a closed world centered on earth to an infinitely large universe of undifferentiated matter with no obvious place for humans was an immense journey with complex causes.

The regular movements of heavenly bodies and the obvious importance of the sun for life on earth made astronomy a vital undertaking for both scientific and religious purposes in many ancient societies. Astronomers in ancient Greece carefully observed the heavens and learned to calculate and to predict the seemingly circular motion of the stars and the sun about the earth. The orbits of the planets were more difficult to explain, for the planets seemed to travel both east and west across the sky at various times and with no regularity that could be mathematically understood. Indeed, the very word *planet* comes from a Greek word meaning "wanderer."

We now know that all the planets simultaneously orbit the sun at different speeds and are at different distances from the sun. The relative positions of the planets thus constantly change; sometimes other planets are "ahead" of the earth and sometimes "behind." In the second century A.D., the Greek astronomer Ptolemy attempted to explain the planets' occasional "backward" motion by attributing it to "epicycles"—small circular orbits within the larger orbit. Ptolemy's mathematical explanations of the imagined epicycles were extremely complex, but neither Ptolemy nor medieval mathematicians and astronomers were ever able fully to account for planetary motion.

Ancient physics, most notably the work of Aristotle (384–322 B.C.), explained the fact that some objects (such as cannonballs) fall to earth but others (stars and planets) seem weightless relative to the earth by presuming that objects are made up of different sorts of matter. Aristotle thought that different kinds of matter had different inherent tendencies and properties. In this view, all earthbound matter (like cannonballs) falls because it is naturally attracted to earth—heaviness being a property of earthbound things.

In the Christian era, the Aristotelian explanation of the universe was infused with Christian meaning and purpose. The heavens were said to be made of different, pure matter because they were the abode of the angels. Both earth and the humans who inhabited it were changeable and corruptible. Yet God had given human beings a unique and special place in the universe. The universe was thought to be literally a closed world with the stationary earth at the center. Revolving around the earth in circular orbits were the sun, the moon, the stars, and the planets. The motion of all lesser bodies was caused by the rotation of all the stars together in the crystal-like sphere in which they were embedded.

A few ancient astronomers theorized that the earth moved about the sun. Some medieval philosophers also adopted this heliocentric thesis (*helios* is the Greek word for *sun*), but it remained a minority view because it seemed to contradict both common sense and observed data. The sun and stars *appeared* to move around the earth with great regularity. Moreover, how could objects fall to earth if the earth was moving beneath them? Also, astronomers detected no difference in angles from which observers on earth viewed the stars at different times. Such differences would exist, they thought, if the earth changed positions by moving around the sun. It was inconceivable that the universe could be so large and the stars so distant that the earth's movement would produce no measurable change in the earth's position with respect to the stars.

Several conditions of intellectual life in the sixteenth century encouraged new work in astronomy and led to revision of the earth-centered world view. The most important was the humanists' recovery of and commentary on ancient texts. Now able to work with new Greek versions of Ptolemy, mathematicians and astronomers noted that Ptolemy's explanations for the motions of the planets were imperfect and not simply inadequately transmitted, as they had long believed. Also, the discovery of the New World dramatically undercut the assumption that ancient knowledge was superior and specifically undermined Ptolemy's authority once again, for it disproved many of his assertions about geography.

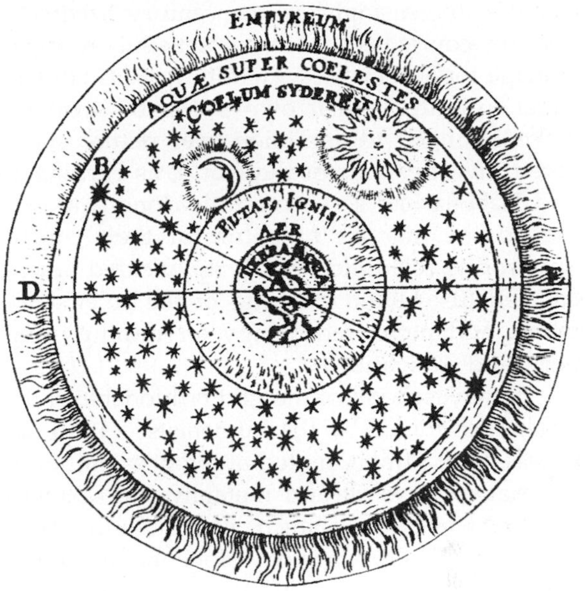

A Medieval Concept of the Universe The universe is organized here in concentric circles, with a realm of fire (Empyreum) outermost. The most respected astronomical theories of the day placed the moon and sun in circular orbits between the earth and stars, not among the stars as pictured here. *(From Gerald E. Tauber,* Man's View of the Universe *[Crown, 1979])*

The desire to explain heavenly motions better was still loaded with religious significance in the sixteenth century and was heightened by the immediate need for reform of the Julian calendar (named for Julius Caesar). Ancient observations of the movement of the sun, though remarkably accurate, could not measure the precise length of the solar year (365 *and* one-fourth days). By the sixteenth century, the cumulative error of this calendar had resulted in a change of ten days: The spring equinox fell on March 11 instead of March 21. An accurate and uniform system of dating was necessary for all rulers and their tax collectors and recordkeepers but was the particular project of the church, because the calculation of the date of Easter was at stake.

Impetus for new and better astronomical observations and calculations arose from other features of the intellectual and political landscape as well. Increasingly as the century went on, princely courts became important sources of patronage for and sites of scientific activity. Rulers eager to buttress their own power by symbolically linking it to dominion over nature sponsored investigations of the world, as Ferdinand and Isabella had so successfully done, and displayed the marvels of nature at their courts. Sponsoring scientific inquiry also yielded practical benefits: better mapping of the ruler's domains and better technology for mining, gunnery, and navigation.

Finally, schools of thought fashionable at the time, encouraged by the humanists' critique of Scholastic tradition, hinted at the possibilities of alternative physical and metaphysical systems. The first was Paracelsianism, named for the Swiss physician Philippus von Hohenheim (1493–1541), known as Paracelsus. Paracelsus offered an alternative to the theory, put forth by the ancient master, Galen (ca. 131–ca. 201), that the imbalance of bodily "humors" caused illness. He substituted a theory of chemical imbalance.

Neo-Platonism, the second school of thought, had a more systematic and far-reaching impact. Neo-Platonism, a revival primarily in Italian humanist circles of certain aspects of Plato's thought, contributed directly to innovation in science because it emphasized the abstract nature of true knowledge and thus encouraged mathematical investigation. This provided a spur to astronomical studies, which, since ancient times, had been concerned more with mathematical analysis of heavenly movements than with physical explanations for them. Also, like Paracelsianism, Neo-Platonism had a mystical dimension that encouraged creative speculation about the nature of matter and the organization of the universe. Neo-Platonists were particularly fascinated by the sun as a symbol of the one divine mind or soul at the heart of all creation.

Nicolaus Copernicus, as this portrait reflects, was both a cleric and a mathematical astronomer. The deliberate symbolism in the picture suggests that, after Copernicus, there was some tension between these two roles. *(The Mansell Collection)*

INRI
Non parem Pauli gratiam requiro
Veniam Petri neq; posco, sed quam
In crucis ligno dederas latroni
Sedulus oro.

The Copernican Challenge

Nicolaus Copernicus (1473–1543), son of a prosperous Polish merchant, pursued wide-ranging university studies in philosophy, law, astronomy, and mathematics—first in Cracow in Poland and then in Bologna and Padua in Italy. In Italy he was exposed to Neo-Platonic ideas. He took a degree in canon law in 1503 and became a cathedral canon in the bishopric of Ermland, where he pursued his own interests in astronomy. When the pope asked Copernicus to assist with the reform of the Julian calendar, Copernicus replied that reform of the calendar required reform in astronomy. His major work, *De Revolutionibus Orbium Caelestium* (*On the Revolution of Heavenly Bodies*), was dedicated to the pope in the hopes that it would help with the task of calendar reform—as indeed it did. The Gregorian calendar, issued in 1582 during the pontificate of Gregory XIII (r. 1572–1585), was based on Copernicus's calculations.

Copernicus postulated that the earth and all the other planets orbit the sun. He did not assert that the earth does in fact move around the sun but offered the heliocentric system as a mathematical construct, useful for predicting the movements of planets, stars, and the sun. However, he walked a thin line between making claims

Copernicus's Preface to *On the Revolution of Heavenly Bodies*

In this dedicatory letter to the pope, Copernicus explains his desire to assist with calendar reform. Principally, however, he seeks to justify his novel conclusions. He not only cites ancient authority for the movement of the earth but also stresses the mathematical nature of the problem and of his solution.

To the Most Holy Lord, Pope Paul III

I may well presume, most Holy Father, that certain people, as soon as they hear that in this book about the Revolutions of the Spheres of the Universe I ascribe movement to the earthly globe, will cry out that, holding such views, I should at once be hissed off the stage. . . . How I came to dare to conceive such motion of the Earth, contrary to the received opinion of the Mathematicians and indeed contrary to the impression of the senses, is what your Holiness will rather expect to hear. So I should like your Holiness to know that I was induced to think of a method of computing the motions of the spheres by nothing else than the knowledge that the Mathematicians are inconsistent in these investigations. . . . Mathematicians are so unsure of the movements of the Sun and the Moon that they cannot even explain . . . the constant length of the seasonal year.

. . . I pondered long upon this uncertainty of mathematical tradition. I . . . read again the works of all the philosophers on whom I could lay a hand to seek out whether any of them had ever supposed that the motions of the spheres were other[wise]. I found first in Cicero that Hicetas [of Syracuse, fifth century B.C.] had realized that the earth moved. . . . Mathematics are for mathematicians, and they, if I be not wholly deceived, will hold that my labors contribute somewhat . . . to the Church. . . . For under Leo X, the question of correcting the ecclesiastical calendar was . . . left undecided.

Source: Thomas S. Kuhn, *The Copernican Revolution* (Cambridge, Mass.: Harvard University Press, 1985), pp. 137–143.

for mathematical and physical reality. He had searched in ancient sources for thinkers who believed the earth did move. Other astronomers familiar with his work and reputation urged him to publish the results of his calculations. But not until 1542, twelve years after finishing the work, did he send *De Revolutionibus* to be published; he received a copy just before his death the next year. (See the box, "Copernicus's Preface to *On the Revolution of Heavenly Bodies*.")

Copernicus's colleagues were right: His work was immediately useful. Copernicus's schema made possible a simpler explanation of all planetary motion. Copernicus accounted for most backward motion without resorting to epicycles. But Copernicus still assumed that the planets traveled in circular orbits, so he retained some epicycles to account for the circular motion.

By positing the earth's movement around the sun but also retaining features of the old system, such as circular orbits, Copernicus faced burdens of explanation not faced by Ptolemy. In general, however, the Copernican account of planetary motion was simpler than the Ptolemaic account. It appealed to other astronomers of the age because it was useful and because it highlighted the harmony of heavenly motion, which remained a fundamental physical and metaphysical principle. Accessible only to other astronomers, Copernicus's work only slowly led to conceptual revolution, as astronomers worked with his calculations and assembled other evidence to support the heliocentric theory.

The most important reason why Copernican theory only gradually led to fundamental conceptual change was that Copernicus did not

MILESTONES OF THE SCIENTIFIC REVOLUTION

1543	Copernicus, *On the Revolution of Heavenly Bodies*
	Vesalius, *On the Fabric of the Human Body*
1576	Construction of Brahe's observatory begins
1591	Galileo's law of falling bodies
1609	Kepler's third law of motion
1610	Galileo, *The Starry Messenger*
1620	Bacon, *Novum Organum*
1628	Harvey, *On the Motion of the Heart*
1632	Galileo, *Dialogue on the Two Chief Systems of the World*
1637	Descartes, *Discourse on Method*
1660	Boyle, *New Experiments Physico-Mechanical*
1668	Cavendish, *Grounds of Natural Philosophy*
1687	Newton, *Principia*

resolve the physical problems his theory raised. If Copernicus was right, earth would have to be made of the same stuff as other planets. How then would Copernicus explain the motion of objects on earth—the fact that they fall to the earth—if it was not in their nature to fall toward the heavy, stationary earth? In Copernicus's system, the movement of the earth caused the *apparent* motion of the stars. But if the stars did not rotate in their crystalline sphere, what impelled all other heavenly bodies to move?

Copernicus was not as troubled by these questions as we might expect him to be. Since ancient times, mathematical astronomy—the science of measuring and predicting the movement of heavenly bodies—had been far more important than, and had proceeded independently of, physical explanations for observed motion. Nevertheless, as Copernicus's own efforts to buttress his notion that the earth moves reveal, his theories directly contradicted many of the supposed laws of motion. The usefulness of his theories to other astronomers meant that the contradictions between mathematical and physical models for the universe would have to be resolved. Copernicus himself might be best understood as the last Ptolemaic astronomer, working within inherited questions and with known tools. His work itself did not constitute a revolution, but it did initiate one.

The First Copernican Astronomers: Brahe and Kepler

In the first generation of astronomers after the publication of *De Revolutionibus* in 1543 we can see the effects of Copernicus's work. His impressive computations rapidly won converts among fellow astronomers. Several particularly gifted astronomers continued to develop the Copernican system. Thus, by the second quarter of the seventeenth century, they and many others accepted the heliocentric system as a reality and not just as a useful mathematical fiction. The three most important astronomers to build on Copernican assumptions, and on the work of each other, were the Dane Tycho Brahe (1546–1601), the German Johannes Kepler (1571–1630), and the Italian Galileo Galilei (1564–1642).

Like generations of observers before him, Tycho Brahe had been stirred by the majesty of the regular movements of heavenly bodies. After witnessing a partial eclipse of the sun, he abandoned a career in government and became an astronomer. Brahe was the first truly post-Ptolemaic astronomer because he was the first to improve on the data that the ancients and all subsequent astronomers had used. Ironically, *no* theory of planetary motion or mathematics to explain it could have reconciled the data that Copernicus had used: They were simply too inaccurate, based as they were on naked-eye observations, even when errors of translation and copying, accumulated over centuries, had been corrected.

In 1576 the king of Denmark showered Brahe with properties and pensions enabling him to build an observatory, Uraniborg, on an island near Copenhagen. At Uraniborg Brahe improved on ancient observations with large and very finely calibrated instruments that permitted precise measurements of celestial movements by the

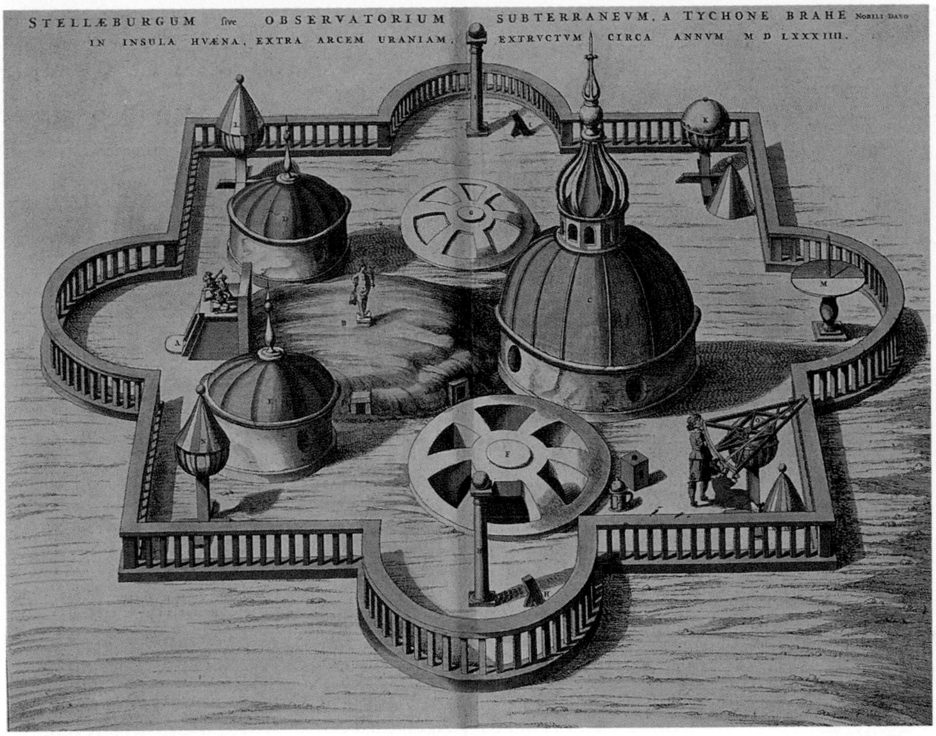

STELLÆBURGUM ſive OBSERVATORIUM SUBTERRANEVM, A TYCHONE BRAHE Nobili Dano
IN INSULA HVÆNA, EXTRA ARCEM URANIAM, EXTRVCTVM CIRCA ANNVM M D LXXXIIII.

Tycho Brahe's Observatory Brahe's fame was initially established by his observation and measurement of a new star in 1572, but his enduring contribution to astronomy was the meticulous collection of data by means of the instruments assembled at Uraniborg. *(The Fotomas Index)*

naked eye. His attention to precision and frequency of observation produced results that were twice as accurate as any previous data had been.

As a result of his observations, Brahe agreed with Copernicus that the various planets did rotate around the sun, not around the earth. He still could not be persuaded that the earth itself moved, for none of his data supported such a notion. Brahe's lasting and crucial contribution was his astronomical data. They would become obsolete as soon as data from use of the telescope were accumulated about a century later. But in the meantime, they were used by Johannes Kepler to further develop Copernicus's model and arrive at a more accurate heliocentric theory.

Kepler was young enough to be exposed to Copernican ideas from the outset of his training, and he quickly recognized in Brahe's data the means of resolving the problems in Copernican analysis. Though trained in his native Germany, Kepler went to Prague, where Brahe spent the last years of his life after a quarrel with the Danish king, and became something of an apprentice to Brahe. After Brahe's death, Kepler kept his mentor's records of astronomical observation and continued to work at the imperial court as Rudolf II's court mathematician.

Kepler's contribution to the new astronomy, like that of Copernicus, was fundamentally mathematical. In it, we can see the stamp of the Neo-Platonic conviction about the purity of mathematical explanation. Kepler spent ten years working to apply Brahe's data to the most intricate of all the celestial motions—the movement of the planet Mars—as a key to explaining all planetary motion. Mars is close to the earth but farther from the sun than is the earth. This combination produces very puzzling and dramatic variations in the apparent movement of Mars to an earthly observer.

The result of Kepler's work was laws of planetary motion that, in the main, are still in use.

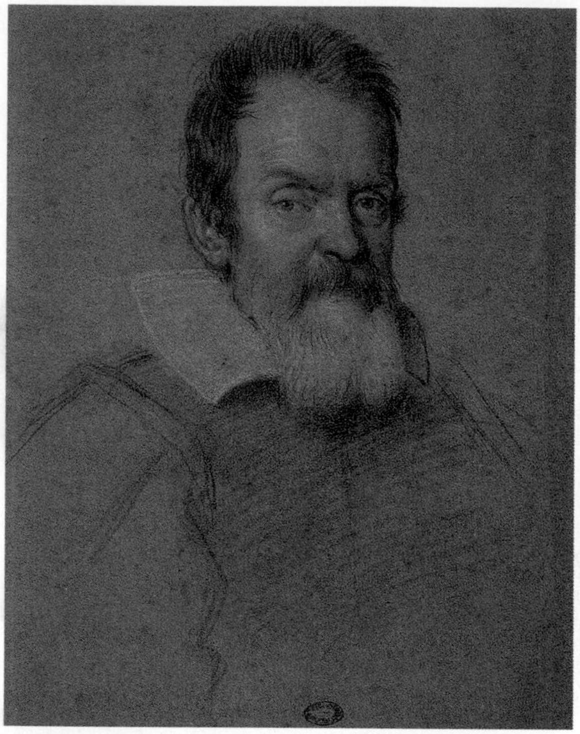

Galileo Galileo built his telescope himself after hearing that such an instrument had been built by a Dutch lens-maker. We do not know precisely what combination of practical insight and imaginative leap led him to look at the heavens, but we can speculate that his lifelong adherence to Copernican theory convinced him that there was something out there to see. *(Biblioteca Marucelliana, Florence)*

First, Kepler eliminated the need for epicycles by correctly asserting that planets follow elliptical and not circular orbits. Elliptical orbits could account—mathematically and visually—for the motions of the planets when combined with Kepler's second law, which described the *rate* of a planet's motion around its orbital path. Kepler noted that the speed of a planet in its orbit slows proportionally as the planet's distance from the sun increases. A third law demonstrated that the distance of each planet from the sun and the time it takes each planet to orbit the sun are in a constant ratio.

Kepler's work was a breakthrough because it mathematically confirmed the Copernican heliocentric hypothesis. In so doing, the work directly challenged the ancient world view, in which heavenly bodies constantly moved in circular orbits around a stationary earth. Hence, Kepler's laws invited speculation about the properties and motion of heavenly and terrestrial bodies alike. A new physics would be required to explain the novel motions that Kepler had posited. Kepler himself, in Neo-Platonic fashion, attributed planetary motion to the sun:

> [the sun] is a fountain of light, rich in fruitful heat, most fair, limpid and pure . . . called king of the planets for his motion, heart of the world for his power. . . . Who would hesitate to confer the votes of the celestial motions on him who has been administering all other movements and changes by the benefit of the light which is entirely his possession?[1]

Galileo and the Triumph of Copernicanism

Galileo Galilei holds a pre-eminent position in the development of astronomy for several reasons. He provided compelling new evidence to support Copernican theory, and he contributed to the development of a new physics—or, more precisely, mechanics—that could account for the movement of bodies in new terms. Just as important, his efforts to publicize his findings and his condemnation by the church spurred popular debate about Copernican ideas in literate society and helped to determine the course science would take.

Born to a minor Florentine noble family, Galileo studied medicine and mathematics at the University of Pisa and became professor of mathematics there in 1589 at the age of 25. He had already completed important work on mechanics and within three years was given a chair at the University of Padua, where Copernicus had once studied. He continued work in mechanics during the 1590s but did not publish the results of his experiments until much later. Instead, he became famous for the results of his astronomical observations, which he began in 1609 and first published the next year. *Sidereus Nuncius* (*The Starry Messenger*, 1610) described in lay language the results of his scrutiny of the heavens with a telescope that he had built.

Galileo was the first person that we know who used a telescope to look at the sky. In *The*

Galileo Challenges the Authority of Aristotle

This document is from* Letters on Sunspots *(1613), Galileo's correspondence with a German astronomer about the "blemishes" of the sun. The letters discuss the limitations of received knowledge and illustrate Galileo's personal audacity and the confidence in new learning felt by investigators several decades after Copernicus. Notice that Copernicus's challenge to Aristotle's physics has become a straightforward challenge to the entire Aristotelian world view.

[The traditional philosophers] go about defending the inalterability of the sky, a view which Aristotle himself perhaps would abandon in our age.... Well, if alteration were annihilation, [they] would have some reason for concern; but since it is nothing but mutation, there is not reason for such bitter hostility to it. It seems to me unreasonable to call "corruption" in an egg that which produces a chicken.

These men are forced into their strange fancies by attempting to measure the whole universe by means of their tiny scale. Our special hatred of death need not render fragility odious. Why should we want to become less mutable?... Besides... we abase our own status too much and do this not without some offense to Nature (and I might add to divine Providence), when we attempt to learn from Aristotle that which he neither knew nor could find out, rather than consult our own senses and reason. For she, in order to aid our understanding of her great works, has given us two thousand more years of time and sight twenty times as acute as that which she gave Aristotle.

Source: Stillman Drake, *The Discoveries and Opinions of Galileo* (New York: Doubleday, 1957), pp. 141–143.

Starry Messenger, he documented sighting new (previously invisible) stars, another blow to the authority of ancient descriptions of the universe. He also noted craters and other "imperfections" on the surface of the moon as well as the existence of moons orbiting the planet Jupiter. Three years later, he published his observations of sunspots. Sunspots are regions of relatively cool gaseous material that appear as dark spots on the sun's surface. For Galileo, the sunspots and the craters of the moon constituted proof that the heavens were not perfect and changeless but rather were like the supposedly "corrupt" and changeable earth. His telescopic observations also provided further support for Copernican heliocentrism because they revealed that each heavenly body rotated on its axis: Sunspots, for example, could be tracked across the visible surface of the sun as the sun rotated. (See the box, "Galileo Challenges the Authority of Aristotle.")

Galileo's principle contribution to mechanics lay in his working out of an early theory of inertia. As a result of a number of experiments with falling bodies (balls rolling on carefully constructed inclines—not free-falling objects that, according to myth, he dropped from the Leaning Tower of Pisa), Galileo ventured a new view of what is "natural" to bodies. Galileo's view was that uniform motion is as natural as a state of rest. In the ancient and medieval universe, all motion needed a cause, and all motion could be explained in terms of purpose. "I hold," Galileo countered in 1624, "that there exists nothing in external bodies... but size, shape, quantity and motion."[2] Galileo retained the old assumption that motion was somehow naturally circular. Nevertheless, his theory was a crucial step in explaining motion according to new principles and in fashioning a world view that accepted a mechanical universe devoid of metaphysical

Galileo Confronts the Church

His work increasingly under attack after the publication of* Letters on Sunspots, *Galileo defended himself by criticizing the claim that biblical authority could decide matters of astronomy. This dangerous line of argument not only argued for a separation of theology and science but also presumed to evaluate the work of theologians and even offered an interpretation of biblical passages. In this document, from an essay couched as a letter to his patron Christina of Lorraine, Galileo broaches these ideas.

But I do not feel obliged to believe that . . . God who has endowed us with senses, reason and intellect has intended to forgo their use and by some other means to give us knowledge which we can attain by them. . . . This must be especially true in those sciences of which but the faintest trace . . . is to be found in the Bible. Of astronomy, for instance, so little is found that none of the planets except Venus are so much as mentioned. . . .

Now, if the Holy Spirit has purposely neglected to teach us propositions of this sort as irrelevant to the highest goal (that is, to our salvation), how can anyone affirm that it is obligatory to take sides on them, and that one belief is required by faith, while another side is erroneous? . . . I would assert here something that was heard from [a respected cleric]: . . . "the intention of the Holy Ghost is to teach us how to go to heaven, not how heaven goes."

Moreover, we are unable to affirm that all interpreters of the Bible speak with divine inspiration, for if that were so there would exist no differences between them about the sense of a given passage. Hence [it would be wise] not to permit anyone to usurp scriptural texts and force them in some way to maintain any physical conclusion to be true, when at some future time the senses . . . may show the contrary. Who . . . will set bounds to human ingenuity? Who will assert that everything in the universe capable of being perceived is already . . . known?

Source: Stillman Drake, *The Discoveries and Opinions of Galileo* (New York: Doubleday, 1957), pp. 183–187.

purpose. These theories were published only toward the end of his life, however. His astronomical theories were the more influential at the time.

Galileo's works were widely read, and his work became common currency in the scientific societies already flourishing in his lifetime and in courtly circles where science was encouraged. In 1610, Galileo became court mathematician to Cosimo de' Medici, the grand duke of Tuscany (r. 1609–1620), as a result of the fame brought by *The Starry Messenger.* Soon after his arrival, however, rumors that "Galileists" were openly promulgating heliocentrism led to an investigation and, in 1616, the official condemnation of Copernicus's works by the inquisition in Rome. This condemnation allowed room for maneuver. After meeting personally with the pope, Galileo was assured that he could continue to use Copernican theory, but only as a theory.

In 1632 Galileo issued a bold response to that limitation. *Dialogue on the Two Chief Systems of the World* was perhaps the most important single source for the popularization of Copernican theory. The work consists of a dialogue among three characters supposedly debating the merits of Copernican theory. Simplicio, the character representing the old world view, was—as his name suggests—an example of ignorance, not wisdom. In this work, Galileo expresses his supreme confidence—bordering on arrogance—

in his own powers and in human power generally to use the senses and reason to understand the physical world.

By publishing the *Dialogue* Galileo was defying the papal ban on advocating Copernicanism. In an earlier work, *Letter to the Grand Duchess Christina* (1615), Galileo had also been impolitic. In the *Letter,* he had trespassed on the church's authority to interpret the Scriptures (see the box, "Galileo Confronts the Church"). He was tried for heresy and forced to condemn his "errors" in 1633, though Pope Urban VIII (r. 1623–1644) intervened to give him the light sentence of house arrest at his villa in Tuscany. There, until his death in 1642, Galileo continued his investigations of mechanics.

The Scientific Revolution Generalized

Galileo's work found such a willing audience because Galileo, like Kepler and Brahe, was not working alone. Dozens of other scientists were working energetically on old problems from the fresh perspective offered by the breakthroughs in astronomy. Some were analyzing the nature of matter, now that it was supposed that all matter in the universe was somehow the same despite its varying appearances. Many of these thinkers addressed the metaphysical issues that their investigations inevitably raised.

The Promise of the New Science

No less a man than Francis Bacon (1561–1626), lord chancellor of England during the reign of James I, wrote a utopian essay extolling the benefits of science for a peaceful society and for human happiness. In *New Atlantis,* published one year after Bacon's death, Bacon argued that science would produce "things of use and practice for man's life."[3] In *New Atlantis* and in *Novum Organum* (1620) Bacon revealed his faith in science by advocating patient, systematic observation and experimentation to accumulate knowledge about the world. He argued that the proper method of investigation "derives axioms from . . . particulars, rising by gradual and unbroken ascent, so that it arrives at the most general axioms of all. This is the true way but untried."[4]

Bacon himself did not undertake experiments, though his widely read works were influential in encouraging both empirical method and inductive reasoning. Indeed, Bacon was a visionary. Given the early date of his writings, it might even seem difficult to account for his enthusiasm and confidence. In fact, Bacon's writings reflect the widespread interest and confidence in science within his elite milieu that was founded largely on the interests of the state. In another of his writings he argued that a successful state should concentrate on effective "rule in religion *and nature,* as well as civil administration."[5]

Bacon's writing reflected the fact that an interest in exploring nature's secrets and exercising "dominion over nature" had become an indispensable part of princely rule. Princely courts were the main source of financial support for science and a primary site of scientific work during Bacon's lifetime. Part of the impetus for this development had come from the civic humanism of the Italian Renaissance, which had celebrated the state and service to it and had provided models both for educated rulers and for cultivated courtiers. The specific turning of the rulers' attention to science and to its benefits for the state reflected the scope of princely resources and ambitions: the desire of rulers for technical expertise in armaments, fortification, building projects in general, navigation, and mapmaking.

The promise of the New World and the drive for overseas trade and exploration especially encouraged princely support of scientific investigation. A renowned patron of geographical investigation, from mapmaking to navigation, was Henry, prince of Wales (d. 1612), son of James I. Prince Henry patronized technical experts such as experienced gunners and seamen as well as those with broader and more theoretical expertise. One geographer at his court worked on the vital problem of calculating longitude, sketched the moon after reading and emulating Galileo's work with the telescope, and—in a spirit of empiricism often associated with Bacon—compiled information about the new territory Virginia, including the first dictionary of any Native American language.

A Collection of Naturalia Displays of exotica, such as these specimens in Naples, symbolized the ruler's authority by suggesting his or her power over nature. *(From Ferrante Imperato,* Dell' Historia Naturale *[Naples, 1599]. By permission of the Houghton Library, Harvard University)*

Science was an ideological as well as a practical tool for power. Most courts housed collections of marvels, specimens of exotic plants and animals, and mechanical contrivances. These demonstrated the ruler's interest in investigation of the world—his or her status, in other words, as an educated person. These collections and the work of court experts enhanced the ruler's reputation as a patron and the image of the ruler's power. Galileo was playing off such expectations when he named some of his newly discovered bodies "Medician Stars."

Exploring the secrets of nature became a tool for rulers and an honorable activity for scholars and courtiers. By the beginning of the seventeenth century, private salons and academies where investigators might meet on their own were another major site of scientific investigation. These too had their roots in the humanist culture of Italy, where circles of scholars without university affiliations had formed. They were an important alternative to princely patronage—a ruler's funds might wax and wane according to his or her other commitments. Also, private organizations could avoid the hierarchical distinctions that were inevitable at court.

The earliest academy dedicated to scientific study was the Accadèmia Segreta ("Secret Academy") founded in Naples in the 1540s. The members pursued experiments together, in order, in the words of one member, "to make a true anatomy of the things and operations of nature itself."[6] During the remainder of the sixteenth century and on into the seventeenth, such academies sprang up in many cities. The most celebrated was the Accadèmia dei Lincei, founded in Rome by an aristocrat in 1603. Its most famous member, Galileo, joined in 1611. The name "Lincei," lynx, was chosen because of the legendary keen sight of that animal, an appropriate mascot for "searchers of secrets."

Galileo's notoriety and the importance of his discoveries forced acceptance or rejection of Copernicanism on all communities. Throughout the seventeenth century, specific investigation of natural phenomena would continue in increasingly sophisticated institutional settings. The flowering of scientific thought in the seventeenth century occurred because of the specific innovations in astronomy and the general spread of scientific investigation that had been achieved by the end of Bacon's life.

Scientific Thought in France, 1600–1650: Descartes and a New Cosmology

Philosophers, mathematicians, and educated elites engaged in lively debate and practical investigation throughout Europe in the first half of the seventeenth century, but in France questions about cosmic order were being posed at a time of political disorder. The years following the religious wars saw the murder of Henry IV, another regency, and further civil war in the 1620s. In this environment, questions about order in the universe and the possibilities of human knowledge took on particular urgency. It is not surprising that a Frenchman, René Descartes (1596–1650), created the first fully articulated alternative world view.

Descartes's work emerged in dialogue with a circle of other French thinkers. His work became more influential among philosophers and lay people than the work of some of his equally talented contemporaries because of its thoroughness and rigor, grounded in Descartes's mathematical expertise, and because of Descartes's graceful, readable French. His system was fully presented in his *Discours de la méthode* (*Discourse on Method*, 1637). This work was intended to be the centerpiece of a series of scientific treatises, including works on optics and geometry. Descartes described some of his intellectual crises in *Meditations* (1641).

Descartes accepted Galileo's conclusion that the heavens and the earth are made of the same elements. In his theorizing about the composition of matter, he drew on ancient atomic models that previously had not been generally accepted. His theory that all matter is made up of identical bits, which he named "corpuscles," is a forerunner of modern atomic and quantum theories. Descartes believed that all the different appearances and behaviors of matter (for example, why stone is always hard and water is always wet) could be explained solely by the size, shape, and motion of "corpuscles." Descartes's was an extremely mechanistic explanation of the universe. It nevertheless permitted new, more specific observations and hypotheses and greater understanding of inertia. Because he reimagined the universe as being filled with "corpuscles" free to move in any direction, "natural" motion no longer seemed either circular (Galileo's idea) or toward the center of the earth (Aristotle's idea). The new understanding of motion would be crucial to Isaac Newton's formulations later in the century.

René Descartes had been given the best of traditional educations. From the Jesuits he had learned not only scholastic logic and rhetoric but also, perhaps for purposes of debate, Galileo's new discoveries. *(Royal Museum of Fine Arts, Copenhagen)*

Central to Descartes's appeal was his substitution of a new kind of certainty for traditional methods and conclusions. The collapse of the old explanations about the world made Descartes and other investigators doubt not only what they knew but also their capacity to know anything at all. Their physical senses—which denied that the earth moved, for example—had been proved untrustworthy. In his various works, Descartes depicts and then firmly resolves the crisis of confidence that the new discoveries about the universe had produced.

Descartes's solution was to re-envision the human rational capacity, the mind, as completely distinct from the world—that is, as distinct from the human body—and the betraying sense data it offers. In a leap of faith, Descartes presumed that he could count on the fact that God would not have given humans a mind if that mind were to betray them. For Descartes, God became the guarantor of human reasoning capacity, and humans, in Descartes's view, were distinguished by that capacity. This is the significance of his famous claim "I think, therefore I am."

For himself and others like him, Descartes achieved a resolution of the terrifying doubt about the world—a resolution that exalted the role of the human knower. The Cartesian universe was one of mechanical motion—not purpose or mystical meaning—and the Cartesian human being was pre-eminently a mind that could apprehend that universe. In what came to be known as "Cartesian dualism," Descartes was proposing that humans are detached from the world yet at the same time can be objective observers of the world. (See the box, "Descartes's Meditations.")

Important implications followed from Descartes's ambitious view of human reason. One was the emphasis on deductive reasoning, which naturally followed from his philosophical rejection of sense data. Descartes believed that fundamental knowledge of the world is the product of the divine capacity for reasoning alone. In actuality, he did rely on sense data; he did undertake experiments and urged his readers to keep careful records of their thoughts, observations, and conclusions. But, like the mathematician he was, he urged that science "[keep] the right order for one thing to be deduced from that which precedes it."[7] In the short run, Descartes's embrace of absolute certainty proved very useful to the advancement of knowledge because with a positive sense of purpose—even within the limits of deductive reasoning—natural philosophers could tolerate enormous uncertainty and speculate fruitfully about specific problems.

Descartes's views also had enormous psychological utility for his elite audience. His vision of the enhanced position of the individual knower, and of the power of the knower's reason, were attractive to philosophers (Galileo's self-confidence comes to mind). They also were attractive to educated lay people who sought in science an affirmation of their own status in the world—which could now be expressed in terms of intellectual power and power over nature, rather than only as political power. Descartes was careful not to advocate the "madness" of applying reason to changing the state. The state alone had made humans civilized, he maintained; and although he and other thinkers had to rebuild knowledge of the universe from its foundations, he believed it was "unreasonable for an individual to conceive the plan of reforming a state by changing everything from the foundations."[8]

Similar possibilities for human perception were being suggested in other areas of creative endeavor. Renaissance painters, who utilized the principles of linear perspective, presented views of the world as detached still life—more distant and distinct than the world ever was in real life. A similar detachment was evident in the memoirs and essays of writers such as Michel de Montaigne (1533–1592). Descartes's view of rationality, however, was the most radical detachment of all, for Descartes claimed objectivity for his perspective. Descartes's assumption that humans could achieve objective knowledge about the world rejected contemporaneous trends suggesting that human knowledge was relative, a matter of where an observer happened to stand in time, in culture, in space—or in emotion.

Though much of Cartesian physics would be surpassed by Newton at the end of the century, Descartes's assumption about the objectivity of the observer would become an enduring part of scientific practice. The sense of detachment from the world also fostered a belief in humans' ability to control nature. In our own time, we have become aware of the possible limits of our ability to control nature. In Descartes's day, the most radical aspect of his thought was the reduction of God from being an active presence in the world to the position of guarantor of knowledge. Later generations of scientists would be fearful of Descartes's system because it seemed to encour-

Descartes's Meditations

In the* Meditations *Descartes describes the personal crisis that led him to doubt everything except the existence of God and his capacity to think. This passage from the meditation "Of True and False" reveals the mind-body dualism that distinguishes Descartes's thought as well as the role of God as the guarantor for human reason.

I have been well accustomed these past days to detach my mind from my senses, and have accurately observed that there are very few things that one knows with certainty regarding corporeal objects, that there are many more which are known to us respecting the human mind, and yet more still regarding God Himself; so that I shall now without any difficulty abstract my thoughts from the consideration of . . . objects, and carry them to those which, being withdrawn from all contact with matter, are purely intelligible. And certainly the idea which I possess of the human mind inasmuch as it is a thinking thing, and not extended in length, width, and depth, nor participating in anything pertaining to body, is incomparably more distinct than is the idea of any corporeal thing. And when I consider that I doubt, that is to say, that I am an incomplete and dependent being, the idea of a being that is complete and independent, that is of God, presents itself to my mind with so much distinctness and clearness—and from the fact alone that this idea is found in me, or that I who possess this idea exist, I conclude so certainly that God exists and that my existence depends entirely on Him . . . that I do not think that the human mind is capable of knowing anything with more evidence and certitude. And it seems to me that I now have before me a road which will lead us from the contemplation of the true God . . . to the knowledge of the other objects of the universe.

Source: The Philosophical Works of Rene Descartes, trans. Elizabeth S. Haldane and G. R. T. Ross, in Mortimer Adler, ed., *Great Books of the Western World,* vol. 28 (Chicago: Encyclopaedia Britannica, 1990), p. 315.

age "atheism." In fact, a profound faith in God was necessary for Descartes's creativity in imagining his new world system—but the system did work without God. Although Descartes would have been surprised and offended by charges of atheism, he knew that his work would antagonize the church. He had moved to Holland to study in 1628, and his *Discourse* was first published there.

A contemporary of Descartes, Blaise Pascal (1623–1662), drew attention in his writings and in his life to the limits of scientific knowledge. Son of a royal official, Pascal was perhaps the most brilliant mind of his generation. A mathematician like Descartes, he stressed the importance of mathematical representations of phenomena, built one of the first calculating machines, and invented probability theory. He also carried out experiments to investigate air pressure, the behavior of liquids, and the existence of vacuums.

Pascal's career alternated between periods of intense scientific work and religious retreat. Today he is well known for his writings that defended Jansenism, an austere strain of Catholicism, and explored the human soul and psyche. His *Pensées* (*Thoughts,* 1657) consists of the published fragments of his defense of Christian faith, which remained unfinished at the time of his early death. Pascal's appeal for generations after him may lie in his assumption that matters of faith and of feeling must also be open to investigation. His most famous statement, "The heart has its reasons which the reason knows not," can be read as a statement of the limits of the Cartesian world view.

Science and Revolution in England

The new science had adherents and practitioners throughout Europe by 1650. Dutch scientists in the commercial milieu of Holland, for example, had the freedom to pursue practical and experimental interests. The Dutch investigator Christiaan Huygens (1629–1695) worked on a great variety of problems, including air pressure and optics. He invented and patented the pendulum clock in 1657, the first device accurately to measure small units of time, essential for a variety of measurements.

England, however, because of the political revolution that occurred there, was a unique environment for the development of science in the middle of the century. Religious and political struggle in England took place at a time when scientific questions were also to the fore. Thus, differing positions on science became part and parcel of differing positions on Puritanism, church hierarchy, and royal power. Scientific investigation and speculation were spurred by the urgency of religious and political agendas. Scientific, along with political and religious, debate was generally encouraged by the collapse of censorship beginning in the 1640s.

In the 1640s, natural philosophers with Puritan leanings were encouraged in their investigations by dreams that science, of the practical Baconian sort, could be the means by which the perfection of life on earth could be brought about and the end of history, the reign of the saints preceding the return of Christ, accelerated. Their concerns ranged from improved production of gunpowder (for the armies fighting against Charles I) to surveying and mapmaking. Perhaps the best-known member of this group was Robert Boyle (1627–1691). In his career we can trace the evolution of English science through the second half of the seventeenth century.

Boyle and his colleagues were theoretically eclectic, drawing on Cartesian mechanics and even Paracelsian chemical theories. They attacked the university system, still under the sway of Aristotelianism, and proposed widespread reform of education. They were forced to moderate many of their positions, however, as the English revolution proceeded. Radical groups such as the Levelers used Hermeticism and the related Paracelsianism as part of their political and religious tenets. The ancient doctrine of Hermeticism, revived since the Renaissance, claimed that matter is universally imbued with divine (or magical) spirit. The Levelers and others believed that each person was capable of a godly life and divine knowledge without the coercive hierarchy of officials of church and state.

Boyle and his colleagues responded to these challenges. They gained institutional power, accepting positions at Oxford and Cambridge. They formed the core of the Royal Society of London, which they persuaded Charles II to recognize and charter upon his accession to the throne in 1660. They worked to articulate a theoretical position that combined the orderliness of mecha-

Boyle's Air Pump This illustration from Boyle's major work implies that the device could easily be assembled and used. But Boyle himself failed to make the pump work every time, and only Huygens, of all other scientists, also produced a working model. *(Edinburgh University Library)*

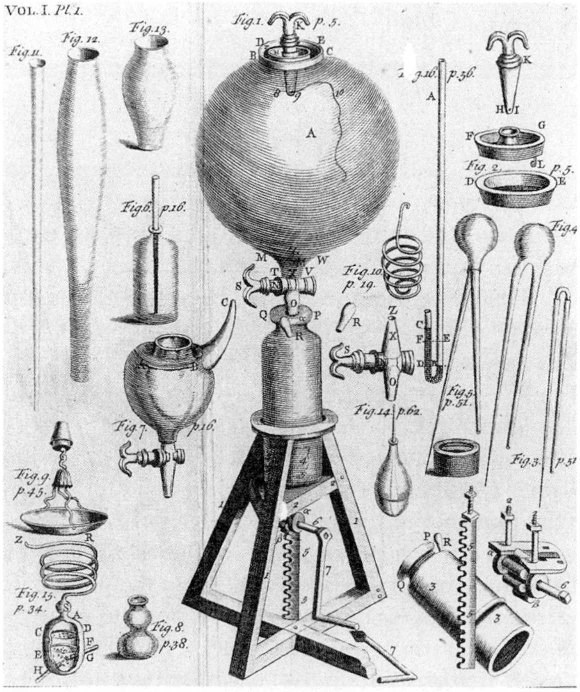

nism, a continued divine presence in the world, and a Baconian emphasis on scientific progress. This unwieldy set of notions was attractive to the educated elite of their day who wanted the certainties of science without losing all of the authoritarian aspects of the old Christian world view.

Their most creative contribution, both to their own cause and to the advancement of science, was their emphasis on and refinement of experimental philosophy and practice. In 1660 Boyle published *New Experiments Physico-Mechanical.* The work described the results of his experiments with an air pump that he had designed, and it laid out general rules for experimental procedure. Descartes had accounted for motion by postulating that "corpuscles" of matter act on each other, thereby eliminating the possibility of a vacuum in nature. Recent experiments on air pressure suggested otherwise, however, and Boyle's air pump confirmed their findings.

Boyle's efforts to demonstrate that a vacuum could exist—by evacuating a sealed chamber with his pump—were not successes by modern standards because they could not readily be replicated. Boyle tied the validity of experimental results to the agreement of witnesses to the experiment—a problematic solution, for only investigators sympathetic to the experiment usually witnessed the results. Boyle's self-serving definition of experimental success inevitably narrowed the scope of scientific investigation.

The Newtonian Synthesis: The Copernican Revolution Completed

The Copernican revolution reached its high point with the work of the Englishman Isaac Newton (1642–1724), who was born the year Galileo died. Newton completed the new explanation for motion in the heavens and on earth that Copernicus's work had initiated and that Kepler, Galileo, and others had sought. In Newton's career, we can see how different was the climate for science by the second half of the seventeenth century. Unlike Copernicus, who usually worked alone on traditional problems, Newton entered Cambridge University as a student in 1661. At Cambridge, Copernicanism was studied, the benefits of scientific investigation were debated, and much attention was focused on the problems of Descartes's explanations of matter.

Like all the other natural philosophers before him, Newton was as concerned by questions of metaphysics as by physics. In the 1680s, he devoted himself primarily to the study of church history, theology, and alchemy. As a student at Cambridge he was strongly influenced by the work of a group of Neo-Platonists who were critical of Cartesian dualism, which posited God as a cause of all matter and motion but removed God as an explanation for the behavior of matter. Their concerns were both religious and scientific. As Newton says in some of his early writing while a student, "however we cast about we find almost no other reason for atheism than this [Cartesian] notion of bodies having . . . a complete, absolute and independent reality."[9] He reflected his mentors' concern to harmonize science with a securely Christian world view following the "excesses" of the English revolution. Meanwhile, they were all uncertain how to account for motion in a world filled with matter, as Descartes had posited. The experiments of Robert Boyle in creating a vacuum shed further doubt on Descartes's schema.

Isaac Newton combined his scientific skepticism and his religious certainty to posit the existence of gravity—a mysterious force that accounts for the movement of heavenly bodies. Others had speculated about the existence of gravity, but Newton's genius was the mathematical computation of the laws of gravity and planetary motion, which he combined with a fully developed concept of inertia. The concept of inertia as so far elaborated by Galileo, Descartes, and others suggested the need for the concept of gravity. Otherwise, if a planet was "pushed" (say, in Kepler's view, by the "motive force" of the sun), it would continue along that course forever unless "pulled back" by something else.

In 1687 Newton published *Philosophia Naturalis Principia Mathematica* (*Mathematical Principles of Natural Philosophy*). In this mathematical treatise—so intricate that it was inaccessible to lay people, even those able to read Latin—Newton lays out his laws of motion and expresses them as mathematical theorems that can be used to test future observations of moving bodies. Then he demonstrates that these laws also apply to the

Isaac Newton Pictured here about fifteen years after the publication of the *Principia,* Newton was also one of the developers of calculus. The cumbersome mathematics he still relied on in the *Principia,* however, has led one scholar to ponder: "What manner of man he was who could use as a weapon what we can scarcely lift as a burden."[10] *(National Portrait Gallery, London)*

solar system—confirming the data already gathered about the planets and even predicting the existence of an as-yet-unseen planet. His supreme achievement was his law of gravitation, with which he could predict the discovery of the invisible planet. This law states that every body—indeed every bit of matter—in the universe exerts over every other body an attractive force proportional to the product of their masses and inversely proportional to the square of the distance between them. Newton not only accounted for motion but definitively united heaven and earth in a single scheme and created a convincing picture of an orderly nature.

Neither Newton nor anyone else claimed that his theorems resolved all questions about motion and matter. Exactly what gravity is and how it operates were not clear, as they still are not. Newton himself was troubled by his lack of understanding of gravity except in mathematical terms (see the box, "Newton on God and Gravity"). He couched the *Principia* as a mathematical treatise, rather than as a general treatise in philosophy, because he felt he could make no systematic claims, such as did Descartes, because of the unsolved problem of gravity. After its publication, he experienced periods of severe depression, leading to a nervous breakdown in 1693.

Newton's laws of motion are still taught because they still adequately account for most problems of motion. The fact that so fundamental a principle as gravity remains unexplained in no way diminishes Newton's achievement but is clear evidence about the nature of scientific understanding: Science provides explanatory schemas that account for many—but not all—observed phenomena. When a scientific explanation ceases to account satisfactorily for enough data, it collapses of its own weight. No schema explains everything, and each schema contains open doorways that lead to further discovery and blind alleys that lead to mistaken impressions. Newton, for example, during his most productive years studied alchemy. He assumed that the spiritual forces that somehow accounted for gravity would mysteriously work on metals so that they might "quickly pass into gold."[11]

Other Branches of Science

The innovations in astronomy that led to the new mechanistic view of the behavior of matter did not automatically spill over to other branches of science. Developments in astronomy were very specific to that field; innovation came at the hands of skilled practitioners after the ancient and medieval inheritance had been fully assimilated and its errors made undeniable. Other branches of science followed their own paths, though all were strongly influenced by the mechanistic world view.

In chemistry, the mechanistic assumption that all matter was composed of small, equivalent parts was crucial to understanding the properties and behavior of compounds (combinations of elements). But knowledge of these small units of matter was not yet detailed enough to be of much

Newton on God and Gravity

Most of Newton's **Principia** *consists of observations about the mechanical properties of matter, astronomical data, and, above all, mathematical descriptions and proofs. The last section of the work, however, contains some general material about the nature of scientific reasoning and the role of God. In this passage, Newton moves from describing the qualities of God necessary to explain the complexities of the universe to commenting on the appropriate limits to scientific speculation.*

This most beautiful system of the sun, planets, and comets, could only proceed from the counsel and dominion of an intelligent and powerful Being.... We know him only by his most wise and excellent contrivances of things; and final causes; we admire him for his perfections; but we reverence and adore him on account of his dominion: for we adore him as his servants; and a god without dominion, providence and final causes, is nothing else but Fate and Nature. Blind metaphysical necessity... could produce no variety of things....

Hitherto we have explained the phenomena of the heavens and of our sea by the power of gravity, but we have not yet assigned the cause of this power. This is certain, that it must proceed from a cause that penetrates to the very centers of the sun and the planets, without suffering the least diminution of its force.... But hitherto I have not been able to discover the cause of [the] properties of gravity from phenomena, and I frame no hypotheses; for whatever is not deduced from the phenomena is to be called an hypothesis; and hypotheses, whether metaphysical or physical, whether of occult qualities or mechanical, have no place in experimental philosophy.

Source: Mathematical Principles of Natural Philosophy, trans. Andrew Motte and revised by Florian Cajori (Berkeley: University of California Press, 1934), in Mortimer Adler, ed. *Great Books of the Western World,* vol. 32 (Chicago: Encyclopaedia Britannica, 1990), pp. 369–371.

use in advancing chemistry conceptually. Nevertheless, the flawed conceptual schema did not hold back all chemical discovery and development. Lack of understanding of gases, and of the specific elements that make them up, for example, did not prevent the development and improvement of gunpowder. Indeed, unlike the innovations in astronomy, eventual conceptual innovation in chemistry and biology owed a great deal to the results of experiment and the slow accumulation of data.

A conceptual leap forward was made in biology in the sixteenth and seventeenth centuries. Because biological knowledge was mostly a byproduct of the practice of medicine, biological studies had been and remained very practical and experimental. But the discovery of *On Anatomical Procedures,* a treatise by Galen, encouraged dissection and other practical research. Andreas Vesalius (1514–1564), in particular, made important advances by following Galen's exhortation to anatomical research. Born in Brussels, Vesalius studied at the nearby University of Louvain in Belgium, and then at Padua, where he was appointed professor of surgery. He ended his career as physician to Emperor Charles V and his son, Philip II of Spain. In his teaching at Padua he embodied newly discovered Galenic precepts by doing dissections himself rather than giving the work to technicians. In 1543 he published versions of his lectures as an illustrated compendium of anatomy, *De Humani Corporis Fabrica* (*On the Fabric of the Human Body*). The results of his dissections of human corpses, revealed in this work, demonstrated a number of errors in Galen's knowledge of human anatomy, much of which had been derived from dissection of animals. Neither Vesalius nor his immediate successors questioned overall Galenic theory about the functioning of the human body—any more than Copernicus had utterly rejected Aristotelian physics.

The slow movement from new observation to changed explanation is clearly illustrated in the career of the Englishman William Harvey (1578–1657). Much like Vesalius, Harvey was educated first in his own land and then at Padua, where he benefited from the tradition of anatomical research. He also had a career as a practicing physician—in London and at the courts of James I and Charles I.

Harvey postulated the circulation of the blood—postulated rather than discovered because, owing to the technology of the day, he could not observe the tiny capillaries where the movement of arterial blood into the veins occurs. After conducting on animals vivisectional experiments that revealed the actual functioning of heart and lungs, he reasoned that circulation must occur. He carefully described his experiments and his conclusions in *Exercitatio Anatomica de Motu Cordis et Sanguinis in Animalibus* (1628), usually shortened to *De Motu Cordis* (*On the Motion of the Heart*).

Harvey's explanation of bodily functions in light of his new knowledge initially remained within the Galenic tradition. (See the feature, "Weighing the Evidence: Scientific Diagrams and Texts," on pages 736–737.) But by the end of his life, Harvey's own adjustments of Galenic theory were suggesting new conceptual possibilities. His work inspired additional research in physiology, chemistry, and physics. Robert Boyle's efforts to understand vacuums can be traced in part to questions Harvey raised about the function of the lungs and the properties of air.

Science and Society

Scientists wrestled with questions about God, human capacity, and the possibilities of understanding the world every bit as intently as they attempted to find new explanations for the behavior of matter and the motion of the heavens. Eventually, the profound implications of the new scientific posture began to affect thought and behavior throughout society. Once people no longer thought of the universe in hierarchical terms, questioning the hierarchical organization of society became easier. Once all matter was thought of as equal, thinking of all people as equal became easier. Once people questioned the authority of traditional knowledge about the universe, the way was clear for them to begin to question traditional views of the state and social order.

Such profound changes of perspective happened gradually. In the short term, Louis XIV and other rulers actually welcomed the new science for its practical value, and the practice of science remained wedded to religion. The advances in science did lead to revolutionary cultural change; but, until the end of the seventeenth century, traditional institutions and ideologies circumscribed this change.

The Rise of Scientific Professionalism

Institutions both old and new supported the new science developing in the sixteenth and seventeenth centuries. Some universities were the setting for scientific breakthroughs, but court patronage, a well-established institution, also sponsored scientific activity. The development of the Accadèmia dei Lincei, to which Galileo belonged, and other academies was a step toward modern professional societies of scholars, although these new organizations depended on patronage.

In both England and France, royally sponsored scientific societies were founded in the third quarter of the century. The Royal Society of London, inaugurated in 1660, received royal recognition but no money and remained an informal institution sponsoring amateur scientific interests as well as specialized independent research. The Académie Royale des Sciences in France, established in 1666 by Jean-Baptiste Colbert, Louis XIV's minister of finance (see page 677), sponsored research and supported chosen scientists with pensions. These associations were extensions to science of traditional kinds of royal recognition and patronage. Thus, the French Académie was well funded but tightly controlled by the central government of Louis XIV, and the

Royal Society of London received little of Charles II's precious resources or his scarce political capital.

One important role of academies and patrons was to support the publication of scientific work. The Accadèmia dei Lincei published two of Galileo's best-known works. The Royal Society of London published its fellows' work in *Philosophical Transactions of the Royal Society*, beginning in 1665.

The practice of seventeenth-century science took place in so many diverse institutions—academies, universities, royal courts—that neither *science* nor *scientist* was rigorously defined. Science

Astronomers Elisabetha and Johannes Hevelius were one of many collaborating couples among the scientists of the seventeenth century. Women were usually denied pensions and support for their research when they worked alone, however. *(From Hevelius,* Machinae coelestis. *By permission of the Houghton Library, Harvard University)*

as a discipline was not yet detached from broad metaphysical questions. Boyle, Newton, Pascal, and Descartes all concerned themselves with questions of religion, and all thought themselves not as scientists but, like their medieval forebears, as natural philosophers. These natural philosophers were among the elite who met in aristocratic salons to discuss literature, politics, or science with equal ease and interest. Nevertheless, the beginning of the narrowing of the practice of science to a tightly defined, truly professional community is evident. Robert Boyle and his fellow advocates of experimentalism, for example, claimed that their procedures alone constituted true science.

One kind of exclusion that began to be practiced toward the end of the seventeenth century was that of women. The importance of court life and patronage to the new science, however, at first enabled women to be actively involved. Women ran important salons in France, aristocratic women everywhere were important sources of patronage for scientists, and women themselves were scientists.

Noblewomen and daughters of gentry families had access to education in their homes, and a number of such women were active scientists—astronomers, mathematicians, and botanists. The astronomer Maria Cunitz (1610–1664), from Silesia, learned six languages with the support and encouragement of her father, who was a medical doctor. Later, she published a useful simplification of some of Kepler's mathematical calculations.

Margaret Cavendish, duchess of Newcastle (1623–1673), wrote several major philosophical works, including *Grounds of Natural Philosophy* (1668). She was a Cartesian but was influenced by Neo-Platonism. She believed matter to have "intelligence" and thus disagreed with Cartesian dualism, but she criticized English philosophers with whom she agreed on some matters because, like Descartes, she distrusted sense knowledge as a guide to philosophy.

Women were proposed as members of and were accepted in Italian academies regularly; but they were excluded from formal membership in the academies in London and Paris, though they could use the academies' facilities and received prizes from the societies for their work. One reason for the exclusion of women was the limited amount of patronage available: Coveted positions automatically went to men. Moreover, the hierarchical distinction signified by gender made the exclusion of women a useful way to define the academies as special and privileged.

Margaret Cavendish was aware of the degree to which her participation in scientific life depended on informal networks and on the resources available to her because of her aristocratic status (see the box, "Margaret Cavendish Challenges Male Scientists"). In her play *The Female Academy* (1661), she depicts an institution solely for the education of women. Interestingly, men's efforts to attack women's education in the play are far more energetic than women's efforts to compete with men.

The New Science and the Needs of the State

The new natural philosophy had implications for traditional notions about the state. The new world view that all matter was alike and answerable to discernible natural laws gradually undermined political systems resting on a belief in the inherent inequality of persons and on royal prerogative. By the middle of the eighteenth century, a fully formed alternative political philosophy would argue for more "rational" government in keeping with the rational, natural order of things. But the change came slowly, and while it was coming, the state of Louis XIV and other rulers found much to admire and make use of in the new science.

New technical possibilities were very attractive to governments and members of ruling elites. Experiments with vacuum pumps had important applications in the mining industry. The astronomy professor at Gresham College in London was required to teach navigation, and other professors at Gresham worked with naval architects to improve the design of ships.

Governments also sponsored purely scientific research. The French Académie des Sciences sponsored the construction of an astronomical observatory in Paris. A naval expedition to

Margaret Cavendish Challenges Male Scientists

In her preface to her earliest scientific work, **The Philosophical and Physical Opinions** *(1655), Cavendish addresses scholars at Oxford and Cambridge universities with deceptive humility. She implies that the seeming limitations of women's abilities are in fact the consequence of their exclusion from education and from participation in affairs.*

Most Famously Learned,

I here present to you this philosophical work, not that I can hope wise school-men and industrious laborious students should value it for any worth, but to receive it without scorn, for the good encouragement of our sex, lest in time we should grow irrational as idiots, by the dejectedness of our spirits, through the careless neglects and despisements of the masculine sex to the female, thinking it impossible we should have either learning or understanding, wit or judgment, as if we had not rational souls as well as men, and we out of a custom of dejectedness think so too, which makes us quit all industry towards profitable knowledge, being imployed only in low and petty imployments which take away not only our abilities towards arts but higher capacities in speculations, so that we are become like worms, that only live in the dull earth of ignorance, winding ourselves sometimes out by the help of some refreshing rain of good education, which seldom is given us, for we are kept like birds in cages, to hop up and down in our houses . . . ; thus by an opinion, which I hope is but an erroneous one in men, we are shut out of all power and authority by reason we are never employed either in civil or martial affairs our counsels are despised and laughed at and the best of our actions are trodden down with scorn, by the over-weening conceit men have of themselves and through a despisement of us.

Source: Moira Ferguson, ed., *First Feminists: British Women Writers, 1578–1799* (Bloomington and New York: Indiana University Press and The Feminist Press, 1985), pp. 85–86.

Cayenne, in French Guiana, led to refinements of the pendulum clock but had as its main purpose progressive observations of the sun to permit the calculation of the earth's distance from the sun.

The sponsorship of pure science is evidence of both the adaptability of institutions and the complexity of change. Members of the elite, such as Colbert in France, recognized the opportunity not only for practical advances but also for prestige and—most important—confirmation of the orderliness of nature. It is hard to overestimate the psychological impact and intellectual power of this fundamental tenet of the new science—namely, that nature is an inanimate machine that reflects God's design not through its purposes but simply by its orderliness. Human beings could now hope to dominate nature in ways not possible before. Dominion, order, control—these were the goals of ambitious and powerful rulers in the seventeenth century.

Thus, in the short run, the new science supported a vision of order that was very pleasing to a monarch of absolutist pretensions. Louis XIV energetically sponsored scientific investigation by the Académie des Sciences and reaped the benefits in improved ships, increasingly skillful military engineers, and new and improved industrial products. For these purposes, he ignored the political writers of his day whose theoretical support for absolutism was so important for his political power at home and his activist foreign policy.

Science and Royal Power This painting memorializes the founding of the French Académie des Sciences and the building of the royal observatory in Paris. This celebration of the institutions' openings reveals Louis XIV's belief in their importance, both symbolic and practical. *(Château de Versailles/Laurie Platt Winfrey, Inc.)*

Religion and the New Science

Because of Galileo's trial, the Catholic church is often seen as an opponent of scientific thought, and science and religion are often seen as antagonists. But this view is an oversimplification. Indeed, scientific thought remained closely tied to religion during the seventeenth century.

Both religion and the Catholic church as an institution were implicated in scientific advancement from the time of Copernicus. Copernicus himself was a cleric, and many philosophers and scientists active in the early seventeenth century were clerics. This is not surprising, for most research in the sciences to this point had occurred within universities sponsored and staffed by members of religious orders. Moreover, religious and metaphysical concerns were central to the work of virtually every scientist. The entire Cartesian edifice of reasoning about the world, for example, was founded on Descartes's certainty about God. God's gift of the capacity to reason was the only certainty that Descartes claimed. Copernicus, Kepler, and other investigators perceived God's purpose in the mathematical regularity of nature. In addition, traditional Christian views of operations and purpose of the universe were evident in the work of all scientists from Copernicus to Newton—from Galileo's acceptance of perfect circular motion to Newton's theological writings.

It is true that the new astronomy and mechanics challenged specific tenets of faith and the Catholic church's role in shaping and controlling matters of knowledge and faith. Adjusting to a new view of nature in which God was less immanently and obviously represented was not easy for the church, for several reasons. First of all, the church itself mirrored the hierarchy of the old view of the universe in its own hierarchy of believers, priests, bishops, popes, and saints. Moreover, in its sponsorship of institutions of higher learning, the church was the repository of the old view. In the inevitable scientific disagreements spawned by the new theories and discoveries, the church was both theoretically and literally invested in the old view.

Nevertheless, the church's condemnation of Galileo shocked many clerics, including many who were scientists themselves, as well as three of Galileo's judges, who voted for leniency at his trial. Over the course of the centuries, many apparent conflicts between scientific arguments and sacred teachings had been resolved with great intelligence and flexibility. The rigid response of the church hierarchy to Galileo's challenge must be seen in the context of the Protestant Reformation, which, in the minds of the pope and others, had demonstrated the need for a firm response to any challenge. Galileo seemed threatening because he was well known, wrote for a wide audience, and—like the Protestants—presumed on the church's right to interpret the Scriptures.

The condemnation of Galileo had a chilling effect on scientific investigators in most Catholic regions of Europe. They could and did continue their research, but many could publish results only by smuggling manuscripts to Protestant lands. Many of the most important empirical and theoretical innovations in science occurred in Protestant regions after the middle of the seventeenth century.

Protestant leaders, however, at first were not receptive to Copernican ideas because they defied scriptural authority as well as common sense. In 1549, one of Martin Luther's associates wrote:

> The eyes are witnesses that the heavens revolve in the space of twenty-four hours. But certain men, either from love of novelty or to make a display of ingenuity, have concluded that the earth moves. . . . Now it is want of honesty and decency to assert such notions publicly and the example is pernicious. It is part of a good mind to accept the truth as revealed by God and to acquiesce in it.[12]

Protestant thinkers were as troubled as Catholics by the metaphysical problems that the new theories seemed to raise. In 1611, one year after the publication of Galileo's *Starry Messenger*, the English poet John Donne (1573–1631) reflected in "An Anatomie of the World" on the confusion about human capacities and social relationships that Copernican astronomy caused:

> [The] new Philosophy calls all in doubt,
> The Element of fire is quite put out;
> The Sun is lost, and th'earth, and no man's wit
> Can well direct him where to look for it.
> . . . .
> 'Tis all in pieces, all coherence gone;
> All just supply, and all Relation:
> Prince, Subject, Father, Son, are things forgot,
> For every man alone thinks he hath got
> To be a Phoenix, and that then can be
> None of that kinde, of which he is, but he.[13]

The dilemma of accounting in religious terms for the ideas of Copernicus and Descartes became more urgent for Protestants as the ideas acquired an anti-Catholic status after the trial of Galileo in 1633, and as they became common scientific currency by about 1640. The development of the new science in the mid-seventeenth century coincided with religious and political upheavals throughout Europe. Religious, political, and scientific viewpoints became inextricably mixed. A religious certainty about divine force that could account for the motion of bodies in a vacuum enabled Newton to develop his theories on motion and gravity. In short, religion did not merely remain in the scientists' panoply of explanations; it remained a fundamental building block of scientific thought, just as it remained central to most scientists' lives.

The Mechanistic World Order and Human Affairs at the End of the Century

Traditional institutions and ideologies checked the potential effects of the new science for a time, but by the middle of the seventeenth century, political theory was beginning to show the impact of the mechanistic world view. Political philosophers viewed neither the world nor human society as an organic whole in which each part was distinguished in nature and function from the rest. Thomas Hobbes, John Locke, and others reimagined the bonds that link citizens to each other and to their rulers.

Because of the political turmoil in England, Thomas Hobbes (1588–1679) spent much of his productive life on the Continent. After the beginnings of the parliamentary rebellion, he joined a group of royalist émigrés in France. He met Galileo and lived for extended periods in Paris, in contact with the circle of French thinkers that included Descartes. Like Descartes, he theorized about the nature and behavior of matter; he published a treatise on his views in 1655.

Hobbes is best known today for *Leviathan* (1651), his treatise on political philosophy. *Leviathan* applies to the world of human beings Hobbes's mostly Cartesian view of nature as composed of "self-motivated" atomlike structures. Hobbes viewed people as mechanistically as he viewed the rest of nature. In his view, people were made up of appetites of various sorts—the same kind of innate forces that drove all matter. The ideal state, concluded Hobbes, is one in which a strong sovereign controls the disorder that inevitably arises from the clash of desires. Unlike the medieval philosophers, Hobbes did not draw analogies between the state and the human body (the king as head, judges and magistrates as arms, and so forth). Instead, Hobbes compared the state to a machine that "ran" by means of laws and was kept in good working order by a skilled technician—the ruler.

Hobbes's pessimism about human behavior and his insistence on the need for order imposed from above reflect, like the work of Descartes, a concern for order in the wake of political turmoil. This concern was one reason he was welcomed into the community of French philosophers, who were naturally comfortable with royalty as a powerful guarantor of order. But Hobbes's work, like theirs, was a radical departure because it envisions citizens as potentially equal and constrained neither by morality nor by natural obedience to authority.

Another Englishman, John Locke (1632–1704), offered an entirely different vision of natural equality among people and of social order. Locke's major works, *Essay on Human Understanding* (1690) and *Two Treatises on Government* (1690), reflect the experimentalism of Robert Boyle, the systematizing rationality of Descartes, and other strands of the new scientific thought. In the *Essay*, Locke offers a view of human knowledge that is more pragmatic and utilitarian than the rigorous mathematical model of certainty used by many other philosophers. He argues that human knowledge is largely the product of experience. He agrees with Descartes that reason orders and explains human experience. But he thinks that reason does not necessarily perceive reality as it really is but rather perceives reality in a limited way that is nevertheless useful. Unlike Descartes, Locke thinks there are limits to what human reason can achieve, but Locke offers a more optimistic vision of the possible uses of human reason. Whereas Descartes was interested in mentally ordering and understanding the world, Locke was interested in humans' functioning in the world.

Locke's treatises on government reflect his notion of knowledge based on experience as well as his particular experiences as a member of elite circles in the aftermath of the English revolution. A trained physician, he served as personal physician and general political assistant to Anthony Ashley Cooper (1621–1683), Lord Shaftsbury, one of the members of Parliament most opposed to Charles II's pretensions to absolutist government. When James II acceded to the throne in 1685, Locke remained in Holland, where he had fled to avoid prosecution for treason. He became an adviser to William of Orange and returned to England with William and Mary in 1688. Locke's view of the principles of good government, then, came to reflect many of the features of English government after the Glorious Revolution as well as a general confidence in human reason and knowledge.

Unlike Hobbes, Locke argues that people are capable of restraint and mutual respect in their pursuit of self-interest. The state arises from a contract that individuals freely enter into to protect themselves, their property, and their happiness from possible aggression by others. They can invest the executive and legislative authority to carry out this protection in monarchy or any other governing institution, though Locke believed the English Parliament was the best available model. Because sovereignty resides with the people who enter into the contract, rebellion against abuse of power is justified. Thus, Locke frees people from arbitrary bonds of authority to the state and to each other.

Locke's experience as a member of the elite of his society is apparent in his emphasis on private property, which he considers one of the fundamental human rights. Indeed, there is no place in his political vision for serious disagreement about the nature of property. Locke even found a justification for slavery. He also did not consider women to be political beings in the same way as men. The family, he felt, was a separate domain from the state, not bound by the same contractual obligations.

Locke's dismissal of women from the realm of politics and of questions of power and justice from the family was not an accident. The ability of Locke and many other seventeenth-century thinkers to imagine a new physical or political order was constrained by the prevailing view of gender as a "natural" principle of order and hierarchy. Gender distinctions are in the main socially ascribed roles that are easily misinterpreted as "natural" differences between women and men. Although Margaret Cavendish (see the box on page 729) and other women disputed the validity of such distinctions, men frequently used them. Locke's use of gender as an arbitrary organizing principle gave his bold new political vision a claim to being "natural." The use of gender-specific vocabulary to describe nature itself had the effect of making the new objective attitude toward the world seem "natural." Works by seventeenth-century scientists are filled with references to nature as a woman who must be "conquered," "subdued" or "penetrated."

Traditional gender distinctions limited and buttressed most facets of political thought, but in other areas, the fact of uncertainty and the need for tolerance was embraced. Another of Locke's influential works was the impassioned *Letter on Toleration* (1689). In it he argues that religious belief is fundamentally private and that only the most basic Christian principles need be accepted by everyone. Others went further than Locke by entirely removing traditional religion as a fundamental guarantor of morality and order. Fostering this climate of religious skepticism were religious pluralism in England and the irrationality of religious intolerance—demonstrated by Louis XIV's persecution of Protestants.

Pierre Bayle (1647–1706), a Frenchman of Protestant origins, argued that morality can be wholly detached from traditional religion. Bayle cited as an example of morality the philosopher Baruch Spinoza (1632–1677). Spinoza believed the state to have a moral purpose and human happiness to have spiritual roots. Yet he was not a Christian at all but a Dutch Jew who had been ejected from his local synagogue for supposed atheism. One need hardly be a Christian of any sort in order to be a moral being, Bayle concluded.

Bayle's skepticism toward traditional knowledge was more wide ranging than his views on religion. His best-known work, *Dictionnaire historique et critique* (*Historical and Critical Dictionary*, 1702), was a compendium of observations about and criticisms of virtually every thinker whose works were known at the time, including recent and lionized figures such as Descartes and Newton. Bayle was the first systematic skeptic, and he relentlessly exposed errors and shortcomings in all received knowledge. His works were very popular with elite lay readers.

Bayle's fellow countryman Bernard de Fontenelle (1657–1757), secretary to the Académie des Sciences from 1699 to 1741, was the greatest popularizer of the new science of his time. His *Entretiens sur la Pluralités des Mondes* (*Conversations on the Plurality of Worlds*, 1686) was, as the title implies, an informally presented description of the infinite universe of matter. It went through numerous editions and translations. As secretary to the Académie, Fontenelle continued his work as popularizer by publishing descriptions of the work of the Académie's scientists. He died one month short of his hundredth birthday. At his death in 1757 it was said that "the Philosophic spirit, today so much in evidence, owes its beginnings to Monsieur de Fontenelle."[14]

Summary

Fontenelle is a fitting figure with whom to end a discussion of the Scientific Revolution because he represents, and worked to accomplish, the transference of the new natural philosophy into political and social philosophy—a movement we know as the "Enlightenment." The Scientific Revolution began, as innovation in scientific thinking often does, with a specific research problem whose answer led in unexpected directions. Copernicus's response to traditional astronomical problems led to scientific and philosophical innovation because of his solution and because of the context into which it was received.

Other scientists, following Copernicus, built on his theories, culminating in the work of Galileo, who supported Copernican theory with additional data and widely published his findings. The Frenchman Descartes was the first to fashion a systematic explanation for the operations of nature to replace the medieval view. The political and intellectual climate in England, meanwhile, encouraged the development of experimental science and inductive reasoning. Isaac Newton provided new theories to explain the behavior of matter and expressed them in mathematical terms that could apply to either the earth or the cosmos; with his work, traditional astronomy and physics had been overturned.

Rulers made use of the new science for the practical results it offered despite the ideological challenge it presented to their power. By the end of the seventeenth century, the hierarchical Christian world view grounded in the old science was being challenged on many fronts. A fully articulated secular world view would be the product of the Enlightenment.

Notes

1. Quoted in Thomas Kuhn, *The Copernican Revolution* (Cambridge, Mass.: Harvard University Press, 1985), p. 131.
2. Quoted in Margaret C. Jacob, *The Cultural Meaning of the Scientific Revolution* (Philadelphia: Temple, 1988), p. 18.
3. Quoted ibid., p. 33.
4. Quoted in Alan G. R. Smith, *Science and Society in the Sixteenth and Seventeenth Centuries* (New York: 1972), p. 72.
5. Quoted in Jacob, *Cultural Meaning*, p. 32 (emphasis added).
6. Quoted in Bruce T. Moran, ed., *Patronage and Institutions: Science, Technology and Medicine at the European Court* (Rochester: The Boyden Press, 1991), p. 43.
7. Quoted in Jacob, *Cultural Meaning*, p. 59.
8. Quoted ibid.
9. Quoted ibid., p. 89.
10. Quoted in Smith, *Science and Society*, p. 130.
11. Quoted in Jacob, *Cultural Meaning*, p. 25.
12. Quoted in Kuhn, *The Copernican Revolution*, p. 191.
13. *Complete Poetry and Selected Prose of John Dunne*, ed. John Hayward (Bloomsbury, England: Nonesuch Press, 1929), p. 365; quoted in Kuhn, *The Copernican Revolution*, p. 194.
14. Quoted in Paul Edwards, ed., *The Encyclopedia of Philosophy*, vol. 3 (New York: Macmillan, 1967), p. 209.

Suggested Reading

General Surveys

Debus, Allen G. *Man and Nature in the Renaissance.* 1978. A survey of developments in science and medicine during the two centuries leading up to the seventeenth-century revolution; its special contribution stems from Debus's emphasis on Paracelsianism and alchemy.

Hall, A. Rupert. *The Revolution in Science, 1500–1800.* 1983. A thorough introduction to all scientific disciplines that de-emphasizes the larger context of scientific development but explains many of the innovations in detail.

Kearney, Hugh. *Science and Change.* 1971. A readable general introduction to the scientific revolution.

Kuhn, Thomas. *The Copernican Revolution.* 1985. A readable treatment of the revolution in astronomy that also lucidly explains the Aristotelian world view; important for setting Copernicus's work in the context of the history of astronomy; the first thing to read to understand the Copernican revolution.

———. *The Structure of Scientific Revolutions.* 1970. A pathbreaking work that argues that all scientific schemas are systems of explanation and that science progresses by shifting from one general paradigm to another, not from error to "truth."

Mandrou, Robert. *From Humanism to Science.* 1978. A general intellectual history of the period 1450–1650 that sets the Scientific Revolution in the context of broader intellectual, social, and economic currents.

Merchant, Carolyn. *The Death of Nature: Women, Ecology and the Scientific Revolution.* 1980. An important corrective interpretation that focuses on the changing definition of nature—particularly how nature became something to be dominated and consumed—and the way in which this definition reinforced negative cultural views of women.

Thomas, Keith. *Religion and the Decline of Magic.* 1971. An exploration of the changing character of religious belief and "superstitious" practice; finds roots outside of science for changing, increasingly secular world views.

Westfall, Richard S. *The Construction of Modern Science: Mechanisms and Mechanics.* 1977. A general treatment of the Scientific Revolution that emphasizes and explains the mechanistic world view.

Individual Scientists

Bordo, Susan R. *The Flight to Objectivity: Essays on Cartesianism and Culture.* 1987. A collection that studies Descartes's work as a metaphysical and psychological crisis and discusses implications of Cartesian mind-body dualism.

Cohen, I. Bernard. *The Newtonian Revolution.* 1987. A brief introduction to Newton and the meaning of his discoveries; a good place to start on Newton.

Drake, Stillman. *Galileo at Work: His Scientific Biography.* 1978. A detailed chronological study that reveals Galileo's character and illuminates his scientific achievements.

Frank, Robert G., Jr. *Harvey and the Oxford Physiologists.* 1980. An explanation of Harvey's work in the context of traditional Galenic medicine and a discussion of the community of scholars who accepted and built on Harvey's innovations.

Redondi, Pietro. *Galileo Heretic.* 1987. A careful account of Galileo's confrontation with the church.

Shapin, Steven, and Simon Schaffer. *Leviathan and the Air-Pump.* 1985. One of the most important studies of seventeenth-century science: traces the conflict between Cartesian science, as represented by Hobbes, and experimental science, in the work of Boyle; and shows the relationship of Hobbes and Boyle to their respective contexts as well as some of the political, cultural, and philosophical implications of each school of thought.

Political, Social, and Cultural Contexts for Science

Hunter, Michael. *Science and Society in Restoration England.* 1981. A study that sets English science in its political and cultural contexts; critical of Webster's classic study (see below).

Jacob, Margaret C. *The Cultural Meaning of the Scientific Revolution.* 1988. An account that moves from the Scientific Revolution through the industrial transformation of the nineteenth century, sketching the relationship of developments in science, metaphysics, and technology to the political and social history of the various eras.

———. *The Newtonians and the English Revolution.* 1976. A work that links the development of Newtonian science to its political and social context and examines the simultaneous evolution of religion that could accept the new science yet maintain traditional perspectives.

Moran, Bruce T., ed. *Patronage and Institutions: Science, Technology and Medicine at the European Court.* 1991. A work that looks at royal courts as shaping and sustaining institutions for science from the early sixteenth century onward.

Schiebinger, Londa. *The Mind Has No Sex?* 1989. An examination of the participation of women in the practice of science and an explanation of how science began to reflect the exclusion of women in its values and objects of study—above all, in its claims about scientific "facts" about women themselves.

Webster, Charles. *The Great Instauration.* 1975. A classic study that links the development of the modern scientific attitude to the Puritan revolution in England.

Weighing the Evidence

SCIENTIFIC DIAGRAMS AND TEXTS

Look at this scientific diagram, reproduced from William Harvey's *De Motu Cordis* (*On the Motion of the Heart*), first published in 1628. It illustrates one of Harvey's experiments establishing the function of the valves in the veins and, ultimately, the circulation of the blood. Harvey applied tourniquets with pressure sufficient to block the passage of venous blood out of the arm but not so tightly as to restrict the arteries, which are deeper in the arm. Arterial blood, trying to return to the heart, caused distension of the veins.

Figure 4 shows that a vein remains empty (between points L and M) if, after compressing the vein with a finger (L), one draws that finger toward the heart past the next valve. Even pushing backward on a bulging valve (Figure 3, point O) cannot refill with blood a vein thus emptied. Hence, venous blood moves only in the direction of the heart, assisted by the valves.

The information in the diagrams is presented in a way that strikes us as straightforward, almost simplistic. Two disembodied hands (adorned with elegant cuffs) manipulate the veins with ease. Precisely how the veins are made visible is illustrated by the clenched fist and the tourniquet applied above the elbow. We view illustrations of this kind as evidence of the straightforward nature of scientific truth. Of course the diagram is convincing to a modern audience, because Harvey was right: The blood *does* circulate, returning to the heart through the veins, assisted by the valves. But to Harvey, the diagram was neither straightforward nor convincing by itself. The experiments were only a small part of the evidence that Harvey assembled for the circulation of the blood. He also gave painstaking explanations in an accompanying text that is studded with appreciative references to the physicians and anatomists of past centuries.

> It will not be foreign to the subject if I here show further, from certain familiar reasonings, that the circulation is matter both of convenience and necessity. In the first place [as Aristotle says], since death is a corruption which takes place through the deficiency of heat, and since all living things are warm, all dying things cold, there must be a particular seat and fountain, a kind of home and hearth, where the . . . original of the native fire is stored and preserved; whence heat and life are dispensed to all parts as from a fountainhead. Now, that the heart is this place [and] that all passes in the manner just mentioned, I trust no one will deny. *(William Harvey,* On the Motion of the Heart and Blood in Animals, *trans. Robert Willis, in Mortimer J. Adler, ed.,* Great Books of the Western World, *vol. 26 [Chicago: University of Chicago Press, 1990], p. 296.)*

The work of Harvey and of his forerunner Vesalius (see page 725) provides an opportunity to note the slow process by which accumulated observations gradually undermine accepted scientific explanations. No observation is obvious; none automatically leads to the conclusions that we now find convincing. Scientific diagrams like those of Harvey and Boyle (page 722) may seem merely facile confirmation of what we now know, until we view them in the context of other evidence of contemporary scientific practice.

Harvey's work challenged Galenic anatomy and, like Copernicus's discoveries, created new burdens of explanation. According to Galenic theory, the heart and the lungs helped each other to function. The heart sent nourishment to the lungs through the pulmonary artery, and the lungs provided raw material for the "vital spirit," which the heart gave to blood to produce and sustain life. The lungs also helped the heart to sustain its "heat." Like "vital spirit," "heat" was considered necessary to living organisms. It was understood to be an innate property of organs, just as "heaviness," in traditional physics, was considered an innate property of earth-bound objects. One chamber of the heart was supposedly reserved for the cleansing of venous blood—thought to be entirely separate from the "nour-

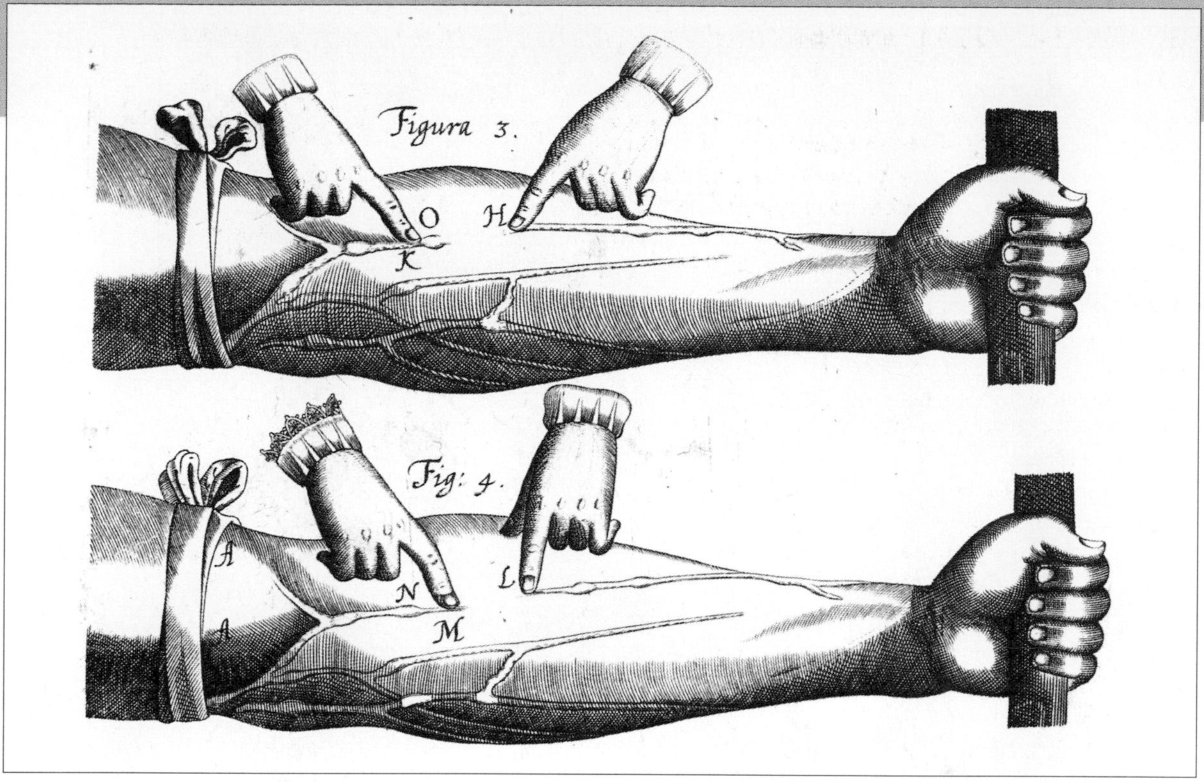

Harvey's Demonstration of the Function of Valves *(The Wellcome Institute Library, London)*

ishing" blood pumped out by the heart—of its waste products.

Harvey's experiments and vivisections revealed that all of the blood pumped by the heart circulates through the lungs and that all of the chambers of the heart are involved in pumping blood. After observing the volume of blood pumped out by the heart, and by devising experiments like the one illustrated here, Harvey theorized the circulation of blood and the return of blood to the heart through the veins.

But Harvey did not leap to a new conceptualization of the body's functions. He came to think of the heart in terms consonant with the new mechanistic notions about nature—as a pump to circulate the blood. But to Harvey the heart was never only that. Consider the passage shown opposite from *De Motu*; it immediately follows his descriptions of these experiments.

Harvey adjusted but did not abandon Galenic theories concerning how "heat" and "vital spirit" were made. His discovery of the pulmonary transit—the passage of blood from the heart, through the lungs, and back to the heart—meant that he had to adjust the accustomed view of the relationship of the heart to the lungs. The lungs, for example, had been thought to "ventilate" the heart by providing air to maintain "heat" (rather like bellows on a fire) and by drawing off heat to cool the heart as necessary. In light of the pulmonary transit, Harvey suggested that the lungs carried out some of these functions for the blood, helping it to concoct the "vital spirit." Only in this context could the heart be thought of as a machine, circulating this life-giving material around the body.

As the passage from *De Motu* suggests, Harvey continued to believe that the "heat" of the heart was essential to its function; the heart, the seat of "native fire," was where the blood returned to receive its "heat." Thus, paralleling his understanding of the heart, he began to conceive of the blood as a carrier of sorts, but he also continued to think of it in terms of Galenic innate qualities. Harvey's discoveries led to a revolution in biology and medicine in part because so much of Galenic physiology was tied to mistaken notions about how the blood moved and how it related to other organs. Science, however, is made up of interpretation as well as discovery, and Harvey's views remind us that no scientific conclusion is "obvious."

CHAPTER 20

Europe on the Threshold of Modernity, ca. 1715–1789

In the summer of 1762, Catherine of Russia engineered a coup against her husband, Tsar Peter III. He was overthrown and killed, and Catherine, known as "the Great," ruled alone as empress for most of the rest of the century. No single political figure can justifiably dominate our vision of the eighteenth century as Louis XIV did the seventeenth. Catherine the Great of Russia, however, represents many of its political trends. She was an "enlightened" monarch, educated in the French intellectual tradition now known as the "Enlightenment" and in some ways committed to a program of reform and wise rule that would have been inconceivable to Louis XIV. Most important, her reign exemplifies the fact that, in the eighteenth century, the Russian Empire became a powerful player in European affairs.

The single figure most representative of this century was not a ruler, however, but a political thinker and writer: the philosopher Voltaire. A prolific writer, critic, and reformer in his own society, France, Voltaire was lionized by European elites that included Catherine the Great and other rulers. The Russian empress admired him from a distance. It is said that she banished a statue of him to the attic of one of her palaces out of an almost personal anger when the French Revolution began to follow a course that she deplored and for which she vaguely blamed Voltaire, who by that time was dead. Voltaire is an apt symbol for the age not because of his personal influence—which, though considerable in literate circles, hardly approached the cataclysmic proportions that Catherine presumed—but rather because he reflects the emergence of an informed body of public opinion,

John Cleveley II, *George III Reviewing the Fleet at Spithead* (detail).

critical of the prevailing political system, that existed outside the corridors of power. In the eighteenth century the relationship between governments and the governed was changing: Subjects of monarchs were becoming citizens of nations.

Catherine the Great and other rulers self-consciously tried to use Enlightenment precepts to guide their efforts at governing. They had mixed success, however. Powerful interests opposed their efforts at reform, and their own hereditary and autocratic power was incompatible with Enlightenment perspectives. Elites still sure of their power, as well as the traditional interests of states, dominated eighteenth-century politics. Nevertheless, profound changes in economic, social, and political life began in this period. Economic growth spurred population growth, which in turn stimulated industry and trade. The increasing economic and strategic importance of overseas colonies made them important focal points of international conflict. Dramatic political and social change beginning at the end of the century had its roots in the intellectual, economic, and social ferment of eighteenth-century life.

The Enlightenment

One of Isaac Newton's countrymen wrote the following epitaph for the English scientist:

> Nature and Nature's Laws lay hid in Night.
> God said, "Let Newton be," and all was Light.

The most important works of Enlightenment philosophy reflected the intellectual confidence that Newton's work generated. The poet's assertion that "all was Light," however, requires scrutiny.

The phrase evokes the determination and confidence of an intellectual elite that felt that it did have a new key to truth. In this sense, the Enlightenment was nothing less than the transfer into general philosophy and political and social thought of the intellectual revolution that had already taken place within the physical sciences. But, like the Scientific Revolution, the Enlightenment was not only sweeping in its impact but specific in its content. In this so-called Age of Reason, *reason* had specific meanings and philosophers' speculations had particular goals.

Enlightenment philosophy occurred in the specific context of increasingly widespread publication and new opportunities in literary societies, clubs, and salons for the exchange of views. This context shaped the outline of Enlightenment thought, which was for the most part an elite set of preoccupations. It also determined the radicalism of the Enlightenment, by helping to ensure that an entire level of society would share in attitudes that were fundamentally critical of that society.

Voltaire and the Enlightenment

The Enlightenment was not so much a body of thought as it was an intellectual and social movement. Originating in France, it consisted, first, of the application to political and social thought of the confidence in the intelligibility of natural law that theoretical science had recently achieved. Enlightenment thinkers combined confidence in the intelligibility of the world and its laws with confidence in the human capacity to discern and work in concert with those laws. The former confidence was Newton's legacy; the latter confidence was the legacy of Descartes and Locke. The most dramatic effect of confidence was the desacralizing of social and political bonds—a new belief that society can be grounded on rational foundations to be determined by humans, not arbitrary foundations determined by God.

A wide range of thinkers participated in Enlightenment; in France, they were known as *philosophes,* a term meaning not a formal philosopher but rather a thinker and critic. To most philosophes, the main agenda was clear. For too long, humans had been mired in ignorance. Rather than thinking of themselves as thinkers, they thought of themselves as sinners. Arbitrary laws and institutions oppressed them. Lack of proper education and the tyranny of the church condemned them to ignorance. French thinkers singled out the Catholic church as the archenemy, because of its opposition to their positive views of human nature and because it controlled much education and was still a force in political life.

The following passage from Voltaire's *Dictionnaire philosophique* (*Philosophical Dictionary,* 1764) is typical of his work in its casual format and biting wit and is also typical of the venomous Enlightenment view of the church. The dictionary entry for "authority" is not about authority in general but focuses on the arbitrary authority of the church:

A hundred times [you clerics] have been spoken to of the insolent absurdity with which you condemned Galileo, and I shall speak to you for the hundred and first . . . I desire that there be engraved on the door of your holy office: Here seven cardinals assisted by minor brethren had the master of thought of Italy thrown into prison at the age of seventy, made him fast on bread and water, because he instructed the human race.

The life of Voltaire (1694–1778), the most famous of the philosophes, spanned the century. Born François-Marie Arouet to a middle-class family, he took the pen name Voltaire in 1718, after one of his early plays was a critical success. He was educated by the Jesuits, whom he despised but admired for their teaching methods. He produced a vast array of written work: plays, epic poems, novelettes—some of which have explicit philosophical or political content—as well as philosophical tracts. Voltaire moved in courtly circles. Mockery of the regent, the duke of Orléans, led to a year's imprisonment in 1717, and an exchange of insults with a leading courtier some years later led to enforced exile in England for two years.

Voltaire The philosophe's intelligence and wit are captured in this superb likeness by the contemporary sculptor Houdon. *(Courtesy of the Board of Trustees of the V&A)*

After returning from England, Voltaire published his first major philosophical work. *Lettres philosophiques* (*Philosophical Letters,* 1734) revealed the influence of his English sojourn and helped to popularize Newton's achievement. The empirical tradition in English philosophy profoundly influenced Voltaire. To his confidence in the laws governing nature he added cautious confidence in humans' attempts to establish truth. From Locke's work he drew confidence in human educability tempered by awareness of the finite nature of the human mind. These elements gave Voltaire's philosophy both its passionate conviction and its practicality.

Voltaire portrayed England as a more rational society than France. The English government had a more workable set of institutions, the economy was less crippled by the remnants of feudal privilege, and education was not in the hands of the church. He was particularly impressed with the religious and intellectual toleration evident in England. (See the box, "Voltaire on England's Commercial Success.")

After the publication of his audacious *Lettres,* Voltaire was again forced into exile from Paris, and he resided for some years in the country home of a woman with whom he shared a remarkable intellectual and emotional relationship: Emilie, marquise du Châtelet (1706–1749). Châtelet was a mathematician and a scientist. She set to work on a French translation of Newton's *Principia* while Voltaire worked at his accustomed variety of writing, which also included a commentary on Newton's work. Because of Châtelet's tutelage, Voltaire became more knowledgeable about the sciences and more serious in his efforts to apply scientific rationality to human affairs. He was devastated by her sudden death in 1749.

Voltaire on England's Commercial Success

In this excerpt from* Philosophical Letters*, Voltaire compares British trade and seapower with the commercial activities of the German and French elites, who scorn trade in order to engage in aristocratic pretentiousness and court politics. Voltaire's wit, his admiration for England, and his penchant for criticizing irrationalities of all sorts are evident.

Commerce, which has brought wealth to the citizenry of England, has helped to make them free, and freedom has developed commerce in its turn. By means of it the nation has grown great; it is commerce that little by little has strengthened the naval forces that make the English the masters of the seas. . . . Posterity may learn with some surprise that a little island with nothing of its own but a bit of lead, tin . . . and coarse wool became, by means of its commerce, powerful enough to send three fleets at one time to three different ends of the earth.

All this makes the English merchant justly proud; moreover, the younger brother of a peer of the realm does not scorn to enter into trade. . . . [In Germany], they are unable to imagine how [an aristocrat could enter trade since they have] as many as thirty Highnesses of the same name, with nothing to show for it but pride and a coat of arms.

In France anybody who wants to can [act the part of marquis] and whoever arrives in Paris with money to spend and a [plausible name] may indulge in such phrases as "a man of my rank and quality" and with sovereign eye look down upon a wholesaler. . . . Yet I don't know which is the more useful to a state, a well-powdered lord who knows precisely what time the king gets up in the morning . . . and who gives himself airs of grandeur while playing the role of slave in a minister's antechamber, or a great merchant who enriches his country.

Source: Ernest Dilworth, trans. and ed., *Voltaire: Philosophical Letters* (New York: Bobbs-Merrill, 1961), pp. 39–40.

Shortly afterward, he accepted the invitation of the king of Prussia, Frederick II, to visit Berlin. His stay was stormy and brief because of disagreements with other court philosophers. He resided for a time in Geneva, until his criticisms of the city's moral codes forced yet another exile on him. He spent most of the last twenty years of his life at his estates on the Franco-Swiss border, where he could be relatively free from interference by any government. These were productive years. He produced his best-known satirical novelette, *Candide,* in 1758. It criticized aristocratic privilege and the power of clerics as well as the naiveté of philosophers who took "natural law" to mean that the world was already operating as it should.

Voltaire's belief that one must struggle to overturn the accumulated habits of centuries is also reflected in his political activity. Voltaire became involved in several celebrated legal cases in which individuals were pitted against the authority of the church, which was still backed by the authority of the state. The most famous case was that of Jean Calas (1698–1762), a Protestant from southern France who was accused of murdering his son, allegedly to prevent him from converting to Catholicism. Calas maintained his innocence until his execution in 1762. Voltaire saw in this case the worst aspects of religious prejudice and injustice and worked tirelessly to establish Calas's innocence as a matter of principle and so that his family could inherit his property. In pursuit of justice in these cases and in criticism of his archenemy the church, Voltaire added a stream of straightforward political pamphlets to his literary output. He also worked closer to home, initiating agricultural reform on his estates and working to improve the status of peasants in the vicinity.

In 1778, Voltaire died in Paris. He had returned there, to great public acclamation, to direct one of his plays. By then, he was no longer leader of the Enlightenment in strictly intellectual terms. Thinkers and writers more radical than he had earned prominence during his long life and had dismissed some of his beliefs, such as the notion that reform could be introduced by a monarch. But Voltaire had provided a crucial stimulus to French thought with his *Lettres philosophiques.* His importance lies also in his embodiment of the critical spirit of eighteenth-century rationalism: its confidence, its increasingly practical bent, its wit and sophistication. Until the end of his life, Voltaire remained a bridge between the increasingly diverse body of Enlightenment thought and the literate elite audience.

MAJOR WORKS OF THE ENLIGHTENMENT

1721	Montesquieu, *Persian Letters*
1734	Voltaire, *Philosophical Letters*
1748	Montesquieu, *The Spirit of the Laws*
	Hume, *Essay Concerning Human Understanding*
1758	Voltaire, *Candide*
1751–65	Diderot, *The Encyclopedia*
1762	Rousseau, *The Social Contract*
1764	Voltaire, *Philosophical Dictionary*
1776	Smith, *The Wealth of Nations*
1784	Kant, *What Is Enlightenment?*
1792	Wollstonecraft, *A Vindication of the Rights of Woman*
1795	Condorcet, *The Progress of the Human Mind*

The Variety of Enlightenment Thought

Differences among philosophes grew as the century progressed. In the matter of religion, for example, there was virtual unanimity of opposition to the Catholic church among French thinkers, but no unanimity about God. Voltaire was a theist—believing firmly in God, creator of the universe, but not a specifically Christian God. To some later thinkers, God was irrelevant—the creator of the world, but a world that ran continuously according to established laws. If the world were a machine, then God was the watchmaker. Some philosophes were atheists, arguing that a universe that ran according to discoverable laws needs no higher purpose and no divine presence to explain, run or justify it. In Protestant areas of Europe, in contrast to France, Enlightenment thought was often less hostile to Christianity.

Questions about social and political order, as well as about human rationality itself, were also pondered. Charles de Secondat (1689–1755), baron of Montesquieu, a French legist, combined the belief that human institutions must be rational with Locke's assumption of human educability. Montesquieu's treatise *L'Esprit des lois* (*The Spirit of the Laws,* 1748) was published in twenty-two printings within two years. In it Montesquieu maintained that laws were not meant to be arbitrary rules but derived naturally from human society: The more evolved a society was, the more liberal were its laws. This notion provided a sense of the progress possible within society and government and deflated Europeans' pretensions vis-à-vis other societies, for a variety of laws could equally be "rational" given differing conditions. Montesquieu is perhaps best known to Americans as the advocate of the separation of legislative, executive, and judicial powers that later became enshrined in the American Constitution. To Montesquieu, this scheme seemed to parallel in human government the balance of forces observable in nature and seemed best to guarantee liberty.

The "laws" of economic life were also investigated. In France, economic thinkers known as *physiocrats* proposed ending "artificial"—that is, feudal and seigneurial—control over land use in order to free productive capacity and permit the freer flow of produce to market. The freeing of restrictions on agriculture, manufacture, and trade was proposed by the Scotsman Adam Smith in his treatise *An Inquiry into the Nature and Causes of the Wealth of Nations* (1776).

Smith (1723–1790), a professor at the University of Glasgow, is best known in modern times as the originator of "laissez-faire" economics: the assumption that an economy will regulate itself without interference by government and, of more concern to Smith, without the monopolies and other economic privileges common in his day. Smith's schema for economic growth was not merely a rigid application to economics of faith in natural law. His ideas grew out of an optimistic view of human nature and human rationality that was heavily indebted to Locke. Humans, Smith believed, have drives and passions that they can direct and govern by means of reason and inherent sympathy for one another. Thus, Smith said, in seeking their own achievement and well-being, they are often "led by an invisible hand" to simultaneously benefit society as a whole.

Throughout the century, philosophers of various stripes disagreed about the nature and the limits of human reason. Smith's countryman and friend David Hume (1711–1776) was perhaps the most radical in his critique of the human capacity for knowing. He was the archskeptic, taking Locke's view of the limitations on pure reason to the point of doubting the efficacy of sense data. His major work in which he expounded these views, *Essay Concerning Human Understanding* (1748), led to important innovations later in the century in the work of the German philosopher Immanuel Kant but were, at the time, almost contrary to the prevailing spirit of confidence in empirical knowledge. Hume himself separated this work from his other efforts in moral, political, and economic philosophy, which were more in tune with the prevailing views of the day.

The Encyclopédie This ambitious work attempted to bring together the current knowledge in philosophy, the arts, the sciences, and in agriculture and industry. This depiction of shipbuilding is one of the technical illustrations from the encyclopedia. *(From* Encyclopédie, ou Dictionnaire Raisonné des Sciences, des Arts, et des Métiers. *Courtesy, Dover Publications)*

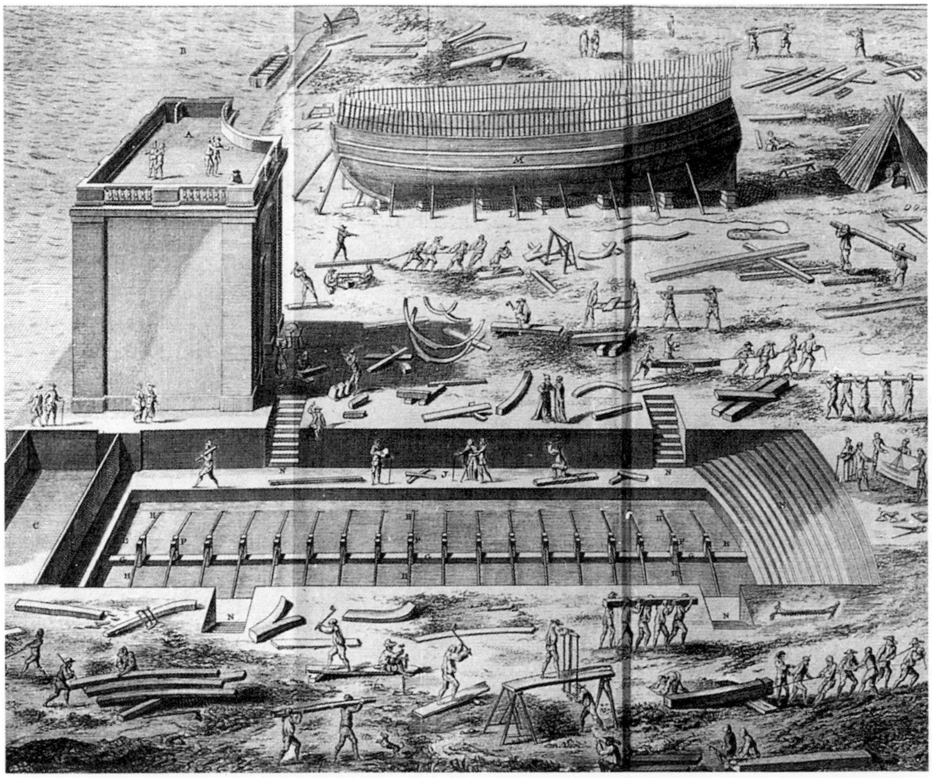

D'Alembert on the Progress of Human Knowledge

Jean le Rond d'Alembert (1717–1783), an accomplished mathematician, was coeditor, with Denis Diderot, of the **Encyclopédie.** *As this excerpt from his* **Essay on the Elements of Philosophy** *reveals, the energy and optimism of much Enlightenment thought rested on awareness of the historic changes that had transformed society, culture, and science since the sixteenth century.*

The middle of the sixteenth century saw a rapid change in the religion and the disposition of a great part of Europe; . . . the rivalry stirred up by [the issues of religion] extended knowledge in every direction; and the light, kindled amidst error and discord, has shone on the very subjects which seem the furthest removed from these controversies. Finally, Descartes, in the middle of the seventeenth century, founded a new philosophy, at first passionately attacked, then surreptitiously espoused, and today reduced to its useful and true elements.

. . . If the present state of our knowledge is examined without bias, the progress of philosophy amongst us cannot be gainsaid. Natural science acquires new riches daily; . . . the true nature of the world has been discovered, developed and perfected . . . The invention and the use of a new method of philosophy, the kind of enthusiasm that accompanies discoveries, a certain grandeur of ideas that the spectacle of the universe induces in us, all these causes have brought about a lively intellectual ferment. This ferment . . . has turned its attention with a sort of violence to everything that comes before it, like a river that has burst its banks. Now men seldom come back to a subject they have long neglected except to revise . . . accepted ideas.

Source: J. F. Lively, *The Enlightenment* (New York: Barnes and Noble, 1966), pp. 3–5.

Mainstream confidence in empirical knowledge and in the intelligibility of the world is evident in the production of the *Encyclopédie* (*Encyclopedia*), a seventeen-volume compendium of knowledge, criticism, and philosophy assembled by leading philosophes in France and published there between 1751 and 1765. The volumes were designed to contain state-of-the-art knowledge about arts, sciences, technology, and philosophy. The guiding philosophy of the project, set forth by its chief editor, Denis Diderot (1713–1784), was a belief in the advance of human happiness through the advance of knowledge (see the box, "D'Alembert on the Progress of Human Knowledge"). The *Encyclopédie* was a kind of history of the advance of knowledge as well as a compendium of known achievements. It was revolutionary in that it not only intrigued and inspired intellectuals but assisted thousands of government officials and professionals. Catherine the Great remarked in a letter that she consulted its pages to find guidance concerning one of her reform schemes.

The encyclopedia project illustrates the political context of Enlightenment thought as well as its philosophic premises. The Catholic church placed the work on the Index of prohibited books, and the French government might have barred its publication but for the fact that the official who would have made the decision was drawn to Enlightenment thinking. Many other officials, however, worked to suppress it. By the late 1750s, losses in wars overseas had made French officials highly sensitive to political challenges of any kind. Thus, like Voltaire, the major contributors to the *Encyclopédie* were lionized by certain segments of the elite and persecuted by others in their official functions.

The *Encyclopédie* reflects the complexities and limitations of Enlightenment thought on another score—the position of women. One might expect that the Enlightenment penchant for challenging received knowledge and traditional social and political hierarchies would lead to revised views of women's abilities and rights. Indeed, some contributors blamed women's inequality with men not on any deficiencies in women but rather on the customs and laws that had kept women from education and the development of their abilities. However, other contributors blamed women, and not society, for the inequality women suffered, or they argued that women had talents that fit them only for the domestic sphere.

Both positions were represented in Enlightenment thought as a whole. The assumption of the natural equality of all people provided a powerful ground for arguing the equality of women with men. Some thinkers challenged Locke's separation of family life from the public world of free, contractual relationships (see the box, "An English Feminist Criticizes Unenlightened Views of Women"). Most advocated increased education for women, if only to make them more fit to raise enlightened children. By the end of the century, the most radical thinkers were advocating full citizenship rights for women and equal rights to property along with enhanced education.

The best-known proponent of those views was an English woman, Mary Wollstonecraft (1759–1797). She assumed that most elite women would devote themselves to domestic duties, but she argued that without the responsibilities of citizenship, the leavening of education, and economic independence, women could be neither fully formed individuals nor worthy of their duties. Working women, she concluded, needed these rights simply to survive.

A more limited view of women's capacities was one element in the influential work of Jean-Jacques Rousseau (1712–1778). Like Locke, Rousseau could conceive of the free individual only as male, and he grounded his critique of the old order and his novel political ideas in an arbitrary division of gender roles. Rousseau's view of women was linked to a critique of the artificiality of elite, cosmopolitan society in which Enlightenment thought was then flourishing and in which aristocratic women were fully involved. Rousseau believed in the educability of men but was as concerned with issues of character and emotional life as with knowledge. Society—particularly the artificial courtly society—was corrupting. The true citizen had to cultivate virtue and sensibility, not manners, taste, or refinement. Rousseau designated women as guarantors of the "natural" virtues of children and nurturers of the emotional life and character of men—but not as fully formed beings in their own right.

Rousseau's emphasis on the education and virtue of citizens was the underpinning of his larger political vision, set forth in *Du Contrat social* (*Social Contract,* 1762). He imagined an egalitarian republic—possible particularly in small states such as his native Geneva—in which men would consent to be governed because the government would determine and act in accordance with the "general will" of the citizens. The "general will" was not majority opinion but rather what each citizen *would* want if he were fully informed and were acting in accordance with his highest nature. The "general will" became apparent whenever the citizens met as a body and made collective decisions, and it could be imposed on all inhabitants. This was a breathtaking vision of direct democracy—but one with ominous possibilities, for Rousseau rejected the institutional brakes on state authority proposed by Locke and Montesquieu. Also, the demands of citizenship in such a political order, in contrast to simple obedience under a monarchy, necessitated, for Rousseau, the subordination of women's lives to those of male citizens.

Rousseau's emphasis on the private emotional life anticipates the romanticism of the early nineteenth century. It also reflects Rousseau's own experience as the son of a humble family, always sensing himself an outcast in the brilliant world of Parisian salons. He had a love-hate relationship with this life, remaining attached to several aristocratic women patrons even as he decried their influence. His own personal life did not match his prescriptions for others. He completely neglected to give his own four children the nurturing and education that he argued were vital; indeed, he abandoned all of them to a foundling home. He was nevertheless influential as a critic of an elite society still dominated by status, patronage, and privilege. Rousseau's work

An English Feminist Criticizes Unenlightened Views of Women

Both male and female writers criticized the failure of some Enlightenment thinkers to view ideas about women with the same skepticism and rationalism that they brought to other subjects. One of the earliest was the Englishwoman Mary Astell (1666–1731). In this excerpt from **Some Reflections on Marriage** *(1700), Astell criticizes, in an ironic tone, negative assessments of women's capacities, Locke's separation of the public and private spheres, and the denial to women of the rights that men enjoy in public life.*

'Tis true, through want of learning, and that of superior genius which men, as men, lay claim to, she [the author] was ignorant of the natural inferiority of our sex, which our masters lay down as self-evident and fundamental truth. She saw nothing in the reason of things to make this either a principle or a conclusion, but much to the contrary.

If they mean that some men are superior to some women, this is no great discovery; had they turned the tables, they might have seen that some women are superior to some men. . . .

Again, if absolute sovereignty be not necessary in a state, how comes it to be so in a family? Or if in a family why not in a state, since no reason can be alleged for the one that will not hold more strongly for the other? If the authority of the husband, so far as it extends, is sacred and inalienable, why not that of the prince? The domestic sovereign is without dispute elected and the stipulations and contract are mutual; is it not then partial in men to the last degree to contend for and practice that arbitrary dominion in their families which they abhor and exclaim against in the state? For if arbitrary power is evil in itself, and an improper method of governing rational and free agents, it ought not to be practiced anywhere.

Source: Moira Ferguson, ed., *First Feminists* (Bloomington: Indiana University Press, 1985), pp. 191–193.

reflects to an extreme degree the tensions in Enlightenment thought generally: It was part of elite culture as well as its principal critic.

The Growth of Public Opinion

It is impossible to understand the significance of the Enlightenment without an analysis of how it was a part of public life. Most of the philosophes were of modest origin. They influenced the privileged elite of their day because of the social and political environment in which their ideas were elaborated. Indeed, the clearest distinguishing feature of the Enlightenment may be the creation of an informed body of public opinion that stood apart from court society.

Increased literacy and access to books and other print media are an important part of the story. Perhaps more important, the kinds of reading that people favored began to change. We know from inventories made of people's belongings at the time of their death (required for inheritance laws) that books in the homes of ordinary people were no longer just traditional works such as devotional literature. Ordinary people were reading secular and contemporary philosophical works. As the availability of such works increased, reading itself was evolving from a reverential encounter with traditional material to a critical encounter with new material. Solitary reading for reflection and pleasure was becoming more widespread.

The Growth of the Book Trade As literacy continued to become more widespread, book ownership also dramatically increased in the eighteenth century. A wide range of secular works, from racy novelettes to philosophical tracts, was available in print. *(Musée des Beaux-Arts de Dijon)*

Habits of reading and responding to written material were changed not only by increased opportunities to do so but also by changes in the social environment. In the eighteenth century, forerunners of the modern lending libraries made their debut. In Paris, for a fee, one could join a *salle de lecture* (literally, a "reading room") where the latest works were available to any member. Booksellers, whose numbers increased dramatically, found ways to meet readers' demands for inexpensive access to reading matter. One might pay for the right to read a book in the bookshop itself. In short, new venues encouraged people to see themselves not just as readers but as members of a reading public. The most famous of these venues are the French salons, where Voltaire and others read their works aloud and discussed them.

In Paris, certain women of noble rank invited courtiers, bureaucrats, and intellectuals to meet regularly in their homes. An invitation to a salon was highly prized by members of the literate elite, and the salons were fiercely competitive with each other. The ideas discussed in these gatherings constituted much of the informed political opinion of the day. Salons represented an alternative to court life for many elite men who previously might have aspired only to a role at court. An important dimension of political life now existed outside court and government.

Various clubs, local academies, and learned and secret societies copied some features of the salons of Paris. Hardly any municipality was without a private society that functioned both as a forum for political and philosophical discussion and as an elite social club. Here mingled doctors, lawyers, local officials—some of whom enjoyed the fruits of the political system in offices and patronage. In Scotland, universities were flourishing centers of Enlightenment thought, but political clubs in Glasgow and Edinburgh enriched debate and the development of ideas.

In all these arenas, Enlightenment ideas became the encouragement for and the legitimation of a type of far-reaching political debate that had never before existed, except possibly in England during the seventeenth century. Understanding the Enlightenment involves understanding the milieu in which these ideas were received. The first and greatest impact of the Enlightenment, particularly in France, was not the creation of a program for political or social change but the creation of a culture of politics that could generate change.

Art in the Age of Reason

The Enlightenment had reverberations in all aspects of cultural life. Just as the market for books and the reading public expanded, so did the audience for works of art in the growing leisured urban circles of Paris and other great cities. The modern cultured public—a public of concertgoers and art-gallery enthusiasts—began to make its first appearance. The brilliant and sophisticated courts around Europe continued to sponsor composers, musicians, and painters by providing both patronage and audiences. Yet some performances of concerts and operas began to take place in theaters and halls outside the courts and were more accessible to the public.

Beginning in 1737, one section of the Louvre palace in Paris was devoted annually to public exhibitions of painting and sculpture (though by royally sponsored and approved artists). In both France and Britain, public discussion of art began to take place in published reviews and criticisms: The role of art critic was born. Works of art were also sold by public means, such as auctions. As works became more available by such means, demand grew and production increased.

In subject matter and style these various art forms exhibited greater variety than works in preceding centuries had shown. We can nevertheless discern certain patterns and tendencies in both the content and the form of the art in the century. A revival of classical subjects and styles evoked what were thought to be the pure and timeless values of classical heroes. This art revealed the influence of Enlightenment thought by assuming the educability of its audience. Classical revival architecture illustrated a belief in order, symmetry, and proportion. Americans are familiar with its evocations because it has been the architecture of their republic, but even churches were built in this style in eighteenth-century Europe.

Another trend in art and literature was a fascination with nature and with the seemingly "natural" in human culture—less "developed" or historically distant societies. One of the most

Classical Revival Architecture celebrated order, balance, and proportion. The church of Ste-Genevieve in Paris, begun in 1764, imitates Roman architecture. Now known as the Pantheon, it later became a memorial to great Frenchmen—including Voltaire, who is buried there. *(Scala/Art Resource, NY)*

popular printed works in the middle of the century was the supposed translation of the poems of Ossian, a third-century Scots Highland poet. Early English, German, Norse, and other folk tales were "discovered" (in some cases invented) and published. Many of these went through several editions during the century.

The fact that folk life, other cultures, and untamed nature itself began to be celebrated just when they were being more definitively conquered is very revealing. (See the feature, "Weighing the Evidence: Gardens," on pages 774–775). The early poetry of Scotland, for example, was celebrated just as the Scottish Highlands were being punished by the English because of the clans' support for a rival claimant to the English throne. Many of the bards who had carried on the oral traditions of each clan were executed because of the political threat that their traditions embodied. Once purged of any threat, the exotic image of another culture (even the folk culture of one's own society) could be a source of imagination and create a sense of distance from which to measure one's own sophistication. Thus, both ancient and exotic subjects reinforced a sense of dominance and control.

A related trend in music, the arts, and literature has been called the cult of "sensibility." Partly, this was a stylistic challenge to rococo design in architecture and decorative arts—furniture, china, and so forth. Rococo art was seen to represent the playful eroticism and excess of aristocratic culture and court life. There was a new emphasis on more simple, dramatic, and emotive themes in art, literature, and music. The classical movement in music, embodied in the works of Austrians Franz Josef Haydn (1732–1809) and Wolfgang Amadeus Mozart (1756–1791), saw the clarification of musical structures, such as the modern sonata and symphony, and enabled melody to take center stage.

Another glorification of "sensibility" was a further move toward the exploration of private emotion. Much literature at the end of the century was devoted to exploring the private world of individuals—not the ironic self-exploration of Montaigne, two centuries earlier (see page 648), but the exploration of personal feelings. The inner life nurtured by literacy and by a need to retreat from the elaborate artifice of court life made possible a fuller exploration of emotion than would have been imaginable before. The novel became an increasingly important genre. In English literature the novels of Samuel Richardson (1689–1761)—*Pamela,* (1740) and *Clarissa* (1747–1748)—explored personal psychology and passion. Rousseau followed Richardson's lead in structuring his two novels.

The Enlightenment and French Society

It is one of the seeming paradoxes of the Enlightenment that critical thought about society and politics flourished in France, an autocratic state with institutionally privileged elites. Yet in France there was a well-educated elite, a tradition of scientific inquiry, and a legacy of cultured court life that, since the early days of Louis XIV, had become the model for all Europe. French was the international intellectual language, and France was the most fertile center of elite cultural life. Both Adam Smith and David Hume, for example, spent portions of their careers in Paris and were welcomed into the salons. In fact, the French capital was an environment that encouraged debate and dissent precisely because of the juxtaposition of the new intellectual climate with the difficulties the French state was facing and the institutional rigidities of its political system—a system that excluded many talented and productive members of the elite from its privileged circles.

In the last decades of the reign of Louis XIV (d. 1715), many thoughtful French people criticized the direction the French state was taking. They began to question the point of foreign wars that yielded ever-diminishing returns. The intoxicating congruence of stability, effective government, national interest, and the personal glory of the monarch began to break apart. It continued to break down as the eighteenth century progressed.

Louis XIV was followed on the throne by his 5-year-old great-grandson, Louis XV (r. 1715–1774). During the regency, nobles clamored for the establishment of councils so that they could become more active partners in government. Likewise, the supreme law courts, the parlements, reclaimed the right of remonstrance—the right to object to royal edicts and thus to exercise some control over the enactment of law. Throughout Louis XV's reign, his administration tended to be in conflict with the parlements, particularly as royal ministers tried to cope with France's financial crises. Louis XIV had left the nation financially exhausted and in need of more money and new and more reliable ways to get money. During Louis XV's reign the pressures of further wars intensified the need for wholesale reform. The parlements, however, representing the privileged interests of officeholders, mounted effective opposition to all measures to reform taxation.

Parlementary power was one of very few institutional brakes on royal authority. Thus, ordinary property holders who had little in common with privileged officeholders and nobles might nevertheless agree with opposition to royal attempts to tax them. Moreover, the Crown itself provided little leadership. Louis XV displayed none of the kingly qualities of his great-grandfather. He was not pleasant or affable, and he was lazy. By the end of his reign, he was roundly despised. He did not give the "rationality" of royal government a good name.

Public opinion came down on both sides of this conflict between the monarch and the parlements. A number of ministers under Louis XV and his grandson Louis XVI (r. 1774–1793) shared Enlightenment views of the efficiency of creating economic change from the top and the rationality of doing away with feudal privileges such as the exemption of the nobility from taxation. However, the role of consultative bodies and the separation of powers beloved of Montesquieu were much prized, and the parlements were the only institutions that could legitimately check monarchial powers.

Not surprisingly, from about the middle of the century, public opinion, nurtured in salons and other new settings, was proposing a variety of ways to enhance representation, consultation, and reform. There were calls for the moribund Estates General (last called in 1614) as well as for the establishment of new councils or local, decentralized representative assemblies. The workability of these proposals is less important than the simple fact that they were made. By the time an Estates General was finally called in the wake of further financial problems in 1788, the habit of carrying on political analysis and criticism of government outside the actual corridors of power had given rise to a volatile situation.

European Rulers and European Society

Mindful of the lessons to be learned from the revolution in England and the achievements of Louis XIV, European rulers in the eighteenth century continued their efforts to govern with greater effectiveness. Some—like the rulers of Prussia and Russia—were encouraged in their efforts by Enlightenment ideas that stressed the need for reforms in law, economy, and government, and in the main they (like Voltaire) believed that monarchs could be agents for change. In Austria, significant reforms, including the abolition of serfdom, were made. The changes were uneven, however, and at times owed as much to traditional efforts at better government as to enlightened persuasions.

In all cases, rulers' efforts to govern more effectively meant continual readjustments in relationships with traditional elites. Whether or not elites could formally participate in the governing process by means of established institutions such as the English Parliament, royal governments everywhere were still dependent on their participation. Enlightened monarchs were changing their view of themselves and their image from the diligent but self-aggrandizing image of Louis XIV to that of servant of the state. In this light, the monarchy was moving to undermine the dynastic claim to rule by refounding it on a utilitarian basis, from traditional monarchial rule toward a new notion of the state as separate from the ruler.

Monarchy and Constitutional Government in England

After the deaths of William (d. 1702) and Mary (d. 1694), the British crown passed to Mary's sister, Anne (r. 1702–1714) and then to a collateral line descended from Elizabeth, sister of the beheaded Charles I. Elizabeth had married Frederick, Elector Palatine (and had reigned with him briefly in Bohemia at the outset of the Thirty Years' War), and her descendants were Germans, now electors of Hanover. The new British sovereign in 1714, who reigned as George I (r. 1714–1729), was both a foreigner and a man of mediocre abilities. Moreover, his claim to the throne was immediately contested by Catholic descendants of James II, who attempted to depose him in 1715.

A second attempt to depose the Hanoverian kings in 1745 was more nearly successful. The son of the Stuart claimant to the throne, Charles (known in legend as Bonnie Prince Charlie), landed on the west coast of Scotland with French assistance and marched south into England with surprising ease. Scotland had been formally united with England in 1707 (hence the term "Great Britain" after that time), but Charles found support among the poor and disaffected wherever he marched and drew most of his army from the Highland clans. Gaelic-speaking, often still Catholic, living as cattle-herders, and marauding against each other and against the Lowlands—the clans were in many respects outside the bounds of the Scottish, now the British, state.

When Charles's army was defeated and many Highland chieftains were killed at the battle of Culloden in April 1746, the British government used the opportunity to destroy Highland culture. Traditional practices, from wearing tartans to carrying the accustomed personal daggers and even playing bagpipes, were forbidden. Control of land was redistributed to break the social and economic bonds of clan society. Thousands of Highlanders died—at the battle itself or from wounds that the British refused to treat, in prisons or deportation ships in the aftermath of the battle, by deliberate extermination by the British, or from starvation in the winter following the battle.

Great Britain was not an admirable state on all counts. Nevertheless, Enlightenment admiration for the stability and flexibility of British society was not wholly misplaced. The events of the seventeenth century had reaffirmed both the need for a strong monarchy and the role of Parliament in defending elite interests. The power of Parliament had recently been reinforced by the Act of Settlement, by which the Protestant heir to Queen Anne had been chosen in 1701. By excluding the Catholic Stuarts from the throne and establishing the line of succession, this document reasserted that Parliament determined the legitimacy of the monarchy. The act also claimed greater parliamentary authority over foreign and domestic policy in the wake of the bellicose William's rule.

Noteworthy in the eighteenth century were the ways in which cooperation evolved between monarchy and Parliament as Parliament became a more sophisticated and secure institution. Political parties—that is, distinct groups within the elite favoring certain foreign and domestic policies—came into existence. Two groups, the Whigs and the Tories, had begun to form during the reign of Charles II (d. 1685). The Whigs (named derisively by their opponents with a Scottish term for horse thieves) had opposed Charles's pro-French policies and his efforts to tolerate Catholicism and wholly opposed his brother and successor James II. Initially, the Whigs favored an aggressive foreign policy against continental opponents—above all, France. The Tories (also derisively named—for Irish cattle-rustlers) tended to be staunch Anglicans uninterested in Protestant anti-Catholic agitation. They tended to have a conservative view of their own role, favoring isolationism in foreign affairs and an attitude of deference toward monarchial authority. Whigs represented the interests of the great aristocrats or wealthy merchants or gentry. Tories represented the interests of provincial gentry and the traditional concerns of landholding and local administration.

The Whigs were the dominant influence in government through most of the century to 1770. William and Mary and Queen Anne favored Whig religious and foreign policy interests. The loyalty of many Tories was called into question by their support for a Stuart, not Hanoverian, succession in 1714. The long Whig dominance of government was also ensured by the talents of Robert Walpole, a member of Parliament who functioned virtually as a prime minister from 1722 to 1742.

Walpole (1676–1745) was from a minor gentry family and was brought into government in 1714 with other Whig ministers in George I's new regime. An extremely talented politician, he took advantage of the mistakes of other ministers over the years and, in 1722, became both the first lord of the treasury and chancellor of the exchequer.

The Destruction of the Highlanders Although English rulers had previously attacked individual clans, Highland culture maintained its independence until the uprising of 1745. For the first time, clansmen were decisively beaten in battle by British troops, who used the tactics of volley fire and disciplined bayonet charge. *(The Royal Collection © 1993 Her Majesty Queen Elizabeth II)*

There was not yet any official post or title of "Prime Minister," but the great contribution of Walpole's tenure was to create that office in fact, if not officially. He chose to maintain peace abroad where he could and thus presided over a period of recovery and relative prosperity that enhanced the stability of government. He was helped in his role as go-between for king and Parliament by George I's own limitations. The king rarely attended meetings of his own council of ministers and, in any case, was hampered by his ignorance of English. Gradually, the Privy Council of the king became something resembling a modern Cabinet dominated by a prime minister. By the end of the century the notions of "loyal opposition" to the Crown within Parliament and parliamentary responsibility for policy had taken root.

In some respects, the maturation of political life in Parliament resembled the lively political debates in the salons of Paris. In both cases, political life was being legitimized on a new basis. In England, however, that legitimation was enshrined in a legislative institution, which made it especially effective and resilient.

Of course, Parliament was not truly representative. Because of strict property qualifications, only about 200,000 adult men could vote. In addition, representation was very uneven. Some constituencies with only a few dozen voters sent members to Parliament. Many of these "pocket boroughs" were under the control of (in the pockets of) powerful local families who could intimidate the local electorate, particularly in the absence of secret ballots. Moreover, patronage and the influence of those within the system remained central to government. Walpole governed in part by directing the flow of royal patronage—army commands, bishoprics, and other posts—into the hands of political allies. England was in no sense a democracy. Still, Parliament did manage to survive as the focal point for political life, and it provided a smoother transition to wider participation than did less formal mechanisms or more narrow institutions such as existed in France.

"Enlightened" Monarchy

Arbitrary monarchial power might seem antithetical to tenets of Enlightenment thought that stressed the reasonableness of human beings and their capacity to discern and act in accord with natural law. Yet monarchy seemed an ideal instrument of reform to Voltaire and to many of his contemporaries. The work of curtailing the influence of the church, reforming legal codes, and eliminating barriers to economic activity might be done more efficiently by a powerful monarch than by other means then available, particularly because there was great confidence in the power of education to transform an individual (in this case, a ruler) and in the accessibility of the principles of reason. Historians have labeled a number of rulers of this era "enlightened despots" because of the arbitrary nature of their power and the enlightened or reformist uses to which they put it.

One of the best-known claimants to the title "enlightened" monarch was Frederick II of Prussia (r. 1740–1786), "the Great." Much of the time, Frederick resided in his imperial electorate of Brandenburg, near his capital Berlin. His scattered states, which he extended by seizing new lands, are referred to as "Prussia," rather than as "Brandenburg-Prussia," because members of his family were now kings of Prussia thanks to their ambitions and the weakness of the Polish state of which Prussia had once been a dependent duchy. In many ways, the Prussian state *was* its military victories, for Frederick's bold moves and the policies of his father, grandfather, and great-grandfather committed the resources of the state to a military presence of dramatic proportions. Prussia was a state on the European stage only because of the degree of that commitment.

The institutions that constituted the state and linked the various provinces under one administration were dominated by the needs of the military. Frederick II's father, Frederick William (r. 1713–1740), had added an efficient provincial recruiting system to the state's central institutions, which he also further consolidated. But in many other respects, the Prussian state was in its infancy. There was no tradition of political participation—even by elites—and little chance of cultivating any. Nor was there any political or social room for maneuver at the lower part of the social scale. The rulers of Prussia had long ago traded the support of the aristocracy for the aristocracy's claim to what amounted to a renewed feudal control of their own lands. The rulers relied on nobles for local administration and army commands. Thus, there was a stark limit to the kinds of social, judicial, or political reforms that Frederick could personally hope to carry out.

Frederick tried to introduce improved agricultural methods and simultaneously to improve the condition of peasants, but he met stiff resistance from noble landholders. He did succeed in abolishing serfdom in some regions. He tried to stimulate the economy by sponsoring state industries and trading monopolies, but there were not enough resources or initiative from the tightly controlled merchant communities to create much economic expansion. Simplifying and codifying the inherited jumble of local laws was a goal of every ruler. A law code published in 1794, after Frederick's death, was partly the product of his efforts.

Frederick's views of the role of Enlightenment thought reflect the limitations of his situation. One doesn't have to lead a frontal assault on prejudices consecrated by time, he thought; instead, one must be tolerant of superstition because it will always have a hold on the masses. Perhaps his most distinctive "enlightened" characteristic was the seriousness with which he took his task as ruler. He was energetic and disciplined to a fault. In his book *Anti-Machiavel* (1741) he argued that a ruler has a moral obligation to work for the betterment of the state. He styled himself as the "first servant" or steward of the state. However superficial this claim may appear, in his energy and diligence he compares favorably to Louis XV of France, who, having a much more wealthy and flexible society to work with, did much less.

Describing Frederick as "enlightened" masks the degree to which his activities reflected as

Frederick the Great is pictured here returning from military maneuvers. Frederick's self-imposed work as king included arduous travel throughout his domains to check on local conditions and monitor local governments. *(Staatliches Schlösser und Gärten, Potsdam-Sans Souci)*

much the traditional goals of security and prosperity as the impetus of "enlightened" thinking. Indeed, some of the most thoroughgoing administrative, legal, and economic reforms were accomplished in rival Austria entirely within such a traditional framework, during the reign of Maria Theresa (r. 1740–1780), the daughter of Emperor Charles VI (r. 1711–1740).

Maria Theresa was a remarkable ruler in her diligence and determination. She overcame difficulties that surrounded her accession, survived the near dismemberment of Austrian territories in the wars that marked her reign, and embarked on an energetic reform program to shore up the weaknesses in the state that the conflicts had revealed. The Austrian monarchy was still a highly decentralized state. Maria Theresa worked to streamline and centralize administration, finances, and defense. She created new centralized governing councils and, above all, reformed the assessing and collection of taxes so that the Crown could better tap the wealth of its subjects. She established new courts of justice and limited the exploitation of serfs by landlords. In general, she presided over an effort to bypass many of the provincial and privatized controls on government still in the hands of great nobility. She accomplished all of this without being in any way "enlightened." For example, she had a traditional fear of freedom of the press and insisted on orthodoxy in religious matters. Her son, Joseph II, is an interesting contrast.

Self-consciously "enlightened," Joseph II (r. 1780–1790) carried out a variety of reforms that his mother had not attempted, including freedom of the press and limited freedom of religion. Some of his reforms were particularly dramatic, such as virtual abolition of the death penalty and encouragement of widespread literacy. Like Frederick the Great, Joseph regarded himself as a servant of the state. During his ten-year reign, the political climate in Vienna began to resemble that in Paris, London, and other capitals where political life was no longer simply confined to court life.

Many of Joseph's reforms, however, were simply extensions of his mother's. For example, he extended further legal protection to peasants and eventually abolished serfdom in all Habsburg lands. And in some ways he was less successful than Maria Theresa had been. Though persuaded of the benefits of enlightened government, he was by temperament an inflexible autocrat, whose methods antagonized many of his most powerful subjects. In the name of "rational" administration, he tried to extend Austrian institutions to the kingdom of Hungary—including the use of the German language for official business. He also tried to bypass the authority of the representative Estates in the Austrian Netherlands in order to achieve some of his aims. In this action reminiscent of his ancestor Philip II of Spain, Joseph II revealed that the curious blend of "enlightenment" and traditional absolutism was not greater than the sum of its parts. Joseph's policies provoked simmering opposition and open revolt in a number of his lands, and some of his reforms were repealed even before his death.

Catherine the Great and the Empire of Russia

Another ruler with a claim to the title "enlightened despot" was Catherine, empress of Russia (r. 1762–1796). Catherine was one of the ablest rulers in the eighteenth century and perhaps the single most able of all the rulers of imperial Russia. She combined intelligence with vision, diligence, and the ability to handle people and choose advisers. Her intelligence and political acumen were obvious early in her life in Russia simply from the fact that she survived at court. In 1745 she had been brought to Russia from her native Germany to marry the heir to the Russian throne. She was brutally treated by her husband.

Catherine the Great was the true heir of Peter the Great in her abilities, policies, and ambitions. Under Catherine, Russia was committed to general European affairs in addition to its traditional territorial ambitions. In situations involving the major European powers, Russia tended to ally with Britain (with which it had important trading connections including the provision of timber for British shipbuilding), and with Austria (against their common nemesis, Turkey), and against France, Poland, and Prussia. In 1768 Catherine initiated a war against the Turks from which Russia gained much of the Crimean coast. She also continued Peter's efforts to dominate the weakened Poland. She was aided by Frederick the Great, who proposed the deliberate partitioning of Poland to satisfy his own territorial ambitions as well as those of Russia and Austria, with which he competed. In 1772, Poland was gobbled up in the first of three successive "grabs" of territory (Map 20.1). Warsaw itself was in Prussian hands, but Catherine gained all of Beloruss, Lithuania, and Ukraine. Thus, like any successful ruler of her age, Catherine counted territorial aggrandizement among her chief achievements.

Nevertheless, Catherine counted herself a sincere follower of the Enlightenment. While young, she had received an education that bore the strong stamp of the Enlightenment. Like Frederick, she attempted to take an active role in the intellectual community, corresponding with Voltaire over the course of many years and acting as patron to Diderot. One of Catherine's boldest political moves was the secularization of church lands. Although Peter the Great had extended government control of the church, he had not touched church lands. She licensed private publishing houses and permitted a burgeoning periodical press. The numbers of books published in Russia tripled during her reign. This enriched cultural life was one of the principal causes of the flowering of Russian literature that began in the early nineteenth century.

The stamp of the Enlightenment on Catherine's policies is also clearly visible in her attempts at legal reform. In 1767 she convened a legislative commission and provided it with a guiding document, the *Instruction,* which she had authored (see the box, "Catherine the Great's Instructions for Legal Reform"). The commission was remarkable because it included representatives of all classes, including peasants, and provided a place for the airing of general grievances. Catherine hoped for a general codification of law as well as reforms such as the abolition of torture and capital punishment—reforms that made the

Catherine the Great One of the ablest rulers of the century, Catherine as a German princess had been brought to Russia to marry another German, Peter of Holstein-Gottorp, who was being groomed as heir to the Russian throne. There had been several Russian monarchs of mixed Russian and German parentage since the time of Peter the Great's deliberate interest in and ties with other European states. *(Wernher Collection, Mondadori, Milan)*

Instruction radical enough to be banned from publication in other countries. She did not propose changing the legal status of serfs, however, and class differences made the commission unworkable in the end. Most legal reforms were accomplished piecemeal and favored the interests of landed gentry. Property rights were clarified and strengthened; judicial procedures were streamlined but constructed to include legal privileges for the gentry.

Like the Austrian rulers, Catherine undertook far-reaching administrative reform to create

Map 20.1 The Partition of Poland and the Expansion of Russia Catherine the Great acquired modern Lithuania, Belarus, and Ukraine, which had once constituted the duchy of Lithuania, part of the multiethnic Polish kingdom.

more effective local units of government. Here again, political imperatives were fundamental, and reforms in local government strengthened the hand of the gentry. The legal subjection of peasants in serfdom was also extended as a matter of state policy to help win the allegiance of landholders in newly acquired areas—such as Ukrainian territory gained in the partition of Poland. Gentry in general and court favorites in particular, on whom the stability of her government depended, were rewarded with estates and serfs to work them.

In Russia as in Prussia and Austria, decline of the peasantry occurred because the monarch wanted to win the allegiance of the elites who lived from their labor. Russia was in a formative stage in another sense as well. It was trying to incorporate new peoples, such as the Tatars in the

Catherine the Great's Instructions for Legal Reform

Catherine consulted Voltaire and other philosophes concerning her project for legal reform. The finished document was boldly liberal in many respects but also consistent with the realities of Russian politics, including Catherine's power. These excerpts from the introductory sections show the influence of both Montesquieu and general Enlightenment notions but fully support Catherine's autocratic power.

(5) For those laws have the greatest conformity with nature whose particular regulations are best adapted to the situation and circumstances of the people for whom they are instituted.
(9) The sovereign is absolute; for there is no other authority but that which centers in his single person that can act with a vigor proportionate to the extent of such a vast dominion [as the Russian Empire].
(11) Every other form of government whatsoever would not only have been prejudicial to Russia, but would even have proved its entire ruin.
(13) What is the true end of monarchy? Not to deprive people of their natural liberty; but to correct their actions in order to attain the *supreme good.*
(14) The form of government, therefore, which best attains this end and at the same time sets less bounds than others to natural liberty is that which coincides with the views and purposes of rational creatures. . . .
(15) The intention and the end of monarchy is the glory of the citizens, of the state, and of the sovereign.
(16) But, from this glory, a sense of liberty arises in people governed by a monarch, which may produce in these states as much energy in transacting the most important affairs and may contribute as much to the happiness of the subjects as even liberty itself.

Source: W. F. Reddaway, *Documents of Catherine the Great* (New York: Russell and Russell, 1931), pp. 215–217.

Crimea, and to manage its relationship with border peoples such as the Cossacks. Catherine's reign was marked by one of the most massive and best-organized peasant rebellions of the century. Occurring in 1773, the rebellion expressed the grievances of the thousands of peasants who joined its ranks and called for the abolition of serfdom. The revolt took its name, however, from its Cossack leader, Emelian Pugachev (d. 1775), and reflected the dissatisfaction with the Russian government of this semiautonomous people.

The dramatic dilemmas faced by Catherine illustrate both the promise and the costs of state formation throughout Europe. State consolidation permitted the imposition of internal peace, of coordinated economic policy, of reform of justice, but it came at the price of greater—in some cases much greater—control and coercion of the population. Thus, we can see from the alternative perspective of Russia the importance of the political sphere that was opening up in France and was being consolidated in England. It was in that environment, rather than in Russia, that the Enlightenment philosophy could find most fertile ground.

States in Conflict

In the eighteenth century a new constellation of states emerged to dominate politics on the Continent. Along with the traditional powers—England, France, and Austria—were Prussia in central Europe and Russia to the east. Certain characteristics common to all these states account for their dominance. None is more crucial than their various abilities to field effective armies. Traditional territorial ambitions accounted for many wars in the eighteenth century, but the increasing importance of overseas trade and colonization was the most important source of conflict between England and France.

A Century of Warfare: Circumstances and Rationales

The large and small states of Europe continued to make war on each other for both strategic and dynastic reasons. The expense of war, the number of powerful states involved, and the complexities of their interests meant that wars were preceded and carried out with complex systems of alliances and were followed by the adjustments of many borders and the changing control of many bits of territory. We can distinguish certain consistent interests of the major states, however, and some of the circumstances within which all of the states acted.

States fought over territory that had obvious economic and strategic value. A fight over the Baltic coastline, for example, absorbed Sweden and Russia early in the century. Often these conflicts were carried out in arbitrary ways that revealed the dynastic view of territory that still existed. Although rational and defensible "national" borders were important, collecting isolated bits of territory was also still normal. The wars between European powers became extremely complex strategically. France, for example, might choose to strike a blow against Austria by invading an Italian state in order to use the conquered Italian territory as a bargaining chip in eventual negotiations. The principal diplomatic alignment remained the rivalry between France and the Habsburgs, but with the constantly changing involvement of lesser states.

Dynastic claims were not merely strategic ploys but also major causes of war. Indeed, the fundamental instability caused by hereditary rule accounts for many of the major wars of the eighteenth century. The century opened with the War of Spanish Succession, and later the succession of the Austrian Habsburgs would be the cause of a major continental war.

The state of military technology, tactics, and organization also shaped the outcomes of conflicts. In the eighteenth century, weapons and tactics were increasingly refined. More reliable rifles were used. A bayonet that could slip over a rifle barrel and not block the muzzle was invented. Coordinated use of bayonets required even more assured drill of troops than volley fire alone to ensure disciplined action in the face of enemy fire and charges. Artillery and cavalry forces were also subjected to greater standardization of training and discipline in action. Increased discipline of forces meant that commanders could exercise meaningful control over a battle for the first time. Thus, battles had the potential for being massive clashes of forces in the open that could be well enough managed to be decisive. Much fighting of the sixteenth and seventeenth centuries had been materially costly, and the outcome had depended on the slow business of capturing fortresses.

An equally important result of new equipment and tactics was that war became a more expensive proposition than ever before and an ever-greater burden on a state's resources and administration. It became increasingly difficult for small states such as Sweden to compete with the forces that others could mount. Small and relatively poor states, such as Prussia, that did support large forces did so by means of an extraordinary bending of civil society to the economic and social needs of the army. In Prussia, twice as many people were in the armed forces, proportionally, as in other states, and a staggering 80 percent of meager state revenue went to support the army.

Most states introduced some form of conscription in the eighteenth century. In all regions, the very poor often volunteered for army service to improve their lives. However, conscription of peasants, throughout Europe but particularly in Prussia and Russia, imposed a significant burden on peasant communities and a sacrifice of productive members to the state. Governments everywhere supplemented volunteers and conscripts with mercenaries and even criminals, as necessary, to fill the ranks without tapping the wealthier elements of the community. Thus, common soldiers were increasingly seen not as members of society but as its rejects. Said Frederick II, "Useful hardworking people should [not be conscripted but rather] be guarded as the apple of one's eye," and a French war minister agreed that armies had to consist of the "scum of people and of all those for whom society has no use."[1] Brutality became an accepted tool of governments managing such groups of men. From the eighteenth century, the army increasingly became an instrument of social control used to manage and make use of individuals who otherwise would have had no role in society.

But the costs and logistics of maintaining these forces had other outcomes as well. Wars could still be won or lost not on the battlefield but on the supply line. Incentive still existed to bleed civilian populations and to exploit the countryside. Moreover, when supply lines were disrupted and soldiers were not equipped or fed, the armies of a major power could be vulnerable to the small and "unmodernized" armies of lesser states. Finally, neither good generalship nor the discipline of soldiers could be guaranteed, yet both were crucial to success. Culloden, in 1746, was the first battle in which the British army was able decisively to defeat the fierce charge and hand-to-hand fighting of Highland clansmen by holding its position and using disciplined volley fire. Warfare was increasingly professional but was still an uncertain business with unpredictable results.

The Power of Austria and Prussia

Major continental wars had a marked impact on the balance of power among states in western and central Europe. The first of these, now known as the "War of Austrian Succession," began in 1740. Emperor Charles VI died that year without a male heir, and his daughter Maria Theresa succeeded him. Charles VI had worked to shore up his daughter's position as his heir by means of an act called the "Pragmatic Sanction," first issued in 1713. He had negotiated carefully to persuade allies and potential opponents to accept it. The question was not whether a woman could rule, for many women had ruled and did rule other states. A new ruler about whom there was any doubt—a woman, child, or any distant relative might raise doubts—opened the door for rival dynastic claims. Taking advantage of Habsburg vulnerability, in 1740 Frederick II of Prussia invaded the wealthy Habsburg province of Silesia, to which he had a hereditary claim of sorts.

Maria Theresa proved a much more tenacious opponent than Frederick anticipated. In the end, he was lucky to be able to hold onto Silesia, which was at some distance from Maria Theresa's other territories. Although Austrian forces were never able to dislodge Frederick, they did best most of the forces ranged against them by their perpetual opponent, France, and by other German states allied with Frederick. In a preliminary peace signed in 1745, Frederick was confirmed in possession of Silesia, but the imperial throne was returned to the Habsburgs—given to Maria Theresa's husband, who reigned as Francis I (r. 1745–1765). A final treaty in 1748, the Treaty of Aix-la-Chapelle, ended all the fighting that had continued since 1745—mostly by France on the Continent and simultaneous fighting by France and Britain overseas.

The gainers were Prussia and Austria. Austria came out ahead because its succession had not been disrupted and its lands had not been dismembered. Prussia, because of the annexation of Silesia and the psychological imprint of victory, emerged as a power of virtually equal rank to the Habsburgs in Germany. Frederick II was now well placed to make further territorial gains.

Not surprisingly, the power of Prussia provoked the outbreak of the next major war. Indeed, the unprecedented threat that Austria now felt from Prussia caused a veritable revolution in alliances across Europe. So great in Austrian minds was the change in the balance of power that Austria was willing to ally with France, its traditional enemy, in order to isolate Prussia. In the years before what would later be known as the "Seven Years' War" (1756–1763), Austrian officials began to approach France to propose a mutual defensive alliance. Sweden and Russia, with territory to gain at Prussia's expense, joined the alliance system. Sweden wanted to regain territory along the Baltic Sea, and Russia coveted east Prussia, which bordered Russian territory.

Frederick initiated hostilities in 1756, hoping, among other outcomes, to prevent consolidation of the new alliances. Instead, he found that he had started a war against overwhelming odds. What saved him was limited English aid. The English, engaged with France in the overseas conflict known as the "French and Indian War," wanted France to be heavily committed on the Continent. Also helpful to Frederick was Russia's withdrawal from the alliance against him when a new ruler took the throne there in 1762, and at key moments the Prussian army managed two very important successes. Prussia managed to emerge intact—though strained economically and demographically.

The results of the war confirmed Prussia and Austria as the two states of European rank in German-speaking Europe. Their rivalry would dominate German history until the late nineteenth century. The war also demonstrated how fragile even successful states could be and revealed something about what it took for them to be successful. Military victory and the reputation that went with it—even at great cost—could allow a ruler a place on the European stage. The nearness of Prussia's escape also revealed that fortune had a great deal to do with the rise of this state.

The Atlantic World: Trade, Colonization, Competition

The importance of international trade and colonial possessions to the states of western Europe grew dramatically in the eighteenth century. Between 1715 and 1785, Britain's trade with North America rose from 19 to 34 percent of its total trade, and Britain's trade with Asia and Africa rose from 7 to 19 percent of its total. By the end of the century, more than half of all British trade was carried on outside of Europe; for France, the figure was more than a third.

The economic importance of colonies and trade was reflected in the strategic importance of overseas possessions and trading outposts during the century. For the first time, tensions abroad fueled major conflicts between European states. Public opinion, particularly in Britain and France, became increasingly sensitive to colonial issues. Governments were quicker to respond to challenges and perceived threats.

European commercial and colonial energies were concentrated in the Atlantic world in the eighteenth century, because there the profits were greatest. The population of British North America grew from about 250,000 in 1700 to about 1.7 million by 1760. The densely settled New England colonies provided a market for manufactured goods from the mother country, though they produced little by way of raw materials or bulk goods on which traders could make a profit. The colonies of Maryland and Virginia produced tobacco; the Carolinas, rice and indigo (a dyestuff). England re-exported all three throughout Europe at considerable profit.

The French in New France, numbering only 56,000 in 1740, were vastly outnumbered by the British colonists. Nevertheless, the French successfully expanded their control of territory in Canada. Settlements sprang up between the outposts of Montreal and Quebec on the St. Lawrence River. Despite native resistance, the French extended their fur trapping—the source of most of the profits that New France generated—west and north along the Great Lakes, consolidating their hold as they went by building forts. They penetrated as far as the modern Canadian province of Manitoba, where they cut into the British trade run out of Hudson Bay to the north. The French also contested the mouth of the St. Lawrence River and the Gulf of St. Lawrence with the British. The British held Nova Scotia and Newfoundland, the French held parts of Cape Breton Island, and both states fished the surrounding waters.

The commercial importance of all of these holdings, as well as those in Asia, was dwarfed by the European states' Caribbean possessions, however. The British held Jamaica and Barbados; the French, Guadaloupe and Martinique; the Spanish, Cuba and San Domingo; and the Dutch, a few small islands. Sugar produced by slave labor was the major source of profits, along with other cash crops such as coffee, indigo, and cochineal (another dyestuff). The concentration of shipping to this region indicates the region's importance. By the 1760s, the British China trade occupied seven or eight ships. In the 1730s, British trade with Jamaica alone drew three hundred ships. The tiny Dutch possession of Guiana on the South American coast required twice as many visits by Dutch ships as the Dutch East India Company sent into Asia.

The economic dependence of the colonies on slave labor meant that the colonies were tied to their home countries not with a two-way commercial exchange but with a three-way "triangle" trade (Map 20.2). Certain European manufactures were shipped to western ports in Africa, where they were traded for slaves. The enslaved Africans were then shipped to South America, the Caribbean, or North America (see the box, "An African Recalls the Horrors of the Slave Ship"), where planters bought and paid for them with profits generated by sugar and tobacco. Sugar and tobacco were then shipped back to the mother country to be re-exported at great profit throughout Europe. A variety of smaller exchanges also took place. For example, timber from British North America was traded in the Caribbean for sugar or its byproducts molasses and rum. Individual planters in the colonies were not the only ones whose fortunes and status depended on these networks. Merchants in cities such as Bordeaux in France and Liverpool in England were also heavily invested in the slave trade and the re-export business.

The proximity and growth of French and British settlements in North America ensured conflict. The Caribbean and the coasts of Central and South America were strategic flashpoints as well. At the beginning of the eighteenth century, several substantial islands remained unclaimed by any power. The British were making incursions along the coastline claimed by Spain and were trying to break into the monopoly of trade between Spain and Spain's vast possessions in the region.

Great Britain and France: Wars Overseas

In the eighteenth century, England became the dominant naval power in Europe. Its navy protected its far-flung trading networks, its merchant fleet, and the coast of England itself. England had strategic interests on the Continent as well, however. England's interest lay in promoting a variety of powers on the Continent, none of which (or no combination of which) posed too great a threat to England, to its coastline, or to its widespread trading system. From across the Channel, the French appeared a particular threat. They assembled a fleet on more than one occasion and actually dispatched one fleet to aid the cause of rival claimants to the British throne.

A second, dynastic consideration in continental affairs was the electorate of Hanover, the large principality in western Germany that was the native territory of the Hanoverian kings of England. Early in the century especially, the interests of this German territory were of particular importance to the Hanoverian kings and were a significant element in British foreign policy. Unable to field a large army, given their maritime interests, the British sought protection for Hanover in alliances and subsidies for allies' armies on the Continent. The money for these ventures came from the profits on overseas trade.

After the death of Louis XIV in 1715, England's energies centered on colonial rivalries with France, its greatest competitor overseas. There were three major phases of conflict between England and France in colonial regions. The first two were concurrent with the major land wars in Europe: the War of Austrian Succession (1740–1748) and the Seven Years' War (1756–1763). The third phase coincided with the rebellion of British colonies in North America—the American Revolution—beginning in the 1770s. France was inevitably more committed to affairs on the Continent than were the British. The French were able to hold their own successfully in both arenas during the 1740s, but by 1763 they had lost many of their colonial possessions to the English.

In the 1740s, France was heavily involved in the War of Austrian Succession while Britain vied with Spain for certain Caribbean territories. Both France and England also tested each other's strength in scattered colonial fighting, which began in 1744 and produced a few well-balanced gains and losses. Their conquests were traded when peace was made in 1748.

Tension was renewed almost immediately at many of the strategic points in North America. French and British naval forces harassed each other's shipping in the Gulf of St. Lawrence. The French reinforced their encirclement of British colonies with more forts along the Great Lakes and the Ohio River. When British troops (at one point led by the colonial commander George Washington) attempted to strike at these forts, beginning in 1754, open fighting between the French and the English began.

In India, meanwhile, both the French and the British attempted to strengthen their commercial

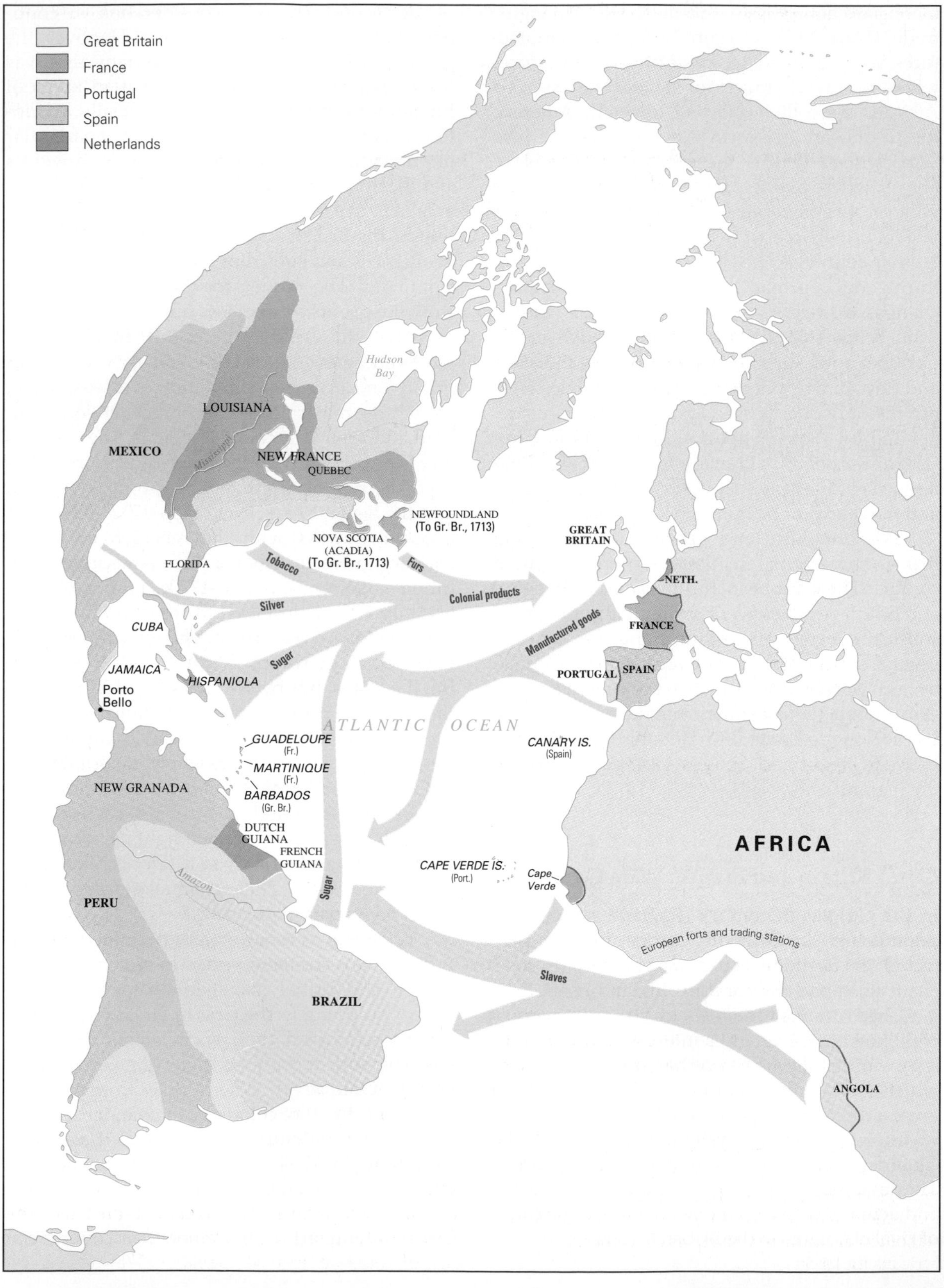

Great Britain
France
Portugal
Spain
Netherlands
Hudson Bay
LOUISIANA
MEXICO
Mississippi
NEW FRANCE
QUEBEC
NEWFOUNDLAND
(To Gr. Br., 1713)
NOVA SCOTIA
(ACADIA)
(To Gr. Br., 1713)
FLORIDA
Tobacco
Furs
Colonial products
GREAT BRITAIN
NETH.
Silver
FRANCE
Manufactured goods
CUBA
Sugar
SPAIN
PORTUGAL
JAMAICA
HISPANIOLA
Porto Bello
ATLANTIC OCEAN
GUADELOUPE
(Fr.)
MARTINIQUE
(Fr.)
BARBADOS
(Gr. Br.)
CANARY IS.
(Spain)
NEW GRANADA
DUTCH GUIANA
FRENCH GUIANA
AFRICA
Amazon
CAPE VERDE IS.
(Port.)
Cape Verde
PERU
Sugar
European forts and trading stations
Slaves
BRAZIL
ANGOLA

An African Recalls the Horrors of the Slave Ship

Olaudah Equiano (ca. 1750–1797) was one of the few Africans sold into slavery in the Americas to leave a written record of his experiences. An Ibo from the Niger region, he first experienced slavery as a boy when kidnapped from his village by other Africans. But nothing prepared him for the brutality of the Europeans who bought and shipped him to Barbados, in the British West Indies. He eventually regained his freedom and received an education.

The first object which saluted my eyes when I arrived on the [African] coast was the sea and a slaveship . . . waiting for its cargo. . . . When I was carried on board I was immediately handled, and tossed up, to see if I were sound, by some of the crew. . . . I was soon put down under the decks, and there I received such a salutation in the nostrils as I had never experienced in my life; so that, with the loathsomeness of the stench . . . I became so sick and low that I was not able to eat. . . . I now wished for the last friend, death, to relieve me; but soon, to my grief, two of the white men offered me eatables; and, on my refusing to eat, one of them held me fast by the hands and laid me across, I think, the windlass, and tied my feet while the other flogged me severely.

One day, when we had a smooth sea and a moderate wind, two of my wearied countrymen, who were chained together, preferring death to such a life of misery, somehow made through the nettings and jumped into the sea; immediately another dejected fellow who [was ill and so not in irons] followed their example. . . . Two of the wretches were drowned, but they got the other and afterwards flogged him unmercifully for thus attempting to prefer death to slavery. In this manner we continued to undergo more hardships than I can now relate. Many a time we were near suffocation for want of fresh air. . . . This, and the stench of the necessary tubs, carried off many.

Source: Philip D. Curtin, *Africa Remembered* (Madison: University of Wisconsin Press, 1967), pp. 92–96.

footholds by making military and political alliances with local Indian rulers. The distintegration of the Mogul Empire facilitated this move, heightening competition among Indian rulers, and reflected a new level of ambition on the part of the European powers in their struggle with each other. A British attack on a French convoy provoked a declaration of war by France in May 1756—three months before fighting in the Seven Years' War broke out in Europe. For the first time, a major war between European nations had started and would be fought in their empires, signifying a profound change in the relation of these nations to the world.

The French had already committed themselves to an alliance with Austria and were increasingly involved on the Continent after Frederick II initiated war there in August 1756. Slowly, the drain of sustaining war both on the Continent and abroad began to tell, and Britain scored major victories against French forces after an initial period of balanced successes and failures. The French lost a number of fortresses on the Mississippi and Ohio rivers and on the Great Lakes and, finally, the interior of Canada with the fall of Quebec and Montreal in 1759 and 1760

Map 20.2 The Atlantic Economy, ca. 1750 The "triangle trade" linked Europe, Africa, and European colonies in the Americas. The most important component of this trade for Europe was the profitable plantation agriculture that depended on enslaved Africans for labor.

(Map 20.3). In the Caribbean, the British seized Guadaloupe, the main French sugar-producing island. Superior resources in India enabled the British to take several French outposts, including Pondicherry, the most important. The sheer cost of involvement on so many fronts meant that French troops were short of money and supplies. They were particularly vulnerable to both supply and personnel shortages—especially in North America—not only because they were weaker than the British at sea but also because the territory they had occupied and fortified remained sparsely settled and dependent on the mother country for food.

By the terms of the Peace of Paris in 1763, France regained Guadaloupe. In India, France retained many of its trading stations but lost its political and military clout. British power in India was enhanced not only by French losses but also by victories over certain local rulers; in the interior Britain now controlled lands that had never before been under the control of any European power. The British also held Canada. They emerged as the pre-eminent world power among European states.

Economic Expansion and Social Change

The eighteenth century was an era of dramatic change, though that change was not always apparent to those who lived through it. The intellectual and cultural ferment of the Enlightenment laid the groundwork for domestic political changes to come, just as British victories in the Seven Years' War shifted the balance of power abroad. More subtle and potentially more profound changes were occurring in the European countryside, however; population, production, and consumption were beginning to grow beyond the bounds that all preceding generations had lived within and taken for granted.

More Food and More People

Throughout European history, there had been a delicate balance between available food and numbers of people to feed. Population growth had accompanied increases in the amount of land under cultivation. From time to time, however, population growth surpassed the ability of the land to produce food, and people became malnourished and prey to disease. In 1348 the epidemic outbreak of bubonic plague known as the "Black Death" struck just such a vulnerable population in decline.

There were few ways to increase the productivity of land. Peasants safeguarded the fertility of the land by alternately cultivating some portions while letting others lie fallow or using them as pasture. Manure provided fertilizer, but during the winter months livestock could not be kept alive in large numbers. Limited food for livestock meant limited fertilizer, which in turn meant limited production of food for both humans and animals.

After the devastating decline of 1348, the European population experienced a prolonged recovery, and in the eighteenth century the balance that had previously been reached began to be exceeded for the first time. Infant mortality remained as high as ever. No less privileged a person than Queen Anne of England outlived every one of the seventeen children she bore, and all but one of them died in infancy. Population growth occurred because of a decline in the death rate for adults and a simultaneous increase in the birthrate in some areas owing to earlier marriages.

Adults were living longer, partly because of a decline in the incidence of the plague. However, the primary reason why adults were living longer, despite the presence of various epidemic diseases, was that they were better nourished and thus better able to resist disease. More and different kinds of food were being produced. The increase in the food supply also meant that more new families could be started.

Food production increased because of the introduction of new crops and other changes in agricultural practices. The cumulative effect of these changes was so dramatic that historians have called them an "agricultural revolution." The new crops included fodder, such as clover, legumes, and turnips, which did not deplete the soil and could be fed to livestock over the winter. The greater availability of animal manure, in turn, boosted grain production. The potato, intro-

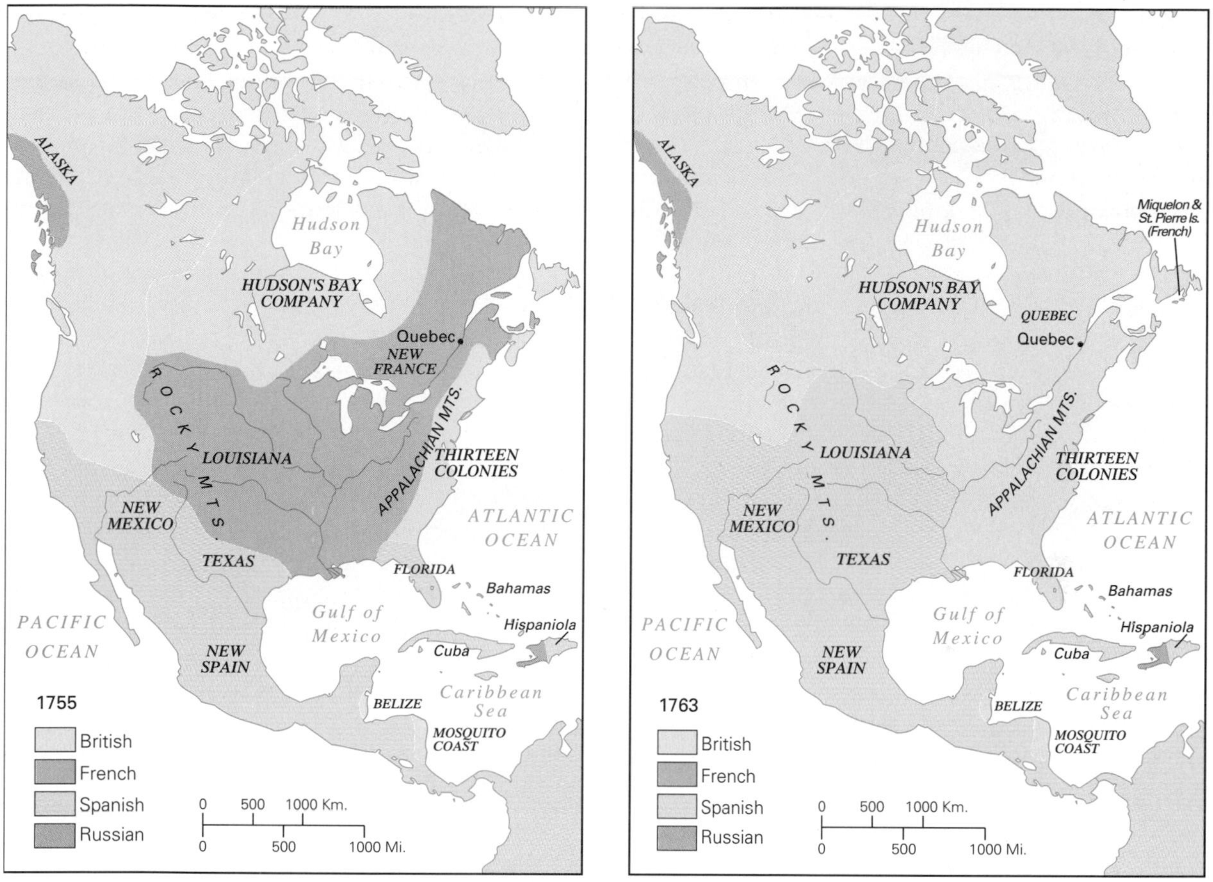

Map 20.3 British Holdings in North America The British colonies on the Atlantic coast were effective staging posts for the armies that ousted the French from North America by 1763. However, taxes imposed on the colonies to pay the costs of the Seven Years' War helped spark revolt—the American Revolution—a decade later.

duced from the Americas in the sixteenth century, produced food for human consumption. The potato is nutrient-dense and can feed more people per acre than can grain. In certain areas, farming families produced potatoes to feed themselves while they grew grain to be sold and shipped elsewhere.

More food being produced meant more food available for purchase. The opportunity to buy food freed up land and labor. A family that could purchase food might decide to convert its farm into a dairy farm. In such a case, many families might be supported from a piece of land that had supported only one family when used for traditional agriculture. Over a generation or two, a number of children might share the inheritance of what had previously been a single farm, yet each could make a living from his or her share, and population could grow as it had not done before.

For centuries farmers had known about many of the crops used for fodder. The fact that the planting of these crops and other changes were long in coming and happened in scattered areas reflects certain political and economic conditions. A farmer had to have control over land in order to institute change. In the traditional open-field system, peasants had split up all land in each community so that each family might have a piece of each field. Making dramatic changes was

Changes in Agriculture This photograph of enclosed farmland in England shows remnants of the long furrows of the open field system, in which each peasant family worked its share of the village's fields. Enclosure had been imposed gradually since the sixteenth century. *(Cambridge University Collection)*

hard when an entire community had to act together. Most important, changing agriculture required capital for seed and fertilizer and for the greater number of people and animals needed to cultivate the new crops. Few rural dwellers had spare capital. Few were inclined to take risks with the production of food and trust the workings of the market. The bad condition of roads alone was reason enough not to rely on distant markets.

Yet where both decent roads and growing urban markets existed, some farmers were willing to produce for urban populations. Cities demanded not only grain but also specialized produce such as dairy products and fruits and vegetables. Thus, farmers had an incentive to make changes such as to dairy farming. Urbanization and improved transportation networks also encouraged agriculture. Human waste produced by city dwellers—known as "night soil"—could be collected and distributed in the surrounding agricultural regions to further increase soil fertility. By the late eighteenth century, pockets of intensive, diversified agriculture existed in England, northern France, the Rhineland in Germany, the Po Valley in Italy, and Catalonia in Spain.

In other areas, changes in agriculture were often accompanied by—indeed caused by—a shift in power in the countryside. Generally, it was wealthy landlords rather than ordinary peasants who had the capital to invest in change and who could cope with the risks of doing so. Where the traditional authority of the village to regulate agriculture was weak, peasants were vulnerable. In England, a combination of weak village structure and inducements to landlords to convert agriculture into more trading wealth created a climate that encouraged landlords to treat land speculatively. To make their holdings more profitable, they raised the rents that farmers paid. They changed cultivation patterns on the land that they controlled directly. They appropriated the village common lands, a process known as "enclosure," and used them for cash crops such as sheep (raised for their wool).

Thus, the agricultural revolution created resources of food to sustain people in Europe generally, but it did not create prosperity. The growth of population did not mean that most people were better-off. Indeed, many people were driven from the land by these changes. Peasants in eastern Europe produced grain for export to the growing urban centers in western Europe, but usually by traditional methods. But in eastern and western Europe, the power and profits of the landlords were a major force in structuring the rural economy.

The Growth of Industry

Agricultural changes forced change in other areas of economic and social life. As more food was grown with less labor, that labor was freed to do other productive work. If there was enough other work to be had—say, making other products that people needed—then the nonagricultural population could continue to grow. If population grew, more and more consumers would be born, and the demand for more goods would help continue the cycle of population growth, changes in production, and economic expansion. This is precisely what happened in the eighteenth century. A combination of forces increased the numbers of people who worked at producing a few essential materials and products (Map 20.4).

There was a dramatic expansion in cottage industry in the eighteenth century, for reasons that were closely related to the changes in the agricultural economy. All agricultural work was seasonal, demanding intensive effort and many hands at certain times but not at others. The labor demands of the new crops meant that an even larger number of people might periodically need nonfarm work in order to make ends meet. Rural poverty, whether as a result of traditional or new agricultural methods, made manufacturing work in the home attractive to more people.

Overseas trade stimulated the expansion of production by spurring the demand in Europe's colonies for cloth and other finished products and spurring the demand at home for manufactured items, such as nails to build the ships on which trade depended. The production of cloth expanded also because heightened demand led to changes in the way cloth was made. Wool was increasingly combined with other fibers to make less expensive fabrics. By the end of the century wholly cotton fabrics were being made cheaply in Europe from cotton grown in America by slave labor.

Steady innovation in production played an important part in the expansion of production because it meant that products were being aimed at a broad market. In the Middle Ages, weavers produced a luxury-quality cloth, and their profits came not from demand, which was relatively low, but from the high price that consumers paid. In the eighteenth century, cloth production became a spur to a transformed industrial economy because cheaper kinds of cloth were made for mass consumption. Producing more became important, and innovations that promoted productivity were soon introduced.

A crucial innovation was increased mechanization. The invention of machines to spin thread in the late eighteenth century brought a marked increase to the rate of production and profound changes to the lives of rural workers who had been juggling agricultural and textile work according to season and need. The selected areas of England, France, and the Low Countries where the new technologies were introduced were on the verge of a massive industrial transformation that would have dramatic social consequences.

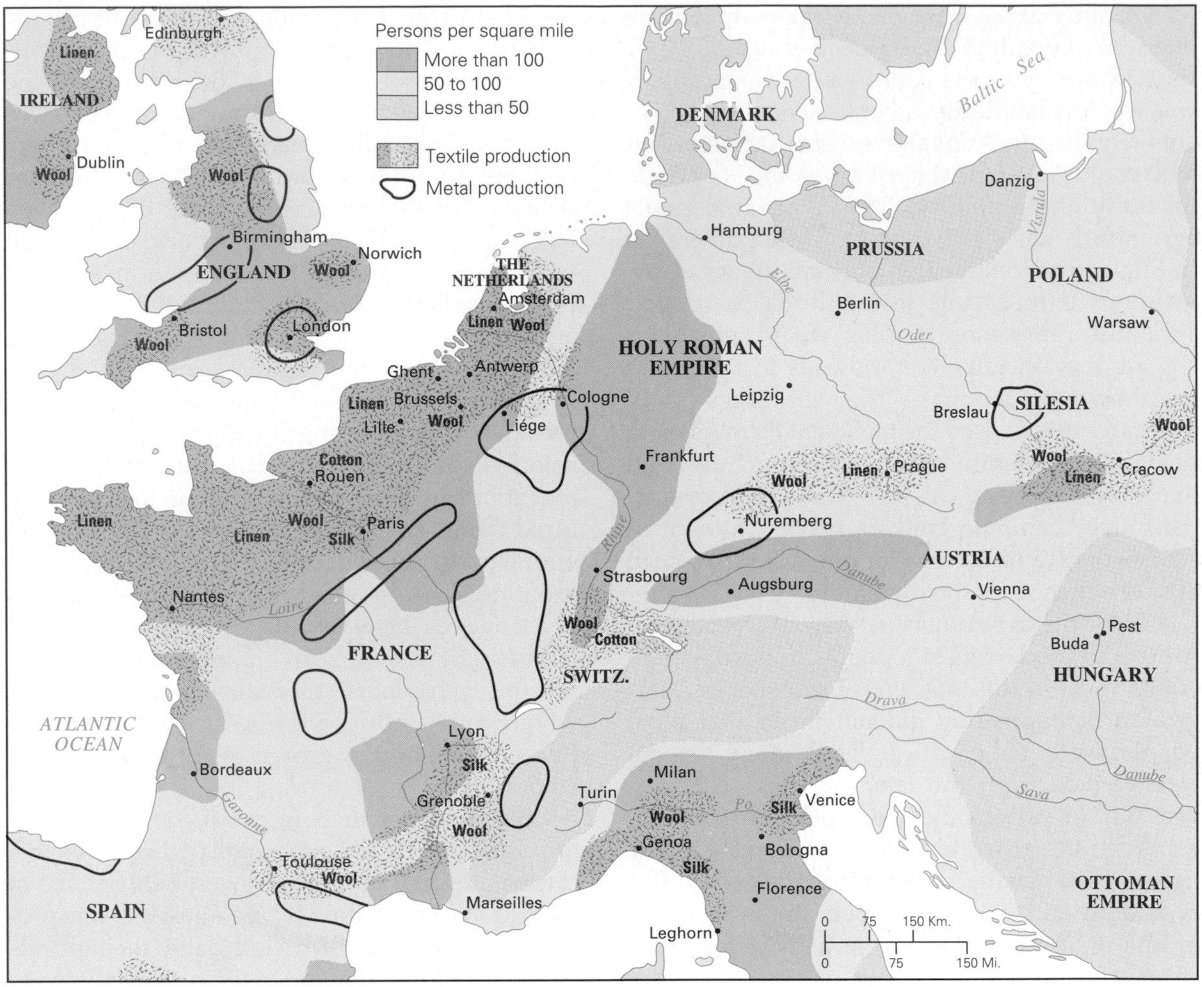

Map 20.4 Population and Production in Eighteenth-Century Europe The growth of cottage industry helped to support a growing population. With changes in agriculture, more land-poor workers were available in the countryside to accept work as spinners, knitters, and weavers.

Control and Resistance

The economic changes of the century produced resistance and adaptation by ordinary people and, at times, direct action by state authorities. Sometimes ordinary people coped in ways that revealed their desperation. In many cities, numbers of abandoned children rose greatly because urban families, particularly recent immigrants from the countryside, could not support their offspring. The major cities of Europe put increasing resources into police forces and city lighting schemes. Charitable institutions run by cities, churches, and central governments expanded. By 1789, for example, there were more than two thousand *hôpitaux*—poorhouses for the destitute and ill—in France. The poor received food and shelter but were forced to work for the city or were forced to live in poorhouses against their will. Men were sometimes taken out of poorhouses and forced to become soldiers.

Resistance and adaptation were particularly visible wherever the needs of common people were at odds with the state's desire for order and

Domestic Industry This picture of women spinning while a family member works a knitting machine is an idealized vision of cottage industry. This interpretation, in which there are no children to watch and no food cooking to tend, represents elite notions about the benefits of domestic industry. *(The British Museum/The Fotomas Index)*

for revenue. Both order and revenue were at issue on the high seas, for example, after piracy was suppressed. Life on the seas was an increasingly vital part of west European economic life, and it began to resemble life on land in the amount of compulsion it included. English-speaking seamen alone numbered about thirty thousand around the middle of the century. The state impinged on the lives of sailors by means of impressment gangs. Sailors in port were always vulnerable to forcible enlistment in the navy, particularly during wartime. A drowsy sailor sleeping off a night of celebrating with new-gotten wages could wake up to find himself aboard a navy ship. Press gangs operated throughout England and not just in major ports, for authorities were as interested in controlling "vagrancy" as in staffing the navy. Merchant captains occasionally filled their crews by such means, particularly when sailing unpopular routes.

Compulsion existed aboard ship also. Sailors could be subjected to brutal discipline and appalling conditions. Seamen attempted to improve their lot by trying to regulate their relationship with ships' captains. Contracts for pay on merchant ships were becoming more regularized, and seamen often negotiated their terms very carefully, including, for example, details about how rations were to be allotted. Sailors might even take bold collective action aboard ship. The English-language term for a collective job action—*strike*—comes from the sailing expression "to strike sail," meaning to lower the sails so that they cannot fill with wind. Its use dates from the eighteenth century, from "strikes" of sailors protesting unfair conditions.

Seafaring men were an unusual group because they were a large and somewhat self-conscious community of workers for wages. Not until industrialization was in full swing a century later would a similar group of workers exist within Europe itself. But economic and political protest by ordinary people on the Continent also showed interesting parallel changes even though strike activity itself would await the large wage labor force of industrialization. Peasant revolts in the past had ranged from small-scale actions against local tax officials to massive uprisings suppressed by an army. The immediate goals of the rebels were usually practical. They aimed not to eliminate taxation altogether but to limit its extent or to protest the collection of a particularly burdensome tax. The political rationale behind such actions was not a hope that the system could be changed but rather a hope that it could be adjusted to operate more fairly. Where there was a revolutionary vision, it was usually a utopian one—a political system with no kings, landlords, taxes, or state of any kind.

Peasant revolts continued to be commonplace and to follow those patterns in the eighteenth century. They were also driven by the localized unemployment caused by agricultural reforms or by objections to press gangs. In certain cases, the peasants, like the sailors, began to confront the state in new ways. Peasants often attacked not state power but the remnants of feudal power wielded by landlords: forced labor, compulsory use of mills, and the remnants of seigneurial authority. They also increasingly marshaled whatever legal devices they could to keep control over their land and thwart landlords' efforts to enclose fields and plant cash or fodder crops. This important, though subtle, change was important because it signaled an effort to bring permanent structural change to economic and legal relationships and not simply a temporary redress of grievances. (See the box, "The Condition of Serfs in Russia.")

In the Pugachev rebellion during the reign of Catherine in Russia are evident both old and new approaches to resisting authority. Pugachev proclaimed himself the legitimate tsar and set up a quasi-imperial court. The movement began among the Ural Cossacks but eventually included thousands of people with traditional grievances against the regime: Cossacks resisting absorption by the state, miners and other poor workers, peasants, and rebellious dissidents. The rebels thus represented a mixture of traditional grievances and acted under the rubric of "tsarist" legitimacy. The rebels' demands were utopian—the elimination of all landlords, all state officials, and all taxation. Less idealistic and with a more modern ring were their demands to end serfdom and their attempts to set up an alternative administration in the areas they controlled. They also tried to assemble a creditable army—inevitably the weak spot of popular uprisings.

Summary

It is important not to exaggerate the degree to which circumstances of life changed in the eighteenth century. The economy was expanding and the population growing beyond previous limits, and the system of production was being restructured. But these changes happened incrementally over many decades and were not recognized for the fundamental changes they were.

Most of the long-familiar material constraints were still in place. Roads, on which much commerce depended, were generally impassable in bad weather. Shipping was relatively dependable and economical—but only relatively. Military life reflected traditional economic and environmental constraints. Despite technological changes and developments of the administrative and economic resources of the state to equip, train, and enforce discipline, the conduct of war was still constrained by problems of transport and supply

The Condition of Serfs in Russia

Generally, the condition of agricultural workers was worst in eastern Europe, where political and economic forces kept them bound in serfdom. In **A Journey from St. Petersburg to Moscow** *(1790), the reform-minded nobleman Alexander Radishchev (1749–1802) describes an encounter with a serf who, like most serfs, was forced to work the lord's lands at the expense of his own.*

A few steps from the road I saw a peasant plowing a field. It was now Sunday, [about midday]. The ploughing peasant, of course, belonged to a landed proprietor, who would not let him pay a commutation tax. The peasant was plowing very carefully. The field . . . was not part of the master's land. He turned the plow with astonishing ease.

"God help you," I said, walking up to the ploughman, who, without stopping, was finishing the furrow he had started. . . . "Have you no time to work during the week, then, and can you not have any rest on Sundays, in the hottest part of the day, at that?"

"In a week, sir, there are six days, and we go six times a week to work on the master's field; in the evening, if the weather is good, we haul to the master's house the hay that is left in the woods. . . . God grant that it rains this evening. If you have peasants of your own, sir, they are praying for the same thing."

"But how do you manage to get food enough [for your family] if you have only the holidays free?"

"Not only the holidays, the nights are ours too."

"Do you work the same way for your master?"

"No, sir, it would be a sin to work the same way. On his fields there are a hundred hands for one mouth, while I have two for seven mouths: you can figure it out for yourself."

Source: Alexander Radishchev, *A Journey from St. Petersburg to Moscow,* trans. Leo Wiener, ed. Roderick Page Thaler (Cambridge, Mass.: Harvard University Press, 1958); quoted in Robert and Elborg Forster, eds., *European Society in the Eighteenth Century* (New York: Harper and Row, 1969), pp. 136–139.

that would have been familiar to warriors two centuries before.

Similarly, though some rulers were inspired by precepts of the Englightenment, all were guided by traditional concerns of dynastic aggrandizement and strategic advantage. One new dimension of relations between states was the importance of conflict over colonies abroad, but the full economic and strategic impact of British colonial gains would not be felt until the next century.

The most visible and dramatic change would happen first in politics, where goals and expectations nurtured by Enlightenment philosophy clashed with the rigid structure of the French state and triggered the French Revolution. The Enlightenment was not simply an intellectual movement that criticized society. It also encompassed the public and private settings where "enlightened" opinion flourished. The revolutionary potential of Enlightenment thought came from belief in its rationality and from the fact that it was both critical of its society but fashionable to practice.

Note

1. Quoted in M. S. Anderson, *Europe in the Eighteenth Century,* 3d ed. (London, Longman, 1987), pp. 218–219.

Weighing the Evidence

GARDENS

What is a garden? We first think of intensely cultivated flower gardens, such as the famous Rose Garden at the White House. We usually don't think of the yards around houses as gardens, yet that is what they are. The landscaping around most ordinary American homes derives from English landscape gardening of the eighteenth century and after—a fact that is reflected in the British custom of calling the "yards" around their homes "gardens." Like most of the art forms that we see habitually, the garden, reproduced in the American backyard, is difficult to analyze or even to think of as an art form. Like the buildings they surround, however, gardens have much to tell us about human habits and values. Let us examine their eighteenth-century ancestors for evidence of contemporaries' attitudes toward nature and their relationship with it.

Look at the two English-style gardens illustrated here. The first is next to the Governor's Mansion in Williamsburg, the capital of the English colony of Virginia. Construction of this garden began at the end of the seventeenth century; the photograph shows the restored gardens that tourists may visit today. The second garden, from the private estate of West Wycombe in England, looks very different—much more like a natural landscape. The engraving reproduced here dates from the 1770s. The two gardens represent distinct epochs in the development of the garden, hence the differences between them. However, each of these gardens in its own way celebrates human domination of nature.

This symbolic domination of nature is more obvious to us in the Williamsburg garden. The lawns and hedges are trimmed in precise geometrical shapes and are laid out, with the walkways, in straight lines. This "palace garden" was a small English variant of the classical garden developed in France—most spectacularly at Versailles Palace—and then imitated throughout Europe during the seventeenth century. At Versailles, the garden is so vast that at many points all of nature visible to the eye is nature disciplined by humans.

We can think of such gardens as pieces of architecture, because that is how they were originally conceived: The design originated in the enclosed courtyard gardens of the homes of classical antiquity. The straight lines and squared

The Governor's Mansion and Formal Gardens at Williamsburg, Virginia
(© Robert Llewellyn)

Landscape Garden at West Wycombe, England *(Courtesy of the Trustees of the British Museum)*

shapes of these gardens mimic the buildings they are attached to. In fact, these seventeenth- and eighteenth-century gardens were usually laid out as an extension of the building itself. Notice the wide staircase that descends from the central axis of the Governor's Mansion into the central walkway of the garden. Other architectural details, such as the benches positioned at the ends of various walkways, add to the sense of the garden as an exterior room. Elsewhere, this sense was enhanced by the construction of devices such as grottoes, such as that at Versailles (see page 681). The garden symbolizes the taming of nature into a pleasing vision of order and regularity.

The later, eighteenth-century garden represents even greater confidence in the human relationship with nature, although it does not appear to do so at first glance. The extensive gardens at first seem to be nature itself plus a few added details, such as the statuary, and a few improvements, such as the grass kept trim by the workers in the foreground. Our familiarity with such landscapes—in our own suburban yards—keeps us from immediately perceiving how contrived such a landscape is. Nature, however, does not intersperse dense stands of trees or clumps of shrubbery with green expanses of lawns. Nor does nature conveniently leave portions of a hillside bare of trees to provide a view of the water from the palatial house, to the left on the hill. Note also that the waterfall cascading over rocks and statuary flows from an artificial lake, neatly bordered by a path.

This kind of garden reflects Enlightenment optimism about humans' ability to understand and work with nature. Such gardens were asymmetrical: Paths were usually curved, and lakes and ponds were irregularly shaped, as they would be in nature. Trees and shrubs were allowed to maintain their natural form. Nevertheless, this landscaping conveys a powerful message of order. Humans cannot bend or distort nature to their own ends, but they can live in harmony with it as they manage it and enjoy its beneficence. People were freed from regarding nature as hostile and needing to be fought. In this garden, one lives with nature but improves upon it. The workers cutting the grass do not detract from the engraving but rather make the scene more compelling.

This brand of landscape gardening appeared in English colonies across the Atlantic by the end of the eighteenth century. One of the best examples is at Monticello, Thomas Jefferson's Virginia estate, first designed in the 1770s and constructed and improved over the remainder of Jefferson's life (1743–1826). If you tour Monticello, you will notice a curving garden path bordered by flowers in season, with mature trees scattered here and there. Jefferson, we know, planned every inch of this largely random-looking outdoor space, just as he planned the regimented fruit and vegetable garden that borders it. The older classical style of the Williamsburg garden is partly explained by its earlier date and also because this more aggressively controlling style lasted longer in the American colonies than in Europe, perhaps because "nature" seemed more wild and still more formidable in the New World. You might wish to consider the curious blend of "nature" and order that is evident in the landscapes we create and live with today.

Suggested Reading

General Surveys

Anderson, M. S. *Europe in the Eighteenth Century, 1713–1783.* 3d ed. 1987.

Doyle, William. *The Old European Order, 1660–1800.* 1978.

Treasure, Geoffrey. *The Making of Modern Europe, 1648–1780.* 1985. Three general histories covering political, social, economic, and cultural developments; each has an extensive bibliography.

The Enlightenment

Chartier, Roger. *The Cultural Uses of Print in Early Modern France.* 1987. A discussion of changes in reading habits and in the uses of printed materials throughout the eighteenth century in France.

Darnton, Robert. *The Literary Underground of the Old Regime.* 1982. One of several important works by Darnton on the social history of print culture.

Fox-Genovese, Elizabeth. "Women and the Enlightenment." In Renate Bridenthal et al., eds., *Becoming Visible: Women in European History.* 2d edition, 251–278. 1987. A discussion of the role of women in the Enlightenment and various thinkers' attitudes toward women and gender.

Gay, Peter. *The Enlightenment: An Interpretation.* 2 vols. 1966–1969. A detailed study of Enlightenment thought by one of its foremost modern interpreters.

———. *Voltaire's Politics.* 1959. A lively introduction to Voltaire's career as a political and social reformer.

Hampson, Norman. *The Enlightenment.* 1968. A useful general survey.

Hazard, Paul. *The European Mind.* 1935. An older but still useful interpretation that depicts a European intellectual crisis between 1680 and 1715.

State Building and Warfare

Carsten, F. L. *The Origins of Prussia.* 1982. An introduction to the growth of the Prussian state in the seventeenth and eighteenth centuries.

Ford, Franklin. *Robe and Sword.* 1953. A path-breaking though controversial study of the consolidation of aristocratic power in France in the eighteenth century.

Gagliardo, John. *Enlightened Despotism.* 1968. A general introduction to the concept and to the rulers of the era.

Hubatsch, Walter. *Frederick the Great.* 1981. A recent biography that illuminates Frederick's system of government.

Kennedy, Paul. *The Rise and Fall of British Naval Mastery.* 1976. The authoritative work on the rise of British seapower from the sixteenth century to modern times.

Madariaga, Isobel de. *Russia in the Age of Catherine the Great.* 1981. The best recent biography of Catherine.

See also the works by Evans, Howard, Geoffrey Parker, Riasanovsky, and Vierhaus cited in Chapter 18.

Early Modern Economy and Society

Cipolla, Carlo. *Before the Industrial Revolution.* 1976. The most comprehensive single treatment of the development of the European economy and technology through this period.

De Vries, Jan. *The Economy of Europe in an Age of Crisis, 1600–1750.* 1976. Essential reading for understanding the changes in Europe's economy and in its trade and colonial relationships throughout the world.

Gullickson, Gay. *Spinners and Weavers of Auffay.* 1986.

Gutman, Myron P. *Toward the Modern Economy.* 1988. Two works that focus on specific communities in western Europe and thus provide compelling, detailed analyses of the changes in the European economy in the seventeenth and eighteenth centuries.

Hufton, Olwen. *The Poor of Eighteenth-Century Paris.* 1974. An analysis of the lives of the poor and the responses of the state.

Laslett, Peter. *The World We Have Lost.* 1965. An innovative study of premodern society and culture, emphasizing the differences in habits and values that separate our society from preindustrial times.

Parry, J. H. *Trade and Dominion: The European Overseas Empires in the Eighteenth Century.* 1971. A reliable survey of developments.

PLUS DE ROI
PATRIE
EGALITE
LIBERTE

CHAPTER 21

Revolutionary Europe, 1789–1815

One day in early July 1792, a troop of national guardsmen from the city of Marseilles in southern France marched into Paris, singing as they came:

Allons enfants de la patrie, Le jour de gloire est arrivé! Contre nous de la tyrannie L'étendard sanglant est levé!	(Come, children of the nation, The day of glory is at hand! Against us is raised The bloody standard of tyranny!)

Their song quickly became famous as the *Marseillaise*, and three years later was officially declared the French national anthem. This choice is appropriate, for the French Revolution, which was unfolding that July, profoundly shaped the growth and character of modern France.

Today the Revolution is considered the initiation of modern European as well as modern French history. The *Marseillaise* had been composed some months earlier by a French army captain in Alsace, where French troops were facing Austrian and German forces. Events in France reverberated throughout Europe because the overthrow of absolute monarchy threatened other monarchs. Revolutionary fervor on the part of ordinary soldiers compensated for inexperience, and France's armies unexpectedly bested many of their opponents. By the late 1790s, the armies of France would be led in outright conquest of other European states by one of the most talented generals in European history: Napoleon Bonaparte. What he brought to the continental European nations that his armies eventually conquered was a fascinating amalgam of imperial aggression and revolutionary fervor. Europe was transformed both by the changing balance of power and by the spread of revolutionary ideas.

Scene of August 10, 1792, by Gérard.

Revolution is a messy business. Understanding the French Revolution means understanding not only how it began but also the complicated course it took and why, together with the significance of those events. Part of the Revolution's significance lay in the power of symbols, such as the *Marseillaise*, to challenge an old political order and to legitimate a new one. Challenges to the power of the king were not new, but the Revolution overthrew his right to rule at all. The notion that the people constituted the nation, were responsible as citizens, and had some right to representation in government replaced a system of government by inherited privilege. Louis XVI was transformed from the divinely appointed father of his people to an enemy of the people, worthy only of execution. But on the day in 1792 the men from Marseilles marched into Paris, none of this was clear.

The Age of Revolution

"I am a citizen of the world," wrote John Paul Jones, a captain of the fledgling United States Navy, in 1778. He was writing to a Scottish aristocrat, apologizing for the conduct of men under his command who had raided the lord's estate while conducting coastal raids against the British Isles during the American Revolution. Jones (1747–1792) himself was a Scotsman. He had begun a life at sea as a boy. He was one of the thousands of cosmopolitan Europeans who were familiar with European cultures on both sides of the Atlantic. As a sailor, Jones literally knew his way around the Atlantic world. He was a "citizen of the world" in another sense as well. When the Scotsman, Lord Selkirk, wrote back to Jones, he expressed surprise that his home had been raided because he was sympathetic to the American colonists. Like Jones, he said, he was a man of "liberal sentiments."[1] Both Jones and Lord Selkirk felt they belonged to an international society of gentlemen who recognized certain principles regarding just and rational government that grew out of the Enlightenment.

In the Atlantic world of the late eighteenth century, both practical links of property and trade and shared ideals about "liberty" were important shaping forces. The strategic interests of the great European powers were also always involved. Thus, when the American colonists actively resisted British rule and then in 1776 declared their independence from Britain, there were many consequences: British trading interests were challenged, French appetites for gains at British expense were whetted, and illusive notions of "liberty" seemed more plausible and desirable. The victory of the American colonies in 1783, followed by the creation of the United States Constitution in 1787, further heightened the appeal of liberal ideas elsewhere. There were other attempts at liberal reform, notably in Ireland and the Netherlands, but the American Revolution had the most direct impact on later events in France because the French had been directly involved in the American effort.

Revolutionary Movements Around Europe

While the British government was facing the revolt of the American colonies, it also confronted trouble closer to home. The war against the American colonies was not firmly supported by Britons. Like many Americans, many Britons had divided loyalties, and many others were convinced that the war was being mismanaged. The prosecution of the war against the American colonies proceeded amid calls for reform of the ministerial government.

In this setting, a reform movement in Ireland began to spring up in 1779. The reformers demanded greater autonomy from Britain. Inspired by the American rebels, they were in an alliance of sorts with British politicians who were suspicious of Crown and ministers. Like the Americans, Irish elites felt like disadvantaged junior partners in the British Empire. They chafed over British policies that favored British imperial interests over those of the Irish ruling class—for example, the exclusion of Irish ports from much trade in favor of English and Scottish ports and the granting of political rights to Irish Catholics so that they might fight in Britain's overseas armies.

Protestant Irish landlords, threatened by such policies, expressed their opposition not only in parliamentary but also in military ways. Following the example of the American rebels, middle- and upper-class Anglo-Irish set up a system of locally sponsored voluntary militia to resist British troops if necessary. The Volunteer Movement was undercut but not wiped out when greater parliamentary autonomy for Ireland was granted in 1782, following the repeal of many restrictions on Irish commerce. Unlike the Americans, the Irish elites faced an internal challenge to their own authority—the Catholic population whom they had for centuries dominated. That challenge forced them to reach an accommodation with the British government.

Meanwhile, a political crisis with constitutional overtones was also brewing in the Netherlands. Tensions between the aristocratic stadtholders of the house of Orange and the merchant oligarchies of the major cities were heightened during the American Revolution, because the Dutch were then engaged in a commercial war against the British, to whom the stadtholder was supposed to be sympathetic. The conflict ceased to be wholly traditional for two reasons. First, the representatives of the various cities, calling themselves the Dutch "Patriot" party, defended their position in the name of the traditional balance of powers within the Netherlands as well as with wider claims to "liberty" like those of the American revolutionaries. Second, the challenge to traditional political arrangements widened when middling urban dwellers, long disenfranchised by these oligarchies, demanded "liberty" too—that is, political enfranchisement in the cities—and briefly took over the Patriot movement. Just as many Irish rebels accepted the concessions of 1782, many "Patriot" oligarchs in the Netherlands did nothing to resist an invasion in 1787 that restored the power of the stadtholder, the prince of Orange, and thereby ended the challenge to their own control of urban government.

Both the Irish "volunteers" and the Dutch "Patriots," though very limited movements, echoed the American rebels in practical and ideological ways. Both were influenced by the economic and political consequences of Britain's relationship with its colonies. Both were inspired by the success of the American rebels and their thoroughgoing claims for political self-determination.

The American Revolution and the Kingdom of France

As one of Britain's greatest commercial and political rivals, France naturally was drawn into Britain's struggle with its North American colonies. The consequences for France were momentous for two reasons. First, the cost of French aid for the American rebels was so great that it helped accelerate a financial crisis in the French monarchy. Second, French involvement directly exposed many French aristocrats and common soldiers to the "enlightened" international com-

Marie-Joseph, Marquis de Lafayette, is depicted commanding troops during the American Revolution. Called the "hero of two worlds," Lafayette returned to France to become one of the most important aristocratic reformers during the French Revolution. He favored a constitutional monarchy and opposed republican rule. *(Jean-Loup Charmet)*

munity to which John Paul Jones felt he belonged, though the absolute monarchy of France turned a cold shoulder toward "liberal" ideas.

Rivalry with Great Britain gave France a special relationship with the American colonies and their fight for independence. In the Seven Years' War (1756–1763), the French had lost many of their colonial settlements and trading outposts to the English. Stung by this outcome, certain courtiers and ministers pressed for an aggressive colonial policy that would regain for France some of the riches in trade that Britain was threatening to monopolize. The American Revolution seemed to offer the perfect opportunity.

The French extended covert aid to the Americans from the very beginning of the conflict in 1775. After the first major defeat of British troops by the Americans—at the battle of Saratoga in 1777—France formally recognized the independent United States and established an alliance with them. The French then committed troops as well as monetary support for American forces. John Paul Jones's most famous ship, the *Bonhomme Richard*, was purchased and outfitted in France at French government expense, as were many other American naval vessels during the war. French support was decisive. In 1781 the French fleet kept reinforcements from reaching the British force besieged at Yorktown by George Washington. The American victory at Yorktown ended the war and won recognition of the colonies' independence.

The effect of the alliance on France was complicated. Aid for the Americans saddled France with a debt of about 1 million *livres* (pounds), which represented as much as one quarter of the total debt that the French government was trying to service. A less tangible impact of the American Revolution was also important. About nine thousand French soldiers, sailors, and aristocrats participated in the war. For many, the war was simply employment. For others, it was a quest of sorts. For them, the promise of the Enlightenment—belief in the rationality of men, natural rights, and natural laws by which society should be organized—was brought to life in America.

Exposure to the American conflict occurred at the French court too. Beginning in 1775, a permanent American mission to Versailles lobbied hard for aid and later managed the flow of that assistance. The chief emissary of the Americans was Benjamin Franklin (1706–1790), a philosophe by French standards, whose writings and scientific experiments were already known to French elites. His talents—among them, a skillful exploitation of a simple Quaker-like demeanor—succeeded in promoting the idealization of America at the French court.

The United States Constitution and the various state constitutions and the debates surrounding them were all published in Paris and were much discussed in salons and at court. America became the prototype of what Enlightenment philosophy said was possible. America was hailed as the place where the irrationalities of inherited privilege did not prevail. A British observer, Arthur Young (1741–1820), noted at the time that "the American revolution has laid the foundation of another in France, if [the French] government does not take care of itself."[2]

By the mid-1780s, there was no longer a question of whether the French regime would experience reform but rather what form the reform would take. The royal government was almost bankrupt. A significant minority of the politically active elite was convinced of the fundamental irrationality of France's system of government. Nevertheless, the cataclysmic proportions that the French Revolution eventually reached raise questions about the position of the monarchy and why less drastic change did not happen. A dissatisfied elite and a financial crisis do not necessarily lead to revolution. Why did the French government—the *Ancien Régime*, or "Old Regime," as it became known after the Revolution—not take care of itself?

The Crisis of the Old Regime

The Old Regime was brought to the point of crisis in the late 1780s by three factors: (1) an antiquated system for collecting revenue, as well as old and recent debts; (2) institutional constraints on the monarchy that defended privileged interests; and (3) elite public opinion that envisioned thoroughgoing reform and pushed the monarchy in that direction. Another factor was the ineptitude of the king, Louis XVI (r. 1774–1793).

Louis came to the throne in 1774, a year before the American Revolution began. He was a kind, well-meaning man better suited to carry out the finite responsibilities of a petty bureaucrat than to be king. The queen, the Austrian Marie Antoinette, was unpopular. She was regarded with suspicion by those for whom the alliance with Austria had never felt natural. She too was politically inept, unable to negotiate the complexities of court life, and widely rumored to be selfishly wasteful of royal resources despite the realm's financial crises.

The fiscal crisis of the monarchy had been a long time in the making and was an outgrowth of the system in which the greatest wealth was protected by traditional privileges. At the top of the social and political pyramid were the nobles, a legal grouping that included warriors and royal officials. In France, nobility conferred exemption from much taxation. Thus, the royal government could not directly tax its wealthiest subjects.

This situation existed throughout much of Europe, a legacy of the individual contractual relationships that had formed the political and economic framework of medieval Europe. Unique to France was the strength of the institutions that defended this system. Of particular importance were the royal law courts, the parlements, which claimed a right of judicial review over royal edicts. All the Parlementaires—well-educated professional lawyers and judges—were noble and loudly defended the traditional privileges of all nobles. Louis XV (d. 1774), near the end of his life, had successfully undermined the power of the parlements by a bold series of moves. Louis XVI, immediately after coming to the throne, buckled under pressure and restored the parlements to full power.

Deficit financing had been a way of life for the monarchy for centuries. After early efforts at reform, Louis XIV (d. 1715) had reverted to common fund-raising expedients such as selling offices, which only added to the weight of privileged investment in the old order. England had established a national bank to free its government from the problem, but the comparable French effort early in the century had been undercapitalized and had failed. Late in the 1780s, under Louis XVI, one-fourth of the annual operating expenses of the government was borrowed, and half of all government expenditure went to paying interest on its debt.

Sois satisfaite, il va rejoindre Maurepas

Criticism of Marie Antoinette In a satirical engraving from 1787, the Queen toasts the dismissal of a reforming minister. She wears a famous diamond necklace that had caused scandal and widespread criticism of the monarchy two years before; it was a gift from a cardinal with whom the queen was wrongly accused of having an affair. *(Musée Carnavalet/Jean-Loup Charmet)*

Short-term economic crises added to the cumulative problem of government finance. During Louis's reign there were several years of disastrously poor harvests, and throughout the reign there was a downturn in the economy. The weakness of the economy proved to be a crucial component in the failure of overall reform.

The king employed able finance ministers who tried to institute fundamental reforms, such as replacing the tangle of taxes with a simpler system in which all would pay and eliminating local tariffs, which were stifling commerce. The parlements and many courtiers and aristocrats, as well as ordinary people, resisted these policies. Few trusted the "free market" (free from traditional trade controls) for grain; most feared that speculators would buy up the grain supply and people would starve. Trying to implement such reforms in a time of grain shortage almost guaranteed their failure. Moreover, many supported the parlements out of self-interest and because they were the only institution capable of standing up to the monarchy.

Not all members of the elite joined the parlements in opposing reform. The imprint of "enlightened" public opinion shaped in salons and literary societies was apparent in the thinking of some aristocrats, who believed that the government and the economic system as a whole needed reform and debated the nature and extent of reform needed.

In 1787, the king called an "Assembly of Notables"—an ad hoc group of elites—to support him in facing down the parlements and proceeding with some reforms. He found little support

Mocking the Old Regime This cartoon from 1789 depicts a robed judge, a clergyman in vestments, and the king himself, whip in hand, "riding" the wretched representative of the common people. The figures in the cartoon brandish documents that proclaim their traditional privileges. By 1789 the fundamental bases of Old Regime society were under attack. *(The Bettmann Archive)*

even among men known to be sympathetic to reform. Some did not support particular reforms, and many were reluctant to allow the monarchy free rein. Others, reflecting the influence of the American Revolution, maintained that a "constitutional" body such as the Estates General, which had not been called since 1614—needed to make these decisions.

Ironically, nobles and clergy who were opposed to reform supported the call for the Estates General, for they assumed that they could control its deliberations. The three Estates met and voted by "order"—clergy (First Estate), nobles (Second Estate), and commoners (Third Estate)—each meeting and voting separately. It was assumed that the votes of the clergy and nobles would nullify whatever the Third Estate might propose.

In 1788, popular resistance to reform in the streets of Paris and mounting pressure from his courtiers and bureaucrats induced Louis to summon the Estates General. On Louis's orders, deputies to the Estates General were elected by intermediate assemblies chosen by wide male suffrage. Louis assumed there was widespread loyalty to the monarchy in the provinces, and he wished to tap into it by means of this voting. Louis also agreed that the Third Estate should have twice as many deputies as the other two Estates, but he did not authorize voting by head rather than by order, which would have brought about the dominance of the Third Estate. Nevertheless, he hoped that the specter of drastic proposals put forth by the Third Estate would frighten the aristocrats and clergy into accepting some of his reforms. (See the box, "Louis XVI's Subjects State Their Grievances.")

Louis faced a critical situation when the Estates General convened in May 1789. As ever, he faced immediate financial crisis. He also faced a constitutional crisis. There was already a sense of legitimacy about the Estates General, about the role of the Third Estate, and about the authority of the Third Estate to enact change. Political pamphlets abounded arguing that the Third Estate deserved enhanced power because it carried the mandate of the people. The most important of them was *What Is the Third Estate?* (1789) by Joseph Emmanuel Sieyès (1748–1836), a church official from the diocese of Chartres. The sympathies of Abbé Sieyès, as he was known, were with the Third Estate—his career had suffered because he was not noble. Sieyès argued that the Third Estate represented the nation because it did not reflect special privilege.

Among the deputies of the first two Estates—clergy and nobility—were men, like the marquis de Lafayette (1757–1834), who were sympathetic to reform. More important, the elections had returned to the Third Estate a large majority of deputies who reflected the most radical political thought possible for men of their standing. Most were lawyers and other professionals who were functionaries in the government but, like Sieyès, of low social rank. They frequented provincial academies, salons, and political societies. They were convinced of their viewpoints and determined on reform and had little stake in the system as it was. When this group convened and met with resistance from the First and Second Estates and from Louis himself, they seized the reins of government and a revolution began.

1789: The Revolution Begins

The three Estates met at Versailles, but the opening of the Estates General was celebrated first in Paris with a solemn procession and religious services attended by all the participants—the last public ritual of the Old Regime. The three Estates marched separately—the clergy arrayed in magnificent vestments, the nobles decked out in furs and velvet, the "commoners" dressed in simple black bringing up the rear. Neither this staged portrayal of social distinctions, nor the spectacularly presented king and queen, nor the religious symbolism that linked monarchy to divine order could conceal the political conflicts.

As soon as the three Estates began to meet, the conflicts surfaced. The ineptness of the Crown was immediately clear. On the first day of the meetings, Louis and his ministers failed to introduce a program of reforms for the deputies to consider. This failure raised doubt about the monarchy's commitment to reform. More important, it allowed the political initiative to pass to the Third Estate. The deputies boldly challenged the Crown's insistence that the three Estates meet and vote separately. Deputies to the Third Estate refused to be certified (that is, to have their credentials officially recognized) as members of only

Louis XVI's Subjects State Their Grievances

Before each meeting of the Estates General, French subjects drew up lists of grievances that they hoped the Estates would address. The grievances in 1789 reveal the perennial concerns of unfair taxation and other economic burdens. They also reveal both faith in the king and a consciousness of the Estates as an embodiment of the "nation." The complaints cited here, offered by ordinary villagers, were often sophisticated but not revolutionary.

Excerpts from Grievances of the Inhabitants of Erceville (North of Orléans)

The said inhabitants hope that the goodness of the King, in whom they put all their confidence, and the enlightenment of the Estates-General will reform the abuses which have crept into finances, so that the money collected from them no longer passes through so many hands, but goes directly to the treasury to provide for the needs of the state. . . .

The said inhabitants observe that they alone have been charged with the mass of taxes, while their [landlord], who farms much of the land in the parish, enjoys total exemption, although he has had a great part of the land planted with woods, which are populated by game that devastates the rest of the countryside . . . wherefore they ask that . . . without any distinction of title or rank, the said [lord] be taxed like them.

[The inhabitants] petition that all taxes be abolished which were not consented to by the Nation assembled . . . and that in the future no tax can be established with the consent of the whole Nation assembled in the Estates-General.

Excerpts from Grievances of the Inhabitants of Lion-en-Sullias (South of Orléans)

Let it please [the king] to have the Estates-General assemble often and to alleviate their woes and their misery by granting them a discharge from the obligations of the [many different taxes] with which they are burdened, substituting a single tax in kind at a rate in proportion to the scanty harvests they collect on their infertile ground. . . .

Relying on His Majesty's paternal goodness, they dare to hope that he . . . will exempt their sons and domestics from militia service in order to let them attend to the cultivation of the land.

Source: Philip Dawson, ed., *The French Revolution* (Englewood Cliffs, N.J.: Prentice-Hall, 1967), pp. 25–26, 30–32.

the Third Estate rather than as members of the Estates General as a whole.

For six weeks the Estates General was unable to meet officially, and the king did nothing to break the impasse. During this interlude, the determination of the deputies of the Third Estate strengthened. More and more deputies were won over to the notion that the three Estates should meet together and that the reform process must begin in the most systematic way: France must have a written constitution.

By the middle of June, more than thirty reformist members of the clergy were sitting jointly with the Third Estate, which had invited all deputies from all three Estates to meet and be certified together. On June 17, the Third Estate simply declared itself the National Assembly of France. The issue of credentials would no longer be bothered with. At first, the king did nothing, but when the deputies arrived to meet on the morning of June 20, they discovered they had been locked out of the hall. Undaunted, they assembled instead in a nearby indoor tennis court and produced the document that has come to be known as the "Tennis Court Oath." It was a collective pledge to meet until a written constitution had been achieved. Only one deputy refused to support it. Sure of their mandate, the deputies had assumed the reins of government.

The king continued to handle the situation with both ill-timed self-assertion and attempts at compromise. As more and more deputies from the First and Second Estates joined the National Assembly, Louis "ordered" the remaining loyal deputies to join it too. Simultaneously, however, he ordered troops to come to Paris. He feared disorder in the wake of the recent disturbances throughout France and believed that any challenge to the legitimacy of arbitrary monarchial authority would be disastrous.

The appeal for armed assistance stirred unrest in the capital. Paris, with a population of about 600,000 in 1789, was one of the largest cities in Europe. There were thousands of workers in all trades plus thousands more—perhaps one-tenth of the inhabitants—jobless recent immigrants from the countryside. Paris was the political nerve center of the nation—the site of the publishing industry, salons, the homes of Parlementaires and royal ministers. The city was both extremely volatile and extremely important to the stability of royal power. The king's call for troops aroused Parisians' suspicions. Some assumed that there was a plot afoot to starve Paris and destroy the National Assembly. Already they considered the Assembly to be a guarantor of acceptable government.

It took little—the announcement of the dismissal of a reformist finance minister—for Paris to erupt in demonstrations and looting. Crowds besieged City Hall and the royal armory, where they seized thousands of weapons. A popular

The Tennis Court Oath It was raining on June 20 when the deputies found themselves barred from their meeting hall and sought shelter in the royal tennis court. Their defiance created one of the turning points of the Revolution; the significance was recognized several years later by this painting's artist. *(Photographie Bulloz)*

Storming the Bastille The crowd was convinced that the Bastille held political prisoners as well as a large supply of arms. In fact, it held neither. Thousands of Parisians—including artisans and shopkeepers and not merely desperate rabble—surrounded the fortress and forced the garrison to surrender. *(Photographie Bulloz)*

militia formed as citizens armed themselves. Armed crowds assailed other symbols and sites of royal authority, including the huge fortified prison, the Bastille, on the morning of July 14. Like the troops at the armory, the guards at the Bastille were not given an order to fire on the crowds. The garrison eventually surrendered, convinced that it would be allowed to go free; instead, several members were murdered by the crowd.

The citizens' victory was a great embarrassment to royal authority. The king immediately had to embrace the popular movement. He came to Paris and in front of crowds at City Hall donned the red and blue cockade worn by the militia and ordinary folk as a badge of resolve and defiance. This symbolic action signaled the legitimation of politics based on new principles.

Encouraged by events in Paris, inhabitants of cities and towns around France staged similar uprisings. In many, the machinery of royal government completely broke down. City councils, officials, and even Parlementaires were thrown out of office. Popular militias took control of the

Declaration of the Rights of Man and the Citizen

Each of the articles of the Declaration was a response to some feature of Old Regime society or law that was now deemed unacceptable.

Preamble: The representatives of the French people, organized as a National Assembly, believing that the ignorance, neglect, or contempt of the rights of man are the sole cause of public calamities and the corruption of governments, have determined to set forth in a solemn declaration the natural, inalienable, and sacred rights of man. . . .

(1) Men are born and remain free and equal in rights. Social distinctions may be founded only upon the general good.
(2) The aim of all political association is the preservation of the natural and imprescriptible rights of man. These rights are liberty, property, security, and resistance to oppression.
(3) The principle of all sovereignty resides essentially in the nation. No body or individual may exercise any authority which does not proceed directly from the nation.
(6) Law is the expression of the general will. Every citizen has the right to participate personally, or through his representative, in its formation. It must be the same for all. . . . All citizens, being equal in the eyes of the law, are equally eligible to all dignities and to all public positions and occupations, according to their abilities, and without distinction except that of their virtues and talents.
(11) The free communication of ideas and opinions is one of the most precious rights of man. . . .
(13) A common contribution is essential for the maintenance of the public forces and for the cost of administration. This should be equitably distributed among all the citizens in proportion to their means.

Source: James Harvey Robinson, *Readings in European History* (Boston: Ginn, 1906), pp. 409–411.

streets. There was a simultaneous wave of uprisings in rural areas. Most of them were the result of food shortages, but their timing added momentum to the more strictly political protests in urban areas. These events forced the members of the National Assembly to work energetically on the constitution and to pass legislation to satisfy popular protests against economic and political privileges.

On August 4 the Assembly issued a set of decrees abolishing the remnants of powers that landlords had enjoyed since the Middle Ages, including the right to compel peasants to labor for them and the bondage of serfdom itself. Although largely symbolic, because serfdom and forced labor had been eliminated in much of France, these changes represented a dramatic inroad into the property rights of the elite as they had been traditionally construed. They were hailed as the "end of feudalism." A blow was also struck at established religion by abolishing the tithe. At the end of the month, the Assembly issued a "Declaration of the Rights of Man and the Citizen," a bold assertion of principles condemning the old order. (See the box, "Declaration of the Rights of Man and the Citizen.")

In September, the deputies debated the king's role in a new constitutional government. Deputies known as "monarchists" favored a government rather like England's, with a two-house legislature, including an upper house representing the hereditary aristocracy and a royal right to veto legislation. More radical deputies favored a single legislative chamber and no veto power for the king. After deliberation, the Assembly reached a compromise. The king was given a three-year suspensive veto—the power to suspend legislation for the sitting of two legislatures. This was still a formidable amount of power but a drastic limitation of the king's formerly absolute sovereignty.

Again, Louis resorted to troops. This time, he called them directly to Versailles, where the Assembly sat. News of the troops' arrival provoked outrage, which heightened with the threat of another grain shortage. Women in street markets in Paris, early on the morning of October 5, noticed food shortages and took immediate collective action. "We want bread!" they shouted at the steps of City Hall. Women commonly led protests over bread shortages, because they procured food for their families. This protest, however, went far beyond the ordinary. A crowd of thousands gathered and decided to go to Versailles, accompanied by the popular militia (now called the "National Guard"), to petition the king directly for sustenance.

At Versailles, they presented a delegation to the National Assembly, and a joint delegation of the women and deputies was dispatched to see the king. Some of the women fell at the feet of the king with their tales of hardship, convinced that the "father of the people" would alleviate their suffering. He did order stored grain supplies distributed in Paris, and he also agreed to accept the constitutional role that the Assembly had voted for him.

The march ended on an odd note as the National Guard replaced much of the royal guard around the person of the king. That night the National Guard saved the king's life when members of the crowd broke into the palace and managed to kill two members of the royal guard still in attendance outside the queen's chamber. The king agreed to return to Paris, so that he could reassure the people. But the procession back to the city was a curious one. The entire royal family was escorted by militia and city people, and the severed heads of the killed guardsmen were carried on pikes.

The king was now in the hands of his people. Already, dramatic change had occurred as a re-

Women's March on Versailles The Parisian marketwomen marched the twelve miles to Versailles, some provisioning themselves with tools, stolen firearms, and horses as they left the capital. *(Jean-Loup Charmet)*

sult of a complex dynamic among the three Estates, the Crown, and the people of Paris. The king was still assumed to be the fatherly guardian of his people's well-being; but his powers were now limited, and his authority was badly shaken. The Assembly had begun to govern in the name of the "nation" and, so far, had the support of the people.

The French Revolution, 1789–1791

May 5, 1789	Meeting of Estates General
June 17, 1789	Third Estate declares itself the National Assembly
June 20, 1789	Tennis Court Oath
July–August 1789	Storming of the Bastille (July 14); Great Fear in the countryside; abolition of feudalism (August 4); Declaration of the Rights of Man and of the Citizen (August 27)
October 5–6, 1789	Women's march on Versailles; Louis XVI's return to Paris
July 1790	Civil Constitution of the Clergy
June 1791	Louis XVI attempts to flee Paris; is captured and returned
September 1791	New constitution is implemented; Girondins dominate newly formed Legislative Assembly

The French Revolutions

The French Revolution was a complicated affair. It was a series of changes driven not by one group of people but by several groups. Even among elites convinced of the need for reform there was a wide range of opinion. The people of Paris continued to be an important force for change. Country people also became active, primarily in resisting changes forced on them by the central government.

All of the wrangling within France was complicated by foreign reaction. Managing foreign war soon became a routine burden for the fragile revolutionary governments. In addition, there were the continuing problems that had precipitated the Revolution in the first place: the indebtedness of the government, economic difficulties, and recurrent shortages of grain. Finally, the Revolution itself was an issue in that momentum for further change was created once the traditional arrangements of royal government had been altered.

The First Phase Completed, 1789–1791

At the end of 1789, Paris was in ferment, but for a time the forward progress of change blunted the threat of disastrous divisions between king and Assembly and between either of those and the people of Paris. The capital continued to be the center of lively political debate. Salons continued to meet; academies and private societies proliferated. Deputies to the Assembly swelled the ranks of these societies or helped to found new ones. Several would be important throughout the Revolution—particularly the Jacobin Club, named for the monastic order whose buildings the members used as a meeting hall.

These clubs represented a wide range of revolutionary opinion. Some focused on economic policies that would directly benefit common people. Women were active in some of the more radical groups (see the box, "Parisian Women in Revolutionary Clubs"). Monarchists dominated other clubs. Initially like salons and debating societies of the Enlightenment era, the clubs increasingly became both sites of political action and sources of political pressure on the government. These clubs, other gathering places, and a bevy of popular newspapers—in addition to debates in the Assembly—constituted the vigorous political life in the capital.

Parisian Women in Revolutionary Clubs

Women were active on their own or working with men in demonstrations and protests and also in political clubs. In March 1791 Etta Palm d'Aedlers read the following proposals to the Society of the Friends of Truth, the first club open to women. D'Aedlers was active in revolutionary politics until 1793, when she emigrated to avoid persecution during a radical phase of the Revolution.

My fellow citizens . . . [throughout France] armed citizens united to defend the consitution. Do you not believe, gentlemen, that these wives and mothers of families could join together . . . to make the constitution loved? . . . Would it not be useful to form, in each section of the capital, a patriotic society of *citoyennes* (women citizens), female friends of the truth? Each circle of citoyennes would meet . . . as frequently as they believed useful and following their own particular rules. . . .

These circles of women could be charged with overseeing the establishment of wet nurses. . . . Young women, from the country, arriving in this huge capital without friends [and] without work [are] prey to all kinds of seduction [and] the innocent victims confided to these creatures are condemned to . . . countless infirmities.

These societies of citoyennes could be charged, in addition, with supervising public education. Zealous women patriots would take care to teach children the rights of men, respect and obedience for the law, the duty of citizens, the decrees of the National Assembly, [and] the revered names of France's regenerators instead of legends of the saints and the almanac of miracles.

A fund could be formed for indigent women [and the citoyennes could] designate commissioners [from their group] charged with keeping a register of those who asked for their assistance [and with] going into humble dwellings to inform themselves and [bring] consolation along with aid to their unfortunate brothers.

Source: Darlene Gay Levy, Harriet Branson Applewhite, and Mary Durham Johnson, *Women in Revolutionary Paris, 1789–1795* (Urbana: University of Illinois Press, 1979), pp. 68–71.

The broad front of revolutionary consensus began to break apart as the Assembly forged ahead with decisions about the constitution and with policies necessary to remedy France's still-desperate financial situation. The largest portion of the untapped wealth of the nation lay with the Catholic church, an obvious target for anticlerical reformers. The deputies did not propose to dismantle the church, but they did make sweeping changes. They kept churches intact and retained the clergy as salaried officials of the state. They abolished all monasteries and pensioned the monks and nuns to permit them to continue as nurses and teachers where possible. The Assembly seized most of the vast properties of the church and declared them national property to be sold for revenue.

Economic and political problems ensued. Revenue was needed faster than the property could be inventoried and sold, so government bonds (*assignats*) were issued against the eventual sale of church properties. Unfortunately, in the cash-strapped economy, the bonds were treated like money, their value became inflated, and the government never realized the hoped-for profits. A greater problem was the political divisiveness generated by the restructuring of the church. Many members of the lower clergy, living as they did near ordinary citizens, were among the most reform-minded of the deputies. Their daily lives and work might have gone on much as before, but their independence vis-à-vis the state was over. These clergy were willing to go along with many changes, but the required oath of loyalty to the state challenged clerical identity and seemed overly intrusive.

The "Civil Constitution of the Clergy," as these measures were called, was passed by the Assembly in July 1790 because the clerical deputies opposing it were outvoted. More than half of the clergy did take the oath of loyalty. Those who refused, concentrated among the higher clergy, were in theory thrown out of their offices. A year later (April 1791) the pope declared that clergy who had taken the oath were suspended from their offices. Antirevolutionary sentiment grew among thousands of French people, particularly among rural people, to whom the church was still important. This religious opposition helped to undermine the legitimacy of the new government.

Meanwhile, the Assembly proceeded with administrative and judicial reform. The deputies abolished the medieval provinces as administrative districts and replaced them with uniform *départements* (departments). They declared that local officials would be elected—a revolutionary dispersal of power that had previously belonged to the king.

As work on the constitution drew to a close in the spring of 1791, the king decided that he had had enough. Royal authority and government had been virtually dismantled. Louis had always lived in splendid isolation in Versailles, but he now was a virtual prisoner in the Tuileries Palace in the very heart of Paris. Afraid for himself and his family, he and a few loyal aides and troops worked out a plan to flee to the eastern border of France. The king and the members of his immediate family set out incognito on June 20, 1791. However, the royal party missed a rendezvous with a troop escort and was stopped along the way—and recognized—in the town of Varennes.

Louis and his family were returned to Paris and lived under lightly disguised house arrest. The circumstances of his flight were quickly discovered. He had intended to invade France with Austrian troops if necessary. He and the queen had sent money abroad ahead of themselves. He had left behind a document condemning the constitution. Thus, in July 1791, just as the Assembly was completing its proposal for a constitutional monarchy, the constitution it had created began to seem unworkable because the king was not trustworthy.

Editorials and popular demonstrations against the monarchy echoed these sentiments. In an incident known as the "Massacre of the Champ (Field) de Mars," government troops led by Lafayette charged citizens gathered in a public demonstration organized by certain clubs against the monarchy. The government of the National Assembly fired on the demonstrators, and about fifty died. This incident both reflected and heightened tensions between moderate reformers satisfied with the constitutional monarchy—such as Lafayette—and those who were openly republican and hoping to eliminate the monarchy.

On September 14, the king swore to uphold the constitution. He had no choice. The event became an occasion for celebration, but the tension between the interests of the Parisians and the provisions of the new constitution could not be glossed over. Though a liberal document for its day, the constitution reflected the views of the elite deputies who had created it. The right to vote, based on a minimal property qualification, was given to about half of the adult men. (See the box, "Declaration of the Rights of Woman.") However, these men only chose electors, for whom the property qualifications were higher. The electors in turn chose deputies to national bodies and also local officials. Although in theory any eligible voter could be an elected deputy or official, the fact that elite electors voted candidates into office reduced the likelihood that ordinary citizens would be national deputies or local officials. The "Declaration of Rights" that accompanied the constitution reflected a fear of the masses that had not existed when the Declaration of the Rights of Man and the Citizen was promulgated in 1789. Freedom of the press and freedom of assembly, for example, were not fully guaranteed.

Very soon after the constitution was implemented, the fragility of the new system became clear. The National Assembly declared that its members could not serve in the first assembly to be elected under the constitution. Thus, the

Declaration of the Rights of Woman

Authored in 1791 by Olympe de Gouges (1748?–1793), a butcher's daughter from southwestern France, this document and its author's career reflect the complexity of political life during the Revolution. Gouges's advocacy of women's rights represents the extension to women of the broad-based challenge to tradition that the Revolution embodied. Gouges dedicates the Declaration to the queen, drawing on the tradition of aristocratic patronage. Ironically, given Article 10, Gouges died on the scaffold for her revolutionary sympathies.

Man, Are you capable of being just? It is a woman who poses the question; you will not deprive her of that right at least. Tell me, what gives you sovereign empire to oppress my sex? . . . Bizarre, blind, bloated with science and degenerated—in a century of enlightenment and wisdom—into the crassest ignorance, he wants to command as a despot a sex which is in full possession of its intellectual faculties; he pretends to enjoy the Revolution and to claim his rights to equality in order to say nothing more about it.

(1) Woman is born free and lives equal to man in her rights. Social distinctions can be based only on the common utility.

(2) The purpose of any political association is the conservation of the natural and imprescriptible rights of woman and man; these rights are liberty, property, security, and especially resistance to oppression.

(4) Liberty and justice consist of restoring all that belongs to others; thus, the only limits on the exercise of the natural rights of woman are perpetual male tyranny; these limits are to be reformed by the laws of nature and reason.

(10) No one is to be disquieted for his very basic opinions; woman has the right to mount the scaffold; she must equally have the right to mount the rostrum. . . .

Source: Darlene Gay Levy, Harriet Branson Applewhite, and Mary Durham Johnson, *Women in Revolutionary Paris, 1789–1795* (Urbana: University of Illinois Press, 1979), pp. 87–91.

members of the newly elected Legislative Assembly, which began to meet in October 1791, lacked any of the cohesiveness that would have come from collective experience. Also, unlike the previous National Assembly, they did not represent a broad range of opinion but were mostly republicans.

The Legislative Assembly was dominated by republican members of the Jacobin Club. They were known as "Girondins," after the region in southwestern France from which many of the club's leaders came. The policies of these new deputies and continued pressure from the ordinary citizens of Paris would cause the constitutional monarchy to collapse in less than a year.

The Second Revolution and Foreign War, 1791–1793

An additional pressure on the new regime soon arose: a threat from outside France and a war to counter the threat. The most antirevolutionary aristocratic émigrés, including the king's brothers, had taken refuge in nearby German states and were planning to invade France. The emperor and other German rulers did little actively to aid the émigrés. Austria and Prussia, however, in the "Declaration of Pilnitz" of August 1791, declared that as a concession to the émigrés they would intervene if necessary to support the monarchy in France.

The threat of invasion, when coupled with distrust of the royal family, seemed more real to the revolutionaries in Paris than it actually was. Many deputies actively wanted war. They assumed that the outcome would be a French defeat, which would lead to a popular uprising that would rid them—at last—of the monarchy. In April 1792, under pressure from the Assembly, Louis XVI declared war against Austria. From this point, foreign war would be an ongoing factor in France's revolution—not only because of the threat of foreign invasion but also because of deliberate decisions to take war abroad in order to safeguard the revolution at home.

At first, the war was a disaster for France. The army had not been reorganized into an effective fighting force after the loss of many aristocratic officers and the addition of newly self-aware citizens. On one occasion, troops insisted on putting an officer's command to a vote. The French lost early battles in the Austrian Netherlands, but the Austrians did not press their advantage and invade France because they were preoccupied with problems in eastern Europe.

The defeats heightened criticism of the monarchy and pressure for dramatic change. Under the direction of the Girondins, the Legislative Assembly began to press for the deportation of priests who had been leading demonstrations against the government. The Assembly abolished the personal guard of the king and ordered provincial national guardsmen, including those from Marseilles, to come to Paris. The king's resistance to these measures, as well as fears of acute grain shortages owing to a poor harvest and the needs of the armies, created further unrest. Crowds staged dramatic marches near the king's palace, physically confronted him, and forced him to don the "liberty cap," a symbol of republicanism.

By July 1792, tensions had become acute. The grain shortage was severe, German troops committed to saving the royal family were threatening to invade, and, most important, the populace was better organized and more determined than ever before. In each of the forty-eight "sections" of Paris a miniature popular assembly thrashed out all the events and issues of the day just as deputies in the nationwide Legislative Assembly did. Derisively called *sans-culottes*, "without knee

THE FRENCH REVOLUTION, 1791–1793

April 1792	France declares war on Austria
August 10, 1792	Storming of the Tuileries; Louis XVI arrested
September 21, 1792	National Convention declares France a republic
January 21, 1793	Louis XVI is executed

Louis XVI in 1792 The king, though a kindly man, had neither the character nor the convictions necessary to refashion royal authority symbolically as the Revolution proceeded. When Parisian crowds forced him to wear the "liberty cap," the monarchy was close to collapse. *(Metropolitan Museum of Art, The Elisha Whittelsey Collection, The Elisha Whittelsey Fund, 1962)*

pants," because they could not afford elite fashions, the ordinary Parisians in the section assemblies included shopkeepers, artisans, and laborers. Their new political organization enhanced their influence with the Assembly, the clubs, and the newspapers in the capital. By late July most sections of the city had approved a petition calling for the exile of the king, the election of new city officials, the exemption of the poor from taxation, and other radical measures.

In August, they took matters into their own hands. On the night of August 9, they ejected the officials from City Hall in order to install representatives of their own choosing. Then, they stormed the Tuileries Palace. The king lost his nerve. He did not order his remaining guards to fire on the huge crowd, and they were overwhelmed. The royal family was imprisoned in one of the fortified towers in the city.

The storming of the Tuileries inaugurated the second major phase of the Revolution: the establishment of republican government in place of the monarchy. The people of Paris now physically dominated the Legislative Assembly. Some deputies had fled. Those who remained agreed under pressure to dissolve the Assembly and make way for another body to be elected by universal manhood suffrage. On September 20, that assembly—known as the "Convention"—began to meet. The next day, the Convention declared the end of the monarchy and began to work on a constitution for the new republic.

Coincidentally, on the same day, French forces won their first real victory over the German forces that had attempted to invade France. Though not a decisive battle, it was a profound psychological victory. A citizen army had defeated the professional force of a ruling prince. The victory bolstered the republican government and encouraged it to put more energy into the wars. Indeed, maintaining armies in the field became increasingly a factor in the delicate equilibrium of revolutionary government. The new republican regime let it be known that its armies were not merely for self-defense but for the liberation of all peoples in the "name of the French Nation."

The Convention faced the divisive issue of what to do with the king. Louis had not done anything truly treasonous, but some of the king's correspondence, discovered after the storming of the Tuileries, provided the pretext for charges of treason. The Convention held a trial for him, lasting from December 11, 1792, through January 15, 1793. He was found guilty by an overwhelming vote (683 to 39), reflecting the fact that the republican government would not compromise with monarchy. Less certain was the sentence: Louis was condemned to death by a narrow majority, 387 to 334.

The consequences for the king were immediate. On January 21, 1793, Louis mounted the scaffold in a public square near the Tuileries and was beheaded. The execution split the ranks of the Convention and soon resulted in the breakdown of the institution itself.

The Faltering Republic and the Terror, 1793–1794

In February 1793, the republic was at war with virtually every state in Europe, except Russia. Moreover, the regime faced massive and widespread counter-revolutionary uprisings within France. Vigilance against internal as well as external enemies seemed necessary. Nevertheless, for a time, the republican government functioned adequately. In April 1793, for example, it passed the first "Law of the Maximum," which guaranteed a stable maximum price for bread, the price of which had increased to the point that urban people could barely afford it.

The Convention established an executive body, the Committee of Public Safety. In theory, this executive council was answerable to the Convention as a whole. As the months passed, however, it acted with greater and greater autonomy not only to institute various policies but also to eradicate internal and external enemies. The republican government began to disintegrate.

The first major narrowing of control came in June 1793. Pushed by the Parisian sections, a group of extreme Jacobins purged the Girondin deputies from the Convention and arrested many of them. The Girondins were republicans who favored an activist government in the people's behalf, but they were less radical than the Jacobins, less insistent on central control of the Revolution, and less willing to share power with the citizens of Paris. After the purge, the Convention still met, but most authority was held by the Committee of Public Safety.

New uprisings against the regime began. Added to counter-revolutionary revolts by peasants and aristocrats were new revolts by Girondin sympathizers. As resistance to the government mounted and the foreign threat continued, a dramatic event in Paris led the Committee of Public Safety officially to adopt a policy of political repression. A well-known figure of the Revolution, Jean Paul Marat (1743–1793), publisher of a radical republican newspaper very popular with ordinary Parisians, was murdered on July 13 by Charlotte Corday (1768–1793), a young aristocratic woman who had asked to meet with him. Shortly afterward, a long-time member of the Jacobin Club, Maximilien Robespierre (1758–1794), joined the Committee and called for "Terror"—the systematic repression of internal enemies. He was not alone in his views. Radicals in the section assemblies of Paris led demonstrations to pressure the government into making Terror the order of the day.

Robespierre himself embodied all the contradiction of the policy of Terror. He was an austere, almost prim, man who lived very modestly—a model, of sorts, of the virtuous, disinterested citizen. The policies followed by the government during the year of his greatest influence, from July 1793 to July 1794, included generous, rational, and humane policies to benefit ordinary citizens as well as the policy of official Terror. (See the box, "Robespierre Justifies the Terror.")

Terror meant the use of intimidation to silence dissent. Since the previous autumn, the guillotine had been at work against identified enemies of the regime, but now a more energetic apparatus of terror was instituted. A "Law of Suspects" was passed that allowed citizens to be arrested simply on vague suspicion of counter-revolutionary sympathies. (See the box, "A Citizen of Paris Suffers Under the Terror.") Revolutionary tribunals and an oversight committee made arbitrary arrests and rendered summary judgment. In October, a steady stream of executions began, beginning with the queen, imprisoned since the storming of the Tuileries the year before. The imprisoned Girondin deputies followed, and then the process continued relentlessly. In Paris, there were about 2,600 executions from 1793 to 1794.

Around France, approximately 14,000 executions were the result of verdicts from revolution-

THE FRENCH REVOLUTION, 1793–1794

February 1793	France declares war on Britain, Spain, and the Netherlands
June 1793	Radical Jacobins purge Girondins from the Convention
July 1793	Robespierre assumes leadership of Committee of Public Safety
July 1793–July 1794	Reign of Terror
July 1794	Robespierre guillotined

Robespierre the Incorruptible A lawyer who had often championed the poor, Robespierre was elected to the Estates General in 1789 and was a consistent advocate of republican government from the beginning of the Revolution. His unswerving loyalty to his political principles earned him the nickname "the Incorruptible." *(Musée des Beaux-Arts, Lille)*

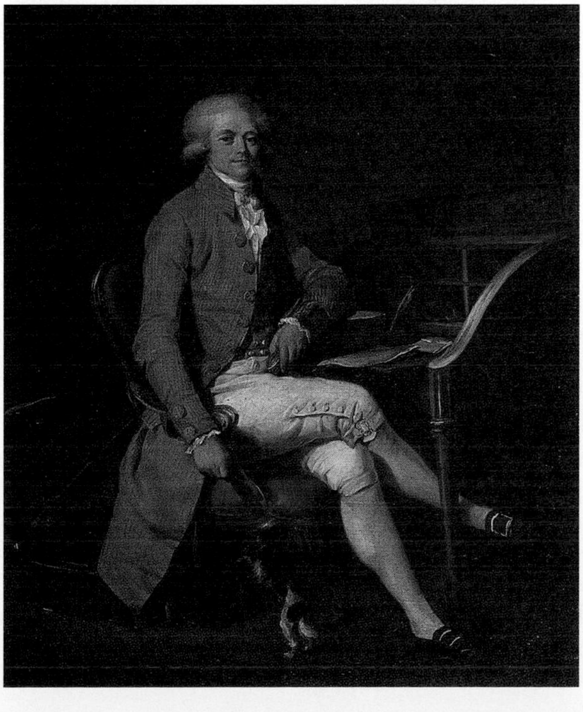

Robespierre Justifies the Terror

In this excerpt from a speech before the Convention in December 1793, Robespierre justifies the revolutionary government's need to act in an extra-constitutional manner. He echoes Rousseau's notion of a highly abstract sense of the public good. He also warns against challenges to the Revolution within France posed by foreign powers.

The defenders of the Republic must adopt Caesar's maxim, for they believe that "nothing has been done so long as anything remains to be done." Enough dangers still face us to engage all our efforts. It has not fully extended the valor of our Republican soldiers to conquer a few Englishmen and a few traitors. A task no less important, and one more difficult, now awaits us: to sustain an energy sufficient to defeat the constant intrigues of all the enemies of our freedom and to bring to a triumphant realization the principles that must be the cornerstone of public welfare. . . . Revolution is the war waged by liberty against its enemies; a constitution . . . crowns the edifice of freedom once victory has been won and the nation is at peace. . . . The principal concern of a constitutional government is civil liberty; that of a revolutionary government, public liberty. [A] revolutionary government is obliged to defend the state itself against the factions that assail it from every quarter. To good citizens revolutionary government owes the full protection of the state; to the enemies of the people it owes only death.

Is a revolutionary government the less just and the less legitimate because it must be more vigorous in its actions and freer in its movement than ordinary government? . . . It also has its rules, all based on justice and public order. . . . It has nothing in common with arbitrary rule; it is public interest which governs it and not the whims of private individuals.

Thanks to five years of treason and tyranny, thanks to our credulity and lack of foresight . . . Austria and England, Russia, Prussia, and Italy had time to set up in our country a secret government to challenge the authority of our own. . . . We shall strike terror, not in the hearts of patriots, but in the haunts of foreign brigands.

Source: George Rudé, ed., *Robespierre* (Englewood Cliffs, N.J.: Prentice-Hall, 1967), pp. 58–63.

ary tribunals. Another 10,000 to 12,000 people died in prison. Ten thousand or more were killed—usually by summary execution—after the defeat of counter-revolutionary uprisings. For example, 2,000 people were summarily executed in Lyon when a Girondin revolt collapsed there in October. The repression in Paris, however, was unique because of the city's role in the nation's political life. The aim of the repression was not merely to stifle active resistance; it was also to stifle simple dissent. The victims in Paris included not merely aristocrats or former deputies but sans-culottes. The radical Jacobins wanted to seize control of the Revolution from the Parisian citizens who had helped them to power.

The Terror notwithstanding, the government of the Committee of Public Safety was effective in providing direction for the nation at a critical time. It instituted the first mass conscription of citizens into the army (*levée en masse*), and an effective popular army came into existence. In the autumn of 1793, this army won impressive victories. Accomplishments in domestic policy included an extended Law of the Maximum that applied to other necessary commodities other than bread. Extensive plans were made for a system of free and universal primary education. Slavery in the French colonies was abolished in February 1794. Divorce, first legalized in 1792, was made easier for women to obtain.

A Citizen of Paris Suffers Under the Terror

The apparatus of the Terror meant that ordinary citizens could be arrested for the slightest offense. Here, a woman describes her arrest, which led to months of grim imprisonment. (She was eventually released only because she persuaded the authorities that she was pregnant.)

For a long time I have had to feed the members of my household on bread and cheese and . . . tired of complaints from my husband and my boys, I was compelled to go wait in line to get something to eat. For three days I had been going to the same market without being able to get anything, despite the fact that I waited [all day]. After the distribution of butter on the twenty-second, . . . a citizen came over to me and said I was in a very delicate condition [and I answered] "You can't be delicate and be on your legs for so long . . . " He replied that I needed to drink milk. I answered that I had men in my house and couldn't nourish them on milk [and that] if he . . . was sensitive to the difficulty of obtaining food, he would not vex me so, and that he was an imbecile and wanted to play despot, and no one had that right.

I was arrested [on the spot and] was led to the Revolutionary Committee [of the section] where I was called a counterrevolutionary and was told I was asking for the guillotine because I told them I preferred death to being treated ignominiously. . . . I was asked if I knew whom I had called a despot . . . and I was told that he was the commander of the post. I said he was more [a commander] beneath his own roof than anyone, given that he was there to maintain order and not to provoke bad feelings. For [these] answers, I was told that I had done three times more than was needed to get the guillotine and that I would be explaining myself before the Revolutionary Tribunal.

Source: Darlene Gay Levy, Harriet Branson Applewhite and Mary Durham Johnson, *Women in Revolutionary Paris, 1789–1795* (Urbana: University of Illinois Press, 1979), pp. 267–68.

In the name of "reason," traditional rituals and rhythms of life were changed. One reform of long-term significance was the introduction of the metric system of weights and measures. Although people continued to use the old familiar measures for a very long time, the change was eventually accomplished, leading the way for change throughout Europe. Equally "rational" but not as successful was the elimination of the traditional calendar. The traditional days, weeks, and months were replaced by 40-day months and *decadi* (10-day weeks with one day of rest). All saints' days and Christian holidays were eliminated. The years had already been changed—Year I had been declared with the founding of the republic in the autumn of 1792.

Churches were rededicated as "temples of reason." Believing that outright atheism left people with no basis for personal or national morality, Robespierre sought instead to promote a cult of the Supreme Being. The public festivals organized around either principle were solemn civic ceremonies intended to ritualize and legitimize the new political order.

These and other innovations of the regime were not necessarily welcomed. The French people generally resented the elimination of the traditional calendar. In the countryside, there were massive peasant uprisings over loss of poor relief, community life, and familiar ritual. Divorce law and economic regulation were a boon especially to urban women, but women's participation in sectional assemblies and in all organized political activity—which had been energetic and widespread—was banned in October 1793. The regime thereby removed one competing source

A Victim of the Terror Manon Phlipon (1754–1793), Madame Roland, led one of the most influential Parisian salons and was married to an important Girondin deputy. She was arrested and guillotined along with other Girondins in 1793; her last words on the scaffold were: "Oh Liberty, what crimes are committed in thy name!" *(Photographie Bulloz)*

of popular power. It also, simultaneously, sought to ground its legitimacy in a larger framework of order. The seemingly "natural" exclusion of women might make the new system of government appear part of the "natural" order. (See the feature, "Weighing the Evidence: Political Symbols," on pages 814–815.)

The Committee and the Convention were divided over religious and other policies, but the main policy differences concerned economic matters: how far to go to assist the poor, the unemployed, and the landless. Several of the temperate critics of Robespierre and his allies were guillotined because they differed with them on policy and on the continuing need for the Terror itself. Their deaths helped to precipitate the end of the Terror because Robespierre's power base was so narrowed that it had no further legitimacy.

Deputies to the Convention finally dared to move against Robespierre in July 1794. French armies had scored a major victory over Austrian troops on June 26, so there was no longer any need for the emergency status that the Terror had thrived on. In late July (the month of Thermidor, according to the revolutionary calendar), the Convention voted the arrests of Robespierre, the head of the Revolutionary Tribunal in Paris, and their closest associates and allies in the city government. On July 28 and 29, Robespierre and the others—about a hundred in all—were executed, and the Terror ended.

Thermidorian Reaction and the Directory, 1794–1799

After the death of Robespierre, the Convention reclaimed many of the executive powers that the Committee of Public Safety had seized. The Convention dismantled the apparatus of the Terror, repealed the Law of Suspects, and forced the revolutionary tribunals to adopt conventional legal procedures. The Convention also passed into law some initiatives, such as expanded public education, that had been proposed in the preceding year but not enacted.

The stability of the government, however, was threatened from the outset. Counter-revolutionary uprisings in western France during the autumn of 1794 were joined by landings of émigré troops the following June. These challenges were put down. There were also popular uprisings against the Terror throughout France. Officials of the previous regime were lynched, and pro-revolutionary groups were massacred by their fellow citizens.

The people of Paris tried to retain influence with the new government. With the apparatus of Terror dismantled, the Convention was unable to enforce controls on the supply and price of bread. Thus, economic difficulties and a hard winter produced famine by the spring of 1795. In May, crowds marched on the Convention, chanting "Bread and the Constitution of '93," referring to the republican constitution drafted by the Convention but never implemented because of the Terror. The demonstrations were met with force and were dispersed.

Fearful of a renewed, popularly supported Terror, or even of desperate popular support for a royalist uprising, the Convention drafted a new constitution that limited popular participation, as had the first constitution of 1791. The new plan allowed fairly widespread (but not universal) male suffrage, but only for electors, who would choose deputies for the two houses of the legislature. The property qualifications for being an elector were very high, so all but elite citizens were effectively disenfranchised.

In the fall of 1795, as the Convention was preparing to dissolve so that new elections might proceed, a final popular uprising shook Paris. The Convention anticipated the trouble, and when a crowd of 20,000 or more converged on the Tuileries Palace, the officer in charge ordered his troops to fire. Parisian crowds never again seriously threatened the government, although living conditions worsened as food prices soared. The army officer who issued the command to fire was Napoleon Bonaparte.

A new government began under the provisions of the new constitution. It was called the "Directory" for the executive council of five men chosen by the upper house of the new legislature. To avoid the concentration of authority that had produced the Terror, the members of the Convention had tried to enshrine separation of powers in the new system. However, because of unsettled conditions throughout France, the governments under the Directory were never stable and never free from attempted coups and extra-constitutional maneuvering.

The most spectacular challenge, the "Conspiracy of Equals," was led by extreme Jacobins who wanted to restore popular government and aggressive economic and social policy on behalf of the common people. The conspiracy ended with arrests and executions in 1797. When elections in 1797 and 1798 returned many royalist as well as Jacobin deputies, the Directory resorted to force to forestall challenges to its authority: Many deputies were arrested, sent into exile, or denied seats.

By 1799, conditions had once again reached a critical juncture. France was again at war with a coalition of states and was faring badly in the fighting. The demands of the war effort, together with other economic woes, were bringing the government again to the brink of bankruptcy. The government seemed to be losing control of the countryside; there were continued royalist uprisings and local political vendettas as well as outright banditry.

Members of the Directory had often turned to sympathetic army commanders to carry out the arrests and purge of the legislature. They now invited General Napoleon Bonaparte to help them form a government that they could more strictly control. Two members of the Directory plotted with Napoleon to seize power on November 9, 1799. Following the coup, Napoleon was expected to yield active governing authority to the two other men. But as had often happened in the Revolution, neither the course of events nor their outcome could be predicted or controlled.

THE FRENCH REVOLUTION, 1794–1799

August 1794	Thermidorian reaction begins
October 1795	Directory is established
November 1799	Napoleon seizes power

The Napoleonic Era

Napoleon Bonaparte (1769–1821) was the kind of person who gives rise to myths. He was talented, daring, and ruthless. He was also charming and charismatic. His audacity, determination, and personal magnetism enabled him to profit from the political instability and confusion in France and ensconce himself in power. Once in power, he stabilized the political scene by enshrining in law the more conservative gains of the Revolution. He also used his power and his abilities as a general to continue wars of conquest against France's neighbors.

Napoleon's troops, in effect, exported the Revolution when they conquered most of Europe. Law codes were reformed, governing elites were opened to talent, and public works were undertaken in most states under French control. Yet French conquest also meant domination, pure and simple, and involvement in France's rivalry with Britain. The Napoleonic era left Europe an ambiguous legacy—war and its complex aftermath and revolution and encouragement to further change.

Napoleon: From Soldier to Emperor, 1799–1804

Napoleon was from Corsica, a Mediterranean island that had passed from Genoese to French control in the eighteenth century. The second son of a large gentry family, he was educated at military academies in France, and he married the beautiful and politically well-connected widow Joséphine de Beauharnais (1763–1814), whose aristocratic husband was a victim of the Terror.

Napoleon steered a careful course through the political turmoil of the Revolution. By 1799, however, he was well known and popular because of his military victories. He demonstrated his reliability and ruthlessness when he ordered troops guarding the Convention to fire on the Parisian crowd, but his greatest victories had been against France's foreign opponents. In 1796 and 1797 he had conquered all of northern Italy, forcing Austria to relinquish that territory as well as to cede control of the Austrian Netherlands, which revolutionary armies had seized in 1795. He then commanded an invasion of Egypt in an attempt to strike at British influence and trade connections in the eastern Mediterranean. The invasion produced no long-term gains for France in the region, but spectacular victories ensured Napoleon's reputation. By the end of the 1790s, Napoleon had demonstrated that he was an enormously skilled general, that he could produce victories when the nation needed them, and that he was personally ambitious, perhaps at the expense of French interests.

His two partners in the new government after the November coup soon learned of his great political skill. By cleverly manipulating members of the old legislature, he gained the formal acceptance of a new constitution that he had designed. After its approval, there was a national plebiscite, and his constitution was overwhelmingly approved. He was to be first among equals in a three-man executive—First Consul, according to borrowed Roman terminology—but he actually ruled alone with the advice of a Senate.

Napoleon was careful to cultivate goodwill and to avoid heavy-handed displays of power. Perhaps most important to the success of his increasingly authoritarian regime was his effort to include, among his ministers, advisers, and bureaucrats, men of many political stripes—Jacobins, reforming liberals, even former Old Regime bureaucrats. He welcomed many exiles back to France, including all but the most ardent royalists. He thus stabilized his regime by healing some of the rifts among the ruling elites. Napoleon, however, could be ruthless. Between 1800 and 1804, he imprisoned, executed, or exiled dozens of individuals for alleged Jacobin agitation or royalist sympathies. His final gesture to silence royalist dissent came in 1804 when he kidnapped and coldly murdered a Bourbon prince who had been in exile in Germany.

By the terms of the Treaty of Amiens in 1802, he made peace with Britain, France's one remaining enemy. The fragile and short-lived peace only papered over the two countries' commercial and strategic rivalries, but it gave Napoleon breathing room to establish his rule more securely in France. One of the most important steps had been accomplished a year earlier by means of the Concordat of 1801. The aim of this treaty with the pope was to solve the problem of church-state relations that for years had caused antirevolutionary rebellions. The agreement allowed for the resumption of Catholic worship and the continued support of the clergy by the state, as well as for the more dramatic changes accomplished by the Revolution. Church lands that had been sold were guaranteed to their new owners. Protestant churches were also allowed and their clergy was paid, although Catholicism was recognized as the "religion of the majority of Frenchmen." Later, Napoleon granted new rights to Jews also. In many respects, the Concordat re-established the church, but church control of civil affairs such as marriage was limited. French people were no longer necessarily under the church's power.

The law code that Napoleon established in 1804 was much like his accommodation with the church in its mixture of revolutionary gains and reaction against them. It reflected the revolutionary legacy in its guarantee of equality before the law and its requirement for the taxation of all social classes, and it put another nail in the coffin of feudalism by enshrining modern forms of property ownership and civil contracts. But neither the code nor Napoleon's political regime fostered

The Coronation of Napoleon A grand coronation was staged complete with carefully managed political symbolism. The pope was present, for example, but Napoleon took the crown from him and placed it on his own head. He then crowned his wife, Joséphine. *(Louvre © Photo R.M.N.)*

individual rights. Fathers' control over their families was enhanced. Women lost all of the rights they had gained during the Revolution. Divorce was no longer permitted except in rare instances. Women lost all property rights when they married, and they generally faced legal domination by fathers and husbands.

Napoleon helped to put the regime on better financial footing by establishing a national bank. The Bank of France, modeled on the Bank of England, provided capital for investment and could help the state manage its money and return to a system of hard coinage. He also took an active role in streamlining and further centralizing the administrative system set up by the first wave of revolutionaries in 1789.

Some of these legal and administrative changes occurred after the final political coup that Napoleon undertook—declaring himself emperor. This was a bold move, but Napoleon approached it dexterously and was successful. Long before he declared himself emperor, Napoleon had begun to live like one and to sponsor an active court life. The empire was proclaimed in May 1804 with the approval of the Senate; it was also approved by a plebiscite. The plebiscite sustained the myth that Napoleon was faithful to the Revolution, but in truth all power was in Napoleon's hands. Members of Napoleon's family were given princely status, and a number of his favorites received various titles and honors. The titles brought no legal privilege but signaled social and political distinctions of great importance. Old nobles were allowed to use their titles on this basis.

Many members of the elite, whatever their persuasions, tolerated Napoleon's claims to power because he safeguarded many revolutionary gains and reconfirmed their own status. War soon resumed against political and economic enemies—principally Britain, Austria, and Russia—and Napoleon's success in the field continued. Because military success was central to the political purpose and self-esteem of elites, Napoleon's early successes as emperor further enhanced his power.

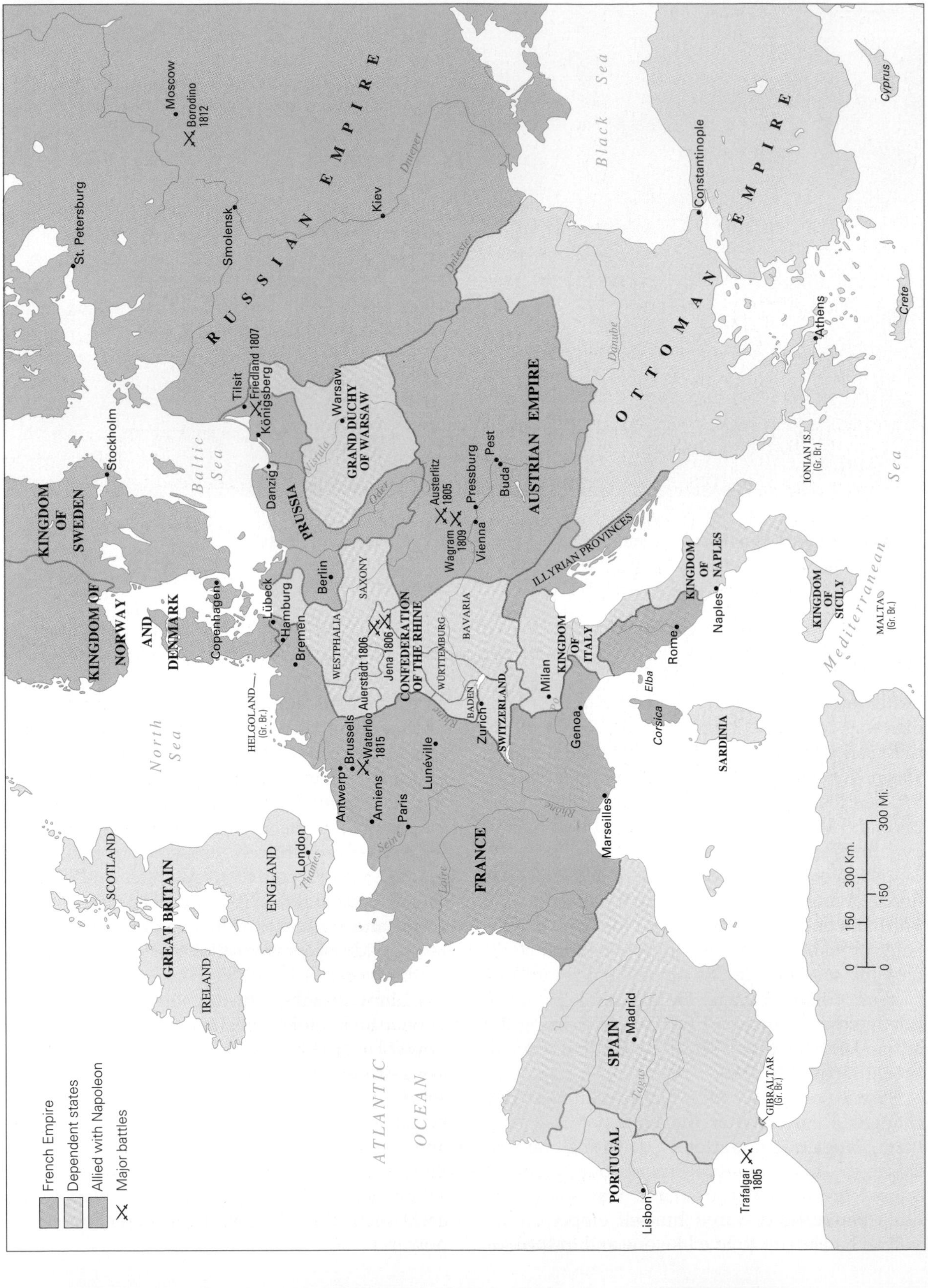
French Empire
Dependent states
Allied with Napoleon
Major battles
RUSSIAN EMPIRE
St. Petersburg
Moscow
Borodino 1812
Smolensk
Kiev
Dnieper
Dniester
Black Sea
OTTOMAN EMPIRE
Constantinople
Cyprus
Crete
Athens
Danube
KINGDOM OF SWEDEN
Stockholm
Baltic Sea
Tilsit
Friedland 1807
Königsberg
Warsaw
GRAND DUCHY OF WARSAW
Vistula
Danzig
PRUSSIA
Oder
Berlin
SAXONY
AUSTRIAN EMPIRE
Austerlitz 1805
Wagram 1809
Pressburg
Vienna
Pest
Buda
ILLYRIAN PROVINCES
IONIAN IS. (Gr. Br.)
KINGDOM OF NORWAY AND DENMARK
Copenhagen
Lübeck
Hamburg
Bremen
WESTPHALIA
Auerstädt 1806
Jena 1806
CONFEDERATION OF THE RHINE
WÜRTTEMBURG
BAVARIA
BADEN
SWITZERLAND
Zurich
KINGDOM OF ITALY
Milan
Genoa
KINGDOM OF NAPLES
Naples
Rome
Elba
Corsica
SARDINIA
KINGDOM OF SICILY
MALTA (Gr. Br.)
Mediterranean Sea
HELGOLAND (Gr. Br.)
North Sea
Brussels
Waterloo 1815
Antwerp
Amiens
Paris
Lunéville
Rhine
Seine
Loire
Rhône
Po
FRANCE
Marseilles
SCOTLAND
GREAT BRITAIN
ENGLAND
London
Thames
IRELAND
ATLANTIC OCEAN
SPAIN
Madrid
Tagus
PORTUGAL
Lisbon
Trafalgar 1805
GIBRALTAR (Gr. Br.)
0 150 300 Km.
0 150 300 Mi.

Conquering Europe, 1805–1810

Napoleon maintained relatively peaceful relations with other nations while he consolidated power at home, but the truces did not last. Beginning in 1805, Napoleon conquered most of continental Europe (Map 21.1). Tensions with the British had quickly re-escalated. In 1803, Britain resumed aggression against French shipping, and Napoleon countered by seizing Hanover, the ancestral German home of the English king. Then Napoleon seized several Italian territories and extended his influence in other German states. By 1805, all the states of Europe were threatened. Austria was alarmed by his power in Italy. England was at war on the high seas with Spain and Holland, which Napoleon had forced to enter the fray. Napoleon began to gather a large French force on the northern coast of France, ostensibly to invade England.

The British fleet, commanded by Horatio Nelson (1758–1805), intercepted the combined French and Spanish fleets that were to have been the invasion flotilla and inflicted a devastating defeat off Cape Trafalgar, on October 21, 1805. The victory ensured British mastery of the seas and, in the long run, helped ensure Napoleon's defeat. In the short run, the defeat at Trafalgar paled for the French beside Napoleon's impressive victories on land. Even as the French admirals were preparing for battle, Napoleon had abandoned the plans to invade England and in August had begun to march his army east through Germany.

In December 1805, after some preliminary, small-scale victories, Napoleon's army confronted a Russian force near Austerlitz, north of Vienna. Tsar Alexander I (r. 1801–1825) led his own troops into a battle that he ought to have avoided. Austrian reinforcements could not reach him in time, and French armies shattered the Russian force. The battle of Austerlitz was Napoleon's most spectacular victory. Austria sued for peace.

Map 21.1 Napoleonic Europe, ca. 1810 France dominated continental Europe after Napoleon's victories. Though French control would collapse quickly after defeats in Russia and Spain in 1812, the effects of French domination were more long-lasting.

In 1806 Napoleon faced the remaining resistance—chiefly Prussia and Russia. He defeated the Prussians at Jena and at Auerstädt. He then followed the Russians east and, several months later, conquered them at Friedland in east Prussia. At their own doorstep, the Russians had to acknowledge their defeat and negotiate a peace.

In July 1807, the two emperors—Napoleon and Alexander—met with great ceremony near Tilsit, in east Prussia. Prussia was virtually dismembered by the treaty, but Napoleon tried to work out terms to make Russia into a contented ally. His hold on central Europe would not be secure with Russia as an enemy, nor would the anti-British economic system that he envisioned—the "Continental System"—be workable without Russian participation.

French forces were still trying to subdue Spain, which had been a client state since its defeat by revolutionary armies in 1795 but was resisting outright rule by a French-imposed king. After a relatively successful campaign to quash resistance in Spain in 1808, Napoleon turned his attention to a more formidable enemy: Austria. Napoleon won the battle of Wagram in July 1809 but did not totally defeat Austria. Austria, like Russia, accepted French political and economic hegemony in a sort of alliance.

By 1810, Napoleon had transformed many of the European states into allied and dependent states. The only exceptions were Britain and the parts of Spain and Portugal that continued to resist France with British help. The impact of French hegemony varied from state to state, depending on the nature of a state's links with France and on the effects of Napoleon's Continental System on a state's economy.

The states least affected by French hegemony were the most powerful in their own right: Austria and Russia. After Wagram, Austria was more a nonbelligerent rather than an ally. Russia, whose principal trading relationships had long been with Britain, was a reluctant partner that Napoleon hoped only to neutralize. At the other extreme were territories that had been incorporated into France. These included the Austrian Netherlands, territory along the Rhineland, and territories in Italy that bordered France. These regions were occupied by French troops and were treated as though they were départements of France itself.

In most other regions, some form of French-controlled government was in place, usually headed by a member of Napoleon's family. In both Holland and northern Italy, where "sister" republics had been established after French conquests under the Directory, Napoleon imposed monarchies. Rulers were also imposed in the kingdom of Naples and in Spain. Western German states of the Holy Roman Empire that had allied with Napoleon against Austria were organized into the Confederation of the Rhine, with Napoleon as its "Protector." After a thousand years, the Holy Roman Empire ceased to exist. After the victory of Friedland and the negotiations with the tsar at Tilsit, two more states were created out of Prussian territory and given French-controlled governments: the kingdom of Westphalia in central Germany and the duchy of Warsaw.

All of the states that France dominated were run by a combination of external French control and local rule. Governing these various regions would have been impossible without the active involvement of local elites. The makeup of the ruling groups varied from place to place, as did the degree to which they were sympathetic to the reforms that Napoleon typically introduced. Generally, however, Napoleonic domination meant constitutional government that guaranteed equality under the law, legal reforms, diminished church power, and the abolition of feudalism and serfdom. Political dissent was suppressed, but careers in government and the military were thrown open to all talented men in the elite as they had been in France. Infrastructure reforms—improved roads, bridges, sewage systems, and educational systems—were widespread and were among the most lasting of Napoleon's legacies.

The economic consequences of Napoleon's Continental System were mixed. The Continent was in theory closed to all British shipping and British goods. The effects were widespread but uneven. Smuggling to evade controls on British goods became a major enterprise. Regions that had been dependent on long-distance trade with Britain or its colonies or dependent on the British carrying trade suffered in the new system, as did overseas trade in general when Britain gained dominance of the seas after Trafalgar. Peasants and landlords in many regions that produced grain for export suffered, and some cities dependent on overseas trade experienced catastrophic decline. However, the closing of the Continent to British trade, combined with increases in demand resulting from the need to supply Napoleon's armies, spurred the development of continental industries, at least in the short run. This industrial growth, enhanced by the improvement of roads, canals, and the like, formed the basis for further industrial development.

Whatever its benefits, the Napoleonic empire was expensive. The Napoleonic Wars were costly in both money and human life. The increased tax burden on ordinary people wiped out savings from the suppression of feudal dues and from economic growth. The empire sowed the seeds of its own destruction: Many regions chafed at the economic hardships it caused, and elites everywhere were exposed to the new ideology of nationalism exported by the French armies. In the long run, the period of enforced reform encouraged liberal ideas among elites. In future years, these people would be crucial to furthering constitutional rule and other reforms. More immediately, their self-confidence and national pride increased their impatience and dissatisfaction with French domination.

Defeat in Russia and Spain, 1812

Napoleon's success in battle stemmed from a combination of strategic innovations and audacity. Napoleon organized his forces into independent corps. Each corps included infantry, cavalry, and artillery. Organized in these workable units, his armies could travel quickly by several separate routes and converge in massive force to face the enemy. Numbers were important to success, but so were discipline, control of troop movements, and determination to follow up initial gains. When Napoleon located his enemy, he massed troops at a battle site and used them in battle as deliberately as he had ordered the cannon to fire on the Paris crowd in 1795.

Leadership on the battlefield came from a loyal and talented officer corps that Napoleon had fashioned by welcoming returning aristocrats and favoring rising new talent. The final ingredient in the success formula was the high morale of French troops under Napoleon. Confidence led to aggressiveness on the battlefield and helped ensure victory. Napoleon's

English nemesis, Arthur Wellesley (1769–1852), duke of Wellington, once remarked that Napoleon's presence on a battlefield was worth forty thousand men.

Recruiting soldiers and supplying the army were crucial to military success, as they had always been. Napoleon's forces consisted of draftees and volunteers. As the wars dragged on, recruits were thrown into battle with little training, casualty rates rose, and margins of victory became slim. Provisioning his forces was always Napoleon's weakness. Getting the fast-traveling corps of soldiers to a site was far easier than transporting food, reserves of ammunition, and other supplies. Bold victories enabled Napoleon's troops to live off the countryside much of the time and to wait for supplies to catch up with them. But when the enemy attacked his supply lines, when the distances traveled were very great, when the countryside was impoverished, or when battles were not decisive, Napoleon's ambitious strategies proved unworkable. In varying degrees, these conditions prevailed in Russia and Spain.

Russia was a particularly weak link in the chain of alliances and subject states. Russian landowners and merchants were angered when their vital trade in timber for the British navy was interrupted and when supplies of luxury goods, brought in British ships, began to dwindle. A century of close alliances with German ruling houses made alliance with a French ruler extremely difficult politically for Alexander I.

It was Napoleon, however, who ended the alliance by provoking a breach with Russia. He suddenly backed away from an arrangement to marry one of Tsar Alexander's younger sisters and accepted the Austrian princess Marie Louise instead (he had reluctantly divorced Joséphine in 1809 because their marriage had not produced an heir). He seized lands along the German Baltic seacoast belonging to a member of Alexander's family. When Alexander threatened rupture of the alliance if the lands were not returned, Napoleon mounted an invasion. Advisers warned him about the magnitude of the task he seemed so eager to undertake—particularly about the preparations needed for winter fighting in Russia.

The campaign against Russia began in June 1812. It was a spectacular failure. Napoleon had gathered a force of about 700,000 men—about half from France and half from allied states—a force twice as large as Russia's. The strategy of quickly moving and assembling massive forces could not be implemented because simply assembling so many men along the border was already the equivalent of gathering them for battle. Also, sustaining them thereafter was beyond the capacity of the supply system.

As the French armies began to march across sparsely populated Russian farmland, their supply systems were already overwhelmed. The armies walked some 500 miles, over two months, before they fought the principal battle of the campaign, at Borodino, west of Moscow. By that time, the rigors of the march had virtually evened the odds for the Russians. One hundred thirty thousand men on each side faced each other and endured staggering losses of about 40,000 each. The French claimed victory because they controlled the battlefield at day's end, but they had not broken and overwhelmed the enemy's forces.

The French occupied and pillaged Moscow but found scarcely enough food and supplies to sustain them. Alexander, safe in St. Petersburg, sent Napoleon defiant messages saying that the French could seize all the land or cities they wanted but he would never surrender. When Napoleon finally led his troops out of Moscow late in October, after an uncharacteristic period of indecisiveness, the fate of the French forces was all but sealed. Winter was approaching, and discipline had almost completely broken down. Napoleon marched south to reach warmer and better-provisioned Ukraine but was turned back by Russian forces. The French then began to retreat north and west out of Russia, the way they had come.

Those who did not die in battle died of exposure or starvation or were killed by Russian peasants when they wandered away from their units. Some survived by defecting to the Russian side. Artillery was abandoned. Even the stolen treasures of the Kremlin—Napoleon's only fruits of victory—were abandoned along the road. Of the original 700,000 French troops, less than 50,000 made it out of Russia.

Napoleon left his army before it was fully out of Russia. A coup attempt in Paris prompted him to return to his governing duties before the French people realized the extent of the disaster

The French Army Flees Russia Napoleon's engineers built bridges for a night crossing of the Berezina River (in Belarus), which blocked the French retreat. The remainder of the army was saved from annihilation, but as in the rest of the Russian campaign, the cost was high: wagons and provisions, as well as thousands of wounded soldiers, were abandoned on the Russian side. Many of the engineers died of exposure. *(Musée de l'Armée)*

in Russia. The collapse of his reign had begun, spurred by a coincidental defeat in Spain.

Spain had been a particularly reluctant ally. Spain and the Spanish overseas empire were vulnerable to British naval strength. Since 1808, Spain had been largely under French domination, with Napoleon's brother Joseph as king. A rebel Cortes, however, continued to meet in territory that the French did not control, and British troops were never expelled from the Iberian Peninsula. In 1812, as Napoleon was beginning his move against Russia, the collapse of French control accelerated. By the time Napoleon was back in Paris at the turn of the new year, Joseph had been expelled from Spain, and an Anglo-Spanish force led by the duke of Wellington was poised to invade France.

The End of Napoleon?

Napoleon's most able generals rallied what remained of his troops and held off Prussian and Russian forces until April 1813, when Napoleon could return to Germany from France with a new army made up of raw recruits. But Prussia and Russia mobilized their forces, and news of Wellington's victories in Spain emboldened Austria to join them. Napoleon's strength began to collapse. With Britain willing to subsidize the allied armies, and Tsar Alexander determined to destroy Napoleon, the allies were able to invade France. They forced Napoleon to abdicate on April 6, 1814. Napoleon was exiled to the island of Elba, off France's Mediterranean coast, but was still treated somewhat royally. He was installed as the island's ruler and was given an income drawn on the French treasury.

Meanwhile, the restored French king was having his own troubles. Louis XVIII (r. 1814–1824) was the brother of the executed Louis XVI; he took the number eighteen out of respect for Louis XVI's son, who had died in prison in 1795. He was not cut out for the demanding task of resuming monarchial rule after a revolution. He had been out of the country and out of touch with its circumstances since the beginning of the Revolution. Though forced to acknowledge that he could not rule as his brother had once done, Louis XVIII conceded the principles of constitutional government with little sincerity and in extremely limited form. In addition to the delicate task of establishing his own legitimacy and resolving constitutional questions, he faced enormous practical problems, including the pensioning off of thousands of soldiers now unemployed and still loyal to Napoleon.

Napoleon, bored and almost broke on his island kingdom (the promised French pension never materialized), took advantage of the circumstances and returned surreptitiously to France on February 26, 1815. His small band of attendants was joined by the soldiers sent by the king to prevent him from advancing to Paris. One of Napoleon's greatest generals fell weeping into his arms instead of arresting him as he had been ordered. Louis XVIII abandoned Paris to the returned emperor.

Napoleon's triumphant return lasted only one hundred days. His reappearance galvanized the divided allies, who had been haggling over a peace settlement, into unity. Napoleon tried to strike first, but he lost against English and Prussian troops in his first major battle at Waterloo (in modern Belgium) on June 18, 1815. His troops were of poor quality and were outnumbered, and his own direction of the battle faltered. When Napoleon reached Paris after the defeat, he discovered the government in the hands of an ad hoc committee that included the marquis de Lafayette. Under pressure, he abdicated once again. He was exiled to the tiny, remote island of St. Helena in the South Atlantic, from which escape would be impossible. He died there in 1821.

Napoleon's return to power, though brief, was nevertheless important. It reflects the degree to which his power was always rooted in military adventurism and in the loyalty of soldiers and officers. Hundreds of his best-trained veterans chose to die on the battlefield of Waterloo rather than to accept surrender. Napoleon's return to power also demonstrates the fragility of the legitimacy claimed by both Napoleon and Louis XVIII. His bravado suggests the importance of personal qualities to the success of an authoritarian regime. But the swiftness of his collapse suggests that although the empire under Napoleon may have seemed an enduring solution to the political instability of the late 1790s, its legitimacy and security were as uncertain as the legitimacy and security of the revolutionary governments.

The Impact of Revolution on France and the World

The process of change in France between 1789 and 1815 was so complex that it is easy to overlook the overall impact of the Revolution. Superficially, the changes seemed to come full circle—with first Louis XVI on the throne, then Napoleon as emperor, and then Louis XVIII on the throne. Even though the monarchy was restored, however, the Revolution changed the fundamental premises of political life in France and was an impetus to challenges to the existing order elsewhere.

The Significance of Revolution in France

The French monarchy was restored in 1815, but the Revolution had discredited absolute monarchy in theory and practice. The restored constitutional monarchy governed with only a small group of representatives of the elite, but their participation slowly widened during the nineteenth century. An important legacy of the Revolution was thus new principles on which to base a government: the right of "the people," however narrowly defined, to participate in government and to enjoy due process of law.

There was fundamental disagreement, however, about which people were worthy of inclusion in the political process and the degree to which the government might govern in their interests. There was a significant philosophical difference between many republicans and reformers who had supported the Revolution in its initial stages. The latter argued for access to government by the politically sophisticated elite and for the freeing of the economy from traditional constraints. There were two different notions about who constituted "the people" and about government's obligations to the people. The more inclusive view and the more activist posture would be reinstated by revolutionary action later in the nineteenth century (see Chapter 22). Neither notion included a vision of women as citizens coequal with men.

Other legacies of the Revolution included a centralized political system. The nation was divided into départements, rather than provinces. For the first time, a single code of law applied to all French people. Most officials—from départe-ment administrators to city mayors—were appointed by the central government until the late twentieth century. The conscientious attention of the government—at various stages of the Revolution—to advances for France generally reflects the positive side of this centralization. The government sponsored national scientific societies, a national library and archives, and a system of teachers' colleges and universities. Particularly under Napoleon, there was a spate of canal- and road-building.

Napoleon's legacy, like that of the Revolution itself, was mixed. His self-serving reconciliation of aristocratic pretensions with the opening of careers to men of talent helped to ensure the long-term success of revolutionary principles from which the elite as a whole profited. However, it applied mostly to his favorite institution—the army. His reconciliation of the state with the Catholic church helped to stabilize his regime and to ensure some revolutionary gains. But he could not eliminate the antirevolutionary bent of the church as a whole, and the church continued to be a reactionary force in France. The Napoleonic Code was a uniform system of law for the nation. But while it guaranteed equality under the law for men, it enshrined political and legal inferiority for women.

Whatever the concrete gains of the Revolution and Napoleon's rule, Napoleon's overthrow of constitutional principles worsened the problem of political instability. Although Louis XVIII acknowledged the principle of constitutionalism at the end of the Revolution, it was on fragile footing. Indeed, the fragility of new political systems was one of the most profound lessons of the Revolution. There was division over policies, but even greater division over legitimacy—that is, the acceptance by a significant portion of the politically active citizenry of a particular system or of a particular government's right to rule.

Politics, the Revolution revealed, takes place in part on a symbolic level. What is acceptable and what is legitimate are expressed not only in words but also symbolically. The symbols are effective because they link a specific political system to a broader, fundamental system of values. The religious symbolism used by the monarchy, for example, linked royal government to divine order. Similarly, the public cults of reason and of the Supreme Being that Robespierre promoted during the Terror were attempts to link patriotism and support of the government to universal principles. Other, more limited, symbols were constantly in use: the red and blue cockades that supporters of the National Assembly put in their caps; the "liberty cap" that Louis XVI donned on one occasion; various representations of the abstract notion of "Liberty" in newspapers and journals widely available at the time.

Before the Revolution started, there was a significant shift in notions about political legitimacy. The deputies who declared themselves to be the National Assembly in June 1789 already believed that they had a right to do so. In their view, they represented "the nation," and their voice had legitimacy for that reason. The shift reflects not the innate power of ideas but the power of ideas in context. The deputies brought to Versailles not only their individual convictions that "reason" should be applied to the political system but also their experience in social settings where those ideas were well received. In their salons, clubs, and literary societies, they had experienced the familiarity, trust, and sense of community that are essential to effective political action.

The deputies' attempt to transplant their sense of community into national politics was not wholly successful. Factions, competing interests, and clashes of personality can be fatal to an insecure system. The National Assembly had scarcely inaugurated a secure system when its deputies undermined its workability by making themselves ineligible to hold office under the new constitution. The king also actively undermined the system because he disagreed with it in principle. The British parliamentary system, by comparison, though every bit as elitist as the narrowest of the representative systems during the French Revolution, had a long history as a workable institution for lords, commoners, and rulers. This shared experience was an important counterweight to differences over fundamental issues, so that Parliament as an institution both survived political crises and helped solve them.

The legitimacy of the National Assembly was real and reveals the startling degree to which politics in France had already undergone fundamental change. But the course of the Revolution reveals the weight of previous conditions and experience. Both before and after the Revolution, professional bureaucrats handled much of the business of government. The revolutionaries overturned the monarchy's arbitrary claim to power; but, paradoxically, that arbitrary claim continued to shape politics because it helped to justify the equally sweeping claims to power advanced by the Committee of Public Safety. The Committee's arbitrary power over life and death equaled that of the monarchy at its worst. The revolution thus left a powerful yet ambiguous legacy for France. Politics was established on a new footing, yet still lacking were the practical means to achieve the promise inherent in the new principles.

The Impact of the Revolution Overseas

The legacy of the Revolution overseas was powerful and complex. Warfare between Britain and the French-dominated continent had echoes overseas. The British tried to take advantage of French preoccupation with continental affairs by seizing French colonies and the colonies of the French-dominated Dutch. They were largely successful. In 1806, they seized the Dutch colony of Capetown—crucial for support of trade around Africa—as well as French bases along the African coast. In 1811, they grabbed the island of Java. In the Americas, French sugar colonies in the Caribbean were particularly vulnerable to English seapower. The British readily seized Martinique, Guadaloupe, and other islands while Napoleon was executing his brilliant victories on the Continent after 1805. The sugar island of Haiti was an exception to this pattern of French losses because British aggression there occurred in the context of a local revolution.

In Haiti, the Revolution itself, and not merely the strategic moves of great powers, had an impact. The National Assembly in Paris delayed abolishing slavery in French colonies—despite the moral appeal of such a stance—because of pressure from the white planters on Haiti and out of fear that the financially strapped French government would lose some of its profitable sugar trade. But the example of revolutionary daring in Paris and confusion about ruling authority that occurred as the Assembly and the king wrangled invited challenges to authority in the colonies.

White planter rule in Haiti was challenged first by wealthy people of mixed European and African descent and then by a full-fledged slave rebellion, beginning in 1791. Britain sent aid to the rebels when it went to war against the French revolutionary government in 1793. Only when the republic was declared in Paris and the Convention abolished slavery did the rebels abandon alliances with France's enemies and attempt to govern in concert with the mother country.

France, however, never regained control of Haiti. Led by a former slave, François Dominique Toussaint-Louverture (1743–1803), the new government of Haiti tried to run its own affairs, though without formally declaring independence from France. Napoleon, early in his rule, decided to tighten control of the profitable colonies by reinstituting slavery and ousting the independent government of Haiti. In 1802, French forces fought their way onto the island. They captured Toussaint-Louverture, who died shortly thereafter in prison. But in 1803 they were forced to leave by another rebellion prompted by the threat of renewed slavery.

The French Revolution and Napoleonic rule had a great impact on Spanish colonies in the Americas also, and for many of the same reasons as in Haiti. The confusion of authority in Spain enabled some Spanish colonies to govern themselves independently in all but name. Like the British North American colonies, the Spanish colonies wanted freedom from the closed economic ties the mother country tried to impose.

The liberal ideas that had helped spawn the French Revolution spurred moves toward independence in Spanish America. There were also echoes of radical republican ideology in some of the events in Spanish America. For example, participants in two major rebellions in Mexico espoused the end of slavery and generally championed the interests of the poor against local and Spanish elites. The leaders of these self-declared revolutions were executed (in 1811 and 1815), and their movements were crushed by local elites in alliance with Spanish troops. The efforts of local elites to become self-governing—the attempted liberal revolutions—were little more successful. Only Argentina and Paraguay broke away from Spain at this time. But as in Europe, there was a legacy of both limited and more radical revolutionary activity.

The View from Britain

Today the city of Paris is dotted with public monuments that celebrate Napoleon's victories. One of the main train stations is the Gare (Station) d'Austerlitz. A column in a city square, crowned with a statue of Napoleon, was made from the metal of enemy cannon captured at Austerlitz.

In London, another set of events and another hero is celebrated. In Trafalgar Square stands a statue of Lord Nelson, the British naval commander whose fleet destroyed a combined French and Spanish fleet in 1805. Horatio Nelson (1758–1805) remains a figure of mythic proportions in British history.

Trafalgar looms large in British history in part because Nelson was killed during the battle. More significant, the battle ensured British mastery of the seas, which forced Napoleon into economic policies that strained French ties to France's allies and satellites. Virtually unchallenged seapower enabled the British to seize colonies formerly ruled by France and its allies. Trafalgar also reflects the stature Britain had already attained as a seapower. The British victory was the result not only of superior tactics and high morale but also of superior seafaring technology and skill.

Britain's seizure of French possessions expanded British trading networks overseas. The struggles against Napoleon also enhanced British trading networks and strategic dominance closer to home, particularly in the Mediterranean. As long as the British had been involved in trade with India, the Mediterranean had been important for economic and strategic reasons. It marked the end of the land route for trade from the Indian Ocean. Its eastern coastline was dominated by the Ottoman Empire, which itself played a role in Indian affairs and was a counterweight in European politics to Russia and other powers to the north. Especially after Napoleon's aggression in Egypt, the British redoubled their efforts to control important strategic outposts in the Mediterranean, such as ports in southern Italy and on the island of Malta.

Since the late eighteenth century, the British had steadily made other gains abroad. In 1783 Britain had lost control of thirteen of its North American colonies; however, it had more successfully resolved the Irish rebellions. Similarly, in the Caribbean, British planter families, like Irish elites, were willing to accept tighter rule from the mother country in return for greater security against the enslaved subject population. Much of the autonomy of British traders in India also gave way to tightened control by British governing agents in the wake of challenges from local rulers.

The British economy would expand dramatically in the nineteenth century as industrial production expanded. The roots for that expansion were being laid in this period in the countryside of Britain, where changes in agriculture and in production were occurring. These roots were also laid in Britain's overseas possessions by the profits made there and also, increasingly, by the control of sources of raw materials, notably raw cotton raised in India. The control of the export of Indian cotton expanded significantly during the revolutionary period as part of an expanding trading system that included China, the source of tea.

However, economic expansion was not the sole motive for British aggression. In fact, economic expansion was often the product of increased British control of particular regions or sea lanes, and the reasons for it were as much strategic as economic. Not every conquest had direct economic payoffs, but British elites were sure that strategic domination was a desirable step, wherever it could be managed. One Scottish landholder, writing in the opening years of the nineteenth century, spoke for many when he said that Britain needed an empire to ensure its greatness and that an empire of the sea was an effective counterweight to Napoleon's empire on land. Much as the French were at that moment exporting features of their own political system, the British, he said, could export their constitution wherever they conquered territory.

Thus, England and France were in fact engaged in similar phases of expansion in this period. In both, the desire for power and profit drove policy. In each, myths about heroes and about the supposed benefits of domination masked the state's self-interest. In both, the effects of conquest would become a fundamental shaping force in the nineteenth century.

The Funeral of Lord Nelson, January 8, 1806 Nelson had been mortally wounded on the deck of his flagship at the Battle of Trafalgar in October. Rather than being buried at sea, as was the custom, his body was returned to London for an impressive state funeral, commemorated here in a contemporary engraving. *(National Maritime Museum, London)*

Summary

The French Revolution was a watershed in European history because it successfully challenged the principles of hereditary rule and political privilege on which all European states had hitherto been governed.

The Revolution began when a financial crisis forced the monarchy to confront the desire for political reform by a segment of the French elite. Political philosophy emerging from the Enlightenment and the example of the American Revolution moved the French reformers to action. In its initial phase, the French Revolution established the principle of constitutional government and ended many of the traditional political privileges of the Old Regime.

The Revolution moved in more radical directions because of the intransigence of the king, the threat of foreign invasion, and the actions of republican legislators and Parisian citizens. Its most radical phase, the Terror, produced the most effective legislation for ordinary citizens but also the worst violence of the Revolution. A period of unstable conservative rule that followed the Terror ended when Napoleon seized power.

Though Napoleonic rule enshrined some of the gains of the Revolution, it also subjected France and most of Europe to the great costs of wars of conquest. After Napoleon, the French monarchy was restored but forced to accept many limitations on its power as a result of the Revolution. Indeed, hereditary rule and traditional social hierarchies remained in place in much of Europe, but they would not be secure in the future. The legacy of revolutionary change would prove impossible to contain in France or anywhere else.

Notes

1. Quoted in Samuel Eliot Morison, *John Paul Jones: A Sailor's Biography* (Boston: Little, Brown, 1959), pp. 149–154.

Weighing the Evidence

POLITICAL SYMBOLS

During the French Revolution, thousands of illustrations in support of various revolutionary (or counter-revolutionary) ideas were reproduced on posters, on handbills, and in pamphlets. Some satirized their subjects, such as Marie Antoinette, or celebrated revolutionary milestones, such as the fall of the Bastille. The etching here of the woman armed with a pike, dating from 1792, falls into this category. Other pictures symbolized or reinforced various revolutionary ideals. The representation from 1795 of Liberty as a young woman wearing the liberty cap does so.[1]

An Armed Citizen, ca. 1792 *(Bibliothèque Nationale, Cabinet des estampes)*

Political images like these are an invaluable though problematic source for historians. Let us examine these two images of women and consider how French people during the Revolution might have responded to them. To understand what they meant to contemporaries, we must know something about the other images that these would have been compared to. We must also view the images in the context of the events of the Revolution itself. Immediately, then, we are presented with an interpretive agenda. How ordinary and acceptable was this image of an armed woman? If women were not citizens coequal with men, how could a woman be a symbol of liberty? What, in short, do these political images reveal about the spectrum of political life in their society?

The woman holding the pike stares determinedly at the viewer. Many details confirm what the caption announces: This is a French woman who has become free. In her hat she wears one of the symbols of revolutionary nationhood: the tricolor cockade. The badge around her waist celebrates a defining moment for the revolutionary nation: the fall of the Bastille. Her pike itself is inscribed with the words "Liberty or death!"

The woman appears to be serving not merely as a symbol of free women. She comes close to being the generic image of a free citizen, willing and able to fight for liberty—an astonishing symbolic possibility in a time when women were not yet

1. This discussion draws on the work of Joan Landes, "Representing the Body Politic: The Paradox of Gender in the Graphic Politics of the French Revolution," and Darlene Gay Levy and Harriet B. Applewhite, "Women and Militant Citizenship in Revolutionary Paris," in Sara E. Melzer and Leslie W. Rabine, eds., *Rebel Daughters: Women and the French Revolution* (New York: Oxford University Press, 1992), pp. 15–37, 79–101.

treated equally under the law or granted the same political rights as the men of their class. Other images prevalent at the time echo this possibility. Many contemporary representations of the women's march on Versailles in 1789 (see page 790) show women carrying arms, active in advancing the Revolution. By the time this image was created (most likely in 1792), many other demonstrations and violent confrontations by ordinary people had resulted in the creation of dozens of popular prints and engravings that showed women acting in the same ways as men.

Repeatedly during 1792, women proposed to the revolutionary government that women be granted the right to bear arms. Their request was denied, but it was not dismissed out of hand. There was debate, and the issue was in effect tabled. Nevertheless, women's actions in the Revolution had created at least the possibility of envisaging citizenship with a female face.

The image of liberty from 1795 does not reflect the actions of women but rather represents their exclusion from political participation. It is one of a number of images of Liberty that portray this ideal as a passive, innocent woman, here garbed in ancient dress, surrounded by a glow that in the past had been reserved for saints. Liberty here is envisaged as a pure and lofty goal, symbolized as a pure young woman.

Late in 1793, during the Terror, women had been excluded from formal participation in politics with the disbanding of women's organizations. They had gained no political rights under the Directory, which re-established some of the limited gains of the first phase of Revolution. The justification offered for their exclusion in 1793 was borrowed from Rousseau: It is contrary to nature for women to be in public life (see page 746). Women "belong" in the private world of the family, where they will nurture male citizens. Women embody ideal qualities such as patience and self-sacrifice; they are not fully formed beings capable of action in their own right.

"Liberty" as a Young Woman, ca. 1795 *(S. P. Avery Collection, Miriam and Ira D. Wallach Division of Art, Prints, and Photographs, The New York Public Library, Astor, Lenox, and Tilden Foundations)*

Such notions made it easy to use images of women to embody ideals for public purposes. A woman could represent Liberty precisely because actual women were not able to be political players.

The two images shown here thus demonstrate that political symbols can have varying relationships to "reality." The pike-bearing citizen is the more "real." Her image reflects the way actual women acted, and it represents a way of thinking about politics that became possible for the first time because of their actions. The other woman reflects not the attributes of actual women but an ideal type spawned by the use of arbitrary gender distinctions to legitimize political power. In these images we can see modern political life taking shape: the sophistication of its symbolic language; the importance of abstract ideas such as liberty and nationhood; as well as the grounding of much political life in rigid distinctions between public and private, male and female.

2. Quoted in Owen Connelly, *The French Revolution and Napoleonic Era* (New York: Holt, Rinehart and Winston, 1979), p. 32.

Suggested Reading

General Surveys

Connelly, Owen. *French Revolution/Napoleonic Era.* 1979. A clear and readable survey that devotes equal time to the Revolution and to Napoleon.

Sutherland, D. M. G. *France, 1789–1815.* 1986. A dense and detailed treatment, with extensive bibliography, that emphasizes the revolutionary over the Napoleonic period.

Thompson, John. *The French Revolution.* 1951. A classic liberal interpretation of the Revolution.

Recent Interpretations of the Revolution

Baker, Keith Michael, ed. *The French Revolution and the Creation of Modern Political Culture.* 1987. A collection of essays by diverse scholars emphasizing the Revolution as a period of change in political culture.

Furet, François. *Interpreting the French Revolution.* 1981. The major work by the outstanding French scholar of the Revolution of the current generation, written in reaction to liberal and to Marxist interpretations.

Hunt, Lynn. *The Family Romance of the French Revolution.* 1992. A study of political ideology and symbolic politics emphasizing the vast cultural consequences of killing the king and queen.

———. *Politics, Culture and Class in the French Revolution.* 1984. A survey and assessment of other interpretations of the Revolution, emphasizing the role of symbols and symbolic politics.

Kennedy, Emmet. *A Cultural History of the French Revolution.* 1989. An ambitious interpretation of the Revolution as a period of cultural change.

Landes, Joan. *Women and the Public Sphere in the Age of the French Revolution.* 1988. An analysis of the uses of gender ideology to fashion the new political world of the revolutionaries.

Manceron, Claude. *The Age of the French Revolution.* 1986. An innovative, multivolume study of the experience of the Revolution, beginning in the 1770s, told by means of biographical vignettes.

Origins and Preconditions of the Revolution

Censer, Jack, and Jeremy D. Popkin. *Press and Politics in Pre-Revolutionary France.* 1987. A work that is helpful in understanding the context of opposition to the monarchy before the outbreak of the Revolution.

Chartier, Roger. *The Cultural Origins of the French Revolution.* 1991. An interpretation of intellectual and cultural life in the eighteenth century with a view to explaining its revolutionary results; has a good bibliography.

Lefebvre, Georges. *The Coming of the French Revolution.* Translated by R. R. Palmer. 1947. The greatest of several works by this French historian; a readable Marxist interpretation that remains useful.

Palmer, R. R. *The Age of Democratic Revolution.* 2 vols. 1959. A study of the American and European revolutionary movements and their reciprocal influences; detailed, erudite, but immensely readable.

The Phases of Revolution, 1789–1791

Godeschot, J. *The Taking of the Bastille, July 14, 1789.* 1970. An explanation of the circumstances and significance of the seizure of the Bastille.

Rudé, George. *The Crowd in the French Revolution.* 1959. A classic Marxist assessment of the importance of common people to the progress of the Revolution.

Tackett, Timothy. *Priest and Paris in Eighteenth-Century France.* 1977. A study of rural Catholic life before the Revolution and after the impact of the Civil Constitution of the Clergy.

The Phases of Revolution, 1791–1794

Jordan, D. P. *The King's Trial.* 1979. A thorough and readable study of Louis XVI's trial and its importance.

Palmer, R. R. *Twelve Who Ruled.* 1941. A study of the principal figures of the Terror by one of the greatest American historians of the French Revolution.

Patrick, A. *The Men of the First French Republic.* 1972. A study of the Girondins—their identity and their coherence as a political faction.

Soboul, Albert. *The Sans-Culottes.* 1972. A study of the workers of Paris who were active in the Revolution, by Georges Lefebvre's successor as the foremost Marxist historian of the Revolution.

The Phases of Revolution, 1795–1799

James, C. L. R. *The Black Jacobins.* 1938. The classic study of the Haitian revolution in the context of events in Europe.

Sydenham, M. *The First French Republic, 1792–1804.* 1974. A useful survey of the relatively neglected phases of the Revolution.

Napoleon and Napoleonic Europe

Bayly, C. A. *Imperial Meridian.* 1989. A new study of the developing British Empire in the context of both European and world affairs; has an extensive bibliography.

Connelly, Owen. *Blundering to Glory: The Campaigns of Napoleon.* 1992. A new assessment of Napoleon's military achievements by an expert on Napoleonic warfare.

Holtman, Robert B. *The Napoleonic Revolution.* 1967. The standard survey of Napoleonic government.

Markham, Felix. *Napoleon.* 1963. The best biography in English of Napoleon.

CHAPTER 22

Restoration, Reform, and Revolution, 1814–1848

The French Revolution and the wars it unleashed challenged the existing European state system and the social and political arrangements of the Old Regime. The victors in 1814 wanted to create abroad a world congenial to their interests. At home, monarchy and aristocracy attempted to reassert, to "restore," their authority. Historians often call the period from 1814 to 1832 in Europe the "restoration." The state system, challenged and undermined nearly from the beginning, by 1848 had been substantially transformed.

The great powers tried to re-establish as much of the old European state system as possible. The international arrangements of the victorious powers—Austria, Great Britain, Prussia, and Russia—were soon challenged by the outbreak of nationalism. Nationalists aimed either to create larger political units, as in Italy and Germany, or to win independence from foreign rule, as in Greece.

Domestically, the attempt to set the clock back was of limited success. The conservatism of European rulers and their opposition to change were at odds with the new dynamism of European society. Europe was not static. Its population increased from around 190 million in 1800 to 280 million by midcentury. Population growth and the development of industry created large cities where there had been small towns or nothing at all. Factory manufacturing was not yet the main means of manufacture even in England, but it was clear that factories would eventually dominate the production of goods. Meanwhile, romanticism, liberalism, and other systems of thought were redefining the relationships of the individual to society.

Peter Fendi,
Guards on Maneuvers, 1839

Congress of Vienna Beginning in September 1814, representatives of the powers met in Vienna and hammered out a European settlement. The representatives attending were all of noble lineage, symbolizing the attempt at restoring aristocratic power in the post-Napoleonic era. *(Louvre/Giraudon/Art Resource, NY)*

European statesmen in 1814 consciously tried to forestall revolution, but within less than a generation, they were challenged by waves of violence and revolution. Revolutionaries did not win all their goals, and in many cases the forces of order crushed them. Yet major intellectual, social, and political changes had occurred by midcentury.

The Search for Stability: The Congress of Vienna

The defeat of Napoleon put an end to French dominance in Europe. The victorious Great Powers—Austria, Great Britain, Prussia, and Russia—convened in September 1814 an international conference in Vienna to make peace. In drawing up the peace terms, the victors wanted to create advantageous territorial changes for themselves and to provide for long-term stability on the European continent. Although many small powers attended the Congress of Vienna, their role was reduced to ratifying the large states' decisions. Having faced a powerful France, which had mobilized popular forces with revolutionary slogans and revolutionary principles, the victors decided to erect an international system that would remove such threats. One way to do so was to restore the European order that had existed before the French Revolution. Thus, following principles of "legitimacy and compensation," they redrew the map of Europe (Map 22.1). Rulers who had been overthrown were restored to their thrones. In France, the eldest surviving brother of Louis XVI became King Louis XVIII. In Spain, Ferdinand VII was restored to the throne from which Napoleon had toppled him and his father. The restoration, however, was not quite as complete as its proponents said it was. Since the Revolution, certain new realities had to be recognized. Napoleon had consolidated the German and Italian states; the process was acknowledged in the former with the creation of a loose German Confederation. New states that could not be dismembered had emerged.

Negotiations at the Congress of Vienna strengthened the territories bordering France, enlarged Prussia, created the kingdom of Piedmont-Sardinia, joined Belgium to Holland, and provided the victors with spoils and compensation for territories bartered away. Russia's

Map 22.1 Europe in 1815 The map of Europe was redrawn at the Congress of Vienna.

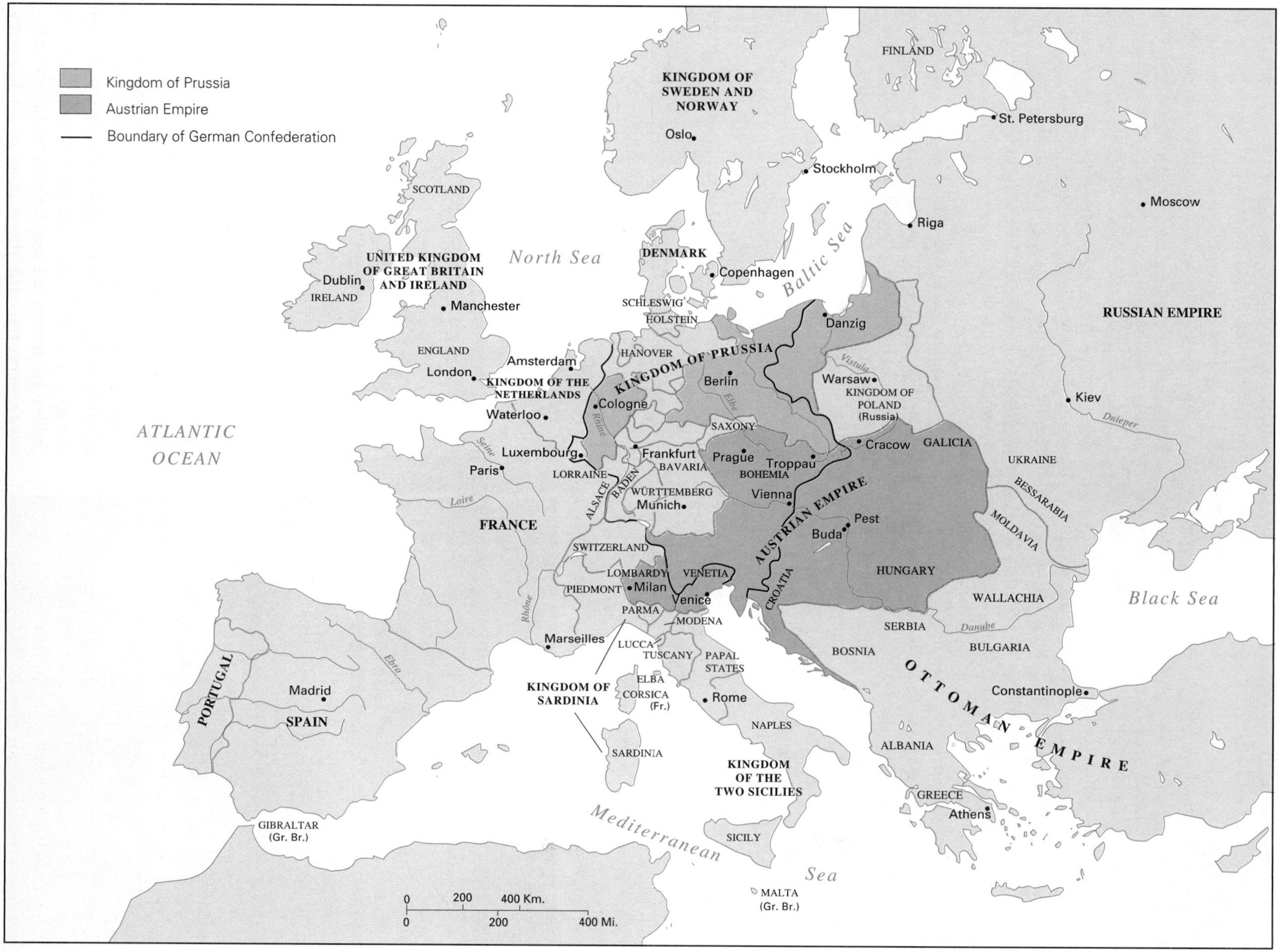
Kingdom of Prussia
Austrian Empire
Boundary of German Confederation
KINGDOM OF SWEDEN AND NORWAY
FINLAND
St. Petersburg
Oslo
Stockholm
Moscow
Riga
SCOTLAND
UNITED KINGDOM OF GREAT BRITAIN AND IRELAND
Dublin
IRELAND
Manchester
North Sea
DENMARK
Copenhagen
Baltic Sea
SCHLESWIG
HOLSTEIN
RUSSIAN EMPIRE
Danzig
ENGLAND
London
Amsterdam
HANOVER
KINGDOM OF PRUSSIA
Berlin
Vistula
Warsaw
KINGDOM OF POLAND (Russia)
Kiev
Dnieper
KINGDOM OF THE NETHERLANDS
Cologne
Rhine
Elbe
Waterloo
ATLANTIC OCEAN
SAXONY
Seine
Luxembourg
Frankfurt
BAVARIA
Prague
BOHEMIA
Troppau
Cracow
GALICIA
UKRAINE
Paris
LORRAINE
ALSACE
BADEN
WÜRTTEMBERG
Munich
Vienna
AUSTRIAN EMPIRE
BESSARABIA
Loire
FRANCE
Pest
Buda
MOLDAVIA
SWITZERLAND
LOMBARDY
VENETIA
HUNGARY
PIEDMONT
Milan
Venice
CROATIA
WALLACHIA
Black Sea
PARMA
Rhône
MODENA
SERBIA
Danube
Marseilles
LUCCA
TUSCANY
PAPAL STATES
BOSNIA
BULGARIA
PORTUGAL
Ebro
Madrid
SPAIN
KINGDOM OF SARDINIA
ELBA
CORSICA (Fr.)
Rome
OTTOMAN EMPIRE
Constantinople
NAPLES
ALBANIA
SARDINIA
KINGDOM OF THE TWO SICILIES
GREECE
Athens
GIBRALTAR (Gr. Br.)
Mediterranean Sea
SICILY
MALTA (Gr. Br.)
0
200
400 Km.
0
200
400 Mi.

reward for its contribution to the war effort was most of Poland and all of Finland, which had belonged to Sweden. Sweden was compensated for the loss of Finland by being given Norway, formerly held by Denmark, which had adhered to the Napoleonic alliance longer than the victorious Great Powers thought was appropriate. Austria received northern Italy to compensate for the loss of Belgium and the loss of parts of Poland to Russia and to strengthen its position in general. Prussia was also allowed annexations in compensation for giving up parts of Poland. England acquired a number of colonies and naval outposts. Thus, the map of Europe was changed by conservative statesmen even as they proclaimed their loyalty to the prerevolutionary past.

The leading personality at the Congress of Vienna was the Austrian foreign minister, Prince Clemens von Metternich (1773–1859), who presided over the meetings. An aristocrat in exile from the Rhineland, which had been annexed by revolutionary France, he had gone into the service of the Habsburg empire and risen to become its highest official. Personal charm, tact, and representation of a state that at the time was satiated made Metternich seem a disinterested statesman. His influence at the Congress was great.

Metternich The consummate statesman and aristocrat, Metternich tried to quell revolution at home and abroad. Some called his era the Metternichean age. *(The Royal Collection © 1993 Her Majesty Queen Elizabeth II)*

At the Congress of Vienna, the Quadruple Alliance—Austria, Great Britain, Prussia, and Russia—agreed to cooperate to prevent any future French aggression. They also planned to meet periodically to resolve all European issues—creating what was known as the "Concert of Europe."

Already at Vienna Count Charles Talleyrand (1754–1838), the wily French foreign minister, was able to insinuate himself into the councils of the Great Powers. The desire of Russia and Prussia for sizable territorial gains alarmed both Austria and Great Britain, and France joined them in limiting Russian and Prussian ambitions. At Talleyrand's insistence, France was counted as one of five Great Powers.

The Concert of Europe, including France, continued to function, and several meetings were held to discuss subsequent crises and to try to resolve them in a way satisfactory to the powers involved. Underlying the cooperation of the states was a concept of a common European destiny.

Ideological Confrontations

The international and domestic political system established in 1815 was modified by a series of challenges, even revolts, culminating in Europe-wide revolutions in 1848. The order established in 1815 was inspired by conservatism. Its challengers advocated competing ideologies: romanticism, liberalism, nationalism, and socialism.

Conservatism

The architects of the restoration justified their policies with doctrines based on the ideology of conservatism, emphasizing the need to preserve the existing order. As a coherent movement, conservatism sprang up during and after the French Revolution to support resistance to the forces of change. Not until the old order faced serious challenges in the late eighteenth and early nineteenth centuries did there emerge an ideology

Edmund Burke Defends Traditional Institutions

In 1790, Edmund Burke penned his defense of France's Old Regime. Traditional institutions that had stood the test of time, Burke insisted, should be preserved. His writings were the most reasoned argument on behalf of the conservative cause and became a classic source of conservatism.

In states there are often some obscure and almost latent causes, things which appear at first view of little moment, on which a very great part of its prosperity or adversity may most essentially depend. The science of government being, therefore, so practical in itself, and intended for such practical purposes, a matter which requires experience, and even more experience than any person can gain in his whole life, however sagacious and observing he may be, it is with infinite caution that any man ought to venture upon pulling down an edifice which has answered in any tolerable degree for ages the common purposes of society, or on building it up again without having models and patterns of approved utility before his eyes. . . .

Society is, indeed, a contract. It is not a partnership in things subservient only to the gross animal existence of a temporary and perishable nature. It is a partnership in all science, a partnership in all art, a partnership in every virtue and in all perfection. As the ends of such a partnership cannot be obtained in many generations, it becomes a partnership not only between those who are living, but between those who are living, those who are dead, and those who are to be born. Each contract of each particular state is but a clause in the great primeval contract of eternal society, linking the lower with the higher natures, connecting the visible and invisible world, according to a fixed compact sanctioned by the inviolable oath which holds all physical and all moral natures each in their appointed place. This law is not subject to the will of those who, by an obligation above them, and infinitely superior, are bound to submit their will to that law.

Source: "Reflection on the Revolution in France," in *The Works and Correspondence of Edmund Burke,* vol. 4 (London: Francis & John Rivington, 1852), pp. 200, 229–230.

justifying traditional authority. Before the American and French revolutions, the existing political institutions appeared to be permanent.

Edmund Burke (1729–1797), an English statesman and political theorist, launched one of the first intellectual assaults on the French Revolution. The revolutionary National Assembly had proclaimed ancient prerogatives superseded by the rights of man and principles of human equality based on appeals to natural law. In *Reflections on the Revolution in France* (1790), Burke said that such claims were abstract and dangerous and that the belief in human equality undermined the social order. Government should be anchored in tradition, he argued. No matter how poorly the French monarchy and its institutions had served the nation, they should be preserved; their very longevity proved their usefulness (see the box, "Edmund Burke Defends Traditional Institutions"). Burke's writings were widely read and influential on the Continent.

A more extreme version of conservatism was the counter-revolutionary or ultra-royalist ideology. Unlike Burke, who was willing to countenance some change, counter-revolutionaries and ultra-royalists wanted to restore society to its prerevolutionary condition. The most extreme counter-revolutionaries were those who had personally experienced the upheavals of the Revolution. Count Joseph de Maistre (1753–1821), a Savoyard (from the Franco-Italian border region) nobleman whose estates were occupied by the invading French, described monarchy as a God-given form of government in his *Considerations on France in 1796.* In his opinion, any attempt to abolish or even limit it was a violation of divine law. According to de Maistre and his fellow reactionaries, the authority of church and state was necessary to prevent human beings from falling into evil ways. De Maistre advocated stern government control, including the generous use of the death penalty, to keep people loyal to throne and altar.

In Germany, the influential thought of Georg Wilhelm Friedrich Hegel (1770–1831), philosophy professor at the University of Berlin, was interpreted by many of his disciples as a defense of the conservative order re-established by the Restoration. In Hegel's view, history was propelled from one stage to another by the "world spirit" incarnate in the dominant power. Just as Rome had fulfilled divine plans by dominating the ancient world, so Napoleon, when he entered Jena in 1806, was hailed by Hegel as a "world soul." The emperor's fall, however, convinced Hegel that the true world soul was incarnate in the victorious allies, particularly Prussia. The state, Hegel said, showed "the march of God in the world"; the existing power, reactionary and authoritarian, was divinely ordained.

Conservativism was also influenced by romanticism, with its glorification of the past, taste for pageantry, and belief in the organic unity of society. But by no means were all conservatives romantics. Metternich, for instance, saw his work as the attempt of an enlightened mind to restore the world that had been undermined by the emotional turmoil of the French Revolution.

Romanticism

The long-lived romantic movement emerged in the 1760s as a rebellion against rationalism and persisted until the 1840s. Many contradictory strands came together in romanticism. It was primarily a movement in the arts. Writers, painters, composers, and others consciously rebelled against the Enlightenment and its values. In contrast to the philosophes with their emphasis on reason, romantics praised emotion and feeling. Jean-Jacques Rousseau's strong appeal to sentiment was taken up by the German writer Johann Wolfgang von Goethe (1749–1832), who declared that "Feeling is everything." Goethe's *Sorrows of Young Werther* (1774), the most widely read book of the era—Napoleon had a copy by his bedside—depicted the passions of the hero, who, depressed by unrequited love, kills himself. Many readers dressed in "Werther clothes"—tight black pants and an open yellow shirt—and in some cases emulated the tragic hero by committing suicide.

Whereas the Enlightenment had studied nature for the principles that it could impart, romantics worshiped nature for its inherent beauty. The German composer Ludwig van Beethoven (1770–1827) wrote his *Pastoral* Symphony in praise of nature. The English poets William Wordsworth (1770–1850) and Samuel Taylor Coleridge (1772–1834) treated untamed wilderness as a particular subject of wonder. Wordsworth saw nature as a true teacher (see the box, "William Wordsworth Prefers Nature to Bookish Learning"). Fellow Englishman Joseph Turner (1775–1851) displayed the raw passions of the sea in his paintings *Fire at Sea* (1834) and *Snowstorm, Steamboat Off a Harbour's Mouth* (1842). To paint the latter, Turner is said to have tied himself to a ship's mast and braved a snowstorm for four hours.

In pursuit of the authentic and the ancient, and in pursuit of feeling rather than rationality, many romantics rediscovered religion. In some areas of Europe, popular religion had anticipated the artists' and intellectuals' romantic sensibilities. France experienced a revival of Catholicism. In the German states, pietism, which emerged in the seventeenth and eighteenth centuries, emphasized the personal relationship of the individual to God, unimpeded by formal theology or religious authorities. The influence of pietism, with its emphasis on feeling and emotion, spread throughout central Europe in schools and churches.

In England, emotionalism in religion expressed itself in the popularity of Methodism. Founded in the 1730s by the English preacher John Wesley (1703–1791), this movement emphasized salvation by faith. To Methodists, religion was a personal matter and was expressed in highly emotional terms. Appealing especially to the poor and desperate, Methodism by the 1790s had gained 70,000 members, and within a generation it quadrupled its flock.

Turner: St. Augustine's Gate Painted about 1793–1794, this work reflects the romantics' love of ruins and their passion for the Middle Ages, another age of faith. *(Yale Center for British Art, Paul Mellon Collection)*

The classicism of the Enlightenment had required an audience well versed in the traditional texts. Since the mid-eighteenth century, however, the reading public had grown to include people without access to elite culture. In 1815 few books printed in France had press runs larger than a thousand copies; by the 1840s, runs of three thousand copies were common. Readership had expanded. Appeals to emotion and sentiment were congenial to these new audiences. Many works depicted life as it was really lived. Thus, a new interest developed in folklore and rustic life. Many painters chose the latter as a subject matter. An earlier era had mythologized country life; the romantic in loving detail painted its realistic charms. Romantics deemed the life of the peasant to be worthy of literary and artistic attention.

The eighteenth century had denigrated the Middle Ages, but romantics celebrated the medieval period. Sir Walter Scott (1771–1832) in Scotland and Victor Hugo (1802–1885) in France celebrated chivalry and the age of faith in such popular works as *Ivanhoe* (1819) and *The Hunchback of Notre Dame* (1831). Painters frequently had as their theme Gothic buildings or ruins. Architects imitated the Gothic style in both private and public buildings.

The romantics sought displacement not only in time but also in place. The exotic had great appeal to them. Recently conquered Algeria in North Africa provided exotic scenes for French painters, among them Eugène Delacroix (1798–1863) and Jean Ingres (1780–1867).

After the French Revolution, nobles and monarchs ceased sponsoring art on a grandiose scale and were expected to conduct their lives soberly. Instead of the royal patronage, artists had to depend on members of the new middle classes to buy paintings and books and attend plays and musical performances. Earning a livelihood was always difficult for artists, but now it became more so. Forced to live marginally, artists cultivated the image of the starving genius living the life of a bohemian—a gypsy. In their lifestyles and their work, they deliberately rejected the

William Wordsworth Prefers Nature to Bookish Learning

Born and reared in England's Lake District, an area of great natural beauty, William Wordsworth was one of the foremost romantic poets. In this poem, probably written in 1798, he turns his back on his university days and embraces the instinctual appreciation of nature.

The Tables Turned

An Evening Scene . . .

Up! up! my Friend, and quit your books;
Or surely you'll grow double:
Up! up! my Friend, and clear your looks;
Why all this toil and trouble?

. . . .

Books! 'tis a dull and endless strife:
Come, hear the woodland linnet,
How sweet his music! on my life,
There's more of wisdom in it.

. . . .

One impulse from a vernal wood
May teach you more of man,
Of moral evil and of good,
Than all the sages can.

. . . .

Enough of Science and of Art;
Close up those barren leaves;
Come forth, and bring with you a heart
That watches and receives.

Source: William Knight, ed. *The Poetical Works of William Wordsworth* (Edinburgh: William Paterson, 1882), pp. 238–240.

conventions of society. The romantic period gave rise to the notion of the artistic genius, alienated from society, loyal only to art.

Romanticism exalted the incarnation of energy in mythical figures. In the dramatic poem *Faust,* Goethe retold the legend of a man who sold his soul to the devil in exchange for worldly success. In the poetic drama *Prometheus Unbound,* the English romantic poet Percy Bysshe Shelley (1792–1822) celebrated Prometheus, who stole fire from the gods and gave it to human beings. In much the same spirit, many romantics exalted Napoleon, who had overthrown kings and states. Delacroix, who witnessed the July Revolution of 1830 in Paris, celebrated the heroism and passion of the revolutionaries in *Liberty Leading the People* (1830). (See the feature, "Weighing the Evidence: Revolutionary Art," on pages 850–851.)

In the eighteenth century Mary Wollstonecraft had analyzed the social arrangements that reinforced male domination and female subservience (see page 746). The romantics provided a critique of relations between the sexes. The French writer Amandine-Aurore Dupin (1804–1876), better known by her pen name, George Sand, spoke for the emancipation of women from the close supervision of their husbands, fathers, and brothers (see the box, "George Sand Stands Up for Women's Rights"). In her personal life, Sand practiced the freedom she preached, dressing like a man, smoking cigars, and openly pursuing affairs with the writer Prosper Mérimée (1803–1870), the poet Alfred de Musset (1810–1857), and the composer Frédéric Chopin (1810–1849). The English writer Mary Ann Evans (1819–1892), like George Sand, also adopted a male pen name, George Eliot. She conducted her life in a nonconformist manner, living with a married man. The adoption of male pen names by both writers attests to the hostility that intellectal women still faced.

Romantics of many stripes declared their determination to overthrow the smug present and create a new world. Victor Hugo called for "no

George Sand Stands Up for Women's Rights

Married while young to a much older man, George Sand found marriage stultifying. Both the legal system and the social conventions of the day made it hard for a woman to leave an indifferent or even abusive husband. In her semi-autobiographical novel* Indiana *(1832), Sand protested the conditions imposed on women. In the preface to the second edition of* Indiana, *she indicated her motives for writing the novel.

I wrote *Indiana,* and I was justified in writing it; I yielded to an overpowering instinct of outcry and rebellion which God had implanted in me. God who makes nothing that is not of some use, even the most insignificant creatures, and who interposes in the most trivial as well as in great causes. But what am I saying? Is this cause that I am defending so very trivial, pray? It is the cause of half of the human race, nay, of the whole human race; for the unhappiness of woman involves that of man, as that of the slave involves that of the master, and I strove to demonstrate it in *Indiana.* . . .

I wrote *Indiana* with a feeling not deliberately reasoned out, to be sure, but a deep and genuine feeling that the laws which still govern woman's existence in wedlock, in the family and in society are unjust and barbarous. I had not to write a treatise on jurisprudence but to fight against public opinion; for it is that which postpones or advances social reforms. The war will be long and bitter; but I am neither the first nor the last nor the only champion of so noble a cause, and I will defend it so long as the breath of life remains in my body.

Source: George Sand, *Indiana,* trans. George Burnham Ives (Chicago: Academy Press, 1978), pp. 5–6 from preface to 2d ed.

more rules, no more models" to constrain the human imagination. Romantic painters and musicians consciously turned their backs on the classical tradition in both their choice of subject matter and their style. Old methods were discarded for new ones. The English poet George Gordon, Lord Byron (1788–1824), declared war on kings, on established religion, and on the international order; he died while fighting for the independence of Greece.

Nationalism

The ideology of nationalism emerged in, and partly shaped, this era. Nationalism is the belief that people derive their identity from their nation and owe their nation their primary loyalty. A list of criteria for nationhood is likely to include a common language, religion, and political authority, as well as common traditions and shared historic experiences.

Some nineteenth-century nationalists found any one of those criteria sufficient. Others insisted that all of them had to be present before a group could consider itself a nation.

In an era that saw the undermining of traditional religious values, nationalism offered a new locus of faith. To people who experienced the social turmoil spawned by the erosion of the old order, nationalism held out the promise of a new community. Nationalism became an ideal espoused as strongly as religion. The Italian nationalist Giuseppe Mazzini (1805–1872) declared that nationalism was "a faith and mission" ordained by God. The religious intensity of nationalism's appeal helps explain why nationalism attracted so many people.

Many forces shaped nationalism. Its earliest manifestation, cultural nationalism, had its origins in Rousseau's ideas of the organic nature of a people. Johann Gottfried Herder (1744–1833), Rousseau's German disciple, elaborated on Rousseau's ideas, declaring that every people has a "national spirit." To explore the unique nature of this spirit, intellectuals all over Europe began collecting folk poems, songs, and tales. In an effort to document the spirit of the German people, the Grimm brothers, Jacob (1785–1863) and Wilhelm (1786–1859), collected fairy tales and published them between 1812 and 1818; among the better known are "Little Red Riding Hood" and "Snow White."

Political nationalism, born in the era of the French Revolution, injected urgency and passion into the new ideology. In the 1770s, French aristocrats resisted attempts by the French monarchy to impose taxes, claiming that they embodied the rights of "the nation" and could not be taxed without its consent. Thus, the concept of nation was given general currency. When revolutionary France was attacked by neighboring countries, ruled by kings and dukes, the Legislative Assembly called on the French people to rise and save the nation. The realm of the king of France had become the French nation.

In reaction to the threat posed by the French, intellectuals in Germany and Italy embraced the spirit of nationalism. In Germany, the philosopher Johann Gottlieb Fichte (1762–1814) in his *Addresses to the German Nation* delivered after Prussian defeat at Jena, called on all Germans to rise up against Napoleon. He argued that Germans were endowed with a special genius that had to be safeguarded for the well-being of all humankind. In Italy, the writer Vittorio Alfieri (1749–1803) challenged France's claim to have the right to lead the peoples of Europe. That right, Alfieri insisted, properly belonged to Italians, the descendants and heirs of ancient Rome.

Culture could also be invoked for the purpose of throwing off a foreign yoke and shaping a newly independent state. In the 1810s, as part of a campaign to free Greece from the Turks, Greek intellectuals re-issued the classics of ancient Greek literature and "purified" the Greek language, ridding it of developments in popular speech over two millennia, to resemble more closely its classical antecedent. They wanted to remind their countrymen and countrywomen that they were the sons and daughters of Hellas.

Except during the French Revolution and the Napoleonic era, early-nineteenth-century nationalism was generous and cosmopolitan in its outlook. Herder and Mazzini believed that each of Europe's peoples was destined to achieve nationhood and that the nations of Europe would then live peacefully side by side. The members of groups like Young Germany and Young Italy were also members of Young Europe. Many nationalists in the 1830s and 1840s were also committed to the ideal of a "Europe of free peoples." Victor Hugo even envisioned a "European republic" with its own parliament.

Liberalism

Liberalism was a direct descendant of the Enlightenment's critique of eighteenth-century absolutism. Nineteenth-century liberals believed that individual freedom was best safeguarded by the reduction of government powers to a minimum. They wanted to impose constitutional limits on government, to establish the rule of law, to sweep away all restrictions on individual enterprise—specifically, state regulation of the economy—and to ensure a voice in government for men of property and education. Liberalism was influenced by romanticism, with its emphasis on individual freedom and the imperative of the human personality to develop to its full potential. Liberalism was also affected by nationalism, especially in multinational autocratic states like Austria, Russia, and the Ottoman Empire, in which free institutions could be established only if political independence were wrested from, respectively, Vienna, St. Petersburg, and Constantinople.

Liberalism was both an economic and a political theory. In 1776, Adam Smith (1723–1790), the influential eighteenth-century Scottish economist, published *An Inquiry into the Nature and Causes of the Wealth of Nations,* a systematic study of the economic knowledge of his era. Smith advocated freeing national economies from the fetters of the state (see the box, "Adam Smith Describes the Workings of the Market Economy"). Under the mercantilist system, prevalent until the end of the eighteenth century throughout Europe, the state regulated the prices and conditions of manufacture (see page 678). Smith argued for letting the free forces of the marketplace shape economic decisions. In France, advocates of nonintervention by government in the economy were called supporters of *laissez faire* (to

Adam Smith Describes the Workings of the Market Economy

In* An Inquiry into the Nature and Causes of the Wealth of Nations, *Adam Smith stressed how the economy can expand and society as a whole benefit if all participants try to maximize their own interests. Characterized by a mixture of theory and down-to-earth examples, his writings are still a pleasure to read.

Whoever offers to another a bargain of any kind, proposes to do this. Give me that which I want, and you shall have this which you want, is the meaning of every such offer; and it is in this manner that we obtain from one another the far greater part of those good offices which we stand in need of. It is not from the benevolence of the butcher, the brewer, or the baker, that we expect our dinner, but from their regard to their own interest. We address ourselves, not to their humanity, but to their self-love, and never talk to them of our own necessities, but of their advantages. Nobody but a beggar chooses to depend chiefly upon the benevolence of his fellow-citizens. (Vol. 1, p. 17)

Every individual is continually exerting himself to find out the most advantageous employment for whatever capital he can command. It is his own advantage, indeed, and not that of the society, which he has in view. But the study of his own advantage naturally, or rather necessarily, leads him to prefer that employment which is most advantageous to the society. (Vol. 2, p. 32)

Source: Adam Smith, *An Inquiry into the Nature and Causes of the Wealth of Nations* (London: W. Strahan, 1776).

leave alone, to let run on its own). Adam Smith was the most widely read and influential proponent of this policy.

A basic idea underlying Smith's economic theory was that economic self-interest was compatible with and even advantageous to the general interest. According to Smith, entrepreneurs will discover that they can increase profits by lowering prices and thereby selling more. Greed will thus benefit the community, for people will be able to buy goods at low prices. Consequently, an individual entrepreneur's drive for profit benefits society as a whole. The economy is driven to the benefit of all as if "by an invisible hand." Although disadvantages from allowing the marketplace to regulate itself were to appear, the competitive drive for profits, as Smith predicted, expanded the "wealth of nations."

Wages and employment were also seen as subject to the laws of supply and demand. Thomas Malthus (1766–1834), an Anglican minister, published in 1798 *An Essay on the Principle of Population.* Malthus posited that if employers paid their workers higher salaries, the workers living better-off would marry earlier and have more children, thus glutting the labor market and driving wages down. Workers, Malthus suggested, are "themselves the cause of their own poverty."

The third giant among the classical economists was the retired English stockbroker David Ricardo (1772–1823), who set forth his ideas in *Principles of Political Economy* (1817). Ricardo saw that capitalists' major expenses were wages and that to be competitive capitalists had to keep depressing wages. According to the school of classical economics, the economy is driven by laws, and intervention of any sort will only worsen the situation.

Liberals in the political realm argued that political power must be limited to prevent despotism. Enlightened eighteenth-century monarchs had declared that the purpose of their rule was to promote the public good. In even more ringing terms, the French Revolution had proclaimed that the purpose of government was to ensure the happiness of humankind. As Thomas Jefferson (1743–1826), another child of the Enlightenment, asserted in the Declaration of Independence (1776), among the "unalienable rights" of man were "life, liberty, and the pursuit of happiness." The purpose of government was to safeguard and promote those rights.

The Enlightenment had posited "natural law" as the basis of government. French liberals in the nineteenth century continued to see human liberty as founded on natural law, but their English counterparts were more empirical in outlook. Jeremy Bentham (1748–1832) argued that the purpose of government was to provide "the greatest happiness of the greatest number" and that governments should be judged on that basis. Bentham and his disciples believed that the test of government was its usefulness; they were known as "utilitarians." Democracy was implicit in Bentham's philosophy: The greatest number could ensure its own happiness only by voting for its rulers. John Stuart Mill (1803–1873), a disciple of Bentham, warned against the tyranny of the majority and emphasized the need to respect minority opinions. More clearly than Bentham, Mill advocated universal suffrage, not excluding women.

Many liberals, however, especially in the first half of the nineteenth century, feared the masses and therefore vigorously opposed democracy. The French liberal Benjamin Constant (1767–1836) denounced democracy as "the vulgarization of despotism"; the vote, he declared should be reserved for the well-off and educated. When less fortunate Frenchmen denounced the property requirements that prevented them from voting, the liberal statesman François Guizot (1787–1874) smugly replied, "Get rich."

Liberal ideas were popular with the bourgeoisie, who found it intolerable that they—the creators of society's wealth and knowledge—were denied a role in governance. Economic liberalism was also congenial to merchants and manufacturers who wished to produce wealth without the interference of the state.

In the second half of the century, however, it became clear to many people that the laws of the marketplace could not be allowed to operate without intervention. To protect workers and consumers, some controls on market forces were needed. In politics, the basic tenets of the liberal credo—the sanctity of human rights, freedom of speech and freedom to organize, the rule of law and equality before the law, and the abolition of torture—eventually became so widely accepted that even conservative and socialist opponents of liberalism accepted them as fundamental rights.

Socialism

The notion that human happiness can best be assured by the common ownership of property had been suggested in earlier times by individuals as different as the Greek philosopher Plato (427?–347 B.C.) and Sir Thomas More (1478–1535), author of *Utopia.* Troubled by the condition of the working classes, thinkers in Britain and France came to espouse theories that, beginning in the 1820s, were called "socialist." Socialists believed that the "social" ownership of property, unlike private ownership, would benefit society as a whole. During the first half of the nineteenth century, most workers, even in industrializing England, were artisans. It was in a later era that socialism would address the issues raised by industry.

In 1796, during the French Revolution, Gracchus Babeuf (1760–1797), a minor civil servant, participated in the Conspiracy of Equals (see page 801). The Revolution, however haltingly, had brought political equality to its citizens, but it had failed to bring economic equality. Babeuf decided to resort to revolution to bring about a communist society—a society in which all property would be owned in common and private property would be abolished. Work would be provided for everyone; medical services and education would be free to all. Babeuf's plot was discovered, and he was guillotined, but his theories and example of conspiratorial revolutionary action would influence later socialists.

Several other important French thinkers made contributions to what eventually became European socialism. Curiously, a French aristocrat, a member of a distinguished noble family, Henri de Saint-Simon (1760–1825), emphasized the need "to ameliorate as promptly and as quickly as possible the moral and physical existence of the most numerous class." The proper role for the state, Saint-Simon declared, was to ensure the welfare of the masses. The course of history, he suggested, was in the direction of expertise. No longer could people rule on the basis of their birth. Rather, Europe should be governed by a council of artists and scientists who would oversee the economy and ensure that everyone enjoyed a minimum level of well-being.

Young intellectuals who gravitated to Saint-Simonism took on the master's faith in the capacity of technology to transform society. They became the dynamic entrepreneurs and engineers who in the 1850s would build up the French banking, investment, and rail systems. Still later, Saint-Simonism would inspire technocracy, the notion that social problems can be resolved by the application of technology.

Another important contribution to socialist thought came from thinkers who tried to imagine an ideal world. They were later derisively dismissed as dreamers, as builders of utopias, fantasy worlds (the Greek word *utopia* means "no place"). Their schemes varied, but they shared the view that property should be owned in common and should be used for the common good. They also believed that society should rest on principles of cooperation rather than competitive individualism.

One of the earliest and most influential utopians was the Welsh mill-owner Robert Owen (1771–1859). In New Lanark, Scotland, beginning in 1800 he ran an economically successful cotton mill. He also provided generously for his workers, including guaranteeing them a job and a decent education for their children. In his writings Owen suggested the establishment of self-governing communes owning the means of production. Essentials would be distributed to all members according to their needs. Owen's ideas for the new society included equal rights for women.

Owen received little support from fellow manufacturers and political leaders. In 1824 he decided to establish in New Harmony, Indiana, an ideal new society that was to be a model for others. Within four years of its founding, New Harmony ran into economic difficulty and was torn by internal dissension. Disheartened, Owen abandoned the community and returned to England.

Another influential contributor to early socialist theory was the Frenchman Charles Fourier (1772–1837), a clerk and salesman. He wrote out in great detail what the future society would look like. It would consist of cooperative organizations called "phalanxes," each with 1600 inhabitants who would live in harmony with nature and with each other. Everyone would be assured gainful employment. Work would be made enjoyable by rotating jobs and by sharing pleasurable and unpleasurable tasks. Cooperative communes often faced the issue of who would carry out the unpleasant tasks. Fourier thought that because children presumably enjoy playing with dirt, they should be put in charge of picking up the garbage.

Fourier's belief in equality of the sexes gave him an important female following. In Belgium, the activist Zoé Gatti de Gamond (1806–1854) cofounded a phalanx for women. She believed that if women could be assured of economic well-being, other rights would follow. Inspired also by Fourier, Flora Tristan (1801–1844) was an effective spokesperson for workers' rights. In her

Flora Tristan An early socialist thinker and writer, Flora Tristan propagandized for socialism and the emancipation of women. She called women "the proletariat of the proletariat." In her last writing she declared that "the most oppressed man can oppress one being, his wife." *(Jean-Loup Charmet)*

book *Union Ouvrière* (*Workers' Union*), she suggested that all workers should contribute to establish a "Worker's Palace" in every town. In the palace, the sick and disabled would have shelter and the workers' children could be given a free education. Tramping throughout France, she spread the word of workers' solidarity and self-help.

There were other approaches. The French socialist journalist Louis Blanc (1811–1882) saw in democracy the means of bringing into existence a socialist state. By securing the vote, the common people could win control over the state and have it serve their needs. The state could be induced to buy up banks, insurance companies, and railway systems and set up a commercial and retail chain that would provide employment for workers and goods and services at prices unaffected by the search for profits. Once the workers controlled the state by the ballot, the state in turn would establish social workshops where the workers were responsible for production and supervision of business matters. Society should be established in such a way that it would be possible to "Let each produce according to his aptitudes and strength; let each consume according to his need."

Blanc's contemporary Auguste Blanqui (1805–1882) suggested a more violent mode of action. He advocated the seizure of the state by a small, dedicated band of men who were devoted to the welfare of the working class and would install communism, the equality of all. Blanqui was a perpetual conspirator, confined to state prisons for much of his long life. His ideas strengthened the notion of class warfare, and his own life served as a symbol of this struggle. The thought and example of Blanqui and the other socialists would play a major role in shaping the thinking of the most important socialist of the nineteenth century, Karl Marx (see page 881).

Restoration and Reform

After the collapse of Napoleon, the governing classes of the old regime returned to power, proclaiming their intention to restore the old order—a nearly impossible goal to achieve. The turmoil of the revolutionary era had upset old ruling dynasties. The new political order allowed some forms of popular participation, and the political boundaries of Europe were redrawn. The new ideologies of romanticism, nationalism, liberalism, and socialism emerged to challenge the existing order. Yet efforts at restoration appeared successful until at least 1830.

In central and eastern Europe, from the German states to Russia, the political systems established in 1815 would persist virtually unchanged in spite of challenges. In western Europe, important transformations would occur by the 1830s as reaction gave way to reform. Then in 1848, widespread revolutions would break out on the Continent (see Map 22.2). The language of liberalism and nationalism and even the newer idiom of socialism would be heard on the barricades, in popular assemblies, and in parliamentary halls.

France

The most dramatic restoration was that of the Bourbons in France. In 1814 Louis XVIII was installed on the throne by the victorious coalition of Great Powers that had exiled Napoleon to Elba. Louis (r. 1814–1824) had barely established his rule when Napoleon escaped to the French mainland and was acclaimed by the French people. Louis fled, but Napoleon's restored regime lasted only one hundred days, ending in defeat at the battle of Waterloo. This time, Napoleon was exiled to St. Helena, a barren island in the South Atlantic, where he remained until his death in 1821. The victorious allies re-entered Paris with Louis XVIII, who reclaimed the throne in July 1815.

Louis XVIII had granted France a charter. Liberals considered such a grant ominous, for what the king gave he could presumably also revoke. Yet the charter had many reassuring provisions. Political and religious liberties and legal equality were confirmed. The new constitution provided for a parliament with an elected lower house, the Chamber of Deputies, and an appointed upper house, the Chamber of Peers. The restoration turned the clock back, not to 1789 but closer to 1791, when the country had briefly enjoyed a constitutional monarchy. Louis XVIII stands out among European rulers because he realized that compromises with the principles of popular sovereignty proclaimed by the French Revolution were necessary. His intention was to "popularize the monarchy" and "royalize the nation." However, the exiled noblemen who re-

Daumier: Rue Transnonain, April 15, 1834 In this lithograph, the artist Daumier portrays the victims of government repression. In Lyon during riots, national guard members, believing they heard shots from a building, entered it and at random shot and stabbed its inhabitants. *(Babcock Bequest. Courtesy of Museum of Fine Arts, Boston)*

turned with him thwarted this worthy goal. Opposed to new ideas, they were determined to win back all their old privileges and prerogatives.

In an effort to win over the people who had benefited from the sale of confiscated church and aristocratic property, Louis's charter guaranteed the ownership of property acquired during the Revolution. However, the returned émigrés and spokesmen of the church challenged these terms, demanding the return of their lost properties. Returning aristocrats also reclaimed their previous positions in the army and administration from men identified with the revolutionary and Napoleonic regimes.

The most extreme reactionaries strengthened their position when liberals were blamed for the assassination in 1820 of the duke who was second in line to the throne. The press was fettered; suffrage, already limited, was further restricted, and a new law allowed the government to imprison without trial anyone suspected of conspiracy.

When Louis was succeeded by his ultra-reactionary brother, Charles X (r. 1824–1830), the extreme reactionaries came into their own. The new king encouraged passage of an indemnity bill to pay the émigrés for property lost during the Revolution and Napoleon's regime. Bourgeois and lower-class taxpayers were outraged. Many of them resented the increased power granted the clergy and were shocked by the introduction of the death penalty for acts deemed sacrilegious. Charles X's dissolution of the National Guard, one of the bastions of the middle class, further alienated the bourgeoisie.

Frustration mounted with the economic downturn of 1827, marked by poor harvests and more unemployment in the cities. The regime of Charles X was becoming increasingly unpopular. Liberal parliamentary majorities refused to accept the reactionary ministers the king appointed. On July 26, 1830, after the humiliating defeat of his party at the polls, the king issued a set of decrees suspending freedom of the press, dissolving the Chamber of Deputies, reducing the number of deputies, and stiffening property qualifications for voters in subsequent elections. The king appeared to be engineering a coup against the existing political system.

The first to protest were the Parisian journalists and typesetters, directly threatened by the censorship laws. On July 28, others joined the protest and began erecting barricades across many streets. After killing several hundred protesters, the king's forces lost control over the city. The uprising, known as "the three glorious days," drove the king into exile.

Alarmed by the crowds' clamor for a republic, the liberal opposition—consisting of some of the leading newspaper editors and liberal deputies—quickly drafted the duke of Orléans, Louis Philippe (1773–1850), to occupy the throne. Known for his liberal opinions, Louis Philippe was the son of Philippe l'Égalité, who had voted for the execution of his cousin Louis XVI and had served in the revolutionary army. The idea of a republic frightened the middle classes because it evoked memories of the Terror. A liberal constitutional monarchy was more in tune with their goals. They were better organized than the republicans and prevailed on the Chamber of Deputies to invite Louis Philippe to accept the throne.

Louis Philippe proclaimed himself "King of the French," thus seeming to acknowledge that he reigned at the behest of the people. Freedom of the press was reinstated, suffrage was extended to twice as many voters as before, 200,000 men. Nevertheless, the so-called July Monarchy—named after the July revolution that had brought it into power—disappointed some of its supporters, especially the lower classes.

Shortly after the revolution, a downturn in the economy caused another increase in unemployment. Then came an epidemic of cholera (which affected most of Europe). Also contributing to the unsettled atmosphere was labor agitation. In the silk-producing city of Lyon, for instance, artisans who were exasperated by their worsening prospects staged bloody uprisings in 1831 and 1834. In the countryside there were rumors of mass arson. In the face of unrest, the monarchy often resorted to severe repression.

Liberal institutions functioned less well than people hoped they would function. When the government and the king were criticized, they resorted to censorship. Parliament was essentially a rubber stamp. The most advanced liberals demanded that suffrage be broadened, but the government was unyielding. Inaugurated by revolution, in a few years it would face revolution.

Great Britain

Unlike the rest of Europe, Great Britain enjoyed considerable constitutional guarantees and a parliamentary regime. Yet English liberals and radicals found the government retrograde and repressive. Traumatized by the French Revolution, the governing groups clung to the past, certain that advocates for change were Jacobins in disguise. Change seemed to invite revolution.

The social unrest that beset England as it faced serious economic dislocation triggered repression. The outbreak of peace in 1815 led to a sudden drop in government expenditures, the return into the economy of several hundred thousand men who had been away at war, financial disarray, and a drop in prices. There was much discontent among the poor. The middle classes were demanding parliamentary reform. Both middle and lower classes were incensed by the clear economic advantages that the landed classes, dominating Parliament, had secured for themselves in 1815 in passing the Corn Law. This legislation imposed high tariffs on imported "corn"—that is, various forms of grain. It thus shielded the domestic market from international competition and allowed landowners to reap huge profts at the expense of consumers. All these issues were cause for demonstrations, petitions, protest marches, and other challenges to the authorities.

In August 1819, sixty thousand people gathered in St. Peter's Fields in Manchester to demand universal suffrage for men and women alike, an annual Parliament, and other democratic reforms. The crowd was peaceful and unarmed, but when a speaker whom the government considered a rabble-rouser took to the podium, the mounted militia charged foward to arrest him. In the ensuing melee, eleven people were killed and four hundred wounded. The British public was shocked by this use of violence against peaceful demonstrators. Parliament responded in autumn 1819 by passing the Six Acts, which outlawed freedom of assembly and effectively imposed censorship.

Although continuing conservative policies, the government throughout the 1820s began to embrace change. The disabilities that prevented Catholics from holding any government position and from serving in Parliament were removed in

1829. In other ways a more just order was introduced. The number of crimes punishable by death was reduced to just one, homicide. Prison reforms were made. Sir Robert Peel (1788–1850), heir to a manufacturing fortune and an enthusiastic reader of Bentham's works, was the driving force behind many of these reforms. Becoming home secretary (thus in charge of internal security) in 1828, the following year he organized an efficient London police force, known ever after as "bobbies" in his honor, to control crime and contain popular protests. The Poor Law of 1834, though harsh toward the poor, forcing them into workhouses if they were physically able, was an acknowledgment of a national responsibility for the underprivileged.

The major political problem facing Britain in the early nineteenth century was the composition of Parliament. It did not reflect the dramatic population shifts that had occurred since the seventeenth century. Industrialization had transformed mere villages into major cities—Manchester, Birmingham, Leeds, Sheffield; but those cities had no representation in Parliament. Localities that had lost population, however, were still represented. In districts known as "pocket boroughs," single individuals owned the right to a seat in Parliament. In districts known as "the rotten boroughs," a handful of voters elected a representative.

News of the July revolution in Paris encouraged liberals to push for reform and made some conservatives reluctant to oppose reform for fear of suffering the same fate as the hapless Charles X. In 1831 the liberal Whig government of Earl Grey (1764–1845), a hereditary peer who nevertheless was well attuned to the demands of the middle classes, introduced a reform bill abolishing or reducing representation for sparsely populated areas while granting representation for the populous and unrepresented cities. The bill also widened the franchise by lowering property qualifications to include many middle-class men.

People of more modest means enthusiastically supported the measure, believing that they too eventually would be enfranchised. The House of Commons approved the bill, but the House of Lords defeated it. Throughout England acts of violence threatening the social order greeted the failure of the bill to become law. The

"Peterloo" Massacre In August 1819 at St. Peter's Fields in Manchester, a crowd demanding parliamentary reform was charged by government troops, leading to bloodshed. Many English people derided the event and called it "Peterloo." *(Public Record Office)*

government was eager to see the law passed. When it threatened to have the king appoint enough new peers to pass the law, the House of Lords finally passed what came to be known as the "Great Reform Bill of 1832."

The reform was not particularly radical. Only the upper layers of the middle class were enfranchised. The number of voters increased from 286,000 to 650,000 out of a total population of 4 million adult males. Although the old franchise had not excluded women from the vote, the new law did so. Despite its shortcomings, the reform demonstrated the willingness of the political system to acknowledge the increasing economic importance of manufacturing. Parliament became a more representative forum whose composition better reflected the shift of economic power from agricultural landowners to the industrial and commercial classes. The bill passed as a result of nationwide agitation; its passage revealed the ability of the political system to bring about reform peacefully.

Parliament justified the population's newfound faith in its efficacy by undertaking several more reforms. Opposition to slavery had been voiced since the eighteenth century. Parliament took heed in 1833 and abolished slavery in the British Empire, foregoing on humanitarian grounds the still-obvious financial rewards.

Parliament's ability to bring about change stimulated support for Chartism, a movement intended to transform England into a democracy. In 1838 political radicals with artisan and middle-class support drew up a "people's charter" calling for universal male suffrage, equal electoral districts, salaries and the abolition of property qualifications for members of Parliament, the secret ballot, and annual general elections. Chartism won wide support among men and women in the working class. A petition drive to persuade Parliament to adopt the people's charter collected 1.2 million signatures in May 1839 and 3.3 million signatures three years later, but Parliament refused to act.

Winning mass support during particularly hard economic years, Chartism lost followers during a temporary economic upswing. The movement also fell under the sway of advocates of violence, who scared off many artisans and middle-class supporters. Although Chartism failed, it drew public attention to an integrated democratic program whose main provisions would be adopted piecemeal over the next half-century.

In 1839 urban businessmen founded the Anti–Corn Law League for the purpose of abolishing the Corn Law of 1815, which was increasing the price of grain. The Corn Law was unpopular with manufacturers who favored cheap food, because low food prices would allow them to pay low wages. It was also unpopular with workers, who wanted cheap bread. The anti–Corn Law movement proved more effective than Chartism because it had the support of the middle classes. Parliament, alarmed by the threat of famine due to the bad harvest of 1845, repealed the Corn Law in 1846.

In the end, repeal did not affect the price of grain. Nevertheless, repeal of the Corn Law was a milestone in British history, demonstrating the extent to which organized groups could bring about economic and social reform by putting pressure on Parliament. It also underscored what the Great Reform Act of 1832 had already revealed: Political and economic power was shifting away from the landed gentry to the urban industrial classes, and the British political system responded more flexibly to this change than did the political systems of the Continent. When revolution broke out on the Continent, it did not cross the English Channel.

Spain

In Spain, where the term *liberal* was first coined, the fate of liberals prefigured what would happen elsewhere in continental Europe. In 1812 a national parliament, the Cortes, elected during the Napoleonic occupation, had issued a democratic constitution that provided for universal manhood suffrage and a unicameral legislature that would control government policy. Supporters and admirers of the constitution in Spain and elsewhere were known as "liberals," or friends of liberty.

The Bourbon king Ferdinand VII (r. 1808, 1814–1833) was overthrown by Napoleon. In 1814 he returned to power, promising to respect the 1812 constitution. But Ferdinand was by temperament hostile to the new order, and he was a believer in the divine right of kings. He had no real intention of abiding by the constitution of 1812, a document drawn up by the educated middle classes and reflecting their anticlericalism and desire for power. Ferdinand drew his support from the aristocracy and from segments of the general population still loyal to the call of throne and altar. Liberals were arrested or driven into exile.

Ferdinand's plan to restore Spain to its earlier prominence included a reassertion of control over Spain's American colonies. The Spanish dominions had been restless in the eighteenth century, for they had witnessed the advent of an independent United States and the French occupation of Spain itself. The dominions refused to recognize the Napoleonic regime in Madrid and became increasingly self-reliant. Their attitude did not change when French control of Spain ended. Ferdinand refused to compromise with the overseas territories. He declined to grant them local autonomy and commercial freedoms such as the right to trade with whomever they pleased. Instead, he gathered an army to subdue the rebellious colonies. Some liberal junior officers, declaring the army's loyalty to the constitution of 1812, won support from the rank and file, which balked at going overseas. This military mutiny coinciding with a sympathetic provincial uprising produced the "revolution of 1820," the first major assault on the European order established in 1815 at the Congress of Vienna. Ferdinand appealed to the European powers for help. France intervened on his behalf and crushed the uprising.

Ferdinand restored his reactionary regime but could not regain Spain's American colonies. The British, sympathetic to the cause of Latin American independence and eager for commercial access to the region, made clear their opposition to reconquest. The British navy's dominance of the seas made Britain's opposition effective. The United States, meanwhile, had recognized the independence of the Latin American republics and wished to see their independence maintained. In 1823 President James Monroe (r. 1817–1825) issued the Monroe Doctrine, proclaiming U.S. opposition to any European colonization or intervention in the affairs of independent republics in the Americas. The United States had no military power to back this proclamation, but the British navy effectively enforced it. By 1825, all Spain's colonies on the mainland in Central and South America had won their freedom.

Upon Ferdinand's death in 1833, Spain was torn by competing claims to the succession. Liberals supported his infant daughter. Conservatives supported his brother. A civil war between these factions led to extreme cruelty on both sides. The moderates and liberals won, but the military gained the upper hand in governing. A Cortes and what appeared to be constitutional government were established, but real power lay in the hands of the army, representing a small oligarchy of the business and landowning classes. Several successive officers served as dictators of the country, replacing each other in a series of coups. One of them, General Ramón Narváez (1799–1868), brutally ran the country from 1844 to 1851. When he was on his deathbed, he was asked whether he forgave his enemies. He answered, "I have no enemies. I have shot them all!"

EUROPEAN REVOLUTIONS, 1820–1831

January 1820	Spain
July 1820	Naples
August 1820	Portugal
March 1821	Piedmont; Greece
December 1825	Russia
July 1830	France
August 1830	Belgium
September 1830	Brunswick; Saxony; Hesse-Cassel
November 1830	Poland
February 1831	Revolt in Piedmont, Modena, and Parma; revolt in Papal States

Austria and the German States

The Austrian empire's farflung territories seemed to its Habsburg rulers to require a firm hand. Liberalism, which challenged imperial power, could not be countenanced. Nor, in this multinational empire, could nationalism be tolerated. The emperor, Francis I (r. 1806–1835), was opposed to any change; his motto was "Rule and change nothing." Prince Metternich, Francis's chief minister, viewed the French Revolution of 1789 and its aftermath as a disaster and believed his task was to hold the line against the threat of revolution. Quick to interpret protests or the desire for change as a threat to the fundamental order, Metternich established a network of secret police and informers to spy on the imperial subjects and keep them in check.

In most of the German states, the political order was authoritarian and inflexible. The west German states of Baden, Württemberg, and Bavaria had been granted constitutions by their rulers, although effective power remained in the hands of the ruling houses. The king of Prussia had repeatedly promised a constitution, but none had materialized. A central, representative, united Diet would not meet until 1847. Prussia was ruled by an alliance of the king and the *Junkers,* the landowning aristocrats who staffed the officer corps and the bureaucracy. Both were efficient enough to serve as models for the rest of Europe. Where Prussia lagged by liberal standards was in its political institutions.

Throughout the German states, the urban middle classes, intellectuals, journalists, university professors, and students were frustrated with the existing system. They were disappointed by the lack of free institutions and the failure of the patriotic wars against Napoleon to create a united Germany. University students formed *Burschenschaften,* or brotherhoods, whose slogan was "Honor, Liberty, Fatherland." Conservatives saw the agitation of these young Germans as a threat to the existing order. Metternich imposed a policy of reaction on the Germanic Confederation and had it adopt the Carlsbad Decrees in July 1819, establishing close supervision over the universities, censorship of the press, and dissolution of the youth groups. Wholesale persecution of liberals and nationalists followed. The Prussian king dismissed his more enlightened officials.

The outbreak of revolution in Paris in 1830 inspired further political agitation. The authoritarian ruler of the state of Brunswick was forced to resign. Under pressure, his successor and the rulers of Saxony, Hanover, and Hesse-Cassel promulgated new constitutions. Mounting opposition to local despots and agitation for national unity led to the prosecution of outspoken liberals. Many associated with the "young Germany" movement fled abroad, particularly to Paris. Reaction was maintained, and the free development of liberal ideals was prevented in Germany.

Italy

Austria exercised considerable power over Italy through its possession of Italian territory. Some had been acquired in the eighteenth century; some, like Lombardy and Venetia, was acquired in 1815. Austria had dynastic ties to several ruling houses in the central part of the peninsula and political alliances with others, including the papacy. The only ruling house to be free of Austrian ties—and hence eventually looked to by nationalists as a possible rallying point for the independence of the peninsula—was the Savoy dynasty of Piedmont-Sardinia.

Italy consisted of eight political states, and it was in Austria's interest to maintain disunity. Many Italian rulers—notably the papacy, the kingdom of Naples, and the central Italian duchies—imposed repressive policies, knowing that they could count on Austrian assistance in case of a popular uprising. Metternich's interventions to crush liberal rebellions generated hatred of Austria among Italian liberals and nationalists.

Austria's most dramatic intervention in the affairs of Italy was undertaken on behalf of Ferdinand IV of Naples (r. 1759–1806, 1815–1825). He swore loyalty to a constitution in 1812 (closely patterned on that of Spain) but reneged when he was restored to power. Inspired by the recent events in Spain, Italian military officers demanding restoration of the constitution staged a revolt in July 1820. The revolution soon spread from the mainland to Sicily. Ferdinand appealed to the Great Powers, which entrusted Austria with the task of restoring the king. Austria did so with speed and brutality.

The political backwardness of the Italian states cannot be wholly blamed on Austria. Piedmont, which was free of Austrian influence, nevertheless embraced reaction. When the royal house of Savoy returned to power in 1815, it nullified all laws passed under the French and banned from government service all officials who had served the French. The Jesuits were put in charge of education and censorship.

Throughout Italy, there was resistance to the restoration. Liberal journalists favored a constitutional system. The Carbonari (literally "charcoal burners," suggestive of men of simple occupations), a nationalist conspiratorial group that had been formed to fight the French occupation, after 1815 targeted the restoration regimes. In March 1821, liberal-minded young army officers in Piedmont, inspired by the examples of Spain and Naples, proclaimed their support of a constitution and their desire to evict Austria from Italy. The movement, essentially military, did not win much popular support. Piedmontese loyal to the monarch Charles Felix (r. 1821–1831), with the help of Austria, crushed the uprising.

A decade later, under the impact of the July revolution in Paris, the same forces came to the fore. An uprising broke out in Piedmont, then spread to the Papal States and Modena. The revolt was aimed at the authoritarian rulers of the various Italian states, but it was also in support of a united Italy. Led by intellectuals and some members of the middle classes, the uprisings lacked a popular base and were fragmented by the participants' primary loyalties to their individual states and cities. The Austrians promptly crushed the hopes for the liberty and unity of Italy.

Russia

By far the most autocratic of the European states was tsarist Russia. Since 1801 it had been ruled by Alexander I (r. 1801–1825), an enigmatic character whose domestic policy vacillated between liberalism and reaction and whose foreign policy vacillated between brutal power politics and apparently selfless idealism. Alexander's policies puzzled his contemporaries. When the Congress of Vienna gave additional Polish lands to the tsar, he demonstrated his liberalism to the world (and curried favor with his new subjects) by granting Poland a liberal constitution. But he offered no such constitution to his own people. He and his council discussed terms for the abolition of serfdom in 1803 and again in 1812, but like so many of his plans this one was not implemented. Although he earnestly desired freedom for the serfs, the tsar was unwilling to impose any policy detrimental to the interests and privileges of the landed gentry.

Toward the end of his rule, Alexander became increasingly authoritarian and repressive, probably in recognition of growing opposition. Western liberal ideas, including constitutionalism, were adopted by Russian military officers who had served in western Europe, by Russian Freemasons who had corresponded with Masonic lodges in western Europe, and by Russian intellectuals who read Western liberal political tracts. These groups formed secret societies with varying programs. Some envisioned Russia as a republic, others as a constitutional monarchy; but all shared a commitment to the abolition of serfdom and the establishment of a freer society.

Alexander died in December 1825, leaving ambiguous which of his brothers would succeed him. Taking advantage of the confusion, the military conspirators declared in favor of the older brother, Constantine, in the belief that he favored a constitutional government. The younger brother, Nicholas, claimed to be the legal heir. The St. Petersburg garrison rallied to the conspirators' cause. The officers, taking their cue from the Spanish uprising of 1820, believed that the military could bring about change on its own in a country in which popular participation in governance was unknown.

Nicholas I, Emperor of Russia Acceding to the throne at the same time as the Decembrist uprising, Nicholas was haunted by the danger of revolution and ran a repressive regime. *(The Fotomas Index)*

The military uprising in the Russian capital was badly coordinated with uprisings planned in the countryside. The "Decembrist uprising," as it was called, quickly failed. Nicholas crushed it. He had the leaders executed, sent to Siberia, or sent into exile.

Though opposed to autocracy, the Decembrist conspirators were solidly in the Russian tradition in their attempt to impose modernity on

Russia from above. In spite of its tragic end, throughout the nineteenth century the Decembrist uprising served as an inspiration to Russians resisting tsarist oppression.

Coming to the throne after crushing a revolt, Nicholas I (r. 1825–1855) was obsessed with the danger of revolution and was determined to suppress all challenges to his authority. He created a stern, centralized bureaucracy to control all facets of Russian life. He originated the modern Russian secret police called the "Third Section"; it was above the law—a state within the state.

Russia's single most overwhelming problem was serfdom. Economically, serfdom had little to recommend it; free labor was far more efficient. Moreover, public safety was threatened by the serfs' dissatisfaction with their lot. During Nicholas's thirty-year reign there were over six hundred peasant uprisings, half of them quelled by the military. Nicholas understood that serfdom had to be abolished for Russia's own good, but he could envision no clear alternative to serfdom. Emancipation, he believed, would only sow further disorder. Except for a few minor reforms, he did nothing. Nicholas's death, followed by Russia's defeat in the Crimean War, eventually brought to an end the institution that had held nearly half of the Russian people in bondage.

The Ottoman Empire

In its sheer mass, the Ottoman Empire continued to be a world empire. It extended over three continents. In Africa it ran across the whole North African coast. In Europe it stretched from Dalmatia (on the Adriatic coast) to Constantinople. In Asia it extended from Mesopotamia (present-day Iraq) to Anatolia (present-day Turkey). But it was an empire in decline, having difficulty maintaining its institutions and seriously challenged from within by nationalist movements and from outside by foreign threats.

The Ottoman bureaucracy, once the mainstay of the government, had fallen into decay. In the past, officials had been recruited and advanced by merit; now lacking funds, Constantinople sold government offices. Tax collectors ruthlessly squeezed the peasantry. The Janissaries, in the past an elite military force, by the eighteenth century had become an undisciplined band that menaced the peoples of the Ottoman Empire—especially those located at great distances from the close control of the capital.

In the 1790s, some rulers began to recognize the need to curb the army. But the rebellious Janissaries, after strangling the reform-minded Sultan Selim III (r. 1789–1807), forced the new ruler, Mahmud II (r. 1808–1839), to retract most of the previous improvements. The worst features of the declining empire were restored.

Most of the Ottoman empire was inhabited by Muslims, but in the Balkans Christians were in the majority. Ottoman officials usually treated Christians no differently from the way they treated their Muslim neighbors. But the Christian subject people found in their religion a means of collectively resisting a harsh and at times capricious rule. Some of the Christian peoples in the Balkans looked back nostalgically to earlier eras—the Greeks to when they had formed a great civilization or the Serbs to when they had possessed their own state. The ideas of nationalism and liberty that triggered changes in western Europe also stirred the peoples of the Balkans.

The Serbs were the first people to revolt successfully against Ottoman rule. A poor, mountainous region, Serbia suffered greatly from the rapaciousness of the Janissaries. In protest a revolt broke out in 1804. At first the Ottomans were able to crush the uprising, but in 1815 they had to recognize one of its leaders, Milosh Obrenovich (r. 1815–1839), as governor and allow the formation of a national assembly. In 1830, under pressure from Russia, which took an interest in fellow Slavs and members of the Orthodox faith, Constantinople recognized Milosh as hereditary ruler over an autonomous Serbia.

The Greeks' struggle led to complete independence from Ottoman rule. Greeks served as administrators throughout the Ottoman lands and, as merchants and seafarers, traveled widely throughout the Mediterranean world and beyond. They had come into contact with the ideas of the French Revolution, wanted to revive their homeland, and thus formed a conspiratorial group, the Philike Heteira, or Society of Friends, which was dedicated to restoring the independence of Greece. Greek peasants were not particularly interested in politics, but they were hostile to the Turks, who had accumulated vast landholdings at their expense. This in part motivated the Greek peasants to join an anti-Turkish campaign.

The revolt started in 1821. Greeks killed large numbers of defenseless Turks in the Morea, in the Peloponnesus. The Turkish authorities hanged the Greek patriarch in Constantinople and massacred or sold into slavery the population of the Aegean island of Chios. The war continued in fits. By 1827, the Ottomans, aided by their vassal Mehemet Ali (1769–1849) of Egypt, controlled most of the Balkan peninsula. The rest of Europe, excited by the idea of an independent Greece restored to its past greatness, widely supported the Greek movement for freedom. The Great Powers intervened in 1827, sending their navies to intercept supplies intended for the Ottoman forces. At Navarino Bay, the Turkish navy fired on the allies, who returned fire and sank the Ottoman navy. With the destruction of Ottoman power, the independence of Greece was ensured. In 1830 an international agreement spelled out the independence of Greece.

In the 1820s and 1830s, local agitation and several Russian military interventions weakened Ottoman control over Wallachia and Moldavia (future Romania). Constantinople lost its right to name the governors of the provinces. It had to reduce its fortifications there, and from 1828 to 1834 Russian troops occupied the provinces.

Losing influence in the Balkans, the Ottoman Empire was also challenged elsewhere. In Egypt, Mehemet Ali modernized his army and used it to wrest Syria away in 1831. He threatened to march against his overlord, the sultan. Britain and Russia, concerned lest the Ottoman Empire collapse and thus threaten the balance of power, intervened on its behalf. Constantinople won back Syria but in 1841 had to acknowledge Mehemet Ali as the hereditary ruler of Egypt. The survival of the Ottoman Empire was beginning to depend on the goodwill of the Great Powers. One of them, France, in 1830 attacked and conquered Algeria, depriving the empire of its westernmost outpost.

The Revolutions of 1848

From France in the west to Poland in the east, at least fifty separate revolts and uprisings shook the Continent in 1848 (Map 22.2). They were triggered as much by discontent as by the hope for change. The economic depression of 1845–1846 played an important role in undermining the existing regimes. Agricultural disasters were accompanied by an industrial downturn, creating massive unemployment. Municipal and national governments seemed unable to deal with the crowding, disease, and unsanitary conditions that were worsening tensions already running high in the cities. People were discontented and ready to heed those who called for the overthrow of the existing regimes.

France

Once again the spark for revolution was ignited in Paris and spread from there to the rest of the Continent. Economic crisis had a severe impact in the French capital. In some occupations as many as half of the people were out of work. The price of bread had shot up to over one franc a pound (less than the daily consumption of a male laborer); a franc was roughly a day's pay for the average male worker. Given any provocation, thousands of workers might pour into the streets to protest the government's indifference to their desperation.

Meanwhile, liberals were agitating for the expansion of suffrage. When political meetings were forbidden in 1847, they resorted to banquets featuring long-winded toasts indistinguishable from political speeches. Such a banquet was scheduled for Paris on February 22 to celebrate the birthday of George Washington—an icon to French liberals. When the government banned the meeting, mass demonstrations by students and workers broke out. Unlike the British with their professional urban police, the French had no forces trained in crowd control. The government called in the military, whose tactics were more appropriate to engaging an enemy army than to containing civilian demonstrators. On February 23, soldiers guarding the Ministry of Foreign

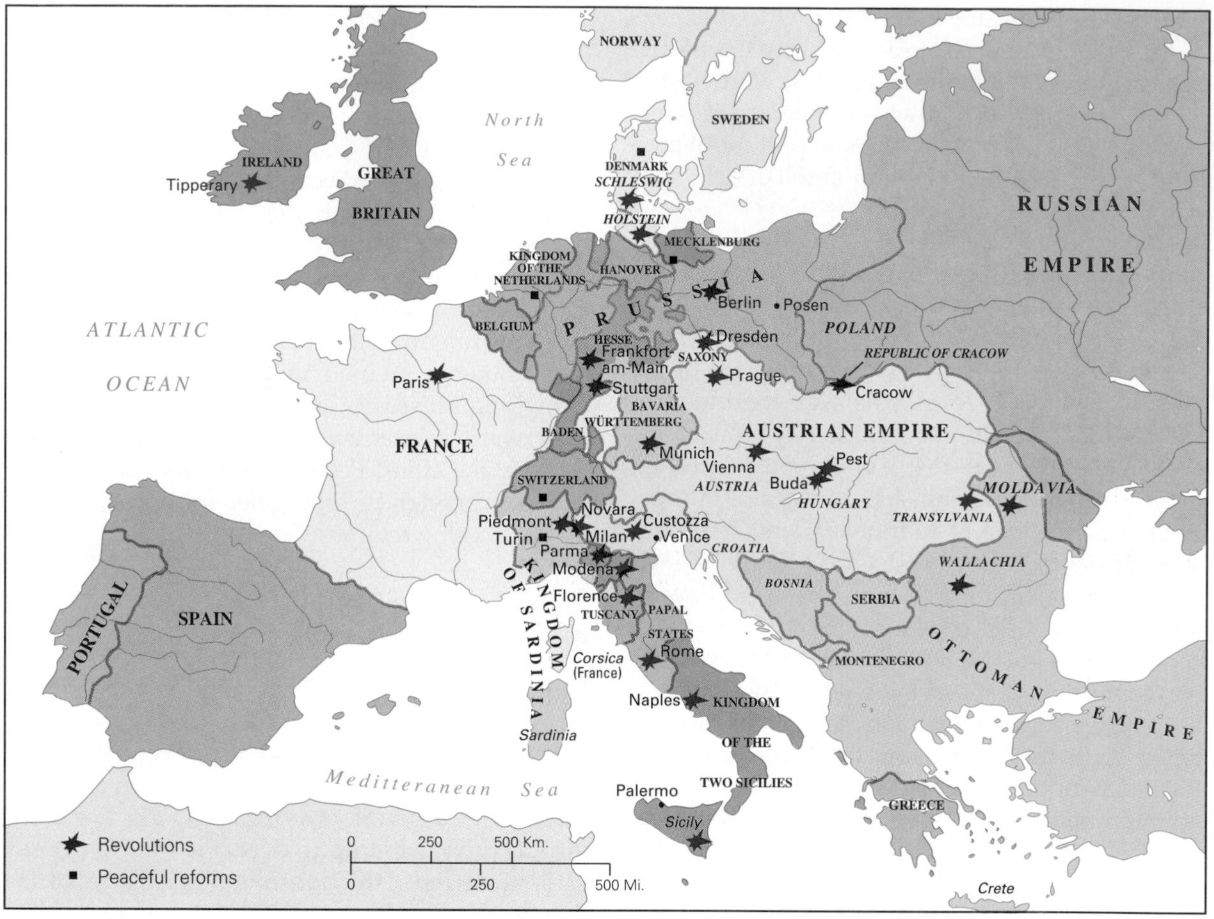

Map 22.2 Major Revolutions and Reforms, 1848–1849 In no other year had as many revolts broken out simultaneously; in many cases the revolutions led to reforms and new constitutions.

Affairs panicked and shot into a crowd; fifty-two people died.

Word spread that the government was shooting at the people. To protect themselves, residents of the traditionally revolutionary neighborhoods near the Bastille erected barricades. On February 24, police and army posts were attacked, and the royal palace was surrounded. The National Guard, a civilian force recruited from the artisans and the middle class and charged with restoring order, had become sympathetic to the protesters and refused to fight the populace. Louis Philippe resigned as king and fled for London under the pseudonym "Mr. Smith." The royalists were clearly discredited.

The abruptness of the king's resignation left the opposition forces in disarray. The opposition shared one goal—the extension of suffrage—but otherwise diverged sharply. Liberals accepted the monarchy but were offended by its corruption, manipulation of elections, and overly restrictive suffrage. More radical elements favored a democratic republic. Socialists' prime goal was a government that would ensure social justice.

The new regime, hastily organized under the pressure of a mob invasion of the Chamber of Deputies, lacked uniformity in its makeup or ideas. The provisional government consisted of well-known liberal opponents of the July Monarchy such as the poet Alphonse de Lamartine (1790–1869) and the journalist Alexandre Ledru-Rollin (1807–1874). Under pressure from the radicals, socialist journalist Louis Blanc (see page 832) and a worker known only as Albert joined the government. At first the liberal supporters of constitutional democracy and the radical republicans committed to economic justice for the underprivileged cooperated with each other. Under the strain of events, however, the coalition had fallen apart by late spring.

Bowing to pressure from the poor and unemployed of Paris, who resorted to demonstrations and occupied City Hall, the government established national workshops and a commission headed by Louis Blanc to study the problems of the poor. The national workshops were not a substitute for the capitalist order, as Louis Blanc had intended, but were a stopgap measure to enable the unemployed to earn a livelihood. They nevertheless represented the most ambitious plan that any French government had yet undertaken to combat the misery of the poor.

The new republic was quick to institute other reforms. It abolished slavery in the colonies and the death penalty for political crimes. Imprisonment for debt ceased, and the workday was limited to ten hours in Paris, eleven hours in the départements. The most radical move was the adoption of universal male suffrage. Men in 1789 had identified citizenship as a distinctly male prerogative, and they continued to do so.

In the general euphoria over human liberties, women asserted their rights. A new woman's newspaper, *La Voix des Femmes (The Voice of Women),* argued for equal pay, political rights, and educational opportunities. But when women's political clubs operating under the paper's auspices petitioned for the vote, the revolutionary government abolished them. In light of women's active role at the barricades that had toppled the monarchy, this was a bitter disappointment.

The first universal-manhood elections took place in April. The results were surprising. Nearly everyone expected enfranchisement of the poor and uneducated to bring about the election of radicals and outsiders. Most of France's population, however, consisted of rural peasants. Although there were some radical peasants, particularly in the south, most peasants distrusted the radicalism of the capital and resented the tax increases needed to support social programs. At the polls, peasants tended to vote for their social superiors: the local landowner, notary, or lawyer. Even Paris elected mostly moderate deputies. The new National Assembly elected by popular vote did not look much different from that of the July Monarchy. Most members were landowners and lawyers; among the new deputies, there were only seventeen workers and no peasants.

The government that emerged was more moderate than the conservative turnout at the polls would have justified but was at loggerheads with the radical workers in Paris. Under conservative pressure, the Assembly in May disbanded the national workshops, which were expensive to run and accomplishing little, though they provided a livelihood for more than half of the male working-class population of Paris. At the news of

Revolutionary Women In this cartoon, entitled "The Divorced Women," Daumier ridicules women who fought for their rights in the Revolution of 1848. They are seen as divorced, deprived of male companionship, and probably therefore crazed. This kind of depiction was one of many ways in which women were discouraged from participating in politics. *(Jean-Loup Charmet)*

The June Days of 1848

In 1831 and 1832, Alexis de Tocqueville traveled throughout the United States and later analyzed American society in **Democracy in America** *(1835, 1840). In 1848, he observed the revolution in France firsthand and wrote this eyewitness account of the bloody confrontation between workers and government troops.*

I come at last to the insurrection of June, the most extensive and the most singular that has occurred in our history, and perhaps in any other.

What distinguished it also, among all the events of this kind which have succeeded one another in France for sixty years, is that it did not aim at changing the form of government, but at altering the order of society. It was not, strictly speaking, a political struggle, in the sense which until then we had given to the word, but a struggle of class against class, a sort of Servile War.

This formidable insurrection was not the enterprise of a certain number of conspirators, but the revolt of one section of the population against another. Women took part in it as well as men. While the latter fought, the former prepared and carried ammunition; and when at last the time had come to surrender, the women were the last to yield.

These women went to battle with, as it were, a housewifely ardour: they looked to victory for the comfort of their husbands and the education of their children. They took pleasure in this war as they might have taken pleasure in a lottery.

Source: The Recollections of Alexis de Tocqueville, trans. and ed. Alexander Teixeira de Matos and J. P. Mayer (New York: Meridian, 1959), pp. 150–151.

the closings, people who depended on the workshops rose up in despair. After days of fighting in which 1500 were killed and 12,000 arrested, government forces gained control of the city. Passionate feelings on both sides led to savagery: Corpses were mutilated, and severed heads were paraded through the streets. Both the liberal commentator Alexis de Tocqueville (1805–1859) and the socialist Karl Marx called the June uprisings class warfare between the poor and the rich. (See the box, "The June Days of 1848.")

The defeat of the insurgents revealed that universal suffrage had enabled the government to mobilize moderate public opinion against radicalism in Paris. The advent of railroads had enabled the government to muster military support from outside the city. Thereafter, it would be far more difficult for radical Parisian crowds to dictate policies to the rest of the country.

People had entered into the revolution in February with confidence, but the June uprisings transformed the situation. The propertied classes, feeling menaced by the poor, looked to the authorities for security. Of the several candidates for president in 1848, Louis Napoleon (1808–1873), a nephew of Napoleon Bonaparte, appealed to the largest cross-section of the population. The bourgeoisie was attracted by the promise of authority and order. Peasants disillusioned by the tax policies of the republic remained loyal to the memory of Napoleonic glory. Workers embittered by the government's repression of the June uprisings were impressed by Louis Napoleon's vaguely socialistic program.

Louis Napoleon received nearly three times as many votes as all his opponents combined. His government was conservative, composed of men of the old order. Three years later, Louis

Celebrating the Revolution of 1848 in Vienna In the early stages of the Austrian revolution, enthusiasm crossed class lines. In this painting simple artisans and wealthy burghers mingle on top of a barricade. The sense of solidarity was, however, to be short-lived. *(Historisches Museen der Stadt Wien)*

Napoleon dissolved the National Assembly by force and established a personal dictatorship. In 1852 he declared himself Emperor Napoleon III.

Austria

In Austria, news of the overthrow of Louis Philippe and of agitation in the German states prompted demonstrations and petitions calling for a constitution and the dismissal of Metternich, the symbol of the reactionary order. In the face of growing opposition, Metternich resigned, and the army withdrew from Vienna, which appeared to have fallen under the control of students and workers. On March 15, 1848, the imperial court, surrounded by crowds of students and workers, announced its willingness to issue a constitution. Even more important was the decision to abolish serfdom. There had been fear of a serf uprising, but the relatively generous terms of the emancipation mollified the peasantry.

The promised constitution was issued, but it was drafted by the emperor rather than by representatives of the people. It was probably acceptable to the male middle classes because it enfranchised them, but students and workers who favored popular sovereignty opposed it. Mass demonstrations and an invasion of the prime minister's office prompted the court to leave Vienna for Innsbruck on May 17.

The government also faced revolts in the non-German parts of the empire: in Italy, Hungary, the Czech lands, and Croatia. In March, Vienna acquiesced to Hungary's demands; thereafter Hungary was joined to the Austrian empire by personal union to the emperor. Constitutional government was established in Hungary, but participation in the political process was limited to Magyars, who were the single largest ethnic group but were only 40 percent of the population. The other peoples of Hungary—Romanians, Slovaks, Croats and Slovenes—did not want to live under Magyar rule; they preferred the more distant rule of German Vienna.

Many nationalities rallied to the Austrian empire in 1848 for their own reasons—fear of falling under German rule in Bohemia, fear of Magyar rule in Hungary—and the empire survived. There was no solidarity among the various nationalities that rose up against Vienna's rule. The empire had been able to practice a policy of divide and rule, yet the dangers nationalism posed to its survival were also revealed.

The revolution in Austria and its possessions was suppressed as soon as the royal court was able to gather military forces and send them against the rebels. General Alfred Windischgratz (1787–1862) bombarded Prague into submission in June and Vienna in November. By August 1849, the rebellious Hungarians had been crushed. A reactionary regime under Prince Felix von Schwarzenberg (1800–1852) re-established absolutist rule over the empire.

Italy

In the years before 1848, Italy was in the grip of unrest and the expectation of some great change. Economic hardship triggered social turmoil. The pope was not only a religious leader but also secular ruler of the Papal States. In 1846, when Pius IX (r. 1846–1878) was elected, Italians hoped for change. Pius appeared to be a liberal and a supporter of Italian national unification. In January 1848, revolution forced the king of Sicily to grant a constitution to his subjects. The Sicilian revolution was the first to erupt in Europe, but it was news of the Paris uprising in February that stimulated further revolutions in Italy.

Emboldened by news of the revolution in Vienna, Italians then under Austrian rule revolted, forcing the Austrians to evacuate their Italian possessions. The middle classes, though eager to be free of Austrian rule, saw working-class radicals as a threat. They believed that annexation to nearby Piedmont would provide security from both Austria and the lower classes. The king of Piedmont, Charles Albert (r. 1831–1849), reluctantly decided to unite Italy under his throne if doing so would prevent the spread of radicalism to his kingdom. On March 24, 1848, he declared war on Austria but was defeated in July at the battle of Custozza and had to sue for an armistice.

The pope had expressed sympathy for Italian unification but provided no support for the cause. Republicans, disappointed by the pope's abandonment of the national cause and a liberal program, forced the pope to flee. In January 1849 they declared the Roman Republic. Hope ran high that it would become the capital of a united republican Italy. Giuseppe Mazzini was to be a member of the governing triumvirate.

In Piedmont, meanwhile, Charles Albert's desire to bring the radical movement under control by defeating the Austrians tempted him to declare war on Austria once again, in March 1849. The outcome for Piedmont was even worse than it had been a year earlier. Within six days its army was defeated. Humiliated, Charles Albert resigned his throne to his son, Victor Emmanuel II (r. 1849–1878).

The Austrians quickly reconquered their lost provinces and helped restore their puppets to power. Louis Napoleon, the newly elected president of France, eager to curry favor with Catholic voters, sent French troops to Rome, restoring the pope to power in July 1849. Nevertheless, profound liberal and even revolutionary ideas—constitutional government, universal suffrage, abolition of the remnants of the Old Regime—had been expressed and in some cases implemented, though briefly. Most reforms were rescinded, but Piedmont's liberal constitution, the *Statuto*, implemented in 1848, was retained and later became the constitution of a united Italy.

The German States

News of the February uprising in Paris also acted as a catalyst for change in the German states. In response to large public demonstrations in the grand duchy of Baden in southwestern Germany, the duke—reluctant to suffer the same fate as Louis Philippe—dismissed his conservative prime minister and installed a government sympathetic to the aspirations of middle-class liberals. The forces of change seemed irresistible. As the king of Württemberg observed, "I cannot mount on horseback against ideas." The wisest course appeared to be compromise. He and many of his fellow dukes and princes changed their governments, dismissing their cabinets and instituting constitutions. Bavaria's King Ludwig I (r. 1825–1848), who had scandalized the court by his public liaison with a dancer, found himself without supporters when public demonstrations broke out. He abdicated in favor of his son.

Prussia was conspicuous for being untouched by the revolutionary wave. But when news of Metternich's fall reached Berlin on March 16, middle-class liberals and artisans demonstrated for reforms. To appease his subjects, King Frederick William IV (r. 1840–1861) appointed a liberal Rhenish businessman to head a new government.

Except for King Ludwig of Bavaria, none of the monarchs in Germany lost their thrones. All were able to weather the storm by accepting significant changes. Representative government was introduced, and suffrage was extended, though it was still restricted to men of property. Government, no longer the exclusive preserve of the aristocracy, was opened to men from the liberal professions and the business classes.

By the fall of 1848, a royalist reaction had begun to take shape in Prussia. In October, facing a workers' uprising triggered by economic despair, the king brought soldiers into Berlin, declared a state of siege, and dissolved the assembly. The Prussian reassertion of royal power, though partial, was a signal for other German rulers to use courage and dismiss their liberal ministers.

The revolutionary outbreaks in the German states in 1848 were triggered by dissatisfaction with local economic and political conditions, not by agitation for German unification. But once the revolutions had taken hold, preoccupying the two largest powers, Prussia and Austria—which both opposed unification lest it reduce their control—the question of unification quickly came to the fore.

In March 1848, a self-appointed national committee invited five hundred prominent German liberals to convene in Frankfurt to begin the process of national unification. In addition to fulfilling a long-standing liberal dream, a united nation would consolidate the liberal victory over absolutism.

The gathering called for suffrage based on property qualifications. The poor and the artisan classes were thus excluded from the political process and alienated from the evolving new order. The vast majority of those elected to the first all-German National Assembly in 1848 came from the liberal professions; one quarter were lawyers, only four were artisans, and one was a peasant. The liberals rejoiced that they controlled the new parliament, but it was unrepresentative and lacked broad popular support.

The first all-German–elected legislature met in May 1848 in the Paulskirche in Frankfurt to pursue the unification of Germany. It faced the thorny issue of the shape of this new Germany: Which regions should be included and which excluded? The most ambitious plan envisioned a *Grossdeutschland*, or large Germany, consisting of all the members of the Germanic Confederation, including the German-speaking parts of Austria and the Germanized western parts of Bohemia. Such a solution would include many non-Germans, including Poles, Czechs, and Danes. The proponents of *Kleindeutschland*, or small Germany, saw their solution as a more likely scenario for national unity, although it would exclude many Germans. They succeeded in the end, largely because the reassertion of Austrian imperial power in the fall of 1848 made the areas under Vienna's control ineligible for inclusion.

The Frankfurt assembly formed a provisional government in June 1848. The individual states, however, including the most important ones, Prussia and Austria, did not recognize the assembly's authority, so it was utterly powerless. The minister of war could not raise any soldiers, and the minister of finance could not impose taxes. The United States, enthusiastic about a new republic consciously modeled on its own, was one of the few nations to accept an ambassador from the all-German government.

The parliament also lacked the power to transfer authority from the individual states to itself. It might have succeeded if it had called for a national uprising against the princes, but the liberals in Frankfurt were loathe to do so. They distrusted the populace and feared working-class opposition. Force was still in the hands of the traditional authorities. At one point, when the parliament was invaded by radicals, it survived only by calling on Prussia to restore order. Its longevity apparently depended on how long the king of Prussia would tolerate it.

The Frankfurt parliament brought its work to an end by drawing up a constitution at a most unpropitious moment—spring 1849, after conservatives had regained the upper hand in most German states and in Austria. Having opted for the *Kleindeutsch* solution, the parliament offered the throne to Frederick William IV, king of Prussia. Although the king was not a liberal, he ruled the largest state within the designated empire. If power had to be used to promote and protect German unity, he possessed it in the form of the Prussian army. But Frederick William feared that accepting the throne would lead to war with Austria. Believing in the principle of monarchy, he also did not want an office offered by representatives of the people. Lacking an alternative plan in case their offer was refused, most members of the Frankfurt parliament went home. A rump parliament and a series of uprisings in favor of German unity were crushed by the Prussian army.

So German unification failed. Liberalism was unable to bring about German unity; other means would be required to do so. The liberals' failure to carry out their program weakened their cause for a long time to come.

Summary

The revolutions of 1848 released many of the forces for change that had been gathering strength since 1815. In spite of the Congress of Vienna's effort to restore the old order after Napoleon's fall, the generation after 1815 established a new order. The ideas of change that had powered the French Revolution of 1789 continued to shape an era that claimed to be rolling history back to prerevolutionary times. Liberalism contested authoritarianism. Nationalism challenged existing borders in an attempt to create new political entities. Liberalism and socialism gave new economic models that would shape the rest of the nineteenth century and beyond.

The generation after 1815 experienced revolutions frequently and broadly. These uprisings usually failed, and the forces of order were able to recapture power. Yet the status quo was altered. In many cases absolutist rulers had to grant constitutions and accept ministers who were not their choice. Even though most of these arrangements were temporary, they established an important precedent.

Rather than representing the restoration of an earlier epoch, these years, with demands for broadened political participation, suggested the outlines of the era that would follow. Popular agitation brought down two royal houses in France and in 1848 seemed to threaten most of the others in Europe. In Britain, popular movements dating from the 1820s led to the enlargement of the franchise and the undermining of landed interests. The principle of popular sovereignty that the French Revolution of 1789 had represented was adopted in France in 1848 with the establishment of universal male suffrage.

Nationalism arose in these years. The desire for national independence and unity was voiced in Italy, Germany, Hungary, Poland, and the land of the Czechs. The second half of the century would contend with the forces of nationalism that first appeared after 1814.

The middle classes found their position strengthened after 1848. They did not dominate the political system, but their influence was growing with the growth of entrepreneurship. Middle-class professionals were recruited into the civil services of states determined to streamline their operation in order to withstand revolution more effectively. Revolutionary fervor waned after 1848, but change was to occur—though in different ways.

Suggested Reading

General Surveys

Hobsbawm, E. J. *The Age of Revolution, 1789–1848.* 1962. A compellingly argued book that describes the era as being dominated by two simultaneous revolutions, the French Revolution and the Industrial Revolution.

Langer, William L. *Europe in Social Upheaval, 1832–52.* 1969. A huge but easy-to-read history providing a strong emphasis on the social aspects of these years.

The Search for Stability

Kissinger, Henry. *A World Restored.* 1957. A study by a future U.S. secretary of state who emphasizes the efforts of diplomats to build an international order resistant to revolution.

Nicolson, Harold. *The Congress of Vienna.* 1946. An account by a prominent British diplomat who provides colorful sketches of the diplomats at Vienna.

Palmer, Alan. *Metternich.* 1972. The best one-volume life in English of the dominant statesman of the era.

Ideological Confrontations

Anderson, Benedict. *Imagined Communities.* 1983. A noted anthropologist underscores the extent to which a nation is an "imagined community."

Carlisle, Robert B. *The Proffered Crown: Saint-Simonianism and the Doctrine of Hope.* 1987. A work that shows the originality of Saint-Simonian thought and its continuity after the founder's death.

Grana, Cesar. *Bohemian vs. Bourgeois: French Society and the Man of Letters in the Nineteenth Century.* 1964. A consideration of the intellectual origins of the notion of artist as rebel.

Harrison, J. F. C. *Quest for the New Moral World: Robert Owen and the Owenites in Britain and America.* 1969. A good biography that views the movement as affected by contemporary religious notions of a coming millennium.

Kedourie, Elie. *Nationalism.* 1960. An account that describes the German romantics as developers of modern nationalism and creators of an essentially pernicious force.

Porter, Roy, and Mikulas Teich, eds. *Romanticism in National Context.* 1988. An up-to-date series of essays on romanticism in different national settings.

Restoration and Reform

Brock, Michael. *The Great Reform Act.* 1973. An account that emphasizes the sense of crisis on the eve of the Great Reform Act.

Church, Clive. *Europe in 1830: Revolution and Political Change.* 1983. A view of the end of the restoration period, punctured by the revolutions of 1830, from a European-wide perspective.

Collingham, H. A. C. *The July Monarchy: A Political History of France.* 1988. An account of the divisions in France that continued in spite of the new king's well-meaning efforts.

Jardin, André, and André-Jean Tudesq. *Restoration and Reaction, 1815–1848.* 1988. A general survey of France.

Jones, Gareth Stedman. *The Languages of Class: Studies in English Working-Class History, 1832–1982.* 1983. A work that considers the Chartists a movement of the politically disenfranchised seeking a voice within the political system.

Kann, Robert A. *A History of the Habsburg Empire, 1526–1918.* 1977. A work that examines the problems of maintaining the multinational empire.

Lincoln, W. Bruce. *Nicholas I: Emperor and Autocrat of All the Russias.* 1978. A biography of the tsar, revealing the ruler's dedication to preserve the autocratic regime and its values.

More, Charles. *The Industrial Age: Economy and Society in Britain, 1750–1985.* 1989. A survey of British economic and social history.

Pinkney, David H. *The French Revolution of 1830.* 1972. The standard work on the subject.

Sheehan, James J. *German History, 1770–1866.* 1989. A survey of the variety and contrast of the German experience.

Sked, Alan. *The Decline and Fall of the Habsburg Empire, 1815–1918.* 1989. A brief, clear study stressing the very real threat the revolutions of 1848 posed to imperial survival.

Woodward, Sir Llewellyn. *The Age of Reform, 1815–1870.* 2d ed. 1962. A strong political narrative of British history.

Woolf, Stuart Joseph. *A History of Italy, 1700–1860.* 1979. A consideration of the problems of political divisions in Italian life.

The Revolutions of 1848

Agulhon, Maurice. *The Republican Experiment.* 1983. A work that stresses how the splits between different political groups made it difficult for revolutionary goals to succeed.

Ginsborg, P. *Daniele Manin and the Venetian Revolution of 1848–1849.* 1979. An account portraying a heroic opponent of Habsburg rule as a representative of the local bourgeoisie.

Price, Roger. *The French Second Republic: A Social History.* 1972. An account suggesting that divisions in French society produced the revolution of 1848 and that local elites asserting their interests caused its demise.

———. *The Revolutions of 1848.* 1989. A general history of the European revolutions describing them as the result of discontent with an economic and political system out of tune with the needs and desires of most peoples.

Sheehan, James J. *German Liberalism in the Nineteenth Century.* 1978. The standard work revealing the difficulties that German liberals faced as early as the first half of the nineteenth century.

Snell, John L. *The Democratic Movement in Germany, 1789–1914.* 1976. A long and detailed work emphasizing the existence over a long period of time of a democratic and liberal movement.

Stadelmann, Rudolf. *Social and Political History of the German 1848 Revolution.* 1975. An account in which both the outbreak and the unraveling of the 1848 revolution are attributed to social and political forces.

Weighing the Evidence

REVOLUTIONARY ART

In an era of social and political turmoil how do authorities legitimate their newly won power? How do contemporaries explain and understand the chaotic events they experience? Historians find art a useful means by which to understand how an event was viewed; sometimes the art serves as a kind of photographic record. Of the many artists who depicted the Paris revolution of July 1830, Eugène Delacroix (1798–1863) provided the most powerful rendering of this event with the painting illustrated here, *Liberty Leading the People*.

An eyewitness to the revolution, Delacroix created his dramatic work at the end of the year. For contemporaries the huge 8′6″-by-10′8″ canvas captured the mood of the revolution. The painting mobilizes powerful images and myths celebrating and legitimating the revolution. We may examine it as an allegory of the event. If *Liberty Leading the People* has limited value as a depiction of the actual uprising, it is invaluable in telling us how the artist and the government that bought and displayed the painting wanted the revolution of 1830 to be understood.

During the Old Regime, the symbol of the state was an effigy of the monarch. Once the king was removed, the state had to be personified in a different fashion. After the French Revolution of 1789, the state usually was personified as a woman. (See Chapter 21's feature, "Weighing the Evidence: Political Symbols," on pages 814–815.) The enemies of the Revolution of 1789, suggesting that the new regime lacked refinement, derogatorily characterized the new republic as "Marianne," the common name implying a woman of easy virtue. To spite these reactionaries, supporters of the republic accepted the name and depicted the new regime as Marianne.

With a Phrygian cap, a mark bestowed on free slaves in ancient Rome, Marianne symbolizes the republic, liberty, and democracy. After the Revolution of 1789, as moderates sought to assert control, painters and sculptors often omitted the Phrygian cap and dressed Marianne in more clothing. Notice that in this painting of 1830, Liberty wears a prominent Phrygian cap. The radical nature of the revolution is emphasized too by Liberty's relative undress and her carrying of a rifle. The headdress of the female worker at her feet also suggests a Phrygian cap.

Dominating the painting, in its very center, is the tricolor, the national flag of France. Under the Old Regime, the king displayed the coat of arms of the royal house, the *fleur-de-lis* ("flower of the lily"). Red and blue were the colors of the city of Paris. The revolutionaries adopted them in July 1789 in cockades they displayed on their hats, and when the king decided also to wear the cockade with his own color (white), a national emblem was created. France was the first nation to adopt a national flag, in 1792. Proudly displayed during the revolutionary and Napoleonic periods, the tricolor was proscribed under the Restoration. Its reappearance in 1830 connected this uprising to the Revolution of 1789, with its promises of liberty at home and national glory abroad.

The central figure represents liberty, but might we also view her as a depiction of one of the women who participated in the revolt? Delacroix rendered into high art the representation of women at the barricades that was common in the lithographs and prints of the era. Women did play a role, by digging up the cobblestones and building barricades, but few women seem to have been in the thick of the fighting. Yet many contemporaries believed that women had fought heroically. At the onset of the revolt, according to stories at the time and later myths, one of them was the first victim of Charles X's forces. Given the widely held view of women as weak and defenseless, such an account was intended to reflect negatively on Charles X's regime and also to encourage the men of Paris to rise up. If a woman had risen up against tyranny, could men do any less?

The painting depicts broad participation of Frenchmen in the 1830 revolution. Notice the

Delacroix: Liberty Leading the People *(Giraudon/Art Resource, NY)*

bourgeois on the left. The supposed participation of bourgeois was reassuring to those who feared that the revolt was the work of the mob. Delacroix may have wanted to celebrate the bourgeois national guard, which played an important role in the revolution—though in its latter part. Like many of his bourgeois contemporaries, Delacroix had particular sympathy for the guard because he believed it had kept the revolution under control and had prevented it from further excesses.

Notice too the images that evoke youthful participation in the revolution and its promise of a new beginning. Delacroix includes both an armed street urchin and a student. We have little evidence of street urchins participating in the revolt, however. And although students indicated their support for the cause, they were absent from the worst fighting in the first two days and seem to have played a role only when it was safe to do so. Most of the participants were too young to have experienced the Revolution of 1789, although many had known the Napoleonic era. Indeed, a very large number of the participants in the 1830 uprising were veterans from Napoleon's wars. They were seasoned fighters, and their skills account for their defeat of the armed forces sent against them.

The regime purchased Delacroix's enormous canvas, now in the Louvre Museum, and put it on display at the official salon exhibition in 1831. Its size and drama seemed effectively to legitimate the July Monarchy. But, reflecting growing conservatism and fears of armed insurrections, the government withdrew *Liberty Leading the People* from public display after a few months. In the 1860s, the self-confident Second Empire, for which revolution seemed but a distant threat, again put on public display the painting that had come to incarnate the July Revolution.

CHAPTER 23

The Industrial Transformation of Europe

Industrial revolution is what Frenchmen in the 1820s called the great economic changes then underway in Great Britain. Eventually, that expression entered the general vocabulary to describe the advances in production that occurred first in England and were dominating most of western Europe by the end of the nineteenth century. Many economic historians now emphasize how gradual and cumulative the changes were and question the appropriateness of the term. Indeed, it seems best to discuss the changes not as an industrial revolution but as a continuous process of economic transformation.

Industrial development left its mark on just about every sphere of human activity. Scientific and rational methods altered production. Economic activity became increasingly specialized. The unit of production changed from the family to a larger and less personal group. Significant numbers of workers left farming to enter mining and manufacturing, and major portions of the population moved from a rural to an urban environment. Machines and the use of capital replaced or supplemented manual labor.[1]

The economic changes physically transformed Europe. Greater levels of production were achieved and more wealth was created than ever before. Factory chimneys belched soot into the air. Miners in search of coal, iron ore, and other minerals cut deep gashes into the earth. Cities, spurred by industrialization, grew quickly, and Europe became increasingly urban.

Industrialization simultaneously created unprecedented advancement and opportunity as well as unprecedented hardships and social problems. Various groups tried various strategies to strike a balance between the positive and negative effects. Many entrepreneurs and their sympathizers stood

The world's first iron bridge, ca. 1780, in Shropshire, western England.

for liberal principles based on classical economics. Workers, with a growing sense of solidarity, struggled for their common interests. Out of the socialist ideologies of the early part of the nineteenth century, Karl Marx forged a militant ideology to address the needs of the industrial working class.

Setting the Stage for Industrialization

No one can say with certainty which conditions were necessary for the industrialization of Europe. Nevertheless, we do know why industrialization did *not* spread widely to the rest of the world. A certain combination of conditions—geographical, cultural, economic, commercial, demographic—helped make industrialization possible in Europe.

Why Europe?

A fortunate set of circumstances seems to explain why Europe was the stage for industrial development. Since the Middle Ages, political transformations in western Europe reduced risk and uncertainty while encouraging productive investment. With the development of legal due process, rich merchants did not run the risk of having their wealth confiscated—as they did, for instance, in the Ottoman Empire. The unfolding of state power in Europe reduced the frequency of brigandage—still common in many parts of the world—and thus encouraged trade. Discrepancies in risk are apparent in the differences in interest rates in the eighteenth century: 3 percent in England, 36 percent in China.

In Europe, disparities of wealth, though serious, were less extreme than in non-European societies; thus, there was a better market for goods. At the time Western Europe industrialized, the average yearly income per person was equivalent to $500—more than the amount in many non-Western societies even today. And nearly half of the population was literate, again a very high proportion compared to non-Western societies.

In Europe, late marriages and limited family sizes restrained population growth, so the society was rarely overwhelmed by the pressures of population. In India and China, by contrast, population growth was so dramatic that society had to be fully engaged to feed the people and could not be readily mobilized for other production.

Europe enjoyed a measure of diversity unknown elsewhere. Diversity meant a culture that tolerated and eventually encouraged innovation. Competitiveness drove states to try to catch up with each other and by emulation to wipe out competitive advantages. Governments actively encouraged industries and commerce to enrich a country and make it more powerful than its neighbors. Challenges to dominant religious and political powers had brought some religious diversity—a rarity outside the West, where large territories tended to be dominated by a single ruler and faith.

None of these factors alone explains why industrialization occurred, but their combination seems to have facilitated the process when it did occur.[2] The industrialization of Europe radically transformed power relationships between the industrial West and nonindustrial Africa, Asia, and South America. By the end of the nineteenth century the latter were overwhelmed by the economic and military power of the former. Within Europe, power shifted to the nations that were most industrial. Britain was the first to industrialize, and it was the dominant political power throughout the nineteenth century. Britain was widely admired and seen not only as an economic model but also as a political and cultural model. As France had been the dominant power in the eighteenth century and the United States would be in the second half of the twentieth century, so Britain dominated the nineteenth, a stellar accomplishment for a small island nation.

Transformations Accompanying Industrialization

A number of transformations preceded or accompanied and helped define the industrializing era. Changes in commerce, agriculture, demographics, and transportation, if not always creating the preconditions of industrial development, were at least the major stimuli making them possible.

Changes in agriculture increased the productivity of the land. Farmers more frequently used fertilizer, and they rotated their crops to ease the exhaustion of the soil. New, more efficient plows enabled them to cultivate more land than ever before. In the eighteenth century, new crops that provided high yields even in poor soil were introduced into Europe: maize (corn) and potatoes from the Americas.

The wealth created by agriculture allowed for investment in industry and for expenditures on infrastructure, such as roads and canal systems, useful to industry. A wealthier landed class could purchase manufactured goods such as iron plows and even machine-woven textiles, thus providing an impetus for industry. Most important, the new crops and the more efficient cultivation of traditional ones increased the capacity to feed a growing population and freed many people to go to the city and work in the industries.

In the seventeenth century, European trade had increased significantly, enriching businessmen and making them aware of the fortunes to be made by marketing goods that were in demand not just locally but even far away. A new dynamic ethos took hold of businessmen eager to venture into new fields of economic endeavor.

Population grew during the years of the industrial transformation. The first spurt occurred before the effects of industrialization could be widely felt. Then the population of Europe increased dramatically throughout the industrial era: From 1750 to 1850 it grew by 100 percent. The growth was largely due to a lowering of the death rate. Infant mortality had been very high from diseases such as smallpox and tuberculosis. Although none of these diseases had been medically conquered, improved standards of living after midcentury, such as greater food intake, enabled children to better resist killer diseases. Improved employment opportunities led to earlier marriages and thus higher fertility. Most of the population increase occurred in the countryside. This growing group of people supplied the labor force for the new industries and provided the large surge in consumers of various industrial goods.

Transportation improved significantly in the eighteenth century. Better roads were built; coaches and carriages were constructed to travel

Steam Locomotive: "The Rocket" The engineer George Stephenson (1781–1848) displayed the advantages of the locomotive over a stationary engine by using a locomotive to pull a wagon. His son, Robert Stephenson (1803–1859), gave the locomotive its first demonstration in 1829, when the "Rocket" ran a 1½-mile course at a speed of 15 miles an hour for a total distance of 60 miles. *(From Gustav Reder,* The World of Steam Locomotives *[Éditions Office du Livre])*

faster and carry larger loads. Government and private companies built canals linking rivers to each other or to lakes. Road- and canal-building were important preconditions for industrialization, hastening and cheapening transportation and making possible the movement of raw materials to manufacture and from there to market without too great an increase in the price of the finished good. In England these transformations occurred simultaneously with industrialization; on the Continent they were actual precursors to economic change.

In England, industrialization preceded railbuilding; yet once railroad expansion occurred, beginning in the 1830s, the order for iron rails, steam engines, and wagons sustained and advanced industrial growth. On the Continent railbuilding promoted industrialization, notably in Germany and later in Italy.

Industrialization and European Production

Several important technical advances powered European industry, and breakthroughs in one field often led to breakthroughs in other fields. Increased rates of production created new pressures for the invention of new technologies and, surprisingly, they usually emerged. The first two industries to be affected by major technical breakthroughs were textiles and iron. New forms of energy powered the machinery; novel forms of directing labor and organizing management further enhanced production. At first limited to the British Isles, industry spread to the Continent, although unevenly and at diverse times.

Advances in the Cotton Industry

A series of inventions in the eighteenth century led the way to the mass manufacture of textiles. One of the earliest was the flying shuttle, introduced in Britain in 1733 by John Kay (1704–1764). It accelerated the weaving process to such an extent that it increased the demand for thread. This need was met in the 1760s by James Hargreaves (d. 1778), who invented the spinning jenny, a device that spun thread from wool or cotton. Improved spinning machines, such as Samuel Crompton's "mule," made the spinning jenny increasingly efficient, and by 1812 one spinner could produce as much yarn as two hundred had made before the invention of the jenny. In 1769 Richard Arkwright (1732–1792), a barber and wigmaker, invented the water frame. This huge machine, powered by horses or by a waterfall, was installed in a single establishment with three hundred employees—the first modern factory. In 1777 Arkwright had James Watt construct a steam engine to operate the frame. With these innovations, cotton manufacturing increased 130-fold between 1770 and 1841.

In the past, finished cloth had been soaked in buttermilk and spread out in the meadows to be bleached by the sun. That method was hardly practical for the unprecedented quantities of cloth rolling out of the factories. The introduction of sulfuric acid solved the problem. It was a far more economical bleach than buttermilk and sunlight, and it could be produced in commercial quantities. It in turn was replaced in the 1790s when the Frenchman C. L. Berthollet (1748–1822) discovered the bleaching powers of chlorine gas. Entrepreneurs or artisans made many of the other industrial inventions, but the breakthroughs in bleaching demonstrated that increasingly industry would be fueled by advances in scientific knowledge and training.

The cotton-manufacturing industry in England represented another important first. With cotton manufacture, for the first time in history a staple industry was based on a natural resource that was not domestically provided. Grown mainly in the American South, cotton was transformed into cloth in England.

Manufactured cotton was comfortable to wear and easy to wash and became so cheap that it competed effectively with all handmade textiles. The popularity of cotton may have improved public health as well, for it enabled people to own several changes of clothing and keep them clean. Everyone was eager to buy British cottons. The increased demand for the raw material put pressure on the cotton growers in the American South. To meet this demand, they opened up new land.

In 1793, Eli Whitney (1765–1825) invented the cotton gin, a device that mechanically removed the seeds from cotton. The cotton gin meant that more cotton could be processed and thus more could be grown. It heightened the profitability of

British Cotton Manufacture Machines simultaneously performed various functions. The carding machine (front left) separated cotton fibers, readying them for spinning. The roving machine (front right) wound the cotton onto spools. The drawing machine (rear left) wove patterns into the cloth. Rich in machines, this factory needed relatively few employees; most were women and children. *(The Granger Collection, New York)*

the American southern plantation economy, and that situation increased the attractiveness of slave labor. The second half of the eighteenth century marked the height of the slave trade. In that fifty-year period, approximately 3 million Africans were forcibly transported to the New World.

The cotton industry in England is an example of how manufacturing has an impact locally and also produces a ripple effect across the oceans. Among those benefiting overseas were American farmers, cotton traders, and merchants, as well as consumers of English cotton cloth around the world. Elsewhere, people were adversely affected—in Africa, where slaving raids increased, and in India, where local spinners were driven out of business.

In ways beneficial and not, people were interconnected by the cotton trade; later other products would also link economies of various nations and peoples. No longer, as in preindustrial trade, were all goods locally made, nor did the consumer meet producers and buy from them. Increasingly, specialization became the norm. Those best fit performed a particular function efficiently and productively. The results were high production and low price for the finished product.

Iron, Steam, and Factories

Charcoal had traditionally fueled the smelting of iron. England, however, ran out of wood before other European countries did and needed an alternative source of fuel. There was plenty of coal, but it contained impurities, particularly sulfur, which contaminated the materials with which it came into contact. In 1708, Abraham Darby (1677–1717), an English ironmaster, discovered that coal in a blast furnace could smelt iron without the attending complications. His discovery triggered the use of coal in the iron industry. In 1777, the introduction of a steam engine to operate the blast furnace considerably increased its efficiency. In 1783, a steam engine was used to drive a forge hammer to shape the iron; three years later, a steam engine rolled the iron into

MAJOR INVENTIONS OF THE INDUSTRIAL TRANSFORMATION

1708	Use of coke in blast furnaces by Abraham Darby
1712	Steam-operated water pump by Thomas Newcomen
1733	Flying shuttle by John Kay
1764	Spinning jenny by James Hargreaves
1769	Water frame by Richard Arkwright
1769	Improved steam engine by James Watt
1776	Steam engine–operated machinery by James Watt
1779	The "mule" by Samuel Crompton
1784	Chlorine gas as a textile bleach by Claude Berthollet
1793	Cotton gin by Eli Whitney

sheets. With these innovations, the output of the English iron industry doubled between 1788 and 1796 and again in the following eight years.

The increased supply of iron stimulated other changes. Relatively cheap and durable iron machines replaced wooden machines, which wore out rapidly. The new machines fueled further manufacturing breakthroughs. Improvements in manufacturing methods and techniques led to the production of ever larger amounts of goods, usually at lower prices. Industrial change started with cotton but was continued and sustained by breakthroughs in the use of iron and coal.

Before the age of industry, the basic sources of power were humans, animals, wind, and water. Humans and animals were limited in their capacity to drive the large mills needed to grind corn or operate a sawmill. Wind was unreliable because it was not constant. Water-driven mills depended on the seasons—streams dried up in the summer, froze in the winter. And water mills could be placed only where there was a waterfall. Clearly what was needed was a power source that was constant and that could be located just about anywhere. The steam engine, invented and improved on in England, met that need and stoked England's industrial growth.

The steam engine was first used to pump out coal mines. As mining shafts were dug ever deeper, water in the mines became an increasing hindrance. In 1712 Thomas Newcomen (1663–1729) invented a steam-operated water pump. Its use spread rapidly. The first steam engine in the Americas was a Newcomen engine installed in New Jersey in 1753. James Watt (1736–1819) improved on the Newcomen engine considerably, making it twice as efficient in energy output. Eventually he made it capable of converting the reciprocating motion of the piston to rotary motion. This breakthrough enabled the steam engine to power a variety of machines. Thus, mills that had been powered by water or wind could be operated by steam engines. Further changes improved Watt's engines—most notably, the invention of the powerful and energy-efficient high-pressure steam engine. The use of steam engines spread in England, to the Continent, and to the United States.

The steam engine centralized the workplace. With the machine as a central power source, it became practical and commonplace to organize work in a central factory. The location of a factory where it was most convenient eliminated the expense of transporting raw materials to be worked on at a power source such as a waterfall. The central factory also reinforced work discipline. These factories were large, austere edifices inspired sometimes by military architecture and therefore resembling barracks. With the introduction of blast furnaces and other heat-producing manufacturing methods, the tall factory chimney became a common sight on the industrial landscape.

Although the machine age was inaugurated in the eighteenth century and spurred the proliferation of factories and large plants, these were still rather uncommon phenomena. As late as the 1860s more than half of the energy needs of manufacturing in Great Britain and the United States were supplied by people, animals, and wind- and water-operated machines. But the steam engine was clearly the wave of the future.

Factories ranged in size from food-manufacturing operations that were small to textile mills that were quite large. In the first half of the nineteenth century, the average number of employees in both English and French textile mills was between 200 and 300. Some plants were huge, but by midcentury the small workshop, worked by the owner and his relatives or by a handful of employees, was still the most common site of manufacturing in England. English production became truly industrial only after 1850. But long before that, it had become clear that the mechanized factory had overwhelming advantages and that handmade products would face increasing difficulty competing.

The steam engine powered a dramatic growth in production. It increased the force of blast furnaces and the mechanical power of forging iron and spinning and weaving machinery. In Britain, cotton production increased 200-fold between 1740 and 1840, more than 400-fold between 1840 and 1860. Assisted by machines, workers were enormously more productive than when they depended on hand-operated tools. At the beginning of the eighteenth century, spinning 100 pounds of cotton took 50,000 worker-hours; by 1825, it took only 135—a 370-fold increase in productivity capacity per worker.

Newcomen Engine Thomas Newcomen, an ironmonger, produced the first successful operating steam engine in 1712. Steam was introduced into a cylinder that was then cooled, creating a partial vacuum. The pressure of the atmosphere forced the piston down, pulling down one end of the beam, creating a pumping stroke. The engine could make as many as fourteen pumping strokes a minute. *(The Fotomas Index)*

Inventions and Entrepreneurs

The industrial age was triggered by inventions, and it was sustained by the continued flow of new ones. In the decade 1700–1709, 22 patents were issued in England; by 1840–1849, 4581 had been issued. Something revolutionary in human history was occurring. People were seeing in their lifetime sizable increases in productivity, both in the factory and on the farm. Rather than clinging to traditional methods, many entrepreneurs consciously and persistently challenged them and attempted to find new ways of improving production. Invention itself seems to have been invented in this age of invention.

Industry did not just happen. The early entrepreneurs not only applied considerable technical skills to their production but also dealt with workers and other employees. They were salesmen selling the goods they produced. They were financiers taking risks to finance building and expand their factories. They were managers and accountants.

Most of the early industrialists belonged to merchant families. In England, very few were landed noblemen, industrial workers, or artisans. However, in the iron industry, it was not uncommon for metalworkers to build up a modest iron mill and then enlarge it. That was also the case with potters. Josiah Wedgwood (1730–1795), who pioneered the industrial manufacturing of china, came from a long line of artisan potters and is a good example of a self-made man. The thirteenth child of a potter, who died when Josiah was 9 years old, he went to work for his brother as an apprentice and gradually established himself on his own. Richard Arkwright was a barber before his invention of the water frame brought him a knighthood and a personal fortune of half a million pounds. Many entrepreneurs began as farmers, then became involved in the putting-out system, and then graduated to industrial manufacture. A disproportionate number of the early manufacturers were university educated, a fact suggesting that even in the early stages of industry, scientific knowledge was valuable. In fact, the self-made man was more a myth than a rule. Most entrepreneurs came from relatively privileged backgrounds.

Entrepreneurs such as Arkwright and Watt pioneered innovations and became famous, but most who advanced the cause of industrial production were not particularly inventive. They just replicated methods of production that had proved profitable to others. Truly successful entrepreneurs, however, seemed to share one attribute: They were driven by a nearly insatiable appetite for innovation, work, and profit. Near the mid-nineteenth century mark, one of the most successful French textile tycoons advised his son, "One seeks by means of imagination, by means of effort, to surpass one's neighbor; therefore, work, work, always work."

Entrepreneurs took the financial risk of investing in new types of enterprises. Most entrepreneurs by themselves or with a partner ran a single plant, but some even in the early stages ran several plants. In 1788, Richard Arkwright and his partners ran eight mills. Some enterprises were vertically integrated, controlling production at the various stages. The Peels in England owned enterprises ranging from spinning to printing and even banking. The entrepreneurs' dynamism and boldness fostered the growth of the British industrial system, making the small nation the "workshop of the world."

Britain's Lead in Industrial Innovation

Britain led the way industrially for many reasons. It was the first European country to have a standard currency, tax, and tariff system. It enjoyed the most emancipated labor. Serfdom was long gone, and although England was by no means an egalitarian society, it accommodated some movement between the classes. Ideas and experiments were readily communicated among entrepreneurs, workers, and scientists. Although other countries had scientific societies, several societies in England brought together theoreticians and practical businessmen—for example, the Lunar Society in Birmingham and the Literary and Philosophical Society in Manchester.

England was far more open to dissent than were other European countries at the time. The lack of conformity was reflected in religion, and also in a willingness to try new methods of production. In fact, the two often went together. A large proportion of British entrepreneurs were Quakers or belonged to one of the dissenting (non-Anglican) religious groups—for instance, the ironmaking Darby family, the engineer of the steam engine James Watt, and the inventor of the "mule" Samuel Crompton (1753–1827). Perhaps they were accustomed to questioning authority and treading new paths. They were also well educated and, as a result of common religious bonds, were prone to provide mutual support, including financial.

England had dominated international trade since the seventeenth century. This trade provided capital for investment in industrial plants. The world trade network also ensured that England had a market beyond its borders, and because aggregate demand was relatively high, mass manufacture was feasible. The international network built up by trade also enabled Britain to import raw materials for its industry, the most important of which was cotton.

Britain earlier than its competitors had a national banking system that could provide capital to industries in areas where it was needed. In addition to numerous London banks lending mainly in the capital, there were by 1810 six hundred provincial banks. The banking system reflected as much as it contributed to the growth of the economy. Banking could flourish because Britons had wide experience in trade, had accumulated considerable amounts of wealth, and had found a constant demand for credit.

Geographically, Britain was also fortunate. Coal and iron were located close to each other. A long and narrow island, Britain had easy access to the sea—no part of the country was more than 70 miles from a seacoast. This was a strategic advantage, for water was by far the cheapest means of transportation. Compared to the Continent, Britain had few tolls, and goods could easily move around.

On the whole, English workers were better off than their continental counterparts. They were more skilled, earned higher wages, and had discretionary income to spend on manufactured goods when they became available. But because their wages were higher than wages on the Continent, there was an incentive for English business owners to find labor-saving devices.

Population growth in England—in part the result of industrial growth—increased by 8 percent in each decade in the second part of the eighteenth century. This growing population provided markets for goods. The most rapid growth occurred in the countryside, causing a steady movement of people from rural to urban areas. The presence of this work force was another contributing factor in England's readiness for change.

The timing of the industrial transformation in Britain was also influenced by plentiful harvests in the years 1715–1750, creating low food prices and thus making possible low industrial wages. The demand for industrial goods was reasonably high. Farmers with good earnings could afford to order the new iron manufactured plows. It is likely that much of the income from farming helped bring changes associated with industrialization such as population growth, improvements to the transportation system, and the increasing availability of capital for investment. Thus, each change triggered more change, and the cumulative effect was staggering (Map 23.1).

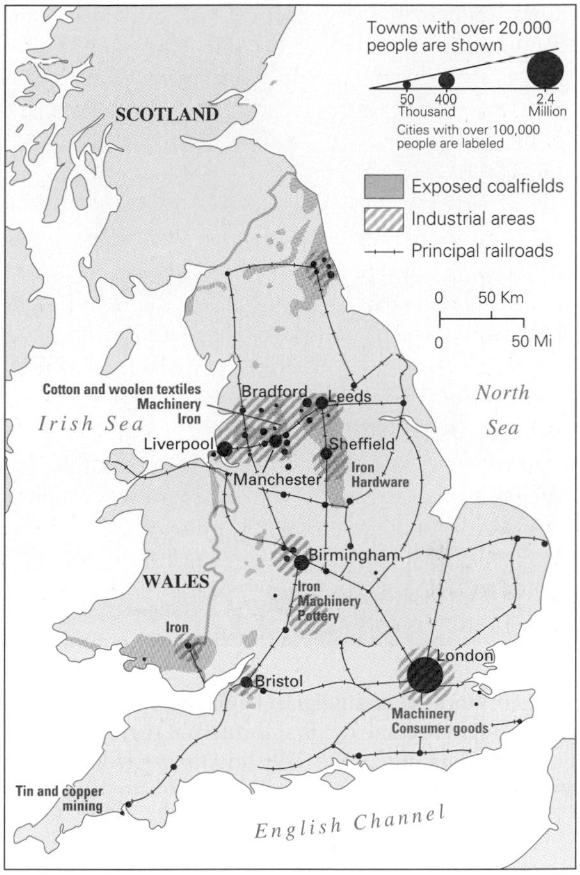

Map 23.1 The Industrial Revolution in England, ca. 1850 Industry developed in the areas rich in coal and iron fields. Important cities sprang up nearby and were linked to each other by a growing rail network.

The Spread of Industry to the Continent

The ideas and methods changing industry in England spread by emulation and by the direct movement of people. Visitors from the Continent came to England, studied local methods of production, and returned home to set up blast furnaces and spinning works inspired by British design. The German engineer August Borsig (1804–1854), after studying steam engines in England, built the first German steam engine in 1825 and the first German locomotive in 1842. Some visitors even resorted to industrial espionage, smuggling blueprints of machines out of Britain. Although a law in England forbade local artisans from emigrating, some did leave, including entrepreneurs who helped set up industrial plants in France and Belgium. By the 1820s English technicians were all over Europe—in Belgium, France, Germany, and as far east as Austria.

Belgium was the first country on the Continent to industrialize, perhaps because, like England, Belgium had iron and coal in proximity. Belgium also had a long tradition of working cloth and iron and could readily adapt new methods to increase production of both. Belgium's location on the route between England and Germany fostered the development of railroads. And rail-building facilitated industrialization not only by providing fast and cheap transportation but also by stimulating the iron industry. In 1840, there were 200 miles of rail in Belgium; twenty years later, there were 1200 miles of rail. Belgium was the most densely equipped in rails of any European country. The Belgian government encouraged industrial modernization by building railroads and investing in the shipping industry. In the early years it kept tariffs high to protect nascent industries; later it negotiated free-trade

Women Working in a Belgian Mine Shaft Belgium had a great deal of coal, which allowed it to become the first industrial region on the Continent. Women and children worked frequently in the risky and taxing work of mining. *(The Granger Collection, New York)*

agreements providing expanded markets for its manufacturers.

In the eighteenth century France seemed a more likely candidate for economic growth than Britain. France's overseas trade was growing faster than Britain's. In 1780, France's industrial output was greater than Britain's, though production per person was less. In the nineteenth century, however, while Britain's industry boomed and it became the workshop of the world, France lagged behind. Historians have suggested several reasons. The war and revolutions of the late eighteenth century were certainly contributing factors. They slowed economic growth and cut France off from the flow of information and new techniques from Britain. Moreover, in the 1790s, when the French peasants pressured for legislation to ease their situation, the revolutionaries responded positively. Thus, the peasantry was somewhat relieved from its misery and comfortable enough to feel no urgency to leave the land and provide the cheap and ready labor that Britain had. Further, the Napoleonic Code of 1804 abolished primogeniture, so that when a peasant died, his younger sons were not forced off the land.

French population growth lagged behind other countries'. Between 1800 and 1914, the population of France grew at half the average rate of the rest of the Continent. In England during this period much of the labor that left the land and worked the factories and mills came from the rural population explosion; but no such phenomenon occurred in the French countryside, and thus the labor force in France was not as available for industrial growth.

Traditionally, France had produced high-quality luxury goods, and French entrepreneurs who sought to emulate English accomplishments faced serious difficulties. Iron and coal in France were not close together. Labor was still quite cheap, so there was no incentive to invest in labor-saving machines because goods still could be manufactured inexpensively by hand. Soon, however, French manufacturers found themselves facing British competition. By being the first to industrialize, the British had the advantage of being able to manufacture goods and to corner markets efficiently and relatively cheaply. The French were the first to feel the negative effects of being an industrial latecomer.

Although France's growth rate was lower than that of its neighbors, the French economy experienced slow but nearly constant growth throughout the nineteenth century. From 1810 to 1850, both the production of coal and the consumption of raw cotton quintupled. In 1830 France had 130 machines, by 1852, 16,000. In ceramics, glass, porcelain, and paper manufacturing, France was a pioneer. Most French manufacturing, however, remained small; the typical firm had a handful of employees. Production by artisans, rather than by mass industrial production, continued longer there than in England or Germany. Compared to other industrial nations, France experienced lower economic growth. But if the growth figures take population into account, then the French did better than Great Britain and only slightly less well than Germany.

The invasions of Germany by Napoleon caused considerable destruction, but they also brought some positive economic benefits. The example of the French Revolution led to important changes in the socioeconomic situation. Restrictive guilds were abolished. The French occupiers suppressed the small German states with their many tariffs and taxes, established a single unified legal system—which survived even after 1815—and introduced a single standard of measurement based on the metric system.

Government in Germany played an important role in the adoption of improved methods of manufacturing. The Prussian state, eager for industrial development, sent an official to England to observe the puddling process (the method by which iron is freed of carbon) and bring that know-how back to Prussia. The Prussian government promoted industrial growth by investing in a transportation network to carry raw materials for processing and finished goods to their markets. To spur both trade and industrial growth, Prussia took the lead in creating a customs union, the Zollverein. By 1834 a German market embracing eighteen German states with a population of 23 million had been created.

German industrial growth accelerated dramatically in the 1850s. Massive expenditures on railways created a large demand for metal, which pressured German manufacturers to enlarge their plant capacities and increase efficiency. Germany was not yet politically unified, but the German middle classes saw economic growth as the means by which their country could win a prominent place among Europe's nation-states. Germany's growth was phenomenal. Germany successfully emulated Britain, overtook France, and toward the end of the nineteenth century served as a pioneer in the electrical engineering and chemical industries. If France experienced the disadvantages of being a latecomer, Germany reaped the benefits of that situation. The Germans were able to avoid costly and inefficient early experimentation and adapt the latest methods; moreover, Germany entered fields that Britain had neglected.

In the first half of the nineteenth century, a number of European states were aware of the momentous economic transformations occurring around them but did little to embrace those changes. Even by the end of the century, progress remained slow in many areas of Europe. As long as Russia retained serfdom (until 1861), it would lack the mobile labor force needed for industrial growth. And until late in the century, the ruling Russian aristocracy hesitated to adopt an economic system in which wealth was not based on land. In Austria, Bohemia was the only important industrial center; otherwise, Austria was heavily agrarian. Moreover, culturally Austria was suspicious of change, remaining traditional in its outlook. A rail line built there in 1830 operated horse-drawn carriages until 1860.

The impoverished southern Mediterranean countries experienced little economic growth. With mostly poor soil, their agriculture yielded little surplus. Spain, lacking coal and access to coal and other energy sources, could not easily diversify its economic base. There was some industry in Catalonia, especially around Barcelona, but it was limited in scope and had little impact on the rest of the country. Italy was still industrially underdeveloped in the middle of the nineteenth century. There were modest advances, but growth was too slow to have a measurable positive impact on the Italian economy. In 1871, 61 percent of the population of Italy was still agrarian. The economic backwardness of these countries was reflected in their high illiteracy rates. At

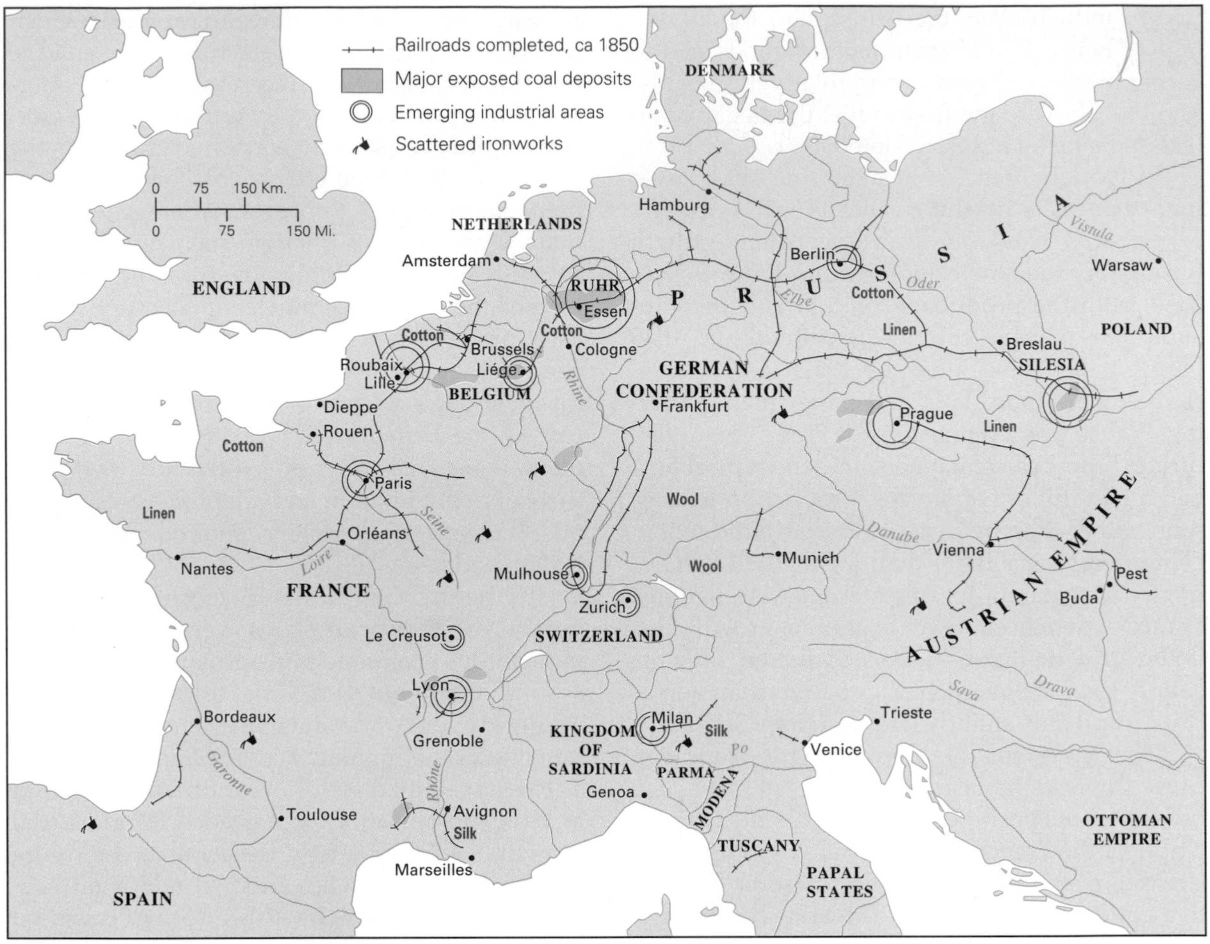

Map 23.2 Continental Industrialization, ca. 1850 Despite the fact that industry had begun on the Continent by the mid-nineteenth century, it was still sparse there, as was the rail network.

midcentury, illiteracy was around 75 percent in both Italy and Spain, between 90 and 95 percent in Russia.

Although by midcentury only a few European nations had experienced industrialization to any great extent, many more would do so by the end of the century, pressured by severe competition from their more advanced neighbors (Map 23.2; Figure 23.1). The potential threat was political and military as well as economic, for the industrialized nations represented military might and superiority. As compared to the non-European world, the European continent in the nineteenth century had acquired a distinct material culture that was increasingly based on machine manufacture or recognized to be in the process of becoming so.

The Transformation of Europe and Its Environment

Industry changed the traditional methods of agriculture, commerce, trade, and manufacture. It also transformed people's lives, individually and collectively. It altered how they made a livelihood, where and how they lived, and how they thought of themselves. Industry's need of people with specialized skills created new occupations. Because industry required specialization, the range of occupations that people took up expanded dramatically.

The advent of industry transformed the way society functioned. Until the eighteenth century, the basis of influence and power was hereditary privilege, which meant aristocratic birth and land. The aristocracy did not disappear overnight. In the late eighteenth century, however, it was challenged by a rising class of people whose wealth was self-made and whose influence was based on economic contributions to society rather than on bloodlines. Increased social mobility opened opportunities even for some workers. Industrialization transformed both the manmade and the natural environment. Cities grew dramatically as a result of industrialization, and Europeans faced urban problems and the polluting of their air and water.

Urbanization and Its Discontents

A sociologist at the end of the nineteenth century observed, "The most remarkable social phenomenon of the present century is the concentration of population in cities."[3] The number and size of cities grew as never before. The major impetus for urban growth was the concentration of industry in cities and the resulting need of large numbers of urban workers and their families for goods and services (Figure 23.2).

Industrialization was not the only stimulus. France provides many examples of urban growth with little industry. Increased commercial, trading, and administrative functions led to the growth of cities such as Toulouse, Bordeaux, and Nancy. Neither Holland, Italy, nor Switzerland experienced much industry in the first half of the nineteenth century, yet their cities grew. In general, however, industry transformed people from rural to urban inhabitants. People wanted to live near their work, and as industries concentrated in cities so did populations.

Urban growth in some places was dramatic. In the entire eighteenth century, London grew by only 200,000; but in the first half of the nineteenth century, it grew by 1.4 million, more than doubling its size. Liverpool and Manchester experienced similar growth in the same period. By 1851, England was a predominantly urban society, the first country to have as many people living in cities as in the countryside. For Germany that

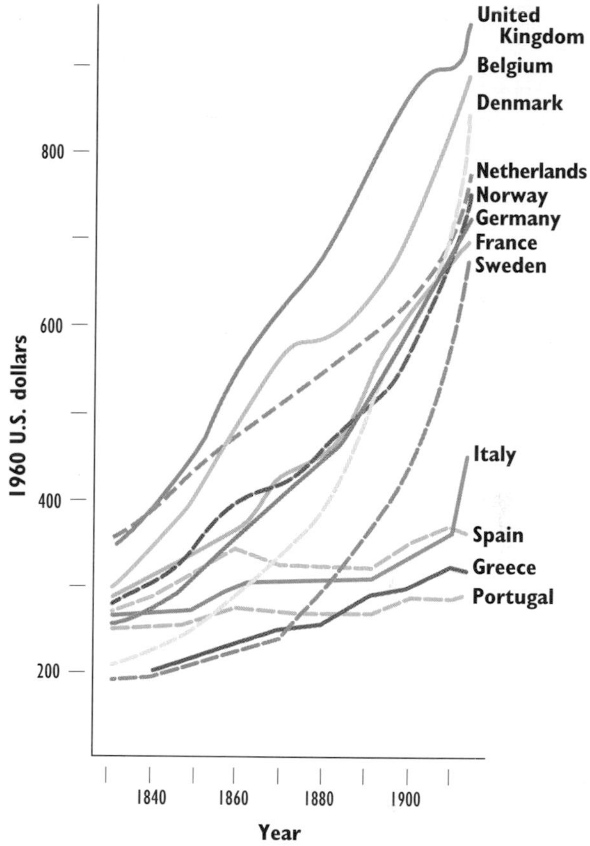

Figure 23.1 The Increase in Gross National Product per Capita in Principal European Countries, 1830–1913 The countries that industrialized rapidly—such as the United Kingdom in particular, and also Belgium, France, and Germany—experienced dramatic increase in per capita income during the nineteenth century. Other countries such as Greece and Portugal economically trailed the industrial leaders, and per capita income remained essentially flat. (*Source:* Norman J. G. Pounds, *An Historical Geography of Europe, 1800–1914* [New York: Cambridge University Press, 1985], p. 32. Used by permission of Cambridge University Press.)

date was 1891, and for France it was 1931. Although the proportion of people who were urban varied from place to place, the trend was clear and has continued (Map 23.3).

In some cases industry was located in the countryside where there was no town, and the increasing size of the factory led to the development of a city. The steelworks in Le Creusot,

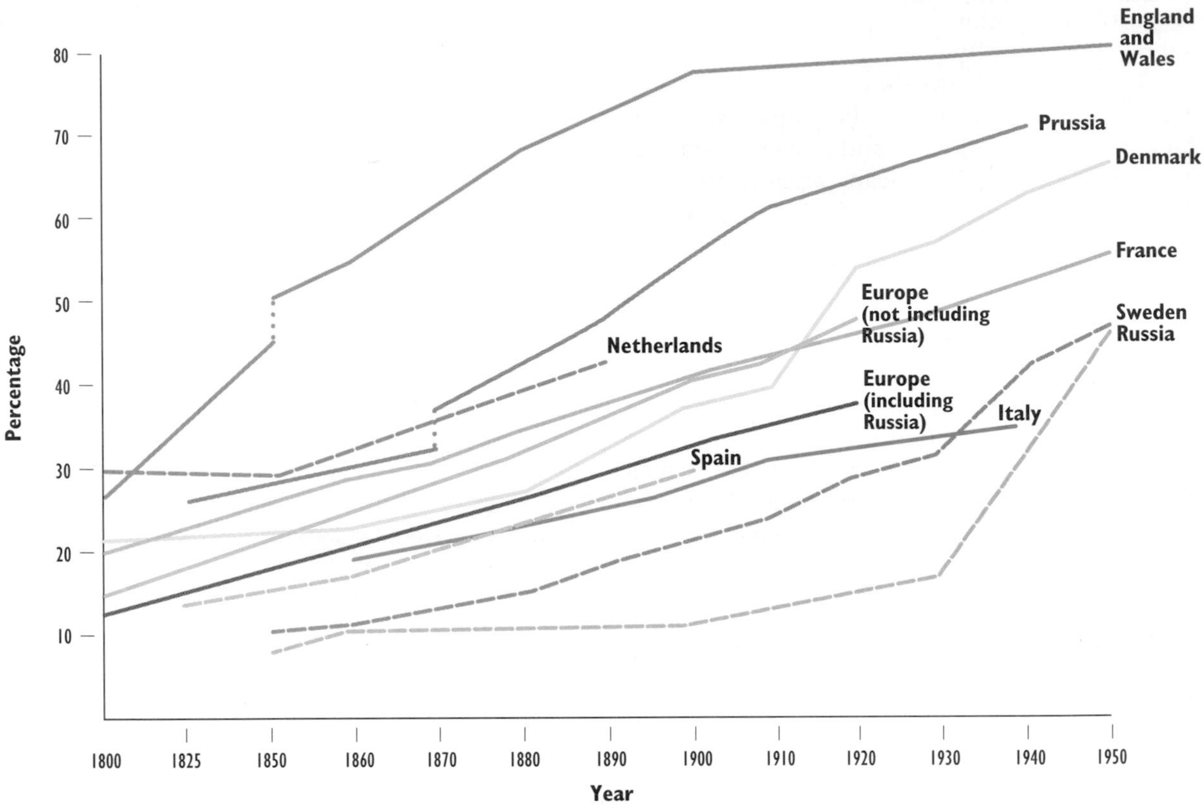

Figure 23.2 Percentages of Urban Population in European Countries, 1800–1950 By 1850 half the population of England lived in cities. On the other hand, the development of an urban population was far slower in agricultural Russia. And the Netherlands, which experienced slow industrialization but had an urban tradition, continued to have a fairly high proportion of city dwellers. (*Source:* Paul M. Hohenberg and Lynn Hollen Lees, *The Making of Urban Europe, 1000–1950* [Cambridge, Mass.: Harvard University Press, 1985], p. 219. Copyright © 1985. Used by permission of Harvard University Press.)

France, followed that pattern. In 1846 Le Creusot had 6000 inhabitants; in 1860, 16,000; by 1875, 25,000. In other cases industry gave rise to dramatic growth in a once-modest town—for instance, the west German town of Essen. In 1850 Essen had 9000 inhabitants; a half-century later its population had increased 30-fold. Occasionally, industry actually led to people leaving a city as manufacturers located on the outskirts of urban areas or as subcontracting increased the work of people involved in the putting-out system. But such an outward flow was unusual.

As urban growth was governed in part by the pace of industry, it also contributed to the continuing development of industry. Large cities provided convenient markets for goods and a labor pool for manufacturing. The concentration of people encouraged the exchange of ideas. A large city was likely to have scientific societies and laboratories in which engineers and scientists could discuss new ideas and new inventions that would spur industrial production. After midcentury, the progress in industrialization increasingly was driven by scientific and technical breakthroughs made in urban environments.

With the growth of cities came a multitude of urban ills. In the first half of the nineteenth century, the countryside was usually the healthiest region to live. Mortality rates were higher in the cities than in the countryside. In the 1840s, England as a whole had a death rate of 22 per thousand, but Liverpool averaged 39.2 and Manches-

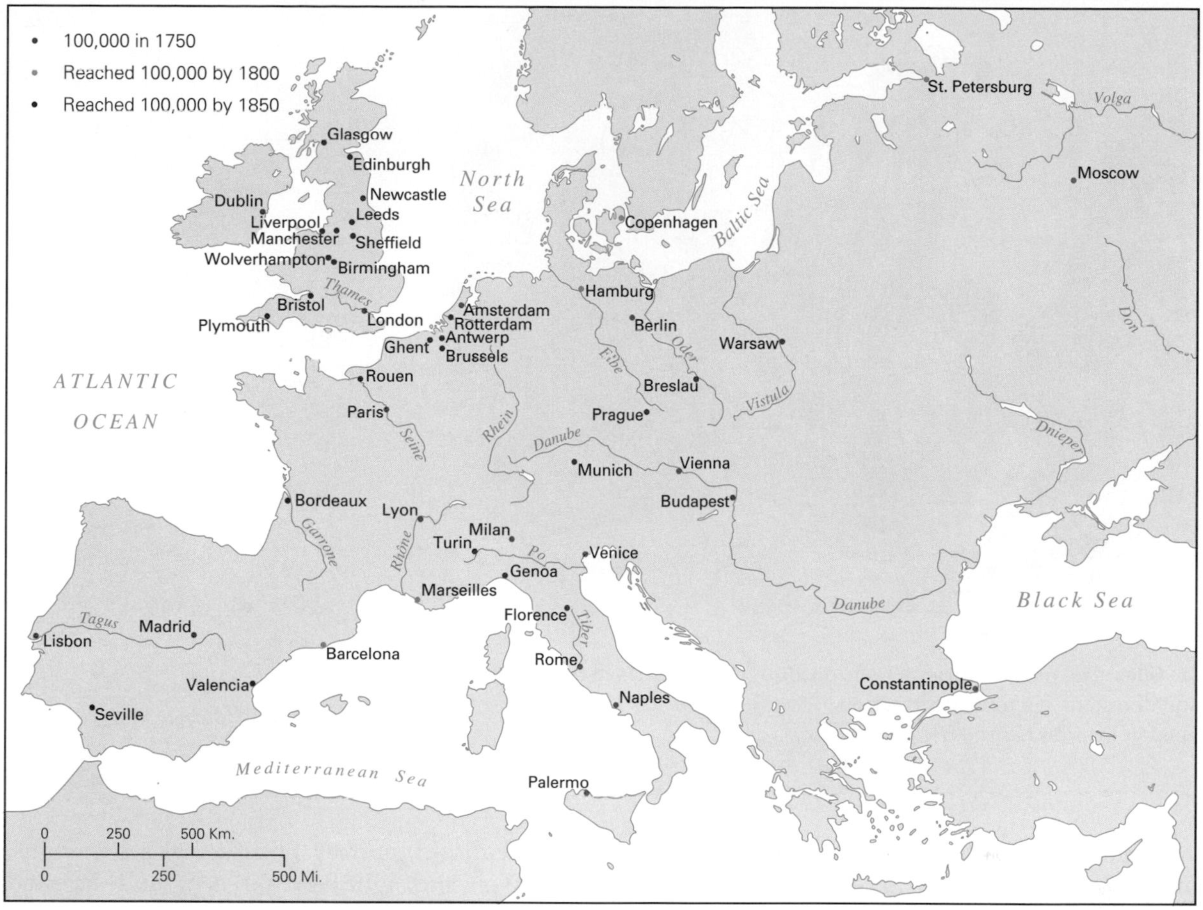

Map 23.3. Cities Reaching Population Level of 100,000 by 1750, 1800, and 1850 In 1750 the largest cities owed their existence to factors other than industry, but increasingly thereafter the development of industry determined the growth of cities. England, the leading industrial nation, contained many of the largest cities. (*Source:* Data from Tertius Chandler, *Four Thousand Years of Urban Growth: An Historical Census* [Lewistown, N.Y.: St. David's University Press, 1987], pp. 22–24.)

ter 33.1. In France national mortality rates were around 22 per thousand, but in some French cities the rate was as high as 35 per thousand. There was a dramatic social inequality in the face of death. Including the high child mortality rate, the average age at death for the gentry in Liverpool in 1842 was 35; for laborers it was 15. In 1800, boys living in urban slums were 8 inches shorter than their more fortunate contemporaries.

The rapid growth of the cities caught local authorities unprepared, and in the early stages of industrialization city life was particularly severe for the poor. Urban slums developed. The most notorious London slum was St. Giles, which became a tourist attraction because of its squalor (see the box, "Friedrich Engels Describes an Urban Slum"). In many cities, large numbers of people were crammed into small areas. The houses were built back to back on small lots and had insufficient lighting and ventilation. Overcrowding was the norm. One study of a working-class parish in central London in midcentury showed three quarters of the families living in single rooms. On one particular street, between 12 and 20 people were sleeping in each room. In Preston in 1842, 2400 persons slept three to a bed. The proximity of buildings blocked out sunlight. In the 1840s, from 12 to 15 percent of people in Manchester and Liverpool were living in cellars.

St. Giles The most notorious London slum was St. Giles, whose human squalor made it a tourist attraction. *(From Thomas Beames,* The Rookeries of London. *Courtesy Harvard University Library)*

Sanitation was rudimentary. A single privy in a courtyard was likely to serve dozens of tenants—in some notorious cases in England and France, a couple hundred. Waste from the privy might drain through open sewers to a nearby river, which was likely to be the local source of drinking water. Or the privy might be connected to a cesspool from which wastewater would seep and contaminate nearby wells. Some tenants lacked toilets and relieved themselves in the street. In the 1830s, people living in the poorest sections of Glasgow stored human waste in heaps along their houses and sold it as manure.

In manufacturing towns factory chimneys spewed soot, and everything was covered with dirt and grime. Smoke and fog created the famous London fog, which not only reduced visibility but posed serious health risks. City streets were littered with refuse; rotting corpses of dogs and horses were common. In 1858, the stench from sewage and other rot was so severe that the British House of Commons had to suspend its sessions.

In midcentury the city fathers of Marseilles described the center of their French city as "covered with old, narrow houses that are in ruins, where air and light hardly reach, [and] infected sewers spread epidemics." It is not surprising that cholera swept the city and other European urban centers. In the 1830s one of the first epidemics of modern times swept Europe, killing 100,000 in France, 50,000 in England. The cholera epidemic of 1854 killed 150,000 Frenchmen. Typhoid fever hit mostly the poor but did not spare the privileged. Queen Victoria of England nearly died of it, and her husband Prince Albert did.

Water was scarce and dirty. Piped water was reserved for the rich. The poor had to supply themselves from public fountains or wells and often carry water a considerable distance. In Birmingham in the middle of the century, out of 40,000 houses only one-fifth had running water. French cities were usually worse; some of the major ones had only about two gallons of public water available per person a day.

For most of its denizens, the city provided a crowded and squalid environment. Only in the second half of the nineteenth century would any attempts be made to bring some order to the chaos of urban life.

Friedrich Engels Describes an Urban Slum

In 1845 the young socialist Friedrich Engels, who was destined to be Karl Marx's literary partner, published **The Condition of the Working Class in England.** *Having lived in England in 1842–1844, Engels on his return to Germany provided a lively description of the hardships facing the English industrial working classes. Critics then and later noted that Engels, motivated by socialist zeal, at times exaggerated the misery he encountered. His description of the urban slum, however, was corroborated by many of his contemporaries. In this selection he describes St. Giles, one of the worst slums of London.*

St. Giles is situated in the most densely-populated part of London.... It is a confused conglomeration of tall houses of three or four stories. The narrow, dirty streets are just as crowded as the main thoroughfares, but in St. Giles one sees only members of the working classes. The houses are packed from cellar to attic and they are as dirty inside as outside. No human being would willingly inhabit such dens. Yet even worse conditions are to be found in the houses which lie off the main road down narrow alleys leading to the courts. These dwellings are approached by covered passages between the houses. The extent to which these filthy passages are falling into decay beggars all description. There is hardly an unbroken windowpane to be seen, the walls are crumbling, the door posts and window frames are loose and rotten. The doors, where they exist, are made of old boards nailed together. Indeed in this nest of thieves doors are superfluous, because there is nothing worth stealing. Piles of refuse and ashes lie all over the place and the slops thrown out into the street collect in pools which emit a foul stench. Here live the poorest of the poor. Here the worst-paid workers rub shoulders with thieves, rogues and prostitutes.

Source: Friedrich Engels, *The Condition of the Working Class in England,* trans. and ed. W. O. Henderson and W. H. Chaloner (Stanford, Calif.: Stanford University Press, 1968), pp. 33–34.

The Working Classes and Their Lot

In 1842, a middle-class observer traveling in industrial Lancashire noted that around the mills and factories had developed a "population [which] like the system to which it belongs is NEW.... hourly increasing in breadth and strength."[4] A French countess, using the pen name Daniel Stern, wrote in her memoirs of France in the 1830s and 1840s that in this era had emerged "a class apart, as if it were a nation within the nation," working in factories and mines, called "by a new name: the industrial proletariat."[5]

As industry advanced and spread, more and more people depended on it for a livelihood. In the putting-out system, when there was an agricultural downturn, a cottager could spend more time on hand labor, and when there was a slack in demand for hand labor, the cottager could devote more time to the land. But people living in industrial cities were totally dependent on manufacture for a livelihood; they did not have such flexibility. The working class was particularly vulnerable to downturns in the economy.

Most factory work was heavy and dirty in grim plants with primitive machinery. Sixteen-hour days were common. Child labor was widespread. Because there were no safety provisions, the workers were prone to accidents—especially new workers unaccustomed to work routines, or experienced workers untrained on new machines. Factory owners made no effort to protect their workers against dangerous substances or dangerous circumstances. Mercury used in hat manufacturing gradually poisoned the hatmakers and often led to dementia. There were sound reasons to speak of "mad hatters." Lead used in paints and pottery also had a devastating impact on workers' health. Metal grinding caused serious health problems. In Sheffield in 1842, three quarters of the cutlery workers had lung disease by the age of 40. In the 1840s, the military rejected four out of ten rural vounteers because of some health deficiency; in the industrializing cities the rate of rejection was 90 percent. In the industrial area of Saint-Etienne in France from 1836 to 1847, the average life expectancy of a miner was 37 years, but that of a farmer was 59.

Did industrialization improve the workers' lot? Perhaps the question is answered by another question: What would the workers have done without industrial employment? They could have continued working as farmers or farm hands or as artisans spinning and weaving by hand. But certainly in England in the eighteenth century, men and women rushed from the countryside to the cities to work in the factories. A population explosion was preventing many of them from having enough land to make a living, and improved farming methods were lessening the need for farm hands. It is not clear that these workers could have made a living if they had remained in the country.

From the beginning, industrialization increased wealth. "Optimist" historians argue that some of the new wealth trickled down to the lower levels of society. "Pessimist" historians say that that downward flow did not necessarily occur. Statistics, however, suggest that in Britain by the 1840s the workers' lives had improved. Their real income improved by 40 percent between 1800 and 1850. In part this advance was due to an increase in the numbers of skilled workers, whose wages were higher than the wages of their unskilled counterparts. Workers benefited not only from higher earnings but from the relatively low prices of many basic goods. In London, the price of 4 pounds of household bread fell from 15 pennies at the beginning of the nineteenth century to 8½ pennies in the 1830s. As the cost of cloth declined, there was a marked improvement in the dress of working-class people. On the Continent, the lot of workers improved a little later than in Britain, but the process followed the same pattern. In Germany workers' wages did not increase appreciably between 1800 and 1829, but by 1850 they had increased by 25 percent and by 1870 by another 50 percent.

For the early years of industrialization, information on workers' income and expenses is incomplete. The best evidence comes from Britain,

Child Labor in the Industrial Era Children were used often in mining; their small size made them particularly "convenient" for carting coal in narrow shafts. *(The Bettmann Archive)*

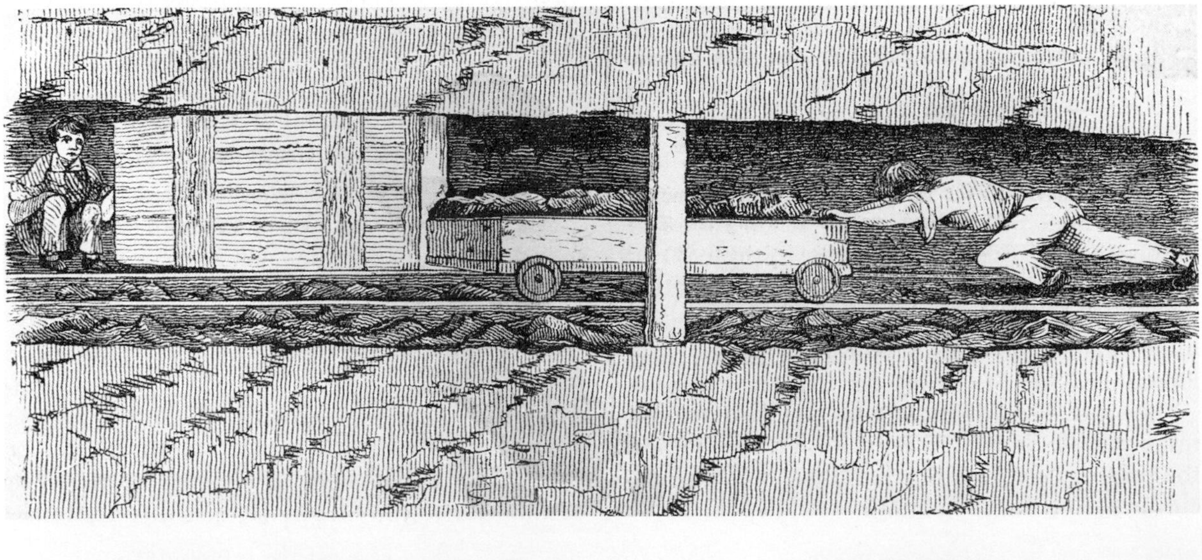

where an average family needed at least 21 shillings a week to escape from poverty. Skilled workers, who were in demand, might earn as much as 30 shillings a week, but most workers were unskilled. In Manchester in the mid-1830s, workmen producing coarse calicoes earned only between 6 and 8 shillings a week. And neither skilled nor unskilled workers were assured of regular employment. Economic depression and slumps led to mass layoffs. Injured workers could sicken and die. Women who were the main breadwinners did not receive wages high enough to meet a family's total needs. A young, healthy, skilled male worker might earn 30 shillings; but if he became ill or when he aged, as he became less productive, his wages fell, or the manufacturer might cut wages, as often happened. Thus, if women and children did not always need to work to help the family meet its minimum needs, at some point they usually did have to pitch in.

Incomes were so low that workers normally spent between two-thirds and three-fourths of their budget on food (Table 23.1). Those who lived in rural areas might raise chickens or pigs or have a plot of potatoes. Bread was the largest single item consumed, varying between one and two pounds a day per person. In Britain and Germany people also ate a lot of potatoes. A little bacon or other meat gave flavor to the soup in which people dipped their bread or potatoes, but meat was rarely consumed for its own sake. Because men were the main breadwinners and tended to have the most strenuous occupation, they received the choice piece of meat and the largest amount of food. Women and children ate what was left.

Table 23.1 An 1832 Estimate of a Worker's Weekly Budget

	Shillings	Pence*
Rent, fuel, candle	3	0
Soap, soda, starch		5½
Sand, black lead, beeswax		3
White washing cottage		½
Flour for bread	3	9
Flour for puddings		8
Eggs		3½
Milk		11
Oatmeal		6½
Treacle	1	2
Tea, coffee		10½
Meat (5 lbs.)	2	6
Vegetables		7
Salt, pepper, mustard, vinegar		2
Beer		10½
Water		1
Schooling for 2 children		6
Reading		2
Wear & tear of household goods		6
Clothing	2	10
Total	20 shillings or one pound	

*12 pence = 1 shilling

Note: This worker, compared to most workers, is quite well off. His children go to school, he spends money on reading matter, and he consumes quite a bit of meat. Nevertheless, he spends 13 shillings, or two-thirds of his weekly income, on food and drink.

Source: Estimate by Humphrey Boyle in 1832 of laboring family budget in Leeds, reproduced in B. W. Clapp et al., eds., *Documents in English Economic History* (London: Bell & Sons, 1976), p. 449.

Industrialization and the Family

Industrialization dramatically changed the character of the working-class family and household. Especially in the textile industries, factory owners preferred to employ children and women. They were thought to be more pliable than men, and their wages were considerably lower. Women generally received from 30 to 50 percent of men's wages; children, from 5 to 25 percent. In 1839 Thomas Heath, a weaver in Spitalfields, a London neighborhood, earned 15 shillings a week, his wife but 3 shillings.

Women working in factories, away from home, had to find ways of taking care of their infants. An older child, sometimes but 5 or 6 years old, would be entrusted with the care of her or his sibling. A newborn might be sent to a "baby-farm," to individuals in the countryside who were paid to take care of the child. Very often these babies were neglected, and their mortality

The Young Girl in the Factory

Reformers in Parliament, among them Michael Sadler, denounced the appalling conditions in the factories. Sadler was appointed to head a commission to hold hearings; workers appeared before it giving vivid descriptions of their lot. Public and parliamentary outrage at the conditions revealed by these hearings led to the Factory Act of 1833. Among the witnesses was Elizabeth Bentley, a 23-year-old weaving machine operative, who gave the following testimony.

What age are you?—23. . . .

What time did you begin to work in a factory?—When I was 6 years old. . . .

What were your hours of labor? . . . —From 5 in the morning till 9 at night, when they were thronged.

For how long have you worked that excessive length of time?—For about half a year.

What were your usual hours of labor when they were not so thronged?—From 6 in the morning till 7 at night.

What time was allowed for your meals?—40 minutes at noon. . . .

Your labor is very excessive?—Yes, you have no time for anything.

Suppose you flagged a little, or were too late, what would they do?—Strap us. . . .

Girls as well as boys?—Yes.

Severely?—Yes. . . .

Did you live far from the mill?—Yes, two miles.

Had you a clock?—No, we had not. . . .

Were you generally there in time?—Yes; my mother has been up at four o'clock in the morning and at two o'clock; the colliers used to go to their work at about three or four o'clock, and when she heard them stirring she has got up out of her warm bed, and gone out and asked them the time; and I have sometimes been at Hunslet Car at 2 o'clock when it was steaming down with rain, and we have had to stay till the mill was opened [at 5 A.M.].

Source: Great Britain, *Sessional Papers, House of Commons,* Hearing of June 4, 1832, vol. XV (1831–1832), pp. 195–197.

rate was extremely high. In many cases, baby-farming was but a camouflaged form of infanticide. Mothers who were unable to use those sorts of child care and needed to keep their children calm at home during their absence drugged their children with mixtures of opium, readily available from the local druggist.

The new industry found employment for children once they were over the age of 5 or 6. Their size made them useful for certain jobs, such as reaching under machines to pick up loose cotton. Because of their small hands they were also hired as "doffers," taking bobbins off frames and replacing them. Elizabeth Bentley began working as a doffer in 1815 at the age of 6. At the age of 23, when she testified before a parliamentary commission, she was "considerably deformed . . . in consequence of this labor" (see the box, "The Young Girl in the Factory"). Child labor, of course, did not start with the industrial transformation; it had always existed. What was new was the harsh industrial discipline imposed on the children.

Although children were common in British textile industries, overall less than 10 percent of working children were in industry. Most were in agriculture or the service sector. In the early stages of industrialization, children were primarily employed in textile mills to pick up waste and repair broken threads. As technological improvements reduced both, the need for children lessened.

Improved technology and the growth of industries other than textiles increased the employment of adult men. In iron and later steel plants, physical strength was essential. Despite the high labor costs that resulted when men were employed, managers had no choice but to hire them. However, in France, where textiles were still the predominant product after the turn of the nineteenth century, women made up two-thirds of the work force as late as 1906.

During the era of industrial transformation the mortality rate of women was higher than men. Usually physically lighter than boys and often underfed, young girls were faced with heavy labor that undermined their health. In 1842, 18-year-old Ann Eggley, a mineworker since the age of 7, hauled carriages loaded with ore weighing 800 pounds, for 12 hours a day. She testified to a parliamentary commission that she was so tired from her work that when she came home she often fell asleep before even going to bed. In addition to factory work, women did virtually all housework and were physically depleted by frequent childbearing. Isabel Wilson, another mineworker, testified that she had given birth to ten children and had had five miscarriages. These women—worn out, exhausted, vulnerable to disease—faced premature death. This situation changed only toward the end of the nineteenth century, and today women outlive men.

In some cases, industrialization meant a transformation in the authority structure of workers' households, undermining the influence of the male head of household. A woman could make a living independent of her spouse, and children at a reasonably early age could emancipate themselves from their parents and make a go of it working in a factory or a mine. These options were not possible in agriculture or in the putting-out system. Although the options were available, and contemporaries sometimes denounced industry for dissolving family bonds, the family remained an effective work unit. As in the putting-out system, often whole families were hired as a group to perform a specific function.

Wives and children contributed in other ways to the household budget—by making the clothes, raising a pig, tending a potato patch, and performing daily household chores. Grandparents often moved from the country to live with the family and take care of children. A study of Verviers, an industrial city in eastern Belgium, showed that at midcentury a sizable number of grown children continued living with their parents and contributing to the financial well-being of the family unit. In the steel-manufacturing city of Solingen in western Germany, a cutlery worker known as Fritz B., the subject of a sociological study in 1851, lived with his wife and four children. All were contributing either in cash or in labor to the family's well-being. Although industry had the potential to undermine traditional family structures, the historical evidence is that the family adjusted and survived the challenges posed by the new economic system.

Table 23.2 Coal Production in Industrializing Nations

	Millions of tons	Kilograms per inhabitant
1700	4	26
1750	7	16
1800	16	76
1830	30	120
1860	129	390

Source: Based on B. R. Mitchell, "Statistical Appendix, 1700–1914," in Carlo Cippola, ed., *The Fontana Economic History of Europe*, vol. 4 (London: Collins, 1973), pp. 747 and 770; and Norman J. G. Pounds, *An Historical Geography of Europe, 1500–1840* (New York: Cambridge University Press, 1979), pp. 268–269.

The Land, the Water, and the Air

Industrialization impinged seriously on the environment, transforming the surface of the earth, the water, and the air. To run the new machinery, coal was mined in increasing amounts (Table 23.2) Iron and other minerals were also extracted in increasing amounts.

To extract coal and other minerals, miners dug deep tunnels. Millions of tons of earth, rock, and other debris were removed from underground. This material, plus slag and other waste from the factories, created mounds that at times covered acres of land, creating new geological formations. In one district in England in 1870, a million cubic yards of soda waste occupied 50 acres.

The exploitation of coal ushered in the modern age of energy use, in which massive amounts of nonrenewable resources are consumed. With axes and saws people cut down trees, depleting forests to supply the wood needed to build shafts for coal, iron, and tin mines, or to make the charcoal necessary for glassmaking. Between 1750 and 1900, increasing industrial and agricultural needs led to the clearing of 50 percent of all the forests ever cleared. Many of Europe's major forests disappeared or were seriously diminished. Deforestation in turn sped up soil erosion.

Industry changed the physical environment in which people lived. Forests, lakes, rivers, and air—as well as people themselves—showed the harmful effects of industry. Centrifugal pumps drained large marshes in the Fenland in eastern England. A contemporary lamented, "The wind which, in the autumn of 1851 was curling the blue water of the lake, in the autumn of 1853 was blowing in the same place over fields of yellow corn." Factories dumped waste ash into rivers, changing their channels and making them considerably shallower. Because of pollution from industrial and human waste, by 1850 no fish could survive in the lower Thames River. Smoke and soot darkened the skies, intensifying the fog over London and other cities. Foul odors from factories could be detected at several miles' distance. In addition to being unpleasant, various air pollutants caused cancer and lung disease.

Responses to Industrialization

People in the new industrial classes living at subsistence levels were disquieting evidence of the impact of industrialization. What should be done about the working classes—or for them? These new classes developed their own sense of a common interest and fate. The result was a resounding cry for political and social democracy that began in the first half of the nineteenth century and became increasingly insistent. Many solutions were proffered. The proposals became powerful ideologies shaping the nineteenth and twentieth centuries, not only in Europe but also in most of the non-European world.

Economic Liberalism

The classical economists of the late eighteenth and early nineteenth centuries (see page 828) argued in favor of laissez faire, the policy of nonintervention by the government in the economy. The laws of supply and demand, they contended, if allowed to operate unhindered, would provide for the well-being of both the individual and society. Their arguments formed the basis of what was known as "economic liberalism."

Building on earlier liberals' advocacy of laissez-faire policies, others more directly and even more uncompromisingly argued against any government action to improve the conditions of the working classes. The British social theorist Herbert Spencer (1820–1903) took to extremes the lessons of classical economics. Although he lived on inherited money, he unabashedly asserted that wealth reflected innate virtue and poverty indicated innate vice. According to Spencer, the state should guarantee the right of everyone to pursue freedom as long as the pursuit did not infringe on others. In *Social Statics* (1851), Spencer opposed relief for the poor on the grounds that it unfairly deprived some—the rich—of their property. He also argued that schooling was outside the purview of the state.

Applying to human society Charles Darwin's principle of "natural selection" (see page 941), Spencer was a Social Darwinist. In 1864 he coined the expression "survival of the fittest." Society, he believed, should be established in such a way that the fittest would survive. The weak, poor, and thus improvident were not worthy of survival, and if the state helped them survive—such as by providing education—it would only perpetuate the weak and unfit. Spencer's harsh doctrine was widely acclaimed.

The classical economists' theories had a large audience. Popularizers spread the gospel of free enterprise, teaching the advantages of the capitalist system while justifying the conditions of the wealthy. They were particularly prevalent in Britain. Among them, Samuel Smiles (1812–1904) was widely read. Originally a physician, Smiles turned to popular education and in 1859 published *Self-Help,* one of the most influential books of the nineteenth century. In *Self-Help* he argued that the poor people's remedy lay in their own

Manchester, England, 1851 A small, unimportant town of 20,000 in the 1750s, Manchester—as a result of industrialization—had 400,000 inhabitants in 1850. In this 1851 painting, the polluted industrial city is contrasted with its idealized rural suburb. *(The Royal Collection © 1993 Her Majesty Queen Elizabeth II)*

hands. If they lived thrifty, industrious lives, the good life would come to them. The improvement of the human condition was dependent not on society but on the character of the individual. Smiles's works sold a quarter-million copies in Britain by the end of the century and were translated into many languages.

Many of those who basically favored laissez-faire policies, including some classical economists, criticized some aspects of the market economy. The Scottish economist Adam Smith (1723–1790) warned that the market tended to form monopolies, and he suggested that government intervene to prevent this situation. According to Smith, not all human needs could be provided by the marketplace; the government needed to supply education, road systems, and an equitable system of justice. The liberal thinker and government reformer Jeremy Bentham (1748–1832) was fearful of an overly intrusive government but also saw government as a possible force for good, to ensure the greatest happiness for the greatest number. Edwin Chadwick (1800–1895) advocated government intervention to ensure public sanitation and care for the poor; as a government official he worked to implement these twin goals.

John Stuart Mill (1806–1873), the leading British economic and political thinker at midcentury, in the first edition of his *Principles of Political Economy* (1848), voiced strong support for laissez-faire economics. The individual if left alone could carry on economic functions better than the government, Mill insisted. In subsequent editions, however, he remarked that the state had an obligation to intervene in the face of human misery. There were also many human needs that the free market could not address satisfactorily. Once wealth was produced, he noted, its distribution was subject to traditions and to decisions made by those in power. Thus, presumably, wealth could be shared by society as a whole. Toward the end of his life, Mill seemed to be leaning toward socialism.

The liberal economists' views on the virtues of laissez-faire policy gradually changed. In the face of unsanitary urban conditions, child labor, and other alarming results of industrialization, the state around midcentury began to intervene in areas of concern that would have been unthinkable a half-century earlier.

The Growth of Working-Class Solidarity

Hardest hit by economic changes, workers sought to improve their conditions by organizing and articulating their needs. In the preindustrial economy, artisans and craftsmen lived in an accepted hierarchy with prescribed rules. They began by serving for a certain number of years as apprentices to a master, then became journeymen, and finally with hard work and good fortune became masters of their trade. As tradesmen with common interests, they tended to band together into brotherhoods, promising each other help and trying to influence their working conditions.

These early workers' associations expanded their spheres of influence. In France by the seventeenth century, the brotherhoods, known as *compagnonages,* included people from more than one craft. In England, there were national networks for particular crafts, and through the "tramping system" people out of work could go to another town and receive assistance and sometimes work from their fellow tradesmen.

Guilds were urban institutions, and with industrialization they gradually declined. Manufacturing occurred not only in cities but on their outskirts and even in the countryside, and thus guilds became irrelevant to the new methods of production. Moreover, guilds were frequently attacked by the new economic liberals, who viewed them as constraints to trade and the free flow of labor. In France, the revolutionaries abolished the guilds and all workers' coalitions. In Britain throughout the eighteenth century Parliament passed various acts against "combinations" by workmen.

While guilds faded in importance, the solidarity and language born of the guild continued to shape workers' attitudes throughout much of the nineteenth century. New experiences also reinforced the sense of belonging to a group and sharing common aspirations.

Cultural forces reinforced workers' sense of solidarity. The common language of religion and common religious practice created a bond among English workers, and many religious groups were born as a result. Some historians believe that the growth of Methodism in England in the 1790s was a response to economic conditions. Emphasis on equality before God fueled the sense of injustice in a world where some were privileged and living in luxury while others were condemned to work with their children for a pittance. Religious cults flourished in an environment of despair punctuated by hopes of deliverance. Joanna, a self-proclaimed prophet active in the 1810s in England, announced both salvation and the coming of a new world of material wellbeing. In France, workers believed the new society would come about by their martyrdom; like Jesus, the workers would suffer and from their suffering would emerge a new, better society. Ideas of social justice were linked in the countryside with religious broadsides speaking of "Jesus the worker." Religious themes and language continued to be important in labor organization for many years.

Other cultural factors fostered the workers' sense of shared purpose. Housing was increasingly segregated. Workers lived in low-rent areas—in slums in the center of cities or in outlying areas near the factories. Thus, many workers lived close together, in similar conditions of squalor and hardship. Entrepreneurs who built factories or established mineworks in the countryside had to provide housing in order to attract and retain workers. Although this housing may have been better than what was available in the cities, it nevertheless reinforced the workers' solidarity and sense of commonality.

Workers grew close to each other by spending their leisure time together, drinking in pubs, attending popular theaters and new forms of popular entertainment such as the circus, or attending various traditional blood sports such as boxing or cockfights. Popular sports emerged in the 1880s. Sporting events were attended only by workers, and the participants came from the working classes. Soccer developed in England at this time.

Social institutions also fostered class unity. In the eighteenth century marriage was usually within a particular craft. By the nineteenth century it became more common for workers to marry across their crafts, thereby strengthening

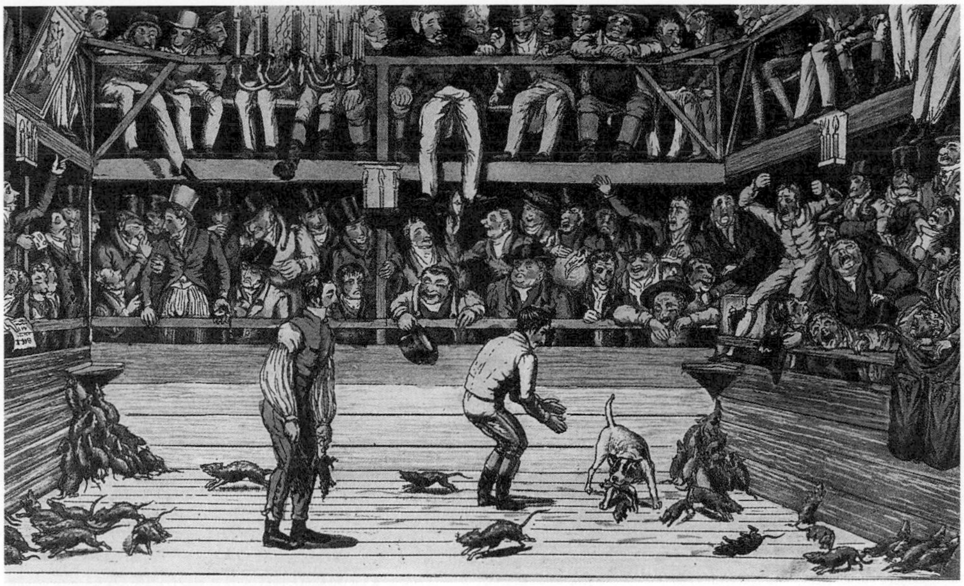

Leisure Activity for the Working Poor Some harsh forms of entertainment turned up in the industrial period. By the hundreds, working-class spectators came to see the celebrated dog "Billy" kill a hundred rats at one time at the Westminster Pit in London in 1822. *(The British Library)*

the sense of solidarity that encompassed the working classes as a whole.

Faced with the uncertainties of unemployment and job-related accidents, in addition to disease and other natural catastrophes, workers formed so-called friendly societies in which they pooled their resources to provide mutual aid (see the box, "Rules of the Mechanics' Friendly Institution"). These societies, descendants of confraternities and benefit organizations of the Middle Ages and Renaissance, combined business activity with feasts, drinking bouts, and other social functions.

Friendly societies had existed as early as the seventeenth century, but they became increasingly popular and important after industrialization. Their strength in an area often reflected the degree to which the area was industrialized. First started to provide aid for workers in a particular trade, they soon included members in several crafts. They federated into national organizations, so that a worker who moved to a new town could continue his membership in his new locale. Connected by common membership in friendly societies, workers expressed group solidarity beyond their individual occupations. Though far from accomplished, a working class was in the making.

Collective Action

Militant and in some cases violent action strengthened workers' solidarity. In politics, workers expressed common grievances, and some of their disappointments in the political arena underscored their common situation.

In the face of hardships, workers organized for collective action. In 1811–1812, English hand weavers, faced with competition from mechanized looms, organized in groups claiming to be led by a General Ned Ludd. In the name of economic justice and to protect their livelihood, the "Luddites," as the general's followers were called, smashed machines or threatened to do so. To bring the Luddite riots under control, twelve thousand troops were dispatched; and in January 1813, the authorities excecuted ten people for Luddism. Similarly, in Saxony in eastern Germany in the 1830s and 1840s, weavers went on machine-crushing campaigns. These movements

Rules of the Mechanics' Friendly Institution

By paying regular dues, the members of friendly societies built up funds that could be used in case of illness, death, or unemployment. The rules adopted by the Mechanics' Friendly Institution in 1824 in Leeds were typical.

Rule First: The different orders of Mechanics to be admitted members of this Institution are to be Model Makers, Smiths, Filers, Joiners, and Wood and Iron Turners, engaged in the making of Steam Engines only, and Machinery for the preparing and spinning of Flax, Tow, Hemp, Cotton, Woollen, Worsted, or Silk; and every person who has not worked five years at one or more of the Branches above stated, by the time he is twenty-one years of age, must be considered ineligible, except one son of any of the members of this Society, who shall be admitted on the same terms as those who may have served five years. . . .

Any person who shall become a member of this Institution to be relieved in distress and death, shall pay three half-pence per week; and any person wishing to be relieved in sickness, shall pay threepence per week. . . .

Every member of this Institution shall contribute towards the support of it, as above stated, to be paid every meeting night to the stewards; and when that sum is found insufficient, the same shall be made known to the Institution, and the contributions advanced to meet the demand. . . .

Every member when visited with sickness or lameness which renders him incapable of following his employment, and which is not occasioned by drunkenness, fighting, or anything contrary to the true intent and meaning of these Rules, shall be relieved by the stewards with one and sixpence per day, during the time of his sickness or lameness, for the space of six calendar months; at the end of which time he shall receive one shilling per day for the term of two years. Should he still continue sick, his case shall be referred to a committee.

Source: "Rules of the Mechanics' Friendly Institution, as Agreed upon by the Deputies from the Different Branches, Convened at Leeds, August 16th, 1824" (Bolton, 1824), in J. T. Ward and W. Hamish Fraser, eds., *Workers and Employers: Documents on Trade Unions and Industrial Relations in Britain Since the Early Nineteenth Century* (New York: Archon Press, 1980), pp. 27–28.

revealed the militance of labor and its willingness to resort to violence.

In Lyon, France, in 1831 and 1834, fair wages for piecework was the cause for workers' uprisings. When the silk merchants lowered the amount they would pay, the workers rose up, bearing banners proclaiming "Live Working or Die Fighting." Troops were brought in to restore order to the riot-torn city. Although conditions of the silk trade had been the immediate impetus for the uprising, the workers appealed for help to their fellow workers in other trades.

Labor agitation in much of Europe increased in the 1840s; a major strike wave involving twenty thousand workers broke out in Paris in 1840. In the summer of 1842, an industrial downturn in England led to massive unemployment and rioting. In the summer of 1844 in Silesia, in eastern Prussia, linen handloom weavers who, desperate because of worsening conditions brought on by competition from machine-made cotton fabrics, attacked the homes of the wealthy. In 1855 in Barcelona, the government tried to dissolve unions, and fifty thousand workers went on strike carrying banners that warned "Association or Death."

Many of the friendly societies, concerned with the well-being of their members, also confronted their members' working conditions and acted very much as labor unions would. They or-

The New Discipline of the Factory System

The new factories regimented the work force and were likely to impose stiff penalties for infractions of the rules. This document lists some of the regulations of the Berlin Foundry and Engineering Works of the Royal Overseas Trading Co. of 1844.

The normal working day begins at all seasons at 6 A.M. precisely and ends, after the usual break of half an hour for breakfast, an hour for dinner, and half an hour for tea, at 7 P.M., and it shall be strictly observed....

The doorkeeper shall lock the door punctually at 6 A.M., 8:30 A.M., 1 P.M., and 4:30 P.M.

Workers arriving 2 minutes late shall lose half an hour's wages; whoever is more than 2 minutes late may not start work until after the next break, or at least shall lose his wages until then.

Repeated irregular arrival at work shall lead to dismissal. This shall also apply to those who are found idling by an official or overseer, and refuse to obey their order to resume work....

All conversation with fellow-workers is prohibited....

Natural functions must be performed at the appropriate places....

It goes without saying that all overseers and officials of the firm shall be obeyed without question, and shall be treated with due deference. Disobedience will be punished by dismissal.

Immediate dismissal shall also be the fate of anyone found drunk in any of the workshops....

The gatekeeper and the watchman, as well as every official, are entitled to search the baskets, parcels, aprons, etc. of the women and children who are taking the dinners into the works, on their departure, as well as search any worker suspected of stealing any article whatever....

A free copy of these rules is handed to every workman, but whoever loses it and requires a new one, or cannot produce it on leaving, shall be fined 2½ silver groschen.

Source: S. Pollard and C. Holmes, eds., *Documents of European Economic History*, vol. 1 (New York: St. Martin's Press, 1968), pp. 534–536.

ganized strikes and provided support to members while they were on strike. Unions were illegal in Britain until 1825, in Prussia until 1859, and in France until the 1860s. The advantages offered by unions were well understood. As a French workers' paper declared in 1847, "If workers came together and organized . . . nothing would be able to stop them." They would be able to ensure their conditions of work by having an organized force that could threaten to withhold labor if the employer did not grant decent wages and acceptable conditions. Unions made workers a countervailing force to the factory owners.

Discipline in the factory was often severe (see the box, "The New Discipline of the Factory System"). Workers had to conform to rigid rules not only in the workplace but also away from it. Workers in some factories were forbidden to read certain newspapers, had to attend religious services, and could marry only with the owners' permission. Workers resisted these attempts at control and resented the employers' intrusiveness. They wanted autonomy, they wanted to be free of outside regulation, and unions provided a means to ensure that freedom.

The process of unionization was difficult. By midcentury, many countries had passed laws supporting employers against the workers. Censorship and the use of force against organized strikes were not uncommon. Population growth made it difficult for workers to withhold labor lest they be replaced by others only too willing to take their place. Foreign workers—for example, the Irish who streamed into England and the Belgians and Italians who streamed into France—were often desperate for work and not well informed about local conditions.

In many countries, workers formed unions before unions were legalized. Most were centered around a single craft or a single industry. In Britain, however, there were early attempts to organize unions on a national basis. In 1834, Welsh socialist Robert Owen (1771–1858) helped launch the Grand National Consolidated Trades Union. The organization's goal was to use the principles of cooperation to unite all of labor against the capitalist system. Internal strife and government repression kept this organization from succeeding. Not until 1860 was a federal structure created for the British unions—the Trade Union Congress.

Unionization This certificate of membership is for the earliest professional union in Britain, the Amalgamated Society of Engineers. With references to classical antiquity, British inventors, and various trades, the document highlights the nobility of the trade. *(E. T. Archive)*

In Germany in 1848 the General Workers' Brotherhood was founded. Its first members were people from many walks of life, but gradually its membership included workers only. Most of the members were craftsmen and artisans: skilled workers such as cigar makers, book printers, typesetters. The year after its founding, the General Workers' Brotherhood had 15,000 members and 170 locals. After 1859, when labor unions were legalized, they grew significantly.

The composition of union membership evolved over time. Because labor unions originated in the crafts tradition, the earliest members were skilled craftsmen who organized to protect their livelihood from the challenge that industrialization posed. The craftsmen were usually literate and were usually long-time residents of their communities. They provided the labor movement with much of its leadership and organization. Skilled craft workers played a strong role in developing a sense of class consciousness. The language and institutions that they had developed over decades and sometimes over centuries became the common heritage of workers in general.

Workers looked to political action as the means by which to improve their situation. In the 1830s and 1840s English workers agitated for the right to vote; they saw voting as a way to put themselves on equal footing with the privileged and to win better conditions. The failure to win the vote in 1832 with the passage of the Great Reform Bill disappointed many workers, and they heavily backed the Chartist movement of the 1840s. Symptomatically, Chartism won its greatest support in the industrial areas.

In France, urban laborers who had played an important part in the various stages of the Revolution continued to shape political events. In July 1830, workers helped topple the Bourbon monarchy and bring Louis Philippe (r. 1830–1848) to the throne. They insisted that their labor had created the wealth of the nation and that their self-sacrifice had brought in a freer government. Workers were disappointed by their failure to win political representation under the July

Monarchy, and their sense of betrayal strengthened their class solidarity vis-à-vis the wealthy, privileged upper classes.

Politically, workers played a major role in the European revolutions of 1848. They demonstrated and helped bring down the July Monarchy in France. In Germany and Austria, they participated as organized groups in the initial successful uprisings against the established orders. Workers also influenced the course of the revolutions. However vague their ideas, European workers showed that their organizations were legitimate representatives of the people and that the lot of the worker should be the concern of government. In general, workers upheld the ideal of a moral economy—one in which all who labored got a just wage and a minimum level of well-being was assured to all.

The working classes were never a monolithic group. They consisted of people with varying skills, responsibilities, and incomes. (See the feature, "Weighing the Evidence: Workers' Wages," on pages 886–887.) Craftsmen with valuable skills were the segment that employers most respected and favored in pay and in working conditions. In contrast, unskilled workers were poorly paid, harshly treated, and often given only temporary work. Many skilled workers looked with contempt on the unskilled.

If both sexes worked side by side, there was little solidarity between them. Men worried that women were undermining their earning power by accepting lower wages. They often excluded women from their unions. They even went on strike to force employers to discharge women.

Foreign workers were heartily despised. British workers were hostile to their Irish colleagues, the French to the Belgians and Italians in their midst. The hostility often led to fisticuffs. In London anti-Irish riots were common.

Thus, many forces fostered disunion among the working classes in the nineteenth century, and unity among workers was far from achieved. Nevertheless, various experiences, including the spread of industry, broadened and deepened workers' sense of a common fate and goal.

The middle classes came to believe that all workers formed a single class. By the mid-nineteenth century, they had developed a clear fear of workers, not only as individuals but as a group, as a class. It was not unusual for members of the elite to refer to workers as "the swinish multitude" or, as the title of a popular English book put it, *The Great Unwashed* (1868). In France reference was alternately made to "the dangerous classes" and "the laboring classes." Not just workers but even the privileged seemed to see relations between the groups as a form of class war.

Marx and Marxism

Socialism provided a powerful language for the expression of working-class interests. Many of the workers who were enfranchised in the later part of the century joined political parties espousing this doctrine. Socialism in various forms existed before Karl Marx came on the scene. Saint-Simon, and Fourier in France, and Owen in Great Britain, were the foremost prophets of socialism (see pages 830–832). Marx drew on their theories and gave them a very special twist, and in the end his became the dominant form of socialism.

Karl Marx (1818–1883), the son of a lawyer, grew up in the Rhineland, in western Germany, an industrializing area that was particularly open to political ideas and agitation. The Rhineland had been influenced by the ideas of the French Revolution and was primed for political agitation. As a young man Marx studied philosophy at the University of Berlin and joined a group known as the "Young Hegelians," self-declared disciples of the idealist philosopher G. W. F. Hegel (1770–1831) (see page 824). Marx showed an early interest in political liberty and socialism. In 1842–1843 he edited a newspaper that spoke out for freedom and democracy in Germany. The following year in Paris, he met several of the French socialist writers. Marx presented his views forcefully and passionately. Even as a young man, he was perceived by his contemporaries as bright but unyielding in his determination.

Because of his radical journalism, he was exiled from the Rhineland and lived briefly in Paris, then Brussels. In 1849, he settled in London, where he lived for the rest of his life, dedicated to establishing his ideas on what he viewed as scientific bases. He was never able to provide well for his family, which constantly lived on the brink of poverty. Of the six children born to the Marx household, three died in infancy. His modest income came from writing for the *New York*

Karl Marx Through his writings and agitation, Marx transformed the socialism of his day and created an ideology that helped shape the nineteenth and twentieth centuries. *(The Bettmann Archive)*

Daily Tribune and from funds provided by his friend and collaborator Friedrich Engels (1820–1895).

In 1848, Marx and Engels published the *Communist Manifesto* (see the box, "The Communist Manifesto"). A pamphlet written for the Communist League, a group of Germans living in exile, the manifesto was an appeal to the working classes of the world. The league deliberately called itself "Communist" rather than "Socialist." Communism was a radical program, bent on changing property relations by violence; socialism was associated with more peaceful means of transformation. The pamphlet was too late and too obscure to influence the revolutions of 1848. However, it laid out Marx's basic ideas, calling on the proletariat to rise—"You have nothing to lose but your chains"—and create a society that would end the exploitation of man by man.

A number of political and polemical works flowed from Marx's pen, but most of them remained unpublished during his lifetime. The first volume of his major work, *Capital*, was published in 1867; subsequent volumes appeared posthumously. Marxism, the body of Marx's thought, is complex and sometimes contradictory. It is written in an obscure style, difficult to penetrate. But certain basic concepts resound throughout and were embraced by Marx's followers.

Marx agreed with Hegel and many of his contemporaries that human history has a goal. Hegel believed that the goal was the realization of the world spirit. Marx believed that it was the abolition of capitalism, the victory of the proletariat, the disappearance of the state, and the ultimate liberation of all humankind.

Whereas Hegel thought that ideas govern the world, Marx insisted that material conditions determine it. Hegel said that truth evolves by a "dialectic method": A person states a proposition and then states its opposite; from the clash of the two emerges a synthesis that leads to a higher truth. Marx called his philosophy "dialectic materialism." Copying Hegel, he posited a world of change but said that it was embedded in material conditions, not in a clash of ideas. Ideas, to Marx, were but a reflection of the material world.

Marx grouped human beings into classes based on their relationship to factories and machines—the means of production. Capitalists were one class, because they owned the means of production. Workers were a separate class—the proletariat—because they did not own any of the means of production and their income came only from their own hands. Because these two classes had different relationships to the means of production, they had different—in fact, antagonistic—interests and were destined (Marx believed) to engage in a class struggle.

Some of Marx's contemporaries lamented the increasing hostility between workers and capitalists. Marx, however, saw the conflict as necessary to advance human history, and he validated his thesis by the study of the past. In the Middle Ages, he pointed out, the feudal class dominated society but eventually lost the struggle to the commercial classes. Now, in turn, the capitalists were destined to be overwhelmed by the rising proletariat. As Marx and Engels proclaimed in the opening of the *Communist Manifesto*, "The history of all hitherto existing society is the history of class struggles."

In the study of history and economics, Marx found not only justification for but irrefutable

The Communist Manifesto

The **Communist Manifesto** *provides a preview of the major themes that would inform Marx and Engels's later writings: the concept of class formation and class antagonism, the privileged role of the proletariat, and the inevitability of the proletariat's success.*

The history of all hitherto existing society is the history of class struggles.

Freeman and slave, patrician and plebeian, lord and serf, guild-master and journeyman, in a word, oppressor and oppressed, stood in constant opposition to one another, carried on an uninterrupted, now hidden, now open fight, that each time ended, either in a revolutionary reconstitution of society at large, or in the common ruin of the contending classes. . . .

In ancient Rome we have patricians, knights, plebeians, slaves; in the Middle Ages, feudal lords, vassals, guild-masters, journeymen, apprentices, serfs; in almost all of these classes, again, subordinate gradations.

The modern bourgeois society that has sprouted from the ruins of feudal society, has not done away with class antagonisms. It has but established new classes, new conditions of oppression, new forms of struggle in place of the old ones. . . .

Society as a whole is more and more splitting up into two great hostile camps, into two great classes directly facing each other: Bourgeoisie and Proletariat. . . .

With the development of industry the proletariat not only increases in number; it becomes concentrated in greater masses, its strength grows and it feels that strength more.

The advance of industry, whose involuntary promoter is the bourgeoisie, replaces the isolation of the laborers, due to competition, by their revolutionary combination, due to association. The development of modern industry, therefore, cuts from under its feet the very foundation on which the bourgeoisie produces and appropriates products. What the bourgeoisie therefore produces, above all, are its own grave-diggers. Its fall and the victory of the proletariat are equally inevitable.

Source: Karl Marx and Friedrich Engels, *The Communist Manifesto* (1848; reprint, New York: International Publishers, 1948), pp. 9, 17, 21.

proof of the "scientific" basis of his ideas. Capitalism was creating the forces that would supplant it. The large industrial plants necessitated an ever-larger work force with an increasing sense of class interest. The increasingly competitive nature of capitalism would inevitably drive an increasing number of enterprises out of business, and there would emerge a form of monopoly capitalism, abusive of both consumers and workers. As a result of ever-more savage competition, more businesses would fail, and consequently more workers would become unemployed. Angered and frustrated by their lot, workers would overthrow the system that had abused them for so long: "The knell of private property has sounded. The expropriators will be expropriated." The proletariat would take power and to solidify its rule would temporarily exercise the "dictatorship of the proletariat." Once that had taken place, the state would wither away. With the coming to power of the proletariat, the history of class war would end. Ironically, Marx, who spent his life writing about the nature and history of social change, envisaged a time when change would cease, when history, as it were, would stop.

In looking at the structure of society in his day, Marx saw the proletariat as the most deprived class. In coming to power, it would overthrow the existing forms of oppression. Thus, the proletariat was the agent that would free humankind. Once that freedom had been accomplished, the ideal society would prevail.

Many protested the evils of industrialism but Marx was able to describe economic change in dramatic terms as a necessary stage for humankind to traverse on its way to liberation. The suffering of the workers was not in vain; rather, it was a necessary process, part of the drama that would finally lead to human emancipation. Unlike some of the utopians who deplored industrialism, Marx accepted it and saw it as part of the path that history was fated to take.

Although the utopians had spent an inordinate amount of time drawing up the minutiae of their ideal society, they had not clearly indicated the nature of the process that would bring it into being. Marx, in contrast, spent his lifetime drawing up what the process would be but said little about the nature of the new society.

Marx's study of economics and history proved to him that the coming of socialism was not only desirable—as the utopians had thought—but inevitable. The laws of history dictated that capitalism would collapse, having created within itself the means of its own destruction—namely, the rising proletariat. By proclaiming his brand of socialism as scientific, Marx gave it the aura it needed to become the faith for millions of people. For to declare ideas "scientific" in the nineteenth century, when science was held in such high esteem, was a promising way of gaining a popular following for them.

Summary

The industrial transformation altered the face of Europe. It changed the nature of work for large numbers of Europeans. Increasingly fewer people worked in agriculture, more in manufacturing. Machines replaced human energy in the workplace. Population patterns changed; cities grew dramatically, and for the first time European cities had over a million inhabitants.

The massing of workers in factories and urban areas called attention to their misery and also to their potential power. To wrest a better life for themselves, workers began to express their solidarity as workers. They organized into groups that were more broadly based and therefore more powerful than past workers' groups had been. As workers began to think of themselves as a group, the dominant groups within society began to perceive them as such.

Confronted by the realities of industrialization, many people changed their intellectual convictions. It was obvious that the laissez-faire system could not meet many workers' needs. Classical liberal economists revised their orthodoxy; the state became more interventionist, trying to remove some of the worst abuses.

Drawing on earlier strands of socialism, Karl Marx articulated this ideology in a new and compelling way. Marxism gave a powerful voice to the new proletarian class that industrialization had created, and it was to cast a shadow far into the next century.

Notes

1. Phyllis Deane, *The First Industrial Revolution* (Cambridge, England: Cambridge University Press, 1965), p. 1.
2. These ideas are provocatively developed by E. L. Jones, *The European Miracle: Environments, Economies and Geopolitics of Europe and Asia* (Cambridge, England: Cambridge University Press, 1981).
3. Adna Ferrin Weber, *The Growth of Cities in the Nineteenth Century: A Study in Statistics* (New York: Macmillan, 1899; Ithaca, N.Y.: Cornell University Press, 1963), p. 1.
4. W. Cooke Taylor, *Notes of a Tour in the Manufacturing Districts of Lancashire, in a Series of Letters to His Grace the Archbishop of Dublin* (London, 1842), pp. 4–6, quoted in E. P. Thompson, *The Making of the English Working Class* (New York: Vintage, 1963), p. 191.
5. Marie de Flavigny d'Agoult [Daniel Stern], *Histoire de la Révolution de 1848,* 2d ed., vol. 1 (Paris, 1862), p. 7, quoted in Theodore S. Hamerow, *The Birth of a New Europe: State and Society in the Nineteenth Century* (Chapel Hill: University of North Carolina Press, 1983), pp. 206–207.

Suggested Reading

General Surveys

Jones, E. L. *The European Miracle.* 1981. A broad comparative work considering the forces leading to the industrialization of the West.

Landes, David S. *Prometheus Unbound.* 1969. A standard work emphasizing technological and cultural factors as explanations for industry.

Mokyr, Joel. *The Lever of Riches: Technological Creativity and Economic Progress.* 1990. A work that provides a comparative study of Western and Chinese technology, emphasizing cultural elements as explanations for the industrialization of the West.

Industrialization of Britain

Brown, Richard. *Society and Economy in Modern Britain, 1700–1850.* 1991. A work pointing out that British development was gradual, varied regionally, and was unequally spread.

Mathias, Peter. *The First Industrial Nation: An Economic History of Britain, 1700–1914.* 1969. A consideration of the unique combination of factors that explain Britain's pioneering role as an industrializer.

The Spread of Industry to the Continent

Milward, A., and S. B. Saul. *The Development of the Economies of Continental Europe.* 1977. An examination of the relationship between the availability of capital, labor, and technology and the speed of industrial development.

Pollard, Sidney. *Peaceful Conquest.* 1981. A reminder that although industrialization started in England, it occurred not throughout the whole country but only in specific regions; likewise when industry spread to the Continent, it spread only to specific regions.

Pounds, Norman J. G. *An Historical Geography of Europe, 1800–1914.* 1985. A consideration of the impact of geographic factors in shaping industry and how industry changed the physical face of Europe.

Sylla, Richard, and Gianni Toniolo, eds. *Patterns of European Industrialization.* 1991. A volume describing the patterns of industrialization in a comparative perspective.

The Industrial Transformation of Society

Alter, George. *Family and the Female Life Course: The Women of Verviers, Belgium, 1849–80.* 1988. A reminder that women were usually not continuously in the industrial work force but entered and exited according to family needs.

Anderson, Michael S. *Family Structure in Nineteenth Century Lancashire.* 1971. A study of the industrial town of Preston, revealing a family system far more resilient than the system usually described by contemporaries.

Brimblecombe, Peter. *The Big Smoke: A History of Air Pollution in London Since Medieval Times.* 1987. An account of the causes of pollution and the attempts to control it.

Hohenberg, Paul M., and Lynn Hollen Lees. *The Making of Urban Europe, 1000–1950.* 1985. A good general introduction to the impact of industry on urbanization, emphasizing less the pathology of cities and more their resilience.

Hopkins, Eric. *Birmingham: The First Manufacturing Town in the World, 1760–1840.* 1989. An account that emphasizes the extent to which the city and its industry depended on manufacture by hand rather than by machine.

Lawton, Richard, and Robert Lee. *Urban Population Development in Western Europe from the Late Eighteenth to the Early Twentieth Century.* 1989. A country-by-country study of urban growth.

Nardinelli, Clark. *Child Labor and the Industrial Revolution.* 1990. A work that describes child labor as being not as harsh as some contemporaries claimed and rather a rational adjustment to existing economic conditions.

Ponting, Clive. *A Green History of the World.* 1991. A work that includes some remarks on the impact of early industry on the European environment.

Tilly, Louise, and Joan Scott. *Women, Work and Family.* 1978. A description of the family wage economy in which all members contributed to the economy of the family, especially in the early stages of industrialization.

Turner, B. L., et al. *The Earth as Transformed by Human Action: Global and Regional Changes in the Biosphere over the Past 300 Years.* 1990. A work that includes some information on the nineteenth-century impact of industry on the environment.

Responses to Industrialization

Furet, François. *Marx and the French Revolution.* 1988. A consideration of the impact of the French Revolution on Marx.

Himmelfarb, Gertrude. *The Idea of Poverty: England in the Early Industrial Age.* 1983. A work that describes the image of the poor among Victorian middle-class observers.

Kolakowski, Leszek. *Main Currents of Marxism.* Vol. 1, *The Founders.* 1978. A work that traces the intellectual background of Marx's thought and the nature of the original synthesis he created.

Mazlish, Bruce. *The Meaning of Karl Marx.* 1984. An easy-to-read introduction to the man and his thought, emphasizing the shaping of both by the era in which Marx lived.

Moss, Bernard H. *The Origins of the French Labor Movement, 1830–1914: The Socialism of Skilled Workers.* 1976. A work that traces the origins of labor militancy among artisans.

Sewell, William H., Jr. *Work and Revolution in France: The Language of Labor from the Old Regime to 1848.* 1980. An account that stresses continuity in the development of the French working class from the time of the Old Regime to the mid-nineteenth century.

Thompson, E. P. *The Making of the English Working Class.* 1963. A work that emphasizes cultural factors that encouraged the development of working-class consciousness in England.

Weighing the Evidence

WORKERS' WAGES

In 1869 the Chamber of Commerce of Verviers, a town in eastern Belgium, published a report on workers' wages. In the seventeenth century, Verviers, located on the Vesdre River, had become a major producer of woolens. The river provided water for power, for washing the cloth, and for carrying away industrial waste. Thus, the site was ideal for finishing textiles, and the merchants of Verviers drew upon the labor of spinners and weavers in the surrounding farm areas. With a population of 4,500 in the mid-seventeenth century, Verviers had 10,000 inhabitants by the end of the eighteenth.

Two local entrepreneurs brought the Englishman John Cockerill to town. In 1802 he set up the first spinning machine on the Continent and in 1816 the first steam engine in Belgium. Thirty years later, Verviers boasted forty factories and the population had increased to 23,000.

Industrialization transformed the people's lives in many ways. The table of wages reveals the existence of a variegated, hierarchical work force with clear, separate functions and specified salaries. It indicates the uneven ways in which people benefited from industry, depending on their skills, age, and gender.

For example, this list allows us to compare the wages of industrial workers and artisans. Industry made it difficult for the artisans to survive; unable to compete with machine manufacture, many had to give up their trade or tighten their belts to make ends meet. The new machine age, however, created an increased demand for the services of some artisans. Early in the nineteenth century the new machines eliminated hand spinning, for example, but inexpensive yarn at first increased the demand for handloom weavers. Notice that handloom weavers ("hand weavers" in the table) were relatively well paid in 1836. This is due to the uneven introduction of mechanical production. Weaving of high quality woolens proved to be more difficult to mechanize than cotton goods. Power looms did not become common in Verviers until the 1860s, and we see the relative wages of handloom weavers decline in 1869. Joiners and ironsmiths not only did the work they had traditionally done but found new opportunities building and repairing machines. The ironsmiths, joiners, and carpenters of Verviers were all paid better than other workers.

We may note several things about the impact of industry on the labor force. Notice the specialized descriptions of occupations in the textile industry. Among the factory workers we find some significant wage discrepancies. Compare, for example, the wages of the nonspecialized laborer to the wages of the other industrial workers.

Changes in technology, productivity, labor supply, and market demand for certain goods changed the relative wages of workers. Thus the relative wages of jobs changed between 1836 and 1869. Notice that a wool washer in 1869 was making 174 percent more than a wool washer made in 1836, but in the same period the wages paid to a warper had increased by 300 percent.

Let us next consider women in the labor force. Notice that the list is divided into "male occupations," "female occupations," and finally "children's occupation." Work is divided according to gender and age. Look at the list of women's industrial occupations. The absence of spinning female occupations in this list is significant. Spinning had been a female occupation since antiquity, but the spinning machines in Verviers were tended by men. Notice how little differentiation is evident; far fewer industrial occupations are listed for women than for men. Also look at the wages. Women's wages were all equally depressed, with the one exception of menders' wages, hovering in 1836 around .7 francs but climbing by 1869 to 2.25 francs, an increase of over 300 percent. Among men's occupations the spread of salaries was far greater. In 1869 the highest-paid women (menders) received 40 percent more than the lowest-paid women in 1836 (scourers), but the highest-paid men (ironsmiths) received 138 percent more than the lowest-paid men (wool washers) in 1836. By 1869 the wage

Wage Differentials in Verviers, Belgium, 1836–1869

		Wages (francs per day)				
		1836	1846	1856	1863	1869
Male Occupations	Ironsmith*	1.73	2.25	2.50	3.00	3.87
	Carpenter*	1.90	2.25	2.65	2.87	3.50
	Dyer	1.40	1.46	1.60	2.60	3.37
	Spinner	1.80	1.90	2.90	3.12	3.40
	Carder	1.47	1.75	2.30	3.25	3.30
	Tanner*	1.83	2.00	2.25	3.00	3.25
	Warper	0.80	0.95	1.57	1.65	3.25
	Hand weaver*	1.97	1.70	2.85	3.00	3.00
	Joiner*	1.98	2.00	2.25	2.75	3.00
	Tenterer	—	1.25	1.40	2.34	3.00
	Presser	1.47	1.78	1.78	2.15	3.00
	Machine weaver	—	—	—	—	2.75
	Comber	0.84	1.27	1.50	1.75	2.65
	Fuller	1.40	1.50	1.75	2.30	2.67
	Laborer	—	1.25	1.50	1.87	2.50
	Wool washer	1.15	1.25	1.40	1.75	2.25
Female Occupations	Mender	0.73	0.80	1.10	1.40	2.25
	Wool sorter	0.98	1.08	1.70	1.85	2.00
	Gigger	0.75	0.80	0.80	1.25	2.00
	Burler	0.77	1.00	1.20	1.70	1.80
	Seamstress*	0.73	0.80	1.10	1.40	—
	Scourer	0.70	0.75	0.85	1.35	1.62
Children's Occupation	Piecener	—	0.70	0.90	1.10	1.60

*Artisans. (Those not starred were industrial workers.)

Source: Chamber of Commerce of Verviers, *Rapport général sur la situation du commerce et de l'industrie en 1868* (Verviers, 1869), p. 69; repr. in George Alter, *Family and the Female Life Course—The Women of Verviers, Belgium, 1849–1880* (Madison: University of Wisconsin Press, 1988), p. 103. Used by permission.

gap had somewhat diminished for both men and women, but it was still far larger for men (72 percent) than for women (28 percent).

Some male artisans consistently received wages higher than the wages of many machine operators—consider the wages of carpenters, for example. But notice the one female artisan occupation: seamstress. Although a seamstress was probably quite skilled, she was paid no more than the women in the factories. Special crafts, still prized for some men, were not given much monetary value when practiced by women.

Note the wage differences overall between male and female workers. In 1836 the average female worker received wages equivalent to 53.2 percent of the average male worker's wages. By 1869, there was some improvement: the difference had declined by 11 percentage points; still, women earned 64 percent of men's pay.

The table lists only one occupation for children: piecener. Small and nimble, children were paid to fix broken threads. They worked in many other capacities as well. Some were paid wages by their employers; others helped their parents in a factory or workshop. The wages of some adults probably included compensation for their children's labor.

We can learn much from a statistical table such as this about the impact of industrialization on the labor force. Some workers benefited, and others were harmed by the adoption of industry; over time workers experienced changes in their circumstances. If statistical tables are informative on such issues, they also have their limits. They do not tell us how workers interpreted and understood their experience. As workers suffered daily hardships, they had to try to make sense of their changing world.

CHAPTER 24

New Configurations of Power, 1850–1880

In the generation after 1848, several new nation-states emerged, changing the map of Europe, while other states developed new political institutions. To meet the demand for popular participation in government that had been so dramatically expressed in 1848, every European state, except for the Ottoman and Russian empires, found it necessary to have a parliament. Rare before midcentury, such institutions became common thereafter. No longer was the demand for popular participation seen as a threat to the existing political and social order. In fact, popular participation, or the appearance of such participation, gave the existing order a legitimacy it had not enjoyed since the French Revolution.

These political transformations occurred in an era of unprecedented economic growth and prosperity, which started with the discovery of gold in California in 1848. The increased supply of gold allowed for the expansion of credit, which led to the founding of new banks and mass investments in growing industries. The iron output of Britain, France, and Germany tripled in the years between 1850 and 1870. During this same period the standard of living of every class rose significantly in industrializing nations. Unlike the hungry and turbulent 1840s, the more prosperous decades inaugurated an "age of optimism" in which the elites tried to re-establish their power in new ways.

Also during this period, nationalism emerged for the first time as a decisive force in European affairs. In the first half of the century, international relations had been dominated by the congress system, in which representatives of the major European states met periodically to preserve the balance

Entry into Paris of Queen Victoria and Prince Albert during state visit of August 18, 1855. Accompanied by Napoleon III and the Empress Eugénie.

of power. This order disappeared in the second half of the century, to be replaced by outbreaks of violence as political leaders pursued the narrow interests of their state. Instead of negotiation, brute military force, or the threat of its use, was employed to resolve international conflict. The new age was dominated not by ideals but force, announced the Prussian chancellor Otto von Bismarck, the main practitioner of what became known as *Realpolitik*—a policy in which war became a regular instrument of statecraft.

The Changing Scope of International Relations

The Crimean War and its aftermath shaped European international relations for several decades. A new level of mutual suspicion arose, leading nations to pursue narrow self-interest while ignoring the concerns of the other major actors in the international system.

Crimean War This photograph shows the interior of the Sevastapol fortress after it had been battered into surrender. The Crimean War was the first conflict to be documented by photographers. *(Courtesy of the Board of Trustees of the Victoria & Albert Museum)*

The Crimean War as a Turning Point

The Crimean War had many causes. Principally, however, it was ignited by the decision of French and British statesmen to contain Russian power in the Balkans and keep it from encroaching on the weakening Ottoman Empire. Russian pretensions to have the right to intervene on behalf of the Christians in the Ottoman Empire had led to war between the two states in October 1853. The defeat of the Ottoman navy at Sinope in November left the Ottoman Empire defenseless, bringing British and French intervention.

British and French statesmen had considerable interest in the conflict. Since early in the century, Britain had feared that the collapse of the Ottoman Empire would lead Russia to seek territorial gains in the Mediterranean. Such a move would challenge Britain's supremacy. The British government was also propelled to take an aggressive stance by an explosion of public sentiment against Russia. Meanwhile, the French emperor, Napoleon III, viewed defeat of Russia as a way to eclipse one of the states most dedicated to preserving the existing European borders. He wanted to undermine existing power relations, hoping that a new order would somehow lead to increased French power and influence. Napoleon also imagined that fighting side by side with Britain could lay the foundation for Anglo-French friendship. So England and France rushed to defend the Ottoman Empire and declared war on Russia in March 1854.

The war was poorly fought on all sides. Leadership was woefully inadequate, and there were five times more casualties from disease than from enemy fire. The Russians had a standing army of a million but never managed to use more than a fraction of that number due largely to poor communications and supply systems. In Britain, failures in military supplies and leadership were denounced in the press and in Parliament. For the first time the press played an active role in reporting war, and photography brought to readers at home the gruesome realities of battle.

One of the few heroic figures to emerge from this conflict was Florence Nightingale (1820–

Florence Nightingale in the Crimean War

Florence Nightingale used her influential family connections to win an appointment to the Crimean battlefield. Once there, she organized nursing for the wounded and was able to secure additional personnel and medical supplies for her hospital. In this letter, Nightingale describes the plight of the wounded in an army lacking sufficient supplies.

We have no room for corpses in the wards. The Surgeons pass on to the next, an excision of the shoulder-joint—beautifully performed and going on well—ball lodged just in the head of the joint, and fracture starred all round. The next poor fellow has two stumps for arms—and the next has lost an arm and leg. As for the balls, they go in where they like, and do as much harm as they can in passing. That is the only rule they have. The next case has one eye put out, and paralysis of the iris of the other. He can neither see nor understand. But all who can walk come into us for Tobacco, but I tell them that we have not a bit to put into our own mouths. Not a sponge, nor a rag of linen, not anything have I left. Everything is gone to make slings and stump pillows and shirts. These poor fellows have not had a clean shirt nor been washed for two months before they came here, and the state in which they arrive from the transport is literally *crawling*. I hope in a few days we shall establish a little cleanliness. But we have not a basin nor a towel nor a bit of soap nor a broom—I have ordered 300 scrubbing brushes. But one half the Barrack is so sadly out of repair that it is impossible to use a drop of water on the stone floors, which are all laid upon rotten wood, and would give our men fever in no time. . . .

I am getting a screen now for the Amputations, for when one poor fellow, who is to be amputated tomorrow, sees his comrade today die under the knife it makes impression—and diminishes his chance. But, anyway, among these exhausted frames the mortality of the operations is frightful.

Source: Letter to Dr. William Bowman, November 14, 1854, in Sue M. Goldie, ed., *"I Have Done My Duty": Florence Nightingale in the Crimean War, 1854–56* (Iowa City: University of Iowa Press, 1987), pp. 37–38.

1910), who organized a nursing service to care for the British sick and wounded. Later, her wartime experience allowed her to pioneer nursing as a professional calling (see the box, "Florence Nightingale in the Crimean War").

The war ended in December 1855 when Russia surrendered the fortified port of Sevastopol after a long, bitter siege. The Russians were reluctant to admit defeat, but the threat of Austro-Prussian entry into the war on the side of the Western allies convinced them to sue for peace.

The Crimean War killed three-quarters of a million people—more than any European war between the end of the Napoleonic wars and World War I. The slowness with which each side mobilized, the lack of planning and foresight in staging battles, the large number of fatalities from causes other than enemy fire—all were reminiscent of hostilities from earlier eras. It was a particularly futile, senseless war whose most important consequence was political, for it unleashed dramatic new changes on the European continent.

The Congress of Paris and Its Aftermath

The former combatants met in Paris in February 1856 to work out a peace treaty; their decisions shaped relations among European states for the next half-century. Unfortunately, the settlement pleased no one. The peace treaty forbade Russia from having a fleet in the Black Sea and forced it to withdraw from Moldavia and Wallachia, where it had enjoyed the right of intervention since the 1830s. Russian statesmen, especially discontented, were bent on revising the map of Europe. The tsar had expected Austrian assistance in the war in return for his help in crushing the Hungarian rebellion in 1849. Instead, Austria's leaders had not only withheld aid but even threatened to join the Western alliance, and Russian officials denounced Austrian "betrayal." Nor did French leaders feel their nation had benefited. Although holding the congress in Paris flattered the emperor's pride, no other clear advantages emerged for France. The north Italian state of Piedmont, which had joined the allies, gained from the congress only a vague statement on the unsatisfactory nature of the existing situation in Italy. Prussia was invited to attend the congress only as an afterthought and hence also felt slighted.

Although the war seemed to have sustained the integrity of the Ottoman Empire, the peace settlement undermined it indirectly by dictating reforms in the treatment of its Christian populations. These reforms weakened the empire's ability to repress growing national movements and opened the door to the eventual independence of the Balkan states. British political leaders, disappointed by the heavy sacrifices of the war, moved toward isolationism in foreign policy. Austrian policymakers, who had hoped to gain the aid of Britain and France in preserving the Habsburg empire, found them instead to be hostile, thereby encouraging the forces undermining it. At the time the peace treaty was signed, not many people foresaw the tragic results that would flow from it.

In the past the congress system had tried to ensure that no major power was dissatisfied enough to subvert the existing distribution of power, but the Crimean War and the peace treaty markedly changed that situation. For example, in the first half of the century the international order had been upheld in part by the cooperation of the rulers of the conservative eastern powers: Russia, Austria, and Prussia. Now these powers were rivals, and their competition contributed to growing instability in the international system. By and large, the decisions reached in Paris were either disregarded or unilaterally revised. Furthermore, this new international climate allowed the emergence of new states without international sanction.

Italian Unification

In the words of Prince von Metternich of Austria, Italy was nothing but a "geographic expression." The revolution of 1848 had revealed an interest in national unification, but the attempt had failed. Few predicted that within a dozen years what many believed to be impossible would succeed. Idealists like Giuseppe Mazzini (1805–1872) had preached that Italy would be unified by its people, who would rise and establish a free republic. Instead, it was unified by royalty, by war, and by the help of a foreign state. Although ideals were not absent from the process of unification, cynical manipulation and scheming also came into play.

After the failed 1848 revolution, various Italian rulers resorted to repression. In Modena, the Habsburg duke, Francis V (r. 1846–1859), jailed liberals, closed the universities, and personally caned passersby who did not tip their hat to him. In the Papal States, men were imprisoned for "appearing inclined to novelty." Pope Pius IX, who initially had appeared sympathetic to Italian unification, opposed it as soon as he realized it was attainable only by war against Catholic Austria. Italian nationalists viewed him as a traitor as he became a firm opponent of both liberalism and nationalism. In Naples, the government was so weak it established its authority by working with organized crime. In Parma, the duke was assassinated in 1854—to the relief of his people—and the attempted uprising that accompanied this desperate act was suppressed by three thousand Austrian troops sent in by the duke's ally, the Habsburgs.

Compared to this dismal record, the kingdom of Piedmont in northern Italy appeared stable and successful. It was the only Italian state that kept the liberal constitution it had adopted during the 1848 revolution, and it welcomed political refugees from other Italian states. Economically, it was a beacon to the rest of Italy, establishing modern banks and laying half the rail lines in the peninsula.

Since the late eighteenth century, some Italians had called for a *risorgimento,* a political and cultural resurrection of Italy. By the mid-nineteenth century the idea was actively supported by a small, elite group of the educated middle class, urban property owners, and members of the professional classes, who were open to nationalist arguments. For merchants, industrialists, and professionals, a unified state would provide a larger stage on which to pursue their ambitions. Individuals from these groups established the National Society, a grassroots unification movement. This organization increasingly looked to Piedmont to lead the peninsula toward national unity.

Cavour Plots Unification

The statesman who was to catapult Piedmont into a position of leadership in the dramatic events leading to Italian unification was Count Camillo di Cavour (1810–1861). The son of a Piedmontese nobleman and high government official, he grew up speaking French, the language of the court and of formal education in Piedmont, and mastered Italian only as an adult. Well-traveled, Cavour knew more about Britain and France than about Italy. He was sympathetic to the aspirations of the middle class and saw in Britain and France models of what Italy ought to become, a liberal and economically advanced society.

Short, fat, and myopic, Cavour hardly cut a heroic figure. Yet he was ambitious, hardworking, and driven to succeed. In 1850 he joined the government of Piedmont. Two years later he was appointed prime minister. He shared the general enthusiasm of the middle classes for an Italian nation, but his vision probably did not include the entire Italian peninsula, only the north and the center, which then could dominate the rest of the peninsula in a loose federation. One fateful lesson he had learned from the failures of 1848 was that foreign help, especially French assistance, would be necessary to expel the Austrians from the peninsula.

When the Crimean War broke out in 1854, Cavour steered Piedmont to the allied side, hoping to advance his cause. He sent twenty thousand troops to the Crimea, one-tenth of whom died. This act gained him a seat at the Congress of Paris, where his presence boosted the kingdom's prestige—and where he and Napoleon III had an opportunity to meet and size up each other.

Napoleon III favored the cause of Italian liberation from Austrian rule and some form of unification of the peninsula. Austria had been France's traditional opponent; destroying Austria's power in Italy would presumably promote

Camillo di Cavour, Unifier of Italy A wily politician, Cavour had a rapid rise to power, becoming prime minister of Piedmont in 1852 at the age of 42. By diplomacy and warfare Cavour was able to unify Italy under the ruling dynasty of Piedmont, the House of Savoy. *(Scala/Art Resource, NY)*

France's. Thus the French emperor and the Piedmontese prime minister, both desirous of changing the map of Europe, each for his own reasons, secretly met in July 1858 at Plombières, a French spa, to discuss how Italian unity might be achieved. They agreed that Piedmont would stir up trouble in one of Austria's Italian territories in an effort to goad the Austrians into war. France would help the Piedmontese expel Austria from its Italian possessions, and the new Piedmont, doubled in size, would become part of a confederation under the papacy. In exchange, the French emperor demanded the cession of Nice and Savoy (see the box, "Cavour and Napoleon III Plot War").

This demand presented difficulties: Savoy was the heartland of the Piedmont kingdom, the area from which the royal house came; and the city of Nice was clearly Italian in nationality. France's other demand was that the king of Piedmont, who represented the House of Savoy, the

Cavour and Napoleon III Plot War

In July 1858 Cavour and Napoleon III met at Plombières to plot war against Austria with the intention of evicting it from Italy. Italy's borders were to be reorganized, giving Piedmont additional territory, and France was to receive compensation for its assistance. On July 24, Cavour outlined the contents of the agreement in a letter to the king of Piedmont, a cynical display of realpolitik.

. . . [T]ogether we began to go through the Italian States, in search of those grounds for war which were so difficult to find. After we had traveled the whole length of the peninsula without success, we came almost unawares upon Massa and Carrara, and there discovered what we had been trying so hard to find. When I had given the Emperor an exact description of that unfortunate country, of which he already had a pretty clear idea anyway, we agreed on getting in a petition from the inhabitants to Your Majesty asking for his protection and even requesting the annexation of these Duchies to Sardinia. Your Majesty would not accept the proposed surrender, but would support the cause of these oppressed populations by addressing a haughty and menacing note to the Duke of Modena. The Duke, confident of Austrian support, would reply in an impertinent manner. Thereupon, Your Majesty would occupy Massa, and the war would begin. . . .

What would be the aim of the war?

The Emperor freely agreed that the Austrians must be driven out of Italy altogether, leaving them not an inch of land this side of the Alps and the Isonzo. . . .

After we had settled the future fate of Italy, the Emperor asked me what France would get, and if Your Majesty would cede Savoy and the County of Nice.

Source: Cavour to Victor Emmanuel, July 24, 1858, in David Thomson, ed., *France: Empire and Republic, 1850–1940* (New York: Harper, 1968), pp. 322–324.

oldest reigning house in Europe, allow his 15-year-old daughter to marry the emperor's 38-year-old dissipated cousin. To accept these terms seemed a betrayal of national honor and conventional morality. But such scruples gave way to political ambition, and Cavour assented.

War between Austria and Piedmont began in April 1859. By June the combined Piedmontese and French forces had routed the Austrians at Magenta and Solferino. Instead of pressing on, Napoleon III decided to end the fighting. Several developments motivated his decision. First, he was truly shocked by the bloodshed he witnessed on the battlefield, and he was alarmed by the Prussian mobilization on the Rhine on behalf of Austria. Second, his plans for Italy were threatening to develop in unforeseen directions. To the south of Piedmont, popular revolts in August and September had broken out against the local rulers. Both revolutionaries and the local elites, fearing victory by the other side, appealed for annexation to Piedmont, creating a larger and more independent state than Napoleon had anticipated. These factors led Napoleon to sign an armistice with the Austrians, allowing Austria to keep part of Lombardy and all of Venetia and to participate in an Italian Confederation. Cavour was outraged by Napoleon's betrayal of their agreement and resigned as prime minister; he returned to office, however, in January 1860.

Unification Achieved

The overthrow of the Austrian-backed rulers in Parma, Modena, and Tuscany led these areas in 1859 to vote in plebiscites to join Piedmont. Farther south, in central Italy, agitation against the misrule of the papacy also inclined those regions toward the more enlightened Piedmont.

Cavour had envisioned no more than a united northern Italy. However, unanticipated events in the south dramatically changed that vision. The centuries-old misgovernment of Naples led to an uprising, further abetted and encouraged by the revolutionary firebrand Giuseppe Garibaldi (1807–1882), a rival of Cavour who had developed a large popular following and who also favored unification. In May 1860, with but a thousand poorly armed, red-shirted followers, he set sail for Sicily to help the island rise up against its Bourbon ruler. Winning that struggle, Garibaldi's forces crossed to the mainland. Victory followed victory, and enthusiasm for Garibaldi grew. His army swelled to 57,000 men, and he won the entire kingdom of Naples.

Threatened by the advance of Garibaldi's power and fearing that Garibaldi's influence would reach into the Papal States, Cavour sent his army into the area in September 1860. This action, a brutal attack on a weak state that had not harmed Piedmont, was viewed by many Catholics as aggression against the spiritual head of their church. However, as Cavour explained to his parliament, political necessity required it. The interests of the state of Piedmont and the about to-be-born Italy superseded traditional morality.

Although Garibaldi was a republican, he was convinced that Italy could best achieve unity under the king of Piedmont, and he willingly submitted the southern part of Italy, which he controlled, to the king, Victor Emmanuel II (r. 1849–1878). Thus by November 1860, Italy lay united under Piedmontese rule. The territories that came under Piedmontese control affirmed their desire to be part of the new Italy by plebiscites based on universal male suffrage. By huge majorities, the populations voted affirmatively. Undoubtedly there was a lot of pressure from the occupying army and from the upper classes, who marched the people dependent on them—workers, employees, tenant farmers—to the polls. Voting was not secret, and fraud was widespread. But in an age increasingly drawn to democracy, the plebiscite provided legitimacy to the new state and won sympathy from liberally inclined states abroad.

Still to be joined to the new state were Austrian-held Venetia in the northeast and Rome and its environs, held by the pope with the support of a French garrison. But within a decade, a propitious international situation enabled the fledgling

Gamba: The Plebiscite of the Annexation of the Campagna Romana This 1861 painting by Enrico Gamba (1831–1883) celebrated the annexation of central Italy. People of all walks of life are seen marching enthusiastically in front of and behind the flag of the kingdom of Piedmont, under whose domain Italy was united. *(Comune di Genova, Servizio Beni Culturali)*

country to acquire both key areas. Austria was defeated in the Austro-Prussian War in 1866, and Venetia was ceded to Italy. Then the Franco-Prussian War forced the French to evacuate Rome, which they had occupied since 1849. Rome was joined to Italy and became its capital in 1870. With that event, unification was complete (Map 24.1).

The Problems of Unified Italy

National unity had been achieved, but it was frail. The nation was divided between the modernizing north and the traditional south. The uprisings in the south that had led to their inclusion in a united Italy were motivated more by hatred of the Bourbons than by fervor for national union. And once the union occurred, the north behaved like a conquering state—sending its officials to the south, raising taxes, and imposing its laws. Southerners resented the central control and the north's lack of empathy for their needs. In 1861 an uprising of disbanded Neapolitan soldiers and brigands broke out. To crush the revolt, half the Italian army was sent south; the civil war lasted five years and produced more casualties than the entire effort of the *risorgimento.*

Other major divisions remained. In 1861 only 2.5 percent of the population spoke the national language, Florentine Italian. The economy also remained divided. The north was far more industrialized than the rural south. In the south, child mortality was higher, life expectancy was lower, and illiteracy reached the 90 percent mark. The two regions seemed to belong to two different nations.

Piedmont dominated Italy; the new country even adopted its constitution. This constitution limited suffrage to men of property and education, less than 2 percent of the population. Further, although parliamentarism was enshrined in the constitution, Cavour's maneuvering as prime minister had kept governments from being answerable to the parliament. Shifting majorities meant that the government could cajole and bribe the opposition, transforming previous foes into supporters. This system of manipulation, known as *trasformismo,* characterized Italian government for many years. However, although Italian parliamentarism was far from complete, a liberal state recognizing legal equality and freedom of association had been established, providing more freedom for its citizens than the peninsula had seen for centuries.

German Unification

Like Italy, Germany began as a collection of polities, originally loosely united in the Holy Roman Empire and then, after 1815, equally loosely organized in the German Confederation. As did Piedmont in Italy, Prussia, the most powerful of the German states, led the unification movement. And just as Italy had in Cavour a strong-willed leader who imposed his will on events, so did German unification have a ruthless and cunning leader: Otto von Bismarck, prime minister of Prussia.

In 1848 German unification under Prussian leadership had appeared likely, but the process aborted when the king of Prussia refused to accept a throne offered by an elected assembly. When national unity was ultimately achieved, it was not as a result of popular decision but by the use of military force and the imposition of Prussian absolutism over the whole country.

The Rise of Bismarck

Metternich had always treated Prussia as a privileged junior partner. After his fall in 1848, however, rivalry erupted between the two German states, each trying to use for its own aggrandizement the desire for national unity that had become manifest during the revolution of 1848.

In March 1850, Prussia invited various German rulers to a meeting in Erfurt to consider possible unification under its sponsorship. Austria, which had been excluded, insisted that the "Erfurt Union" be dissolved and that Prussia remain in the German Confederation. Austrian leaders backed their demands with the threat of war; at a meeting in Olmütz in November, Prussia had to scuttle the Erfurt Union and accept Austrian leadership in Germany. The Prussians dubbed this event the "humiliation of Olmütz," and many were determined to redress their disadvantageous situation in Germany. At that time, however, the Prussian military was not strong enough to challenge Austria. But this situation changed under the new Prussian king, William I

Map 24.1 The Unification of Italy, 1859–1870 Piedmontese leadership and nationalist fervor united Italy.

(r. 1861–1888), who was committed to expanding the size and effectiveness of the army. He wanted to reduce the reserve army, increase the professional army, and expand the training period from two to three years. These measures needed parliamentary approval, but the parliament, which was dominated by the liberals, opposed the increased costs.

When the parliament refused to accept the king's proposals, he dissolved it. It was immedi-

GERMAN UNIFICATION

1862	Bismarck appointed prime minister of Prussia
January 1864	Austria and Prussia attack Denmark and occupy Schleswig and Holstein
June 1866	Austro-Prussian War
July 3, 1866	Prussia wins Battle of Sadowa
1867	The North German Confederation
March–July 1870	Crisis over Hohenzollern candidacy for Spanish throne
July 13, 1870	Interview at Ems and publication of Ems dispatch
July 19, 1870	France declares war on Prussia
September 1, 1870	Prussia victorious at Battle of Sedan
January 18, 1871	The German Empire declared in the Hall of Mirrors in Versailles.

ately re-elected, with an even stronger liberal majority. The issues were not purely technical or military, but rather who should govern the country—the king or the elected representatives. To get his way, the king appointed Otto von Bismarck as prime minister to implement his program of reforms.

The new head of government was a Junker, a Prussian aristocrat known for his reactionary attitudes, who had opposed the liberal movement in 1848. Then, as Prussian emissary to the German Confederation, he had challenged Austrian primacy. Bismarck smarted at the humiliation of Olmütz and sought to heighten Prussian power in Germany. Devoted to his monarch, he was also determined to expand Prussian power and influence in Germany and Europe. He faced down the parliament, telling the Budget Commission in September 1862, "The position of Prussia in Germany will be decided not by its liberalism but by its power . . . not through speeches and majority decisions are the great questions of the day decided—that was the mistake of 1848–49—but by 'iron and blood.'"[1]

Bismarck tried to win over the liberals by suggesting that with military force at its disposal, Prussia could lead German unification. But the liberals resisted, and the Parliament voted against the military reforms. Ignoring the elected assembly, Bismarck decided to carry out the military measures anyway and to collect the taxes that would make them possible. The citizens acquiesced and organized no resistance.

Several factors explain why Bismarck prevailed. The liberals who opposed him represented the business and professional classes who had received the vote as a result of the 1848 revolution. They had not implemented effective political or social programs, and they did not enjoy mass support. Had they wished to mobilize large segments of the population on behalf of their principles, they could not have done so.

Neither the Prussian king nor Bismarck's fellow aristocrats were nationalists. They believed in a strong Prussia, but they feared that a united Germany would dilute Prussian power and influence. German unification had been part of the liberals' program, not the conservatives'.

German liberals were faced with a dilemma: Did they value nationhood or the principles of liberty more? Fellow liberals elsewhere lived in existing nation-states, where statehood had preceded the development of liberalism. Even in Italy, the liberals had been faced by a less harsh dilemma, for unification was led by the liberal state of Piedmont. That was not the case in Germany, where the natural leader, Prussia, had a long tradition of militarism and authoritarianism. To be effective in opposition to Bismarck, German liberals would have had to join with the working classes, but they feared them and held themselves aloof from such an alliance.

Prussian Wars and German Unity

Having established the supremacy of royal power in Prussia, Bismarck was ready to enlarge Prussia's role in Germany at the expense of Austria. The provocation was a crisis over Schleswig-

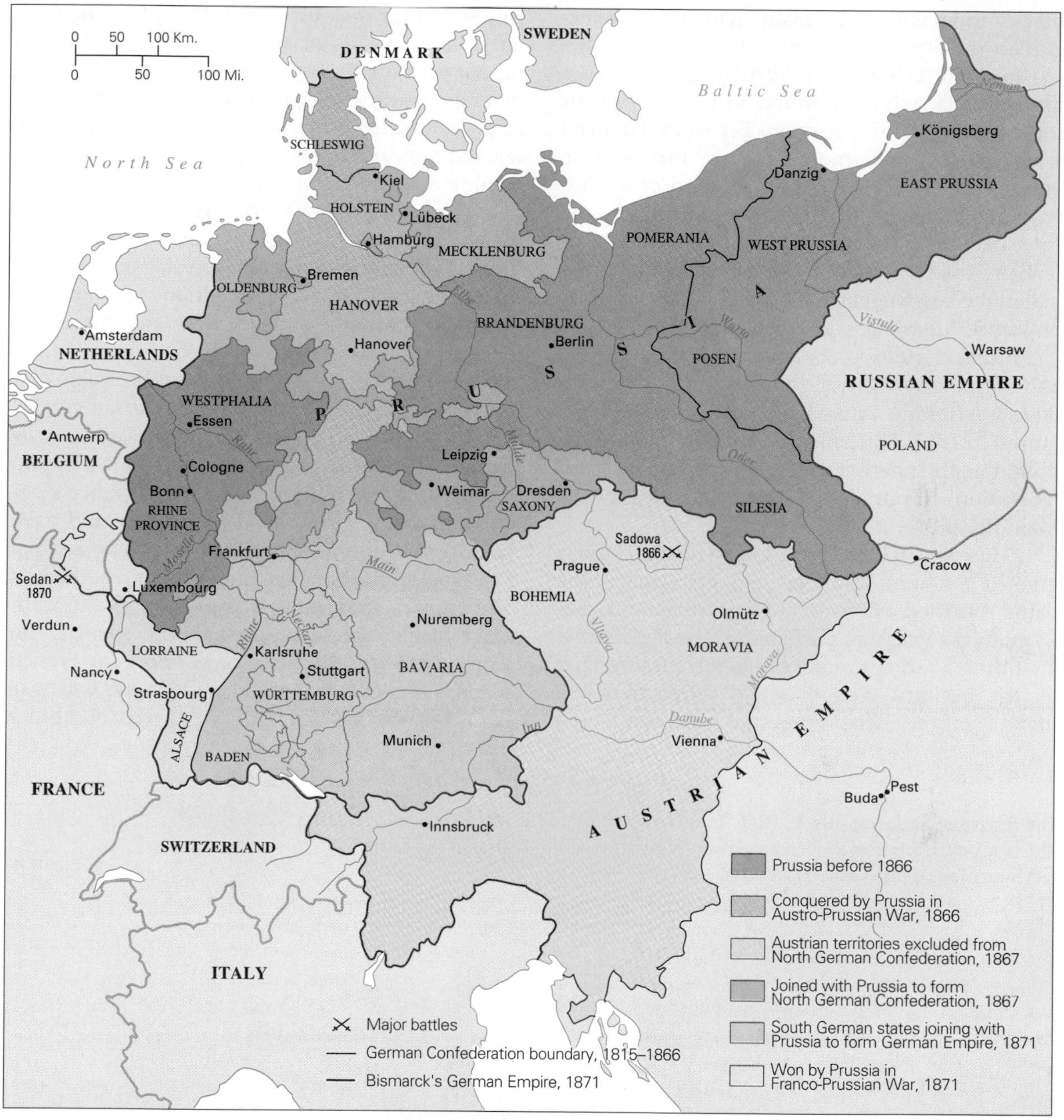

Map 24.2 The Unification of Germany A series of military victories made it possible for Prussia to unite Germany under its domain.

Holstein (Map 24.2). These two provinces, ethnically and linguistically German (except for northern Schleswig), were ruled by the Danish king. The Danes, demonstrating the same nationalism other European states were experiencing, moved to establish central control over these duchies in violation of earlier treaty commitments. Especially offensive to Germans was the decision to install Danish schools and institutions in Holstein, a solidly German-speaking duchy. The Austrians and Prussians, on behalf of the German Confederation, went to war against Denmark and won a quick, cheap victory. Prussia occupied Schleswig, and Austria took Holstein.

Joint military action in no way united Prussia and Austria, who continued to be bitter rivals for domination of Germany. Bismarck believed war was the only means to win this contest, and conflicts over the administration of Schleswig and Holstein provided the opportunity. In June 1866, with no declaration of war, Prussia attacked Austrian-administered Holstein and defeated the Austrian army at Sadowa (Königgratz) on July 3. Austria sued for peace.

Prussia annexed its smaller neighbors who had supported Austria, thus creating a contiguous state linking Prussia with the Rhineland, acquired in 1815. This enlarged Prussia intended to dominate the newly formed North German Confederation, comprising all the states north of the Main River.

After the battle of Sadowa, Bismarck was greeted as a hero. Elections held on the day of the battle returned a conservative pro-Bismarck majority to the Prussian parliament. The legislature, including a large number of liberals mesmerized by the military victory, voted retroactively to make legal the illegal taxes that had been levied since 1862 for the purpose of upgrading the military. Enthusiastic at the prospect that Prussia might now successfully lead German unity, these liberals readily compromised their principles. They rationalized that national unity ought to be gained first, and liberal constitutional institutions could be secured later. They proved to be wrong.

The unification of Germany, like that in Italy, was facilitated by a favorable international situation. The Crimean War had estranged Russia from Austria. In 1850, Austrian resistance to Prussian attempts to lead Germany had been backed by Russia, but in 1866 Austria stood alone. Moreover, when the Austro-Prussian War broke out, France was certain of Austrian victory and saw no need to intervene. However, Austria's defeat meant a strong, enlarged Prussia on France's eastern border, threatening France's position as a Great Power. Although it would have been opportune for France to intervene against Prussia while it was fighting Austria, the French emperor was indecisive and in the end did nothing. He also had been lulled into security by vague Prussian promises of support for French plans to annex Luxembourg. Once the war was won, however, Bismarck reneged on these

The Battle of Sadowa, July 3, 1866 In this important battle, the Prussians defeated Austria, eclipsing it as a German power. Now the road to Prussian supremacy in Germany lay open. *(Giraudon/Art Resource, NY)*

promises. British statesmen likewise did not intervene in the unification process. Disillusioned by the results of the Crimean War, they were in an isolationist mood. Besides, Britain was sympathetic to the rise of a fellow Protestant power.

Bismarck hoped that the southern German states would eventually merge with the North German Confederation. For the time being, he allowed them to remain outside the new body, but he obliged them to sign a military treaty with Prussia. Economically, they continued to be dependent as a result of the Zollverein (the customs union). Many southerners favored unity, especially business people who saw in it the hope of improving the economy. And German nationalists, north and south, saw the realization of a decades-long dream.

The Franco-Prussian War and Unification

French leaders, however, were determined to prevent German unity. They feared the loss of French influence in the southern German states that had traditionally been France's allies. Moreover, since the mid-seventeenth century, French security had been linked to a weak and divided Germany.

Since France was not disposed to be an idle bystander to German unification, both Berlin and Paris anticipated war. And war came soon enough, precipitated by a crisis over the Spanish succession. In 1868, a military coup had overthrown the Spanish queen Isabella, and the new authorities offered the throne to a Catholic member of the Hohenzollerns, the reigning Prussian monarch's family. The French viewed this candidacy as an unacceptable continued expansion of Prussian power and influence. Fearing a two-front war with Prussia on the east and Spain on the south, they were outraged and insisted the Hohenzollerns refuse the proffered throne. As passions heated, Bismarck was elated at the prospect of war. But the Prussian king was not. On July 12, 1870, he withdrew the young prince's candidacy, removing the cause for war. Bismarck was bitterly disappointed.

The French had won considerable prestige in getting their way—but, not satisfied at the withdrawal of the Prussian candidacy, they pushed their luck further. On July 13 the French ambassador met the king of Prussia at Ems and asked for confirmation that the Hohenzollern candidacy had been withdrawn. William provided these assurances, but the ambassador further demanded guarantee that no Hohenzollern would ever again be a candidate to the Spanish throne. Unable to provide any further concessions without a serious loss of prestige, the Prussian king refused the French demand.

William telegraphed an account of his meeting to Bismarck. The chancellor, who had been discouraged at the lost chance of war with France, was heartened by the opportunity this message provided. He edited what became known as the Ems dispatch, making the exchange between king and ambassador seem more curt than it actually had been; then he released it to the press. As he hoped, the French interpreted the account as a deliberate snub to their ambassador. Faced by a flood of emotional demands for redress of the imagined slight to French national honor, Napoleon III declared war.

The Prussians led a well-planned campaign. An army of 384,000 Prussians was rushed by rail to confront a force of 270,000 Frenchmen. The French had the advantage of better rifles, but the Prussians were equipped with heavier guns, which at a distance could pulverize French positions. Within a few weeks, Prussia won a decisive victory at Sedan, taking the French emperor prisoner on September 2. The French did not accept defeat readily and continued the struggle, despite difficult odds. Infuriated by the continuation of the war, the Prussians resorted to extreme measures, even targeting civilians. They took hostages and burned down whole villages, and they laid siege to Paris, starving and bombarding its beleaguered population.

Throughout Germany the outbreak of the war was accompanied by general enthusiasm for the Prussian cause. Exploiting this popular feeling, Bismarck called on the other German states to accept the unification of Germany under the Prussian king. Reluctant princes, such as the king of Bavaria, were bought off with bribes. On January 18, 1871, the German princes met in the hall of mirrors of the Versailles palace, symbol of past French greatness, and acclaimed William I as German emperor.

In May 1871, the Treaty of Frankfurt established the peace terms. France was forced to give up the provinces of Alsace and Lorraine and to

William I Proclaimed Ruler of the German Empire at Versailles, 1871 After a series of military victories, Prussia unified Germany. In this 1885 painting by Anton von Werner (1843–1915), the King of Prussia is proclaimed emperor of Germany by the other kings. Depicted as standing in the front, among the kings, is Otto von Bismarck, the Prussian statesman who carefully orchestrated the event. *(Bismarck Museum, Friedrichsruh)*

pay a heavy indemnity of five billion francs. These harsh terms embittered the French, leading many to desire revenge and establishing a formidable barrier to future relations between France and Germany.

The Character of the New Germany

German unity had been forged by a series of wars—against Denmark in 1864, Austria in 1866, and France in 1870—and lacked the popular democratic base that had been present in Italy. Because the military had played such a crucial role in the formation of the new German state, it maintained a dominant role in the new society that followed. Italian unity had been sanctioned by plebiscites and a vote by an elected assembly accepting the popular verdict. The founding act of the new German state was the meeting of the German rulers on the soil of a defeated neighbor. Thus the rulers placed themselves above elected assemblies and popular sanction.

The constitution of the new Germany was remarkably democratic on the surface, however. It provided for an upper, appointed house, the Bundesrat, representing the individual German states, and a lower house, the Reichstag, which was elected by universal manhood suffrage. The latter was a surprising concession from Bismarck, the authoritarian aristocrat. But he knew the liberals lacked mass support and gambled that, with appropriate appeals, he would be able to create majorities that could be manipulated for his purposes.

The dominant state in the new Germany was, of course, Prussia, which also had two-thirds of its population. Within the Bundesrat, Prussia had 17 of the 43 seats and could block any legislation it opposed with the aid of only a few other states. The king of Prussia occupied the post of emperor, and the chancellor and other cabinet members were responsible not to parliament but to him. He alone could make foreign policy and war, command the army, and interpret the constitution. The authoritarianism of Prussia had been projected onto all of Germany.

The emergence of a strong, united Germany disrupted the European balance of power. In February 1871, the British political leader Benjamin Disraeli observed that the unification of Germany was "a greater political event than the French revolution of last century. . . . There is not a diplomatic tradition which has not been swept away. You have a new world.... The balance of power has been entirely destroyed."[2] Germany had become the dominant power on the Continent.

Precarious Supranational Empires

In an age of nationalism that saw two new nation-states emerge—Italy and Germany—those European states that were multinational found themselves in an increasingly precarious position. The Habsburg and Ottoman empires of central and eastern Europe consisted of a multitude of peoples speaking different languages, holding different religious beliefs, and having different historical traditions. In the past such multinational states had been quite normal in Europe, but in the nineteenth century they became increasingly anomalous. The peoples living under the authority of Vienna and Constantinople became more and more restive.

Facing this severe challenge, the Austrian and Ottoman empires attempted to strengthen themselves by restructuring their institutions. To some extent these efforts succeeded, although the Ottoman Empire, the weaker of the two, and beset by hostility from the other Great Powers, suffered loss of territory and status.

The Dual Monarchy in Austria-Hungary

Austrian statesmen sensed the vulnerability of their empire. By 1860 they had lost much of their Italian possessions; they confronted sullen resistance from the Magyars in Hungary, still resentful they had not won independence in 1848; and they faced the bitter struggle for German supremacy with Prussia. To give his government credibility, in February 1861, Emperor Francis Joseph (r. 1848—1916) issued what were known as the February Patents, which liberalized the government, guaranteed civil liberties, and provided local self-government and an elected parliament.

The need to concentrate on safeguarding the remaining territories was clear (Map 24.3). By 1866 the Austrian Habsburgs were no longer a German or Italian power (Venetia had been handed over to a united Italy). The strongest challenge to Habsburg rule came from Hungary, where a powerful minority, the Magyars, controlled the country. A broad spectrum of Magyars insisted on self-rule, a claim based on age-old historic rights and Vienna's initial acceptance of autonomy in 1848. Since Magyar cooperation was crucial for the well-being of the Habsburg empire, the government entered into lengthy negotiations with Magyar leaders in 1867. The outcome was a compromise that created a new structure for the empire that lasted until 1918. The agreement divided the Habsburg holdings into Austria in the west and Hungary in the east. Each was independent, but they were linked by the person of the emperor of Austria, Francis Joseph, who was also king of Hungary. Hungary had full internal autonomy and participated jointly in imperial affairs—state finance, defense, and foreign relations. The new state created by the compromise was known as the dual monarchy of Austria-Hungary.

The emperor of the new state of Austria-Hungary had come to the throne as an 18-year-old in that year of crisis, 1848. Francis Joseph was a well-meaning monarch who took his duties seriously. He diligently attended to the mass of bureaucratic paperwork, but he lacked imagination and did little more than try to conserve a disintegrating empire coping with the modern forces of liberalism and nationalism. His upbringing was German, he lived in German-speaking Vienna, and he headed an army and a bureaucracy that was mostly German, but Franz Joseph was markedly cosmopolitan. He spoke several of his subjects' languages and thought of himself as the emperor of all his peoples. In both halves of the empire, he was a much-loved, regal figure who provided a visible link and embodied the state in which they lived. In part, the empire was held together by him.

The compromise confirmed Magyar dominance in Hungary. Although numerically a minority, Magyars controlled the Hungarian parliament, the army, the bureaucracy, and other state institutions. They opposed self-rule by the Croats, Serbs, Slovaks, Romanians, and others in the kingdom and attempted a policy of Magyarization—teaching only Magyar in the schools, conducting all government business in Magyar, and giving access to government positions only to those fully assimilated in Magyar culture. This

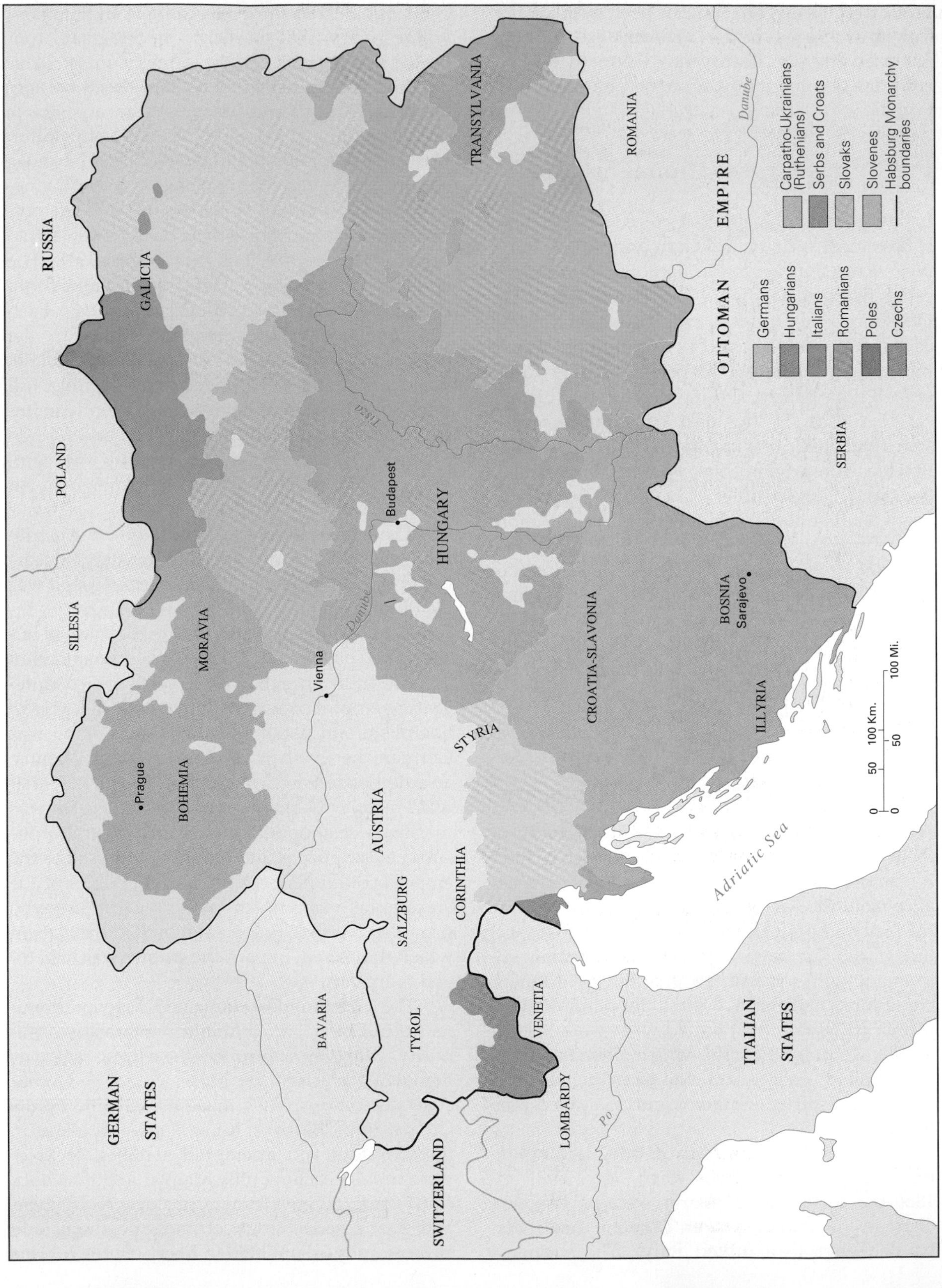

GERMAN STATES
SWITZERLAND
BAVARIA
TYROL
SALZBURG
CORINTHIA
VENETIA
LOMBARDY
Po
ITALIAN STATES
Adriatic Sea
AUSTRIA
STYRIA
BOHEMIA
Prague
Vienna
Danube
MORAVIA
SILESIA
POLAND
GALICIA
RUSSIA
HUNGARY
Budapest
Tisza
TRANSYLVANIA
ROMANIA
Danube
CROATIA-SLAVONIA
BOSNIA
Sarajevo
ILLYRIA
SERBIA
OTTOMAN EMPIRE
Germans
Hungarians
Italians
Romanians
Poles
Czechs
Carpatho-Ukrainians (Ruthenians)
Serbs and Croats
Slovaks
Slovenes
Habsburg Monarchy boundaries
0 50 100 Km.
0 50 100 Mi.

arrangement created frustrations and resistance among the various nationalities under their rule.

The terms of the compromise also gave the Hungarians a voice in imperial foreign policy. Magyars feared that Slavic groups outside the empire, who had or would form independent states, would inspire the nationalities under their control to revolt. To prevent that, the Hungarians encouraged an expansionist foreign policy into the Balkans, which the monarchy willingly embraced. Having lost its influence in Germany, Austria-Hungary found in the Balkans an area in which to assert itself. The policy was fraught with risks and, by bringing more discontented Slavs into the empire, led to hostility with other states.

The Decline of the Ottoman Empire

At midcentury the Ottoman Empire was still one of the largest European powers, but it faced unrest within its borders and threats by the expansionist designs of its neighbors (Map 24.4). The ailing empire was commonly referred to as "the sick man of Europe." Over the next twenty-five years, the empire shed some of its territory and modernized its government, but nothing could save it from decline in the face of nationalist uprisings in its Balkan possessions.

As early as the 1840s, the Ottoman Empire had begun various reform movements to bring more security to its subjects. Known as the *Tanzimat,* these changes were initiated by Sultan Abdul Mejid (r. 1839–1861), with the help of his able prime minister, Reshid Mustafa Pasha (1800–1858). Reshid had served as the Ottoman ambassador in London and Paris and was familiar with Western institutions, which he admired and wished to emulate. The reforms tightened control over the janissaries, the traditional military elite that had become a marauding force in the countryside. They also introduced security of property, equality of taxation, and equality before the law regardless of religion. Government officials—who previously had been free to collect taxes arbitrarily, sending the required amount to the central government and keeping the rest—were given fixed salaries and subjected to regular inspections from the imperial capital. These reforms were strengthened after the Crimean War by further imperial edicts. Contacts with the West encouraged Turks to think of transforming their empire into a more modern, Westernized state. Some young intellectuals were impatient with the rate of change, however, and critical of the sultan. Unable freely to express their opinions at home, some went into exile in the late 1860s to Paris and London. Their hosts called them the "Young Turks," an expression that became synonymous with the desire for change and improvement.

Map 24.3 Austria-Hungary in 1878 A multinational state, the Austrian-Hungarian empire acquired Bosnia in 1878, bringing more dissatisfied peoples under its rule. Tensions in the Balkans would lead to the outbreak of war in 1914.

After these initial reform efforts, however, the central government began to turn away from reform, and in 1871 the sultan decided to assert his personal rule. His inability successfully to wage war and hold onto the empire led to dissatisfaction, and in the spring of 1876 rioters demanded and won the establishment of constitutional government. Within less than a year, however, the new sultan, Abdul Hamid II (r. 1876–1909), dismissed the constitutional government and reverted to personal rule.

Part of the administration's problem was financial. The Crimean War had forced the empire to borrow money abroad. The easy terms of foreign credit lured the sultan into taking out huge loans to finance some extravagant projects. By 1875 more than half the annual income of the empire went to pay the interest on the debt. In spite of a drought and famine, the authorities raised taxes, increasing opposition within the realm.

Opposition to the government continued to grow, fueled by nationalist fervor. At the beginning of the nineteenth century, the Ottoman Empire had extended as far west as Algeria, through the Balkans, and eastward to the Persian Gulf. Ottoman subjects spoke many languages and practiced many religions. To varying degrees they were restive. The empire tolerated religious diversity and did not persecute people because of their religion. But the central administration had lost control over its officials in the provinces, who were often corrupt and tyrannical. In particular, much of the Balkan region was isolated from any benign control Constantinople might

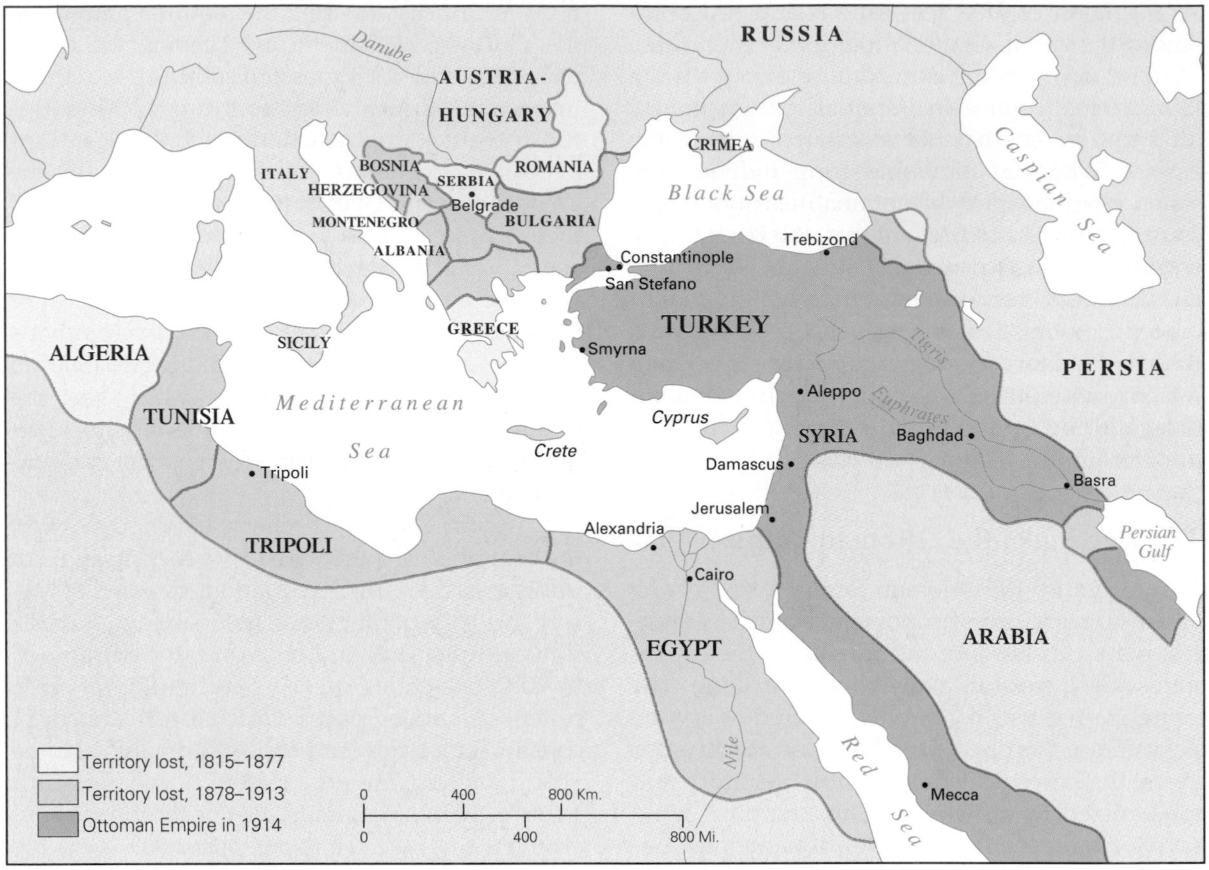

Map 24.4 The Decline of the Ottoman Empire Throughout the nineteenth century, the Ottoman empire was reduced in size as nationalist movements wrested independence from Constantinople and foreign powers annexed territories.

have wished to exercise. Christians, a majority of the population in the Balkans, blamed their suffering on Islamic rule, and many were inspired by the 1821 Greek war of independence to seek their own independence.

The Romanians, for example, who lived mainly in the twin provinces of Moldavia in the north and Wallachia in the south, began to express nationalist sentiments in the late eighteenth century. These sentiments were nurtured by Western-educated students, who claimed for their fellow countrymen illustrious descent from Roman settlers of antiquity. News of revolution in Paris in 1848 helped trigger a revolt in both provinces demanding unification and independence. This uprising was quickly crushed by the Turks.

The 1856 Peace of Paris removed Russia's right of protection over the two principalities and provided for a referendum to determine their future. Forbidden by international agreement from uniting, the principalities chose a local nobleman, Alexander Cuza (r. 1859–1866), as ruler of each territory. Thus they were separate legally but united under one ruler. In 1861, the Ottoman Empire under pressure from the Romanians recognized the union of the two principalities into the single, autonomous state of Romania, and in 1878, at the Congress of Berlin, full independence was granted. Thus, in less than a quarter-century, two provinces of the Ottoman Empire merged and gained full sovereignty.

The path to independence was much more violent for the Bulgars. Influenced by neighboring Serbia and encouraged by the Russians, who after the Crimean War were willing to use nationalism to upset the existing international order, revolutionary committees spread propaganda and agitated against Ottoman rule. An uprising in Bulgaria broke out in May 1876. The rebels attacked not only symbols of Ottoman authority but also peaceable Turks living in their midst. The Ottoman army, aided by local Turk volunteers, quickly re-established Ottoman authority. Incensed by the massacre of fellow Muslims, the volunteers resorted to mass killing, looting, and burning of Christian villages. A shocked Europe provided an outpouring of sympathy for the Bulgar Christian victims. The "Bulgarian horrors" made the continuation of Turkish rule unacceptable.

The Bulgar problem was resolved by the Balkan wars of 1876–1878, which were provoked by the uprising of the westernmost Ottoman provinces of Bosnia and Herzegovina. Since many of the inhabitants of these two provinces were Serbs, they had the sympathy of their neighbor, Serbia, which believed it could unify the southern Slavs. Together with the neighboring mountain state of Montenegro, Serbia declared war on the Ottoman Empire. They were savagely defeated by the Turks.

Russia, which saw itself as the protector of the Slavic peoples and wanted to weaken the Ottoman Empire, reacted to the Bulgarian horrors by also declaring war on the empire, in April 1877. At first progress was slow, then the Russians broke through the Turkish lines and forced the sultan to sue for peace. The resulting Treaty of San Stefano, signed in March 1878, excluded the Ottoman Empire from Europe and created a huge, independent Bulgaria as essentially a Russian satellite.

The British, Austrians, and French were shocked at the extent to which the San Stefano treaty favored Russia. Under their pressure, the European powers met in Berlin in 1878 to reconsider the treaty. The Congress of Berlin reduced the size of the Bulgarian territory, allowing the rest to revert to Constantinople. Bosnia and Herzegovina were removed from Ottoman rule and put under that of Austria-Hungary. Constantinople had to acknowledge the legal independence of Serbia, Montenegro, and Romania and the autonomy of Bulgaria. The British insisted on

Nationalistic Uprising in Bulgaria In this 1879 lithograph, Bulgaria is depicted in the form of a maiden—protected by the Russian eagle, breaking her chains, and winning liberty from the Ottoman empire. *(St. Cyril and Methodius National Library, Sofia)*

being given nearby Cyprus to administer, an outpost from which they might prevent further challenges to the existing balance of power.

Thus Turkey was plundered, not only by its enemies but also by powers that had intervened on its behalf. When France complained that it received no compensation, it was suggested that it grab Tunisia, another territory under Ottoman rule. Russia, which had signed an alliance with Romania and promised to respect its territorial integrity, refused to honor its obligations and took southern Bessarabia from its ally. The work of the congress reflected the power politics that now characterized international affairs. Statesmen shamelessly employed force against both foe and friend for the aggrandizement of their own state. Neither morality nor international law restrained ambition.

Stability in Victorian Britain

Midcentury was a period of unprecedented wealth and security for Britain as the population as a whole began to share in the economic benefits of the industrial revolution. Britain enjoyed both social and political peace. The political system was not challenged as it had been in the generation after the Napoleonic wars. The self-assured, even smug, political elite—merchants, industrialists, and landowners—developed a political system reflecting liberal values.

Parliamentary Government

Although suffrage was still very restricted, the parliamentary system became firmly established, with a government clearly responsible to the elected legislature. The importance of Parliament was symbolized by the new, imposing building, finished in 1850 on the site of previous parliamentary buildings but of a splendor and size that was unprecedented. The form of parliamentary government developed in its halls after midcentury represented a model that was the envy of much of the Western world. Parliament consisted of an upper, hereditary House of Lords, and a lower, elected House of Commons. Increasingly, the cabinet became answerable to Parliament.

In the twenty years after 1846, five different parties vied for power. Depending on the issue, parties and factions coalesced to support particular policies. After 1867, however, a clear two-party system emerged: Liberal and Conservative (Tory), both with strong leadership. This development gave the electorate a distinct choice. The Conservatives were wedded to preserving traditional institutions and practices, while the Liberals tended to be open to change.

Gladstone, Disraeli, and the Two-Party System

Heading these parties were two strong-minded individuals who dominated British political life for over a generation: William E. Gladstone (1809–1898), a Liberal, and Benjamin Disraeli (1804–1881), a Conservative. Gladstone came from an industrial family and married into the aristocracy; Disraeli was the son of a Jewish man of letters who had converted to Christianity. His father's conversion allowed him to be a candidate and sit in Parliament (before the 1850s Jews could not be members of Parliament). Prior to heading their parties, Gladstone and Disraeli both served in important cabinet positions. They were master debaters; Parliament and the press hung with interest on their every word. Each was capable of making speeches lasting five hours or more and of conducting debates that would keep the house in session until 4 A.M. The rivalry between the two men was a kind of sport that thrilled the nation and made politics a popular pastime.

The Conservatives' electoral base came from the landed classes, Anglicans, and from England, rather than the rest of the United Kingdom. The Liberals' base came from the middle classes, from those belonging to the variety of Christian groups other than the Church of England, and from Scotland and Wales. In the House of Commons both parties had a large number of members from the landed aristocracy, but increasingly cabinet members were chosen for their political competence rather than their family background. Aristocratic birth was no longer a requirement for reaching the pinnacle of power, as Gladstone and Disraeli so clearly illustrated.

The competition for power between Liberals and the Conservatives led to an extension of the suffrage in 1867. The Second Reform Bill lowered property qualifications, extending the vote from 1.4 to 2.5 million electors out of a population of 22 million, and gave new urban areas better representation by equalizing the electoral districts. Although some members of Parliament feared that these changes would lead to the common masses capturing political power—"a leap into the dark," one member called it—in fact no radical change ensued. Extending the vote to clerks, artisans, and other skilled workers made them feel more part of society, and thus bolstered the existing system. John Stuart Mill, then a member of Parliament, was inspired to support the cause of women's suffrage by his late wife, the feminist and essayist Harriet Taylor Mill (1807–1858), but that cause failed.

With the increased size of the new electorate, parties became stronger. Strong party systems meant a clear alternation of power between the Liberals and the Conservatives. With a clear majority and minority party, the monarch could no longer play favorites in choosing a prime minis-

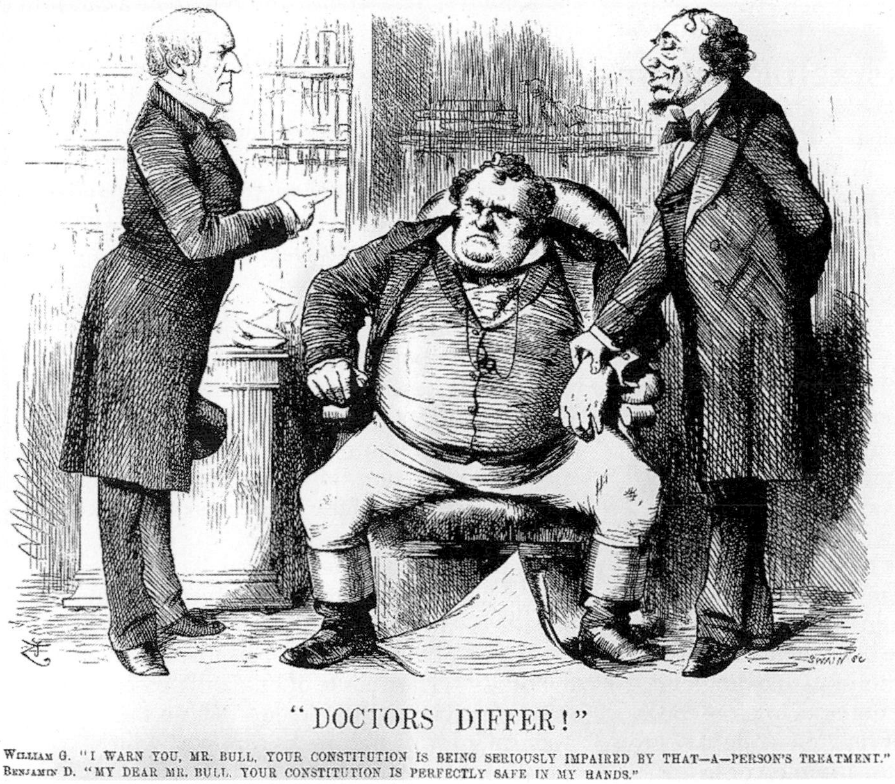

SWAIN SC
"DOCTORS DIFFER!"
WILLIAM G. "I WARN YOU, MR. BULL, YOUR CONSTITUTION IS BEING SERIOUSLY IMPAIRED BY THAT—A—PERSON'S TREATMENT."
BENJAMIN D. "MY DEAR MR. BULL, YOUR CONSTITUTION IS PERFECTLY SAFE IN MY HANDS."

Gladstone and Disraeli This *Punch* cartoon shows the two eternal political rivals vying for the right to minister to the needs of John Bull, the figure symbolizing England. *(Mary Evans Picture Library)*

ter. The leader of the majority party had to be asked to form a government. Thus, even though Queen Victoria (r. 1837–1901) detested Gladstone, she had to ask him to form governments when the Liberals won parliamentary elections. (See the feature, "Weighing the Evidence: An Engraving of the British Royal Family," on pages 918–919.)

The creation of a mass electorate also meant that politicians had to make clear appeals to the public and its interests. In the past, oratory had been limited to the halls of Parliament, but after the electoral reforms, it occurred in the public arena as well. Public election campaigns became part of the political scene in England. The democratic "American" style of campaigning increasingly appealed to the common man. Also borrowed from across the seas was the "Australian ballot"—the secret ballot—adopted in 1872. This removed opportunity for intimidation of the lower-class voters by their employers, landowners, or other social superiors. In 1874 the first two working-class members of Parliament were elected, sitting as Liberals. Although their victory represented a very modest gain for workers' representation, it presaged the increasingly democratic turn England was to take (see the box, "Disraeli Proclaims 'Tory Democracy'").

France: From Empire to Republic

Unlike Britain, which gradually metamorphosed into a parliamentary democracy, France took a more tumultuous path. A series of severe jolts—revolutions and war—overthrew existing political systems and inaugurated new ones. Each time the French seemed to have democracy within reach, the opportunity slipped away. Luckily, however, authoritarianism was equally elusive.

Disraeli Proclaims "Tory Democracy"

Benjamin Disraeli understood that his party, if it were to succeed in a changing Britain, had to be concerned with the lot of the poor. By espousing "Tory democracy," the Conservatives could still win and retain political power in an increasingly democratic society.

Gentlemen, the Tory party, unless it is a national party, is nothing. . . . It is not a confederacy of nobles, it is not a democratic multitude; it is a party formed from all classes of the realm—classes alike and equal before the law, but whose different conditions and different aims give vigour and variety to our national life. . . . Now, I have always been of the opinion that the Tory party has three great objects. The first is to maintain the institutions of this country—not from any sentiment of political superstition, but because we believe that the principles upon which a community like England can alone safely rest—the principles of liberty, of order, of law, and of religion—ought not to be intrusted to individual opinion or to the caprice and passion of the multitudes, but should be embodied in a form of permanence and power. . . . Another object of the Tory party . . . is the elevation of the condition of the people. The attention of public men should be directed to the condition of the people. . . . It concerns the state of the dwellings of the people, the moral consequences of which are not less important than the physical. It concerns their enjoyment of some of the chief elements of nature—air, light, and water. It concerns the regulation of their industry, the inspection of their toil. . . .The people of England possess every personal right of freedom . . . social, not political improvement is the object at which they should aim. . . .

Source: Speech of June 24, 1872, in T. E. Kebbel, ed., *Selected Speeches of the Late Right Honorable the Earl of Beaconsfield,* vol. 2 (London: Longmans, Green, 1882), pp. 524–525, 531–532.

The People's Emperor, Napoleon III

The constitution of the Second French Republic provided for a single four-year presidential term. Frustrated by this limitation of power, Louis Napoleon by a coup d'état extended his presidency to a ten-year term in 1851. The following year, he called for a plebiscite to confirm him as Napoleon III, emperor of the French. Both of these moves were resisted in the countryside, particularly in the south, but the resistance was put down by massive repression.

In the rest of the country, huge majorities of voters endorsed first the prolonged presidency and then the imperial title. The new emperor seemed different from his predecessors. He believed in the principle of popular sovereignty (he maintained universal male suffrage, introduced in 1848), he did not pretend to reign by divine grace, and he repeatedly tested his right to rule by an appeal to the popular vote. He seemed to combine order and authority with the promises of the Revolution—equality before the law, careers open to talent, and the abolition of hereditary rights.

The midcentury period was an era of prosperity that benefited most Frenchmen, including urban workers and peasants. Louis Napoleon, in his youth the author of a book on pauperism, introduced government measures congenial to labor. On the one hand, workers were required to maintain a booklet in which their conduct was to be recorded by their employers; on the other hand, however, they were granted some initial rights to organize strikes, and labor unions were virtually legalized. The emperor expressed empathy for improving the workers' lot, and the government initiated a few concrete measures, such as providing some public housing. Although slum clearance during the rebuilding of

Paris drove many from their homes to the outskirts of cities, it did provide healthier towns for those who stayed behind, and the ambitious urban projects provided work for many (see page 935). Other public works projects, such as the building of ports, roads, railroads, and monumental public buildings, also created jobs. Railroads in France increased tenfold and provided the means for peasants to market their harvests more widely. By and large the peasantry supported Louis Napoleon. Not only were they a cautious group, preferring stable authority, but they saw in the emperor—the heir to the great Napoleon—an incarnation of national glory.

Not all Frenchmen supported the emperor; many republicans could not forget that he had usurped the constitution of 1848. In protest, some had gone into exile, including the poet Victor Hugo. Trying to win over the opposition, Napoleon made some concessions in 1860, easing censorship and making his government more accountable to the parliament. Instead of winning him new support, however, this liberalization allowed the expression of mounting opposition. A coordinated republican opposition rebuked the economic policies of the empire, notably the decision to sign a free-trade treaty with England. Although this policy helped the wine and silk exporters, it left iron and textile manufacturers unprotected. Businessmen in these fields rallied their workers against the imperial regime. A number of other issues—widespread hostility to the influence of the Catholic church and the desire for more extensive freedoms of expression and assembly—also helped forge a republican alliance of the middle classes and workers. This alliance was particularly powerful in the large cities and in some southern regions notorious for their opposition to central government control. Republicanism was better organized than it had been previously and had a more explicit program, and its proponents were better prepared to take over the government, if the opportunity arose, than was the case in earlier years.

By 1869 the regime, which declared itself a "liberal empire," had fully evolved into a constitutional monarchy, responsible to the Legislative Corps, the lower house of the parliament. In a plebiscite in May 1870, Frenchmen supported the liberal empire by a vote of five to one. The empire might have endured, but two months later Napoleon III rashly declared war against Prussia over the imagined slight to French national honor precipitated by the Ems dispatch. Defeat brought down the empire. In September, at news of the emperor's capture, the republican opposition in the Legislative Corps declared a republic. It continued the war but had to sign an armistice in January 1871.

Napoleon III This is an example of official art glorifying the emperor. The emperor is framed by a Roman statue on his right and the imperial eagle on his left, both symbols of strength and glory. *(Château de Versailles/Giraudon/Art Resource, NY)*

The leader of the new government was an old prime minister of Louis Philippe, Adolphe Thiers (1797–1877). To sign a definite peace, the provisional government held elections. The liberals, known as republicans since they favored a republic, were identified with continuing the war; the conservatives, mostly royalists, favored

The Principles of the Paris Commune

While surrounded by government troops, the Paris Commune issued an official program clarifying its principles. The declaration asserts the Commune's right to rule Paris and the right of self-rule for all other municipalities plus the right to intervene in the economy to ensure the well-being of the general citizenry.

Once more Paris labours and suffers for the whole of France, for whom she prepares by her battles and intellectual, moral, administrative, and economic regeneration, glory and prosperity.

What does she demand?

The recognition and consolidation of the Republic, the only form of government compatible with the rights of the People and with the free, regular development of society.

Paris reserves to herself liberty to bring about as may seem good to her administrative and economic reforms which the people demand, and to create such institutions as may serve to develop and further education, production, exchange, and credit; to universalise power and property according to the necessities of the moment, the wishes of those interested, and the data furnished by experience.

Unity, such has been imposed upon us up to the present by the empire, the monarchy, and parliamentary government, is nothing but centralisation, despotic, unintelligent, arbitrary, and onerous.

Political unity, as desired by Paris, is a voluntary association of all local initiative, the free and spontaneous co-operation of all individual energies with the common object of well-being, liberty and security of all.

The Communal Revolution, begun by popular initiative on the 18th of March, inaugurated a new era of experimental, positive, and scientific politics.

It marks the end of the old governmental and clerical world, of militarism, of bureaucracy, of exploitation, of jobbing in monopolies, of privileges, to which the proletariat owes its slavery and the country its misfortune and disasters.

Our mission is to accomplish the modern Revolution, the greatest and most fruitful of all those which have illuminated history.

It is our duty to fight and conquer.

Source: Declaration of April 19, 1871, in Stewart Edwards, ed., *The Communards of Paris* (Ithaca, N.Y.: Cornell University Press, 1973), pp. 81–83.

peace. Mainly because of their position on this issue, the royalists won a majority from a country discouraged by defeat.

The Paris Commune

The new regime had no time to establish itself before it was confronted in the spring of 1871 by an uprising that shook France and reminded the rest of Europe of revolutionary dangers. The uprising was called the Paris Commune, a name that harked back to 1792–1794, when the Paris crowds had dictated to the government. The Commune insisted on its right to home rule. It was greeted by both radicals and conservatives as a workers' revolt that sought to establish a workers' government. Marx described it as the "bold champion of the emancipation of labor . . ." However, although labor discontent played a role in the Paris Commune, other forces also contributed to its outbreak. Primarily the uprising was triggered by the Prussian siege of Paris during the Franco-Prussian war. Parisians, who had suffered because of the siege, rose up against the new French government. They were angered at the lack of concern for their economic needs and the lack of recognition for their courage in withstanding the Prussians. Paris had become radicalized during the siege: The rich had evacuated the city, leaving a power vacuum quickly filled by the lower classes. Under their pressure, the Commune, composed largely of artisans, began governing the city (see the box, "The Principles of the Paris Commune").

In March 1871, the Commune declared itself free to carry out policies without hindrance from the central government in Versailles. The government sent forces to crush the Commune, and they massacred 25,000 people, arrested 40,000, and deported several thousand more. Although the savagery of this repression indicated that the Commune was viewed as unacceptably radical, it was, in fact, quite moderate. It sought free universal education, a fairer taxation system, a minimum wage, and disestablishment of the official Catholic church.

Nonetheless, the crushing of the Paris Commune and some of its sister communes in southern France, which were also asserting local autonomy, signified the increasing power of the centralized state. The emerging modern state had vast power and could squelch popular revolts that in the past had seriously threatened regimes. Western Europe would not again witness a popular uprising of this magnitude.

The Third Republic

Despite its brutality, the crushing of the Commune by Thiers' new government reassured many Frenchmen. "The Republic will be conservative, or it will not be," declared Thiers. The question now at hand was what form the new government would take.

The monarchist majority was split between those favoring a restoration to the throne of the Bourbon heir, the grandson of Charles X, and those favoring the Orléanist heir, grandson of Louis Philippe. The partisans of both sides were finally able to compromise and agreed to offer the throne to the elderly and childless Bourbon pretender. However, he insisted he would become king only if the *tricouleur*—the flag of the Revolution, which long since had become a cherished national symbol—were discarded and replaced by the white flag of the house of Bourbon. The monarchists realized their project was unfeasible; their plan was thus scuttled and France remained a republic. The republic, as Thiers put it, "is the regime which divides us the least."

By 1875, the parliament had approved a set of basic laws that became the constitution of the Third Republic. Ironically, a monarchist parliament had created a liberal, democratic parliamentary regime. The parliament was to consist of two chambers: the Chamber of Deputies, elected by universal male suffrage, and the Senate, chosen indirectly by local officials. The two houses sitting jointly elected the president, who was to occupy essentially a ceremonial role as chief of state. The head of government, the premier, and his cabinet were responsible to the parliament.

Manet: The Barricade In this 1871 painting, Edouard Manet catches a scene from the Paris Commune of 1871. With barricades, the communards are trying to protect themselves from the onslaught of government troops. Although fewer than a thousand government soldiers died, over 25,000 communards were killed. *(Reproduced by courtesy of the Board of Directors of the Budapest Museum of Fine Arts)*

At first, the government personnel were all royalists, but in successive elections republicans gained control of every branch of government. By 1880, both chambers of the parliament and the president were republicans, and the republican system of government was launched.

Russia and the Great Reforms

By the 1840s, concern about the archaic nature and structure of Russian government was growing. Many officials lamented the tendency of a timid bureaucracy to lie and mislead the public. There were calls for *glasnost*—greater openness—which became the leading motif for the great reforms of the 1860s. Defeat in the Crimean War made the reassessment of Russian institutions imperative.

The Abolition of Serfdom

The chief problem that needed to be addressed was serfdom. For a very long time educated opinion had denounced it as immoral. But that was not the principal reason for its abolition. Serfdom was abolished because it presented clear political disadvantages in both the domestic and international domains. The new tsar, Alexander II (r. 1855–1881), feared that if the abolition of serfdom was not mandated from above, it would occur from below—by a violent serf rebellion that would sweep away everything in its path, including the autocracy itself.

Serfdom also presented a challenge to Russia's place in the world. Defeat in the Crimean War had seemed to show that if Russia depended for its defense upon a soldiery of serfs rather than free men, it would be unable to survive in an increasingly competitive international situation. The Russian army would be more powerful if it consisted of soldiers who had a stake in their society rather than men who were tied to lifetime servitude. In addition, the victorious Western states had won in part because their industrial might translated into more and better guns, ammunition, and transportation. Industrial progress required a mobile labor force, not one tied to the soil by serfdom. For many educated Russians, the defeat in the Crimea revealed general Russian backwardness. To catch up with the West, Russia needed to rid itself of its timeworn institutions, particularly serfdom.

In April 1861, the tsar issued a decree freeing the serfs (see the box, "The Tsar Demands the Freeing of the Serfs"). It was a radical measure to emancipate 22 million people from a system that allowed them to be bought and sold, separated from their families, and treated in the cruelest ways imaginable. The emancipation represented a compromise with the gentry, which had reluctantly agreed to liberate its serfs but insisted on compensation. As a result, the newly liberated peasants had to reimburse the government with mortgage payments lasting fifty years. The peasants received some land, but its value was vastly overrated and it was insufficient to live on. To make ends meet, the freed peasants continued working for their former masters. Thus the emancipation proclamation disappointed the peasants; they could not believe it was genuine. In fact, the declaration was accompanied by massive peasant uprisings that had to be put down by force.

The mortgage payments and taxes imposed upon the peasants by the central government were to be paid by the local commune, the *mir.* The commune determined how the land was to be used, and it paid collectively for the mortgage and taxes on the land. As a consequence, the commune was reluctant for the peasants to leave the land, and they could do so only with its permission. Freed from serfdom, the peasants nonetheless still suffered many constraints.

The tsar and his advisers feared the large mass of uneducated peasants as a potential source of anarchy and rebellion. Thus they depended on the *mir* to preserve control even though the commune system had some inherent economic disadvantages. Increased productivity benefited the commune as much as the individual peasant; hence there was little incentive for land improvement, and yield remained low.

Reforms in Russian Institutions

Alexander was called the "tsar emancipator" by his contemporaries, but he was wedded to the principles of autocracy. His aim in abolishing serfdom and introducing other reforms was to modernize and strengthen Russia and stabilize his rule. Like most Russians, Alexander believed that only the firm hand of autocracy could hold

The Tsar Demands the Freeing of the Serfs

In January 1861, Tsar Alexander II addressed the Council of State, an advisory body that he had asked four years earlier to prepare a draft law emancipating the serfs. After this forceful speech, a workable proposal emerged and was implemented six weeks later.

The matter of the liberation of the serfs, which has been submitted for the consideration of the State Council, I consider to be a vital question for Russia, upon which will depend the development of her strength and power.

My predecessors felt all the evils of serfdom and continually endeavored, if not to destroy it completely, to work toward the gradual limitation of the arbitrary power of the estate owners.

Already in 1856, before the coronation, while in Moscow I called the attention of the leaders of the nobility of the Moscow guberniia to the necessity for them to occupy themselves with improving the life of the serfs, adding that serfdom could not continue forever and that it would therefore be better if the transformation took place from above rather than from below. . . .

I have the right to demand one thing from you: that you, putting aside all personal interests, act not like estate owners but like imperial statesmen invested with my trust. Approaching this important matter I have not concealed from myself all those difficulties that awaited us and I do not conceal them now.

Source: Speech of January 28, 1861, in George Vernadsky et al., eds., *A Sourcebook for Russian History from Early Times to 1917*, vol. 3.

together a large, ethnically diverse country. The peasant uprisings that accompanied emancipation only confirmed these beliefs. Clearly, however, the sudden freedom of 22 million illiterate peasants threatened to overwhelm existing institutions, and some changes had to be made.

Although he surrendered no powers, Alexander did promulgate a number of reforms, changing the government and the judicial and military systems so they could more effectively deal with all the changes in Russian society.

Government reform had paramount importance. In merely fifty years, the Russian population had increased from 36 to 59 million and it had become increasingly difficult to administer this vast country. By midcentury, the Ministry of Internal Affairs was demanding 16,697,421 reports annually from the provinces. Overcentralized, with a poorly trained civil service, the government was unable to cope effectively with the problems of its people. Emancipation of the serfs exacerbated this need; suddenly a large number of people, freed from their owners' control, were in need of services. Thus in 1864 a law was passed providing for local governments, or *zemstvos,* at the village and regional level, giving Russians the authority and the opportunity to use initiative in local matters. The powers of the zemstvos, however, were circumscribed; the local organs had to pay for prescribed services before they could spend money on education, public health, and road systems; less than one-fifth of their funds could be disbursed on these services. The zemstvos were also forbidden to debate political issues. They were largely controlled by the gentry and not particularly democratic. Their decisions could be overridden or ignored by local officials appointed by the tsar. Some hoped that zemstvos could become the basis for Russian self-government at the national level, the creation of an all-Russian zemstvo, but such hopes were firmly squelched by the tsar, who believed in the divine right to rule and jealously insisted on his right to undivided and undiminished absolutism. Nonetheless, the zemstvos were an attempt to modernize an overburdened central government.

The tsar also created an independent judiciary that ensured equality before the law, public jury trials, and uniform sentences. Russian political leaders recognized that public confidence in the judiciary was a prerequisite for the development of commerce and industry. Businessmen would no longer fear arbitrariness and could develop enterprises in greater security.

In addition, prepublication censorship was abolished. Under the previous tsar, Nicholas, strict government control had permitted only ideas that conformed to government opinion and policy to be expressed. Such censorship prevented the central government from being well informed about public opinion or about the effects of its policies on the country. Under Alexander, openness in the press was viewed as a remedy for corruption and misuse of power. People could be punished only for specific violations after publication, and they would face trial in an independent court.

Reform also extended to the Russian army. Its structure and methods became more Western. Military service, previously limited to peasants, became the obligation of all Russians. All men submitted to a lottery, and those with an "unlucky" number entered the service. The length of service was drastically cut, and corporal punishment was abolished. Access to the officer corps was to be by merit rather than by social connection. The Ministry of War also established a larger system of reserves that enabled Russia to mobilize a larger army with more modern weapons in case of war.

Although the tsarist regime remained autocratic and repressive, it did institute several key reforms. A new page had been turned in Russian history.

Summary

New configurations of power appeared on the European chessboard as new states were created through warfare or the threat of force. But if liberal nationalists in the early nineteenth century had believed that Europe would be freer and more peaceful if each people had a separate nation, they were proved sadly wrong. The balance of power was severely shaken as Italy and Germany emerged from the center of Europe and Romania and Bulgaria were carved out of the dying Ottoman Empire in the east.

Both these new states and those already established were faced by the choice between some form of federalism or centralized rule. In the process of unification, Italy and Germany could have opted for a loose federal union, but both Piedmont and Prussia chose central control. And the crushing of the Paris Commune spelled the doom of those who wanted a France of decentralized self-governing units. Strong, centralized governments increasingly became the norm.

Even so, there was a redistribution of power at the center. France and Britain became increasingly democratic in these years, answerable to a growing electorate. To achieve legitimacy, governments had to appear to be enjoying the consent of their peoples. Hence all European rulers except those of the Ottoman and Russian empires had found it necessary to have a parliament. True, in many states parliaments had only limited powers, but once they were in place, it could be argued—and was—that more power should be shifted toward them and that they should be elected by an expanded electorate.

Two major changes that liberals in 1848 had agitated for had become reality: freer political institutions and the organization of nation-states. Although neither of these was fully implemented everywhere, both certainly appeared to have been successfully established.

In international relations, although interaction between the states had deteriorated with the demise of the congress system, no general war had broken out since the Crimean War; the military encounters of the period had limited goals and duration. So there appeared to be many signs of progress, and Europeans could easily believe they were living in an age of optimism.

Notes

1. Quoted in Otto Pflanze, *Bismarck and the Development of Germany,* vol. 1 (Princeton: Princeton University Press, 1990), p. 184.
2. Quoted in William Flavelle Monypenny and George Earle Buckle, *The Life of Benjamin Disraeli: Earl of Beaconsfield,* vol. 2 (London: John Murray, 1929), pp. 473–474.

Suggested Reading

Changing Scope of International Relations

Pearton, Maurice. *The Knowledgeable State: Diplomacy, War and Technology since 1830.* 1982. Emphasizes the contribution of general breakthroughs in science, technology, and social organization to military matters.

Rich, Norman. *Why the Crimean War? A Cautionary Tale.* 1985. Argues that the war was caused by the Western powers' decision to eliminate the Russian threat to the Ottoman Empire.

Italian Unification

Grew, Raymond. *A Sterner Plan for Italian Unity.* 1963. Studies the role of the National Society in advancing the cause of unification.

Hearder, H. *Italy in the Age of the Risorgimento, 1790–1870.* 1983. Considers regional variations in the peninsula and analyzes the debates among varying protagonists of the risorgimento.

Smith, Dennis Mack. *Cavour and Garibaldi, 1860.* 1954. Contrasts the heroic, but sometimes naive, Garibaldi with the master manipulator, Cavour.

———. *The Making of Italy, 1796–1870.* 1968. Considers the long-term forces leading to Italian unity.

———. *Cavour.* 1985. Debunks the notion that the Italian statesman was a liberal nationalist who carried out a carefully planned strategy to unite the peninsula.

Woolf, Stuart. *A History of Italy, 1700–1860.* 1979. Provides a long-term view of the place of unification in Italian history.

German Unification

Hamerow, Theodore S. *The Social Foundations of German Unification, 1858–1871.* 2 vols. 1969 and 1972. Reveals the essentially middle-class support for the program of German unification.

Howard, Michael. *The Franco-Prussian War: The German Invasion of France, 1870–71.* 1961. Reveals some of the more "modern" aspects of the war, including a willingness to target civilians.

Pflanze, Otto. *Bismarck and the Development of Germany.* I: *The Period of Unification, 1815–1871.* 1990. Emphasizes Bismarck's flexibility and ability to improvise to accomplish long-range goals.

Sheehan, James. *German Liberalism in the Nineteenth Century.* 1978. Emphasizes the environment that conditioned the shaping of liberalism in a country that unified late and had to deal with a fast-emerging working class.

Precarious Supranational Empires

Jelavich, Charles and Barbara. *The Establishment of the Balkan National States, 1804–1920.* 1977. Traces the emergence of independent states from the Ottoman Empire.

Shaw, Stanford J. *History of the Ottoman Empire and Modern Turkey.* II: *Reform, Revolution and Republic: The Rise of Modern Turkey, 1808–1975.* 1977. Emphasizes the success of reform in the Ottoman Empire and sees its decline as essentially due to foreign aggression.

Sked, Alan. *The Decline and Fall of the Habsburg Empire, 1815–1918.* 1989. Provides a revisionist interpretation, concentrating on the strengths of the empire.

Stability in Victorian Britain

Blake, Robert. *Disraeli.* 1966. The authoritative biography of the Victorian statesman who helped shape the British parliamentary system.

Evans, Eric J. *The Forging of the Modern State—Early Industrial Britain, 1783–1870.* 1983. Considers the development of political parties for the period covered in this chapter.

Wilson, A. N. *Eminent Victorians.* 1990. Has a chapter devoted to Gladstone that emphasizes his idealism and devotion to great causes.

France: From Empire to Republic

Greenberg, Louis. *Sisters of Liberty: Marseilles, Lyon, Paris, and the Reaction to a Centralized State, 1868–1871.* 1971. Reminds us that the Commune did not break out only in Paris but also in several provincial French cities and insists that local self-government was at least as important a goal to the Communards as their social program.

Smith, William H. C. *Napoleon III.* 1972. Provides a sympathetic view of Napoleon III as a staunch believer in popular sovereignty who was devoted to the welfare of his people.

Williams, Roger L. *The French Revolution of 1870–1871.* 1969. Describes the Commune as the continuation of the French revolutionary tradition.

Russia and the Great Reforms

Kolchin, Peter. *Unfree Labor: American Slavery and Russian Serfdom.* 1987. The most recent study of Russian serfdom, of particular interest to American readers.

Lincoln, W. Bruce. "The Problem of *Glasnost* in Mid-Nineteenth Century Russian Politics." *European Historical Quarterly* 11 (April 1981): 171–188. Considers the origins of the concept in the Russian bureaucracy.

———. *In the Vanguard of Reform.* 1982. Argues that the great reforms originated in the 1840s.

———. *Great Reforms.* 1990. Shows the reforms to be part of a general program of modernization.

Weighing the Evidence

AN ENGRAVING OF THE BRITISH ROYAL FAMILY

Why were Queen Victoria and her family depicted in the manner shown in this popular engraving? The illustration might well have been of an upper-middle-class family. Note the family's attire. The queen is soberly dressed; her husband, Prince Albert, is wearing a dark business suit; the children are simply dressed. The image extends from the royal family to the rest of England, depicted as a simple farm, some cottages, and a grouping of common people. Notice the crown hovering over this idyllic scene. Victoria's reign was the longest of any British monarch; the manner in which she conducted herself, and her subjects' image of her, shaped the monarchy and people's expectations of it.

Illustrations of this type familiarized the British with their monarch. Surrounded by her husband and children, the queen seemed to have an endearing common touch. In the past representations of the monarchy had suggested power and intimidation. The aura of the close-knit, nuclear royal family, akin to the families of the queen's middle-class subjects, suggested a serenity that was reassuring to those subjects.

Such prints provided a new way of looking at royalty and reflected a change in the character of the monarchy. Victoria's family life was in strong contrast to that of her predecessors. Her grandfather George III (r. 1760–1820) had bouts of insanity. Her uncle George IV (r. 1820–1830) was a notorious philanderer. He was cruel to his wife, Caroline, started divorce proceedings against her, and barred her from being queen when he was crowned king. There were public demonstrations in favor of the wronged spouse.

George IV and his brothers, the Duke of Clarence (later to be William IV [r. 1830–1837]) and the Duke of Kent (Victoria's father), were bigamists. They fathered a large brood of illegitimate children and they were notorious womanizers and spendthrifts and were involved in various public scandals.

The character of Victoria's three predecessors and of the various other men in line to the throne had strengthened opposition to the monarchy. Public outrage at their excesses had led to a call for the abolition of the monarchy. When the 18-year-old Victoria came to the throne, it would have been difficult to imagine that she would upon her death leave the monarchy considerably strengthened.

The image of Victoria shown here intentionally contrasts her reign to the reigns of her predecessors. Victoria is surrounded by four of her children (eventually she would have nine). Her predecessors had died leaving no legitimate direct heirs and thus endangering the regular succession to the throne. The engraving announces that the royal line is assured. English people wary of a female ruler can find solace in knowing that Victoria would be succeeded by one of her sons. Later, Victoria's children and their progeny would intermarry with the rest of Europe's royalty, and by the end of her reign most of Europe's crowned heads would be related to one another.

Although Victoria's uncles and father were wastrels and bankrupts, the queen and her husband lived frugally by royal standards and conducted an exemplary family life. Under the wise administration of Prince Albert, royal wealth increased; he carefully administered various royal estates and investments. Instead of being subject to various debtors, the British royal house became one of the wealthiest landowners in Great Britain, achieving financial independence and winning social prestige. Among the large landowning magnates of Britain, the royal house became the most prominent.

The model royal family appealed to the growing middle class of Victorian society. Consider how the simple terms in which the monarch is depicted here and in many other illustrations reflect the increasingly democratic spirit of the

Illustration from *A Book of English Song*

era. The ruler and her family appear in a common scene. Victoria is queen, but she also is a mother and wife. There is no sign here of pomp and ceremony.

Given the disrepute into which the monarchy had fallen and the rise of republican sentiment, the coming to the throne of a woman in 1837 may have substantially lessened antimonarchial sentiment. The last woman to rule England had been one of its greatest monarchs, Elizabeth I (r. 1558–1603), who had provided stability and brought glory to her kingdom. There was also a certain gallantry toward a young woman coming to the throne. Victoria's apparent frailty stirred men's desire to protect the queen. Also, because of her gender she was seen as less of a threat to constitutional liberties.

Under Victoria's rule the process of Britain becoming a constitutional monarchy was completed. Although Victoria's predecessors had been openly partisan, the queen cultivated the image of being above party, a symbol of national unity and the state. Fellow monarchs in central and eastern Europe exercised greater power, but after World War I they were toppled. In Britain, monarchy in its constitutional form endured. Victoria established a pattern of public and private behavior by which members of subsequent generations of the British royal family were to be judged.

ALLSOP
WINE MERC

The Age of Optimism, 1850–1880

As industrialization spread throughout western Europe, greater productivity led to increased wealth for many social groups and nations. The late nineteenth century was an era shaped to a large extent by a growing middle class filled with optimism and convinced it was living in an age of progress. The successful application of science and technology to social problems gave many people confidence in the human ability to change the world for the better.

People controlled their environment to a degree never before possible. On the land they increased the fertility of the soil; to the burgeoning cities they brought greater order. Scientists used new methods to study and combat disease. Public authorities founded schools, trained teachers, and reduced illiteracy. Transportation and communication rapidly improved.

The new age of materialism that industry created led artists and writers to stress the tangible world around them. They advocated improving it, but they also described it realistically, eschewing myths and idealistic flights of fancy. A number of intellectuals strongly denounced the materialism and smugness of the age, stressing the meanness and ignorance that lay just beneath the surface.

In fact, not all of society benefited from the fruits of progress. The new wealth was far from equally shared. Eastern and southern Europe changed little, and even in the western part a large group of the population still lived in great misery. If some cities carried out ambitious programs of urban renewal, others continued as slums. Public sanitation programs did not affect the majority of Europeans who lived in rural areas. Despite spectacular advances in science, much of the population maintained a traditional belief in

Atkinson Grimshaw, *Liverpool Quay by Moonlight* (detail), 1887 supernatural intervention. Still, the tone of the age was set by the ascending middle classes in western Europe, which embraced change and optimistically believed that the era was heading toward even greater improvements.

Industrial Growth and Acceleration

Beginning in the 1850s, Europeans experienced an unprecedented level of economic expansion. Manufacturers created new products and employed new sources of energy. An enlarged banking system provided new sources of credit that funded the expansion. Science was systematically employed to research new methods of manufacture. A revolution in transportation speedily delivered goods and services to distant places. For many Europeans, daily life was profoundly changed by technical innovations.

The "Second Industrial Revolution"

The interrelated cluster of economic changes that occurred in the generation after 1850 is often called the "second industrial revolution." It was characterized by a significant speedup in production and by the introduction of new materials such as mass-produced steel, synthetic dyes, and aluminum. Manufacturers replaced the traditional steam engine with stronger steam-powered turbines and with completely new forms of energy—petroleum and electricity.

The invention of new products and methods of manufacture spurred this industrial expansion. The second part of the nineteenth century has often been called the "age of steel." Up to then, steel production had been limited by the expense involved in its manufacture, but in 1856, Sir Henry Bessemer (1813–1898) discovered a much cheaper method, which produced in twenty minutes the same amount of steel previously produced in twenty-four hours. Ten years later, William Siemens (1823–1883) in England and Pierre Martin (1824–1915) in France developed an even better technique of steel production, the open-hearth process. The Thomas-Gilchrist method, invented in 1878, made possible the use of phosphor-laden iron ore, which previously had been economically unfeasible. The results were dramatic. In Great Britain, steel production increased fourfold, and the price of steel fell by more than 50 percent. Increased steel production made possible the expansion of the rail system, the creation of a steamship fleet, and an explosive growth in the building industry. No longer was steel a rare alloy used only for the finest swords and knives; it became the material that defined the age.

Significant changes in the supply of credit further stimulated economic expansion. Discovery of gold in California and Australia led to the inflow of huge amounts of the precious metal to Europe, expanding the supply of money and credit. This led to the establishment of the modern banking system.

Each advance made possible further changes. Increased wealth and credit accelerated further expansion of industrial plants and the financing of an ambitious infrastructure system of roads, railroads, and steamships, which in turn boosted trade. Between 1800 and 1840, the value of world trade had doubled. In the twenty years following 1850, it increased by 260 percent.

By the 1880s important scientific discoveries increasingly fueled industrial improvements. Electricity began to be more widely used, replacing coal as a source of energy. Synthetic dyes revolutionized the textile industry, as did alkali in the manufacture of soap and glass.

This new era of prosperity and technical prowess celebrated itself at the Great International Exhibition at the Crystal Palace in London in 1851. Presided over by Queen Victoria's consort, Prince Albert, the exhibition was the first of many international expositions proudly displaying the new world of invention and plenty. Among the 100,000 objects the Crystal Palace proudly displayed were some of the newest products of the industrial age—turbine engines and sophisticated printing presses. The luxuries available to the wealthy classes were also displayed: fancy vases, overstuffed furniture, pianos, reproductions of various paintings and statuary from ancient and modern times, ranging from the sublime to the utterly garish. Although most visitors left with a great sense of pride in their contemporaries' accomplishments, there were also reasons for unease. The cannons of the Prussian arms manufacturer Krupp were part of the display, a grim reminder that industry was now producing instruments of death at record

The Crystal Palace The largest building made of glass and steel frame at the time, the Crystal Palace became a prototype for many buildings of the second half of the nineteenth century, such as railroad stations and department stores. The Crystal Palace symbolized the era of progress and its hopes for a world improved by technology. *(Courtesy of the Trustees of the British Museum)*

levels. The British part of the exposition proudly displayed an elephant and other exotic objects from Britain's empire in India—an empire acquired and maintained by force. Britain's ascendancy was ensured not only by its economic prowess but also by domination of other peoples.

Transportation and Communications

One of the principal reasons for the success of the Crystal Palace Exhibition was the railroad system, which brought huge numbers of provincials and foreigners to London. This system, begun in the first industrial revolution, grew dramatically in the middle decades of the nineteenth century. When the engineer Robert Stephenson (1803–1859) demonstrated the feasibility of the steam locomotive, the "Rocket," in 1829, it ran on a track that was one-and-a-half miles long. In 1840, Europe had a total of 1700 miles of rails. Ten years later, there were 14,500 miles, and by 1880 the total railroad mileage was 102,000 (Map 25.1). In 1888 the *Orient Express* line opened, linking Constantinople to Vienna and from there to the rest of Europe. Distance was conquered by speed as well: By midcentury trains ran 50 miles per hour, ten times as fast as when they were invented. The cost of rail transport steadily decreased, allowing in turn for its greater use. Between 1850 and 1880 in Germany, the number of rail passengers increased tenfold and the volume of goods eightyfold. In France and Great Britain, the increases were only slightly less impressive.

Nothing seemed to stop the rail lines. Even the Alps were pierced with railroad tunnels, eight miles long at Mont Cenis in 1870, and ten miles long at St. Gothard in 1882. Suspension bridges crossed rivers and other impasses; in England the Clifton Bridge, which opened in 1862 over the Avon River, was 245 feet high and

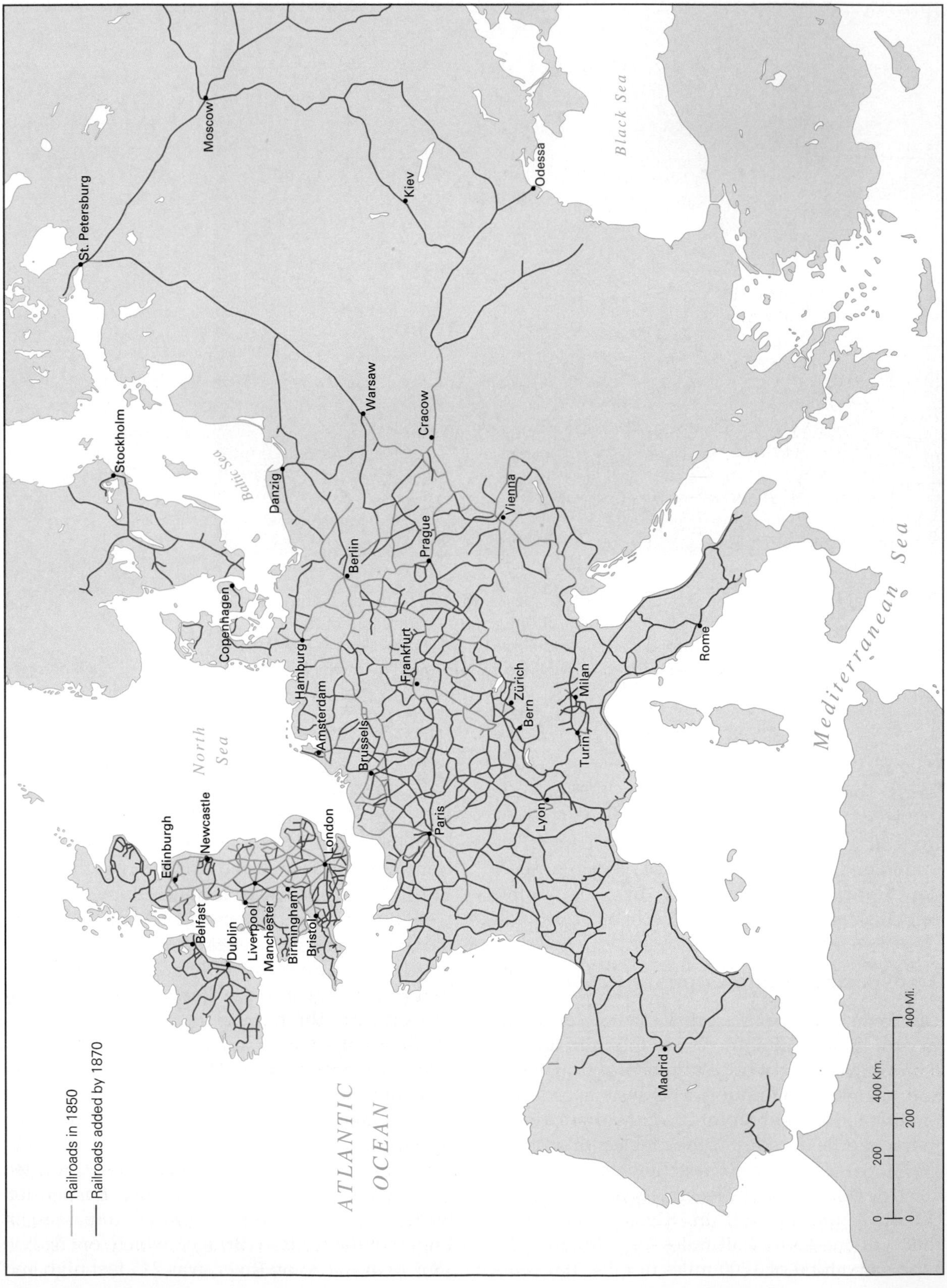
Railroads in 1850
Railroads added by 1870
ATLANTIC
OCEAN
North
Sea
Baltic Sea
Black Sea
Mediterranean Sea
St. Petersburg
Moscow
Kiev
Odessa
Stockholm
Warsaw
Cracow
Danzig
Berlin
Prague
Vienna
Copenhagen
Hamburg
Amsterdam
Brussels
Frankfurt
Zürich
Bern
Milan
Turin
Rome
Paris
Lyon
London
Edinburgh
Newcastle
Belfast
Dublin
Liverpool
Manchester
Birmingham
Bristol
Madrid
0
200
400 Km.
0
200
400 Mi.

The Railroad Inaugurates a New Age

William M. Thackeray (1811–1863), a journalist and one of the major Victorian novelists, founded **Cornhill Magazine** *in 1859. In this selection, he describes how the world has changed as a result of the introduction of railroads.*

The vision had disappeared off the silver, the images of youth and the past are vanishing away! We who have lived before railways were made, belong to another world. In how many hours could the Prince of Wales drive from Brighton to London, with a light carriage built expressly, and relays of horses longing to gallop the next stage? Do you remember Sir Somebody, the coachman of the Age, who took our half-crown so affably? It was only yesterday; but what a gulf between now and then! *Then* was the old World. . . . But your railroad starts the new era, and we of a certain age belong to the new time and the old one. We are of the time of chivalry. . . . We are of the age of steam. . . . Towards what new continent are we wending? to what new laws, new manners, new politics, vast new expanses of liberties unknown as yet, or only surmised? I used to know a man who had invented a flying-machine. "Sir," he would say, "give me but five hundred pounds, and I will make it. It is so simple of construction that I tremble daily lest some other person should light upon and patent my discovery." Perhaps faith was wanting; perhaps the five hundred pounds. He is dead, and somebody else must make the flying-machine. But that will only be a step forward on the journey already begun since we quitted the old world. . . .

We who lived before railways, and survive out of the ancient world, are like Father Noah and his family out of the Ark. . . . We who lived before railways are antediluvians—we must pass away. We are growing scarcer every day; and old—old—very old relicts of the times when George was still fighting the Dragon.

Source: William M. Thackeray, "De Juventute," in *Roundabout Papers* (New York: Worthington Co., 1891), pp. 57–58.

had a span of 702 feet. A new age had dawned, as the British novelist William Thackeray recognized (see the box, "The Railroad Inaugurates a New Age").

Ocean transportation also changed dramatically. In 1869, the Suez Canal opened, linking the Mediterranean to the Red Sea and the Indian Ocean. It reduced by 40 percent the distance between London and Bombay. More efficient ships were developed; by midcentury the clipper ship could cross the Atlantic in fourteen days. Steamships were also built, although they did not dominate ocean traffic until the 1890s. By 1880, European shipping carried nearly three times the cargo it had thirty years earlier.

The optimism born of conquering vast distance was reflected in a popular novel by the French writer Jules Verne (1828–1905), *Around the World in Eighty Days* (1873). The hero, Phineas Fogg, not only traveled by balloon and many other untraditional means, such as llama and ostrich, but also used the modern steam locomotive and the steamship to accomplish in eighty days a feat that took Magellan's crew nearly three years to complete in the sixteenth century. Even as late as the 1840s, prior to the steamship, locomotive, and the Suez Canal, such a trip would have taken at least eleven months.

Map 25.1 European Rails, 1850 and 1870 During the mid-nineteenth century, European states built railroads at an increasing rate, creating a dense network by the 1870s.

The Suez Canal Opened in 1869, the canal significantly shortened the voyage by ship from Europe to East Asia. The Suez Canal exemplified the speeding up of transportation and communication in the second half of the nineteenth century. *(Archiv für Kunst und Geschichte, Berlin)*

The new speed, plus advances in refrigeration, changed food transport. Formerly, refrigeration could be achieved only with natural ice, cut out of frozen ponds and lakes, but in the 1870s the introduction of mechanical ice-making machines that used ammonia made the process much less cumbersome. By the 1880s dairy products and meat were being transported vast distances by rail and even across the seas by ship. Thanks to these advances, the Americas and Australia, rich in grasslands, could not only feed themselves but also provide much of Europe's needs. Cheap transport lowered the cost of food and made possible a far more varied diet for Europeans.

Regular postal service was also a child of the new era of improved transportation. In 1840, Britain instituted a postage system based on standard rates. Replacing the earlier practice in which the recipient paid for the delivery of a letter, the British system enabled the sender to buy a stamp—priced at the low rate of one penny—and drop the letter into a mailbox. It was collected, transported speedily by the new railroads, and delivered. The efficiency and low cost of mail encouraged massive increase in its use. In Great Britain the number of letters mailed in a year increased from 7 per person per year in 1840 to 32 by 1880.

In the late 1830s the telegraph was invented, and by 1849 2,000 miles of telegraph wire were laid on the European continent. By 1859, the total was 42,000 miles; by 1864, 80,000. By 1865, transoceanic cables connected the Americas to Europe. Suddenly news from distant parts of the globe—of earthquakes, revolutions, or the outbreak of war—could reach Europe within minutes. In 1875, Alexander Graham Bell (1847–1922) invented a machine capable of transmitting the human voice by electrical impulses; in 1879 the first telephones were installed in Germany; two years later they appeared in France.

The speedy linking of distant areas within the nation and between nations called attention to the need to standardize time. Up to now, countries typically had innumerable time zones; each town established its time according to the location of the sun. Railroad traffic made these quaint differences a source of annoyance to travelers and railroad officials, and it became imperative to have a standard time for each nation. The electric telegraph made it possible to set that time to the second.

IMPROVEMENTS IN COMMUNICATIONS

1820s	The omnibus is introduced in France
1829	Robert Stephenson runs the "Rocket"
1833	Invention of the telegraph
1840	Introduction of the penny stamp
1850s	Clipper ships
	Invention of the tramway
1863	Building of underground railroad in London
1865	Transoceanic telegraph cable installed
1869	Opening of Suez Canal
1875	Alexander Graham Bell invents the telephone

Changing Conditions among Social Groups

Industrial advances transformed the traditional structure of European society. Fewer people worked the land; more worked in industry. Wealth became far less dependent on ownership of land. An individual could become wealthy by owning a factory or a bank, or by inventing a new machine. Thus the social and political influence of the landed aristocracy waned. To varying degrees, this influence now had to be shared with a growing middle class. Generally, life for both industrial and farm workers improved in this period. However, there were great disparities; many people continued to suffer from profound deprivation.

The Declining Aristocracy

Always a small, exclusive group, the European aristocracy in the nineteenth century represented less than 1 percent of the population. There were regional variations; in Bavaria and Bohemia, nobles accounted for less than one-tenth of 1 percent of the population, while in Hungary they represented 5 percent. Many of those of noble birth were quite poor and economically indistinguishable from their nonnoble neighbors. Others owned vast estates and were fabulously wealthy. The duke of Sutherland in Britain and the Esterhazy family in Hungary owned over one million acres; Count Orloff in Russia half that amount.

Some ennoblements were of recent origin. In England, most titles were less than a hundred years old, having originally been conferred to individuals honored for service to the state, the arts, or the economy. In France both Napoleons had ennobled persons they wished to honor. In Germany, Bismarck ennobled the Jewish banker Gerson Bleichröder (1822–1893) for helping finance the wars of the Prussian state and for relieving the German chancellor of personal financial worries by making profitable investments for him.

Distinctions between aristocrats and members of the upper middle class became increasingly blurred; noble families in financial straits often married their children to the offspring of wealthy merchants. And many nobles who previously had shunned manufacture participated in the new economy by becoming industrialists and bankers. Idle members of the nobility were now somewhat rare. Rather, they appeared eager to prove useful. Although many still lived on huge estates and enjoyed a lavish lifestyle, others were far more restrained than their ancestors and might be mistaken for successful business people.

In spite of these changes, nobles continued to play important roles in a number of countries. In Prussia, some of the wealthiest industrialists came from the highest aristocracy—among them Prince Henckel von Donnersmarck and the duke of Utjest. The heavily aristocratic officer corps played an important role in running the Prussian state and unified Germany. In France about a quarter to a fifth of French officers were aristocrats, and they were also visible in the diplomatic corps. In Britain officers, diplomats, and high-ranking civil servants were usually of noble birth.

In Austria and Russia, aristocratic origin was the norm for government service.

Despite the political egalitarianism that swept Europe in the aftermath of the French Revolution and the rapidly changing social structure engendered by industrialization, the power of the aristocracy did not disappear. Decline was slow, and the nobility survived by adopting new strategies, such as intermarrying with the upper ranks of the middle class or proving its usefulness through government service and participating in business and finance. Nonetheless, nobles no longer asserted privileges based exclusively on birth. In most European states such a claim had become an anachronism.

The Expanding Middle Classes

Up to the eighteenth century, society had been divided by legally separate orders based on birth. In the nineteenth century, it became more customary to classify people by their economic function. The "middle class" was the group that belonged neither to the nobility nor to the peasantry nor to the industrial working class. The term was amorphous, including people as diverse as wealthy manufacturers, country physicians, and bank tellers. Given this diversity, it has become common to use the plural and think of all these people as forming the "middle *classes.*" Another term frequently used to describe these classes is *bourgeois,* which originated in the twelfth and thirteenth centuries when a new wealthy class based on urban occupations emerged. Its members were called burghers, or bourgeois. The term was widely used in France beginning in the seventeenth century for the middle classes and in the nineteenth century it became interchangeable with "middle class."

The nineteenth century has often been described as "the bourgeois century." Although such a description may be too broad, certainly after the midcentury mark it is appropriate to use as a shorthand term to describe the dominance of the bourgeois elites. This situation was especially prevalent in western Europe, where the middle classes helped fashion much of society.

The middle classes expanded dramatically after the middle of the century. The increase in trade and manufacture spawned increased numbers of entrepreneurs and managers, while the development of a more complex society created the demand for more engineers, lawyers, accountants, and bankers. New standards of comfort and health demanded more merchants and doctors. Urban improvements in the generation after the midcentury mark created a need for architects, contractors, and speculators, among others.

The middle and lower levels of middle-class society grew most rapidly as business, the professions, and government administration created more jobs. In the 1870s, about 10 percent of urban working-class people reached lower-middle-class status by becoming storekeepers, lower civil servants, clerks, or salespeople.

Faster growth occurred for the white-collar workers than their blue-collar counterparts. As industries matured, the increasing use of machinery and better industrial organization meant that fewer additional workers and more clerks and bureaucrats were needed. Large import-export businesses, insurance companies, and department stores provided opportunities of this kind. So did the expansion of government services. In the second half of the nineteenth century, France increased its teacher corps by 80,000 and hired 50,000 more postal employees. The men and women staffing these new positions often came from modest backgrounds. For the son or daughter of peasants to become village postmaster, schoolteacher, or clerk in a major firm signified social ascension, however modest. And for the family, such a position, even more than income, meant joining the lower stratum of the middle class. That accessibility to its ranks was certainly one of the strengths of the middle class. It was an ever-growing class whose promise of social respectability and material comfort exercised a compelling force of attraction over the lower classes.

In midcentury Britain the middle class represented 15 percent of the population; by 1881, 25 percent. Elsewhere, the proportion was lower; in 1881 in Italy the middle classes represented 7 percent of the population, in France, 14 percent, but there also it was growing in number and well-being as the economy expanded.

A growing subgroup of the middle classes consisted of members of the professions, those whose prestige rested on the claim of exclusive expertise in a particular field. In the early nineteenth century, requirements for exercising a profession varied, depending on the country. In France and Prussia, for example, government regulation stipulated the necessary qualifications to practice medicine; in England anyone might practice it, although at his own risk. As the professions attempted to create a monopoly for themselves and eliminate rivals, they established more standards and requisites. Medical doctors, for instance, began requiring specialized education to distinguish themselves from herbalists, midwives, bone-setters, healers, and other rivals, and insisted on their exclusive right to exercise their profession.

Although the professionalization of medicine did not create better doctors immediately, as the science of medicine taught at universities improved, so did the preparation and expertise of doctors. Similarly, in other professions, such as law, architecture, and engineering, common standards and requirements facilitated professional practice. By midcentury either professional associations or the state itself accredited members of the professions. Women had limited access to these professions; typically their opportunities were confined to lower teaching positions. After the Crimean War, as a result of Florence Nightingale's efforts, nursing became an increasingly popular profession for women.

The growing role of the state in society led to the growth of bureaucracies. Increasingly, civil servants were selected by merit rather than through patronage. By the eighteenth century, Prussia had instituted a civil service examination system. After the Revolution, France instituted educational requirements for certain government corps; and by the 1880s it established civil service exams for the rest of government service. Beginning in 1870, Britain introduced the civil service examination and eliminated patronage.

Middle-Class Lifestyles

The standard of living of the growing middle classes varied considerably, from the wealthy entrepreneur who bought a chateau, or had a copy of one built, to the bourgeois who dwelled in a modest apartment. But they all lived in new standards of comfort. Their homes had running water, upholstered furniture, and enough space to provide separate sleeping and living quarters. They had several changes of clothing and consumed a varied diet that included meat and dairy products, sugar, coffee, and tea. They read books and subscribed to newspapers and journals. They were taken care of by servants.

Having at least one servant was a requisite for anyone who wished to be counted among the middle class. Most servants were female, and they were often seriously disadvantaged. Their hours were overly long: A six-and-one-half-day week was not uncommon. Housed in either the basement or the attic, servants experienced extremes of cold, heat, and humidity. Often young and vulnerable, they were frequently subjected to physical or sexual abuse by the the master of the house, his sons, or the head of the domestic staff. A good proportion of the rise in urban illegitimacy came from domestic servants. Many servants were fired when they became pregnant, others abandoned their children, and the most desperate resorted to infanticide. Certainly not all servants were subject to such a fate, and for all its risks, domestic employment was an attractive form of employment for impoverished rural women. It provided free housing, food, and

Servants in a Middle-Class Home The prosperity of this home is revealed by its having at least four servants. The butler, the only male in this picture, received higher pay and status than the women domestics. The clock on the wall suggests that this home was run with attention to punctuality. *(From* A Hundred Years Ago, *Colin Ford and Brian Harrison [B. T. Batsford, Inc.])*

clothing and allowed the servant to save a sum equivalent to an amount between one-third and one-half of a worker's yearly wages. These savings often served as a dowry and allowed the young woman to make an advantageous match.

By the beginning of the twentieth century, servants were still common among bourgeois households, but they were fewer in proportion to the population as a whole. In 1861 in Barmen, Germany (present-day Wuppertal), 16 percent of the population consisted of domestics; by 1911 it was but 2.5 percent. As various service industries developed, the need for servants decreased. With the growth of cab services, for instance, a family could dispense with a coachman and stable boy. And many families went without servants. Toward the end of the century, domestics' wages rose as competing forms of employment vied for their service, and only the upper layers of the bourgeoisie still employed domestic help.

In a number of cities suburban living became fashionable. The wealthy lived in large, imposing houses; the less well-off lived in smaller houses with a garden for privacy and quiet. Some owned two homes—one in the city and one in the countryside, providing respite from the rushed urban environment.

For further relief from the crowded cities, visits to resorts became popular. Throughout Europe, resort towns sprang up, devoted principally to the amusement of the well-off. It became fashionable to "take the waters"—bathing in hot springs and drinking the mineral waters thought to have special attributes—and gamble in resorts such as Baden-Baden in Germany and Vichy in France. For the first time, tourism became big business. Thomas Cook (1808–1892), an Englishman, organized tours to the Crystal Palace exhibition. Discovering the large market for travel tours, he began running tours in England and on the Continent. In the eighteenth century the European tour had been a custom of the aristocracy, but now many members of the middle classes demanded this experience as well. They visited the monuments, museums, and sights their guidebook told them were required viewing. Beginning in 1835, a German publisher, Karl Baedeker (1801–1859), issued a successful tourist guide to the Rhine, followed by guidebooks to various European countries and the Middle East. The Baedeker guides were eagerly purchased and provided the pattern for the multitude of guidebooks that followed.

The middle classes shared certain attitudes about the conduct of their lives. They believed their successes were due not to birth but to talent and effort. They wanted to be judged by their merits, and they expected their members to abide by strict moral principles. Their lives were supposed to be disciplined, especially with regard to sex and drink. The age was called "Victorian" because the middle class in Britain saw in the queen who reigned for two-thirds of the century a reflection of their own values. "Victorian morality," preached but not always practiced, was often seen as hypocritical. Yet as the middle classes increasingly dominated society, their values became the social norms. Public drunkenness was discouraged, and anti-alcoholic movements vigorously campaigned against drinking. Public festivals were regulated, making them more respectable and less rowdy. In several countries, societies for the protection of animals agitated against blood sports such as cock and bull fights.

In spite of their differences in education, wealth, and social standing, most of the bourgeoisie could be distinguished by common dress and common habits of speech and general deportment. Bourgeois men dressed somberly, in dark colors, avoiding any outward signs of luxury. Clothing that fit closely and avoided decoration reflected an adjustment to the machine age, where such dress hampered activity. It also reflected a conscious attempt to emphasize the frugal and achievement-oriented attitudes of the bourgeois in contrast to what was seen as the frivolous nobility.

Bourgeois conventions regarding women's dress were less reserved. Extravagant amounts of colorful cloth used to fashion huge, beribboned hoop dresses reflected the newfound wealth of the middle classes and confirmed their view of women as ornaments whose lives were to be limited to the home and facilitated by servants. This era was dominated by domesticity, by the ideal of the home. The wife was to provide her family a shelter from the storms of daily life (see the box, "Advice on Running the Middle-Class Household"). While the man was out in the secular world earning a living and advancing his career, the bourgeois woman was to run her household. She decorated the house, changed curtains with

Advice on Running the Middle-Class Household

In 1861, Isabella Mary Mayson Beeton (1836–1865) published **Mrs. Beeton's Book of Household Management,** *which was outsold only by the Bible. The popular book provided middle-class women advice on running their households and reflected the values they held on discipline, frugality, and cleanliness.*

As with the commander of an army, or the leader of an enterprise, so is it with the mistress of a house. Her spirit will be seen through the whole establishment; and just in proportion as she performs her duties intelligently and thoroughly, so will her domestics follow in her path. Of all those acquirements, which more particularly belong to the feminine character, there are none which take a higher rank, in our estimation, than such as enter into a knowledge of household duties; for on these are perpetually dependent the happiness, comfort, and well-being of a family. . . .

Early rising is one of the most essential qualities which enter into good Household Management, as it is not only the parent of health, but of innumerable other advantages.

Cleanliness is indispensable to health, and must be studied both in regard to the person and the house, and all that it contains. . . .

Frugality and economy are home virtues, without which no household can prosper. . . .

A housekeeping account-book should invariably be kept, and kept punctually and precisely.

Source: Isabelle Mary Mayson Beeton, *Mrs. Beeton's Book of Household Management* (London: S. O. Beeton, 1861), pp. 1, 2, 6.

the seasons and the styles, supervised the servants, kept the accounts, supervised the children's homework and religious education, and was involved in charitable works. In the decades around the midcentury, the assumption that there were two separate spheres—one male and public, the other female and private—reached its apogee.

In spite of the relatively passive role assigned to women, many bourgeois women were, of course, very active. Many were involved in philanthropic causes, helping the sick and the poor. In England, Josephine Grey Butler (1828–1906), a member of a family of reformers, fought for the spread of education to impoverished women. She also waged a fierce battle against prostitution.

Many bourgeois women also helped their husbands or fathers in the office, the business, or the writing of scientific treatises. Others achieved success in their own terms, running their own businesses, writing, painting, teaching. Many knew how to take advantage of the very impediments placed in their way. Rosa Bonheur (1822–1899), who because of her gender was not allowed to attend nude sketching sessions at her art school, concentrated on painting animals and became the best-known painter of domestic animals in the nineteenth century.

Expanding businesses and school systems provided some employment opportunities for women; by the 1890s, two-thirds of primary school teachers in England and half the post office staff in France were women. Slowly, secondary and university education was made available to young women. In Europe the first university to admit women was the University of Zurich in Switzerland in 1865. Although British universities admitted women, the University of London did not grant them degrees until after 1878, and the most prestigious British institutions, Oxford and Cambridge, did not grant degrees to women until after World War I. In spite of discriminatory laws, harassment by male students, and intitial obstruction by professional

Josephine Grey Butler An important Victorian reformer, Butler agitated for several causes, most notably abolition of the Contagious Diseases Act. This act empowered the police to arrest any woman it suspected of prostitution and to force her to be examined for venereal disease. Largely as a result of Butler's efforts, this act was repealed in 1886. *(Fawcett Library/Mary Evans Picture Library)*

and accrediting groups, there were a few female doctors and lawyers in England by the 1870s and on the Continent in the following decades.

Symbolic of the developing consumer interest among the middle classes was the department store, introduced in Paris in 1852. It had the advantage of sheltering under one roof a large assortment of goods that previously were available only in separate specialty stores. The price of each item was marked, avoiding the endless haggling that occurred in the market. The stores bought goods in mass and thus could sell them at low prices. The first department store in Paris, which served as a model for others in France and abroad, was named "Bon Marché" (the good buy). Filled with items of all sorts for the comforts of the emerging bourgeoisie, the department store was a symbol of the new opulence of the middle classes and created standards of consumption for them and those less fortunate who wished to emulate them.

The department store would not have been possible in another age. Thus, it serves as a summary of the various technical and social changes in the more prosperous parts of Europe at this period. Industrial innovation had lowered the price of glass and steel, so that these new, huge commercial emporiums could be built at reasonable cost. Railroads brought customers from outside the city and trams and omnibuses from within it (see page 937). The new penny press provided advertising for the department store, which in turn supported the emergence of this new medium. The expansion of the postal system facilitated catalog sales and the mailing of goods to customers. And the generally higher incomes available to Europeans allowed them to purchase more than just the necessities. A phenomenon began that became predominant in the West a century later—the consumer society.

The Workers' Lot

The increased prosperity and greater productivity of the period gradually improved the conditions of workers in the generation after 1850. Their wages and standard of living rose, and they enjoyed more job security. In Britain the earning power of the average worker rose by one-third between 1850 and 1875.

The workers' increased income enabled them to enjoy a better diet. In France the average number of calories consumed per adult male increased by one-third between 1840 and 1890. In Britain, between 1844 and 1876, per capita consumption of tea tripled, that of sugar quadrupled. The quality of food as well as the amount also improved; people consumed more meat, fish, eggs, and dairy products.

For the first time, workers were able to put money aside to tide them over in hard times. By 1870, two million Frenchmen had savings accounts. By the 1860s, one million people in England subscribed to post office savings accounts established especially for those of limited means.

Legislation gradually reduced the length of the workweek. The British workweek, which typically had been 73 hours in the 1840s, was reduced to 56 hours in 1874. In France it was reduced to 10 hours a day, in Germany to 11. But these improvements were accompanied by an increased emphasis on efficiency at the workplace. Fewer informal breaks were allowed as industrialists insisted on greater worker efficiency. New machines increased the tempo of work, frequently leading to accidents and exhaustion.

Such transformations were accompanied by changes in workers' leisure patterns. Some types of leisure that previously had been limited to the upper classes became available to workers. The introduction of rail connections to resort towns such as Brighton in England or Trouville and Dieppe in France enabled workers to visit such places on excursion trips. Workers had more spending money, and new music and dance halls, popular theaters, and other forms of public entertainment sprang up in response.

Although workers knew their lot had improved, they were also aware that a vast gulf still existed between them and the middle and upper classes. In the 1880s in the northern French industrial city of Lille, the combined estate of 20,000 workers equaled that of an average industrialist. In Paris the gluttonous rich ate multicourse meals; the leftover scraps from their plates found a ready market among the poor, who bought them for a few centimes from specialized vendors. Life expectancies still varied dramatically according to income; in Berlin in the mid-1850s life expectancy for the middle-class person was 54, for a laborer it was 42.

Although a few members of the working class were able to improve their condition by entering the lower levels of the middle class, most remained mired in the same profession as their fathers and grandfathers. Poverty was still pervasive. In the 1880s about one-third of Londoners were living at or below the subsistence level. Various industrial and urban diseases, such as tuberculosis, were common among workers. Compared to the healthier, better-fed, and better-housed middle classes, the workers continued living in shabby and limited circumstances.

The Transformation of the Countryside

Before the nineteenth century, change in the countryside had been nearly imperceptible, but beginning in midcentury it was radically transformed. Especially in western Europe, an increasing number of people left the land. In 1850, one-fifth the population of Britain was in agriculture; by 1881 only 11 percent were. The decrease of the agricultural population led in many places to labor shortages and therefore higher wages for farm hands.

Agriculture became increasingly efficient, and the food supply increased significantly. Fewer people working the land fed more people. The population of Europe nearly doubled in the years between 1800 and 1880, and yet it was fed better than ever before. More land was put under the plow. Sweden's acreage more than doubled, Italy's grew more than one-half, Germany's and Hungary's by more than one-third. In Italy and Denmark, land was reclaimed from marshes, in Holland from the North Sea. Not only was more land cultivated but the yield per acre increased. In 1760 an agricultural worker in England could feed himself and one other person; by 1841 he could feed himself and 2.7 others. The German population grew by 59 percent between 1816 and 1865, but agricultural output grew twice as fast.

These higher yields were due to an increased use of manure, augmented in the 1870s by saltpeter imported from Chile and, beginning in the 1880s, by chemical fertilizers manufactured in Europe. Innovations in tools also improved productivity. The sickle, which required the laborer to crouch to cut the grass or wheat, was replaced by the long-handled scythe, which allowed the field hand to stand and use the full weight of the body to swing the instrument through the grain. This new method increased efficiency fourfold. And in the 1850s steam-driven threshing machinery was introduced in some parts of western Europe. Industrial labor-organization techniques, the insistence on regularity in the workplace, and specialization also contributed to greater productivity on the land.

Improved roads and dramatically expanded rail lines enabled farmers to extend their markets. No longer did they need to produce only for the local area; they could depend on a national market and beyond for customers. In Brittany, in western France, a rail line to Paris led to a rapid increase in dairy cattle. The demand for farm products rose, and so did the price on many items, thus improving the lot of the farmer.

While the prices of farm products rose, that of industrial products fell, so farmers could pur-

Steam-powered Thresher This image shows the thresher being operated in the French countryside in 1860. It would be decades before this kind of technology became a common sight in Europe, but it was already a harbinger of the change coming to the rural world. *(Bibliothèque Nationale)*

chase machinery to work the farm and also items providing personal comfort and convenience such as cast-iron stoves. Medium and larger farmers did particularly well. For the first time, many had credit available to them, and some of the vagaries of farming were buffered by the availability of fire and weather insurance.

Life in the countryside became less insular. Not only did rail lines connect the farm to the city, but a national school system brought teachers into the village. Local dialects and in some cases even distinct languages that peasants had spoken for generations were replaced by a standardized national language. Postal systems brought catalogs of consumer goods from the cities to the countryside. Local provincial costumes became less common as styles adopted in the cities spread to the countryside via these catalogs. The farm girls who went to the cities as maids to work in middle-class homes returned to the village with urban and middle-class notions of comfort. The military draft brought the young men of the village into contact with urban folk and further spread urban values to the countryside.

These trends had a striking effect in western Europe. Eastern Europe, in contrast, was hardly touched at all by them. In Russia agriculture remained backward; the average yield per acre in 1880 was one-quarter that of Great Britain. There was a large surplus of population on the land that was underemployed and contributed little to the rural economy. In the Balkans, most peasants were landless and heavily indebted; many lived isolated and unaffected by the forces of modernity.

Urban Problems and Solutions

By 1851 the majority of English people lived in cities; by 1891 the majority of Germans. In 1850, 400,000 people lived in Berlin; the number doubled in the next twenty years and yet again in the next twenty years, reaching 1.6 million in 1890. Although London's rate of growth slowed after midcentury, no other city saw as large an addition of people—1.9 million. To cope with urban growth and its attendant problems—epidemics, crowding, traffic jams—cities developed public health measures and introduced planning and rebuilding programs. They adapted the new technologies to provide such urban amenities as streetlights, public transportation, water and sewer systems, and police forces. Cities gradually became safer and more pleasant places to live.

City Planning and Urban Renovation

Most of Europe's cities had begun as medieval walled cities and had grown haphazardly into major industrial centers. Their narrow, crooked streets could not accommodate the increased trade and daily movement of goods and people, and traffic snarls were common. City officials began to recognize that broad, straight avenues would resolve the traffic problem and also bring sunlight and fresh air into the narrow and perpetually dank lanes and alleys. In the 1820s, London saw the first ambitious street-widening initiative. On Regency Street, old hovels were torn down and replaced with fancy new houses; the poor were usually displaced. Later projects followed this pattern.

The most extensive program of urban rebuilding took place in midcentury Paris. Over a period of eighteen years, Napoleon III and his aide, Baron Georges Haussmann (1809–1891), transformed Paris from a dirty medieval city to a beautiful modern one. Broad, straight avenues were carved through what had been dingy slums. The avenues were lined with trees and graced with elegant houses. Enhancing the city were public monuments and buildings, such as the new opera house. The tremendous costs of this ambitious scheme kept the city of Paris in debt for decades. In addition, the slum-removal program drove tens of thousands of the poorest out of the city to its outskirts, leading to greater social segregation than had previously been the case. (See the feature, "Weighing the Evidence: A Map of Haussmann's Paris," on pages 952–953.)

Haussmann's extensive work in Paris served as a model for other cities, and although none rebuilt as extensively, many made signficant improvements. Many European cities began to reflect a beauty and order that they had previously lacked.

The Introduction of Public Services

Beginning in midcentury, government at the central and local level helped make cities more livable by legislating sanitary reforms and providing public transportation and lighting. Medical practitioners in the 1820s had observed that disease and higher mortality were related to dirt and

The Ringstrasse, Vienna To provide easier transportation in a congested city, the Austrian government destroyed the fortifications surrounding the city and in their place built a ring-like broad avenue with elegant public buildings and private mansions. *(Historisches Museen der Stadt, Wien)*

lack of clean air, water, and sunshine. Since diseases spreading from the poorer quarters of town threatened the rich and powerful, there was a general interest in improving public health by clearing slums, broadening streets, and supplying clean air and water to the cities.

As with other reforms, England led the way. The foremost sanitary reformer was the lawyer and civil servant Edwin Chadwick (1800–1895), who authored important reforms that became the basis for legislation. The Public Health Bill of 1848 established national standards for urban sanitation and required cities to regulate the installation of sewers and the disposal of refuse. The 1875 Health Act required cities to maintain certain basic health standards such as water and drainage. Armed with these laws, local municipalities took the initiative: The city of Birmingham cleared fifty acres of slums in the 1870s, for example. Sanitary reform laws in France were less progressive than in England but also moved in the direction of improved urban sanitation. An 1850 law, for example, allowed cities to regulate the quality of rental housing.

London was also a leader in supplying public water. Paris and many other cities copied London in extending such services. Berlin had a municipal water system in 1850, but it took several decades before clean water was available in every household. As late as the 1870s, Berlin's sewage was carried in open pipes. In Paris, which typically led France in innovations, 60 percent of the houses had running water in 1882. The French capital did not have a unitary sewer system until the 1890s.

As running water into the home became a standard rather than a luxury, bathing became more common. The English upper classes had learned the habit of daily baths from their colonial experience in India; on the Continent it was not the custom until about the third quarter of the nineteenth century. French artist Edgar Degas (1834–1917) frequently painted bath scenes portraying the new European habit.

All these changes had a direct impact on the lives of city dwellers. Life became healthier, more comfortable, and more orderly. Between the 1840s and 1880, London's death rate fell from 26 per thousand to 20 per thousand. In Paris for the same period the decline was from 29.3 to 23.7 per thousand. There was a more immediate decline in the incidence of diseases associated with filthy living conditions. Improved water supplies provided a cleaner environment and reduced the prevalence of water-borne diseases such as cholera and typhoid.

Other improvements also contributed to an improved quality of life. With the introduction of urban transportation, city dwellers no longer had to live within walking distance of their work.

Public Transportation in Berlin A few years after this photograph was taken, horses were dispensed with, as trams were electrified and buses were motorized.
(Landesbildstelle, Berlin)

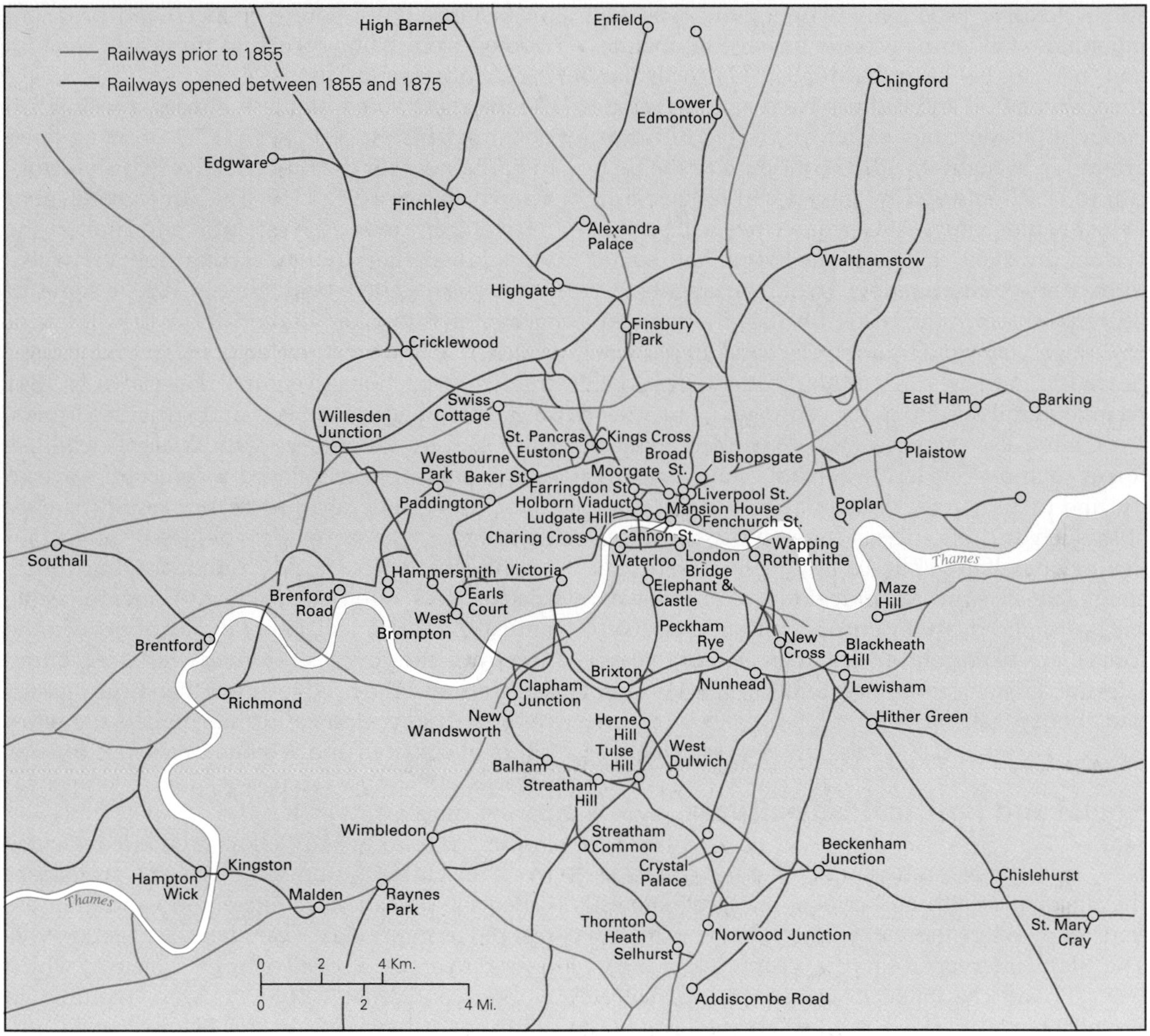

Map 25.2 The Development of London Railways, 1855–1875 The British capital became the railhead for a growing number of rail lines. To connect the many railroad stations, an underground, or subway, was built. (*Source: Mid-Victorian Britain, 1851–1875,* by Geoffrey Best. Copyright © 1972. Used by kind permission of Weidenfeld & Nicolson.)

This led to a decrease in population density and eventually helped make the city a healthier place to live. In the 1820s France instituted omnibus service, a system of horse-drawn carriages available to the public on fixed routes. Other cities followed—Hamburg in 1843, Berlin in 1846. In the 1850s the tram was introduced. A carriage drawn on a rail line, it could pull larger loads of passengers faster than the omnibus. Because of the many rail stations in London and the difficulty of quickly getting from one station to another, London built an underground railway in 1863, the predecessor of the subway system (Map 25.2).

These improvements enabled workers to move out of the inner city and relocate to the less dense and less expensive suburbs. The bicycle also became a serious means of transportation for some city dwellers. By the mid-1880s, there were nearly 100,000 bicycles in Great Britain.

Street lighting by oil had been introduced in the eighteenth century in major cities, but it was still a luxury, used only when there was no moonlight. Oil lamps were expensive to operate and had to be lit individually. Gas was far cheaper than oil and did not need as much care. Gaslights made cities easier and safer to move around in at night. In 1813, London was the first city to be illuminated by gas; Berlin followed in 1816; by midcentury 34 German cities had such a system; by 1860, 250 German towns had some form of street illumination. The first gaslights appeared in Paris in the 1820s, by 1844 the city had 65,000 gas lamps. The first electrical lights appeared in Paris in 1875, although they were not common until the end of the century.

Cities also significantly expanded police forces to impose order, to control criminal activity, and to discourage behavior deemed undesirable, such as dumping garbage on the street, relieving oneself in public, or singing loud, raucous songs late at night. At midcentury, London was the best-policed city in Europe with a 5,000-man force. Paris had around 3,000 men. Twenty years later the French capital had 6,000, while London had about 8,000.

Social and Political Initiatives

New institutions and groups emerged to tackle the unequal wealth and critical urban problems that followed in the wake of economic growth. The state intervened in the economy in new ways. Private charitable groups sprang up. And a Socialist party emerged, exclusively dedicated to ameliorating the lot of the worker.

State Intervention in Welfare

The difficult conditions industry imposed on workers led to debates in several countries about the need for the state to protect the workers. The growing militancy of organized labor also seemed to make it imperative for the established authority to meet the workers' needs. Some found it difficult to justify government intervention in the free operation of market forces. The conditions of work, like the price of goods, they believed, could best be regulated by the laws of supply and demand; the state ought to remain aloof from all economic transactions. But the laws of supply and demand proved unable to prevent, for instance, very young children and pregnant women from being forced to do heavy work in the factories and mines.

To right some of these abuses, the English philanthropist Robert Owen (1771–1858) agitated in Parliament for the first effective British factory act, which passed in 1819. This act forbade labor for children under the age of 9 and limited the workday of children over that age to twelve hours a day. Then, beginning in 1833, a series of factory acts further limited the work hours of children and women in factories and mines and funded inspections to enforce these laws. In 1841 in France, medical experts and social reformers, provoked by the widespread physical debilities among children, convinced a reluctant government to legislate against factory work for children under 8 and provide a degree of protection for those between 8 and 16. But no funding for inspectors was voted, so the law was unenforceable until 1874, when legislators finally approved the necessary funding. Confronted with a declining birthrate and the need to strengthen itself against rival Germany, France further limited the work hours of children and women in a series of laws between 1892 and 1905. Workmen's compensation became law in 1898.

In Prussia, an 1839 law prohibited factory work for children under the age of 9 and established the precedent for state intervention in the rest of Germany. Ten years later, legislation was passed to create a social security system to which workers and their employers were required to contribute. Beginning in the 1840s, Prussia limited a city's right to refuse welfare support to its poor. Laws passed in the 1890s protected workers from harsh conditions and limited the hours of women.

States also became involved in the fight against disease and epidemics. Norway and Sweden introduced mandatory vaccination for smallpox in 1810 and 1816, respectively. England followed in 1867 and Germany in the 1870s.

Fear of social upheaval and the rising strength of socialist political parties also prompted governments to act. In France moderate bourgeois liberals attempted to defuse class war by advocating "Solidarism," insisting on the responsibility of each class and individual for its fellow citizens. In Germany, after unification, the government wanted to show workers the benefits

Bismarck Favors Social Reforms

In 1881, Bismarck submitted to the parliament a law insuring all mine and factory workers with annual income of less than 2000 marks against accidents. This was followed by the Sickness Insurance Law of 1884 and the Old Age and Invalidity Law of 1887. Having banned the Socialist party in 1878, Bismarck decided it was important to introduce measures that signaled concern for the workers. This mixture of humanitarian concern and political calculation is shown in this 1881 speech introducing the first of these reforms.

For the last fifty years we have been talking about the social question. Since the Socialist Law was passed, I have been repeatedly reminded, in high quarters as well as low, of promise I then gave that something positive should be done to remove the causes of Socialism. . . .

Whosoever has looked closely into the state of the poor in large towns, or into the arrangements made for paupers in country communes, and has seen for himself how—even in the best-managed villages—a poor wretch is sometimes treated when weakly and crippled, must admit that any healthy operative, contemplating that spectacle, is fully justified in exclaiming: "It is simply horrible that a human being should be treated worse than a dog in his own house!" I say, therefore, our first object in bringing forward this bill is to ensure kindlier treatment to this class of the poor. . . .

Source: Moritz Busch, *Bismarck,* vol. 2, trans. William Beatty-Kingston (New York: Scribner, 1891), pp. 219–223.

they could gain from the new state so they would abandon the growing Socialist party and support the kaiser's government. It embarked on a deliberate program to tame the workers and win their support for the existing political and economic institutions. Thus, in the 1880s the new German government provided a comprehensive welfare plan that included health insurance and old-age pensions (see the box, "Bismarck Favors Social Reforms"). Although local governments in many European states had provided welfare services in various forms, Germany was the first to recognize a national responsibility, and German social programs became models for the rest of Europe.

In addition to the welfare initiatives by state and city governments, middle and upper classes worked to better the workers' lot. Concern among these groups and individuals arose from a mixture of pity for workers' condition, religious teachings about their responsibilities for the less fortunate, and fear of the consequences of unrelieved misery. In Paris, for example, three thousand private charitable organizations were founded between 1840 and 1900; their combined outlay in aid equaled the public charity available. In London, in 1890 six million pounds, more than the total budget of many European states, was employed on behalf of the poor.

Women contributed heavily to volunteer charity work. By the end of the nineteenth century, as many as half a million English women contributed their time to provide charity to the less fortunate. In Sweden by the 1880s, women had founded refuges for the destitute, old-age homes, a children's hospital, an asylum for the mentally handicapped, and various societies to promote female industry. In Spain various religious orders, devoted to provide free education to the poor, flourished in the 1880s.

In Catholic and Protestant countries, the Christian churches traditionally had identified with the rights of employers and seemed to ignore the lot of the workers. However, a number of Christians, lay and clerical, began to emphasize the need to address social issues. In Germany, Bishop Wilhelm Von Ketteler (1811–1877) preached the need for the well-off to take responsibility for the less privileged. His message was taken up in France, Italy, and Spain among what became known as "social Catholics." In England, Protestants' concern for the poor was demonstrated by the founding of the Salvation Army in 1878. Religious groups also hoped they could win converts by demonstrating their concern to the less privileged.

Increasingly, states, municipalities, volunteer groups, and churches accepted responsibility for the well-being of their peoples. This trend marked the beginning of an evolution that would eventually spread in scope and lead to the welfare state in much of twentieth-century Europe.

Educational and Cultural Opportunities

At the beginning of the century, governments took little responsibility for providing education. The upper classes educated their children with private tutors, parents from more modest economic groups taught their children the little they knew, and the poor attended the few schools—usually one-room schools—provided by charitable and religious groups. In England the education of the masses became a national responsibility after the Second Reform Bill of 1867. This legislation extended the vote to the artisan classes and prompted a movement to ensure that the new voters were educated. In 1870 the English government began to provide significant subsidies for education, to set educational standards, and to provide a national inspection system to enforce them. England and France initiated mandatory primary school education in the 1880s. In Britain, one million children attended school in 1865; by 1880 more than three million attended.

Public education included not only reading, writing and arithmetic but other skills as well. By insisting on punctuality, on carrying out repetitive skills such as copying letters, words, or sentences, schools made it easier for people to fit into the emerging industrial society. Obedience and the respect for authority learned at school shaped the soldiers and factory workers of the future. And regardless of political inclination, each regime took advantage of its control of the educational system to inculcate in the young the love of country and of its form of government.

Secondary education was, on the whole, available only to the privileged few in the upper middle classes. It confirmed their social status and won them access to the universities and the professions. To a very small number from the lower middle classes, secondary school attendance provided the means to ascend socially. University education validated the positions of sons of the elite and offered access to positions of influence for the sons of the middle class. The lower middle class was sparsely represented in universities, and the children of workers and peasants were totally absent.

Public education occurred not only in the schools but also through other institutions, which made culture available to the masses in new ways. Between 1840 and 1880, the number of large libraries in Europe increased from 40 to 500; and by the late 1870s England had over 66 public lending libraries. The French national public library, the Bibliothèque nationale, was established in Paris in the 1860s. The building, constructed of iron and glass, was considered radical at the time. It was an impressive monument to the desire to make reading available to an expanded public. Many provincial cities, as well as the glittering capitals of Europe, were also endowed with new libraries.

Museums and art galleries, which in the previous century had been open only to a select few, gradually became accessible to the general public. The first museum to open to the public was the Louvre in Paris after the French Revolution. The rest of Europe lagged behind in making the cultural heritage available to the masses. The British Museum was extremely restrictive; only the wealthy and the well-connected could gain access, for there was widespread fear of the possible disorder and destruction that the "vulgar classes" might cause if they were allowed to visit the galleries of the British Museum. But the sedate manner in which the crowds behaved during the Crystal Palace exposition reassured the authorities, and finally in 1879 the museum was opened daily without restrictions.

Culture in an Age of Optimism

The improving economic and material conditions buoyed European thinkers. Many believed that men and women were becoming more enlightened, and they expressed faith in humankind's ability to transform the world with new scientific and technical breakthroughs. The world seemed knowable and perfectible. This new faith both undermined the certainties of traditional religion and advanced secularism. The arts reflected these new values, too, emphasizing realism and science—as well as an underlying foreboding of the dark side of this "age of optimism."

Darwin and the Doctrine of Evolution

By midcentury, most thinkers accepted the notion of change and transformation of society—and by analogy of the natural environment. The French thinker Auguste Comte (1798–1857) championed the notion that human progress proceeded by developmental stages. Human progress was a law of nature leading men and women irresistibly to the final and highest stage of development, the positive, or scientific stage. Widely read throughout Europe and Latin America, Comte's writings helped gird the era's faith in science, and the very progress science made seemed to confirm its precepts. Comte's philosophy, which he called positivism, dominated the era. While the romantics had emphasized feeling, positivists upheld the significance of the measurable, the palpable, that which could be scientifically understood. Their methods, they were confident, would assure the continued progress of mankind. Science had proven that the world was evolving to ever higher forms.

In the field of geology, the Englishman Charles Lyell (1797–1875) maintained that the earth was far older than the biblical story of Genesis suggested. He argued that its geological formations—the mountains, valleys, and seas—had been subject to natural forces that, over hundreds of thousands, even millions, of years, had transformed them. Most educated people accepted his theory, which led many to wonder if it might also be true that the animal kingdom had evolved gradually over long periods of time.

Charles Darwin With the publication of *On the Origin of Species by Means of Natural Selection* (1859), Darwin provided a grand interpretation of how species evolved. The dramatic breakthrough made by observation and study won him fame as a scientist. He is undoubtedly the dominating scientific figure of the nineteenth century. *(The Mansell Collection)*

Although evolution in the biological realm had been suggested as early as the end of the eighteenth century, Charles Darwin (1809–1882) was the first to offer a plausible explanation of the process. As the naturalist on an official British scientific expedition in the 1830s, he had visited the Galápagos Islands off the coast of South America. On these islands he found species similar to but different from those on the mainland and even different from each other. Could they be the result of separate creation? Or was it more likely that in varying environments they had adapted differently? Darwin theorized that species that are closely related compete for food and living space. In this struggle, those in each species that are better adapted to the environment have the

Darwin's Basic Laws of Evolution

In **On the Origin of Species by Means of Natural Selection** *(1859) Darwin explained his theories of evolution. Writing in an age of vast transformations, he could imagine the mutability of all nature, including species, over time. And, like his contemporaries, he could imagine that evolution would lead to improvement, to increasing "perfection" of various species.*

A religious man, who lost much of his faith as a result of his scientific work, he was anxious to reassure Christians that evolution could be seen as part of the divine plan.

Nothing at first can appear more difficult to believe than that the more complex organs and instincts have been perfected, not by means superior to, though analogous with, human reason, but by the accumulation of innumerable slight variations, each good for the individual possessor. Nevertheless, this difficulty, though appearing to our imagination insuperably great, cannot be considered real if we admit the following propositions, namely, that all parts of the organisation and instincts offer, at least, individual differences—that there is a struggle for existence leading to the preservation of profitable deviations of structure or instinct—and, lastly, that gradations in the state of perfection of each organ may have existed, each good of its kind. The truth of these propositions cannot, I think, be disputed....

As geology plainly proclaims that each land has undergone great physical changes, we might have expected to find that organic beings have varied under nature, in the same way as they have varied under domestication. And if there has been any variability under nature, it would be an unaccountable fact if natural selection had not come into play....

There is grandeur in this view of life, with its several powers, having been originally breathed by the Creator into a few forms or into one; and that, whilst this planet has gone cycling on according to the fixed law of gravity, from so simple a beginning endless forms most beautiful and most wonderful have been, and are being evolved.

Source: Charles Darwin, *On the Origin of Species by Means of Natural Selection,* 6th ed., vol. 2 (1872; reprint, New York: Appleton, 1923), pp. 267–268, 279, 305–306.

advantage over the others and are more likely to survive. These surviving members of the species, Darwin claimed, pass on their desirable adaptive traits to their offspring, while the others die off. Darwin described this continuous process as a "struggle for existence," in which only the fittest endure. He called the mechanism that explained the evolution and development of new species "natural selection," a process that was imperceptible but continuous (see the box, "Darwin's Basic Laws of Evolution").

Darwin's theory of the inevitability of evolution in nature echoed the era's belief in change and its conviction that the present represented a more developed stage of the past. His work was seen as confirming the notion that species—and societies—were preordained to evolve toward progressively higher stages. Science seemed to confirm the era's faith in progress.

Darwin at first avoided the question of whether human beings, too, were affected by the laws of evolution. To do so would be to question humanity's uniqueness, its separation from the rest of creation by its possession (in the Christian view) of a soul. But in *Descent of Man* (1871), Darwin did confront this issue, clearly stating his belief that humanity, too, was subject to these natural laws. The recognition that human beings were members of the animal kingdom like other species disturbed him, and the admission, he wrote "is like confessing a murder." Nonetheless, scientific truth took precedence over all other considerations.

Many Christians were shocked by these assertions, and some denounced the new scientific findings. Some argued that science and faith belonged to two different worlds. Others claimed that there was no reason why God could not create the world through natural forces. In the long run, however, Darwinism seemed to undermine the certainties of religious orthodoxies by showing their incompatibility with scientific discovery.

Physics, Chemistry, and Medicine

Dramatic scientific breakthroughs occurred in the nineteenth century, confirming the prevalent belief that human beings could control the environment. In physics, laws regarding electricity and magnetism were articulated by Michael Faraday (1791–1867) and James Clerk Maxwell (1831–1879) in the 1830s and 1850s, respectively. Their work established the field of electrical science. In the 1840s, Hermann von Helmholtz (1821–1894) in Germany and James Joule (1818–1889) in Great Britain defined the nature of energy in the laws of thermodynamics. In chemistry, new elements were discovered almost every year, and individual findings contributed to the understanding of larger patterns. In 1869, Russian chemist Dmitri Mendeleev (1834–1907) developed the periodic table, in which the elements are arranged by their atomic weight. He left blank spaces for elements still unknown but that he predicted would be discovered. Within ten years three of these elements were discovered, proving that science is not only knowledge that can be experimentally tested but that it can also have predictive value. Such triumphs further enhanced its prestige.

Prolific research yielded discoveries in one field of knowledge that could be transferred to another. For example, chemists produced new dyes, enabling biologists to color slides of microorganisms and better study their evolution. Scientific breakthroughs also led to technical achievements that had industrial uses; for instance, inventions in chemistry led to the development of the first artificial fertilizers in 1842 and to synthetic dyes in the 1850s.

Science also became increasingly specialized. In the eighteenth century, the scientist had been a learned amateur practicing a hobby. In the nineteenth century, as the state and industry became increasingly involved in promoting scientific research, the scientist became a professional, employed by a university, a hospital, or some other institution. Scientific ideas were disseminated by scientific journals and by meetings of scientific associations and congresses. International scientific cooperation became common.

Around the midcentury mark, a number of important breakthroughs occurred in medicine. Before the development of anesthesia, surgical intervention had been nearly impossible. Only the bravest patients being served by the swiftest surgeons could undergo even modest surgical procedures. In the 1840s, however, the introduction of ether and then chloroform allowed people to undergo more extensive surgery.

Increasingly, the experimental method in science was applied to medicine, and as a result physicians became concerned not simply with treating diseases but discovering their origins. Louis Pasteur (1822–1895) achieved notable breakthroughs when he discovered that microbes, small organisms invisible to the naked eye, cause various diseases. Pasteur also pioneered certain methods of disease prevention. He discovered, for example, that the body could resist a strain of disease when vaccinated by a weaker form of the bacilli that caused it. This discovery led to the widespread vaccination of people against smallpox and of animals against anthrax. Further, Pasteur discovered that heating milk to a certain temperature killed disease-carrying organisms. This process, called *pasteurization,* reduced the incidence of certain diseases that were particularly harmful to children.

In England, the surgeon John Lister (1827–1912) developed an effective disinfectant, carbolic acid, to kill the germs that caused gangrene and other infections in surgical patients. Eventually, midwives and doctors began to reduce the incidence of the puerperal fever that killed so many women after childbirth by washing their hands and sterilizing their instruments. Lister's development of germ-free procedures transformed the science of surgery. By reducing the patient's risk, more ambitious surgery could be attempted. The first surgical kidney removal took place in 1876; the first successful brain surgery in modern times three years later.

The increasingly scientific base of medicine and its visible success in combating disease improved its reputation. The medical profession began to control access to its ranks by establishing powerful professional associations: The British Medical Association was founded in 1832, the German Association in 1872. Medical journals were established to spread scientific knowledge. Although these advances did not immediately reduce the death rate, progress had begun.

Birth of the Social Sciences

The scientific method, so dramatically effective in uncovering the mysteries of nature, was also applied to the human enterprise. Just as the secrets of nature were unlocked, the workings of society, it was thought, could be understood in a scientific manner.

No field in the human sciences flourished as much in the nineteenth century as history. In an era undergoing vast transformations, many people became interested in change over time. They were eager to employ the methods of the scientist to explore their past. The father of modern historical writing is Leopold von Ranke (1795–1886). Departing from the tradition of earlier historians, who explained the past as the fulfillment of some overall purpose—God's will, the liberation of humanity, or some other goal—Ranke insisted that the role of the historian was to "show how things actually were." Like a scientist, the historian must be objective and dispassionate. By viewing humankind in different eras and environments, historians could arrive at a better understanding of humanity.

This perspective transformed the study of history into a dicipline with recognizable common standards of evidence. Historians studied and interpreted historical documents; they collected and published their findings; they founded professional organizations and published major journals.

Other social sciences also developed in this period. Anthropology, the comparative study of people in differing societies, had been the subject of speculative literature for hundreds of years. The increased contacts with non-European societies in the nineteenth century increased anthropological curiosity. In 1844 the Society of Ethnology was founded in Paris; the Anthropological Society was also founded in Paris, in 1859, followed in the 1860s by societies in London, Berlin, and Vienna. Consisting of medical doctors, biologists, and travelers, these societies speculated on the causes of the perceived differences between human races. The Paris society was dominated by the medical doctor Paul Broca (1824–1880) and other physicians, who saw in biological structure the explanation for differences between human groups, thus giving apparent "scientific" backing to the era's racism. They used their findings to demonstrate that non-Europeans were condemned to an existence inferior to the white races.

In Britain, the main anthropological theorist was Edward Tylor (1832–1917). The son of a brass manufacturer, he traveled because of ill health and came into contact with non-European peoples, who aroused his curiosity. He believed that the various societies of mankind were subject to discoverable scientific laws. Tylor was strongly influenced by the evolutionary doctrines of his day. Just as one could presumably travel back in time and find humankind increasingly unsophisticated, so Tylor posited, as one became distanced from Europe, humankind also became increasingly primitive. The contemporary African was at a level of development similar to that of Europeans in an earlier era. Although Tylor was not a racist—since he did not believe that the conditions of non-Europeans were due to biology, but were rather a function of their institutions—he did think non-Europeans were at a developmental stage inferior to Europeans. Although they disagreed on the causes, both racists and evolutionists thus believed in the superiority of the European over other races.

Anthropology gradually gained recognition and legitimacy as a profession. In 1872 in France, Broca founded a journal emphasizing physical anthropology. In 1876 he founded a school of anthropology with six chaired professors. In Britain in 1884, Tylor—who was so closely identified with anthropology it was called "Mr Tylor's science"—was appointed to the first university chair in anthropology in his country.

Sociology was a term originally coined by Comte. A number of ambitious thinkers, among them the English "social philosopher" Herbert Spencer, had considered how individuals are affected by the society in which they live. In the 1840s various social reformers published detailed statistical investigations revealing relationships between, for instance, income and disease and death rates. A few decades later, the theoretical principles underlying sociology were spelled out. Among the first to do so was Emile Durkheim (1858–1917), who insisted that sociology was a verifiable science. He occupied the first chair of sociology at a French university in 1887. A few years later he founded a journal of sociology and gathered around him a coterie of disciples who ensured the success of sociology as a professionalized discipline.

Whereas in the past, history, anthropology, and sociology were the purview of amateurs, now professional historians, anthropologists, and sociologists were engaged full time in research and teaching at universities or research institutes. The professionalization that had occurred in medicine and physics also transformed the social sciences. Professionalization and specialization led to significant advances in several disciplines, but it also led to the fragmentation and compartmentalization of knowledge. People of broad learning and expertise became far less common.

The Challenge to Religion

The scientific claims of the era seemed to clash with the traditions of religion. A number of scientists, including Darwin himself, found their Christian faith undermined by theories on evolution. Although the large majority of Europeans continued to be strongly influenced by traditional religious beliefs, they appeared less confident than in earlier eras.

After the revolutions of 1848, religion was seen as a bulwark of order. In France, Napoleon III gave the Catholic church new powers in education, and the bourgeoisie flocked to church. In Spain, moderates who had been anticlerical began to support the church, and in 1851 they signed a concordat declaring Roman Catholicism "the only religion of the Spanish nation." In Austria in 1855, the state surrendered to the bishops full control over the clergy, the seminaries, and the administration of marriage laws.

In 1848, the papacy had been nearly overthrown by revolution and in 1860 it lost most of its domains to Italy. Thus Pope Pius IX became a sworn enemy of liberalism, and in 1864, in the *Syllabus of Errors,* he condemned a long list of what he perceived to be modern errors, among them "progress," "liberalism," and "modern civilization." To establish full control over the clergy and believers, the Lateran Council in 1870 issued the controversial doctrine of infallability, declaring that the pope, when speaking officially on faith and morals, was infallible. This doctrine became a target of anticlerical opinion.

The political alliance the Catholic church struck with reactionary forces meant that when new political groups came to power they moved against the church. In Italy, since the church had discouraged national unification, conflict raged between the church and the new state. In Germany, Catholics had either held on to their regional loyalties or favored unification under Austrian auspices. When Protestant Prussia unified Germany, Chancellor Bismarck viewed the Catholics with suspicion as unpatriotic and started a campaign against them, the *Kulturkampf* ("cultural struggle").

In France the republicans, who finally won the upper hand over monarchists in 1879, bitterly resented the church's support of the monarchist party. They were also strongly influenced by Comte's ideas of positivism, believing that France would not be a free country until the power of the church was diminished and its nonscientific or antiscientific disposition was overcome. The republican regime reduced the role of the church in education as well as some other clerical privileges.

Greater religious tolerance, or perhaps it was increasing religious indifference, led to more acceptance of religious diversity. In 1854 and 1871, England opened university admission and teaching posts at all universities to non-Anglicans. Anti-Catholicism, at times a popular and virulent movement, declined in the 1870s. In France, too, the position of religious minorities improved. Some of the highest officials of the Second Empire were Protestants, as were some early leaders of the Third Republic and some important business leaders and scientists.

Legal emancipation of Jews, started in France in 1791, subsequently spread to the rest of the

Continent. England removed restrictions on Jews when the House of Commons, in 1858, and the House of Lords the following decade allowed Jews to hold a parliamentary seat. In the 1860s Germany and Austria-Hungary granted Jews the rights of citizenship. Social discrimination continued, however, and Jews were not accepted as social equals in most of European society. Although some Jews occupied high office in France and Italy, in Germany and Austria-Hungary they had to convert before they could aspire to such position. In other fields, access was easier. Some of the major banking houses were founded by Jews, the Rothschilds and the Warburgs, for instance.

In the expanding economy of western Europe, where the condition of most people was improving, the enhanced opportunity of a previously despised minority aroused relatively little attention. In other parts of Europe, Jews were not as fortunate. When they seized economic opportunities in eastern Europe and moved into commerce, industry, and the professions, they were resented. Acts of violence against them, called pogroms, broke out in Bucharest, the capital of Romania, in 1866 and in the Russian seaport of Odessa in 1871. Although economic rivalries may have fueled this anti-Semitism, they do not completely explain it. In most cases anti-Jewish sentiment occurred in the areas of Europe least exposed to liberal ideas of human equality and human rights.

The emphasis on science and reason transformed religion in the nineteenth century, but, as the continued anti-Semitism showed, it was by no means always in the direction of increased tolerance or weakening of religious fervor. On the contrary, in certain cases religiosity grew. In France there were frequent reported sightings of the Virgin Mary. A shepherdess claimed to have seen and spoken with her at Lourdes, which became an especially important shrine whose waters were reputed to heal the lame and the sick. In 1872, construction of a rail line allowed 100,000 people a year to visit the town.

Church attendance continued to be high, especially in rural areas. In England villagers usually attended church, many twice or more each Sunday. Children dutifully attended Sunday schools. Advances in printing made it possible to distribute large quantities of cheap religious tracts to a sizable and avid readership. The faithful eagerly engaged in proselytizing, sending large numbers of missionaries to all corners of the globe.

Art in the Age of Material Change

The new era of technology, science, and faith in progress was reflected in the arts. Some artists optimistically believed they could more accurately depict reality by adopting the methods of the scientist, cooly describing their subject. A minority, however, were disillusioned by the materialism of the age and warned against its loss of values.

Photography had a direct impact on painting. Various experiments in the late eighteenth century, plus the inventions of the Frenchman Louis Daguerre (1789–1851), made the camera relatively usable in the 1830s. It was still a large, cumbersome object, however, until the dry plate and miniature camera were introduced in the 1870s. Twenty years later, with the invention of celluloid film, it came into wide use. Unlike paintings and portraits, photography was accessible to the public. And photographic services were in high demand; by the 1860s, 30,000 people in Paris made a living from photography and allied fields. Many Europeans became amateur photographers—Queen Victoria and Prince Albert had a darkroom at Windsor Castle.

The ability of photography to depict a scene with exactitude had a significant impact on art. On the one hand, it encouraged artists to be true to reality, to reproduce on the canvas a visual image akin to that of a photograph. On the other hand, other artists felt that such realism was now no longer necessary in their sphere. However, the great majority of the public, which now had wide access to museum exhibitions, was accustomed to photographic accuracy and desired art that was accessible and understandable. Realistic works of art met this need, at least superficially.

Discarding myths and symbols, many artists described the world as it actually was or appeared to them—a world without illusions, everyday life in all its grimness. The realist painter Gustave Courbet (1819–1877) proclaimed himself "without ideals and without religion" (see the box, "Gustave Courbet Describes *The Stone Breakers*"). His fellow Frenchman, Jean-

Courbet: The Stone Breakers This realistic 1849 painting depicts the rough existence of workers' lives. The bleakness of the subject matter and the style in which it was carried out characterized much of the realistic school of art. *(Staatliche Kunstsammlungen, Dresden/The Bridgeman Art Library, London)*

François Millet (1814–1875), held a similar opinion. Instead of romanticizing peasants as earlier artists had, his paintings reveal the harsh physical conditions under which they labored. In England the pre-Raphaelites took as their model the painters of Renaissance Italy prior to Raphael, who presumably had depicted the realistic simplicity of nature. In painting historical scenes, these artists emphasized meticulous research of the landscape, architecture, fauna, and costumes of their subjects. To paint the Dead Sea in *The Scapegoat,* Holman Hunt (1827–1910) traveled all the way to Palestine so that the site would be accurately portrayed.

In the past, artists had been concerned about composition and perspective. But under the influence of photography, they began to paint incomplete, off-center pictures. Edgar Degas' *Orchestra of the Paris Opera* looks as if it has been cropped, with only half of a musician showing on each edge and the top half of the ballet dancers missing.

On April 15, 1874, six artists—Edgar Degas (1834–1917), Claude Monet (1840–1926), Camille Pissarro (1830–1903), Auguste Renoir (1840–1919), Alfred Sisley (1839–1899), and Berthe Morisot (1841–1895)—opened an exhibition in Paris that a critic disparagingly called "impressionist," after the title of one of Monet's paintings, *Impression: Sunrise.* The impressionists were influenced by new theories of physics that claimed images were transmitted to the brain as small light particles that the brain then reconstituted. The impressionists wanted their paintings to capture what things looked like before they had been "distorted" by the brain. In their search for realism, impressionist painters ceased painting in their studios and increasingly went outdoors to paint objects exactly as they looked when light hit them at a certain angle. Monet, for example, emphasized outdoor painting and the need for spontaneity, for reproducing subjects without the preconception of how they had been depicted in earlier work but rather exactly how

Gustave Courbet Describes *The Stone Breakers*

After studying for a decade in Paris, Gustave Courbet, the son of a wealthy farmer, returned in 1849 to his hometown of Ornans in the Franche-Comté, near Switzerland. There he painted one of his best-known works, **The Stone Breakers*****, a powerful example of realist art. In a letter to his friend Jules Champfleury (the pen name of Jules Husson), an author, socialist agitator, and champion of realism, Courbet described his canvas and the conditions surrounding its creation.***

Stonebreakers is composed of two very pitiable figures: one is an old man, an old machine grown stiff with service and age. His sunburned head is covered with a straw hat blackened by dust and rain. His arms, which look sprung, are dressed in a coarse linen shirt. In his red-striped vest you can see a tobacco box made of horn with copper edges. At the knee, resting on a straw mat, his drugget pants, which could stand by themselves, show a large patch; through his worn blue socks one sees his heels in his cracked wooden clogs. The one behind him is a young man about fifteen years old, suffering from scurvy. Some dirty linen tatters are his shirt, exposing his arms and his sides. His pants are held up by a leather suspender, and on his feet he has his father's old shoes, which have long since developed gaping holes on all sides. . . . The figures are seen against the green background of a great mountain that fills the canvas and across which move the shadows of clouds. Only in the right-hand corner, where the mountain slopes, can one see a bit of blue sky.

I made up none of it, dear friend. I saw these people every day on my walk. Besides, in that station one ends up the same way as one begins. The vine growers and the farmers, who are much taken with this painting, claim that, were I to do a hundred more, none would be more true to life.

Source: To Champfleury, Ornans, February–March 1850, in Petra ten-Doeschate-Chu, trans. and ed., *Letters of Gustave Courbet* (Chicago: University of Chicago Press, 1992), pp. 92–93.

the colors and shapes hit the eye. Monet was particularly interested in painting several views of the same object to underscore that there was no single correct depiction of a subject but that it depended on viewpoint, weather, and time of day.

The school of realism also influenced literature, especially the novel. In realist novels, life was not glorified or infused with mythical elements; the stark existence of daily life was seen as a suitable subject. Charles Dickens (1812–1870), who came from a poor background and had personally experienced the inhumanity of the London underworld, wrote novels depicting the lot of the poor with humor and sympathy. The appalling social conditions he described helped educate his large middle-class audience on the state of the poor. And like his middle-class contemporaries—for by the pen he became a member of this class—he also provided numerous examples of individuals who by hard work were able to rise above their circumstances.

Another realist, the French novelist Gustave Flaubert (1821–1880), consciously debunked the romanticism of his elders. His famous novel, *Madame Bovary,* describes middle-class life as bleak, boring, and meaningless. The heroine seeks to escape the narrow confines of provincial life by adulterous and disastrous affairs.

Emile Zola (1840–1902), another Frenchman, belonged to the naturalist school of literature. The writer, Zola declared, should be like a surgeon or chemist, providing a scientific cause and record of human behavior. In his Rougon-Macquart series, which describe in detail the experience of several generations of a family, Zola's major theme is the impact of environment and

Monet: Boulevard des Capucines In 1873 Claude Monet painted this scene of one of the new broad Paris streets. He used only a few brush strokes of dark paint to suggest the presence of people, including their dress and facial expressions. Spots of colored pigment conveyed a whole impression without providing a detailed illustration. *(The Nelson-Atkins Museum of Art, Kansas City, Missouri [Purchase: The Kenneth A. and Helen F. Spencer Foundation Acquisition Fund] F72–35)*

heredity on the life of degradation and vice of his characters. His characters seem locked in a Darwinian struggle for survival; some doomed by the laws of biology to succeed and others to succumb.

The Russian novelist Leo Tolstoy (1828–1910) brought a new perspective to the historical novel in *War and Peace.* Instead of a heroic approach to battle, he showed the individual caught in forces beyond his control. Small and insignificant events, rather than major ones, seem to govern human destiny. Another Russian novelist often associated with the realist school, Feodor Dostoyevsky (1821–1881), aimed to portray realistically the psychological dimensions of his characters in novels such as *Crime and Punishment* (1866), *The Idiot* (1868), and *The Brothers Karamazov* (1879–1880).

Although material progress was generally celebrated in this era, a number of intellectuals reacted against it. They were alarmed by the prospect of the popular masses achieving political power by winning the vote and by mass production and consumption. They denounced the smug and the self-satisfied, who saw happiness in acquisition and consumption. Some condemned the age in severe terms. Dostoyevsky denounced the materialism and egotism of the West, decribing its civilization as driven by "trade, shipping, markets, factories." In Britain—the nation that seemed to embody progress—the historian Thomas Carlyle (1795–1881) denounced his age as not that of progress but of selfishness. Parliamentarianism he saw as a sham, and he called for a strong leader to save the nation from endless palavers and compromises. Unlike most of his contemporaries who saw in material plenty a sign of progress, Carlyle saw the era as one of decline, bereft of spiritual values.

Another Englishman, John Ruskin (1819–1900), looked back to the Middle Ages as an ideal era in human history. People then did not produce with machines, but exercised a fine sense of craftsmanship. People then supposedly had a better sense of community and labored for the common good. Ruskin was one of the founders of the arts and crafts movement, which emphasized the need to produce goods for daily use with an eye for beauty and originality. "Industry without art is brutality," Ruskin warned.

In France, republicans saw in the ostentation of the Second Empire a sign of depravity and decline. Defeat in war in 1870 and the outbreak of the Commune furthered a mood of pessimism among many intellectuals. Flaubert intensely detested his own age, seeing it as petty and mean. The characters in Zola's Rougon Macquart novels are constantly headed downward in mental faculties, social position, and morality.

Thus, all was not optimistic in this age of optimism. If many people celebrated what they viewed as an age of progress, some claimed that under the outer trappings of material comfort there lay a frightening ignorance of aesthetic, moral, and spiritual values.

Summary

During the middle decades of the nineteenth century, the advances in industry created an era of material plenty, providing more riches and comforts to a larger population than ever before. It was a self-confident age that believed in progress and anticipated further improvements in its material and intellectual environment.

Economic changes transformed the class structure of many European countries, and middle-class values and tastes defined the second half of the century. The new wealth and technologies led to improvements in both the countryside and the cities; in both, life became more comfortable and safer. Governments provided new services such as public education, cultural facilities, and expanded welfare services.

The material changes in society were reflected in intellectual currents. Change and evolution were embraced as an explanation for the origin of species. A new confidence in scientific research led to many scientific and technical breakthroughs. Novelists and painters aimed to dissect as scientists the world around them, creating realism in the arts. Some intellectuals, however, revolted against a certain crass self-satisfaction that imbued the bourgeoisie, and they criticized an age that worshiped industry and materialism.

Progress, as Europeans were to learn in a later era, was two-edged; the very forces that improved life for many also threatened it. The same breakthroughs in chemistry that led to the development of artificial fertilizers also provided more powerful military explosives. The expansion of education and reduction of illiteracy meant not only an end to ignorance but also the creation of a public that could more easily absorb messages of hate against a rival nation or against religious or ethnic minorities at home. Material progress and well-being continued, but there were new forces in the shadows that would ultimately undermine the comforts, self-assurance, and peace of this age.

Suggested Reading

General Surveys

Hearder, Harry. *Europe in the Nineteenth Century, 1830–1880.* 2d ed. 1988. A broad survey of this period.

Hobsbawm, Eric J. *The Age of Capital, 1848–1875.* 1979. Particularly strong on social and economic developments.

Rich, Norman. *The Age of Nationalism and Reform, 1850–1890.* 1970. Emphasizes the growing confidence in human progress in these years.

Economic Growth

Milward, A. S., and S. B. Saul. *The Development of the Economies of Continental Europe, 1850–1914.* 1977. Has good chapters on economic developments in the second half of the nineteenth century.

Ville, Simon P. *Transport and the Development of the European Economy, 1750–1918.* 1990. Describes the importance of transportation in the modernization of Europe.

Social Change

Blum, Jerome. *The End of the Old Order in Rural Europe.* 1978. A broad, comparative study of the position of the peasantry in nineteenth-century Europe.

Cocks, Geoffrey, and Konrad H. Jarausch, eds. *German Professions, 1800–1950.* 1990. Describes the relationship between the professions and the state.

Geison, Gerald L., ed. *Professions and the French State, 1700–1900.* 1984. Considers the development of the various professions in France.

Grew, Raymond, and Patrick J. Harrigan. *School, State and Society—The Growth of Elementary Schooling in Nineteenth Century France.* 1991. Reveals the constantly growing demand for education throughout the nineteenth century and the spread of formal schooling to the whole country.

Hurt, J. S. *Elementary Schooling and the Working Classes, 1860–1918.* 1979. Studies the impact of compulsory education on the British working class.

Mayer, Arno. *The Persistence of the Old Regime—Europe to the Great War.* 1981. Argues for the persistence of the aristocracy throughout the nineteenth century.

Pilbeam, Pamela. *The Middle Classes in Europe, 1789–1914.* 1990. Reviews the formation and values of the bourgeoisie in four continental European nations.

Thompson, F. M. L. *The Rise of Respectable Society—A Social History of Victorian Britain, 1830–1910.* 1988. Depicts considerable social mobility and well-being in Britain in the second half of the nineteenth century.

Weber, Eugen. *Peasants into Frenchmen: The Modernization of Rural France, 1870–1914.* 1976. A lively description of the process by which the French peasantry was modernized.

Women's Experience

Peterson, M. Jeanne. *Family, Love, and Work in the Lives of Victorian Gentlewomen.* 1989. Offers a revisionist examination of the view that women were passive in the Victorian era.

Prochaska, F. K. *Women and Philanthropy in Nineteenth Century England.* 1980. Reveals the important role women played in charity work throughout the century.

Robertson, Priscilla. *An Experience of Women and Change in Nineteenth Century Europe.* 1982. Describes the private lives of bourgeois women in the nineteenth century, emphasizing the differing cultural traditions of various nations.

Smith, Bonnie G. *Ladies of the Leisure Class—The Bourgeoises of Northern France in the Nineteenth Century.* 1981. Emphasizes the separate world of domesticity bourgeois women created and maintained.

Urban Development

Briggs, Asa. *Victorian Things.* 1989. Provides an amusing and instructive history of the various new objects that became part of consumer culture.

Lees, Andrew. *Cities Perceived: Urban Society in European and American Thought, 1820–1940.* 1985. Depicts how various writers in Europe and the United States perceived their cities.

Miller, Michael B. *The Bon Marché—Bourgeois Culture and the Department Store, 1869–1920.* 1981. Views the first and largest department store in Paris as both manifestation and promoter of bourgeois culture.

Olsen, Donald J. *The City as a Work of Art—London, Paris, Vienna.* 1986. Compares and contrasts how these cities evolved in the nineteenth century.

Pinkney, David. *Napoleon III and the Rebuilding of Paris.* 1958. The standard work on the urban renewal of Paris.

Science and Medicine

Bowler, Peter J. *Evolution—The History of an Idea.* Rev. ed. 1989. Written by a scientist, who examines the history and development of the concept while evaluating the scientific merit of the debates.

Burrow, J. W. *Evolution and Society: A Study in Victorian Social Theory.* 1966. Considers the impact of the evolutionary paradigm in the social sciences.

Chadwick, Owen. *The Secularization of the European Mind in the Nineteenth Century.* 1973. Considers the rise and spread of secular attitudes at the cost of religion.

Desmond, Adrian, and James Moore. *Darwin.* 1991. A lengthy and interesting biography of the great scientist.

Youngson, A. J. *The Scientific Revolution in Victorian Medicine.* 1979. A record of innovation in British medicine.

Art

Clark, T. J. *Image of the People: Gustave Courbet and the 1848 Revolution.* 1973. Explores the impact of the sociopolitical environment on Courbet's paintings and the audiences' reactions to them.

Pool, Phoebe. *Impressionism.* 1985. Studies the origins, accomplishments, and legacies of impressionism.

Weisberg, Gabriel P., ed. *The European Realist Tradition.* 1982. A multinational study revealing the pervasiveness of realism in European art.

Weighing the Evidence

A MAP OF HAUSSMANN'S PARIS

Look at this map of Paris between 1850 and 1870. The city population had grown significantly. Between 1800 and 1850 it doubled from half a million to 1 million and by 1870 had increased to 1.8 million. Paris needed room to expand. Notice the areas annexed in 1860. Neither the Tollhouse Wall dating from 1784 to 1791 nor the Fortress Wall of the 1840s was able to contain the city.

Notice the broad, straight avenues that Baron Haussmann laid out. They cut through what still was essentially a medieval city of narrow, crooked streets bordered by a motley group of crowded buildings of different materials and varied heights and depths. The old streets and buildings were torn down to make way for broad avenues bordered by elegant apartment houses of uniform height and style.

Why were the streets widened? There were many reasons. Consider the political advantages of broad streets. Paris had experienced many popular uprisings, most recently in 1848. People could easily barricade narrow streets, but not wide ones. Soldiers could move quickly along broad avenues to control areas where they might be challenged.

Consider the forces that made it imperative to improve the traffic flow. Increasing numbers of people, horses, and carriages were contributing to traffic congestion. And the city felt the impact of industry and the railways. The large amount of wares produced by developing industry, brought in and out of Paris by the expanding rail system, represented an ever-increasing amount of cargo. The horse-drawn wagons that delivered and picked up products from the rail stations added to the traffic. Both pedestrians and carriages could proceed only slowly and with difficulty. A great amount of time was spent just moving through the maze of narrow Parisian streets. The width of the new streets allowed the construction of sidewalks, segregating pedestrian from carriage movement and contributing to more rapid street traffic and safety for the pedestrians. In addition to broader streets, Haussmann provided an additional means to move people and goods more efficiently—the railway built around Paris. Many of the new boulevards connected the rest of the city to the railway stations. See, for example, the large boulevards from the Gare de l'Est and the Montparnasse stations.

The new, broad avenues were also a public health measure. Narrow streets and the houses that bordered them were dark, crowded, and airless—not that different from London streets (see the illustration of St. Giles on page 868). Disease-producing organisms, such as the tuberculosis bacillus, had not yet been discovered, but since the 1820s health officials and social reformers had observed that people living in dark, crowded areas were more prone to disease than were those living in more open, airy environments. Haussmann's wide, new avenues brought in fresh air and daylight and contributed to an improvement in public health.

Other measures to safeguard public health were also instituted. Notice the aqueducts to bring more water into the city for drinking, washing, and street cleaning. A new sewer system brought to nearly every city street an underground drain that conducted rain and wastewater out of the city and thus reduced the pools of stagnant water in the streets and the foul smells produced by the old, ill-functioning drainage system.

The new Paris provided leisure facilities. Note the new parks the city established, the Bois de Boulogne and the Bois de Vincennes. These parks also were built with health and social issues in mind. In the mid-nineteenth century it was understood that green space provided "lungs for the city," increasing its oxygen supply. And parks provided space for leisure activities. The rich could promenade, go on a carriage outing, and ride on horseback, and even the very poorest could take a walk or have a picnic. Note the location of the parks, however—in the pe-

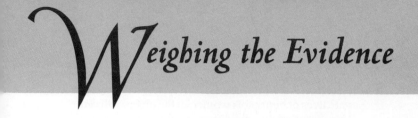

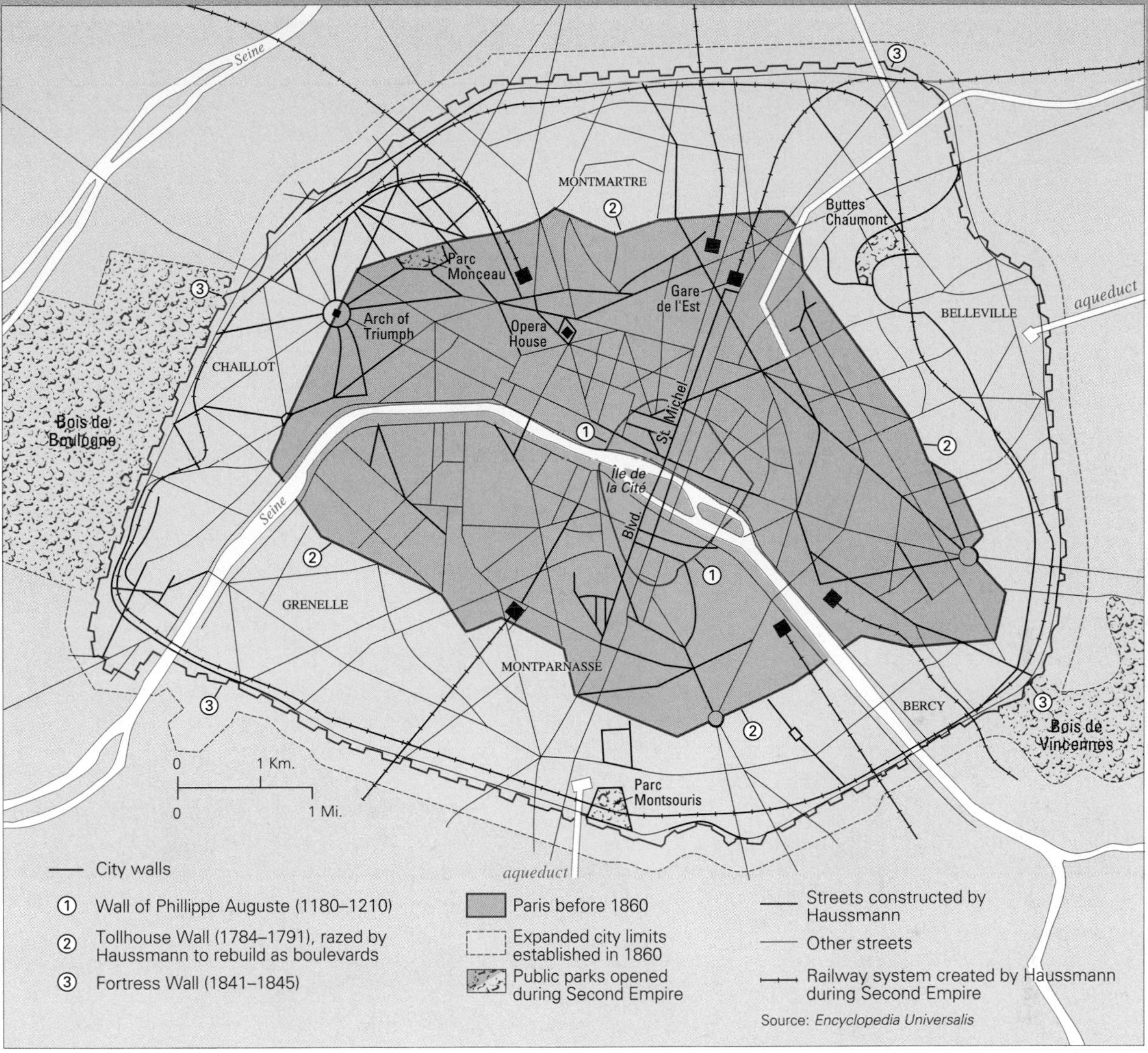

Haussmann's Paris

riphery and thus out of reach to many Parisians. London's centrally located parks and housing in the center of the city had been developed at the same time. By the mid-nineteenth century, however, there was no space for such large projects in central Paris.

The need for public works projects such as these had been evident for a few decades. Why, then, were they finally accomplished in this era? Between 1850 and 1870 the French economy was expanding. Private as well as public income was rising. With increased revenues, central and local administrations could assume greater responsibilities. Officials were optimistic about future growth and willing to finance ambitious public works with long-term public loans. Moreover, an urban program such as Haussmann's required tearing down people's houses and seizing land by the exercise of rights of eminent domain. In a parliamentary system, where disgruntled property owners are also voters, such actions are especially troublesome. But the authoritarian regime of Napoleon III was immune to such controversy.

Although the French capital has changed, especially since the 1960s, the Paris that Baron Haussmann built is essentially intact, with its large boulevards, imposing public buildings, and delightful public parks. It became a model for other cities to emulate.

CHAPTER 26

The Coming Conflict, 1880–1914

The years preceding the outbreak of World War I are often called *"la belle époque"*—the beautiful era. For many people these years continued to be prosperous. The arts flourished and were celebrated. Parliamentary government continued to spread, and more nations seemed to be adapting to democracy as suffrage was extended. To a large extent the trends of progress and increased well-being continued, yet hand-in-hand with them came troubling new tendencies. Several developments in the generation before 1914 undermined and threatened all the accomplishments of these years.

In many societies, governing became more complex as populations increased. The population of Europe jumped from 274 million in 1850 to 423 million in 1900 to 460 million by 1914. A larger population coupled with extended suffrage meant that more people participated in the political system, but it became harder to find consensus. The example of democracy in some countries led to frustration in the autocratic ones at their failure to move toward freer institutions. Although many people's lives had improved materially, many grew impatient that conditions had not improved faster, and some groups were frustrated by their exclusion from the political system.

Intellectuals revolted against the smug self-assuredness of earlier years. They no longer felt certain that the world was knowable, stable, subject to comprehension and, ultimately, mastery by rational human beings. Some jettisoned rationality, imagining that they had made strides in sophistication by glorifying emotion, irrationality, and, in some cases, violence. The works of painters and writers seemed to anticipate the impending destruction of world order.

Italian strikers in 1890s.
Pellizza da Volpedo Giuseppe,
study for *The Fourth Estate* (detail).

Anxieties of various sorts beset many Europeans and were manifest in a variety of ways. Ethnic minorities became the target of hatreds. Overseas, non-Europeans were forcibly put under white domination as European states embarked on a race for empire throughout the world. Within the European continent, states increasingly felt insecure, worried that they would be subject to attack. They established standing armies, shifted alliances, drafted war plans, and, utlimately, went to war.

Politics and Culture in an Age of Doubt

Many of the beliefs and institutions that had seemed so solid in the "age of optimism" found themselves under attack in the subsequent generation. Forces hostile to liberalism became increasingly vocal. In the arts and philosophy, the earlier confidence was replaced by doubt, relativism, and a desire to flee the routines of everyday life.

The Erosion of the Liberal Consensus

By the mid-nineteenth century, liberalism appeared to be the ascending ideology, and liberals assumed that with the passage of time an increasing number of people would be won over to their way of looking at the world. However, toward the end of the century, liberalism faced serious challenges. Liberal principles eroded within the liberal camp, and in addition, various ideas and movements—some new, some rooted in the past—contributed to the undermining of the liberal consensus. Prominent among these were socialism, anarchism, a new political right, racism, and anti-Semitism.

The undermining of the liberal consensus began among liberals themselves, who, in the face of changing circumstances, retreated from some of their basic tenets. For example, one of the principal emphases of liberalism had always been free trade. But under the pressure of economic competition, liberals supported tariffs at home and created closed markets for the mother country overseas in the empire.

Historically, liberals had typically stood for an expansion of civil liberties, yet several groups were denied their rights. Power remained an exclusively male domain, and liberal males saw nothing improper or inconsistent in continuing to deny women both the vote and free access to education and professional advancement. In the face of labor agitation, many liberals no longer unconditionally supported civil liberties and favored instead the violent crushing of strikes.

Similarly, liberals had always upheld the sanctity of private property, but under the pressure of events, they abandoned this principle as an absolute goal. To ensure workers' safety, they instituted limits on employers by passing legislation on working conditions. In some countries, they supported progressive income taxes, which many perceived as a serious invasion of private property. When it became clear that a free market was unable to meet many human needs, welfare programs were instituted in several countries. These reforms were intended to strengthen the state by winning support from the broader masses. But, together with a willingness by liberals themselves to breach their fundamental principles, these measures also revealed the apparent inability of liberal ideology to deal with the problems of the day.

The Rise of Socialism and Anarchism

Among the groups challenging the monopoly of power and liberal ideology of the middle classes were the socialist parties, both Marxist and non-Marxist, whose goal was to win the support of workers by espousing their cause. Socialists varied in their notions of how their goals should be achieved; some thought they could be achieved gradually and peacefully; others were dedicated to a violent overthrow of capitalist society.

In England, where the Liberal party was more open to the needs of workers than in other European states, a separate socialist party, the Independent Labour party, was established relatively late, in 1893. It was not until the 1920s that this party gained any particular electoral success. Some of Britain's major social reformers belonged to the Fabian Society, founded in 1884. The Fabians criticized the capitalist system for being inefficient, wasteful, and unjust. They believed that by gradual, democratic means, factories and land could be transferred from the private sector to the state, which would employ them for the benefit of society as a whole. Socialism was a desirable system that would replace capitalism because it was more efficient and more just. It would come into being not through class war but through enlightened ideas. This gradualist approach became the hallmark of British socialism.

In Germany there were two socialist parties in the 1860s. The first, founded in 1863 by Ferdinand Lassalle (1825–1864), viewed universal suffrage as the means of assuring the workers' well-being. A competing party, formed in 1868 and influenced by Marx, called for a workers' revolution. In 1875 the two socialist parties unified around a common program.

Unification did not prevent the party from being split a few years later by a debate soon to be echoed in all European socialist parties. A German socialist leader, Eduard Bernstein (1850–1932), who had been in England and soaked up the influence of the Fabians, argued in a book with the telling English title *Evolutionary Socialism* (1898) that Marx had been wrong to suggest that capitalism would necessarily collapse and lead to the increasing wretchedness of the working class. Its record had indicated otherwise. The capitalist economy had in fact expanded and been able to provide for steadily improved conditions. Workers would not need to seize power by some cataclysmic act. Rather, by piecemeal democratic action they could gradually win increasing power and legislate on behalf of their interests. Since he argued for a revision of Marxist theory, Bernstein was labeled a "revisionist."

Opposing Bernstein in this great debate was the party theoretician Karl Kautsky (1854–1938). Although Kautsky agreed that the workers' lot had not worsened, he insisted that workers were relatively worse off. In Germany, he argued, workers could come to power only if they first overthrew autocracy. A violent revolution would thus be necessary to institute socialism.

Although the party officially rejected revisionism and seemed to embrace the doctrine of a violent proletarian revolution, it in fact practiced the former. The German Socialist party had become a part of established society, with its newspapers, party bureaucracy, and headquarters; it had gained a vested interest in society and was not ready to overthrow it. Nevertheless it continued to espouse a militant ideology of class war.

Similarly ambiguous developments occurred in neighboring France. One of Marx's French disciples, Jules Guesde (1845–1922), founded a socialist party with a strong working-class membership devoted to carrying on a workers' revolution. Opposing his brand of socialism was Jean Jaurès (1859–1914), an idealistic schoolteacher who saw socialism as an ethical system. Unlike the Marxists, he did not regard the advent of socialism as inevitable but rather as desirable to bring about a more equitable and just society. Jaurès believed that socialism could be achieved in cooperation with the more enlightened members of the middle classes, and he abhorred the vocabulary of class warfare so frequently voiced by Guesde. In 1905 the socialist parties led by Guesde and Jaurès merged, and Jaurès became virtual party leader. Although Jaurès' brand of gradual democratic socialism influenced the daily functioning of the newly unified party, the French Socialist party formally continued to adhere to Guesde's doctrines of revolution and class

Jean Jaurès The leader of the French socialist party, Jean Jaurès, addresses a meeting in 1913. A charismatic figure, he was one of France's greatest orators. *(Roger-Viollet)*

war. In 1914, on the eve of the outbreak of world war, a nationalist incensed by Jaurès' call on his government to avoid war assassinated him.

Another movement that declared its mission to be the liberation of the downtrodden was anarchism, which proclaimed that humans could be free only when the state had been abolished. According to anarchist theory, in a stateless society people would naturally join together in cooperative communes and share the fruits of their labor. Although many anarchists believed their goal could be reached by enlightening people, others were more impatient and hoped to speed up the process by making direct attacks on existing authority. The Russian nobleman Michael Bakunin (1814–1876), frustrated at the authoritarianism of his homeland, became a lifelong anarchist. He challenged tsarism at home and participated in the 1848 revolutions throughout Europe. He viewed all governments as repressive and declared war on them: "The passion for destruction is also a creative passion." His ideas were particularly influential in Italy, Spain, and parts of France, especially among the artisan classes.

Many anarchists of this period wanted to bring about the new society by "propaganda of the deed." An attack on the bastions of power, these anarchists believed, could bring about the dissolution of the state. They formed secret terrorist organizations that assassinated heads of state or those close to them. Between 1894 and 1901, the president of France, a prime minister of Spain, the empress of Austria, the king of Italy, and the president of the United States (McKinley) were killed by anarchists. These murders tarnished the image of anarchism. More important, they produced no particular improvement in the lot of the working-class people, on whose behalf these campaigns were supposedly launched.

Without accepting the anarchists' methods, some in the labor movement shared their hostility toward parliamentary institutions. A working-class program, they argued, could be implemented only by a pure workers' movement such as unions. Workers should eschew the political arena and concentrate on direct workers' action. According to this line of thought, known as syndicalism (after the French word for unions), workers should amass their power in unions, and at the right moment carry out a general strike, crippling capitalist society and bringing it down. Syndicalism was particularly popular in the Mediterranean countries, where its more militant form, anarchosyndicalism, radicalized labor and made a sizable segment of the labor force hostile to parliamentarism.

European socialism attempted also to have an international presence. In 1864, Marx had participated in the founding of the International Workers' Association, which fell prey to internal dissension and dissolved after a few years. Known as the First International, it was followed by a more robust organization, the Second International, in 1889. The International met yearly and debated issues of concern to socialists in general, including the worsening relations among European states. As early as 1893 the International called on European states to resolve their conflicts by mandatory arbitration. In 1907, sensing impending war, the International called on the workers to strike and refuse military service. The International saw itself as a bulwark of peace; it did not realize that once war broke out, Europeans, including socialists, would be swept up in nationalist fervor and would willingly go to war. Although most socialists advocated peace at home and abroad, many others had also contributed to a militant discourse by emphasizing class war.

The New Right, Racism, and Anti-Semitism

The traditional opponents of liberalism on the political right were the conservatives, wedded to preserving the existing order. Beginning in the 1880s, however, a "new right" emerged that was populist and demagogic. Although conservatives had been wary of nationalism, the new right embraced it. Traumatized by industry, democracy, and social egalitarianism, many in this new right rejected doctrines of human equality and embraced racist ideologies.

Racist thinking was common in the nineteenth century. Many Europeans believed human races were not only different physiologically but also—as a result of these differences—differently endowed in intelligence and other qualities (see Chapter 25). Europeans were basically ethnocentric, convinced they were the epitome of humankind while members of other races belonged to lesser groups. In midcentury, the Frenchman

Arthur de Gobineau (1816–1882) published his *Essay on the Inequality of Human Races,* declaring that race "dominates all other problems and is the key to it." Biologists and early anthropologists made similar statements, thus giving racism a scientific aura. Throughout the second half of the nineteenth century, race was thought to be the principal explanation for the differences that were discovered among human groupings. Some races were relegated to near subhuman levels. For example, the British anatomist Robert Knox (1798–1862) declared that the Africans lacked the "grand qualities which distinguish man from animal."

These racist ideas helped fuel anti-Semitism. For centuries Jews had been the object of suspicion and bigotry. Originally, the basis of the prejudice was religious. However, as early as the Middle Ages, there were arguments that "Jewish blood" was different. And with the popularization of pseudoscientific racist thinking in the nineteenth century, Jews were commonly viewed as a separate, inferior race, unworthy of the same rights as the majority of the population.

Historically, Christians had relegated the Jews in their midst to marginal positions. In the Middle Ages, when land was the basis of wealth and prestige, Jews had been confined to such urban trades as cattle trading and moneylending. They incurred high risks by lending money: They often were not paid back and faced unsympathetic courts when they tried to collect their due. To counteract these risks, Jewish moneylenders charged high interest rates that gave them reputations as usurers and made them increasingly disliked.

The emancipation of the Jews, which began in France with the Revolution and spread to Germany and Austria by the 1860s, provided them opportunities they had not had before, and some members of society found it hard to adjust to the prominence a few Jews had gained. Since their prominence and success occurred concurrently with the wrenching social transformations brought by industrialization and urbanization, anti-Semites pointed to the Jews as the perpetrators of these unsettling changes.

Many people perceived Jews as prototypical of the new capitalist class. Although most Jews were of modest means, resentment of the rich often was aimed at Jews. In the earlier part of the century, many anti-Semites were often socialists, speaking on behalf of the working class. Later they came from among the petty bourgeois, small shopkeepers and artisans, who felt threatened by economic change.

Political movements based on anti-Semitism were founded in the 1880s. They depicted Jews as dangerous and wicked and called for the exclusion of Jews from political and governmental power and from certain professions. In some cases they even suggested that Jews be expelled from the state. The mayor of Vienna, Karl Lueger (1844–1928), was elected on an anti-Semitic label. In Berlin, the emperor's chaplain, Adolf Stöcker (1835–1909), founded an anti-Semitic party, hoping to make political inroads among the working-class supporters of socialism. In France, Edouard Drumont (1844–1917) published one of the best-sellers of the second half of the nineteenth century, *Jewish France,* which attributed all the nation's misfortunes to the Jews.

In Russia, the tsarist government, beset by political difficulties, organized and encouraged pogroms, or mass attacks, on Jews in the 1880s, forcing them to flee westward. Court circles openly proclaimed that these campaigns were intended to obliterate the Jewish presence within the empire. "One-third will emigrate, one-third will convert, and one-third will perish," declared the tsar's closest adviser. Although such extreme results were not reached—two thousand Jews were killed—the terror drove two million Jews into exile. In later years, other violent outbreaks were also to occur in Russia.

In the face of growing hostility, some Jews speculated that they would be safe only in their own nation. The Austrian Jewish journalist Theodore Herzl (1860–1904), outraged by the Dreyfus affair in France, in which a Jewish officer was imprisoned on trumped-up charges of treason, founded the Zionist movement. He advocated establishing a Jewish state in the Jews' ancient homeland of Israel. In the beginning, the Zionist movement won a following only in eastern Europe, where the Jews were particularly ill-treated.

Various manifestations of anti-Semitism revealed the weakness of the principle of toleration, one of the basic ideas of liberalism. It became eminently clear that racism, with its penchant for irrationality and violence, could easily be aroused.

Irrationality and Uncertainty

In contrast to the confidence in reason and science that characterized the midcentury period, the era starting in the 1890s wrestled with the issues of irrationality and uncertainty—in philosophy, in science, in the arts, even in religion. The positivism of the earlier era had emphasized the surface of reality but neglected inner meaning and ignored the emotive and intuitive aspects of life. By the 1890s, a neoromantic mood, emphasizing emotion and feeling, stirred major intellectual movements.

The intellectuals who matured in the 1890s, and thus are known as "the generation of 1890," emphasized the extent to which irrational forces guide human beings and their relation to each other. Nonetheless, they remained strongly affected by the positivists, to the extent that they adopted their scientific methods to study irrationality, hoping to find ways to make human beings more rational. Following this group came those intellectuals who matured around 1905, known as the "generation of 1905." Like their seniors, they believed human beings were irrational and the world was unknowable, but they did not express any regret at this condition. Rather, they glorified it.

Freud in 1909 Although much of Sigmund Freud's career still lay ahead of him, he already had established a reputation as the founder of modern psychology. *(Sigmund Freud Copyrights/Mary Evans Picture Library)*

The intellectual trends of the 1890s are exemplified in the work of Sigmund Freud (1856–1939), the founder of psychoanalysis. He believed that people were motivated not only by observed reality but also by their unconscious feelings and emotions. Whereas earlier physicians had described hysteria as a physical ailment, Freud saw its roots as psychological, the result of unresolved inner conflicts. Although Freud's work was influenced by rational methods, he recognized that irrational forces played a significant role in human behavior. Reflecting the concerns of his contemporaries, Freud hoped that understanding these forces would make people more rational.

In philosophy, the tension between reason and emotion was expressed in the work of the German philosopher Friedrich Nietzsche (1844–1900), who proclaimed that rationality had led humankind into a meaningless abyss. Reason would not resolve human problems, nor would any preconceived ideas. In an often-quoted phrase, Nietzsche declared that "God is dead." With no God, humankind was free of all outside constraints, free to overthrow all conventions. Nietzsche admonished his readers to challenge existing institutions and verities and create new ones. However, he realized that such nihilism offered great temptations to inflict unspeakable horrors. According to Nietzsche, only a "superman" could resist these temptations. Nietzsche's call for restraint reflected a hesitation to embrace the full implications of his philosophy. Unfortunately, his warnings were not always heeded. Nietzsche's ideas spread throughout Europe by the turn of the century and were reflected not only in philosophy but also in art and literature.

In contrast to Nietzsche, the French philosopher Henri Bergson (1859–1940) reflected the values of the generation of 1905. He argued that science—and life, for that matter— must be interpreted not rationally but intuitively. "Science," Bergson declared, "can teach us nothing of the

The Limits of Intellect

In Creative Evolution *(1907), a widely heralded work that influenced a whole generation of European intellectuals, the French philosopher Henri Bergson spearheaded the revolt against intellectualism, arguing that intuition was a far better guide.*

We see that the intellect, so skillful in dealing with the inert, is awkward the moment it touches the living. Whether it wants to treat the life of the body or the life of the mind, it proceeds with the rigor, the stiffness and the brutality of an instrument not designed for such use.... *The intellect is characterized by a natural inability to comprehend life.*...

Instinct, on the contrary, is molded on the very form of life. While intelligence treats everything mechanically, instinct proceeds, so to speak, organically. If the consciousness that slumbers in it should awake, if it were wound up into knowledge instead of being wound off into action, if we could ask and it could reply, it would give up to us the most intimate secrets of life. For it only carries out further the work by which life organizes matter—so that we cannot say, as has often been shown, where organization ends and where instinct begins....

Our eye perceives the features of the living being, merely as assembled, not as mutually organized. The intention of life, the simple movement that runs through the lines, that binds them together and gives them significance, escapes it. This intention is just what the artist tries to regain, in placing himself back within the object by a kind of sympathy, in breaking down, by an effort of intuition, the barrier that space puts up between him and his model. It is true that this aesthetic intuition, like external perception, only attains the individual. But we can conceive an inquiry turned in the same direction as art, which would take life in *general* for its object, just as physical science, in following to the end the direction pointed out by external perception, prolongs the individual facts into general laws.

Source: Henri Bergson, *Creative Evolution,* trans. Arthur Mitchell (New York: Holt Rinehart & Winston, 1911), pp. 165, 177, 248–249, 263–271.

truth; it can only serve as a rule of action." Meaningful truths could best be understood emotively, such as the truth of religion, literature, and art (see the box, "The Limits of Intellect").

The scientists of this period seemed to underscore the philosophers' conclusions. In 1905, Albert Einstein (1879–1955) proposed the theory of relativity, which undermined the certainties of Newtonian physics. Einstein's theory demonstrated that time and space are not absolute but exist relative to the observer. Much of the research in atomic theory also revealed variations and unexplained phenomena. For example, the work of German physicist Max Planck (1858–1947) in quantum theory showed that energy was neither absorbed nor emitted continuously, but rather discontinuously. Some scientists no longer shared the self-confidence that their colleagues had maintained half a century earlier, finding it increasingly difficult to believe in ultimate certainties.

In the arts, the idea of being avant-garde took hold among creative people. Being misunderstood and breaking the taboos of society and the conventions of one's craft seemed to be signs of artistic creativity. Artistic movements proclaimed idiosyncratic manifestos and constantly called for the rejection of existing forms of expression and the creation of new ones. The symbolists in France and Italy, the expressionists in Germany, the futurists in Italy, and the secessionists in Austria all reflected the sense that they were living through a fractured period.

In protest against the assembly-line culture of their day, intellectuals emphasized that which was different and unique. Unlike earlier art,

Munch: The Scream Painted in 1893, this work seems to illustrate the fear and horror that some intellectuals experienced at the end of the nineteenth century. *(Edvard Munch,* The Scream, *1893. Tempera and oil pastel on cardboard. 91 x 73.5 cm. Photo: J. Lathion, Nasjonalgalleriet, Oslo. Copyright Munch Museum, Oslo, 1993)*

which had a clear message, the art of this era did not. Many artists no longer believed their role was to portray or spread ideals; rather, they tended to be introspective and even self-absorbed. Although the public at large found it more difficult to decipher the meaning of the new art, a number of art patrons confirmed the avant-garde artists' talent and insight.

Unlike the realists who preceded them, artists in the 1890s surrendered to neoromanticism, trying to investigate and express inner forces. As Paul Gauguin (1848–1903) noted, the purpose of painting was to communicate not how things looked but the emotions they conveyed. Unlike the impressionists, who believed that the artist should reproduce what the world looked like, the new generation wanted to go deeper and interpret the world. The Russian Wassily Kandinsky (1866–1944) asked viewers of his art to "look at the picture as a graphic representation of a mood and not as a representation of objects." Artists appeared to be examining the hidden anxieties of society. Gustave Moreau (1826–1898) displayed monsters, creations of nightmare, byproducts of the unconscious. The Austrian artist Egon Schiele (1890–1918) and the Norwegian painter Edvard Munch (1863–1944) emphasized scenes of violence, fear, and sheer horror.

Religion, too, felt the effects of these intellectual trends. Although large numbers of people still held traditional religious beliefs and followed traditional practices, indifference to organized religion spread. In urban areas of western Europe, church attendance declined; as these areas urbanized, they became increasingly secular. But with the decline of traditional Christian practices, various forms of mysticism became more widespread. Some people were attracted to non-Western religions like Buddhism and Hinduism, and to other mystical beliefs. These attitudes may have reflected a loss of faith in Western culture itself. As the century came to an end, a number of intellectuals argued that their culture, like the century, was destined for decline.

The New Imperialism

The age of empire building that started in Europe in the sixteenth century seemed to have ended by the mid-eighteenth century. Then, in the 1880s, the European states launched a new era of expansionism and conquered an unprecedented amount of territory. In only twenty-five years, Europeans seized ten million square miles and subjugated half a billion people—one half of the non-European population of the world. European expansion was also manifest in a massive movement of people; between 1840 and 1914, between 30 and 35 million Europeans moved overseas, mainly to Australia, the United States, Canada, and Argentina (Map 26.1).

The spurt of ambitious conquest is often called the "new imperialism" to differentiate it from the earlier era of empire building. Whereas the earlier imperialism focused on the Americas, nineteenth-century imperialism centered on Africa and Asia. And unlike the earlier period, the new imperialism occurred in an age of mass participation in politics and was accompanied by expressions of popular enthusiasm.

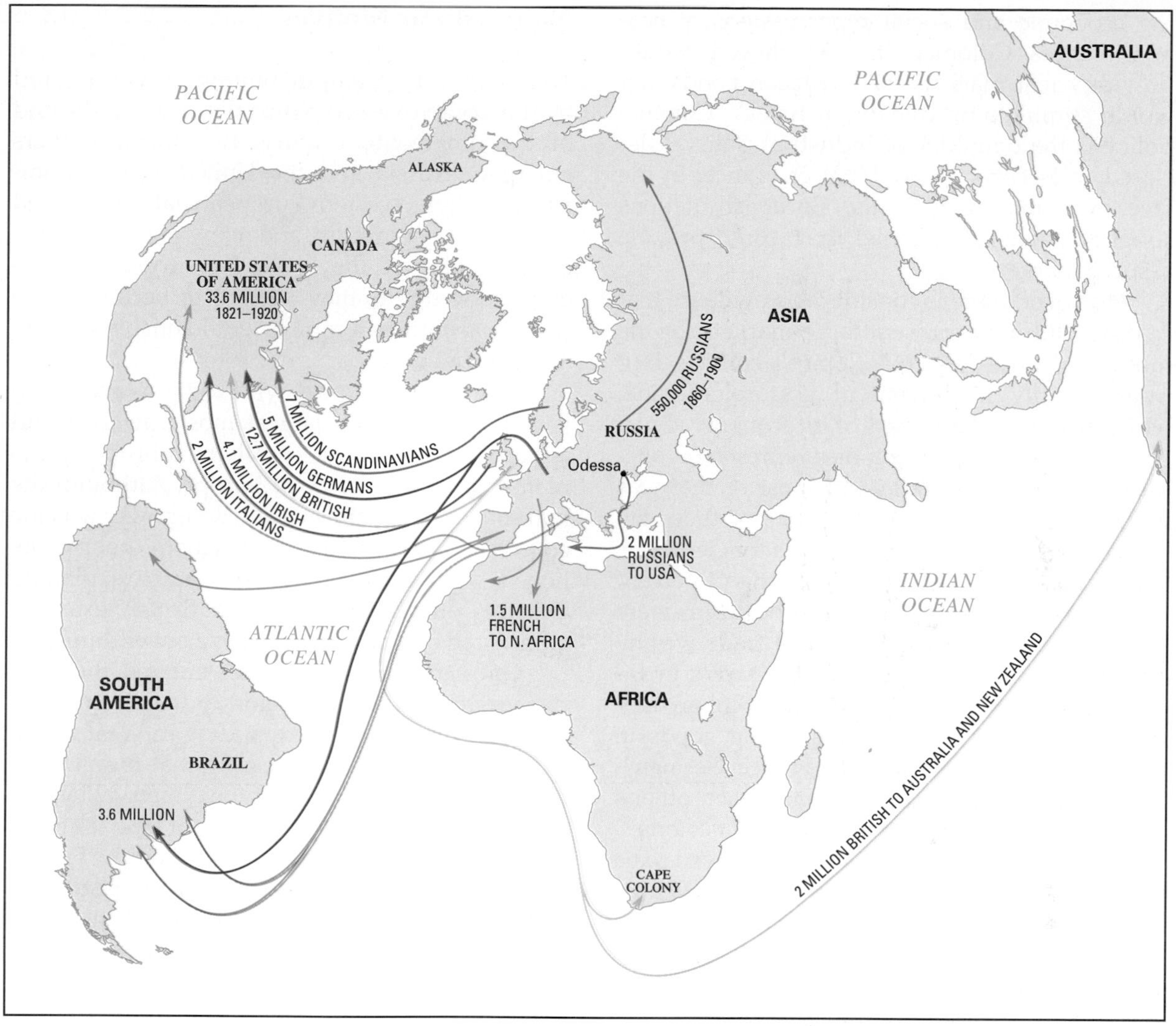

Map 26.1 European Migrations, 1820–1910 Throughout the nineteenth century, millions of Europeans left home for overseas; most headed for the United States. (*Source:* Reproduced from *THE TIMES ATLAS OF WORLD HISTORY*, 3d ed., by kind permission of Times Books. Some data from Eric Hobsbawm, *The Age of Empire, 1875–1914* [New York: Pantheon, 1987].)

Economic and Social Motives

The hope of profit overseas contributed to a large degree to the dynamic of the new imperialism. When the explorer Henry Stanley (1841–1904) returned from Africa in the late 1870s, he told the Manchester Chamber of Commerce, "There are forty million people beyond the gateway of Congo, and the cotton spinners of Manchester are waiting to clothe them." However, many Europeans had unrealistic notions of the potential markets that might be available to them. French explorers and statesmen spoke of a western Sudan inhabited by "two hundred million" people—a sixtyfold exaggeration of the real situation. Nonetheless, such illusions of huge markets were instrumental in stirring an interest in empire.

Certain economic anxieties beset European states, and colonization seemed to resolve them. There had been an economic downturn in the 1870s, and many political leaders worried about the economic and social repercussions of economic crises. Colonies, it was believed, would provide eager markets for European goods that would stimulate production at home. "Colonial policy is the daughter of industrial policy," declared Jules Ferry (1832–1893) of France. In the face of rising tariff walls, European nations sought to establish colonies that would provide assured markets.

However, there is considerable evidence that colonies did not represent large markets for the mother countries. In 1914, France's colonies represented only 12 percent of its foreign trade, which was not a large part of its economy. Great Britain's trade with its colonies represented one-third of its foreign trade, but most of that was with the settlement colonies and not those acquired through direct conquest. As for Germany, her colonial trade represented less than 1 percent of her exports. Even when protective tariffs were imposed in colonies, monopoly of trade was by no means secured. In spite of the tariffs in Indochina, French imports to the Asian colony represented only 40 percent of entering goods in 1914. And despite rising tariffs, France, Germany, and Great Britain continued being each other's main customers, rather than that of their colonies.

Although export to the colonies proved to be economically unprofitable, it was difficult to argue with those who contended that the colonies would turn out to be profitable in the long run. So while the colonies were not necessary to the capitalist system—as Marxist critics argued—the belief in colonial profitability was certainly present.

Some proponents of empire, known as social imperialists, argued that possession of an empire could resolve social as well as economic issues. It would give employment to the working classes and thus keep them satisfied with their lot. The British imperialist Cecil Rhodes (1853–1902) claimed that Britain's empire was saving the country "from a murderous civil war." An empire could be an outlet for a variety of frustrations at home, especially for those nations that believed they suffered from overpopulation. German and Italian imperialists frequently argued that their nations needed colonies to settle their growing poor. Once the overseas territories were acquired, however, few found them attractive for settlement.

Nationalistic Motives

To a large extent, empire building was triggered by the desire to assert national power. At the end of the nineteenth century, two major powers emerged, Russia and the United States. Compared to them, western European nations seemed small and insignificant, and many of their leaders believed that if they were to survive the inevitable struggle, they needed to become large territorial entities. Empires would enable them to achieve that goal.

The British Empire, with India as its crown jewel, constituted the largest, most powerful, and apparently wealthiest of all the European domains. It was the envy of Europe. Although the real source of Britain's wealth and power was the country's industrial economy, many people believed possession of a vast empire explained Britain's success. And so the British example stimulated other nations to carve out empires.

Once the European states entered the fray, they excited mutual suspicion and fear. When the French appeared to be expanding in West Africa in the 1890s, the British, fearing that they would be cut off from the trade of the Niger valley, aggressively conquered huge tracts of land that previously had been of little interest. And the French had started off their conquests believing that they had to get to the Niger before the British did. Thus the scramble for Africa was triggered by European rivalries, by fear of being excluded from an opportunity that would never return. Similarly in Asia, Britain annexed Burma in 1885 under the impression that France was about to annex it. And France expanded in Indochina in the 1880s and 1890s for fear the British would beat them to the punch.

France, defeated by Prussia in 1870, found in its colonies proof that it was still a Great Power. Germany and Italy, which formed their national identity late, cast a jealous eye on the British and French empires and decided that if they were to be counted as Great Powers, they too would need overseas colonies. King Leopold II (r. 1865–1909) of Belgium spun out various plans to acquire colonies to compensate for his nation's small size. And Britain, anxious at the emergence of rival economic and political powers in the late nineteenth century, found in its colonies a guarantee for the future. If colonies were to become the base of power, no state wanted to be without them.

In the race for colonies, worldwide strategic concerns stimulated expansion. Because the Suez Canal assured the route to India, the British established a protectorate over Egypt in 1882. And then, in 1900, fearing that a rival power might threaten their position by encroaching on the Nile, they established control over the Nile valley all the way south to Uganda. Russian expansion southward into central Asia toward Afghanistan was intended to avert a British takeover of this area, while the British movement northwestward to Afghanistan had the opposite intention—to prevent Russia from encroaching on India. The "great game" played by Russia and Britain in central Asia lasted the entire nineteenth century, ending only in 1907.

The strategic imperative also functioned with regard to areas continguous to an acquired territory, which were viewed as vital for the protection of the original colony. European statesmen decided that these adjoining regions must not fall to rival powers or become staging areas for attacks by the local peoples on the colonial power. Such concerns help explain why France, after conquering Algeria in 1830, turned on Tunisia in 1884 and Morocco in 1911, and why Britain, wanting to safeguard its position in India, forcibly annexed Burma in 1885. In the second half of the nineteenth century, Russia continuously pushed southward and eastward, annexing much of central Asia and eastward at the cost of China, creating a large contiguous territory reaching to the Pacific.

The Highlanders' Charge at the Battle of Futtehpore Imperialist propaganda entered various forms of media, including children's books. Imperialist themes were particularly popular among boys' books. This is an illustration from the frontispiece of a 1911 book for juveniles, *Heroes of Modern India*. *(The Collection of J. M. MacKenzie)*

Much of this expansion was due to the desire to control the frontiers of newly acquired areas. And once these frontiers had been brought under control, there were, of course, turbulent new frontiers that had to be brought under control. Such a process also explains the constant westward movement of the United States at the same time. As the Russian foreign minister said of such an incentive for expansion, "The chief difficulty is to know where to stop." The imperial powers rarely did.

The bitter rivalry among the Great Powers helps explain the division of the globe, but it also protected some regions from falling under European domination. In an effort to contain their rivalry in southeast Asia, Britain and France established Siam (Thailand) as a buffer state. China's sovereignty was seriously violated when Russia took large chunks of territory as it moved southward and eastward, and the Western powers seized "treaty ports" and insisted on the right of their merchants and missionaries to move freely. Yet most of China survived because the European powers held each others' ambitions in check. No state alone could conquer all of China; none would allow another to do so either.

Given all the reasons Europeans expressed on behalf of empire, one might imagine that far-flung areas overseas were acquired as a result of a policy determination in the capitals of Europe.

However, that was not always the case. The local situation and "the man on the spot," the European official dispatched overseas, often determined the pace and direction of empire building. In 1883, British Prime Minister Gladstone sent General Charles Gordon (1833–1885) to the Sudan to supervise the withdrawal of British troops who had only temporarily entered the country. Gordon disregarded orders and tried to overthrow the local political religious leader, the Mahdi, who counterattacked, laid siege to Khartoum, entered the city, and killed Gordon. In the face of public outrage over the killing, the British annexed the Sudan. A parallel incident in Indochina also highlighted how disobedient officials, hungry for action, created unexpected situations—opportunities, perhaps—for colonial annexation. In 1883, France dispatched Commander Henri Rivière (1827–1883) to the southern part of Vietnam, already under French authority. Exceeding his orders, Rivière marched northward and was massacred. When news reached Paris, the National Assembly unanimously voted an expedition of 20,000 men, who more than avenged the hapless commander. They brought northern Vietnam under French control.

Other Ideological Motives

In addition to the search for profit and nationalistic pride, overseas empire building was at times swayed by altruism—or at least, a strong sense of mission was used to rationalize imperialism.

Influenced by Darwin and his theory of the struggle for survival, many argued that just as competition among species existed in nature, so also did a struggle for survival among groups exist in human society. Dubbed "Social Darwinists," these thinkers envisioned a world of fierce competition. They believed that the most serious struggle was among the races; and in this struggle the white race was destined to succeed, the nonwhites to succumb. At the same time that Europeans were making substantial material progress as a result of the industrial revolution, their widescale expansion overseas brought them into contact with Africans and Asians who had not created an industrial economy. They assumed that the dramatic disparity between their own material culture and that of the overseas peoples was proof of their innate superiority. Africans and Asians were seen as primitive, inferior peoples, still in their evolutionary "infancy." (See the feature, "Weighing the Evidence: The Layout of the British Museum," on pages 988–989.)

Social Darwinists claimed that the law of nature dictated the eclipse of weaker races and the victory of the stronger and presumably better race. Lord Salisbury (1830–1903), the British prime minister, declared that the nations of the world could be divided between "the living and the dying," the former replacing the latter. Others saw an obligation of the white man to dominate and lead the "lesser breeds" to a "higher stage." The British bard of imperialism, Rudyard Kipling (1865–1936), celebrated this view in his poem "White Man's Burden" (1899), which, incidentally, bid the United States to partake in the imperial race by colonizing the Philippines:

Take up the White Man's burden—
Send forth the best ye breed—
Go bind your sons to exile
To serve your captives' need. . . .

Each nation was certain that providence had chosen it for a colonial mission. Cecil Rhodes declared that he thought God wanted him to "paint as much of the map of Africa British as possible." His superior, Secretary of Colonies Joseph Chamberlain (1836–1914), exulted that "the British race is the greatest governing race the world has ever seen." France, its leaders announced, had a civilizing mission to fulfill in the world; Jules Ferry, its prime minister, declared it the duty of his country "to civilize the inferior races" (see the box, "Ferry's Arguments in Favor of Empire"). Although European states were colonial rivals, they also believed they were engaged in a joint mission overseas. Empire building underscored the belief in a common European destiny, as opposed to the ascribed savagery and backwardness of non-Europeans.

Pointing to historic antecedents, imperialists colored their activities with a hue of heroism. Many Europeans found satisfaction in the thought that their country performed feats equal or superior to those of ancient Rome or the Crusaders, spreading "civilization" to far-flung empires. Colonial literature celebrated white men of action who, by their heroism, conquered and administered what had been large kingdoms or empires in Africa and Asia. Novelists like Kipling

Ferry's Arguments in Favor of Empire

In asking the French parliament in July 1885 to vote funds for a colonial expedition, Prime Minister Ferry provided a broad range of reasons why France should acquire overseas possessions.

For a country such as ours, which is obliged by the very nature of its industry to devote itself to exports on a large scale, the colonial question is a matter of finding outlets for those exports. When one founds a colony, one is supplying an outlet for trade....

There is another matter, another order of ideas, with which I must also deal—as briefly as possible, I assure you—and this is the humanitarian and civilizing aspect of the matter....

Let us speak clearer and more frankly. It must be openly said that the superior races have rights over the inferior races....

I repeat that the superior races have a right because they have a duty. They have a duty to civilise the inferior races....

And then there is the political aspect of the matter....

A policy of colonial expansion is being engaged in by all European powers. We must do likewise. If we do not, then we shall meet the fate—not that we here shall meet it but our children and grandchildren will—which has overtaken other nations which played a great role on the world's stage three centuries ago but which today, for all their power and greatness in the past, are now third- or fourth-rate powers.

Source: Henri Brunschwig, *French Colonialism, 1871–1919*, trans. W. G. Brown (London: Pall Mall Press, 1966), pp. 76–78, 80.

empasized the superiority and heroism of white men over perfidious, cowardly "natives."

Missionary groups also were motivated by strong ideals favoring expansion. David Livingstone (1813–1873), a missionary doctor who had explored central and East Africa in the 1850s, had come across slave caravans and other practices that he found shocking. If the area were opened to commerce, he proclaimed, then Christianity and civilization would follow. His *Travels* and posthumous *Last Journals* were widely read by the British public, and they seemed to suggest that Africa would be vastly improved if it were "opened" to European contact. Missionaries were gripped by the notion of millions of heathens in Africa and Asia who should be converted to Christianity. They welcomed European expansion to ensure the spread of Christianity.

Missionaries also unwittingly created conditions that invited European intervention. Often they went to lands that were inhospitable and even hostile. In societies where the indigenous religion sanctioned the existing social and political structures, local leaders perceived as a threat and a menace European missionaries who preached a different religion. The execution of French missionaries in Vietnam in 1851 and 1852 led to the prompt intervention of the French navy; Emperor Napoleon III saw this action as a convenient way to win support from Catholics at home. The killing of missionaries in China also brought intervention by European powers. In addition to demanding the right of missionaries to travel freely in China, the European powers also demanded in 1860 the right of traders to move about freely and forced the Chinese government to cede to them treaty ports. In 1886 the murder of British missionaries in the kingdom of Buganda, in East Africa, fixed British interest on the area and eventually led to its conquest. In Madagascar, competition between British Protestant and French Catholic missionaries for influence over the Malagasy queen precipitated French military intervention and conquest in 1896.

Colonial acquisitions triggered public support for further expansion of the empire—support that was expressed by the founding of various colonial societies. Britain's Primrose League, which supported empire as well as other patriotic goals, had one million members. In Germany, the German Colonial Society, founded in 1888, had 43,000 members by 1914. The French and Italian groups were limited in size but had influential contacts with policymakers. Colonial societies generally drew their membership from the professional middle classes, who were quite open to nationalist arguments—civil servants, professors, and journalists. These societies produced a steady stream of propaganda favoring empire building.

Conquest, Administration, and Westernization

As a result of the industrial revolution, Europeans had achieved superior weapons technology, making them virtually invincible in a colonial conflict. One remarkable exception was the defeat of the Italians in Adowa in 1896, when the Italians faced an Ethiopian force that was not only superior in numbers but better armed.

Conquest was often brutal. In September 1898, British-led forces at the battle of Omdurman slaughtered 20,000 Sudanese. From 1904 to 1908, an uprising in southwest Africa against German rule led to the killing of an estimated 60,000 of the Herero people; the German general, who had expressly given an order to exterminate the whole population, was awarded a medal by William II.

In many colonies resistance continued long after conquest had officially been declared. Continuous skirmishes, in somes cases full-scale wars, were fought. Britain annexed Burma in 1886, but it then faced wide-scale rebellion for five years. In Indochina, the French were confronted with the "Scholars' Revolt," led by mandarins who refused the protectorate; it took twenty years to defeat the uprising. In West Africa, France declared the Ivory Coast to be a French possession in the 1890s; it was 1916 before the whole territory was "pacified" (Map 26.2).

In the first few years, the Europeans ran a haphazard administration, undermanned and underfunded; in 1913 Germany spent ten times more on its postal service than on its colonies. Colonial governments could also be brutally insensitive to the needs of the indigenous peoples. To save money, France in the 1890s put large tracts of land in the French Congo under the administration of private rubber companies, which systematically and brutally coerced the local people to collect rubber. When the scandal broke in Paris, the concessionary companies were abolished and the French state re-established its control.

The most notorious example of exploitation, terror, and mass killings was connected with the Belgian Congo. King Leopold II of Belgium had acquired it as a personal empire and mercilessly exploited it and its people. An international chorus of condemnation finally forced the king to disgorge his empire and put it under the administration of the Belgian government, which abolished some of the worst features of Leopold's rule.

Brutal and exploitive, imperialism spread Western institutions, technology, and values. In an effort to exploit the economic potential of their colonies, Europeans introduced various Western technologies. By 1914, Great Britain had built 40,000 miles of rail in India—nearly twice as much as in Britain. In India and Egypt, the British erected hydraulic systems that irrigated previously arid lands. Colonials built cities often modeled on the European grid system. In some cases they were graced with large, tree-lined avenues, and some neighborhoods were equipped with running water and modern sanitation. Schools, patterned after those in Europe, taught the imperial language and spread Western ideas and scientific knowledge—although only to a small percentage of the local population.

The European empire builders created political units that had never existed before. Although there had been many efforts in the past to join the Indian subcontinent under a single authority, the British were the first to accomplish this feat (Map 26.3). By a common administration, rail network, and trade, Britain imparted to Indians a sense of a common condition, leading in 1885 to the

Map 26.2 Africa in 1914 European powers in the late nineteenth century conquered most of Africa. Only Liberia and Ethiopia were left unoccupied by 1914.

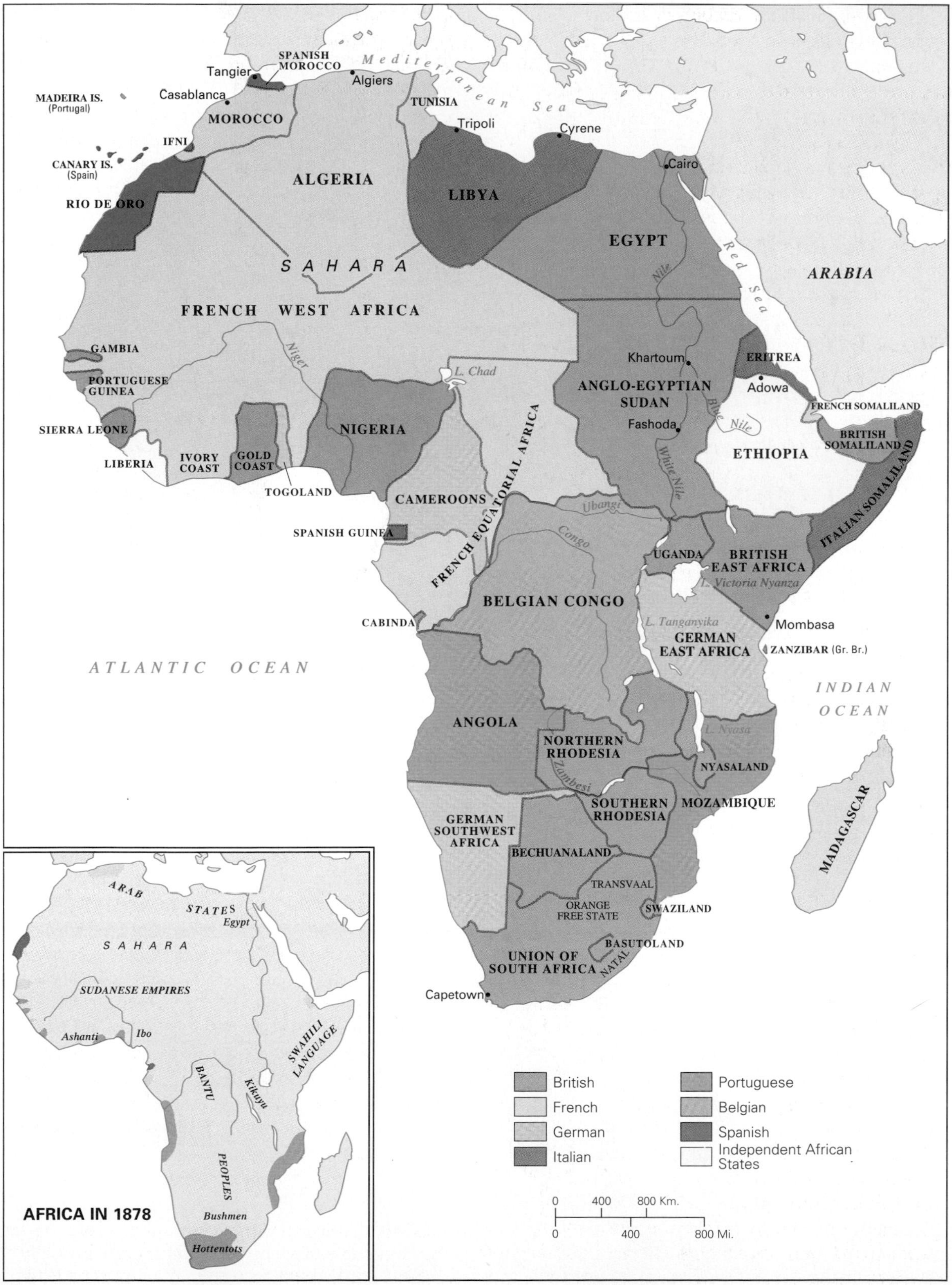
SPANISH MOROCCO
Tangier
Mediterranean Sea
Algiers
MADEIRA IS. (Portugal)
Casablanca
MOROCCO
TUNISIA
Tripoli
Cyrene
IFNI
CANARY IS. (Spain)
ALGERIA
Cairo
LIBYA
RIO DE ORO
EGYPT
SAHARA
Red Sea
Nile
ARABIA
FRENCH WEST AFRICA
GAMBIA
Niger
Khartoum
ERITREA
L. Chad
PORTUGUESE GUINEA
Adowa
ANGLO-EGYPTIAN SUDAN
FRENCH SOMALILAND
SIERRA LEONE
NIGERIA
Fashoda
Blue Nile
BRITISH SOMALILAND
LIBERIA
IVORY COAST
GOLD COAST
ETHIOPIA
White Nile
TOGOLAND
CAMEROONS
FRENCH EQUATORIAL AFRICA
Ubangi
ITALIAN SOMALILAND
SPANISH GUINEA
Congo
UGANDA
BRITISH EAST AFRICA
L. Victoria Nyanza
BELGIAN CONGO
CABINDA
Mombasa
L. Tanganyika
GERMAN EAST AFRICA
ZANZIBAR (Gr. Br.)
ATLANTIC OCEAN
INDIAN OCEAN
ANGOLA
L. Nyasa
NORTHERN RHODESIA
NYASALAND
Zambesi
SOUTHERN RHODESIA
MOZAMBIQUE
MADAGASCAR
GERMAN SOUTHWEST AFRICA
BECHUANALAND
TRANSVAAL
ORANGE FREE STATE
SWAZILAND
BASUTOLAND
UNION OF SOUTH AFRICA
NATAL
Capetown
ARAB STATES
Egypt
SAHARA
SUDANESE EMPIRES
Ashanti
Ibo
SWAHILI LANGUAGE
BANTU
Kikuyu
PEOPLES
Bushmen
Hottentots
AFRICA IN 1878
British
French
German
Italian
Portuguese
Belgian
Spanish
Independent African States
0 400 800 Km.
0 400 800 Mi.

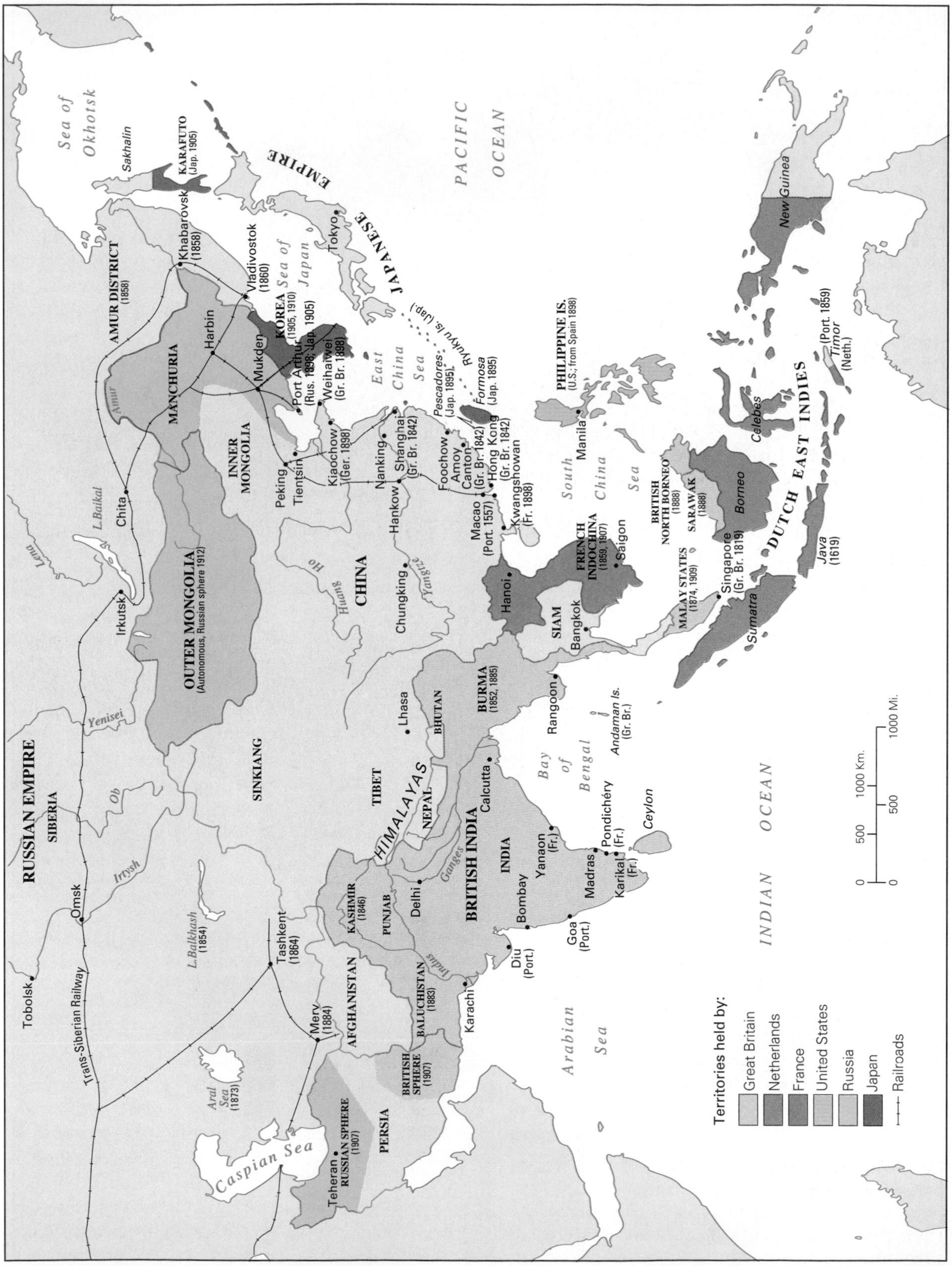
RUSSIAN EMPIRE
SIBERIA
Sea of Okhotsk
Sakhalin
KARAFUTO (Jap. 1905)
Khabarovsk (1858)
AMUR DISTRICT (1858)
Vladivostok (1860)
Sea of Japan
Tokyo
JAPANESE EMPIRE
PACIFIC OCEAN
KOREA (1905, 1910)
Port Arthur (Rus. 1898; Jap. 1905)
Weihaiwei (Gr. Br. 1898)
Harbin
Mukden
MANCHURIA
Amur
INNER MONGOLIA
OUTER MONGOLIA (Autonomous, Russian sphere 1912)
Chita
L.Baikal
Irkutsk
Lena
Yenisei
Ob
Irtysh
Omsk
Tobolsk
Trans-Siberian Railway
L.Balkhash (1854)
Tashkent (1864)
Merv (1884)
Aral Sea (1873)
Caspian Sea
Teheran
RUSSIAN SPHERE (1907)
PERSIA
BRITISH SPHERE (1907)
AFGHANISTAN
BALUCHISTAN (1883)
KASHMIR (1846)
PUNJAB
SINKIANG
TIBET
Lhasa
HIMALAYAS
NEPAL
BHUTAN
BURMA (1852, 1885)
Rangoon
BRITISH INDIA
INDIA
Delhi
Ganges
Indus
Karachi
Diu (Port.)
Bombay
Goa (Port.)
Madras
Yanaon (Fr.)
Pondichéry (Fr.)
Karikal (Fr.)
Calcutta
Ceylon
Bay of Bengal
Andaman Is. (Gr. Br.)
Arabian Sea
INDIAN OCEAN
CHINA
Huang Ho
Yangtze
Chungking
Hankow
Nanking
Peking
Tientsin
Kiaochow (Ger. 1898)
Shanghai (Gr. Br. 1842)
Foochow
Amoy
Canton
Hong Kong (Gr. Br. 1842)
Kwangshowan (Fr. 1898)
Macao (Port. 1557)
East China Sea
Pescadores (Jap. 1895)
Formosa (Jap. 1895)
Ryukyu Is. (Jap.)
PHILIPPINE IS. (U.S.; from Spain 1898)
Manila
South China Sea
Hanoi
FRENCH INDOCHINA (1859, 1907)
Saigon
SIAM
Bangkok
MALAY STATES (1874, 1909)
Singapore (Gr. Br. 1819)
BRITISH NORTH BORNEO (1888)
SARAWAK (1888)
Borneo
Sumatra
Java (1619)
Celebes
DUTCH EAST INDIES
Timor (Port. 1859) (Neth.)
New Guinea
0 500 1000 Km.
0 500 1000 Mi.
Territories held by:
Great Britain
Netherlands
France
United States
Russia
Japan
Railroads

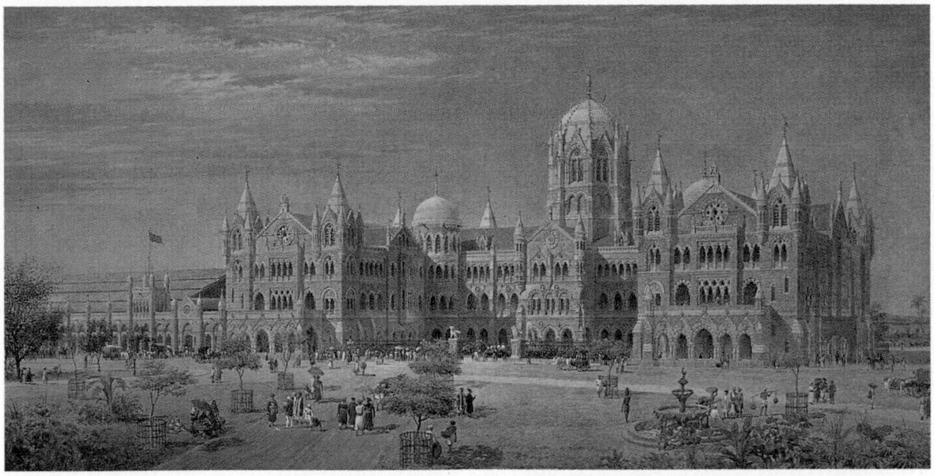

Victoria Terminus, Bombay Europeans' tendency to transfer values and institutions to their colonies included the export of architectural style. Various traditional European architectural styles, mainly the neo-Gothic that was so popular in nineteenth-century England, shaped this edifice, completed in 1888. *(The British Library, Oriental and India Office Collections)*

founding of the India Congress party. Initially this party demanded reforms within the British colonial system; eventually it became the major nationalist group. The Congress party platform included the demand for constitutional government, representative assemblies, and the rule of law—concepts all based on Western theory and practice.

It is far from certain that conquest was the best or only manner of ensuring the limited Westernization that occurred. Japan escaped European subjugation and on its own was able to copy the West far more extensively than the colonized peoples. European conquest and threat of conquest (as in Japan) spread Western institutions and values to much of the rest of the world.

The transformations that Europeans wrought confirmed their belief that they were agents of progress, building a new and better world. Europeans arrogantly believed they knew what was best for other people; and they accepted force as a means of dealing with others.

Map 26.3 Asia in 1914 China, Siam (Thailand), and a portion of Persia were the only parts of Asia still independent after the great powers, including the United States and Japan, subjugated the continent to alien rule.

The Democratic Powers

By the end of the nineteenth century, most of Europe's political systems floundered in crisis, unable to respond to change. The major powers with democratic institutions—Great Britain, France, and Italy—confronted volatile public opinion and had difficulty winning broad consensus for their policies. To varying degrees, they struggled with new challenges that emerged from an expanded electorate that, at times, became frustrated by the failure of the system to resolve their demands. Contrary to democratic precepts that differences be resolved by the ballot and legislation, many people, both in government and out, were willing to resort to extraparliamentary means, including violence, to see their interests prevail.

Great Britain

In Great Britain, the Reform Bill of 1884 transformed the political landscape by doubling suffrage to five million—giving the vote to two of every three adult males. The appeal of this enlarged electorate tempted politicians to make demagogic promises, leading to frustration when they were not met. It also made it more difficult to establish compromise in a Parliament that was no longer represented by a fairly limited class of people with common interests and values. Faced with a number of issues, the British political system proved unable to resolve them peacefully and—uncharacteristically—had to resort to force or the threat of force.

As in earlier periods, Ireland proved to be a persistent problem. The political consciousness of the Irish had risen considerably, and they seethed under alien rule. In an attempt to quell Irish opposition in 1886, Prime Minister Gladstone proposed autonomy, or "home rule" for Ireland. There were many objections to such a plan, the most serious being that if Ireland ruled itself, the local Protestant majority in Ulster, the northeast part of the island, would be overwhelmed and likely to fall under the control of the larger majority of Catholics making up the population of Ireland as a whole. "Home rule is Rome rule," intoned the supporters of Ulster Protestantism. Among Gladstone's own Liberals, many opposed changing the existing relationship between England and its possession. They seceded from the Liberals and formed the Unionist party, which, in coalition with the Conservatives, ruled the country from 1886 to 1905. When the Liberals returned to power in 1906, they again proposed home rule. In 1911, the House of Commons passed a home-rule bill, but it was obstructed in the House of Lords and was not supposed to go into effect until September 1914.

In the process of debating the Irish issue, many segments of British society showed they were willing to resort to extralegal and even violent means. Fearing Catholic domination, Protestants in northern Ireland armed themselves, determined to resist home rule. In the rest of Ireland, Catholic groups armed, too, insisting on the unity of the island; they were ready to fight for home rule for the whole of Ireland. The Conservative party in Britain, which opposed home rule, called on Ulster to revolt. British officers threatened to resign their commissions, rather than fight Ulster. The behavior of the Conservatives and the army indicated a breakdown of order and authority, a disregard for tradition by two of its bulwarks. Only the outbreak of war in 1914 delayed a showdown over Ireland and then for only a few years.

Once back in power in 1906, the Liberals committed themselves to a vast array of social reforms but were frustrated by the difficulty of getting their program through the House of Lords. The feisty Liberal chancellor of the Exchequer, David Lloyd George (1863–1945), expressed his outrage that the will of the people was being thwarted by a handful of magnates in the House of Lords, sitting there not by election but by hereditary right.

The Liberals' social reform program included old-age pensions. To finance them, Lloyd George proposed raising income taxes and death duties and establishing a tax on landed wealth. A bill with these measures easily passed the House of Commons in 1909 but was stymied in the upper chamber, where many members were prominent landowners. Although the House of Lords technically had the power to amend or reject a bill passed by Commons, for nearly 250 years it had been understood that it did not have the right to reject a money bill. Nonetheless, motivated by economic self-interest and personal spite against the Liberals, a majority in the House of Lords disregarded the convention and voted against the bill. This decision created a major constitutional crisis.

The government wanted not only to pass its bill but to reduce the power of the House of Lords. In 1911 it sponsored a bill, quickly passed by the House of Commons, to limit the House of Lords to a suspensive veto. This would mean that a bill defeated in the House of Lords could be prevented from going into effect for only a predetermined period—in this case, two years. The House of Lords, of course, would not pass such a law. Finally, however, at the request of the government, the king threatened to appoint four hundred new lords. Under this threat the House of Lords passed the bill. During the debate over the bill, Conservatives—the representatives of British traditionalism and the upholders of decorum—resorted to brawling and refused to let the prime minister speak. It was the first time in British parliamentary history that such an act of defiance had occurred.

The British Parliament, considered the model for supporters of free institutions, had shown itself unable to resolve issues in a reasoned manner. Violence in language and deed had been introduced into its halls; and only the threat of destroying the integrity of the upper house had forced a resolution.

Violence also appeared in another unlikely place: the women's suffrage movement. Most liberal males, when speaking of the need to extend human liberty, had excluded the female gender. Toward the end of the nineteenth century, that, too, was challenged. Women began to organize into groups devoted to winning the vote but had little initial success. In 1903, Emmeline Pankhurst (1858–1928) and her two daughters founded the Women's Social and Political Union, whose goal was immediate suffrage.

Angered and frustrated by their lack of progress, the suffragettes, led by the Pankhursts, began in 1906 a more militant program of protest—disturbing proceedings in Parliament, breaking windows at the prime minister's residence, slashing canvases at the National Gallery, burning down empty houses, dropping acid into mailboxes, and throwing bombs. There were even threats on the lives of the prime minister and king. Understandably impatient, the suffragettes were in no mood for negotiations and compromise, and the government treated them with unaccustomed harshness. Suffragettes who were arrested often engaged in hunger strikes. Fearing they would die, the authorities force-fed the women. Female protesters were also physically attacked by male thugs (see the box, "Pankhurst on Women's Rights"). That women would resort to violence, and that men in and outside of the government would resort to force against them, seemed to show how widespread the cult of force had become.

Modern Inquisition This 1910 poster protested the force feeding of suffragettes on hunger strike. It invited voters to reject the Liberal government, guilty of what suffragettes viewed as state torture. *(Library of Congress)*

France

The Third Republic, founded in 1870 after France's humiliating military defeat at the hands of the Prussians, also continued to face an ongoing series of crises. Challenged by enemies on the political left and right who continually called for the abolition of democracy, the regime found itself buffeted from all sides.

The French government itself contributed to an unstable political situation by its lack of effective leadership. The need to build coalitions among the several parties in the parliament rewarded those politicians who had moderate programs and were flexible. Thus there was little premium on holding strong ideas and commitments, and the prime minister was often more a conciliator than a leader. Moreover, lackluster leadership appealed to republicans, who continued to fear that a popular leader might—as Louis Napoleon had in 1851—exploit his support to make himself dictator.

The regime seemed to lurch from scandal to scandal. The most notorious was the Dreyfus affair. In October 1894, Captain Alfred Dreyfus (1859–1935) of the French army was arrested and charged with passing military secrets to the German embassy. Dreyfus seems to have attracted suspicion because he was the only Jewish officer on the general staff. The evidence was flimsy—a

Pankhurst on Women's Rights

In 1908 the suffragettes, led by Emmeline Pankhurst, issued a handbill calling on the people of London to "rush" Parliament and win the vote for women. The legal authorities interpreted this as threatening the peace, and several suffragettes, including Pankhurst, were put on trial. They put up a spirited defense, in which Pankhurst movingly explained her motives for leading the suffragette cause.

I want you to realise how we women feel; because we are women, because we are not men, we need some legitimate influence to bear upon our law-makers.

Now, we have tried every way. We have presented larger petitions than were ever presented for any other reform, we have succeeded in holding greater public meetings than men have ever had for any reform, in spite of the difficulty which women have in throwing off their natural diffidence, that desire to escape publicity which we have inherited from generations of our foremothers; we have broken through that. We have faced hostile mobs at street corners, because we were told that we could not have that representation for our taxes which men have won unless we converted the whole of the country to our side. Because we have done this, we have been misrepresented, we have been ridiculed, we have had contempt poured upon us. The ignorant mob at the street corner has been incited to offer us violence, which we have faced unarmed and unprotected by the safeguards which Cabinet Ministers have. We know that we need the protection of the vote even more than men have needed it. . . .

If you had power to send us to prison, not for six months, but for six years, for sixteen years, or for the whole of our lives, the Government must not think that they can stop this agitation. It will go on. . . .

We are here not because we are law-breakers; we are here in our efforts to become law-makers.

Source: F. W. Pethick Lawrence, ed. *The Trial of the Suffragette Leaders* (London: The Women's Press, 1909), pp. 21–24.

letter written in a handwriting that some thought resembled that of Dreyfus, although other experts testified it was not that of the young officer.

This letter, and materials that later turned out to be forged, led the French army to court-martial Dreyfus and sentence him to life imprisonment on Devil's Island (see the box, "A Letter from Prison"). By March 1896, the general staff had evidence that it was another officer, Major Esterhazy, who was actually the spy. But to reopen the case would be to admit the army had made an error, and the general staff refused to do so.

By late 1897, when the apparent miscarriage of justice became widely known, French society split over "the affair." The political left, including a large number of intellectuals, argued for a reopening of the case. For them it was crucial that justice be carried out. The army and its supporters, right-wing politicians, royalists, and Catholics, argued that the decision should not be changed. As the bulwark against internal and foreign threats, the army should be above challenge, and the fate of a single man—guilty or innocent—was immaterial.

The affair unleashed a swirl of controversy and rioting, which led the government to order a retrial in 1899. But the court again found Dreyfus guilty—this time with "extenuating circumstances" and the recommendation that he be pardoned. Finally, in 1906, Dreyfus was fully exonerated. He ended his days as a general in the army that had subjected him to so much suffering.

A Letter from Prison

During his years of imprisonment, Dreyfus and his wife, Lucie, exchanged hundreds of letters. In this letter written before he embarked on his journey to Devil's Island, Dreyfus struck themes that were frequently reiterated in their correspondence.

Dépôt de Saint-Martin-de-Ré,
January 21, 1895

Ma bonne chérie:

Yesterday they gave me your sad letter, and then your telegram, to which I replied. How wretched we are! I think that no one in the world has ever suffered as we two. You know there are times when I am sorry that I promised you to live. After my conviction I had prepared everything for my death. I was ready to appear before God, my conscience clear and at peace. You could have vindicated my memory quite as well, and you would not have suffered as much at the thought of my own torment. . . .

What is essential, my dear, and what must be the object of your every thought, is to discover the truth, by every means possible, by using our whole fortune. Money is nothing, honor is all. . . .

Take every care of your health, my dear, you need all your strength. Think of the children before you think of me. They need you, and they have only you now. You must not give yourself up to your grief. You have a task too lofty and too noble still to fulfill. . . .

Alfred

Source: Donald C. McKay, ed. and trans., *The Dreyfus Case, by the Man—Alfred Dreyfus, and His Son—Pierre Dreyfus* (New Haven, Conn.: Yale University Press, 1937), pp. 78–79.

The strong encouragement Catholics gave to those who supported the original verdict confirmed the republicans' belief that the church was a menace to the regime. The Radical party, the strongest supporters of Dreyfus, won the elections in 1899. In spite of its title, the Radical party favored moderate social reforms. It was uncompromising, however, in its anticlericalism, determined to wreak vengeance on the Catholics and end the influence of the church once and for all. In 1905, the parliament passed a law separating church and state, thus ending the privileged position the Catholic church had enjoyed. Violent language and physical confrontations on both sides accompanied this separation. Catholics trying to prevent state officials from entering churches to take required inventories sometimes resorted to force, using weapons or, in one case, a bear chained to the church. Armed soldiers broke down church doors and led monks away.

Labor problems also triggered repeated confrontations with the government. Increased labor militancy produced long, drawn-out strikes, which in 1904 led to the loss of four million labor-days. There was agitation in the countryside, too, particularly in 1907 in the Midi, the south of France. This region suffered from a crisis in the wine industry caused by disease, competition from cheap foreign wines, and fraud. Frustration led to revolt. Troops were sent to the Midi, where they killed dozens and won for the government the title "government of assassins."

Italy

The third major power to use parliamentary government in Europe also had grave problems.

Although unification took place in 1860, Italy found genuine unity elusive; the country was plagued by regionalism, social strife, and an unrepresentative political system. The central government was continually tested in the south by assertive regionalism and brigandage. Poverty and general backwardness made the area resistant to most government programs.

The parliamentary system that had been established in 1860 was far from satisfactory. Property qualifications limited suffrage to less than 3 percent of the population. And as a result of the persistence of trasformismo—the practice by which government corrupted and co-opted the opposition—electoral choice was shortcircuited.

Between 1870 and 1890 the Italian government introduced some important reforms, but it was difficult to improve the general standard of living for a people undergoing rapid population growth. In the fifty years after unification, population increased from 25 to 35 million, and the country had limited resources to deal with such growth. In the south, a few wealthy landowners held large latifundia, private estates, while the majority of the peasants were landless and forced to work the land for minimum wages. In the north, industrialization had started, but the region was not rich in coal or iron. To be competitive, industry paid very low wages, and the workers lived in abject misery.

Conditions on the land and in the factory led to widespread protests, followed by stern government repression. In 1893, a Sicilian labor movement won the adherence of 300,000 members, who seized land and attacked government offices. The government responded with massive force and declared martial law. In 1896, with unrest spreading throughout the peninsula, the government placed half of the provinces under military rule. A cycle of violence and counterviolence gripped the nation. In May 1898, labor protests in the northern industrial city of Milan against previous government repression led to brutal retaliation. In this general atmosphere of violence, an anarchist killed King Umberto I on July 29, 1900.

After the turn of the century, a new prime minister, Giovanni Giolitti (1842–1928), tried to bring an end to the upheaval. He used government force more sparingly and showed a spirit of cooperation toward the workers. Trying to broaden his popularity by an appeal to nationalist fervor, Giolitti launched an attack on Libya in 1911, wresting it from the Ottoman Empire. The territory was arid and bereft of economic promise, but its conquest was championed as a test of national virility and the foundation of national greatness. The imperialists proudly proclaimed force the arbiter of the nation's future.

Domestically, the nation also returned to force. A wave of workers' discontent seized the nation again, and in June 1914 a national strike led to rioting and seizure of power in many municipalities, including Bologna. In the Romagna, an independent workers' republic was proclaimed. It took 100,000 government troops ten days to restore order. The workers' restlessness and the apparent difficulty of keeping them under control led some nationalist right-wing extremists to form "volunteers for the defense of order," anticipating the vigilante thugs who were to make up the early bands of Italian fascism.

The Autocracies

Four major autocracies dominated central and eastern Europe: Germany, Austria-Hungary, the Ottoman Empire, and Russia. If the democracies were faced with difficulties in these years, the autocracies faced even more severe challenges. At least the democracies had governments accountable to their people through periodic elections and a parliamentary system. Although many groups in the parliamentary regimes grew impatient at the slowness of change, theoretically at least they could believe that someday their goals would be realized. Not so in the autocracies, where the monarchs asserted final authority. The challenges to the autocracies were severe, leading to broad popular challenges to the German imperial system, the reduction of Austria-Hungary into a nearly ungovernable empire, and revolution in the Russian and Ottoman empires.

Germany

Although Germany had a parliament, the government was answerable to the kaiser, not the people's electoral representatives, and Prussia, the most reactionary part of the country, continued to dominate.

To rule effectively, Chancellor Otto von Bismarck maneuvered and intrigued to quell opposition. In the face of socialist growth, he used an attempt to assassinate the emperor as the excuse to ban the Socialist party in 1879. He succeeded in simultaneously winning over conservative agrarian and liberal industrial interests by supporting tariffs on both imported food stuffs and industrial goods. He also turned against the Catholics, who were lukewarm toward Protestant Prussia, persecuting them and their institutions. These measures, however, did not prevent the growth of the Socialist and Catholic Center parties.

Unfortunately for Bismarck, whose tenure in office depended on the goodwill of the emperor, William I died in 1888, to be succeeded first by his son Frederick, who ruled only a few months, and then by his grandson, William II (r. 1888–1918). The young Kaiser William intended to rule as well as reign, but he was ill fit to govern. Convinced of his own infallibility, he bothered to learn very little. Born with a crippled hand, William seemed to want to compensate for this infirmity by appearing forceful, even brutal. He hated any hints of limitation to his powers, announcing, "There is only one ruler in the Reich and I am he. I tolerate no other." A restless individual, William changed uniforms eight times daily and traveled ceaselessly among his seventy-five castles and palaces. Shocked by Bismarck's proposals of reprisals against the Socialists, the kaiser dismissed him. But he also did so to rid himself of a formidable, intimidating individual.

The emperor was determined that Germany become a world power and conduct a foreign policy that would have a global impact. He wanted Germany to have colonies, a navy, and major influence among the Great Powers. This policy, *Weltpolitik,* greatly troubled Germany's neighbors, partly because they were having difficulty adjusting to the emergence of a new, assertive power in central Europe and partly because German moves were accompanied by the kaiser's bombastic threats. Within Germany, however, Weltpolitik won support. Steel manufacturers and shipbuilders received lucrative contracts; workers seemed assured of employment.

Although the nationalist appeals impressed many Germans, the nation could not be easily managed. The emperor's autocratic style was challenged, and his behavior was increasingly viewed as irresponsible.

William II The German emperor liked to be viewed in a heroic and military posture. His crippled left hand is turned away from the viewer. *(Landesbildstelle, Berlin)*

In the elections of 1912, one-third of all Germans voted for the Socialist party. Thus the largest single party in the Reichstag was committed to the downfall of the capitalist system and autocracy. Labor militancy also reached new heights. In 1912, one million workers—a record number—went on strike. More and more Germans pressed for a parliamentary system with a government accountable to the people's elected representatives.

The emperor could not tolerate criticism of his behavior. He had come to Bismarck's conclusions and frequently talked about using the military to crush socialists and the parliament. These thoughts were echoed in the officer corps and in government circles. To some observers it seemed likely that the days of German autocracy were numbered—or that there would be a violent confrontation between the army and the people.

Austria-Hungary

The neighboring Austro-Hungarian Empire also continued to face a series of crises. In an age of intense nationalism, a multinational empire was an anomaly, as the emperor himself acknowledged. Although the relationship between the two parts of the empire was regulated by the agreement of 1867, the agreement did not prevent conflict between Austria and Hungary, particularly over control of their joint army. The insistence on separate Hungarian interests had developed to such a degree that, had it not been for the outbreak of the world war, Hungary probably would have broken loose from the dual monarchy.

In the Hungarian half of the empire, the Magyars found it increasingly difficult to maintain control. Other nationalities, opposed to Magyarization—the imposition of the Magyar language and institutions—insisted on the right to use their own languages in the schools and administration. The Hungarian government resorted to censorship and jailings to silence nationalist leaders. In the Austrian half of the empire, the treatment of nationalities was less harsh, but the government was equally strife-ridden.

There were no easy solutions to the many conflicts that the empire faced. Since much of the national agitation was led by middle-class intellectuals, the Habsburg government introduced universal male suffrage in 1907 in an effort to undercut their influence. However, the result was an empire even more difficult to govern. It became nearly impossible to find a workable majority within a parliament that included thirty ethnically based political parties.

The virulence of debate based on nationality and class divisions grew to ridiculous extremes. Within the parliament, deputies threw inkwells at each other, rang sleigh bells, and sounded bugles. Parliament ceased to be relevant. By 1914, it had been dissolved and so had several regional assemblies. Austria was being ruled by decree. Emperor Francis Joseph feared the empire would not survive him.

The Ottoman Empire

In the generation before 1914, no political system in Europe suffered from so advanced a case of dissolution as the Ottoman Empire, undermined by both secessionist movements within its own borders and aggression from other European powers. Sultan Abdul Hamid II (r. 1876–1909) ruled the country as a despot and authorized mass carnage against those who contested his rule, earning him the nickname the "Great Assassin."

Young, Western-educated Turks—the "Young Turks"—dismayed at one-man rule and the continuing loss of territory and influence, successfully overthrew Abdul Hamid in a coup in July 1908. They established a government responsible to an elected parliament. The Young Turks believed they could stem the loss of territory by establishing firmer central control. Their efforts, however, had the opposite effect. The various nationalities of the empire resented the attempts at "Turkification," the imposition of Turkish education and administration. Renewed agitation broke out in Macedonia, Albania, and among the Armenians. The government carried out severely repressive measures to end the unrest, killing thousands of Armenians.

For foreign powers, the moment seemed propitious to plunder the weakened empire. In 1911, Italy occupied Libya, an Ottoman province. Greece, Bulgaria, and Serbia—impatient to enlarge their territory—formed an alliance, the Balkan League, which in 1912 prosecuted a successful war against the empire. Albania became independent, and Macedonia was partitioned among members of the league. Thus the empire lost most of its European possessions, except for the capital, Constantinople, and a narrow strip of surrounding land.

Russia

Through the Great Reforms of the 1860s, the Russian autocracy had attempted to resolve many of the problems facing its empire and people. But the reforms and the major social changes of the period unleashed new forces, making it even more difficult for the tsars to rule.

The needs of a modernizing country led to an increase in the number of universities and students. However, the newly educated Russian youths began almost instantly an ardent, sustained critique of autocracy. In the absence of a large group upholding liberal, advanced ideas, university students and graduates, who came to be known as the *intelligentsia,* saw it as their mission to transform Russia. In the 1870s, university youths by the thousands organized a populist movement, hoping to bring change to the countryside.

These youthful idealists intended to educate the peasants and make them more politically aware. But they were met by suspicion from the peasantry and repression by the government. Large numbers of populists were arrested and put on trial. Frustrated at the difficulty of bringing about change from below by transforming the people, disaffected young radicals formed the People's Will, which turned to murdering public officials to hasten the day of revolution.

Although the regime intensified repression, it also sought to broaden its public support. In 1881, Tsar Alexander II decided to establish an advisory committee that some thought would eventually lead to a parliamentary form of government. In March 1881, as he was about to sign the decree establishing this committee, the tsar was assassinated by members of the People's Will.

The new ruler, Tsar Alexander III (r. 1881–1894), who had witnessed his father's murder, ascribed the deed to his father's leniency. By contrast, he was determined to uphold autocracy firmly. He had some of his father's reforms watered down, thus reducing local self-rule.

When Alexander's son, Nicholas II (r. 1894–1917), succeeded his father on the throne in 1894, he declared he would be as autocratic as his father. However, he lacked the methodical, consistent temperament such a pledge required. A pleasant man, he wanted to be liked, and he lacked the forcefulness to carry out a coherent policy for his troubled country.

Since the Great Reforms, serious problems had accumulated that threatened the stability of the regime. In the countryside the situation worsened steadily as the population exploded and the pressure on the land increased. The provisions that had accompanied the freeing of the serfs left considerable discontent. The peasants were not free to come and go as they pleased; they had to have the permission of the village council. Agriculture remained inefficient, far inferior to that of western Europe; hence the allotted land was insufficient to feed the peasants, creating a constant land hunger, or demand for more land.

The attempted modernization of Russia had changed it more dramatically and rapidly than any other central or eastern European state. In the 1890s the minister of finance, Sergei Witte (1849–1915), launched an ambitious railroad-expansion program, which triggered a broader program of industrial development. Although Russia remained largely agrarian and backward, pockets of industrial growth were created. Some factories and mining concerns were unusually large, with as many as six thousand employees. When workers grew incensed at their condition and insistent on winning the same rights and protection that existed in western Europe, they engaged in massive strikes that crippled industry.

Political dissatisfaction with the autocracy grew. Members of the expanding middle classes began to clamor that, like their contemporaries in western Europe, they should be given the opportunity to participate in governance. And parts of the aristocracy also demanded a right to political participation.

Various revolutionary groups committed to socialism continued to flourish. The heirs to the populists were the Social Revolutionaries, who emerged as a political force in the 1890s. They believed that the peasants were the force that would bring socialism to Russia. In 1898 the Russian Social Democratic party was founded. A Marxist party, it promoted the industrial working class as the harbinger of socialism. In 1903, that party split between the Mensheviks and the Bolsheviks. The Mensheviks insisted that Russia had to go through the stages of history Marx had predicted—that it had to witness the full development of capitalism and its subsequent collapse before socialism could come to power. The Bolsheviks, a minority group, were led by Vladimir Lenin (1870–1924), a zealous revolutionary and revisionist Marxist. Rather than wait for historic forces to undermine capitalism, he insisted that a revolutionary cadre could seize power on behalf of the working class. Lenin favored a small, disciplined, conspiratorial party, like the People's Will, while the Mensheviks favored a more open, democratic party (see the box, "A Conspiratorial Revolutionary Party").

At the turn of the century these groups were still quite small and played a limited role in the mounting opposition to tsarism. But popular opposition soon grew in the face of Russian military

Building of the Trans-Siberian Railway Financed by foreign loans, the rail line connected the eastern part of the empire with the rest of Russia, heightening Russian interest in eastern Asia. The 5000-mile railway fueled Russian economic development and in 1904 spurred conflict with Japan. *(The Bettmann Archive)*

ineptness in the war against Japan, which had broken out in February 1904 in a dispute over control of northern Korea. Antagonism to the tsarist regime escalated as a result of social tensions, heightened by an economic slowdown.

Beginning in January 1905, a series of demonstrations, strikes, and other acts of collective violence began. Together, they were dubbed "the revolution of 1905." One Sunday in January 1905, 400,000 workers seeking redress of their grievances gathered in front of the tsar's palace. Rather than hear their protests, officials had the soldiers fire on them. "Bloody Sunday" angered the populace. The tsar, instead of being viewed as an understanding, paternal authority, had become the murderer of his people. Unrest spread to most of the country. As reports reached Russia of more defeats in the war with Japan, the regime's prestige was further undermined. By September 1905, Russia had to sue for peace and admit defeat. Challenged in the capital, where independent workers' councils called *soviets,* had sprung up, the government also lost control over the countryside, the site of widescale peasant uprisings.

Fearing that his regime was at stake, Nicholas hoped to split the forces challenging tsarism by meeting the demands for parliamentary government, granting major constitutional and civil liberties including freedom of religion, speech, assembly, and association. At the end of October, the tsar established an elective assembly, the Duma, with restricted male suffrage and limited political power. It was far from the Western-style parliament that the liberals within Russia had desired, but it quickly became the arena for criticism of autocracy. The tsar became annoyed, and hoping to create a more pliant instrument, suspended the assembly, changing its electoral base and its rules of operations.

A new prime minister, Peter Stolypin (1862–1911), tried to win support for the regime by a series of reforms, including improvement in the lot of the peasantry: The government reduced the peasants' financial obligations; the power of the commune was weakened; and local self-rule was extended to the peasants. Some peasants were now better off, but others were annoyed by the economic disparities that the reforms had estab-

A Conspiratorial Revolutionary Party

The Russian Socialist party was racked by internal debates over the direction and means by which a socialist revolution could be created. The majority favored a broad-based socialist party, but in his 1902 essay "What Is to Be Done?" Lenin explained why revolution in Russia could succeed only if it were made by a cadre of professional revolutionaries, organized into a tightly knit conspiratorial group.

We must have a committee of professional *revolutionaries* . . . irrespective of whether they are students or working men. I assert: 1) That no movement can be durable without a stable organization of leaders to maintain continuity; 2) that the more widely the masses are drawn into the struggle and form the basis of the movement, the more necessary it is to have such an organization and the more stable it must be—otherwise it is much easier for demagogues to sidetrack the more backward sections of the masses; 3) that the organization must consist chiefly of persons engaged in revolution as a profession; 4) that in a country with a despotic government, the more we *restrict* the membership of this organization to persons who are engaged in revolution as a profession and who have been professionally trained in the art of combating the political police, the more difficult will it be to catch the organization; and 5) the *wider* will be the circle of men and women of the working class or of other classes of society able to join the movement and perform active work in it. . . .

It is . . . argued against us that the views on organization here expounded contradict the "principles of democracy."

Ponder a little over the real meaning of the high-sounding phrase . . . and you will realize that "broad democracy" in party organization, amidst the gloom of autocracy and the domination of the gendarmes, is nothing more than a *useless and harmful toy*. It is a useless toy, because as a matter of fact, no revolutionary organization has ever practiced *broad* democracy, nor could it, however much it desired to do so.

Source: Lenin, "What Is to Be Done?" *Collected Works*, vol. 4 (New York: International Publishers, 1929), pp. 198–199, 210, 212.

lished. So rural dissatisfaction remained widespread.

The workers also were still highly dissatisfied. Labor unrest mounted: in 1912 there were 725,000 strikers, by the first half of 1914, there were twice that number. When the French president visited St. Petersburg on the eve of the outbreak of the war, barricades were rising in the workers' neighborhoods.

The Coming War

Instability and upheaval characterized international relations in the years between 1880 and 1914. However, there was nothing inevitable about the outbreak of war. Good common sense dictated against it, and intelligent people predicted that in the new modern era, war had become so destructive that it was unthinkable. Finally, no European state wanted a war, although the Great Powers carried on policies that brought them to its brink.

Power Alignments

Germany enjoyed an unchallenged position in the 1870s and 1880s. It was united in an alliance with the two other eastern conservative states—Russia and Austria-Hungary—in the Three Emperors' League, formed in 1873 and renewed by treaty in 1884. And it was part of the Triple

Alliance with Austria and Italy. France was isolated, without allies. Britain, with little interest in continental affairs, appeared to be enjoying a "splendid isolation."

However, Germany's alliance system was not free from problems. Two of its allies, Austria-Hungary and Russia, were at loggerheads over control of the Balkans. How could Germany be the friend of both? To reassure the Russian government, wary of apparent German preference for Austria, Bismarck signed the Reinsurance Treaty in 1887, assuring Russia that Germany would not honor its alliance with Austria if the latter attacked Russia. After Bismarck's resignation in 1890, Emperor William allowed the Reinsurance Treaty to lapse. Alarmed, the Russians turned to France and, in January 1894, signed the Franco-Russian Alliance, by which each side pledged to help the other in case either was attacked by Germany.

Cover Page of German Army League newspaper One of many nationalist movements, the League ran organized campaigns for increases in German army expenditures. The newspaper enjoyed a circulation of over 300,000. The engraving suggests that just as Germans had to rally for the fatherland in 1813 and 1870, so they may again have to defend it. *(From* The German Army League, *Marilyn Shevin Coetzee [Oxford University Press])*

The Great Powers were now divided into two alliances, the Triple Alliance and the Dual (Franco-Russian) Alliance. Britain formally belonged to neither. But if it favored any side, it would be the German-led alliance. Britain's strongest challengers in the world in the 1880s and 1890s were France and Russia. Both rivaled Britain for influence in Asia, while France challenged Britain for control of Africa.

However distrust of Germany soon led Britain and France to resolve their difficulties overseas. In 1904, Britain and France signed an understanding, or entente, resolving their rivalries in Egypt; and in 1907, Great Britain and Russia regulated their competition for influence in Persia (present-day Iran) with the Anglo-Russian Entente. Now Europe was loosely divided into two groups: the Triple Alliance of Germany, Austria-Hungary, and Italy; and the Triple Entente of Great Britain, France, and Russia.

The Momentum for War

Only under the stress of a series of crises did these alignments solidify to the point where their maintenance became a goal for their members, and they were willing to go to war to save them. France's attempts to take over Morocco led twice to conflict with Germany. In 1905, Germany insisted that an international conference discuss the issue and deny France this kingdom adjacent to its colony of Algeria. In 1911, when France grabbed Morocco anyway, Germany accepted the situation only after extorting compensation from the French, who deeply resented what they viewed as German bullying.

Britain also began to view Germany as a serious international menace. Over the years, Britain had developed a navy equal to none. An island nation, dependent on international trade for its economic survival, Britain saw its navy as a necessity. Wishing to challenge Britain's supremacy on the seas, however, Germany began building its own navy in the 1890s. Both countries began building powerful armored fighting ships called dreadnoughts.

The heightened international rivalry forced the European states to increase their arms expenditures. Between 1875 and 1914, Germany increased its arms expenditure by 230 percent, Britain by 189 percent, and France by 109 percent. Many political leaders viewed this escalating arms race as a form of madness. British Foreign Secretary Sir Edward Grey (1862–1933) warned that if it continued, "it will submerge civilization." But no way was found to stop it.

It was territorial rivalry between Austria and Russia that finally led to international disaster. For decades there had been growing enmity between the two empires for control over the Balkans (Map 26.4). In 1903, following a bloody military coup that killed the king and queen of Serbia, a pro-Russian party took control of the Serbian government. It spread anti-Austrian propaganda and sought to unify under its banner the Slavs living in the Balkans, including those under Austrian rule. As a result, many Austrian officials were convinced that the survival of the Austro-Hungarian Empire required that Serbia be destroyed. Talk of an attack on Serbia filled the Austrian court in 1914.

On June 28, 1914, the heir to the Habsburg throne, Archduke Francis Ferdinand, visited Sarajevo in Austrian-ruled Bosnia. Some young Bosnian nationalists, hostile to Austrian rule, who had been trained and armed by a Serb terrorist group called the Black Hand, assassinated the archduke and his wife.

The assassination of the heir to the throne provided Austria with an ideal pretext for military action. The German kaiser, fearing that failure to support Vienna would lead to Austrian collapse and a Germany bereft of any allies, urged Austria to attack Serbia (see the box, "Another Step Closer to War"). On July 23, Austria issued an ultimatum to Serbia, deliberately worded in such a way as to be unacceptable. When Serbia refused the ultimatum, Austria declared war on July 28.

Perceived self-interest motivated each state's behavior in the ensuing crisis. Although in the past Russia had failed to protect Serbia, now it was determined to help. Russian great power status demanded that it not allow its client state to be humiliated, much less obliterated. In the past the French government had acted as a brake on Russian ambitions in the Balkans. But increasingly after 1911, France feared isolation in the face of what it perceived as growing German aggressiveness. Its only ally on the continent was Russia. To remain a great power, France needed to preserve its friendship with Russia, and this time it apparently did not discourage Russian determination to aid Serbia. Russia, presuming French aid, mobilized its huge armies.

Germany could not allow Austria, its only ally, to be destroyed, and therefore it mobilized and declared war on Russia. Assuming that France would come to the aid of Russia, Germany

Map 26.4 The Balkans in 1914 By 1914 the Ottoman empire was much diminished, containing virtually none of Europe. Political boundaries did not follow nationality lines. Serbia was committed to unite all Serbs at the expense of the Austro-Hungarian empire.

MAJOR DIPLOMATIC ALLIANCES AND AGREEMENTS

1873	Three Emperors' League (Germany, Austria-Hungary and Russia)
1879	Alliance between Germany and Austria
1882	Triple Alliance (Germany, Austria and Italy)
1884	Renewal of Three Emperors' League
1887	Re-insurance Treaty (Germany and Russia)
1894	Franco-Russian Alliance
1904	Anglo-French Entente
1907	Anglo-Russian Entente

invaded France through Belgium. The British, concerned by the threat to their ally France, and outraged by the violation of Belgian neutrality to which all the great powers had been signatories since 1839, declared war on Germany. Events had hurtled forward between the Austrian declaration of war on Serbia on July 28 and the British decision on August 4. Europe was at war. Eventually so would be much of the world.

Summary

On the surface, the years from 1880 to 1914 seemed comfortable. More people than ever before enjoyed material advantages and an improved standard of living. Literacy spread. Death rates went down; life expectancy rose. But because a revolution of rising expectations had been created, people grew more demanding, in-

Capture of Assassin of Archduke Francis Ferdinand A Bosnian, Gavril Princip, was arrested minutes after he had assassinated the archduke and his wife, on June 28, 1914. This political murder unleashed World War I. *(Gernsheim Collection, Harry Ransom Humanities Center, University of Texas, Austin)*

Another Step Closer to War

Listening to Austrian officials arguing for severe measures against Serbia for its alleged complicity in the assassination of the archduke, the German ambassador in Vienna, Heinrich Leonhard von Tschirschky, advocated caution. Tschirschky's dispatch of June 30 to the German imperial chancellor recording his efforts was shown to William II who, irritated, called for immediate retribution. On July 5, the German government sent a message to Vienna lending support for any action Austria might wish to take against Serbia. Often labeled a "blank check," this message encouraged the Austrians to wage war against Serbia.

The text on the left is Tschirschky's dispatch. That on the right is the Kaiser's comments on the margins of the document.

The Ambassador at Vienna to the Imperial Chancellor
Vienna, June 30, 1914

Count Berchtold told me today that *everything* pointed to the fact that	I hope not.
the threads of the conspiracy to which the Archduke fell a sacrifice, *ran together at Belgrade.* The affair was so well thought out that very young men were intentionally selected for the perpetration of the crime,	Now or never.
against whom *only a mild punishment could be decreed.* The Minister spoke very bitterly about the Serbian plots. I frequently hear expressed here, even among serious people, the wish that *at last a final and fundamental reckoning should be had with the Serbs.* The Serbs should first be presented with a number of demands, and in case they should not accept these, energetic measures should be taken. I *take opportunity of every such occasion to advise quietly but very impressively and seriously against too hasty steps.* First of all, they must make sure what they want to do, for so far I have heard only indefinite expressions of opinion. Then the chances of every kind of action should be carefully weighed, and it should be kept in mind that Austria-Hungary does not stand alone in the world, that it is her duty to think not only of her allies, but to take into consideration the entire European situation, and especially to bear in mind the attitude of Italy and Roumania on all questions that concern Serbia.	Who authorized him to act that way? That is very stupid! It is none of his business, as it is solely the affair of Austria, what she plans to do in this case. Later, if plans go wrong, it will be said that Germany did not want it! Let Tschirschky be good enough to drop this nonsense! The Serbs must be disposed of, *and* that right *soon!*
von Tschirschky	Goes without saying; nothing but truisms.

Source: Max Montgelas and Walter Schüking, eds. *Outbreak of the World War,* trans. Carnegie Endowment for International Peace (New York: Oxford University Press, 1924), p. 61.

sisting in sometimes violent ways on their political and economic rights. Maybe it was no accident that intellectuals like Freud and artists like Munch and Moreau suggested that there was a hidden, secret dimension of life beneath surface appearances. Behind the façade of smugness and conformity lay many irrational and violent fantasies.

Although optimism was probably the most common mood of the era, it was not universally shared. Intellectuals spoke of decadence and decline. Statesmen, worried about the future of their countries and hoping to avoid the threat of decline, resorted to drastic measures: empire overseas and armed competition in Europe. Among European thinkers and statesmen, force was widely accepted as a means to an end.

No one wanted the world war that broke out. All the countries involved assumed they were entering a local conflict. But each side had a large standing army with millions of men and much modern equipment. And Europe's network of alliances led inexorably to the larger conflict. If there were some leaders who feared war, more dreaded the consequences of not fighting, believing that war would save their regimes from the internal challenges they were facing. Few could foresee the dire consequences of such a choice.

Suggested Reading

General Surveys

Gilbert, Felix. *The End of the European Era, 1890 to the Present.* 1979. Sees the years from 1890 to 1914 as helping to shape the rest of the twentieth century.

Hobsbawm, Eric. *The Age of Empire, 1875–1914.* 1987. A fine survey, emphasizing social change, by a leading British historian.

Romein, Jan. *The Watershed of Two Eras—Europe in 1900.* 1978. A long and at times challenging study of the generation straddling the turn of the century.

Politics and Culture in an Age of Doubt

Gay, Peter. *Freud—A Life for Our Time.* 1988. An admiring study by a prominent historian and trained psychoanalyst.

Geary, Dick. *European Labor Protest, 1848–1939.* 1981. A brief, clearly written work that emphasizes the deradicalization of labor.

Hughes, H. Stuart. *Consciousness and Society: The Reorientation of European Social Thought, 1890–1930.* 1979. A classic on changes in European social thought.

Joll, James. *The Second International, 1889–1914.* 1955. A brief, well-written history of the successes and failures of the international socialist organization.

Katz, Jacob. *From Prejudice to Destruction, 1700–1933.* 1980. A survey of two centuries of European anti-Semitism.

Schorske, Carl E. *Fin de Siècle Vienna—Politics and Culture.* 1980. A critically acclaimed work on the arts and social and political thought in the Habsburg capital at the turn of the century.

Teich, Mikulas, and Roy Porter, eds. *Fin de Siècle and Its Legacy.* 1990. A collection of critical essays summarizing the cultural trends at the end of the century.

The New Imperialism

Baumgart, Winfried. *Imperialism—The Idea and Reality of British and French Colonial Expansion, 1880–1914.* 1989. A comparative study, emphasizing the political aspects of imperialism.

Betts, Raymond F. *The False Dawn—European Imperialism in the Nineteenth Century.* 1975. An elegantly written survey by one of the most authoritative historians of the subject.

Davis, Lance E., and Huttenback, Robert A. *Mammon and the Pursuit of Empire.* 1988. A careful statistical study that shows British imperialism overall not to have been a profitable venture.

Headrick, Daniel R. *The Tentacles of Progress—Technology Transfer in the Age of Imperialism, 1850–1940.* 1988. Considers the extent and limits of technology transfer from the West to its empire.

Moch, Leslie Page. *Moving Europeans: Migration in Western Europe since 1650.* 1993. An up-to-date survey that puts the large nineteenth-century waves of migration in historic perspective.

Pakenham, Thomas. *The Scramble for Africa.* 1991. A long but colorful narrative of the European conquest of Africa, emphasizing personalities.

The Democratic Powers

Brédin, Jean-Denis. *The Affair: The Case of Alfred Dreyfus.* 1986. The most authoritative account, written by a prominent French lawyer, covers both the details of the affair and its context.

Clark, Martin. *Modern Italy, 1872–1982.* 1984. Contains some fine chapters on the decades before the war, emphasizing the difficulties of governing a society as divided and diverse as Italy.

Feuchtwanger, E. J. *Democracy and Empire, Britain, 1865–1914.* 1985. While describing the challenges to the existing order, emphasizes the resilience of British institutions.

Harrison, J. F. C. *Late Victorian Britain, 1875–1901.* 1990. Considers how different social classes experienced the social and economic transformations of the era.

Levine, Philippa. *Victorian Feminism.* 1987. Shows that Victorian women were involved in several campaigns for their rights, including the suffragette movement.

Mayeur, Jean-Marie, and Madeleine Réberioux. *The Third Republic—From Its Origins to the Great War, 1871–1914.* 1987. The most up-to-date survey of France in these years, emphasizing the emergence of republican government and the challenges it faced.

Thayer, John A. *Italy and the Great War, Politics and Culture 1870–1915.* 1964. Surveys Italy's political and cultural life in these years.

Townshend, Charles. *Political Violence in Ireland.* 1983. Concentrates on violence in Ireland since 1848, stressing its social and economic origins.

The Autocracies

Bridge, F. R. *The Habsburg Monarchy among the Great Powers, 1815–1918.* 1990. Contrary to most works on the Habsburg empire, this praises Austrian leaders for preserving the empire as long as they did.

Kohut, Thomas A. *Wilhelm II and the Germans—A Study in Leadership.* 1991. A psychohistorical study, analyzing the German emperor's youth and unsatisfactory relations with his parents.

Lieven, Dominic. *Russia's Rulers Under the Old Regime.* 1989. Presents a study of Russia's aristocracy and its attitudes toward most public issues in the nineteenth century.

Rogger, Hans. *Russia in the Age of Modernization, 1881–1917.* 1983. Concentrates on Russian institutions in the generation prior to the revolution.

The Coming War

Joll, James. *The Origins of the First World War.* 1984. A clear, concise, readable history emphasizing strategic interests and nationalist passions leading to the outbreak of the war.

Kennedy, Paul. *The Rise and Fall of the Great Powers, 1500 to 2000.* 1987. Masterfully summarizes the factors that led to the shifting fates of the Great Powers.

Massie, Robert K. *Dreadnought—Britain, Germany and the Coming of the Great War.* 1991. A very long but lively discussion of Anglo-German affairs in the generation leading up to the war. The author emphasizes the leading personalities involved.

Weighing the Evidence

THE LAYOUT OF THE BRITISH MUSEUM

The British Museum was founded in the mid-eighteenth century when the government acquired some private collections. The museum increased the size of its collections, largely through donations, bringing in objects from around the world. In its early years the museum was located in a converted private mansion; then in 1847, to house its growing collection, the museum moved into a monumental building with a neoclassical façade. Until the 1830s public access was limited to the upper classes, mainly the learned. By the mid-nineteenth century, however, a million people a year were visiting the museum. Displays of materials gathered from non-European cultures drew particularly large audiences.

Consider how the exhibits reflected British imperialism. In the first half of the nineteenth century, objects from Oceania, reflecting British activities in the Pacific, were acquired. African materials became more plentiful with the British conquest of much of Africa after the 1880s; the British military expedition to Nigeria in 1897 led to the acquisition of the fabulous Benin bronzes.

While imperial adventures were shaping the museum collection, the museum in turn was supporting imperialism. Museum officials declared that increased knowledge about regions overseas would fuel enthusiasm for the imperial venture and make the British people better fit to rule their new subjects.

The manner in which the British Museum displayed some of its possessions reflected the intellectual currents of the times. In the late eighteenth and early nineteenth centuries the museum grouped its non-European objects with "natural history"; non-Europeans were associated with nature, with the beasts of the earth. Running out of space, the museum moved the natural history collection to a separate Natural Museum in South Kensington, and in the 1880s ethnography, the branch of anthropology devoted to human cultures, constituted a separate collection.

The late-nineteenth-century plan of the upper floor of the museum shown here reflects the racial views of imperial Britain. After climbing the stairs from the ground floor, we start at the room labeled 1, the Anglo-Saxon Room, which celebrates England's early history. Then comes the Waddesdon Bequest Room, which houses various artifacts of ancient and medieval English and European history (the room is named after the Rothschild mansion where the collection was previously housed). Next we arrive at the Medieval Room itself. Using the route most visitors would then take, we come to the Asiatic Saloon, filled with pottery, porcelain, and other works of art from Japan, China, Persia, and India.

What is the significance of this juxtaposition of rooms? The British and other Europeans had developed an ethnocentric view of the human races, believing that the white race was by far superior to all others. This belief seemed confirmed by the material accomplishments of Europeans, especially impressive in the nineteenth century. Of the non-Europeans, Asians had won the grudging respect of the British and other Europeans. China, with its thousands of years of recorded history and sophisticated government structures, was one of several Asian societies that impressed them. Because many African societies lacked a written culture and had government and religious systems dramatically different from the Europeans', the British and other Europeans often considered Africans ignorant and primitive.

Biologists, anthropologists, and others speculating about the human races offered two different explanations for racial variations. These hypotheses competed with each other for public acceptance. According to the first, biology determined the level of civilization of each people. According to the second, different peoples were at different levels of development. In this view, Europeans were most developed, Africans least; but eventually Asians and Africans would progress and reach a level akin to that of Europeans. In the meantime non-Europeans illustrated European life at earlier stages of development.

It is interesting that the Asiatic Saloon, with its swords, shields, and other elaborate Asian

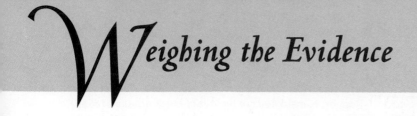

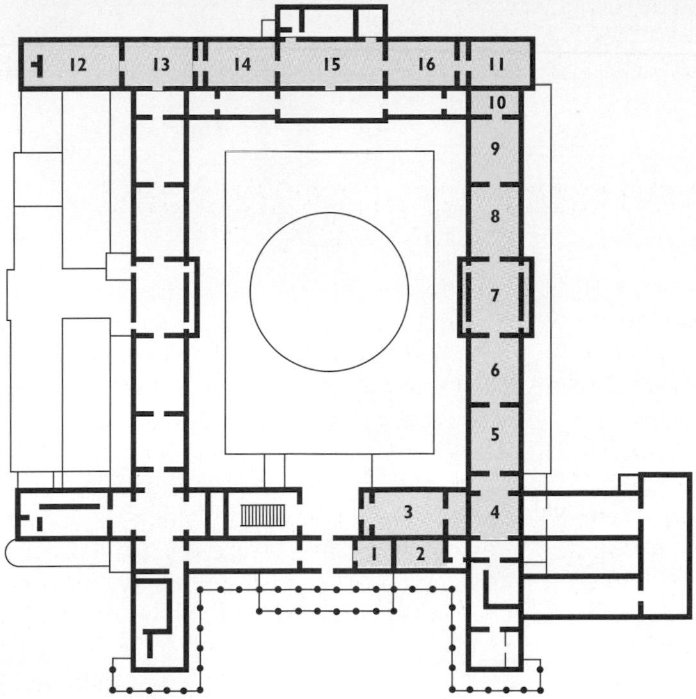

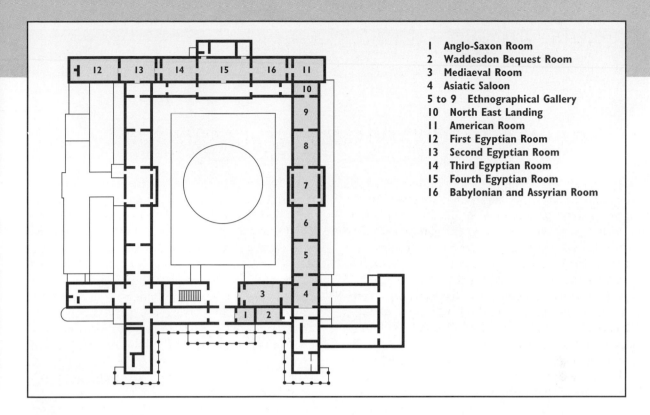

Plan of the Upper Floor of the British Museum, ca. 1880 *(Based on map in Henry C. Shelley,* The British Museum: Its History and Treasures *[Boston: L.C. Page, 1911], pp. 274–275.)*

objects, was next to the Medieval Room. The positioning invites consideration that some nineteenth-century Asian societies were at a level of development akin to medieval England.

An empty corridor separated this part of the museum from the Ethnographic Gallery, giving visitors the sense that what they would view was separate from medieval England and selected Asian societies. The Ethnographic Gallery displayed objects from Asia, Oceania, Africa, and the Americas. They tended to be objects of daily life such as household wares, weapons, and clothing. The stress was on their simplicity and primitiveness—presumably reflections of the primitive culture of their makers. The objects were not differentiated chronologically; pre-Columbian artifacts from the Americas were displayed beside modern African crafts. Ethnographic items were seldom dated, implying that the peoples who created them did not develop and had no history. The museum guidebook invited nineteenth-century viewers to consider how close the development of these peoples was to that of the earliest Europeans.

After passing through the Ethnographic Gallery, a visitor would arrive at the North East Landing and then enter the American Room. It contained items from Eskimos, native Americans, and other peoples whom Victorians considered "primitives," but it also included artifacts from the Aztecs and Incas, whom the British considered to be highly developed.

The Aztec and Inca collections abutted the room devoted to two ancient civilizations with monumental architecture, the Babylonian and Assyrian Room. Next came four Egyptian rooms. In the nineteenth century the greatness of ancient Egyptian culture was recognized. The British Museum allotted ancient Egypt ample space far removed from what were seen as the "primitive" peoples represented in the Ethnographic Gallery.

In 1972 the ethnographic collection was moved out of the British Museum and now constitutes a separate Museum of Mankind. With the loss of empire and the decline of confidence in the superiority of the white race, the old uses for the objects collected overseas had become obsolete.[1]

1. I am grateful to Thomas Prasch, Indiana University, for his help and advice and for making available to me two of his unpublished papers on this subject.

CHAPTER 27

War and Revolution, 1914–1919

Coming after a century of relative peace and apparent progress, World War I constituted a dramatic turning point for Western civilization. It was not simply the fact of full-scale war that proved so significant, or even the war's immediate results, remarkable though they were. The war had a deeper impact because of the way it was fought, the experience it entailed; much about that experience was so new that it could scarcely have been imagined before 1914. A far wider and more destructive war would follow within a generation, but it was during World War I, known to contemporaries as "the Great War," that the old European order began to dissolve and Europe began to lose its predominant place in the world. After World War I it would no longer be possible to believe in progress, rationality, and the privileged place of Western civilization in the same way again.

The war proved such a turning point because the fighting, which had been expected to produce a quick result, instead bogged down in a stalemate during the fall of 1914. By the time it finally ended, in November 1918, the war had strained the whole fabric of life, affecting virtually everything, from economic organization to literary vocabulary, from journalistic techniques to the role of women. Long-standing empires and dynasties fell apart, so the political and territorial map had to be fundamentally redrawn after the war was over.

Although the war solved at least some of the problems that had caused it in the first place, it introduced new problems as well, and several of its most significant effects were unrelated to its causes. Most notably, the difficulties of war led to a communist revolution in Russia that had an

Paul Nash,
The Menin Road

incalculable impact on the subsequent history of the twentieth century. So it is essential to distinguish what the war settled from what was left unresolved in the aftermath. In the same way, it is necessary to ask to what extent, and in what ways, World War I simply accelerated processes already under way and in what sense it was a rupture, introducing new possibilities—for both good and ill.

The Unforeseen Stalemate, 1914–1917

When the war began in August 1914, enthusiasm and high morale, based on expectations of quick victory, marked both sides. But fighting on the crucial western front led to a stalemate by the end of 1914, and the particularly brutal encounters of 1916 made it clear that this had become a very different war from what most had expected in 1914. By early 1917 the difficult experience of war forced deeper questions about what it was all for—and whether it was worth the price.

August 1914: The Domestic and Military Setting

Although some, like Helmuth von Moltke (1848–1916), chief of the German general staff, worried that this would prove a long, destructive war testing the very fabric of Western civilization, the outbreak of fighting early in August produced a wave of euphoria and a remarkable degree of domestic unity. To many, war came almost as a relief; at last, the issues that had produced tension and intermittent crisis for the past decade would find definitive solution. Especially among educated young people, this settling of accounts seemed to offer the prospect of renewal, even a kind of redemption, for themselves and their societies. The war promised an escape from the stiflingly respectable bourgeois world and, in response to the common danger, an end to the petty bickering and divisiveness of everyday politics.

In all the belligerent countries, an unexpected display of patriotism from the socialist left fed the sense of domestic unity and the high morale that went with it. Defying their long-standing rhetoric about international proletarian solidarity, members of the socialist parties of the Second International rallied to their respective national war efforts almost everywhere in Europe. To socialists and workers, national defense against a more backward aggressor seemed essential to the eventual creation of socialism. French socialists had to defend France's democratic republic against autocratic and militaristic Germany; German socialists had to defend German institutions, and the strong socialist organizations that had proven possible within them, against repressive tsarist Russia. The German Socialists' vote for war credits in the Reichstag on August 4 dramatically symbolized the failure of the Second International to prevent working-class involvement in a European war.

In France, the government had planned, as a precaution, to arrest about a thousand trade union and socialist leaders in the event of war, but no such arrests seemed necessary when the war began. Instead, the order of the day was *Union Sacrée* (Sacred Union), which even meant Socialist participation in the new government of national defense. In Germany, the watchword was *Burgfrieden* (Fortress Truce), which meant agreement to suspend labor conflict for the duration of the war, although here no Socialist was invited to join the war cabinet.

The high spirits of August were possible because so few Europeans could foresee what they were getting into. It would be "business as usual" as the British government put it—no shortages, no rationing, no massive government intervention. There was little inkling of the total mobilization to come or of what the war would cost.

Before the war began, the forces of the Triple Entente outnumbered those of Germany and Austria-Hungary. Russia had an army of over 1 million men, the largest in Europe, and France had 700,000. Britain, which did not introduce conscription until 1916, had about 250,000. Germany led the Central Powers with 850,000;

Map 27.1 Major Fronts of World War I Although World War I included engagements in East Asia and the Middle East, it was essentially a European conflict, encompassing fighting on a number of fronts. A vast territory was contested in the east, but on the western front, which proved decisive, fighting was concentrated in a relatively small area.

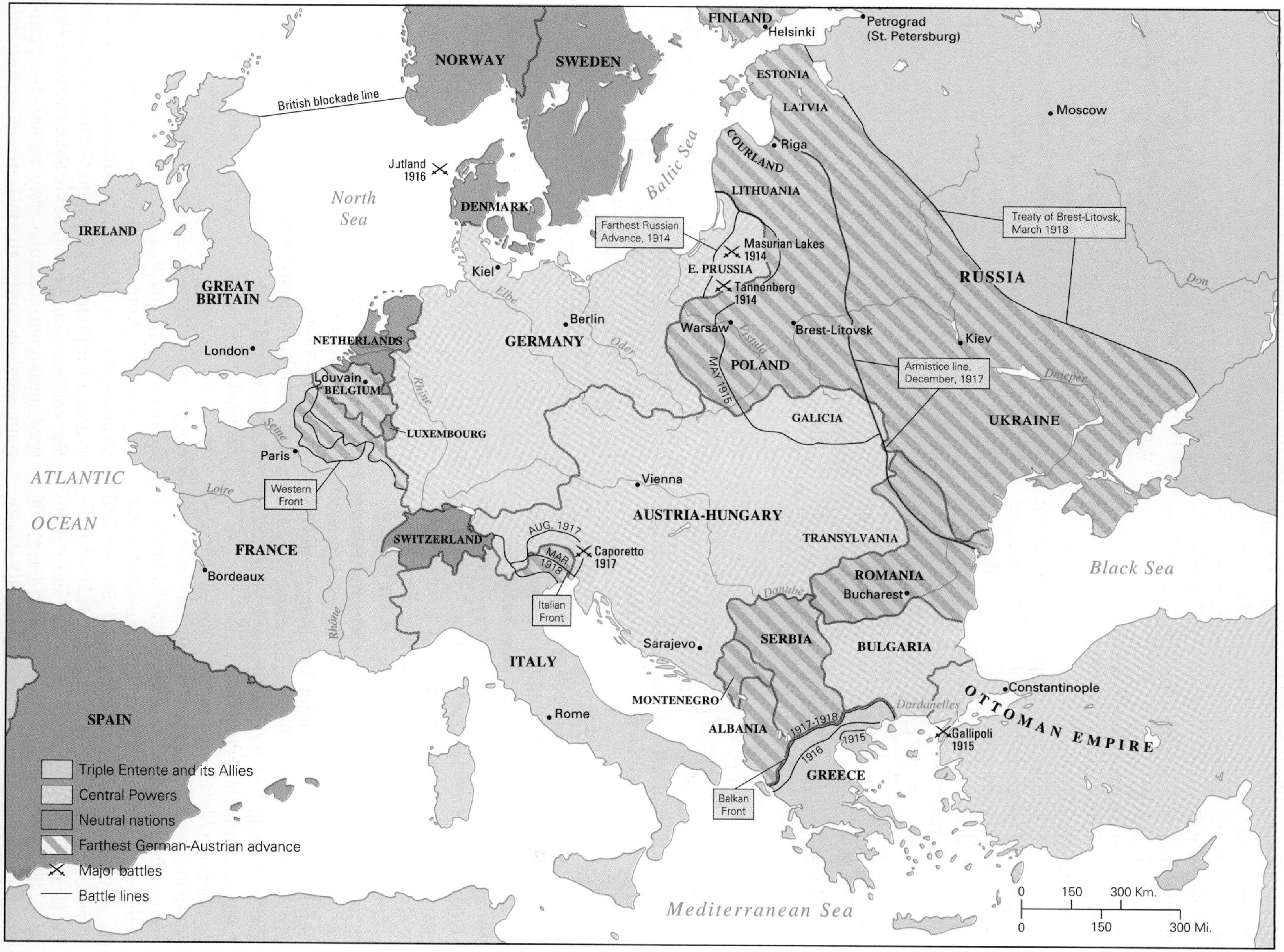

FINLAND
Helsinki
Petrograd (St. Petersburg)
NORWAY
SWEDEN
ESTONIA
LATVIA
Moscow
British blockade line
Riga
COURLAND
Jutland 1916
Baltic Sea
North Sea
LITHUANIA
DENMARK
IRELAND
Farthest Russian Advance, 1914
Masurian Lakes 1914
Treaty of Brest-Litovsk, March 1918
Kiel
E. PRUSSIA
RUSSIA
GREAT BRITAIN
Elbe
Tannenberg 1914
Don
Berlin
Warsaw
Brest-Litovsk
Vistula
Kiev
London
NETHERLANDS
GERMANY
Oder
MAY 1915
POLAND
Armistice line, December, 1917
Dnieper
Louvain
BELGIUM
Rhine
GALICIA
UKRAINE
Seine
LUXEMBOURG
Paris
Vienna
ATLANTIC
Loire
Western Front
OCEAN
AUSTRIA-HUNGARY
SWITZERLAND
AUG. 1917
MAR. 1918
Caporetto 1917
TRANSYLVANIA
FRANCE
Bordeaux
ROMANIA
Black Sea
Danube
Bucharest
Italian Front
Rhône
Sarajevo
SERBIA
BULGARIA
ITALY
Constantinople
OTTOMAN EMPIRE
MONTENEGRO
Dardanelles
SPAIN
Rome
ALBANIA
1917-1918
1915
Gallipoli 1915
1916
GREECE
Balkan Front
Triple Entente and its Allies
Central Powers
Neutral nations
Farthest German-Austrian advance
Major battles
Battle lines
Mediterranean Sea
0 150 300 Km.
0 150 300 Mi.

Austria-Hungary contributed 450,000. Though outnumbered, the Central Powers had potential advantages in equipment, coordination, and speed over their more dispersed adversaries, so the outcome was hardly a foregone conclusion when the fighting began.

After the war had started, a second tier of belligerents intervened one by one, expanding its scope and complicating the strategic alternatives. The entry of the Ottoman Empire on the side of the Central Powers in November 1914 extended the war to Turkey and on to the Middle East. Italy, after dickering with both sides, finally committed itself to intervention on the side of the Entente with the secret Treaty of London of April 1915, which specified the territorial compensation that Italy was to receive in the event of Entente victory—primarily Italian-speaking areas that still remained within Austria-Hungary. In September 1915, Bulgaria entered the war on the side of the Central Powers, seeking territorial advantages at the expense of Serbia, which had defeated Bulgaria in the Second Balkan War in 1913. In much the same way, Romania intervened on the side of the Entente, in August 1916, hoping to gain Transylvania, then part of Hungary.

Thus the war was fought on a variety of fronts (Map 27.1), and this, combined with uncertainties about the role sea power might play, led to ongoing debate among military decision makers about strategic priorities. Because of the antagonism that the prewar German naval buildup had caused, some expected that Britain and Germany would quickly be drawn into a major naval battle, which might well decide the war. Britain promptly instituted an effective naval blockade on imports to Germany, but the great showdown on the seas never materialized. Even the most significant naval encounter between them, the battle of Jutland in 1916, was indecisive. Despite the naval rivalry of the prewar years, World War I proved fundamentally a land war.

Germany faced not only the long-anticipated two-front war against Russia in the east and France and Britain in the west; it also had to look to the southeast, given the precarious situation of its ally Austria-Hungary, fighting Serbia and Russia, and then also Italy, and eventually Romania as well. On the eastern front, Germany managed decisive victories during 1917 and 1918, forcing first Russia, then Romania, to seek a separate peace. But it was the western front that proved decisive.

Into the Nightmare, 1914

With the lessons of the wars of German unification in mind, both sides had planned for a short war based on rapid offensives, a war of movement. According to the Schlieffen Plan, drafted in 1905, Germany would concentrate first on France, devoting but one-eighth of its forces to containing the Russians, who were bound to need longer to mobilize. After taking just six weeks to knock France out of the war, Germany would then concentrate on Russia. The strategy for France crafted by General Joseph Joffre (1852–1931) similarly relied on rapid offensives. The boys would be home by Christmas—or so it was thought.

Although German troops encountered more opposition than expected from the formerly neutral Belgians, they moved rapidly through Belgium into northern France during August. By the first week of September they had reached the Marne River, threatening Paris and forcing the French government to retreat south to Bordeaux. But the French and British under Joffre counterattacked September 6–10, forcing the Germans to fall back and begin digging in along the Aisne River. By holding off the German offensive at this first battle of the Marne, the Entente had undercut the Schlieffen Plan—and with it, it turned out, any chance of a rapid victory by either side.

During the rest of the fall of 1914, each side tried—unsuccessfully—to outflank the other. When, by the end of November, active fighting ceased for the winter, a military front of about three hundred miles had been established, all the way from Switzerland to the coast of the North Sea in Belgium (Map 27.2). And this line failed to shift more than ten miles in either direction over the next three years. So on the western front the result of the first six weeks of fighting in 1914 was not gallant victory by either side but a grim and unforeseen stalemate.

Virtually from the start, the war took a destructive turn that few had predicted. In northern France in September 1914, the Germans fired on the cathedral at Reims, severely damaging the roof and nave, because they believed—apparently correctly—that the French were using one

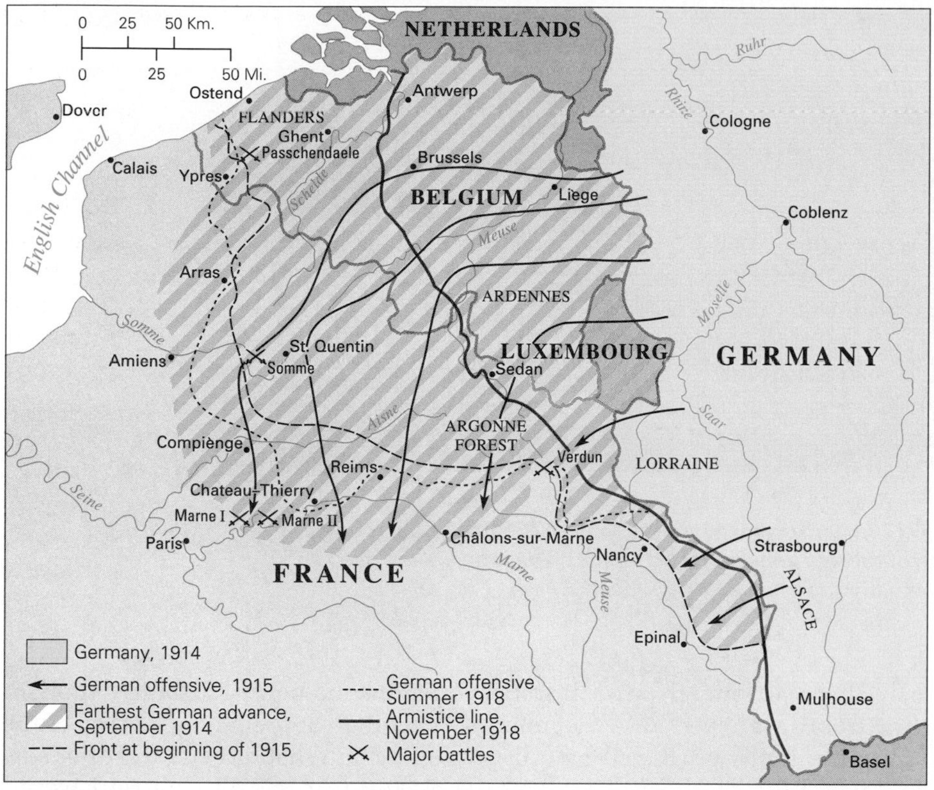

Map 27.2 Stalemate and Decision on the Western Front On the western front, in northern France and Belgium, trench warfare developed and the most famous battles of the war were fought. Notable sites included Verdun, Passchendaele, and the Marne and Somme rivers.

of the cathedral's towers as an observation post. If this could happen, at the very outset, to one of the great Gothic monuments in Europe, who could say what else this war might bring?

The two sides were forced to settle into a war of attrition relying on the elaborate network of defensive trenches. Although they were separated by as much as five miles in some places, enemy trenches were sometimes within shouting distance, so there was occasionally banter back and forth, even attempts to entertain the other side. But the trenches quickly became almost unimaginably grim—filthy, ridden with rats and lice, noisy and smoky from artillery fire, and foul-smelling, partly from the odor of decaying bodies.

As defensive instruments, however, the trenches proved quite effective, especially because each side quickly learned to take advantage of barbed wire, mines, and especially machine guns to defend its positions. A mass of barbed wire, perhaps three to five feet high and thirty yards wide, guarded a typical trench. The machine gun had been developed before the war as an offensive weapon; few anticipated the decided advantage it would give the defense. But with machine guns, it proved possible to defend trenches even against massive assaults—and to impose heavy casualties on the attackers.

In 1916 the tank was introduced as an antidote to the machine gun, but, as skeptics had warned, it proved too ungainly to be widely effective. Although the French used tanks to their advantage when at last it became possible to mount a decisive offensive in 1918, they were not crucial to the outcome of the war.

Though the defensive trenches had formidable advantages, neither side could give up the

Passchendaele, Belgium, 1917 After several months of intense shelling and fighting, autumn rains turned much of the war zone into a sea of mud. The mud was so deep and widespread that soldiers actually drowned in it. *(Trustees of the Imperial War Museum)*

vision of a decisive offensive to break through on the western front. Thus the troops were periodically called on to go "over the top" and then across "no man's land" to assault the enemy trenches. Again and again, however, such offensives proved futile, producing incredibly heavy casualties: "Whole regiments gambled away eternity for ten yards of wasteland."[1]

For the soldiers on the western front the war became a nightmarish experience in a hellish landscape. Bombardment by new, heavier forms of artillery not only threatened the enemy more directly but devastated the terrain in the war zone with craters, which then became muddy, turning the landscape into a near swamp (see the box, "Into the Trenches"). Beginning early in 1915, tear gas, chlorine gas, and finally mustard gas found use on both sides. Although the development of gas masks significantly reduced the impact of this menacing new chemical warfare, the threat of poison gas added another nightmarish element to the experience of those who fought the war.

The notions of patriotism, comradeship, duty, and glory that had been prevalent in 1914 gradually dissolved as those in the trenches experienced the unforeseen horrors of warfare on the western front. A French soldier, questioning his own reactions after battle in 1916, responded with sarcasm and irony: "What sublime emotion inspires you at the moment of assault? I thought of nothing other than dragging my feet out of the mud encasing them. What did you feel after surviving the attack? I grumbled because I would have to remain several days more without *pinard* [wine]. Is not one's first act to kneel down and thank God? No. One relieves oneself."[2]

Although the Germans had been denied their quick victory in the west, by the end of 1914 they occupied much of Belgium and almost one-tenth of France, including major industrial areas and mines producing most of France's coal and iron. On the eastern front, as well, the Germans won some substantial advantages in 1914—but not a decisive victory.

The first season of fighting in the east suggested that the pattern there would not be trench warfare but rapid movement across a vast but thinly held front. When the fighting began in August, the Russians came more quickly than anticipated, confronting an outnumbered German force in a menacing, if reckless, invasion of east Prussia. But by mid-September German forces under General Paul von Hindenburg (1847–1934) and his chief of staff General Erich Ludendorff (1865–1937) repelled the Russian advance, taking a huge number of prisoners and seriously demoralizing the Russians.

As a result of their victory in east Prussia, Hindenburg and Ludendorff emerged as heroes,

Into the Trenches

As the initial offensives on the western front turned into stalemate, ordinary soldiers on both sides began to experience unprecedented forms of warfare in an eerie new landscape. Writing home to his family from France in November 1914, a young German soldier, Fritz Franke (1892–1915), sought to convey what this new war was like. He was killed six months later, in May 1915.

Yesterday we didn't feel sure that a single one of us would come through alive. You can't possibly picture to yourselves what such a battlefield looks like. It is impossible to describe it, and even now, when it is a day behind us, I myself can hardly believe that such bestial barbarity and unspeakable suffering are possible. Every foot of ground contested; every hundred yards another trench; and everywhere bodies—rows of them! All the trees shot to pieces; the whole ground churned up a yard deep by the heaviest shells; dead animals; houses and churches so utterly destroyed by shellfire that they can never be of the least use again. And every troop that advances in support must pass through a mile of this chaos, through this gigantic burial ground and the reek of corpses.

In this way we advanced on Tuesday, marching for three hours, a silent column, in the moonlight, toward the Front and into a trench as Reserve, two to three hundred yards from the English, close behind our own infantry.

There we lay the whole day, a yard and a half to two yards below the level of the ground, crouching in the narrow trench on a thin layer of straw, in an overpowering din which never ceased all day or the greater part of the night—the whole ground trembling and shaking! There is every variety of sound—whistling, whining, ringing, crashing, rolling . . . [ellipses in the original] the beastly things pitch right above one and burst and the fragments buzz in all directions, and the only question one asks is: "Why doesn't one get me?"

Source: A. F. Wedd, ed., *German Students' War Letters,* translated and arranged from the original edition of Dr. Philipp Witkop (London: Methuen, 1929), pp. 123–124.

and they would play major roles in German public life thereafter. Hindenburg, the senior partner, became chief of staff of the entire German army in August 1916, but the able and energetic Ludendorff remained at his side. Ludendorff proved to be the key figure as this powerful duo assumed undisputed control of the whole German war effort, both military and domestic.

Seeking a Breakthrough, 1915–1917

After the campaigns of 1915 proved inconclusive, German leaders decided to concentrate in 1916 on a massive offensive against the great French fortress at Verdun, intending to inflict a definitive defeat on France. To assault the fortress, the Germans gathered 1220 pieces of artillery for attack along an eight-mile front. Included were thirteen "Big Bertha" siege guns, weapons so large that nine tractors were required to position each of them; a crane was necessary to insert the shell, which weighed over a ton. The level of heavy artillery firepower that the Germans applied at Verdun was without precedent in the history of warfare.

German forces attacked on February 21, taking the outer defenses of the fortress, and appeared poised for victory. The tide turned, however, when General Philippe Pétain (1856–1951) assumed control of the French defense at Verdun. Pétain had the patience and skill necessary to organize supply for a long and difficult siege.

Paul von Hindenburg and Erich Ludendorff The talents of Hindenburg (left) and Ludendorff meshed effectively to carry them from success on the eastern front in 1914 to a predominant role in the German war effort. They are shown here at a reception in honor of Hindenburg's seventieth birthday in October 1917. *(Archiv für kunst und Geschichte, Berlin)*

Moreover, he proved able, through especially considerate treatment, to inspire affection and confidence among his men. By mid-July the French army had clearly repelled the German offensive, although only in December did it retake the outer defenses of the fortress. The French had held in what would prove the war's longest, most trying battle—one that killed 600,000 men on both sides. The battle of Verdun would remain for France the epitome of the horrors of World War I.

Meanwhile, early in July, the British led a major attack at the Somme River that was similarly bloody—and that affected Britain much as Verdun affected France. On the first day alone the British suffered 60,000 casualties, including 21,000 killed. Fighting continued into the fall, but the offensive proved futile in the end. One-third of those involved, or over 1 million soldiers, ended up dead, missing, or wounded. Of these, 400,000 were British, 200,000 French, and 500,000 German.

Dominated by the incredibly costly battles at Verdun and the Somme, the campaigns of 1916 marked the decisive end to the high spirits of the summer of 1914. Both sides suffered huge losses—and apparently for nothing. By the end of 1916, the front had shifted only a few miles from its location at the beginning of the year.

In light of the frustrating outcome so far, the French turned to new military leadership, replacing Joffre with Robert Nivelle (1856–1924), who promptly sought to prove himself with a new offensive during the spring of 1917. Persisting even as it became clear that this effort had no chance of success, Nivelle provoked increasing resistance among French soldiers, some of whom were simply refusing to follow orders by the end of May.

With the French war effort in danger of collapse, the French government replaced Nivelle with General Pétain, the hero of the defense of Verdun a year earlier and the obvious person to restore morale. Pétain managed to re-establish discipline by adopting a conciliatory approach—improving food and rest, visiting the troops in the field, listening, offering encouragement, urging patience, even dealing relatively mercifully with most of the resisters themselves. To be sure, many of the soldiers who had participated in this near-mutiny were court-martialed, and over 3400 were convicted. But of the 554 sentenced to death, only 49 were actually executed.

After the failure of the Nivelle offensive, the initiative again fell to the British, under General Douglas Haig (1861–1928), who was convinced, despite skepticism in the British cabinet, that Nivelle's offensive had failed simply because of tactical mistakes. Beginning near Ypres in Flanders on July 31, 1917, and continuing until November, the British attacked, but, as before, the effort yielded only minimal territorial gains—about fifty square miles—at a horrifying cost—including 240,000 British casualties. Known as the battle of Passchendaele, the British offensive of 1917 ranks with the battles of Verdun and the Somme as the bloodiest of the war.

1917 as a Turning Point

Meanwhile, the Germans, feeling that the Russians could not hold out much longer, decided to concentrate on the eastern front in 1917, in an effort to knock Russia out of the war at last. This intensified German military pressure helped spark revolution in Russia, and in December 1917 a new revolutionary regime asked for a separate peace. The defeat of Russia freed the Germans at last to concentrate on the west, but by this time France and Germany had a new ally.

On April 6, 1917, the United States finally entered the war on the side of the Entente, in response to Germany's controversial use of submarines. Germany lacked sufficient strength in surface ships to respond to Britain's naval blockade, whether by attacking the British fleet directly or by mounting a comparable blockade of the British Isles. So the Germans decided to use submarines to interfere with shipping to Britain. Submarines, however, were too vulnerable to be able to surface and confiscate goods, so the Germans had to settle for sinking suspect ships with torpedoes. In February 1915 they declared the waters around the British Isles to be a war zone and served notice that they would torpedo not only enemy ships but also neutral ships carrying goods to Britain.

The German response was harsh, but so was the British blockade, which violated a number of earlier international agreements about the rights of neutral shipping and the scope of wartime blockades. The British had agreed that only military goods such as munitions and the raw materials needed for military manufacture, as opposed to nonmilitary goods such as ordinary food and clothing, were to be subject to confiscation. Yet in blockading Germany, the British refused to make this distinction, prompting the sarcastic German quip that Britannia not only rules the waves, but waives the rules.[3]

In May 1915 a German sub torpedoed the *Lusitania,* a British passenger liner, killing almost 1200 people. The act produced widespread indignation. Indeed, partly because 128 of those killed were Americans, U.S. President Wilson issued a severe warning, which contributed to the German decision in September 1915 to pull back from unrestricted submarine warfare. But in this war of attrition, the flow of supplies became ever more critical. As German suffering under the British blockade increased, pressure steadily mounted within Germany to put the subs back into action.

The issue provoked bitter debate among German leaders. Chancellor Bethmann-Hollweg and the civilian authorities opposed resumption out of fear it would provoke the United States to enter the war. But Ludendorff and the military finally prevailed, partly with the argument that even if the United States did intervene, U.S. troops could not get to Europe in sufficient numbers, and in sufficient haste, to have a major impact. Germany announced the resumption of unrestricted submarine warfare on January 31, 1917, and the United States responded with a declaration of war on April 6.

Many on both sides doubted that U.S. intervention would make a decisive difference; most assumed that it would take at least a year for the American presence to materialize in force—an assessment that proved accurate. Still, the entry of the United States gave the Entente at least the promise of more fighting power. And the United States seemed capable of renewing the sense of purpose on the Entente side, showing that the war had a meaning that could justify all the unexpected costs and sacrifice.

The Experience of Total War

As the war dragged on, the distinction between the military and civilian spheres blurred. Suffering increased on the home front, and unprecedented governmental mobilization of society proved necessary to wage war on the scale that had come to be required. Because it became "total" in this way, the war affected not simply international relations and the power balance but also culture, society, and the patterns of everyday life.

Hardship on the Home Front

The war meant food shortages, and thus malnutrition, for ordinary people in the belligerent countries, although Britain and France, with their more favorable geographical positions, suffered considerably less than others. Germany was especially vulnerable and promptly began suffering under the British naval blockade. With military needs taking priority, the Germans quickly encountered shortages of the chemical fertilizers, farm machinery, and draft animals necessary for agricultural production. The government began rationing bread, meat, and fats during 1915. The increasing scarcity of foodstuffs produced sharp increases in diseases like rickets and tuberculosis and in infant and childhood mortality rates in Germany during the war.

The need to pay for the war inevitably produced economic dislocations as well. Government borrowing covered some of the cost for the short term, but to cover the rest, governments all over Europe found it more palatable to inflate the currency, by printing more money, than to raise taxes. The notion that the enemy would be made to pay once victory had been won seemed to justify this decision. But this way of financing the war meant rising prices and severe erosion of purchasing power for ordinary people all over Europe. In both France and Germany, the labor truce of 1914 gave way to increasing strike activity during 1916.

With an especially severe winter in 1916–1917 adding to the misery, there were serious instances of domestic disorder, including strikes and food riots, in many parts of Europe during 1917. In Italy, major strikes developed in Turin and other cities over wages and bread supplies. The revolution that overthrew the tsarist autocracy in Russia that same year began with comparable protests over wartime food shortages.

The strains of war even fanned the flames in Ireland, where an uneasy truce over the home-rule controversy accompanied the British decision for war in 1914. Partly because of German efforts to stir up domestic trouble for Britain, unrest built up again in Ireland, culminating in the Easter Rebellion in Dublin in 1916. The brutality with which British forces crushed the uprising intensified demands for full independence—precisely what Britain would be forced to yield to the Irish Republic shortly after the war.

Moreover, new technologies had expanded warmaking capacities in ways that made civilians ever less immune to wartime violence. Most dramatically, an entirely new aspect of warmaking, bombing from aircraft, directly assaulted civilians. Although bombing began with an immediate military aim—to destroy industrial targets or to provide tactical support for other military units—it quickly became clear that night bombing, especially, might demoralize civilian populations. As early as 1915, German airplanes were bombing English cities, provoking British retaliation against cities in the German Ruhr and Rhineland areas. These raids had little effect on the course of the war, but they showed that new technologies could make warfare more destructive even for civilians.

Domestic Mobilization

Once it became clear, by the end of 1914, that the war would not be over quickly, leaders on both sides began to realize that victory could not be achieved on the battlefield alone but required the mobilization of all of their nations' resources and energies. So World War I became a total war, involving the whole society, not just the military.

In imposing their naval blockade on Germany, the British refused to accept the distinction between military and nonmilitary goods because they sensed that this would prove a new, more total kind of war in which that distinction dissolved. They realized the blockade would not affect Germany's immediate strength on the battlefield, but they believed—correctly—that it could damage Germany's long-term war-making capacity. The blockade proved significant because Germany had not made effective economic preparations—including stockpiling—for this long war of attrition.

In peacetime, Germany had depended on imports of food, fats, oils, and chemicals, including the nitrates needed for ammunition. With the onset of war, these commodities were immediately in short supply, as was labor. Thus Germany seemed to need stringent economic coordination and control. By the end of 1916, Germany had developed a militarized economy, with all aspects of economic life coordinated for the war effort. Under the supervision of the military, state agencies, big business, and the trade unions were brought into close collaboration. The new system included rationing, price controls, and compulsory labor arbitration, as well as a national service law enabling the military to channel workers into the jobs deemed most important for the war effort.

In the Trenches A German poster from 1917 invites the people of Frankfurt to express their gratitude by making special Christmas donations for the German forces at the front. *(Trustees of the Imperial War Museum)*

Forced to provide for an unexpectedly long war, the Germans did not hesitate to exploit the economy of occupied Belgium, requisitioning foodstuffs even to the point of causing starvation among the Belgians themselves. They forced 62,000 Belgian workers to work in German factories under conditions of virtual slave labor. Although this practice was stopped in February 1917, by then nearly a thousand Belgian workers had died in German labor camps.

The most influential feature of Germany's war economy was the Kriegsrohstoffabteilung (KRA), or war raw materials office, established under the authority of the War Ministry to provide the raw materials essential to the war effort. Led initially by the able Jewish industrialist Walther Rathenau (1867–1922), this agency came to symbolize the unprecedented coordination of the German economy for war. Recognizing as early as the fall of 1914 that Germany lacked the raw materials for a long war, Rathenau devised an imaginative program that included the development of synthetic substitute products and the creation of new mixed (private and government) companies to allocate raw materials. The KRA's effort was remarkably successful—a model for later economic planning and coordination.

Although Germany presents the most dramatic example of such domestic coordination, the same pattern was evident everywhere, even in France, with its economic individualism and distrust of an interventionist state. In Britain, Lord Herbert Kitchener, appointed war secretary in August 1914, was at first almost alone in envisioning the need to began planning immediately for a long and exhausting war. But although he spearheaded a major expansion of the British army, he proved ineffective in organizing supply and, by 1915, was widely blamed for Britain's serious ammunition shortages.

The central figure in Britain's domestic organization for war proved to be David Lloyd George (1863–1945), appointed to the newly created post of minister of munitions in 1915. During his year in that office, ninety-five new factories opened and the shortages of guns and ammunition soon ceased. In fact, types of ammunition that had formerly taken a year to manufacture were now being produced in weeks, even days. His performance as munitions minister made Lloyd George seem the one person who could organize Britain for victory. He became war secretary in June 1916, following Kitchener's death, and then, in December 1916, succeeded Asquith as prime minister. From there he would direct the British war effort to its victorious conclusion.

Accelerating Socioeconomic Change

Everywhere the war effort rapidly accelerated the long-term process of socioeconomic change associated with industrialization. Guaranteed government orders for war materiel fueled industrial expansion. In France, the Paris region now became a center of heavy industrial production for the first time. The needs of war spawned new technologies—advances in food processing

Domestic Mobilization and the Role of Women

Early in 1917, the British writer Gilbert Stone published a remarkable collection of statements intended to illuminate the new experiences that British women were encountering in the workplace. The following passage by Naomi Loughnan, a well-to-do woman who worked in a munitions factory, makes it clear that the new work experience during the war opened the way to new questions about both gender and class.

Engineering mankind is possessed of the unshakable opinion that no woman can have the mechanical sense. If one of us asks humbly why such and such an alteration is not made to prevent this or that drawback to a machine, she is told, with a superior smile, that a man has worked her machine before her for years, and that therefore if there were any improvement possible it would have been made. As long as we do exactly as we are told and do not attempt to use our brains, we give entire satisfaction, and are treated as nice, good children. Any swerving from the easy path prepared for us by our males arouses the most scathing contempt in their manly bosoms.... Women have, however, proved that their entry into the munitions world has increased the output. Employers who forget things personal in their patriotic desire for large results are enthusiastic over the success of women in the shops. But their workmen have to be handled with the utmost tenderness and caution lest they should actually imagine it was being suggested that women could do their work equally well, given equal conditions of training—at least where muscle is not the driving force. This undercurrent of jealousy rises to the surface rather often, but as a general rule the men behave with much kindness, and are ready to help with muscle and advice whenever called upon. If eyes are very bright and hair inclined to curl, the muscle and advice do not even wait for a call.

The coming of the mixed classes of women into the factory is slowly but surely having an educative effect upon the men. "Language" is almost unconsciously becoming subdued. There are fiery exceptions who make our hair stand up on end under our close-fitting caps, but a sharp rebuke or a look of horror will often bring to book the most truculent.... It is grievous to hear the girls also swearing and using disgusting language. Shoulder to shoulder with the children of the slums, the upper classes are having their eyes prised open at last to the awful conditions among which their sisters have dwelt. Foul language, immorality, and many other evils are but the natural outcome of overcrowding and bitter poverty. If some of us, still blind and ignorant of our responsibilities, shrink horrified and repelled from the rougher set, the compliment is returned with open derision and ribald laughter.... On the other hand, attempts at friendliness from the more understanding are treated with the utmost suspicion, though once that suspicion is overcome and friendship is established, it is unshakable.

Source: Naomi Loughnan, "Munition Work," in Gilbert Stone, ed., *Women War Workers: Accounts Contributed by Representative Workers of the Work Done by Women in the More Important Branches of War Employment* (New York: Thomas Y. Crowell, [1917]), pp. 35–38.

and medical treatment, for example—that would carry over into peacetime.

With so many men needed for military service, women were called on to assume new economic roles—running farms in France, for example, or working in the new munitions factories in Britain (see the box, "Domestic Mobilization and the Role of Women"). During the course of the war, the number of women employed in Britain rose from 3.25 million to 5 million. In Italy,

New Roles for Women The needs of wartime brought more women than ever into the work force. Women were especially prominent in the munitions industry that Lloyd George built up in Britain. These women are at work in a British shell factory in May 1918. *(Trustees of the Imperial War Museum)*

200,000 women had war-related jobs by 1917. Women also played indispensable roles at the front, especially in nursing units.

Wartime opportunities intensified the debate over the overall sociopolitical role of women that the prewar movement for women's suffrage had stimulated. The outbreak of war led some antiwar feminists to argue that women would be better able than men to prevent wars, which were essentially masculine undertakings. Women should have full access to public life not because they could be expected to respond as men did, but because they had a distinctive—and valuable—role to play. On the other hand, by giving women jobs and the opportunity to do many of the same things men had done, the war undermined the stereotypes that had long justified restrictions on women's political roles and life choices.

For many women, doing a difficult job well, serving their country in this emergency situation, afforded a new sense of accomplishment, as well as a new taste of independence. Freed from male domination, women were now much more likely to have their own residences, to go out in public on their own, eating in restaurants, even smoking and drinking. Yet the pressures of war also created tension as women looked to new opportunities yet still felt responsible for traditional family roles (see the box, "Women at the Front: Conflicting Obligations").

Propaganda and the "Mobilization of Enthusiasm"

Because the domestic front was crucial to sustaining a long war of attrition, it became ever more important to shore up civilian morale as the war dragged on. The result was the "mobilization of enthusiasm"—the conscious manipulation of collective passions by national governments on an unprecedented scale. Everywhere there was extensive censorship, even of soldiers' letters from the front. Because of concerns about civilian morale, the French press carried no news of the battle of Verdun, with the horrifying number of

Women at the Front: Conflicting Obligations

Vera Brittain (1893–1970) gave up her university studies in 1915 to enlist as a nurse in the British armed services. She served throughout the war—in London, in Malta, and at the front in France. In* Testament of Youth, *first published in 1933, she explores the special difficulties faced by women in wartime military service as the strains of war began to cause privation back home.

This despondency at home was certainly making many of us in France quite alarmed: because we were women we feared perpetually that, just as our work was reaching its climax, our families would need our youth and vitality for their own support. . . . [A]s the War continued to wear out strength and spirits, the middle-aged generation, having irrevocably yielded up its sons, began to lean with increasing weight upon its daughters. Thus the desperate choice between incompatible claims—by which the women of my generation, with their carefully trained consciences, have always been tormented—showed signs of afflicting us with new pertinacity. . . .

Early in April [1918] a letter arrived from my father to say that my mother had "crocked up" and had been obliged . . . to go into a nursing home. . . . "As your mother and I can no longer manage without you," he concluded, "it is now your duty to leave France immediately and return to Kensington."

I read these words with real dismay, for my father's interpretation of my duty was not, I knew only too well, in the least likely to agree with that of the Army. . . . What was I to do? I wondered desperately. There was my family, confidently demanding my presence, and here was the [German] offensive, which made every pair of experienced hands worth ten pairs under normal conditions. . . .

Half-frantic with the misery of conflicting obligations, I envied Edward his complete powerlessness to leave the Army whatever happened at home. . . .

. . . What exhausts women in wartime is not the strenuous and unfamiliar tasks that fall upon them, nor even the hourly dread of death for husbands or lovers or brothers or sons; it is the incessant conflict between personal and national claims which wears out their energy and breaks their spirit.

Source: Vera Brittain, *Testament of Youth: An Autobiographical Study of the Years 1900–1925* (New York: Penguin, 1989), pp. 401–402, 421–423.

casualties it involved. In addition, systematic propaganda included not only patriotic themes but also attempts to discredit the enemy, even through outright falsification of the news. British propaganda helped draw the United States into the war in 1917.

At the outset of the war, the brutal behavior of the German armies in Belgium made it easy for the French and the British to develop anti-German propaganda. Having expected to pass through neutral Belgium unopposed, the Germans were infuriated by the Belgian resistance they encountered. At Louvain late in August 1914 they responded to alleged Belgian sniping by shooting a number of hostages and setting the town on fire, destroying the famous old library at the university. This notorious episode led the London *Times* to characterize the Germans as "Huns," a reference to the Mongolian tribe that began invading Europe in the fourth century. Stories about German soldiers eating Belgian babies began to circulate.

In October 1914 ninety-three important German intellectuals, artists, and scientists signed a manifesto, addressed to "the World of Culture," justifying Germany's conduct in Belgium and larger purposes in the war. To a point, such gestures stemmed from expected forms of patriotism, but as passions heated up, major intellectuals on both sides—from the German theologian Adolf von Harnack (1851–1930) to the French philosopher Henri Bergson (1859–1941)—began denigrating the culture of the enemy and claiming a monopoly of virtue for their own side.

This unprecedented propaganda combined with the unexpected destruction and loss of life to give the war an increasingly catastrophic aura. This was no mere adjustment in the traditional balance of power; so great were the strains of war, in fact, that the sense of common involvement in a single civilization, or a single European state system based on an accepted set of rules, began to weaken. Some came to believe that real peace with an adversary so evil, so different, was simply not possible. Thus, there must be no compromise, but rather total victory, no matter what the cost.

But just as chauvinistic propaganda fanned the fires of war, war-weariness produced a countervailing tendency to seek a "white peace," a peace without victory for either side. Both sets of impulses were at work as Europeans began debating war aims in earnest in 1917, at a time when dramatic events were changing the war's meaning for contemporaries. The most significant was the Russian Revolution, which developed from wartime difficulties, but which then fundamentally affected the nature of the war.

Civilian Suffering The war affected civilians in many ways, but those who happened to live in the area of most intense fighting, in Belgium and northern France, suffered most directly. This British poster urges contributions to a charity helping Belgians whose means of livelihood had been damaged or destroyed. *(Trustees of the Imperial War Museum)*

Two Revolutions in Russia: March and November, 1917

The old European order finally cracked in Russia in 1917. Revolution against the tsarist autocracy seemed first to lay the foundations for parliamentary democracy. But by the end of the year, the Bolsheviks, the smallest and most extreme of Russia's major socialist parties, had taken power, an outcome that was hardly conceivable when the revolution began.

The Wartime Crisis of the Russian Autocracy

The Russian army performed better than many had expected during the first year of the war, and even as late as June 1916, it was strong enough for a successful offensive against Austria-Hungary. Russia had industrialized sufficiently by 1914 to sustain a modern war, and the country's war production increased significantly by 1916. But Russia suffered from problems of leadership and organization—in transportation, for example—that made it less prepared for a long war than the other belligerents. Even early in 1915, perhaps a fourth of Russia's newly conscripted troops found themselves sent to the front without weapons, instructed simply to pick up rifles and supplies from the dead.

As problems mounted, Tsar Nicholas II (1868–1918) assumed personal command of the army in August 1915, but his absence from the capital, Petrograd, only accelerated the deterioration in government and deepened the bitter divisions within the ruling clique. With the tsar away, the illiterate but charismatic Siberian monk Grigori Rasputin (c. 1872–1916) emerged as the key political power within the circle of the German-born Empress Alexandra (1872–1918). He won her confidence because of his alleged ability to control the bleeding of her hemophiliac son, Alexis, the heir to the throne. Led by Rasputin, those around the empress made a shambles of the state administration. Many educated Russians, appalled at what was happening, assumed—incorrectly—that pro-German elements at court were responsible for the eclipse of the tsar and the resulting government chaos. Asked one Duma deputy of the government's performance, "Is this stupidity, or is it treason?"

Finally, late in December 1916, Rasputin was assassinated by aristocrats seeking to save the autocracy from these apparently pro-German influences. This act indicated how desperate the situation was becoming, but it made no decisive difference.

By the end of 1916, the immediate difficulties of war had combined with the strains of rapid wartime industrialization to produce a revolutionary situation in Russia. The country's urban population had increased rapidly, and now, partly because of transport problems, the cities faced severe food shortages. Strikes and demonstrations spread from Petrograd to other cities during the first two months of 1917. In March renewed demonstrations in Petrograd, spearheaded by women protesting the lack of bread and coal, led to revolution.

The March Revolution and the Failure of the Provisional Government

At first, the agitation that began in Petrograd on March 8, 1917, appeared to be just another bread riot. Even when it turned into a wave of strikes, the revolutionary parties expected it to be crushed by the government troops stationed at the Petrograd garrison. But when called out to help the police break up the demonstrations, the military generally avoided firing at the strikers. Within days, the soldiers were sharing weapons and ammunition with the workers; the garrison was going over to what now was clearly becoming a revolution.

Late in the afternoon of March 12, leaders of the strike committees, delegates elected by factory workers, and representatives of the socialist parties formed a soviet, or council, following the example of the revolution of 1905, when such soviets had first appeared. Regiments of the Petrograd garrison also began electing representatives, soon to be admitted to the Petrograd Soviet, which officially became the Council of Workers' and Soldiers' Deputies. This soviet was now the ruling power in the Russian capital. It had been elected and was genuinely representative—though of a limited constituency of workers and soldiers. Following the lead of Petrograd, Russians elsewhere promptly began forming soviets, so that over 350 local units were represented when the first All-Russian Council of Soviets met in Petrograd in April. The overwhelming majority of their representatives were Mensheviks and Socialist Revolutionaries; only about one-sixth were Bolsheviks.

On March 14, a committee of the Duma, recognizing that the tsar's authority had been lost for good, persuaded Nicholas to abdicate, then formed a new provisional government. Particularly because it derived from the Duma elected in 1907, under extremely limited suffrage, this government was supposed to be strictly temporary, to pave the way for an elected constituent assembly, which would establish fully legitimate governmental institutions.

In light of the strains in the autocratic system that had produced the revolution of 1905 after the Russo-Japanese War, it was hardly surprising that the system would shatter now, in light of this far more trying war and the resulting disarray within the tsarist government. Russia had apparently had, at long last, the bourgeois political revolution necessary to develop a Western-style parliamentary democracy. Even from an orthodox Marxist perspective, this was the revolution to expect, and Marxists could only help consolidate bourgeois democracy. The longer-term pursuit of socialism could take place within that new political framework. These, however, were anything but orthodox times, and the March revolution proved only the beginning.

Although the fall of the tsarist order produced widespread relief, Russia's new leaders faced difficult questions about priorities. Many, both inside and outside Russia, believed that the revolution's immediate purpose was to revitalize the Russian war effort. Yet war-weariness was widespread, and there were pressures to get on with domestic political change—which would be difficult in the context of war. Moreover, the provisional government had to operate with the potentially more radical Petrograd Soviet, the keystone of the network of soviets across the country, looking over its shoulder.

At first the Petrograd Soviet was perfectly willing to give the provisional government a chance to govern. In this bourgeois revolution, it was not up to socialists and workers to take responsibility by participating directly in government, though they could offer support, especially against any attempt at counterrevolution. Even among the Bolsheviks, there was widespread support for conciliation and at least short-term acceptance of the new government. Although the Bolshevik leader, Vladimir Lenin (1870–1924), took a different tack, he was in exile in Switzerland and could not yet make his will prevail.

Given its chance by the Petrograd Soviet, the provisional government took important steps toward Western-style liberal democracy, establishing universal suffrage, civil liberties, autonomy for ethnic minorities, and labor legislation, including provision for an eight-hour workday. But the government failed in two key areas, fostering discontents that the Bolsheviks soon exploited. First, the new government persisted in fighting the war. Second, it dragged its feet on agrarian reform.

The provisional government's determination to renew the war effort stemmed from genuine concern about Russia's obligations to its allies, about the country's national honor and position among the great powers. Moreover, the longstanding goal of Russian diplomacy—an outlet to the Mediterranean Sea through the Dardanelles Strait—seemed within reach if a revitalized Russia could continue the war, contributing to an Allied victory. The educated, well-to-do Russians who led the new government expected that ordinary citizens, now free, would fight with renewed enthusiasm, like the armies that had grown from the French Revolution over a century before. But these leaders failed to grasp how desperate the situation of ordinary people had become.

The March revolution grew from unrest in the cities, but in the aftermath the peasantry gradually moved into action as well, seizing land, sometimes burning the houses of their landlords. By midsummer, a full-scale peasant war seemed to be in the offing in the countryside, and calls for radical agrarian reform became increasingly insistent. Partly from expediency, partly from genuine concern for social justice, the provisional government promised that a major redistribution of land would be forthcoming, but it insisted that the reform be carried out legally—not by the present provisional government, but by a duly elected constituent assembly.

Calling for elections would thus seem to have been the first priority, but the new political leaders kept putting it off, waiting for the situation to cool off before relinquishing power to a newly elected assembly. In fact, however, the situation did not allow the luxury of playing for time. As unrest grew in the countryside, the authority of the provisional government diminished and the soviets gained in stature. But what role were the soviets to play?

The Bolsheviks Come to Power

In the immediate aftermath of the March revolution, the Bolsheviks had not seemed to differ substantially from their rivals within the socialist movement, at least on the matters of most immediate concern—the war, land reform, and the character of the revolution itself. But the situation began to change in April when Lenin returned from exile in Switzerland, thanks partly to the help with transportation that the German military provided. The Germans assumed—correctly, it turned out—that the Bolsheviks would help undermine the Russian war effort. Largely through the force of Lenin's leadership, the Bolsheviks soon assumed the initiative.

Lenin, born Vladimir Ilich Ulianov, came from a comfortable upper-middle-class family

Lenin as Leader Although he was in exile during much of 1917, Lenin's leadership was crucial to the Bolshevik success in Russia. In this famous photo, he is shown speaking in Moscow in 1920. Leon Trotsky stands next to the podium, at the right side of the picture. *(Bettmann/Hulton)*

and was university-educated and trained as a lawyer. But after an older brother was executed in 1887 for participating in a plot against the tsar's life, Lenin followed him into revolutionary activity. He was arrested for the first time in 1895, then exiled to Siberia. After his release in 1900, he made his way to western Europe, and there he remained, except for brief return to Russia during the revolution of 1905, until the renewal of revolution in 1917.

The Bolshevik party was identified with Lenin from its beginning in 1903, when it emerged from the schism in Russian Marxist socialism. Because of his emphases, Bolshevism came to mean discipline, organization, and a special leadership role for a revolutionary vanguard. Lenin proved effective because he was a stern and somewhat forbidding figure, disciplined, fiercely intelligent, sometimes ruthless. As a Bolshevik colleague put it, Lenin was "the one indisputable leader . . . a man of iron will, inexhaustible energy, combining a fanatical faith in the movement, in the cause, with an equal faith in himself."[4]

Still, when Lenin began taking the initiative in 1917, he astonished even many Bolsheviks at first. He held that the revolution was about to pass from the present bourgeois-democratic to a socialist phase, involving dictatorship of the proletariat in the form of government by the soviets. It was time, then, for active opposition to the provisional government, and this meant both criticism of the war, as fundamentally imperialist, and calls for the distribution of land from the large estates to the peasants. This latter measure had long been identified with the Socialist Revolutionaries; most Bolsheviks had envisioned collectivization and nationalization instead.

But what Lenin envisioned was anything but "socialism in one country," with embattled, relatively backward Russia trying to create a socialist order on its own. Rather, a Bolshevik-led revolution in Russia would provide the spark to ignite the proletarian revolution smoldering elsewhere in Europe, especially in Germany. Although some Bolsheviks remained skeptical, Lenin's strategic vision promptly won acceptance among most of his colleagues.

In April 1917, moderate socialists still had majority support in the soviets, so the Bolsheviks sought to build gradually, postponing any decisive test of strength. But events escaped the control of the Bolshevik leadership in mid-July when impatient workers, largely Bolshevik in sympathy, took to the streets of Petrograd on their own. The Petrograd Soviet refused to support the uprising, and the provisional government had no difficulty getting military units to put it down, killing two hundred in the process. Though the uprising had developed spontaneously, Bolshevik leaders felt compelled to offer public support, and this gave the government an excuse to crack down on the Bolshevik leadership in the aftermath. Lenin managed to escape to Finland as a number of his colleagues suffered arrest and imprisonment.

With the Bolsheviks on the defensive, counterrevolutionary elements in the Russian military decided to seize the initiative with a march on Petrograd in September. In resisting this attempted coup, the provisional government, now under Alexander Kerensky (1881–1970), a young and charismatic Socialist Revolutionary, had to rely on whoever could offer help, including the Bolsheviks. Bolshevik propaganda led the soldiers under the command of the counterrevolutionaries to refuse to fight against the upholders of the revolution in Petrograd. Within days, the Bolsheviks won their first clear-cut majority in the Petrograd Soviet, then shortly gained majorities in most of the other soviets as well.

During the fall of 1917, the situation became more spontaneously revolutionary, eluding control by anyone. People looted food from shops; peasants seized land, sometimes murdering their landlords; within the Russian military desertions and the murder of officers increased.

With the Bolsheviks at last the dominant power in the soviets, and with the government's control diminishing, Lenin, from his hideout in Finland, began urging the Bolshevik central committee to prepare for armed insurrection. Although some found this step unnecessarily risky, the majority accepted Lenin's argument that the provisional government would continue dragging its feet, inadvertently giving right-wing officer leagues time for another counterrevolutionary coup.

Although his views prevailed, Lenin himself remained in hiding, so the task of organizing the seizure of power fell to Leon Trotsky (1870–1940), who skillfully modified Lenin's aggressive stance. Whereas Lenin had advocated that the Bolsheviks rise in their own name, in opposition to the provisional government, Trotsky linked the insurrection to the cause of the soviets and played up its defensive character, against the ongoing danger of a counterrevolutionary coup. With the political center at an impasse, the only alternative to such a coup seemed to be a Bolshevik initiative to preserve the Petrograd Soviet, by now the sole viable institutional embodiment of the revolution and its promise. Trotsky's interpretation led people seeking not a Bolshevik revolution, but simply to defend the Soviet, to support the Bolsheviks' initiative.

During the night of November 9, armed Bolsheviks and regular army regiments occupied key points in Petrograd, including railroad stations, post offices, telephone exchanges, power stations, and the national bank. When it proved able to mount only token resistance, the provisional government collapsed. Kerensky escaped by morning and mounted what quickly proved a futile effort to rally troops at the front for a counterattack against the Bolsheviks. In contrast to the March revolution, which had taken about a week, the Bolsheviks took over the capital, overthrowing the Kerensky government, literally overnight, and almost without bloodshed. A wave of popular euphoria followed (see the box, "Revolutionary Discipline at the Winter Palace, November 1917"). But though the Bolsheviks had taken Petrograd, they would need three more years and a civil war to extend their control across the whole Russian empire.

However, the revolution's immediate prospects, and the wider impact it might have, were bound up with the course of the war. Would the Bolshevik Revolution in Russia prove the spark for revolution elsewhere in war-weary Europe, as Lenin anticipated? If not, could a Bolshevik regime survive in Russia on its own?

The Russian Revolution and the War

Having stood for peace throughout the revolution, the Bolsheviks promptly moved to get Russia out of the war, agreeing to a separate peace with Germany in December 1917. They hoped that Russia's withdrawal would speed the collapse of the war effort on all sides and that this, in turn, would intensify the movement toward revolution elsewhere in Europe. The Russian Revolution, they believed, was but a chapter in a larger story, proceeding from war to wider revolution. As Lenin said to Trotsky, "If it were necessary for us to go under to assure the success of the German revolution, we should have to do it. The German revolution is vastly more important than ours." Indeed, said Lenin to the Communist party congress of March 1918, "It is an absolute truth that we will go under without the German revolution."[5]

Still, the Bolsheviks did not have to wait passively for events elsewhere to unfold. They could help spark wider revolution by demonstrating the imperialist basis of the war, with all its hardships. After assuming control in November, they published the tsarist government's secret documents concerning the war—the treaties and understandings specifying how the spoils were to be divided in the event of victory. In doing so, the

Revolutionary Discipline at the Winter Palace, November 1917

John Reed (1887–1920), an American journalist and communist leader from Portland, Oregon, was in Russia during the fall of 1917, when the second revolution began. His enthusiastic first-hand account, which drew the praise of Lenin himself, conveys the drama and excitement of the revolutionary events. In the following passage, he describes the revolutionary crowd storming the palace of the tsars in Petrograd at the height of the November revolution.

Carried along by the eager wave of men we were swept into the right hand entrance, opening into a great, bare, vaulted room, the cellar of the East wing, from which issued a maze of corridors and stair-cases. A number of huge packing cases stood about, and upon these the Red Guards and soldiers fell furiously, battering them open with the butts of their rifles, and pulling out carpets, curtains, linens, porcelain plates, glassware. . . . [ellipses in original] One man went strutting around with a bronze clock perched on his shoulder; another found a plume of ostrich feathers, which he stuck in his hat. The looting was just beginning when somebody cried, "Comrades! Don't touch anything! Don't take anything! This is the property of the people!" Immediately twenty voices were crying, "Stop! Put everything back! Don't take anything! Property of the people!" Many hands dragged the spoilers down. Damask and tapestry were snatched from the arms of those who had them; two men took away the bronze clock. Roughly and hastily the things were crammed back in their cases, and self-appointed sentinels stood guard. It was all utterly spontaneous. Through corridors and up staircases the cry could be heard growing fainter and fainter in the distance, "Revolutionary discipline! Property of the people. . . ." [ellipses in original]

We crossed back over to the left entrance, in the West wing. There order was also being established. "Clear the palace!" bawled a Red Guard, sticking his head through an inner door. "Come comrades, let's show that we're not thieves and bandits. Everybody out of the Palace except the Commissars, until we get sentries posted."

Source: John Reed, *Ten Days That Shook the World* (New York: New American Library, Signet, 1967), pp. 105–106.

Bolsheviks hoped to show ordinary people elsewhere that this had been, all along, a war on behalf of capitalist interests. This Bolshevik effort added fuel to the controversy already developing in all the belligerent countries over the war's purpose and significance.

The New War and the Entente Victory, 1917–1918

Because the stakes of the war changed during 1917, the outcome, once the war finally ended in November 1918, included consequences that Europeans could not have foreseen in 1914. Thus German defeat brought revolution against the monarchy and the beginning of a new democracy. Thus grandiose new visions competed to shape the postwar world.

The Debate Over War Aims

The French and British governments publicly welcomed the March revolution in Russia, partly because they expected Russia's military performance to improve under new leadership, but also because the change of regime seemed to have highly favorable psychological implications. With Russia no longer an autocracy, the war could be portrayed—and experienced—as a crusade for democracy. At the same time, the March revolution could only sow confusion among the many Germans who had understood their own war effort as a matter of self-defense against reactionary Russia. But the November revolution required a deeper reconsideration for all the belligerents.

Entente war aims agreements, like the secret Treaty of London that brought Italy into the war in 1915, had remained secret until the Bolsheviks published the tsarist documents. Products of old-style diplomacy, those agreements had been made by a restricted military and foreign policy elite within the governing circles of each country; not only the general public but also the elected parliaments were generally not aware of what they involved. The public debate over war aims that developed in 1917 thus became a debate over decision making as well, stimulating calls for greater popular involvement, which seemed sure to diminish the possibility of such wars in the future. In addition, there were exhortations for all the parties in the present war to renounce annexations and settle for a white peace. It was time to call the whole thing off and bring the soldiers home.

Seeking to counter such sentiments, especially the Russian contention that the war was not worth continuing, the idealistic U.S. president, Woodrow Wilson (1856–1924), insisted on the great potential significance of an Allied victory. First in his State of the Union speech of January 1918, and in several declarations thereafter, Wilson developed the "Fourteen Points" that he proposed should guide the new international order (see the box, "A Meaning to the War: Wilson's Fourteen Points"). Notable among them were open diplomacy, free trade, reduced armaments, self-determination, a league of nations, and a recasting of the colonial system, recognizing that the indigenous populations had rights equal to those of the colonizers.

Lenin and Wilson, then, offered radically different interpretations of the war, with radically different implications for present priorities. Yet they had something in common compared to the old diplomacy. Together, they seemed to represent a whole new approach to international relations—and the possibility of a more peaceful

WORLD WAR I AND ITS AFTERMATH

August 1914	Fighting begins
September 1914	French forces hold off the German assault at the Marne
August–September 1914	German victories over the Russians in the battles of Tannenberg and Masurian Lakes
May 1915	Italy declares war on Austria-Hungary
February–December 1916	Battle of Verdun
May 1916	Naval battle of Jutland
July–Nov 1916	Battle of the Somme
January 1917	Germans announce resumption of unrestricted submarine warfare
March 1917	First Russian Revolution: fall of the tsar
April 1917	U.S. declaration of war
July 1917	German Reichstag war aims resolution
November 1917	Second Russian Revolution: the Bolsheviks take power
March 1918	Treaty of Brest-Litovsk between Germany and Russia
March–July 1918	Germany's last western offensive
July 1918	Second battle of the Marne
July–November 1918	French-led counter-offensive
November 1918	Armistice: fighting ends
January 1919	Peace Congress convenes at Paris
June 1919	Victors impose Treaty of Versailles on Germany

A Meaning to the War: Wilson's Fourteen Points

After the United States entered the war in April 1917, President Woodrow Wilson sought to play down conventional national interests and emphasize wider, more idealistic purposes. His key statement proved to be his 1918 State of the Union address, during which he offered his famous Fourteen Points.

It will be our wish and purpose that the processes of peace, when they are begun, shall be absolutely open and that they shall involve and permit henceforth no secret understandings of any kind. The day of conquest and aggrandizement is gone by; so is also the day of secret covenants entered into in the interest of particular governments and likely at some unlooked-for moment to upset the peace of the world....

... What we demand in this war, therefore, is nothing peculiar to ourselves. It is that the world be made fit and safe to live in; and particularly that it be made safe for every peace-loving nation which, like our own, wishes to live its own life, determine its own institutions, be assured of justice and fair dealing by the other peoples of the world as against force and selfish aggression. All the peoples of the world are in effect partners in this interest; and for our own part we see very clearly that unless justice be done to others it will not be done to us. The program of the world's peace, therefore, is our program; and that program, the only possible program, as we see it, is this:

I. Open covenants of peace, openly arrived at, after which there shall be no private international understandings of any kind but diplomacy shall proceed always frankly and in public view....

V. A free, open-minded, and absolutely impartial adjustment of all colonial claims, based upon a strict observance of the principle that in determining all such questions of sovereignty the interests of the populations concerned must have equal weight with the equitable claims of the government whose title is to be determined....

XIV. A general association of nations must be formed under specific covenants for the purpose of affording mutual guarantees of political independence and territorial integrity to great and small states alike....

Source: The Public Papers of Woodrow Wilson, V. War and Peace: Presidential Messages, Addresses, and Public Papers (1917–1924) (New York: Harper & Brothers, 1927; New York: Kraus Reprint, 1970), vol. 1, pp. 158–159, 161.

world. Thus, they found an eager audience among the war-weary peoples of Europe.

Despite the unforeseen strains of the war, Sacred Union in France did not weaken substantially until April 1917, with General Nivelle's disastrous offensive. But then, as near-mutiny began to develop within the army, rank-and-file pressures forced Socialist leaders to demand clarification, then revision, of French war aims. Suddenly French government leaders found themselves under considerable pressure to endorse the notion that the war had idealistic and democratic purposes. Growing doubts about the government's goals threatened to turn into active opposition to the war.

The same pressures were at work in Germany, where antiwar sentiment grew within the Social Democratic party (SPD), finally leading the antiwar faction to split off and form the Independent Socialist party (USPD) in April 1917. A large-scale debate on war aims, linked to considerations of domestic political reform, developed in the Reichstag by the summer of 1917, culminating in the Reichstag war aims resolution of July 19. Affirming that Germany's purposes were solely defensive, the measure passed by a solid 60 percent majority. So Germany, too, seemed open to a white peace; indeed, it was not clear, by mid-1917, that the German people were prepared to push on to victory in a war with aggressive, annexationist aims.

But just as the dramatic events of 1917 interjected important new pressures for moderation and peace, pressures leading in the opposite direction also mounted as the war dragged on. Something in the old European order seemed to have changed irrevocably; this war might prove only the beginning of a new era of intense international competition, in which the old rules would no longer apply. War aims grew more grandiose as it began to seem that this war offered a precious opportunity to secure advantages for the more contentious world that would follow, and that would surely entail further war before long.

The shape of the present war convinced top German government and military officials that Germany's geography and dependence on imports made it especially vulnerable in a long war. The purpose of the war for Germany increasingly seemed the conquest of what would be needed to fight the next war on a more favorable footing. Responding in February 1918 to calls for a white peace, General Ludendorff stressed that "If Germany makes peace without profit, it has lost the war." Germany, insisted Ludendorff, must win the military and economic basis for future security—to "enable us to contemplate confidently some future defensive war."[6]

Many in German government circles felt that Germany had to win control of the Belgian coast to achieve the parity with Britain necessary for peace. German security seemed to require a more favorable situation in the east as well, including control over Russian Poland and Lithuania and Courland (western Latvia) on the Baltic Sea.

When, in response to the Russian request for an armistice, Germany was able to establish the terms of peace with Russia, it became dramatically clear how radically annexationist Germany's war aims had become. The outcome of negotiations during early 1918 at Brest-Litovsk, in German-occupied Poland, was a dictated peace that Russia finally had no choice but to accept. Germany was to annex 27 percent of Russia's European territory, including the agriculturally valuable Ukraine, 40 percent of its population, 75 percent of its iron and coal. All the German Reichstag parties, except the Socialists, accepted the terms of the treaty, which, in fact, produced a new wave of enthusiasm for a victorious peace after the disillusionment that had led to the Reichstag war aims resolution of July 1917.

France, less vulnerable geographically than Germany, tended to be more modest. But news of the terms the Germans had imposed at Brest-Litovsk inflamed the French, lending credence to the notion that France must push on to definitive victory in order to secure substantial advantages against an ongoing German menace.

The Renewal of the French War Effort

The domestic division in France that followed the failure of Nivelle's offensive reached its peak during the fall of 1917. In November, with pressures for a white peace intensifying and France's ability to continue fighting in doubt, President Raymond Poincaré called on Georges Clemenceau (1841–1929) to lead a new government. The 76-year-old Clemenceau was already known as a "hawk"; his appointment portended a stepped-up prosecution of the war, using whatever measures were necessary to achieve a decisive victory. And his message was simple as he appeared before the Chamber of Deputies on November 20, 1917: "If you ask me about my war aims, I reply: my aim is to be victorious." For the remainder of the war, France was under the virtual dictatorship of Clemenceau and his cabinet.

Clemenceau moved decisively on both the domestic and military levels. By cracking down on the antiwar movement—imprisoning antiwar leaders, suppressing defeatist newspapers—he produced an undeniable stiffening of morale. Choosing a new commander of all Allied forces in the west, Clemenceau bypassed Pétain and picked General Ferdinand Foch (1851–1929). From Clemenceau's perspective, Pétain was too passive, even defeatist. After some initial friction, Clemenceau let Foch have his way on the military level, and the two proved an effective leadership combination.

The German Gamble, 1918

As the campaign of 1918 began, Germany seemed in a relatively favorable military position: Russia had been knocked out at last, and American troops were yet to arrive. Moderates in Germany wanted to take advantage of the situation to work out a compromise peace while there was still a chance. But the military leadership persuaded Emperor William II that Germany could still win a definitive victory on the western front if it struck quickly and decisively, before U.S. help could arrive. Germany would be out of reserves by summer, so the alternative to decisive victory in the west would be total German defeat. In shunning the moderates' calls for a compromise peace, the German leadership opted for all or nothing.

And the Germans came very close to pulling it off. From March to June 1918, they seized the initiative with four months of sustained and effective attacks. By May 30, they had again reached the Marne, where they had been held off in 1914, and again Paris, only thirty-seven miles away, had to be evacuated. Even as late as mid-July, Ludendorff remained confident of victory, but by mid-August it was becoming clear that Germany lacked the manpower to exploit the successes of the first several months of 1918.

Those successes had caused mutual suspicion between the French and the British at first, but under Foch's leadership the Western allies eventually managed fuller and more effective coordination. By mid-1918, American involvement was also becoming a factor. On June 4, over a year after the U.S. declaration of war, American troops went into action for the first time, bolstering French forces along the Marne. Even this was a small operation, in which the American performance was amateurish, when compared to that of their battle-seasoned allies. But as the Allied counterattack proceeded, 250,000 U.S. troops were arriving per month, considerably boosting Allied morale and battlefield strength.

Germany lost the initiative for good during the second battle of the Marne, which began on July 15 with yet another German attack. Foch commenced a sustained counterattack on July 18, using tanks to good advantage, and never lost the initiative thereafter. By early August, the whole western front began to roll back. With astonishing suddenness, the outcome was no longer in doubt, although most expected the war to drag on into 1919. Few realized how desperate Germany's situation had become.

Military Defeat and Political Change in Germany

By late September, it was clear to Ludendorff that his armies could not stop the Allied advance, so he informed the government on September 29 that to avoid invasion, Germany had to seek an immediate armistice. Hoping to secure favorable peace terms and to make the parliamentary politicians take responsibility for the defeat, Hindenburg and Ludendorff asked that a government based on greater popular support be formed. A leading moderate, Prince Max von Baden (1867–1929), became chancellor, and the Reichstag again became significant after its eclipse during the virtual dictatorship of the military. Prince Max promptly replaced Ludendorff with General Wilhelm Groener (1867–1939), who seemed more democratic in orientation. By now it was clear that ending the war could not be separated from the push for political change in Germany.

After securing a written request for an armistice from Hindenburg, Prince Max sent a peace note to President Wilson during the night of October 3, asking for an armistice based on Wilson's Fourteen Points. During the month that followed, Prince Max engineered a series of measures, passed by the Reichstag and approved by the emperor, which reformed the constitution, abolishing the three-class voting system in Prussia and making the chancellor responsible to the Reichstag. At last Germany had a constitutional monarchy, but would that be enough? President Wilson encouraged speculation that Germany could expect better peace terms if William II were to abdicate and Germany were to become a republic. But if the emperor, and even the monarchy itself, could not survive, was Germany to become a parliamentary democracy on the Western model, or was there to be more radical change, perhaps inspired by the Russian example?

A radical outcome seemed a real possibility during late 1918 and early 1919. As negotiations for an armistice proceeded during October, the continuing war effort produced instances of mutiny in the navy and breaches of discipline in the army. By early November, workers' and soldiers' councils were being formed all over the country, just as in Russia the year before. In Munich, on November 7, antiwar socialists led an uprising of workers and soldiers that expelled the king and proclaimed a new Bavarian republic, which sought its own peace negotiations with the Allies. In Berlin on November 9, thousands of workers took to the streets to demand immediate peace, and the authorities could not muster enough reliable military force to move against them.

The senior army leadership grew concerned that the collapse of governmental authority would undermine the ability of army officers even to march their troops home. So Hindenburg and Groener persuaded the emperor to abdicate. Having lost the support of the army, William II accepted the inevitable and left for exile in the Netherlands.

With the German right, including the military, in disarray, and with even the centrist parties discredited by their support for what had become an annexationist war, the initiative now passed to the socialists. They, at least, had been in the forefront of the movement for peace. But the socialists had divided in 1917, mostly over the question of response to the war. To many leftist socialists, the fact that the reformist mainstream of the SPD had supported the war for so long had discredited the party irrevocably. The most militant of these leftist socialists, led by Karl Liebknecht (1871–1919) and Rosa Luxemburg (1870–1919), envisioned using the workers' and soldiers' councils as the basis for a full-scale revolution, more or less on the Bolshevik model.

The SPD, on the other hand, clung to its reformist heritage and insisted on working within parliamentary institutions. A Bolshevik-style revolution was neither appropriate nor necessary under the circumstances Germany now faced. Partly to head off the extreme left, SPD moderates proclaimed a parliamentary republic on November 9, just hours before the revolutionaries proclaimed a soviet-style republic. The next day the soldiers' and workers' councils in Berlin elected a provisional executive committee, to be led by the moderate socialist Friedrich Ebert (1871–1925). As the new republic sought to consolidate itself, the radical leftists continued to promote further revolution during December and January. So the end of the war meant for Germany a leap into an unfamiliar democratic republic, which had to establish itself in conditions not only of military defeat and economic hardship but also of incipient revolution on the extreme left.

Birth from military defeat was especially disabling for this new republic because the German people were so little prepared for the defeat when it came. The vigorous censorship and control of public opinion had kept the public from any grasp of Germany's real situation as the war sped to conclusion. Thus the request for an armistice early in October came as a shock. At no time during the war had Germany been invaded from the west, and by mid-1918 the German army had seemed on the brink of victory. It seemed inconceivable that Germany had lost a military decision, plain and simple. Thus the "stab in the

Rosa Luxemburg Long a leader within the radical wing of the German Social Democratic party, Luxemburg was in the center of the revolutionary activity in Berlin after the war. She and her colleague Karl Liebknecht were murdered after their capture by antirevolutionary forces in January 1919. *(Courtesy Centraine Archiwum KCPZPR, Warsaw, Poland)*

back" myth, the notion that political intrigue and revolution at home had undermined the German military effort, developed to explain what seemed an inexplicable defeat. This notion would prove a heavy burden for Germany's new democracy to bear.

The Outcome and the Impact

After the armistice officially ended the fighting on November 11, 1918, those responsible for a formal peace settlement faced unprecedented challenges. The war's casualties included the Habsburg and Ottoman empires, as well as the Hohenzollern and Romanov dynasties, so the peacemakers had to deal not just with defeated adversaries but with a changed political and territorial order in much of Europe and beyond. And the volatile sociopolitical situation in the wake of war and revolution inevitably colored their deliberations.

To make peace was to restore order, though necessarily on a new basis. But the distintegration of the old order had produced a sense of vulnerability that would be hard to overcome. The number of casualties, the advent of terrifying new weapons, the destruction of famous old monuments—all gave the war an apocalyptic aura that heightened its psychological impact. After all that had happened since August 1914, it was not obvious what a restoration of peace and order would require.

The Costs of War

Raw casualty figures do not begin to convey the war's human toll, but they afford some sense of the magnitude of the catastrophe that had befallen Europe and much of the world. Estimates differ, but it is generally agreed that from 10 to 13 million military men lost their lives, with another 20 million wounded. In addition, between 7 and 10 million civilians died as a result of the war and its hardships. In the defeated countries, especially, food shortages and the resulting malnutrition continued well after the end of the fighting (see the box, "A Difficult Ending").

Germany suffered the highest number of military casualties, but France suffered the most in proportional terms. Two million Germans were killed, with another 4 million wounded. Military deaths per capita for France were roughly 15 percent higher than for Germany—and twice as severe as for Britain. Of 8 million Frenchmen mobilized, over 5 million were killed or wounded. Roughly 1.5 million French soldiers, or 10 percent of the active male population, were killed—and this in a country already concerned about demographic decline. The other belligerents suffered less, but still in great numbers. Among the military personnel killed were 2 million Russians, 500,000 Italians, and 114,000 Americans.

Especially after "the great illusion" of European superiority and inevitable progress, this unprecedented bloodletting deeply affected the European self-image. It was the worst loss of life Europe had suffered since the Black Death of the fourteenth century. Although World War II would be far more destructive, its psychological impact was in some ways less, for the illusions had been shattered by World War I.

Economic costs were heavy as well. In addition to the privations suffered during the years of war, Europeans found themselves reeling from inflation and saddled with debt, especially to the United States, once the war was over. Although the immediate transition to a peacetime economy did not prove as difficult as many had feared, the war and its aftermath produced an economic disequilibrium that lingered, helping to produce a worldwide depression by the end of the 1920s.

The Search for Peace in a Revolutionary Era

The war had begun because of an unmanageable nationality problem in Austria-Hungary, and it resulted not simply in military defeat for Austria-Hungary but in the breakup of the Habsburg system. Thus, for much of east-central Europe, the end of the war brought bright hopes for self-determination, to enable peoples like the Czechs, Slovaks, Poles, Serbs, and Croats at last to control their own destinies. Even before the peacemakers began deliberating their fate in January 1919, some of the ethnic groups of the region had begun creating a new order on their own. For example, a popular movement of Czechs and Slovaks created a new Czechoslovak republic on October 29, 1918, and a new Yugoslavia and an independent Hungary similarly emerged from sponta-

A Difficult Ending

Shortages of food and other materials made the domestic situation in both Germany and Austria-Hungary truly desperate by the last year of the war. The following passages from the diary of Anna Eisenmenger, a middle-class Austrian woman, give a sense of the dislocations that resulted from the war—and make it clear that the war's end late in 1918 resulted in no immediate improvement in the lives of beleaguered central Europeans.

October 25, 1918. . . . For a long time we have only been getting a part of the food due to us on our ration cards. The doctors have discovered that, even if we got the whole of our ration, this would only be sufficient to meet one-fourth of the food requirements of an adult person weighing 11 stone. Aunt Bertha, out of an excessive and misguided conscientiousness, has insisted on living exclusively on the official food rations; in consequence she is now ill with softening of the bones—a striking proof that to obey the food laws is equivalent to suicide. Karl's letter proved to me that, in spite of our privations in the Hinterland, we are no longer in a position to feed our armies. If the War is to end soon, as Karl declares and as I pray to God it may, I shall have to provide for another three hungry stomachs in addition to Wolfi and his ailing mother. . . .

October 26, 1918. . . . To-day I traveled outside the boundaries of Vienna for the first time after a long interval. On the trams there were only women conductors, who did their work quietly and efficiently. . . . Only women were working in the fields, except for a boy or an old man here and there and sometimes a few Russian prisoners of war. . . .

March 15, 1919. Five months after the Armistice we housewives are suffering more acutely than in the worst war years. . . .

Thousands of invalids, women, children and infants, are perishing of hunger and cold. There are no longer any swaddling bands in which to wrap the newly-born. People use paper, if they have any, or old scraps of material. . . .

We only exist thanks to charitable gifts from abroad, and the American food parcels in particular have saved the lives of many of us Viennese.

Source: [Anna Eisenmenger], *Blockade, The Diary of an Austrian Middle-Class Woman, 1914–1924* (London: Constable Publishers, 1932), now in Jere Clemens King, ed., *The First World War* (New York: Harper & Row, 1972), pp. 247–258. The above passages are from pp. 248–249, 251, 256–257.

neous, indigenous movements. Some of these new nations were amalgams of different ethnic groups that found cooperation advantageous now, but that might disagree in the future. Moreover, many of these countries lacked traditions of self-government, and they had reason to feud among themselves. With the Habsburg system no longer imposing one form of stability, a power vacuum seemed likely in this potentially volatile part of Europe.

The triumph of a revolutionary regime in Russia immeasurably complicated the situation, because in the unsettled conditions of the former Habsburg territories, as in Germany, the revolution seemed poised to spread in the wake of defeat—precisely according to the script the Russian revolutionaries were reading to the world. The Bolsheviks, still a precarious minority within Russia in 1918, continued to bank on immediate revolution elsewhere in Europe until 1920. Shortly after taking power, they had rechristened themselves "Communists," partly to jettison the provincial Russian term *bolshevik,* but especially to underline their sharp distinction from the old reformist socialists of the Second International. Communism meant revolution along Russian lines. The Russian Communists influenced revolutionaries elsewhere both by force of example and by actively seeking to spread the revolution.

Outside Russia, the greatest communist success in the wake of the war was in Hungary, where a communist regime under Béla Kun (1885–1937) governed Budapest and other parts of the country from March to August 1919, before it was put down by Allied-sponsored forces from Romania. At about the same time, separatist communist republics lasted for matters of months in the Slovak part of Czechoslovakia and in the important German state of Bavaria. Even in Italy, which had shared in the victory, Socialists infatuated with the Bolshevik example claimed that the labor unrest of 1919–1920 was the beginning of full-scale revolution.

Fears that the Russian Revolution might spread helped fuel foreign intervention in Russia beginning in June 1918, when 24,000 French and British troops entered the country. Military concerns, as the war with Germany continued, helped to dictate intervention at this point, but such intervention continued after the armistice of November 1918, becoming overtly anticommunist. A series of thrusts, involving troops from fourteen countries at one time or another, struck at Russia from diverse points on its huge border. To some degree that effort served the cause of the counterrevolutionary Whites, especially members of the old elites dispossessed by the Bolsheviks, who challenged the communist control of the Russian empire in what became a brutal civil war during 1918–1920. There was never a coordinated strategy between the Whites and the foreign troops, but foreign intervention was intended to help topple the new regime and undercut its effort to export revolution.

The fourth of the major prewar regimes to disappear with defeat was the Turkish Ottoman Empire, which had controlled much of the Middle East in 1914. During the war the British, especially, encouraged Middle Eastern Arabs to revolt against the Turks, suggesting that independence, perhaps even a single Arab kingdom, might follow from a defeat of the Ottoman Empire. The Arab revolt that developed in the Arabian peninsula in 1916 did not achieve its major military aims, though it endured, causing some disruption to the Turkish war effort. Its success was due partly to the collaboration of a young British officer, T.E. Lawrence (1888–1935), who proved an effective military leader and an impassioned advocate of the Arab cause.

But British policy toward the Arabs was uncertain and contradictory. Concerned about the Suez Canal, the British government sought to tighten its control in Egypt by declaring it a protectorate in 1914, causing increased anti-British sentiment. One of the various secret wartime deals among the Allies, the Sykes-Picot Agreement of May 1916, named for the British and French diplomats who negotiated it, projected a division of the Ottoman territories of the Middle East into colonial spheres of influence. France would control Syria and Lebanon, while Britain would rule Palestine and Mesopotamia, or present-day Iraq.

Potentially complicating the situation in the region was Zionism, the movement to win a Jewish state in Palestine. Led by Chaim Weizmann (1874–1952), a remarkable Russian-born British chemist, Zionists reached an important milestone when British foreign secretary Arthur Balfour (1848–1930) cautiously announced in the Balfour Declaration of November 1917 that the British government "looked with favor" on the prospect of a "Jewish home" in Palestine. At this point, British leaders sympathetic to Zionism saw no conflict in embracing the cause of the Arabs against the Ottoman Turks at the same time; indeed, collaboration between Arabs and Jews, each seeking self-determination, could be expected.

In the heat of war, the British, especially, established their policy for the former Ottoman territories of the Middle East without careful study. Thus, they made promises and agreements that were not entirely compatible. After the war, new problems would quickly ensue from the effort of the victors to spearhead a new order in the Middle East.

The Peace Settlement

The peace conference took place in Paris, beginning in January 1919. Its labors led to five separate treaties, with each of the five defeated states, known collectively as the Paris peace settlement.

The Arab Cause T.E. Lawrence (middle row, second from the right) and Prince Faisal (foreground) attended the Paris Peace Conference, where they sought support for the creation of an independent Arab kingdom from former Ottoman Turkish holdings in the Middle East. *(Trustees of the Imperial War Museum)*

The first and most significant was the Treaty of Versailles with Germany, signed in the Hall of Mirrors of the Versailles Palace on June 28, 1919. But treaties were also worked out, in turn, with Austria, Bulgaria, Hungary, and finally Turkey, in August 1920.

This was to be a dictated, not a negotiated, peace. Germany and its allies were excluded, as was renegade Russia. The passions unleashed by the long war had dissolved the possibility of a more conciliatory outcome, a genuinely negotiated peace. Having won the war, France, Britain, the United States, and Italy were to call the shots on their own, with the future of Europe and much of the world in the balance. Spokesmen for many groups—Slovaks and Croats, Arabs and Jews—were in Paris as well, however, seeking a hearing for their respective causes. For example, both the Arab Prince Faisal (1885–1933), who would later become king of Iraq, and Colonel T.E. Lawrence were there to plead for an independent Arab kingdom.

The fundamental challenge at the peace conference was to reconcile the conflicting visions of the postwar world that had emerged by the end of the war. On the one hand, Wilson, the idealist from across the sea, represented the promise of a new order that could give this terrible war a lasting meaning. His vision stimulated considerable enthusiasm among Europeans. Indeed, adulation followed the American president as he toured parts of Europe en route to the peace conference. Clemenceau, on the other hand, was a hard-liner concerned with French security and dismissive of the new diplomacy. Since becoming prime minister in 1917, he had stressed that only a permanent preponderance of French military power over Germany, and not some utopian league of nations, could guarantee a lasting peace. The negotiations at Paris centered on this fundamental difference between Wilson and Clemenceau. Although Britain's Lloyd George took a hard line on certain issues, he also sought to mediate, helping engineer the somewhat awkward compromise that resulted. When, after the peace conference, he encountered criticism for the outcome, Lloyd George replied, "I think I did as well as might be expected, seated as I was between Jesus Christ and Napoleon Bonaparte."[7]

In Article 231 of the final treaty, the peacemakers sought to establish a moral basis for their treatment of Germany by assigning responsibility for the war to Germany and its allies. On this basis, the Germans would be made to pay reparations to reimburse the victors for the costs of the war. The determination to make Germany pay for what had become a fabulously expensive war was one of the factors militating against a compromise peace by 1917. Thus the peacemakers found it essential to fix a reparations responsibility, although the amount that Germany was to pay was not established until 1921.

In addition, Germany was forced to dismantle much of its military apparatus. For example, the army was to be limited to 100,000 men, all of them volunteers. The treaty severely restricted the size of the German navy as well, and Germany was forbidden to manufacture or possess military aircraft, submarines, tanks, heavy artillery, or poison gas.

France took back Alsace and Lorraine, the provinces it had lost to Germany in 1871 with its defeat in the Franco-Prussian War. But for France, the crucial provision of the peace settlement in 1919 was the treatment of the adjacent Rhineland section of Germany itself. For fifteen years Allied troops were to occupy the west bank of the Rhine River in Germany—the usual military occupation of a defeated adversary. But this would only be temporary. The long-term advantage for France was to be the permanent *de*militarization, on the part of Germany itself, of the Rhineland—including all German territory west of the Rhine and a strip of fifty kilometers along its east bank. Germany, in other words, was to maintain no troops on this part of its own soil. In the event of hostilities, French forces could march unopposed into this economically vital area of Germany.

The overall territorial settlement cost Germany almost 15 percent of its prewar territory, including major iron- and coal-producing regions, as well as about 10 percent of its prewar population (Map 27.3). But the great bitterness that immediately developed in Germany over the terms of the peace stemmed above all from a sense of betrayal. In requesting an armistice, German authorities had appealed to Wilson, who seemed to be saying that the whole prewar international system, not one side or the other, had been to blame for the current conflict. Wilson's emphasis had not been on war guilt and reparations. In 1919, however, the peacemakers treated Germany according to very different principles, so for Germans the terms of the peace greatly intensified the sting of defeat.

French interests also helped shape the settlement in east-central Europe. Wilsonian principles called for self-determination, but in this area of great ethnic complexity, ethnic differences were not readily sorted out geographically. Was it best to countenance proliferation and fragmentation of ethnic groups, or to foster consolidation in an effort to build larger states, which might have a better chance of maintaining their independence and succeeding economically?

Worrying little about the problematic principle of self-determination, the French approached the situation in east-central Europe in terms of their own strategic concerns. So that Germany would again face potential enemies on both east and west, the French envisioned building a network of allies—to include the new Polish state, surely, but possibly also Czechoslovakia, Yugoslavia, and Romania as well. These states would be weak enough to remain under French

Map 27.3 The Impact of the War: The Territorial Settlement in Europe and the Middle East The defeat of Russia, Austria-Hungary, Germany, and Ottoman Turkey opened the way to major changes in the map of east-central Europe and the Middle East. A number of new nations emerged in east-central Europe, but in the Arab world the end of Ottoman rule meant not independence but new roles for European powers.

Boundaries of German, Russian, and Austro-Hungarian empires in 1914
Areas lost by Austro-Hungarian Empire
Areas lost by Russian Empire
Areas lost by German Empire
Areas lost by Bulgaria
Areas lost by Ottoman Empire
Demilitarized Zones
Boundaries of 1926
Areas controlled under mandates from the League of Nations, 1920
FINLAND
NORWAY
SWEDEN
Oslo
Helsinki
Leningrad (St. Petersburg)
Stockholm
Tallinn
ESTONIA
North Sea
GREAT BRITAIN
DENMARK
Copenhagen
Baltic Sea
Riga
LATVIA
Memel
LITHUANIA
Vilnius
RUSSIAN EMPIRE
(Became Union of Soviet Socialist Republics, 1922)
Volga
NETHERLANDS
Amsterdam
Danzig
POLISH CORRIDOR
EAST PRUSSIA
GERMANY
RUHR
Cologne
Brussels
BELGIUM
Berlin
POLAND
Warsaw
Paris
Seine
LUX.
Rhine
Weimar
Frankfurt
Elbe
Oder
Vistula
FRANCE
LORRAINE
ALSACE
Loire
Strasbourg
Prague
CZECHOSLOVAKIA
GALICIA
Kiev
Don
Ural
Dnieper
Geneva
Berne
SWITZ.
Vienna
AUSTRIA
S. TYROL
Budapest
HUNGARY
BESSARABIA
Locarno
Milan
Po
Rhone
Venice
Trieste
Genoa
Rapallo
Zagreb
CROATIA
ROMANIA
Belgrade
ITALY
YUGOSLAVIA
Bucharest
Danube
Corsica
Rome
SERBIA
BULGARIA
Sofia
MONTENEGRO
(To Yugoslavia 1921)
Black Sea
Batum
Baku
Sardinia
Naples
ALBANIA
Kars
Istanbul (Constantinople)
Ankara
TURKEY
Tabriz
GREECE
Izmir (Smyrna)
Sicily
Athens
PERSIA (IRAN)
Annexed by Turkey 1939
Aleppo
SYRIA
(French Mandate)
Tigris
Euphrates
TUNISIA
(French)
Mediterranean Sea
Crete
Cyprus
(Gr.Br.)
Baghdad
IRAQ (MESOPOTAMIA)
(British Mandate)
Kut el Amara
Beirut
Damascus
PALESTINE
(British Mandate)
Amman
Jerusalem
TRANSJORDAN
(British Mandate)
Basra
KUWAIT
(Gr. Br.)
Suez Canal
Cairo
NEUTRAL ZONES
NEJD (SAUDI ARABIA)
LIBYA
(Italian)
EGYPT
(Independent 1922)
Red Sea
Nile
Riyadh
Medina
0 200 400 Km.
0 200 400 Mi.

The Victors and the Peace In June 1919 the leaders of the major victorious powers exude confidence after signing with Germany the Treaty of Versailles, the most important of the five treaties that resulted from the Paris Peace Conference. From the left are David Lloyd George of Britain, Georges Clemenceau of France, and Woodrow Wilson of the United States. *(The Bettmann Archive)*

influence but strong enough to replace Russia as a force against Germany. Yet to maximize the size and strength of these countries was to combine more than one nationality grouping within each; some of those national groups were more numerous and thus, almost inevitably, more advantaged than others (Table 27.1).

The new Czechoslovakia was not only an amalgam of Czechs and Slovaks, but also encompassed a substantial number of Germans and Magyars. Indeed, Germans, mostly from the old Bohemia, made up 22 percent of the population of Czechoslovakia. Yugoslavia was even more complex, encompassing not only Serbs and Croats, but also Slovenes, Macedonians, Albanians, and other minorities. But French policymakers were so determined to foster a strong Czechoslovakia and a strong Yugoslavia that they ordered the French police to force the spokesmen for Slovak and Croat separatism to leave Paris as the conference deliberated.

Partly as a result of these French priorities, Poland, Czechoslovakia, Yugoslavia, and Romania ended up as large as possible, either by the fusion of ethnic groups or by the incorporation of minorities that, on ethnic grounds, belonged with neighboring states. Austria, Hungary, and Bulgaria, on the other hand, found themselves diminished (Map 27.4). What remained of Austria, the German part of the old Habsburg empire, was prohibited from choosing to join Germany, an obvious violation of the Wilsonian principle of self-determination.

Concern to contain and weaken communist Russia was also at work in the settlement in east-central Europe. A band of states in east-central Europe, led by France, could serve not only as a check to Germany but also as a shield against Russia. Romania's aggrandizement came partly at the expense of the Russian empire, as did the creation of the new Poland. Finland, Latvia, Estonia, and Lithuania, all part of the Russian empire for over a century, now became independent states (see Map 27.3).

Wilson had been forced to compromise with French interests in dealing with east-central Europe, but he achieved a potentially significant success in exchange—the establishment of a League of Nations, embodying the widespread hopes for a new international order. According to the League covenant worked out by April, disputes among member states were no longer to be settled by war but by mechanisms established by the League. Other members were to participate in sanctions, from economic blockade to military action, against a member that went to war in violation of League provisions.

How could Wilsonian hopes for a new international order be squared with the imperialist system, which seemed utterly at odds with the ideal of self-determination? It seemed an important step that German colonies and Ottoman territories were not simply taken over by the victors, in the old-fashioned way, but fell under the authority of the League, which then assigned them as mandates to one of the victorious powers, which was to report back to the League annually. There were various classes of mandates, based on how prepared for sovereignty the area was taken to be. In devising this system at the peace confer-

Table 27.1 Minorities in the New Nation-States

Country	Population	Principal Minorities	
Czechoslovakia	14,700,000 (including 6,500,000 Czechs and 3,000,000 Slovaks)	German	3,250,000
		Magyar	700,000
		Ruthene	400,000
		Polish	70,000
Estonia	1,700,000	Russian	170,000
		German	17,000
Finland	3,600,000	Swedish	300,000
Hungary	8,700,000	German	500,000
Latvia	2,000,000	German	65,000
Lithuania	2,500,000	German	100,000
Poland	32,000,000	Ukrainian and Byelorussian	6,000,000
		German	800,000
Romania	18,800,000	Magyar	1,500,000
		German	750,000
		Ukrainian	600,000
		Russian	400,000
		Bulgarian	360,000
Yugoslavia	14,000,000 (including 5,500,000 Serbs, 4,500,000 Croats, 1,000,000 Slovenes)	Macedonian	600,000
		German	500,000
		Magyar	500,000
		Albanian	500,000
		Muslim/Turkish	700,000

Source: The Origins of the Second World War in Europe (Origins of Modern Wars Series), by P. M. H. Bell. Used by permission of the publisher, Longman Group UK.

ence, the Western powers formally recognized for the first time that non-Western peoples under Western influence had rights and interests of their own and that, in principle, they were progressing toward independence.

Still, the mandate approach to the colonial question was a halting departure at best. Although Britain granted considerable sovereignty to Iraq in 1932, the victorious powers generally operated as before, assimilating the new territories into their existing systems of colonial possessions. After the hopes raised in the Arab world during the war, this outcome produced a sense of betrayal among Arab leaders, who had counted on full-scale independence. Continuing Arab unrest provoked, most notably, a revolt against the French presence in Syria, put down only at considerable expense to the French during the mid-1920s. So though the colonial system remained, the war and its aftermath gave an important impetus to anticolonial sentiment, in the Arab world and elsewhere. This emerging anticolonialism added uncertainty to the postwar order.

In fact, much remained uncertain after the peacemakers had done their work; the outcome of the war, even with the terms of peace settled, seemed strangely inconclusive. In the band of nine east-central European states from Finland to Yugoslavia, the peace settlement left about 19 million people, almost 20 percent of the population, as national minorities. The incongruities of the settlement prompted Marshal Foch to proclaim, "This is not peace. It is an armistice for twenty years."[8]

Map 27.4 Ethnicity in East-Central Europe, 1919 Ethnic diversity made it hard to create homogeneous nation-states in east-central Europe. The new states that emerged after World War I mixed ethnic groups, and ethnic tensions would contribute to future problems.

The most basic question was whether the three principal victors had the resolve, and the capacity, to preserve the new order they had solidified at Paris. After being so badly weakened and scarred by the war effort itself, was France capable of the leadership its new position in Europe implied? How active was Britain prepared to be on the Continent, especially to sustain France in this new position? Would the United States remain actively involved in Europe?

Debate over that issue promptly developed in the United States as President Wilson sought Senate ratification of the peace treaty, which entailed U.S. membership in the League of Nations as well as commitments to France and Britain. Wilson's opponents worried especially that League membership would compromise U.S. sovereignty. Although it was not clear, at this point, how significant the departure from the old international system was to be, other nations found it easier to ratify the treaty and join the League. U.S. reluctance stemmed especially from the isolationist backlash that developed as Americans increasingly questioned whether the U.S. had been wise to become involved, for the first time, in a war in Europe. Late in 1919, at the height of the debate, Wilson suffered a disabling stroke. The Senate then refused to ratify the peace treaty, thereby keeping the United States out of the League of Nations. By 1920 the United States seemed to be pulling back from the leadership role it had been poised to play in 1918.

American hesitation stemmed partly from the doubts about the wisdom of the peace settlement that quickly developed in both Britain and the United States. During the peace conference, a member of the British delegation, the economist John Maynard Keynes (1883–1946), resigned to write *The Economic Consequences of the Peace* (1920), which helped undermine confidence in the whole settlement. Keynes charged that the shortsighted, vindictive policy of the French, by crippling Germany with a punishing reparations burden, threatened the European economy and thus the peace of Europe over the long term. For some, then, the challenge was not to enforce the Versailles treaty but to revise it. This lack of consensus about the legitimacy of the peace made it especially hard to predict what the longer-term outcome of the war would be.

Summary

By destroying the Habsburg empire and the imperial regime in Germany, World War I seemed to have solved the immediate problems that caused it. More generally, the war accelerated processes, involving everything from technological development to women's suffrage, that many deemed progressive.

Yet the war also produced new tensions and revealed possibilities that seemed considerably less benign. Despite all the hopes for a peaceful new order, the novel forms of warfare introduced during World War I portended a dangerous and even terrifying new era. To be sure, a measure of terror unimaginable after World War I accompanied the advent of the nuclear age a generation later, but the experience of World War I was the turning point, the end of an earlier innocence. Thanks to modern technology, which had been central to the West's confident belief in progress, Europeans had now experienced machine-gun fire, poison gas attacks, and the terror-bombing of civilians from airplanes.

In a more general sense, the war unleashed irrational passions and demonstrated that European civilization was more fragile than it had seemed. Such episodes as the partial destruction of the Reims cathedral gave the war an apocalyptic quality, and the transition to peace did not overcome the new sense of vulnerability that resulted.

The war touched virtually everyone, but it marked for life those who knew the nightmarish experience of the trenches. At first, traditional notions of glory, heroism, and patriotic duty combined with images of fellowship and regeneration to enable the soldiers to make a certain sense of their wartime experience. But as the war dragged on, such sentiments gradually eroded, giving way to resignation and cynicism (see the feature, "Weighing the Evidence: The Poetry of World War I," on pages 1028–1029).

Beckmann: The Night In this painting from 1918–1919, the German expressionist Max Beckmann (1884–1950) drew on medieval art and a complex personal symbolism to convey the violence, insecurity, and hardship that surrounded Germany's defeat in 1918. *(Kunstsammlung Nordrhein-Westfalen)*

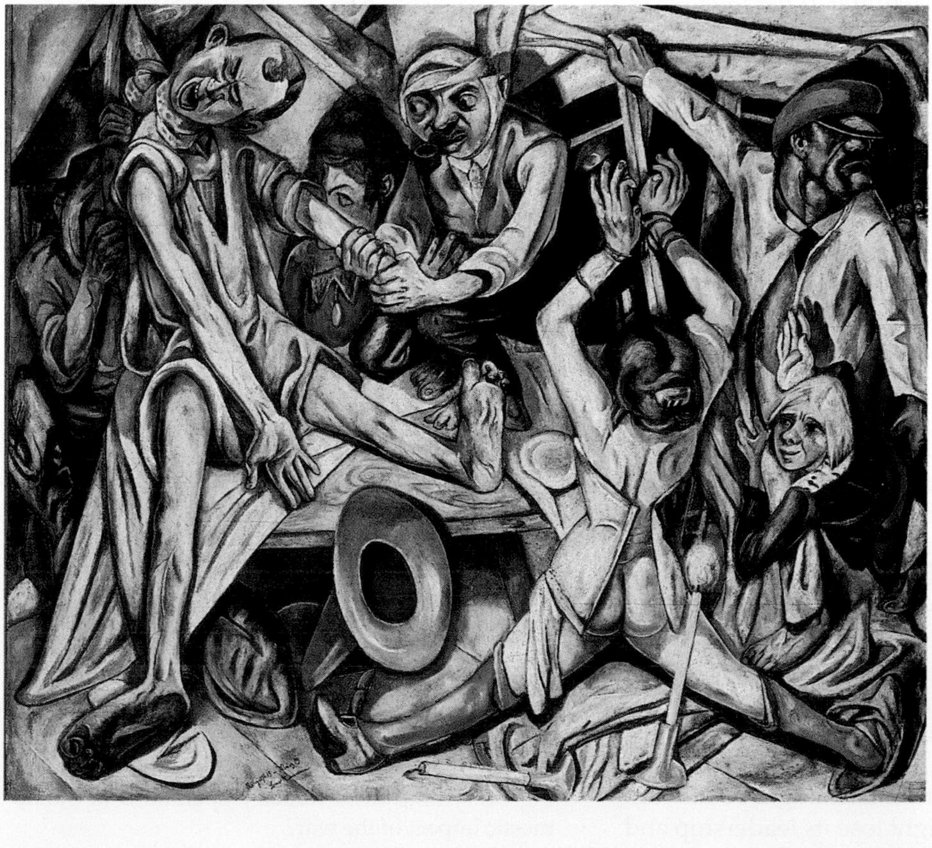

After the war was over, many of those who had fought it felt a sense of ironic betrayal; their prewar upbringing, the values and assumptions they had inherited, had not equipped them to make sense of what they had witnessed. But the quest for meaning continued, and beginning in the late 1920s a wave of writings about the war appeared. Many were memoirs, such as *Goodbye To All That* by the English writer Robert Graves (1895–1985) and *Testament of Youth* by Vera Brittain (1893–1970), who had served as a British army nurse at the front. The most famous exploration of the war was the antiwar novel *All Quiet on the Western Front* (1929) by German writer Erich Maria Remarque (1898–1970), which sold 2.5 million copies in twenty-five languages in its first eighteen months in print.

Although Remarque had seen front-line action, his novel said more about the growing feeling of disillusionment after the war than it did about the actual experience of those in the trenches. An element of myth-making was creeping into these efforts to give meaning to the war experience by the end of the 1920s. Still, there was something undeniably genuine in the laments of loss of innocence, in the sense of belonging to a "lost generation," that marked many of these writings. Not only were many friends dead or maimed for life, but all the sacrifices seemed to have been largely in vain, a sentiment that fueled determination to avoid another war in the future.

What followed from the war, most fundamentally, was a new sense that Western civilization was neither as secure nor as superior as it had seemed. The celebrated French poet Paul Valéry (1871–1945), speaking at Oxford shortly after the war, observed that "we modern civilizations have learned to recognize that we are mortal like the others. We had heard . . . of whole worlds vanished, of empires foundered. . . . *Elam, Nineveh, Babylon* were vague and splendid names; the total ruin of these worlds, for us, meant as little as did their existence. But *France, England, Russia* . . . these names, too, are splendid. . . . And now we see that the abyss of history is deep enough to bury all the world. We feel that a civilization is as fragile as a life."[9] Valéry went on to warn that the coming transition to peace would be even more difficult and disorienting than the war itself. So traumatic might be the convulsion that Europe might lose its leadership and be shown up for what it was in fact—a pathetically small corner of the world, a mere cape on the Asiatic land mass. Astounding words for a European, yet even Valéry, for all his foresight, could not predict what Europe would go through in the decades to follow.

Notes

1. Thus wrote the German poet Ivan Goll in 1917; quoted in Modris Eksteins, *Rites of Spring: The Great War and the Birth of the Modern Age* (Boston: Houghton Mifflin, 1989), p. 144.
2. The remarks of Raymond Joubert, as quoted in John Ellis, *Eye-Deep in Hell: Trench Warfare in World War I* (Baltimore: Johns Hopkins University Press, 1989), p. 104.
3. Brian Bond, *War and Society in Europe, 1870–1970* (New York: Oxford University Press, 1986), p. 114.
4. By A. N. Potresov, as quoted in Richard Pipes, *The Russian Revolution* (New York: Random House, Vintage, 1991), p. 348.
5. Both statements are quoted in Koppel S. Pinson, *Modern Germany: Its History and Civilization,* 2d ed. (New York: Macmillan, 1966), p. 337.
6. Quoted in Arno J. Mayer, *Political Origins of the New Diplomacy, 1917–18* (New York: Random House, Vintage, 1970), p. 135.
7. Quoted in Walter Arnstein, *Britain Yesterday and Today: 1830 to the Present,* 6th ed. (Lexington, Mass.: D.C. Heath, 1992), p. 266.
8. Quoted in P. M. H. Bell, *The Origins of the Second World War* (London and New York: Longman, 1986), p. 14.
9. Paul Valéry, *Variety,* 1st series, (New York: Harcourt, Brace, 1938), pp. 3–4.

Suggested Reading

General Surveys

Ferro, Marc. *The Great War 1914–1918.* 1973. Combines a narrative of events with a feel for the war experience, based on the expectations and perceptions of those involved.

King, Jere Clemens, ed. *The First World War.* 1972. A documentary history, with selections on an array of topics, from military operations to trench life, from diplomacy and peacemaking to the role of women in the war.

Robbins, Keith. *The First World War.* 1985. An accessible, balanced, and comprehensive treatment, covering everything from military operations to the domestic impact of the war.

Winter, J. M. *The Experience of World War I.* 1989. An ideal introductory work that proceeds via concentric circles from politicians to generals to soldiers to civilians, then to the war's longer-term effects.

Fighting the War

Ellis, John. *Eye-Deep in Hell: Trench Warfare in World War I.* 1989. A compelling account of life and death in the trenches, covering topics from trench construction to eating, drinking, and sex. Includes striking photographs.

Hough, Richard. *The Great War at Sea, 1914–1918.* 1983. A survey of naval operations, featuring the British navy. Includes photographs.

Kennett, Lee. *The First Air War, 1914–1918.* 1991. A vivid account of the new flying machines, those who flew them, and their diverse wartime roles, from reconnaissance to combat.

War and Society

Bond, Brian. *War and Society in Europe, 1870–1970.* 1986. Lucid, well-balanced survey of the relationship between war and society, with particular attention to the two world wars.

Brayborn, Gail, and Penny Summerfield. *Out of the Cage: Women's Experiences in Two World Wars.* 1987. Comparative study of the impact of the two world wars on women, relying especially on direct testimony. Considers not only the workplace but also everyday experience, from home life and health to courtship and marriage.

Higonnet, Margaret Randolph, et al., eds. *Behind the Lines: Gender and the Two World Wars.* 1987. Sophisticated essays on the role of women during the two world wars, concerned especially with the impact of war on gender definition.

Kocka, Jürgen. *Facing Total War: German Society, 1914–1918.* 1984. Using concepts of class and monopoly capitalism in a flexible way, a leading German historian analyzes the impact of the war on German society.

Marwick, Arthur. *The Deluge: British Society and the First World War.* 1970. A lively account by a leading British social historian, conveying what it was like to live in Britain during the war and tracing the enduring impact of wartime social changes.

The Russian Revolution

Fitzpatrick, Sheila. *The Russian Revolution, 1917–1932.* 1982. An ideal introductory work that places the events of 1917 in the sweep of Russian history.

Pipes, Richard. *The Russian Revolution.* 1991. A detailed, comprehensive study, critical of the Bolshevik takeover as a mere coup, as opposed to a genuinely revolutionary transformation. Argues that a tendency toward terror followed from the nature of the revolution itself.

Ulam, Adam B. *The Bolsheviks: The Intellectual, Personal and Political History of the Triumph of Communism in Russia.* 1968. Focuses on Lenin and his central role in shaping the strategy that brought the Bolsheviks to power.

Von Laue, Theodore H. *Why Lenin? Why Stalin? Why Gorbachev? The Rise and Fall of the Soviet System,* 3d ed., 1993. A widely used survey. Accents the larger context of international preoccupations and power relations that helped shape the revolution and the system that developed from it.

War Aims, Diplomacy, and Peacemaking

Mayer, Arno J. *The Politics and Diplomacy of Peacemaking: Containment and Counterrevolution at Versailles, 1918–1919.* 1967. Emphasizes the impact of domestic political concerns and fears of spreading revolution on thinking about the end of the war and the aims of the peace.

———. *Political Origins of the New Diplomacy, 1917–18.* 1970; first pub. 1959. Influential account of the war aims debate; analyzes the competing efforts of Wilson and Lenin to redefine the meaning of the war.

Nicolson, Harold. *Peacemaking 1919.* 1965. A classic account, critical of the treaty, by a junior member of the British delegation.

Rowland, Peter. *David Lloyd George: A Biography.* 1975. Lively, balanced—one of the best one-volume treatments of Lloyd George, including his role as a wartime leader and a major architect of the peace.

Sharp, Alan. *The Versailles Settlement: Peacemaking in Paris, 1919.* 1991. A brief, clear, and balanced overview that seeks to do justice to the magnitude of the task the peacemakers faced.

Memory and Cultural Impact

Eksteins, Modris. *Rites of Spring: The Great War and the Birth of the Modern Age.* 1989. Original and provocative exploration of the relationship between culture and the war experience. Good on the difference between the actual experience of the war and the memory fabricated after the fact.

Fussell, Paul. *The Great War and Modern Memory.* 1975. Widely admired study of the attempts to forge the new language, through literature, necessary to make sense of the British war experience.

Mosse, George L. *Fallen Soldiers: Reshaping the Memory of the World Wars.* 1990. Shows how the encounter with mass death in World War I led to new ways of sanctifying and justifying war.

Wohl, Robert. *The Generation of 1914.* 1979. Probes the common features in the experience of educated young people in France, Britain, Germany, Italy, and Spain.

Weighing the Evidence

THE POETRY OF WORLD WAR I

We don't normally think of poetry and war together, and World War I, with its unexpected brutality and hardship, may seem the least poetic of wars. Yet even during the war, soldiers like the Englishmen Rupert Brooke (1887–1915) and Wilfred Owen (1893–1918) sought to shape their experiences into poetic imagery. What does such poetry tell us about what the war meant to those who fought it? How has poetic testimony affected our understanding of the place of World War I in the Western experience?

In Brooke's wartime poetry what strikes us first is his gratitude that his generation had come of age at this dramatic historical moment:

> Now, God be thanked Who has matched us with His hour,
> And caught our youth, and wakened us from sleeping

But why would a young man like Brooke welcome war? He seemed to envision release, deliverance—but from what?

When the war broke out, Brooke promptly volunteered, even pulling strings to get into a combat unit. Seeing action for the first time, in Belgium in October 1914, he was excited by the intensity of battle and pleased by his own calm self-control. Back in England for further training shortly thereafter, he wrote several sonnets, including "Peace," the one reproduced here, expressing his feelings about the war. But he died of blood poisoning on the way to battle in April 1915—without ever fully experiencing trench warfare.

Although most of the young Englishmen who took up arms with such enthusiasm in 1914 assumed that their country was in the right, that Germany was at fault, they did not worry much about the purposes of the war or the larger historical impact it might have. Brooke understood that the war would not accomplish all that was claimed for it, but he was grateful for the personal experience it made possible. Somehow it meant "peace," as the title of his sonnet suggests, and even cleanliness:

> To turn, as swimmers into cleanness leaping,
> Glad from a world grown old and cold and weary

Brooke's sense of deliverance responded to personal frustrations, yet he spoke for others of his generation who also were finding it difficult to assume a place in adult society at that particular time. Though they came from educated, upper-middle-class families, they were contemptuous of the routines and compromises of the respectable, everyday world to which they were expected to adjust. Thus Brooke welcomed the chance to

> Leave the sick hearts that honour could not move,
> And half-men, and their dirty songs and dreary

Yet those of Brooke's generation were equally troubled by their own uncertainty about values and commitments—to marriage, career, a place in society. Thanks to the overwhelming, inescapable reality of the war, values that had seemed empty—honor, country, duty, fellowship—now seemed meaningful after all. To his

---

ANTHEM FOR DOOMED YOUTH

What passing-bells for these who die as cattle?
—Only the monstrous anger of the guns.
Only the stuttering rifles' rapid rattle
Can patter out their hasty orisons.
No mockeries now for them; no prayers nor bells;
Nor any voice of mourning save the choirs,—
The shrill, demented choirs of wailing shells;
And bugles calling for them from sad shires.

What candles may be held to speed them all?
Not in the hands of boys but in their eyes
Shall shine the holy glimmers of goodbyes.
The pallor of girls' brows shall be their pall;
Their flowers the tenderness of patient minds,
And each slow dusk a drawing-down of blinds.

Wilfred Owen

PEACE

Now, God be thanked Who has matched us with His hour,
  And caught our youth, and wakened us from sleeping,
With hand made sure, clear eye, and sharpened power,
  To turn, as swimmers into cleanness leaping,
Glad from a world grown old and cold and weary,
  Leave the sick hearts that honour could not move,
And half-men, and their dirty songs and dreary,
  And all the little emptiness of love!

Oh! we, who have known shame, we have found release there,
  Where there's no ill, no grief, but sleep has mending.
    Naught broken save this body, lost but breath;
Nothing to shake the laughing heart's long peace there
  But only agony, and that has ending;
    And the worst friend and enemy is but Death.

Rupert Brooke

Rupert Brooke (1887–1915)
(The Mansell Collection)

surprise and relief, Brooke found that he himself was capable of courage, commitment, and sacrifice. With its promise of cleanliness and renewal, the war was worth even its highest price, which was merely death.

Unlike Brooke, Wilfred Owen hated the war from the start. He was quickly struck by its sheer ugliness, as manifested in the landscape, the noise, the language of the soldiers themselves. Yet he served with distinction, was decorated for bravery, and was killed by machine-gun fire just one week before the armistice in November 1918.

Owen, then, experienced the reality of World War I in a way that Brooke did not. The sonnet here, "Anthem for Doomed Youth," was written during September and October of 1917, after the war had come to entail a terrible bloodletting. Thus Owen sought to shape sentiments very different from Brooke's—a sense of waste, of loss, of incongruity between suffering endured and results achieved. Whereas Brooke had brushed aside the possibility of death, Owen saw death as relentless, carrying off a generation of innocent youth, dying like cattle.

In a sense, even the dignity of death had become a casualty of the war. Thus Owen mixed funeral images with the new horror that this war had brought forth: The only mourning was "The shrill, demented choirs of wailing shells." Mocking the ongoing effort to sweeten the reality of death at the front through reference to nobility and sacrifice, Owen drowned out his initial suggestion of bells with the new and awful sounds of machine-gun fire:

—Only the monstrous anger of the guns.
Only the stuttering rifles' rapid rattle

Quite apart from its military and political outcome, World War I has assumed a particular place in our collective memory, thanks partly to those like Brooke and Owen who managed to frame their wartime experiences in the memorable language of poetry. At first, Brooke's poetry helped to justify the alarming slaughter to those who began questioning the war's purpose as it claimed the lives of their sons. Yet by now we find it hard to grasp the ideals that inspired his poetic testimony, for they were in one sense consumed by the war and the era of violence that it began. We still live in the world that emerged from that war, so Owen, with his cynicism and sense of tragedy, is far more our contemporary. Brooke may still reveal for us something of the innocence that was lost, but it is especially through Owen's way of conveying the tragedy, the sense of betrayal and lost innocence, that World War I has continued to haunt the memory of Western civilization.

TEPPICHLAGER
Schuhwarenhaus Lauter
ANTIQUARIAT
Herren Friseur Damen
Fleischwaren.
PROTHESEN.
SPORTBANK
EISENWAREN.
HALTESTELLE DER STRASSENBAHN
MOABIT
ODOLZAHNPASTA

CHAPTER 28

The Illusion of Stability, 1919–1930

Because the war shattered so many old conventions, Europeans experienced a sense of liberation and openness once it was over. The result was a decade of extraordinary cultural vitality as Europeans reached out to embrace the new, from movies and sports to art deco and American jazz. But insecurity lurked beneath the new freedom and vitality. In light of all the disruption and novelty, many wanted simply to return to normal—although it was not clear what that would entail. After all that had changed—from political systems to the role of women—it was not possible to return to the prewar European order. So attempts to find new bases of order, in everything from architecture to the international economy, were central to the 1920s.

Although the immediate disruptions of wartime carried over to 1923, a more hopeful era of relative prosperity and international conciliation followed, continuing until 1929. It seemed, briefly, that European civilization had managed to surmount the disruptions unleashed by the war. Even in Germany, where the new democracy got off to a rocky start, political stability seemed on its way by the later 1920s. Although the Treaty of Versailles continued to rankle the Germans, Germany gradually patched things up with the victors in the war. And though the new communist regime in the Soviet Union remained a potentially disruptive force, it had to suspend its effort to spearhead wider revolution.

Nevertheless, in Italy the democracy that had emerged in the nineteenth century gave way to the first regime to call itself fascist, and some of the new democracies in east-central Europe did not survive the decade. Even in the more established democracies of Britain and France, tensions

Street life in Berlin.
Nikolaus Braun,
Strassenszene (detail, 1921).

came close to the surface. Thus, when the Great Depression began at the end of the decade, serious sociopolitical strains developed throughout most of the Western world. The restabilization of the 1920s proved only an illusion.

The Postwar Setting: Toward Mass Society

Common involvement in the war blurred class lines and accelerated the trend toward what contemporaries began to call "mass society." Not only was political democracy spreading, but ordinary people were increasingly setting the cultural tone, partly through new mass media like film and radio. To some, the advent of mass society portended a welcome revitalization of culture and a more authentic kind of democracy, but others saw only a debasement of cultural standards and a susceptibility to populist demagoguery. At the same time, it was not clear that democracy could take root and flourish in central and east-central Europe without social change to dilute the power of old social elites.

Economic Readjustment and the New Prosperity

As many had feared, the problems of readjustment to peace caused wild economic swings in the first few years after the war. The downturns were relatively short, however, and by the later twenties, Europe was enjoying renewed prosperity, with newer industries such as chemicals, electricity, and advanced machinery in the forefront. Automobiles, available to a few before the war, began to be mass-produced. In France, the production of automobiles shot up dramatically, from 40,000 in 1920 to 254,000 in 1929. The needs of war had stimulated innovations that helped fuel this renewed economic growth. The civilian air industry, for example, developed rapidly during the 1920s by taking advantage of wartime work on aviation for military purposes. But wartime innovation was carried over only selectively. In their effort to return to normal, governments were quick to dismantle wartime planning and control mechanisms.

This eagerness to get back to business as usual masked problems that lay beneath the relative prosperity of the twenties. If new industries prospered, old ones declined in the face of new technologies and stronger foreign competition. And such decline posed challenges that no industrialized society had faced before. This phenomenon was most obvious in Britain, where the textile, coal, shipbuilding, and iron and steel industries responsible for Britain's earlier industrial pre-eminence were now having trouble competing. Rather than investing in new technologies, these older industries sought to survive by demanding government protection and by imposing lower wages and longer hours on their workers. At the same time, however, British unions resisted the mechanization necessary to make these older industries more competitive.

If the structural decline of older industries was clearest in Britain, inflation and its psychological impact was most prominent in Germany and France. The German hyperinflation of 1923 will be discussed later in this chapter, in connection with the fortunes of the Weimar Republic. In France inflation was far less dramatic, but it affected French perceptions and priorities in significant ways between the two world wars. For over a century, from the Napoleonic era to the outbreak of war in 1914, the value of the French franc had remained stable. But the war started France on an inflationary cycle that shattered the security of its many small savers—those, like teachers and shopkeepers, who had been the backbone of the Third Republic. To repay war debts and rebuild war-damaged industries, the French government continued to run budget deficits, and thereby cause inflation, even after 1918. Runaway inflation threatened during 1925 and 1926, but the franc was finally restabilized in 1928, though at only about one-fifth its prewar value.

On the international level, war debts and reparations strained the financial system, creating problems with the financing of trade. Yet adjustments were made during the course of the twenties, and most of the time the international exchange system seemed to be returning to equilibrium. In retrospect, however, the strains that would lead the international capitalist system into crisis and depression by the end of 1929 are all too apparent.

Work, Leisure, and the New Popular Culture

The wartime spur to industrialization produced a large increase in the industrial labor force all over Europe, and a good deal of labor unrest accompanied the transition to peacetime. Some of that agitation challenged factory discipline and authority relationships. Yet restabilization was soon achieved because much of the advanced working class came to accept productivism as a societal goal. Seeking to re-establish authority on a new basis for the competitive postwar world, business leaders and publicists fostered a new cult of efficiency and productivity after the war. There was much interest in Taylorism, the earlier time-and-motion studies of the American Frederick W. Taylor (1856–1915), and Fordism, the possibilities for mass production, based on mass consumption, that Henry Ford (1863–1947) had pioneered in the United States.

In light of the major role women had played in the wartime labor force, women's suffrage proved irresistible in Britain, Germany, and much of Europe, though not France or Italy. In Britain, where the demand for women's suffrage had earlier provoked such controversy, the suffrage was readily conceded in 1918, partly because women no longer seemed a threat to the political system. Once given the vote, British women simply flowed into the existing parties, dissolving earlier hopes—and fears—that women's suffrage would mean a specifically feminist political agenda.

Although female employment remained higher than before the war, many women were willing to stay at home, yielding their jobs to the returning soldiers. The need to replace the men killed in the war lent renewed force to the traditional notion that women served society, and fulfilled themselves, by marrying and rearing families. This notion was symptomatic of the widespread desire to return to normal after the disruptions of the war years.

Mass consumption was the reverse side of the mass production that made possible the new prosperity of the 1920s. As it became possible to mass-produce the products of the second industrial revolution, more people could afford automobiles, electrical products like the radio and phonograph, and clothing of synthetic fabrics, made possible by innovations in chemistry. First came rayon, which had been produced in small quantities since 1891, but which began to be mass-produced only during the 1920s. The advent of rayon was of particular symbolic importance; in this new artificial form, silk, which had long been one of the trappings of wealth, was now within the means of ordinary people.

With the eight-hour day increasingly the norm, growing attention was devoted to leisure as a positive source of human fulfillment—for everyone, not just the wealthy. Ordinary people began to have the time, and the means, to take vacations. European beach resorts grew crowded. An explosion of interest in soccer among Europeans paralleled the growth of baseball and football in the United States. Huge stadiums, seating as many as 240,000, were built across Europe.

The growth of leisure was linked to the development of mass media and mass culture. During the early twenties, radio became a commercial venture, reaching a mass audience in Europe, as in the United States. Although movies had begun to emerge as vehicles of popular entertainment even before the war, they came into their own during the 1920s, when the names of film stars became household words for the first time.

The rapid development of film showed that new, more accessible media could nurture extraordinary innovation. Germany led the way with such films as *The Cabinet of Dr. Caligari* (1920), *Metropolis* (1927), and *The Blue Angel* (1930), but the Russian Sergei Eisenstein (1898–1948) became perhaps the most admired filmmaker of the era with *Potemkin* (1925), his brilliant portrayal of the Russian Revolution of 1905. Other new cultural forms, from jazz, newly imported from the United States, to art deco, popularized by a decorative arts exhibition in Paris in 1925, similarly helped give the decade a distinctive flavor. Although Paris held its own as a European cultural center, Berlin emerged from within the unsettled conditions of postwar Germany to rival Paris for cultural leadership during what Germans called "the Golden Twenties" (see the box, "The Gay Subculture in Weimar Berlin").

The vogue of American jazz was central to a new interest in the United States. America meant not only no-nonsense efficiency but also a vital popular culture, expressed even in advertising, which now seemed a genuine cultural form,

Weimar Cinema This poster advertises Fritz Lang's film *Metropolis*, which explored the dehumanization and exploitation of the modern city. *(Schulz-Neudamm,* Metropolis, *1926. Lithograph, 83 x 36 ½". The Museum of Modern Art, New York. Gift of Universum Film Aktiengesellschaft.)*

appropriate to the developing age of mass consumption. A black woman from St. Louis, Josephine Baker (1906–1975), moved to Paris in 1925 to become a sensation as a cabaret singer and nightclub dancer. But such cultural migration worked both ways. The actress Marlene Dietrich (1901–1992), famous as Lola Lola in *The Blue Angel,* was among a number of German film celebrities who went to Hollywood.

Exploiting the new popular fascination with air travel, the American Charles Lindbergh (1902–1974) captured the European imagination in 1927 with the first solo flight across the Atlantic. Lindbergh's feat epitomized the affirmative side of the twenties—the sense that there were new worlds to conquer, that they could be conquered, and that there still were heroes, despite the ironies of the war and the ambiguities of the peace.

A World Safe for Democracy?

By the time it ended, at least, the war was advertised as paving the way for democracy, and the fall of the monarchies in Russia, Germany, and Austria-Hungary seemed, especially, to create opportunities. But even where democracy was already established, as in Britain, France, and Italy, there seemed a chance to broaden it by expanding political access to those previously on the fringes. As it happened, however, hopes for democracy were frustrated and undermined in much of Europe during the twenties and early thirties.

Even before the war was over, the Bolshevik Revolution had overwhelmed whatever democratic promise attached to the first revolution in Russia. In Italy, hopes for democratic renewal gradually receded as a new regime, hostile to parliamentary democracy, triumphed by the mid-1920s. In east-central Europe, new democracies seemed to take root after the war, but except in Czechoslovakia, where traditions were most favorable, the practice of parliamentary government did not bear out the promise of the immediate postwar period. Democracy seemed divisive and ineffective, so one country after another adopted a more authoritarian alternative during the twenties and early thirties.

Poland offers the most dramatic example. Although its democratic constitution of 1921 established a cabinet responsible to a parliamentary majority, the parliament fragmented into numerous parties so that instability proved endemic from the start. Indeed, Poland had fourteen different ministries from November 1918 to May 1926, when the coup d'état of Marshall Josef Pilsudski effectively ended parliamentary government in favor of an authoritarian regime, stressing national unity. This suppression of democracy came as a relief to many Poles—and was even welcomed by the trade unions. After Pilsudski's death in 1935, a group of colonels ruled Poland until the country was invaded by Nazi Germany in 1939.

Democracy proved hard to manage in east-central Europe partly because of special economic difficulties resulting from the breakup of the Habsburg system. New national borders meant new economic barriers, disrupting long-standing economic relationships. Centers of relative industrial strength like Vienna and Budapest found themselves cut off from their traditional markets and sources of materials. In what was now Poland, Silesians had long been oriented toward Germany, Galicians toward Vienna, and those in eastern Poland toward Russia; the creation of the Polish nation-state was not in itself sufficient to form a cohesive economic unit.

The countries of east-central Europe remained overwhelmingly agrarian, and this, too, proved unconducive to democracy. Land reform that accompanied the transition to democracy made small properties the norm in much of the region. But these units were often too small to be efficient, so where land was redistributed agricultural output actually decreased, most dramatically in Romania and Yugoslavia. When agricultural prices declined by the late 1920s, many of those peasants had no choice but to sell out to larger landowners. What had seemed a progressive and democratic reform thus failed to provide a stable agrarian smallholder base for democracy. There were important peasant political parties, but rather than offer a positive program, they merely reflected peasant resentment of the industrial workers and the "parasitical" middle classes of the cities.

The tendency to jettison democracy in favor of more authoritarian alternatives in east-central Europe stemmed partly from the attraction of fascism, which emerged first in Italy in the immediate aftermath of the war. The term *fascism* was derived from the ancient Roman fasces, the bundle of rods surrounding an ax that guards carried at state occasions as a symbol of power and unity. Stressing solidarity and discipline, fascism was hostile to liberal individualism and multiparty parliamentary democracy. But it also opposed the Marxist socialists, with their emphasis on class struggle and the special role of the working class. Thus fascism is generally placed on the "right" of the political spectrum. Yet fascism was not merely conservative, although conservatives sought to exploit it. In Italy fascism claimed to embody the new dynamism and vitality derived from the war experience, yet it also seemed, to some, to offer precisely the new form of order that was necessary after the war.

Josephine Baker During the 1920s, America began influencing European culture and entertainment as never before. Baker, a black dancer from St. Louis, was a major reason. She created an instant sensation in the cabarets of Paris and also became famous in Germany. *(Bettmann/Hulton)*

Both communism and fascism were new, and no one knew what they would mean to the na-

The Gay Subculture in Weimar Berlin

Imperial Berlin had been a somewhat stodgy capital, but it became the center of a remarkable cultural flowering during the Weimar period. Among the star attractions was a gay subculture centering on clubs so famous that they attracted even prim British tour groups by the late twenties. The emergence of this subculture reflected the new freedom that some Germans found exhilarating, others threatening. Among the best-known gay cabaret songs was "The Lavender Lay" (Das Lila-Lied), which became popular in 1928. It was sung to a fox-trot tune.

How civilized / That we're despised / And treated as something taboo, / Though wise and good, 'cause our selfhood / Is special through and through. / We're classified / Fit to be tried, / For the law forbids us too. / Since we're of different stripe, / They malign and fine our type.

REFRAIN:

After all, we're different from the others / Who only love in lockstep with morality, / Who wander blinkered through a world of wonders, / And find their fun in nothing but banality. / We don't know what it is to feel that way, / In our own world we're sisters and we're brothers: / We love the night, so lavender, so gay, / For, after all, we're different from the others! /

Why the quarrels / Others' morals / Foist on us, torment bringing? / We, near and far, / Are what we are. / They'd love to see us swinging. / But still we think / Were we to swing, / You'd soon hear them complain, / For, sad their plight, / In just one night, / Our sun would shine again. / For equal rights we fought our bitter war! / We *will* be tolerated, and never suffer more!!

Source: Laurence Senelick, ed., *Cabaret Performance,* vol. 2: *Europe 1920–1940* (Baltimore: Johns Hopkins University Press, 1993), pp. 89–90.

tions or peoples that embraced them. But these two movements expanded political options and thus made the political framework in Europe more complex and unstable during the 1920s.

Communism and the Continuing Experiment in Russia

The postwar period began in the context of hopes for—and fears of—further revolution all over Europe. Having actually made a revolution, the Russian communists enjoyed extraordinary prestige on the European left and significantly influenced leftist priorities. At the same time, however, their success promptly produced a split in the international socialist movement, which seriously weakened the left.

In making their revolution in 1917, the Bolsheviks had not envisioned having to go it alone; their revolution was to spark revolution elsewhere. But what would become of the new communist regime in Russia if revolution elsewhere was *not* forthcoming? What might it accomplish on its own?

Consolidating Communist Power

Even after leading the revolution that toppled the provisional government in November 1917, the Bolsheviks could not claim majority support. When the long-delayed elections to select a constituent assembly were finally held a few weeks after the revolution, the Bolsheviks ended up with fewer than one-quarter of the seats, while the Socialist Revolutionaries won a clear majority. But over the next three years the Communists, as the Bolsheviks renamed themselves, gradually consolidated their power, outmaneuvering their potential rivals and establishing a centralized and nondemocratic communist regime. Power lay not with the soviets, and not with some coalition of socialist parties, but solely with the Communist party. The Communists also established centralized control of the economy, subjecting workers to more rigorous discipline.

During its first years, the new communist regime encountered a genuine emergency that seemed especially to require a monopoly of power. For over two years it had to fight a brutal civil war against counterrevolutionary Whites, representing people who had been dispossessed by the revolution or who had grown disillusioned with the Communists. The Whites drew support from foreign intervention and from separatist sentiment, as several of the non-Russian nationalities of the old Russian Empire sought to defect, freeing themselves from Russian and communist control.

The counterrevolutionary assault seriously threatened the young communist regime and the territorial basis of the state it had inherited from the old Russian Empire. In the final analysis, however, the Whites proved unable to rally much popular support. Peasants feared, plausibly enough, that a White victory would mean a restoration of the old order, including the return of their newly won lands to the former landlords. By the end of active fighting in November 1920, the new communist regime had not only survived but had regained most of the territory it had lost early in the civil war (Map 28.1).

The need to launch the new communist regime in this way, fighting counterrevolutionaries supported by foreign troops, significantly affected Communist perceptions and priorities. Separatist sentiment might continue to feed counterrevolutionary efforts, so the new regime exerted careful control over the non-Russian nationalities. The Ukraine, for example, had been the base for anticommunist activity as an independent republic under Menshevik leadership beginning in 1918, so in retaking the area in 1920 the Communists sought to bury all hopes for Ukrainian self-determination.

Even after the end of active fighting, the communist government had trouble re-establishing control over Georgia, Azerbaijan, and Russian Armenia, in light of the strong separatist sentiment in those areas. Thus, when the Union of Soviet Socialist Republics (U.S.S.R.) was finally organized in December 1922, it was only nominally a federation of autonomous republics; strong centralization from the communists' new capital in Moscow was the rule from the start.

International Communism and the Comintern

Although they had to concentrate on the civil war in the period from 1918 to 1920, the Russian communists founded the Third, or Communist, Inter-

Tatlin: Monument to the Third International
Vladimir Tatlin created this model for a monument to the Third International, or Comintern, during 1919 and 1920. He envisioned a revolving structure, made of glass and iron, and twice as tall as the later Empire State Building. Although the monument was never built, Tatlin's bold, dynamic form symbolized the utopian aspirations of the early years of the communist experiment in Russia. *(David King Collection)*

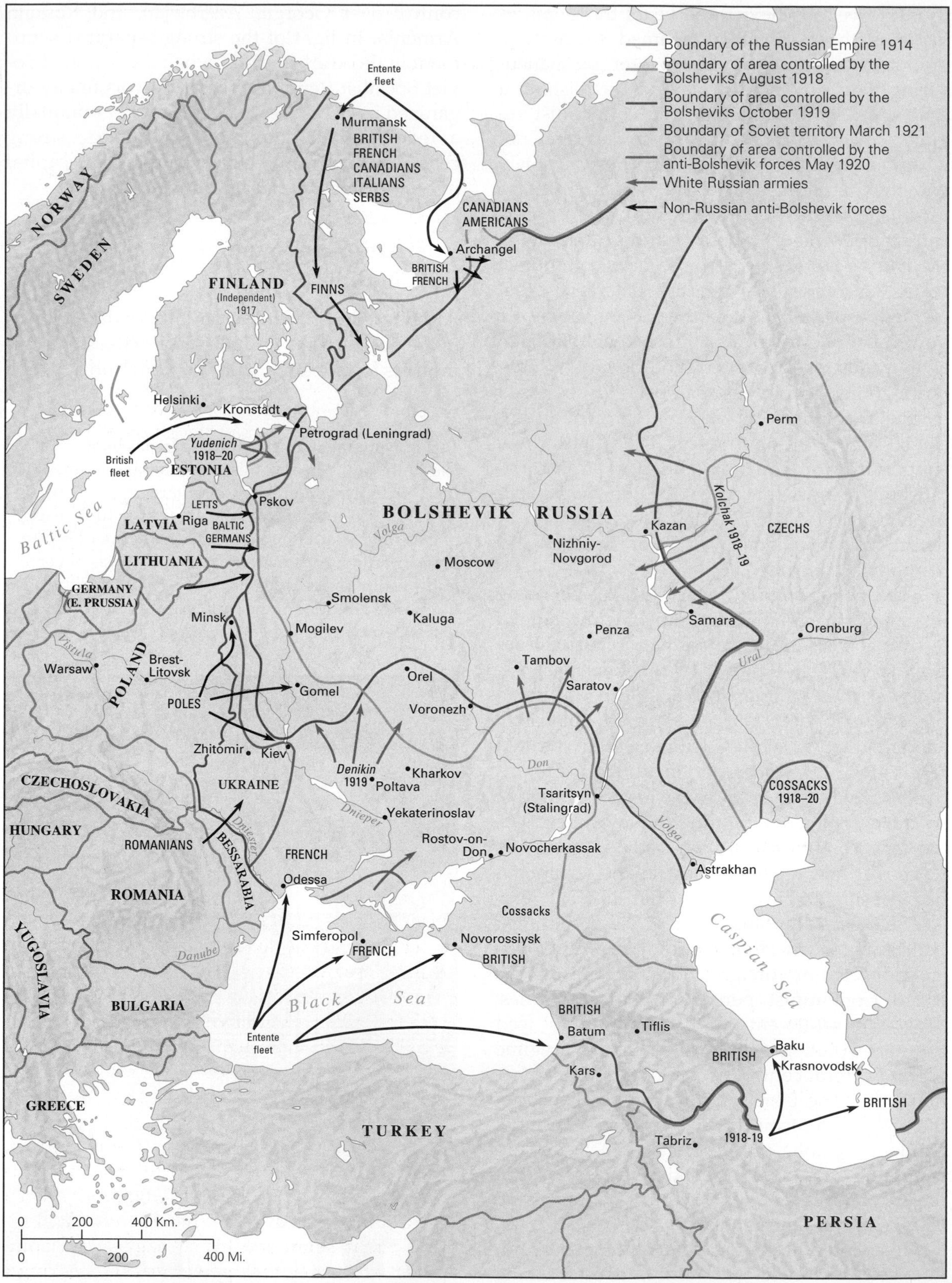
Boundary of the Russian Empire 1914
Boundary of area controlled by the Bolsheviks August 1918
Boundary of area controlled by the Bolsheviks October 1919
Boundary of Soviet territory March 1921
Boundary of area controlled by the anti-Bolshevik forces May 1920
White Russian armies
Non-Russian anti-Bolshevik forces
Entente fleet
Murmansk
BRITISH
FRENCH
CANADIANS
ITALIANS
SERBS
CANADIANS
AMERICANS
Archangel
BRITISH
FRENCH
NORWAY
SWEDEN
FINLAND
(Independent)
1917
FINNS
Helsinki
Kronstadt
Petrograd (Leningrad)
Yudenich
1918–20
British fleet
ESTONIA
Baltic Sea
LETTS
Pskov
LATVIA
Riga
BALTIC GERMANS
LITHUANIA
GERMANY
(E. PRUSSIA)
BOLSHEVIK RUSSIA
Volga
Kazan
Nizhniy-Novgorod
Moscow
Kolchak 1918–19
CZECHS
Perm
Smolensk
Kaluga
Minsk
Mogilev
Samara
Penza
Orenburg
Ural
Vistula
Warsaw
Brest-Litovsk
POLAND
POLES
Gomel
Orel
Tambov
Saratov
Voronezh
Zhitomir
Kiev
Denikin
1919
Kharkov
Poltava
Don
CZECHOSLOVAKIA
UKRAINE
Tsaritsyn
(Stalingrad)
COSSACKS
1918–20
HUNGARY
ROMANIANS
BESSARABIA
Dniester
Dnieper
Yekaterinoslav
Rostov-on-Don
Novocherkassak
Volga
Astrakhan
FRENCH
Odessa
ROMANIA
Cossacks
YUGOSLAVIA
Simferopol
FRENCH
Novorossiysk
BRITISH
Danube
Caspian Sea
Black Sea
BULGARIA
BRITISH
Batum
Tiflis
Entente fleet
Baku
BRITISH
Krasnovodsk
Kars
GREECE
BRITISH
TURKEY
Tabriz
1918-19
PERSIA
0
200
400 Km.
0
200
400 Mi.

A Marxist Critique of Communism

Karl Kautsky (1854–1938) was long recognized as the leading spokesman for orthodox Marxism within the German Social Democratic party, the most influential Marxist party in the world during the era of the Second International. Thus it is striking that he harshly criticized Leninist Bolshevism, or communism, as a heretical departure that could lead only to disaster. Kautsky's volume, **Terrorism and Communism**, *written in 1919, was central to a volley of charges and countercharges that pitted him first against Lenin, then against Trotsky.*

The hereditary sin of Bolshevism has been its suppression of democracy through a form of government, namely, the dictatorship, which has no meaning unless it represents the unlimited and despotic power, either of one single person, or of a small organization intimately bound together.... It is easy to begin a dictatorship as it is to begin war, if one has the State power under control. But when once such steps have been taken, it is as difficult at will to stop the one as the other....

...wherever Socialism does not appear to be possible on a democratic basis, and where the majority of the population rejects it, its time has not yet fully come. Bolshevism, on the other hand, argues that Socialism can only be introduced by being forced on a majority by a minority.... The Bolsheviks are prepared, in order to maintain their position, to make all sorts of possible concessions to bureaucracy, to militarism, and to capitalism, whereas any concession to democracy seems to them to be sheer suicide. And yet that alone offers any possibility... of leading Russia along paths of economic progress and prosperous development towards some higher form of existence....

...Bolshevism... adds the attempt to split up all other Socialist parties which have still remained in unity—so long as they do not prove to have a Bolshevik majority. Such is the meaning of the Third International....

...since the rise of the Soviet Republic, a new wedge has been driven through the Socialist ranks of Germany by Bolshevik propaganda, which has demanded that our Party should relinquish the essential claims of democracy....

Source: Karl Kautsky, *Terrorism and Communism: A Contribution to the Natural History of Revolution* (Westport, Conn.: Hyperion Press, 1973), pp. 217–218, 220–222, 226. (Reprint of the first English edition, published in 1920.)

national—commonly known as the Comintern—in March 1919, to make clear their break with the seemingly discredited strategies of the Second International. Through the Comintern, the Russian communists expected to translate their success in Russia into leadership of the international socialist movement. At the same time, however, many old-line Marxists elsewhere found it hard to swallow the notion that the leadership of European socialism had passed to the Bolshevik leaders of backward Russia (see the box, "A Marxist Critique of Communism").

From its founding in March 1919 until the spring of 1920, as a wave of leftist political agitation and labor unrest spread throughout Europe, the Comintern actively promoted the wider revolution that Lenin and his colleagues had anticipated when they took power in 1917. Seeking to

Map 28.1 Foreign Intervention and Civil War in Revolutionary Russia, 1918–1920 By mid-1918 the new communist regime was under attack from many sides, by both foreign troops and anticommunist Russians. Bolshevik-held territory shrank during 1919, but over the next year the Red Army managed to regain much of what had been lost and to secure the new Communist state. Anton Deniken, Alexander Kolchak, and Nicholas Yudenich commanded the most significant counterrevolutionary forces. (*Source:* Adapted from THE TIMES ATLAS OF WORLD HISTORY, 3d ed., by kind permission of Times Books.)

win mass support under communist leadership, the organization accented leftist solidarity and reached out to the rank and file in the labor unions, whether communist or not. By the spring of 1920, however, it seemed clear that further revolution was not imminent. Thus, Comintern leaders quit worrying about immediate support and began concentrating on improving organization and discipline for a more protracted revolutionary struggle.

The Russians felt that poor organization and planning had undercut the immediate revolutionary possibility elsewhere in Europe during 1919 and 1920. Thus the Comintern would cut through all the revolutionary romanticism and rhetoric to show the others what the Leninist strategy, or communism, meant in fact. The Russians themselves would have to call the shots, because what communism meant, above all, was tight organization and discipline.

The second Comintern congress, during the summer of 1920, devised twenty-one points, or conditions to be fulfilled by a socialist party seeking affiliation with the Comintern (see the box, "Toward the Socialist Split: Conditions for Membership in the Comintern"). Most notably, any such party had to accept the Comintern's authority, adopt a centralized organization, and purge its reformists. The result of the Comintern's more aggressive claim to leadership was a lasting schism in the European socialist movement by early 1921, for the Comintern attracted some, but not all, of the members of the existing socialist parties. All over the world those parties split between "communists," who chose to affiliate with the Comintern, and "socialists," who rejected Comintern leadership. These socialists still claimed to be Marxists, but they were not Leninists; they rejected the Russian Bolshevik strategy for taking political power.

Many European socialists had difficulty assessing the options objectively, even though the Comintern sought to make them unmistakably clear. The Russian communists enjoyed cult status because they had made a real revolution, while elsewhere socialists had talked and compromised, even getting swept up in wartime patriotism. When, for example, the French socialist party considered the matter at its national congress in December 1920, about 70 percent of the delegates opted for the Comintern and the twenty-one points, while a minority walked out to form a new socialist party. But as the implications of Comintern membership became clearer over the next few years, the balance shifted to favor the socialists. Membership in the French Communist party, which stood at 131,000 in 1921, declined to 28,000 by 1932.

By late 1923 the Comintern finally concluded that revolution elsewhere could not be expected any time soon. For the foreseeable future, the Comintern declared, the entire communist movement must nurture the new Soviet Union, the homeland of communists everywhere. There was no difference between Soviet interests and the long-term interests of the international communist movement, so Comintern policy and Soviet foreign policy were indistinguishable. And with further revolution indefinitely postponed, the immediate enemy was not capitalism or the bourgeoisie, but the socialists, the communists' rivals for working-class support.

The communists' incessant criticism of the socialists, whom they dubbed "social fascists," seriously demoralized and weakened the European left. But these priorities meant that communism, though still an uncertain and potentially disruptive element, posed no immediate threat of revolution by the late 1920s.

From Lenin to Stalin

Although it managed to win the civil war, the communist regime was clearly in crisis by early 1921, partly because of "war communism," the rough-and-ready controlled economy that the war effort seemed to make necessary. With industrial production only about one-fifth the 1913 total, there were strikes in the factories, and peasants were resisting further requisitions of grain. Finally, in March 1921, sailors at the Kronstadt naval base mutinied, suffering considerable loss of life as governmental control was reestablished.

With the very survival of the revolution in question, Lenin replaced war communism with the New Economic Policy, or NEP, in March 1921. Although transport, banking, heavy industry, and wholesale commerce remained under state control, the NEP restored considerable scope for private enterprise, especially in the retail sector and in agriculture. The economy

Toward the Socialist Split: Conditions for Membership in the Comintern

Meeting in July and August 1920, the Comintern established twenty-one conditions for membership. Its Russian leaders were seeking to assume the leadership of international socialism—on terms that, from their point of view, would overcome the ambiguities that had compromised the effectiveness of the Second International before the war. The following were among the most pointed of the twenty-one conditions.

2. Every organization desiring to belong to the Communist International must steadily and systematically *remove* from all responsible posts in the labor movement, in the party organization, editorial boards, trade unions, parliamentary fractions, cooperative societies, municipalities, etc., all reformists and followers of the "center," and have them replaced by communists, even at the cost of replacing, at the beginning, "experienced" leaders by rank-and-file workingmen. . . .

12. Parties belonging to the Communist International must be built on the principle of democratic *centralism.* At the present time of acute civil war, the communist party will only be able fully to do its duty when it is organized in the most centralized manner. . . .

13. The communist parties of those countries where the communists' activity is legal shall make periodical cleanings (re-registration) of the members of the party organizations, so as to systematically cleanse the party from the petty bourgeois elements who inevitably attach themselves to it. . . .

16. All decisions of the congresses of the Communist International, as well as the decisions of its Executive Committee, are binding on all parties affiliated with the Communist International. . . .

17. . . . Every party that wishes to join the Communist International must bear the name *Communist party* of such-and-such country. . . . Every rank-and-file worker must clearly understand the difference between the communist parties and the old official "social democratic" or "socialist" parties which have betrayed the cause of the working class.

Source: Helmut Gruber, ed., *International Communism in the Era of Lenin: A Documentary History* (Garden City, N.Y.: Doubleday Anchor, 1972), pp. 241–246.

quickly began to revive and by 1927 was producing at prewar levels.

But what about the longer term? If revolution elsewhere was no longer on the horizon, what room was there for building a socialist order in the Soviet Union, which was still relatively backward economically, and which still bore the scars of the upheavals of the last decade? Certain measures to address the country's relative backwardness were obvious: The new regime engineered rapid improvements in literacy, for example. But the Marxist understanding of historical progress required industrialization, so debate focused especially on the scope for industrial development in the Soviet Union and its relationship to the creation of socialism.

This debate about priorities became bound up with questions about the leadership of the new regime. Lenin suffered the first of a series of strokes in May 1922, and then died in January 1924, setting off a struggle among his possible successors. In the combination of reasoned debate and political infighting that ensued, three basic positions emerged.

The "leftist" perspective was identified especially with Leon Trotsky, architect of the new Red

Lenin's Doubts About Stalin

Even after a series of strokes left him partially incapacitated, Lenin continued to influence Soviet communism through written communications. He even gave his wife, the influential leader Nadezhda Krupskaya (1869–1939), some notes to be placed before the first party congress that would follow his death. The following were among Lenin's notes of December 1922 and January 1923.

Com[rade] Stalin has, having become Secretary General, concentrated enormous power in his hands and I am not at all certain that he is capable of utilizing this power with sufficient caution. Com[rade] Trotsky, on the other hand . . . is probably the most able man in the present CC [Central Committee] but at the same time he possesses an exaggerated self-confidence and an exaggerated attraction to the purely administrative side of affairs.

These two traits of the able leaders of the present CC might quite innocently lead to a split; if our Party does not take steps to prevent this, the split can occur unexpectedly. . . .

Stalin is too rude and this defect, which can be freely tolerated in our midst and among us Communists, can become an intolerable defect in one holding the position of Secretary General. Because of this, I propose that the comrades consider ways and means by which Stalin can be removed from this position and another man selected, a man who, above all, would differ from Com[rade] Stalin in only one quality, namely, greater tolerance, greater loyalty, greater kindness and more considerate attitude toward his comrades, less capricious temper, etc. This circumstance could appear to be a meaningless trifle. I think, however, that from the viewpoint of preventing a split and from the viewpoint of what I have written above concerning the relationship between Stalin and Trotsky, this is not a trifle, or if it is one, then it is a trifle which can acquire a decisive significance.

Source: Warren B. Walsh, ed., *Readings in Russian History*, vol. 3: *The Revolutionary Era and the Soviet Period*, 4th ed., revised (Syracuse, N.Y.: Syracuse University Press, 1963), pp. 735–736.

Army that had won the civil war and by most measures Lenin's heir apparent. Although he favored tighter economic controls to speed industrial development, Trotsky insisted that the Soviet Union should continue to concentrate on spreading the revolution to other countries. There was simply no way the Soviet Union could build socialism on its own.

On the "right," Nikolai Bukharin wanted to concentrate on the gradual development of the Soviet Union, based on a more open and conciliatory strategy than Trotsky envisioned. Much of the NEP should continue—no longer to confront an emergency but to create the preliminary conditions for genuine socialism in Russia. The way to industrialize successfully was not by tightening controls, squeezing a surplus from agricultural producers, as Trotsky proposed, but by allowing them to profit, thereby building up purchasing power.

Bukharin's position seems to have accorded with Lenin's final thinking as well. And Lenin, by the time of his death, had developed considerable misgivings about the man who would win this struggle for direction within the fragile new Soviet regime (see the box, "Lenin's Doubts About Stalin").

The victory of Joseph Stalin (1879–1953), born Josef Djugashvili into a lower-class family in Georgia, in the Caucasian region, proved crucial to twentieth-century history—and decisive for the fate of Soviet communism. From the position of party secretary that he had assumed in 1922, he gradually established his control within the Soviet system by 1929. Faced with rivals on the left and right, Stalin adopted a tack that was "cen-

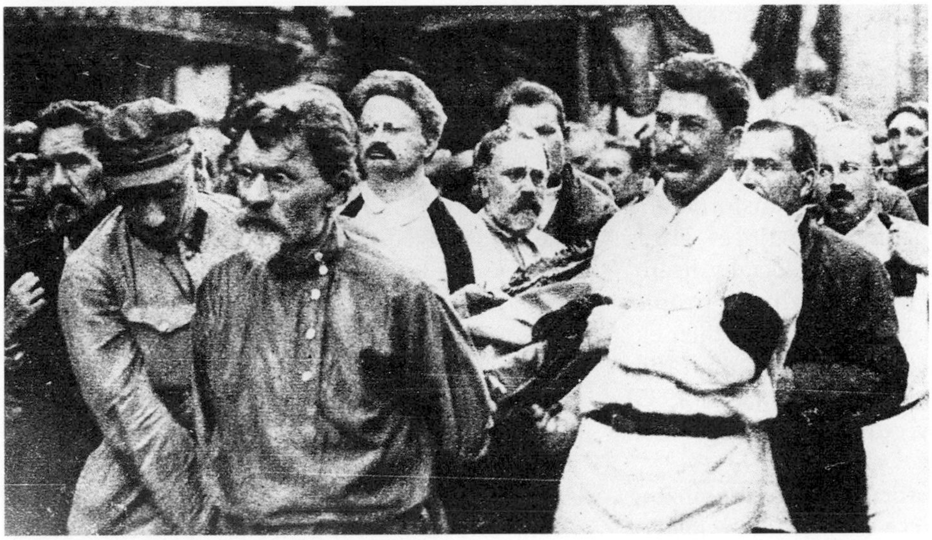

Rivals for the Soviet Leadership In July 1926 in Moscow, Soviet leaders carry the coffin of Feliks Dzerzhinsky, the first head of the secret police. Among them are Trotsky (with glasses, center left), Stalin (right foreground), and Bukharin (with mustache, at far right), rivals for the Soviet leadership after Lenin's death. The winner, Stalin, would eventually have his two competitors killed. *(David King Collection)*

trist" in one sense, but based less on a serious weighing of economic possibilities than on tactical maneuvering, playing his rivals off against each other. Though he lacked Trotsky's charisma, Stalin proved a master of backstage political maneuvering. Knowing little of economics, he projected a "can-do" attitude that enabled him to accuse those more skeptical, like Trotsky, of lack of faith in the Soviet working class.

Stalin first outmaneuvered the left; Trotsky and his allies were removed from positions of power, and Trotsky himself was finally forced into exile in 1929. Bitterly critical of Stalin to the end, he was finally murdered by Stalin's agents in Mexico in 1940. Stalin took on Bukharin and the right more gradually, but ultimately just as decisively.

Stalin's victory over the right was bound up with his decision for crash industrialization, favoring heavy industry, and based on forced agricultural collectivization. The pivotal year was 1929. The first of the Soviet five-year plans had already been adopted in 1927, but now, in 1929, its goals for industrial production were revised upward, to be attained through immediate collectivization of agriculture. In embarking on this program, Stalin created a sense of crisis and emergency, but also heroic challenge and achievement, that made further opposition from the right difficult.

Emphasizing will and determination, Stalin played up the great historical drama surrounding the Soviet experiment, with its almost incredible targets and goals. Suggestions that the pace could not be maintained only proved grist for Stalin's mill: "No, comrades," he told a workers' conference early in 1931, "the tempo must not be reduced. On the contrary, we must increase it as much as is within our powers and capabilities. . . . To slow the tempo would mean falling behind. And those who fall behind get beaten. . . . Do you want our socialist fatherland to be beaten and to lose its independence? . . . We are fifty or a hundred years behind the advanced countries. We must make good this distance in ten years. Either we do this or they will crush us."[1]

Stalin's program of rapid industrialization called forth an attempt to mobilize and control society without precedent in Western history. Although the economic sphere was crucial, this mobilization affected the whole shape of the regime—including, for example, cultural and artistic policy.

During the 1920s, the possibility of building a new socialist society in the Soviet Union had attracted a number of modernist artists, who assumed that artistic innovation went hand in hand with the radical socioeconomic transformation the communists were seeking to engineer. These artists wanted to make art more socially useful and more central to the lives of ordinary people. With Soviet cultural officials welcoming their experiments, such Soviet artists as Vladimir Tatlin (1885–1956) and Kasimir Malevich (1878–1935) developed striking new cultural forms between 1919 and 1929.

But in 1929 Soviet officials began mobilizing the cultural realm to serve the grandiose task of building socialism in one country. No longer welcoming experiment and innovation, they demanded "socialist realism," which portrayed the achievements of the ongoing Soviet revolution in an inspiring, romantically heroic light. Modernism, in contrast, they denounced as decadent and counterrevolutionary.

In retrospect, it is clear that a Stalinist revolution *within* the Soviet regime began in 1929, but where it was to lead was by no means certain—not even to Stalin himself. Still, the Soviet Union was pulling back, going its own way, by the end of the twenties. For the foreseeable future, the presence of a revolutionary regime in the old Russia would apparently be less disruptive for the rest of Europe than it had first appeared.

The Crisis of Liberal Italy and the Creation of Fascism

Although Soviet communism was something new, it had developed from within the established tradition of Marxist socialism. The pedigree of fascism, which emerged in Italy at about the same time, was much less clear. Its undisputed leader, Benito Mussolini (1883–1945), had begun as a socialist, but by the end of the war he had left the socialist mainstream behind and was looking for a new constituency, especially among young war veterans who claimed that political renewal could follow from the Italian war experience. The new fascist movement that Mussolini forged in March 1919 proved violent and disturbing, yet it attracted considerable support among those disillusioned with parliamentary politics and hostile to the Marxist left.

The Shape of the Postwar Crisis in Italy

The war proved especially controversial in Italy because the Italians could have avoided it altogether. No one attacked, and the country could have received significant territorial benefits just by remaining neutral. Yet it seemed to many, including leading intellectuals and educated young people, that Italy could not stand idly by in a European war, especially one involving Austria-Hungary, which still controlled significant Italian-speaking areas. To participate in this major war, in which Italian national interests were very much at issue, would be the test of Italy's maturity as a nation. In May 1915, Italy finally intervened on the side of the Triple Entente. The government's decision stemmed not from vague visions of renewal but from the commitment of tangible territorial gains, primarily at the expense of Austria-Hungary, that France and Britain made to Italy with the secret Treaty of London in April.

Despite the near collapse of the Italian armies in October 1917, Italy lasted out the war, making a creditable overall showing and some contribution to the victory. Supporters of the war felt that this success could lead to a thoroughgoing renewal of Italian public life. Yet many Italians had been skeptical of claims for the war from the outset, and the fact that it proved so much more difficult than expected hardly won them over. To Socialists, Catholics, and those loyal to the longtime liberal political leader Giovanni Giolitti, intervention itself had been a tragic mistake. Thus, despite Italy's participation in the victory, division over the war's significance immensely complicated the Italian political situation after the war was over.

The situation became even more volatile when Italy did not manage all the gains expected at the Paris Peace Conference. Italy got most of what it had been promised in the Treaty of London, but appetites increased with the dissolution of the Austro-Hungarian Empire. To some Italians, the disappointing outcome of the peace conference simply confirmed that the war had been a mistake, its benefits not worth the costs. But others were outraged at what seemed a denigration of the Italian contribution by France, Britain, and the United States. Thus the outcome fanned resentment of Italy's allies, but also of the country's political leaders, who seemed too weak to deliver on what they had promised.

Whatever Italy's prospects at the peace conference, the established political leaders did not do well at renewing the political system in light of the war experience. The last gasp of the old liberal politics was Giovanni Giolitti, who returned for a final stint as prime minister in 1920, at the age of 78. But Giolitti, who had been especially adept at piecing together parliamentary majorities before the war, found the situation much less manageable now, partly because Italy, in a spirit of democratic reform, had adopted proportional representation to replace the old system of small, single-member constituencies in 1919. The new system meant a greater premium on mass parties and party discipline at the expense of the one-to-one bargaining at which Giolitti had excelled. But the new mass politics quickly reached an impasse—partly because of the stance of the Italian Socialist party.

In contrast to the French and German parties, the Italian Socialists had never supported the war, and they did not buy the notion that the war experience was somehow the key to political renewal in the aftermath. So rather than reaching out to discontented war veterans, Socialist leaders talked of imitating the Bolshevik Revolution. During 1919 and 1920, the Italian situation seemed at least potentially revolutionary. A wave of quasi-revolutionary labor unrest included several imposing national strikes and finally a series of factory occupations during September 1920. But despite their revolutionary rhetoric, Italian Socialist leaders did not understand what Leninism involved in practice, and they did not carry out the planning and organization that might have made an Italian revolution possible.

The established political system was at an impasse, and the Socialist party seemed at once too inflexible and too romantic to lead some sort of radical transformation. It was in this context that fascism emerged, claiming to offer a "third way." It emerged, inevitably, in opposition to the Socialists and the socialist working class, because of conflict over the meaning of the war and the kind of transformation Italy needed. And this antisocialist posture made fascism open to exploitation by narrowly reactionary interests. By early 1921 some landowners in northern and central Italy were footing the bill as bands of young fascists drove around the countryside in trucks, beating up workers and burning down socialist meeting halls. But fascist spokesmen claimed to offer something other than mere reaction, a new politics that would prove better than Marxist socialism at pursuing the long-term interests of the working class.

At the same time, important sectors of Italian industry, having grown rapidly thanks to government orders during the war, looked with apprehension toward the more competitive international economy that seemed on the horizon now that the war was over. With its relative lack of capital, markets, and raw materials, Italy seemed to face an especially difficult situation. Nationalist thinkers and spokesmen for big business questioned the capacity of the present parliamentary system to provide the vigorous leadership that Italy especially seemed to need. Prone to short-term bickering and partisanship, ordinary politicians lacked both the vision to pursue Italy's long-term international economic interests and the will to impose the necessary discipline on the domestic level. Thus the government had been relatively weak in responding to the labor unrest of 1919 and 1920 (see the box, "Toward Fascism: Alfredo Rocco on the Weakness of the Liberal Democratic State").

In postwar Italy, then, there was widespread discontent with established forms of politics, but those discontented were socially disparate, and some of their aims were not entirely compatible. Some had been socialists before the war, others nationalists hostile to socialism. While some envisioned a more intense kind of mass politics, others thought the masses already had too much power. Still, the discontented agreed on the need for an alternative to *both* conventional parliamentary politics and conventional Marxist socialism, and it was widely felt that the germs of that alternative could be found in the Italian war experience. What would be necessary to translate these

Toward Fascism: Alfredo Rocco on the Weakness of the Liberal Democratic State

As Italy's minister of justice from 1925 to 1932, the Italian legal scholar Alfredo Rocco (1875–1935) spearheaded the construction of the new fascist state. Speaking in November 1920, he revealed why he would seek to replace parliamentary democracy with a new, stronger form of government. Rocco was troubled, most immediately, by the apparent weakness of the liberal state in the face of strikes by unions, or syndicates, of public-service employees. But the deeper problem was liberal individualism, linked to shortsighted pursuit of personal advantage.

There is a crisis within the state; day by day, the state is dissolving into a mass of small particles, parties, associations, groups and syndicates that are binding it in chains and paralysing and stifling its activity: one by one, with increasing speed, the state is losing its attributes of sovereignty. . . . The conflict of interests between groups and classes is now being settled by the use of private force alone. . . . The state stands by impassively watching these conflicts which involve countless violations of public and private rights. This neutrality which, in liberal doctrine, was intended to allow free play for economic law in the clash of interests between the classes is now being interpreted as allowing the state to abandon its essential function of guardian of public order and agent of justice. . . .

. . . The eighteenth-century reaction against the state . . . came to a head politically in the explosion of the French Revolution. . . . From that time onwards, the claims of individualism knew no bounds. The masses of individuals wanted to govern the state and govern it in accordance with their own individual interests. The state, a living organism with a continuous existence over the centuries that extends beyond successive generations and as such the guardian of the immanent historical interests of the species, was turned into a monopoly to serve the individual interests of each separate generation. . . .

The state must return to its traditions, interrupted by the triumph of liberal ideology, and treat the modern syndicates exactly as it treated the medieval corporations. It must absorb them and make them part of the state. . . . On the one hand, syndicates must be recognized as essential and on the other they must be placed firmly beneath the control of the state, which must lay down their precise functions. . . . But above all, it is necessary to change them from aggressive bodies defending particular interests into a means of collaboration to achieve common aims.

Source: Adrian Lyttelton, ed., *Italian Fascisms from Pareto to Gentile* (New York: Harper & Row, Harper Torchbooks, 1975), pp. 269, 273–276, 280.

discontents and aspirations into a new political force?

Benito Mussolini: From Socialist Journalist to Fascist Prime Minister

Benito Mussolini came from the Romagna region of central Italy, his father a blacksmith and a socialist, his mother a teacher. Mussolini was moderately well educated, and taught French for a time, but he also became active in socialist journalism, demonstrating such talent that he became editor of the Socialist party's national newspaper, *Avanti!*, in 1912, when only 29 years old. At that point many saw him as the fresh face needed to revitalize Italian socialism, bogged down between sterile intransigence and bland reformist compromise.

Benito Mussolini The founder of fascism is shown with other fascist leaders in 1922, as he becomes prime minister of Italy. Standing at Mussolini's right (with beard) is Italo Balbo, later a pioneering aviator and fascist Italy's air force minister. *(UPI/Bettmann Newsphotos)*

His concern with such renewal had made Mussolini an unorthodox socialist even before 1914, and when the European war broke out, he was prominent among those on the Italian left who began to call for Italian intervention. The fact that socialists in France, Germany, and elsewhere had immediately rallied to their respective national war efforts suggested that the old socialism, based on international proletarian solidarity, required a thoroughgoing recasting. The war itself could be the foundation for radical change in Italy. But the Socialist party refused to follow, remaining neutralist and aloof, so Mussolini found himself cut off from his earlier constituency.

However, through his new newspaper, *Il popolo d'Italia* (The People of Italy), Mussolini promptly emerged as a leading advocate of Italian participation in the war. He saw military duty once Italy intervened, and after the war was over he was the most credible person to translate the war experience into a new form of politics.

But after founding the fascist movement in March 1919, Mussolini became embroiled in periodic disputes with important sectors of his movement, especially as fascism gathered force in violent reaction against the socialist labor movement by 1921. Although leading young fascist militants wanted fascism to replace the established parliamentary system with a wholly new political order, Mussolini seemed prone to use fascism simply as his personal instrument as he jockeyed for power within the existing system. So when his maneuvering finally won him the prime minister's post in October 1922, it was not at all clear that a change of regime, or a one-party dictatorship, was in the offing.

At that point, Mussolini, like most Italians, emphasized normalization and legality. Fascism had apparently been absorbed within the political system, perhaps to provide an infusion of youthful vitality after the war. With Mussolini as prime minister, there would be changes, but not revolutionary changes. Government would become more vigorous and efficient; the swollen Italian bureaucracy would be streamlined; the trains would run on time. But those who had envisioned more sweeping change were frustrated that nothing more had come of fascism than this.

The Matteotti Murder and the Commitment to a New Regime

In June 1924 the murder of Giacomo Matteotti (1885–1924), a moderate socialist parliamentary deputy, sparked a crisis that forced fascism to begin replacing the existing system with a regime of its own. Shortly after a speech denouncing fascist violence, Matteotti was killed by fascist thugs. A great public outcry followed, and the key question for Italians in the months that followed concerned the responsibility of the government—and especially Mussolini himself—for the crime. Many of those from the establishment who had tolerated Mussolini as the man who could keep order now deserted him. A growing chorus called for his resignation.

Mussolini sought at first to be even more conciliatory and reassuring. Other fascists, however, saw the crisis as a precious opportunity for fascism to end the compromise with the old order, to force the opposition to the shadows, and to commit itself to creating a whole new political system. The more serious of these radicals condemned the Matteotti murder and stressed that further violence could only be counterproductive. But the only way fascism could survive—and justify its continued existence—was by committing itself to a definite course of serious change.

The crisis came to a head on December 31, 1924, when thirty-three militants called on Mussolini to demand that he make up his mind. The way out of the crisis was not to delimit the scope of fascism but to expand it. And Mussolini himself would have to accept responsibility for the fascist revolution, including its violent excesses. He was not an ordinary prime minister but the leader of fascism, *Il Duce,* and in that role he would have to implement the fascist revolution.

Finally at a crossroads, without his customary room for maneuver, Mussolini agreed to a more radical course. Addressing the Chamber of Deputies a few days later, on January 3, 1925, he defiantly claimed the "full political, moral, and historical responsibility for all that has happened," including "all the acts of violence."[2] He then promised to accelerate the transformation that he had initiated with his agitation for intervention in 1914 and 1915. And now began the creation of a new fascist state, although the compromises continued and the direction was never as clear as committed fascists desired.

Innovation and Compromise in Fascist Italy

Early in 1925, the Fascist government began to undermine the existing liberal system by imprisoning or exiling opposition leaders and outlawing the other parties and the nonfascist labor unions. But fascism was seeking not simply a monopoly of power; the new fascist state was to be totalitarian, all-encompassing, limitless in its reach. Under the old liberal regime, the fascists charged, the state had been too weak to promote the national interest, and the society had been too fragmented to enable the Italian nation to achieve its potential. So Mussolini's regime expanded the state's sovereignty and mobilized the society to create a deeper sense of national identity and solidarity among Italians. Thus, for example, a new system of labor judges settled labor disputes, replacing the right to strike. And the Fascist party fostered new forms of participation in organizations it devised for youth, for leisure-time activities, and the like.

The centerpiece of the new fascist state was corporativism, based on mobilization of people as producers, through organization of the workplace. Groupings based on occupation, or economic function, were gradually to replace parliament as the basis for political participation and decision making. Beginning in 1926, corporativist institutions were established in stages until a Chamber of Fasces and Corporations at last replaced the old Chamber of Deputies in 1939.

In constructing the corporative state, the fascists claimed a grandiose mission to offer the world a third way beyond both outmoded democracy and misguided communism. The practice of corporativism during the 1930s never lived up to such rhetoric, but the effort to devise new forms of political participation and decision making, as an alternative to parliamentary democracy, was central to fascism's self-understanding and its quest for legitimacy.

Despite the commitment to a new regime, however, fascism continued to compromise with pre-existing elites and institutions. The accommodation was especially evident in the arrangements with the Catholic church that Mussolini worked out in 1929, formally ending the dispute between the church and the new Italian state that went back to the national unification of the nineteenth century. With the Concordat and the Lateran Pact, Mussolini restored the sovereignty of the Vatican and conceded the church autonomy in education and supremacy in marriage law. This settlement of an old and thorny dispute afforded Mussolini a good deal of prestige abroad, as well as among nonfascist Italians. At the same time, the compromise seemed to imply a kind of endorsement of Mussolini's government on the part of the church and the establishment in Italy.

But such a compromise with a traditional institution displeased many fascists, who complained that it was hardly consistent with the totalitarian pretensions of fascism to give this powerful, nonfascist institution an autonomous role in Italian public life. Such complaints led to a partial crackdown on Catholic youth organizations in 1931, as Mussolini continued trying to juggle traditionalist compromise and revolutionary pretension.

By the end of the 1920s, then, it remained unclear whether Italian fascism was a form of revolution or a form of restoration. It could be violent and disruptive, dictatorial and repressive, and it inspired movements with at least some common characteristics elsewhere in Europe. But Mussolini in power did not seem all bad, and there were signs he was becoming more responsible.

France, Britain, and the Ambiguous Fruits of Victory

While Russia and Italy tried new political forms, France and Britain remained the leading democracies in Europe. Victory in the war seemed to have confirmed their values and institutions. Of the major European countries, they seemed the best positioned to confront postwar sociopolitical challenges. In retrospect, however, new strains and missed opportunities are evident in the experience of each during the 1920s.

Moreover, it was up to France and Britain to spearhead international restabilization, but it was not clear they had the will and the resources to make the new international order work. Cooperation between them was essential, yet sometimes their differences—in geography, in values, and in perceptions—seemed to doom them to work at cross-purposes.

France and the Paradox of Victory

Victory in the Great War seemed to belie all France's prewar concerns about decadence and decline and to confirm the fundamental solidity of French ways. In the immediate aftermath of the war, French leaders were confident in dealing with radical labor unrest and aggressive in translating the battlefield victory into a dominant position on the European continent. But despite the victorious outcome, the war itself, with its tremendous loss of French life, had produced a widespread but unspoken conviction that the country could not withstand another such challenge. The renewed confidence thus proved hollow. On the domestic level, confidence meant complacency—and thus a failure to address socioeconomic problems under the conditions of relative political stability and economic prosperity during the 1920s. At the same time, the underlying will to back up France's position of international leadership was missing.

As before the war, the Radicals set the tone for the Third Republic during the 1920s. Representing ordinary people, from schoolteachers to shopkeepers to lower-level bureaucrats, they could still be counted on to defend the now traditional ideas of liberty and equality, and to support the republic against the church, the army, or any threat to political democracy. But where socioeconomic matters were concerned, the Radicals were anything but radical. Thus, when a moderately leftist alliance, led by the Radicals, won the parliamentary elections of 1924 and replaced the conservative cabinet elected in 1919, there was no dramatic change in the French government's domestic priorities.

Although some in prewar France had worried about falling behind rapidly industrializing Germany, the victory seemed to have vindicated France's more cautious, balanced economy, with its blend of industry and agriculture. Thus the prewar mistrust of rapid industrial development continued. Rather than foster a program of economic modernization that might have afforded the basis for genuine security, the French pulled back even from the measure of state responsibility for the economy that had developed during the war.

To be sure, in France, as elsewhere, the 1920s were a decade of relative prosperity. Led by the oil and electricity industries, the economy grew at an annual rate of 4.6 percent between 1923 and 1929, double the prewar rate. Industrial production by 1929 was 40 percent higher than it had been in 1913. But, with the exception of Britain, other Western economies grew more rapidly during the 1920s, and the opportunity that growth afforded to modernize the French economy was not seized. Although government grants helped rebuild almost eight thousand factories, most were simply rebuilt as they were before the war. Moreover, the working class benefited little from the relative prosperity of the twenties. Housing remained poor, wages failed to keep up with inflation, and France continued to lag behind other countries in social legislation.

Despite the bravado of the immediate postwar period, France remained relatively static in the aftermath of victory, and the veneer of renewed self-confidence gradually peeled away to reveal defensiveness and resignation. The defensive mentality found physical embodiment in the Maginot Line, a system of fortifications on the country's eastern border. Remembering the defensive warfare of World War I, and determined to preclude the sort of invasion France had suffered in 1914, Marshal Pétain and the military convinced France's political leaders to adopt a defensive strategy based on a fortified line. The Maginot system was conceived in 1925, begun in 1929, and reached at least preliminary completion in 1935, when it extended along France's border with Germany from Switzerland to the Ardennes Forest at the border with Belgium.

This defensive system was not without military justification, but it also was not consistent with the other major strands of French military and diplomatic policy. To replace the earlier link with Russia, France had developed an alliance system in east-central Europe—involving Poland, Czechoslovakia, Romania, and Yugoslavia—but if France emphasized defense behind an impregnable system of forts, what good were French security guarantees to these new allies? Though understandable, the French desire to defend, to preserve, to avoid another war, was not consistent with the role that France set out to play in Europe after its victory in 1918.

Restoration and Innovation in Britain

In Britain, as in France, the illusion of restoration after the war masked changes and tensions that would cause problems later. Rather than realistically assessing Britain's prospects in the more competitive international economy, British leaders sought to return to the prewar situation, based on the gold standard, with London the world's financial center. For many Britons, the government's announcement in 1925 that the pound was again freely convertible to gold at 1914 exchange rates was the long-awaited indication that normality had returned at last.

Yet the return to 1914 exchange rates overvalued the pound relative to the U.S. dollar, making British goods more expensive on export markets and making it still more difficult for aging British industries to compete. Moreover, Britain no longer had the capital to act as the world's banker. By trying to do so, Britain became all the more vulnerable when the international economy reached a crisis in 1929.

The British political system remained stable between the wars, although it opened up in one significant sense as Labour gradually became a governing party. In the 1922 parliamentary elections, won by the Conservatives, the Labour vote surpassed the Liberal total for the first time. The gap widened in the elections of December 1923, when none of the parties won an absolute majority. Although the Conservatives still held the most seats, the Liberals threw their support to Labour, hoping, apparently, that an all-Labour government might discredit itself through poor performance. So the Labour party, under Ramsay MacDonald (1866–1937), formed Britain's first Labour—and nominally socialist—government in January 1924.

The coming of Labour to power wrought a significant expansion of the governmental elite to incorporate those, like MacDonald himself, with genuinely working-class backgrounds. And the new government promptly devised an innovative program of municipal housing at controlled rents. But the advent of a Labour government meant nothing like a socialist transformation of the British economy, despite hopes—and fears—that it would. Such a transformation was neither intended nor possible, given MacDonald's need for Liberal support. Rather than seek ways of controlling the economy, the new government continued the dismantling of wartime controls that was already in progress.

Labour reached another milestone in the 1929 elections, when for the first time it passed the Conservatives to become the country's largest party, although it still lacked an absolute majority. It got a second chance to govern, again under Ramsay MacDonald, from 1929 until 1931, but again its scope for new directions was limited. In this ambiguous interwar period, which revolved around a three-party political system, the significance of the growing strength of Labour remained uncertain. Not until the immediate aftermath of World War II would Labour have a chance to begin seriously transforming Britain on its own.

Stanley Baldwin The most important British leader of the 1920s, the Conservative prime minister Stanley Baldwin had an engaging modesty and a gift for direct communication that made him popular with wide sectors of the electorate. *(UPI/Bettmann Newsphotos)*

The rise of Labour was striking, but it was the Conservative leader, Stanley Baldwin (1867–1947), who set the tone for British politics between the wars in three stints as prime minister, in 1923, 1924 to 1929, and 1935 to 1937. Although he was the wealthy son of a steel manufacturer, Baldwin deliberately departed from the old aristocratic style of British conservative politics. More down-to-earth and pragmatic than his predecessors, he was the first British prime minister to use radio effectively, and he made an effort to foster good relations with the workers. Yet Baldwin's era was one of growing social tension.

With exports declining, unemployment remained high in Britain throughout the interwar period, never falling below 10 percent. The coal industry, though still the country's largest employer, had become a particular trouble spot in the British economy. As coal exports declined, British mineowners became ever more aggressive in their dealings with labor, finally, in 1926, insisting on a longer workday and a wage cut of 13 percent to restore competitiveness. The result was a coalminers' strike in May that promptly turned into a general strike, involving almost all of organized labor, or about 4 million workers, in the most notable display of trade-union solidarity Britain had ever seen. For nine days the British economy was at a virtual standstill. But threats of arrest and a growing public backlash forced the union leadership to back down, accepting a compromise. The miners continued the strike on their own, but they finally returned to work six months later at considerably lower wages.

Although for somewhat different reasons, Britain and France both failed during the 1920s to take advantage of what would soon seem, in retrospect, to have been a precious opportunity to adjust their economies, to heal social wounds, and thereby to create a deeper consensus and a more meaningful democracy. The lost opportunity would mean growing social tensions once the relative prosperity of the twenties had ended.

Enforcing the Versailles Settlement

In the aftermath of World War I, France was unquestionably the dominant power on the European continent, and until well into the 1930s it boasted the strongest army in the world. Yet even in the early twenties there was something artificial about that strength; thus the shrillness, the defensiveness, and finally the resignation that marked French thinking and French policy.

In light of Germany's stronger demographic and industrial base, French security seemed to require certain measures to tip the short-term scales in its favor. By imposing German disarmament and the demilitarization of the Rhineland, the Versailles treaty gave France immediate military advantages. Yet each of these measures was in some ways artificial. How long could they be maintained, once the passions of war had died down, and once Germany no longer seemed such a threat? Much depended on agreement between France and Britain, but during the 1920s Britain pulled back from the Continent somewhat, just as it had after other major European wars.

British leaders felt compelled to address problems in the British Empire, especially after the war had stimulated anticolonial sentiment in Egypt, India, and elsewhere. But Britain especially wanted to avoid getting dragged into the uncertain situation in east-central Europe, where vital British interests did not seem to be at stake. As France developed its alliance system in that region, the British grew wary of close ties and clear agreements with the French.

Even when Western Europe was at issue, Britain was reluctant to get closely linked to France, which seemed unnecessarily vindictive and bellicose. Indeed, the Versailles treaty increasingly seemed counterproductive to the British, who placed great store in the League of Nations and in the international arms reduction effort prominent by the later 1920s. So France found itself with ever less support from its wartime allies as it sought to enforce the peace settlement. As the provisions of Versailles were gradually revised, France lost the advantages it had gained by defeating Germany. By the mid-1930s, a note of fatalism and resignation had crept into French thinking.

At first, France felt confident enough to go it alone if necessary. In response to German foot-dragging in paying reparations, Prime Minister Raymond Poincaré decided to get tough in January 1923. Declaring the Germans in default, he sent French troops at the head of an international force to occupy the Ruhr industrial area and force German compliance. But the move backfired. The costs of this military intervention more than offset the increase in reparations that France received, so the French government had to raise taxes to pay for the venture. Moreover, the move further alienated the British, whose lack of support bordered on active hostility.

The Ruhr occupation of 1923 proved the last time the French dared to go it alone to enforce the postwar settlement, defying the opinions of others as necessary. Its counterproductive outcome led the French to try a more conciliatory policy, and by 1924 a new, more conciliatory era began.

In both France and Britain, elections in 1924 produced victories for the moderate left, ending the conservative nationalist dominance that had resulted from the first postwar elections. In each country, international relations was a major issue in the elections, and the victories of the moderate left portended a more conciliatory tack. But the scope for international reconciliation depended considerably on the course of the new democracy in Germany.

The Weimar Republic in Germany: A Candle Burning at Both Ends

With the Weimar Republic of 1918–1933, Germany experienced a full-fledged parliamentary democracy for the first time, but that democracy had great difficulty establishing its legitimacy, and it reached an impasse when confronted with the depression by 1930. As a result of this impasse, the Nazi leader Adolf Hitler (1889–1945) got a chance to govern early in 1933. He immediately began creating a new regime, the Third Reich, intended as the antithesis of Weimar democracy. But though Hitler and the Nazis were bitterly hostile to the republic and exploited its weaknesses, they were not directly responsible for its failure. So we will wait until the next chapter to consider Nazism in detail. To understand why the new German democracy failed, we must examine the Weimar Republic on its own terms, remembering that no one knew where its failure would lead.

Because its failure led to Nazism, the Weimar Republic has been much scrutinized. What might its leaders have done differently to produce a more viable democracy at this point in German history? Are the republic's immediate problems enough to explain its failure, or was some longer-term German aversion to democratic institutions crucial as well? Certainly many Germans were skeptical of this new regime, although many came around to support it, at least as the lesser of evils. But whether that kind of support afforded the resiliency a democracy needs to weather a crisis was by no means clear.

Germany's Cautious Revolution

The Weimar Republic had two strikes against it virtually from the outset: It was born of national defeat, and it was forced to take responsibility for the harsh and dictated Treaty of Versailles in 1919. During its first years, moreover, the regime encountered severe economic dislocation, culminating in hyperinflation by 1923, as well as ideological polarization that threatened to tear the country apart.

Although Germany had strong military and authoritarian traditions, the initial threat to the new democracy came not from the right, disoriented and discredited, but from the left, stimulated by the Russian example. Those seeking further revolution, and those who feared it, could easily equate the proclamation of a German republic in November 1918 with the first revolution in Russia; as in Russia, the new, more democratic order could prove a mere prelude to communist revolution.

Spearheaded by Karl Liebknecht and Rosa Luxemburg in Berlin, revolutionary unrest reached its peak in Germany during December 1918 and January 1919. But even after Liebknecht and Luxemburg were captured and murdered in January, there remained a serious chance of further revolution through May 1919, and commu-

Leftist Agitation in Berlin, January 9, 1919 The possibility of further revolution dominated the first months of the new Weimar Republic. *(Bildarchiv Preussischer Kulturbesitz)*

nist revolutionary agitation continued to flare up until the end of 1923.

As it turned out, there was no further revolution, partly because the parallel between Germany and Russia carried only so far. The new German government had made peace, whereas the leaders of the provisional government in Russia had sought to continue the war. Moreover, those who ended up controlling the councils that sprang up in Germany during the fall of 1918 favored political democracy, not communist revolution, and thus they supported the provisional government.

Still, the revolutionary minority constituted a credible threat. And the new government made repression of the extreme left a priority—even if it meant leaving in place some of the institutions and personnel of the old imperial system. In November 1918, at the birth of the new republic, the moderate socialist leader Friedrich Ebert had agreed with General Groener to preserve the old imperial officer corps to help prevent further revolution.

But when the regular army, weakened by war and defeat, proved unable to control radical agitation in Berlin in December, it seemed that the republic would have to take extraordinary measures to defend itself from the revolutionary left. With the support of Ebert and Groener, Gustav Noske (1868–1946), the minister of national defense, began to organize the Free Corps, irregular volunteer paramilitary groups to be used against the left. Noske, who was a Socialist, but one long supportive of the military, noted that "somebody will have to be the bloodhound—I won't shirk the responsibility."[3]

During the first five months of 1919, the government unleashed the Free Corps to crush leftist revolutionary movements all over Germany, often with wanton brutality. In relying on right-wing paramilitary groups, the republic's leaders were playing with fire, but the immediate threat at this point came from the left. In 1920, however, the government faced a right-wing coup attempt, the Kapp Putsch. The army declined to defend the republic, but the government managed to survive the challenge thanks largely to a general strike by leftist workers. The republic's early leaders had to juggle both extremes because, as one of them put it, the Weimar Republic was "a candle burning at both ends."

With the advent of the republic in 1918, Germany experienced a dramatic political revolution, but it proved to be *only* a political revolution. It did not entail significant change in the social hierarchy or in economic relationships. There was no program to break up the cartels, with their concentrations of economic power. Even on the level of government personnel, continuity was more striking than change. There was no effort to build a loyal republican army, and no attempt to purge the bureaucracy and the judiciary of antidemocratic elements from the old imperial order. Thus, those who ran the new government day-to-day were often skeptical of democracy, even hostile to the new regime.

In light of the republic's eventual failure, the willingness of its early leaders to leave intact so much from the old order has made them easy targets for criticism. It can be argued, however, that the course they followed—heading off the extreme left, reassuring the established elites, and playing for time—was the republic's best chance of success. The new regime established its legitimacy by inertia, much like the Third Republic in France, which had similarly been born of defeat. In the event of an early crisis, however, a republic consolidating itself in this cautious way was likely to find few active defenders.

The Difficulties of a Multiparty System

Those who proclaimed Germany a republic promptly arranged elections for a constituent assembly, which were held in January 1919. In February, the assembly convened at Weimar, seat of what seemed the best traditions of German culture, to draft a constitution. The assembly selected Ebert to be the republic's first president, and Ebert called upon one of his Socialist colleagues to form the new regime's first cabinet.

In the January elections, the Socialists had won 163 of the 421 seats—a large plurality of the vote, but not a majority. Indeed, no single party ever won an absolute majority during Weimar years, so government was always by party coalition. The second and third largest vote-getters in 1919—the Catholic Center party, with 89 seats, and the German Democratic party (DDP), with 75 seats—were also committed to the new republic and joined with the SPD to form the "Weimar coalition."

Hopes for the consolidation of the new democracy in Germany rested especially with these three parties, yet there was something curious about the position of each. The DDP included a number of prestigious intellectuals as well as professionals and progressive businessmen. A decent, rational party, it proved unable to broaden its constituency, and its strength declined steadily after its promising beginning in 1919. The Center party was based on common Catholic religious affiliation, but it was socially heterogeneous and tended to fragment on key socioeconomic issues. And because it was not seeking to reach out to Protestants, the Center party was unlikely to become the broadly based moderate party the republic needed.

The socialists of the SPD had led the creation of the republic, but their role proved especially difficult. By taking responsibility for governing under these extraordinary circumstances, and, more particularly, by repeatedly cracking down on the extreme left, the SPD became easy prey to attacks from the Communists, who were seeking to win over the SPD's rank-and-file support. So the SPD's leaders had to insist that they, too, were socialists, with a special attachment to the working class. And though the SPD would participate in several Weimar governments, the party had to avoid becoming too closely identified with this bourgeois republic.

The results of the first regular Reichstag elections, held in dramatic circumstances in June 1920, brought the dilemmas facing all supporters of the republic—but especially the Socialists—starkly into the open. Fearing an electoral backlash, the government established in 1919 had been reluctant to hold elections just after it had been forced to accept the widely resented Versailles treaty. Its foot-dragging lent support to the Kapp Putsch of March 1920. But in this still volatile situation, the general strike that helped defeat the putsch took on a revolutionary character. After this leftist agitation, too, was crushed—through another application of Free Corps violence—the government felt secure enough to hold the elections. After all, it had just stood firm against major threats from both the right and the left. But when the parliamentary elections finally took place in June 1920, the Weimar coalition suffered a significant defeat, dropping from 76 to 47 percent of the seats. The results of this election, like many of those that followed, indicated a lack of consensus and a troubling tendency toward polarization and extremism in the German electorate.

After their defeat in the 1920 elections, the three Weimar coalition parties—the parties most committed to democratic institutions—were never again to achieve a parliamentary majority. Polarization to the left favored the Communists. To the right, the situation was more complex. On the extreme right, the National Socialists, or Nazis, were noisy and often violent, but they did not attract much electoral support until 1930. More damaging to parliamentary democracy for most of the Weimar period was the right-wing Nationalist party (DNVP), which played on nationalist resentments and fears of socialism and offered only the most tenuous support for democratic institutions. Also leaning to the right was the German People's Party (DVP), but it was

THE TWENTIES

March 1919	Founding of the Italian fascist movement
November 1920	End of fighting in the Russian civil war
October 1922	Mussolini becomes Italian prime minister
January 1923	French-led occupation of the Ruhr
January 1924	First Labor Government in Britain
January 1924	Death of Lenin
August 1924	Acceptance of the Dawes Plan on German reparations
October 1925	Locarno Agreements
May 1926	Pilsudski's coup d'état in Poland
May 1926	Beginning of general strike in Britain
August 1929	Acceptance of the Young Plan on German reparations
October 1929	Death of Stresemann

more flexible and seemed to represent the best hope of broadening the republic's base of support.

Gustav Stresemann and the Years of Tentative Consolidation

All was not necessarily lost for the republic when the three Weimar coalition parties were defeated in 1920. Others, unsupportive or hostile at first, might be gradually won over. After the death of President Ebert in 1925, Paul von Hindenburg, the emperor's field marshal, was elected president. That a conservative military leader from the old order would assume this role suggested to skeptics that the new regime was legitimate—and a worthy object for German patriotism. But the individual who best exemplified this scope for conversion was the leader of the DVP, Gustav Stresemann (1878–1929), who as chancellor, and especially as foreign minister, proved the Republic's leading statesman.

Stresemann was conservative in background and instinct. Early in 1918, for example, he was among the many to acclaim the annexationist treaty of Brest-Litovsk, and he was sufficiently frustrated with the new republic by 1920 tacitly to acquiesce in the Kapp Putsch. But the volatility that still marked German politics during 1920 suggested that the alternative to the new republic would not be the conservative monarchy that he still preferred in principle but increasing polarization leading to the triumph of the extreme left. Moreover, it had become clear by 1920 that the new democratic republic was not likely to be revolutionary on the socioeconomic level. It made sense, then, to work actively to make the new regime succeed; the alternative could be much worse. Moreover, within the framework that the new republic afforded, Germany could pursue its international aims, most immediately the revision of Versailles and a return to great power status. So although Stresemann was never emotionally attached to democratic ideals, he came to accept the republic and did his best to make it work.

Stresemann moved to center stage under the most difficult of circumstances. By the summer of 1923, Germany's response to the French occupation of the Ruhr had transformed an already serious inflationary problem, stemming initially from wartime deficit spending, into one of the great hyperinflations in history. At its height, when it took 4.2 trillion marks to equal a dollar, Germans were forced to take wheelbarrows of paper currency to buy ordinary grocery items. Simply printing the necessary currency was a severe strain for the government.

In August 1923, with the inflation raging out of control, Stresemann became chancellor. During his pivotal three-month tenure, he managed to stabilize prices, partly by spearheading a major currency reform and partly by drastically reducing government spending. Within months Germany was back on its feet, exporting more and again growing economically. But even more dramatically than in France, the rampant inflation, and the readjustment necessary to control it, wiped out the life savings of ordinary people, while serving the interests of speculators and those in debt, including some large industrialists. This inequity left scars that remained even as Germany enjoyed a measure of prosperity in the years that followed.

Germany surmounted the immediate inflationary crisis partly because of the more conciliatory attitude developing among the other powers. By November of 1923 even the French agreed that an international commission should review the reparations question, specifying realistic amounts based on Germany's ability to pay. During the summer of 1924, a commission led by the American financier Charles G. Dawes produced the Dawes Plan, which remained in force until 1929. The plan worked well by pinpointing revenue sources, lowering payments, providing loans, and securing the stability of the German currency.

At the same time, Stresemann understood that better relations with the victors, starting with France, had to be a priority if Germany was not only to overcome the present crisis but also to return to the councils of the great powers. French foreign minister Aristide Briand (1862–1932) shared Stresemann's desire for improved relations, and together they engineered the new, more conciliatory spirit in international relations evident by 1924. Its most substantial fruit was the Locarno Agreement of October 1925. France and Germany accepted the postwar border between the two countries, which meant that Germany gave up any claim to Alsace-Lorraine. France, for its part, renounced the sort of direct military intervention in Germany that it had attempted with the Ruhr invasion of 1923 and agreed to begin withdrawing troops from the Rhineland ahead of schedule. On the other hand, Germany now freely accepted France's key advantage, the demilitarization of the Rhineland, and Britain and Italy now explicitly guaranteed the measure.

By accepting the status quo in the west, Stresemann was freeing Germany to concentrate on the east, where he envisioned gradual but substantial revision in the territorial settlement that had resulted from the war. Especially with the creation of Poland, that settlement had come partly at Germany's expense. Stresemann, then, was pursuing German interests, not subordinating them to some larger European vision; but he was willing to compromise and, for the most part, to play by the rules as he did so.

With the Locarno treaty, the victors accepted Germany as a diplomatic equal for the first time since the war. Germany's return to good graces culminated in its entry into the League of Nations in 1926, further evidence of conciliation that was widely welcomed. Indeed, Stresemann and Briand were joint winners of the Nobel Peace Prize for 1926.

Still, Stresemann had already discovered that even successes in dealing with Germany's former enemies could prove costly to him and his party in the volatile German political climate. Beginning in 1924 the German Nationalist party continually exploited German resentments by criticizing Stresemann's compromises with the victors of 1918—in accepting the Dawes Plan, for example. Stresemann concluded that the only way to overcome this domestic political volatility was to complete the revision of the Versailles treaty as quickly as possible. But his negotiations continued to agitate the German electorate.

With the expiration of the Dawes Plan in 1929, the Young Plan, spearheaded by American businessman Owen D. Young, removed Allied controls over the German economy but also required that Germany pay reparations until 1988. The annual amount was less than Germany had been paying, and it was expected that this plan constituted a permanent, and reasonable, settlement. The Young Plan produced considerable resentment in Germany nevertheless, leading, once again, to political gains on the right.

Hopes for Peace Foreign ministers Aristide Briand (left) of France and Gustav Stresemann of Germany spearheaded the improved international relations that bred optimism during the later 1920s. *(UPI/Bettmann Newsphotos)*

The political controversy that surrounded Stresemann, a German conservative pursuing conventional national interests, indicates how volatile the German political situation remained, even with the dramatically improved economic and diplomatic climate of the later 1920s. Still, Stresemann's diplomatic successes were considerable, and his death in October 1929, at the age of 51, was a severe blow to the republic.

The End of the Weimar Republic

Although Weimar Germany was considerably better off in 1929 than it had been in 1923, the political consensus remained weak, the political party system remained fragmented, and unstable coalition government remained the rule. The onset of the economic depression by the end of 1929 produced problems that Germany's fragile new democracy proved unable to handle. The pivotal issue was unemployment insurance, which became a tremendous financial burden for the government as unemployment grew. As it happened, a Socialist chancellor, Hermann Müller

(1876–1931), was leading the government when the Depression began, and as the crisis deepened, his party demanded increases in insurance coverage. When they failed to convince their coalition partners, the Müller government resigned in March 1930. That proved to be the end of normal parliamentary government in Weimar Germany.

To replace Müller, President Hindenburg called upon the Center party's Heinrich Brüning (1885–1970), who proposed to the Reichstag a hard-nosed, deflationary economic program, intended to stimulate exports by lowering prices. Brüning was typical of middle-class opinion in his fear of inflation, his distaste for unemployment insurance, and his belief that Germany could not afford public works projects to pump up demand—the obvious alternative to his deflationary policy. Still, Brüning's program encountered opposition not only from socialists but also from conservatives, who were beginning to sense the chance to undermine the republic altogether. As a result, Brüning could get no parliamentary majority. Rather than resign, he invoked Article 48, the emergency provision of the Weimar constitution, which enabled him to govern under presidential decree.

When this expedient provoked strenuous protests, Brüning dissolved the Reichstag and held new elections in September 1930. The SPD and the Center party held their own, but the two other republican parties, the DDP and the DVP, lost heavily. The big winners were the two extremes. The Communists gained 23 seats, for a total of 77 deputies in the Reichstag; the National Socialists did even better, climbing from the 12 seats they had garnered in 1928 to 107.

Brüning continued to govern, still relying on President Hindenburg and Article 48 rather than majority support in the Reichstag. His efforts climaxed in December 1931 with a series of deflationary measures that, among other things, further raised taxes and decreased government spending, even for unemployment benefits. But the impact on the economy was disappointing.

In May 1932, Hindenburg's advisers finally persuaded him to dump Brüning in favor of an antidemocratic conservative. The republic was becoming a mere shell covering the back-room manipulation and dealing in Hindenburg's circle. But the results of the elections that followed in July 1932 proved the republic's death knell. The Nazis won 37.3 percent of the vote (230 seats), and the Communists 14.3 percent (89 seats). Together, the two extremes controlled a majority of the seats in the Reichstag, and each refused to work in coalition with any of the mainstream parties. Although he resisted for months, Hindenburg found it difficult not to give Adolf Hitler, as the leader of the largest party in the Reichstag, a chance to govern. He finally called upon Hitler to form a government in January 1933.

It became clear almost immediately that the outcome of the Weimar crisis was a dramatic change of regime, the triumph of Hitler and Nazism. But though the Nazis had always wanted to destroy it, the Weimar Republic failed on its own—or collapsed from within—because of its structural problems. It was not a viable, working institution that the Nazis overthrew. Nor was the Republic's failure the result of sabotage by antidemocratic elements left untouched in the cautious revolution of 1918–1920. Such elements existed, and they were not above sabotage, but what ultimately mattered was the weakness of the postwar German political consensus, which brought first instability, then virtual paralysis.

During the brief and tortured history of the republic, there were twenty different cabinets, lasting an average of eight and a half months each. By the early thirties, the system had reached an impasse and thus seemed incapable of confronting a major socioeconomic crisis. This experience of instability, divisiveness, and finally paralysis reinforced the perception, which had long been strong in Germany, that parliamentary democracy was petty, divisive, and ineffective. By 1932, the majority of the German electorate had simply lost confidence in the institutions of parliamentary democracy. Even those who voted for the Nazis at that point were not clear what they might be getting instead, but, in light of economic depression and political impasse, it seemed time to try something else.

The Search for Meaning in a Disordered World

For all its vitality, the new culture of the 1920s had something shrill, or brittle, about it; the frenetic pace masked a deeper sense that things had started to come apart and might well get worse.

So the feeling of release and excitement combined with an anxious longing for stability, for a return to order. The war had accelerated the long-term "modernization" process toward large industries, cities, and bureaucracies, and toward mass politics, society, and culture. That process was positive, even liberating, in certain respects, but it was also disruptive and disturbing. Thus the emphases of intellectuals and artists differed dramatically in the 1920s.

Anxiety, Alienation, and Disillusionment

Concern about the dangers of the emerging mass civilization was especially clear in the *Revolt of the Masses* (1930), by the influential Spanish thinker José Ortega y Gasset (1883–1955). Ortega concluded that contemporary experience showed that ordinary people were intolerant and illiberal, incapable of creating standards, and content with the least common denominator. Communism and fascism indicated the violent, intolerant, and ultimately barbaric quality of the new mass age. But Ortega found the same tendencies in American-style democracy. Much of Europe seemed to be moving toward the mass politics and culture of the United States, but, as far as Ortega was concerned, that was a symptom of the deeper problem, not a solution.

Concern with cultural decline was part of a wider pessimism about the condition of the West, which stood in stark contrast to the belief in progress, and the attendant confidence in Western superiority, that had been essential to Western self-understanding before 1914. The German thinker Oswald Spengler (1880–1936) made concern with decline almost fashionable with his bestseller of the immediate postwar years, *The Decline of the West* (1918), which offered a cyclical theory purporting to explain how spirituality and creativity were giving way to a materialistic mass-based culture in the West.

To Sigmund Freud, the eruption of violence and hatred during the war and after indicated a deep, instinctual problem in the human makeup. In his gloomy essay *Civilization and Its Discontents* (1930), he suggested that the progress of civilization entails the bottling up of aggressive instincts, which are directed inward, as guilt, or left to erupt in violent outbursts. This notion raised fundamental questions not only about the idea of progress but also about the plausibility of the Wilsonian ideals that had surrounded the end of the war. Perhaps, with civilization growing more complex, the Great War had been only the beginning of a new era of hatred and violence.

The sense that there is something incomprehensible, even nightmarish about modern civilization, with its ever more complex bureaucracies, technologies, and cities, found vivid expression in the works of the Czech Jewish writer Franz Kafka (1883–1924), most notably in the novels *The Trial* and *The Castle,* published posthumously in the mid-twenties. In a world that claimed to be increasingly rational, Kafka's individual is the lonely, fragile plaything of forces utterly beyond reason, comprehension, and control. In such a world, the quest for law, or meaning, or God is futile, ridiculous.

Especially in the unsettled conditions of Weimar Germany, the anxiety of the 1920s tended to take extreme forms, from irrational activism to a preoccupation with death. There was a striking increase in suicides among students, even before the Depression. Youthful alienation prompted the novelist Jakob Wassermann (1873–1934) to caution German young people in 1932 that not all action is good simply because it is action, that feeling is not always better than reason and discipline, and that youth is not in itself a badge of superiority.

Recasting the Tradition

Expressions of disillusionment revealed something about human experience in the unsettled new world, but they were sometimes morbid and self-indulgent. Other cultural leaders sought to be more positive; the challenge was not to give vent to new anxieties but to find antidotes to them. One direction was to recast traditional categories—in the arts, in religion, in politics—to make them relevant to contemporary experience. Although not all were optimistic about human prospects, an array of figures found such a renewal of tradition to be the best hope for responding to the disarray of the postwar world.

Even modernist artists sought to consolidate earlier gains, to pull things back together after the headlong experiment of the years before 1914. In music composers as different as Igor Stravinsky (1882–1971) and Paul Hindemith (1895–1963) adapted earlier styles, although often in a somewhat ironic spirit, as they sought to weave new means of expression into familiar forms. The overall tendency toward neoclassicism during the period was an effort to give musical composition a renewed basis of order.

One of the most striking responses to the anxieties of this increasingly secular age was a wave of neo-orthodox religious thinking, most prominent in Protestants like the Swiss theologian Karl Barth (1886–1968). In his *Epistle to the Romans* (1919), Barth reacted against the liberal theology, the attempt to marry religious categories to secular progress, that had become prominent by the later nineteenth century. The war, especially, had seemed to shatter the liberal notion that the hand of God was at work in history, and Barth emphasized the radical cleft between God and this, the human world of history, sunken in sin. Recalling the accents of Augustine and Luther, he portrayed humanity as utterly lost, capable only of a difficult relationship with God, through faith, grace, and revelation.

Croce's Antifascism Already widely known as a philosopher of art, the Italian thinker Benedetto Croce began speaking out against fascism in 1925. His subsequent efforts to revitalize liberal democracy helped inspire the Italian resistance to fascism and made him one of the world's most respected intellectuals. *(UPI/Bettmann Newsphotos)*

With democracy faring poorly in parts of Europe, and with fascism and communism claiming to offer superior alternatives, some sought to make new sense of the democratic tradition. In Italy, Benedetto Croce (1866–1952) agreed with critics that the old justifications for liberal democracy, based on natural law or utilitarianism, were deeply inadequate, but he also became one of Europe's most influential antifascists. He insisted that the most significant innovations in modern thought show us why democratic values, institutions, and practices are still appropriate. We human beings are free, creative agents of a history that we make as best we can, without quite understanding what will result from what we do. Humility, tolerance, and equal access to political participation are essential to the process whereby the world is endlessly remade.

The new political challenges also stimulated fresh thinking within the Marxist tradition. By showing that Marxism could encompass consciousness as well as economic relationships, the Hungarian Georg Lukács (1885–1971) invited a far more sophisticated Marxist analysis of capitalist culture than had been possible before. Lukács accented the progressive role of realistic fiction and attacked the disordered fictional world of Kafka, which seemed to abandon all hope for human understanding of the forces of history. Though more eclectic, the Institute for Social Research, founded in Frankfurt, Germany, in 1923, gave rise to an influential tradition of criticism of capitalist civilization in what came to be known as the Frankfurt School. These innovations helped give the Marxist tradition a new lease on life in the West, even as it was developing in unforeseen ways in the Soviet Union.

The Search for a New Tradition

While some sought renewal from within the tradition, others insisted that a more radical break was needed—but also that the elements for a viable new cultural tradition were available.

Reflecting on the situation of women writers in 1928, the British novelist Virginia Woolf

Tradition and Women: The Conditions of Independence

Speaking in 1928 about the situation of women writers, Virginia Woolf raised questions that were relevant to all women seeking the opportunity to realize their potential. Indeed, her reflections about the value of difference, and the need for particular traditions, inspired those seeking equal opportunity for decades to come. And her question about why we know so little about women's lives in the past—in the Elizabethan age of the later sixteenth century, for example—helped stimulate later historians to ask precisely the questions she envisioned about the experience of ordinary people.

Woman . . . pervades poetry from cover to cover; she is all but absent from history. . . .

Occasionally an individual woman is mentioned, an Elizabeth, or a Mary; a queen or a great lady. But by no possible means could middle-class women with nothing but brains and character at their command have taken part in any one of the great movements which, brought together, constitute the historian's view of the past. . . . What one wants . . . is a mass of information; at what age did she marry; how many children had she as a rule; what was her house like; had she a room to herself; did she do the cooking; would she be likely to have a servant? All these facts lie somewhere, presumably, in parish registers and account books; the life of the average Elizabethan woman must be scattered about somewhere, could one collect it and make a book of it. . . .

But whatever effect discouragement and criticism had upon their writing—and I believe they had a very great effect—that was unimportant compared with the other difficulty which faced them (I was still considering those early nineteenth-century novelists) when they came to set their thoughts on paper—that is that they had no tradition behind them, or one so short and partial that it was of little help. For we think back through our mothers if we are women. It is useless to go to the great men writers for help, however much one may go to them for pleasure. . . . The weight, the pace, the stride of a man's mind are too unlike her own for her to lift anything substantial from him successfully. . . .

. . . [W]omen have sat indoors all these millions of years, so that by this time the very walls are permeated by their creative force, which has, indeed, so overcharged the capacity of bricks and mortar that it must needs harness itself to pens and brushes and business and politics. But this creative power differs greatly from the creative power of men. And one must conclude that it would be a thousand pities if it were hindered or wasted, for it was won by centuries of the most drastic discipline, and there is nothing to take its place. It would be a thousand pities if women wrote like men, or lived like men, or looked like men. . . . Ought not education to bring out and fortify the differences rather than the similarities?

Source: Virginia Woolf, *A Room of One's Own* (San Diego: Harcourt Brace Jovanovich, 1929), pp. 45–47, 79, 91.

(1882–1941) showed how women in the past had suffered from the absence of a tradition of writing by women. By the 1920s, women had made important strides, but Woolf suggested that further advance required a more self-conscious effort by women to develop their own tradition. Most basically, women needed greater financial independence so that they could have scholarships, the leisure of cultivated conversation, the privacy of "a room of one's own." Woolf also envisioned a new sort of historical inquiry, focusing on how ordinary women lived their lives, that could show contemporary women where they have come from—and thus deepen their sense of who they are (see the box, "Tradition and Women: The Conditions of Independence").

Ernst: Forest (1927) Seeking to let the subconscious manifest itself, surrealist painters produced eery, ambiguous, sometimes troubling images, like the "forest" paintings by Max Ernst (1891–1976). Insisting that "the artist is a spectator, indifferent or impassioned, at the birth of his work," Ernst devised special techniques to break down conscious control. *(Staatliche Kunsthalle, Karlsruhe)*

A very different effort to establish a new tradition developed in Paris in the early twenties as the poet André Breton (1896–1966) spearheaded the surrealist movement in literature and the visual arts. Surrealism grew directly from Dada, an artistic movement that had emerged in neutral Zurich and elsewhere during the war. Radically hostile to the war, Dada artists developed shocking, sometimes nihilistic forms to deal with a reality that now seemed senseless and out of control. Some made collages from gutter trash; others indulged in nonsense or relied on chance. By the early 1920s, however, the surrealists felt it was time to create a new and deeper basis of order after the willful disordering of Dada. Having learned from Sigmund Freud about the subconscious, they sought to adapt Dada's novel techniques—especially the use of chance—to gain access to the subconscious, which they believed contains a deeper truth, without the overlay of logic, reason, and conscious control.

But other artists, seeking to embrace the modern industrial world in a more positive spirit, found surrealism merely escapist. Among them was Walter Gropius (1883–1969), a pioneering modernist architect and leader of the influential German art school, the Bauhaus, during the 1920s. (See the feature, "Weighing the Evidence: Modern Design,"on pages 1066–1067.) Gropius held that it was possible to establish new forms of culture, even "a new tradition," that could be affirmative and reassuring in the face of the postwar cultural disarray. Rather than putting up familiar neoclassical or neo-Gothic buildings, "feigning a culture that has long since disappeared," we must face up to the kind of civilization we have become—urban, industrial, technological, democratic, mass-based, efficient. If we pick and choose among the elements of our new machine-based civilization, we can again have a culture that works, an "integrated pattern for living."[4]

This "constructive," promodern impulse was particularly prominent in Germany, but it could be found all over—in the modernists of the Russian Revolution, in the French painter Fernand Léger (1881–1955), in the Swiss architect Le Corbusier (1887–1965). Whereas many of their contemporaries were at best ambivalent about the masses, these artists sought to bring high art and mass society together in the interests of both. And they welcomed the new patterns of life that seemed to be emerging in the new world of mass production and fast-paced cities.

Summary

The 1920s proved a contradictory period of vitality and despair, pacifism and violence, restabilization and instability. The era began with bright hopes for democracy, yet the outcome of the democratic experiment in east-central Europe was disappointing. In Germany as well, the new democratic republic remained on the defensive, then failed to weather the economic depression that began in 1929. Even Italy, heir by the 1920s to a respectable tradition of democracy, gave rise to the troubling new phenomenon of fascism. A hopeful new spirit of international conciliation drew France and Germany closer together by the end of 1925, but France and Britain seemed to draw further apart.

Despite tensions and doubts, however, the disruptions of the immediate postwar years had apparently been surmounted by early 1929, when restabilization seemed to have taken hold in Europe. Even Germany, Italy, and the Soviet Union, the most volatile and potentially disruptive of the major countries, seemed to be settling down. Still, it would all come apart over the next decade, leading to political extremism and another major war. In light of that outcome, the successes, even

Léger: Three Women With their sleekly impersonal forms, Fernand Léger's paintings suggested that human beings could fit comfortably into the mass machine age that was emerging. This work dates from 1921. *(Léger, Fernand,* Three Women (Le grand dejeuner), *1921. Oil on canvas, 6'¼" x 8'3". The Museum of Modern Art, New York. Mrs. Simon Guggenheim Fund.)*

the vitality, of the 1920s appear superficial, and the unrecognized tensions stand out. Thus the importance of taking the decade on its own terms. But while the vitality, the renewed prosperity, and the diplomatic good will were all real, so were the unresolved problems that made the twenties a prelude to the more difficult thirties, when the notion that Europe had returned to normal came to seem but a fairy tale.

Notes

1. Quoted in Martin McCauley, *The Soviet Union Since 1917* (London and New York: Longman, 1981), pp. 72–73.
2. Benito Mussolini, speech to the Italian Chamber of Deputies, January 3, 1925, from Charles F. Delzell, ed., *Mediterranean Fascism, 1919–1945* (New York: Harper & Row, 1970), pp. 59–60.
3. Quoted in Robert G. L. Waite, *Vanguard of Nazism: The Free Corps Movement in Postwar Germany, 1918–1923* (New York: W. W. Norton, 1969), pp. 14–15.
4. Walter Gropius, *Scope of Total Architecture* (New York: Collier Books, 1962), pp. 15, 67.

Suggested Reading

General Surveys

Ansprenger, Franz. *The Dissolution of the Colonial Empires.* 1989. Covers the whole decolonization process but is stronger than most surveys on the impact of World War I and the events of the interwar period.

Kitchen, Martin. *Europe Between the Wars: A Political History.* 1988. A clear narrative of international and domestic political developments.

Sontag, Raymond J. *A Broken World, 1919–1939.* 1971. Comprehensive survey by a master historian. Concerned especially with domestic politics and international relations but includes developments in science and the arts.

Political Restoration

Carsten, F. L. *Revolution in Central Europe, 1918–1919.* 1972. A straightforward study emphasizing Germany, Austria, and Hungary. Accents the failure to overcome conservative forces and to lay the foundations for successful democracy.

Maier, Charles S. *Recasting Bourgeois Europe: Stabilization in France, Germany, and Italy in the Decade After World War I.* 1975. An important but somewhat difficult study showing how European elites sought new bases of stability, especially through new authority relationships in industry, during the 1920s.

Marquand, David. *Ramsay MacDonald.* 1977. Thorough and balanced account of the controversial career of Britain's first Labour prime minister.

Trachtenberg, Marc. *Reparation in World Politics: France and European Economic Diplomacy, 1916–1923.* 1980. A detailed but readable study questioning the widespread view that France imposed an unreasonable reparations burden on Germany after World War I.

The Soviet Union

Cohen, Stephen F. *Bukharin and the Bolshevik Revolution: A Political Biography, 1888–1938.* 1975. A sympathetic and influential biography of the leading Soviet "moderate," who lost out to Stalin in the power struggle of the later twenties.

———. *Rethinking the Soviet Experience: Politics and History Since 1917.* 1985. Explains how the Soviet regime came to be understood as a totalitarian system, as opposed to a contingent historical outcome with scope for different directions.

Conquest, Robert. *Stalin: Breaker of Nations.* 1991. A readable biography that assesses Stalin's career in light of the bankruptcy of the Soviet system by 1991.

Lewin, M[oshe]. *Russian Peasants and Soviet Power: A Study of Collectivization.* 1975. A pioneering account of the process leading to the decision for forced collectivization by 1929.

———. *The Making of the Soviet System: Essays in the Social History of Interwar Russia.* 1985. Essays by a leading social historian. Especially strong on agriculture and the peasantry.

Stites, Richard. *Revolutionary Dreams: Utopian Visions and Experimental Life in the Russian Revolution.* 1989. A vivid account of the utopian aspirations that gave the new communist regime emotional force from 1917 to 1930.

Tucker, Robert C. *Stalin as Revolutionary, 1879–1929: A Study in History and Personality.* 1973. A pioneering account of Stalin's early years and rise to power, probing the sources of the elements of character and personality that helped shape his subsequent rule.

European Fascism

Carsten, F. L. *The Rise of Fascism.* 1971. A straightforward narrative, widely used as an introduction to the problem of European fascism.

Griffin, Roger. *The Nature of Fascism.* 1991. Sophisticated but accessible effort to identify the core of aspirations, stemming especially from the new situation created by the war and the Russian Revolution, that led to the fascist movements of the interwar period.

Payne, Stanley G. *Fascism: A Comparative Approach Toward a Definition.* 1980. On the basis of recent research, seeks a handle on the overall problem of European fascism.

Fascism in Italy

De Grand, Alexander. *Italian Fascism: Its Origins and Development.* 2d ed. 1989. An accessible overview, providing a good sense of the heterogeneity of both the purposes and the policies of Italian fascism.

Forgacs, David, ed. *Rethinking Italian Fascism: Capitalism, Populism and Culture.* 1986. An important collection of essays, reflecting critical rethinking of conventional approaches and interpretations.

Lyttelton, Adrian. *The Seizure of Power.* 2d ed. 1988. Based on pioneering archival research, this book offers a detailed dissection of the complex process through which the fascist movement took control of Italy.

Mack Smith, Denis. *Mussolini: A Biography.* 1983. A lively, critical account, and the most important biography of Mussolini in English.

Sarti, Roland. *Fascism and the Industrial Leadership in Italy, 1919–1940: A Study in the Expansion of Private Power Under Fascism.* 1971. Carefully researched study demonstrating the cat-and-mouse relationship between the fascist regime and big business.

Segré, Claudio. *Italo Balbo: A Fascist Life.* 1987. A readable biography of one of the most colorful of Mussolini's lieutenants.

Tannenbaum, Edward. *The Fascist Experience: Italian Society and Culture, 1922–1945.* 1972. A comprehensive study of life in fascist Italy.

Webster, Richard A. *The Cross and the Fasces.* 1960. Traces the development of Christian democracy in Italy from the late nineteenth century through its interaction with fascism to its triumph after World War II.

Weimar Germany

Diehl, James M. *Paramilitary Politics in Weimar Germany.* 1977. Probing account of the rise and normalization of political violence, showing how it helped undermine the Weimar Republic.

Gay, Peter. *Weimar Culture: The Outsider as Insider.* 1970. Provides a good sense of the conflicting impulses—the embrace of modernity, the nostalgia for wholeness, the sense of foreboding—that made German culture so intense and vital during the 1920s.

Kolb, Eberhard. *The Weimar Republic.* 1988. Provides a good overall survey, then pinpoints the recent trends in research and the questions at issue among historians of the period.

Laqueur, Walter. *Weimar: A Cultural History, 1918–1933.* 1980. A comprehensive, well-balanced survey, especially good on expressionism.

Schrader, Bärbel, and Jürgen Schebera. *The "Golden" Twenties: Art and Literature in the Weimar Republic.* 1988. A superbly illustrated study that gives a good sense of complexity and contradiction of German culture in the 1920s.

Stern, Fritz. *The Politics of Cultural Despair: A Study in the Rise of the Germanic Ideology.* 1961. A classic work focusing on three thinkers of the German radical right; shows how their resentment of the modernization process fed antidemocratic sentiment in Germany.

Turner, Jr., Henry Ashby. *Stresemann and the Politics of the Weimar Republic.* 1963. A well-balanced study of the most important German statesman of the Weimar period.

Willett, John. *Art and Politics in the Weimar Period: The New Sobriety, 1917–1933.* 1978. A lively, complex study that plays up the effort of German cultural innovators to make art constructive by combining it with work, production, and everyday life.

Weighing the Evidence

MODERN DESIGN

Led by Walter Gropius, the Bauhaus of Weimar Germany became the most influential art school of the twentieth century. As the incubator of modern architecture and design, it helped determine what the "modern world" would look like. And it did so consciously, believing it could help us embrace as our own the unnerving new world of machines, mass production, and rapid transit. But many, especially in the unsettled conditions of Weimar Germany, found the Bauhaus style alienating and threatening. Bauhaus artists seemed to foster all that was negative in the emerging world of industry and technology, impersonal cities and large bureaucracies. When the Nazis came to power in 1933, they promptly closed the Bauhaus down.

Things made by the Bauhaus, from chairs to housing projects, still look "modern"—but why? How do they symbolize or manifest modernity? Do these new forms lead us to affirm the modern world, or are they alienating and repelling?

We note first that the Bauhaus stressed clean lines, simple and precise forms. In designing the chair shown here, Marcel Breuer tried to eliminate everything extraneous to the function of the chair as an object to sit in. The Bauhaus's own building, illustrated here, has none of the classical or Gothic ornament—the columns and pediments, the gargoyles and pointed arches—that had long seemed essential to architecture. Notice the extensive use of glass and steel. Bauhaus architects sought to use the new materials and construction techniques that industrialization made possible. On the one hand, Bauhaus design seems coolly impersonal; on the other, utilitarian and functional.

Marcel Breuer, Chair, Tubular Steel and Black Fabric, 1925–1926 *(Bauhaus Archiv, Berlin)*

In evaluating these pioneering modern forms, we must ask what the Bauhaus architects and designers were reacting against. In the nineteenth century, historical revivals dominated architecture, but by the 1920s such historical references seemed irrelevant, even dishonest. Why should banks look like Greek temples? Why should modern universities copy Gothic guild halls? According to the Bauhaus, it was time we faced up to the fact that the industrial age has cut us off from the old tradition. At first, the experience of disruption may be troubling, but we can develop an honest, satisfying, distinctively modern style based on the possibilities and patterns of the industrial world itself.

If the modern world is one of mass culture and mass society, perhaps even the best artists need to rethink the purpose of what they do. Students at the Bauhaus were taught that art was no longer something to be venerated in a museum or acquired by a cultivated and wealthy elite. Rather, art was to be socially useful. No longer was there to be a rigid distinction between art objects and utilitarian objects. Bauhaus artists placed great emphasis on the design of ordinary things for everyday use, from desk lamps to textiles to chairs. No longer was art to express the personality of the artist. Reacting against the romantic cult of individual self-expression, the Bauhaus stressed teamwork and impersonal design. Moreover, by using new materials, mass production, and even prefabrication, artists could play a newly democratic role—in designing, for example, housing projects that would give ordinary working people more light and fresh air than older urban buildings provided. Projects like the one shown here, built for employees of the Siemens electrical company, could be constructed affordably because they stressed the efficient use of materials and avoided irrelevant ornamentation.

Mass production, efficiency, and the purging of ornaments, however, did not have to undermine beauty. According to the Bauhaus, beauty in the modern world is seen in sleekly impersonal precision, clarity, and economy of means. From the Bauhaus perspective, Breuer's chair and the Siemens housing project are beautiful because they are efficient and functional.

Others, however, found the impersonal art of the Bauhaus to be cold and materialistic. Some, including the Nazis, labeled it "international" and "Bolshevik" as well. As far as such critics were concerned, the Bauhaus was simply giving in to the tyranny of the machine.

The cultural historian Peter Gay has argued that "what Gropius taught, and what most Germans did not want to learn, was . . . that . . . the cure for the ills of modernity is more, and the right kind of modernity."[1] Surely it is true that many Germans were particularly nostalgic and resistant to change during the 1920s. But perhaps the Bauhaus was too quick to assume that in the modern world we have no choice but to start over; perhaps it underestimated the need for continuity with our cultural traditions.

The kind of thinking nurtured at the Bauhaus led to the urban renewal and freeway projects that, by the end of the 1960s, had radically altered the face of many American cities, destroying much that had connected the present with the past. We continue to wrestle with what tradition means in the face of modernity and change, but we are now less likely to assume that we can do without the old, the visible embodiments of a living tradition.

In the aftermath of World War I, however, Walter Gropius and his colleagues at the Bauhaus thought it would be healthier and more honest to make a clean break with the past. They set out with missionary fervor to derive a wholly new tradition from the modern industrial world. And controversial though they were, their designs were instrumental in giving "modern" its characteristic look.

The Bauhaus Building, Dessau, 1925–1926 *(Vanni/Art Resource, NY)*

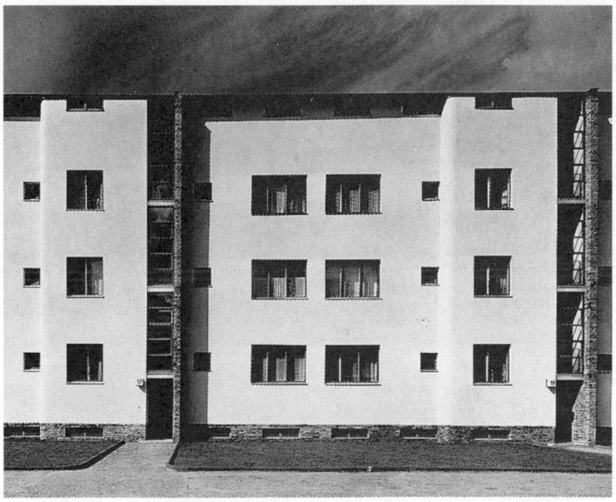

Housing Complex for Siemens Company Employees, Berlin, 1929 *(Bauhaus Archiv, Berlin)*

1. Peter Gay, *Weimar Culture: The Outsider as Insider* (New York: Harper & Row, 1970), p. 101.

CHAPTER 29

The Tortured Decade, 1930–1939

Economic depression, political polarization, and the increasing threat of a new European war dominated the 1930s. For most of the 1920s, the complicated mechanisms used to realign the international economy after the war seemed to be working. But by 1929, they were beginning to backfire, helping to trigger the Great Depression. During the early 1930s the Depression intensified sociopolitical strains all over the Western world. In Germany, it helped undermine the Weimar Republic and gave a major impetus to Nazism. The rise to power of the Nazi leader, Adolf Hitler, intensified the ideological polarization in Europe, and his policies produced a series of diplomatic crises that eventually led to a new European war.

German Nazism paralleled Italian fascism in important respects, but differed from it in others. At about the same time, the direction of Stalin's communist regime in the Soviet Union seemed to converge, in some ways, with German Nazism. So although they started from opposite ends of the political spectrum and seemed to have radically different aims, Stalinism and Nazism are sometimes lumped together as instances of totalitarianism. Both apparently sought total government control over all aspects of life in society. But though the term *totalitarianism* has become central to twentieth-century political language, it proves a tricky concept indeed, and whether it is correct to lump Stalinist communism with Nazism remains controversial.

However they are to be characterized, the new political regimes of the 1930s stood opposed to the parliamentary democracy that seemed well established in Britain, France, and elsewhere. Such parliamentary democracy had long seemed the direction of progressive political change, but in the

Execution of soldiers by a firing squad during the Spanish civil war.

face of the new regimes of the 1930s the democratic movement appeared to lose its momentum.

The Great Depression

Although the stock market crash of October 1929 in the United States helped usher in the world economic crisis of the early 1930s, it had this effect only because the new international economic order after World War I was especially fragile. By October 1929, in fact, production was already declining in all the major countries except France, though for different reasons in each.

The economies of Germany and the states of east-central Europe remained especially vulnerable after World War I, and in the newly interdependent economic world, their weaknesses magnified problems that started elsewhere. The crash of the U.S. stock market led to a restriction of credit in central Europe, which triggered a more general contraction in production and trade. Facing cruel dilemmas, policymakers proved unable to master the situation for the first few years of the crisis. The consequences—both human and political—were profound.

Sources of the Economic Contraction

Throughout the 1920s, finance ministers and central bankers had difficulty juggling the economic imbalances that had resulted from the war, especially the war debts to the United States and the reparations that Germany was required to pay France, Britain, and Belgium. The shaky new system they developed depended on U.S. bank loans to Germany, funneled partly by international agreements but also drawn by high interest rates. By 1928, however, U.S. investors were rapidly withdrawing their capital from Germany in search of the higher returns that could be made in the booming U.S. stock market. This tightened credit in Germany. And then the crash of the U.S. market in October 1929 deepened the problem by forcing suddenly strapped American investors to pull still more of their funds out of Germany. This process continued over the next two years, weakening the major banks in Germany and the other countries of central Europe, which were closely tied to the German economy. In May 1931 the bankruptcy of Vienna's most powerful bank, the Credit-Anstalt, made it clear that a crisis of potentially catastrophic proportions was in progress.

Despite attempts at adjustment on the international level, fears of bank failure or currency devaluation led to runs on the banks and currencies of Germany and east-central Europe. To resist the withdrawal of capital, government policymakers raised interest rates. This measure was not sufficient to stem the capital flight, but by restricting credit still more, it further dampened domestic economic activity.

Finally, the Germans seemed to have no choice but to freeze foreign assets—that is, to cease allowing conversion of assets held in German marks to other currencies. In this atmosphere, investors seeking the safest place for their capital tried to cash in currency for gold—or for British pounds, which could then be converted to gold. This flight to gold, however, soon put such pressure on the British currency that Britain was forced to devalue the pound and sever it from the gold standard in September 1931. This proved the definitive end of the worldwide system of economic exchange based on the gold standard.

The absence of a single standard of exchange, combined with various currency restrictions, made foreign trade more difficult and uncertain, thereby diminishing it further. So did the scramble for tariff protection that proved one widespread response to the developing crisis. Britain, for example, adopted a peacetime tariff for the first time in nearly a century with the Import Duties Act of 1932, which imposed a 10 percent tax on most imports.

The decline of trade spread depression throughout the world economic system. By 1933 most major European countries were able to export no more than two-thirds, and in some cases as little as one-third, of the amount they had sold in 1929. Losses from international bank failures contracted purchasing power and credit and furthered the downward spiral, until by 1932 the European economies had shrunk to a little over half their 1929 size. This was the astonishing outcome of the illusory prosperity of the 1920s.

Consequences and Responses

The Depression was essentially a radical contraction in economic activity; with less being produced and sold, demand for labor declined

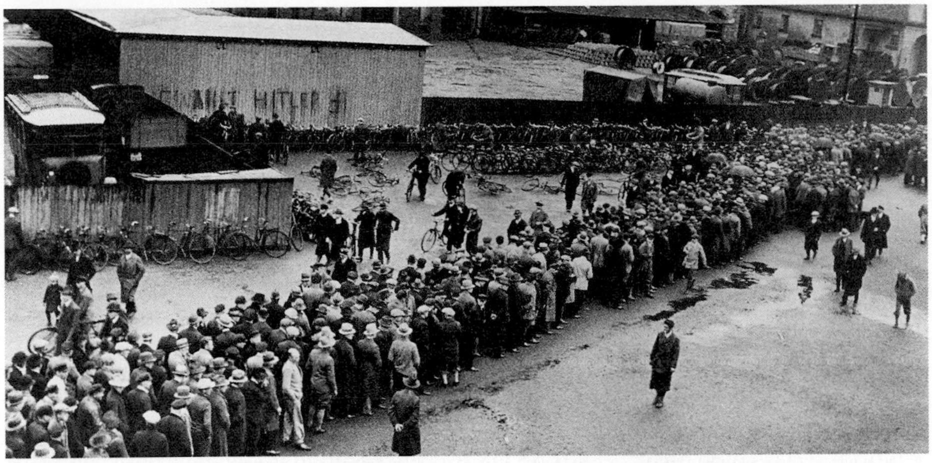

Unemployment in Weimar Germany With pro-Nazi graffiti in the background, Germans seeking work line up in front of an employment office in Hannover during the early 1930s, when the Depression was most severe. *(Archiv fur Kunst und Geschichte, Berlin)*

sharply. In Germany, industrial production by early 1933 was only half what it had been in 1929; roughly 6 million Germans, or one-third of the labor force, were unemployed.

Although its timing and severity varied, the Depression profoundly affected the lives of ordinary people throughout the Western world (see the box, "Poverty in the Emerging Consumer Society"). Unemployment produced widespread malnutrition, which led, in turn, to sharp increases in such diseases as tuberculosis, scarlet fever, and rickets. Even those who hung on to jobs suffered from growing insecurity. In his aptly titled *Little Man, What Now?* (1932), the German novelist Hans Fallada (1893–1947) explored the effects of the Depression on members of the lower middle class—store clerks, shopowners, civil servants. Such people were first resentful, then resigned, as their dreams of security, of "order and cleanliness," fell apart.

During the first years of the Depression, central bankers everywhere sought to balance budgets in order to reassure investors and stabilize the currency. Under the existing circumstances of economic contraction and declining tax revenues, balancing the budget meant reducing government spending. In addition, governments responded to the decline in exports by forcing wages down, seeking to enhance competitiveness abroad. But by cutting purchasing power at home, both these measures reinforced the contraction in economic activity.

Economic policymakers based their responses on the "classical" economic model that had developed from the ideas of Adam Smith in the eighteenth century. According to this model, a benign "invisible hand" ensured that a free-market price for labor, for capital, and for goods and services would produce an ongoing tendency to economic equilibrium. A downward turn in the business cycle was a normal and necessary adjustment; government interference would only upset this self-adjusting mechanism.

By 1932, however, it was clear that the conventional response was not working, and governments began seeking more actively to stimulate the economy. In the United States, Franklin Roosevelt defeated the incumbent, Herbert Hoover, in 1932 with the promise of a New Deal—a commitment to increase government spending to restore purchasing power. In fascist Italy, a state entity created to infuse capital into failing companies proved a reasonably effective basis for collaboration between government and business, partly because it was a pragmatic response to the Depression, not a specifically fascist innovation. After Hitler came to power in 1933, Hjalmar Schacht (1877–1970), the German finance minister, mounted an energetic assault on the economic problem. Government measures sealed off

Poverty in the Emerging Consumer Society

During the Depression, the Left Book Club, an important movement of left-leaning British intellectuals, commissioned George Orwell (1903–1950) to write a report on the conditions of unemployed miners in the north of England. Published in 1937, Orwell's study offered pioneering insights into the dynamics of relative poverty in the modern world. In this excerpt, Orwell shows how the beginnings of the consumerist revolution affected responses to the Depression.

Twenty million people are underfed but literally everyone in England has access to a radio. Whole sections of the working class who have been plundered of all they really need are being compensated, in part, by cheap luxuries which mitigate the surface of life.

... [I]t may be that the psychological adjustment which the working class are visibly making is the best they could make in the circumstances. They have neither turned revolutionary nor lost their self-respect; merely they have kept their tempers and settled down to make the best of things on a fish-and-chip standard. The alternative would be God knows what continued agonies of despair; or it might be attempted insurrections which, in a strongly governed country like England, could only lead to futile massacres and a régime of savage repression.

Of course the post-war development of cheap luxuries has been a very fortunate thing for our rulers. It is quite likely that fish and chips, art-silk stockings, tinned salmon, cut-price chocolate ..., the movies, the radio, strong tea and the Football Pools have between them averted revolution. Therefore we are sometimes told that the whole thing is an astute maneuver by the governing class ... to hold the unemployed down. What I have seen of our governing class does not convince me that they have that much intelligence. The thing has happened, but by an unconscious process—the quite natural interaction between the manufacturer's need for a market and the need of half-starved people for cheap palliatives.

... [T]he less money you have, the less inclined you feel to spend it on wholesome food.... When you are unemployed, which is to say when you are underfed, harassed, bored and miserable, you don't *want* to eat dull wholesome food. You want something a little bit "tasty." ... Unemployment is an endless misery that has got to be constantly palliated.

Source: George Orwell, *The Road to Wigan Pier* (New York: Berkley Medallion, 1961), pp. 84–85, 88–89.

the German mark from international fluctuations, stimulated public spending, partly on rearmament, and kept wages low. By 1935 Germany was back to full employment. This success added tremendously to Hitler's popularity.

But in the democracies the Depression proved particularly intractable. Although Britain saw some recovery by the mid-1930s, it was especially the rearmament of the later 1930s, financed by borrowing, or deficit spending, that got the British economy growing again. The Depression, and the halting responses of the democracies in dealing with it, enhanced the prestige of the new regimes in Germany, Italy, and the Soviet Union, which seemed either to have avoided the economic crisis or to be dealing with it more creatively. Capitalism seemed to be on trial—and so, increasingly, did parliamentary democracy.

The Stalinist Revolution in the Soviet Union

Seeking to build "socialism in one country," Joseph Stalin led the Soviet Union during the 1930s through one of the most astounding trans-

Promoting Industrial Growth With the turn to crash industrialization by 1929, the Soviet regime harnessed art to inspire enthusiastic participation in the common effort to build an industrial economy. The mix of images in this poster from about 1932 suggests that, working together, the state and the people were rapidly raising the country's socioeconomic level. *(David King Collection)*

formations the world had ever seen. It mixed change and achievement with brutality and terror in bizarre and often tragic ways. The resulting governmental system, which gave Stalin unprecedented power, proved crucial to the outcome of the great experiment that began with the Russian Revolution of 1917. But whether the fateful turn of the 1930s had been implicit in the Leninist revolutionary model all along, or stemmed mostly from unforeseen circumstances and Stalin's idiosyncratic personality, remains uncertain.

Crash Industrialization and Forced Collectivization

Stalin's strategy entailed rapid industrialization accompanied by compulsory collectivization in agriculture. By forcing peasants into large, government-controlled farms, political leaders could control agricultural pricing and distribution. On that basis, the government could squeeze a surplus from agriculture to be sold abroad, earning money to buy the equipment needed to build factories, dams, and power plants.

Beginning in 1930, the peasants were forcibly herded into collectives. So unpopular was this measure that many peasants killed their livestock or smashed their farm implements rather than have them collectivized. During the first two months of 1930, as many as 14 million head of cattle were slaughtered, resulting in an orgy of meat eating and a shortage of draft animals. In 1928, there had been 60 million cattle in the Soviet Union; by 1934 there were only 33.5 million.

Collectivization served, as intended, to squeeze from the peasantry the resources needed to finance industrialization. But it was carried out with extreme brutality. What was being squeezed was hardly a "surplus," because the state's extractions cut into subsistence. So while Soviet agricultural exports went up in the years after 1930, large numbers of peasants literally starved to death. The great famine that developed during 1932–1933 resulted in between 5 and 6 million

Carrying out the Stalinist Revolution

Lev Kopelev (b. 1912), who came from a middle-class Jewish family, was an enthusiastic Communist as a young man. Believing the Soviet Communist party embodied the progressive movement of history, he eagerly assisted in the forced collectivization drive of the early 1930s, which caused such suffering and death in his native Ukraine. But after World War II he became critical of Soviet communism, and he was finally exiled from the Soviet Union in 1980.

Our great goal was the universal triumph of Communism, and for the sake of that goal everything was permissible.... And to hesitate or doubt about all this was to give in to "intellectual squeamishness" and "stupid liberalism," the attributes of people who "could not see the forest for the trees."

... I saw what "total collectivization" meant—how ... mercilessly they stripped the peasants in the winter of 1932–33. I took part in this myself, scouring the countryside, searching for hidden grain, testing the earth with an iron rod for loose spots that might lead to buried grain. With the others, I emptied out the old folks' storage chests, stopping my ears to the children's crying and the women's wails. For I was convinced that I was accomplishing the great and necessary transformation of the countryside; that in the days to come the people who lived there would be better off for it; that their distress and suffering were a result of their own ignorance or the machinations of the class enemy; that those who sent me—and I myself—knew better than the peasants how they should live, what they should sow and when they should plow.

In the terrible spring of 1933 I saw people dying from hunger. I saw women and children with distended bellies, turning blue, still breathing but with vacant, lifeless eyes....

Nor did I lose my faith. As before, I believed because I wanted to believe. Thus from time immemorial men have believed when possessed by a desire to serve powers and values above and beyond humanity....

Any single-minded attempt to realize these ideals exacts its toll of human sacrifice. In the name of the noblest visions promising eternal happiness to their descendants, such men bring merciless ruin on their contemporaries.... They become unprincipled liars and unrelenting executioners, all the while seeing themselves as virtuous and honorable militants—convinced that if they are forced into villainy, it is for the sake of future good, and that if they have to lie, it is in the name of eternal truths.

Source: Lev Kopelev, *No Jail for Thought* (London: Secker & Warburg, 1977), pp. 11–13.

deaths, over half of them in the Ukraine. This "terror-famine" went unrecorded in the Soviet press (see the box, "Carrying out the Stalinist Revolution").

By 1937 almost all agriculture took place on collective farms—or on state farms set up in areas not previously under agriculture. However, restrictions on private plots and livestock ownership were eased slightly after 1933, and partly as a result agriculture rebounded and living standards began to rise. By the late 1930s, moreover, significant increases in industrial output had established solid foundations in heavy industry, including the bases for military production.

Soviet propaganda, including art in the official socialist realist style, glorified the achievements of the new Soviet industrial and agricultural workers. "Stakhanovism," named for a coal miner who heroically exceeded his production quota, became the term for the prodigious economic achievements that the regime came to expect as it proclaimed to the world the superiority of the communist system. Indeed, the fact that in the Soviet Union state management seemed to produce results while much of the world languished in depression helps explain the prestige of communism among intellectuals and others during the 1930s, and in developing countries later.

But this forced development program created many inefficiencies, and whatever its successes, the human costs were tremendous. The country could probably have done at least as well, with much less suffering, through other strategies of industrial development. Moreover, Stalin's program entailed a departure from certain socialist principles—egalitarianism in wages, for example—that the regime had taken very seriously during the late 1920s. By 1931, bureaucratic managers, concerned simply with maximizing output, were openly favoring workers in certain industries. To ensure labor discipline, new labor laws established harsh punishments for absenteeism or tardiness and severely limited the freedom of workers to change jobs. There was no collective bargaining and no right to strike.

From Opposition to Terror

Stalin's radical course, with its brutality and uncertain economic justification, quickly provoked opposition. During the summer of 1932, a group centered around M. N. Ryutin (1890–1937) circulated among party leaders a two-hundred-page tract calling for a retreat from Stalin's economic program and a return to democracy within the party. It advocated readmitting those who had been expelled—including Stalin's archenemy, Leon Trotsky. Moreover, the document strongly condemned Stalin personally, calling for his removal from the party leadership. In an astonishing statement, Ryutin even referred to Stalin as "the evil genius of the Russian Revolution, who, motivated by a personal desire for power and revenge, brought the Revolution to the verge of ruin."[1]

Stalin promptly had Ryutin and his immediate associates expelled from the party, then arrested and imprisoned. But especially as the international situation grew menacing during the 1930s, he became ever more preoccupied about the possibility of further opposition. Both Germany and Japan exhibited expansionist aims that might threaten Soviet territories. Trotsky from exile might work with foreign agents and Soviet dissidents to sabotage the Soviet development effort.

In 1934 the assassination of Sergei Kirov (1888–1934), party leader of Leningrad (the former Petrograd), gave Stalin an excuse to intensify the crackdown against actual and potential opponents. Though not conclusive, the evidence suggests that Stalin was himself responsible for killing Kirov, a popular moderate who seemed a plausible rival. In any case, the event served Stalin's interests by creating a sense of emergency justifying extraordinary measures. The eventual result was a series of bizarre show trials, deadly purges, and, ultimately, a kind of terror, with no one safe from arrest by the secret police.

Between 1936 and 1938, famed Bolshevik veterans like Bukharin and major functionaries like Genrikh Yagoda (1891–1938), who had just been removed as chief of the secret police, confessed to a series of sensational trumped-up charges: that they had been behind the assassination of Kirov, that they would have killed Stalin if they had gotten a chance, that they constituted an "anti-Soviet, Trotskyite center," spying for Germany and Japan, and preparing to sabotage Soviet industry in the event of war.

The authorities extracted these confessions partly through torture and partly through threats to the families of the accused. But some, at least, offered false confessions because they believed they were serving the revolution in doing so. The revolution had required all along a willingness to compromise one's personal scruples, including conventional middle-class concerns about personal honor and dignity. Even though they were false, these confessions could help the communist regime ward off the genuine dangers it faced. So in confessing, the accused would still be serving the long-term cause, which they still believed to be bigger than Stalin and the compromises of the moment. What some could not see—or admit—was that the triumph of Stalinism was fatally compromising the original revolutionary vision.

Almost all the accused, including Bukharin and others central to the revolution, were convicted and executed. The few who refused, even in the face of torture, to play their assigned roles and confess could not be put on public trial. Among them was Ryutin, who was shot in secret early in 1937.

But the show trials were very public, surrounded by great propaganda. And the unending talk of foreign intrigues, assassination plots, and "wrecking"—all intended to undo the heroic achievements of the Soviet Union—inevitably affected the perceptions of the Soviet people. There seemed a vast conspiracy at work, responsible, among other things, for the shortages and economic mishaps that had accompanied the crash industrialization program.

Meanwhile, a purge of the army in 1937 wiped out its top ranks, with 35,000 officers—half the entire officer corps—shot or imprisoned, in response to unfounded charges of spying and treason. The Communist party underwent several purges, culminating in the great purge of 1937 and 1938. Over half the 1,966 delegates to the congress of the Communist party in January 1934 were shot over the next few years. In particular, the purge of the party got rid of the remaining "old Bolsheviks," those who had been involved in the revolution in 1917 and who thus retained a certain independence. By 1939, Stalin loyalists constituted the entire party leadership.

Although it centered on the party, the purge process touched virtually everyone as the net widened by 1938. Everybody knew someone who had been implicated, so everyone felt some measure of vulnerability to arrest, to be followed by execution or exile to forced-labor camps. Moreover, there was a random, arbitrary quality to the purges, so there was no way to be sure what was punishable or who was "guilty." Ordinary people were thus tempted to denounce others, if only to demonstrate their own loyalty and conscientiousness.

The final toll was staggering. Of the approximately 160 million people in the Soviet Union, something like 8.5 million were arrested during 1937 and 1938, and of these perhaps 1 million were executed by shooting. Half the total membership of the Communist party—1.2 million people—was arrested; 600,000 were executed, and the vast majority of the rest died in forced-labor camps. Altogether, the several purges resulted in approximately 8 million deaths. The death toll from all of Stalin's peacetime policies between 1929 and 1939, including the forced collectivizations, was perhaps 20 million. Even Hitler and the Nazi regime did not match this appalling total.

Communism and Stalinism

This fateful turn in the development of the communist regime in the Soviet Union proved to be one of the pivotal events of modern history. Some insist that Stalin was pursuing a deliberate, coordinated policy, seeking to create an all-encompassing system of control. Others argue that though Stalin's ultimate responsibility is undeniable, he was simply responding on an improvised basis to a situation that became chaotic as the communists tried to carry through a revolution in a backward country.

Virtually from the beginning of its power, the Communist party had attracted careerists and opportunists, and thus there were bitter differences among party leaders over what party membership should entail. Was membership to be limited to a trained and committed elite, who would need to purge the party of opportunists periodically, or was the party to be a mass-based vehicle for socialist education? The concern to root out potential opponents during the 1930s gave various factions an opportunity to have it out with their enemies. Stalin sometimes held back before lending his support to one side or the other. But even if the chain of events did not stem from a coherent policy, Stalin took advantage of it and, by 1939, had crushed all actual or potential opposition. In a sense, the outcome was the triumph of Stalin over the Communist party, which had held on to the original Bolshevik ideal of collective leadership by a revolutionary vanguard.

Obviously Stalinism was one possible outcome of Leninist communism, but was it the logical, even the inevitable, outcome? Leninism had accented centralized authority and the scope for human will to force events, so it may have created a framework in which Stalinism was likely to develop. On the other hand, Stalin's personal idiosyncracies and growing paranoia seem to have been crucial for the Soviet system to develop as it did by the end of the 1930s.

Stalin had won his position from within the Communist party, based on his backroom political skill, not his popular appeal. Although a special aura came to surround him by the end of the thirties, he remained essentially the chief bureaucrat, referring to the surviving fragments of the Marxist-Leninist blueprint as he oversaw the process of revolutionary implementation. So even as he concentrated power in his hands, Stalin's style of leadership remained decidedly different from that of Mussolini and Hitler, who based their power on personal charisma and a direct relationship with the people.

Hitler and Nazism in Germany

Beset with problems from the start, the Weimar Republic lay gravely wounded by 1932. Various antidemocratic groups competed to replace it. The winner was the Nazi movement, led by Adolf Hitler, who became chancellor in January 1933. Nazism took inspiration from Italian fascism, but Hitler's regime proved far more dynamic—and more troubling—than Mussolini's.

To understand where Nazism came from, it is necessary to examine, and distinguish among, motives and purposes. For example, the substantial voting support the Nazis gained by 1932 was essential in giving Hitler a chance to govern. But to understand why so many Germans voted for the Nazis is not to understand why Hitler ended up using power as he did. Nor can we explain Nazism simply by invoking power and opportunism, convenient though such categories are, because the most troubling aspects of Nazism, from personal dictatorship to the extermination of the Jews, stemmed from a wider vision of the world, radiating from Hitler himself.

Nazism was not conventionally revolutionary, in the sense of mounting a frontal challenge to the existing socioeconomic order. Some of its accents were traditionalist and even antimodernizing. But in the final analysis Nazism was anything but conservative. Indeed, it constituted a direct assault on what has long been held as the best of the Western tradition.

The Rise of Nazism

The National Socialist German Workers' party (NSDAP), or Nazism, emerged from the turbulent situation of Munich just after the war. A center of the movement for further leftist revolution, the city also became a hotbed of the radical right, nurturing a number of new nationalist, militantly anticommunist political groups. One of them, a workers' party founded under the aegis of the right-wing Thule Society early in 1919, attracted the attention of Adolf Hitler, who soon gave it his personal stamp.

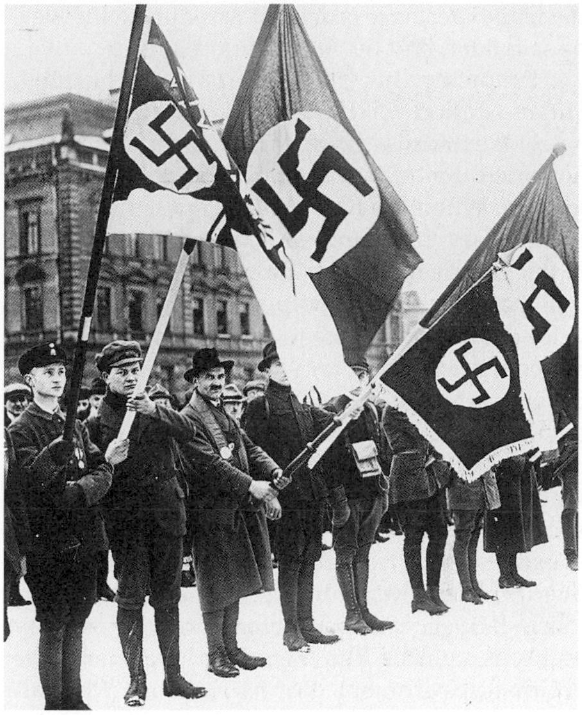

Early Nazism Although Nazism did poorly in national elections before the Depression, the movement attracted a loyal and militant membership, in which young people were especially numerous. Here young Nazis parade with banners in 1923. *(© Harlingue-Viollet)*

Hitler had been born not German but Austrian, the son of a lower government official. As a young man he had gone to Vienna, hoping to become an artist, but he failed to gain admission to the Viennese Academy of Fine Arts. By 1913 he had become a German nationalist hostile to the multinational Habsburg empire, and he emigrated to Germany to escape service in the Austrian army. He was not opposed to military service per se, however, and when war broke out in 1914, he immediately volunteered for service in the German army.

Corporal Hitler experienced firsthand the fighting at the front and, as a courier, performed bravely and effectively. Indeed, he was in a field hospital being treated for gas poisoning when the war ended. Although his fellow soldiers considered him quirky and introverted, Hitler found the war experience crucial; it was during the war, he said later, that he "found himself."

Following his release from the hospital, Hitler worked for the army in routine surveillance of extremist groups in Munich. In this role he joined the infant German Workers' party late in 1919. When his first political speech at a rally in February 1920 proved a resounding success, Hitler began to believe he could play a special political role. From this point, he gradually developed the confidence to lead a new nationalist, anticommunist, and anti-Weimar movement, especially when more plausible leaders seemed inept during the Kapp Putsch of 1920.

But Hitler jumped the gun in November 1923 when, with Erich Ludendorff at his side, he spearheaded the Beer Hall Putsch in Munich, an abortive attempt to launch a march on Berlin to overthrow the Republic. On trial after this effort failed, Hitler gained greater national visibility as he denounced the Versailles treaty and the Weimar government. But *Mein Kampf* (My Battle), the political tract that he wrote while in prison during 1924, sold poorly. To most, Hitler was simply a right-wing rabble-rouser whose views were not worth taking seriously.

His failure in 1923 convinced Hitler that he should exploit the existing political system, but not challenge it directly, in his quest for power on the national level. Still, the NSDAP did not want to be just another political party, playing by the same rules as the others within the Weimar system. Thus, for example, it maintained a paramilitary arm, the Sturmabteilung (SA), which provoked a good deal of antileftist street violence.

By 1928, Nazi membership was increasing, but the Nazis were still peripheral to national politics, attracting only 2.6 percent of the vote in the Reichstag elections of that year. However, in the elections of September 1930, the first since the onset of the Depression, they increased their share dramatically to 18.3 percent of the vote. When elections were held again in July 1932, their vote exploded to 37.3 percent, enough to make them the largest party in the Reichstag.

Both the Nazis and the Communists gained electoral support as unemployment grew, but the Germans voting for the Nazis were not simply those most threatened economically. Nor did the Nazi party appeal primarily to the uneducated or socially marginal. Rather, the party served as a focus of opposition for those now alienated from the Weimar Republic itself. Although the Nazis did relatively poorly among Catholics and industrial workers, they put together a broad, fairly diverse base of electoral support, running from artisans and small shopkeepers to university students and civil servants. Still, that support was shallow. The Nazi vote in 1932 was largely a protest vote, reflecting the hope that Nazism, or Hitler himself, portended something new and more effective. Although Nazism was clearly anticommunist, anti-Weimar, and anti-Versailles, its positive program remained vague.

As the crisis of the Weimar Republic deepened in 1932, conservative fear of a Marxist outcome played into Hitler's hands. By May 1932, when Heinrich Brüning's government fell, President Hindenburg was relying heavily on a narrow circle of advisers who wanted to take advantage of the Nazis' mass support for conservative purposes. Two of those advisers, Franz von Papen (1878–1969) and General Kurt von Schleicher (1882–1934), each got a chance to govern, but neither succeeded. By January 1933, each had grown hostile to the other, and Papen lined up a new coalition that he proposed to Hindenburg to replace Schleicher's government. Hitler would be chancellor, Papen himself vice chancellor, and Alfred Hugenberg (1865–1951), the leader of the Nationalist party, finance minister. For months, Hindenburg had resisted giving Hitler a chance to govern. But he felt this combination might work to establish a parliamentary majority, box out the left, and contain Nazism. So Hindenburg turned to Hitler, who became chancellor at last on January 30, 1933.

The Consolidation of Hitler's Power

When Hitler became chancellor, it was not obvious that a change of regime was beginning. Like his predecessors, Hitler could govern only with the president's approval, and governmental institutions like the army, the judiciary, and the diplomatic corps, though hardly bastions of democracy, were not in the hands of committed Nazis. But though an element of caution and cultivated ambiguity remained, a revolution quickly began, creating a new regime, the Third Reich.

On February 23, just weeks after Hitler became chancellor, a fire engulfed the Reichstag building in Berlin. It was set by a young Dutch communist acting on his own, but it seemed to suggest that a communist uprising was imminent. This sense of emergency afforded the new Hitler government an excuse to restrict civil liberties and imprison leftist leaders, including the entire Communist parliamentary delegation. Even in this atmosphere of crisis the Nazis could not win a majority in the Reichstag elections of March 5. But support from the Nationalists and the Center party enabled the Nazis to win Reichstag approval for an enabling act granting Hitler the power to make laws on his own for the next four years, bypassing both the Reichstag and the president.

Although the Weimar Republic was never formally abolished, the laws that followed fundamentally altered government, politics, and public life in Germany. The other parties were either outlawed or persuaded to dissolve so that in July 1933 the Nazi party was declared the only legal party. When President Hindenburg died in August 1934, the offices of chancellor and president were merged, and Germany had just one leader, with unprecedented power in his hands. Members of the German armed forces now swore loyalty to him personally.

During this period of power consolidation, Hitler acted decisively but carefully, generally accenting normalization. To be sure, his methods occasionally gave conservatives pause. In an especially dramatic episode, he had several hundred people murdered in the Blood Purge of June 30, 1934. Although Hitler used the occasion to settle a number of old scores, the purge was directed against the SA, led by Ernst Röhm (1887–1934). Because Röhm and the SA had had pretensions of controlling the army, his removal seemed evidence that Hitler was taming the radical elements in his own movement, bringing the Nazi revolution to an end. In fact, however, this purge led to the ascendancy of the Schutzstaffel, or SS, the select Nazi elite, led by Heinrich Himmler (1900–1945). Linked to the Gestapo, the secret police apparatus, the SS became the institutional basis for the most troubling aspects of Nazism. So whereas the Blood Purge seemed to indicate Hitler's willingness to work with established institutions like the army, over the longer term it proved a step to radical measures barely conceivable in 1934.

Hitler's World View

In achieving the chancellorship and in expanding his power thereafter, Hitler showed himself an adept politician, but he was hardly a mere opportunist, seeking to amass power for its own sake. Power was only the instrument for the grandiose transformation he believed necessary.

Hitler acted on the basis of a world view that coalesced by about 1924—and that remained extremely important to him (see the box, "Hitler's World View: Nature, Race, and Struggle"). This is not to say that he was an original thinker or that his ideas were true—or even plausible. But he sought to make systematic sense of things, and the most disturbing features of his political activity stemmed directly from the resulting world view. His most committed followers shared some of those ideas, although for some fanatical loyalty to Hitler himself was more important. The central components of Hitler's world view—geopolitics, biological racism, anti-Semitism, and Social Darwinism—were by no means specifically German. They could be found all over the Western world by the early twentieth century.

Geopolitics claimed to offer a scientific understanding of world power relationships based on a mechanistic geographical determinism. In his writings of the 1920s, Hitler warned that Germany faced imminent decline unless it confronted its geopolitical limitations. To remain fully sovereign in the emerging new era of global superpowers like the United States, Germany would have to act quickly to expand its territory. Otherwise it would end up like Switzerland or the Netherlands.

For decades German imperialists had argued about whether Germany was better advised to seek overseas colonies or to expand its reach in Europe. As Hitler saw it, Germany had lost World War I because it had failed to make a clear choice. Now choice was imperative, and current geopolitical thinking seemed to indicate the direction for the essential German expansion. Far-flung empires relying on naval support were said to be in full decline. The future lay with dense, land-based states—unified, geographically contiguous, with the space necessary for self-sufficiency. By expanding eastward, into Poland and the western part of the Soviet Union, including the Ukraine, Germany could conquer

Hitler's World View: Nature, Race, and Struggle

Hitler outlined his beliefs and aims in* Mein Kampf, *which he wrote while in prison in 1924. The following passages reveal the racism, the anti-Semitism, and the emphasis on nature and struggle that formed the core of his world view.

No more than Nature desires the mating of weaker with stronger individuals, even less does she desire the blending of a higher with a lower race, since, if she did, her whole work of higher breeding, over perhaps hundreds of thousands of years, might be ruined with one blow.

Historical experience . . . shows with terrifying clarity that in every mingling of Aryan blood with that of lower peoples the result was the end of the cultured people. . . .

Here, of course, we encounter the objection of the modern pacifist, as truly Jewish in its effrontery as it is stupid! "Man's rôle is to overcome Nature!"

Millions thoughtlessly parrot this Jewish nonsense and end up by really imagining that they themselves represent a kind of conqueror of Nature. . . .

. . . [T]his planet once moved through the ether for millions of years without human beings and it can do so again some day if men forget that they owe their higher existence, not to the ideas of a few crazy ideologists, but to the knowledge and ruthless application of Nature's stern and rigid laws. . . .

Those who want to live, let them fight, and those who do not want to fight in this world of eternal struggle do not deserve to live. . . .

In the Jewish people the will to self-sacrifice does not go beyond the individual's naked instinct of self-preservation. . . .

If the Jews were alone in the world, they would stifle in filth and offal; they would try to get ahead of one another in hate-filled struggle and exterminate one another. . . .

Source: Adolf Hitler, *Mein Kampf* (Boston: Houghton Mifflin, Sentry, 1943), pp. 286–289, 299, 301–302.

the living space, or *Lebensraum,* necessary for agricultural-industrial balance—and ultimately for self-sufficiency.

Though limited and mechanistic, this geopolitical way of thinking had a certain plausibility, especially in light of the German vulnerabilities that had surfaced during the war. The other three strands of Hitler's world view were much less plausible, though each had become prominent during the second half of the nineteenth century. Biological racism insisted that built-in racial characteristics determine what is most important about any individual. Anti-Semitism went beyond racism in claiming that Jews play a special and negative role. The fact that the Jews were dispersed and often landless indicated that they were different—and parasitical. Finally, Social Darwinism, especially in its German incarnation, accented the positive role of struggle—not among individuals, as in a prominent American strand, but among racial groups.

The dominant current of racist thinking labeled the "Aryans" as healthy, creative, superior. Originally the Sanskrit term for "noble," *Aryan* came to refer simply to speakers of Indo-European languages. By the late nineteenth century, however, the term had become supremely ill defined. In much racist thinking, Germanic peoples were somehow especially Aryan, but race mixing had produced impurity—and thus degeneration. Success in struggle with the other races was the ultimate measure of vitality, the only proof of racial superiority for the future.

Hitler brought these themes together by emphasizing that humanity is not special, but simply part of nature, subject to the same laws of struggle and selection as the other animal species. Humanitarian ideals are thus dangerous illusions. As he put it to a group of officer cadets in 1944:

Nature is always teaching us . . . that she is governed by the principle of selection: that victory is to the strong and that the weak must go to the wall. She teaches us that what may seem cruel to us, because it affects us personally or because we have been brought up in ignorance of her laws, is nevertheless often essential if a higher way of life is to be attained. Nature . . . knows nothing of the notion of humanitarianism, which signifies that the weak must at all costs be protected and preserved even at the expense of the strong.

Nature does not see in weakness any extenuating reasons . . . on the contrary, weakness calls for condemnation.[2]

To Hitler, the Jews were not simply another of the races involved in this endless struggle. Rather, as landless parasites, they had played a special historical role, embodying the principles—from humanitarianism to class struggle—that were antithetical to the healthy natural struggle among unified racial groups. "Jewishness" was bound up with the negative, critical intellect that dared suggest things ought to be not natural but just, even that it was up to human beings to change the world and make it just. The Jews were the virus keeping the community from a healthy natural footing. Marxist communism, embodying divisive class struggle as well as utopian humanitarian ideals, was fundamentally Jewish.

The central features of Nazism in practice, from personal dictatorship to the extermination of the Jews, followed from Hitler's view of the world. First, the racial community must organize itself politically for this ceaseless struggle. Individuals are but instruments for the success of the racial community. Parliamentary democracy, reflecting short-term individual interests, fostered selfish materialism and division, thereby weakening that community. The political order must rest instead on a strong, charismatic leader, united with the whole people through bonds of common blood.

Nazi Aims and German Society

Although Hitler's world view provided the underlying momentum for the Nazi regime, it did not specify a consistent program that could be implemented all at once. Moreover, the regime sometimes found it necessary to adopt short-term expedients that conflicted with its long-term aims. Thus it was possible for Germans living under Nazi rule in the 1930s to embrace aspects of Nazism in practice without seeing where it was all leading.

Hitler's special leadership function was based on a charismatic relationship with the German people, a nonrational bond resting ultimately on common race. But to create a genuine racial community, or *Volksgemeinschaft,* it was

Hitler and Children Adolf Hitler was often portrayed as the friend of children. This photograph accompanied a story for an elementary school reader that described how Hitler, told it was this young girl's birthday, picked her from a crowd of well-wishers to treat her "to cake and strawberries with thick, sweet cream." *(From* Jugend um Hitler, *Heinrich Hoffman © "Zeitgeschichte" Verlag und Vertriebs-Gesellschaft Berlin. Reproduced with permission. Photo courtesy Wiener Library, London)*

Nazism as Totalitarian Populism

Nazism embodied the resentments that some felt in the face of modernist culture and cultural sophistication in general. In a speech in 1937, Hitler's propaganda minister, Joseph Goebbels, played on such resentments while claiming that art had to be coordinated by the Nazi regime. In the exhibition to which he refers, the Nazis had displayed examples of modern painting as unfavorably as possible, to dramatize the "degeneracy" of modern art.

How deeply the perverse Jewish spirit had penetrated German cultural life is shown in the frightening and horrifying forms of the "Exhibition of Degenerate Art" in Munich, arranged as an admonitory example. We have been frequently attacked in the so-called world press on account of this exhibit. . . .

Does this now signify a narrowing of the much-discussed artistic freedom? If so, then only when the artist should have the right to withdraw from his times and its demands and lead an eccentric life outside the community of the people. That, however, cannot and ought not to be. The artist stands in the midst of his nation. . . .

Art is a function of the life of the people and the artist its blessed endower of meaning.

And just as the leadership of the state claims for itself the political guidance of other areas of the people's life, likewise does it make the same claim here. . . .

At the congress held last year. . . . The responsibility for the . . . degeneration in art was in large measure laid at the door of art criticism. . . . It did not judge artistic development in terms of a healthy instinct linked to the people, but only in terms of the emptiness of its intellectual abstractions. . . .

. . . While the taste of the so-called cultural persons, precisely because they are cultured and have read so much, was exposed to the most manifold ill will and therefore also to fluctuations, the taste of the broad masses has always remained the same. . . . Their joy in the healthy and the strong is still naïve, untroubled, and sensuously moved. They still feel with the heart, and this heart does not stand in the shadow of an all-knowing, all-perceiving mind which in the end is also destructive and doubtful of all.

Source: George L. Mosse, *Nazi Culture: Intellectual, Cultural and Social Life in the Third Reich* (New York: Grosset & Dunlap, 1968), pp. 152–154, 156.

necessary to unify society and instill Nazi values, thereby making the individual feel part of the whole—and ultimately an instrument to serve the whole (see the box, "Nazism as Totalitarian Populism"). This entailed more or less forced participation in an array of Nazi organizations, from women's groups to the Hitler Youth, from the Labor Front to the Strength Through Joy leisure-time organization.

Common participation meant shared experiences such as weekend hikes and the weekly one-dish meal. Even the most ordinary, once-private activities took on a public or political dimension. Moveover, the Nazis devised unprecedented ways to stage-manage public life, using rituals like the Hitler salute, symbols like the swastika, new media like radio and film, and carefully orchestrated party rallies—all in an effort to foster this sense of belonging. (See the feature, "Weighing the Evidence: Film as Propaganda," on pages 1102–1103.)

Did the Nazis succeed in drawing ordinary Germans into their orbit? The matter remains sensitive and difficult. Hitler's regime enjoyed considerable support, but even after Hitler was well entrenched in power, most Germans did not grasp the regime's deeper dynamic. Certainly some welcomed the sense of unity, the feeling of belonging and participation, especially after what had seemed the alienation and divisiveness of the Weimar years. Moreover, Hitler himself was immensely popular, partly because of his personal charisma, partly because his apparently decisive leadership seemed a welcome departure from the near paralysis of the Weimar parliamentary system. But most importantly, before the coming of war in 1939, he seemed to go from success to success, surmounting the Depression and repudiating the major terms of the hated Versailles treaty.

The skillful work of Hitler's propaganda minister, Joseph Goebbels (1897–1945), played on these successes to create a "Hitler myth," which made Hitler seem at once heroic and a man of the people, even the embodiment of healthy German ideals *against* the excesses and corruptions of the Nazi party. This myth became central to the Nazi regime, but it merely provided a façade behind which the real Hitler could pursue deeper, longer-term aims. These aims were not publicized directly, because the German people did not seem ready for them. In this sense, then, support for Hitler and his regime was broad but shallow during the 1930s.

Moreover, resistance increased as the regime became more intrusive. Youth gangs actively opposed the official Hitler Youth organization as it became more overbearing and militaristic by the late 1930s. But people resisted especially by minimizing their involvement with the regime, retreating into the private realm, in response to the Nazi attempt to make everything public.

Did such people feel constantly under threat of the Gestapo, the secret police? In principle, the Gestapo could interpret the will of the *Führer,* or leader, and decide whether any individual citizen was "guilty" or not. And the Gestapo was not concerned about due process; on occasion it simply bypassed the regular court system. But the Gestapo did not terrorize Germans at random. Its victims were generally members of specific groups, people suspected of active opposition, or people who protected those the Gestapo had targeted. It did not become as intrusive as its Soviet counterpart, the NKVD, became during the height of the Stalinist terror in the late 1930s.

Moreover, changes and contradictions in Nazi goals allowed considerable space for personal choices. For example, the Nazis claimed to embrace traditional family values. During the 1920s, they had emphasized the woman's role as wife and mother and deplored the ongoing emancipation of women evident in Germany as elsewhere after the war. Once Hitler came to power, concerns about unemployment reinforced these views. During the summer of 1933, the government began offering interest-free loans to help couples set up house if the woman agreed to leave the labor force. Moreover, efforts to increase the German birthrate reinforced the emphasis on child rearing in Nazi women's organizations. Nonetheless, the size of the family continued to decrease in Germany as elsewhere in the industrialized world during the 1930s.

And beginning in 1936, when rapid rearmament began to produce labor shortages, the regime did an about-face and began seeking to attract women back to the workplace, especially into jobs central to military preparation. These efforts were not notably successful, and by 1940 the military was calling for conscription of women into war industries.

Further, the Nazis valued the family only insofar as it was congruent with the "health" of the racial community, so efforts to promote that health also compromised traditional family values. The regime regulated marriage and sought actively to eliminate the "unhealthy," those deemed unfit. Just months after coming to power in 1933, Hitler brushed aside the objections of Vice Chancellor Franz von Papen, a Catholic, and engineered a law mandating the compulsory sterilization of persons suffering from certain allegedly hereditary diseases.

The Nazi regime also began immediately to single out the Jews, although Nazi policy toward them remained an improvised hodgepodge prior to World War II. Within weeks after Hitler became chancellor in 1933, new restrictions limited Jewish participation in the civil service, in the professions, and in German cultural life—and quickly drew censure from the League of Nations. The Nuremberg Laws, announced at a party rally in 1935, included prohibition of sexual relations and marriage between Jews and non-Jewish Germans. Beginning in 1938, the Jews had to carry special identification cards and to add "Sarah" or "Israel" to their given names.

Although Hitler and other Nazi leaders claimed periodically to be seeking a definitive solution to Germany's "Jewish problem," this led only to sporadic attempts to force German Jews to emigrate during the 1930s. About 60,000 of Germany's 550,000 Jews emigrated during 1933 and 1934, and perhaps a fourth had gotten out by 1938. The fact that the regime stripped emigrating Jews of their assets made emigration more difficult, because other countries were unwilling to take in substantial numbers of penniless Jews.

On November 9, 1938, the Nazis used the assassination of a German diplomat in Paris as the pretext for staging the *Kristallnacht* (Crystal Night) pogrom, during which almost all the synagogues in Germany and about 7,000 Jewish-owned stores were destroyed. Between 30,000 and 50,000 relatively prosperous Jews were arrested and forced to emigrate after their property was confiscated. Although the German public had generally acquiesced in the earlier restrictions on Jews, this pogrom caused considerable shock among many Germans, who drew the line at this wanton violation of private property.

Concentration camps—supplementary detention centers—had become a feature of the Nazi regime virtually at once, but prior to 1938 they were used primarily to hold political prisoners. As part of the Crystal Night pogrom, about 35,000 Jews were rounded up and sent to them, but most were soon released as long as they could document their intention to emigrate. When World War II began in 1939, the total camp population was about 25,000. The physical extermination of the Jews began only during the war, in newly constructed death camps in Poland.

However, the killing of others deemed superfluous or threatening to the racial community began earlier, with the so-called euthanasia program initiated under volunteer medical teams in 1939. Its aim was to eliminate chronic mental patients, the incurably ill, and those with severe physical handicaps. Those to be eliminated were primarily ethnic Germans, not Jews or foreigners. Although the regime did all it could to make it appear that the victims had died naturally, a public outcry developed, especially among relatives and church leaders. Thus the program had to be discontinued in 1941, but by then it had claimed between 80,000 and 100,000 lives.

The euthanasia program was based on the sense, fundamental to radical Nazism, that readiness for war was the real norm for society. In war, societies send individuals to their deaths and, on the battlefield, make difficult distinctions among the wounded, letting some die while saving others to fight another day. Struggle necessitates selection, which requires overcoming humanitarian scruples—the notion that "weakness" calls for special societal protection. Thus it was desirable to kill even ethnic Germans who were deemed unfit, as "life unworthy of life."

Preparation for war was the core of Nazism in practice. The conquest of living space in the east would make possible a more advantageous agricultural-industrial balance, thereby providing not only the self-sufficiency necessary for sovereignty but also the land-rootedness necessary for racial health. Such a war of conquest would strike not only the Slavic peoples of the region but also communism, centered in the Soviet Union.

The point of domestic reorganization was to marshal the community's energies and resources for this war. Because business interests generally seemed congruent with Nazi purposes, Nazi aims seemed to require no revolutionary assault on business elites or the capitalist economy. But the Nazis had their own road to travel, and beginning in 1936 they proved quite prepared to bend the economy, and to coordinate big business, to serve their longer-term aims of war-making.

The Nazi drive toward war during the 1930s entailed foreign policy revision at first, and this necessarily involved the other European powers, each trying to understand Hitler's Germany in terms of the increasingly polarized political context of the period. Before considering the fortunes of Hitler's foreign policy, we must consider fascism as a wider phenomenon—and the efforts of the democracies, on the one hand, and the Soviet Union, on the other, to come to terms with it.

Fascist Challenge and Antifascist Response

Communism, fascism, and Nazism departed from the parliamentary democracy that had been the West's political norm. Each seemed subject to violence and excess, yet each had features that some found attractive. Especially in the difficult socioeconomic circumstances of the 1930s, the presence of these new political systems caused polarization all over Europe.

Yet communists and adherents of the various forms of fascism were bitterly hostile to each other, and beginning in 1934 communists sought to join with other antifascists to defend democracy. This effort led to new antifascist coalition governments in Spain and France. In each case, however, the Depression restricted maneuvering room, and these governments ended up furthering the polarization they were seeking to avoid. By 1940 democracy had fallen in Spain, after a brutal civil war, and even in France, in the wake of military defeat. As the 1940s began, democracy appeared to be in full retreat.

The Reorientation of Fascist Italy

Mussolini's regime in Italy continued to emphasize its corporativist direction, the intent of which was to involve people in political decision making based on their roles in the national economy. But though corporativist institutions were gradually constructed, with great rhetorical fanfare, fascism became bogged down in ambiguous compromise with prefascist elites and institutions by the middle of the 1930s. Italian businessmen, cautious and suspicious of Mussolini, sought to maintain their autonomy against the fascist effort to subordinate business to the political sphere. And generally they succeeded. Partly because of the opposition of conservative business leaders and traditional bureaucrats, the corporative institutions never developed into genuine vehicles of mass participation through the workplace. If anything, in fact, they served simply to regiment the working class. Mussolini offered assurances that, despite the necessary compromises, fascism's corporativist revolution was continuing, but those seeking a new corporative state became sharply critical of the obvious inadequacies of the new system.

Mussolini was never merely the instrument of the established Italian elites, but neither was he a consistent ideologue like Hitler, forcing his regime in a certain direction. By the early 1930s, he sometimes seemed satisfied with the cult that came to surround him as he juggled the various contending forces in fascist Italy. But he was increasingly frustrated by the limitations he had encountered on the domestic level. On the international level, however, the new context after Hitler came to power offered him some welcome space for maneuver. So as the fascist revolution in Italy bogged down, Mussolini began concentrating on foreign policy.

THE DIPLOMATIC REVOLUTION OF THE 1930s

January 1933	Hitler becomes German chancellor
October 1933	Germany withdraws from the League of Nations
March 1935	Hitler announces rearmament in defiance of the Versailles Treaty
April 1935	Britain, France, and Italy meet at Stresa
October 1935	Italy invades Ethiopia
March 1936	Remilitarization of the Rhineland
July 1936	Beginning of the Spanish civil war
March 1938	The Anschluss: Germany absorbs Austria
September 1938	Munich Conference ends Sudetenland crisis
March 1939	Dismemberment of Czechoslovakia
August 1939	Nazi-Soviet nonaggression pact
September 1, 1939	German invasion of Poland
September 3, 1939	Britain and France declare war on Germany

Though Italy, like Germany, remained dissatisfied with the territorial status quo, it was not obvious that fascist Italy and Nazi Germany had to end up in the same camp. For one thing, Italy was anxious to preserve an independent Austria as a buffer with Germany, whereas there was considerable sentiment among Germans and Austrians for the unification of the two countries. Such a greater Germany might then threaten the gains Italy had won at the peace conference at the expense of Austria. When, in 1934, Germany seemed poised to absorb Austria, Mussolini helped stiffen the resistance of Austria's leaders and played a part in forcing Hitler to back down.

Imperialism, Ideology, and Foreign Policy

The ideological polarization of the 1930s affected foreign policy considerations everywhere, but nowhere more than in France. In October 1935 a "Manifesto of the Intellectuals" defending Italy's aggression in Ethiopia appeared in a number of French newspapers. Most of the 850 signatories came from the right, but some well-known centrists were included as well. The manifesto indicates the concerns that had come to dominate foreign policy debates by the mid-1930s—and that contributed to polarization in France.

At a time when Italy is being threatened with sanctions which could lead to a war without precedent, we, as French intellectuals, wish to declare before world opinion that we want neither sanctions nor war. . . .

They do not hesitate to treat Italy as guilty . . . on the pretext of protecting the independence of a mixture of savage tribes. . . .

The Great Powers should surely have abandoned their own colonial mission from the outset, if they wished without hypocrisy to prevent Rome from pursuing the fulfillment of those projects which she honestly planned and openly prepared, in regions of Africa where she long ago acquired incontestable rights.

And so we see with some amazement a people, whose colonial empire covers one-fifth of the globe, oppose the justifiable ambitions of a young Italy, and thoughtlessly adopt the dangerous fiction of the absolute equality of nations. . . .

Geneva provides . . . a false judicial universalism, which puts on an equal footing the superior and the inferior, civilized man and the barbarian. . . . For it is in the name of equality that sanctions are formulated which, in order to impede the civilizing conquest of one of the most backward countries in the world . . . would not hesitate to unleash a universal war, and to coalesce all kinds of anarchy and disorder against a nation in which some of the essential virtues of humanity at its highest level have been affirmed, revived, organized, and strengthened over the last fifteen years.

This fratricidal conflict would be not only a crime against peace but an unpardonable outrage against Western civilization, which was in the past and is now the only valid future open to the human race.

Source: David Thomson, ed., *France, Empire and Republic, 1850–1940: Historical Documents* (New York: Walker, 1968), pp. 354–357.

Mussolini even warned that Nazism, with its fundamentally racist orientation, posed a significant threat to the best of European civilization.

As it began to appear that France and Britain might have to work with the Soviet Union to check Hitler's Germany, French and British conservatives pushed for good relations with Mussolini's Italy to provide ideological balance. So Italy was well positioned to play off both sides as Hitler began shaking things up on the international level after 1933. In 1935, just after Hitler announced significant rearmament measures, unilaterally repudiating provisions of the Versailles treaty for the first time, Mussolini hosted a meeting with the French and British prime ministers at Stresa, in northern Italy. In a move clearly intended to contain Germany, the three powers agreed to resist "any unilateral repudiation of treaties which may endanger the peace of Europe."

However, Mussolini was already preparing to extend Italy's possessions in East Africa to encompass Ethiopia (Abyssinia), assuming that the French and British, who needed his support against Hitler, would not offer significant opposition. Ethiopia had become a League of Nations member in 1923—sponsored by Italy, but opposed by Britain and France because it still practiced slavery. After a border incident in December 1934, Italian troops invaded in October 1935, prompting the League to announce sanctions against Italy.

These sanctions were applied haphazardly, largely because France and Britain wanted to avoid irreparable damage to their longer-term relations with Italy. In any case, the sanctions did not deter Italy, whose forces prevailed through the use of aircraft and poison gas by May 1936. But they did make Italy receptive to German overtures in the aftermath of its victory. And the victory made Mussolini more restless. Rather than seeking to play again the enviable role of European balancer, he almost immediately began lending Italian support—both men and materiel—to the antidemocratic nationalists in the Spanish civil war, thereby further alienating democratic opinion elsewhere.

Conservatives in Britain and France continued to push for accommodation with Italy, hoping to revive the "Stresa Front" against Hitler. Some even defended Italian imperialism in East Africa. (See the box, "Imperialism, Ideology, and Foreign Policy.")

But Italy continued its drift toward Germany. Late in 1936, Mussolini spoke of a new Rome-Berlin axis for the first time. During 1937 and 1938 he and Hitler exchanged visits. Finally, in May 1939, Italy joined Germany in an open-ended military alliance, the Pact of Steel, but Mussolini made it clear that Italy could not be ready for a major European war before 1943.

To cement this developing relationship, fascist Italy adopted anti-Semitic racial laws modeled on Germany's, even though Italian fascism had not originally been anti-Semitic and indeed had attracted Jewish Italians to its membership in about the same proportion as non-Jews. Although the imperial venture in Ethiopia had been popular among the Italian people, the increasing subservience to Nazi Germany displeased even many committed fascists. Such opposition helped keep Mussolini from immediate intervention when war broke out in September 1939. But in the wake of stunning Nazi successes by May 1940, Italy finally intervened, expecting to gain territorial advantage at the expense of France at relatively low cost. Mussolini was not expecting a long war, for which he knew Italy was unprepared. But a long and difficult war was forthcoming, and by July 1943 the poor Italian performance had led not only to military defeat but to the collapse of the fascist regime itself.

Hitler and Mussolini Personal meetings between the two dictators helped cement the good relations that culminated in the Pact of Steel between Germany and Italy in 1939. *(Hugo Jaeger, Life Magazine © Time Warner, Inc.)*

Fascism and the Popular Front Response

The influence of Hitler's regime extended far beyond fascist Italy. With its apparent dynamism and success, Nazi Germany stimulated interest in fascism among those elsewhere who were disaffected with democracy and hostile to communism. But the line between fascism and conservative authoritarianism grew muddy in the volatile political climate of the thirties. To some, any retreat from democracy appeared a step toward fascism.

In east-central Europe, political distinctions became especially problematic. Movements like the Arrow Cross in Hungary and the Legion of the Archangel Michael in Romania modeled themselves on the Italian and German prototypes. But the antidemocratic governments in Hungary and Romania, as in Poland, Bulgaria, and Yugoslavia, were authoritarian traditionalist, not really fascist. Still, many government leaders welcomed the closer economic ties with Germany that Hitler's economics minister, Hjalmar Schacht, engineered. The difference between authoritarianism and fascism remained clearest in Austria, where Catholic conservatives undermined democracy during 1933 and 1934. They were actively hostile to the growing pro-Nazi agitation in Austria, partly because they wanted to keep Austria independent.

In France, various nationalist, anticommunist, and anti-Semitic leagues gathered momentum during the early 1930s. They covered a spectrum from monarchism to outspoken profascism, but together they seemed to constitute at least a potential threat to French democracy. In February 1934, in fact, right-wing demonstrations against the Chamber of Deputies provoked a bloody clash with police and forced a change of ministry. As it began to seem that even France might be vulnerable to fascism, those from the center and left of the political spectrum began to think about working together to keep fascism from spreading further. The communists, especially, took the initiative by promoting "popular fronts" of all those seeking to save democracy from fascism.

This was a dramatic change in strategy for international communism. Even as Hitler was closing in on the German chancellorship in the early thirties, German Communists, following Comintern policy, continued to attack their socialist rivals rather than seek a unified response to Nazism. From the communist perspective, fascism represented the crisis phase of monopoly capitalism, so a Nazi government would actually be useful to strip away the democratic façade hiding class oppression in Germany. But when the new Hitler government promptly outlawed the German Communist party and arrested all the Communists it could find, and when the demonstrations in Paris in February 1934 made it seem that even France might "go fascist," the Comintern abruptly changed direction. The threat of fascism was so pressing that the Communists had to begin actively promoting electoral alliances and governing coalitions with Socialists and even liberal democrats to resist its further spread. From 1934 until 1939, Communists everywhere consistently pursued this "popular front" strategy.

But by the mid-thirties it was becoming ever harder to be sure what was fascist, what was dangerous, what might lead where. As fears intensified, perceptions became as important as realities. Popular front governments, intended to preserve democracy against what appeared to be fascism, could seem, to conservatives, to be leaning too far to the left. Ideological polarization made democracy extraordinarily difficult. The archetypal example proved to be Spain, where a tragedy of classical proportions was played out.

From Democracy to Civil War in Spain

Spain became a center of attention in the 1930s, when its promising new parliamentary democracy, launched in 1931, led to civil war in 1936 and the triumph of a repressive authoritarian regime in 1939. The country's earlier effort at constitutional monarchy had fizzled by 1923, when King Alfonso XIII (1886–1941) supported a new military dictatorship. But growing opposition led first to the resignation of the dictator in 1930 and then, in April 1931, to the end of the monarchy and the proclamation of a republic. The elections for a constituent assembly that followed in June produced a solid victory for a coalition of liberal democrats and Socialists, as well as considerable hope and expectation.

The optimism began to break down first because the leaders of the new republic dragged their feet on land reform, which seemed necessary especially in southern Spain, where large estates worked by landless day laborers remained the rule. A significant agrarian reform law was passed in 1932, but the new government was slow to implement it, partly because of budgetary concerns in the difficult context of the Depression, but also because the government's leaders concentrated on checking the power of the Catholic church and the military. Feeling betrayed, Socialists and agricultural workers became increasingly radical, producing growing upheaval in the countryside. Radicalism on the left made it harder for the moderates to govern and, at the same time, stimulated conservatives to become more politically active.

A conservative, or right-wing, coalition (the CEDA) under José Maria Gil Robles (1898–1980) grew in strength, becoming the largest party in parliament with the first regular elections, held in November 1933. In light of its parliamentary strength, the CEDA had a plausible claim to a government role, but it was kept from participation in government until October 1934. It seemed to the left, in the ideologically charged atmosphere of the time, that the growing role of the CEDA was a prelude to fascism. To let the CEDA into the government would be to hand the republic over to its enemies.

In retrospect, the charge of fascism seems inappropriate. Gil Robles himself warned that the persistent use of the "fascist" epithet prevented the possibility of rational discussion and eventual peace in Spain. A strong Catholic from the traditional Spanish right, Gil Robles refused to endorse the democratic republic as a form of government, but he and the CEDA were willing to work within it. So the Spanish left may have been too quick to see the CEDA as fascist—and to react when the CEDA finally got its government role. On the other hand, Mussolini and Hitler had each come to power more or less legally, from within parliamentary institutions. The German left has been criticized for its passive response to the advent of Hitler; the Spanish left wanted to avoid the same mistake.

Thus, during the fall of 1934, the left responded to the opening of the government to the CEDA with quasi-revolutionary uprisings in Catalonia and Asturias, where a miners' commune was put down only after two weeks of heavy fighting. In the aftermath, the right-leaning government of 1935 began undoing some of the reforms of the left-leaning government of 1931–1933, though still legally, within the framework of the parliamentary republic.

In February 1936, a popular front coalition to ward off fascism won a narrow electoral victory, sufficient for an absolute majority in parliament. As would be true in France a few months later, electoral victory produced popular expectations that went well beyond the essentially defensive purposes of the popular front. Hoping to win back the leftist rank and file and head off what seemed a dangerous attempt at revolution, the new popular front government began to implement a progressive program, now including the land reform that had been promised but not implemented earlier. But it was too late to undercut the growing radicalization of the masses.

The Spanish Civil War In August 1936, shortly after the outbreak of fighting, militiamen loyal to the Republic surrendered to insurgent Nationalist troops at the Somosierra Pass on the Guadarrama front north of Madrid. *(From* Spanish Civil War, *Raymond Carr, [W.W. Norton, 1986])*

A wave of land seizures, encouraged by socialist radicals, began in March, followed by a quasi-insurrectionary strike movement, the most extensive in Spanish history, which took on a clearly revolutionary character during June and July. To many, the government's inability to keep order had become the immediate issue. By the early summer of 1936, leaders of the democratic republic had become isolated between the extremes of left and right, each preparing an extralegal solution.

Finally, in mid-July, several army officers initiated a military uprising intended as a coup to seize power. Soon led by General Francisco

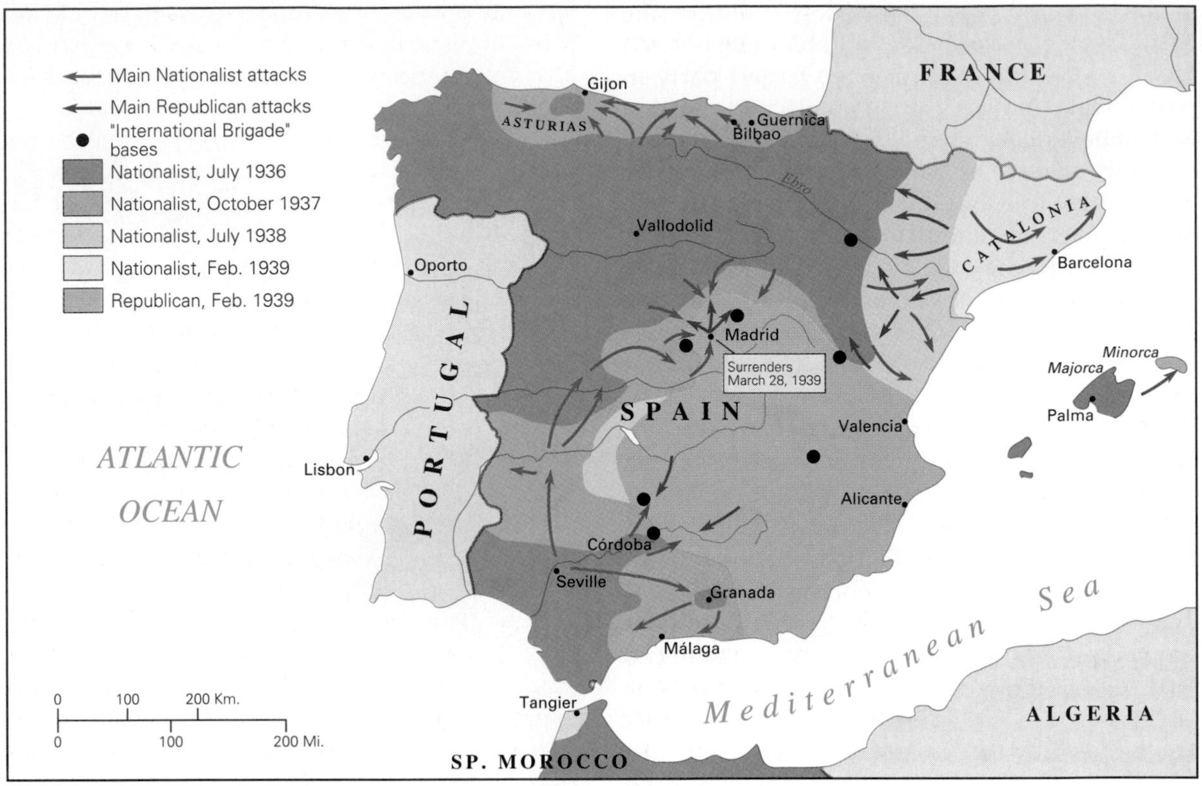

Map 29.1 The Spanish Civil War, 1936–1939 The Nationalist insurgents quickly took over most of northern and eastern Spain in 1936, and then gradually expanded their territory. The fall of Madrid early in 1939 marked the end of fighting. The revolutionary effort of 1936–1937 within the Republican zone was centered in Barcelona. (*Source:* Adapted from THE TIMES ATLAS OF WORLD HISTORY, 3d ed., by kind permission of Times Books.)

Franco (1892–1975), these Nationalist insurgents took control of substantial parts of Spain, but elsewhere they failed to overcome the resistance of the Republican Loyalists, those determined to defend the republic. So the result was not the intended military takeover but a brutal civil war (Map 29.1). The substantial Italian fascist and Nazi German intervention on the Nationalist side by the end of 1936 intensified the war's ideological ramifications. At the same time, the remarkable, often heroic resistance of the Loyalists captured the imagination of the world. Indeed, 40,000 volunteers came from abroad to fight to preserve the Spanish republic.

It proved a war of stunning brutality on both sides. Loyalist anticlericalism led to the murder of twelve bishops and perhaps one-eighth of the parish clergy in Spain. On the other hand, the German bombing of the Basque town of Guernica on a crowded market day in April 1937, represented unforgettably in Pablo Picasso's painting, came to symbolize the brutality and suffering of the whole era.

Republican Loyalists assumed that Franco and the Nationalists represented another instance of fascism. In fact, however, Franco was no fascist, but rather a traditional military man whose leadership role did not rest on personal charisma. He was an authoritarian emphasizing discipline, order, and Spain's Catholic traditions.

Still, in their effort to rally support during the civil war, Franco's forces found it expedient to take advantage of the appeal of the *Falange,* a genuinely fascist movement that had emerged under the leadership of the charismatic young José Antonio Primo de Rivera (1903–1936). Although extremely weak by the time of the election in February 1936, the Falange grew rapidly in opposition to the leftist radicalism that followed the popular front victory. As street fighting between left and right intensified that spring, the Republic arrested José Antonio, as he was called, and thus he was in prison when the civil war began.

José Antonio decided his best hope was alliance with the military. Although he was contemptuous of their shortsighted conservatism, he felt their very absence of ideas, "their abysmal political mediocrity," afforded an opening for the Falange to provide direction, a genuine alternative. But it worked out the other way. In November 1936, José Antonio was tried and executed for conspiring to overthrow the republic, and the Nationalists promptly began using the trappings of the Falange, including the memory of José Antonio, to increase their popular appeal.

Meanwhile, the Republicans had to fight a civil war while dealing with continuing revolution in their own ranks. Developing especially in Catalonia from the uprisings of 1936, that revolution was not communist but anarchist and syndicalist in orientation. The Communists, true to popular front principles, insisted that this was no time for such "infantile leftist" revolutionary experiments. What mattered, throughout the Republican zone, was the factory discipline necessary to produce essential war materiel. So the Communists, under Stalin's orders, were instrumental in putting down the anarchist revolution in Catalonia in June 1937.

Under these extraordinary circumstances, the Communists, at first a distinct minority on the Spanish left, gradually gained the ascendancy on the Republican side, partly because they were disciplined and effective, partly because the help the Soviets offered enhanced their prestige. But, again, the Soviets became involved to help prosecute the civil war, not to make a revolution. When all was said and done this single-minded prosecution of the civil war did not prove enough to defeat the military insurgency, despite the considerable heroism on the Loyalist side. The war ended with the fall of Madrid to the Nationalists in March 1939. General Franco's authoritarian regime governed Spain until his death in 1975.

In Spain, as in Weimar Germany, the initial lack of consensus in a new republic made parliamentary democracy difficult, and the wider ideological framework magnified the difficulties. With the political boiling point so low, the left and the right each viewed the other in extreme terms and assumed that extraordinary responses to the other were necessary. Thus the tendency of

Picasso: Guernica In perhaps the best-known painting of the twentieth century, Pablo Picasso conveyed horror and outrage in response to the Nazi bombing of the village of Guernica in 1937, during the Spanish civil war. *(Pablo Picasso,* Guernica *[1937, May–early June]. Oil on canvas. © SPADEM, Paris/ARS, New York)*

Léon Blum The French Socialist leader appears in an enthusiastic moment after the Popular Front victory in 1936. He was about to become France's first socialist prime minister, but in that role he encountered one dilemma after another. By 1938, the high spirits of 1936 had dissolved. *(Archives Ringart)*

the left to view even conservatives operating within a parliamentary framework as "fascist." And each side was relatively quick to give up on a democratic republic that seemed to be tilting too far in the other direction.

France in the Era of the Popular Front

In France, as in Spain, concern to arrest the spread of fascism led to a popular front coalition, here including Socialists, Communists, and Radicals, that governed the country from 1936 to 1938. Although it did not lead to civil war, the popular front was central to the French experience of the 1930s, producing polarization and resignation, and undermining confidence in the Third Republic.

Beginning in 1934, the French Communists took the initiative in approaching first the Socialists, then the Radicals, to develop a popular front coalition against fascism. In reaching out to the Radicals, the Communists stressed French patriotism and made no demand for significant economic reforms. Stalin gave this effort a major push in 1935 when, in a stunning change in the communist line, he stressed the legitimacy of national defense and explicitly approved of French rearmament.

In the elections of April and May 1936, the popular front won a sizable majority in the Chamber of Deputies, putting the Socialists' leader, Léon Blum (1872–1950), in line to become France's first socialist prime minister. The Communists pledged full support of the new Blum government but, to avoid fanning fears, they did not participate directly. However, despite the popular front's moderate and essentially defensive aims, the situation quickly began to polarize after the elections.

Fearing that the new Blum government would be forced to devalue the French currency, thereby diminishing the value of assets denominated in francs, French investors immediately began moving their capital abroad. At the same time, the popular front victory produced a wave of enthusiasm among workers that escaped the control of popular front leaders and culminated late in May in a spontaneous strike movement, the largest France had ever seen. By June 4 it had spread to all major industries nationwide. Although the workers' demands—for collective bargaining, a forty-hour week, and paid vacations—were not extraordinary, the movement involved sit-down strikes as well as the normal walk-out form and thus seemed to have a quasi-revolutionary character. The major trade union confederation, the Communists, and most Socialists, including Blum himself, saw the strikes as a danger to the popular front, with its more modest aims of defending the republic, and eagerly pursued a settlement.

That settlement, the Matignon Agreement of June 8, 1936, was a major victory for the French working class. Having been genuinely frightened by the strikes, and now reassured that the popular front government would at least uphold the law, French industrialists were willing to make significant concessions. For now, at least, they could best protect their interests by following the government's lead. So the workers got collective bargaining, elected shop stewards, and wage increases as a direct result of Matignon, then a forty-hour week and paid vacations among the reforms promptly passed by parliament.

In the enthusiasm of the summer of 1936, there were other reforms as well, but after that the popular front was forced onto the defensive. Two problems undermined its energy and cohesion: the noncooperation of French business and the Spanish civil war. In each case, the cautious response of Blum, the Socialist prime minister, is striking.

Blum was a respected socialist intellectual, but his performance in office seems classic confirmation of the notion that intellectuals do not make good practical politicians. Critics cite his introspection, his need for esteem, his desire to conciliate rather than dominate, his optimistic faith in the good intentions of others. But he faced a situation with little maneuvering room in 1936. From the outset he stressed that he had no mandate for revolution, and as France's first Socialist prime minister, he felt it essential to prove that a Socialist could govern responsibly.

Thus Blum did not respond energetically to the capital flight, even though it produced serious currency and budgetary difficulties. At first, he simply tried to persuade French capital holders to repatriate their assets, instead of devaluing the franc or imposing exchange controls, measures that he worried would further alienate investors. When this proved unsuccessful, he finally was forced to devalue in September 1936, but with only limited results. Perhaps, as critics suggest, he should have acted more aggressively to overhaul the French banking and credit system. But Blum shied away from any such drastic measures, both to prove he could be responsible and to avoid antagonizing business. And it is surely possible that a more energetic stance would only have confirmed business fears and thus made things worse.

On the economic issue, it was the popular front against the conservative business establishment, but the dilemmas surrounding the Spanish civil war undermined the popular front itself. The key question was whether the French government should help the beleaguered Spanish republic, at least by sending supplies. Although he initially favored such help, Blum changed his mind under pressure from three sides. The Conservative government of Stanley Baldwin in Britain was against it. So was the French right; some even suggested that French intervention would provoke civil war in France as well. Moreover, the Radicals in his own coalition were generally opposed to helping the Spanish republic, so intervention would jeopardize the popular front itself. Thus, rather than help supply the Spanish republic, Blum promoted a nonintervention agreement among the major powers, including Italy and Germany.

However, many Socialists and Communists within the popular front disliked Blum's nonintervention policy, especially as it became clear that Mussolini and Hitler were violating the nonintervention agreement. As Blum stuck to nonintervention, the moral force of the popular front dissolved. On this issue especially, Blum's caution, his desire to conciliate, is easily criticized. Nonetheless, he faced a genuine dilemma; as a leader seeking to preserve the democratic republic against a possible threat from the right, it could seem a plausible priority to avoid involvement in an ideological civil war abroad.

Blum's first government lasted about a year. He got a brief second chance in 1938, but by then the popular front was simply disintegrating. A new government under the Radical Edouard Daladier (1884–1970), still nominally a creature of the popular front, began dismantling some of the key gains of 1936, even attacking the forty-hour week. Citing productivity and national security concerns, Daladier did all he could to attract capital back to France. And he had considerable success. French investors who had remained nervous about Blum now had more confidence in the government's economic course.

On the other hand, Daladier's policies produced a serious rift with Blum and a sense of betrayal among the workers, who watched the gains they had won in 1936 gradually slip away. Those gains had outstripped what the popular front had stood for in the first place. And though such a better deal for French workers was overdue, it would have been easier to absorb during the more prosperous twenties than now, in a context of serious economic difficulty. As it happened, the workers' relatively extreme expectations made French businessmen and conservatives even more hostile to the popular front than they otherwise would have been. Indeed, those on the French right began blaming the workers' gains—like the five-day week—for slowing French rearmament. Rather than work shifts, the argument went, the workers insisted on a "double Sunday," or two-day weekend, so the provision for a five-day week cut into the production necessary for rearmament. Although such charges were not entirely fair, they indicated how poisoned the atmosphere in France had become in the wake of the popular front.

As France began to face the possibility of a new war, the popular front was widely blamed for French weakness. When war came at last, resignation and division were prevalent, in contrast with the patriotic unity and high spirits of 1914. It was partly for that reason that France was so easily defeated by Germany in 1940. And partly for the same reason, when France fell the democratic Third Republic fell with it, and the country opted for an authoritarian alternative.

The Coming of World War II, 1933–1939

Still under the long shadow of World War I, most Western leaders were determined to preserve the peace during the two ensuing decades. But the peace settlement that had followed the war created new problems and, despite promising adjustments during the 1920s, many remained when Hitler came to power in 1933. And Hitler had consistently trumpeted his intention to overturn that settlement. What scope was there for peaceful revision? Could Hitler be stopped by threat of war? Should he be?

Restoring German Sovereignty, 1935–1936

During his first years in power, through 1936, Hitler could be understood as merely restoring German sovereignty, revising a postwar settlement that had been misconceived in the first place. However uncouth and abrasive he might seem, it was hard to find a basis for opposing him. Yet in commencing German rearmament in 1935, and especially in remilitarizing the Rhineland in March 1936, Hitler fundamentally reversed the power balance established in France's favor at the peace conference.

France's special advantage had been the demilitarization of the entire German territory west of the Rhine River and a fifty-kilometer strip on the east bank. The measure had been reaffirmed at Locarno in 1925, now with Germany's free agreement, and it was guaranteed by Britain and Italy. Yet on a Saturday morning in March 1936, that advantage disappeared as German troops moved into the forbidden area. The French and British acquiesced, uncertain what else to do. After all, Hitler was only restoring Germany to full sovereignty.

But Hitler was not likely to stop there. As a result of the war and the peace, three new countries—Austria, Czechoslovakia, and Poland—bordered Germany. In each, the peace settlement had left trouble spots involving the status of ethnic Germans; in each the status quo was not necessarily sacrosanct.

Austria, Czechoslovakia, and Appeasement

As early as 1934, Hitler had moved to encompass his homeland, Austria, but strenuous opposition from Italy led him to back down. The developing understanding with Italy by 1936 enabled Hitler to focus again on Austria—initiating the second, more radical phase of his prewar foreign policy. On a pretext in March 1938, German troops moved into Austria, which was promptly incorporated into Germany. This time Mussolini was willing to acquiesce, and Hitler was genuinely grateful.

The Treaty of Versailles had explicitly prohibited this *Anschluss,* or unity with Germany, though that prohibition violated the principle of self-determination. It was widely believed in the West that most Austrians favored unity with Germany—and this perception was no doubt correct. The Anschluss could be justified as revising a misconceived aspect of the peace settlement.

Czechoslovakia presented quite a different situation. Although it had preserved democratic institutions, the country suffered from significant nationality problems. It included restive minorities of Slovaks, Magyars, Ruthenians, Poles, and—concentrated especially in the Sudetenland, along the German and Austrian borders—about 3.25 million Germans. After having been part of the dominant nationality in the old Habsburg empire, those Germans were frustrated with their minority status in the new Czechoslovakia, especially because they seemed to suffer disproportionately from the Depression. Hitler's agents actively stirred up their resentments. And Nazi Germany, with its economic and diplomatic successes, was bound to be attractive to many in this German population.

Leading the West's response, when Hitler began making an issue of Czechoslovakia, was Neville Chamberlain (1869–1940), who followed Stanley Baldwin as Britain's prime minister and foreign minister in May 1937. An intelligent, vigorous, and public-spirited man from the progressive wing of the Conservative party, Chamberlain has long been derided as the architect of the "appeasement" of Hitler at the Munich conference of 1938, which settled the crisis over Czechoslovakia. Trumpeted as the key to peace, the Munich agreement proved but a step to the war that broke out less than a year later. Yet though it failed, Chamberlain's policy of appeasement stemmed not from cowardice or mere drift and certainly not from some unspoken pro-Nazi sentiment.

Rather than let events spin out of control, as seemed to have happened in 1914, Chamberlain sought to master the difficult international situation through creative bargaining. The excesses of Hitler's policy resulted from the mistakes of Versailles; redo the settlement on a more realistic basis, and Germany would behave responsibly. The key, Chamberlain felt, was to pinpoint the sources of Germany's frustrations and, as he put it, "to remove the danger spots one by one."

Moreover, in Britain as elsewhere, there were some who saw Hitler's resurgent Germany as a bulwark against communism, which might spread into east-central Europe—especially in the event of another war. Indeed, the victor in another war might well be the revolutionary left. To prevent such an outcome was worth a few concessions to Hitler.

Although the Czechs, led by Eduard Beneš (1884–1948), made some attempt to liberalize their nationality policy, by April 1938 they were becoming ever less sympathetic to Sudeten German demands for autonomy, especially because a threat of German intervention seemed to accompany them. Tensions between Czechoslovakia and Germany mounted, and by late September 1938 war appeared imminent, despite Chamberlain's efforts to mediate (see the box, "Toward Appeasement: The Longing for Peace"). Both the French and the British began mobilizing, with French troops manning the Maginot Line for the first time.

A 1924 treaty bound France to come to the aid of Czechoslovakia in the event of aggression. Moreover, the Soviet Union, according to a treaty of 1935, was bound to assist Czechoslovakia if the

Germany Absorbs Austria, 1938 With the defeat and dismemberment of the Habsburg Empire, Austria was left a small, landlocked country after World War I. Most Austrians would have welcomed unification with Germany, but the peacemakers specifically prohibited any such step. As it happened, Austria was unified with Germany on Hitler's terms with the *Anschluss* of March 1938. Here Austrians look on as German troops march into Salzburg. *(Hulton-Deutsch)*

Toward Appeasement: The Longing for Peace

Late in September 1938, the crisis that developed over Germany's demands on Czechoslovakia produced an emotional roller coaster for Europeans. Central to the continuing effort to preserve the peace was the British prime minister, Neville Chamberlain, who flew to Germany twice to meet with Hitler before the crisis reached its climax. At first, Chamberlain thought he had found a formula for peace, but then Hitler upped his demands. Thus, Chamberlain's tone was somber when he addressed the British people by radio shortly after his second trip, on September 27, at what proved the height of the crisis.

First of all I must say something to those who have written to my wife or myself in these last weeks to tell us of their gratitude for my efforts and to assure us of their prayers for my success. Most of these letters have come from women—mothers or sisters of our own countrymen. But there are countless others besides—from France, from Belgium, from Italy, even from Germany, and it has been heartbreaking to read of the growing anxiety they reveal. . . .

If I felt my responsibility heavy before, to read such letters has made it seem almost overwhelming. How horrible, fantastic, incredible it is that we should be digging trenches and trying on gas masks here because of a quarrel in a far-away country between people of whom we know nothing. It seems still more impossible that a quarrel which has already been settled in principle should be the subject of war.

I can well understand the reasons why the Czech Government have felt unable to accept the terms which have been put before them in the German memorandum. Yet I believe after my talks with Herr Hitler that, if only time were allowed, it ought to be possible for the arrangements for transferring the territory that the Czech government has agreed to give to Germany to be settled by agreement under conditions which would assure fair treatment to the population concerned. . . .

However much we may sympathise with a small nation confronted by a big and powerful neighbor, we cannot in all circumstances undertake to involve the whole British Empire in war simply on her account. If we have to fight it must be on larger issues than that. . . . [I]f I were convinced that any nation had made up its mind to dominate the world by fear of its force, I should feel that it must be resisted. . . . but war is a fearful thing, and we must be very clear, before we embark on it, that it is really the great issues that are at stake. . . .

For the present I ask you to await as calmly as you can the events of the next few days. As long as war has not begun, there is always hope that it may be prevented, and you know that I am going to work for peace to the last moment. Good night.

Source: Neville Chamberlain, *In Search of Peace: Speeches (1937–1938)* (London: Hutchinson, 1939), pp. 274–276.

French did so. And throughout the crisis, the Soviets pushed for a strong stand in defense of Czechoslovakia against German aggression. For both ideological and military reasons, however, the British and French were not anxious for a war on the side of the Soviet Union. The value of the Soviet military was uncertain, at best, at a time when the Soviet officer corps had just been purged.

By September, Hitler seemed eager to smash the Czechs by force, but when Mussolini proposed a four-power conference, he was persuaded to talk again. At Munich late in September, Britain, France, Italy, and Germany settled the matter, with Czechoslovakia—and the Soviet Union—excluded. Determined not to risk war over what seemed Czech intransigence, the British ended up agreeing to what Hitler had wanted all along—not merely autonomy for the Sudeten Germans but German annexation of the Sudetenland.

The Munich agreement specified that all Sudeten areas with German majorities be transferred to Germany; plebiscites were to be held in areas with large German minorities, and Hitler pledged to respect the sovereignty of the newly diminished Czechoslovak state. Chamberlain and his French counterpart, Edouard Daladier, each returned home to a hero's welcome, having transformed what had seemed certain war to, in Chamberlain's unforgettable phrase, "peace in our time."

Rather than settle the nationality questions bedeviling Czechoslovakia, the Munich settlement only provoked further unrest. First, disputed areas with large Polish and Hungarian populations fell to Poland and Hungary, respectively. Each proved eager to exploit the new weakness of Czechoslovakia. Then unrest stemming from Slovak separatism afforded a pretext for Germany to send troops into Prague in March 1939. The Slovak areas were spun off as a separate nation, while the Czech areas became the Protectorate of Bohemia and Moravia. Less than six months after the Munich conference, most of what had been Czechoslovakia landed firmly within the Nazi orbit (Map 29.2). It was no longer possible to justify Hitler's actions as seeking to unite all Germans in one state.

The Illusion of Peace Neville Chamberlain, returning home to Britain from Munich to a hero's welcome, waves the peace declaration that was supposed to have brought "peace in our time." This was late September 1938. Less than a year later, Europe was again at war. *(Hulton-Deutsch)*

Poland, the Nazi-Soviet Pact, and the Coming of War

With Poland, the German grievance was still more serious, for the new Polish state had been created partly at German expense. Especially galling to Germans was the Polish corridor, which cut off East Prussia from the bulk of Germany in order to give Poland access to the sea. The German city of Danzig was left a "free city," supervised by the League of Nations.

Disillusioned by Hitler's dismemberment of Czechoslovakia, and angered by the Germans' menacing rhetoric with respect to Poland, Chamberlain announced in the House of Commons on March 31, 1939, that Britain and France would intervene militarily in the event of a threat to Poland's independence. Chamberlain was not only abandoning the policy of appeasement; he was making a clear commitment to the Continent, of the sort that British governments had resisted since 1919. He could do so partly because Britain was rapidly rearming; by early 1940, in fact, Britain was spending nearly as large a share of its national income on the military as Germany was.

Although most have seen in Chamberlain's statement an overdue indication of backbone and commitment, revisionist historians have suggested that such a guarantee to Poland was an overreaction, precluding negotiation over genuinely problematic German-Polish border issues. By May 1939, however, Hitler seems to have been determined to settle the Polish question by force in any case, though he stressed how limited and reasonable German aims were in an effort to localize the conflict. Germany simply wanted Danzig and German transit across the corridor; it was the Polish stance that was rigid and unreasonable. Hitler seems to have believed that Polish

Map 29.2 The Expansion of Nazi Germany, 1936–1939 Especially with the remilitarization of the Rhineland in 1936, Hitler's Germany began moving, step by step, to alter the European power balance. In September 1939 the Soviet Union also began annexing territory, capitalizing on its agreement with Germany the month before.

intransigence would alienate the British and French, undercutting their support. And as the crisis developed by mid-1939, doubts were increasingly expressed, on all sides, that the British and French were really prepared to aid Poland militarily—that they had the will "to die for Danzig."

Although they had been lukewarm to Soviet proposals for a genuine military alliance, Britain and France began to negotiate with the Soviet Union more seriously during the spring and summer of 1939. But doubts about the value of a Soviet alliance continued to gnaw at Western leaders. For one thing, Soviet troops could gain access to Germany only by moving through Poland or Romania, neither of which was willing to grant such passage. Poland and Romania each had territory gained at the expense of Russia in the postwar settlement, so the British and French, suspicious of Soviet designs on both, were reluctant to insist that Soviet troops be allowed to pass through them.

Even as negotiations between the Soviet Union and the democracies seemed to continue, the Soviet Union came to its own agreement with Nazi Germany on August 22, 1939, in a pact that astonished the world. Each of them had been denouncing the other, and although Hitler had explored the possibility of Soviet neutrality in May, serious negotiations began only that August, when the Soviets got the clear signal that a German invasion of Poland was inevitable. It now appeared that no Soviet alliance with Britain and France could prevent war. Under these circumstances, a nonaggression pact with Germany seemed better to serve Soviet interests than a problematic war on the side of Britain and France. So the Soviets agreed with the Germans that each would remain neutral in the event that either became involved in a war with some other nation.

The Soviet flip-flop stemmed partly from disillusionment with the British and French response to the accelerating threat of Nazism. The democracies seemed no more trustworthy, and potentially no less hostile, than Nazi Germany. Moreover, a secret protocol to the Nazi-Soviet Pact apportioned major areas of east-central Europe between the Soviet Union and Germany. Thus the Soviets soon regained much of what they had lost in the wake of World War I, when Poland, Finland, and other states had been created or aggrandized with territories that had been part of the Russian Empire.

The Nazi-Soviet Pact seemed to give Hitler the free hand he wanted in Poland. With the dramatic change in alignment, the democracies were surely much less likely to intervene. But Chamberlain, again determined to avoid the hesitations of 1914, publicly reaffirmed the British guarantee to Poland on August 25. Britain would indeed intervene in the event of a German attack. And after Hitler ordered the German invasion of Poland on September 1, the British and French responded with a declaration of war on September 3.

With each step on the path to war, Hitler had vacillated between apparent reasonableness and wanton aggressiveness. Sometimes he accented the plausibility of his demands in light of problems with the postwar settlement; sometimes he seemed actively to be seeking war. Even in invading Poland, he may still have been hoping to localize hostilities. But he was certainly willing to risk a more general European war, and the deepest thrust of his policy was toward a war of conquest—first against Poland, but ultimately against the Soviet Union. War was essential to the Nazi vision, and only when the assault on Poland became a full-scale war did the underlying purposes of Nazism became clear.

Summary

The 1930s made a cruel mockery of the hopes for restabilization that had followed World War I. The Depression and the challenges from new political regimes called both capitalism and democracy into question. Hitler's Germany, especially, presented an unprecedented challenge to the European order, but in the ideologically polarized context of the period others found it difficult to respond. Led by Britain, the democracies began to resist unequivocally only in 1939.

The most important new political systems of the interwar period—Italian fascism, German Nazism, and Stalinist communism—were dictatorial and hostile to liberal democracy, but they were not merely authoritarian in the old-fashioned, predemocratic sense. They were clearly novel, and they had some features in common. Their common direction is often summed up as "totalitarian," a useful though problematic term.

In each of the three regimes, the totalitarian direction meant expanding the sovereignty of the state and mobilizing ordinary people, forcing new forms of mass participation in public life. The political was to become all-encompassing, breaking down the distinction between public and private. Thus Mussolini's oft-quoted boast that there was "nothing outside the state" in fascist Italy, and thus the proclamation of Robert Ley, head of the Nazi Labor Front, that "the private citizen has ceased to exist."

The common totalitarian direction is important, but it glosses over differences, especially in origins and purposes, that are at least as important. Racism and anti-Semitism, in some ways the core of radical Nazism, were not central to Italian fascism. On the other hand, the corporativist thrust central to Italian fascism carried the regime well beyond the superficially comparable institutions of Nazi Germany. Racism and corporativism stemmed from very different frustrations with the modern democratic order. It is striking that many Italian fascists disliked the increasingly close ties with Nazi Germany after 1935 because they found Nazism not simply a more dynamic form of fascism but something uniquely German—and negative.

In practice, Nazism and Stalinism were far more extreme than Italian fascism, so comparison of these two regimes is central to any attempt to understand the troubling political experience of the 1930s. Again, whatever the convergence in practice, the difference in origins and purposes must not be forgotten.

Twisted though it became, the Marxist vision of human liberation, based on long-standing Western values, was still manifest in the ongoing Soviet revolution during the 1930s. And though the revolutionary enthusiasm of its origins had largely disappeared in the Soviet Union by the 1970s, it was still present in the 1930s, and it underlies some of the fervid excess of those years. Committed communists believed that extreme measures were necessary if they were to carry out, in the difficult conditions the Soviet Union faced, a transformation that would eventually benefit all mankind. Nazism never claimed a comparably universal aim. Indeed, with its emphasis on racial determinism and natural struggle, Hitler's world view was the antithesis of the humanistic tradition that found in Marxism one coherent, if extreme, manifestation. More generally, Hitler's radical Nazism was fundamentally antithetical to basic Western values, which emphasize the worth of human life and the dignity of every individual.

But whatever the differences in values and intentions, the final reckoning must rest on the results. Stalin's way of implementing the Marxist revolution made individual human lives expendable, just as they were for Hitler. Thus the outcome of both Stalinism and Nazism was mass murder on a horrifying scale.

Notes

1. Quoted in Robert Conquest, *The Great Terror: A Reassessment* (New York: Oxford University Press, 1990), p. 24.
2. Quoted in Helmut Krausnick et al., *Anatomy of the SS State* (New York: Walker, 1968), p. 13.

Suggested Reading

The Great Depression

James, Harold. *The German Slump: Politics and Economics, 1924–1936.* 1986. Weaves economics and politics to explain the Depression in Germany and the economic recovery after Hitler came to power in 1933.

Kindleberger, Charles. *The World in Depression, 1929–1939.* Revised and enlarged ed. 1986. An important revisionist work arguing that the Depression stemmed from difficulties in the international exchange system rather than from problems and responses in the United States.

Skidelsky, Robert. *Politicians in the Slump: The Labour Government of 1929–1931.* 1967. Searching analysis of the inability of Britain's Labour government to respond effectively to the mass unemployment of the first years of the Depression.

Stalinism and the Soviet Union

Conquest, Robert. *The Harvest of Sorrow: Soviet Collectivization and the Terror-Famine.* 1986. Dramatic, pioneering account of the deportation and forced collectivization of peasants that proved the cornerstone of the Stalinist revolution of 1929–1933.

———. *The Great Terror: A Reassessment.* 1990. Updated edition of an influential work first published in 1968. Offers a gripping account of the Stalinist purges of the 1930s, emphasizing Stalin's personal responsibility.

Getty, J. Arch. *Origins of the Great Purges: The Soviet Communist Party Reconsidered, 1933–1938.* 1985. Challenges the notion that the purges, show trials, and terror of the thirties were parts of a single totalitarian system orchestrated by Stalin. Argues that they were ad hoc responses to disparate pressures.

Kuromiya, Hiroaki. *Stalin's Industrial Revolution: Politics and Workers, 1928–1932.* 1988. Avoids debates about whether the Stalinist route to industrialization was necessary and explains how the crash industrialization was actually accomplished.

Tucker, Robert C. *Stalin in Power: The Revolution from Above, 1928–1941.* 1990. The second volume of the author's acclaimed study of Stalin, but stands on its own. Provides a superb account of the crash industrialization and forced collectivization that led to the Stalinist regime.

Hitler and Nazism

Bessel, Richard, ed., *Life in the Third Reich.* 1987. Essays on the connections between the Nazi regime and German society. An ideal introductory work.

Bracher, Karl Dietrich. *The German Dictatorship: The Origins, Structure, and Effects of National Socialism.* 1970. A comprehensive synthesis by a major German authority.

Fest, Joachim C. *The Face of the Third Reich: Portraits of the Nazi Leadership.* 1970. Perceptive collective biography of the major Nazi hierarchs, highlighting common personal weaknesses.

———. *Hitler.* 1975. Generally recognized as the best full-scale biography of Hitler.

Jaeckel, Eberhard. *Hitler's World View: A Blueprint for Power.* 1981. Influential account of the combination of racism, anti-Semitism, and Social Darwinism that structured Hitler's thinking—and ultimately the aspirations of the Nazi regime.

Kershaw, Ian. *The "Hitler Myth": Image and Reality in the Third Reich.* 1987. Explores the often contradictory image of Hitler created in Nazi propaganda.

———. *The Nazi Dictatorship: Problems and Perspectives of Interpretation.* 2d ed. 1989. Excellent historiographical account of the major issues and recent controversies concerning the Nazi regime in practice.

Koonz, Claudia. *Mothers in the Fatherland: Women, the Family, and Nazi Politics.* 1987. A thoughtful, readable study accenting the active role of women in implementing Nazism within German society, especially on the grassroots level in welfare, education, and leisure activities.

Mosse, George, ed. (with commentary). *Nazi Culture: Intellectual, Cultural and Social Life in the Third Reich.* 1966. Varied documents on numerous aspects of German life under Nazism.

Noakes, J[eremy], and G[eoffrey] Pridham, eds. *Nazism: A History in Documents and Eyewitness Accounts, 1919–1945.* 2 vols. 1990. An invaluable collection of documents on all aspects of Nazism, usefully arranged with running commentary by the editors.

Peukert, Detlev J. K. *Inside Nazi Germany: Conformity, Opposition, and Racism in Everyday Life.* 1987. Among the best of recent efforts to understand Nazi Germany by depicting how Nazism affected the everyday lives of ordinary people.

Stephenson, Jill. *Women in Nazi Society.* 1975. Pioneering work on what Nazism meant for women's status and opportunities. Shows that by the late 1930s, German women were neither better nor worse off than women elsewhere in the West.

Comparative Approaches to the Dictatorships

Bullock, Alan. *Hitler and Stalin: Parallel Lives.* 1992. A lengthy yet gripping comparative account by a master of the biographical approach to history.

Menze, Ernest A., ed. *Totalitarianism Reconsidered.* 1981. A collection of essays examining the uses and limitations of "totalitarianism" as an interpretive category.

France and Spain

Carr, Raymond. *The Spanish Tragedy: The Civil War in Perspective.* 1977. An accessible account, blending narrative with analysis and commentary. Particularly useful on the politics of the Nationalist zone.

Colton, Joel. *Leon Blum: Humanist in Politics.* 1987. First pub. 1966. Sympathetic but carefully balanced biography, featuring dilemmas stemming from Blum's background as a socialist intellectual.

Fraser, Ronald. *Blood of Spain: An Oral History of the Spanish Civil War.* 1986. Based on interviews with participants, this book provides a running history of the war and the revolutionary efforts that accompanied it.

Jackson, Julian. *The Popular Front in France: Defending Democracy, 1934–38.* 1988. Combines narrative with thematic chapters on the most controversial issues surrounding the popular front experience.

Payne, Stanley. *The Spanish Revolution.* 1970. Focuses on the disintegration of the second Spanish republic and the coming of the civil war.

Diplomacy and the Coming of War

Bell, P. M. H. *The Origins of the Second World War in Europe.* 1986. A well-organized and nicely balanced survey.

Cameron, Donald Watt. *How War Came: The Immediate Origins of the Second World War, 1938–1939.* 1989. Detailed but readable narrative account, based on thorough research.

Overy, R. J., and Andrew Wheatcroft. *The Road to War.* 1989. Without questioning Hitler's ruthlessness and ultimate responsibility, the authors challenge standard views of the causes of World War II by recreating the particular situations and perspectives of each country.

Weinberg, Gerhard L. *The Foreign Policy of Hitler's Germany.* Vol. 1, *Diplomatic Revolution in Europe, 1933–1936,* and vol. 2, *Starting World War II, 1937–1939.* 1970, 1980. Comprehensive study focusing on the key decisions and those who made them. Emphasizes Hitler's aims and German initiatives in the process that led to war.

Weighing the Evidence

FILM AS PROPAGANDA

One of the extraordinary pieces of evidence from the Nazi period is *Triumph of the Will*, a documentary film on the sixth Nazi party rally, which took place September 4–10, 1934, in the historic city of Nuremberg, by this time the official site for such party rallies. Directed by a talented young woman, Leni Riefenstahl (b. 1902), *Triumph of the Will* has long been recognized as one of the most compelling propaganda films ever made. What can we learn from this film about how the Nazis understood and used propaganda? What was the Nazi regime trying to convey in sponsoring the film, with the particular images it contained?

A sense of the scope for political propaganda was one of the defining features of the Nazi movement virtually from its inception. In his quest for power Hitler allotted an especially significant role to his future propaganda minister, Joseph Goebbels. Both Hitler and Goebbels saw that new media and carefully orchestrated events might be used to shape the political views of masses of people.

The Nazi party held the first of what would become annual conventions in Nuremberg in 1927. From the start, these meetings were rallies of the faithful, intended to give the Nazi movement a sense of cohesion and common purpose; but they increasingly became carefully staged propaganda spectacles, with banners and searchlights, parades and speeches. When, by 1934, the regime had completed the task of immediate power consolidation, it seemed time to seize the potential of the film medium to carry the spectacle beyond those present in Nuremberg. The intention to make a film thus influenced the staging of the 1934 rally. Film would transform the six-day event into a single potent work of art.

As seen in *Triumph of the Will*, the Leader . . .

When Hitler came to power, Goebbels, as propaganda minister, assumed control of the German film industry, and he was particularly jealous of his prerogatives in this sphere. If there was to be a film of one of the Nuremberg rallies, he assumed that he would be in charge. So he objected strenuously when Hitler decided that Riefenstahl, who was not even a party member, should film the 1934 rally.

Already popular as an actress, Riefenstahl had established her own film-making company in 1931, before she turned 30. Her first film won the admiration of Hitler, who sought her out and eventually proposed that she direct the film of the party rally. Although she was an artist with no special interest in politics, Riefenstahl, like many Germans, believed at this point that Hitler might be able to revive Germany's fortunes. So despite considerable reluctance, she bowed to Hitler's persistence and agreed to do the film—though only after she was guaranteed final control over editing. Her relations with Goebbels remained strained, but Hitler continued to support her as she made *Triumph of the Will*.

Riefenstahl developed the 107-minute film by editing sixty-one hours of footage that covered everything from Hitler's arrival and motorcade to the closing parades and speeches. As depicted on film, the party rally does not convey an overt ideological message. We hear Hitler not attacking Jews or glorifying conquest but simply trumpet-

. . . and the Disciplined, Tightly Knit Community of Followers *(Both photos from the Museum of Modern Art/Film Stills Archive)*

ing German renewal. What strikes us in Riefenstahl's portrayal are the unity and epic monumentality that Nazism had apparently brought to Germany thanks to Hitler's leadership.

The film opens as Hitler emerges from dramatic cloud formations to arrive by airplane, descending from the sky like a god. He appears throughout the film as an almost superhuman figure, even, as in the shot shown here, as inspired, possessed, uncanny. Above all, he is a creator who shapes reality by blending will and art, forging masses of anonymous individuals into one people, one racial community, ready for anything. Those individuals seem, from one perspective, to lose their individuality in a monolithic mass, as in the shot of the parade grounds. But their sense of involvement in grandiose purposes charges them emotionally, even gives them a kind of ecstasy. The symbols, the massed banners, the ritualistic show of conformity, all strengthened this sense of participation in the new people's community. But unity and community were not ends in themselves; the film exalted military values and depicted a disciplined society organized for war.

Triumph of the Will extended participation in the spectacle to those who were not actually present in Nuremberg. But the film chiseled the sprawling event into a work of art, so seeing the film was in some ways more effective than being there. The Nazis looked for every means possible to involve the whole society in ritualistic spectacles that could promote a sense of belonging and unity. In addition to film, they made effective use of radio, even subsidizing purchase of radio sets, or "people's receivers." Such new media were to help ordinary Germans feel a more meaningful kind of belonging than had been possible under the democracy of the Weimar Republic. But this was only an emotional kind of involvement, not the active participation of free citizens invited to make rational choices.

Triumph of the Will had its premiere in March 1935, with Hitler in the audience. It won several prizes in Germany and abroad but enjoyed only mixed success with the German public, especially outside the large cities. For some, it was altogether *too* artistic, and the Nazi regime did not use it widely for overt propaganda purposes. Still, the Nazis commissioned no other film about Hitler, for *Triumph of the Will* captured the way he wanted to be seen. Indeed, Hitler praised the film as an "incomparable glorification of the power and beauty of our Movement."

ACH OSTEN
НА ВОСТОК

CHAPTER 30

The Era of the Second World War, 1939–1949

The war that began with the German invasion of Poland in 1939 ended up convulsing the world as none ever had before. World War II proved far more destructive than World War I and more truly global in scope. By the end of 1941, it had grown to encompass Japan, allied with Germany and Italy, and aggressively seeking an empire in East Asia and the Pacific. In World War I, Japan had played only a secondary role, on the side of Britain. Japan's far greater involvement in World War II brought the full brunt of the war to Asia and the Pacific and dramatically changed the war's overall shape. Moreover, because the war expanded as it did, it profoundly affected the place of Western civilization in the world. Yet the Japanese became involved late in 1941 only because of the outcome in Europe to that point, and ultimately it was the European theater that proved decisive.

The war led to the defeat of the Axis powers—first Italy, then Germany, and finally Japan—and it left fascism utterly discredited. In this sense, the war overcame the forces that had caused it. But the experiences it entailed and the outcomes it produced changed the world forever. Indeed, it brought much of the old Europe to collapse and ruin. Symptomatic of this decline, the European overseas empires began seriously unraveling even during the war. Of the European states, only the Soviet Union emerged enhanced from the war—and it was radically enhanced, thrust into a world role that would have been inconceivable just a few years before.

The war spawned new forms of death and destruction that continued to haunt the world after it ended. The Nazis began systematically murdering the Jews of Europe in specially constructed extermination camps. Britain and the United States firebombed major cities such as Dresden and Tokyo,

Soviet poster from 1943 proclaiming the USSR's western offensive.

causing massive destruction and loss of life. And the war ended when the United States used a new weapon of unprecedented destructiveness—the atomic bomb—to force the surrender of Japan.

The ironic outcome of the war in Europe was a new cold war between the United States and the Soviet Union, former allies in the victorious struggle against Nazi Germany. By the end of the 1940s, Europe was divided between these antagonistic superpowers. And the new atomic age was especially terrifying because each immediately raced for the advantage in nuclear weapons.

The Nazi Triumph, 1939–1941

Instead of the enthusiasm of 1914, the German invasion of Poland on September 1, 1939, produced a grim sense of foreboding, even in Germany. Well-publicized incidents like the German bombing of civilians during the Spanish civil war and the Italian use of poison gas in Ethiopia suggested that the frightening new technologies introduced in World War I would now be used on a totally different scale, making this a much uglier war, more directly involving civilians.

Still, as in 1914, there were hopes that this new war could be localized and brief—that it would not become a "world war." Hitler was not expecting a protracted war with Britain. In light of the Nazi-Soviet Pact, war between Germany and the Soviet Union seemed unlikely. And isolationist sentiment in the United States made U.S. intervention doubtful.

Rather than a long war, Hitler and the Germans expected a *Blitzkrieg*, or "lightning war." And at first events seemed to confirm German expectations. When Poland fell after just over a month, Hitler publicly offered peace to Britain and France, seriously thinking that might be the end of it. The British and French refused to call off the war, but from 1939 through 1941 the Nazis won victory after victory and began building their own "new order" in Europe.

Initial Conquests and "Phony War"

The Polish army was large enough to have given the Germans a serious battle. But in adapting the technological innovations of World War I, Germany had developed a new military strategy based on rapid mobility. This *Blitzkrieg* strategy employed swift, highly concentrated offensives based on mobile tanks covered with concentrated air support, including dive-bombers that struck just ahead of the tanks. In Poland this strategy proved decisive. The French could offer only token help, and the last Polish unit surrendered on October 2. The speed of the German victory stunned the world.

Meanwhile, the Soviets began cashing in on the pact they had made with Nazi Germany a few weeks before. It offered a precious opportunity to undo the parts of the World War I settlement that had significantly diminished the western territories of the former Russian Empire, thereby damaging the interests and defenses of the new Soviet state. On September 17, with the German victory in Poland assured, Stalin sent Soviet forces into Poland. Soon Poland was again divided between Germany and Russia, as it had been before 1914. Stalin looked next to the Baltic states of Estonia, Latvia, and Lithuania, which had been within the Russian Empire before World War I. The Nazi-Soviet agreement had assigned Lithuania to the German orbit, but the Germans agreed to let the Soviets have it in exchange for an additional slice of Poland. Although they were initially let off with treaties of mutual assistance, Estonia, Latvia, and Lithuania were incorporated as republics within the Soviet Union during the summer of 1940.

When Finland proved less pliable, the Soviets invaded in November 1939. In the ensuing "Winter War," the Finns held out bravely, and only by taking heavy casualties did the Soviets manage to prevail by March 1940. These difficulties seemed to confirm suspicions that Stalin's purge during the mid-thirties had substantially weakened the Soviet army. Still, by midsummer 1940 the Soviet Union had regained much of what it had lost during the upheavals surrounding the earlier revolution.

In the West, little happened during the strained winter of 1939–1940, known as the "Phony War." Then, on April 9, 1940, the Germans attacked Norway and Denmark in a surprise move to pre-empt a British and French scheme to cut off the major route for the shipment of Swedish iron ore to Germany. Denmark fell virtually at once, while the staunch resistance in

The Fall of France: A Strange Defeat?

Just after the defeat of France in 1940, Marc Bloch (1886–1944), a well-known historian of medieval Europe, tried to explain his country's poor performance against Nazi Germany. He argued that the inadequacies of France's military leadership stemmed from a more general complacency and lack of dynamism in French society. Bloch became active in the French resistance in 1942 and was captured, tortured, and killed by the Nazis in 1944. His book was published only after his death.

Let us . . . have the courage to admit that what has so far been conquered in our land is precisely the life of our dear dead towns. The leisurely rhythm of their days, their crawling motor-buses, their sleepy officials, the time lost in their soft atmosphere of lethargy, the lazy ease of their café-life, their local politics and petty trades, their empty libraries, their taste for the past, and their mistrust of anything that may shake them out of their comfortable habits. These are the things that have succumbed before the hellish onslaught of that "dynamic" Germany whose aggression was backed by the resources of a national life organized on the principle of the hive. If only to preserve what can, and ought to, be of value in our great heritage, we must adapt ourselves to the claims of a new age. The donkey-cart may be a friendly and a charming means of transport, but if we refuse to replace it with the motor car, where the motor car is desirable, we shall find ourselves stripped of everything—including the donkey. But if we are to set about building the new, we must first acquire the necessary knowledge. If our officers failed to master the methods of warfare imposed upon them by the contemporary world, that was largely because, in the contemporary world, our middle classes, from which they were drawn, had been willing to keep their eyes lazily shut to the facts. If we turn back on ourselves we shall be lost.

Source: Marc Bloch, *Strange Defeat: A Statement of Evidence Written in 1940* (New York: W. W. Norton, 1968), pp. 126, 149.

Norway was effectively broken by the end of April. The stage was set for the German assault on France.

The Fall of France

The war in the West began in earnest on May 10, 1940, when the Germans attacked France and the Low Countries. They launched their assault on France through the Ardennes Forest, above the northern end of the Maginot Line, terrain so difficult the French had discounted the possibility of an enemy strike there. As in 1914, northern France quickly became the focus of a major war pitting French forces and their British allies against invading Germans. But this time, in startling contrast to World War I, the Battle of France was over in less than six weeks, a humiliating defeat for the French. What had happened? Could the defeat be explained in military terms alone, or did it stem from underlying weaknesses in French society? (See the box, "The Fall of France: A Strange Defeat?")

The problem for the French was not lack of men and materiel, but strategy: how men and materiel were used. For example, Germany had, at best, no more than a slight numerical advantage in tanks. But in France, as in Poland, Germany took advantage of mobile tanks and dive-bombers to mount rapid, highly concentrated offensives. Germany achieved the essential breakthrough partly because the French command underestimated the speed with which the German army could move through Belgium.

French strategy, in contrast, was based on lessons learned during World War I. Anticipating another long, defensive war, France dispersed its tanks among infantry units along a broad front. Once the German tank column broke through the French lines, it quickly cut through northern France toward the North Sea. France's poor showing convinced the British that rather than commit troops and planes to a hopeless battle in France, they should get out and regroup for a longer global war. Finally 200,000 British troops—as well as 130,000 French—escaped German encirclement and capture through a difficult evacuation at Dunkirk early in June.

By mid-June, just five weeks after the fighting began, France had been thoroughly defeated. As the French military collapsed, the French cabinet resigned, to be replaced by a new government under Marshal Philippe Pétain, the hero of Verdun. That government first asked for an armistice, then engineered a change of regime. The parliament voted by an overwhelming majority to give Pétain exceptional powers, including the power to draw up a new constitution. So ended the parliamentary democracy of the Third Republic, which seemed responsible for France's weakness. The Third Republic gave way to the more authoritarian Vichy regime, named after the resort city to which the government retreated as the Germans moved into Paris. The end of the fighting in France resulted in a kind of antidemocratic revolution, but one in which the French people, stunned by military defeat, at first acquiesced.

According to the armistice agreement, the French government was not only to cease hostilities but also to collaborate with the victorious Germans. However, French resistance began immediately. In a radio broadcast from London on June 18, Charles de Gaulle (1890–1970), the youngest general in the French army, called on French forces to rally to him to continue the fight against Nazi Germany. The military forces stationed in the French colonies, as well the French troops that had been evacuated at Dunkirk, could form the nucleus of a new French army. Under the circumstances of military defeat and political change, de Gaulle's appeal seemed quixotic at best, and most French colonies went along with what seemed the legitimate French government at Vichy. And for the new Vichy government, de Gaulle was a traitor. Yet a new Free French force grew from de Gaulle's remarkable appeal, and its role later in the war helped overcome the humiliation of France's quick defeat in 1940.

What next for Hitler and the Germans, who seemed virtually invincible after their conquest of France? Ultimately decisive would be the assault on the Soviet Union in June 1941, but two chains of events after the Battle of France influenced the timing of the assault—perhaps in a crucial way. Britain proved a more implacable foe, and Italy a more burdensome friend, than Hitler had expected.

Winston Churchill and the Battle of Britain

With the defeat of France, Hitler seems to have expected the British, now apparently vulnerable to German invasion, to come to terms. But the British, having none of it, found a new spokesman and leader in Winston Churchill (1874–1965), who had replaced Neville Chamberlain as prime minister when the German invasion of western Europe began on May 10. Although Churchill had been prominent in British public life for years, his career to this point had not been noteworthy for either judgment or success. He was obstinate, difficult, something of a curmudgeon. Yet he rose to the wartime challenge, becoming one of the notable leaders of the modern era. In speeches to the House of Commons during the remainder of 1940, he uttered perhaps the most memorable words of the war as he sought to dramatize the situation and inspire his countrymen. Some, hoping for a negotiated settlement with Germany as the Battle of France ended, objected to Churchill's rhetoric, but his dogged promise of "blood, toil, tears, and sweat" helped rally the English people, so that later could he say, without exaggeration, that "this was their finest hour."

After the fall of France, Britain moved to full mobilization for a protracted war. Churchill consolidated economic policy under a small committee that promptly gave Britain the most thoroughly coordinated war economy of all the belligerents. Between 1940 and 1942, Britain produced more tanks, aircraft, and machine guns than Germany did. In 1941, Britain adopted a National Service Act that subjected men aged 18 to

British Resistance At the height of the German bombing of Britain in 1940, Winston Churchill surveys the damage in London. *(Hulton-Deutsch)*

50 and women aged 20 to 30 to military or civilian war service. The upper age limits were subsequently raised to meet the demand for labor. Almost 70 percent of the 3 million people added to the British work force during the war were women.

Britain, then, intended to continue the fight even after France fell. Hitler weighed his options, then decided to attack. In light of British naval superiority, he hoped to rely on aerial bombardment to knock the British out of the war without an actual invasion. The ensuing Battle of Britain culminated in the nightly bombing of London from September 7 through November 2, 1940, killing 15,000 and destroying thousands of buildings. But the British held. Ordinary people holed up in cellars and subway stations, while the fighter planes of the Royal Air Force fought back effectively, inflicting heavy losses against German aircraft over Britain.

Although the bombing continued into 1941, the British had withstood the worst the Germans could deliver, and Hitler began looking to the east, his ultimate objective all along. In December 1940, he ordered preparations for Operation Barbarossa, the assault on the Soviet Union. Rather than continuing the attack on Britain directly, Germany planned to use submarines to cut off shipping—and thus the supplies the British needed for a long war. Once Germany had defeated the Soviet Union, it would enjoy the geopolitical basis for world power, while Britain, as an island nation relying on a dispersed empire, would sooner or later be forced to come to terms.

Italian Intervention and the Spread of the War

Lacking sufficient domestic support, and unready for a major war, Mussolini had been forced to look on as the war began in 1939. But as the Battle of France neared its end, it seemed safe for Italy to intervene, sharing in the spoils of what seemed certain victory. Thus in June 1940, Italy entered the war, expecting to secure territorial advantages in the Mediterranean, starting with Corsica, Nice, and Tunisia at the expense of France. Eventually Italy hoped to supplant Britain as well, even taking the Suez Canal.

Although Hitler and Mussolini got along remarkably well, their relationship was sensitive. When Hitler seemed to be proceeding without

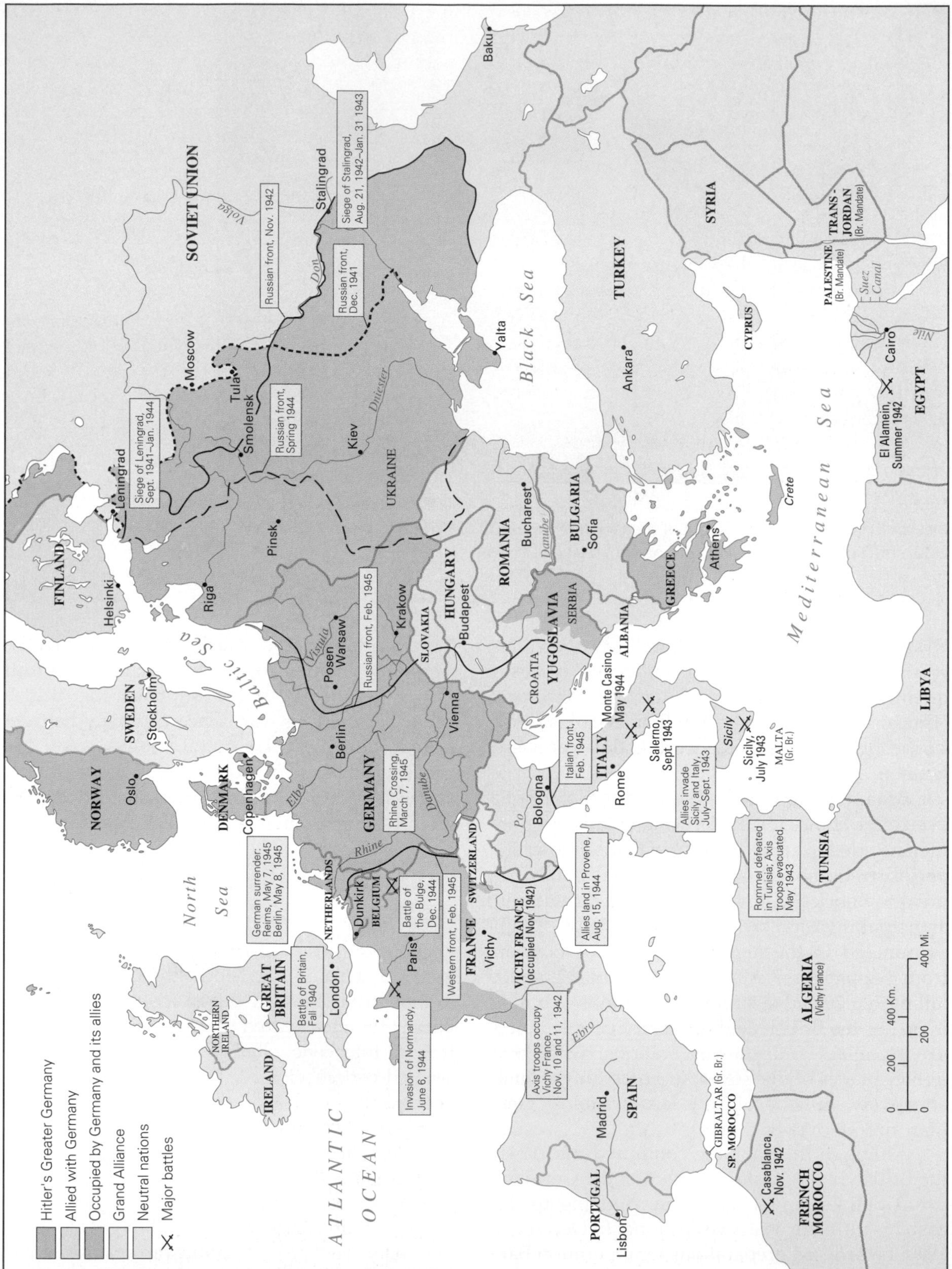

Hitler's Greater Germany
Allied with Germany
Occupied by Germany and its allies
Grand Alliance
Neutral nations
Major battles
ATLANTIC OCEAN
North Sea
Baltic Sea
Black Sea
Mediterranean Sea
SOVIET UNION
FINLAND
NORWAY
SWEDEN
DENMARK
GREAT BRITAIN
NORTHERN IRELAND
IRELAND
NETHERLANDS
BELGIUM
GERMANY
FRANCE
VICHY FRANCE (occupied Nov. 1942)
SWITZERLAND
ITALY
SPAIN
PORTUGAL
SP. MOROCCO
FRENCH MOROCCO
ALGERIA (Vichy France)
TUNISIA
LIBYA
EGYPT
PALESTINE (Br. Mandate)
TRANS-JORDAN (Br. Mandate)
SYRIA
TURKEY
CYPRUS
GREECE
ALBANIA
YUGOSLAVIA
CROATIA
SERBIA
BULGARIA
ROMANIA
HUNGARY
SLOVAKIA
UKRAINE
GIBRALTAR (Gr. Br.)
MALTA (Gr. Br.)
Sicily
Crete
Oslo
Stockholm
Helsinki
Copenhagen
Riga
Leningrad
Moscow
Tula
Smolensk
Stalingrad
Baku
Kiev
Pinsk
Yalta
Berlin
Posen
Warsaw
Krakow
Vienna
Budapest
Bucharest
Sofia
Athens
Ankara
Cairo
London
Dunkirk
Paris
Vichy
Bologna
Rome
Madrid
Lisbon
Volga
Don
Dniester
Vistula
Elbe
Rhine
Danube
Po
Ebro
Nile
Suez Canal
Siege of Leningrad, Sept. 1941–Jan. 1944
Russian front, Spring 1944
Russian front, Nov. 1942
Russian front, Dec. 1941
Siege of Stalingrad, Aug. 21, 1942–Jan. 31 1943
Russian front, Feb. 1945
Rhine Crossing, March 7, 1945
German surrender: Reims, May 7, 1945 Berlin, May 8, 1945
Battle of Britain, Fall 1940
Battle of the Bulge, Dec. 1944
Western front, Feb. 1945
Invasion of Normandy, June 6, 1944
Axis troops occupy Vichy France, Nov. 10 and 11, 1942
Allies land in Provene, Aug. 15, 1944
Italian front, Feb. 1945
Monte Casino, May 1944
Salerno, Sept. 1943
Allies invade Sicily and Italy, July–Sept. 1943
Sicily, July 1943
Rommel defeated in Tunisia; Axis troops evacuated, May 1943
El Alamein, Summer 1942
Casablanca, Nov. 1942
0 200 400 Km.
0 200 400 Mi.

Italy during the first year of the war, Mussolini grew determined to show his independence and finally, in October 1940, ordered Italian forces to attack Greece. However, the Greeks mounted a strong resistance, thanks partly to the help of British forces from North Africa.

Meanwhile, Germany had established its hegemony in much of east-central Europe without military force, often by exploiting grievances over the outcome of the peace conference in 1919. In November 1940, Romania and Hungary formally committed to the Axis camp, and Bulgaria followed a few months later. But in March 1941, just after Yugoslavia had similarly committed to the Axis, a coup overthrew the pro-Axis government in Yugoslavia, and the new Yugoslav government prepared to aid the Allies.

By this point Hitler had decided it was expedient to push into the Balkans with German troops, both to reinforce the Italians and to consolidate Axis control of the area. The war's geographical extent was expanding, and its stakes were increasing, but the Germans continued to meet every challenge. By the end of May 1941 they had taken Yugoslavia and Greece (Map 30.1).

Meanwhile, the war had spread to North Africa and the Middle East because of European colonial ties. The native peoples of the area sought to take advantage of the conflict among the Europeans to pursue their own independence. Iraq and Syria became involved as Germans operating from Syria, administered by Vichy France, aided anti-British Arab nationalists in Iraq. But most important proved to be North Africa, where Libya, an Italian colony since 1912, lay adjacent to Egypt, where Britain still had a strong presence.

In September 1940 the Italian army drove 65 miles into Egypt, initiating almost three years of fighting across the North African deserts. A British counteroffensive from December 1940 to February 1941 drove the Italians back 340 miles into Libya, prompting Germany to send some of its forces from the Balkans into North Africa. Under General Erwin Rommel (1891–1944), the famous "Desert Fox," Axis forces won remarkable successes in North Africa from February to May 1941. But successful though they had been by this point, the German forays into the Balkans and North Africa had delayed the crucial attack on the Soviet Union.

Map 30.1 World War II: European Theaters Much of Europe saw fighting at one time or another during World War II, although different fronts were important at different times.

The Assault on the Soviet Union and the Nazi New Order

In ordering preparations for Operation Barbarossa in December 1940, Hitler decided to risk attacking the Soviet Union before knocking Britain out of the war. Then he invaded the Balkans and North Africa in what may have been

Forgive Me, Comrade . . . On June 23, 1941, the day after Nazi Germany attacked the Soviet Union, the London *Daily Mail* published this cartoon depicting Hitler's betrayal of his 1939 pact with Stalin. (Daily Mail, *London, 23 June 1941. Reprinted with permission)*

an unnecessary diversion. In retrospect, it is easy to pinpoint that particular combination as his fatal mistake. But in light of the Soviet purges of the thirties and the poor performance of the Soviet army in 1939 and 1940, Hitler had reason to believe the Soviet Union would crack relatively easily. Western military experts had come to similar conclusions, estimating that German forces would need but six weeks to take Moscow. And if Germany were to defeat the Soviet Union with another *Blitzkrieg,* it could gain control of the oil and other resources required for a longer war against Britain and, if necessary, the United States.

So the Nazi assault on the Soviet Union was not ill considered. Ultimately, however, it failed, and its failure was the decisive fact of World War II. Although supplies from its new Allies—Britain and eventually the United States—helped the Soviet forces to prevail, the most important factor was the unexpected strength of the Soviet military effort.

Before they were defeated, the Germans penetrated well into the Soviet Union, achieving the apex of their power in 1942. German conquests by that point enabled Hitler to begin actually constructing the new European order he had dreamed of. Although in western Europe the Nazis generally sought the collaboration of local leaders, in Poland and the Soviet Union the new order meant brutal subjugation of local populations. Now, and only now, did the Nazis begin physically exterminating the Jews of Europe in specially constructed death camps.

An Ambiguous Outcome, 1941–1942

Attacking the Soviet Union on June 22, 1941, German forces achieved notable successes during the first month of fighting, partly because Stalin was so unprepared for this German betrayal. Ignoring warnings of an impending German assault, he had continued to live up to his end of the 1939 bargain with Hitler, even supplying the Germans with oil and grain. After the attack, Russia's defenses were at first totally disorganized, and by late November, German forces were within twenty miles of Moscow.

But the Germans were ill equipped for Russian weather, and as an early and severe winter descended, the German offensive bogged down. In December, the Soviets mounted a formidable surprise counterattack near Moscow. The German *Blitzkrieg,* which had seemed a sure thing in July, had failed; Germany might still prevail, but a different strategy would be required.

Although their initial assault had stalled, the Germans still had the advantage. They kept the key city of Leningrad under brutal siege until late in the war. And during the summer of 1942, they mounted another offensive, concentrating farther south, and moved even farther east than the year before, reaching Stalingrad in November. But this proved the deepest penetration of German forces—and the zenith of Nazi power in Europe.

Hitler's New Order

By the summer of 1942, Nazi Germany dominated the European continent as no power ever had before (Map 30.2). German military successes made it possible—indeed, essential—for the Nazi regime to begin building a new order in the territories under German domination. Satellite states in Slovakia and Croatia, and client governments in Romania and Hungary, owed their existence to Nazi Germany and readily adapted themselves to the Nazi system. Elsewhere in the Nazi orbit, some countries proved eager collaborators; others did their best to resist; still others were given no opportunity to collaborate but were ruthlessly subjugated instead.

The Nazis' immediate aim was simply to exploit the conquered territories to serve the continuing war effort. Precisely as envisioned, access to the resources of so much of Europe made Germany considerably less vulnerable to naval blockade than it had been during World War I. France proved a particularly valuable source of

Map 30.2 The Nazi "New Order" in Europe, 1942
At the zenith of its power in 1942, Nazi Germany controlled much of Europe. Concerned most immediately with winning the war, the Nazis sought to coordinate the economies of their satellite states and conquered territories. But they also began establishing what was supposed to be an enduring new order in eastern Europe. The inset shows the location of the major Nazi concentration camps and of the six extermination camps the Nazis constructed in what had been Poland.

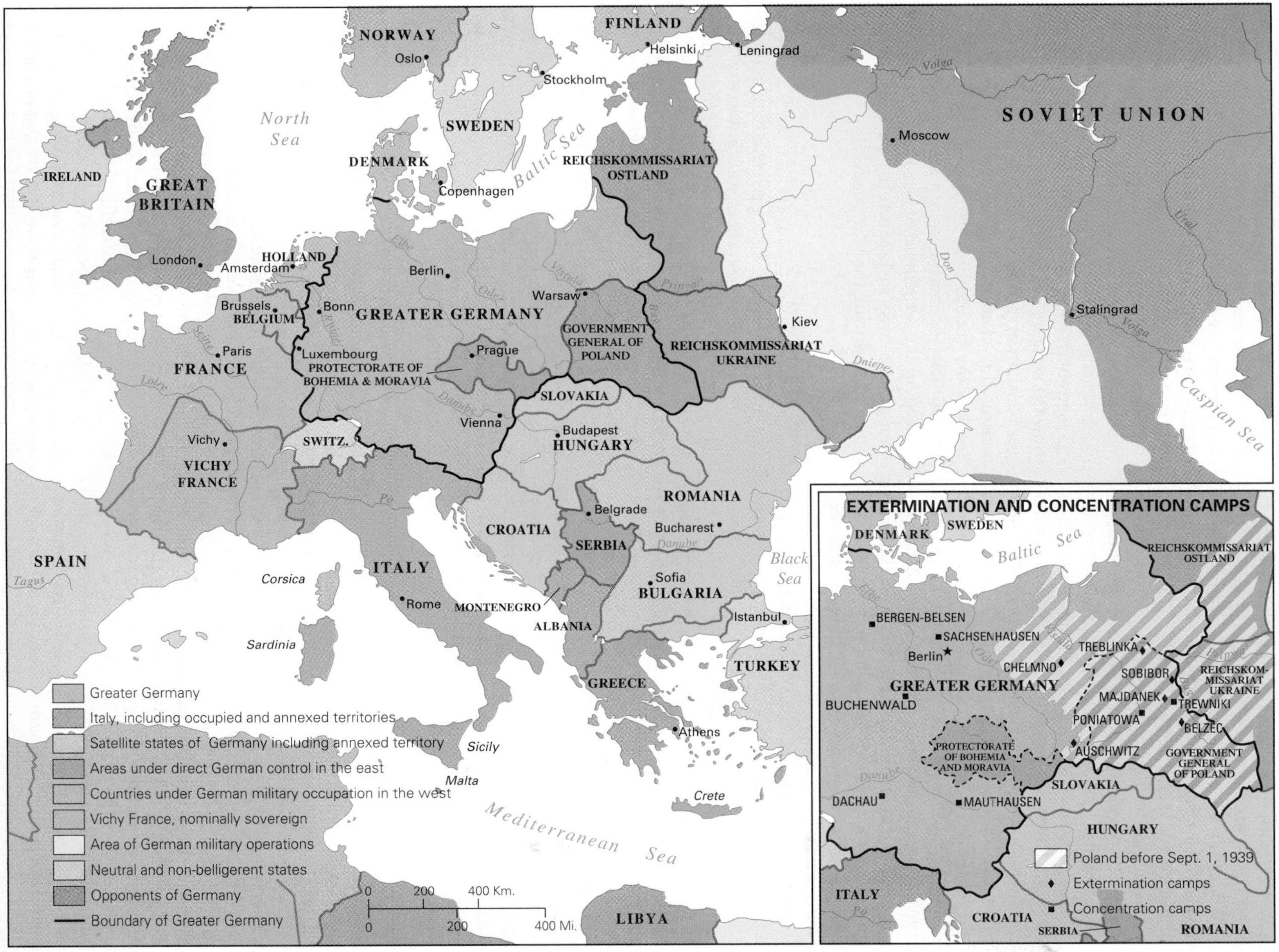

SOVIET UNION
FINLAND
NORWAY
SWEDEN
DENMARK
IRELAND
GREAT BRITAIN
HOLLAND
BELGIUM
FRANCE
VICHY FRANCE
SPAIN
SWITZ.
GREATER GERMANY
PROTECTORATE OF BOHEMIA & MORAVIA
REICHSKOMMISSARIAT OSTLAND
GOVERNMENT GENERAL OF POLAND
REICHSKOMMISSARIAT UKRAINE
SLOVAKIA
HUNGARY
ROMANIA
CROATIA
SERBIA
BULGARIA
MONTENEGRO
ALBANIA
ITALY
GREECE
TURKEY
LIBYA
Helsinki
Leningrad
Oslo
Stockholm
Moscow
Copenhagen
London
Amsterdam
Berlin
Warsaw
Brussels
Bonn
Kiev
Stalingrad
Paris
Luxembourg
Prague
Vienna
Budapest
Vichy
Belgrade
Bucharest
Sofia
Rome
Istanbul
Athens
North Sea
Baltic Sea
Black Sea
Caspian Sea
Mediterranean Sea
Corsica
Sardinia
Sicily
Malta
Crete
Volga
Ural
Don
Dnieper
Pripyat
Vistula
Oder
Elbe
Bug
Rhine
Danube
Seine
Loire
Po
Tagus
Greater Germany
Italy, including occupied and annexed territories
Satellite states of Germany including annexed territory
Areas under direct German control in the east
Countries under German military occupation in the west
Vichy France, nominally sovereign
Area of German military operations
Neutral and non-belligerent states
Opponents of Germany
Boundary of Greater Germany
0 200 400 Km.
0 200 400 Mi.
EXTERMINATION AND CONCENTRATION CAMPS
DENMARK
SWEDEN
Baltic Sea
REICHSKOMMISSARIAT OSTLAND
BERGEN-BELSEN
SACHSENHAUSEN
Berlin
TREBLINKA
CHELMNO
SOBIBOR
REICHSKOM-MISSARIAT UKRAINE
GREATER GERMANY
MAJDANEK
TREWNIKI
BUCHENWALD
PONIATOWA
BELZEC
PROTECTORATE OF BOHEMIA AND MORAVIA
AUSCHWITZ
GOVERNMENT GENERAL OF POLAND
SLOVAKIA
DACHAU
MAUTHAUSEN
HUNGARY
ITALY
CROATIA
SERBIA
ROMANIA
Poland before Sept. 1, 1939
Extermination camps
Concentration camps

raw materials; by 1943, for example, 75 percent of French iron ore went to German factories.

But the deeper purposes of the war were also clear in the way the Nazis treated the territories under their control, especially in the difference between east and west. In western Europe, there was plenty of brutality, but Nazi victory still led to something like conventional occupation under regular military commanders. The Germans tried to enlist the cooperation of local authorities in countries like Denmark, the Netherlands, and France, though with mixed results. And though the Nazis thoroughly exploited the economy of France, for example, it never became clear what role France might play in Europe after a Nazi victory. However, in Poland and later in the conquered parts of the Soviet Union, there was no pretense of cooperation, and it immediately became clear what the Nazi order would entail.

After the conquest of Poland, the Germans annexed the western part of the country outright and promptly executed, jailed, or expelled members of the Polish elite—professionals, journalists, business leaders, and priests. The Nazis prohibited the Poles from entering the professions and restricted even their right to marry. All the Polish schools and most of the churches were simply closed.

In the rest of Poland, administered by a German governor-general, Nazi policy was slightly less brutal at first. Most churches remained open, and Poles were allowed to practice the professions, but the Nazis closed most schools above the fourth grade, as well as libraries, theaters, and museums as they sought to root out every expression of Polish culture. Whether the Poles in this area were to be exterminated, enslaved, or shipped off to Siberia was much debated, but the decision was postponed—to be made after the victory (see the box, "Toward the Nazi New Order").

With the conquest of Poland, Nazi leaders proclaimed that a new era of monumental resettlement in the east had begun for Germany. By mid-1941, 200,000 Germans had been relocated into the part of Poland annexed to Germany, primarily on farms. During the fall of 1942, the SS began arresting and expelling peasants from the rest of Poland to make way for further German resettlement. By 1943 perhaps 1 million Germans had been moved into what had been Poland.

After the assault on the Soviet Union, Hitler made it clear that the entire east as far as the Ural Mountains was to be opened for German settlement. War veterans were to be given priority, partly because the German settlers would have to be especially tough, a bulwark against the Slavs who would be concentrated east of the Urals. To prepare for German colonization, Himmler told SS leaders that Germany would have to exterminate 30 million Slavs in the Soviet Union. After the German invasion, the SS promptly began executing prisoners of war, as well as any Soviet leaders they could find. However, the Nazis expected that several generations would be required for the settlement of European Russia, and here, in contrast to Poland, the program barely got started during the war years.

The Holocaust

Conquest of the east also gave the Nazis the opportunity for a more radical solution to the "Jewish problem" than they had attempted before. Under the cover of war, they began actually exterminating the Jews within their orbit. Thus began the process, and the experience, that has come to be known as the Holocaust.

When and why this policy was chosen remains controversial. Although prewar Nazi rhetoric occasionally suggested the possibility of actual physical destruction, the Nazi goal of a "final solution" to the "Jewish problem" seemed to mean forced emigration. The conquest of Poland, with a Jewish population of 3 million, gave the Nazis control over a far greater number of Jews than ever before. In 1940, as part of their effort to create a new order in Poland, the Nazis began confining Polish Jews to ghettos set up in Warsaw and five other cities. No one knew what was to become of these Jews at first. Himmler and the SS were making tentative plans to develop, after the Nazi victory, a kind of superghetto for perhaps 4 million Jews on the island of Madagascar, at that point still a French colony. However, as the ghettos grew ever more crowded and difficult to manage, Nazi officials in Poland began pressing for a more definitive policy.

In 1940, Hitler seemed to endorse the Madagascar plan, but he cultivated ambiguity on the operational level—and he left no paper trail. So the precise chain of events that led to a more radi-

Toward the Nazi New Order

After Nazi Germany conquered much of Poland in 1939, the SS assumed major responsibility for creating a new Nazi order in the conquered territories. In a memorandum dated May 15, 1940, and endorsed by Hitler, the SS leader Heinrich Himmler offered "some thoughts on the treatment of the alien population in the east." The passages that follow make clear the racist basis of Nazi wartime policy.

In our treatment of the foreign ethnic groups in the east we must . . . fish out the racially valuable people from this mishmash, take them to Germany and assimilate them there.

. . . The non-German population of the eastern territories must not receive any education higher than that of elementary school with four forms. The objective of this elementary school must simply be to teach: simple arithmetic up to 500 at the most, how to write one's name, and to teach that it is God's commandment to be obedient to the Germans and to be honest, hard-working, and well-behaved. I consider it unnecessary to teach reading.

There must be no schools at all in the east apart from this type of school. Parents who wish to provide their children with a better education both in the elementary school and later in a secondary school, must make an application to the higher SS and Police Leader. . . . If we recognize such a child as being of our blood then the parents will be informed that the child will be placed in a school in Germany and will remain in Germany indefinitely. . . .

. . . [T]he moment the children and parents arrive in Germany they should not be treated in school and life as outcasts but—after changing their names and despite being treated with vigilance—should be integrated into German life on the basis of trust. The children must not be made to feel rejected; for, after all, we believe in our own blood, which through the mistakes of German history has flowed into a foreign nation, and are convinced that our ideology and ideals will find an echo in the souls of these children which are racially identical to our own. . . . Abusive expressions such as "Polack" or "Ukrainian" and such like must be out of the question. . . .

After these measures have been systematically implemented during the next ten years, the population of the General Government will inevitably consist of an inferior remnant. . . . This population will be available as a leaderless laboring class and provide Germany with migrant and seasonal labor for special work projects (road-building, quarries, construction); even then they will get more to eat and have more from life than under Polish rule. . . .

Source: J. Noakes and G. Pridham, *Nazism: A History in Documents and Eyewitness Accounts, 1919–1945,* vol. 2 (New York: Schocken, 1990), pp. 932–934.

cal approach will no doubt remain uncertain. The evidence suggests, however, that Hitler ordered the physical extermination of the Jews early in the spring of 1941, before the German assault on the Soviet Union in June. By the fall, the Nazis were actively impeding further Jewish emigration from the occupied territories. And they were sending large numbers of German and Austrian Jews to the ghettos in Poland.

With the invasion of the Soviet Union, special SS "intervention squads" were assigned to get rid of Jews and Communist party officials. By late November, the Nazis had killed 136,000 Jews, most by shooting, in the invaded Soviet territories. But as it became obvious that such mass shooting was impractical, Nazi leaders began devising a more systematic and impersonal method of mass extermination. Late in July 1941, Reinhard Heydrich of the SS began developing a detailed plan, which he explained in January 1942 at a conference of high-ranking officials at Wannsee, a suburb of Berlin. The conference had been postponed from November, and by now the Nazis were already implementing Heydrich's plan for the extermination of the Jews.

The Nazis took advantage of the methods, and especially the deadly Zyklon-B gas, that had proven effective during the euthanasia campaign in Germany. By March 1942 they had constructed several large extermination camps with gas chambers and crematoria, intended to kill Jews and dispose of their bodies as quickly and efficiently as possible. And now they began the full-scale mass killing, targeting first the Polish Jews who had already been confined to ghettos. Once the apparatus for mass extermination had been constructed, the ghettos became mere way stations on the way to the death camps. The Nazis brutally suppressed attempts at resistance, like the Warsaw ghetto uprising of April and May 1943.

During the course of the war the Nazis constructed six full-scale death camps, although not all were operating at peak capacity at the same time. All six were located in what had been Poland (see inset, Map 30.2). Brutal though they were, the concentration camps in Germany, such as Dachau, Buchenwald, and Bergen-Belsen, were not extermination camps, although many Jews died in them late in the war.

The largest of the six death camps was the Auschwitz complex, which became the principal extermination center in 1943. The Nazis shipped Jews from all over Europe to Auschwitz, which was killing about 12,000 people a day at the peak of its operation in 1944. Auschwitz was one of two of the extermination camps that included affiliated slave-labor factories, in which Jews most able to work were literally worked to death. Among the companies profiting from the arrangement were two of Germany's best-known, Krupp and IG Farben.

The Jews typically arrived at one of the camps crammed into cattle cars on special trains.

Life and Death in the Nazi Camps Images from the Nazi concentration camps have haunted the twentieth century. The overwhelming majority of those sent to the camps were Jews, who encountered a nightmare world of barbed wire and SS brutality, malnutrition and disease, dehumanization and death. *(Brown Brothers)*

Camp personnel, generally SS medical doctors, subjected new arrivals to "selection," picking some for labor assignments and sending the others, including most women and children, to the gas chambers. Camp personnel made every effort to deceive the Jews who were about to be killed, to lead them to believe they were to be showered and deloused. Even in camps without forced-labor factories, Jews were compelled to do much of the dirty work of the extermination operation. But under the brutal conditions of the camps, those initially assigned to work inevitably weakened; most were then deemed unfit and put to death.

The Nazis took every precaution to hide what was going on in the death camps. The SS personnel involved were sworn to silence. Himmler insisted that if secrecy was to be maintained, the operation would have to be quick—and total, to include women and children, "so that no Jews will remain to take revenge on our sons and grandsons." Indeed, Himmler constantly sought to accelerate the process, even though it required scarce labor and transport facilities desperately needed for the war effort.

Himmler and the other major SS officials, such as Rudolf Höss, the commandant at Auschwitz, or Adolf Eichmann, who organized the transport of the Jews to the camps, cannot be understood simply as sadists who enjoyed humiliating their victims. Rather, they took satisfaction in doing what they believed was their duty without flinching, without signs of weakness. Addressing a group of SS members in 1943, Himmler portrayed the extermination of the Jews as a difficult "historical task" that they, the Nazi elite, must do for their racial community: "Most of you know what it means to see a hundred corpses piled up, or five hundred, or a thousand. To have gone through this and—except for cases of human weakness—to have remained decent, that has made us tough. This is an unwritten, never to be written, page of glory in our history."[1]

However, as Himmler's casual reference to "cases of human weakness" suggests, some among the SS camp guards failed to live up to this image and indulged in wanton cruelty, humiliating their helpless victims. For some, the extermination process became the occasion to act out sadistic fantasies. But though this dimension is surely horrifying, the bureaucratic, factory like nature of the extermination process is in some ways more troubling.

Despite the overriding emphasis on secrecy, reports of the genocide reached the West almost immediately in 1942. Especially at first, however, most tended to discount them as wartime propaganda of the sort that many had believed during World War I, when stories about Germans eating Belgian babies had circulated. Skepticism about extermination reports was easier because there were a few concentration camps, most notably Theresienstadt in what had been Czechoslovakia, which housed Jews who had been selected for special treatment for some reason. These camps were not used for extermination and were not secret; the Red Cross was even allowed to inspect Theresienstadt several times. Those outside, and the German people as well, were led to believe that all the Jews were being interned, for the duration of the war, in camps like these, much as Japanese-Americans were being interned in camps in the western United States at the same time. But even as the evidence grew, Allied governments, citing military priorities, refused pleas from Jewish leaders in 1944 to bomb the rail line into Auschwitz.

The Nazis' policy of actually murdering persons deemed undesirable or superfluous did not start with, and was not limited to, the Jews. In addition to the euthanasia program of 1939 through 1941 (described in Chapter 29), the war afforded the Nazis the chance to do away with an array of other "undesirables," from communists and homosexuals to Gypsies and Poles. So the most radical and appalling aspect of Nazism did not stem from anti-Semitism alone. This must not be forgotten, but neither must the fact that the Jews constituted by far the largest group of victims—perhaps 5.7 to 6 million, almost two-thirds of the Jews of Europe. (See the feature, "Weighing the Evidence: Holocaust Testimony," on pages 1146–1147.)

Collaboration and Resistance

In rounding up Jews for extermination, and in establishing their new order in Europe, the Nazis found willing collaborators among some of the countries within their orbit. Croatia, the most thoroughly Nazi of the satellite states, was eager to round up Jews and Gypsies, as well as to attack

Serbs, on its own. Romania, too, was happy to deliver foreign-born Jews to the Germans, though it dragged its feet when the Germans began demanding acculturated Romanian Jews.

But degrees of collaboration varied widely across Europe. In Denmark, Norway, and the Netherlands, where they thought racial kinship would matter, the Nazis never found sufficient support to make possible genuinely independent collaborationist governments. In Denmark and the Netherlands, governments put up a façade of cooperation but still managed to foster resistance. Denmark did especially well at resisting the German effort to round up Jews, as did Italy and Bulgaria.

Vichy France was somewhere in the middle, and thus has remained especially controversial. When the Vichy regime was launched during the summer of 1940, there was widespread support for Marshal Pétain, its 84-year-old chief of state. Pétain claimed he could maximize French sovereignty and shield his people from the worst aspects of Nazi occupation. On the other hand, the Vichy government claimed at first to be implementing its own "national revolution," to return, it claimed, to authority, discipline, and tradition after the shambles of the Third Republic. Vichy's revolution was anti-Semitic and hostile to the left, so it seemed compatible, up to a point, with Nazism. And at first Germany seemed likely to win the war. Thus Pétain's second-in-command, Pierre Laval (1883–1945), was willing to collaborate actively with the Nazis. As a result, the Vichy regime ended up doing much of the Nazis' dirty work for them—rounding up workers for forced shipment to German factories, hunting down members of the anti-German resistance, and picking up Jews to be sent to the Nazi extermination camps.

After the war, Pétain, Laval, and others were found guilty of treason by the new French government. Because of his advanced age, Pétain was merely imprisoned, while Laval and others were shot. But the shame of Vichy collaboration continued to haunt the French, deepening the humiliation of the defeat in 1940.

Though the Nazis found some willing collaborators, the great majority of those living under German occupation came to despise the Nazis as their brutality became ever clearer. Nazi rule meant pillage; it meant rounding up workers for forced labor in Germany; it meant randomly killing hostages in reprisal for resistance activity. In an extreme case, the Germans destroyed the Czech village of Lidice, killing all its inhabitants, in retaliation for the assassination of SS security chief Reinhard Heydrich.

Clandestine movements of resistance to the occupying Nazi forces gradually developed all over Europe. In western Europe, resistance was especially prominent in France and, beginning in 1943, northern Italy, which was subjected to German occupation after the Allies defeated Mussolini's regime. But the anti-German resistance was strongest in Yugoslavia, Poland, and the occupied portions of the Soviet Union, where genuine guerrilla war against the Germans and their collaborators produced the highest civilian casualties of World War II. The Polish resistance achieved some notable successes in sabotaging roads and railroads, although it met disastrous defeat when it sought to tackle the Germans head-on in Warsaw in 1944.

The role of the resistance proved most significant in Yugoslavia, where the Croatian Marxist Josip Broz, taking the pseudonym Tito (1892–1980), forged the opponents of the Axis powers into a broadly based guerrilla army. Its initial foe was the inflated Croatian state that the Germans, early in 1941, carved from Yugoslavia and entrusted to the pro-Axis Croatian separatist movement, the Ustashe. But Tito's forces soon came up against a rival resistance movement, led by Serb officers, that tended to be pro-Serb, monarchist, and anticommunist. By 1943, Tito led 250,000 men and women in what had become a brutal civil war, one that deepened ethnic divisions and left a legacy of bitterness. Tito's forces prevailed, enabling him to create a communist-led government in Yugoslavia late in the war.

In France and Italy as well, communists played a leading role in the wartime resistance movements. Thus the communists overcame the disarray that followed from the Nazi-Soviet Pact of 1939 and, in each country, enjoyed a level of prestige after the war that would have been unthinkable earlier.

In the French case, there could have been conflict between the indigenous resistance, with its significant communist component, and the Free French under Charles de Gaulle, operating outside France until August 1944. But it is striking how well they were able to work together. Still, de Gaulle took pains to cement his own leadership in the overall struggle. Among the measures to this end, he decreed women's suffrage for France, partly because women were playing a major role in the resistance. After the liberation of France in 1944, he sought to control a potentially volatile situation by disarming the resistance as quickly as possible.

The western European resistance movements are easily romanticized, their extent and import overstated. Compared to regular troops, resistance forces were poorly trained, equipped, and disciplined. In France, fewer than 30 percent of the nearly 400,000 active resisters had firearms in 1944. But though the Allies never tried to use them in a systematic way, the resistance movements made at least some military contribution, especially through sabotage. And they boosted national self-esteem for the longer term, helping countries humiliated by defeat and occupation make a fresh start after the war.

Defending the Soviet Union This typical Soviet wartime poster seeks to rally popular support for the Soviet war effort against Nazi Germany in 1942. The caption reads, "Follow this worker's example. Produce more for the front." *(Trustees of the Imperial War Museum)*

Toward the Soviet Triumph

The import of what happened elsewhere in Europe depended on the outcome of the main event, the German invasion of the Soviet Union. Although the German Sixth Army, numbering almost 300,000 men, reached Stalingrad by late 1942, the Germans could not achieve a knockout (see the box, "Stalingrad: The Diary of a German Soldier"). The Soviets managed to defend the city in what was arguably the pivotal military engagement of World War II. While some Soviet troops fought street by street, house by house, others counterattacked, encircling the attacking German force. Hitler refused a strategic retreat, but his doggedness backfired. By the end of January 1943, the Soviets had captured what remained of the German force, about 100,000 men, very few of whom survived to return to Germany. Perhaps 240,000 German soldiers died in the battle of Stalingrad or as prisoners afterward. But the price to the Soviets for their crucial victory was far greater: 1 million Soviet soldiers and civilians died at Stalingrad.

Although the Germans resumed the offensive on several fronts during the summer of 1943, the Soviets won the tank battle of Kursk-Orel in July, and from then on Soviet troops relentlessly moved west, forcing the Germans back. By February 1944, Soviet troops had pushed the Germans back to the Polish border, and the outcome of the war was no longer in doubt.

The Soviet victory in what proved the decisive front of World War II was incredible, in light of the upheavals of the thirties and the low esteem in which most held the Soviet military in 1941. Portraying the struggle as "the Great Patriotic War" for national defense, Stalin managed to rally the Soviet peoples as the Germans attacked. Rather than emphasize communist themes, he recalled the heroic defenses mounted against

Stalingrad: The Diary of a German Soldier

The following excerpts from the diary of a soldier named Wilhelm Hoffman reveal the changing German mood during 1942, as the Nazis penetrated deeply into the Soviet Union, then met disastrous defeat at Stalingrad. The writer himself did not survive the battle; his closing curse was his last diary entry.

July 29. The company commander says the Russian troops are completely broken, and cannot hold out any longer. To reach the Volga and take Stalingrad is not so difficult for us. The Führer knows where the Russians' weak point is. Victory is not far away....

August 2.... What great spaces the Soviets occupy, what rich fields there are to be had here after the war's over!...

September 26. Our regiment is involved in constant heavy fighting. After the [grain storage] elevator was taken the Russians continued to defend themselves just as stubbornly. You don't see them at all, they have established themselves in houses and cellars and are firing on all sides, including from our rear—barbarians, they use gangster methods....

October 14. It has been fantastic since morning: our aeroplanes and artillery have been hammering the Russian positions for hours on end; everything in sight is being blotted from the face of the earth....

October 22. Our regiment has failed to break into the factory. We have lost many men; every time you move you have to jump over bodies.... Who would have thought three months ago that instead of the joy of victory we would have to endure such sacrifice and torture, the end of which is nowhere in sight?...

The soldiers are calling Stalingrad the mass grave of the [German army]....

October 27. Our troops have captured the whole of the Barrikady factory, but we cannot break through to the Volga. The Russians are not men, but some kind of cast-iron creatures; they never get tired and are not afraid of fire. We are absolutely exhausted; our regiment now has barely the strength of a company....

November 21. The Russians have gone over to the offensive along the whole front. Fierce fighting is going on. So, there it is—the Volga, victory and soon home to our families! We shall obviously be seeing them next in the other world.

December 14. Everybody is racked with hunger. Frozen potatoes are the best meal, but to get them out of the ice-covered ground under fire from Russian bullets is not so easy.

December 26.... The soldiers look like corpses or lunatics, looking for something to put in their mouths. They no longer take cover from Russian shells; they haven't the strength to walk, run away and hide. A curse on this war!

Source: Vasili I. Chuikov, *The Battle for Stalingrad* (New York: Holt, Rinehart and Winston, 1964), pp. 248–254.

invaders in tsarist times, including the resistance to Napoleon in 1812.

The invading Germans gained access to major areas of Soviet industry and oil supply, and by the end of 1941 the country's industrial output had been cut in half. Yet the Soviet Union was able to weather this blow and go on to triumph. Help from the outside contributed a little, but only 5 to 15 percent of Soviet supplies came from the West. Between 1939 and 1941, before the German invasion, Soviet leaders had begun building a new industrial base east of the Urals, out of reach of German attack. Once the invasion began, moreover, the plant and equipment of 1,500 enterprises was dismantled and shipped by rail for reassembly farther east. Then, beginning in 1942, thousands of new factories were constructed in eastern regions as well.

Moreover, the earlier purges of the armed forces proved to do less long-term damage than outside observers had expected. If anything, the removal of so many in the top ranks of the military hierarchy made it easier for talented young officers like Georgi Zhukov (1896–1974), who would become the country's top military commander, to move quickly into major leadership positions.

When the United States entered the war in December 1941, the Soviets were fighting for their lives. They immediately began pressuring the United States and Britain to open another front in Europe, preferably by landing in northern France, where an Allied assault could be expected to have the greatest impact. But the Allies did not invade northern France and open a major second front until June 1944. By then the Soviets had turned the tide in Europe on their own.

A Global War, 1941–1944

European colonial links spread the war almost at once, most dramatically to North Africa but also to East Asia and the Pacific. The Soviet Union also had interests in Asia and the Pacific, where it had long bumped up against the Japanese. During the 1930s, the United States had also become involved in friction with Japan. By 1941 President Franklin Roosevelt was openly favoring the anti-Axis cause, though it took a surprise attack by the Japanese in December 1941 finally to bring the United States into the war.

Japan and the Origins of the Pacific War

As a densely populated island nation lacking the raw materials essential for industry, Japan had been especially concerned about foreign trade and spheres of economic influence as it modernized after 1868. By the interwar period, the Japanese had become unusually reliant on exports of textiles and other products. During the world economic crisis of the thirties, when countries all over the world adopted protectionist policies, Japan suffered from increasing tariffs against its exports. This situation tilted the balance within Japanese ruling circles from free-trade proponents to those who favored a military-imperialist solution.

To gain economic hegemony by force, Japan could choose either of two directions. The northern strategy, concentrating on China, would risk Soviet opposition as well as strong local resistance. The southern strategy, focusing on southeast Asia and the East Indies, would encounter the imperial presence of Britain, France, the Netherlands, and the United States.

Japan opted for the northern strategy in 1931, when it took control of Manchuria, in northeastern China. But the Japanese attempt to conquer the rest of China, beginning in 1937, led only to an impasse by 1940. Japanese aggression in China drew the increasing hostility of the United States, a strong supporter of the Chinese nationalist leader Chiang Kai-shek (1887–1975), as well as the active opposition of the Soviet Union. Clashes with Soviet troops along the border between Mongolia and Manchuria led to significant defeats for the Japanese in 1938 and 1939. The combination of China and the Soviet Union seemed more than Japan could handle.

By 1941, however, Germany's victories in Europe had seriously weakened Britain, France, and the Netherlands, the major European colonial powers in southeast Asia and the East Indies. This seemed a precious opportunity for Japan to shift to a southern strategy. To keep the Soviets at bay, Japan agreed to a neutrality pact with the Soviet Union in April 1941. Rather than worry about China and the areas of dispute with the Soviet Union, the Japanese would seek control of southeast Asia, a region rich in such raw materials as oil, rubber, and tin—precisely what Japan lacked.

Japan had already joined with Nazi Germany and fascist Italy in an anticommunist agreement in 1936. In September 1940, the three agreed to a formal military alliance. For the Germans, alliance with Japan was useful to help discourage U.S. intervention in the European war. Japan, for its part, could expect the major share of the spoils of the European empires in Asia. However, diplomatic and military coordination between Germany and Japan remained minimal.

The United States began imposing embargoes of certain exports to Japan in 1938, in response to the Japanese aggression in China. After Japan had assumed control of Indochina, nominally held by Vichy France, by the summer of 1941, the United States imposed total sanctions, and the British and Dutch followed, forcing Japan to begin rapidly drawing down its oil reserves. Conquest of the oil fields of the Dutch East Indies now seemed a matter of life and death to the Japanese.

These economic sanctions brought home how vulnerable Japan was and heightened its determination to press forward aggressively now, when its likely enemies were weakened or distracted. But the Japanese did not expect to achieve a definitive victory over the United States in a long, drawn-out war. Rather, Japanese policymakers anticipated, first, that their initial successes would enable them to grab the resources needed for a longer war if necessary, and, second, that Germany would defeat Britain, leading the U.S. to accept a compromise peace allowing the Japanese what they wanted—a secure sphere of economic hegemony in southeast Asia.

Some Japanese leaders—diplomats, businessmen, naval officers, and even the emperor and some of his circle—were dismayed by the prospect of war with the United States. But as the influence of the military grew during the 1930s, it had become ever more difficult for those opposing Japan's new imperialist direction to make themselves heard. By 1941, a conformist confidence in victory was demanded, and dissenters dared not speak out. From then until the war ended, doubters were labeled defeatists or traitors and might even be assassinated by extremist army officers.

The Japanese finally provoked a showdown on December 7, 1941, with a surprise attack on Pearl Harbor, a U.S. naval base in Hawaii. The next day, Japanese forces seized Hong Kong and Malaya, both British colonies, and Wake Island and the Philippines, both controlled by the U.S. The United States promptly declared war; in response, Hitler kept an earlier promise to Japan and declared war on the United States. World War II was now unprecedented in its geographical scope.

Much like their German counterparts, Japanese forces got off to a remarkably good start. By the summer of 1942, Japan had taken Thailand, the Dutch East Indies, the Philippines, and the Malay Peninsula. Having won much of what it had been seeking, it began devising the Greater East Asia Co-Prosperity Sphere, its own new order in the conquered territories.

The United States in Europe and the Pacific

During the first years of the war in Europe, the United States under President Franklin Roosevelt had hardly been a disinterested bystander. At this point the United States did not have armed forces commensurate with its economic strength; in 1940, in fact, its army was smaller than the Belgian army. But the United States could be a supplier in the short term, and if it chose to intervene, it could become a major player over the longer term. With the Lend-Lease Act of March 1941, intended to provide war materiel without the economic dislocations of World War I, the United States lined up on the side of Britain against the Axis powers. (Lend-lease was extended to Russia in September 1941, three months after the Nazi attack.) In August 1941, a meeting between Churchill and Roosevelt aboard a cruiser off the coast of Newfoundland produced the Atlantic Charter, the first tentative agreement about the aims and ideals that were to guide the anti-Axis war effort.

But though President Roosevelt was deeply committed to the anti-Axis cause, isolationist sentiment remained strong in the United States. It took the Japanese attack on Pearl Harbor in December to bring the United States into the war as an active belligerent. By May 1942, the United States had joined with Britain and the Soviet Union in a formal military alliance against the Axis powers.

The two democracies had joined with Stalin's Soviet Union in a marriage of expediency, and mutual suspicions marked the relationship from the start. Initially, Britain and the United States feared that the Soviet Union might even seek a separate peace, as Russia had in World War I. The Soviets, for their part, worried that these newfound allies, with their long-standing anticommunism, might hold back from full commitment, or even seek to undermine the Soviet Union.

In response to pressure from Stalin, Britain and the United States agreed to open a second front in Europe as soon as possible. But the Nazis dominated the Continent, and so opening a second front required landing troops from the outside. It proved far more difficult to mount an effective assault on Europe than either Churchill or Roosevelt anticipated in 1942. The resulting de-

THE ERA OF WORLD WAR II

September 1, 1939	Germany invades Poland
May 10, 1940	Germany attacks the Netherlands, Belgium, and France
June 22, 1941	Germany attacks the Soviet Union
August 1941	Churchill and Roosevelt agree to the Atlantic Charter
December 7, 1941	Japanese attack on Pearl Harbor
January 1942	Wannsee Conference; Nazi plan for the extermination of the Jews
August 1942–February 1943	Battle of Stalingrad
November 1942	Allied landings in North Africa
January 1943	Casablanca Conference
April–May 1943	Warsaw Ghetto revolt
July 1943	Soviet victory in Battle of Kursk-Orel
July 1943	Allied landings in Sicily; fall of Mussolini; Italy asks for an armistice
November 1943	Teheran Conference
June 6, 1944	D-Day: Allied landings in Normandy
February 1945	Yalta Conference
April 30, 1945	Suicide of Adolf Hitler
May 7–8, 1945	German surrender
June 1945	Founding of the United Nations
July–August 1945	Potsdam Conference
August 6, 1945	U.S. atomic bombing of Hiroshima
August 14, 1945	Japanese surrender
March 1947	Truman Doctrine speech
August 1947	India becomes independent
May 1948	Founding of Israel
June 1948–May 1949	Berlin blockade and airlift
August 1949	First Soviet atomic bomb
September 1949	Founding of the Federal Republic in West Germany
October 1949	Founding of the People's Republic of China

lays furthered Stalin's suspicions that his allies were only too eager to have the Soviets do the bulk of the fighting against Nazi Germany—and weaken themselves in the process.

The United States agreed with its new allies to give priority to the war in Europe. But because it had to respond to the direct Japanese assault in the Pacific, the United States was not prepared to act militarily in Europe right away. However, it quickly played a major role in supplying the British with the ships needed to overcome German submarines, which seriously threatened shipping to Britain by 1942.

In the Pacific theater, in contrast, it was immediately clear that the United States would bear the brunt of the Japanese assault. Although the Japanese went from one success to another during the first months of the war, they lacked the long-term resources to exploit their initial victories. In May 1942, the battle of Coral Sea—off New Guinea, north of Australia—ended in a stalemate, stopping the string of impressive Japanese successes. Then in June, the United States defeated the Japanese navy for the first time in the battle of Midway, northwest of Hawaii. After the United States stopped attempted Japanese advances in the Solomon Islands and New Guinea early in 1943, U.S. forces began steadily advancing across the islands of the Pacific toward Japan (Map 30.3).

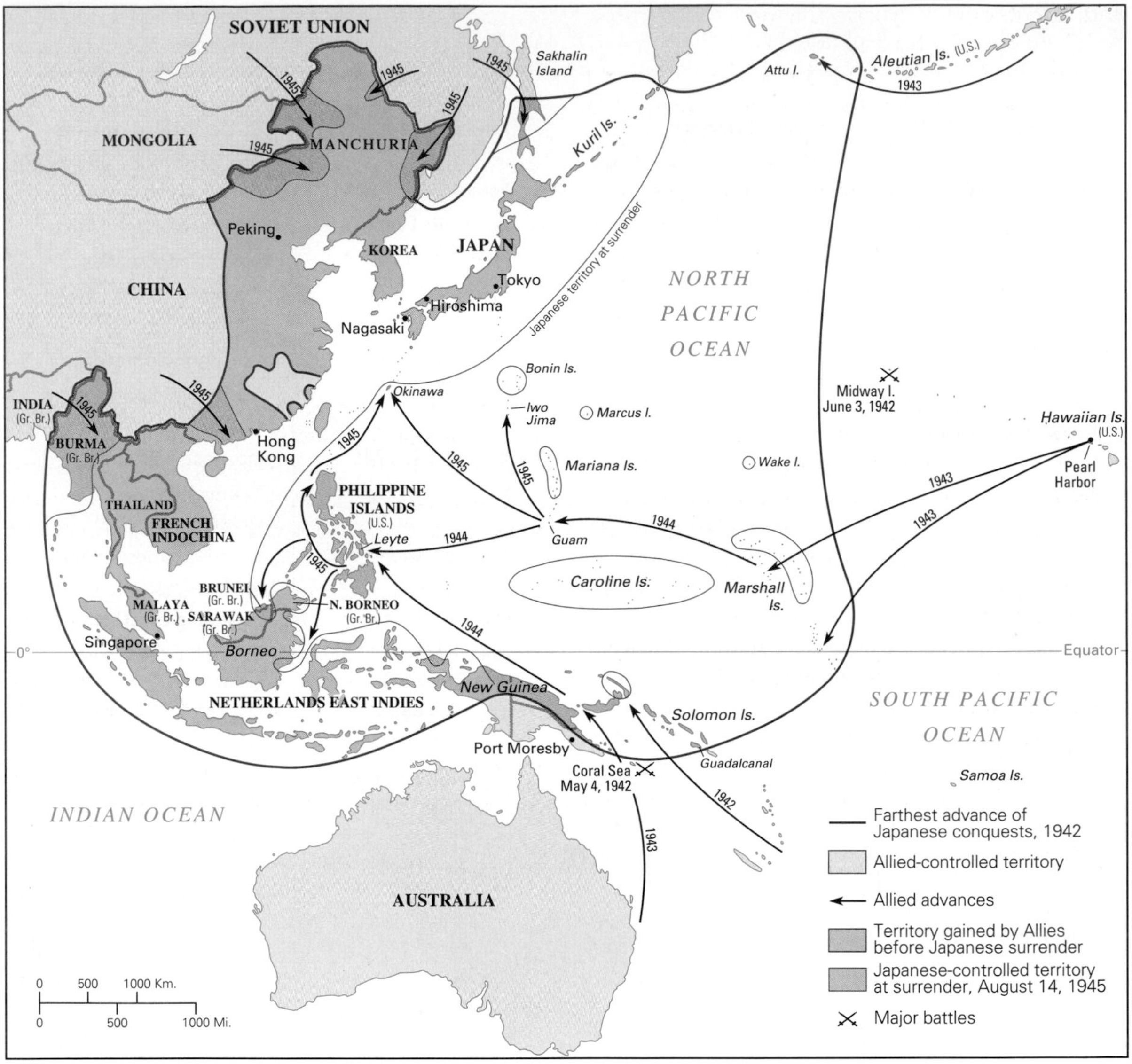

Map 30.3 The War in East Asia and the Pacific After a series of conquests in 1941 and 1942, the Japanese were forced gradually to fall back before U.S. forces. However, when the war abruptly ended in August 1945 the Japanese still controlled much of the territory they had conquered.

The Search for a Second Front in Europe

As the Soviet army fought the Germans in the Soviet Union, the United States and Britain tried to determine how they could help tip the scales in Europe, now an almost impregnable German fortress. Stalin kept urging a direct assault across the English Channel, which, if successful, would have the greatest immediate impact. Churchill, however, advocated burrowing into the underbelly of the Axis empire by seeking access to the Mediterranean, first by winning control of North Africa. And it was that strategy that the Allies tried first, starting in 1942.

In North Africa the initial Italian assault on Egypt in 1940 led to eighteen months of attack and counterattack across the desert. But after Axis forces under Rommel pushed 570 miles east by June 1942, the British held at El Alamein, in Egypt, and then began a counterattack that forced the Axis troops to begin what proved a definitive retreat. As this British counterattack proceeded, American and additional British forces landed at several points on the coasts of Morocco and Algeria, weakly defended by Vichy France, in November 1942. Joined by Free French troops, they, too, steadily advanced, squeezing Rommel's Axis forces, until, by May 1943, the Allies had won control of North Africa.

But North Africa was valuable for the Allies only as a staging ground for an attempt to penetrate Europe from the south. Meeting at Casablanca, Morocco, in January 1943, Churchill and Roosevelt agreed that British and American forces would proceed from North Africa to Sicily and on up through Italy. The Soviets, still pushing for an invasion across the English Channel into France, objected that the Germans could easily block Allied advance through the long, mountainous Italian peninsula.

Crossing from North Africa, Allied troops landed in Sicily in July 1943, leading to the ouster and arrest of Mussolini and the collapse of the fascist regime. Supported by King Victor Emmanuel III, the Italian military commander formed a new government to seek an armistice. Meanwhile, Allied forces moved on to the Italian mainland, but the Germans quickly occupied much of Italy in response. They even managed a daring rescue of Mussolini and re-established him as puppet leader of a new rump republic in northern Italy, now under German control. Just as the Soviets had warned, the Germans were sufficiently successful in blocking the Italian peninsula that the Allies got as far as Rome only nine months later, in June 1944. So Churchill's strategy of assaulting Europe from the south proved less than decisive.

Only when Churchill, Roosevelt, and Stalin met for the first time, at Teheran, Iran, in November 1943, did they agree that the next step would be to invade western Europe from Britain. Preparations had been under way since early 1942. Finally, Allied troops crossed the English Channel to make an amphibious landing on the beaches of Normandy, in northern France, on June 6, 1944, known to history as D-Day.

The success of the D-Day invasion opened a major second front in Europe at last. Now American-led forces from the west and Soviet forces from the east worked systematically toward Germany. The one substantial German counterattack in the west, the Battle of the Bulge in December 1944, slowed the Allies' advance, but on March 7, 1945, Allied troops crossed the Rhine River.

By June 1944, when Allied forces landed at Normandy, Soviet forces had already crossed the 1939 border with Poland as they moved steadily westward. But in August the Soviets stopped before reaching Warsaw, and the major Soviet thrust began cutting south, through Romania, which surrendered in August, and on into the Danube valley in Hungary and Yugoslavia during the fall. The Soviets resumed their advance westward through Poland and toward Germany only in January 1945.

Now, with the defeat of Germany simply a matter of time, Allied concern shifted to the shape of the postwar order. Churchill, especially, worried about the implications of the Soviet advances in east-central Europe and the Balkans. As a supplement to the D-Day landings, he wanted to strike from Italy through Yugoslavia into east-central Europe. But the Americans resisted; Churchill's priorities, they felt, reflected old-fashioned concerns over spheres of influence that were no longer appropriate. So the Allies concentrated instead on a secondary landing in southern France in August 1944. This assault, in which Free French forces were prominent, led quickly to the liberation of Paris. But because the Allies made both their landings in France, and not in southeastern Europe, the Western democracies were involved only in the liberation of western Europe. It was the Soviets alone who drove the Germans from east-central Europe and the Balkans. This fact, and the resulting geographical distribution of military strength, fundamentally affected the postwar order in Europe (Map 30.4).

The Shape of the Allied Victory, 1944–1945

The leaders of the Soviet Union, Britain, and the United States sought to mold that postwar order at two notable conferences in 1945. They brought different aspirations for the postwar world, but

D-Day, 1944 Allied forces land at Normandy, early in the morning of June 6, 1944, at last opening a major second front in Europe. *(National Archives, Washington)*

they also had to face the hard military realities that had resulted from the fighting so far: Each had armies in certain places, but not in others. Those military realities led to the de facto division of Europe into spheres of influence among the victors.

The most serious question the Allies faced concerned Germany, which would soon be forced to surrender unconditionally. Germany was widely held responsible for the two world wars, as well as for Nazism with all its atrocities—including the extermination camps, discovered with shock and horror by the advancing Allied armies in 1945. How should Germany be treated?

In the Pacific theater, as in Europe, the way the war ended had major implications for the postwar world. The United States decided to use an atomic bomb, forcing Japan into prompt and unconditional surrender. The suddenness of the ending helped determine the fate of the European empires in Asia.

Yalta: Shaping the Postwar World

When Stalin, Roosevelt, and Churchill met at Yalta, a Soviet Black Sea resort, in February 1945, Allied victory was assured. Yet Yalta has long been surrounded by controversy, because the concessions made there to Stalin seem in retro-

Map 30.4 Allied Victory in Europe Although Allied landings in Italy and France contributed to the victory, it was ultimately the Soviet drive from the east that was decisive in defeating Nazi Germany. By early 1945 it was becoming clear that the shape of the postwar order in Europe would depend in part on the location of the troops of each of the victors.

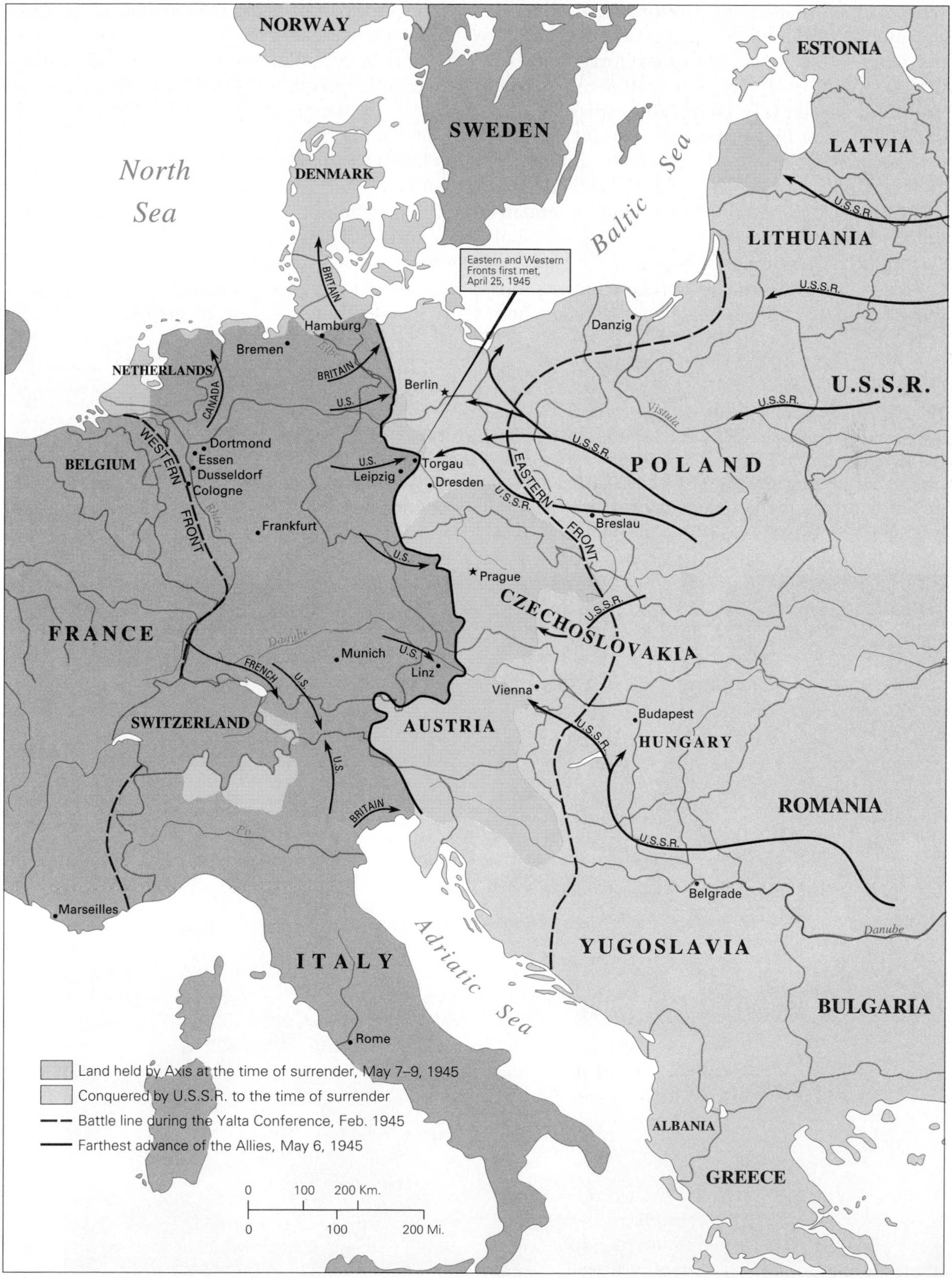
NORWAY
SWEDEN
ESTONIA
LATVIA
LITHUANIA
DENMARK
North Sea
Baltic Sea
Eastern and Western Fronts first met, April 25, 1945
BRITAIN
Hamburg
Bremen
NETHERLANDS
CANADA
Danzig
Berlin
U.S.
U.S.S.R.
U.S.S.R.
Vistula
Elbe
U.S.S.R.
POLAND
WESTERN FRONT
Dortmund
Essen
Dusseldorf
Cologne
BELGIUM
Torgau
Leipzig
Dresden
EASTERN FRONT
Breslau
Rhine
Frankfurt
Prague
CZECHOSLOVAKIA
FRANCE
Danube
Munich
Linz
FRENCH
Vienna
Budapest
SWITZERLAND
AUSTRIA
HUNGARY
ROMANIA
Po
Belgrade
Marseilles
Danube
YUGOSLAVIA
ITALY
Adriatic Sea
BULGARIA
Rome
ALBANIA
GREECE
Land held by Axis at the time of surrender, May 7–9, 1945
Conquered by U.S.S.R. to the time of surrender
Battle line during the Yalta Conference, Feb. 1945
Farthest advance of the Allies, May 6, 1945
0 100 200 Km.
0 100 200 Mi.

spect to have consigned east-central Europe to communist domination and opened the way to the dangerous cold war of the next forty years. At the time, however, the anticipation of victory produced a relatively cooperative spirit among the Allies. Thus, they firmed up plans for military occupation of Germany in separate zones, for joint occupation of Berlin, and for an Allied Control Council, composed of the military commanders in chief, which would make policy for all of Germany by unanimous agreement.

Each of the Allies had special concerns, but there was not yet a rigid east-west division, and each got much of what it was seeking at Yalta. Roosevelt was eager for Soviet help against Japan as soon as possible, and he won Soviet commitment to an agreement tentatively worked out earlier. In exchange for territorial concessions in Asia and the Pacific, Stalin agreed to declare war on Japan within three months of the German surrender.

Churchill, on the other hand, worried about the future of Europe in light of the American intention, which Roosevelt announced at Yalta, to maintain occupation troops in Europe for only two years after the war. To help balance Soviet

The Big Three at Yalta With victory over Nazi Germany assured, Churchill, Roosevelt, and Stalin were in reasonably good spirits when they met at Yalta, a Black Sea resort in the Soviet Union, in February 1945. Important sources of friction among them were evident at the meeting, but the differences that led to the later cold war did not seem paramount at this point. The Yalta conference proved to be the last meeting of the three leaders. *(F.D.R. Library)*

power on the Continent, Churchill felt it essential to restore France as a great power. To this end, he urged that France be granted a share in the occupation of Germany and a permanent seat on the Security Council of the proposed new United Nations. Roosevelt agreed, even though he had little use for Charles de Gaulle and French pretensions.

It seemed to the Americans that both Britain and the Soviet Union remained too wedded to traditional conceptions of national interests as they sought to shape the postwar world. Hence, one of Roosevelt's major priorities was to get British and Soviet commitment to the United Nations before the three allies began to disagree over particular issues. He won that commitment at Yalta, but only by giving in to Churchill on the sensitive matter of British colonies.

Because anti-imperial sentiment had worked to Japan's advantage in Asia, the United States had pestered Britain on the colonial issue since early in the war. Roosevelt had even asked Churchill in 1941 about British intentions in India. So prickly was Churchill that he proclaimed in 1942, "I have not become the King's First Minister in order to preside over the liquidation of the British Empire." It was agreed at Yalta that the British Empire would not be subject to an anticipated measure to bring former colonies under United Nations trusteeship after the war.

Provision for the territories formerly held by the Nazis in east-central Europe was but one of the questions on the table at Yalta. By this time the division of former Axis territory into spheres of influence was already becoming evident, and, in light of the location of Allied troops, the alignment was probably inevitable. In Italy, where U.S. and British troops held sway, the two democracies had successfully resisted Stalin's claim for a share in the administration. In east-central Europe, on the other hand, the Soviet army was in control. Still, the United States, with its vision of a new world order, refused simply to accept a division into spheres of influence and insisted that democratic principles be applied everywhere. At Yalta this American priority led to an awkward compromise over east-central Europe; the new governments in the area were to be both democratic and friendly to the Soviet Union.

Most important to the Soviets was Poland, with its crucial location between Russia and Germany. Although the Soviets insisted that Communists lead the new Polish government at the outset, they compromised by allowing a role for the noncommunist Polish government in exile in London. They also promised free elections in Poland. The three Allies agreed that the Polish-Soviet border would be the line established after World War I. Poland would gain substantial German territory to its west to make up for what it would lose to the U.S.S.R. to its east (Map 30.5).

In addition, the United States and Britain were to have a role in committees set up to engineer the transition to democracy in the rest of east-central Europe. However, only the Soviets had troops in the area, and those committees proved essentially powerless. But though the sources of future tension were already at work at Yalta, they generally remained hidden by the high spirits of approaching victory.

Victory in Europe and the Beginning of the Cold War

Although the tide had turned in 1943, Germany managed to continue the war by exploiting its conquered territories and by more effectively allocating its domestic resources for war production. Thanks partly to the efforts of armaments minister Albert Speer, war production increased sharply between 1941 and 1944, so Germany still had plenty of weapons even as the war was ending. But Germany encountered two crucial bottlenecks that finally crippled its military effort: It was running out of military manpower, and it was running out of oil.

Although it made effective use of synthetics, the Nazi war machine depended heavily on oil from Romania. However, late in August 1944, Soviet troops crossed into Romania, taking control of the oil fields. In addition, from the middle of 1944 on, U.S. and British planes successfully bombed German oil installations.

From the start of the war, some, especially in Britain, insisted that bombing could destroy the economic and psychological basis of the enemy's ability to wage war. Beginning in 1942, British-led bombing attacks destroyed an average of half the built-up area of seventy German cities, sometimes producing huge firestorms. The bombing of the historic city of Dresden in February 1945 killed more than 135,000 civilians in the most

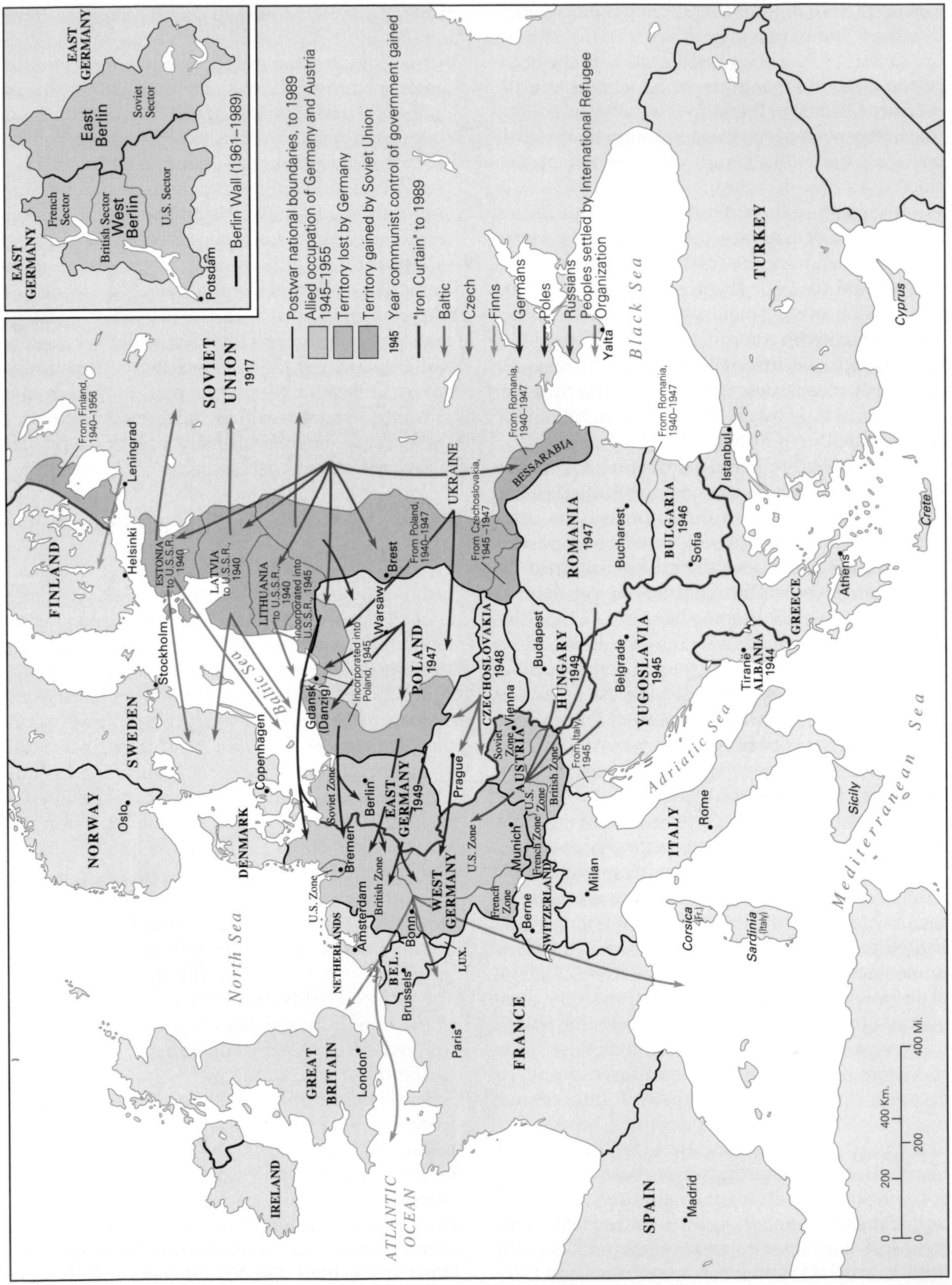
EAST GERMANY
East Berlin
Soviet Sector
French Sector
British Sector
West Berlin
U.S. Sector
Potsdam
Berlin Wall (1961–1989)
Postwar national boundaries, to 1989
Allied occupation of Germany and Austria 1945–1955
Territory lost by Germany
Territory gained by Soviet Union
1945 Year communist control of government gained
"Iron Curtain" to 1989
Baltic
Czech
Finns
Germans
Poles
Russians
Peoples settled by International Refugee Organization
FINLAND
Helsinki
Leningrad
From Finland, 1940–1956
SOVIET UNION 1917
ESTONIA to U.S.S.R., 1940
LATVIA to U.S.S.R., 1940
LITHUANIA to U.S.S.R., 1940
Incorporated into U.S.S.R., 1945
Incorporated into Poland, 1945
UKRAINE
BESSARABIA
From Romania, 1940–1947
From Poland, 1940–1947
From Czechoslovakia, 1945–1947
Brest
Warsaw
POLAND 1947
Gdansk (Danzig)
Baltic Sea
Stockholm
SWEDEN
NORWAY
Oslo
Copenhagen
DENMARK
North Sea
Soviet Zone
Berlin
EAST GERMANY 1949
Bremen
U.S. Zone
British Zone
Amsterdam
NETHERLANDS
Bonn
WEST GERMANY
BEL.
Brussels
LUX.
French Zone
U.S. Zone
Munich
Prague
CZECHOSLOVAKIA 1948
Vienna
Soviet Zone
AUSTRIA
U.S. Zone
French Zone
British Zone
From Italy, 1945
Budapest
HUNGARY 1949
ROMANIA 1947
Bucharest
BULGARIA 1946
Sofia
Black Sea
Yalta
From Romania, 1940–1947
Istanbul
TURKEY
Cyprus
Crete
Athens
GREECE
Tiranë
ALBANIA 1944
Belgrade
YUGOSLAVIA 1945
Adriatic Sea
Rome
ITALY
Sicily
Mediterranean Sea
Milan
Berne
SWITZERLAND
Corsica (Fr.)
Sardinia (Italy)
FRANCE
Paris
London
GREAT BRITAIN
IRELAND
ATLANTIC OCEAN
SPAIN
Madrid
0 200 400 Km.
0 200 400 Mi.

destructive air assault of the war in Europe. But despite this widespread destruction, such bombing did not undermine morale or disrupt transport and production to the extent expected. Despite steady Allied bombing, Germany increased its war production during 1943 and 1944.

The more precise targeting favored by U.S. strategists proved more effective. In May 1944, the United States began bombing oil fields in Romania and refineries and synthetic oil plants in Germany. Because of the resulting oil bottleneck, Germany lacked enough fuel even to train pilots, so that by 1945 German industry was producing more aircraft than the German air force could use. Though its proponents consistently overestimated its value, strategic bombing made a significant contribution to the Allied war effort by the end.

Russian troops moving westward finally met U.S. troops moving eastward at the Elbe River in Germany on April 26, 1945. With his regime now thoroughly defeated and much of his country in ruins, Hitler committed suicide in his military headquarters on April 30, 1945. The war in the West finally ended with the German surrender to General Eisenhower at Reims, France, on May 7 and to Marshal Zhukov at Berlin on May 8. The world celebrated the end of the fighting in Europe, but an element of uncertainty surrounded the Allied victory because East-West differences were increasingly coming to the fore within the anti-German alliance.

Between the Yalta Conference in February 1945 and the next meeting of the three Allied leaders, in July 1945, differences over east-central Europe hardened into the beginnings of a cold war between the Western democracies and the Soviet Union. Whereas the United States envisioned a world order based on the ongoing cooperation of the three victors, the Soviet Union gave top priority to creating a buffer zone of states friendly to the Soviet Union in east-central Europe, especially as a bulwark against Germany, which had invaded—and devastated—the Soviet Union twice within living memory. Especially in Poland, the Soviets were determined to have their own way. When the new Communist-led Polish government held elections in January 1947, it rigged them to guarantee a favorable outcome.

Map 30.5 The Impact of World War II in Europe As a result of World War II the Soviet Union expanded its western borders and Poland shifted westward at the expense of Germany. Territorial changes added to the wartime disruption and produced a flood of refugees. The cold war division of Europe did not depend on immediate territorial changes, but soon Germany itself came to be divided along east-west lines.

The United States refused to acquiesce as the Soviets established this sphere of influence in east-central Europe. Whatever the realism of their alternative vision of the postwar world, the Americans can hardly be blamed for refusing to write off the peoples of east-central Europe to unwelcome Soviet hegemony. But U.S. policymakers failed to grasp the historical and strategic basis for Soviet priorities and assumed the Soviets were primarily trying to spread communism. As a result, the cleft between the emerging superpowers widened and became more dangerous.

While seeking this sphere of influence in east-central Europe, Stalin did not push for revolution in western Europe and gave the British a free hand to settle the civil war between communists and anticommunists in Greece. Communists in Italy and France, strengthened by major roles in their respective resistance movements, were directed to work within broad-based democratic fronts rather than try to take power. Although no formal deal was made, Stalin saw this moderate position in western and southern Europe as something of an exchange with the West for a free hand in east-central Europe.

The Potsdam Conference and the Question of Germany

The shape of the postwar era rested above all on the fate of Germany. At Potsdam, just outside Berlin, the leaders of the United States, Britain, and the Soviet Union met from July 17 to August 2, 1945, under dramatically different circumstances than at Yalta just months before. With Hitler dead and Germany defeated, there was no longer a common military aim in Europe to provide unity. And of the three Allied leaders who had been at Yalta, only Stalin remained. President Roosevelt had died in April, so Harry Truman represented the United States. In Britain,

The Coming of the Atomic Age

Albert Einstein (1879–1955), born of Jewish parents in Germany, became famous for his work in theoretical physics on the eve of World War I. When Hitler came to power in 1933, Einstein happened to be in the United States, and he never returned to Germany. Although Einstein was the most famous scientist in the world by the late 1930s, he was not in any direct sense the father of the atomic bomb. Indeed, even early in 1939, he doubted that a bomb based on atomic energy could be devised. But conversations with colleagues convinced him not only that such a bomb might be possible but that Nazi Germany might well develop it first. Thus Einstein wrote to President Roosevelt on August 2, 1939, to urge that the United States begin exploring the possibilities in earnest.

F. D. Roosevelt
President of the United States
White House
Washington, D.C.

Sir:

Some recent work by E. Fermi and L. Szilard, which has been communicated to me in manuscript, leads me to expect that the element uranium may be turned into a new and important source of energy in the foreseeable future. Certain aspects of the situation seem to call for watchfulness and, if necessary, quick action on the part of the Administration. I believe, therefore, that it is my duty to bring to your attention the following facts and recommendations.

In the course of the last four months it has been made probable—through the work of Joliot in France as well as Fermi and Szilard in America—that it may become possible to set up nuclear chain reactions in a large mass of uranium, by which vast amounts of power and large quantities of new radium-like elements would be generated. Now it appears almost certain that this could be achieved in the immediate future.

This new phenomenon would also lead to the construction of bombs, and it is conceivable—though much less certain—that extremely powerful bombs of a new type may thus be constructed. A single bomb of this type, carried by boat or exploded in a port, might very well destroy the whole port together with some of the surrounding territory. However, such bombs might very well prove to be too heavy for transportation by air. . . .

In view of this situation you may think it desirable to have some permanent contact maintained between the Administration and the group of physicists working on chain reactions in America. . . .

I understand that Germany has actually stopped the sale of uranium from the Czechoslovakian mines which she has taken over. That she should have taken such early action might perhaps be understood on the ground that the son of the German Under-Secretary of State, von Weizsäcker, is attached to the Kaiser Wilhelm Institute in Berlin, where some of the American work on uranium is now being repeated.

Yours very truly,

A. Einstein

Source: Otto Nathan and Heinz Norden, eds., *Einstein on Peace* (New York: Simon and Schuster, 1960), pp. 294–296.

Churchill's Conservatives lost the general election during the first days of the conference, so Clement Attlee (1883–1967), the new Labour prime minister, assumed the leadership of the British delegation.

The task for the Allies at Potsdam was to implement their earlier agreements about Germany, which now depended on the Allied occupying forces even for its day-to-day survival. The Allies had agreed that Germany was to be forced to surrender unconditionally, but it was not yet clear what would be done with the country over the longer term. For a time U.S. policymakers had even considered destroying Germany's industrial capacity in perpetuity. However, cooler heads understood that the deindustrialization, or "pastoralization," of Germany would not be in anyone's economic interests. Moreover, as the democracies grew increasingly suspicious about Soviet intentions, an economically healthy Germany seemed necessary to help in the balance against the Soviet Union.

For their part, the Soviets wanted to weaken Germany for the long term but also to exploit its resources by exacting heavy reparations. The United States and Britain accepted the Soviet proposal that Germany's eastern border with Poland be shifted substantially westward, to the line formed by the Oder and Neisse rivers. As a result of this arrangement, the geographical area of Germany, quite apart from the later division between east and west, was reduced by about 20 percent, to the advantage of Poland and the Soviet Union.

Although each of the Allies had responsibility for administering its own occupation zone, they were supposed to coordinate their activities, to make possible a common policy toward Germany. This effort was to include de-Nazification, demilitarization, and an assault on concentrations of economic power—to root out what seemed the sources of Germany's antidemocratic and aggressive tendencies. But disagreements over economic policy soon undermined the pretense of joint government. Thus East-West differences, already affecting events in east-central Europe, came to affect the settlement in Germany as well.

The Atomic Bomb and the Capitulation of Japan

In the Pacific, Japan had been forced onto the defensive by September 1943, but during 1944 it mounted two major counterattacks to challenge the Americans' newly won naval supremacy. The Japanese wanted especially to prevent American reconquest of the Philippines, which would cut Japan off from its vital raw materials further south. But the naval battles of 1944 led only to further Japanese defeat. The resulting losses of ships, coupled with increasing shortages of fuel, had virtually crippled the Japanese navy by the end of the year. U.S. forces encountered only token naval resistance when they began invading Okinawa in April 1945.

However, as the situation grew more desperate for Japan, Japanese ground soldiers and aircraft pilots fought ever more fiercely, often fighting to the death, or taking their own lives, rather than surrendering. Thus the U.S. conquest of Okinawa required the most bitter combat of the entire Pacific war.

Finally taking Okinawa in June, U.S. forces got close enough for air raids on the Japanese home islands. But though the United States was now clearly in control, it seemed likely that an actual invasion of Japan would be necessary to force a Japanese surrender. That invasion might cost the United States as many as 1 million additional casualties, because the Japanese could be expected to fight even more desperately to defend their own soil. It was especially for this reason that the Americans decided to end the war in an altogether different way, by using atomic bombs.

In 1939 scientists in several countries, including Germany, began advising their governments that new, immensely destructive weapons based on thermonuclear fission were theoretically possible. The German economics ministry began seeking uranium as early as 1939, but Hitler promoted jet- and rocket-propelled terror weaponry instead, especially the V-2 rocket bombs that the Germans began showering on England in the fall of 1944. Still, fear that the Nazis were developing atomic weapons lurked behind the Allied effort to produce an atomic bomb as quickly as possible (see the box, "The Coming of the Atomic Age").

Although the British were the first to initiate an atomic weapons program, by late 1941 the Americans were building on what they knew of British findings to develop their own crash program, known as the Manhattan Project. Constructing an atomic bomb proved far more difficult and costly than most had expected in 1941, and it took a concerted effort by the United States to have atomic weapons ready for military use by mid-1945.

The U.S. decision actually to use the atomic bomb, dropping two of them on Japanese civilians, has been one of the most controversial of

Hiroshima, September 1945 The U.S. bombing of Hiroshima was instrumental in ending the war with Japan, but it also ushered in the new terrors of the atomic age. The advent of such destructive weapons seemed to mark a definitive change in human affairs. *(UPI/Bettmann Newsphotos)*

modern history. The decision fell to the new president, Harry Truman, who had known nothing of the bomb project when Roosevelt died in April 1945. During the next few months, Truman listened to spirited disagreement among American policymakers. Was it necessary actually to drop the bomb to force the Japanese to surrender? Especially because the ultimate victory of the United States was not in doubt, some thought it would be enough simply to demonstrate the new weapon to the Japanese.

By July, when the Allies met at Potsdam, the United States was prepared to use the bomb, but President Truman first warned Japan that if it did not surrender at once, it would be subjected to destruction immeasurably greater than Germany had just suffered. The Japanese decided to ignore the American warning, although the United States had begun area-bombing Japanese cities a few months before. The bombing of Tokyo in March produced a firestorm that gutted one-fourth of the city and killed over 80,000 people. In light of the Japanese refusal to surrender, the use of the atomic bomb could seem the logical next step.

An American pilot released the first atomic bomb 32,000 feet above Hiroshima at 8:15 in the morning on August 6, 1945. It exploded after 45 seconds, 2,000 feet above the ground, killing 80,000 people outright and leaving tens of thousands more to die in the aftermath. Three days later, on August 9, a second atomic bomb was exploded over Nagasaki, killing perhaps 50,000 people. Although sectors of the Japanese military held out for continued resistance, the emperor finally surrendered on August 15. The bombing of civilians had discredited the Japanese military, which not only had proven unable to defend the country but had systematically misled the Japanese people about the country's prospects.

The war in the Pacific ended more suddenly than had seemed possible just a few months before. The Europeans had little opportunity to reassert their control in the colonial territories they had earlier lost to the Japanese. This proved advantageous to the various national liberation or decolonization movements that had developed in Asia during the war.

In Burma and the Dutch East Indies, the Japanese had encouraged anticolonial sentiment, even helping local nationalists create patriotic militias. After the war, the Dutch were never able to re-establish their control against the Indonesian nationalists the Japanese had helped build up in the East Indies. But even when its target was Japanese occupation, resistance intensified local nationalism and produced hostility to the former colonial masters, as well as to the Japanese. British troops returned to Malaya and Singapore in time to accept the Japanese surrender, but they eventually came into conflict with local forces that they themselves had helped to develop against the Japanese.

In Asia and the Pacific, then, Japanese occupation provoked resistance that quickly fed anticolonialism. In 1945, Japan had been defeated, but the war had weakened the old Western imperialism, and it was not clear what would follow.

Disruption, Destruction, and Death

World War II left 50 to 60 million people dead—three times as many as World War I. About that same number were left homeless for some length of time, or found themselves forced onto the mercies of others as refugees. The Soviet Union and Germany suffered by far the highest casualty figures; for each, the figure was considerably higher than in World War I. An appalling 23 million Soviet citizens died, of whom 12 to 13 million were civilians. Germany lost 5 to 6 million, including perhaps 2 million civilians.

In contrast, casualty rates for Italy, Britain, and France, were lower than in World War I. Italy suffered 200,000 military and 200,000 civilian deaths. Total British losses, including civilians, numbered 450,000, to which must be added 120,000 from the British Empire. Despite its quick defeat, France lost more lives than Britain, because of the ravages of German occupation: the 350,000 deaths among French civilians considerably exceeded the British figure, which was closer to 100,000.

The United States lost 300,000 servicemen and 5,000 civilians. Figures for Japan are problematic, partly because the Japanese claim that 300,000 of those who surrendered to the Soviets in 1945 have remained unaccounted for. Apart from this number, 1,740,000 Japanese servicemen died from 1941 to 1945, more from hunger and

Reconstruction Begins Shortly after the end of the war, women in Berlin pass pails of rubble along a line to a dump. Wartime bombing had severely damaged cities throughout much of Europe, although destruction was greatest in Germany. *(Hulton-Deutsch)*

disease than from combat, and 300,000 civilians died in Japan, most from U.S. bombing.

But this war was not confined to the major powers. Armed forces in east-central Europe also suffered substantial losses, perhaps 300,000 to 400,000 each for Hungary, Yugoslavia, Poland, Austria, and Romania. In addition, up to 1.5 million from the Yugoslav resistance died in fighting that took on the dimensions of a civil war.

Although bombing did not have the expected effect on morale or production, it destroyed buildings and left huge areas of major cities in rubble by the end of the fighting. This destruction, in turn, left hundreds of thousands homeless and contributed to the unprecedented uprooting of peoples that marked the era of World War II.

During the war, Jews, Poles, and others deemed undesirable by the Nazis had been rounded up and shipped to ghettos or camps, and the great majority had died. Of those Jews who were still alive when the Nazi camps were liberated, almost half died within a few weeks. Even those who managed to return home sometimes faced pogroms there; forty Jews were killed in the worst of them, at Kielce, in Poland.

The redrawing of Germany's borders contributed to the huge wave of refugees just after the war. To guarantee the permanence of the new territorial configuration of Poland, the Soviets and Poles began expelling ethnic Germans from the historically German areas that were now to become Polish. Some 10 million Germans were forced out, so that by 1958 only about 1 million Germans were left living in these areas. Similarly, the Czechs were expelling the Germans living in the Sudetenland area of Czechoslovakia by 1947. So a flood of German refugees was forced to move west after the war, into the shrunken territory of the new Germany. They were among the 16 million Europeans who were permanently uprooted and transplanted between 1939 and 1947.

Victory and Defeat, Hope and Despair

Even after the fighting stopped in 1945, astonishing changes continued as the forces unleashed by the war played themselves out. Most immediately, differences between the Soviets and the Western democracies promptly shattered the wartime alliance, producing the division of Germany and a bipolar Europe. Thus the conclusion of World War II led directly to the danger of a third world war, which might involve nuclear weapons and threaten the very survival of life on Earth.

In addition to the dramatic changes in Europe, the wider effects of the war brought to the forefront a whole new set of issues, from anticolonialism to the Arab-Israeli conflict to the spread of communism within the non-Western world. These issues would remain central for decades, but by 1949 it was possible at least to discern the contours of the new postwar world, a world with new sources of hope but also with conflicts and dangers that had hardly been imaginable in 1939.

The Division of Germany

An immediate priority for the victorious Allies in Germany was de-Nazification. In the western zones, Germans were required to attend lectures on the virtues of democracy and to view the corpses of the victims of Nazism. The most dramatic instances of de-Nazification, however, were the Nuremberg trials of August 1945 through October 1946, the most famous of a number of war crimes trials held in Germany and the occupied countries after the war. Although Hitler, Himmler, and Goebbels had committed suicide, the occupying authorities apprehended for trial an assortment of twenty-four individuals who had played important but very different roles in the Third Reich. All but three were convicted of war crimes and "crimes against humanity." Twelve were sentenced to death, of whom ten were ultimately executed.

Questions about their legitimacy dogged the Nuremberg trials from the start. To a considerable extent the accused were being judged against law made after the fact. The notion of "crimes against humanity" remained vague. Moreover, even insofar as a measure of international law was in force, it was arguably binding only on states, not individuals. But in light of the unprecedented atrocities of the Nazi regime, there was widespread agreement among the victors that the Nazi leaders could not be treated simply as defeated adversaries.

The Legacy of Nazism As part of the de-Nazification effort in Germany after the war, Allied authorities required Germans to view the corpses of some of those who had died at the hands of the Nazis. This photo shows Germans in Nuremberg filing past the open coffins of 161 Polish Jews shot by SS troops in the woods outside the city. *(UPI/Bettmann Newsphotos)*

The effort to apprehend the perpetrators of Nazi atrocities continued in Germany and elsewhere, but the concern of the Western Allies to root out the sources of Germany's apparent waywardness faded as communism, not Nazism, came to seem to be the immediate menace.

By the terms of the Potsdam agreement, military government in the German occupation zones was to be coordinated by the Allied Control Authority, but because East-West differences immediately surfaced, this body proved ineffective. Thus decisions were made not in the coordinated way initially envisioned, but within each zone, by the military commander, responsible to his own government.

Disagreements over economic policy proved the major source of the split. At Potsdam, the West had accepted Soviet demands for German reparations, but rather than wait for German payments, the Soviets began removing German factories and equipment for reassembly in the Soviet Union. To assure that they got their due, the Soviets wanted access to the economic resources not simply of the Russian occupation zone but of the whole of Germany. The United States and Britain, in contrast, gave priority to economic reconstruction and quickly began integrating the economies of the western zones for that purpose.

Friction developed from 1945 to 1948 as the West insisted on reduced reparations and a higher level of industrial production than the Soviets wanted. Finally, as part of their effort to spur economic recovery, the United States and Britain introduced a new currency without Soviet consent. Stalin's response, in June 1948, was to blockade the city of Berlin, cutting its western sectors off from the main Western occupation zones, almost two hundred miles west. The Western Allies responded with a massive airlift that kept their sectors of Berlin supplied for almost a year, until May 1949, when the Soviets finally backed down.

The fragile Potsdam agreement about Germany had gradually disintegrated. The pretense of Allied collaboration, sustained for a while after 1945, disappeared altogether by 1948, when two separate states clearly began emerging from the Allied occupation zones. The growing split with the Soviet Union reinforced the determination of the United States and Britain to get the Western zones back on their feet as quickly as possible. Western Germany must become a viable state—economically, politically, and even militarily.

The Western occupying powers began restoring local government immediately after the war, to create the administrative framework necessary to provide public utilities and food distribution. Gradually a governing structure was built from the ground up in the Western zones, which were increasingly coordinated, so that by 1949 it was possible to restore government on the national level.

With Allied support, a "parliamentary council" of German leaders met during 1948 and 1949 and produced a document that, when ratified in September 1949, became the "basic law" of a new Federal Republic of Germany. This founding document was termed simply the "basic law," as opposed to the constitution, to emphasize the provisional character of the new West German state. For the same reason, the capital was placed in the small, provincial city of Bonn, which was obviously no substitute for Berlin. As far as many West Germans were concerned, the advent of a new state limited to the west did not foreclose the future reunification of Germany. But as it became clear that a new state was being created in the Western zones, and that Germany was thus to be at least temporarily divided, the Soviets settled for a new state in their zone, in eastern Germany. Thus the Communist-led German Democratic Republic, with its capital in East Berlin, was born in October 1949.

The "Iron Curtain" and the Emergence of a Bipolar World

In east-central Europe, only Yugoslavia and Albania had achieved liberation on their own, and the communist leaders of their resistance movements had a plausible claim to political power. Elsewhere, the Soviet army had provided liberation, and the Soviet military presence remained the decisive political fact as the war ended. In much of the region, authoritarianism and collaboration had been the rule for a decade or more, so there was no possibility of returning to a clearly legitimate prewar political order. To be sure, each country had local political groups, some representing former governments in exile, that now claimed a governing role, but their standing in relation to the Soviet army was uncertain.

Under these circumstances, the Soviets were able to work with local communists to install new communist-led regimes friendly to the Soviet Union in most of east-central Europe. But though Churchill warned as early as 1946 that "an iron curtain" was descending from the Baltic to the Adriatic, the process of Soviet power consolidation was not easy, and it took place gradually, in discrete steps over several years (see the box, "Discerning the Iron Curtain"). Only in 1948 did the communists, facing serious losses in upcoming elections, assume outright power in Czechoslovakia. But by 1949 there were communist governments, relying on Soviet support, in Poland, Czechoslovakia, East Germany, Hungary, Romania, and Bulgaria, with Yugoslavia and Albania also communist but capable of a more independent line.

Communism might have spread still farther in Europe, and perhaps beyond, but the West drew the line over Greece. There, as in Yugoslavia, an indigenous, communist-led resistance movement had become strong enough to challenge for political power by late 1944. But when it sought to oust the monarchial government that had just returned to Greece from exile, the British intervened, helping the monarchy put down the communist uprising. Although Stalin gave the Greek communists little help, communist guerrilla activity continued, thanks partly to

Discerning the Iron Curtain

Winston Churchill, out of office and touring the United States, sought to specify the contours of the postwar international situation in a speech at Westminster College in Fulton, Missouri, on March 5, 1946. To characterize the developing division of Europe, Churchill referred to "an iron curtain," a term that attracted immediate attention and dramatically affected public opinion in both the United States and western Europe. Soviet historians dated the beginning of the cold war from this speech.

A shadow has fallen upon the scenes so lately lighted by the Allied victory. Nobody knows what Soviet Russia and its Communist international organization intends to do in the immediate future, or what are the limits, if any, to their expansive and proselytizing tendencies. . . . We understand the Russian need to be secure on her western frontiers from all renewal of German aggression. We welcome her to her rightful place among the leading nations of the world. . . . It is my duty, however, to place before you certain facts. . . .

From Stettin in the Baltic to Trieste in the Adriatic, an iron curtain has descended across the Continent. Behind that line lie all the capitals of the ancient states of central and eastern Europe. Warsaw, Berlin, Prague, Vienna, Budapest, Belgrade, Bucharest, and Sofia, all these famous cities and the populations around them lie in the Soviet sphere and all are subject in one form or another, not only to Soviet influence but to a very high and increasing measure of control from Moscow. . . . The Russian-dominated Polish government has been encouraged to make enormous and wrongful inroads upon Germany, and mass expulsions of millions of Germans on a scale grievous and undreamed of are now taking place. The Communist parties, which were very small in all these eastern states of Europe, have been raised to pre-eminence and power far beyond their numbers and are seeking everywhere to obtain totalitarian control. . . .

. . . I do not believe that Soviet Russia desires war. What they desire is the fruits of war and the indefinite expansion of their power and doctrines. But what we have to consider here today while time remains, is the permanent prevention of war and the establishment of the conditions of freedom and democracy as rapidly as possible in all countries. . . .

From what I have seen of our Russian friends and allies during the war, I am convinced that there is nothing they admire so much as strength, and there is nothing for which they have less respect than for weakness, especially military weakness.

Source: Winston S. Churchill, *His Complete Speeches, 1897–1963,* vol. VII, *1943–1949,* ed. Robert Rhodes James (New York: Chelsea House, 1974), pp. 7290–7292.

support from Tito's Yugoslavia. In 1946 a renewed communist uprising escalated into civil war.

As the cold war developed, both the Soviet Union and the United States began taking a more active interest in the Greek conflict. After the financially strapped Labour government in Britain pulled back from its involvement early in 1947, the United States stepped in to support the Greek monarchy against the communists. American policymakers feared that communism would progress from the Balkans through Greece to the Middle East. Greece seemed the place to draw the line. Thus, in March 1947, President Truman announced the Truman Doctrine, which committed the United States to the "containment" of communism throughout the world. American advisers now began re-equipping the anticommunist forces in Greece. Faced with this determined opposition from the West, Stalin

The Soviet View of the Cold War

In a speech in Poland in September 1947, Andrei Zhdanov (1896–1948) applied Marxist categories of analysis to the new situation created by World War II in an effort to explain the developing cold war. Zhdanov was a powerful figure in the hierarchy of the Soviet Communist party, and his views were widely regarded as authoritative.

The end of the Second World War brought with it big changes in the world situation. . . . The decisive role played by the Soviet Union in the vanquishing of the fascist aggressors sharply altered the alignment of forces between the two systems—the Socialist and the Capitalist—in favor of Socialism. . . .

Of the capitalist powers, only one—the United States—emerged from the war not only unweakened, but even considerably stronger economically and militarily. . . .

But the end of the war confronted the United States with a number of new problems. The capitalist monopolies were anxious to maintain their profits at the former high level. . . . But this meant that the United States must retain the foreign markets which had absorbed American products during the war, and moreover, acquire new markets, inasmuch as the war had substantially lowered the purchasing power of most of the countries. . . .

. . . United States policy envisages a broad program of military, economic and political measures, designed to establish United States political and economic domination in all countries marked out for American expansion, to reduce these countries to the status of satellites of the United States. . . .

But America's aspirations to world supremacy encounter an obstacle in the U.S.S.R. . . . Accordingly, the new expansionist and reactionary policy of the United States envisages a struggle against the U.S.S.R. . . .

Realization of the strategical plans for future aggression is connected with the desire to utilize to the utmost the war production facilities of the United States, which had grown to enormous proportions by the end of World War II. American imperialism is persistently pursuing a policy of militarizing the country. . . .

The strategical plans of the United States envisage the creation in peacetime of numerous bases . . . situated at great distances from the American continent and designed to be used for aggressive purposes against the U.S.S.R. . . .

Source: U.S. Congress, House Committee on Foreign Affairs, *The Strategy and Tactics of World Communism,* supplement I: "One Hundred Years of Communism, 1848–1948" (Washington: U.S. Government Printing Office, 1948), pp. 212, 214–215, 220–221.

pulled back, but the Greek communists, with their strong indigenous support, were not defeated until 1949.

Thus the wartime marriage of expediency between the Soviet Union and the Western democracies fell apart in the war's aftermath. Only in Austria, jointly occupied by the Soviets and the Western democracies, were the former Allies able to arrange the postwar transition in a reasonably amicable way. The Soviets acquiesced in the neutralization of a democratic Austria as the occupying powers left in 1954. Elsewhere, Europe was divided into two antagonistic power blocs. The antagonism between the two superpowers became more menacing when the Soviets exploded their first atomic bomb in August 1949, intensifying the postwar arms race. By then, in fact, the United States was on the way to the more destructive hydrogen bomb. The split between these two nations, unmistakable by 1949, established the framework for world affairs for the next forty years (see the box, "The Soviet View of the Cold War").

The United Nations and the New World Agenda

Starting with the Atlantic Charter conference of 1941, Roosevelt had sought to assure that the common effort against the Axis would lead to a firmer basis for peace, to be framed through a new international organization after the war. At a conference at Dumbarton Oaks in Washington in September 1944, the United States outlined the structure of a new United Nations. Seeking to design a more effective body than the discredited League of Nations, Roosevelt proposed that the United States, Britain, the Soviet Union, and China play a special role as members of a Security Council, which would form a directing nucleus for the new international body. At Yalta a few months later, Churchill persuaded Roosevelt that France, too, should have a permanent seat on the Security Council.

By the end of the war, several international meetings had used the United Nations title. The United Nations Monetary and Financial Conference at Bretton Woods, New Hampshire, in July 1944 brought together delegates from forty-four nations to deal with the problems of currency and exchange rates that would accompany the end of emergency wartime conditions. Although it produced only recommendations that had to be ratified by the individual states, the conference indicated a new determination to cooperate on the international level after the failures of the interwar period. And the outcome of the conference, the Bretton Woods Agreement, laid the foundation for international economic exchange in the noncommunist world for the crucial quarter-century of economic recovery after the war. In addition, the conference gave birth to the International Monetary Fund and the International Bank for Reconstruction and Development, which became pillars of the global economic order.

At a conference in San Francisco from April to June 1945, delegates from almost fifty anti-Axis countries translated the principles discussed at Dumbarton Oaks into a charter for the new United Nations. As Roosevelt had envisioned, the major powers were given a privileged position in the organization as permanent members of the Security Council, each with veto power. But it was hoped that the United Nations would institutionalize the spirit of cooperation that had developed among those who had struggled against the Axis during the war. To dramatize its departure from the League of Nations, which had been based in Geneva, and which the United States had refused to join, the United Nations was headquartered in New York. In July 1945, the American Senate approved U.S. membership in the international body almost unanimously.

The creation of the United Nations afforded hope for the future, but the virtually simultaneous advent of the cold war cast a heavy shadow over the new organization. At the same time, other dramatic changes, stemming from forces unleashed partly by World War II, suggested that, with or without the cold war, the new postwar world would be hard to manage. Events in India in 1947, in Israel in 1948, and in China in 1949 epitomized the new hopes and uncertainties that had emerged directly from World War II.

Fearing a Japanese attack on India, the United States pressured Britain into a conciliatory stance toward the growing movement for Indian independence, spearheaded by the charismatic spiritual leader Mohandas Gandhi (1869–1948). In March 1942, the British government pledged that as soon as the war was over, India would be granted independence, under a constitution that the Indians could devise for themselves. During the remainder of the war, Britain cracked down on Indian dissidents demanding immediate independence, but once the war was over the British lacked the will and the financial resources to do anything but abide by their earlier pledge. Thus Britain acquiesced in Indian independence, proclaimed on August 15, 1947. Allowing independence to India, long the jewel of the British Empire, raised questions about Britain's role in the postwar world and portended a wider disintegration of the European colonial system. There would be new countries, many of them poor—and resentful of Western imperialism. What would that mean for the new United Nations?

Questions about the fate of the Jews, who had suffered so grievously during World War II, were inevitable as well. Almost two-thirds of the Jews of Europe had been killed, and many of the sur-

Toward Independence for India An apostle of nonviolence, Mohandas Gandhi (right) inspired the movement for Indian independence from Britain. He is seen here in 1946 with Jawaharlal Nehru (1889–1964), who would become prime minister when India achieved independence the next year. *(UPI/Bettmann Newsphotos)*

vivors either had no place to go or had concluded that they could never again live as a minority in Europe. Many insisted that they must have a homeland of their own. For decades such Zionist sentiment had centered on the biblical area of Israel, in what had become, after World War I, the British mandate of Palestine. Jewish immigration to the area accelerated during the interwar period, but it caused increasing friction between the Jews and the Palestinian Arabs.

Concerned about access to Middle Eastern oil, the British sought to cultivate good relations with the Arab world after the war. Thus they opposed further immigration of Jews to Palestine, as well as proposals to carve an independent Jewish state from the area. The United States, however, was considerably more sympathetic to the Zionist cause. As tensions built, Jewish terrorists blew up the British headquarters in Jerusalem, and the British decided to abandon what seemed a no-win situation. In September 1947, they announced their intention to withdraw from Palestine, leaving its future to the United Nations. In November the UN voted to partition Palestine, creating both a Jewish and a new Arab Palestinian state (Map 30.6).

Skirmishing between Jews and Arabs became full-scale war in December, and in that context the Jews declared independence as the new state of Israel on May 14, 1948. When fighting ended in 1949, the Israelis had conquered more territory than had been envisioned in the original partition plan, and the remaining Arab territories fell to Egypt and Jordan, rather than forming an independent Palestinian state. Thus was born the new state of Israel, partly a product of the assault on the Jews during World War II. Yet it was born amid Arab hostility and Western concerns about oil.

In 1949, the communist insurgency in China under Mao Zedong (Mao Tse-tung) finally triumphed over the Chinese Nationalists under Chiang Kai-shek, who were forced to flee to the island of Taiwan. During the war, the Communists had done better than the Nationalists at identifying themselves with the Chinese cause against both Japanese and Western imperialism. And after their victory, the Chinese Communists enjoyed great prestige among other "national liberation" movements struggling against Western colonialists. To many in the West, however, the outcome in China by 1949 simply intensified fears that communism was poised to spread in the unsettled postwar world.

At the same time, the Chinese revolution undermined Roosevelt's conception of the United Nations. The United States had long supported Chiang Kai-shek as a bulwark against Japan and a source of stability in Asia. And at Roosevelt's insistence, China had been accorded a permanent seat on the UN Security Council as the war was ending. Even after being forced from the mainland in 1949, the militantly anticommunist Chinese nationalists retained their permanent Security Council seat until 1971, when the communist People's Republic of China was admitted to the UN—and assumed China's seat on the Security Council. The obviously artificial role that the Nationalists played for so long damaged the credibility of the new United Nations.

Map 30.6 The Partition of Palestine and the Birth of the State of Israel In November 1947 the United Nations offered a plan to partition the British mandate of Palestine, but complications immediately arose. The Jews of the area won their own state, Israel, but the Palestinian Arabs did not. Thus tensions continued in the area.

Summary

After earlier wars there had been restorations, or at least attempts at restoration. But after the fighting ended in 1945, restoration was out of the question as the forces unleashed by the war played themselves out. By 1949 the division of Europe, the advent of nuclear weapons, and the symptomatic events in India, Israel, and China made it clear that the world's agenda had been radically transformed in the ten years since the beginning of World War II.

Dwarfed by the two new superpowers, the old European states seemed destined to play a diminished role in world affairs. It quickly became clear that the costs of the war had left even Britain, a full partner in the Allied victory, too weak to remain a great power. Almost at once, the Europeans began retreating from their longstanding imperial roles, though not without kicking, screaming—and more bloodshed. At the same time, it was clear by 1949 that non-Western nations would now be playing a more prominent role in world affairs.

Although the war opened a new universe of problems and possibilities, it brought to a close an era of European history dominated by fascism. As a result of the war, the two major fascist powers collapsed and fascist forms of politics stood discredited. But Nazism and fascism continued to haunt the Western mind, especially with the discovery of the Nazi extermination camps. It was not clear, moreover, whether Germany and Italy, and, for that matter, much of the rest of Europe, would be able to develop effective democratic political systems amid defeat and destruction.

So whereas there had been, for a while, some illusion of stability after World War I, it was obvious after World War II that the world would never be the same, that the old Europe was gone forever. Indeed, much of its proud culture, on the basis of which Europe had claimed to lead the world, lay in the ruins of war, apparently exhausted. What could Europeans still believe in? What role could Europe play in Western civilization, and in the wider world, after all that had happened?

Notes

1. Quoted in Karl Dietrich Bracher, *The German Dictatorship: The Origins, Structure, and Effects of National Socialism,* trans. Jean Steinberg (New York: Praeger, 1970), p. 423.

Suggested Reading

General Surveys

Calvocoressi, Peter, Guy Wint, and John Pritchard. *Total War: Causes and Courses of the Second World War.* 2d ed., revised. 2 vols. 1989. New edition of a standard, readable work.

Campbell, John, ed. *The Experience of World War II.* 1989. Focusing on the experience of those touched by the war, this collaborative volume covers everything from prisoners of war to the uses of the arts for propaganda purposes. A handsome volume in a large format, with superb illustrations and maps.

Keegan, John. *The Second World War.* 1989. A detailed but accessible study featuring military operations. Well illustrated.

Parker, R. A. C. *Struggle for Survival: The History of the Second World War.* 1990. An accessible, comprehensive, and well-balanced survey. Especially good on debates over strategy and the wider implications of the strategies chosen.

Willmott, H. P. *The Great Crusade: A New Complete History of the Second World War.* 1989. Focuses especially on military operations. Seeks to deflate notions of German military excellence.

Wright, Gordon. *The Ordeal of Total War, 1939–1945.* 1968. Masterly synthesis of all aspects of the war experience, from the battlefield to the scientific laboratory, from the Nazi "new order" to the coming of the cold war.

The Home Front

Harrison, Mark. *Soviet Planning in Peace and War, 1938–1945.* 1985. Shows how Soviet economic planners responded to invasion in 1941, enabling the Soviet Union to defeat Nazi Germany and emerge from the war as a great power.

Milward, Alan S. *War, Economy and Society, 1939–1945.* 1979. A detailed study of the economic adjustments that the war necessitated—and that sustained the long years of fighting.

Pelling, Henry. *Winston Churchill.* 1974. Among the best single-volume biographies of Churchill. Balanced and readable.

Summerfield, Penny. *Women Workers in the Second World War: Production and Patriarchy in Conflict.* 1989. Shows how the disruptions of war affected women's opportunities and self-understanding.

Collaboration and Resistance

De Gaulle, Charles. *The Complete War Memoirs of Charles de Gaulle.* 3 vols. in one. 1955, 1959, 1960. Revealing personal account of de Gaulle's remarkable role as leader of the Free French forces during World War II.

Delzell, Charles F. *Mussolini's Enemies: The Italian Anti-Fascist Resistance.* 1961. An exhaustive account of Italian resistance activities, proceeding region by region.

Lacouture, Jean. *De Gaulle.* Vol. 1: *The Rebel, 1890–1944.* 1990. First volume of a standard biography, detailed but accessible. Shows how de Gaulle's maverick qualities enabled him to play his special role during the war.

Paxton, Robert O. *Vichy France: Old Guard and New Order.* 1975. A widely admired study that assesses Vichy claims to have shielded Frenchmen from the worst features of Nazi occupation.

Sweets, John F. *Choices in Vichy France: The French Under Nazi Occupation.* 1986. Based on a local study, this book emphasizes the wide scope and diverse forms of resistance.

Wilhelm, Maria de Blasio. *The Other Italy: Italian Resistance in World War II.* 1988. A readable, sympathetic account, focusing on various sides of the complex experience in thematically organized chapters.

The Holocaust

Gilbert, Martin. *The Holocaust: A History of the Jews of Europe During the Second World War.* 1986. A comprehensive but straightforward account, making effective use of the testimony of those involved.

Hilberg, Raoul. *The Destruction of the European Jews.* Revised and definitive ed. 3 vols. 1985. Pioneering, detailed account of the Holocaust, based on exhaustive research. Especially revealing on the administrative mechanics of the process.

Langer, Lawrence L. *Holocaust Testimonies: The Ruins of Memory.* 1991. A sensitive, sophisticated analysis of oral testimonies on the Holocaust by a leading expert on Holocaust literature.

Laqueur, Walter. *The Terrible Secret: Suppression of the Truth about Hitler's "Final Solution."* 1982. Raises the gnawing questions about who knew what, and when, about the extermination of the Jews. Without exonerating policymakers who might have responded more effectively, the author shows how difficult it was to comprehend what seemed incomprehensible.

Lifton, Robert Jay. *The Nazi Doctors: Medical Killing and the Psychology of Genocide.* 1986. A major expert on the psychology of extreme situations seeks to understand the large number of German medical doctors who played central roles in Nazi programs of mass killing.

Marrus, Michael. *The Holocaust in History.* 1987. An ideal introduction to the major issues. Readable and balanced.

Wyman, David S. *The Abandonment of the Jews: America and the Holocaust, 1941–1945.* 1984. Focuses on the limits of the American response, despite the scope for a more concerted rescue effort.

Yahil, Leni. *The Holocaust: The Fate of European Jewry.* 1990. A clear and comprehensive account that accents the underlying continuity in Nazi policy and assesses the Jewish response.

Wider Impact

Fussell, Paul. *Wartime: Understanding and Behavior in the Second World War.* 1989. Explores the rationalizations and euphemisms, the contempt and subversion, that enabled U.S. and British fighting men to deal with the horrors of World War II.

Laqueur, Walter. *A History of Zionism.* 1989. Surveys the five decades of European Zionist activity that helped bring about the establishment of the state of Israel.

Marrus, Michael R. *The Unwanted: European Refugees in the Twentieth Century.* 1985. Pioneering account of the rise of the refugee phenomenon as a major but neglected aspect of modern political disruptions.

Rhodes, Richard. *The Making of the Atomic Bomb.* 1988. An acclaimed study that combines science, politics, and personality in an especially dramatic way.

The Coming of the Cold War

LaFeber, Walter. *America, Russia, and the Cold War, 1945–1984.* 5th ed. 1985. Considers the cold war in the wider context of U.S. economic concerns and relations with Russia. Accents the contradictions and limits of U.S. policy.

Nadeau, Remi. *Stalin, Churchill, and Roosevelt Divide Europe.* 1990. Focuses on the failure of the U.S. to support British desires to head off Stalin during the war, when there were still alternatives to the military configuration that led to the cold war split of 1945–1948.

Paterson, Thomas G. *On Every Front: The Making and Unmaking of the Cold War.* 1992. Updated edition of a highly regarded survey.

Yergin, Daniel. *Shattered Peace: The Origins of the Cold War.* Revised ed. 1990. Readable, balanced narrative, focusing especially on the bases of American policy.

Weighing the Evidence

HOLOCAUST TESTIMONY

There were loud announcements, but it was all fairly restrained: nobody did anything to us. I followed the crowd: "Men to the right, women and children to the left," we had been told. The women and children disappeared into a barrack further to the left and we were told to undress. One of the SS men—later I knew his name, Küttner—told us in a chatty sort of tone that we were going into a disinfection bath and afterwards would be assigned work. Clothes, he said, could be left in a heap on the floor, and we'd find them again later. . . .

The queue began to move and I suddenly noticed several men fully dressed standing near another barrack further back, and I was wondering who they were. And just then another SS man (Miete was his name) came by me and said, "Come on, you, get back into your clothes, quick, special work." That was the first time I was frightened. Everything was very quiet, you know. And when he said that to me, the others turned around and looked at me—and I thought, my God, why me, why does he pick on me? When I had got back into my clothes, the line had moved on and I noticed that several other young men had also been picked out and were dressing. We were taken through to the "work-barrack," most of which was filled from floor to ceiling with clothes, stacked up in layers. . . . You understand, there was no time, not a moment between the instant we were taken in there and put to work, to talk to anyone, to take stock of what was happening . . . [ellipses in the original] and of course never forget that we had no idea at all what this whole installation was for. One saw these stacks of clothing—I suppose the thought must have entered our minds, where do they come from, what are they? We *must* have connected them with the clothes all of us had just taken off outside . . . [ellipses in the original] but I cannot remember doing that. I only remember starting work at once making bundles.[1]

This is the voice of Richard Glazar, recalling when, as a young Jewish student from Prague, he arrived at the Nazi extermination camp at Treblinka in October 1942. Glazar was telling his story in 1972 to the British journalist Gitta Sereny, who had been covering the trial in Germany of the commandant of the Treblinka camp, Franz Stangl. Seeking to understand Stangl, Sereny tracked down a number of those who had come into contact with him, including survivors like Glazar.

Glazar's recollections are part of a rich body of testimony by Jewish survivors of the Holocaust, testimony that is often moving, gripping, terrifying. Some accounts offer direct personal recollections. Others integrate personal remembrance into literature. Still others use the insights of social psychology in an effort to explain the special features of the camp experience.

Even with all this evidence, we wonder if we can ever really grasp what millions of Jews experienced at the hands of the Nazis in the extermination camps. But listening to witnesses like Glazar, we gain some sense of the uncertainty and fear, the suffering and humiliation, that helped define that experience. And we recognize the determination, the affirmation of life, that marked the Jewish response.

We may be surprised at Glazar's insistence that "we had no idea at all what this whole installation was for." Didn't the Jews understand what the camps held for them? In fact, some Jews had a better idea than others, but in most cases only through rumor, and no one could know the whole story as it was unfolding. Over a year before, Glazar's family had sent him to work in the country, where they assumed he would be safe, so he had been relatively isolated. But what one knew, or could surmise, also depended on what one was prepared to believe was possible, what the world could hold. Some simply could not believe the rumors.

Once they were in the camps, however, the Jews could only come to terms with the unprece-

1. The testimony of Richard Glazar is from Gitta Sereny, *Into That Darkness: An Examination of Conscience* (New York: Random House, Vintage Books, 1983), pp. 176–179, 183.

Arrival at the Auschwitz Extermination Camp *(UPI/Bettmann Newsphotos)*

dented situation as best they could. Let us listen further to Glazar, whose insights into the minds of the SS overseers help us better to grasp the terrible capriciousness of the situation:

> One must not forget their incredible power, their autonomy within their narrow and yet, as far as we were concerned, unlimited field; but also the isolation created by their unique situation and by what *they*—and hardly anyone else even within the German or Nazi community—had in common. Perhaps if this isolation had been the result of good rather than evil deeds, their own relationship towards each other would have been different. As it was, most of them seemed to hate and despise each other and do anything—almost anything—to "get at" each other. Thus, if one of them selected a man out of a new transport for work, in other words to stay alive at least for a while, it could perfectly easily happen . . . that one of his rivals . . . would come along and kill that man just to spite him. . . . All this created a virtually indescribable atmosphere of fear. The most important thing for a prisoner at Treblinka, you see, was not to make himself conspicuous.

But what, then, can be said about the human attributes that such conditions called forth—and that enabled some, at least, to survive?

> Our daily life? It was in a way very directed, very specific. . . . [I]t was essential to fill oneself completely with a determination to survive; it was essential to create in oneself a capacity for dissociating oneself to some extent from Treblinka; it was important *not* to adapt completely to it. . . .
>
> It wasn't *ruthlessness* that enabled an individual to survive—it was an intangible quality, not peculiar to educated or sophisticated individuals. Anyone might have it. It is perhaps best described as an overriding thirst—perhaps, too, a *talent* for life, and a faith in life.

Glazar, of course, was speaking thirty years later, and despite the engaging spontaneity of his testimony, he may have forgotten things, or the experiences of the intervening years may have colored his memory. Moreover, he could only tell what he recalled through the categories of language, which may be inadequate to convey, to those who were not there, what it was like to be sent to the Nazi extermination camps. Perhaps survivors called upon, years later, to put their recollections into words are bound to impose too much order, even to romanticize, by using categories their listeners can understand—or want to hear. Glazar was clearly stretching to find the words. Does "talent for life" ring true? We will continue to wonder.

As for Glazar himself, he escaped from Treblinka in an uprising in August 1943, and then made his way to Germany, where he managed to survive the war disguised as a foreign laborer. When Sereny reached him in 1972, he was living in Switzerland, working as an engineer.

1977

CHAPTER 31

A Tentative Stability: Europe in a Bipolar World, 1949–1980

Both halves of Europe had to operate within the bipolar framework that defined the cold war era, but the Western and Soviet blocs each confronted different challenges and evolved in very different ways. Although the Soviet Union faced serious difficulties, the communist regime emerged from World War II with renewed legitimacy. It had proven itself in an extraordinary way, first surviving the Nazi onslaught, then contributing decisively to the Allied victory, and finally leading the country to superpower status in the aftermath. Battered though it was, the Soviet Union seemed to offer its citizens hope for the future.

But the extension of Soviet control over what became the satellite states of east-central Europe compromised the prestige the Soviet Union had won during World War II. At first the local communists in charge clearly depended on Soviet support. It remained to be seen whether these new communist regimes could move in their own directions, perhaps developing innovative forms of socialism, and eventually establish their legitimacy.

In Western Europe just after the war, there was considerable sense of exhaustion, with cities in rubble, economies broken down, and cultural traditions under a cloud after fascism, defeat, and collaboration. Also evident, however, were the renewed determination and fresh ideas that soon led to a dramatically successful postwar reconstruction.

That reconstruction rested on a new consensus that government must play a more active role in promoting both economic growth and social welfare. An implicit promise of growth and, eventually, shared prosperity helped Western Europe start afresh, and by the 1960s that promise was

Red Square, Moscow: military parade marking sixtieth anniversary of the Russian Revolution.

realized to a remarkable extent. The outcome of postwar reconstruction was a long period of relative prosperity, stability, and peace. Hand in hand with these came, however, a diminished international role for Western Europe, as the two superpowers made the key decisions and as the former European colonies achieved independence.

Partly because of this economic success, the renewal of democracy proved less difficult than many had expected immediately after the war. However, changing circumstances by the early 1970s threatened the consensus that the postwar prosperity had made possible. The Soviet system also achieved certain successes during the fifties and sixties, but its efforts to outgrow its Stalinist framework were halting, and by the end of the seventies the system was becoming rigid and stagnant. In both East and West, new directions associated with an array of new leaders began taking shape by the early 1980s, radically changing the terms of the long postwar settlement.

The Search for Cultural Bearings

The events from World War I to the cold war added up to an unprecedented period of disaster for Europe. Europeans were bound to ask what had gone wrong, and what could be salvaged from the ruins of a culture that had made possible the most destructive wars in history, as well as fascism, totalitarianism, and the Holocaust. In addition to the immediate economic and political uncertainties of the late forties, Europeans faced the potentially devastating combination of the cold war and the atomic age. In their most pessimistic moods, people all over the West worried that the modern world would inevitably tilt toward tyranny, oppression, and dehumanization, a fear chillingly portrayed in George Orwell's novel *Nineteen Eighty-Four,* published in 1949. Human beings might prove powerless to resist.

Absurdity and Commitment in Existentialism

The mood of despair found its classic expression in the work of Samuel Beckett (1906–1989), especially his plays *Waiting for Godot* (1952) and *Endgame* (1957). Through Beckett's characters, we see ourselves going through the motions, with nothing worth saying or doing, ludicrously manipulating the husks of a worn-out culture. The only redeeming element is the comic pathos we feel as we watch ourselves. (See the feature, "Weighing the Evidence: Theater of the Absurd," on pages 1184–1185.)

The same sense of despair and anxiety led to the vogue of existentialism, a movement that marked philosophy, the arts, and popular culture from the later forties until well into the 1950s. Existentialism developed from the ideas of the German thinker Martin Heidegger (1889–1976), especially *Being and Time* (1927), one of the most influential philosophical works of the century. Though it was a philosophy of sorts, existentialism was most significant as a broader cultural tendency, finding expression in novels and films. The existentialists explored what it means to be a human being in a world cast adrift from its cultural moorings, with no accepted guideposts, standards, or values to rely on.

The most influential postwar existentialists were Albert Camus (1913–1960) and Jean Paul Sartre (1905–1980), each of whom had been involved in the French resistance, Camus in a particularly central role as editor of an underground newspaper. For both, an authentic human response to a world spinning out of control entailed engagement, commitment, responsibility—even though every action is fraught with risk for the individual (see the box, "The Appeal of Existentialism").

Rather than accept the bleak, ludicrously comic vision of Beckett's plays, Camus sought to show how we might go on living in a positive, affirmative spirit, even in an absurd world, even after all that had happened. Conventional values like friendship and tolerance could be made usable again, based on the simple fact that we human beings are all caught up in this unmasterable situation together. People suffer and die, but as we come together to help as best we can, we might at least learn to stop killing each other.

Camus split from Sartre in a disagreement over the ongoing value of Marxism and the communist experiment in the Soviet Union. Though he remained intellectually independent, Sartre found potential for human liberation in the working class, in communist parties, even in the Soviet Union itself, which he saw as the strongest alter-

Sartre and de Beauvoir Among the most influential intellectual couples of the century, Jean-Paul Sartre and Simone de Beauvoir emerged as leaders of French existentialism by the later 1940s. See the boxes on pages 1152 and 1189. *(G. Pierre/Sygma)*

native to U.S. imperialism. By the fifties, he was portraying existentialism as fundamentally a way to revitalize Marxism.

On the other hand, Camus, who had started as a Communist in the 1930s, had grown disillusioned even before the war, and his major political tract, *The Rebel* (1951), was partly an attack on Marxism and communism. Establishing new bases for human happiness and solidarity meant recognizing limits to what human beings could accomplish, limits even to our demands for freedom and justice. These were precisely the limits that the new political movements of the century had so disastrously overstepped. Communism, like fascism, was part of the problem, not the solution.

Marxists and Traditionalists

Sartre was among the many European intellectuals who believed that Marxism had gotten a new lease on life from the resistance. As they saw it, Marxism could be revamped for the West, without the Stalinist excesses that had resulted from the special difficulties facing the Soviet Union.

In Italy, as in France, the communists' major role in the resistance enhanced their prestige, preparing the way for the extraordinary posthumous influence of Antonio Gramsci (1891–1937), who had been one of the founders of the Italian Communist party in the early 1920s but who had spent most of the fascist period in prison. His *Prison Notebooks,* published during the late 1940s, became influential throughout the world and helped make Marxism a powerful force in postwar Italian culture. Seeking to learn the lessons of the fascist triumph in Italy, Gramsci pointed the way to a flexible communist strategy, attuned to the special historical circumstances of each country.

By the late forties, however, others, like Camus, held that Marxism was inherently flawed and denied that any recasting could overcome its deficiencies. Damaging revelations about the excesses of Stalinism during the thirties seemed to confirm this view. Prominent intellectuals like Arthur Koestler (1905–1983) and Ignazio Silone (1900–1978), who had earlier believed in communism, said they had been mistaken and insisted that Marxism, despite its initial appeal, would inevitably lead to the kind of tyranny that had developed in the Soviet Union.

Despite this wave of denunciations during the early years of the cold war, Marxism re-

The Appeal of Existentialism

In a lecture in 1945, Jean Paul Sartre offered the classic explanation of the fundamental existentialist tenet: "Existence precedes essence"—we human beings simply find ourselves existing, without some "human nature" that tells us what we are or might become.

What do we mean by saying that existence precedes essence? We mean that man first of all exists, encounters himself, surges up in the world—and defines himself afterwards. If man as the existentialist sees him is not definable, it is because to begin with he is nothing. He will not be anything until later, and then he will be what he makes of himself. . . . If . . . it is true that existence is prior to essence, man is responsible for what he is. Thus, the first effect of existentialism is that it puts every man in possession of himself as he is, and places the entire responsibility for his existence squarely upon his own shoulders. And, when we say that man is responsible for himself, we do not mean he is responsible only for his own individuality, but that he is responsible for all men. . . .[N]othing can be better for us unless it is better for all. . . .
. . . I am creating a certain image of man as I would have him be. In fashioning myself I fashion man. . . .

It is nowhere written that "the good" exists, that one must be honest or must not lie, since we are now upon the plane where there are only men. . . . [M]an . . . cannot find anything to depend upon either within or outside himself. . . . one will never be able to explain one's actions by reference to a given and specific human nature; in other words, there is no determinism—man is free, man *is* freedom.

Source: Jean Paul Sartre, *Existentialism and Humanism,* trans. Philip Mairet (Brooklyn, N.Y.: Haskell House, n.d.), pp. 28–30, 33–34. (First pub. in French in 1946; first English ed. 1948)

mained influential through the 1970s, although it proved more effective as a critique of the culture surrounding capitalism than as a blueprint for change. The best-known spokesman for renewed radicalism on both sides of the Atlantic during the late sixties and early seventies was Herbert Marcuse (1898–1979), who explored the cultural mechanisms through which capitalism perpetuates itself in *One-Dimensional Man* (1964).

At the same time, however, the powerful denunciations of the Stalinist gulag, or forced-labor-camp system, by the exiled Soviet writer Alexander Solzhenitsyn (b. 1918) stimulated another wave of anticommunist thinking by the mid-1970s. By the end of the decade, Marxism, no matter how updated and "Western," was coming to seem increasingly irrelevant to the industrial democracies of western Europe.

Those hostile to Marxism often insisted that the West had to reconnect with older traditions if it was to avoid further horrors like those it had just been through. Especially in the first years after the war, many, like the French Catholic thinker Jacques Maritain (1882–1973), held that only a return to religious traditions would suffice. For the American-born British writer T. S. Eliot (1888–1965), the essential return to tradition had to embrace family and locality, as well as religion. Without a return to tradition, Eliot warned, the West could expect more excesses like fascism and totalitarianism in the future.

Others, like the German Gustav Radbruch (1878–1949) and the Italian Guido de Ruggiero (1888–1948), appealed to the natural law tradition. A belief in absolute values seemed the only antidote to the relativism and nihilism that seemed to have found their most dramatic manifestation in modern totalitarianism.

The Intellectual Migration and Americanism

The extraordinary migration of European artists and intellectuals to the United States to escape persecution during the thirties and forties profoundly affected the cultural life of the postwar period. An array of luminaries arrived on American shores, from the composer Igor Stravinsky to the theoretical physicist Albert Einstein, from the architect Walter Gropius to the radical social theorist Herbert Marcuse.

Before this cultural cross-fertilization, America had remained slightly provincial, sometimes proudly and self-consciously so. All the direct contact with the Europeans by the 1940s helped propel the United States into the Western cultural mainstream. No longer could "Western" culture be identified primarily with Europe. In some spheres—painting, for example—Americans were now confident enough to claim the leadership for the first time.

With the abstract expressionism of the later forties, American painters began creating visual images the like of which had never been seen in Europe. In comparison with the raw, energetic painting of Jackson Pollock (1912–1956), the work of the Europeans seemed merely "pretty"—and the newly brash Americans were not shy about telling them so. New York began to supplant Paris as the art capital of the Western world.

But the American achievement owed something to European existentialism, and it became possible only because so many of the most innovative European painters had come to New York, where the Americans had been able to learn their lessons at close hand. At the same time European painters like Jean Dubuffet (1901–1985) in France and Francis Bacon (1910–1992) in Britain created new forms of their own—sometimes playful, sometimes brutal—as they sought the visual imagery that Western culture seemed to need after the era of fascism and war (see the box, "A Whimsical Art for a New Beginning").

Some Europeans were eager to embrace what seemed distinctively American, because America had remained relatively free of the political ideologies that seemed to have led Europe to totalitarianism and ruin. By the fifties there was much talk of "the end of ideology," with America pointing the way to a healthier alternative, combining technology, value-free social science, and scientific management. Whereas the old European way led either to mere theorizing, to political extremism, or to polarization and impasse, the American approach got results by tackling problems one at a time, so that they could be solved by managerial or technical experts. "America" meant can-do optimism and continued progress,

Bacon: Pope I Seeking to confront the horror and suffering of the era, Francis Bacon combined distorted figures and images from past art. Here he adapts a famous painting of Pope Innocent X by the seventeenth-century painter Diego Velásquez to suggest the contemporary world's anxiety and uncertain responsibility. *(Francis Bacon,* Pope I, *1951. Oil on canvas. 77 ¾ x 53 ⅞". The Art Gallery, Aberdeen.)*

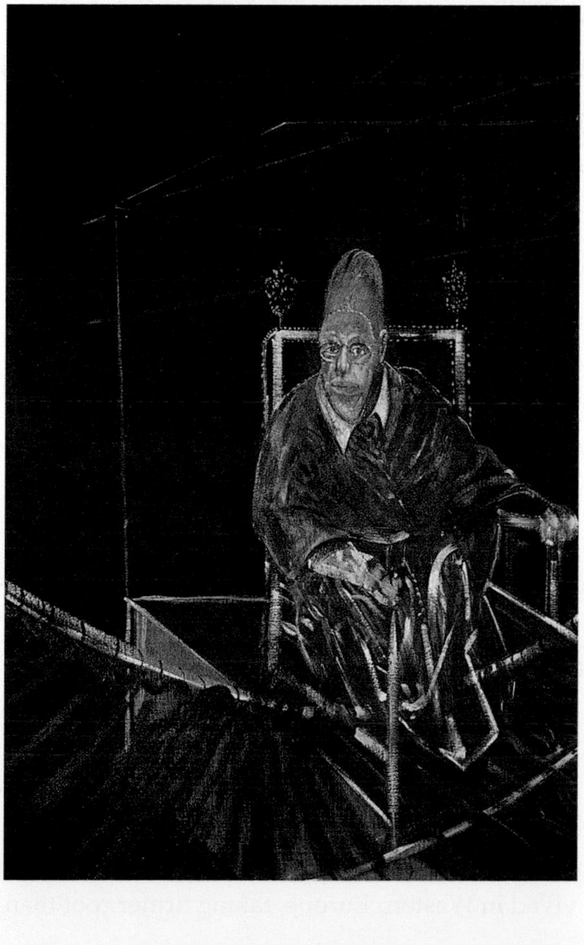

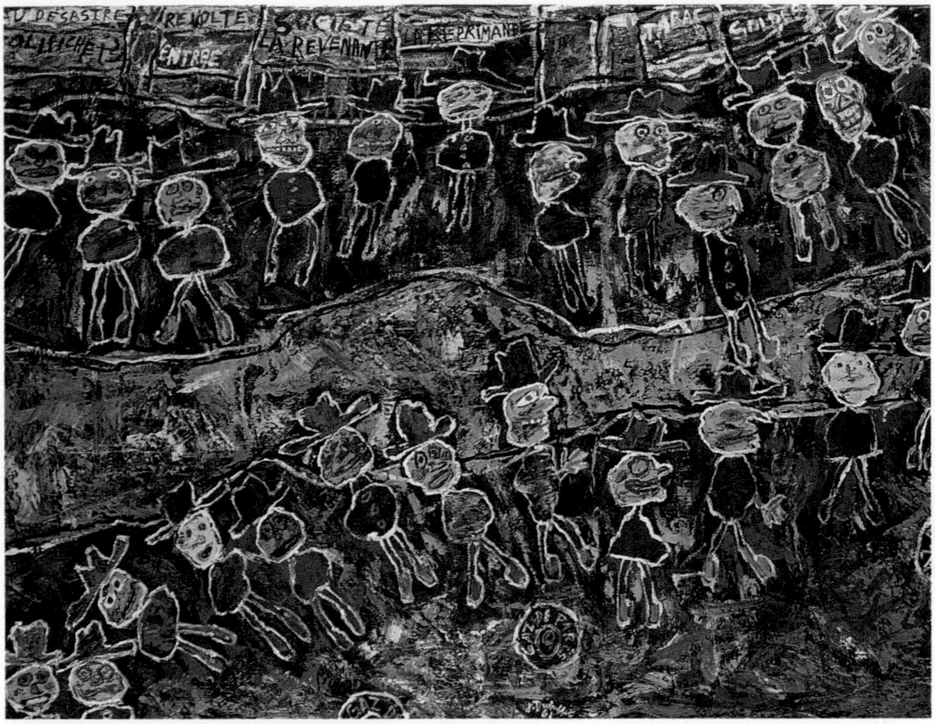

Dubuffet: Spinning Round Seeking to depart from the European tradition of sophisticated, well-made art, Jean Dubuffet developed imagery that was at once crude and primitive, playful and whimsical. *(Dubuffet, Jean,* Spinning Round, *1961. ARS Tate Gallery, London, Great Britain)*

as opposed to the despair that had become fashionable in some European cultural circles.

Such Americanism fed the notion that Europe needed a clean break based on technological values. If such a break was necessary, however, what was to become of the European tradition, for centuries the center of gravity of the West, and until recently dominant in the world? Did anything distinctively European remain, or was Europe doomed to lick its wounds in the shadow of America? These questions lurked in the background, but first Europeans faced the difficult task of economic and political restoration.

Prosperity and Democracy in Western Europe

By 1941, democracy seemed to be dying on the European continent, yet after World War II it revived in Western Europe, taking firmer root than most had thought possible in 1945. The postwar situation was so unsettled that no one, not even stable and victorious Britain, could simply return to normal or apply an earlier model. Everywhere governments became more active in promoting economic growth and social welfare. And success at economic reconstruction provided one necessary precondition for the more favorable experience with democracy after the war. Prosperity was not the only factor, however.

From Economic Reconstruction to Economic Miracle

It is hard to imagine how desperate the situation in much of Western Europe had become by 1945. Major cities like Rotterdam, Hamburg, and Le Havre lay largely in ruins, and normal routines suffered radical disruption. Production had declined to perhaps 25 percent of the prewar level in Italy, to 20 percent in France, and to a mere 5

A Whimsical Art for a New Beginning

The French painter Jean Dubuffet sought to break from conventional ideals and techniques, which he found outmoded and irrelevant. He believed he could point the way to the new visual imagery the culture needed. It would be whimsical, playful, ordinary, often clumsy, yet liberating.

I have the impression that a complete liquidation of all the ways of thinking, whose sum constituted what has been called humanism and has been fundamental for our culture since the Renaissance, is now taking place, or, at least, going to take place soon.

I think the increasing knowledge of the thinking of so-called primitive peoples, during the past fifty years, has contributed a great deal to this change, and especially the acquaintance with works of art made by those peoples. . . .

. . . It may be that refinement, cerebrations, depth of mind, are on their side, and not on ours. . . .

. . . [T]he culture of the Occident . . . drifts further and further from daily life. It is confined to certain small and dead circles. . . . It no longer has real and living roots.

For myself, I am for an art which would be in immediate connection with daily life . . . and which would be a very direct and very sincere expression of our real life and our real moods. . . .

[O]ccidental culture . . . believes that there are beautiful objects and ugly objects, beautiful persons and ugly persons. . . . Not I. . . . This idea is for me stifling and revolting. . . .

Painting now . . . can illuminate the world with wonderful discoveries, can endow man with new myths and new mystiques, and can reveal, in infinite number, unsuspected aspects of things, and new values not yet perceived.

Here is, I think, for artists, a much more worthy job than creating assemblages of shapes and colors pleasing for the eyes.

Source: Jean Dubuffet, "Anticultural Positions," lecture at the Arts Club of Chicago, December 1951, as excerpted in Wylie Sypher, *Loss of the Self in Modern Literature and Art* (New York: Random House Vintage, 1962), pp. 171, 174–175; and Dore Ashton, ed., *Twentieth-Century Artists on Art* (New York: Pantheon, 1985), p. 124.

percent in southern Germany. Cigarettes, often gained through barter from American soldiers, served widely as a medium of exchange.

Although the U.S. commitment to help reconstruct Europe was not originally a cold war measure, the developing cold war context made it seem all the more necessary for the United States to help the Europeans get their economies running again as quickly as possible. The key was the Marshall Plan, first outlined in 1947 by General George Marshall, the U.S. secretary of state, which channeled over $11 billion in aid to Western Europe by 1951. The need to rebuild afforded Europeans a chance to start over, using the most up-to-date methods and technologies. Though rebuilding strategies differed, the Western European countries made remarkable recoveries.

The new German government cut state aid to business and limited the long-standing power of cartels. The state was permitted to intervene in the economy only to assure free competition. In France, on the other hand, many were determined to use government to modernize the country, thereby overcoming the weakness that had led to defeat. So virtually at once after the war, France adopted a flexible, pragmatic form of government-led economic planning.

In 1946 Jean Monnet (1888–1979) launched the first of the French postwar economic plans, which brought government and business leaders

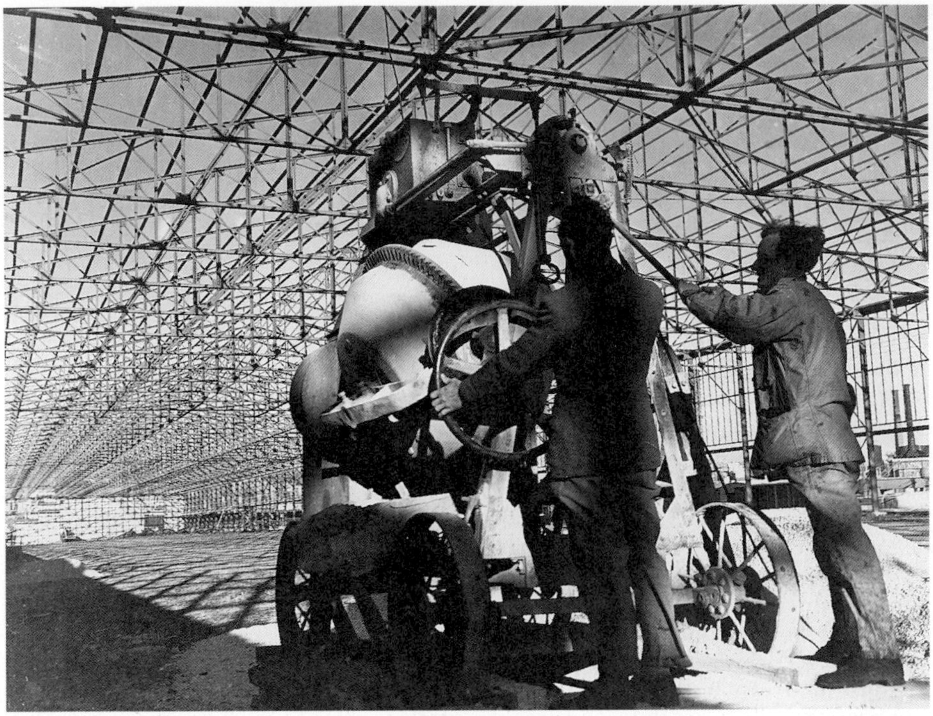

Postwar Reconstruction Rebuilding rapidly after the war, Western Europeans were often able to take advantage of new materials and technologies. Thus many of the Western European economies returned to competitiveness more quickly than most had believed possible in 1945. Here, in 1949, workmen in Marseilles make concrete for a new warehouse, one of many under construction all over France at the time. *(The Bettmann Archive)*

together to agree on production targets. Economic planning enabled France to make especially effective use of the capital that the Marshall Plan provided. French industrial production returned to its prewar peak by 1951, and by 1957 had risen to twice the level of 1938.

Strong and sustained rates of economic growth were achieved throughout much of Western Europe through the mid-1960s. From 1953 to 1964, annual rates of growth averaged 6 percent in Germany, 5.6 percent in Italy, and 4.9 percent in France. Britain, however, lagged considerably, averaging only 2.7 percent growth annually during that same period.

As part of the new postwar consensus, labor was supposed to be to brought more fully into economic decision making. In France, the trade unions joined the planning process. In Germany the co-determination law of 1951 provided for labor participation in management decisions in heavy industry, and labor representatives were given access to company books and full voting memberships on boards of directors. This measure ultimately made little difference in the functioning of the affected firms, but it helped head off any return to trade-union radicalism.

During the first years of rapid economic growth, the labor movement remained fairly passive in Western Europe, even though wages stayed relatively low. After an era of depression, fascist repression, and war, workers were grateful simply to have jobs, free trade unions, and at least the promise of greater prosperity in the future. By the 1960s, however, it seemed time to redeem that promise; labor began demanding—generally with success—to share more fully in the new prosperity. Now, rather abruptly, much of Western Europe assumed the look of a consumer society, with widespread ownership of, for example, automobiles and televisions.

The Creation of the British Welfare State

Churchill's inspired leadership of Britain during the darkest days of the war made him perhaps the most admired leader of the twentieth century. Yet when Britain held its first postwar elections, in July 1945, Churchill's Conservatives suffered a crushing loss to the Labour party, led by Clement Attlee (1883–1967). Even early in the war most Britons came to take it for granted that major socioeconomic changes would follow from victory, and Labour seemed better equipped to deliver on that promise.

Greater collective responsibility for the wellbeing of all British citizens seemed appropriate in light of the shared hardships that the war had imposed. Moreover, the successes of government planning and control in response to the wartime emergency suggested that once the war was over, government could assume responsibility for the basic needs of the British people, guaranteeing full employment and providing a national health service. But only after the Labour victory in the 1945 elections did formal legislation begin putting these aspirations into practice, creating the British welfare state.

Although some expected, and others feared, that the result would be a form of socialism, establishing a welfare state did not undermine the capitalist economic system. The Labour government nationalized some key industries, but 80 percent of the British work force remained employed in private firms in 1948. Moreover, even under Labour, the British government did not seek the kind of economic planning role that government was playing in France. Britain relied on monetary and fiscal policy to coordinate its economy, much like the United States.

The core of the British departure in 1945 was not nationalization but a set of social welfare measures that significantly affected the lives of ordinary people. These included old-age pensions; insurance against unemployment, sickness, and disability; and allowances for pregnancy, child rearing, widowhood, and burial. The heart of the system was free medical care, to be provided by a National Health Service, created in November 1946 and operating by 1948.

Whatever the desirability of such a welfare state in principle, could Britain afford it over the long term? The costs of waging war had seriously eroded the country's economic strength. During the later 1940s, neither the government nor the people of Britain quite grasped the change in the country's prospects that had followed from World War II.

The Rebirth of Democracy in West Germany

The new Federal Republic of Germany held its first election under the basic law in August 1949, initiating what proved a successful experience with parliamentary democracy. Because Germany's effort at democracy after World War I had failed, with tragic results, the question of why the new Bonn republic succeeded is one of the most important in modern history.

The international economic climate was considerably more favorable after World War II. This time, the victors sought to help get Germany back on its feet as quickly as possible, partly to counter the Soviet Union but also because they had learned from past mistakes. It was also crucial that the Germans themselves worked hard to avoid the errors of the past. Leaders now better understood the need to compromise, to take responsibility for governing the whole nation.

To avoid the instability that had plagued the Weimar Republic, the creators of the new government strengthened the chancellor in relation to the Bundestag, the lower house of parliament. In the same way, the basic law helped establish a stable party system by discouraging splinter parties and by allowing the courts to outlaw extremist parties. On that basis, the courts outlawed both the Communist party and a neo-Nazi party during the formative years of the new German democracy.

The Bonn republic proved more stable than the earlier Weimar Republic partly because the political party system was now considerably simpler. Two mass parties, the Christian Democratic Union (CDU) and the Social Democratic party (SPD), were immediately predominant, although a third, the much smaller Free Democratic party (FDP), proved important for coalition purposes.

Konrad Adenauer (1876–1967), head of the CDU, the largest party in 1949, immediately emerged as postwar Germany's leading statesman. A Catholic who had been mayor of Cologne under Weimar, he had withdrawn from active politics during the Nazi period, but he reemerged after the war to lead the council that drafted the Basic Law. As chancellor from 1949 until 1963, he oriented the new German democracy toward Western Europe and the Atlantic bloc, led by the United States.

The new bipolar world confronted West Germany with a cruel choice. By accepting the bipolar framework, the country could become a full partner within the Atlantic bloc. By trying instead to straddle the fence, it could keep open the possibility that Germany could be reunified as a neutral and disarmed state. The choice was made in the early 1950s when the outbreak of war in Korea intensified the cold war, and the United States pressured West Germany to rearm and join the Western bloc.

Konrad Adenauer As chancellor from 1949 to 1963, Adenauer played a central role in cementing democracy in the new West Germany. *(UPI/Bettmann Newsphotos)*

Although some West Germans resisted, Adenauer led the Federal Republic into the Atlantic alliance in 1955. Thus the country implicitly accepted not only U.S. leadership but also the division of Germany. Adenauer was eager to anchor the new Federal Republic to the Western democracies, partly to buttress the new democracy in West Germany. But he also wanted to cement the U.S. guarantee to Europe in the face of what seemed an ongoing Soviet threat to German security.

By the late 1950s the West German economy was recovering nicely, and the country was a valued member of the Western alliance. Adenauer's CDU seemed so potent that the other major party, the SPD, appeared to be consigned to permanent—and sterile—opposition. Frustrated with its outsider status, the SPD began to shed its Marxist trappings in an effort to widen its appeal. Prominent among those pushing in this direction was Willy Brandt (1913–1992), who became mayor of West Berlin in 1957, and who would become the party's leader in 1963. At its watershed national congress at Bad Godesberg in 1959, the party officially gave up talk of the class struggle and adopted a more moderate program.

Adenauer stepped down in 1963 at the age of 87, after fourteen years as chancellor. The contrast with Weimar, which had known twenty-one different cabinets in a comparable fourteen-year period, could hardly be more striking. The Adenauer years proved to Germans that liberal democracy could mean stable and effective government, economic prosperity, and foreign policy success. Still, Adenauer had become somewhat authoritarian by his later years, and it was arguable that after fourteen years the danger for Germany was not instability but too much stability, too much reliance on one man.

During the years from 1963 to 1969, the CDU proved it could govern without Adenauer, and the SPD came to seem ever more respectable, even joining as junior partner in a government coalition with the CDU in 1966. Finally, in October 1969, new parliamentary elections brought Brandt to the Chancellorship, and the SPD became responsible for governing West Germany for the first time since the war. Its ability to work effectively within the overall framework of the Bonn republic proved essential for the consolidation of the new German democracy.

In becoming West Germany's first postwar Social Democratic chancellor, Brandt sought to provide a genuine alternative to the CDU without undermining the consensus that had developed around the new regime since 1949. He wanted especially to improve relations between West Germany and the Soviet bloc, but this required a more independent foreign policy than Germany had followed under Adenauer and his successors. For a socialist chancellor seeking to prove his respectability, this *Ostpolitik*, or opening to the East, was a bit risky, but Brandt pursued his policy with skill and success, winning broad support among Germans.

In treaties with the Soviet Union, Czechoslovakia, and Poland, West Germany accepted the main lines of the postwar settlement. Thus Germany apparently gave up any claim to the former German territory east of the Oder-Neisse line, now in Poland. Brandt also managed to improve relations with East Germany. After the two countries finally agreed to mutual diplomatic recognition, each was admitted to the United Nations in 1973. Brandt's overtures made possible closer economic ties between them, and even broader opportunities for ordinary citizens to interact across the east-west border.

With his opening to the East, Brandt was not seeking to compromise Germany's important place in the Atlantic alliance. But his success proved that within the framework of its larger Western orientation, West Germany could take the initiative and develop a more flexible and balanced policy. And whereas every major foreign policy initiative during the Weimar Republic had caused political polarization, Brandt's *Ostpolitik* was widely popular and helped deepen the postwar consensus in West Germany.

Democracy without Revolution in France and Italy

In both France and Italy, communists had played major roles in the resistance movements and might conceivably have made a bid for power as the war was ending. But Moscow, concerned with the larger picture in Europe, called for the moderate route of participation in coalitions instead, not least because the presence of Western troops in these countries gave the leverage to noncommunists. And the U.S. intervened persistently to minimize the communists' role as new democracies took root in both nations after 1945.

When the first parliamentary elections were held in the new Fourth Republic in France in 1946, the Communists won the largest number of seats, and their support continued to rise until 1949. Partly because of pressure from the United States, however, they were forced out of the coalition government in 1947, and after 1949 their strength began leveling off. During the years that followed, the French Communist party proved particularly inflexible and unimaginative, maintaining strict subservience to the Soviet Union.

With the liberation of France in August 1944, Charles de Gaulle, the leader of the Free French, had immediately assumed the dominant political role. But he led France only until January 1946, when he withdrew from active politics after a bruising battle over the shape of the new French constitution. Seeking to avoid the political bickering of the Third Republic, de Gaulle advocated stronger presidential authority and less power for the deputies in the lower house of parliament. When the French people finally accepted a constitution that portended a return to the style of government of the Third Republic, de Gaulle stepped aside, holding himself in reserve, as he saw it, for the inevitable moment when the flawed new republic would prove unable to deal with a crisis.

Just as de Gaulle had feared, government in the new Fourth Republic depended, as before, on multiparty coalitions, which required considerable political energy simply to put together a stable majority. The Fourth Republic became something of a laughingstock as governments rose and fell every six months, on the average, over its twelve-year life. In important respects, however, decision making in the new French state changed as the nonpolitical, technocratic side of the French state gained power in areas such as economic planning.

This technocratic side of the French state survived the fall of the Fourth Republic in 1958, when de Gaulle returned to an active political role at a moment of political crisis, stemming from France's war to maintain control of Algeria. Although he became prime minister within the Fourth Republic, it was clear that his return portended a change of regime. The French legislature promptly gave de Gaulle's government full powers for six months, including a charge to

The Return of de Gaulle Disillusioned with the political squabbles of the early Fourth Republic, General Charles de Gaulle retired from public life in 1946. But he believed his country would need his leadership again. He returned to power in 1958, with France in turmoil over the Algerian War, and spearheaded the creation of the Fifth Republic. *(Keystone/Sygma)*

draft a new constitution, which was then approved by referendum in the fall of 1958. The result was the new Fifth Republic, based on a stronger executive, a president elected independently of the Chamber.

Italy's political challenge, after more than twenty years of fascism, was even more dramatic than France's. Shortly after the war, the Italians adopted a new democratic constitution and voted to end the monarchy, thereby making Italy a republic for the first time. But much depended on the balance of political forces, which quickly crystallized around the Christian Democratic party (DC), oriented toward the Catholic church, and the Communist and Socialist parties. The international context strongly favored the Christian Democrats, who promptly assumed the dominant political role. As the cold war developed, the United States intervened as necessary to support the Christian Democrats as the chief bulwark against the Communists. Many Italian moderates and conservatives with little attachment to the church supported the DC for the same reason.

Initially, and well into the 1970s, the Christian Democrats' share of the vote remained relatively stable at around 40 percent in national parliamentary elections. The DC was invariably the largest single party, yet not a majority, so it was forced to work in coalition with smaller parties. Beginning in the early sixties, with the much-trumpeted "opening to the left," this could even include the Socialist party (PSI), which typically won 10 to 15 percent of the vote in national elections. This total fell far behind that of the Communist party, which for decades remained the second largest at 25 to 35 percent. The relative strength of the political parties established the framework for the curious combination of surface instability and deeper stability—or immobility—that came to characterize the new Italian democracy. Domination by the Christian Democrats was the fundamental fact of Italian political life until the early 1990s.

The Communists remained the strongest opposition party, but unlike their counterparts in France, the Italian Communists did not settle for a role of opposition and protest. Led by Palmiro Togliatti (1893–1964), they followed the path that Gramsci had indicated and sought to make their presence felt in as many areas of Italian life as possible. Wherever they found popular discontents, they offered diagnoses and solutions in an effort to persuade ever-wider circles of Italians that they offered a superior grasp of the overall Italian situation. Their aim was gradually to establish their legitimacy, and they had considerable success, garnering the support of intellectuals, journalists, and publishers, organizing profit-making cooperatives for sharecroppers, and winning local and regional elections. At one time or another, they ran many of Italy's local and regional governments, often for years at a time, and they generally did well at it. Heavily communist Bologna, for example, was widely considered one of the best-governed cities in Europe.

At the same time, the Italian Communist party established its relative independence from Moscow. In a widely discussed document published in 1964, Togliatti deplored the slow pace of liberalization in the Soviet Union and insisted that greater "polycentrism" was necessary to overcome the stagnation of communism in the West. Communism did not have to entail the Stalinist features that still marked the system in the Soviet Union and its satellites.

But as the years after World War II turned to decades, the Communists' successes forced awkward questions to the fore. What was the party trying to do on the national level, and how long was it supposed to take? Could a communist party function as a governing party within a democratic political system?

Western Europe and the World

By the early 1950s, the old Europe seemed dwarfed by the two global superpowers and, for the foreseeable future, divided by the conflict between them. The colonial networks that had symbolized European predominance unraveled rapidly at the same time. One obvious response to the fall of Europe was some form of European unity: A unified Europe might eventually have the clout to stand as a global superpower in its own right. Nationalism, in contrast, had kept Europe a collection of small, squabbling states—and had led to disaster.

Although the steps toward European unity did not go as far as visionaries had hoped, they established lasting foundations by the late 1950s—and they served European prosperity and security well. As a result of that success, a common European outlook gradually developed, portending, perhaps, a renewed role of leadership for Europe in world affairs.

NATO and the Atlantic Orientation

As the Soviets tightened their grip on the satellite states of east-central Europe, fears of Soviet expansion into Western Europe led to the creation of the North Atlantic Treaty Organization (NATO) under U.S. leadership in April 1949. NATO pooled the forces of its member countries under a unified command, and in this sense went

Ban the Bomb As nuclear tension escalated during the 1950s, some built air-raid shelters; others took to the streets in antinuclear protest. The protest movement was especially prominent in Britain, where the noted philosopher Bertrand Russell (1872–1970) played a central role. Here, seated at right, he awaits arrest during a sit-in demonstration outside the British Defense Ministry. *(Hulton-Deutsch)*

The Importance of National Sovereignty

In a speech on French radio and television in 1963, President Charles de Gaulle explained why, even in the radically new postwar world, France had to be responsible for its own defense.

. . .[I]mbued once more with the spirit of renovation, in the full flush of invention, production, and economic growth, provided with solid institutions, released from colonial bonds, France finds herself, for the first time in half a century, with a free spirit and free hands. And thus she can and must play throughout the world the role that belongs to her. . . .

. . . [W]ithin the Atlantic Alliance—indispensable so long as the ambitions and threats of the Soviets are raised—our country, while combining its defense with that of its allies, intends to . . . contribute to the common effort something quite different from the soulless and powerless assistance of a people that would no longer be responsible for themselves. This leads us to provide ourselves with the modern means of ensuring our security. . . . I mean, of course, atomic weapons. It is true that our American allies possess in this respect a colossal power, capable of throwing into chaos all or part of the Soviet empire. . . .

. . . [T]he possible adversary is himself equipped with enormous means of the same kind. This being the case, no one, nowhere, can know in advance whether, in the event of a conflict, the atomic bombs would or would not be used at the start by the two principal champions; whether, if they did use them, they would use them in Central and Western Europe only, without striking each other directly and immediately. . . . [I]n light of this enormous and inevitable uncertainty, France must herself have the means of directly reaching any State that would be her aggressor. . . .

In sum, our country, perpetually threatened, finds itself once again faced with the necessity of possessing the most powerful weapons of the era. . . . "It is useless," say some. "It is too costly," say others. These voices France listened to, sometimes and to her misfortune, notably on the eve of the two world wars. . . . But this time we shall not allow routine and illusion to invite invasion of our country.

Source: Major Addresses, Statements, and Press Conferences of General Charles de Gaulle, May 19, 1958–January 31, 1964 (New York: French Embassy, Press and Information Division, n.d.), pp. 224–226.

beyond the usual peacetime military alliance. This Atlantic bloc assumed definitive shape only in 1955, when it encompassed the newly rearmed West Germany. The prospect of German rearmament made the French nervous at first, but between 1950 and 1954 they came to agree that, even if it had to mean German rearmament, the best course for French security was to integrate the western part of a divided Germany into the U.S.-led Western bloc.

NATO was intended specifically to prevent any Soviet expansion in Europe. Yet the Soviets had considerable superiority in conventional forces, which had ready access to Western Europe. As a balance, the United States offered its nuclear superiority; indeed, the American nuclear guarantee was the cornerstone of the NATO alliance. Thus it seemed crucial for the United States to maintain its superiority in nuclear weapons, a fact that helped fuel the continuing arms race and nuclear buildup. However, as the Soviet Union developed the capacity for a nuclear strike at the United States, Europeans began asking whether the Americans could be counted on to respond with nuclear weapons to a *conventional* Soviet attack on Western Europe. The Americans might hesitate, now that the United States was vulnerable to Soviet nuclear retaliation. Did it make sense, then, for Western Europeans to rely on the United States as the ultimate guarantor of their defense? (See the box, "The Importance of National Sovereignty.")

The Varieties of Decolonization

The advent of a new world configuration, with a circumscribed place for Europe, found dramatic expression in the rapid disintegration of the European colonial empires after World War II (Map 31.1). The process of decolonization was varied and uneven, partly because the local independence movements differed but also because the interests of Europeans varied. Where there were large numbers of European settlers, the colonial powers were reluctant to yield to independence forces. But everywhere they were more likely to yield if they could negotiate their withdrawal with local moderates, thereby preserving property rights and the possibility of continued influence.

After World War II, five major European colonial powers remained—Britain, France, Belgium, the Netherlands, and Portugal. In all five colonialism became a major and divisive issue. The overriding question was whether any of them could still afford imperial pretensions, especially in the face of growing local opposition.

The war proved a major catalyst for anticolonialist independence movements throughout the world. In southeast Asia and the Pacific, the quick Japanese conquests revealed the vulnerability of France, the Netherlands, and Britain. And it was not colonial reconquest that marked the end of the war, but the atomic bomb and the victory of the United States, which took a dim view of conventional European colonialism.

The effort of the Netherlands to regain control of the Dutch East Indies led to four years of military struggle against the Indonesian nationalist insurgency. Although most independent observers felt they could not win, the Dutch were reluctant to relinquish control of the East Indies, which had been in Dutch hands since the seventeenth century. Especially after the humiliations of defeat and occupation during World War II, the imperial role still meant a good deal to the Netherlands. The struggle lasted from 1945 to 1949, when the Dutch finally had to yield as their former colony became independent Indonesia.

Unlike the Netherlands, Britain was still a great power in the twentieth century, and its empire had seemed essential to its stature. Though Churchill had staunchly defended Britain's imperial role, Attlee's postwar Labour government began the decolonization process, which was no doubt irreversible by the time the Conservatives returned to power in 1951. Although India, the crown jewel of the empire, had won its independence in 1947, many Britons still envisioned extending Commonwealth status to the former British colonies as a way of retaining economic ties and political influence. But the Commonwealth idea proved to have little appeal for Britain's former colonies; the British Commonwealth became little more than a voluntary cooperative association. Despite illusions and hesitations, however, Britain proved the most realistic of the European colonial powers, grasping the need to compromise and work with emerging national leaders.

Nevertheless, even Britain decided to resist in 1956, when it provoked an international crisis over the status of the Suez Canal in Egypt. Once a British protectorate, Egypt had remained under heavy British influence even after nominally becoming sovereign in 1922. But a revolution in 1952 produced a new government of Arab nationalists, led by the charismatic Colonel Gamel Abdul Nasser (1918–1970). In 1954, Britain agreed with Egypt to leave the Suez Canal zone within twenty months, though the zone was to be international, not Egyptian, and Britain was to retain special rights there in the event of war. In 1956, however, Nasser announced the nationalization of the canal, partly so that its revenues would fall to Egypt, to be used to finance public works projects.

Led by the Conservative Anthony Eden (1897–1977), Britain decided on a showdown. Eden won the support of Israel and France, each of which had reason to fear the pan-Arab nationalism that Nasser's Egypt was now spearheading. Israel had remained at odds with its Arab neighbors since its founding in 1948, and Nasser was helping the Arabs who were beginning to take up arms against French rule in Algeria.

Late in 1956, Britain, Israel, and France orchestrated a surprise attack on Egypt. After the Israelis invaded, the British and French bombed military targets, then landed troops to take the

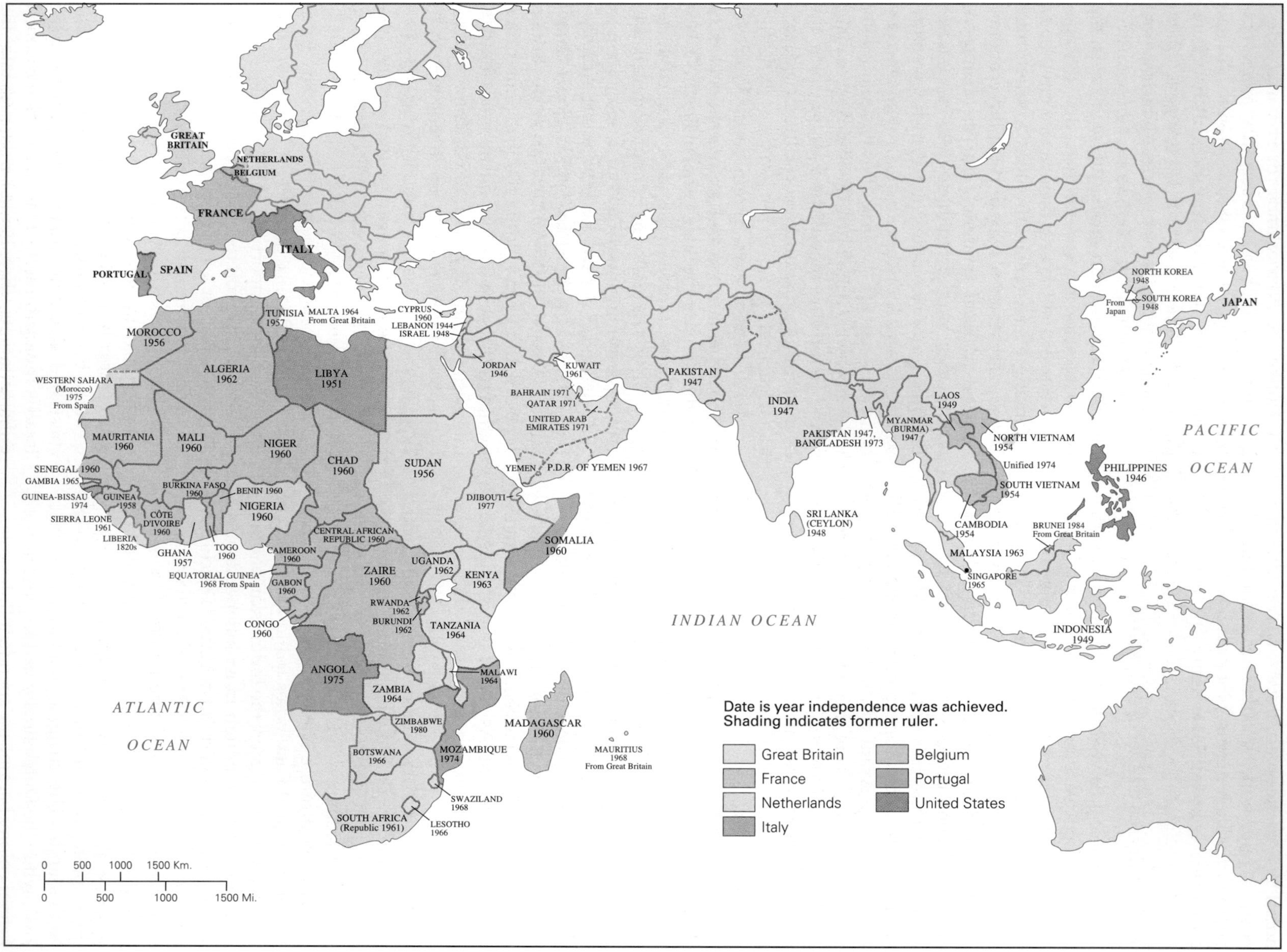
GREAT BRITAIN
NETHERLANDS
BELGIUM
FRANCE
ITALY
PORTUGAL
SPAIN
TUNISIA 1957
MALTA 1964 From Great Britain
CYPRUS 1960
LEBANON 1944
ISRAEL 1948
MOROCCO 1956
ALGERIA 1962
LIBYA 1951
WESTERN SAHARA (Morocco) 1975 From Spain
JORDAN 1946
KUWAIT 1961
BAHRAIN 1971
QATAR 1971
UNITED ARAB EMIRATES 1971
YEMEN
P.D.R. OF YEMEN 1967
PAKISTAN 1947
INDIA 1947
PAKISTAN 1947, BANGLADESH 1973
MYANMAR (BURMA) 1947
LAOS 1949
NORTH VIETNAM 1954
Unified 1974
SOUTH VIETNAM 1954
CAMBODIA 1954
NORTH KOREA 1948
SOUTH KOREA 1948
From Japan
JAPAN
PACIFIC OCEAN
PHILIPPINES 1946
BRUNEI 1984 From Great Britain
MALAYSIA 1963
SINGAPORE 1965
INDONESIA 1949
SRI LANKA (CEYLON) 1948
INDIAN OCEAN
MAURITANIA 1960
MALI 1960
NIGER 1960
CHAD 1960
SUDAN 1956
SENEGAL 1960
GAMBIA 1965
GUINEA-BISSAU 1974
GUINEA 1958
SIERRA LEONE 1961
LIBERIA 1820s
CÔTE D'IVOIRE 1960
GHANA 1957
TOGO 1960
BURKINA FASO 1960
BENIN 1960
NIGERIA 1960
CENTRAL AFRICAN REPUBLIC 1960
CAMEROON 1960
EQUATORIAL GUINEA 1968 From Spain
GABON 1960
CONGO 1960
ZAIRE 1960
RWANDA 1962
BURUNDI 1962
UGANDA 1962
KENYA 1963
TANZANIA 1964
DJIBOUTI 1977
SOMALIA 1960
ANGOLA 1975
ZAMBIA 1964
MALAWI 1964
ZIMBABWE 1980
MOZAMBIQUE 1974
BOTSWANA 1966
SWAZILAND 1968
LESOTHO 1966
SOUTH AFRICA (Republic 1961)
MADAGASCAR 1960
MAURITIUS 1968 From Great Britain
ATLANTIC OCEAN
0 500 1000 1500 Km.
0 500 1000 1500 Mi.
Date is year independence was achieved.
Shading indicates former ruler.
Great Britain
France
Netherlands
Italy
Belgium
Portugal
United States

canal. But the troops met stubborn Egyptian resistance, and the British and French encountered decisive defeat in the diplomatic maneuvering that accompanied the outbreak of fighting. World opinion, including both the United States and the Soviet Union, opposed the Anglo-French-Israeli move. The Suez crisis of 1956 proved the last time the old European powers sought to act on their own, by the old rules, within the new bipolar framework. The outcome demonstrated not only how limited the reach of the Western European states had become but also that nations like Egypt, formerly subservient to Europeans, could be a factor in their own right.

Still, the outcome in 1956 did not convince France to abandon its struggle to retain Algeria. And that struggle proved the culmination of the most dramatic, wrenching experience that any European country was to have with decolonization. The process started, however, in Indochina, in southeast Asia.

Led by the communist Ho Chi Minh (1890–1969), the Indochinese anticolonialist movement gained strength resisting the Japanese during the war, then, before the French could return, established a base in northern Vietnam in 1945. Although the French re-established control in the south, negotiations between the French and the Vietnamese nationalists seemed at first to be moving toward some form of self-government for Vietnam. However, there was considerable opposition in France, especially within the army, to giving in to the Vietnamese independence movement. In 1946, French authorities in Indochina deliberately provoked an incident to undercut negotiations and start hostilities. Eight years of difficult guerrilla war followed, creating a major drain on the French economy.

With its strongly anticolonialist posture, the United States was unsympathetic to the French cause at first. However, the communist takeover in China in 1949 and the outbreak of war in Korea in 1950 made the French struggle in Indochina seem a battle in a larger war against communism in Asia. By 1954, the United States was covering 75 percent of the cost of the French effort in Indochina. Nonetheless, when the fall of the fortified area at Dien Bien Phu in May 1954 signaled a decisive French defeat, the United States decided to pull back and accept a negotiated settlement. Partly at the urging of its European allies, the United States had concluded that the Soviet threat in Europe must remain its principal concern.

Shortly after the fall of Dien Bien Phu, Pierre Mendès-France (1907–1982), a vigorous, reforming politician from the old Radical party, became France's prime minister with a promise to end the war. He engineered independence for Vietnam in 1955. The solution, however, entailed north-south partition to separate the communist and anticommunist forces, pending elections to unify the country. The anticommunist regime the United States sponsored in the south resisted holding the elections, so the country remained divided. Only in 1975, after a brutal war with the United States, would the communist heirs of those who had led the fight against the French assume the leadership of a unified Vietnam.

In France, the defeat in Indochina left a legacy of bitterness, especially among army officers, many of whom felt that French forces could have won had they not been undercut by politicians at home. When the outcome in Indochina emboldened Arab nationalists in North Africa to take up arms against the French colonial power, the French army was anxious for a second chance, and the French government was willing to give it to them. The French agreed to independence for Tunisia and Morocco by 1956, but only so that they could concentrate their military forces in Algeria, where the stakes seemed high enough for a showdown. Algeria had been French since 1830, and it had a substantial European minority, totaling over a million, or 10 percent of the total population.

Although France gradually committed 500,000 troops to Algeria, the war bogged down into what threatened to become a lengthy stalemate, with increasing brutality on both sides. As it drained French lives and resources, the war became a highly volatile political issue in France. Things came to a head during the spring of 1958 when the advent of a new ministry, rumored to favor a compromise settlement, led to violent demonstrations, engineered by the sectors of the

Map 31.1 From Colonialism to Independence During a thirty-year period after World War II, the European empires in Africa, Asia, and the Pacific gradually came apart as the former colonies became independent nations.

The French in Algeria As nationalist opposition to French rule in Algeria gathered force in 1956, French authorities sought to root out the forces of rebellion. Here, in May 1956, French troops march away arrested suspects after sweeping through the Arab quarter of Algiers in a search for rebels, guns, ammunition, and subversive literature. *(UPI/Bettmann Newsphotos)*

French army in Algeria. Military intervention in France itself seemed likely to follow—and with it the danger of civil war.

It was at this moment of genuine emergency that Charles de Gaulle returned to spearhead the change to the Fifth Republic. Those of the French right, determined to hold Algeria, welcomed de Gaulle as their savior. But de Gaulle fooled them, working out a compromise with the nationalist rebels that ended the war and made Algeria independent in 1962. No doubt only de Gaulle could have engineered this outcome without provoking still deeper political division in France.

The anticolonial movement in Algeria gave rise to a more radical new political order than had been the case in Tunisia and Morocco. The new Algerian government's policy of expropriation and nationalization led most of the French settlers to relocate to France.

All over Europe, the colonialist impulse, which had still been significant immediately after World War II, waned noticeably by the end of the 1950s. The economic successes of Germany and Italy, both free of colonialist expenses, suggested to Europeans that they would be better off without colonies, particularly if maintaining them required a heavy military burden.

But there remained resistance, and considerable variation, as the colonies of sub-Saharan Africa moved toward independence during the fifties, sixties, and seventies. Outcomes depended on the number and intransigence of white settlers, on the extent to which local elites had emerged, and on the confidence of the Europeans that they could retain their influence if they acquiesced in independence. Of the major imperial powers in the region, Britain had done best at preparing local leaders and proved the most willing to work with indigenous elites. The two smaller countries, Belgium and Portugal, were less certain they could maintain their influence, and they proved the most reluctant to give up imperial status.

The transition was smoothest in British West Africa, where the Gold Coast achieved independence as Ghana, first as a dominion within the Commonwealth in 1957, then as a fully independent republic in 1960. There were few British settlers in that part of Africa, and the small, relatively cohesive African elite favored a moderate transition, not revolution. On the other hand, where British settlers were relatively numerous, as in Kenya or Rhodesia, the transition to independence proved much more difficult. The very presence of Europeans had impeded the development of cohesive local elites, so movements for independence in those areas tended to become more radical, threatening the expropriation of European-held property.

The British had to use 50,000 troops and police to put down a major rebellion in Kenya from 1951 to 1956. This episode helped convince the British that the cost of maintaining colonial rule was simply too high, and they gradually developed a compromise that led to independence for Kenya in 1963. In Southern Rhodesia, however, intransigent European settlers resisted the British government's effort to promote a comparable compromise. A white supremacist government declared its independence from Britain in 1965, fueling a guerrilla war. The Africans won independence as Zimbabwe only in 1980.

Nowhere was decolonization messier than in the two largest Portuguese colonies in Africa, Mozambique and Angola. Partly because of its own economic weakness, Portugal had run the most repressive of the African colonial regimes, with elements of the earlier system of forced labor lingering into the 1960s. Portuguese intransigence radicalized the independence movement, which took advantage of help from the communist world to resist the colonizers militarily. Finally, by 1974, sectors of the Portuguese military, weary of a multifaceted colonial war they lacked the resources to win, engineered a political coup at home. The new government promptly washed its hands of the debilitating colonialist struggle, granting independence to both Mozambique and Angola in 1975. In each of the new countries, communist-supported radicals had won the upper hand within divided anticolonialist movements, but the struggles themselves, and the sudden departure of the Portuguese, left considerable socioeconomic disarray.

The process of decolonization led to a remarkable transformation in the quarter-century after World War II. Forms of colonial rule that had been taken for granted before World War I stood discredited, virtually without defenders, by the late twentieth century. But decolonization hardly offered a neat and definitive solution. New political boundaries often stemmed from the way Europeans had carved things up, rather than from indigenous ethnic or national patterns. Moreover, questions remained about the longer-term economic relationships between the Europeans and their former colonies.

In some areas, reasonably good relations, compatible with Western interests, promptly developed, although the leader of Ghana, Kwame Nkrumah (1909–1972), used the term *neocolonialism* to suggest that more subtle forms of Western exploitation had replaced direct colonial rule. Nonetheless, attempts by the former colonies to do without economic ties to the West often proved counterproductive.

The reaction against Eurocentrism that accompanied the turn from colonialism was not confined to those who had been subjected to European imperialism. Even in the West there was much interest, for example, in the work of Frantz Fanon (1925–1961), a black intellectual from Martinique who became identified especially with the cause of the Algerian rebels. In *The Wretched of the Earth* (1961), Fanon called on the peoples of the non-Western world to go their own way, based on their own values and traditions, in light of the spiritual exhaustion of the West (see the box, "Anticolonialism and the Reaction Against the West").

European Economic Integration and the Common Market

As the old colonialism increasingly fell into disrepute, many found in European unity the best prospect for the future. Although hopes for full-scale political unity were promptly frustrated, the movement for European integration gradually achieved significant fruit in the economic sphere, especially through the European Economic Community (EEC), or Common Market, established in 1957.

The impetus for economic integration came especially from a new breed of "Eurocrats," technocrats with a supranational European outlook. Two remarkable French leaders, Jean Monnet and Robert Schuman (1886–1963), set the pattern. Schuman came from Lorraine, which had passed between France and Germany four times between 1870 and 1945. After serving as a German officer in World War I, he was elected to the

Anticolonialism and the Reaction Against the West

In the conclusion to* The Wretched of the Earth, *Frantz Fanon gave strong voice to the antipathy toward the West that accompanied the anticolonial movement.

Leave this Europe where they are never done talking of Man, yet murder men everywhere they find them.... For centuries they have stifled almost the whole of humanity in the name of a so-called spiritual experience. Look at them today swaying between atomic and spiritual disintegration....

...[T]he European game has finally ended; we must find something different. We today can do everything, so long as we do not imitate Europe, so long as we are not obsessed by the desire to catch up with Europe....

Two centuries ago, a former European colony decided to catch up with Europe. It succeeded so well that the United States of America became a monster, in which the taints, the sickness, and the inhumanity of Europe have grown to appalling dimensions....

Today we are present at the stasis of Europe....

The Third World today faces Europe like a colossal mass whose aim should be to try to resolve the problems to which Europe has not been able to find the answers.

...[I]f we want humanity to advance a step further, if we want to bring it up to a different level than that which Europe has shown it, then we must invent and we must make discoveries.

Source: Frantz Fanon, *The Wretched of the Earth* (New York: Grove, 1968), pp. 311–315.

French Chamber of Deputies in 1919 as Lorraine was returned to France. Monnet, on the other hand, served as an official of the League of Nations while a young man just after World War I. He quickly became convinced that the League was too much a collection of existing, unequal nations; peace and cooperation required stronger rules and institutions to transcend parochial national interests.

As French foreign minister after World War II, Schuman was responsible for a 1950 plan to coordinate French and German production of coal and steel. The Schuman Plan quickly encompassed Italy and the Benelux countries as well to become the European Coal and Steel Community (ECSC) in 1951. Monnet served as the ECSC's first president. From this position, he pushed for more thoroughgoing economic integration, and the successes of the ECSC led directly to the Common Market (see the box, "Practical Thinking and European Integration").

The effort was boosted by the 1956 Suez crisis, which dramatized Europe's dependence on Middle Eastern oil. In light of this long-term vulnerability, economic unity seemed essential to the very survival of Europe. It helped, too, that in 1957 the Soviet Union launched *Sputnik I,* the first artificial satellite, suggesting that unless the nations of Western Europe could work together, they were in danger of falling ever further behind the superpowers in advanced technology.

In March 1957, leaders of France, Germany, Italy, Belgium, the Netherlands, and Luxembourg signed the Treaty of Rome, establishing the EEC. Subsequently ratified by the parliaments of the member nations, the treaty took effect on January 1, 1958. Over the next two decades the EEC's membership gradually expanded to include Denmark, Ireland, Britain, Greece, Spain, and Portugal (Map 31.2).

The immediate aim of the EEC was to broaden markets and facilitate trade by eliminating customs duties within the Common Market and establishing a common tariff on imports from the rest of the world. For each of the parties to the EEC, tariff reduction entailed the advantage of access to wider markets abroad, but also the risks of new competition in its own domestic market. So it was hard to be sure who might gain and who might lose from the move toward a common market. However, the EEC promptly proved advantageous to so many that tariff reduction proceeded well ahead of schedule. By 1968 the last internal tariffs had been eliminated.

With tariffs dropping, trade among the member countries nearly doubled between 1958 and 1962. French exports of both automobiles and chemicals to Germany increased more than eightfold. Partly because the increasing competition stimulated dynamism and productivity, industrial production within the EEC increased at a robust annual rate of 7.6 percent during that time.

The overall goal of the EEC—to enable goods, capital, and labor to move freely among the member countries—required some coordination of the social and economic policies of the member states. How did that requirement square with the sovereignty that those states retained? To what extent was the Common Market to be a new whole, greater than the sum of its parts, as opposed to a mere federation of existing states? Until the mid-sixties, as the Common Market went from one success to another, the initiative lay with the supranational Eurocrats, who wanted to pursue economic growth and efficiency without reference to parochial national concerns. The next twenty years, however, proved a period of fits and starts for the Common Market, as its supranational reach bumped up against continuing national sovereignty.

In the mid-sixties President de Gaulle forced some of the underlying uncertainties about the Common Market to the fore. Though he had willingly turned from the old colonialism, de Gaulle was not prepared to compromise French sovereignty, and he was not persuaded that European integration, along the lines of the Common Market, offered the best course for postwar Europe. With the end of the Algerian War in 1962, France began playing an assertively independent role in international affairs. De Gaulle recognized the communist People's Republic of China, curtailed the French role in NATO, and began developing an independent French nuclear force (see the box, "The Importance of National Sovereignty," on page 1162).

Jean Monnet A leading French technocrat, Monnet spearheaded economic planning in France and economic cooperation and integration in Europe. His efforts led to the European Common Market, which gradually developed into the wider European Community. Monnet sought especially to cement close economic ties between France and Germany to overcome the frictions that had been a major source of war in his own lifetime. He and West German chancellor Adenauer greatly admired each other, and cooperation between France and Germany was central to the success of the Common Market. *(Archives/Sygma)*

This determination to assert France's sovereignty inevitably led to friction between de Gaulle and the supranational Eurocrats of the Common Market. Matters came to a head in 1965, when a confrontation developed over a matter of agricultural policy. The immediate result was a

Practical Thinking and European Integration

Jean Monnet insisted that European unity would grow not from idealistic pronouncements but from technical solutions to specified problems, taken one at a time. In the following passages from his memoirs, he outlines the thinking that led him to help create the European Coal and Steel Community.

In places like London, New York, and Washington, where the big decisions are made, my first talks have always been with people who cannot afford to make mistakes—bankers, industrialists, lawyers, and newspapermen. What others say may be colored by imagination, ambition, or doctrine. I certainly respect their influence, but I base my judgement on the wisdom of practical men. . . .

Experience had taught me that one cannot act in general terms, starting from a vague concept, but that anything becomes possible as soon as one can concentrate on one precise point which leads on to everything else. . . .

If only the French could lose their fear of German industrial domination, then the greatest obstacle to a united Europe would be removed. A solution which would put French industry on the same footing as German industry, while freeing the latter from the discrimination born of defeat—that would restore the economic and political preconditions for the mutual understanding so vital to Europe as a whole. It could, in fact, become the germ of European unity. . . .

The joint resources of France and Germany lay essentially in their coal and steel, distributed unevenly but in complementary fashion over a triangular area artificially divided by historical frontiers. . . . Coal and steel were at once the key to economic power and the raw materials for forging weapons of war. This double role gave them immense symbolic significance. . . . To pool them across frontiers would reduce their malign prestige and turn them instead into a guarantee of peace.

Source: Jean Monnet, *Memoirs* (Garden City, N.Y.: Doubleday, 1978), pp. 271, 286, 292–293.

compromise, but de Gaulle's tough stance served to check the increasing supranationalism that had been evident in the Common Market until then. As the economic context became more difficult during the 1970s, it became still harder to maintain the cohesion of the EEC. So though the Common Market proved an important departure, it did not overcome the older forms of national sovereignty and give the Western European states a new place in the world.

The Soviet Union and the Communist Bloc

By the late 1950s, there were increasing concerns in the West that the Soviet Union, though rigid and inhumane in important respects, could do some things very well—and might have significant advantages in the race with the capitalist democracies. While still making jokes about "made in Japan," Westerners worried about producing enough scientists and engineers to match the Soviets. Nonetheless, flaws in the political and economic system that had emerged under

Map 31.2 Military Alliances and Multinational Economic Groupings in the Era of the Cold War The cold war split was reflected especially in the two military alliances: NATO, formed in 1949, and the Warsaw Pact, formed in 1955. Each side also had its own multinational economic organization, but the membership of the EEC, or Common Market, was not identical to that of NATO. Although communist, Yugoslavia remained outside Soviet-led organizations, as did Albania for part of the period.

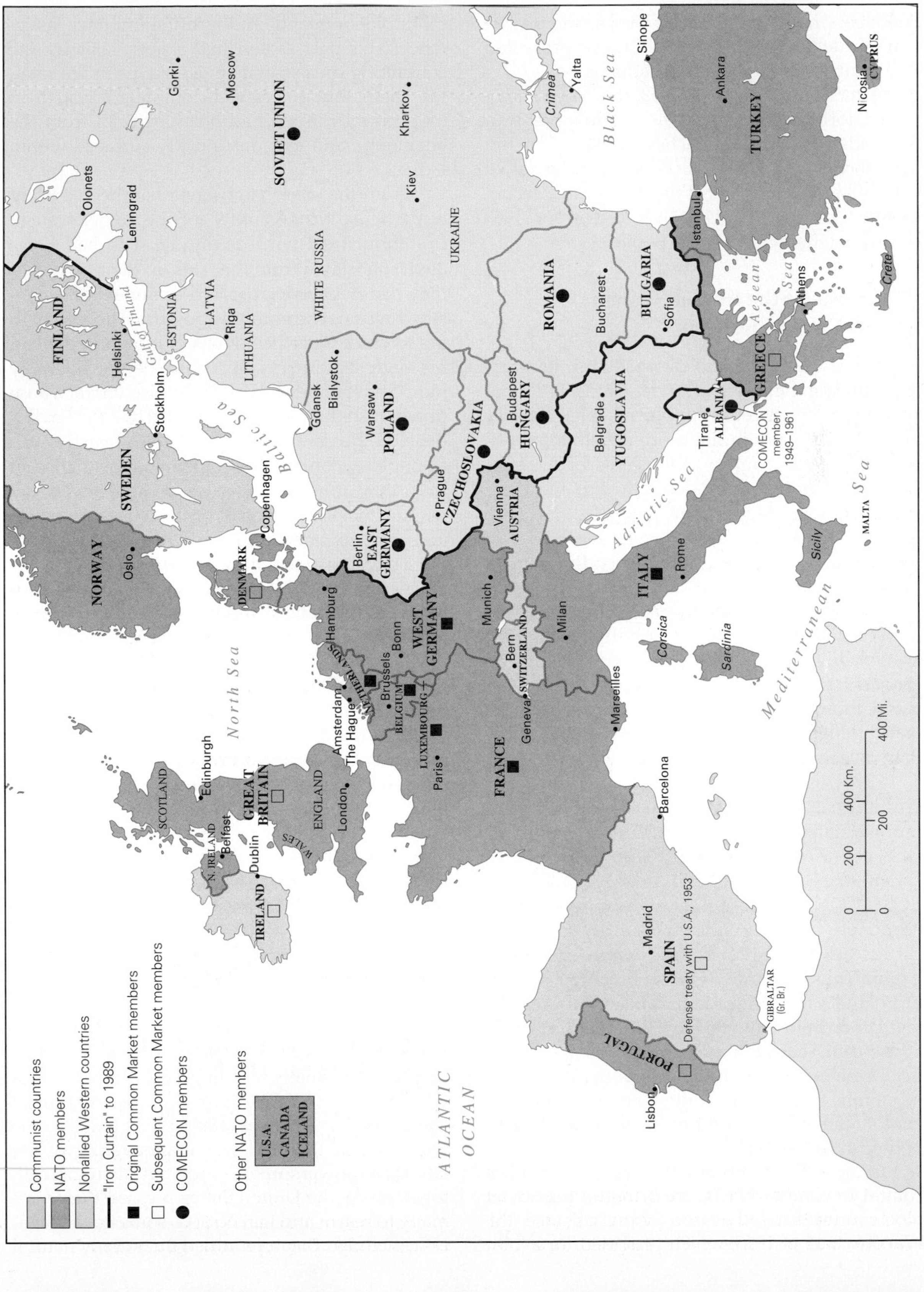
Communist countries
NATO members
Nonallied Western countries
"Iron Curtain" to 1989
Original Common Market members
Subsequent Common Market members
COMECON members
Other NATO members
U.S.A.
CANADA
ICELAND
ATLANTIC OCEAN
North Sea
Baltic Sea
Gulf of Finland
Black Sea
Aegean Sea
Adriatic Sea
Mediterranean Sea
NORWAY
Oslo
SWEDEN
Stockholm
FINLAND
Helsinki
DENMARK
Copenhagen
IRELAND
Dublin
N. IRELAND
Belfast
SCOTLAND
Edinburgh
GREAT BRITAIN
WALES
ENGLAND
London
NETHERLANDS
Amsterdam
The Hague
BELGIUM
Brussels
LUXEMBOURG
FRANCE
Paris
Marseilles
Geneva
SWITZERLAND
Bern
WEST GERMANY
Bonn
Hamburg
Munich
EAST GERMANY
Berlin
POLAND
Warsaw
Gdansk
Bialystok
CZECHOSLOVAKIA
Prague
AUSTRIA
Vienna
HUNGARY
Budapest
YUGOSLAVIA
Belgrade
ALBANIA
Tiranë
COMECON member, 1949–1961
GREECE
Athens
ROMANIA
Bucharest
BULGARIA
Sofia
TURKEY
Istanbul
Ankara
Sinope
CYPRUS
Nicosia
Crete
ITALY
Milan
Rome
Corsica
Sardinia
Sicily
MALTA
SPAIN
Madrid
Barcelona
Defense treaty with U.S.A., 1953
PORTUGAL
Lisbon
GIBRALTAR (Gr. Br.)
SOVIET UNION
Leningrad
Olonets
Moscow
Gorki
Kharkov
Kiev
Yalta
Crimea
ESTONIA
LATVIA
Riga
LITHUANIA
WHITE RUSSIA
UKRAINE
0 200 400 Km.
0 200 400 Mi.

Stalin continued in the Soviet Union, and its system of satellites in east-central Europe presented the country with some new dilemmas.

After Stalin's death in 1953, there was a sporadic effort to make the Soviet system more flexible under Nikita Khrushchev (1894–1971). But Khrushchev was ousted in 1964, and the Soviet suppression of the reform movement in Czechoslovakia during the "Prague Spring" of 1968 confirmed the rigidity of the Soviet system.

Dilemmas of the Soviet System in East-Central Europe

In light of the losses and destruction it had suffered during the war, the Soviet Union could not afford to relax or return to normal even after its victory. Especially in the more developed western part of the country, thousands of factories and even whole towns lay destroyed, and there were severe shortages of everything from labor to housing. In addition, the developing cold war seemed to require that military spending remain high.

At the same time, the Soviet Union faced the unprecedented challenge of solidifying the new system of satellite states it had put together in east-central Europe. Except in Yugoslavia and Albania, those communist regimes depended more on ongoing occupation by the Soviet Red Army than on genuine popular support.

Partly in response to U.S. initiatives in Western Europe, the Soviets sought to mold the communist states in east-central Europe into a secure, coordinated bloc of allies. In the economic sphere, the Soviets founded a new organization, COMECON, as part of their effort to reorient the economies of the satellite states away from their earlier ties to the West and toward the Soviet Union. Thus, for example, whereas only 7 percent of Poland's foreign trade had been with the Soviet Union before the war, by 1951 the figure was 58 percent. Through such mechanisms as artificial pricing of imports and exports, these new economic relationships often entailed outright exploitation of the satellite states for the benefit of the Soviet Union.

In the military-diplomatic sphere, the Soviets sought to counter NATO by bringing the Soviet bloc countries together in a formal alliance, the Warsaw Pact of 1955, which provided for a joint military command and mutual military assistance. This pact established a new basis for the continuing presence of Soviet troops in the satellite states, but the Soviet-dominated system in east-central Europe had been artificial from the beginning, and tensions quickly surfaced within it.

From the start, Yugoslavia had been a point of particular vulnerability for the Soviet system. Communist-led partisans under Tito had liberated Yugoslavia from the Axis on their own, and they had not needed the Red Army to begin constructing a new communist regime. Tito was willing to work with the Soviets, but because he had his own legitimacy, he could be considerably more independent than those elsewhere whose power rested on Soviet support. Thus the Soviets deemed it essential to bring Tito to heel, lest his example encourage too much independence in the other communist states. When Soviet demands, including control of the Yugoslav police and army, became intolerably meddlesome from the Yugoslav point of view, Tito broke with the Soviet Union altogether in 1948. Yugoslavia then began developing a more flexible socialist economic system, with greater scope for local initiatives. Soviet leaders worried that others, too, might seek their own particular directions, causing the Soviet satellite system to fall apart.

The initial response to Tito's defection in 1948 was a crackdown on the potential for independence or opposition throughout the Soviet bloc. In the Soviet Union itself, a major target was the army, which enjoyed great prestige after its victory in World War II. Its top commander, Marshal Zhukov, was reassigned from Berlin to an obscure post. As during the 1930s, Stalin relied especially on the secret police, which executed those suspected of deviation, inspiring fear even among those closest to Stalin.

As arrest and execution of prominent communist leaders continued in the satellite states, opposition strikes and demonstrations developed as well, finally reaching a crisis point in East Germany in 1953. The East German communist leader, Walter Ulbricht (1893–1973), had become worried that the cold war maneuvering of the two superpowers might undercut his regime altogether. As the United States pressed West Germany to rearm and join NATO, some Soviet leaders concluded that a reunified but strictly neutral and disarmed Germany would be better for Soviet security than the integration of West Germany into a military alliance against the Soviet Union. German reunification, however, would entail free elections, which the East German Communists could not hope to win. Seeking to head off any such scenario, Ulbricht intensified the industrial development of East Germany, to make his country too valuable an economic ally for the Soviet Union to sacrifice. The resulting pressure on labor produced growing opposition, which came dramatically to a head in East Berlin in June 1953.

A workers' protest against a provision to increase output or face wage cuts promptly led to political demands, including free elections and the withdrawal of Soviet troops. Disturbances spread from East Berlin to the other major East German cities. Though this spontaneous uprising was not well coordinated, Soviet troops and tanks had to intervene to put down the movement and save the Ulbricht government. The East German example helped stimulate strikes and antigovernment demonstrations elsewhere in the Soviet bloc, convincing Soviet leaders that something had to give. But at this point, shortly after Stalin's death, the leadership of the Soviet Union was still being sorted out.

THE ERA OF THE COLD WAR

1945	Labour victory in Britain
1947	Marshall Plan
1949	Formation of NATO
1951	Formation of the European Coal and Steel Community
1953	Death of Stalin
1953	Workers' revolt in East Germany
1955	West Germany joins NATO
1955	Warsaw Pact
1956	Khrushchev speech to the twentieth party congress
1956	Suez crisis
1956	Hungarian reform movement crushed
1957	Sputnik I launched
1957	Treaty of Rome establishes Common Market
1958	Beginning of Fifth Republic under de Gaulle
1959	Bad Godesberg conference: reorientation of German socialism
1961	Berlin Wall erected
1962	Cuban missile crisis
1964	Ouster of Nikita Khrushchev
1968	Days of May uprising in France
1968	Prague Spring reform movement crushed
1969	Willy Brandt becomes West German chancellor
1973	First OPEC oil crisis begins
1978	Kidnapping and assassination of Aldo Moro in Italy

De-Stalinization Under Khrushchev

Although a struggle for the succession followed Stalin's death, the nature of the struggle itself portended some departure from the extremes of Stalinism. The political infighting entailed a reasonable degree of give and take, as opposed to terror and violence. To be sure, the contestants quickly ganged up on the hated secret police chief, Lavrenti Beria, who was tried and executed in a matter of months, but this was part of their agreed-upon effort to limit the role of the secret police. Moreover, although one of the eventual losers was sent to Siberia to run a power station, and another was made ambassador to Outer Mongolia, it was a major departure that the winner, Nikita Khrushchev, had neither of them exiled or executed.

Although he had not been Stalin's heir apparent, Khrushchev gradually established himself as the new leader by building up patronage networks and playing off factions. Slightly crude, even something of a buffoon, he won out by 1955 partly because his opponents repeatedly underestimated him. Although his period of leadership was brief, it was eventful indeed—and was in some ways the best hope the Soviet system was to have.

At a closed session of the Soviet Communist party's twentieth national congress in February 1956, Khrushchev made a dramatic late-night speech denouncing the "cult of personality" that had developed around Stalin and the criminal excesses that had been central to the Stalinist system (see the box, "Denouncing the Crimes of Stalinism"). Khrushchev's immediate aim was to undercut his hard-line rivals, but he also insisted that key features of Stalinism had amounted to an unnecessary deviation from Marxism-Leninism. So the advent of Khrushchev suggested there might be liberalization and reform.

At the same time, however, the growing popular discontent in the satellite states placed the whole system in crisis. In the face of the East German uprising of 1953, the Soviets backed off from hard-line Stalinism, making room for more moderate communists they had previously shunned, like the Hungarian Imre Nagy (1896–1958) and the Pole Wladislaw Gomulka (1905–1982). Khrushchev even sought to patch things up with Tito, exchanging visits with him in 1955 and 1956. In his speech to the party congress in 1956, Khrushchev condemned Stalin's treatment of Tito and suggested that different countries might take different routes to communism.

To keep their new system together, the Soviets apparently had to allow greater flexibility among the satellite states. But could liberalization be contained within the larger framework of Soviet leadership, or were openness and innovation bound to threaten the system itself? In Poland beginning in June 1956, strikes against wage cuts took on a political character, finally provoking the intervention of Soviet troops by October. Nonetheless, the Soviets found they could work with the moderate communist Gomulka, who favored reform within Poland but was quite loyal to the Warsaw Pact as a bulwark against Germany. By the fall of 1956, however, the events in Poland had helped stimulate comparable demonstrations in Hungary, where reformers led by the moderate communist Nagy took advantage of the liberalizing atmosphere by mid-1956 to begin making dramatic changes.

The Hungarians dismantled their collective farms and moved toward a multiparty system and democratic coalition government. Then they called for Soviet troops to withdraw, enabling Hungary to exit the Warsaw Pact and become neutral. These were not changes within the system, but changes that would undermine the system itself. So when a democratic coalition government was set up by November, the Soviets finally used tanks to crush the Hungarian reform movement. Thousands were killed during the fighting or executed in the aftermath, and 200,000 Hungarians fled to the West.

Yet even the crackdown in Hungary did not mean a return to the old days of Stalinist rigidity throughout the Soviet bloc. The Soviets understood that the system had to become more palatable, but they had made it clear to would-be reformers that liberalization had to be kept within certain limits and not challenge the system itself, especially communist monopoly rule and the Warsaw Pact.

Hungary's new leader, János Kádár (b. 1912), collectivized agriculture more fully than before, but he also engineered a measure of economic decentralization, allowing scope for local initiatives and market mechanisms. There was eventually an amnesty for political prisoners, as well as considerable liberalization in cultural life, so that Hungary came to enjoy freer contact with the West than the other satellites.

Even where hard-liners remained predominant, as in East Germany and Romania, differences arose. Although Romania under Nicolae Ceausescu (1918–1989) remained one of the most repressive communist states, it grew relatively independent from the Soviet Union in matters of foreign and economic policy. And Ceausescu fostered autonomy by playing up the ethnic difference between the Romanians, Latin in background, and the Slavic peoples of much of the Soviet bloc.

In light of East Germany's special situation, on the other hand, its communist leaders had every reason *not* to try to distance themselves from the Soviets by playing up nationalism and distinctiveness. Walter Ulbricht, who remained in power until his retirement in 1971, concentrated on central planning and heavy industry in orthodox fashion, but he made the East German economy the most successful in the Soviet bloc.

Still, because that economic growth was built on low wages, East German workers were tempted to emigrate to West Germany as the West German economic miracle gleamed ever brighter during the fifties. The special situation of Berlin, in the heart of East Germany yet still divided among the occupying powers, made such emigration relatively easy, and 2.6 million East Germans left for the West between 1950 and 1962.

Denouncing the Crimes of Stalinism

In his speech to the Soviet Communist party's national congress in 1956, Nikita Khrushchev repeatedly contrasted Stalin with Lenin, seeking to make it clear that Stalinism had been an unfortunate and unnecessary deviation, not the logical outcome of the communist revolution. Khrushchev's denunciation of Stalin produced considerable commotion in the hall.

. . . [I]t is impermissible and foreign to the spirit of Marxism-Leninism to elevate one person, to transform him into a superman possessing supernatural characteristics. . . .

Such a belief about a man, and specifically about Stalin, was cultivated among us for many years. . . .

While ascribing great importance to the role of the leaders and organizers of the masses, Lenin at the same time mercilessly stigmatized every manifestation of the cult of the individual. . . .

Stalin originated the concept "enemy of the people." . . . [T]his term made possible . . . the most cruel repression, violating all norms of revolutionary legality, against anyone who in any way disagreed with Stalin, against those who were only suspected of hostile intent, against those who had bad reputations. . . . In the main . . . the only proof of guilt used, against all norms of current legal science, was the "confession" of the accused himself; and, as subsequent probing proved, "confessions" were acquired through physical torture against the accused. . . .

Arbitrary behavior by one person encouraged and permitted arbitrariness in others. Mass arrests and deportations of many thousands of people, execution without trial and without normal investigation created conditions of insecurity, fear and even desperation. . . .

Lenin used severe methods only in the most necessary cases, when the exploiting classes were still in existence and were vigorously opposing the revolution. . . .

Source: The Anti-Stalin Campaign and International Communism: A Selection of Documents, edited by the Russian Institute, Columbia University (New York, Columbia University Press, 1956), pp. 2, 4, 12–14, 17.

With a population of only 17.1 million, East Germany could not afford to let this hemorrhaging continue. Thus, in August 1961 the Ulbricht regime erected the infamous Berlin Wall, a looming reminder that despite periodic thaws in East-West relations, the iron curtain remained in place and the cold war continued to define the era.

From Liberalization to Stagnation

The most intense phase of the cold war ended with the death of Stalin in 1953. In his speech to the twentieth party congress in 1956, Khrushchev repudiated the previous Soviet tenet that the very existence of Western capitalist imperialism made a military showdown with the communist world inevitable. Both sides began talking of "peaceful coexistence." Despite summit conferences and sporadic efforts at better relations, however, friction between the Soviet Union and the United States continued.

Indeed, a new peak of tension was reached in October 1962 when the Soviets placed missiles in Cuba, which had developed close ties with the Soviet Union after the 1959 revolution led by Fidel Castro (b. 1926). Although the United States had offensive missiles in Turkey, adjacent to the Soviet Union, the Soviet attempt to base missiles in Cuba seemed to the United States an intolerable challenge. Military confrontation seemed a distinct possibility, but President John Kennedy (1917–1963) managed an effective combination of resistance and restraint in responding to the Soviet move. Finally, the Soviets withdrew their missiles in exchange for a U.S. promise not to seek to overthrow the communist government in Cuba. The outcome was essentially a victory for the United States, which retained its offensive missile capacity adjacent to the Soviet Union. The Cuban missile crisis was the closest the superpowers came to armed confrontation during the cold war period.

At the same time, it became increasingly clear that international communism was not the monolithic force it had once seemed. The most dramatic indication was the Sino-Soviet split, which developed during the fifties as the Chinese communists solidified their regime. In the long struggle that led to their victory in 1949, the Chinese communists had often had no choice but to go their own way, and during the 1940s, especially, Stalin had been quite willing to subordinate any concern for their cause to Soviet national interests. After taking power in 1949, the Chinese communists pursued their own path to development, without worrying about the Soviet model. With some justification, the Soviets feared that the independent, innovative Chinese might be prepared to challenge Soviet leadership in international communism. By the early sixties, Chinese communism proved appealing especially in the non-Western world, though it attracted dissident communists in the West as well. The split within world communism, and the antagonism between China and the Soviet Union, added another layer of uncertainty to the cold war era.

As a domestic leader, Khrushchev proved mercurial and erratic, but he was an energetic innovator, willing to experiment. He jettisoned the worst features of the police state apparatus, including some of the infamous Siberian prison camps, and offered several amnesties for prisoners. He also liberalized cultural life and gave workers greater freedom to move from one job to another. The economic planning apparatus was decentralized somewhat, affording more scope for local initiatives and placing greater emphasis on consumer goods. The government expanded medical and educational facilities and, between 1955 and 1964, doubled the nation's housing stock, substantially alleviating a severe housing shortage.

Although living standards remained low, Khrushchev's reforms helped produce a noticeable improvement in the lives of ordinary people by the early 1960s. Even his claim in 1961 that the Soviet Union would surpass the Western standard of living within twenty years did not seem an idle boast. After all, the Soviets had launched *Sputnik I* in 1957, assuming the lead in the ensuing space race. They followed by putting the first human being in space in 1961. Such achievements suggested that even ordinary Soviet citizens had reason for optimism.

Although Khrushchev had some important successes to his credit, he also made enemies with his erratic reform effort, and this led to his ouster and forced retirement in October 1964. After the unending experiment in the economy, his opponents wanted to consolidate, to return to stability and predictability. But not until 1968 did it become clear that the liberalization and innovation of the Khrushchev era were over.

By early 1968 a significant reform movement had developed within the Communist party in Prague, the capital of Czechoslovakia. Determined to avoid the fate of the Hungarian effort in 1956, the reformers emphasized that Czechoslovakia was to remain a communist state and a full member of the Warsaw Pact. But within that framework, they felt, it should be possible to invite freer cultural expression, to democratize procedures within the Communist party, and to broaden participation in public life.

However, efforts to reassure the Soviets about the limits of the reform movement's aims alienated some of its supporters, who stepped up their demands as a result. As earlier in Hungary, the demand for change seemed to outstrip the intentions of the movement's organizers. Finally, Soviet leaders in Moscow decided to crack down. In August 1968, Soviet tanks moved into Prague to crush the reform movement, precisely what its leaders had been seeking to avoid.

The end of the "Prague Spring" closed the era of relative flexibility and cautious innovation in the Soviet bloc that had begun as early as 1953. A period of relative stagnation followed under Leonid Brezhnev (1906–1982), a careful, consensus-seeking bureaucrat. Although efforts toward détente and arms control made news during the seventies, the Soviets found it ever harder to match the West in economic growth and technological innovation.

The End of the Prague Spring In Prague in August 1968, Soviet tanks crush the reform movement in communist Czechoslovakia that had flowered that spring. This outcome dashed hopes for liberalization within the Soviet Bloc. *(Sygma)*

Democracy and Its Discontents, 1968 and After

A kind of breaking point was reached in 1968 in Western Europe as well. On one level, democracy had succeeded remarkably, but by the late sixties it became clear that political alienation had been building up beneath the surface of prosperity and stability. This dissatisfaction now erupted, surprising the many observers who had overestimated the solidity of the new democracy. Although new economic difficulties beginning in 1973 also affected the European political mood, the breaking point was reached earlier, when prosperity was at its height.

The shock waves from the movements of protest that began in 1968 continued throughout the seventies, as new issues came to the fore, and new political alignments and forms of political action developed. Expectations had been raised, so that while reform efforts accomplished a good deal, the level of alienation remained high. As the new politics sometimes turned to terrorist violence, the ability of governments to keep order became a major issue, and it sometimes seemed that the postwar political consensus, the basis for two decades of success since the war, was about to come apart.

1968–1973: New Strains in West European Politics

The most dramatic eruption of radical political protest was the "Days of May" uprising that shook France during May 1968. Although it did not have the revolutionary consequences that seemed possible at first, it finally forced de Gaulle's resignation in 1969, and it proved a watershed for the political left in France and elsewhere.

The movement was partly a reaction against the priorities of de Gaulle's Fifth Republic—especially the preoccupation with France's international role. But it was also a response to the unevenness in the modernization effort that had seemed necessary to support that role. The commitment to technocratic values had produced impressive economic growth, but many felt left out as France's economic success became more visible. Despite all the growth, public services had been neglected, and problems in such areas as housing and education continued—or even worsened.

The French university system affords a telling example. Enrollment in French universities more than doubled between 1939 and 1960, then more than doubled again between 1960 and 1967. Apart from a few highly selective *grandes écoles,* the institutions of the state-run university system were open to anyone who passed the same exam, and it was not considered politically feasible to limit enrollments by restricting access. Instead, the government tried to build to keep up with demand—thereby creating vast, impersonal institutions with professors and administrators increasingly inaccessible to students. But overcrowding persisted, and the value of a university degree diminished, leaving students with uncertain job prospects.

The uprising of 1968 started with university students, who sought to reach out to others, especially industrial workers, by framing their critiques of the system very broadly. But though the movement grew strong enough to shake the government, it did not focus discontents as effectively as it might have. Above all, the failure of working class and union activists to rally behind the student cause limited the movement's effectiveness.

Although the students themselves settled for relatively limited concessions, the student rising brought home to the government that the university system needed a complete overhaul—and that faculty and students had to be involved in the changes. Over the next several years, the Education Ministry spearheaded a significant reform effort, breaking existing institutions into smaller units, with more local control over budgets and instructional methods. At the same time, however, faculty and student participation in institutional governance tended to politicize French universities, some of which became communist strongholds, others strongholds of the right. And this caused friction with the education bureaucrats in Paris.

In Italy, comparable frustration with the political system developed during the sixties, as little seemed to result from the decade's great hope for renewal, the "opening to the left," which brought the Socialists into governments led by the Christian Democrats. And as in France, that frustration produced a powerful wave of radicalism by the end of the sixties, although in Italy its major manifestations were different. Most notable was the labor militancy that developed during the "hot autumn" of 1969 and continued into the early seventies.

Especially in the industrial sectors of northern Italy, this wave of strikes and other labor actions was notable for the novelty of its methods and demands. The workers sought not just higher wages but power over the organization of work in the factory, even a major say in the investment decisions of the companies involved. Moreover, the working-class rank and file often took the initiative in these labor actions, reflecting a new determination to do things themselves, without waiting for the established leftist parties or trade unions to call the shots. Those institutions had come to seem simply large, unresponsive bureaucracies like the others.

By the early seventies, the workers had won considerable power, and their innovations attracted the interest of the left in countries all over Europe. As the economic climate steadily deteriorated after 1973, however, the employers gradually regained the initiative. By the end of the decade, the workers again found themselves on the defensive.

At first glance, the parties of the Marxist left might appear the likely beneficiaries of the popular discontent that came to the surface during the late 1960s. But in France the effort to draw the lessons of 1968 deepened divisions within the Communist party and initiated a growing disenchantment with Marxism among French intellectuals. French communism seemed old and stale to many of those, especially young people, who believed the promise of 1968 could still be translated into substantial change. On the other hand, the French Socialist party, overshadowed by the communists since the war, gained dramatically during the 1970s as it claimed the mantle of the new left that had emerged in 1968. The situation in Italy was more complex, but the forms of protest in 1969 indicated growing alienation from a political establishment that now seemed to include the established left.

The Oil Crisis and the Changing Economic Framework

As the political situation in Western Europe became more volatile, events outside Europe made it clear how interdependent the world had become—and that the West did not hold all the trump cards. In the fall of 1973, Egypt and Syria attacked Israel, seeking to undo the losses they had suffered in a brief war in 1967. Although the assault failed, the Arab nations of the oil-rich Middle East came together in the aftermath to retaliate against the Western bloc for supporting Israel. By restricting the output and distribution of the oil they controlled, the Arab-led Organization of Petroleum Exporting Countries (OPEC) produced a sharp increase in oil prices and a severe economic disruption in Western Europe, which was heavily dependent on Middle Eastern oil. By January 1975 the price of oil was six times what it had been in 1973, before the embargo, and this increase remained a source of inflationary pressure throughout the Western world until the early 1980s.

The immediate European response to the oil embargo dramatized the limits of the economic integration so far achieved through the Common Market. When OPEC imposed especially harsh measures on the Netherlands, which had taken a strong stand in support of Israel, the other nations of the Common Market dealt separately with the cartel rather than stand together.

The 1970s proved to be an unprecedented period of "stagflation"—sharply reduced rates of growth combined with inflation and rising unemployment. The economic miracle that had transformed much of Western Europe had clearly ended, partly because the European economies were subject to growing competition from non-Western countries, most notably Japan. Everywhere the labor movement was on the defensive in light of increasing global competition, techno-

Oil, the West, and the World Spearheaded by several oil-rich Arab states, OPEC drove up world oil prices by restricting production during the 1970s. The power of the oil cartel made it clear that decisions by non-Westerners could vitally affect the industrialized West. OPEC delegates are shown here in Algiers in 1975. *(Sygma)*

logical change, and high unemployment. These more difficult economic circumstances deepened the disaffection evident by the late 1960s and intensified the challenge to the democratic political order.

Democracy in the Fragile Seventies

How adaptable were the postwar democracies in Germany, France, and Italy? In Germany, the Socialists had clearly been integrated into a modified two-party system as a governing party by the mid-seventies. In France and Italy, in contrast, the left sought ways to escape what seemed increasingly sterile opposition. Yet in each country there were also questions about the legitimacy or viability of the ruling conservatives.

In France, the first question was whether the unique persona of Charles de Gaulle was necessary to the functioning of the Fifth Republic, and even to the cohesion of the conservative coalition that had governed France since 1958. Even before de Gaulle's retirement in 1969, his eventual successor, Georges Pompidou (1911–1974), worked to move the informal Gaullist party, and the regime itself, away from exclusive identification with de Gaulle. And beginning in 1969, the steady leadership of Pompidou and his successor cemented both the legitimacy of the Fifth Republic and the ongoing role of the Gaullist coalition. To be sure, the conservative Gaullists became increasingly unpopular during the troubled 1970s and were at last defeated in 1981. But the alternative to them emerged from within the Fifth Republic and did not challenge the system itself. The system survived the departure of de Gaulle and established its ongoing legitimacy.

The situation in Italy was more dramatic. The severity of the economic downturn and the growth of terrorism produced a genuine crisis of the Italian state by the mid-seventies, yet the dominant Christian Democrats seemed increasingly concerned with shortsighted political patronage and dealing. Italian public life desperately needed revitalization, yet only the Communists seemed strong enough to provide an alternative, or at least some novel departure. Since the war, the Communists had done well at organization and governance on the local and regional levels, so they had gradually built up a significant measure of credibility in postwar Italian life. In the parliamentary elections of 1976 they won 34.4 percent of the vote, a new high.

Seeking to translate that support into a more significant national role, the Communists under Enrico Berlinguer (1922–1984) offered what they called a "historic compromise." Although they knew this strategy would alienate their more militant followers, they offered to participate in a coalition government with the Christian Democrats, sharing responsibility for the measures necessary to deal with the growing emergency. But though there was much negotiation and talk, the Christian Democrats outmaneuvered the Communists, who got little for their willingness to compromise.

Although Italians welcomed Communist effectiveness in local government, many were reluctant to entrust the Communists with power on the national level. The Communists' aims for the longer term remained unclear. Moreover, a Communist role in the national government would surely raise questions about Italy's place in NATO.

The fruitlessness of the historic compromise strategy led Italian communism to an impasse by the end of the 1970s. Support among younger people and intellectuals declined noticeably, and the Communist party's share of the vote in national elections fell from its 1976 peak. But if communism, for better or worse, could not mount a credible strategy for revitalizing Italian politics, Italy seemed stuck with an endless reshuffling of ministries dominated by Christian Democrats, a system that looked unstable on the surface but that was in fact stagnant, breeding increasing political alienation and cynicism.

Across Western Europe during the 1970s, frustration with the political immobility that seemed even to have neutralized the established left gave rise to novel forms of political action, some extreme and violent. Terrorism grew to alarming proportions, especially in Italy and Germany, reaching a peak in 1977 and 1978. Terrorists in such groups as the Red Brigades in Italy and the Baader-Meinhof gang in Germany assassinated a number of prominent public officials and businessmen, including the long-time Italian Christian Democratic leader Aldo Moro (1916–1978). By the late seventies, left- and right-wing extremism fed each other, and it was right-wing terrorists who were responsible for the worst episode of the era, a bombing in the railway station in Bologna, Italy, that killed eighty-five people in August 1980.

But political frustration also found more productive outlets, as new coalitions developed around newly politicized issues—from abortion to the environment—that had not been associated with the Marxist left. In Italy, initiatives from below led to popular referenda on particular issues—which offered a way of breaking the stranglehold of the Christian Democrats and the other political parties. Use of the referendum tactic forced the Italian parliament to enact one of the most liberal abortion laws in Europe in 1978.

In Germany, the Green movement formed by peace and environmental activists during the late 1970s took pains to avoid acting like a conventional party. Concerned that Germany, with its central location, would end up the devastated battleground in any superpower confrontation, the Greens opposed deployment of additional U.S. missiles on German soil and called for an alternative to the endless arms race. The SPD, as the governing party in an important NATO state, seemed unable to confront this issue effectively and lost members as a result.

Re-evaluating the Welfare State

Governments all over Western Europe accepted greater responsibility for social welfare after the war. Much publicity surrounded the British welfare state, but by the early 1970s the percentage of the British economy devoted to public expenditure for welfare, public housing, and education—18.2 percent—was about average for the industrialized nations of the West. Sweden had the highest figure at 23.7 percent.

In Sweden, as in Britain, the economy remained fundamentally capitalist, based on private ownership; its nationalized, or government-run, sector was not large by European standards. But the system of social insurance in Sweden was the most extensive in Europe, and the government worked actively with business to promote full employment and to steer the economy in directions deemed socially desirable. Moreover, the welfare state came to mean a major role for the Swedish trade unions, which won relatively high wages for workers and even enjoyed a quasi veto power over legislation.

Government welfare measures were costly. By the early seventies, 40 percent of Sweden's national income went for taxes to finance the system—the highest rate of taxation in the world. And in Sweden as elsewhere the economic strains of the 1970s made the welfare state harder to manage. By the mid-seventies, moreover, there were growing doubts that a welfare state could nurture the initiative and productivity needed for success in the increasingly competitive global economy. Sweden rather suddenly found itself less competitive, both because its wages were so high and because it was not keeping abreast of technological developments. Swedish efforts to adjust to the changing circumstances simply accelerated the dissolution of the postwar consensus around the welfare state. By 1980, unemployment and efforts to cut government spending led to the most severe labor unrest the country had experienced since the war.

In Britain, a dramatic assault on the welfare state developed at the same time. Until the early 1970s, Britain retained the consensus on the government's role in social welfare that had emerged with the end of the war. The Conservatives had accepted the essentials of the system when they returned to power from 1951 to 1964. But that consensus began to come apart during the 1970s.

During the first two decades after the war, the British economy grew at an annual rate of only 2.8 percent, less than half the rate in Germany and Italy. Even as growth slowed all over Western Europe during the mid-seventies, the British economy continued to lag, still growing at less than half the average rate of the other industrial democracies. Between 1968 and 1976, the country lost 1 million manufacturing jobs. By the mid-seventies economic decline threatened to shatter Britain's postwar settlement, because there was no consensus over how to apportion the pain of the greater austerity that the situation seemed to demand.

During the 1970s, each of Britain's two major political parties made a serious effort to deal with the situation, but neither proved effective. The Conservatives got their chance between 1970 and 1974 with the government of Edward Heath (b. 1916), whose failure is especially significant because he was an energetic moderate with a good deal of technocratic expertise. Whatever he tried provoked widespread strikes in response; a major miners' strike was the immediate cause of his electoral defeat in 1974.

But Labour did no better when its turn came from 1974 to 1979. Government efforts to limit wage increases soon produced an open rupture with the unions. A wave of strikes during the winter of 1978 and 1979 battered the government, contributing to its defeat by the Conservatives in the elections of 1979. The growing split between the Labour party and the trade-union movement made the party's future course uncertain.

The Conservatives, on the other hand, were prepared to offer Britain a decided change in direction by 1979. With the defeat of the moderate Heath in 1974, the Conservative party moved to the right, away from consensus over the welfare state. The election of the militantly conservative Margaret Thatcher (b. 1925) as party leader in 1975 was a turning point. When she became prime minister in 1979, it was clear that Britain had embarked on a radically different course.

Summary

The bipolar framework of the years from 1949 to 1980 limited the political options of the nations in both halves of the newly divided Europe. The result was an uneasy stability throughout the period. In Western Europe, that stability helped democracy take firm root. The more delimited international role meant that certain kinds of questions that had proven especially divisive between the wars did not come up. An exception was the Algerian question for France, which proved a serious threat to French democracy. But that was a legacy of the older colonialism, and de Gaulle had the skill and the prestige to remove the issue from center stage while maintaining a democratic framework. Although some variation proved possible for the nations of the Soviet bloc, the monolithic unity demanded by communism imposed stability in a potentially volatile part of Europe, especially by keeping long-standing ethnic rivalries in check.

In Western Europe the shared experience of wartime led to a new social compact based on greater government responsibility for social welfare. That consensus provided a foundation for democracy, which became solidly established in Western Europe during the first two decades after the war. Moreover, the implicit promise of growing prosperity for all made possible greater cooperation between business and labor.

By 1968, however, strains began to appear, and slower economic growth during the 1970s jeopardized the postwar settlement. Even in the context of increasing prosperity, a diffuse discontent had developed among many Western Europeans, who felt left out as the real decisions were made by party leaders, technocratic planners, EEC Eurocrats, or the executives of multinational corporations, beyond the purview of genuinely democratic institutions. Thus the quest for new forms of political participation that began in 1968 and continued throughout the 1970s.

The bipolar world rested on a kind of balance between the superpowers. And though significant political discontents surfaced in both halves of divided Europe in 1968, Western Europe came to take for granted a substantial measure of prosperity and political legitimacy, while Eastern Europe was not so fortunate. That imbalance threatened to undermine the uneasy stability that characterized the era from 1949 to the end of the 1970s.

Suggested Reading

General Surveys

Kesselman, Mark, et al. *European Politics in Transition.* 1987. A superior text on postwar European politics, with separate sections on Britain, France, West Germany, Italy, Sweden, and the Soviet Union.

Laqueur, Walter. *Europe in Our Time: A History, 1945–1992.* 1992. A comprehensive, well-balanced survey by a leading authority on twentieth-century Europe.

Cultural and Intellectual History

Hughes, H. Stuart. *Between Commitment and Disillusion: The Obstructed Path and the Sea Change, 1930–1965.* 1987. New edition of two previously published works by an influential intellectual historian. *The Sea Change* covers the intellectual migration from Europe to America.

Stromberg, Roland N. *After Everything: Western Intellectual History Since 1945.* 1975. A survey, good on the forties and fifties, less sympathetic on the innovations of the later sixties and thereafter.

Restabilization and Economic Growth

Hogan, Michael J. *The Marshall Plan: America, Britain, and the Reconstruction of Western Europe, 1947–1952.*

1987. Concerned especially with U.S. policy toward Europe; emphasizes the American desire for a neocapitalist world system based on free trade.

Kuisel, Richard F. *Capitalism and the State in Modern France: Renovation and Economic Management in the Twentieth Century.* 1981. A careful and thorough study tracing the emergence of economic planning and a technocratic ethos in France.

Maier, Charles S. *In Search of Stability.* 1987. A collection of essays on the wider sociopolitical context of economic policies in the twentieth century. Several of the essays contrast the two postwar periods in illuminating ways.

Milward, Alan S. *The Reconstruction of Western Europe, 1945–51.* 1984. An influential account that emphasizes the importance of European initiatives, as opposed to American help, in making the postwar economic boom so durable.

Postwar Government and Politics

Bark, Dennis L., and David R. Gress. *A History of West Germany.* Vol. 1: *From Shadow to Substance, 1945–1963;* vol. 2: *Democracy and Its Discontents, 1963–1988.* 1989. Offers a favorable account of West Germany's democracy and its Atlantic and European roles in the face of ongoing suspicion and criticism.

Ginsbourg, Paul. *A History of Contemporary Italy: Society and Politics, 1943–1988.* 1990. A comprehensive survey especially good on the radical postwar socioeconomic transformation in Italy.

Lacouture, Jean. *De Gaulle.* Vol. 2: *The Ruler, 1945–1970.* 1991. A readable account of de Gaulle's role as French political leader.

Larkin, Maurice. *France Since the Popular Front: Government and People, 1936–1986.* 1988. A comprehensive survey that focuses on the interaction between political life and socioeconomic change.

Morgan, Kenneth O. *The People's Peace: British History 1945–1990.* 1992. A thorough survey that seeks to avoid overemphasis on decline and pessimism. Accents the relative peace and stability of the period.

Turner, Henry Ashby, Jr. *Germany from Partition to Reunification.* 1992. A fair-minded treatment of both East and West Germany. Explains the collapse of communism in East Germany and reunification.

Europe and the World

DePorte, A. W. *Europe Between the Superpowers: The Enduring Balance.* 2d ed. 1986. An excellent analysis of the cold war framework. Emphasizes the importance of the division of Germany, which provided the foundation for the tense period of bipolar peace that followed the war.

Hanrieder, Wolfram F. *Germany, America, Europe: Forty Years of German Foreign Policy.* Updated ed. 1991. A major work on the place of West Germany in the cold war era. Updated edition considers the import of German reunification.

Holland, R. F. *European Decolonization, 1918–1981: An Introductory Survey.* 1985. A sensitive survey. Comprehensive but gives particular attention to the British experience.

Mommsen, Wolfgang J., and Jürgen Osterhammel, eds. *Imperialism and After: Continuities and Discontinuities.* 1986. A collection of essays by leading scholars. Analyzes the informal means through which European influence continued even after the end of formal imperial control.

European Integration and the Common Market

Brinkley, Douglas, and Clifford Hackett, eds. *Jean Monnet: The Path to European Unity.* 1991. A collection of essays on Monnet's central role in the movement toward European integration after World War II.

Hackett, Clifford. *Cautious Revolution: The European Community Arrives.* 1990. An effective blend of history with prescription, suggesting how the European Community could become capable of unified political decision.

Pinder, John. *European Community: The Building of a Union.* 1991. Combines a historical account of the development of EC institutions with a balanced assessment of the prospects for full-fledged European federation.

The Soviet Union and the Soviet Bloc

Hosking, Geoffrey. *The First Socialist Society: A History of the Soviet Union from Within.* Enlarged ed. 1990. Looks at family, religion, nationality, and the experience of factory workers in an effort to portray the lives of ordinary Soviet citizens.

Linden, Carl A. *Khrushchev and the Soviet Leadership: With an Epilogue on Gorbachev.* Updated ed. 1990. Especially good on the internal political maneuvering that eventually led to Khrushchev's ouster. Includes a useful epilogue on the course from Khrushchev's ambiguous legacy to Gorbachev's reform effort.

Rothschild, Joseph. *Return to Diversity: A Political History of East Central Europe Since World War II.* 1989. A straightforward survey that makes sense of the differences as well as the similarities among the Soviet bloc countries during the cold war.

Stokes, Gale, ed. *From Stalinism to Pluralism: A Documentary History of Eastern Europe Since 1945.* 1991. A collection of documents, with effective commentaries. Includes the disintegration of communism in 1989 and the immediate aftermath.

Ulam, Adam. *Expansion and Coexistence: A History of Soviet Foreign Policy, 1917–1967.* 2d ed. 1974. A major survey of Soviet foreign policy, especially strong on the fifties and sixties. Unsympathetic to the Soviet Union but also critical of the U.S. response.

Weighing the Evidence

THEATER OF THE ABSURD

Characters in garbage cans. A toy dog with three legs. Ragged, clownlike protagonists confined to a room with windows so high they would have to climb a ladder to see out of them. Hamm, the master, can't stand up. Clov, his servant, can't sit down. An absurd scenario—but that's the point. These scenes from Samuel Beckett's *Endgame* exemplify the dramatic form that became well known during the 1950s as Theater of the Absurd. But why present absurdity on stage? Why did some of Europe's most gifted writers choose to write absurdist drama at this point in the history of Western civilization?

When *Endgame* was first performed in London in 1957, the Irish-born Beckett was already well known for his *Waiting for Godot*, which had premiered in Paris four years earlier. Although he had written some important fiction before the war, these plays established him as one of the leading avant-garde writers in Europe. Among absurdist playwrights, only the Romanian-born French writer Eugène Ionesco was as influential as Beckett.

HAMM:
(Pause.)
What time is it?
CLOV:
The same as usual. . . .
HAMM:
Apart from that, how do you feel?
CLOV:
I don't complain.
HAMM:
You feel normal?
CLOV *(irritably)*:
I tell you I don't complain.
HAMM:
I feel a little queer.
(Pause.)
Clov!
CLOV:
Yes.
HAMM:
Have you not had enough?
CLOV:
Yes!
(Pause)
Of what?
HAMM
Of this . . . this . . . thing.
CLOV:
I always had.
(Pause.)
Not you?
HAMM *(gloomily)*:
Then there's no reason for it to change.
CLOV:
It may end.
(Pause.)
All life long the same questions, the same answers.

Theater of the Absurd was often funny, but in Beckett's plays especially, the humor is grim, self-conscious, pathetic. *Endgame* presents the winding-down of a civilization reduced to a few ludicrous remnants as it approaches its end. Writing in the 1950s, during the early years of the nuclear era, Beckett associated the approaching end with images of nuclear war, but the absurdity of the human condition in the play is not simply the result of the nuclear threat. Indeed, *Endgame* suggests that it might better for the human race to die out altogether.

Whatever its ending might entail, the culture Beckett portrays is worn-out and exhausted. Once-sustaining values like friendship, love, beauty, and order have decayed, become hollow, merely empty words. Beckett suggests that we have come late, that there is nothing we can really believe in, nothing meaningful for us to do. Yet the characters in *Endgame* are reluctant to let go, so they drag it out, absurdly, pathetically, self-consciously going through the motions.

Hamm, the master, takes some satisfaction in manipulating the husks of his worn-out culture, especially in the rhetorical games he plays as he makes up an absurd, endless story. His servant, Clov, plays along, but in a resigned, cynical spirit, lamenting the dreary repetition: "All life long the same questions, the same answers." "Why this farce, day after day?"[1] But his absurd interdependence with Hamm keeps him playing along.

The deadly sameness is punctuated by efforts to create order or find meaning that are themselves comic, absurd. At one point Hamm proposes that a rational observer, watching them long enough, might understand what human life

1. All excerpts from Samuel Beckett, *Endgame* (New York: Grove Press, 1958). Used by permission.

is all about, might even conclude that it has some purpose—so "perhaps it won't all have been for nothing." But then Clov has a flea, and then Hamm has to correct Clov's syntax, and then Hamm enjoys the momentary satisfaction of urinating. Again and again the notion that things might have meaning, or make sense, falls away, recognized as having been a ludicrous idea in the first place.

But though time itself seems to have flattened into a static sameness, late in the play the characters finally face the possibility of the end. Clov at last envisions leaving, ending his tortuous interdependence with Hamm. But the end would entail only the bleakest sort of deliverance: "I open the door of the cell and go. I am so bowed I see only my feet, if I open my eyes, and between my legs a little trail of black dust. I say to myself the earth is extinguished though I never saw it lit." Perhaps to leave is simply to abandon for good our traditional values and beliefs, so that at last we quit tormenting ourselves with them. Clov would leave trailing their black ashes. Yet there is nothing outside—nothing, perhaps, but death itself. Or to end may mean starting over, but would the new world be any better, or would it end up turning in the same absurd groove?

Even as Beckett was writing, not everyone saw the human condition—or the state of Western civilization—in such bleak terms. The early 1950s saw a religious revival throughout the Western world, and even intellectuals who accepted absurdist premises found more reason for hope than Beckett did. Albert Camus emphasized that we human beings make the world meaningful, and human life valuable, precisely as we come together to do what we can in the face of a world that never quite makes sense to us. Still others simply sought to get down to the practical tasks at hand. The year that saw the first performance of *Endgame,* 1957, also saw the launching of the Common Market, which the practical visionary Jean Monnet viewed as a new beginning for Western Europe.

Hamm (seated) and Clov *(Photo Pic/The Billy Rose Theatre Collection/The New York Public Library for the Performing Arts)*

Yet Beckett's plays have reached a wide audience, and many whose sense of the world is not ultimately so bleak have found the theatrical experience he offers deeply significant, even strangely satisfying. Perhaps Beckett offers a kind of catharsis, enabling us to come to terms with one side of our cultural experience in light of the disillusionments of the twentieth century. After experiencing Beckett's world, we go on with our lives, defying Beckett's way of portraying what we are doing.

The American poet Archibald MacLeish, speaking in 1969, portrayed Beckett's absurdist vision of the 1950s as a kind of cultural nadir, expressing "the diminishment of man" after all the horrors of the era of the two world wars.[2] Yet the increasing political activism of the 1960s indicated to MacLeish that a new generation all over the Western world was reacting passionately against that sense of diminishment. Despite the disasters of the recent past, there remained much that human beings might do to shape a better world.

2. Archibald MacLeish, "The Revolt of the Diminished Man," *Saturday Review,* June 7, 1969, pp. 16–19, 61.

CHAPTER 32

Europe, the West, and the World in the Late Twentieth Century

Between 1978 and 1982, an array of new leaders broke with familiar patterns and pointed the way, perhaps, to a different future. There was a dramatic change in the papacy in 1978; a militant conservative became British prime minister in 1979; a socialist was elected president of France in 1981. Then the death of Leonid Brezhnev in 1982 opened the way for a reform effort in the Soviet Union that had stunning consequences. At the same time, an unknown electrician in the shipyards of Gdansk, Poland, emerged in 1980 to play a different kind of leadership role, in perhaps the most remarkable story of all. The advent of such new leaders did not present an obvious pattern at first, but within a decade of 1982, Europe and the world had been transformed in a way that would have seemed inconceivable just a few years before.

The postwar order had rested on a kind of balance between the communist states and the capitalist democracies. The East held the immediate military advantage in Europe, but the West had what proved overwhelming advantages in political legitimacy and economic prosperity. These advantages produced increasing imbalance by the 1970s, and during the 1980s the postwar order changed radically as the whole Soviet system unraveled. By 1989 the cold war was coming to a dramatic end, perhaps making possible a different place for Europe in the world.

At the same time, however, the Western democracies were finding it difficult to deal with the unprecedented economic challenges of the late twentieth century. The apparent limits of government power produced

Kaiser Wilhelm Church, Berlin. Bombed in World War II and rebuilt in modern style, incorporating the original tower as a visible reminder of the recent past.

increasing disillusionment with national politics. Some pulled back to emphasize ethnic identity; others looked to supranational organizations like the Common Market, where the key decisions increasingly seemed to be made.

Challenges of Affluence in Western Europe

Despite the setbacks encountered in the 1970s, the postwar economic growth produced increasing prosperity, but also some disruptive changes in patterns of life. And though strong growth returned in much of Western Europe by the early 1980s, it was uneven, confined to certain sectors and regions. By the end of the 1980s, prosperity mixed with ongoing worries about international competition, technological unemployment, and environmental constraints in a small and crowded continent.

Many of the trends important in Europe were visible in the United States during the same period. The widening gap between rich and poor, the weakening of organized labor, the growing prominence of women in the work force, the increasing concern about child care—all were characteristic of Western civilization in general by the late twentieth century. But there were some instructive differences in the ways the different nations of the West dealt with these issues.

The Changing Economies: Prosperity, Imbalance, Limitation

By the early eighties there was greater prosperity in Western Europe, but for a smaller proportion of the people, as unemployment reached levels not seen since the Great Depression. Even after solid growth resumed by 1983, unemployment hovered stubbornly at 9 or 10 percent throughout much of Western Europe, with 13 percent the norm in some older industrial areas. These figures would have seemed unimaginable fifteen years before and were much higher than the rates of 5 to 7 percent typical of the United States during the same period.

The unevenness of prosperity often translated into regional disparity. In both Germany and Britain, economic decline especially afflicted older manufacturing areas in the north, which suffered "deindustrialization" as factories closed and relatively high-paying factory jobs disappeared. Newer, high-technology firms and service industries were more likely to be found in the south—in the Stuttgart area of Germany, for example, or, in Britain, along the M4 corridor, the highway from London west through the rapidly growing triangle of Swindon, Newbury, and Reading.

The advent of new technologies in a context of increasing global competition produced some new winners, but it also entailed worrisome changes in the structure of unemployment. Such technologies created opportunities for new firms able to start from scratch, without the problems of outmoded plant and equipment, or redundant workers, that older competitors faced. A good example was Benetton, an Italian clothing firm founded in 1964 that quickly made good use of computer technology in all aspects of its operation. But Benetton was so successful partly because it needed fewer workers. And, more generally, manufacturing jobs were lost as competition forced the industrial sector to become more efficient through computers and automation. In the Belgian steel industry technological advance cost 25,000 jobs between 1978 and 1985.

Changing labor patterns reinforced the decline of organized labor, which was decidedly on the defensive throughout Western Europe by the 1980s. In Italy, the outcome of a labor dispute with the giant automaker Fiat in 1980 shifted the balance of power decisively back to management and proved a watershed in labor relations. The increasing danger of unemployment undercut the leverage of the unions, but so did more general changes in the Western European economies. As the economy grew more complex, workers were ever less likely to understand themselves as members of a single, unified working class.

The decline of the labor movement was part of a wider deterioration in the prestige of traditional institutions and approaches. One cost of that decline was a kind of alienation, a loss of ties to the community. Though most obvious among unemployed youth in older industrial areas, it was reflected in a more general loss of civility in many reaches of social interaction. One prominent example was the disturbing problem of soccer hooliganism—the drunken, rowdy, often violent behavior of fans behaving almost like street

Overcoming Gender Limitations

The renewed feminism that became prominent by 1970 took inspiration from* The Second Sex*, a pioneering work by the French existentialist Simone de Beauvoir (b. 1908), first published in 1949. Even while valuing sexual difference, she showed the scope for opening the full range of human choices to women.

. . . [T]he nature of things is no more immutably given, once for all, than is historical reality. If woman seems to be the inessential which never becomes the essential, it is because she herself fails to bring about this change. . . .

To decline to be the Other, to refuse to be a party to the deal—this would be for women to renounce all the advantages conferred upon them by their alliance with the superior caste. Man-the-sovereign will provide woman-the-liege with material protection and will undertake the moral justification of her existence; thus she can evade at once both economic risk and the metaphysical risk of a liberty in which ends and aims must be contrived without assistance. Indeed, along with the ethical urge of each individual to affirm his subjective existence, there is also the temptation to forgo liberty and become a thing. . . .

If a caste is kept in a state of inferiority, no doubt it remains inferior; but liberty can break the circle. Let negroes vote, and they become worthy of having the vote; let woman be given responsibilities and she is able to assume them. . . .

. . . [T]here will be some to object that . . . when woman is "the same" as her male, life will lose its salt and spice. . . . [A]ssuredly there are certain forms of the sexual adventure which will be lost in the world of tomorrow. But this does not mean that love, happiness, poetry, dream, will be banished from it.

. . . New relations of flesh and sentiment of which we have no conception will arise between the sexes. . . .

. . . [T]here will always be certain differences between man and woman; her eroticism, and therefore her sexual world, have a special form of their own and therefore cannot fail to engender a sensuality, a sensitivity, of a special nature.

Source: Simone de Beauvoir, *The Second Sex* (New York: Random House Vintage, 1989), pp. xxv, xxvii, 728–731.

gangs. Though especially associated with Britain, the phenomenon grew all over Western Europe during the 1980s. In a particularly ugly incident at an international match in Belgium in 1985, British fans from Liverpool attacked the fans of the opposing Italian team, causing a stadium wall collapse that resulted in thirty-eight deaths.

Critics linked this loss of civility to the values of aggressive market capitalism that set the tone for the 1980s and beyond. The renewed premium on the unbridled pursuit of self-interest seemed to undermine any identification with the larger national community. But even if such diagnosis was convincing, it did not point to a cure.

The Changing Role of Women

Economic change affected social patterns, creating new opportunities but also new challenges for governments. Employment among women had declined after the war with the renewed emphasis on traditional roles. But it began rising steadily during the 1950s, then accelerated during the 1960s. From the early sixties to 1988, the percentage of women aged 25 to 34 in the labor force rose from 38 to 67 in Britain, from 42 to 75 in France, and from 49 to 87 in Germany. The greatest job growth during this period was in the service sector—in government, schools, and hospitals, for example—and many of these new jobs went to women.

The increasing prominence of women in the workplace combined with the more aggressive political consciousness of the late sixties to produce a new feminist movement, comparable to the earlier movement for women's suffrage (see the box, "Overcoming Gender Limitations"). All over Western Europe, feminists forced issues like abortion, day care, and gender discrimination onto the political stage.

In Western Europe, as in the United States, a remarkable baby boom had followed the end of the war and carried into the early 1960s. However, the birthrate declined rapidly thereafter, so that family size diminished markedly by 1990. In Italy, where changes in lifestyle accompanying the new prosperity were especially dramatic, the number of births in 1987 was barely half the number in 1964, when the postwar baby boom reached its peak. Fears about population decline and the need for women to make up the labor shortfall led Western European governments to begin providing for day care to enable women to combine paid employment with raising a family. A national commitment to combine productive working parents with effective development for children seemed the key to future productivity.

France set the pace, making quality day care available to all during the 1980s. Government subsidy kept costs within reach for ordinary working families. In addition, 95 percent of French children aged 3 to 6 were enrolled in the free public nursery schools available by the early 1990s. Comparable figures for Italy (85 percent) and Germany (65 to 70 percent) were also high, although Britain lagged at 35 to 40 percent. The increasing reliance on government-supported child care both reflected and reinforced a decline in the socializing role of the traditional family. Demographic and economic patterns seemed to dictate change in this direction, and no one could be sure what the long-term consequences would be.

Mass Society and Popular Culture

By the mid-sixties, the new affluence had produced a secular, consumerist society throughout Western Europe, seriously altering patterns of life. As an old and crowded continent, Europe could not easily adapt to the automobile, and traffic threatened to choke the already congested European city centers. The increasing designation of pedestrian-only areas by the 1970s eased the problem, but the automobile raised ongoing questions about the impact of prosperity on the fragile continent.

Growing prosperity meant the democratization of leisure, increasingly enjoyed in the privacy of the home rather than in a public café, pub, or theater. Television was virtually universal in households across Europe by the beginning of the eighties. Still, spectator sports grew ever more popular at the same time, with soccer the undisputed king. And prosperity meant not only paid vacations of three to four weeks but also that increasing numbers of Western Europeans could afford to spend them away from home, often at crowded beach resorts.

Secularization diminished the once central role of the churches in popular culture, which had long revolved around religious festivals and holy days. Regular church attendance declined steadily. In assuming responsibility for social welfare, the state had taken over much of the charitable role that the churches had long played. Seeking to change with the times, the Catholic church undertook a notable modernization effort under the popular Pope John XXIII (r. 1958–1963). But under his more conservative successors, the church became caught up in controversy, especially over women's issues, and was clearly on the defensive by the last decade of the century.

Government, Society, and Social Mobility

As the example of day care suggests, the strong government role in society continued across Western Europe into the 1990s, even expanding to respond to new issues. In Italy reforms during the 1970s made available a wider range of state services than ever before, from kindergarten and medical care to sports and recreational facilities. In general, the government role remained considerably stronger in Europe than in the U.S. Europeans had difficulty understanding how measures like government-sponsored health care could cause such controversy among Americans.

But if government social services remained popular, Europeans encountered what seemed

Encountering the Limits of the Welfare State

The expanded role for government after the war produced mixed results. In 1979 a group of British public-sector employees gave voice to the element of disillusionment that many had come to feel.

The ways in which we interact with the state are contradictory—they leave many people confused. We seem to need things from the state, such as child care, houses, and medical treatment. But what we are given is often shoddy or penny-pinching, and besides, it comes to us in a way that seems to limit our freedom, reduce the control we have over our lives. The tenant of a council house, pleased enough to obtain a tenancy, could still say plenty about inadequate maintenance and restrictive rules and regulations, for instance. As state workers, perhaps voting Labour, we may have hopes that a Labour administration is in the working person's interest. Yet we find that as manual workers employed by a Labour-controlled council or government, we are as overworked and underpaid as we would be in a private firm. . . .

As socialists we're always taught that somehow services provided by the state are better than those from the private sector. . . . And this seems to be true, but only up to a point. Somehow what we get is never quite what we asked for. The waiting lists for hospital beds were always too long; gradually charges began to be introduced for this and that. Another example is the promise of the new towns after the war—which made Britain famous for town planning, but were somehow, when it came to it, bleak social deserts to live in. It is not just that state provision is inadequate, under-resourced and on the cheap. The way it is resourced and administered to us doesn't seem to reflect our real needs. . . .

Source: The London Edinburgh Weekend Return Group (A Working Group of the Conference of Socialist Economists), *In and Against the State,* revised and expanded ed. (London: Pluto Press, 1990), pp. 8–9.

the limits to the role of government by the 1980s (see the box, "Encountering the Limits of the Welfare State"). In France the active government role in the economy had continued to produce successes through the sixties. France's state sector was the spearhead of efficiency. But by the early eighties, it was encountering precisely the problems that had come to dog Britain's state sector by the seventies. State-owned firms seemed to need ever higher prices, ever more generous subsidies, to stay afloat.

"Privatization" became the watchword in France, Britain, and Italy. When the Italian government sold the auto maker Alfa-Romeo to Fiat in 1987, productivity went up, despite a no-layoff agreement, because privatization removed Alfa-Romeo from the political patronage system that accompanied state ownership.

Continuing pressure for still more social mobility focused especially on access to government-supported higher education, the chief vehicle for upward mobility based on merit. In France, university admission required passing the *baccalauréat* exam at the end of secondary school. The percentage of the age group that reached this threshold grew from 1 percent in 1900 to 5 percent in 1949, then up to 23 percent by 1974. In Italy the number of university students increased sixfold from the late thirties to the late sixties, partly the result of an open enrollment policy. In Germany, on the other hand, higher education was still restrictive, elitist, and authoritarian at the end of the 1960s, but under pressure from the left the university system quadrupled in size by the mid-seventies.

Everywhere, however, the development of a mass-based university system produced new dilemmas. In France, demands for reform of higher education had been central to the uprising of 1968, but subsequent government efforts to decentralize the system produced widespread opposition from students and faculty by the 1980s. The government's proposal to give individual universities the right to choose their own students provoked protests and strikes, the most notable of which, in 1986, involved 400,000 demonstrators and violent clashes with police. Such opposition forced the government to abandon much of its reform effort.

Those resisting reform did not want institutional competition and differentiation, which would make some degrees worth less than others and undermine the equality of all faculty as civil servants. Such resistance reflected the reverse side of social mobility, the considerable status anxiety among students and faculty, especially those in the humanities and social sciences. As French universities had become institutions of mass education, the market value of the state diploma had declined substantially, as had the prestige of the faculty. For those opposed to reform, fear of loss outweighed the possibility of gain from a more competitive system. The French experience with university reform made it clear that mobility and security, equality and excellence, opportunity and merit meshed uneasily. Each was surely desirable, but the democratic societies of the West found it difficult to address the tensions among them.

The Political Sphere: Normalization and Disillusionment

The 1980s saw the consolidation of democracy, which had become the unchallenged norm. In Germany, France, and Italy, socialism had apparently been domesticated for good. And though conservatives began eliminating aspects of the welfare state in Britain and Sweden, the left and the right sounded more and more alike in much of Western Europe by the end of the 1980s. The left had come to accept the market economy, while the right had come to accept basic welfare measures and an ongoing socioeconomic role for a slimmed-down state.

Although an indifferent consensus set the political tone by the early 1990s, some the issues Europeans faced—the role of immigrants or the scope of the Common Market—seemed to have the potential for disruption. At the same time, revelations of corruption and ineffectiveness produced growing disillusionment with politics and government across Western Europe.

The Democratic Consensus and Its Limitations

Beginning in the mid-seventies, Portugal, Spain, and Greece quickly established workable democracies after periods of dictatorial rule. Following the death of Francisco Franco in 1975, almost forty years after his triumph in the Spanish civil war, democracy returned to Spain more smoothly than most had dared hope. As Spain modernized after World War II, the repressive Franco regime became increasingly unpopular, but there was considerable uncertainty about what might follow it. Some even feared a return to civil war. But Franco established that a restoration of the monarchy would follow his death, and King Juan Carlos (b. 1938) served as an effective catalyst in the transition to democracy.

When the first democratic elections in Spain since the civil war were held in 1977, the big winners were a democratic centrist party and a moderate socialist party. The extremes of both left and right did poorly. When the Socialists won a majority of the seats in parliament in the next elections, in 1982, a moderate Socialist replaced the centrist leader as prime minister. The transition suggested that Spain had quickly found its way to an effective two-party system. Meanwhile, the new constitution of 1978 dismantled what was left of the Franco system, so that, for example, Catholicism was no longer recognized as the official religion of the Spanish state.

A comparable transition from military rule to democracy took place in Portugal and Greece. Like Spain, each sought to help cement a long-term commitment to democracy by seeking entry into the EEC, and each was accepted by the end of the 1970s. For all three, EEC membership became a pillar of the solidifying democratic consensus.

The normalization of democracy was linked to the domestication of the socialist left. In Germany, the Socialists led the government for thirteen years until meeting electoral defeat in 1982. By that point, Socialists and Conservatives agreed on the essentials; there was room for disagreement only about degrees. The turn to moderation that the Socialists had begun in the late 1950s had been completed, leaving Germany essentially with a two-party system. The strength of the Green party, which had first seemed to offer a new political direction, leveled off during the 1980s at 10 to 15 percent of the vote—significant, but hardly a breakthrough.

In France and Italy, too, the left became increasingly domesticated, although it was not obvious by the early 1990s that either country had settled into a two-party system like Germany's. At first, in the early 1980s, revitalized socialist parties in both France and Italy seemed poised to marginalize the communists and reorient government. This was especially true in France, where in 1981 the Socialist leader, François Mitterrand (b. 1916), was elected president and a Socialist-led coalition won a clear majority in the assembly elections that followed. These election results produced widespread enthusiasm. The French Socialists had built up support during the 1970s by claiming the mantle of the "new left" and promising to promote a more participatory kind of democracy at all levels. The French Communist party, meanwhile, seemed increasingly irrelevant. By the early 1980s, the Communists could garner only 10 to 12 percent of the vote, about half the support the Socialists enjoyed.

Assuming the presidency in 1981, Mitterrand insisted that he was not seeking merely to prove that French Socialists could govern responsibly; rather, he offered a major reform program intended to create the first genuinely democratic socialism. Though Mitterrand strengthened individual rights and enhanced local government, reforms with a more specifically socialist cast proved problematic. The government promptly increased the state's share of French industry from 15 to 35 percent by taking over, for example, the largest French producers of aluminum, petrochemicals, and electronic equipment. It quickly became clear, however, that the aim of state ownership was not to redistribute power or wealth but to enhance competitiveness and focus investment on future technological winners.

King Juan Carlos of Spain Picked by Francisco Franco to be his successor, Juan Carlos played a central role in engineering the transition to democracy in Spain by the early 1980s. He is shown here in 1988. *(T. Graham/Sygma)*

Moreover, Mitterrand's initial economic efforts produced inflation and unemployment. During the 1980s, he gradually abandoned his talk of socialism in the face of economic and political pressures. By the end of the decade, he was questioning the relevance of long-standing socialist tenets and playing up the virtues of entrepreneurship, the profit mechanism, and free-market competition. What mattered most was that France had to operate, like the other industrial democracies, in an increasingly competitive international economy.

By the early 1990s, the French Socialists seemed to have lost their distinctive identity and sense of purpose; some even got caught up in corruption scandals. Moreover, although France was still one of postwar Europe's great success stories, unemployment remained stubbornly high. When legislative elections were held in 1993, the ruling Socialists were so unpopular that they met massive defeat at the hands of the conservatives. The Socialists had proven they could work within the system, but they had gradually discredited themselves at the same time. It remained to be seen if they would eventually return to power in the normal course of things, or if their defeat portended a more fundamental shakeup of the French political system.

In Italy, too, change on the left was central to political development during the 1980s, when a "second economic miracle" made Italy the world's fifth largest economy by most measures. By the early 1980s, both the Christian Democrats and the Communists were losing electoral support. The Christian Democrats' message seemed ever less relevant as Italy became an increasingly secular society. Moreover, as the Italian Communists declined, and especially as communism in the Soviet bloc weakened by the end of the 1980s, support for Christian Democracy as a bulwark against communism no longer seemed crucial.

For their part, the Communists ended up in disarray after getting so little for their effort during the 1970s to play a more central governmental role. During the early eighties they moved toward greater democracy within the party and stepped up their criticisms of the Soviet system, at last producing an open break with the Soviet Union. Finally, as communism collapsed in the Soviet bloc at the end of the decade, the party renamed itself the "Democratic Party of the Left," dropping the term *communist* altogether. With their role and even their political identity uncertain, the Communists' share of the vote in national parliamentary elections steadily declined.

It seemed at first that in Italy, much as in France, a revitalized Socialist party would not only supplant the Communists but offer a viable alternative to the reigning government party. During the mid-eighties, a Socialist served as Italy's prime minister for the first time, though still within a coalition dominated by Christian Democrats. By the early 1990s, however, hopes for the Socialists had dissipated. Not only did the party have little distinctive to offer, but it was heavily involved in a nationwide corruption scandal that began convulsing the country in 1992.

That scandal spread to implicate major figures from other parties, including the Christian Democrats, in a system of kickbacks to finance the political parties. Some leaders were accused of ties to organized crime. As the political system came to seem not only ineffective but rotten, disgust among Italians grew, threatening the Italian state itself.

One manifestation was the growing prominence of regionalist leagues in the north, which protested the exploitative nature of the national state and the continuing burden that the south seemed to impose on the Italian nation. The most important, the Lombard League, commanded almost 25 percent of the vote in the prosperous region of Lombardy, centered in Milan.

But in the wake of scandal and disillusionment, Italians also began a wholesale political housecleaning on the national level. By 1993, some were speaking of a "revolution of the judges," as members of Italy's relatively independent judiciary spearheaded the corruption investigations that brought the politicians to heel. Those politicians who had sought reform, such as the Christian Democrat Mario Segni, gained a wide audience, and referenda changed the electoral system to weaken the parties and make the politicians more responsive to the public. The system of domination by party bosses seemed to be ending at last, but what new form of democracy would replace it remained unclear.

Thatcher and the Assault on the Welfare State

On becoming prime minister in Britain's new Conservative government in 1979, Margaret Thatcher made it clear that she meant to pursue a definite agenda without worrying much about compromise, consensus, or social harmony. She lived up to her word, becoming one of the most remarkable—and controversial—political leaders of the century.

The daughter of a prosperous provincial grocer, Thatcher started her own law practice before going into politics. In 1959 she won election to the House of Commons, then in 1970 was given a cabinet post in Edward Heath's new conservative government. But Thatcher soon challenged Heath's moderate course and took the party clearly to the right as she assumed the leadership in 1975.

As prime minister, Thatcher promised to confront head-on Britain's economic decline. This required, she insisted, that Britain turn decisively from the values and practices of the welfare state. It was essential to foster a new "enterprise culture" by restoring the individual initiative that had been sapped, as she saw it, by decades of dependence on the government. Thatcher took it for granted that the free market, undistorted by government intervention, produced economic efficiency and thus, in the long term, the greatest social benefit.

In light of the socioeconomic difficulties Britain faced by the late 1970s, Thatcher's message had broad appeal across the social spectrum, but it also served as a catalyst for new political alignments. Thatcher had no particular affection for Britain's traditional upper classes, who seemed to have been too willing to compromise with Labour and the unions. So the Conservative party increasingly lost its aristocratic vestiges and appealed to the upwardly mobile, entrepreneurial middle class. Thatcher herself combined conservatism and innovation in her own characteristic way. It was striking, for example, that though she was Britain's first female prime minister, she was hostile to the feminist movement and seemed to go out of her way to avoid bringing other talented women into her government.

With Labour increasingly isolated, identified with decaying inner cities and old industrial regions, Thatcher easily won re-election in 1983 and 1987. By the time of her departure late in 1990, she was the longest-serving British prime minister of the century. Thus she had a chance to carry out her assault on the welfare state.

Three immediate priorities followed directly from Thatcher's overall strategy. First, her government made substantial cuts in taxes and corresponding cuts in spending for education, national health, and public housing. Second, the government fostered privatization, selling off an array of state-owned firms from Rolls Royce to British Airways. The government even sold public housing to tenants, at as much as 50 percent below market value, a measure that helped Thatcher win considerable working-class support. Third, Thatcher curbed the power of the labor unions, which were already on the defensive in this period of high unemployment.

Thatcher and Mitterrand The Conservative British prime minister and the socialist French president were prominent among the new leaders who spearheaded an array of innovations during the pivotal 1980s. They are shown here meeting in France in 1987. *(Michel Philippot/Sygma)*

Several new laws curtailed trade-union power, and Thatcher refused to consult with union leaders as her predecessors had done since the war. A showdown was reached with the yearlong coal miners' strike of 1984 and 1985, one of the most bitter and violent strikes of the century in Europe. The strike's failure in the face of government intransigence further discredited the labor movement and enhanced Thatcher's prestige. Still, the violent encounters between police and picketing strikers, carried nationwide on TV, indicated the cracks in the relative social harmony that Britain had long enjoyed.

In addition, riots by unemployed youths broke out in several major industrial cities in 1981 and again in 1985. On one issue, however, the

Thatcher government managed a meeting of the minds with discontented city dwellers. Even before Thatcher took office, increasing immigration from Britain's former colonies was being blamed for a variety of social ills, from unemployment to urban crime. In the 1979 electoral campaign, Thatcher's Conservatives took a hard line on the immigration issue, then spearheaded the Nationality Act of 1982 that restricted nonwhite immigration from the former British colonies.

With her nationalist bent, Thatcher resisted the growing power of the multinational EEC. But her rigid posture on this issue, coupled with what seemed an increasingly arrogant, strident tone, provoked growing opposition even within her own party, which finally dumped her as party leader, and thus as prime minister, late in 1990.

Controversy over the significance of the Thatcher years mounted after her departure. On the plus side, her efforts helped boost the competitiveness of British industry; productivity grew at an average annual rate of 4.5 percent in Britain from 1979 to 1988, 50 percent above the average of the other industrial democracies. This striking improvement stemmed partly from the attack on the trade unions, which had impeded productivity growth by protecting redundant labor. Even critics admitted that Thatcher's policies, especially this willingness to curb the unions, produced a significant change in British attitudes in favor of enterprise and competition. Privatization became more extensive than had been expected when Thatcher took office in 1979, while the number of new businesses reflected a revival of entrepreneurship—apparently the basis for better economic performance over the longer term.

Despite the upturn of the 1980s, however, the British economy was again in relative decline by 1990, suffering unusually high inflation. Whatever the gains during the Thatcher years, the gap between rich and poor widened and the old industrial regions of the north were increasingly left behind. More generally, the civility and sense of community that others had long admired in the British seemed a notable casualty of the Thatcher revolution. Defenders insisted that the harmony had already dissolved by the late 1970s—and that Thatcher had offered the only way of reversing the economic decline that was destroying the British social fabric.

In Britain, as all over Western Europe, the need to operate within the competitive world economy seemed increasingly to offer a limited range of public policy options. Thus Mitterrand's Socialists in France had ended up sounding like capitalists, and thus the Green movement, though it spread elsewhere from Germany, seemed unable to spearhead fundamental political realignment. At the same time, however, several long-simmering political issues that came to the fore by the early 1990s seemed potentially explosive enough to force some significant political rethinking. There was growing resentment of immigrants and foreign workers; and there was resistance to the continuing thrust toward European integration. These issues had such resonance partly because the end of the cold war in the early 1990s fundamentally altered the framework in which virtually every issue had to be considered.

The Soviet Bloc: Crisis, Innovation, Dissolution

By the early eighties, the system hammered out by Stalin and his successors still seemed firmly entrenched in the Soviet Union and its satellites in east-central Europe, despite a lackluster period under the aging leadership of Leonid Brezhnev and his allies. Yet crises were building in both the Soviet Union and Poland, producing forces for change that finally engulfed the whole communist bloc. In one sense, the process began with Solidarity, an independent trade union that emerged in Poland in 1980 to challenge the communist system. But no one had forgotten the fate of the earlier reform movements in Hungary and Prague; whatever pressures might develop in the satellite states, the outcome would depend on the Soviet response.

So in another sense, the death of Brezhnev in 1982 and the beginning of a concerted reform effort in the Soviet Union in 1985 were the decisive moments. By the end of the 1980s, the forces for change in Poland and the Soviet Union had intersected, causing the whole communist system to come apart. The dangerous but stable bipolar world that had emerged from World War II had suddenly vanished. What would replace it remained unclear.

Gorbachev, *Glasnost,* and *Perestroika*

The Soviet economy had had some success in building a heavy industrial base. The achievements of their space program and their ability to compete in the postwar arms race suggested that the Soviets could do well at science, engineering, and technology as well. Moreover, the development of Soviet society had entailed a significant social transformation, overcoming illiteracy and radically expanding access to education and to certain of the professions. Nonetheless, though the communists had made a genuine revolution, concern grew by the end of the 1970s that a crisis was engulfing the whole Soviet system.

The Soviet Union had developed an especially centralized and inflexible kind of command economy, involving methods of accounting and resource allocation that proved increasingly ineffective. The results of the agriculture plan of 1976 to 1980 were especially disappointing. The persistent shortages of many consumer goods, understandable during the transformation to an industrial society, seemed increasingly intolerable. Perhaps most telling was the fact that the Soviet Union was falling behind in high technology, which increasingly required the freedom to experiment and exchange ideas that was notably lacking in the rigid Soviet system. And as that system bogged down, the expense of the arms race with the United States dragged ever more seriously on the Soviet economy.

For all its terrible excesses, Stalin's regime had continued to galvanize some measure of genuine idealism during his lifetime. But by the 1970s, the Soviet system had settled into narrow routine or outright corruption. Its major functionaries were increasingly a class apart, enjoying access to special shops and other privileges. Brezhnev himself took enormous pleasure in his collection of expensive automobiles.

The death of Brezhnev in November 1982 made possible the rise of Mikhail Gorbachev (b. 1931), who became party secretary in March 1985 and who represented a new generation beyond those who had been groomed for party careers during the Stalinist thirties. He quickly charted a reform course—attracting the admiration of much of the world.

Gorbachev's effort encompassed four intersecting initiatives: arms reduction; liberalization in the satellite states; *glasnost,* or "openness"; and *perestroika,* or "restructuring." This was to be a reform *within* the Soviet system. The notion that reform might mean abandoning communism, giving up the Communist party's monopoly on power or embracing a free-market economy, was simply beyond what anyone thought possible at first. The reformers still took it for granted that communism could point the way beyond Western individualistic capitalism, with its crime, its drugs, its shallow consumerism. So a measure of idealism guided the reformers' efforts. But they had to make communism work.

Gorbachev understood that "openness" was a prerequisite for "restructuring." The freedom to criticize was essential to check abuses of power, which, in turn, was essential to overcome the cynicism of the workers and improve productivity. Openness was also necessary to gain the full participation of the country's most creative people, whose contribution was essential if the Soviet Union was to become competitive in high technology.

BEYOND THE COLD WAR

1979	Margaret Thatcher becomes prime minister of Britain
1979	First direct elections to European parliament
1980	Formation of Solidarity in Poland
1981	Mitterrand elected president of France
1982	Death of Leonid Brezhnev in the Soviet Union
1985	Gorbachev comes to power in the Soviet Union
1986	Explosion at Chernobyl nuclear power plant
1989	Collapse of communism in east-central Europe
1990	Reunification of Germany
1991	Collapse of communism in the Soviet Union; dissolution of the Soviet Union
1991	Beginning of fighting in Yugoslavia
1991	Maastrict agreement expanding scope of the EC

The main thrust of restructuring was to depart from the rigid economic planning mechanism by giving local managers more autonomy. The alternative did not have to mean privatization or a return to free-market capitalism. It could mean, for example, letting workers elect factory managers. But any restructuring was bound to encounter resistance, especially from those with careers tied to the central planning apparatus.

From Solidarity to Democracy in Poland

Meanwhile, in several of the satellite states, opposition had continued beneath the surface even after the crushing of the Prague reform effort in 1968. The pivotal case proved to be Poland, where an opposition movement crystallized around Solidarity, the trade-union movement formed in 1980. Intellectuals helped give it direction, but Solidarity developed especially from the energy and courage of workers on the Baltic coast, under the leadership of a shipyard electrician named Lech Walesa (b. 1944).

There was already a tradition of labor militancy on the Baltic coast of Poland, where strikes demanding free, genuinely representative trade unions had developed in 1970. Dissident intellectuals emphasized the wider import of such grassroots efforts, which challenged the logic of the communist system without attacking it directly. By the late 1970s intellectuals in Czechoslovakia and Hungary had come to see the prospects for change in similar terms. The Czech writer Václav Havel (b. 1936) noted that after 1968 there was no hope of reforming the state or the Communist party through direct political action. So hopes for change depended on people organizing themselves, doing things for themselves, outside the structures of the party-state, in diverse, independent social groupings. The state, as Havel put it, might be forced to accept "an incremental de facto reduction in the areas of its total control" (see the box, "Power from Below: The Impact of Living the Truth").

Because it had retained some tradition of labor militancy, Poland offered the greatest scope for this sort of change, but an extra ingredient from an unexpected quarter also affected the situation in Poland, perhaps in a decisive way. In 1978 the College of Cardinals of the Roman Catholic church departed from long tradition and, for the first time since 1522, elected a non-Italian pope. But even more startling was the fact that the new Pope was from Poland, behind the iron curtain. This was Karol Cardinal Wojtyla, the archbishop of Cracow, who took the name John Paul II.

In Poland the Catholic church had managed some degree of compromise with the communist regime, in contrast to Hungary and Croatia, where resistance had led to repression. Thus the Polish church had remained the most tangible institutional alternative to communism and the focus of Polish national self-consciousness in the face of Soviet domination. The new pope's visit to Poland in 1979 had an electrifying effect—providing, in fact, the catalyst for the founding of Solidarity in August 1980.

Solidarity emerged as the spearhead of a nonviolent strike movement centered on the vast Lenin shipyard in Gdansk, formerly the German Danzig. Demanding, above all, the right to form their own independent trade unions, 70,000 workers took over the shipyards, winning support not only from their intellectual allies but also from the Catholic church.

After over a year of negotiation, compromise, and broken promises, the tense situation came to a head in December 1981, when the government under General Wojciech Jaruzelski (b. 1923) declared martial law and outlawed Solidarity, imprisoning its leaders. Strikes in protest were crushed by military force. Soviet intervention was a firm possibility—but proved unnecessary.

So much for that, it seemed. Another lost cause, another reform effort colliding with inflexible communist power in east-central Europe, as in 1953, 1956, and 1968. But this time, it was different.

The ideas of Solidarity continued to spread underground. Walesa remained a powerfully effective leader, able to keep the heterogeneous movement together. Then the advent of Gorbachev in 1985 changed the overall framework of the communist bloc, for Gorbachev was convinced that the essential restructuring of the Soviet system required reform in the satellites as well. So as the Polish economy, already in difficulty by 1980, reached a crisis in 1987, Solidarity began renewing its efforts.

When proposed price increases were rejected in a referendum, the Polish government imposed

Lech Walesa and Solidarity A shipyard electrician, Walesa spearheaded the dissident Polish trade union, Solidarity, formed in 1980, and then emerged from prison to lead the movement that eventually toppled the communist regime in Poland in 1989. He is shown here leading a protest during a strike at the Lenin shipyards in Gdansk in August 1988. *(Sygma)*

them by fiat. Strikes demanding the relegalization of Solidarity followed during the spring of 1988. The government again responded with military force, but Solidarity-led strikes in August forced government leaders to send signals that they might be prepared to negotiate. With the economy deteriorating, the government recognized that it could no longer govern on its own.

The "Round Table" negotiations that followed early in 1989 proved pivotal. When they began, Walesa and his advisers wanted primarily to regain legalization for Solidarity within the communist-dominated system, still under Jaruzelski. In exchange, they assumed, they would have to help legitimate a rigged election to approve painful but necessary economic measures. But as the negotiations proceeded, the government gave ever more in exchange for Solidarity's cooperation. Not only did it consent to legalize Solidarity, but it agreed to make the forthcoming elections free enough for the opposition genuinely to participate.

The elections of June 1989 produced an overwhelming repudiation of Poland's Communist government. Even government leaders running unopposed failed to win election as voters simply crossed out their names. In the aftermath of the elections, President Jaruzelski had difficulty assembling a new communist-led government, so he finally gave Solidarity a chance to lead. Not all members of the opposition felt it wise to accept government responsibility under such difficult economic circumstances, but finally Tadeusz Mazowiecki (b. 1927), Walesa's choice and one of the movement's most distinguished intellectuals, agreed to form a government.

The chain of events in Poland culminated in one of the extraordinary events of modern history—the negotiated end of communist rule. That a communist government might give up power voluntarily had been utterly unforeseen. It happened partly because the Soviet Union under Gorbachev was seeking reform and thus had become much less likely to intervene militarily. It also mattered that the Polish Catholic church was available to act as mediator, hosting meetings, reminding both sides of their shared responsibilities in the difficult situation facing their country.

Power from Below: The Impact of Living the Truth

Considering the scope for change in the communist world by the late 1970s, Václav Havel imagines a conformist grocer who routinely puts a sign in his window with the slogan "Workers of the world, unite!" simply because it is expected. That same grocer, says Havel, has the power to break the stifling sociopolitical system, which ultimately rests on those innumerable acts of everyday compliance.

Let us now imagine that one day something in our greengrocer snaps and he stops putting up the slogans merely to ingratiate himself. He stops voting in elections he knows are a farce. He begins to say what he really thinks at political meetings. . . .

By breaking the rules of the game, he has disrupted the game as such. He has exposed it as a mere game. He has shattered the world of appearances, the fundamental pillar of the system. He has upset the power structure by tearing apart what holds it together. . . . He has shown everyone that it *is* possible to live within the truth. Living within the lie can constitute the system only if it is universal. The principle must embrace and permeate everything. There are no terms whatsoever on which it can coexist with living within the truth, and therefore everyone who steps out of line *denies it in principle and threatens it in its entirety*. . . .

And since all genuine problems and matters of critical importance are hidden beneath a thick crust of lies, it is never quite clear when the proverbial last straw will fall, or what that straw will be. This . . . is why the regime prosecutes, almost as a reflex action preventively, even the most modest attempts to live within the truth.

Source: Václav Havel et al., *The Power of the Powerless: Citizens Against the State in Central-Eastern Europe* (Armonk, N.Y.: M. E. Sharpe, 1985), pp. 39–40, 42.

By some accounts, General Jaruzelski, who seemed for most of the 1980s to be just another military strongman, willing to do the Soviets' bidding, had proven a national hero for his grace, perhaps even ingenuity, in yielding power to the opposition. But most important was the courage, the persistence, and the vision of Solidarity itself.

The Anticommunist Revolution, 1989–1991

The Polish example suggested to anticommunists all over the Soviet bloc that the communist system was open to challenge. As a result, anticommunism spread through east-central Europe by means of the domino effect that had preoccupied the Soviets from the start, ultimately toppling the Soviet satellite system.

Though antigovernment strikes and demonstrations took place throughout the region, the end of the established communist order in East Germany, Hungary, Czechoslovakia, Bulgaria, and Albania was more peaceful than anyone would have dreamed possible a few years before. Starting with Hungary, these countries essentially followed the model established in Poland and negotiated the transfer of power from the communist leadership to an opposition group. In Czechoslovakia, the transition was so peaceful that it was promptly dubbed the "Velvet Revolution." The signal exception was Romania, where the communist dictator Nicolae Ceausescu's bloody crackdown on the reform movement provoked an armed revolt that finally overthrew the government. The opposition executed Ceausescu and his wife on Christmas Day 1989.

Though the outcome was relatively peaceful, the possibility of violent crackdown was never far from the surface. Just months before, in June 1989, the communist leadership in China had used massive force to crush a comparable movement for democracy in Tiananmen Square in Beijing. As the opposition movement grew in East Germany early in the fall, with weekly demonstrations in Leipzig attracting 300,000 people, the East German communist leader Erich Honecker (b. 1912) began preparing for such a "Chinese solution" in his country. But a dramatic appeal for nonviolence by local opposition leaders in Leipzig helped persuade the police to hold off. At the same time, Gorbachev, visiting Honecker in October, called for moderation. Gorbachev still believed that reform offered the best hope for saving the system. Honecker was soon forced out of the East German leadership in favor of more reform-minded communists.

A marked increase in illegal emigration from East Germany to the West had been one manifestation that discontent was reaching the breaking point. If the reform-minded communists in East Germany were to have any chance of turning the situation around, they had to relax restrictions on travel and even grant the right to emigrate. Thus they immediately began preparing legislation to both ends, amid a host of reforms intended to save the system. Finally, on November 9, 1989, the regime in East Germany did what had long seemed unthinkable: It opened the Berlin Wall, which was promptly dismantled altogether. Germans now traveled freely back and forth between east and west.

This liberalization effort proved too late, however; events outraced the control of even the most innovative and flexible of the East German communists. East Germans no longer aimed simply at reforming the communist system but at ending it altogether. As it even became possible to contemplate German reunification, the communist system in the East quickly dissolved. Decisive steps toward reunification followed almost immediately during 1990. (See the feature, "Weighing the Evidence: Current Events as History," on pages 1222–1223.)

The opening of the Berlin Wall in November 1989 signaled the end of the cold war. The immediate result in the West was euphoria, but no one could doubt that a still more difficult task lay ahead. To be sure, reformers in the former Soviet bloc countries claimed to want individual freedom, political democracy, and free-market capitalism. But it would be necessary to build these on the ruins of the now-discredited communist regimes and their command economies, a task that no one had ever confronted before.

Meanwhile, in the Soviet Union, what began as a restructuring of the communist system became a struggle for survival of the system itself. The disintegration of the communist regimes in east-central Europe showed that communism, even if apparently entrenched, did not embody the irreversible logic of history. During 1990 and 1991, the situation in the Soviet Union evolved with extraordinary speed, producing a revolution as stunning as any the West had known.

The much-trumpeted *glasnost* produced greater freedom in Soviet culture and politics, but Gorbachev sought to avoid alienating hard-line Communists, so he compromised, watering down the economic reforms essential to *perestroika.* The result proved an unfortunate set of half measures. Because so little was done to force the entrenched Soviet bureaucracy to go along, the pace of economic reform was lethargic. Yet the change that did take place was sufficient to interrupt the chain of command through which the state plan had been carried out in the Soviet system. The essential structures of the command economy weakened, but free-market forms of exchange among producers, distributors, and consumers did not emerge to replace them.

By 1989, with the economic situation deteriorating, and with people free to discuss alternatives as never before, the communist system itself was clearly in jeopardy. Soviet citizens felt betrayed by their earlier faith that Soviet communism was leading to a better future. A popular slogan spoke sarcastically of "seventy years on the road to nowhere."

Even during the Gorbachev era, in 1986, an accidental explosion at the Soviet nuclear power plant at Chernobyl, in the Ukraine, contaminated food supplies and forced the abandonment of villages and thousands of square miles of formerly productive land. Later estimates suggested that the radioactivity released would eventually kill or hasten the death of at least 100,000 Soviet citi-

Gorbachev and Yeltsin The two leaders appear together in August 1991, just after the failure of an attempted coup by Soviet hard-liners. After the coup attempt, as it became clear that Gorbachev's effort to reform Soviet communism had stalled, the initiative passed to Yeltsin, who was determined to replace the communist system altogether. *(De Keerle/Grochowiak/Sygma)*

zens. For two and a half weeks after the accident, Gorbachev had reverted to old-fashioned Soviet secrecy in an effort to minimize what had happened. As a result, the eventual toll was far greater than it need have been. The accident and its aftermath seemed stark manifestation of all that was wrong with the Soviet system—its arrogance and secrecy, its premium on cutting corners to achieve targets imposed from above.

By early 1990, Soviet citizens were actively discussing once unthinkable possibilities like privatization and a market economy. At the same time, the Soviet Communist party began to disintegrate, losing 4 million members in the eighteen months up to July 1991. By mid-1990, moreover, the union of the Soviet republics that had been engineered in the very different circumstances of 1922 tottered on the verge of collapse. Lithuania led the way in calling for outright independence. But the stakes were raised enormously in June 1990 when the Russian republic, the largest and most important in the U.S.S.R., began following Lithuania's lead.

In June 1990 the newly elected chairman of Russia's parliament, Boris Yeltsin (b. 1931), got the Russian republic to declare its sovereignty, thereby pushing the form of the Soviet Union itself to the center of discussions. But Yeltsin had wider motives. He had grown impatient with the slow pace of economic and political change, and by threatening that Russia might go its own way, he hoped to force Gorbachev's reform effort beyond the present impasse. As a further challenge to Gorbachev, Yeltsin dramatically resigned from the Communist party during the televised twenty-eighth congress in July 1990. When, in June 1991, free elections in the Russian republic offered the first clear contest between Communists determined to preserve the system and those seeking to replace it, the anticommunist

Yeltsin was elected the republic's president by a surprising margin.

By late 1990 the danger the whole system might collapse raised the possibility that communist hard-liners would intervene to restore the system on their terms, perhaps deposing Gorbachev in the process. As the situation polarized, Gorbachev sought to make himself indispensable to both sides, even to play them against each other, but he ended up alienating both and found himself increasingly isolated as a result.

After tilting toward the hard-liners late in 1990, Gorbachev sought a return to reform after Yeltsin's dramatic election as president of Russia in June 1991. Late in July, Gorbachev prepared a new union treaty that would have given substantial powers, including authority over taxation, to the constituent republics. He also engineered a new party charter that jettisoned much of the Marxist-Leninist doctrine that had guided communist practice since the revolution.

These measures promised the radical undoing of the Soviet system, and now the hard-liners finally struck back, initiating a coup in August 1991. They managed to force Gorbachev from power—but only for a few days. As the world held its breath, Yeltsin, supported by ordinary people in Moscow, stood up to the conspirators. Key units of the secret police, charged to arrest Yeltsin and other opposition leaders, refused to follow orders, prompting the Soviet army, already divided, to back off from the conspirators' plan to take Moscow. The coup quickly fizzled, but the episode galvanized the anticommunist movement and radically accelerated the pace of change.

Although Gorbachev was restored as head of the Soviet Union, the undisputed winner was Yeltsin, who immediately spearheaded an effort to dismantle the party apparatus before it could regroup. Spontaneous anticommunist demonstrations across much of the Soviet Union toppled statues of Lenin and dissolved local party networks. In a referendum in December 1991, Ukraine, the second most populous Soviet republic, overwhelmingly voted for independence.

Although the dissolution of the Soviet empire was liberating in one sense, it raised a new set of problems at the same time. What was to become of the 27,000 nuclear weapons stationed in

The Fall of Lenin During the revolutions in east-central Europe and the Soviet Union, anticommunist forces toppled statues of communist heroes to dramatize the fall of the communist order. Here, with the aid of a giant crane, a colossal statue of Lenin is taken from its pedestal in Bucharest, Romania, in March 1990. *(Patrick Forestier/Sygma)*

four of the Soviet republics? Moreover, as the economic situation deteriorated, individual republics began setting up obstacles to economic exchange with the others, keeping what they produced for themselves. Some new form of coordination and unity seemed essential. Thus late in December 1991, the leaders of Russia, Ukraine, and Byelorussia (Belarus) spearheaded the creation of a new Commonwealth of Independent States, which replaced the Soviet Union with a much looser confederation of eleven of the fifteen former Soviet republics. Late in December, Gorbachev finally resigned, paving the way for the official dissolution of the Soviet Union on January 1, 1992 (Map 32.1).

To underline the change, the capital of the new commonwealth was placed not in Moscow but in Minsk, the capital of Belarus. Still, Moscow remained the capital of the Russian republic, and it was not clear how much power the new commonwealth would have in light of Russia's great relative strength. In the following years, disagreements about defense and economic policy and the disposition of nuclear weapons raised questions about the commonwealth's future.

On the Ruins of the Communist System

All over the formerly communist part of Europe, calls for Western-style democracy accompanied the end of the old order. But the area had had little experience with the give and take of democratic politics, and the fragile new political systems found themselves responsible for the difficult transition from a command to a free-market economy. Transition under these difficult circumstances promptly raised questions of political legitimacy. In Russia there was increasing tension between President Boris Yeltsin and the parliament, which included many who resisted Yeltsin's push toward a free-market economy.

Throughout the region, the overriding question was whether the end of communism meant the advent of democracy or the emergence of new forms of dictatorship. Although the communist label had been abandoned, by 1992 those in power in Lithuania, Romania, Bulgaria, and the dominant Serbian part of Yugoslavia were former communists whose commitment to democracy remained suspect. In Romania, for example, part of the old Communist party apparatus managed to regroup and assume the dominant role after the revolutionary crisis of late 1989 had passed. Prospects for genuine democracy seemed better in Hungary, Poland, and Czechoslovakia, although in each the effort to practice democratic politics promptly produced new tensions.

In Poland, Solidarity, which had lived up to its name so remarkably during the years of struggle, began to splinter as it assumed the task of governing. After falling out with Mazowiecki, Walesa decided to run for president and won a decisive victory in the election of December 1990. During the electoral campaign, he showed a tendency toward bullying and demagoguery that led some to worry that his triumph portended dictatorship. However, others felt that he alone had the stature to accelerate the painful transition and make it work.

Postcommunist Poland's first parliamentary elections in October 1991 produced a parliament fragmented among twenty parties, none strong enough to muster more than 12 percent of the vote. Poland seemed doomed to a weak parliament capable of forming only precarious, easily fragmented coalitions—a situation that might invite an ever-more authoritarian approach from the president.

Political prospects rested in large part on the success of the economic transition. Although Poland and the rest of the former communist bloc seemed at first to offer investment opportunities for Western capitalists, it quickly became clear that their economies were close to chaos. Poland, especially, sought to privatize former state-owned businesses as quickly as possible, but here, as elsewhere, the transition entailed unemployment, inflation, and widespread corruption. Some former communist functionaries turned themselves into capitalists, taking over state-owned companies, and quickly got rich, provoking widespread popular resentment. Still, though initial hopes were disappointed, some significant Western investment and business expertise flowed especially into Poland and Hungary, suggesting that, with time, each might find competitive advantages and become full participants in the international economy.

The economy was the overriding issue, but political freedom opened up divisive new questions across the former Soviet bloc. For example, the eclipse of communism in Poland initially

Map 32.1 The Dissolution of the Soviet Union As crisis gripped the Soviet system by the late 1980s, the republics of the Soviet Union began declaring first their sovereignty, then their independence. Most of the fifteen republics that had made up the Soviet Union became part of a much looser confederation in 1991 and 1992.

seemed to portend a major role for the Catholic church, which had been so important as an alternative focus during the communist period. But angry debate followed when, in 1990, the Mazowiecki government ordered that children be taught religion in the schools and the head of the Polish church called for an end to the "communist-inspired" separation of church and state. An effort to pass a strong antiabortion bill in time for a visit by Pope John Paul II in 1991 caused more heated debate; public opinion polls indicated that a majority of Poles favored abortion rights.

So despite the drama of the anticommunist revolution of 1989 through 1991, it remained unclear what would result from it. Freedom, democracy, and free-market economics were hardly panaceas. The citizens of the formerly communist countries had to come to terms with the new political and economic challenges in their own way.

Europe and the West After the Bipolar Peace

The dissolution of the Soviet system meant the swift, unexpected end of the cold war, which had defined the era since World War II. But by the end of the 1980s the world configuration was changing not only because of the collapse of the Soviet bloc. Though it could claim, in one sense, to have won the cold war, the United States had also declined in relative strength from the unprecedented pre-eminence it had enjoyed after World War II. So the end of the cold war meant not unchallenged U.S. hegemony but a new universe of possibilities and uncertainties.

The new framework seemed to invite Western Europe to become a superpower in its own right, so a push for further European integration

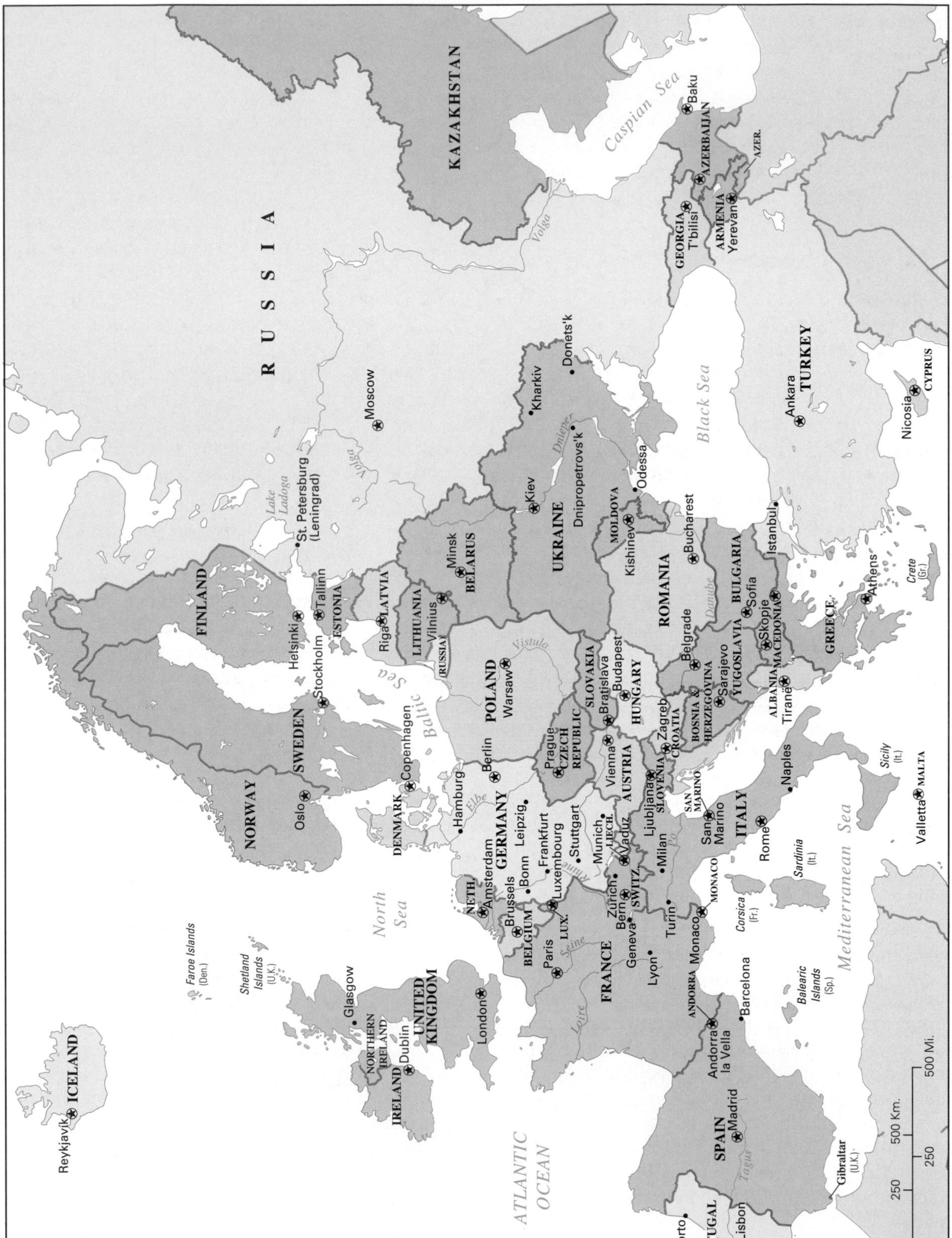
RUSSIA
KAZAKHSTAN
Caspian Sea
Baku
AZERBAIJAN
AZER.
GEORGIA
T'bilisi
ARMENIA
Yerevan
Volga
Moscow
St. Petersburg (Leningrad)
Lake Ladoga
Donets'k
Kharkiv
Dnieper
Dnipropetrovs'k
Odessa
Black Sea
TURKEY
Ankara
CYPRUS
Nicosia
FINLAND
Helsinki
Tallinn
ESTONIA
LATVIA
Riga
LITHUANIA
Vilnius
RUSSIA
BELARUS
Minsk
Kiev
UKRAINE
MOLDOVA
Kishinev
ROMANIA
Bucharest
Danube
BULGARIA
Sofia
Istanbul
Athens
Crete (Gr.)
GREECE
MACEDONIA
Skopje
YUGOSLAVIA
Belgrade
Sarajevo
BOSNIA & HERZEGOVINA
ALBANIA
Tiranë
CROATIA
Zagreb
HUNGARY
Budapest
SLOVAKIA
Bratislava
POLAND
Warsaw
Vistula
Baltic Sea
SWEDEN
Stockholm
NORWAY
Oslo
Copenhagen
DENMARK
CZECH REPUBLIC
Prague
Berlin
Hamburg
Elbe
GERMANY
Leipzig
Frankfurt
Stuttgart
Munich
Bonn
Amsterdam
NETH.
Brussels
BELGIUM
Luxembourg
LUX.
Rhine
LIECH.
Vaduz
AUSTRIA
Vienna
Ljubljana
SLOVENIA
SAN MARINO
San Marino
ITALY
Rome
Naples
Milan
Po
Turin
Zürich
Bern
SWITZ.
Geneva
MONACO
Monaco
FRANCE
Paris
Seine
Lyon
Loire
Corsica (Fr.)
Sardinia (It.)
Sicily (It.)
MALTA
Valletta
Mediterranean Sea
Balearic Islands (Sp.)
Barcelona
ANDORRA
Andorra la Vella
SPAIN
Madrid
Tagus
Gibraltar (U.K.)
PORTUGAL
Lisbon
Porto
ATLANTIC OCEAN
North Sea
UNITED KINGDOM
London
Glasgow
NORTHERN IRELAND
IRELAND
Dublin
Shetland Islands (U.K.)
Faroe Islands (Den.)
ICELAND
Reykjavík
0 250 500 Km.
0 250 500 Mi.

accompanied the end of the cold war. But obstacles remained, stemming especially from traditional concerns about national sovereignty. At the same time, different forms of multinational organization, from a newly revitalized United Nations to a grouping of the world's seven leading industrial democracies, suggested other ways of reconfiguring power relationships (Map 32.2).

The Changing International Framework

As the potential threat from the Soviet Union dissolved, the United States inevitably lost some of its leverage in Europe because American support no longer seemed essential for European security. Despite a renewed military buildup during the 1980s, the United States, by the early 1990s, could no longer claim the same kind of leadership in any case. The role of superpower had taken its toll on the United States, just as it had on the U.S.S.R. These two had been the big winners of World War II, yet the subsequent arms race burdened the budgets of both countries, while the war's major losers, Germany, Japan, and Italy, pulled back from any great power role to prosper as never before. In terms of productivity and living standards, the United States was in relative decline compared to Japan and much of Western Europe by the 1990s. Suffering from mounting budget deficits, and shifting from net creditor to net borrower in its international accounts, it lost some of its economic leverage—and thus some of its capacity to lead.

The ambiguities of the new international situation came to the fore during the first major crisis of the post–cold war period, the Persian Gulf War that the United States spearheaded against Iraq in 1990 and 1991. With superpower rivalry no longer an issue, the United States assembled a wide-ranging coalition that reversed an Iraqi takeover of Kuwait. Though the United States led successfully, it had to pass the hat among its prosperous allies to pay for the Gulf War, and those called on to contribute seemed unlikely to settle for such arrangements again. This was especially true of Japan and Germany, both of which had been limited to a circumscribed sphere of action within the international framework of the cold war era. Now, with the lid off, each was bound to reassess its international role.

Among the Japanese, this rethinking sometimes assumed a strongly nationalist cast. Japan might translate its economic power into a more independent military-strategic role, perhaps leading an East Asia bloc encompassing the other increasingly prosperous nations of the region. Or Japan might be content to work closely with the United States, its fellow Pacific power, or simply to work within multinational organizations. Much depended on how others dealt with Japan, especially in light of the resentment—and the protectionist sentiment—that Japan's success in international trade produced in both Europe and the United States.

On the European side, much depended on Germany, whose prospects seemed radically enhanced with the end of the cold war. Most immediately, the collapse of communism in east-central Europe made possible the reunification of Germany in 1990. Despite some nervousness, the four postwar occupying powers gave their blessing as the leaders of the two countries negotiated the incorporation of the east into the Federal Republic. The division of Germany had been central to the postwar settlement; the speed with which it was overcome astonished the world.

Although some in West Germany were hesitant about immediate reunification, especially because of the economic costs that seemed likely, West German Chancellor Helmut Kohl (b. 1930) took the initiative to complete the process as quickly as possible. By early 1990 emigration of East Germans to the west had become a flood. West German law treated these Germans as citizens, entitled to social benefits, so their arrival in such numbers presented a considerable financial burden. It thus seemed imperative for West Germany to regularize the situation as quickly as possible, assuming responsibility for the east and restoring its economy.

Reunification prompted nervousness about the role the new Germany, already a major economic power, might seek to play in Europe and the world. Because 30 percent of the territory of present-day Poland had been taken from Ger-

Map 32.2 Europe After the Cold War The reunification of Germany and the break-up of the Soviet Union, Yugoslavia, and Czechoslovakia fundamentally altered the map of Europe by the early 1990s.

many after World War II, the Poles were especially concerned. However, Germany remained cautious and eager to prove its good intentions by continuing to support the movement toward European integration. At the same time, reunification contributed to some unexpected problems on the domestic level that limited the new Germany's freedom of maneuver.

Reunification was simply more costly than Kohl had expected in 1990, and thus the German government found it hard to keep some of the promises it had made, in the initial euphoria of reunification, to those in the east. When, in 1993, the government pulled back from its promise of wage equality between east and west, workers in the former East Germany mounted the most serious strikes the Federal Republic had experienced since the war. Moreover, the strains and costs of reunification contributed to the growing controversy over the role of immigrants in Germany by the early 1990s.

To atone for the crimes of the Nazi period, the Federal Republic adopted an especially liberal and generous asylum law. In addition, Germany actively recruited foreign workers during the decades of economic boom and labor shortage that followed the war. By 1993 Germany had a large foreign population of 6.4 million, and 60,000 new arrivals were seeking asylum in Germany every month. This wave of immigration provoked resentment and sometimes violence among Germans who felt that foreigners and asylum-seekers were getting a better deal than ordinary citizens such as themselves. In 1992 alone, there were two thousand attacks on foreigners, some of them fatal. Those responsible for such attacks were often "skinheads," young people with uncertain economic prospects who claimed to admire Nazism. Their violence provoked massive counter-demonstrations by Germans eager to disavow it, but the new volatility of German domestic politics made it difficult for Germany to play a more assertive international role.

Supranational Initiatives and Global Issues

The push toward European integration had been renewed earlier in the 1980s, but the end of the cold war added urgency to the process. Most immediately, the role of the Common Market in coordinating aid to the former communist countries suggested that it needed its own foreign policy to match its growing responsibilities.

From the start, proponents of European integration had hoped that the Common Market could promote greater uniformity in areas like tax policy and business law, in which national differences constituted barriers to full-scale economic integration. Although a full customs union had technically been achieved by the late 1960s, national policies continued to compromise the open market, especially by coddling certain companies to give them a competitive advantage. For domestic political reasons, national governments sometimes confined their purchases to national firms or granted subsidies to domestic producers, thus enabling them to offer artificially lower prices to compete with foreign firms.

Still, movement toward the full-scale integration of the member economies continued by fits and starts. After another oil crisis in 1979, and amid increasing concern about "Eurosclerosis," or lack of innovation and competitiveness, the EEC's twelve members committed themselves in 1985 to the measures necessary to create a true single market with genuinely free competition by the end of 1992. Not only were goods, services, and money to circulate freely among the twelve member countries, but there would be uniform product standards, as well as equal competition for the government contracts of each country.

By the late 1980s, the thrust toward economic integration increasingly assumed a political dimension. A European Parliament had developed from the assembly of the European Coal and Steel Community by 1962, though it had little importance at first. The provision for direct election to this body, which had formerly comprised delegations from the national parliaments, greatly increased its stature when the first such elections were held in 1979.

After the merger of the governing institutions of the several European supranational organizations in 1967, the term "European Community," or EC, gradually replaced "Common Market" to indicate the institutional web that had emerged since the launching of the European Coal and Steel Community in 1951. By the late eighties the European Community included a network of interlocking institutions, variously seated in Brussels, Strasbourg, and Luxembourg.

French Farmers in Protest In June 1992 French farmers protest a threatened cut in agricultural subsidies by blocking a freeway near Paris with farm equipment and piles of grain. *(Patrick Durand/Sygma)*

Among them the European Parliament and the European Court of Justice played increasingly important roles.

Meeting at Maastrict, in the Netherlands, in December 1991, the members of the EC buttressed the powers of the European Parliament, agreed to move toward a common policy of workers' rights, and committed to a common currency and central banking structure by 1999. But Maastrict required the approval of the EC members, and in one country after another the ensuing debate over European integration proved more intense and divisive than EC proponents had expected. Many were nervous about the implications of the reunification of Germany for the operations of the EC. The organization had earlier seemed a way to contain Germany within a larger Europe, but now, with Germany aggrandized, the EC might become a vehicle for unwelcome German domination.

Moreover, the creation of an internal customs union, benign though it seemed, did not commit the EC to freer trade with nonmember countries like the United States and Japan. French farmers, especially, relied on a system of government supports that shielded them from U.S. competition. Conversely, high EC agricultural subsidies undercut the chance for Americans to sell their agricultural products in Europe. In 1992 the possibility that the French government would lower those supports, partly in response to pressures from the United States, caused massive demonstrations by French farmers.

Despite these fits and starts, the EC seemed poised to play an expanding role in the post–cold war world. In addition, there were other supranational alignments that might prove even more important. The leaders of the seven leading industrial democracies—the United States, Japan, Germany, France, Italy, Britain, and Canada—began meeting regularly in 1975, first to wrestle with the impact of the OPEC oil price shock. Their meetings grew steadily in importance thereafter, and by the early nineties, this "Group of 7" (G7) had become, in a sense, "the world's executive committee." The end of the cold war seemed to portend not the unipolar hegemony of the United States but a concert of the industrial democracies, with four Western European countries among the major players.

In addition, the World Bank and the International Monetary Fund played ever more visible roles, helping to keep the industrial economies synchronized and the less-developed economies on a free-market path. These organizations could strongly influence domestic policies—by refusing, for example, to lend to countries that were spending heavily on defense. Even the United Nations, overshadowed for decades by superpower rivalry, got a new lease on life with the end of the cold war, becoming more active and winning greater respect. As the UN returned to prominence, however, questions arose about the composition of the Security Council, which still reflected Roosevelt's wartime vision of fifty years before. Did it make sense for Britain and France to have permanent Security Council seats but not Germany and Japan? Some suggested that the less-developed world needed greater representation on the Security Council—and in the whole network of multinational organizations.

International cooperation took on greater urgency because a growing concern with the global environment produced an increasing sense of world interdependence. Such problems as global warming, the destruction of rain forests, and the deterioration of the ozone layer were inherently supranational in scope. Yet environmental concerns complicated relations between the industrialized nations, concentrated in the West, and much of the non-Western world. Countries seeking to industrialize encountered environmental constraints that had not been at issue when the West industrialized. The challenge for the West was to foster protection of the environment without imposing on the non-Western world limitations on economic growth that the West had not had to accept.

At the same time, changing demographic and economic patterns suggested that North-South tensions between the prosperous countries of the northern hemisphere and the poorer countries in the Third World might replace the East-West tensions of the cold war. World population reached 5.5 billion in 1993, doubling in forty years. This was the fastest rate of world population growth ever, and by the 1990s virtually all of the growth was in the Third World. The population of Europe was growing at only 0.2 percent per year, and in several countries the population was actually declining (Map 32.3).

Demographic pressure in the less-developed countries contributed to the increasing immigration to western Europe that made Africans selling hats, figurines, and sunglasses familiar fixtures in European cities by the early 1990s. But as Europeans faced problems of their own, immigration became a divisive political issue. The problem of how to respond to the needs of poorer countries with burgeoning populations would clearly be central to the new world that was gradually coming into focus with the end of the cold war.

The weakening of national sovereignty and the new scope for supranational organization made possible more grandiose forms of abuse as well as greater scope for constructive change. When it broke in 1991, the scandal surrounding the Bank of Credit and Commerce International (BCCI), a multinational bank nominally based in Luxembourg, brought home how vulnerable the world had become in an age of instant communications and global financial networks. For several years BCCI had dealt in drugs, illegal arms, terror, and money-laundering on a colossal international scale, corrupting prominent individuals throughout the world. Revelations of its operations suggested the need for more sophisticated forms of international regulation and accounting. But how the international community might organize itself for such purposes remained unclear.

In the Shadow of History: The Experiment Continues

The rapid change since 1945 raised new questions for Europeans about the meaning of their distinctive history and traditions. Some worried that prosperity necessarily entailed "Americanization," the unwelcome sameness of mass consumerist culture. For the formerly communist countries of east-central Europe, the challenge was to find a positive way of reconnecting with their own national histories after decades of Soviet

Map 32.3 World Population Density Most of Europe remains densely populated, but the explosive population growth of the late twentieth century took place especially in the poorer countries of Asia, Africa, and Latin America. (*Source:* Data from *World Atlas*, 2d ed. [Chicago: Rand McNally, 1992]; cited in *Facts on File 1993* [New York: Facts on File, 1993], pp. 2–6.)

More than 500/mi²
(More than 200/km²)
Bahrain
Bangladesh
Belgium
Burundi
El Salvador
Germany
Haiti
India
Israel
Jamaica
Japan
Korea, South
Lebanon
Netherlands
Philippines
Rwanda
Sri Lanka
Taiwan
Trinidad and Tobago
United Kingdom
Vietnam
250–500/mi²
(100–200/km²)
Albania
Armenia
China
Cuba
Cyprus
Czech Republic
Denmark
Dominican Republic
France
Hungary
Indonesia
Italy
Korea, North
Kuwait
Luxembourg
Moldova
Nepal
Nigeria
Pakistan
Poland
Portugal
Romania
Slovakia
Slovenia
Switzerland
Thailand
125–249/mi²
(50–99/km²)
Austria
Azerbaijan
Belarus
Bosnia/Herzegovina
Brunei
Bulgaria
Costa Rica
Croatia
Egypt
Gambia
Georgia
Ghana
Greece
Guatemala
Ireland
Lesotho
Lithuania
Macedonia
Malawi
Malaysia
Morocco
Myanmar (Burma)
Sierra Leone
Spain
Swaziland
Syria
Togo
Tunisia
Turkey
Uganda
Ukraine
Yugoslavia
25–124/mi²
(10–49/km²)
Afghanistan
Algeria
Argentina
Belize
Benin
Bhutan
Brazil
Burkina Faso
Cambodia
Cameroon
Chile
Colombia
Côte d'Ivoire
Djibouti
Ecuador
Equatorial Guinea
Eritrea
Estonia
Ethiopia
Finland
Guinea
Guinea-Bissau
Honduras
Iran
Iraq
Jordan
Kenya
Kyrgyzstan
Laos
Latvia
Liberia
Madagascar
Mexico
Mozambique
New Zealand
Nicaragua
Norway
Panama
Paraguay
Peru
Qatar
Senegal
Somalia
South Africa
Sudan
Sweden
Tajikistan
Tanzania
United Arab Emirates
United States
Uruguay
Uzbekistan
Venezuela
Yemen
Zaire
Zambia
Zimbabwe
Less than 25/mi²
(Less than 10/km²)
Angola
Australia
Bolivia
Botswana
Canada
Central African Republic
Chad
Congo
French Guiana
Gabon
Greenland (Den.)
Guyana
Iceland
Kazakhstan
Libya
Mali
Mauritania
Mongolia
Namibia
Niger
Oman
Papua New Guinea
Russia
Saudi Arabia
Suriname
Turkmenistan
Western Sahara

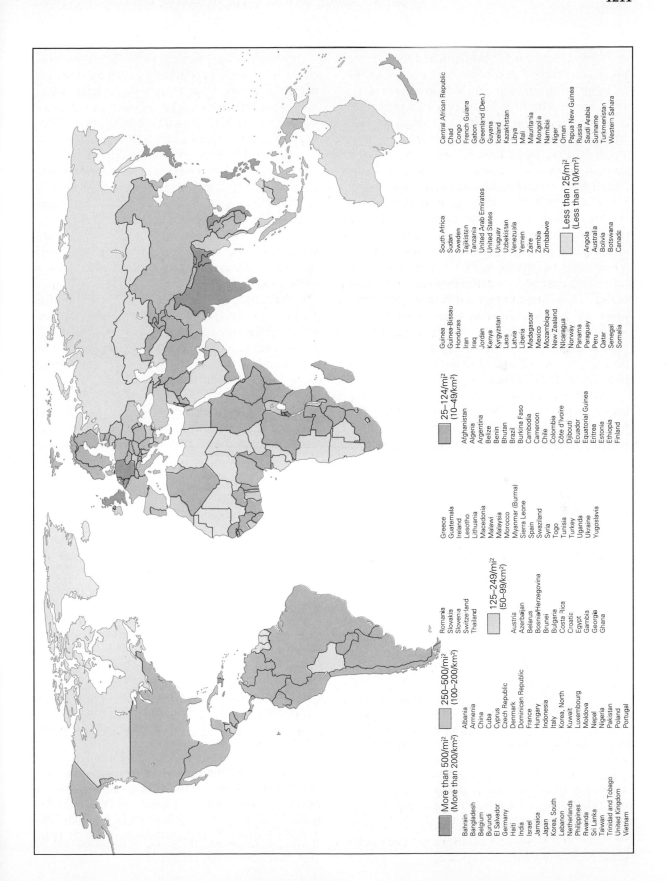

Kiefer: Osiris and Isis The German artist Anselm Kiefer combined unusual materials to create haunting images that often suggested the horrors of recent history. In this work from 1985 to 1987, the interpenetrating layers of human culture include images of ruin and death, hope and resurrection. *(Anselm Kiefer,* Osiris und Isis, *1985–87. Mixed media on canvas, 150 x 220½ x 6½". San Francisco Museum of Modern Art. Purchased through a gift of Jean Stein by exchange, the Mrs. Paul L. Wattis Fund, and the Doris and Don Fisher Fund. Photo: Ben Blackwell)*

domination and communist ideology. In many cases, this return of history and memory meant a renewed emphasis on ethnic identity, which sometimes produced conflict and repression.

Although the shadow of fascism and war remained, Europe had experienced a radical transformation in the half-century since World War II, a transformation that had cut it off from its own tradition. Visible remains of Europe's history, including its difficult recent past, lurked as bits and pieces in present experience, and the contemporary relationship to the tradition grew increasingly uncertain, even ironic. This ambiguous relationship found striking expression in architecture and painting by the last decades of the century.

During the first two decades after the war, modernist architecture, turning from tradition to embrace the modern industrial age, had triumphed at last, transforming cities throughout the world. By the 1980s, however, architects were turning from modernism to postmodernism, a glitzy way of building with ambiguous or ironic references to a tradition that was still present, even if those living within it were not quite sure what to make of it.

This uneasy contemporary relationship with the past, especially the traumatic past of the earlier twentieth century, took more pointed form in the neo-expressionism prominent in German and Italian painting during the 1980s. Artists like Anselm Kiefer (b. 1945) and Sandro Chia (b. 1946) created striking images that reflected the ongoing search for commitment and meaning in the context of an unmastered past.

Europe and the American Challenge

The center of gravity of Western civilization had changed before, gradually shifting from the eastern Mediterranean to the north Atlantic, but its location became especially uncertain with the dramatic changes surrounding World War II. Having weakened itself disastrously in the two world wars, Western Europe found itself dependent on the United States, first for its economic recovery, then for its defense. For decades after 1945, Europe seemed to have no choice but to follow the U.S. lead. Such subservience troubled some Europeans, and a kind of love-hate relationship with the United States developed in Western Europe during the late twentieth century.

Even after Europe's postwar economic recovery, the United States continued to set the pace in high-technology industries, prompting concerns that Europe would become a mere economic satellite of the United States. Europe seemed to be caught in a dilemma: To retain its distinctiveness over the long term, it apparently had to become, in the short term, more like America. The French writer Jean-Jacques Servan-Schreiber (b. 1924) made this case in his widely discussed book *The American Challenge,* first published in France in 1967 and quickly recognized as the classic statement of postwar Europe's ambivalent attitude toward Americanization. Haunted by the decline of earlier civilizations, he warned that if Europeans failed to become sufficiently dynamic to compete with the Americans, Europe would gradually sink into decadence without ever understanding why or how it happened (see the box, "Europe and the American Challenge").

By the 1980s, much of Western Europe had caught up with the United States in standard of living, and the Western Europeans set the pace in confronting some of the new problems that resulted from ongoing socioeconomic change. Confined to a small, fragile continent, Europeans pioneered the environmental movement, and they often took the initiative in responding to new social challenges, as with the French day-care system. The end of the cold war freed Europe from its dependence on America and perhaps opened still greater scope for leadership.

Nonetheless, concerns about Americanization deepened. By the late 1980s, consumerism and the widening impact of American popular culture—from blue jeans and American TV to shopping malls and theme parks—suggested a growing homogenization in the capitalist democracies. A Euro-Disneyland was built in the heart of France. Tangible reminders of Europe's distinctive past remained, but the growing "heritage industry" in Britain and elsewhere suggested that they were merely commodities to be packaged like any other.

Technology and the Fragile European Environment

With the disintegration of the Soviet bloc, it became clear that the years of communism had produced environmental degradation on an appalling scale. The Stalinist determination to industrialize quickly had combined with the Marxist faith in human mastery and progress to produce this result, and those who came after were left to clean up as best they could. But in Western Europe as well, the impact of rapid economic growth on the European landscape and cityscape had provoked concern since the late 1960s.

The number of automobiles in Western Europe increased from 6 million in 1939 to 16 million by 1959 to 42 million by 1969. Almost overnight, traffic and air pollution fundamentally changed the face of Europe's old cities. In 1976 five caryatids that had supported the Eastern Portico of the Erectheum Temple on the Acropolis in Athens since the fifth century B.C. had to be replaced by replicas and put in a museum to save them from the rapid decay that air pollution was causing. There was talk of the "melancholy of progress" as the dimensions of the conflict between economic prosperity and the tangible monuments of Europe's history became clear.

The historic natural setting proved just as vulnerable. By the early 1980s acid rain had damaged one-third of the forests of West Germany, including the famous Black Forest of the south-

Europe and the American Challenge

Writing in 1967, the French writer Jean-Jacques Servan-Schreiber worried that dependence on America would deprive European civilization of its distinctiveness, vitality, and purpose.

Today's generation faces a . . . clear choice of building an independent Europe or letting it become an annex of the United States. The sheer weight of American power is pushing our hesitant countries along the path of annexation, and the point of no return may be reached before today's ten-year-olds are able to vote.

It is still possible for us to catch up, but there is a great deal of dead weight to overcome. . . . [P]erhaps it is asking too much of Europeans to adapt to global competition, shake themselves loose from entrenched national habits, pull together dispersed resources, adjust to severe new rules of management, and stop wasting precious men and capital. Is it reasonable to ask an old continent to show the vitality of a new nation—especially when the satellization of Europe is accompanied, at least initially, by a rising standard of living and by only a very gradual reduction in our freedom of thought? . . .

There is no way of leaving the "economic area" to the Americans so that we can get on with political, social, and cultural areas in our own way, as some people would like to believe. There is no such compartmentalization in the real world. . . .

A few leading firms, subsidiaries of American corporations, would decide how much European workers would earn and how they would live. . . .

. . . [T]hese managers . . . will take a majority interest in, and then control, the firms that dominate the market in publishing, the press, phonograph recording, and television production. The formulas, if not all the details, of our cultural "messages" would be imported. . . .

There is no excuse for Europeans to be passive or complacent, for they are free to examine the American experience critically. . . .

If Europe decides to do this, she would greatly improve the chances of building a decent world, one that could reconcile the unity of modern industrial society with the variety of national cultures that compose it. A polycentric world would ensure a growing exchange of goods and ideas, and the continuing competition between human societies that has always been the condition of human progress. Would an isolated Egypt, Greece, or Rome have done any better than the Mayas trapped in their jungle?

Source: Jean-Jacques Servan-Schreiber, *The American Challenge* (New York: Avon, 1969), pp. 175–180.

west. Water pollution was a major problem from the Rhine to the Mediterranean.

During much of the seventies and eighties, environmental concerns focused on the difficult question of nuclear power, which solved certain environmental problems while posing the risk of still more serious ones. By 1990, the West's greatest proponent of nuclear power was France, which was getting 70 percent of its electricity from nuclear plants and was projecting a goal of 100 percent by 1995. The French could boast that they had experienced no major safety problems and that by using nuclear power they were overcoming the problems of fossil fuels, from acid rain to global warming. In much of Europe, however, there was decisive movement away from nuclear power, even before the Soviet nuclear accident at Chernobyl in 1986. In Germany, the

Concern for the Earth Environmental pollution was a major problem throughout the industrialized world by the last years of the twentieth century, but it was almost catastrophic in parts of the former Soviet bloc. In this photo from Czechoslovakia in 1990, a toxic waste dump stands out in the foreground, while the factory in the background is barely visible through the polluted air. *(Shepard Sherbell/Saba)*

Greens led demonstrations in 1977 that forced the government drastically to decrease its plans for nuclear power. In Austria a referendum banned nuclear power altogether in 1978.

Ethnic Conflict and Tribalism

As the European Community and other supranational organizations became more prominent, forces in the opposite direction—subnational, ethnic, tribal—grew more powerful at the same time, producing conflict from Northern Ireland to Yugoslavia, from Spain to Lithuania. Such ethnic conflict was not new, but especially in the Soviet bloc, it had been kept largely submerged in the rigidly bipolar world of the cold war. To end the cold war was to remove the lid on long-standing ethnic hatreds.

In several of the republics of the former Soviet Union, autonomy and democracy led quickly to intolerance of ethnic minorities. In east-central Europe, Hungary complained of the treatment of the Hungarian minority in Romania, and Czechoslovakia, which had been widely admired for its peaceful, civilized departure from communism, promptly split on ethnic lines. The Slovak minority broke away to form an independent republic at the beginning of 1993. In Yugoslavia, ethnic and religious conflict produced not only the disintegration of the country but also a multi-sided war among Serbs, Croats, and Bosnian Muslims during the early 1990s (Map 32.4).

Indeed, the brutality and hatred that characterized the fighting in the former Yugoslavia brought to an abrupt end the optimism that had surrounded the ending of the cold war. The Serbs were widely accused of "ethnic cleansing," intended to rid Bosnia of its Muslim inhabitants. And the European Community, which had seemed poised to play a more active international role, proved unable to orchestrate a solution to the conflict.

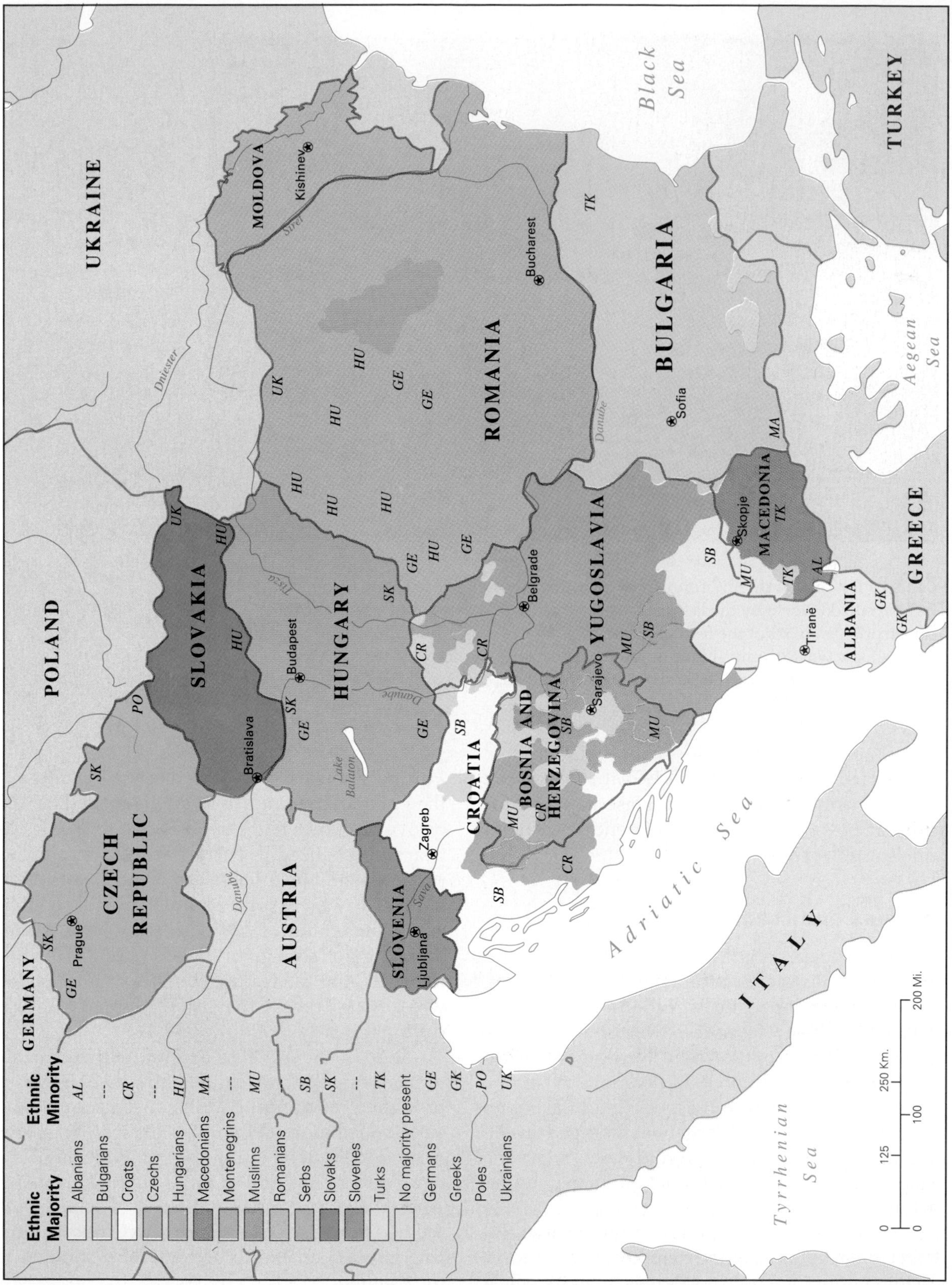
Ethnic Majority
Ethnic Minority
Albanians AL
Bulgarians --
Croats CR
Czechs --
Hungarians HU
Macedonians MA
Montenegrins --
Muslims MU
Romanians --
Serbs SB
Slovaks SK
Slovenes --
Turks TK
No majority present
Germans GE
Greeks GK
Poles PO
Ukrainians UK
0 125 250 Km.
0 100 200 Mi.
GERMANY
POLAND
UKRAINE
CZECH REPUBLIC
Prague
SLOVAKIA
Bratislava
AUSTRIA
HUNGARY
Budapest
Lake Balaton
MOLDOVA
Kishinev
ROMANIA
Bucharest
BULGARIA
Sofia
SLOVENIA
Ljubljana
CROATIA
Zagreb
BOSNIA AND HERZEGOVINA
Sarajevo
YUGOSLAVIA
Belgrade
MACEDONIA
Skopje
ALBANIA
Tiranë
GREECE
TURKEY
ITALY
Black Sea
Aegean Sea
Adriatic Sea
Tyrrhenian Sea
Danube
Dniester
Siret
Tisza
Sava

Detention in Bosnia, August 1992 As the civil war in the former Yugoslavia escalated, Serbs removed Muslims from a large part of Bosnia-Herzegovina and interned many of them in primitive, overcrowded camps, including this one in the Manjaca region of Bosnia. Such haunting images from Bosnia helped shatter the optimism that briefly accompanied the end of the cold war. *(Patrick Robert/Sygma)*

Ethnic conflict was most tragic in east-central Europe, but it grew in Western Europe as well, suggesting that its sources were widespread. Beginning in 1969, the British had to use troops in Northern Ireland to keep order in the face of ongoing threats from Irish Catholics seeking the end of British rule and unification with the Republic of Ireland. The result was polarization between Protestants and Catholics that defied solution into the 1990s. In Spain the restoration of democracy gave the long-restive Basque and Catalan minorities the chance to press openly for autonomy. Even in Belgium, there was growing antagonism between Flemish-speaking Flemings and French-speaking Walloons by the early 1990s.

Map 32.4 Ethnic Conflict in East-Central Europe Much of east-central Europe, and particularly the Balkans, has long been an area of complex ethnic mixture. The end of communist rule opened the way to ethnic conflict, most tragically in what had been Yugoslavia. This map shows ethnic distribution in the region in the early 1990s.

The grievances of ethnic minorities were often real enough, but because ethnicity meshed poorly with geography and political borders, the growing emphasis on ethnic identity was necessarily a source of instability. With the breakup of the communist bloc in east-central Europe, there was some renewed appreciation for the Habsburg system—for what it might, at least, have accomplished. As a prominent aspect of Europe's recent history, it served as a reminder that there might be alternatives to ethnic or national loyalties, that the ethnically homogeneous nation-state was not necessarily progressive, or the foreordained goal of history.

The hostility to immigrants that became a major political issue by the early 1990s seemed related to the eruption of ethnic awareness and conflict. In Britain and France, such sentiment was often racist, directed against nonwhite immigrants from former colonies. As reaction against refugees and foreign workers grew in Germany, the German parliament voted in 1993 to eliminate all foreigners' rights to seek asylum there. Many Germans of the political left criticized the government for turning from Germany's special responsibility after Nazism, but the claims of immigrants and refugees confronted all the Western democracies with difficult questions about governmental responsibility, national sovereignty, and the meaning of citizenship.

All over Western Europe, immigration proved such a volatile issue because of the persistence of high unemployment, the result of technological change and increasing global competition. The combination of ethnic conflict, regionalism, and anti-immigrant sentiment reflected a diminishing sense of community, a growing intolerance for diversity, that might damage the effectiveness of the European political systems in the future. This concern cast a shadow over the democracy that had apparently emerged victorious from the cold war.

The Uncertain Triumph of Democratic Capitalism

The end of the cold war, the discrediting of communism, and the domestication of socialism all seemed to mean the triumph of political democracy and some form of free-market capitalism. The superiority of both to the Soviet alternatives were all but universally recognized by the early 1990s. But though there was a good deal of self-congratulation in the West at first, victory did not satisfy for long, for there was growing uneasiness about democratic capitalism, despite its undoubted advantages over the Soviet system. What followed the West's victory in the cold war was not a period of untroubled confidence but a deeper questioning of the capitalist democracy that had triumphed.

In light of the Western political experience so far, few denied that what had proven to work best, and afforded the only basis for political legitimacy, was representative democracy based on universal suffrage, within an open, pluralistic society guaranteeing individual freedom. There must be freedom not only to inquire and to criticize but also to pursue individual advantage within a market economy. On the other hand, that free-market system had to be bounded by some measure of government responsibility for social welfare. Although the socialist left had won reforms that were now central to the consensus around democratic capitalism, it had abandoned much of what it had stood for—from class struggle and revolution to the goal of state ownership and a centrally planned economy. Socialism could apparently serve only as the mildly left-leaning party within the framework of capitalist democracy.

The resulting narrowing of the political spectrum promised consensus and stability, but it also meant a restriction of the scope for constructive collective action through the political process. And this gave pause as the capacity of the democratic political order to match the force of international capitalism seemed increasingly in question. As global competition intensified, the logic of capitalism seemed ever more relentless, fundamentally determining community well-being. It could require plant closings, and it increasingly called forth political bidding to attract the businesses that alone could provide the jobs and pay the taxes. New multinational groupings like the G7 managed to keep the international economy in bounds, but the relationship between triumphant capitalism and triumphant democracy remained uneasy.

Participation in the national political process came to seem less significant as the range of political choices contracted and as it became clear that many of the key decisions were being made elsewhere, often by multinational corporations or supranational organizations, outside the sphere of national politics and government. By the early 1990s, political disillusionment was growing all over Europe, in light of the apparently diminished scope for constructive public action. One symptom was declining voter turnout. Decreasing interest in politics meant an increasing emphasis on private concerns and satisfactions. So it remained unclear whether modern democracy could deal with the challenges facing the advanced capitalist economies in this era of global economic competition.

Conclusion: Western Civilization in a Global Age

Though it seemed only a balance of terror at the time, the cold war had provided a measure of order and security to the years from 1949 to 1989. As the end of the bipolar world led to new uncer-

Old and New in Contemporary Europe Especially with the transformation of Europe since World War II, new styles of life intersect with living artifacts from the past to form sometimes ironic combinations. Here, in a neighborhood in Milan, Italy, teenagers wearing blue jeans and backpacks seem oblivious to the legacies of Roman antiquity and Christianity that are prominent around them. *(© 1993 George Steinmetz)*

tainties and dangers, nostalgia for the stability of the cold war era was not long in coming. But the chance for a different configuration of the West and a more central role for Europe meant opportunity as well as uncertainty. And it stimulated some rethinking about what the Western tradition had meant—and might mean for the future.

The West was now part of a world that, in one sense, was dramatically less Eurocentric than it had been just a half-century before. Events in the West competed for attention with OPEC meetings, Japanese economic decisions, or the struggle against apartheid in South Africa. Decisions vitally affecting Europeans might be made anywhere. A planetary culture, a threatened environment, and an interdependent international economy required people to think and react in global terms as never before.

Nonetheless, for better or worse, institutions and ideals that had emerged from within Western civilization existed throughout much of the world, if only to provide a standard or direction. To be sure, the ideal of individual freedom in an open society remained imperfectly realized even in the West, and political democracy and market capitalism were continuing experiments, not finished solutions that others could adopt wholesale. But Westernization had been fundamental to the global experience of the twentieth century, and the West could not avoid playing a distinctive role in the future (see the box, "The Universal West: Experiment, Openness, Possibility").

The Universal West: Experiment, Openness, Possibility

V. S. Naipaul (b. 1932) was born and raised in Trinidad, part of a family of Indian Hindu descent, then went to London in the 1950s, gradually establishing himself as an important novelist. Speaking in New York in 1990, he sought to pinpoint the values that have made Western civilization at once unique and universal. He began by reflecting on his own non-Western background.

We were a people of ritual and sacred texts. . . . But it couldn't be said that we were a literary people. Our literature, our texts, didn't commit us to an exploration of our world; rather they were cultural markers, giving us a sense of the wholeness of our world, and the alienness of what lay outside. I don't believe that, in his family, anyone before my father would have thought of original literary composition. That idea came to my father in Trinidad with the English language . . . in spite of the colonial discouragements of the place. . . .

The universal civilization has been a long time in the making. It wasn't always universal; it wasn't always as attractive as it is today. The expansion of Europe gave it for at least three centuries a racial tint, which still causes pain. In Trinidad I grew up in the last days of that kind of racialism. And that, perhaps, has given me a greater appreciation of the immense changes that have taken place since the end of the war, the extraordinary attempt of this civilization to accommodate the rest of the world, and all the currents of that world's thought. . . .

. . . [T]he idea of the pursuit of happiness . . . is at the heart of the attractiveness of the civilization to so many outside it or on its periphery. . . . It is an elastic idea; it fits all men. It implies a certain kind of society, a certain kind of awakened spirit. I don't imagine my father's parents would have been able to understand the idea. So much is contained in it: the idea of the individual, responsibility, choice, the life of the intellect, the idea of vocation and perfectibility and achievement. It is an immense human idea. It cannot be reduced to a fixed system. It cannot generate fanaticism. But it is known to exist; and because of that, other more rigid systems in the end blow away.

Source: V. S. Naipaul, "Our Universal Civilization," reprinted in *The New York Review of Books*, January 31, 1991, pp. 22, 25.

The Columbian Quincentenary of 1992, which had been expected to be a festive celebration, proved a more somber occasion because the reflection it produced brought home how tragically history operates. The "rise of the West," the "progress of Westernization," the spread of the white Europeans throughout the globe no longer seemed evidence of God's will, or providence, or reason, or progress, or even "development." Rather than indulge in self-congratulation, many pondered the costs and the losses of the spread of Western civilization to the Americas. Such thinking even produced a backlash against the study of Western civilization—no doubt understandably, after the long tradition of glorification.

But that challenge made it clearer that the point of such study was not to celebrate Western civilization but to understand it critically as the matrix that continued to shape not only the West but the world. That tradition entailed much that might be criticized, and its present outcome entailed much that might be changed, but understanding had to come first. The invitation to think freely about the Western tradition, to criticize it, and to build a better future on it, rested on precisely that tradition—and is perhaps its most fundamental legacy.

Suggested Reading

The New Society in Western Europe

Ardagh, John. *France in the 1980s.* 1983. From the perspective of the early 1980s, a leading observer of French society offers a lively survey of the changes in French life since the war.

Barkan, Joanne. *Visions of Emancipation: The Italian Workers' Movement Since 1945.* 1984. A sympathetic account of the influential postwar Italian labor movement. Provides a good feel for the experience of factory workers and makes sense of their demands for autonomy.

Bridenthal, Renate, et al., eds. *Becoming Visible: Women in European History.* 1987. A major collection of essays on women's history, including seven that deal with twentieth-century topics. Jane Jenson's "Both Friend and Foe: Women and State Welfare" offers an illuminating comparative study of women and the welfare systems in Britain and France in the post–World War II period.

Craig, Gordon A. *The Germans.* 1991. A distinguished historian of modern Germany places the recent German experience in historical perspective. First published in 1982, but with a new afterword for the 1991 edition.

Hollifield, James F., and George Ross, eds. *Searching for the New France.* 1991. A collection of essays on topics from political structure and foreign policy to immigration and higher education.

Kramer, Jane. *Europeans.* 1988. By focusing on concrete episodes and personalities, this European correspondent for *The New Yorker* provides a good sense of the connection between the lives of ordinary people and larger public and historical issues.

Marwick, Arthur. *British Society Since 1945.* 1990. A lively, comprehensive survey, accenting the change to a consumer culture in the sixties, but with due emphasis on the conservative transformation of the 1980s.

Ruggie, Mary. *The State and Working Women: A Comparative Study of Britain and Sweden.* 1984. A sophisticated comparative study that seeks to explain why women have achieved greater economic equality in Sweden than in Britain.

Sorlin, Pierre. *European Cinemas, European Societies 1939–1990.* 1991. Emphasizes the themes of urbanization, immigration, and gender. Contrasts European with U.S. filmmaking.

Tipton, Frank B., and Robert Aldrich. *An Economic and Social History of Europe from 1939 to the Present.* 1987. A well-balanced survey that covers the whole of Europe.

Williams, Shirley. *A Job to Live: The Impact of Tomorrow's Technology on Work and Society.* 1985. A prominent British political leader's searching analysis of the implications of technological innovation for both employment and democratic politics.

Democracy and Its Discontents in Western Europe

Bell, D.S., and Byron Criddle. *The French Socialist Party: The Emergence of a Party of Government.* 2d ed. 1988. An accessible and sympathetic account of the transformation of the Socialist party that enabled it to assume a major role in French politics by the 1980s.

Fulbrook, Mary. *The Divided Nation: A History of Germany, 1918–1990.* 1992. A solid survey, incorporating the East German revolution of 1989 and the subsequent reunification of Germany.

Hughes, H. Stuart. *Sophisticated Rebels: The Political Culture of European Dissent, 1968–1987.* 1988. Elegant essays on diverse aspects of recent European political culture, focusing on the scope for dissent.

Jenkins, Peter. *Mrs. Thatcher's Revolution.* 1988. Accents the positive changes that resulted from Thatcher's attempt to confront the British socioeconomic crisis.

Maier, Charles, ed. *Changing Boundaries of the Political: Essays on the Evolving Balance Between the State and Society, Public and Private in Europe.* 1987. Though uneven and sometimes difficult, this is a useful collection of essays on an important and elusive topic. Good, for example, on the changing politics of health care.

Riddell, Peter. *The Thatcher Era and Its Legacy.* 1991. A leading British financial journalist offers a generally positive assessment of the economic impact of Thatcher's innovations.

Singer, Daniel. *Is Socialism Doomed? The Meaning of Mitterrand.* 1988. Analyzes the ambiguities and contradictions in Mitterrand's political stance and concludes that socialism must be reinvented more fundamentally.

Young, Hugo. *The Iron Lady: A Biography of Margaret Thatcher.* 1989. A full-scale and readable biography that challenges Thatcher's consistency and questions her achievement.

The Transformation in Eastern and East-Central Europe

Garton Ash, Timothy. *The Magic Lantern: The Revolution of '89 Witnessed in Warsaw, Budapest, Berlin, and Prague.* 1990. Firsthand testimony on the fall of communism by a British intellectual with close contacts among anticommunists in east-central Europe.

Weighing the Evidence

CURRENT EVENTS AS HISTORY

The dismantling of the Berlin Wall in November 1989 was a defining episode in the revolution that toppled communism in east-central Europe and ended the cold war era. As that revolution unfolded, television images and journalistic chronicles conveyed events to a fascinated, astonished world. Men and women caught up in those events knew they were making history, and people following the story as it happened knew they were watching history being made.

In one sense, of course, history is being made around us all the time, and our overall historical understanding endlessly expands to encompass new "current events." However, the dramatic revolution of 1989 raised a series of questions about how we incorporate such events into our understanding of history. As the photograph here suggests, the dismantling of the Berlin Wall was a media event; we could see it happening.

> Hindsight is also a disadvantage. Perhaps the most difficult thing of all for the historian to recapture is the sense of what, at a given historical moment, people did not know about the future. *(Timothy Garton Ash, "Refolution in Hungary and Poland,"* New York Review of Books, *August 17, 1989, p. 9.)*
>
> If there were uncertainties about the post-revolutionary transitions in Poland and Hungary, they were nothing compared to those in East Germany, no, in Germany as a whole. The West German government, which for decades had urged the East German regime to let the people go, was now delighted but also appalled by the consequences of the regime doing precisely that. For the people were coming to West Germany at a rate which threatened to overwhelm their housing market and welfare state, and, above all, to provoke a domestic political backlash. *(Timothy Garton Ash,* The Magic Lantern: The Revolution of '89 Witnessed in Warsaw, Budapest, Berlin, and Prague *[New York: Random House, 1990], p. 76.)*

But the meaning of what was happening was hardly obvious. The fall of the wall suggests an end to the most repressive features of communism, but it also suggests something quite different—the reunification of Germany. So how do we fit this very public and visible event into the larger sweep of modern history?

As was true in 1989, it is journalistic writers, not historians, who provide the initial chronicle of the events we live through. In the period that led to the anticommunist revolution of 1989, Timothy Garton Ash, a British writer with wide contacts among opposition intellectuals in east-central Europe, proved unusually successful at making sense of events as they occurred. His solid grounding in the history of the region enabled him to explain the developing opposition movement and to assess its prospects. But his more general historical sensitivity, his sense of how things happen, also served him well. He kept in mind what he notes in the first passage here—that those involved, including observers like himself, did *not* know what later historians would know about the events in progress.

Seeking to place the fall of the Berlin Wall in historical perspective, Garton Ash looked into both the past and the future. East German opposition leaders had been seeking not the fall of communism or the reunification of Germany but simply an end to the repressiveness within East Germany that the wall epitomized. They were still hoping to create a viable socialist alternative, more humane than the free-market capitalism of the West. Yet events escaped their control, and with the opening of the wall the quest for reform became a movement for reunification, including the embrace of West German capitalism.

Because the fall of the wall was simply part of the West's continuing history, Garton Ash was quick to emphasize that what might result from it remained uncertain. In the second passage here, he notes that reunification could produce unforeseen problems for the Federal Republic, the former West Germany. Moreover, it was hardly clear what the fall of the wall and German re-

Watching the Wall Come Down *(Reuters/Bettmann Newsphotos)*

unification would mean for Germany's neighbors in east-central Europe or for Germany's overall place in the world.

In the years before 1989 Garton Ash traveled widely in east-central Europe and wrote a number of articles seeking to explain that something potentially momentous was stirring there. But at each moment, he understood that there were myriad possibilities, some tragic, some disappointing, some happier, but none perfect. Because he was so sensitive to the open-endedness of history, Garton Ash was better able than most to expect the unexpected. Thus he suggested in June 1989 that Hungary's communist leaders might give up power more or less voluntarily, an outcome that still seemed almost inconceivable. Yet it happened within months.

Still, Garton Ash took care not to claim prophecy. No one could know what would result, in the longer term, from the fall of communism in east-central Europe—and by 1991 in the Soviet Union as well. What would follow could only be part of the continuing experiment.

Although we are constantly reinterpreting the past in light of new experiences, the revolution of 1989 presented a particular challenge because it forced us to reconsider the significance of some of the pivotal events of the twentieth century. The collapse of communism put the Russian Revolution of 1917 in a different light. And the abrupt end of the cold war radically altered our perspective on the Allied victory in 1945 and the subsequent division of Europe. For decades, 1945 had seemed to constitute a permanent watershed in the history of the West. But with the end of the cold war, Germany reunified and ethnic conflict returned, so we had to think again about what had, and had not, changed with the era of the two world wars that had ended in 1945.

Although Soviet-style communism seemed discredited for good by the early 1990s, much remained uncertain in the formerly communist part of Europe. The meaning of the revolution of 1989, its import and place in history, depended on subsequent history, on what had not happened yet. Indeed, trying to make sense of those events made it clearer that at no point within history does the meaning of such events become fixed. The world changes, so we keep taking a fresh look at our history. In a sense, in fact, what we make of it is up to us—as we, too, help to continue the experiment.

At first it is a little unnerving to realize that we must continually change our historical account as we interpret contemporary events. Isn't this to invite relativism, even to offer a license to interpret history any way we like, perhaps to serve our own political purposes? But on further reflection, we recognize that to live in this world, to act effectively within it, we need to understand it. Thus, we try to approach even the very recent past in a genuinely historical way, not to confirm what we already think we know, but to learn as much as we can.

———. *The Uses of Adversity: Essays on the Fate of Central Europe.* 1990. Essays on the tensions and responses that helped bring about the fall of communism in east-central Europe.

Goldman, Marshall I. *Gorbachev's Challenge: Economic Reform in the Age of High Technology.* 1987. Written during the early years of Gorbachev's reform effort but good at pinpointing both the reasons for that effort and the obstacles that ultimately frustrated it.

———. *What Went Wrong with Perestroika.* 1991. Focuses on the incongruity between the successful political restructuring, which went beyond what Gorbachev intended, and the inadequate economic reform.

Gorbachev, Mikhail. *Perestroika: New Thinking for Our Country and the World.* 1987. The Soviet leader's blueprint for reform, offering visionary proposals for change in both the Soviet system and international relations.

Havel, Václav. *Disturbing the Peace: A Conversation With Karel Hvížďala.* 1991. Part autobiography, part history, part philosophy, part personal testimony. Demonstrates the moral vision that made Havel so effective as a leader in the Czech opposition to communism.

———. *Summer Meditations.* 1992. The first post–communist era president of Czechoslovakia reflects on the nature of politics and on the new situation facing east-central Europe after the fall of communism.

Hosking, Geoffrey. *The Awakening of the Soviet Union.* Enlarged ed. 1991. Seeks to understand the Gorbachev reform effort from the perspective of ordinary people. Accents the potential for autonomy and initiative that would enable Soviet citizens to carry the reform effort beyond the intent of its leaders.

Kornai, János. *The Road to a Free Economy: Shifting from a Socialist System: The Example of Hungary.* 1990. Accessible study of the transition from a command to a market economy, by a leading expert on the socialist economies of east-central Europe.

Laba, Roman. *The Roots of Solidarity.* 1991. Seeks to show that workers, as opposed to the Polish intelligentsia, were the driving force behind the Solidarity movement.

Vaksberg, Arkady. *The Soviet Mafia.* 1991. A bitterly critical account, showing how systematic corruption by Communist party officials drastically complicated the transition to a capitalist economy in the former Soviet Union.

Toward the Post–Cold War Era

Albert, Michel. *Capitalism Against Capitalism.* 1993. Examination by a French economist and business leader of the changing face of democratic capitalism. Assesses the options for France in light of the contrasting approaches of Germany and the United States.

Krause, Axel. *Inside the New Europe.* 1991. An accessible account of the continuing movement toward European integration, based on interviews with leading businessmen, politicians, and Eurocrats. Shows why the integration movement can seem threatening to ordinary people in light of increasing global economic competition.

Treverton, Gregory. *America, Germany, and the Future of Europe.* 1992. By treating the historical background of European-American relations after the cold war, this book shows why the United States seems bound to play a diminished role in Europe.

Chapter Opener Credits

Chapter 1: Egyptian Expedition of The Metropolitan Museum of Art, Rogers Fund, 1915. (15.5.1)
Chapter 2: Louvre © Photo R.M.N.
Chapter 3: The Ancient Art & Architecture Collection
Chapter 4: Museum of Thessaloniki
Chapter 5: Mike Yamashita/Woodfin Camp & Associates
Chapter 6: Scala/Art Resource, NY
Chapter 7: Scala/Art Resource, NY
Chapter 8: R.W. Schlegelmilch/Thames and Hudson Ltd.
Chapter 9: National Museum of Ireland
Chapter 10: Tapissérie de la Reine Mathilde, Ville de Bayeux
Chapter 11: Sonia Halliday Photographs
Chapter 12: The British Library. Ms. C, VII, f. 41
Chapter 13: Bibliothèque Nationale
Chapter 14: Scala/Art Resource, NY
Chapter 15: Trans. no. V/C 31(2). Courtesy Department of Library Sciences, American Museum of Natural History
Chapter 16: Siegfried Lauterwasser
Chapter 17: MAS, Barcelona
Chapter 18: Michael Holford
Chapter 19: Museum of the History of Science, Oxford/The Bettmann Archive
Chapter 20: Private collection/John Webb Photography
Chapter 21: Jean-Loup Charmet
Chapter 22: The Hermitage, Inv. No. 4753, Oil on canvas, 26 x 37½″
Chapter 23: Spectrum Colour Library
Chapter 24: The Royal Collection © 1993 Her Majesty Queen Elizabeth II
Chapter 25: The Tate Gallery/Art Resource, NY
Chapter 26: Arborio Mella
Chapter 27: Trustees of the Imperial War Museum
Chapter 28: Berlinische Galerie, Museum für Moderne Kunst Photographie und Architecktur
Chapter 29: Keystone Press
Chapter 30: Courtesy Bison Books, London
Chapter 31: Alain Nogues/Sygma
Chapter 32: Hideo Kurihara/© Tony Stone Worldwide

Text Credits

Chapter 1: p. 3: Sumerian poem from *History Begins at Sumer: Thirty-nine Firsts in Man's Recorded History,* 3d revised edition by Samuel Noah Kramer. Copyright © 1981, pp. 91, 94. By permission of University of Pennsylvania Press. **pp. 15, 17, 23, 26:** Boxes from Pritchard, James B., *Ancient Near Eastern Texts Relating to the Old Testament,* 3d ed. Copyright © 1969 by Princeton University Press. Reprinted by permission of Princeton University Press. **p. 34:** "A Hittite King Analyzes Politics," From *The Hittites,* 3d ed. by O. R. Gurney, pp. 175–176. Copyright © 1975. Reproduced by permission of Penguin Books Ltd.

Chapter 2: All Biblical quotations are from The Revised English Bible. Copyright © Oxford University Press and Cambridge University Press, 1989. Reprinted by permission. **p. 45:** "An Assyrian King Attacks Phoenicia and Jerusalem," from Pritchard, James B., *Ancient Near Eastern Texts Relating to the Old Testament,* 3d ed. Copyright © 1969 by Princeton University Press. Reprinted by permission of Princeton University Press. **p. 60:** "Cyrus and His Subjects' Gods," From Pritchard, James B.; *Ancient Near Eastern Texts Relating to the Old Testament,* 3/e. Copyright © 1969 by Princeton University Press. Reprinted by permission of Princeton University Press. **p. 70:** "A Greek Goddess Speaks to a Mortal," from THE ODYSSEY by Homer, trans. R. Fitzgerald. Copyright © 1961, 1963 by Robert Fitzgerald and renewed 1989 by Benedict R. C. Fitzgerald. **p. 73:** "Homeric Society," from THE ILIAD by Homer. Copyright © 1974 by Robert Fitzgerald. Used by permission of Doubleday, a division of Bantam Doubleday Dell Publishing Group, Inc.

Chapter 3: p. 87: "An Oracle Establishes Sparta's Government," from "Life of Lycurgus," by Plutarch in *Plutarch on Sparta,* translated by Richard J.A. Talbert. Translation copyright © 1946 J. A. Talbert, 1988. Reprinted by permission of Penguin Books Ltd. **p. 93:** Quotes reprinted from Charles Rowan Beye, *Ancient Greek Literature and Society,* Second Edition. Copyright © 1987 by Cornell University. Published 1987 by Cornell University Press. **p. 96:** "The Archaic World View: 'Look to the End'," from *The Histories,* translated by Aubrey de Sélincourt. Copyright © the Estate of Aubrey de Sélincourt, 1958. Reproduced by permission of Penguin Books Ltd. **p. 100:** "The Debate on Democracy," from "The Suppliant Women," by Euripides, from *The Complete Greek Tragedies,* edited by Richmond Lattimore and David Grene. Copyright © 1958. Reprinted by permission of The University of Chicago Press. **p. 103:** "A Wealthy Woman Gives a Speech," from *Lysias,* translated by W.R.M. Lamb, pp. 667–671. Copyright © 1926 by Harvard University Press. **p. 110:** "Socrates' Defense," from *The Last Days of Socrates* translated by Hugh Tredennick, 1954, 1959, 1969. Reproduced by permission of Penguin Books Ltd. **p. 112:** "'Man Is a Political Animal'," adapted from *The Politics of Aristotle,* edited and translated by Ernest Barker, copyright © 1946. Reprinted by permission of Oxford University Press.

Chapter 4: p. 124: "Virtues and Vices of Alexander the Great," from *The Campaigns of Alexander* by Arrian, translated by Aubrey de Sélincourt. Copyright © the Estate of Aubrey de Sélincourt, 1958. Reproduced by permission of Penguin Books Ltd. **p. 134:** "An Alexandrian Procession," from *The Hellenistic World from Alexander the Great to the Roman Conquest: A Selection of Ancient Sources in Translation* by M.M. Austin. Copyright © 1981. Used by permission of Cambridge University Press. **p. 140:** "Jason and Medea," from *Voyage of the Argo* by Apollonius of Rhodes, translated by E. V. Rieu. Copyright © E. V. Rieu, 1959, 1971. Reproduced by permission of Penguin Books Ltd. **p. 144:** "A Seleucid Queen Helps the City of Iasos," adapted from the translation in *The Hellenistic Age from the Battle of Ipsos to the death of Kleopatra VII,* edited and translated by Stanley M. Burstein. Copyright © 1985. Used by permission of Cambridge University Press. **p. 146:** "Early Stoic Ethics and Politics," reprinted with the permission of The Free Press, a Division of Macmillan, Inc., from GREEK AND ROMAN PHILOSOPHY AFTER ARISTOTLE, edited by Jason L. Saunders. Copyright © 1966 by Jason L. Saunders. **p. 148:** "The Jews Struggle over Hellenism," from I Maccabees, *The Anchor Bible, vol. 41,* translation, notes, and commentary by Jonathan A. Goldstein. Copyright © 1976 by Jonathan A. Goldstein. Used by permission of Doubleday, a division of Bantam Doubleday Dell Publishing Group, Inc.

Chapter 5: p. 155: Excerpt from *The Aeneid of Vergil* translated by Allen Mandelbaum, copyright ©1971. Reprinted by permission of Bantam Books, a division of Bantam Doubleday Dell Publishing Group, Inc. **p. 164:** "The Rape of Lucretia," from *The Early History of Rome* by Livy, translated by Aubrey de Sélincourt, introduction by R.M. Ogilvie. Copyright © 1960, the Estate of Aubrey de Sélincourt, 1960. Reproduced by permission of Penguin Books Ltd. **p. 174:** "The Law of the Twelve Tables," from *Roman Civilization, Sourcebook I: The Republic,* edited by Naphtali Lewis and Meyer Reinhold. Copyright © Columbia University Press, New York. Reprinted with the permission of the publisher. **p. 176:** "A Roman Triumph," from *Roman Civilization, Sourcebook I: The Republic,* edited by Naphtali Lewis and Meyer Reinhold. Copyright © Columbia University Press, New York. Reprinted with the permission of the publisher. **p. 181:** "Aftermath of the Battle of Cannae," from *The Rise of the Roman Empire* by Polybius, translated by Ian Scott-Kilvert. Copyright © Ian Scott-Kilvert, 1979. Reproduced by permission of Penguin Books Ltd. **p. 186:** "Cato the Censor on Agriculture," from *Roman Civilization, Sourcebook I: The Republic* edited by Naphtali Lewis and Meyer Reinhold. Copyright © Columbia University Press, New York. Reprinted with the permission of the publisher.

Chapter 6: All Biblical quotations are from The Revised English Bible. Copyright © Oxford University Press and Cambridge University Press, 1989. Reprinted by permission. **p. 195:** "Tiberius Gracchus on Rome's Plight," from *Roman Civilization: Selected Readings, Volume I: The Republic,* 3d ed., by Meyer Reinhold & Naphtali Lewis. Copyright © 1990 Columbia University Press, New York. Reprinted with the permission of the publisher. **p. 202:** "Cicero Against Catilina," from *Selected Political Speeches* by Cicero, translated by Michael Grant. Copyright © Michael Grant Publications Ltd., 1969. Reproduced by permission of Penguin Books, Ltd. **p. 206:** "Augustus: The Offficial Story," from *Res Gestae Divi Augusti: The Achievements of the Divine Augustus* edited by P. A. Brunt and J. M. Moore, copyright © 1967. Reprinted by permission of Oxford University Press. **p. 207:** "Augustus: A Skeptical View," from *The Annals of Imperial Rome* by Tacitus, translated by Michael Grant. Copyright © Michael Grant Publications Ltd., 1956, 1959, 1971. Reproduced by permission of Penguin Books Ltd. **p. 217:** "Suicide," from *The Annals of Imperial Rome* translated by Michael Grant. Copyright © 1988. Reproduced by permission of Penguin Books Ltd.

Chapter 7: p. 249: "Perception and Prejudice: A Roman on the Huns," from *The Later Roman Empire (A.D. 354–378)* by Ammianus Marcellinus, edited and translated by Walter Hill. Translation copyright © Walter Hill, 1986. Reproduced by permission of Penguin Books Ltd. **p. 250:** "A King and a Bishop: The New Order in Gaul," from *Christianity and Paganism, 350–750: The Conversion of Western Europe,* edited and translated by J.N. Hillgarth, p. 76. Copyright 1986. By permission of Penguin Books Ltd. **p. 257:** "Basic Principles of Roman Law," reprinted by permission of Duckworth from Justinian's INSTITUTES. Introduction and translation © 1987 by Peter Birks and Grant McLeod. Published 1987 by Cornell University Press. **p. 262:** "Melania the Younger: The Appeal of Monasticism to Women," reprinted by permission of Edwin Mellen Press. **p. 265:** "The Moment of Augustine's Spiritual Awakening," from *Confessions* by Saint Augustine, translated by R. S. Pine-Coffin. Copyright © R.S. Pine-Coffin, 1961. Reproduced by permission of Penguin Books Ltd.

Chapter 8: pp. 278 and 285: "The Failure of the Umayyads" and "Muslim and Byzantine Insults," from *Islam: From the Prophet Muhammed to the Capture of Constantinople,* vol. 1, by Bernard Lewis. Copyright © 1974 by Bernard Lewis. Reprinted by permission of HarperCollins Publishers, Inc.

Chapter 10: p. 347: "The Expansion of Cultivated Land," from *The Expansion of Cultivated Land from Rural Economy and Country Life in the Medieval West* by Georges Duby, translated by Cynthia Postan. Copyright © 1968. Reprinted by permission of Hodder & Stoughton Limited. **p. 381:** "The Death of a Hero," from *Beowulf, A Verse Translation into Modern English* by Edward Morgan. Copyright © 1967. Reprinted by permission of the author.

Chapter 11: p. 397: "Innocent III on His Rights and Powers," from THE CRISIS OF CHURCH & STATE 1050–1300, by Brian Tierney © 1964, 1992. Used by permission of the publisher, Prentice-Hall/A Division of Simon & Schuster, Englewood Cliffs, N.J. **p. 405:** "Selections from Magna Carta," from *Magna Carta* by J.C. Holt. Copyright © 1969. Reprinted by permission of Cambridge University Press. **p. 413:** "Pronouncements of the Fourth Lateran Council on Heresy," from *Documents of the Christian Church,* 2d ed., by Henry Bettenson. Copyright © 1963. Reprinted by permission of Oxford University Press. **p. 421:** "Thomas Aquinas's Proof for the Existence of God," used by permission of the A.C. Pegis Estate.

Chapter 12: p. 443: "The Battle of Crécy," from *Chronicles* by Jean Froissart, translated by Geoffrey Brereton (Penguin Classics, 1968). Translation copyright © Geoffrey Brereton, 1968. Reproduced by permission of Penguin Books Ltd. **p. 453:** "Saint Catherine of Siena Criticizes the Popes in Avignon," translated in *Babylon on the Rhone: A Translation of Letters by Dante, Petrarch, and Catherine of Siena on the Avignon Papacy* by Robert Coogan. Copyright © 1983. Used by permission of the author. **p. 459:** "The Black Death," from THE DECAMERON by Giovanni Boccaccio, translated by Mark Musa and Peter Bondanella. Translation copyright © 1982 by Mark Musa and Peter Bondanella. Introduction copyright © 1981, 1982 by Thomas Bergin. Used by permission of Dutton Signet, a division of Penguin Books USA Inc. **p. 461:** "Christians, Flagellants, and Jews," from *Chronicles* by Jean Froissart, translated by Geoffrey Brereton (Penguin Classics, 1968). Translation copyright © Geoffrey Brereton, 1968. Reproduced by permission of Penguin Books Ltd. **p. 467:** "The Rising of 1381," from R. B. Dobson, *The Peasant's Revolt of 1381,* 2d ed. Copyright © 1983. Reprinted by permission of Macmillan Ltd.

Chapter 13: p. 477: "The Efficient Merchant," From *Medieval Trade in the Mediterranean World,* edited by Robert S. Lopez and Irving Raymond. Copyright © 1955 by Columbia University Press, New York. Reprinted with the permission of the publisher. **p. 491:** "Louis XI and the Art of Government," reprinted by permission of D.C. Heath. **p. 502:** "A European View of the Ottoman Empire," portions of pages 126, 127, 129, and 134–135 from PURSUIT OF POWER: VENETIAN AMBASSADORS' REPORTS ON SPAIN, TURKEY, AND FRANCE IN THE AGE OF PHILLIP II, 1550–1600 by James C. Davis. Copyright © 1970 by James C. Davis. Reprinted by permission of HarperCollins, Publishers, Inc. **p. 504:** "The Expulsion of the Jews," reprinted by permission of Carmi House.

Chapter 14: p. 513: Quote from the play, *Ecerinis,* from *Art and Politics in Late Medieval and Early Renaissance Italy, 1250–1500,* edited by Charles M. Rosenberg. © 1990 by the University of Notre Dame Press. Used by permission. **p. 515:** "Petrarch Responds to His Critics," from "On His Own Ignorance and That of Many Others," by Petrarch from *The Renaissance Philosophy of Man,* edited by Ernst Cassirer, Paul Oskar Kristeller, and John H. Randall. Copyright © 1948. Reprinted by permission of the University of Chicago Press. **p. 518:** "Cassandra Fedele Defends Liberal Arts for Women," reprinted by permission of State University of New York. **p. 525:** "Giorgio Vasari on the History of Art," from *The Lives of Artists, Vol. 1,* by Giorgio Vasari, translated by George Bull. Copyright © George Bull, 1965. **p. 526:** Poem extract from the *Italian Renaissance Reader* by Julia Bondanella and Mark Musa. Copyright © 1987 by Julia Conaway Bondanella and Mark Musa. Used by permission of New American Library, a division of Penguin Books USA Inc. **p. 540:** "Giovanni Della Casa on the Perfect Gentleman," from the Portable Renaissance Reader, edited by James B. Ross and Mary Martin McLaughlin. Copyright 1953, renewed © 1981 by Viking Penguin Inc. Used by permission of Viking Penguin, a division of Penguin Books USA Inc.

Chapter 15: p. 551: "Pegalotti on Travel to the East," from *Medieval Trade in the Mediterranean World,* edited by Robert S. Lopez and Irving Raymond. Copyright © 1955 by Columbia University Press, New York. Reprinted with the permission of the publisher. **p. 558:** "Albuquerque Defends the Portuguese Empire," from *Albuquerque, Caesar of the East,* by Earle and Villiers, Warminster, 1990. Reprinted by permission of Aris & Phillips Ltd. **p. 574:** "The New World and the Old," from *General History of the Things of New Spain: Florentine Codex,* edited and translated by J. O. Anderson and Charles E. Dibble, Part 1, pp. 96–97. Copyright 1950. Reprinted by permission of the School of American Research Press.

Chapter 16: p. 585: "Martin Luther's Address to the Christian Nobility of the German Nation," from *Documents Illustrative of the Continental Reformation,* edited by Beresford James Kidd, copyright © 1967. By permission of Oxford University Press.

p. 595: "The Peace of Augsburg," from *Documents Illustrative of the Continental Reformation,* edited by Beresford James Kidd, copyright © 1967. By permission of Oxford University Press. **p. 608:** "Ignatius Loyola's Spiritual Exercises," from David Englander, Diana Norman, Rosemary O'Day, and W. R. Owens, eds. *Culture and Brief in Europe 1450–1600: An Anthology of Sources* (Oxford, England: Basil Blackwell in association with the Open University, 1990), pp. 241–242. Reprinted by permission.

Chapter 17: **p. 650:** "Montaigne Discusses Barbarity in the New World and the Old," from *The Complete Essays of Montaigne,* translated by Donald M. Frame. Copyright © 1948. Reprinted by permission of the publisher, Stanford University Press.

Chapter 19: **p. 715:** "Galileo Challenges the Authority of Aristotle," from *The Discoveries and Opinions of Galileo* by Stillman Drake. Copyright © 1957. Reprinted by the permission of Doubleday, a division of Bantam Doubleday Dell Publishing Group, Inc. **p. 716:** "Galileo Confronts the Church," from *The Discoveries and Opinions of Galileo* by Stillman Drake. Copyright © 1957. Reprinted by the permission of Doubleday, a division of Bantam Doubleday Dell Publishing Group, Inc. **p. 721:** "Descartes's Meditations," from *The Philosophical Works of Rene Descartes,* trans. by Elizabeth S. Haldane and G. R. T. Ross, reprinted in *Great Books of the Western World,* edited by Mortimer Adler. Copyright © 1990. Reprinted by permission of Cambridge University Press. **p. 725:** "Newton on God and Gravity," from Isaac Newton, Florian Cajori, ed., *Mathematical Principles of Natural Philosophy and His System of the World,* edited and translated by Andrew Motte. Copyright © 1934, © renewed 1962 by the Regents of the University of California. Reprinted by permission of the University of California Press.

Chapter 20: **p. 742:** "Voltaire on England's Commercial Success," reprinted with the permission of Macmillan Publishing Company from PHILOSOPHICAL LETTERS by Voltaire and translated by Ernest Dilworth. Copyright © 1961 by Macmillan Publishing Company. **p. 759:** "Catherine the Great's Instructions for Legal Reform," from *Documents of Catherine the Great* by W. F. Reddaway. Reprinted by permission of Cambridge University Press.

Chapter 21: **p. 792:** "Parisian Women in Revolutionary Clubs," copyright 1980 by the Board of Trustees of the University of Illinois. Used with the permission of the University of Illinois Press. **p. 794:** "Declaration of the Rights of Woman," copyright 1980 by the Board of Trustees of the University of Illinois. Used with the permission of the University of Illinois Press. **p. 798:** "Robespierre Justifies the Terror," from the book ROBESPIERRE, by George Rude, Editor, © 1967. Used by permission of the publisher, Prentice-Hall/A Division of Simon & Schuster, Englewood Cliffs, N.J.

Chapter 23: **p. 869:** "Friedrich Engels Describes an Urban Slum," reprinted by permission of Stanford University Press and Basil Blackwell Publishers from Friedrich Engels, *The Condition of the Working Class in England,* translated and edited by W. O. Henderson and W. H. Chaloner. Copyright © 1968. **p. 878:** "Rules of the Mechanics' Friendly Institution," from *Workers and Employers: Documents on Trade Unions and Industrial Relations in Britain Since the Early Nineteenth Century,* edited by J. T. Ward and W. Hamish Fraser. Copyright © 1980. Reprinted by permission of Macmillan Press Ltd. **p. 879:** "The New Discipline of the Factory System," from *Documents of European Economic History* by Holmes & Pollard. Copyright © 1968. Reprinted with permission of St. Martin's Press, Incorporated, and Hodder & Stoughton Limited. **p. 883:** "The Communist Manifesto," reprinted by permission of International Publishers.

Chapter 24: **p. 891:** "Florence Nightingale in the Crimean War," reprinted from *"I have Done my Duty": Florence Nightingale in the Crimean War, 1854–56* by Sue M. Goldie by permission of the University of Iowa Press and Manchester University Press. Copyright 1987 by Sue Moriarty. **p. 894:** "Cavour and Napoleon III Plot War," from FRANCE: EMPIRE AND REPUBLIC, 1850–1940 by David Thomson. Copyright © 1968 by David Thomson. Reprinted by permission of HarperCollins, Publishers, Inc. **p. 912:** "The Principles of the Paris Commune," reprinted from "The Declaration of April 19, 1871" in *The Communards of Paris, 1871,* edited by Stuart Edwards. Copyright © 1987 by Thames & Hudson Ltd., London. Used by permission of the publishers, Cornell University Press, and Thames & Hudson Ltd.

Chapter 25: **p. 948:** "Gustave Courbet Describes *The Stone Breakers,*" from *Letters of Gustave Courbet,* translated and edited by Petra ten-Doeschate-Chu. Reprinted by permission of the publisher, The University of Chicago Press.

Chapter 26: **p. 975:** "A Letter from Prison," reprinted by permission of Curtis Brown, Ltd. Copyright © 1937 renewed Weitzner and Jacquese Weil. **p. 981:** "A Conspiratorial Revolutionary Party,"reprinted by permission of International Publishers. **p. 985:** "Another Step Closer to War," from *Outbreak of the World War* edited by Max Montgelas and Walter Schüking, translated by Carnegie Endowment for International Peace. Copyright © 1924. Reprinted by permission of Carnegie Endowment for International Peace.

Chapter 27: **p. 1002:** "Domestic Mobilization and the Role of Women," from *Women War Workers: Accounts Contributed by Representative Workers of the Work Done by Women in the More Important Branches of War Employment,* edited by Gilbert Stone. Copyright © 1917. Reprinted by permission of HarperCollins, Publishers, Inc. **p. 1017:** "A Difficult Ending," from *Blockade: The Diary of an Austrian Middle-Class Woman, 1914–1924,* by Anna Eisenmenger, copyright © 1932. Reprinted by permission of Constable & Co.

Chapter 28: **p. 1036:** "The Gay Subculture in Weimar Berlin," Senelick, Laurence, ed. *Cabaret Performance,* Vol. II. PAJ Publication, © 1993 by The Johns Hopkins University Press. **p. 1039:** "A Marxist Critique of Communism," reprinted by permission of Hyperion Press. **p. 1041:** "Toward the Socialist Split: Conditions for Membership in the Comintern," from *International Communism in the Era of Lenin: A Documentary History,* edited by Helmut Gruber. Copyright © 1972. Used by permission of Doubleday, a division of Bantam Doubleday Dell Publishing Group, Inc. **p. 1042:** "Lenin's Doubts About Stalin," from Warren B. Walsh, ed., *Readings in Russian History, 4th edition, vol. 3: The Revolutionary Era and the Soviet Period* (Syracuse: Syracuse University Press, 1963), pp. 735–736. By permission of the publisher. **p. 1061:** "Tradition and Women: The Conditions of Independence," from *A Room of One's Own* by Virginia Woolf, copyright © 1929 by Harcourt Brace & Company and renewed 1957 by Leonard Woolf. Reprinted by permission of the publishers, Harcourt Brace & Company and The Hogarth Press.

Chapter 30: **p. 1115:** "Toward the Nazi New Order," from NAZISM: A HISTORY IN DOCUMENTS AND EYEWIT-

NESS ACCOUNTS, vol. II, by J. Noakes and G. Pridham. Copyright © 1988 by Department of History and Archaeology, University of Exeter. Reprinted by permission of Pantheon Books, a division of Random House, Inc. **p. 1132:** "The Coming of the Atomic Age," copyright © 1960 by The Estate of Albert Einstein. Reprinted by permission of Simon & Schuster, Inc.

Chapter 31: p. 1152: "The Appeal of Existentialism," reprinted by permission of Haskell House Publishers. **p. 1170:** "Practical Thinking and European Integration," from *Memoirs* by Jean Monnet. Copyright © 1978. Reprinted by permission of Doubleday, a division of Bantam, Doubleday, Dell Publishing Group. **pp. 1184–1185:** Excerpts from *Endgame* from the book *Endgame,* copyright © 1958 by Grove Press, copyright renewed © 1986 by Samuel Beckett. Used with the permission of Grove/Atlantic Monthly Press.

Chapter 32: p. 1189: "Overcoming Gender Limitations," from THE SECOND SEX by Simone DeBeauvoir, trans. H. M. Parshley. Copyright 1952 and renewed 1980 by Alfred A. Knopf, Inc. Reprinted by permission of the publisher, Alfred A. Knopf, Inc., and Jonathan Cape. **p. 1214:** "Europe and the American Challenge," copyright © 1975 by Éditions Denoël. English translation copyright © 1968 by Atheneum House, Inc. Reprinted by permission of Georges Borchardt, Inc. **p. 1220:** "The Universal West: Experiment, Openness, Possibility," from "Our Universal Civilization," by V. S. Naipaul, *The New York Review of Books,* January 31, 1991, pp. 22, 25. Reprinted by permission of Wylie, Aitken & Stone.

Index

An Invitation to Respond

We would like to find out a little about your background and about your reactions to *Western Civilization: The Continuing Experiment.* Your evaluation of the book will help us to meet the interests and needs of students in future editions. We invite you to share your reactions by completing the questionnaire below and returning it to *College Marketing, Houghton Mifflin Company, 222 Berkeley Street, Boston, MA 02116.*

1. How do you rate this textbook in the following areas?

	Excellent	*Good*	*Adequate*	*Poor*
a. Understandable style of writing	______	______	______	______
b. Physical appearance/ readability	______	______	______	______
c. Fair coverage of topics	______	______	______	______
d. Comprehensiveness (covered major issues and topics)	______	______	______	______
e. "Weighing the Evidence" sections	______	______	______	______
f. Presentation of maps and artwork	______	______	______	______

2. Can you comment on or illustrate your above ratings? ______________

3. What chapters or feature did you particularly like? ______________

4. How useful did you find the timeline? ______________

5. What chapters or features did you dislike or think should be changed?

____

____

____

6. What material would you suggest adding or deleting?

____

____

____

7. Are you a student at a community college or a four-year school?

____

8. Do you intend to major in history?______________________

____

9. Did you use the *Study Guide* that accompanies this textbook?

____Yes ____No

10. We would appreciate any other comments or reactions you are willing to share. ______________________________

____

____